# HANDBOOK OF RESEARCH

# ON TEACHING

# THE ENGLISH LANGUAGE ARTS

## SECOND EDITION

# HANDBOOK
# OF RESEARCH ON
# TEACHING THE
# ENGLISH LANGUAGE ARTS

## SECOND EDITION

*Sponsored by the International Reading Association
and the National Council of Teachers of English*

EDITED BY

**JAMES FLOOD**
*San Diego State University*

**DIANE LAPP**
*San Diego State University*

**JAMES R. SQUIRE**
*Silver Burdett & Ginn*

**JULIE M. JENSEN**
*University of Texas at Austin*

 LAWRENCE ERLBAUM ASSOCIATES, PUBLISHERS
2003   Mahwah, New Jersey                    London

KH

| | |
|---|---|
| Senior Acquisitions Editor: | Naomi Silverman |
| Editorial Assistant: | Stacey Mulligan |
| Cover Design: | Kathryn Houghtaling Lacey |
| Textbook Production Manager: | Paul Smolenski |
| Full-Service Compositor: | TechBooks |
| Text and Cover Printer: | Edwards Brothers, Inc. |

This book was typeset in 9/11 pt. ITC Garamond Roman, Bold, and Italic.
The heads were typeset in Novarese, Novarese Medium, and Novarese Bold Italic.

Lawrence Erlbaum Associates, Inc., Publishers
10 Industrial Avenue
Mahwah, New Jersey 07430

**Library of Congress Cataloging-in-Publication Data**

Handbook of research on teaching the English language arts / edited by
    James Flood . . . [et al.].—2nd ed.
        p.   cm.
    "Sponsored by the International Reading Association and the National
    Council of Teachers of English."
    Includes bibliographical references and indexes.
    ISBN 0-8058-3786-8 (hardcover : alk. paper)—ISBN 0-8058-4518-6 (paper)
        1. Language arts.   2. English language—Study and teaching.   I. Flood, James.
    II. International Reading Association.   III. National Council of Teachers of English.

    LB1576 .H234   2003
    428'.007073—dc21                                          2002011444

Printed in the United States of America
10  9  8  7  6  5  4  3  2

10/19/06

# CONTENTS

## Part I

## HISTORICAL AND THEORETICAL PERSPECTIVES FOR ENGLISH LANGUAGE ARTS TEACHING AND LEARNING   1

v

## Part IV

## ENVIRONMENTS FOR ENGLISH LANGUAGE ARTS TEACHING   499

## Part V

## RESEARCH ON TEACHING SPECIFIC ASPECTS OF THE ENGLISH LANGUAGE ARTS CURRICULUM 685

# LIST OF CONTRIBUTORS

JoBeth Allen, University of Georgia
Donna E. Alvermann, University of Georgia
Arthur N. Applebee, State University of New York, Albany
Gwynne E. Ash, University of Delaware
Lori Assaf, University of Texas, Austin
Kathryn H. Au, University of Hawaii
Lawrence Baines, Mesa State College
Aretha F. Ball, Stanford University
James F. Baumann, University of Georgia
Michael D. Beck, BETA, Inc.
June Birnbaum, Rutgers University
David Bloome, Vanderbilt University
Fenice B. Boyd, University of Buffalo, SUNY
Rita S. Brause, Fordham University
Cynthia H. Brock, The University of Nevada Reno
Betram Bruce, University of Illinois, Champaign
Fredrick R. Burton, Witchiffe Alternative Middle School
Robert C. Calfee, Standford University
Robert F. Carey, Rhode Island College
Pamela S. Carroll, Florida State University
Jeanne S. Chall, Harvard University
Marilyn Chambliss, University of Maryland, College Park
Marie M. Clay, University of Auckland, New Zealand
Carole Cox, California State University
Bernice E. Cullinan, New York University
Anne E. Cunningham, University of California, Berkeley
Mary E. Curtis, Boys' Town Reading Center
Karin Dahl, The Ohio State University
Thomas G. Devine, University of Lowell
Anne Dipardo, University of Iowa
Carol N. Dixon, University of California, Santa Barbara
John Dixon, Educational Consultant
Janice A. Dole, University of Utah
Anne Haas Dyson, University of California, Berkeley
Brian Edmiston, The Ohio State University
Janet Emig, Rutgers University
Patricia E. Enciso, The Ohio State University
Nancy Farnan, San Diego State University
Marcia Farr, University of Illinois, Chicago
Roger Farr, Indiana University
Edmund J. Farrell, University of Texas, Austin
Bob Fecho, University of Georgia
Joan T. Feeley, The William Paterson College of New Jersey

Douglas Fisher, San Diego State University
Sheila Fitzgerald, Michigan State University
James Flood, San Diego State University
Sarah Warhauer Freedman, University of California, Berkeley
Nancy Frey, San Diego State University
Lee Galda, University of Georgia
Allan A. Glatthorn, East Carolina University
Yetta M. Goodman, University of Arizona
Judith L. Green, University of California, Santa Barbara
Patricia R. Grogan, University of Dayton
Jane Hansen, University of New Hampshire
Violet J. Harris, University of Illinois, Urbana-Champaign
Jerome C. Harste, Indiana University
Patricia A. Herman, Kamehameha Schools
Elfrieda H. Hiebert, University of Colorado
George Hillocks, Jr., University of Chicago, Professor Emeritus
Richard E. Hodges, University of Puget Sound
James V. Hoffman, University of Texas, Austin
George C. Hruby, University of Georgia
Sarah Hudelson, Arizona State University
Roselmina Indrisano, Boston University
Angela M. Jaggar, New York University
Julie M. Jenson, University of Texas, Austin
Edward J. Kame' enui, University of Oregon
John S. Kania
James L. Kinneavy, University of Texas, Austin
Charles K. Kinzer, Vanderbilt University
Susan S. Klein, U.S. Department of Education
Diane Lapp, San Diego State University
Lora L. Lawson, The Ohio State University
Kevin Leander, Vanderbilt University
James Levin, University of Illinois, Champaign
Cindy Mall, University of Illinois
Debra Bayles Martin, San Diego State University
Miriam Martinez, University of Texas, San Antonio
Robert J. Marzano, Mid-Continent Regional Educational Laborato
Jana M. Mason, University of Illinois, Urbana-Champaign
John S. Mayher, New York University
Susan I. McMahon, National-Louis University
Paula Menyuk, Boston University
Dianne L. Monson, University of Minnesota

Lesley Mandel Morrow, Rutgers University
Miles Myers, National Council of Teachers of English
Nancy Nelson, Louisiana State University
Thomas Newkirk, University of New Hampshire
James W. Ney, Arizona State University
Donna M. Ogle, National-Louis University
Jean Osborn, University of Illinois, Urbana-Champaign
Jeanne R. Paratore, Boston University
Scott G. Paris, University of Michigan/CIERA
Elizabeth Patterson, University of Texas, Austin
Charles W. Peters, University of Michigan
Gay Su Pinnell, The Ohio State University
Leslie Poynor
Gordon M. Pradl, New York University
Robert E. Probst, Georgia State University
Alan C. Purves, State University of New York, Albany
Louise M. Rosenblatt, New York University
Nancy L. Roser, University of Texas, Austin
Leo P. Ruth, University of California, Berkeley
Rachel Salas, Texas A&M University, Corpus Christi
Diane Lemonnier Schallert, University of Texas, Austin
Patricia L. Scharer, The Ohio State University
Sam L. Sebesta, University of Washington
Barbara L. Seidl, The Ohio State University
Margaret Sheehy, The Ohio State University

Daniel L. Shouse, East Carolina University
John Simmons, Florida State University
Carl B. Smith, Indiana University
Karen Smith, Arizona State University
Michael W. Smith, Rutgers University
James R. Squire, Silver Burdett & Ginn
Steven A. Stahl, University of Georgia
Keith E. Stanovich, University of Toronto
Patricia Lambert Stock, Michigan State University
Sandra Stotsky, Harvard Graduate School of Education
Dorothy S. Strickland, Rutgers University
Elizabeth Sulzby, University of Michigan
W. H. Teale, University of Illinois, Chicago
Shane Templeton, University of Nevada, Reno
Robert J. Tierney, The Ohio State University
Gail E. Tompkins, California State University, Fresno
Eileen Tway
Richard L. Venezky, University of Delaware
Betty Jane Wagner, National-Lewis University
Arlette I. Willis, University of Illinois, Urbana-Champaign
M. C. Wittrock, University of California, Los Angeles
Karen K. Wixson, University of Michigan
Paula Wolfe, University of Arizona
David B. Yaden, Jr., University of Southern California
Amy Zaharlick, The Ohio State University

# PREFACE

Preface to the *Handbook of Research on Teaching the English Language Arts*

The second edition of a *Handbook* for teaching must satisfy the expectations of those who have used the first edition, not only in correcting errors and omissions, but by reviewing significant studies of recent vintage. The editors have attempted to do so by revising or deleting existing chapters and by adding 18 new contributions.

The basic purpose—that of providing an integrated perspective on the teaching of the English language arts—remains the same, as does the organization of the *Handbook* itself. Thus, the *Handbook* opens with a consideration of historical and theoretical perspectives on how the English language arts are taught and learned.

Part II focuses on bodies of research that influence decision making; Part III with the characteristics of learners at various developmental levels that may influence what and how we learn.

Part IV deals with environments for teaching the English language arts, the nature of classrooms, the ways in which teachers are educated, and how they may be encouraged to grow in applying research and in participating in research on their own. Research in using instructional materials needed for effective teaching is also included.

Part V focuses on the content of the English language arts, the strategies and skills basic to learning the subject, and on present and future directions for teaching the English language arts.

Prominent scholars, researchers, and professional leaders provide the chapters in each section and review past and present developments, issues, and controversies. They also identify priorities for English language teaching and learning. Authors have been encouraged to develop their own points of view; no attempt has been made to maintain a unified perspective beyond that implied in the organization of the *Handbook*.

## ACKNOWLEDGMENTS

The editors are grateful for the willingness of authors to serve the sponsoring organizations, the National Council of Teachers of English, and the International Reading Association. We also thank the article readers whose incisive comments assisted the authors in preparing the text. We thank the editors of the sponsoring organizations, staff members at San Diego State University, and those who assisted us at Lawrence Erlbaum Associates, Inc.

We also want to thank Naomi Silverman of Erlbaum and Joan Irwin for their continued support of this project as well their tireless efforts to see it to fruition. A special thanks to Paul Smolenski of Erlbaum for his excellent editorial skills and to Kelly Moore for her assistance in getting the project started. Finally, we give a special thank you to Nancy Frey for her assistance with EVERY facet of this project. We couldn't have done it without her.

Informal teaching of the English language arts is central to the success of our schools and the future of our society. We hope that this *Handbook* will continue to remind readers of the number of ways to make their teaching more informed.

James Flood
Diane Lapp
James R. Squire
Julie M. Jensen

# HANDBOOK OF RESEARCH

# ON TEACHING

# THE ENGLISH LANGUAGE ARTS

## SECOND EDITION

# HISTORICAL AND THEORETICAL PERSPECTIVES FOR ENGLISH LANGUAGE ARTS TEACHING AND LEARNING

# •1•

# THE HISTORY OF THE PROFESSION

## James R. Squire
### Silver Burdett & Ginn

Although its antecedents date back 2,500 years, teaching the English language arts in today's schools has been shaped largely by the forces of the last century. Teachers in classical Greece emphasized rhetoric. The medieval trivium of grammar, rhetoric, and logic formed the core of an education provided for future churchmen or noblemen. Not until the rise of the common school did teaching reading, writing, and spelling in the mother tongue occupy the major attention of schoolmasters (Smith, 1985; Venezky, 1984). The literature that was studied in academies and the early grammar schools was usually written in Greek or Latin. Indeed, major universities, like Oxford, did not offer a degree in English until 1896. Psalters, ABC's, and Hornbooks, used for beginning lessons in the mother tongue in colonial America, were based on 16th- and 17th-century British models and taught the rudiments of language through religious and moralistic content (Smith, 1985; Squire, 1988; Venezky, 1984). Primers containing fragments from the Bible or from established literary works used to teach reading in a one-classroom school were well established by 1790, when Noah Webster's spelling books appeared. Developed as a way of seeking standardization of variant English spellings, the Webster spellers became the most widely used texts for teaching reading as well as spelling (Robinson, 1977; Smith, 1985). Spelling and reading thus became associated in teaching English for the next half century (Goodman, Freeman, Murphy, & Shannon, 1988). Webster's intent was to standardize spelling, but the result in terms of instruction was to link beginning reading with pronunciation and with words.

For three quarters of a century from the first edition in 1836, the graded McGuffey readers became so widely used that an estimated two million copies were published. This primer series controlled vocabulary and provided graded levels of difficulty to satisfy the requirements of the multigrade level classrooms of the time; they thus established the pattern for subsequent elementary school textbook series. Graded spellers to accompany each reader were soon published, thus linking reading and spelling, and establishing the concept of grade level standards

in the two subjects. The early moralistic content in elementary school readers yielded to informational content (to make the books seem more relevant to children) and then to the literary, often presented in fragments and snippets, and the tradition that textbook content defined curriculum content was implanted in American education (Robinson, 1977; Smith, 1985; Venezky, 1984).

By the early years of this century, a substantial number of educational publishers had arisen, each offering schools diverse yet similar basal reading and spelling programs based on the mold that had emerged (Chall & Squire, 1993). Twentieth-century authors were to add workbooks and ancillary material and expand terse teachers' manuals into expensive teacher editions with reproduced pages, questions and answers, and teaching support materials, which limited the preparation and planning needed by the teacher. A pattern of instruction that relied on basal readers was well established by 1930 (Mavrogenes, 1985). By 1980, it would be followed by more than 90% of American classrooms (Institutional Tracking Service, 1980). Spelling programs were developed independently of the readers from early in this century and normally were selected and used independently by schools. Reading and spelling thus formed the core of elementary school education in the language arts; writing and grammatical study came later.

Curiously, textbooks dealing with writing in the elementary school did not appear until early in this century, and then focused on penmanship, manuscript form, and elements of grammar and usage (Burrows, 1955). Indeed, not until the mid-1960s was composition stressed below the high school levels, and only during the 1980s and 1990s has writing shared a priority with reading in the primary school (Chall, Conard, & Harris, 1977; Graves, 1978). As the recent emphasis on the total writing process has grown, proponents have increasingly urged that the teaching of spelling, grammar, usage, and other skills be embedded within the overall process, although evidence that teachers are moving in this direction remains scant (Applebee, Langer, & Mullis, 1986a; 1986b; 1986c).

As school enrollments expanded during the early years of this century, children were separated into age/grade level classrooms, each with its own teacher (Smith, 1985). Earlier stress on oral reading in elementary school instruction (with some emphasis on phonics and alphabetic method) yielded to silent reading, the result partially of research in pedagogy, partially of the publication of silent reading tests, and partially, perhaps, from the emphasis on "economy of time" and practicality during the first quarter of the century (adults do their reading silently—why should students be taught orally?) (Judd & Buswell, 1922; Smith, 1985). The result: less emphasis on word analysis and decoding methods; more on whole words, meaning fluency (Chall & Squire, 1988). Further, with spelling instruction so carefully limited to pronunciation and oral usage, the close tie between readers and spellers was broken and independent spellers began to appear. Until the late 1960s, elementary school classrooms and the readers and spellers used in them followed this general approach.

## ORIGINS OF SECONDARY SCHOOL ENGLISH

Until the first quarter of the 20th century, content in secondary school English classrooms focused largely on the study of major literary works, primarily those mandated for college entrance (Mason, 1960b; Piché, 1967; Rosewall, 1965). President Charles Eliot of Harvard University, for example, recommended a celebrated 5-foot shelf of books that he felt all Americans should know. Until World War I, and for a time thereafter, few students other than the college-bound completed high school. Hence, college requirements predominated in determining the high school English curriculum. The National Conference on Entrance Examinations for Colleges formed in 1894 and the Committee of Ten in 1892 were influential in identifying the literary works to be read and in recommending universal completion of an English curriculum designed to develop understanding, expression, and familiarity with good literature (Applebee, 1974). The result, early in the century, was an increase in literary studies, particularly studies of major English writers, and a decrease in independent courses of rhetoric, grammar, and analysis. English as a subject combining literature with teaching of all essential skills thus became established (Applebee, 1974), although separate high school courses in literature and composition, sometimes even in grammar, are found as late as 1968 (Smith, 1932, 1939; Squire & Applebee, 1968). The teaching of reading for all children, however, was largely ignored as a subject for secondary school, although remedial or corrective reading was a matter of continuing concern. Children were to be taught to read in the grammar school; they then read to learn in the secondary. Those reading skills that were addressed inevitably related to literary analysis. Required works read by all were largely traditional, as George Norwell, then state supervisor for New York, demonstrated in 1950 when he reported the reactions of New York students to 5,000 selections that regularly appeared in junior and senior high school anthologies (Olson, 1969).

In 1911, the National Council of Teachers of English (NCTE) was organized, largely to protect high school departments against slavish adherence to college requirements (Hosic, 1921; Hook, 1979). For the next 75 years, its book lists for high school, junior high, and elementary schools sought to advance wide reading by children and young people (Applebee, 1974; Fay, 1968; Hook, 1979; Mason, 1960a). Some freedom of choice by teachers and schools was thus encouraged, and growth in nonacademic curricula and the requirements for acculturating millions of new Americans led to some relaxation in the procrustean yardstick of college requirements. Still, the rise of freshman composition courses and entrance examinations in writing, coupled with the continued emphasis of the College Entrance Board (CEEB) on Scholastic Aptitude Tests (SAT), so influential in determining entrance requirements, meant that the requirements of college preparation were never far from crucial professional consideration, even as nonacademic English programs emerged to satisfy other needs (Applebee, 1974; Hays, 1936; see also the Commission on English's review of the impact of tests in 1931). From interpretations of college requirements have come the theme-a-week, ultimately ossified into "the five-paragraph essay," with its stress on expository writing, which has held unity, coherence, and emphasis to be the greatest value in writing. To understand the uniqueness of this stress in American English teaching, see reports from international assessment of writing (Purves & Takala, 1982).

Instruction in English grammar was particularly strong in junior high schools, where the need for teaching a Latin-based schoolroom grammar was created by the heavy Latin enrollments in Grade 9. Learning Latin by grammatical methods, students encountered difficulties if they did not command the grammar of their native tongue. Speech education, or the teaching of speaking and listening, was much talked about in professional conferences (as it is today), but rarely applied in the classroom perhaps because specialists in oral language left the National Council of Teachers of English to form their own association in 1922 (Veith, 1952). A curriculum in speech education for all young people beyond the primary level has been little more than a desired goal. Indeed, as late as 1968, a national study reported that as few as 15% of pupils graduating from high school had any formal instruction in speech (Squire & Applebee, 1968). Jewett's review of 238 courses of study also confirmed the emphasis on traditional literature, English grammar, and some composition (1958).

Reading remains a major focus of the elementary school language arts curriculum, requiring as much as half of all instructional time in language arts and around 40% of all textbook expenditures (Squire, 1988). Grammar dominated the junior high school until the 1960s, and literature the high school (85% of the instructional time) (Squire & Applebee, 1968). This has been the prevailing pattern until recent reform movements. (See Applebee, 1974; Applebee, 1978; Squire & Applebee, 1968.)

## MAJOR CURRICULUM REFORMS

If the revolt against college domination of the curriculum early in the 20th century represented one significant thrust that influenced subsequent decisions in English teaching, other forces also impacted teaching decisions. For example, the Clapp report (1926) was part of an Economy of Time Movement, which emphasized minimum essentials and emerged shortly after World War I. It directed attention to language competencies needed in various occupations (Applebee, 1974). These were the first of many attempts to emphasize the functional aspects of English teaching and efficiency in teaching, much as did the Effective Schooling studies of the 1970s and 1980s (Applebee, 1974). Both movements raised questions about the practicality of the content to be emphasized and the ways in which time tended to be wasted in schools. And both occurred as schools sought to adjust curriculum and instruction to strong waves of immigrant children.

From the Hosic report on reorganization of high school English in 1917 to Dora V. Smith's evaluation of schools in 1933, professional leaders tried to define priorities. Smith, for example, reported more children conjugating English verbs in six tenses than engaged in all other English activities combined (1932). These early attempts to define functional aspects of the subject led to Stormzand and O'Shea's efforts to define the essentials of language as distinct from niceties (1924), to O'Rourke's attempt to define minimum essentials (1934), and ultimately, to Robert C. Pooley's (1946) efforts to classify instruction in English grammar and usage into elements to be emphasized, elements to be taught, if possible, and elements to receive no instruction. The recommendations were carried to the schools through the *English Journal*, a professional periodical owned by W. Wilbur Hatfield, then executive secretary of NCTE, which became the official journal of the Council. But its stress on high school concerns led C. C. Certain in 1927 to found *Elementary English* (now *Language Arts*) to give voice to problems of teaching the language arts in the elementary school. Certain's journal became the official organ for NCTE's elementary section 2 years later (Petty, 1983), and changes in lower level curriculum are more easily traced from that time. The inclusion of pedagogical considerations of reading as well as of the other language arts within the same journal led Council leaders ultimately to promote consideration of integrated language arts within the classroom (Hook, 1979; Smith, 1952). Still, the continued domination of Council meetings by secondary school concerns led Certain, Harry A. Greene, and Emmett Betts to found the National Conference for Research in English (NCRE) in 1933 to provide for gatherings of those concerned with educational research, particularly research in reading and the other language arts (Petty, 1983). Indeed, for the next 3 decades, NCRE normally met with the American Educational Research Association (AERA), perhaps one of the reasons why research findings did not loom large in discussions of English teaching during the early years. NCRE tried to publicize findings regularly in *Elementary English*, but the journal reached few secondary school teachers, and not all of those in English Education. In 1996 NCRE changed its name to the National Conference on Language and Literacy (NCRLL), a change representing a growing concern with reading as well as developmental values.

## THE EXPERIENCE CURRICULUM

The teaching of the English language arts during the 1930s and 1940s was only partially touched by experimentation then underway in progressive education in American schooling. But the significant lesson—that young people taught by content-free educational methods stressing higher thought processes did as well or better in higher education than students graduated from more rigid content-bound programs—had little impact on national decision making, largely because the findings were not released until the early 1940s when Americans were more occupied with World War II than with improving education (Aikin, 1942). NCTE's leaders did embrace the functional emphasis in Progressive Education (PEA) and the concern with the individual student (Simmons, Shadiow, & Shafer, 1990), but did not retreat from an interest in subject matter. More influential than the PEA—perhaps the most influential title in English teaching during the century—was the 1935 publication, *An Experience Curriculum in English*, by the NCTE Commission on the Curriculum, edited by W. Wilbur Hatfield, then secretary-treasurer of the Council and editor of the *English Journal*. The report stressed the importance of experiences in literature and language and experiences through literature and language. Although isolated instruction in reading, grammar, literature, and writing would continue for the next 50 years, professional leaders from the late 1930s began to talk about the project method, about integrating the language arts in "meaningful" classroom activities, about "functional teaching" of English, and about correlating English studies with those in other subjects. Almost 2 decades later, another commission, this time headed by Dora V. Smith, popularized concern for integrated language arts (i.e., reading, writing, speaking, listening) (Smith, 1952) and published four volumes to illuminate how this integrated language arts philosophy could influence curriculum in schools and in teacher education (Broening, 1956; Grommon, 1963; Mackintosh, 1954). The term "language arts" rose to professional popularity among elementary school teachers at this time, since it suggested the integration of skills and experiences; English, the term still used in the high school, suggested subject matter, and often, subject matter taught in isolation. Today's concern with "whole language" and integration of reading and writing dates back to such curriculum efforts.

## SKILL IN READING

The stress on language activities and experiences and on children's literature in the elementary school, which marked much of the profession, if not the teaching, during the 1940s through the 1960s, made reading specialists increasingly dissatisfied with the quality of instruction. Too little attention was being directed to basic skills. The rise of standardized tests and the development of age-grade norms in reading provided evidence that many children were not developing needed competence in basic reading skills (a development increasingly apparent with the children from lower socioeconomic groups with their characteristic problems in learning language). Early NCTE meetings frequently saw as many debates on "skills" versus experience-oriented instruction as do our conventions today. Paul Witty, a highly regarded advocate of an experience curriculum, was seen as one who wanted to teach "the whole child," while Stella Center, an early leader in teaching the skills of reading, was concerned more with "the hole in the child" (Hook, 1979).

Dissatisfied with the state of skill instruction in the early 1950s, and unable to find an adequate voice for their views within NCTE and its journals, a group of national reading specialists joined with a group of remedial reading teachers that had formed a separate association shortly after World War II—the National Association of Remedial Teachers in 1946 and the International Council for the Improvement of Reading Instruction in 1947. The bulletin of the latter association became *The Reading Teacher* in 1951, and the two groups merged to form the International Reading Association (IRA) in 1955 (Jerrolds, 1977). Many reading specialists who had been active in the NCTE elementary section left the organization. Initially concerned with the curriculum in reading skills and remedial reading, with NCTE remaining the major center for those interested in children's literature, oral language, and writing, IRA has grown over the past 45 years to be a broadly based association with an extensive publishing program dealing with all aspects of the English language arts. Further, from the very beginning, its affiliated associations included Canadian chapters, and it has focused on international concerns both in its journals and in a biennial World Congress on reading. *The Reading Teacher*, its journal for elementary school, and the *Journal of Adolescent and Adult Literacy* for secondary school teachers, have consistently provided guidelines for reading instruction. Over the past 40 years, these journals have been particularly influential in suggesting methods and strategies for teaching reading.

The teaching of reading has continued to be influenced by commercial instructional materials, with Komokski reporting by the mid-1970s that more than 90% of all classroom teaching decisions were influenced by the textbooks (EPIE Institute, 1977). The widespread use of basal reading programs from the early years of the century, and particularly the development beginning in 1930 of modern graded basals by leaders like William S. Gray, Arthur Gates, and David H. Russell, provided detailed manuals of teaching strategies (some say too detailed), which were followed extensively, sometimes even blindly and sluggishly, by classroom teachers. By 1980, virtually all K–6 classrooms were using such manuals (ITS, 1980) and were often organizing much of the language arts instruction around the basal programs. However, recent criticism of the uses of basal reading approaches, concentrating on their overemphasis on skill drills and underemphasis on literary and language processing experience, suggests that today's elementary school classrooms are changing (Anderson, Hiebert, Scott, & Wilkinson, 1985; Goodman et al., 1988).

Almost 2 decades of debate between those advocating a skills approach and those promoting a experience approach seems to be resulting in a consensus that a balanced approach involving both is likely to achieve the best results (Honig, 1996; Snow, 1997).

## COMPOSITION AND RHETORIC

Although the teaching of rhetoric and writing historically has been a significant dimension of English, the emergence of concern with contemporary rhetorics and with the relationship of instruction in grammar and usage to writing (or the lack of such relationship) dates mostly from the founding of the Conference on College Composition and Communication (CCCC) in 1949 within NCTE, and to the influence of its annual meeting and its quarterly journal. Initially focused on college freshman composition and on preparation for it, the CCCC served as a national center within the profession for those concerned with the teaching of writing throughout the Kindergarten through college curriculum. CCCC leaders were responsible for publication of *The State of Knowledge about Composition* in 1963, a review of research that forcefully rejected grammar-based approaches in improving children's writing (Braddock, Lloyd-Jones, & Schoer, 1963). The CCCC conference and its journal provided a way of communicating to schools information about the newer grammars and rhetorics that were advanced in the 1960s and 1970s. Members of the organization lobbied vigorously for stronger preparation of high school and elementary school teachers in writing (Committee on the National Interest, 1961, 1964). As recently as 25 years ago, half of the nation's high school teachers of English had not studied composition beyond freshman composition, and almost no elementary teacher had formally studied language development or the teaching of writing. That such conditions largely have changed today is due in no small measure to the efforts of CCCC leaders.

## TEACHER EDUCATION

During the early part of the 20th century, many elementary school teachers had been educated in the 2-year normal schools and lacked extensive course work in the subject matter of English or its teaching. Donald Durrell noted, for example, that in 1930, when he began teaching at Boston University, not a single course on teaching reading was offered in the nation's colleges (Squire, 1988). Emphasis on preparation of language arts teachers and stronger certification standards in the subject began earnestly after World War II when NCTE and later IRA provided concrete recommendations to state certification authorities for strengthening preparation for teaching subject matter. (See Austin, Morrison, & Kenny, 1961; Committee on National Interest, 1964; Grommon, 1968.)

The strengthening of certification standards for teaching in elementary school and the rising interest in research in reading and the other language arts led during the 1930s and 1940s to the rise of major university centers for preparing teachers, administrators, and faculty for teacher training. During this period, many universities developed laboratory schools or demonstration centers, making it possible for would-be teachers and administrators to study and sometimes participate in the proper teaching of English language arts. A few of the university centers developed such powerful philosophies that they influenced an entire generation of teacher educators and classroom teachers. At the University of Chicago, for instance, William S. Gray, supported by Ralph Tyler, Helen Robinson, Hilda Taba, Guy Buswell, and others, created in reading education a distinct point of view, not only through their graduate programs, but through such publications as an annual summary of research in reading (Gray, 1933–1960), and through an influential and unique 25-year series of summer reading conferences at the University of Chicago.

Perhaps the strongest influence on teaching the other language arts was the program Dora V. Smith administered at the University of Minnesota, which stressed the importance of children's literature and meaningful language arts teaching. The experiments in progressive education at Ohio State University, and, particularly, its laboratory school, led by Paul Witty, Lou LaBrant, and Edgar Dale, were probably the most significant influences on introducing free reading. Teachers College, Columbia University, given its base in New York and its distinguished faculty in curriculum and instruction, became both a national center for training teachers and educational leaders in reading, with Arthur Gates and, later, Roma Gans and Ruth Strang, and a center for the English communication arts, where Lennox Gray and Francis Shoemaker, during the 1940s and 1950s, perpetuated a communication arts model based on the philosophy of Suzanne Langer (1942), furthered by the multimedia theories of Marshall McLuhan (1964). These centers were important not only for stimulating bodies of research and theory published at the time, but for training teacher educators, school administrators, and young research professors who sallied forth to schools of education and teacher training institutions across the land during expansion of higher education in the 1950s. Thus was the influence of William S. Gray or Arthur Gates spread throughout the nation, as were the unique points of view of Dora V. Smith or Lennox Gray on the teaching of English. Many teachers were educated during the 1960s and 1970s by professional leaders whose attitudes had been shaped at these university centers. Their importance to the history of teaching and learning the English language arts was profound, but today few such centers continue.

With a decline in interest in teacher education during the 1960s and 1970s, centers for research in English and reading became less common. Individual leaders, not institutional centers, became more common. Laboratory schools were closed. Teacher training moved into the public school classroom so as to become more "realistic," and beginning teachers were often denied an opportunity to see theory in practice. Thus, the kind of advanced study of theory, research, and practice in teaching reading, writing, literature, and oral language with teams of high level educators has been lost during the recent decades, and the views associated with any particular center for study have been less influential.

Recent federally supported centers, such as the Center of the Study of Reading at the University of Illinois at Urbana-Champaign, seemed to open a new era to today's graduate students. Cognitive psychologists concerned with comprehension and the thinking process gathered at Illinois, and their work for a time dominated professional discussions about reading. The attitudes of large numbers of today's educational leaders have also been influenced by the philosophies that emerged at the Illinois center, as others were influenced by the programs at the Center for the Study of Writing (University of California at Berkeley) and the Center for the Learning and Teaching of Literature (State University of New York at Albany). Such institutions may again assert the kind of leadership once associated with the earlier institutional centers. Indeed, some of the more influential of recent publications have come from such centers. (See Anderson et al., 1985; Applebee, Langer, & Mullis, 1985; 1986a; 1986b; 1986c; 1988.)

Further, a renewed concern about the quality of the nation's teachers and the ability of American schools to attract outstanding young teachers has led to calls for the reform of teacher education, such as in the Holmes Report (Olson, 1987), and the Carnegie Commission on Teacher Education (*A Nation Prepared*, 1986). The recent development centers such as the Center for English Learning and Achievement at the New York State University at Albany are devoting much attention to teacher preparation (Langer, 1944). It seems likely that reform effort, which stresses sound academic preparation as well as pedagogy, will exert a critical influence on education for several years.

## ACADEMIC REFORM

Despite the work of the early centers in improving aspects of the English language arts, a report on the state of the profession in 1960, read into the Congressional Record as part of the deliberations leading to an extension of the National Defense Education Act of 1958 to include English, called for teacher institutes, curriculum development, and research to strengthen the teaching of the "bed rock" subject in the schools. Squire and others reported at that time that half of the nation's teachers of English were ill-prepared in the subject (Committee on the National Interest, 1961).

The late 1950s and early 1960s were marked by a school reform movement in which Nobel Laureates and professors in academic subjects worked with teachers to provide new instructional materials in an attempt to strengthen academic achievement, mostly notably in school mathematics, sciences, and foreign languages. NCTE joined with the Modern Language Association (MLA) and other college English associations to identify "The Basic Issues in the Teaching of English" that needed to be resolved and that required federal support (Modern Language Association, 1959; Squire, 1963). Reform efforts in English focused largely on funding research and curriculum development projects (Project English), and on support for 3 years of summer training institutes for teachers (see Shugrue, 1968). Stronger preparation in English was stressed in nationally oriented projects (Shugrue & Everett, 1968).

A "Spiral Curriculum" model, advanced by Jerome Bruner (1960), stressed that children could be introduced early to mature concepts, then repeatedly and systematically re-exposed to the ideas as they matured (Bruner, 1960). This model of learning appealed to professors who wished to strengthen the teaching of subject matter and led to a strengthening of instructional components in composition and language in the elementary school and to some attempts to strengthen literary content. Conant's (1959) widely emulated report on high schools stressed the need for 4 years of English and for a strong writing program. Extensive federally sponsored research, which has continued since that day, supported such influential studies as Loban's 13-year study of language development, Strickland's analysis of the importance of informing language arts teaching by concepts from language and linguistic research (Strickland, 1962); Hanna's linguistically based analysis of the regularity of English orthography in spelling (Hanna, Hanna, Hodges, & Rudolph, 1966); and the First Grade Reading Studies (Bond & Dykstra, 1967), where a series of comparisons of classroom teaching pointed to a need for many approaches to beginning reading even while emphasizing the value of early phonics instruction.

At this time, also Chall (1967) reviewed research in beginning reading and added her powerful call for "code-oriented," not "meaning-oriented" beginning reading instruction. Although her findings seemed initially controversial to those addicted to meaning emphasis in beginning reading instruction, they had a profound influence on subsequent materials and methods. The summer institutes for teachers of the English language arts were based on a tripod model of curriculum (language, literature, composition) with separate courses in each subject taught by academic professors following a pattern developed and pioneered in 1962 by the CEEB's Commission on English (Gerber, 1963). The institute thus provided a way of educating members of academic college departments about schools and teachers and about recent scholarly developments in the disciplines (Commission on English, 1965). From this effort came a stress on basic skills and basic content in the elementary school, ultimately to include writing, spelling, some grammar, and attention to the study of literature in depth and to rhetoric in the high school (Shugrue, 1968). The long-range effects of Project English thus can be seen more in powerful research studies and in the education of teacher leaders than in curriculum development, although the units, courses, and books developed at such diverse English curriculum centers as Hunter College, Florida State University, University of Nebraska, and University of Oregon did for a time dominate professional discussion (Simmons, et al., 1990). More recent concerns over curriculum change has focused less on teaching content and more on how students learn. The shift in view became particularly pronounced in the 1980s and thereafter as researchers concerned with process turned their attention away from controlled laboratory research and more to human learning in the classroom (Squire, 1999).

## LITERATURE

Historically, the curriculum in literature has consisted of great works from traditional western literature deemed suitable for reading by boys and girls. Many of the works were moralistic, much as was the content of early basal readers. *Silas Marner* and *A Tale of Two Cities* were seen as excellent ways of inculcating Victorian values, then under siege, as were many standard selections, e.g., "Abou Ben Adam," "Say Naught the Struggle Not Availeth," and "The Chambered Nautilus." Like university scholars early in the century, teachers emphasized literary history or the backgrounds of literature (the togas of Rome, the theatres of Shakespeare, the lives of the Romantic poets). When Smith conducted her field studies of secondary English school teaching in the late 1930s, she found the teaching of literature dominated by the selections existing within the large anthology (Smith, 1941), as the single resource, largely developed as an economic measure during The Great Depression to make worthwhile literature available to students in the classroom. Such anthologies, like the basal reading programs in the elementary school, tended to provide a relatively uniform national curriculum in literature for Grades 7–12, the more so since two anthology programs,

Scott Foresman's *Literature and Life*, first published in 1922–24, and Harcourt Brace Jovanovich's *Adventures* series, first published in 1932, have dominated secondary school English classrooms for the past 50 years (Applebee, 1974; Searles, 1942).

School libraries often could not be supported at that time and inexpensive paperback editions of works did not appear widely until after World War II. The college entrance requirements of earlier years remained the most important determinant of content (Applebee, 1974), much as the elementary school reader provided the literary curriculum for the lower level. Yet, anthologies and readers were useful, also, in providing for a prescreening of selections so that only those judged appropriate for the young might be included in course offerings, and schools and teachers could avoid the censorship issues that surfaced strongly in the McCarthy era and have continued ever since (Association of American Publishers, American Library Association, Association for Supervision and Curriculum Development, 1981; Committee on Right to Read, 1962; Jenkinson, 1979; Moffett, 1988). Thus, many of today's readers and anthologies contain works adapted to be more acceptable to schools (Goodman et al., 1988). Further, instructional purpose increasingly required books tailored to special groups of learners. Vocabulary control and graded readability criteria led to more and more selections being written or rewritten specifically for school programs.

Literary scholarship changed in the nation's universities late in the 1930s and 1940s when Brooks and Warren (1938) and Wellek and Warren (1949) forced attention to works themselves and to internal interrelationships of language and metaphor within the selections. This emphasis on text—the insights of "The New Criticism"—found support for teaching in the CEEB Institute of the early 1960s, which, at about the time that literary ventures at universities were turning away from exclusive concern with text, succeeded in directing the attention of school teachers and examiners to a study of texts in depth. The Advance Placement program in literature, also sponsored by CEEB, furthered such emphasis by the kind of test questions asked on its examinations (Commission on English, 1965). Thus, the study of major works in depth came to secondary school teaching. (See, particularly, the recommendations of Lynch & Evans, 1983.) Among the more influential literary scholars was Shakespearean student Northrup Frye, whose *Anatomy of Criticism* (1957) defined the importance of metaphor in learning literature, and whose *Educated Imagination* (1964) provided guidance to teachers in schools seeking to expand literary education. Of unique importance also during this period of academic reform was the John Hay Fellow Program, which provided a selected number of outstanding teachers with advanced work in literature at outstanding graduate schools. Directed by historian, Charles Keller, the John Hay program developed an informed alumni association that provided opportunities for teachers from diverse school districts to discuss teaching in the school. The interdisciplinary humanities course, introduced in many high schools during the 1960s, probably owes its origin to the work of these teachers (Applebee, 1974).

Largely unnoticed during the period was work on the reader's response to literature initiated by Richards (1929) and Rosenblatt (1938). Influential initially on researchers rather than on classroom teachers (Purves & Beach, 1972; Squire, 1964), concern with the response of the reader did not emerge widely in schools until a professional reaction to the formalism of the academic reform movement occurred during the late 1960s (Squire & Applebee, 1968). Subsequent publication of another seminal work from Rosenblatt (1978) and release of major new research works (Beach, 1993; Cooper, 1982; Farrell & Squire, 1990 and Purves & Beach, 1972) led teachers to think again about the reader in relation to the literary text. The State of California also recommended major attention to children's response to literature, not merely to literature per se (California State Department of Education, 1987). But advocates of more traditional approaches continued to argue for greater stress on the traditional curriculum (Ravitch & Finn, 1987) and a major new concern emerged: how to also include multicultural literary experiences. Indeed, the 1999 presidential address at NCTE called specifically for a reawakening of interest in the plurality of our students (Harste, 1999).

## URBAN SCHOOL REFORM

The academic reform of the late 1950s and early 1960s was short lived, even though it formed the impetus for redirecting an entire generation of English teachers. Rising concern with educating children from lower socioeconomic groups in reading and language led to the massive "Great Society" programs of the Lyndon Johnson administration and to various federal programs, which sought to equalize opportunity for all (Corbin & Crosby, 1965; Jewett, 1964). Because language deprivation is an almost universal characteristic of children reared in poverty, many federal and state initiatives of this period emphasized headstart programs in reading and language, multimedia approaches, expanded library services, special tutoring, and similar initiatives in urban schools.

Also important for the classroom teacher was an increased awareness of special problems in teaching bilingual children both within the general classroom and in special classes (Allen, 1966). The Association for Teachers of English to Speakers of Other Languages (TESOL) was formed in 1966 in a series of conferences sponsored by NCTE, IRA, Modern Language Association (MLA), and the Speech Association of America (Hook, 1979). The continued increase of new Americans entering classrooms during the 1970s and 1980s, particularly Americans speaking Hispanic and Asian languages, mandated a new commitment to multiculturalism (Harste, 1999). One of the ways that professional associations responded to the new needs was through formation of special interest subgroups. Witness, for example, the organization of spring conferences by the same organization; the extensive preconvention and postconvention programs of such organizations as IRA and NCTE; as well as the formation of special "job-alike" associations such as the Conference on English Education (CEE), the Conference for Secondary School English Department Chairpersons, and the NCTE assemblies for literature and research (Hook, 1979, p. 263). English teaching had become so complex it required specialization. Each special interest group required its own programs and publications. Leaders of NCTE increasingly chose to view the association as a national forum for all groups and individuals interested in English, rather than an organization with a unified viewpoint. The conferences, assemblies, and expanded activities were seen as a way of responding to diverse educational interests, and moving conferences around the nation, a way of serving a diversity of teachers (Hook, 1979, p. 205).

But the Coleman Report in 1966 suggested that schooling had little influence on the learning of such children, and the debate over its findings stimulated extensive attempts to define exactly how the classroom teacher does influence learning. Thus, Edmonds (1979), Rosenshine and Stevens (1984), and Berliner and Rosenshine (1977), among others, led teams into schools that were achieving instructional goals in reading and (sometimes) writing and reported on the characteristics of effective schooling. Initially, most such studies were in urban schools, but later studies extended the findings to schools of all kinds. Instructional leadership, direct instruction, time-on-task, and stress on academic achievement were found to be characteristic of quality instruction in these studies (Denham & Lieberman, 1980), and teachers everywhere struggled to apply these ideas to their teaching. A decade earlier, Squire and Applebee had conducted a similar survey of successful high school English programs in the United States and England (1968, 1969), and their results, like the more widely publicized studies of effective teaching in the elementary school, provided similar teaching modes.

Also influential in the urban school reform efforts were anecdotal descriptions of teaching in the slums and of responding to individual children. Among the more influential were titles by Kozol (1968), Herndon (1971), and Kauffman (1965). Most of the writings of these so-called "Romantic Critics" emphasized the teaching of the language arts.

## TESTING AND ACCOUNTABILITY

Both in their assessment of successful teaching and in their recommendations for school improvement, educational leaders seeking to improve instruction in reading and instruction in language and writing were influenced by the increase in academic testing that began to pervade the schools in the 1960s and 1970s. Criterion-referenced assessment measures focused on specific skills were developed for elementary school reading; national, statewide, and districtwide accountability of pupil competence assessment in reading (Valencia & Pearson, 1987) became commonplace in 48 of the states by the early 1980s. Process assessment of growth in reading as well as product assessment emerged as matters of educational concern. Samplings of student writings were assessed in two thirds of the states (Applebee, Langer, & Mullis, 1986b).

The National Assessment of Educational Progress (NAEP), first from a base with The Education Commission of the States and later with Educational Testing Service, published national "report cards" every 5 or 6 years on how schools were doing in reading, writing, and other subjects. The data initially indicated a perceptible improvement in scores as the teaching effectiveness movement took hold, but continued to show low scores by minority children and children of low socioeconomic status. Only in the 1986 reading assessment did the improvement halt (Applebee, Langer, & Mullis, 1988).

Given the emphasis on skill development in reading and writing as part of "back to the basics," and the single level of purpose of most instruments used in assessments, small wonder that our classrooms tended more and more to emphasize skill development and drill and practice. Public criticism of schooling drove administrators to rely on test score improvement in responding to critics, and the tests themselves drove teachers to overemphasize specific skills. "Mastery Learning" as a teaching model seems to fit the demand (Bloom, 1982). So extensive did skill drill become in American schools that the Commission on Reading of the National Academy on Education (NAE) reported in 1985 that 80% of the time devoted to reading at the primary level was spent on skill drills (Anderson et al., 1985). Durkin (1983) and Applebee (1978) also reported a low level of teaching based on their classroom observations.

But if the academic formalism of the early 1960s led, on the one hand, to a counter-effort in which students engaged in drills and testing, it also stimulated an interest in productive language (Applebee, 1978; Durkin, 1983). To counter an overemphasis on "basics," many teachers sought interactive programs. (See Moffett, 1968). Alternative schools, or "storefront schools," stressing "open education," emphasized expression during the late 1960s and early 1970s. Natural language activities were introduced into elementary classrooms and free electives replaced the standardized high school English curriculum. During this interval, some secondary schools reported offering as many as 272 different courses, many of short duration (Hillocks, 1972; Squire & Applebee, 1968). Teachers, encouraged to offer courses reflecting their own interests, tried to interest the young with such relevant English courses as "The Cookery of the Midwest," "Broadway Musical Comedy," "The History Plays of Shakespeare," or "Women I," "Women II," and "Women III."

The excesses of the new freedom defeated itself. In schooling, as in life, one cannot sustain freedom without discipline. The extreme liberalism of many experiments seemed to strengthen the belief that children did need skills and were not acquiring them. Doubt had been planted, of course, concerning the value of teaching subject matter unrelated to children's needs. In 1966, the Anglo-American Seminar at Dartmouth College provided opportunity for 60 international professors, teacher eductors, and teachers to review the teaching of the English language arts for 3 intensive weeks. The seminar occurred at a moment of watershed in the history of English teaching. Americans were just completing a series of curriculum projects known as Project English, which, for the most part, attempted to apply academic reforms in literature, grammar, and composition to the classroom. The British were struggling between twin philosophies—a basic literary outlook associated with literary critic F. R. Leavis and the Cambridge school (Frank Whitehead, Dennis Thomson, Dennis Harding, David Holbrook), and the views of leaders from the London Institute of Education, who emphasized the power of writing in transforming learning (James Britton, Harold Rosen, Nancy Martin). In the long run, the London group became ascendent in England and their influence can be seen in publications of the next decade as well as in reports from the New Hampshire conference. (See Her Majesty's Stationery Office, 1975; Squire & Applebee, 1969).

The recommendations from the Dartmouth Seminar called for a growth model of learning stressing creativity, expressive writing, and response to literature (Muller, 1967). Given the climate of the time, the recommendations were slow to reach fulfillment, but some of the views found fruit in the interactive model of teaching proposed by James Moffett and his fellows (1968; Moffett & Wagner, 1976) and in the emphasis on responding to literature associated with Alan Purves (1973). Literature teaching, however, was never again to dominate professional life as it did earlier in our history; composition and composing increasingly attracted attention. Those who sought more naturalistic teaching, based on the experience of pupils, were encouraged by an independent series of studies by James Britton (1970; Britton, Martin, McLeod, & Rosen, 1975) and Louise Rosenblatt (1978).

## WRITING AS PROCESS

The Dartmouth Seminar had stressed the creativity inherent in writing and how writing could contribute to an individual's growth. Meanwhile, rhetoric again began to loom large in college scholarly inquiries and "new rhetorics" began to attract attention, among them the work by Francis Christensen (Applebee, 1974; Moffett, 1968), and the publications by James Britton and colleagues (Britton, 1970; Britton et al., 1975). Emig's seminal study of the composing process appeared at about the same time, focusing the profession's attention on how children learn to write, not on what they write (Emig, 1971). Moffett and Britton, almost as effective as international analysts as they were as researchers or philosophers, continued to stress the importance of writing in learning. Donald Murray (1986) and Mina Shaughnessy (1977) helped a generation of teachers clarify their thinking about the process of composing, and Donald Graves (1978) popularized such concepts with elementary teachers.

In 1974, James Gray initiated a writing project at the University of California at Berkeley that stressed the re-education of teachers in composition. Gray's 6-week and 8-week institutes concentrated on teachers writing for other teachers, and, thus, teaching one another. Extended a year or two later to a series of statewide California institutes, and, ultimately, to 152 other institutes or writing projects in 46 states and 6 foreign countries, plus the Department of Defense Schools around the world, the Writing Project network reached at its peak some 60,000 elementary and secondary school teachers annually (Gray, 1987).

At the least, writing projects have provided an instrument to communicate concern about, and experiences with, teaching writing and new research in composing. Follow-up programs, a quarterly newsletter, and a national alumni association, formed within the National Council of Teachers of English, help to maintain the excitement of being a writing teacher. Similar projects at the University of Iowa, at Bread Loaf in Vermont (and in England), in New Jersey, and elsewhere, have also been influential, particularly in the Midwestern and New England regions.

The impact on the profession in focusing attention on writing as central to English teaching and then to the teaching of all subjects has been incalculable.

## COMPREHENSION OF READING

If the teaching of reading in the 1960s and 1970s concentrated on specific skills, teaching in the 1980s stressed the teaching of comprehension. Cognitive psychologists studying human learning in the mid-1960s found themselves focusing on language learning, since it is through language that a person develops concepts. Researchers in psycholinguistics, such as Kenneth Goodman and Frank Smith, directed attention to the interrelationships of oral and written language (Smith, 1971). Such work contributed strongly to insights into the processes of writing, but, even more, to research on the processes of comprehension. The 1976 creation by the federal government of a Center for the Study of Reading at the University of Illinois provided a focus for much of the work of the cognitive psychologists (so much so that initially some reading people feared that the Center was not being controlled by "specialists in reading"). Through a series of reports, conferences, and publications at the Center and related to the Center's work has come new insights into comprehension that have informed today's teaching: the importance of prior knowledge, text structure, and writing and speaking in relation to text (Flood, 1984; Pearson, Barr, Kamil, & Mosenthal, 1984). This version sees reading less as a collection of specific skills to be mastered than as an integrated sequence of processes closely associated with writing. Further, study of the processes of comprehension led to awareness of metacognition, the reader's awareness of what he is learning and his ability to assess his own progress. The impact on today's teaching can be gleaned in part by noting the heavy stress placed on comprehension in today's textbooks as contrasted with yesterday's, and by the concern expressed by professional leaders over the failure of some teachers to apply the findings of research in comprehension (Durkin, 1983; Mason & Osborn, 1983). Although many assessment instruments still focus on specific skills, leaders in reading are now calling for tests focusing on comprehension, and some experimental changes are under way (Squire, 1987). The impact on how the profession views the teaching of reading has been manifest. Just contrast today's IRA convention programs with the programs of the 1950s, or review the new history of reading comprehension published by IRA (Robinson, Faraone, Hittleman, & Unruh, 1990.)

Much of the research on comprehension has stressed the interrelationship of the language arts—the importance of early experiences with literature to beginning reading, say, or the value of writing after reading as a way of encouraging students to process the ideas they acquired. The result has been heightened interest in interrelating the language arts, most particularly seen in the whole language movement in primary as well as secondary classrooms with its rejection of traditional basal instruction (Goodman et al., 1988). The research available suggests that integrated whole language approaches may be more effective in the initial stages of teaching reading, but not subsequently as skill development is stressed (Stahl & Miller, 1988). But the conflict between whole language advocates who stress construction of meaning and skill-oriented specialists who stress decoding continues. Almost certainly the current movement will result in more balanced stress on literature, writing, and oral language, and less emphasis on separate instruction in language skills, spelling, or grammar (Snow, 1997).

## ORAL LANGUAGE

Far less research has been devoted to the teaching of speaking and listening than to the other language arts. In the early years of the 20th century, departments of English celebrated "Better Speech Days" as a way of emphasizing clarity in communication, but this interest largely waned after specialists in oral language left NCTE in 1922 to form their own organization, the Speech Association of America, now the Speech Communication Association (Applebee, 1974; Hook, 1979). For many years research in oral language was mostly initiated by university speech departments and seldom filtered down to teachers of English Language Arts since the latter were educated in departments of English and education.

Speaking and listening were emphasized as two of the four language arts by the Commission on the English Curriculum in 1952 (Smith, 1952) and 1948. The Conference on College Composition and Communication brought together college faculty members interested in oral as well as written communication (Hook, 1979), but oral language seldom has received the stress in schools or in the research accorded to writing, reading, and literature. As late as 1968, Squire and Applebee reported almost all high school teachers of English professing to assume responsibility for speech education, but only 15% of the graduating seniors were found to have completed course work in oral English.

Indeed, until the most recent decades, much of the research in oral language that affected classroom teaching was conducted by structural linguists and their followers, who believed deeply that oral language was *the* language, and that writing and reading were secondary. "There is no language apart from the speaker active in expression," wrote Charles C. Fries, and his grammar studies along with those of Marckwardt, Allen, McDavid, and others focused on oral language—oral pattern practice, variations in spoken dialects, and audiolingual approaches (Marckwardt, 1963). Such pedagogy proved to be particularly influential in teaching English as a second language. For teaching native-language speakers, one of the more influential pedagogical reports reflecting these views was Robert C. Pooley's *Teaching English Usage*, which stressed oral practice in establishing appropriate expression (1946).

The rise of transformational grammar with its emphasis on self-generation of expression, the Dartmouth Seminar with its stress on individual creation through language (Wilkinson, 1970), and particularly recent concern with the integration of the language arts and the reawakening of interest in the emergence of literacy, have given new emphasis to oral language, particularly in relation to the other language arts (see Pinnell and Jaggar, this edition). Loban's monumental 12-year study of the development of competence in oral language not only provided a base study on children's competence in oral language, but pointed up many critical interrelationships (Loban, 1976). In recent years cooperative learning, reciprocal teaching and response-oriented teaching of literature have renewed interest in oral processing of ideas and in the ways in which oral language processing can contribute to improved comprehension and written communication (Cazden, 1988). In addition, the discovery by Heath and others that at-risk children frequently lack opportunity in school or out of school to exchange ideas orally with others seems to be leading to a new emphasis in our classrooms (Heath, 1983). So does concern with early literacy and developmental teaching.

## TEACHING CONDITIONS

Concern with teaching during past decades has also meant concern with teaching conditions. Crucial, perhaps, to the teaching of the English language arts has been the repeated concern with class size, teacher–pupil ratios, library and classroom book supply, censorship, certification of teachers (see the previous discussion on teacher education), and the quality of teachers. The American Federation of Teachers and the National Education Association have been instrumental in seeking improved salaries; but NCTE, IRA, and the American Association of School Librarians (AASL) have addressed such critical subject issues as the size of classes and the instructional materials needed.

Class size has concerned English teachers for more than 50 years. Certainly, if teachers are to read children's writing regularly and hold conferences with individual children, the number of pupil contacts must be manageable. (Committee on National Interest, 1961). Research has seldom shown that smaller classes result in more effective instruction (Braddock et al., 1963; U.S. Department of Education, 1988), but the effort to demonstrate the importance of a low teacher to pupil ratio continues. Many instructional leaders feel that overly heavy teaching loads contribute to "teacher burnout." Most recognize the importance of teacher–student ratios that permit conferencing. Given that annotation of a single student theme to improve thinking requires at least 10 minutes per theme (Dusel, 1956), secondary school teachers with 105–200 students early found it impossible to assign and annotate papers on a regular basis. Leaders seeking to increase the amount of writing in our classrooms have generally supported smaller classes. Certainly, those who believe in interaction recognized the need for class sizes that stimulate the exchange of ideas. The NCTE repeatedly has resolved in annual convention that no more than four classes of 25 students each be established as a standard teaching load (Hook, 1979). IRA adopted a similar policy at its 1999 convention.

Censorship has been a continuing concern of teachers of literature. Communities have objected even to traditional titles, based at different times on political issues, profanity, morality, ethnic stereotypes, and so on (Jenkinson, 1979). Working especially closely with ALA's Freedom of Information Office, the National Council of Teachers of English throughout its history has insisted that the suitability of any work for student reading must be judged in relation to the student's level of development and in relation to critical appraisals of the worth of the selection (see Applebee, 1974, p. 221). During the 1960s, the Council, under the leadership of Edward Gordon, developed an extended form for parents to request reconsideration of a book—a widely used instrument that did much to decrease casual protests.

In 1961, Squire and others reported that more than 10 million children were attending elementary schools without central libraries, resulting in a widespread effort to create a better collection of books during the next 2 decades (Committee on National Interest, 1961). Today, the concern is less with the libraries and textbooks themselves (most schools have improved schoolwide collections) than with their use and with the supply of books for children from lower socioeconomic groups (Anderson et al., 1985; Chall, 1967).

The importance of providing time for conferencing and adequate staff development, the need for effective supervision, and the importance of reducing interruption to academic instruction are other recent concerns about the conditions of teaching (Committee on National Interest, 1964). A related effort sought to ensure an adequate supply of up-to-date textbooks for all children (Association of American Publishers & National Education Association, 1972; Denham & Lieberman, 1980). Perhaps most important has been the increased awareness during recent years for improving the morale of teachers and for attracting better qualified teachers to the classroom (Anderson et al., 1985; Goodlad, 1985). "Teacher empowerment" was the "buzzword" of the late 1980s, apparent in professional as well as union associations, so much so that at times the term seems to suggest a new sentimentalism. Still, the renewed focus on teaching is overdue (Myers, 1985). And the work of the Holmes Commission and the Carnegie Commission on Teacher Education (1987) seeks to assure schools of better teachers (Olson, 1987). An improvement in salaries and strengthened recruitment efforts have also characterized the recent efforts to achieve excellence in the schools.

## THE INTERNATIONALIZATION OF ENGLISH TEACHING

The early years of the 20th century saw the teaching of English in America, Canada, England, and other English-speaking countries develop almost independently, albeit derived from many British models. But cross-national communication began in earnest after World War II and most of today's teaching is strongly influenced by ideas initiated in other countries. From its inception, the IRA has been international with vigorous professional Canadian leadership and has sponsored a biennial series of international conferences from Singapore to Dublin. TESOL brought together teachers concerned with English as a Second Language (ESL) and English as a First Language (EFL) teaching through the world (Hook, 1979). The formation of the British National Association of Teachers of English (NATE) in 1965, and the Canadian Council of Teachers of English (CCTE) in 1968, provided associations to further cross-national dialogue (See, for example, Squire, 1966). The Anglo American Dartmouth Seminar in 1966 saw the organization of an international steering committee that planned subsequent international conferences such as those held at York University in 1970, Melbourne in 1976, Ottawa in 1978, and Awkland in 1990. An International Federation of English Associations has been formed to maintain communication from country to country and to plan international conferences on a multiyear cycle. International exchanges of beginning teachers have been sponsored by such institutions as the University of Connecticut, Florida State University, and Rutgers; and the National Writing Project at Berkeley has held workshops in three other countries. Further, the International Assessment of Educational Progress, operating out of Stockholm, has provided comparative studies of the teaching of reading, literature, and writing (Purves, 1974; Purves & Takala, 1982; Thorndike, 1974). These efforts have informed teachers of new ideas for teaching the English language arts from every country, and have made available internationally the resources of gifted teachers like Marie Clay in language development, Eva Malmquist in reading, Dorothy Heathcote in drama, James Britton in writing, and Louise Rosenblatt in literature.

## THE EXCELLENCE REFORM MOVEMENT

Alarmed at falling test scores, reports of educational deprivation, and vocal public criticism of American schools, the United States Department of Education in 1983 issued *A Nation at Risk*, a painfully written call for educational reform, lest the nation condemn itself to "drowning in a sea of mediocrity" (National Commission on Excellence, 1983). Supported by 28 major studies of the quality of teaching, the most influential of which were by Goodlad (1985) and Sizer (1986), and an estimated 480 separate task forces and committees appointed by states, professional societies, and large school districts, the "Excellence Reform Movement," as it has been tagged, sought to improve the teaching of basic skills in reading and writing as well as in mathematics and to strengthen the academic content of the school. The Secretary of Eduction publicly introduced the report with support from the President of the United States, and called for an end to "the dumbing down" of textbooks (Bell, 1989). The Holmes Group and a Carnegie Task Force called for reform of teacher education (Carnegie Commission, 1987; Olson, 1987). The National Academy of Education published a monograph on improving reading instruction and reading in content areas (Anderson et al., 1985). Report after report pointed to the significance of writing in improving comprehension and thinking (Graves, 1978). Especially significant has been concern with improving basic literacy for children at risk (Chall, 1985; Venezky, Kaestle, & Sum, 1987). Much of the previous decade's work in writing and thinking and writing across the curriculum led to increased calls for writing in every subject as a way of improving learning (Corbett, 1987; Squire, 1967). Trying to direct attention to outstanding teachers and teaching, the NCTE initiated a Centers of Excellence program to direct attention to classrooms and schools regularly achieving excellence. So focused had been the claims for attention to reading and writing in English classrooms that it appeared for a time that literature might suffer. Articulate advocates of strong programs in literature, however, particularly those seeking programs in traditional literature, began to emphasize the importance of cultural literacy and of familiarizing children and young people with the best that has been known and thought in the world (California State Department of Education, 1987; Hirsch, 1987; Ravitch & Finn, 1987; Squire, 1967). A National Assessment on Cultural Literacy revealed some American children less familiar with Bible stories, legends and myths, and traditional literature than many would wish (Applebee, Langer, & Mullis, 1978).

Widespread as the efforts to promote cultural literacy in the first phase of the reform movement (Westbury & Purves, 1988), falling test scores in reading as well as questionable progress in writing convinced many educators that basic literacy required more direct attention (Snow, 1997). In California, which had been at the forefront in promoting literature-based reading, pupil performance fell from 14th of all states to 48th (Honig, 1996). The reasons are complex and related in part to the decline in consultant staff and the inability of schools to provide assistance to teachers. Many educators, including the former superintendent Honig, felt the declining performance resulted from the lack of attention to longevity competencies.

## PROCESS VERSUS CONTENT

Conflict between the content of English education and the processes of language learning continue to spark professional debate. Do we teach the skills of reading or the process of comprehension? Is rhetoric our subject or the processes of composing? Should we teach literature or focus on response to literature? William Bennett, Secretary of Education in 1987 and 1988, stressed the importance of content in literature as well as in reading and composition (Bennett, 1979), yet a coalition of English Associations (NCTE, MLA, College English Association, CCCC, CEE, and others) meeting for 3 weeks during the summer of 1987, asserted the importance of process in learning language and responding to literature, and the value of looking at instruction in relation to the growing capacities of readers and writers and not in relation to inert content alone. Their report, released in early 1989, stimulated new debate in professional discussion (Lloyd-Jones & Lunsford, 1989).

During the 1990s, spurred by the U.S. Office of Education, professional leaders sought to redefine goals and standards for teaching language and literacy. A clear understanding of outcomes and assessment of the desired outcomes were expected to result in higher quality instruction and curriculum. Through its state and local affiliates, NCTE led by its Executive Director Miles Myers, sponsored scores of regional discussion groups on the conferences (Standards, 1996). And ultimately NCTE and IRA nationally agreed on blueprint standards for developing language and literature.

## VIEWING ENGLISH TEACHING FROM BOOKS

One way of ascertaining current and developing views of the profession of the teaching of the English language arts is to look at widely read books that have defined the role of the teacher at different times. During the past half century, the conception of what a teacher of English is and does appears to have progressed from early, oversentimentalized portraits of Mr. Chips (Hilton, 1934), or Miss Dove (Patton, 1954), to the pixilated Miss Gurney in the popular 1950s television series, "Mr. Peepers," or to Bel Kaufmann's giddy *Up the Down Staircase* (1965), to the repressed sexuality of Blanche Dubois (Williams, 1980). Is it the centrality of our subject in education that leads to so much satirization of English teaching? Two profoundly influential portraits of the elements in a language arts classroom set the standard for a generation of teachers. Lou LaBrant's *We Teach English* (1951) provided an assertion of value for secondary teachers. And Neil Postman and Samuel Weingartner (1969) perhaps best reflected the values of the romantic critics in *Teaching As Subversive Activity*. Important personal credos with respect to teaching English have appeared by Moffett (1968), Macrorie (1970), G. B. Harrison (1962), and others. These views have shaped what thousands of teachers think and feel about the teaching of the English language arts, and, perhaps more accurately than any school survey or research, reflect how many feel about the profession today.

## THE PROFESSION FACES THE FUTURE

Teachers of the English language arts today face new responsibilities as they look at their changing classrooms. The aging white population coupled with increasing minorities in our schools point to critical new priorities. The very young children currently in our society seem to represent a new kind of pluralism. The traditional "ideal" family now embraces only 6% of our households, and two thirds of the world's immigration is still to the United States (Hodgkinson, 1988). Further, the problems of poverty loom large. If we had faced continued problems in teaching basic English skills to the children of poverty (Chall, 1985; Venezky et al., 1987), the fact that 40% of today's children are poor—13 million—necessitates continued attention to literacy (Hodgkinson, 1988). The recent emphasis on strengthening academic requirements may only exacerbate the problems of schooling. We are becoming a nation in which one out of three children is nonwhite. English will remain our national language, but teaching it will be a continued challenge, particularly when tomorrow's language arts classrooms will become steadily more Asian, more Hispanic, more African American, and less white. The growing economic and cultural influence of these nonwhite American cultures should support sound efforts in our schools. But our inability thus far to recruit large numbers of nonwhite teachers, particularly teachers from new American cultural groups, may not bode well for the future. Nor may our persistent concern with a narrow definition of "cultural literacy." At a time when the cultural antecedents of America are changing, our school curriculum in English must also be prepared to change (Harste, 1999). Fortunately, the historical resiliency of teachers of the English language arts and their professional leaders should help to face the challenge.

## References

Aikin, W. M. (1942). *The story of the eight year study*. New York: Harper & Row.

Allen, H. B. (1966). TENES: *A survey of the teaching of English to non-English speakers*, Urbana, IL: National Council of Teachers of English.

Anderson, R. A., Hiebert, E., Scott, J., & Wilkinson, I. (1985). *Becoming a nation of readers*. Champaign, IL: National Academy of Education, National Institute of Education, Center for the Study of Reading.

Applebee, A. (1974). *Tradition and reform in the teaching of English: A history*. Urbana, IL: National Council of Teachers of English.

Applebee, A. (1978). *Writing in the secondary school*. Urbana, IL: National Council of Teachers of English.

Applebee, A., Langer, J., & Mullis, I. (1985). *The reading report card*. Princeton, NJ: Educational Testing Service.

Applebee, A., Langer, J., & Millis, I. (1986a). *Learning to be literate in America*. Princeton, NJ: Educational Testing Service.

Applebee, A., Langer, J., & Mullis, I. (1986b). *The writing report card*. Princeton, NJ: Educational Testing Service.

Applebee, A., Langer, J., & Mullis, I. (1986c). *Writing trends across the decades*. Princeton, NJ: Educational Testing Service.

Applebee, A., Langer, J., & Mullis, I. (1988). *Who can read*. Princeton, NJ: Educational Testing Service.

Association of American Publishers, American Library Association, & the Association for Supervision and Curriculum Development. (1981). *Limiting what students should read*. Washington, DC: Association of American Publishers.

Association of American Publishers, & National Education Association. (1972). *Selecting instructional materials for purchase*. Washington, DC: National Education Association.

Austin, M., Morrison, C., & Kenny, H. J. (1961). *The torchlighters*. Cambridge, MA: Harvard University Press.

Beach, R. (1993). *A teachers introduction to reader response theories*. Urbana, IL: National Council of Teachers of English.

Bell, T. (1989). *The thirteenth man, a Reagan cabinet memoir*. New York: The Free Press.

Bennett, W. (1979). *To reclaim a legacy: A report on the humanities in higher education*. Washington, DC: National Endowment for the Humanities.

Berliner, D. C., & Rosenshine, B. (1977). The acquisition of knowledge in the classroom. In R. C. Anderson, R. J. Spiro, & W. E. Montague (Eds.), *Schooling and the acquisition of knowledge*. Hillsdale, NJ: Lawrence Erlbaum Associates.

Bloom, B. (1982). *Human characteristic and school learning*. New York: McGraw-Hill.

Bond, G., & Dykstra, R. (1967, Winter). The cooperative research programs in first grade reading instruction. *Reading Research Quarterly, 2*, 5–41.

Braddock, R., Lloyd-Jones, R., & Schoer, L. (1963). *Research in written composition*. Urbana, IL: National Council of Teachers of English.

Britton, J. (1970). *Language and learning*. Portsmouth, NH: Heinemann/Boynton.

Britton, J., Martin, N., McLeod, A., & Rosen, H. (1975). *The development of writing abilities*. London: Macmillan.

Broening, A. (1956). *The English language arts in the secondary school*. New York: Appleton-Century-Crofts.

Brooks, C., & Warren, R. P. (1938). *Understanding poetry*. New York: D. Appleton Century.

Bruner, J. (1960). *The process of education*. Cambridge, MA: Harvard University Press.

Burrows, A. T. (1955). Composition: Prospect and retrospect. In H. A. Robinson (Ed.), *Reading and writing instruction in the United States: Historical trends*. Urbana, IL: ERIC and International Reading Association.

California State Department of Education. (1987). *Handbook for planning an effective literature program*. Sacramento, CA: Author.

Carnegie Commission on Teacher Education. (1986, May 21). A nation prepared: Teachers for the 21st century. *Chronicle of Higher Education, 32*, 43-51.

Cazden, C. (1988). *Classroom discourse: The language of teaching and learning*. Portsmouth, NH: Heinemann.

Chall, J. S. (1967). *The great debate*. New York: McGraw-Hill. Also, revised 1984.

Chall, J. S. (1985). *Growth in reading ability*. New York: McGraw-Hill.

Chall, J. S., Conard, S., & Harris, S. (1977). *An analysis of textbooks in relation to falling SAT scores*. New York: College Entrance Examination Board.

Chall, J. S., & Squire, J. R. (1993). Publishing and textbooks. In P. D. Pearson et al. (Eds.), *Handbook of research in reading* (2nd ed.). New York: Longman.

Clapp, J. M. (1926). *The place of English in American life*. Chicago, IL: National Council of Teachers of English.

Coleman, J. (1966). *Equality of educational opportunity*. Washington, DC: U.S. Government Printing Office.

Commission on English. (1931). *Examining the examination in English*. Cambridge, MA: Harvard University Press.

Commission on English. (1965). *Freedom and discipline in English*. New York: College Entrance Examination Board.

Committee on the National Interest. (1961). *The national interest and the teaching of English: A report on the status of the profession*. Urbana, IL: National Council of Teachers of English.

Committee on the National Interest. (1964). *The national interest and the continuing education of teachers: A report on the status of the profession of English*. Urbana, IL: National Council of Teachers of English.

Committee on the Right to Read of National Council of Teachers of English. (1962). *The students' right to read*. Urbana, IL: National Council of Teachers of English.

Conant, J. B. (1959). *The American high school today*. New York: McGraw-Hill.

Cooper, C. (1982). *Researching response to literature and the teaching of literature: Points of departure*. Norwood, NJ: Ablex.

Corbett, E. P. J. (1987). Teaching composition: Where we've been and where we're going. *College Composition and Communication, 38*, 444-452.

Corbin, R., & Crosby, M. (1965). *Language programs for the disadvantaged*. Urbana, IL: National Council of Teachers of English.

Denham, C., & Lieberman, A. (1980). *Time to learn*. Washington, DC: National Institute of Education and U.S. Department of Education.

Durkin, D. (1983). *Is there a match between what elementary teachers do and what basal manuals recommend* (Technical Report No. 44). Urbana, IL: Center for the Study of Reading, University of Illinois.

Dusel, W. (1956). *Determining an efficient load in English*. San Leandro, CA: Central California Council of Teachers of English.

Edmonds, R. (1979). Effective schools for the urban poor. *Educational Leadership, 37*, 15-34.

Emig, J. (1971). *The composing process of twelfth grades*. Urbana, IL: National Council of Teachers of English.

EPIE Institute. (1977). *Report on a national study of the nature and quality of instructional materials most used by teachers*. (EPIE Report No. 78). New York: Educational Products Information Exchange.

Farrell, E. J., & Squire, J. R. (Eds.). (1990). *Transactions with Literature*. Urbana, IL: National Council of Teachers of English.

Fay, R. S. (1968). *The reform movement in English teaching, 1910-1917* (Doctoral dissertation, Harvard University). (University Microfilms No. 68-12,068)

Flood, J. (Ed.). (1984). *Promoting reading comprehension: Cognition, language, and structure of prose*. Newark, DE: International Reading Association.

Frye, N. (1957). *The anatomy of criticism*. Princeton, NJ: Princeton University Press.

Frye, N. (1964). *The educated imagination*. Bloomington, IN: Indiana University Press.

Gerber, J. C. (1963). The 1962 summer institutes of the Commission on English. *PMLA, 78*, 9-25.

Goodlad, J. (1985). *A place called school*. New York: McGraw-Hill.

Goodman, K. S., Freeman, S., Murphy, S., & Shannon, P. (1988). *Basal reader report card*. Des Moines, IA: Richard Owen.

Graves, D. F. (1978). *Balance the basics and let them write*. New York: Ford Foundation.

Gray, J. (1987). *The Bay Area writing project, model of university-school collaboration*. Berkeley: University of California.

Gray, W. S. (1933, February). Summary of reading investigations. *Journal of Educational Research, 21*, 401-424. (Published annually in this journal until 1960 and thereafter by International Reading Association).

Grommon, A. H. (1963). The education of teachers of English for American schools and colleges. New York: Appleton-Century-Crofts.

Grommon, A. H. (1968). A history of the preparation of teachers of English. *The English Journal, 57*(4), 484-527.

Hanna, P., Hanna, J. S., Hodges, R. E., & Rudolph, Jr., E. H. (1966). *Phonemegrapheme correspondencies as cues to spelling improvement*. Washington, DC: U.S. Department of Health, Education, and Welfare.

Harrison, G. B. (1962). *The profession of English*. New York: Harcourt, Brace, & World.

Hatfield, W. W. (Ed.). (1935). *An experience curriculum in English*. New York: D. Appleton-Century.

Harste, J. (1999). *Curriculum, multiple literacies, and democracy: What if English/language arts teachers really cared?* 1999 Presidential address at NCTE, Denver, CO.

Hays, E. (1936). College entrance requirements in English: Their effects on the high schools. *Contributions to Education, No. 675*. New York: Teachers College, Columbia University.

Heath, S. B. (1983). *Ways with words*. Cambridge, England: Cambridge University Press.

Her Majesty's Stationery Office. (1975). *A language for life: Report of the committee of inquiry under chairmanship of Sir Alan Bullock*. London: Author.

Herndon, J. (1971). *The way it's spozed to be*. New York: Simon & Schuster.

Hillocks, G. (1972). *Alternatives in English: A critical appraisal of elective programs*. Urbana, IL: National Council of Teachers of English.

Hilton, J. (1934). *Goodbye Mr. Chips*. Boston: Little, Brown.

Hirsch, E. D. (1987). *Cultural literacy*. Boston: Houghton Mifflin.

Hodgkinson, H. L. (1988, October). Using demographic data for long range planning, *Phi Delta Kappan, 70,* 166–170.

Honig, W. (1996). *Teaching our children to read: The importance of skills in a comprehensive reading programs.* Thousand Oaks, CA: Corwin Press.

Hook, J. N. (1979). *A long way together.* Urbana, IL: National Council of Teachers of English.

Hosic, J. F. (1917). *Reorganization of English in the secondary schools.* (Bulletin No. 2). Washington, DC: Government Printing Office.

Hosic, J. F. (1921). The National Council of Teachers of English. *English Journal, 10*(1), 1–10.

Institutional Tracking Service. (1980). Reading/language arts. White Plains, NY: Author.

Jenkinson, E. B. (1979). *Censors in the classroom: The mind benders.* Carbondale, IL: Southern Illinois University Press.

Jerrolds, R. W. (1977). *Reading reflections: The history of the International Reading Association.* Newark, DE: International Reading Association.

Jewett, A. (1958). *English language arts in American high schools* (Bulletin No. 13). Washington, DC: U.S. Office of Education.

Jewett, A. (1964). *Improving the English skills of culturally different youth.* Washington, DC: U.S. Department of Health, Education, and Welfare.

Judd, C. H., & Buswell, G. T. (1922). *Silent reading.* Chicago, IL: University of Chicago.

Kaufmann, B. (1965). *Up the down staircase.* Englewood Cliffs, NJ: Prentice Hall.

Kozol, J. (1968). *Death at an early age.* Boston: Houghton Mifflin.

LaBrant, L. L. (1951). *We teach English.* New York: Harcourt Brace.

LaBrant, L. L. (1961). The uses of communication media. In M. Willis (Ed.), *The guinea pigs grow up.* Columbus, OH: Ohio University Press.

Langer, J. (1944). A response-approach to the teaching of literature. Albany: Center for English Learning and Achievement, State University of New York.

Langer, S. (1942). *Philosophy in a new key.* Cambridge, MA: Harvard University Press.

Lloyd-Jones, R., & Lunsford, A. (1989). *The English coalition conference: Democracy through language.* Urbana, IL: National Council of Teachers of English and Modern Language Association.

Loban, W. D. (1976). *Language development: Kindergarten through grade twelve* (Research Report No. 18). Urbana, IL: National Council of Teachers of English.

Lynch, J., & Evans, B. (1983). *High school English textbooks: A critical examination.* Boston: Little, Brown.

Mackintosh, H. K. (1954). *Language arts for today's children.* New York: Appleton-Century-Crofts.

Macrorie, K. (1970). *Uptaught.* New York: Hayden.

Marckwardt, A. H. (1963). Research in the teaching of English language and linguistics (a summary). In R. W. Rogers (Ed.), *Proceedings of the Allerton Park Conference on Research in the Teaching of English.* Unpublished U.S.O.E. Project #G-1006.

Mason, J. (1960a). *The National Council of Teachers of English— 1911–1926.* Unpublished doctoral dissertation, George Peabody College of Education. (University Microfilms No. 62-5681).

Mason, J. (1960b). The teaching of literature in American high schools, 1885–1900. In R. C. Pooley (Ed.), *Perspectives in English.* New York: Appleton-Century-Crofts.

Mason, J., & Osborn, J. (1983). *When do children begin reading to learn. A survey of practices in grades two to five* (Technical Report No. 261). Urbana, IL: Center for the Study of Reading, University of Illinois.

Mavrogenes, N. A. (1985). *William Scott Gray: Leader of teachers and shaper of American reading instruction.* Unpublished doctoral dissertation, University of Chicago.

McLuhan, M. (1964). *Understanding media: The extensions of man.* New York: McGraw-Hill.

Modern Language Association, National Council of Teachers of English, College English Association, & American Studies Association. (1959). The basic issues in the teaching of English. *PMLA, 74,* 1–12.

Moffett, J. (1968). *Teaching in a universe of discourse.* Boston, MA: Houghton Mifflin.

Moffett, J. (1988). *Storm in the mountains: A case study of censorship, conflict, and consciousness.* Carbondale, IL: Southern Illinois University Press.

Moffett, J., & Wagner, B. J. (1976). *A student centered language arts curriculum, grades K-12* (2nd ed.). Boston: Houghton Mifflin.

Muller, H. (1967). *The uses of English.* New York: Holt, Rinehart, & Winston.

Murray, D. (1986). *Writing to learn.* New York: Holt, Rinehart, & Winston.

Myers, M. (1985). The need for a new professionalism. In M. Chorny (Ed.), *Teacher as learner* (pp. 107–120). Calgary, Alberta: Language in Curriculum Project, University of Calgary.

National Commission on Excellence. (1983). *A nation at risk: The imperative for educational reform.* Washington, DC: U.S. Department of Education.

Norvell, G. (1950). *The reading interests of young people.* Boston: D.C. Heath.

Olson, J. W. (1969). The nature of literature anthologies in the teaching of high school English, 1917–1957. Unpublished doctoral dissertation, University of Wisconsin. (University Microfilms No. 69-22-454).

Olson, L. (1987). An overview of the Holmes Group. *Phi Delta Kappan, 68,* 619–621.

O'Rourke, L. J. (1934). *Rebuilding the English curriculum to involve greater mastery of essentials.* Washington, DC: The Psychological Institute.

Patton, F. (1954). *Good morning, Miss Dove.* New York: Dodd Mead.

Pearson, P. D., Barr, R., Kamil, M., & Mosenthal, P. (Eds.). (1984). *Handbook of research on reading.* New York: Longman.

Petty, W. J. (1983). *A history of the national conference on research in English.* Urbana, IL: National Council of Teachers of English.

Piche, G. L. (1967). *Revision and reform in secondary school English curriculum 1870–1900.* Unpublished doctoral dissertation, University of Minnesota.

Pooley, R. C. (1946). *Teaching English usage.* New York: Appleton-Century-Crofts.

Postman, N., & Weingartner, S. (1969). *Teaching as a subversive activity.* New York: Delacorte.

Purves, A. C. (1974). *Literature education in ten countries.* New York: Wiley.

Purves, A., & Beach, R. (1972). *Literature and the reader.* Urbana, IL: National Council of Teachers of English.

Purves, A. C. et al. (Eds.). (1973). *Responding—A literature program for grades 7-12.* Boston, MA: Ginn.

Purves, A. C., & Takala, S. (1982). An international perspective on the evaluation of written composition. In A. C. Purves & S. Takala (Eds.), *Evaluation in education: An international review series* (pp. 207–290). New York: Pergamon Press.

Ravitch, D., & Finn, C. E. (1987). *What do our seventeen-year olds know? A Report on the First National Assessment of History and Literature.* New York: Harper & Row.

Ravitch, D. (Ed.). (1995). *Debating the future of American standards.* Washington, DC: The Brookings Institute.

Richards, I. A. (1929). *Practical criticism.* New York: Harcourt Brace.

Robinson, H. A., Faraone, V., Hittleman, D., Unruh, E. (1990). *Reading comprehension instruction 1783-1987*. Newark, DE: International Reading Association.

Robinson, H. A. (Ed.). (1977). *Reading and writing instruction in the United States: Historical trends*. Urbana, IL: ERIC and International Reading Association.

Rosenblatt, L. (1938). *Literature as exploration*. New York: Progressive Education Association. 4th ed., Modern Language Association, 1982.

Rosenblatt, L. (1978). *The reader, the text, and the poem*. Carbondale, IL: Southern Illinois University.

Rosenshine, B., & Stevens, R. (1984). Classroom instruction in reading. In P. D. Pearson (Ed.), *Handbook of research on reading*. New York: Longman.

Rosewall, P. T. (1965). *A historical survey of recommendations and proposals for the literature curricula of American secondary schools since 1892*. Lincoln: University of Nebraska.

Searles, J. F. (1942). *Some trends in the teaching of literature since 1900 in American high schools*. Unpublished doctoral dissertation, University of Wisconsin.

Shaughnessy, M. (1977). *Errors and expectations: A guide for teachers of writing*. New York: Oxford University Press.

Shugrue, M. F. (1968). *English in a decade of change*. New York: Pegasus.

Shugrue, M., & Everett, E. (1968). English teacher preparation study. *English Journal, 57*(4), 475-483.

Simmons, J. S., Shadiow, L., & Shafer, R. E. (1990). History of the teaching of English in the United States. In R. E. Shafer, J. Britton, & K. Watson (Eds.), *Teaching and learning English worldwide*. Clevedon, Avon, England: Multilingual Matters, Ltd.

Sizer, T. (1986). *Horace's compromise*. Boston: Houghton Mifflin.

Smith, D. V. (1932). *Instruction in English* (Bureau of Education, Bulletin No. 17). Washington, DC: U.S. Government Printing Office.

Smith, D. V. (1939). *Evaluating instruction in secondary school English*. New York: Appleton-Century-Crofts.

Smith, D. V. (1941). *Evaluating instruction in secondary school English*, Chicago: National Council of Teachers of English.

Smith, D. V. (Ed.). (1952). *The English language arts*. New York: Appleton-Century-Crofts.

Smith, F. (1971). *Psycholinguistics and reading*. New York: Holt, Rinehart, & Winston.

Smith, N. B. (1985, 1934). *American reading instruction*. Newark, DE: International Reading Association.

Snow, C. (1997). *Preventing reading difficulties*. Boston, MA: National Academy on Education.

Squire, J. R. (1963). College English departments and professional efforts to improve English teaching. *PMLA, 78* (4), 36-38.

Squire, J. R. (1964). *The response of adolescents to four short stories*. Urbana, IL: National Council of Teachers of English.

Squire, J. R. (1966). *A common purpose*. Urbana, IL: National Council of Teachers of English.

Squire, J. R. (1967). English at the crossroads: The national interest report plus eighteen. *The English Journal, 52*(6), 381-397.

Squire, J. R. (Ed.). (1987). The state of assessment in reading. *The Reading Teacher, 40* (themed issue).

Squire, J. R. (1999). Language arts. In G. Cawelti, *Handbook of research on improving student achievement*. Arlington, VA: *Education*.

Squire, J. R. (1988). Studies of textbooks: Are we asking the right questions. In P. Jackson (Ed.), *Contributing to educational change*. Berkeley, CA: McCutchan.

Squire, J. R., & Applebee, A. (1968). *High school English instruction today: The national study of high school English*. New York: Appleton-Century-Crofts.

Squire, J. R., & Applebee, A. (1969). *Teaching English in the United Kingdom*. Urbana, IL: National Council of Teachers of English.

*Standards for the English language arts*. (1996). Urbana, IL: National Council of Teachers of English and International Reading Association.

Stahl, D. (1965). *A history of the English curriculum in American high schools*. Chicago, IL: Lyceum Press.

Stahl, S. A., & Miller, P. D. (1988). *The language experience approach for beginning reading*. Unpublished research report, Western Illinois University, Macomb, IL.

Stormzand, M. J., & O'Shea, M. V. (1924). *How much English grammar?* Baltimore: Warwick & York.

Strickland, R. (1962). *The language development of children, its relationship to the language of reading textbooks, and the quality of reading of selected school children*. Bloomington, IN: School of Education, Indiana University.

Strickland, R. (1969). *Language arts in the elementary* school (3rd ed.). Boston: D.C. Heath.

Thorndike, R. (1974). *Reading education in ten countries*. New York: Wiley.

U.S. Department of Education. (1988). *Class size and public policy: Politics and panaceas*. Washington, DC: Author.

Valenica, S., & Pearson, P. D. (1987). Time for a change. *The Reading Teacher, 40,* 726-733.

Veith, D. P. (1952). *A historical analysis of the relations between English and speech since 1910*. Unpublished doctoral dissertation, Teacher College, Columbia University, New York.

Venezky, R. L. (1984). History of reading research. In P. D. Pearson (Ed.), *Handbook of research on reading* (pp. 3-35). New York: Longman.

Venezky, R. L., Kaestle, C. F., & Sum, A. M. (1987). *The subtle danger.* Princeton, NJ: Educational Testing Service.

Wellek, R., & Warren, R. (1949). *Theory of literature*. New York: Harcourt Brace.

Westbury, A., & Purves, A. (1988). Cultural literacy and the idea of general education. *National Society for the Study of Education Eighty-Seventh Yearbook, Part II*. Chicago: University of Chicago Press.

Wilkinson, A. (1970). The concept of oracy. *English Journal, 59,* 70-77.

Williams, T. (1980). *A streetcar named desire*. New York: New Directions.

# HISTORICAL CONSIDERATIONS:
# AN INTERNATIONAL PERSPECTIVE

## John Dixon
### Educational Consultant

### History as Living Present

> I went to a one-room school through eighth grade. We had countywide examinations, the purpose of which I am not quite sure [about]. What I do recall is that it was a real feather in a teacher's cap to have his or her eighth-grade pupils score at or near the top of that list. At any rate, the other eighth-grade students and I spent every afternoon of the last two months of the school year in the entryway asking each other questions from every standardized achievement test that the teachers could get their hands on. I have no doubt that every other entry to every other one-room school was similarly occupied by eighth graders hot in pursuit of the knowledge embedded in standardized tests.
>
> Robert Dykstra (1987)

History invites us both to record what happened and to ask why. It suggests we study small-scale institutions, like classrooms, and ask how what goes in them is related to what goes on in bigger institutions, like school boards, subject associations, state legislatures, national offices of education—and, wider still, in the society at large, or internationally.

Why did Robert Dykstra's teachers take county tests so seriously? What alternatives had they access to? What power had they, individually or as a group, to propose an alternative? How common was their experience? What, if anything, has happened since in that county to change the tests, the alternatives, or who has power to decide? What conflicts, if any, have there been over different models of education? History invites you to ask such questions.

Once you begin to ask them, and only then, historical research becomes usable, fascinating, and never-ending. This brief article must start, then, by prompting you to look at what's going on in your classroom, in your school and board, and to ask questions; to realize that you, like Robert Dykstra, are a part of history and therefore need to ask how you were formed as a student, and equally, perhaps, how you are being formed as a teacher now.

## FORMATIVE EXPERIENCES OF
## THE OLDER GENERATION

Retired teachers roughly aged 70 (and I am one of them) went to school in the 1930s and early 1940s: in the Depression years, for the most part. The times were hard, with little cash for education. They reached their teens during a world war; some of the oldest fought in it. Education faced specific, narrow demands. Many went to college immediately after the war, however, and with luck caught the feeling that humanity was capable after all of building a better world.

Looking into a sample of their schools in the 1930s, Dora V. Smith saw "methods conditioned by desks nailed to the floor"; it is a powerful image. "Question and answer procedures with the teacher in command, and recitation around the class of sentences written out at home the night before represent by far the most common activities of the average high school class in New York State" (1941). "Regimentation of pupils was the rule; individualization, the exception." For a handful to be sent out into the entry to ask each other questions, then, would still have been a radical innovation.

Literature was the major element in English courses for the secondary schools (Applebee, 1974). In half the junior high schools, this meant the study of a literary anthology textbook, which successive presidents of the National Council of Teachers of English (NCTE) worked hard to write and disseminate, in order to encourage wider reading. Unfortunately, in many cases that one anthology was all the school could afford in the 1930s. It easily became the dominating book, and its assignments the inevitable goal of reading. In New York, 60% of teachers in Dora Smith's 1941 sample testified that what determined their classroom practices was the textbook available, not the official course of study.

Senior high school kept to the study of classic works; half the schools in a national sample had no other method of organizing the course, just the list of texts (Smith, 1933). Following the recent "unit" method, schools would give up on average 4 weeks to the study of *Julius Caesar, Macbeth*, or *As You Like It*, for instance; some allowed as much as 9 weeks for the one text. Of the 30 most frequently used texts, not one was contemporary.

What was the force behind this curriculum? It was the early traditions of college entrance exams. Apart from the omission of the "Bunker Hill Oration," 25 to 40 years had passed "with little change in the requirements except to add a few more titles in kind plus the nineteenth century novel" and possibly an 11th grade program in American literature. In 1931, the College Entrance Examination Board found that the best two predictors of college achievement were the new Scholastic Achievement Test, on the one hand, and the high school record, on the other. Read candidly, this result might have suggested radical change in their own examinations. But, though their "restricted text exam" finally was set aside 10 years later, they still hung on, like colleagues elsewhere in the English-speaking world, to their right to "test the candidate's ability to paraphrase or to make a precis, or to interpret the subtler qualities of a poem read at sight," by whatever methods their examiners were accustomed to.

Also in 1931, the Board concluded that English teachers in the lower levels "cannot afford to ignore the value of these [standardized] tests in classroom work" and recommended "recurrent" practice throughout the year. (So young Dykstras were actually getting off lightly.)

For Dora Smith, "no impression remains more vivid after conferences with hundreds of teachers throughout the country than the fear [sic] under which they labor because of the requirements (real or imaginary) of the institutions higher up" (1933). A characteristic result was "deadly and uninteresting routine" (1941).

## A Model of External Domination

Teachers and students were dominated, then, by higher institutions, by textbooks or set texts, and by tests or exams. How could this model be so widespread? After all, since its foundation in 1911 NCTE had given the various "clubs" and "associations" of English teachers both a national voice and a forum for discussion. In the 1930s alone, the pages of "English Journal" had been open to many new ideas, including:

• The Committee for Film or "Photoplay Appreciation" (beginning 1932).
• The early work of the Radio Committee (beginning 1936).
• An invited series, for instance, on Hemingway, Dos Passos, and contemporary Left-Wing literature in 1933. (Applebee, 1974).

In a major report in 1936, NCTE recommended, among other things, the abandonment of formal grammar teaching, except as an elective for seniors, and a curriculum based on "selected experiences," each unit forming an "organic whole." (Hatfield, 1935).

A minority of classrooms were affected by these and other "progressive" ideas, as we shall see, but the majority were not. To realize why, takes an act of historical imagination. First, let's imagine the social constraints: whole regions thrown onto the poverty line or starvation; more than one in three unemployed and job opportunities shrivelling; savage cutting of salaries and funds for education—the days "of crisis and chaos" with which the 1930s began (DeBoer, 1932). Thus, within that ambience, the inexorable clinging on to recognizable results: success with college entry tests.

Consider then the teachers and their preparation, solidly based on college Anglo-Saxon and Middle English, for a start; on an academic tradition modelled on the study of the ancient classics. Admittedly, a sizable minority had the initiative to set up flourishing extracurricular programs in drama, journalism and debate; there was still no feedback, however, about their work in class. After all, what recognition would such activities get in standardized tests for college entrance, "an examination system that takes cognizance chiefly of facts and skills" (Smith, 1941).

Teachers who persisted had "to meet, study and assimilate several new psychologies, at least one new sociology, and a score of isms. We have had to grapple with such concepts as 'the child centred school,' the activity program, the socialized recitation, the project method, correlation, two- and three-track plans, and the unit plan . . . all movements . . . [that] have added immeasurably to the science and art of teaching" (Pooley, 1939). Against "local insistence upon more formal elements of instruction," and without adequate institutions to prepare themselves for revolutionary changes in class, most teachers, not surprisingly, felt a growing chasm between practice and theory, which they were powerless to deal with (Applebee, 1974).

Historical circumstances like these have almost inevitable outcomes. Without special support, teachers (like students) learn to accept the targets set them from above, and getting through the textbook assignments becomes yet another imposed task, for teachers as well as students. Thus, authority comes to rest in tests and exams, and status depends on who comes out on top. It is a model of external domination—but then, for over a decade, almost everyone felt inescapably fettered and chained by economic and social forces. You had to learn to endure.

If you had support and unusual enterprise, you joined the groups who resisted: who escaped the "serfdom" of college entrance by exam, who struggled to democratize school and classroom, who looked for "experiences" relevant to adolescents, who took modern, American literature and media seriously. But with so much to learn at once, only exceptional teachers and students could swim against the tide, and then with difficulty.

## Alternative Models in the 1930s

When Dora V. Smith spotted the desks nailed to the floor, she clearly had other possibilities in mind—desks (or chairs) that could be moved, grouped and arranged according to the classroom activity. Her critical observer role (like ours today) depended on a knowledge of alternatives that had been important in her own formation.

Indeed, from the 1910s there had been a concerted movement across the English-speaking world to escape from the limited horizons—and achievements—of a test-dominated model. Here, for example, is a liberal inspector in the United Kingdom Board of Education describing the kind of elementary school practices that he and his colleagues were hoping to promote in 1914:

The good modern school will have a generous course in English. The children will not only be taught to read aloud, but will have plenty of practice, in *reading for enjoyment and for information* . . . [The] children will read *six or seven [books] or even more* in each year, and those supplied to the older children will include standard books in travel and fiction . . . Children will be taught to consult books for reference and in their later years will *look up and prepare the subject matter of their essays themselves.* Composition, a starved subject under the old conditions . . . will be practised throughout the school, *orally or in written form* or both, and the children will take as naturally to *recording their ideas* with the pen as to uttering them in speech . . . [In] all the best schools, much will be made of English poetry, no longer in the shape of a formal recitation lesson, but by the children reading and learning numerous poems *often chosen by themselves* (from personal archives; my emphases).

The stress is on real books (not practice readers); on recording their own ideas (not reproducing the teacher's or the text's), using speech (as well as writing); on choosing poems individually, and on preparing subject matter by themselves (not being told by teacher). Clearly, behind this model there is a whole new philosophy. (See also the chapter by Goodman on alternative modes of testing, this edition.)

In the 1910s and immediately after World War I, there were international exchanges and practical contributions to a model along these lines. At that time the Child Study movement with Froebel, Montessori, and others gradually had set up a wide interest in children's development, in their questions and responses, the stories and poems they became involved in, their ways of thinking, and the choices they were capable of making. New ideas on adolescence spreading through the United States from the 1900s, raised questions about the ways high school subjects like English might be affecting a vital phase in students' lives. New aspirations for active participation in democracy (Dewey, 1916) promoted a move to individual rather than class work, and to extensions of student choice and autonomy. All this was submerged in the classrooms of the Depression years, surviving only as a minority aspiration.

## INTERLUDE: COLLEGE AND SCHOOLS IN THE FIFTIES

Most of us 70-year-olds went through college in the 1940s just before another revolution, the "new criticism." By the early 1950s, according to Welleck (1953), it predominated among younger staff members in the United States and would come to dominate graduate training, sweeping aside the historical, philological, and genre courses that had originally won English studies a place in the university. So some of our generation may have felt themselves no sooner graduated than obsolete.

About the same period, academic critics opened up on the progressive movement: *Crisis in Education* (Bell, 1949), *Quackery in the Public Schools* (Lynd, 1953), *Educational Wastelands* (Bestor, 1955). The call from college was for "minds made free by discipline" (Applebee, 1974). Finally, as the Cold War intensified and political witch hunts began, progressivism was linked with "communism."

In line with a new focus on the academically gifted, the Advanced Placement Program was established, including from 1955 a series of exams. In English, these immediately established textual analysis and "new" criticism as major new goals (for underprepared teachers).

In 1957, however, the growing excitement in the United States about courses for "Students of Superior Ability" turned into a wave of shock: the Soviet Union had launched the first rocket into space, the Sputnik. "Only massive upgrading of the scholastic standards of our schools will guarantee the future prosperity and freedom of the Republic" wrote Admiral Rickover (1958). How would a new generation respond?

## FORMATIVE EXPERIENCES OF TEACHERS NOW IN THEIR PRIME

This generation went to school in the 1960s and early 1970s, during a worldwide economic boom. In their early years money, was thrown—recklessly at times—into new education projects to try to secure "massive upgrading" of standards. Yet while they were still in elementary school, the nation fell into turmoil, positively through the Civil Rights movement, negatively through the war in Vietnam. Volunteer, be conscripted, or protest? This group faced inexorable choices, the men especially. For some of the women, on the other hand, there were new horizons, through the resurgence of the Women's Rights Movement. But before this age group were all through college in the 1970s, the advanced capitalist economies felt the first jolt in what was to become a long-term crisis of overproduction.

Surveying the best of their high schools in the mid-1960s, Jim Squire and Roger Applebee found "little reason for rejoicing" (1968). Each school had been selected because of outstanding English students (generally NCTE award winners) but, significantly, that gave little indication of the strength of the English department. For this reason, the mainstream practices and norms that were observed probably stand for what was then going on in many average to above average schools across the country.

Half the class time was spent in literary studies. *Macbeth* and *Julius Caesar* were studied in half the college preparatory classes; *Hamlet*, *Silas Marner*, *The Scarlet Letter*, *A Tale of Two Cities*, and *The Return of the Native*, in 40%. In these classes, then, authors were still dead, and formed a rather odd canon. But with two-, three- and five-track systems of instruction there was wide variation in the texts on offer. (Was it because of the *teachers'* formative experiences that, after Shakespeare, *The Grapes of Wrath* was the next "most significant text" listed by students?)

How about the teaching? Research observers attended, more often than not, talks by the teacher (or a student) on the age in which the work was written, the writer, the literary genre (in abstraction from the given text), or simply isolated facts. Analytical reading (dealing with a play line by line, for example) were rare: When it happened, the observers noted, it often lead to a more emotional response with greater sophistication.

Associated with these talks, there were oral questions from the teacher that were often self-defeating, curtailing discussion and interest, and were frequently answered by the teachers themselves. Students were expected to accept the thematic interpretation, to answer an assigned series of questions, and possibly to follow a mimeographed study guide.

As well as factual quizzes on the text, there were writing assignments. Much of the writing was superficial. Some questions invited imaginative construction beyond the text ("William Dane confesses . . .")—a "questionable" approach, according to the observers, who were happier to report the national impact of advanced placement tests. The latter ensured that, in honors classes at least, the analytical study of a particular poem or passage was attempted.

After a decade of pressure for advanced academic courses, targeted on the "gifted" (i.e., the students most able to teach themselves and each other), how can these classroom practices be explained? Perhaps the answer lay in the model of reform itself. A test-led change in classroom practices still leaves teachers passive and dominated by external demands. Outstanding individuals escape, it's true, but the majority feel no energies released in *them* for changing habitual ways of working with students. And without workshop discussion and practice, there was no vehicle for such changes at the time. This helps to explain the important finding that "outstanding" teaching had not

spread throughout a department; it could only do so if teachers were accustomed to taking joint initiatives and organizing work together.

The results of a test-led curriculum were inevitably most clearly observable in writing instruction. Little or no thought was being given as to how a student's writing ability could be improved. Thus "for most teachers [in the sample], correcting papers is synonymous with teaching writing." Actually one third of papers collected were not corrected, and in a further third corrections were limited to gross errors in spelling and usage. Only 17% of the teachers said that their comments were designed to teach writing and thinking.

What teachers had learned from testing was a negative point of view, a search for student error. But this was reinforced by the composition–grammar texts they used: these had twice as many pages on grammar, usage, and mechanics as on units beyond the sentence. Many teachers had rejected the books available, according to the observers, but not, it seems, the stance.

The remaining 30% or so of the time in class was spent on "confused" language programs, on developmental reading programs, or (occasionally) on speech. Confusion over language was only to be expected: Lynch and Evans (1963) had found that most textbooks taught the same content at every grade level. As to reading development, while department chairs agreed that the fundamental purpose was to help students become active and critical readers, the only vehicle widely used was the packaged system, a prescribed set of texts and assignments.

By contrast, when this age group entered college in the early 1970s, they found the profession split. Radical questions were being asked: "The subject of English in this country has been used to inculcate a white, Anglo-Saxon, Protestant ethic . . . My own feeling is that the game is just about played out" (Fisher, 1969).

Colleges responded in the early 1970s by adopting a mixed program. On the one hand, they added new electives: women's studies, African American literature, ethnic literatures, film studies, psychoanalysis and literature, the literature of adolescence, science fiction. On the other hand, they preserved the standard period studies, either as a requirement or an advised course for the English major (Ohmann, 1976). Presumably, it was this evasion of theoretical issues that opened the floodgates in the 1980s.

These, then, were some of the formative experiences of the generation now in their prime. Naturally, there was variation (for better, and for worse); but the pattern above is easily recognizable to a teacher in the 1950s and early 1960s, whether in Australia, Canada, or the United Kingdom. In those countries, the focus on academic students and exam targets was probably more insistent, if anything, and the practices that resulted were in many ways comparable.

In retrospect, one might say that there was a price to be paid for the 1950s' aggressive rejection of "progressive" aspirations, of their quest for individual choice, for student (and teacher) autonomy, for independent projects, and for active learning. The staleness of many high school programs was perhaps a significant factor in shaping the outbreak of radical, even anarchic, college protest that spread across the United States in the later 1960s, and linked up with other, worldwide movements.

## A NEW MODEL EMERGING

So far I have taken two generations of teachers, and briefly sketched some mainstream traditions that may have shaped their current practices. In retrospect, U.S. observers of the 1930s and the 1960s clearly pointed to a model of dominated teaching, whether by tests, textbooks, or canonical texts. Indeed, over the same period, it would not be difficult to present evidence showing the same model at work throughout the English-speaking world. Not surprisingly, then, there are currently teachers, departments, and even whole regions still working to that model (generally under the new banner of an "objectives-driven" curriculum, "objectively measured").

Equally, during the past 2 or 3 decades, some readers will have experienced, however briefly, a sharply opposed model of teaching, in terms of:

- The purposes of teacher–student (and student–student) dialogue (Barnes, 1976).
- The initiatives allowed for in student writing, and the roles of teacher and fellow students in response to what's written (Britton, 1967; Emig, 1971; Graves, 1983).
- The multicultural choices and purposes underlying what is read, listened to, or viewed, and the active roles taken by students in such "readings" and the discussions that follow (Meek, Wardlow, & Barton, 1977, Thompson, 1987).
- The place of speech (oracy), role play, and drama within such work (Heathcote, 1980) [All references could be multiplied.]

Taken singly, these changes have their parallels and forerunners in exceptional classrooms of the earlier period, especially in elementary schools. What is significantly different today is the kind of theoretical frame available to integrate the planning, practices, and evaluation of English "lessons." Even in the last 2 decades, new ways have been discovered of making explicit—and thus differentiating among—students' achievements in using speech and writing for personal and social ends. (And in consequence, there has been a devastating critique of traditional assumptions behind "measuring" instruments.)

Even more important, however, has been the breakthrough in forms of teacher education. Extended "workshops," summer schools, writing (and reading) project networks have developed forms in which teacher-students make active contributions, experiencing for themselves the break from dominated classrooms. Since the 80s some teachers have become partners in research, and empowered teachers in turn empower their students (Boomer, 1982).

In most countries, these changes affect a minority. It is easier and cheaper for central administrators in the advanced economies to apply tests, make international comparisons, and, in a period of economic depression, to call on teachers nationally for better "output." So, in societies with greater wealth than ever before, an historical struggle continues. Will education, perhaps the central example today of social enterprise, win through to a new plateau in the "western democracies"? This history is still in the making, and, whether active or passive, we are part of it right now.

## REFLECTIONS IN THE YEAR 2000

"Will education . . . win through to a new plateau," or not? The question still stands, a decade later, and in parts of the UK, Australia, and Canada, the answer today is decidedly more pessimistic. Why is that so? What has happened in the wider societies to swing the balance against the emerging model? If we don't face that question, I believe, any strategies for changing the teaching of English will hold out little hope of success.

First, Australia, Canada, and the UK have suffered critical economic setbacks in the 1990s; in response they have become dependent economies, relying on multinational firms to bring in new capital and enterprise. Thus, whether at the state or national level, governments are aiming to provide a skilled workforce shaped to attract new business. That's the new international message. This does imply a massive investment in education, it's true, bringing university degrees and diplomas within reach of the majority in those coutries, for the first time. But at a price. In the education ministries the technocrats ride high, and their ideology focuses on "student output," "measurable standards" and "teacher/school efficiency." At its worst—in England and Wales—a top-down model turns ministers into managers of the biggest firm in the country, resolutely laying down curricular requirements, testing the outcomes (at 7, 11, 13, and 16), putting schools into league tables, and calling those at the bottom to account. Target standards are set, and just in case schools don't meet them, national packages—for "literacy" and "numeracy"—are promulgated. The model will be recognizable, I assume, in several states of the U.S. where it was pioneered. And ironically, with the United States riding a long economic boom, technocratic models are widely endorsed, politicians being more interested in spreading standardized tests than in investing in a drive for greater creativity in education.

However, as we agreed at IFTE 1999, there's still widespread conflict within the prevailing ideology. After all, this same workforce is already beginning to face a further revolution in electronic communication, and who knows what lies beyond that a decade on? Ministers in the leading industrial countries recognize that they depend on a national climate of "innovation" and "adaptability." Widespread 'resourcefulness' and 'enterprise' are actually vital, if their states are to ride a crescendo of complex, volatile, and unpredictable changes, not only economic, but cultural and social too. Thus, it's not surprising that France has recently instituted a drive for "student autonomy" and "local flexibility"; the Netherlands, after a fierce struggle, is heading in the same direction; and the recent Japanese report on "The Frontier Within" passionately urges education to pursue "personal and creative self-realization."

With the media (propelled by information technology) as massively growing enterprises, what does all this imply for students of English—and their teachers, across an ever-expanding world of English-speakers? Politicians have hardly begun to ask such questions: They are currently trapped in the short term. But it's not impossible to foresee a phase beyond their current naive managerialism. Over the next decade, aren't we likely to see some English-speaking states thinking again about the suppression of teacher/student initiatives and enterprise—in the longer term interests of their workforce. When they do, one or two ministries will gain an edge by striking new alliances with the subject assocations. Politicians will be forced to harness teachers' pioneering energies again, simply to leaven the lump the ministries themselves are creating. And when one state or country starts, the rest may well be goaded to follow.

If so, there's still a serious challenge to our several associations, and to IFTE in particular. Can English stay static, locked in models of the 70s and 80s, as it often is? What about the overlaps with drama, media and cultural studies: How can we place and relate this emerging new domain? And how are we to reconstruct that central category, literature? Here's a real test to our own abilities to pioneer and adapt. What's more, in an era of increasing globalization and Internet dialogue, it seems ridiculous for any national association to go it alone.

The answer isn't going to be easy. We certainly can't look to the universities for anything like consensual guidelines. So that major project needs time and deliberation on the widest scale. But meanwhile I suggest there are two domains where answers are more readily available internationally. Suppose we raise again the question put by Jimmy Britton to the first international conference, Dartmouth 1966, "What at our best have we (and our students) been doing in 'English'?—English at its most wide-ranging, resourceful and enterprising?"

Much of this work is already recorded, I believe, on video and film, and in substantial documentary reports built up over the last 2 decades. What IFTE will have to harness is a network of university centers (closely linked with teachers in schools), where such materials can be internationally collated, sifted, and published. National associations will have a key role to play in discussing first drafts. The work can be staged and momentum built up. But the prime focus is clear: to show in detail how students and teachers can work together to maximize the progress of individuals and groups—whatever the staging point in their development. And, after 3 decades of intensive work, we can now add the vital corollary: How at our best have we learned to assess and promote such work?

# References

## Historical Background

Applebee, A. N. (1974). *Tradition and reform in the teaching of English*. Urbana, IL.: National Council of Teachers of English.

Bell, B. I. (1949). *Crisis in education*. New York: H. Renergy.

Bestor, A. (1955). *Educational wastelands*. Urbana, IL: Univ. of Illinois Press.

DeBoer, J. J. (1932, January). The materials of the English curriculum. *English Journal, 21,* 68–69.

Dewey, J. (1916). *Democracy and education*. New York: Macmillan.

Dyskra, R. (1987). Introduction. In J. R. Squire (Ed.), *The dynamics of language learning*. Urbana, IL: ERIC Clearinghouse.

Fisher, J. (1969). Movement in English. (ADE Bulletin 22) New York: Modern Language Associates.

Hatfield, W. W. (1935). An experience curriculum in English. New York: D. Appleton Century.

Lynch, J. J., & Evans, B. (1963). *High school English text-books: A critical examination*. Boston: Little, Brown.

Lynd, A. (1953). *Quackery in the public schools*. New York: Grosset & Dunlap.

Ohmann, R. (1976). *English in America*. New York: Oxford University Press.

Pooley, R. C. (1939, May). Varied patterns of approach in the teaching of literature. *English Journal*.

Rickover, H. G. (1959). *Education and freedom*. New York: Dutton.

Smith, D. (1933). *Instruction in English*. Washington, DC: Government Printing Office.

Smith, D. (1941). *Evaluating instruction in secondary school English*. Chicago: National Council of Teachers of English.

Squire, J. R., & Applebee, R. K. (1968). *High school English instruction today*. New York: Appleton-Century-Crofts.

Welleck, R. (1953). Literary scholarship. In M. Curti (Ed.), *American scholarship in the twentieth century*. Cambridge: Harvard University Press.

## Pioneers of Current Developments

Barnes, D. (1976). *From communication to curriculum*. London: Penguin.

Boomer, G. (1982). *Negotiating the curriculum*. Sydney: Ashton Scholastic.

Britton, J. N. (1967). (Ed.). *Talking and writing*. London: Methuen.

Emig, J. (1971). *The composing process of twelfth graders*. Urbana, IL: National Council of Teachers of English.

Graves, D. (1983). *Writing: Teachers and children at work*. Portsmouth, NH: Heinemann.

Heathcote, D. (1980). *Exploring the theatre and education*. London: Heinemann.

Meek, M., Wardlow, A., & Barton G. (1977). (Eds.). *The cool web: The pattern of children's reading*. London: Bodley Head.

Wagner, B. J. (1976). *Dorothy Heathcote: Drama as a learning medium*. Washington, DC: National Education Association.

Thompson, J. (1987). *Understanding teenagers' reading*. New York: Nichols.

# LINGUISTICS AND TEACHING
# THE LANGUAGE ARTS

## Paula Menyuk
### Boston University

The study of linguistics has long had an influence on the teaching of English Language Arts in this country. Linguistic theory has experienced changes over this period of influence. One of the more dramatic changes occurred some 30 years ago when the field was remarkably influenced by a theory of generative grammar (Chomsky, 1965). Since that time there have been periodic changes to the description of language introduced by generative grammar. The latest description is Chomsky, 1995. Despite changes, the underlying notion of language knowledge being a set of rules that allows us to comprehend and produce an infinite number of utterances has not changed.

Theories of language prior to the 1960s were influenced by behaviorists' hypotheses about learning. Language was described as a set of learned habits and was acquired by learning these habits through stimulus, response, and reward conditions. Current theories of language acquisition are largely influenced by the theory of generative grammar and hold that language knowledge is acquired by an active learner. At the same time that theories of language acquisition changed from passive to active models of learning so did theories of cognitive development. This was largely due to the work of Piaget (1970). Only those influences arising from generative grammar, in its various forms, will be discussed since current linguistic influences on teaching the language arts all stem from this dramatic change.

The following aspects of current linguistic theory seem most germane to the teaching of the language arts: (a) theoretical positons now held about the nature of language knowledge and its acquisition, (b) research about the process of acquiring language knowledge and application of this linguistic knowledge in learning, and (c) research about how differing sociocultural experiences can affect what the child knows about language when entering school. These aspects are studied by linguists,

psycholinguists, and sociolinguists and are the topics covered in this chapter. The implications of theory in each of these areas for practice will be touched on.

## LANGUAGE KNOWLEDGE AND ACQUISITION

All linguistic theories, both current and past, have described language as an arbitrary, symbolic system comprised of units at different levels that are embedded into each other. When speaking, sounds are combined to produce words, words are combined to produce utterances and utterances are combined to produce discourse. In comprehending language, these units are used to get at the meanings of words, utterances, and discourse. Language is used to represent categories and relations that people find important to talk about. Because language is such an arbitrary and symbolic system, questions arise about what language knowledge is and about what causes acquisiton of this knowledge.

### Nature of Language Knowledge

Theories of the nature of language knowledge are really theories about the nature of human minds. Thus, when it was held that language knowledge consisted of a number of habits that were learned, then humans were conceived as having the ability to learn habits and associate these with certain situations. Humans could imitate, memorize, and generalize language behaviors just as they learned other behaviors such as how to ride a bicycle. Current theorizing paints a different picture. Humans have a unique, species-specific, ability to test various hypotheses about the structure of language, to develop rules of a particular language and remember them, and to use these rules to generate appropriate language in various circumstances (Pinker, 1994).

The distinction between these two positions often pointed to is that the first seems to depict the human as a passive learner whereas the second conceives of the human as an active learner. The fact that a person is considered an active learner in current linguistic and psycholinguistic theories suggests that efforts to teach language to human learners should actively engage them in the learning process. Such active engagement consists of providing opportunities to test hypotheses about the language, rather than simply requiring that learners memorize bits of language for use in certain situations. Asking children to judge the goodness of sentences that do and do not violate linguistic rules, to complete sentences that require a dependent and logical clause ("because," "although," and "if-then" clauses), and to combine sentences (for example, "The man walked." "He walked to the store." becomes "The man walked to the store.") are a few activities that require such hypothesis testing.

Current linguistic theorists all agree that language knowledge is generative rather than memorized. However, langage acquisition does not simply take place by creation of language on the part of the child, as nativists might suggest, but also includes the important role that input can play in acquisition (Schieffelin & Ochs, 1986). This emphasis on input as well as on innate abilities has obvious importance for teachers of the language arts. If acquisition of language knowledge and use of that knowledge depend on receiving appropriate input at certain times, then teachers have an important role to play.

The child's acquisition of language is described as the acquisition of a set of language rules. These rules are acquired because of the biological structure of humans and the discourse situations in which language is presented to the child. The human infant is designed to process or test hypotheses, and remember language input in particular ways. As the child develops, these hypotheses about how language is structured are modified by particular language input. In other words, the set of rules available to the child changes as the child develops and recognizes what are and are not permissable structures in his or her particular language. The evidence of developmental change is clear in the types of utterances and discourse understood and produced at various ages. The child of 3 years is markedly different in language knowledge from the 1-year-old child; the 5 year old is remarkably different from the 3 year old; the 10 year old from the 5 year old; and so on, until some adult level of knowledge is achieved.

Not only does the child's structural knowledge change in time, but, also, his or her knowledge of how to use structures for the purposes of communication and learning changes (Menyuk, 1988). This latter knowledge has been termed *pragmatic knowledge*. Because there are systematic changes in knowledge that have been described in numerous books on language development, materials for teaching language can be designed to fit the varying developmental levels of the children within a classroom. Children will vary in terms of the sophistication of their linguistic knowledge and also in the ways in which they can use this knowledge. Table 3.1 presents a few examples of structural and pragmatic knowledge at the ages previously cited.

TABLE 3.1. Examples of Language Knowledge and Use at Various Ages

| Ages | Knowledge | Use |
|---|---|---|
| 1 year | Word or jargon phrase Shoe or Wuzzat shoe. | Command, request, state Shoe!, Shoe?, Shoe. |
| 3 years | Embedded sentences I see the boy who's there. | Polite requests Can I have a cookie? |
| 5 years | Complement sentences I know that he'll come. | Bargaining If you give me a ____, I'll . . . |
| 10 years | Figurative language He's as hungry as a lion. | Riddles What has 4 wheels . . . |

## Causes For Language Development

As stated, some arguments have been raised about the causes for developmental changes in knowledge of language structure and use. There are those who hold that these changes are solely due to the child 's innate ability to acquire knowledge of the structure of a language. Because of the constraints on the structures in all languages, the so-called universals of language, all children learn the rules of the language in the same sequence and at, approximately, the same time (Wexler & Cullicover, 1980).

There are others who hold that acquisition of such knowledge is based on certain cognitive abilities. Categorization abilities explain the acquisition of vocabulary (Clark, 1983). Information processing abilities, for example, the ability to determine and remember the distributional characteristics of categories such as nouns, verbs, and adjectives in sentences, are said to explain the acquisition of the structural aspects of language (Siegler, 1998). If this is the way word meaning and syntax structure is acquired, then such theorizing has implications for teaching. For example, it might be the case that teachers should teach certain cognitive prerequisites before teaching certain vocabulary and sentence structures. However, there is little evidence to indicate that teaching these so-called prerequisites will lead to the acquisition of language knowledge. Rather than teaching certain readinesses, thought should be given to how language can be taught directly. Knowledge of the sequences in language development can be directly useful in planning language activities for the child. Information about the role of input in producing this sequence might be directly useful in designing the circumstances in which language is presented to the child.

For example, it is clear that the child's acquisition of pragmatic knowledge is a product of "motherese" or of how mothers interact with their infants. Mothers support their infant's communication interaction by providing frames for them to interact within (like peek-a-boo games) and by encouraging them to take a turn (Bruner, 1985). This behavior has been described by Bruner as "scaffolding" and within the child's "zone of proximal development"; that is, the zone in which one who is more expert guides the learner (Vygotsky, 1978), and, in this way, extends the child's knowledge of, at least, how to communicatively interact. Such interaction, in addition, can provide children with the opportunity to test their hypotheses about language. Such opportunities can, indirectly, lead to the acquisition of structural knowledge.

Similarly, communicative interaction in the classroom, during which students and teachers take turns, can provide the school-age child with the opportunity to test hypotheses about language. Now that "school age" is getting younger and younger, it is important that what is known about very early language development and the conditions that facilitate it, is also known by preschool language teachers. In addition the principles of presenting the language to be acquired clearly, meaningfully, and with a great deal of background support is useful for teaching students of all ages. The following discussion provides some examples of making the language knowledge to be acquired clear and meaningful.

There are some who suggest that there are direct effects of caregivers' input on children's acquisition of lexical and structural as well as pragmatic knowledge because such input is simplified and clarified by the use of contextual information. Pointing to named objects and by only naming objects in the child's presence has been shown to help in early vocabulary acquisition (Snow, 1986). These techniques can be used in later vocabulary acquisition as well when visual support for new vocabulary items or structures are presented as the vocabulary and structures are being presented. Communicative interaction can be crucial for the acquisition of structural knowledge because it is through *discourse* that hypotheses about structural knowledge can be tested. For example, it is through discourse by and with others that the child determines the appropriate use of anaphora in storytelling (Hickman, 1985). If anaphora is used inappropriately, the discourse will not be understood and the listener will question the meaning of the discourse. How one negates a sentence or forms a question are also determined in discourse, and by the same means; that is, by observing whether the sentence is or is not comprehended (Foley & Van Valin, 1984). In this latter view, what the child learns are the relations between forms and functions rather than simply a set of abstract linguistic rules. All these theorists point to the importance of communicative interaction in language development.

Input provides support by acknowledging the contributions of the child *and*, in addition, provides data from which the child can draw conclusions about the structure and use of the language. As stated, such input can also extend the child's knowledge by having a more expert language user interact with the child within that child's zone of proximal development. For example, it has been observed that mothers shift from requesting actions on objects ("Roll the ball!") to requesting information ("Do you want the ball?") from their infants during the second year of life (Menyuk, Liebergott, & Schultz, 1995). They apparently do so as soon as their infants give some indication that they understand a number of lexical items. Such requests are then within the infant's zone of proximal development. However, this shift also presents a greater challenge to the language learner because it requires knowledge of language apart from the ordinary context (decontextualized knowledge) of what one ordinarily does with a ball. The child is required to attend to the language per se to achieve an appropriate response, and, in this way, learns more about language.

Theories of language acquisition that stress the innate aspect of development and those that stress the importance of input on that development, have obvious importance for the teaching of the language arts. The former stress the importance of keeping in mind the developmental changes that occur in the child's linguistic competence due to innate and cognitive factors. The latter stress the importance of communicative *interaction* as a vehicle for language growth.

## THE ACQUISITION PROCESS

The process by which language is acquired has been described as one of developing strategies for mapping meaning onto a fast fading signal. In hearing individuals this signal is an acoustic one. The process has also been described as one that changes in the degree to which there is reliance on the context for interpretation of that signal. At the beginning stages of acquisition, the infant is highly dependent on the surface structure (the acoustics) of the signal for deriving meaning, and the context in which it is heard. At later stages, higher order knowledge (or rules) allows the child to chunk and interpret the signal with minimal use of the acoustic signal per se. At this stage the child is imposing meaning on the signal. At the beginning stages of development, the infant is highly dependent on context for the interpretation of the meaning of a word or phrase. At later stages of development the child achieves a decontextualized knowledge of the meaning of the signal.

The process of achieving decontextualized knowledge of language is a gradual one. For example, in first learning the meaning of a word, a child relies heavily on having present the item or action that is denoted by the word. Mothers initially talk about the "here and now." Later, the child understands the meaning of the word in all linguistic and situational contexts. Relying heavily on situtional context first and then linguistic context alone applies to the learning of all aspects of language. It takes the child a long time to achieve such knowledge for the complex aspects of language such as passive structures and relativized sentences. Early on, children rely on real world knowledge to understand passive sentences such as "The baby was fed by the mother" and relative sentences such as "The boy who read the book ran away." Later in development, they understand these structures in contexts where real world knowledge does not help comprehension. This is the case in reversible passives ("The boy was chased by the girl.") and relatives that separate the subject from the verb ("The boy who kissed the girl ran away."). It is not until the middle childhood years that such knowledge becomes conscious and can be deliberately used in speaking and writing (Karmiloff-Smith, 1979). Being able to metaprocess language (*to bring to conscious awareness what one knows about language*) is a product of this decontextualization process. Such metaprocessing begins early with simple structures. Many of the activities in which the child engages in school, such as following directions and learning to read, require metaprocessing abilities. Therefore, teachers need to keep in mind the limits of the young child's decontextualized knowledge of language (see also Sulzby, this edition).

Various psycholinguistic models of language processing have been presented that might account for the developmental processes previously described (Carroll, 1986). One model, a parallel processing model, seems to be most explanatory of the developmental changes (for example, Marslen-Wilson & Tyler, 1980). Such a model describes the language processer as accessing all aspects of the language (phonological, lexical, and syntactic) as soon as some meaningful chunk has occurred. At the beginning stages of the process the phonology and meaning of a single word is probably accessed and some predictions made about what may follow depending on context and real world knowledge. However, as more data are collected, the word might be incoporated into a meaningful phrase, and as still more data are collected, the chunk becomes the clause and complete sentence. The young child's chunks would be smaller and more limited (limited in the sense of lexical and syntax knowledge) than those of the older child, and, therefore, processing would be slower and also more limited. Nevertheless, even the young child attempts to access all levels of language while trying to map meaning onto the signal. In fact, the child needs all levels of language present to process effectively. Isolating aspects of language from each other places a burden on the young child's limited processing ability, and teachers should be aware of this.

This model of the process of language acquisition has both developmental and process implications. The developmental implications are that there are limits in the amount and type of language that can be processed at various ages, and there also are limits on the *conditions* under which language can be processed. The processing implications are that the conditions that provide the most favorable opportunities for language interpretation are those that provide materials that are within the child's competence limits, and do so under conditions where both the context of the situation and the context of the language allow the child to access units from all levels of the language. At later stages of development such props to understanding need not be present.

## APPLICATION OF LINGUISTIC KNOWLEDGE

Teachers of the language arts are concerned with how oral language knowledge is applied in the acquisition of written language knowledge. Psycholinguistic theories have clearly impacted on theories of reading and writing. Current theories hold that the process of reading requires bringing to conscious knowledge what one knows about various levels of language. This, in turn, requires that the child have thorough knowledge of the units (sounds, words, and structures) that are being read so they can be easily brought to conscious awareness. The parallel processing model for language acquisition previously described has been applied to the reading process with one addition. In the reading process the child must *initially* translate the written word into an oral language word so that meaning can be mapped onto the written signal. Just as in oral language processing, when this translation takes place, all levels of language knowledge are accessed and used to predict what might follow in the sequence (Perfetti & McCutchen, 1987). Once the child becomes familiar with this translation process with a set of words and structures, this process takes place automatically with that particular set of words and structures. As the material to be read becomes more complex phonologically, lexically, and

syntactically, this process of first conscious awareness and then automaticity is repeated. It is repeated throughout life as the reader approaches text that is unfamiliar in structure and topic (Menyuk, 1983).

Earlier, I described the developmental process of decontextualization of oral language knowledge. Because reading requires bringing language units to conscious awareness, such decontextualized knowledge is required in reading. This suggests that practice in achieving awareness of linguistic units of varying size and complexity can be a bridge to reading. Kindergarten teachers engage children in such awareness tasks on the phonological level (rhyming and segmentation) but such practice can be carried out with language units at all levels throughout the school years. The domain in which such practice can occur should change as the children achieve more and more complex knowledge of oral language units (Menyuk, 1988). This practice can be carried out not only in the oral language mode but also in reading and writing. Written language provides even greater opportunity to think and talk about language units because these units do not disappear when they're in writing.

The relation between reading and writing has been described as being analogous to the relation between listening and speaking. This implies that writing development is highly dependent on reading. To some extent that is true. However, writing is more highly dependent on oral language knowledge in its beginning stages than it is on reading (Perera, 1986). That is, beginning writing once past the handwriting and spelling problems stage (the mechanics stage) appears to be talking in written form. Children, initially, write what they say. Thus, in the early stages, writing accesses speech in its phonological, lexical, semantactic, and discourse forms. In the more mature stages of writing, speech and writing forms become more and more dissimilar. The forms used in writing become similar to those found in reading and, therefore, probably dependent on frequent reading of varied literary forms.

To interpret and remember what we have read, and to write so that others can interpret and remember what we have written requires knowledge that goes beyond that of linguistic knowledge. Cognitive strategies of gist extraction, inferencing, organization, use of schema (world knowledge), and planning are some of the cognitive strategies that must be used in effective reading and writing (Rumelhart, 1981; Flower & Hayes, 1980). It also should be obvious that to map meaning onto written text and to generate meaning always requires accessing the various aspects of language. In order to map meaning accurately onto written text and to generate comprehensible text, this access process must be constantly monitored. Thus, throughout the development of reading and writing, linguistic knowledge is constantly called on. In the emphasis on cognitive strategies in reading and writing this fact may be ignored, but the language arts teacher must constantly be aware of it. In fact, the problem for the language arts teacher is to teach both aspects of these written language processes so that students can determine the relations between them. Stages in the development of reading and writing, to which a number of researchers have pointed, are presented in Table 3.2. The accomplishments selected at each stage for presentation in the table attempt to make clear the relation of these processes. Emergent literacy involves knowing

TABLE 3.2. Some Stages in the Development of Reading and Writing

| Reading | Writing |
| --- | --- |
| Emergent literacy | Scribbling |
| Print awareness | Writing equals saying |
| Decoding | Spelling related to saying |
| Reading for literal meaning | Writing and saying integrated |
| Inferencing while reading | Writing from readers' point of view |

that text conveys language while scribbling suggests that the child is attempting to reproduce this relation. Print awareness and attempting to write what you say indicate that children are becoming aware of segments on the page that convey words. Decoding and spelling indicate the child's awareness of sounds within segments. Reading for literal meaning and writing what you say indicate that as children become more accomplished in reading and writing connected discourse, they see the relation between these two processes. Finally, when children become more accomplished readers and writers, they become aware of the relation between what the text can accomplish and what they need to try to accomplish when they produce text.

## SOCIOLINGUISTICS AND TEACHING THE LANGUAGE ARTS

Different children come to school with different levels of knowledge about language structure and use. That is, some children are more linguistically mature than others when they enter school. In addition, children bring with them different sociolinguistic experiences. In particular, they bring with them different notions about the purpose of language use, different rules of conversational interaction, and different rules of discourse organization. When the children come from sociolinguistic backgrounds that are similar to that of the teachers', then these differences create few problems in communicative interactions in the school. When children come from sociolinguistic backgrounds that are markedly different from that of their teachers, then difficulties can arise. More and more children are now entering school with knowledge of a language other than English, and sociolinguistics differences in language use or pragmatic knowledge. Some of these problems can be avoided if teachers, and particularly language arts teachers, are aware of the nature of the distinctions that exist both in language knowledge and language use. The latter differences will be discussed first.

Differences in expectations about classroom communication on the part of teachers and students can be very disruptive of the learning that is supposed to be going on. Several studies of such communication indicate discrepancies between teacher and child expectations in common classroom communications due to sociolinguistic differences. For example, in show-and-tell situations the teacher expects the child to follow the expected format of telling. This format is one of sequential narration of a story with a setting, episodes, and conclusion presented, in other words, in a story grammar format (Mandler, 1983). Some children from minority sociolinguistic backgrounds use a different format, one similar to that used in cultures in which oral stories are used to relate the history and culture of the people. This format includes lengthy departures from the sequence, and then return to it (van Keulen, Weddington, & DeBose, 1998). Further differences exist between minority children and some majority teachers in terms of how turn-taking should occur in a classroom (Ogbu, 1978).

The most common situation in mainstream classrooms is that of teacher as lecturer and guide. Classroom communication is usually one way—the teacher giving directions and asking questions and the students answering. Such interaction is contrary to the expectations of children from minority sociolinguistic groups, who expect more of a shared situation in the classroom.

There are other roles that teachers can and do take. One role is that of guide and learner (Heath, 1985). The term that is used to describe this situation is "reciprocal teaching" (Brown, Palinscar, & Armbruster, 1987; Cole & Hall, 1982). In this situation, teachers shift from being experts to being guides, then coaches, and, finally, learners along with the children.

All of the above findings point to differences in discourse styles that can affect classroom interactions and, therefore, the teaching of language arts to minority children. In addition to differences in discourse styles, children from different sociolinguistic groups can come to school with varying degrees of knowledge of the English language and varying degrees of decontextualized knowledge of language. In sum, these children may have a different set of structural rules as well as a different set of pragmatic rules. These differences can obviously affect how ready these children are to engage in learning the English language arts.

The patterns of language input discussed previously that are said to be necessary for language development do not occur in all sociocultural environments (Ochs & Schieffelin, 1984). Despite these differences in input, all children throughout the world acquire language. However, much of the sociolinguistic research with children from nonmajority sociocultural backgrounds indicates that differences in patterns of caregiver–child communicative interaction may be the source of differences in degree of decontextualized knowledge of language that a child has on entering school (Heath, 1983). As pointed out previously, such decontextualized knowledge, which leads to the ability to metaprocess language, is necessary for many school tasks. The ability to metaprocess language is particularly crucial in learning to read and write. Differences in metaprocessing abilities can be overcome. There is at least one study indicating that if children who use a dialect other than standard English are given the same experiences in phonological awareness that standard English-speaking children are given, they can learn to read as successfully as children from the majority culture (Piestrup, 1973).

Children who come to school with limited knowledge of English pose a different kind of problem to the teacher of English language arts. If decontextualized knowledge of the language is needed in reading, writing, and other school tasks, it is clear that children with little English will have difficulty completing these tasks in English. This is especially so if they also have little or no decontextualized knowledge of their own language. The educational implications for these children are a matter of great argument, and the research carried out thus far leaves more questions than answers (Krashen, 1996; Willig, 1982). Sociolinguistic research, however, has indicated that bilingualism perse can give the child a cognitive advantage in decontextualized knowledge of language (Hakuta, Ferdman, & Diaz, 1987). Therefore, educational programs that foster bilingualism in children, may put them at a cognitive advantage in learning to read, write, and use language creatively. Two-way bilingual programs in first grade, in which children from two linguistic backgrounds learn each other's language, have had some success (Genesee, 1989). Simultaneous teaching of literacy in the child's home and school languages provides some promise as well (Homza, 1995).

## IMPLICATIONS FOR TEACHING

Throughout this chapter I have referred to what I believe are the important contributions of linguistic, psycholinguistic, and sociolinguistic research to the teaching of the English language arts. They will be summarized here. First, such research has provided information about the patterns of language development and language use in both majority and minority group children. This information can be used in the selection of developmentally appropriate materials and contexts for teaching. Second, the research has shown the conditions under which language is learned and grows. Communication *interaction* between the child and more mature users of the language is vital for such growth. Linguistic meta-abilities are best learned when children are asked to actively think and talk about language. Third, this research also has shown that metaprocessing abilities are crucial to learning to read and write. Finally, research has shown that there are important differences in different sociocultural groups that should affect how these students are taught. There are variations in styles of communication interaction, the important context for language learning. There are also differences in experiences with decontextualized use of language. These differences can adversely affect learning of reading and writing, but adverse effects can be overcome with appropriate attitudes and teaching.

## *References*

Brown, A., Palinscar, A., & Armbruster, B. (1987). Inducing comprehension fostering abilities in interactive learning situations. In H. Mandl, N. Stein, & T. Trabasso (Eds.), *Learning and comprehension of texts* (pp. 273-304). Hillsdale, NJ: Lawrence Erlbaum Associates.

Bruner, J. (1985). Vygotsky: A historical and conceptual perspective. In J. V. Wertsch (Ed.), *Culture communication and cognition* (pp. 21-34). Cambridge, England: Cambridge University Press.

Carroll, D. (1986). *Psychology of language.* Monterey, CA: Brooks/Cole.

Chomsky, N. (1965). *Aspects of the theory of syntax.* Cambridge, MA: MIT Press.

Chomsky, N. (1995). *The minimalist program.* Cambridge, MA: MIT Press.

Clark, E. (1983). Meanings and concepts. In J. Flavell & E. Markman (Eds.), *Handbook of child psychology, Vol. III* (pp. 787-840). New York: Wiley.

Cole, M., & Hall, W. (1982). A model system for the study of learning disabilities. *Quarterly Newsletter of the Laboratory of Comparative Human Cognition, University of California, San Diego, 4,* 39-66.

Flower, L., & Hayes, J. (1980). The dynamics of composing: Making plans and juggling constraints. In L. N. Gregg & E. R. Steinberg (Eds.), *Cognitive processes in writing* (pp. 31-50), Hillsdale, NJ: Lawrence Erlbaum Associates.

Foley, N., & Van Valin, R. (1984). *Functional syntax and universal grammar.* Cambridge, England: Cambridge University Press.

Genesee, F. (1989). Second llanguage learning through immersion: A review of United States programs. *Review of Educational Research, 55,* 541-561.

Hakuta, K., Ferdman, B. M., & Diaz, R. M. (1987). Bilingualism and cognitive development: Three perspectives. In S. Rosenberg (Ed.), *Advances in applied psycholinquistics, Vol. II* (pp. 284-319). Cambridge, England: Cambridge University Press.

Heath, S. B. (1983). *Ways with words.* Cambridge, England: Cambridge University Press.

Heath, S. B. (1985). The cross-cultural study of language acquisition. *Papers on research in child language development, Vol. 24.* Stanford, CA: Stanford University.

Hickman, M. (1985). The implications of discourse skills in Vygotsky's developmental theory. In J. Wertsch (Ed.), *Culture, communication and cognition* (pp. 236-257). Cambridge, England: Cambridge University Press.

Homza, A. (1995). Developing biliteracy in a bilingual first grade writing work shop. Unpublished doctoral dissertation, Boston University, MA.

Karmiloff-Smith, A. (1979). Language development after five. In P. Fletcher & M. Garman (Eds.), *Language acquisition: Studies in first language development* (pp. 307-324). Cambridge, England: Cambridge University Press.

Krashen, S. (1996). *Under attack: The case against bilingual education.* Culver, CA: Language Education Associates.

Mandler, J. M. (1983). Representation. In J. Flavell & E. Markman (Eds.) *Handbook of child psychology, Vol. III* (pp. 420-494). New York: Wiley.

Marslen-Wilson, W., & Tyler, L. (1980). The temporal structure of spoken language understanding. *Cognition, 8,* 1-71.

Menyuk, P. (1983). Language development and reading. In T. Gallagher & C. Prutting (Eds.), *Pragmatic issues: Assessment and intervention* (pp. 151-170). San Diego, CA: College Hill Press.

Menyuk, P. (1988). *Language development: Knowledge and use.* New York: Addison-Wesley & Longman.

Menyuk, P., Liebergott, J., & Schultz, M. (1995). *Early language development in full-term and premature infants.* Hillsdale, NJ: Lawrence Erlbaum Associates.

Ogbu, J. (1978). *Minority education and caste.* New York: Academic Press.

Ochs, E., & Schieffelin, B. (1984). Language acquisition and socialization: Three stories and their implications. In R. Levine (Ed.), *Culture theory: Essays on mind, self, and emotion* (pp. 276-320). Cambridge, England: Cambridge University Press.

Perera, K. (1986). Language acquisition and writing. In P. Fletcher & M. Gatman (Eds.), *Language acquisition: Studies in first language development (2nd ed.)* (pp. 494–518). Cambridge, Cambridge University Press.

Perfetti, C., & McCutchen, D. (1987). Schooled language competence: Linguistic abilities in reading and writing. In S. Rosenberg (Ed.), *Advances in applied psycholinguistics, Vol. 2* (pp. 105–141). Cambridge, England: Cambridge University Press.

Piaget, J. (1970). Piaget's theory. In P. Mussen (Ed.), *Manual of child psychology, VI* (pp. 705–730). New York: Wiley.

Piestrup, A. (1973). *Black dialect interference and accommodation of reading instruction in first grade*. (Monographs of the Language Behavior Research Laboratory No. 4). Berkeley CA: University of California, Berkeley.

Pinker, S. (1994). *The language instinct: How the mind creates language*. New York: Morrow.

Rumelhart, D. E. (1981). Schemata: The building blocks of cognition. In J. T. Guthrie (Ed.), *Comprehension and teaching: Research reviews* (pp. 3–26). Newark, DE: International Reading Association.

Schieffelin, B., & Ochs, E. (1986). *Language socialization across cultures*. New York: Cambridge University Press.

Siegler, R. (1998). *Children's thinking (3rd ed.)*. Upper Saddle River, NJ: Prentice-Hall.

Snow, C. (1986). Conversations with children. In P. Fletcher & M. Gatman (Eds.), *Language acquisition: Studies in first language development (2nd ed.)* (pp. 69–89). Cambridge, England: Cambridge University Press.

van Keulen, J., Weddington, G., & DeBose, C. (1998). *Speech, language, learning and the African-American child*. Boston: Allyn & Bacon.

Vygotsky, L. (1978). *Mind in society*. Cambridge, MA: Harvard University Press.

Wexler, K., & Cullicover, P. W. (1980). *Formal principles of lanquaqe acquisition*. Cambridge, MA: MIT Press.

Willig, A. (1982). The effectiveness of bilingual education [Review of report]. *NABE Journal, 6,* 1–19.

# · 4 ·

# A PSYCHOLOGICAL ANALYSIS OF WHAT TEACHERS AND STUDENTS DO IN THE LANGUAGE ARTS CLASSROOM

*Diane Lemonnier Schallert*
University of Texas, Austin

*Debra Bayles Martin*
San Diego State University

Those of us who have the word "psychologist" as part of our professional description (like Diane) often experience some version of the following scenario:

I am reading students' papers as I fly home from a conference and my neighbor in the cramped quarters of our seat says, "Where do you teach?" I name my university and my neighbor replies, "So what do you teach, then?" and I say, "Courses on the psychology of learning and on psycholinguistics." Or my neighbor asks, "What department?" and I say, "Educational Psychology." The word "psychology" is enough to trigger a long personal story of emotional trauma or a troubled childhood. Or else, the person says, "I had better be careful. You're probably analyzing me even now, right?" Although I usually demur and deflect the conversation to some other topic, in some ways the person is right, for a psychologist IS interested in what makes people tick, in how individuals respond to their environment and make meaning of their life experiences. Further, a psycholinguist will have the additionally annoying habit of being interested not just in what the person is saying but in how it is being said. The constructs and findings that crowd my readings are fascinating to me, especially when I can find them useful in understanding real human experiences.

Those of us who identify ourselves as "teacher educators" (like Debra) may have a slightly different experience:

It happens sometimes that my plane companion is herself a teacher (perhaps *she* is grading papers) and when I ask what she teaches, she says, "I teach fourth grade," or "I teach eighth grade language arts." What fun it is to discuss details of classroom life, to joke about educational psychologists (many teachers report unflattering memories of the educational psychology course in their teacher preparation programs), and to find out how she guides her students through reading and writing. Questions come fast: What are your students like? How do they get along? What do you think of their parents, the school's neighborhood, your fellow teachers and principal? What do you do to get your boys to love to read? Is it ever hard to get them to STOP reading or writing?

In this chapter, we offer our scholarly response were our imaginary seatmate to ask what about the field of psychology might be relevant to her as a teacher. To set the stage, we offer an overview of the metatheoretical orientations that have captured the imagination of psychologists interested, as we are, in language and learning phenomena. We then describe four general topics of interest to the language arts teacher. The first of these deals with the productive research on the role of motivation and emotion in learning situations. In the second section, we consider how attention has been described and what it means to develop expertise in a domain. Next, the portrayal of learners as active, strategic meaning makers points to the role of prior knowledge in any learning or comprehension situation. With the fourth section, we connect learning and meaning making to the thinking and research on language and culture.

# ONE POSSIBLE LENS ON THE 100-YEAR-OLD STORY ABOUT PSYCHOLOGY

The history of something, be it of a place, an object, or an idea, is not always inherently interesting, we will admit. The sort of reverential description of the past in some textbooks can often seem irrelevant to things current. Perhaps it is simply a sign of our own aging that we now enjoy contemplating how *ideas* grow, transmute, live, and die, and how what was once popular a decade or more ago is now viewed so differently. The process of change, with its intricate weaving of causal and casual influences that leads to an ephemeral present, is one concern that learning theorists share with historians.

## The Legacy of a Behaviorist Perspective

From our *fin de siecle* perspective, it is convenient that the American version of psychology's history fits rather well within the 100 years of the 20th century. The 50-year mark can serve as a major divide, with the first half of the century taken up by the intellectually vigorous, and sometimes contentious, debate associated with *behaviorism*. Behavior theory, with its emphasis on the relationship between environmental events and outwardly observable responses, has waned in importance in psychology (Robins, Gosling, & Craik, 1999). Yet, the principles and perspectives developed from this view of learning will likely remain an important part of psychology's story for years to come. In addition, at least two interests pursued by psychologists from that era still intrigue us today. The first has to do with how we develop an emotional repertoire to our experiences, something that behavior theorists also considered in the extensive research program on classical conditioning. The second interest encompasses the question of how motivation insinuates itself into learning of every kind. Although pursued now by researchers who would perhaps be loath to acknowledge any legacy from the behaviorists, still that early interest in principles of reinforcement is easy to connect to the topic of motivation.

## The Rise of the Cognitivists

By the early 70s, Behaviorism was regularly cast as the big, bloated monolith against which a new, robust, and exciting Cognitive Perspective offered so much more in terms of describing how the mind works (Gibson, 2000). Robins, Gosling, and Craik (1999) reported that the topics discussed in the main psychology journals and in the dissertations indexed by the psycINFO database show a clear crossover from behaviorist to cognitive influences at the beginning of the 70s and an ever-widening gap from that point forward. We did not notice at the time that with the decline of a behavior theory perspective and the rise of a cognitive approach, interest in the topic of learning per se, that is, a change in people's behavioral and cognitive repertoire, also waned. Cognitive psychologists studied memory, not learning, and proposed theories of information processing and knowledge representation, not knowledge acquisition. It was not until the middle 80s that cognitive psychologists turned their direct attention to learning (Shuell, 1986).

What, then, was the essence of a cognitive perspective? The individual was said to be active rather than passive, to act upon and re-work and transform input rather than simply receive environmental stimuli to trigger responses. When we discuss the next school of thought in psychology's history, we note the major role ascribed to prior knowledge, surely the most important way in which an individual could be said to be active in interacting with the world. However, one of the first interests in a cognitive perspective was in describing how the mind did its work. The dominant metaphor for this discussion was that of the computer. Although today we may shy away from the mechanistic description offered by the computer metaphor (even in the futuristic world of Star Trek, Mr. DATA has no emotions), its early use helped us attend to certain learner characteristics previously overlooked. Indeed, many psychological models continue today to exploit the computer metaphor, proposing a view of the human mind as a system with interactive and parallel processes operating within the constraints of limits on working memory capacity. Of course, when we think of the mind only as an information processing system, our view of how people learn, how they become literate, and how they respond to one another and to the world at large is somewhat obscured. Still, the perspective reminds us to be appreciative of the special challenges that any newcomer to a task faces simply by virtue of how the mind deploys its resources.

In Table 4.1, we depict a series of timelines with the decades of the century listed horizontally. We tried to give a sense of perspective on the history of psychology by showing the decades in lighter or darker shades. The first panel is meant to indicate how, from the perspective of the 70s, with the first 50 years of psychology's rise still very much present in our consciousness and the future decades merely foreshadowed, psychologists preferred to portray the field as consisting of two schools of thought, Behavior Theory and Cognitive Theory.

## Cognitivists Divided: The Rise of a Constructivist Perspective

By the middle 80s, researchers and thinkers were beginning to make distinctions WITHIN the cognitivist perspective. The heroic perspective that had been the champion some 15 years was enduring ever more telling blows. For example, Faigley (1986) labeled the schools of thought in the field of rhetoric as Expressivist, Cognitivist, and Sociocultural views of the process of writing; and in his carefully consensual language, it is easy to read the criticism that writing researchers were beginning to level at the now less preferred cognitive perspective. A little later, McCarthey and Raphael (1992) discussed how classroom instruction connecting reading and writing was differently envisioned from different theoretical foundations. For them, the most rigid, teacher-controlled, and contextually insensitive approach was represented by what they called "cognitive information processing theories." Similarly, in a discussion of the

TABLE 4.1. Characterizing the History of Psychological Views of Learning

**Panel 1:**

| 1900 | 1910 | 1920 | 1930 | 1940 | 1950 | 1960 | **1970** | 1980 | 1990 | 2000 |

Behavior Theory Era           Cognitive Theory Era

←-------------------------------------------→    ←----------------------------→

**Panel 2:**

| 1900 | 1910 | 1920 | 1930 | 1940 | 1950 | 1960 | 1970 | **1980** | 1990 | 2000 |

Behavior Theory Era        Cognitive Era

                           Constructivist Era

←-------------------------------------------→    ←-----→ ←----------→

Mechanistic              Meaning Making

←-----------------------------------------------→ ←-------------→

**Panel 3:**

| 1900 | 1910 | 1920 | 1930 | 1940 | 1950 | 1960 | 1970 | 1980 | 1990 | **2000** |

Behavior Theory Era        Information-
                                Processing Era

                                     Construct-
                                     ivist Era

                                               Socio-
                                               Construct-
                                               ivist Era

←----------------------------------------→ ←----------→ ←----------→ ←-------→

Mechanistic                             Meaning Making

←----------------------------------------------→ ←----------------→

Individually–focused                     Cultural/Social focus

←----------------------------------------------------------→ ←-----→

philosophical roots of constructivist views of learning, Prawat and Floden (1994) presented information processing models as dependent on a mechanistic world view, one in which the task of the human "cognizer" is to respond to the regularities afforded by the input. Information processing, the darling of the early cognitivists, was being relegated to the same status as behaviorist explanations. In Panel 2 of Table 4.1, we show how in the 80s psychological inquiry reflected three schools of thought—the behaviorist, cognitivist, and constructivist—with the first two offering a more mechanistic view of how the mind works.

How could a school of thought that had made "active" its centerpiece be criticized for being potentially as mechanistic as behaviorism? As Bruner (1990) explained in his characteristically trenchant account of the Cognitive Revolution

emphasis began shifting from "meaning" to "information," from the *construction* of meaning to the processing of *information*. These are profoundly different matters. The key factor in the shift was the introduction of computation as the ruling metaphor and of computability as a necessary criterion of a good theoretical model. Information is indifferent with respect to meaning (p. 4).

To re-invigorate the Cognitive Revolution, as Bruner would say, it became necessary in the late 1980s to separate Cognitive from Constructivist perspectives, to distinguish the person as information processor from the person as meaning maker. Granted, some of constructivism's roots predated the split between the behaviorist and cognitive schools of thought, as witnessed by the powerful examples of memory's reconstructive nature presented by Sir Frederic Bartlett (1932) and of children's sense-making by Jean Piaget (1932). However, in the psychological literature, the modern resurgence can be traced to the seminal work on constructive and reconstructive processes involved in comprehension and memory published by Bransford and colleagues (Bransford & Johnson, 1972; Bransford, 1979; Bransford, 1984). Additionally, the theoretical grounding of the early schema theorists (Anderson, 1977; Rumelhart & Ortony, 1977; Schank & Abelson, 1997) provided a description of knowledge use that put interpretation at the heart of cognition.

The essence of the Constructivist perspective is the central role ascribed to a person's own construction of meaning. In this view, *to construct* means *to build*, and *to construct meaning* means to build a new cognitive structure out of what is available in one's knowledge. Constructing meaning is a matter of the intentional, or goal-directed, interpretation that the individual is making of whatever situation is encountered. The person is guided by answers to the following questions: What is the task here? What are my goals as they relate to this task? What do I perceive as others' goals for me? What strategies should I use to reach my goals? What background knowledge am I reminded of in this situation? How can I make a coherent "story" to account for what I see in the current situation? Thus, in a constructivist account of the moment-by-moment experience of a person, the meaning constructed necessarily reflects the individual's own perspective, past experience, and interpretation of the task. When we elaborate on particular key constructs in the sections that follow, we focus on two that clearly owe their prominence to the constructivist perspective: the role of prior knowledge in comprehension, learning, and any form of language use; and the agentive, intentional, and strategic nature of human functioning.

## All Things Social: Socioconstructivist Perspective on the Mind

By the late 80s, just as we might have settled into a view of psychology's past schools of thought as comprised of "behaviorism-cognitivism-constructivism," another shake-up was brewing. At first included as one of the giant figures of constructivism, Vygotsky (1978) was recognized as having presented some radically different ideas indeed. We attribute to him and to others (e.g., Bahktin, 1981, 1990; Bruner, 1990; Cole & Engestrom, 1993; Leont'ev, 1981; Wells, 1999; Wertsch, 1991) who helped develop socioconstructivist theories our current enchantment with all things cultural. From the perspective of the new millennium, the early years of psychology now seem to have focused on trying to better understand how humans function as *individuals*, as the separate, unique nexus for forces working on functioning and as the repository of memories, abilities, goals, personality tendencies, and motivations. Even the constructivist perspective remains closer to information processing and to behaviorist notions on this dimension.

While constructivist and socioconstructivist perspectives share a strong similarity in terms of how the learner is said to construct interpretations of ongoing events, actively making sense of language and life, the socioconstructivist perspective also includes the cultural/social/historical milieu into which every person is born and lives. From a socioconstructivist perspective, we attend to the cultural meaning of the situation in which learning is taking place and to the social practices and power differentials that influence teachers and learners in learning situations. Nieto (1999) beautifully summarizes the socio-cultural perspective on learning and education, explaining that

learning develops primarily from social relationships and the actions of individuals that take place within particular sociopolitical contexts. That is to say, learning emerges from the social, cultural, and political spaces in which it takes place, and through the interactions and relationships that occur among learners and teachers (p. 2).

In Table 4.1, increased differentiation within the post-behaviorism era is depicted by lines that now represent four schools of thought on the process of learning and how the mind works—Behaviorism, Cognitivism, Constructivism, and Socioconstructivism.

Having considered psychological perspectives on learning up to the millennial divide, we would be remiss if we did not make some predictions about what may come next in the story. One possible plot line focuses again on individuals and their motivational and cognitive experiences, but from within a socioconstructivist perspective. In a consideration of the role of individual cognition in distributed systems, Salomon (1993).

argued that the total dismissal of individuals' cognitions in favor of situated and distributed cognitions provides only frozen pictures of states that neither develop nor grow. To account for changes and developments in the performance of joint, distributed systems, one has to consider the role played by individual partners (p. 134).

The reciprocality of the influence of social systems and of the individuals constituting and being constituted by those systems seems to represent a viable future direction. A second line of development may include constructs from complexity theory, a theory that represents human endeavors as complex adaptive systems where humans construct islands of meaning at the border between chaos and order. The concept of adaptability and the individual's desire to impose order and predictability on the world seem crucial as areas of future inquiry. At the same time, there is value in considering human functioning as a dynamic system, one in which opportunistic and chance juxtapositions influence the sense-making that individuals experience (Kunnen & Bosma, 2000; Van der Maas & Molenaar, 1992; Van Geert, 1994).

## THE EMOTIONAL AND MOTIVATIONAL CHARACTER OF LEARNING

Psychologists, we freely admit, often pursue wonderfully esoteric searches whose findings may fail to address teachers' calls for direct classroom application. However, one area of prolific development that does have immediate relevance to schooling is the work exploring the role of human motivation and emotion in learning contexts. We begin with emotions because there is less to say about them and also because descriptions of the emotional nature of learning easily lead into a discussion of motivation.

### The Emotional Side

As intellectual a pursuit as it may seem, learning is fraught with emotions. Students may experience anticipatory eagerness for a learning situation or be filled with dread at the possibility of failure about to be publicly experienced. They can feel pride or shame once they finish a learning task, they can be caught up in the excitement and enjoyment of an activity, or they may suffer from boredom and ennui as a learning task unfolds. Models of the effect of moods on cognitive processing such as the mood-as-information model of Schwarz (1990) describe how different affective states influence processing by encouraging the learner to adopt different strategies in processing information from the environment. Individuals experiencing negative mood states are likely to adopt a systematic, vigilant style of information processing, highly focused on the input material. By contrast, a positive mood state seems to foster more global, simplifying processing strategies. Because of its powerful interrupt effect (Lewis, 1992), shame is a particularly debilitating emotion and yet one that learners of all ages, degrees of academic success, and perhaps cultural backgrounds can experience. Some researchers have reported that shame could be experienced even by high achieving students; some were able to rebound from the shame experience and invest more effort in the learning situation, while others felt defeated. In addition, learners often report feelings of anxiety and worry, particularly in situations involving some sort of verbal performance such as in writing apprehension (e.g., Cleary, 1991; Larson, 1985), speech apprehension (Daly & Stafford, 1984), and foreign language anxiety (e.g., Horwitz & Young, 1991).

Lest we paint too dark a picture, we should consider also the positive consequences that can come from strong negative emotions. Students who have experienced shame may prove resilient and strive hard to succeed in subsequent tasks (Turner & Schallert, in press). Pekrun (1992) developed a model of the role of emotions in motivation for academic endeavors that considers how negative emotions can help learners be more effective.

Also, there are positive emotions associated with enjoyment and deep involvement in learning. Csikszentmihalyi (1990) described a particular kind of internal psychological state that he calls "flow" referring to the rapt attention one invests in certain tasks. A person in flow becomes so involved in a task that an awareness of passing time, distracting stimuli, or the ruminations of self-consciousness recedes into the background. In a particularly thorough investigation of what it means for a reader to be lost in a book, Nell (1988) described the psychological, physiological, textual, and social factors of *ludic* reading, that is, of reading for pleasure in a state reminiscent of flow. Schallert and Reed (1997) considered how certain characteristics of text and context can pull a reader into a state of involvement so deep that hours may pass before the reader returns to reality. As they stated, "involvement while reading is pleasurable, enough so that previously involved readers will take a chance with an unknown text to repeat the experience" (p. 81). In other words, the experience of flow is its own motivator, being sought out by learners for its own sake.

## The Motivational Side

Consideration of the positive psychological state of flow brings us to motivation, because one way to think about flow and enjoyment is to think of them as prime indicators of intrinsic motivation. Educators have an understandable bias of valuing intrinsic over extrinsic motivation, of preferring the learner who engages in an academic task willingly and eagerly over the learner who seems to need extrinsic incentives (even threats!) to get started. Yet, we have noticed that when educators discuss motivation, they often conflate a broad array of motives that psychologists have found useful to distinguish. For example, just because a student seems dedicated to schoolwork and seems to need little outside inducement to tackle assignments does not mean the student is intrinsically motivated in the theoretical sense. Two lines of motivation research have been particularly applicable to education. First is the work emanating from Atkinson's (1957, 1964) theory of achievement motivation. Second are views of motivation as derived from basic human needs (Ryan & Deci, 2000).

In the first line of work, achievement motivation is portrayed as the multiplicative function of expectancies and values. One is said to be motivated to persist and to invest effort in a situation to the degree that one expects success in accomplishing a task and that one values success in that realm. Elaborations on Atkinson's simple formulations have been many. Such constructs as self-efficacy (Bandura, 1986; Pintrich & De Groot, 1990), academic self-worth (Covington & Omelich, 1979),

self-regulation (Zimmerman & Martinez-Pons, 1990), and academic risk-taking (Clifford, 1991) have all generated their own prolific literatures. Deriving also from this work is the idea of motivational orientations, a concept we find especially helpful for teachers.

Beginning with a simple distinction between individuals with a performance orientation and those with a mastery orientation in academic tasks (Dweck & Leggett, 1988), more recently the construct of motivational orientations is presented as independent dimensions that are task-specific and context-sensitive. Dweck and Leggett (1988) proposed that students' motivation seems linked to their perception of themselves as learners and the potential of a task to support or refute that self-view. They identified two cognition-affect-behavior patterns in children. One group of learners tended to avoid tasks they deemed too challenging, or, if they met a challenge during a task, their performance deteriorated and they expressed negative self-cognitions. These were termed maladaptive or "helpless" learners. In contrast, the more adaptive "mastery-oriented" learners seemed to thrive on challenges, and maintained effective efforts toward a task when they were actually failing at it. These learners even coached themselves through difficult aspects of a task, often "bootstrapping" themselves to success.

This pattern seems to play out in classrooms. Many new teachers assume that maladaptive responses are associated with students who have struggled with prior learning tasks, and have thus "learned" to avoid further embarrassment and pain. Saving face in these conditions, while painful to observe, seems to make a kind of sense to the caring teacher. Unfortunately, the maladaptive response appears frequently among students who are clearly bright and skilled, students the teacher "knows" can accomplish a given task and yet choose to avoid it. In puzzling out this behavior, Dweck and Leggett (1988) suggested that "the goals individuals are pursuing create the framework within which they interpret and react to events" (p. 256). They differentiated between *performance goals* (goals that individuals pursue to gain favorable judgments of their competence and to avoid negative evaluations), and *learning goals* (goals concerned with increasing personal competence in an area).

More recently, the idea that motivational orientation is a trait characteristic of individuals that they carry into most learning situations has changed. Now we see motivational orientations as separate dimensions that can change with different tasks and in response to different evaluative environments (Ames, 1992; Harackiewicz, Barron, Tauer, Carter, & Elliot, 2000). It is clear that teachers influence the sorts of goals that students adopt by how they arrange for feedback and communicate their views about the relative importance of outcomes versus learning processes (Ames & Archer, 1988). It is also possible, and in some views, advantageous, to be both performance and mastery oriented. The first orientation is associated with high success on achievement outcome measures and the second with enjoyment, interest, and the likelihood of re-engaging the same content or task in the future (Harackiewicz, et al., 2000).

This brings us to the second, also extremely prolific, line of research on motivation, derived from theories of basic human needs (Lepper & Hoddell, 1989; Ryan & Deci, 2000). This line of work is the one most educators are likely considering when they bemoan their students' lack of motivation, or make distinctions between intrinsic and extrinsic motivation. The classic question defining this approach to motivation was not so much how to promote intrinsic motivation but about whether extrinsic rewards would harm intrinsic motivation. For example, Lepper, Greene, and Nisbett (1973) reported that children lost interest in an activity that they had initially enjoyed when they received attractive rewards for engaging in the task. A lively debate ensued, culminating in the 90s with a thorough meta-analysis by Cameron and Pierce (1994) suggesting that the evidence in support of the harmful effects of extrinsic rewards was more flimsy than often reported, to which Lepper, Keavney, and Drake (1996) responded. To anyone who has ever worried about the moral overtones associated with "bribing" children into doing their school tasks, we recommend this literature. What is interesting about it, however, is that it deals less with how to foster intrinsic motivation than one might like, especially in situations where there is little or no intrinsic motivation to begin with.

A more recent consideration of extrinsic and intrinsic motivation is the work on self-determination theory (Ryan & Deci, 2000). Rather than positing two separate categories of motivation, this view designates them as ends of an underlying continuum that measures the degree to which the learner is choosing, or "self-determining," to be engaged in a particular task. The need for autonomy drives individuals to seek choice in task engagement, even when the task is onerous. The intrinsic motivation end of the continuum represents situations when individuals willingly and eagerly choose to do something; they experience no initial reluctance and do not need to force themselves to begin the task. What is particularly useful about self-determination theory, however, is the rich ways it describes motivations that deviate from the purest sort of intrinsic engagement in a task for its own sake. Deci and Ryan (1985) proposed that there are different degrees to which learners identify with the goals of a task. Thus, a task that one enters into only for the extrinsic consequences it yields is very different from a task that one sees as important and valuable, even if not inherently pleasurable. The major underlying dimension reflected in different motivational processes is that of autonomy and choice: "Students can perform extrinsically motivated actions with resentment, resistance, and disinterest, or, alternatively, with an attitude of willingness that reflects an inner acceptance of the value or utility of a task" (Ryan & Deci, 2000, p. 55).

Recent classroom trends in language arts echo findings from motivational research such as those noted by Turner (1995), who found that open tasks that allowed choice and problem solving were more likely to foster motivation than closed tasks that required one answer and specified procedures. Response-based literature circles (e.g., Galda, Cullinan, & Strickland, 1993; Nystrand & Gamoran, 1991; Raphael & McMahon, 1994; Short & Pierce, 1990), writing workshops (e.g., Atwell, 1987; Calkins, 1994; Graves, 1983), CORI (concept-oriented reading instruction, Guthrie & McCann, 1997), and other similar approaches are commonly recommended in teacher education texts and journals as motivating and engaging interventions to encourage student literacy development across grades and contexts. Much remains to be studied regarding the effects of these interventions on student attitudes, motivation, and achievement, however (Morrow & Gambrell, 2000).

## ATTENTIONAL CONSTRAINTS AND THEIR ROLE IN SMOOTH, EXPERT-LIKE LANGUAGE PROCESSING

Over time, it has become apparent that the metaphor of information processing is inadequate for the complex, variable, and emotional tasks of responding to text, learning to read and write, or taking on the role of teacher. However, there is one aspect of the metaphor that has survived and still provides a compelling reminder of the difficulties that learners encounter when new to a skill or to a way of thinking. That aspect, referred to typically as "the constraints on attentional capacity," emphasizes how the perceptual and attention systems have key "pinch" points that limit the way we can take in information from our world (Baddeley, 1986; Just & Carpenter, 1992; and Samuels, 1988). Even though the architecture of the mind is often portrayed as a system of interactive, parallel processes allowing for multiple pathways and connections (cf., Kintsch, 1988; Rumelhart, 1991), nevertheless, there seem to be clear limits about what we can pay attention to consciously at any one moment in time.

In undertaking any new learning task, a learner is constrained by limited cognitive resources. As the learner engages in the subprocesses of a task, attention must be allocated across all demands, especially those aspects least familiar. At some point, the learner experiences overload, and must relinquish attention to some part of the task. This often results in a less-than-ideal, novice-like performance. Happily, the occurrence of overload rarely remains constant. With experience and practice, components of the task that once required major chunks of cognitive capacity can become so well learned that they can be accomplished automatically or with little attention devoted to them. This is one of the more predictable shifts that result as one acquires expertise in a domain. Thus, more accomplished drivers, cooks, readers, and writers share at least one characteristic in that many components of their task have become routine or automatic so that greater resources can be devoted to more complex aspects. As various aspects of a task are automatized, the task becomes, in a real sense, "easier" for the learner (Samuels, 1988).

An example often used to describe the tremendous impact on performance associated with limits on attentional resources is that of driving, and in particular, learning to drive a car. For the novice driver, every part of learning to drive is new: inserting the key into the ignition, turning the wheel, easing on the gas pedal, knowing where the brake is, etc. All these parts occur as separate tasks, each presenting some challenge to a beginning driver. Eventually each of the tasks associated with starting the car becomes automatized and interconnected. However, starting the car is just one of the many chunks of the more complex task of driving. It is a wonder that there is no special area of psychology devoted to an understanding of how driving skills are acquired, or on what to do about the problem of the driving disabled!

This phenomenon is also apparent when observing beginning readers. For those who quickly recognize the phonologic and alphabetic principles of language, decoding becomes simpler, allowing them to attend to the greater message in the text and to increase their familiarity with text patterns, story elements, and even new vocabulary terms (Stanovich, 1986). Reading becomes enjoyable, and something in which these students willingly engage. By comparison, for students who fail to automatize decoding skills, each reading act is difficult—fraught with numerous attentional demands. Predictably, students who experience "reading" under these conditions often avoid the very practice that would help them better automatize decoding skills (Juel, 1988). These "Matthew" effects, so named by Stanovich (1986) after the biblical parable in which the "rich get richer," have always seemed a bitter irony. Those who require the greatest resources to deal with the difficult part of a task find they must allocate precious attentional resources to ALL aspects of the task, rather than just to the difficult parts.

Thus, some beginning readers seem to grasp, rather quickly, the phonologic and alphabetic notions underlying reading. Children who have learned to attend to the sound patterns in words through exposure to nursery rhymes, word play, and being read to regularly seem to grasp more readily the alphabetic principle—that letters can represent sounds in words. For those who have already "automatized" the ability to hear the separate sounds in words (phonemic awareness), assigning those sounds/phonemes to particular letter configurations probably requires less active attention, thereby freeing them to notice frequently recurring letter patterns and other print conventions in their reading. In contrast, beginning readers who have not internalized the notion of separate sounds in words are faced with a much more demanding task—discovering and attending to the separate sounds (phonemes) in words at the same time as they are associating particular letter configurations with those sounds. In this view, it is no wonder that measures of young children's phonemic awareness reliably predict reading success well beyond first grade (Blachman, 2000). Indeed, word recognition challenges become an ongoing and reliable indicator of reading difficulty, not just for beginning readers, but for older readers as well (Blachman, 2000; Kim & Goetz, 1994).

The principle of attentional capacity has also been applied to writing acquisition and development, suggesting that writing requires the coordination of many sub-components, each of which requires practice before it can be performed without taking up an undue proportion of available capacity. For example, Jones and Christensen (1999) analyzed the difficulties some young writers experience and hypothesized that at least in part, fluency in the physical act of handwriting was lacking. By providing a specialized intervention simply focused on getting students to "solve" the handwriting problem early, Jones and Christensen found that young writers who had fallen behind their peers were able to catch up when it came to the quality of what they were writing.

The notion of information processing limits offers important applications for teaching. When students are introduced to new domains of knowledge and to the complexities of new academic tasks, there is likely to be an initial period during which the task requires concentrated care and effort, often yielding only

paltry performance. It is easy to appreciate that a learner could need strong motivation to persevere through initial stages of task acquisition. The same would be true for students attempting to refine a subprocess of a larger skill, who, when paying greater attention to a part of the process, exhibit a decline in the overall quality of work (e.g., paying so much attention to correct spelling that the creativity and flow of the message suffers). With patience and practice, the subprocess is automatized and integrated into the overall task, and greater performance in both the subprocess and the overall task is noted. Happily, most adolescents exhibit exactly the needed motivation when learning to drive, but what about that required for learning to read and write, or learning to read and write in a second language? These present special challenges not only for learners but also for teachers who seek to support learners through the sometimes drawn-out process of gaining expertise in academic endeavors.

## THE LEARNER AS ACTIVE, INTENTIONAL, AND STRATEGIC CONSTRUCTOR OF MEANING

As we previously mentioned in our description of the history of psychologological views of learning and literacy, one of the powerful ideas that intrigued educational psychologists when they became dissatisfied with the mechanistic perspective on human functioning, as represented by the information processing and behaviorist views, was the description of the learner as meaning maker. The essence of the constructivist perspective lies in its portrayal of learners as organic rather than mechanistic sense-makers. We have already cited some of the early psychological work on constructive and reconstructive processes in comprehension and memory. Here, we want to emphasize two concepts that continue to interest educational psychologists and that we believe inform how real students in real classrooms make sense of instruction: the role of prior knowledge, and the intentional and strategic nature of learning.

### What is the Good of Having "Prior" Knowledge?

There is a sense in which the claim that what one already knows influences the quantity and quality of what one can learn is now so taken for granted that it is difficult to appreciate anew the special contribution such a view makes to our understanding. And yet, the powerful idea gave teachers and researchers a different perspective from which to explain why someone might fail to learn or understand: not because of low intelligence or a deficiency in the ability to engage the basic comprehension processes, but because of missing or unactivated background knowledge presupposed by the new input (Bransford, 1979, 1984). Nevertheless, the concept continues to occupy psychologists and educational researchers because, though it may seem sensible in broad outline, it is not always clear what prediction to make in particular situations, and there continue to be interesting controversies in the ideas (Alexander, Schallert, & Hare, 1991; Schallert, 1991).

For example, although there are several demonstrations that more knowledgeable individuals understand better and remember more from information presented to them than less knowledgeable individuals (cf., Pritchard, 1990; Walker, 1987), in certain learning situations, prior knowledge can actually interfere with learning. Alvermann, Smith, and Readance (1985) found that, when learning new science information that conflicted with what they already held to be true, students in the condition in which they were not reminded of their prior knowledge performed better than students who considered and wrote about what they currently knew about the topic. Spiro (1980) demonstrated that individuals can compartmentalize conflicting information, and thus manage to hold incompatible ideas. In research on science education, much has been made of how difficult it is to change individuals' conceptions of what they believe to be true about natural phenomena (Perkins & Simmons, 1988; Pintrich, Marx, & Boyle, 1993). Entrenched ideas lead learners, and not just struggling readers, to see the text as confirming what they already believe rather than as an invitation to expand, elaborate, or change their existing views (Nissani & Hoefler-Nissani, 1992). Thus, although it is almost always an advantage to have more rather than less knowledge in an area in which one is attempting to read or learn something new, there are special challenges associated with the difficult task of changing one's mind. This is especially true when, as often happens, the text materials used to present the new information are neither considerate, in the sense of being clear, or coherent (Armbruster, 1984; Beck, McKeown, Sinatra, & Loxterman, 1991), nor good examples themselves of the sort of integrative, open-inquiry, or critical stance that we often proclaim as worthy goals for our students (Rukavina & Daneman, 1996).

A second puzzle that has fascinated educational psychologists is how exactly to characterize the knowledge that we bring to bear in new learning and comprehension situations. The major contrast that has been made is between the schema, or knowledge structure, metaphor and the connectionist, parallel-distributed, neural net model. "Schema" is a theoretical label for cognitive structures posited as the basic unit of knowledge and described as an organized, interconnected set of nodes that represent abstracted regularities in one's experience (cf., Anderson, 1977; Anderson & Pearson, 1984; Rumelhart & Ortony, 1977; Schallert, 1982, 1987; Schank & Abelson, 1977; Tierney & Cunningham, 1984). As useful and intuitive a construct as it proved, it has received some vigorous attacks (cf., Beers, 1987; Sadoski, Paivio, & Goetz, 1991; Spiro, Vispoel, Schmitz, Samarapungavan, & Boerger, 1987). One of the more essential problems with the metaphor of knowledge as structures was that knowledge was portrayed as static, fully-formed structures rather than as constructed, probabilistic, and incomplete open systems responsive to the vagueries of the input. Connectionist models, by contrast, make the claim that one's knowledge is represented in patterns of connections, in interrelationships (one might say, in associations) between empty nodes, rather than as structures (Rumelhart, 1991). Kintsch (1988) and others who have investigated his construction–integration model have made productive use of the idea that knowledge is represented as connections. However, as Alexander et al. (1991) implied, there is perhaps a way

to make use of the strengths that both of these models offer so as to offset any disadvantages they may have. In their framework, one's knowledge always is in one of two states, a tacit or an explicit one. Tacit knowledge may best be represented as a net of spreading activation, as in the connectionist model. This tacit knowledge is the basis from which individuals construct in a responsive, dynamic way the knowledge structure (schemata) they may need in their explicit knowledge to make sense of new text, new input, new situations.

Finally, there has been a surprising proliferation of terms, as in *background knowledge, domain knowledge, schema, content knowledge, procedural and declarative knowledge*, that has not helped the field maintain a clear grasp on what we mean by the underlying construct of prior knowledge. This was the goal that Alexander and colleagues (1991) had when they proposed their tacit–explicit framework, to provide conceptual coherence to the field and delineate the nuances of meanings related to knowledge terms. In their review of 2 decades of work on knowledge, they proposed that explicit knowledge was comprised of two major interactive planes, conceptual knowledge and metacognitive knowledge, drawing from a sea of tacit knowledge and influenced by sociocultural knowledge that acts as a "pervasive filter through which all experiences and understandings must pass" (p. 325). In addition to the distinction between explicit and tacit knowledge and to the inclusion of sociocultural knowledge as a pervasive influence, their model was unusual in including metacognitive knowledge as a part of prior knowledge. Thus, what influences learners is not just particular conceptions they are able to construct from their tacit knowledge but also their knowledge of how to learn, of themselves as learners, and of their plans and goals. Three recent developments are connected to metaconitive knowledge: the work on learners' beliefs about learning and the nature of knowledge, what are sometimes referred to as epistemological beliefs (Schommer, 1994; Schraw, 2000), instructional interventions that encourage strategic views of interacting with text such as Reciprocal Teaching (Palincsar & Brown, 1984) and Questioning the Author (Beck, McKeown, Hamilton, & Kucan, 1997), and the work on teacher beliefs, ranging from interactions between beliefs and instructional decisions (cf., Clandinin, 1986; Clark & Peterson, 1986; Cochran-Smith & Lytle, 1990; Richardson, 1994, 1996) to work on exploring and changing beliefs through literacy autobiographies and other techniques (Carter & Doyle, 1996).

## Learning as an Intentional, Strategic Act

In its everyday meaning of the word, construction usually takes place with plans in hand, with teams of workers assigned to tasks in their area of expertise, and with inspectors whose job it is to certify that the plans have been followed and that the building meets "code." In developing a view of learners as active meaning makers, psychologists made use of the idea of learners who reflect on their own learning and manage their learning processes to meet their goals. Like building inspectors, learners monitor their current learning to see if they are following their plans on a trajectory to their goals. Positive outcomes of the monitoring allow learners simply to continue whatever they are currently doing. Monitoring that detects potential problems sends learners on a search for more effective strategies to meet their goals, or it may lead to changed goals.

This self-reflective, self-managing process is what we mean by metacognition. Although there are still debates about what the term exactly encompasses, Paris and Winograd (1990) provided a sensible conceptualization, presenting metacognition as the interacting processes of self-appraisal and self-management. In addition, they connected metacognition to motivation and affect. Self-appraisal can result in exactly the kinds of powerful emotional outcomes that we were describing in an earlier section, fear and shame, or pride and joy. Self-management may require effort, the "will" as well as the "skill" to engage in those strategies that will allow one to reach one's goals (Weinstein & Mayer, 1985). Finally, Paris and Winograd connected what has traditionally been seen as an individualistic concern to the social and cultural context in which the learning is occurring. In their view, metacognitive messages about the difficulty of tasks, about how one should approach them, about how well a learner is performing so far, and what the learner should expect given past experiences often come from important others like teachers, parents, and peers. Thus, Paris and Winograd closed their insightful description of metacognition with a consideration of several instructional interventions that encourage learners to become more metacognitively sophisticated by way of social exchanges about learning: direct explanation, scaffolded instruction, cognitive coaching, and cooperative learning.

Before we close our discussion of what it means to be an active, strategic learner, we want to bring into our discussion three final points. First, current psychological conceptions of metacognitive processes are more about learners becoming strategic than about them having a well-stocked "bag" of strategies (Paris, Lipson, & Wixson, 1983; Paris, 1988). It has been a perennial and frustrating aspect associated with attempts at helping learners become more strategic, that the strategies acquired are often context-glued and show little transfer to other possible applications. Instead of focusing on strategies per se isolated from their context of use, it may be more generative to encourage learners when they encounter difficulties to consider their goals and to assess whether they seem on the path to reaching those goals.

Second, it is also important, we believe, in our enthusiasm for anything self-reflective to remember that there are occasions when even the usually good and effective learner does not appear to be very strategic. Garner (1990) pointed out several of these occasions. Echoing our discussion of experts and attentional capacity, when learners have well-developed, rich, interconnected knowledge, they sometimes so easily make sense of new information that the effort-demanding deployment of conscious strategic processes is not needed (Brown, 1988). Also, it is important to remember that adults may label young learners as nonstrategic when in fact, what differs between them are the goals they each have for the learning situation, the values they place on particular tasks. Many adolescent learners show themselves to be quite strategic in how they manage to avoid expending effort at academic tasks without getting into too much trouble with teachers and parents. Garner pointed to additional reasons why strategic approaches may not be taken: Young and older learners may not be good at monitoring their learning, they may have so little knowledge in a new area that they cannot tell yet whether they are successful or what to do to help themselves succeed, and they may be in classroom situations that do not encourage sophisticated, goal-directed strategy use. Thus, becoming a strategic learner depends on the learner's conception of topics relevant to the to-be-learned new skill or information, prior knowledge, as it does on the conception of the learning task itself.

Finally, the relationship between strategies and knowledge offers an interesting puzzle. Not only does it seem true, as we previously presented, that more knowledgeable individuals are sometimes found to be more and sometimes found to be less strategic. Alexander, Graham, and Harris (1998) proposed a model of developing expertise that they specifically tied to the change in strategies that more expert individuals in a particular domain adopt when compared to individuals who are only being acclimated to the domain. As they claimed, "the course of strategy development is not strictly aligned with chronological age, as much as it is with the experiences and schooling that are often age-associated" (p. 136).

## THE IMPORTANCE OF LANGUAGE AND CULTURE IN LEARNING

So far, in our description of the contributions that psychological explorations have made to our understanding of learning and literacy, we have considered learning in terms of its emotional and motivational aspects, its attentional demands, and its active, meaning-making character. Although we have referred to how the social and cultural context can influence all of these processes, we have not yet focused specifically on the primary tool by which learning and schooling, at least in our culture, occurs, that is, language. Wells (1999) opened his book on dialogic inquiry with a quote from Halliday (1993) that truly underscores how critical this primary tool is now considered to be:

When children learn language, they are not simply engaging in one type of learning among many; rather, they are learning the foundations of learning itself. The distinctive characteristic of human learning is that it is a process of making meaning—a semiotic process; and the prototypical form of human semiotic is language (p. 93 in the original).

Much of the most exciting work in current educational research involves a focus on how language participates in and mediates learning, a view that is often framed in terms of Vygotsky's (1978) sociocultural theory of human development.

Wertsch (1991) identified three major themes in Vygotsky's work that support much of what has come to be known as the sociocultural or socioconstructivist influence in educational research. First among these is Vygotsky's advocacy of genetic or developmental inquiry, by which he did *not* mean a focus on the contribution of heredity to individual differences, but rather a focus on the origin and evolution of processes. Vygotsky's genetic inquiry was historical in nature, seeking to explain how one developmental process holds the emerging roots to the next stage in development and growth, and how that growth unfolds. Thus, his interest was in the actual process of learning, not in the final end product of something learned.

Another important theme in Vygotsky's (1978) work, deriving logically from the first, is his explication of the social, cultural nature of learning, especially as seen in young children's internalization of language and in studies of learning within the Zone of Proximal Development. His claim was that higher level processes were always first demonstrated in interaction with others and only then appropriated and internalized, so that "the specific structures and processes of intrapsychological functioning can be traced to their genetic precursors on the interpsychological plane" (Wertsch, 1991, p. 89). Much of the research on early reading and writing acquisition has reflected this theme as researchers have broadened their focus from what individual children are doing (cf., Gentry, 1987) to careful documentation of the interactions between young children and their caregivers, their teachers, and their peers for insight into social and cultural influences on literacy development (cf., Dyson, 1995; Snow, 1983; Wertsch & Hickmann, 1987). Recent work has broadened this lens even further, to include ever-widening circles of sociocultural inquiry (see Gee, 2000 for a brief review of past and current directions).

A third theme derives from Vygotsky's description of the mediating role of artifacts or tools in human activity and learning. Distinguishing between technical tools and psychological tools, Vygotsky noted that technical tools allow humans to effect change upon an object (e.g., digging in the ground with a stick) whereas psychological tools involve symbol systems (e.g., verbal and written language) and allow individuals to represent and consider objects independently of their physical presence (e.g., using the symbols c-a-t to represent the verbal sounds for /cat/, the concept of "cat", or to refer to a particular cat). For Vygotsky, an individual's appropriation and use of the psychological tool of language were key to learning. As individuals engage in any language-based activity, whether it be a conversation with another person or with an author, they make use of a mediational mean that they can only have appropriated from their sociocultural milieu. As Wertsch (1991) stated, "Instead of locating mental functioning in the individual in isolation, Vygotsky locates it in the individual functioning together with a mediational means" (p. 92).

As Wertsch (1991) points out, Vygotsky wrote at the time of the Russian Revolution and died at a young age (before his 40s), before he could fully work out how language functions as a mediational tool. In current sociocultural formulations, much is made of the contributions of another Russian thinker, Bakhtin (1981, 1990), and his views on the essentially dialogic nature of every utterance. This dialogic character refers to the intertextual nature of language, oral or written, to how "real" utterances indicate and point to other utterances and by so doing, connect to the social and cultural world.

A view that places such emphasis on language and on the sociocultural basis of the learning process is certain to offer a number of intriguing educational implications, especially when contrasted with the dominantly transmissive instruction long practiced by many educators. We will describe three particular areas of current concern for educators: the role of dialogue and social interaction, the centrality of inquiry-based instruction, and the importance of cultural practices.

## The Role of Dialogue and Social Interaction in Learning

In many classrooms, oral interaction patterns commonly follow an IRE pattern (Cazden, 1988; Mehan, 1985) of teacher initiation, student response, teacher evaluation. Although such participation patterns show in each utterance the dialogic echoes of other utterances and although these ways of using language can be described fruitfully from a socioconstructivist perspective, such approaches to classroom discourse do little to support learners in the construction and representation of their own meaning (Wells, 2000). Classrooms in which most of the public talk is of this type are often dull and unmotivating places. By contrast, many educators have begun to emphasize the value of authentic conversations in the classroom, discussions that allow wonder (Townsend, 1991), that encourage student-to-student as much as student–teacher exchanges (Hammer, 1995), and that invite students to connect their personal knowledge and experiences with that of others through discovering and articulating links between and across texts (text-to-text); links between texts and themselves (text-to-self), and connections from texts to life in a larger sense (text-to-world) (Keene & Zimmermann, 1997).

This thinking also extends to the importance of oral modeling for instructing children in reading comprehension and writing processes. The underlying concept of this approach holds that as teachers make apparent their own thinking processes through language, students are able to appropriate or "borrow" particular words and phrases to guide their own thinking (as in the cognitive apprenticeship of Rogoff, 1990, or reciprocal teaching of Palincsar & Brown, 1984), eventually undertaking similar processes without the need of external models. The same principle holds for encouraging students to share their thought processes aloud, both during and after problem solving occurs. A number of studies have examined how concepts and ideas evolve through discussion and how student contributions become increasingly more sophisticated and complex in settings where articulation of personal meanings and connections is valued and supported (e.g., book clubs, McMahon & Raphael, 1996; CORI, Guthrie & McCann 1997; Alvermann et al., 1996).

## The Centrality of Inquiry-based Instruction in Learning

Franklin's summary of knowledge as created and recreated "in the discourse between people doing things together" (cited in Wells, 2000) aptly captures the focus of a number of investigations of the value of active learning as expressed in project-based curricula, cooperative learning strategies (cf., Kagan, 1990; Slavin, 1983), and inquiry-based curriculum (Heald-Taylor, 1996; Monson & Monson, 1994). Because learning is an integral part of participating in the activities of a community and mastering the tools and practices that enable one to do so effectively, Wells (1999, 2000), Harste (Monson & Monson, 1994) and others have suggested that schools might most productively be organized with inquiry at the heart of the curriculum. Encouraging an inquiry stance involves raising authentic questions within experiences common to students' lives. An inquiry curriculum is based on questions students wonder and care about on their own (Townsend, 1991) or are willing to entertain because an enthusiastic and knowledgeable teacher has invited them to consider possible answers (Hammer, 1995). As students interact with one another to answer these questions, they both create and refine knowledge, communicating personal biases and positions. For example, Dodson (2000) found that students reflected in their utterances one of two underlying stances. On one hand, their ways of expressing themselves, their very words, reflected a sense of being open to others' input, and a willingness to change their minds, whereas other comments had a presentational quality, a sense of certainty and unwillingness to entertain other ideas.

## The Importance of Cultural Practices in Learning

The notion that there are accepted "ways to learn" within a given culture is extremely important for educators, especially given the wonderful diversity represented within any group of students. One of the contributions of the socioconstructivist perspective has been to allow us to appreciate the constitutive role that discourse practices and the sociocultural context play in a learning situation, a role that is always easier to see when participants in an activity bring with them different experiences and expectations. There have been several influential authors who have sensitively described the special challenges facing all participants, but especially those in the less powerful position, whenever activities are co-joined by individuals representing very different cultural foundations.

For example, Au (1997) described more than 2 decades of work with students of native Hawaiian ancestry highlighting the ways in which teachers, particularly teachers of European ancestry, had learned to adapt their ways of interacting with children as they conducted literacy lessons. Adopting patterns of talk that were sensitive to the ways that these students carried on discussions of stories in their family context allowed the teachers to be much more effective. For their part, the students showed gains not only in terms of literacy achievement but also in terms of enjoyment and, of what Au called "ownership" of reading and writing.

A second example is Heath's (1983) yearlong ethnography of a small town, with her careful description of three different cultures in contact. Her detailed, vivid depiction of the talk engaged in by adults and children showed how everyday "in family" talk did or did not easily match the language and learning practices that the children encountered in school. Ways of thinking about school and about learning, and of talking their way in and through school were connected to their cultural roots, and, for some children, became the contact zone in which they battled and often lost the struggle to acquire literacy. Moll, Tapia, and Whitmore (1993) described yet another situation in which individuals make use of funds of knowledge that their cultural crossings necessitate both in everyday contexts as well as the classroom.

Thus, our views of learning are increasingly informed by an appreciation for the more invisible aspects of context that influence learners, the sociocultural experiences that have led participants in a new setting to have expectations of each other and of themselves as they engage in an activity. Note that in these views, the idea of culture is meant to apply to more than just the national, gender, or ethnic groupings that one might supply on a census form. Every group we join (willingly or not so willingly) leaves some mark, even if only that we know better how we want to resist and combat the group's influence. In this sense, we are all multicultural beings, bringing with us as we enter new groups the residue of other groups we have experienced, expressed in how we think, feel, and most of all, talk.

Helping students recognize what counts as learning and knowledge in a particular setting is an important part of the educational enterprise. Current views of learning and of how learners appropriate literate practices encourage teachers to construct supportive classroom environments that allow for peer interaction, authentic conversations among students and teachers, and opportunities for learners to connect across space and time (e.g., via Internet connections and other technological advances). Thus, the classrooms of educators exploring sociocultural views of learning will be anything but silent, and anything but isolated.

## CONCLUSION

So we return to the imaginary teacher with whom we opened this chapter, the one who asked about current psychological research and what it might offer a language arts teacher. Having described psychology's contribution in terms of four broad areas that are currently generating much interest, we want to give a quick assessment of the enlightened educator of today, one who enters the language arts classroom with a more refined understanding of learning and development than educators of any previous generation. Today's language arts teacher likely views literacy learning as a complex social interaction. Today's teacher recognizes the importance of emotion in learning, and knows there are a number of implications for strong emotions, both negative and positive. In planning various learning activities, this teacher seeks to engender in the classroom an environment conducive to "flow," hoping that once students experience the joy of literacy, they will return to literate practices again and again, of their own accord. Even when flow seems unlikely, today's teacher has an awareness of the role that motivation plays in learning, a regard that plays out in consistent planning to support students in adopting a learning rather than performance orientation and to provide for student choice and autonomy within lessons.

Today's teacher is aware of the aptness of the notion of limited capacity as it relates to the attentional resources of students, appreciating how new tasks can require great effort that may not result in immediately satisfying results for students.

The teacher of today expects and even enjoys the wide variety of different meanings students will construct as they interact with new learning opportunities, and finds ways to enter into the students' conceptions respectfully even while guiding them to consider the best representations of the disciplines. Today's teacher also knows that students are active and strategic learners and seeks to support their growing sophistication in thinking about their own thinking and analyzing the success of their efforts all the while creating an environment that values increased personal understanding and competence over performance.

Today's teacher also sees learning and, in fact, all human interactions as occurring in a rich cultural context with language as a pervasive, powerful, and constitutive tool for meaning making. Thus, this teacher is likely to be particularly sensitive to practices in the classroom that replay damaging power differentials along cultural, gender, ethnic, and linguistic lines, and to attempt to replace them with more benign practices. Today's teacher is likely to encourage students to interact verbally throughout their day with peers, with teachers, with themselves (through writing and through inner contemplation). This teacher encourages students to recognize the wonderful diversity represented by the experiences of each class member and communicates regard not only for shared understandings, but also for the places and spaces where differences encourage new problem-solving goals.

What can today's teacher expect from the research community of educational psychologists in the next few years? As identified by Pintrich (2000), four themes have characterized recent inquiry in educational psychology, and we believe they will probably continue to inform our views of teaching and learning. These include the following:

1. A focus on the individual learner.
2. A broadened view of the "individual in context" (p. 223).
3. The extension of study variables to include broader outcomes of schooling.

4. The use of nontraditional models and constructs to explore new avenues of inquiry.

Although many studies have focused on the learner as an individual (and such focus remains a critical area for inquiry), other researchers have extended the view to include a number of social interactions and contextual issues. We believe future research will include ever-increasing efforts to describe, explain, and perhaps even predict the complex interactions of motivational, cognitive, social, emotional, and cultural factors in real-life settings. More and more, we believe teachers will see themselves and their students in the writings of psychological inquiry, lessening the sense of distance between research producer and consumer. This is also true as an increasing number of teachers engage in action research, undertaking informed and systematic inquiry about their own teaching and knowing, and sharing those insights with others who share their interests and concerns.

Today's teacher is concerned with outcomes of schooling that go beyond traditional inquiries about learning, cognition, and motivation to include affect, values, caring, mental health, adjustment, adaptation, and social issues. This concern is mirrored in the work of a number of educational psychologists, and we believe, will continue to offer important insights regarding what we mean by the concept of "schooling" and ways that the construct can be altered to reflect individual and societal goals.

Finally, we applaud recent trends toward the use of nontraditional models and constructs to understand learning and development, especially as they are rigorously applied and challenged. New models and constructs can be particularly helpful as we consider "how to conceptualize classrooms, peer groups, and communities as units of analyses" (Pintrich, 2000, p. 223). What will psychological inquiry offer today's teacher in another 10 years? If the past decade is any indicator, tomorrow's teachers may take for granted a theoretical framework that articulates the complexity of human learning and interaction in an increasingly clear and cogent manner.

# References

Alexander, P., Graham, S., & Harris, K. (1998). A perspective on strategy research: Progress and prospects. *Educational Psychology Review, 10,* 129–153.

Alexander, P. A., Schallert, D. L., & Hare, V. C. (1991). Coming to terms: How researchers in learning and literacy talk about knowledge. *Review of Educational Research, 61,* 315–343.

Alvermann, D. E., Smith, L. C., & Readance, J. E. (1985). Prior knowledge activation and the comprehension of compatible and incompatible text. *Reading Research Quarterly, 20,* 420–436.

Alvermann, D. E., Young, J. P., Weaver, D., Hinchman, K. A., Moore, D. W., Phelps, S. F., Thrash, E. C., & Zalewski, P. (1996). Middle and high school students' perceptions of how they experience text-based discussions: A multicase study. *Reading Research Quarterly, 3,* 244–267.

Ames, C. (1992). Classrooms: Goals, structures, and student motivation. *Journal of Educational Psychology, 84,* 261–271.

Ames, C., & Archer, J. (1988). Achievement goals in the classroom: Students' learning strategies and motivational processes. *Journal of Educational Psychology, 80,* 260–267.

Anderson, R. C. (1977). The notion of schemata and the educational enterprise. In R. C. Anderson, R. J. Spiro, & W. E. Montague (Eds.), *Schooling and the acquisition of knowledge* (pp. 415–431). Hillsdale, NJ: Lawrence Erlbaum Associates.

Anderson, R. C., & Pearson, P. D. (1984). A schema-theoretic view of basic processes in reading comprehension. In P. D. Pearson (Ed.), *Handbook* of Reading Research (pp. 255–291). New York: Longman.

Armbruster, B. B. (1984). The problem of "inconsiderate text." In G. G. Duffy, L. R. Rohler, & J. Mason (Eds.), *Comprehension instruction* (pp. 202–217). New York: Longman.

Atkinson, J. W. (1957). Motivational determinants of risk-taking behavior. *Psychological Review, 64,* 359–372.

Atkinson, J. W. (1964). *An introduction to motivation.* Princeton, NJ: Van Nostrand.

Atwell, N. (1987). *In the middle*. Portsmouth, NH: Heinemann.

Au, K. H. (1997). Ownership, literacy achievement, and students of diverse cultural backgrounds. In J. T. Guthrie & A. Wigfield (Eds.), *Promoting literacy engagement: Motivational, strategic reading through integrated instruction* (pp. 168-182). Newark, DE: International Reading Association.

Baddeley, A. D. (1986). *Working memory*. New York: Oxford University Press.

Bakhtin, M. M. (1981). *The dialogic imagination* (C. Emerson & M. Holquist, Trans.). Austin: University of Texas Press.

Bakhtin, M. M. (1990). *Art and answerability* (V. Liapunov, Trans.). Austin: University of Texas Press.

Bandura, A. (1986). *Social foundations of thought and action: A social cognitive theory*. Englewood Cliffs, NJ: Prentice-Hall.

Bartlett, F. C. (1932). *Remembering: A study in experimental and social psychology*. Cambridge: Cambridge University Press.

Beck, I. L., McKeown, M. G., Hamilton, R. L., & Kucan, L. (1997). *Questioning the author: An approach for enhancing student engagement with text*. Newark, DE: International Reading Association.

Beck, I. L., McKeown, M. G., Sinatra, G. M., & Loxterman, J. A. (1991). Revising social studies text from a text-processing perspective: Evidence of improved comprehensibility. *Reading Research Quarterly, 26,* 251-276.

Beers, T. (1987). Schema-theoretic models: Humanizing the machine. *Reading Research Quarterly, 22,* 369-377.

Blachman, B. A. (2000). Phonological awareness. In M. L. Kamil, P. B. Mosenthal, P. D. Pearson, & R. Barr (Eds.), *Handbook of reading research,* (Vol. 3, pp. 483-502). Mahwah, NJ: Lawrence Erlbaum Associates.

Bransford, J. D. (1979). *Human cognition: Learning, understanding, and remembering*. Belmont, CA: Wadsworth.

Bransford, J. D. (1984). Schema activation and schema acquisition: Comments on Richard C. Anderson's remarks. In R. C. Anderson, J. Osborn, & R. J. Tierney (Eds.), *Learning to read in American schools: Basal readers and content texts* (pp. 259-272). Hillsdale, NJ: Lawrence Erlbaum Associates.

Bransford, J. D., & Johnson, M. K. (1972). Contextual prerequisites for understanding: Some investigations of comprehension and recall. *Journal of Verbal Learning and Verbal Behavior, 11,* 717-726.

Brown, A. L. (1988). Motivation to learn and understand: On taking charge of one's own learning. *Cognition & Instruction, 5,* 311-321.

Bruner, J. (1990). *Acts of meaning*. Cambridge, MA: Harvard University Press.

Calkins, L. M. (1994). *The art of teaching writing*. Portsmouth, NH: Heinemann.

Cameron, J., & Pierce, W. D. (1994). Reinforcement, reward, and intrinsic motivation: A meta-analysis. *Review of Educational Research, 64,* 363-424.

Carter, K., & Doyle, W. (1996). Personal narrative and life history in learning to teach. In J. Sikula (Ed.), *Handbook of research on teacher education* (2nd ed., pp. 120-142). New York: Macmillan.

Cazden, C. (1988). *Classroom discourse*. Portsmouth, NH: Heinemann.

Clandinin, D. J. (1986). *Classroom practice: Teacher images in action*. London: Falmer.

Clark, C., & Peterson, P. (1986). Teachers' thought processes. In M. Wittrock (Ed.), *Handbook of research on teaching* (3rd ed., pp. 255-296). New York: Macmillan.

Cleary, L. M. (1991). Affect and cognition in the writing processes of eleventh graders. *Written Communication, 8,* 473-507.

Clifford, M. M. (1991). Risk taking: Empirical and educational considerations. *Educational Psychologist, 26,* 263-298.

Cochran-Smith, M., & Lytle, S. L. (1990). Research on teaching and teacher research: The issues that divide. *Educational Researcher, 19,* 2-10.

Cole, M., & Engestrom, Y. (1993). A cultural approach to distributed cognition. In G. Salomon (Ed.), *Distributed cognitions* (pp. 1-46). New York: Cambridge University Press.

Covington, M. V., & Omelich, C. L. (1979). Effort: The double-edged sword in school achievement. *Journal of Educational Psychology, 71,* 169-182.

Csikszentmihalyi, M. (1990). *Flow: The psychology of optimal experience*. New York: HarperCollins.

Daly, J. A., & Stafford, L. (1984). Correlates and consequences of social-communicative anxiety. In J. A. Daly & J. C. McCroskey (Eds.), *Avoiding communication: Shyness, reticence, and communication apprehension* (pp. 125-143). Beverly Hills, CA: Sage.

Deci, E. L., & Ryan, R. M. (1985). *Intrinsic motivation and self-determination in human behavior*. New York: Plenum.

Dodson, M. M. (2000). Monologic and dialogic conversations: How preservice teachers socially construct knowledge through oral and computer-mediated classroom discourse. In T. Shanahan & F. V. Rodriguez-Brown (Eds.), *Forty-ninth Yearbook of the National Reading Conference* (pp. 137-152). Chicago: National Reading Conference.

Dweck, C. S., & Leggett, E. (1988). A social-cognitive approach to motivation and personality. *Psychological Review, 95,* 256-273.

Dyson, A. H. (1995). Writing children: Reinventing the development of childhood literacy. *Written Communication, 12,* 4-46.

Faigley, L. (1986). Competing theories of process. *College English, 48,* 527-542.

Galda, L., Cullinan, B. E., & Strickland, D. S. (1993). *Language, literacy and the child*. New York: Harcourt Brace.

Garner, R. (1990). When children and adults do not use learning strategies: Toward a theory of settings. *Review of Educational Research, 60,* 517-529.

Gee, J. P. (2000). Discourse and sociocultural studies in reading. In M. L. Kamil, P. B. Mosenthal, P. D. Pearson, R. Barr (Eds.), *Handbook of reading research* (Vol. 3, pp. 195-207). Mahwah, NJ: Lawrence Erlbaum Associates.

Gentry, R. (1987). *Spel . . . is a four-letter word*. Portsmouth, NH: Heinemann.

Gibson, K. R. (2000). Corroboration. *American Psychologist, 55,* 271.

Graves, D. (1983). *When children write*. Portsmouth, NH: Heinemann.

Guthrie, J. D., & McCann, A. D. (1997). Characteristics of classrooms that promote motivations and strategies for learning. In J. T. Guthrie & A. Wigfield (Eds.), *Promoting literacy engagement: Motivational, strategic reading through integrated instruction* (pp. 128-148). Newark, DE: International Reading Association.

Halliday, M. A. K. (1993). Towards a language-based theory of learning. *Linguistics and Education, 5,* 93-116.

Hammer, D. (1995). Student inquiry in a physics class discussion. *Cognition and Instruction, 13,* 401-430.

Harackiewicz, J. M., Barron, K. E., Tauer, H. M., Carter, S. M., & Elliot, A. J. (2000). Short-term and long-term consequences of achievement goals: Predicting interest and performance over time. *Journal of Personality and Social Psychology, 92,* 316-330.

Heald-Taylor, R. G. (1996). Three paradigms for literature instruction in grades 3 to 6. *The Reading Teacher, 49*(6), 456-466.

Heath, S. B. (1983). *Ways with words: Language, life, and work in communities and classrooms*. Cambridge, England: Cambridge University Press.

Horwitz, E. K., & Young, D. J. (1991). *Language anxiety: From theory and research to classroom implications*. Englewood Cliffs, NJ: Prentice-Hall.

Jones, D., & Christensen, C. A. (1999). Relationship between automaticity in handwriting and students' ability to generate written text. *Journal of Educational Psychology, 91*, 44–49.

Juel, C. (1988). Learning to read and write: A longitudinal study of 4 children from first through fourth grades. *Journal of Educational Psychology, 80*(4), 437–447.

Just, M., & Carpenter, P. (1992). A capacity theory of comprehension: Individual differences in working memory. *Psychological Review, 99*, 122–149.

Kagan, S. (1990). *Cooperative learning resources for teachers.* San Juan Capistrano, CA: Resources for Teachers.

Keene, E. O., & Zimmerman, S. (1997). *Mosaic of thought: Teaching comprehension in a reader's world.* Portsmouth, NH: Heinemann.

Kim, Y. H., & Goetz, E. T. (1994). Context effects on word recognition and reading comprehension of poor and good readers: A test of the interactive–compensatory hypothesis. *Reading Research Quarterly, 29*, 178–187.

Kintsch, W. (1988). The role of knowledge in discourse comprehension: A construction–integration model. *Psychological Review, 95*, 163–182.

Kunnen, E. S., & Bosma, H. A. (2000). Development of meaning making: A dynamic systems approach. *New Ideas in Psychology, 18*, 57–82.

Larson, R. (1985). Emotional scenarios in the writing process: An examination of young writers' affective experiences. In M. Rose (Ed.), *When a writer can't write* (pp. 19–42). New York: Guilford.

Leont'ev, A. N. (1981). The problem of activity in psychology. In J. V. Wertsch (Ed.), *The concept of activity in Soviet psychology* (pp. 37–71). Armonk, NY: Sharpe.

Lepper, M. R., & Hodell, M. (1989). Intrinsic motivation in the classroom. In C. Ames & R. Ames (Eds.), *Research on motivation in education, Vol. 3: Goals and cognitions* (pp. 73–105). San Diego, CA: Academic Press.

Lepper, M. R., Greene, D., & Nisbett, R. E. (1973). Undermining children's intrinsic interest with extrinsic rewards: A test of the "overjustification" hypothesis. *Journal of Personality and Social Psychology, 28*, 129–137.

Lepper, M. R., Keavney, M., & Drake, M. (1996). Intrinsic motivation and extrinsic rewards: A commentary on Cameron and Pierce's meta-analysis. *Review of Educational Research, 66*, 5–32.

Lewis, M. (1992). *Shame: The exposed self.* New York: Free Press.

McCarthey, S. J., & Raphael, T. E. (1992). Alternate perspectives of reading/writing connections. In J. W. Irwin & M. Doyle (Eds.), *Reading/writing connections: Learning from research* (pp. 2–30). Newark, DE: International Reading Association.

McMahon, S. I., & Raphael, T. E. (Eds.). (1996). *The Book Club connection: Literacy learning and classroom talk.* New York: Teachers College Press.

Mehan, H. (1985). The structure of classroom discourse. In T. van Dijk (Ed.), *Handbook of discourse analysis,* (Vol. 3). London: Academic Press.

Moll, L. C., Tapia, J., & Whitmore, K. F. (1993). Living knowledge: The social distribution of cultural resources for thinking. In G. Salomon (Ed.), *Distributed cognitions: Psychological and educational considerations* (pp. 139–163). Cambridge, England: Cambridge University Press.

Monson, R. J., & Monson, M. P. (1994). Literacy as inquiry: An interview with Jerome C. Harste. *The Reading Teacher, 47*, 518–521.

Morrow, L. M., & Gambrell, L. B. (2000). Literature-based reading instruction. In M. L. Kamil, P. B. Mosenthal, P. D. Pearson, & R. Barr (Eds.), *Handbook of reading research* (Vol. 3, pp. 563–586). Mahwah, NJ: Lawrence Erlbaum Associates.

Nell, V. (1988). The psychology of reading for pleasure: Needs and gratifications. *Reading Research Quarterly, 23,* 6–50.

Nieto, S. (1999). *The light in their eyes: Creating multicultural learning communities.* New York: Teachers' College.

Nissani, M., & Hoefler-Nissani, D. M. (1992). Experimental studies of belief dependence of observations and of resistance to conceptual change. *Cognition & Instruction, 9,* 97–111.

Nystrand, M., & Gamoran, A. (1991). Instructional discourse, student engagement, and literature achievement. *Research in the Teaching of English, 25,* 261–290.

Palincsar, A. S., & Brown, A. L. (1984). Reciprocal teaching of comprehension-fostering and comprehension-monitoring activities. *Cognition and Instruction, 1,* 117–175.

Paris, S. G. (1988). Models and metaphors of learning strategies. In C. E. Weinstein, E. T. Goetz, & P. A. Alexander (Eds.), *Learning and study strategies: Issues in assessment, instruction, and evaluation* (pp. 299–321). San Diego, CA: Academic Press.

Paris, S. G., & Winograd, P. (1990). How metacognition can promote academic learning and instruction. In B. F. Jones & L. Idol (Eds.), *Dimensions of thinking and cognitive instruction* (pp. 15–51). Hillsdale, NJ: Lawrence Erlbaum Associates.

Paris, S. G., Lipson, M. Y., & Wixson, K. K. (1983). Becoming a strategic reader. *Contemporary Educational Psychology, 8,* 293–316.

Pekrun, R. (1992). The impact of emotions on learning and achievement: Towards a theory of cognitive/motivational mediators. *Applied Psychology: An International Review, 41,* 359–376.

Perkins, D., & Simmons, R. (1988). An integrative model of misconceptions. *Review of Educational Research, 58,* 303–326.

Piaget, J. (1932). *The language and thought of the child.* London: Routledge.

Pintrich, P. R. (2000). Educational psychology at the millennium: A look back and a look forward. *Educational Psychologist, 35,* 221–226.

Pintrich, P. R., & De Groot, E. (1990). Motivational and self-regulated learning components of classroom academic performance. *Journal of Educational Psychology, 82,* 33–40.

Pintrich, P. R., Marx, R. W., & Boyle, R. A. (1993). Beyond cold conceptual change: The role of motivational beliefs and classroom contextual factors in the process of conceptual change. *Review of Educational Research, 63,* 167–199.

Prawat, R. S., & Floden, R. E. (1994). Philosophical perspectives on constructivist views of learning. *Educational Psychologist, 29,* 37–48.

Pritchard, R. (1990). The effects of cultural schemata on reading processing strategies. *Reading Research Quarterly, 25,* 273–295.

Raphael, T. E., & McMahon, S. I. (1994). Book Club: An alternative framework for reading instruction. *The Reading Teacher, 48,* 102–116.

Richardson, V. (1994). The consideration of beliefs in staff development. In V. Richardson (Ed.), *Teacher change and the staff development process: A case in reading instruction.* New York: Teachers College Press.

Richardson, V. (1996). The role of attitudes and beliefs in learning to teach. In J. Sikula, (Ed.), *Handbook of research on teacher education* (2nd ed., pp. 102–119). New York: Macmillan.

Robins, R. W., Gosling, S. D., & Craik, K. H. (1999). An empirical analysis of trends in psychology. *American Psychologist, 54,* 117–128.

Rogoff, B. (1990). *Apprenticeship in thinking: Cognitive development in context.* New York: Oxford University Press.

Rukavina, I., & Daneman, M. (1996). Integration and its effect on acquiring knowledge about competing scientific theories from text. *Journal of Educational Psychology, 88,* 272–287.

Rumelhart, D. (1991). The architecture of mind: A connectionist approach. In M. I. Posner (Ed.), *Foundations of cognitive science* (pp. 133–159). Cambridge, MA: The MIT Press.

Rumelhart, D. E., & Ortony, A. (1977). The representation of knowledge in memory. In R. C. Anderson, R. J. Spiro, & W. E. Montague

(Eds.), *Schooling and the acquisition of knowledge* (pp. 99-135). Hillsdale, NJ: Lawrence Erlbaum Associates.

Ryan, R. M., & Deci, E. L. (2000). Intrinsic and extrinsic motivations: Classic definitions and new directions. *Contemporary Educational Psychology, 25*, 54-67.

Sadoski, M., Paivio, A., & Goetz, E. T. (1991). Commentary: A critique of schema theory in reading and a dual coding alternative. *Reading Research Quarterly, 26*, 463-484.

Salomon, G. (1993). No distribution without individuals' cognition: A dynamic interactional view. In G. Salomon (Ed.), *Distributed cognitions* (pp. 111-138). New York: Cambridge University Press.

Samuels, S. J. (1988). Decoding and automaticity: Helping poor readers become automatic at word recognition. *The Reading Teacher, 41*, 756-760.

Schallert, D. L. (1982). The significance of knowledge: A synthesis of research related to schema theory. In W. Otto & S. White (Eds.), *Reading expository material* (pp. 13-48). New York: Academic Press.

Schallert, D. (1987). Thought and language, content and structure in language communication. In J. R. Squire (Ed.), *The dynamics of language learning* (pp. 65-79). Urbana, IL: ERIC Clearninghouse.

Schallert, D. L. (1991). The contribution of psychology to teaching the language arts. In J. Flood, J. M. Jensen, D. Lapp, & J. R. Squire (Eds.), *Handbook of research on teaching the English language arts* (pp. 30-39). New York: Macmillan.

Schallert, D. L., & Reed, J. H. (1997). The pull of the text and the process of involvement in one's reading. In J. T. Guthrie & A. Wigfield (Eds.), *Promoting literacy engagement: Motivational, strategic reading through integrated instruction* (pp. 68-85). Newark, DE: International Reading Association.

Schank, R. C., & Abelson, R. P. (1977). *Scripts, plans, goals, and understanding: An inquiry into human knowledge structures*. Hillsdale, NJ: Lawrence Erlbaum Associates.

Schommer, M. (1994). An emerging conceptualization of epistemological beliefs and their role in learning. In R. Garner & P. A. Alexander (Eds.), *Beliefs about text and instruction with text* (pp. 25-40). Hillsdale, NJ: Lawrence Erlbaum Associates.

Schraw, G. (2000). Reader beliefs and meaning construction in narrative text. *Journal of Educational Psychology, 92*, 96-106.

Schwarz, N. (1990). Feelings as information: Informational and motivational functions of affective states. In E. T. Higgins & R. Sorrentino (Eds.), *Handbook of motivation and cognition: Foundations of social behavior* (Vol. 2, pp. 527-561). New York: Guilford.

Short, K. G., & Pierce, K. M. (Eds.). (1990). *Talking about books: Creating literate communities*. Portsmouth, NH: Heinemann.

Shuell, T. J. (1986). Cognitive conceptions of learning. *Review of Educational Research, 56*, 411-436.

Slavin, R. E. (1983). *Cooperative learning*. New York: Longman.

Snow, C. E. (1983). Literacy and language: Relationships during the preschool years. *Harvard Educational Review, 53*, 165-189.

Spiro, R. J. (1980). Accommodative reconstruction in prose recall. *Journal of Verbal Learning and Verbal Behavior, 19*, 84-95.

Spiro, R. J., Vispoel, W. L., Schmitz, J. G., Samarapungavan, A., & Boerger, A. E. (1987). Knowledge acquisition for application: Cognitive flexibility and transfer in complex content domains. In B. C. Britton & S. Glynn (Eds.), *Executive control processes* (pp. 177-199). Hillsdale, NJ: Lawrence Erlbaum Associates.

Stanovich, K. E. (1986). Matthew effects in reading: Some consequences of individual differences in the acquisition of literacy. *Reading Research Quarterly, 21*, 360-407.

Tierney, R. J., & Cunningham, J. W. (1984). Research on teaching reading comprehension. In P. D. Pearson (Ed.), *Handbook of reading research* (pp. 609-655). New York: Longman.

Townsend, J. S. (1991). *A study of wondering discourse in three literature class discussions*. Unpublished doctoral dissertation, University of Texas, Austin.

Turner, J. C. (1995). The influence of classroom contexts on young children's motivation for literacy. *Reading Research Quarterly, 30*, 410-441.

Turner, J. E., Husman, J., & Schallert, D. L. (In press). The Importance of Student Goals & Academic Context: Investigating the Precursors and Consequences of Experiencing Shame upon Students' Subsequent Motivational Behavior & Academic Achievement. *Educational Psychologist*.

Van der Mass, H., & Molenaar, P. (1992). A catastrophe-theoretical approach to cognitive development. *Psychological Review, 99*, 395-417.

Van Geert, P. (1994). *Dynamic systems of development: Change between complexity and chaos*. New York: Harvester Wheatsheaf.

Vygotsky, L. (1978). *Mind in society: The development of higher psychological processes* (M. Cole, V. John-Steiner, S. Scribner, & E. Souberman, Eds. and Trans.). Cambridge, MA: Harvard University Press.

Walker, C. H. (1987). Relative importance of domain knowledge and overall aptitude on acquisition of domain-related information. *Cognition & Instruction, 4*, 25-42.

Weinstein, C. E., & Mayer, R. E. (1985). The teaching of learning strategies. In M. C. Wittrock (Ed.), *Handbook of research on teaching* (3rd ed.). New York: Macmillan.

Wells, G. (2000). Dialogic inquiry in education: Building on the legacy of Vygotsky. Retrieved from: http://www.oise.utoronto.ca/~gwells/NCTE.html

Wells, G. (1999). *Dialogic inquiry: Toward a sociocultural practice and theory of education*. New York: Cambridge University Press.

Wertsch, J. V. (1991). A sociocultural approach to socially shared cognition. In L. B. Resnick, J. M. Levine, & S. D. Teasley (Eds.), *Perspectives on socially shared cognition* (pp. 85-100). Washington, DC: American Psychological Association.

Wertsch, J. V., & Hickmann, M. (1987). Problem solving in social interaction: A microgenetic analysis. In M. C. Hickmann (Ed.), *Social and functional approaches to language and thought* (pp. 251-265). Orlando, FL: Academic Press.

Zimmerman, B., & Martinez-Pons, M. (1990). Student differences in self-regulated learning: Relating grade, sex, and giftedness to self-efficacy and strategy use. *Journal of Educational Psychology, 82*, 51-59.

# CHILD DEVELOPMENT

## Marie M. Clay
### University of Auckland, New Zealand

In 1991 the International Reading Association and the National Council of Teachers of English produced a Handbook of Research on Teaching the English Language Arts. It is a comprehensive guide to what we know about literacy teachers, the processes involved in learning to read and write, and language arts instruction. The articles explore most aspects of language arts from the history of the profession to ethnographic research, child development, and learning, to teacher preparation and evaluation, and classroom environments. Part I covers theoretical bases for English Language Arts teaching in related disciplines, like Linguistics, Psychology, Anthropology, Literary Theory, and Child Development, and the last named was the chapter that I was asked to write. I was pleased to do this because Developmental Psychology is my academic discipline, and my commitment is first and foremost to the child as learner.

Perhaps a brief introduction would help readers to understand why some of the legitimate activities of the researchers do not necessarily lead to changes in the classroom activities of teachers. The theorists and researchers must push the boundaries of understanding how children change and why they succeed; teachers must teach tomorrow and the next day:

• When the two disciplines share common interests in oral language, writing and reading, the developmental psychologists seek explanations, explore competing alternatives, and describe trends of change over time in literacy behaviors. Educators, on the other hand, try to use the ideas of informed experts to optimize opportunities for enhanced development in effective programs. Developmental psychologists need questions that will lead to a breakthrough in understanding; literacy educators need answers that can be built into practice.

• Developmental theories are constructed from research findings, strongly influenced by the research designs that are required to separate out this from that. Many times the researcher's questions are not asked with teaching in mind; they are asked to clarify complex and challenging issues.

• Teaching is about moving children of very different competencies as far as possible over a change process lasting usually a school year; the developmental psychologist is often exploring overarching explanations that hold over much longer periods of time, and trying to explain what causes developmental change.

• Teaching is about the interactions of child with task, of teacher with child, and child with child, and how interactions need to be different with different children. However, interactions are hard to study and have been largely avoided by researchers who find it more informative to measure outcomes.

There are good reasons why these two groups of people interested in children and their learning should create distance between their activities. But if the two sets of activities do not, in the end, line up and present the same picture (i.e., agree with each other), then either or both of their formulations are wrong or misleading. The focus of the two lenses must present the same view.

Theories in developmental psychology and theories about teaching the English language arts are furthest apart when developmental psychology has nothing to say about teaching, when it attends focally to the evidence that the child constructs his own knowledge, and when it fails to address the roles assigned by society to teachers. Conversely, when teaching is seen as the delivery into children of content and skill by didactic instruction, or the use of teacher-proof curricula that calls for no developmental wisdom, or nothing more than publishers' programs, these positions ignore the highly relevant insights about children's learning that exist in developmental psychology. The work of both disciplines is closely allied when researchers document in precise ways the effects on children of real-world interactions and when they search for theoretical explanations of how and why children's responses change over time. The two disciplines have shared interests in recent studies of parent-child interaction, tutoring by novice tutors, adults talking with children especially in schools (Cazden, 1988), all of which show

how the apprentice learner gradually assumes a self-monitored role.

The child study movement of the early 1900s emerged from the innovation and international interchange of the 1930s as developmental psychology (Senn, 1975). Like the parent discipline of psychology, it placed high value on empirical evidence gained under controlled conditions and theories grounded in data. The methodological and theoretical uniqueness and challenge of a developmental orientation (Baltes, 1983) are reflected in its goals, namely

- To describe change over time in behaviors, abilities, and processes.
- To explain what occurs.
- To optimize opportunities for enhanced development.

Optimization may call for interventions that establish external or internal resources to allow for optimal development, or programs that modify problematic behavior. A diversity of philosophical, theoretical, and methodological orientations are found at the cutting edge of current debates (Lerner, 1983), but there is a major focus today on internal, cognitive, strategic, and affective variables as prior and causative. Learning contexts influence behaviors and cognitive processes in important ways, and the problem of how to study the process of learning during interactions is a challenge to researchers.

Interpreted broadly, formal education fits comfortably into this goal of optimization: Its central enterprise can be seen as a myriad of interventions in children's lives during formative years of change. Educational researchers also record cumulative change over time as children learn, with their empirical evidence ranging from that gained under controlled conditions (evaluation or assessment) to telling accounts in individual biographies. In such descriptive research, learning is conceptualized broadly as something that occurs in or out of school, with or without instruction. Such research recognizes that some changes in children occur under the control of historical and societal factors, others are determined by the child's selection of what to attend to, many are brought about in interaction with significant others, and some result from what is delivered more formally in classroom programs.

There is no clear distinction between the two disciplines when educational researchers pursue questions to the level of explanatory theory tested against competing alternatives, or when developmental psychologists test theories in interventions in the real world of schools. More commonly, developmental psychologists focus more on research designs and questions that will yield explanations and educational researchers attend to effective optimization as a goal. There is a search for both a better explanation and a more effective program.

Since 1970, the need of societies to solve problems by changing the next generation of school children produced different research pressures in psychology and education, complicating the transfer of information between them. Education received calls for accountability and for higher standards while hearing arguments to narrow its focus, which seemed blind to what was known about child development; while developmental psychology broadened its scope from highly controlled experimental studies to consider the ecologies within which children learned (Bronfenbrenner, 1979). In part this led to a more culturally aware and activist stance, and involvements in interventions with underprivileged children (Weikart, Rogers, Adcock, & McClelland, 1971).

In this chapter, brief comment on research interests shared by the two disciplines in oral language, writing, and reading is followed by a more general analysis of congruence and communicative distance between them.

## THE ACQUISITION OF LANGUAGE

### Oral Language

Language acquisition has been richly generative of challenges to educators. It is clearly cumulative, its foundation is laid before entry to school, and most of it is completed in interaction with significant others but without direct instruction (Lindfors, 1987). Preschoolers use it to code cognitive stores of information and acquire processes for accessing that information. They derive order and structure for language from massively different and diverse samples, test and refine their values for production, and are barely conscious of any of these processes. The learning is often initiated by the child, although adults and older children may pace the learning and provide appropriate information that the child is able to use. It does not proceed by accurate performance with the use of correct grammar. This is important, because how would the brain construct self-monitoring and self-correction processes if it never made an imperfect response? By being partially correct, the child progresses to more control over complexity in the use of language. Accuracy is the outcome, not the process, of learning.

In the 1960s as psychologists came to terms with the linguists' conceptual approaches to syntax, attention to detailed protocols of individual progress placed the spotlight on the importance of interrelationships between parts of the utterance and the organization of language on several levels. When linguists began to explore the links between structure and meaning, developmental psychologists found themselves in familiar territory with knowledge about cognition and how we understand language. As interest turned to the pragmatics of language use, it was easy for educators to recognize the influence of familiar contextual variables—settings, home influences, cultural factors, discourse factors, dialect differences. By 1975, oral language was seen in rich perspective, with important implications for teaching, for the valuing of cultures, and for bilingual education. Since then, the interactions of language, culture, and education have received attention as ethnomethodological approaches have been tested and refined (Heath, 1983), cultural factors explored (Au & Kawakami, 1984), and classroom discourse analyzed (Cazden, 1988).

Perhaps because children seem to have well-formed response systems for comprehending and producing language prior to entering school, the continuing development of oral language during schooling is not often seen by teachers to be important. In fact individual differences in oral language achievement vary greatly. While teachers see oral language as central to writing and reading acquisition, they often do not recognize the need to foster its further development. Multicultural or bilingual challenges in most English-speaking countries have led to a new awareness of oral language issues, which may direct more attention to the ways in which the language of the child at home undergoes further development during schooling.

## Writing

Three slim volumes appeared by 1978 with detailed observations of young children writing (Clay, 1975; Graves, 1978; Read, 1975). Graves placed prime emphasis on the observation of the writing processes used by children who were encouraged to be writers. Read discovered children who analyzed the sounds they could hear in their own pronunciation of sentences and invented a writing system for themselves. Clay collected weekly writing samples from an age cohort of children in five schools throughout their first year of school. An area that had been confined by beliefs about motor incoordination, having to be correct, needing to read before you could write, and getting images of spellings into the brain, began to expand with new vigor. Today even preschool children are seen as writers. Attention focussed on

- How to look at children's writing.
- How to look for processes of change.
- How to evaluate change.

Writing acquisition had surprising similarities to oral language. Children made responses that were systematic rather than random, and they occurred across children, even across countries and languages (Ferreiro & Teberosky, 1982; Goodman, 1990) as if children were operating on rules they had discovered for themselves. Children were hard to shift from such positions pointing to cognitive involvements. Questions were needed to elicit the rules or assumptions that children were using. Researchers could almost see cognitive processes in operation as they recorded children in classrooms composing messages and monitoring their oral production against their written composition at sound, sound cluster, word, or phrase level within the text as a whole, using recursive strategies of reviewing and revising (Graves, 1983; King & Rentel, 1979).

## Reading

By analogy reading acquisition might have been viewed constructively, i.e., something that the child put together, except that reading instruction has a long history of polarized theoretical positions. In lay minds, there are two superficial descriptions of beginning reading instruction, one at the letter level (phonics) and one at the word level (sight vocabulary). A wealth of writing on communication, information, and linguistic theory (Miller, 1951) showed how language transmits information on several levels. Research directed the attention of teachers to variables that found no place in the stripped-down versions

of decoding and sight vocabulary theories—research on children's syntactic errors in reading, the role of context and meaning, the links within stretches of texts called cohesive variables (Chapman, 1983), and memory experiments that showed how children related prior experience to new text. These research results were consistent with textual approaches to reading and writing.

Strategic reading is seen by many educators as something that older readers learn: rereading to comprehend (Garner, Wagoner, & Smith, 1983), skimming ahead for organizational structure, using context to process unfamiliar words (Potter, 1982), summarizing text to ensure understanding and remembering (Palincsar & Brown, 1984), and comprehension monitoring (Wagoner, 1983). That earlier forms of each of these strategies occur in the young reader (Baker, 1984; Clay, 1979) if instruction allows for it, is inconsistent with the advocacy of "decoding first and comprehension later." Unlike oral language and writing research, there have been few continuous longitudinal studies of reading processes in formation, with a result that young speakers and writers are seen as building their competencies and young readers receive them from their teachers and/or texts. The weight of research on early reading is on how cognition and teaching interact at the level of phonological awareness, to the neglect of other levels of language knowledge that might be powering the progress. Recent attention to the interactions of reading with writing may take us out of this strange situation (Langer, 1986). [See chapter by Tierney, this edition, on longitudinal studies.]

---

# THE CONTRIBUTION OF DEVELOPMENTAL THEORY

---

In the first half of the 20th century psychoanalytic theory with its focus on the study of the individual child provided a strong developmental emphasis for the education of young children of in British education from the time of Susan Isaacs (1935) to the Plowden (1967) report. In the United States, the strong influences on education from psychology were from associationist or behavioral theories, which could be applied to children being instructed in groups; at that time developmental psychology studied children's development before they went to school and in their out-of-school lives. In contrast to Britain and the United States, the Soviet Union's developmental psychology was directed, even in the 1930s, to pedagogical issues (although it only reached Western countries in translation to the 1960s) and work from that period is central to important research on children's learning today (Vygotsky, 1962, Wertsch, 1985).

For 50 years Piaget's theory of cognitive development evolved, expanded, and provided an approximation to a theory that might account for all development and learning, an "inclusive model" (Cairns & Valsiner, 1984). Children not only carried out cognitive operations, but used processing strategies, coded experiences, and compiled records of experiences stored as memory schemas. Piaget's description of assimilatory and accommodation processes presents teachers with the option of going with the child or against the child in one-to-one teaching, but provides only very general guidance for the design of day-to-day cumulative instruction of groups for children in classrooms (Goodman, 1990). Critical evaluation of the contribution of Piagetian theory to teaching has led to the concept of the competent preschooler (Donaldson, 1979) and to theories that challenge the role of conflict in cognitive change (Bryant, 1982, 1984).

Current analysis of Vygotsky's theory is focused not on his concept of inner speech, only partially on his social theory, and mostly on his concept of the zone of proximal development. His challenge to current teaching practice is that he sanctions shared activity between tutor and learner so that the learner can complete more difficult tasks with help that he would not complete on his own. He is supported in the beginning but gradually takes over the entire task. The help of the expert becomes unnecessary as learners become able to assume control. Education does not have to be an activity on which the child must always work solo on unseen material. Although these ideas can be easily fitted to concepts of teaching, they do not reflect the depth of the theory that claims that the shared and supported activity allows the child to construct some inner generating system, which will initiate and manage learning of this kind independently on future occasions.

Many abilities are now regarded in developmental psychology as "alterable variables" and potential targets for education. Researchers study the procedures children use to get to solutions, like cognitive strategies and self-monitoring (Flavell, 1982), and provide explanations of how we understand speech and texts arguing that 'scripts' have causal effects on achievement (Schank & Abelson, 1977). Even intelligence is seen as a matter of dynamic processes, rather than fixed static states (Sternberg, 1984; Pintrich, Cross, Kozma, & McGeachie, 1986).

How do developmental theories influence teachers' assumptions about children? The explanations provided, particularly in language and cognitive areas, have created for teachers vocabulary and knowledge structures that allow them to think beyond what the child does to what may be occurring in children's heads. It is the purpose of scientific study to go beyond the detailed variability of individual differences and the surface plausibility of what is observed, to less obvious phenomena and more general statements of relationships. This is a position to be treated very seriously. Education needs to know why developmental psychology works in the ways it does.

However, the need to test particular developmental theories on certain age groups has led to an uneven spread of information with most attention going to the preschool years (ages 4 to 6), followed by the early elementary years (ages 6 to 9), and the intermediate years (ages 9 to 12) (McCandless & Geis, 1975), and with adolescence a poorly researched age group. Recent research on infants and toddlers has overcome an earlier neglect, and lifespan developmental psychology is theoretically strong but empirically young. Such coverage serves early childhood education well but not schooling in later years.

Theories of child development influence teachers' assumptions about why children behave the way they do, rather than their decisions about how and what to teach. There are particular risks when the theories applied belong to another historical time, arose from a different knowledge base, and may be

distorted by the time-warp. For example Wertsch (1985) had to use Soviet authorities who wrote long after Vygotsky's death to explicate Vygotsky's work; Gesell's attempt to characterize the mismatch between some children's learning needs and instruction demands is used today to exclude children from instruction and so from opportunities to learn. Bloom's (1971) theory of how the scores of average achievers can be lifted two standard deviations by teaching in certain ways can be applied as a concept of mastery learning that looks like pouring content into empty vessels more demandingly.

## THE CONTRIBUTION OF METHODOLOGY

In the area of methodology, the two professional areas can negotiate concurrent rather than derivative exchanges. A question in education may be explored by the newest methodology and the best available analytic logic in developmental psychology at the point of beginning the investigation. "Join our team, and when we get there you will know as much as we do and avoid the lag in the transfer of information," could be a useful idea.

Critical for more effective interchange between the two disciplines is a need to appreciate the logical linkages between theoretical issues, research designs, statistical analyses, and interpretations (Baltes, Reese, & Nesselroade, 1977; Bryant & Bradley, 1985; Pintrich et al., 1986). Theory testing and experimental controls in psychology are necessary to answer some kinds of questions for which observational and participant observation methodologies are not alternatives, because they address important but different questions.

Experimental or longitudinal studies that compare age groups can only produce descriptions or change in children consistent with discreet stages. Gradual change in process or knowledge, which teachers find a better match to what they see in classrooms, is more likely to emerge from intensive longitudinal studies of change over short intervals.

Where developmental psychology has paid detailed attention to what happens in the course of development, with manipulative and precise measurement of change in children's responses, it provides good models for education, and for teachers to monitor whether good outcomes are occurring. Ideas of where, when, and how to begin teaching, of the changes that may be expected over time, of the track that most children take, of the variability to be expected, and of different developmental paths to the same outcomes could emerge from developmental research designed for this purpose.

Piaget's clinical method, used to study children's cognitions in depth, had an important impact on the acceptability of talking to children about their understanding. (Ferreiro & Teberosky, 1982; Karmiloff-Smith, 1979). Roger Brown (1973) and his eminent students began a search for description of language acquisition with in-depth data from the language of three children. The new emphases required careful recording of daily change, small scale manipulations, and analyses of particular features, trying to model the inner structure to account for the outer behaviors. Studies in the Soviet Union of sensory features used a similar kind of detailed observation, asking what was behind the behavior change.

Longitudinal research is highly relevant to the understanding of change over time needed in education; it is essential for the study of prediction, for understanding the origins of individual differences, and for the evaluation of outcomes of educational programs (Sontag, 1971). It is a method too rarely used, and almost never applied to a total cohort of children across the whole normal curve, varying in age as they do in real classrooms and under the normal school conditions within which children are taught. Yet descriptive data of learning processes in classrooms is very useful in education (Nicholson, 1984). If teachers became researchers of change over time in the day-to-day, small-scale sense this could enrich assessment and evaluation of children's progress.

Detailed description of process changes in successful learners may well provide teachers with appropriate guides for what the poor learners need to be taught to do in what education regards as 'basic' subjects (Clay, 1985).

## DIFFERENT PRIORITIES

While there are many points of congruence between the two disciplines, there are many reasons for communicative distance to arise between research on teaching the English language arts and research in developmental psychology. A recognition of some of these reasons may improve the potential for dialogue between two important areas of research endeavour.

### Questions and Answers

While developmental psychology must take time to pose its questions and systematically test its explanations in a scientific way, education must act on today's best available knowledge for current programs and tomorrow's plan for changes. Teachers need answers to build into practice; psychologists want questions that lead to breakthroughs in understanding. Researchers in both disciplines will be problem solving in similar areas but with different goals. What counts as relevant is different and is liable to lead one group to ignore what the other group is finding out.

### Selecting the Subjects

Teachers must deal with all children; they present the kind of diversity that developmental psychology seeks to control in its research designs. Teachers face the average majority, extreme subgroups, and particular individuals with learning challenges all at the same time. In order to obtain a clear test of an hypothesis, developmental psychologists select appropriate samples of children. Their findings may be clear but will usually apply only to some of the children in a mixed classroom who have to be taught today, and only extremely rarely to all of them. This problem can lead to impatience on the part of educators with psychological research and an unwillingness to consider its findings.

### "The Whole Learner" Versus "Particular Processes"

The teacher's job is to work with all aspects of the child's functioning impinging on a single task. Teachers know that it is the individual child who interacts in some holistic way with the specific task at a particular time. Developmental psychology tries, in its advocacy, to remember the whole organism, and research has been directed to the links between perception and reading, cognition and language, culture and learning, classroom discourse and child learning, and contexts and outcomes. However, it is the nature of the developmental psychologist's work to search for explanations in specialized areas, to tease out the specific, eschew the complex, explicate processes, avoid global theory, and oppose unwarranted generalization, thus tending to exclude holistic theories.

## COMMON RESEARCH PROBLEMS

### Achievement Outcomes Do Not Define Curricula Inputs

Research findings of what children typically do at selected ages describe in sequences of achievements, which are the outcomes of learning. Those error-free end-results, which are the outcome of many false starts, half-correct processes, and much self-correction en route to a recognizable product or achievement, have sometimes been built into curricula by educators in their perfected form. The appropriate research questions relate to how this "now perfect performance" was acquired, and records of the changes that took place en route to perfect performance will provide a better guide for the curricula of learning than study of the perfect outcomes of instruction.

Education is not about putting in the outcomes; it is about knowing what inputs, in what contexts, give rise to the desired achievement outcomes. In current debates about phonological segmentation in reading, metacognitive awareness in oral language, or the importance of correctness in writing, the distinction is not made between where you begin and where you end, but between inputs that give rise to outcomes.

For example, if the child learner constructs knowledge from learning interactions, then finding that competent readers score well on tests of phonological awareness do not imply that one should teach phonics, but, rather, that one should study change over time in younger children and document the sequences of interactions by which they reach that final tested state. Perhaps, like language acquisition, there are many inputs of different kinds that can contribute to the desired outcome. The fact that most children learn to read in very different instructional programs suggests that this may be the case. Developmental psychology is rich in understandings of this problem in a slightly different form. It accepts that change over time must be studied on individuals who change over time. Language acquisition research has illustrated how individuals learn from different language samples on different time scales, taking different paths to similar goals of talking fluently. What they need to learn cannot be interpolated from the average scores of separate samples of 3-, 4-, 5-, 6- and 7-year-olds. In the school years, it has been common for designers of educational interventions to try to achieve change in individuals on the basis of evidence derived from cross-sectional norms. Differences between individuals do not describe what is required to achieve change within or by individuals, and interventionists in both disciplines have often failed to recognize this (Montada & Filipp, 1976). A normative description of change is a gross approximation and does not provide a satisfactory basis for designing an instructional sequence.

## Interactions Are Hard to Study

Riegel (1979), impressed by the dialectical world view of developmental psychology, chided the discipline for describing either the responses of the adult (parent or teacher) or the child during learning interactions and not doing the harder task of studying the interactions themselves. Two design and analysis problems are that interactions occur in sequences, and that any one response affects the subsequent responses of either or both parties. (That is, of course, one description of instruction.) Research designs in behavioral psychology, language acquisition research, the studies of Bruner (Bruner & Sherwood, 1976; Bruner & Garton, 1978), classroom discourse, and ethnomethodological research could be the source of innovative methodologies for interaction research. An emphasis on the sensitive observation of children shifts easily to the observation of interactions, and a new guide to the observation of interactions (Bakeman & Gottman, 1986) will be helpful.

## SOME FINAL THOUGHTS

### A Beginning Has Been Made

Vygotsky's theories (1962; Wertsch, 1985) of the support system provided by others for the learner at the growing edge of their competence (Bruner, 1986) come almost as a confirmation of recent developments (Au & Kawami, 1984; Clay, 1985; Palincsar & Brown, 1984) and adults have been shown to work in this way tutoring preschool children (Wood, Bruner, & Ross, 1976). "Teachers scaffold budding reading skills through prompts and examples and then foster individual control of reading by gradually removing social supports" (Pintrich et al., 1986). There is more than a scaffold involved, however, because the learning in the language and cognitive areas leaves the learner not only with the production of performance but with the inner structures and functions capable of generating these (Karmiloff-Smith, 1986).

### Updating the Knowledge Base

A somewhat disturbing claim in recent years has been that we can predict very little about the way an individual will change from infancy to adulthood (Lipsitt, 1982), or about the way selected behaviors will be achieved from one historical era to another (Baltes et al., 1977; Elder, 1974; Lerner, 1983). Group predictions often do not hold up for individuals, and they do not hold up even for groups if the social contexts in which we learn are undergoing change. These claims are disturbing because education operates on assumptions about accumulating expertise and continual change in expected directions during childhood (Kagan, 1983), and the degree and direction of expected change are derived from the average majority. Awareness of such claims implies that knowledge about children gained from research should be checked at quite short intervals, since today's research populations may be responding differently than the original research populations. Replication studies should be funded, as neither discipline would want its outdated information to limit the learning opportunites of today's children. This becomes more important today because an hypothesis currently receiving some attention from developmental psychologists is that schooling may influence cognitive development in important ways.

## References

Au, K., & Kawakami, A. (1984). Vygotskian perspectives on discussion processes in small group reading lessons. In P. Peterson, L. Wilkinson, & M. Hallinan (Eds.). *The social context of instruction: Group organization and group processes.* New York: Academic Press.

Bakeman, R., & Gottman, J. M. (1986). *Observing interaction: An introduction to sequential analysis.* Cambridge: Cambridge University Press.

Baker, L. (1984). Children's effective use of multiple standards for evaluating their comprehension. *Journal of Educational Psychology, 76,* 588–597.

Baltes, P. B. (1983). Lifespan developmental psychology: Observations on history and theory revisited. In R. M. Lerner (Ed.). *Developmental psychology: Historical and philosophical perspectives* (pp. 79–111). Hillsdale, NJ: Lawrence Erlbaum Associates.

Baltes, P. B., Reese, H. W., & Nesselroade, J. R. (1977). *Lifespan developmental psychology: Introduction to research methods.* Monterey, CA: Brooks/Cole.

Bloom, B. (1971). Mastery learning. In J. H. Block (Ed.). *Mastery learning: Theory and practice.* New York: Holt, Rinehart, & Winston.

Bronfenbrenner, U. (1979). *The ecology of human development.* Cambridge: Harvard University Press.

Brown, A., & Palincsar, A. S. (1982). Inducing strategic learning from text by means of informed self-control training. In S. J. Samuels (Ed.). *Issues in reading diagnosis (Special Issue), Topics in Learning and Learning Disabilities, 2,* 1–17.

Brown, R. (1973). *A first language: The early stages.* Cambridge: Harvard University Press.

Bruner, J. S., & Sherwood, V. (1976). Early rule structure: The case of peek-a-boo. In J. S. Bruner, A. Jolly, & K. Sylva. *Play: Its role in development and evolution.* Harmondwoth, England: Penguin.

Bruner, J. S., & Garton, A. (Eds.). (1978). *Human growth and development.* Oxford, England: Clarendon Press.

Bruner, J. S. (1986). *Actual minds: Possible worlds.* Cambridge, MA: Harvard University Press.

Bryant, P. E. (1982). The role of conflict and agreement between intellectual strategies in children's ideas about measurement. *British Journal of Psychology, 73,* 243–252.

Bryant, P. E. (1984). Piaget, teachers and psychologists. *Oxford Review of Education, 10*(3), 251–259.

Bryant, P., & Bradley, L. (1985). *Children's reading problems.* Oxford, England: Blackwell.

Cairns, R. B., & Valsiner, J. (1984). Child psychology. In M. R. Rozenweig & L. W. Porter (Eds.). *Annual Review of Psychology, 35,* 553–578.

Cazden, C. B. (1988). *Classroom discourse: The language of teaching and learning.* Portsmouth, NH: Heinemann.

Chapman, L. J. (1983). *Reading development and cohesion.* London: Heinemann.

Clay, M. M. (1975). *What did I write?* Auckland: Heinemann.

Clay, M. M. (1979). *Reading: The patterning of complex behaviour.* Auckland: Heinemann.

Clay, M. M. (1985). *The early detection of reading difficulties.* Auckland: Heinemann.

Donaldson, M. (1979). *Children's minds.* New York: W. W. Norton.

Elder, G. H. (1974). *Children of the great depression.* Chicago: University of Chicago Press.

Ferreiro, E., & Teberosky, A. (1982). *Literacy before schooling.* Portsmouth, NH: Heinemann.

Flavell, J. J. (1982). On cognitive development. *Child Development, 53,* 1–10.

Garner, R., Wagoner, S., & Smith, T. (1983). Externalizing question-answer strategies of good and poor comprehenders. *Reading Research Quarterly, 16,* 439–447.

Goodman, Y. (1990). *Literacy development: Psychogenesis and pedagogical implications.* Newark, DE: International Reading Association.

Graves, D. H. (1978). *Balance the basics: Let them write.* New York: Ford Foundation.

Graves, D. (1983). *Teachers and children at work.* Portsmouth, NH: Heinemann.

Heath, S. B. (1983). *Ways with words.* Cambridge, England: Cambridge University Press.

Isaacs, S. (1935). *Children we teach.* London: University of London Press.

Kagan, J. (1983). Developmental categories and the premise of connectivity. In R. M. Lerner (Ed.). *Developmental psychology.* Hillsdale, NJ: Lawrence Erlbaum Associates.

Karmiloff-Smith, A. (1979). *A functional approach to child language.* Cambridge, England: Cambridge University Press.

Karmiloff-Smith, A. (1986). From meta-processes to conscious access: Evidence from children's metalinguistic and repair data. *Cognition, 23,* 95–147.

King, M., & Rentel, V. (1979). Towards a theory of early writing development. *Research in the Teaching of English, 13*(3), 243–253.

Langer, J. A. (1986). *Children reading and writing: Structures and strategies.* Norwood, NJ: Ablex.

Lerner, R. M. (1983). (Ed.). *Developmental psychology: Historical and philosophical perspectives.* Hillsdale, NJ: Lawrence Erlbaum Associates.

Lindfors, J. W. (1987). *Children's language and learning.* (2nd ed.). Englewood Cliffs, NJ: Prentice-Hall.

Lipsitt, L. P. (1982). Infancy and life-span development. In T. M. Field, A. Huston, H. C. Quay, L. Troll, & G. E. Finlay (Eds.). *Review of Human Development.* New York: Wiley.

McCandless, B. R., & Geis, M. F. (1975). Current trends in developmental psychology: In H. W. Reese (Ed.). *Advances in child development and behaviour* (pp. 1–8). New York: Academic Press.

Miller, G. (1951). *Language and communication.* New York: McGraw-Hill.

Montada, L., & Fillip, S. H. (1976). Implications of life-span developmental psychology for childhood education. In H. W. Reese (Ed.). *Advances in child development and behaviour* (pp. 253–266). New York: Academic Press.

Nicholson, T. (1984). Experts and novices: A study of reading in the high school classroom. *Reading Research Quarterly, 14*(4), 436–451.

Palincsar, A. S., & Brown, A. L. (1984). Reciprocal teaching of comprehension monitoring activities. *Cognition and Instruction, 2,* 117–175.

Pintrich, P. R., Cross, D. R., Kozma, R. B., & McGeachie, W. J. (1986). Instructional psychology. In M. R. Rozenweig & L. W. Porter, *Annual Review of Psychology* (pp. 611–654). Palo Alto, CA: Annual Reviews.

Plowden, B. (1967). *Children and their primary schools.* London: Her Majesty's Stationery Office.

Potter, F. (1982). The use of linguistic context: Do good and poor readers use different strategies? *British Journal of Educational Psychology, 52,* 16–23.

Read, C. (1975). *Children's categorizations of speech sounds in English.* (Research Report 17). Urbana, IL: National Council of Teachers of English.

Riegel, K. F. (1979). *Foundations of dialectical psychology: Some historical and ethical considerations.* New York: Academic Press.

Schank, R. C., & Abelson, R. P. (1977). *Scripts, plans, goals and understanding.* Hillsdale, NJ: Lawrence Erlbaum Associates.

Senn, M. J. E. (1975). Insights on the child development movement in the United States. *Monograph of the Society for Research in Child Development, 40*(3).

Sontag, L. W. (1971). The history of longitudinal research: Implications for the future. *Child Development, 42,* 987–1002.

Sternberg, R. J. (Ed.). (1984). *Mechanisms of cognitive development.* New York: W. H. Freeman.

Vygotsky, L. S. (1962). *Thought and language.* Cambridge, MA: MIT Press.

Wagoner, S. (1983). Comprehension monitoring: What it is and what we have to know about it. *Reading Research Quarterly, 18,* 328–346.

Weikart, D. P., Rogers, L., Adcock, C., & McClelland, D. (1971). *The cognitively-oriented curriculum.* Urbana, IL: University of Illinois.

Wertsch, J. V. (1985). *Vygotsky and the social formation of mind.* Cambridge, MA: Harvard University Press.

Wood, D., Bruner, J. S., & Ross, G. (1976). The role of tutoring in problem-solving. *Journal of Child Psychology and Child Psychiatry, 17,* 89–100.

# ANTHROPOLOGY AND RESEARCH ON TEACHING THE ENGLISH LANGUAGE ARTS

## David Bloome
### Vanderbilt University

The application of anthropological perspectives offered educational researchers new lenses for understanding teaching. Perhaps most influential were studies of cultural diversity in classrooms that raised questions about the ethnocentrism of taken-for-granted pedagogical practices, assessment, and curricular design (e.g., Bloome, 1989; Cazden, John, & Hymes, 1972; Erickson & Mohatt, 1982; Gilmore, 1987; Goldenberg, 1987; Guthrie, 1985; Heath, 1983; Michaels, 1981, 1986; Scollon, 1988; Trueba, Jacobs, & Kirton, 1990). These studies were influential because they provided alternatives to deficit models, and focused attention on cultural differences in classrooms as a key construct in the pursuit of educational equity (e.g., Au, 1980; Cook-Gumperz, Gumperz, & Simons, 1981; De & Gregory, 1997; Delgado-Gaitan, 1989; Heath & Thomas, 1984; Moll & Diaz, 1987; Soliday, 1997; Willett, Solsken, & Wilson-Keenan, 1998). Among the methodological influences of these studies and similar studies are cross-cultural comparative studies (e.g., Spindler & Spindler, 1987a; Hymes, 1996; Schieffelin & Gilmore, 1986), and the use of ethnographic methods and techniques including participant observation and long-term field work in a small number of educational settings (for a review see Zaharlick & Green, 1991, this edition).[1]

However, as I have argued elsewhere (Bloome, 1991), perhaps the most important contribution of the relationship of anthropology to research on teaching the English language arts has been to call into question taken-for-granted foundational constructs used in educational research. This includes definitions of education, language, literacy, literature, learning, and culture. Calling into question taken-for-granted constructs and modes of representation in educational research allows for the unpacking of the "common sense," opening them up for cultural analysis and critique. (See Geertz, 1983 for a discussion of the cultural dynamics of common sense. See also Marcus & Fischer, 1986 for one model of anthropology as cultural critique.)

Although the contributions of applying anthropology to research on teaching the English language arts are substantial, it is also the case that the relationship of anthropology and research on teaching is more complex than just *applying* anthropology. The one way direction of influence (from anthropology to education) is no longer appropriate as the only framework for understanding anthropology *and* research on teaching the English language arts.

One complexity involves recent internal debates within anthropology, prompted in part by the "linguistic turn" in anthropology and the social sciences in general, postmodernist, and poststructuralist revisionings of anthropology, and by incorporation of critical social theory (for further discussion see Clifford & Marcus, 1986; González, 1999; Harris, 1999; Kuznar, 1997; Levinson & Holland, 1996; Said, 1979, 1985; Tyler, 1987). For some anthropologists, these debates threaten to destroy anthropology as a scientific endeavor (e.g., Kuznar, 1997; Harris, 1999), for others, such as Moore (1997), it is controversy that has produced anthropological knowledge over its 150 year history. He provides a partial list of five "basic insights into human nature"

---

[1] The terms "ethnography and ethnographic research" are used to refer to anthropologically grounded research and to qualitative research in general (whether grounded in anthropology or not). In this paper, I use ethnography and ethnographic research to refer to research grounded in anthropology, and I use the term qualitative research to refer to methods of doing research that may appear similar to anthropologically based research but lack the same theoretical framing. It is also important to make a distinction between "ethnography" and "ethnographic research." The first refers to an in-depth full study of a community, grounded in anthropological theory. Ethnographic research, by contrast, refers to the use of constructs, methods, and techniques associated with anthropological ethnography, but not necessarily a fully developed study of a community.

produced by anthropology and its controversies.

- Race does not account for variations in human behavior.
- Other cultures are not "fossilized" representatives of earlier stages in human evolution.
- There is a complex dialectic between individual and culture in every society. Individuals are shaped by and shape the culture they experience.
- Culture is not a thing of "shreds and patches," but neither is it a smoothly integrated machine. Different elements of culture meet the adaptive requisites of human existence, express the creativity of human actors in their use of symbols, and reflect the transmitted experiences of humanity.
- Our knowledge of other peoples is shaped by our own cultural experience. There is nothing simple about understanding another culture (p. 274).

Although many anthropologists might agree with Moore's partial list of basic insights, the list can still be critiqued both with regard to content (e.g., is "race" a viable construct even if it is not connected to behavior) and language (e.g., to whom does the "Our" refer to). The point of presenting the list is not to present an uncontested set of constructs but to illustrate a position taken by some anthropologists who do not view current controversies as debilitating or destructive.

Among the generative insights produced by recent debates are the concepts of multiplicity (multiple and sometimes contradictory "truths"), heteroglossia (multiple and potentially discordant voices and audiences), partiality (recognition that any description or explanation can only ever be partial), the ubiquitousness of power relations, and the necessity of reflexivity (serious interrogation of one's own and others' actions, interpretations, roles, relationships, representations, and constructions). These concepts, along with recent debates, hold promise for more sensitive, reflexive, and less hierarchical understandings of people and culture (e.g., Atkinson, 1990; Hammersly & Atkinson, 1983) with similar implications for educational research, policy, and practice (e.g., Eisenhart, 1999; Gitlin, 1994). Further, the concepts suggest the need for a different relationship between anthropology and educational research than solely that of "application." At the very least, they call for a transformation from the hierarchical relationship of a "basic" discipline to an "applied" field to a horizontal relationship at every level: theory, method, practice, and social action. One example of a movement toward a "horizontal" relationship are the chapters in Gitlin's (1994) edited volume where a broad range of educational researchers and other scholars create dialogues between theoretical constructs about power and method generated in disciplinary fields of anthropology and sociology with theoretical constructs generated through educational praxis.

A second complexity that makes difficult the construct of "applying anthropology to research on teaching" is the adaptation and transformation of anthropological constructs by educational researchers and educators. Over the past several decades, there has been a growing dialogue among educational researchers and anthropologists with regard to the study of classrooms. It is not just that the Council on Anthropology and Education has grown[2] and includes a large number of researchers located in Schools/Colleges of Education and who received their doctorates in Schools/Colleges of Education, it is also the redefinition of anthropological theory and modes of inquiry applied to the study of teaching (see Green & Bloome, 1998). Such redefinition derives at least in part from the difference in positions that educational researchers hold. Whereas anthropologists can limit their concern to building anthropological understandings and theory, educational researchers have explicit obligations to improve educational processes and institutions and often have dual integrated roles as researchers and educators (for example, as teacher educators and teachers). Through praxis, a history of applying anthropological theories and methods, transformative pedagogies, and attention to the particularities of specific classrooms and communities, educational researchers have generated new directions for and understandings of teaching, literacy, and the English language arts (see Delgado-Gaitan, 1993; Egan-Robertson & Bloome, 1998).

Also different from academic anthropologists, educational researchers and educators work in a multidisciplinary environment where integration of perspectives for a specified purpose is commonplace. Perhaps most noteworthy with regard to the integration of perspectives has been the redefinition of "learning" (discussed later) generated through juxtaposition of cultural, social, historical, psychological, sociolinguistic, and literary theoretical discussions. For educational researchers, the questions to ask about anthropological constructs that might be useful in the study of teaching include how such constructs reshape and are reshaped by theoretical constructs from other disciplines.

In sum, the discussion of anthropology *and* research on teaching the English language arts needs to include both the *application* of anthropology to research on teaching as well as the *dialogic* relationship between anthropology/anthropologists and educational researchers.

In this chapter, I focus on the (re)definition of a small number of key constructs, referencing both anthropological research and educational research (research conducted by researchers affiliated with the field of education) that either is anthropologically based or that employs anthropological constructs within a multidisciplinary framework or as part of action-oriented research. Other constructs could have been included had there been sufficient space. Unlike the first edition of this manuscript (Bloome, 1991), I have prefaced each construct with the phrase "The problem of _____." Each construct is changing too rapidly and is the site of too much debate to suggest that the space occupied by the construct can be described as stable, uncontested, or unproblematic.

---

[2]The Council on Anthropology and Education (CAE), which merged with the American Anthropological Association (AAA) in 1984, has a current membership of 977 (no membership figures available before 1996). In 1968, only one session was organized by CAE for the AAA conference and only a handful of people met in various coordinating teams and committees (information from AAA and Kathleen DeMarrais, CAE historian, personal communication, February 2000).

## THE PROBLEM OF CULTURE

Anthropological perspectives vary in their definition of culture (Moore, 1997). Tylor (1871) defined culture as "that complex whole which includes knowledge, belief, art, morals, law, custom, and any other capabilities and habits acquired by man as a member of society" (Peacock, 1986, p. 3). Similar definitions can be found in many anthropological textbooks and introductions to the cultural foundations of education (e.g., Pai & Adler, 1997). Anthropologists have attended less to surface features of culture as definition and more to underlying processes, structures, and dynamics as definition. In brief, among the perspectives taken are: *functionalism* (e.g., Malinowski, 1922) where attention is focused on how a cultural system functions to meet the needs of people; *structuralism* (e.g., Levi-Strauss, 1963) where attention is focused on how underlying themes (usually thought of as binary oppositions) structure cultural phenomena; *psychological anthropology* (e.g., Spindler, 1978; Whiting & Whiting, 1975) where attention is focused on the relationship of the individual and the culture; *cognitive anthropology* (e.g., Frake, 1969; Goodenough, 1981; Quinn & Holland, 1987), where attention is focused on shared cultural models and the standards people hold for perceiving, believing, evaluating, communicating, and acting; *symbolic analysis* (e.g., Geertz, 1973) where attention is focused on the meaning and significance of what people do; and *linguistic anthropology* (e.g., Duranti, 1997; Gumperz, 1986; Gumperz & Hymes, 1972; Hymes, 1974), where attention is focused on the relationship of language and culture. Different perspectives are not necessarily taken as mutually exclusive.

One can point to commonalities in the various approaches to culture. Culture is learned and shared. It is taken for granted. It is studied holistically. Care is typically taken to avoid reification of a culture, and to distinguish between "culture" and race, ethnicity, and nationality, although there are certainly complex relationships among these processes (cf., Goldberg, 1993).

One of the major debates regarding definitions of culture has been its location—in the head or in the doing. Keesing (1987) writes:

[A] cognitive view of culture, while potentially allowing us to interpret the distribution and variability of knowledge and the situational co-construction of shared worlds, renders it difficult to capture the publicness and collectiveness of culture as symbol systems (Geertz, 1972). As Varenne (1984, p. 291) has perceptively written in critically assessing "individualist" theories of culture, the collective tradition of a people is in an important sense external, and transcendent in relation to any individual; such a cultural tradition "is *always already there*. It is in this sense that ideology, or culture, is an external social fact that is part of the environment of individuals. To the extent that it is part of the environment, it is something to which individuals will adapt and against which they may react..." (p. 372) [original emphasis]

Geertz (1973) gives an extended discussion of an alternative to conceptions of culture as in the head.

Culture, this acted document, is public, like a burlesqued wink or a mock sheep raid. Though ideational, it does not exist in someone's head; though unphysical, it is not an occult entity... Once human behavior is seen as (most of the time; there *are* true twitches) symbolic action—action which like phonation in speech, pigment in painting, line in writing, or sonance in music, signifies—the question as to whether culture is patterned conduct or a frame of mind or somehow the two mixed together, loses sense. The thing to ask about a burlesqued wink or a mock sheep raid is not what their ontological status is. It is the same as that of rocks on one hand and dreams on the other—they are things of this world. The thing to ask is what their import is: what is it, ridicule or challenge, irony or anger, snobbery or pride, that, in their occurrence and through their agency, is getting said (p. 10).

It may be difficult for those raised in Western cultures (and others) with an emphasis on individualism and with the hegemony of psychological explanations of behavior (especially in education, see McDermott & Hood, 1982; McDermott, 1999) to conceive of human phenomena being located outside of the individual without defining that phenomena as mystical or ethereal. Nonetheless, it is in understanding definitions of culture as more than in-the-head phenomena that the potential exists for anthropological research on teaching the English language arts to provide an alternative to the extant psychological perspectives of teaching.

In addition to these various definitions and debates, questions need to also be raised about culture as a productive process. On one hand, culture produces meanings, guides actions, assigns identities, makes particular events possible, structures social relationships and power relations among people, etc., while on the other hand people produce culture and transform it. What people do in their production of culture is not monolithic, indeed the production of culture may be highly contested. Such conflicts may be explicit or involve forms of resistance not consciously tied to transformation of cultural institutions. Thus, any definition of culture is problematized at least at three levels. First, there is the problem of identifying what exactly is shared and how things mean and come to have significance, by whom, when, where, and how; and who contests such assumptions about what is shared, its significance and meaning. Second, although related to the first, there is the problem of culture as "situated" versus broad-based. Cultural ideologies and social structures that operate at a macro level (e.g., national, Western/European) and their material realizations (e.g., the layout of cities, physical structures, widespread traditions and social practices, military campaigns, governmental organization, etc.) constitute a level of culture that profoundly influences what people do and what meanings are assigned to actions, people, objects. But it is also the case that people, through their face-to-face interactions (and similar interactions) constitute culture, both reproducing it (that is, invoking extant cultural practices) and transforming it (through adaptation to the particulars of the event and/or through explicit transformations tied to resistance or other forms of praxis). While situated views of culture and macro views are not necessarily antithetical, the practical constraints of conducting research often require one to choose between them as an initial framework; and doing so may make an important difference in the knowledge and insights yielded. Similarly, a third way in which the construct of culture is problematized is that determining which definition(s) of culture to employ is a political choice. The term "culture," like any key construct, is itself highly charged and contested. It is part of a system of cultural meanings, actions, and social relationships that are implicated when the term is used. There is no neutrality nor stability in cultural description.

The warrant then for educational researchers is not to ask what the culture of an English language arts classroom is, as if one could fix a moment in time and count that as its culture, but rather to ask how a particular classroom and the events in it defines/is part of/contributes to the evolving and contested cultural dynamics of education, of the community more broadly speaking, and of the particular classroom itself (as an important social setting in its own right) and what the consequences are of those dynamics both for the particular people involved (teachers and students) and for all of those with a stake in what they do, how they do it, and what meaning and significance it has. The methodological warrant is to create a "telling case" (Mitchell, 1984). In addition, educational researchers have to ask questions about the meaning and consequences of having engaged in the study of a classroom's culture, including the legitimacy of claiming authority to write up a cultural description of others.

## THE PROBLEM OF EDUCATION

Anthropologists often define education as cultural transmission (e.g., Gearing, 1973; Spindler, 1963), passing a culture from one generation to the next. Building on education as cultural transmission, Spindler and Spindler (1987b) define education as a "calculated intervention in the learning process" (p. 30). As Hymes (1996) points out, a major contribution of anthropologically based research has been to remind researchers and educators that education does not only occur in classrooms and that education within schools is connected to the broader society.

Cross-cultural studies of education, including cross-national, studies in nonWestern societies, and studies in settings that have eschewed traditional Western-style schooling, provide important perspectives for (a) understanding variation and possibility in education, (b) correcting stereotypes held by dominant Western societies of others' educational system (e.g., Eisemon & Hallett, 1989), including minority groups living in the midst of Western societies (e.g., Boyarin, 1992), as well as (c) revealing "invisible" cultural processes in Western schooling. While societies with or without formal schooling may explicitly teach and may teach abstract knowledge, Mead (1970) points out that a contrast can be made between conceptions of education as seeking to learn versus seeking to teach. The difference is not an issue of motivation, but rather of cultural organization and transmission. Firth (1936) describes the difference in his study of the Tikopia.

The cardinal points of education in a native society such as the Tikopia are its continuity in both temporal and a social sense, its position as an activity of kinsfolk, its practicality—not in the sense of being directed to economic ends, but as arising from actual situations in daily life—and its nondisciplinary character. A certain subordination to authority is required and is sometimes impressed by forcible and dramatic methods, but these are sporadic and the individual is a fairly free agent to come and go as he likes, to refuse to heed what is being taught him. All this is in direct contrast to a system of education for native children wherever it is carried out under European tutelage. Such consists usually of periodic instruction while segregation, intermitted by intervals of relaxation and rejoining of the normal village life, and imparted not by kinsfolk of the children but by strangers, often from another area, even when non-Europeans. This instruction is given not in connection with practical situations of life as they occur, but in accord with general principles, the utility of which is only vaguely perceived by the pupils. Moreover it is disciplinary, the pupils are under some degree of direct restraint and may even suffer punishments for neglect of appointed tasks (p. 134).

The equation of education with schooling leads not only to limited possibilities in imagining role relationships, organization, the structure of knowledge, and sites for education, it downgrades the importance of nonschool locations for learning, despite studies showing the importance of such settings (e.g., Heath, 1983; Schieffelin & Gilmore, 1986; Taylor, 1983). It also creates an open space that can be filled by schooling in the name of education. For example, in the name of education schools and related institutions have attempted to colonize homes and communities as additional sites for schooling (e.g., Bloome, 1997; McDermott, Goldman, & Varenne, 1984).[3] The issue of what counts as an educational site is not just a matter of whether the site provides access to cultural capital, but it is also an issue of control and struggle about what constitutes an "educated" person (Levinson & Holland, 1996) and the distribution of symbolic capital that accompanies such labeling.

Whether in schools or nonschool settings, education involves socialization. Socialization is a constructed, interactive process rather than a deterministic one (Mehan, 1980). Parents, teachers, and others seek to help children become members of their society (although not necessarily compliant ones, for example see Trujillo, 1996), and they take actions to do so based on their historical experiences, their understandings of how children learn, and their assessment of the particularities of the situations with which they are faced. Children are not passive, they act on their world to understand it (to fit in, to create a place for themselves, and/or to change it). Children, based on what parents, teachers, and others do, and on the results of their own actions, construct models of how the world operates, and what is expected of them and of others (which to some extent are shared models with peers and adults). Children are participants in constructing meaning and the outcomes of the educational events in which they participate. Although research attention has primarily focused on children, socialization is a lifespan process. Throughout one's life, members of a cultural group act to

---

[3]I use the term "colonize" to suggest a takeover of the social space through processes of redefining the space and shifting its institutional location, the people in the space, and what activities they should be engaged in, and placing the space and in the people in it under surveillance (even if indirect). Thus, parents with young children become (through encouragement, social pressure, and family literacy programs) teachers of reading at home to their children, and their failure to do so, and report doing so, to teachers and school-home liaison workers can have consequences for how they are defined as parents.

conform and inform each other's public behavior (Schieffelin & Ochs, 1986).

Socialization occurs at many levels. At deeper levels, less accessible to conscious reflection and attention, in Western societies, individualism is an important ideology shaping many beliefs, feelings, activities, and understandings across a wide range of endeavors. Individualism is evident, among other places, in dominant Western religions (e.g., individual salvation), government (e.g., one person, one vote), sports (e.g., the superstar), economies (e.g., free market), and schooling (e.g., individual instruction and achievement). Individualism is taken for granted, learned not as an explicit focus of a curriculum but because it is deeply and broadly embedded in the organization and structure of events and institutions in which people participate on a daily basis. It is part of the "common sense" without which one is at risk of being defined as deviant.

With regard to the English language arts, questions need to be asked about how people are socialized as students of the English language arts, what underlying and hidden cultural ideologies are embedded in the teaching and classroom practices that make up daily life in the language arts classroom, and in the definition of the explicit curriculum. For example, how does what happens in the language arts classroom influence what students think language is and how it is or should be used? How language is interpreted? How does what happens in the language arts classroom define students as individuals? As a group? As members of a speech community? How does the language arts classroom define and give interpretation to those who are not there (e.g., students in other tracks, schools, or who do not go to school)? How does what happens in a language arts classroom construct borders between the academic world and the world of the students' home community? In our study of writing for the Mass-Observation Project (Sheridan, Street, & Bloome, 2000) we found that language arts instruction (especially writing, spelling, and grammar instruction) may be playing an important role in creating (and legitimizing) a hierarchical structure regarding who is and can be a "writer."

Also of concern to anthropologically based research is differentiation in how socialization occurs and its consequences within and across groups. Questions need to be asked about how what happens in the language arts classroom structures and gives meaning to differentiation with regard to gender, race and ethnicity, sexual orientation, and class, among other ways that predominate in Western society for differentiating people as members of social groups. Part of what complicates the issue of socialization and differentiation is that it is not the differentiation per se, but the social construction of the categories and the meanings that are given to both the categorization and the differentiation, along with the consequences of that differentiation both for the members of the social group and others.

## THE PROBLEM OF LANGUAGE

From the perspective of sociolinguistic ethnography, language use can be framed as communicative competence within a speech community. According to Cazden (1972), the first presentation of Hymes' paper "On Communicative Competence" was in June 1966. Hymes laid out three assumptions underlying the framing of language as communicative competence.

1. Each social relationship entails the selection and/or creation of communicative means considered specific and appropriate to it by its participations.
2. The organization of communicative means in terms of social relationships confers a structure that is not disclosed in the analysis of the means separately.
3. The communicative means available in a relationship conditions its nature and outcome (Hymes, 1971, p. 60).

Hymes ties communicative competence directly to issues of equality in education, particularly for people from outside the dominant cultural and linguistic groups (Hymes, 1996). Rather than describing their language as deficient, their language is described as a consequence of setting, function, means of language behavior, and of social and power relationships within and across settings. It is not that a particular language is inherently inferior, but rather that the symbolic value of the language has been socially constructed as inferior, similarly so, with multilingualism; and in both cases technocratic and pseudoscientific explanations have often been called on to justify the inferiority.

[O]ne should note the widespread assumption that a brain has room for only one language. If that were true for Americans, they would have to be classed as biologically deficient, since multilingualism is normal in the rest of the world. Note the frequent opinion that difference of language is divisive. Difference of language is not itself divisive; it can become a symbol of conflict in certain economic and political circumstances. A good way to make a language a symbol of conflict is to repress it (Hymes, 1996, p. 210).

From the perspective of sociolinguistic ethnography (and closely related perspectives), questions can be asked about how children learn to use language(s) appropriately in classrooms to interact with teachers and peers and to engage in academic tasks (e.g., DeStefano, Pepinsky, & Sanders, 1982; Erickson 1982a; Green & Wallat, 1981; Wallat & Green, 1979). Questions can also be asked about the nature of the language(s) made available in classrooms, and how that language (or languages) is differentiated across schools, classrooms, and groups (e.g., Borko & Eisenhart, 1989; Collins, 1986; Eder, 1986). Questions can be asked about the differences that emerge between the language(s) used by students from the dominant cultural and linguistic groups and other students, and how those differences are treated, as well as the relationship of language(s) in and out of the classroom (e.g., Gilmore, 1986; Heath, 1982b, 1983; Miller, Nemoianu, & DeJong, 1986; Taylor, 1983).

Although the construct of language use as communicative competence has been an effective one in generating important questions for educational research, criticism of the construct of "appropriateness" (an important aspect of the concepts of communicative competence and speech community) has led to additional important questions. In brief, should the framework for understanding language use in classrooms be the pursuit of language use and behavior that is appropriate to the social setting, or should the framework be more sensitive to multiple and differing agendas that may exist in any setting, power relations among participants, and potential resistance behaviors (cf., Fairclough, 1992, 1995; Luke, 1995)? An analogous critique has been made of the construct of speech community from the perspective of the study of women and language. The notion of a speech community, with a single set of rules for the appropriate use of language can obfuscate understanding the use of language by women and others in less powerful positions. Thus, the argument is made that the construct of a speech community needs to be revised to incorporate all of the social, cultural, and political complexities and conflicts that characterize social relationships across genders, cultures, races, ethnicities, etc. (cf., Coates & Cameron, 1988 ).[4]

Some social linguists, linguistic anthropologists, and educational researchers have promoted the use of the critical analysis of discourse as a framework for analysis of language events (e.g., Fairclough, 1989, 1995; Ivanic, 1994; Luke, 1995), and related instructional practices and curriculum materials have been generated for use in language arts classrooms (e.g., Janks & Ivanic, 1992; Mellor, Patterson, & O'Neill, 1991; Morgan, 1997). An underlying assumption of the critical analysis of discourse is that the use of language reflects and produces power relations at multiple levels including among individuals, groups, and institutions. A second assumption is that language use can be analyzed to reveal power relations and language can be used to transform power relations.

While the question of whether communicative competence, critical analysis of discourse, or similar language frameworks provide a more theoretical sound framework may be of importance to anthropological and social theorists, for educational researchers it is the tension created by the juxtaposition of these views that can be important. For example, in a study of the language of teaching in a junior college business class taught by an African American teacher to predominately African American students, Foster (1995) found that simultaneously the language was geared to providing access and to critiquing the dominant economic system. Further, Foster found that while at the surface level the language of the classroom maintained what looked to be a traditional classroom structure and climate, at a deeper level the language created an alternative set of social relationships between the teacher and the students characterized by caring, high standards, and connection to community. Fosters' research shows how the tensions between the frameworks of a critical analysis of discourse and the ethnography of communication can be used productively to create insightful descriptions that hold potential both for theoretical understandings of classrooms as sites of cultural dynamics and for improving classroom practice.

One of the problems addressed by anthropologists and educational researchers building on anthropological perspectives is the teaching of standard English, a major component of most English language arts classrooms. The teaching of standard English is viewed by some educators as fundamental to academic development. While many reject the assumption of an inherent relationship between a particular dialect of language and thinking and learning, another rationale for the teaching of standard English has been to provide students with access to the dominant culture and economic spheres. For many English teachers, the teaching of standard English is synonymous with the teaching of Grammar,[5] and is not a choice but a mandate from the government. From an anthropological view, the teaching of standard English (indeed, the standardization and teaching of any language), is closely tied to political processes related to nationalism and the hegemony of dominant classes (e.g., Collins, 1991; Grillo, 1989).

It has long been known that standardization of languages accompanies movements for political autonomy, in particular movements for national autonomy and consolidation.... The general issue, however, is that linguistic unification and standardization is always *imputed* as well as real, counterfactual as well as factual (Bakhtin, 1981; Heath, 1980). The result of political centralization, the rise of great cities, and the stabilizing of literary norms in the service of print-capitalism, language standardization is an undeniable aspect of life in modern nation states. Yet it is also an official representation, an official definition of speaking practices (as good and bad), an attempt to impose a class dialect on an always complex array of social dialects. The standard *qua* ideal is not an illusion, or simple play of power, yet it is part of a system of class hegemony, of ruling-class legitimization. A partial truth which is the official truth, it is an attempt to universalize the particular and class-bound, an attempt which has various sources of strength and points of tension or weakness (Collins, 1991, pp. 233–234).

For educational researchers building on anthropological perspectives, an understanding of the cultural, historical, and political contexts of the standardization of language is important but not sufficient to creating a critique and a set of directions that hold promise for transforming the teaching of Grammar in ways that are counter hegemonic while providing a broad range of opportunities through education for students from diverse cultural and linguistic backgrounds. The problem of language, for educational researchers, is not one just of applying anthropological frameworks, but of the lack of attention to language (not to be confused with attention to Grammar) in the language arts curriculum, in teacher education, and even in the education of educational researchers.

## THE PROBLEM OF LITERACY

Anthropologically based research has been concerned with definitions of literacy, the relationship of literacy to other cultural processes, and the relationship of schooling and literacy.

---

[4]The critique of the constructs of "appropriateness" and of "speech community" may not necessarily reflect the complexity that Hymes has ascribed to them (Hymes, 1996) or the complex relationship between researcher and researched embedded in Hymes' conception of sociolinguistic research (see Rampton, 1992). Thus, while there are still differences between the frameworks provided by sociolinguistic ethnography and critical discourse analysis, for example, there is much more consistency and shared goals than critics might seem to be suggesting.

[5]In this chapter, I use Grammar (upper case G) to refer to the teaching of prescriptive uses and forms of language, I use grammar (lower case g) to refer to syntax.

Heuristically, definitions of literacy can be divided into two models. Street (1984, 1995b) labels them autonomous models and ideological models. Autonomous models conceptualize literacy as a technology, a set of cognitive skills, that are relatively stable and decontextualized (autonomous). Acquiring literacy, from the perspective of autonomous models, is like acquiring a set of cognitive and linguistic tools that are used for a broad range of purposes including the accumulation of knowledge, and communication over distance and time. From the perspective of autonomous models, one set of questions to ask about literacy is what the consequences are of the acquisition of literacy both by a society/social group and by individuals. Goody (1968; Goody & Watt, 1968) has suggested that the consequences include the development of bureaucratically based societies, government based on laws, schools, libraries, and linear history. Others have suggested that the acquisition of literacy is related to a series of cognitive processes associated with

providing definitions, making all assumptions and premises explicit, and observing the formal rules of logic produc[ing] an instrument of considerable power for building an abstract and coherent theory of reality . . . the predominant features of Western culture and for our distinctive ways of using language and our distinctive modes of thought (Olson, 1977, p. 105).

Ideological models conceptualize literacy as a set of cultural practices (e.g., Baynham, 1995; Gee, 1996; Street, 1984, 1995b), ways of using written language, that may and do vary across cultures and settings. Literacy practices (i.e., cultural practices that involve written language) reflect and help constitute the cultural ideology of a social group; as such, they get part of their meaning and significance from the broad range of cultural dynamics of the social group. Further, just as any set of cultural practices evolves and changes, so too do literacy practices. People adopt and adapt literacy practices from a broad range of situations and institutions for use elsewhere, and they do so both in overt and covert ways (Street, 1993). From the perspective of ideological models, there is no predetermined set of linguistic, cognitive, or social processes that define literacy and the relationship of written language to other modes of communication such as oral language (how they differ, how they are integrated, for what uses and in what settings one mode is used versus another, who can use what mode of communication, when, where, and for what). From the perspective of ideological models, autonomous models of literacy are themselves a set of cultural practices for the use of written language that have been assigned hegemonic status (in the sense of marginalizing or not even acknowledging the existence and meaningfulness of other literacy practices (Auerbach, 1992). The discussion of literacy that follows builds on the conception of literacy as a set of cultural practices.

How a person or a group interprets written language (comprehension) reflects broader cultural themes. It is not just a matter of the use of culturally based knowledge for interpretation, but rather, what is considered to be culturally appropriate norms for how to use written text to construct meaning, when, where, and by whom (Bloome, 1987; Green, 1990). Scollon and Scollon (1981) suggest that Western cultures restrict interpretation to the text and standardized interpretations, whereas other cultures may vary in the degree to which they do so. Reder and Green (1983) make a similar point in their study of literacy practices in an Alaskan fishing village, showing how the literacy practices in which people engaged defined them as insiders or outsiders.

One contribution of ideological models of literacy is to provide an alternative way to visualize literacy. From the perspective of an autonomous model and from most psychological models, literacy is visualized/defined as the interaction between a solitary text and a solitary reader or writer (what Bloome, 1983, has called an isolated configuration of reading and writing). Such a model often implies an "ideal" reader or writer, against whom the adequacy of actual readers and writers can be evaluated (and thus legitimate literacy testing as if the testing were not a way of structuring power relations or promulgating a particular ideology (see Collins, 1991; Hill & Parry, 1989). Bloome (1987), building on Heath's (1982a) definition of a literacy event, argues that all literacy events involve social relationships among the participants involved in the literacy event itself (e.g., the members of a reading group) and only potentially between authors and readers. He further argues that the social relationships of the literacy event always drive the construction of meaning and significance of any written text. In brief, meaning does not exist outside of a complex set of social relationships and cultural-historical dynamics that surround, and are inscribed in the text, and are produced through how people simultaneously engage a text and each other.

One of the dynamics associated with literacy is social identity. From the perspective of an autonomous model, identity is located along a continuum from illiterate to literate to highly literate. The degree to which a person can demonstrate acquisition of a particular set of literacy behaviors in a particular setting provides the identity, a function typically provided by schools and examinations.[6] From a cultural practices view of literacy, the relationship between literacy practices and identity is more complex. Within any particular institution that foregrounds a prescribed set of literacy practices (for example, a university), there may be a series of differentiated positions (identities) that participants can take up, assign, and contest. (The available positions may also vary across different literacy practices within an institution.) The cultural norms that define how an academic essay should be written—the language used, topics covered, stance, distance, purpose, relationship of author to audience, conditions under which it is written, its footing, where it should be written, when, with whom, etc.—provide the author with an identity (Ivanic, 1994). Ivanic (1994) shows that the identity assumed for particular literacy practices, such as the writing of an academic essay, may require some students to give up or background their identities as members of nondominant cultural and linguistic groups as well as their gendered identity.

---

[6]The acceptance of an autonomous model of literacy by schools leads to the social reality of identities created along the continuum of illiterate to highly literate, both producing and reflecting a set of privileges and power relations structured across classes (cf., Erickson, 1984).

Anthropologically based studies of literacy and schooling[7] have shown how the literacy practices of schooling differ from those of many communities (especially nonwhite, nonmiddle-class communities) often resulting in cross-cultural difficulties (e.g., Heath, 1983). Studies have also shown how the organization of literacy practices in schooling structures' access to educational opportunities (e.g., Michaels, 1981, 1986), creates identities based on progress through a literacy curriculum (e.g., Anderson-Levitt, 1996), produces cultural trauma and learning disabilities (Trueba, 1988), among other social and cultural effects. To some extent, these studies have led educators to develop models of instruction often referred to as "culturally relevant teaching" in which one component of the pedagogical model is the accommodation and validation of students' cultural knowledge and experiences in the classroom (e.g., Ladson-Billings, 1994).

Another construct derived from anthropological and historical studies of literacy and schooling is "schooled literacy" (Collins, 1991; Cook-Gumperz, 1986; Street & Street, 1991). In brief, schooled literacy refers to literacy practices oriented to the objectification of language and the engagement and completion of literacy practices for the primary purpose of teaching and evaluating performance (cf., Street & Street, 1991). Bloome (2001) writes:

Schooled literacy practices often lack substance, and when they do include substance, there is little reason to attend to the substance or view it as having much importance (Applebee, 1984; Street, 1994; Street & Street, 1991). For example, students often have to copy assignments from textbooks or answer questions at the end of a textbook chapter. What matters is completing the assignment and getting the correct answer, not the substance of the text; it is a phatic exercise (Bloome, Puro, & Theodorou, 1989). The result is that the literacy practices presented as having value have no substance, and the literacy practices that have substance (family and community practices) have no value.

Bloome (2001; Sheridan, Street, & Bloome, 2000) links schooled literacy to the creation of a writing hierarchy, created through Grammar instruction, a narrow range of writing opportunities and genres, and the establishment and teaching of an elitist literary canon. As a consequence of the writing hierarchy, most people come to believe that they are not writers, a status reserved for an elitist few.

The problem of literacy for educational researchers building on anthropological perspectives is how to create a social space in, through, and outside of schooling, that opens up academic literacy practices both to critique and to broader participation in ways that eschew its elite-forming function. One direction has been to conceptualize academic disciplines as cultural communities with a set of cultural practices, including literacy practices (Street, 1995a). Membership in the academic communities requires acquisition of (socialization to) those cultural practices that define the community. By articulating what the literacy practices are of an academic community/discipline, educational researchers can critique the ways in which those practices marginalize others while at the same time identifying and designing avenues by which others might join. Part of what is crucial in the study of academic disciplines is attention to the power relationships within an academic community and between an academic community and other communities, and how literacy practices are implicated in those power relations (and how transformation of literacy practices might help transformation of power relations).

## THE PROBLEM OF LITERATURE

One of the decisions English faculty usually make, whether at a college, high school, or elementary school, is what literature to include as part of the curriculum. Debates over what to include can be viewed as a debate over what counts as the literary cultural capital of the society and what value or priority is given to the literary domain compared with other domains. However, beyond the choice of stories and books are questions about the location of literature, and who gets to decide what is and what is not literature.

In a classic article, Bohannon (1971) describes her attempt to tell *Hamlet* to the Tiv in West Africa. She was unable to tell the story as she wanted because their understanding of stories—what could and could not be in a story, how a story would be organized, and the relationship of a story to the real world—differed from Bohannon's. They continually interrupted her and at the end of her telling, concluded, "[Y]ou must tell us some more stories of your country. We, who are elders, will instruct you in their true meaning, so that when you return to your own land your elders will see that you have not been sitting in the bush, but among those who know things and who have taught you wisdom" (p. 25). Since Bohannon lacked authority among the Tiv to decide what is and what is not literature and what the nature of literature should be, at that time and place, she had to yield to their definition of literature.

From an anthropological perspective, the issue is not merely what books or stories are chosen as literature, but who gets to do the choosing, as well as how, when, and under what circumstances and what meanings are assigned to those choices. Underlying definitions of literature is the organization of story as narrative and of narrative performance. Children, through their interaction with parents, teachers, peers, and others, learn culturally specific ways of organizing, understanding, and performing narratives as well as adapting the narratives they encounter to new situations and to a broad range of social and communicative purposes (e.g., Bauman, 1982; Bauman & Briggs, 1990; Cook-Gumperz & Green, 1984; Heath & Branscombe, 1986). When diverse cultural groups, each with their own definition of literature, come into contact in educational settings, there is the potential for conflict reflecting relations of inequality among the cultural groups. The definitions held by less powerful groups are liable to be viewed as alien or not valid and given token or no visibility. That is, less powerful groups may not be "entitled"

---

[7] "Schooling" here refers to Western style public/state secular schools (and similar private schooling), not necessarily to religious schools or alternative schools that have deliberately eschewed traditional schooling practices.

to tell their stories, to have their stories be part of the literature, or told in their way. Hymes (1996), reflecting on the nature of narrative in society, writes:

The narrative use of language seems universal, potentially available to everyone and to some degree inescapable. Humanity was born telling stories, so to speak, but when we look about us, we find much of humanity mute or awkward much of the time. The right to think and express thought in narrative comes to be taken as a privilege, as a resource that is restricted, as a scarce good, so that the right to unite position and personal experience in public is a badge of status and rank. My account is to be listened to because I am an *x*, yours is of no interest because you are only *y* (p. 119).

For educational researchers building on anthropological perspectives, part of the problem of literature is reconceptualizing it within the study of folklore, ethnopoetics, and cultural performance; that is, removing the construct of literature from the outdated hierarchy of high and low culture, lifeless text, and extending the construct of literature to what ordinary people do in their everyday lives with narrative.

## THE PROBLEM OF LEARNING

Although it may be "common sense" to view them so, teaching and learning are not necessarily complementary constructs. Teaching does not imply learning. Teachers engage in teaching and students engage in studenting (cf., Green & Dixon, 1993; Heras, 1993). That is, teachers enact the role of "teacher," engaging in those cultural behaviors that define what they are doing as teaching, while students engage in a complementary set of cultural behaviors that define them as "students," together producing a cultural event known as "lesson" (cf., Bloome, Puro, & Theodorou, 1989). From this perspective, at least part of the meaning of classroom events and practices is in the public production of the event and of the identities of the participants.

Although from a different anthropological perspective, Anderson-Levitt's (2001) approach to research on the teaching of reading similarly does not view teaching and learning as inherently related constructs. She views the study of teaching as the study of shared cultural knowledge (both explicit and implicit/tacit) that guides how teachers act and interpret others' actions in classroom settings. [Cultural knowledge is not shared equally or fully. See Anderson-Levitt 2001] for a fuller discussion of how cultural knowledge is "shared".) Anderson-Levitt argues that cultural knowledge for teaching is shared at some level cross-nationally, while at other levels it is shared particular to a nation or more localized community. One advantage of Anderson-Levitt's approach is that it allows the concept of culture to be applied to a professional community. Becoming a teacher, then, is not so much a matter of acquiring skills and strategies that enhance student learning (although that may be a byproduct) as it is acquiring a shared cultural knowledge base that allows one to know how to act and think like a teacher and claim a teacher identity. A teacher puts at risk his or her identity as a teacher if he or she does not act in a way consistent with the shared cultural knowledge within a community of teachers.

The redefinition of teaching as shared cultural knowledge within a community of teachers, and as teaching and studenting as a cultural production of a "lesson," shifts questions about classrooms from the effectiveness of particular teaching behaviors or of a curricular or instructional design to questions about how teachers and students come to acquire the cultural knowledge needed to appropriately participate in "lessons," how teachers and students collaborate in the production of a cultural event and of cultural meanings, and how teachers and students produce identities for themselves.

With regard to learning, as recent as 1982, Erickson lamented the lack of interest by anthropologists in "taught cognitive learning," referring in large to the "deliberative teaching and learning of cognitive subject matter, wherever this occurs throughout the life cycle (and whether inside or outside of school)" (1982b, p. 150). The anthropological study of learning shifts the definition of learning from an internal process located in an individual, to a social process located historically among people engaged in cultural practices defined as "learning" with resultant changes in the nature of participation over time (cf., Lave & Wegner, 1991). Changes in participation over time can refer to an individual's movement from one type and level of participation to another, to changes in the way a group conducts itself internally and in relation to other groups, and to the restructuring of the nature and organization of knowledge, including the use of extant knowledge in new ways and settings or for new purposes.

One direction in the use of anthropological perspectives in studies of learning is as part of a multidisciplinary approach heavily grounded in ethnographic studies of learning in school and nonschool studies (e.g., John-Steiner, 1994; Moll, 1992, 2000; Scribner & Cole, 1981). This direction is often referred to as sociohistorical psychology, cultural psychology, sociocultural studies of the mind, or Vygotskian/Neo-Vygotskian. (Although the labels index important differences among perspectives, for the purpose of this chapter they are treated as parts of a single, broad direction.) Part of what is promulgated in these studies is rejection of dualisms related to culture and cognition, individual and social group, empiricism and ideology, among others, as these dualisms are viewed as constraining how learning might be defined, how learning is related to culture, and how learning might be studied.

Building on a framework associated with sociohistorical psychology and cultural psychology, Moll's studies of writing instruction and academic learning provide an illustrative case of the redefinition of learning and how such redefinition can lead to changes in instructional practice (Moll & Diaz, 1987; see also Moll, 1990). When teachers brought knowledge of and from the community (what Moll, Amanti, Neff, & González, 1992, call "funds of knowledge") into the classroom and made it available for student use in writing and other academic learning, students could change how they participated in instructional events and practices, part of which included the production of artifacts (e.g., essays) that they had not previously been able to produce. What Moll provides is an example not only of student learning, but also of teacher learning as the nature of the teachers' participation in classroom instruction changed over time. What changes is not just the knowledge base that students use for participation, but the "tools" they have for their participation. "Tools" refers to both material and intellectual practices for mediating the social, cultural, and cognitive dynamics of events, as well as the relationships between individuals and the social worlds in which they find themselves.

For educational researchers, building on anthropological perspectives involves more than contesting definitions of learning. Underlying the contesting of definitions of learning are assumptions about what constitutes legitimate instructional practice, a learning environment, and assessment. One direction has been to examine how classroom environments can be transformed to provide a broad range of learning opportunities based on anthropologically based understandings of learning and of educational equity (e.g., Collins & Green, 1992; Yeager, Floriani, & Green, 1998). Another direction has been to redefine instructional practices, curriculum, and educational goals from an anthropological perspective (e.g., Curry & Bloome, 1998; Egan-Robertson, 1998; Erickson, 1999; Mercado, 1998; Torres, 1998). In the research conducted within both of these directions, through the collaboration of university researchers and teacher researchers, insights about learning derive from the ethnographic study of deliberate attempts to transform classroom education based on anthropological perspectives. In brief, a circle is created in which anthropological understanding of learning, literacy, literature, language, and culture are used to generate transformative classroom situations that are then studied ethnographically, leading to an enhanced understanding of learning, literacy, literature, language, and culture at both a micro and macro level.

## FINAL COMMENTS

The general mission of anthropology in part can be said to be to help overcome the limitations of the categories and understandings of human life that are part of a single civilization's partial view (Hymes, 1980, p. 2).

In 1991, it could be said that despite calls for anthropologically based research on teaching the English language arts, with the exception of a relatively small number of studies, there was more promise than substance. While there have been additional studies and attention to anthropologically based research on the English language arts, it still remains mostly promise. (In 1994, Delamont and Atkinson (1995) made a similar argument.) One function of such studies would be to redefine and problematize constructs that are foundational to the English language arts. Another function would be to make it more possible to address issues of social justice in and through education as they manifest themselves in a culturally and linguistically diverse society. In considering the relationship of anthropology *and* research on teaching the English language arts, and what would be necessary to move from promise to substance, it is not simply a matter of more anthropologically based studies or more calls for applying anthropology. Certainly, the lack of study of language, literacy, literature, culture, and learning from anthropological perspectives in the education of teachers and educational researchers is one obstacle. Another obstacle lies in the *application* relationship of anthropology to research on teaching the English language arts. While *application* can and should constitute part of the relationship, an *application* relationship inherently defines the *applier* as an "other" who is limited in how the world might be defined. The relationship also needs to be constituted by joint action by educational researchers, anthropologists, and educators on the teaching of the English language arts, as a means of critique, theorizing, and for constructing new possibilities.

## ACKNOWLEDGMENTS

I want to acknowledge Kathryn Anderson-Levitt, James Collins, and Brian Street for comments on an earlier version of this manuscript. I also want to acknowledge Angela Saylor for technical assistance. Whatever problems and flaws remain are my sole responsibility.

## *References*

Anderson-Levitt, K. (1996). Behind schedule: Batch-produced children in French and U.S. classrooms. In B. A. Levinson, D. E. Foley, & D. C. Holland (Eds.), *The cultural production of the educated person: Critical ethnographies of schooling and local practice* (pp. 57–78). Albany, NY: State University of New York Press.

Anderson-Levitt, K. (2001). *Teaching cultures: Knowledge for teaching first grade in France and the United States.* Cresskill, NJ: Hampton Press.

Applebee, A. (1984). *Contexts for learning to write: Studies of secondary school instruction.* Norwood, NJ: Ablex.

Atkinson, P. (1990). *The ethnographic imagination: Textual constructions of reality.* New York: Routledge.

Au, K. (1980). Participation structures in a reading lesson with Hawaiian children. *Anthropology and Education Quarterly, 11*(2), 91–115.

Auerbach, E. (1992). Literacy and ideology. *Annual Review of Applied Linguistics, 12,* 71–85.

Bakhtin, M. (1935/1981 trans.). Discourse in the novel. In M. Holquist (Ed.), *The dialogic imagination.* Austin, TX: University of Texas Press.

Bauman, R. (1982). Ethnography of children's folklore. In P. Gilmore & A. Glatthorn (Eds.), *Children in and out of school* (pp. 172–186). Washington, DC; Center for Applied Linguistics.

Bauman, R., & Briggs, C. (1990). Poetics and performance as critical perspectives on language and social life. *Annual Review of Anthropology, 19,* 59–88.

Baynham, M. (1995). *Literacy practices.* London: Longman.

Bloome, D. (1983). Reading as a social process. In B. Hutson (Ed.), *Advances in reading/language research, 2,* 165–195. Greenwich, CT: JAI Press.

Bloome, D. (1987). Reading as a social process in a middle school classroom. In D. Bloome (Ed.), *Literacy and schooling* (pp. 123-149). Norwood, NJ: Ablex.

Bloome, D. (1989). Beyond access: An ethnographic study of reading and writing in a seventh grade classroom. In D. Bloome (Ed.), *Classrooms and literacy* (pp. 53-107). Norwood, NJ: Ablex Publishing Corporation.

Bloome, D. (1991). Anthropology and research on teaching the English language arts. In J. Flood, J. Jensen, D. Lapp, & J. Squires (Eds.), *Handbook of research on teaching the English language arts* (pp. 46-56). New York: Macmillan.

Bloome, D. (1997). This is literacy: Three challenges for teachers of reading and writing. *Australian Journal of Language and Literacy, 20*(2), 107-115.

Bloome, D. (2001). Boundaries on the construction of literacy in secondary classrooms: Envisioning reading and writing in a democratic and just society. In E. B. Moje & D. O'Brien (Eds.), *Constructions of literacy: Studies of teaching and learning in secondary classrooms*. Mahwah, NJ: Lawrence Erlbaum Associates.

Bloome, D., Puro, P., & Theodorou, E. (1989). Procedural display and classroom lessons. *Curriculum Inquiry, 19*(3), 265-291.

Bohannon, L. (1971). Shakespeare in the bush. In J. P. Spradley & D. W. McCurdy (Eds.), *Conformity and conflict: Readings in cultural anthropology* (pp. 13-23). Boston: Little, Brown.

Borko, H., & Eisenhart, M. (1989). Reading ability groups as literacy communities. In D. Bloome (Ed.), *Classrooms and literacy* (pp. 107-134). Norwood, NJ: Ablex.

Boyarin, J. (Ed.). (1992). *The ethnography of reading*. Berkeley: University of California Press.

Cazden, C. (1972). Preface. In C. Cazden, V. John, & D. Hymes (Eds.), *Functions of language in the classroom* (pp. vii-ix). New York: Teachers College Press.

Cazden, C., John, V., & Hymes, D. (Eds.). (1972). *Functions of language in the classroom*. New York: Teachers College Press.

Clifford, J., & Marcus, G. (Eds.). (1986). *Writing culture*. Cambridge, England: Cambridge University Press.

Coates, J., & Cameron, D. (Eds.). (1988). *Women in their speech communities*. London: Longman.

Collins, E., & Green, J. (1992). Learning in classroom settings. Making or breaking a culture. In H. Marshall (Ed.), *Redefining student learning: Roots of education change* (pp. 59-86). Norwood, NJ: Ablex.

Collins, J. (1986). Differential instruction in reading groups. In J. Cook-Gumperz (Ed.), *The social construction of literacy* (pp. 117-137). New York: Cambridge University Press.

Collins, J. (1991). Hegemonic practice: Literacy and standard language in public education. In C. Mitchell & K. Lueiles (Eds.), *Rewriting literacy: Culture and the discourse of the other* (pp. 229-254). New York: Benjamin & Garvey.

Cook-Gumperz, J. (Ed.). (1986). *The social construction of literacy*. New York: Cambridge University Press.

Cook-Gumperz, J., & Green, J. (1984). A sense of story: Influences on children's storytelling ability. In D. Tannen (Ed.), *Coherence in spoken and written discourse* (pp. 201-218). Norwood, NJ: Ablex.

Cook-Gumperz, J., Gumperz, J., & Simons, H. (1981). *School-home ethnography project*. Final report to the National Institute of Education. Washington, DC: Department of Education.

Curry, T., & Bloome, D. (1998). Learning to write by writing ethnography. In A. Egan-Robertson & D. Bloome (Eds.), *Students as researchers of culture and language in their own communities*. Cresskill, NJ: Hampton Press.

De, E. N., & Gregory, D. U. (1997). Decolonizing the classroom: Freshman composition in a multicultural setting. In C. Severino, J. Guerra,
& J. Butler (Eds.), *Writing in multicultural settings* (pp. 118-132). New York: The Modern Language Association of America.

Delamont, S., & Atkinson, P. (1995). *Fighting familiarity: Essays on education and ethnography*. Cresskill, NJ: Hampton Press.

Delgado-Gaitan, C. (1989). Classroom literacy activity for Spanish-speaking students. *Linguistics and Education, 1*(3), 285-297.

Delgado-Gaitan, C. (1993). Researching change and changing the researcher. *Harvard Educational Review, 63*(4), 389-411.

DeStefano, J., Pepinsky, H., & Sanders, T. (1982). Discourse rules for literacy learning in a classroom. In L. Wilkinson (Ed.), *Communicating in the classroom* (pp. 101-130). New York: Academic Press.

Dunkin, M. J., & Biddle, B. J. (1974). *The study of teaching*. New York: Holt, Rinehart, & Winston.

Duranti, A. (1997). *Linguistic anthropology*. Cambridge, England: Cambridge University Press.

Eder, D. (1986). Differences in communicative styles across ability groups. In L. Wilkinson (Ed.), *Communicating in classrooms* (pp. 245-264). New York: Academic Press.

Egan-Robertson, A. (1998). "We must ask our questions and tell our stories": Writing ethnography and constructing personhood. In A. Egan-Robertson & D. Bloome (Eds.), *Students as researchers of culture and language in their own communities* (pp. 261-284). Cresskill, NJ: Hampton Press.

Egan-Robertson, A., & Bloome, D. (Eds.). (1998). *Students as researchers of culture and language in their own communities*. Cresskill, NJ: Hampton Press.

Eisenhart, M. (1999). Reflections on educational intervention in light of postmodernism. *Anthropology & Education Quarterly, 30*(4), 462-465.

Eisemon, T., & Hallet, M. (1989). The acquisition of literacy in religious and secular schools. In D. Bloome (Ed.), *Classrooms and literacy* (pp. 264-288). Norwood, NJ: Ablex.

Erickson, F. (1982a). Classroom discourse as improvisation: Relationships between academic task structure and social participation structure in lessons. In L. Wilkinson (Ed.), *Communicating in the classroom* (pp. 153-181). New York: Academic Press.

Erickson, F. (1982b). Taught cognitive learning in its immediate environments: A neglected topic in the anthropology of education. *Anthropology and Education Quarterly, 13*(2), 149-179.

Erickson, F. (1984). School literacy, reasoning, and civility. *Review of Research in Education, 54*, 525-546.

Erickson, F. (1999). Culture in society and in educational practices. In J. A. Banks & C. A. McGee Banks (Eds.), *Multicultural education: Issues and perspectives* (3rd ed., pp. 32-59). New York: Wiley.

Erickson, F., & Mohatt, G. (1982). Cultural organization of participation structures in two classrooms of Indian students. In G. Spindler (Ed.), *Doing the ethnography of schooling: Educational anthropology in action* (pp. 132-175), Prospect Hts., IL: Waveland Press.

Fairclough, N. (1989). *Language and power*. London: Longman.

Fairclough, N. (1992). *Discourse and social change*. Cambridge, England: Polity.

Fairclough, N. (1995). *Critical discourse analysis*. London: Longman.

Firth, R. (1936). *We, the Tikopia: A sociological study of kinship in primitive Polynesia*. Boston: Beacon Press.

Foster, M. (1995). Talking that talk: The language of control, curriculum and critique. *Linguistics and Education, 7*(2), 129-150.

Frake, C. (1969). The ethnographic study of cognitive systems. In S. Tyler (Ed.), *Cognitive anthropology* (pp. 28-40). New York: Holt, Rinehart, & Winston.

Gage, N. L. (Ed.). (1963). *Handbook of research on teaching*. Chicago: Rand McNally.

Gearing, F. O. (1973, reprinted 1984). Toward a general theory of cultural transmission. *Anthropology and Education Quarterly, 15*(1), 29–37.

Gee, J. P. (1996). *Social linguistics and literacies: Ideology in discourses* (2nd ed.). London: Taylor & Francis.

Geertz, C. (1972). Deep play: Notes on the Balinese cockfight. *Daedalus, 10*(1), 1–37. (Reprinted in C. Geertz [1973] *The interpretation of cultures.* New York: Basic Books).

Geertz, C. (1973). *The interpretation of culture.* New York: Basic Books.

Geertz, C. (1983). *Local knowledge: Further essays in interpretive anthropology.* New York: Basic Books.

Gilmore, P. (1986). Sub-rosa literacy: Peers, play, and ownership in literacy acquisition. In B. Schieffelin & P. Gilmore (Eds.), *The acquisition of literacy: ethnographic perspectives* (pp. 155–170). Norwood, NJ: Ablex.

Gilmore, P. (1987). Sulking, stepping, and tracking: The effects of attitude assessment on access to literacy. In D. Bloome (Ed.), *Literacy and schooling* (pp..). Norwood, NJ: Ablex.

Gitlin, A. (Ed.). (1994). *Power and method: Political activism and educational research.* New York: Routledge.

Goldberg, D. T. (1993). *Racist culture: Philosophy and the politics of meaning.* Oxford, England: Blackwell.

Goldenberg, C. (1987). Low-income Hispanic parents' contributions to their first-grade children's word recognition skills. *Anthropology and Education Quarterly, 18*(3), 149–179.

González, N. (1999). What will we do when culture does not exist anymore? *Anthropology & Education Quarterly, 30*(4), 431–435.

Goodenough, W. (1981). *Culture, language, and society.* Menlo Park, CA: Benjamin/Cummings.

Goody, J. (Ed.). (1968). Literacy in traditional societies. Cambridge, England: Cambridge University Press.

Goody, J., & Watt, I. (1968). The consequences of literacy. In J. Goody (Ed.), *Literacy in traditional societies.* Cambridge, UK: Cambridge University Press.

Green, J. (1990). Reading is a social process. In J. Howell, A. McNamara, & M. Clough (Eds.), *Social context of literacy.* Canberra, Australia: ACT Department of Education.

Green, J., & Bloome, D. (1998). Ethnography and ethnographers of and in education: A situated perspective. In J. Flood, S. Heath, & D. Lapp (Eds.), *A handbook for literacy educators: Research on teaching the communicative and visual arts.* New York: Macmillan.

Green, J., & Dixon, C. (1993). Talking knowledge into being: Discursive and social practices in classrooms. *Linguistics and Education, 5*(3–4), 231–240.

Green, J., & Wallat, C. (1981). Mapping instructional conversations—A sociolinguistic ethnography. In J. Green & C. Wallat (Eds.), *Ethnography and language in educational settings* (pp. 161–207). Norwood, NJ: Ablex.

Grillo, R. (1989). *Dominant languages: Language and hierarchy in Britain and France.* Cambridge, England: Cambridge University Press.

Gumperz, J. (1986). *Discourse strategies.* New York: Cambridge University Press.

Gumperz, J. J., & Hymes, D. (Eds.). (1972). *Directions in sociolinguistics: The ethnography of communication.* New York: Holt, Rinehart, & Winston.

Guthrie, G. P. (1985). *A school divided: An ethnography of bilingual education in a Chinese community.* Hillsdale, NJ: Lawrence Erlbaum Associates.

Hammersly, M., & Atkinson, P. (1983). *Ethnography: Principles in practice.* London: Tavistock.

Harris, M. (1999). *Theories of culture in postmodern times.* Walnut Creek, CA: Altamira Press.

Heath, S. (1980). Standard English: Biography of a symbol. In T. Shopen & J. Williams (Eds.), *Standards and dialects in English* (pp. 3–31). Cambridge, MA: Winthrop.

Heath, S. (1982a). Protean shapes in literacy events. In D. Tannen (Ed.), *Spoken and written language* (pp. 348–370). Norwood, NJ: Ablex.

Heath, S. (1982b). What no bedtime story means: Narrative skills at home and at school. *Language in Society, 11*(1), 49–76.

Heath, S. (1983). *Ways with words.* New York: Cambridge University Press.

Heath, S., & Branscombe, A. (1986). The book as narrative prop in language acquisition. In B. Schieffelin & P. Gilmore (Eds.), *The acquisition of literacy: Ethnographic perspectives* (pp. 16–34). Norwood, NJ: Ablex.

Heath, S. B., & Thomas, C. (1984). The achievement of preschool literacy for mother and child. In H. Goelman, A. Oberg, & F. Smith (Eds.), *Awakening to literacy* (pp. 51–72). London: Heinemann.

Heras, A. I. (1993). The construction of understanding in a sixth grade bilingual classroom. *Linguistics and Education, 5*(3 & 4), 275–300.

Hill, C., & Parry, K. (1989). Autonomous and pragmatic models of literacy: Reading assessment in adult education. *Linguistics and Education, 1*(3), 233–284.

Hymes, D. (1971). On linguistic theory, communicative competence, and the education of disadvantaged children. In M. L. Wax, S. Diamond, & F. O. Gearing (Eds.), *Anthropological perspectives on education* (pp. 51–66). New York: Basic Books.

Hymes, D. (1974). *The foundations of sociolinguistics: Sociolinguistic ethnography.* Philadelphia: University of Pennsylvania Press.

Hymes, D. (1980). *Language in education: Ethnolinguistic essays.* Washington, DC: Center for Applied Linguistics.

Hymes, D. (1996). *Ethnography, linguistics, narrative inequality: Toward an understanding of voice.* London: Taylor & Francis.

Ivanic, R. (1994). I is for interpersonal: Discoursal construction of writer identities and the teaching of writing. *Linguistics and Education, 6*(1), 3–17.

Janks, H., & Ivanic, R. (1992). Critical discourse awareness and emancipatory discourse. In N. Fairclough (Ed.), Critical language awareness (pp. 305–331). London: Longman.

John-Steiner, V. (1994). *Sociocultural approaches to language and literacy: An interactionist perspective.* Cambridge, England: Cambridge University Press.

Keesing, R. M. (1987). Models, "folk" and "cultural": Paradigms regained? In D. Holland & N. Quinn (Eds.), *Cultural models in language and thought* (pp. 369–393). New York: Cambridge University Press.

Kuznar, L. A. (1997). *Reclaiming a scientific anthropology.* Walnut Creek, CA: Altamira Press.

Ladson-Billings, G. (1994). *The dreamkeepers: Successful teachers of African-American children.* San Francisco: Jossey-Bass.

Lave, J., & Wegner, E. (1991). *Situated learning: Legitimate peripheral participation.* Cambridge, England: Cambridge University Press.

Levi-Strauss, C. (1963). *Structural anthropology.* New York: Basic Books.

Levinson, B. A., & Holland, D. (1996). The cultural production of the educated person: An introduction. In B. A. Levinson, D. E. Foley, & D. C. Holland (Eds.), *The cultural production of the educated person: Critical ethnographies of schooling and local practice* (pp. 1–56). Albany, NY: State University of New York Press.

Luke, A. (1995). Text and discourse in education: An introduction to critical discourse analysis. In M. Apple (Ed.), *Review of research in education, 21,* Washington, DC: AERA.

Malinowski, B. (1922). *Argonauts of the Western Pacific.* London: Routledge.

Marcus, G. E., & Fischer, M. M. (1986). *Anthropology as cultural critique: An experimental moment in the human sciences*. Chicago: University of Chicago Press.

McDermott, R. (1999). Culture is not an environment of the mind. *The Journal of the Learning Sciences, 8*(1), 157–169.

McDermott, R., Goldman, S., & Varenne, H. (1984). When school goes home: Some problems in the organization of homework. *Teachers College Record, 85*(3), 391–409.

McDermott, R. P., & Hood, L. (1982). Institutionalized psychology and the ethnography of schooling. In P. Gilmore & A. Glatthorn (Eds.), *Children in and out of school* (pp. 232–249). Washington, DC: Center for Applied Linguistics.

Mead, M. (1970). Our education emphases in primitive perspective. In J. Middleton (Ed.), *From child to adult: Studies in the anthropology of education* (pp. 1–13). Garden City, NY: The Natural History Press.

Mehan, H. (1980). The competent student. *Anthropology and Education Quarterly, 11*(3), 131–152.

Mellor, B., Patterson, A., & O'Neill, M. (1991). *Reading fictions*. Cottesloe, Australia: Chalkface Press.

Mercado, C. (1998). When young people from marginalized communities enter the world of ethnographic research—Scribing, planning, reflecting, and sharing. In A. Egan-Robertson & D. Bloome (Eds.), *Students as researchers of culture and language in their own communities*. Cresskill, NJ: Hampton.

Michaels, S. (1981). "Sharing time": Children's narrative styles and differential access to literacy. *Language in Society, 10*(3), 423–442.

Michaels, S. (1986). Narrative presentations: An oral preparation for literacy with first graders. In J. Cook-Gumperz (Ed.), *The social construction of literacy*. Cambridge, England: Cambridge University Press.

Miller, P., Nemoianu, A., & DeJong, J. (1986). Early reading at home: Its practices and meaning in a working classroom community. In B. Schieffelin & P. Gilmore (Eds.), *The acquisition of literacy: Ethnographic perspectives* (pp. 3–15). Norwood, NJ: Ablex.

Mitchell, J. C. (1984). Typicality and the case study. In R. Ellen (Ed.), *Ethnographic research: A guide to general conduct* (pp. 238–241). New York: Academic Press.

Moll, L. (Ed.). (1990). *Vygotsky and education: Instructional implications and applications of sociohistorical psychology*. Cambridge, England: Cambridge University Press.

Moll, L. C. (1992). Literacy research in community and classrooms: A sociocultural approach. In R. Beach, J. L. Green, M. L. Kamil, & T. Shanahan (Eds.), *Multidisciplinary perspectives on literacy research* (pp. 211–244). Urbana, IL: NCRE/NCTE.

Moll, L. (2000). Inspired by Vygotsky: Ethnographic experiments in education. In C. Lee & P. Smagorinsky (Eds.), *Vygotskian perspectives on literacy research* (pp. 256–268). Cambridge, England: Cambridge University Press.

Moll, L., & Diaz, R. (1987). Teaching writing as communication: The use of ethnographic findings in classroom practice. In D. Bloome (Ed.), *Literacy and schooling*. Norwood, NJ: Ablex.

Moll, L., Amanti, C., Neff, D., & González, N. (1992). Funds of knowledge for teaching: Using a qualitative approach to connect homes and classrooms. *Theory Into Practice, 31*, 132–141.

Moore, J. D. (1997). *Visions of culture: An introduction to anthropological theories and theorists*. Walnut Creek, CA: Altamira Press.

Morgan, W. (1997). Critical literacy in the classroom: The art of the possible. *London: Routledge*.

Olson, D. (1977). From utterance to text: The bias of language in speech and writing. *Harvard Education Review, 47*(3), 257–281.

Pai, Y., & Adler, S. (1997). *Cultural foundations of education* (2nd ed.). Upper Saddle River, NJ: Merrill.

Peacock, J. L. (1986). *The anthropological lens: Harsh light, soft focus*. Cambridge, England: Cambridge University Press.

Quinn, N., & Holland, D. (1987). Culture and cognition. In D. Holland & N. Quinn (Eds.), *Cultural models in language and thought* (pp. 3–40). New York: Cambridge University Press.

Rampton, B. M. H. (1992). Scope for empowerment in sociolinguistics? In D. Cameron, E. Frazer, P. Harvey, M. B. H. Rampton, & K. Richardson (Eds.), *Researching language: Issues of power and method* (pp. 29–61). London: Routledge.

Reder, S., & Green, K. (1983). Contrasting patterns of literacy in an Alaska fishing village. *International Journal of the Sociology of Language, 42*, 9–39.

Said, E. (1979). *Orientalism*. New York: Vintage Books.

Said, E. (1985). Orientalism reconsidered. In F. Barker, P. Hulme, M. Iversen, & D. Loxley (Eds.), *Europe and its others: Proceedings of the Essex conference on the sociology of literature* (Vol. 1, pp. 14–27). Colchester, England: University of Essex.

Schieffelin, B. B., & Gilmore, P. (Eds.). (1986). *The acquisition of literacy: Ethnographic perspectives*. Norwood, NJ: Ablex.

Schieffelin, B., & Ochs, E. (1986). Language socialization. *Annual Review of Anthropology, 15,* 163–191.

Scollon, R. (1988). Storytelling, reading, and the micropolitics of literacy. In J. E. Readence & R. S. Baldwin (Eds.), *Dialogues in literacy research: Thirty-seventh yearbook of the National Reading Conference* (pp. 15–34). Chicago: National Reading Conference.

Scollon, R., & Scollon, S. (1981). *Narrative/literacy and face in interethnic communication*. Norwood, NJ: Ablex.

Scribner, S., & Cole, M. (1981). *The psychology of literacy*. Cambridge, MA: Harvard University Press.

Sheridan, D., Street, B., & Bloome, D. (2000). *Writing ourselves: Literacy practices and the Mass-Observation Project*. Cresskill, NJ: Hampton Press.

Soliday, M. (1997). The politics of difference: Toward a pedagogy of reciprocity. In C. Severino, J. Guerra, & J. Butler (Eds.), *Writing in multicultural settings* (pp. 261–272). New York: The Modern Language Association of America.

Spindler, G. (Ed.). (1963). *Education and culture*. New York: Holt, Rinehart, & Winston.

Spindler, G. (Ed.). (1978). *The making of psychological anthropology*. Berkeley: University of California Press.

Spindler, G. D., & Spindler, L. S. (Eds.). (1987a). *Interpretive ethnography of education: At home and abroad*. Hillsdale, NJ: Lawrence Erlbaum Associates.

Spindler, G. D., & Spindler, L. S. (1987b). Issues and applications in ethnographic methods. In G. D. Spindler & L. S. Spindler (Eds.), *Interpretive ethnography of education: At home and abroad* (pp. 1–7). Hillsdale, NJ: Lawrence Erlbaum Associates.

Street, B. (1984). *Literacy in theory and practice*. New York: Cambridge University Press.

Street, B. (Ed.). (1993). *Cross-cultural approaches to literacy*. Cambridge, England: Cambridge University Press.

Street, B. (1994). Struggles over the meaning(s) of literacy. In M. Hamilton, D. Barton, & R. Ivanic (Eds.), *Worlds of literacy* (pp. 15–20). Clevedon, North Somerset: Multilingual Matters.

Street, B. (1995a). Academic literacies. In D. Baker, C. Fox, & J. Clay (Eds.), *Challenging ways of knowing in maths, science and English*. Brighton, England: Falmer Press.

Street, B. (1995b). *Social literacies*. London: Longman.

Street, B., & Street, J. (1991). The schooling of literacy. In D. Barton & R. Ivanic (Eds.), *Writing in the community* (pp. 143–166). London: Sage.

Taylor, D. (1983). *Family literacy*. Exeter, NH: Heinemann.

Torres, M. (1998). Celebrations and letters home: Research as an ongoing conversation among students, parents, and teacher. In A. Egan-Robertson & D. Bloome (Eds.), *Students as researchers of culture and language in their own communities* (pp. 59-68). Cresskill, NJ: Hampton Press.

Trueba, H. (1988). English literacy acquisition: From cultural trauma to learning disabilities in minority students. *Linguistics and Education: An International Research Journal, 1*(2), 125-152.

Trueba, H., Jacobs, L., & Kirton, E. (1990). *Cultural conflict and adaptation: The case of Hmong children in American society*. New York: Falmer Press.

Trujillo, A. (1996). In search of Aztl★n: Movimiento ideology and the creation of a Chicano worldview through schooling. In B. A. Levinson, D. E. Foley, & D. C. Holland (Eds.), *The cultural production of the educated person: Critical ethnographies of schooling and local practice* (pp. 119-149). Albany, NY: State University of New York Press.

Tyler, S. A. (1987). *The unspeakable: Discourse, dialogue, and rhetoric in the postmodern world*. Madison, WI: University of Wisconsin Press.

Tylor, E. (1871/1958). *Primitive culture*. New York: Harper & Row.

Varenne, H. (1984). Collective representation in American anthropological conversations about culture. *Current Anthropology, 25*(3), 281-299.

Wallat, C., & Green, C. (1979). Social rules and communicative contexts in kindergarten. *Theory Into Practice, 18*(4), 275-284.

Whiting, B. B., & Whiting, J. M. (1975). *Children of six cultures: A psychocultural analysis*. Cambridge, MA: Harvard University Press.

Willett, J., Solsken, J., & Wilson-Keenan, J. (1998). The (Im)possibilities of constructing multicultural language practices in research and pedagogy. *Linguistics and Education, 10*(2), 165-218.

Yeager, B., Floriani, A., & Green, J. (1998). Learning to see learning in the classroom. In A. Egan-Robertson & D. Bloome (Eds.), *Students as researchers of culture and language in their own communities*. Cresskill, NJ: Hampton Press.

Zaharlick, A., & Green, J. (This Edition). Ethnographic research.

# LITERARY THEORY

## Louise M. Rosenblatt
### New York University

Assumptions concerning literature underlie at least tacitly any teaching of literature and any research on the teaching of literature. What texts fall under the heading of literary? What are appropriate ways of interpreting literary texts? Consciously or unconsciously, teachers are guided by answers to such questions, answers often assimilated automatically from their own education or from the established practices in their field. Basic to literature teaching are not only assumptions about the learning process but also assumptions about the nature of the reading process and the relationship between the reader and the text. Ultimately, the underlying theoretical implications involve such matters as assumptions about the nature of language and its relation to how human beings know their world, or "reality"—the problem philosophers term epistemology or the theory of knowledge.

Such problems, now grouped under the heading of literary theory, or sometimes critical theory, have occupied thinkers since Plato and Aristotle, especially at times of cultural and intellectual change. In the United States, since the late 1960s and early 1970s, literary theory has been increasingly discussed in professional journals and publications, and it has emerged as a distinct field of academic specialization. Proponents of various alternative theories are competing for representation in graduate and undergraduate university departments. Since such theories ultimately have implications for teaching and research, this chapter will sketch the major outlines of recent developments in this highly controversial field. In such short compass, only very reductive accounts are possible.

In addition to works cited, fuller bibliographies may be found in the following surveys of literary theory listed in References: *Bedford Glossary of Critical and Literary Terms*, 1997; *Johns Hopkins Guide to Literary Theory*, 1994; *Encyclopedia of Contemporary Literary Theory*, 1993; *Encyclopedia of Rhetoric and Composition*, 1996; *Encyclopedia of Aesthetics* (1998).

## DOMINANT THEORIES BEFORE 1950

In the colleges, only the Greek and Latin literatures were at first deemed proper for study, and they were approached primarily as objects of grammatical, rhetorical, or philological analysis. When, for various reasons, the shift was made to English texts, there was no problem following the model of the philological study of literature in the German universities. Philology was the main concern of Francis Child when in 1896 he was appointed the first professor of English literature at Harvard. Moreover, his reading list included works in what today would be considered fields other than literary, such as history or philosophy. When later in the century courses were introduced that focused more on works now defined as imaginative, concern for scholarship dictated, in addition to textual analysis, largely a biographical and historical approach.

The Romantic movement in England had produced a body of theory that, on the one hand, supported this view of the literary work as primarily a reflection of the writer's biography and times. On the other hand, the Romantic view of the organic nature of art, with its emphasis on the poem as a poem, derived from Kant and other German philosophers mainly through the writings of Coleridge, did not fit easily into the scientific or scholarly academic scheme. An influential theoretical strand in both the universities and schools was Matthew Arnold's (1880) neoclassical emphasis on the potentialities of literature as the transmitter of ethical and spiritual ideals, and of the critic as concerned with propagating "the best that is known and thought in the world."

As the study of English and American literature became an accepted part of the American college and university curriculum in the early decades of the 20th century, these, not always consistent, approaches contributed to shaping the program. Linguistic and textual analysis, the study of Anglo-Saxon, the history of literary periods and movements, the concern for objective scholarship, and the concentration on works deemed good or great characterized the usual English program. The graduate school emphasized especially scholarly research and historical accuracy. The undergraduate program sought to promote knowledge of the canon, viewed largely in terms of great writers and literary periods.

Certain assumptions concerning the study of literature can be discerned as having prevailed over the whole educational spectrum until recent decades. The general assumption was that competent readers could interpret the text and agree on the author's intended meaning, on "what the text meant." A pedagogical result of these theoretical assumptions was the college classroom lecture in which the instructor expounded and analyzed the work and its background. Classroom recitations and written examinations were designed to establish whether the student had acquired this knowledge.

From the earliest days, the dominance of factually oriented literary study and research in the universities led some to complain that the values of literature as an art were being neglected, and to defend the acceptability of criticism as an academic subject. An indication of the continuing struggle is that a historian of the "profession of literature" (Graff, 1987) uses the title "Scholars versus Critics" for chapters covering the years from 1915 to 1965.

## Literature in the Schools

Long before literature in English was introduced into the college curiculum, literary texts were being used in schools in teaching reading and were being justified as a means of inculcating moral and social attitudes. Histories of the teaching of English in the schools (e.g., Applebee, 1974, 1996), histories of American education (e.g., Cremin, 1961), and accounts of the academic profession (Berlin, 1984, 1987; Graff, 1987) show that the treatment of literature over the K–12 spectrum has not necessarily reflected developments in the universities. In the early 20th century, when emphasis shifted from college preparation to a more democratic concern for the general student, professional educators turned away from the academic model offered by the colleges. Emphasis on the personal and social needs and interests of the individual student, and on education as a process of growth emerged in the 1920s and reached its height as the progressive education movement in the 1930s and the early 1940s. Except for a few colleges (e.g., Sarah Lawrence and Bennington), progressive ideas influenced teaching methods and curriculum mainly in the schools. However, pressures from the growing demands of mass education led in the 1950s to the movement for education for "life adjustment" that contradicted the progressive concern for the development of critical thinking. Not until the 1960s do we find a convergence of attitudes among school and college theorists (Applebee, 1974, pp. 107–245). The present chapter is concerned primarily with the emergence of the New Criticism, its dominance in the midcentury, and the continuing theoretical reaction against it in recent decades.

A difficulty to be faced is that in many of the writings to be discussed, ambiguities arise from unnoticed slippages in the use of the term, text: sometimes to refer to the physical paper-and-ink artifact, sometimes to the syntax, the pattern of the inked signs, and sometimes to the interpretation, the work.

## THE NEW CRITICISM: FORMALIST ANALYSIS

In the late 1930s, a group calling themselves the New Critics emerged, and by the midcentury they had gained academic preeminence in the universities. The prevalent concern with the history of literature and with literature as a reflection of biographical and social factors, the New Critics claimed, led to neglect of literature as an art. They reacted also against the Romantic emphasis on the personality of the author and the critic. The New Critics urged an impersonal "intrinsic" analysis of "the poem itself," as an autonomous entity, instead of study of "extrinsic" biographical or historical materials. Their attacks on "the affective fallacy" decried the concern with the reader's response (Wellek & Warren, 1949; Wimsatt & Beardsley, 1954).

The New Critics called for an objective approach to the work. The poem was presented as an autonomous entity embodying its meaning and existing in its own right as a unified system whose workings could be objectively studied and analyzed. Thus, the central concern was no longer the message, its ethical or intellectual import or its relation to author and social context. Interest turned rather to analysis of a formal structure. Though this approach was in various ways new, it developed to an extreme one component of the traditional approach, the emphasis on formal analysis.

In *Understanding Poetry*, an anthology for the college introductory course, Cleanth Brooks and Robert Penn Warren (1938) set forth a technique of "close reading" that exemplified the New Criticism. Explication of the text demanded categorization of genre, analysis of such matters of technique as the structure of the work (the relation of its parts to the whole), verse forms, patterns of imagery and metaphor, and definitions of the technical means by which effects such as irony were produced. The potential personal significance for the student reader was not stressed.

In the following decades, other anthologies by these and other authors and theoretical writings supporting this approach enjoyed increasing success. In 1949, Wellek and Warren's *Theory of Literature* provided theoretical support for the formalist position. Various competing critical positions—e.g., the Chicago neo-Aristotelians, such as Crane (1952), or the myth or "archetypal" critics, such as Northrop Frye (1957), also enjoyed high prestige. By the midcentury, however, the New Criticism was dominant in the universities.

In the 1950s and 1960s, formalist approaches to literature were increasingly imposed on the earlier traditional historical patterns of program organization in the colleges. Introductory courses (and anthologies) were usually organized by genres, with organization by periods left to advanced courses for majors. Graduate studies reflected a similar division between formalist critical concerns and historical or linguistic research. Despite the infiltration of alternative practices, to be described, this pattern still predominates, as college catalogues and the sales of college "introduction to literature" texts demonstrate.

## "READER RESPONSE" THEORIES

### Reaction Against the New Criticism

In the late 1960s, the unrest in the universities generated by the Vietnam War and the feeling that formalist criticism was propagating an endless flow of sterile explications of literary works opened the way for the propounding of alternative views on the literary work and on critical method. In the 1970s and 1980s, a multiplicity of journals, books, and conference reports on controversial problems of literary criticism and interpretation produced a wide range of theoretical positions. By 1980, literary theory had emerged as a distinct field of academic specialization, increasingly seeking representation in university departments of English, first in graduate schools and in scattered instances in undergraduate courses.

### The "Reader Response" Spectrum

The New Critics tacitly accepted the traditional view of the text as an entity embodying a determinate message or meaning. Rejection of this assumption was a major point of agreement among the various competing literary theories in the late 1980s. No matter by what philosophic paths they had arrived at their differing positions, and no matter how different the implications derived, they saw the reader as involved in the process of making meaning. Hence in 1980, the editors of anthologies of the new literary theories grouped them loosely under the label, "reader response." By that time, however, they were being differentiated under a variety of overlapping labels, such as structuralist, poststructuralist, feminist, Marxist.

These theories fall into still other groupings when considered from the point of view of their implications for teaching and research. Especially significant is how they resemble or differ in their conception of the interpretive process and their treatment of aspects of the complex reader-text relationship.

One group of theorists emphasizes the role and responses of the reader, and will be labeled "reader-oriented." Another grouping derives from emphasis on formal analysis, and will be labeled "text-oriented." A third group focuses on the interrelationship between reader and text, and will be labeled "reader-plus-text-oriented."

### Reader-Oriented Theories

The reader emerges as paramount in psychoanalytically oriented theories. For Holland (1975), applying "ego psychology" developed by followers of Freud (e.g., Erikson, 1963), the reader's personality, manifested in an "identity theme" or "defense mechanism," dominates the interaction with an ultimately passive text. The reader's characteristic modes of adaptation and defense—expectations, desires, fantasies—shape the reader's interpretation. Although theoretically the constraints of the text are recognized, attention is focused mainly on the reader's response as a means of discovering the reader's identity theme. Although more eclectic psychologically, Bleich (1975, 1978) also makes the reader's response the central object of analysis and the source of self-understanding. Bleich's titles, *Readings and Feelings* and *Subjective Criticism*, underline his reaction against the impersonality of classrooms dominated by traditional or New Criticism approaches. He stresses various ways of eliciting students' primary emotional responses and distrusts the distancing effect of the intellectual aspects of interpretation. Instead of the orthodox concern with objectivity of interpretation, he maintains the emphasis on the reader by postulating a process of negotiation for a consensus among readers in the classroom. More recently, he has tended toward a greater emphasis on the contextual aspect.

### Text-Oriented Theories

From the early 1970s to the early 1980s, the structuralists were considered the bringers of a new theoretical emphasis. After about 1975, they were displaced as a center of attention by the poststructuralist "deconstructionists." Both are rooted in the French tradition stemming from the linguist, Saussure (1966). His stress on the arbitrary relationship between the sign and the signified, the word and its object, gave rise to a dyadic view of language as a closed system. This focused on the underlying codes, rules, and conventions, which he termed *langue*, that could be abstracted and analyzed apart from actual speech, termed *parole*. The anthropologist Levi-Strauss applied to cultures a process of analysis similar to the formal structural analysis that linguists applied to language.

The influence of the structuralist movement on literary theory became apparent in the early 1970s in the United States in the writings, e.g., of Chatman, 1978; Culler, 1975; Riffaterre, 1978; and Scholes, 1974. Jakobson (1960) with roots in Russian formalism, was a powerful ally. Rejecting historical and interpretive approaches, they brought to literature the type of formal analysis linguists applied to language. Just as the linguists were interested in abstract syntactic patterns of language, so the structuralist critics were interested, not in explication of meaning as conceived by individual readers, but in revealing underlying syntactic and rhetorical conventions and codes.

To this view of language the poststructuralists (Hartman, 1975; de Man, 1979; Fish, 1980; and Scholes, 1985) brought an extreme philosophical relativism, derived largely from contemporary French writers (Derrida, 1976; Barthes, 1974) and their forebears Heidigger and Nietzsche (see Passmore, 1985). They rejected the rationalist tradition of Western culture and the idea of the connection between experience and knowledge. Traditionally, the assumption has been that the sign or word referred to a thing, that language mirrored reality. Questioning the referential and mimetic aspects of language, some poststructuralists carried the idea of the indeterminancy of language—the idea that there is no single, unvarying meaning of a text—to the point of such phrasings as "the unreadability" of texts. They developed a deconstructionist technique of reading, especially exemplified in the writings of Derrida (1976, 1978), based on the assumption that every text contained its own contradiction and could be shown to self-deconstruct. Moreover, the poststructuralist philosophic views led to a Nietzschean denial of the importance of the individual. Language and cultural codes are seen to dominate, or "write," both author and reader. Thus, despite being originally grouped with the reader-response critics, both the structualists and the poststructuralists carried to an even greater extreme the New Critics' neglect of the reader's contribution.

Stanley Fish (1980), probably the most widely read reader-response theorist in the 1980s, started from a scholarly New Critical position and moved through various stages from simple discovery of the reader's activity to poststructuralism. Recognizing the universality of the interpretive act, he ends up attributing authority for the interpretive process to neither the reader nor the author but to the "interpretive communities" to which they belong and which psychologically impose impassible limits on their interpretations. This leads to a sociological interest in the politics of the literary profession. Fish sees no practical implications for teaching flowing from his theory.

From the late 1970s on, increasing criticism of the poststructuralists' and deconstructionists' antihumanism declared that it cut off the literary work from the world, banished the author, devalued the personal moral and emotional responses of the reader, and ruled out traditional historical and biographical critical approaches (Abrams, 1977; Booth, 1988; Graff, 1987; Rosenblatt, 1978; Searle, 1977; Todorov, 1987; Wellek, 1986). Deconstructionists countered with complex theoretical arguments that sometimes qualified their position (Derrida, 1988; Miller, 1987).

## Reader-Plus-Text-Oriented Theories

Theorists who fall under this heading still may differ in their interpretation of these terms and in their emphasis on one or the other. Grouped under the label of "reception theory," the German theorists, Iser (1978) and Jauss (1982) stem from phenomenological philosophy (see Passmore, 1985). Iser, who has been more widely read in the United States, maintains an awareness of the roles of both reader and text in his account of the reading process. The text is seen as setting particular requirements for an "implied reader," but also having gaps that the reader must fill. Different readers will therefore "concretize" the text differently. Each will seek to create a consistent structure and at the same time accommodate the shifting perspectives presented by the text. When challenged, Iser acknowledged that for him the "text" is ultimately fixed and determinate.

Jauss is the originator of "reception theory," a new type of literary history that involves the reader-text relationship. He investigated "the horizon of expectations" that readers at a particular time and place bring to a text. This involves primarily the contextual and intertextual influences on the interpretive process.

Mailloux (1989, 1998) developed a Pragmatist version of reception theory, "rhetorical hermeneutics." This traces the interpretive history of how cultural elements such as events, texts, figures, are rhetorically established in different contexts for different purposes.

The transactional theory (Rosenblatt, 1938, 1978, 1995) draws on Pragmatist philosophers (Dewey, 1929; James, 1890; Peirce, 1932, 1933). Rosenblatt rejects the reader response label as too often interpreted simply as a critical approach with personal response as its end product, whereas she sees it as the matrix within which any critical approach is selected. Since the term "interaction" as generally used assumes the reader and text to be separate, completely defined entities acting on one another, she adopts "transaction" from Dewey and Bentley (1949). This designates a spiral reciprocal relationship in which each conditions the other. Thus, the text and the "self" of the reader are conceived as flexible sequentially affecting the emerging meaning. The importance of the cultural or social context is stressed, but transactional theory sees the convention or code, as, e.g., in language, always individually internalized, hence always having both cognitive and affective aspects. Each reader draws on a personal reservoir of linguistic and life experiences. The work is constituted during the actual transaction between the equally essential reader and text.

Instead of the prevalent dualistic, either-or, view of literary and nonliterary, poetic and nonpoetic as contradictory opposites, the transactional theory presents the concept of a continuum of possible readings of the same text even by the same reader at different times. Different purposes produce different stances, ranging from the "efferent" extreme to the "aesthetic" extreme, depending on the proportion of attention the reader accords to cognitive and affective aspects of sense. In the efferent reading, attention is focused predominantly on abstracting out, analyzing, and structuring what is to be retained after the reading, e.g., factual information or analysis. In an aesthetic reading, attention is focused predominantly on what is being lived through during the reading, the ideas and feelings being evoked and organized as the work corresponding to the text. This evocation constitutes the work that is the object of interpretation and evaluation.

Although agreeing that there is no single "correct" meaning for a text, the transactional theory rejects the deconstructionists' extreme relativism, and maintains that agreement on criteria of validity of interpretation permits deciding that some interpretations are better, have more "warranted assertibility," than others (Dewey, 1938; Rosenblatt, 1994).

Many readings fall near the middle of the continuum, making it important for the reader to learn to handle the affective aspect according to whether the purpose is efferent or aesthetic, and to apply appropriate criteria of evaluation. A political speech, for example, may have a powerful emotional impact, yet should be judged by efferent criteria as to supporting evidence and logic. A poem might be valued for its emotional, rather than logical or factual, consistency.

When the reader response movement developed in the 1970s and 1980s, Rosenblatt's *Literature as Exploration* (1938) was recognized as the first statement of the reader response approach (Tompkins, 1980, p. XXVI) and has gone through five editions. Although after the midcentury the New Criticism dominated in the colleges, this book and *The Reader, The Text, The Poem* (1978, 1994) continued to be influential in the schools (Applebee, 1974, pp. 123–25, 131, 1996. See also the other references to Rosenblatt, This Edition).

## Feminist, African American, Multicultural, Marxist, and Other Critics

Various critical groups were at first listed under the general rubric of reader response, since all recognize the reader's construction of meaning, but they differentiated themselves by their special concerns. Some were especially interested in the influences of social or cultural context. Some focused on the politics of interpretation in actual critical practice. Such groups, like the formalists, neglect the individual reader's response and tend to be text-oriented, typically seeking to influence the selection of works read and/or the point of view from which the reader should respond, interpret, and evaluate. They sometimes find deconstructionists reading strategies useful for revealing hidden assumptions that support the status quo, and sometimes draw on Foucault's (1980) theories about power. Nevertheless, their social-historical emphases, political aims, and acceptance of the reader as a factor contributed to the "marginalization" of deconstruction in the 1990s.

The following citations represent a few of the overlapping categories or labels that have emerged since the 1970s. Recent national and world events have increased the fluidity of issues and labels. For example, various groups have reacted against multicultural hyphenizations such as African American, Hispanic American, or Asian American, both as ignoring internal cultural differences and as suggesting second-class citizenship. Generally, the criticism has resulted in greater emphasis on American unity in diversity, labelled here as cultural pluralism.

Feminist: Butler (1993), Fetterly (1977), Flynn and Schweickart (1986), Fox-Genovese (1998), Gilbert and Gubar (1979), Sedgwick (1990), Showalter (1977, 1985), Walker (1983), Woolf (1929).

African American: Baker (1988), Christian (1985), Gates (1984), Hurston (1979), Locke (1925).

Marxist: Eagleton (1983), Jameson (1991), Williams (1977).

Postcolonial: Bhabha (1991), Rosaldo (1989), Said (1983), Spivak (1987).

Cultural Pluralists: Appadurai (1996), Cheung (1997), Gubar (2000), Powell (1999), Weaver (1997).

The extraordinary academic preoccupation with theory during the past half-century, now diminishing, has affected the intellectual climate in the universities. Concern with the problem of indeterminacy of linguistic interpretation has contributed to a certain breaking down of boundaries between literary study and other disciplines. Also, other disciplines, e.g., history and economics, have had to assimilate the discovery that they, too, use the language in ways usually thought as "literary" (Geertz, 1973, 1995; Greenblatt, 1982; McCloskey, 1987; White, 1987).

## CONTINUING CONTROVERSIES: EDUCATIONAL IMPLICATIONS

While theoretical controversialists in the graduate liberal arts departments have only in recent decades paid much attention to educational implications, educators concerned with the preparation of teachers or with actual work in the schools had been carrying on their own line of development in professional journals and conferences, in experimental projects, and in education courses. Repercussions from the various types of literary theory occurred, although developments in the psychology of learning created receptivity particularly to response theories that are reader-oriented or reader-plus-text-oriented. Their influence has been evident not only in theories of the teaching of literature, but also the theory of the reading process, the theory of composition, and curriculum theory. In short, these approaches have strong professional backing. The situation is by no means stable, however, and controversy continues, even moving into new arenas.

The changing socioeconomic and political context has made education an important political issue. All levels of the educational establishment are under attack from a wide range of points of view. Some, reacting against emphasis on the student reader, or threatened by the stress on developing the individual's critical abilities, are calling for concentration on skills. Some are demanding the teaching of literature as a transmitter of traditional values; others are advocating the teaching of a common body of information about frequently mentioned literary and other works; and others are seeking to change the canon to reflect the diverse minority groups in our society. Literary theorists belonging to the various categories sketched in this chapter are not only competing among one another, but are also facing the public challenge. Because the theoretical controversies have been mainly addressed to professional peers, and—under the influence of the poststructuralists or deconstructionists— were often expressed in highly esoteric discourse, the various positions are often being interpreted in caricatured form in the media for the general public.

The degree of influence of the reader- and reader-plus-text theories on actual educational institutions has been uneven, greatest in the earlier grades, less evident in the high schools and, if state "standards" are an indication, greater in some states than others. There has in many instances been an infiltration of changes in classroom procedures, selection of works read, and use of varied media. Publishers' lists of textbooks have evidenced awareness of this increasingly important trend. However, recent legislation has reinforced the dominance of the traditional approaches. Especially in the economically deprived inner city schools, the traditional approaches still dominate.

A history of the teaching of English (Applebee, 1974, 1996) reports in all periods dissatisfaction at the lack of success in achieving the humanistic goals of literature teaching that schools profess and the failure to understand that the traditional approach conflicts with these aims. Literature is treated as primarily a body of knowledge *about* literary works rather than as a series of experiences. To produce readers capable of critically evoking literary works for themselves and deriving the pleasures and insights claimed for literary study evidently requires different methods and a different educational climate from the traditional teacher-dominated explication of literary texts.

Accounts of the theoretical developments in the past half-century have tended to designate the theories in terms of methods of interpretation without making explicit their pedagogical implications. When the competing theoretical positions are looked at from that point of view, the division falls elsewhere than between, on the one hand, traditional historicism and New Critical formalism, and on the other hand, the newer theories. For educational purposes, the division falls between the text-oriented theories—traditional, New Critical, structuralist, poststructuralist, deconstructionist—on the one hand, and on the other, the reader-oriented and reader-plus-text-oriented theories.

Text-oriented theories tend most readily to continue traditional approaches to the teaching of literature. New formulations of literary conventions can be taught, and radical deconstructive methods of analysis of content can be imparted without changing anything in the traditional teacher-dominated and text-centered classroom. Similarly, the curriculum can be changed or new items introduced into the reading lists without affecting instructional methods.

Reader-oriented and reader-plus-text-oriented theories, in their agreement that readers must draw on past experiences in order to evoke the literary work, tend directly and indirectly to challenge traditional methods of literature teaching. Readers are encouraged to pay attention to their own literary experiences as the basis for self-understanding or for comparison with others' evocations. This implies a new, collaborative relationship between teacher and student. Emphasis on the reader need not

exclude teaching criteria of valid interpretation or application of various approaches, literary and social, to the process of critical interpretation and evaluation.

## Ethics of Indoctrination

Agreement that the teaching of literature has social and political implications has not produced widespread discussion of educational ethics, especially the problems of covert and overt indoctrination and censorship. Attention has been focused rather on the politics of gaining control of the academic institution. Some support the teacher's explicit affirmation of a social or political point of view. For example, some religious fundamentalist or Marxist theorists call for a revision of the curriculum in those terms. Others contend that the preservation of our democracy demands explicit affirmation of the democratic values of the importance of individual human beings and their right to freedom of thought and expression: Given such explicit basic values, the student can participate through literary experiences in a diversity of worlds and systems of values, can become acquainted with diverse interpretive frames of reference, and can be helped to critically develop a personal hierarchy of values that recognizes the democratic rights of others.

# References

Abrams, M. H. (1979). *How to do things with texts.* Partisan Review, 46, 566–588.

Abrams, M. H. (1977). The limits of pluralism: Deconstructive angel. *Critical Inquiry, 3,* 425–38.

Abrams, M. H. (1953). *The mirror and the lamp: Romantic theory and the critical tradition.* New York: Oxford University Press.

Applebee, A. N. (1974). *Tradition and reform in the teaching of English: A history.* Urbana, IL: National Council of Teachers of English.

Applebee, A. N. (1996). *Curriculum as conversation: Transforming traditions of teaching and learning.* Chicago: University of Chicago Press.

Appadurai, Arjun (1996). *Modernity at large: Cultural dimensions of globalization.* Minneapolis, MN: University of Minnesota Press.

Arnold, M. (1880). *Essays in criticism.* New York: Macmillan.

Baker, H. (1988). *Afro-American poetics.* Madison, WI: University of Wisconsin Press.

Barthes, R. (1974). *S/Z* (R. Miller, Trans.) New York: Hill and Wang.

*Bedford glossary of critical and literary terms* (1997). R. Murfin and S. M. Ray (Eds.). Boston: Bedford.

Berlin, J. A. (1987). *Writing instruction in American colleges 1900–1985.* Carbondale, IL: Southern Illinois University Press.

Berlin, J. A. (1984). *Writing instruction in nineteenth-century American colleges.* Carbondale, IL: Southern Illinois University Press.

Bhabha, H. K. (1991). *Nation and narration.* New York: Routledge.

Bleich, D. (1978). *Subjective criticism.* Baltimore: Johns Hopkins University Press.

Bleich, D. (1975). *Reading and feelings: An introduction to subjective criticism.* Urbana, IL: National Council of Teachers of English.

Booth, W. C. (1988). *The company we keep.* Berkeley, CA: University of California Press.

Brooks, C., and R. P. Warren, (Eds.) (1938). *Understanding poetry.* New York: Henry Holt.

Butler, J. (1993). *Bodies That Matter: On the Discursive Limits of Sex.* New York and London: Routledge.

Chatman, S. (1978). *Story and discourse.* Ithaca, NY: Cornell University Press.

Cheung, King-Kok (1997). *Words matter: Conversations with Asian American Writers.* HonoluluL University of Hawaii Press in association with UCLA Asian American Studies Center, Los Angeles.

Christian, B. (1985). *Black feminist criticism: Perspectives on black women writers.* New York: Pergamon.

Crane, R. S. (Ed) (1952). *Critics and criticism: Ancient and modern.* Chicago: University of Chicago Press.

Cremin, L. A. (1961). *The transformation of the school: Progressivism in American education.* New York: Vintage Books.

Culler, J. (1975). *Structuralist poetics: Structuralism, linguistics, and the study of literature.* Ithaca, NY: Cornell University Press.

de Man, P. (1979). *Allegories of reading.* New Haven, CT: Yale University Press.

Derrida, J. (1976). *Of grammatology.* (G. C. Spivak, Trans.). Baltimore: Johns Hopkins Press.

Derrida, J. (1988). *Limited, Inc.* Evanston, IL: Northwestern University Press.

Derrida, J. (1978). *Writing and difference.* (Alan Bass, Trans.). Chicago: University of Chicago Press.

Dewey, J. (1929). *The quest for certainty.* New York: Minton Balch.

Dewey, J. & Bentley, A. F. (1949). *Knowing and the known.* Boston: Beacon Press.

Eagleton, T. (1983). *Literary Theory: An Introduction.* Minneapolis: University of Minnesota Press.

*Encyclopedia of contemporary literary theory* (1993). I.R. Makaryk (Ed.). Toronto, Canada: University of Toronto Press.

Enos, T. (Ed.) (1996) *Encyclopedia of rhetoric and composition.* T. Enos (Ed.). New York: Garland.

Erikson, E. H. (1963). *Childhood and society*. New York: W. W. Norton.

Fetterly, J. (1977). *The resisting reader: A feminist approach to American fiction*. Bloomington, IN: Indiana University Press.

Fish, S. (1980). *Is there a text in this class? The authority of interpretive communities*. Cambridge, MA: Harvard University Press.

Flynn, E. A., and P. Schweickart, (Eds.) (1986). *Gender and reading: Essays on readers, texts, and contexts*. Baltimore: Johns Hopkins University Press.

Foucault, M. (1980). In C. Gordon (Ed.), *Power/knowledge: Selected interviews and other writings*. New York: Random House.

Fox-Genovese, E. (1988). *Within the plantation household*. Chapel Hill, NC: University of North Carolina Press.

Frye, N. (1957). *The anatomy of criticism*. Princeton, NJ: Princeton University Press.

Gates, H. L. (1984). *Black literature and literary theory*. New York: Methuen.

Geertz, C. (1973). *The interpretation of cultures*. New York: Basic Books

Geertz, C. (1995). *After the fact*. Cambridge, MA: Harvard University Press.

Gilbert, S. and S. Gubar. (1979). *The madwoman in the attic: The woman writer and the nineteenth-century literary imagination*. New Haven: Yale University Press.

Graff, G. (1987). *Professing literature*. Chicago: University of Chicago Press.

Groden, M. and M. Kreiswirth, (Eds.) (1994). *Johns Hopkins guide to literary theory and criticism*. Baltimore: Johns Hopkins University Press.

Greenblatt, S., (Ed.) (1982). *The power of forms in the English Renaissance*. Norman, OK: Pilgrim Books.

Gubar, S. (2000). *Critical Condition: Feminism at the Turn of the Century*. New York: Columbia University Press.

Hartman, G. (1975). *The fate of reading*. Chicago: University of Chicago Press.

Holland, N. (1975a). *5 readers reading*. New Haven, CT: Yale University Press.

Hurston, Z. N. (1979). *I love myself when I am laughing*. Old Westbury, NY: Feminist Press.

Iser, W. (1978). *The act of reading: A theory of aesthetic response*. Baltimore: Johns Hopkins University Press.

Iser, W. (1974). *The implied reader*. Baltimore: Johns Hopkins University Press.

Jakobson, R. (1960). Linguistics and poetics. In T. A. Sebeok (Ed.), *Style in language*, pp. 350–377. Cambridge, MA: MIT Press.

James, W. (1890). *The principles of psychology*. New York: Henry Holt.

Jameson, F. (1972). *The prison-house of language*. Princeton, NJ: Princeton University Press.

Jameson, F. (1991). *Postmodernism or the cultural logic of late capitalism*. Durham, NC: Duke University Press.

Jauss, H. R. (1982). *Toward an aesthetic of reception*. Minneapolis: University of Minnesota Press.

Kelley, M. (Ed.) (1998). *Encyclopedia of Aesthetics*. New York and Oxford: Oxford University Press, (1998).

Locke, A. (1925). *The New Negro*. New York: Boni.

Mailloux, S., et. al. (1989). *Rhetorical power*. Ithaca, NY: Cornell University Press.

Mailloux, S. (1998). *Reception histories: Rhetoric, pragmatism, and American cultural politics*. Ithaca, NY: Cornell University Press.

McCloskey, D. N. (1987). *The rhetoric of economics*. Madison, WI: University of Wisconsin Press.

Miller, J. H. (1987). *The ethics of reading*. New York: Columbia University Press.

Millet, K. (1970). *Sexual politics*. New York: Doubleday.

Passmore, J. A. (1968). *A hundred years of philosophy*. Harmondsworth: Penguin Books.

Passmore, J. A. (1985). *Recent philosophers*. La Salle, IL: Open Court Publishing.

Peirce, C. S. (1932, 1933). *Collected papers*. P. Weiss & C. Hartshorne (Eds.). Cambridge, MA: Harvard University Press.

Powell, T. B. (Ed.) (1999). *Beyond the binary: Reconstructing cultural identity in a multicultural context*. New Brunswick, NJ: Rutgers University Press.

Rosaldo, R. (1989). *Culture and truth*. Boston: Beacon.

Riffaterre, M. (1978). *Semiotics of poetry*. Bloomington, IN: Indiana University Press.

Rorty, R. (1979). *Philosophy and the mirror of nature*. Princeton, NJ: Princeton University Press.

Rosenblatt, L. M. (1938). *Literature as exploration*. New York: Appleton-Century.

Rosenblatt, L. M. (1978, 1994). *The reader, the text, the poem: The transactional theory of the literary work*. Revised paperback edition. Carbondale, IL: Southern Illinois University Press.

Rosenblatt, L. M. (1995). *Literature as exploration*. Fifth edition. New York: Modern Language Association.

Said, E. W. (1983). *The world, the text and the critic*. Cambridge, MA: Harvard University Press.

Saussure, F. de (1966). *Course in general linguistics* (W. Baskin, Trans.). New York: McGraw-Hill.

Scholes, R. (1985). *Textual power: Literary theory and the teaching of English*. New Haven, CT: Yale University Press.

Scholes, R. (1974). *Structuralism in literature*. New Haven, CT: Yale University Press.

Searle, J. (1977). *Reiterating the differences: A reply to Derrida*. Glyph I (pp. 198–208). Baltimore: Johns Hopkins University Press.

Sedgwick, E. K. (1990). *Epistemology of the closet*. Berkeley, CA: University of California Press.

Showalter, E. (Ed.) (1985). *The new feminist criticism: Essays on women, literature, and theory*. New York: Pantheon.

Showalter, E. (1977). *A literature of their own*. Princeton, NJ: Princeton University Press.

Spivak, G. C. (1987). *In other worlds*. New York: Methuen.

Suleiman, S. R., & Crosman, I. (Eds.) (1980). *The reader in the text*. Princeton, NJ: Princeton University Press.

Todorov, T. (1987). *Literature and its theorists*. (C. Porter, Trans.). Ithaca, NY: Cornell University Press.

Tompkins, J. (Ed.) (1980) *Reader-response criticism*. Baltimore: Johns Hopkins University Press.

Walker, A. (1983). *In search of our mothers' gardens*. New York: Harcourt Brace Jovanovich.

Weaver, J. (1997). That the people might live: Native American literatures and Native American community. New York: Oxford University Press.

Wellek, R. (1986). *American criticism, 1900-1950, Vol. 6 of a history of modern criticism*. New Haven, CT: Yale University Press.

Wellek, R., & Warren, A. (1949). *Theory of literature*. New York: Harcourt Brace.

White, H. (1987). *The content of the form*. Baltimore: Johns Hopkins University Press.

Williams, R. (1977). *Marxism and literature*. Oxford: Oxford University Press.

Wimsatt, W. K., & Beardsley, M. (1954). *The affective fallacy*. In W. K. Wimsatt (Ed.), *The verbal icon: Studies in the meaning of poetry*. Lexington: University of Kentucky Press.

Woolf, V. (1929). *A room of one's own*. New York: Harcourt.

# ·8·

# THE TAO OF INSTRUCTIONAL MODELS

## Lawrence Baines
### Mesa State College, Grand Junction, Colorado

## Edmund J. Farrell
### University of Texas, Austin

*And this Way of nature is the way in which all things come into being out of darkness into light, then pass out of light back into darkness, the two principles—light and dark—being in perpetual interaction, and in variously modulated combinations, constituting this whole world of "ten thousand things."*

*The light and the dark of this system of thought are named respectively yang and yin, which are words referring to the sunny and the shady sides of a stream. Yang is of the sunny side; yin the shady. On the sunny side there is light, there is warmth, and the heat of the sun is dry. In the shade, there is the cool, rather moist, light, hot, and dry: earth and sun in counteraction. These are associated, further, with the female and the male as the passive and active principles. There is no moral verdict here intended; neither principle is better than the other, neither "stronger" than the principles on which all the world rests, and in their interaction they inform, constitute, and decompose all things.*
—Campbell (1973, p. 118–119)

Loosely translated, *Tao* is a Chinese word that means "the way of Nature." If anything can be learned from surveying trends of curriculum over the past 200 years, it is that the *tao* of instructional models is a constant fluctuation between the yang of student-centered instruction and the yin of content knowledge. While many proponents of content (such as Bennett, 1993, 1995; Finn, 1994; Sowell, 1994) view an emphasis on a common curriculum as essential to ameliorating both economic inequities and incivility in society, many progressive educators criticize them on the grounds that they too heavily rely on ephemeral, unconnected "factoids." The extent to which classrooms actually are traditional, teacher-centered domains or more progressive, student-centered places is even under debate. Hirsch (1996)

claims that student-centered learning exercises "virtually totalitarian intellectual dominion over not just schools of education but a large percentage of policymakers and the general public as well" (p. 237), while Cuban (1984) has found that, in 90 years of classroom practice (1890–1980), teacher-centered learning has been overwhelmingly dominant and almost "impervious" to change (p. 260).

At times, shifts in curricular models can give teachers a sense of déjà vu, as reforms become formulated, grow in popularity, diminish, then seemingly rise again, phoenix-like when the pendulum begins to swing back from yang to yin. Where once the utterances of John Dewey, Ralph Tyler, Franklin Bobbit, Helen Parkhurst, or James Conant held sway, the writings of

Howard Gardner, Harry Wong, Ted Sizer, James Banks, or Seymour Papert have begun to reign. And so it goes.

Like old soldiers who never die, curricular reforms may eventually fade away, though sometimes their more enduring aspects mutate with emerging phenomena in surprising ways. For example, who would have believed that Mager's (1962) conception of the behavioral objective would "have legs" 30-something years after his thin volume first appeared? Despite Mager's total absence from the *Handbook of Research on Teaching the English Language Arts* (Flood, Jensen, Lapp, & Squire, 1991) and *Research on Teaching* (Wittrock, 1986), his formulation of the behavioral objective is still in evidence on thousands of lesson plan formats and teacher evaluation instruments in the country.

In many states, the evaluation instrument for teachers is still reliant on "the Mager objective," though the subject-area standards for states, especially in the language arts, generally advocate generic, student-centered orientations. While most English teachers would prefer to bury Mager's particular contribution than praise it, the "TSWBAT" (the student will be able to) form of the behavioral objective illustrates the difficulty in predicting which educational reforms will retain some sparkle and which will rapidly lose their luster.

In the first section, we review some recent instructional theories and discuss how pressures of accountability and increased accessibility through technology have affected the language-arts curriculum. Then, we highlight some recent research from the neurosciences and their implications for instruction in that curriculum.

In the second section, we briefly explicate three major instructional models—mastery, heritage, and process—and discuss the emergence of an overarching educational goal for our time—social mobility. Finally, we discuss the increasing complexity of the English language arts curriculum and the volatile microenvironment of the secondary language arts classroom.

## SECTION 1: RECENT THEORY INTO PRACTICE

One of the most important, perhaps most neglected, influences on learning is a teacher's ability to engage students so that learning is enduring, intellectually stimulating, and useful. Most proponents of constructivism, an educational theory currently in vogue, would suggest that a teacher use the knowledge and dispositions that students bring into the classroom as a launching point for learning. Terms associated with constructivism include *critical thinking, life-long learning, metacognition, problem solving, hands-on learning, empowerment*, and the ubiquitous *facilitation*. One problem with constructivism has been its slippery, potentially polymorphic nature. According to constructivism, learning is contingent and situational, and highly dependent on the constituency of the students in the classroom and their momentary dispositions. Thus, a teacher who is a constructivist might teach a freshman-level English class quite differently from a teacher who wants to ensure that her students study *Romeo and Juliet* and *The Grapes of Wrath* before moving on to composition and grammar.

Despite the seeming popularity of constructivism in the literature, Csikszentmihalyi (1984, 1993, 1996) has documented that even the most gifted students spend little time pursuing their unique talents during the school day. Most teens spend far more of their waking hours watching television (9% of their time) than grooming (5%), reading (3%), or working on an endeavor close to their hearts (3%) (Csikszentmihalyi, Rathunde, & Whalen, 1993, p. 220). The available evidence (Baines, 1998b; Sarason, 1990; Sizer, 1997; Welsh, 1987) suggests that many students are frustrated and bored with school. In this regard, it seems little has changed since Coleman (1961) noted over 30 years ago that most students would gladly trade good grades and brains for the chance to be a popular sports hero or cheerleader. Nevertheless, the specter of accountability forces a particular subject-matter focus as well as a strongly teacher-oriented instructional style that could limit (or eliminate) the time available for students to delve into academic areas that truly interest them.

Despite the wealth of data that substantiates that quality of instruction can make a difference in student learning (Darling-Hammond, & Sykes, 1999; National Commission on Teaching and America's Future, 1996; National Center for Research on Teacher Learning 1994), the perception remains in many circles that quality of instruction has no effect on learning. Robert Hutchins' maxim that anyone with a degree should be able to teach has oft been repeated, even by supposedly pro-education policy elite such as Leon Bottstein (1997), president of Bard College. Concerning quality of instruction, Bottstein writes, "What should be avoided is the corruption of the study of English, history, and mathematics by the mixing in of pedagogical science, curriculum strategy, and classroom management.... There is nothing to be taught that can't be better taught on the job" (p. 123).

A central issue at present has to do with the degree to which teachers of the English language arts have "ownership" of the curriculum and of subsequent instructional strategies. One of the many reports emanating from the English Coalition Conference of 1987 speaks of the established dominance of the lecture-and-recitation mode of teaching:

In recent years many states, regions, and local school boards have used this model to dictate curriculum and either directly or indirectly dictate the instructional models that will be used to reach curricular goals. This model dictates not only expected student outcomes, usually in terms of isolated learner behaviors, but often teacher behaviors which presumably will help learners master language objectives (*English for the 90's and Beyond*, p. 5).

Whereas most secondary teachers still use a strongly teacher-centered approach (National Assessment of Educational Progress, 1992), instructional models that incorporate long stretches of time expressly for reading and writing during the day, popularized by Atwell (1987), Reif (1991), Slavin (1996), and Slavin and Fashola (1998), have penetrated both elementary and middle schools. Even commercial programs, such as *Accelerated Reader*, mandate that teachers devote large chunks of class time to reading trade books and that students be given some choice in selecting books to be read (Davies & Beaucamps,

1998; Rich 1998). As appealing as some curricular innovations might be, Greenspan (1997) argues that the determining factor in learning always should be the entirety of the learning experience, not simply a collection of discrete bits of information. "Affect and interaction, rather than the acquisition of specific information and skills, are the foundation of learning," writes Greenspan (p. 224).

## Accountability

Inspired by Frederick Taylor's well-financed plans to apply "scientific management theory" to factories, schools in the 1920s began to be thought of as akin to businesses that should be held accountable for their efficiency and the quality of their "product," namely, the intellectual and social development of students (Cremin, 1988). The emphasis for accountability has intensified over time and is in evidence today in even the most well-to-do suburban schools. "States and districts are demanding scores and statistics that can be used to judge schools—while politicians, the news media, and interest groups eagerly take on the judging" (Keller, 1998).

Today, most discussions concerning schools abound in industrial metaphors—"school plant planning," "teacher load"—and with concerns—"efficiency," "accountability" "zero-based budgeting"—derived principally from an historic alliance with business (for documentation and perspectives on this alliance see Callahan, 1962; McNeil, 1988; Spring, 1972). In schools as in factories, bells regulate time, the principal/foreman (front office) administrates away from the assembly line (classroom), and the products (students) are recycled (retained) or are shipped out to the public (graduate). Under this model, knowledge is segmented into discrete subjects, and at the bell, students move along, conveyor-belt fashion, from one station to another where they are analogically "processed" by teachers.

The trend is for the job security and advancement of superintendents, principals, and teachers to be dependent on how students' latest scores on standardized tests stack up with baseline projections. As a result, many schools begin preparing for a late spring achievement exam on the first day of class in mid-August. In such schools, the curriculum for the year is largely dictated by the perceived content of the anticipated exam.

As more and more school districts move to comprehensive accountability systems (principals evaluated on schoolwide, district, and even statewide data; teachers rated on comparative classroom results; and the fates of students dependent on individual scores), the pressure to perform well on high-stakes tests will continue to escalate. Unfortunately, many standardized tests still give little diagnostic help for students who fail to do well on them, a criticism of standardized tests raised by Dewey (1916, 1963) decades ago. Furthermore, achievement tests rarely provide surprising results, as any perusal of the socio economic status of parents and the performance of their children will attest. About accountability, Berliner and Biddle (1995) write, "When considered from the perspective of America's neediest children, accountability programs are little

more than ceremonies for awarding prizes, honors, and extra finances to America's best-supported schools, which serve its most privileged students" (p. 199).

Berliner and Bidwell's contention that accountability systems have rarely yielded dividends for anyone other than the well-off seems well supported by reports of threatened or actual state takeovers in Philadelphia, Newark, Miami, and other urban areas where large pockets of high poverty and high crime exist (Quality Counts, 1998, January 8; Kozol 1991). Yet, state takeovers are not restricted to the inner city, which has no corner on poverty. Takeovers have recently been threatened for rural schools as well, such as Alexander High School in east Oktibbeha County, Mississippi, a state that ranks 50th in terms of amount of educational expenditures per pupil. The achievement scores for students attending Alexander High are among the lowest in Mississippi, which make them among the lowest in the nation (Mississippi Department of Education, 1998).

Over the past decade, many state departments of education have learned that takeovers can be fraught with unexpected complications. To legitimize a new regime, the first step in a takeover usually involves firing most, if not all, the teachers and administrators. Because Oktibbeha County is not a place individuals seek out for vacation, entertainment, or quality of life, its revenues are meager. Laying off most of the staff who are local residents would squeeze the county budget still harder. Furthermore, the state will be challenged to attract new teachers and administrators to a rural school whose pay is among the lowest in the nation and which has just been identified as deficient academically. Most good teachers can easily find more attractive offers.

Another outcome that has accompanied some state takeovers is the reformulation of the school day to eliminate "electives," such as physical education (or recess), music, art, and after-school sports. While the impetus to reformulate the curriculum may be grounded in concern over achievement, the reality is that electives provide the only bright spots in the day for many students. Although research findings showing that the arts and kinesthetics may enhance academic achievement may not be overwhelming (Begley, 1996; Caine, Caine & Crowell, 1994; Davenport & Forbes, 1997; Rose & Nichol, 1997), eliminating activities students consider worthwhile seems an illogical way to increase their academic motivation. If a student does not encounter success through traditional subjects, it does not make sense to eliminate other subjects in which he or she may still learn and succeed (Csikszentmihalyi, 1990).

The current obsession with accountability and achievement scores has had a profound, immeasurable effect on the curriculum and instruction of the language arts. In a school environment that elevates the learning of specific skills—understanding the main idea, writing an expository paragraph, and spelling—over other less documentable aspects of the language arts, the danger is that poetry, mythology, contemporary fiction, oral communications, critical listening, and anything else that doesn't show up on paper-and-pencil tests, may soon be considered frivolous and therefore expendable.

Recent school-based reform projects, many of which originated out of observational studies in the schools, are restructuring the roles and responsibilities of teachers and, in some cases, redesigning the curriculum. Networks of affiliated schools support these grassroot endeavors: Mortimer Adler's Paideaia Group, Theodore Sizer's Coalition of Essential Schools, John Goodlad's National Network for Educational Renewal, the National Education Association's Mastery in Learning Project, Howard Gardner's Key School (and related offspring of the Multiple Intelligences movement), and the American Federation of Teacher's Research-in-to-Practice Practitioners Network.

## Accessibility

One aspect of curriculum that has changed dramatically over the past century is increased accessibility through electronic technologies. As the student-per-computer ratio continues to drop and more and more schools get wired to the Internet, teachers soon will be able to provide students with materials that once would have been thought impossible. While radio, film, television, video, and even overhead projectors, in their inceptions, were erroneously hailed as innovations that would fundamentally alter the delivery system for education (Baines, 1997), there are several reasons to believe that computers and the Internet will endure and eventually become integrated into the landscape of the public school.

Perhaps most important, computers do not compete with previous technologies—they incorporate them. With computers, a student may watch television, edit films, download clips of new musical releases from a favorite band, and project images and text against a wall-size screen. Further, a student can do research, author papers and projects, send e-mail, and post writings to a Web site. Unlike most earlier technologies, computers can leave a tangible and comprehensive paper trail, a crucial consideration in an age of accountability.

While most of the benefits of increased accessibility may seem self-evident, the realm of available curricular materials can be greatly expanded with the proper equipment and training. For example, every play and sonnet ever written by Shakespeare is available somewhere on the Internet, and the number of Web sites and commercial CD-ROMs created for particular authors, works of literature, and aspects of language—composition, grammar, usage, spelling—have burgeoned exponentially. Lesson plans, national and state standards, model student projects, and dialogue with colleagues are a point and click away for any teacher with access to the Internet.

Accessibility can also be enhanced through technology for students who have special needs. For example, a student who has a visual impairment can have a text read to him or her via computer-generated voices. A student whose first language is not English could use a computer to better understand difficult parts of literary texts. As many states continue to opt for mainstreaming, increased accessibility to course materials for students with special needs becomes a significant factor in both the quality and the content of instruction.

A possible third effect of increased accessibility through technology is a growing reliance on teacher-centered instruction and passive learning styles (Tweedle, Adams, Clarke, Scrimshaw, &

Walton, 1997). A computer-generated virtual experience simulating a hike through a forest is an experience that students can have more cheaply and more viscerally by putting on their boots and going for a long walk in the woods. The point is that sometimes increased accessibility through technology frames the learning situation in ways that reduce human interactions and supplant vital, but imperfect, real experience. While technology can significantly expand the realm of possibilities for curriculum, it may not always provide the optimal learning experience.

## Searching for a Biological Basis for Curriculum

One of the more interesting trends in curriculum is the effort to tie it to developments in the neurosciences (Jacobson, 1998). To be sure, much of the interest in attempting to align curriculum with brain-healthy learning has to do with the contention that the brain is an elastic organism whose growth is highly dependent on inputs from the environment.

Rosenzweig was one of the first scientists to report that animals in enriched environments developed larger brains, a different neurochemistry, and improved ability to learn (Rosenzweig & Bennet, 1979). Later, Rosenzweig (1996) concluded that animals in nurtured environments demonstrate a more active and more organized behavior when confronted with unfamiliar situations than do animals in impoverished conditions.

The work of Diamond (1988) has taken Rosenzweig's work a step farther by actually showing how the physical dimensions of the brains of animals can be molded through the manipulation of various aspects of the environment. Diamond writes, "The neurons in the cerebral cortex exhibit an impressive amount of plasticity . . . every part of the nerve cell from soma to synapse alters its dimensions in response to the environment" (p. 156). Diamond found that the cortical neurons located in the brains of rats grew in response to a stimulating environment, while they decreased in size when provided less sensory input. Increased levels of stimulation resulted in structural changes in brains of rats at all ages. In other words, the life experiences of a rat somehow affected the physical structure of its brain. Regarding the relationship between experience and the architecture of the brain, Pribram (1991) has written, "Brain processes undergo a dynamic matching procedure until there is a correspondence between the brain's microprocessors and those in the sensory input" (p. xxii).

Other brain research has revealed that brain cells follow Darwin's "survival-of-the-fittest" theory of genetics, with neurons fighting each other for dominance and only the strongest remaining (Edelman, 1987, 1994). Neurons that successfully survive, in turn, seek to attract more neurons to their group, so that stronger synapses and a larger structure of cells emerge as a result. In this way, an individuals' brain evolves in accordance with life experiences.

Through the use of Positron Emission Tomography (PET), researchers (Peterson, Fox, Posner, Mintun, & Raichle, 1988; Posner, Petersen, Fox, & Raichle, 1988; Posner & Raichle, 1994) have shown that different areas of the brain are affected when an individual reads a word on a page in contrast to when he or she listens to it. In one set of experiments Peterson, Fox, Snyder, & Raichle (1990), found words that were read activated "several regions of striate and extrastriate cortex," while the words presented auditorily "activated an entirely separate set of areas in temporal cortex bilaterally." Indeed, according to Shaywitz, Bennet, et al. (1995), "It is now possible to isolate specific components of language and, at the same time, to relate these language processes to distinct patterns of functional organization in the brains of neurologically normal individuals" (p. 609).

In most of us, verbal functions are located in cortical regions of the left hemisphere, and nonverbal functions (such as spatial skills) "tend to be lateralized to the right hemisphere" (Rugg, 1995, p. 561). When we use language, then, we activate particular parts of the brain associated with words and thoughts, and when we decide how we want to rearrange the furniture, we activate another part of the brain. According to Collins (1991), "Learning and training are experiential factors that sculpt the functional architecture of the brain" (p. 13).

The research in neuropsychology and neurobiology seems to substantiate, through science, the points made in quite different ways by Britton (1981), Emig (1971), Heath (1982), Hillocks (1986), Moffett (1968), and by other recent researchers (Sikula, 1996). The environment has an indelible impact on what one learns, how one learns it, and how one feels about that learning.

Only a few, sad examples exist of what happens to children when they are denied the opportunity to use language during the critical stages of brain growth. Wills (1993) describes the language deprivation of Genie, a severely abused girl who had very little opportunity to use or hear words until age 13, when she was rescued from her family. Apparently, Genie's father strapped her to a potty seat during the day, placed her in a straitjacket-type sleeping bag at night, and forbade that anyone ever speak with her. As a result, Genie could not speak and could comprehend little. Even after being given intensive social and academic rehabilitation following her rescue, she had only limited success with learning language.

In contrast to Genie, who lived with all her senses intact, Helen Keller lost sight and hearing from a severe fever at the age of 19 months. According to Wills, one reason for the differences in the language skills shown by Keller and Genie might be attributable to the presence of the teacher, Anne Sullivan, whose "firm and patient insistence that she [Helen Keller] phrase her thoughts using the appropriate grammatical constructions" (p. 288).

In today's sensory-rich, multimedia environment, research in the neurosciences has repeatedly found the role of language to be critical for appropriate development of thinking skills. The theories of brain development espoused by neuroscientists from Terrence Deacon (1997) to Steven Pinker (1994) are predicated on the premise that language promotes complex and abstract thinking processes, which, in turn, foster brain growth and cognitive development. As the Genome Project pushes toward the goal of mapping every gene in the human body, formulating curriculum on the basis of biological predispositions, now a movement only in a seedling stage, may come to full fruition in the decades ahead.

## SECTION 2: CURRICULAR MODELS

By their nature, curriculum models imply instructional models. In his introduction to *Three Language-Arts Curriculum Models*, Mandel (1980) discriminates among a competencies model, which he equates with the mastery learning of language skills; a heritage model, in which the values and traditions of the culture are transmitted; and a process or student-centered model, in which emphasis is on the language processes that lead to the individual growth of each student. (For an earlier discussion of these models, see Dixon, 1967, pp. 1–13.) About the relation of instruction to this curricular triad, Mandel writes, "whatever the pedagogical choice might be, all pedagogical paradigms, if understood correctly, are devoted to process, competencies, and heritage" (p. 4). He discriminates as follows among the three:

Whereas a competencies model can fairly clearly state behavior expected to occur . . . , a process approach focuses more on watchfulness, the observation of what is developing at a given moment of instruction and then the harnessing of its energy. . . . In the heritage model, the underlying assumption is that the way to acquire skills and knowledge is to submit to something larger than oneself, that is to the culture. By culture I mean traditions, history, the time-honored values of civilized thought and feeling . . . and the skills that make it possible to share in one's culture and to pass it on. (p. 8)

After asserting that it is reasonable to assume that particular models will be best suited for specific kinds of learning, Mandel concludes his introduction by calling "for a true and strict eclecticism: selection from what appears to be the *best* in various doctrines, methods, or styles" (p. 12).

Despite Mandel's plea that teachers select methodology, the reality is that popular reform movements and urgent edicts from the state often take precedence over what might be construed as the "highest and best use" of time in English class. For example, hosts of English teachers in Texas during the 1980s were required to view a series of videotapes in which a very serious, red-haired woman named Madeline Hunter explained effective teaching practices. That year, most Texas teachers were also required to write each day's activities in the "lesson cycle" format suggested by Hunter and were evaluated on an observation instrument that assessed the degree to which their lessons adhered to the Hunter model. Those select three or four teachers per school who received the highest scores on their evaluations received a bonus equivalent to 10% of their annual salary. Today, few beginning teachers would know the name of Madeline Hunter, though her legacy remains alive in the numerous school districts that continue to evaluate teachers on how well they adhere to the routine of "establishing set" through that of "closure and extension."

### Mastery Learning Model

While not a mastery learning program per se, the Hunter model shares some similarities with such programs: It assumes that nearly all students can learn the basic school curriculum, it derives its authority from research in human learning and human behavior, and it is highly structured. Further, Hunter (1985) has said that Mastery Teaching is among the several names by which her program is known. Unlike other mastery programs, however, it appears to focus more on teachers' instructional strategies than on students' progress through a sequence of formative and summative tests.

Mastery teaching derives much of its theoretical basis from Carroll (1963), and its popularity from Bloom (1968, 1971, 1974, 1976, 1981), who claims that as high as 95% of all students can master content and skills if they are given the instructional time they need. Motivational features are that all students can expect success from their efforts, that students assume considerable responsibility for evaluating their own progress, and that errors are accepted as a natural part of the learning process.

Mastery learning requires that instructional objectives be clearly formulated and that course content be broken into small discrete units for learning. The units are organized hierarchically to permit mastery at increasing levels of complexity. The teacher normally introduces a new unit to the whole class in accordance with his or her customary teaching style (style of presentation is not prescribed in mastery learning programs). Following the unit introduction, the teacher provides students with instructional materials for applying the new concepts.

To determine each student's level of understanding (formative evaluation), the teacher develops brief, ungraded, student-scored diagnostic progress tests. Results from the tests keep both teacher and student apprised of the student's progress toward mastery of instructional objectives. A summative test determines grades, which are noncompetitive in that any student mastering the unit within the designated instructional time is given an *A*. Until a student demonstrates mastery on the summative test, he or she is given an *I* (incomplete). (Students who master the unit quickly are given "enrichments," which permit them to pursue more intensely or broadly the material covered on formative tests.) Based on performance on the test, a student is given additional instructional material. These "correctives," which differ from the teacher's group instruction, may include supplementary print or audiovisual materials, academic games, small-group study sessions, affective exercises, and peer tutoring. This cycle of diagnostic test—corrective instruction continues until students have achieved mastery.

A principal variant of Bloom's Learning for Mastery Model (LFM) is Keller's (1968) Personalized System of Instruction (PSI), which finds its theoretical basis in B. F. Skinner's operant conditioning. Conceptually related to Bloom's LFM is the Exemplary Center for Reading Instruction (ECRI), a program that has been taught to teachers at sites throughout the nation. Founded in 1966 in Salt Lake City, Utah, and directed by Ethna Reid, ECRI "is a total language arts instructional program. It provides instruction simultaneously in reading, oral language, spelling, comprehension, and other activities in a highly structured, systematic pattern that ensures mastery" (Reid, 1986, p. 511).

Within special education, mastery learning is the overwhelming choice of instructional models, and most IEPs (Individualized Education Plan) involve extensive checklists of activities and skills. Indeed, some elementary and middle schools have even initiated pull-out programs for nonspecial education students, programs designed to remediate perceived weaknesses in students experiencing academic difficulties.

In general, evidence suggests mastery learning programs have been reasonably successful in increasing the percentage of students who master the basic curriculum in the subjects investigated (Block & Burns, 1976). Nevertheless, criticism has been advanced that the programs are overly structured, even mechanistic; that they fail to develop proficiency in speaking or listening skills; that they lead to decreased motivation in highly competitive (usually high ability) students; that they imply too narrow a view of education, giving too little attention to creativity; that they make unrealistic demands on teachers (Stallings & Stipek, 1986, pp. 745–746); and that they are inappropriate for learning certain processes, for example, writing, "because it would be difficult to ascertain at what point the student has 'mastered' the ability to write" (Guam Department of Education, 1987, p. 3). In short, mastery learning does not handle complexity well, nor does it consider the social environment of the classroom, including the attitudes, interests, or motivations of students.

## The Heritage Model

Evidenced early in American education was concern for transmitting the values and traditions of the culture. Applebee (1974) reports that Webster purposefully designed his *Blue-Backed Speller*, published in 1783, "to foster the unity and common culture which he sensed that the nation lacked" (p. 3). Since Webster's time, any number of individuals, committees, and commissions have sensed that the nation has lacked a common culture and criticized the schools for not providing it (Applebee, 1974, *passim*). With respect to teaching English, teachers have most often fallen under attack when literature programs have been found wanting. This criticism is usually founded on the belief that there exists a core of literary works that has enduring value through brilliance of content, style, or ethics, and that these works are accessible to and understandable by virtually all students. (For works reflecting this position, see for example, Adler, 1940; Lynch & Evans, 1963; Ravitch & Finn, 1987; Stone, 1961; Van Doren, 1943.)

Proponents of the heritage model often recommend that teachers themselves make the selections from among the multitude of critically acclaimed literary works. The Commission on English of the College Entrance Examination Board (1965) suggested that in the secondary school, the curriculum in literature be determined by departmental consensus and that it consist mainly of American and English literature. In one way or another, writers such as Cheney (1987), Hirsch (1987), and Ravitch and Finn (1987) have decried the collapse of the high school literary canon. For example, Ravitch and Finn present charts comparing books that students in 1986 had reported reading in public school to books that students over two decades earlier had reported being assigned (Anderson, 1964). Despite the charge that schools have contributed to an attrition in literary standards, the charts appear to reflect considerable stability in the curriculum. For example, 33% of students reported reading *Tale of Two Cities* in school in 1963, as compared to 21% in 1986; 33% in 1963 had read *The Red Badge of Courage*, as compared to 30% in 1986; 32% in 1963 had read *The Scarlet Letter*, as compared to 39% in 1986.

Like Hirsch (1996, 1987), Ravitch and Finn (1987) attribute students' weakest performances to the education profession's belief "that *what* children learn is unimportant compared to *how* they learn; . . . that skills can be learned without content . . ." (p. 17). The contention of many proponents of the heritage model is that students who lack sufficient background knowledge are culturally handicapped, incapable of carrying on complex transactions in conversation or reading.

Although desire for the schools to transmit a literary heritage through "great" works of literature has been recurrent for the past century, specification of books for particular grades has become ever more problematic for levels beyond the local: The corpus of potential literature grows steadily with time, and the clientele of public education is far more diverse than it was early in the nation's history. In recognition of these facts, neither the Commission on English (1965) nor members of the Anglo-American Conference at Dartmouth (Muller, 1967) would specify particular works to be taught to all students, relying instead on the judgments of teachers in local schools. Nevertheless, the 100 best works of literature as selected by one group or another are discussed at great length from time to time in the pages of magazines such as *Newsweek, Time,* and *The New Republic* and in the pages of newspapers and academic journals.

Responding to the perceived dearth of curricula promulgating a heritage model, ex-Commissioner of Education William Bennett published a set of books that harkened back to a morally unambiguous, largely mythical past. That Bennett edited a set of briskly selling volumes, including *The Book of Virtues* (1993), *The Book of Virtues for Young People* (1997), *Adventures from the Book of Virtues* (1996), *The Children's Book of America* (1998), *The Children's Book of Heroes* (1997), and *The Children's Book of Virtues* (1995) among others, would seem to indicate that the heritage model still elicits strong responses from a significant number of Americans (see also Hirsch's set of books organized by grade level, such as *What Your First Grader Should Know, 1997* ).

## The Process Model

More student centered than either the mastery or heritage models, the process model for instruction asks that the teacher establish the most favorable conditions wherein students can make meaning for themselves. Rather than requiring that students master a set body of content or skills before progressing further, or that as a part of their heritage they become familiar with specific authors and works, the process model places a premium on diversity, on the varied ways by which individuals, each unique, construct knowledge from experience.

Louise Rosenblatt, James Moffett, and James Britton are three major theorists who advocate a process approach in the teaching of the English language arts. Although Rosenblatt's work has long been read and discussed in college methods courses on the teaching of English, her "transactional approach" to literature appears to also have greatly influenced literature programs in the elementary and secondary schools. According to Rosenblatt, teachers need to provide students a broad range of literature, including works, both present and past, that reflect cultures quite different from the students' own. Teachers should not, however, force young people to confront "classics" in which archaic language or ways of life confound their understanding. Such works can await students' greater maturity: "To force such works upon the young prematurely defeats the long-term goal of educating people to a personal love of literature sufficiently deep to cause them to seek it out for themselves at the appropriate time" (Rosenblatt, 1983, p. 218). The test is whether the child or adolescent is intellectually and emotionally ready for what the book has to offer.

Rosenblatt offers less an instructional model for English language arts than a set of attitudes, an approach or stance, that she believes teachers should adopt toward the teaching of literature. The teacher of literature referred to in her work—flexible, undogmatic, compassionate, well-versed in literature, and familiar with the methods and major findings of the social sciences—seems more the ideal teacher of English than the one most often observed (Goodlad, 1984; Powell, Farrar, & Cohen, 1985; Squire & Applebee, 1968).

To accommodate student variability, Moffett and Wagner (1992) propose a student-centered language arts curriculum that would promote the "three things that are hardest for the schools to bring about . . . individualization, interaction, and integration" (p. 46). The curriculum would foster individualization by allowing students to select and sequence their own activities and materials; interaction, by arranging for students to teach each other; integration, by interweaving subjects so that students could synthesize knowledge structures in their own minds (p. 25). The student-centered classroom would ideally permit students "access at any time to any activity, book, person, medium, materials, and methods" (p. 29).

The implied teachers for the curriculum that Moffett advocates would have to be creative, self-assured, and highly tolerant. Like the teachers of literature implied in Rosenblatt's work, they would need to be broadly educated, familiar with concepts, methods, and resources in the social and physical sciences as well as in the humanities. However, unlike Rosenblatt's implied teachers, they would not give print literature a privileged place in the curriculum: It would compete with content from other subjects for students' attention. Rather than being concerned principally with students' mastery of discrete skills or their familiarity with a cultural or literary heritage, teachers would be primarily interested in helping students gain control over language through using it in increasingly sophisticated ways. "Through reading, writing, and discussing whole, authentic discourses—and using no textbooks—students can learn better everything that we consider of value in language and literature than they can by the current substantive and particle approach" (Moffett, 1968, p. 7). Because students would be going in diverse and sometimes unpredictable directions, teachers would not be able to rely on set lesson plans or sequences of instruction. The classroom would be active and at times filled with noise.

Like Moffett, Britton deals with the whole spectrum of the English language arts, though not from as complete a conceptual model and not in the detail that Moffett provides. In the past, Britton's research on composition has most strongly affected the English curriculum, particularly in elementary and middle schools. According to Britton (1972), the process of composing in writing should be wedded to that of reading, and both should be related to students' spoken language (p. 159). Elementary teachers should not use graded readers, which isolate a "sight vocabulary" from the child's speech vocabulary. Talk is the most likely means by which students first investigate, explore, and organize new fields of interest. "Talk . . . prepares the environment into which what is taken from reading may be accommodated: and from that amalgam the writing proceeds" (p. 166).

Britton believes that the emphasis in language arts instruction should be on students' psycholinguistic development rather than on their mastery of skills or familiarity with works of literature that ostensibly help constitute their cultural heritage. Britton wants teachers to engage students in a full spectrum of language activities—reading, writing, listening, and speaking. Moreover, he wants language in the classroom to be used for real purposes, not for "dummy runs." Britton's work emphasizes that students need more opportunities and stronger incentive to choose their own audiences so as "to be able, when the occasion arises, to write as someone with something to say to the world in general" (p. 192).

## Social Mobility

The fluctuating nature of instructional models is due in no small part to the paradoxical demands of American schools, which usually attempt to foster democratic values, such as equality, while espousing the virtues of living in a highly competitive, capitalistic society. Indeed, teachers are expected to maximize student potential on an individual basis, while ensuring a certain level of minimum competencies for all. Although certified by the state as experts in their subject areas and mandated to implement the state's curriculum, teachers are expected to be also knowledgeable about national standards. Meanwhile, the locus of authority to hire, fire, and evaluate resides with administrators within the local school, who also have the power to modify curriculum, to moderate instruction, and to set boundaries regarding instructional methods. The degree to which a teacher allows the myriad curricular pressures to influence decision making in the classroom has much to do with what he or she considers to be the goals of a public education.

Labaree (1997) describes three defining goals of American education—democratic equality, social efficiency, and social mobility. The goal of democratic equality has as its roots the Common School Movement of the 1830s, when the idea of universal schooling for all Americans was touted as a way to "solve the major social, economic, and political problems of society" (Spring, 1986; p. 81). The goal of social efficiency has

both cultural and practical attributes. By being socially efficient, schools ideally produce model citizens by teaching democratic values and providing a common core of learning for students, all the while maximizing the fiscal contributions of taxpayers. Despite the lofty goals of social efficiency and democratic equality, the goal of social mobility—and by implication economic mobility—seems to have emerged as the overarching mission of American schooling in the new millennium. As Goodlad (1997) has noted, "Preparing for parenthood and citizenship has taken second place, well behind preparing for work, in the implicit expectations for schooling and higher education and in the rhetoric of reform" (p. 101).

The mission of advancing social mobility has exerted tremendous influence on curricular and economic decisions. For example, administrators often rationalize paying millions of dollars to wire their schools for the Internet on the grounds that students must learn to function within the world of work and that "the Internet is becoming perhaps the primary medium for business transactions in the emerging Information Age" (Cummins and Sayers, 1997, p. 175). If social mobility has become the primary goal of education, then measures must be formulated to ensure that students are graduating with the appropriate credentials. Seen in this light, popular programs such as the International Baccalaureate Program, Advanced Placement Programs, dual-enrollment programs, and recent forays in public education by private concerns—Disney, Whittle/Edison, Nobel Education Dynamics, and school vouchers—become possible indicators of heightened public concern over students' future social mobility. In the drive to verify student competence, most states have begun to mandate high school exit exams. Incredibly, as many as 20% of high schools now require students in honors classes to take Advanced Placement exams (Sandham, 1998), while states are increasingly linking spending on public colleges to indices of the campuses' performance (Schmidt, 1998).

DeTocqueville (1966) once wrote, "A time [is] approaching in which freedom, public peace, and social stability will not be able to last without education" (p. 528). The quest for marketable credentials has altered the emphasis in many schools from what is to be learned to what evidence has been gathered.

## The Ever-expanding Language Arts

Certainly, one of the difficulties of teaching the language arts in the 21st century will be in getting a handle on exactly what should constitute a course of study. Even though *What is English?* (Elbow, 1990) seemed poised to offer a reply, it wound up adding to the list of questions. Recently, the English language arts have been characterized as possessing eight components—language, literature, composition, speech and drama, critical thinking, technology, media literacy, and interdisciplinary studies (Baines, 1998a; Britton & Chorney, 1991; Smagorinsky, 1996).

Because of the complexity of the curriculum (or curricula) of the English language arts, any single instructional model, particularly a monolithic one, will perforce distort what takes place in the classroom. First, the enormous content and the myriad skills traditionally associated with the subject are not stable (e.g., literature accretes, and knowledge about how students attain literacy steadily alters as a consequence of scholarship); second, like other areas of the curriculum, the English language arts are subject to cultural influences and trends (on this point, see Applebee, 1974; Glatthorn, 1980; Squire, 1977); third, the curriculum involves the performance of thousands of teachers and millions of students, each of whom brings to the classroom peculiarities in aptitudes, interests, and life experiences. In short, the curriculum and the instructional modes it implies are dynamic and resist verbal encapsulation.

Despite the apparent expansion of the language arts as cited in the professional literature and despite the growth of fringe interest groups such as the Institute for Media Literacy and The Association for Expanded Perspectives on Learning, the newest components of the language arts have had some difficulty in establishing footholds in real elementary and secondary classrooms. For example, the finding three decades ago that most classrooms spend only 1.3% of class time on mass media (Squire & Applebee, 1968) probably has not changed much over time. Indeed, the foci of most classrooms today likely remains on reading and writing, the "bedrock" subjects of schooling (Squire, 1995). Certainly, even by themselves, reading and writing are difficult enough to teach well (Farrell, 1991; E. Farrell, personal communication, 1998), though, as this chapter earlier indicated, the computer may place an increasingly critical role in that teaching.

With regard to literature, a teacher must consider the state-adopted suggestions, the textbook, "classic works," young adult and children's literature, contemporary best sellers, students' reading levels, books-on-hand in the school storeroom, parental concerns, local standards of decorum, and student motivation. The complexity of the decision-making process in regard to the choices available in literature and reading alone should not be underestimated. In the subcategory of "classic works," for example, Bloom (1994) lists over 550 authors (often, with multiple numbers of books listed under each author) as necessary reading for a basic understanding of 20th century literature. And "classic works" compose only one subtopic subsumed under literature, which is one of eight major headings in the cosmos of the language arts (the other seven being language, composition, media literacy, technology, critical thinking, interdisciplinarity, and speech and drama). Furthermore, if a teacher receives too much adverse parental criticism for having students read a certain book (especially a story involving ghosts, dreams, or witches), it is likely that he or she might eventually opt for titles that do not provoke as much commotion.

All this is not to deny the value of words like "mastery teaching," "heritage," or "process" in suggesting curricular emphases at a given time. But curricula might be described in other ways. For example, Goodlad (1977) hypothesized that five curricula exist simultaneously in the schools: the *ideal curriculum*, what scholars propose be taught; the *formal curriculum*, what has been mandated by a controlling agency, such as the state or local district; the *perceived curriculum*, what teachers believe they are teaching; the *operational curriculum*, what observers actually see being taught; and the *experiential curriculum*, what students believe they are learning.

Certainly Goodlad's ideal curriculum as envisioned by leaders within the profession is oft at odds with the observed operational curriculum. Despite emphasis by researchers on the importance of both process and practice in writing (see, e.g., Britton, 1978; Emig, 1971; Graves, 1983; Moffett, 1981; Tate, 1987), Applebee (1981) found in an observational study of writing in the content areas of two midwestern high schools that only 10% of observed time in English classes was devoted to writing of at least paragraph length and that the amount of time devoted to prewriting activities averaged just over three minutes. Summaries of research on written composition (Braddock, Lloyd-Jones, & Schoer, 1963; Hillocks, 1986) report little relationship between instruction in formal grammar and students' proficiency in writing; yet in analyzing observational data from his national study of 38 elementary and secondary schools, Goodlad (1984) concluded that in English language arts the dominant emphasis throughout was on teaching basic language skills and mastering mechanics—capitalization, punctuation, paragraphs, . . . parts of speech, etc. These were repeated in successive grades of the elementary years, were reviewed in the junior high years, and reappeared in the low track classes of the senior high schools (p. 205).

## Navigating the Microenvironment

In general, because of the complexities of the subject and the traditional role of local boards in establishing curricula, state departments of education and national organizations such as the National Council of Teachers of English and The International Reading Association have opted to elucidate generic rather than specific standards with regard to objectives in the language arts. Even though most states have formulated separate "standards" for English language arts, one reading them readily becomes aware of overlaps between the profession's and the states' standards. For example, according to the state of Massachusetts, "Lifelong learners construct and convey meaning by reading, writing, speaking, listening, viewing, and presenting effectively. They access, analyze, evaluate, and apply knowledge and experiences for a variety of purposes, audiences, and situations" (Massachusetts Department of Education, 1998). The first three competency goals for the language arts in North Carolina (Public Schools of North Carolina, 1998) are as follows:

"Competency Goal 1: The learner will use strategies and processes that enhance control of communication skills development.

Competency Goal 2: The learner will use language for the acquisition, interpretation, and application of information.

Competency Goal 3: The learner will use language for critical analysis and evaluation."

The third and fourth standards of the NCTE/IRA national standards are that "Students apply a wide range of strategies to comprehend, interpret, evaluate, and appreciate texts. . . ." and "Students adjust their use of spoken, written, and visual language (e.g., conventions, style, vocabulary) to communicate effectively with a variety of audiences and for different purposes" (NCTE/IRA, 1997, p. viii).

For all the billions of dollars spent on formulating standards and in developing instruments to assess their attainment, what really matters is what happens when a teacher closes the door to the classroom and begins to teach and how students respond to that teaching. Below are listed possible factors that might influence learning for a particular day:

**Teacher variables**: Assessment of achievement for the reporting period, how success as measured by the state, knowledge of the subject matter, competence with various teaching methods, knowledge of standards, principal's views on education, possible evaluation of the lesson by an outside administrator, university and practicum experiences, talent with classroom management, disposition of the school board, priorities of the superintendent, opinion of the head of the department, curriculum guides, teachers' guides, involvement with a parent-advisory committee, work load, class size, familiarity with diverse populations, knowledge of special needs of students, community values, and relationships with parents and fellow teachers.

**Student variables**: age, gender, race, socio-economic background, peer influence, attitude towards school, relationship with teacher, sociability, proximity to distractions, time of day, support from family or other adults, in-class support (such as special education teachers, teachers' aides, or bilingual education teachers), class size, other classes, stage of development, interest in subject matter, previous experience with subject matter, previous grades, and after-school obligations, such as work, sports, or clubs.

**Classroom variables**: Textbooks (old or up-to-date), availability of computers, Internet-access, furniture, temperature, interruptions (such as announcements or fire drills), proximity of bathrooms, visual and olfactory appeal, and other equipment, such as an overhead machine, blackboard, or VCR.

Tracking the actual curriculum (or experiential curriculum as Goodlad calls it) in a particular classroom at a specific point in time would require consideration of a complex series of interactions involving variables related to the teacher, student, and classroom. Despite increased micromanaging from both the federal government (Bernstein, 1998) and state departments of education (*Education Week*, 1997, January 22), most

teachers are still free to teach the language arts in any way they wish, as long as student achievement scores remain sufficiently high. Undeniably, the American public continues to look to standardized tests as the way to provide the index of quality for instructional models. At the beginning of the twenty-first century, the ideal curriculum is apparently an instructional model that can provide maximal student achievement at the cheapest possible cost.

When foresters consider the growth pattern of a particular tree, they refer to its microenvironment, that is, the conditions under which one particular tree exists, day-in and day-out. A large tree in the forest receives much sunshine, has plenty of room to spread its branches, has access to sufficient water, and experiences few difficulties with pests such as termites. A smaller tree in the same forest lives in the shadow of the large tree, and, as a result, experiences less sunshine, receives less water, and withstands more assaults from pests. The two trees have very different microenvironments, though they exist within feet of each other in the same forest.

As difficult as it is for a teacher to conceptualize instructional models on an individual basis, it is through each student's microenvironment that he/she comes to know the language arts. Although accountability, styles of instruction, accessibility, and curricular models all may affect the growth and development of a students' learning, these factors pale in comparison to the influence of the human relationship that is established with peers and with the teacher. About the latter Bloom (1987) has written, "No real teacher can doubt that his task is to assist his pupil to fulfill human nature against all the deforming forces of convention and prejudice" (p. 20).

Although it may be appealing to create a model of a masterful teacher with formidable content area knowledge and incredible instructional prowess, anyone who has ever taught in public schools for more than fifteen minutes knows that such a superteacher under certain conditions could be doomed in a classroom. In truth, the most valuable assets for a teacher are a sense of humor, charisma, determination, compassion, common sense, and an unbridled enthusiasm for the language arts. Given these traits, a teacher may move on to the *tao* of instructional models.

# References

Adler, M. (1940). *How to read a book: The art of getting a liberal education.* New York: Simon & Schuster.

Anderson, S. (1964). *Between the Grimms and "The Group": Literature in Anderson High schools.* Princeton, NJ: Educational Testing Service.

Applebee, A. N. (1974). *Tradtion and reform in the teaching of English: A history.* Urbana, IL: National Council of Teachers of English.

Applebee, A. N. (1981). *Writing in the secondary school: English and the content areas.* (Research report No. 21). Urbana, IL: National Council of Teachers of English. ED 197347.

Atwell, Nancy (1987). *In the middle.* Portsmouth, NH: Heinneman.

Baines, Lawrence (1997, March). Future schlock, *Phi Delta Kappan,* 493-498.

Baines, Lawrence (1998a, February). From tripod to cosmos: A new metaphor for the language arts. *English Journal,* 24-35.

Baines, Lawrence (1998b). It's just too damn boring. Manuscript in preparation, unpublished research.

Baines, Lawrence (1998c). The future of the written word. In Simmons, J., and L. Baines (Eds). *Language study in middle school, high school, and beyond.* Newark, DE: International Reading Association.

Banks, James (1991). Multicultural literacy and curriculum reform, *Educational Horizons,* vol. 69, 135-140.

Begley, Sharon (1996, February 19). Your child's brain; Hows kids are wired for music, math, and emotions, *Newsweek.*

Bennett, William (Ed.) (1993). *The book of virtues.* New York: Simon & Schuster.

Bennett, William (Ed.) (1995). *The moral compass*. New York: Simon & Schuster.

Berliner, David, & Bruce, Biddle (1995). *The manufactured crisis*. White Plains, NY: Longman.

Bernstein, Mark (1998, January 21). The tyranny of a national curriculum. *Education Week*. Available: http://www.edweek.com

Birkerts, Sven (1994). *The Gutenberg elegies*. New York: Fawcett Columbine.

Block, J., & Burns, R. (1976). Mastery Learning. *Review of Research in Education, 4*, 3-49.

Bloom, Alan (1987). *The closing of the American mind*. New York: Simon & Schuster.

Bloom, B. (1968). Learning for mastery. *Evaluation Comment, 1*(2). University of California at Los Angeles: Center for the Study of Evaluation of Instructional Programs.

Bloom, B. (1971). Mastery learning and its implications for curriculum development. In E. W. Eisner (Ed.), *Confronting curriculum reform* (pp. 17-49). Boston: Little, Brown.

Bloom, B. (1974). An introduction to mastery learning theory. In J. H. Block (Ed.), *Schools, society, and mastery learning* (pp. 4-14). New York: Holt, Rinehart & Winston.

Bloom, B. (1976). *Human characteristics and school learning: A theory of school learning*. New York: McGraw Hill.

Bloom, B. (1981). *All our children learning*. New York: McGraw Hill.

Bloom, Harold (1994). *The western canon*. Orlando: Harcourt Brace.

Bottstein, Leon (1997). *Jefferson?s children*. New York: Doubleday.

Braddock, R., Lloyd-Jones, R., & Schoer, L. (1963). *Research in written composition*. Urbana, IL: National Council of Teachers of English.

Britton, James (1970). *Language and learning*. New York: Viking.

Britton, J. (1972). *Language and learning*. Harmondsworth, Middlesex, England: Penguin Books Inc. (First published by Allen Lane, The Penguin Press, 1970).

Britton, J. (1978). The composing processes and the functions of writing. In C. Cooper & L. Odell (Eds.), *Research on composing* (pp. 13-28). Urbana, IL: National Council of Teachers of English.

Britton, James, & Merron, Chorny (1991). Current issues and future directions. In *Handbook of research on teaching the English language arts*, Flood, J., J. Jensen, D. Lapp, & J. Squire (Eds.), 110-122.

Caine, Geoffrey, Renate, Caine, & Sam, Crowell (1994). *Mindshifts*. Tucson, AZ: Zephyr Press.

Callahan, Raymond (1962). *Education and the cult of efficiency*. Chicago: University of Chicago Press.

Campbell, Joseph (1973). *Myths to live by*. New York: Bantam.

Carroll, J. (1963). A model for school learning. *Teachers College Record, 64*, 723-733.

Cheney, L. V. (1987). *American memory: A report on the humanities in the nation's public schools*. Washington, DC: U.S. Government Printing Office.

Coleman, J. (1961). *The adolescent society*. New York: Free Press of Glencoe.

Collins, R. (1991). Basic aspects of functional brain metabolism. In D. Chadwick & J. Whelan (Eds.) *Exploring brain functional anatomy with positron tomography*, 6-22. New York: John Wiley.

Commission on English. (1965). *Freedom and Discipline in English*. Princeton, NJ: College Entrance Examination Board.

Cremin, Lawrence (1988). *American education, the metropolitan experience, 1876-1980*. New York: Macmillan.

Csikszentmihalyi, M., & Larsen, R. (1984). *Being adolescent*. New York: Basic Books.

Csikszentmihalyi, M. (1993a). *The evolving self*. New York: Harper Perennial.

Csikszentmihalyi, M., Rathunde, K., & Whalen, S. (1993b). *Talented teens*. New York: Cambridge.

Csikszentmihalyi, M. (1996). *Creativity*. New York: Harper Collins.

Cuban, Larry (1984). *How Teachers Taught*. New York: Longman.

Cummins, Jim, & Dennis Sayers (1997). *Brave New Schools*. New York: St. Martin?s.

Darling-Hammond, Linda, & Gary Sykes (in press). *Teaching as the learning profession*. San Francisco, CA: Jossey-Bass.

Davenport, Donna, & Cheryl, Forbes (1997, Winter). Writing movement/dancing words: A collaborative pedagogy. *Education, 118*(20), 293-302.

Davies, Merrill, & Connie, Beaucamps (1998). The effect of Accelerated Reader on the reading achievement of secondary school students. Berry College. Unpublished research.

Deacon, Terrence (1997). *The symbolic species*. New York: W. W. Norton.

DeTocqueville, Alexis (1966). *Democracy in America*. New York: Harper & Row.

Dewey, John (1916). *Democracy and education*. New York: Macmillan.

Dewey, John (1963). *Experience and education*. New York: Collier Books.

Diamond, Marian (1988). *Enriching heredity*. New York: Free Press.

Dixon, J. (1967). *Growth through English: A report based on the Dartmouth seminar*. Reading, England: National Association for the Teaching of English.

Edelman, Gerald (1987). *Neural Darwinism*. New York: Basic Books.

Edelman, Gerald (1994). *Bright air, brilliant fire*. New York: Basic Books.

*Education Week* (1997, January 22). Quality counts: A report card on the caondition of public educaiton in the 50 states. *Education Week, 16*. Available: http://www.edweek.com.

*Education Week* (1998, January 8). Quality counts: The urban challenge. *Education Week, 17*(7). Available: http://www.edweek.com.

Elbow, Peter (1990). *What is English*? New York: Modern Language Association.

Emig, Janet (1971). *The composing processes of twelfth graders*. Urbana, IL: NCTE.

Farrell, Edmund (1991). What is English? *Journal of Teaching Writing, 10*(2), 111-122.

Farrell, Edmund (1998). Personal communication.

Finn, Chester (1994). *We must take charge*. New York: Free Press.

Flood, James, Julie, Jensen, Diane, Lapp, & Jim, Squire (1991). *Handbook of research on teaching the English language arts*. New York: Macmillan.

Glatthorn, A. A. (1980). *A guide for developing an English curriculum for the eighties*. Urbana, IL: National Council of Teachers of English.

Goodlad, John (1977). What goes on in our schools. *Educational Researcher 6*, 3-6.

Goodlad, John (1984). *A place called school: Prospects for the future*. New York: McGraw Hill.

Goodlad, John (1997). *In praise of education*. New York: Teachers College Press.

Graves, D. H. (1983). *Writing: Teachers and children at work*. Exeter, NH: Heinemann.

Greenspan, Stanley (1997). *The growth of the mind*. Reading, MA: Addison-Wesley.

Guam Department of Education. (1987). *Teaching for Mastery*. Draft copy. Agana, Guam.

Heath, Shirley (1983). *Ways with words*. New York: Cambridge.

Hillocks, George (1986). *Research on written composition*. Urbana, IL: ERIC Clearninghouse on Reading and Communication Skills.

Hirsch, E. D. (1987). *Cultural literacy*. New York: Doubleday.

Hirsch, E. D. (1996). *The schools we need and why we don't have them.* New York: Doubleday.

Hirsch, E. D. (1997). *What your first grader needs to know.* New York: Doubleday.

Hunter, M. (1985). What's wrong with Madeline Hunter? *Educational Leadership, 42,* 57–60.

Jacobson, Linda (1998, April 8). Education policymakers embrace brain findings. *Education Week.* Available: http://www.edweek.com.

Keller, Bess (1998, May 20). In Age of Accountability, Principals Feel the Heat, *Education Week.* Available: http://www.edweek.com.

Keller, F. (1968). Goodbye, teacher... *Journal of Applied Behavior Analysis, 1,* 79–89.

Kosslyn, Stephen, Thompson, W. Irene, K. & Alpert N. (1995, November 30). Topographical representations of mental images in the primary visual cortex. *Nature,* 496–498.

Labaree, David (1997). *How to succeed in school without really learning.* New Haven, CT: Yale University Press.

Lynch, J., & Evans, B. (1963). *High school English textbooks: A critical examination.* Boston: Little, Brown.

Mager, Robert (1962). *Preparing instructional objectives.* Belmont, CA: Fearon-Pitman Publishers.

Mandel, B. J. (Ed.). (1980). *Three language-arts curriculum models: Pre-kindergarten through college.* Urbana, IL. National Council of Teachers of English.

Massachusetts Department of Education (1998). Massachusetts Curriculum Framework for English and the language arts. Available: http://www.doe.mass.edu/doedocs/frameworks/englishTOC.html

McNeil, L. (1988). Contradictions of control, part I: Administrators and teachers. *Phi Delta Kappan, 69*(5), 333–339.

Mississippi Department of Education (1998). *Office of student assessment: Mississippi state test scores.* Available: http://mdek12.state.ms.us/.

Moffett, James (1968). *Teaching the universe of discourse.* Boston: Houghton-Mifflin.

Moffett, J. (1981). *Active voice, A writing program across the curriculum.* Upper Montclair, NJ: Boynton/Cook.

Moffett, J., & Wagner, B. J. (1992). *Student-centered language arts and reading, K-13: A handbook for teachers* (3rd. ed.) Boston: Houghton Mifflin.

Muller, H. (1967). *The uses of English.* New York: Holt, Rinehart & Winston.

National Assessment of Educational Progress (1992). *Trends in home and school contexts for learning.* Washington, D.C.: U.S. Department of Education (NCES 92070).

National Center for Research on Teacher Learning (1994). *Findings on learning to teach.* Lansing, MI: Michigan State University.

National Commission on Teaching & America?s Future (1996). *What matters most: Teaching for America's future.* New York: National Commission on Teaching & America's Future.

N.C.T.E./I.R.A. (1997). Standards for the English language arts. In P. Smagorinsky, *Standards in practice 9–12,* viii–ix. Urbana, IL: NCTE.

Peterson, S., Fox, P., Posner, M., Mintun, M., & Raichle, M. (1988). Positron emission tomographic studies of the cortical anatomy of single-word processing. *Nature, 331,* 585–589.

Peterson, S., Fox, P., Snyder, A., & Raichle, M. (1990). Activation of extrastriate and frontal cortical areas by visual words and word-like stimuli. *Science, 24,* 1041–1044.

Pinker, Steven (1994). *The language instinct: How the mind creates language.* New York: William Morrow.

Posner, M. I., Petersen, S. E., Fox, P. T., & Raichle, M. E. (1988). Localization of cognitive operations in the human brain. *Science, 240,* 1627–1631.

Posner, M. I., & Raichle, M. E. (1994). *Images of mind.* New York: Scientific American Library.

Postman, Neil (1996). *The end of education.* New York: Alfred A. Knopf.

Powell, A. G., Farrar, E., & Cohen, D. K. (1985). *The shopping mall high school.* Boston: Houghton Mifflin.

Pribaum, K. (1991). *Brain and perception.* Hillsdale, NJ: Lawrence Erlbaum.

Public schools of North Carolina (1998). *English Language Arts: K12 Standard Course of Study and Grade Level Competencies.* Available: http://www.dpi.state.nc.us/Curriculum/languagearts/index.html

Ravitch, D., & Finn, C. E., Jr. (1987). *What do our 17-year-olds know? A report on the first national assessment of history and literature.* New York: Harper & Row.

Reid, E. R. (1986). Practicing effective instruction: The exemplary center for reading instruction approach. *Exceptional Children, 52*(6) 510–519.

Rich, Pamela (1998). The Effects of Accelerated Reader on the Reading Achievement of Fourth Graders. Unpublished research, Berry College.

Rief, Linda (1991). *Seeking diversity.* Portsmouth, NH: Heinneman.

Rose, Colin and Malcolm Nicholl (1997). *Accelerated learning for the 21st century.* New York: Dell.

Rosenzweig, M., & Bennett, R. (1972). Cerebral changes in rats, exposed individually to an enriched environment. *Journal of Comparative and Physical Psychology, 80,* 304–313.

Rosenzweig, M. (1979). Responsiveness of brain size to individual experience. In M. Hagn, C. Jensen, and B. Dudek (Eds.) *Development and evolution of brain size,* 263–293. New York: Academic Press.

Rosenzweig, M. (1996). Aspects of the search for neural mechanisms of memory. *Annual Review of Psychology, 47*(96), 1–32.

Rugg, Michael (1995, February). La difference vive. *Nature,* 561–562.

Sandham, Jessica (1998, May 13). More Students in AP Courses Find They Can't Escape the Test, *Education Week.* Available: http://www.edweek.com.

Sarason, Seymour (1990). *The predictable failure of educational reform.* San Francisco: Jossey-Bass.

Shaywitz, Bennett et al. (1995, February). Sex differences in the functional organization of the brain for language. *Nature,* 607–609.

Sikula, John (1996, March 7). Educational improvement requires increased funding. *Teacher Education Reports,* 6–8.

Sizer, Theodore (1997). *Horace?s Compromise.* Wilmington, MA: Houghton-Mifflin.

Slavin, Robert (1996). *Education for all.* Royesford, PA: Swets & Zeitlinger Publishers.

Slavin, Robert, & Olatokundo, Fashola (1998). *Show me the evidence.* Thousand Oaks, CA: Corwin Press.

Smagorinsky, Peter (1996). *Standards in practice 9–12.* Urbana, IL: NCTE.

Sowell, Thomas (1994). *Inside American education.* New York: Free Press.

Spring, J. H. (1972). *Education and the rise of the corporate state.* Boston: Beacon Press.

Spring, Joel (1986). *The American School 1642–1985.* New York: Longman.

Squire, J. R. (Ed.). (1977). *The Teaching of English: The seventy-sixth yearbook of the national society for the study of education. Part I.* Chicago: University of Chicago Press.

Squire, James, & Applebee, R. (1968). *High school English instruction today.* New York: Appleton-Century-Crofts.

Squire, James (1995). Language arts. In G. Calwelti (Ed.), *Handbook of research on improving student achievement*. Arlington, VA: Educational Research Service.

Stallings, J., & Stipek, D. (1986). Research on early childhood and elementary school teaching programs. In M. C. Wittrock (Ed.), *Handbook of research on teaching* (3rd. ed., pp. 727-753). New York: MacMillan.

Stone, G. W., Jr. (Ed.). (1961). *Issues, problems, and approaches in the teaching of English*. New York: Holt, Rinehart, & Winston.

Tate, G. (Ed.). (1987). *Teaching composition: 12 bibliographical essays*. Fort Worth: Texas Christian University Press.

Tweedle, Sally, Anthony Adams, Stephen Clarke, Peter Scrimshaw, and Shona Walton (1997). *English for tomorrow*. Philadelphia, PA: Open University Press.

Van Doren, M. (1943). *Liberal education*. New York: Henry Holt.

Welsh, Patrick (1987). *Tales out of school*. New York: Viking.

Wittrock, Merlin (Ed.) (1986). *Handbook of research on teaching*. New York: Macmillan.

Wills, Christopher (1993). *The runaway brain*. New York: Basic Books.

# · 9 ·

# WHO HAS THE POWER? POLICYMAKING AND POLITICS IN THE ENGLISH LANGUAGE ARTS

*Leo P. Ruth*

*University of California, Berkeley*

> Since the initiation of the public school system ... national leaders have periodically issued statements of a "literacy crisis" and have launched reform programs designed to eliminate illiteracy.
>
> —Harvey Graff (1987)

Educational standards, testing, and literacy issues in general have held center stage in much of the political debate in the final decades of the 20th century. Specifically, issues in teaching and testing in the English language arts have been marked by clashes between public officials—who had the power but not the knowledge to create sound policy—and educators—who had the knowledge but not the power to prevail. Consequently, federal and state mandates have increasingly replaced practitioner knowledge and educational research as the main forces guiding school program development.

In the mid-90s, for example, the California Legislature passed laws requiring public schools to teach beginning reading with a focus on explicit phonics and spelling, initially isolated from context. The new laws mandated use of skills-based reading programs and required the retraining of teachers in a phonics-based curriculum. One of the laws designated a portion of the state's Goals 2000 money for professional development programs in reading. It set up a process to prepare a list of approved inservice providers whom schools and districts could hire with these special funds. When the list was completed in the spring of 1998, the state had screened out the inservice programs of "many of the most widely respected literacy scholars and consultants in the field" (*The Council Chronicle*, 1998, June, p. 3). Other states also moved toward legislating phonics-based teaching of reading, and in the fall of 1997, a federal version of the

prescriptive California legislation, titled The Reading Excellence Act, passed the U.S. House of Representatives, but it died in the Senate.

These intrusive mandates prompted the National Council of Teachers of English to enact a resolution "On Continued Government Intrusion into Professional Decision Making" at its annual convention in the fall of 1998. In essence, the resolution protested the ever-increasing encroachment of state and federal mandates on the content of early instruction in reading and on specification of "reliable, replicable research" based on a narrow definition of literacy. The resolution declared "that neither Congress nor any federal or state agency should establish a single definition of reading and writing or restrict the type of research used in funding criteria for preservice or inservice teacher education and professional development programs" (*The Council Chronicle*, Special Supplement, 1999, February, p. 2). The body of this chapter explores the political conditions that instigated this resolution.

Policymaking has always been conducted in a sociopolitical context. Contributing to the development of that context were sweeping distortions in reports in the media on language arts issues such as early grade reading instruction, bilingual education, multicultural literature, and the Ebonics controversy. How the media generated superficial and inaccurate perceptions that led federal and state policymakers to move in risky directions is highlighted in Gene Maeroff's *Imaging Education* (1998). One of the studies he included documents the strong negative slant of reporting and its impact on policy.

[c]onsistently unbalanced accounts in the media contribute to a general perception of crisis, and crises allow little time for careful reflection and analysis. In such an atmosphere, prudent discussions of the issues give way to the compulsion for immediate solutions. Public officials, pressured to respond, might try something—anything—to improve their education system, and in their haste, focus on the wrong problem, the wrong solution (Ogle & Dabbs, in Maeroff, 1998, p. 91).

The media have not been kind to schooling in general or to the English language arts in particular. They have fostered the prevailing mood of the 90s, a pervasive sense of doom, which conveys the notion that we are a culture in decline. Leon Botstein (1997) describes the era as one marked by diminished confidence in the ability of government to act constructively to solve social problems. This attitude nourishes a turn toward simplistic ideas about the benefits of less governance and unregulated reliance on market forces. The once huge investment in the development of quality education systems and other public services crumbled in the 90s as the California-initiated crusade against taxes spread throughout the nation.

Botstein (1997) finds a "deadly combination of nostalgia for yesterday and pessimism about today" (p. 29) in the language of those critics who conjure bleak images of a golden age undone by years of massive error and mismanagement at various levels of governance. Botstein refutes this view of American cultural history, concluding that "selective memory, willful distortion, and even downright falsehood combined to generate a pessimistic account of history" (p. 16). Given this doomsday atmosphere, people are inclined to believe that today's literacy standards are lower, that teachers are less rigorous and less well trained. The outpouring of negative prose about standards and achievement makes the reporting of any good news automatically suspect. This mistrust in turn makes the public susceptible to political machinations and untested quick-fix remedies. Easy to castigate, literacy education has become more politicized than ever as a favorite topic of candidates for local, state, and national elected office. Politically, the basic subjects make ideal low-risk, high-yield rhetorical issues.

The public system of education has repeatedly been declared a failure, but several scholars have demonstrated that the condition of schooling in America is not nearly as debased as is commonly alleged. These educational researchers have sought to counter the abundant misinformation about schooling with facts that have been either ignored or distorted. The titles of their publications indicate their thrust: *The Manufactured Crisis: Myths, Fraud, and the Attack on America's Schools*, David Berliner and Bruce Biddle (1995); *Setting the Record Straight: Responses to Misconceptions About Public Education in the United States*, Gerald W. Bracey (1997). Bracey's book, for example, lays out data pertinent to 18 concerns. He addresses issues such as the SAT score decline, international comparisons, reading rankings, teacher accountability, results of choice and charter experiments, and so forth. Jeff McQuillan in *The Literacy Crisis: False Claims, Real Solutions* (1998) also refutes, with statistical evidence, the claims that U.S. students are among the worst readers in the world and that progressive, holistic approaches to reading instruction have failed.

Peter Schrag (1997) was one of the rare journalists to publish a supportive article in the popular press. Titled "The Near-Myth of Our Failing Schools," his analysis in *The Atlantic Monthly* argues that the truth about public school quality is far more complex than the ideologically inspired "rhetoric of alarm" (p. 72) allows to be considered. Schrag alerts the public to misleading statistical comparisons, to misleading historical comparisons, and to parental ambiguity about tougher standards for their students. Meanwhile, Larry Cuban, a Stanford scholar who has studied the patterns of school reform in the past hundred years, has observed that "[r]eforming schools in the United States requires the manufacturing of a crisis and the severe scolding of educators" (1997, p. 92). The terrible cost of this strategy is an erosion of public confidence every time it is used.

There is good reason for the policymakers' obdurate refusal to take a more balanced view of the conditions of American schooling. As a political strategy, the rhetoric of crisis, of decline and failure, sets the stage for employing the rhetoric of reform. Policies labeled "reforms" presuppose legitimacy and assure support.

This chapter inquires into the roots of policymaking in the English language arts. Policymaking is essentially a political process of negotiating arrangements to attain power and influence over the conduct of curriculum in the English language arts. Policymaking occurs by means of the multilayered and largely decentralized governing systems that compete with one another for ascendance. Three levels—federal, state, and local district units—as well as professional associations and special interest groups, all vie with one another to formulate policy for the English language arts. Sometimes the several levels of governance work together; sometimes they work independently; sometimes they clash as adversaries. All levels of the system are interrelated by a complex web of laws and regulations and ingrained traditions of custom and prior practice. At each of these levels of governance, many special interest groups and individuals also compete for influence.

The present composition of the English language arts as a school subject has evolved through the political struggles of various professional and social interests seeking to use the school to express particular purposes and values. For example, the roots of elementary reading instruction derive from the religious concerns of colonial times. New England Puritans who felt obliged to teach their children how to read the Bible made reading a priority subject for home instruction. But because reading also was important for knowing society's laws, it very quickly became a subject of concern within the arena of government. The Massachusetts Bay Colony passed a law in 1642 that empowered the selectmen (the board of town officers) to remove from their parents any children who had not been taught "to read and understand the principles of religion and the capital laws of this country" (quoted, in modern spelling in Cremin, 1970, p. 124, cited by Monaghan & Saul, 1987, p. 86).

The tangled paths of policy influences are so difficult to follow that they can easily lead the analyst into confusion and frustration. However, as the historian Sheldon Rothblatt

(1988) asserts "modern culture exists on diversity, flexibility, and individual initiative" and "we should not therefore expect much agreement about an ideal type called an 'educated person'" (p. 20). Nor, adds Rothblatt, should we assume that in the past there once was common agreement about the norms of cultural literacy. Gerald Graff (1989) also challenges the "myth of the lost cultural consensus" popularized by former Secretary of Education William J. Bennett and in best-selling books like those by E. D. Hirsch, Jr. (1987), and Allan Bloom (1987). On the contrary, the maintenance of a commonly agreed upon vision of the English language arts as a field of study grows more difficult as the field evolves, as social conditions change, and as government intervention increases.

This chapter describes how the members of these varied spheres of interest seek to exercise power and influence over the English language arts through the political processes of policymaking. The chapter concludes with an examination of the pivotal role of the "grass roots" policymaker, the teacher, and with a set of recommendations about establishing policy analysis as a field of study in English language arts education.

## MISSING: STUDIES OF POLICY ANALYSIS IN ENGLISH LANGUAGE ARTS

### A Neglected Area of Research

Even though there is an intense public focus on what English language arts teachers do, few educational policy analysts have examined the curriculum choices in English language arts as policy decisions and consequential political acts. The interrelated issues of policy, power, and politics in constructing the English language arts curricula have received scant attention in either the theoretical or research literature of English education. With few exceptions, scholars in the English language arts do not analyze the complex interplay of individuals, social groups, and governmental structures in shaping the policy decisions that form the political economy of the English language arts.

There is a sociopolitical-historical context in which the content, procedures, and organization of an English language arts program are structured and function that needs to be studied. These are the types of questions that might be answered in programs of study in policy analysis in English education. Who has power to decide what knowledge will be transmitted in English language arts classrooms? What is the nature of this knowledge and where does it come from? In whose interest is it selected, organized, evaluated, and presented? Who decides what the processes of instruction are to be in English language arts classrooms?

But policy analysis is not yet a field of study in the English language arts. There is no recognized set of research activities and no identifiable group of researchers who practice them. There exist only scattered articles, and a few books that deal with some aspects of politics and policymaking, which taken together still do not really constitute the "literature" of a recognizable field (Berlin 1987; Blau, 1998; Clifford, 1987; Fraatz,

1987; Goodman, 1998; Graff & Warner, 1989; Moffett, 1988; Monaghan & Saul, 1987; North, 1987; Ohmann, 1987; Pearson, 1997; Routman, 1996; Shannon, 1991; Shor, 1986; Taylor, 1998; Winkeljohann, 1973).

In the absence of a substantive research tradition in policy analysis within English language arts scholarship, the chapter draws on the general literature of policy analysis and curriculum studies to define the relationships of power, influence, and politics and to provide information about their interrelation and operation at the three levels of governance—federal, state, and local (Beyer & Apple, 1988; Chrispeels, 1997; Cizek, 1999; Popkewitz, 1987a, 1987b; Spring, 1985, 1988; Wirt & Kirst, 1982; Wirt & Kirst, 1997).

## POLICY, POWER AND INFLUENCE DEFINED

Before moving on, it is necessary to define several terms that recur throughout this chapter. Educational *policy* is made by anyone who has the power to prescribe a particular plan or course of action for others to follow. *Power* means having the authority to make demands and set constraints on any of the people occupying various roles in an educational system. In this chapter, power generally refers to the ability of a policymaker to affect, influence, or control what happens in English language education. Although the term *influence* (as a word) is related to power, it embraces a different set of working relationships between the actors in a decision-making event. The difference between an exercise of power and an exercise of influence is largely strategic, hinging on the appeal to authority that the policymaker adopts to get people to follow rules and plans that they themselves did not devise.

Chrispeels (1997), through study of a decade of reforms in California schools, explains more precisely how educational policy gets implemented. She draws on a body of prior work (McDonnell & Elmore, 1987 and McDonnel, 1994) to identify "five classes of policy instruments—mandates, inducements, capacity-building, system-changing, and hortatory which contribute to policy implementation in different ways depending on the policy goals and context" (p. 455). Chrispeels (1997) defines these "instruments" as

*Mandates* are enacted by a higher level of government, require action by a lower jurisdictional level.... *Inducements* are rewards (usually additional funding) provided as components of federal and state policy to increase the likelihood that a mandate or a valued policy goal will be carried out at the local level.... *Capacity-Building* policies ... are designed to enhance the resources or professional skills needed to accomplish policy goals. *System-changing* policies alter who has the authority to distribute valued goods and services. *Hortatory* or symbolic policy, according to McDonnell (1994)... often "appeal[s] to values, and ... [relies] on positive symbols and images" in an effort to motivate and mobilize people to act (p. 478).

These tactics or methods involved in managing units of the educational system constitute the *politics* of policymaking. The section on policymaking at the state level will focus on how these tactics have been and continue to be used in California reform movements.

## POWER AND INFLUENCE
## OF PROFESSIONAL ASSOCIATIONS

### The National Council of Teachers of English

For many people "politics" connotes dubious practices. Thus, it is not surprising that until the turbulent late 60s and early 70s, many members of the English profession innocently declared themselves to be "above politics." Even many of the leaders in English language arts believed themselves to be "apolitical." Yet the history of any organized profession is necessarily a history of political arrangements.

The National Council of Teachers of English (NCTE) was founded in 1911 in a protest against the prevailing political arrangement that supported college domination of the high school English curriculum (Applebee, 1974). Historically the NCTE has taken an active role in policymaking, beginning with James Hosic's report on the reorganization of English in the secondary schools in 1917. Throughout its history, the various leaders of the NCTE, on behalf of its members, have periodically articulated important values, goals, and processes for teaching the English language arts that the profession desired to pursue. These policy statements were prepared with the intention of guiding the thinking of other professionals, legislators, jurists, bureaucrats, and citizens.

A policy analyst would construe these texts as political in nature, but the English profession itself, until very recently, was less likely to interpret its work from a political perspective. Thus, it was not until the time of the volatile, consciousness-raising movements of the 60s and 70s, that politics surfaced in the organizational rhetoric. The NCTE Board of Directors took official notice in 1975 of its political function by establishing the standing committee called Support for the Learning and Teaching of English (SLATE). This committee on social and political concerns "seeks to influence public attitudes and policy decisions affecting the teaching of the English language arts . . . [to] publicize policies adopted by the NCTE membership . . . [and to] help create an environment for free and responsible teaching and learning," according the SLATE membership leaflet (n.d.).

SLATE publishes the *SLATE Newsletter*, which offers practical suggestions dealing with current issues, e.g., guidelines for review of protested materials, tips for influencing public policy, and so forth. SLATE also publishes the Starter Sheet Series on sociopolitical topics and the Fact Sheet Series that provides research-based information on controversial areas in the English language arts. In 1998, a Political Advocacy Booth became a standard feature of the annual convention and the spring conference. Here members are invited to indicate willingness to advocate for English language arts educational issues.

***The national interest and the teaching of English.*** The major professional effort to influence public policy in English studies at the national level comes through the leadership of the NCTE. The direct efforts of NCTE leaders to influence national legislation and national policy intensified in the decade of the 60s when the focus of American education moved from state and local districts to Washington, D.C. James Squire (1967), then

Executive Secretary of NCTE, described the scene during those years in his *Eight Year Report 1960–1967*:

Beginning almost "hat in hand" outside each USOE office, the Executive Secretary and Council leaders (with support and encouragement of loyal members within) built solid and substantial relationships within the Office of Education, the United States Information Agency, and other government groups. Our mission has been to improve the teaching of English, and Council members have responded magnificently. Despite continued national disputes over federal-local control, the Council has clearly stood for strengthened English instruction (p. 16).

The development of *categorical aid* became a powerful tool of federal influence and control. For example, initially, the 1958 National Defense Education Act (NDEA) contained financial aid for the improvement of mathematics, science, and foreign languages; thus these subjects became linked with national policy objectives. But the NDEA had failed to link English to the "national interest." The situation called for a dramatic lobbying effort on the part of the English profession, and it came in a report on *The National Interest and the Teaching of English* (1961) produced by the NCTE Committee on National Interest chaired by the newly appointed Executive Secretary of the Council, James Squire. This policy report made what Applebee (1974) has called "a direct and shrewd presentation of the importance of English to the national welfare, coupled with a startling documentation of instructional inadequacies" (p. 199). Although the NDEA was not broadened in 1961 to include English, the Council's efforts did succeed in attracting funds from the United States Office of Education to initiate Project English (Hook, 1979).

Project English established at major universities curriculum study centers that developed and tested a number of curricular patterns drawing on help from classroom teachers. Project English also sponsored some 50 or more basic research projects, including a series of cooperative studies of beginning reading instruction that came to be known as the First Grade Studies. The Project established also a small number of demonstration centers, and it sponsored a series of semiannual conferences on such issues as teaching English to "culturally different" youth. According to Squire (1987), one of these conferences on research in the teaching of English (Carnegie Institute of Technology, 1962), developed recommendations that "defined for years the priorities used by the Cooperative Research Branch of the U.S. Department of Health, Education, and Welfare in allocating research funds" (p. 387).

In 1964, the NCTE's Committee on National Interest issued a second report on *The National Interest and the Continuing Education of Teachers of English*. This volume described in great detail the inadequacy of the preparation of many secondary teachers of English and most elementary school teachers. Finally, in response to the Project English activity and to the National Interest reports, the National Defense Education Act was broadened in 1964 to include English, reading, and the teaching of English to second language speakers. Hook (1979) sums up NCTE's role in national policy formation: "It is certain that NCTE had firmly assumed a leadership role and, through its publications, conferences, and supplying of personnel, had demonstrated to Congress, USOE, and other groups some of the kinds of changes that were needed to teach more effectively a subject basic to almost all other learning..." (p. 198).

This National Interest episode illustrates the power of moral and political suasion that an active national professional association can marshall to influence the policymakers at the federal level. It illustrates how a national association when it is in a sense "accredited" with the authority to make "official" statements can function to define issues, provide ideas, and prompt the officials who have the actual power to determine policy. This episode in the history of curriculum policy in the English language arts suggests that such policy is made in a variety of arenas and at a variety of levels.

Squire (1967) foresaw the consequences of the shift of federal funding to the states and the political burdens it would place on many state English councils ill-prepared to advance policy proposals at the state level. He said:

We seem to be facing a relentless effort to channel federal funds and federal projects through individual state departments of education. Yet in far too few of our states are the leaders of English—elementary, secondary, and college—ready to speak in a united voice. How the Council meets this responsibility will depend in large measure on the effectiveness of our affiliated state associations (p. 18).

Nevertheless, professional associations in the English language arts at the national level—notably, the NCTE and the IRA—have continued into the millennium to influence the shaping of curriculum policies, determination of research agendas, and appropriation of funds. This influence has been attained largely through the ongoing dialogue that NCTE and IRA national and state councils maintain about the content of English, reading, and other language arts through journals and other publications, conferences, commissions, special task forces, and targeted lobbying efforts both in Washington, D.C. and in some state capitals. Ongoing coverage of policy issues, state and federal legislation, convention resolutions, opinion pieces by members, and affiliate council news appears in NCTE's *The Council Chronicle*, published five times a year and IRA's *Reading Today*, published bimonthly.

***NCTE policy documents.*** The range of its hortatory texts can be seen in a sampling of NCTE's policy documents issued over a period of 80 years. For the most part, these works achieve their power and influence by appealing to the intellectual authority of reason, logic, evidence, ethics, and human conscience. The titles suggest the extent of policy concerns: the Hosic Report written in collaboration with the National Education Association and the U.S. Bureau of Education, *Reorganization of English in Secondary Schools* (1917); Hatfield's *An Experience Curriculum in English* (1935); Smith's *Basic Aims of English Instruction* (1942); Smith, Broening, and Perrin's five volumes on the English curriculum (1952–1965) developed under the auspices of NCTE's Commission on the English Curriculum; *The Basic Issues in the Teaching of English* (1958) formulated in collaboration with the Modern Language Association (MLA), American Studies Association (ASA), and the College English Association (CEA); Squire's *The National Interest and the Teaching of English* (1961); *The Student's Right*

*to Read* (1960); Corbin and Crosby's *Language Programs for the Disadvantaged* (1965); Dixon's *Growth Through English* (1967), a report of the Anglo-American Seminar on the Teaching of English (Dartmouth Conference) as co-sponsor with the MLA and the National Association of Teachers of English, England (NATE); the CCCC's policy statement on "Students' Right to Their Own Language" (adopted 1972; published 1974); Mellon's *The National Assessment and the Teaching of English* (1975); Purves' *Common Sense and Testing in English* (1975); Hillock's *The English Curriculum Under Fire: What Are the Real Basics?* (1982); *Standards for the Assessment of Reading and Writing* (1994); *Standards for the English Language Arts* (1996), and others.

In an effort to provide breadth of vision to the "minimum competency" movement, the NCTE joined with a set of representatives from a number of educational associations in 1979 to develop a general statement on "The Essentials of Education." In 1982 the NCTE followed with its own statement on "The Essentials of English." Between 1995 and 1997, NCTE published three series of materials related to standards: The *Standards Exemplar Series* (3 books), the *Standards in Practice Series* (4 books), the *Standards Consensus Series* (6 books). The *1999-2000 NCTE Catalog* listed some 38 guidelines and position statements covering a variety of professional issues relating to reading, writing, censorship, nonsexist use of language, gender-balanced curriculum, bilingual education, and so forth. In keeping with the technology of the times, NCTE established its Web site (www.ncte.org), making issues text files available to be freely downloaded.

***Shifting boundaries within NCTE.*** Sociologists have observed in the life of organizations the tendency to move in cycles of differentiation and integration. This process is evident in the organizational development of the field of the English language arts. As the profession of English teaching grew in complexity and size, a division of labor occurred, with numerous specializations, distinctions, and factions appearing. As the teaching of English has matured as a profession, it has tended to divide into specialized professional bodies, sometimes as sub-groups within a parent organization, but often as independent organizations. For example, separate—but sometimes overlapping—constituencies have been organized in professional associations to speak for English, reading, speech, drama, journalism, modern languages (including English), teaching English as a second language, and so forth. Each of these organizations functions to define and maintain power over the boundaries of its curriculum area and over the qualifications of its practitioners. Thus, establishing a new curriculum domain, provides a new political arena where its members determine what policy issues matter and how to interact with the larger body politic. This chapter, however, is limited to the policymaking activities of the NCTE and the IRA.

As an organization grows larger, there tends to be an increase in differentiation as perceived interests of members diverge. The result of this process of micropolitics in NCTE is reflected in the table of contents of its annual directory, which shows the Council's structure by educational level in three sections: elementary, secondary, and college. Other permanent divisions in the

Council are commissions related to subject interests: composition, curriculum, language, literature, media, and reading. Other permanent NCTE substructures, defined by the special interests of professional role, are called conferences: the Conference for Secondary English Department Chairpersons; the Conference on College Composition and Communication; and the Conference on English Education. Still other permanent substructures called assemblies relate to various areas of the English language arts curriculum and profession. Standing committees deal with certain enduring issues of the profession, while a range of task-oriented committees address current, relatively short-term concerns. Collectively, these varied agencies contained within a single organizational structure provide a range of social arenas where curriculum issues and questions are identified and professional policies are negotiated.

Paradoxically, even as any large organization responds to the differences in backgrounds, interests, roles, and functions of its members, it must also seek to unite them internally for their greater good. Outside of its own membership, it must also seek alliance or coalition with other professional organizations or governmental entities sharing a core of policy interests. Differentiation and partition of function often lead to conflict, lack of coordination, and loss of control. The response to differentiation is an attempt to overcome differences by providing mechanisms for communication, collaboration, even re-integration. The history of NCTE then is partly a history of collaborative efforts with other organizations, with governmental bodies, and with special interest groups such as the "whole language movement" among elementary language arts teachers.

***The development of rival positions.*** There are policymaking groups, both inside and outside of our profession, that represent to one another rival or contrary positions in their conceptions of what content and arrangements are most desirable for the field of English language arts. In curriculum theory, this divergence could mean "skills" versus "whole language" approaches, or "subject-centered" versus "student-centered" approaches, and so forth. In organizational theory, this divergence could mean "open" classroom versus "structured" classroom, or "preformulated objectives" versus "expressive outcomes," and so forth. As two opposite strains of belief develop in a conceptual area, the tensions that arise may be dispelled in several ways:

1. An agreement may be reached to divide the conceptual territory, resulting in a form of complementarity in content as viewed from the perspective of the whole curriculum.
2. The strains may be played out in competition for power and resources.
3. One strain may be ignored for a time, remaining latent until conditions change to favor it.

Rival positions may develop within virtually any domain of the English language arts—the so-called "reading wars" provide a notable example. The sociologist Kai Erikson (1976) theorizes, in another context, that a line of conceptual divergence, which he calls an *axis of variation* (p. 82), is part of the natural order of things in any culture. He suggests that polarities function to draw attention to the meaningful contrasts in a culture. The tendency toward development of rival positions within the English language arts is evident at many points in the history of the subject.

The tendencies toward differentiation and integration that have characterized NCTE's history took a turn toward integration in the first gathering of the Coalition of English Associations. In 1984, a Coalition of English Associations met at NCTE headquarters to develop a statement, "Some Plain Truths About Teaching English," to speak to the neglect of English studies in the reform reports of that time. By 1987, the foundations had been laid for the Coalition to draft a policy statement about the teaching of English language arts, which evolved from a 3-week "summit meeting" (July 6–24, 1987), attended by some 60 representatives of all levels of schooling from eight major language arts professional associations: NCTE, MLA, CCCC, CEA, the Association of Departments of English (ADE), the College Language Association (CLA), the Conference on English Education (CEE), and the Conference for Secondary School English Department Chairpersons (CSSEDC). The formal conference report, *The English Coalition Conference: Democracy Through Language* (Lloyd-Jones & Lunsford, 1989), calls for a restructuring of the way the English language arts are taught at all levels of instruction.

As Wayne Booth says in the Foreword to the Coalition report, "our colleagues in English . . . travel under many different names: language arts, communications studies, media studies, linguistics, composition, rhetoric, and so on" (Lloyd-Jones & Lunsford, 1989, p. viii). Thus, the Coalition Conference provided an important forum for uniting constituencies within the field of English who "were not, for the most part, accustomed to talking with one another," (p. xviii) to deliberate about the common goals of teaching the English language arts that apply to all levels from elementary classes to doctoral programs.

## The International Reading Association

The process of differentiation and integration in the NCTE turned toward differentiation in the late 1940s. Some professionals specializing in reading became dissatisfied with NCTE's lack of attention to the area of reading in programs and services. Thus a divergence of interests led to formation of the International Reading Association (IRA), chartered in 1953, which arose from the merger of the International Council for the Improvement of Reading Instruction (ICIRI) formed in 1948 and the National Association of Remedial Teachers (NART) formed in 1947. The unification that formed IRA was completed on December 31, 1955, when ICIRI and NART closed their books (Jerrolds, 1979).

Monaghan and Saul (1987) have traced the forces that helped the IRA to grow rapidly in its membership. They point out that the existence of the field's theoretical base—as defined through the work of its early scholars, William S. Gray, Arthur Gates, David Russell, and others—provided a core of knowledge useful to the founding of a professional organization. In contrast, no comparable, coherent theoretical knowledge base was yet available for writing during this period. Composition, as an academic field for the development of theory and research, was not to take substantive form until the mid-70s.

The growth of reading as a profession was abetted unintentionally by the publication of Rudolf Flesch's *Why Johnny Can't Read* (1955), according to Monaghan and Saul (1987). Even though the leaders of the reading profession denounced the book, it nevertheless created a public furor and helped to give reading instruction its high visibility. The polarized debate aroused public concern, which in turn influenced policy decisions for funding and for the establishment and certification of experts in reading. This context of concern contributed to the growth of the ranks of professionals and the influence of IRA. During this period, the position of "reading specialist" began to emerge as a new field of expertise. By 1956 there were reading specialists in both schools and colleges, and by 1960 seven states had sanctioned the certification of reading specialists as a specific profession (Monaghan & Saul, 1987). The growth of the professionalization of reading instruction was also helped by the massive infusion of resources directed to it by President Johnson's Great Society policies. The Elementary and Secondary Education Act (ESEA) of 1965 provided more than a billion dollars to help disadvantaged children. Because no school subject was considered more important than reading, a substantial portion of the funding of ESEA was earmarked for remedial programs in reading under the Title I provision of the Act.

***Early IRA policy on response to issues.*** In contrast to the more direct role of NCTE in generating policy statements for English, the history of the IRA indicates that a number of IRA leaders sought to avoid taking policy stands because they "believed that it was best to avoid dissension" (Jerrolds, 1979, p. 145). One concludes from Jerrolds' history that it was the rare IRA president who entered into any sort of "controversy." Thus, President Donald L. Cleland's support for the "Right to Read" project in 1969 was an exception to the typical IRA leadership stance of nonalignment on policy issues. IRA established its first legislative committee in 1972.

IRA's first resolution committee was established in 1962 in response to Arthur I. Gates' urging of the leadership to respond to then current criticisms of the teaching of reading. Jerrolds (1979) reports on this first committee's restrictions on the content of resolutions:

[It] saw as its purpose the task of aiding the IRA in speaking out to educators and laypersons, nationally and internationally, with regard to critical issues in the teaching of reading. They decided to make a distinction between controversial issues and wholesale assaults on the reading program. The committee felt that controversial issues reflected honest differences of opinion; they were debatable and would not be the subject of resolutions by the IRA (p. 101).

According to Jerrolds (1979), the resolutions committee decided to answer only the "gross exaggerations" and "assaults" that could do "damage to the field of reading" (p. 101). It also agreed that resolutions would not attack persons or organizations and would be stated in general terms. But when the committee did consider a resolution recommending "that producers

of reading materials and devices make their publicity and advertising conform to professional standards of ethics and avoid exaggerated or unwarranted claims" (p. 101), this forthright position seemed to go too far for Gates, who served as advisor to the committee. He wrote, "I feel until the line of action and general intention of the International Reading Association in such matters are clear the committee should be cautious" (quoted in Jerrolds, 1979, p. 101).

The organization heeded Gates's advice: During the next two administrations the "resolutions" committee was called the "timely issues" committee; thereafter, it once again became a "resolutions" committee, but it continued to move very cautiously until the end of the 70s.

***Recent IRA policy on response to issues.*** In 1979, the IRA Board adopted its initial position statement on "minimum competencies" opposing the use of a single assessment as a basis to determine promotion or graduation. Since then, the IRA has regularly adopted and circulated board position statements and general assembly resolutions. During the 90s, the IRA became more active in its advocacy of policy, placing a representative in Washington, D.C. to disseminate information to legislators and other policymakers. Richard Long keeps watch on legislative developments relating to literacy and reports his findings in a column, "Washington Update" appearing regularly in IRA's bimonthly newspaper, *Reading Today*.

IRA's policy statements have ranged across such matters as "Misuse of Grade Equivalents" (1981), "Courts Should Not Make Reading Policy" (1981), "Ethnic Minorities in Teaching Materials" (1988), "Reading Assessment" (1988), "Textbook and Reading Program Censorship" (1988), "Role of Phonics in Reading Instruction" (1997), "Phonemic Awareness and the Teaching of Reading" (1998), "Learning to Read and Write: Developmentally Appropriate Practices for Young Children" (a joint position statement of IRA and the National Association for the Education of Young Children (NAEYC; 1998), and "Using Multiple Methods of Beginning Reading Instruction" (1999).

In developing its most recent policy document, "High Stakes Assessment Statement," IRA turned to its new technology to gather reactions to its draft form. Its writers posted the statement in the "Critical Issues" section of IRA's electronic journal *Reading Online* (www.readingonline.org). Readers were invited to review it and make comments. The final version presented in the form of a question-and-answer dialog decries unthinking acceptance of high-stakes testing. It calls for a "common sense" look at the way testing is used in schools today. It emphasizes the point that "to be opposed to large-scale, high-stakes testing is not to be opposed to assessment or accountability. It is a call to align our purposes and goals with our methods" (*Reading Today*, 1999, p. 27).

IRA has moved beyond its early practice disdaining political advocacy to the point where it issues timely position statements on literacy issues. Yet its primary goals remain focused on improving the quality of reading instruction through the study of the reading process and teaching techniques and the dissemination of reading research through conferences, journals, and the internet (www.reading.org). When he was the director of

IRA's Division of Research and Development, Alan A. Farstrup, who later became Executive Director, explained IRA's role as a forum for clarification of ideas:

There are many, widely varying points of view and philosophies represented within the Association. I view the Association as a forum for the competition and clarification of these ideas and philosophies rather than as an institution whose job it is to advocate specific points of view unless there is a strong consensus across the entire membership with regard to particular issues. Certainly when the question revolves around matters of basic literacy and the importance of literacy we can all agree on the correct stance to adopt. When the issues revolve around contrasting, underlying philosophies of education—for example whether we should insist on highly structured teacher directed lessons or whether we should follow an approach where the teacher is not as directive— then the Association's role as an open forum becomes very important (Personal Communication, April 4, 1989).

***Major policy texts on reading.*** Several of the major policy statements about reading have come from outside the IRA. Other agencies have moved to fill the policy vacuum left by IRA's historic policy of nonalignment with the various positions on reading instruction. For example, in 1969, when James E. Allen, Jr., United States Commissioner of Education, sought information that would guide his proposed Right-to-Read program, he turned to the Committee on Reading, a special task force of the National Academy of Education (NAE). Six years later, the Committee issued its report, *Toward a Literate Society* (Carroll & Chall, 1975), with a number of policy recommendations for "a national strategy for attacking the reading problem," (p. 27) which included recommendations for legislative and administrative actions at federal, state, and local levels.

The next major policy document to appear was the *Yearbook of the National Society for the Study of Education, Becoming Readers in a Complex Society* (Purves & Niles, 1984), under the joint editorship of Alan Purves, a past president of the NCTE and Olive Niles, a past president of the IRA. In it are a number of policy positions advanced from the individual perspectives of the contributors rather than as official representations of viewpoints of their respective professional associations.

Seeking that ever-elusive consensus on research-based principles for teaching reading, the National Academy of Education sponsored another major policy document on reading, *Becoming a Nation of Readers* (Anderson, Hiebert, Scott, & Wilkinson, 1985). It was developed by the Commission on Reading of the NAE, this time with the sponsorship of the National Institute of Education (NIE) and with research support from the Center for the Study of Reading (CSR), which also prepared the manuscript.

As the "reading wars" intensified in the 90s, the National Research Council once again embarked on a project to seek out the "substantial agreed-upon results" of empirical research "that could form a basis for breaching the differences among the warring parties" (p. v). The resulting 400-page comprehensive synthesis of research, *Preventing Reading Difficulties in Young Children* (Snow, Burns, & Griffin, 1998) was followed a year later by a reader friendly brief treatment intended for parents and teachers, *Starting Out Right: A Guide to Promoting Young Children's Reading Success* (Burns, Griffin, & Snow, 1999).

Although the IRA may not have sponsored the major policy documents on reading, it has not been without influence on the curriculum in reading. Most of the leading reading experts are members. They are doing the seminal research in the field, and according to Goodman, Shannon, Freeman, and Murphy (1988), they are writing the reading curricula of the nation under contract to the publishers of basal readers. The IRA joined with the NCTE to develop two major standards documents: *Standards for the Assessment of Reading and Writing* (National Council of Teachers of English and International Reading Association, 1994) and *Standards for the English Language Arts* (National Council of Teachers of English and International Reading Association, 1996).

## POLITICS AND THE STANDARDS DEVELOPMENT PROCESS AT NCTE AND IRA

When the Goals 2000 agenda (described in the following) called for the creation of national and state content and performance standards for what students know and can do in nine subject areas, it initiated the political process to establish national standards for English language arts. The Standards Project for English Language Arts was originally financed by the Fund for Improvement and Reform of Schools and Teaching of the U.S. Office of Research and Improvement. The Project was conceived as a 3 year collaborative effort of the Center for the Study of Reading, the International Reading Association, and the National Council of Teachers of English beginning in September 1992.

In our profession there are many competing views and commitments about the nature and processes of English language arts. Consequently, the leadership of the Standards Project inaugurated a broad-based grass roots approach to develop theory and research-based content and process standards with the consensus of teams of teachers around the country. For 18 months the Standards Project weathered widespread differences within the profession to come up with a draft consensus document. This product provoked a number of critiques inside the profession and attracted a devastating rejection from the U.S. Department of Education. In 1994 the Department of Education halted the Standards Project funding on the grounds that it had not made "substantial progress toward meeting its objectives." The proposed standards "are vague and often read as platitudes," and they focus too much on process rather than content, declared Janice Anderson, the interim director of the funding agency (as quoted by Marzano & Kendall, 1997, p. 32). Miles Myers, former executive director of NCTE, concluded that what the Department of Education sought was a "behaviorist" rather than a "constructivist" standards document and failed to "appreciate *both* the products and processes of language" (April 1, 1994 Memo to NCTE Executive Committee as quoted in Milner, 1997, p. 135).

In 1994, even though action on standards had shifted from the national scene to the states with the Republican control of Congress, the NCTE and the IRA agreed to underwrite financially the completion of the standards. According to Milner (1997), the leadership of NCTE and IRA considered it worthwhile to proceed with development of a document that could provide a model for states and local districts. Milner recounts the convolutions of the whole development process through to its successful completion in 1996 with the NCTE/IRA *Standards for the English Language Arts.*

Immediately upon their release, the Standards met a barrage of criticism in the press. They were faulted for their lack of "benchmarks" or behavioral objectives for each grade level and their omission of booklists. Most commonly they were called vague. The NCTE and the IRA decided to fire back at the critics, according to the *Council Chronicle* (June, 1996). One month after their release, the two organizations ran a quarter-page reply to the critics headlined "Sense about Nonsense—Critics of English Standards Miss the Point" (p. 16). Few of the media critics understood the function of the Standards as guidelines and principles, leaving details for development at state and local levels. However, Rick Segal, Director of Microsoft Corporation's Education On-Line did see the point when he commented

What is particularly impressive about the standards for the English language arts is the degree to which they accommodate changes in language, and cultural progress, including technology. Without unduly restricting curriculum or methods, the standards provide a lens for educators, administrators, parents, and the community at large to focus their discussions and choices for the language education of students (*Council Chronicle*, 1996, June, p. 4).

In 1997, the General Educational Development (GED) Testing Service of the American Council on Education (ACE) completed a review of the NCTE/IRA standards, the New Standards Project, the reading and writing frameworks of the U.S. Department of Education's National Assessment of Educational Progress (NAEP), the College Board's Pacesetter Project, and the National Writing Project. The GED's test specialists also looked at the English language arts documents from a selected sample of 10 states (*Council Chronicle*, April, 1997). They found "'remarkable' similarities between national and state documents; . . . they also found 'strong parallels' between the U.S. Department of Education's NAEP tests and the NCTE/IRA standards" (p. 5).

Miles Myers (1997) described the standards movement in NCTE as part of an overall effort to understand and explain the "new literacy of interpretation and understanding" and its programs in K-12 schools. He asserts that the profession has met the challenge of developing standards and materials for the new literacy despite politically motivated criticisms about emphasis on multicultural themes in literature and the absence of test items and mandates to teach specific grammatical items in particular grades. However, he acknowledges that despite these efforts to make the new literacy more understandable, many state policymakers still don't use the standards document to guide them. They continue to make dubious fundamental changes in English language arts curriculum and its assessment.

***The new standards project and literacy assessment.*** Pearson, Spalding, and Myers (1998) describe the background and development of the Literacy Unit of the New Standards Project that continues to devote itself to using assessment as an

"engine of reform" (p. 55) in our schools. Its architects—Lauren Resnick of the Learning, Research and Development Center at the University of Pittsburgh, Daniel Resnick of Carnegie Mellon University, and Mark Tucker of the Center for the Education and the Economy, Washington, D.C.— built a conceptual framework based on the idea that "the problem is not that teachers teach to the test but that teachers need tests worth teaching to" (p. 55). Hence, New Standards has sought to develop new broader, more authentic forms of assessment in reading, speaking, writing, science, and mathematics. The Literacy Unit of New Standards contracted with NCTE during the years 1991–1996 to carry forward its work. These new performance assessments were to be based on the content standards under development in various professional organizations. In the case of the Literacy Unit this meant working with the draft versions of the content standards being developed jointly by the National Council of Teachers of English and the International Reading Association, according to Pearson, Spalding, and Myers (1998).

In its ambitious program to reform American schools through the development of high standards and worthy assessment, the project enlisted 24 partners, including 17 states and seven large school districts. These became the proving grounds for the New Standards for engaging students and teachers in the design and trial of performance tasks, portfolios, exhibits, and ultimately a "reference examination" (Pearson, Spalding, & Myers, p. 75) that consists of multiple choice and short task components.

In summing up what they learned from the New Standards work, Pearson, Spalding, and Myers (1998) discuss several impressions, but the following observation is key:

Our experience with teachers in New Standards underscores the importance of teacher knowledge and the construct of a community of professional judgment. We found that at every stage along the way—from task development, to implementation, to scoring—the key element in whatever success we experienced was bringing teachers together to examine and to wrestle with, both collaboratively and dialectically, the question of what counts as evidence of quality in student work. . . . We also learned a lot about sustaining a reform effort. New Standards was, and to a degree still is, nothing short of an attempt to reform the instructional landscape of schools in the United States (pp. 77-78).

This very brief account of New Standards appears here as an interesting example of policymakers from different realms coming together to achieve certain reform goals. The actors came from professional associations, foundations, university research units, state education offices, and schools. At play in this enterprise were four of the five "instruments" described by Chrispeels (1997): inducements, capacity-building, system-changing, and hortatory texts. Missing in this voluntary association were mandates.

***Mandates from outside the profession.*** Outside the profession of the English language arts there are policymakers within the three levels of governance who have authority to mandate both broad and specific public policies impinging upon the English language arts. These policymaking agents include U.S. presidents and secretaries of education at the national level, state governors and legislators, state school boards and state superintendents of instruction, local school boards, local administrators, community pressure groups, jurists, testmakers, textbook publishers, unions, private foundations, and university academics. These policymakers collaborate or compete to attain the political arrangements they desire, making deals to shape the dominant trends in public educational policy. During the last 25 years, these agents have often moved in the name of accountability to constrain the discretionary powers of teachers as "grass roots" policymakers in the school.

## POWER AND CONTROL AT THE FEDERAL LEVEL

### The Power of the Presidential Office

The federal government does not have the power to control local public schools directly. But it does have the constitutional authority to control the spending of federal money. Thus, it has the power to advance its policies though the inducement of funding. If a state school system is reluctant to adopt certain programs, materials, or curricula, the federal government can "persuade" that system to adopt these changes by granting it money. According to Joel Spring (1985), the pattern that emerged in the 1970s found the American school system functioning under three levels of control: federal, state, and local. State governments imposed regulations and requirements on local districts, which in turn administered these regulations and requirements in terms of local needs. Additionally, the federal government intervened in state and local educational policies by providing the money and planning for innovative programs under provisions of the Elementary and Secondary Education Act (ESEA) and, later, under ESEA amendments such as the Bilingual Education legislation.

Until the establishment of Title VI of the 1964 Civil Rights Act as part of President Johnson's Great Society, the United States Office of Education (USOE) had traditionally defined its role as a servant of the state and local educational systems. Given the doctrine of local control and the opposition to federal control, the Office of Education disbursed money usually with a minimum of requirements and regulation. However Title VI established the precedent for using federal funds as a means of controlling state and local educational policy, completely reversing the traditional relationship. Title VI required the withholding of federal funds from institutions practicing racial, religious, or ethnic discrimination. In 1972, Title IX of the Higher Education Act extended federal protection of civil rights to include means of ending sex discrimination and further expanded the activities of the Office of Education into writing guidelines to end discrimination in schools.

At the end of the Carter administration, the U.S. Office of Education became a separate Department of Education in 1980, with cabinet status for its secretary. President Reagan came to office in 1980 favoring termination of the Department of Education. He cut its budget and staff, rendering its continued existence precarious. Reagan wanted to reduce federal power over local school systems by giving greater administrative control to state and local governments. His administration sought to achieve this objective by revoking existing rules and regulations and by reducing the level of enforcement. Within a year of President Reagan's election, the Department of Education had revoked 30 sets of rules governing 19 programs. Joel Spring (1985) sees in this circumstance an important political lesson

in the real power of the presidential office to control and shape educational policies. Congress can pass legislation, and the courts can make decisions regarding education, but how that legislation is carried out and how the court decisions are applied depend on the actions of the executive branch of the federal government (p. 197).

*Federal involvement with research.* In the early 1970s policymakers began to argue that past educational policy and programs had failed because research had not been conducted before implementation. Thus, during the administration of President Richard Nixon in the early 70s came the establishment of the National Institute of Education (NIE), created as a vehicle to make wise use of available government funds for educational research. By designating priority areas, the NIE established a new research agenda in reading and writing for the educational community. To overcome problems of fragmented educational research, the USOE had earlier established (circa 1966) a total of 14 centers and 20 laboratories to mount large-scale research on major educational concerns. But once established, the regional laboratories and the R & D centers found survival precarious as successive administrations struggled to gain control of these institutions against congressional resistance. By 1988 there remained only 6 labs and 10 R & D centers to sponsor the bulk of federally funded educational research. Among the R & D centers were separate centers for the study of reading, writing, and literature.

The power of the presidential office to shape educational policies through controls implemented by federal education agencies is especially evident in the history of the fate of educational research under several administrations. The story of shifting federal priorities with increasing trends toward politicization of research agendas is traced in a collection of articles (Justiz & Bjork, 1988) published for the American Council on Education. These articles track the development of a succession of federal agencies charged with initiating, funding, and overseeing research conducted in the nation's institutions of higher education. In 1988, Clark and Astuto reported that the level of support for the unsolicited grants programs has shrunk to the $1.0 million level of 1956, when the Cooperative Research Program was first funded.

*The U.S. secretary of education.* The chief agent in executing the presidential agenda for education is the Secretary of the Department of Education. Terrel H. Bell, who held this position in the Reagan administration, remarked, "We could have changed the course of history in American education if the President had stayed with the issue through the implementation phase of the school reform movement" (quoted in Miller, 1987, p. 1), upon reviewing his years of service under President Reagan. Bell rather quietly appointed the National Commission on Excellence in Education on August 26, 1981, naming as chairman, David Gardner, then president of the University of Utah. Given the Reagan administration's agenda for dismantling the Department of Education, its curtailment of federal spending, and its advocacy of controversial polices, such as tuition tax credits and school prayer, many of the members of the Commission were dubious about its prospects, according to Lynn Olson (1988) who has studied early drafts of *A Nation at Risk*, staff memoranda, letters, and other Commission papers hitherto unavailable.

When it came out in April 1983, the Commission's report, *A Nation at Risk: The Imperative for Educational Reform* jolted the nation with its grim message about a "rising tide of mediocrity" in our educational system. This report had a major impact on education even though many of its recommendations were not realized. Its recommendations focused on five areas:

1. Stronger content in high school as reflected in Five New Basics that included 4 years of English.
2. More rigorous and measurable standards and higher expectations for academic performance and student conduct.
3. More time, more effectively used for learning the New Basics.
4. Better prepared, better rewarded and more highly respected teachers.
5. Public commitment to providing leadership and funding necessary to achieve these reforms.

The report set off reverberations through the states, and many of its recommendations were echoed in a flurry of further reform reports. Coming out the year before the presidential election, the report afforded a useful vehicle to Reagan for projecting an image of himself as a friend of education. Guthrie and Koppich (1988) describe how he seized the moment:

For the first time in any significant way since the days of Theodore Roosevelt, the nation experienced effective use of the Presidential "bully pulpit". President Reagan was quick to recognize the significance of *A Nation at Risk* and the intense public concern it had awakened. He made repeated statements regarding the importance of renewed educational rigor to the nation's future. He admonished state and local officials, as well as parents and educators, to make the changes necessary to restore America's schools to their past levels of prominence. He was careful to specify, however, that the financial burden of reform, if there was any, should be borne by states and localities (p. 29).

## Nationwide Reform Movements

*A demand for rigor.* The publication of *A Nation at Risk* prompted a wave of top-down education reform during the Reagan presidency, consisting mainly of state mandates to raise academic standards (e.g., California was pushed to require 4 years of English). States attempted to increase rigor by boosting graduation requirements, expanding student achievement testing, and introducing teacher testing. Most of these reforms were intended to cost little in the way of new money.

*Restructuring.* By the late 1980s the failure of this initial top-down reform strategy mounted and motivated a second wave of education reform called *restructuring*. This countermovement to change one school at a time encouraged decentralized governance, more participative styles of school management, more active, constructivist styles of school learning, and more varied forms of assessment. Wirth (1992) reported 40 or more approaches to the restructuring concept, however, he cited a 1990 MIT study on minority education that estimated that "probably no more than 1 to 2 percent of American schools are involved in some kind of restructuring" (p. 107).

*Systemic reform.* Meanwhile at the state level of governance, centralizing forces were introducing complex statewide educational reforms that came to be known as *systemic* reform. This policy approach attempts to bring coherence to all educational components—curriculum, textbooks, testing, teacher preparation—much as described in then California State Superintendent of Instruction Honig's policies of "alignment" described later in this chapter. Top-down broad-scale systemic reform has increasingly moved governors, state superintendents, and state legislatures into new power relations as policymakers for local schools, diminishing the strength of local control.

*Private management of schools.* Traditionally, concepts of ownership and profit have been missing from education. But a decade of berating American education has resulted in the promotion of even so drastic a reform as the idea that perhaps government should get out of schooling. A widely held belief that free market forces invariably produce better results than governmental institutions is countered by *Hard Lessons: Public Schools and Privatization* (Ascher, Fruchter, & Berne, 1996) a Twentieth Century Fund report that provides strong evidence that privatization is being oversold, often used as a desperate but inadequate solution to underfunded urban public schools. They conclude that no empirical evidence to date demonstrates the superiority of private management of schools. Ernest R. House (1998) explains in *Schools for Sale* why the market is an untrustworthy instrument of change. He describes how politically driven proposals to employ market forces of vouchers, competition, and privatization fail because they ignore how schools work and how students learn.

## Standards-Based Reform

Centralizing forces emerged at the federal level when Congress passed the Goals 2000 Educate America Act (1994). The legislation closely reflected the six national goals for education that were first announced by President Bush and the nation's governors (among them then Governor Bill Clinton of Arkansas). President Clinton made standards-based reform a central feature of his educational policy. The Goals 2000 legislation was designed to refocus federal education support to promote national standards and a system of assessment of student achievement. The legislation contained language making it clear that federal funding would go to those states emulating the "voluntary" national goals, standards, and tests. Goals 2000 was amended in 1996, and it may be amended again as the dominant political forces regroup. The national testing provisions remained unoeffled until 2001. Nevertheless, the Act generated enormous momentum in professional associations (including NCTE), state agencies, and local districts for developing content standards and assessment systems.

Although the Goals 2000 program had strong bipartisan support reaching back to the first Bush administration, by the mid-90s it was being attacked by both ends of the political spectrum. Conservatives claimed it erodes local control and is intended to instill in students state-sanctioned attitudes, values, and beliefs. Progressive educators argued that the standards driven reform is an attempt to centralize power over education. They considered standards and high-stakes testing to be misguided control mechanisms that consume scarce funds without addressing the real problems of educating a diverse society for the 21st century (Clinchy, 1997). *One Size Fits Few* (Ohanian, 1999) expresses one progressive language arts teacher's counter argument against the folly of attempting to inject externally developed standards into the realities of everyday life in modern multicultural classrooms. She argues that "America's teachers don't need national committees to grade their worth. We need local teachers to reflect on their own experiences, to figure out how the students, the curriculum, and even the bureaucracy interact in a process we call education" (p. 151).

### Equity and opportunity to learn standards.

Because of the enormous variability of student experiences in U.S. schools, a strong equity argument supports the standards movement. Porter (1995) identifies the origin of opportunity to learn standards: "The initial motivation for OTL standards stems from an equity concern that high-stakes assessments of student achievement are fair only if students have an adequate opportunity to learn the content assessed in those high-stakes tests" (p. 41). In a democratic society it is unjust that students of different races or that students who happen to live in a poor urban district instead of an affluent suburb should have unequal educational experiences.

Early in the standards movement, questions arose about equality of access to qualified teachers, resources and technologies, and safe, well-maintained schools. Clearly all students in America do not start from an equal base of support. Thus, the notion of "opportunity to learn standards" or "delivery standards" arose in contrast to "content" standards that focused on "what students know and can do." The proponents of this view argue that content and performance standards enforced apart from delivery standards might result in misused test scores and practices damaging to disadvantaged students. They contend it does no good to require uniform standards without setting up an equal playing field that makes the performance demands feasible and fair for all participants.

The original Goals 2000 legislation took a "fairly soft stand" (Porter, 1995, p. 42) on opportunity to learn standards. At the national level such standards would be voluntary. The states were expected to create OTL standards, but these would not be reviewed or approved at the federal level. The partisan split in Congress over OTL—the Democrats want them; the Republicans want them dropped—presages a weakening, if not elimination as long as the Republicans are in power. Porter concludes (1995) that "while the federal role in OTL standards does not appear to be headed toward heavy influence on what states will

do, several states seem persuaded on their own to take OTL standards seriously" (p. 62).

### The "pain of standards".

When President Clinton and 117 leaders—28 governors, 21 state school superintendents, and 34 executives—assembled in an education summit in October 1999, all states except Iowa had detailed academic standards. Although more than half of the states test students on the standards, only 16 reward or sanction schools on the basis of their pupils' achievement. At the 1996 summit, only 14 states had developed standards. The increase in state participation had been stimulated by federal funding. Richard Lee Colvin (1999, October 1) of the *Los Angeles Times* explained that

The president has given teeth to the standards movement through changes to the $8-billion Title I program that aids disadvantaged students. The administration now requires states to have standards against which to measure the progress of schools receiving that money. By next year [2000], states that get the federal funds must have tests based on those standards that show how different types of students compare.... Another issue that must be addressed is the growing achievement gap between minority students on the one hand and white and Asian students on the other (p. A17).

The impressive acceleration of state standards adoption has yet to deliver. Participants acknowledged that the emphasis on standards had not yet transformed teaching and learning. Many states were reporting failure of students to meet state objectives, leading to the temptation, some participants feared, to water down rigorous standards and eliminate tests. Louis V. Gestner, the chairman of I.B.M. and co-chair of the conference with Wisconsin Governor, Tommy G. Thompson, said in an interview that

the current gathering will focus on what he call "the pain," which he defines as the sting that teachers, principals, and students feel when they realize that they are now being held accountable for their performance and will be disciplined accordingly (Steinberg, 1999, p. A16).

According to Jacques Steinberg of the *New York Times*, the conference briefing book assembled by Gerstner and Thompson discloses the states' experience with standards, "warts and all."

They write for example that many states have crammed their standards with so many topics to memorize as to paralyze students, and then have written tests that bear no connection to the standards (p. A16).

David Hoff (1999), writing in *Education Week*, reported that now tests tied to high standards are starting to deliver bad news.

[M]any parents, civil rights activists, and educators are questioning the wisdom of standardizing the curriculum and relying on test scores for such decisions as student promotion and high school graduation (p. 9).

In the same issue of *Education Week* Zehr (1999) reported that a lawsuit, *GI Forum, et al. v. Texas Education Agency*, has been filed against the Texas graduation exam. A federal district court will hear arguments that the Texas Assessment of Academic Skills violates the constitutional and civil rights of black and Hispanic students. The exam containing three parts—reading, writing and mathematics—is intended to encompass what students have learned by the end of ninth grade. The failure rate in February 1997 among blacks and Hispanics was more than twice that of whites. Because minority students are "disproportionately negatively affected" (p. 14), the counsel for the plaintiffs, Albert H. Kauffman, argues that the Texas test violates the due process clause of the 14th Amendment of the U.S. Constitution and Title VI of the Civil Rights Act of 1964. The case could set a new precedent with national repercussions.

## POWER AND CONTROL AT THE STATE LEVEL

### Growth of State Power

The Tenth Amendment to the Constitution of the United States specifies that "the powers not delegated to the United States by the Constitution, nor prohibited by it to the States, are reserved to the States respectively, or to the people." Since the Constitution makes no reference to education, this function is reserved to the states. The provision of state constitutions coupled with this Amendment have been taken to mean that the burden of policymaking for schools falls on state governments. But for most of this century, school management, finance, and politics were local issues. Although the state held the constitutional authority to oversee public education, it did not exercise its full powers until recent decades, leaving it to the boards at local levels to create the basic policies governing schools. Education was hardly ever "big news."

After 1965 the shift of power from the local authority to the state was dramatic and swift. Ironically, the federal government created the conditions for this expansion of state power with the infusion of funds from the Elementary and Secondary Education Act (ESEA) of 1965 and the need to create mechanisms to approve local projects. Wirt and Kirst (1982) document the striking increase in state legislated control of education. The main areas of regulation included state administration of federal grants and finance, programs for children with special needs, requirements for accountability, and efforts to stimulate experimentation. The growth of accountability mandates illustrates one area of expansion in state control. Wirt and Kirst (1982) report that between 1966 and 1976, 35 states passed laws mandating various forms of accountability dealing with teacher evaluation, assessment of curricula to meet state standards, setting of objectives for local education authorities, and minimum competency standards for high school graduation. Some 4,000 reports about these activities were published in this period. Wirt and Kirst (1982) assert that "local control as a value and operational fact has declined to the vanishing point" (p. 196). Today the state is increasingly inclined to oversee all state educational business. The initiators of policy at the state level usually include the legislature, the governor, and the chief state school officer.

### The Legislature and the Governor As Policymakers

By the beginning of the 1980s educational issues had climbed to the top of the list of priorities in the state legislatures across the land. The states responded swiftly and intensively to *A Nation at Risk* and other reports on the decline of education. Between 1982 and 1984, over 200 state commissions were formed to review the status of education and make recommendations for its improvement. Many state legislatures immediately enacted omnibus education bills. California's reform vehicle, Senate Bill 813, contained more than 80 provisions. There proved to be a remarkable similarity from state to state in the rhetoric of the educational excellence movement and its realization through the provisions of state-level educational reform legislation.

During the last 2 decades, there has been a notable uniformity in educational policies across the states. Some analysts ascribe this consistency in practice as arising from the fact that the governors and state legislators share a common pool of resources to draw on for guidance in determining the policy stances they will take. Joel Spring (1988), for example, attributes this nationalization of state policies to the work of three organizations: the National Governors' Association, the Council of Chief State School Officers, and the Education Commission of the States. He illustrates how uniformity in policy between states occurs through the strengthening of ties between governors in the activities of an agency such as the Education Commission of the State (ECS) in its development of task force reports such as *Action for Excellence*. ECS was founded in 1965 as a "non-profit, nationwide interstate compact. The primary purpose of the commission is to help governors, state legislators, state education officials and others to develop policies to improve the quality of education at all levels" (Green, 1987, p. iv).

In 1986, the National Governors' Association under the leadership of Governor Lamar Alexander of Tennessee (later named Secretary of Education by President George Bush) issued its own school reform report, *Time for Results*. In it the state governors signaled their intention to began a national initiative to align standards and tests. The governors' ideas were to take even more significant shape when in July 1990, President Bush and the 50 state governors formed the National Education Goals Panel (NEGP) to assess and report progress toward achievement of six national goals as part of the America 2000 program. What came next under President Clinton has been described previously in the standards based reform section.

### "Reforms" California Style: A Cautionary Tale

What has happened in California in 1977 and 1998 could be a harbinger of the future in other states (Pearson, 1999, p. 245).

. . . the truth of the matter is that kinds of statewide curriculum decisions currently being made in California and the highly charged political atmosphere in which they are being made also are occurring or are likely to occur in a host of other nations, states, cities, and individual schools (International Reading Association Board of Directors *Reading Today*, October, 1999, p. 3-4).

*A turbulent policy context.* California has the largest state school system in the nation, with a student population of more than 5 million. By the mid-90s one fourth of the school population was comprised of students whose first language was not English. One third of the state's half million first graders begin school speaking only limited English or no English. By 1993, more than half of the state's high school graduates were non-white, a record unmatched by any other state (Schrag, 1998).

In the 90s, the status of California's underfunded system plummeted. Yet, just after World War II California was considered a model for the nation with its much admired, well-supported public education system and its nearly free higher education of state universities and community colleges. But following the tax-cutting Proposition 13 in 1978 and a host of other voter initiatives since then, California has regressed to become one of the most socially backward states in the nation. In 1994, Californians voted to exclude all illegal alien children from public schools. In 1996 they voted to prohibit every form of race- or gender-based affirmative action in public employment contracting and in education. And in June 1998 Californians voted to eliminate bilingual education.

*Curriculum by Consensus: 1984–1994.* Traditionally, the states have allowed curriculum content specifications to be developed at the local level. The state education office has sometimes specified course titles and issued advisory curriculum frameworks. Major curriculum instruments were only loosely related, having been developed within different administrative units of a state department. State achievement tests developed in one unit were not always closely aligned with the curriculum frameworks and the textbook specifications generated in other units. This was the case in California, until a policy of "curriculum alignment" was adopted. The criticism of local district standards in reform documents such as *A Nation at Risk* spurred the efforts of state departments of education to adopt new more stringent methods of influencing local academic efforts.

Chrispeels (1997) has analyzed 10 years of policy initiatives to reform curriculum in California's schools. She describes the nature of her study as follows:

By examining the types of policy instruments used, comparing the policy texts and juxtaposing these to the written and oral texts of educators from this region, the study shows how the enactment of policies over this period created a coherent policy system for California educators, built the capacity of local leaders to shape and interpret these policies and influenced classroom practices. The analysis made visible how these three factors—coherence, capacity building, and changed practices—sustained local educators in pursuing alternative assessment even when a policy void was created at the state level by the veto of funding for the new assessment system (p. 453).

Chrispeel's work explains the interrelationships of the California frameworks, textbook selection, assessment, and professional development. The frameworks served an important hortatory purpose in guiding reform. Drawing on the latest research about teaching and learning, the frameworks provided guidelines on how to create more student-centered classrooms with students actively engaged in constructing knowledge. To speed adoption of recommended practices and build teacher capacity, curriculum projects housed at various campuses were established. To build the cadre of classroom leaders in the English language arts, the California Writing Project and The Literature Project were founded.

Chrispeels (1997) does an intertextual analysis of a variety of policy texts beyond the frameworks to show how

local actors were involved in new ways of governance, innovation, and capacity building. These policy initiatives were seen as supporting an interactive and developmental policy process between local stakeholders and state policymakers ... thus redefining who counted as leaders in their region.... [D]istricts and schools served as models of exemplary practice that were to be used by the state to guide its policy development, not merely as implementers of state policies.... As administrators and teachers worked to implement the policies, they were engaged in joint construction of the policies through their own interpretations and sense-making (pp. 462–463).

Even though the capacity building reforms were moving ahead and many teachers had participated in the curriculum projects, critics felt that changes in classrooms were not happening fast enough. So policymakers looked at an assessment system and saw that while teachers were being invited to change their ways, students were still being tested on discrete points of knowledge. The policymakers recognized the need to move the testing system into alignment with the curriculum. Thus arose the need to create the innovative California Learning Assessment System.

When these reforms were taking place, California's most influential education leader was not the governor but the state superintendent of instruction. Bill Honig came into this office with a plan for reform that he hoped to foster. Honig's reform efforts in the English language arts begun in 1983 came to fruition in the *English Language Arts Framework for California Public Schools, Grades K-12* (California State Department of Education, 1987). The *Framework* endorsed among other things:

- A literature-based English language arts program for all students, giving attention to a range of thinking processes through focus on ethical, aesthetic, and cultural values.
- The integration of listening, speaking, reading, and writing and the teaching of language skills in meaningful contexts.
- A school environment where teachers of all subjects encourage students to read widely, to write frequently, and to listen and speak effectively.
- Teacher preparation programs in the English language arts that ensure that teachers are prepared to implement an effective program of instruction.
- Assessment of the full range of goals of the language arts program with alternative methods other than the common sta1ndardized tests.

Once the *English Language Arts Framework for California Public Schools.* (Framework) was in place, the adoption of instructional materials compatible with it became the next step. That adoption process was completed in June 1988. The policy implications of this adoption were reviewed in the NCTE *Council-Gram* (January, 1989):

The [California] board of education in that influential state has adopted a policy of switching from basal readers to literature-based textbooks to help its three-million-plus elementary students learn to read. Further, it has cut its purchases of workbooks and flash cards used for drill by about one-fourth. "Such material was seen as taking time away form direct reading and writing," David S. Wilson reported in the *New York Times* October 19 [1988], "The decision to rely on anthologies and novels in original form rather than [on] what were portrayed as less imaginative, 'dumbed-down' texts is expected to influence other states and the plans of book publishers," Wilson added, noting that 10 percent of the country's textbook purchases are made by California. [The state board] is also requiring publishers to label any stories that have been adapted or abridged. And the board has "encouraged teachers to give students more time to read in class" (p. 6).

The reform strategies completed so far made sense to the English language arts profession because there had been extensive involvement of teachers from all levels in the development of standards and curriculum. The next adjustment needed was in the state mandated English language arts achievement tests. An English Language Arts Assessment Task Force recognized the influence of traditional tests as a significant barrier to the full implementation of the innovative *Framework*. Unless assessment measures and practices were revised to focus on literature-based, student-constructed expression of meaning, classroom practices were likely to remain rooted in a formalistic, specific skills-based approach. Development committees for a new kind of test went to work around the state. The result was a revolutionary, performance-based, teacher-developed integrated test of reading and writing, which allowed for various modes of initial response to a story, and even provided time for group discussions about it.

In 1993, California administered the first version of its innovative California Learning Assessment System (CLAS) program to about 1 million students in Grades 4, 8, and 10, and in 1994 the state offered a revised version. This was the start of something new in California assessment, but it was difficult to implement smoothly in its initial phase without more preparation of teachers and the public to understand its sound but radical approaches. By 1994, adverse political fallout had killed the whole program.

Almost immediately, CLAS became a target for the state's right-wing, who denounced the test as "subjective," as encouraging an "invasion of privacy," as being "uneconomical." This group was quick to find suspicious messages in the multicultural literature passages accompanying reading questions. Issues of race ran through the challenges to the content of the multicultural readings. A small, well-organized group of people led a sophisticated assault on CLAS. Their rhetoric disparaged the testmakers as professional educators. The professional expertise and testimony of the state's teacher consultants and other English language arts authorities were denigrated and dismissed as subjective and supportive of bad language and immoral content. They shrewdly co-opted the credibility of the concerned parent stance, insisting that they spoke "as California parents" interested in promoting objectivity in state testing. Yet their linkages with national ultraconservative organizations were evident in the spokespeople they assembled to appear before state board of education and legislative committee hearings. Themes

of fear and conspiracy evident in certain national conservative discourse about schooling surfaced in the public statements of the group.

Within 3 months, a few parents with conservative political agendas derailed the CLAS test that had been under development for 4 years. Then Governor Pete Wilson, one of a legion of possible Republican candidates for president, yielded to the ultraconservative political pressure and vetoed the legislation that would have continued the program, bringing to an end 10 years of long-term, consistent, comprehensive policies in the English language arts. Loss of leadership in the state senate and in the state superintendent's office, a change in the agenda of the governor, a poor showing on the National Assessment of Education Progress (NAEP) reading test and some other factors all contributed to the end of CLAS. But the story does not end here. Besides the longitudinal document analysis, Chrispeels (1997) also conducted a longitudinal study of implementation of the states' policies in 25 districts in San Diego County. She was interested in finding out what happened when the state shifted its policy direction. She found that "local school districts were continuing and expanding efforts to implement CLAS-like alternative assessments, while at the same time not abandoning traditional forms of testing student knowledge and skills" (p. 465). Surveys and interviews revealed that participants in professional development academies "had internalized the major concepts of the California Curriculum Frameworks.... [T]hey also valued the use of these [nontraditional teaching] strategies that improved learning for students.... [They] valued the need for more diverse ways of assessing what children know and are able to do" (p. 471).

***Curriculum by mandate: 1994–????.*** Electoral cycles shift who is in power, who decides curriculum and assessment policy. When Republican Governor Pete Wilson took office in 1991, the most visible and potent policymaker in education was the elected state superintendent, Bill Honig, who had run the schools during his 10 years in office. But a legal shift in the power balance of the state educational leadership has altered the policy origins of the plethora of policy initiatives that intend to radically change what happens in California classrooms, especially in English language arts. Asimov (1999) describes what happened:

Wilson quietly... transform[ed] 11 little-known gubernatorial appointees to the state Board of Education into a powerful policy-setting body that supersedes the elected superintendent and all but asks the governor how it should vote.... In the past year alone, Wilson's board reinstated phonics instruction, changed how math will be taught, installed a new state achievement test, established grade-by-grade academic standards and refused to consider school district requests to teach in languages other than English—all Wilson priorities (pp. A1, A11).

For most of its history, the Board had been in the background, adopting the state superintendent's recommendation. In 1991 with a new Republican governor in office, the Board (largely appointees of the immediately previous conservative Republican governor) took an unprecedented step in hiring its own lawyer to sue the superintendent for control of the schools. The Board and the governor had clashed with Superintendent Honig over a number of issues. "In 1993, the State Court of Appeals ruled that the superintendent must carry out Board policies, not the other way around" (Asimov, 1999, p. A11). Since this ruling, Wilson tripled the Board's budget to $1.6 million and doubled its staff to eight, while he cut the Department of Education's budget by 19% (Asimov, 1999).

This background is important because it provides insight into how politicized the process of developing language arts standards and frameworks has become under the purview of this Board. Decisions about what knowledge can be put before students and teachers in California schools, especially in the area of reading in the primary grades is at the center of California school politics. The construction of new policy texts, standards, frameworks, and advisories in English language arts, must be seen as a political process for allocating competing values as well as a technical process for selecting content.

The new policy initiatives in English language arts called for balanced and comprehensive reading and writing programs. To achieve this goal, the policy process between 1993–1999 would rely on (according to Chrispeels' [1997] analytic framework), a variety of policy mechanisms: legislative mandates, monetary inducements, and capacity building professional development programs. Unlike earlier frameworks and guidelines, the new mandates made a matter of law the content of English language arts instruction as spelled out in the new standards statements and content frameworks. Legislation was adopted to require "new" approaches to the teaching of early reading: the so-called "balance" meant concentrating on teaching phonics, phonemic awareness, decoding, word-attack skills, sound-symbol relationships, the structure of English, and spelling, all as explicit and discrete skills.

The policy directives also required teacher and preparation programs to be modified to include skills-based instruction in reading. The directives also specified the skills content of training programs that a school district must provide to be able to receive state and Goals 2000 funds. This is where the in-service provider scenario noted at the beginning of this chapter fits into to this account of policy developments in California. A provision of Assembly Bill 1086 (1997) specifically prohibits any in-service program that advocates "inventive" spelling or "embedded phonics" with being paid for by state funds. Providers must sign an "assurance clause," swearing to abide by the laws' prohibitions. Ohanian (1999) offers a telling account of how she and other distinguished members of NCTE and IRA were "banned in California" (pp. 96–99) when they submitted their course prospectus to become in-service providers.

The new policy texts for English language arts teaching in California are *English-Language Arts Content Standards for California Public Schools: Kindergarten Through Grade 12* (California State Department of Education, 1998) and *Reading Language Arts Framework for California Schools: Kindergarten Through Grade Twelve* (California State Department of Education, 1999). The introduction to the *Content Standards* represents this publication as a "strong consensus on the skills, knowledge, and abilities that all students should be able to master at specific grade levels during 13 years in the California public school system" (p. v). Who participated in the consensus is unclear, but who is responsible for its underlying mandate is crystal clear. These content standards were constructed

in accordance with *Education Code* section 60603, as added by Assembly Bill 265 (Chapter 975, Statutes of 1995), the Leroy Greene California Assessment of Academic Achievement Act, there will be performance standards that "define various levels of competence at each grade level . . . [and] gauge the degree to which a student has met the content standards." The assessment of student mastery of these standards is scheduled for no later than 2001 (p. v).

A late draft version of the *Framework* (June 12, 1998) reached the offices of IRA and prompted a response from the IRA Board of Directors in *Education Today* (International Reading Association Board of Directors, 1999, October/November), which outlined several areas of concern. They found an over-emphasis on decoding in the primary grades that offset the degree of balance found in the *Standards*. The draft expressed a limited view of comprehension centered on story structure. It lacked an adequate discussion of the writing process at all levels. Its detailed and prescriptive approach severely impinged on the rights and judgment of local districts and school boards. The board also took issue with the assessment model that emphasized pre- and post-testing specific skills in isolation. The Board further expressed its dismay over the neglect of multicultural literature in a state as diverse as California.

In the same issue, the president of the National Reading Conference (NRC) issued a statement that found wanting the narrow scope of the research base relied on to justify the emphasis of decoding in early grades. The NRC, devoted to the dissemination of literacy research in any form does not endorse particular theoretical perspectives. Missing from the reference list were many of the most notable names in reading research that one finds in standard works such as the *Handbook on Reading Research, Volumes I and II*.

The final draft of the *Framework* was approved by the State Board of Education at its December 1998 meeting. The published version released by the State Printing Office in 1999 awaits further review by the profession.

Among the cluster of new policy documents in California is one little known to the teaching profession, which provides the blueprint for holding schools and teachers accountable, *Steering by Results: A High Stakes Rewards and Intervention Program for California Schools and Students* (California State Department of Education, 1998). The major provisions of this document mandated by SB 1570 and completed in the waning days of the Wilson administration were enacted into law in 1999 during the new Democratic Governor Gray Davis's early days in office. The 40-member Commission on Rewards and Intervention is comprised of business people, professors, superintendents, directors of agencies, parents, and one classroom teacher. The Commission recommended developing a school performance index based on a state assessment test. The first year of testing would serve as a baseline for the school. The second year, the school would be categorized as one of the following types: Exemplary School, High Performing School, School on the Move, School in Need of Improvement, or Low Performing School. Along with this index of accomplishment, the Commission would establish a rewards program for successful schools and an intervention program to assist Schools in Need of Improvement and Low Performing Schools.

Gray Davis, as so many politicians in recent years, made education his chief priority. So after taking office in January 1999, he presented a legislative package of four education bills and won their approval by March. These bills included school accountability, a high school exit exam, peer assistance and review, and teacher and principal training programs in reading as well as summer reading academies for struggling readers, K-4. All became effective in summer of 1999 except the exit exam, which became effective January 1, 2000.

The school accountability bill put into law a version of the recommendations of the Rewards and Intervention Committee. Under this plan schools are ranked based on the tests in The Standardized Testing and Reporting program, commonly known as STAR. Currently, the only component of STAR is the multiple-choice, norm-referenced Stanford Achievement Test, 9th edition, commonly known as SAT 9 and described in the following. That test was administered in the late spring of 1999. On the basis of results from this test, 430 schools were identified as Low Performing Schools and received grants to fund the drafting of plans for improvement. Schools that fail to improve for 2 consecutive years face closing, the reassignment of teachers, and the dismissal of the principal (Colvin, 1999, October 1).

A logical progression of policy implementation would seem to move in stages first through development of standards, then creation of a framework, followed by development of an assessment closely aligned to its progenitors. High stakes uses of assessment data would be held in abeyance until all the pieces of the reform program were in place. That is not the way implementation of the new curriculun and assessment system has worked out in California. Once CLAS was dead, legislation soon followed to replace it, but the implementation of the newly mandated Standardized Testing and Reporting (STAR) system was slow to materialize. Finally, in 1998 at Governor Wilson's insistence, the state hastily undertook a new state testing program, the third one in less than a decade. Even though standards on which to base a state test had not yet completed, the California State Board of Education perversely adopted an "off-the-shelf" standardized commercial test, the Stanford Achievement Test, 9th edition (SAT 9) that was not the choice of the majority of school administrators in California.

The test forms administered in 1998 and 1999 were not aligned with California's standards or curriculum frameworks, which were then still under development when the deal for the SAT 9 was cut. Despite the fact that the SAT 9 does not test what is taught in California classrooms at any level, 4 million students in Grades 2 through 11 including all nonEnglish speaking students were required to take the test in these years. The 1999 form had an "augmented" section that included items aligned to standards, but not yet taught. These items were included to set benchmarks against which measurements could be taken in subsequent test administrations.

Colvin (1999), in referring to ranking and sanctioning of schools under Davis' accountability index, reports that "Such severe penalties, to be meted out at first, based solely on test scores, worry many educators, because many schools lack qualified teachers or other resources" (p. A17). There is ample evidence of lack of resources to be found in *Paradise Lost: California's Experience, America's Future*. Peter Schrag (1998)

demonstrates how the politics of retrenchment have taken their toll on education, libraries, social services, and social ethics. Schrag notes that California's schools are now in the bottom quarter of the nation in their physical condition, in public funding, and in test scores. A decade of tight budgets has produced crowded classrooms, unmaintained buildings, inadequate textbooks (too few and too old), reductions in course offerings, and layoffs of librarians, counselors, and nurses.

Intensifying the effects of severely overcrowded classrooms in California is the deteriorating physical environment. The General Accounting Office in two surveys prepared for Congress in 1996 found "California school facilities as being in the worst physical shape of any state, overall, excepting only the notoriously derelict schools of the District of Columbia" (Schrag, 1998, p. 71). The per pupil funding for California schools went from 6th or 8th in the nation in the 60s to 41st in the 90s. By 1995 to 1996, California was spending 20% below the national average on schooling (Schrag, 1998, pp. 15, 66). Slim budgets have resulted in a shocking lack of instructional material and computers: The NEA and the Association of American Publishers, for example, estimated that "54% of California teachers don't have enough textbooks to send home with their students" (Schrag, 1998, p. 68). Schrag provides telling examples of the materials shortages:

There are still reference works on California school shelves that have Eisenhower as president, science encyclopedias published in 1955 that speak hopefully about how one day man might fly to the moon, colonial era geography books that know nothing about Zaire or Zimbabwe, and etiquette books advising girls not to try to beat boys at their games (p. 67).

By the mid-90s public library service hours had declined 40% and "the state was dead last in its per capita library services" (Schrag, 1998, p. 101). It is hardly surprising that *Education Week*'s (January 22, 1997) report card on the condition of education in the 50 states summed up California's system, "once [a] world-class system, is now third-rate" (quoted in Schrag, 1998, p. 87).

The conditions in California suggest that setting standards and enacting tough accountability will not lead to the educational improvement desired unless basic weaknesses in the system are confronted. Outmoded notions of learning theory embedded in conceptions of curriculum that ignore recent research on cognitive development will not aid the recovery of learning in California schools no matter how strong the policy mandates. The research base in cognitive-science studies and applied work in early literacy is bursting with knowledge about how children learn; however, today's top-down curriculum policymaking embargoes use of much of that knowledge for enlightened practice in literacy development in California.

***Involvement in policymaking versus following mandates.*** Chrispeel's (1997) work shows how a consistent system of instructional guidance—including frameworks, curricular materials, capacity-building inservice projects, and appropriate accountability assessments—is fundamental to a long-term policy strand. For a decade, educational policy development in California was not top-down. There was interaction between state and local levels, and teachers and administrators were deeply involved in the policymaking and implementation process, e.g., framework development, textbook selection, piloting and scoring of CLAS. This high-quality involvement helped to develop teacher leaders and made gains toward professionalizing teaching. Districts had liberty to set standards and explore a variety of ways to assess learning. This model fostered a professional stance that included developing standards and assessments of student performance that were tailored to the needs of the individual student and the school.

If the primary goal of high-level policy decisions is largely to promote local initiative, California now seems embarked on the opposite policy course. Top-down mandates are legion. For example, teacher participation in the development of policy texts is minimal. Although the *Standards* and the *Framework* went through a pro forma field review process, the California Association of Teachers of English and the California Reading Association were not officially involved, unlike the collaborative process of developing the earlier frameworks. It seems emblematic of the policymakers' low regard for professional expertise in California that they selected Edward J. Kame'ennui and Deborah C. Simmons, *both from the University of Oregon*, to be the "primary authors" of the *California Framework in English Language Arts*. The trend in the new policy cycle seems to be one of excluding teachers from the policymaking processes in developing curriculum and approaches to accountability. The many kinds of sanctions now in place signal an expectation that teachers and administrators are merely to follow directives.

## State Control by Testing

***Politics of reform by testing.*** Educational testing has become a medium of political struggle in nation and state. In the 90s, more than ever before, it became necessary to grapple with the political character of educational testing. California furnishes a prime example of how politicians and special interest groups co-opted the testing debate to serve their own interests of claiming power and authority over curriculum. Tests are at the center of exercising power over curriculum and people. Popkewitz (1987a) states, "Power is exercised through the ability to assign categories that provide identity to those to whom the categories are to be applied. The techniques of sorting, classifying, and evaluating of people enable the exercise of sovereignty" (p. ix). Tests are now used to sort, classify, and evaluate students for placement, promotion, graduation, or college admission; teachers and administrators for certification, accountability, reward, or dismissal; school systems for accountability, reward, censure, or allocation of resources. The widespread replacement of human judgment by tests in decision-making processes in education results from practices where "Policymakers have mandated that the [test] results be used *automatically* to make such decisions" (Madaus, 1988, p. 87). Such has not always been the case.

George Madaus (1988) describes the evolution of the use of test results to inform policy. From the 1920s to the 1960s standardized tests had little or nothing to do with state or federal policy. But in the 1950s and 1960s the large expenditures for curriculum development and compensatory programs led federal and state policymakers to request student test data to appraise the effectiveness of these programs. So test scores began to be used as a primary indication of educational attainment. More recently the various educational reform reports have used National Assessment of Educational Progress (NAEP) and Scholastic Aptitude Test (SAT) data both to portray the mediocre state of American education and to lobby for programs to address the weaknesses. According to Madaus, the data from standardized tests have become an important source of the negative descriptions of the status of American education.

Where standardized tests once served primarily as indicators of achievement, they now have become the primary instrument of accountability. From the 1960s onward state legislatures have used such tests as a mechanism of power to leverage reforms. This growing use of tests in the policy sphere was revealed by a 50-state survey of reform measures conducted by *Education Week* in 1985: Thirty-seven states already had some type of assessment program, and six additional states were considering such a program (Madaus, 1988). By 1999, as previously reported all states but Iowa had some form of standards-based assessment system.

Now that the evolution to test-based accountability is virtually complete, various scholars are observing the occurrence of unintended policy consequences. Koretz (1988) questions these "unintended costs:"

[W]e must face the fact that test-based accountability has not always worked as advertised . . . there are disturbing signs that it has substantial unintended costs. In making measurement-driven educational policy a cornerstone of the reform movement, we have made a more powerful change in the educational system than many people anticipated (p. 48).

Madaus (1988), too, has noted the costs of measurement-driven policy, declaring that "It is testing, not the 'official' stated curriculum, that is increasingly determining what is taught, how it is taught, what is learned, and how it is learned" (p. 83).

***A profile of state testing at the century's end.*** Educational Testing Service (ETS) issued a Policy Information Report, *Testing in America's Schools* (Barton & Coley, 1994) that gives a profile of state testing in 1992 through 1993. The report observed that "the nation is entering an era of change in testing and assessment" with "greater use of performance assessment, constructed response questions, and portfolios." The report continues: "However, . . . the multiple-choice, machine-scored approach is still very much dominant" (p. 3). The report states that "seventy percent of tests given in statewide systems are multiple-choice" (p. 4) and that "testing is one of the levers being used to raise achievement standards" (p. 5).

In 1999, ETS issued another Policy Information Report, *Too Much Testing of the Wrong Kind: Too Little of the Right Kind in K-12 Education*. Barton (1999), who wrote this report, acknowledges the efforts to broaden tests beyond multiple-choice items to include open-ended questions, "performance" assessments, and portfolios. But, he says, "the assessment reform movement has slowed over issues of reliability and measurement error. . . . *Most* of the testing today is not much changed from what it was a dozen years ago" (p. 4). Barton argues, "Improving testing is important because testing has become, over the last 25 years, the approach of first resort of policymakers" (p. 5). Even though testing is slowly being aligned to new higher content standards, problems still exist. As Barton continues:

[T]esting is often an instrument of public policy to affect schools, to grade schools, to scold schools, and to judge whether other improvements in the educational system are having the desired effect. Most of these tests have not been validated for these purposes (p. 8).

(Clearly this is the case with the SAT 9 in California.)

Most tests are constructed to measure the knowledge a student has acquired. They have not been designed for the accountability purposes for which they are now regularly used; they are not designed, for example, as measures of teachers capabilities (p. 9).

Barton argues the case for moving from the intrusive testing of every student to sample-based assessments and assessments aligned to content standards and the curricula actually being taught, ironically as California once had not so long ago. Barton concludes his report:

Americans must demand higher standards in testing, as they are demanding higher standards in education generally. Standardized testing, used properly, may tell us whether the standards-based reforms are working. In and of itself, testing is not the treatment (p. 32).

The National Center for Fair & Open Testing (FairTest) issued a report card on state assessment systems, *Testing Our Children* (Neill & Staff of FairTest, 1997). FairTest attempted to evaluate assessment systems in all 50 states in light of standards derived from *Principles and Indicators for Student Assessment Systems* (National Forum on Assessment, 1995), developed by a coalition of education and civil rights groups. Among the major findings in 1997 were the following:

- While most states now have content standards, many state tests are not based on their standards, and many important areas in their assessments are not assessed [California in 1999].
- Most states rely too heavily on multiple-choice testing and fail to provide an adequate range of methods for students to demonstrate their learning [California in 1999].
- A majority of states (33) use norm-referenced tests, which compare students to a reference group and not to achievement on state standards [California in 1999].
- Seventeen states use a single test as a requirement for high school graduation violating widely recognized standards for good assessment practice, ensuring unfair treatment of many students and increasing the likelihood that narrow tests will dictate curriculum and instruction [California is moving in this direction with yet-to-be-developed exit test for 2004].

As the documents just cited demonstrate, the use of large-scale achievement tests as instruments of educational policy is growing. Some states are using such tests to make high-stakes decisions for tracking, promoting, and graduating individual students. To assure that such tests are used properly and fairly,

Congress charged the National Academy of Sciences through its National Research Council to study this situation and to make written recommendations. The Council's report, *High Stakes: Testing for Tracking, Promotion, and Graduation* (Heubert & Hauser, 1999) offers the following principles of appropriate use based on "established professional standards:"

Tests that are valid for influencing the classroom practice, 'leading' the curriculum, or holding schools accountable are not appropriate for making high-stakes decisions about individual student mastery unless the curriculum, the teaching, and the test(s) are aligned.

Tests are not perfect. Test questions are a sample of possible questions. . . . Moreover, a test score is not an exact measure of a student's knowledge or skills. . . . Thus, no single test score can be considered a definitive measure of a student's knowledge.

An educational decision that will have a major impact on a test taker should not be made solely or automatically on the basis of a single test score.

Research shows that students are typically hurt by simple retention and repetition of a grade in school without remedial and other instructional support services. In the absence of effective services for low performing students, better tests will not lead to better educational outcomes (p. 3).

The Council further recommends:

students [should] have been taught the knowledge and skills upon which they will be tested. We . . . recommend that test users respect the distinction between genuine remedial education and teaching narrowly to the specific content of a test. At the same time, all students should receive sufficient preparation for the specific test so their performance will not be adversely affected by unfamiliarity with its format or by ignorance of appropriate test-taking strategies (p. 7).

***Getting past the exam.*** In principle the official standardized tests are supposed to provide neutral, "objective" assessments of student accomplishment in locally determined curricula in the English language arts. In practice, however, these state mandated tests are norm-referenced tests created for purposes other than ones they are made to serve. California's current use of the SAT 9 is a prime example of the this form of misuse. Students are measured against a reference population on content not aligned with the California standards or framework. Then the results are wrongly used to rank districts and make decisions about individual students in clear violation of the kinds of established professional standards presented previously.

Given the uses of high-stakes tests in many states, it is not surprising to find that both students and teachers consider preparation for these tests to have priority over other school goals in language arts that are unrelated to the tests. As long as the states use "off-the-shelf" commercial tests that are not aligned directly to their standards, these tests will actually constitute a covert national language arts curriculum affecting local selection of content, student work strategies, and the nature of the teacher-student interaction. The local course of study in the English language arts is reshaped to fit the state mandated test policy, focusing on what is needed to pass the test, with a consequent loss of attention to the broad social or personal goals the English language arts might serve in the local community.

Teachers are sometimes quite explicit in letting students know that the real objective of the course is to pass the exam rather than to master the subject under study.

Quoting a high school English department chairman, Madaus (1988) offers a telling example of the corrupting effects of accountability testing in the area of English language arts in the Georgia Regents' Testing Program, a program designed to assess minimum competencies in reading and writing on the part of college preparatory students. The department chair speaks:

Because we are devoting our best efforts to getting the largest number of students past the essay exam . . . , we are teaching to the exam, with an entire course, English III, given over to developing one type of essay writing, the writing of a five-paragraph argumentative essay written under a time limit on a topic about which the author may or not have knowledge, ideas, or personal opinions (p. 96).

The Georgia Regents' Test may or may not now still exist. But the type of survival behavior represented in the anecdote surely does exist elsewhere when teachers face the prospect of getting through one more ill-conceived high-stakes test. Such a test transfers control over the curriculum to the testing agency. Madaus (1988) considers this shift of power from the local education authority to the state to be well understood by the policymakers who are mandating school rankings and graduation and promotion tests, but he believes that the implications of this shift "have not received sufficient attention and discussion" (p. 98) by members of the profession.

## POWER AND CONTROL AT THE LOCAL DISTRICT LEVEL

Americans in most communities exercise control over their schools through some type of appointed or elected board of education whose members are supposed to represent the population at large. These boards of education formulate educational policy, which is then administered by a central office headed by the local district superintendent. The line of administrative power reaches into each elementary or secondary school through the building principal who has responsibility for administering school policy at that level.

In addition to the increases in state and federal involvement in policy issues relating to school curricula, as previously noted, there has also been an increase in regulation of local district practices as a result of judicial decisions. Such increases in policy activity at the federal and state levels have meant a decline of power at the local level. Wirt & Kirst (1982) have described the 1970s as a time when local control became much more limited as "the political web surrounding the school district tightened and included many more participants" (p. v). One result of the burgeoning development of new power groups during the last 25 years is that

the local superintendent has lost his once pre-eminent position in setting the district agenda and controlling decision outcomes. The superintendent and school board have become a reactive force, trying to juggle diverse and changing coalitions across different issues (pp. 20–21).

## Local Pressure Groups and Textbook Selection

The social composition and political world of each local district varies; the complex issues of power and control also vary from community to community. Parent groups, taxpayer associations, and other special interest constituencies have become ever more strident in their efforts to influence and shape the educational policies adopted by local school boards. Materials and procedures within the area of the English language arts increasingly have become a favorite target of powerful pressure groups. Ardent speakers arise in various local board meetings to champion a favored teaching method—phonics versus whole language; or to warn against "invidious" instructional approaches—journal writing and discussions of values; or to challenge "humanistic" textbook selections. The dynamics of the complex U.S. political system as it involves the interaction of special interest groups, school officials, local politicians, and even, the courts is especially well revealed in the case of textbook selection, which is still a local matter even though there may be state constraints on the range of choices.

In most states, a local textbook selection committee comprised of educators (teachers and administrators) from a county or a district administrative unit traditionally has selected the textbooks and library books used in the elementary schools. At the secondary level the textbook selection may be made within subject departments at the school site. Generally, these choices become major concerns of the community and the school board only when a local individual or group protests the content.

What happened when a raging protest erupted over local textbook choices is recounted in James Moffett's (1988) *Storm in the Mountains*. Moffett provides a fully documented history of the efforts of certain local citizens to protest the adoption of language arts and reading textbooks in 1974 in Kanawha County, West Virginia. Here began what George Hillocks, Jr. has called "the most prolonged, intense, and violent textbook protest this country has ever witnessed" (cited in Moffett, 1988, p. 26). Moffett's dramatic account of this firestorm of protest led by fundamentalist groups offers more than the usual censorship case study. His detailed analysis of the underlying psychology and motives of the protestors enriches his insightful history of how a local censorship case came to have broad national policy effects.

The Kanawha County protestors lost in the courts, but they won a larger victory, according to Moffett (1988):

The fact that nothing like it has occurred since gives a good indication of how effective it was: [N]o publisher has dared to offer to schools any textbooks of a comparable range of subjects and ideas and points of view to those the protestors vilified and crippled in the market. Theoretically returned to Kanawha County schools, they may as well not have been. In many other ways the bitter controversy closed up its own school system as much as it did textbook editorial offices (p. 26).

Defeats in the courts have not discouraged would-be censors of school material. According to a *Council-Grams* (Books Old and New Raise Censors Ire, 1988) summary of censorship activities, People for the American Way, a civil liberties group, in its annual report, *Attacks on Freedom to Learn* (1988), cited 157 attempts at censorship, about a third of them successful. A second report on censorship from the American Library Association and the American Association of School Administrators has estimated the number of challenges to library books and school materials has increased by 168% within the last 5 years. Despite decisions such as the following, by the U.S. Supreme Court, efforts at censorship seem to be increasing:

We hold that local school boards may not remove books from school library shelves simply because they dislike the ideas contained in those books and seek by their removal to prescribe what shall be orthodox in politics, nationalism, religion, or other matters of opinion. (U.S. Supreme Court, *Board of Island Union Free School District v. Steven A. Pico*, 1982) (cited in Spring, 1985, p. 256).

## Court Decisions and Local Book Selection

Most English teachers probably do not consider themselves to be in jeopardy of losing their positions when they select literary works for use in class or as outside reading. Yet certain school boards have dismissed teachers for making "improper" choices of literature, such as Vonnegut's "Welcome to the Monkey House" or Salinger's *Catcher in the Rye* or stories that contain "dirty" words. Algeo and Zirkel (1987) have reviewed seven cases involving lawsuits in which the courts were asked to review a teacher's termination or nonrenewal as a violation of legal rights to academic freedom in the selection of literary works. Their review of decisions in state and federal courts reveals a split in the courts over the extent of the English teacher's academic freedom in choosing literature to teach. During the 1980s, English language arts teachers (as well as social studies and science teachers) found increasing numbers of legal challenges to their freedom of choice in book selection on the grounds that their adoptions were infringing on the constitutional rights of some children to free exercise of religion.

In one case, a small group of Tennessee parents from a fundamentalist Christian faith objected, on religious grounds, to the 1986 district-adopted basal readers for Grades 1 to 8 because they allegedly contained sacrilegious and unAmerican doctrine. To these parents, *Goldilocks* portrayed secular humanism, *Cinderella* and *King Arthur* contained dangerous portrayals of magic and supernatural acts, and *The Wizard of Oz* favorably depicted witchcraft. When the district refused the parents' request for an alternative reading program and suspended the students for refusing to use the adopted reading textbooks, the parents withdrew their children from the schools and instituted a law suit.

The district court judge agreed with the parents, and although he didn't require the district to provide alternative textbooks, he did order school officials to allow these students to "opt out" of reading instruction. An appeals court judge, in reversing that decision, held that requiring public school students to study textbooks duly selected by school authorities did not create an unconstitutional burden under the First Amendment right to free exercise of religion. Yet even though the parents' complaint was ultimately dismissed, it could not have been easy to conduct school business as usual during the 2 years of this burdensome litigation process. (*Mozert v. Hawkins County Board of Education, 1986 & 1987*)

In another such lawsuit, an Alabama judge not only ruled that the textbooks challenged by a group of parents violated the First Amendment by promoting a religion of secular humanism, but he also ordered the books removed from the schools. The appeals judge, reversing this decision, held that even assuming secular humanism *was* a religion, the use of these books did not violate the students' First Amendment rights. The original decision, if upheld, would have posed an even more serious threat to school authority because it ordered the elimination of curriculum materials for *all* students, not just the excusing of the offended individuals from using them (*Smith v. Board of School Commissioners of Mobile County, 1987*).

Many educators are concerned about the impact of legal cases that threaten to proscribe the range of texts that can be introduced into classrooms. Jenkinson (1987) observes that even though relatively few cases reach the courts, dozens of protests over textbooks occur throughout the United States each month at the local level. Thus, the specter of protests leading to lengthy and costly litigation through the courts may very well threaten to weaken the determination of publishers, school officials, and teachers to defend their textbook decisions. Self-censorship or overly conservative selection policies then loom as an unfortunate consequence of fear of potential court action. Donelson (1987) quotes an American Civil Liberties Union document, *Censorship in the South: A Report of Four States, 1980-85*, which suggests that

[S]elf censorship may be widespread. A Louisiana librarian wrote, "My main observation is that teachers, librarians, media personnel, and supervisors practice self-censorship—if let's do it for them before they do it to us" (p. 210).

The process whereby self-imposed censorship and a more conservative text selection policy can enter state and local deliberation in choosing texts can be seen in the response of one state level administrator to the *Mozert* decision. In his review of that case, Charles L. Glenn (1987), director of equal educational opportunity for the Massachusetts Department of Education calls for "flexibility of approach and parental choice." Mr. Glenn argues:

Why fight with parents over whether their children will read a particular story, if there is another one they find more acceptable that will achieve the same result? I have read the *Wizard of Oz* aloud to my children several times, but I can't see that we have any business making a free public education dependent on accepting that particular book (p. 455).

Taking local school systems to court can lead to policy decisions with broad-ranging consequences for the freedom of editorial choice of authors in developing the content textbooks and for the freedom of professionals in selecting textbooks at all levels of authority. It may become increasingly difficult for publishers and schools to sponsor the degree of intellectual freedom that the distinguished historian, Lawrence A. Cremin (Olson, 1988), has insisted must be preserved. Interviewed by Lynn Olson of *Education Week*, Cremin carefully challenged the popular view that the public school should be totally reflective of the local sentiments and that local citizens should have full control of it. He declared that this arrangement works only to a certain degree:

[A] free society owes it to its children to have the schools at a certain point begin to make the children aware of points of view, to make the children aware of knowledge, to make the children aware of phenomena and experience that they will not get in their families or in their neighborhoods (p. 5).

It does seem obvious that in a mobile society many children will end up living elsewhere and be unprepared for the divergent views they may encounter in new environments unless schools have prepared them to be open minded, active, thoughtful learners in a democratic society.

## THE POWER OF THE COURTS AS A POLICY AGENCY

The Supreme Court and other federal courts have never questioned the principle that education is a function of the states. Thus for many years the federal courts did not review educational practices unless they violated provisions of the United States Constitution. The decades of the 1960s and 1970s, however, initiated a period of court mandated reform as the federal judiciary expanded the scope of its review of educational practices. Examining trends in educational policy, Yudorf, Kirp, van Geel, and Levin (1982) have concluded that during the past 35 years "decisions once made by school administrators and local boards of education have increasingly become the province of the courts" (p. xxiii). They further noted two trends in these developments: "As the reach of law expands, distinctions between law and politics begin to blur. . . . What has diminished is dependency on professional expertise" (p. 813). For example, the courts now address questions once left to professionals: What language shall we teach in our classrooms? How much attention must we pay to the home language of the child?

### The Lau Decision and Bilingual Programs

The courts have ruled that "the primary task of the schools is to teach standard English, and that other languages and 'black English' are to be used as means to achieve that goal" (Spring, 1985, p. 260). In the case of *Lau et al. v. Nichols et al.*, 1974, the Supreme Court ruled that the lack of special instruction to help non-English-speaking students learn standard English violated Title VI of the 1964 Civil Rights Code:

It seems obvious that the Chinese-speaking minority receives fewer benefits than the English-speaking majority from the respondents' school system which denies them a meaningful opportunity to participate in the educational program—all earmarks of the discrimination banned by the regulations (cited in Spring, 1985, p. 260).

The Supreme Court did not specify bilingual education as the only solution to the problem found by the Court, but the original regulations issued by the U.S. Department of Education did focus on the provision of bilingual programs. What began as a pedagogical problem became a volatile social policy issue with many political overtones, prompting bitter controversy and further litigation.

### The Ann Arbor Decision on Black English

Although the Supreme Court did not specify a remedy for the situation covered by the *Lau* decision, the U.S. District Court of Michigan did provide a remedy in a case involving children from non-standard English backgrounds. After reviewing the evidence, the court argued that there is a possible relationship between poor reading ability and the school's failure to take into account the home language of African American children. Therefore, in the case of *Martin Luther King Junior Elementary School Children et al. v. Ann Arbor School District* on July 12, 1979, Judge Charles W. Joiner directed the school system to develop within 30 days a plan to identify children speaking black English and to "use that knowledge in teaching such students how to read standard English" (cited in Spring, 1985, p. 260).

Many regarded this ruling, which came to be known as the Ann Arbor Decision, as establishing an important precedent in the education of African American students who are dialect speakers (Farr, 1980). But what has happened since the Ann Arbor decision? Has it been effective? Nicholas Bountress (1987), who had earlier written two articles describing the significance of the Ann Arbor Decision, conducted a computer search of the literature 10 years later to answer these questions. He turned up no new information, only "repetitive discussions of the case itself." Bountress reports that "while the plan had been implemented, no information was gathered and disseminated that indicated whether or not teacher attitudes had been altered or pupil performance had been improved" (p. 19).

Thus, a unique opportunity for gathering information that might improve the educational progress of dialect-speaking children was lost, according to Bountress (1987), who concluded:

Judge Joiner's ruling did provide public recognition of black English and demonstrated that the nation's legal system can intervene when the schools allow dialectal interference to disrupt the progress of minority children. However, two crucial lessons remain. The courts cannot legislate teacher sensitivity nor can they develop more effective educational programs (p. 19).

The Ann Arbor experience suggests that judicial decisions are not self-activating. It remains for the educational profession itself, as the ultimate policymakers, to act to sustain the life and force of the judicial intent behind this or any other court mandate.

## POWER AND INFLUENCE OF SPECIAL INTEREST GROUPS

Outside of the court system and the other federal, state, and local educational governance structures already discussed in this chapter, there are myriad special interest groups seeking to wield influence over the English language arts curriculum to make it serve the interests and ideologies of their constituencies. Previous sections have shown how religious special interest groups have organized to attempt to influence critical decisions about the English curriculum. But besides the various religious bodies there are a great many other special interest groups seeking to influence what is taught in school: corporations, business organizations, publishers, private foundations, accrediting agencies, universities, parent-teacher associations, advocates for students with special needs, teachers' organizations, professional associations, organized community pressure groups, and nonaffiliated individuals. Representatives of these various constituencies lobby the lawmakers and bureaucrats at all levels of governance to fight for their moment in the curriculum. Sometimes the special interest groups enter the political arena of educational policymaking as allies, sometimes as combatants.

## THE ULTIMATE POLICYMAKERS: TEACHERS IN ENGLISH LANGUAGE ARTS

### Moment-By-Moment Policymakers

The making of laws and regulations does not end the policymaking process. Laws and regulations are not self-executing. Janet White (1988) has observed that "The primary teacher, when in sole charge of a class, has the power to reshape the whole curriculum." Clark (1988) contends that "Teachers are policymakers, although they are not recognized as such in most of the literature on educational policymaking" (p. 177). Teachers make curriculum decisions moment by moment that directly affect students:

It makes little difference what the secretary of education says works, what the governor includes in his program, or what the school board adopts for the district administration to implement, *if* none of these actions affects what happens between the teacher and the student (Clark, 1988, p. 177).

Wise (1988) explains why the intrusive, legislated rationalistic models of planning and supervision do not work:

Because students are not standardized in their needs, stages of development, home environments, preconceptions, or learning styles, a given stimulus does not produce a predictable response. A teacher must make decisions based on knowledge of the student, of the subject matter, and of pedagogy to create the right conditions of learning. Appropriate instructional decisions must be made at the point of service delivery (p. 332).

Policies that attempt to tighten control of what happens in classrooms by standardizing instructional planning, supervision, and evaluation fail because these well-intentioned rationalistic models erode teacher professionalism and autonomy, emphasize narrow, measurable goals, and lead to a decline in the quality of education for all students, according to Wise (1979).

Larry Cuban (1986) observed that in spite of a century of reform efforts, the durable core of teaching practice has not changed. He suggests that because most such "well-intentioned and highly motivated" reformers have been nonteachers, they were simply unable to take into account the "survival needs" of teachers in a demanding teaching environment. Cuban says:

[U]ntil state policymakers and national cheerleaders for change understand clearly the consequences for teachers of the reforms they propose, those reforms are likely to prove counterproductive for students and for the teaching profession. And the would-be reformers will continue to thrash about blindly, seeking clear-cut solutions to irreconcilable dilemmas arising from the structural conditions within which teachers labor (p. 11).

A belated recognition of the teacher's power to shape curriculum has finally led some reformers to look to the teacher at the local school site to discover how reforms might be brought to life. According to John Goodlad (1987), there is a growing body of evidence that the familiar top-down, linear approach to change with its "pathological emphasis on accountability" will not work. He sees an alternative to this authoritarian approach:

One-way directives are replaced by multiple interactions; leadership by authority is replaced by leadership by knowledge; following rules and regulations is replaced by providing more room for decision making; mandated behavior is replaced by inquiring behavior; accountability is replaced by high expectations, responsibility, and a level of trust that includes freedom to make mistakes . . . educational improvement calls for increasing the authority and decision-making space of the large numbers of individuals who constitute the base of the pyramid. . . . Empowering principals and teachers—those closest to the processes of students' learning . . . (p. 4).

In other words, it requires a teacher to make the actual classroom decision that activates any policy received from any level of authority.

The act of choosing a story or a method of teaching writing constitutes a policy decision about what knowledge and culture and what processes of thinking will be emphasized to students. The act of selecting a particular item of nonstandard English usage for children to learn to eliminate or replace with a valued standard form inevitably involves incorporating prior values and interests into instruction. Likewise, the act of choosing a particular literary work and the strategies for teaching it is an act that has potential for shaping and organizing the social and cultural consciousness of the children so instructed. Thus, the act of designing an English language arts program—tacitly, if not consciously—engages curriculum decision makers at every level of occurrence in social, philosophical, and political decisions about what counts as knowledge of value.

Different intellectual traditions and social values underlie the debates between scholars, legislators, and citizens about what forms of literacy to develop in English classrooms. Thus, divergent—sometimes incompatible, often unstated assumptions—shape emerging policies affecting allocation of academic learning time, specification of teacher competencies, content and frequency of achievement testing, and standards and expectations for English language arts courses.

In concluding his address to the Third International Conference for the Teaching of English in Sydney, Australia in 1980, James Britton (1982) proposed a toast to the 1980s as the "decade of the teacher."

As we have developed our view of learning as interactive, and that of curriculum as negotiable; as we have recognised the dramatic effect of intentions upon performance, by teachers as well as by student; as it has become clear that teaching consists of moment-by-moment interactive behavior, behavior that can only spring from inner conviction—I think we are, perhaps for the first time ready to admit that what the teacher can't do in the classroom can't be achieved by any other means (Britton, 1982, p. 11).

In a similar vein, Milbrey McLaughlin (1987), speaking in the language of policy analysis, asserted "policy-directed change ultimately is a problem of the smallest unit" (p. 171). Gene Maeroff (1988) added his voice to these sentiments. In his book, *The Empowerment of Teachers: Overcoming the Crisis of Confidence*, he declares that "if elementary and secondary education in America improves, it will be, more than anything else, because of the part teachers play" (p. 1). In the end, the question is what part should the teacher in English language arts play in policymaking? Certain writers are saying it is now the time for English language arts teachers to seize control of the direction of school reform. Books like *Deciding to Lead: The English Teacher As Reformer* (Wolfe & Antinarella, 1997) and *You Can Make a Difference: A Teacher's Guide to Political Action* (Keresty, O'Leary, & Wortley, 1998) suggest ways for teachers to take the lead as policymakers.

## RECOMMENDATIONS

It is unfortunate that no strong theory and no coherent field of policy studies in the English language arts have yet been developed. As social conditions change, as governmental interventions increase, and as teacher participation in policymaking advances, such studies are more sorely needed than ever. But the entire field of policy studies in education is still young, and those who have pioneered this field have not directed their attention to the English language arts. Little attention to the study of policymaking has come from within the profession, possibly because many members of the English profession have tended to resist involving themselves with politics and policymaking, preferring to direct their attention to what they consider loftier matters. Hence, the field of English language arts is rarely studied either by members within its own profession, or by scholars outside of it. However, a study group on research in English education has recognized the knowledge gap in policy studies and the importance of investigating such issues:

"[W]e have little research from an English Education perspective on how the socio-political climate constrains teachers from testing to censorship, from curricular control to professional autonomy (Angelotti, Brause, Mayher, Pradl, & Appleby, 1988, pp. 234–235).

It would seem that the more profound a profession's understanding of policymaking activity, the less likely will that profession be at the mercy of plausible but mistaken policy applications from without. The more thoroughly a profession understands its own history, the less likely will that profession embrace the illusions that await the ill-informed. If a profession is to advance to higher ground, it must understand where it has stood before. As a case in point, Gerald Graff, who has studied the institutional history of literary studies, assesses the "cultural literacy" controversy from the breadth of his historical perspective, concluding that

because [the] defenders of the past [such as Education Secretary Bennett, Allan Bloom, and E. D. Hirsch] know little about the actual past [of humanities education], they are unaware that the diagnoses they offer were already clichés a hundred years ago, and that the cures they have recommended have been repeatedly tried and have always led to futility (Graff & Warner, 1989, pp. 1–2).

In the absence of any tradition of policy studies in the English language arts, the policy initiative is too often left open to anyone who dares seize it. Who should decide the key policy questions in the English language arts? The ongoing dialogue about policy issues in relation to the concreteness of real classrooms could inject new vitality into the profession. Whoever makes such policy decisions shapes the education of our future citizens, especially the cultural literacy they may attain.

The initial question still remains: Who has the power to decide what is good policy for the English language arts? If the answer is the English profession, then the professional community has no choice but to recognize its need to consider matters of strategy, politics, and public relations, leading to the exercise of power. Kirst (1984) puts the matter bluntly: "When a constituency is so well organized that it becomes a lobby, it has power" (p. 55). Most important, if the profession is to exercise its power wisely and effectively at all levels of governance, it must make room for the establishment of policy study as a legitimate field of inquiry within English education.

## References

Algeo, A. M., & Zirkel, P. A. (1987). Court cases on teaching literature in the secondary schools. *Educational Horizons, 65,* 179–182.

Anderson, R. C., Hiebert, E. H., Scott, J. A., & Wilkinson, I. A. G. (1985). *Becoming a nation of readers: The report of the commission on reading.* Champagne, IL: Center for the Study of Reading, University of Illinois.

Angelotti, M., Brause, R., Mayher, J., Pradl, G., & Appleby, B. (1988). On the nature and future of English education: What the grayhair's gathering was really about. *English Education, 20,* 230–244.

Applebee, A. N. (1974). *Tradition and reform in the teaching of English: A history.* Urbana, IL: National Council of Teachers of English.

Ascher, C., Fruchter, N., & Berne, R. (1996). *Hard lessons: Public schools and privatization.* New York: The Twentieth Century Fund Press.

Asimov, N. (1999, January 4). Pete Wilson's unintended gift to his successor: Outgoing governor remade state Board of Education. *San Francisco Chronicle, 1,* 11.

Barton, P. E. (1999). *Too much testing of the wrong kind, too little of the right kind* (A Policy Information Perspective). Princeton, NJ: Policy Information Center, Educational Testing Service.

Barton, P. E., & Coley, R. J. (1994). *Testing America's schools* (Policy Information Report). Princeton, NJ: Policy Information Center, Educational Testing Service.

Berlin, J. A. (1987). *Rhetoric and reality: Writing instruction in American colleges, 1900–1985*. Carbondale, IL: Southern Illinois University Press.

Berliner, D., & Biddle, B. (1995). *The manufactured crisis: Myths, fraud, and the attack on America's public schools*. Reading, MA: Addison-Wesley.

Beyer, L. E., & Apple, M. W. (Eds.) (1988). *The curriculum: Problems, politics, and possibilities*. Albany, NY: State University of New York Press.

Blau, S. (1998). Toward the separation of school and state. *Language Arts, 75*, 132–136.

Bloom, A. (1987). *The closing of the American mind: How higher education has failed democracy and impoverished the souls of today's students*. New York: Simon and Schuster.

Books old and new raise censors' ire (1988, November). *NCTE Council-Grams, 6*.

Botstein, L. (1997). *Jefferson's children: Education and the promise of American culture*. Garden City, NY: Doubleday.

Bracey, G. W. (1997). *Setting the record straight: Responses to misconceptions about public education in the United States*. Alexandria, VA: Association for Supervision and Curriculum Development.

Britton, J. (1982). Opening address: English teaching retrospect and prospect. In R. D. Eagleson (Ed.), *English in the eighties* (pp. 1–12). Adelaide, Australia: Australian Association for the Teaching of English (Heinemann & Boynton/Cook).

Bountress, N. G. (1987). Educational implications of the Ann Arbor decision. *Educational Horizons, 66*, 18–19.

Burns, M. S., Griffin, P., Snow, C. E. (1999). *Starting out right: A guide to promoting children's reading success*. Washington, DC: National Academy Press.

California State Department of Education (1987). *English language arts framework for California public schools, kindergarten through grade twelve*. Sacramento, CA: Author.

California State Department of Education (1998). *English language arts content standards for California public schools, kindergarten through grade twelve*. Sacramento, CA: Author.

California State Department of Education (1998). *Steering by results: A high-stakes rewards and intervention program for California schools and students*. Sacramento, CA: Author.

California State Department of Education (1999). *Reading language arts framework for California public schools, kindergarten through grade 12*. Sacramento, CA: Author.

Carroll, J. B., & Chall, J. S. (Eds.) (1975). *Toward a literate society: The report of the committee on reading of the national academy of education*. New York: McGraw Hill.

Chrispeels, J. H. (1997). Educational policy implementation in a shifting political climate: The California experience. *American Education Research Journal, 34*, 453–481.

Cizek, G. J. (Ed.) (1999). *Handbook of educational policy*. New York: Academic Press.

Clark, R. W. (1988). Who decides? The basic policy issue. In L. N. Tanner (Ed.), *Critical issues in curriculum: The Eighty-seventh yearbook of the National Society for the Study of Education: Part I* (pp. 175–205). Chicago: University of Chicago Press.

Clifford, G. J. (1987). *A sisyphean task: Historical perspectives on the relationship between writing and reading instruction* (Technical Report No. 7). Berkeley, CA: University of California, Center for the Study of Writing.

Clinchy, E. (Ed.) (1997). *Transforming public education: A new course for America's future*. New York: Teachers College Press.

Colvin, R. L. (1999, October 1). Education standards fail to deliver, governors concede. *The Los Angeles Times*, pp. A1, A17.

Corbin, R., & Crosby, M. (Eds.) (1965). *Language programs for the disadvantaged. The Report of the National Council of Teacher's of English Task Force on Teaching English to the Disadvantaged*. Champaign, IL: National Council of Teachers of English.

Cuban, L. (1986). Persistent instruction: Another look at constancy in the classroom. *Phi Delta Kappan, 68*, 7–11.

Cuban, L. (1997). The end of the federally driven standards movement in U.S. school reform? In E. Clinchy (Ed.), *Transforming public education: A new course for America's future* (pp. 92–96). New York: Teachers College Press.

Darling-Hammond, L. (1988, April 20). In Commentary: Thinking about education: On the "cult of efficiency" in schools. *Education Week*, 20.

Dixon, J. (1967). *Growth through English Set in the Perspective of the Seventies* (1st ed.). Yorkshire, UK: National Association for the Teaching of English.

Donelson, K. (1987). Six statements/questions from the censors. *Phi Delta Kappan, 69*, 208–214.

Erikson, K. T. (1976). *Everything in its path: Destruction of community in the Buffalo Creek flood*. New York: Simon & Schuster.

Farr, M. (Ed.) (1980). *Reactions to Ann Arbor: Vernacular black English and education*. Washington, DC: Center for Applied Linguistics.

Flesch, Rudolf. (1955). *Why Johnny can't read and what you can do about it*. New York: Harper & Row.

Flygare, T. J. (1987). Some thoughts about the Tennessee textbook case. *Phi Delta Kappan, 68*, 474–475.

Fraatz, J. M. B. (1987). *The politics of reading: Power, opportunity, and prospects for change in America's public schools*. New York: Teachers College Press.

GED testing service compares national, state standards (1997, April) *The Council Chronicle, 6*, 5.

Glenn, C. L. (1987). Textbook controversies: A "Disaster for public schools"? *Phi Delta Kappan, 68*, 451–454.

Goodlad, J. I. (1987). Structure, process, and agenda. In J. I. Goodlad (Ed.), *The ecology of school renewal: The eighty-sixth yearbook of the National Society for the Study of Education: Part I* (pp. 1–20). Chicago: University of Chicago Press.

Goodman, K., Shannon, P., Freeman, Y., & Murphy, S. (1988). *Report card on basal readers*. Katonah, NY: Richard Owen.

Goodman, K. S. (Ed.) (1998). *In defense of good teaching: What teachers need to know about the "reading wars"*. York, ME: Stenham.

Goodson, I. F. (1988). *The making of curriculum: Collected essays*. London: Falmer Press.

Graff, H. J. (1987). *The legacies of literacy: Continuities and contradictions in western culture and society*. Bloomington, IN: Indiana University Press.

Graff, G., & Warner, M. (Eds.) (1989). *The origins of literary studies in America*. New York: Routledge.

Green, J. (1987). *The next wave: A synopsis of recent education reform reports* (Advance Copy, Report No. TR-87-1). Denver, CO: Education Commission of the States.

Guthrie, J. T. (Ed.) (1984). *Responding to "A Nation at Risk": Appraisal and policy guidelines*. Newark, DE: International Reading Association.

Guthrie, J. W., & Koppich, J. (1988). Exploring the political economy of national education reform. In W. L. Boyd & C. T. Kerchner (Eds.), *The politics of excellence and choice in education: The 1987 yearbook of the politics of Education Association* (pp. 25–47). New York: Falmer Press.

Hatfield, W. W. (1935). *An Experience Curriculum in English*. New York: D. Appleton-Century.

Heubert, J. P., & Hauser, R. M. (Eds.) (1999). *High stakes: Testing for tracking, promotion, and graduation*. Washington, DC: National Academy Press.

Hillocks, G., Jr. (Ed.) (1982). *The English Curriculum Under Fire: What are the real basics?* Urbana, IL: National Council of Teachers of English.

Hirsch, Jr., E. D. (1987). *Cultural literacy: What every American needs to know*. Boston: Houghton Mifflin.

Hoff, D. J. (1999, September 22). Standards at crossroads after decade. *Education Week, 19*, 1, 9.

Hook, J. N. (1979). *A long way together: A personal view of NCTE's first sixty-seven years*. Urbana, IL: National Council of Teachers of English.

House, E. R. (1998). *Schools for sale: Why free market policies won't improve America's schools, and what will*. New York: Teachers College Press.

In the states: California switches to literature-based reading texts (1989, January). *NCTE Council-Grams*, 6.

International Reading Association Board of Directors. (1999, October/ November). Draft framework sparks controversy. *Reading Today*, 3-4.

Jenkinson, E. B. (1987). The significance of the decision in "Scopes II." *Phi Delta Kappan, 68*, 445-450.

Jerrolds, B. W. (1979). *Reading reflections: The history of the International Reading Association*. Newark, DE: International Reading Association.

Justiz, M. J., & Bjork, L. G. (Eds.) (1988). *Higher education research and public policy*. New York: American Council on Education (Macmillan).

Keresty, B., O'Leary, S., & Wortley, D. (1998). *You can make a difference: A Teacher's guide to political action*. Portsmouth, NH: Heinemann.

Kirst, M. W. (1984). *Who controls our schools? American values in conflict*. New York: W. H. Freeman.

Kirst, M. W. (1989). Who should control the schools? Reassessing current policies. In T. J. Sergiovanni & J. H. Moore (Eds.), *Schooling for tomorrow: Directing reforms to issues that count* (pp. 62-89). Boston: Allyn & Bacon.

Koretz, D. (1988). Arriving in Lake Woebegon: Are standardized tests exaggerating achievement and distorting instruction? *American Education, 12*, 8-15, 46-52.

Lloyd-Jones, R. & Lunsford, A. A. (Eds.) (1989). *The English coalition: Democracy through language*. Urbana, IL: National Council of Teachers of English.

Lusi, S. F. (1977). *The role of state departments of education in complex school reform*. New York: Teachers College Press.

Madaus, G. F. (1988). The influence of testing on the curriculum. In L. N. Tanner (Ed.), *Critical issues in curriculum: The eighty-seventh yearbook of the National Society for the Study of Education* (pp. 83-121). Chicago: University of Chicago Press.

Maeroff, G. I. (1988). *The empowerment of teachers: Overcoming the crisis of confidence*. New York: Teachers College Press.

Maeroff, G. I. (1998). *Imaging education: The media and schools in America*. New York: Teachers College Press.

Marzano, R. J., & Kendall, J. S. (1997). National and state standards: The problems and the promise. *National Association of Secondary School Principals Bulletin, 81*, 26-41.

McLaughlin, M. W. (1987). Learning from experience: Lessons from policy implementation. *Educational Evaluation and Policy Analysis, 9*, 171-178.

McQuade, E. P. (1989, January). A story at risk: the rising tide of mediocre education coverage (Kappan Special Report). *Phi Delta Kappan, 70*, K1-K8.

McQuillan, J. (1998). *The literacy crisis: False claims, real solutions*. Portsmouth, NH: Heinemann.

Mellon, J. C. (1975). *National assessment and the teaching of English*. Urbana, IL: National Council of Teachers of English.

Miller, J. A. (1987, October 28). Bell recounts tenure as chief of ED in book. *Education Week*, 1.

Milner, J. O. (1997). The development of English standards: Using a flat structure in a hierarchical world. *The Clearing House, 70*, 129-135.

Mitchell, D. E., & Iannaccone, L. (1980). *The impact of California's legislative policy on public school performance* (Monograph No. 5, California Policy Seminar). Berkeley, CA: University of California, Institute of Governmental Studies.

Moffett, J. (1988). *Storm in the mountains: A case study of censorship, conflict, and consciousness*. Carbondale, IL: Southern Illinois Press.

Monaghan, E. J., & Saul, E. W. (1987). The reader, the scribe, the thinker: A critical look at the history of American reading and writing instruction. In T. S. Popkewitz (Ed.), *The formation of school subjects: The struggle for creating an American institution* (pp. 85-122). London: The Falmer Press.

*Mozert v. Hawkins County Bd. of Educ.*, 827 F.2d 1058 (6th Cir. (Tenn.), Aug. 24, 1987).

Myers, M. (1977). Standards in the English language arts: Meeting the challenge. *National Association of Secondary School Principals Bulletin, 81*, 42-48.

Meyers, M., & Spalding, E. (Eds.) (1997). *Assessing student performance* (Series: Grades K-5, Grades 6-8, Grades 9-12). Urbana, IL: National Council of Teachers of English.

National Council of Teachers of English Committee on the National Interest (1961). *The national interest and the teaching of English*. Urbana, IL: National Council of Teachers of English.

National Council of Teachers of English and International Reading Association (1996). *Standards for the English language arts*. Urbana, IL & Newark, DE: Author.

National Council of Teachers of English & International Reading Association (1994). *Standards for the assessment of reading and writing*. Urbana, IL & Newark, DE: Author.

NCTE returns fire on critics. (June, 1996). *The Council Chronicle, 5*, 1, 4, 15.

NCTE to you: Information, news, announcements (1989). *Language Arts, 66*, 347-348.

National Forum on Assessment (1995). *Principles and indicators for student assessment systems*. Cambridge, MA: National Center for Fair & Open Testing.

Neill, M., & Staff of FairTest. (1997). *Testing our children: A report card on state assessment systems*. Cambridge, MA: National Center for Fair & Open Testing.

North, S. M. (1987). *The making of knowledge in composition: Portrait of an emerging field*. Upper Montclair, NJ: Boynton/Cook.

Ohanian, S. (1999). *One size fits few: The folly of educational standards*. Portsmouth, NH: Heinemann.

Olson, L. (1988, March 16). History: "A lamp to light the present" [Interview with Lawrence A. Cremin] *Education Week, 5*, 20.

Olson, L. (1988, April 27). Inside "A Nation at Risk": A view from the cutting room floor. *Education Week, 1*, 22-23.

Ogle, L. T., & Dabbs, P. A. (1998). The media's mixed record on reporting test results. In G. I. Maeroff (Ed.), *Imaging education: The media and schools in America* (pp. 85-100). New York: Teachers College Press.

Ohmann, R. (1987). *Politics of letters*. Middletown, CT: Wesleyan University Press.

Pearson, P. D. (1997, February). The politics of reading research and practice. *The Council Chronicle, 7*, 24, 8.

Pearson, P. D. (1999). A historically based review of *Preventing Reading Difficulties in Young Children*. *Reading Research Quarterly, 34,* 231–246.

Pearson, P. D., Spalding, E., & Myers, M. (1998). Literacy assessment as part of new standards. In M. Coles & R. Jenkins (Eds). *Assessing reading 2: Changing practice in classrooms* (pp. 54–79). London: Routledge.

Popkewitz, T. S. (1987a). *Critical studies in teacher education: Its folklore, theory, and practice*. London: Falmer Press.

Popkewitz, T. S. (1987b). Knowledge and interest in curriculum studies. In T. S. Popkewitz (Ed.), *The formation of school subjects: The struggle for creating an American institution*. London: Falmer Press.

Porter, A. (1995). The uses and misuses of opportunity-to-learn standards. In D. Ravitch (Ed.), *Debating the future of American education: Do we need national standards and assessments?* (pp. 40–65). Washington, DC: The Brookings Institute.

Position statement decries high-stakes assessment (August–September, 1999). *Reading Today, 17,* 27.

Purves, A. N., & Niles, O. (Eds.) (1984). *Becoming readers in a complex society: The eighty-third yearbook of the National Society for the Study of Education: Part I*. Chicago: University of Chicago Press.

Rothblatt, S. (1988). General education on the American campus: A historical introduction in brief. In I. Westbury & A. C. Purves (Eds.), *Cultural literacy and the idea of general education: The eighty-seventh yearbook of the National Society for the Study of Education: Part II* (pp. 9–29). Chicago, IL: University of Chicago Press.

Routman, R. (1996). *Literacy at the Crossroads: Crucial talk about reading, writing and other teaching dilemmas*. Portsmouth, NH: Heinemann.

Schrag, P. (1997, October). The near-myth of our failing schools. *The Atlantic Monthly,* 72–80.

Schrag, P. (1998). *Paradise lost: California's experience, America's future*. New York: The New Press.

Shannon, P. (1991). Politics, policy and reading research. In R. Barr, M. L. Kamil, P. B. Mosenthal, & P. D. Pearson (Eds.), *Handbook of reading research: Volume II* (pp. 147–167). New York: Longman.

Shor, I. (1986). *The culture wars: School and society in the conservative restoration, 1969–1984*. Boston: Routledge & Kegan Paul.

*Smith v. Board of School Commissioners of Mobile County,* 827 F.2d 684 (11th Cir. (Ala.) Aug. 26, 1987).

Snow, C. E., Burns, M. S., & Griffin, P. (1998). *Preventing Reading Difficulties in Young Children*. Washington, DC: National Academy Press.

Spring, J. (1985). *American education: An introduction to social and political aspects* (3rd ed.). New York: Longman.

Spring, J. (1988). *Conflict of interests: The politics of American education*. New York: Longman.

Squire, J. R. (1967). *The eight year report of the executive secretary*. Champaign, IL (Urbana): National Council of Teachers of English.

Squire, J. R. (1987). Retrospect and prospect. In J. R. Squire (Ed.), *The dynamics of language learning: Research in reading and English* (pp. 387–393). Urbana, IL: ERIC Clearinghouse on Reading and Communication Skills.

Steinberg, J. (1999, September 30). Educators focus on 'pain' of standards. *The New York Times,* p. A16.

Taylor, D. (1998). *Beginning to read and the spin doctors of science: The political campaign to change America's mind about how children learn to read*. Urbana, IL: National Council of Teachers of English.

Teachers reveal limits of their decision making (1988, November). *NCTE Council-Grams,* 5.

White, J. (1988). *Changing practice: A collaborative study between SCDC national writing project and the NFER department of language: Part one: (September 1986–February 1988)*. Slough, England: National Foundation for Education and Research.

Winkeljohann, R. (Ed.) (1973). *The politics of reading: Point-counterpoint*. Urbana, IL: ERIC Clearinghouse on Reading and Communication Skills.

Wirt, F. M., & Kirst, M. W. (1982). *Schools in conflict: The politics of education*. Berkeley, CA: McCutchan.

Wirt, F. M., & Kirst, M. W. (1997). *The political dynamics of American education*. Berkeley, CA: McCutchan.

Wirth, A. G. (1992). *Education and work for the year 2000: Choices we face*. San Francisco: Jossey-Bass.

Wise, A. E. (1979). *Legislated learning: The bureaucratization of the American classroom*. Berkeley, CA: University of California Press.

Wise, A. E. (1988). Legislated learning revisited. *Phi Delta Kappan, 69,* 328–333.

Wolfe, D., & Antinarella, J. (1997). *Deciding to lead: The English teacher as reformer*. Portsmouth, NH: Heinemann & Boynton/Cook.

Yudorf, M. G., Kirp, D. L., van Geel, T., & Levin, B. (1982). *Kirp and Yudorf's educational policy and the law: Cases and materials* (2nd ed.). Berkeley, CA: McCutchan Publishing.

Zehr, M. A. (1999, September 29). Texas testing trial has potential to set new precedent. *Education Week, 19,* 1, 14.

# ·10·

# TRENDS AND ISSUES IN RESEARCH IN THE TEACHING OF THE ENGLISH LANGUAGE ARTS

*Karen Smith*
Arizona State University

*Patricia Lambert Stock*
Michigan State University

In the first *Handbook of Research on Teaching the English Language Arts* (1991), James H. Britton and Merron Chorny introduce a discussion of current trends and future directions with a call for an overarching conception of the subject English. According to Britton and Chorny (1991), some 50 American and British scholars set the stage for the development of such a unifying theory in the 1966 Dartmouth Seminar on the Teaching and Learning of English when they replaced (a) a view of English that focused on product with a view that focused on process, (b) a view of language learning as a means to literacy with a recognition of the role of language in all learning, and (c) a sense of the learner as a passive receiver with a recognition of learning as an activity to be pursued (p. 110). After reconstructing a stage set at Dartmouth, Britton and Chorny go on to propose the unifying theory for which they call:

In the act of using language to explore their own experiences and develop their own ideas, students would be encouraged within the class community to acquire self-knowledge and world-knowledge in the course of learning to use and understand language (pp. 110–111).

Although Dartmouth has come to symbolize what Joseph Harris (1997) calls a "Copernican shift from a view of English as something you *learn about* to a sense of it as something you *do*." (p. 1), not long after the seminar, other researchers began to raise important questions about Dartmouth's impact on the teaching of English. They asked whether in shifting professional attention from English as something one learns to English as something one does, educators had not also emphasized the importance of personal uses of language in learning at the expense of social uses of language and society's investment in language learning. These critics questioned whether the "personal growth" theorists—as they came to be called—whose views of subject English were widely circulated in three printings of John Dixon's *Growth Through English* (1967, 1969, 1974) had not, in fact, trivialized personal uses of language in their overemphasis on them, deflected attention from social uses of language, and obscured the power politics entailed in language teaching and learning (e.g., Berlin, 1982; Berthoff, 1971; Griffith, 1988; Harris, 1997). While some critics have regarded "growth theory" and "process pedagogy"—both of which gained currency after Dartmouth—as antithetical to researchers' current concern with social origins and community-based uses of language and with the larger culture's investment in language learning and use, others regard Dartmouth's influential legacies as seamless precursors to current concerns.

Whether we understand the discussions of some 60 scholars who gathered at Wye Plantation just over 20 years later in rural Maryland "to chart directions for the study of English in the twenty-first century" as reactions to or extensions of the Dartmouth Seminar, the focus of the 1987 English Coalition Conference was not on developing a unifying theory of subject

English but on the diverse origins and uses of the English language arts. Participants at Wye concerned themselves with the social constructions of language learning and language use that educators need to understand, respect, and draw upon if they are to teach increasing numbers of increasingly diverse students to live fulfilling lives in a multicultural society and to make satisfactory livings in a global economy (Jones & Lunsford, 1989). Different in tone and flavor from discussions at Dartmouth, those undertaken at Wye Plantation named goals like the following ones for the teaching of English: (a) to make critical literacy possible for all students, (b) to enable students to use language to articulate their own points of view, and (c) to encourage students to respect different points of view.

As participants in the English Coalition Conference identified situations and issues that teachers of the English language arts must consider to accomplish these goals, those focusing on elementary education drew attention to the structure and lifestyles of families, as well as to the media and technologies; others focusing on secondary education dramatized perspectives and experiences that students in a multicultural society bring with them to school; and still others focusing on higher education noted the importance of engaging students actively in courses that use theory and research to focus not only on the uses of language but also on the value-laden nature of those uses and their political effects. Before discussion ended, participants in the English Coalition Conference concluded that the goals they hoped to accomplish in schools depended on "a fresh view of the field" of English studies.

To gain that fresh view of the field, researchers have looked for theoretical insights to disciplines like those discussed in this section of the handbook (linguistics, psychology, child development, anthropology, and literary theory) and to integrative and interdisciplinary studies that Clifford Geertz (1983) reminds us are changing the way we think about the way we think now. Across the 1990s, in its move away from a search for unifying theory to a concern with understanding diverse experiences, diverse interpretations of experiences, and the limits of theory, scholarship in the teaching of the English language arts has taken its place within the larger body of what has come to be called post-modern scholarship in the academy and professions.

Referring to the writing of scholars in various fields whose work speaks to and with the work of researchers in the teaching of the English language arts, we set the stage for this essay about current trends and future directions for research and teaching in the English language arts by drawing attention to the broader intellectual context in which that research and teaching has been conducted over the last decade, and we go on to illustrate how this intellectual movement has influenced research and the teaching of subject English.

## POSTMODERNISM

(Parts of the discussion of postmodernism have appeared in Stock, 1996.) In preparation for a discussion of postmodernism, Pauline Marie Rosenau (1992) equates modernism "with one of its major currents, that which incorporates the Enlightenment

heritage and urges the social sciences in a positivist direction" (p. 5). Rosenau's description of the Enlightenment project and postmodernity's disillusionment with it are ones familiar to researchers in the teaching of the English language arts.

Modernity entered history as a progressive force promising to liberate humankind from ignorance and irrationality, but one can readily wonder whether that promise has been sustained. As we in the West approach the end of the twentieth century, the "modern" record—world wars, the rise of Nazism, concentration camps (in both East and West), genocide, world-wide depression, Hiroshima, Vietnam, Cambodia, the Persian Gulf, and a widening gap between rich and poor (Kamper & Wulf, 1989)—makes any belief in the idea of progress or faith in the future seem questionable. Post-modernists criticize all that modernity has engendered: the accumulated experience of Western civilization, industrialization, urbanization, advanced technology, the nation state, life in the "fast lane." They challenge modern priorities: career, office, individual responsibility, bureaucracy, liberal democracy, tolerance, humanism, egalitarianism, detached experiment, evaluative criteria, neutral procedures, impersonal rules, and rationality (Jacquard, 1978; Vattimo, 1988) (pp. 5–6).

Disillusioned with the Enlightenment project, postmodern thinkers in the social and natural sciences, the humanities, the arts, and in practice professions like English education have called into question both modern accomplishments and modern understandings. Researchers have questioned not only what we know, what constitutes knowledge, how we can produce knowledge, and on what foundational basis we can confirm the knowledge we produce, but also the relationship between the production of knowledge and knowledge in action.

Scholars like Thomas Kuhn (1970), in fields once regarded as at a distance from the work of English language arts teaching, as well as researchers and teachers of the English language arts, like Lester Faigley (1992), remind readers:

The foundational concepts associated with artistic judgment such as "universal value" and "intrinsic merit," with science such as "truth" and "objectivity," and with ethics and law such as "rights" and "freedoms" suddenly have no meaning outside of particular discourses and are deeply involved in the qualities they are alleged to be describing (Faigley, 1992, p. 8).

The intellectual historian David A. Hollinger (1995) illustrates Faigley's point in a discussion of Edward Steichen's photographs exhibited in the Museum of Modern Art in the name of *The Family of Man* (1955), Hollinger writes:

Although this great exhibition, and the book based upon it, no doubt stimulated feelings of human solidarity across many dividing lines, today's celebrants of human diversity are quick to find fault with it. Steichen's pictures of Asians and Africans growing up, marrying, struggling through their adult lives at work and at home seem to reduce the population of the globe to a set of mirrors for the narrower world of middle-class liberal males of Steichen's milieu. Steichen . . . achieved a species wide view by limiting the range and depth of human differences (p. 53).

In light of anti-foundational, anti-essentialist critiques of Enlightenment claims for the power of reason, present-day scholars are turning away from studies designed to produce knowledge of universal truths. Some who have announced the end of the author, the death of the subject, and the impossibility of theory, claim that all representation—upon which theory-building depends—is misleading. Arguing that representations do nothing more than represent other representations, the French philosopher Jean Baudrillard (1983) would likely describe Edward Steichen's *Family of Man* photographs as copies of Steichen's images of his own experience, facsimiles of events that shaped Steichen's lived life, representations of the observations that Steichen was able to make.

According to the cultural historian Todd Gitlin (1989), postmodernists like Baudrillard adopt a blase attitude because they believe that "they have seen it all" and that nothing really new is possible (p. 103). Since they believe there is no truth, they find that all that is left is the play of words and meaning. Other postmodern thinkers, a group Pauline Marie Rosenau contrasts with the skeptics by calling them the affirmatives—a group in which we would place researchers into the teaching of the English language arts—find this skeptical position the luxury of a privileged class of intellectuals.

In an interview, Cornel West—philosopher of religion and theorist of African American Studies—takes dramatic exception to Baudrillard's intellectual stance and in so doing voices concerns of many post-modern thinkers who are not content to spend their intellectual energies in word play:

Baudrillard seems to be articulating a sense of what it is to be a French, middle-class intellectual, or perhaps what it is to be middle class generally. Let me put it in terms of a formulation from Henry James that Frederic Jameson has appropriated: there is a reality *that one cannot not know*. The ragged edges of the Real, of *Necessity*, not being able to eat, not having shelter, not having health care, all this is something that one cannot not know. The black condition acknowledges that. It is so much more acutely felt because this is a society where a lot of people live a Teflon existence, where a lot of people have no sense of the ragged edges of necessity, of what it means to be impinged upon by structures of oppression. To be an upper-middle-class American is actually to live a life of unimaginable comfort, convenience, and luxury. Half of the black population is denied this, which is why they have a strong sense of reality (West, 1988, p. 277).

## ENGLISH LANGUAGE ARTS EDUCATION IN POSTMODERN TIMES

As critical of the failures of the Enlightenment project and the positivist program for science as their skeptical counterparts, during the 1990s, postmodern English language arts educators have begun addressing these "ragged edges of the Real" by producing a body of praxis-oriented scholarship designed to enable teaching and learning of increasingly diverse students in a rapidly changing culture and to better understand what difference difference makes (Dyson et al., 1995, 1997a) for teachers and learners in multicultural, post-colonial societies in which new information technologies are not only redefining literacy and literature but also the ways in which they are taught, learned, and used.

Like *praxis*-oriented postmodern scholars in other fields of endeavor, during the past decade English language arts

educators have concerned themselves with what counts as knowledge, with how that knowledge is produced, with who produces it, and with how it does and doesn't benefit students and the larger society in which we live. In complex studies—many of them conducted collaboratively with teachers, students, families, school administrators, representatives of community agencies, and policy makers—language arts researchers have designed and published inquiries that draw attention to the situation-specific nature of teaching and learning and to multiple views of what counts as effective teaching and learning. Simultaneously, an increasing number of teacher-researchers have moved center stage to conduct and publish studies aimed at answering the questions that perplex them and to provide portraits of teaching and learning that "you had to be there" to have seen. Of special significance among these studies are ones that question predominant methods of educational inquiry and tests of validity, that advance new methods of inquiry and validity, and that find public expression in narrative genres, genres closer in texture and spirit to both the dramas of classroom life and the body of knowledge these teachers teach.

## THE PROBLEMS OF REPRESENTATION

Known best for her influential books *Landscapes of Learning* (1978) and *The Dialectic of Freedom* (1988), in an article in *English Education* (1994), Maxine Greene draws readers' attention to one of the challenges of particular concern to researchers who are charged with describing, explaining, and constructing theories of teaching and learning that depend on their observations and interpretations:

Many of us are beginning to recognize that representation in its traditional sense has had to do with the exercise of power. It has been, ordinarily, arbitrary and dependent on false assumptions. This applies not merely to the taking for granted of the referential status of words, images, symbols, and the like. It also applies to any person's being thought to be representative of a gender, category, ethnic group, as if there were "essences" to be embodied or exemplified (1994, p. 209).

Grappling with the problematics of representation, English language arts researchers have not only demonstrated that children reared in diverse cultural communities come to school diversely prepared to talk, listen, read, write, and design but also that the learning experiences of children reared in the same cultural contexts differ from one another (e.g., Delpit, 1995; Fishman, 1988; Gonzalez et al., 1995; Heath, 1983; Mahiri, 1998; Moll, 2000; Purcell-Gates, 1995; Rose, 1995; Street, 1995; Taylor & Dorsey-Gaines, 1988). Extensive discussion of issues these and other researchers raise is found in the July 2000 issue of *English Education*, the journal of the National Council of Teachers of English (NCTE) Conference on English Education (CEE). In this issue, Nancy Mellin McCracken (2000) provides a context and background for a report issued by the CEE Commission on Teacher Education for Teachers of Urban, Rural, and Suburban Students of Color. Writing for the commission, Lois Matz Rosen and Dawn Abt-Perkins (2000) indicate the need for the study that produced the report:

The National Center for Educational Statistics (1997) reports in their 1993–94 survey of teaching that blacks, Hispanics, and other minority students accounted for thirty-two percent of the K-12 school population in the U.S. while nearly eighty-seven percent of the teachers were white (p. A-22). Moreover, the racial and cultural difference between students and teachers is predicted to expand. As the number of school-age children from different circumstances continues to increase, few minority teachers are attracted to the teaching profession as indicated by the 1992–93 data on college graduates who enter teaching (p. 114). Similar differences exist in socio-economic levels and language backgrounds: the majority of teachers are middle-class, come from rural and suburban backgrounds, and are mono-lingual in English, while increasingly large numbers of their students live in poverty in urban areas and come from home environments where English is not the primary language of communication (Gomez, 1993). Equally disturbing is the fact that teacher educators share the racial, ethnic, and socio-economic characteristics of their pre-service teachers (pp. 251–252).

In an effort to advance productive dialogue about the mismatch between the cultural backgrounds of students and their teachers, Rosen and Abt-Perkins go on to do four things:

1. Outline the understandings and guiding principles for practices that the commission proposes as a result of its study of research conducted in a variety of academic disciplines and practical settings.
2. Describe a variety of programmatic reforms and promising practices for the development of cross cultural awareness and understanding.
3. Name lingering issues and persistent dilemmas that students, teachers, schools, and families face in multicultural settings.
4. Propose future actions with promise to increase cross cultural understanding and appreciation.

In addition, Rosen and Abt-Perkins provide an extensive, annotated bibliography of research into the issues that inspired the commission's work.

In other articles in the July 2000 issue of *English Education*, Arlette Ingram Willis (2000) argues that the best preparation she can provide her English education students for the work they will do in schools is not preparation in methods of teaching and best practices. Rather, Willis argues, her goal is to inform and broaden students' understanding of their own and others' cultures. Marcella Fleischman Pixley and Laura Schneider VanDerPloeg (2000) discuss the racial conflicts that result when they invite their students in rural Connecticut and the Bronx to "talk" with one another online. Kris Gutierrez (2000) discusses issues of cross cultural understandings and misunderstandings in the context of opportunities that teachers have and do not have for useful lifelong learning opportunities. Writing as seventh-grade school teacher, Cammie Kim Puidokas (2000) dramatizes the life of students and teacher in a multicultural inner-city school. Reminding those who wish to advance more promising practices for teaching and learning in a multicultural society, Puidokas cautions English educators about how studies conducted from the perspective of outsiders looking

in might be regarded by those being studied. Voicing similar concerns, Carol Lee (2000) warns teachers and researchers not to equate culture with color when she writes: "Culture is not a corner that only colored people occupy" (p. 310).

A number of studies currently informing English educators' about the cultural and linguistic resources that students from diverse backgrounds bring with them to school have been conducted in urban settings in homogeneous cultural communities (e.g., Barton & Hamilton, 1998; Cushman, 1998; DeStigter, 2001; Farr, 1994; Mahari, 1998; Michie, 1999; Peck, Flower, & Higgins, 1995). Other urban literacy studies have been conducted in school communities in which students come together from a variety of cultural backgrounds (e.g., Dyson & Genishi, 1994; Flesicher & Schaafsma, 1998; Freedman, Simons, Kalnin, Casareno, 1999; Heath, McLaughlin, & Milbrey, 1993; Stock, 1993). Another group of studies refocuses English educators' attention on students' rights to their own language.[1] This body of work has received extensive public attention as a result of the decision concerning language variation announced by the school board of Oakland, California (1996), which inspired what has come to be known as the Ebonics Debate. In response to widespread misinformation and media coverage of the school board's decision, 13 national organizations concerned with issues of language diversity and education (among them, American Association for Applied Linguistics, American Dialect Society, Center for Applied Linguistics, Linguistic Society of America, National Alliance of Black School Educators, National Council of Teachers of English, Teachers of English to Speakers of Other Languages) formed the Coalition on Language Diversity in Education. In the conference, *Language Diversity and Academic Achievement in the Education of African American Students*, the coalition assembled some 50 national leaders in language, education, and public policy to present their research and propose continuing investigation of language variation and use.

In the proceedings emerging from the conference, *Making the Connection: Language and Academic Achievement among African American Students* (Adger, Christian, & Taylor, 1999), 10 scholars draw attention to trends and issues that participants identified. John R. Rickford introduces the collection (1999) with an overview of the issues of concern to educators interested in language diversity and the academic achievement of African American students. Reviewing research on variation in language structure and style in classroom discourse, Courtney Cazden (1999) calls for additional research into language use and students' opportunities to participate in academic settings. Kelli Harris-Wright (1999) and Walt Wolfram (1999) describe school curricula that make productive use of language variation by making both students' Ebonics proficiency and Standard English usage subjects of study. John Baugh (1999) draws attention to the inadequacy of teachers' preparation in language variation and notes the promise of programs like one that Terry Meier (1999) describes. In their contributions A. G. Hilliard, III (1999) and Anna F. Vaughn-Cooke (1999) indicate that the same

---

[1] Here, of course, we allude to the publication *Students' Right to their own Language*, published in 1974 by the Conference on College Composition and Communication of the National Council of Teachers of English.

issues that are at stake in the Ebonics curriculum debate are also at stake in the assessment of language learning.

Drawing attention to policy statements on language variation developed in the United States, including the National Language Policy developed by the Conference on College Composition and Communication of the National Council of Teachers of English (NCTE), Geneva Smitherman (1999) notes that the Ebonics Debate inspired renewed interest in these statements. Smitherman goes on to observe that professional organizations' development of policy statement is a scholarly activity with potential long-term as well as immediate public consequences. Concluding the collection is Orlando Taylor's (1999) public testimony before the United States Senate Committee on Appropriations, Subcommittee on Labor, Health, and Human Services and Education shortly after the Oakland School Board's decision initiated the Ebonics Debate. In his testimony, Taylor addresses the work of language scholars to the concerns of policymakers and the public at large.

The articles in *Making the Connection* and those in the recent March 2001 *English Journal* that focus on language learning and teaching are also rich bibliographic resources that document the publication, since 1996, of a number of studies on language variation.

Another set of public policies that focuses English educators' attention on language are those emerging from "English for the Children" initiatives, a new phase of English-only activism. Recently proponents of English for the Children have campaigned in California, Arizona, Colorado, Massachusetts, and New York—and succeeded in California and Arizona—to dismantle bilingual education programs. In these settings, even if teachers are able to speak students' native languages, they may only use English to instruct students. Scholars and policy makers who oppose this development offer as support for their opposition research which demonstrates (1) that high levels of proficiency and literacy in a native language contributes to second language proficiency (Carlisle, 1994; Collier & Thomas, 1996; Hudelson, 1987; Krashen, 1996; Ramirez, 1991); (2) that it may take up to 2–3 years to acquire oral communication skills in a second language, and up to 4–6 years to acquire a level of proficiency for understanding English in its instructional uses (Collier, 1989; Cummins, 1981). Educators and scholars who oppose English for the Children legislation argue that it disadvantages linguistic minority students by preventing them from drawing upon both their linguistic and cultural resources (Crawford, 1999; Gutierrez, Baquedano-Lopez, & Asato, 2000; Paredes, 2000; Stritikus & Garcia, 2000).

Focusing attention on individual learners in a variety of communities, researchers have called into question not only misunderstandings of the relationships between language, aptitude, and learning and essentialist understandings of race, class, and gender but also categorical conceptions of children (e.g., at-risk, underprepared, learning disabled) that function all too often as disabling labels (e.g., Au, 1998; Ball, 2000; Carger, 1996; Cazden, 1988; Gutierrez & Stone, 2000; Lee, 1997; Mahiri, 1998; Moll, 2000; Nieto, 2000; Purcell-Gates, 1995).

In *What Difference Does Difference Make* (1994), Anne Haas Dyson gives voice to a set of questions that has inspired considerable research in the English language arts during the 1990s:

> How amidst the differences represented in any one classroom, do we as educators allow "the child" a place of integrity in the curricular landscape? How do we keep from reducing children to categories based on race, ethnicity, or gender, or worse, rendering great sweeps of children as "at risk" deviants from an imagined norm (pp. 25–26)?

In a study that examines simultaneously occurring social practices in classrooms, Kris Guitierrez and Lynda Stone (2000) confront the "imagined norm" that Dyson names. Revealing differences between teachers' goals for instruction (official scripts) and student literacy practices that sometimes contradict, sometimes resist teachers' goals (counterscripts), Gutierrez and Stone conclude that students' resistant discourse often gives voice to concerns that teachers' learning goals fail to address (p. 10). In an observation reminiscent of the findings of Shirley Brice Heath's (1983) groundbreaking study of children and families in two Piedmont communities, Guitierrez and Stone observe that language practices valued in students' home communities can be undermined when schooling does not take students' cultural backgrounds into account. And they argue for the study of counterscripts that can reveal what students know and value and the meanings they make of literacy tasks assigned in school (pp. 150–164). In earlier studies, that documented the mismatch between cultural strengths that African American children bring with them to the classroom and their teachers' expectations, Hale-Benson (1986) and Taylor and Dorsey-Gaines (1988) offered the same valuable insights and arguments as Guitierrez and Stone.

Jacqueline Irvine (1990) attributes the all too frequent failure of educators to make productive use of what Luis Moll has called students' "funds of knowledge" to "prescriptive ideologies and prescriptive structures that are premised on normative belief systems" (p. 13). Susan Ohanian (1999) supports Irvine's claim in a book length argument. A number of researchers have dramatized Ohanian's claim that *One Size Fits Few* in case studies of individual students' experiences in school (Allen, Michalove, & Shockley, 1993; Parker, 1997; Purcell-Gates, 1993; Voss, 1996). For example, in *Of Borders and Dreams: A Mexican-American Experience of Urban Education*, Chris Carger (1996) presents a probing portrait of Alejandro Juarez, Jr., a Mexican American youth, his family, and their frustrating experiences in negotiating the bureaucracy of one school system. Carger attributes the problems that the bilingual, bicultural child of her study faces to differences between home and school literacy, lack of funding for programs that might build bridges between home and school, and also to an "us" and "them" climate in which part of Alejandro's schooling took place.

In order to help teachers construct learning experiences that acknowledge and build on the language and literacy practices valued in students' home communities and to redress experiences like Alejandro Juarez Jr.'s, a number of researchers in the English language arts have conducted ethnographic studies designed to identify community values and cultural practices (e.g., Egan-Robertson & Bloome, 1998; Green & Dixon, 1993; Tuyay, Jennings, & Dixon, 1995). Recognizing culture as the product of multiple voices, creative human actions, and changing circumstances, these researchers work closely with teachers in an effort to develop culturally responsive curricula that invite dynamic interactions among teachers and students, schools and communities.

In another kind of effort designed to address the current mismatch between the cultural backgrounds of the majority of the nation's students and their teachers, Susan Florio-Ruane (1994) convened the Autobiography Club. Interested in learning whether preservice teachers' reading of autobiographies composed by individuals with diverse ethnic backgrounds might enable them to identify with individuals from diverse cultural communities, Florio-Ruane invited a group of preservice teachers to read and discuss six autobiographies written by individuals whom John Ogbu (1987) would call "voluntary" and "involuntary" immigrants to the United States. In an analysis of club members' informal, dinnertime conversations, Florio-Ruane notes a reality seldom mentioned in research reporting on efforts to bridge cultural divides: "in an effort to manage conflict . . . the group may back away from difficult and contested ideas" (p. 35).

Unique among inquiries of teachers and researchers working to study similarities and differences among their own and their students' understandings is David Schaafsma's (1993) phenomenological study, *Eating on the Street*. Schaafsma's study reports on a summer teaching project in which six teachers (three men, three women; three European American, three African American; three reared in working-class families, three reared in professional families) react differently to their students' eating snacks while walking to visit a local museum. After a troubling discussion in which the teachers told one another what they believed to be appropriate behavior for children, Schaafsma, one of the teachers involved, interviewed his colleagues and documented the experiences and understandings that shaped them as individuals, teachers, and colleagues working in an urban setting with children suffering the problems of persistent poverty. For the teachers in Schaafsma's study, the answer to the question *What Difference Does Difference Make?* (1995) is: A significant difference.

In the article and book that ask that question, Anne Haas Dyson claims that just as teachers understand students' actions differently as a result of their prior experiences, researchers' portrayals of students are rooted in their understandings and experiences. Even as she calls on teachers and researchers to develop deep, rich portraits of children, portraits that eschew "imagined norms," Dyson reminds her fellow researchers:

In making the child deeper, richer, we are also expanding our own identity as teachers. For the constructed child is indeed made in our image. And there are many of us who have trouble seeing ourselves—and our mothers—in the child of the past twenty years; social circumstance and cultural frames guide our ways of living with and loving children. It may be time to talk less of "empowering" and more of recognizing the power that exists in a newly reconstructed child, one with social skill and cultural roots needing curricular space. Of course, this child too is a construct, one to be reconceived by educators of the future, as they respond to other historical and cultural conditions and, indeed, to other children swimming over the boundaries of the past (1995, p. 26).

Acknowledging that the children of her research are children of her construction, Dyson names another problem of representation that has led post-modern researchers in English education to work to shape complex understandings of students and teachers, of learning and teaching: the inevitable inadequacy of one individual's (the researcher's) constructive descriptions of another (the researched).

Outlining some dimensions of the problem, Maxine Greene (1994) writes:

[D]escription, like language itself, is contingent on vantage point, or on location, or on gender, or on class, or on ethnicity. Description, after all is a human activity; it does not come down from "nowhere," nor does it point to some non-human reality beyond. . . . [I]n these post-modern times, neither artist nor philosopher [nor English educator] is capable of representing what is objectively "out there" (p. 207).

Rather, each of us represents phenomena, events, and persons as we see them, from our various vantage points.

In books and articles that describe, explain, and account for teachers and learners, for teaching and learning, a number of researchers have not only addressed the problem of representation directly but have also composed poly-vocal inquiries that incorporate multiple perspectives to address the problem (e.g., Carger, 1996; Dyson et al., 1995; Fleischer, 1995; Lather, 1991; Schaafsma, 1993; Stock, 1995).

## THE RESEARCHER AND THE RESEARCHED

Reflecting on case studies and ethnographic studies that she has conducted, Cathy Fleischer (1995) documents concerns she shares with other researchers in the English language arts whose work represents others. Invoking anthropologists James Clifford and Clifford Geertz, Fleischer writes:

James Clifford asks some important questions about representation, questions which seemed appropriate to my work: in an ethnography, "who speaks? who writes? when and where? with or to whom? under what institutional and historical constraints?" (1986, p. 13). Such questions highlight not only the difficulty—some would say the impossibility—of representing others fairly accurately, but also the political implications of even trying to do so.

Geertz (1988) raises similar issues but in somewhat different terms. For him the major problem ethnographers face—that of persuading their audiences—has resulted in what he calls issues of one's signature entering the writing. Geertz is concerned with more than whether or not an author is a trustworthy person. He is concerned with how an author enters a text, who the author of the text is, what an author does to convince a readership that she has "been there." The "moral certainty" involved in such questions leads Geertz to a specific conclusion: In today's world, he tells us, "the burden of authorship seems suddenly heavier" (p. 138). He goes on to say,

How you know you know is not a question they [anthropologists] have been used to asking in other than practical, empiricist terms. . . . How words attach to the world, texts to experience, works to lives, is not one they have been used to asking at all (p. 135).

For Geertz this raises questions both of the ethics of ethnographic approaches (is it decent?) as well as of the possibility of such an undertaking (is it possible?) (p. 115).

Addressing the questions Clifford and Geertz raise, and drawing on lessons she gleans from feminist research, Fleischer reflects on a case study she conducted and coauthored with a student and wonders whether researchers, even when students join in their research, ever adequately understand another's worldview; whether researchers who conduct inquiries with students and then go on to publish accounts of that research do not, in effect, reduce the significance of their students' perspectives on the research.

Like Fleischer, postmodern ethnographer Stephen Tyler (1986) has struggled with similar issues of representation and proposed a way to rethink representational research.

It [ethnographic research] foregrounds dialogue as opposed to monologue and emphasizes the cooperative and collaborative nature of the ethnographic situation in contrast to the ideology of the transcendental observer. In fact, it rejects the ideology of "observer-observed," there being nothing observed and no one who is observed. There is instead the mutual, dialogical production of a discourse, of a story of sorts. We better understand the ethnographic context as one of cooperative story making that, in one of its ideal forms, would result in a polyphonic text, none of whose participants would have the final word in the form of framing story or encompassing synthesis—a discourse on the discourse. It might be just the dialogue itself, or possibly a series of juxtaposed paratactic tellings of a shared circumstance ... or perhaps only a sequence of separate tellings in search of a common theme ... (p. 126).

Some English language arts educators have worked to conduct and publish the kind of poly-vocal studies Tyler describes (e.g., Draper, Puidokas, Schaafsma, & Widmer, 2000; Dyson et al., 1995; Dyson et al., 1997; Fishman & McCarthy, 2000; Fu, 1995; Graham, Hudson-Ross, Adkins, McWhorter, & Stewart, 1999; Vinz, 1995). In these studies, voices speculate rather than reach consensual conclusions (Fleischer, 1995, p. 62) and move to blur the boundaries between researcher and researched.

In *What Difference Does Difference Make*, for example, 12 urban teachers join Dyson (1997) as speakers. Teachers' conversations dramatize the challenges confronting urban educators. Dyson's thematic discussions highlight the dimensions of the challenges. Photographs of the teachers' students add semiotic depth to the essay's intertextual argument. In effect, researcher and researched "evoke" rather than represent phenomena under study in experienced teachers' tea-time discussions of their work in culturally diverse schools (Tyler, 1986, p. 126). In another study, Ruth Vinz (1995), working with the teaching logs of four first-year teachers, audiotapes of the teachers' group meetings, observations of their classes, and audiotapes of interviews with them, presents a richly textured portrait of the confusion and insights, struggles and achievements of newcomers to teaching. Acknowledging both the impossibility of replicating lived experience and the inadequacy of cause–effect reasoning to account for teaching and learning, Vinz allows readers to accompany her in an archeological "dig" as she moves back and forth in time and space and between and among artifacts and experiences, uncovering their dimensions and tracing their connections.

In still another study conducted by teacher educators and their former students, Sylvia Robbins and Jean Ketter (1996)

describe how teachers and students experience working together differently. As they do so, Robbins and Ketter draw readers' attention to another concern of postmodern scholarship: the limitations of theory to account for, explain, and predict teaching and learning.

## THEORY AND PRACTICE

Pleased by the prospect of introducing a group of preservice students to the highly recommended and regarded as theoretically sound practices of collaboration and portfolio assessment, Robbins and Ketter collaborated in planning two, independently taught teacher education courses. In an effort to make their separate courses a coherent learning experience for jointly enrolled preservice teachers, they asked their students to prepare one set of portfolios that both might use for evaluation purposes. Not only did Robbins and Ketter collaborate in planning their courses, but they also invited students to join them in determining the elements to be included in their portfolios and the criteria for portfolio evaluation. What they discovered is that two teachers' collaboratively designed, theoretically sound portfolio assessment results in anxiety-filled learning experiences for students.

Because students had been "apprenticed" in classroom cultures with "traditional assumptions about the role of teachers, the nature of language learning and the purposes of education" (Ritchie & Wilson, 1993, p. 76), they found it difficult to "see" through their shared culture the assumptions about language learning and assessment we were asking them to critique. [O]n the other hand, [we] had experienced an equally powerful apprenticeship in a culture promoting alternative assessment, and had difficulty, at first, "deciphering" or even recognizing the students' gestures of resistance (p. 82).

The stumbling blocks Robbins and Ketter faced when they collaborated to build community with their students and to integrate instruction and assessment in their teacher education courses draws attention to the fact that moving theory into practice is considerably more complex for practicing teachers than it is often purported to be.

Currently persuasive theory in language arts education argues, for example, that portfolios of students' work completed over time and in fulfillment of different tasks within one or several courses of study constitute authentic sites—especially when students have some control over portfolio contents—for both students and teachers to make sense of students' learning. Similar theory argues for the benefits of collaboration between and among teachers and students. Both these theoretical practices, however, assume others that often go unnamed. They assume, for example, that teachers and their students share communal values and motives, that they invest language and actions with common meanings (Fish, 1980). The reality is—of course—that classrooms of teachers and students in our society often do not begin their work together as members of communities with shared language and values. Such communities must be built, and building them in the course of one term, or one semester, or one year is neither easy, nor in some cases possible. As a result, educational theories—some of them in conflict with one another, others dependent on circumstances that do not exist—with their claims to universal powers of explanation and prediction, are problematic in practice.

Making this point, with reference to another example of teacher–student collaboration, Anne DiPardo (1996) writes:

Perhaps the rosy interest in teacher collaboration is of a piece with our longing for the 'good society' (Bellah et al., 1991), a place where concern for the individual and the whole are held in productive and humane balance. But as with that wider yearning, collaboration rubs against powerful precedents, challenging assumptions and modes of being with long tenacious roots. . . . Before we can think meaningfully about promoting teacher collaboration, we need to set aside romantic notions of what collaboration could or should be. We find no neatly delineated causes and effects in the gritty day-to-day of teachers' lives, just the ambiguities and vicissitudes that characterize real teaching and learning (McDonald, 1992) (p. 111).

Drawing readers' attention to still another problematic fault line in foundational conceptions of theory, Marilyn Wilson and Sharon Thomas (1995) question the predictive power of a learning theory that most English educators, including themselves, find persuasive. Questioning theory that correlates readers' comprehension of texts with their prior experiences of subjects discussed in those tests, Wilson and Thomas write:

It would seem that prior experience of situations and arguments presented in texts, do not always help students develop generally-agreed-upon meanings of those texts. Rather, the nature of readers' background knowledge, shaped as it is by an intricate web of cultural myths, emotional experiences, and prior assumptions, may actually prevent students from understanding texts as teachers might expect them to (p. 63).

Responsible teachers, Wilson and Thomas report that the lessons they learned when studying what they call their students' idiosyncratic interpretations "have prompted [them] to recast the theoretical construct *prior knowledge* into a constellation of lenses [that they] can invite students to draw upon when [students] have difficulty constructing meaning" (p. 63).

Further explorations in the "problematics of theory" may be found in *The Practice of Theory*, Ruth E. Ray's (1993) discussion of teacher research in composition studies as an important theory-building enterprise. Along with Patricia Harkin (1991), Ray argues that the knowledge practitioners create is superior in many ways to that created by university researchers in established disciplines:

Free of the constraints of disciplinary practices and ideologies which make university researchers blind to alternative explanations for phenomena, teacher-researchers are "postdisciplinary" in their ability to admit contradictions and deal with "overdetermined" situations in which complex phenomena are typically reduced to a single, cause-effect relationship (p. 71).

Ray's argument resonates with those of other researchers in the English language arts who acknowledge the tension between university-initiated inquiries into teaching and learning and the realities of school-life (e.g., Russel & Flynn, 1992; Sirotnik & Goodlad, 1988). It also serves as a telling introduction

to the published research of practicing teachers who are contributing to the knowledge base on teaching (Cochran-Smith & Lytle, 1999), influencing classroom teaching (Atwell, 1998; Barbiari, 1995; Glover, 1999; Rief, 1992; Smith, 1993), confronting the ethics of research as it has been practiced in education (e.g., Allen, Michalove, & Shockley, 1993; Graham et al., 1999; Hollingworth, 1994; Mortensen & Kirsch, 1996), highlighting mismatches between teachers' expressed theories and teaching practices (e.g., Hines, 1995; White & Smith, 1994), and calling into question teacher educators' conviction that theory(ies) emerging from traditionally conducted research can and should underlie the practice of different teachers, at different times, in different places.

Making it clear that they appreciate the powerful potential of what Elizabeth Bruss (1982) has called "beautiful theories," teacher-scholars acknowledge that explanatory, predictive theories in practice professions reveal that they are theories not descriptions of reality when they are exposed to the "unbearable lightness of being" (Kundera, 1984).

## THE NARRATIVE TURN

Acknowledging the limits of theory's power to explain and predict phenomena as complex as teaching and learning, a number of researchers in the English language arts (e.g., DeStigter, 2001; Fu, 1995; Gallas, 1994; Mahiri, 1998; Rose, 1995; Stock, 1995) have turned to anecdote, story, and narrative to capture the complexities of teaching and learning and to highlight anomalies that are too often overlooked in studies aimed at identifying generalizations about learners and learning. Focusing on texts (events) of daily life and lived experiences, on local knowledge (Geertz, 1983), on contingent understandings (Rorty, 1979), on personal testimonies (Felman & Laub, 1992), and on the direct experience of individuals and communities (Rose, 1995), these researchers "produce anti-positivist, anecdotal empiricism that savors detail and reserves a special place for what is unique in every life" (Rosenau, 1992, p. 83). Some of these researchers (e.g., Barone, 1995; Fu, 1995; Gallas, 1994) turned to narrative as a means of documenting the experiences of underrepresented individuals and groups; others, as a means of teacher preparation (e.g., Jipson & Paley, 1994; Wilson & Ritchie, 1994).

Karen Gallas (1994) turned to narrative to document how her students make sense and communicate their understandings of the world. Dialogical productions, Gallas' narratives are products of her interactions with students in a particular context over time. Gallas' stories do not pretend to be neutral representations of research findings, rather they are conditions of meaningfulness which John Clifford (1986) claims ". . . simultaneously describe real classroom events and make additional moral, ideological, and even cosmological statements. . . ." (pp. 98–99). Acknowledging the subjective nature of her research, Gallas argues that powerful and important understandings emanate from the intimate and changeable relationships that develop in classrooms and that her narratives function as evidence of the claims she makes. For Gallas, they are "embarrassing footnotes," stories grounded in amazement, metaphor, ambiguity, imagination, and sometimes, pain (p. 11).

As aware of the power of the storyteller as she is persuaded of the importance of testimony, Gallas describes her research as ongoing, self-conscious examination of subjective work. Negotiating between her roles as "participant" and "observer," Gallas locates her research data in both the stories she tells and the theoretical traditions that guide her thinking about children, classrooms, and literacy learning (1994, p. 7).

Across the 1990s, other researchers of the teaching of the English language arts turned to narrative for other purposes. Scholars, like David Schaafsma, draw upon theorist of narrative (e.g., Bakhtin, 1981; Bruner, 1986, 1990; Chambers, 1984; Clifford, 1986; Coles, 1989; Egan, 1986; Gates, 1989; Geertz, 1973; Mitchell, 1981; Noddings & Witherell, 1991; Polokow, 1985; Shuman, 1986; Silko, 1978; Volisinov, 1986; Wells, 1986; White, 1984) to better understand the stories students tell as they write and respond to published literature and to uncover the sources of teachers' expectations of students. Researchers, like Joseph Trimmer, whose edited collection *Narration as Knowledge: Tales of the Teaching Life* includes stories of teaching told by a number of well-known English language arts educators (among them, Chris Anson, Patricia Shelley Fox, Toby Fulwiler, Sharon Hamilton, Lad Tobin, Victor Villanueva, Jr., Ruth Vinz) to reveal how teachers use "devices of storytelling (scene, dialogue, point of view) to render moments that suggest an educational encounter" (1997, xii). Theorists, like Patricia Lambert Stock (1993, 1995, 2001), argue that narrative forms like the anecdote are not "mere" evidence of—but in fact valuable accounts of—teaching and learning. Based on her interviews of diverse individuals born between 1900 and 1980, Deborah Brandt (1998) highlights the methodological usefulness of narrative as an interpretative tool for probing current conditions of literacy teaching and learning and persistent stratification of opportunities for literacy learning as well as escalating standards across the 20th century for what counts as literacy. Scholars like Jane Tompkins (1996), whose memoir *A Life in School: What the Teacher Learned*, draw the attention of larger audiences in English studies to the uses of narrative as a means of inquiry.

Still other researchers turn to narrative to draw attention to how they develop a perspective on the roles they play in the stories they tell (Chiseri-Stater, 1996; Stock, 1995), and to who is telling the story about whom (Brodkey, 1989). In one such study, Dangling Fu (1995) foregrounds the speech, writing, and drawings of four Laotian refugee adolescents, recent immigrants to the United States. Positioning herself as a student of these four individuals, Fu constructs a collaborative text born of shared inquiry into the nature of literacy and learning across a dramatic range of cultural and linguistic borders.

From the outset, Fu is interested in her young informants—Tran, Paw, Cham, and Sy—as "individuals" and not merely "representations" of Loatian culture. She allows the four teenagers to dictate the story of their own lives, following their lead as they relate their personal histories, share anecdotes about their family, interpret classroom assignments—or, as is sometimes the case, remain silent. She devotes considerable textual space to these individual accounts, and though she self-consciously mediates between cultures, selecting and editing the conservations and compositions that will represent an other's reality, the fact that her informants' divergent accounts of a shared past, express different desires for their new life in America, and relate their stories with varied skill in their second language leaves little doubt but that, in speaking for others, Fu has positioned herself as a student of the other (Sullivan, 1996, pp. 110–111).

Convinced that teachers' reconstructions and examinations of their own learning experiences enable them to develop effective practices for literacy teaching, David Wilson and Joy Ritchie (1994) invite their teacher preparation students to compose stories about their own learning and teaching experiences. After reading Wilson and Ritchie's re-telling of her stories and insights, Carol Gulyas—one of their former students—chose to retell her own story (1994). Explaining why, Gulyas writes:

The story they have told is based on statements I made a number of years ago as I was beginning to move through my teacher education courses. Although their telling of my story is accurate and honest, I'm not that person anymore. My stories have changed, and I have changed as I continue to reflect on my life and as I gain more experience as a classroom teacher. I am now authoring my own story (p. 189).

Responding to the fact that some students' learning is constrained because they do not find familiar figures in the books they read in school or familiar stories of their experience in schoolroom discussions, some teachers use imaginative literature as texts in their courses and some teach imaginative literature in a fashion that allows students to figure their personal experiences into communal interpretations of literary works. Jan Jipson and Nicholas Paley (1994) explain why they use imaginative literature as texts in courses in social and historical foundations of education, educational research, and curriculum theory. In an essay they compose as a dialogue, Jipson and Paley allude to their personal experiences and encounters with literature to support their practice. Avowed postmodern thinkers, they argue that practicing teachers have as much to learn from imaginative literature and from attending to the gaps and silences between self and other in dialogic exchanges as they do from mono-logically constructed texts that erase difference and invisibility.

While a number of scholars have drawn our attention to the politics of scholarship in our field during the last 10 years, others have directed our attention to pedagogical models that create what Jay L. Robinson (1990) has called habitable places for learning, places where teachers and students can be in conversations with themselves and others, where prior experiences and understandings are shared, where meanings are negotiated, where possible worlds can be imagined, where new worlds can begin to be created within the curriculum.

## CREATING HABITABLE SPACE FOR LEARNING

At the time of the Dartmouth Conference and for the two decades thereafter, research into the teaching of the English language arts shifted from an emphasis on the expertise of teachers, teachers' movements through parts of classroom lessons, and the development of teacher-proof instructional materials to an emphasis on how individual learners use language to make meaning and accomplish goals. Pedagogies developed that asked students to read texts silently for sustained periods of time and to write about their reading in personal journals (e.g., Fader, 1968; Fulwiler, 1980; Manning & Manning, 1984). These pedagogies also asked students to choose their own writing topics and to write to discover, explore, and revise their ideas and understandings about those topics (e.g., Atwell, 1987; Butler & Turbill, 1984; Calkins, 1986; Graves, 1983; Macrorie, 1988). More recently, research in the teaching of the English language arts has shifted from an emphasis on individual students' uses of language to develop their own ideas and to acquire self-knowledge to learners' uses of language to explore and negotiate meanings in view of one another, in earshot of one another. Pedagogies have been developed that ask students to read in community, to write in collaboration, to construct the public place in which they can talk and write, listen and read to communicate with one another.

As the emphasis on exploring the personal has shifted to an emphasis on exploring the social, as a focus on the student as meaning maker and the teacher as facilitator has shifted to an emphasis as the student and the teacher as partners in meaning making, the classroom has been redefined as a site for conversation, for sharing of diverse views and perspectives, for entertaining diverse meanings, for negotiating common ones. Pedagogies have been designed to bring teachers and their students into conversation with one another and to engage teachers and students in conversations already underway, conversations alive and well in students' and teachers' cultural communities, conversations alive and well in disciplines and fields of study. These models assume that goals for teaching and learning and effective methods of instruction are culturally sensitive ones and that high standards for learning do not translate into uniform demonstrations of learning. Many acknowledge the potential of the English language arts curriculum to advance social justice and equity. Some invite students and teachers to question the ways that social systems such as race privilege, gender dominance, corporate interests work in the society in which they live.

In most cases, educators who have developed or written about these models (e.g., Applebee, 1996; Edelsky, 1999; Fleischer, 2000; Ladson-Billings, 1994; Mahari, 1998; McCormick, 1994; Pradl, 1996; Robinson & Stock, 1990) argue for active, critical learning that begins with students' prior knowledge and experience, is inquiry-oriented, asks students not only to learn subject matter but also to shape knowledge by using customary and creative methods of inquiry, requires critical thinking and creative expression, and results in public demonstrations of learning that are appropriate to the learners involved and the materials being studied. These educators' reform agenda are not radical in that they do not propose to throw out the Enlightenment baby with the bathwater; they have not promised that education will ensure economic success for individuals and society. Instead these educators recommend that individuals with disparate understandings come together in what Jay L. Robinson calls habitable spaces to learn how to conduct the kinds of conversations that will advance human understanding and enable humane interaction. In creating such spaces, these educators argue, as Robinson does, that it may be possible for students to learn the kinds of literacy upon which a democracy depends.

The terms *civic literacy* and *civil literacy* are meant to name capacities for the uses of the written word that promote certain ways of communicating "to achieve freedom in dialogue" [Greene, 1988, xii] to enable both "personal fulfillment and the emergence of a democracy dedicated to life and decency" [Greene, 1988, xii]. The first names collectively the responsibilities of citizenship in a democracy; the second names a mode of conducting dialogue that holds some promise of achieving decency in our conversations, in our dialogues, as we inevitably encounter conflicts that can threaten to separate us (Robinson, in Fleischer & Schaafsma, 1998, 22).

Two recent publications highlight the ways in which curriculum is being reconceived as conversation to accomplish such aims: Arthur Applebee's *Curriculum as Conversation* (1996) and Patricia Lambert Stock's *The Dialogic Curriculum* (1995). The argument that underlies Applebee's book is rooted in two ongoing conversations in the field, one about the nature of language learning and the other about curriculum. As he brings these two conversations together, Applebee offers a new vision of curriculum that stresses knowledge-in-action. Arguing that the curriculum in most high school English classes focuses on what educators consider most worth knowing, Applebee argues that such a curriculum reflects a fundamental misconception about the nature of knowledge and learning and strips knowledge of the contexts that give it meaning and vitality. Such a curriculum, Applebee claims, teaches students about the traditions of the past rather than about how they may enter into and participate in present and future traditions. Applebee's own vision of curriculum places emphasis on knowledge-in-action, which he contends, is at the heart of all living traditions. This knowledge, he says

arises out of participation in ongoing conversations about things that matter, conversations that are themselves embedded within larger traditions of discourse that we have come to value (science, the arts, history, literature, and mathematics) (Applebee, 1996, p. 3).

For Applebee, the development of curriculum must become the development of culturally significant domains for conversation; and instruction, a matter of helping students learn to participate in conversations within those domains.

Stock's (1995) book traces a year in the life of two classes of 12th-grade students and teachers who work together to uncover diverse and common themes in their life experiences by composing and sharing their growing up stories and reading the stories of published authors whose ethnic heritages match those of the learners. Reading and writing multiple texts and exploring their experiences in light of one another's experiences and those of the published authors', students and teachers discuss how the similarities and differences in their lived lives have led them to the ideas, understandings, and concerns that shape their identities.

While Stock's, like Robinson's, conception of curriculum as conversation is indebted to John Dewey who argued that conversation is a necessary component of critical pedagogy, Carole Edelsky's conception of curriculum, like Applebee's, is based on ongoing conversations in the field. In *Making Justice Our Project* (1999), Edelsky proposes a curricular model based on conversations about whole language and critical pedagogy. Like earlier critiques of progressive theories and practices that flourished in the 1970s and 1980 (e.g., reader response theory, writing process theory), Edelsky's is not a call for the abandonment of one theory for another, rather it is a call for the retheorizing of whole language theory in the light of critical pedagogy. Claiming that whole language does not go far enough in promoting an education for justice and equity, for ending systematic classism, racism, sexism, and other systems of domination, Edelsky argues that the first step in putting an end to systems of domination that inhibit democracy is to learn to *see them*—"to see how systematic (not idiosyncratic) privilege linked to a system driven by profit prevents people from participating equally and meaningfully; i.e., from having a democracy" (p. 14).

*Making Justice Our Project* presents stories of educators committed to bringing together whole language and critical pedagogy, which, according to Edelsky means among other things, highlighting the relationship of language and power; foregrounding the political, sociological, historical character of language and reading practices. Edelsky suggests that rather than talking about whole language as perspective-in-practice, we might talk about it as a set of commitments in practice; and instead of talking about accepting and celebrating students' interpretations and compositions of texts, we might talk about analyzing the positions texts offer (whether authored by students or others) and the already-available readings culture offers.

In her work, Gloria Ladson-Billings (1997) names the shortcomings of critical theory to guide the preparation and practice of teachers just as Edelsky has named what she sees to be the shortcoming of whole language theory. Arguing that critical theory does not meet the needs of individuals oppressed because of race, Ladson-Billings writes: "[S]cholars of color in a variety of fields have begun to challenge the 'universal' applicability of critical theory to their specific social, political, educational and economic concerns" (p. 131). Just as Edelsky does not call for the abandonment of whole language theory, Ladson-Billings does not call for doing away with critical theory. Rather she suggests that critical theorists bring race to the foreground by making race "problematic and open to critique" (p. 134). Presenting the stories of eight teachers who have problematized race, in her book *The Dreamkeepers: Successful Teachers of African American Children*, Ladson-Billings dramatizes the complex social systems at work in classrooms. She also reveals the benefits of culturally relevant pedagogy that helps students achieve academic success while also enabling them to maintain and be proud of their African American identity.

Many of the narratives written in the 1990s that help us to envision pedagogies of possibility, hope, and dreams are in a family with Ladson-Billings' story of the dreamkeepers. All resonate with Applebee (1999), when he claims: "I think we have reached a point in research in teaching of English where we have a fairly widespread consensus about the nature of effective teaching and learning, within a fairly well elaborated sociocognitive or socio-cultural frame" (p. 363). That said, Applebee points out challenges we have yet to address: developing a pedagogy that recognizes and respects cultural differences in forms

of authority and ways of teaching and learning as well as issues raised by policymakers and critics of the schools.

Others working in the English language arts have also invoked the conversation metaphor to draw the attention of researchers and teacher educators to the dynamics of classroom interactions and the realities of teaching and learning in the settings in which human beings teach and learn. Kathleen McCormick (1994) calls for active dialogue about reading among teachers and researchers of reading, contemporary literary, and cultural studies, so they begin to understand the dialectical relationship that exists among cognitive, expressivist, and social-cultural models of reading, and Cathy Fleischer (2000) demonstrates how literacy teachers can use strategies developed by veteran community organizers to engage community members in classrooms and to improve the quality and accuracy of public discussions of education.

## POLICY MANDATES AND THE ENGLISH LANGUAGE ARTS

While a number of English educators who have moved away from essentialist views of knowing have used the metaphors of borders, dreams, possibilities, and conversation to represent their belief that education is about the creation of knowledge that is made in action and in the company of others, public discussion of education has been conducted, for the most part, in the metaphors of business and industry (e.g., productivity, measured outcomes, standards, and quality control) that became the language of educational policy-making in the early part of the century (Callahan, 1962).

In *Reinventing Education: Entrepreneurship in America's Public School*, for example, Louis Gerstner, Jr. (1994) CEO of IBM—together with Roger Semerad, Denis Doyle, and William Johnston—refers to students as human capital, describes the relationship between teachers and the communities they serve as that of "buyers and sellers," recommends measuring school productivity "with unequivocal yardsticks" (p. 69), and insists on "absolute standards" (p. 70). Commenting on *Reinventing Education*, Susan Ohanian (2000) draws attention to the business metaphors of which it is composed, noting that they bespeak a conception of knowledge as fixed and education as uniformly realized. Ohanian places the argument of the book in a family of responses to the declared crisis in education as reportd in government documents like *A Nation at Risk* (National Commission on Excellence in Education, 1983), *America 2000*, and *Goals 2000*.

Whether this crisis in education is real or manufactured (Berliner & Biddle, 1995), the mandated policies that have emerged from these government reports stand in stark contrast to research conducted in the field of English language arts and to the epistomological and ideological thought that informs them. Summarizing the recommendations of *The Nation at Risk* in terms of three dominant themes (raise standards, measure results, and hold people accountable for their performance), literacy educator James Hoffman (2000) asserts that essentialist ways of thinking about reform are undemocratic—a threat to teachers and students:

Centralization and control are the reality in education as we enter the 21st century. Two hundred years of democratic and grass roots traditions in educational decision making have been abandoned in just a decade. Is there a threat to American Society from its schools? Yes, there is…. As a literacy educator, I see this threat represented in the proliferation of reductionist curricula for reading, in the silencing of professional dialogue and debate, in the marginalizing of minority positions and people, in a muting of voices in the texts our students are expected to read, and a stern control over the "correct" interpretations of these already bland texts (p. 617).

The results of numerous educational policies legislated in the 1990s—mandates that control teachers' actions both directly and indirectly—can be found in standardized testing plans that shape curriculum; state curriculum frameworks for reading and writing that produce detailed scripts and specifications for what is taught, how it is taught, and when it is taught; state-level legislation that requires specific methods of instruction; and federal legislation that defines the kind of research that can be used to prove programs "effective" (Hoffman, p. 620).

Willis and Harris (2000) offer a critique of mandated policies and literacy learning and teaching. They argue that the ideological domination and conformity driving these mandates serve effectively to revictimize the most needy children, the very children they are developed to help:

[These mandates relinquish] the responsibility and accountability of literacy proponents to acknowledge the socio-historic barriers of literacy's past. Moreover, the current disregard for the cultural politics of literacy research, which is being used to maintain an illusion of an equal educational system, has failed to suggest the importance of creating more culturally responsive, inclusive, and transformative literacy learning and teaching (p. 80).

*Standards for the English Language Arts: A Publication by the Profession for the Profession* published by the National Council of Teachers of English (NCTE) and the International Reading Association (IRA; 1996), is an interesting example of a document that attempts to meet a government mandate with public education's commitment to access and equity in mind. Noting the uselessness of content standards unless they are coupled with opportunity to learn standards, the first section of the *Standards* document highlights the correlation between student performance and socioeconomic status. In effect, the NCTE/IRA *Standards* argue that students and teachers cannot be held solely accountable for the educational problems we face. Defining standards as guidelines rather than normative measures, the document provides flexible descriptions of what students should know and be able to do by the time they leave high school, rather than delineating a body of knowledge that must be taught or mastered subject by subject, grade by grade. In an attempt to show how these standards can function as guidelines and not mandates, the *Standards* document also provides a set of classroom vignettes that may be used at local levels by educators, parents, and interested others for the purpose of talking about the schools they want and the learning they hope for their young people. Because NCTE and IRA insisted on linking achievement standards to opportunity-to-learn standards, avoided naming grade level indicators of achievement,

and refused to name a standardized list of books to be read by all students at each grade level, the federal government withdrew financial support for the development of the *Standards* document. When released, the document was criticized by the public because it did not provide detailed descriptions of information and skills that all students should know, and it was criticized from within the profession by members like Lois Weiner (1995, May). Crediting NCTE and IRA with naming conditions necessary for students to achieve the standards its members defined, Weiner argues that the standards movement does not accommodate the richness and complexity of the organizations' educational principles.

Coincident with the standards debate were others about the teaching of reading. As early as 1994, California politicians were naming the improvement of reading scores as goals of their political agenda. Subsequently, they translated political platforms into law. In fall of 1995, the California legislature passed two bills mandating that phonics instruction be used to teach reading. In 1996, Governor Pete Wilson proposed an annual budget of $100 million for skills-based reading instruction. By September 1997, the California legislature had passed seven separate reading bills; among other things these bills allocated funds from the *Goals 2000* program to support phonics instruction and funded phonics training for teachers (Lemann, 1997).

At the same time that California policymakers were promoting particular means of teaching reading to all students that are grounded in behaviorally based psychometric research (Putney, Green, Dixon, & Kelly, 1999), others were joining the movement. Similar legislation was developed in other states and at the national level. In 1998, a National Reading Panel (NRP) was formed and charged by Congress "to assess the status of research-based knowledge including the effectiveness of various approaches to teaching children to read" (p. 1). The panel offered the following description of the standard it would use to evaluate research:

The highest standard of evidence for such a claim is the experimental study, in which it is proved that treatment can make such changes and affect such outcomes. Sometimes when it is not feasible to do a genuine experiment, a quasi-experimental study is done. This type of study provides a standard of evidence that, while not as high, is acceptable to many investigators. To sustain a claim it is necessary that there be experimental or quasi-experimental studies of sufficient size or number, and scope (in terms of population served), and these studies be moderate to high quality (p. 6 of section 5).

As public policy moved to mandate the body of research that would inform the teaching of reading, critics called into question the efficacy of legal definitions of reading, reading practices, reading research (e.g., Allington & Woodside-Jiron, 1998; Goodman, 1998), the validity of claims about the "crisis in reading," the wisdom of equating phonics instruction with reading instruction (e.g., Coles, 1998; McQuillan, 1998), and the limitations of public endorsement of one research paradigm (e.g., Putney, Green, Dixon, & Kelly, 1999; Willis & Harris, 1997, 2000). Fundamental to each of these criticisms is the objection to the ways that policy mandates strive for standardization and uniformity of thought and actions. These public policy efforts fail to promote socially just and equitable opportunities of all literacy learners and teachers and therefore revictimize the most needy children (Willis & Harris, 2000).

Because the same schools of thought that underlie much of the legislation on standards and reading can be found in public discussion calling for the elimination of bilingual educational programs, and narrow definitions of what constitutes fair use of intellectual property, to name just a couple issue of concern to English language arts educators, the profession has begun to grapple with the role the profession should play in the development of government policies. Some members of the profession argue that we must find ways to work together. Miles Myers (1994), former Executive Director of NCTE, argues that the United States federal government will not provide sufficient resources to support public education if it can have no influence over the forms that education takes and that issues of equity must be addressed by the profession as well as the courts. Acknowledging the controversial nature of English language arts educators' direct participation in policy formation, Myers writes:

Participation in public policy projects always involves one in dilemmas, complexities, uncertainties, and sometimes questionable outcomes. Involvement always carries with it responsibility, a responsibility to recognize that "perfect" procedures and techniques cannot guarantee "perfect" uses. Others believe that these various standards projects may be one of the last chances for the K-12 public system of this country (p. 75).

Willis and Harris (2000) also acknowledge that literacy teaching and learning and politics will continue to be inextricably interwoven and must be addressed by and among educators and politicians. However, their recommendation is not without conditions. Calling explicitly for public discussion among policymakers and literacy educators, Willis and Harris argue that discussions of literacy practice, materials, and research must address issues of equity, issues that confront race, class, and gender in equities, issues that challenge the taken-for-granted paradigms that inform language and literacy practices and policy mandates.

## CLOSING REMARKS

During the next decade, as English educators continue to grapple with the pedagogical and political issues confronting teachers and students in a multicultural society in an era of breathtaking change, in a postcolonial world moving toward economic globalization, in an information era of dramatic technological development, we will continue to explore the social nature of language learning and use and the social dimensions of thought and learning. We expect that we will also expand a research agenda that has productively informed us about the learning needs of diverse students to include the need to speak more effectively to local, state, and national policymakers. We have learned from one another that the subject English lies not just in the study of already published texts but also in the development and use of texts that accomplish personal and communal goals. And we have learned about the interconnectedness of the personal and the social, of the social nature of personal thought and language use. Just as we have developed and shared with one another instructional practices and programs that advance choice, voice, and empowerment and conducted research that has taught us much about the politics of representation, the nature of *praxis*, and the power of dialogue, we will need to learn how better to explain our work and its value to others. An English educators work to accomplish this challenge, we predict they we will turn and return to narrative and story, both real and imaginative, as means of exploring intellectual, moral, and ethical dilemmas through the eyes of particular individuals at particular times in particular places.

More than a few of the researchers we have discussed in this essay are charting the directions that we believe our research will take during the next decade as we seek to bridge rivers that divide us (e.g., Applebee, 1996), enlist the public in our project (e.g., Fleischer, 2000), and rededicate ourselves to the development of a democracy yet to be realized (e.g., Edelsky, 1999; Hoffman, 2000; Stock, 1995; Willis & Harris, 2000).

## *References*

Adger, C. T., Christian, D., & Taylor, O. (Eds.). (1999). *Making the connection: Language and academic achievement among African American students*. Washington, DC: Center for Applied Linguistics.

Allen, J., Michalove, B., & Shockley, B. (1993). *Engaging children: Community and chaos in the lives of young literacy learners*. Portsmouth, NH: Heinemann.

Allington, R., & Woodside-Jiron, H. (1998). Thirty years of research in reading . . .: When is a research summary not a research summary? In K. Goodman (Ed.), *In defense of good teaching* (pp. 143–158). York, ME: Stenhouse.

Applebee, A. (1996). *Curriculum as conversation: Transforming traditions of teaching and learning*. Chicago, IL: University of Chicago Press.

Applebee, A. (1999). Building a foundation for effective teaching and learning of English: A perspective on thirty years of research. *Research in the Teaching of English, 33,* 352–366.

Atwell, N. (1987). *In the middle: New understandings about writing, reading and learning*. Portsmouth, NH: Boyton/Cook.

Atwell, N. (1998). *In the middle: New understandings about writing, reading and learning*. Portsmouth, NH: Heinemann.

Au, K. (1998). Constructivist approaches, phonics, and the literacy learning of students of diverse backgrounds. *National Reading Conference Yearbook, 47,* 1–21.

Bakhtin, M. (1981). *The dialogic curriculum*. (C. Emerson & M. Holquist, Eds.). Austin, TX: University of Texas Press.

Ball, A. (2000). Teachers developing philosophies on literacy and their use in urban schools: A Vygotskian perspective on internal activity and teacher change. In C. Lee & P. Smagorinsky (Eds.), *Vygotskian perspective on literary research: Constructing meaning though collaborative inquiry* (pp. 226–255). New York: Cambridge University Press.

Barbiari, M. (1995). *Sounds from the heart*. Portsmouth, NH: Heinemann.

Barone, T. (1995). Persuasive writing, vigilant readings, and reconstructed characters: the paradox of trust in educational storysharing. In J. Hatch & R. Wisniewski (Eds.), *Life history and narrative* (pp. 63–74). Washington, DC: The Falmer Press.

Barton, D., & Hamilton, M. (1998). *Local literacies.* New York: Routledge.

Baudrillard, J. (1983). *Simulations* (P. Foss, P. Patton, & P. Beitchman, Trans.). New York: Semiotext(e).

Baugh, J. (1999). Considerations in preparing teachers for linguistic diversity. In C. Adger, D. Christian, & O. Taylor (Eds.), *Making the connection: Language and academic achievement among African American students* (pp. 81–95). Washington, DC: Center for Applied Linguistics.

Bellah, R. (with others). (1991). *The good society.* New York: Vintage.

Berlin, J. (1982). Contemporary composition: The major pedagogical theories. *College English, 44,* 765–777.

Berliner, D., & Biddle, B. (1995). *The manufactured crisis: Myths, fraud, and the attack on America's public schools.* Reading, MA: Addison-Wesley.

Berthoff, A. (1971). The problem of problem solving. *College Composition and Communication, 22,* 237–242.

Brandt, D. (1998). Sponsors of literacy. *College composition and communication, 49,* 165–185.

Britton, J., & Chorny, M. (1991). Current issues and future directions. In J. Flood, J. M. Jensen, D. Lapp, & J. Squire (Eds.), *Handbook of research on teaching the English language arts* (pp. 110–120). New York: Macmillan.

Brodkey, L. (1989). On the subjects of class and gender in "The Literacy Letters." *College English, 51,* 125–141.

Bruner, J. (1986). *Actual minds, possible worlds.* Cambridge, MA: Harvard University Press.

Bruner, J. (1990). *Acts of meaning.* Cambridge, MA: Harvard University Press.

Bruss, E. (1982). *Beautiful theories.* Baltimore, MD: Johns Hopkins University Press.

Butler, A., & Turbill, J. (1984). *Towards a reading-writing classroom.* Rozelle, Australia: Primary English Teaching Association.

Callahan, R. (1962). *Education and the cult of efficiency.* Chicago, IL: University of Chicago Press.

Calkins, L. (1986). *The art of teaching writing.* Portsmouth, NH: Heinemann.

Carger, C. (1996). *Of borders and dreams: A Mexican-American experience of urban education.* New York: Teachers College Press.

Carlisle, R. (1994). Influences of L1 writing proficiency on L2 writing proficiency. In R. A. Devillar, C. Faltis, & J. Cummins (Eds.), *Cultural diversity in schools: From rhetoric to practice* (pp. 161–188). Albany, NY: SUNY Press.

Cazden, C. (1988). *Classroom discourse: The language of teaching and learning.* Portsmouth, NH: Heinemann.

Cazden, C. (1999). The language of African American students in classroom discourse. In C. Adger, D. Christian, & O. Taylor (Eds.), *Making the connection: Language and academic achievement among African American students* (pp. 31–52). Washington, DC: Center for Applied Linguistics.

Chambers, R. (1984). *Story and situation: Narrative seduction and the power of fiction.* Chicago: University of Chicago Press.

Chiseri-Stater, E. (1996). Turning in upon ourselves: Positionality, subjectivity, and reflexivity in case study and ethnographic research. In P. Mortensen & G. Kirsch (Eds.), *Ethics & representation in qualitative studies of literacy* (pp. 115–133). Urbana, IL: National Council of Teachers of English.

Clifford, J. (1986). On ethnographic allegory. In J. Clifford & G. Marcus (Eds.), *Writing culture: The poetics and politics of ethnography* (pp. 98–212). Berkeley, CA: University of California Press.

Cochran-Smith, M., & Lytle, S. (1999). The teacher research movement: A decade later. *Educational Researcher, 28*(7), 15–25.

Coles, G. (1998). *Reading lessons: The debate over literacy.* New York: Hill & Wang.

Coles, R. (1989). *The call of stories: Teaching and the moral imagination.* Boston: Houghton Mifflin.

Collier, V. (1989). How long: A synthesis of research on academic achievement in a second language. *TESOL Quarterly, 23,* 509–531.

Collier, V., & Thomas, W. (1996). *Effectiveness in bilingual education.* Orlando, FL: National Association of Bilingual Education.

Crawford, J. (1999). *Bilingual education: History, politics, theory and practice.* Los Angeles, CA: Bilingual Educational Services.

Cummins, J. (1981). The role of primary language development in promoting educational success for language minority students. In California State Department of Education, *Schooling and language minority students: A theoretical framework* (pp. 3–44). Los Angelas, CA: California State Department of Education.

Cushman, E. (1998). *The struggle and the tools: Oral and literate strategies in an inner-city community.* Albany, NY: SUNY Press.

Delpit, L. (1995). *Other people's children: Cultural conflict in the classroom.* New York: The New York Press.

DeStigter, T. (2001). *Literacy, democracy, and the forgotten students of Addison High: Reflections of a citizen teacher.* Urbana, IL: National Council of Teachers of English.

DiPardo, A. (1996). Seeking alternatives: The wisdom of collaborative teaching. *English Education, 28,* 109–126.

Dixon, J. (1967). *Growth through English: A Record based on the Dartmouth Seminar 1966.* Reading, England: NATE, 1967.

Dixon, J. (1969). *Growth through English.* New York: Oxford University Press.

Dixon, J. (1974). *Growth through English* (3rd Ed.). London: NATE, 1974.

Draper, A., Puidokas, C. K., Schaafsma, D., & Widmer, K. (2000). The St. Dymphna project: Engagements with democracy and teaching English. In *English Education, 33,* 51–72.

Dyson, A. H. (with the San Francisco East Bay Teacher Study Group). (1997). *What difference does difference make: Teacher perspectives on diversity, literacy, and the urban primary school.* Urbana, IL: National Council of Teachers of English.

Dyson, A. H. (1994). Confronting the split between "the child" and children: Toward new curricular visions of the child writer. *English Education, 26,* 12–28.

Dyson, A. H., Bennett, A., Brooks, W., Garcia, J., Howard-McBride, C., Malekzadeh, J., Pancho, C., Rogers, L., Rosenkrantz, L., Scarboro, E., Stringfield, K., Walker, J., & Yee, E. (1995). What difference does difference make? Teacher reflections on diversity, literacy, and the urban primary school. *English Education, 27,* 77–139.

Dyson, A. H., & Genishi, C. (1994). *The need for story: Cultural diversity in classroom and community.* Urbana, IL: National Council of Teachers of English.

Edelsky, C. (Ed.). (1999). *Making justice our practice: Teachers working toward critical whole language practice.* Urbana, IL: National Council of Teachers of English.

Egan, K. (1986). *Teaching as storytelling: An approach to teaching and curriculum in the elementary school.* Chicago: The University of Chicago Press.

Egan-Robertson, A., & Bloome, D. (Eds.). (1998). *Students as researchers of culture and language in their own communities.* Cresskill, NJ: Hampton Press.

Fader, D. (1968). *Hooked on books: Program and proof.* New York: Berkley.

Faigley, L. (1992). *Fragments of rationality: Postmodernity and the subject of composition*. Pittsburgh: University of Pittsburgh Press.

Farr, M. (1994). En los dos idiomas: Literacy practices among Chicago Mexicanos. In B. Moss (Ed.), *Literacy across communities* (pp. 9–47). NJ: Hampton Press.

Felman, S., & Laub, D. (1992). *Testimony: Crises of witnessing in literature, psychoanalysis, and history*. New York: Routledge.

Fish, S. (1980). *Is there a text in this class?: The authority of interpretative communities*. Cambridge, MA: Harvard University Press.

Fishman, A. (1988). *Amish literacy: What and how it means*. Portsmouth, NH: Heinemann.

Fishman, S., & McCarthy, L. (2000). *Unplayed tapes: A personal history of collaborative teacher research*. Urbana, IL: National Council of Teachers of English.

Fleischer, C. (1995). *Composing teacher research: A prosaic history*. New York: State University of New York Press.

Fleischer, C. (2000). *Teachers organizing for change*. Urbana, IL: National Council of Teachers of English.

Fleischer, C., & Schaafsma, D. (1998). *Literacy and democracy*. Urbana, IL: National Council of Teachers of English.

Florio-Ruane, S. (1994). The future teachers' autobiography club: Preparing educators to support literacy learning in culturally diverse classrooms. *English Education, 26*, 52–66.

Freedman, S., Simons, E., Kalnin, J., Casareno, A., & The M-Class Teams (Eds.). (1999). *Inside city schools: Investigating literacy in multicultural classrooms*. New York: Teachers College Press.

Fu, D. (1995). *"My trouble is my English:" Asian students and the American dream*. Portsmouth, NH: Heinemann.

Fulwiler, T. (1980). Journals across the disciplines. *English Journal, 69*, 14–22.

Gallas, K. (1994). *The languages of learning: How children talk, write, dance, draw, and sing their understanding of the world*. New York: Teachers College Press.

Gates, H. L. (1989). "Narration and cultural memory in the African-American tradition." In L. Goss & M. Barnes (Eds.), *Talk that talk: An anthology of African-American storytelling* (pp. 15–19). New York: Simon & Schuster.

Geertz, C. (1973). *The interpretation of cultures*. New York: Basic Books.

Geertz, C. (1983). *Local knowledge: Further essays in interpretative anthropology*. New York: Basic Books.

Gerstner, L. (with Semerad, R., Doyle, D., & Johnston, W.). (1994). *Reinventing education*. New York: Dutton.

Gitlin, T. (1989). Postmodernism: Roots and politics. *Dissent, 36*, 100–108.

Glover, M. (1999). *A garden of poets*. Urbana, IL: National Council of Teachers of English.

Gomez, M. L. (1993, Fall). Prospective teachers' perspectives on teaching diverse children: A review with implications for teacher education and practice. *The Journal of Negro Education, 62*, 459–474.

Gonzalez, N., Moll, L., Floyd-Tenery, M., Rivera, A., Rendon, P., Gonzales, R., & Amanti, C. (1995). Funds of knowledge for teaching in Latino households. *Urban Education, 29*(4), 443–470.

Goodman, K. (1998). Comments on the reading excellence act (U.S.) [Electronic version]. *Reading Online*. Retrieved from http://www.readingonline.org/critical/ACT.html

Graham, P., Hudson-Ross, S., Adkins, C., McWhorter, P., & Stewart, J. (1999). *Teacher/mentor: A dialogue for collaborative learning*. New York: Teachers College Press, and Urbana, IL: National Council of Teachers of English.

Graves, D. (1983). *Writing: Teachers and children at work*. Portsmouth, NH: Heinemann.

Green, J., & Dixon, C. (1993). Talking knowledge into being. Discursive and social practices in classrooms. *Linguistics and Education, 5*(3&4), 231–239.

Greene, M. (1978). *Landscapes of learning*. New York: Teachers College Press.

Greene, M. (1988). *The dialectic of freedom*. New York: Teachers College Press.

Greene, M. (1994). Postmodernism and the crisis of representation. *English Education, 26*, 206–219.

Griffith, P. (1988). The discourses of English teaching. *English Education, 20*, 191–205.

Gulyas, C. (1994). Reflections or Telling Stories: A response to "Resistence, revision, & representation." *English Education, 3*(26), 189–194.

Gutierrez, K. (2000). Teaching and learning in the 21st century. *English Education, 32*, 290–298.

Gutierrez, K., Baquedano-Lopez, P., & Asato, J. (2000). "English for the children": The new literacy of the old world order, language policy and educational reform [Electronic version]. *Bilingual Research Journal, 24*(1&2). Retrieved from http://brj.asu.edu/v2412/

Gutierrez, K., & Stone, L. (2000). Synchronic and diachronic dimensions of social practice: An emerging methodology for cultural-historical perspectives on literacy learning. In C. Lee & P. Smagorinsky (Eds.), *Vygotskian perspective on literary research: Constructing meaning though collaborative inquiry*. New York: Cambridge University Press.

Hale-Benson, J. (1986). *Black children: Their roots, culture, and learning styles*. Baltimore, MD: Johns Hopkins University Press.

Harkin, P. (1991). The postdisciplinary politics of lore. In P. Harkin & J. Schilb (Eds.), *Contending with words: Composition and rhetoric in a postmodern age* (pp. 124–138). New York: Modern Language Association.

Harris, J. (1997). *A teaching subject: Composition since 1966*. Upper Saddle River, NJ: Prentice-Hall.

Harris-Wright, K. (1999). Enhancing bidialectalism in urban African American students. In C. Adger, D. Christian, & O. Taylor (Eds.), *Making the connection: Language and academic achievement among African American students* (pp. 53–60). Washington, DC: Center for Applied Linguistics.

Heath, S. (1983). *Way with words: Language, life, and work in communities and classrooms*. Cambridge, England: Cambridge University Press.

Heath, S., & McLaughlin, M. (Eds.) (1993). *Identity and inner-city youth: Beyond ethnicity and gender*. New York: Teachers College Press.

Hilliard, III, A. G. (1999). In Language, diversity, and assessment—Ideology, professional practice, and the achievement gap. In C. Adger, D. Christian, & O. Taylor (Eds.), *Making the connection: Language and academic achievement among African American students*. Washington, DC: Center for Applied Linguistics.

Hines, M. B. (1995). Complicating the coherence quest(ions): What's theory got to do, got to do with it? *English Education, 27*, 240–257.

Hoffman, J. (2000). The de-democratization of schools and literacy in America. *The Reading Teacher, 53*(8), 616–623.

Hollinger, D. A. (1995). *Postethnic America: Beyond multiculturalism*. New York: Basic Books.

Hollingworth, S. (1994). *Teacher research and urban literacy education: Lessons and conversations in a feminist key*. New York: Longman.

Hudelson, S. (1987). The role of native language literacy in the education of language minority children. *Language Arts, 64*(8), 827–840.

Irvine, J. (1990). *Black students and school failure*. Westport, CT: Greenwood.

Jipson, J., & Paley, N. (1994). Literature/curriculum//authority/absence: An axiomatic conversation. *English Education, 26,* 220-235.

Jones, R., & Lunsford, A. (1989). The English coalition conference: Democracy through language. Urbana, IL: National Council of Teachers of English, and New York: Modern Language Association.

Kamper, D., & Wulf, C. (Eds.). (1989). *Looking back on the end of the world.* New York: Semiotext(e).

Krashen, S. (1996). *Under attack: The case against bilingual education.* Culver City, CA: Language Education Association.

Kuhn, T. (1970). *The structure of scientific revolutions.* Chicago: University of Chicago Press.

Kundera, M. (1984). *The unbearable lightness of being.* New York: Harper & Row.

Ladson-Billings, G. (1994). *The dreamkeepers: Successful teachers of African-American children.* San Francisco, CA: Jossey-Bass.

Ladson-Billings, G. (1997). I know why this doesn't feel empowering: A critical race analysis of critical pedagogy. In P. Freire, J. Fraser, & D. Macedo (Eds.), *Mentoring the mentor: A critical dialogue with Paulo Freire* (pp. 127-141). New York: Peter Lang.

Lather, P. (1991). *Getting smart: Feminist research and pedagogy with/in the postmodern.* New York: Routledge.

Lee, C. (1997). Bridging home and school literacies: A model of culturally responsive teaching. In J. Flood, S. B. Heath, & D. Lapp (Eds.), *A handbook for literacy educators: Research on teaching the communicative and visual arts* (pp. 330-341). New York: Macmillan.

Lee, C. (2000). Understanding in the most fundamental way. *English Education, 32,* 308-311.

Lemann, N. (1997). The reading wars. *The Atlantic Monthly, 280*(5), 128-134.

Macrorie, K. (1988). *The I-search paper.* Portsmouth, NH: Boynton/Cook.

Mahiri, J. (1998). *Shooting for excellence.* New York: Teacher College Press and Urbana, IL: National Council of Teachers of English.

Manning, G., & Manning, M. (1984). What models of reading make a difference? *Reading World, 23,* 375-380.

McCormick, K. (1994). *The culture of reading and the teaching of English.* Manchester, England: Manchester University Press.

McCracken, N. M. (2000). Muted dialogues: Seeking a discourse for preparing to teach across race, class, and language. *English Education, 32,* 246-250.

McDonald, J. P. (1992). *Teaching: Making sense of an uncertain craft.* New York: Teachers College Press.

McQuillan, J. (1998). *The literacy crisis: False claims, real solutions.* Portsmouth, NH: Heinemann.

Meier, T. (1999). The case for Ebonics as part of exemplary teacher preparation. In C. Adger, D. Christian, & O. Taylor (Eds.), *Making the connection: Language and academic achievement among African American students.* Washington, DC: Center for Applied Linguistics.

Michie, G. (1999). *Holler if you hear me: The education of a teacher and his students.* New York: Teachers College Press.

Mitchell, W. J. T. (Ed.). (1981). *On narrative.* Chicago: University of Chicago Press.

Moll, L. (2000). Inspired by Vygotsky: Ethnographic experiments in education. In C. Lee & P. Smagorinsky (Eds.), *Vygotskian perspective on literary research: Constructing meaning though collaborative inquiry.* New York: Cambridge University Press.

Mortensen, P., & Kirsch, G. (1996). *Ethics & representation in qualitative studies of literacy.* Urbana, IL: National Council of Teachers of English.

Myers, M. (1994). NCTE's role in standards projects. *English Education, 26,* 67-76.

National Commission on Excellence in Education. (1983). *A nation at risk: The imperative for educational reform.* Washington, DC: U.S. Government Printing Office.

National Council of Teachers of English, & International Reading Association. (1996). *Standards for the English language arts: A publication by the profession for the profession.* Urbana, IL: National Council of Teachers of English.

National Reading Panal. (1999). Interim Report [Online]. http://www.nationalreadingpanel.org/Publications/Interim_Report/section5.htm.p6.

National Reading Panal. (2001). Summary [Online]. http://www.nichd.nih.gov.publications/nrp/intro.htm.pg.1

Nieto, S. (2000). *Affirming diversity: The sociopolitical context of multicultural education.* Reading, MA: Addison-Wesley.

Noddings, N., & Witherell, C. (Eds.). (1991). Stories lives tell: Narrative and dialogue in education. New York: Teachers College Press.

Ogbu, J. (1987). Variability in minority school performances: A problem in search of an explanation. *Anthropology and Education Quarterly, 18,* 312-334.

Ohanian, S. (1999). *One size fits few: The folly of educational standards.* Portsmouth, NH: Heinemann.

Ohanian, S. (2000). Goals 2000: What's in a name? *Kappan, 81*(5), 344-355.

Paredes, S. (2000). How proposition 227 influences the language dynamics of a first- and second-grade mathematics lesson [Electronic version]. *Bilingual Research Journal, 24*(1&2). Retrieved from http://brj.asu.edu/v2412/

Parker, D. (1997). *Jamie: A literacy story.* York, ME: Stenhouse.

Peck, W. C., Flower, L., & Higgins, L. (1995). Community literacy. *College composition and communication, 46,* 199-222.

Pixley, M. F., & VanDerPloeg, L. (2000). Learning to see: White. *English Education, 32,* 278-289.

Polokow, V. (1985). "Whose stories should we tell? Critical phenomenology as a call to action." *Language Arts, 62,* 1-16.

Puidokas, C. K. (2000). Spinning the web: Relationships, talk, and learning in a diverse classroom. *English Education, 32,* 299-307.

Pradl, G. M. (1996). *Literature for democracy: Reading as a social act.* Portsmouth, NH: Boyton/Cook.

Purcell-Gates, V. (1993). I ain't never read my own words before. *Journal of Reading, 37,* 210-219.

Purcell-Gates, V. (1995). *Other people's words: The cycle of low literacy.* Cambridge, MA: Harvard University Press.

Putney, L., Green, J., Dixon, C., & Kelly, G. (1999). Conversations: Evolution of qualitative research methodology: Looking beyond defense to possibilities. *Reading Research Quarterly, 34*(3), 368-377.

Ramirez, J. D. (1991). *Final report: Longitudinal study of structured English immersion strategy, early-exit, and late-exit bilingual education programs.* Washington, DC: U.S. Department of Education.

Ray, R. E. (1993). *The practice of theory: Teacher research in composition.* Urbana, IL: National Council of Teachers of English.

Rickford, J. R. (1999). Language diversity and academic achievement in education of African American students—An overview of the issues. In C. Adger, D. Christian, & O. Taylor (Eds.), *Making the connection: Language and academic achievement among African American students.* Washington, DC: Center for Applied Linguistics.

Rief, L. (1992). *Seeking diversity: Language arts with adolescents.* Portsmouth, NH: Heinemann.

Ritchie, J. S., & Wilson, D. E. (1993). Dual apprenticeships: Subverting and supporting critical teaching. *English Education, 25,* 67-83.

Robbins, S., & Ketter, J. (with others). (1996). Revising the language of classroom-based assessment: Multiple perspectives on a portfolio experiment in teacher education. *English Education, 28,* 77-108.

Robinson, J. (1990). *Conversations on the written word: Essays on language and literacy.* Portsmouth, NH: Boynton/Cook.

Robinson, J. (1998). Literacy and lived lives: Reflections on responsibilities of teachers. In C. Fleischer & D. Schaafsma (Eds.), *Literacy and democracy: Teacher research and composition studies in pursuit of habitable spaces*. Urbana, IL: National Council of Teachers of English.

Robinson, J., & Stock, P. L. (1990). The politics of literacy. In J. Robinson (Ed.), *Conversations on the written word: Essays on language and literacy*. Portsmouth, NH: Boyton/Cook.

Rorty, R. (1979). *Philosophy and the mirror of nature*. Princeton, NJ: Princeton University Press.

Rose, M. (1995). *Possible lives: The promise of public education in America*. New York: Penguin Books.

Rosen, L., & Abt-Perkins, D. (2000). Preparing English teachers to teach diverse student populations: Beliefs, challenges, proposals for change. *English Education, 32*, 251-266.

Rosenau, P. M. (1992). *Post-modernism and the social sciences*. Princeton, NJ: Princeton University Press.

Russel, J., & Flynn, R. (1992). *School-university collaboration*. Bloomington, IN: Phi Delta Kappa Educational Foundation.

Schaafsma, D. (1993). *Eating on the street: Teaching literacy in a multicultural society*. Pittsburgh, PA: University of Pittsburgh Press.

Shuman, A. (1986). *Storytelling rights: The uses of oral and written texts by urban adolescents*. London: Cambridge University Press.

Silko, L. M. (1978). *Ceremony*. New York: Knopf.

Sirotnik, K., & Goodlad, J. (1988). *School-university partnerships in action*. New York: Teachers College Press.

Smith, K. (1993). *A descriptive analysis of the responses of six students and their teacher in literature study sessions*. Unpublished doctoral dissertation, Arizona State University, Tempe, AZ.

Smitherman, G. (1999). Language policy and classroom practices. In C. Adger, D. Christian, & O. Taylor (Eds.), *Making the connection: Language and academic achievement among African American students*. Washington, DC: Center for Applied Linguistics.

Steichen, E. (1955). *The family of man*. New York: Museum of Modern Art.

Stock, P. L. (1993). The function of the ancedote in teacher research. *English Education, 25*(4), 173-187.

Stock, P. L. (1995). *The dialogic curriculum: Teaching and learning in a multicultural society*. Portsmouth, NH: Boynton/Cook.

Stock, P. L. (1996). Post-modern scholarship: Contributions from a practice profession. *English Education, 28*, 227-251.

Stock, P. L. (2001). Toward a theory of genre in teacher research: Contributions from a reflective practitioner. *English Education, 33*(2), 100-114.

Street, B. (1995). *Social literacies: Critical approaches to literacy in development, ethnography and education*. Reading, MA: Addison-Wesley.

Stritikus, T., & Garcia, E. (2000). Education of limited English proficient students in California schools: An assessment of the influence of Proposition 227 on selected teachers and classrooms [Electronic version]. *Bilingual Research Journal, 24*(1&2). Retrieved from http://brj.asu.edu/v2412/

Sullivan, P. (1996). Ethnography and the problem of the "other." In P. Mortensen & G. Kirsch (Eds.), *Ethics & representation in qualitative studies of literacy* (pp. 115-133). Urbana, IL: National Council of Teachers of English.

Taylor, D., & Dorsey-Gaines, C. (1988). *Growing up literate: Learning from inner-city families*. Portsmouth, NH: Heinemann.

Taylor, O. (1999). Testimony of Orlando L. Taylor on the subject of "Ebonics." In C. Adger, D. Christian, & O. Taylor (Eds.), *Making the connection: Language and academic achievement among African American students*. Washington, DC: Center for Applied Linguistics.

Tompkins, J. (1996). *A life in school: What the teacher learned*. New York: Addison-Wesley.

Trimmer, J. (1997). *Narration as knowledge: Tales of the teaching life*. Portsmouth, NH: Boynton/Cook.

Tuyay, S., Jennings, L., & Dixon, C. (1995). Classroom discourse and opportunities to learn: An ethnographic study of knowledge construction in a bilingual third grade classroom. *Discourse Processes, 19*(1), 75-110.

Tyler, S. (1986). Post-modern ethnography: From document of the occult to occult document. In J. Clifford & G. E. Marcus (Eds.), *Writing culture: The poetics and politics of ethnography* (pp. 122-140). Berkeley, CA: University of California Press.

United States Department of Education, National Center for Education Statistics. (1997). *America's teachers: Profile of a profession*, 1993-94 (pp. 97-460). Washington, DC: Author.

Vattimo, G. (1988). *The end of modernity: Nihilism and hermeneutics in post-modern critique*. London: Polity.

Vaughn-Cooke, A. F. (1999). Lessons learned from the Ebonics controversy—Implications for language assessment. In C. Adger, D. Christian, & O. Taylor (Eds.), *Making the connection: Language and academic achievement among African American students*. Washington, DC: Center for Applied Linguistics.

Vinz, R. (1995). Opening moves: Reflections on the first year of teaching. *English Education, 27*, 158-207.

Volisinov, V. N. (1986). *Marxism and the philosophy of knowledge*. (L. Matejka & I. R. Titunik, Trans.). Cambridge: Harvard University Press.

Voss, M. (1996). *Hidden literacies*. Portsmouth, NH: Heinemann.

Weiner, L. (1995, May). Democracy, pluralism, and the teaching of English. *English Education, 27*, 140-145.

Wells, G. (1986). *The meaning makers: Children learning language and using language to learn*. Portsmouth, NH: Heinemann.

West, C. (1988). Interview with Cornel West. In A. Ross (Ed.), *Universal Abandon? The politics of postmodernism* (pp. 269-286). Minneapolis, MN: University of Minnesota Press.

White, B., & Smith, M. (1994). Metaphors in English education: Putting things in perspective. *English Education, 26*, 157-176.

White, J. B. (1984). *When words lose their meaning*. Chicago: University of Chicago Press.

Willis, A. (2000). Keeping it real: Teaching and learning about culture, literacy, and respect. *English Education, 32*, 267-277.

Willis, A., & Harris, V. (1997). Expanding the boundaries: A reaction to the First-Grade Studies. *Reading Research Quarterly, 32*, 439-445.

Willis, A., & Harris, V. (2000). Political acts: Literacy learning and teaching. *Reading Research Quarterly, 35*(1), 72-88.

Wilson, D., & Ritchie, J. (1994). Resistance, revision, and representation: Narrative in teacher education. *English Education, 26*, 177-188.

Wilson, M., & Thomas, S. (1995). Holy smoke! I missed something here: Cultural experience and the construction of meaning. *English Education, 27*, 56-64.

Wolfram, W. (1999). Repercussions from the Oakland Ebonics controversy—The critical role of dialect awareness programs. In *Making the connection: Language and academic achievement among African American students*. Washington, DC: Center for Applied Linguistics.

# METHODS OF RESEARCH ON ENGLISH LANGUAGE ARTS TEACHING

# ·11·

# UNDERSTANDING RESEARCH ON TEACHING THE ENGLISH LANGUAGE ARTS: AN INTRODUCTION FOR TEACHERS

*Sandra Stotsky*
*Harvard Graduate School of Education*

*Cindy Mall*
*University of Illinois*

In everyday life, we often do research to find practical solutions for immediate problems; we look for something that "works," even if we don't really know why it works. The immediate purpose of academic research in education, however, is to seek empirical evidence for explanatory generalizations, or theories, about the relationships among teaching practices, learning processes, and educational outcomes. The larger purpose of academic research is the development of theoretical knowledge.

Theoretical knowledge consists of systematically formulated and organized generalizations that explain the nature or behavior of a particular phenomenon. In the English language arts, these explanatory generalizations, or theories, constitute our knowledge about what happens as language teachers and language learners interact, what their interactions mean to them, why they take place, and what effects they have on the quality of language learning. The purpose of these theories is not only to explain what we can observe but also to predict what will or might happen. In essence, a theory is an educated "guess" about cause and effect for a particular phenomenon. A theoretical model derived from a theory tries to organize all the seemingly relevant elements of the phenomenon in a way that may account for its occurrence, and the model serves as a guide in formulating hypotheses for empirical studies of the phenomenon.

The purpose of much of the research in the English language arts is to determine how valid a particular theory is in explaining a particular phenomenon. The more validity a theory has, the more support it has, the more researchers can use it to guide further research, and the more teachers can rely on it as a general guide for pedagogical practice. Nevertheless, no matter how much explanatory strength a theory has, for example, no matter how much empirical evidence has been obtained to support the theory, theories in the English language arts, as in other areas, are always tentative. Problems constantly arise or new facts are discovered, that do not seem to be explained by existing theories. Moreover, our ability to understand any educational phenomenon is always limited by the complexity of human behavior. Every theory is simply the best explanation we have at the moment for a particular educational question or concern. Thus, academic research on teaching the English language arts is a continuous, never-ending process of systematic inquiry for enhancing the explanatory power of theoretical discourse on language teaching and learning.

This chapter is intended to give K–12 teachers an introduction to understanding the basic categories and functions of research in teaching the English language arts, as academic research is generally understood. It was designed with the assumption that most teachers do not have extensive backgrounds in understanding educational research. It was also designed to highlight, as much as possible, studies that tell us something about teaching or the teacher's role in the learning process in order to compensate for the fact that there have been relatively few studies since the 1960s devoted to the teacher's role in stimulating student learning in the English language arts (Peters, 1987). Although much of the research in the English language arts is addressed chiefly to other researchers or doctoral students (e.g., the research on planning processes in composing), or is of primary concern to public policymakers or educational administrators (e.g., large program evaluations), the illustrative research in this chapter was selected, as much as possible, for its potential appeal to classroom teachers or curriculum developers.

The chapter begins with a brief overview of what research is and what it is not. It then describes the two basic modes of academic inquiry—conceptual work and empirical research—with a discussion of empirical research in the English language arts divided into two categories: qualitative and quantitative methods. It concludes by suggesting how teachers might recognize these major categories of research in classroom-oriented studies and how they might go about determining the theoretical value of a study's findings. However, the chapter also suggests why the usefulness of a particular study to a particular practitioner may not necessarily depend on the theoretical value of its findings. Thus, the overall purpose of this chapter is to help teachers become more intelligent consumers of, as well as participants in, educational research.

## WHAT IS RESEARCH?

Academic research on teaching the English language arts is a planned, methodical exploration of some aspect of language teaching and learning. Regardless of the nature of the question or problem the researcher is investigating, researchers plan what they are going to do and proceed by systematically gathering data of some kind to address the question or problem. Data are facts. Sometimes they may be easily established and verified by others (e.g., the works of literature that secondary school teachers recommend for whole class instruction, as in Stotsky and Anderson, 1990). Or they may have a subjective quality and their status as facts depends on what researchers report they have observed (e.g., how students with different levels of reading ability participated in informal literature discussion groups, as in Wollman-Bonilla, 1994). Or they may be quantities resulting from criteria or instruments that assess the quality of language teaching and learning, as in Sadoski, Willson, and Norton, 1997. But researchers do more than provide their readers with data to inspect (e.g., a list of the readings certain teachers assign their classes; a detailed description of how particular sixth graders responded to their teacher's invitation to talk informally about what they had read; or the combination of instructional variables associated with large gains in writing. They also interpret the meaning of these data. Researchers then suggest how their findings contribute to the development of theoretical knowledge about the process of language teaching and language learning and the effects of this process on the students' development as a speaker, listener, reader, and writer of the English language.

In the English language arts, as in other subject areas, one must distinguish a research study from instructional materials that operationalize the pedagogical implications of research findings. For example, a workbook on the editing process by Epes and Kirkpatrick (1987) provides exercises designed to help adult basic writers discover whether they are most prone to overlooking either missing words, missing endings, or reversed letters. The exercises are based on many years of teaching, joint research (e.g., Epes & Kirkpatrick, 1978), and Epes' (1985) in-depth case study of 26 unskilled adult students, all of which suggested that unskilled adult writers show different patterns of errors in their writing. While the material in Epes and Kirkpatrick's workbook is clearly derived from their research findings, it is not the research itself. A bibliography (as in Epes and Kirkpatrick's workbook) or an introductory section should suggest the body of research on which an instructional text is based.

It is also important to distinguish academic research from field-testing instructional material. Before mass distribution of newly created instructional material, field-testers for publishing companies attempt to determine the material's usability in selected classrooms representative of the intended market. Their goal is to find out if the material needs to be revised (and made more useful), not if the the theoretical knowledge that the material was designed to reflect should be revised. Field-testing is also done by teachers. As Calkins (1985) points out, many of the studies conducted by teacher researchers in their own classrooms are also examples of field-testing. Teachers often try out their own or others' ideas in their own classrooms. But, Calkins suggests, "Will this work in my classroom?" is not an academic research question.

One must also distinguish academic research from what is referred to as "advocacy-oriented research" or "action research." In this kind of classroom-based work, a self-designated teacher researcher shapes a classroom lesson to achieve a particular self-chosen social or political goal. It is done for the purpose of "altering social relationships" in the classroom, which Harste (1992) asserts is the larger goal of literacy research. For example, Enciso (1994) used literature discussion in a fifth-grade classroom to bring up the topic of race and racism, which the children had not brought up themselves, in order to make them aware of the color of their skin and to shape their "cultural identities." However, as the co-directors of the National Reading Research Center (1995) comment, it is not clear that researchers who engage in advocacy-oriented research "can know what is enabling, or empowering, for others" and can "instill a certain sense of empowerment within those who participate in our studies." Their comments point to the flaw in such so-called research; its purpose is not to find answers to questions about an issue or problem in teaching or learning but to act on the belief that the answers to the questions are already known.

Finally, one must distinguish academic research from personal narratives describing a successful teacher's philosophy, approach, and experiences in the classroom, such as Eliot Wigginton's (1985) account of the *Foxfire* project, or Nancie Atwell's (1987) book on teaching writing and reading in a middle school. Books or articles of this nature can stimulate other practitioners' thinking, provide them with much useful pedagogical advice, and offer rich insights for researchers to use in creating or revising theory. But in themselves, they do not constitute academic research, a form of inquiry characterized by, among other things, the professional detachment of the inquirer, the systematic collection and write-up of data to address an explicit problem or question, and the use of a codified methodology (Chilcott, 1987).

Good research provides teachers with concepts to think with and ideas to think about. It also raises questions to stimulate their thinking about what they see or do in the classroom. But its purpose is not to propose a specific solution to a particular teacher's classroom problems, to advocate a particular pedagogical practice, or to provide instructional materials for teachers or students. Rather, its purpose is to enhance a teacher's ability to make intelligent instructional decisions. It is from this general perspective that teachers should examine academic research.

## THE BASIC MODES OF ACADEMIC INQUIRY IN TEACHING THE ENGLISH LANGUAGE ARTS

In order to understand the nature of empirical research on teaching the English language arts, it is useful to distinguish first the two basic modes of academic inquiry. In its categorization of doctoral dissertations for determining awards each year (e.g., *Educational Researcher*, 1988, p. 30), the American Educational Research Association (AERA) suggests two broad categories of academic inquiry concerned with the improvement of the educational process: conceptual and empirical work.

### Conceptual Inquiry

Conceptual work is theoretical or philosophical in nature and is usually referred to as scholarship rather than research. It focuses on an examination of the assumptions and conditions that shape teaching and learning and on the formulation of broad principles for models of teaching and learning. It may draw insights from the results of existing empirical research, but it is not concerned with gathering new data from systematic observations to provide evidence for support of its propositions. The work of John Dewey (1938) is a prime example of conceptual inquiry in the field of education. He saw a need for active learning within a coherent intellectual framework, and he stressed the development of a curriculum that moved progressively in the direction of a "more objective intellectual scheme of organization" from roots in the student's experience. But Dewey did not actually gather data from classroom observations to show that experience-based activities could lead to better and more meaningful learning than formal text-based discussion. We accept or reject his ideas according to how sensible, insightful, and well-reasoned we judge them to be.

The work of James Moffett (1968) is a notable example in the field of composition teaching. He proposed principles for developing a series of composition assignments that he believed could, over time, enhance growth in abstract thinking. Although he showed examples of student writing to illustrate the use of his principles in actual writing assignments, he, too, did not gather data from classrooms to show that the use of the principles he articulated did, in fact, improve student thinking.

### Empirical Research

In contrast to purely conceptual work, empirical research focuses on the collection, analysis, and interpretation of data that can be sensed or experienced in some way, either to answer research questions, to test hypotheses derived from theories, and/or to develop hypotheses or theories. Examples of different forms of empirical research, according to the AERA, are experimental research, survey research, participant observational research, audiovisual recording analysis, in-depth interviewing, and empirical historiography.

Although North (1987) distinguishes four "communities" of empirical researchers in the field of composition (experimentalists; clinicians, or case study researchers; formalists, or model-builders; and ethnographers), most educational researchers have in recent years grouped various methods for empirically investigating questions of interest in English language arts into two basic categories of methods. This chapter uses the terms "qualitative" and "quantitative" to designate these two groups of methods because they seem to be the most commonly used terms in recent articles, including those in *Educational Researcher*, an official journal of the AERA. However, the terms qualitative, holistic, phenomenological, hypothesis-generating, participant-observational, ethnographic, longitudinal, humanistic, naturalistic, field-based, interpretivistic, or hermeneutical are often used interchangeably, even though some researchers do not see them all as interchangeable; unfortunately, no clear definitions can be found that distinguish among all these various terms. Similarly, the terms positivistic, scientific, hypothesis-testing, or quantitative are also often used interchangeably. However distinct these two groups of methods may be in theory and in practice, a question we will return to later, all methods can contribute to the development of theoretical knowledge in teaching the English language arts.

In the next section, we look at the general features of these two broad categories of methods. Other chapters deal separately with various types of studies using these methods (see, for example, the chapters on case studies or ethnographic studies), and readers should consult these chapters for further illustrations and more detailed explanations of these specific types.

### Qualitative Methods

Researchers use qualitative methods to investigate how language teaching and language learning take place in the complexity of their natural settings. They may explore the process of language teaching and language learning as these occur in the classroom, the home, or the community. Qualitative methods, by definition, feature qualitative data—the researcher's description of what participants do or say about themselves and their activities in an educational setting. Studies featuring qualitative methods tend to focus on small numbers of participants and a thorough understanding of small, complete units of social interaction; hence, "thick" descriptions, or masses of details, are a salient characteristic of these studies. Researchers then analyze and interpret these details and often formulate categories for classifying their data. If their studies are not theory-based, they may propose tentative generalizations based on their data, and these tentative generalizations may be referred to as "grounded theory" because the theory has been derived from the data.

For example, Florio and Clark (1982) observed an elementary classroom to find answers to the following questions: "What opportunities for writing do students find in school? How is writing used by students to meet those opportunities? How do students come to differentiate among the functions of writing and the forms appropriate to them? What role does the teacher play in this process? What other contextual forces are operant" (p. 116)? After lengthy observations and an analysis of what they saw and heard, they concluded that, among other things, they could identify four different purposes for student writing in this classroom: students wrote to participate in community, to know themselves and others, to demonstrate academic competence, and to occupy free time. By providing categories for understanding how the teacher and her students used and talked about writing in this classroom, this study contributes to the formulation of a theory about the social meaning of written literacy in the classroom.

Studies featuring qualitative methods tend to be exploratory in nature. Sometimes qualitative researchers do not decide in advance all the aspects of the phenomenon under investigation they will explore; they hope to discover possibly important aspects that may not have been noted yet. On the other hand, sometimes they explore the possible significance of features that have been noted but which have not yet been considered relevant to an understanding of a particular phenomenon. For example, Wong (1988) examined teacher/student talk in writing conferences at an engineering school over a 3-month period. The descriptive research she had reviewed found that teachers tend to initiate talk in writing conferences, despite a view by eminent teachers of writing that the writing conference should be more like a "natural conversation," with both parties initiating talk. Wong hypothesized that a writing conference might be less dominated by the teacher if students had more technical knowledge than their tutors with respect to the content of their writing. She discovered from this small case study involving two tutors and four tutees that this variable seemed to have some influence on the teacher/student conference; students writing technical papers did engage in more give-and-take dialogues than did the students in the research Wong had reviewed. Thus, her study contributes to a better understanding of why conferences do not seem to be natural conversations and helps in the elaboration of a "complete theory of conferencing for guiding instruction" (p. 459).

Researchers using qualitative methods not only make their own interpretation about what they see and hear, they frequently explore what the language learning and teaching activities mean to the participants as well (although researchers using quantitative methods may also examine this). They try to discover the participants' point of view, thoughts, and feelings and why they think, feel, or behave as they do. For example, Hudson (1986) asked 20 children in several elementary grades to tell her whether the pieces of writing they had done at home and at school over the course of several months were self-sponsored or school-sponsored. By obtaining the children's perceptions of their own writing, she found that many children often did

not distinguish assignments given by the teacher from those they wrote on their own, seeing many school assignments as self-sponsored if they had a personal interest in them. Hudson did not determine whether or not their teachers had kindled their interest in the school assignments they perceived as self-sponsored, but she was able to conclude that the traditional dichotomy between self-sponsored and school-sponsored writing may be misleading, and that students' personal investment in their writing may not depend on their having chosen the topic themselves. Hudson also found a much wider variety of purposes for writing in the classroom than Florio and Clark (largely because she asked the children for their perception of their purposes and categorized what she found in a different way), suggesting the importance of multiple descriptive studies of a commonly observed phenomenon.

## Quantitative Methods

Studies featuring quantitative methods are apt to be concerned with the discovery of broad principles of language teaching and learning that will hold across many students, classrooms, or schools. These studies are usually characterized by a testable theory, concrete data obtained by a reproducible methodology, and a methodology that allows confirmation or disconfirmation of the theory (Becker, 1987). In order to make valid generalizations across many students, classrooms, or schools, quantitative researchers may use representative populations or randomly chosen subjects in experimental and control groups, or carefully constructed comparison groups. Drawing on the results of other relevant research to shape and justify their specific focus of interest, they decide in advance on all the variables to be examined, specify the relationships among them that are to be investigated, and measure them (statistically) in prescribed ways (Howe, 1988). A study using a quantitative method usually proceeds by systematically manipulating its specific variables to test the predictions made by the theory informing the study. Quantitative methods, by definition, feature quantified data (facts) expressed as quantities so that objective measurements are possible.

Hillocks' (1986) integrative review of research in written composition provides an examination of many well-done studies using quantitative methods. As part of a meta-analysis, a statistical treatment of the quantified findings of experimental studies with similar purposes and variables that makes the results of each individual study interpretable in relation to the others, Hillocks showed that studies exploring the effects of similar writing strategies or modes of writing instruction produced similar amounts of gain in students, despite differences in the individual studies with respect to such contextual variables as population and grade level. (For example, students in sentence-combining studies showed about the same amount of improvement in their writing, despite differences among these studies in the classroom setting.) This indicated that the findings of well-designed experimental studies in composition may be generalized across varied instructional contexts; for example, sentence-combining activities may have a beneficial effect on writing in any classroom.

Not all studies using quantitative methods focus directly on cause and effect relationships. Many such studies are correlational rather than experimental. They seek to discover whether one entity is related to another, and if so, how or to what extent. Researchers may then try to infer cause and effect, but must do so carefully. For example, a study by Anderson, Wilson, and Fielding (1986) found a relationship between outside-of-school book reading and reading achievement in fifth-grade students. In itself, this study cannot establish a causal relationship between outside-of-school book reading and reading achievement. But it still can suggest that teachers and parents might assign a "higher priority" to outside-of-school book reading, and it does provide a rationale for a rigorous study comparing an experimental curriculum stressing outside-of-school reading with one not doing so.

It is important to note that not all quantitative research is oriented to the validation of theory; in fact, a great deal of it in and outside of academic settings does not directly concern theory at all. Some of it is conducted to assess instructional programs. Descriptive data are frequently gathered and quantified to provide a vast variety of factual information, such as faculty or student profiles. Other kinds of studies without a theoretical orientation also use quantitative methods. They can provide useful information on matters of interest to researchers or scholars. Studies on word frequencies, or studies detailing the objective characteristics of oral or written texts, such as parts of speech, types of words, misspelled words, or level of word difficulty, are among the best examples. For example, the data in Stotsky, 1997, on the nature and scope of the reading vocabulary in current basal readers for grades 4 and 6 help raise questions about the capacity of these readers to accelerate students' growth in reading ability. Often these collections of data are used in other research or for creating instructional materials, such as vocabulary or spelling textbooks.

## ARE QUANTITATIVE AND QUALITATIVE METHODS INCOMPATIBLE?

Howe (1988) argues that no incompatibility between quantitative and qualitative methods exists in theory or in practice. In an examination of qualitative and quantitative methods with respect to the design of a study, the analysis of data, and the interpretation of results, Howe suggests that differences exist primarily in the assumptions researchers are willing to make and in how much attention they pay to "closely experienced" data—data based on their own observations and their own understanding of their interactions with participants in the research setting. There are, in fact, many commonalities among the methods used for empirical research.

To begin with, both categories of methods can be used to enhance theoretical knowledge. On one hand, empirical studies can be pre-theoretical, and their findings can help to create theory. As Jacob (1988) notes in an examination of six academic "traditions" that emphasize descriptive studies, all these traditions see descriptive studies preceding the testing of specific theories and hypotheses. On the other hand, empirical

studies can be based on theory, and their findings can help to strengthen, revise, or disconfirm it. Case study research, as Calkins (1985) points out, as well as experimental research, is often, if not usually, theory-based, and can contribute to the confirmation, revision, or disconfirmation of theory (e.g., the case studies by Wong, 1988, and Epes, 1985).

Second, as Jacob notes, all researchers are interested in minimizing or controlling bias despite differences in how they obtain their data or in the kind of data they collect. Jacob notes that even qualitative researchers want to report their data as objectively as possible, even when they report on subjective aspects of behavior as participant-observers-researchers who not only observe their subjects but interact with them and, possibly, influence them.

Third, all researchers collect, analyze, and interpret data. No facts of any kind ever interpret themselves. Moreover, all researchers present their data to the reader in some form. A researcher's argument is always based on evidence available to the reader, with a careful exploration of alternative explanations of the data (Howe, 1988).

Finally, studies using either quantitative and qualitative methods to investigate teaching in the English language arts can take place in the classroom or in other natural settings. Both kinds of methods can also be used in laboratory settings.

It may be the case that studies using qualitative methods do not, in general, focus on an assessment of the quality of teaching and learning activities. They may more often seek to describe the process of language teaching and learning in its natural settings and to understand the meaning of what happened in the classroom from both the researcher's and the participants' perspectives. It may also be the case that studies using quantitative methods do not, in general, focus on all the details of various contexts for language teaching and learning. They may more often seek to discover the precise role of individual elements in the process of language teaching and learning in order to determine their influence on the quality of language learning. Nevertheless, Kantor, Kirby, and Goetz (1981) note: "Quantitative strategies can be associated with investigation of processes, grounded theory, and close examination of contexts, while qualitative approaches can serve the study of outcomes, hypothesis testing, and generalizable conclusions" (p. 295). Thus, each group of methods does not necessarily cluster around a completely different set of interests, and methods from both groups can be, and are, combined for purposes often associated with one or the other group.

Jacob (1988), too, concludes that "researchers are presented with a range of research options, not just an all-or-nothing approach between qualitative research and positivistic research" (p. 23). And, indeed, more and more studies on the English language arts today use both qualitative and quantitative methods. Researchers may creatively combine the case-study method of investigation with some of the advantages of a quantified study as Epes (1985) did in a model case study; using 26 carefully selected subjects in comparison groups, Epes was able to test hypotheses and tentatively establish causal relationships. Researchers can also codify and quantify classroom observations and use comparison groups based on seemingly important differences to explore possible causal factors. For example,

Wendler, Samuels, and Moore (1989) conducted observations of three groups of elementary school teachers (teachers who had received an award for excellence in teaching, teachers with a master's degree, and a group of teachers with significantly fewer years of teaching experience and reading courses) to determine the amount of time they spent on comprehension instruction using basal readers and to see if there were differences among them in the use of the best comprehension instruction practices suggested by research. Finding that all three groups spent very little time on pre-reading activities and direct comprehension instruction, the researchers were able to conclude that graduate-level course work in reading may not be influencing comprehension instruction in the way it should and suggested we need to find out why.

Witte (1987) also believes that the field of composition research is "large enough . . . to make good use of both qualitative and quantitative methodologies and to embrace both the logic of discovery and the logic of validation" (p. 207). Moreover, he feels that it must do both if the field of research is "to meet its obligations to itself *and* to the larger social context which sustains it" (p. 207).

In sum, both qualitative and quantitative methods are useful, are used together, and should be used together in empirical research on the English language arts. Moreover, both qualitative and quantitative methods can be used in both pre-theoretical and theoretically motivated research. Both groups of methods serve both functions of empirical research—studies using qualitative methods may be theory-based, and studies using quantitative methods may be pre-theoretical. This suggests that what teachers should first note when reading research on teaching the English language arts is not what methodology the study uses, or whether the data are qualitative or quantitative in nature, but rather how the study contributes to the development of theoretical knowledge and how well scientific reasoning is demonstrated in its design and in the analysis, presentation, and interpretation of its findings. As Stotsky (1989) concluded in a review of several recent books on teaching the English language arts, the value of theoretical knowledge and scientific thinking may well be what is at stake in the controversy about which empirical methods are more or less useful for research on teaching the English language arts.

## DETERMINING THE THEORETICAL VALUE OF A STUDY'S FINDINGS

As we have previously suggested, perhaps the most important question for teachers to ask when reading a classroom-oriented study on teaching the English language arts is how it contributes to the development of theoretical knowledge. To answer that question, they need to ascertain whether the study is pre-theoretical or based on theory. Pre-theoretical studies help us to create theories, while theory-based studies help us to validate theories and build a knowledge base. Teachers need to ask: Is a study exploratory and pre-theoretical, one in which the researcher seeks to describe what is happening in a particular educational setting and to generate questions or explanations

for further research as in Stotsky, 1997? Do its findings contribute to the construction of theory, to the formulation of a tentative generalization that might explain its findings? Or does a study begin with a formulated theory and seek to gather evidence that validates the theory? Do its findings contribute to the strengthening of a theory, to the revision or confirmation of a formulated theory that predicted the findings?

Teachers may determine the theoretical value of a study's findings by distinguishing theory-based studies from pre-theoretical studies. Any empirical study can give teachers insights and useful ideas for the classroom, as we shall point out. But studies whose findings clearly validate an articulated theory about a particular phenomenon should probably carry more weight than pre-theoretical studies about that phenomenon, all other things being equal. This is particularly the case when the theory-based studies have resulted in converging evidence, or similar findings, using a variety of methodologies, teachers, and students as in Hillocks, 1986 and in Sadoski et al., 1997. And theories that account for all available evidence or that have been validated by a great deal of empirical evidence from a variety of sources and types of studies deserve more consideration than theories with little or no empirical evidence to validate them. Thus, when administrators or curriculum makers wish to develop recommendations for formal policy in English language arts, or when researchers wish to propose directions for future research, or when teachers consider making basic changes in classroom practices, they should pay especial attention to research whose findings provide strong empirical evidence to validate a comprehensive theory. The larger the body of research whose findings support the theory, the greater its explanatory power, and the more fruitful a practical translation of its pedagogical implications should be.

Although it is beyond the scope of this chapter to enumerate and explain in detail the questions educators might use to determine whether a study in the English language arts is pre-theoretical or theoretically-motivated, the following questions may be useful.

1. What exactly seems to be the purpose of the study? Does it seek to describe language teaching and learning in one specific context and to generate generalizations after data have been collected (as in Florio and Clark's study)? Or does it seek to validate a proposed principle of language teaching and learning (as in Wong's study)? The first kind of study is pre-theoretical: the second, theory-based.
2. Does the study begin with a series of questions or a statement of the researcher's focus of interest (as in Florio and Clark's study)? If so, it *may* be pre-theoretical: however, researchers sometimes phrase their hypotheses in the form of questions so that the presence of questions does not necessarily indicate a pre-theoretical study. If a study begins with specific hypotheses (as in Epes' study), then it is theoretically motivated.
3. Is the study informed by an explicit theoretical framework? If so, the study is theoretically motivated. If not, the study *may* be pre-theoretical. (Sometimes a theoretically motivated study is poorly written up and the reader can find little, if any, mention of its particular theoretical framework.)

Needless to say, a researcher's methodology should flow from his or her purpose for a study. If the methodology of a study is not guided by what the researcher seeks to do, then the study is conceptually flawed. And if the researcher's methodology is based on his or her values or beliefs, rather than on the purpose for the study, then rational discussion is not possible.

It is often not easy to determine exactly how a study contributes to the development of theoretical knowledge, for example, whether it seeks to create or confirm theory. Teacher discussion groups can be especially helpful. As teachers talk to each other about their understanding of the same study, the meaning of research concepts can be illuminated and the researcher's goals and reasoning process clarified. Comparing individual interpretations of a research report in teacher discussion groups may be the most fruitful way for teachers of the English language arts to learn how to interpret research.

## HOW ACADEMIC AND CLASSROOM INQUIRY AND PRACTICE ARE RELATED

For policy-making purposes or basic changes in pedagogical practices, educators should pay close attention to studies whose findings strengthen theoretical knowledge about teaching the English language arts. However, the usefulness of a particular study to a classroom teacher is not necessarily determined by the study's orientation to theory and the theoretical value of its findings. According to Chilcott (1987) and Calkins (1985), most school ethnographic studies lack a theoretical basis. Their findings, therefore, do not contribute to the strengthening of an articulated theory; at best they contribute only to the formulation of a tentative generalization. Nevertheless, classroom descriptions can give (and have given) teachers stimulating and useful ideas. For example, elementary grade teachers can learn about a remarkable classroom project and the kinds of civic writing even young children can do from the description of the model imaginary community called "Betterburg" that second-grade students planned, organized, and managed in their classroom for the school year under the direction of their teacher (Florio & Frank, 1982).

The findings of experimental research support articulated generalizations about students or classrooms across specific contexts; they do not tell us about specific students or specific contexts. Nevertheless, they can be directly useful to individual practitioners. For example, the results of the studies on reciprocal teaching and guided cooperative learning by Palinscar and Brown (1983) and Brown and Palinscar (1986) suggest the value of a variety of group learning procedures for improving reading comprehension. Teachers can easily adapt these procedures for their own classrooms, and probably many have done so.

Even the fruits of conceptual inquiry can serve teachers directly as a source of inspiration and guidance. For example, Dewey's ideas on the value of experiential learning within an articulated and organized intellectual framework served as the primary academic source for the writing curriculum Wiggenton designed around the publication of the journal *Foxfire*. Wiggenton drew on relatively little, if any, empirical

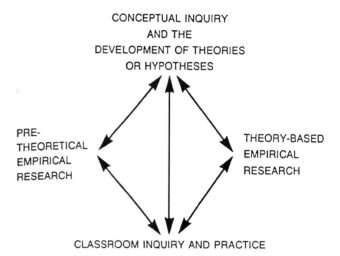

FIGURE 11.1. The relationship of the functions of empirical research to conceptual inquiry, the development of theories or hypotheses, and classroom inquiry and practice.

research to guide his thinking about classroom and community-based learning activities for his Appalachian Mountain students. Moffett's ideas have also directly influenced many teachers, such as Dellinger (1982), who developed a series of assignments and activities for teaching composition to her high school students that reflects almost wholly the use of the principles Moffett proposed.

Figure 11.1 shows the reciprocal nature of the relationship between the basic modes of academic inquiry and classroom inquiry and practice. At the base of the figure is the classroom where the teaching of the English language arts takes place. Teachers often do practical problem solving in their own classrooms without reference to academic inquiry, and the practical research they do can be very useful to other teachers. But their questions can serve as a stimulus for pre-theoretical empirical research, purely conceptual inquiry, and theoretically motivated empirical research, as the three arrows suggest. In return, the insights and findings of all modes of academic inquiry (whether or not this inquiry is based on the classroom teacher's questions) can stimulate teachers' thinking by expanding the contexts and the constructs they use for viewing their work in their own classroom.

Figure 11.1 also shows how the two functions of empirical research are related to conceptual inquiry and the development of theory. As the figure suggests, pre-theoretical research can contribute to conceptual inquiry and the formulation of hypotheses or theoretical generalizations (grounded theory). Reciprocally, theoretical thinking can lead to further exploratory, pre-theoretical research. Hence, the bi-directional arrow. As the figure also shows, empirical research also proceeds from hypotheses or formulated theories and seeks evidence to validate them. The findings of this research may support or disconfirm these hypotheses or theories and provide a rationale for further theory-based empirical research (or even further exploratory pre-theoretical research). Hence, the bi-directional arrow here as well. It is important to note that theoretical generalizations can be formulated without prior pre-theoretical research and do not necessarily result in empirical research.

In theory and in practice, therefore, as Fig. 11.1 suggests, all modes and functions of academic inquiry can be useful to teachers. In turn, all modes and functions of academic inquiry can and should be responsive to teachers' questions and concerns. For teachers are not simply pragmatic or eclectic in all they choose to do in the classroom. For the most part, they are highly principled with respect to the goals of formal education. Their ideas about how they think students learn to become informed, self-sufficient, and responsible citizens through their English language arts programs are as worthy of consideration as are the ideas of academic researchers.

## JUDGING THE USEFULNESS OF RESEARCH FINDINGS FOR CLASSROOM PRACTICE

We have discussed how teachers might determine the theoretical value of a study's findings. But we have not suggested how they might judge their usefulness for their classroom. Whether or not a study is pre-theoretical or theoretically motivated, the following questions may be helpful.

First, how applicable are the study's concepts to the teacher's classroom? The educational level of the study may make a considerable difference. Concepts useful at the elementary school level may have little meaning for adult learners, while those useful for adult learners may be inappropriate for young children. On the other hand, teachers may still wish to consider the adaptability of any concept for different educational levels.

Second, are the location of the teacher's school (rural, urban, or suburban), class size, and the students' level of ability in English similar to the school's setting, class size, and student ability in the study? Clearly, teachers should be cautious about applying the findings from any one study if their classroom differs substantially from the classroom in the study.

Third, are only small numbers of students involved in the study? If so, teachers should exercise caution unless a study's findings are consistent with those from a large body of research. If the study is unique, and its findings have not been replicated in any way, then the pedagogical implications of its findings should be considered with extreme tentativeness. One study should be seen as only a possible piece of a puzzle, with firm knowledge accumulating only slowly over time as evidence comes in from a variety of sources and types of studies.

Fourth, is other research negatively portrayed? A study should be able to stand on its own merits. If the researchers appear biased, both the conceptualization of the study and the interpretation of the data may be affected.

Fifth, are the teachers in the study criticized or demeaned in some way? Are they portrayed as resistant to new ideas? Does the researcher appear to believe that his or her ideas are the "correct" ones? Such a stance is patronizing to teachers, even if the researcher is also a teacher. But more importantly, negative attitudes toward teachers may also signal a bias in the interpretation of a study's findings. For example, most, if not all, studies of the differences between school talk and home talk have viewed these differences as sources of conflict that prevent students from learning in school. These studies then imply that teachers need to adjust their curricula accordingly. The possibility that differences between home and school talk have no necessary bearing on school learning, or that differences between the two may even stimulate school learning, has not been explored and might well be. While no professional practice is above examination and criticism, it is useful for teachers to note whether the researcher explored alternative explanations for negatively interpreted findings, and whether evidence was provided to show that what the researcher found actually influences student achievement.

Sixth, are some or all of the students in the study portrayed negatively? Does the researcher appear to believe that some or all of the students are inherently racist, sexist, or ethnocentric by virtue simply of the color of their skin, their gender, or their ethnicity? This is a new and growing problem in English language arts research. For example, some studies assume that students whom they label "European-American" are inherently racist because they are white and that they are complicit in racism if they believe that it is caused by individual prejudice only (e.g., Beach, 1994) or fail to make direct references to racial identity and racial conflicts in discussions of a literary work (e.g., Enciso, 1994). The situation would be similar for gender studies in which the researcher appears to assume that all male students are inherently sexist whether or not they articulate sexist views or demonstrate sexist behaviors, or for studies on the use of multicultural literature in which the researcher assumes that the students' dislike of a particular work is an indication of ethnocentrism rather than a result of either not understanding the work or authentic boredom with the work. When a researcher has made assumptions that beg the research question, teachers need to question the validity of the study's results.

Seventh, are teachers urged to adopt specific practices on the basis of one study? As our discussion of empirical research implied, the findings of any one study are apt to be too context-specific or too general for blanket recommendations and for unqualified or automatic application to any one classroom. Even if a body of similar research findings supports strong generalizations about the effects of a particular classroom practice, no generalization necessarily applies to all classrooms in exactly the same way. Ultimately, what is best for particular students can best be determined by the teacher's professional judgment in light of what the best evidence suggests.

Finally, is the study well conceived and implemented? In Stotsky (1996), I note the common types of problems I found in qualitative studies submitted for consideration to *Research in the Teaching of English* during my tenure as editor of the journal. The problems appeared in their conceptual framework, their design, the selection of participants, the researcher's role in the classroom and relationship to the teacher, the validity of the interpretation offered, the presentation of the results, and the conclusions drawn. Although studies using quantitative methods also have problems, studies using qualitative methods have become much more frequent in the English language arts than quantitative studies and pose more problems in their planning, execution, and presentation than do the others. Before accepting the results of a qualititative study or the advice the researcher offers on the basis of it, teachers need to consider whether the study is seriously flawed by the problems elaborated in this chapter and in Chap. 9 in Stotsky (1999).

## CONCLUDING REMARKS

Serious educational research in the English language arts is only about 100 years old. Today, educators have the opportunity to gain insights and information from studies using a broad array of methodologies. Moreover, given the complexities of any research with human beings, teachers can legitimately expect researchers to use all methods of research and to gather both qualitative and quantitative data for investigating questions in teaching the English language arts. To deserve serious consideration, any specific conclusions about the teaching of the English language arts should be supported by a variety of pre-theoretical and theoretically motivated studies.

Teachers have many complex questions for researchers to address such as: What are ways to assess growth in reading and writing ability? How can parents assist their children's development as readers and writers? Do the results of a literature-based approach to reading instruction differ from the results of other approaches? Why are more boys than girls remedial readers and writers, and what can the schools do about it? What are the effects on reading and writing achievement in English if a young nonEnglish-speaking child's native language is used for beginning reading and writing instruction? Such questions require a variety of research methodologies as well as many different studies using similar methodologies, if teachers are to have confidence in the conclusions of these studies.

However, it is worth keeping in mind that findings from different studies on the same topic may just as easily be inconsistent or contradict each other as converge (Mathison, 1988). And they may just as easily support or contradict teachers' intuitions or experiences. Mixed findings do not invalidate academic research, nor do findings that contradict teachers' intuitions invalidate their judgment. To the contrary, mixed findings provide new and useful information, and they suggest how complex the problem is. The best wisdom suggests that we should not expect one or two studies, no matter how well done, to provide answers to complex questions of classroom practice in teaching the English language arts. In the final analysis, how teachers read and interpret research on teaching the English language arts depends on the respect researchers and teachers have for each other, the respect researchers have for other researchers, and the respect researchers have for the moral and intellectual goals that most teachers have for their students.

## References

Anderson, R., Wilson, P., & Fielding, L. (1986). *Growth in reading and how children spend their time outside of school* (Tech. Report No. 389). Urbana-Champaign, IL: University of illinois, Center for the Study of Reading.

Arwell, N. (1987). *In the Middle: Writing, reading, and learning with adolescents.* Portsmouth, NH: Boynton/Cook, Heinemann.

Beach, R. (1994, November). *High school students' responses to portrayal of racial discrimination in short stories.* Unpublished paper distributed at the annual conference of the National Council of Teachers of English, Orlando, FL.

Becker, H. (1987). The importance of a methodology that maximizes falsifiability: Its applicability to research about Logo. *Educational Researcher, 16*(5), 11-16.

Brown, A., & Palinscar, A. (1986). *Guided, cooperative learning and individual knowledge acquisition* (Tech. Report No. 372). Urbana-Champaign, IL: University of Illinois, Center for the Study of Reading.

Calkins, L. (1985). Forming research communities among naturalistic researchers. In B. McClelland & T. Donovan (Eds.), *Perspectives on research and scholarship in composition.* New York: Modern Language Association.

Chilcott, J. (1987). Where are you coming from and where are you going? The reporting of ethnographic research. *American Educational Research Journal, 24*(2), 199-218.

Dellinger, D. (1982). *Out of the heart: How to design writing assignments for high school courses.* The National Writing Project, Berkeley, CA: University of California.

Dewey, J. (1938). *Experience and education.* New York: Macmillan.

*Educational Researcher.* (1988, January–February). p. 30.

Enciso, P. (1994, November). Cultural identity and response to literature: Running lessons from *Maniac Magee. Language Arts, 71,* 524-533.

Epes, M. (1985). Tracing errors to their soruces: A study of the encoding processes of adult basic writers. *Journal of Basic Writing, 4,* 4-33.

Epes, M., & Kirkpatrick, C. (1978). *Investigating error in the writing of nontraditional college students.* (ERIC Document Reproduction Service No. ED 168 018.)

Epes, M., & Kirkpatrick, C. (1987). *Editing your Writing.* New York: Prentice-Hall.

Florio, S., & Clark, C. (1982). The functions of writing in an elementary classroom. *Research in the Teaching of English, 16*(2), 115-130.

Florio, S., & Frank, J. (1982). Literacy and community in the classroom: A case study of Betterburg. In B. Beyer & R. Gilstrap (Eds.), *Integrating Writing and Social Studies, K-6* (pp. 31-42). Boulder, CO: Social Science Education Consortium.

Harste, J. (1992). Foreword. In R. Beach, J. Green, M. Kamil, & T. Shanahan (Eds.), *Multidisciplinary perspectives on literacy research* (pp. ix-xiii). Urbana, IL: National Council of Teachers of English.

Hillocks, G. (1986). *Research on written composition: New directions for teaching.* Urbana, IL: NCRE and ERIC Clearinghouse on Reading and Communication Skills.

Howe, K. (1988). Against the quantitative–qualitative incomplitiability thesis or dogmas die hard. *Educational Researacher, 17*(8), 10-16.

Hudson, S. (1986). Context and children's writing. *Research in the Teaching of English, 20*(3), 294-316.

Jacob, E. (1988). Clarifying qualitative research: A focus on traditions. *Educational Researcher, 17*(1), 16-24.

Kantor, K., Kirby, D., & Goetz, J. (1981). Research in context: Ethnographic studies in English education. *Research in the Teaching of English, 15,* 293-310.

Mathison, S. (1988). Why triangulate? *Educational Researcher, 17*(2), 13-17.

Moffett, J. (1968). *Teaching the universe of discourse*. Boston: Houghton Mifflin.

North, S. (1987). *The making of knowledge in composition: Portrait of an emerging field*. Montclair, NJ: Boynton/Cook.

Palinscar, A., & Brown, A. (1983). *Reciprocal teaching of comprehension-monitoring activities* (Tech. Report No. 269). Urbana-Champaign, IL: University of Illinois, Center for the Study of Reading.

Peters, W. (Chair). (1987). *Effective English teaching: Concept, research, and practice*. CEE Commission on Research in Teacher Effectiveness. Urbana, IL: National Council of Teachers of English.

Sadoski, M., Willson, V., & Norton, D. (1997, February). The relative contributions of research-based composition activities to writing improvement in the lower and middle grades. *Research in the Teaching of English, 31*(1), 120–150.

Stotsky, S. (1989). How to restore the professional status of English teachers: Three useful but troubling perspective [Essay review of *Consensus and dissent: Teaching English past, present, and future; Effective English teaching: concept, research, practice; and Working together: A guide for teacher-researchers*]. *College English, 51*(7), 750–758.

Stotsky, S. (1996, June). Problems in qualitative manuscripts submitted to *Research in the Teaching of English*. *English International, 4*(1), 11–14.

Stotsky, S. (1997). Why today's multicultural basal readers may retard, not enhance, growth in reading. In L. R. Putnam (Ed.), *Readings on language and literacy: Essays in honor of Jeanne S. Chall* (pp. 259–286). Cambridge, MA: Brookline Books.

Stotsky, S., & Anderson, P. (1990). *Works of literature recommended for whole-class instruction by New England Area teachers of English*. Report of research for the New England Association of Teachers of English.

Wendler, D., Samuels, S., & Moore, V. (1989). Comprehension instruction of award-winning teachers, teachers with master's degrees, and other teachers. *Reading Research Quuarterly, 24*(4), 382–398.

Wigginton, E. (1985). *Sometime a shining moment: The Foxfire experience*. New York: Doubleday.

Witte, S. (1987). [Review of Research on Written Composition New Directions for Teaching] G. Hillocks, Jr., *College Composition and Communication, 38*(2), 202–207.

Wollman-Bonilla, J. (1994, October). Why don't they "just speak?" Attempting literature discussion with more and less able readers. *Research in the Teaching of English, 28*(3), 231–258.

Wong, I. (1988). Teacher-student talk in technical writing conferences. *Written Communication, 5*(9), 444–460.

# ·12·

# TEACHER PROFESSIONALISM AND THE RISE OF "MULTIPLE LITERACIES": HOW TO DESCRIBE OUR SPECIALIZED KNOWLEDGE?

*Anne DiPardo*
*University of Iowa*

Talk of teacher "professionalization" is much in the air these days—in local efforts to give teachers a greater say in decision making and governance (Clift, Johnson, Holland, & Veal, 1992; Clift, Veal, Holland, Johnson, & McCarthy, 1995; Fullan & Hargreaves, 1996; Wilson & Daviss, 1994), as well as in national calls to raise initial licensure requirements and restructure career opportunities (National Board for Professional Teaching Standards (NBPTS), 1989; National Center for Education Statistics (NCES), 1999). In common usage, the term "Professional" meanwhile remains as vague as it is reified. "He acted so unprofessionally," we might say of a backbiting colleague; or, in recounting an instance of top-down management, "It was an affront to my professionalism." More substantively, what do we mean when we say that teaching is more than a mere job—that it is properly described as a *profession*? Does "professionalism" rest primarily in autonomy and empowerment, the judgments of outsiders, or perhaps some combination of both? What particular things might "professionalism" mean in the context of English/language-arts teaching? How to describe what literacy educators understand and enact in ways that communicate authority and a clear sense of purpose?

## "PROFESSIONALISM" AND "SPECIALIZED KNOWLEDGE"

The word "professionalism" has been the subject of much debate over the years, its meaning shifting along with changing times and ideologies. Several decades ago, the sociologist Talcott Parsons (1968) predicted that the power of the capitalist titans would soon disappear, with professionals emerging as a transcendent national influence. Parsons envisioned professionals as both enlightened and ethical—possessing specialized bodies of knowledge, learning from one another through mutual interaction and associations, providing altruistic service to the whole of humankind, and intervening where colleagues' performance slips below desired norms. Parsons maintained that the proliferation and rising power of the professions would place greater influence in the hands of universities, charged with providing "formal technical training accompanied by some institutionalized mode of validating both the adequacy of the training and the competence of trained individuals" (p. 536). For Parsons, professional preparation involved heads as well as hands, "giving prominence to an *intellectual* component—that is ... primacy to the valuation of cognitive rationality as applied to a particular field" (p. 536). Parsons regarded medicine and law as prototypes, models to all the applied professions in terms of specialized training, collegial support, and commitment to serving the good of humankind above economic self-interest (p. 541).

Revisionist sociologists would later take issue with Parsons's arguments. Some noted that the particulars of this "specialized training" (just *how* long and *how* intellectual?) were left unduly vague in Parsons's formulation (Freidson, 1970). Magali Sarfatti Larson (1977) argued that such vagueness masked a hidden agenda of the professions: a desire to control their own domains, dictating what members of their fields should know, fencing out those who do not follow the sanctioned training and induction rituals. For Larson, professions achieve respect and status not through the lofty passage Parsons envisioned, but by creating exclusive markets for their services and keeping competitors at bay—that is, by creating a "monopoly of expertise in the market [and] monopoly of status in a system of stratification" (p. xvii). For monopolist critics such as Larson, professionalism has an underside, providing power to silence alternative voices and diminish the quality of service to clients.

Whether grounded in altruism and "cognitive rationality" or a more self-interested desire for market control, the quest for professional status has inevitably involved staking claims to bodies of "specialized knowledge." In an influential book on the history of medicine, Paul Starr (1982) traced the ascendance of doctors to early reforms in medical education, stimulated by a host of social and economic factors, and brought to fruition by Abraham Flexner's 1910 report on the uneven quality of physician training. As medical education became more standardized and scientific, argues Starr, doctors achieved new levels of legitimacy—assuming an air of authority that engendered popular trust, thereby ensuring their economic well-being and political influence. Historian Elizabeth Lunbeck (1994) has meanwhile explored the rise of psychiatry, grounding her analysis of psychiatrists' claims to specialized knowledge in Michel Foucault's (1980) notion of disciplinary control as derived through the power moves of labeling and categorizing.

While the nature of professionals' "specialized knowledge" remains the subject of analysis and debate, its importance in terms of authority and prestige endures. For scholars since Parsons, such knowledge may be suspect or indisputable, its authority achieved through systematic data or rhetorical sleights of hand; but if a group of workers is to acquire and maintain professional status, they must be perceived as possessing specialized understanding that distinguishes them from their untrained counterparts. What does this imply, then, for our thinking about the professionalization of teaching? Given that a claim to "specialized knowledge" remains a hallmark of professionalism, how to characterize the understandings one must acquire in learning to teach—and in learning to do so with distinction?

## TEACHERS' "PROFESSIONAL KNOWLEDGE"

"Special schooling for teachers is neither intellectually nor organizationally as complex as that found in the established professions," observed Dan Lortie (1975, p. 58). While the work of teachers is nearly as old as humankind, Lortie perceived a paucity of systematic studies of teaching and learning that might guide the efforts of novices. For Lortie, the "specialized study" of classroom learning had a short and undistinguished history, with little connection to the intellectual mainstream:

Early study of education was isolated from scholarship; attempts to integrate it with disciplines like psychology have lasted only a few decades. Nor do we find an equivalent to the centuries of codified experience encountered in law, engineering, medicine, divinity, architecture, and accountancy; no way has been found to record and crystallize teaching for the benefit of beginners ... what meaningful record exists of the millions of teaching transactions that have occurred since the City on the Hill?" (pp. 58–59).

While Lortie may have exaggerated the historical basis of knowledge in other professions and diminished that of teachers, the perception remains that teacher educators lack an agreed-upon conceptual framework and knowledge base. Lieberman and Miller (1992) concur that "the knowledge base in teaching is weak; there is simply no consensus (as there is in medicine and law) about what is basic to the practice of the profession" (p. 3). This lack of generalizable knowledge has added fuel to conservatives' criticisms of teacher preparation programs. Echoing charges made by James Koerner (1962) nearly 30 years earlier, Rita Kramer (1991) came away from her visits to colleges of education convinced that prospective teachers would be better off focusing on discipline-based knowledge. "How to teach English literature should be the concern of professors of English," she writes, "not experts in curriculum and instruction" (p. 219). Kramer places esteemed literary scholars to the one side, their claim to specialized knowledge unquestioned even in the midst of challenges to the traditional canon and formalist approaches to literary understanding; on the other, well-meaning but misguided education professors, experts in nothing, replacing rigor and solid foundations with airy talk of equity and caring.

Such critiques have exacerbated the already low status afforded teacher preparation at many American universities. For education professors Frances Maher and Mary Kay Tetreault (1999), this prestige problem reflects an unfortunate split in higher education "between the world of knowledge and the world of pedagogy":

People view the work of scholars, articulated through the academic disciplines, as a corpus of knowledge to be presented to students; the means of presentation is considered unimportant. Pedagogues, on the other hand, are seen as concentrating on the learning process, which is without content; when they call for attention to student learning, they are accused of "watering down" real knowledge (p. 40).

The perceived split—between knowing a field of study and knowing how to teach—is as enduring as it is unfortunate, one of those reductionist dichotomies John Dewey warned of many decades ago (1938/1963).

Recent years have seen efforts to describe in more precise and compelling terms the melding of disciplinary, pedagogic, and interpersonal understandings that constitute the specialized professional knowledge effective teachers possess, formulations emanating most notably from bodies such as the Holmes Group (1995), the National Board for Professional Teaching Standards (1989), and the National Council for Accreditation of Teacher Education (1995). Shulman (1987) has termed this melding "pedagogical content knowledge," defining it as "that special amalgam of content and pedagogy that is uniquely the province of teachers, their own special form of professional understanding" (p. 8). For Shulman, teachers' knowledge reaches well beyond what can be learned within the walls of the academy, to understandings of learners, classroom organization, curriculum, and school and district contexts. Pedagogical content knowledge encompasses all this and more, comprising "the distinctive bodies of knowledge for teaching," that which distinguishes "the understanding of the content specialist from that of the pedagogue" (p. 8).

Shulman allowed that the precise contours of this melding were still being articulated, an enterprise that has informed the subsequent work of the National Board for Professional Teaching Standards (NBPTS). The NBPTS's statement of "What Teachers Should Know and Be Able To Do" reflects an integrated commitment to student learning, habits of reflexive thinking, commitment to learning communities, as well as a deep understanding of one's chosen field of study:

The fundamental requirements for proficient teaching are relatively clear: a broad grounding in the liberal arts and sciences; knowledge of the subjects to be taught, of the skills to be developed, and of the curricular arrangements and materials that organize and embody that content; knowledge of general and subject-specific methods for teaching and for evaluating student learning; knowledge of students and human development; skills in effectively teaching students from racially, ethnically, and socioeconomically diverse backgrounds; and the skills, capacities and dispositions to employ such knowledge wisely in the interest of students (NBPTS, 2000a, p. 1).

These conceptions cast teachers' "specialized knowledge" as at once practical and conceptual, reminiscent of what psychologists have called "situated knowledge" (Kennedy, 1999; Lave, 1988). In keeping with the belief that teachers must know in a special way—that "they must know in the context of practice" (Lampert & Ball, 1999, p. 38)—the NBPTS casts the value of disciplinary knowledge in terms of its relevance to students. That is, what teachers need to know must be seen as directly linked to what students need to learn, and how such learning can best be accomplished. Although such specialized knowledge is enriched by theory, it is increasingly seen as much more than a set of abstractions that can be mastered apart from young people, classrooms, and schools (Darling-Hammond, 1997; Darling-Hammond, Berry, Haselkorn, & Fideler, 1999; Sykes, 1999; Thompson & Zeuli, 1999).

If disciplinary knowledge remains crucial, the emphasis is increasingly on understanding how such bodies of knowledge are made and revised by human beings functioning in particular cultural and historic contexts (Thompson & Zeuli, 1999; Wertsch, 1991). This concern with understanding the knowledge-making process is reflected in the NBPTS' proposition that "accomplished teachers have a rich understanding of the subject(s) they teach and appreciate how knowledge in their subject is created, organized, linked to other disciplines and applied to real-world settings." Disciplinary knowledge is to be both respected and critiqued, as teachers communicate regard for its value while also using it as a site for developing "the critical and analytical capacities of their students" (NBPTS, 2000b, p. 2).

Despite such efforts to professionalize teaching by more clearly formulating the necessary knowledge base, considerable skepticism remains. Arguably, the process of such formulation is still in its infancy (Carter, 1996), marked by competing purposes and "contrasting epistemologies" (Tom & Valli, 1996, p. 373). Doubts concerning the adequacy of teacher knowledge remain prevalent among policymakers and the public, fueled by news of impending teacher shortages, failing schools, and dropping test scores. A recent survey by the National Center for Education Statistics (NCES, 1999) found that only 20% of new

teachers describe themselves as feeling adequately prepared, that too many are teaching outside their subject-area specializations, and that professional development activities do little to enhance their knowledge once in the field.

Linda Darling-Hammond (1996) observes that efforts to professionalize teaching have historically met with widespread criticism (following Cremin, 1965). As in Dewey's day, when the progressive aspiration to teach for understanding called for teachers of exceptional aptitude and training, Darling-Hammond observes a problem in recruiting sufficient numbers of talented and strongly prepared practitioners. Citing the standardizing influences that displaced Dewey's progressive ideals, Darling-Hammond cautions that teachers risk bureaucratic control from above where they do not adhere to conceptually grounded standards of their own choosing. While allowing that appropriate practice "cannot be reduced to rules and lodged in concrete" (p. 269), Darling-Hammond argues that a failure to stipulate a common body of necessary knowledge ensures the continuing de-professionalization of teaching:

A profession is formed when members of an occupation agree that they have a knowledge base, that what they know relates directly to effective practice, that being prepared is essential to being a responsible practitioner, and that unprepared people will not be permitted to practice. Until members of the profession band together to articulate and enforce standards, the debate will continue (p. 288).

Darling-Hammond (1997) likens this lack of an agreed-upon knowledge base to the infancy of medical education, before the 1910 Flexner Report called for higher standards and greater curricular consistency. Teachers can meaningfully respond to demands for increased accountability only as they define and defend their "strong and widely shared base of knowledge," she writes, knowledge "clearly related to improved learning and . . . a strong and widely shared commitment to the welfare of all children that is enacted in partnership with parents and communities" (p. 302).

If we acknowledge that teachers' professional knowledge rests in a dynamic interplay between understandings about teaching, experience in an academic field of study, insight into what students need to know, and an ethic of collaborative care, what are the implications for English educators? How to describe "English" as a discipline, and how to characterize its enactment in the public school classroom? How to delineate the professional knowledge that literacy educators should hold in common, and its translation into a vision of what students should learn?

## KNOWING ABOUT LITERACY

English teachers recount a generic tale of struggling to explain their work to strangers; the setting may be a grocery store line or a community gathering, but airplanes seem an especially common site. Seat belts are snapped in place in preparation for take-off, and the person in the neighboring seat turns in greeting. "And what do you do for a living?" he asks. Then, grimacing, "Ah, an *English* teacher. Better watch my grammar." A bit into the flight come remembrances of works he still loves to hate—*Silas Marner, Julius Caesar, The Scarlet Letter*. If pressed, however, the stranger reveals a strong distaste for what he knows of the new pedagogic wave—whole language, ebonics, multicultural literature. He may wince at memories of his own literary and grammatical training, but he remains a traditionalist at heart, preferring to think that literacy means one thing, and still the *same* one thing it meant when he suffered through high school English. He bemoans slipping standards, but applauds the determined pedagogues still out there, transmitting the best that has been thought and said to the next generation of American citizens and workers.

Meanwhile, research into reading and writing practices both in and out of school has revealed a more textured landscape, suggesting that "literacy" is best imagined in the plural. Embedded in diverse contexts, shaped by culture, gender, and class, literacies are conceived as multiplistic, complicating discussions of what it means to prepare workers and citizens for the demands of a new millennium. For former National Council of Teachers of English (NCTE) Executive Director Miles Myers (1996), emerging societal and workplace landscapes demand more sophisticated literacies, redefining "minimal" in ways that up the ante for teachers and students alike. Myers emphasizes the growing need for workers and citizens with a high tolerance for ambiguity, a penchant for weighing diverse points of view, and for understanding parts in the context of systemic wholes. An ability to decode for literal meaning is no longer enough; what Myers calls "critical/translation" literacy involves finding places to stand among competing perspectives, understanding the social, cultural, and historic influences that shaped particular texts, and fitting one's own writing to the rhetorical demands of occasion and audience.

Literacy, then, is increasingly conceptualized in ecological terms, as embedded in social-cultural practices that must be continually interpreted and negotiated (Barton, 1994). According to this expanded vision, literacy learning is also political, as diverse students maintain their own ways with words even as they acquire the "genres of power" (Street, 1995) that allow entrance into educational and economic opportunities. Increasingly, literacy is seen not as a body of knowledge but a flexible tool, while literacy learning is conceptualized as guided practice across varied rhetorical contexts. The New London Group (1996), an international assemblage of leading scholars, describes this dynamic, versatile, de-stabilized status of literacy and literacy learning:

Local diversity and global connectedness mean not only that there can be no standard; they also mean that the most important skill students need to learn is to negotiate regional, ethnic, or class-based dialects; variations in register that occur according to social context; hybrid cross-cultural discourses; the code switching often to be found within a text among different languages, dialects, or registers; different visual and iconic meanings; and variations in the gestural relationships among people, language, and material objects (p. 69).

The notion of multiple literacies is connected to social constructivist conceptions that have come to supplant behavioristic, transmission-oriented models of teaching and learning. Martin Nystrand (1997) calls this new mode "dialogic," involving a conception of knowledge "not as previously formulated by someone else but rather as continuously regenerated and co-constructed among teachers and learners and their peers" (p. 89). Influenced by the work of Vygotsky (1978) and neo-Vygotskian activity theorists (Forman, Minick, & Stone, 1993), this new conception emphasizes vital dialogue over "long lists of facts, points, and obligatory principles to teach" (Nystrand et al., p. 106). Recitation and one-way transmission are supplanted by "a seemingly vague process of 'negotiated meanings' and 'transforming understandings' in open-ended discussion and instructional 'conversations'" (p. 89).

Also drawing on the metaphor of curriculum as "conversation," Arthur Applebee (1996) argues that meaningful learning takes place where students come to recognize "culturally significant domains for conversation," and "learn to participate in conversations within those domains" (p. 3). In contrast to E. D. Hirsch's (1987) conception of "cultural literacy," which emphasizes the acquisition of discrete facts, Applebee points to the primacy of exploring relationships among ideas, of understanding knowledge as both shaped by cultural tradition and subject to challenge and reassessment. Hirsch's curricular critique, with its concrete lists and promise of firmer cultural ground, has been enthusiastically embraced by the general public. Meanwhile, observes Applebee, progressive educators have failed to codify adequately what they know and are working to accomplish, as "lively vignettes have replaced serious attempts at consensus about the structure and content of schooling" (p. 37).

Reductionist notions have permeated the popular conversation about literacy, as has insistence on accountability measures that emphasize bits and pieces of forgettable knowledge. Schools are political places largely because everyone has spent lots of time in them and therefore feels like something of an educational expert (Sarason, 1971/1996). Add to this the public's generally low tolerance for ambiguity, as well as the determination of those casting the issues in simplified either/or terms (Dewey, 1938/1963), and English/language arts teachers face some strong popular opinions about what they should be doing. In other words, the public is poised to doubt that literacy educators' specialized understandings are somehow greater than their own; in fact, they seem increasingly inclined toward dictating what "literacy" is and how teachers should be going about their work. Complicating all this, of course, is the historically low status afforded teacher knowledge generally, and the fact that our field's vision of the nature of literacy has grown ever more nuanced and complex. Not all of us embrace this new vision, to be sure; at least since the Dartmouth conference of 1966, observers have noted an internal divide between teachers who see English as something one *does*, and those who see it as a body of information one can come to *know*—great books, literary criticism, rhetorical forms, and so on (Harris, 1991). If discussions of our work in the public arena are too often organized around deceptive dichotomies, the same could be said of our own debates. The simplistic polarities of these arguments obscure more fundamental questions: What are students to take away from their years of textual study and instruction in writing? What sorts of literate abilities are we striving to foster, and toward what ends?

While some continue to conceptualize the specialized knowledge of literacy educators as a body of information to be transmitted to students, others are arriving at a more integrated, activity-driven characterization, one that honors the multiple uses of literacy in the world beyond school and the complexities of engaging young people in its practice. How to describe this expanded definition of literacy in ways that will compete with lists of "what every American needs to know"? How to communicate to the public the grounded fit between these new conceptions of literacy and progressive language arts pedagogy—that what English educators understand about literacy suggests mastery through conversation and hands-on practice, not transmission of discrete facts and canonical texts? How to speak with a united professional voice in the midst of inevitable disagreement within our own ranks? As the controversy over the NCTE/International Reading Association (IRA) Standards suggests, these are challenges more easily named than mastered.

## PROFESSIONAL KNOWLEDGE AND THE NCTE/IRA STANDARDS

Popular dissatisfaction with the NCTE/IRA Standards derives from the fact that "multiple literacies" is not a notion readily translated into catchy sound bites or measurable goals. When the Standards were released in 1996 (NCTE/IRA, 1996a), the Associated Press, *The Washington Post*, *USA Today*, and *The New York Times* all quoted Michael Cohen, a senior advisor to the Secretary of Education, who called the document "very vague and very general" (Tabor, 1996, p. A12; NCTE, 1996). "There is no specific call for first-grade readers, phonics or Faulkner," began the article in *The New York Times*; "No demand for sentence diagramming or Dante":

Instead, a long-awaited report on national standards for English language instruction gives only general guidelines. It says, for example, that by the time they finish high school, American students should have read a "wide range of literature" and be able to communicate with a "variety of audiences," using books and newspapers as well as computer databases. They should be able to use a library and write and critique texts (Tabor, 1996, p. A12).

Where were the expected reading lists, benchmarks, and recommended teaching techniques, critics asked—the prescriptive verbs "should" or "ought"? (*New York Times* Editorial Staff, 1996). What about complaints from employers and parents that "many high school graduates cannot read or write effectively, use poor grammar and have little knowledge of literature"? (Tabor, 1996, p. A12). Arguing that curricular decisions are best made locally, NCTE President Beverly Chin hinted at the expanded vision of literacy informing the Standards: "'The key thing is that we use language in order to communicate and think,'" she explained. "'We want all students to be able to use language effectively. This document furthers our vision of what literacy means'" (Tabor, 1996, p. A12). In *USA Today*, Chin characterized this vision as "the kind of complex, real-world literacy . . . students should be encouraged to develop" (Henry, 1996, p. 1A).

A few weeks after the release of the Standards, NCTE and IRA leaders published an "advocacy advertisement" in the national pages of *The New York Times*, criticizing journalists' coverage of the Standards and charging that "many also attack the professionalism of English/language arts teachers" (NCTE/IRA, 1996b, p. A14). Again, NCTE and IRA leaders attempted to elaborate this enlarged definition of "literacy":

The standards recognize that our definition of "basic" must be expanded if our students are to assume responsible roles as parents, workers, and community members in the 21st century. Students must interpret and evaluate a range of superb literature; write for many purposes and for many audiences; use computers to find information and communicate effectively; and think critically about film, television, and other visual media . . . The standards are emphatically not designed to create a centrally regulated national curriculum or a simplistic and expensive national system of testing. Many critics think such approaches are "silver bullet" solutions that can be fired at every school and every learner. These critics are missing the main point: teachers need a shared vision of a new, more rigorous literacy, and they need support from parents and their communities to help students achieve it.

This notion of a "new, more rigorous literacy" implicitly referenced research documenting the reading and writing challenges of the world beyond school, but neither the public nor the press was particularly receptive. "Two education groups today are proposing to change the meaning of literacy," began the front-page story in *USA Today* upon the Standards' release (Henry, 1996). In the minds of many, literacy had not changed along with changes in the wider world, thereby necessitating fresh curricular approaches; rather, a disturbingly vague new definition was being proposed by NCTE and IRA. In national press coverage, literacy educators were widely regarded as lacking firm beliefs or systematic knowledge, as talking of complex skills and negotiated meaning while ignoring calls for benchmarks and measurable criteria.

What to say to a public that longs for reassuring explanations that resonate with what they already believe about literacy learning? To politicians, whose interest in educational matters is reaching unprecedented intensity? To present and prospective teachers, who face a future in which policymakers seem increasingly determined to supply the specifics perceived as lacking in the NCTE/IRA Standards? While complete self-regulation may not be an appropriate goal for teachers, the ability to stipulate the contours of best practice remains a basic hallmark of professionalism. Teachers must work in partnership with parents and communities, but it is also important that they speak with credible, authoritative voices of their own. Even as the Standards articulated a need for learners to have multiple literacies at their disposal, fitting their written productions to the rhetorical demands of audience and occasion, such a fit eluded the Standards writers themselves. Given the growing gap between this "new, more rigorous literacy" and the public's desire for concrete specifics, how to ensure that English/language arts teachers have a say—that in this complicated age of multiple literacies, they are perceived as professionals possessing trustworthy specialized knowledge?

## THE MULTIPLE LITERACIES NEEDED BY ENGLISH/LANGUAGE ARTS PROFESSIONALS

Admittedly, a perceived lack of specialized knowledge is not a problem faced by English educators alone. Teachers have long been said to lack codified, generalizable knowledge, and teacher education programs seen as lacking intellectual centers, what Parsons called "cognitive rationality as applied to a particular field" (1968, p. 536). Though amply grounded in compelling theory and research, the notion of "multiple literacies" has likewise fallen short in the public's conception, dismissed all too easily as vague and insubstantial. Much else enters the mix, to be sure—fears of cultural and linguistic pluralism, a new passion for accountability, and a desire for yardsticks by which inferior outcomes can be identified and remedied. Part of what politicians wanted from the Standards was a way to foster our nation's global competitiveness, an aspiration perhaps never fully embraced by English educators. In any case, if seen as an effort to explain a profession's conception of literacy to the general public, the NCTE/IRA Standards must be regarded as less than fully satisfying.

English educators can scarcely be described as a homogeneous group, and while many were receptive to the Standards, the response was by no means unanimous. Some joined the chorus of voices calling the document excessively vague (Maloney, 1997; Zorn, 1997), while others questioned the very idea of English/language arts teachers embarking on such a venture (Kohn, 1999; Ohanian, 1997, 1999). In a ringing critique, Susan Ohanian (1997) took issue with both the Standards and their underlying premise:

I, for one, am uneasy about all this blather about teachers as professionals. Professionalism has a lot to answer for, particularly when it employs a language to shut out people who don't belong to the guild. I'm thinking here of doctors and lawyers and people who write Standards documents. People who worry about being professionals seem to spend a lot of time thinking about tests and outcomes. Me? I'd rather be known as a nurturer, somebody who always has an eye out for the bird in the window, a person who has enough faith in kids and books to believe that tomorrow will take care of itself (pp. 34–35).

Professionalism does have its lesser-acknowledged suspect side. Along with those who have countered Talcott Parsons' rosy optimism, perhaps we should all worry a bit more about the monopolistic aspect of professionalism colliding with an ethic of client care (Larson, 1977). Perhaps we do not wish to be just like doctors and lawyers, yet we long for a bit more respect, believing that increased authority would help us better serve students and lead more satisfying work lives. In the end, the alternative—having someone else make the key decisions for us—seems scarier than whatever seductions professionalism might present. Given the current climate, a belief that "tomorrow will take care of itself" may indeed not be enough.

We inhabit a contradictory school reform landscape, and these conversations about professionalization and standards are rife with unnamed tensions (Little, 1993). Even as many are calling for the professionalization of teaching, undergirded by enhanced initial preparation and opportunities for continuing growth, others insist on increased government intervention and oversight—more student testing, more reconstitution of low-achieving schools, more centralized control of research dollars—all communicating a general lack of trust in what teachers know and do. Even the basic question of whether English/language arts teachers are best seen as subject-area specialists or versatile generalists is increasingly unresolved. Rubbing against the grain of discipline-specific initiatives—standards, advanced licensure options, and so on—are an array of calls for blurring disciplinary boundaries. Middle school language-arts educators are under particular pressure to imagine curricula in interdisciplinary or integrated terms (Beane, 1997; Carnegie Council, 1989), often with little acknowledgment that much else in their career experience has communicated clear boundaries—discipline-specific training programs, membership in organizations such as NCTE, and professional-development opportunities that emphasize the teaching of literature and writing (DiPardo, 1999). While interdisciplinary teaching seems particularly well suited to current conceptions of literacy, disciplinary boundaries are so time honored (Grossman & Stodolsky, 1994, 1995; Siskin, 1994; Siskin & Little, 1995) that attempts to blur or eliminate them carries a further risk of a perceived diminishment of specialized knowledge, and with it a loss of professionalism.

In calling for more professional working conditions for teachers, Secretary of Education Richard Riley (1999) recently emphasized the need for the kind of joint discussion time that has long characterized the work of doctors and lawyers. On the one hand, these ideas would seem ideally matched to the notion of multiple literacies, with its emphasis on the joint construction of meaning, and on understanding how texts and readings are shaped by different angles of vision (Myers, 1996; New London Group, 1996). If students are to engage in such shared exploration, it certainly makes sense for teachers to model these activities in their daily work (Clift et al., 1995; Sarason, 1996/1971; Tharp, 1993). But here, too, are tensions and contradictions—rhetoric that emphasizes collaboration and community, but practices that measure success and failure on an individual basis for teachers and students alike. Literacy educators may wax enthusiastic over the idea of Bakhtinian dialogism (Bakhtin, 1981), but the rising clamor is for outcomes assessment, and outcomes are most readily assessed in the context of an autonomous, individualistic conception of literacy and its teaching. The world of standardized testing and policymaking is an uneasy match with the multiple-literacies vision of things—a vision honoring ambiguity, competing perspectives, and eluding uniformity in both enactment and explanation. Where these expanded conceptions of literacy and literacy learning are dismissed as insubstantial, so too are English/language arts educators' claims to professionalism.

The challenge of conveying the specialized understandings English/language arts teachers bring to their work remains a matter of structural and economic urgency. If the notion of "multiple literacies" is seen as soft-headed and vague, then research informed by it will not be publicly funded, and materials that reflect it will not be published. Many of us hold the continuing hope that career ladders will become available for teachers who desire them, providing opportunity for expert practitioners to move into school- and district-based leadership roles. It is imperative that these voices reflect the best insights of the profession, that they look ahead to the world students will inherit, not backwards to an imagined past. Our profession's collective efforts to explain the foundation and nature of our work will help ensure that our most well-informed, thoughtful teachers are heard in local governance.

How might English educators bolster their professionalism by communicating what they know—and, more important, want students to learn—to policymakers and the general public? Lest the challenge seem hopelessly complex, it is well to remember that the current school reform landscape, with its often tacit contradictions and competing agendas, is the very sort of text English/language arts educators are best suited to reading. Comprehending the obstacles blocking their paths to professionalism seems an easy task for people accustomed to talk of the multiplistic and political nature of literacy. As we advise students that effective discourse is all about understanding context and audience and gearing one's approach accordingly, why not up the ante for our own dialogue with the public? As students of literature, English educators are uncommonly skilled at holding competing points of view simultaneously in mind, finding places to stand among an array of possibilities. Practiced in complex thinking in a world with a generally low tolerance for ambiguity, most of us have not fully realized ways to convert this turn of mind to political advantage.

Teacher educators can lay a professional foundation by engaging prospective teachers in lively discussion of competing conceptions of literacy, the need to be clear about their fundamental purposes, and persuasive in articulating those purposes to the general public. Meanwhile, literacy educators at all levels need to model this kind of rhetorical skill to novices, seeking out opportunities to explain themselves to skeptics, and to explore the real world uses of literacy beyond school in ways that can usefully inform instructional approaches. In addition to supporting NCTE's national advocacy efforts, more of us need to commit to intensified involvement at the state and local levels as well. When NCTE passed a resolution at its 1998 annual convention stating that "neither Congress nor any federal or state agency should establish a single definition of reading or writing," (NCTE, 1998) many of us experienced a certain temptation to rest in the satisfaction of a collective voice. But we tend to find sooner or later that such relief is temporary, doing little to prepare us for the snags and roadblocks increasingly cropping up in our local paths—where the challenges are just as great, the stakes immediate, and like-minded company often harder to find.

Around the time that the NCTE/IRA Standards were released, I agreed to join my local school district's strategic planning committee. Our deliberations began benignly enough, with review of the "belief statements" included in the prior strategic plan. Our facilitator wanted to know if the new team still believed in them, assuring us that if even one member had the slightest reservation, any of the statements would be eliminated. Many

were the usual platitudes—"all students can learn," "everyone has a right to feel safe," "challenge enhances learning," and so on. Then we came upon this one, with its unmistakable echoes of E. D. Hirsch: "The survival of our civilization depends upon the transmission of a common core of knowledge." The room grew still as I voiced my objections, then angrily vocal. How could I, an English educator of all people, take issue with a statement so undeniably true? How could the district proceed with curriculum review absent such a statement? Don't I believe in teaching Shakespeare and Chaucer? What would I say to low-income parents, who were sure to read such a statement as ensuring basic literacy? After a much longer debate than anyone would have preferred, the statement stayed in with only slight modifications.

Three years later at the annual update meeting of our committee, we were asked to review the belief statements once again. "The survival of our civilization depends upon citizens' possession of a shared core of knowledge," read the slightly revised statement. My fellow committee members glanced uneasily my way, anticipating another windy speech on how my field just doesn't think of "literacy" in quite this way anymore. But this time a high school principal spoke first. It seemed that parents and teachers had approached him, asking what the statement was intended to say and accomplish. He realized that he couldn't come up with a clear paraphrase, nor, on further reflection, could the other members of our committee. No longer distracted by my talk of an expanded definition of literacy, they decided they didn't quite know what the statement meant after all, and it was thrown out.

I teach courses in literacy theory and research, and I enjoy lots of opportunities to talk with students about changing literacy demands and the complexities of the current school reform climate. But when pressed, I could not satisfactorily explain to a committee of community members, policymakers, and teachers how the "transmission of a common core of knowledge" was a notion out of sync with current conceptions of literacy, and why they should trust me on this. Worse still, I forgot to listen adequately, or to pose searching questions in return, questions that might have helped them detect the shaky foundation of a definition of "literacy" they had mistaken as sturdy. For a few moments, I found myself yearning to be back at my university office, with all those books lined up alphabetically on my shelves, Britton and Dewey looking down in tacit agreement. Community involvement had seemed such a good idea at the time, but that was before I had come to anticipate these unexpected challenges, this yawning conceptual gap. I realized that I still have a lot to learn by way of rhetorical skill, but then I suspect we all do. The challenges ahead are substantial, but our literate understandings prepare us—and our professionalism depends on our continuing (if sometimes stumbling) efforts to articulate what we know and why it matters.

## ACKNOWLEDGMENTS

Thanks to Michael Millender, Bonnie Sonnek, Stacy Haynes Moore, and Jane Hansen.

# References

Applebee, A. (1996). *Curriculum as conversation: Transforming traditions of teaching and learning.* Chicago: University of Chicago Press.

Bakhtin, M. (1981). *The dialogic imagination.* Austin, TX: University of Texas Press.

Barton, D. (1994). *Literacy: An introduction to the ecology of written language.* Cambridge, MA: Blackwell.

Beane, J. (1997). *Curriculum integration: Designing the core of democratic education.* NY: Teachers College Press.

Carnegie Council on Adolescent Development (1989). *Turning points: Preparing American youth for the 21st century.* NY: Carnegie Corporation.

Carter, K. (1996). Teachers' knowledge and learning to teach. In J. Sikula, T. Buttery, & E. Guyton (Eds.), *Handbook of research on teacher education* (pp. 291-310). New York: Macmillan.

Clift, R., Johnson, M., Holland, P., & Veal, M. (1992). Developing the potential for collaborative school leadership. *American Educational Research Journal, 28,* 877-908.

Clift, R., Veal, M., Holland, P., Johnson, M., & McCarthy, J. (1995). *Collaborative leadership and shared decision making: Teachers, principals, and university professors.* New York: Teachers College Press.

Cremin, L. A. (1965). *The genius of American education.* New York: Vintage Books.

Darling-Hammond, L. (1996). Teachers and teaching: Signs of a changing profession. In J. Sikula, T. Buttery, & E. Guyton (Eds.), *Handbook of research on teacher education* (pp. 267-289). New York: Macmillan.

Darling-Hammond, L. (1997). *The right to learn: A blueprint for creating schools that work.* San Francisco: Jossey-Bass.

Darling-Hammond, L., Berry, B., Haselkorn, D., & Fideler, E. (1999). Teacher recruitment, selection, and induction: Policy influences on the supply and quality of teachers. In L. Darling-Hammond & G. Sykes (Eds.), *Teaching as the learning profession: Handbook of policy and practice* (pp. 183-232). San Francisco: Jossey-Bass.

Dewey, J. (1963). *Experience and education.* New York: Macmillan. (Original work published in 1938).

DiPardo, A. (1999). *Teaching in common: Challenges to joint work in classrooms and schools.* New York & Urbana, IL: Teachers College Press & NCTE.

Flexner, A. (1910). *The Flexner report on medical education in the United States and Canada 1910.* Princeton, NJ: The Carnegie Foundation for the Advancement of Teaching.

Forman, E., Minick, N., & Stone, C. A. (Eds.). (1993). *Contexts for learning: Sociocultural dynamics in children's development.* New York: Oxford University Press.

Foucault, M. (1980). *Power/knowledge: Selected interviews & other writings, 1972-1977* (C. Gordon, ed.). New York: Pantheon.

Freidson, E. (1970). *Profession of medicine.* New York: Dodd & Mead.

Fullan, M., & Hargreaves, A. (1996). *What's worth fighting for in your school?* New York: Teachers College Press.

Grossman, P. L., & Stodolsky, S. S. (1994). Considerations of content and the circumstances of secondary school teaching. In L. Darling-Hammond (Ed.), *Review of Research in Education, 20,* 179-221.

Grossman, P. L., & Stodolsky, S. S. (1995). Content as context: The role of school subjects in secondary school teaching. *Educational Researcher, 24,* 5-11.

Harris, J. (1991). After Dartmouth: Growth and conflict in English. *College English, 53*(6), 631-646.

Henry, T. (1996, March 12). 'Real-world' literacy urged. *USA Today,* p. 1A.

Hirsch, E. D. (1987). *Cultural literacy: What every American needs to know.* Boston: Houghton Mifflin.

Holmes Group (1995). *Tomorrow's schools of education.* East Lansing, MI: author.

Kennedy, M. (1999). The role of preservice teacher education. In L. Darling-Hammond & G. Sykes (Eds.), *Teaching as the learning profession: Handbook of policy and practice* (pp. 54-85). San Francisco: Jossey-Bass.

Koerner, J. D. (1962). *The miseducation of American teachers.* Boston: Houghton Mifflin.

Kohn, A. (1999). *The schools our children deserve: Moving beyond traditional classrooms and "tougher standards."* Boston: Houghton Mifflin.

Kramer, R. (1991). *Ed school follies: The miseducation of America's teachers.* New York: The Free Press.

Lampert, M., & Ball, D. (1999). Aligning teacher education with contemporary K-12 reform visions. In L. Darling-Hammond & G. Sykes (Eds.), *Teaching as the learning profession: Handbook of policy and practice* (pp. 33-53). San Francisco: Jossey-Bass.

Larson, M. S. (1977). *The rise of professionalism: A sociological analysis.* Berkeley: University of California Press.

Lave, J. (1988). *Cognition in practice: Mind, mathematics, and culture in everyday life.* Cambridge: Cambridge University Press.

Lieberman, A., & Miller, L. (1992). *Teachers: Their world and their work.* New York: Teachers College Press.

Little, J. W. (1993). Teachers' professional development in a climate of educational reform. *Educational Evaluation and Policy Analysis, 15,* 129-151.

Lortie, D. (1975). *Schoolteacher: A sociological study.* Chicago: University of Chicago Press.

Lunbeck, E. (1994). *The psychiatric persuasion: Knowledge, gender, and power in modern America.* Princeton, NJ: Princeton University Press.

Maher, F., & Tetreault, M. (1999). Knowledge versus pedagogy: The marginalization of teacher education. *Academe, 85*(1), 40-43.

Maloney, H. (1997). The little Standards that couldn't. *English Journal, 86*(1), 86-90.

Myers, M. (1996). *Changing our minds: Negotiating English and literacy.* Urbana, IL: National Council of Teachers of English.

National Board for Professional Teaching Standards (1989). *Toward high and rigorous standards for the teaching profession: Initial policies and perspectives of the National Board for Professional Teaching Standards.* Detroit: National Board for Professional Teaching Standards.

National Board for Professional Teaching Standards (2000a). *What teachers should know and be able to do.* Retrieved from: <http://www.nbpts.org>.

National Board for Professional Teaching Standards (2000b). *The five propositions of accomplished teaching.* Retrieved from: <http://www.nbpts.org>.

National Center for Education Statistics (1999). *Teacher quality: A report on teacher preparation and qualifications.* Washington, DC: U.S. Department of Education.

National Council for Accreditation of Teacher Education (1995). *Standards, procedures, and policies for the accreditation of professional education units.* Washington, DC: author.

National Council of Teachers of English (1998). *Resolution on continued government intrusion into professional decision making.* Urbana, IL: NCTE.

National Council of Teachers of English/International Reading Association (1996a). *Standards for the English/language arts*. Urbana, IL & Newark, DE: NCTE/IRA.

National Council of Teachers of English/International Reading Association (1996b, April 12). Sense about nonsense: Critics of English standards. (Advertisement.) *The New York Times*, p. A14.

National Council of Teachers of English (1996). Standards response (NCTE web site). <http://www.ncte.org/Standards/response.html>.

New London Group (1996). A pedagogy of multiple literacies: Designing social futures. *Harvard Educational Review, 66,* 60-92.

New York Times Editorial Staff (1996, March 14). How not to write English. *The New York Times*, editorial page.

Nystrand, M. (with Gamoran, A., Kachur, R., & Prendergast, C.) (1997). *Opening dialogue: Understanding the dynamics of language and learning in the English classroom*. New York: Teachers College Press.

Ohanian, S. (1997). Insults to the soul. *English Journal, 86*(5), 32-35.

Ohanian, S. (1999). *One size fits few: The folly of educational standards*. Portsmouth, NH: Heinemann.

Parsons, T. (1968). Professions. In D. L. Sills (Ed.), *International encyclopedia of the social sciences (vol. 12)*. New York: Macmillan & The Free Press.

Riley, R. (1999). Remarks as prepared for delivery, NCES Press Conference: A report on teacher preparation and qualifications. Washington, DC: U.S. Department of Education.

Sarason, S. B. (1996). Revisiting *"The culture of the school and the problem of change."* New York: Teachers College Press. (Original work published 1971).

Shulman, L. S. (1987). Knowledge and teaching: Foundations of the new reform. *Harvard Educational Review, 57,* 1-22.

Siskin, L. S. (1994). *Realms of knowledge: Academic departments in secondary schools*. Washington, DC: Falmer Press.

Siskin, L. S., & Little, J. W. (1995). *The subjects in question: Departmental organization and the high school*. New York: Teachers College Press.

Starr, P. (1982). *The social transformation of American medicine*. New York: Basic Books.

Street, B. (1995). *Social literacies: Critical approaches to literacy in development, ethnography and education*. New York: Longman.

Sykes, G. (1999). Teacher and student learning: Strengthening their connection. In L. Darling-Hammond & G. Sykes (Eds.), *Teaching as the learning profession: Handbook of policy and practice* (pp. 341-375). San Francisco: Jossey-Bass.

Tabor, M. (1996, March 12). New guidelines on English a sketch, not a blueprint. *The New York Times*, p. A12.

Tharp, R. (1993). Institutional and social context of educational practice and reform. In E. A. Forman, N. Minnick, & C. A. Stone (Eds.), *Contexts for learning: Sociocultural dynamics in children's development* (pp. 269-282). New York: Oxford University Press.

Thompson, C., & Zeuli, J. (1999). The frame and the tapestry: Standards-based reform and professional development. In L. Darling-Hammond & G. Sykes (Eds.), *Teaching as the learning profession: Handbook of policy and practice* (pp. 54-85). San Francisco: Jossey-Bass.

Tom, A. R., & Valli, L. (1996). Professional knowledge for teachers. In J. Sikula, T. Buttery, & E. Guyton (Eds.), *Handbook of research on teacher education* (pp. 373-392). New York: Macmillan.

Vygotsky, L. (1978). *Mind in society*. Cambridge, MA: Harvard University Press.

Wertsch, J. (1991). *Voices of the mind: A sociocultural approach to mediated action*. Cambridge, MA: Harvard University Press.

Wilson, K. G., & Daviss, B. (1994). *Redesigning education*. New York: Henry Holt.

Zorn, J. (1997). The NCTE/IRA Standards: A surrender. *English Journal, 86*(1), 83-85.

# ·13·

# THE DESIGN OF EMPIRICAL RESEARCH

*Robert C. Calfee*
*Stanford University*

## *Marilyn Chambliss*
*University of Maryland, College Park*

Empirical research is a systematic approach for answering certain types of questions. Through the collection of evidence under carefully defined and replicable conditions, social science researchers seek to discover the influence of factors that affect human thought and action, and to understand when and why these influences occur. Nonempirical research spans a wide range of approaches, including mathematical, logical, historical, and legal, many of which support empirical techniques.

The empirical tradition plays a significant role in creating and validating social and psychological theories about how people think and act. In language arts, for instance, data-based research has supported models that link reading and writing as social acts (e.g., Nystrand, 1989; 1990; Spivey, 1997). No longer are readers and writers perceived as lost in their own thoughts, but instead as communicating with one another through written text.

Empirical research also searches for answers to practical questions. A high school English teacher seeks to improve her students' understanding of formal arguments. A middle school teacher aims to encourage his students toward more analytic comprehension. A remedial reading teacher wants to improve vocabulary instruction so that students score higher on standardized tests. While these questions are informed by scholarship and conceptual analysis, the primary goals are pragmatic.

Empirical research is disciplined (Cronbach & Suppes, 1969). It is distinguished "by the ways observations are collected, evidence is marshaled, arguments are drawn, and opportunities are afforded for replication, verification, and refutation" (Shulman, 1988, p. 4). The essential criterion for judging empirical evidence, from a research perspective, is *validity*; the researcher must be able to defend the interpretation of the evidence against counter-interpretations.

Empirical research is often equated with statistics and experimentation, in contrast to qualitative methods and naturalistic inquiry. We think this contrast is misleading for several reasons. First, it leads a researcher to concentrate on methodology rather than conceptualization. Second, it implies that the researcher must choose between what are often characterized as "hard" and "soft" approaches. Third, it overlooks the fact that virtually all significant educational problems call for a mix of methods, and all require rigorous conceptualization and creative design. Shulman (1988) advises novice researchers, "Become *skilled and experienced* in at least two methodologies..., become *aware* of the rich variety of methods of disciplined inquiry..., [and] do not limit your education to methodology alone" (p. 16). Our notion of empirical research design will encompass a full range of systematic approaches directed toward both theoretical and practical questions. The most appropriate starting point for a research project is a problem: questions unanswered by a previous investigation, a pragmatic need, a theoretical puzzle. Conceptualization and design focused on the problem should then determine the methods. Conceptualization represents the researcher's efforts to understand and analyze the structure of a research question. Design covers the various strategies for planning data collection.

We take our audience to be varied: researchers, college teachers of research methods, and high school teachers who rely on research as a guide to practice, among others. Based on our estimate of who is most likely to use the *Handbook*, we focus on a graduate student who is planning a dissertation. This individual is probably a practitioner who has returned for advanced work, who is interested in a study aimed toward practical outcomes, but who is prodded by her advisor to consider generalizability and theoretical implications. This chapter addresses the activities required for a research project: problem identification and conceptualization, surveying of the research literature with an informed and critical eye, construction of a research plan, data collection and analysis, and the interpretation and presentation of the findings, the latter with an eye to practical applications. We assume that a reader is already familiar with basic concepts of social science and educational research.

The chapter has four sections. The first explores the task of framing a research question. The next three sections describe the principles of research design, the process of constructing a design, and the task of interpretation. To demonstrate practical application of the concepts, we introduce a vignette early in the chapter that we will employ throughout the four sections. We include relatively few references; a sampling of the variety of methods texts available as of this writing would include Berliner and Calfee (1996, especially chapters by Behrens & Smith, Jaeger and Bond, and Hambleton), Creswell (1994), Gall, Borg, and Gall (1996), Jaeger (1997), Krathwohl (1997; also Calfee, 2001), and Thomas (1998). All of these volumes tackle the issues of conceptualization and design, placing methodology (quantitative and qualitative) at the service of problem solving.

## RESEARCH STRATEGY: MOVING FROM ANSWER TO QUESTION

It is tempting to begin a research project by thinking, "I'd like to prove that. . . ." Especially in the educational sciences, we tend to be advocates of particular positions and actions. "Spelling tests are bad (or good)." "English teachers should (or should not) know a good deal of linguistics." "Student motivation is (or is not) critical in a writing assignment." And so on. Such hypotheses are entirely appropriate starting points for inquiry, but developing a research problem requires a fundamental shift in thinking toward "I wonder what will happen. . . ." A small switch, but with major implications. For instance, the earlier proposals now take shape as questions. "Under what conditions are spelling tests bad or good?" "What are the effects of more or less linguistic preparation on the thinking and behavior of English teachers?" "In what ways do higher or lower levels of motivation affect students' responses to different types of writing assignments?"

These questions all open Pandora's box; they challenge the researcher to explore a universe of possibilities. No longer is the task to compare one condition with another, but to think about a broad array of situations, outcomes, and individuals. Spelling tests come in a variety of flavors, and may help with some tasks (new spelling tests) and not others (writing assignments), for some students (compulsives) but not others (impulsives). How to grapple with the infinite possibilities? The simple answer is that *design* is an essential tool. In this section, we describe three critical tasks for constructing a research design: framing the research question, selecting a context for the study, and thinking forward to how you will defend your interpretation of the findings. The serial nature of print forces us to present these in sequence, but they are actually interactive and recursive.

## Framing an Answerable Question

The initial phase in empirical research is the formulation of a workable scientific question, one that is answerable by objective evidence. For instance, imagine yourself as the high school teacher mentioned at the beginning of the chapter. You want to help your ninth graders to learn to write well reasoned and coherent arguments. You have recently become familiar with Toulmin's (1958) concept of argument, and this structure has become critical in your thinking. Toulmin proposed that all arguments have three basic parts: a claim, or assertion, what English teachers think of as a thesis statement; evidence offered to support the claim; and warrants, or principles about how to link the evidence more or less explicitly to the claim. In addition to the basic structure, complex arguments also present qualifications, counterarguments, and rebuttals.

It has taken you some time to understand what Toulmin means by a "warrant." Claims, evidence, and even counterarguments and rebuttals, seemed much more straightforward. Describing warrants as the underlying reasoning that links the claim to the evidence and either makes or breaks the argument, Toulmin suggested that warrants can be expressed as general statements, such as "If this evidence, then this claim;" or "Evidence such as this entitles one to draw a conclusion or make a claim such as this."

The relationships among claims, evidence, and warrants become clearest in simple arguments. Think about an argument that claims, "Wolves often represent evil in folk tales." It offers as evidence, "In various folktales, wolves terrorize and almost kill three little pigs, a little girl wearing a red coat and her sick grandmother, and a little Russian boy and his pets." The warrant would be something like "Any character that terrorizes and almost kills innocent people and animals represents evil." Alternatively, imagine the same claim with slightly different evidence. "A smart pig, a woodcutter, and a grandfather boil, chop up, or shoot wolves who are intent on eating weaker characters." Stating the warrant for this second argument reveals a problem with its evidence that you may have already noticed: "Any character who is destroyed by a more powerful character before killing weaker characters represents evil." The warrant is almost nonsensical given what we all know about the representation of evil in literature, and stating it explicitly seems almost silly. We all know that good evidence should exemplify the claim in simple arguments and that it succeeds in the first instance but fails in the second. Where stating the warrants becomes crucial is when the connections between evidence and claim are not obvious, when they need to be explained or defended against various counterarguments.

Now imagine an editorial claiming, "World political systems have converged on a single model that combines socialistic economics and democratic politics." Most of the editorial presents as evidence world events where socialistic economics and democratic politics were both present. The editorial explains how each of these events warrants the claim by describing how socialistic economics and democratic politics have combined. These explanations help the reader decide whether each of the world events indeed exemplifies the relationship between economics and politics stated in the claim. The editorial also counterargues that certain events demonstrate socialistic economics within a totalitarian political system, but notes in rebuttal that these events have occurred sporadically, accompanied by strong protests from the world community. The Toulminian framework applies to a range of situations in politics, history, literature, and so on—and also to research methods.

Analyzing several written arguments has led you to realize that focusing attention on warrants could help students highlight the reasoning present in their reading and writing. You are particularly interested in exploring whether having them state warrants explicitly helps them evaluate how well the evidence in the arguments that they write supports their claims.

In addition to applying the Toulmin model to your instruction, you want to explore the social aspects of reading and writing (Spivey, 1997). You believe that all writing is dialogic, involving at a minimum the communication between an author and a reader. Your experience suggests that students have mastered the argument genre when they can use it to query and critique an author's ideas (Mathison, 1998) and can anticipate readers' responses to their own writing (Rubin, 1998).

You ponder several issues, including the following:

- What is the essence of a good argument?
- What do my students already know about the concept of argument?
- How might I effectively teach all of my students to comprehend, critique, and compose various types of arguments?

Let's look at the researchability of each of these questions. The first question cannot be answered empirically because the answer depends on value judgments—"good" is the fly in the ointment. In *Argument Revisited; Argument Redefined: Negotiating Meaning in the Composition Classroom* (Emmel, Resch, & Tenney, 1996), the authors debate the "goodness" of three argument models: Toulmin's model (e.g., Fulkerson, 1996), a classical model that retains the contrast between deduction and induction (e.g., Gage, 1996), and a Rogerian argument model seen as being less confrontational than either of the other two approaches (e.g., Brent, 1996). Reading this debate and studying the scholarship of other philosophers, you decide that the Toulmin model best matches the writing curriculum in your school district, and so you choose it as the "best." However, you know that you must be prepared to defend your choice from critics who disagree, believing other argument models to be superior.

The second and third questions, in contrast, both provide starting points for empirical study. For instance, students' responses to the question, "What makes this argument strong?" may reveal their thinking processes. Observing the results of different instructional approaches on student performance can provide evidence about the third question.

The key to establishing the researchability of a question is to ask yourself, "Assuming that I collect evidence of one sort or another, and obtain a particular set of results, to what degree can I make a convincing argument when I interpret the findings in relation to the original question?" Addressing this issue demands that you step outside your own convictions and develop skills as a self-critic; it helps to find a "friendly enemy" along the way, someone interested in your problem, and willing to work hard at destroying your line of argument. Defending your interpretations against alternative explanations is the essence of the research enterprise, and is the central theme of this chapter.

## Finding the Evidence

Once a question has appeared on the screen, the researcher must decide what evidence is relevant to the question, how to gather it, and how to analyze and interpret the data. It helps to know the territory: What do you already know about research on comprehension of argument texts, about comprehension and composition in general, about effective instructional practices, and so on? Another task is review of the literature, which can seem a daunting task. By selecting a few "best evidence" papers as starting points and working backwards from there (Krathwohl, 1997, chap. 6; Slavin, 1986), you can sometimes shape the job into manageable proportions. You should also bring your professional knowledge and experience into the mix.

You must then reach decisions about *what* data to collect, along with *how* and *where* to carry out this task, and from *whom*. We will cover the *what* of data collection later as a design task, but a few fundamental matters deserve immediate consideration. First, should you focus on numbers or "stuff" (observations, interviews, and so on)—quantitative or qualitative? In fact, you don't have a choice! Empirical data are inherently qualitative, and it takes a uniquely human act—*measurement*—to assign numbers to observations. A student essay begins as "stuff," but you can count the number of words, calculate the average sentence length, or ask a panel of judges to assign one or more rubric-based values to the work. Whether you decide to measure and how you decide to do it is a conceptual matter.

A second dimension to *what* is "how much?" A useful guiding principle is *triangulation*, which means to consider different ways of collecting data for each construct in the study. If you are interested in student writing, then looking at different facets (length, coherence, mechanics) of each composition makes sense. You might also accumulate other artifacts (student notes and outlines) and indicators (e.g., ask students to talk about the compositions and how they planned and produced them). If this amalgam of information produces a consistent picture, then your argument is increasingly believable.

The *how* of data collection encompasses two overlapping strategies; the researcher can either *observe* or *intervene* with the intent of *describing* or *experimenting*. Imagine a young boy examining an ant hill. One moment he is the naturalist, observing the hectic activity in the insect community. Suddenly compelled to intervene, he pokes a twig into the hole and watches the ants' responses.

To observe or to intervene? Most texts on research methodology separate these two approaches, one section on naturalistic approaches and a second on experiments. *Experimental*, *quantitative*, and *statistical* are often bound together in one package, and contrasted with *naturalistic*, *qualitative*, and *descriptive*. Fortunately, the joining of quantitative and qualitative methods is becoming more commonplace (Krathwohl, 1997). Both approaches are clearly empirical, in the sense that they both rely on evidence. Moreover, the various strategies are independent;

you can design a naturalistic investigation that uses quantitative methods, or an experimental study that employs qualitative assessments. Quantifying observations allows the researcher to employ statistical techniques for summarizing information and conducting inferential analyses (how closely related or disparate are two sets of evidence). The richness of qualitative information, on the other hand, may allow the researcher to delve into underlying processes and explore complex hypotheses. For instance, measuring the length of two sets of compositions may reveal substantial and trustworthy differences; students taught about warranting may write substantially more than students without such instruction. Student interviews may resist quantification, but suggest to the researcher how instruction led students to write longer essays. For instance, suppose several students tell you something like this: "I knew that if I just wrote my main point and a few details you wouldn't like my paper, so I just rambled around—that's kinda what you mean by that 'warrant' thing." The interview results may not be what you hypothesized, but they connect the quantitative information with the instructional treatment.

The *where* of data collection is frequently tied with the *who*. Traditionally, "real" classroom situations have been contrasted with laboratory environments, the latter presumably "unreal." More recently, close collaboration between classroom teacher and researcher has been contrasted with researcher imposed designs (Freedman, Simons, & Kalnin, 1999). These contrasts can be misleading. Researcher imposed designs implemented within either classrooms or laboratories are supposed to eliminate extraneous fluctuations in conditions, whereas the classroom is a "wild and crazy" place. The practical value of researcher imposed designs and laboratory findings is often questioned, whereas teacher designed, classroom based research is presumed to be directly applicable. Neither stereotype stands close scrutiny.

One can find many examples of untrustworthy laboratory research and excellent instances of classroom-based investigations. The practical significance of a study depends on the quality of the research rather than the characteristics of the setting. An important bridge between these extremes is the *design experiment*, in which systematic variations are tried out in different classrooms through collaborations between teachers and researchers, a range of quantitative and qualitative indicators serving to inform the teams (Brown, 1992; Collins, 1994). The design experiment technique, although still in the early stages of development, illustrates the linkage of methodological distinctions that previously seemed altogether contradictory.

Evidence is trustworthy to the extent that it holds up against attack from others; research has much in common with law. Earlier we introduced validity as of central importance. You will also encounter the concept of *control*; in social science research, control refers to the researcher's efforts to ensure the validity of the interpretations, the trustworthiness of the argument, the generalizability of the findings.

One essential contributor to adequate control is *design*, which refers to the steps in identifying the contextual factors that influence performance, planning the conditions of data collection so that these factors are adequately represented, and ensuring that the plan allows defensible generalizability of the findings—you can argue that the findings are trustworthy,

replicable, and usable. Later in the chapter we introduce the concepts of *factors* and *factorial design* as one strategy for establishing adequate control.

Enough abstractions. Let us now show how these concepts might apply to the vignette, starting with *where* and *who*. Suppose you discover that two teachers in your school employ different approaches to argument instruction—one fairly traditional, the other more innovative. The traditional teacher relies on lecture and discussion to cover thesis/support forms of argument and assigns a five paragraph essay with the claim or thesis in the introductory paragraph, three paragraphs of evidence or support, and a conclusion that summarizes the argument. The second teacher leads students through several forms of argument including those with counterarguments and rebuttals. This teacher emphasizes the role of warrants in linking evidence to a claim and directs students continually to identify and question their thinking. She integrates comprehension and composition in each lesson.

You have the makings of a natural experiment. The plan seems simple enough; your task as researcher will be to visit classrooms and describe what you see. On reflection, you realize that the reality is more complex. For instance, your questions and your presence may have influenced both teachers and students. These effects are not necessarily "bad," but they illustrate how research almost always entails some intervention.

You then begin to think about a planned experiment, with classes assigned to contrastive treatments, one traditional and the other more innovative. This approach resembles the studies covered in Chapter NN on *Major Research Programs*. This plan also seems simple enough at first. You construct materials for the two instructional treatments, select measures to assess performance at the beginning and end of the study, and decide on appropriate statistical tests.

Your advisor raises questions. First, she warns that the two treatments appear to be *confounded*. Don't think that your ideas are being denounced. Confounding is a technical term describing a condition where two or more dimensions or factors vary simultaneously. In your plan, the two treatments differ in several ways, including the goals (five paragraph compositions vs. analytic essays), the reading materials (none vs. some), the teaching approach (lecture vs. discussion), and student activities (individual vs. group assignments), to name a few. If the results favor the innovative approach, how can you identify the critical elements? Second, how can you be sure that the treatments are implemented as you intend? Third, what if the measures do not mesh with critical elements of the instruction? You begin to understand that, even in a planned experiment, you may have to play the naturalist's role, documenting in detail what happens during instruction for both classes.

## Making Sense of the Evidence

The study is now complete—you are satisfied with the design, and the data are in the bag. You have completed the analyses. You have almost finished the job—or have you?

Unfortunately, data do not answer questions; people do. For evidence to have meaning, you must deal with several issues. How far can you trust the evidence; how far can you generalize the findings; how convincingly can you persuade others of your interpretation? The basic point is simple: You should reflect on what you will say in response to various outcomes—*before you collect the data*. You can organize this task around two options: The findings confirm your expectations or they surprise you. The reason for this exercise is equally simple: It helps you refine your research design.

Suppose the results turn out as you predicted. You document that students in the novel treatment for analyzing and composing arguments are more likely to participate vigorously in classroom discussions about one another's arguments and prepare coherent arguments for their classroom assignments than those in the traditional approach. What does this result mean? Your argument appears straightforward; the innovative approach is superior, supporting your convictions about what students need to learn and how they can best learn it.

The researcher's task is seldom so simple. You should expect challenges. How else might the results be interpreted? This question is both practically and theoretically important. The intent is to establish the *validity* of the findings, to ensure that the interpretation holds up to close scrutiny. You are probably familiar with the concept of validity as it applies to testing: Validity is the extent to which a test measures what it is supposed to measure. In fact, recent thinking (Messick, 1995) about validity has taken a different turn: "Validity is the strength of the argument that a particular test outcome means what the tester says that it means" (page 742). Would the same conclusion hold if the student were given a different test at a different time or by a different tester? What alternative conclusions might fit the data? In a word, do the warrants hold up?

Research validity comes down to the same issue—the validity of a study is the strength of the argument that a particular finding means what the researcher says that it means. Meeting this challenge is seldom easy. The researcher is usually close to the problem and invested in the expected conclusion. Imagining other possibilities does not come readily.

One remedy is to ask colleagues for alternatives. You will be surprised at the creative ideas that emerge from this exercise. For instance, the novelty of your favored approach may invigorate both teachers and students; what will happen when the method becomes humdrum? Instruction can be highly dependent on the larger context. Would your approach work as well for teachers and students who were accustomed to a lecture/recitation format? The technique worked for this class, but will students apply the ideas in other classes and situations? The approach takes extra work; if another teacher decides to try it with modifications, what critical features need to be kept in order for the treatment to remain effective?

On the other hand, suppose the results do not come out as expected? You may have difficulty imagining this outcome. Given all your planning, thinking, and work, how could this happen! But it does. The most frequent disappointment occurs when an innovative treatment produces little or no effect, when the *null hypothesis* (no difference) cannot be rejected. This result can come about for either or both of two reasons. First, the treatment may actually not be effective—hard to accept, but possible. Second, student performance may vary so widely that random fluctuations swamp the effect. It's like a slot machine, which "costs" you on each play; you do not immediately

notice the loss because sometimes you win and sometimes you lose. A well-conceived research design allows you to identify extraneous sources of variability in performance, so that you can tell whether you have won or lost.

We have laid out three elements, but as noted earlier, planning an empirical investigation is not a step-by-step process, despite what you may have learned in high school (and even college). The process begins with a question. You wrestle with the details, and the shape of the question changes. You think about how to interpret various outcomes, and the design takes a different form, which leads you back to your original conceptualization. Each element has distinctive features, but the process is recursive and interactive. When you read a research report, it may resemble bowling; the investigator sets the pins, throws the ball, and counts how many pins fall. Reality is different. "Some of the most excellent inquiry is free ranging and speculative in its initial stages, trying what might seem to be bizarre combinations of ideas and procedures, restlessly casting about..." (Cronbach & Suppes, 1969, p. 16). But threading through all the elements is one critical theme—design.

## PRINCIPLES OF DESIGN

This section of the chapter develops the foundational concepts of research design. Any field of study evolves in stages or paradigms, often beginning with the careful examination of intuitive experiences and ideas and the increasingly careful collection of evidence. Data patterns emerge, often to vanish or transmute. Eventually the patterns lead to the formulation of theoretical ideas, which are valuable because they explain and enlighten the evidence. Along the way, investigators must rely on informed guesses. Educational research is in this middle stage today. Educators do not yet have powerful theories and so must still rely on informed guesses to guide their work. Disciplined planfulness is crucial. Hence, our focus in this chapter on research design.

We first explain the three fundamental barriers that design techniques help surmount: *lack of construct validity, confounding,* and *extraneous variability*. Then we discuss four fundamental principles: the *concept of design*, the *elements of design, connection of the elements,* and *integration around a theme*. We will employ a technical vocabulary that has evolved over the past several decades; the critical terms are shown in Fig. 13.1. This table should be helpful as you proceed through the chapter.

### Three Fundamental Barriers

In conducting a research study, the researcher must keep in mind three critical issues—construct validity, confounding, and uncontrolled variability—that can undermine the merit of the outcomes. Design methods safeguard against these threats.

The *construct validity* of a research study, as for a test, refers to the trustworthiness of various interpretations of the evidence; does the finding mean what you think it means, where "it" is the construct? Validity can be compromised in several ways, but most of the shortcomings arise from a failure to think through the path that leads from the initial question to the final interpretation. The concept of test validity is a useful metaphor.

- **FACTOR:** A variation in treatment conditions, in subject characteristics, or in instrumentation, that is identified by the researcher to achieve control over the performance outcomes in a study; also referred to as an *independent variable*.

- **LEVEL OF A FACTOR:** A particular choice or selection from the possible variations in a factor.

- **MEASURE:** Result of observation or measurement of performance under specified conditions; also referred to as a *dependent variable*.

- **TREATMENT FACTOR:** Variation in environmental conditions under direct control of the researcher. *Amount of time allowed for revising a draft* is a treatment factor; *5, 10,* and *30 minutes are levels*.

- **PERSON FACTOR:** Pre-existing characteristics of a person or group, identified by the researcher in designing a plan for selecting a sample for investigation. *Undergraduate major* is a person factor; *English, Engineering,* and *Political Science* are levels.

- **OUTCOME FACTOR:** Facet used in designing a measurement package (e.g., test, observation, interview, or questionnaire). *Writing topic* is an outcome factor; *contemporary writing styles, earthquake preparation,* and *world conflicts* are levels.

- **NUISANCE FACTOR:** A variation included in the design of an investigation to ensure adequate control, not necessarily because of conceptual or practical importance. *Class period* is a nuisance factor; *early* and *late morning* and *afternoon* are levels.

FIGURE 13.1 Technical vocabulary for research design terminology.

Suppose a student's test score indicates that she reads two grade levels below expectation. The validity of the test for this decision can be questioned in several ways: Is the test suitable for this purpose? Were the testing conditions appropriate? What other evidence is available? What are the costs and benefits of the decision for the student? Does the evidence say something about "reading" or about the test and testing conditions?

Similar questions can be posed for a research study. The principles are the same; the construct validity of the findings depends not only on the data but on the interpretation. Is the plan of the study adequate? To what extent does the context allow generalization to other situations? How does the finding mesh with other studies? What are the cost-benefit implications of various decisions springing from the study? The more you know about the answers to these questions, the more secure will be the construct validity. One purpose of research design is to increase the chances that outcomes are trustworthy. As Cronbach (1988) puts it, "Validators should do what the detached scientist would do; [the key ingredient is] a vigorous, questing intellect. . . ." (p. 14)

The second barrier, *confounding*, occurs when the effect of the primary factor cannot be separated from the confounded factor, in which instance the findings are completely compromised. Consider how confounding might arise in your study if you select two teachers, one assigned to each instructional approach in a different class of students. Suppose you find a striking difference in student outcomes. The finding can result from the teacher, the students, the program, or some combination of the three. Given these possibilities, the evidence cannot

be interpreted with any confidence. This difficulty is virtually impossible to repair after the fact.

Confounding is the major shortcoming of designs that contrast an innovative approach and a traditional method, the classical experimental-control technique. A quarter century ago, Cronbach (1963) pointed out the severe limitations of this design, but it still appears with great regularity in the empirical literature. Any comparison of two groups means confounded variables, and hence is subject to multiple interpretations. Our advice, if you consider such a study, is to give the matter further thought. A more complex design can separate the confounded variables. Qualitative descriptions of classroom life during both the innovation and its contrast can also help in interpreting confoundings.

*Uncontrolled variability*, the third concern, occurs when unintended fluctuations obscure answers to the research question. Eliminating unwanted variability is essential because of the critical importance of variability in educational research. On the one hand, systematic or explainable variability is the payoff. You predict that performance under the novel treatment will differ from the traditional approach, presumably because of the treatment. On the other hand, unexplained variability is the gauge against which systematic differences are measured; large differences in student performance within the two conditions may obscure the treatment effect.

Your job is to plan a design and arrange conditions so that systematic variability is maximized and unexplained variability is minimized. Suppose, for instance, that writing scores (rated on a 1–10 rubric scale) under one approach range from 8 to 10, while they range from 3 to 5 in the other approach. This difference passes the eyeball test. On the other hand, if scores range from 6 to 10 in the treatment group and 5 to 9 in the control group, you are well advised to wonder about the possibility that the differences are due to chance. In this second example, suppose that most girls score 9 or 10 in the first group, while boys in both groups range around 5 to 8. Now your interpretation takes a different turn; the treatment appears to make a difference, but only for girls.

Control encompasses the various methods employed to strengthen validity. Chief among these methods is design, although other issues are also important. For instance, if your findings are to be generalized to other situations, the evidence should presumably be based on a *random sample* from some population of interest, or at least you should know how nonrandom the data are. Social science research typically relies on "handy" random samples. You have access to teachers and students in a particular school, not exactly a chance selection, but typical of schools in the area. Some teachers will cooperate with you; others will not. Or you may search for a "purposive" sample, a situation selected because it meets conditions important for your hypotheses. These constraints and decisions may limit the generalizability of your findings. What should you do? In these and other instances, the important point is to *be aware* of these constraints, and to *document* events for yourself and your audience. The reader can then assess the degree to which the failure to achieve absolute randomness—which is both impossible and unnecessary—compromises your argument.

A second nondesign control issue is the maintenance of *uniformity* during data collection. A well constructed design provides control over certain variables, but other conditions are likely to be free floating. For instance, suppose your study spans a 5-week period. Consult the calendar—what upcoming events may influence instruction or assessment? If the critical posttest is scheduled on the day before a big football game, students may not give full attention to the task. What is happening in the lives of students and teachers during the study? If several students know that they are moving in 2 months, their engagement in the program may be lessened. If one teacher is in the midst of a divorce or fighting with the Internal Revenue Service, this may not be the best time for a new program—nor, for that matter, to handle a traditional approach.

These scenarios exemplify the difficulty of establishing uniformity. You should nonetheless make every effort to keep conditions constant, while remaining sensitive to discrepancies, and documenting them. Like randomness, uniformity is an ideal seldom attainable. Problems arise when you do not detect these variations and when you fail to report them. Unrecognized sources of variation arise from such conditions, and they can cloud the picture when you ignore their effects.

## The Concept of Design

Thus far we have outlined the steps in conceiving a design from question to answer. We have discussed three threats that design can defuse. But a crucial question remains: What does a good research design look like?

A well-planned design is the key to separating treatment effects from and lowering background noise. It is the best protection against lack of validity, confoundings, and extraneous variability. Textbooks on research design often stress the procedures and mechanics of the design task, along with complementary statistical methods of analysis of variance. We will start instead with the underlying principles of design, which apply equally to descriptive and experimental investigations, to quantitative and even qualitative approaches.

Many human endeavors rely on the concept of design, sometimes through recognition and appreciation of naturally occurring patterns, more often through creation and construction. As Simon (1981) notes, design is the feature that distinguishes between the natural and the artificial, between happenstance and the artifices of humankind. All designs have three essential ingredients (Chambliss & Calfee, 1998). First is a set of distinctive elements, what Simon calls "nearly decomposable components." Second are the linkages that bind individual elements together. Third is the theme that gives overall shape and meaning to the enterprise.

Toulmin's argument model actually illustrates the design concept nicely. The *theme* comes from the claim, which sets the author's overall purpose and guides the remainder of the argument. The *elements* are the sources of evidence, the concrete statements chosen by the author to support the claim. The warrants are the *linkages* that bind the evidence to the claim and join the separate parts into a coherent whole. The three characteristics of good design are present in Toulmin's model, which serves as the conceptual framework for your study.

Now let us turn to the application of design principles for a research study. The elements include the factors that influence performance: the treatment or environmental variations, differences between individuals, and various methods for assessing performance. The elements are linked by one of two relationships, "crossing" or "nesting," described in the following. The theme encompasses the overarching objectives of the research guided by questions or hypotheses. A design with these three characteristics will generate a data structure to inform your research questions in a well controlled—i.e., trustworthy and generalizable—fashion.

## Factorial Elements

A factor is a variable that the researcher defines and controls in order to evaluate its influence on performance (see Fig. 13.1). Some factors can be directly controlled; others depend on careful observation of natural variations. In your study, for instance, initial reflections turn up several candidates as factors for inclusion in the design: argument type, instructional method, prior student experience with arguments, age and sex of students, teacher experience with the genre, teacher and student beliefs about the social nature of reading and writing, and choice of a written or oral test.

As suggested earlier, your best strategy at the outset is to cast a wide net—brainstorm, think divergently. The idea is not to create a shopping list of every conceivable variable, but to identify a range of factors that may substantially influence performance or inform your understanding of the phenomenon.

Novice researchers tend to begin with one or two factors of central interest, relying on "randomness" to handle other effects. Such a strategy leaves much to chance. Keep in mind the following principle: *If you ignore factors that influence performance, variability from these sources does not disappear; instead, it confuses the picture.* In a well-controlled study, the researcher pins down important sources of variability, to ensure that systematic effects stand out clearly against background noise.

For practical purposes, we distinguish three primary types of factors: treatment factors; person or individual-difference factors; and outcome factors (see Fig. 13.1). A fourth category, nuisance or "control" factors, is also useful in preparing a design.

A *treatment factor* is an environmental facet directly controllable by the researcher. Argument type, social interaction, and task might serve as treatment factors in your study. You decide to introduce students to the two types of arguments depicted in Fig. 13.2: a simple version where all the evidence supports a single claim, and a complex form where different facets of a claim are supported by different pieces of evidence. You arrange two types of social interaction: one in which students work together to analyze the two types of arguments and another in which the teacher models the analysis through lectures. Finally, you give students practice with one or two tasks—either reading only or both reading and writing. You have defined three treatment factors, each with two variations.

The primary goal of identifying various factors is to assess the importance of these variations each in its own right—the

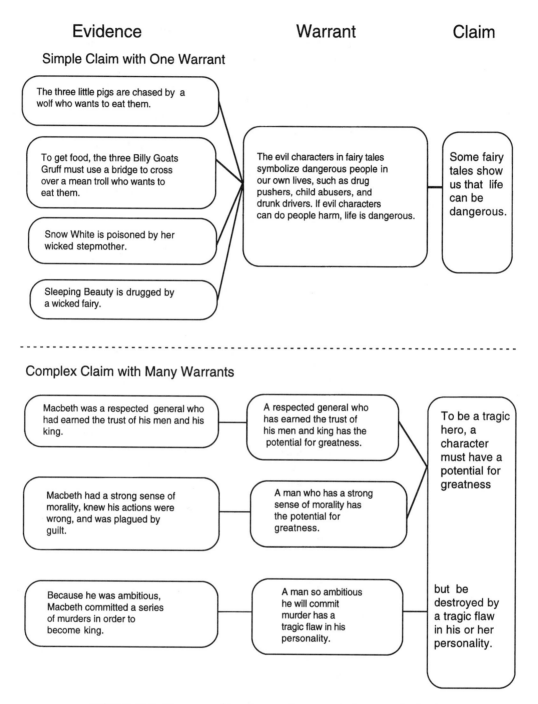

FIGURE 13.2. Diagrams of two types of argument structure: A simple claim with one warrant and a complex claim with many warrants.

*main effect* of the variation. To what extent do students perform differently on simple and complex arguments? Do the student interactions and teacher's role make a difference?

In a *factorial design*, the research plan includes all combinations of the factors. Including the combinations can increase the cost of the study, although not that much. For instance, suppose you have identified two factors. You could do two studies, one for each factor, a total of four different conditions. If you combine the two factors—two times two equals four, the same number of conditions.

The real payoff from a factorial design is that you can also assess the *interaction* among factors. An interaction occurs when the effect of one variable depends on conditions associated with another factor. For instance, simple arguments may not require social interaction, but complex arguments may be more easily acquired under this condition. Main effects and interactions are critical outcomes from factorial designs, and we will return to this matter in a later section.

A *person factor* is an intrinsic characteristic of an individual or group. Age, sex, ability, and prior experience are examples. These factors should be taken into account when selecting teachers, students, and classes, either because you have a theoretical interest in the effects or to control extraneous variability. For instance, if you know that some students have been taught about arguments while others are unfamiliar with the concept, then you should include student experience as a design factor. If you know that some teachers understand the argument genre better than others, then you should include teacher understanding as a factor as well. Interactions can also occur among person factors. It is possible that students with no prior instruction about arguments would benefit from having a teacher who understands the argument genre, but that the teacher understands the genre well would matter much less for students with prior instruction.

Interactions are also assessable from combinations of treatment and person factors. For instance, more experienced students may not benefit from social interactions, while novices do much better in a group than when left on their own. This particular effect exemplifies an aptitude–treatment interaction, in which students respond to variation in a treatment factor differentially depending on person characteristics (Cronbach & Snow, 1977).

*Outcome factors* direct the choice of measures in an investigation. Like treatment factors, they can often be directly manipulated by the researcher, although this opportunity is frequently overlooked. The tendency is to select an off-the-shelf instrument without thinking about its relation to the research questions. Suppose your school administers a standardized comprehension test. Shouldn't you employ this test to assess the relative effectiveness of the two programs? In making this decision, you face some trade-offs. On the one hand, most standardized tests use rather vague expository passages, not the argument genre, and they tap the students' ability to recognize, not to reflect or to compose. Because of these limitations, you could construct measures that directly assess students' ability to handle argument structures, that demonstrate their ability to craft a persuasive text, and that reveal attitudes and confidence about these tasks. On the other hand, standardized tests are proven instruments with established reliability and validity estimates, while your measure has not been submitted to tests of reliability and validity. You might use the standardized test as an index of general student ability, and your own measure for a more focused look at students' composition of arguments.

Because you expect factors such as teacher understanding or social interaction to affect student performance, it would be important that you describe the instruction that each teacher provides and the social interaction that actually occurs. You can collect detailed field notes that record teacher and student dialogue or videotape class sessions and analyze the amount and quality of social interaction. It is not uncommon, for example, for students to spend small group time discussing social roles rather than analyzing a complex written text together, an unintended event that could muddy your results if you have not collected descriptive data during implementation.

Beside deciding on the factors for your design, you also need to choose the levels for each factor. Sometimes the decision is straightforward; if sex is a factor, then male and female are obvious choices. For a factor like undergraduate major, the range of options is greater, and the selection requires more thoughtfulness. If revision time is a treatment variable, the number of options is virtually infinite. Think first about the relation between this factor and performance. For instance, does performance increase steadily with time? Might it increase for a while and then tail off? Or perhaps, beyond a certain point, further time might actually lead to a poorer outcome? For each possibility, what are your best estimates of candidate values?

What instructional options emerge in your study? We suggested earlier that you might either have students analyze arguments in small groups or have teachers teach the argument structure directly. On reflection, what about a level (a condition) that combines the two? Now the factor has three levels (Fig. 13.3). But how are lecture and group work to be combined? Students

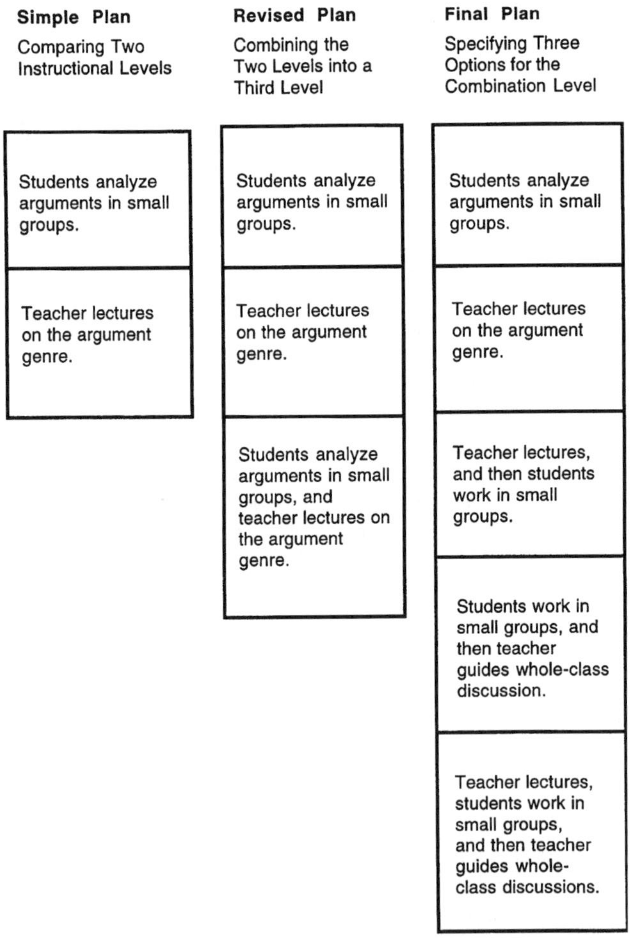

| Simple Plan<br>Comparing Two<br>Instructional Levels | Revised Plan<br>Combining the<br>Two Levels into a<br>Third Level | Final Plan<br>Specifying Three<br>Options for the<br>Combination Level |
|---|---|---|
| Students analyze arguments in small groups. | Students analyze arguments in small groups. | Students analyze arguments in small groups. |
| Teacher lectures on the argument genre. | Teacher lectures on the argument genre. | Teacher lectures on the argument genre. |
| | Students analyze arguments in small groups, and teacher lectures on the argument genre. | Teacher lectures, and then students work in small groups. |
| | | Students work in small groups, and then teacher guides whole-class discussion. |
| | | Teacher lectures, students work in small groups, and then teacher guides whole-class discussions. |

FIGURE 13.3. Choosing levels for an instructional factor from a simple plan with two levels to a final plan with options for five levels.

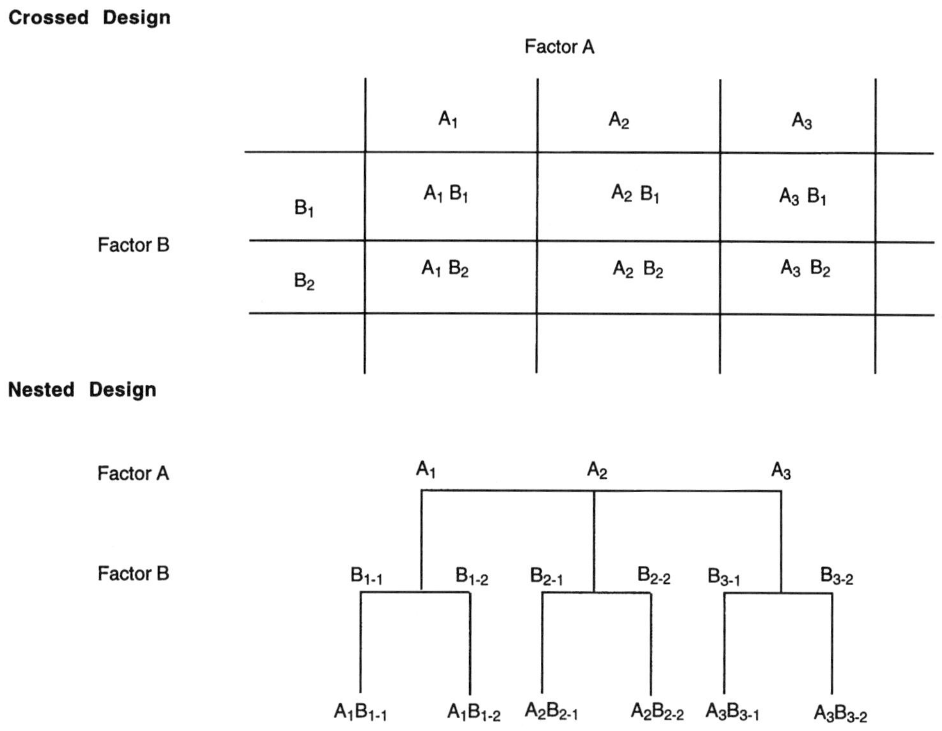

**Crossed Design**

Factor A

|  |  | $A_1$ | $A_2$ | $A_3$ |
|---|---|---|---|---|
| Factor B | $B_1$ | $A_1 B_1$ | $A_2 B_1$ | $A_3 B_1$ |
|  | $B_2$ | $A_1 B_2$ | $A_2 B_2$ | $A_3 B_2$ |

**Nested Design**

Factor A    $A_1$    $A_2$    $A_3$

Factor B    $B_{1\text{-}1}$    $B_{1\text{-}2}$    $B_{2\text{-}1}$    $B_{2\text{-}2}$    $B_{3\text{-}1}$    $B_{3\text{-}2}$

$A_1 B_{1\text{-}1}$    $A_1 B_{1\text{-}2}$    $A_2 B_{2\text{-}1}$    $A_2 B_{2\text{-}2}$    $A_3 B_{3\text{-}1}$    $A_3 B_{3\text{-}2}$

FIGURE 13.4. Two types of linkages: Crossed and nested.

might first analyze arguments in small groups with minimal guidance and then end the session with a teacher-guided discussion. Another approach could be to lecture the students about argument structures and then have them practice in small groups. A third approach could be to begin with lecture followed by group work and ending with a guided discussion. Which plan should you employ in the design? The answer depends on your resources and your judgment about what you can learn from each plan. If you are looking for the grand design and you have limited resources, you will have a difficult time managing the entire design; far better to prioritize by thinking about the most interesting choices for a preliminary study.

## Building a Factorial Design

The simplest way to construct a design from factors is to combine them as though they were Lego blocks—put all the pieces together. This strategy works well as a start, but you also need to know about some refinements. Two factors can be joined in either of two ways: *crossed* (every level of the first factor is combined with every level of the second factor) or *nested* (the levels of the second factor differ at each level of the first factor). The contrast, shown in Fig. 13.4, parallels the difference between a matrix and a hierarchy. In a matrix, every level on the first dimension is combined with every level of the second dimension. In a hierarchy, while the lower levels may have a common thread, they do not connect to other points at the same level. When a set of factors is crossed, you can assess the main effects of each factor as well as the interactions among them. When

factors are nested, only the main effects can be evaluated, because the design does not include combinations of the two factors.

These methods for connecting factors have two advantages. First, like Lego blocks or Tinker toys, they combine in virtually infinite ways to join any number of factors. While the previous definitions express relations between a pair of factors, any number of factors may be joined by combinations of crossing and nesting.

Second, the methods ensure that any factorial design is free from confounding, that the effects of any two factors are independent of one another. This assurance has two caveats. First, each combination must include an equal (or proportionate) number of observations. For instance, suppose you divide a writing class into high and low achievers (the achievement factor) crossed with boys and girls (the sex factor). You are likely to find many more high girls and low boys than the other two combinations, which means that the design is partly confounded; "boys" means (in part) "low achieving," and contrariwise. Second, the strategy does not guarantee that any given factor is not confounded with other factors *not* in the design. Low-achieving may also mean "from poor families," for instance. You can often predict such patterns in advance. By selecting your sample according to a design that you have prepared, you can collect data that allow you to separate the various facets.

How does the researcher decide whether to cross or nest a particular pair of factors in planning a design? The linkage can depend on the situation. Suppose you have initially spent time in several classrooms observing comprehension and composition instruction. During your observations and teacher

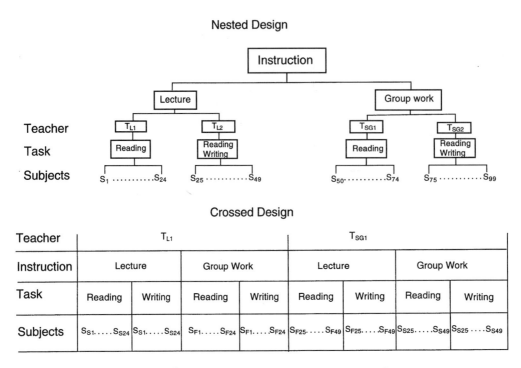

FIGURE 13.5. Linking INSTRUCTION, TEACHER, TASK, and SUBJECTS into alternative designs.

interviews, you discovered that the teachers who are candidates for the study seem to prefer different types of instruction. One group, whom you decide to call "Group L," prefers traditional teacher-led lecture and discussion while the second group, "Group SG," favors small group student-centered instruction.

Figure 13.5 shows two alternate sets of linkages for creating a design that acknowledges these teacher differences. The top panel shows a design that is primarily hierarchical. Believing that teachers will be more effective if your instruction matches their preferences, you assign teachers $L_1$ and $L_2$ to the lecture condition and teachers $SG_1$ and $SG_2$ to the small group condition. Note from the figure that students are nested within teacher and task; a particular student receives only one type of instruction and one type of task from the same teacher.

This hierarchical design does not allow you to see what might happen when instruction mismatches teacher preferences. Perhaps teachers will be even more motivated by instruction that differs from their usual style than instruction that matches what they already do. The design in the second panel is more crossed than nested. In this design, one teacher with a lecture preference and a second teacher with a small group preference teach both types of instruction. Furthermore, whether they are lecturing or facilitating small groups, all teachers provide instruction in both comprehension and composition. Like the hierarchical design, however, students are nested within teacher. Teacher $L_1$ lectures in the spring to one group of students and provides small group work to next year's group of students in the fall. Teacher $SG_1$ reverses this pattern.

An important consideration in planning a design is the decision about how to assign individuals or groups to various treatment combinations. The issue often appears in research texts as the choice of a *between-subject* or *within-subject* plan, but is better described as crossing versus nesting of persons with other design factors. Both of the designs in Fig. 13.5 nest students within teacher, a common design in educational research. All of the students in a class receive the same instruction, which differs from the students in another teacher's class, a between-subjects design. However, every student participates in comprehension and composition instruction in the crossed design, a within-subjects plan.

The decision to nest or cross persons with other factors reflects both practical and theoretical considerations. Practically speaking, the researcher sometimes has little choice. For instance, individual-difference factors like sex or personality dictate that individuals be nested within the levels of a factor. A person is either male or female, impulsive or reflective. Treatment factors can generally be crossed with person factors, and sometimes it makes sense to do so. If a treatment combination takes only a minute or two to administer and the student is available for an hour, the researcher should probably administer as many conditions as possible. This decision means crossing the student with several factors.

Crossed and nested person designs provide qualitatively different information. If each student is tested under a single condition, the researcher cannot assess how individuals react to different combinations. When each individual is tested under several conditions, then contrasts in performance are measurable. To be sure, the researcher must then attend to performance changes due to the testing itself. People improve with practice; they also become fatigued over time. Several techniques (e.g., counterbalancing through Latin Square designs, Cobb, 1998) permit control over these influences, but the key issue remains the researcher's sensitivity to such ancillary factors.

## Theme

The final ingredient in a design is the conceptual framework that guides selection of the factors and decisions about how to combine them. While we have placed this topic at the end of our list, it is actually of paramount importance. The thematic foundation of a research study requires knowledge of the territory, experience in dealing with the issues, and a large dollop of intuition and art. On the other hand, the task can also be guided by systematic strategy, for which Simon (1981) gives counsel. Although some systems appear complex on the surface, Simon argues all are fashioned around a relatively small set of separable components, each with a distinctive internal structure, each linked in simple ways to one another (Calfee, 1981). We applied this notion earlier to the composing of a written argument and the planning of the sample study. It also applies more generally to the conceptualizing of virtually any research problem.

The key is to look for the joints that divide a complex system into a small number of simpler entities. Carving a turkey is a metaphor. A turkey can pose quite a challenge to the novice carving the Thanksgiving bird. The trick is to find the joints, so the carver can divide a big job into relatively small ones. Think about *messes, lumps, chunks.* If you carve a problem into a lot of little pieces, you will be overwhelmed by the details. If you try to handle the problem as a whole, you will be confused by the apparent complexity. Human beings can effectively handle a few items at a time; the key is to keep it simple—more to the point, make it simple.

How do you know when you have hit a joint in a conceptual domain? We suggest that when the technical language and relations in one chunk differ from those in another chunk, you have found a starting point. The previous discussion about selecting treatment, person, and outcome factors illustrates this point; we "talked" differently about the choices within each of these domains. Locating the chunks, then, is the key to analysis of a complex question; it also lays the foundation for synthesis, for relating the chunks to one another.

Let us apply this reasoning to the previous vignette. Your initial thinking about argument was fuzzy and complex. You saw the issues as one dimensional: The best method seemed obvious. But then you were soon burdened by technical details of control. Try looking for a few joints, which will allow you to divide the big problem into manageable chunks that organize the details. You have already moved in this direction by focusing on two thematic areas: forms of argument and styles of integrated instruction. Both areas have a distinctive technical base; each can be considered as an entity in its own right.

You can apply the divide-and-conquer principle to each of the two domains. For instance, how might you subdivide the complexities of instruction—pedagogical method, materials, and management? The answer is implicit in the question. Divide the big chunk into a handful of distinctive subchunks, and decide which are critical to your research question. To be sure,

the chunks will then need to be re-related to one another, but the capacity to assess interactions is inherent in the technology of factorial design.

## CREATING THE DESIGN

This section discusses how the previous concepts and procedures apply to construction of a specific research plan. This is the time when you move from divergent to convergent thinking, from strategy to tactics.

You have identified two thematic issues: how your students process arguments and instructional strategies that help students improve both how they comprehend the claim in a writer's argument and how they support a claim in their own writing. You have posed researchable questions for each issue. What processes do ninth graders use as they work their way through a written argument? How do they use their knowledge about arguments (if any) when they write? Both of these questions are descriptive. Your instructional question is: What combination of social interaction and teacher direction will improve student skills? This question implies an intervention.

How do you formalize a plan of action? You have several options, but certain principles can guide your decisions. First, the thematic chunks—how students process arguments and instructional approaches—need to be expanded into operational factors. Second, you might consider two or three bite-sized investigations rather than putting all of your eggs into a single basket. Third, keep the ultimate goal in mind, and be careful not to drown in details. The factors selected for the design should support the thematic foundations of the study, while ensuring that the design controls significant sources of extraneous variability. The following sections offer some practical advice about preparing a plan.

### Big Picture and First Steps

The first word of advice is to remember where you are going, and to keep moving in that direction—unless you have a good reason to chary. You have shaped the elements of a plan; an image of the research problem is taking shape in your mind's eye. How should you proceed next? One approach is to plan a full-scale experiment. Another is to develop a series of mini-studies. A third is to initiate a naturalistic investigation of observation, interview, and assessment. Our recommendation is that you work at all levels of this continuum, but especially the middle, collecting preliminary data while also refining your thoughts about the big picture—even if you never get around to it.

Developing a conceptual framework requires abstract thinking, but it can also be aided in practical ways. For instance, a graphic layout can help you document the emergence of your research plan. Figure 13.6 shows a midstream road map that might fit your project. The matrix arranges the two thematic elements as column headings; the rows show the factorial categories central to any research plan. Imagine the sketch as a structure for laying out ideas; the entries in the

| | Description of Comprehension Processes | Method of Instruction |
|---|---|---|
| Treatments | Argument differences | Task differences for teachers & students<br><br>Comprehension & composition |
| Subjects | Different levels of expertise | Different levels of expertise |
| Outcomes | Performance measures | Performance measures<br><br>Transfer measures<br><br>Satisfaction measures<br><br>Field notes |

FIGURE 13.6. An overall design for describing comprehension processes and instructing comprehension and composition of arguments.

figure are illustrative. Creating the plan is a dynamic enterprise; use "Post-Its," or record your thoughts on a word processor. Ask colleagues for comment and criticism. Be flexible; the one constancy in research design is change; to be sure, funding agencies may not always appreciate this advice.

Our second recommendation is that, as your plans take shape, you spend time in the research context (e.g., classrooms, teachers, and students), looking and listening, trying out your ideas and procedures and materials in realistic settings. This suggestion does not assume you have an empty head; to the contrary, what you see and hear will be guided by the conceptual framework spread around the walls of your study area. But before the design is cast in stone, check the context. Approach this task with explicit questions in mind. What are the major sources of evidence? What variations are especially critical? Where are you least certain and most confused? What questions should you pose to informants? What answers do you expect, and how can you follow up for further clarification?

These early forays into the field can make substantial demands on research methodology. You are still framing the research question. You are still developing the instruments. The decisions you base on early descriptive work are critical and will determine the shape of the subsequent study. Yet in making these decisions you must rely on relatively unreliable evidence.

We might do well in social science research to adopt a more organic and decision-oriented approach, a more deliberative and interactive process: "Given what I have learned thus far, what is the most sensible direction for my next move?" Custom (and

the reliance on the set-piece proposal) often leads the novice researcher (as well as others) to persist with an original course of action even when it is clear that things are not going as planned. Research is a problem-solving activity and depends on flexibility and response to feedback for success.

## Evolution of a Strategy

Following classroom visits and reflection on the issues, you begin to construct your research plan. Studying the charts around your walls, you may feel overwhelmed. Too many factors, too many combinations, too much data to assemble and interpret. Simon's suggestion to search for parsimony is now the remedy.

Our experience suggests that the initial stage of an instructional study (after the "walking around" phase) is often most effectively directed toward the development of a descriptive system designed to uncover psychological processes—cognition, behavior, and motivation. The description stage informs your research questions and gives you valuable information for designing instruction. The second stage explores the impact of instructional interventions, not to demonstrate the efficacy of a particular approach, but to gain an understanding of the relation between instruction and learning. The following two sections illustrate ideas for pursuing a strategy crafted along these lines.

## Description of Comprehension Processes

Figure 13.7 depicts a plan for the description phase. The plan incorporates three psychological tasks: (a) identify the author's purpose, (b) search for the author's claim and evidence, and (c) use the warrants to integrate the parts into a mental representation of the author's argument. Your knowledge of comprehension research (e.g., Chambliss, 1995; Meyer & Freedle, 1984) suggests to you that these tasks are basic to effective comprehension. Some factors, like author's purpose, have specific variations for each task. For example, the contrast between informational and argumentative purposes will show whether students recognize when an author intends to support a point, the first task. The general factors apply to all three components. For instance, individual differences in reading achievement are likely to influence student performance in all three tasks, and must be included to control extraneous variability and evaluate interactions.

## The Instructional Study

Figure 13.8 lays out a plan for instructional factors. This design has two parts, the first intended to aid students to comprehend the argument schema, and the second to assist them in composing an argument text. As in Fig. 13.7, the plan is designed as a matrix crossing the two components with the three general factorial categories. Factors for the comprehension component depend on outcomes from the description study, which reveal areas where students have difficulty. Factors for the

| Comprehension Processes | | | |
|---|---|---|---|
| **Identify Author's Purpose** | **Search for Author's Claim and Evidence** | **Integrate Parts to Represent Author's Argument** | |
| **Specific Factors** | | | **General Factors** |
| Text Structure<br><br>*Argument or informational* | Claim Presence<br><br>*Claim present or absent*<br><br>Evidence Presence<br><br>*Support or superfluous information* | Argument Structure<br><br>*Simple claim/individual warrants or simple claim/one warrant or complex claim/individual warrants.*<br><br>Warrant Presence<br><br>*Warrant explicit or implicit* | Text Replicates<br><br>*2 examples of each text type (e.g., two arguments and two informational texts.)*<br><br>Order<br><br>*For all crossed designs, the order of the factors (e.g., Argument first or second.)* |
| Text Knowledge<br><br>*Know text schemata or not* | Argument Knowledge<br><br>*Know how to find argument parts or not* | Argument Structure Knowledge<br><br>*Know argument structures or not* | Vocabulary Skills<br><br>*Grade level or not*<br><br>Prior Experience<br><br>*Present or not* |
| Identify Text Type<br><br>*Paper/pencil comprehension measure Videotape of class work Student compositions* | Identify Argument Parts<br><br>*Paper/pencil comprehension measure Videotape of class work Student compositions* | Summarize the Argument<br><br>*Paper/pencil comprehension measure Videotape of class work Student compositions* | Vocabulary Scores<br><br>*Standardized reading subtests Classroom vocabulary tests*<br><br>Prior Experience Questions<br><br>*Student Interview Student Records Teacher Interview* |

Row labels at left: Treatment Factors, Person Factors, Outcome Factors.

FIGURE 13.7. A design for describing the comprehension of arguments.

composition component are adapted from Nystrand's (1989) reciprocity model whereby writers' choices are continuously affected by what they presume will be the response of readers: choosing a rhetorical pattern, translating the pattern to print, and reviewing according to the needs of the audience.

A few words about the structure of this particular design. Teaching presumably has lasting effects. Different students are assigned to each instructional combination; in this instance, students *must* be nested in a factor. In making these and other decisions, basic design principles provide the basis for moving from initial conceptualization toward the final plan.

## DATA ANALYSIS

This chapter centers on the role of design in the research enterprise, and we have neither the mandate nor the space to say much about the tasks of dealing with the evidence once it is in hand. A few points directly relevant to design do merit attention, however. First, whatever the nature of the evidence, some common principles undergird the job of data analysis. Two of these principles will be mentioned in the following. The point here is that the principles are the same whether

| | **Processes to be Taught** | | |
| --- | --- | --- | --- |
| | **Comprehend Author's Argument** | **Compose Own Argument** | |
| | **Specific Factors** | | **General Factors** |
| Treatment Factors | Instructional Content<br><br>*Identify text type, find claim and evidence, and integrate to match text* | Instructional Content<br><br>*Choose a rhetorical pattern, translate the pattern to print, and review according to the needs of the reader throughout* | Teacher Tasks<br><br>*Lecture or small group instruction or a combination*<br><br>Student Tasks<br><br>*Individual practice or small group practice or whole class practice or a combination* |
| Person Factors | Argument Knowledge<br><br>*Know argument type or not*<br><br>Reading Skills<br><br>*Level of decoding skills*<br>*Level of vocabulary skills* | Argument Knowledge<br><br>*Know argument type or not*<br><br>Writing Skills<br><br>*Level of spelling skill*<br>*Level of sentence mechanics skill*<br>*Level of paragraph development skills* | Prior Experience<br><br>*Earlier experience with arguments or not*<br><br>*Earlier experience with whole class, small group and/or individual work or not* |
| Outcome Factors | State Author's Point in Argument Text<br>*Accurately or not*<br><br>State Speaker's Point in Class Discussion<br>*Accurately or not*<br><br>State Speaker's Point in Political Speech<br>*Accurately or not* | Write an Argument<br><br>*Competently or not*<br><br>Prepare a Debate<br><br>*Competently or not* | Fill Out Motivation Questionnaire<br>*High or low interest*<br><br>Fill Out Prior Experience Questionnaire<br>*High or low prior experience*<br><br>Teacher Field Notes<br>*Instruction implemented as planned or not* |

FIGURE 13.8. A design for instructing students to comprehend and compose arguments.

the evidence is quantitative or qualitative, whether in the form of numbers, field notes, interviews, pictures, videotapes, or whatever. The tools and techniques may differ from one type of evidence to another, but managing the path from data collection to interpretation places similar demands on the researcher.

One job is *summarization*, pulling together trends in the evidence. For numbers, the trends are represented by basic terms like *mean*, *variance*, and *correlation*. The customary tactic today is to load the numbers into a computer, which generates "descriptive statistics." For the "raw observations" typical of qualitative evidence, the usual approach is to immerse yourself in the data, transcribing recordings, constructing thick notebooks with numerous post-its and multicolored highlightings. Both of these tactics carry important messages. The researcher dealing with numbers is well advised to "explore the data," to study frequency distributions, prepare scatterplots, and look for unusual events. The field of *exploratory data analysis* (Behrens & Smith, 1996) provides a range of systematic techniques for guiding these tasks. The researcher exploring qualitative evidence is equally well advised to look for trends analogous to those found in statistical methods. Central tendencies—what are the typical elements in the data set? Variability—what kinds of deviations from typicality do you find? Correlations—in what ways do parallel trends seem to emerge? You may not be able to attach precise summary indices to these trends, but you can certainly convince the reader of their existence. Arguments based solely on anecdotes rest on perilous ground.

We mentioned earlier that factorial designs provide the basis for assessing both main effects and interactions. To remind you, main effects reflect differences that emerge as you move from one level to another of a factor, such as the differences between males and females, or between writing by the individual versus small group tasks. Interactions describe patterns associated with factorial combinations; girls might do better than boys when writing as individuals, while boys do better than girls in group settings. Statistical procedures such as analysis of variance generate indices for identifying reliable differences associated with main effects and interactions. An exact parallel does not exist for qualitative methodologies, but the researcher can still examine the evidence for such patterns and develop an argument to support various conclusions. In doing so, the researcher may find himself or herself falling back on numbers, something like the following example:

In 70% of the small group protocols, boys expressed a competitive stance on the writing task, whereas girls voiced a more cooperative slant. These trends were supported in the interview data. When I talked with students after individual writing assignments, competitive-cooperative motivations were mentioned by only 15% of the students.

A final remark on data analysis—personal computers now make available incredible power for "feeling the data." The graphic representation of numeric data is an integral part of virtually every contemporary statistics package, and statistics textbooks are beginning to catch up with the programs. On the qualitative side, programs like NUD*IST and Atlas-TI (for background, see Weitzman & Miles, 1995) now provide researchers with powerful tools for discovering and representing patterns in nonnumeric data sets.

## INTERPRETATION

We now make another pass at a question raised earlier: With the data in hand, how does a researcher interpret and generalize the findings? Again, the critical issue is validity—the trustworthiness of the interpretations. This task of establishing validity comprises two subtasks: internal validity and external validity (Campbell & Stanley, 1966; Cook & Campbell, 1979; Porter, 1997). Internal validity addresses the question, "To what degree can I trust the evidence that I have within my grasp?" External validity asks, "To what degree can I extend the findings to other situations?"

The matrix in Fig. 13.9 extends the concepts of internal and external validity to reflect the design perspectives laid out in this chapter. The matrix is organized around factors controlled by the design and uncontrolled "free floating" factors. The first test of validity, *conceptual clarity*, depends on the design factors. Now that the data are in, how clearly can you tell what happened? To what degree do the factors appear as compelling representatives of the constructs (the underlying concepts) that you chose to represent the research question? To what degree can you make sense of patterns in the data? Complex interactions may be appealing when you first think about a problem, but they can also render interpretation difficult. To what extent did the treatments work as intended? Secrest, West, Phillips, Redner, and Yeaton (1979) refine this point: "The essence of construct validity is that one has a good understanding of the conceptual meaning of the treatment.... It refers to our interpretation of the treatments, not the treatments themselves" (p. 17). For instance, you may discover that when you form small group writing teams, the interactions do not take shape as you intended. You had in mind the construct of *cooperation*, but your qualitative observations reveal variations that include cooperation, competition, and a lot of "parallel play." The research is not a failure if you learn something from the results.

The second validity test, *situational stability*, is the degree to which the evidence allows you to project the basic findings with confidence to other contexts, without modification of the original design. What about the influence of factors that you decided to ignore; either directly or through interactions, how may they influence the outcome? If the sample of participants is too small or too homogeneous, then you may not be able to extend the findings. If the instruments are too specialized, you may again be hesitant to recommend your results to others.

The next two categories go beyond the details of your original design to extension of the underlying principles. Researchers seldom limit their interpretive scope to a particular study. You are interested not just in the program that you have developed, whatever shape it may take in the final design, but in the concepts that undergird this program. Researchers aspire to broadly generalizable statements, and here the issue of validity takes a different shape.

Figure 13.9 has two entries under this heading. First is *conceptual match*. In going beyond the original conditions, while staying close to the original conception, how safe are you in projecting your results? The key here is again the clarity of the original conceptualization, and the degree to which the conditions can be implemented in a similar manner in a different context.

Your argument program shows considerable promise on its test flight. The program employs a student-centered approach, with techniques for working in groups to comprehend and critique an author's argument. The instruction incorporates a group planning guide and graphic organizers that students can use to represent an author's reasoning. Teachers receive intensive staff development in the concepts and the procedures. A colleague plans to implement the program in a different setting, but must modify it to fit local conditions. What are the

|  | Conditions Within Immediate Domain of Study<br><br>(design remains constant) | Conditions Beyond Domain of Study<br><br>(design changes; underlying concepts remain constant) |
|---|---|---|
| **Factors Within the Design** | CONCEPTUAL CLARITY<br><br>(Affected by the design factors)<br><br>* Clarity of concepts<br><br>* Size and simplicity of effects<br><br>* Inadvertent confounding | CONCEPTUAL MATCH<br><br>(Affected by the replicability of underlying concepts)<br><br>* Repeatability of plan<br><br>* Interactions<br><br>* Faithfulness to plan |
| **Factors Outside the Design** | SITUATIONAL STABILITY<br><br>(Affected by the effect of factors in the situation)<br><br>* Extraneous factors, direct and interactive<br><br>* Reliability of measures<br><br>* Size of sample; number of observations | SITUATIONAL MATCH<br><br>(Affected by the degree of similarity between situations)<br><br>* Presence of new conditions and contexts<br><br>* Reliance on new tests<br><br>* Different people and groups |

FIGURE 13.9. Factors both within a design and within a situation that affect the trustworthiness of interpretations.

boundaries? Surely, the program is not limited to specific wording or format. If staff development has to be reduced from a week to 2 days, what to keep and what to jettison?

Next comes the *situational match*, which is related to what Cronbach (Cronbach, Glesser, Nanda, & Rajaratnam, 1972) labeled *generalizability*. Suppose a user wants to change the program and apply it to a different situation—what are the chances that the results apply under these circumstances? Your program has been tested under one set of conditions, with certain factors under control. The students are from middle-class backgrounds, the classes are relatively small, the teachers are experienced professionals, and resources are available for staff development and collegial interactions. Can the findings be applied in situations where these conditions do not hold? If the treatment is powerful, then the variation in local contexts should not matter. An investigation should ideally provide linkages that inform judgments about the transferability of the findings.

Answers to these questions require human judgment. Informed judgment is enhanced when you understand the conceptual issues. Interpretation is generally a matter of pattern detection, a task in which the human mind excels.

## FINAL THOUGHTS

Research is problem solving—with real problems. Empirical data are part of the process, though not necessarily the most significant element. Educational and social science research are particularly demanding because the theoretical foundations are weak—and because researchers tend to overlook the theoretical tools that are available (Suppes, 1974). But "the times are a-changing," and rapidly. Cognition and social cognition, the practical emphasis on educating rather than training, and the challenge of helping every individual realize his or her full potential—the road ahead is exciting and demanding.

Educational and social science research is still in the "sleepwalking" phase (Koestler, 1968). Even the best of our theories are heuristic more than formal, and we must often rely on experience and intuition. Success depends most frequently on doing several things right rather than the one best answer (Slavin, 1986; Tyack, 1974). Cronbach (1975) paints a dim prospect for generalizable research in education, portraying a hall of mirrors with infinitely complex and intricate interactions.

The problems are clearly daunting, but we are optimistic. Whether as producer or consumer of empirical research, you should consider the "divide and conquer" strategy. A series of modest but well-designed studies is likely to be more informative than a single humongous effort. Critical experiments are rare in our business; any single investigation may provide one or two insights—often from a mistake that suggests what *not* to do.

While we do not recommend a fixed algorithm for planning empirical research, the strategy exemplified in the vignette often works quite well. First, learn as much as you can about the territory through a descriptive study. Your goal is to focus on person factors such as motivation and psychological processes as well as factors that are present in the situation. Then experiment; try out a series of instructional treatments, perhaps one or two chunks at a time. Innovations are difficult to implement, and you are more likely to succeed by proceeding in phases. It is important to assess the actual implementation and to examine in detail the full range of potential effects (positive and negative). You may not be able to complete an indepth evaluation for every participant, but you can usually select a few individuals for "thick" study, for contrast with the thinner data from the entire group.

Our main message throughout is the essential importance of *design*—basic building blocks, linkages, and an overarching theme. These components assume different shapes in different stages of an investigation, but if you build on them consistently, they give coherence and unity to the effort. You are likely to learn something from the experience, and to gain satisfaction from the enterprise.

# References

Behrens, J. T., & Smith, M. L. (1996). Data and data analysis. In D. C. Berliner & R. C. Calfee (Eds.), *Handbook of educational psychology* (pp. 945-989). New York: Macmillan.

Berliner, D. C., & Calfee, R. C. (1996). *Handbook of educational psychology*. New York: Macmillan.

Brent, D. (1996). Rogerian rhetoric: Ethical growth through alternative forms of argumentation. In B. Emmel, P. Resch, & D. Tenney (Eds.), *Argument revisited; Argument redefined: Negotiating meaning in the composition classroom* (pp. 73-96). Thousand Oaks, CA: Sage.

Brown, A. L. (1992). Design experiments: Theoretical and methodological challenges in creating complex interventions in classroom settings. *The Journal of the Learning Sciences, 2,* 141-178.

Calfee, R. C. (1981). Cognitive Psychology and Educational Practice. In D. Berliner (Ed.), *Review of Educational Research*. Washington, DC: American Educational Research Association.

Calfee, R. C. (2001). Social science methodology: quo vadis. A Review of *Methods of Educational and Social Science Research: An Integrated Approach*. In *Issues in Education, 5,* 309-318.

Campbell, D. T., & Stanley, J. C. (1966). *Experimental and quasi-experimental designs for research*. Chicago: Rand McNally.

Chambliss, M. J. (1995). Text cues and strategies successful readers use to construct the gist of lengthy written arguments. *Reading Research Quarterly, 30,* 778-807.

Chambliss, M. J., & Calfee, R. C. (1998). *Textbooks for learning: Nurturing children's minds*. Malden, MA: Blackwell.

Cobb, G. W. (1998). *Introduction to design and analysis of experiments*. New York: Springer-Verlag.

Collins, A. (1994). Toward a design science of education. In E. Scanlon & T. O'Shea (Eds.), *New directions in educational technology*. New York: Springer-Verlag.

Cook, T. D., & Campbell, D. T. (1979). *Quasi-experimentation: Design and analysis issues for field settings*. Chicago: Rand McNally.

Creswell, J. W. (1994). *Research design: Qualitative and quantitative approaches*. Thousand Oaks, CA: Sage.

Cronbach, L. J. (1963). *Evaluation for course improvement. Teachers College Record, 64,* 97-121. Also in R. W. Heath (Ed.), *New curricula*. New York: Harper & Row, 1964.

Cronbach, L. J. (1975). Beyond the two disciplines of scientific psychology. *American Psychologist, 30,* 116-127.

Cronbach, L. J. (1988). Five perspectives on the validity argument. In H. Wainer & H. I. Braun (Eds.), *Test validity*. Hillsdale, NJ: Lawrence Erlbaum Associates.

Cronbach, L. J., Glesser, G. C., Nanda, H., & Rajaratnam, N. (1972). *The dependability of behavioral measurements: Theory of generalizability for scores and profiles*. New York: Wiley.

Cronbach, L. J., & Snow, R. E. (1977). *Aptitudes and instructional methods/A handbook for research on interactions*. New York: Irvington.

Cronbach, L. J., & Suppes, P. (Eds.). (1969). *Research for tomorrow's schools: Disciplined inquiry for education*. New York: Macmillan.

Emmel, B., Resch, P., & Tenney, D. (Eds.) (1996). *Argument revisited; argument redefined: Negotiating meaning in the composition classroom*. Thousand Oaks, CA: Sage.

Freedman, S. W., Simons, E. R., & Kalnin, J. S. (1999). *Inside city schools: Investigating literacy in multicultural classrooms*. New York: Teachers College Press.

Fulkerson, R. (1996). The Toulmin model of argument and the teaching of composition. In B. Emmel, P. Resch, & D. Tenney (Eds.), *Argument revisited; argument redefined: Negotiating meaning in the composition classroom* (pp. 45-72). Thousand Oaks, CA: Sage.

Gage, T. (1996). The reasoned thesis: The E-word and argumentative writing as a process of inquiry. In B. Emmel, P. Resch, & D. Tenney (Eds.), *Argument revisited; argument redefined: Negotiating meaning in the composition classroom* (pp. 3-18). Thousand Oaks, CA: Sage.

Gall, M. D., Borg, W. R., & Gall, J. P. (1996). *Educational research: An introduction, 6th Ed.* White Plains, NY: Longman.

Jaeger, R. M. (Ed.). (1997). *Complementary methods for research in education, 2nd Ed.* Washington, DC: American Educational Research Association.

Koestler, A. (1968). *The sleepwalkers*. New York: Macmillan.

Krathwohl, D. R. (1997). *Methods of educational and social science research: An integrated approach*. Menlo Park, CA: Addison Wesley.

Mathison, M. A. (1998), Students as critics of disciplinary texts. In N. Nelson & R. C. Calfee (Eds.), *The reading-writing connection/Ninety-seventh yearbook of the National Society for the Study of Education* (pp. 249-265). Chicago: The National Society for the Study of Education.

Messick, S. (1995). Validity of psychological assessment: Validation of inferences from persons' responses and performances as scientific inquiry into score meaning. *American Psychologist, 50,* 741-749.

Meyer, B. J. F., & Freedle, R. O. (1984). Effects of discourse type on recall. *American Educational Research Journal, 21,* 121-143.

Nystrand, M. (1989). *A social-interactive model of writing. Written Communication, 6,* 66-85.

Nystrand, M. (1990). Sharing words: The effects of readers on developing writers. *Written Communication, 7,* 3-24.

Porter, A. C. (1997). Comparative experiments in educational research. In R. Jaeger (Ed.), *Complementary methods for research in education (2nd Ed.),* (pp. 521-586). Washington, DC: American Educational Research Association.

Rubin, D. L. (1998). Writing for readers. In N. Nelson & R. C. Calfee (Eds.), *The reading-writing connection/Ninety-seventh yearbook of the National Society for the Study of Education* (pp. 53-73). Chicago: The National Society for the Study of Education.

Secrest, L., West, S. G., Phillips, M. E., Redner, R., & Yeaton, W. (1979). Introduction. In L. Secrest (Ed.), *Evaluation studies review annual, Vol. 4.* Beverly Hills, CA: Sage.

Shulman, L. S. (1988). Disciplines of inquiry in education: A new overview. In R. Jaeger (Ed.), *Complementary methods for research in education (2nd Ed.)* (pp. 71-116). Washington, DC: American Educational Research Association.

Simon, H. A. (1981). *The sciences of the artificial* (2nd edition). Cambridge, MA: MIT Press.

Slavin, R. (1986). Best evidence synthesis: An alternative to meta-analytic and traditional reviews. *Educational Researcher, 15(9),* 5-11.

Spivey, N. N. (1997). *The constructivist metaphor.* San Diego, CA: Academic Press.

Suppes, P. (1974). The place of theory in educational research. *Educational Research, 3,* 3-10.

Thomas, R. M. (1998). *Conducting educational research: A comparative view.* Westport, CT: Bergin & Garvey.

Toulmin, S. E. (1958). *The uses of argument.* Cambridge: Cambridge University Press.

Tyack, D. B. (1974). *The one best system; A history of American urban education.* Cambridge, MA: Harvard University Press.

Weitzman, E. A., & Miles, M. B. (1995). *Computer programs for qualitative data analysis.* Thousand Oaks, CA: Sage.

# WHAT LONGITUDINAL STUDIES SAY ABOUT LITERACY DEVELOPMENT/WHAT LITERACY DEVELOPMENT SAYS ABOUT LONGITUDINAL STUDIES

### Robert J. Tierney and Margaret Sheehy
#### Ohio State University

Perhaps no other research approach has more potential to answer the complex development questions that should undergird curriculum. Indeed, longitudinal studies have illuminated our thinking about literacy development in ways that have startled theorists and often challenged key assumptions of touted approaches. Amidst a flurry of political polemics and pronouncements about literacy development, longitudinal research oftentimes yields surprises and unmasks presuppositions—especially a review of such research. And, especially, if such research is examined in terms of the assumptions about literacy and society including the sociopolitical nature of what counts as research or, within a research study, what counts as data/evidence or the lens that might be used to illuminate development.

In preparation for the original review (Tierney, 1992), a great deal of time was spent gathering information about longitudinal research: scanning the research for examples of longitudinal research on particular topics of relevance to the language arts and reviewing discussions of research methodologies for some tenets by which longitudinal studies might be conducted and reviewed. At the time, neither a substantial review of longitudinal research dealing with methodological issues nor a thorough review of those longitudinal studies pertaining to reading and writing development existed. Most discussions of research in the social sciences included a mere mention of longitudinal research; and with a few exceptions, reviews of reading and writing research only incidentally mentioned the extent

to which longitudinal studies have been pursued. Perhaps this should have come as no surprise. For longitudinal studies are expensive to pursue and are apt to be viewed as unrewarding if a rapid turnaround in research is an investigator's goal. This may account for the enormous number of cross-sectional studies comparing students at different ages rather than studies of the same students at these ages.

As with the previous review, the current review examines longitudinal studies of readers and writers. Again, most discussions of research in literacy development included a mere mention of longitudinal research. Instead, there continues to be an enormous number of cross-sectional studies comparing students at different ages or studies of short instructional treatments rather than studies of the same students where full consideration is given to development. In addition, most reports of longitudinal studies do not exist in the mainstream research outlets. For the current review, an ERIC search was done using key terms "longitudinal, literacy, and research" from 1992 to 1998 resulting in 225 hits, 30 of which were studies published in journals, and not necessarily research journals. Of these 30 articles, only those that detailed the methods taken to arrive at the conclusions are included in this review. Too, other research was included, including journal articles that did not come up in the ERIC search and research published in books. Not included as "longitudinal studies of literacy development" are studies that occurred over time that describe uses, processes, or co-constructions of literacy but do not chart development of these uses or social processes according to a stated unit of analysis over time.

A review runs the risk of effecting an illusion of a developmental progression of research and knowledge. In this review, we have fabricated a quilt, of sorts, from the available material—research represented in journals and books. We laid out these "patches" of material in what seemed manageable categories. In this act, each patch was plucked from the history that produced it. Thus, we risk re-presenting a neatly sewn history, one where one study leads to another and knowledge progresses steadily forward. This is not the case. In fact, in this chapter, we find that research is revisiting old haunts—particularly a consistent theme across time: the development of phonemic awareness. We see this as a historical–political phenomenon, and not as a natural progression of research. At the same time, a line of research previously silent is being afforded space in journals—biliteracy research and research that attempts to bridge or understand differences in literacies used in homes and in schools. Some of this research has, in our minds, destabilized previously assumed stabilities: the individual and literacy.

The question that guided this review—How does literacy develop?—has, in most the research reviewed, been looked at in terms of stabilities. Some of the recent research, however, suggests that literacy has to be seen as "literacies," which at every turn is not a set of skills and abilities but situated systems of language and language activities at play in powerful webs of discourse. Thus, an individual may become adept at the use of literacies only to the extent that there is possibility for a multitude of literacy performances. From this perspective, what longitudinal research has to say about literacy development, and what literacy development has to say about longitudinal research should not be seen as a developmental progression that reveals in ever more provocative and sophisticated ways readers' and writers' development over time. Perhaps the political climate in which we write this review will best make this point. As we write, a standards movement across the United States has mandated phonics instruction to occur in specific ways; teachers' practice in some states is scripted; and education professors in California are prohibited from using particular books. Indeed, what counts as research and what counts as literacy depends to a large degree on affordances and constraints the politics around education—and literacy, in particular—support researchers, teachers, and developing readers' and writers' literate endeavors. In this particular historical moment, what counts as research and literacy, at legislative levels, is affording particular literacy practices above others. In past and much of present longitudinal research, literacy was not theorized within political contexts. If anything striking has occurred between the time of the original review and this one, it is that literacy can no longer be understood outside the political discourses that constitute the various ways it becomes defined through a number of culturally and politically situated social practices.

Having situated this review (its patches plucked as they are outside their various histories) within the historical moment we have outlined, this chapter examines longitudinal studies of reading and writing growth with two major questions: How do readers and writers develop? and What are some of the methodological considerations involved in longitudinal studies?

## LONGITUDINAL STUDIES DIRECTED AT THE STUDY OF READING AND WRITING IN THE EARLY YEARS

Over the past 40 years, studies of children's initial encounters with print and beginning school experiences represented the majority of longitudinal studies conducted. Especially in the past 20 years, there appeared several case studies of young children and observational studies of several children that examined reading and writing development across time. The antecedents of such studies seem to be rather a mixed set. Some of them have their roots similar to those pursued by developmental psychologists who were predominant in the period from 1910 to 1930. For example, in the early part of the 20th century a number of maturational psychologists detailed the early development of young children. For instance, based on his observations of several children at various ages and the same children at different times, Gesell (1925, 1928, 1940) detailed what he termed a reading gradient—a scale that represented the book handling and related behaviors that were typical of children at different ages. Likewise, toward proposing development sequences to early writing development and reading, Hildreth (e.g., 1932, 1934) engaged in various observational analyses over time and correlational studies of reading and writing development of students from 3- to 6-years old and elementary age students in conjunction with looking at opportunities to practices and individual differences. Other studies have their roots in more clinically oriented studies based on the case history of the students who had incurred difficulty in learning to read. In this regard, the work of Vernon (1957) in England, Schonell (1956) in Australia and Monroe (1932) in the United States may be most notable. Still others have their roots in case studies that focused on readers' response to storybooks. Finally, many have roots that stem from a reaction to or movement away from correlational studies that compared skills considered to be related to later reading achievement with each other (e.g., Barrett, 1965; Dykstra, 1966). The 1990s, however, saw a return to correlational studies that predicted phonological awareness and the role of decontextualized language of preschool children in their reading achievement beyond third grade.

A landmark study is Durkin's (1966) longitudinal research of early readers in which she examined the impact of home experiences on later reading achievement in hopes of attaining answers to several questions: How many children learn to read before they start school? Do they have any traits that distinguish them from other children? What are their family backgrounds? What do their families report about how they learned to read? Do they stay ahead as they move through the grades? Durkin found 49 children out of 5,103 in Oakland, California and 180 children out of 4,465 in New York who could read a list of primary level words at the beginning of first grade. The early readers were retested at least once a year for several years and the results on these tests were related to various factors in the preschool situation as well as to measures such as IQ, sex, data from personality tests, teacher ratings, and interviews with parents. In addition, the progress of the early readers was compared with that of equally bright students who were not early readers. Furthermore, a number of these early readers were selected for case studies. Several of Durkin's findings served to challenge popular beliefs about early reading experiences. Her studies in "no way corroborate the pessimistic predictions about the future achievement of early readers" (p. 133). After 6 years of schooling, early readers maintained their advantage. Her findings also challenged the belief that IQ, socioeconomic factors, and other traits were effective predictors of success. Neither IQ nor selected personality traits nor other measures suggested a particular advantage for any of these factors. Instead, what proved to be salient were an array of factors related to how parents and siblings encouraged, nurtured, and responded to the reading interests of these children. Durkin stressed that what appeared to be important was "the presence of parents who spend time with their children; who read to them; who answer their questions and their requests for help; and who demonstrate in their own lives that reading is a rich source for relaxation, information and contentment" (p. 136). She also stressed that a great deal of the early readers' interest in print and learning to read was tied to their interest in learning to "print and spell," and their curiosity about what words "say."

In addition to being partially replicated (Tobin & Pikulski, 1988), several lines of research addressed some of the same issues raised by Durkin. In particular, a number of studies examined through parents' diaries, parent–child and teacher–child interactions and other data during young children's storybook reading experiences. Dorothy White's *Books Before Five*, originally published in 1954, represents one of the earliest, best known diary accounts of story reading. White's diary describes a 3-year period (from ages 2 to 5) of her daughter's story reading experience. White's diary chronicles her daughter's response to a caring parent who shares various books with her daughter and notes sensitively the nature of her responses including acquisition of written language, but especially meaning making. As Somerset (1954) points out in the foreword, there are two sets of issues explored implicitly throughout and explicitly on occasion in the diary:

we find on the intellectual side the following lines clearly marked: a gradual understanding of the meaning of drawings and pictorial symbols, growth in comprehending the meaning of words, the growth of memory, the emergence of the distinction between "real" and "pretend," "true" and "untrue." On the aesthetic side, too, we find a great deal of interesting material: the joy in sounds and words, in rhymes and rhythms, and a dawning perception of literary form not only in verse but even in prose stories. And, of course, many phases of a child's emotional life—its joys, its fears, its likes and dislikes, its interests—are to be found illustrated in these pages (p. xvi).

Over the past 20 years, a number of other parents have told the story of their child's development as a reader and writer in conjunction with story reading. In 1979, Butler described her reflections of her grandchild, Cushla, and the role of story reading on her ongoing cognitive and social development. In 1980, Bissex described the literacy development of her son, Paul, in conjunction with his early reading and writing development. In 1983, Crago and Crago reported the preschool discoveries of their daughter, Anna, as she encountered pictures and texts. In 1989, Wolf offered a case study of her daughter, Lindsey, from 3 years 2 months to 4 years 6 months of age.

Apart from diary studies, a number of longitudinal studies of parent–child interaction together with studies involving repeated readings of storybooks have led to a gradual refinement in understanding of the nature and role of story reading and especially its significance to ongoing literacy development. For example, a study by Ninio and Bruner (1978) with children 8 to 18 months suggests a rich but rather routinized dialogue between parent and child occurs during story reading. As Ninio and Bruner stated, the interactions around books had a "structured interactional sequence that had the texture of dialogue" (p. 6) with the parent's dialogue centering on labeling and the child smiling, pointing, vocalizing, and acquiring the turn-taking rules underlying such dialogues. Investigations by Snow (1983) and Snow and Goldfield (1982) indicate that this type of routinized interaction with parents affords children the security whereby they can link ideas from these experiences. Snow's studies and studies by Teale (1984), Teale and Sulzby (1987), Sulzby (1985), Teale and Martinez (1986b, October), Teale and Sulzby (1986a), Teale and Sulzby (1986b), Teale and Sulzby (1987), Teale, Martinez, and Glass (1988) suggest that routine does not mean mindless repetition. In repeated readings of a storybook children move from elaboration and labeling to a concern with motive and causal issues. Teale (1984) has noted that they shift their focus from character identification to what the characters are doing. Furthermore, the nature of the social interactions between child and parent shift as the child assumes more responsibility for the reading. Describing the changes in the language and social interaction that took place over a 14-month period in a mother–child dyad reading of a counting book, Teale and Sulzby (1987) found important shifts in responsibility as the child gained more and more control over the task. In fact, after 8 months of the mother initiating the reading, the child spontaneously read the material.

In an effort to detail children's use of text cues, a number of studies focused on how children respond to and use print as a source for making meaning across repeated story readings. For example, Cochran-Smith (1984) described in some detail the behaviors of children enrolled in a nursery school over a period of 18 months. According to Cochran-Smith the study demonstrated that the students "were coming to know . . . a great deal about print" (p. 252). The 3- to 5-year olds knew reading and writing were integral and meaningful parts of the everyday world and were effective ways to accomplish many of their own purposes and needs. Furthermore, they knew how to organize and use print, relate print to oral language, relate their own knowledge to decontextualized print of storybooks, achieve and apply understandings, and integrate the use of reading and writing into their lives.

Other studies examined in more detail the shifts that occur in students' use of text cues across time. For example, Sulzby (1985), reported a longitudinal study in which the "emergent reading" attempts of 24 children at the beginning and end of their kindergarten year were compared and examined against similar data acquired from repeated readings with storybooks by 2-, 3-, and 4-year-olds. By using a classification scheme to characterize the reading behaviors of children, Sulzby demonstrated the extensive repertoire of strategies students acquired as a result of storybook reading and the types of changes that occurred across time but seemed relatively stable across books. Sulzby contends, as several of these researchers who have pursued longitudinal studies have stressed, literacy is not learned by rote procedures but occurs in conjunction with negotiations between the child, parent, text, and other features of context.

Adopting a slightly different orientation, Pappas and Brown (1987) explored in detail the extent to which 27 kindergartners were developing an understanding of the register of shared reading including the linguistic awarenesses necessary to understand stories. As they stated,

learning to read is fundamentally an extension of the functional potential of language. During the preschool years young children . . . learn to adjust their linguistic choices to meet the features of particular social contexts—the setting, the participants, and the specific task at hand. To become literate, however, the young child has to come to terms with certain important characteristics of written language—its sustained organization, its characteristic rhythms and structures, and the disembedded quality of written language. Thus, an essential aspect of the extension of the functional potential of language involves young children's coming to understand that the registers of written language are different from those of speech (pp. 160–161).

Rather than focus on children's role-like word-by-word response to the repeated reading of a story, Pappas and Brown focused on the children's approximations of the author's wordings and extrapolations from the story. Across repeated readings Pappas and Brown found that children made extensive use of extrapolations and approximations and their use seemed integral to their realizations of the potentials of written language (including their constructing an understanding of the social conflicts and plans of characters pertaining to the story). What is noteworthy is the socio-semiotic perspective adopted by Pappas and Brown. Their analyses bring to the fore the social nature of literacy and literacy learning, as well as the extent to which meaning making is constructive. As they concluded,

While young children's reading-like behavior in previous research might have been explained in terms of rote memory, the results reported in this study indicate that this is not the case. The ontogenesis of the registers of written language appears to be just as much a constructive process as we have seen in other areas of children's cognitive/linguistic development (Pappas & Brown, 1987, p. 175).

Along similar lines, Yaden, Smolkin, and Conlon (1989) were interested in the hypothesis that "story reading may provide an opportunity for children not only to explore many aspects of the book itself, but also to acquire new ways of communicating, and to sharpen, refine, and compare their own view of the world with the perspectives they encounter in books" (p. 207). To this end, they reported studies in which the questions and inquiries of preschoolers (3 to 5 years) regarding print and pictures have been described. On a weekly basis for periods of one and two years, they collected, transcribed, and analyzed the questions and inquiries of nine children. Children's questions were classified as pertaining to graphic forms, word meaning, story text, pictures and book conventions. Their findings suggested that over 1 or 2 years, even the least inquisitive child would ask over 1,000 questions and these represented a full range of question types. While most students asked questions about pictures, some students moved toward asking questions about the story text. At no time did students ask many questions about the conventions of books. While the researchers tended to decline from suggesting trends or developmental patterns (due to the variations that were found across students, the story selections themselves, and the interactional style of parents, and other variables), the researchers concluded that storybook reading offered children a foundation from which they might begin to "master" reading. As they stated,

Perhaps it is safest to say that story books provide a variety of information about the way print communicates meaning and represents the sounds of oral language, just as environmental print may influence children's acquisition of print knowledge. In another way, exposing children to as many sources of written information in the environment as possible before school cannot help but give them the kind of foundation needed for successful mastery of this most complicated human invention (Yaden, Smolkin, & Conlon, 1989, p. 211).

Studies of literacy acquisition have not been restricted to children's responses to story reading. Apart from a number of cross-sectional studies of different children at different ages (e.g., Goodman, 1986; Hiebert, 1978), a few longitudinal studies exist that focus on the link between what is commonly referred to as "print awareness" and reading ability. The key tenet underlying such pursuits is the notion that children acquire an understanding of literacy as a result of their interactions with everyday print. As Goodman (1986) argued, environmental print encounters are at the root of the child developing a model for the features of written language. As she stated, "the development of print awarenesses in environmental contexts is the root of literacy most common to all learners and the most well developed in the preschool years" and serves to facilitate the child's development of "a model . . . which includes rules about the features of written language in situational contexts" (p. 7). One example is a study by Kontos (1988) who examined the relationship between print awareness and reading achievement from the beginning of preschool to the end of first grade for 47 subjects. Print awareness measures included a battery of tests directed at various aspects of print and book awareness (Clay, 1982) along with a researcher constructed measure of the children's knowledge of the communicative functions of print. Other measures included a test of knowledge of sound–symbol correspondence, writing measure, and a prereading phonics inventory. Across six time periods from spring of the preschool year to fall of first grade the intercorrelations between these variables and their relationship to performance on the Metropolitan

Reading Test and California Test of Basic Skill (involving a composite score based on several tests including tests of component skills) were determined. Despite the fact that some of her reading measures were similar to the measures of reading subskills used as predictors, print awareness, especially as measured by Clay's battery of tests, did emerge as a significant predictor. Kontos argued that the role of print awareness seemed to be intertwined with the role of other literary knowledge and skills.

The aforementioned research on print awareness has its corollary in studies of early writing development. For example, Bloodgood (1999) examined the role of name writing and its relationship to other literacy development across 67 3-, 4- and 5-year-olds. Using Hildreth's (1936) 7-point scale (no representation, scribble, linear scribble, separate units, mock letters, name generally correct, consistent first name, fluent first and last name), Bloodgood revealed the interface between name writing and other facets of literacy development (e.g., alphabet knowledge, word recognition, and concept of word, etc.) as well as the extent to which letters from students names accounted for the children's "random" choice of characters that they chose to write.

Research on writing development has been another major area for study. In the past 20 years this area of research has received a great deal of attention as researchers began asking questions about the child's conceptions of written language rather than concentrating on how well the letters and words are formed and conventions adopted. In this regard, the work of Ferreiro and Teberosky (1982), which is more cross-sectional than longitudinal, has been most seminal. Based on their analyses of children's writing at various ages, they described the hypotheses that were governing children's writing. Central to their work was the thesis that children operate according to certain assumptions (e.g., writing is a way of representing speech and objects, a principle of minimal quantity in terms of number of letters, a principle of individual variation of letters within words, the syllabic principle) that they construct and upgrade to account for new encounters. To date, a number of researchers have offered a longitudinal perspective on the understandings children acquire as they write. Several past researchers have offered several examples of how young children's writing develops across time. Bissex's (1980) and Baghban's (1984) case studies of their children are devoted primarily to tracing their early writing development. Graves (1982) has offered rich descriptions of writing development across time as students begin writing and conferencing with others. The longitudinal studies of Sulzby and her colleagues (1983b, 1985a; Sulzby, Barnhart, & Heishima, 1988; Sulzby & Teale, 1985) support the findings that have emerged from the aforementioned studies. While highlighting the active and constructive nature of meaning making by the child, they argue that children's writing might be informed more by adult conventions than previous research supported. In a similar vein, Read (1971, 1975), Chomsky (1979), Beers and Henderson (1977), and Zutell (1978) have described in some detail students' spelling development including the linguistic understandings and principles that inform children's spelling adeptness, explorations, and appropriation of conventional spelling.

Taken together, the longitudinal research on early reading and writing to date has confirmed some beliefs at the same time as it has added definition and stimulated a number of issues. The view of the child as an active meaning maker constructing his or her own hypotheses in the context of daily negotiations with print and others is substantiated repeatedly. Left unanswered is how such constructions are achieved. Some of the key factors seem to have been identified, but their interrelationship and the mechanisms students use to construct these hypotheses seem relatively undefined. What seems most promising are those studies that have adopted a more expansive, differentiated view of literacy that is situation-based—namely, studies that have been willing to address the complex configurations of variables that constitute literacy events.

Rowe (1987), in conjunction with exploring the nature of literacy learning across an 8-month period with 3- and 4-year olds enrolled in a daycare situation, pursued detailed analyses in hopes of understanding the saliency of interactions with others and prior experiences in literacy learning. Her analyses prompted her to hypothesize that the links and negotiations children have with their own and other's past experience was central to their ongoing literacy learning. As she stated:

as children formed new communicative goals, they flexibly combined various aspects of their existing knowledge, or linked their existing knowledge to available demonstrations, to construct situation-based hypotheses which were their communicative goals (p. 110).

In accordance with this view, Rowe (1987) suggested that literacy events in the classrooms

provided opportunities for children to observe another at work, to talk with that person in order to expand and develop their ideas, to observe again, and often to incorporate new ideas into their own texts. Sometimes children used the demonstrations of others as starting points for developing their own ideas.... At other times, children chose to use available demonstrations conservatively; that is, they chose to stick as close to the demonstration as possible until they felt they understood it fully.... It was by observing the demonstrations of others, by exchanging meanings in conversation, and by authoring their own texts that children formed shared meanings about literacy (p. 106).

Rowe's work has a number of parallels with the work by Dyson (e.g., 1983, 1985, 1986, 1988; 1992) who has explored the role of the tensions that occur as various texts (oral, written, drawings) and ideologies (writing workshops) transact. As she stated,

children's major developmental challenge is not simply to create a unified text world but to move among multiple worlds, carrying out multiple roles and coordinating multiple space/time structures. That is, to grow as writers of imaginary worlds and, by inference, other sorts of text worlds as well, children must differentiate, and work to resolve the tensions among, the varied symbolic and social worlds within which they write—worlds with different dimensions of time and space (1988, p. 356).

It is noteworthy that the studies of both Rowe and Dyson extrapolated their principles of literacy learning based on detailed analyses of both individuals and groups across different literacy situations. These leanings concur with the implications drawn in conjunction with longitudinal pursuits by Galda, Pellegrini, and Cox (1989) and Pellegrini, Galda, Dresden, and Cox (1991) in which a determination of the relationship among play and literacy development were assessed. They hypothesized that the language of reading lessons and linguistic verbs in symbolic play share features involving talking about words and using them to represent meaning. Drawing on Vygotsky, the researchers assumed "that early writing originates in symbolic play and travels a developmental route through drawing to writing." The authors explain that in symbolic play, children divorce meaning from objects; using language to redefine meaning is necessary in writing. A drawing of a car or the written word car at this stage represents the object, not the word car. In a second order symbolization, the written word represents the oral word. Consistent with this theory, they hypothesized that the symbolic transformations at $3\frac{1}{2}$ years-of-age should predict writing status 1 year later because symbolic play provides the basis for using written symbols. The authors predicted, also, that the use of process and process-contrastive linguistic verbs in peer discourse should predict facility with the lexicon of reading events as measured by the Concepts of Print Test (Clay, 1982) because both constructs are concerned with the lexicon of reading events. More exactly, the language or reading lessons and linguistic verbs used in symbolic play share design features to the extent that they both involve talking about words and using words to represent meaning. To explore these hypotheses, 7 boys and 5 girls were observed and audio recorded for 15 minutes during free play periods nine times per year in a university lab school. A variety of data were gathered and assessments used. They found that within Years 1 and 2, the use of linguistic verbs were positively intercorrelated, but Concepts of Print was not significantly correlated with transformations or highest level of writing. Linguistic verbs predicted children's performance on the Concepts of Print Test "to the extent that linguistic process and linguistic process-contrastive verbs were positive and significant predictors. Linguistic idiomatic verbs were not significantly related" (p. 231). Symbolic transformations, however, predicted children's emergent writing status. Accordingly, the authors concluded that "The ability to write words should be related to representational competence in play because both indicate children's ability to use signifiers to convey meaning" (pp. 230–231).

As children navigate these multiple worlds using their own emerging principles, there is some disagreement as to the role of adult conventions. In particular, whereas some researchers verge on the view that literacy learning involves acquiring adult conventions, other researchers contend that literacy should be viewed as emerging. In accordance with this latter position, literacy is viewed as involving respect for what and how literacy is negotiated in different situations rather than how literacy measures up to adult conventions. What seems to distinguish this view is that literacy can be viewed as open to refinement or closed with static conventions. Accordingly, literacy involves refinement, invention, and development in conjunction with pursuing the power to negotiate meanings in different contexts rather than being tied to eventually acquiring a standard set of conventions for so doing. On the one hand, it might be useful to pursue a view of literacy that somewhat merges the two positions. An amalgamation of such views might suggest that literacy has many of the features of "jazz" music—a mixture of improvisations, inventions, allusions, variations, and standard themes inspired by the combination of players and context. On the other hand, it may be that we simply do not, as yet, understand the extent to which conventions may be embedded in sets of relations available to children, caregivers, and teachers within larger political contexts. While young children may improvise and invent literacy within their communities, once they attend school, improvisation is not rewarded equally across races and classes (see, for instance, Delpit, 1995; Luke, 1995/1996). Understandings of literacy development within situated plays of power involving curriculum, materials, standards movements, and sociocultural processes of race, class, and gender are wide open for exploration.

## LONGITUDINAL STUDIES OF LITERACY ACQUISITION DURING THE BEGINNING SCHOOL YEARS

Early longitudinal studies of writing development during the beginning school years represent rather disparate concerns and approaches, and some of these studies further complicate the invention/conventions debate. Hilgers (1987) studied four children repeatedly as they evaluated pieces of writing in hopes of gleaning developmental trends in the standards students used to evaluate their texts and how they applied these criteria. In general, the students' aesthetic response (i.e., whether or not they liked a piece) was the most prevalent criteria used by all four students across this period. While Hilgers suggested there were no clear developmental trends, students, with age, tended to increase in the number of criteria that they employed as well as the time that they spent evaluating essays. In terms of how and when students employed criteria, the trends were not straightforward. Some students applied criteria during planning, others during revision, or both. Furthermore, students tended to use certain skills in their own writing prior to employing that same skill as a basis for evaluating essays. Oftentimes, opportunities to discuss certain skills seemed tied to their use.

Rentel and King (1983) studied written narrative texts elicited from a population of 36 children stratified by sex, socioeconomic class, dialect, and school at intervals of 4 months over the children's first 4 years of schooling. A subsample of the texts of 16 of these children was then used as the basis for an examination of coherence in the students' narratives. Specific to their study, the data revealed that students developed what the researchers deemed to be a coherent text at a very young age and that differences in the coherence of these texts was linked to their use of identity and similarity relationships for purposes of tying together events. Of relevance to the potential of longitudinal studies to inform developmental appreciations, their comments regarding these findings are noteworthy. As Rentel and King stated:

Children marshal their linguistic resources and bend them to the task of writing almost in defiance of the law of adult expectations. From second grade onward, the sample of children's texts we investigated thwarted our expectations about levels of coherence we could expect within them. Our expectation was that cohesive harmony scores would improve gradually over a period of several years. They did not. Cohesive harmony scores increased significantly from the point at which children could navigate the rudiments of a fictional narrative—for most, at the beginning of second grade. We expected roughly parallel emergence of identity and similarity relations in children's texts. Identity and similarity relations followed a course separate from each other in the sense that identity relations took precedence in children's earliest texts, while similarity relations came to dominate their fourth-grade texts. We expected that reiteration would be an important chain-forming relation in children's first stories, but would gradually diminish as a chain-forming strategy. It did not; instead, reiteration was a basic chain-forming strategy from the outset of writing and grew in its importance as a chain-forming resource over the entire four years of development we studied (p. 31).

Based on a case study of a first grade child, Sipe (1999) contended that shifts in writing development were influenced by a pull of conventional forms, the social nature of writing, topic choice, and by the influence of the teacher. As Sipe observed across a year, shifts in the boy's writing involved (a) using environmental print resources, to linking what he knew to what others knew and requesting less help; (b) focusing on encoding, to focusing on the message; (c) getting lost in revision at letter and word levels, to automaticity in revision at phrase and sentence levels; (d) knowing a meager stock of words, to a large stock of known words, automatization of subroutines, and increased fluency; (e) verbalizing his actions, to not speaking aloud; (f) acquiring case knowledge with sudden breakthroughs, to making analogies and applying knowledge across cases; and, finally, (g) having diffuse spatial organization and serial order, to controlled spatial organization and serial order.

Dyson (1992) suggested that conventions, a social construction, are imposed on writers through such ideological pedagogies as "writing workshops" and process writing. This imposition is embedded in power relationships for which the first grade composer she observed once a week for 4 months and twice a week for 6 months, created "stages of performance." Citing her earlier work, she writes,

Learning to write in school involves figuring out—and gaining entry into—the range of social dialogues enacted through literacy, including the assumed relationships among writers and their audiences (Dyson, 1992, p. 6).

Jameel, an African American boy, used culturally relevant language such as music, repetition, and rhyme in his composing processes. He did not always find his audience helpful and negotiating the multiplicity of roles his audience played was tense. When his teacher asserted a stance that emphasized conventions, it confused his performances. Dyson illustrates how Jameel blended genres, a blending that points to ways literacy genres could open up to allow for cultural performances. Jameel used his strong storytelling style and musical sense of language

as stages to perform. Dyson notes that orality and musicality are part of the dialogic properties of language.

Kamberelis (1992), taking the position that children make transitions to conventional forms, hypothesized that two mixed-level relationships between writing and reading were potential indices of transitional knowledge in emergent literacy. He qualifies "writing" as that which is made up of alphabetic print.[1] A level mixture, Kamberelis explains, is internal disequilibrium experienced when different levels of sophistication of reading and writing are operating. For instance, disequilibrium may be experienced if a child knows more convention strategies in writing than in reading, or vice versa. Hence, "a mixed-level relationship is a relationship comprised of a low-level writing form paired with a higher level reading form or vice versa" (p. 371). He predicted that low-level writing/high-level reading would involve an unsophisticated form of alphabet writing combined with an advanced form of reading and would index transitional knowledge. In this case, random and patterned letter strings would be paired with reading written monologue style. Similarly, high-level writing/low-level reading would also index transitional knowledge. Writing would include invented spellings and conventional orthography but reading would be characterized as an oral monologue style, written, or a mix of the two. Oral and written monologues are re-enactments of printed messages that do not involve decoding the print but, rather, involve enactment of the message using nonprint clues and memory for text. An oral monologue is conversational.

Offering an approach that enabled understanding not only of the sociality of forms but of the social negotiation of power, Wilde et al. (1992) conducted a 2-year study of the writing processes of Tohono O'odham children in Grades 3 and 4. The researchers' overarching purpose was,

not merely to understand the influences on the writing of these particular children but also to suggest how all children learn to write, learn through writing, and learn about writing (p. 3).

To these ends, the researchers observed and interviewed 10 children the first year and 6 of these same children in the second year of their schooling on the Tohono O'odham Reservation. Teachers and parents were also interviewed and researchers recorded observations about the classroom after each session, including details of curriculum and instruction. Data included 278 texts, fieldnotes, 63 videotapes, 46 writing assessment interviews, 32 concept of writing interviews, 9 teacher interviews, and 13 parent interviews. A profile emerged over 2 years: Writing is influenced by (a) societal views about literacy; (b) the nature of the social community inside and outside the classroom; and (c) the ways schools and classrooms are organized.

Kasten's analysis, as part of the Tohono O'odham study, revealed children's development of resourcefulness. Kasten analyzed field notes accompanying 278 texts for the nature and function of oral language used during composition and the use

---

[1] Kamberelis's hypothesis rests on the notion that Sulzby's classification scheme is "more or less" hierarchical. If variation does occur, the levels on which Kamberelis hypothesis is based could not be held constant, either for individuals or across individuals. The use of the hierarchy is interesting, however, and would be interesting to continue exploring. If the heirarchy were found stable, however, a further difficulty in testing Kamberelis's hypothesis is finding a large enough sample of transitional readers and writers fitting the needed characteristics. That only 13 of 26 students indicated transition does not seem strong evidence of a mixed-level relationship indexing transition to conventional reading or writing.

of classroom resources. She found that children used resources 575 times. The children most often used human resources, to spell a word, for instance, and less often, used inanimate resources. In the second year, students used classroom resources more often in one of the teacher's classes, and less often in another teacher's classroom. The use of resources led directly to changes in text. Kasten concludes:

Classroom management styles, availability and accessibility of resources, and teacher encouragement are all factors in how students solve their writing problems within their community. In this context, control over writing grows, and the confidence to become a writer is established (Kasten, 1992, p. 103).

Wilde analyzed 1,896 invented spellings out of 13,793 words in 215 stories written by the 6 children. She analyzed four spelling features: rounded vowels, unstressed vowels, double consonants, and inflectional suffixes. Over the 2 years, the children improved on these features more than the other eight features she examined. Wilde reports three major findings: First, that children's spellings "progressed beyond what could be called 'emergent' or even 'developing' into something more like 'high level' or 'refined.' Any interpretation of children's invented spellings must always be seen in the larger context . . . that includes the extent to which knowledge of dictionary spellings has replaced invention." Second, there is logic to invented spelling and omitted letters are not random. And third, a "decrease in the frequency of invented spelling was often also accompanied by an improvement in the quality of those that remained" (p. 146).

Vaughan examined one girl, Anna's, development over the 2 years. In third grade, Anna had conceptions of writing and of herself as a writer; her sense of audience depended on genre (for instance, her audience seemed clear in a letter, less clear in narrative); she used dialogue; she used varied sentence structures; and used punctuation marks mostly appropriately. Too, Anna liked writing narratives but didn't like to revise and what she did revise were surface level revisions. As in Kasten's observations, Vaughan, too, observed the differences in writing communities between Anna's third and fourth grade years and relates Anna's development to the changes in the community. In fourth grade, the class was encouraged to talk about their writing, and Anna became more aware of what her listeners needed from her as a writer, which influenced her revision growth. By the middle of fourth grade, Anna's stories were longer and more complex, syntactically and semantically.

Wilde (1992) presented a case study of a boy, Gordon, in these 2 years. An early "concept of writing" interview revealed Gordon's lack of sophistication about writing: he liked stories if they were interesting and was aware of the impression that spelling and handwriting had on readers. In the third grade, when writing assignments were restrictive, Gordon showed an understanding of his teacher as audience, to such a degree that one assignment was largely copied from an encyclopedia. From the first half to the second half of third grade, Gordon's writing did not change much in terms of use of appropriate spelling and words per story, per sentence, or clause. Gordon's punctuation, however, decreased in approriateness. Wilde found

this was due to omission of punctuation as Gordon tended to use only periods. Wilde suggested this is "a context induced variable" (p. 186), rather than a developmental regression. In fourth grade, Gordon began to speculate on what makes a story good. Gordon was interactive in third grade and continued to be in the fourth. As story topics were often unassigned in the fourth grade classroom, Gordon wrote on a range of topics. In fourth grade, Gordon's syntactic complexity increased and his spelling and punctuation continued to develop. Gordon began to use hyphens and quotation marks. By the second half of the fourth grade, Gordon's stories were longer as were sentences and clauses; his spellings were generally appropriate, and the words he used most frequently were always spelled correctly; and the percentage of conventional punctuation varied from 25 to 100% as he sometimes omitted periods, often omitted commas, and had partial control of quotation marks.

Taken together, these studies show development of children not only as individuals but across two distinctly different writing contexts. It seems the children developed as writers particularly because the fourth-grade classroom not only involved students in wide varieties of writing, but because socializing over writing was encouraged and made part of the fourth-grade teacher's curriculum.

Several longitudinal studies of reading and writing development describe the stages students pass through as they learn to read and write in school. Clay (1982), for example, pursued a longitudinal study of children during their first year of school in New Zealand. She collected weekly records of reading (including running records of their oral reading of books that they were assigned to read) for a sample of 100 children from six schools, and administered a battery of 17 tests (tests of language skills, auditory and visual perception, a reading readiness battery) within 2 weeks of school entry, midyear, and when each child was 6 years old. In hopes of attaining a comparative perspective on the data, Clay examined the data across three ability groups (high, middle, and low). Her conclusions served two purposes: a description of the strategies of successful readers and a developmental description of the stages they pass through. Good readers, she observed, manipulate a "network of language, spatial, and visual perception cues and sort these implicitly but efficiently, searching for dissonant relations and best-fit solutions. Redundancy in cue sources allows for confirming checks and acts as a stimulus to error correction" (1982, p. 28). In terms of stages, she claimed that children move from a reliance on information from their oral language experience and knowledge of situation to the use of an expanded set of cues that include visual dimensions, word knowledge, and letter–sound associations. As she stated, cues from these sources for a long time are "piece meal, unreliable and unstable" but become efficient as the use of these cueing systems simultaneously become more differentiated. In accordance with these conclusions and other findings, she argued for maintaining a difficulty level of approximately 95% accuracy so that students will be challenged to apply a range of cues rather than rely on a limited repertoire or for which success is dependent on a restricted use of cues, for example, an overreliance on auditory cues.

Emerging from Clay's findings and studies of writing development is the view of children as intuitively sophisticated language users who access a variety of knowledge about language as they develop as readers and writers. Not surprisingly, a corollary to these findings comes studies of spelling acquisition (e.g., Beers & Henderson, 1977; Zutell, 1978), which suggest that young children approach spelling as extremely intuitive language users who enlist a variety of cuing systems as they learn the English orthographic system. Similarly, Y. Goodman (1976) drawing from various miscue analysis studies of readers over time stresses that "all systems of language must be intact in order for the reader to understand that reading is language and that the purpose of reading is to get at the author's message" (p. 126). She also cautions that development may not be "gradually and continuously in an upward direction for one reader" (p. 126) but is likely to involve a sequence of rises and declines pending the transaction of various elements including personal, emotional, and physical factors and the experiential background of the reader in relationship to the setting, content, plot, characterization, theme, and style of the material.

A number of studies have tended to adopt and be restrained by a priori models of reading development and a focus on decoding. A longitudinal study launched by the Center for the Study of Reading at the University of Illinois in 1985 examined both comprehension and decoding. The primary focus of the Illinois study was on how children develop the ability to comprehend. As Meyer, Waldrop, and Hastings (1989) stated,

How do children develop the ability to comprehend over time? In the process of ferreting out answers to this question, several more focused research questions have emerged. What kinds of home experiences contribute to the development of reading comprehension ability? What is the nature of these activities? What sort of things do children do independently that contribute to the development of reading comprehension ability? How much reading instruction is there in the lower elementary grades? What are the characteristics of this instruction? How do activities in the home and the school jointly influence the development of children's reading comprehension ability (p. 12).

To answer these questions, the research team at Illinois adopted a tentative model of comprehension development that they had been testing. Their model assumed that various home and school factors together with student aptitude and student initiated activity combined to influence reading comprehension development. In all, the model included six general constructs (home background characteristics, students' ability at the time that they entered school, the characteristics of the instructional materials, teacher's management and instructional style, home support for literacy development, and independent reading), which were measured in different ways at different times in accordance with some important a priori decisions. For example, they decided to exclude any measure of independent reading prior to the third grade, and decided to characterize teaching style in terms of micro-level analyses of decoding activities and silent reading activities rather than other features such as shared reading, reading–writing experiences, conferencing, and story talk. The Illinois team did extensive observations of classrooms as well as extensive use of questionnaires and published tests. Perhaps due to the size of their sample, none of their measures of basic abilities were what might be termed open-ended—for example, their measures of reading comprehension included

cloze procedures, multiple-choice items, and so on, but did not include any type of free recall or miscue analysis. Their measures of decoding did not include a measure that addresses the students' use of decoding strategies in context.

The first cohort included 240 students from the three districts selected for study. The schools from which they were drawn represented a suburban school with diverse ethnic mix and two small midwestern towns. While the reading programs in each school differed somewhat, they appeared to be traditional given their alignment with a basal approach and their orientation to the teaching of skills. Using analysis procedures that sought to create a path model with a certain "goodness of fit" (in conjunction with factor analysis techniques to accommodate the use of multiple measures), the research team generated a model of the interrelationship between variables that maximized the variance accounted for at each grade level. As the researchers pointed out, the "model we are presenting is not the only possible model for these interrelationships, but it is the one obtained when we applied the criteria and diagnostic/revision procedures described" (Meyer et al., 1989, p. 41).

Their findings seemed to support and extend some of the findings of other research. Home factors emerged as closely related to end-of-year achievement and, at Grade 2 interacted with teacher behavior. Not surprising, the entry level achievement of students predicted success at the end of each grade level and, beginning in the first grade, interacted with teaching practices to affect achievement—in other words, as they stated, "What teachers do appears to be influenced by the skills the pupils bring with them" (p. 49). Also, the relationship between decoding attainment, reading comprehension, and activities that focus on letters or texts became complex by the end of the second grade. As Meyer, Wardrop, and Hastings pointed out, the decoding and comprehension appeared to be more distinct variables by the end of the second grade. That is, decoding activities tended to be less clearly related with reading comprehension and sometimes appeared to be negatively correlated. Indeed, decoding had a limited and sometimes negative relationship to comprehension by Grade 2. In general, these data point to an issue—the nature of the relationship between decoding and reading development—that has been an important facet of a number of longitudinal studies in reading.

A number of studies have attempted to sort out the precise nature of the interrelationships between component skills and reading, as well as how the development of these skills interface with different instructional experiences. Taken together, these studies, to which we now turn, seem to be suggesting that phonics appears to bear a relationship with reading that changes across time and that does not appear to be causal. By the end of the second grade, the relationship between phonics and reading for meaning is slight. Furthermore, there appears to be no advantage and some disadvantages for emphasizing phonics over reading for meaning. Students who are encouraged to read for meaning have comparable phonic segmentation and superior reading for meaning abilities to students who have received a strict phonics emphasis.

To assess the viability of a model of literacy acquisition that posits decoding as crucial, Juell, Griffith, and Gough (1986) studied changes in the pattern of relationship of scores on various tests across 80 students during Grades 1 and 2 who were enrolled either in classrooms using a basal approach or in classrooms receiving daily synthetic phonics on top of the basal reading material.

We begin with the simple view of reading . . . that reading is composed of (a) decoding and (b) listening comprehension. This is not to suggest that either of the components, decoding and listening comprehension, is simple in itself but to argue that these two skills are the critical components of reading. That is, we suppose that reading crucially involves decoding, the ability to translate print into linguistic form. But we do not suppose that decoding alone is sufficient for reading. Having derived the linguistic form represented in print, the reader must then comprehend that form. To do this, we suppose that the reader employs the same mechanisms, the same knowledge of morphology, syntax, semantics and pragmatics that are used in the comprehension of spoken language in order to understand decoded print. We recognize that written text has certain distinctive characteristics from speech with differential impact upon the comprehension process . . . But we are inclined to agree with those researchers who emphasize the commonality of the demands of written and spoken language upon the comprehender. Thus, we believe that given perfection in decoding, the quality of reading will depend entirely on the quality of the reader's comprehension; if the listening comprehension is poor, then his reading comprehension will be poor, no matter how good his decoding (p. 244).

In terms of data collection, a battery of tests were given either at the beginning of Grade 1 or periodically during Grades 1 and 2. Some of the measures represented a standard fare of published tests; others seem somewhat limited. For example, ciphering knowledge was based on the students' ability to pronounce non-sense words; exposure to print was assessed in terms of the number of words the students had confronted in their basals. What was apparent in their analyses was some specificity of effects. In particular, phonemic awareness tended to be most clearly related to those tasks which, in a restrictive sense, seem tied to phonemic awareness, such as spelling-sound knowledge. Furthermore, its relationship to reading comprehension, perhaps due to a ceiling effect, became quite diminished by the end of the second grade. Whereas those studies which have tended to focus on phonemic awareness to the exclusion of other variables suggest a strong relationship between phonemic segmentation and reading achievement; those studies which have looked at some of the "other variables" suggest a more tempered and sometimes different viewpoint.

Take, if you will, some of those studies that have attempted to sort out the relationship between decoding and reading in the context of different instructional approaches. For example, Calfee and Piontkowski (1981) pursued a longitudinal study of the acquisition of decoding skills of 50 first graders in 10 classrooms. The design, which included four categories of data diagnostic decoding tests—oral reading, comprehension measures, standardized achievement test, and classroom observations—allowed for an investigation of the patterns of reading acquisition of "component skills" during regular classroom instruction and to examine the relationship of these patterns to the instructional program. In terms of the relationship between component skills and reading acquisition, there appeared to be some transfer from decoding to oral reading and comprehension, but not vice versa. In other words, those students who were

comprehending successfully may or may not have had the same level of decoding skills. In terms of the effects of instruction, the results were somewhat predictable. Student performance on the various tests suggested that students learned what they were taught. In particular, target students in the reading for meaning programs tended to perform better on reading passages than in response to isolated words; target students in the programs emphasizing phonics performed better on decoding tasks rather than reading passages. The findings from this study underline the impact of differences in instructional emphases and illustrate the power of longitudinal studies to inform our understanding of development. As Calfee and Piontkowski (1981) argued in the closing statement of their study:

Understanding how readers become "good" or "poor" readers is not impossible, but it requires longitudinal, multivariate data with appropriate information about teaching styles and programs. Such research will not only clarify our knowledge of the acquisition of reading; it is also likely to yield the practical tools for assessment and instruction (p. 372).

A number of studies adopted the multivariate viewpoint advocated by Calfee and Piontkowski and the possibility that the pattern of relationships between variables would vary with differences in instruction. Perfetti, Beck, Bell, and Hughes (1987) reported the results of a longitudinal study of the relationship between phonemic knowledge and reading for first graders ($N = 82$) in different instructional programs (basal with readiness, basal without readiness, and a direct code teaching method). Various measures were included throughout the year to assess phonemic knowledge, word reading, and curriculum progress. At four points throughout the year phonemic blending and analysis were tested while other tests were less frequent. In general, the results suggested that those students who were given opportunities to read achieved more progress and were as able to perform adequately on the decoding tasks; students who received an emphasis on decoding made less progress and their decoding abilities did not necessarily transfer to reading. Based on partial time-lag correlations, the authors argued that reading gains had a reciprocal relationship with an ability to phonemically analyze (deletion task, e.g., remove the "k" sound from cat), but reading contributed to the ability to delete, which in turn contributed to reading rather than the ability to delete making a contribution by itself. As they stated:

What is clear is that learning to read can begin in a variety of ways, most of which may require only minimal explicit knowledge of speech segments. Thus, the rudimentary ability to manipulate isolated segments may be necessary for significant progress in reading. However, it is reading itself, we suggest, that enables the child to be able to analyze words and to manipulate their speech segments. It is not that the reader performs such manipulations on the orthography. Rather, learning some orthographic principles through reading enables the discoveries, including the alphabetic principle, can happen without direct instruction as well as with it. Although the direct teaching of the code may have some consequences for analytic phonemic knowledge, they are fairly subtle. Children taught by direct code instruction do not seem to learn any more (or less) about deletion than do other children. However, their improvement in decoding may depend less on phonemic analytic abilities than does the improvement of children not taught coding directly (pp. 317–318).

Likewise, in a 15-month longitudinal study that began with children aged 3 years, Maclean, Bryant, and Bradley (1987) found a strong and specific relationship between knowledge of nursery rhymes and the development of phonological skills—particularly the detection of rhyme and alliteration, which remained significant when differences in IQ and social background were "controlled."

It is interesting to note that studies by Mason (1980) and by Maclean, Bryant, and Bradley (1987) made a similar argument based on their pursuit of the origins of phonological awareness. Mason (1980; Mason & McCormick, 1979; 1981) reported a number of studies in which she examined the reading development of students enrolled in informal preschool and nursery school situations. Based on parent questionnaires describing the children's interests in words, letters, and learning to read and tests directed at letter and word recognition and word learning, Mason (1980) argued that the progress that students appeared to make in knowledge of reading and skill in recognizing and reading words could best be described as involving three levels of development. She stated:

The first level is denoted by children's ability to read at least one printed word, usually their name or a few signs and labels. They can also recite the alphabet, recognize a few letters, and may print letters. At the second level, they read a few short and very common words from books, print, and spell short words and begin to try reading new words by looking at the first consonant. At the third level, they notice and begin to use the more complex letter–sound congruences and letter–pattern configurations. Thus, first level children recognize words by context, second-level children begin to use letter and word–sound cues, and third-level children rely on a sounding-out strategy to identify words (pp. 515–516).

Mason defines third-level children as readers; first and second-level children as prereaders. Vellutino and Scanlon (1987) reached similar findings regarding the interrelationship between phonic segmentation and reading ability. Vellutino and Scanlon (1987) compared the relationship of oral reading scores (acquired at the end of first and second grade) and IQ, various phonemic segmentation measures, vocabulary and syntactic abilities. Word recognition, phonemic segmentation (especially consonant substitution) abilities and use of contextual cues proved to be better predictors of oral reading performance than vocabulary measures and syntactic skills at the end of Grades 1 and 2.

In a slightly different vein, Stanovich, Cunningham and West (1981) have suggested that the interrelationship between automaticity of word recognition varies across time. Stanovich et al. adopted a longitudinal approach in hopes of assessing changes in automaticity of letter and word recognition across skilled and less skilled readers in the first grade; and developing an understanding of its development and role in reading improvement. An automated process was defined as "one that can take place while attention is directed elsewhere." Across two experiments various measures of response times were obtained at different times of the year (late September, mid-February, and April for experiment one; December and April for experiment two) for two groups of first graders ($n = 24$ for experiment one and $n = 24$ for experiment two). The data from experiment one suggested

that for both skilled and less skilled readers there was little difference in their automaticity between February and late April indicating "a flattening out by the end of first grade" (p. 64). In experiment two, Stanovich et al.'s data confirmed the possibility that the chief difference between skilled and less skilled readers by the end of first grade was speed of recognition rather than automaticity. As they point out, the results are consistent with Ehri and Wilce (1979) who argued that success in reading should be assessed in regard to three criteria: accuracy, automaticity, and speed. And from their results, they argue, one could conceptualize these as stages beginning with accuracy.

Research regarding literacy development and the development of phonemic awareness in the 1990s tended to compare development within different pedagogical contexts. Morris (1993) tested whether beginning consonant knowledge facilitates concept of word in text, which, in turn, facilitates phoneme segmentation, which, in turn, facilitates word recognition. Drawing on observations from his earlier studies, he sought a "clearer developmental formulation of the relationship between concept of word and phoneme awareness" (p. 135). Fifty three suburban Chicago kindergarten children in two teacher's classrooms, with different pedagogical approaches to the teaching of reading, were tested, in 2-month intervals, on five tasks:

1. Alphabet awareness that had limited use in the study because the children had high alphabet recognition prior to entering kindergarten.
2. Beginning consonant sound of dictated words.
3. Finger-point reading sentences under line drawings and finger-point reading at various points, and after examiner modeling, a few sentences while reading with the examiner a five-page storybook.
4. Moving a block while pronouncing separate phonemes in words.
5. Reciting 10 words as the examiner pointed to them along with 10 basal words.

As a group, the children conformed to the predicted sequence of word recognition development. Individually, 20 of the 53 students did not fit the predicted developmental sequence. Growth was not significantly different between instructional settings. Morris wrote:

The theoretical position put forth and tested in the present study offers a different perspective on beginning reading instruction. Although the crucial role of phoneme segmentation in printed word learning is not challenged in this study, the results suggest that a stable concept of word in text can actually facilitate a child's awareness of the sequential sounds within words. If one acknowledges this "facilitator" role of concept of word, then it follows that reading instruction of a certain kind (that which leads beginners to map spoken words to written words in text) need not await the presence of phoneme segmentation skill, but rather can precede it (or at least be taught in conjunction with it) (p. 149).

Chapman (1996), collecting the writing samples of six children in a whole language, first-grade classroom, presented an analysis of the phonemic awareness of one boy who entered school not knowing the alphabet and having few book-reading experiences with adults at home. Offering nine examples of writing over 9 months of school, Chapman attributed the boy's increasing phonological awareness evident in changes in the boy's texts to the cultural practices of literacy in the classroom that enabled the boy to invent spellings, and in that invention, demonstrate his phonemic awareness.

Treiman (1993) collected data from 43 first-grade children in a mostly white and middle-class whole language classroom. The children were in one teacher's class, 2 different years. Treiman's premise was that "Just as learning to read words is an important part of reading comprehension, so learning to spell is an important part of writing" (p. 3). She collected writing samples at the start and end of the school year. Analysis involved: (a) pairing the words with spoken words in the child's diction; (b) omitting words that couldn't be paired with spoken words—that is, when she couldn't figure out what conventional spelling was associated with a child's spelling—those words were omitted from analysis; (c) inferring breaks between words, where children did not have spaces; (d) transcribing words according to how they sounded in isolated speech rather than as they sounded when said because she assumed "children spell words as they sound when said alone rather than as they sound in connected speech" (p. 9); and (e) matching letters in a linguistic phonemic transcription with spoken word spellings.

Her analytic transcription considered spelling, pronunciation, match between spelling and pronunciation, conventional spelling, the name of the child, and the date produced. In answer to her question, "How do children spell each phoneme," she concluded that at least three processes seemed to be involved in spelling a word: analyzing the spoken word into smaller units, remembering the identity and order of the units, and assigning a grapheme to each unit.

MacIntyre and Freppon (1994), drawing on data from two previous studies, one by Dahl and Freppon (1995), charted the pattern of acquisition and use of alphabetic knowledge of six children in skills-based and whole language classrooms during their kindergarten and first grade years. Alphabetic knowledge included knowledge of the graphemic and phonemic nature of written language, grapheme/phoneme correspondence, and use of graphophonics as a tool for reading and writing. The researchers sought a pattern of the acquisition and use of alphabetic knowledge of the six children as they developed as readers and writers in both skills-based and whole language classrooms. The children, all from low-income homes in an urban community, were assessd for literacy knowledge at the beginning of kindergarten and the end of Grade 1. Three children from the two types of instructional classrooms who matched on pre- and post-measures and on levels of achievement (most experienced, less experienced, least experienced) were randomly selected for the study. Each was determined to have no alphabetic knowledge at the beginning of kindergarten, and they each learned to read and write by the end of first grade. MacIntyre and Freppon observed in the two classroom types twice a week from October of kindergarten through the end of the children's first-grade year. They sat near the observed child and recorded what the child and teacher said as well as students' interactions. They also noted materials the child was using. The teachers were interviewed informally about their beliefs and practices. "The goal of analysis was to identify each observed child's knowledge and use of the alphabetic system across contexts during both years of school" (p. 401). To this end, they coded field notes and transcripts of audio recordings for "talk and action related to each child's use of the system" (p. 401). Their coding categories included: graphemic knowledge, phonemic knowledge, knowledge of sound/symbol correspondences, experimentation with (attention to) sound/symbol correspondences, effective use of sound/symbol correspondences, emergent reading behavior, emergent writing behavior, and level of invented spelling. They found all six children exhibited the same chronological acquisition pattern. The progression was: sound sense (hearing and matching sounds); sound–symbol sense; self-initiated experimentation with the alphabetic system; successful use of the alphabetic system, with assistance; and successful, independent use of the alphabetic system. Differences in the 2-year study were not in how fast or how well children learned the alphabetic system, but in what children did with their knowledge. All three children in the whole language instructional setting read literature and wrote extensively on self-selected topics. The children in the skills-based setting exhibited alphabetic knowledge while working with words in isolation or in sentences in basal readers. The authors documented that the whole language classroom offered more engaged literacy experiences.

In a related study, Dahl, Scharer, Lawson, and Grogan (1999) documented and analyzed the phonics teaching and learning in eight whole language first-grade classrooms from October through May. Their observations complement the aforementioned findings and contrast sharply with the suggestion that whole language teachers offer first graders limited learning opportunity with phonics (e.g., Stahl, Duffy-Hester, & Stahl, 1998). Dahl, Scharer, Lawson, and Grogan (1999) demonstrate that students of varying reading ability within these classes made substantial growth across a variety of reading ability indicators. Furthermore, they tied these observations to the learning opportunities that teachers "flexibly" enlisted. In terms of phonics, strategy development as well as foundational concepts in conjunction with contextualized learning opportunities are more differentiated per customized adjustments for individual students.

Rohl and Pratt (1995) studied the relationship between phonological awareness and verbal working memory in the development of reading and spelling. They note that phonological awareness and verbal working memory have been proposed as causal factors in the acquisition of literacy; yet, phonological memory and phonological memory may be related, "as both may be dependent on a common latent phonological ability" (pp. 327–328). Phonological awareness was measured by tests of onset and rime, phonemic segmentation, and phoneme deletion. The authors noted that less is known about what is measured by verbal working memory tests. The authors posited that phonological awareness influences automatic word recognition, and verbal working memory could play a part before and during automaticity of word recognition. Seventy six children (46 boys and 37 girls) from three schools in lower-middle class schools in Perth, Australia, were administered a battery of tests three times in 2 years: the beginning of Grade 1, the end of Grade 1, and the tail end of Grade 2. The battery included three verbal working memory tests, three phonological awareness tests, and six reading and spelling tests. From means, standardizations, and maximum scores of phonological awareness tests, the authors concluded that many pre-reading children were aware of phonological categories of onset and rime and that while children could categorize words based on onset and rime, few could segment whole syllables phonemically. Factor analyses were performed to examine whether measures hypothesized to tap processing in the articulatory loop of verbal working memory loaded on a different factor from those measures designed to tap processing in the articulatory loop. Across the three testing times, a similar pattern was obtained. The authors concluded that the articulatory loop and central executive components of verbal working memory are related but distinct. As Rohl and Pratt stated, "tests which required children to repeat verbal sequences exactly as spoken by the experimenter consistently loaded on a separate factor from those which required children to repeat sequences in reverse order . . . [and] results of hierarchical multiple regression analyses showed that backwards repetition made some contributions to reading and spelling that were independent of simple repetition" (p. 351). Rohl and Pratt further concluded that "whilst the phonological awareness variables made contributions to reading and spelling which were independent of verbal working memory, verbal working memory did not contribute to reading and spelling in Grade 2 independently of end of Grade 1 phonological awareness when onset and rime and simple and compound phonological awareness were all controlled" (p. 351). They concluded also that while phonological awareness may be an independent causal factor in reading and spelling, verbal working memory may be subsumed under phonological awareness tasks. Too, phonemic segmentation contributed to reading and spelling over sound categorization and phoneme deletion contributed above sound categorization and phonemic segmentation.

The sheer number of longitudinal studies of beginning reading that have focused on the acquisition of decoding skills suggest not only certain preoccupations but a political context fostering such concerns. First, research has tended to be preoccupied with decoding to the exclusion of other literacy understandings. There are a host of facets of being literate that have barely been touched on. They include: children's emotional responses to literacy tasks, aesthetic development, view of interpretative authority, genre, cognitive processes such as self-questioning, on-line thinking, the student's use of multiple sources of information, criteria for self-selection, self-assessment, and the role discursive affordances and constraints play in all literacy processes.

## HOME AND SCHOOL STUDIES

In the last 20 years, a major field of longitudinal research has opened up—inquiring about language and literacies in children's homes. While much early longitudinal work occurred in homes, the current home studies tend to involve literacies in low-income homes or in homes of nondominant cultures. This move is important because a great deal of understandings of language and literacy development derive from white, middle-class homes and may assume uses of language that are culturally irrelevant in diverse settings. (e.g., Taylor, 1983; Cairney, 1945; Cairney & Munsie, 1992; Delgado-Gaitin, 1992).

The Home-School Study of Language and Literacy Development is an ongoing study undertaken by several teams of researchers (i.e., Beals, DeTemple, & Dickinson, 1994; Dickinson & Tabors, 1991; Snow, Tabors, Nicholson, & Karland, 1995) with low-income families in the Boston area. "The basic hypothesis of the Home-School Study of Language and Literacy Development is that early development of skill with decontextualized language will be related to reading comprehension abilities when children are in the middle grades of school" (Snow, 1991, p. 5). The home-study project in Boston is too voluminous to review in full. It is premised on the idea that a particular kind of language use—decontextualized language—enables comprehension. Snow (1991) explains that there is a particular kind of discourse that plays in literacy, and it involves "decontextualized" language, which Snow defines as language used to convey information to an audience at a distance, rather than face-to-face, when "contextualized" oral language is used. Snow contends that decontextualized language occurs among all classes and does not necessarily involve discussions around books. Thus, she and other researchers involved in this study recorded the language of 80 children and their families in their homes and at their school settings from the time the children were 3 years, with the intention of collecting data until the children are 10 years old. The researchers predicted that decontextualized language would not be significant in the battery of tests the children received yearly, in their homes and schools, until they were in the fourth grade when their experiences with literacy would more actively involve comprehension. They argue that "school literacy outcomes in Grades 1 and 2 may be quite strongly related to preschool print skills, whereas school literacy outcomes in Grades 4 and higher, when reading comprehension becomes an important factor, may be more strongly related to oral decontextualized language skills" (p. 6). The "Model of Relationships Between Language and Literacy Development" the researchers developed shows no interconnections between print and comprehension in children's early years. As such, "reading" in first grade appears merely a decoding process. Observations of reading in many classrooms, however, would reveal guided reading and book sharing, which include the semantic cueing system in reading. Data are being collected, annually, in more than 80 low-income families' homes as well as in participant children's schools. Home data consist of (a) interviews with mothers; (b) children playing with a toy provided by the researcher; (c) mothers reading two, researcher-provided books, to their children; (d) a report of a past experience that mothers elicit from their children; and (e) mealtime recordings of conversations. School data consist of (a) spontaneous talk between the teacher and child; (b) videotaped group book readings; (c) a report about something that occurred at home, elicited by the teacher; (d) activities of all children in the class are noted every half-hour; (e) displays of environmental print noted; (f) researchers' curriculum rating; (g) teacher interviews; and (h) teachers' ratings of children's oral language. School recordings are coded. A test battery is administered at the children's homes when they are in kindergarten. Another battery, administered in school, include oral language tasks, a narrative production task, picture description, definitions, comprehension, vocabulary, and spelling tests.

Different researchers involved in the study have presented different results. Dickinson and Tabors (1991), for instance, concentrating on 5-year-olds, found support for the model of decontextualized talk as influential in literacy development; found that homes and schools contribute to early language and literacy skills; and found that vocabulary, story understanding, definitional skill, and print knowledge "seem to be correlating with similar home and preschool predictors" (p. 42). They further conclude that studies examining single settings such as book reading at home may have overemphasized the importance of such settings when other kinds of talk in other settings may also have contributed to literacy support. Beals, DeTemple, and Dickinson (1994), whose data reflect a cohort of 38 children when they were 3-, 4-, and 5-years old, tested the hypothesis that verbal interaction in early childhood would be a precursor of later cognitive and linguistic activity when the children were in kindergarten. Of the variety of data mentioned earlier, this research reports only mealtime talk, home book reading, and school book reading. At age 5, this cohort of children were administered the PPVT to measure receptive vocabulary; a story comprehension task; a narrative production task; and print skills assessments. The researchers found that the proportion of explanatory talk and the number of narratives occurring during mealtime talk when children were age 4 correlated positively with PPVT scores at age 5. The amount and proportion of non-immediate talk (decontextualized talk) at age 3 correlated with the children's Concepts About Print scores. The amount of non-immediate talk in book reading at age 3 correlated with a child's ability to tell a story, and children who provided information without assistance had better story comprehension. From the school book-reading data, the researchers determined that challenging talk at age 4 carries over to story comprehension at age 5; nonimmediate talk at age 4 correlated with PPVT scores; and specific content of talk and not overall amount of talk is what is crucial. Total amount of talk about a book at age 4 is unrelated to vocabulary or story comprehension.

Along somewhat similar lines, a 5-year study by Linda Baker, Robert Serpell, and Susan Sonnenschein, as well as other contributors, explored the interrelationships between sociocultural contexts in conjunction with looking at preschool home experiences and emergent literacy competencies related to different aspects of reading development, including word recognition, comprehension, and motivation. Participants (initially 43 but eventually 24) were caregivers and children (including equal numbers of males and females of African American and European American descent) drawn from 6 schools in communities associated with varying income levels in the Baltimore area. The children were all born in 1988 and were scheduled to begin kindergarten in 1993–94. A focal point of the research was the overlap between home and

school and how they might interact to support literacy development especially across African American families and European American families varying in income level. The initial data collection included an "ecological inventory" of socialization activities and resources derived from interviews, diaries maintained by caregivers, and observations; ethnohistories developed to detail the parent and teacher beliefs, values, and practices; co-constructive processes through which children appropriate literacy resources based on interviews and videotaped observations; and assessments of a range of developing literacy competencies, including orientation to print, narratvie competence, phonological awareness, motivation, and word recognition in the later grades. As they stated:

A general hypothesis guiding our research is that children from different sociocultural groups may have different home experiences because of the characteristics of their niche (such as, parent belief about child development, available material resources, and general activity patterns of the family) that can lead to differences in subsequent reading development.

Their findings suggested that children may receive different degrees of certain types of literacy experiences and that these "niches" appear to be related to income level and the advantages that some children may have over others across all three years of schooling. Where literacy is a source of enterntainment versus skill those niches are significantly more highly correlated with the development of literacy competencies (orientation to print, narrative competence in Year 1 and word recognition in Year 3 as well as motivation to read). These niches were most closely related to low-income situations.

The ongoing contribution of meaningful reading experiences versus an isolated skill emphasis also emerges from their analyses of the interrelationship of various measures acquired across Grades 1 through 3. Whereas othographic knowledge and phonological knowledge were not found to make a significant contribution to word recognition in Grade 3, nursery rhyme knowledge and frequency of activities such as storybook reading, visits to the library and abc book reading did. As the author concluded:

providing children with enjoyable print-related interactions with a variety of genre of books is likely to be of more lasting value than enforced practice on isolated letters and sounds. (Baker, Mackler, Sonnenschein, Serpell, & Fernandez-Fein, 1998, p. 9)

Looking more broadly on home influences, Weinberger (1996) traced the influence of early literacy experiences on later development. She was a teacher in a nursery school in England where she collected data on 24 boys and 18 girls. The children were white and all but one spoke English as a first language. Twenty-seven came from working-class homes, and 15 from middle–class homes. She collected data over 5 years at 2-year intervals. Data consisted of an interview with parents in their homes when the children were 3-years old. She garnered information about family background, literacy resources and activities, access to reading material, book ownership, experience of being read to, parents' approaches to reading and writing with their children, and details of children acting like readers and writers. When the children were 5, they were given school entry assessments of vocabulary, writing (writing their first name and copying a phrase), letter knowledge (children were presented with letters out of sequence), access to stories at home (parents were asked if they read with their children at home and how often), and their uses of books at school (the teacher recorded her observations of whether children chose books and looked at them voluntarily). At age 7, children and parents were interviewed to update family information from previous contacts. Outcome measures included: (a) the child's level of reading book; (b) assessment of literacy difficulty including their placement on Young's Group Reading Test; (c) a writing score that included story writing and expository writing and the level of independence in these tasks; (d) levels reached on Standardized Assessment Tasks for English; and (e) anecdotal information from their teachers regarding problems. What Weinberger considers significant in her study was not statistically significant. She states that children's favorite books prior to school may not be statistically significant but they are educationally significant. She found that children who read well were those whose literacy was well resourced at home.

Purcell-Gates' (1995) case study of the literacy learning of an urban Appalachian mother and child, over 2 years in a clinical reading context that encapsulated, too, home and community contexts, is rich data for the field of literacy—especially in terms of class and cultural issues. Purcell-Gates is critical of a middle-class world view of literacy, and this criticism is supported by the experiences of Jenny and her son, Donny (a second grader for 2 years during the study), who did not learn to read even though they live in print rich worlds. Purcell-Gates explores the world of illiteracy, from the perspective of the participants in her ethnographic study. One can see Donny's literacy development as part of two worlds: a school that does not seem to see either Donny or his mother, and their home world, which is not mediated by print. Purcell-Gates calls for a consideration of one's assumptions regarding children's literacy experiences prior to schooling and the need to address an expanded consideration of literacy practices when children's situations that are tied to class and culture may not have enabled the learning of implicit rules of literacy practiced in schools.

Biliteracy research has stressed the importance of a home–school bridge including its social, political, and economic character. Moll's (1992) research with teachers who document and make use of literacies or "funds of knowledge" used in Latino homes, posits that curriculum becomes reduced in schools of children from working class families. As teachers document how knowledge is enacted and built in homes of Latinos, they come to see that language use is cultural practice, and cultural practices build social networks among communities. Biliteracy home–school bridges play out very differently in research. Moll takes a "strengths" view of knowledge sources and treats literacy as cultural practice. He also locates the teacher centrally in bridging home and school cultural practices.

Biliteracy research opens up provocative ways of viewing not only biliteracy but literacy, in general. Valdés (1998) writes, "the teaching of English is not neutral . . . the key tenet of the discourse of ESL teaching—that it is possible to just teach

language—is untenable because it is impossible to separate English from its many contexts" (p. 15). Valdés asked, "Why is it that so many non-English-background students fail to learn English well enough to succeed in school?" (p. 4). She documented how two girls recently immigrated from Honduras and Mexico negotiated their ways in United States schools. At ages 12 and 13, neither knew much English when they arrived in California. Teachers' pedagogies fell flat in ESL classes. Critical thinking questions and engagements were usurped by time communicating how to fold paper, for instance, which exhausted teachers and didn't build necessary comprehension skills in the students. The students were used to strict teachers and considered those who seemed nice, weak rather than kind. Class sizes were 35 to 38. Teachers had little mechanisms for figuring out how much English students knew and could not easily evaluate their instruction, either. In the first year, Elisa was quiet and spent a lot of time on her work, whereas Lilian was energetic and out of her seat a lot. The teacher felt Lilian had a learning problem and might need special education. In English class the first year, students were not given advanced organizers to help them know what to listen to and language seemed to be directed at more fluent speakers of English. Little practice in oral English occurred. They pointed at objects and drew and colored shapes for their direct language instruction. By the end of the year, neither girl had progressed much. Elisa, however, was pushed by her mother to use English. Elisa approached the ESL teachers and asked to be let into regular classes, even enlisting the researcher's help. Elisa didn't get into classes on her merits; she had to finish her class materials. The next year, though, when an abundance of immigrant students arrived at the school, Elisa was able to attend a regular math class due to overcrowding in the ESL program. Once admitted to regular math, much language was needed and she had great difficulty writing the longer prose necessary for problems. Lilian learned less English because it tangled too greatly with her identity to accept teachers' definitions of her as her own. She later moved and attended an ESL program all day long, which meant not mixing with many students other than ESL students. Lilian's mother did not know how American schools worked and she, herself, had not known social mobility growing up. Lilian never did escape "the ESL ghetto" (p. 12), did not finish high school, and knows only enough English to work at a fast food restaurant. Elisa, who could not get out of ESL on her own, enlisted, again, the help of the researcher to get into another school. She later enrolled in a college-bound program.

Valdés's research shows how difficult it is to study literacy "development" in classrooms where practices arrest development. Her work points to the increasing visible problem of seeing literacy development as an accomplishment outside of the sociopolitical nature of schools. What home and school literacy research has in common is that it redefines literacy as cultural practice and, by no means, monocultural practice. Nonetheless, monocultural literacy is put forth through curricula and mechanisms of standardized tests. Thus, home and school research does three things: it complicates singular and stable definitions of literacy by providing description of the numerous uses and economies of literacy in specific cultures; it makes visible the middle-class assumptions of literacy; and it leaves researchers, educators, and policymakers with an unanswered question: If it is schooling that administers certificates of status in the form of standardized literacies, how can these be made available to all cultures?

## LONGITUDINAL STUDIES OF READING AND WRITING IN LATER YEARS

The number of longitudinal research studies quickly diminishes as the focus becomes the student moving through the elementary school, high school, or college. As the child's learning moves away from beginning reading and writing, extrapolations about development have tended to depend almost solely on comparisons of sophisticated and less sophisticated learners, experts and novices, good and poor, knowledgeable and less knowledgeable or younger and older students. Such dichotomous comparisons have offered researchers worthwhile descriptions of what students might aspire to, but they have offered only highly speculative insights into how a student might advance his own learning toward the aspirations which were set. Indeed, an interesting ramification of this void are educational practices that naively pursue the eradication of those behaviors associated with novice-like performance or that assume that expert-like behavior can be explicitly taught by carefully mimicking such behavior. What seems missing are those understandings and appreciations of student behaviors that emerge when researchers follow development of the same individual across time and when researchers ask themselves to identify the students' views of literacy.

There do seem to be a some exceptions to this trend. First, there are a number of case studies of readers and writers. For example, Bissex (1980) extended the case study of her son through his elementary schooling experience. Numerous case studies have been pursued of professional writers by biographers. Holland (1975) offered case studies of a college student's reading. Petrosky (1976) and Cooper (1985) have pursued case studies of readers' responses to stories. These tend to be more descriptive than biographical so that a longitudinal perspective is less forthcoming.

## STUDIES INVOLVING A LONGITUDINAL METHODOLOGY AND PERSPECTIVE

Essentially only a small number of studies exist that adopt what might be viewed as longitudinal methodology and longitudinal perspective. Studies by Wells (1986) and Loban (1967) are among the most notable. Beginning with children at the age of 15 months and continuing with a subsample of these children through the end of elementary school, Wells reported his attempt to address the question: Why were some children, usually lower in socioeconomic status, failing to become literate and failing at school? Wells chronicles their language development by referring to data acquired by interviews, tape-recorded conversations, and assessments by the teacher. A number of recurring themes developed. One theme is the notion that children need to be equal partners in conversation if they are to

succeed. He argued that the types of partnership that parents have with children are lacking from schools. As Wells stated, "schools are not providing an environment that fosters language development. For NO child was the language experience of the classroom richer than that of the home—not even for those believed to be 'linguistically deprived' " (p. 87). He argued that a child's contributions should be taken seriously, that he or she should be viewed as and encouraged to be an active meaning maker.

A second theme was tied to what Wells described as the most striking finding from his longitudinal study—namely, that achievement of children varied little from the time they entered elementary school to the time they ended. Students who were assessed as high at age 5 were high at age 10. Moreover, the explanation for differences entering school seemed governed by the values developed for literacy. Wells argued that it was not the mechanics of literacy that were important, but the purposes for reading and writing that the child had acquired.

A third major theme developed by Wells was that the single most important activity that parents could pursue was reading or telling stories:

We are the meaningmakers—every one of us; children, parents, and teachers. To try to make sense, to construct stories, and to share them with others in speech and in writing is an essential part of being human. For those of us who are more knowledgeable and more mature—parents and teachers—the responsibility is clear; to interact with those in our care in such a way as to foster and enrich their meaning–making (p. 222).

While Wells' longitudinal study has no counterpart in other countries, a longitudinal study conducted by Loban in the 50s and 60s has numerous parallels. Loban (1967) pursued a 13-year longitudinal study of over 200 students during the entire course of their schooling (kindergarten through Grade 12). The study was concerned with the use and control of language, the rates of growth and interrelationships of language abilities. As Loban stated:

From the outset, the basic purpose of the research has been to accumulate a mass of longitudinal data on each aspect of linguistic behavior, gathering the information in situations identical for each subject and using a cross-section of children from a typical American city so that findings could be generalized to any large urban area (Loban, 1967, p. 1).

In particular, Loban delineated patterns of growth in language and details on how proficiency was acquired. Taped oral interviews and a wide range of tests and inventories including lists of books read were used to measure reading achievement, listening ability, written language abilities, as well as ability and fluency in oral language (on an annual basis). Loban found similar findings to Wells in that later success followed from earlier achievements. Just as Wells argued that later success was dependent on the quality of home experience, so Loban argued that a strong oral language base, especially the ability to use language flexibly, seemed to be tied to a student's success as a reader and writer. As Wells also found there appeared to be marked differences in the oral language of students in families of lower socioeconomic status. Like Wells, Loban lamented what appeared to be the gulf between home and school that seemed to detract from facilitating ongoing language learning.

## LONGITUDINAL STUDIES OF DIGITALLY BASED LITERACIES

Longitudinal studies of the emergence of digitally based literacies by individuals and groups have extended the vistas of literacy research. Certainly, we have a growing body of critiques on the impact of these technologies on the nature of text and societal development. But, detailed examinations of literacy development for groups have been restricted to studies such as analyses of engagement of groups on websites, listservs, etc.

In terms of studies of the impact of technology on the literacies of individuals, Tierney has been engaged in a long-term study and follow up of a rather unique set of children who had almost unlimited access to state of the art software (including hypertext in the Apple Classroom of Tomorrow) at a high school in Columbus, Ohio. In particular, a series of papers by Tierney and his colleagues (Tierney, 1996; Tierney, Bond, & Bresler, 1998; Tierney, Kieffer, Whalin, Desai, & Moss, 1990; Tierney, Stowell, & Desai, 1990) report the exploration of the impact of high computer access on selected high school students across 4 years of high school as well as in their experiences after graduation. A major focus of their longitudinal study was an examination of literacy acquisition tied to viewing digital technologies as different medium with semiotic, cognitive, and social dimensions. In particular, they focused on the extent to which computers afforded students alternative ways to represent ideas, access different learning routines, achieve various outcomes, and prompt various collaborations.

The students selected for the case studies represented the first two cohorts of students to complete the high school program offering high computer access and several students who were graduates from various classes. These students represented a cross-section of students in terms of ability and came from primarily working-class homes of a variety of racial origins. The physical arrangement of the high school classrooms was largely self-contained. Most of the classroom periods were taught in one of three or four rooms involving team-teaching situations (e.g., science and math; English and history). Within each classroom, each student had various workspaces that afforded opportunities for individual or group computer use, printers and other media, and access to a range of software available over the 4 years. For example, in their science class or history class, they might pull together projects using PageMaker, HyperCard, and SuperCard, using a mix of scanned images, video, and multilevel stacks of ideas. They also had access to computers at home where they could pursue classwork or projects that they decided to initiate themselves. Researchers' observations and interviews served as the cornerstone for delving into the nature of literacy acquisition.

Emerging as key areas for consideration were major shifts in students' thinking about text, attitudes toward text, and approach to the representation of ideas. Whereas students in Years 1 and 2 tended to approach their composition from brainstormed lists of ideas that were then used to develop drafts and be refined, in Years 3 and 4 they developed stacks from their vision of the dynamics and visual dimensions of their texts. The students in the high access classroom explored images, sound tracks, and text interconnected in very complex ways (i.e., multifaceted, multilayered ways) using a smorgasbord of image, sound, and print. The researchers were able to demonstrate that the technology increased the likelihood of students' being able to pursue multiple lines of thought and entertain different perspectives. The technology allowed students to embed ideas within other ideas, as well as to explore other forms of multilayering and interconnections between ideas. The students spent a great deal of time considering how ideas laid out—that is, how the issues that they wrestled with could be explored across an array of still pictures, video segments, text segments, and sound clips. The introduction of desktop publishing, scanning capabilities, and hypermedia contributed to some major shifts in how students represented ideas and approached the integration of ideas from various sources. The graphic capabilities of technology afforded the students a means of developing and testing theories at the same time as it became a way to pilot and assess the potential of certain technologies for such purposes. Furthermore, the shifts in approach to representing ideas continued beyond their high school years to their studies at tertiary institutions and in jobs they pursued outside of school. With the technology they were able to do things they might not have otherwise done and were astutely aware of the potential utility of these tools for their own advancement and, in turn, their families'. They also seemed to have a sense of their own expertise, a recognition of various functions technology could serve as well as an appreciation of the skills they needed, including the ability to work with others. The researchers found that students had goals for technology that transcended the classroom (e.g., all of the students viewed the expertise as affording them advantages in the workplace or college, some had begun using their computer expertise to help family members with projects or for their own profit), and the use of the computers assumed a role that might be best described as socially transforming.

The researchers demonstrated that the students became independent and collaborative problem solvers, theorists, communicators, recordkeepers, and learners with the computers. They developed a repertoire of abilities to explore possibilities that were either too cumbersome or difficult to attain without the technology. The researchers predicted that longitudinal studies of societal engagement with these new literacy genres could possibly set the stage for some shifts in how literacy abilities are defined, affecting outcomes of literacy development.

## CONCLUDING REMARKS

In the introduction we argued that longitudinal studies were crucial to the advancement of our understanding of how literacy develops. To date, research on reading and writing has been dominated by extrapolations about development based on a comparison of literacy learners at different ages, ability levels, and so on. We have stressed that such comparisons may be problematic if our goal is to understand how a literacy learner advances from one age to another or from one ability to another, etc. A number of the longitudinal researchers attest to the fact that when they studied the same literacy learners across time that their hunches about development were often challenged and subsequently revised. Some were taken aback with the speed with which literacy developed, the repertoire of literacy learning abilities children had and used at very young ages, the flattening out of certain literacy learnings, the extent to which the relationship between certain variables changed across time, and the extent to which some variables remained closely related to the child's literacy learning across time. At the same time, case studies of diverse cultures that are frequently looked past in schools reveal how slowly literacy develops when uses for literacy assume a middle class family existence.

Repeatedly researchers seem to be sensitive to the child's active construction of meaning-making systems and ongoing negotiation of meanings. Across the various studies the picture of meaning making that emerges is one in which the child is not becoming a meaning maker; the child is already a meaning maker. Some meaning makers, though, do not make meaning of school literacies that are culturally incongruent with their own and they need explicit instruction regarding implicit rules they don't have access to. When classroom culture is engaging, meanings seem to be negotiated by the child using a variety of cues and systems simultaneously, and the child's increasing facility with these cues and systems comes from being involved with experiences that challenge the child in the context of making meaning to use these cues, skills, and systems. Meaning making, once seen as a natural entity of the child, is now seen as dependent on a meaningful context where, when help is needed from a more knowledgeable expert, it is made available.

Despite the fact that longitudinal research seems essential to answer questions regarding how literacy develops, such pursuits are neither straightforward nor problem-free. Indeed, longitudinal research seems plagued by many of the same problems of any research pursuit. Studies are limited by the researchers' view of literacy, selected biases, and awareness (or lack of awareness) of previous research. These can shape the questions that are asked, the variables included for study, the methods used to assess these variables, and the procedures for analysis and interpretation. Across the various studies relatively widespread use was made of instruments that lacked precision or offered a somewhat distorted glimpse of the variable being assessed. In some cases the method used to assess a predictor variable given one name seemed to closely match that used to assess a criterion variable given another name. Obviously, some of the problems seem unavoidable—particularly, problems devising methods of measuring or describing facets of literacy at an early age or facets that seem amorphous.

Longitudinal research is riddled with problems related to the interpretation of findings. In a number of studies, researchers had a tendency to move from statements about relationships between variables to statements of causality. In a number of cases, a license to make causal inferences seemed to arise whenever multiple regression procedures and the use of path models were enlisted to afford a "best fit." Researchers should be reminded that, regardless of the sophistication of the statistical analyses, these data remain correlational. The limitations surrounding the use of path analysis procedures is not restricted to just ascribing causality. The use of path analysis models oftentimes preclude the consideration of alternative constellations of variables or ways of configuring relationships that are less straightforward. Researchers using path analysis should acknowledge the extent to which their approach adopts an a priori model that is then validated, rather than a more open-ended approach to modeling a configuration of variables. Wells (1986), in the introduction to the *Meaning Makers*, stated:

there can be no true stories. The evidence is never so complete or so ambiguous as to rule out alternative interpretations. The important criteria in judging the worth of a story are: does it fit the facts as I have observed them and does it provide a helpful basis for future action (p. xiii)?

It should be stressed that longitudinal research is not excluded from the various problems associated with generating reasonable interpretations. Just as in any study, there are constraints on the generalizability of findings to other sites, subjects, times, and so on. There may be a danger of assuming that comparisons across age levels, cultures, genders, classes, and abilities will avail themselves. Certainly longitudinal studies do not involve making inferences based on a comparison of the responses of different individuals, but despite the fact that the individuals might be the same, the context, including time, is not. If the individual can perform only as context allows, and if contexts for schooling are ever more restrictive and prescriptive, then research and literacy instruction reduces possibilities for an individual's, and oftentimes, a whole culture's literacy development. What longitudinal literacy research says about literacy development, and what literacy development has to say about research is that they are both delimited by the historical-political discourses that afford and constrain particular literacy practices. One has to question focusing the lens solely on learners, texts, and their immediate social environments, and development may be better understood as contextual affordances for performance.

# References

Baghban, M. J. M. (1984). *Our daughter learns to read and write: A case study from birth to three.* Newark, DE: International Reading Association.

Barrett, T. (1965). The relationship between measures of prereading, visual discrimination and first grade reading achievement: A review of the literature. *Reading Research Quarterly, 1,* 51-76.

Beals, D. E., DeTemple, J. M., & Dickinson, D. K. (1994). Talking and listening that support early literacy development of children from low-income families. In D. K. Dickinson (Ed.), *Bridges to literacy: Children, families, and schools* (pp.19-40). Cambridge, England: Blackwell.

Beers, J. W., & Henderson, E. H. (1977). A study of developing orthographic concepts among first graders. *Research in the Teaching of English, 2*, 133-148.

Bissex, G. L. (1980). *Gnys at wrk: A child learns to write and read.* Cambridge, MA: Harvard University Press.

Bloodgood, J. W. (1999). What's in a name? Children's name writing and literacy acquisition. *Reading Research Quarterly, 34*(3), 342-367.

Bridges Bird, L. (1992). Self in the writings of Tohono O'odham children. In Y. M. Goodman & S. Wilde (Eds.), *Literacy events in a community of young writers* (pp. 64-86). New York: Teachers College Press.

Butler, D. (1979). *Cushla and her books.* London: Hodder and Stoughton.

Cairney, T. H., & Munsie, L. (1992). *Beyond tokenism: Parents as partners in literacy.* Melbourne: Australian Reading Association.

Cairney, T. H. (1995). Family literacy: Moving toward new partnerships in education. *Australian Journal of Language and Literacy, 17*, 4.

Calfee, R., & Piontkowski, D. (1981). The reading diary: Acquisition of decoding. *Reading Research Quarterly, 16*, 346-373.

Chapman, M. L. (1996). The development of phonemic awareness in young children: Some insights from a case study of a first grade writer. *Young Children, 51*, 31-37.

Chomsky, C. (1979). Approaching reading through invented spelling. In L. B. Resnick & P. A. Weaver (Eds.), *Theory and practice of early reading, Vol. 2,* Hillsdale, NJ: Lawrence Erlbaum Associates.

Cochran-Smith, M. (1984). *The making of a reader.* Norwood, NJ: Ablex.

Clay, M. M. (1982). *Observing young children: Selected papers.* Exeter, NH: Heinemann.

Clark, M. M. (1976). *Young fluent readers.* London: Heinemann.

Cooper, C. (1985). *Researching response to literature and the teaching of literature: Points of departure.* Norwood, NJ: Ablex.

Dahl, K., & Freppon, P. A. (1995). A comparison of innercity children's interpretations of reading and writing instruction in the early grades in skills-based and whole language classrooms. *Reading Research Quarterly, 30*, 50-87.

Dahl, K., Scharer, P., Lawson, L., & Grogan, P. (1999). Phonics instruction and student achievement in whole language first-grade classrooms. *Reading Research Quarterly, 34*(3), 312-341.

Delpit, L. (1995). Other people's children: Cultural conflict in the classroom. New York: The New Press.

Dickinson, D. K., & Tabors, P. O. (1991). Early literacy: Linkages between home, school and literacy achievement at age five. *Journal of Research in Childhood Education, 6*(1), 30-47.

Durkin, D. (1966). *Children who read early.* New York: Teachers College Press.

Dykstra, R. (1966). Auditory discrimination abilities and beginning reading achievement. *Reading Research Quarterly, 1*, 5-34.

Dyson, A. H. (1983). The role of oral language in early writing. *Research in the Teaching of English, 17*, 1-30.

Dyson, A. H. (1985). Individual differences in emerging writing. In M. Farr (Ed.), *Advances in writing research, Vol. 1: Children's early writing development* (pp. 59-126). Norwood, NJ: Ablex.

Dyson, A. (1988). Negotiations among multiple worlds: The space/time dimensions of young children's composing. *Research in the Teaching of English, 22*(4), 355-390.

Dyson, A. H. (1992). The case of the singing scientist: A performance perspective on the "Stages" of school literacy. *Written Communication, 9*(1), 3-47.

Ehri, L. C., & Wilce, L. S. (1979). Does word training increase or decrease interference in a Stroop task? *Journal of Experimental Child Psychology, 27*, 352-364.

Ferreiro, E., & Teberosky, A. (1982). Literacy before schooling. Exeter, NH: Heinemann.

Galda, L., Pellegrini, A. D., & Cox, S. (1989). A short-term longitudinal study of preschoolers' emergent literacy. *Research in the Teaching of English, 23*(3), 292-309.

Gesell, A. L. (1925). *The mental growth of the preschool child.* New York: Macmillan.

Gesell, A. L. (1928). *Infancy and human growth.* New York: Macmillan.

Gesell, A. L. (1940). *The first five years of life.* New York: Harper & Bros.

Goodman, Y. M. (1986). Children coming to know literacy. In W. H. Teale & E. Sulzby (Eds.), *Emergent literacy: Writing and reading* (pp. 1-14). Norwood, NJ: Ablex.

Graves, D. (1982). Patterns of child control of the writing process. In R. D. Walshe (Ed.), *Donald Graves in Australia.* Exeter, NH: Heinemann.

Hiebert, E. H. (1978). Preschool children's understandings of written language. *Child Development, 49*(1), 231-234.

Hildreth, G. (1932). Success of young children in number and letter construction. *Child Development, 3*, 1-14.

Hildreth, G. (1934). Reversals in reading and writing. *Journal of Educational Psychology, 25*(1), 1-20.

Hildreth, G. (1936). Developmental sequences in name writing. *Child Development, 7*, 291-303.

Hilgers, L. L. (1986). How children change as critical evaluators of writing: Four three-year case studies. *Research in the Teaching of English, 20*(1), 36-55.

Holland, N. (1975). 5 readers reading. New Haven, CT & London: Yale University.

Juell, C., Griffith, P. L., & Gough, P. B. (1986). Acquisition of literacy: A longitudinal study of children in first and second grade. *Journal of Educational Psychology, 78*(4), 243-255.

Kamberelis, G. (1992). Markers of cognitive change during the transition of conventional literacy. *Reading and Writing: An Interdisciplinary Journal, 4*(4), 365-402.

Kasten, W. C. (1992). Speaking, searching, and sharing in the community of writers. In Y. M. Goodman & S. Wilde (Eds.), *Literacy events in a community of young writers* (pp. 87-103). New York: Teachers College Press.

Kontos, S. (1988). Development and interrelationships of reading knowledge and skills during kindergarten and first grade. *Reading Research and Instruction, 27*(2), 13-28.

Loban, W. (1967). *Language ability: Grades ten, eleven, and twelve.* (USOE Cooperative Research Project No. 2387 Contract No. EI-4-10-31). ERIC ED 0014477. Berkeley: University of California. (ERIC Document Reproduction Service No. ED 0014477).

Luke, A. (1995/96). Text and discourse in education: An introduction to critical discourse analysis. In M. W. Apple (Ed.), *Review of research in education.* Washington, DC: American Educational Research Association.

MacIntyre, E., & Freppon, P. A. (1994). A comparison of children's development of alphabetic knowledge in a skills-based and a whole language classroom. *Research in the Teaching of English, 28*(4), 391-417.

Maclean, M., Bryant, P., & Bradley, L. (1987). Rhymes, nursery rhymes and reading in early childhood. *Merrill-Palmer Quarterly, 33*(3), 255-282.

Mason, J. M. (1977b). Suggested relationships between the acquisition of beginning reading skills and cognitive development. *Journal of Educational Research, 70,* 195-199.

Mason, J. (1980). When do children begin to read: An exploration of four year old children's letter and word reading competencies. *Reading Research Quarterly, 15,* 203-227.

Mason, J., & McCormick, C. (1979). *Testing the development of reading and linguistic awareness* (Tech. Rep. No. 126). Urbana: University of Illinois, Center for the Study of Reading.

Mason, J., & McCormick, C. (1981). *An investigation of prereading instruction: A developmental perspective* (Tech. Rep. No. 224). Urbana: University of Illinois, Center for the Study of Reading.

Meyer, L. A., Waldrop, J. A., & Hastings, C. N. (1989). *Interim report of trends from a longitudinal study of the development of reading comprehension ability.* Champaign, IL: Center for the Study of Reading.

Moll, L. C. (1992). Bilingual classroom studies and community analysis: Some recent trends. *Educational Researcher, 1*(2), 20-24.

Monroe, M. (1932). *Children who cannot read.* Chicago: University of Chicago Press.

Morris, D. (1993). The relationship between children's concept of word in text and phoneme awareness on learning to read: A longitudinal study. *Research in the Teaching of English, 27*(2), 133-154.

Ninio, A., & Bruner, J. S. (1978). The achievement and antecedents of labelling. *Journal of Child Language, 5,* 5-15.

Pappas, C. C., & Brown, E. (1987). Learning to read by reading: Learning how to extend the functional potential of language. *Research in the Teaching of English, 21*(2), 160-184.

Pellegrini, A. D., Galda, L., Dresden, J., & Cox, S. (1991). A longitudinal study of the predictive relations among symbolic play, linguistic verbs, and early literacy. *Research in the Teaching of English, 25*(2), 219-235.

Perfetti, C. A., Beck, I., Bell, L. C., & Hughes, C. (1987). Phonemic knowledge and learning to read are reciprocal: A longitudinal study of first grade children. *Merrill-Palmer Quarterly, 33,* 283-319.

Petrosky, A. R. (1976). The effects of reality perceptions and fantasy on response to literature: Two case studies. *Research in the Teaching of English, 10,* 239-256.

Purcell-Gates, V. (1995). *Other people's words: The cycle of low literacy.* Cambridge, MA: Harvard University Press.

Read, C. (1971). Pre-school children's knowledge of English phonology. *Harvard Educational Review, 41,* 1-34.

Read, C. (1975). Children's categorizations of speech sounds in English. (NCTE Research Report #17). Urbana, IL: National Council for Teachers of English.

Rentel, V., & King, M. (1983). A longitudinal study of coherence in children's written narratives (Report for the National Institute of Education, NIE-6-81-0063).

Rohl, M., & Pratt, C. (1995). Phonological awareness, verbal working memory and the acquistion of literacy. *Reading and Writing: An Interdisciplinary Journal, 7,* 327-360.

Rowe, D. W. (1987). Literacy learning as an intertextual process. In J. E. Readence & R. Scott Baldwin (Eds.), *Research in literacy: Merging perspectives.* Rochester, NY: National Reading Conference.

Schonell, F. J. (1956). Diagnostic and attainment testing. London: Oliver & Boyd.

Sipe, L. R. (1999). Transitions to the conventional: An examination of a first grader's composing process. *Journal of Literacy Research.*

Snow, C. E. (1983). Literacy and language: Relationships during the preschool years. *Harvard Educational Review, 53,* 165-189.

Snow, C. E. (1991). The theoretical basis for relationships between language and literacy development. *Journal of Childhood Education, 6*(1), 5-10.

Snow, C. E., & Goldfield, B. A. (1982). Building stories: The emergence of information structures from conversation. In D. Tannen (Ed.), *Analyzing discourse: Text and talk* (pp. 127-141). Georgetown University Round Table on Languages and Linguistics. Washington, DC: Georgetown University Press.

Snow, C. E., Tabors, P. O., Nicholson, P. A., & Karland, B. F. (1995). SHELL: Oral language and early literacy skills in kindergarten and first-grade children. *Journal of Research in Childhood Education, 10*(1), 37-48.

Somerset, H. C. D. (1954). Forward. In D. White, *Books before five.* Westport, CT: Heinemann.

Sonnenschein, S., Baker, L., Serpell, R., & Schmidt, D. (in press). Reading is a source of entertainment: The importance of the home perspective for children's literacy development. In K. Roskos & J. Christie (Eds.), *Literacy and Play.* Mahwah, NJ: Lawrence Erlbaum Associates.

Stahl, S., Duffy-Hester, A., & Stahl, K. A. D. (1998). Everything that you wanted to know about phonics (but were afraid to ask). *Reading Research Quarterly, 33,* 338-355.

Stanovich, K. E., Cunningham, A. E., & West, R. F. (1981). A longitudinal study of the development of automatic recognition skills in first graders. *Journal of Reading Behavior, 13*(1), 57-74.

Sulzby, E. (1985a). Children's emergent reading of favorite storybooks: A developmental study. *Reading Research Quarterly, 20,* 458-481.

Sulzby, E., & Teale, W. H. (1985). Writing development in early childhood. *Educational Horizons, 64,* 8-12.

Sulzby, E., Barnhart, J., & Hieshima, J. (1988). Forms of writing and re-reading from writing: A preliminary report. In J. Mason (Ed.), *Reading/writing connections.* Boston: Allyn & Bacon.

Taylor, D. (1983). *Family literacy: Young children learning to read and write.* Portsmouth, NH: Heinemann.

Teale, W. H. (1984, November). *Learning to comprehend written language.* Paper presented at the annual convention of the National Council of Teachers of English: Detroit, MI. (ERIC Document Reproduction No. ED 255-871)

Teale, W. H., Martinez, M. G., & Glass, W. L. (1988). Describing classroom storybook reading. In D. Bloome (Ed.), *Learning to use literacy in educational settings.* Norwood, NJ: Ablex.

Teale, W. H., & Martinez, M. (1986, October). *Connecting writing: Fostering emergent literacy in kindergarten children.* Paper presented at the Reading/Writing Acquisition Conference, University of Illinois, Champaign-Urbana.

Teale, W. H., & Sulzby, E. (1986a). Emergent literacy as a perspective for examining how young children become writers and readers. In W. H. Teale & E. Sulzby (Eds.), *Emergent literacy: Writing and reading* (pp. vii-xxv). Norwood, NJ: Ablex.

Teale, W. H., & Sulzby, E. (1987). Literacy acquisition in early childhood: The roles of access and meditation in storybook reading. In D. A. Wagner (Ed.), *The future of literacy in a changing world.* New York: Pergamon Press.

Teale, W. H., & Sulzby, E. (Eds.) (1986b). *Emergent literacy: Writing and reading.* Norwood, NJ: Ablex.

Tierney, R. J. (1987). The engagement of thinking processes: A preliminary study of selected Apple Classroom of Tomorrow students. Report prepared for Apple Computer, Inc., Cupertino, CA.

Tierney, R. J. (1992). Studies of reading and writing growth: Longitudinal research on literacy acquisition. In J. Flood, J. Jensen, D. Lapp, & J. R. Squire (Eds.). *Handbook of research on teaching the language arts.* New York: Macmillan.

Tierney, R. J. (1996). Redefining computer appropriation: A five year longitudinal study of ACOT students. In C. Fisher (Ed.), *Education and technology: Reflections on a decade of* experience in classrooms. San Francisco: Jossey-Bass.

Tierney, R. J., Bond, E., & Bresler, J. (1998). *Computer appropriation and developing literacies: A follow up study.* National Reading Conference, Austin, TX.

Tierney, R. J., Kieffer, R. D., Whalin, K., Desai, L. E., & Moss, A. G. (1990). Computer acquisition: A longitudinal study of the influence of high computer access on students' thinking, learning, and interactions. Report for Apple Computer, Inc., Cupertino, CA.

Tierney, R. J., Kieffer, R., Desai, L., Stowell, L., et al. (1990, July 6). *The influence of hypertext on students' thinking.* Paper presented at ACOT R&D Open House, Advanced Technology Group, Apple Computer.

Tierney, R. J., Stowell, L., & Desai, L. (1990, April 16). *Assessing the assessment of literacy learning, problem solving, and knowledge change.* Paper presented at the American Educational Research Association Annual Conference, Boston.

Tobin, A. W., & Pikulski, J. J. (1988). A longitudinal study of the reading achievement of early and non-early readers through sixth grade. In J. E. Readence & R. Scott Baldwin (Eds.), *Dialogues in literacy research.* Chicago, IL: National Reading Conference.

Torrey, J. W. (1969). Learning to read without a teacher: A case study. *Elementary English, 46,* 550-556, 658.

Treiman, R. (1993). *Beginning to spell: A study of first-grade children.* New York: Oxford University Press.

Valdés, G. (1998). The world outside and inside schools: Language and immigrant children. *Educational Researcher, 27*(6), 4-18.

Vaughan, S. (1992). Bringing it all together: Anna writing in a community of writers. In Y. M. Goodman & S. Wilde (Eds.), *Literacy events in a community of young writers* (pp. 148-174). New York: Teachers College Press.

Vellutino, F. R., & Scanlon, D. M. (1987). Phonological coding, phonological awareness and reading ability: Evidence from a longitudinal and experimental study. *Merrill-Palmer Quarterly, 33*(3), 321-363.

Vernon, M. (1957). Backwardness in reading: A study of its origins. Cambridge, England: Cambridge University Press.

Vygotsky, L. S. (1978). *Mind in society.* Cambridge, MA: Harvard University Press.

Vygotsky, L. S. (1981). The genesis of higher mental functions. In J. V. Wertsch (Ed.), *The concept of activity in Soviet psychology* (pp. 144-188). White Plains, NY: M. E. Sharpe.

Weinberger, J. (1996). A longitudinal study of children's early literacy experiences at home and later literacy development at home and school. *Journal of Research in Reading, 19*(1), 14-24.

Wells, C. G., & Raban, B. (1978). *Children learning to read* (Final Rep. to the Social Science Research Council). University of Bristol, Bristol, England.

Wells, G. (1986). *The meaning makers: Children learning language and using language to learn.* Portsmouth, NH: Heinemann.

Wilde, S. (1992). Spelling in third and fourth grade: Focus on growth. In Y. M. Goodman & S. Wilde (Eds.), *Literacy events in a community of young writers* (pp. 125-147). New York: Teachers College Press.

Wilde, S., Goodman, Y. M., Bridges Bird, L., Gespass, S., Kasten, W. C., Vaughan, S., & Weatherill, D. (1992). The research story: Context, methodology and findings. In Y. M. Goodman & S. Wilde (Eds.), *Literacy events in a community of young writers* (pp. 17-63). New York: Teachers College Press.

Yaden, Jr., D. B., Smolkin, L. B., & Conlon, A. (1989). Preschoolers questions about pictures, print, convention, and story text. *Reading Research Quarterly, 24*(2), 188-214.

Zutell, J. (1978). Some psycholinguistic persepctives on children's spelling. *Language Arts, 55*(7), 844-850.

# ·15·

# CASE STUDIES: PLACING LITERACY PHENOMENA WITHIN THEIR ACTUAL CONTEXT

## June Birnbaum
### Rutgers University

## Janet Emig
### Rutgers University

## Douglas Fisher
### San Diego State University

Within the past 30 years, case study as a mode of inquiry has gained increased credibility in English language arts research. A scan of the literature reveals hundreds of inquiries in which researchers recount how children acquire and develop language, as well as hundreds of others that characterize their histories and processes as speakers, listeners, writers, and readers. Still other studies have examined individual issues, texts, concepts, programs, and curricula. This chapter provides an overview of case study inquiry, the history of case study research, the use of case studies in literacy research, and concludes with a discussion of trends and future directions.

## CASE STUDY INQUIRY

Although traditional, quantitative approaches to measurement are appropriate for evaluating activities and behaviors that can be counted or measured, they are less effective in analyzing complex, multidimensional characteristics of a phenomenon. For this reason, qualitative approaches such as observations, open-ended interviews, and case studies are often selected as a way to situate findings within a specific context. The advantage of a qualitative approach is that it allows a more in-depth exploration of the research questions. This chapter focuses on one specific type of qualitative inquiry, case studies.

Case study is defined here, following Yin (1981), as an empirical study that investigates a contemporary phenomenon within its real-life context when the boundaries between phenomenon and context are not clearly evident and when multiple sources of evidence are used. In addition, to qualify as a case study, the data must be in some way representative of the phenomenon under scrutiny. As Shulman (1986) cautions, an exclusive description of an individual or event does not qualify as a case study.

Whereas some researchers consider the case an object of study (e.g., Stake, 1995) and others consider it a methodology (e.g., Merriam, 1988), a case study is an examination of a bounded system. By bounded system, we mean that the case or cases being studied are fixed in time and place and have identifiable confines such as a program, an event, an activity, or an individual.

Lincoln and Guba (1985) set forth other crucial characteristics and advantages of case study as a mode of inquiry. Contrasting naturalistic with positivistic inquiries, they note that case study inquirers tend to reconstruct the respondent's constructions (*emic* inquiry), whereas positivistic inquirers "tend toward a construction that they bring to the inquiry a priori" (*etic* inquiry). Case studies build on the reader's tacit knowledge, thus providing "a measure of vicarious experience because case study presents a holistic and lifelike description, like those readers normally encounter in their experience of the world. Case studies are effective in demonstrating the interplay between inquirer and respondent. They provide the reader opportunities to probe for internal consistency. The case study provides what Stake (1994) defines as "thick description," so necessary for judgments of transferability. They provide a grounded assessment of context.

Researchers who use case study approaches hope to identify what is common as well as what is unique about the case. However, the end product of a case study regularly results in something unique. As Stake (1994) points out, this uniqueness is likely to be related to:

• The nature of the case.
• Its historical background.
• The physical setting.
• Other contexts, including economic, political, legal, and aesthetic.
• Other cases through which this case is recognized.
• Those informants through whom the case can be known. (p. 238)

As with other forms of research, researchers who use case study methodology must first decide on the research questions. They must then decide on the unit of analysis. This is often a difficult task as researchers ask themselves about data they might collect from individual students, classrooms, schools, or communities. Once the unit of analysis has been decided, most researchers use purposeful sampling to identify the case(s). Purposeful sampling provides the researcher an opportunity to obtain different perspectives on the issue, problem, process, situation, or event. Purposeful sampling can also increase variance and thus improve the validity of the findings.

Following the sampling decision, the researcher decides on the types of evidence or data that will be collected. It is not uncommon for case study researchers to use a variety of data collection procedures, including observations, interviews, records reviews, and others. Collecting this array of data lets the case tell its own story (Carter, 1993). Although we are not sure that a case can tell its own story or tell that story well, we do know that, with sufficient data, researchers can assist in relating a story that is reflective of the phenomenon as it occurred in a specific setting.

One of the ways that researchers ensure that the story they relate is valid is through triangulation. In case study work, triangulation is generally considered a process in which researchers use multiple perceptions to clarify meanings. In other words, researchers look either across cases or across types of data collected for evidence of the phenomenon (see Janesick, 1994 for additional information on triangulation).

## THE HISTORY OF CASE STUDY RESEARCH

The neurologist Oliver Sacks, in the preface to his *The Man Who Mistook His Wife for a Hat* (1985), traces case study back to Hippocrates, the first physician, and credits Hippocrates with creating the concept of case study through his presentations of diseases as having a course "from their first intimations to their climax or crisis, and thus to their fatal or happy resolution." Sacks suggests, in fact, that the origin of case study can be found, even earlier, in "that universal and prehistorical tradition by which patients have always told their stories to doctors."

In his historical overview, Sacks regards the late 19th century as the high point in the writing of "richly human clinical tales" with the case studies of neurologist Hughlings Jackson (1931) and of the psychoanalyst Sigmund Freud (1956) as exemplars. Within the 20th century A. R. Luria is, in Sacks' opinion, the greatest writer of case study. Luria's case studies of such brain-damaged veterans of World War I as *S* (1972) and *Z* (1960) are famous instances.

Within the 20th century, Penfield and Perot (1963), Sherrington (1940), and Bettelheim (1950) have also produced case studies of importance within the fields of neurology and psychiatry, as has Sacks (1989) himself. In light of this history, it is not surprising that North (1987) in his taxonomy of our field places case study inquirers in a category he terms "clinicians."

Prior to Strang, Robinson, and Emig, case study was not regarded as a legitimate mode of inquiry in English language arts research. A major reason for its lack of status was the domination in the post-World War II period by behaviorist psychology, with its tenet that only large-scale experimental studies conducted under ostensibly controlled and context-stripped conditions provided validity and generalizability of findings (Mishler, 1979).

At first, perhaps consequently, individual case researchers worked in isolation, at times idiosyncratically, without models. Some current surveyors of the field seem unaware in their critiques of early work of this pervading domination by behaviorism, and early difficulty in getting case studies published in the reputable journals of any of the social sciences. Now, however, not only is case study honored, but the case for case study is being made with greater and greater sophistication (Creswell, 1998; Lincoln & Guba, 1985; Neuman & McCormick, 1995; Stake, 1994; Yin, 1994). This change seems to reflect a general dissatisfaction with experimental research as expressed by a National Institute of Education-sponsored committee on teaching, testing, and learning: "we need ways of describing that are more informative and insightful than percentiles or stanines. . . . As we have indicated, descriptive materials are important starting points for much scientific work and for teaching" (Tyler & White, 1979, p. 363).

## THE USE OF CASE STUDIES IN LITERACY RESEARCH

Studies of children's language acquisition and development have classically proceeded as case study. Perhaps in part because of the difficulty in finding large numbers of subjects, investigators have studied a few children—frequently their own—as the most available source of data (e.g., Piaget, 1930; Weir, 1970). With the exception of Piaget, case studies of bilingualism occurred earlier than those focusing on monolinguistic acquisition and development—English and Chinese, for example (Chao, 1951). Other bilingual studies include Bowermann's (1973) of Finnish, Rydin's (1971) of Swedish, and Tolbert's (1971) of Spanish.

The goal of these investigations has been to make apt intra- and inter-linguistic characterizations of how children develop and use language. For the most part longitudinal, many exhibit the characteristics delineated by Lincoln and Guba (1985) as those marking successful case study reporting:

- Repeated purposeful probing.
- Ongoing sampling design.
- Hypothesis generation that is fluid, refined, and grounded.
- Nonexploitive sharing of findings with subjects, or at least, when the subjects are very young, with the subjects' families.

Studies of exceptional language development range from those examining the highly gifted to those examining students with disabilities or children who have been abused. Primary accounts of brilliant writers can take the form of autobiography (Welty, 1984; Sartre, 1964); or occur as exemplars often supporting a general thesis, as with Gardner's (1983) examination in *Frames of Mind: A Theory of Multiple Intelligences* of the extraordinary linguistic abilities of the poets T. S. Eliot and Stephen Spender. Classic among studies of students with disabilities is Luria and Yudovich's (1971) examination of Russian twins; of the socially isolated, Itard's (1962) study of the Wild Boy of Aveyon; and of the abused, Curtiss' (1977) study of Genie.

## Listening

Perhaps because of the formidable methodological challenges involved, there have been, to our knowledge, no discrete case studies of listening and attending behaviors and processes involving subjects with normal hearing. A very few studies involving partially or totally deaf students have, however, been made (e.g., Nelson, 1985). Sacks (1989) provides a case study of the status of "sign" as a symbolic modality within the deaf community.

## Invented Spelling

Because invented or transitional, temporary spelling can be regarded developmentally as a common precursor of abilities to write, so this brief account logically precedes a discussion of the use of case study in the domain of writing. Beginning with Read (1971) a number of parent/scholars conducted studies of how their children "invented" the orthographic systems of American English. Noteworthy here is Bissex's (1980) study of her son, Paul, making "thick" documentation by collecting and analyzing all texts he produced between the ages of 4 and 9, from signs on his bedroom door, to original newspaper and school writing. In a more formal classroom setting, Sipe (1998) describes the process and procedures used by a first grader during writing and attempting to spell words.

## Writing

Emig (1969) was the first researcher to make a case study of the composing processes of successful English-speaking student writers; Brown (1965) had previously studied how a prototypical French school boy learned to write. Using protocol analysis, Emig examined the processes of eight 12th graders as they wrote in what she called the reflexive and extensive modes. Through interviews she also collected the writing histories of these students. She set her findings against the dicta in the most widely used composition and rhetoric handbooks and developed a tentative profile of the composing processes of 17 year olds. Her case study of Lynn became the prototype for over 1,000 case studies of nonprofessional writers from the ages of 4 and 5 (Dyson, 1988) to 79 (Harrienger, 1988). Others who looked at successful student writers include Berkenkotter, Huckin, and Ackerman (1988), Calkins (1983), Chapman (1996), Fu and Townsend (1999), Lenski (1998), Mishel (1974), and Stallard (1974).

Pianko (1977) and Perl (1979) examined the composing processes of less skilled writers—specifically, college freshmen—as did Sommers (1980), who focussed on their revising practices. Holbrook (1968) had conducted very sophisticated case studies of 13 D-stream, or supposedly limited ability, 16-year-olds in a Cambridgeshire, England, comprehensive school, studies that were accompanied by a psychiatrist's analysis of emotional growth represented by selected student texts. Contributing importantly and eloquently to this set is the intellectual autobiography of Rose (1989), against a powerful analysis of like students whom he teaches in the Writing Center at UCLA.

In recent studies, the processes and outcomes of writing have been examined with greater and greater thoroughness (Hull, 1989; Sipe, 1998). Representative here is Kamler (1980), who scrutinized the complex interaction among Jill, 7-year-old writer; her teacher; a single piece of writing; and the climate for writing within Jill's Second grade classroom. Bell (1999) described in detail a one-to-one writing conference between a graduate student tutor and the person receiving tutoring in a writing center. Kim (1998) described a second-language student's writing process and development over the course of 2 years.

As inquiries into linguistic and specifically writing processes developed, more and more methodological procedures were devised, many with concomitant, not unexpected uses of technology. Perhaps Weir (1970), who audiotaped the presleep soliloquies of her son, Anthony, was among the first here. Pianko (1977) may have been the first to videotape her subjects as they composed. For the time, a most dramatic use of technology was Glassner's (1981) procedure of having his subjects undergo EEGs as they composed, with the record of their brain waves subsequently analyzed by a computer program that divided these into right- and left-brain activities. In the past decade, writing and revising on computers has become a focus of inquiry (Haas, 1990; Jones & Pellegrini, 1996).

The writing across the curriculum movement, in which teachers of subjects other than English involve students in writing to learn, began in the late 1960s with the work of the London Schools' Council under the direction of James Britton and Harold Rosen. The illustrative documents published by the team used mini-case studies to exemplify how writing could help teach the concepts of science (Medway, 1973) and social studies (Martin, 1980). In the United States, Goodkin (1982) made case studies of instructors of nursing, business, and chemistry within a community college to show the uses of writing in teaching such subjects. McCarthy (1987) analyzed the differing, even conflicting, demands made on a college freshman by examining writing requirements in his composition, literature, and biology classes.

One of the most perceptive and thorough efforts to deploy case study in examining the writing of children is represented by the work of Dyson (1983, 1987, 1992, 1995, 1999). She states the thesis she is exploring as follows:

Children's major developmental challenge is not simply to create a unified text but to move among multiple worlds, carrying out multiple roles and coordinating multiple space/time structures (Dyson, 1988, p. 2).

## Reading

In 1910, Huey wrote, "We have surely come to the place where we need to know just what the child normally does when he reads, in order to plan a natural and economic method of learning to read" (p. 9). Yet in the next half century, few heeded what was a clear call for case study. In Johnston's (1985) survey of the methods used to understand reading disabilities, he cited one case study by Morgan in 1896 on congenital word blindness and Olson's (1938) recommendation of case study as the most scientific method available. Yet Johnston concluded nearly 50 years later that case studies remained underrepresented in the literature.

Robinson (1975) and Venezky (1984) provided some reasons for reading researchers' reluctance to engage in case study. With the advent of standardized tests around 1920, researchers moved away from the more difficult and time-consuming task of studying natural reading behavior and toward tightly controlled experimental and correlational studies based in laboratories. Often these experimental psychologists valued the elegance of their design over the relevance of their findings for reading classrooms. Others viewed case studies as "soft science" and too untidy to report in the prescribed format of many of the reading journals.

Kamil (1984) acknowledged the prevailing distrust of naturalistic inquiry into reading but forecast the growth of descriptive and ethnographic studies and a tendency to use case studies in conjunction with experimental research as complementary modes of investigation. Indeed, recent studies have included postexperimental interviews to augment the investigators' interpretations of their quantitative data (e.g., Bloodgood, 1999; Lehr, 1988). In fact, the editors of the *Handbook of Reading Research (Volume III)* (Kamil, Mosenthal, Pearson, & Barr, 2000) elected to include several chapters focused on qualitative research given the "greater impact that qualitative methodologies have had" (p. xi). These editors elected not to include chapters on quantitative research methods due to "the lack of similar impact of quantitative methodologies" (p. xi).

Beyond the addition of case studies to quantitative investigations, a number of case studies in reading have been published within the past several decades. For example, Ryndak, Morrison, and Sommerstein (1999) used a case study approach to document the literacy achievements of a student with a significant disability in a general education classroom. Greenberg (1997–1998) documented the reading development of Betsy, an adult nonreader in her fifties, and compares this with children who are beginning to read. Finally, Chapman (1996), described the development of phonemic awareness as she analyzed data from a first-grade writer. During the past 2 decades, an important outgrowth of the early-reader studies has been the many investigations of emergent literacy from infancy to the onset of conventional reading and writing behaviors. Many of them have been based on an ethnographic or case study design, and, in some instances employ both (e.g., Chapman, 1996; Crago, 1993).

Clearly, since the early 1970s the number of case studies in reading has grown dramatically, matching the increased use of naturalistic inquiry in all areas of language development. These case studies tend to address an area, or cross over several areas, including:

- Instructional programs and practices.
- Factors associated with successful reading achievement.
- Observations of readers' response to literature.

In spite of the relative paucity of case studies prior to the 1970s, each of these areas had been addressed in at least one case study earlier in the century. Each was undertaken by investigators with closer ties to the classroom than to the laboratory and each of the researchers was or has emerged as a major figure in the field: Gray, Robinson, Durkin, and Squire. We will describe these studies briefly and then review recent exemplars that have extended areas of inquiry.

## INSTRUCTIONAL PROGRAMS AND PRACTICE

In 1933, W. S. Gray published his monograph concerning the outcomes of a multiyear program to improve reading instruction in five Chicago schools. Data included participant-observers' diaries and field notes from conferences and interviews with school personnel and students concerning organization and instruction, yearly reading scores, and students' reading diaries. Ongoing analysis of the data led to refinement in the improvement program. The cyclical nature of collecting data, analyzing them, revising questions and/or hypotheses and collecting new data—the hallmark of case study—was, as Venezky (1984) commented, unique at that time. More recently, case studies have been used to examine teachers' beliefs about literacy instruction (Thomas & Barksdale-Ladd, 1997), literacy instruction in inclusive environments for students with disabilities (Mathes & Torgesen, 1998), and community literacy (Davis, 1996).

## READING ACHIEVEMENT

In 1946, H. M. Robinson published *Why Pupils Fail in Reading*, a study of 30 subjects, ages 6 to 15, of normal intelligence but with low reading scores. A team of medical, psychological, and reading specialists and social workers studied the readers and their families. Additional data came from scores on standardized reading tests, filmed eye movements, and oral reading samples. The multiple evaluations of each subject, followed by reexamination of results to modify treatment, exemplifies the triangulation of data that is another hallmark of case study.

Two decades later, in 1966, D. Durkin published *Children Who Read Early: Two Longitudinal Studies*, based on her California investigations of first-grade early-readers and her New York study of first-grade readers and nonreaders. As Durkin notes, her experiences in the California study, begun in 1958, led her to modify the design of her second study while retaining her original research questions. Her second study of 158 subjects included 30 nonreaders as well as readers for intensive study through parent interview, questionnaires, teacher rating, personality tests as well as intelligence and reading tests. In addition to presenting data for the entire group, Durkin included brief case studies of several subjects.

Apart from her results from this study, Durkin contributed much to the evolution of case study research and to studies of early literacy. First, she recognized the impact of the observer's presence on natural behavior. Second, she acknowledged changes in attitude toward early reading that occurred between 1958 and 1961. Her use of the results of her first study to refine the design and instrumentation of her second study while retaining her original questions is typical of case study (Lincoln & Guba, 1985). Finally, she provided the foundation for subsequent case studies of early readers and writers such as Chapman (1996), Clark (1976), Fu and Townsend (1999), Sipe (1998), Torrey (1969), and Yeoman (1990).

## RESPONSE TO LITERATURE

The third area of inquiry—readers' response to literature—led researchers to widen their focus of inquiry to include readers' psychological and emotional responses especially to literature. Although earlier studies, such as Richards (1942), had examined students' reactions to poems upon completion, Squire's (1964) was the first to attempt to examine their reactions while reading. Squire studied the responses of 52 ninth- and tenth-graders to four stories by stopping each reader at five points in the story to explore his or her response while reading as well as upon completion.

To complement his findings from the large group, Squire selected 13 students for case studies. In addition to the quantitative and response data obtained for all of the students, information concerning the 13 focus students was obtained from interviews from school personnel and observations of the students in their classrooms. Although Squire did not present his case studies in his monograph, his frequent reference to them as confirmatory evidence illustrates their value.

The use of case studies to explore the nature of readers' response to literature has also proliferated since Squire first investigated adolescents' interpretations of short stories. The increased interest parallels the shift in theories of literacy criticism, mirroring developments in cognitive psychology and linguistics, and the recognition of the active role of the reader in constructing the meaning of the text (e.g., Iser, 1978; Farnan & Kelly, 1993; Rosenblatt, 1938, 1978; Sipe, 1997). As

Rosenblatt's dates indicate, she recognized the active nature of the transaction between the reader and the text decades before other response theorists.

Although many studies have reported investigations of response to literature, most have not been case studies as defined in this chapter (e.g., Applebee, 1977, Beach & Wendler, 1987; Brown, 1977; Hickman, 1980; Purves & Beach, 1972; Studier, 1981). The case studies can be divided into age-related categories.

Preschool studies have included observations of children's changing response to repeated readings of favorite stories (Baghban, 1984; Snow & Ninio, 1986; Yaden, 1988). Case studies of primary, elementary, and middle school students' response to literature have ranged from repeated observations of kindergarten students' browsing patterns in the library (Martinez & Teale, 1988); analysis of a second grader's corpus of writing for stylistic devices that seemed influenced by her reading of literature (Temple, Burris, Nathan & Temple, 1988); a study of a mainstreamed eighth grader's explorations of literature in a class where personal response was encouraged after years of being in skills-oriented classes where correct completion of dittos was valued (Atwell, 1988); and a comparative study of teachers of literature-based reading classes, who believed in whole language, with those who still believed in a subskills philosophy while trying to use a literature-centered approach (Zarrillo, 1989).

At the presecondary level, two studies merit attention, because each represents the two lines of inquiry suggested by Purves and Beach (1972). These are the cognitive and affective states of the reader and the context for reading a text as influences on reader response. Galda (1982) exemplifies the first avenue of investigation and Atwell (1987) represents the second.

Galda examined the responses of three fifth graders to two novels during individual and group discussions of each novel. Using transcripts from the discussions, Galda found that all three subjects tended to evaluate characters and their actions. Further analysis, based on the findings of Applebee (1977) and Petrosky (1976), revealed subtle differences in the overall responses of each of the subjects. These ranged from one subject's typical piece-meal, subjective interpretation of each text, which precluded virtual experiencing of the text, to another's ability to enter the story world and interpret it as a whole.

Acting as a teacher researcher, Atwell (1987) published a study of her eighth-grade student's yearlong progress in a reading–writing workshop where connections between the two processes were fostered. Against this background, Atwell presented case studies of five students and their changes in attitudes and behaviors as they explored literature and their own writing.

At the secondary and postsecondary levels, case studies have focused on either readers' cognitive and affective states or on the context (i.e., stimulus, setting, purpose) as influences on reader response—two areas recommend for research by Purves and Beach (1972). Holland (1975), Petrosky (1976), and Washburn (1979) exemplify the first approach, and Marshall (1987) and McCarthy (1987) exemplify the second.

Holland used psychoanalytic measures to search for adult readers' personal identity themes and then compared their interpretations of literary texts, obtained in repeated interviews, with their psychological profiles. He concluded that readers' internal states markedly influenced their perception and interpretation of texts. Petrosky, like Holland, used psychoanalytic measures to profile ninth-grade readers but added Piaget's theory of stage development as an additional framework for his study of four readers' response to fiction and poems. His analysis of their twice-weekly interviews during a 3-month period revealed that readers' level of cognitive development as well as their emotional state combined to influence their interpretation of texts. Washburn furthered this line of research by using a Kelly Repertory Grid to elicit the personal construct system of four high school seniors. He videotaped them as they read four short stories and verbalized their responses, then videotaped their reactions and explanations of their earlier videotaped behaviors.

## MULTIPLE EMPHASES DOCUMENTED IN CASE STUDIES

Not all current case studies fall neatly into the categories dividing the first generation of case studies. Instead many studies overlap two or more areas as investigators recognized the connections among language processes and the need to broaden their scope of inquiry to obtain data from as many sources as possible. For example, Wells (1986) drew six case studies from his observations of 32 children as they advanced from 15 months to 10 years and another 128 from 3 or 5 years to 10 years. His data included observations of progress in oral language acquisition, parent–child communication, students' reading and writing development profiles across the period, general academic histories, and exit interviews that included story-telling ability and self-projections about their future. Thus, Well's conclusions about his six subjects were contextualized by his broader ethnographic research as well as his analysis of these children's histories.

Birnbaum's (1982) study of the reading and writing behaviors of fourth and seventh graders offers another example of not only the merging of categories but the need in case study to adjust the initial design to address emerging data. The initial purpose of the yearlong study had been to investigate the reading and writing processes, products, and histories of good readers and writers. The design included at least 40 hours of in-class observation of each subject in language arts activities, multiple videotaped episodes of silent reading and writing behaviors, two audiotaped reading and writing episodes, interviews with parents, teacher, and the students, as well as a review of academic records at the end of data collection. Early data analysis revealed differences in student levels of proficiency; therefore, the focus of the study shifted from a search for shared characteristics for all subjects to a search for differential patterns. As both Wells and Birnbaum illustrate, the broader the scope of inquiry, the less likely that the study can be neatly pigeonholed. The distinguishing feature of these second generation case studies is that they probed beyond scores, printed curricular goals, and scope and sequence charts to observation of instruction and materials and their effects on students. As more case studies in

this area appear, we may move closer to knowing not only what reading programs accomplish but why.

Thus far, reflecting both the assumptions and the emphases of most literature in the field, we have treated case study as an examination or characterization of persons. Yet Yin (1994) notes, in the definition of case study that we espouse that case study investigates phenomena; and in both an actual and a logical sense, persons represent but a subset of phenomena. Within education, other subsets of legitimate phenomena to examine include concepts, issues, curricula, and programs, all of which have also received treatment through case study.

For example, significant issues in the field of English language arts have been examined through case study. One of the most telling and eloquent of these is James Moffett's *Storm in the Mountains* (1988), with its descriptive subtitle "A Case Study of Censorship, Conflict and Consciousness." In his analysis of the vast religious and political complexities of the highly publicized 1974 conflict in Kanawha County, West Virginia, over adoption of a cluster of language arts textbooks, including several he authored, Moffett interweaves historical and media accounts with interviews he holds with many of the parties in the dispute—school board members, politicians, parents, children—interviews that he presents in the form of a dramatic script. He also employs as organizing theme his interpretation of the rhetorical term *agnosis*, thus orchestrating classical and contemporary modes of analysis.

In March 1986, the deaf students at Gallaudet University in Washington, D.C., the sole liberal arts university for the deaf in the world, staged a 7-day uprising when their Board of Trustees selected a hearing president for the school and forced the board to replace her with a deaf president. Through case study Sacks (1989) analyzed this compelling instance of curricular reform, although to characterize the events at Gallaudet merely as an instance of curricular reform would be as inaccurate as to characterize the 1974 events in Kanawha County as an instance of a moment that intertwined issues of theory, research, curriculum, politics, and culture, with consideration of the legitimacy of a communicative modality sign. Sacks served as eyewitness to the events leading within that week to the selection of a president who was deaf, interplaying, as Moffett did for censorship, a rich historical account of sign language with descriptions of the chief participants in the conflict and of their interplay.

The case study of Gallaudet differs from that of Kanawha in major ways, making it worthy of this separate citation. Moffett's account was retrospective, with his return 8 years later to the county to analyze what had transpired. Sacks was present for all the events, serving as an on-site observer, not as an instigator-observer. Also, the issue at Gallaudet was more powerfully one of opposing theories that found their support in research rather than in theology, although in both cases the participants proceeded from deeply held personal beliefs and practices.

## TRENDS AND FUTURE DIRECTIONS

Five trends are currently noteworthy within case study inquiry in the English language arts. First, many recent studies are characterized by greater immediacy, with ongoing, recurrent on-site and in-process observations a steady feature. Second, researchers are providing denser and richer contextualizations for the phenomena and subjects under scrutiny. Third, if indeed a clear demarcation ever separated the domains of case study and ethnography, such a boundary now grows increasingly blurred, even to the point, in some cases, of disappearing entirely. Fourth, case study finds itself as a mode more and more contextualized within multilayered, multidimensional inquiries for which it represents but one source of data and of combined qualitative–quantitative knowing. Fifth, substantive studies that feature, in Dyson's term *symbol-weaving*, as between drawing and writing, or of speaking and signing, are growing more common, appropriate in an era more and more concerned with developmental and neuroscientific insights.

We agree with Geertz (1988) that case studies represent, in his recent metaphor, "theaters of language," quite as significantly as matters of rhetorical stances, decisions, and style as of methods of data collection and analysis. The rhetorical dimensions of case study, how those case studies are literally written, require more explicit acknowledgment and attention, perhaps using as model Geertz's own analysis of the writing of four anthropologists: Levi-Strauss, Malinowski, Benedict, and Evans-Pritchard.

## CONCLUSION

Because case study documents dense and specific human history, the mode may flourish especially under those psychological and political arrangements that honor uniqueness—under, that is, mature democracies and political systems. The status of case study in a culture may well prove then an index not only of investigative but also of societal sophistication.

## References

Applebee, A. (1977). A sense of story. *Theory Into Practice, 16,* 342–347.

Atwell, N. (1987). *In the middle: Writing, reading, and learning with adolescents.* Portsmouth, NH: Heinemann.

Atwell, N. (1988). A special writer at work. In T. Newkirk & N. Atwell (Eds.), *Understanding writing: Ways of observing, learning and teaching K–8.* (2nd ed.). Portsmouth, NH: Heinemann.

Baghban, M. S. M. (1984). *Our daughter learns to read and write: A case study from birth to three.* Newark, DE: International Reading Association.

Beach, R., & Wendler, L. (1987). Developmental differences in response to a story. *Research and education, 21,* 286–297.

Bell, J. H. (1999). Tutoring a provisional student in freshman composition. *Journal of College Reading and Learning, 29,* 194–208.

Berkenkotter, C., Huckin, T. N., & Ackerman, J. (1988). Conventions, conversations and the write: Case study of a student in a rhetoric Ph.D. program. *Research in the Teaching of English, 22,* 9–44.

Bettelheim, B. (1950). *Love is not enough: The treatment of emotionally disturbed children.* Glencoe, IL: Free Press.

Birnbaum, J. C. (1982). The reading and composing behavior of selected 4th and 7th grade students. *Research in the Teaching of English, 16,* 241–260.

Bissex, G. L. (1980). *GNYS at wek: A child learns to write and read.* Cambridge, MA: Harvard University Press.

Bloodgood, J. W. (1999). What's in a name? Children's name writing and literacy acquisition. *Reading Research Quarterly, 34,* 342–367.

Bowermann, J. (1973). *Early syntactic development: A cross-linguistic study with special reference to Finnish.* Cambridge, England: Cambridge University Press.

Brown, G. H. (1977). Development of story in children's reading and writing. *Theory Into Practice, 16,* 357–362.

Brown, R. W. (1965). *How the French boy learns to write.* Champaign, IL: National Council of Teachers of English.

Calkins, L. (1983). *Lessons from a child: On the teaching and learning of writing.* Exeter, NH: Heinemann.

Carter, K. (1993). The place of story in the study of teaching and teacher education. *Educational Researcher, 22,* 5–12.

Chao, Y. R. (1951). The Cantian idiolect: An analysis of the Chinese spoken by a 28-month-old child. In W. J. Fishel. (Ed.), *Semitic and oriential studies.* Berkeley and Los Angeles: University of California Press.

Chapman, M. L. (1996). The development of phonemic awareness in young children: Some insights from a case study of a first-grade writer. *Young Children, 51,* 31–37.

Clark, M. M. (1976). *Young fluent readers: What can they teach us?* London: Heinemann.

Crago, M. (1993). Creating and comprehending the fantastic: A case study of a child from twenty to thirty-five months. *Children's Literature in Education, 24,* 209–222.

Creswell, J. W. (1998). *Qualitative inquiry and research design: Choosing among five traditions.* Thousand Oaks, CA: Sage.

Curtiss, S. (1977). *Genie: A psycholinguistic study of a modern-day "wild child".* New York: Academic Press.

Davis, P. M. (1996). Literacy acquisition, retention, and usage: A case study of the Machiguenga of the Peruvian Amazon. *Reading Research Quarterly, 31,* 353–355.

Durkin, D. (1966). *Children who read early: Two longitudinal studies.* New York: Teachers College Press.

Dyson, A. H. (1983). The role of oral language in early writing processes. *Research in the Teaching of English, 17,* 1–30.

Dyson, A. H. (1987). Individual differences in beginning composing: An orchestrated vision of learning to compose. *Written communications, 4,* 411–442.

Dyson, A. H. (1988). *Drawing, talking and writing: Rethinking writing development* [Occasional Paper No. 3]. Center for the Study of Writing. Berkeley, CA: University of California.

Dyson, A. H. (1992). The case of the singing scientist: A performance perspective on the "stages" of school literacy. *Written Communication, 9,* 3–47.

Dyson, A. H. (1995). The courage to write: Child meaning making in a contested world. *Language Arts, 72,* 324–333.

Dyson, A. H. (1999). Coach Bombay's kids learn to write: Children's appropriation of media materials for school literacy. *Research in the Teaching of English, 33,* 367–402.

Emig, J. A. (1969). *Components of the composing process among 12th grade writers.* Unpublished doctoral dissertation, Harvard University, Cambridge, MA.

Farnan, N., & Kelly, P. R. (1993). Response-based instruction at the middle level: When student engagement is the goal. *Middle School Journal, 25,* 46–49.

Freud, S. (1956). The relation of the poet to daydreaming and Leonardo da Vinci and a memory of his childhood. *Collected Papers* (J. Riviere, Trans.) New York: Basic Books.

Fu, D., & Townsend, J. S. (1999). "Serious" learning: Language lost. *Language Arts, 76,* 404-411.

Galda, L. (1982). Assuming the spectator stance: An examination of the responses of three young readers. *Research in the Teaching of English, 16,* 1-20.

Gardner, H. (1983). *Frames of mind: A theory of multiple intelligences.* New York: Basic Books.

Geertz, C. (1988). *Works and lives: The anthropologist as author.* Stanford, CA: Stanford University Press.

Glassner, B. (1981). *Lateral specialization of the modes of composing.* Unpublished doctoral dissertation, Rutgers University, Newark, NJ.

Goodkin, V. (1982). *The intellectual consequences of writing: Writing as a tool for learning.* Unpublished doctoral dissertation, Rutgers University, Newark, NJ.

Gray, W. S. (1933). *Improving instruction in reading.* (Supplemental Educational Monographs, No. 40). Chicago: University of Chicago Press.

Greenberg, D. (1997-1998). Betsy: Lessons learned from working with an adult nonreader. *Journal of Adolescent & Adult Literacy, 41,* 252-261.

Haas, C. (1990). Composing in technological contexts: A study of notemaking. *Written Communication, 7,* 512-547.

Harrienger, M. (1988). *Discursivity, subjectivity and empowerment: Elderly ill women.* Unpublished doctoral dissertation, Rutgers University, Newark, NJ.

Hickman, J. (1980). Children's response to literature: What happens in the classroom. *Language Arts, 57,* 524-529.

Holbrook, D. (1968). *English for the rejected: Training literacy in the lower streams of the secondary school.* Cambridge, England: Cambridge University Press.

Holland, N. (1975). *Five readers reading.* New Haven, CT: Yale.

Huey, E. B. (1910). *The psychology and pedagogy of reading.* New York: Macmillan.

Hull, G. A. (1989). Research on writing: Building a cognitive and social understanding of composing. In L. B. Resnick & L. E. Klopfer (Eds.), *Toward the thinking of curriculum: Current cognitive research: ASCD Yearbook.* Alexandria, VA: Association for Supervison and Curriculum Development.

Iser, W. (1978). *The act of reading: A theory of aesthetic response.* Baltimore: The Johns Hopkins University Press.

Itard, J. M. G. (1962). *Wild Boys of Aveyon.* Englewood Cliffs, NJ: Prentice-Hall.

Jackson, H. (1931, 1958). In J. Taylor, *Selected writings of Huglings Jackson.*

Janesick, V. J. (1994). The dance of qualitative research design: Metaphor, methodolatry, and meaning. In N. K. Denzin & Y. S. Lincoln (Eds.), *Handbook of qualitative research* (pp. 209-219). Thousand Oaks, CA: Sage.

Jones, I., & Pellegrini, A. D. (1996). The effects of social relationships, writing media, and microgenetic development on first-grade students' written narratives. *American Educational Research Journal, 33,* 691-718.

Johnston, P. H. (1985). Understanding reading disability: A case study approach. *Harvard Educational Review, 55,* 153-177.

Kamil, M. L. (1984). Current traditions of reading research. In P. D. Pearson, R. Barr, M. L. Kamil, & P. B. Mosenthal (Eds.), *Handbook of reading research.* New York: Longman.

Kamil, M. L., Mosenthal, P. B., Pearson, P. D., & Barr, R. (2000). *Handbook of reading research* (volume III). Mahwah, NJ: Lawrence Earlbaum Associates.

Kamler, B. (1980). One child, one teacher, one classroom: The story of one piece of writing. *Language Arts, 57,* 680-693.

Kim, A. C. (1998). A case study of error analysis/syntactic maturity as indicators of second language writing development. *Research and Teaching in Developmental Education, 15,* 79-88.

Lehr, S. (1988). The child's developing sense of theme as a response to literature. *Reading Research Quarterly, 23,* 337-357.

Lenski, S. D. (1998). Strategic knowledge when reading in order to write. *Reading Psychology, 19,* 287-315.

Lincoln, Y., & Guba, E. G. (1985). *Naturalistic inquiry.* Beverly Hills, CA: Sage.

Luria, A. R. (1960). *The mind of a mnemonist: A little book about a vast memory* (L. Solotaroff, Trans). New York: Basic Books.

Luria, A. R. (1972). *The man with a scattered world: The history of a brainwound.* (L. Solotaroff, Trans). New York: Basic Books.

Luria, A. R., & la Yudovich, F. (1971). In J. Simon (Ed.), *Speech and the development of mental processes in the child.* Harmonsworth, Middlesex, England: Penguin Books.

Marshall, J. D. (1987). The effects of writing on student's understanding of literary texts. *Research in the Teaching of English, 21,* 30-63.

Martin, N. (1980). *The Martian report: Case study from government high schools in Western Australia.* Education Dept., Western Australia.

Martinez, M., & Teale, W. H. (1988). Reading in a kindergarten classroom library. *Reading Teacher, 41,* 568-572.

Mathes, P. G., & Torgesen, J. K. (1998). All children can learn to read: Critical care for the prevention of reading failure. *Peabody Journal of Education, 73,* 317-340.

McCarthy, L. (1987). A stranger in a strange land: A college student writing across the curriculum. *Research in the Teaching of English, 21,* 233-265.

Medway, P. (1973). *From talking to writing.* (Project: Writing Across the Curriculum). London: London School Council.

Merriam, S. (1988). *Case study research in education: A qualitative approach.* San Francisco: Jossey-Bass.

Mishel, T. (1974). A case study of a twelfth grade writer. *Research in the Teaching of English, 8,* 303-314.

Mishler, E. G. (1979). Meaning in context: Is there any other kind? *Harvard Educational Review, 49,* 1-19.

Moffett, J. (1988). *Storm in the mountains: A case study of censorship, conflict and consciousness.* Carbondale, IL: Southern Illinois University Press.

Nelson, K. (1985). *Making sense: The acquisition of shared meaning.* Academic Press.

Neuman, S. B., & McCormick, S. (Eds.). (1995). *Single-subject experimental research: Applications for literacy.* Newark, DE: International Reading Association.

North, S. M. (1987). *The making of knowledge in composition: Portrait of an emerging field.* Montclair, NJ: Boynton/Cook.

Penfield, W., & Perot, P. (1963). The brain's record of visual and auditory experience: A final summary and discussion. *Brain, 86,* 595-696.

Perl, S. (1979). The composing processes of unskilled college writers. *Research in the Teaching of English, 13,* 317-333.

Petrosky, A. R. (1976). The effects of reality perception and fantasy on response to literature: Two case studies. *Research in the Teaching of English, 10,* 239-257.

Piaget, J. (1930, 1955). *The language and thought of the child* (M. Gabain, Trans.). New York: Meridan.

Pianko, S. (1977). *The composing art of college freshman writers: A description.* Unpublished doctoral dissertation, Rutgers University, Newark, NJ.

Purves, A., & Beach, R. (1972). *Literature and the reader: Research in response to literature, reading interests and the teaching of literature.* Urbana, IL: National Council of Teachers of English.

Read, C. (1971). Pre-school children's knowledge of English phonology. *Harvard Educational Review, 23,* 17-38.

Richards, I. A. (1942). *How to read a page.* New York: Norton.

Robinson, H. M. (1946). *Why pupils fail in reading.* Chicago: The University of Chicago Press.

Robinson, H. M. (1975). Insights from research: Children's behaviors while reading. In W. P. Page (Ed.), *Help for the reading teacher.* Urbana, IL: National Council of Teachers of English.

Rose, M. (1989). *Lives on the boundary.* New York: The Free Press.

Rosenblatt, L. (1938/1983). *The reader, the text, the poem: The transactional theory of the literary work.* Carbondale: Southern Illinois University Press.

Rosenblatt, L. (1978). *Literature as exploration* (4th ed.). New York: Modern Language Association.

Rydin, I. (1971). *A Swedish child in the beginning of syntactic development and some cross-linguistic comparisons.* Unpublished paper on file with Roger Brown, Harvard University, Cambridge, MA.

Ryndak, D. L., Morrison, A. P., & Sommerstein, L. (1999). Literacy before and after inclusion in general education settings: A case study. *Journal of the Association for Persons with Severe Handicaps, 24,* 5-22.

Sacks, O. (1985). *The man who mistook his wife for a hat.* New York: Simon & Schuster.

Sacks, O. (1989). *Seeing voices.* Berkeley, CA: University of California Press.

Sartre, J. (1964). *The words* (B. Frechtman, Trans.). New York: George Braziller.

Sherrington, C. S. (1940). *Man on his nature.* Cambridge, England: Cambridge University Press.

Shulman, L. (1986). Those who understand: Knowledge growth in teaching. *Educational Researcher, 15,* 4-14.

Sipe, L. R. (1997). Children's literature, literacy, and literary understanding. *Journal of Children's Literature, 23,* 6-19.

Sipe, L. R. (1998). Transitions to the conventional: An examination of a first grader's composing process. *Journal of Literacy Research, 30,* 357-388.

Snow, C. E., & Ninio, A. (1986). The contracts of literacy: What children learn from learning to read books. In W. H. Teale & E. Sulzby (Eds.), *Emerging literacy: Writing and reading.* Norwood, NJ: Ablex.

Sommers, N. (1980). Revision strategies of student writers and experienced writers. *College Composition and Communication, 31,* 378-388.

Squire, J. R. (1964). *The reading of adolescents while reading four short stories.* [National Council of Teachers of English research report No. 2] Champaign, IL: National Council of Teachers of English.

Stallard, C. K. (1974). An analysis of the writing behavior of good student writers. *Research in the Teaching of English, 8,* 206-218.

Stake, R. (1994). Case studies. In N. K. Denzin & Y. S. Lincoln (Eds.), *Handbook of qualitative research* (pp. 236-247). Thousand Oaks, CA: Sage.

Stake, R. (1995). *The art of case study research.* Thousand Oaks, CA: Sage.

Studier, C. (1981). Children's response to literature. *Language Arts, 58,* 425-429.

Temple, C., Burris, N., Nathan, R., & Temple, F. (1988). *The beginnings of writing* (2nd ed.). Boston: Allyn & Bacon.

Thomas, K. F., & Barksdale-Ladd, M. A. (1997). Plant a radish, get a radish: Case study of kindergarten teachers' differing literacy belief systems. *Reading Research and Instruction, 37,* 39-60.

Tolbert, K. (1971). *Pepe Joy: Learning to talk in Mexico.* Unpublished paper on file with Roger Brown, Harvard University, Cambridge, MA.

Torrey, J. W. (1969). Learning to read without a teacher: A case study. *Elementary English, 46,* 550-556.

Tyler, R., & White, S. (Eds.). (1979). *Teaching, testing and learning.* Washington, DC: National Council of Teachers of Education.

Venezky, R. L. (1984). This history of reading research. In P. D. Pearson, R. Barr, M. L. Kamil & P. Mosenthal (Eds.), *Handbook of reading research.* New York: Longman.

Washburn, W. V. (1979). *Responding to a literary work of art.* Unpublished Doctoral Dissertation, The University of Calgary, Alberta, Canada.

Weir, R. (1970). *Language in the crib.* The Hague, The Netherlands: Mouton.

Wells, G. (1986). *The meaning makers: Children learning language and using language to learn.* Portsmouth, NH: Heinemann.

Welty, E. (1984). *One writer's beginnings.* Cambridge, MA: Harvard University Press.

Yaden, D. (1988). Understanding stories through repeated read-abouts: How many does it take? *The Reading Teacher, 41,* 556-561.

Yin, R. K. (1981). The case study as a serious research strategy. *Knowledge: Creation, Diffusion, Utilization, 3,* 97-114.

Yin, R. K. (1994). *Case study research: Design and methods* (2nd ed.). Beverly Hills, CA: Sage.

Yeoman, E. (1990). The meaning of meaning: Affective engagement and dialogue in a second language. *Canadian Modern Language Review, 52,* 596-610.

Zarrillo, J. (1989). Teachers' interpretations of literature-based reading. *The Reading Teacher, 43,* 22-28.

# ETHNOGRAPHY AS A LOGIC OF INQUIRY

*Judith L. Green and Carol N. Dixon*
University of California, Santa Barbara

*Amy Zaharlick*
The Ohio State University

The previous version of this chapter concluded with a call for those engaged in ethnographic research in education to contribute to "a critical dialogue about the nature of ethnography in educational settings" (Zaharlick & Green, 1991, p. 223). In the decade since that chapter was published, a critical dialogue has taken place and major changes in the status and understandings of *ethnography in education* have occurred. This critical dialogue has focused in large part around the issue of theory–method relationships related to what does and does not count as ethnography or as the logic of inquiry guiding ethnographic research and reporting.

This chapter will provide a framework for understanding an ethnographic logic of inquiry, so that those joining in the dialogue and those taking up ethnography in education at this point in time may do so in a way that meets the criteria for adequate ethnographic research. While ethnography has been utilized as a research approach by a number of disciplines, the anthropological approach has been the most dominant in education in the United States, and the most systematically and theoretically defined within educational contexts. This approach, has been called anthroethnography by some of those who brought ethnography and education together in its early stages (Spindler & Spindler, 1983). Anthroethnography is ethnography guided by an anthropological perspective. While this term is not generally used today, the underlying principles still guide those engaging in *ethnography in education*.

## THE EYE OF THE STORM: CRITIQUES AND CONCERNS STILL WITH US

The question of what counts as ethnography is not a new question but one that has been part of the ongoing critique of work claiming to be "ethnographic" for at least the past two decades. For example, in 1980, Rist in an article in the *Educational Researcher* argued that much of the work that *claimed* to be ethnographic was in fact observational research, not ethnography. He called this research, "Blitzkreig Ethnography," since it did not meet the requirements of ethnography defined within the field of anthropology. In 1982, Heath argued that researchers did not understand or honor the anthropological traditions that ground ethnographic work, thus calling their research ethnographic when this appellation does not apply.

More than a decade later, Athanases and Heath (1995) reiterated and expanded this concern in relationship to work that has been undertaken in the area of English Language Arts. In their article in *Research in the Teaching of English*, they argue that

Often . . . educational research labeled ethnography has shown little evidence of being guided by what scholars in cultural anthropology and the ethnography of communication have articulated as sound principles to guide the conduct of ethnographic language research. Part of the problem stems from a lack of clarity among educational researchers about the disciplinary roots and principles of ethnography (p. 264).

Underlying the critiques raised by Rist, Heath, Athanases and others is a concern that educators have adopted, and at times co-opted, ethnographic methods, without understanding the theoretical bases as well as the purposes and goals that anthropology (and other disciplines) have for engaging in ethnography. (See Hammersley, 1992; Smith, 1990; and Vidich & Lyman, 1994 for discussions from a sociological perspective.) Two factors lead to this critique. The first is captured in the critiques by Rist (1980) and Athanases and Heath (1995), more than a decade later, and focuses on the issue of observational research claiming the label of ethnography. The second stems from the range of qualitative methods and theoretical stances involving participant observation that have developed within education since the 1980s.

For both bodies of work, the issue is not one of the value of the research undertaken but rather whether it meets the criteria for an adequate ethnography. (For an extended discussion of these issues related to education, see Green & Bloome, 1995.) The reasons for the first set of concerns become visible when we consider ethnographic observations in relationship to observation from other perspectives. As Evertson and Green (1986) have argued, there are a range of approaches to observational research, entailing different ways of recording the phenomena of interest, most of which do not involve ethnography: category systems, descriptive systems, narrative systems, and technological records. Category systems are *closed systems* in which all of the *variables* to be observed are defined a priori and the *data* are recorded by tallying occurrences of particular behaviors or by recording a limited set of a priori codes to represent what is being observed. Only the variables in the system may be included, regardless of whether additional ones become relevant in the setting. Some using category systems have found the need to record additional information through narratives or through descriptive notes that are then used as contextual information. Those using category systems often observe for a limited period of time on a given day (often less than 1 hour) and for a limited times across days. Further, these systems are generally used online (live) to record the behaviors, with no opportunity to verify live coding through a video or audio analysis of the observed events.

Descriptive and narrative systems as well as technological records are *open systems* and entail some form of recording of the flow of activity or interaction so that it can be revisited at later points in time. Descriptive systems may have preset categories that can be combined in a variety of ways to construct systematic descriptions of evolving lessons and to segment streams of behavior. Central to descriptive systems is the use of transcriptions of the flow of talk or activity in the context of the observation, making these systems context specific and leading to a representation of the event or activity that can be examined once the researcher leaves the setting (post hoc). Narrative systems are open systems with no predetermined categories. The researcher records broad segments of activity or of events (activities) in a narrative form to represent the unfolding flow of actions. What is recorded in written form on these systems depends on the observer's perception of what is important to record, how, when and in what ways. The narrative record becomes the event that is analyzed. The nature of the record (e.g., specimen records or narrative accounts of the sequence of activity) and the approach to analysis (e.g., using preset codes or developing grounded codes) depend on the goals of the researcher. Technological records (e.g., audiotapes, videotapes, and photographs) are open systems that record sounds and/or actions within the field of the camera lens or the microphone. These records make post hoc analyses possible but they do not represent all that occurred, and like narrative systems, are influenced by the choice of focus or placement by the researcher. An example of the importance of having either narrative or technological records comes from the work of Marshall and Weinstein (1988). In their study of teacher expectations, they found that two of the teachers' did not fit the prediction, and they reentered the narrative record to reexamine the data. By recontextualizing the data, they found that it was not the existence, or nonexistence, of particular variables but the patterns of use and distribution that made a difference. Without the narrative record as the base for coding, they would not have been able to reexamine why their model did not work for these two teachers.

Narrative systems and technological records *can be* ethnographic tools *when* used as part of *participant observation*. The mere use of such observation approaches, however, does not constitute ethnographic method (Green & Wallat, 1981; LeCompte & Priessle, 1993; Spradley, 1980). For example, Spradley (1980) argues that an ethnographic observer is always a participant but may take up the role along a continuum of ways, moving from full involvement with a social group over time as a participant observer to a more passive role of observer participant. Further, as will become evident in subsequent sections, such observation is undertaken over an extended period of time, guided by theories of culture. As such, ethnographic observations involve an approach that focuses on understanding what members need to know, do, predict, and interpret in order to participate in the construction of ongoing events of life within a social group, through which cultural knowledge is developed (e.g., Agar, 1980; Ellen, 1984; Heath, 1982; Spradley, 1979, 1980). To obtain such information, the ethnographer records field notes, collects and analyzes artifacts produced by members, interviews participants about their interpretations of what is occurring (whenever possible), and if possible makes audio or video records of the observed actions. In this way, the ethnographic observer records the chains of activity, thus making what members accomplish and produce in and through such chains available to examination at a later point in time. (See also, Emerson, Fretz, & Shaw, 1995; Spindler & Spindler, 1987; Spradley, 1979, 1980.)

An observer who enters with a predefined checklist, predefined questions or hypotheses, or an observation scheme that defines, in an *a priori* manner, *all behaviors* or *events* that will be recorded is *not* engaging in ethnography, regardless of the length of the observation or the reliability of the observation system. Further, if the observer does not draw on theories of culture to guide the choices of what is relevant to observe and record, or overlays his or her personal interpretation of the activity observed, they are not engaging in an ethnographic approach from an anthropological point of view. Thus, the problem arises for Rist (1980), Heath (1982), Athanases and Heath (1995) and others when people conducting these forms of observational studies *claim* to be engaging in or doing ethnography, when their research is guided by different goals, methods, and theories. (For a further discussion of the differences related to research on teaching, see Erickson, 1986.)

A similar argument can be applied to some of the work labeled "qualitative" research. Since the 1980s, a broad range of "qualitative" perspectives, driven by a number of different theoretical orientations, has been adopted and/or developed within education (e.g., Denzin & Lincoln, 1994; LeCompte, Millroy, & Priessle, 1992). While some equate these approaches with ethnography since they often share common methods, they do not necessarily meet the tenets or share the goals of ethnography. Erickson (1986) described such approaches in relation to research on teaching in the following manner, stating that they are

alternatively called ethnographic, qualitative, participant observational, case study, symbolic interactionist, phenomenological, constructivist, or interpretive. These approaches are all slightly different, but each bears strong family resemblance to the others. . . . What makes such work interpretive or qualitative is a matter of substantive focus and intent, rather than of procedure in data collection, that is, a research *technique* does not constitute a research *method* (pp. 119-120).

One way of restating the concerns raised is to see them as indicating that methodology is more than technique; it entails theory–method relationships. Such relationships form the basis for constructing knowledge that is the outcome of work of members of what Toulmin (1972) calls an intellectual ecology. Kelly and Green (1998) describe Toulmin's position about scientific knowledge and changes in such knowledge in the following manner:

Analysis of Toulmin also showed that his view of conceptual change [within a discipline] is based on a theory of rationality of science in which science is viewed, not as a universal set of inference rules or commitments to central theories, but as a collective set of commonly held concepts, practices and actions of members of a group called "scientists." Thus, conceptual change can be viewed as a theory of rationality in that it makes visible what counts as reasons for changes in knowledge within a group . . .

[Thus,] [o]ne way to understand Toulmin's argument is to see "Science" as a product of the actions of members of a group (i.e., scientists) who, in the face of a problem-situation, draw on their intellectual history of ideas as well as the social and physical features of the problem-situation to construct understandings of the 'problematic' being explored. From this perspective, new phenomena can be viewed as being talked and acted into being through the actions of members of a scientific community (Knorr-Cetina, 1983, 1995; Latour & Woolgar, 1986) (p. 149).

Given Toulmin's view of the construction of scientific knowledge as the product of actions of members within an intellectual ecology, we can see why Heath (1982), Athanases and Heath (1995), Rist (1980) and others grounded in anthropology[1] raise critiques of work that does not honor the intellectual traditions and history of ideas within their intellectual ecology. In other words, these critics do not see this work as guided by the "set of commonly held concepts, practices and actions" (Toulmin, 1972, as cited in Kelly & Green, 1998, p. 149) that constitute a cultural anthropology or an ethnography of communication perspective. The problems raised can be further understood if we examine the argument about ethnography as constituting a discipline within Education as proposed by Green and Bloome (1995). They argue that there now exists a sufficiently large research community of ethnographers grounded in cultural theory and ethnography of communication traditions within the *field of education* to constitute ethnography as a *discipline* (an intellectual ecology) *within Education*. Given this view of *ethnography-in-education*, both those seeking to take up ethnography in a principled way and those wishing to label their work as ethnography are joining a community of practice and are subject to its criteria for appropriate work. (For a discussion of criteria for qualitative research that builds a similar argument about the need to meet the expectations of different traditions, see Howe & Eisenhart, 1990.)

## WHAT IS ETHNOGRAPHY?

Having considered the critiques and proposed a way of understanding ethnography as the work of an intellectual ecology, we now present a brief introduction to its development across time. This history is part of the cultural knowledge of those engaged in ethnography from an anthropological point of view. It is *cultural knowledge* needed to locate the current developments within Education in the larger intellectual history of ethnography across disciplines.

### Differing Views on Ethnography and Its Historical Development

The answer to what is ethnography is itself contested terrain. Agar (1994) states that "ethnography [is] a term whose Greek roots mean 'folk description'" (p. 54). LeCompte and Priessle (1993), trace its roots as coming "from *ethnos*, or race, people, or cultural group, and *graphia*, which is writing or representing in a specific way a specified field" (p. 1); it is a way of "writing about people" (p. 1). R. F. Ellen, a social anthropologist from the UK, captures the complexity of defining ethnography. His description provides a multifaceted view of this term that makes visible the variations in current usage.

Consider, for example, the word "ethnography." This word is used regularly to refer to empirical accounts of the culture and social organization of particular human populations (as in "an ethnographic monography," "an ethnography"). The implication is that of a completed record, a product. But then the sense alters somewhat if we speak of "ethnography" as opposed to "theory," or of "an ethnographic account" (meaning living people) as opposed to an historical or archaeological account. Different again from all of these is the use of the term to indicate a set of research

---

[1]The same would be true for those working from a sociological perspective, but to date such arguments have been more visible in the UK than in the U.S. (e.g., Atkinson, 1990; Ellen, 1984; Hammersley, 1983, 1992; and Smith, 1990).

procedures, usually indicating intensive qualitative study of small groups through "participant-observation". . . Finally, "ethnography" may refer to an academic subject, a discipline in the wider sense involving the comparative study of ethnic groups. . . . Thus, ethnography is something you may do, study, use, read, or write. The various uses reflect ways in which different scholars have appropriated the term, often for perfectly sound conceptual reasons. We would not wish to suggest that the word be employed in one sense only, even if it were possible to effectively dictate that this should be so. However, it is important to know that the differences, often subtle, exist (1984; pp. 7–8).

In light of Ellen's argument, we see little value in seeking a single point of view. Rather, we argue that it is important to understand the differences in order to make informed decisions about whether the work being undertaken meets the criteria for ethnography defined within education and related fields.

An examination of different research textbooks and review articles also led to the identification of a range of differing views of ethnography's beginnings and its development across time and disciplines. While the views differ in specific details, what emerges from this analysis is the long history that ethnography has had and how it has developed across centuries, shaping and being shaped by emerging disciplines (e.g., anthropology, sociology, and education). In this section, we present the historical picture that emerged when we considered arguments of those working at the intersection of anthropology and education.

Dobbert (1984) argues that ethnography had its origins in the ways that poets, travelers, missionaries, and historians documented and described "strange-seeming peoples" these writers encountered when they traveled and/or lived far from their own national borders. Both Erickson (1986) and Athanases and Heath (1995) take this argument further, relating its origins to the 16th and 17th centuries and changes in its development to shifts in Western intellectual history. Erickson (1986) argues that interpretive theory and ethnography are interrelated.

Interpretive research and its guiding theory developed out of interest in the lives and perspective of people in society who had little or no voice. The late Eighteenth Century saw the emergence of this concern. Medieval social theorists had stressed the dignity of manual labor, but with the collapse of the medieval world view in the sixteenth and seventeenth centuries, the lower classes had come to be portrayed in terms that were at best paternalistic (p. 122).

He ties the further development of ethnography in the 19th century to the emergence of the discipline of anthropology and to interest in colonial expansion and their peoples. He argues that

Another line of interest developed in the late nineteenth century in kinds of unlettered people who lacked power and about whom little was known. These were the nonliterate peoples of the European-controlled colonial territories of Africa and Asia, which were burgeoning by the end of the 19th century. Travelers' accounts of such people had been written

since the beginnings of European exploration in the 16th century. By the late 19th century such accounts were becoming more detailed and complete. They were receiving scientific attention from the emerging field of anthropology. Anthropologists termed these accounts *ethnography*, a monograph-length description of the lifeways of people who were *ethnoi*, the ancient Greek term for "others"—barbarians who were not Greek (p. 123).

Athanases and Heath (1995) provide additional insights into the historical development of ethnography, arguing that

By the early twentieth century, key judgments about what was "good" ethnography established the expectation that the researcher would carry out fieldwork in the local language and represent *what was* within a group, and not *what was not* or *what was in need of change* from an outsider's perspective. [Emphasis in the original] In addition, ethnography continued to rely on close ties with political and economic history and to include descriptions of contextual influences on the cultural and linguistic habits of groups (p. 264).

Dobbert (1984) characterizes this shift as moving from an etic perspective to an emic perspective. She argues that prior to the 1960s, the ethnographer's *own* perspective (an etic or outsider's perspective) on what was being observed framed the description of a group. Since the 1960s, some ethnographers, particularly those guided by cognitive, interpretive, symbolic, or ethnography of communication approaches within anthropology, have become more concerned with grounding their descriptions in the "folk terms" of a group and in identifying the meaning(s) to members of actions and events of everyday life. This is referred to as an emic or an insider's perspective.[2]

Athanases and Heath (1995) identify yet another shift in the 20th century, one that had significant implications for education. They argue that in the 1930s some anthropologists began to study "slices of organizational life within complex societies and encouraged shorter works than the hitherto extensive volumes that had documented lifeways of entire groups" (p. 265). This shift meant that classrooms and small schools became a focus of anthropologists (as well as sociologists). They state further that "by the 1960s and 1970s, such work in the United States was strongly influenced by studies of specific situations for conversation and other types of discourse—oral and written—carried out by ethnomethodologists and sociolinguists (e.g., Cazden, John, & Hymes, 1972)" (p. 265).

This turn meant that ethnographers took a more *topic-oriented* or focused approach to the study of cultural practices, rather than a comprehensive approach, i.e., the study of a whole society Hymes (1982). This shift can be viewed as related to what Ortner (1984) described as a shift to *practice-oriented* theories of cultural activity, with a concern for understanding culture as constituted in and through the everyday practices of members of a social group.[3]

---

[2]Origins of emic—etic are found in the terms phon*emic* and phon*etic*—what is meaningful within a language to the speaker (emic) and external descriptions (etic). (cf., Pike, 1954.)

[3]These shifts are also related to a growing concern in sociology for the need for grounded theory (Glaser & Strauss, 1967; Strauss & Corbin, 1990) that provides a basis for examining the social construction of reality (Berger & Luckmann, 1966), and everyday life of members of a social group (e.g., Heller, 1984; Schutz, 1970).

As this brief history shows, those writing about ethnography tie its evolution to shifts in the history of Western intellectual thought as well as to the development of anthropology and other disciplines (e.g., sociology, education, and social psychology). However, regardless of the view of its origins and development, all agree that ethnography is a complex process that involves the written account of a social group and that such accounts have transformed and become more systematic and scientific in the 20th century. Today, those exploring ethnography as a research approach have a wealth of theoretical perspectives to draw on, each with particular ways of theorizing culture and ethnographic approaches to studying social groups, and thus, what Strike (1974, 1989) calls the expressive potential of a research program.[4] These include: cognitive anthropology (Agar, 1994; D'Andrade, 1995; Frake, 1977; and Spradley, 1980), critical ethnography (Carspecken, 1996); cultural ecology (Ogbu, 1974, 1978, 1982), ethnography of communication (Gumperz & Hymes, 1972; Hymes, 1974; Saville-Troike, 1989); ethnography of experience (Turner & Bruner, 1986); interpretive ethnography in education (Erickson, 1986; Gee & Green, 1998; Gilmore & Glatthorn, 1982; Green & Wallat, 1981; Heath, 1982; Spindler, 1982; Spindler & Spindler, 1987); Linguistic Anthropology (Duranti, 1997), and symbolic anthropology (Geertz, 1973, 1983) among others.

## Locating Educational Ethnography Within the Developing History

According to Spindler (1955), prior to the 1950s, educational ethnography did not exist. In 1954, a conference was held at Stanford University under joint auspices of the School of Education and the Department of Sociology and Anthropology at Stanford and the American Anthropological Association. The purpose of this conference was to explore the interrelationships between education and anthropology. Attending the conference were 22 noted educators and anthropologists. The outcome of the conference was one of the first books on the potential *inter*relationships of these fields. This book, *Education and Anthropology*, was edited by George Spindler (1955). In his overview, Spindler (1955) notes that the participants in these two fields, while sharing a concern for the ultimate improvement of society, had different purposes for ethnography and different problems of import. In the next 2 decades, discussions continued, eventually leading to the sole session on "Ethnography of Schools" organized by John Singleton at the 1968 meetings of the American Anthropological Association and the session chaired by Fred Gearing on "Studies of Complex Societies." Gearing was, at that time, the director of the federally funded Program in Anthropology and Education. Hess (1999) states that it was "out of a meeting to describe the Program in Anthropology and Education that CAE [the Council on Anthropology and Education] was born" (p. 404). The formation of the Council of Anthropology and Education in 1970 also led to the founding of a journal, the *Anthropology and Education Quarterly*, which publishes studies *of education* by anthropologists and studies *in education* by educators grounded in anthropology.

The December 1999 volume (V. 30, Issue 4) of that journal revisits this history and discusses the challenges facing educational ethnography in the future. Issues raised include the meaning, role, and value of the concept of *culture* as an organizing principle of ethnography (González, 1999; Eisenhart, 1999). These articles and reflections also discuss shifts in focus of ethnography (Anderson-Levitt, 1999; Singleton, 1999) and in ways that topics are examined. Such shifts include: ethnohistorical roots of gender ideologies and the historical and material circumstances that shape gender in relation to markets and families (Stambach, 1999); education beyond K-12 settings (Jensen, 1999; Dunn, 1999); and educational reform (Emihovich, 1999). Some articles also address issues in writing *with* or writing *over* voices of participants (Emihovich, 1999); intentions of the researcher (Schram, 1999); types of cultural knowledge studied (Spindler, 1999) and recurrent methodological concerns, e.g., objectivity-subjectivity (Brantlinger, 1999); activism (Brantlinger, 1999); and distance from those studied (Rogers & Swadener, 1999).

The distinction between educators' and anthropologists' goals in engaging in ethnography in relationship to education that was evident in the early years is still important to consider today. Green and Bloome (1995) suggest that to understand the contributions of work at the nexus of ethnography and education, it is necessary to distinguish between ethnography by anthropologists, i.e., *ethnography of education* and ethnography undertaken by educators (e.g., university researchers, teachers, students, and others), i.e., *ethnography in education*. The difference, they argue, is in the questions and purposes for doing ethnography.

What this history makes visible is that the answer to the question, *What is ethnography?*, continues to evolve as new theories and new disciplines develop within and outside of education. It also makes visible, as Green and Bloome (1995) have argued, that the issues raised about what counts as ethnography and who counts as ethnographers transcend the field of Education.

## UNDERSTANDING ETHNOGRAPHY AS A LOGIC OF INQUIRY

In the previous sections, we have described the current context in which those seeking to take up or engage in ethnographic research find themselves. In the remaining sections, we present a set of key underlying principles: *ethnography as the study of cultural practices; as entailing a contrastive perspective*; and *as entailing a holistic perspective*. These principles are central to a range of theoretical positions and can be seen as constituting a *logic of inquiry* for research grounded in a cultural anthropology and ethnography of communication approach. As part of the discussion, we draw methodological implications and present examples of how researchers have used these principles in their research.

---

[4]By research program, Strike means the program of research of an intellectual ecology, not an individual person's research.

Following this, we describe the interactive-responsive process that ethnographers use as they design an ethnographic study, negotiate and renegotiate entry into a site, make ethnographic records, collect ethnographic data, and analyze data related to the questions of interest. This interactive-responsive process guided by these principles constitutes the ethnographer's *logic-in-use*. We also propose a way of representing the logic-in-use so that readers unfamiliar with ethnographic research can understand how theory–method decisions are made in relationship to anticipated and unanticipated questions that develop as an ethnographer seeks understandings of what members need to know, understand, produce, and predict in order to participate in socially and culturally appropriate ways within a social group. We conclude this section with criteria for ethnographic research in education.

## Ethnography As the Study of Culture: A Practice Oriented Approach

As previously discussed, for *cultural anthropology* and *ethnography of communication*, ethnography is a theoretically driven approach involving a contrastive perspective, through which cultural phenomena or cultural practices are studied. Guided by their particular theoretical backgrounds,[5] ethnographers seek understandings of the cultural patterns and practices of everyday life of the group under study from an emic or insider's perspective. Through an interactive and responsive process that is recursive in nature, the ethnographer examines what members need to know, produce, understand, and predict in order to participate as a member of the group. In this way, the ethnographer seeks to "uncover"[6] the principles of practice that guide members' actions within the local group (Frake, 1977, as cited in Spradley, 1980). One way of thinking about this is that the ethnographer seeks to make visible the everyday, often, invisible practices[7] of a cultural group, and to make the familiar or ordinary practices strange (i.e., extraordinary). Thus, the patterns and the principles of practice of members of a social group are viewed as the material resources that ethnographers use to construct a grounded theory of culture. By examining such practices, the ethnographer also seeks understandings of the consequences of membership, and how differential access within a group shapes opportunities for learning and participation. This is an issue particularly relevant in the study of access to education in today's schools.

Just what theory of culture will be constructed depends on the ethnographer's intellectual history and the particular intellectual ecology (and thus the *logic of inquiry*) in which the ethnographer claims membership. To illustrate how the logic-of-inquiry shapes the logic-in-use of an ethnographer, we present an example from a cognitive anthropological perspective. Although Spradley (1980) died in the early 1980s, his work has been influential within education, both for university-based researchers and for secondary school students.[8]

Spradley (1980) proposed viewing culture as more than a fixed cognitive map. He quotes Frake (1977), who argued that

Culture is not simply a cognitive map that people acquire in whole or in part, more or less accurately, and then learn to read. People are not just map-readers; they are map-makers. People are cast out into imperfectly charted, continually revised sketch maps. Culture does not provide a cognitive map, but a set of principles for map making and navigation. Different cultures are like different schools of navigation designed to cope with different terrains and seas (as cited in Spradley, 1980, p. 9).

This view of culture as a set of *principles of practice* that members use to guide their actions with each other suggests that *cultures*, and by implication, *cultural knowledge*, are not fixed but are open to development, modification, expansion, and revision by members as they interact across time and events. Viewed in this way, ethnographers are concerned with developing a descriptive study of a group's customary ways of life at given points in time and from different points of view. Therefore, culture is not a variable or even a set of variables, but a set of practices and principles of practice that are constructed by members as they establish roles and relationships, norms and expectations, and rights and obligations that constitute membership in the local group. To identify these principles of practice, Spradley (1980) proposed a set of conceptual and semantic relationships among and between actors, social situations, and activity that the ethnographer uses as a guide but not a fixed model or "cookbook."

In a book on ethnography for high school students, Spradley and McCurdy (1972) argued that "Cultural knowledge is organized; we discover meaning by grasping the underlying pattern, the implicit frame of reference that people have learned" (p. 59). Cultural knowledge as learned and, at times, implicit has implications for research. The task of the ethnographer, then, is to uncover the ways in which members view their world; how they construct the patterns of life; and how through their actions (and interactions), they construct values, beliefs, ideas, and symbolic-meaningful systems.

---

[5]See for example, the discussion in the introduction to *The Anthropology of Experience* by Victor Turner and Edward Bruner, 1986. These perspectives often differ in how etic and emic descriptions are used, the goals that the ethnographer has, the intellectual community in which they claim membership, and the questions that they seek to explore among other factors that shape their *logic-in-use*.

[6]We use the term uncover rather than find or identify to maintain an archeological metaphor from anthropology. The patterns are constructed by members and the task of the ethnography is to make those visible, that is, to separate the figure from the ground and then to see how they are used in other situations of occurrence.

[7]For a discussion of a turn toward practices in the study of culture within anthropology, see Ortner, 1984.

[8]For more current views of Cognitive Anthropology see Agar, 1994; D'Andrade, 1995. For a theoretical discussion of an alternative to the cognitive anthropological perspective that has come to be known under the label, Symbolic Anthropology, see Geertz (1973), *Local Knowledge*. For critiques of cognitive anthropology see Geertz, 1973, 1983; Gilbert, 1992, and Gilbert and Mulkay, 1984. For a discussion of the critiques of Spradley in education, see Kelly, Chen, and Crawford, 1998.

Central to the task as specified by Spradley (1980; Spradley & McCurdy, 1972) is the need to identify how members of a social group *name* and *categorize* their world. Thus, ethnographers who are guided by Spradley's perspective may begin with what he called a *grand tour* of the local setting or social world of the group to identify who the actors are, with whom they interact, when, where, under what conditions, and with what outcomes. This tour enables the ethnographer to examine the spaces, times, objects, events, acts, and chains of activity, among other aspects, that form a ground for subsequent analyses. By engaging in a process of developing initial categories that members of the group use, the ethnographer identifies ways members name their activities, spaces, actors, objects (artifacts), and interactions with actors, thus locating emic or insider categories. This approach enables ethnographers, wherever possible, to avoid imposing their own etic or outsider categories on what they observed. The exception to this approach comes when members do not have a "name" for the observed practice, activity, or cultural phenomenon. At such points, the ethnographer develops an etic term that *describes* the observed cultural phenomenon.

The analysis from this phase of data collection sets the stage for a more focused examination of particular cultural practices, events, or processes. This focusing process is based on a set of principled decisions that enable the ethnographer to move closer to an emic understanding of the patterns of life within the group. Just what will be observed in this phase depends on what members indicate, through their actions, are culturally marked or significant phenomena to examine, not on what the researcher initially planned. This process continues until the ethnographer has sufficient information to identify principles of practice. This process of focusing, Spradley (1980) calls a *developmental research process* or what we (and others) refer to as the *interactive-responsive process* of ethnography. Such responses are an anticipated part of the ethnographers plan from the outset.

Once data are collected at each stage of the research process, Spradley (1980) proposes a domain analysis approach for examining these data. This approach entails constructing a set of part-whole relationships through the consideration of a set of semantic relationships: *x is a kind of y; a place for y; a step in y; a reason for y; a way of doing y; an outcome of y, among others*. The domain analyses form the basis for constructing taxonomies of cultural terms, practices, and processes. (See Fig. 16.3 later in this chapter for an example of a taxonomy). The goal is not merely to categorize the world, but to construct a cultural "grammar" that may be used by the ethnographer and others in the group without breaking cultural norms and expectations or roles, and relationships, while appearing to meet the rights and obligations of membership. The goal is not to go "native" but to be able to make visible the cultural practices and principles of practice to others who are not members of that group. To accomplish this goal, the ethnographer seeks ways of identifying what members need to know, use, produce, and predict to guide their participation in their everyday world. This approach, therefore, requires a reflexive and recursive approach by the ethnographer, not merely a single instance of identification of a practice.

There are a number of implications of this approach to the study of culture that need to be considered in planning as well as conducting an ethnographic study in education. First, the notion of a developmental research process means that questions are generated and identified across time and events in response to data collection and analysis conducted at different points in the study, with different actors and in different places (spaces). Questions as well as phases and levels of data collection can be proposed in advance, with the understanding that the actual questions relevant to the study within *this* group, and the phases or levels of collection and analysis can only be defined *in the local setting* (in situ). Second, over time observations and participation in the ongoing community are necessary to begin to understand what *counts* as a relevant term, practice, activity, or event, and how participation is entailed within and across such events. Third, the position that the ethnographer takes in negotiating entry and in interacting in the setting is one of *learner*, who studies with people within a local group to seek cultural knowledge that is often implicit or invisible to members. Fourth, what the ethnographer learns can be triangulated with members to see if the analysis matches local cultural knowledge. If there is no match with the understandings of members, it may not mean that the ethnographer is wrong, although this may be a possibility. Since cultural knowledge is often tacit knowledge, by watching the responses of members, ethnographers can assess whether the person with whom they are sharing their interpretation was surprised by the findings, thus suggesting that he or she was unaware of the practice but now affirms the description of the practice as culturally possible (or impossible). Each of these responses can lead to new data collection (e.g., interviewing others) and analyses to assess the adequacy of the description and to clarify, modify, and/or revise the understandings.

One reason that further study may be required is that the person with whom the ethnographer is speaking may not have access to or be aware of the cultural practice, the knowledge required, or the processes involved. This state-of-affairs comes from the fact that *no individual* holds all cultural knowledge; cultural knowledge is of a group, and individuals, depending on what cultural activities and practices they have access to, will have *particular knowledge* of *particular aspects* of a culture. Thus, an ethnographer cannot rely on a single informant to assess the adequacy of the interpretations of the data. Multiple points of view or perspectives are needed. For example, a teacher or group of teachers may not have access to all knowledge about the workings of a school. A principal may not have all knowledge either, but the knowledge that he or she does have will differ from that of the teacher(s) in particular ways, given the rights and obligations of each position. The teacher(s) and principal will not have the same knowledge as the office personnel, who help the teachers, administrators, and community (i.e., parents and others). Further, students will have a particular range of knowledge constructed through their participation in the classroom, the peer group, the school, the home, and the community that differs from that of teachers, administrators, parents, and others. Singularly, each provides a situated view, one that is related to the roles and relationships, norms and expectations, and rights and obligations associated with the ways in which they are positioned within the school community. Collectively their knowledge constitutes a broader picture of cultural practices and processes of the school. However, the study of a single class or school provides only a situated perspective and a comparative approach is needed across different classes or schools to understand *what counts as schooling* within the broader society. Within anthropology, the comparative approach is called ethnology and serves as a basis for comparative generalizations (Hymes, 1996).

The existence of differential access, and thus a situated perspective,[9] is important to understand and to consider in writing a proposal or conducting an ethnographic research study. In the next section, we examine how differences in perspectives and understandings can be productive in the process of uncovering principles of practice across time and events as well as across cultural groups.

## Ethnography As Involving a Contrastive Perspective

In this section, we examine three ways in which a contrastive perspective informs the work of ethnographers: contrast as a basis for triangulating perspectives, data, method, and theory; contrastive relevance as a principled way of making visible emic processes and practices; and frame clashes and rich points as contrastive spaces for identifying cultural knowledge. Each of these ways of viewing what is entailed in a contrastive approach provides particular insights and allows the ethnographer to make visible different aspects and practices of a culture. Just which perspective an ethnographer will use will depend again on his or her approach to the study of culture and the goals of the research. The systematic use of contrastive analysis is one area in which those involved in ethnography *in* and *of* education have contributed theoretically and methodologically to ethnographic methods and to theories of cultural practices.

## Contrast As a Basis for Triangulating Perspectives, Data, Method, and Theory

Corsaro (1981; 1985) proposes four types of contrast that can be used within an ethnographic study: perspective, data, methods, and theory. These types of contrast form the basis for triangulation. Central to the idea of triangulation is the notion that in juxtaposing different perspectives, data, methods, and theories, the ethnographer will be able to make visible the often invisible principles of practice that guide members' actions, interactions, production of artifacts, and construction of events and activity of everyday life.

As discussed in the previous section, juxtaposing perspectives within a setting provides information that the study from one perspective cannot reveal. While such juxtapositions often involve use of different types of data, methods, or theories, using *perspective* as *the point of contrast* makes visible the differences in types of knowledge and access afforded members of a community. It also allows the researcher to identify new sites and

groups to observe so that the repertoire of cultural practices needed by different members of the group can be identified and the consequences of the differences in positions can be explored within and across groups, times, events, and spaces.

To illustrate how triangulation of perspective, data, method, and theory is productive for theory generation, we present an example from the work of Judith Solsken (1992). Solsken contrasted reading in the home with reading across years of schooling in order to construct a literacy biography for individual students and to identify what counted as literate practices in each setting. By contrasting who could read what, when, where, with whom, under what conditions, and for what purposes, she was able to identify patterns in each site (child's room, family homework session, kindergarten and second grade class with female teacher, and first grade class with a male teacher). Thus, she used contrast of practices across actors, times, events, and sites to construct a grounded argument about why one boy in kindergarten said, "No words for me."

She argued on the basis of her observations in the boy's home that he saw literacy as "women's work," since his mother and older sisters were the ones that he observed reading. Because her visits occurred at different points in time across the year before he entered school, she was able to construct a picture of the patterns of literacy work among family members. The father's role in literacy work was not visible to her, leading her to link the boy's comments in the following year (his kindergarten year) to the observed pattern of literacy as gendered work. Additionally, since she traced the boy's literacy development across 3 years of schooling, she was able to see how he responded to a male teacher in first grade as well as to his female teachers (kindergarten and second grade). It was not until he had a male teacher that his engagement in literacy practices in the classroom shifted, and he took up the opportunities for reading and other forms of literacy work more fully.

On the basis of this contrastive analysis, Solsken (1992) argues that

Luke's pattern of categorizing reading and writing by social relations continued into second grade. The major observable change was in his response to having a female teacher again. He did not resist Mrs. Benedict in conferences as he had in kindergarten, but he also did not seek her attention or support as he had Mr. Sullivan's The result was that he devoted more of his attention and energy to peer interaction and to his own interests (p. 179).

The over time look allowed her to build a grounded biography that made visible multiple sources of influence on the student's valuing of literacy as well as what he was willing to take up and display at particular points in time.

In following this student and other across time, Solsken (1992) engaged in all four types of contrast identified by Corsaro (1985) in order to construct a more comprehensive grounded theory of literacy learning and how it is related to other types of learning, including gender and work. Solsken contrasted different theories of literacy in the early years (e.g., emergent literacy, the social construction of literacy, literacy as social status and

---

[9]For a discussion of a situated perspective on literacy learning see Heap, 1991 and others in the volume edited by Baker and Luke (1991), *Toward a critical sociology of reading pedagogy.*

identity) to develop an orienting framework for her study. Her orienting framework built on the work of Anderson, Teale, and Estrada (1980) and Heath (1983) in which literacy events were identified by observing actions and interactions with and about written texts. However, Solsken's contrastive analysis of the ways in which beginning reading had been approached and her initial analyses of her data led to the identification of a "missing" perspective, the role of individual agency in the take up of cultural resources. This way of conceptualizing literacy learning, once identified, became both an orienting theory and an explanatory framework that guided her subsequent questions, methods selection, data collection, and analysis approaches, as well as her interpretation of the data. Her data showed the agency of the child within and across literacy situations[10] and led her to new a conceptualization and explanation of what is entailed in learning to be literate:

each and every literacy transaction is a moment of self-definition in which people take action within and upon their relations with other people. From this perspective, literacy learning would rarely be expected to proceed smoothly or without tension.

The major argument of this book is that the study of beginning literacy in families and in schools must start with the assumption that literacy learning is such a self-defining social act. Adopting this assumption requires that we view children as acting within and upon larger social systems. We tend to associate childhood with innocence, future potential, or even victimization in relation to those systems, but not with agency and choice (p. 8).

Solsken was able to explore the issue of agency, the "missing" perspective, by contrasting data for each individual and for the group across actors, times, events, and sites. She contrasted perspectives (e.g., child reading alone *with* family reading practices in the home) and methods (e.g., videotape records with field notes, prompted literacy activities, interviews, and artifacts). These contrasts enabled her to identify when, where, and under what conditions reading and writing occurred, how it occurred, who participated, and how members viewed and/or understood and valued such practices. Thus, a strategy of contrastive analysis was a central part of her study of literacy at home and at school.

Without the explicit use for multiple forms of contrast, much of the information she obtained would not have been visible and would have constrained her interpretations and understandings of the patterns within the data. This would have led to a more impoverished view of the complexity of literacy practices and literacy learning available to, and taken up by, the individual students she followed across years of schooling. It would also have left unexamined the child's role and agency in the construction of literacy learning. It was not solely the lack of opportunity that led to the student's performance, since a broad range of opportunities were available in the larger social contexts of home and school, but rather, the individual's agency in valuing particular practices at particular points in time.

Her contrastive analyses, therefore, made visible multiple types of emic knowledge, each related to different actors and social situations. Types of knowledge included knowledge of practices as represented in the actions of family members; in the actions and interactions of class members and their teachers; and in the actions of individuals within and across different actors, situations, and times. Additionally, by contrasting different theoretical perspectives she was able to add to the field's understanding of early literacy by making visible the relationships between opportunities for learning and individual take up of such opportunities as well as the contribution of gendered practices to such learning. Thus, for Solsken (1992), triangulation was a key principle of practice that guided her *logic-in-use*.

## Contrastive Relevance As a Principled Way of Making Visible Emic Processes and Practices

Hymes (1977) proposed the concept of contrastive relevance as a principle of practice of ethnographers. He argues that the use of contrastive analysis provides a means of demonstrating functional relevance of the bit of life, or language and actions within that bit. Contrastive relevance, therefore, provides a way of examining and identifying what counts as cultural knowledge, practice, and/or participation constituting a particular "bit of life" within a group. In discussing contrastive relevance and its value to education, Hymes argues that:

We cannot adequately evaluate language development and the use of language that enters into education without attention to the principle of contrastive relevance—to the demonstration of functional relevance through contrast, showing that a particular change or choice counts as a difference within the frame of reference. . . . To discover what is there, what is happening, one seeks to discover what changes of form have consequences for meaning and choices of meaning lead to changes in form. One works back and forth between form and meaning in practice to discover the individual devices and codes of which they are a part (p. 92).

Defined in this way, contrastive analysis depends on analysis of the talk and actions among members from an emic perspective. As in triangulation, this task involves the constant use of contrast to build grounded interpretations. The use of contrastive relevance requires ethnographers to ground their analysis in the choices of words and actions members of the group use to engage with each other within and across actors, events, times, actions, and activity that constitute the social situations of everyday life. (See Gee & Green, 1998 for examples and an extended discussion of discourse analysis in relationship to reflexivity as a basis for contrast from an ethnographic perspective.)

## Rich Points and Frame Clashes As Contrastive Spaces for Identifying Cultural Knowledge

Previously, we discussed the ethnographic understanding that members may not have the same interpretation of all actions or events, given the issue of differential access to different aspects of the social life within a group. Agar (1994) proposes the concept of *rich points* to capture what is made visible through

---

[10]For a discussion of socialization of children that has agency of the child as a contributor to the development of society, see Gaskin, Miller, and Corsaro, 1992.

differences in the frames of reference (what Mehan, 1979, and others call *frame clashes*). For Agar (1994), a rich point can occur within a group; it can happen when visiting a new place; or it can occur when the ethnographer's cultural resources and background do not allow him or her to see and understand the actions and activity within the social group under study from an emic perspective. A rich point, he argues, is a place where *culture happens*. That is, at such points, the ordinary is made extraordinary, since the actor(s) can no longer proceed as usual.

Rich points in an ethnography, therefore, are points at which the differences in understanding, action, interpretation, and/or participation become marked. At such points, the cultural practices and resources that members draw on become visible in their efforts to maintain participation. Two examples of rich points and what each made visible will be presented. The first comes from the work of Green and Harker (1982). In an analysis of an event in a kindergarten classroom called "News & Views" from a year-long ethnography, Green and Harker describe how one of the students read only some of the cues to the activity and not the full range available. In describing the unfolding event, they identified James as reading two sets of cues but not a third set. Their analysis showed that his actions indicated that he viewed the talk as being about a classroom event called News and Views, and that everyone would get a turn to share. However, James' actions showed that he did not read the event as one that was talking about *what we* do *in News & Views*, or as an introduction to that event. Rather, his actions showed that he had read the task as *doing News & Views*; that is, he began to share something. The teacher's statement, "Excuse me, James" and her actions of continuing to present what the task would be to members of the class told James that what they were doing was not News and Views but *getting ready* to do News and Views. Through discourse analysis of pronominal reference, propositional ties present and past reference to activities, events, and actions, and Green and Harker (1982) argue that James was drawing on prior cultural knowledge to take action but not on the action that was under construction. Thus, James anticipated the event that would take place next and acted as if he were in that event.

The contrast between James' actions and the teacher's expectations for action formed a rich point that signaled to James, and other group members, just what was expected and how James, and by implication others, were to participate. It made visible to others in the group, as well as to the ethnographers, what actions were relevant in the local moments. Contrastive analysis of this moment with previous ones provided a basis for understanding the cultural knowledge that James drew on to guide his attempt to begin sharing, i.e., that he would be the first to share given his position in the circle. Further analysis showed that James often invoked norms for participation on the group, e.g., "talk one at a time" even if he did not follow the norms. Thus, James' actions are understandable through contrastive relevance, both in the moment and over time.

The second example is drawn from a year-long ethnography by Tuyay and her colleagues (Tuyay, 1999; Tuyay, Jennings, & Dixon, 1995), who show how rich points are part of a process of shaping opportunities for learning in a bilingual classroom.

While they provide a number of examples to build an understanding of how *opportunities for learning* are constructed in classrooms and how individual actors take up the opportunities in particular ways, one example will be presented here. This example focuses on a small group of students (3 boys), one a bilingual speaker who acknowledged his bilinguality, one a bilingual speaker who preferred to be viewed as an English speaker, and one Spanish dominant speaker. The three boys were working on a collaborative writing project in which they were to compose a fictional planet story. The event was part of a 33-day cycle of activity focusing on the solar system in a variety of ways. This event occurred approximately two thirds of the way through this cycle of activity and was one of the first opportunities in which students were to write fiction based on scientific fact (see also Tuyay, 1999).

As the teacher approached the small group, she noticed that only two of the boys were involved, given that the talk was all in English. The Spanish dominant student was watching but not participating in the composing process. Using Spanish, she asked the group whether the boy who only spoke Spanish knew what they were doing. One of the boys speaking English answered in Spanish that he [meaning the Spanish dominant speaker] was "only playing." In response to this, the teacher asked the boys again in Spanish "¿Cómo puede decir ideas si no sabe lo que está escribiendo? ¿Es possible?" (How can he tell you ideas if he doesn't know what you are writing? Is that possible?) They answered "no" and she then asked "¿Entoncesqué puedes hacer tú?" (So what can you do?). What followed was a shift in language, both oral and written, to include Spanish. The final product the three boys produced was bilingual in form and substance with the Spanish dominant student contributing the illustrations for the story.

This brief exchange (approximately 30 seconds) between the teacher and the three students was a rich point in two ways. First, it made visible to the boys (and the ethnographer) that both languages were a resource for academic work and that the choice of language by two of the students (the bilingual students who chose to speak English) served to exclude one member of the group. Second, because the teacher elected to use Spanish in speaking to the group, it became a rich point in which the three students had an opportunity to clarify the task, as well as the roles and relationships and norms and expectations among members. These actions enabled them to take up new positions as participating members of the group. It also provided an opportunity to revisit classroom rights and obligations for participation and to revise the activity to include all, a right *and* obligation.

Both examples show how rich points are places where the norms and expectations, roles and relationships, and rights and obligations for group membership and participation become visible to members as well as to ethnographic observers. Without such rich points, both researchers and members alike would not have had an opportunity to learn about what *counts as membership* and *appropriate participation*. Further, the second example suggests that issues of access are constructed locally and not just at a macro level by school systems. These examples show how small actions among members may have large consequences for participants, and how actions make visible what counts as appropriate participation and cultural practice. Without contrasting the patterns of discourse and activity across time and events, the nature of these brief interactions as being rich points would not have been visible. Thus, rich points involve examination of what is occurring in the moment and then contrasting the observed moment with what has been seen in similar events across times and actors. In this way the present and historical contexts of actions are part of the ethnographic analysis. Ethnography, therefore, involves a part–whole approach to building a grounded theory of activity and meaningful symbolic systems.

## Ethnography Involves a Holistic Perspective

The problem for those seeking to understand the nature of part–whole relationships within an ethnography is one of understanding what is meant by the term "whole." Some ethnographers argue that "whole" refers to the community level (e.g., Lutz, 1981; Ogbu, 1974), while others argue that "whole" does not equate with size but with the identification of a "bounded" social unit (Erickson, 1977; Gee & Green, 1998). Erickson (1977), for example, argues that ethnographic work is "holistic," not because of the size of the social unit, but because the units of analysis are considered analytically as wholes, whether that whole be a community, a school system . . . or the beginning of one lesson in a single classroom" (p. 59).

Holistic, in this instance, does not mean that a single event can be analyzed and then reported as an ethnography. Nor that a unit of analysis can be viewed as a variable (e.g., culture as a variable, a cultural practice as a variable) that can then be counted and used in a statistical equation. Rather, it means that the analysis must consider how the individual parts relate to the broader whole (e.g., beginnings of other lessons, other aspects of lessons, other aspects of classroom life, and beginnings of other types of speech events outside of the classroom). Thus, an individual event may be analyzed in depth to explore and identify the cultural demands or elements of the event (e.g., the ways in which it is accomplished, the social and academic demands for participation, the roles and relationships among members, and the communicative requirements for participation). However, the exploration will not stop with the analysis of the individual event. Rather, the information obtained from this analysis will be used as the basis for the exploration of other aspects of the culture or phenomenon. In this way, a "piece of culture" can be examined in depth to identify larger cultural issues and elements.

The notion of holistic has methodological implications for the study of everyday life in cultural contexts (e.g., school, home, church, and playground). Observations made of individual "wholes" are compared to other similar wholes and to larger wholes within the group under study. For example, an ethnographer might elect to study reading within the social unit called classroom. Once this decision has been made, the ethnographer would then need to observe the period of classroom life called "reading" by the participants, as well as all other classroom activities to identify the embedded nature of "reading" in other types of events (Green & Meyer, 1991). (For a discussion of how this process works in mathematics, see Moschkovich & Brenner, 2000; and in science, Kelly & Crawford, 1997).

To explore the nature of "reading" in the everyday life-world, or culture, of the classroom, the ethnographer would need to examine the beginning and ending boundaries of events as defined by the actions of the participants in the local setting. Once the boundaries of events are established, the ethnographer would then explore what occurs within the events, both those defined as reading and those in which reading is embedded. These analyses would then be undertaken for a complete cycle of activity. A cycle of activity in a classroom would be a series of purposefully tied events (e.g., completed lessons that form a "unit" of instruction. Unit is used here to refer in an analytic sense of tied events, not in a curriculum sense of a predefined set of instructional activities, although the two may overlap.) The length or boundaries of a cycle depend on how this aspect of culture is defined by the participants and not on predetermined criteria set by the ethnographer. Thus, while *reading* as an activity in the daily life of the classroom might occur throughout the year, it is also composed of *cycles of activity* (e.g., instruction) within the larger whole. Further, within cycles of activity other than those officially labeled as reading, the ethnographer would identify a broad range of literate practices that count as reading in and across disciplines, events, actors, and times. These cycles can be explored in their own right and then the findings compared across instances of occurrence to obtain a more "comprehensive" understanding of "what counts as reading" in the local context for the local participants. (For examples of this type of analysis see the Santa Barbara Classroom Discourse Group, 1992a; 1992b.) In addition, once a unit of observation is determined within the local setting, the ethnographer can take a more focused look at how the local event(s) are accomplished withing reading in the classroom (e.g., contrast high group reading practices with low group reading practices). The focus will depend on the question being explored. The ethnographer might then select a "representative" event and contrast the social and academic demands and structure of the events. (See, for example, Collins, 1987; Cook-Gumperz, 1986; Egan-Robertson, 1998; Erickson, 1982; Rex, Green, & Dixon, 1997; and Rex & McEachen, 1999.)

The part–whole approach to the study of reading from a sociocultural perspective differs from those of other perspectives in which the definition of reading is assumed prior to entry into the context of the study or is assumed to be stable across all instances of occurrence. While the ethnographer may elect to focus on reading and may derive information from the literature about the nature of reading in classroom contexts, the ethnographer will not begin with a preset definition of "reading." Rather, the ethnographer will examine whether participants in the social group have an event called "reading." He or she will then explore how it is accomplished, what counts as reading, when and where it occurs, who can participate, what functions and purposes it serves, and what the outcomes are of participating in the events called reading (e.g., Bloome & Bailey, 1992; Gee, 1996; Heap, 1991). In instances where the cultural group does not have a "formal" event called reading, the ethnographer will make *principled decisions* about how to locate instances of reading in the group under study. The

| TIMELINE OF THE OVERALL ETHNOGRAPHY | | |
|---|---|---|
| Academic Year One | **Academic Year Two** | Academic Year Three |

| CONCEPTUAL PHYSICS: SCIENCE PROJECTS | | | | | | | |
|---|---|---|---|---|---|---|---|
| Project | 1 | 2 | 3 | 4 | 5 | 6 | 7 |
| Dates | 09/07/95-09/29/95 | 10/02/95-10/23/95 | 10/26/95-11/02/95 | **11/06/95-11/21/95** | 11/29/95-12/15/95 | 12/18/95-12/22/95 | 01/08/96-01/22/96 |
| Project topic | Catapult | Circular Motion Space Travel Projectile Motion | Solar Energy | **Musical Instruments** | Optics | History of the Atom | Museum Project |
| Conceptual | Mechanics | Application of | Thermo- | **Sound waves** | Optics | Atomic energy | Enacted |

| MUSICAL INSTRUMENTS PROJECT: KEY EVENTS | | | | | | | | | |
|---|---|---|---|---|---|---|---|---|---|
| 11/06/95 | 11/07/95 | 11/08/95 | 11/09/95 | 11/13/95 | 11/15/95 | 11/16/95 | 11/17/95 | 11/20/95 | 11/21/95 |
| * Simple Harmonic Motion lecture<br>* Pendulum lab<br>* Discussion of graphs | * Graphing (whole class; groups)<br>* Wave lecture<br>* Film on waves | * Wave lecture<br>* Sound lab: turning fork & voice<br>* Demo of FFT<br>* Discussion of labs & projects | * FFT lecture with demo<br>* Sound lab: consonants & vowels | * Light lecture<br>* Sound lab: fundamental & harmonics<br>* Presentaion of lab data | * Review of test<br>* Chapter test<br>* **Intro. of Musical Instrument project**<br>* Discussion of projects | * **Intro. to writing technical papers**<br>* Project time: construction of musical instruments | * Project time: construction of instruments; data collection | * Project time: data collection & measurements | * Preparation for presentation<br>* Student presentations of musical instruments<br>* Optics lecture |

* Kelly & Chen, 1999.

FIGURE 16.1. Timeline situating "Musical Instruments Project" in three years of Ethnography*.

principle of practice guiding this aspect of ethnographic analysis is the concept of part–whole relationships, guided by a practice-oriented perspective on culture. That is, by examining the local practices involving the production and interpretation of "text," the ethnographer constructs a situated view of what counts as literate practices in the local group across actors, times, events, and spaces (see Anderson, Teale, & Estrada, 1980; Barton, 1994; Bloome & Egan-Roberston, 1993; Heath, 1983; and Street, 1984, 1993; for a discussion of the issue of locating literacy events).

The challenge facing the ethnographer in writing about such part–whole relationships is one of finding a way to represent this aspect of the logic-in-use. To illustrate one of the ways in which part–whole relationships have been represented in recent work, we draw on research by Kelly and Chen (1999) who studied the construction of science as sociocultural practices in a high school physics class. Their study examined different dimensions contributing to the writing of a technical paper on the physics of sound (the Musical Instruments Project). These ethnographers used textual analysis of student papers to examine how students used evidence in their papers to make claims, and discourse analysis of how students appropriated and used the scientific practices and content available within and across cycles of activity. Figure 16.1 is their representation of the part–whole relationships from their published article.

As indicated in Fig. 16.1, Kelly and Chen used three levels of mapping to situate the project analyzed, The Musical Instruments Project, in the ongoing academic year, and within the ongoing ethnography (a 3-year study). Each of the three *maps*, while representing different periods of time, provides increasing detail from the Timeline of the Overall Ethnography (Map 1) to the Key Events (Map 3). The *Key Events Map* shows the greatest detail by describing the general range of activity within the Musical Instruments Project and the emic names for types of events within this cycle of activity. Together, the three maps locate when in time[11] particular events occurred and present a general statement about what was undertaken at each point in time. This form of graphic representation makes visible key part–whole relationships that were considered in the analysis and provides evidence of the data used as a basis for interpretation. Thus, this approach to representing relationships among the parts makes visible the *logic-in-use* of these ethnographers for both the larger project and the particular analysis presented in the article. Further, it lays a foundation for understanding important interactive and responsive decisions made in selecting this event as the focus for this article.

---

[11] The concept of being "in time" builds on the argument by Adam (1990) that people within a social group construct time(s) and that it is culturally appropriate to speak of "times" and not "time" in some abstract sense.

## Ethnographic Fieldwork Involves an Interactive–Responsive Approach

As discussed previously, ethnography is not the linear process that is generally associated with many forms of educational research, in which all decisions about a study are made prior to beginning data collection, and analyses are not undertaken until all data are collected. Rather, ethnography is a dynamic, interactive–responsive approach to research, involving a reflexive disposition and a recursive process. Through this process, questions are generated, refined, and revised, and decisions about entry into new settings and access to particular groups, as well as data collection and analysis, are made as new questions and issues arise in situ that need to be addressed.

Central to this reflexive process are the key theoretical and conceptual principles presented previously that guide the ethnographer's research practices. These principles form an *orienting theory* that the ethnographer uses to initiate a project, to take action throughout the project, and to analyze data on which claims about cultural practices will be made. Further, as indicated previously, an ethnographic project entails a developmental research approach that cannot be completely preplanned but that constitutes the basis for the design of the study that emerges from the decisions made across times and events. Additionally, we argue that this process and the emergent design are the result of the reflexive nature of ethnography as well as the ethnographer's logic-in-use. Such changes are an anticipated part of this reflexive, responsive, and contrastive process.

In this section, we revisit this process and explore further how the interactive–responsive approach shapes and reshapes the direction that a study takes. As part of this discussion, we will present a way of graphically representing the logic-in-use, so that decisions about question–theory–method relationships can be made accessible to readers of ethnographically-based research. We argue that the principles that frame the logic of inquiry within cultural anthropology and ethnography of communication form an orienting theory to a *practice-oriented study of culture* that entails a contrastive and reflexive approach, part–whole, relationships, and a holistic perspective.

This framework enables the researcher to enter a context, to ask "what's happening here" in order to unearth or uncover what counts to participants (an emic perspective), and to "bracket" their own cultural expectations about what will occur or what they will "find" (an etic perspective). (For a discussion of how context is viewed across different theoretical perspectives, see Duranti & Goodwin, 1992.) From this orienting theory, culture is not found, it is constructed and written through the theoretical and methodological decisions and actions of the ethnographer as he or she interacts with those within the social group (cf., Clifford & Marcus, 1986; for a discussion in Sociology see Atkinson, 1990). Through these processes and practices, the ethnographer *learns about what counts* to members as relevant issues, processes, practices, events, times, spaces, and values. It also enables the ethnographer to examine who has access to each "bit of life," when, where, under what conditions, with whom, using what artifacts, and with what outcomes. As indicated previously, these decisions and the resultant actions of the ethnographer constitute the ethnographer's *logic-in-use*.

Further, and perhaps critically relevant to education, such actions provide the ethnographer with resources to *learn about the consequences for members* of the patterns of interaction within and across times, actors, events, and practices. Thus, ethnographic research goes beyond *mere description* to ask about the impact on members of their participation in local communities of practice, whether a lesson, a small reading group, a class, a school, or other social institution (e. g., family, peer culture, social clubs, gangs, or religious organizations). As part of this discussion, we draw distinctions among *doing ethnography, adopting an ethnographic perspective*, and *using ethnographic tools* (Green & Bloome, 1983, 1995).

## Representing the Interactive–Responsive Approach as a Logic-in-Use

Decisions to modify the research design are *deliberate decisions* guided by the ethnographer coming to understand what is relevant to members of the group, not what his or her initial plan (or proposal) assumed to be relevant. From this perspective, as the researcher interacts with participants and data, it may become necessary to modify the research design in order to be responsive to the local context. Decisions to modify the initial design, to address new questions, and to seek new data are expected to occur (i.e., they are anticipated in the design), and are grounded in understandings of *what counts* to members obtained through sustained participant observation, and wherever possible, interviews and artifact analysis (see also Ellen, 1984 and Spradley, 1979, 1980). These decisions therefore are purposeful and deliberate. They enable the ethnographer to examine key issues not previously considered or understood to be necessary (e.g., LeCompte, Millroy, & Priessle, 1992; Hammersley & Atkinson, 1995; Heath, 1983; Spradley, 1980; Spindler, 1982).

Figure 16.2, drawn from the work of Castanheira, Crawford, Dixon, and Green (2001), illustrates how an emergent logic-in-use can be graphically represented. We selected this figure for inclusion for two reasons. First, it represents an interactive–responsive research process and makes visible the relationships of an overarching question to the sub-questions used to examine the broader issue, i.e., *what counts as literate practices within and across classes*. Second, it makes visible the decision frame used by these researchers across analyses. The decisions made within each phase of the research process are represented by three different sets of actions: *posing questions, representing data*, and *analyzing events*. The link between the different phases of analysis is represented by overlapping boxes. The overlap is purposeful in that the analysis of one phase leads to new questions, and thus to a new phase of analysis. By overlapping the boxes, these researchers show the interactive–responsive and reflexive nature of ethnographic analysis.

This approach to representing a researcher's or research team's *logic-in-use* can be used for a complete ethnography, or as illustrated here, can be used to take a more topic centered or focused look at the actions of members of a group

<u>Overarching Question:</u> **How can we understand the ways in which the literate practices are shaped, and in turn shape, the everyday events of classroom life, and thus, the opportunities that Simon (and his peers) had for learning?**

**Posing questions:** What events were constructed in these classes? Where, under what conditions, with whom, and with what outcome?

*Representing data:* Constructing time-stamped running record of chains of activity. Creation of two types of event maps. One including phase and sequence units, and one the construction of comparative timelines.

<u>Analyzing events:</u> Review of the comparative timeline to note the flow of activity in each class (Hospitality, Cooking, Machine Shop, English and Math), and to identify what time was spent on and by whom.

**Posing questions:** What did the physical "whole" of the literate environment look like within and across classes? Where was Simon (the focal studetnt) located within these environments?

*Representing data:* C-Video framegrab of each change of camera focus fo get a picture of shifting activity and the literary environment. Construction of comparative physical maps.

<u>Analyzing events:</u> Use of comparative maps to locate Simon in relationship to the group and compare the physical space and literate practices across classes.

**Posing questions:** What was the role of the workbook and other texts in framing the opportunities for learning?

*Representing data:* Domain analysis and taxonomy of the different forms of texts used and the ways in which they were used by teachers and students across classes.

<u>Analyzing events:</u> Comparative analyses of domains analyzed across subject area classes.

**Posing questions:** How was literacy talked and acted into being within and across classrooms? Who was responsible for the text constructed?

*Representing  data:* Transcribing talk into event maps including identifying who talks, contextualization cues, time, and phases of activity.

<u>Analyzing events:</u> Cross-case comparisons of activities and person(s) responsible for change in activity. Domain analysis and taxonomy construction to identify the types of practices across classes and the opportunities they afford.

**Posing questions:** What is the role of the individual in the sociocognitive activities identified?

*Representing data:* Construction of comparative/contradiction tables providing evidence of both the collective and individual practices within and across classes.

<u>Analyzing events:</u> Cross-case comparisons addressing teacher actions/practices that set up and; Simon's interactions across classes.

*Castaheira, Crawford, Dixon & Green, in press.

FIGURE 16.2. Logic of inquiry: Analytic process*.

(see Hymes, 1982; see also Gee & Green, 1998). Building on a distinction by Green and Bloome (1983, 1995), this approach can be viewed as adopting an *ethnographic perspective* that can be used to examine a "bit of life." The issue of concern, given the critical dialogues discussed previously, is the level of claim about cultural practices that can be made through such analyses. Just how an *ethnographic perspective* works to guide analysis of less than the "whole" but remains "holistic" is addressed in what follows. We elected to present this approach to illustrate

how an ethnographic logic-of-inquiry can orient researchers as they examine the artifacts or records of the everyday life of a social group, even when they cannot, or do not, engage in a full ethnographic study.

The data analyzed were obtained from a larger study of literacy across levels of post-secondary schooling by an Australian Team of researchers (Cumming & Wyatt-Smith, 2001). Portions of these data were sent to 10 research communities in different parts of the world, each representing a distinctive theoretical approach to the study of literacy as sociocultural and/or discursive processes. Members of the Santa Barbara Classroom Discourse Group were invited to participate in this comparative study of research approaches. However, since the data sent to each group did not constitute a full ethnography, but rather selected data (1 day) from a larger study, it is important to understand how an ethnographic perspective guided the general approach used by this group.

The Santa Barbara Classroom Discourse Group has developed an approach to *ethnography in education* that they call Interactional Ethnography (Green & Dixon, 1993; Putney, Green, Dixon, Durán, & Yeager, 2000; Santa Barbara Classroom Discourse Group, 1992a; 1992b). This approach usually requires the over time (1 or more years) study of a social group through the integration of ethnography, guided by cultural anthropological theories, and discourse analysis guided by sociolinguistic and interpretive theories of language in use. However, as will be illustrated, this approach makes possible the study of less than the whole community or pattern of life across times and events. By adopting the orienting theories of ethnography and sociolinguistics, the team was able to examine the life inscribed in the words and actions of members of a social group recorded as the "bit of life" on a videotape (see also Gee & Green, 1998).

The data sent to each research community represented a particular postsecondary education population. The Santa Barbara Classroom Discourse Group[12] received artifacts produced by one student on a single day across five of his classes. These data included video records of the five classes, and "official" documents representing the program in which he was participating, the Technical and Advanced Further Education (T.A.F.E.) program (grades 11–12). This program does not exist in the U.S. context, and therefore, necessitated a request for further information in order to locate the videotape record of classroom life and other artifacts in the larger schooling process and to interpret the data from an *emic perspective*. Additionally, to understand how, and in what ways, the data from 1 day were *representative* or *illustrative* of the patterns of life on subsequent days within each class, the research team requested, and obtained, videotape records and artifacts from 2 additional days within the same time period. These data, therefore, formed a corpus that enabled the team to engage in comparative work across classes and across days, to examine what counted as literate practices in each class, and to identify what was *relevant* to do, understand, produce, and predict in the events of each class. Thus, they used an *orienting framework* that can be viewed as an *ethnographic perspective*.

As indicated in Fig. 16.2, their analyses began with an overarching question—*How can we understand the ways in which the literate practices are shaped, and in turn shape, the everyday events of classroom life, and thus, the opportunities that Aaron [the student on the videotapes] and his peers had for learning?* As the study progressed, each analysis raised new questions, which in turn, led to new analyses and interpretations of data. The first analysis involved parallel examination of each of the five classes to locate the events and actors and conditions and outcomes of each event.[13] The second analysis located what was available to be read within the physical space, an aspect that would not have been visible if the team focused solely on Aaron's actions. The literate practices inscribed in the physical world provided a link between local actions and the larger social world (e.g., Barton, 1994; Barton & Hamilton, 1998; Egan-Robertson & Bloome, 1998; Street, 1984). The third analysis examined the artifacts produced and/or available to Aaron as a resource for learning, and how they were used. This analysis brought curriculum designers into the classroom through the artifacts and made visible what counted as *disciplinary knowledge* to those who framed the courses (e.g., English, Hospitality, Mathematics, Food Technology, and Industry Studies: Metal). The fourth analysis examined the patterns of discourse and actions in the events recorded to explore how a particular or situated view of disciplinary knowledge (e.g., English or Mathematics) was talked and acted into being. This analysis involved consideration of how artifacts were used and referenced in the interactions within and across classes (i.e., discipline areas). The final analysis shifted the focus from examining the patterns of interaction at the group level to examining how and what Aaron did in relationship to the group activity and its consequences for him.

As represented in Fig. 16.2, the analyses were guided by the theoretical constructs presented in the previous sections. The team used a contrastive perspective to identify literate practices within and across events of each class and then examined similarities and differences in the practices across the five classes for one student. They explored part–whole relationships among events within a class and across events and days to examine how one event was or was not tied to others and how the practices constructed in one event supported and/or constrained participation in subsequent events. They used emic terms, wherever possible, and took an emic perspective in the analysis of discursive and literate practices to identify what counted as literacy learning or an opportunity to use literacy within and across classes. Figure 16.3 represents a taxonomy of literate practices associated with written texts identified through a domain analysis as suggested by Spradley (1980). This analysis enabled the team to make a *generalized claim* about how differences in instruction were tied to differences in the literate practices used by the teachers and how these were consequential in providing different opportunities for acquiring literacy

---

[12]Members of the Santa Barbara Classroom Discourse Group make a distinction between perspective (angle vision) and perception, what some individual person perceived. This distinction makes it possible to examine everyday activity from a particular point of view or angle of vision without claiming that any particular person held that view. In this way, they were able to take an emic perspective on data provided, without interviewing the participants directly.

[13]Teams of researchers (2–3 each) focused on one of the five classes (English, Mathematics, Hospitality, Food Technology and Industrial Studies: Metal). In addition to the authors of the article, researchers participating on the teams included: Julie Esch, Marli Costa Hodel, Cynthia Hughart, Pedro Paz, Nuno Sena, and Rosemary Staley. These researchers met over an extended period in the summer of 1997 to analyze the data and to explore how an ethnographic perspective could be applied to videotape analysis to make visible cultural practices from an emic perspective.

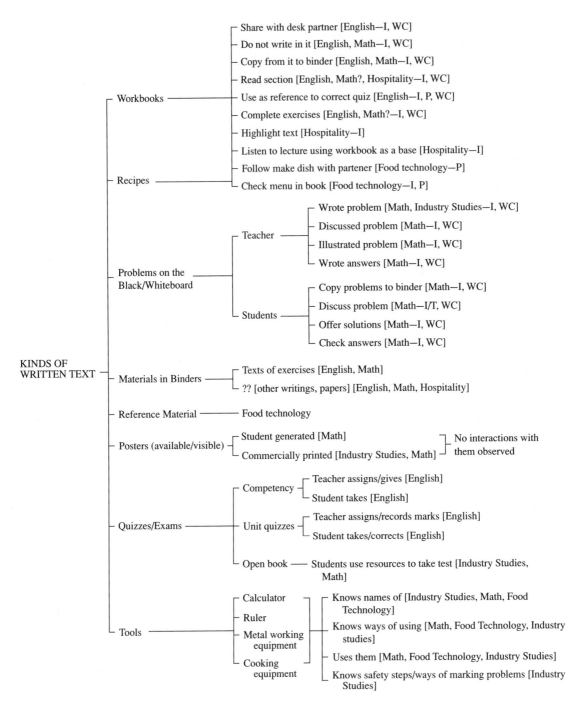

*Castanheira, Crawford, Dixon & Green, in press.
Key: I = Individual, P = pairs, WC = Whole Class, I/T = Individual with Teacher

FIGURE 16.3. Taxonomy of kinds of written texts: A comparative analysis across classes*.

associated with different disciplines. This comparative analysis provided a means of examining differences in access to academic knowledge provided by the actions of the teachers in each class.

Building on Erickson (1977) they viewed the subevents of each class period as constituting a whole. Additionally, they approached these subevents as creating a larger whole (an event) that was a *socially relevant* unit of life within the group. Their analysis, therefore, applied an ethnographic perspective that enabled them to examine who could do (know and/or say) what, to or with whom, using what artifacts, when and where, under what conditions, for what purposes, and with what outcomes. By asking these questions, they were able to identify, for the days they analyzed, the social and academic norms and expectations of group membership, the roles and relationships visible among members, and the rights and obligations entailed by group membership. Through these analyses, they were able to examine the literate practices and demands of each class and to engage in a cross-case analysis of literate practices across classes.

What Fig. 16.2 provides, then, is a representation of the logic-in-use that the research team used in their analyses. This way of representing the complex decisions makes visible to the reader how and why new analyses were needed to build a grounded understanding of the overarching question. These analyses also show how the team addressed the problem posed by the Australian researchers, *How does you research approach inform the study of literacy in classrooms?* By including Figs. 16.1, 16.2, and 16.3, we illustrate how researchers can make visible part–whole relationships, both within the community being studied and within a research project.

## Issues of Appropriateness of the Question and Criteria for Ethnographic Study

The previous sections focused on the principles of practice that constitute a logic of inquiry underlying an ethnographic study, how a researcher's logic-in-use can be represented, and the how it influences what can be known. In this section, we examine two final issues: what constitutes an appropriate ethnographic question and what criteria can be used to guide the development of an ethnographic study.

We begin this section with the assumption that the researcher has chosen a problem that can be examined ethnographically. For those not certain that their problem is appropriate for ethnography, we return to Athanases and Heath's (1995) distinction. They argue that

what was "good" ethnography established the expectation that the researcher would carry out fieldwork in the local language and represent *what was* within a group, and not *what was not* or *what was in need of change* from an outsider's perspective (p. 264).

From the anthropological perspective, ethnography, therefore, is not associated with intervention studies or definitions of what should be. Rather, ethnographic problems are ones that seek understanding of the cultural practices of members of a social group, how those practices shape access and distribution of resources among members within and across times and events, and what the consequences of membership and access are for members of a social group. To study a cultural group, therefore, is not to ask whether individuals are cultured, or if this group's culture leads to disadvantage in contrast to another group. Rather, to study a group *as a culture* is to ask questions about the practices and what they afford members. Just which cultural practices are examined and how they are studied is determined by the questions and problems of interest. For example, Hymes (1977), drawing on work from ethnography of communication, demonstrates how question formulation

within an ethnography differs when the concern is with *social life* rather than *language*. He makes visible this difference by proposing a series of questions from each point of view:

If one begins with social life, then the linguistic aspect of ethnography requires one to ask:

1. What are the communicative means, verbal and other, by which this bit of social life is conducted and interpreted?
2. What is their mode of organization from the standpoint of verbal repertoire or codes?
3. Can one speak of appropriate and inappropriate, better and worse, uses of these means?
4. How are the skills entailed by the means acquired, and to whom are they accessible?

If one starts from language, the ethnography of linguistic work requires one to ask:

1. Who employs these verbal means, to what ends, when, where, and how?
2. What organization do they have from the standpoint of the patterns of social life? (Hymes, as cited in Green & Bloome, 1983, pp. 16–17)

In formulating these differences, Hymes shows how the problem of study shapes the questions asked, and, in turn, the types of data required, as well as serves to foreshadow the types of analyses that will be undertaken. He also makes visible how an anthropological perspective can be used to address different types of questions, each from a particular angle of vision on cultural practices. (For a recent discussion of similar issues see Gee & Green, 1998.)

The importance of an anthropological perspective for educators, therefore, can be seen in the fact that it makes possible examination of the resources students bring to a classroom based on their participation in different cultural groups (e.g., other classrooms, community settings, families, peer groups, church groups, among others). It also makes it possible to understand that their performance in the current classroom draws on cultural knowledge obtained from these other groups. From this perspective, then, each individual brings a repertoire for action constructed by previous opportunities for learning social and academic practices within particular groups. For a discussion of a range of problems that have been addressed through an anthropological approach to ethnography in education, see Bloome (this volume), Green and Bloome, 1995, and Hymes (1996). For early work, see Cazden, John, and Hymes, 1972; Gilmore and Glatthorn, 1982; Green, 1983; Green and Wallat, 1981; and Spindler, 1982.

Having discussed briefly the appropriateness of the problem, we now turn to a discussion of two sets of criteria for engaging in ethnographic research, one proposed in Spindler and Spindler (1987) and one by McDermott (1976). While many have written on this subject, Spindler and Spindler (1987) provide a clear set of criteria closely related to the principles of ethnography presented previously. The 10 criteria can be thought of as part of the logic-of-inquiry of an anthropological approach to ethnography-in-education that the ethnographer needs to consider in planning and undertaking an ethnography.

1. Observations are contextualized, both in the immediate setting in which behavior [action][14] is observed and in further contexts beyond that context, as relevant.
2. Hypotheses emerge in situ, as the study goes on in the setting selected for observation. Judgment on what may be significant to study in depth is deferred until the orienting phase of the field study has been completed. (We assume that the researcher will have searched the literature and defined the "problem" before beginning fieldwork, however much the problem may be modified, or even discarded, as field research proceeds.)
3. Observation is prolonged and repetitive. Chains of events are observed more than once to establish the reliability of observations.
4. The native view of reality is attended through inferences from observation and through the various forms of ethnographic inquiry (including interviews and other eliciting procedures).
5. Sociocultural knowledge held by social participants makes social behaviors [actions] and communication sensible. Therefore, a major part of the ethnographic task is to elicit that knowledge from informant–participants in as systematic a fashion as possible.
6. Instruments, codes, schedules, questionnaires, agenda for interviews, and so forth should be generated in situ as a result of observations and ethnographic inquiry.
7. A transcultural, comparative perspective is present though frequently as an unstated assumption. That is, cultural variation over time and space is considered a natural human condition. All cultures are seen as adaptations to the exigencies of human life and exhibit common as well as distinguishing features.
8. Some of the sociocultural knowledge affecting behavior [actions] and communication in any particular setting being studied is explicit or tacit, not known to some native and known only ambiguously to others. A significant task of ethnography is therefore to make what is implicit and tacit explicit.
9. Since the informant (any person being interviewed) is one who knows and who has the emic, native cultural knowledge, the ethnographic interviewer must not predetermine responses by the kinds of questions asked. The management of the interview must be carried out so as to promote the unfolding of emic cultural knowledge in it most heuristic, *natural* form. This form will often be influenced by emotionally laden preoccupations that must be allowed expression.
10. Any form of technical device that will enable the ethnographer to collect more live data—immediate, natural, detailed behavior [actions]—will be used, such as cameras, audiotapes, videotapes and field-based instruments (Spindler & Spindler, 1987, pp. 18–20).

In framing these criteria, the Spindlers show that the ethnographer does not enter the field without theory, or as a "blank slate" but rather enters in an informed way, while leaving himself or herself open to modifying and revising his or her understandings based on ethnographic analysis and experience. Additionally, they describe an ethnographer as grounded in prior research that guides the initial problem formulation. They also argue that the problem itself, not only method, can and is often modified, revised, or even abandoned based on ethnographic analysis and consideration of what the data show to be culturally relevant or significant. Further, they indicate that decisions about field methods, tools, and schedules of data collection are principled ones, responsive to the needs of the ethnographer as defined in situ. They also make visible the anthropological understanding that *culture* is of a group, not held by any individual. In fact, they argues that some individuals may not have access to particular cultural knowledge, or may have only partial knowledge. The cumulative picture of ethnography that emerges from these criteria, and from the discussion of the principles guiding an anthropological *logic-of-inquiry* is one of a *systematic, conceptually driven* approach to the study of the sociocultural practices and processes of a group. It also demonstrates that the mere use of field methods does not constitute an ethnography or entail an ethnographic perspective. (For a recent discussion of these issues, see Hymes, 1996.)

The criteria proposed by Spindler and Spindler (1987) address the overall conduct of an ethnographic study. However, they do not provide criteria that specify how an ethnographic description of practices can be developed. While different theoretical perspectives within an anthropological approach may vary in the ways in which they identify patterns of practice, McDermott (1976, as cited in Green & Bloome, 1983) argues that ethnographic descriptions need to articulate:

1. How members of a group, through words or gestures, formulate a context.
2. How members act out a context in form as well as content.
3. How contexts are behaviorally oriented to or patterned by members at certain significant times.
4. How members hold each other accountable (p. 15).

These criteria, like those of Hymes (1977) previously presented, hold the researcher accountable to the actions of members and to constructing a *grounded* interpretation of the social and cultural practices from an emic perspective. (See also, Duranti & Goodwin, 1992.) In other words, the ethnographer uses members' actions and words to make visible the patterns of activity and to frame his or her interpretation of what counts as membership and participation within and across time and events for the group being studied. This approach is also referred to as a *situated perspective* (Heap, 1991).

This discussion of criteria shows that within the intellectual ecology of those who engage in ethnography from an anthropological perspective, there are standards of description and accountability that define what *counts as an appropriate account* as well as *appropriate ways* of collecting and analyzing data. These criteria also suggest ways of understanding further

---

[14]We have inserted the term action in brackets wherever behavior is used by Spindler and Spindler because we see what people do with each other as intentional and, for some theories of behavior, behavior does not include or mean intentional actions.

TABLE 16.1. The Research Proposal: Categories and Questions Guiding Decisions

| Categories for Inclusion | Purpose of the Study | Questions Guiding Decisions |
|---|---|---|
| Framing the study | Purpose and rational for the study<br>This category reflects the information and decisions made in framing a study. | What will be studied?<br>What is the rationale for engaging in this study?<br>What issues, interests, or concerns will this study address?<br>What is the educational significance of the proposed study? |
| | Locating the study in the field<br><br>This category reflects the information and decisions made in locating a study in the field. | What information or literature exists from studies in similar cultural settings?<br>What information exists about the processes or phenomena that will be observed (e.g., language, discourse, literacy, language arts, classroom processes, schooling, curriculum, etc)?<br>How do you conceptualize the phenomena to be examined? And, how does it match or vary from existing conceptualizations?<br>What theoretical perspective(s) will you use to guide your research? And, why are they appropriate? |
| Designing the study | Describe population parameters<br>This category includes a description of the group to be studied and the site of the study. | Who will you study? And, why?<br>When and where?<br>Under what conditions? |
| | Describe ways you gained access<br><br>This category includes types of involvement and/or contact you have had or plan to have with the group being studied, as well as the negotiated or social contract that will guide your work with members. | What types of involvement and/or contact have you had with the group that will be studied?<br>What steps will you take to gain access and entry to the group you plan to study (e.g., access to homes, schools, public agencies, people, special ceremonies or service groups)?<br><br>Who will be your contact person (if appropriate)?<br>What type of social contract will you negotiate with the participants (e.g., What will they receive to participate? How will they participate? Will they receive services in return for participation?)<br>How will you address the ethical and human subjects issues (e.g., protection of participants, community)?<br>What types of formal permissions will be needed? How will they be obtained? |
| | Describe the role(s) you plan to assume in the ethnography | In what ways do you plan to study this social group, phenomena, and/or cultural practice?<br>Will you have a co-investigator who is a member of the group or will you need to establish a local consultant, key informant, or advisory group from the local social group?<br>In what ways will you participate in the settings? Which of the following roles will you assume, and why?<br><br>• participant observer<br>• observer participant<br>• interviewer<br>• insider or member of the group (e.g., teacher, specialist)<br><br>With which group in the setting will you be aligned or identified (e.g., students, teachers, administrators, visitors, parents) or will you craft a different role within the group?<br>How will the role(s) you adopt influence access to certain groups and information?<br>How will your role change over time, events, and actors?<br>How will gender issues that might influence access to information and particular settings be considered? |

(*Continued*)

TABLE 16.1. The Research Proposal: Categories and Questions Guiding Decisions (*Continued*)

| Categories for Inclusion | Purpose of the Study | Questions Guiding Decisions |
| --- | --- | --- |
| | Describe the tools and techniques that you plan to use to collect the data | Which of the following field methods (tools and techniques) do you plan to use in the study and how will they be used?<br><br>• field notes (descriptive, personal, theoretical, methodological)<br>• recording devices (e.g., audiotapes, videotapes, still photographs)<br>• interviews (e.g., formal, informal, structured, open-ended)<br>• surveys<br>• questionnaires<br>• artifacts (e.g., materials and objects found in the setting)<br>• types of observations (general, topic-focused, focused on an individual)<br>• natural experiments to explore specific observed phenomena in more "controlled" ways<br>• diaries (e.g., participant research)<br>• other |
| | Describe the schedule for data collection and analysis that you plan to use at the outset of the study | How will the data collection techniques be sequenced?<br><br>What timeline will you use for each type of data you plan to collect?<br>How will you index the data so that you can organize and retrieve information and begin analyses? Will you need:<br><br>• a system for cross referencing data (fieldnotes, videotapes, artifacts, interviews, diaries, experiments, photographs)?<br>• a system for transcribing fieldnotes and video/audiotapes?<br>• a way of recording events observed and the participants, topics, organizational structure, participation structure (constituent phases or major subparts of the event), roles and relationships of participants, content summary to permit data retrieval for comparative analysis within and across events in the study?<br>• time-date code added to your videotapes?<br><br>Will you use a computer data management system (e.g., Ethnograph, Notebook 2, File Maker, Qualog, Nudist, C-Video, or other technological tool)?<br>Do you have a plan for data analysis?<br>Will you do a "pilot" or protoanalysis to explore:<br><br>• theory–method–analysis relationships?<br>• whether the data you collect will provide you with the information needed to answer your questions?<br>• whether the scope and design of the study as initially planned is manageable and feasible?<br>• whether the types of data, length of time, placement of equipment, types of interviews possible, literature, and analysis strategies/techniques (e.g., domain analysis, linguistic/discourse analysis, statistical analysis, content analysis) are the most appropriate ones?<br><br>If you do not include a pilot or protoanalysis, provide a rationale for the theory–method relationships that you propose for data collection and analysis. |

the critiques presented previously and how ethnographic work is different from other forms of observational work, whether or not it involves participant observation or the use of field methods.

## A CLOSING AND AN OPENING: DEVELOPING AN ETHNOGRAPHIC PROPOSAL

We conclude this chapter, by proposing a framework to guide decision making involved in developing a proposal for ethnographic research that builds on the principles identified and on the interactive–responsive nature of ethnography. This framework will pose theory-method issues discussed in this chapter that need to be addressed when writing a proposal. We conclude with this framework to help readers take the next step to move from understanding to taking actions in ways that will enable them to become a members of the intellectual ecology in education we have called *ethnography-in-education*.

Table 16.1 represents the parts of an ethnographic proposal and the questions that researchers need to address as they develop their initial proposal. As indicated in this table, like any research proposal, the ethnographer needs to specify the problem of interest and how the problem is located within the field. These two actions establish the import of the problem, provide a rationale for its study and indicate what the researcher anticipates will be gained from engaging in the study of this issue, interest, or concern. While all studies include a design component, the design of an ethnographic study contains unique elements. Within any study you would describe the population parameters and the tools and techniques that you plan to use to conduct the study. However, in an ethnographic study in which you will be entering a social group to learn about its practices and processes, you will have additional steps and issues to address. These include issues of gaining access to the group, as well as to particular aspects of the cultural world of this group. As part of gaining access, you will also need to negotiate a social contract with the members, a contract that will be renegotiated throughout the developing ethnographic study. You will also need to consider the range of roles and relationships you will assume and/or negotiate at the beginning phase of the study, understanding that these will change across time and events.

Although all proposals will include a schedule for data collection and analysis as well as a description of these processes, and ethnographic study frames a *potential* schedule, one that you anticipate will be revised in situ as issues of cultural relevance of the proposed topic are examined. Viewed in this way, a proposal for an ethnographic study is a beginning point. This fact makes it imperative that the researcher maintain a decision log throughout the study so that the rationale for any changes can be provided and the logic-in-use can be reconstructed, and thus, made visible. Through these actions, the ethnographer in education can describe the theoretical and practical changes needed to address the overarching question from an emic or insider's perspective.

In taking these actions *and* in making visible the principled decisions that were made throughout the interactive-responsive process of the ethnography, the researcher presents a theoretical and methodological argument focusing on (a) how the study was undertaken, (b) why the method(s) were appropriate to use given the question(s) posed, and (c) what can be learned through this approach. In this way, the researcher provides a way of understanding the *expressive potential* (Strike, 1974) of ethnography and thus the contributions that this approach makes to research on the teaching of the English Language Arts and disciplines.

# *References*

Adam, B. (1990). *Time and social theory*. Philadelphia: Temple University Press.

Agar, M. (1980). *The professional stranger: An informal introduction to ethnography*. New York: Academic Press.

Agar, M. (1994). *Language shock: Understanding the culture of conversation*. New York: William Morrow & Co.

Anderson-Levitt, K. M. (1999). Looking back and ahead. *Anthropolgy & Education Quarterly, 30*(4), 430.

Anderson, A. B., Teale, W. B., & Estrada, E. (1980). Low-income children's preschool literacy experience: Some naturalistic observations. *Quarterly Newsletter of the Laboratory of Comparative Human Cognition, 2*(3), 59-65.

Atkinson, P. (1990). *The ethnographic imagination: Textual construction of reality*. New York: Routledge.

Athanases, S. Z., & Heath, S. B. (1995). Ethnography in the study of the teaching and learning of English. *Research in the Teaching of English, 29*(3), 263-287.

Baker, C., & Luke, A. (Eds.). (1991). *Toward a critical sociology of reading pedagogy*. Philadelphia: John Benjamins.

Barton, D. (1994). *Literacy: An introduction to the ecology of written language*. Oxford, England: Blackwell.

Barton, D., & Hamilton, M. (1998). *Local Literacies: Reading and writing in one community*. New York: Routledge.

Berger, P., & Luckmann, T. (1966). *The social construction of reality*. Garden City, NY: Doubleday.

Bloome, D. (this volume). Anthropology and research on teaching the English language arts.

Bloome, D., & Bailey, F. (1992). Studying language through events, particularity, and intertextuality. In R. Beach, J. Green, M. Kamil, & T. Shanahan (Eds.), *Multiple disciplinary perspectives on literacy research* (pp. 181-210). Urbana, IL: NCRE & NCTE.

Bloome, D., & Egan-Robertson (1993). The social construction of intertextuality in classroom reading and writing lessons, *Reading Research Quarterly, 28,* 304-333.

Brantlinger, E. A. (1999). Inward gaze and activism as moral next steps in inquiry. *Anthropology & Education Quarterly, 30*(4), 413-429.

Carspecken, P. F. (1996). *Critical ethnography in educational research: A theoretical and practical guide*. New York: Routledge.

Castanheira, M. L., Crawford, T., Dixon, C., & Green, J. (2001). Interactional ethnography: An approach to studying the social construction of literate practices. *Linguistics and Education, 11*(4), 353-400.

Cazden, C., John, V., & Hymes, D. (Eds.). (1972). *Functions of language in the classroom*. New York: Teachers College Press.

Clifford, J., & Marcus, G. (Eds.). (1986). *Writing culture: The poetics and politics of ethnography*. Berkeley: University of California Press.

Collins, J. (1987). Using cohesion analysis to understand access to knowledge. In D. Bloome (Ed.), *Literacy and schooling* (pp. 67-97). Norwood, NJ: Ablex.

Cook-Gumperz, J. (Ed.). (1986). *The social construction of literacy*. New York: Cambridge University Press.

Corsaro, W. (1981). Entering the child's world: Research strategies for field entry and data collection. In J. L. Green & C. Wallat (Eds.), *Ethnography, and language in educational settings* (pp. 117-146). Norwood, New Jersey: Ablex.

Corsaro, W. (1985). *Friendship and peer culture in the early years*. Norwood, NJ: Ablex.

Cumming, J. J., & Wyatt-Smith, C. M. (2001). *Literacy and the Curriculum: Success in Senior Secondary Schooling*. Melbourne: ACER Press.

D'Andrade, R. (1995). *The development of cognitive anthropology*. Cambridge, England: Cambridge University Press.

Denzin, N. K., & Lincoln, Y. L. (1994). *Handbook of qualitative research*. Thousand Oaks, CA: Sage.

Dobbert, M. L. (1984). *Ethnographic research: Theory and application for modern schools and societies*. New York: Praeger.

Dunn, C. D. (1999). Toward the study of communicative development as a life-span process. *Anthropology & Education Quarterly, 30*(4), 451-454.

Duranti, A. (1997). *Linguistic anthropolgy*. New York: Cambridge University Press.

Duranti, A., & Goodwin, C. (1992). *Rethinking context*. New York: Cambridge University Press.

Egan-Robertson, A. (1998). Learning about culture, language, and power: Understanding relationships among personhood, literacy practices, and intertextuality. *Journal of Literacy Research, 30*(4), 449-487.

Egan-Robertson, A., & Bloome, D. (1998). *Students as researchers of culture and language in their communities*. Cresskill, NJ: Hampton Press.

Eisenhart, M. (1999). Reflections on educational intervention in light of postmodernism. *Anthropology & Education Quarterly, 30*(4), 462-465.

Ellen, R. F. (Ed.). (1984). *Ethnographic research: A guide to general conduct*. Orlando, FL: Academic Press.

Emerson, R. M., Fretz, R. I., & Shaw, L. L. (1995). *Writing ethnographic fieldnotes*. Chicago: University of Chicago Press.

Emihovich, C. (1999). Studying schools, studying ourselves: Ethnographic perspectives on educational reform. *Anthropology & Education Quarterly, 30*(4), 477-483.

Erickson, F. (1977). Some approaches to inquiry in school/community ethnography. *Anthropology & Education Quarterly, 8*(3), 58-69.

Erickson, F. (1982). Classroom discourse as improvisation: Relationships between academic task structure and social participation structure in lessons. In L. C. Wilkinson (Ed.), *Communicating in the classroom* (pp. 153-181). New York: Academic Press.

Erickson, F. (1986). Qualitative Research. In M. Wittrock (Ed.), *The handbook of research on teaching* (3rd ed.) (pp. 119-161). New York: Macmillan.

Evertson, C., & Green, J. (1986). Observation as inquiry and method. In M. Wittrock (Ed.), *The handbook of research on teaching* (3rd ed.) (pp. 162-213). New York: Macmillan.

Frake, C. (1977). Plying frames can be dangerous: Some reflections on methodology in cognitive anthropology. *Quarterly Newsletter of the Institute for Comparative Human Development, 3*, 1-7.

Gaskin, S., Miller, P. J., & Corsaro, W. A. (1992). Theoretical and methodological perspectives in the interpretive study of children. In W. A. Corsaro & P. J. Miller (Eds.), *Interpretive approaches to children's socialization: New directions for child development*. San Francisco: Jossey-Bass.

Gee, J. P. (1996). *Social linguistics and literacies: Ideologies in discourses* (2nd ed.). London: Taylor & Francis.

Gee, J., & Green, J. (1998). Discourse analysis, learning, and social practice: A methodological study. *Review of Research in Education, 23*, 119-169.

Geertz, C. (1973). *The interpretation of cultures: Selected essays*. New York: Basic Books.

Geertz, C. (1983). *Local knowledge: Further essays in interpretive anthropology*. New York: Basic Books.

Gilbert, R. (1992). Text and context in qualitative educational research: Discourse analysis and the problem of contextual explanation. *Linguistics and Education, 4*, 37-57.

Gilbert, G. N., & Mulkay, M. (1984). *Opening pandora's box: A sociological analysis of scientists' discourse*. New York: Cambridge Press.

Gilmore, P., & Glatthorn, A. A. (Eds.). (1982). *Children in and out of school: Ethnography and education*. Washington, DC: Center for Applied Linguistics.

Glaser, B., & Strauss, A. (1967). *The discovery of grounded theory: Strategies for qualitative research*. Chicago: Aldine.

González, N. (1999). What will we do when culture does not exist anymore? *Anthropolgy & Education Quarterly, 30*(4), 431-435.

Green, J. (1983). Teaching as a linguistic process: A state of the art. In E. Gordon (Ed.), *Review of Research in Education, 10*, 151-252.

Green, J., & Bloome, D. (1983). Ethnography and reading: Issues, approaches, criteria and findings. *Thirty-second yearbook of the National Reading Conference* (pp. 6-30). Rochester, NY: National Reading Conference.

Green, J., & Bloome, D. (1995). Ethnography and ethnographers of and in education: A situated perspective. In J. Flood, S. B. Heath, & D. Lapp (Eds.), *Handbook for literacy educators: Research in the communicative and visual arts* (pp. 181-202). New York: Macmillan.

Green, J., & Dixon, C. (1993). Talking knowledge into being: Discursive practices in classrooms, *Linguistics and Education, 5*, 231-239.

Green, J. L., & Harker, J. O. (1982). Gaining access to learning: Conversational, social, and cognitive demands of group participation. In L. Wilkinson (Ed.), *Communicating in the classroom* (pp. 183-221). New York: Academic Press.

Green, J. L., & Meyer, L. A. (1991). The embeddedness of reading in classroom life. In C. Baker & A. Luke (Eds.), *Towards a critical sociology of reading pedagogy* (pp. 141-160). Philadelphia: John Benjamins.

Green, J. L., & Wallat, C. (1981). Mapping instructional conversations—A sociolinguistic ethnography. In J. Green & C. Wallat (Eds.), *Ethnography and languages in educational settings* (pp. 161-195). Norwood, NJ: Ablex.

Gumperz, J. J., & Hymes, D. (Eds.). (1972). *Directions in sociolinguistics: The ethnography of communication*. New York: Basil Blackwell.

Hammersley, M. (Ed.). (1983). *The ethnography of schooling: Methodological issues*. Drieffield, England: Nafferton.

Hammersley, M. (1992). *What's wrong with ethnography*. London: Routledge.

Hammersley, M., & Atkinson, P. (1995). *Ethnography: Principles in practice* (2nd ed.). New York: Routledge.

Heap, J. (1991). A situated perspective on what counts as reading. In C. Baker & A. Luke (Eds.), *Towards a critical sociology of reading pedagogy* (pp. 103-139). Philadelphia: John Benjamins.

Heath, S. B. (1982). Ethnography in education: Defining the essentials. In P. Gillmore & A. A. Glatthorn (Eds.), *Children in and out of school: Ethnography and education* (pp. 35-55). Washington, DC: Center for Applied Linguistics.

Heath, S. B. (1983). *Ways with words: Language, life and work in communities and classrooms.* Cambridge, England: Cambridge University Press.

Heller, A. (1984). *Everyday Life.* Boston: Routledge & Kegan Paul.

Hess, Jr., G. A. (1999). Keeping educational anthropology relevant: Asking good questions rather than trivial ones. *Anthropology & Education Quarterly, 30*(4), 404-412.

Howe, K., & Eisenhart, M. (1990). Standards for qualitative (and quantitative) research: A prolegomenon. *Educational Researcher, 19*(4), 2-9.

Hymes, D. (1974). *Foundations in sociolinguistics.* Philadelphia: University of Pennsylvania Press.

Hymes, D. (1977). Critique. *Anthropology and Education Quarterly, VIII*(2), 91-93.

Hymes, D. (1982). What is ethnography? In P. Gillmore & A. A. Glatthorn (Eds.), *Children in and out of school: Ethnography and education* (pp. 21-32). Washington, DC: Center for Applied Linguistics.

Hymes, D. (1996). *Ethnography, linguistics, narrative inequality: Toward an understanding of voice.* London: Taylor & Francis.

Jensen, J. M. (1999). Creating a continuum: An anthropology of postcompulsory education. *Anthropolgy & Education Quarterly, 30*(4), 446-450.

Kelly, G., & Chen, C. (1999). The sound of music: Constructing science as sociocultural practices through oral and written discourse. *Journal of Research in Science Teaching, 36*(8), 883-915.

Kelly, G. J., Chen, C., & Crawford, T. (1998). Methodological considerations for studying science-in-the-making in educational settings. *Research in Science Education, 28*(1), 23-49.

Kelly, G. J., & Crawford, T. (1997). An ethnographic investigation of the discourse processes of school science. *Science Education, 81*(5), 533-559.

Kelly, G. J., & Green, J. (1998). The social nature of knowing: Toward a sociocultural perspective on conceptual change and knowledge construction. In B. Guzzetti & C. Hynd (Eds.), *Theoretical perspectives on conceptual change* (pp. 145-181). Mahwah, NJ: Lawrence Erlbaum Associates.

Knorr-Cetina, K. (1983). The ethnographic study of scientific work: Towards a constructivist interpretation of science. In K. Knorr-Cetina & M. Mulkay (Eds.), *Science observed: Perspectives on the social study of science* (pp. 115-140). Beverly Hills, CA: Sage.

Knorr-Cetina, K. (1995). Laboratory studies: The cultural approach to the study of science. In S. Jasanoff, G. E. Markle, J. C. Peterson, & T. Pinch (Eds.), *Handbook of science and technology studies* (pp. 140-166). Thousand Oaks, CA: Sage.

Latour, B., & Woolgar, S. (1986). *Laboratory life: The construction of scientific facts.* Princeton, NJ: Princeton University Press.

LeCompte, M. D., & Preissle, J. (1993). *Ethnography and qualitative design in educational research* (2nd ed.). San Diego, CA: Academic Press.

LeCompte, M. D., Millroy, W. L., & Preissle, J. (Eds.). (1992). *The handbook of qualitative research in education.* San Diego, CA: Academic Press.

Lutz, F. (1981). Ethnography: The holistic approach to understanding schooling. In J. Green & C. Wallat (Eds.), *Ethnography and languages in educational settings.* Norwood, NJ: Ablex.

Marshall, H., & Weinstein, R. (1988). Beyond quantitative analysis: Recontextualization of classroom factors contributing to the communication of teacher expectations. In J. L. Green & J. O. Harker

(Eds.), *Multiple perspective analyses of classroom discourse* (pp. 249-280). Norwood, NJ: Ablex.

McDermott, R. P. (1976). Kids made sense: An ethnographic account of the interactional management of success and failure in one first-grade classroom. Unpublished doctoral, disseration, Stanford University, Stanford, CA.

Mehan, H. (1979). Learning lessons: Social organization in the classroom. Cambridge, MA: Harvard University Press.

Moschkovich, J., & Brenner, M. E. (2000). Using a naturalistic lens on mathematics and science cognition and learning. In A. E. Kelly & R. A. Lesh (Eds.), *Research design in mathematics and science education.* Mahwah, NJ: Lawrence Erlbaum Associates.

Ogbu, J. U. (1974). *The next generation: An ethnography of education in an urban neighborhood,* New York: Academic Press.

Ogbu, J. U. (1978). *Minority education and caste: The American system in cross-cultural perspective,* New York: Academic Press.

Ogbu, J. U. (1982). Cultural discontinuities and schooling. *Anthropology and Education Quarterly, 13*(4), 290-307.

Ortner, S. B. (1984). Theory in anthropology since the sixties. *Society for Comparative Study of Society and History, 26,* 126-166.

Pike, K. (1954). *Language in relation to a unified theory of the structure of human behavior.* Orange, CA: Summer Linguistics Institute.

Putney, L., Green, J., Dixon, C., Durán, R., & Yeager, B. (2000). Consequential progressions: Exploring collective–individual development in a bilingual classroom. In P. Smagorinsky & C. Lee (Eds.), *Constructing meaning through collaborative inquiry: Vygotskian perspectives on literacy research* (pp. 86-126). Cambridge, England: Cambridge University Press.

Rex, L., Green, J., & Dixon, C. (1997). Making a case from evidence: Constructing opportunities for learning academic literacy practices. *Interpretations: Journal of the English Teachers Association of Western Australia, 30*(2), 78-104.

Rex, L., & McEachen, D. (1999). "If anything is odd, inappropriate, confusing, or boring, it's probably important": The emergence of inclusive academic literacy through English classroom discussion practices. *Research in the Teaching of English, 34*(1), 65-127.

Rist, R. (1980). Blitzkreig ethnography: On the transformation of a method into a movement. *Educational Researcher, 9*(2), 8-10.

Rogers, L. J., & Swadener, B. B. (1999). Reframing the "field". *Anthropolgy & Education Quarterly, 30*(4), 436-440.

Santa Barbara Classroom Discourse Group (Green, Dixon, Lin, Floriani, & Bradley), (1992a). Constructing literacy in classrooms: Literate action as social accomplishment. In H. Marshall (Ed.), *Redefining student learning: Roots of educational change* (pp. 119-150). Norwood, NJ: Ablex.

Santa Barbara Classroom Discourse Group (Dixon, de la Cruz, Green, Lin, & Brandts), (1992b). Do you see what we see? The referential and intertextual nature of classroom life. *Journal of Classroom Interaction, 27*(2), 29-36.

Saville-Troike, M. (1989). *The ethnography of communication: An introduction* (2nd ed.). Oxford, England: Blackwell.

Schram, T. (1999). Cultural therapy and the explicitness of our intentions. *Anthropolgy & Education Quarterly, 30*(4), 473-476.

Schutz, A. (1970). *On phenomenology and social relations.* Edited and with an introduction by H. R. Wagner. Chicago: The University of Chicago Press.

Singleton, J. (1999). Reflecting on the reflections: Where did we come from? *Anthropolgy & Education Quarterly, 30*(4), 455-459.

Smith, L. (1990). Critical introduction: Whither classroom ethnography? In M. Hammersley, *Classroom ethnography* (pp. 1-12). Milton Keyes, England: Open University Press.

Solsken, J. (1992). *Literacy, gender and work in families and in school.* Norwood, NJ: Ablex.

Spindler, G. (Ed.). (1955). *Education and Anthropology*. Palo Alto, CA: Stanford University Press.

Spindler, G. (1982). *Doing the ethnography of schooling: Educational enthography on action*. New York: Holt, Reinhart, & Winston.

Spindler, G. (1999). Three categories of cultural knowledge useful in doing cultural therapy. *Anthropology & Education Quarterly, 30*(4), 466–472.

Spindler, G., & Spindler, L. (1983). Anthroethnography. *Anthropolgy & Education Quarterly, 14*(3), 191–194.

Spindler, G., & Spindler, L. (1987). *The interpretive ethnography of education: At home and abroad*. Hillsdale, NJ: Lawrence Erlbaum Associates.

Spradley, J. P. (1979). *The ethnographic interview*. New York: Holt, Rinehart, & Winston.

Spradley, J. P. (1980). *Participant observation*. New York: Holt, Rinehart, & Winston.

Spradley, J., & McCurdy, D. (1972). *The cultural experience: Ethnography in complex society*. Chicago: Science Research Associates.

Stambach, A. (1999). Gender-bending anthropological studies of education. *Anthropolgy & Education Quarterly, 30*(4), 441–445.

Strauss, A. L., & Corbin, J. (1990). *Basics of qualitative research: Grounded theory procedures and techniques*. Newbury Park, CA: Sage.

Street, B. (1984). *Literacy in theory and practice*. Cambridge, England: Cambridge University Press.

Street, B. (Ed.). (1993). *Cross-cultural studies of literacy*. Cambridge, England: Cambridge University Press.

Strike, K. A. (1974). On the expressive potential of behaviorist language. *American Educational Research Journal, 11*(2), 103–120.

Strike, K. A. (1989). *Liberal justice and the marxist critique of education*. New York: Routledge.

Toulmin, S. (1972). *Human understanding, Volume 1: The collective use and evolution of concepts*. Princeton, NJ: Princeton University Press.

Turner, V. W., & Bruner, E. M. (1986). *The anthropology of experience*. Chicago: University of Illinois Press.

Tuyay, S. (1999). Exporing the relationships between literate practices and opportunities for learning. *Primary Voices, K-6, 7*(3), 17–24.

Tuyay, S., Jennings, L., & Dixon, C. (1995). Classroom discourse and opportunities to learn: An ethnographic study of knowledge construction in a bilingual third grade classroom. *Discourse Processes, 19*(1), 75–110.

Vidich, A. J., & Lyman, S. M. (1994). Qualitative methods: Their history in sociology and anthropology. In N. K. Denzin & Y. L. Lincoln (Eds.), *Handbook of qualitative research* (pp. 23–59). Thousand Oaks, CA: Sage.

Zaharlick, A., & Green, J. (1991). Ethnographic research. In J. Flood, J. Jensen, D. Lapp, & J. Squire (Eds.), *Handbook on teaching the English language arts* (pp. 205–225). New York: Macmillan.

# TEACHER RESEARCHER PROJECTS: FROM THE ELEMENTARY SCHOOL TEACHER'S PERSPECTIVE

*Fredrick R. Burton*
*Witchiffe Alternative Middle School*

*Barbara L. Seidl*
*The Ohio State University*

It is no secret that positivistic research, which traditionally emphasizes quantitative measures and experimental designs, has not only been ignored by public school teachers, but has alienated them as well. Such traditional research designs have attempted to break down the teaching–learning environment by isolating and controlling its variables. If successful, such experimental procedures yield a design that is "pure" and "findings" that are reported in journals edited by and written for other researchers. However, these studies have failed to make visible the rich complexity of classroom life as children and adults experience it. For many teachers, these studies have findings, but no meaning. And after-all, meanings, not findings are what ultimately make a difference in education.

Fortunately, naturalistic, phenomonological, interpretive, and critical forms of research have made a significant impact on the field of educational research (see, for example, Denzin & Lincoln, *The Handbook of Qualitative Research*, 1994) allowing for multiple reconceptualizations of what constitutes good research. The focus of the teacher researcher movement is one such example. Teacher research as an effort to get teachers "off the bench and into the game" has produced a growing number of independent teacher researchers (e.g., Threatt, et al., 1994) as well as numerous teacher research communities such as the School Research Consortium supported through the National Reading Research Center (Baumann, 1996), Project START (Student Teachers as Researching Teachers), and the Philadelphia Writing Project (Cochran-Smith & Lytle, 1993).

## BACKGROUND OF THE TEACHER RESEARCHER MOVEMENT

The idea that teachers should be active producers of research knowledge is not new (Corey, 1953, 1954; Shumsky, 1958; Wann, 1952) and the roots of teacher research can be seen in earlier forms of action research as promoted by social psychologist Kurt Lewin (McKernan, 1991). Recently, however, the interest in professionalizing teaching (Lieberman, 1988) and in collaboration between universities and schools (Darling-Hammond, 1994; Holmes Group, 1990) has prompted renewed discussion, debate, and clarification around the purposes, methods, and epistemologies of teacher research (Baumann, 1996; Hollingsworth & Sockett, 1994; Olson, 1990; Patterson, Santa, Short, & Smith, 1993; Wilson, 1995; Wong, 1995).

Historically, conceptual work on the teacher researcher focused on the methods or procedures that teachers should use to conduct experiments in their own classrooms. For example, Corey (1954), a follower of Lewin, believed that the intent of the teacher researcher differed from traditional experimental research, the ends being the improvement of practice rather than the discovery of educational laws, but he saw no difference procedurally, defining both as following what he called the "scientific method." These procedures usually involved a linear progression through the following stages:

1. Identification of a problem.
2. Generation of hypothetical solutions.
3. Experimental testing of solutions.
4. Critically examining the results and choosing the best solutions.
5. Retesting.

The emphasis on a set of traditional, positivistic methodological procedures, the teacher researcher roles that accompanied these procedures, and the devaluing of such research within conventional research communities proved to be the demise of this first experiment with action research (Hollingsworth & Sockett, 1994).

Meanwhile, in England, a different foundation was being laid for teacher research, and, to date, much of the theoretical literature regarding teacher research comes from or draws on earlier work from England (May, 1982). Though the work of English scholars like Stenhouse and Elliott (in Hollingsworth & Sockett, 1994) also emphasized a scientific method, their orientation to teacher research was embedded within a tradition of collective teacher autonomy and, thus, "challenged hierarchical models in professional workplaces" (p. 6). This orientation placed teachers as central decision makers and participants in school reform leading both Stenhouse and Elliot to a belief in, "the centrality of teacher-selves in research" (p. 6), a position that eventually, "undermined the kind of objectivity espoused by traditional researchers working with a natural science model" (p. 6).

Thus, the groundwork was laid for a new approach for teacher research leading scholars like May (1982) at the Center for Action Research in Education at the University of East Anglia to distinguish between the teacher-as-research-student and the teacher-as-researcher. The teacher-as-research-student perspective holds that teachers should strive to fit what they do into a traditional experimental framework in much the same way Corey (1953) did with the teachers he worked with in the United States. In contrast to this view, May describes the teacher-as-researcher perspective, grounded in a naturalistic paradigm, as a more desirable approach:

It seems at once clear that the language which the naturalistic paradigm demands of the teacher is that of the everyday practice of teaching. True, the techniques by which data is collected in the process of such research are not part of the everyday practice of most teachers. Nevertheless, they are techniques which may readily be understood and could be used by teachers inclined towards researching the experiences within their classrooms without their having to adopt any narrowly prescriptive theoretical perspectives (p. 281).

In the past, at least in the United States, being a teacher researcher merely meant that with some training and encouragement classroom teachers could also do the same sort of traditional experimental studies that university professors had been doing for decades. However, the work of Schwab (1973), which illuminated the inseparable relationship between curriculum and human deliberation and the concept of teachers as engaging in *knowing-in-action* as described by Schon (1983), engendered new ways of thinking regarding the production and form of teacher knowledge. These influences in combination with new epistemological paradigms (critical, feminist, postmodern,

etc.) opened the door to new forms and purposes for teacher research. As a result, many different conceptions of teacher research have developed, all which act to challenge and redefine basic epistemological questions regarding professional knowledge and teaching practice (Lytle & Cochran-Smith, 1994).

Within the following sections we describe what we believe to be important components of teacher research by: discussing the purpose and the nature of teacher research itself, and considering the psychological processes involved in doing teacher researcher studies.

## DEFINING TEACHER RESEARCHER STUDIES

Simply stated, teacher researcher studies are attempts to illuminate pedagogical acts by researching experience. The aim of the teacher researcher is not to create educational laws (as is sometimes done in the physical sciences) in order to predict and explain teaching and learning. Instead, the teacher researcher attempts to make visible the knowledge that teachers often implicitly employ—knowledge, as described by Posch (1992), that embodies the complex, relational, and constantly negotiated risk between teachers and children in a particular context. This is an emic, or insider, form of knowledge (Lytle & Cochran-Smith, 1994) in which teachers "draw on interpretive frameworks built from their own histories and intellectual interests, and, because the research process is embedded in practice, the relationship between knower and known is significantly altered" (p. 29).

Teacher researchers accomplish this through a process of theorizing. Theorizing, when defined as the articulation and critical examination of directly experienced phenomena leading to increased understanding (Vallance, 1982), is at the very center of doing research as a classroom teacher. This is a view that Stenhouse and Elliot endorsed early in the teacher researcher movement (Hollingsworth & Sockett, 1994) when they concluded that teaching was constant theorizing and that teachers were inevitably researchers. Additionally, Van Manen (1990) described research and theorizing as pedagogic forms of life and therefore inextricably related to teaching pedagogies and decisions. Thus, teaching, theorizing, and research are all intimately bound together.

Teacher researchers believe that they can best serve the larger educational community, as well as their classrooms, by placing at the center of their inquiry the daily challenges and teaching questions that are part of the complicated and demanding context of real classroom life. Rather than embrace the naive empiricism that characterizes a removed, often environmentally controlled, and reductionist approach toward researching teaching and learning, teacher researchers not only observe, but actually manage the multiple demands and constantly shifting factors that characterize educational experiences and necessitate minute-to-minute decision making. Consequently, the knowledge they generate emanates from and is replete with this complexity. Jackson, as early as 1968, recognized the holistic nature of the knowledge that teachers possess and called on teachers to speak as theorizers and researchers within the academic community, stating that:

the growth in our understanding of what goes on in these environments need not be limited to the information contained in the field notes of professional teacher-watchers. In addition to participant observers it might be wise to foster the growth of observant participators in our schools—teachers, administrators, and perhaps even students, who have the capacity to step back from their own experiences, view them analytically, and talk about them articulately (pp. 175, 176).

Although linking the idea of the teacher researcher to the process of theorizing is intriguing, there is still a need to be more exact about what teacher researchers actually do. Drawing on phenomenology, psycholinguistics, Deweyan philosophy, and our own experiences as teacher researchers, we have characterized what teacher researchers actually do as they conduct classroom inquiry (Burton, 1985, 1986). This characterization involves action, reflection, and their reciprocal nature.

## ACTION AND REFLECTION: TEACHER RESEARCHER PROCESSES

We believe that to be a teacher researcher means to be both teacher and learner, a mode of consciousness described by Freire (1985):

I consider it an important quality or virtue to understand the impossible separation of teaching and learning. Teachers should be conscious every day that they are coming to school to learn and not just to teach. This way we are not just teachers but teacher learners. It is really impossible to teach without learning as well as learning without teaching. We cannot separate one from the other; we create a violence when we try. Over a period of time we no longer perceive it as violence when we continually separate teaching from learning. Then we conclude that the teacher teaches and the student learns. That unfortunately is when students are convinced that they come to school to be taught and that being taught often means transference of knowledge (pp. 16–17).

When teachers systematize a way to consider the effects of their teaching on student learning they engage in a process of action and reflection that is the essence of being a teacher researcher or, in Friere's words, a "teacher-learner."

Action within this mode of consciousness is situated within a phenomenological framework (e.g., Stewart & Mickunas, 1974) that argues that to be conscious is to be conscious of a particular phenomenon. As such it can be distinguished from the rote or technical definition that suggests a type of behavior that is ritualistic or a sort of habitual response, because it embodies both intentionality and observation. Teacher researchers experience a sense of meta-awareness about their goals for children and are intentional, or purposeful, in their work. Drawing from multiple possibilities they choose particular pedagogies or make particular curricular decisions to support children's progress.

Action within a teacher researcher's work is not only purposeful, it is also characterized by a style of observation that maintains a necessary degree of uncertainty—observation that Carini (1979) describes as "impressionistic observation." Through observing the effects of their actions, teachers gather impressions that mediate further decisions and prompt more systematized examination of the phenomenon—or in the case

of teaching, student growth. For example, Fred, one of the authors of this chapter, while conducting research in his class, asked Alan, a sandy-haired, freckled 9-year-old to try doing some writing. After a week, he had produced virtually no text. Fred's impression of Alan for the week was that writing was not a way he preferred to express his knowledge (whereas he was quite "fluent" in art and drama).

Fred's intentional action to support Alan's writing and the following observation and impressions of Alan's abilities or preferences represent the beginning of teacher research, but not it's entirety. Teacher researchers must go beyond their actions and their impressions to reflect in a manner that Schutz (1967) best describes:

When, by my act of reflection, I turn my attention to my living experience, I am no longer taking up my position within the stream of pure duration, I am no longer simply living within that flow. The experiences are apprehended, distinguished, brought into relief, marked out from one another, the experiences which were constituted as phases within the flow of duration now become objects of attention as constituted experiences (p. 51).

In order to understand the multiple layers of meaning and the fullness of actions and impressions in his classroom, Fred must reflect on Alan's writing behaviors in a systematic, disciplined manner. As he returned to his reflective journal and discussed his observations and reflections with colleagues, he discovered that his earlier impression of Alan was misdirected. It was only through the processes of acting and reflecting over time that he later began to view Alan as a "methodical" rather than a "reluctant" writer.

Because his actions provide substance for reflections, and because these reflections inform his future encounters with children, there is a reciprocal relationship between the two processes of action and reflection. Action is the content of reflection; reflection is the driving force behind action for it strengthens and gives intentions sustenance and elevates them from their status as mere impressions. Reflection is not merely an act of looking backward to what is known, nor is it an exercise in short-term memory. Instead, it is grounded in the impressions gathered and sifted out while acting in the classroom. These impressions are then systematically reflected on in order to produce fresh, new meanings—that then point to new actions.

## TOOLS FOR TEACHER RESEARCHERS

Whereas the tools that teacher researchers use to conduct their studies may involve quantitative measures, it is more likely that data gathering will involve ways that evoke the qualitative dimensions of classroom life (Baumann, 1996). Tools such as field notes, artifacts, audio and video tape recordings, short- and long-term lesson plans, outside observations by colleagues, and record keeping by students have long been used by anthropologists and others using a naturalistic research paradigm. Field notes, usually the most commonly used form of data gathering, often take the form of teacher journals maintained over time. While there are some very fine examples of different formats and styles for teacher journals (Armstrong, 1980; Bohstedt, 1979; Cochran-Smith & Lytle, 1993; Hubbard & Power, 1993), we will offer some examples and explanations of field notes taken from our own experiences as a teacher researchers. These specific examples come from Fred's inquiry with his class.

Fred's field notes are usually divided into two levels: general narrative notes and what Carini (1979) calls "reflective observations." General narrative field notes are mostly descriptive of the larger classroom context that frames the more specific acts of the children. These notes include information about the nature of long-term (usually 8 to 10 weeks in duration) integrated class studies (e.g., "Folktale Study," "Middle Ages Study") as well as direct and indirect teaching events such as a planned book sharing event, which would sometimes lead to an unplanned discussion of literary structure. These notes also contain Fred's methodological notes to himself, what he calls "thought ramblings," for example, notes concerning how he is feeling about the year or specific times such as his annual frustration with the disruptive nature of having to administer a week of standardized tests to his class. Some examples of his general narrative fieldnotes follow:

4/5—Decided on theme for next week, "The Human Body." There is a twist. Earlier, we studied note-taking and organization. So an information-oriented unit seems logical, however, I'd like the kids to utilize creative reporting methods. I want them to use unique formats and am using existing informational books as models and examples. Some books and their corresponding formats are:

| Book | Format |
| --- | --- |
| Paddle-to-the-Sea | journey |
| Unbuilding and Castle | narrative |
| Wild Mouse | journal |
| Animal Fact/Animal Fable | Q & A |
| All Upon a Sidewalk | journey |
| If You Lived With the Sioux | Q & A |
| Ashanti to Zulu | ABC |
| Charlie Needs a New Cloak | fiction |

I'd like to see kids impart information through narrative. Doing so they would be dealing with informative and poetic functions at the same time. They must attend to information and to the story structure itself. Will go to the Grandview library tonight.

2/6—In order to get the ball rolling on the human body drafts, I gave/made extra time for working on them today. We didn't have read aloud although I did read Tim's published book, *World War II*. His reaction was like most of the authors/kids— impressed, embarrassed, but proud that I was taking the time to read his book to an audience and that I was taking it seriously.

While kids worked on the human body study drafts, I conferenced with 4-6 kids. There was a buzz of talk, but most if it seemed related to their work. About 20-25 minutes into the writing time, I gathered them into the meeting area primarily for the purpose of building momentum. As kids shared, they reinforced on a collective level that we do have a class study—i.e., that each individual is contributing knowledge to the group and through feedback, the group is contributing to individual kids.

2/23—Notes to Myself
Immediate tasks:

1. Revise literary links chart
2. Begin thematic analysis
3. Portrayal
    a. a chronological portrayal of single kid
    b. thematic portrayal
—either way, my purpose is to tell stories that reveal and exemplify my categories, themes, motifs
—tell story of larger context
4. Read
    a. introspective & retrospective analysis
    b. Carini
    c. Spradley

In contrast, reflective observations are focused on specific writing and literary events as well as children and their various projects. They represent an intentional reflective gaze, and, thus, are a form of data analysis as well as actual data. Carini (1979) describes the process that produces reflective observation.

Through description of the person's projects in the world—that is, through the mediums that the person is drawn to and uses and the motifs that recur in his representations, the observer begins to hear the convergent viewpoints offered by the world setting and by time. To do this, the mediums and motifs need to be reflected upon to determine the range of meaning they hold and can preserve. Within this range, it is then possible to describe the particular person's relationship to both medium and motif (p. 63).

Teacher researchers use reflective observations to construct a portrait of a child—specifically attending to multiple contexts to capture their particular strengths, problems, dispositions, and preferences that might inform the teaching decisions to be made. While many reflective observations are a result of specific interactions with children, insight can often come through reflecting on artifacts from children's projects, such as their art work or their written compositions. Many of Fred's field notes contain reflective observations on interactions with children as well as artifacts of their work. Some example of both types follow:

9/26—Alan never seems to be with the group and often plays alone. He has received a lot of attention from me lately, unfortunately, most of this attention has revolved around negative behaviors—e.g., wandering out of the meeting area or simply not starting to work during writing time.

9/28—In an individual writing conference with me, Alan discusses an idea in which he plans to write a modern version of the "Cinderella" story. He appears to be shaping/creating his story as he talks—perhaps through his talk. At one point in the conference, he describes what is going to happen. As he does so, he orally edits and revises and says that certain parts of his description may not actually come out in his writing.

I am glad he wants to share this with me—anything to improve our relationship.

12/11—Alan started an untitled story about 1 and 1/2 months ago, around Halloween. The setting of this story is "trick-or-treat" night. He has created an eerie mood much like (in his words) William Sleator's *Into the Dream*, a book I had read aloud to the class earlier.

2/23—Jane and Kinthia
J and K set about doing a 3-D map of the setting of *The Green Hook*. They started it about 4 weeks ago, right after we finished reading the book. I simply suggested that someone might like to do a project with the book. After brainstorming with the class, J and K decided that the map idea was good. They worked on it steadily over the weeks. Occasionally, the rhythm of their work would be interrupted by a disagreement (see earlier notes) or "acts of God"—e.g., J went to Florida for a week. And now it sits here in the school gym to be viewed tonight during the school "Achievement Fair." It will be interesting to see the comments of the outside "judge."

Although the project is clearly theirs, it certainly has my stamp on it too. After all, I was the one that slowed them down when they were gluing and taping down pine needles to the cardboard. It didn't look very aesthetic.

I was also the one who asked them and encouraged them to revisit the book. They have shown care for the details. Boulder Valley, the mountains, the lake, huts, and the gardens of the original book are all part of their map.

As I observe their project, one other thing seems apparent—i.e., the writing to go with it seems so hurried, they crammed it in on the day that the project was due. Nonetheless, it was done, and I'm not sure that it would have been much different if they would have had more time. As it stands, the writing is primarily descriptive. Captions are done to show, tell, reveal bits about the book. The joy seemed to be in the crafting of the model, not the writing.

3/12—Amy—Analysis of her story, *The Glass Eye*
Background: Since about the last week in January we have been studying the human body. The last 6-7 weeks have consisted of the following general activities in roughly this sequence: 1) choosing a topic; 2) gathering and reading resource books; 3) going through a note taking process; 4) making sketches; 5) more artwork and models with more care; 6) listening to informational books read aloud and used as models; 7) writing drafts of reports using a variety of formats; 8) sharing products along the way; 9) speakers and dissections interwoven; 10) display; and 11) bookmaking and illustrations.

Background on Amy: Amy is a thin, tall girl with dishwater blond, stringy hair. She giggles a lot. I get the impression through our conversations that she has a lot of responsibility at home and also that she has a close family. She walks her younger sister, Caitlin, home everyday.

Reflection on the writing itself: Amy's piece appears to reflect her experience—literary and life. The obvious literary connection is her reference to Beverly Cleary's book, *Dear Mr. Henshaw*, a book we had read aloud and just finished. According to X. J. Kennedy's textbook on literature, this is a literary allusion—i.e., a direct reference to a person, place, or thing in fiction. Kennedy argues that such allusions "enrich" story. Although she hasn't shared it yet, my guess is that the class will notice the allusion.

Her opening, which I think has been influenced by Peter and Sherry, strikes me as particularly effective. Those first 3 lines draw you in as a reader. Looking across her other pieces (e.g., *The Search for the White Stallion's Parents* and *My Sister and the China Horse*), she has not used this direct entry into story through dialogue in the past. Instead, she used an opening similar to that found in many folktales. This willingness to experiment marks a point of growth for her. Other points of interest: passage of time; her description of the hospital based on her experience; the dream as a harbinger; her character names—e.g., Dr. Rock; Nurse Able; Nancy Chin.

Dewey's (in Archambault, 1974) statement that "thought confers upon physical events and objects a very different status and value from those which they possess to a being that does not reflect" (p. 214) captures the role that intentional reflection plays within teacher research. It is this intentional reflection that supports the discovery of previously unseen patterns, and, thus, produces a more complete and complex picture of a child's learning and development and the accompanying curricula and pedagogies that support that growth.

## WHY DO TEACHER RESEARCHER STUDIES?

Teacher research can be seen as a powerful and distinct genre of research (Patterson & Shannon, 1993). As Cochran-Smith and Lytle (1993) contend, the nature and source of teachers' questions, the theoretical frames teachers bring to inquiry, the practical and theoretical utility of what is learned, and the ownership of the research itself distinguish teacher research from other forms of educational research and create a particular epistemological stance. This particular stance positions teacher research at a number of complex intersections including that of theory and practice; of accountability for individual and group progress; and of external and internal sociological influences, to name a few. This is perhaps the most powerful reason for conducting teacher research. As observer-as-participant studies in education, they hold potential for generating insider knowledge useful to educators in a manner that does not disrupt the classroom nor reduce the complexity of the teaching and learning ecology, but instead captures theories of practice and stories of teaching and learning as they occur in real time in real classrooms. Such research offers practicing classroom teachers rich information for improving their own teaching as well as provides valuable theoretical and practical knowledge to the educational community in general.

In addition to providing a particularized form of knowledge, ongoing inquiry, as an orientation to teaching, promotes a continual process of learning and discovery that prevents teaching from becoming a mundane and unexamined routine. Britton (1983) describes the importance of the metacognitive quality of teacher research.

As human beings, we meet every new situation armed with expectations derived from past experiences or, more accurately, derived from our interpretations of past experience. We face the new, therefore not only with knowledge drawn from the past but also with developed tendencies to interpret in certain ways. It is in submitting these to the text of fresh experience—that is, in having our expectations and modes of interpreting either confirmed or disconfirmed or modified that learning, the discovery, takes place (p. 90).

Thus, when teachers engage in research they are also involved in a form of professional development that holds far greater promise for improving their practice than does most external, traditional models of professional inservice. Furthermore, when teachers engage in inquiry together—in collaborative designs or in communities of inquiry—they create powerful structures that support and scaffold greater expertise.

Finally, another reason for fostering teacher researcher inquiry is that these studies may be an important step in defining a paradigm of research that is truly educational rather than being haphazardly adapted from other disciplines. According to Stenhouse (1981), this would be research "in" rather than "on" educational settings or as described by Lytle & Cochran-Smith (1994) "inside/outside, knowledge that calls attention to teachers as knowers and to the complex and distinctly nonlinear relations of knowledge and teaching as they are embedded in local contexts and in relations of power that structure the daily work of teachers" (p. 23). Although research "on" educational settings is undoubtedly necessary (e.g., historical, philosophical, psychological, and sociological studies), research "in" classrooms seeks to understand and to portray the educational intentions of the participants.

## CONCLUSION

Teachers who "research" their own experiences and those of children as well find that their teaching provides substance for their research and that the act of research enriches and illuminates their teaching. Doing research, then, is not something extra that teachers might do. Rather, research is something

teachers must do if they are to become tactful observers and participants in the classroom culture that they are continually helping to create a new with children every day of the school year.

## NOTABLE EXAMPLES OF TEACHER RESEARCH PROJECTS

The following are some notable examples of teacher researcher projects that were initiated and conducted by teachers themselves or in collaboration with colleagues both inside and outside the United States. Some are books comprised entirely of teacher researcher projects.

Armstrong, M. (1980). *Closely observed children*. London: Writers and Readers.

Bissex, G. L., & Bullock, R. H. (Eds.). (1987). *Seeing for ourselves: Case-study research by teachers of writing*. Portsmouth, NH: Heinemann.

Enright, L. (1981). The diary of a primary classroom. In Dixon (Ed.), *A teacher's guide to action research*. London: Grant McIntyre.

Hansen, J., Newkirk, T., & Graves, D. (1985). *Breaking ground: Teachers related reading and writing in the elementary school*. London: Heinemann.

Hudson-Ross, S., & McWhorter, P. (1995). Going back/looking in: A teacher educator and high school teacher explore beginning teaching together. *English Journal, 84*(2), 46-54.

Jensen, I. (1988). *Stories to grow on*. London: Heinemann.

Milz, V. (1980). First graders can write: Focus on communication. *Theory Into Practice, 14*, 179-185.

Mohn, M. (1987). *Working together: A guide for teacher researcher*. Urbana, IL: NCTE.

Paley, V. (1981). *Wally's stories*. Cambridge, MA: Harvard University Press.

Rowlands, S. (1978). Notes from Sherard: Split pins galore. *Outlook, 19*, 18-34.

## *References*

Archambault, R. D. (Ed.). (1974). *John Dewey on education*. Chicago: University of Chicago Press (Phoenix Edition).

Armstrong, M. (1980). *Closely observed children: The diary of a primary classroom*. London: Writers and Readers.

Baumann, J. F. (1996). Conflict or compatibility in classroom inquiry? One teacher's struggle to balance teaching and research. *Educational Researcher, 25*(7), 29-36.

Bohstedt, J. (1979). Old tales for young tellers. *Outlook, 33*, 31-45.

Britton, J. (1983). A quiet form of research. *English Journal, 72*, 89-92.

Burton, J. (1985). *The reading-writing connection: A one year teacher-as-researcher study of third-fourth grade writers and their literary experiences*. Unpublished doctoral dissertation, The Ohio State University Columbus.

Burton, F. (1986). Research concurrents: A teacher's conception of the action research process. *Language Arts, 63*, 718-723.

Carini, P. (1979). *The art of seeing and the visibility of the person*. Grand Fords, ND: University of North Dakota Press.

Cochran-Smith, M., & Lytle, S. L. (1993). *Inside outside: Teacher research and knowledge*. New York: Teachers College Press.

Corey, S. M. (1953). *Action research to improve school practices*. New York: Teachers College Press.

Corey, S. M. (1954). Action research in education. *Journal of Educational Research, 47*, 375-380.

Darling-Hammond, L. (Ed.). (1994). *Professional development schools*. New York: Teachers College Press.

Denzin, N., & Lincoln, Y. (Eds). (1994). *Handbook of qualitative reasearch*. Thousand Oaks, CA: Sage.

Dewey, J. (1974). Why reflective thinking must be an educational aim. In R. D. Archambault (Ed.), *John Dewey on education*. Chicago: University of Chicago Press.

Freire, P. (1985). Reading the word and reading the world: An interview with Paulo Freire. *Language Arts, 62,* 15–21.

Hollingsworth, S., & Sockett, H. (1994). Positioning teacher research in educational reform: An introduction. In S. Hollingsworth & H. Sockett (Eds.), *Teacher research and educational reform: Ninety-third yearbook of the National Society for the Study of Education* (pp. 1–20). Chicago: University of Chicago Press.

Holmes Group. (1990). *Tomorow's schools.* East Lansing, MI: Author.

Hubbard, R. S., & Power, B. M. (1993). *The art of classroom inquiry: A handbook for teacher-researchers.* Portsmouth, NH: Heinemann.

Jackson, P. (1968). *Life in classrooms.* New York: Holt, Rinehart, & Winston.

Lieberman, A. (1988). *Building a professional culture in schools.* New York: Teachers College Press.

Longstreet, W. (1982). Action research: A paradigm. *Educational Forum, 46,* 135–158.

Lytle, S. L., & Cochran-Smith, M. (1994). In S. Hollingsworth & H. Sockett (Eds.), *Teacher research and educational reform: Ninety-third yearbook of the National Society for the Study of Education* (pp. 21–51). Chicago: University of Chicago Press.

May, N. (1982). The teacher-as-researcher movement in Britain. In W. & A. Schubert (Eds.), *Conceptions of curriculum knowledge: Focus on students and teachers.* Special Interest Group on the Creation and Utilization of Curriculum Knowledge.

McKernan, J. (1991). *Curriculum action research: A handbook of methods and resources for the reflective practitioner.* New York: St. Martin's Press.

Olson, M. W. (Ed.). (1990). *Opening the door to classroom research.* Newark, DE: International Reading Association.

Patterson, L., Santa, C. M., Short, K. G., & Smith, K. (1993). *Teachers are researchers: Reflection and action.* Newark, DE: International Reading Association.

Patterson, L., & Shannon, P. (1993). Reflection, inquiry, action. In L. Patterson, C. M. Santa, K. G., Short, & K. Smith (Eds.), *Teachers are researchers: Reflection and action* (pp. 7–11). Newark, DE: International Reading Association.

Posch, P. (1992, April). *Teacher research and teacher professionalism.* Paper presented at the International Conference on Teacher Research, Stanford University, Stanford, CA.

Schutz, A. (1967). *The phenomenology of the social world.* (G. Walsh & F. Lehnert, Trans.) Evanston, IL: Northwestern University Press.

Schwab, J. (1973). The practical: A language for curriculum. *School Review, 81*(4), 501–22.

Schon, D. A. (1983). The reflective practitioner. San Francisco: Jossey-Bass.

Shumsky, A. (1958). *The action research way of learning: An approach to in-service education.* New York: Teachers College Bureau of Publications.

Stenhouse, L. (1981). What counts as research? *British Journal of Educational Studies, 29,* 103–114.

Stewart, D., & Mickunas, A. (1974). *Exploring phenomenology.* Chicago: American Library Association.

Threatt, S., Buchanan, J., Morgan, B., Strier, L. Y., Sugarman, J., Swenson, J., Teel, K., & Tomlinson, J. (1994). In S. Hollingsworth & H. Sockett (Eds.), *Teacher research and educational reform: Ninety-third yearbook of the National Society for the Study of Education* (pp. 222–243). Chicago: University of Chicago Press.

Vallance, E. (1982). The practical uses of curriculum theory. *Theory Into Practice, 21,* 4–10.

Van Manen, M. (1990). *Researching lived experience: Human science for an action sensitive pedagogy.* Albany, NY: University of New York Press.

Wann, D. (1952). Teachers as researchers. *Educational Leadership, 9,* 489–495.

Wilson, S. M. (1995). Not tension but integration: A response to Wong's analysis of researcher/teacher. *Educational Researcher, 24*(8), 19–22.

Wong, E. D. (1995). Challenges confronting the researcher/teacher: Conflicts of purpose and conduct. *Educational Researcher, 24*(3), 22–28.

# ·18·

# TEACHER INQUIRY INTO LITERACY, SOCIAL JUSTICE, AND POWER

## Bob Fecho
University of Georgia

## JoBeth Allen
University of Georgia

Too frequently, parents, teachers, and the general public portray classrooms and schools as separate from the world outside schoolhouse walls in phrases like "out there in the real world" and "wait till you get a taste of life out there." The implication is that the world within classroom walls is somehow different from, probably easier, and perhaps even more just than the world beyond those walls. This portrait of schools as being something other than of the worlds in which they exist creates a false, problematic, and ultimately dangerous frame for imagining pedagogy. By failing to acknowledge the way classrooms are about making meaning of the word and the world (Freire, 1970), we perpetuate a pedagogy of denial that will reify inequities rather than moving society toward more symmetrical relations of power. For anyone who has ever contrasted classroom life to "the real world," we offer the following vignettes.

## Vignette 1

Barbara Michalove, teaching fourth grade in a university town at a school that serves mainly low income families, wrote about how students acted in ways that were less about creating an inclusive community and more about replicating the stereotypes prevalent among adults:

I saw students excluding both the Hispanic students and the students with hearing impairments. Sometimes the exclusion was obvious: The students struggled so they would not be next to Amy when we lined up for recess or lunch. Amy had severe facial imperfections and could hear very little, and her speech was almost unintelligible. Further, she was only with us part of the day, so the kids really didn't get to know her. They treated her as someone with a deformity they might catch if they stood next to her. There was taunting specific to the Mexican students (e.g., "Ricardoo, you smell like doo-doo."). I was surprised and dismayed as I watched a student-written skit shared during writing workshop in which one character referred to another as "a tortilla-eating fool"; the author asked Ricardo to play the character referred to. (Michalove, 1999, p. 23)

## Vignette 2

Griselle Diaz-Gemmati, working with eighth grade students in a multicultural urban setting, saw opportunities for dialogue around complicated issues of race degenerate into sessions that alienated rather than galvanized students. As she wrote:

Then something altered the discussions. I happened to be sitting in on a circle discussion when a major disagreement erupted between two of my top students. The word *nigger* offended the White students in the circle much more than the Black students. Shelly, who is White, brought up this point in the discussion. In not so many words, she let her circle know that it was one of those words everyone knew, but did not use. Nancy, who is Black, resented Shelly's taking offense.

"I don't see what the problem is," she sarcastically responded to Shelly. "No one ever called you guys nothing, but 'Master.'"

Shelly insisted, "Doesn't it bother you to see that vulgarity in print?"

"No, why should it?" retorted Nancy. "We know where we come from."

At this point I asked Nancy if she or people she knew addressed each other by the term *nigger* and how she felt about it.

"It don't bother us. We mean no harm by it."

"Then why does it tick you off when I get offended by it?" Shelly persisted.

"It takes on a different meaning coming from you," Nancy snapped. (Diaz-Gemmati, 1999, p. 62 )

## Vignette 3

Diane Waff, a special education teacher holding "girl talk" sessions with young women in a culturally diverse urban high school, noted how creating communities of trust in informal situations allowed her to learn about and through her students in ways that had impact on more formal academic situations. As she explained her own shift in perspective:

I also stopped trying to interpret their lives by using my own as a backdrop. The girls' journals gave me a lens on a wide variety of personal issues that were not being addressed in the formal classroom setting. Juanita and her sister, Iris, two Latina girls, were poor attenders and chronically late to school. They were not behavior problems, but when they came, I knew I had to spend time fitting them back into the class routine.

When I read their journals, I was able to listen as they shared their hearts. Juanita wrote:

When I met Jose I was afraid to look at him. I was scared to talk to him, and I was scared to kiss him. I've kissed and I've love[d] him. Now I'm going to have a baby and I'm scared I'm going to lose him. My mom says I might lose my baby too. My sister Iris has a baby and she's not going to take care of two babies plus my sisters and brothers. I'm really scared . . . (Waff, 1994, pp. 197–198).

Having read these and other journals by Juanita and her sister, Diane also learned of a fire that essentially left the family homeless. As she went on to write, "Once I learned about their struggles, I understood why they were always absent or unprepared. Buying paper and pencils would not be a high priority item for me either" (Waff, 1994, p. 198).

## RECOGNIZING THE SOCIAL IMPERATIVES

By clustering these three vignettes, we suggest that classrooms are the "real world." Further, the world outside the classroom transacts daily with the world inside the classroom and each reflects, shapes, and is shaped by the other. Such has always been the case. But too few educators, as John Dewey (1938) argued, have considered the ways students' experiences—e.g., cultural identity, socioeconomic circumstances, family language and culture, political issues, religion—transact with their efforts and opportunities to learn. Because the uglier aspects of modern society such as racism, classism, and sexism don't get discussed in complicated ways in many classrooms, there is a tendency to believe that these societal monsters also don't exist there. However, Michalove, Diaz-Gemmati, and Waff—teaching different grade levels in different social contexts with different student populations—didn't invoke issues of controversy and struggle that had never crossed the classroom threshold. They merely brought into the open issues and inequities that previously had been either denied or tacitly condoned.

There is a clear and immediate need for insight into the ways social issues transact with literacy classrooms. Several factors make this insight imperative. One factor is the changing demographics of the United States. In the near future, the number of new immigrants and people of color in the United States will outstrip the number of European Americans. Given this great degree of cultural diversity, schools cannot continue a monocultural approach to learning, if that were ever a viable option. Another factor is that our understanding of what constitutes teaching and learning grows more complex daily. Gulfs in society created by economic disparity such as access to quality education, information technology, and adequate health care are widening. Rapidly changing expectations of the job market (Gee, 2000) call for a flexible and learning-centered workforce, suggesting a pedagogy built on collaborative problem-posing and problem-solving practice, and all members of society need equal access to that pedagogy. Finally, the current repressive environment fostered by programs of high-stakes accountability supported by high-stakes assessment creates situations in classrooms that are rife with unchecked pressure, inequity, and alienation. To ignore these factors is to ignore the future of American education.

## TEACHER RESEARCH

Given this critical need to gain deeper social-contextual understandings of the ways issues of power, equity, and social justice transact with literacy in classrooms, we focused this chapter on what we are learning in those areas from teacher research. Teacher researchers bring unique vantages to research centered on social justice issues. It's not that teachers see better or with more insight than university researchers, but that they see differently. To begin with, teacher researchers don't need to gain access or schedule time in the field; they live in "data world" (Allen & Shockley, 1996). Because of this proximity, teachers are aware of the shared history of the students, the classroom, the school, and the neighborhood. Indeed, the teacher has helped to create that history, and is both actor and observer. Because of this unique positioning, teachers can act from their intense, daily relationships and use them to develop a sense of the ongoing context, developing trust and evolving classroom processes in ways that few outsiders can hope to achieve.

Perhaps most important, the process of inquiry unfolds from the teacher's sense that the dissonance within her or his practice must be embraced and interrogated. Almost without exception, teacher research begins because some student and/or set of circumstances in a classroom compelled a "systematic and intentional" look into practice (Cochran-Smith & Lytle, 1993). The classroom social dynamics spark research questions that then drive subsequent inquiry into those dynamics with a seamlessness that only intimacy with that classroom's struggles can produce.

The pool of teacher research studies from which we wrote this chapter has deepened considerably over the last 15 years. Since the publication of *Reclaiming the Classroom* (Goswami & Stillman, 1987), *The Art of Classroom Inquiry* (Hubbard

& Power, 1993) and *Inside/Outside* (Cochran-Smith & Lytle, 1993)—books that arguably spearheaded the teacher research initiative in the United States—teacher research has proliferated in many directions. The educational community has benefited from teacher research anthologies (e.g., Freedman, Simons, Kalnin, Casereno, & the M-Class Teams, 1999; Banford et al., 1996); books written by a single teacher researching her or his classroom (e.g., Ballenger, 1998; Gallas, 1998; Gaughan, 1997; Goldblatt, 1995; Wilhelm, 1995); edited volumes from various student, teacher, university researcher collaborations (e.g., Allen, 1999; Allen, Cary, & Delgado, 1995; Branscombe, Goswami, & Schwartz, 1992; Graham, Hudson-Ross, Adkins, McWhorter, & Stewart, 1999; Hubbard, Barbieri, & Power, 1998; Hudelson & Lindfors, 1993) and at least one teacher research book series, The Practitioners Inquiry Series of Teachers College Press. There are journals and listservs devoted solely to teacher research, most notably *Teacher Research: The Journal of Classroom Inquiry.* In addition, established journals like *Harvard Educational Review* and *Language Arts* publish teacher research with increasing frequency. Local and electronic teacher research networks such as the North Dakota Study Group, The Philadelphia Teachers Learning Cooperative, National Writing Project sites, the Literacy Education for a Democratic Society inquiry group, the University of Georgia Network for English Teachers and Students, and The Bread Loaf Rural Teacher Network flourish as local and electronic sites of teacher research, as do countless groups in individual schools (e.g., Chandler, 1997).

Pertinent to our intentions here, handbooks of educational research have largely ignored the voices and perspectives of teachers (Cochran-Smith & Lytle, 1993). Recently, however, several handbook or yearbook chapters have illuminated the range of questions, methodologies, and issues related to conducting teacher research and have explored implications for the broader research community (e.g., Baumann, Bisplinghoff, & Allen, 1997; Cochran-Smith & Lytle, 1999; Hollingsworth & Sockett, 1994; Lytle, 2000; Zeichner & Noffke, in press). However, to our knowledge, no one has yet examined the considerable knowledge base being generated by teacher researchers, nor is teacher research commonly integrated in literature reviews by university-based literacy scholars. Because of our own interest in issues of equity and social justice (e.g., Allen, 1999; Allen, Michalove, & Shockley, 1993; Fecho, 1998, 2000) and because of the social imperatives argued earlier, we focus this chapter on the insights into literacy practice and social justice issues *emic* voices provide.

Although much teacher research remains local and/or published in newsletters or other in-house organs (Lytle, 2000), there remains a broad range of more widely published literature. Therefore, we restricted our search in several ways. In addition to identifying equity and social justice issues related to literacy, we included only studies conducted by K–12 teachers in their own schools without coauthorship by university researchers. Our intent was not to discount collaborative studies or university researchers who investigate their own practice— we both have been involved in various aspects of that work—but rather to highlight the unique perspective and voices teachers bring to inquiry. In addition, although we kept in mind Marilyn

Cochran-Smith and Susan Lytle's typology (1993) that includes as teacher research teaching journals, oral inquiries, and essays, we primarily focused on examples that went beyond the reporting of classroom practice and, instead, situated those practices within wider societal and educational discussions. Also, although we never set out with this criterion in mind, all the studies are qualitative in design because that is all we encountered. Finally, with some exceptions, we restricted our search to major book publishers with a record of publishing teacher research, publications of the National Council of Teachers of English, the journals *Teacher Research* and *Harvard Educational Review*, and in-house publications of some long-standing teacher networks. The studies provide a sense of what this research can contribute to current critical discussions of ways to approach "literacy and justice for all" (Edelsky, 1996).

## TEACHER RESEARCH OF SOCIAL JUSTICE ISSUES IN LITERACY CLASSROOMS

Although this section includes five areas of inquiry that we identified, we acknowledge that any categorization is problematic— first because the studies overlap and speak to each other in interesting and complicated ways, and second because there are so many other possible groupings. We hope that the following organization of teacher and student investigations—(a) literacy, language, and power; (b) educational equity; (c) literacy, identity, and power; (d) communities within schools; and (e) school and community intersections—proves a useful point of departure for other ways of organizing these studies.

### Teachers and Students Confront Issues of Literacy, Language, and Power

James Gee (1986) suggested that language arts teachers play a crucial gatekeeping role in our society and could either see themselves as keepers of the museum of language or guides into the complexities of language learning. In particular, he noted that those teachers who failed to view the political nature of their practices opened themselves to being pawns at the hands of those who both saw and exercised their political views of the classroom. Many teachers who take inquiry stances on their practice embrace the concept of classroom as a place where language, literacy, and power intersect in ways that can be enabling or stunting. Accordingly, these teachers seek to understand what it means to teach and research language and literacy in ways that call attention to these political and power issues.

***Talk and silence.*** A key tool for understanding classroom dynamics is listening to students talk. One of the most prolific and influential researchers in this area is Vivian Paley, a teacher who helped teach the educational community not only to listen to young children, but to interpret their worlds in relation to social issues. Hailed by a diverse range of child advocates such as Robert Coles, Derrick Bell, Bruno Bettelheim, and Courtney

Cazden, Paley writes in a direct and engaging manner that appeals to the general public as well as to educators. From her vantage as a kindergarten and preschool teacher in the Laboratory School of the University of Chicago, she has documented, interrogated, and elucidated a broad range of equity and social justice issues. She taught many of us that it is an affront and an injustice to say of our students "I don't see color," when in fact color, gender, religion and other cultural aspects are critical to understanding each child (Paley, 1979). Fifteen years later, she put those insights on the line by engaging in honest and pointed conversation with one of her former students, Sonya, about Paley's limitations as a "white teacher" in *Kwanzaa and Me* (Paley, 1995). And in *The Girl with the Brown Crayon* (1997), Paley demonstrated that the quest for "border crossing" (Giroux, 1992) requires relationships with cultural informants—fellow teachers, children's parents and grandparents, and others—that are honest, open, and self-revealing.

Although all her books include this deep self-reflection, Paley is above all a keen observer of the worlds of children. A transcendent theme across her inquiries is fairness: fairness in the doll house, in dramatic enactments of student stories, in playing, learning, and teaching. In works that build on each other, Paley teaches us how to listen to and talk with children (1981), to understand gender differences and examine our own prejudices about them (1984), and to bring a child from the margins of the classroom into the social circle through story worlds as children dictate and then enact their own stories (1990). Paley (1988) documented the importance of fairness in the child's value system in *Bad Guys Don't Have Birthdays*, but became a powerful actor herself when she made the rule "You can't say you can't play" (1992) and with her children explored the moral implications of that rule. Paley makes visible—and critical—what teachers and society have to learn from her citation of Rabbi Yehuda Nisiah: "The moral universe rests upon the breath of schoolchildren" (Paley, 1999).

From the tradition of Paley, Karen Hankins (1999) skillfully intertwined memories of struggling classmates Bobby and Big Hazel and critique of her own schooling in "the good old days when every child learned to read" with insightful analysis of current teacher attitudes that, if unexamined, may silence their students. Five African American first-grade readers who lived in low-income, high-crime neighborhoods responded to a book about a middle-class African American family with what Hankins first interpreted as disdain and disengagement; as she studied the transcript of the discussion, she learned a great deal about her students and her responsibility to listen across cultural settings. She concluded, "Just as surely as my 2nd grade teacher missed what Bobby and Big Hazel brought to school, just as surely as the teachers at the lunch table miss what 'that kind of kid' brings to 'our' school, I missed what Ivey, Diounte, and Terrence brought to *Storm in the Night*" (1999, p. 71). Hankins provides educators with ways not only to listen, but to hear.

This importance of inquiring into the silence of our students resonates in the work of Richard Meyer (1995) who tells his teaching-life story through a series of classroom narratives. His insights from each demonstrate the power of critical self-reflection. As a student teacher in a New York City Headstart, Meyer was captivated by Leo, a previously silent child, and his

enactment of *Caps for Sale*. Rather than the well-rehearsed literary scene of the peddler wordlessly finessing the return of his hats from the monkeys, Leo used a more direct approach, demanding, "You motherfucking monkeys. You give me back my goddamn hats" (p. 277). This led Meyer to a continuing inquiry regarding home language, school language, and issues of power.

Karen Gallas (1994, 1997) studied the dimensions of silence in the classroom from a variety of perspectives and her work amplifies that of Hankins and Meyer. Within the frame of Gallas' investigations, silence is seen as both trap and power stance, as window and as wall, as defense and as offense. Like Meyer's Leo, Jianna barely spoke at all initially. However, once she shared some family stories that were not considered "appropriate" for the classroom, other children began to open their lives in meaningful ways. When Jianna told "fake" true stories, she opened the class to the role fictional narratives could play for them in addressing "subterranean issues of the community" that were not so easily addressed head on. Gallas reported, "As the children observed me privileging Jianna's attempts by my silent support and as they took on the role of ratifying her speech, their ethics of social inclusion, rather than school notions of inclusion, took control of their responses" (1994, p. 180).

In another case study, this one of a student named Rachel, Gallas (1998) analyzed the ways some students use their silence as a means of controlling the world around them. The silence becomes a stance of power because, as Gallas wrote, "[Rachel] knew I couldn't make her speak" and the girl could consequently confound any invitations to engage. Gallas (1997) noted similar controlling behavior in Denzel, a second grade student in a multiracial, multiethnic, multilingual school, who would neither look nor listen during story time, although he was committed to learning to read. For Gallas, who believed that listening to stories was a necessary road to literacy, this reluctance on the part of Richard to engage at storytelling time created a conflict. In what is all-too-infrequent in any research literature, Gallas reported in detail her many attempts and her repeated failure to reach Denzel, to "bridge the gap between [his] 'now'...and the new worlds of the texts" she valued. However, she did learn from the deep reflection on her interactions with Denzel, and went on to apply and study other ways of reaching students for whom storybooks hold no magic nor meaning.

***Hard talk.*** In Vignette 2, Diaz-Gemmati (1999) illustrated the difficulties of teachers who seek to develop inquiry-based classrooms that reflect democratic ideals. Things get said. People respond. Feelings escalate. In efforts to help students delve into social issues such as racism and sexism, the classroom discourse can alienate students from students, students from teachers, and teachers from colleagues. Both Bob Fecho (2001) and John Gaughan (1996, 1999) spoke to these issues as they recounted classroom experiences that were literature-based inquiries into racism, the former revolving around *Fires in the Mirror* (Deavere Smith, 1993) and the latter around the movie *El Norte* (Nava, 1983). For Gaughan (1996), the revulsion of his student, Misty, toward Latinos was very unsettling, and he explored her feelings with her and with the whole class in an insightful manner through reading, viewing the movie, and extensive writing and sharing. Fecho (2001), as his students inquired into racial tensions between a small sect of Orthodox Jews and mainly Caribbean Americans in a section of New York City, documented the ways colleagues and parents raised concerns about what such study might bring to the surface about Black and Jewish relations. His study shows how he encouraged students through the process of inquiry to interrogate not only the issues of this community, but their own range of prejudices as well. Both Fecho (2001) and Gaughan (1996) demonstrated how confronting complex issues, although anxiety-inducing, creates means for teachers and students to move beyond their entrenched views.

These issues around hard talk are punctuated by the studies of Vicki Zack (1991) and Tricia Taylor (1999). Zack (1991) dealt thoughtfully with the criticism that events like the Holocaust contains horrors not suitable for children, and demonstrated how they can be not only suitable but vital for the individual readers as well as for the collective memory and conscience of a society. The children's sophisticated questions echo those of adults: Why didn't they take action? Why didn't people listen? How could they do that to innocent people? In her classroom, Taylor (1999) confronted a more covert horror when one of her fourth-grade students asked her and the rest of the class, "Is there anyone here who does not have a problem with [homosexuals]?" She had been leading the students for weeks in discussions of social issues, including prejudice, but here her students drew the line. Taylor, however, could not accept that line, even though she suspected that her own views would not be accepted in this conservative, rural area of Georgia. What she hadn't been prepared for was how to handle this situation, nor for the disapproval of her university classmates. She asked, "If I tell my students that I am completely against any type of discrimination, set up a forum so that we may discuss such issues, and bring in literature that addresses discrimination, how can I then deny them the opportunity to discuss homophobia . . . If I ignored intolerance of homosexuals, wouldn't I essentially be condoning it?" (p. 42).

*Language and culture.* Looking at the ways language and culture transact both inside and outside of classrooms is a prevalent theme in the teacher research we reviewed. In particular, researchers from the Brookline Teacher Research Seminar, with its emphasis on listening closely to and learning from the interaction of children, often write about the way language and culture figure into the learning life of the classroom. Jim Swaim (1998) and Anne Phillips (1997) are examples of that Brookline tradition. Swaim's (1998) look at third-grade student Pamela, who created an inclusive community in writing and sharing her re-vision of the world, recalls Karen Gallas' work with Jianna. In a way similar to Jianna, Pamela taught Swaim to listen more closely and to learn from his students. This interaction led Swaim to create a new metaphor for literacy and revision. In her work, Phillips' (1997) case study of a gifted young African American poet from Roxbury reveals how important another pathway—poetry—can be for expressing deep feelings, and how listening helped Phillips and her students understand each other better.

Another Brookline teacher, Cindy Ballenger (1998), inquired into her practice in a Haitian preschool in Boston, posing questions about how language figured into the ways learning occurred across cultural borders. From closely studying the children's interactions in a writing center, she was able to contrast her intended curriculum—the functions of print and how it works in our language system—with the children's "shadow" curriculum, "using letters to represent and interpret their relationships" (1996a, p. 321). She had to understand their purposes and values of print, which were very different from her own and other children she had taught, in order to teach. This insightful analysis also led to a systematic look into storybook sessions (Ballenger, 1996b). What stood out for her was how the children viewed and valued books and book worlds in very different ways—or so she thought at first—than she did as their teacher. Eventually, she realized that the children used books as springboards for talking about their lives, just as many adults do. Understanding the children's actions and responses in relation to their cultural traditions was vital for this understanding.

In a secondary urban classroom in Philadelphia, Bob Fecho (1998, 2000) and his class of African American and Caribbean American students focused on their perspectives regarding home and mainstream codes. Creating a yearlong critical inquiry into language, Fecho documented the ways his students saw language intimately tied to their identity, how a range of perspectives about language existed across his students, and how their ambivalence about learning mainstream power codes transacted with their acquisition of those codes. Crossings of multiple cultural boundaries led Fecho to the understanding that critical inquiry classrooms must be ones where diverse perspectives are not only entertained, but encouraged.

Issues of language and culture are also central to teacher researchers in rural areas. One issue of the *Bread Loaf Rural Teacher Network Magazine* focused on the complex relationships between language and culture. On an isolated island in Alaska, all 90 students and many of their parents and grandparents in the village of Tununak created the Yup'ik encyclopedia project, a bilingual, multimedia archive of tribal stories, knowledge, and skills that has engaged students in deep inquiry into the power of language in their changing society (Dyment, 1997). Through their electronic network, BreadNet, rural teachers have designed several cross-site research projects, such as one on "the language of power" designed by middle and high school teachers Gary Montaño (New Mexico), Sharon Ladner (Mississippi), and Stephen Schadler (Arizona). In this study students discussed online their home languages in relation to the "language of power," or edited English, in order to make informed decisions about the relative uses and value of both (Schadler, Ladner, & Montaño, 1997). Related work has been done by Renee Moore, an African American teacher in rural Mississippi. She and her high school English students and their parents investigated issues of African American culture in relation to their learning of edited English. She has developed a grounded theory of Culturally Engaged Instruction (Moore, 1996).

These studies, taken collectively, remind us of the power that language awareness brings to the classroom. More important, we learn more about the many overt and nuanced ways language, literacy, and power transact almost moment to moment in all classrooms. Particularly, these studies encourage the educational community to inquire into, rather than ignore, the silences and anxiety-producing discussions that occur when subjects of social relevance become part of the classroom agenda. To this effect, we know more about the ways classroom discourses can silence or encourage students, the ways silence can be both disabling and enabling, the ways perceptions of disengagement can shift, and the ways all of this is connected to asymmetrical power relations.

## Teachers and Students Confront Educational Equity Issues

Perhaps owing to their immersion in their contexts, teacher researchers frequently focus on equity issues as they relate to their classrooms and schools. Issues of tracking or other forms of ability grouping merit special attention from teachers, as do choices of materials for classrooms. In addition, some teacher researchers are problematizing privilege and creating opportunities for learners to interrogate their own privilege and what that means for learning, especially in the wake of the violent reactions to alienation in schools across the country.

***Material consequences.*** Teaching from a critical stance, Linda Christensen (1989, 1990, 1993) has inquired into issues such as the hegemony of standard English, the ways learning can flourish in untracked classrooms, and how students make meaning via critical inquiry into the texts of their lives. In this body of work, Christensen provides insight into the ways critical pedagogy works within classrooms. Each snapshot shows how politically steeped theoretical issues get played out in the practice of a teacher who is a critical learner. Christensen and Bill Bigelow (1992a), with whom she team teaches, espouse a mission to be educational and social change agents. They work to create classrooms as centers of equality and democracy, not only within classrooms, but in response to broader social issues. For example, their students role played social injustices and struggles such as the Cherokee Indian Removal and a textile workers strike in 1912; they related those historical injustices to current ones in their lives and then to social movements that have changed American society. They studied the hidden curriculum of obedience and conformity at their own school. When Bigelow realized how powerless students felt in uncovering power without resistance, he designed the "organic goodie simulation" in which they examined power, complicity, and possible ways to resist corrupt social structures.

Bigelow (1992b, 1997) has also used his *emic* stance as a teacher to analyze popular teaching materials. For example, his analysis of the teaching tool *The Oregon Trail* CD-ROM reveals it as "sexist, racist, culturally insensitive, and contemptuous of the earth" (1997, p. 85). He called for both critical computer literacy and for the important role of the teacher in asking questions that prompt students to critique materials. In a similar study, Bigelow (1992b) analyzed how Columbus is portrayed in children's literature, finding blatant examples of distortion and indoctrination. This kind of research, with curriculum materials

the focus rather than teacher/student interactions, nonetheless has profound implications for those interactions.

***Problematizing privilege.*** Teachers who find themselves working with gifted classes or in high schools that reflect largely upper socioeconomic status (SES) student populations are not always comfortable with their own or their students' privilege; therefore some teachers have created learning experiences that problematize privilege. To this purpose, Jeff Schwartz (1992) and a team of high school teachers at affluent Sewickley Academy and economically depressed Clairton High School designed a History of Pittsburgh course in which students conducted original research and corresponded with each other via email about what they were learning. Students struggled to get beyond their economic differences and stereotypes, shared a diverse range of resources, and learned not only about their city, but about themselves and each other.

Mollie Blackburn (1999) and Patricia Goldblatt (1998) both developed inquiries in their gifted classes that allowed students to interrogate their own privilege. Goldblatt (1998) took over a course dubiously titled Third World Literature, changed the title to Postcolonial Literature, and documented the ways the students' initial resistance to reading about other cultures shifted to a realization of the possibilities of understanding diverse perspectives through literature. When Blackburn (1999) was assigned to teach a language arts class for "gifted" sixth graders despite her strong beliefs that academic tracking was wrong, she decided to help her students examine the educational system that privileged them. They read the novel *Queenie Peavy* (Burch, 1987) about a very bright girl who was "from the wrong side of the tracks," and debated whether Queenie would be in their gifted class. This inquiry into socioeconomic status and its intersection with race led the students to some very sophisticated interpretations of why students get into—or are excluded from—gifted classes.

Issues of ability grouping play prominent roles in studies conducted by Joan Cone (1992) and Wilbur Sowder (1993). Cone (1992) essentially opened her advanced placement secondary English class to any student who wished to enter and documented the ways students were able to rise to higher expectations. Sowder (1993) decided to take the same student-centered, discussion-based pedagogy that was emblematic of his advanced placement class and use it with classes labeled as average seventh graders. The pedagogy in both cases focused on establishing layers of talk and proved successful for both teachers despite the perceived differences in abilities.

In some ways, Susan Threatt (1998) took critical pedagogy where it has not gone before. Teaching in a California middle class suburb of Oakland, Threatt raised questions about who needs critical pedagogies and what oppression might look like in suburbia. By problematizing stereotypes of the suburban landscape, she has the educational community wonder what critical pedagogy brings to our understanding of suburban life and the alienation and stratification becoming more and more evident in suburban schools.

The studies in this section begin with two assumptions about schools: one is that they frequently are not places of social equity and the second is that, despite the first condition, schools have great potential for becoming spaces where equity prevails. Therefore, the critique rendered in these studies is not about abandoning our public schools, but instead points in directions that will make those schools more enabling of empowerment for all who enter.

## Teachers and Students Inquire Into Issues of Literacy, Identity, and Power

Social contextual issues of literacy—the ways in which we both shape and are shaped by the texts we encounter and generate—figure prominently in teacher research. Historically, Sylvia Ashton-Warner (1963) taught young children through a "keyword" approach that she developed from listening to and valuing what was important in the lives of Maori children. Her belief that who we are needs to be evidenced in our literacy learning provided a guiding principle on which she based her pedagogy. In problematizing issues of race and gender, current teacher researchers often work in the tradition of Ashton-Warner by providing the opportunity for students to learn about themselves through the investigation of their own textual lives as well as those of others.

*Problematizing race.* Disturbed by the intolerance her predominantly African American fourth-grade students displayed toward Hispanic classmates as well as those with hearing impairments (Vignette 1), Barbara Michalove (1999) created an interdisciplinary immersion into prejudice and discrimination. Through biographies, fiction, a video on the history of intolerance in America, interviews with family members, and shared stories, her students learned not only about the various groups who have been the brunt of discrimination in our country since its inception, but also about themselves. It took time to "circle in" on their own prejudice, but once they did, students were honest in their recognition of intolerance and decisive in their actions. They created rules for their own conduct as they successfully changed their classroom.

Like Michalove, Maria Sweeney (1997) felt personally challenged by Carol Edelsky's concept of "education *for* democracy." She consequently asked her fourth-grade, suburban students "to consider alternative views of events past and present, ... To look for missing or silenced voices" in their reading materials, and to question constantly, "Is this fair? Is this right? Does this hurt anyone? Is this the whole story? Who benefits and who suffers?" (p. 279). As part of this social justice stance, her students studied the end of apartheid and the elections in South Africa. This interdisciplinary, multimedia study led to extensive writing; one piece grew into a play, "No Easy Road to Freedom." They performed it for the rest of the school and community, and urged the audience to get involved with fighting racism by actions such as giving money to the Africa Fund and joining antiracist groups. Like the intensive inquiry in Michalove's classroom, Sweeney's efforts resulted in positive action on the part of her students.

In the immigrant and working class second grade Toronto classroom of Andrew Allen (1997), students took part in an "intentional, developmentally appropriate" approach that nudged them toward a deeper "awareness of social and political issues" (p. 518). Recognizing that his students were often accepting his thoughts and values uncritically, he developed an antiracist/antibias approach that addressed the silencing of student voices. This approach, influenced by Lisa Delpit's (1988) work on power relationships in classrooms, included helping students identify biases in classroom materials, making time for discussion of social issues, and encouraging students to respond to inequities and validate divergent perspectives. Students identified omission and stereotyping in children's literature; learned to name instances of race, class, and gender oppression; and rewrote problematic texts.

*Problematizing gender.* Teacher research networks frequently develop themes of research. We've noted how the Brookline Teacher Research Seminar often focuses on issues of crossing culture. Several teacher researchers of the Philadelphia Writing Project (PhilWP) have centered on the ways gender transacts with literacy instruction within urban classrooms (See Bowers, 1998; Brown, 1998; Pavalko, 1998; Winikur, 1998). In her work, PhilWP teacher researcher Diane Waff (1994; Waff & Yoshida, 1996) has wondered what it means to invite young women to explore their own identities through literacy discussions that go beyond the limitations of classroom literary talk. She established "Girl Talk" sessions with a culturally diverse group of young women of Leadership House, a school within a school comprised of "mildly handicapped special education students" (1994, p. 192). Waff and her students, as Vignette 3 indicates, came to see the power of literacy in terms of creating gender identity. The rich personal talk that characterized these sessions enabled Waff to deepen her sense of the lives of these young women and brought this insight into the classroom. Since males outnumbered females nearly four to one in Leadership House, Waff (1995) eventually brought similar discussions to mixed-gender classrooms, but always with the intent of providing further opportunities for the woman to feel empowered within this male-dominated community.

In a similar fashion, Jennifer Tendero's (1998) detailed and hopeful report on one Write for Your Life Project tells how 14 middle school girls investigated a major social issue in their own lives—teen pregnancy. As teacher, Tendero provided insightful facilitation as these Hispanic and African American girls from one of the poorest, most violent, and least educationally successful areas of the country read articles, novels, and informational books; wrote poems, short stories, and "tips"; and published a 40-page booklet for others in their school encouraging them to wait until they are ready for babies. Tendero presented problems like having boys overpower a meeting—leading to a girls-only rule—and dealing with topics with which the teacher was uncomfortable providing information (e.g., abortion). Framed by Freirian teachings, Tendero's study, like that of Waff (1994), shows the power of literacy in the girls' lives.

Working in a very different setting—an all-girls private school in suburban Ohio—but with similar intention, Maureen Barbieri (1995) studied the ways middle school girls transacted with literature and how such transactions shaped their sense of selves. By immersing these young women in literature that spoke directly to their lives and encouraging them to create their own literary responses, Barbieri created a curriculum that urged her students to inquire into the world by using literature as the focus. Through interrogation of literature, students also came to interrogate their own perspectives on issues such as duplicity, vengeance, and homophobia.

By explicitly problematizing issues of race and gender as played out in diverse classrooms, these studies chart a range of responses to these issues. With particular power, evidence is provided here that thoughtful investigations into issues of gender and race can lead students and teachers into more complicated perspectives that get beyond platitudes and stereotypes. The result is the creation of learning communities that are communities in deed rather than merely in name.

## Teachers and Students Consider Communities Within the School

Teachers, perhaps more than anyone else, understand both the value of creating community in the classroom as well as the complexity of trying to do so. As Paulo Freire and Donaldo Macedo (1996) have suggested, educators need to get beyond the cliches of a "vacuous, feel-good comfort zone" (p. 202) and instead consider the social and dialogical aspects of the classroom. Creating community is not simply a series of activities designed to help class participants feels good about each other, but instead represents a way of knowing that values the manner in which individuals and the group transact with each other in order to make meaning. Many teacher researchers have dedicated themselves to investigating this deep, complex perspective on the creation of community.

***Classrooms as democratic communities.*** Given the student-centered orientation of her pedagogy, it is not surprising that the work of Karen Gallas (1994) also comments on attempts to develop and learn from democratic principles within a learning community. Gallas took on the personal challenge of trying to understand why the "bad" boys in her classroom often silenced other students, contested her authority, and controlled the group dynamics. She worried that these were the children, mirroring deeper messages embedded in society, who would become abusive adults. She studied Alex, Tony, Michael, and Charles, and analyzed their words and actions in light of those of her own "bad boy" son. She asked, as countless other teacher researchers have, "How can I . . . explore their point of view as learners and pull them into the mainstream of the classroom?" (p. 56). Through study of stories—not just their oral and written narratives, but also their stories acted out in plays and playground dramas—she began to understand their behavior and consequently changed her own.

My response has moved from a purely visceral, defensive reaction . . . to one of examining what that child is telling me about his needs as a learner and his view of the world. What I find is that bad boys require, and thrive in a classroom that offers expanded opportunities for creative action in all its forms and deep involvement with the content of the curriculum—*and that is true of all children* (1994, pp. 69–70, italics in original).

By changing the ways she responded to these students, Gallas created a new dynamic that allowed the students to respond differently.

Other teacher researchers have made explicit inquiries into what it means to teach in a classroom based on democratic principles, particularly as adherence to those principles leads to social action. At the high school level, Audrey Sturk (1992) created opportunities for empowerment by encouraging seniors to "question authority, to think for themselves, and to act democratically, responsibly, and compassionately among themselves in the classroom and within our community" (p. 264). For example, in response to Margaret Laurence's (1993) novel dealing with aging, *The Stone Angel*, students launched 13 projects involving interviews of lawyers and senior citizens, working in senior citizen homes, and studying the history of one group whose Arcadian ancestors had been driven from the country. As a result of their actions, including a 20-minute local television program, living conditions were improved and one nursing home was shut down for violation of the law.

Simon Hole (1998) believes in democratic education, but problematized that pedagogy by asking what happens when the democratic decisions of a classroom get in the way of supporting marginalized students. He recounted the experience of a colleague who used a majority vote to determine who would represent the class on the school newspaper. However, conflict arose for the teacher when a young girl who rarely participated overtly in class expressed an interest in writing for the paper. When the young girl was unable to garner enough popular vote, the teacher was caught between her wanting to pull this marginalized learner into the main of the class and her support of the principles and mechanisms of democracy. The piece concludes by suggesting that teaching is more than just following the rote chants of democracy, but more importantly concerns a willingness to grasp the prickly conundrums that the process frequently reveals.

***Classrooms as inclusive literacy communities.*** Almost all of the studies reviewed here give us insight into what it means to create and function in classrooms that are literacy communities. In this section we spotlight teacher researchers who have investigated particular challenges of creating inclusive communities. How do we work together as readers, writers, and "doers"? How do we work across boundaries of power, position, and social hierarchy that inevitably characterize classrooms? Teacher researchers have investigated ways students break down these hierarchies through peer discussion (e.g., Cone, 1993, 1994), small group work (e.g., Cintorino, 1994), and a focus on meaningful literate activity (e.g., Daniel, 1996). In another instance, Carol Stumbo (1992), building on Elliot Wigginton's Foxfire principles, created an oral history magazine in the economically depressed, former mining community of Wheelwright, Kentucky. In so doing, students and teachers needed to establish new relationships and new ways of working in order to carry out their project.

An aspect of investigating the creation of literacy communities that is of critical importance is the questioning of "one size fits all" (de la luz Reyes, 1991) approaches to teaching.

When progressive literacy educators like Donald Graves, Nancie Atwell, and Lucy Calkins and literacy movements like the National Writing Project revolutionized reading and writing instruction, many teachers embraced—and some school districts mandated—more authentic, learner-centered structures such as reading and writing workshop, student-led discussion, and personal response to literature. Some teachers tried and abandoned these new methods as not effective with "these kinds of students." Teacher researchers took a different approach: They studied the problems and promises of progressive pedagogy within their local classroom communities. In so doing, they have provided sociocultural insights into how learners, particularly marginalized students, respond to such pedagogy and what teachers can do to adapt and reinvent pedagogy that is responsive to the specific needs of their students.

Addressing issues surrounding writers workshop, Jo Anne Pryor Deshon (1997), and Karen Evans (1995) examined and then adjusted their instructional practices. As a first-grade teacher in Newark, Delaware, Deshon became uncomfortable with the instruction she was providing her predominantly poor and African American Chapter I students. Through close analysis of these students during writing workshop, she came to understand the negative impact of her scheduling decisions. Since they came back from their Chapter I class in the middle of writing workshop, they wrote in relative isolation during whole class sharing time, and also missed a highly valued time—sharing with a large audience. Like Deshon, Karen Evans (1995) used her research to consider the ways asymmetrical relations of power were affecting the ways her students learned to be writers. Writing workshop in her fifth-grade classroom was "a disaster," but reflecting on its failure led her to get to know and understand her students' worlds. Most were African American, Hispanic, and Native American, and most lived at or near poverty level, and they were not about to write nice, family stories for "the rich, white lady." Evans had to change her thinking about writing instruction to focus on writing that "took place in a larger context that was interesting to students and served a specific purpose" (p. 268) such as writing to prepare for literature discussion groups or on self-selected social studies topics.

In his study of three struggling, urban high school students as they attempted to become authors, Eli Goldblatt (1995) also called attention to the ways mainstream interpretive communities transact with local and marginalized communities. Goldblatt focused on how the power of the institution of writing came into play as these young writers tried to imagine themselves as learners who exercised some control when they transferred thought to paper. Concerned with ways that these writers positioned themselves in relation to this "author-ity," Goldblatt felt that DuBois' (1903) notion of "double consciousness" was evident as these students sought to negotiate a range of public and private discourses. He concluded that we need to build a composition theory and writing pedagogy that carefully considers how cultural conditions affect disenfranchised writers.

Guiding her efforts toward another marginalized community—that of struggling readers and writers—Janet Allen (1995) taught and studied ninth-grade students in a remedial reading class. Drawing on her own and student journals, interviews, photographs, surveys, and other artifacts and field notes, Allen developed case studies and documented her attempts, some successful and some failed, to lead her students to literacy through whole language principles and practices. She documented a myriad of specific teaching strategies such as involving students in researching themselves as readers, visiting bookstores, watching videos, and attending plays related to their reading, and reading with younger students. More important, she showed that while no single strategy was effective with every child, these students who believed themselves to be reading failures began to see themselves not only as students who could read, but as people who could use books to explore their life questions.

In considering notions of learning communities, these studies add to our understanding of the ways students transact with peers and adults as they seek to see themselves as readers, writers, and successful learners in school. In establishing their own identities as learners who are capable of transacting with complicated text in a variety of ways, these students are also establishing a social identity of the classroom as a place of support for all their individual investigations into literacy.

## Teachers and Students Consider the Intersection of Communities and Schools

As teacher researchers better understand the communities created within classroom walls, they also develop insight into the ways these inside communities transact with the larger outside communities of neighborhoods, rural areas, and cities. Such research creates opportunities for schools to embrace more deeply the local cultures that surround them, but are too infrequently celebrated in pedagogy and curriculum. Getting past the simplistic appreciation of ethnic cuisine and dress, teacher researchers wonder what it means to invite the community into the school and to truly explore the possibilities of cultural diversity in substantive and complex ways. Conversely, they investigate the ramifications of failing to engage in such exploration.

***Multiple language communities and schools.*** Cindy Ballenger (1998) sets the tone for this section by showing how one teacher crossed cultural boundaries in order to become a better teacher of her bilingual and bicultural students. In doing so, she informed the educational community about what occurs when teachers and students transact across cultural borders. Ballenger took Delpit's (1995) concerns to heart and thoughtfully investigated what it means to teach "other people's children." By taking deliberate steps to make sense of the Haitian culture of her students through learning from the children and adults of that community, Ballenger developed practical insights into the ways that culture transacted with learning in her preschool classroom. As noted earlier, Ballenger analyzed how cultural differences played out in literacy learning. In addition, she discovered how class management improved when she was able to adapt the more directive vocal styles of the Haitian adults.

In like manner, Howard Banford (1996), Myron Berkman (1996), Iona Whishaw (1994), and Jean Gunkel (1991) learned from their students of other cultures in order to learn with them.

Banford (1996), in working with Maricar—whom he described as a "phantom student," the kind "whose voices are heard little or not at all in whole class discussions," (p. 3)—illustrated how writing workshop allowed a young woman to "bloom" by building on her strengths, letting her cross culture barriers at her own pace, and allowing her to choose to tell the story of her family when it became important for her to do so. Berkman (1996), in a case study conducted in a high school for newly arrived immigrants, analyzed how group discussion and a range of in-class groupings—from all-Spanish to mixed languages to self-chosen—allowed a student, Marisol, to practice language acquisition in a variety of situations. Whishaw (1994) took it upon herself as a student teacher to have nonnative language speakers write poetry in their native language and then pair with an English speaker in order to devise a translation of the poem. These poetic collaborations accessed poetry conventions of the homeland and encouraged problem solving. Finally, Gunkel (1991) examined how Keisuke, a fourth-grade student from Japan, learned both English and "America" in her classroom through dialogue journals, writing workshop, pullout ESL instruction, reading literature at home as well as at school, a hamster, and a study of the New Jersey community. In these studies, teachers demonstrated how investigation into culture is based on a willingness of the teacher to learn from students of that culture.

This willingness is evident in yet another study by Karen Gallas (1994). Imani came to Gallas' classroom from a small country in Africa; like many immigrant children, her language, culture, and lack of any formal education were at first a mystery to Karen and to the other students. How do teachers bridge so many differences, silences, and walls of misunderstanding and distrust? To this end, Gallas studied Imani's dialect, encouraged her to express herself through drawing and movement, and above all made sure that she was always seen as a part of the classroom community, including share time. According to Gallas (1994), "The artistic process enabled Imani and me to speak further about ideas that . . . she would have been unable to pursue in a discussion" (p. 49) due to language differences. For children like Imani, creative action provides a "chance to communicate about themselves and their most important concerns" (pp. 49–50). Linda Rief (1999) makes a similar case for inclusion of the arts to understand community. Her students, through interdisciplinary inquiry, wrote a musical about their community's past (children working in textile mills) and present (gangs who hung out at the abandoned mills).

Christine Igoa (1995) also employed artistic mediums—primarily drawing and creating filmstrips—to help her explore the inner worlds of the immigrant children she taught in her sheltered ESL classes in Hayward, California. The children represented themselves as animals and objects, protecting their vulnerability, but allowing them to be powerful protagonists in their own life stories. Igoa, herself an immigrant from the Philippines, shared important insights about the phenomenon of being uprooted; she recognized that children's emotions and reactions (e.g., silence, curiosity, culture shock, isolation, exhaustion, and loneliness) are a crucial step in relating to children new to this country. Further, Igoa presented her own dialogues with five children in order for readers to hear the children's perspectives in their own voices and to demonstrate how she had to know the children individually in order to teach them.

***School and community connections.*** What stood out for Marci Resnick (1996) was not the ways her school and the surrounding community transacted, but rather how school personnel, through a general attitude of disinvitation, tried to limit parental involvement in the school. Resnick documented her efforts to view parents as resources about the individual histories of their children, as well as resources for learning in the classroom. By seeing parents from a different perspective, Resnick concluded that if "a curriculum of connections between school and families makes sense" then the classroom pedagogy deepens and widens to encompass those beliefs (1996, p. 132). As for so many teachers, what began as a series of activities grew into an epistemological stance.

The importance of reaching out to parents is evident in the work of Deborah Jumpp (1996), Carole Chin (1996), and Betty Shockley (1993), all of whom created ways to involve parents more directly in the life of the classroom. Through portfolio response in Jumpp's inner city high school classes, suggested writing in Chin's urban elementary school, and a set of "parallel practices" in Shockley's first-grade classroom, parents were invited to contribute to the curriculum in meaningful ways. As Jumpp's (1996) parents responded to the work of their children, they became "mediators in their children's learning" and consequently empowered so that they could communicate to her "what they felt their children needed from [the teacher] to improve their writing" (p. 141). In similar fashion, Chin (1996), who became known as "The Teacher Who Gives Parents Homework," documented the ways parents, many of them first generation immigrants, saw these writing assignments as ways to take part in the learning of their children, but also as ways to advance their own study of language. Shockley (1993) invited parents—who responded with overwhelming levels of involvement in this "low SES" school—to share family stories and to read and write with their children three times a week all year in Family Reading Journals. She responded to each entry with a genuine respect for families as equal partners in the literacy education of their children.

Resnick, Jumpp, and Chin were all participants in the Urban Sites Writing Network of the National Writing Project, where issues of community was a dominant theme. Two other Urban Sites participants, Paula Murphy (1994) and Marceline Torres (1998) also reflected community themes through their teacher research. Murphy (1994), in a particularly well-written case study of a 13-year old Latino with reading difficulties, spoke to the importance of understanding the individual story of each child and also sought to interrupt stereotypes of the homeless by describing the care and love evident in this young man's family. Like Tendero (1998), sixth-grade Bronx public school teacher Marceline Torres (1998) got her students involved in self-selected projects investigating "important questions and concerns about the world in which they live" (p. 59) such as drugs, AIDS, teen pregnancy, and homelessness. She also got their parents involved, first by having students dialogue with their parents in "letters home," and second by holding monthly "celebrations" where students presented their research findings to their parents. Family members became valuable resources as, for example, one student interviewed his uncle who had AIDS and another got technical information about the disease from her father who was an X-ray technician.

For Karen Hankins (1998), learning from families began with learning from her own. She blurred the borders between her own experiences and the experiences of her students in work that is important both methodologically and substantively. As she explored and interrogated forgotten, hidden, or never-before-discussed events of her own family, she looked at the lives of her students with deeper, more personal understandings. Her grandfather's loss of his hand in a mill accident and subsequent alcoholism helped her understand how circumstances of hopelessness can lead people to addiction, as it had the families of three children in her room with fetal alcohol/cocaine syndrome; her family's joys, frustrations, and denial about her sister's mental handicaps allowed her to empathize with children with similar problems and their families; and her observations and questions about racial prejudice led her to new insights about crossing cultural borders. Throughout, she showed not only how she learned to see and think differently, but what difference her insights made in how she taught these three children.

In contrast to these very personal entrees into community, Paul Skilton-Sylvester (1994, 1999) described a critical pedagogy he enacted in a third-grade Philadelphia classroom. He documented how students interrogated their own neighborhood by creating a classroom economy called Sweet Cakes Town and exploring such issues as injustice, successful entrepreneurship, homelessness, and cooperation. By problematizing the image of the charismatic teacher, Skilton-Sylvester offers that those of us with less charisma can engage students by directly involving them in substantive and pointed investigations into the workings of their own community. Rather than creating a cult of the individual, the class instead created a culture of inquiry.

Involving students in learning about their own communities is a hallmark of teacher inquiry in organizations like Foxfire, with its many in-house publications such as *Hands On: A Journal for Teachers*, and the Bread Loaf Rural Teacher Network (BLRTN), publishers of a magazine written by rural teachers. The work of teachers in these networks helps students learn of their rich cultural heritages, and in the process, students often delve into equity and social justice issues affecting their communities. For example, Juanita Lavadie (1996), a BLRTN teacher at a Bureau of Indian Affairs school on the Taos Pueblo Reservation, wrote about a schoolwide effort to integrate the culture of the Taos Pueblo into the curriculum. The school staff, two thirds of whom are tribal members, surveyed school and community members to learn not only what various community members might contribute to the curriculum, but also to develop a shared decision-making process for both preserving tribal ways and preparing students for a changing world. In doing so they investigated issues of distribution of ownership, responsibility, and shared commitment to their children's education.

By enlarging the classroom to include the community that has a stake in the learning that occurs in that classroom, these studies create images of places where the voices and experiences of students and parents count in significant ways toward the ways literacy is learned. In addition, by seeing the community as a setting of both advantage and disadvantage, the teacher research described here creates a frame for using community as a window for understanding the actions of the larger, more complex world beyond the neighborhood.

## Directions and Implications

Teacher inquiry, like all research traditions, has it limitations, many of which have been discussed in the professional literature. Concerns include such issues as ethics (Hammack, 1997), hierarchical and political struggle (Herr, 1999), methodology and ways of knowing (Ballenger, 1996c; Fenstermacher, 1994; Huberman, 1996), and what constitutes teacher research (Raphael, 1999). However, we see these concerns not as reasons for disregarding teacher research, but as a means for advancing a dialogue that serves to deepen and strengthen research from an *emic* perspective. We agree with Lytle (2000) when she advises that neither uninterrogated celebrations of teacher research nor critique based on normative research frameworks is useful in discussing or assessing what it means to inquire into one's own practice. All research methodology is simultaneously suspect and enabling; the more we come to understand about the limitations of all educational research, the more we'll know about the necessity of accessing a range of research perspectives, voices, and methodologies.

However, in the spirit of critique inspired by the willingness of teacher researchers to raise questions about their practice, our review of this particular literature raises questions about the impact of teacher research on policy and practice related to equity and social justice issues in schooling. How is what teachers are learning influencing education beyond the individual classroom? How is this information being used by policymakers—or is it—at the school, district, state, and national levels? How are the insights, practices, and recommendations generated in this wealth of research on sociocultural and equity issues being incorporated by university-based researchers—or are they? Even university researchers who support teacher research too frequently limit their citations to other university researchers.

Do our questions demand an impact that is inconsistent with the goals of classroom inquiry? The stated or implied purpose of most teacher research is a very specific focus on the improvement of practice in that researcher's classroom, with the notable exception of schoolwide action research (e.g., Allen, Rogers, Hensley, Glanton, & Livingston, 1999; Calhoun, 1994; Wells et al., 1994). Further, most of the research we reviewed for this chapter, like much other teacher research, is qualitative in nature and does not pretend to imply generalizability. Yet given these local intentions and even honoring the wishes of many teacher researchers to keep their knowledge local, it is puzzling why so much first-hand knowledge seems to be ignored by policymakers and academics. This is especially puzzling when we consider the quality of the work discussed here. We wonder if, similar to the schism that exists for some between qualitative and quantitative research, teacher research is relegated by many academics and policymakers to the margins of acceptable research practice. Or is it simply, like the persistent critique plaguing all educational researchers, that we in the research community have no real impact on teaching and learning (Miller, 1999; Wideen, Mayer-Smith, & Moon, 1998)?

Perhaps we are looking in the wrong places. Perhaps we are thinking of impact in outdated and ineffectual terms—number of citations in research journals, direct links to district policy statements, or influence on textbook content. Some who study school change are suggesting that while official educational policies change rapidly and may give lip service to being "research based," change in practice occurs in a much different manner. It has to be locally constructed. "Truths," even about such widely accepted concerns as providing equity in teaching and learning, are generated one teacher, one classroom, and even one student at a time.

Does this mean that we should expect no influence of the insightful researchers cited in this chapter beyond their own classrooms? Not at all. It means that fostering and following that influence is a much more complex task than previously imagined. Hubbard and Power, who have supported teachers all over the country through publishing their work, are now "channel[ing] our energies away from helping teachers write up their work for academic journals, and towards more political, proactive vehicles" (1999, p. 288). They and others are searching for meaningful forms and forums for increasing the impact of teacher research on policy and practice.

So what might this impact look like? There is a potential for influence not only whenever another researcher, policymaker, or educator reads something written by a teacher researcher, but whenever the teacher next door to Cindy Ballenger asks her, "Why don't these kids like picture books?," or the teacher across the hall from Betty Shockley asks, "How did you get these parents so involved?" There is a potential for influence whenever a teacher reads about what another teacher has learned and responds, not by adopting the exact approach or practice, but by investigating equity and social justice issues and practice in his or her own classroom. There is potential for impact every time school leadership puts their broad commitment to educational equity into action and creates structures wherein teacher researchers have teaching loads and schedules that accommodate rather than limit their capacity to inquire.

There are other questions. The researchers reviewed here are predominantly European American women. Why are there fewer males and teachers of color of either gender conducting teacher research—or are they not being published? This somewhat narrow range—or at least more narrow than it perhaps should be—of researchers raises questions about representation and what interpretations we make through research that largely depends on interpretation. How might an African American or Latina teacher represent children, their language, and their cultures differently than do European American teachers? Given that there are multiple ways of "reading" any data, how can those of us working across cultural boundaries find ways to provide the most insightful and culturally authentic representations of students? When Allen, Michalove, and Shockley (1993) wrote about African American children, one of the children's

teachers, herself African American, took great exception to the use of Shannon's dialect. "You make all Black children sound ignorant when you use that language," she argued. The authors met with her, considered her opinion, but published the study using the children's language. Did they have the right to represent Shannon and the other children this way? Did they have a right not to?

This leads us to ask the entire research community what we are ignoring or misinterpreting by not inviting and hearing other voices as we make sense of classroom-based research. One answer is that we need to look more to in-house publications for these voices. The National Writing Project has been fertile ground for diverse voices, especially in its urban and rural sites. The Bread Loaf Rural Teacher Network includes African American, Native American, Alaskan Native, and Latino/a teachers writing about their schools and communities. Publications such as *Rethinking Schools: An Urban Educational Journal*, *Democracy and Education*, and *Teaching Tolerance Magazine*, while they have national distribution, are somewhat outside of mainstream academic writing. Yet they often contain articles written by teachers dealing with equity and social justice issues; one whole issue of *Rethinking Schools* (Perry & Delpit, 1997) devoted to "The Real Ebonics Debate: Power, Language, and the Education of African American Children" included African American teacher voices, voices conspicuously absent in the national debate.

In addition, we need to actively engage in dialogue across cultures. Part of this query speaks to the greater general diversity of race, ethnicity, and gender to which we've already referred. Specifically, however, we also need to pull students into research roles. Frequently, we who research represent students in our studies—whether we are working across cultural boundaries or not. However, what are we losing by not including them as coresearchers? If teachers provide an *emic* voice on teaching, students must be the voices of learning, and resisting learning (e.g., Branscombe, Goswami, & Schwartz, 1992; Egan-Robertson & Bloome, 1998; Oldfather et al., 1999). How can we enlarge the roles of those who are underrepresented or better understand why some who are members of underrepresented groups elect not to participate?

These questions are critical but they do not diminish the unique and necessary perspectives teachers bring to educational research, theory, and practice. The research in this chapter comments on some of the most compelling issues in educating a diverse society that aspires to democratic principles: the ways literacy and identity are intimately woven together, the ways students come to understand themselves by making meaning of the texts in and of their world, how cultural boundaries are crossed by teachers and students, how difference matters and how understanding of difference matters even more, and what it means to take an inquiry stance on learning. By doing so, it serves as a model of descriptive/interpretive research that takes substantive stances with compassionate perspectives and that in many cases results in changes in teaching and learning.

In risking both their research methodology and their pedagogy, teacher researchers continue to embed their investigations in problems that rise out of the circumstances of their own teaching. Their first audience is most always themselves. However, we are seeing more and more examples of how teachers are sharing this knowledge with others. Given these circumstances, in what ways can the broad educational community in schools, universities, state departments, and other agencies learn from, extend, and employ the insights of teacher researchers to make the literacy education of our children equitable and the applications of their literacies engines of social justice?

# References

Allen, A. (1997). Creating space for discussions about social justice and equity in an elementary classroom. *Language Arts, 74*(7), 518-524.

Allen, J. (1995). *It's never too late: Leading adolescents to lifelong literacy.* Portsmouth, NH: Heinemann.

Allen, J. (Ed.). (1999). *Class actions: Teaching for social justice in elementary and middle school.* New York: Teachers College Press.

Allen, J., Cary, M., & Delgado, L. (1995). *Exploring blue highways: Literacy reform, school change, and the creation of learning communities.* New York: Teachers College Press.

Allen, J., Michalove, B., & Shockley, B. (1993). *Engaging children: Community and chaos in the lives of young literacy learners.* Portsmouth, NH: Heinemann.

Allen, J., & Shockley, B. (1996). Composing a research dialogue: University and school research communities encountering a cultural shift. *Reading Research Quarterly, 31*(2), 220-228.

Allen, L., Rogers, D., Hensley, F., Glanton, M., & Livingston, M. (1999). *A guide to renewing your school: Lessons from the League of Professional Schools.* San Francisco: Jossey-Bass.

Ashton-Warner, S. (1963). *Teacher.* New York: Simon & Schuster.

Ballenger, C. (1996a). Learning the ABCs in a Haitian preschool: A teacher's story. *Language Arts, 73,* 317-323.

Ballenger, C. (1996b). Oral preparation for literature: Text and interpretation in a Haitian preschool. *Teacher Research, 4*(1), 85-103.

Ballenger, C. (1996c). [Review of the book *Teacher research and urban literacy education: Lessons and conversations in a feminist key*]. *Teachers College Record, 97*(4), 660-664.

Ballenger, C. (1998). *Teaching other people's children: Literacy and learning in a bilingual classroom.* New York: Teachers College Press.

Banford, H. (1996). The blooming of Maricar: Writing workshop and the phantom student. In H. Banford, M. Berkman, C. Chin, C. Cziko, B. Fecho, D. Jumpp, C. Miller, & M. Resnick. *Cityscapes: Eight views from the urban classroom* (pp. 3-24). Berkeley, CA: National Writing Project.

Banford, H., Berkman, M., Chin, C., Cziko, C., Fecho, B., Jumpp, D., Miller, C., & Resnick, M. (1996). *Cityscapes: Eight views from the urban classroom.* Berkeley, CA: National Writing Project.

Barbieri, M. (1995). *Sounds from the heart: Learning to listen to girls.* Portsmouth, NH: Heinemann.

Baumann, J., Bisplinghoff, B., & Allen, J. (1997). Methodology in teacher research: Three cases. In J. Flood, S. Heath, & D. Lapp (Eds.). *Handbook of research on teaching literacy through the communicative and visual arts* (pp. 121-143). New York: Macmillan.

Berkman, M. (1996). No problem. We can speak with the hands: Group work in a sheltered high school classroom. In H. Banford, M. Berkman, C. Chin, C. Cziko, B. Fecho, D. Jumpp, C. Miller, & M. Resnick. *Cityscapes: Eight views from the urban classroom* (pp. 25-53). Berkeley, CA: National Writing Project.

Bigelow, W. (1992a). Inside the classroom: social vision and critical pedagogy. In P. Shannon (Ed.), *Becoming political: Readings and writings in the politics of literacy education* (pp. 72-82). Portsmouth, NH: Heinemann.

Bigelow, W. (1992b). Once upon a genocide: Christopher Columbus in children's literature. *Language Arts, 69,* 112-120.

Bigelow, W. (1997). On the road to cultural bias: A critique of *The Oregon Trail* CD-ROM. *Language Arts, 74,* 84-93.

Blackburn, M. (1999). Studying privilege in a middle school gifted class. In J. Allen (Ed.), *Class actions: Teaching for social justice in elementary and middle school* (pp. 72-83). New York: Teachers College Press.

Bowers, B. (1998, April). "Girl" to girls: Literature and learning in a male feminist's classroom. Paper presented at the annual meeting of the American Educational Research Association, San Diego, CA.

Branscombe, A., Goswami, D., & Schwartz, J. (Eds.), (1992). *Students teaching, teachers learning.* Portsmouth, NH: Heinemann.

Brown, S. (1998, April). Learning together and separately: A teacher research group looks at gender. Paper presented at the annual meeting of the American Educational Research Association, San Diego, CA.

Burch, R. (1987). *Queenie Peavy.* New York: Viking.

Calhoun, E. (1994). *How to use action research in the self-renewing school.* Alexandria, VA: ASCD.

Chandler, K. (1997). Emerging researchers: One group's beginnings. *Teacher Research, 4*(2), 73-100.

Chin, C. (1996). "Are you the teacher who gives parents homework." In H. Banford, M. Berkman, C. Chin, C. Cziko, B. Fecho, D. Jumpp, C. Miller, & M. Resnick. *Cityscapes: Eight views from the urban classroom* (pp. 145-163). Berkeley, CA: National Writing Project.

Christensen, L. (1989). Writing the word and the world. *English Journal, 79,* 14-18.

Christensen, L. (1990). Teaching standard English: Whose standard? *English Journal, 80,* 36-40.

Christensen, L. (1993). Tales from an untracked class. *Rethinking Schools, 7*(2), 19-23.

Cintorino, M. (1994, October). Discovering their voices, valuing their words. *English Journal, 83,* 33-40.

Cochran-Smith, M., & Lytle, S. (1993). *Inside outside: Teacher research and knowledge.* New York: Teachers College Press.

Cochran-Smith, M., & Lytle, S. (1999). Relationships of knowledge and practice: Teacher learning in communities. In A. Iran-Nejad & P. D. Pearson (Eds.), *Review of research in education (Volume 24).* Washington, DC: AERA.

Cone, J. K. (1992, May). Untracking advanced placement English: Creating opportunity is not enough. *Phi Delta Kappan,* 712-717.

Cone, J. K. (1993, October). Using classroom talk to create community and learning. *English Journal, 83,* 30-38.

Cone, J. K. (1994). Appearing acts: Creating readers in a high school English class. *Harvard Educational Review, 64*(4), 450-473.

Daniel, P. (1996, March). Inducting an eighth grader into the literacy club. *English Journal, 85,* 32-35.

Deveare Smith, A. (1993). *Fires in the mirror: Crown Heights, Brooklyn, and other identities.* New York: Doubleday.

Delpit, L. (1988). The silenced dialogue: Power and pedagogy in educating other people's children. *Harvard Educational Review, 58*(3), 280-298.

Delpit, L. (1995). *Other people's children: Cultural conflict in the classroom.* New York: The New Press.

Deshon, J. A. P. (1997). Innocent and not-so innocent contributions to inequality: Choice, power, and insensitivity in a first-grade writing workshop. *Language Arts, 74,* 12–16.

Dewey, J. (1938). *Experience and education.* New York: Macmillan.

Diaz-Gemmati, G. (1999). "And justice for all": Using writing and literature to confront racism. In S. Freedman, E. Simons, J. Kalnin, A. Casereno, and the M-CLASS teams, *Inside city schools: Investigating literacy in multicultural classrooms* (pp. 57–76). New York: Teachers College Press.

DuBois, W. E. B. (1903). *The souls of Black folk.* New York: Washington Square Press.

Dyment, H. (1997, Spring/Summer). The Yup'ik encyclopedia of the Paul T. Albert Memorial School. *The Bread Loaf Rural Teachers Network Magazine,* 6–7.

Edelsky, C. (1996). *With literacy and justice for all: Rethinking the social in language and education.* London: Falmer Press.

Egan-Robertson, A., & Bloome, D. (1998). *Students as researchers of culture and language in their own communities.* Cresskill, NJ: Hampton Press.

Evans, K. S. (1995). Teacher reflection as a cure for tunnel vision. *Language Arts, 72,* 266–271.

Fecho, B. (1998). Crossing boundaries of race in a critical literacy classroom. In D. Alvermann, K. Hinchman, D. Moore, S. Phelps, & D. Waff (Eds.), *Reconceptualizing the literacies in adolescents' lives* (pp. 75–101). Mahwah, NJ: Lawrence Erlbaum Associates.

Fecho, B. (2000). Critical inquiries into language in an urban classroom. *Research in the Teaching of English, 34,* 354–381.

Fecho, B. (2001). "Why are you doing this?": Acknowledging and transcending threat in a critical inquiry classroom. *Research in the Teaching of English, 36*(1), 9–37.

Fenstermacher, G. (1994). The knower and the known: The nature of knowledge in research on teaching. In L. Darling-Hammond (Ed.), *Review of research in education (Vol. 20),* (pp. 3–56). Washington, DC: AERA.

Freedman, S., Simons, E., Kalnin, J., Casereno, A., & the M-Class Teams. (1999). *Inside city schools: Investigating literacy in multicultural classrooms.* New York: Teachers College Press.

Freire, P. (1970). *Pedagogy of the oppressed.* New York: Continuum.

Freire, P., & Macedo, D. (1996). A dialogue: Culture, language, and race. In P. Leistyna, A. Woodrum, & S. Sherblom (Eds.), *Breaking free: The transformative power of critical pedagogy* (pp. 199–228). Cambridge, MA: Harvard Educational Review.

Gallas, K. (1994). *The languages of learning: How children talk, write, dance, draw, and sing their understanding of the world.* New York: Teachers College Press.

Gallas, K. (1997). Story time as a magical act open only to the initiated: What some children don't know about power and may not find out. *Language Arts, 74,* 248–254.

Gallas, K. (1998). *"Sometimes I can be anything": Power, gender, and identity in a primary classroom.* New York: Teachers College Press.

Gaughan, J. (1996). Taking a walk in the contact zone. *Teacher Research, 4*(1), 1–11.

Gaughan, J. (1997). *Cultural reflections: Critical teaching and learning in the English classroom.* Portsmouth, NH: Heinemann.

Gaughan, J. (1999). From literature to language: Personal writing and critical pedagogy. *English Education, 31*(4), 310–326.

Gee, J. (1986). Orality and literacy: From *The Savage Mind* to *Ways with Words. TESOL Quarterly, 20,* 719–746.

Gee, J. (2000). Teenagers in new times: A new literacy studies perspective. *Journal of Adolescent and Adult Literacy, 43*(5), 412–420.

Giroux, H. (1992). *Border crossing: Cultural workers and the politics of education.* New York: Routledge.

Goldblatt, E. (1995). *'Round my way: Authority and double consciousness in three urban high school writers.* Pittsburgh, PA: University of Pittsburgh Press.

Goldblatt, P. (1998, November). Experience and acceptance of post-colonial literature in the high school English class. *English Journal, 88,* 71–77.

Goswami, D., & Stillman, P. (1987). *Reclaiming the classroom: Teacher research as an agency for change.* Upper Montclair, NJ: Boynton/Cook.

Graham, P., Hudson-Ross, S., Adkins, C., McWhorter, P., & Stewart, J. (1999). *Teacher mentor: A dialogue for collaborative learning.* New York: Teachers College Press.

Gunkel, J. (1991). "Please teach America": Keisuke's journey into a language community. *Language Arts, 68,* 303–310.

Hammack, F. (1997). Ethical issues in teacher research. *Teachers College Record, 99*(2), 247–265.

Hankins, K. (1998). Cacophony to symphony: Memoirs in teacher research. *Harvard Educational Review, 68*(1), 80–95.

Hankins, K. (1999). Silencing the lambs. In J. Allen (Ed.), *Class actions: Teaching for social justice in elementary and middle school* (pp. 61–71). New York: Teachers College Press.

Herr, K. (1999). Unearthing the unspeakable: When teacher research and political agendas collide. *Language Arts, 77*(1), 10–15.

Hole, S. (1998). Teacher as rain dancer. *Harvard Educational Review, 68*(3), 413–412.

Hollingsworth, S., & Sockett, H. (Eds.). (1994). *Teacher research and educational reform: Yearbook of the NSSE.* Chicago: University of Chicago Press.

Hubbard, R., Barbieri, M., & Power, B. (1998). *We want to be known: Learning from adolescent girls.* York, ME: Stenhouse.

Hubbard, R., & Power, B. (1993). *The art of classroom inquiry: A handbook for classroom researchers.* Portsmouth, NH: Heinemann.

Hubbard, R., & Power, B. (1999). *Living the questions: A guide for teacher-researchers.* York, ME: Stenhouse.

Huberman, M. (1996). Focus on research moving mainstream: Taking a closer look at teacher research. *Language Arts, 73*(2), 124–140.

Hudelson, S., & Lindfors, J. (Eds.). (1993). *Delicate balances: Collaborative research in language education.* Urbana, IL: NCTE.

Igoa, C. (1995). *The inner world of the immigrant child.* New York: St. Martin's Press.

Jumpp, D. (1996). Extending the literate community: Literacy over a life span. In H. Banford, M. Berkman, C. Chin, C. Cziko, B. Fecho, D. Jumpp, C. Miller, & M. Resnick. *Cityscapes: Eight views from the urban classroom* (pp. 133–144). Berkeley, CA: National Writing Project.

Laurence, M. (1993). *The stone angel.* Chicago: University of Chicago Press.

Lavadie, J. (1996, Fall/Winter). Taos Day School: A school-community reform process. *Bread Loaf Rural Teacher Network Magazine,* 30–31.

Lytle, S. (2000). Teacher research in the contact zone. In M. Kamil, R. Barr, P. Mosenthal, & D. Pearson (Eds.). *Handbook of reading research (Volume III)* (pp. 691–718) New York: Longman.

Meyer, R. J. (1995). Stories to teach and teaching to story: The use of narrative in learning to teach. *Language Arts, 72,* 276–286.

Michalove, B. (1999). Circling in: Examining prejudice in history and in ourselves. In J. Allen (Ed.), *Class actions: Teaching for social justice in elementary and middle school* (pp. 21–33). New York: Teachers College Press.

Miller, D. W. (1999, August 6). The black hole of education research. *The Chronicle of Higher Education,* A17–18.

Moore, R. (1996). Between a rock and, a hard place: African Americans and Standard English. ERIC Document No. EDY02593.

Murphy, P. (1994). Antonio: My student, my teacher: My inquiry begins. *Teacher Research, 1*(2), 75-88.

Nava, G. (Director). (1983). *El norte.* [Film].

Oldfather, P., Thomas, S., Eckert, L., Garcia, F., Grannis, N., Kilgore, J., Newman-Gonchar, A., Peterson, B., Rodriguez, P., & Tjioe, M. (1999). The nature and outcomes of students' longitudinal participatory research on literacy motivations and schooling. *Research in the Teaching of English, 34*(2), 281-320.

Paley, V. (1979). *White teacher.* Cambridge, MA: Harvard University Press.

Paley, V. (1981). *Wally's stories: Conversations in the kindergarten.* Cambridge, MA: Harvard University Press.

Paley, V. (1984). *Boys and girls: Superheroes in the doll corner.* Chicago: University of Chicago Press.

Paley, V. (1988). *Bad guys don't have birthdays: The use of storytelling in the classroom.* Cambridge, MA: Harvard University Press.

Paley, V. (1992). *You can't say you can't play.* Cambridge, MA: Harvard University Press.

Paley, V. (1995). *Kwanzaa and me.* Cambridge, MA: Harvard University Press.

Paley, V. (1997). *The girl with the brown crayon.* Cambridge, MA: Harvard University Press.

Paley, V. (1999). *The kindness of children.* Cambridge, MA: Harvard University Press.

Pavalko, S. (1998, April). Play as alternative discourse. Paper presented at the annual meeting of the American Educational Research Association, San Diego, CA.

Perry, T., & Delpit, L. (Eds.), (1997). *The real Ebonics debate: Power, language, and the education of African American children,* a special issue of *Rethinking Schools, 12*(1), 1.

Phillips, A. (1997). Feeling expressed: Portrait of a young poet. *Language Arts, 74*(5), 325-332.

Raphael, T. (1999). What counts as teacher research?: An essay. *Language Arts, 77*(1), 48-52.

Resnick, M. (1996). Making connections between families and schools. In H. Banford, M. Berkman, C. Chin, C. Cziko, B. Fecho, D. Jumpp, C. Miller, & M. Resnick. *Cityscapes: Eight views from the urban classroom* (pp. 115-132). Berkeley, CA: National Writing Project.

Reyes, M. de la luz. (1991). A process approach to literacy instruction for Spanish-speaking students: In search of a best fit. In E. Hiebert (Ed.), *Literacy for a diverse society.* New York: Teachers College Press.

Rief, L. (1999). *Vision and voice: Extending the literacy spectrum.* Portsmouth, NH: Heinemann.

Schadler, S., Ladner, S., & Montaño, G. (1997, Spring/Summer). Inquiring into a language of power. *Bread Loaf Rural Teacher Network Magazine,* 20-22.

Schwartz, J. (1992). On the move in Pittsburgh: When students and teacher share research. In A. Branscombe, D. Goswami, & J. Schwartz (Eds.), *Students teaching, teachers learning* (pp. 107-119). Portsmouth, NH: Boynton/Cook.

Shockley, B. (1993). Extending the literate community. *The New Advocate, 6*(1), 11-24.

Skilton-Sylvester, P. (1994). Elementary school curricula and urban transformation. *Harvard Educational Review, 64*(3), 309-331.

Skilton-Sylvester, P. (1999). Teaching without charisma: Involving third graders as co-investigators of their inner-city neighborhood. In C. Edelsky (Ed.), *Making justice our project: Teachers working toward critical whole language practice* (pp. 144-162). Urbana, IL: NCTE.

Sowder, W. (1993, October). Fostering discussion in the language-arts classroom. *English Journal, 83,* 39-42.

Stumbo, C. (1992). Giving their words back to them: Cultural journalism in Eastern Kentucky. In A. Branscombe, D. Goswami, & J. Schwartz (Eds.), *Students teaching, teachers learning* (pp. 124-142). Portsmouth, NH: Boynton/Cook.

Sturk, A. (1992). Developing a community of learners inside and outside the classroom. In P. Shannon (Ed.), *Becoming political: Readings and writings in the politics of literacy education* (pp. 263-273). Portsmouth, NH: Heinemann.

Swaim, J. (1998). In search of an honest response. *Language Arts, 73*(2), 118-125.

Sweeney, M. (1997). "No easy road to freedom": Critical literacy in a fourth-grade classroom. *Reading & Writing Quarterly, 13,* 279-290.

Taylor, T. (1999). Addressing social justice in class meetings: Can we choose our battles? In J. Allen (Ed.), *Class actions: Teaching for social justice in elementary and middle school* (pp. 34-43). New York: Teachers College Press.

Tendero, J. (1998). Worth waiting for: Girls writing for their lives in the Bronx. *Teacher Research, 5*(2), 10-25.

Threatt, S. (1998, April). Beyond the coin: First steps in the careful consideration of a suburban-based critical pedagogy. Paper presented at the annual meeting of the American Educational Research Association, San Diego, CA.

Torres, M. (1998). Celebrations and letters home: Research as an ongoing conversation among students, parents and teacher. In A. Egan-Robertson, & D. Bloome (Eds.), *Students as researchers of culture and language in their own communities* (pp. 59-68). Cresskill, NJ: Hampton Press.

Waff, D. (1994). Girl talk: Creating community through social exchange. In M. Fine (Ed.), *Chartering urban school reform* (pp. 192-203). New York: Teachers College Press.

Waff, D. (1995). Romance in the classroom: Inviting discourse on gender and power. *The Quarterly of the National Writing Project, 17*(2), 15-18.

Waff, D., & Yoshida, H. (1996). Talking across boundaries: The collaborative construction of identity. *Literacy Networks, 2,* 65-74.

Wells, G., Bernard, L., Gianotti, M., Keating, C., Konjevic, C., Kowal, M., Maher, A., Mayer, C., Moscoe, T., Orzechowska, E., Smiega, A., & Swartz, L. (1994). *Changing schools from within: Creating communities of inquiry.* Portsmouth, NH: Heinemann.

Whishaw, I. (1994, September). Translation project: Breaking the "English only" rule. *English Journal, 84,* 28-30.

Wideen, M., Mayer-Smith, J., & Moon, B. (1998). A critical analysis of the research on learning to teach: Making the case for an ecological perspective on inquiry. *Review of Educational Research, 68*(2), 130-178.

Wilhelm, J. (1995). *"You gotta be the book": Teaching engaged and reflective reading with adolescents.* New York: Teachers College Press.

Winikur, G. (1998, April). Keeping it real. Paper presented at the annual meeting of the American Educational Research Association, San Diego, CA.

Zack, V. (1991). "It was the worst of times": Learning about the Holocaust through literature. *Language Arts, 68,* 42-48.

Zeichner, K., & Noffke, S. (in press). Practitioner research. In V. Richardson (Ed.), *Handbook of research on teaching.* New York: MacMillan.

# SYNTHESIS RESEARCH IN LANGUAGE ARTS INSTRUCTION

*Carl B. Smith*
Indianà University

*Susan S. Klein**
U.S. Department of Education

When William S. Gray was cataloging reading research more than 50 years ago, do you think he could have foreseen the explosion of research in language arts since the end of World War II? Gray's annual summaries of research became a major contribution to the profession, and the annual summary of research in reading has been carried forward over the past 20 years by Sam Weintraub and his associates. Today, it is almost inconceivable that a language arts dissertation or major study would not make use of current annual summaries in reading, English, and instruction.

Summaries and syntheses of research hold treasures for many people besides those who are writing their dissertations. Teachers and administrators who wrestle with daily decisions about curriculum and instruction can find guidance in documents that examine research across numerous studies on the same issue. This chapter defines synthesis research and offers criteria for judging the value of a synthesis paper. It also gives examples of language arts synthesis documents in categories that may be useful to teachers.

Knowledge synthesis is here defined as a cluster of activities often called literature review, research review, interpretive analysis, integrative review, research integration, meta-analysis, state-of-the-art summarizing, evaluation synthesis, or best evidence synthesis. It involves pulling together related extant knowledge from research, evaluation, and practice on specified topics or issues.

## WHERE TO START

English language arts education has so many individual pieces of research that it is difficult for individuals to know where to start when they examine research questions. Under the broad headings of reading, writing, and teaching language arts, each one could generate 10,000 studies, assuming a person had access to all the major research databases, such as ERIC, Psychological Abstracts, Education Index, and so on. Modern computerized search techniques make it possible to refine a library search and thus limit the available studies to the specific interests of the researcher. One can then locate documents that pertain to a question about "the value of prewriting activities on composition performance in the junior high school," and similar narrowly defined topics. But even then, the list of available studies may far exceed the time or the energy that the researcher can devote to analyzing all material. That's where synthesis research enters the picture.

As the number of studies on a particular topic multiply, it becomes increasingly valuable to have and to use resources that summarize or synthesize that research. Then, for example, the annual summary of research in English and the annual summary of research in reading become invaluable. For the same reason handbooks, such as this one, and the *Handbook on Reading Research*, offer educators summarized and synthesized views of

---

*The ideas in this chapter from Dr. Klein are based on "Research and Practice: Implications for Knowledge Synthesis in Education" (Klein, 1989) and do not necessarily reflect the views of her employer, the U.S. Department of Education.

the broad literature. Besides the pertinent studies that answer an individual's research question directly, it is helpful to have the same question seen in a broader perspective through the summaries prepared by individuals and by organizations such as federally funded educational labs and the ERIC/Reading and Communication Skills Clearinghouse.

Cyclical trends in education remind educators of the value of reviewing past research as well as present studies. Doctoral dissertations, for instance, could serve the profession well through their literature reviews by offering syntheses of the topics under consideration and by placing these topics in historical perspective. An historical view of a particular issue might reveal the manner in which old questions keep arising and how research has changed our perception or knowledge of a particular issue. The use of children's literature in the curriculum, for example, and the integration of the language arts were major concerns in the early 1960s and became issues again in the 1980s: A synthesis of that research over those 25 years can give insight into the similarities and the differences of those two issues in two separated decades. Merely reading a half-dozen studies of recent vintage would deprive the researcher of an important perspective and might limit the value of his or her conclusions.

In an article on how to use research evidence from many studies, Light and Pillemer (1984) suggest two major strategies for synthesis research and conflict resolution: "One strategy is to read through the various findings and reach a series of impressionistic conclusions. A second approach is to apply precise analytic procedures to the collection of studies." Among the specific benefits of synthesizing data, they found that it increases the power of the data. It is well known that the larger the sample size, the more likely an effect will be detected as statistically significant. By pooling the information from a number of smaller studies into a single analysis, it is possible to improve the power of statistical tests. As an example, Light and Pillemer discussed two studies that measured the number of books in a child's home and correlated that information with the child's achievement test scores. In the first study, which included homes having mostly fewer than 200 books, there was no noticeable effect on school performance. But when they added a second study asking the same question, they found a significant effect as the number of books in the home rose into the 200 to 400 range. Then there was a significant increase in the achievement scores (p. 181). As the number of books in a home pushed beyond 200, there was a corresponding increase in school grades. But those effects were notieable only when the data from the two studies were meshed together.

Another value of synthesis research is that it helps us to view conflict in a constructive way. Suppose that two studies reveal conflicting outcomes. Synthesis research gives us an opportunity to look for explanations about divergent findings. Were the treatments different in some significant way? Were data collected in a similar fashion? Were the populations different? Thus, conflict acts as a warning to the reviewer, indicating that a more detailed analysis needs to be conducted, Pillemer and Light suggest that an investigator may find a resolution to conflict in other content areas where similar studies have been conducted.

## PURPOSES OF KNOWLEDGE SYNTHESIS

The general purposes of knowledge synthesis are:

1. To increase the knowledge base by identifying new insights, needs, and research agenda that are related to specific topics.
2. To improve access to evidence in a given area by distilling and reducing large amounts of information efficiently and effectively.
3. To help readers make informed decisions or choices by increasing their understanding of the syntheses topic.
4. To provide a comprehensive, well-organized content base to facilitate interpretation activities such as the development of textbooks, training tools, guidelines, information digests, oral presentations, and videotapes.

In the 1975 *Catalog of NIE Education Projects*, Spencer Ward categorized 72 of the 660 catalog entries as knowledge synthesis products. Most of these knowledge synthesis products were developed by the ERIC Clearinghouses and Research and Development (R&D) Centers and Laboratories (Ward, 1976, p. 12). A recent search of the Office of Educational Research and Improvement/National Institute of Education (OERI/NIE) project information database from 1979 to 1988, indicates a wide variety of knowledge synthesis projects ranging from an inexpensive commissioned paper to an elaborate meta-analysis.

An examination of the ERIC *Resources in Education* (RIE) database as of 1988, indicates that 2,030 U.S. Department of Education sponsored documents were classified as Information Analysis Products and/or identified as knowledge synthesis, information analysis, literature review, meta-analysis, integrative analysis, integrative review, evaluation synthesis, or state-of-the-art reviews. (Because all types of ERIC Clearinghouse produced documents are coded as ERIC Information Analysis Products, this total for knowledge synthesis documents is inflated.) This federal contribution represents 12% of all such knowledge synthesis documents in the ERIC RIE database. Putting this in a larger perspective, it is interesting to note that 6% of all documents in both the RIE (16,805) and *Current Index to Journals in Education* (CIJE) (20,891) ERIC database fit this broad knowledge synthesis definition.

In 1977, Ward addressed the problem of the uneven quality of synthesis papers by organizing a conference to plan follow-up research. Information on much of the subsequent R&D is described in *Knowledge Structure and Use: Implications for Synthesis and Interpretation* (Ward & Reed, 1983). In addition to developing useful synthesis products in a wide variety of areas ranging from mathematics to school desegregation, the NIE dissemination group developed models that use a consensus building process for synthesis work. The "Research Within Reach" series supported by this group demonstrated how a consensus process can be used to identify and respond to teachers' questions. The viability of this approach is indicated by *Research Within Reach: Secondary School Reading* (Alvermann, Moore, & Conley, 1988). The dissemination group's most recent R&D on knowledge synthesis was a project by Harris Cooper covering 1982 to 1985. Cooper surveyed knowledge synthesis producers (including authors of ERIC Information Analysis products). Survey questions addressed reviewers' content expertise, knowledge synthesis goals and procedures (Cooper, 1983, 1986a, 1986b). Some of this work is also reflected in *The Integrative Research Review* (Cooper, 1984), which describes how general research methods may be used to guide knowledge synthesis work.

While researchers supported by the NIE dissemination group used meta-analyses and other synthesis approaches for their substantive work, some researchers refined these methods or developed new synthesis approaches. For example, through his work at the Johns Hopkins R&D Centers, Robert Slavin (1986, 1987) developed a knowledge synthesis procedure called "best evidence synthesis." Numerous other researchers, such as Gregg Jackson, Robert Rich, Herbert Walberg, Richard Light, and their colleagues produced many synthesis products and wrote thoughtfully on the synthesis process (Light & Pillemer, 1984; Jackson, 1980; Rich, 1983; Walberg & Haertel, 1980).

## WHAT HAS BEEN LEARNED ABOUT IMPROVING KNOWLEDGE SYNTHESIS?

The profession is starting to learn about the characteristics and potential indicators of quality knowledge synthesis because the federal government has funded a great deal of knowledge synthesis; and individuals are conducting some research on knowledge synthesis practices and examining R&D on knowledge synthesis.

The discussion of these characteristics and indicators will be grouped into four criteria clusters that are based on similar clusters developed by Klein (1976) for the review and selection of knowledge interpretation products such as instructional or training materials. Additional quality indicators were based on results from Klein's 1987 survey of ERIC Clearinghouse knowledge synthesis practices and criteria, a review of research on knowledge synthesis in education and related areas, and discussion with managers of knowledge synthesis work.

### Intrinsic Qualities

The intrinsic quality of a knowledge synthesis document may be judged by experts. Often it is necessary to use different reviewers for these different criteria. For example, it may be advisable to have one or more experts in the content area covered, experts in the knowledge synthesis methodologies used, experts in writing, and educational equity experts for the social fairness criteria.

1. *Nature of Knowledge Synthesis Content.*
   - Is the coverage sufficiently comprehensive and inclusive or at least representative?
   - Is the evidence sufficiently central or pivotal to the topic? (Cooper, 1986b, p. 17)
   - Is the topic not too small or too large for this comprehensive coverage? (Katz, 1986)

   - Is the evidence (information) based on extant research, development, evaluation, and/or practice?
   - Is the evidence sufficiently current and timely and of cutting edge interest?
   - Are significant variables, assumptions, interactions, and analytic questions clearly defined and addressed?
   - Are the evidence, analyses, syntheses, and conclusions accurate and appropriately qualified and interpreted (i.e., with context, size and validity limitations) so that the reader will not reach wrong conclusions?
   - Are the evidence and analyses free of bias with respect to particular views? However, it may be appropriate for the author(s) to take either a neutral or espousal position when stating conclusions and implications (Cooper, 1986b).

2. *Technical Quality.*
   - Were appropriate knowledge synthesis methodological procedures for acquiring, evaluating, analyzing, combining, and describing exact evidence used—whether it was quantitative, qualitative or both?

     There are now many well developed procedures for various types of synthesis for quantitative and qualitative evidence. These are described in many guides on meta-analyses, a book on meta-ethnography (Noblit & Hare, 1988), articles on evaluation synthesis (Chelimsky & Morra, 1984; Slavin, 1986; 1987) and books on research review (Cooper, 1984; Light & Pillemer, 1984).
   - Were these appropriate knowledge synthesis methodological procedures for acquiring, evaluating, analyzing, combining, and explaining the evidence described in the body of the knowledge synthesis or in an easily accessible appendix?
   - Were the context and assumptions for the analytic framework and relevant variables presented so that the syntheses of the evidence is meaningful?
   - Was it clear whether the synthesis was intended to serve as an honest broker or advocate and whether it was intended to present evidence for alternatives or "best" solutions?

     Cooper (1985) pointed out that two of the seven AREA research review award winners from 1978 to 1984 were espousal rather than neutral in their presentations.
   - Is the information balanced in that it resolves, rather than obscures, inconsistencies in the evidence being synthesized? (See Cooper, 1986b, p. 7; Roberts, 1983, p. 479.)

3. *Social Fairness.*
   - Does it adhere to standards for the elimination of social group bias?
   - Does it report relevant information regarding sex, race, ethnicity, age, and socioeconomic status in evidence covered, and in the conclusions?

4. *Communications Quality.*
   - Is the knowledge synthesis well written? Developed logically? Appropriately focused, clear, and organized for the intended readers? Internally congruent and consistent?
   - Does it adhere to document design guidelines for clear writing such as those discussed by Landesman and Reed (1983)?
   - Is the level of detail (parsimony) and terminology appropriate for key audiences?

"As reviewers move from addressing specialized researchers to addressing the general public, they employ less jargon and detail while often paying greater attention to the implications of the work being covered" (Cooper, 1985, p. 7).

- Does it adhere to professional writing standards such as appropriate use of the American Psychological Association style manual, use of requested type size, format, length, permissions relating to copyrighted material, and so on, needed by the publisher?
- Is it dry and mechanical, or interesting and stimulating?
- Are creative formats such as discussing the evidence in terms of alternatives, or in terms of user questions and answers used when appropriate?

## Desirability, Utility, Effectiveness

These criteria can be judged by potential and actual users of the knowledge synthesis.

1. *Desirability.*
   - Is there a need or demand for a current knowledge synthesis on a given topic or would the work be redundant with existing syntheses?
   - Is there a sufficiently large evidence base that would involve many institutions and states?
   - Is the knowledge synthesis likely to address its intended purposes such as increasing knowledge in an area?
   - Do those who are sponsoring the knowledge synthesis work, or doing it, feel that the topic is educationally significant?
2. *Utility Practicality.*
   - Is the product appropriate for its intended users such as specialized scholars, general scholars, practitioners, policymakers or general public? (Dervin, 1983)
   - Is the knowledge synthesis presented in a physically appealing way so that recipients will want to read it?
   - Is the knowledge synthesis product user friendly? For example, is it appropriately self-contained so that its use does not depend heavily on other resources?
   - Is the size of the topic manageable in terms of user comprehension? (Katz, 1986).
   - Is the knowledge synthesis formatted and developed in such a way that it will be accessible to potential users (i.e., a chapter in a handbook or encyclopedia article, or published as an easily available monograph, book, or review journal article?).
   - Is the knowledge synthesis appropriately marketed or better yet, distributed for a sufficiently low cost or for free? (It may be possible to judge user satisfaction to some extent based on sales, but purchases may be limited because of a "thin market" audience or because the document is not part of an established "product line.")
   - Is the knowledge synthesis appropriately linked to one or more knowledge interpretation efforts to increase its visibility and potential utility?

- Does the knowledge synthesis contain a sufficient amount of appropriate interpretations?

  Research suggests that the utility of the knowledge synthesis is generally increased by clear interpretations (Cooper, 1986b), but such interpretations may simplify the information so that scholarly detail is omitted.

3. *Effectiveness.*
   - Can the users comprehend the knowledge synthesis and remember what they have read?
   - Is there any evidence that the readers learned from the knowledge synthesis as indicated by cognitive or behavioral tests?
   - Is there any evidence that the readers confirmed or changed their attitudes about a topic based on the knowledge synthesis?
   - To what extent was knowledge synthesis information used in knowledge interpretations or for direct decision making?
   - To what extent was knowledge synthesis information used to supplement the working knowledge of the reader? (Kennedy, 1983)
   - To what extent has the knowledge synthesis been cited in other work?

## Knowledge Synthesis Development Options

Aside from adhering to the logical technical synthesis procedures suggested in the intrinsic quality criteria, little is known about what constitutes an effective knowledge synthesis process. Thus, the following are provided as exploratory questions rather than quality indicators.

1. *Who Should Do the Knowledge Synthesis?*

   Experts in the content area? Multidisciplinary experts? Experts in synthesis methodology? Experts in writing for specific audiences? Potential knowledge synthesis users? A combination of any of these?

2. *Should Multiple Individuals or Groups Be Involved in the Synthesis Process?*

   Does the use of multiple participants increase the credibility of the work? (Ward, 1983, p. 553).

   If so, should the synthesis process be structured for consensus development and iterative reviews, collaborative work, or adversarial work? (Klein, Gold, Stalford, 1986; Stalford, 1987)

   Glaser (1980, p. 79) suggested the value of developing a state-of-the-art consensus document by iterative reviews and revisions of the drafts by multiple contributors.

   Vian and Johansen (1983, p. 494) suggested ways that computer conferencing may be used for collaborative synthesis work.

   Should the synthesis process be structured to obtain guidance from specific audiences such as potential knowledge synthesis users?

3. *What Systematic Knowledge Synthesis Processes Are Best?*

   Chelimsky and Morra (1984, p. 78) note that one of the characteristics of evaluation synthesis is "that designing backward from the information needed is both feasible and likely to ensure the relevance, timeliness, and use of the work performed." This approach differs from some research syntheses where the topic is determined based on the availability of the data.

## CONCLUSIONS

The questions and criteria provided can help individuals evaluate a particular document. Since purpose, breadth of coverage, and the nature of the analysis all contribute to the value of a synthesis paper, those criteria should be applied as appropriate.

When an important decision about instruction or curriculum development needs to be made about language arts, the decision makers want information. Knowledge synthesis documents offer that kind of summary information. Whether the issue concerns children with specific reading disabilities, process writing strategies, the effect of using children's fiction in a reading program, or the impact of sociocultural influences, there are synthesis studies available. Appended to this chapter are samples of synthesis documents arranged in several frequently used categories. They include only a small fraction of the synthesis papers available in the ERIC database and are presented here merely to indicate the variety that might be useful to language arts educators. (A more complete list of language arts synthesis references is available as a published bibliography from ERIC/RCS, Indiana University, Bloomington, IN 47405.)

## *References*

Alvermann, D., Moore, D., & Conley, M. (Eds.) (1988). *Research within reach: Secondary school reading*. Newark, DE: International Reading Association. (ED 282 187).

Chelimsky, E., & Morra, L. G. (1984). Evaluation synthesis for the legislative user. In W. H. Yeaton & P. M. Wortman (Eds.), *Issues in Data Synthesis*. In New Directions for Program Evaluation, Evaluation Research Society (pp. 75-89). Washington, DC: Jossey-Bass.

Cooper. H. (1984). *The integrative research review: A systematic approach*, Applied Social Research Methods Series (Vol. 2). Newbury Park, CA: Sage Publications.

Cooper, H. (1986a). Literature-searching strategies of integrative research reviewers. A first survey. *Knowledge: Creation, Diffusion, Utilization*, 372-383.

Cooper, H. (1986b). *Moving beyond meta-analysis*. Paper presented at a conference Workshop on the Future of Meta-analysis sponsored by the National Committee on Statistics, Oct. 19-21, Hedgeville, WV.

Cooper, H. (1983). *Six reviews of research on desegregation and black achievement: What they tell about knowledge synthesis*. Paper presented at the American Educational Research Association Annual Meeting, Montreal, Canada.

Cooper, H. (1985). *A taxonomy of literature reviews*. Paper presented at the annual meeting of the American Educational Research Association, Chicago.

Dervin, B. (1983). Information as a user construct: The relevance of perceived information needs so synthesis and interpretation. In S. A. Ward & L. J. Reed (Eds.), *Knowledge Structure and Use: Implications for Synthesis and Interpretation* (pp. 153-184). Philadelphia: Temple University Press.

Glaser, E. M. (1980). Using behavioral science strategies for defining the state-of-the-art. *The Journal of Applied Behavioral Science, 16*, 79-92.

Jackson, G. B. (1980). Methods for Integrative Reviews. *Reviews of Educational Research, 50*(3), 438-460.

Katz, L. G. (1986). Issues in the dissemination of child development knowledge. *Professionalism, Child Development, and Dissemination: Three Papers*, ERIC Clearinghouse on Elementary and Early Childhood Education.

Kennedy, M. M. (1983). Working knowledge. *Knowledge: Creation, Diffusion, Utilization, 5*(2), 193-211.

Klein, S. S. (1976). Toward consensus on minimum criteria for educational products. *Criteria for Reviewing Educational Products* (1978). Educational Products: Information Exchange Institute and the ERIC Clearinghouse on Information Resources, Syracuse, NY. (ED147318)

Klein, S. S., Gold, N., & Stalford, C. (1986). The convening process: A new technique for applying knowledge to practice. *Educational Evaluation and Policy Analysis, 8*(2), 189-204.

Klein S. S. (1989). Research and practice: Implications for knowledge synthesis in education. *Knowledge: Creation, Diffusion, Utilization, 11*(1), 58-78.

Landesman, J., & Reed, L. (1983). How to write a synthesis document for educational practitioners. In S. A. Ward & L. J. Reed (Eds.), *Knowledge structure and use: Implications for synthesis and interpretation* (pp. 576-642). Philadelphia: Temple University Press.

Light, R. J., & Pillemer, D. B. (1984). *Summing up: The science of reviewing research*. Cambridge, MA: Harvard University Press.

National Institute of Education (1975). *Catalog of NIE Education Products* (Vols. 1 & 2). Washington, D.C.: U.S. Department of Health, Education and Welfare.

Noblit, G. W., & Hare, R. D. (1988). *Meta-ethnography: synthesizing qualitative studies*. Qualitative Research Methods Series. Newbury Park, CA: Sage Publications.

Rich, R. (1983). Knowledge synthesis and problem solving. In S. A. Ward & L. J. Reed (Eds.), *Knowledge structure and use: Implications for synthesis and interpretation* (pp. 285-312). Philadelphia: Temple University Press.

Roberts, J. (1983). Quick turnaround synthesis/interpretation for practitioners. In S. A. Ward & L. J. Reed (Eds.), *Knowledge structure and use: Implications for synthesis and interpretation* (pp. 423-486). Philadelphia: Temple University Press.

Slavin, R. E. (1986). Best-evidence synthesis: An alternative to meta-analytic and traditional reviews, *Educational Research, 15*(9), 5-11.

Slavin, R. E. (1987). Best-evidence synthesis: Why less is more. *Educational Researcher, 16*(4), 15.

Stalford, C. B. (1987). Congruence in theory and practice: The convening process and the consensus development program. *Knowledge: Creation, Diffusion, Utilization, 9*(1), 4-18.

Vian, K., & Johansen, R. (1983). Knowledge synthesis and computer-based communications systems: Changing behaviors and concepts. In S. A. Ward & L. J. Reed (Eds.), *Knowledge structure and use: Implications for synthesis and interpretation* (pp. 489-514). Philadelphia: Temple University Press.

Walberg, H. J., & Haertel, E. H. (Eds.) (1980). Research Integration: The state-of-the-art [Entire issue]. *Evaluation in Education, 4*(1).

Ward, S. Summary of results of survey of current NIE synthesis activities (Memorandum to Harold Hodgkinson, Emerson Elliott and NIE Association Directors, March 1, 1976). National Institute of Education, Washington, D.C.

Ward, S. A., & Reed, L. J. (Eds.) (1983). *Knowledge structure and use: Implications for synthesis and interpretation.* Philadelphia: Temple University Press.

# APPENDIX: REPRESENTATIVE SYNTHESIS DOCUMENTS

## Reading

AN: EJ349079
AU: Dehart, Florence E.; Pauls, Leo W.
TI: Computerized Searches on Articles Reporting Reading Research: A Closer Look.
PY: 1987
JN: Reading Horizons; v27 n3 p209-17 Apr 1987
AV: UMI
DE: Databases; Language Usage; Online Searching; Psycholinguistics; Reading Instruction; Reading Research
ID: Computerized Search Services
AB: Compares the terminology used in three different computerized search services—CIJE, LLBA/Online, and PsycINFO—and shows how the choice of terminology used by them impedes retrieval. Suggests compensatory measures. (FL)

AN: ED276970
AU: Manning-Dowd, Alice
TI: The Effectiveness of SSR: A Review of the Research.
PY: [1985]
NT: 8 p.
PR: EDRS Price—MF01/PC01 Plus Postage
DE: Elementary Education; Research Needs
DE: Reading Attitudes; Reading Comprehension; Reading Instruction; Reading Research; Sustained Silent Reading; Teaching Methods
AB: In the past two decades, sustained silent reading (SSR) has gained attention as a component in many schools' reading programs. Some advocates of SSR differ slightly in their recommendations of specific rules, but most agree on the following guidelines: (1) no interruptions; (2) everyone reads, including the teacher; (3) students choose their own reading material; (4) no required reports; (5) a wide variety of reading materials should be available in the classroom; and (6) the time period should be increased gradually. Research conducted to determine the effects of SSR has produced mixed results, but most researchers seem to agree that SSR has a positive effect on reading comprehension and on students' attitudes about reading at all grade levels. However, research is less conclusive on the effect of SSR on students' reading achievement. Of the studies considered, six found SSR to have a significant positive effect on reading scores, whereas five showed no significant improvement. Since SSR appears to positively influence attitudes toward reading, it also appears that its benefits are long range. More research is necessary to determine conclusively the relationship between SSR as a method of reading practice and students' reading achievement. A two-page bibliography concludes the document. (JD)

AN: ED272840
AU: Robinson, Karlen
TI: Visual and Auditory Modalities and Reading Recall: A Review of the Research.
PY: [1985]
NT: 13 p.
PR: EDRS Price—MF01/PC01 Plus Postage.
DE: Comprehension; Learning Processes; Learning Strategies; Memory; Responses; Sensory Integration
DE: Auditory Stimuli; Cognitive Processes; Reading Ability; Reading Research; Recall Psychology; Visual Stimuli
AB: Of particular interest to those exploring student's learning modalities is the relationship between the visual and auditory systems and reading recall. Among the findings of studies that have investigated this relationship are the following: (1) reading competency is dependent as much on auditory processing as on visual processing; (2) when visual and auditory signals are presented simultaneously, subjects generally respond to the visual input and are often unaware that an auditory signal has occurred; (3) auditory stimuli are processed more rapidly than visual stimuli; (4) when preschool children's evaluation and integration of visual and auditory information was compared with that of adults both groups were found to have available continuous and independent sources of information; (5) memory training increases a child's ability to retain stimuli; (6) under audio/video mismatch conditions, memory for audio information is reduced more than memory for video information; however, comprehension and recognition of audio information is similar in the audio only and audio/video match conditions; (7) children recall logical sequences better than illogical ones; and (8) children of all ages show a correspondence between strategy use and metamemory as assessed by verbalization of relationships among pictures during specific questioning; however, when a more typical general question format is used to assess metamemory; strategy use precedes verbalized knowledge of strategy use. In general, most studies show that visual stimuli tend to dominate other modalities in both perceptual and memory tasks. A 3-page list of references concludes the document. (HOD)

AN: EJ325185
AU: Sippola, Arne E.
TI: What to Teach for Reading Readiness—A Research Review and Materials Inventory.
PY: 1985
JN: Reading Teacher; v39 n2 p162-67 Nov 1985
AV: UMI
DE: Child Development; Learning Processes; Primary Education
DE: Learning Readiness; Reading Instruction; Reading Materials; Reading Readiness; Reading Readiness Tests; Reading Research
AB: Reviews literature on different aspects of reading readiness, then presents a reading readiness material analysis inventory constructed according to the findings of the review. Explains how the instrument can be used by educators to compare readiness program materials. (FL)

AN: ED223971
AU: Spangler, Katy
TI: Readability: A Review and Analysis of the Research.

PY: 1980

NT: 51 p.

PR: EDRS Price—MF01/PC03 Plus Postage.

DE: Comparative Analysis; Literature Reviews, Research Design; Research Methodology; Test Reviews

DE: Cloze Procedure; Readability Formulas, Reading Research; Test Interpretation; Test Validity.

AB: This paper reviews seven research studies on the subject of readability. The first study reviewed is itself an extensive review of 30 readability formulas described by George A. Klare. Of these, five formulas considered to be interesting, unusual, or classic on the basis of high validity, simplicity or complexity, common or uncommon variables, and other unusual features were chosen for analysis. The five formulas include those by I. I. Lorge (1939), G. D. Spache (1953, 1974), W. B. Elley (1969), J. R. Bormuth (1966, 1969), and Harris-Jacobson (1975). In addition, the initial research on cloze procedure by W. L. Taylor (1953) is reviewed to give balance to the overview of readability research. Each review consists of an analysis of the research backing the formulas, specifically the theoretical framework, the research design, the results, the author's evaluation, and a summary including comments on the usefulness and the face validity of the formulas. After the reviews, a synthesis of the studies attempts to answer the following questions: (1) What is readability and how is it calculated? (2) How good is the research on readability—what are its strengths and limitations? (3) How do readability measures compare? and (4) What are some practical implications for use of these formulas? (HOD)

AN: EJ297934

AU: Wiesendanger, Katherine D.; Birlem, Ellen D.

TI: The Effectiveness of SSR: An Overview of the Research.

PY: 1984

JN: Reading Horizons; v24 n3 p197–201 Spr 1984

AV: UMI

DE: Program Effectiveness; Research Problems

DE: Reading Improvement; Reading Instruction; Reading Research; Research Utilization; Sustained Silent Reading

AB: Reviews research concerning sustained silent reading and lists factors that are important in determining whether such a reading program is successful. (FL)

## Writing

AN: ED240586

AU: Cronnell, Bruce; And Others

TI: Cooperative Instructional Application of Writing Research. Final Report. Volume Three.

CS: Southwest Regional Laboratory for Educational Research and Development, Los Alamitos, Calif.

PY: 1982

NT: 642 p.; For related documents, see CS 208 143–144

PR: EDRS Price—MF03/PC26 Plus Postage.

DE: Annotated Bibliographies; Basic Skills; Elementary Education; Multiple-Choice Tests; Surveys; Test Items; Test Results; Writing Skills

DE: Achievement Tests; Educational Assessment; Language Arts; Minimum Competency Testing; Writing Evaluation; Writing Research

ID: Theory-Practice Relationship

AB: The last of three volumes studying the relationship between writing research and instruction, this four-part report focuses on writing assessment. The first section details specifications for an instrument assessing student writing samples and the following composition skills: word processing, sentence processing, paragraph development, organizational skill, use of dictionary and reference sources, spelling, and writing mechanics. It also reports on the administration of such an assessment instrument to students from grades 1 to 6 in the Los Angeles Unified School District. The second section discusses specifications for competency based assessment of the following language arts skills: (1) listening, (2) grammar usage, (3) sentence structure, (4) capitalization and punctuation, (5) language expression, (6) spelling, (7) literature, and (8) study skills, media literacy, and nonverbal communication. The third section briefly describes the reading, mathematics, and language proficiency surveys and review exercises administered to entering high school students in the Sacramento City Unified School District, and the final section presents an annotated bibliography of assessment reports. (MM)

AN: ED254848

AU: Davis, David J.

TI: Writing across the Curriculum: A Research Review.

PY: [1984]

NT: 29 p.

PR: EDRS Price—MF01/PC02 Plus Postage.

DE: Higher Education; Learning Theories; Literature Reviews; Writing Processes; Writing Skills

DE: Content Area Writing; Interdisciplinary Approach; Student Attitudes; Teacher Attitudes; Teaching Methods; Writing Research

ID: Writing across the Curriculum

ID: Writing Programs

AB: A review of dozens of journal articles and books on the subject of writing across the curriculum reveals the following basic assumptions that seem to characterize most college writing across the curriculum programs: (1) writing is a complex and developmental process; (2) writing should be used to promote learning; (3) the teaching of writing is the responsibility of the entire academic community and of every teacher; (4) the teaching of writing should be integrated across departmental lines; (5) writing serves several functions in the educational context; (6) the universe of discourse is broad; and (7) the teaching of writing should occur during the entire 4 undergraduate years. Studies also support the assumption that writing increases student learning. It is clear, however, that there is little common agreement on how best to go about fostering writing skills among disciplines operating with quite diverse rhetorical conventions. In addition, few individual faculties seem to have developed a systematic approach giving overall direction to their own practices toward student writing. The apparent broad interest in student writing is accompanied by fragmentation of attitudes, expectations, and practices in that direction. These studies suggest that English departments would serve themselves and the total campus well by seeking ways to cooperate with their colleagues in other disciplines to accomplish what is obviously a widely shared goal—the development of skilled writers. A 33-item reference list is included. (HOD)

AN: ED225147
AU: Faigley, Lester; Skinner, Anna
TI: Writers' Processes and Writers' Knowledge: A Review of Research Technical Report No. 6.
CS: Texas Univ., Austin.
PY: 1982
NT: 71 p.; Prepared through the Writing Program Assessment Project. Figures may not reproduce.
PR: EDRS Price—MF01/PC03 Plus Postage.
DE: Cognitive Processes; Educational Theories; Elementary Secondary Education; Higher Education; Literature Reviews
DE: Prewriting; Revision Written Composition; Writing Composition; Writing Instruction; Writing Processes; Writing Research.
ID: Theory-Practice Relationship
AB: After a short introductory chapter to this literature review on composing processes, the second chapter examines research that covers the timing and content of planning, planning subprocesses, employing planning strategies, and instruction in planning. Studies in the third chapter are divided into two sections, oral and written discourse production and instruction in producing texts. The sections in the fourth chapter deal with research concerning classification systems for revision changes, revising strategies, why writers revise, and instruction on revision. The final chapter deals with studies that outline the kinds of knowledge a writer possesses about language, the conventions of writing, and a particular writing situation. This chapter argues that examining a writer's knowledge is essential to understanding changes in composing and suggests directions for future research. The studies cited in the document are then listed. (JL)

AN: ED280063
AU: Funderburk, Carol
TI: A Review of Research in Children's Writing.
PY: [1986]
NT: 13 p.
PR: EDRS Price—MF01/PC01 Plus Postage.
DE: Cognitive Development; Cognitive Processes; Developmental Stages; Educational Theories; Language Acquisition; Language Arts; Literature Reviews; Prewriting; Research Proposals; Surveys; Teaching Methods; Theory-Practice Relationship
DE: Piagetian Theory; Primary Education; Reading-Writing Relationship; Writing Processes; Writing Research
ID: Invented Spelling; Piaget, Jean
AB: Recent research into the composing processes of children owes much to Piaget's postulate that cognitive development

is linear—that children progress through stages of development whereby tasks are mastered at certain levels of cognitive understanding. The stages of children's writing processes (prewriting, composing, revising), as well as language development, drawing, and reading have been examined by Donald Graves, L. M. Calkins, and Glenda Bissex, among others. In one study, C. Temple, R. Nathan, and N. Burris concluded that children make the same discoveries in the same order. Susan Sowers detailed her observation of a first-grade class; in which she used the techniques of invented spelling, writing conferences, and writing about assigned topics to compile children's writing for publishing. Issues currently being examined include the use of drawing as a prewriting exercise, and the relationships between scribbling, drawing, and talking. The issues of invented spelling and writing before reading have profound implications for new directions in elementary education. A growing amount of research indicates that reading is a highly abstract task and should follow rather than precede writing instruction. Frances Kane's work advocates the progression of thinking, drawing, writing, and reading. The link between Piaget's stages of cognitive development and its writing counterparts is a promising area of research. (NKA)

AN: ED229766
AU: Mosenthal, Peter, Ed.; And Others
TI: Research on Writing: Principles and Methods.
PY: 1983
AV: Longman Inc., 1560 Broadway, New York, NY 10036 ($25.00 cloth).
NT: 324 p.
PR: Document Not Available from EDRS.
DE: Elementary-Secondary Education; Higher Education; observation; Research Needs; Research Problems; Student-Teacher Relationship; Writing Processes; Writing Readiness
DE: Experiments; Holistic Approach; Research Design; Research Methodology; Writing Instruction; Writing Research
AB: Designed to alleviate the confusion caused by the existence of a multiplicity of approaches to writing research, the four parts of this book present explicit discussions of research principles and methods used by researchers actively working within a variety of disciplines. The two chapters in Part 1 describe very broad views of the entire research endeavor. The four chapters in Part 2 show how classical experimental projects are used to examine the processes used by readers in evaluating student composition, the development of writing abilities in children, the writing development of children who are just beginning to write, and the control of writing processes. The three chapters in Part 3 describe the use of observational approaches to study the composing processes of adult writers, the on-the-job writing of workers, and the role of the teacher in the student's writing process. Chapters in Part 4 examine two other approaches, recounting the long tradition of interest in writing disabilities and reviewing approaches to text analysis. (JL)

AN: ED236674
AU: Moss, Kay

TI: The Developmental Aspects of the Writing Processes of Young Children: A Review of Related Research. Instructional Research Laboratory Technical Series #R83003.
CS: Texas A and M Univ., College Station. Instructional Research Lab.
PY: [1982]
NT: 24 p.
PR: EDRS Price—MF01/PC01 Plus Postage.
DE: Elementary Education; Literature Reviews; Teacher Role; Verbal Development; Writing Readiness
DE: Developmental Stages; Language Acquisition; Writing Instruction; Writing Processes; Writing Research
AB: To determine the designs, procedures, and findings of studies related to an investigation of the developmental aspects of the writing processes of children, a literature search was made of documents indexed in "Current Index to Journals in Education" (CIJE) and "Resources in Education" (RIE). A search was also made of the literature in Psychological Abstracts, Comprehensive Dissertation Index, and the Language and Language Behaviors Index. From the analysis it would seem that most of the literature regarding the writing processes of young children has been concerned specifically with developmental aspects. Research conclusions suggest that teachers should question children to help them expand their ideas about writing and options for writing those ideas. Teachers should also encourage other children to set standards for their writing and encourage other children to provide feedback. In particular, the research findings of Donald Graves suggest that children should be encouraged by their teachers to focus on the message rather than on its form and to realize that words are only temporary. His findings also show that informal classroom settings promote writing and that unassigned writing seems to stimulate boys' writing and results in longer compositions. (HOD)

## Integration of Language Arts

AN: ED260409
AU: Froese, Victor; Phillips-Riggs, Linda
TI: Dictation, Independent Writing, and Story Retelling in the Primary Grades [and] Research in Reading and Writing Should be Progressive. A Response to Froese.
PY: 1984
NT: 37 p.; Papers presented at the Colloquium on Research in Reading and Language Arts in Canada (Lethbridge, Alberta, Canada, June 7–9, 1984).
PR: EDRS Price—MF01/PC02 Plus Postage.
DE: Communication Research; Communication Skills; Expressive Language; Language Processing; Language Skills; Research Needs; Research Problems; Speech Communication
DE: Dictation; Integrated Activities; Language Arts; Story Telling; Writing Research; Writing Skills
AB: In addressing selected aspects of the language arts from the context of an integrative language paradigm, this paper focuses on the results of three studies recently completed in Manitoba, which help to shed some light on three modes of expression—dictation, independent writing, and

retelling—in the primary grades. The first part of the paper discusses the background and need for the studies—their purposes, methods and procedures, findings, and conclusions and implications. The second part of the paper is a response by Linda Phillips-Riggs, which outlines the main points of Froese's paper and discusses the weaknesses of his paper and of the three studies. Some research ideas are presented, followed by a conclusion. (EL)

## Summaries of Research

AN: EJ332975
AU: Marshall, James D.; Durst, Russel K.
TI: Annotated Bibliography of Research in the Teaching of English.
PY: 1986
JN: Research in the Teaching of English; v20 n2 p198–215 May 1986
AV: UMI
DE: Language Acquisition; Reading-Writing Relationship; Rhetoric; Writing Evaluation; Writing Processes
DE: Educational Research; English Teacher Education; Language Processing; Literature; Writing Instruction; Writing Research
ID: Writing Contexts
ID: Text Analysis
AB: Describes recent research studies in the areas of writing (contexts, status surveys, instruction, processes, text analysis, assessment rhetoric), language (processing, development, interrelationships, language and schooling), literature, and teacher education. (HOD)

## Children with Disabilities

AN: EJ358541
AU: Barnett, Janette
TI: Research on Language and Communications in Children Who have Severe Handicaps: A Review and Some Implications for Intervention.
PY: 1987
JN: Educational Psychology; v7 n2 p117–28 1987
DE: Language Handicaps
DE: Communication Research; Interpersonal Communication; Nonverbal Communication; Psycholinguistics; Severe Disabilities; Speech Communication
AB: Presents a critical discussion of some contemporary literature on the language development and communication problems of persons with severe handicaps. States that for meaning to be transmitted from one person to another, a social-interactive context is required. Draws implications for caregivers and therapists. (Author/JDH)

AN: EJ344038
AU: Battacchi, Marco W.; Manfredi, Marta-Montanini
TI: Recent Research Trends in Italy: Cognitive & Communicative Development of Deaf Children.
PY: 1986
JN: Sign Language Studies; n52 p210–18 Fall 1986

DE: Foreign Countries; Language Acquisition; Special Education; Total Communication

DE: Cognitive Development; Communication Research; Communicative Competence Languages; Deafness; Exceptional Child Research

ID: Italy

AB: A review of recent research trends in Italy regarding cognitive and communicative development of deaf children indicates that deaf children's potential for communicative and cognitive growth is enormous. This potential may be realized if provision is made for an educational environment based on a multiple code, gestural communication, spoken language, reading, and writing. (CB)

AN: ED223988

AU: Coots, James H.; Snow, David P.

TI: Understanding Poor Reading Comprehension: Current Approaches in Theory and Research.

CS: Southwest Regional Laboratory for Educational Research and Development, Los Alamitos, Calif.

PY: 1980

NT: 28 p.

PR: EDRS Price—MF01/PC02 Plus Postage.

DE: Academic Aptitude; Learning Theories; Reading Rate; Reading Skills

DE: Decoding Reading; Reading Ability; Reading Comprehension; Reading Difficulties; Reading Processes; Reading Research

AB: Two views of the sources of poor reading comprehension are currently distinguishable in the research literature: a decoding sufficiency view and a comprehension skills view. The decoding sufficiency view argues that decoding is the only skill that must be acquired for general language comprehension. The broader, comprehension skills hypothesis argues that a deficiency in any of several basic component skills could thwart reading comprehension mastery. R. M. Golinkoff's major review of studies comparing good and poor comprehenders posited three components of comprehension: decoding, lexical access, and text organization. Research on decoding has yielded some hypotheses relating decoding speed to comprehension, but problems of study design cast some doubt on these conclusions. Research on lexical access ability indicates that poor comprehenders do not typically lack this ability; however, if cognitive overload during reading is more frequent among poor comprehenders, it is likely that lexical access functioning will deteriorate. Most clearly, text organization research has consistently shown that poor comprehenders are word-by-word readers while good comprehenders employ higher level strategies. (JL)

AN: EJ352216

AU: Goodacre, Elizabeth

TI: Reading Research in Great Britain—1985.

PY: 1987

JN: Reading; v21 n1 p16-29 Apr 1987

DE: Elementary Secondary Education; Foreign Countries; Learning Disabilities; Reading Difficulties; Reading Interests; Reading Materials; Reading Tests; Skill Development; Teaching Methods

DE: Educational Technology; Reading Instruction; Reading Research; Reading Skills

ID: Great Britain

AB: Reviews research in the areas of reading standards and tests, reading development, dyslexia and specific reading retardation, and reading materials and interests. (FL)

## Sociocultural Influences

AN: EJ337085

AU: Plant, Richard M.

TI: Reading Research: Its Influence on Classroom Practice.

PY: 1986

JN: Educational Research; v28 n2 p126-31 Jun 1986

DE: Elementary Education; Teacher Responsibility; Teacher Role

DE: Classroom Techniques; Delivery Systems; Reading Research; Research Methodology; Teacher Attitudes

ID: Great Britain

AB: An attempt is made to assess the influence of recent reading research on current classroom practice. It is argued that its overall effect is minimized by a combination of researcher/practitioner disagreement on what constitutes reading, the overreliance by researchers on a particular methodology, and the inadequacy of much of the machinery for dissemination. (Author/CT)

AN: EJ331092

AU: Subervi-Velez, Federico A.

TI: The Mass Media and Ethnic Assimilation and Pluralism: A Review and Research Proposal with Special Focus on Hispanics.

PY: 1986

JN: Communication Research: An International Quarterly; v13 n1 p71-96 Jan 1986

AV: UMI

DE: Ethnic Groups; Research Methodology

DE: Acculturation; Communication Research; Cultural Pluralism, Hispanic Americans; Literature Reviews; Mass Media

AB: Provides an integrated assessment of literature about communication research on Hispanic and other ethnic groups within the context of assimilation and pluralism. (PD)

## Teacher Effectiveness

AN: ED233389

AU: Farr, Marcia

TI: Writing Growth in Young Children: What We Are Learning from Research. The Talking and Writing Series, K-12: Successful Classroom Practices.

CS: Dingle Associates, Inc., Washington, D.C.

PY: 1983

NT: 22 p.

PR: EDRS Price—MF01/PC01 Plus Postage.

DE: Basic Skills; Child Development; Child Language; Elementary Education; Language Experience Approach; Language

Skills; Language Usage; Models; Oral Language; Writing Instruction.

DE: Classroom Research; Developmental Stages; Language Acquisition; Writing Processes; Writing Research; Writing Skills

ID: Theory-Practice Relationship

AB: Prepared as part of a series applying recent research in oral and written communication instruction to classroom practice, this booklet describes several classroom-based studies that have examined children's writing development and synthesizes what they have shown about the process. The first section of the booklet analyzes the term "writing development"; presents a model of literacy acquisition and use devised by J. C. Harste, C. L. Barke, and V. Woodard; and discusses the work of D. H. Graves and his associates in this area. The second section discusses children's transition from oral to written language and reviews the research conducted by M. L. King and V. M. Rentel. The third section examines how written language growth is related to teaching and discusses King's, Rentel's, and Graves' findings on instructional approaches and S. Sowers' work with the concept of scaffolding. (FL)

AN: ED265576
AU: Phelps, Lynn A.; Smilowitz, Michael
TI: Using Research as a Guide for Teaching Interpersonal Communication Competencies.
PY: 1985
NT: 18 p.; Paper presented at the Annual Meeting of the Speech Communication Association (71st, Denver, CO, November 7-10, 1985).
PR: EDRS Price—MF01/PC01 Plus Postage.
DE: Higher Education; Speech Communication; Speech Curriculum; Speech Improvement; Speech Instruction; Speech Skills
DE: Communication Research; Interpersonal Communication; Interpersonal Competence
AB: Twenty years of research in interpersonal communication have provided teachers with a basis for identifying the competencies that should be taught in introductory interpersonal communication courses, including empathy, social composure, and conflict management. However, other issues such as "performance vs. knowledge," the affective dimension, and the situational nature of competency are still being researched and debated. Five suggestions for instructors who teach basic interpersonal communication courses are: (1) review various conceptualizations of interpersonal competence and select factors deemed crucial for students to process, (2) select a basic textbook that treats those factors, (3) encourage students to critically examine their own behaviors, (4) use exercises that provide the opportunity to observe others who process useful skills and that provide opportunities to practice in a nonthreatening environment, and (5) allow students to make their own choices. (DF)

AN: EJ313480
AU: Rupley, William H.; Wise, Beth S.
TI: Methodological and Data Analysis Limitations in Teacher Effectiveness Research: Threats to the External Validity of Significant Findings.

PY: 1984
JN: Journal of Reading Education; v10 n1 p8-18 Fall 1984
NT: The Organization of Teacher Education in Reading, 1917 15th Av., Greeley, CO 80631; $6.00, includes membership.
DE: Classroom Research
DE: Data Collection; Reading Research; Research Methodology; Research Problems; Teacher Effectiveness; Validity
AB: Notes that major changes have occurred in the factors investigated and the data collection procedures employed in teacher effectiveness research and that the generalizability of significant findings continues to be limited by methodological and experimental design problems. (FL)

AN: ED275152
AU: Zamel, Vivian
TI: In Search of the Key: Research and Practice in Composition.
PY: 1983
NT: 14 p.; In: Handscombe, Jean, Ed.; And Others. On TESOL '83. The Question of Control. Selected Papers from the Annual Convention of Teachers of English to Speakers of Other Languages (17th, Toronto, Canada, March 15-20, 1983); see FL 015 035.
PR: EDRS Price—MF01/PC01 Plus Postage.
DE: Classroom Techniques; Diaries; Error Patterns; Higher Education; Research Needs; Second Language Instruction; Writing Composition.
DE: English-Second Language; Writing Exercises; Writing Instruction; Writing Processes; Writing Research
AB: It is important that teachers help students to realize that writing is not simply a product, or a means to an end, but an exploratory, cyclical process. Research has shown that skilled writers conceptualize the effect of their writing as a whole, as a generative process, whereas unskilled writers are distracted by surface-level features and are less aware of the exploratory nature of writing. In light of these findings, methods are proposed for teachers to involve students in the composing process and thereby better prepare them to become independent writers. Some of these activities include: allowing students to be creative and purposeful in their writing; initiating free-writing activities that develop skills for exploring and discovering fresh ideas; and observing students' writing processes closely and noting areas of difficulty. (TR)

## Literature Curriculum

AN: EJ345213
AU: Sawyer, Wayne
TI: Literature and Literacy: A Review of Research.
PY: 1987
JN: Language Arts; v64 n1 p33-39 Jan 1987
AV: UMI
NT: Theme Issue: Literature and Literacy.
DE: Beginning Reading; Children's Literature; Reading Improvement; Reading Strategies
DE: Learning Processes; Learning Theories; Literacy; Literature; Reading Research; Theory-Practice Relationship

AB: Reviews the major theoretical statements regarding the contribution of literature to reading development, noting that they fall into two interwoven strands: the notion of learning to read through literature, and learning to read literature. Evaluates the empirical evidence supporting the claim that literature plays an important role in learning to read. (JD)

AN: ED235506
AU: Sword, Jeane
TI: The What and How of Book Selection: Research Findings.
PY: 1982
NT: 18 p.; Paper presented at the Annual Meeting of the National Council of Teachers of English Spring Conference (1st, Minneapolis, MN, April 15–17, 1982).
PR: EDRS Price—MF01/PC01 Plus Postage.
DE: Elementary Education; Evaluation Criteria; Fiction; Holistic Evaluation; Intermediate Grades; Kindergarten; Oral Reading; Reading Aloud to Others; Resource Materials; Surveys
DE: Children's Literature; Reading Materials; Reading Material Selection; Reading Research; Teacher Attitudes
AB: A review of the literature on read-aloud programs reveals two studies that extensively examine program content and practices and teacher procedures. The first study, conducted in 1969, compiled responses from 582 intermediate teachers of Grades 4, 5, and 6 throughout the United States. The second study, conducted in 1979, surveyed 29 kindergarten teachers in a large northern Minnesota city. Findings from the studies showed that in both kindergarten and intermediate grades the largest category of books teachers read orally to children is fiction. In the intermediate grades study, the quality of teacher selected books was determined by checking the list of titles against two standard bibliographies: "Children's Catalog," and "The Elementary School Library Collections." The kindergarten study used a set of criteria for evaluating the quality of plot, characterization, and style of picture storybooks. In consideration of personal teacher evaluation of a given book, two facts stood out: 85% to 100% of the teachers relied on their own knowledge in book selection; but in regard to quality of literature chosen, only one-fourth to two-fifths of the books selected for the read-aloud programs were categorized as top quality. The most frequently used book selection aids were "The Instructor," for intermediate teachers, and the "Bibliography of Books for Children" for kindergarten teachers. (HOD)

# FICTIVE REPRESENTATION: AN ALTERNATIVE

# METHOD FOR REPORTING RESEARCH

*Donna E. Alvermann*
*George G. Hruby*
University of Georgia

Our starting point is simply that research reports do not have to be boring to read, or for that matter, to write. Too often we hear the complaint that researchers write for themselves, or at most, for a small community of scholars whose interests tend to match their own. As researchers, we also know from personal experience the feeling that comes over us when data collection and analysis are over and the task of writing the "final" report is facing us. It's as if the creative aspects of doing research have ended with the last interview, the last written vignette, the last theoretical memo, and so on. But this need not be the case. Instead, as we will illustrate in this chapter, reporting on research in the field of English Language Arts can be an enlivening, imaginative activity—one that simultaneously helps the researcher and reader interpret qualitative data in ways that begin to approach the richness and complexity of the lived experiences the data are meant to represent.

## PERSPECTIVE AND RATIONALE

Although we do not believe there exists any representational form of lived experience that is capable of fully capturing that experience, we do subscribe to the notion that current conventions for reporting research in the social sciences largely obscure what is of human interest and value about such experience. In making this observation, we draw primarily from the work of scholars in a variety of disciplines who write at the intersections of fiction, social science, ethnography, and cultural studies (e.g., Eisner, 1997; Ellis & Bochner, 1996; Lawrence-Lightfoot & Davis, 1997; Richardson, 1993, 1997; Tierney, 1997). Their work with alternative modes of expression, and particularly their experimentation with fiction as a mode of expression suitable for academic discourse, garnered a good bit of attention in the decade of the '90s.

Critics of this unconventional use of fiction argued that its application in the social sciences threatened the entire research enterprise (Cizek, 1995; Kauffman, 1993). Claiming that it involved the researcher's imagination and thus made any pretense of construct validity a sham, these critics and others like them (e.g., Levine, 1994) argued against turning facts into fiction. Some, like Locke (1992, as cited in Banks & Banks, 1998), grudgingly noted that fiction might have a role in research but only if used within a postmodern framework.

Proponents of bringing techniques used by fiction writers to the research table have redoubled their efforts, largely in light of this criticism. For example, Ellis and Bochner (1996) have written a book that demonstrates the versatility of nontraditional forms of representation, including the fictional and the poetic, for the purpose of reporting research that makes a difference to the reader. To their way of thinking, "interpretive authority ultimately lies with the community of readers who engage the text" (p. 7). Others (Barone, 1995, Barone & Eisner, 1998; Denzin, 1997), have argued that educational storytelling deserves its own textual breathing space. We tend to agree.

In fact, a partial rationale for the stance we have chosen to take in this particular chapter is illustrated in Bochner and Ellis's (1998) introduction to Banks and Banks's (1998) *Fiction and Social Research*, which is part of a series titled *Ethnographic Alternatives* and published by Altamira Press, a division of Sage Publications. In that series, authors purposefully attempt to blur the boundaries between the social sciences and the humanities. In their introduction to *Fiction and Social Research*, the series editors, Bochner and Ellis, wrote:

Taken as a whole, the chapters of *Fiction and Social Research* ask readers to contemplate new possibilities for social research, where the prose is poetically crafted, where the author is construed primarily as a writer rather than exclusively as a researcher, where the reader is invited into the subjective and emotional world of the author, where at least as much attention has been given to the imagination as to the rigor of the inquiry, and where the texts that depict social life have the sound and feel of lived reality, giving context to the lives and actions they detail (pp. 7–8).

Evoking the subjective and emotional texture of the researcher and the researched is largely foreign territory to those of us schooled in the rigors of academic writing for education journals. And, even when we are disposed to try our hand at writing in a more creative style, we frequently lack the experience and literary background (in terms of course work) that novelists, short story writers, and poets bring to their work. In our particular author team, Donna had the requisite academic writing skills and educational background for factually reporting the research she conducted, but she was finding, like Anna Banks (Banks & Banks, 1998), that "facts don't always tell the truth, or a truth worth worrying about" (p. 11). George, on the other hand, whose work prior to entering the doctoral program at the University of Georgia included writing for and editing an award-winning college literary magazine, reporting for a suburban newspaper chain, penning a syndicated new-wave humor column, and writing published and anthologized fiction, was interested in acquiring the skills of an academic writer. It was while working together on a research project (Alvermann & Hruby, 2000) that we began exploring ways to make the written product of our collaborative research more interesting, more accessible, and more aesthetically engaging.

## FICTIVE REPRESENTATION

In this chapter, we focus on how fictive representation—a form of representation that employs the traditional qualities of good storytelling, qualities like character development and figurative language—lends context and depth to the portraits of our research participants and thus makes their actions more believable. As used here, fictive representation allowed us to show rather than tell (Denzin, 1997; Frus, 1994; Wolfe & Johnson, 1973) about what George Hruby learned in his interview with Jerry Harste and Harste's graduate student advisees at Indiana University on the topic of graduate student mentoring in literacy teacher education (Alvermann & Hruby, 2000). Using fictive techniques such as interior monologues and flashbacks, Hruby was an observer of his own acts as researcher as well as an interpreter of Harste's actions. This dramatistic (Burke, 1966) approach to the data allowed us to capture with a certain degree of vividness much of what would have been lost or remained unspoken in a more traditional form of reporting. It also made possible a subtle and nuanced layering of the participants' mentoring experiences. Finally, it contributed to richer readings that forced our sample readers to avoid simple motivational explanations of complex human relationships.

It should be noted that fictive representation is not synonymous with fiction per se, or fictional representation, the latter being a creative fabrication to represent more general delineations of a situated truth or reality (cf. Lawrence-Lightfoot & Davis, 1997). By contrast, *fictive* representation attempts to use the techniques of fiction to frame and present factual data that has been gathered with all of the methodological rigor appropriate to qualitative interview research, but presents this data in an aesthetically effective (and affecting) manner. In this sense, fictive representation attempts to provide the reader the pleasures and engagement found in such similar forms as new journalism, fictionalized history and biography, or the traditional travelogue. All of these forms share the use of fictive and dramatistic technique to make the author's often veiled selectivity (and, after Burke [1966], deflectivity) of the reporting method explicit. Moreover, an author's moral culpability for such choices is usually made explicit as well, often by way of a narrator of dubious reliability (e.g., Thompson, 1971). It must be borne in mind, however, that fictive representation is also equally vulnerable to the sort of criticism new journalism and other analogous forms have received (for a partial review of these strengths and weaknesses, see Denzin, 1997, particularly chapters 2, 5, and 7).

George's visit to Indiana University, Bloomington, spanned 3 days and involved in-depth interviews with Jerome Harste and five of his students. These interviews were tape recorded and the recordings were later transcribed for detailed review and analysis. A group interview with Harste and four of his graduate students was videotaped. George also took extensive notes during and immediately before and after each interview, and kept a record of personal observations of the physical, social, and cultural environments he encountered during his visit to Bloomington. He also collected such local artifacts as photographs, brochures, postcards, receipts, local newspapers, fliers, and other miscellaneous items he thought noteworthy and useful for later rekindling of his memory.

When invited by Donna to be "creative" in his site visit writeup in the manner of the new journalism, George was at first unsure what might prove sufficiently entertaining yet faithfully factual. In order to preserve the integrity of the data, he chose to quote his subjects at length and verbatim from the tape transcripts. His descriptions of events were drawn closely from his field notes. However, for the tone of voice he chose for his report, George initially selected a casual, happily idiosyncratic travelogue narration. His goal was not to attempt the impossible feat of using language to produce an objectively factual representation of an interpersonally constructed moment in time. Rather, George attempted to present an indexical account of his personal impressions of that moment with the added glosses of hindsight. Subsequently, the initial draft was reworked with concessions to stylistic and dramatic effectiveness in pursuit of an engaging account. Constrained by the need to preserve the integrity of the data, George chose to restrict major manipulations of fact to the representation of the narrator.

Thus, emerged a narrator markedly more insecure, neurotic, and defensively caustic–and hopefully more interesting—than the author himself. This narrator plays a jester-like "fool" to the principal subject's "king," and the narrator's inner Imp echoes this narrative device as trickster inside the trickster. Why create such an undependable narrator? Quite simply, for the dramatic tension and textual complexity it provided. Dramatic tensions (and the implicit promise of their resolution) have long been recognized as a basis for reader engagement (Aristotle, 1999; Booth, 1983; Burke, 1969, 1966; Gardner, 1983; Nabokov, 1980; Turner, 1996). The unreliable narrator allowed George as author to construct a dramatic tension between the demands of the interview and the confidence of the interviewer, as well as contrast the seemingly coherent person of the subject with the scattered person of the narrator. The unreliable narrator is also a useful device for contrasting the difference between telling and showing: the narrator *tells* the story, often with a great deal of gratuitous, self-serving spin or, alternatively, naivete, while the author *shows* sufficient discrepancies in this account to tip off the reader to the error, danger, or irony to be recognized. In a work of fiction this is perhaps more obvious; no one confuses Celie for Alice Walker (1992), or Holden Caufield for J. D. Salinger (1991). The narrator is but another, if major, character in a larger story woven by the author.

The tension created between narrator and author is but one manifestation of the unreliable narrator. As Rick Beach pointed out in an earlier critique of this chapter (personal communication, October 27, 1999), another point of tension created by the use of the unreliable narrator is one between the invited or implied audience and the actual reader. Presupposing an audience's knowledge or understanding of narrative conventions, the author is free to play with this tension. Thus, in the narrative that George crafts around his interview with Jerry Harste, the presumed audience would have to know something of the rudimentary conventions of storytelling and to engage in what Rabinowitz (1987) calls the rules of notice and signification for the unreliable narrator convention to work. That is, the presumed audience would have to acknowledge its role in interpreting the text created through the unreliable narrator, thereby playing along with the author's purpose for employing such a convention. If, however, the presumed audience and the actual reader are not one and the same person, a tension could evolve, as in fact it did in one of the responses to the text George created.

Waiving for the purposes of clarity the fiction writer's dictum to "never explain," we emphasize, then, these three caveats:

1. Every effort has been made to preserve the integrity of the data by quoting verbatim and adhering closely to actual events.
2. The reader should distinguish between the narrator and the author.
3. It is the reader's interpretive responsibility to produce the read text–the reading that results from the transaction of the reader and the text cannot be laid at the feet of the author alone (Rosenblatt, 1994).

Beyond that, we can be certain that each reader's response will be appropriate for that particular reading, the mediating constraints of which are beyond our immediate control. We presume our readers are aware that texts that employ fictional techniques have different intentions and place different demands on the reader than do more "purely" informational texts (hence Rosenblatt's [1994] distinction between aesthetic and efferent stances in reading). Similarly, stylistic anomalies like the interpolation of other inter- and intrapersonal voices "layered"

through the main interview, distinguished in the following by italics, should not be perceived as a typographic intrusion to be resisted but as a literary strategy to be judged on the basis of effectiveness.

## IMAGINE HERE A PREFACE...
## GEORGE G. HRUBY

Imagine here a preface in which the writer depicts a graduate student-as-researcher being mentored in his research by a highly regarded academic. Imagine the uncertainty of that graduate student, the trepidation, the intimidation of having to commence a research project on that very subject: to wit, the mentoring of graduate students by academic professionals. Imagine his doubts, second thoughts, and misgivings coalescing into a private counterpoint to the foisted expectations of the role he believes he's expected to play as researcher, that inner perspective taking on a voice all its own. Imagine the dissonance between that voice struggling to retain a dubious autonomy and that more appropriate if less authentic outward voice of polite, postured nice-making. Imagine these voices, and others besides, struggling toward eminence in this graduate student's quest for self-definition as a professional academic researcher researching the development of graduate students' self-definition as professional academics. Just imagine....

## PROFESSOR CARPY

"It's like they say," said Professor Carpy, taking a long drag off his Winston on the walkway outside the Wiggely College of Education, "If you don't stand for something, you'll fall for anything." I nodded dutifully, playing the objective interviewer, but once again I found myself struggling with the Imp. He and my trickster-self were horsing around in my mental vestry while the rest of the congregation, including my serious researcher-self, was trying to pay attention to the sermon.

"You know, you need to take a stand. You have to... That's what I try to make my students do: find out what they stand for. They need to find that out. That's what it's... That's what it's about..."

*Taking a stand. Sly Stone's "Stand." Outstanding student; outstanding in the parking lot smoking cigarettes. "Smoking up good, like a researcher should." Gah, baloney. Isn't that the problem anyway? Too many academics cluttering the discourse with untenable stances. Of no import. And for no reason better than professional self-definition. "Hey, here I am! Look at me! Hey, mom, look at me!!!" Yaaaah! Who is this guy anyway...*

You know, in education there's this notion of eclecticism as scholarship, and I just think that's a bunch of malarkey, really. I just think eclecticism is a disease curable by taking a position, quite frankly. I think one of the problems, you know, I don't know if you've had much experience in working with teachers out in the field, but one of the real problems I think in why teachers can't position themselves as learners is because they don't take a position....

*Take THAT position? Well, bless my sockets! Hush! Enough! Gad, by the time I'm finished here I'm gonna need a shrink. Big brimming bowl of fluoxetine. Must be something about the midwest. I need to watch myself, watch him . . .*

It had been a long first day of interviews, starting with a grueling self-interrogation about 3 A.M. that went on for hours. Then an appropriately institutional breakfast in the student union building where I was quartered. By 8 I was casing the Wiggley College building, locating myself in an empty office to set up my tapes and questions. At 9 it was Anna. At 10 it was Mariana. At 11 it was Sharon. At 12 it was lunch with Professor Carpy himself, which turned out to be an impromptu interview sans notebook or tape recorder. At 1:30 it was Alex. At 2:30 it was Jane. And now, at 3:30, it was Dr. Carpy again, first in his office, then down for a cigarette break to the parking lot. I was punch drunk with interviewing.

*Okay, nod. What's he saying, now? Pay attention. Something about taking a stance. On what? Just listen. Eye contact. Nod. Now you be HYP-no-tized!*

"By [taking a] position I don't mean you've got to be ornery . . . I simply mean you've got to take your best shot at what it is that you think you currently know and then I think you've got to say, you've got to put that on the line and then you've got to look at what happens."

*Strike a pose! Take the . . . Shhh!*

And so this is how it went at Bladderburg University, in the heart of the eastern midwest. My asking anemic questions and looking by turns engrossed and credulous, just like they do on *60 Minutes*, except with all the boring outtakes left in. My own proffered "insights" ham-fisted, off-key, trivial. Much, I presumed, to the private derision of my subjects, thinking me an idiot, which is certainly how I felt. But trying to look sly. Suitably humble, the promising graduate student researcher. Nodding and frowning thoughtfully, Peter Faulk-style, collecting all the pertinent information in spite of my clumsiness and the suspect's dubious estimation of my intellectual wherewithall. The Columbo of qualitative research, that was me.

But meanwhile, off camera, a symphony of distractions performed by the Imp and my trickster-self . . .

*(Columbo starts to leave the room, then turns: Ah, yaah, well, thank you, professor. You've been very helpful. But, ah, just one more question . . .)*

But by taking a position, by anchoring yourself someplace—I don't care, you don't even have to be anchored right, you've just got to be anchored someplace. And then you've got to deal with the data you collect or what happens, what the kids are doing, and you've got to rethink and then . . . it's not . . . You need to criticize where you currently are but also develop your own personal model.

*Anchor, get anchored, collect your data.*

Carpy stepped on his cigarette, making apologetic noises on the subject of quitting, though admitting he knew he wouldn't. He led me to his car to give me a tour of the town. A professor's car, well this side of rattle-trap, but lived-in. I was disappointed not to find any stance-taking bumper stickers on the rear fender. There was an empty pack of Winston's on the floorboard of the passenger seat.

"I think this process is fundamentally observation, reflection, and theorizing, and I think that cycle . . . I want that cycle in place. I don't really care about what, the person's theorizing may in actual fact violate everything I've been doing for years, but I want that cycle in place."

Carpy was the genuine article, all right, and had the potential to be a gristly pain in the ass for the profession. You could see that in a minute. Built solid, like the midwestern, 20th-century industrial-gothic architecture of the campus, he resembled a pastiche of masculine principles: a sinewy shot of George C. Scott, a stoic dollop of Papa Hemingway, and a giddy dash of Fritz Mondale all rolled into one. Wisened eyes. Narrow patrician nose. Silvered beard yellowed with nicotine around the maw. A pain in the ass perhaps, by virtue of his eagerness to call in to question and reconstruct, but there was a weathered kind of generosity about the man, a tolerance approaching kindness. He clearly made an impression. Even the Imp was starting to focus.

*Like Jane's report: "You know, when Carpy comes down the hall in the morning or you see him around, you know, he's always saying the most outlandish things in the loudest voice. It sets a sort of a tone for the graduate students. It kind of promotes a level of comfort. And we have these real informal conversations about the stuff I'm working on, and he just basically asks me a bunch of questions and its deceptive . . . the converstions are deceptively simple because I always feel as if, well, what did he say that was so profound? Well, nothing, except that what he says somehow pushes me against the wall on a notion I'm trying to take somewhere. And he says, well, what about this? You know, and you're stopped dead in your tracks and rethink it."*

Mentoring. When I first heard about what you were up to, I go, what the hell do I know about mentoring? I don't know anything about mentoring. That's my first reaction to all of this, but I suppose I do know some, I don't know. I tend to just live it. I tend to just live the model and I tend to invite students . . . I arrange . . . I guess I put in place structure so that students find the kind of support, experience . . . I assume that the experience of that will sell them on the idea. If it doesn't, that's fine, too.

A light, early spring rain spackling the windshield. Driving across the still winter-bare campus, naked parchment branches, dampened cherry blossoms, wet loam, reawakened turf. Like an oversized cemetery, BU is strewn with moon-beige sandstone monuments, highrise classroom towers, spaced out over seemingly unreasonable distances: the midwestern love of space. We are quiet. I'm feeling vacuously meditative, but I try to sound intelligent.

"Does it seem to transfer through, that structure, to follow them into their professional lives?"

Yeah. It's very . . . I find . . . well, I find that I have connections with graduate students from years and years that I've been . . . that we still maintain conversations in various ways. Last night we had a teleconference with doctoral students who got out of here in the '80s, and they have worked with people and have, you know, have a collective that they're working with. We're now connected over e-mail and I have a study group with new faculty up in Bloodsworthy, some of whom are my doctoral students, and we're inviting other people in to support our writing and our research.

Working together in collectives. That's his thing. Like the story Alex told me:

*"I wrote Carpy and I can't remember what I actually wrote in this inquiry letter, but just said that I was aware of his work and would be interested in working with him and what is he working on now, I think. And he sent me a paper he had just written, and it was just a rough draft, and he said, well, you know, if you're interested in what I'm working on, here's this paper I've just written. So, he was maybe implying I should respond, but he didn't expect a response. So I went through and read it real carefully and there were some wonderful things in it and some things I really questioned . . . things I didn't particularly like . . . very minor things . . . overall I thought it was great. So I just really spent some time analyzing it, taking notes, and then I thought, well, I'll write this up and give it to him. I hesitated for a moment . . . I thought, well, you know he didn't really invite criticism and here I am criticising his paper . . . is this . . . you know, should I do this? And I finally thought, well, if he's a person I really want to work with, he won't mind. And it turned out that he not only didn't mind, but sent back this wonderful encouraging letter saying this is some of the best feedback I've gotten on this paper, thanks a lot, and why don't you tell me what you're doing and meanwhile I told him that I had seen one of his videos. So this exchange started.*

"So, uh, how would you characterize the role you play? If you had to think of a handy descriptor, what might it be? Would you say you're a coach? A choreographer? An instructor? A collegeague? An assistant?"

Carpy's thick frame undulates effortfully under his sweater.

*A benevolent slave-driver? An eager voyeur? A bull in a china shop? An overly self-reflective researcher? Hey, I said: Shhhh!*

Well, you see, the problem is that I don't know that I do any of that very consciously. I tell you what I do is I can be a fairly productive guy myself, right? And I tend to be involved in my own sort of program of research and a lot of people come to participate in that, and I include them. I don't particularly go out of my way to invite people who don't want . . . If they don't want anything to do with me, that's just fine. Nor am I particularly looking at instructing them, in a sense. I mean, I would much prefer to have their perspective. I think I treat people as colleagues, and I think we're enriched by that perspective and try to find out what interests them in what I was doing and what perspective they can bring that can push our thinking forward.

Like his student, Anna, told me,

*He has far great theoretical knowledge than I do, but I'm willing to argue more with him. We have greater debates than I do with other professors. He's revered because I respect him, but he's not revered in the distance way. He really wants to know what I think. And that's been kind of interesting. Because the first time it happened, I thought, okay now, does he really want to know? What's going on here? So I think its been equal footing in that respect. But when I'm sharing my concerns about my project in Bloodsworthy, then it's very much the professor/student role of him saying you should check out this resource or have you ever considered that. And even in those moments where he's asking for my input, it's also a teaching role in the respect that I'll say something and then he will restate it in a clearer way. I always try to listen to how he says things because he says it so much better. But he has a good sense of humor, too, you know. I think it's a very friendly relationship.*

Anna was cool. Nice eyes. All smiles.

But I think, if anything, I'd let the group instruct, not me. I wouldn't . . . I'd let the group talk about what it is we're on to, and work with them . . . bring them into the thought collective, I guess. I use the word thought collective. It's out of Fleck. Rudolph Fleck? And I mean it's . . . I think you've just got to be immersed in the environment. . . . The thing that . . . we were talking about that over lunch, but the thing that always bothers me is that sense of community which I think is very strong and very powerful in the notion . . . and I think which violates academia generally. I think the notion that you don't ever have to work alone is basically a violation of what academia is built on and. . . . But, yet, I think that's really a very powerful part of what it means to be a professional.

Carpy fumbled forth another cigarette as he spoke, burning it off the dashboard lighter.

I think probably what a good graduate program does is connect people to the profession. And I think by connected I mean, you know, connected into a thought collective. But also connected into professional organizations; connected to other people, other groups that are thinking like you. And when I look at the differences between doctoral programs, what I see is, you know, some places just don't work at that. It's just, they go through the program, but they're not. . . . They haven't put in place structures whereby people can talk and form, you know, a group or thought collective bigger than themselves. I mean, it's not . . . I think it's important to connect. I mean, I think it's important to work with students so that they have opportunities where they work to do that. . . . Get into thought groups. People who are working along the same lines but differently. . . . Getting them tied into the profession differently so that they're part of the profession, not just part of a program, but a part of that broader kind of field.

Well, okay, so after a couple of hours of listening to the man and resisting myself, I have to admit I like his style. Indeed, by interview's end, the Imp has been quieted. Not at all the famous sociocultural egghead I'd anticipated. No, an altogether different kind of academic icon. Kinder, gentler, wiser, animated and animating—as a grad student myself I could see Carpy as a mentor. In the course of one day he had safely conducted my inner counterpoint from Schönberg to Bach. I even liked his unrealistic self-deprecation.

Carpy, on the parapet of a local restaurant: "What else do I mean by mentoring? I don't know what mentoring means, but I think it's that working together."

## CODA

At the English Hut, over a sandwich and a beer, between CNN reports and waitress smiles at the bar, pondering my experience at Bladderburg U.

More telling than the truths we perceive and report, are the truths we deny, or worse, cannot muster the perspicuity to warrant.

What do I mean by that? Confronting the taken-for-granted assumptions we never challenge or kickover, I guess. And what brought that to mind? My mentor for a day, of course, Carpy.

You see, I figure a guy like Carpy brings his graduate students into the profession by making a safe thought space for them. He's part of this thought collective, too, of course, but he has a special role. He has, you might say, the metasocial awareness necessary to orchestrate the potential interpersonal dynamics to generate productive work and disciplinary insights. He's reassuring even as he's challenging. In the embrace of that kind of environment, his students can feel more secure in letting go of the thought scaffolds and foundational biases they depend on, that they in fact have held dear as their intellectual selves. To become something more than what we are, we have to let go of the person we've been. Not entirely, but to a much greater degree than our illusory self-continuity suggests. I think about Alex's struggle with his transformation as a professional, and I think of my own. When I was a child, I spoke as a child, but now it's time to put away childish ways and actually do some damage. Or something like that.

I stare blankly at the inflatable news anchor presiding over a muted succession of horrors, many of them for sale, no doubt, at a store somewhere nearby. From the juke box the Shirelles are singing "Will You Still Love Me Tomorrow?" I can't figure out if the waitress is making goo-goo eyes, or if she's just a little tipsy. But the roast beef au jus sandwich is damn good. I stare through the bottom of my glass darkly, and order another. This mentoring research stuff is going to be knotty business, I warn myself.

## WHO DOES THIS ACCOUNT OF "PROFESSOR CARPY" THINK YOU ARE?

Who a film thinks you are is a key concept in film and media studies. It is a concept film theorists technically label *mode of address*. As such, it gets at the question of how viewers are positioned within relations of power associated with race, class, ethnicity, gender, sexuality, age, ability, and so on. Mode of address also gets at how audiences, acting as their own agents, take up and use a film's address to fashion different social and cultural identities. In a series of essays, Elizabeth Ellsworth (1997) uses mode of address, along with psychoanalytic literary criticism, to examine teaching and the teacher–student relationship.

In this chapter, we draw heavily from Ellsworth's (1997) work on mode of address, as applied to pedagogy, to explore what this analytic concept might mean for us as researchers reporting our data using fictive techniques. In a nutshell, who does the text "Professor Carpy" think you (the reader) are? Is there a meaningful distinction to be made between who the narrator thinks you are and who the author thinks you are? And, what is it about mode of address that argues for fictive representation as an academic writing style? Before considering some answers to these questions, a summary of Ellsworth's work on mode of address in pedagogical studies is in order.

### Pedagogy and Mode of Address

Elizabeth Ellsworth was a student of film studies in graduate school before she joined the faculty in curriculum and instruction at the University of Wisconsin, Madison. In her words:

I got hired out of communication arts and into a school of education to teach video production and media criticism for educators. It's been a cross-cultural experience. I didn't speak the language of educational research. I didn't know the stories or characters of the field.

Most alien and alienating of all was having to learn the theories and practices of this new academic world called "curriculum and instruction" in the complete absence of suspense, romance, seduction, visual pleasure, music, plot, humor, tap dancing, or pathos.... What I've learned most from my decade-long encounter with education as an academic field is, I don't want to teach or learn in the absence of pleasure, plot, moving and being moved, metaphor, cultural artifacts, audience engagement and interaction.... That's where mode of address comes in (Ellsworth, 1997, p. 21).

Reading this about Ellsworth prompted us to wonder if there weren't traces of her longings lurking within each of us. Often over the past 2 years while writing up the data from our mentoring project (of which Professor Carpy was a part), we talked about the possibility of using plot, metaphor, cultural artifact, and humor to make our report more interesting and accessible—always, of course, with the half-guilty feeling that we would be writing largely for ourselves, for our own amusement. But need that be the case? Is there no audience for fictive representation as an academic writing style in education research? And if not, how might mode of address be useful as an analytic tool for arguing the value of such a writing style?

According to Ellsworth (1997), mode of address has not been taken up in education but should be. She advocated using it "to shake up solidified and limited ways of thinking about and practicing teaching" (p. 2). Worried about what gets erased or ignored (and at whose expense) when educators act as if there is no mode of address in teaching—as if teaching were a seamless and transparent activity devoid of plot, intrigue, and the lot—Ellsworth has argued that "mode of address is one of those intimate relations of social and cultural power that shapes and misshapes who teachers think students are, and who students come to think themselves to be" (p. 6). Because it is impossible to obtain an exact fit between the perceiver and the perceived, mode of address is more an event than a visible, locatable relationship. In pedagogical terms, mode of address is the space or difference between the *who* the teacher thinks a student is and the *who* that student enacts through her or his verbal responses and nonverbal actions. This difference or "misfit" between address and response is a social space, one which teachers can neither predict nor control, but one which they can use as a resource to feed the questions and curiosities that will forever keep themselves and their practices unsettled.

Applied to our current interest in using certain conventions of new journalism to write a research report, we see the so-called misfit between address and response as a social space in which to negotiate how the stances or positionings of an audience are constituted through different discourses (Beach, 1997; Fiske, 1994). In writing up his report of his interview with Jerry Harste, George avoided a "scientific" discourse in which the audience is distanced for the sake of establishing what would appear to be an objective space between the researcher and the researched. Preferring, instead, a more personal style of writing—one that employs certain rhetorical strategies and tropes common to fiction—George sought to negotiate the space between address and response in ways that kept Fiske's (1994) concept of audiencing fluent. For example, at one point in his write-up, George used a gendered discourse that Donna and Kit (two of his responders) picked up on. In doing so, he destabilized a text that up to that point neither Donna nor Kit had questioned, at least not in terms of their own sense of social identity and social relation to the author.

## Who Does the Text "Professor Carpy" Think I Am?

We propose first to explore this question through Donna's response to George's account of his visit to Indiana University to interview Jerry Harste and several of Professor Harste's doctoral students on the topic of mentoring. In her response, Donna analyzes how George's use of fictive techniques to characterize Harste ("Professor Carpy") and to distill the significance of his mentoring style resulted in a product that packaged "truth" much more memorably for her than would have been the case had George reported the interview data in a conventional form. She also analyzes the text's mode of address. Then, in keeping with our understanding of mode of address as an *event*, we re-explore the same question from the perspective of three new readers, none of whom George had in mind when he initially wrote "Professor Carpy." In each of the three instances, treating mode of address as an *event* signals our belief, after Ellsworth (1997) and Masterman (1985), that it is something that occurs in the social space between the *who* the author imagined or intended the reader to be and the *who* that reader thinks he or she is.

In traditional research exposition, the mode of address presumes an audience of similarly educated scholars. The authors of such pieces take great pains to write with a professional style stressing objectivity, reason, intelligence, authority, and profundity (whether the content deserves such treatment or not). In a sense, academic authors create an implied author who is the very caricature of a scholar. Not for vanity alone is such a voice maintained; the compliment is equally to the reader who is, as noted, presumed to be similarly noble. This academic mode of address is formulaic and required, and so is nearly invisible due to its dependable ubiquity. The result is a standardized discourse form that robs the text of any idiosyncratic humanity that might cast doubt on the implied omniscience of the report. By contrast, in creative narration the mode of address and other stylistic matters are variables to be manipulated for aesthetic and dramatic effect, and idiosyncrasy and humanity are at a premium. A well-practiced evaluator of creative writing, therefore, is one who takes nothing in the text at face value, least of all its mode of address. In traditional academic discourse the author presents him or herself as a scholar and seems to want you to believe the same. In a work of creative writing, the author may well wish for the reader to find the narrator believable, but not necessarily synonymous with the author. The author may also wish the reader to find the narrator an undependable source of information or analysis, and possibly not even a likely target for sympathy (Booth, 1983).

Determining mode of address in works employing fictive techniques, then, is a tricky business. Who the author thinks you are is not the same thing as who the narrator might think you are, if indeed the narrator is presuming a reader at all. And making matters messier, this same indeterminancy that confounds the intentions of the author works in reverse to double the slippage as the reader attempts to determine who the author is, or what the author intends, and who the author thinks the reader is. Since we focus here on the responses of readers, we will refer simply to whom *the text* seems to think a reader is, according to the reader.

***Donna's response.*** George wrote "Professor Carpy" initially with me as his only intended reader in mind. The two of us were in the early stages of our research collaboration on the mentoring project (Alvermann & Hruby, 2000), and we were experimenting with different forms of fictive representation. I found his write-up from the Indiana University interviews to be more interesting and memorable than my recollections of other reports of interview data. This led me to wonder what it was about this style of reporting that prompted me to favor it over more traditional forms. I was put in mind of Kenneth Burke's (1945, 1966) pentad, the five elements of dramatic action and motivation—act, scene, agent, agency, and purpose. That these five elements correlate so closely with a journalist's concern for the who, what, when, where, and why in stories is not surprising. Coupled with balance and distance, the "five w's" are said to foster credibility and acceptance in the reader of a report. Haarsager (1998) described the relationship this way:

> Through the lens of Burke's dramatistic pentad, reporters might be described as trading in words that: 1) name the act (what happened in a thought or deed); 2) name the scene and background of the act; 3) tell what person or kind of person (the agent) performed the act; 4) describe the means or instruments (agency) of the act; and finally, 5) tell why the act happened or was resolved the way it was or will be resolved (the purpose). The combination, and the relative weight given certain of the elements as a rhetorical strategy, also opens a window on the narrator's purpose, motivations, and worldview (p. 57).

However, as noted by James Wertsch (1998), the implications of Burke's pentad for reportorial, literary, and scientific method are more profound than merely a reprise of the journalist's five w's. Burke's pentad provides a "perspective on perspective" for textual analysis (Gusfield, as cited in Wertsch, 1998). Burke's hope is to elude the monistic reductionism that so often bedevils positivistic and critical research in accounting for human behavior. While a purely sociological account of human action would stress the influence of scene (social context), and a psychological account would stress the influence of the individual (agent), a more complex embrace of human action would use all five of the pentad's terminological screens as tools for analysis. Wertsch (1998), a self-confessed Hegalian, claims that to employ more than two of these screens in an analysis is to beget impossible complexity, and so remains wedded to a dialectical analysis employing pairs of perspectives (e.g., the interaction of scene and agent, or agent and agency). But, by presenting his research data in fictive form, George attempted to employ all five. He provided scene (the campus, Carpy's car, a local eatery, etc.), act (the interview with Carpy), agents and counteragents (the researcher and his participants), agency (the interview methodology, active dialogue, reflective monologue), and purpose (research on the mentoring of graduate students in literacy education, trying to get a handle on both the research process and his central subject). In this way he attempted to suggest the multiple motivations behind the actions described in his report. Following Burke (1969), George resisted the urge to clarify the ambiguous, choosing instead to "clearly reveal the strategic spots at which ambiguities necessarily arise" (p. xviii).

Using these elements and various tropes to maintain perceptions of credibility while not losing the power of the narrative, George put a "human face" on the interview data. For instance, he showed, rather than told, what Professor Carpy believed mentoring entailed, and he did this through extensive use of direct quotations, colorful language, and precise wording. With the help of his trickster-self and the Imp, George also opened a window on his own worldviews. By revealing his personal thoughts on the academy, academic research, and mentoring, he made it possible for me to identify and connect with him on several issues. What this connection accomplished in me, as a reader, was a willingness to suspend any doubt that Professor Carpy could be anyone other than the character George showed him to be.

But there is more to be said. Cutting across the various fictive techniques in "Professor Carpy" was a mode of address that acted on me in both predictable and unpredictable ways. Predictably, I took up several of the most obvious positions offered me. As researcher, I applauded Carpy's insistence that graduate students take a stance, that they "anchor themselves someplace"; as mentor, I knew the text wanted me to cringe at the unequal power arrangements that exist between professors and students, and I dutifully acquiesced; as academic, I took up my position as veteran intellectual; and as former doctoral student, I identified with the sense of fraudulence that budding academics almost always feel. Interesting, I mused, that the author knew his reader so well!

Of course, this reader was never only (or fully) who the text imagined, either. At times I would find in "Professor Carpy" the most grating of insinuations. Who does this text think I am, I would whine. Surely, I've not given cause for such allusions. . . . For instance, I bristled at the proffered position of "academic as sociocultural egghead" and subsequently dismissed any attempt by the text to make up for the brush-off. At other times I was unpredictably mellow, so much so in fact that I surprised myself. Take for example how surprised I was at experiencing little or no discomfort with the text's decidedly masculinist mode of address. Later, in reflecting on this unexpected response, I tried to rationalize it. Perhaps, I reasoned, it was due as much to my knowing (or *thinking* I knew) the author as it was to any slippage in my normally intact feminist stance. Or, and this seems more likely, I may simply have found sufficient room in the social space between the text and myself to imagine and try on a new identity. Theories about mode of address being an event, rather than a relatively static concept, would suggest the latter.

***Joel's response.*** Since its initial reading by Donna, "Professor Carpy" has been presented twice: once in a session at the annual meeting of the Invisible College (Alvermann & Hruby, 1998),

and again, in an alternative format session at the National Reading Conference that involved Jerry Harste (Professor Carpy), George, Donna, and three other individuals who were part of the mentoring project (Hruby & Alvermann, 1998). Because we did not take notes on the audience's response to either session, we had no way of retrieving that information for analysis here. Consequently, in preparing to write this section of the chapter, Donna invited one of her colleagues, Joel Taxel, a professor in English Education at the University of Georgia, to read and respond to "Professor Carpy" and then to meet with her to discuss his response.

The meeting between Joel and Donna took place in Joel's office. After some initial awkwardness over the most appropriate form for the encounter, Donna and Joel decided on a conversation, rather than a formal interview. Donna and Joel have known each other professionally for over 18 years, so the informality a conversation offered seemed appropriate. It also seemed appropriate to invite Joel to read Donna's analysis of his response. He graciously agreed to do so, and thus what follows is a jointly constructed response.

Joel began by talking about a session he had attended at a recent meeting of the American Educational Research Association. The session had focused on the pros and cons of writing a dissertation using various modes of fictive representation. Admitting that he was not altogether comfortable with the idea of dissertations becoming stand-alone works of fiction, he was quick to point out that he could see the merits of such an approach if it were embedded in the larger discourse that informed a particular field or discipline. Joel then asked how the text "Professor Carpy" would be presented. When he learned that it was to be part of a chapter in the second edition of *The Handbook of Research on Teaching the English Language Arts* and that it would be situated in such a way that readers would have a context for interpreting it, he was enthusiastic and proceeded to describe several things he found appealing about the piece.

Mostly, Joel was impressed with what he had learned about mentoring as a result of reading "Professor Carpy." He commented on how surprised he was to find that he had never really given much attention to how he mentored—or, if he thought about it at all, he guessed he had seen it as an extension of how he teaches. However, after reading "Carpy" and discovering that he agreed with the professor's insistence on doctoral students taking a stance—any stance—so long as they could defend it, Joel said he was inclined to like the piece even more. Consequently, he said he read it again, looking for more things about mentoring that may have escaped him in the past.

When Donna remarked that Joel was attending more to the content of the text (mentoring) than with the style in which it was written, he nodded in agreement. This observation led to further speculation that the use of fictive techniques to represent social science data may not be as distracting as one might predict. Joel attributed his ability to focus on the content as being partially due to the fact that he was learning something about himself as a mentor by attending to Professor Carpy's philosophical take on the topic.

Joel also commented that he found the piece provocative and insightful. He asked about the author, and when he did not recognize the name, asked more questions about George's background. Joel was particularly interested in whether or not George had given serious thought to writing his dissertation using some of the techniques of new journalism. On learning that George had created the text for a research project that involved experimenting with different forms for writing up one's data, Joel remarked once gain that he found the "Carpy" piece extremely provocative and insightful. He added that he found it a powerful way to draw the reader into the text. He also found it enjoyable reading, something out of the ordinary— something one doesn't typically associate with research reports.

***Margaret and Kit's responses.*** Margaret Hagood and Kit Crowder met each other in a summer session class in 1998. In the summer of 1999, they were together again in a class that focused on the uses of representation in writing up qualitative research. In fact, they are still part of a writing group that grew out of the qualitative research class. Both are also doctoral students at the University of Georgia—Margaret in Reading Education and Kit in Educational Psychology. We asked them to respond to the introductory portion of this chapter and to the "Professor Carpy" piece. Here, we present verbatim segments of their conversation, supplemented in part by notes that Margaret took and by information gathered in a follow-up conversation with her.

Both Margaret and Kit were in agreement that the authors of this chapter assumed that they were good readers and that they were sufficiently steeped in traditional educational research methods to appreciate the authors' interest in presenting an alternative way of reporting research. Beyond that initial point of agreement, the two women's responses held little in common. Kit, for example, responded by pointing out the differences between the mode of address used in the introduction to the chapter and that used in the "Professor Carpy" piece. In her words:

In the introduction, the authors assume I am open-minded about new and various ways to represent data, but they also assume that new forms of data representation should conform to established forms of scholarly writing (e.g., citation). Furthermore, the authors' writing style in the introduction adheres to formal, scholarly prose by stating an argument and then by trying to develop rationally that argument. A sense of humor is not detected, nor do I feel from the introductory portion that this is an insider's piece. I am to be instructed on how this concept works; however, I did not feel the same way about the fictive portion of the chapter. . . . [It] thinks that I, as a reader, am an insider. The authors assume that I am someone who conducts or is interested in reading how educational research is conducted, which means that I am interested in being privy to the researchers' early ramblings of the head, as opposed to just reading the polished version. This understanding between the authors and the reader of how qualitative research works allows the authors to poke fun at and have a sense of humor about qualitative research (e.g., inside jokes, such as being punch drunk with interviews). The authors also think that I am someone interested in academic life and the ways in which professors mentor students. From an insider's perspective, they assume that I have respect for professors and can handle the way that they poke fun at Carpy. But they think that beyond that I can get the point about mentoring.

Margaret, on the other hand, did not draw comparisons between the different modes of address in the introductory and fictive portions of the chapter; nor did she focus on the topic of mentoring, per se. By her account, she read in a holistic manner, attending to how the text positioned her as a knowledgeable and interested reader of research. In Margaret's words:

I read the piece holistically and did not think about differences between the introduction and the fictive portion. . . . The authors assume that I am familiar with the recent thinking about alternative forms of data representation and have been thinking about how to reach a broader audience by writing in more accessible ways than the standard research report procedure. Presenting this information up front, the authors think that I am open to different ways of thinking about research. But to ensure credibility with me as the reader of research, they use citations. . . .

The authors think that I am interested in the personhood of alternative forms of data representation, and by providing an example of their own form of alternative representation, they can show me how the data can be interesting while maintaining its integrity. Through narrative descriptions they present the struggles between the researcher and the researched, participant data and researcher data, faculty and student, mentor and mentee, mentor and person. But they think that I do not need to have these issues explained to me in these terms. Furthermore, they think that I am interested in what goes into a research project so that the people are seen as people and not necessarily as objective observers or inhuman participants. They assume that I think research to be much more than finding the answer to a question posed by the researcher and that observations beyond traditional forms of data collection can be presented in the write-up to reflect this idea. Examples such as Carpy's smoking, Carpy and George's cursing, and George's head musings provide a behind-the-scene portrait that shows the everyday lived experiences of those involved. The authors assume that I will understand these ideas without need of explicit explanations as to their relevance . . .

Both women also responded to how they believed this chapter's mode of address misread them, at least in terms of how they perceived themselves as readers and researchers. Kit, for instance, noted some doubts that she had about the use of fictive techniques to represent data:

I can easily recall the vivid descriptions, but have to revisit the text and filter through all of these details to get at the point of the research on mentoring. . . . When George describes the women he came in contact with in terms of attraction, I read that as a sense of George's power as an interviewer. It made me want to say, "Why don't you listen to what the woman is saying and not think about her eyes and smile?" If I, as the interviewer, had these feelings about the physicality of an interviewee, I would think it a low point of the interview and would try to overcome it. Maybe I am supposed to be bothered by this because it sets me up as a reader of qualitative research. . . . I don't, however, think that as a qualitative educational researcher I am always interested in learning this kind of information; nor am I always willing to do the sifting through of details to get at the heart of the matter.

Like Kit, Margaret expressed some of her own reservations about fictive representation of educational research data:

The authors mention their desire to explore ways to make written products of research more interesting, more accessible, and more aesthetically pleasing. But I don't think myself one to always want to read texts that make ideas more accessible. I also think that they assume that as a reader I find that fiction is more accessible and easier to read than other forms of writing. I do not think this of myself as a reader either. I believe that reading fiction (e.g., works by Toni Morrison), reading theory (e.g., Gayatri Spivak), reading research (e.g., quantum physics) may all qualify as interesting, accessible, and aesthetically pleasing as the reverse of these terms. In other words, I think that the authors assume that I think that reading this research as fiction would be easier than [if it were] written in another way. The conversation that occurred in our writing group over this piece begs to differ with this assumption. One person read the piece . . . [as being] about mentoring while the other read it [as being] about the personhood of representing research. So the piece when discussed, although interesting, was not necessarily easily accessible as anything—fiction or research.

In reflecting on Margaret's and Kit's responses, it bears repeating that the text's mode of address is neither stable nor predictable. For instance, Kit commented at length on how the introductory and fictive portions of the text positioned her differently. Although Margaret did not draw these distinctions, she resisted the fictive representation of the data as a way of making the text more interesting, accessible, and engaging. The responses of both women suggest once again that readers are not positioned by the text alone but in fact act as their own agents in fashioning different positions for themselves. In this instance, Margaret and Kit viewed themselves as competent readers who had an interest in research on educational issues. They also viewed themselves as sufficiently invested in how data are represented (as a result of enrolling in a class on that topic) to take a position relative to the author's mode of address in "Professor Carpy." In using their agency as readers, Margaret and Kit fashioned responses that speak not only about alternative methods for writing up research but also about who they are as people. For instance, their responses gesture toward the emotional as well as the intellectual, and toward the embodied as well as the abstract. In short, in negotiating the text's mode of address, Margaret and Kit reveal aspects of themselves that might not otherwise have surfaced had they been responding to a conventionally written research report.

Our analysis of Margaret's and Kit's responses turned up other points of interest as well. For example, Kit's response to the physicality present in the "Carpy" text contrasted in interesting ways to Margaret's, Joel's, and Donna's responses. Whereas Kit was troubled by the masculinist overtones in references made to the women's eyes and smiles, Donna rationalized her reaction to the same information, and Joel and Margaret did not find (or at least did not mention) any discomfort with the allusions George made to the women's eyes and smiles. It is interesting to note, however, that both Kit and Joel (neither of whom knew George) asked several questions about his physical appearance. Ironically, what may be of importance here is not that Kit responded the way she did to the physicality described in the text, but rather that the text evoked (at least in some of its readers) a visceral response quite different from that which would be expected from traditional research reporting.

Another point worth considering is Margaret's explanation of how fictive representation of the data (at least as it was used in the "Carpy" text) missed the audience on two counts—both as research and as fiction. As she pointed out, this method of reporting research, while interesting, did not make the data any more accessible, and in fact, seemed to invite quite disparate readings of the research. It is important to note here that Margaret and Kit did not have access to the entire chapter's contents when they read the "Carpy" piece. Having only information from a rough draft of the introduction as a scaffold, they were left to their own devices in terms of how they would interpret research written up using fictive techniques. Had they been privy to information subsequently added to the chapter that explained such techniques, it is possible that the text would have been more accessible. We believe the situation to which Margaret has referred demonstrates clearly the need for researchers who use fictive representation to embed it in a manner that gives readers sufficient background information—a point Joel Taxel emphasized in his response to "Professor Carpy."

Finally, from our perspective, the fact that the "Carpy" piece missed its audience might be considered a plus. It could be argued, for instance, that the different readings Margaret and Kit took from the piece made for a more interesting (and possibly more productive) conversation between the two of them. If nothing else, the situation points out how a text that *shows*, rather than *tells*, produces qualitatively different readings. It also stands as a reminder that narrative should not be read as exposition—the form in which research is traditionally written. Not surprisingly, different ways of writing call for different ways of reading.

## FICTIVE REPRESENTATION: AN ACADEMIC WRITING STYLE?

Standardized ways of reporting research are part of the legacy of our field. For decades, language and literacy researchers clung to the styles and formats in scholarly discourse that promised a certain distanced objectivity. The result was a sterile form of reporting in which neither subjects nor researchers were present. With the introduction of ethnographic methods of inquiry in education, researchers attempted to make their participants' presence felt by transforming the data in ways that seemed more "natural" and hence more representative of the participants' everyday meaning-making activities. In truth, however, such transformations may have been more the researchers' stories than the participants' (Bochner & Ellis, 1996; Denzin, 1997). This critique of the modernist goal of representing lived experience, labeled by some as the crisis in representation (Clifford & Marcus, 1986; Denzin, 1994), led to dramatizing narratives as a means of structuring and envisioning data that show, rather than tell about, participants' lives. The products of such experimentation resulted in written reports that also showed how researchers' lives intersected with the lives of the people they studied (Alvermann & Hruby, 2000; Ellis, 1997; Jipson & Paley, 1997; Miller, 1998; Richardson, 1993; Tierney, 1993).

Interest in developing alternative forms for reporting research that make use of various dramatizing techniques are not new. The term *literary journalism*, defined broadly as "extended digressive narrative nonfiction" (Kramer, as cited in Haarsager, 1998, p. 59) has been in use for the last half century. Over 2 decades ago, the well-known historian Hayden White (1978) argued for a greater presence in scholarly journals of "impressionistic, expressionistic, surrealistic, and (perhaps) even actionist modes of representation for dramatizing the significance of data" (pp. 47–48). More recently, a number of scholars in the social sciences have continued to press for a style of research reporting that blurs narrative knowing (Eisner, 1997; Polkinghorne, 1997), sociological telling (Lawrence-Lightfoot & Davis, 1997; Richardson, 1997), poetry (Richardson, 1993), and film making (Trinh, 1992).

Because fictive representation entails writing *through* facts, not *in* facts, it is particularly well suited to reporting research meant to move the reader in ways that cut to the quick. Like Ellsworth (1997), we find ourselves growing weary of academic writing that is ponderous in style, blind to mind-body connections, and devoid of the interpretively pertinent arousals aesthetically crafted language can bring to reading. All of which brings us full circle to mode of address.

To our way of thinking, mode of address—a concept typically given little if any attention in academic writing—has much to offer if for no other reason than it argues the case for using fictive techniques in reporting research. It makes the argument in at least three ways. First, because mode of address concerns itself with lessening the distance between writers and readers, it is inherently useful to researchers *who* are intent on reaching a broad audience, one that extends beyond the academy. The distances that separate researchers from their readers—whether ideological, temporal, social, or geographical—could be lessened considerably if reports were written in light of their desired audiences. We can think of very few forms of writing, other than research reports, that take their readers so much for granted.

Second, mode of address calls attention to the power of storytelling for both the writer and reader. Researchers who use fictive representation to move readers are likely to be moved themselves. Textual encounters with what Ellsworth (1997) describes as those things that make us laugh or cry, that create apprehension, that evoke pathos, or that cause us to question who we think we are in relation to ourselves and others are all part of the humanizing experience made visible by storytelling's mode of address. Neither researchers nor the readers for whom they write are exempt from this process. To act on the assumption that either group is immune to mode of address—the "something" that occurs in the space between the *who* the author imagines the reader to be and the who the reader thinks he or she is—would be unwise indeed.

Third, mode of address also calls attention to how all texts miss their audiences in one way or another. This phenomenon, while not specific to research reports, nevertheless is indicative of how mode of address argues the case for using fictive techniques to move readers. Researchers who use tropes, devices, and structures tend to write reports that do more than "tell it like it is;" they also create textual spaces in which their readers can bring both mind and body to bear on the work produced.

Although critics of this approach might justifiably claim that creating a tolerance for what is "true" using fictional devices only confuses the reader, it could also be argued that such tolerance produces its own kind of critical reading. Moreover, as the American philosopher Kendall Walton (1990) has observed in his work on the foundations of the representational arts, "although fictionality is not truth, the two are perfectly compatible" (p. 42).

Having made a case for inserting fictive techniques into research reports written for a broadened English Language Arts audience, we would be remiss if we failed to point out some of the drawbacks and dangers associated with doing so. For example, it might mean that research topics not amenable to techniques that dramatize narrative events would be increasingly ignored. Alternatively, it might mean that disproportionate attention would be paid to topics that lend themselves to such dramatization. It might also mean that a researcher's skill in writing and his or her ability to tell an interesting story would overshadow the significance of the data being reported. Finally, inserting the techniques of fictive representation into English Language Arts research reports might contribute to a declining credibility for the field's work in general. A public already divided on the merits of such research might be further inclined to discount a form of reporting that proposes to get at "truth" through storytelling (cf. Haarsager, 1998).

All said and done, we return to our starting point—to the notion that research reports do not have to be boring to read, or for that matter, to write. Perhaps the French philosopher Michel Foucault (1984/1985) expressed our sentiments best when he wrote, "There are times in life when the question of knowing if one can think differently than one thinks, and perceive differently than one sees, is absolutely necessary if one is to go on looking and reflecting at all" (p. 8). We have reached that juncture in terms of our own academic writing styles. In exploring different ways of representing data, we have come to value what *showing*, as opposed to *telling*, allows us to do. By using fictive techniques to tell our story, we can maintain the integrity of the research while simultaneously working to give it a sense of the richness of lived experience. Like Ellsworth (1997), we place a premium on modes of address that enable both writers and readers to move and be moved, to mingle fantasies with facts, and to partake of some of the more pleasurable aspects of fictional writing.

## ACKNOWLEDGMENTS

We thank Rick Beach, University of Minnesota, for his generous and helpful comments on an earlier draft of this chapter. We also thank Kit Crowder, Margaret Hagood, and Joel Taxel for taking time out of their busy schedules to read and discuss "Professor Carpy." Their readings of this text provided valuable response data that we used to strengthen our arguments and to question some of our assumptions. Finally, we express our appreciation to Jerome Harste, Indiana University, without whom there would have been no "Professor Carpy," and to the graduate students with whom Jerry worked.

# References

Alvermann, D. E. (in press). Narrative approaches. In M. Kamil, R. Barr, P. Mosenthal, & P. D. Pearson (Eds.), *Handbook of reading research: Volume III*. Mahwah, NJ: Lawrence Erlbaum Associates.

Alvermann, D. E., & Hruby, G. G. (in press). Mentoring and reporting research: A concern for aesthetics. *Reading Research Quarterly*.

Alvermann, D. E., & Hruby, G. G. (1998, April). Professor Carpy: An alternative representation of qualitative interview data. Paper presented at the annual meeting of the Invisible College, San Diego, CA.

Aristotle. (1999). Poetics. In S. Halliwell (Ed.), *Aristotle's Poetics*. Chicago: University of Chicago Press.

Banks, A., & Banks, S. P. (Eds.) (1998) *Fiction and social research*. Walnut Creek, CA: Altamira Press.

Barone, T. (1995). Persuasive writings, vigilant readings, and reconstructed characters: The paradox of trust in educational storysharing. *International Journal of Qualitative Studies in Education, 8,* 63–74.

Barone, T., & Eisner, E. (1998). Arts-based educational research. In R. Jaeger (Ed.), *Complementary methods of educational research* (pp. 73–99). Washington, DC: American Educational Research Association.

Beach, R. (1993). *A teacher's introduction to reader-response theories*. Urbana, IL: National Council of Teachers of English.

Beach, R. (1997). Critical discourse theory and reader response: How discourses constitute reader stances and social contexts. *Reader, 37,* 1–26.

Bochner, A. P., & Ellis, C. (1996). Talking over ethnography. In C. Ellis & A. P. Bochner (Eds.), *Composing ethnography: Alternative forms of qualitative writing* (pp. 13–45). Walnut Creek, CA: Altamira Press.

Bochner, A. P., & Ellis, C. (1998). Series editors' introduction. In A. Banks & S. P. Banks (Eds.), *Fiction and social research* (pp._). Walnut Creek, CA: Altamira Press.

Booth, W. C. (1983). *The rhetoric of fiction* (2nd ed.). Chicago: University of Chicago Press.

Burke, K. (1945). *A grammar of motives*. New York: Prentice-Hall.

Burke, K. (1966). *Literature as symbolic action: Essays on life, literature, and method*. Berkeley: University of California Press.

Burke, K. (1969). *A rhetoric of motives*. University of California Press.

Cizek, G. J. (1995). Crunchy granola and the hegemony of the narrative. *Educational Researcher, 24*(2), 26–28.

Clifford, J., & Marcus, G. E. (1986). *Writing culture*. Berkeley: University of California Press.

Denzin, N. K. (1994). Evaluating qualitative research in the poststructural moment: The lessons James Joyce teaches us. *International Journal of Qualitative Studies in Education, 7,* 295–308.

Denzin, N. K. (1997). *Interpretive ethnography: Ethnographic practices for the 21st century*. Thousand Oaks, CA: Sage.

Eisner, E. W. (1997). The promise and perils of alternative forms of data representation. *Educational Researcher, 26*(6), 4–10.

Ellis, C. (1997). Evocative autoethnography: Writing emotionally about our lives. In W. G. Tierney & Y. S. Lincoln (Eds.), *Representation and the text: Re-framing the narrative voice* (pp. 115–139). Albany: State University of New York Press.

Ellis, C., & Bochner, A. (Eds.). (1996). *Composing ethnography: Alternative forms of qualitative writing*. Walnut Creek, CA: Altimira Press.

Ellsworth, E. (1997). *Teaching positions: Difference, pedagogy, and the power of address*. New York: Teachers College Press.

Fiske, J. (1994). Audiencing: Cultural practice and cultural studies. In N. K. Denzin & Y. S. Lincoln (Eds.), *Handbook of qualitative research* (pp. 189–198). Thousand Oaks, CA: Sage.

Foucault, M. (1985). *The history of sexuality (Vol. 2): The use of pleasure*. (R. Hurley, Trans.). New York: Vintage Books. (Original work published 1984).

Frus, P. (1994). *The politics and poetics of journalistic narrative*. New York: Cambridge University Press.

Gardner, J. (1983). *The art of fiction: Notes on craft for young writers*. New York: Vintage Books.

Haarsager, S. L. (1998). Stories that tell it like it is? Fiction techniques and prize-winning journalism. In A. Banks & S. P. Banks (Eds.), *Fiction and social research* (pp. 51–65). Walnut Creek, CA: Altamira Press.

Hruby, G. G., & Alvermann, D. A. (1998, December). Over-writing: An alternative approach to data analysis and write-up. Paper presented at the annual meeting of the National Reading Conference, Austin, TX.

Jipson, J. A., & Paley, N. (Eds.) (1997). *Daredevil research*. New York: Peter Lang.

Kauffman, L. (1993). The long goodbye: Against personal testimony, or an infant grifter grows up. In G. Greene & C. Kahn (Eds.), *Changing subjects: The making of feminist literary criticism* (pp. 129–146). London: Routledge.

Lawrence-Lightfoot, S., & Davis, J. H. (1997). *The art and science of portraiture*. San Francisco: Joseey-Bass.

Levine, G. (1994). Why science isn't literature: The importance of differences. In A. Megill (Ed.), *Rethinking objectivity* (pp. 65–79). Durham, NC: Duke University Press.

Masterman, L. (1985). *Teaching the media*. London: Comedia.

Miller, M. (1998). (Re)presenting voices in dramatically scripted research. In A. Banks & S. P. Banks (Eds.), *Fiction and social research*. Walnut Creek, CA: Altamira Press.

Nabokov, V. (1980). *Lectures on literature*. New York: Harcourt Brace Jovanovich.

Polkinghorne, D. E. (1997). Reporting qualitative research as practice. In W. G. Tierney & Y. S. Lincoln (Eds.), *Representation and the text: Re-framing the narrative voice* (pp. 3–21). Albany: State University of New York Press.

Rabinowitz, P. (1987). *Before reading: Narrative conventions and the politics of interpretation*. Ithaca, NY: Cornell University Press.

Richardson, L. (1993). Poetics, dramatics, and transgressive validity: The case of the skipped line. *Sociological Quarterly, 35,* 695–710.

Richardson, L. (1997). *Fields of play: Constructing an academic life*. New Brunswick, NJ: Rutgers University Press.

Rosenblatt, L. M. (1994). *The reader, the text, the poem: The transactional theory of the literary work* (2nd ed.). Carbondale, IL: Southern Illinois University Press.

Salinger, J. D. (1991). *Catcher in the rye*. Boston: Little, Brown.

Skelton, T., & Valentine, G. (Eds.) (1998). *Cool places: Geographies of youth cultures*. London: Routledge.

Thompson, H. S. (1971). *Fear and loathing in Las Vegas: A savage journey to the heart of the American dream*. New York: Random House.

Tierney, W. G. (1997). Lost in translation: Time and voice in qualitative research. In W. G. Tierney & Y. S. Lincoln (Eds.), *Representation and the text: Re-framing the narrative voice* (pp. 23–36). Albany: State University of New York Press.

Turner, M. (1996). *The literary mind*. Oxford, England: Oxford University Press.

Trinh, M. T. (1992). *Framer framed*. New York: Routledge.

Walker, A. (1992). *The color purple*. New York: Harcourt Brace Jovonovich.

Walton, K. L. (1990). *Mimesis as make-believe: On the foundations of the representational arts*. Cambridge, MA: Harvard University Press.

Wertsch, J. V. (1998). *Mind as action*. Oxford, England: Oxford University Press.

White, H. (1978). *Tropics of discourse*. Baltimore, MD: Johns Hopkins University Press.

Wolfe, T., & Johnson, E. W. (Eds.) (1973). *The new journalism: An anthology*. New York: Harper and Row.

# · 21 ·

# CONTEMPORARY METHODOLOGICAL ISSUES AND FUTURE DIRECTIONS IN RESEARCH ON THE TEACHING OF ENGLISH

## M. C. Wittrock
### University of California, Los Angeles

Educational research has contributed substantially to our knowledge about the teaching of English, which includes teaching, reading, writing, composition, and literature. The chapters in this section of the *Handbook* make that point clear through their portrayal of the recent history and development of the research contributions to the study of English teaching.

This section also serves as a prologue to the future of teaching English research and as a provocative source of suggestions about future directions in research, directions that include close ties between researchers and teachers, and between research and practice. These directions also focus on understanding how teachers' and students' cognitive and affective processes, their thoughts and feelings, lead to learning and achievement in teaching English.

The focus on understanding how teachers and students use their strategies, background knowledge, and emotions to construct meaning from teaching leads to fundamental changes in the design and conduct of research studies, and to fundamental changes in teaching English, including reading, writing, composition, and literature. We become less interested in standardized testing, norming, ranking, and comparison of students, teachers, classes, schools, and states, because these comparisons do not help us much to understand how teaching functions, how students learn, and how we might improve our teaching and their learning. We also become less interested in simplistic input–output models of teaching (e.g., time correlates positively with achievement), not because they are false, but because they do not lead to an understanding of how and why teaching leads learners to construct meanings and interpretations that enhance their achievement.

We become more interested in learning about the interests, background knowledge, schema, learning strategies, and metacognitive processes of our students. Tests that will provide teachers with these types of information have diagnostic value for designing teaching through understanding student thoughts and emotions. We become more interested in models of teaching that go beyond the products of learning to include the critical role of the teachers and the learners' constructive or generative processes in building meaning as they read and write, as they interpret literature, and as they teach and learn.

## EARLY CONTRIBUTIONS TO EDUCATIONAL RESEARCH

Since the early empirical educational research studies in America in the first half of the 19th century, teaching English and language continues to be a most important area to study. In 1845, after Horace Mann questioned the effectiveness of teaching in the Boston Schools, a subcommittee of the Boston School Committee decided to examine the children from ages 7 to 14 years in the Boston Writing and Grammar Schools (Travers, 1983, pp. 86–87). To measure achievement in writing, which included handwriting, arithmetic, and sometimes algebra, and orthography (spelling), reading, geography, grammar, and history, the subcommittee developed and used printed achievement tests. The scores on these tests were used to rank the Boston Schools and to compare them with one another.

In this survey, measurement and evaluation of student achievement in grammar, writing, and other basic subjects taught in grammar schools began to be used on a large scale basis to provide empirical data about student achievement. At the same time these data were used to evaluate the effectiveness of the Boston Schools.

In New York, Joseph Mayer Rice, a zealous educational reformer, tried unsuccessfully for several years to convince teachers to accept his ideas, which were not supported with data. Rice singled out one school in New York City, generally considered excellent over 25 years, as an example of needed reform. That school's program was designed to "immobilize," "automatize," and "dehumanize" each student, who was required to stare straight ahead, presumably at the teacher, from whom came all knowledge. Speed and efficiency were highly valued in school lessons, which were dominated by drill and practice (Travers, 1983, p. 100).

Even though Rice published these comments widely, including articles in *Forum*, a well-read journal, they received very little attention among the public or among professional educators. Two years later, Rice decided that his comments were probably being treated as the opinion of one person, not as objective or scientific findings. In 1895, Rice decided to collect data about teaching and learning, especially about time to learn and its relation to student achievement. He chose spelling as the subject he would study. After some preliminary research, Rice developed a spelling test, consisting of spelling words embedded in sentences, which he gave to about 13,000 children across the country. He found that differences in achievement across schools serving upper socioeconomic and lower socioeconomic levels were small, but differences across age levels were large. He also found that time on task had almost no positive correlation with learning: 10 to 15 minutes of teaching spelling each day produced about the same achievement as did 40 to 50 minutes of daily spelling teaching.

Rice's empirical research on spelling, and later on arithmetic, led to a series of influential articles on teaching, for which he is still remembered today. His research data also changed his own earlier conceptions of student freedom in schools to emphasize the importance of the teacher in the classroom. Rice's decision to collect data on teaching spelling shows the impact that research can have on the public and on the profession. Those research data from students were more convincing than were his earlier comments about teaching practices, which were discredited as personal opinion, even when they presented jarring accounts of rigid and immobilizing teaching procedures in the public schools.

The central role of English and language teaching and testing in educational research appears again in the seminal work of Edward L. Thorndike. Although he is better known for his research on human learning and transfer, Thorndike led in introducing in America statistics that were being developed in Great Britain. In 1904, he published a book entitled *An Introduction to the Theory of Mental and Social Measurements*. His knowledge of research methods and his ability to gather empirical data to evaluate theories of learning and transfer led to some important changes in teaching language.

Thorndike's identical elements theory of transfer of learning stated that transfer occurred when elements present in an initial learning situation occurred again in a later situation. His theory contrasted sharply with the formal discipline theory of transfer accepted by many teachers of foreign language. Formal discipline theory stated that the mind consisted of faculties, such as memory, reason, and will, which are strengthened by the exercise provided by the most difficult subjects then taught, such as Latin, Greek, and mathematics.

With his identical elements theory to challenge formal discipline theory, and with his knowledge of statistics and research methods to challenge the beliefs of teachers Thorndike (1924) conducted an empirical study on the effects on reasoning of different subjects taken in high school. Mathematics, Greek, and Latin produced no greater reasoning ability then did physical education or drama. However, he found that students in the more difficult courses did have higher reasoning abilities than did other students at the beginning of the study, a factor which he adjusted statistically.

As a result of Thorndike's research on transfer, Latin was largely discredited as a way to increase intelligence and reasoning, and as a way to teach English, or other school subjects. These results decimated the justification for teaching Latin. Without the benefit of Thorndike's expertise in statistics and research methods, the teachers of Latin and English who disagreed with Thorndike were left with the formidable task of mounting equally defensible support for their theories and beliefs. The support was not forthcoming. The study of Latin in high schools declined sharply in the next 20 years, in part because of Thorndike's research.

Thorndike's contributions to the teaching of vocabulary and reading (and to arithmetic) are known and are still influential. Reading consisted of recognizing and comprehending words, he maintained. The comprehensibility of vocabulary was related to its frequency of use in daily life. Thorndike gathered data about the frequencies of words children encounter in reading books, especially classic stories, textbooks, newspapers, and poetry. In 1921, he published the *Teachers Word Book*, which later was expanded (Thorndike & Lorge, 1944).

Throndike's theories of vocabulary in comprehension still influence the teaching of reading of English and foreign languages and still influence our conceptions of sentence and text difficulty, for example, as they occur in readability formulas.

These examples of early contributions show some ways that educational research has contributed to our knowledge about teaching English. They show some of the power of data and research methods to influence teachers and the public, as did Rice's findings about spelling and Thorndike's findings about teaching Latin. They also show how some of the close ties became established between achievement testing and educational research. They imply how difficult it may be to move to more appropriate research methods for understanding teacher and student thoughts and affective processes not measured by conventional achievement or intelligence tests but nevertheless that are critical to understanding and improving teaching English.

## RECENT DEVELOPMENTS

In the early development of empirical educational research, achievement testing and the ranking and evaluation of learners, teachers, schools, and districts were commonly employed research methods. The Boston School Committee used them to study the effectiveness of the Boston Writing and Grammar Schools. Joseph M. Rice employed them to study spelling and to gain public support for his ideas about educational reform. E. L. Thorndike used them to discredit the formal discipline theory of transfer of learning and to change the teaching of foreign language in America.

From these beginnings grew more elaborate and sophisticated empirical methods for conducting educational research. In the 20th century, educational researchers borrowed and adapted research methods from other fields of study. For example, from agriculture came our fundamental elements of experimental design, including experimental groups, control groups, and random assignment of participants. Our basic statistical procedures for analyzing experiments, analysis of variance and analysis of covariance, also came from research on agriculture. These design and statistical techniques were both products of one Englishman, Ronald Fisher.

From biology we obtained correlation techniques (Pearson), path analysis (Sewall Wright), discriminant analysis, and multivariate analysis of variance. From neurology and medicine came the case study. From psychology came a broad array of techniques, including factor analysis, canonical correlation, reliability, validity, Q-sorts, scaling methods, and social interaction analysis. From sociology we derived survey methods, sampling techniques, and latent-structure analysis.

The chapters of this section of the *Handbook* summarize well the progression of recent events in the research on the teaching of English. In these chapters we see how educational researchers used these and other research methods to study and to try to improve the teaching of English.

Educational research progressed from surveys of effective teaching methods in the early 1900s to broadly based curriculum studies in the 1920s, 1930s, and 1940s. In the 1950s and 1960s subject matter-based curriculum reform became prominent. In the 1970s, 1980s, and 1990s, evaluation and policy studies of teaching became widespread in the work of the federally sponsored Research and Development Centers and Regional Laboratories. Throughout these historical developments in the United States, the methods of conducting research described in the previous paragraphs became widely used in research on the teaching of English. These methods led to the current uses of qualitative and observational-descriptive methods, and to the quantitative interventions that characterize contemporary research in the teaching of English.

Before we turn to these concepts, we need to consider a parallel progression of events that involves models of teaching and learning. The research methods I mentioned were employed to study and to test conceptions about English teaching and learning. To understand the changes that occurred in the teaching of English, we need to see the close relations between these conceptions of learning and teaching and the methods of research appropriate for studying them.

The models of learning and teaching English that were dominant in Joseph Rice's times emphasized student verbatim learning and repetition of the teacher's words (Travers, 1983). In those days, there was little concern for student thoughts. E. L. Thorndike, through his model of instrumental learning, stated

that learning was the acquisition of specific behaviors by being rewarded for performing them at the right times and in the right places, which strengthened connections between the situation and the behaviors or responses. Later, B. F. Skinner added to Thorndike's model the concept of reinforcement, which replaced Thorndike's notion of reward as the process of maintaining or increasing behavior, and the concept of behavioral objectives, as a way of knowing when to reinforce behavior. This highly influential conception of learning developed by Thorndike and Skinner again stressed student behaviors, that is, things that can be measured on commonly used tests. The model did not emphasize student and teacher thoughts and feelings, cognitions and affective processes, interpretations, comprehension, images, emotions, learning strategies, motives, metacognitions, or relations between literature and experience. These cognitive and affective processes were not considered appropriate for scientific study because they were difficult or impossible to measure objectively.

However, Thorndike's and Skinner's highly influential models led to a focus on teaching measurable and testable specific behaviors, such as facts, vocabulary, and verbatim information. That narrow focus obtained scientific rigor in research on the teaching of English, but at the expense of ignoring, or at least minimizing its essence, the comprehension and understanding that comes from reading, writing, and speaking.

Because Thorndike's and Skinner's models of learning omitted the constructive or generative nature of language learning, they had great difficulty in explaining basic linguistic events among children and adults. These models could not adequately explain how infants create novel sentences, how the implicit rules of language are learned and applied to construct or to understand an infinite set of rule-governed sentences or utterances. For these reasons, cognitive models of learning arose and supplanted these earlier models. These earlier models, however, still impact the teaching of English through their focus on learning measurable behaviors defined and identified by precise objectives, and taught by reinforcers presented frequently, discriminately, and contingently.

In the late 1950s and increasingly, in the 1960s, cognitive models of learning and knowledge acquisition arose and supplanted the model developed by Thorndike and Skinner. Largely through the pioneering works of Noam Chomsky in linguistics and David Ausubel and others in educational psychology, human learning was conceived as a process of construction of meaning by the learners using their background of experience and their strategies of learning. Student and teacher thoughts and emotions became the center of interest within these cognitive models. In the 1980s and 1990s research on these cognitive and affective processes often emphasized learning in social contexts, in which students and teachers study and learn in groups, such as in collaborative learning. In the teaching of English, these models led to fundamental changes. Comprehension and student interpretations of sentences, stories, texts, and plays came to the foreground. Reading became far more than converting graphemes into phonemes. It became a process of constructing meanings and interpretations of text using one's knowledge and experience.

Research on these cognitive and affective thought processes gained scientific support with the publication of Ericcson and

Simon's (1980) review of "Verbal Reports as Data." In that review, they report the conditions under which verbal reports, such as think alouds and interviews, provide valid, scientifically useful information. For example, concurrent reports of verbal information that use nondirective probes, such as think alouds, produce very little or no distortion in the information they provide about cognitive processes. On the other hand, retrospective reports, such as stimulated recall, introduce substantial distortion in the information they provide about cognitive processes. These results mean that, under the proper conditions, cognitive and affective processes can be scientifically studied, and valid measures of them can be obtained. Behavioral responses are not the only valid or scientifically useful data available from research in the teaching of English.

The developments of conceptions of learning and teaching coupled with the advances in research methods appropriate to study them influenced curricula and instruction in English in fundamental ways.

John Dixon (1991) reports how standardized achievement tests that were used for predicting college achievement influenced the curriculum and the instruction in literature in junior and senior high school. In the 1930s and 1940s, the high school teachers followed the college curriculum, using classics in senior high school and anthologies in junior high school. The methods of instruction emphasized recitation and regimentation.

Later, during the 1950s and 1960s, methods of teaching English in the high schools changed, but there was still an emphasis on learning isolated facts about authors. Teacher-made tests were still centered on facts, rather than on interpretations. Teaching of writing still focused on correcting mistakes in students' grammar and syntax.

In the 1970s, the curriculum and the teaching methods changed further. The introduction of women's studies, ethnic literature, and science fiction in the college curriculum paralleled the introduction of greater student choice in reading, increased student and teacher autonomy in the classroom, independent student projects, and active learning. These college curricular and procedural changes also influenced high school teaching practices.

Dixon calls the model that dominated teaching during the 1970s an "objective-driven" one that emphasized "objective measurement." Teaching English in the high school was still driven by the requirements of the standardized tests, which were used to construct objectives for the teachers to attain. Nonetheless, change was beginning to occur in the high school English classrooms. Student-initiated writing, student interpretations of literature, and active, thoughtful learning began to find a place in the English classroom. These changes paralleled the changes in the study of learning and instruction. Dixon's chapter records well the progression of changes in thinking about teaching English and its impacts on teaching practices in high schools.

This section of the *Handbook* begins appropriately with a thoughtful chapter by Sandra Statsky on the meaning and the purpose of research in the teaching of English. Anne DiPardo, in the second chapter, follows with a discussion of the essential specialized knowledge research produces for a profession engaged in the teaching of English. The next three chapters delve into the design and the conduct of different types of empirical research. Robert Calfee and Marilyn Chambliss describe the basic designs of quantitative research and of qualitative research. Robert Tierney and Margaret Sheehy review in detail the distinctive characteristics and unique contributions of longitudinal research to knowledge about the teaching of English. Fredrick Burton and Barbara Seidl discuss the important contributions of teachers and researchers collaboratively engaged in action research. This section of the *Handbook* concludes with two chapters on the reporting of research and on the syntheses of research. Donna Alvermann and George Hruby argue for fiction as a way to report qualitative research studies. Carl Smith and Susan Klein present some of the impressive results made possible only through the methods for synthesizing research findings across studies. In the following paragraphs I discuss the contributions of each of these chapters.

Sandra Statsky writes an excellent introduction to research on teaching the English language arts. They begin appropriately with the purpose of research, which is to develop explanatory generalizations and theories useful or valid for explaining and predicting phenomena in the teaching of English. Good research improves teachers' abilities to make intelligent decisions about teaching.

Academic research differs from field testing of instructional materials in teachers' classrooms. Academic research differs also from personal narratives, which are not research. The differences that characterize academic research include professional detachment or objectivity, systematic collection of data, and a codified method for conducting research. The authors describe two types of academic research: conceptual inquiry, such as the scholarly writings of educational philosophers, who do not usually gather data; and empirical research, which involves the systematic collection, analysis, and interpretation of quantitative or qualitative data to develop or to test hypotheses and theories. Stotsky considers action research a form of advocacy-oriented classroom investigation that assumes the answers to the problems are known. Action research aims to shape teaching to a specific end by implementing known answers to teaching problems.

Qualitative and quantitative research comprise the two major types of empirical research studies. Qualitative research focuses on reporting the researchers' descriptions and interpretations of the learners' behaviors and cognitions. Qualitative research includes research often called holistic, phenomenological, hypothesis-generating, participant-observational, exploratory, ethnographic, humanistic, naturalistic, field-based interpretive, and hermeneutic. It involves small numbers of subjects. Its data consist of the researchers' own descriptions and interpretations of what they see and hear in the natural situations they observe.

According to the authors, quantitative research focuses on the discovery of the principles of learning and teaching. It tests rather than generates theory. Its data report the behavior and the cognition of learners, not of the researchers. It uses numerical data from representative samples or from random samples of learners, often randomly assigned to systematically different treatments in an experiment. In a carefully controlled way, these treatments compare different methods or ways of teaching English to learners by the manipulation of specific variables that distinguish the otherwise identical conditions of learning. Within specified probability limits, this experimental type of quantitative research establishes cause and effect relations. Quantitative research includes nonexperimental, descriptive research also, which gathers numerical data that describe relationships among correlated variables, such as age and learning.

Stotsky saves for the last part of their chapter one of their most significant contributions to the *Handbook*. That contribution emphasizes the compatibility and the complementarity of qualitative and quantitative research. Both can enhance theories and knowledge. Both try to control bias, to be objective. Both collect, analyze, and interpret data. Both types of research gather data in the classroom or in a laboratory. Both can and often should be used together in a single study. I would add that both contribute to knowledge and to information useful to classroom teachers. In a profession, such as the teaching of English, description and theory generation as well as intervention and theory testing prove essential. Qualitative research and quantitative research make distinctive and complementary contributions.

In her chapter on "Teacher Professionalism and the Rise of Multiple Literacies," Anne Dipardo delves into the tough problems of characterizing the knowledge base of the profession of the teaching of English. Professions must have specialized bodies of knowledge that go beyond intuitions and speculations. In the teaching of English, these specialized bodies of knowledge include useful, research-based principles and theories regarding the subject matter of multiple literacies, its pedagogy, and its classroom practice, which involves the "person" relations between the students and the teacher. But principles and theories in each of those areas provide an insufficient knowledge base for the profession of teaching English. A sufficient knowledge base includes research-based support for specific instructional procedures and curricula that enable teachers to teach multiple literacies to the different learners in their classrooms. That broad and useful knowledge base includes information about these different learners, their cultures, interests, and background knowledge. That same knowledge base also includes useful information about curricula and instructional materials. The knowledge base should be extensive and specialized enough to require years of formal training to learn it and to learn how to use it. By these criteria we have a long way to go in the study of the teaching of multiple literacies. One of our immediate problems in research on the teaching of English comes from the constructivists' cognitive conception of multiple literacies, which differs from the layman's conception of transmission of knowledge. The constructivist's conception emphasizes the learners' construction of knowledge, which laymen find difficult to understand, or at least to appreciate. DiPardo discusses the difficulty in teaching laymen who have a different preconception of the constructivist conception of knowledge acquisition. But she does not suggest a solution to the problem. From cognitive research on the changing of preconceptions of learners we know that they are most difficult to alter. But we also know that preconceptions can be changed by giving the learners problems to solve that show the shortcomings of their

preconceptions and that lead the learners to construct alternative and more useful conceptions.

In this chapter, Anne DiPardo leads us in the proper direction toward a shared vision of a tested, trustworthy specialized knowledge base that will provide the theory and the research a profession needs to guide its practice, in our case the teaching of multiple literacies to different learners.

Robert Calfee and Marilyn Chambliss write their chapter "The Design of Empirical Research" for the graduate student planning a doctoral dissertation on the teaching of English. The design or the planning of empirical research often receives insufficient attention in comparison with the attention given to the analyses of research in handbooks, in graduate research methods courses, and in textbooks.

Empirical research involves the collection of objective evidence under carefully defined and replicable conditions. Its purposes include the determination of factors that affect human thought and action, and the finding of answers to practical questions about teaching. In that sense empirical research differs from scholarship and conceptual analyses that inform practical questions, but that do not answer them specifically. The empirical study of nearly all significant teaching problems involves qualitative and quantitative methods of research in designs that focus on framing the research question, setting an appropriate context to study the problem, and making sense of the data and interpreting its findings. Research findings should be transferable, replicable, and useful to teachers, all of which imply valid results. To be valid, results must mean what the researchers say they mean.

Research design aims to increase the validity of the empirical findings, to reduce the confounding of factors, and to provide control over the factors operating in the study. The validity of the findings refers to their trustworthiness. Confounding refers to the intertwining of the factors, such that one cannot determine the factors that influence the results. Control refers to the elimination of the unintended variations in the procedures or the methods that confuse the findings and complicate their interpretation.

Design, then, plans to maximize the intended differences among the factors we study, and to minimize the unintended differences in the other factors involved in the gathering of the data. As a heuristic for beginning researchers the authors suggest a plan for the conduct of an instructional study. The plan involves conceptualizing and framing the problem, investigating and describing the research context, including developing the tests and the procedures to be used, developing as assessment study, and then conducting the instructional study. The authors provide a useful plan for many researchers that combines qualitative methods with quantitative methods, as suggested by Stotsky in her introductory chapter. Again, *Handbook* authors emphasize the complementarity of quantitative and qualitative methods in research on the teaching of English.

Robert Tierney and Margaret Sheehy examine in depth some of the major contributions of longitudinal research to our understanding of the development of literacies. In contrast to the more frequently used cross-sectional research designs, longitudinal studies follow the same individuals for years. For this reason, longitudinal research produces distinctive contributions not possible in cross-sectional studies, especially in the study of the development of abilities and of achievement. For example, Schaie (1983) used a longitudinal research design to study the finding commonly reported in cross-sectional designs that human intelligence declines quickly from youth to old age. The results of his study, and of other related studies, indicates that from young adulthood a significant decline does not occur until the late 60s (Willis, 1885, p. 821). The cross-sectional designs had shown an early decline because they used increasingly more difficult, renormed tests with the older groups, which made their performances appear to decline early, when no decline had occurred.

Tierney and Sheehy detail some of the distinctive contributions of longitudinal research to the study of the development of literacies. They ask "How do literacies develop?" From longitudinal studies over the past 40 years, they report some provocative and useful findings that often differ markedly from the findings reported in cross-sectional studies of the same phenomena.

First, they report that early readers, who begin to read before school age, 6 years later maintain their advantage over other readers of the same age. Socioeconomic success and IQ do not predict reading success. But parental encouragement and nurturing of reading interest do predict later success at reading. Parents' time invested in teaching their children to read also predicts success at reading years later. These findings differ from the results of cross-sectional studies.

Because of the current political interest in rote and meaningful approaches to the teaching of beginning reading, the findings of longitudinal studies provide especially provocative results. Longitudinal studies show that children do not learn to read by rote. Instead, children learn to read in meaningful ways, through interactions with their parents, texts, and contexts. Reading develops from social meaning-making experiences that begin at home and in preschool settings.

Writing develops in a similar fashion. The child's invented spellings and invented hypotheses again show the constructive nature of meaning-making that provides the basis for the development of writing ability. Young children write to exchange meaning with one another. They compose for the purpose of conveying meaning. In the beginning school years these processes of meaning-making continue to develop. Again, home experiences contribute to the development of comprehension, which is a separate factor from decoding. In longitudinal studies, by the second grade comprehension often correlates negatively with decoding. Even more striking, longitudinal research indicates that phonics instruction does not lead to increased comprehension in the second grade. Instead, early reading for meaning leads to better comprehension in the second grade. By the second grade, phonemic awareness also diminishes in its contribution to comprehension.

These longitudinal data do not imply that instruction in phonics and in phonemic awareness do not contribute to the learning of literacy. Instead these data do show the great importance of meaning-based early instruction that focuses on learning and using phonics and phonemic awareness to construct and to convey meaning. Meaning making, not rote learning, drives the development of literacy.

These impressive findings show how longitudinal data enlighten our understanding of literacy development beyond a narrow focus on phonics and rote learning methods. These data imply that children actively construct meaning, even in their beginning attempts to learn to read and to write. From the very beginning of language learning, children need meaningful, not rote, contexts and instruction to develop their meaning-making abilities, which lie at the core of the development of literacy.

Fredrick Burton and Barbara Seidl discuss the importance of teacher-researcher projects. They feel that teachers tend to ignore research that uses quantitative measures and experimental designs because it isolates variables and loses the complexity of the classrooms, and therefore loses important meanings. They do not discuss the many important contributions over many years of quantitative research to the teaching of reading. Teachers regularly acquire this quantitative research-based knowledge from textbooks, college courses, and teacher development activities. Teachers continually use the rich and extensive curricular and instructional materials developed from our extensive, quantitative research base. Research often produces its impact on practice, not from one study at a time, but through the cumulative effects of many research studies summarized in useful theory, detailed in textbooks, taught in courses, and implemented in curricular materials and instructional procedures.

Burton and Seidl advocate naturalistic, phenomenological, and interpretive research studies, including action research, that focus on improving practice in specific settings, rather than on discovering generalizations that apply across different settings. These action research studies involve teachers as researchers, elucidate teacher knowledge about teaching, and deal holistically with the complexities of the classroom.

In these studies, teacher theorizing and the refinement of teacher theories distinguishes the research. The action research begins with daily challenges, allows teachers to theorize about their teaching, provides ways to experiment with classroom interventions, and obtains feedback in the classroom about the interventions and about the teacher-generated theory or principle of teaching. In that way teachers learn from their teaching, and become active researcher-theoreticians who contribute to their own understanding of teaching.

The authors present admirable goals and workable strategies. These goals and research strategies complement, rather than compete, with other types of research, including quantitative and experimental research or qualitative and descriptive research. In a profession, practitioners have important clinical experiences that can and should contribute to its knowledge and to its practice. The practitioners need ways to study and to learn as they practice. For example, in medicine, general practitioners regularly contribute valuable information about the effectiveness of medicines in the treatment of their patients. In psychology, clinicians provide important insights into our understanding of mental illnesses and their treatments. In education, teachers produce outstanding curriculum materials and instructional procedures for the teaching of many difficult concepts in literacy learning.

We need to remember the importance of understanding the complementary nature of different types of research. We do not have to choose only one type of research. In research on the teaching of literacy, quantitative and qualitative, descriptive and interventional, longitudinal and cross-sectional, theory generating and theory testing, researcher and researcher-teacher methods all play distinctive, important, and complementary roles. They do not compete with one another.

We need to understand and to appreciate the complementary nature of different types of research. We also need to be tolerant of different research methods, and to appreciate the need for researchers and teachers to collaborate with one another in our united effort to develop for our profession a solid research base that produces practical and effective classroom teaching procedures and materials. To construct that solid base for our profession requires the intelligent and sustained work of all its members, including researchers and teachers. In our quest for understanding and improvement of the teaching of literacy we have room for all members of our profession to collaborate in research and to contribute to practice.

In their chapter on "Fictive Representation: An Alternative Method for Reporting Research" Donna Alvermann and George Hruby discuss the reporting of research, especially qualitative research, in the English language arts. They find current expository reports of research dull and uninteresting to people who come to education from other fields, such as theater arts. As an example, they cite a graduate student of film studies, Elizabeth, who accepted a beginning faculty position in a curriculum and instruction program within a department of education at a major midwest state university. In this program she found a total absence of the familiar "suspense, romance, seduction, visual pleasure, music, plot, humor, tap dancing, or pathos" that she liked in her former department where she was a student.

To improve the reporting of research in the teaching of English, in their chapter on "Fictive Representation" Alvermann and Hruby suggest that researchers adopt fiction as the way to write at least parts of their journal articles. These authors believe that fiction stimulates interest and entertainment. A move from exposition to fictional narration, they argue, would provide a different mode of address, broaden the audience for journal articles, and make them more interesting and accessible. To exemplify their argument they present a sample of a report of research about mentoring written as fiction. In another source they comment about fictional reports of quantitative research (Alvermann & Hruby, 2000).

In the communication of theories, models, and principles to lay persons fiction offers some utility, I believe. For example, B. F. Skinner (1948) wrote a novel entitled "Walden Two." In this novel the reader visits a remote and fictional community, called Walden Two, operated according to Skinner's model of operant conditioning, which incorporates his research on positive reinforcement. Although some readers criticized the quality of the writing of the novel, it conveyed to a broad lay audience some of the societal applications and meanings of Skinner's model.

However, the use of fiction for researchers to communicate research findings to one another in journal articles, as suggested by the authors, introduces serious problems and many questions. First, is fiction more accessible than exposition for communicating research among researchers? The authors assume that fiction, familiar to them, compared with exposition, enhances researchers' interest and entertainment in

reading research reports. Yet, when the authors queried some people about the use of fiction to report research, those people found difficulty in reading and interpreting the fictional report they read. For example, Margaret commented that fiction did not increase accessibility and that she and her reading group did not support the authors' assumptions about the advantages of fiction for reporting research.

Second, do researchers want or need fiction to make their journal articles more interesting and better conveyors of meaning? The authors assume that many researchers feel, as they do, that expository reports in journal articles should be written as fictional reports. But fiction is not the only interesting and effective form of writing. Expository reports that clearly state a significant problem, suggest a theory-based approach to its solution, test that approach in a real world setting, and report and interpret the authors' findings often stimulate high interest as they effectively, accurately, and efficiently convey meaning. Because people who enter education from other fields, such as film studies, miss the familiar fictional modes of reporting used in their home fields does not mean that educational researchers should abandon their preferred reporting styles. To turn the argument around, would we expect people in other fields to abandon their reporting styles and adopt exposition when educational researchers join their faculties? Some students initially find some great works of fiction difficult to read with understanding. In school it often takes years of study to learn how to read and to appreciate some of the great works of fiction. Should we rewrite some of the great works of fiction to make them more readable to beginners, or should we teach the beginners how to read these outstanding works?

I think it better to help researchers to learn from one another in the ways that work best for them, not to impose on them ways that others think the researchers should use because other people find them more familiar and more entertaining. We need to remember the primary purposes of reporting research in our profession. These purposes focus on the improvement of the teaching of English language arts through useful applications derived from a solid research base. The form of the journal articles should follow the purposes of the research.

Third, should all research articles be written at a level best for lay persons to read? As a profession grows, its research increases in complexity and in technical sophistication. To do research in a field, to write its results, and to communicate effectively with other researchers requires years of formal training. For example, in the advanced fields of mathematics, biology, chemistry, medicine, and engineering it makes no sense to require researchers to write all their journal articles at the reading level of the layman. The researchers need to communicate accurately and precisely their most complicated findings to other researchers. Although educational research does not embody the technical complexity of these advanced fields and professions, it does embody some complicated vocabulary, methods, procedures, and theories that lay persons cannot be expected to understand or to find interesting. Should these topics be barred from discussion because they do not interest lay persons or beginning educational researchers? We need journal articles written expressly for researchers, just as we need reports, books, essays, and articles written especially for lay persons. One form of writing does not work best for all readers.

Alvermann and Hruby discuss other problems with the use of fiction for reporting research. Will much research be ignored because it does not lend itself to fictional reports? Will the credibility of educational research decline when scholars and researchers outside education, who use other forms of reporting their research, read research reports in education written in fiction? I would add, how will the readers know fiction from nonfiction in a research report? Can we expect schools to introduce into our nation's classrooms new curricula and new types of classroom instruction based on fictional reports of research?

Can other researchers replicate studies reported in fiction? Will fiction function well for the reporting of different types of research, such as qualitative research and quantitative research? We need a common language and a common reporting style to keep our research unified and our researchers communicating with one another, whether they use quantitative methods or qualitative methods.

I think it best to let researchers communicate with one another in the ways that they find most useful. I think it best to write for lay persons in the ways that they find most understandable and most readable.

Finally, Carl Smith and Susan Klein discuss the methods of synthesizing research findings across studies. Contrary to popular understandings, individual research studies rarely directly influence practice. Through the syntheses of research studies, theories and principles either find support or find a lack of it, and then influence practice. From the cumulative results of many studies come a few valid, replicated, and reliable significant findings that we can use for the improvement of the teaching of English.

Smith and Klein discuss the formal methods for synthesizing research studies that can find effects across studies that would not necessarily be found in an individual study. The purposes of these methods of synthesis of research are to increase our knowledge base, to distill large amounts of data, to inform practical decisions through research-base understanding, and to provide a well-organized research base to facilitate interpretations of the data. The authors then discuss what we know about research syntheses, such as literature reviews and meta-analyses, that can improve our understanding of the thousands of studies now available in research on reading, writing, and the teaching of English. After that discussion, the authors append an extensive list of representative recent syntheses that show their contributions to our understanding of a wide variety of topics in language arts. These and related syntheses of research provide valuable links between the original research studies and the development of procedures and curricula for improving the teaching of English language arts in the classroom.

## FUTURE DIRECTIONS

The prologue I have presented in this chapter implies a clear direction for the future. The direction is from assessing student behaviors on achievement tests and intelligence tests and from correlating those behaviors directly with characteristics of the classroom, the school, the home, and the society (Wittrock and Baker, 1991). The direction is toward researching and understanding the cognitive and affective language processes of learners and teachers that mediate achievement in language learning and language teaching (Wittrock, 1974, 1978, 1981, 1983, 1987). The move is from input–output models to cognitive approaches that give ideas about how students and teachers think and feel, about how they use their background knowledge and strategies to generate or construct meaning and interpretations from literature and expository text (Wittrock, 1974, 1990).

The move is toward research that uses case studies and observational methods to study the background knowledge and strategies of learners and teachers (Erickson, 1986). The direction is toward measuring and recording the thought processes of learners as they read and write using process tracing and verbal protocols (Ericsson & Simon, 1980). Process tracing involves methods such as think alouds, retrospective interviews, and stimulated recalls. Verbal protocols are written records of learners' responses during learning that can be used to infer their mental operations.

Another direction is toward measuring the number and quality of ideas, sentences, pictures, and the like, constructed by learners in an experiment or other intervention study, such as one Linden and I (1981) conducted on reading comprehension. In that study, we gathered data from school children to evidence their different thought processes, for example, the sentences and the images that the treatments asked them to generate. Those data enabled us to measure how well the treatments were actually inducing the intended cognitions, and how extensively the induced cognitions were correlated to retention and comprehension. These relations among treatments, thought processes, and comprehension can be analyzed statistically with conditional probability analyses or path analyses and other multivariate regression techniques.

In addition to measuring the learners' and teachers' preconceptions and their thought processes during learning and teaching of English, we need to employ appropriate measures and teach knowledge acquisition, including comprehension (Pearson & Johnson, 1978; McNeil, 1987), semantic maps (Heimlich & Pittelman, 1986), and hierarchical cognitive structures (Naveh-Benjamin, McKeachie, Lin, & Tucker, 1986).

Another move is toward multivariate analyses that are appropriate for relating contexts, preconceptions, and beliefs to thought processes during learning, and to comprehension, retention, and affective responses. Some of these multivariate statistical procedures are already available. See Muthén (1989) and Linn (1986) for discussions of them, including structural equation analyses, meta-analyses and path analyses.

## SUMMARY

In sum, the study of learning and teaching English involves devising methods to research the mental processes of language. These invisible cognitive and affective language processes were avoided by researchers early in the 1900s. With the recent shift to the study of cognition, we have seen parallel innovations in research methods. The combination of a shift to research on cognition and a concomitant development of innovative research methods to study it brings fundamental language processes into the foreground of the scientific study of English teaching. The combination also promises to unite the researchers of teaching and the teachers of English in the study of English teaching.

# References

Alvermann, D. E., & Hruby, G. G. (2000). Mentoring and reporting research. *Reading Research Quarterly, 35*(1), 46-63.

Dixon, J. (1991). Historical considerations: An international perspective. In J. J. Flood, J. M. Jensen, D. Lapp, & J. R. Squire (Eds.), *Handbook of Research on Teaching the English Language Arts* (pp. 18-23). New York: Macmillan.

Erickson, F. (1986). Qualitative methods in research on teaching. In M. C. Wittrock (Ed.), *Handbook of research on teaching* (3rd ed.). (pp. 119-161). New York: Macmillan.

Ericsson, K. A., & Simon, H. A. (1980). Verbal reports as data. *Psychological Review, 87*, 215-251.

Heimlich, J. E., & Pittelman, S. D. (1986). *Semantic mapping: Classroom applications.* Newark, DE: International Reading Association.

Linden, M., & Wittrock, M. C. (1981). The teaching of reading comprehension according to the model of generative learning. *Reading Research Quarterly, 17*(1), 44-57.

Linn, R. (1986). Quantitative methods in research on teaching. In M. C. Wittrock (Ed.), *Handbook of research on teaching* (3rd ed.) (pp. 92-118). New York: Macmillan.

McNeil, J. D. (1987). *Reading comprehension: New directions for classroom practice* (2nd ed.) Glenview, IL: Scott Foresman.

Muthén, B. (1989). Teaching students of educational psychology new sophisticated statistical techniques. In M. C. Wittrock & F. Farley (Eds.), *The future of educational psychology.* Hillsdale, NJ: Lawrence Erlbaum Associates.

Naveh-Benjamin, M., McKeachie, W. J., Lin, Y., & Tucker, D. G. (1986). Inferring students' cognitive structures and their development using the "ordered tree" technique. *Journal of Educational Psychology, 78*, 130-140.

Pearson, P. D., & Johnson, D. D. (1978). *Teaching reading comprehension.* New York: Holt, Rinehart, and Winston.

Schaie, K. M. (1983). The Seattle longitudinal study: A twenty-one year investigation of psychometric intelligence. In K. W. Schaie (Ed.), *Longitudinal Studies of Adult Psychological Development.* (pp. 64-130). New York: Guilford Press.

Skinner, B. F. (1948). Walden two. New York: Macmillan.

Travers, R. M. W. (1983). *How research has changed American schools.* Kalamazoo, MI: Mythos Press.

Thorndike, E. L. (1904). *An introduction to the theory of mental and social measurements.* New York: Science Press.

Thorndike, E. L. (1924). Mental discipline in high school studies. *Journal of Educational Psychology. 15*, 1-22.

Thorndike, E. L., & Lorge, I. (1944). *The teacher's word book of 30,000 words.* New York: Teachers College, Columbia University.

Willis, S. L. (1985). Towards an educational psychology of the older adult learner: Intellectual and cognitive bases. In J. E. Birren & K. W. Schaie (Eds.), *Handbook of the psychology of aging, 2nd Ed.* (pp. 818-847). New York: Van Nostrand Reinhold.

Wittrock, M. C. (1974). Learning as a generative process. *Educational Psychologist, 11*, 87-95.

Wittrock, M. C. (1978). The cognitive movement in instruction. *Educational Psychologist, 13*, 15-30.

Wittrock, M. C. (1981). Reading comprehension. In F. J. Pirozzolo & M. C. Wittrock (Eds.), *Neuropsychological and cognitive processes of reading.* New York: Academic Press.

Wittrock, M. C. (1983). Writing and the teaching of reading. *Language Arts, 60*, 600-606.

Wittrock, M. C. (1987). Process-oriented measures of comprehension. *The Reading Teacher, 734*-737.

Wittrock, M. C. (1990). Generative processes of comprehension. *Educational Psychologist, 24*, 345-376.

Wittrock, M. C., & Baker, E. L. (1991). *Cognition and testing.* Englewood Cliffs, NJ: Prentice-Hall.

Part

## ·III·

# RESEARCH ON LANGUAGE LEARNERS

# WHO REALLY GOES TO SCHOOL? TEACHING AND LEARNING FOR THE STUDENTS WE REALLY HAVE

*Rita S. Brause*
Fordham University

*John S. Mayher*
New York University

We need to understand who our students are by exploring the intimate relationship between their social experiences and their dreams. This knowledge informs our understanding of our students as they function within schools. We will consider the social contexts in which our students live and their unique qualities as learners as these influence their participation and achievement in English language classrooms.

## THE SOCIAL/CULTURAL CONTEXTS IN WHICH OUR STUDENTS LIVE

Most of American society is comprised of people who moved here from other lands. Coming from diverse backgrounds, we were united in our hopes for freedom of opportunity in America. Once here, we sought to become part of American society. Our schooling experiences were intended to unify us as a society (Cremin, 1988), providing us with formal instruction within a uniquely American institution. The government funds public schools with the expectation that schooling will enable students to become responsible, productive citizens within American society.

But American society is changing daily. There are increasing rates of immigration, divorce, unemployment, poverty, crime, homelessness, teenage parenting, and abuse of drugs, alcohol and children. There is concern for nuclear annihilation, depletion of our resources, and environmental pollution. Competition prevails to the exclusion of cooperation; there is a lack of social responsibility. The rich are "obscenely richer and the poor are poorer" (Tobin, 1988, p. 44). Our students live within this complex society and are affected by it whether they live in cities or suburbs, in apartments or on farms. Racial and ethnic diversity has increased substantially in the U.S. in the last 2 decades and is projected to increase even more in the decades to come (*Conditions of Education 1997*, p. 3).

Schools are prominent institutions in that society. We experience school as students, continuing this connection with schooling as adults by watching TV sit-coms and movies set in schools. The popularity of these events suggests the key role of schools in our lives. American public education was established to perpetuate the democratic principles on which our country was founded: freedom and liberty for all, the pursuit of happiness, the constant quest for a "better" life. Embedded in these dreams is a concept of freedom, of equality for all.

Three major issues concerning the social contexts in which our students live will be addressed in this chapter: American Culture; What the Census Tells Us; and School Practices.

### American Culture

There are two competing conceptions of American culture: one advocates cultural homogeneity adopting one common culture by replacing traditions established in other countries; the second advocates cultural pluralism wherein multiple cultures respectfully coexist. The first is labelled the *Melting Pot* metaphor; the second is sometimes called the *American Casserole or Stew*. While these metaphors have been criticized as simplistic (Lieberson & Waters, 1988), they provide us with useful constructs to understand how popular conceptions of the nature of American society influence our students' goals. A third metaphor may be emerging—the mosaic (Banks, 1995) wherein people are both choosing to live separately and traditionally in the U.S., and are often moving back and forth to their country of origin (New York Times, July 19–22, 1998).

***The American melting pot.*** Schools that hold the *melting pot* perspective of equality of opportunity socialize students by transmitting a common, predetermined body of knowledge about the culture as well as about academic content (Cremin, 1988). Recent school reform proposals consistent with this metaphor focus on all students completing a uniform "basic" curriculum and meeting predetermined standards.

Curriculum practices compatible with the melting pot metaphor seek to reduce differences in student background by imposing common experiences with the same books and work books. This has resulted in a *de facto* national curriculum controlled by published texts and tests despite the apparent student differences across school districts and schools. The tests, particularly, are designed to distinguish those who have achieved mastery of an arbitrary set of facts and skills from those who have not. Those who do not score successfully on tests get additional repetition or remedial opportunities to catch up. Success in traditional schools is equated with scores on standardized tests and graduation with age cohorts. Students who adopt the values of the mainstream culture succeed on these standardized tests. The recent passage of a referendum outlawing bilingual education in California has now enshrined assimilation into law by requiring intensive English for all children.

Rodriguez (1982) powerfully relates his experiences of living the melting pot metaphor. He rejected his family's traditions and language for the long-term goal of "becoming American." He spoke only English, ate American dishes, and celebrated American holidays. He believed that to make it in American society, he had to be "melted" to conform with the "mainstream." His family made sure he had access to those traditions, and he was successful in joining the so-called mainstream. But the cost was high. As an adult, he realizes he has *A Hunger of Memory* for the culture he lost, yet he still believes that his route was the correct one to choose.

Schools are subsets of our society; they combine practices that are evident in the larger society with unique rules that make schools distinct. While schools cannot be responsible for the rest of society, educators in schools are accountable for the procedures implemented in those settings. It is clear that schools generally reward students who give evidence of holding the values of our society's middle class. These include abiding by bureaucratic and other traditions, seeking to increase wealth, and competing for recognition particularly through verbal facility or athletic prowess. These values are implicit in schools that venerate tradition without thinking about consequences; encourage competition for grades instead of valuing the learning essential for living; and reward students who are good citizens by following the school rules. Students who either do not realize that there are different values inherent in school than at home, or those who consciously decide not to buy into these values, find themselves in a difficult position. When rules are clear and acceptable to some and either unclear or unacceptable to others, then there is an unfair advantage given to those in the first group. Schools in fact perpetuate the status quo, in the main. Yet schools theoretically seek to provide equal opportunity for all, contradicting the status quo.

The ultimate outcome of such a conflict is that the students who know the rules succeed—and those who do not, do not. Not coincidentally, perhaps, those who know the rules come from homes that are more "mainstream" than the others, thereby the schooling experience serves to credential the "in" group—and keeps the out group at bay—with the appearance of objective criteria. According to McLaren (1989), we blame the students who fail for their failure "rather than looking for ways in which the class and educational systems militate against the success of those who are economically powerless and who are discriminated against by gender and race" (p. 219).

Hirsch (1987) and Ravitch and Finn (1987) implicitly advocate the melting pot metaphor, suggesting there is one body of literary and general cultural knowledge essential for all Americans. When Hirsch's list is used to design curriculum and assessment policies, it institutionalizes the melting pot metaphor. Equality of opportunity is available only to those who choose to follow established or so-called majority practices, foregoing their own individual interests, and their "Roots" in Haley's (1976) term. The freedom implicit in this metaphor is the freedom to be successful by joining the mainstream, established traditions and practices of the elected, powerful governing elite.

***The American casserole.*** In contrast, others have hailed diversity as the hallmark of a democracy. Apple (1986), Aronowitz and Giroux (1988), Gardner (1983) and McNeil (1986) suggest that critical literacy, or divergent thinking, is at the heart of a democratic education. The casserole metaphor values diversity; differences in knowledge; differences in experiences; differences in values and beliefs. These result in a diversity of perspectives shared among all learners. Programs fostering these values are individually negotiated in individual classrooms drawing on the unique experiences of the students and teachers in each setting (Boomer, 1982). Learning cannot be prepackaged nor easily measured by standardized tests; alternative assessment strategies are needed. Equality is realized by all students being equally nurtured and challenged to grow.

As noted in the discussion of the melting pot metaphor, it is by no means accidental that schools have adopted a restricted set of values, skills, and knowledge as they have. The choices made in setting up schools that feature tracking and a standard curriculum reflecting distinctions between those who have the skills and those who do not, have been made by the people who control the schools. Since they are based on choices, then it is possible for other choices to be made that would value plurality rather than uniformity and seek to enhance the strengths each child brings to school rather than labeling many as deficient (Giroux, 1983).

A school that values cultural pluralism or the American casserole metaphor recognizes the unique contributions of individuals, sponsors activities that encourage students to learn-how-to-learn, acquire knowledge, and develop a social conscience (Holmes Group, 1988, p. 2). Recent proposals that are consistent with this view focus on holistic, integrated learning and personal growth of individual students. The individual learner's background knowledge and interests enable individuals to contribute differently to the larger society, the heart of cultural pluralism.

The casserole or American stew is consistent with Hodgkinson's (1988) call for a "pluralistic society," one that simultaneously respects the individual heritage of its members while uniting to work toward a common dream and goal. Bilingual programs that encourage the development of both languages are consistent with the casserole metaphor (Mayher, 1975, for example). This model celebrates each individual's knowledge and helps to enhance knowledge of the world, strategies for understanding the world, and concepts of social responsibility for participation in that world. The equality of opportunity embedded in this model is the professional support provided to each student to guarantee equivalent accomplishments at the end of the program. And the freedom implicit in this metaphor is the freedom to be proud of one's heritage while learning, respecting, and valuing other cultures and backgrounds.

## STUDENTS' OPPORTUNITIES AS SOCIOCULTURAL PHENOMENA

Our students experience American society in diverse ways. Three interdependent aspects of our society influence the equality of opportunity experienced by our students: demographic phenomena, family structure, and economic background. But before trying to use and interpret these data, we must examine their accuracy. The U.S. Census Bureau collects demographic data every 10 years with interim updates. Although cumulatively overwhelming, these statistics provide a limited, biased picture of our students.

The way we, as educators, describe our students both reflects our expectations as we work with them and our implicit social constructs. If we categorize students by the color of clothes they wear, the cost of those clothes, or the length of time worked to pay for those clothes, students would be placed in different groupings. Although we find it convenient to talk about our students by labeling them, we need to acknowledge the effect of such labels, particularly as these influence the quality of each program offered.

Demographic data are collected to quantify the services needed by distinct populations, such as the aged or the newborn. These data are used to plan educational facilities, to provide adequate educational resources, and to monitor program effectiveness as related to educational achievement. They tell us who live where, but they frequently fall short of catching the shifts that happen as suburbs become more and more urban or as exurbs lose their farms to new housing tracts. The ways in which the people are counted then, influence the quantity of services provided and the evaluation of the impact of educational programs on the population. We will first consider the issue of categories used in these reports as these reflect our society's biases and the biases found in our schools.

### Limits of Demographic Data

Biases are revealed in the radically different facilities provided for rich and poor and white and African American. The number of English language programs offered to different students reveal different expectations—for one, power, for the other, dependence. These differences are subtly revealed in the presentation or obfuscation of data. To acquire information presented herein, which is essential for sensitivity to the diversity and magnitude of our current population, required extensive digging. In several cases, numerous data sources need to tapped to extrapolate the information. For example, the economic range in American family incomes, seemingly an easy number to access, was obtained using 3 different sources. The fact that we had difficulty obtaining these data caused us to be suspicious about the categories and their presentation, particularly when these data influence the planning and evaluation of English language-arts programs nationwide.

The labeling of individuals based on ethnicity or race (in contrast to other characteristics such as eye color) reflects an implicit bias in our society. Additionally, any basis for determining ethnicity is highly controversial, being neither objective nor scientific. The 1980 U.S. Census report (U.S. Bureau of Census, 1983) used categories of Black, White and Hispanic noting that "Hispanics can be either Black or White." And the groupings change; in 1987 they named the groups differently: White, Black and Others (U.S. Bureau of the Census, 1987). There is no scientific, objective basis for these categories. The 1980 categories were used in reporting the 1990 Census and the 1997 report on educational statistics (U.S. Bureau of the Census, 1992). Currently the definition of such categories is a hotly debated issue. Some have argued for keeping them as a path to group-specific funding and preferences. Others feel that continued labeling continues to exacerbate the problems of race and racism.

Such categorical distinctions are subject to sociopolitical manipulation as well. The objectivity of the categorical systems suggested by demographers is called in question when data concerning ethnicity and school achievement, for example, are combined in one table. By doing so, a relationship is implied, which is simultaneously an inappropriate and misleading use of statistics. Further, such tables provide encouragement for the perpetuation of biases and stereotypes in assessing the potential for achievement of those students categorized by ethnic labels.

Demographic categories reveal nothing about individuals. Within group variation among students is ignored. Members of the "same" group may vary widely in such factors as goals, experience, feelings, sense of security, and academic proficiencies. Dividing people into such groups frequently magnifies the differences between such groups, rather than revealing commonalities across groups.

"Minority" is a term used in describing the population. The term, however, is not directly related to raw numbers, as evidenced by the fact that women who comprise more than 50% of the population are often characterized as a minority. Further, lumping diverse groups together as "minorities" denies each group its own identity. Using the term sometimes reflects the so-called majority's denigration of another group as a "minority" implying lesser importance.

There have been predictions/warnings that soon there would be a "Minority Majority," an oxymoron. The language games reveal that the majority numbers have not translated into majority power. It is the powerful majority that is disempowering others with the use of these labels. The figures reported are confusing as well. Due in part to the large population, subsamples are used. Each report uses a different database, and comparisons across reports are inappropriate. Some report data in percentages, some round out numbers. Some data are self-reports, others are tabulators' observations. Definitions of terms such as "drop out" are defined in conflicting ways across studies.

## The Educational Misuse of Demography

Standardized tests are used as a basis for assessing student learning. These instruments are inherently flawed in their design and have been found to discriminate against "minority" students. They are designed using a theory that is pervasive, but unsubstantiated: namely, that any group of people will distribute themselves along a normal curve with most falling in the middle, and few at the two extremes. Following the normal curve hypothesis, half of those tested are designated below average. Although these data are purported to be useful only as group data, they are reported with individual student names, and comparisons are constantly presented between students. Thus, students scoring below average are considered educational failures. The scores are also subject to manipulation. Both Koretz (1988) and *Education Week* (Study, 1988) raise doubts about the value of these tests, since districts select tests that their students will score well on. Further, real national comparisons are impossible according to *Education Week*, when "no more than three states use the same national tests" (p. 11).

Yet the press still reports, and many educators discuss, test scores as though they were based on solid criteria. So we are warned that students' SAT scores have declined significantly, bottoming out at 425 on the verbal portion in 1983 (OERI, 1987a); and that only 52% of high school students identified *Raisin in the Sun* as a play about an African American family planning to move into a white suburb (Ravitch & Finn, 1987). These declines make us *A Nation at Risk*, according to the National Commission on Excellence (1983). Although our students are not doing well in school on the barometers used to assess growth as we look at such data, we must always be aware of these limitations of categories and procedures used to generate them. A further irony, of course, from the perspective of 1998, is that the Japanese economy—supposedly the model that put our nation at risk, is now suffering a recession, while ours is booming. Whose school system works better, anyway? Berliner and Biddle (1995) have questioned the whole idea that American schools are in crisis. Their reading of the data suggests that American schools are not perfect, certainly, but neither are they "in crisis."

***What does the census tell us about inequities across race and gender?*** In 1990, the total U.S. population reached a record of 248.7 million. There were 50.5 million students enrolled in 1995 with significant increases noted for the Asian-Pacific Island population and the Hispanic population. The racial/ethnic enrollments in public elementary and

secondary schools are noteworthy: White 64.8%, Black 16.8%, Hispanic 13.5%, Asian-Pacific Islanders 3.7% and American Indian/Alaskan Native 1.1% (*Conditions of Education, 1997*, p. 60). When we consider years of schooling, the *Conditions of Education, 1997* report that of the population aged 25 and above, 86% of White, 75% of Blacks and 53% of Hispanics completed high school; 26% of Whites, 14% of Blacks and 9% of Hispanics completed college (p. 17). While high school drop out rates have declined to 11% in 1996 from 14% in 1977, the ethnic and gender distinctions note 7.3% of Whites, 13% of Blacks and 29.4% of Hispanics; 11.4% men, and 10.9% women (p. 111). The proportion of 18- and 19-year-olds who are attending high school or college rose from 55% in 1986 to 62% in 1996 (p. 15). While we are seeing increasing school enrollment with projected new records in elementary enrollment until 2006, there are discrepancies across ethnic groups. We are becoming a more multiracial society than we ever have been (Orfield & Monfort, 1988).

The fact that the census reports data by ethnicity reveals an implicit assumption that student achievement is influenced by the ethnic group with which they are associated. Thus, students from one group, for example, "Asian-Pacific Island" population, may be expected, as a group, to be significantly different from another group, say "Hispanics" from this reporting.

From the melting pot perspective, those differences are intended to diminish with time. It seems, however, that people are given one label and live with that one for life. It is unclear at which point in a multi-generational perspective, a person whose ancestors immigrated to this country will be considered "American." In fact, only American Indians are native to this land. Yet some are always reminded of their heritage (Italian Americans, for example) while others are not (African Americans, for example). There is an inherent bias in such differential treatments.

Most recently, there has been a move to use the term African American to denote the origins of "Black" people, analogous to the label of Asian American. Although this consistency is long overdue, the purposes of labeling are still suspect, particularly as these ethnic differences correspond to school achievement and school resources. There are two related, but different perspectives to consider in light of these data:

1. Labels and heritage are used to explain causality of differences, assuming hereditary factors.
2. The uniqueness of each individual is concealed by the labels.

There is an implicit effort to make American society homogeneous, despite environmental and personal differences that distinguish individuals in our society. The homogeneity sought reflects the biases/prejudices/values of those in power who seek to mold society in their image. Those who are different are ostracized and denigrated. Since the power elite are mainly while, of Western European heritage, and relatively rich, that model becomes the standard against which others are measured. School goals and, particularly, English-language educators need to address this tension in values present in our society by carefully organizing students and their curriculum to consider the ramifications of such biases.

In the largest school districts, the so-called "minority" population has been steadily increasing. In 1950, 1 in 10 students represented a designated "minority"; in 1980, the "minority" count was 7 of 10 (Bencivenga, 1983). Recently, California reported that more than half of its school children represented "minority" groups. Even more striking are the figures from urban districts. Central city school districts enroll only 3% of the white student population. Such schools "have become almost irrelevant to the nation's white population" (Fiske, 1988, p. 16).

The African Americans, Hispanics, and Asian Americans who collectively have replaced whites in central city schools are to a large extent segregated from each other (Fiske, 1988). Nationwide, urban "children go to schools that are almost totally segregated by race and class. . . . It may well be that the[se] children . . . in . . . underclass schools are even more comprehensively isolated from mainstream middle-class society than were the Black children of the South" (Fiske, 1987, p. 24). A recent report by a New York State Task Force on the Education of children and Youth at Risk concludes that "racism clearly underlines much of the problem" with the schools today (Kolbert, 1988, p. 1).

Nor is the picture much brighter in the suburbs. In many cases, residential shifts and school consolidation have brought "minority" children to many suburban schools, creating tensions that have been "solved" by internal school segregation via tracking (Oakes, 1985). And even where so-called "minority" students are not present in large numbers, Powell, Farrar, and Cohen (1985) and Sedlack, Wheeler, Pullin, and Cusick (1986) point a grim picture of alienation, boredom, and cynicism. The "Shopping Mall High Schools" of the suburbs don't seem to have found the answer any more than their urban counterparts as to how to make the school experience meaningful for their students.

The long-range educational implications of these reports are revealed in the percentages of high school graduates from various groups who have succeeded in school to the extent of enrolling in college. College enrollments have increased, but not equally across ethnic groups (New York Times, 8/30/88, p. A17). The absolute numbers of students in all groups have increased from 1976 to 1986, but the percentage of white high school graduates going to college has gone up from 32.9% to 34.5%, while the percentage of African American graduates enrolling has declined from 33.4% to 28.6% and that of Hispanic graduates from 35.8% to 29.4% during this decade (Chronicle of Higher Ed. Almanac, 1988, p. 81). In 1995, white high school graduates enrolled in college at a rate of 9 percentage points higher than Black and Hispanic counterparts (Conditions of Education, 1997, p. 66).

These differences reflect such contrasts as ethnicity and wealth. When we look at the census categories distinguishing these graduates, we note dramatic differences. "Three out of four Blacks and four out of five Latinos fail to complete high school within four years" (Kolbert, 1988, p. 32).

Despite apparent correlations between ethnicity and school achievement or completion rates, when income data are considered, a very different picture emerges. African American and Hispanic middle-class children "perform like white middle-class children . . . [G]iven the opportunity, youth from every ethnic background can realize their potential" (Hodgkinson, 1988, p.13). Genuine equality of opportunity would result in poor children achieving similarly to their more affluent peers.

Males continue to attend school longer and have slightly higher graduation rates than females. In 1980, 65.8% of females graduated from high school and completed a median of 12.4 years whereas 67.3% of males achieved a median of 12.6 years of schooling (U.S. Bureau of Census, 1983). But unlike the data on ethnic minorities, these gender figures are improving. "As recently as 1960, American colleges and universities were predominantly male preserves. Only 1 in 3 of all students were female. Today half of all college students are women" (Conf. Bd. & U.S. Bureau of Census, 1986, p. 20). Successful high school completion and college enrollments by gender are now generally more equal than any other characteristic used to report demographic data. However, with the end of affirmative action in college admission decisions in California and the decision to end remedial education in New York's City University, we are likely to experience a reversal in the diversity of enrollees and these institutions will become virtually White institutions (New York Times, 6/9/98, p. B7).

## Family Structure and Schooling

Our students do not live in isolation. They are usually members of a family. These family structures exert a powerful influence on our students' education goals and their ability to participate in life at school. The size of the gap between the language and values of the school and those at home predicts the level of success the student is likely to achieve in school. Because the family experience has been such an important predictor of school success, it is essential that educators reconceptualize schooling so that all students, regardless of family background, will have not only access to a high quality education, but be nurtured to succeed in such a setting. This perspective conflicts with those that blame school failure on the students' background rather than taking responsibility for the schools' effects during the 15,000 hours our students are in school. English-language educators need to be knowledgeable about our students' families as a basis for designing successful programs that bridge the gap between experience and expectation, fulfilling our democratic responsibility for equality in educational experience for all.

Part of the reason for the increasingly poor fit between schools and students has been a dramatic shift in the nature of the American family. The traditional American family structure of a "breadwinner father, homemaker mother and two school-aged children . . . now account[s] for only 7% of U.S. households, [it is changing] to a single parent, most often female, with no major job skills (Hodgkinson, 1988, p. 11). In 1990, 59.7% of females with their own children under 6 years of age were in the labor force (Digest, 1997, p. 120). Approximately 25% of children now live in single-parent homes and most of these are poor (Ellwood, 1988). In those homes where there are two parents, most often both are working outside the home in both cities or suburbs. Frequently enrollment in preprimary school programs is connected with parents working outside the home. Between 1986 and 1996 enrollments increased by 27% with increasing numbers, approximately 47%, attending all day compared with 38% in 1986 (Conditions of Education, 1997, p. 61).

One of the important implications of this shift is the extent to which school personnel, from administrators to the individual teacher in a class, have shifted their mental model of who stands behind each child in their class or school. Insofar as we are still thinking of families in Norman Rockwell terms, we may not be able to see our students and their lives with any degree of accuracy. Proposals for increasing homework, for example, assume parental supervision and support. Where that is not forthcoming, a "more homework policy" may actually have the ironic effect of further widening the achievement gap it is intended to narrow.

Other implications for the future can be derived from such data as the increased frequency with which teenagers are giving birth. These children having children most likely come from low-income households and usually have to drop out of school to care for their babies. This perpetuates a vicious cycle in our society. "Early childbearing is highly correlated with lower educational attainment" for both the mother and the child (Wetzel, 1987, p. iv). "Education is associated with parenting skills and child development; the children of teen parents also suffer. They tend to score lower than the children of older parents on standardized intelligence tests and they perform less well in school" (Kenney, 1987, p. 729). "The average education level of parents continues to increase. For example, the percentage of fathers with less than a high school education declined from 43% in 1970 to 19% in 1990 . . . and mothers declined from 38% to 17%. . . . Parents' education was the family characteristic most strongly related to student achievement" (*Conditions of Education, 1997*, p. 5). Our students live in families that have varying economic resources, expectations for schooling, and language traditions. These, in turn, are influenced by the economy at large.

## Economic Background and Schooling

The financial resources available to our students are likely to influence both the breadth and depth of their previous experiences and the time available for continuing to enhance their education (by adults or by themselves). There is a widening gap between the rich and the poor—with the rich getting proverbially richer and the poor getting children. During the 1980s the number of poor school-age children increased by 6% from about 7.2 million to 7.6 million (*Conditions of Education, 1997*). The consequences of such a phenomenon are revealed by the increasing numbers of our students who live in homes (or are homeless) with incomes at or below the poverty level. Six percent of children with 2 married parents were living below the poverty level in contrast to 32% of children living only with their mothers (*Conditions of Education, 1997*, p. 5). Because money is needed for basic survival (food, clothing, and shelter), that becomes a higher priority than education, which is considered a luxury in that context.

Our language-education programs need to be sensitive to our students' economic concerns, particularly focusing on ways to become independent of social service systems. The conflicting values implicit in the individual affluence of people who adopt competitive, independent, entrepreneurial perspectives, in contrast to the unionization of employees who receive the legislated minimum wage needs to be considered within the framework of a democratic society. Literary works need to be studied from a perspective that enlightens the relationship between the individual's power in society and the economic conditions that prevail. The English curriculum needs to be responsive to these issues, reflecting on the impact of society's rules and schools' contribution to the differences across the population, intent on devising alternative practices that might alleviate the poverty our students experience.

Aldrich (1988) notes that fewer than 1% of the population owns 20% of the wealth in our nation. This disproportionate share of economic resources results in a large percentage of people having very limited funds. Income reports are difficult to obtain, and when they are available, quartile rankings disguise the extent of the disparities Aldrich reports. Even so, it is clear that "minorities" are not prospering. In a recent report, grouped by ethnicity 51.6% of the Hispanic population, 40.8% of the African American population and only 17% of the white population fit into the lowest socioeconomic status (SES) quartile. In contrast only 11.8% of the Hispanic population, and 13.1% of the African American population, but 32.5% of the white population are listed in the highest quartile (OERI, 1987b). In a different report, we are told the incomes of "13.5% of the nation (32.5 million Americans) [fall] below the poverty line, with less than 4% of the nation's total disposable income" (Glazer, 1988). Although we do not know the actual figures, the trends are dramatic, and reflect the differential economic support available to our students by ethnic background. White students are more likely to have richer resources available to help them understand the world. They are less likely to be concerned with economic hardships and therefore more free to focus on other matters, *i.e.* education.

Economically advantaged students are increasingly working after school. When considering income, 15.8% of high income and 23% of mid-high income students work in excess of 20 hours per week (*Conditions of Education, 1997*, p. 426). In the main, they do so not to contribute to their family income, but to provide consumer items for their own lifestyle, whether it be designer outfits or gas for their cars. Statistically 20% of female 12th graders and 26.5% of male 12th graders reported working in excess of 20 hours per week with Hispanic students accounting for 25%, White students 23%, American Indian students 22%, and Black students 22% (*Conditions of Education, 1997*, p. 426). While such work may provide valuable experience and a useful taste of employment requirements, it nevertheless distracts from attention to school work and has severely restricted the time available for school-related extracurricular activities.

The dilema that educators face is one of making school and school-related activities sufficiently meaningful and rewarding to compete with the lure of the mall and McDonald's. In schools that have become themselves increasingly like shopping malls (Powell et al., 1985), there is little countervailing pressure against the consumer ethos. For students who have watched as many hours of TV commercials as contemporary students have (Postman, 1987), the power of purchasing solutions to all of life's problems must be directly and energetically addressed by educators if schools are to regain a place of central importance in teenagers' lives. Schools dominated by boring and trivial requirements can hardly compete.

The implications of the impact of these social class phenomena on educational success are still considered controversial. Nevertheless, Jencks et al. (1980) and Bowles and Gintis (1976) have made a compelling case for the conclusion that income levels of parents are the single most important factor in predicting school success. And when low incomes correlate highly with minority status, poor minority students are coming to school with two strikes against them. Median family incomes declined between 1989 and 1993 with ethnicity being a significant factor: Whites averaged $39,300 compared to $24,542 for Blacks and $23,654 for Hispanics. In 1995, Black and Hispanic children were more than twice as likely as White children to live in poverty (*Conditions of Education, 1997*, p. 4).

Even in a time of prosperity and low unemployment (the summer of 1998), those in demand for employment are those who have acquired technical skills in school and/or have some college education. Those students, often students of color, who have not succeeded in school are not succeeding in the job market either. The attempt to limit or eliminate remedial education in colleges will further exacerbate these problems and keep the door to economic success closed for the least prepared members of the population.

One of the consequences of poverty and unemployment is that many students are involved in the drug world in two ways—as users and suppliers. The proportion of high school students who reported using an illicit drug rose from 41% in 1992 to 51% in 1996. Alcohol remains the most often used drug while noting a decline in use within the past 30 days from 72% in 1980 to 51% in 1996 (*Conditions of Education, 1997*, p. 146). Our eighth graders are also involved: 45% report using alcohol, 16% marijuana, and 3% cocaine in the previous year (p. 156). These figures are sobering as we note the devastating effects of these substances on students' brains and lives. As suppliers, they wear beepers to class, responding to buy signals, leaving the school building and their education behind. Money accumulates quickly, easily, and in large denominations. Students feel successful in contrast to their painful experiences in classrooms where they are anonymous, denigrated for their limited academic achievement, isolated from their peers, denied opportunities to participate in decisions affecting their education, and denied access to knowledge essential for becoming self-reliant.

## What Do Parents and Students Expect From Schooling?

Schools are alien places for many of our students. Schools expect different levels of success—some students are deemed "college material" while others are asked what they will do when they "leave school," implying that these students are not expected to graduate. These different treatments are apparent in distinguishing between students of diverse ethnic backgrounds. Students come to accept differential treatment—with some seeing useful models, achieving increasing independence, and getting much encouragement, while others receive isolated drills, are denigrated for their errors, and handicapped from accepting increasing responsibility. These significant differences in treatment and

expectation result in significantly different outcomes. For a select few, school is a very positive experience, resulting in an enhanced self-esteem and access to strategies for lifelong learning. For most it is a negative experience. Some never recover their self-esteem or their inquisitiveness and desire to increase their knowledge with which they entered school. These differences perpetuate the status quo, in that a select few people in our society are rich and respected.

Traditionally, "each generation of Americans achieves a higher level of education than the one before" (Conf. Bd. & U.S. Bureau of Census, 1986, p. 16). Enrollment in school for longer periods of time may be noted in comparing statistics from 1940 when 24.5% of Americans were high school graduates and the median length of schooling was 8.6 years to those in 1996 when 82% of the population graduated from high school, and 20% had bachelor's degrees or higher with the median schooling increasing to 12.9 years (U.S. Bureau of the Census, 1983; Conditions of Education, 1997; Digest, 1997). With high school graduation, an accomplishment of the majority of the population, the importance of all groups obtaining their diplomas is self-evident.

Although overall students are staying in school a longer time and numerically more are achieving high school diplomas, there are dramatic exceptions. "More than half the 300,000 students in the city's high schools failed to qualify for diplomas within four years," (Daley, 1988, p. B4). These figures are troubling for two reasons. We know most of urban students represent large numbers of so called "minorities" and their dropping out reveals the gap between them and the schools. Additionally, the role of education in providing access to the good life is especially important for the "minorities" and the poor who inhabit most urban areas. "The likelihood of dropping out is inversely related to family income and varies directly with parental educational attainment and occupational status" (Wetzel, 1987, p. 17).

When we look at children in different social and economic classes, major differences become apparent. There are many different ways in which our students' school success is influenced by the nature of the support they receive at home. Grant and Sleeter (1988) found students' home backgrounds limited "the school's aspirations for its clients. What the home background did limit was the help parents could give. They told their children to 'get a good education,' 'to do what the teacher says,' most did not know that they should have been telling their children which courses to take, and demanding that teachers do more teaching" (p. 21). Their uninformed view of how schools work deprived their children of important opportunities.

Students and parents believe that schools are organized to help all succeed. They believe that school is the great equalizer where all must attend and all will have similar opportunities to succeed. It is with these implicit beliefs in mind that parents entrust their children to the schools and that students go to school daily. Yet the schools persistently fail to achieve these ends. Students who succeed despite the abundance of negative school experiences, prove they are *Invulnerable* in Anthony and Cohler's terms (1987) and they are persisters in Tinto's (1987) terms, important qualities of Americans. While access to educational opportunities has always been one of the reasons for immigrating to the U.S., for mosaic families who are trying to maintain two cultures and two nationalities, the common values and standards of American schools can pose a threat. One of the questions, therefore, about the move to state and even national standards is whether or not doing so will triumph over the values and aspirations of those communities trying to preserve their traditions. Even coeducation is a threat to such cultures, and the continuation of the common school may be questioned by such dual allegiance citizens.

## The Languages of Home

Another success factor of concern to language educators is the nature of our students' linguistic environments. There are three interdependent dimensions of this issue that are of particular concern: English Dominance, Linguistic Differences, and Background for Literacy.

***English dominance.*** "In 1985, language minority students (from homes where English is not the first language) made up 43 percent of the kindergarten enrollments in the [NYC] public schools" (Reyes, 1987). In 1995, 31% of Hispanic children spoke a language other than English and were categorized as having difficulty speaking English (*Conditions of Education, 1997*, p. 4). Urban schools are more likely to enroll students with limited exposure to English, placing a considerable responsibility on the schools for helping students develop English proficiency. English-language proficiency is no longer exclusively an urban concern, and recent immigrants are spreading to both suburbs and rural areas.

Students who succeed in school are more likely to be English dominant. Only 8% of high school seniors rated themselves as nonEnglish-dominant. Students whose homes and school experiences encourage learning English promote the likelihood that these students will graduate. Schools that provide programs that both value the students' home language, while supporting their acquisition of English proficiency facilitate the possibility that students will succeed in school. We have found such classrooms to be exciting places for students and teachers, accomplishing the dual objective of facilitating the growth of English proficiency while respecting the students' mother tongue (Mayher, 1975). Because English is the dominant language of the nation, it is important for schools to provide programs that support students' learning in ways that are most consistent with current knowledge of factors influencing learning (Bruner, 1986; Kelly, 1955; and Salmon, 1985).

***Linguistic differences.*** The different ways parents talk with their children have dramatic consequences for their participation in English language-arts classrooms. One area where this is particularly dramatic is in the use of "directives." Delpit (1988) provides helpful contrasts as in the following examples:

1. "Boy, get your rusty behind in that bathtub."
2. "Isn't it time for your bath?"

Both of these statements are intended by the parents who utter them to expedite their child's taking a bath. But the first is more typical of the working class home, while the second is more frequently heard in middle-class homes. A child in a working-class home who heard the second would believe he had real options, which the child in the middle-class home would know are illusory. However, when children from working-class homes enter school and hear such questions, they misconstrue the implicit meanings of language prevailing in the classroom. This may result in their being considered a discipline problem, or being placed in a special class for behavior disordered children.

Samples 3 and 4 capture critical characteristics of school language.

3. We're going to take a test.
4. T: Who knows what day it is today?
   S: Friday
   T: Very good.

The teacher who says sample 3 is not taking the test. The collaboration implicit in this statement is deceptive. Rather, the teacher will administer the test, and the students will take the test. Students who ask if the teacher is also going to take the test may be considered insolent, and disciplined for the transgression.

When asking sample 4 the teacher is seeking students who know the answer to so indicate by facing her, raising their hands, and making eye contact (Brause, Mayher, & Bruno, 1985). Students who call out answers are usually either ignored or ostracized. Implicit in this teacher–student interchange is that the teacher knows the answer, and it is the students who have to come up with what's in the teacher's mind. The students need to figure out if the teacher wants them to say the day of the week and/or the date. The teacher is usually not posing a real question—as revealed by the evaluation "Very good". In a real conversation, the teacher would say "thank you," thereby expressing gratitude for the information. Successful students learn to use and interpret language in school that is consistent with the school norms.

There is no necessary superiority or inferiority inherent in such linguistic differences, but schools have fairly rigid value systems that students must adopt to succeed. Rather than assuming that difference always means deficiency, English language educators need to help students have the option of succeeding in mainstream society. The differences between language styles of home and school are significant for many students, and rather than tracking such students away from success, we must find ways to bridge the gaps.

Another linguistic difference that distinguishes homes (both working class and middle class) from schools is the way language is used to discuss issues. Parents in both working-class and middle-class homes talk with their children as they initiate them into the practices and traditions of the community (Heath, 1983; Wells, 1986). They learn how to read books, prepare meals, repair motors, and play ball. When parents engage their children in these activities, they intersperse language as they proceed, sharing ideas and information. These utterances are contextually relevant and purposefully focused on the accomplishment of the activity (with asides on different, but personally important issues, as time permits). It is equally likely that children or adults choose the focus of the talk.

At home there is time and opportunity for implicit negotiation of topics. Parents engage in pleasant, informative conversations with the opportunity for increased understanding, a bonus, as in the following example:

5. Parent: We'll be going to the country on Saturday so you will see your friend Geoffrey again.
   Child: How many days before Saturday?
   Parent: Well today is Thursday, then comes Friday and then Saturday. Do you think you and Geoffrey might go to the river and look for your friends, the ducks?

The most rewarding conversations are ones in which each person tries to understand the other's perspectives, avoiding assumptions, and sharing beliefs freely. All are encouraged to participate collaboratively in the discussion, with no one monopolizing the discussion, and specific opportunities designated for those who haven't gotten a turn to present their views. The focus is on being together, to help each other accomplish something together. Rushing is inconsistent with real conversations that are responsive, engaging, and exciting for all participants. And personal remembrances or connections with experiences in other settings are encouraged. The style is colloquial with technical labels applied retrospectively, and contextually.

Children benefit from these types of conversations enhancing their understanding while becoming increasingly fluent language users. Children who are proficient in conversing with their parents, however, are not necessarily proficient in participating in classroom discussions. There are different ways to talk at home and at school, and these do seem to break along economic lines. When the school is a traditional, teacher-centered experience (Brause & Mayher, 1985) and the home is collaborative, these differences can have an effect on schooling. The conversation in classrooms is very different from family dialogues (as in sample 5). Middle-class parents more deliberately prepare their children to participate in school-type "conversations" as in the following:

6. Parent: Show Grandma how nicely you say the days of the week.

These parents school their children in classroom-type dialogue, in which participants are required to display knowledge about abstract, impersonal information, as the names of the planets in the universe and the plots of stories. Even though at home, the children know the information the parents know, and the children have no personal reason for recalling these arbitrary facts at that particular time, such dialogues as sample 6 are treated as a game. And those who participate in them become good game players. They get experience at school-talk in preparation for school. In such homes, children are encouraged to "play school" and to learn through doing so that the teacher controls who talks, what is said, what is acceptable, what knowledge students are expected to display, and how they are to display it.

Traditional teacher-centered schools demand this kind of understanding. Hull (1985), for example, reported on children being asked to read the teacher's mind as in the following:

7. I'm thinking about being alone—another word beginning with *s* (p. 165).

Unlike home conversations, school-talk is really monologic in quality, since the teacher controls all. Students fill in the blanks in the monologue, as in workbook exercises and tests (Mayher & Brause, 1986). Teachers question students seeking only one acceptable answer. Student questions are considered digressions or attempts to subvert the teacher's control. Students are restricted to regurgitating facts presented in textbooks and teacher statements. They are restricted in their observations, experiences, and focus. They are restricted in the ways in which they can try to make sense of the information being presented. The teacher selects topics for discussion from the curriculum, often resulting in neither the teacher nor the student being personally interested in the topic. There is a constant concern for time—[we need to hurry]—and few students actually get turns-at-talk, with most eavesdropping on the answers of other students whose responses allow the teacher to move the lesson along. The participants frequently remark that they are bored in these settings, they are uninvolved, and forget the facts that they learn exclusively for regurgitation on tests. For students to get opportunities to talk and be successful in traditional classrooms, they must know the rules. But these rules are never explicitly stated, so students who do not know the game frequently violate the teacher's expectations and get penalized for doing so.

Students' homes prepare them differently for school. School experiences are fairly predictable, with the overwhelmingly traditional organization of classrooms, consistent for the past 90 years at least, identified by Cuban (1993), particularly in their valuing of one linguistic dialect over others. If schools are to fulfill the casserole metaphor, and foster a pluralistic society, multiple dialects and languages must be respected, encouraged, and developed, while simultaneously providing access to the variety of mainstream, public English. We need to consider the efficacy of the traditional school practices both in light of current research and theory into language and learning and in light of our students' experiences as successful learners outside of school.

***Background for literacy.*** When considering the homes our students come from, it is instructive to note that 57% of 3 to 5 year olds are read to everyday by a family member, but there are important differences when using ethnic, economic, and social factors. Of the Hispanic children, 39% were read to, in contrast to 44% of Black, and 64% of White children.

When using income as a factor, we note that 46% of homes at or below the poverty level provided this activity, while 61% of homes above the poverty threshold read daily to their children. Two parent homes were more likely (61%) in contrast to one or no parent settings (46%). Mothers' education level also created separate groups: 77% of college graduates, 62% of post-high school, 49% of those with high school diplomas, and 37% of those mothers with less than high school diplomas read to their 3- to 5-year old children on a daily basis (*Conditions of Education, 1997*, p. 142). Children's drawings frequently include words, labels, or comments (Harste, Woodword, & Burke, 1984). From these initial writing efforts, children use their drawings to help them create narratives, alternating between elaborating on the text and the drawing (Graves, 1983). When these drawings and stories are posted on refrigerators at home and shared enthusiastically with friends, children are subtly rewarded and encouraged to enter the literacy club, as when they look at books and tell stories corresponding to the illustrations (Smith, 1988).

On the other hand, homes that are short on paper or space to display children's drawings and stories, provide less support for these activities, which are closely connected to reading and writing (Taylor & Dorsey-Gaines, 1988). Children who are deprived of these opportunities for exploring with literacy at home, live and work in the same classrooms where children are encouraged. This creates a major gap between the experiences of the two groups—and their readiness for more demanding literacy activities. Parents who understand the literacy environment of schools are more likely to specifically select preschool programs that are literacy-oriented, in that they provide the child with opportunities to see others writing and reading, and to engage in those activities with their children (Cochran-Smith, 1983). Such values, implicit in parental choice of program, carry over into the children's learning prior to school and at school. When school activities and goals are respected and valued by parents, children adopt the same values. According to Applebee, Langer, and Mullis, (1988), Chomsky (1972) and Wells (1986), homes that value education prepare children for schooling in a variety of ways such as by having more books and other reading materials.

Wells (1986) conducted an extensive longitudinal study of the language in children's homes. He found that all of the children were equivalent in their language ability when they entered school. A major difference was in their experiences of being read-to. Those who were read-to knew much more about literate language and therefore were able to participate in those types of activities more readily than children without these experiences, and they continued to grow more rapidly as readers and writers through the first 6 years of school.

Anderson, Wilson, and Fielding (1988) studied the out-of-school reading of children in second and fifth grades. They found "staggering differences between children in the amount of reading . . . and that a small difference in the quantity of reading can greatly influence achievement. Time spent reading books was the best predictor of a child's growth as a reader from the second to the fifth grade" (p. 297). However, there are important differences in the achievement by ethnicity. White students' scores exceed those of African American and Hispanic students. Since schooling does not seem to overcome the early differences across these groups, we must reexamine the normal practices of literacy education.

When evaluating the writing of students in grades 3, 7, and 11, an increasing percentage of student writing is evaluated as "satisfactory" or "elaborated," and fewer are receiving the designation of "minimal" or "inadequate" (Applebee et al., 1988, Table 2.4) However, 36% of students in grade 11 are evaluated with the two lowest designations. Considering the length of time these students have attended school, it seems essential to revise teaching practices that do not help students achieve the goals we have set. Rather, differences are perpetuated and magnified, consistent with other schooling practices.

## Schooling Practices

In looking at schooling practices we are making two apparently contradictory arguments:

1. Schools are all the same.
2. Schools are different.

Schools are similar in many respects. They have a curriculum. They administer tests. They are housed in isolated buildings. They are organized by age and neighborhood. They have a predictable range of resources: textbooks, televisions, teachers, blackboards, bookcases. They have similar equipment—chairs and desks. They are staffed with one teacher per classroom. The teacher does the talking and the students do the listening. Schools in one place look like schools in all other places—so much so that Cuban (1993) remarked on the similarity between schools, across the nation and across grades, as well as comparing those in 1890 to those in 1980. These similarities among schools do not reveal the quality of the educational transactions within them. When we look more closely at the organization and structure of our schools and classroom activities, as for example, Brause (1992) we see the enduring nature of educational practices. Inquiries into the impact of these enduring practices on student learning, provide an opportunity for rethinking, reforming or changing practice to create schools where students are empowered and encouraged to learn and grow (see for example, Ames & Miller, 1994, Clark, 1995, Sizer, 1996).

These are the source of the differences among schools. The *people* distinguish one school from another. The life in these buildings embodied in the students, teachers, and administrators can vary widely in background, expectations, and their commitment to equal education for all. These factors strongly influence the nature of the transactions that occur in the schools as noted by one of us (Brause, 1987) returning to one school after 25 years.

In most classrooms, whole class lessons prevail with students answering teacher questions (Goodlad, 1983). During these events, there is a tacit agreement among the participants not to embarrass each other (Powell et al., 1985). Operationalizing that agreement involves students and teachers not asking questions to which the intended respondent does not have the answer. Implicit in such treaties is the belief that there are a finite number of correct answers—and that there is an objective, but predetermined body of knowledge that all should know. Smith (1986) describes such pratices as an *Insult to Intelligence*, but they are central to the normal game of schooling. Students who play the game well, succeed in school; those who do not, do not.

Applebee et al. (1988) note that students in 11th grade read to answer predetermined, externally imposed questions, clearly an outcome of their schooling experiences. All the reasons language educators introduce children to books suggested by Applebee et al. (talk with friends, learn something new, imagine myself in the story, and to relax) decrease in importance as students go through the grades. The one item that almost doubles in student choice is "to answer questions about it." These students who have made it to the 11th grade know that reading in school serves one essential purpose—to prove that they have read by responding to the teacher's questions. These successful students are testwise and schoolwise. Those who are more adept at psyching out the situation and ascertaining the responses that will be more highly valued by the raters are rewarded with higher scores. There is increasing evidence to support the view that this testwiseness is prevalent in so-called mainstream environments. Those in other settings view the task through different lenses and fail to meet the expectations of the test maker who establishes the reward system. In such a context, it is no surprise that students from different backgrounds perform differently on standardized achievement measures.

In some schools teachers are concerned about their students becoming self-respecting learners who use a variety of strategies for acquiring information collaboratively. They have high expectations for themselves and their students. They know their students as individuals, and they are committed to being instrumental in their students' learning while continuing to learn about their students as learners and about the content of their instruction. They search out experiences and materials that are personally meaningful to students, engaging them in the process of learning, helping students individually and collectively to become critically literate. They have confidence in the students' innate abilities to learn and their own ability to help students learn. Programs established in Hawaii's Kamehameha schools (Au, 1980), and Michigan's Perry Preschool Project (Schweinhart, Weikart, & Larner, 1986), for example, provide persuasive evidence of the efficacy of such programs, particularly helping students considered "at risk" to succeed in school. We know the teacher's expectations can have dramatic impact on students' self-concept and learning (Peters, 1971; Rosenthal & Jacobson, 1968).

Programs offered in schools vary. Preschool programs are distinguished by their focus on daycare and autonomous play (Klass, 1986) or socialization and other school-like activities (Cochran-Smith, 1983). Schools establish different tracks for student placement, grouping students with similar scores on standardized tests in the same room. This grouping results in segregation. Some students are relegated to special services, a euphemism for low-expectation groups, and others are guided to advanced placement courses. Erickson and Shultz (1982) document the guidance counselor's role in perpetuating ethnic bias. Gartner and Lipsky (1987) note the disproportionately high representation of "minority" students enrolled in special education courses. They also indicate a paucity of evidence of student success in these programs.

In the 90s more and more policy makers and some educators have adopted the view that the problems of American schools derive from low expectations. They have endorsed a variety of "standards" proposals with the hope that demanding more of students (and teachers) will raise the achievement levels for all. While it seems likely that such higher expectations can make a difference, they will only do so if students are supported with appropriate teaching and materials. Merely setting "higher" standards won't do the trick. Further, the various standards proposals continue to be controversial either because they are too vague to provide much guidance, or because they are being measured by reductive tests that may actually have the effect of limiting student learning. While the long-term effects of the

TABLE 22.1. Enrollments in Honors and Remedial English Programs

| Honors Program | | Remedial Program |
|---|---|---|
| 4.7% | White students | 4.2% |
| 2.2% | Black students | 4.5% |
| 2.1% | Hispanic students | 4.5% |
| 8.3% | Asian & Pacific Island students | 1.6% |
| 2% | American Indian students | 5.2% |

*Note.* From The Conditions of Education: A Statistical Report by OERI, 1987a, Washington, DC: U.S. Government Printing Office. Reprinted with permission.

standards movement can't be determined yet, it seems clear that it is not the panacea some hope for.

Tracking has been studied by Oakes (1985) and Powell et al. (1985) revealing so-called "minority" students are more highly represented in programs that are considered less rigorous. The enrollments in 11th-grade Remedial and Honors English programs are instructive in this regard (Table 22.1).

There are important consequences to student placement. Some programs lead to college admission, others do not. Students who are enrolled in remedial courses and less rigorous programs are denied access to higher education. More importantly, students whose education is viewed as one of remedying their deficient background, rather than an expansion of their experiences, are singularly denigrated by their schooling experiences. "All the national commissions are telling the schools to pick winners, but we need the schools to *create* the winners. . . . We need to make sure that every kid succeeds in school" (Hodgkinson, 1988, p. 14).

Tracking separates and perpetuates differences in students' home backgrounds. The racial segregation embedded in these practices causes us to question all tracking. The effect of these practices handicaps students from kindergarten through grade 12.

Weikart and colleagues (Beruette-Clement, Schweinhart, Barnett, Epstein, & Weikart, 1984; Schweinhart et al., 1986) show the differential effect of children's participation in preschool programs and their achievement in later school grades. Those who participated in the "transactional" model of learning at the Perry Preschool Project at age 3 were followed to the age of 19, with the results indicating lasting benefits of the preschool program in contrast to those who attended no preschool program. Students stayed in school longer, were more likely to go to college, received higher scores on standardized tests, had fewer teenage births, and fewer arrests. A subsequent study (Schweinhart et al., 1986) comparing students in the Perry program with two other programs (the Distar program and a traditional nursery program) found significant differences in the students' sense of responsibility, self-esteem, and similar indicators of success for the students who participated in the transactional, Perry preschool program. School programs differ in their impact on children.

In more traditional schools, students are viewed as empty vessels in need of filling throughout schooling—with the teacher controlling all movement in the room, all topics for discussion, and the assessment of learning. These teachers frequently have low expectations for students achieving in their class or

TABLE 22.2. Characteristics of Students Who Succeed
and Fail

| School Succeeders | School Failures |
|---|---|
| White | "Minority" |
| Suburban | Urban |
| Middle class family | Working class or poor family |
| English proficient | English is a second language |
| Trend to small family | Large family and/or single parent |
| Parent(s) employed | Parent(s) unemployed |
| Stable community | Transient community |
| Expect to succeed | Expect to fail |
| Regular attendance | Frequent absence |
| Spacious school building | Overcrowded school |
| Optimistic teachers | Dispirited teachers |
| Sociable with peers | Socially isolated |
| Teacher knows student names | Students are anonymous |
| "Academic" classes | "Skills" classes |
| Graduate from high school | Dropout prior to high school graduation |

graduating from high school; they have little faith in the students as individuals and do not trust them to be able to work independently, always perceiving the need to move the students in a lock-step process to facilitate monitoring. To accommodate this view, they break the curriculum into arbitrary, atomistic and trivial facts, which they present to the students as truths, in abstraction, and assess their ability to regurgitate information (Gold, 1988; Hull, 1985). These teachers believe they know all they need to know to teach their students, never questioning the efficacy of established practices or the validity of beliefs or strategies.

## Inequality in Our Students' Lives

When we look at students' experiences in schools, there seems to be a problem with operationalizing the concept of equality of opportunity. We note characteristics that tend to distinguish these two groups: those who are succeeding using the schools' value system and those who are failing in that system (see Table 22.2).

School and the real world are one. Historically, public schools have perpetuated society's biases—helping students similar to the power group to succeed while encouraging others who are different from the power group (particularly in physical characteristics) to drop out.

## INTERPRETING THE DATA

Given the undoubted reality that schools are not helping all children get an equal opportunity to participate in the American Dream of access to higher education and economic opportunity, what assessments have been made of this situation and what alternatives have been suggested to help deal with these problems? The analyses vary, but most of them end up blaming the children, their parents, or some other aspect of their social milieu. Further, as Rose (1988) has pointed out, the evaluations themselves frequently exhibit what he calls "cognitive

reductionism," which involves finding a single, and simplistic cause for such problems, which then limits efforts to provide alternative educational environments to help such students catch up.

Some of the evaluations blame the schools. This is the tack taken by The National Commission on Excellence (1983) and by William Bennett and his allies such as Ravitch and Finn (1987) and even Hirsch (1987). In this case, the critique is essentially that schools have failed to have sufficient content in the curriculum, sufficiently high standards for students, and sufficiently professional (i.e., subject-content knowledgeable), teachers. They urge a return to a period when American education worked, although they are vague about when that was, because in that golden age everyone knew more and worked harder. They blame the progressive movement and, particularly, its renewal in the late 1960s for our current problems even though, for example, the NAEP data and studies like those of Goodlad (1983) suggest that the real culprit was the emphasis on atomistic skills of decoding and encoding, of the back-to-basics movement that marked the 1970s conservative response to the 60s.

Most significant of all, however, both the identification of problems and the suggestion for reform embodied in much of the current focus on renewing American education take for granted that so-called "minority" children will never be able to fully participate in the pursuit of educational excellence. Test data and the demographic realities of the lack of success by "minorities" in completing high school and/or higher education are taken at face value to show that since they aren't doing well, it means they can't do well. This version of the self-fulfilling prophecy provides a built-in excuse for school failure, and thereby lets the schools off the hook of responsibility by, in effect, saying, we are not to blame for the low achievements of some students; they simply do not have the potential to succeed.

## Are Schools "Fair"?

The belief in schools can only be sustained if one can assume that the schools and the tests they employ to assess and track students are fundamentally accurate and fair. As noted earlier, this belief is a basic keystone of the American faith in education, a conviction that schools are the great equalizer, the one institution in American society that is both dedicated to and effective at treating every child equally and giving all an equal chance at academic success. While there is no question that schools should, and we believe they could, function that way, we have already cited considerable evidence to show that they just do not do so for all children.

## Who's Responsible?

Rather than continuing to blame the victim—to put the onus of responsibility for failure exclusively on the shoulders of the children (and/or their parents), perhaps it is time to try a new tack. This would recognize that the demographic realities we have described do present new challenges to schools, particularly that of viewing all students, especially children of color, of nonEnglish-speaking backgrounds, or of poor and/or single parent families as likely to succeed. Such an approach would require a significant reconceptualization of the tasks facing schools and of the kinds of education programs required to serve effectively the students who are actually enrolled. It would require school people to recognize that the "drop out" problem is not the result of the inadequate potential of the drop outs, but a powerful statement of the failure of schools to help students achieve academic success.

Such a reconceptualization would demand that schools live up to the educational cliche of starting where the students really are. But it would also demand the abandonment of the more or less overt assumption that students who come to school with backgrounds and motivations different from those of the teacher are thereby permanently and inevitably condemned to low standards of achievement and are more than likely to drop out before completing school. It would also require a renewed commitment not only to equality of opportunity, but to equality of results. This latter is a much more controversial goal since the presumption of the inequality of talent and ability is so pervasive, but unless schools commit themselves to such a goal, the current practices of segregation and tracking will continue to make a mockery of equality of opportunity.

## FROM A PROBLEM TO AN OPPORTUNITY

A commitment to equality of results for schooling must be based on the overwhelming commonalities of our species specific potential for learning. This requires a focus, not on the relatively minor differences that distinguish us from each other, but on the common potential of our genetic endowment as human beings. The fact that children are more alike when they enter kindergarten than they ever are again in school—a conclusion that can be drawn from virtually every study of school achievement—is the most powerful evidence we have that schools are part of the problem, not part of the solution to inequality of achievement.

Those of us in language education know, for example, that, by the time they get to school, all but a minute fraction of the student population have acquired a spoken language system of infinite potential, of normally flexible creativity, and with enormous riches of conceptual understanding. But children whose spoken language system is not English, or whose variety of English is not similar to the regional standard, and/or whose parents have not read to them extensively before they get to school, find themselves immediately behind the literacy eight ball. The statistics further show that virtually all of the remedial programs attempted so far have exacerbated, rather than helped close the literacy gap. Providing an educational environment that will genuinely solve these problems will not be easy, but the preschool and followup data (Au, 1980; Beruette-Clement et al., 1984; Cochran-Smith, 1983 and Schweinhart et al., 1986) show it can be done.

But it won't be done by schools that continue to assume that difference means deficiency. In a genuinely pluralistic society—a real casserole—differences can be celebrated and built on as sources of strength. They can be used to provide a space for the transition to mainstream educational attainment as effective transitional bilingual programs do now. They can be a source of individual pride and group self-esteem, rather than a continued

source of racist and cultural stereotyping. And they can be a source of creating and renewing our commitment to the kind of pluralistic culture that emphasizes our common humanity at its base, as well as our common Americanism as a nation of immigrants who hold common aspirations for ourselves, our children, and our casserole culture.

### From Vision to Reality

Transforming schools is never an easy task as Brause (1992) and Cuban (1993) have shown. Nevertheless, schools do change. Current pressures for accountability and the use of standardized tests to achieve it have changed schools dramatically in the last decade. Our interpretation of the demographic data, however, shows that these changes have been overwhelmingly counterproductive for the most needy of our students. The limited and limiting tests have emphasized and exaggerated the differences among our students. This has had the effect of emphasizing what they cannot do, rather than what they can do. Further, it has labeled them as potential or actual failures and greased the skids toward their early departure from school.

In order to break this vicious cycle, we must take a new look at who our students are and what they can do. We must emphasize their competencies and achievements, constantly striving to expand each student's repertoire, and build on these as the potential foundation for even higher levels of success. We have to believe that excellence is possible for all children, and we have to find approaches to teaching and learning that will narrow the gap between the ideal and the real. If it is *conceivable* that all students can achieve higher levels of critical literacy—to be able to use language as readers, writers, speakers, and listeners with power and imagination and critical acumen—then it should be *achievable* given the power of the oral systems all of them bring with them to school. But it would not be achieved as long as we treat differences as symptoms of negative limits on the potential for achievement, when we continue to assume that children who come to school without the groundwork for literacy under their belts will never be able to catch up, and hold to the belief that our current tests measure unchangeable limits of potential.

### An Uncommon Sense Education for All

The kinds of schools we need for the students we really have—of all colors, of all cultural and linguistic heritages, of both sexes—are what one of us has called uncommon sense schools (Mayher, 1990)—schools that believe in the common human potential of all learners and that build curricula and learning environments that meet the needs of real students by building on their strengths rather than cataloging their deficiencies. Such schools seek excellence for all, not as a pipe dream, but as a commitment to enhancing the common human potential of all students.

The realities they confront of ethnic, racial, and gender stereotyping can be changed by eliminating tracking and developing effective strategies for students of mixed proficiencies, by recognizing and developing effective assessment measures that evaluate children's best work, and by making students partners in the learning process through negotiating the curriculum. When students collaborate with teachers in establishing and implementing the curriculum, there is real dialog in which the interests of students are paramount in identifying the enterprises in which students will engage, and the teacher finds ways to use these experiences to expand students' concepts about the world and strategies for learning. In such a partnership, teams of students design and accept responsibility for accomplishing tasks and collaborating with peers and the teacher in the process of simultaneously accomplishing a project and become increasingly educated. See Boomer (1982) for additional details concerning this concept.

In such schools, everyone not only can learn to use language powerfully in all four modes, but can do so in a framework that helps them learn how to learn, using language and all of the other symbol systems they need to do so. Until we try such approaches we really don't have any idea what the potential for excellence of all students really is. But whatever the possibilities for change in uncommon sense directions, we cannot continue to let the growing number of so-called minority children in our schools serve as the perennial reason to excuse our failures. Their numbers will continue to grow. Our challenge is to use this opportunity to rebuild our schools so that they actually help all children have equal access to the American Dream—to make the American ideal that education should serve to provide equality of access to the good life a reality for our students, not an illusion.

# References

Aldrich, N. W. Jr. (1988). *Old money*. NY: Knopf.

Ames, N. L., & Miller, E. (1994). *Changing middle schools: How to make schools work for young adolescents*. San Francisco: Jossey-Bass.

Anderson, R. C., Wilson, P. T., & Fielding, L. G. (1988). Growth in reading and how children spend their time outside of school. *Reading Research Quarterly, 23*(3), 285-303.

Anthony, E. J., & Cohler, B. J. (Eds.) (1987). *The invulnerable child*. New York: Guilford.

Apple, M. W. (1986). *Teachers and texts: A political economy of class and gender relations in education*. New York: Routledge and Kegan Paul.

Applebee, A. N., Langer, J. A., & Mullis, I. V. S. (1988). *Who reads best? Factors related to reading achievement in grades 3, 7 and 11*. Princeton, NJ: ETS.

Aronowitz, S., & Giroux, H. A. (1988). Schooling, culture, and literacy in the age of broken dreams: A review of Bloom and Hirsch. *Harvard Educational Review, 58*(2), 172-194.

Au, K. H. (1980). Participation structures in a reading lesson with Hawaiian children: Analysis of a culturally appropriate instructional event. *Anthropology and Education Quarterly, 11*, 91-115.

Banks, J. A. (1995). *Handbook of research on multicultural education*. New York: Macmillan.

Bencivenga, J. (1983, March 11). Huge minority enrollment challenges public education. *Christian Science Monitor*, 7.

Berliner, D. C., & Biddle, A. W. (1995). *The manufactured crisis: Myths, fraud, and the attack on America's public schools*. Reading, MA: Addison-Wesley.

Beruette-Clement, J., Schweinhart, L., Barnett, W., Epstein, A., & Weikart, D. (1984). *Changed lives: The effects of the Perry preschool program on youths through age 19*. (Monographs of the High/Scope Educational Research Foundation, 8), Ypsilanti, MI: High/Scope Press.

Boomer, G. (Ed.). (1982). *Negotiating the curriculum: A teacher-student partnership*. Sydney, Australia: Ashton Scholastic.

Bowles, S., & Gintis, H. (1976). *Schooling in capitalist America*. London: Routledge and Kegan Paul.

Brause, R. S. (1987). School days: Then and now. *Anthropology and Education Quarterly, 18*(1), 53-55.

Brause, R. S., Mayher, J. S. (1985). Learning through teaching: Language at home and at school. *Language Arts, 62*(8), 870-875.

Brause, R. S., & Mayher, J. S., & Bruno, J. (1985). *An investigation into bilingual students' classroom communicative competence*. Rosslyn, VA: National Clearinghouse for Bilingual Education.

Brause, R. S. (1992). *Enduring schools: Problems and possibilities*. London: Falmer Press.

Bruner, J. (1986). *Actual minds, possible worlds*. Cambridge, MA: Harvard University Press.

Chomsky, C. (1972). Stages in language development and reading exposure. *Harvard Educational Review, 42*(1), 1-33.

*Chronicle of higher education almanac*. (1998, September 1).

Clark, C. M. (1995). *Thoughtful teaching*. New York: Teachers College Press.

Cochran-Smith, M. (1983). *The making of a reader*. Norwood, NJ: Ablex.

Conference Board & U.S. Bureau of the Census (1986). *How we live: Then and now* (a joint study). Washington, DC: U.S. Government Printing Office.

*Conditions of Education, 1997*. (1997). U.S. Department of Education, National Center for Educational Statistics. (NCES 97-388). Washington, DC: U.S. Government Printing Office.

Cremin, L. (1988). *American education: The metropolitan experience 1876-1980*. New York: Harper & Row.

Cuban, L. (1993). *How teachers taught: Constancy and change in American classrooms 1890-1980* (2nd ed.). New York: Teachers College Press.

Daley, S. (1988, June 21). Hispanic dropout rate is highest in study of New York City schools. *The New York Times*, pp. A1, B4.

Delpit, L. D. (1988). The silenced dialogue: Power and pedagogy in educating other people's children. *Harvard Educational Review, 58*(3), 280-298.

*Digest of Education Statistics, 1997*. (1997). U.S. Department of Education, National Center for Educational Statistics. (NCES 98-015). Washington, DC: U.S. Government Printing Office.

Ellwood, D. T. (1988). *Poor support: Poverty in the American family*. New York: Basic Books.

Erickson, F., & Shultz, J. (1982). *The counselor as gatekeeper: Social interaction in interviews*. New York: Academic Press.

Fiske, E. B. (1987, July 26). Hispanic pupils' plight cited in study. *New York Times*, 24.

Fiske, E. B. (1988, June 23). School integration patterns change. *New York Times*, 16.

Gardner, H. (1983). *Frames of mind: The theory of multiple intelligences*. New York: Basic Books.

Gartner, A., & Lipsky, D. K. (1987). Beyond special education: Toward a quality system for all students. *Harvard Educational Review, 57*(4), 367-395.

Giroux, H. (1983). *Theory and resistance in education*. South Hadley, MA: Bergin & Garvey.

Glazer, N. (1988). *The limits of social policy*. Cambridge, MA: Harvard University Press.

Gold, D. L. (1988, November 2). Some reforms counterproductive for young, group says. *Education Week*, 5.

Goodlad, J. (1983). *A place called school*. New York: McGraw-Hill.

Grant, C. A., & Sleeter, C. E. (1988). Race, class, and gender and abandoned dreams. *Teachers College Record, 90*(1), 19-40.

Graves, D. H. (1983). *Writing: Teachers and children at work*. Exeter, NH: Heinemann.

Haley, A. (1976). *Roots*. Garden City, NY: Doubleday.

Harste, J. C., Woodward, V. A., & Burke, C. L. (1984). *Languages stories and literacy lessons*. Portsmouth, NH: Heinemann.

Heath, S. B. (1983). *Ways with words: Language, life and work in communities and classrooms*. New York: Cambridge University Press.

Hirsch, E. D., Jr. (1987). *Cultural literacy: What every American needs to know*. Boston: Houghton Mifflin.

Hodgkinson, H. (1988). The right schools for the right kids. *Educational Leadership, 45*(5), 10-14.

*Holmes Group Forum*. (1988). *111*(1), 2-3.

Holmes, S. A. (1998, June 7). Census takers will try out new method in California. *New York Times*, 22.

Hull, R. (1985). *The language gap: How classroom dialogue fails*. New York: Methuen.

Jencks, C., Bartlett, S., Corcoran, M., Crouse, J., Eaglesfield, D., Jackson, G., McLelland, K., Mueser, P., Olneck, M., Schwartz, J., Ward, S., & Williams, J. (1980). *Who gets ahead?* New York: Basic Books.

Kelly, G. (1955). *A theory of personality*. New York: Norton.

Kenney, A. M. (1987). Teen pregnancy: An issue for schools. *Phi Delta Kappan, 68*(10), 728-736.

Klass, C. S. (1986). *The autonomous child*. Philadelphia: Falmer Press.

Kolbert, E. (1988, October 22). A NY report says racism creates two tiers of schools. *New York Times*, pp. 1, 32.

Koretz, D. (1988). Arriving in Lake Wobegon: Are standardized tests exaggerating achievement and distorting instruction? *American Education, 12*(2), 8-15.

Lieberson, S., & Waters, M. C. (1988). *From many strands: Ethnic and racial groups in contemporary America*. New York: Russell Sage Foundation.

Mayher, J. S. (1975). *An evaluation of the elementary grades bilingual project*. Unpublished manuscript for the NYC Board of Education and U.S. Office of Education.

Mayher, J. S. (1990). *Uncommon Sense: Theoretical practice in language education*. Portsmouth, NH: Boynton/Cook.

Mayher, J. S., & Brause, R. S. (1986). *Teachers can make a difference*. Presentation at the NCTE Spring Conference, Houston.

McNeil, L. (1986). *Contradictions of control: School structure and school knowledge*. New York: Routledge and Kegan Paul.

McLaren, P. (1989). *Life in schools*. Boston: Longman.

National Commission on Excellence in Education. (1983). *A nation at risk: The imperative of educational reform*. Washington, DC: U.S. Government Printing Office.

*New York Times* (1988, August 30). U.S. reports significant rise in education of workforce, p. A17.

*New York Times* (1988, September 7). U.S. Hispanic population is up 34% since 1980, p. A20.

*New York Times* (1998, June 9). CUNY is sued for vote on remedial courses, p. B7.

*New York Times* Series (1998, July 19-21). Here and there: The pull of tradition, p. 1, ff.

Oakes, J. (1985). *Keeping track: How schools structure inequality*. New Haven, CT: Yale University Press.

Office of Educational Research and Improvement (OERI). (1987a). *The conditions of education: A statistical report, 1987 edition*. (CS 87-365) Washington, DC: U.S. Government Printing Office.

Office of Educational Research and Improvement (OERI). (1987b). *Transition from h.s. to postsecondary education: Analytical studies*. (CS 87-309c) Washington, DC: U.S. Government Printing Office.

Orfield, G., & Monfort, C. (1988). *Racial change and desegregation in large school districts: Trends through the 1986-1987 school year*. Alexandria, VA: National School Boards Association.

Peters, W. (1971). *A class divided*. Garden City, NY: Doubleday.

Postman, N. (1986). *Amusing ourselves to death: Public discourse in the age of show business*. New York: Viking Penguin.

Powell, A. G., Farrar, E., & Cohen, D. K. (1985). *The shopping mall high school: Winners and losers in the educational marketplace*. Boston: Houghton Mifflin.

Ravitch, D., & Finn, C. E., Jr. (1987). *What do our 17-year-olds know? A report on the first national assessment of history and literature*. New York: Harper & Row.

Reyes, L. O. (Compiler). (1987). *Demographies of Puerto Rican/Latino students in NY and the US*. Unpublished manuscript. Aspira of NY Inc.

Rodriguez, R. (1982). *A hunger of memory*. Boston: Godine.

Rose, M. (1988). Narrowing the mind and page: Remedial writers and cognitive reductionism. *College Composition and Communication, 39*(3), 267-302.

Rosenthal, R., & Jacobson, L. (1968). *Pygmalion in the classroom: Teacher expectation and pupils' intellectual development*. New York: Holt, Rinehart & Winston.

Salmon, P. (1985). *Living in time: A new look at personal development*. London: Dent.

Schweinhart, L. J., Weikart, D. P., & Larner, M. B. (1986). A report on the high/scope preschool curriculum comparison study: Consequences of three preschool curriculum models through age 15. *Early Childhood Research Quarterly, 1*(1), 15-45.

Sedlack, M. W., Wheeler, C. W., Pullin, D. C., & Cusick, P. A. (1986). *Selling students short: Classroom bargins and academic reform in the American high school*. New York: Teachers College Press.

Sizer, T. R. (1996). *Horace's Hope: What works for the American high school*. New York: Houghton Mifflin.

Smith, F. (1986). *Insult to intelligence: The bureaucratic invasion of our classrooms*. New York. Arbor House.

Smith, F. (1988). *Joining the literacy club: Further essays into education*. Portsmouth, NH: Heinemann.

Study of southern students' test scores raises doubts on worth of nationally normed exams. (1988, October 26). *Education Week*, p. 11.

Taylor, D., & Dorsey-Gaines, C. (1988). *Growing up literate: Learning from inner-city families*. Portsmouth, NH: Heinemann.

Tinto, V. (1987). *Leaving college: Rethinking the causes and cures of student attrition*. Chicago: U. of Chicago Press.

Tobin, J. (1988, October 23). The rise and fall of the American economy [Review of the *The great u-turn* by B. Harrison & B. Bluestone]. *New York Times Book Review*, 43-44.

U.S. Bureau of the Census (1983). *Characteristics of the population: General social and economic characteristics: U.S. summary*. (PC 80-1-c1). Washington, DC: U.S. Government Printing Office.

U.S. Bureau of the Census (1987). *Estimates of the population of the U.S., by age, sex and race: 1980 to 1986*. (Series p-25, No. 1000) Washington, DC: U.S. Government Printing Office.

U.S. Bureau of the Census (1992). *1990 census of population and housing: Summary social, economic, and housing characteristics*. Washington, DC: U.S. Department of Commerce.

Wells, G. (1986). *The meaning makers: Children learning language and using language to learn*. Portsmouth, NH: Heinemann.

Wetzel, J. R. (1987). *American youth: A statistical snapshot*. New York: The Wm. T. Grant Foundation.

# · 23 ·

# THE DEVELOPMENT OF THE YOUNG CHILD
# AND THE EMERGENCE OF LITERACY

*Elizabeth Sulzby*
University of Michigan

W. H. *Teale*
University of Illinois at Chicago

If we look at the history of education in the United States during the 20th century, we will notice a dearth of information about the reading and writing of young children from birth through kindergarten age during most of that period, even though a few hearty researchers and practitioners (e.g., Hildreth, 1932; Hucy, 1908; Iredell, 1989; see also Mathews, 1966, and Teale & Sulzby, 1986) were pointing to the need to study reading and writing in the pre-first-grade years. Beginning faintly in the mid-1960s, increasing slightly during the 1970s, and burgeoning in the 1980s and early 1990s, research in emergent literacy has itself emerged into a solid area of investigation that differs in approach as well as in age range.

Sulzby (1989, 1991) defines emergent literacy as the "the reading and writing behaviors of young children that precede and develop into conventional literacy." Emergent literacy research treats reading and writing as being interrelated phenomena, with related developmental paths; and treats the young child's literacy development as the relevant object of study (Goodman, 1980, 1984; Mason & Allen, 1986; Teale & Sulzby, 1986). Now as we enter the new century it is commonplace to hear the words emergent literacy in schools or professional meetings or to read them in professional journals or reviews. But, while labels change, Dickinson (1989) and others warn us that instructional practices may move only slowly.

Definitions of term are in flux, both in literacy research and early childhood research, in general. In this chapter, the term *young child* will be used somewhat loosely to denote the child from birth through the end of kindergarten. This is certainly not the end of early childhood, but it is still the boundary,

in general, of instruction based on a model of development that posits the concepts of the young child as being different from conventional concepts. As can be seen from the following, the assumption that all children hold conventional, adult concepts for linguistic units and for literacy practices in first grade is also questionable, but this review ends somewhat arbitrarily at the end of kindergarten and focuses most heavily on the prekindergarten-aged child. The terms *preschool* and *preschooler* have ambiguous meaning. If we refer to children's age, children not yet in kindergarten could be called preschoolers and might not be enrolled in any kind of school; other preschoolers will be enrolled in institutes called preschools that have instructional programs. In the review that follows, terms referring to age and to type of school or child care institutes will be distinguished.

The actual focus of this chapter is on a developmental period for children, rather than merely on their chronological age or institutional affiliation with day cares, preschools, or public schools. It discusses young children prior to their entry into conventional literacy. This period was earlier referred to as "prereading" or "reading readiness" (with children's writing being ignored, for the most part). The shift in terminology signals a shift in conceptions both of young children and of literacy.

The age range is typically from infancy through about age 7, although a few children begin to read and write conventionally as early as 4 or 5, and some do not reach that level of understanding until age 8 or 9. The onset of formal schooling is as variable as is the age range. There are formal lessons in many home settings and there are a variety of attitudes and practices toward instruction in child care, preschool, kindergarten, and first-grade settings—ranging from child-centered programs in which almost all choice is left to the child, through interactive settings in which teachers respond to children's interests and activities, through teacher-centered settings with direct, highly-sequenced instruction.

Teale and Sulzby (1986) provided an extensive history of the shifts in perspective toward the literacy development of young children in the U.S. during the 20th century. They point out that the immediately preceding view toward early literacy, "reading readiness," represented a step forward from a view of young children's literacy as dependent on maturation or neural ripening. Findings from early research in children's maturation were interpreted as providing evidence that a lock-step approach to introducing all children to reading instruction simultaneously with first-grade entry was untenable. Morphett and Washburne (1931) seemed to provide evidence for the need of differentiating instruction according to the mental age of the individual child. While this study was quite flawed and immediately refuted, it was quite influential. Researchers (Betts, 1946; Gates, 1937; Gates & Bond, 1936; Gates, Bond, & Russell, 1939) found, instead, that instruction would begin earlier if methods were changed. This group ushered in the era of reading readiness as the product of experience, and for the next 40 years or so, reading readiness was the model that ruled research in early literacy. The research paradigm was the search for behaviors of the young child that predicted subsequent achievement in instruction in reading.

Models of reading (and writing) have, of course, changed dramatically during the 20th century. A simple way of expressing the difference between the models of reading from the reading readiness perspective and that of emergent literacy is the boundary into conventional reading. From a reading readiness perspective, reading meant an accurate reproduction of the printed words on a page of conventionally spelled words. To put it even more simply, a child was reading when he or she could say and interpret the words in simple texts like basal pre-primers and primers. Prior to that, the child was a prereader and the period was the prereading or readiness period during which the child should be learning the necessary precursors to real reading. Research was the search for what these precursors were, but they were viewed as being different in kind from reading and writing. For example, precursors studied have varied from knowing letter names and sounds to such competencies as maze tracing or balancing on a walking beam (Betts, 1946).

From an emergent literacy perspective, reading begins long before that time and emergent behaviors such as protoreading (Pappas, 1986) or emergent reading (Teale, 1984) are treated as an integral part of reading development. Recently, some researchers (e.g., Sulzby, 1989) have been suggesting that more attention should be paid to the shift from emergent into conventional patterns of reading and writing. The precursors of conventional reading and writing are different under the emergent literacy perspective. They are emergent behaviors and concepts of reading and writing themselves. Examples are children "reading" from books by looking at the pictures or writing by scribbling letters to grandparents.

While emergent literacy is relatively new as an area of research, it has had a vigorous beginning. There have been a number of quite detailed reviews of emergent literacy in the last twenty years (Mason, 1986; Mason & Allen, 1986; Sulzby & Teale, 1991; Teale, 1987; Teale & Sulzby, 1986; McNaughton, 1995) and a number of books containing collections of emergent literacy research studies (Allen & Mason, 1989; Morrow & Smith, 1989; Strickland & Morrow, 1989; Teale & Sulzby, 1986; Yaden & Templeton, 1986). This review will not attempt to go into detail about many of the older studies that have been discussed elsewhere. Instead, this chapter presents a synopsis of what has been learned about children's emergent reading and writing and some of the challenges for future research. The section that follows frames the current research in emergent literacy with its immediate predecessors.

## THE LEGACY OF EARLIER RESEARCH

Many lines of research and theorizing about young children have contributed to today's research in emergent literacy. A major contribution was made by the research in child language acquisition during the 1960s as an aftermath of the so-called Chomskyan Revolution in linguistics. That research revealed that many of the previous explanations of children's language were too simplistic; young children were now seen a being active in their language acquisition, generating hypotheses about how language operates, and testing these hypotheses in linguistic interaction with their parents and other speakers. Children's errors were interpreted as revealing their conceptual understandings of language, picking up on suggestions made earlier by Piaget (1959). Researchers (e.g., Clark, 1978) began to study such phenomena as overgeneralization or overextension and the developmental paths of children's semantic and syntactic behavior, as revealed in their production of language and responses to elicitations based on hypothesized developmental paths. Researchers of early literacy began to turn to language acquisition research and to theories of language as a resource in reconceiving their own studies. In the sections that follow, three other parts of the legacy of earlier studies are reviewed: the studies of early or precocious readers, of metalinguistic awareness, and of environmental print.

### Precocious Reader Studies

This line of research developed relatively early and was not initially informed by the shift in conceptions of child language acquisition or child development in general. Yet its contribution began to provide a missing link in earlier approaches to beginning reading (see Teale, 1978). As early as the mid-1960s, Durkin (1966) was conducting research that focused on children who come to school already reading. In a sense, Durkin was one of the first to operationalize a definition of conventional reading in a manner that would illuminate children's previous development. Her definition, however, was quite traditional, but it was in line with the theory and measurement instruments of the day. Teachers and parents had been reporting that some children came to school already reading. In order to select a sample of such children to study, Durkin used as her criteria the ability to read correctly from a list of common words and the ability to score at a level on a standardized reading test sufficiently high for it to be unlikely that the child was not actually reading conventionally.

Using similar techniques, Durkin (1966), Clark (1976), and Tobin (1981) then used traditional methods to study these precocious or early readers. They interviewed parents about the children's experiences prior to school entry. Durkin (1966) and Clark (1976) found that early readers were quite variable in most characteristics, including I.Q. There was quite a bit of consistency in parents' reports of key experiences: parents read to these children; these were curious children who elicited adult attention and help; and parents enjoyed the company of these children. (See also Stainthorp & Hughs, 1999.)

The early-reader studies were important for at least three reasons:

1. They focused attention on what children knew prior to formal schooling, as did the metalinguistic awareness and environmental print studies.
2. They begin to lay the groundwork for distinguishing the initial onset of conventional literacy, a topic that is just beginning to be investigated currently.
3. They provided the basis for hypotheses about key factors of early experiences that seemed relevant to later reading achievement.

While these studies were only retrospective, they provided a grounding for hypotheses to be investigated in current studies of family literacy that are prospective in nature.

## Metalinguistic Awareness Studies

Early research in children's metalinguistic awareness (Papandropoulou & Sinclair, 1974; Sinclair, Jarvella, & Levelt, 1978) began to provide specific evidence that young children's concepts for terms such as word, letter, sentence, or sound during the preschool and early elementary school years are quite different from mature adult concepts. Reading and writing researchers (e.g., Downing, 1979; Downing & Oliver, 1973–1974; Meltzer & Herse, 1969; Reid, 1966) furthered this research, extending it to show that when children were commonly introduced to formal instruction (which assumed that children's and adults' concepts are isomorphic), usually in first grade, they typically still do not understand metalinguistic terms. This line of research continues to the present day and is represented most strongly in the research of Ferreiro (1985, 1986; Ferreiro & Teberosky, 1982), discussed in the following, and in the work of Clay (1993, 1998) and of McMahon et al. (1996). An interesting study that compares the bilingual, Chinese–English, influences on metalinguistic development is done by W. E. Nagy (1995).

## Environmental Print Studies

At about the same time that researchers in metalinguistic awareness were showing that children knew less than most had presumed and knew it differently, other researchers were showing that quite young children are, in fact, learning about written language from their environment. The studies of environmental print (Goodman, 1980; Hiebert, 1978, 1981; McGee, Lomax, & Head, 1988; Kuby, Aldridge, & Snyder, 1994; Kirkland, 1991) have been quite important in this regard. Hiebert tested 3- and 4-year-old children with familiar written words. These children showed meaningful responses to the words, declining as contextual support was stripped. Goodman and Altweger (1981) showed that children as young as 3, from varying ethnic and socioeconomic backgrounds, showed indications of being aware of print in their environment. Harste, Woodward, and Burke (1984) showed that children in this age range gave semantically appropriate responses to complex parts of common household and restaurant product containers and wrappers. These studies (see also Mason, 1980) showed that children were picking up much information about the functions and features of printed material from their environment. Researchers such as Hiebert (1980, 1981, 1986) urged that these findings be interpreted to mean that children should be involved with print in their environment, in meaningful interactions, during the preschool years. What these earlier studies did not yet do, however, was to investigate the social environment and how adults and children interact with environmental print.

From these lines of early research, a number of implications were being drawn that affected emergent literacy research during the late 1970s and 1980s. First, since children of every socioeconomic level and I.Q. level might become early readers and since parents' memories for early experience showed some consistency, it seemed important to begin studying children's development in process, through observational studies, rather than through predictive or retrospective designs. Second, children's concepts about literacy were seen as being qualitatively different from conventional concepts; tracing the development of those concepts became a new task for research. Third, children were viewed as constructing their concepts from experiences with the environment; it remained the task for research to define and explore the nature of that environment in detail. It should be pointed out also that these lines of research, particularly the last two, can be viewed as part of emergent literacy research and many of those researchers would today use that term to describe their viewpoints.

In the sections that follow, children's emergent reading and writing development will be examined, starting with a look at studies of home literacy.

## LITERACY DEVELOPMENT IN HOMES

Because children are now viewed as entering school with much knowledge about literacy, it was inferred that they gained this knowledge from the home and their parents. Interviews with parents (Clark, 1976; Durkin, 1966; McCormick & Mason, 1986; Tobin, 1981; see also Tobin & Pikulski, 1988; and Bus & van IJzendoorn, 1997) provided evidence of a variety of experiences in the home that were fruitful for research. Furthermore, because children differ in their literary knowledge, it was further speculated that differences in home literacy environments should help explain individual and cultural differences. Conducting studies of home literacy in which researchers actually enter the home, however, is extremely difficult and labor-intensive; it is also quite intrusive, no matter how congenial the researchers might be. Hence there are relatively few studies to review, although they are longitudinal in nature and provide a rich body of knowledge. Some of these studies focused on particular kinds of literacy, such as storybook reading, rather than on the broad question of what the home provides in literacy events and support for development. Because of these difficulties of conducting research in the home, a number of relevant studies have been conducted by bringing parent–child dyads into a laboratory setting and attempting to recreate literacy events similar to those seen in the natural home setting.

Ethnographic techniques seem to be the primary methodological tool for studies that were actually based in the home setting. While researchers attempt to spend as much time in the home as possible, they also solicit the participation of parents as informants. While any given study includes only a few families, across studies the numbers are beginning to be quite impressive. Heath (1983) studied working-class African American and White and "mainstream" families in the Piedmont Carolinas. Taylor (1983) and Taylor and Dorsey-Gaines (1988) studied six middle-income suburban White families and six low-income urban African American families. Baker, Sonnenschein, and Serpell (1999) studied children of various sociocultural groups in urban Baltimore. Teale and colleagues (Anderson, Teale, & Estrada, 1980; Anderson & Stokes, 1984; Teale, 1986) studied six low-income families each from three ethnic groups, Anglo, Hispanic, and African American in the San Diego area. Sulzby and Teale (1987) studied eight families, divided equally between low- and middle-income Anglo and Hispanic families, in the San Antonio area.

Sulzby and Teale (1987, 1991) and Phillips and McNaughton (1990) focused on a particular part of literacy (storybook reading). Commonalities across the other studies included, first, the reports that all children, regardless of ethnicity and socioeconomic background, were included in some kinds of "literacy events," events in which literacy played an integral part. Second, literacy events were functional in nature and only rarely focused on literacy for the sake of learning literacy. Third, each family had some kind of recurring literacy events; literacy events could be classified by type or domain, even though the domains and distributions differed across families.

In addition to varying across families, these domains differed in regard to how closely they appeared to match school-like domains. (See for example, Moschovaki, 1999, and Haden, Reese, & Fivush, 1996.) Researchers in a San Diego study (Teale, 1986) reported nine domains that they described as follows: Daily Living Activities, Entertainment, School-Related Activities, Work, Religion, Interpersonal Communication, Participating in Information Networks, Storybook Time, and Literacy for the Sake of Teaching/Learning Literacy. The social nature of these events from the researchers' reports is obvious and often entails relatively constrained reference to the actual printed text and much use of talk about the social world in which the text plays a part. In many of these events, children are often present but not physically involved with the text; at other times, such as storybook time or school-related events, children are the focus of the involvement with texts.

Heath (1983) reported that children would often be present in events such as newspaper reading or form completion by adults in which the text itself was secondary to both the social interaction and oral discussion about how the text should be interpreted or negotiated. In situations like this, it would be reasoned that children would learn how to use texts functionally to get things done. In contrast, some researchers have reported times in which a text is not even present, yet participants use written language structures or registers. Heath (1986) reported that when families are in cars making trips together, their language becomes more decontextualized as members try to relate or refer to nonpresent events. Scollon and Scollon (1981) showed how their 2-year-old used written language structures and intonation in dictating stories into a tape recorder.

Documenting of differences across domains is not clearcut but is suggestive. Health (1983) documented differences in parental storybook reading styles and how they expected their children to participate in storybook reading. These differences were tied to social class, ethnicity, and age of the child. Working-class African American families in her study did not read storybooks with their young children, although they took part in other literacy events with them. Working-class White families read to their children but began to limit the child's participation from active verbal responding to quiet listening or responding to low-level, literal retelling elicitations when children reached about age 3. Prior to that age, children were encouraged to respond actively and allowed to make imaginative ties to other aspects of their social world. At age 3 and after, children of mainstream families were also expected to listen to longer stretches of a storybook than they did when they were younger, but their imaginative verbal interactions were still encouraged.

One of the most important findings from studies of family literacy is the variability within socioeconomic and ethnic groups (see Miller, Nemoianu, & DeJong, 1986; McGill-Franzen & Lanford, 1994; Baker et al., 1999). First, no group has been found to have a "deprived literacy background," if by that we meant that the children have no literacy. All families studied thus far take part in literacy events, and children are included in these events. This finding matches the finding in elicitation studies that children of all social backgrounds readily show some levels of emergent reading and writing behaviors. Second, these studies have shed light on findings masked by group comparisons that show socioeconomic status (SES) and ethnic group differences. There is great variability within any given group. Just simple participation in a given group does not automatically mean that a child has a particular kind of literacy development. Again, this finding is relevant to the reports of elicitation studies that there are no major differences in the patterns of emergent literacy development.

It has been one of the contributions of emergent literacy research to devise methods so children will demonstrate their emergent literacy. Child language development and cognitive development research has been plagued by criticisms of the artificiality of tasks used and the threat that such task demands underestimate children's knowledge. Many of the tasks and settings used in the following research has grown from observations of the home literacy studies. While our definitions of natural are vague (see Teale, 1984), they seem to involve the criterion that the child seems to do the task without the need for adult pressure, becomes engrossed in the task, and seems to perform with patterns similar to those observed without research intervention. Not all of these studies involve researcher elicitation or structuring, however; naturalistic research occurs in these studies as well.

## READING TO CHILDREN AND CHILDREN READING EMERGENTLY

Storybook reading appears to be a fairly widespread social routine among families of differing backgrounds, across many literate cultures (Bus & van IJzendoorn, 1988; Heath, 1983; Ninio, 1980; Snow & Ninio, 1986; Snow, 1983; Snow & Goldfield, 1983; van Kleeck, Alexander, Virgil, & Templeton, 1996; Wan, 2000). Snow and Ninio (1986) uses the notion of a routine to mean a recurring event that has its own event structure. Young children appear to be very dependent on and comforted by routines in daily living, but routines appear to serve an additional function. They have expected social roles for participants and expected subroutines. Storybooks themselves can be conceived to be social products in which cultural values and concepts about the nature of young children are embedded. Snow and Ninio (1986) claimed that, in the process of reading to their children across ages and times, both Israeli and U.S. parents negotiate social contracts with their children that move children in successive stages from oral interaction about the physical nature of the text (it's for reading and not for eating), closer and closer to responding to the oral reading of the actual words of the text. Sulzby and Teale (1987; Teale & Sulzby, 1987) reported that low- and middle-income Anglo and Hispanic parents in the San Antonio area gradually moved from an oral interactive storybook reading style to a "let's listen to the story" style in which the words of the text were read verbatim. They further reported, however, that each of the eight focal children in their study began to voluntarily reenact the texts independently.

There have been a number of studies (Doake, 1985; Pappas, 1987; Teale, Martinez, & Glass, 1989; Wade & Moore, 1996; De Temple & Tabors, 1996) of children beginning to reenact or read emergently from familiar storybooks. Sulzby (1985a, 1988; Sulzby & Teale, 1987) devised a simple elicitation of asking children to "Read me your book," after books have been read repeatedly to them. Sulzby (1988) reported that children from ages 2 through 5 in a day-care setting almost all responded by reading when asked to after their teachers had read books to them repeatedly. The remainder responded in some appropriate fashion, including reading interactively with an adult. When presented with a favorite book from home after 11 months of day-care storybook reading, however, all the children gave an independent "emergent reading" of the book (except for one child who brought in an obviously new book). (See also Edwards, 1994; Walter, 1994.) Sulzby and Teale (1987) found that low-income incipiently bilingual (Spanish–English) preschoolers also read emergently in both languages at ages 4 and 5. They suggest, in comparing these data with their home literacy study, that children gradually internalize a form of reading that has been socially created from the interaction

between the parent and child. Additionally, this social creation appears to be shaped at least in part by a set of cultural expectations about what the "bedtime story" (Heath, 1983) is or should be.

Storybook reading has become a research arena for the examination of social/cultural differences and interventions (Neuman, 1996; Rodriguez, 1999). Following suggestions from Heath's (1982a, 1982b, 1983; Heath with Thomas, 1984) research, Edwards (1989) found that African American Head Start mothers in Louisiana with very low literacy skills themselves needed to be taught how to read to their children. Whitehurst et al. (1988) were able to train mothers of 21- to 35-month-old toddlers to vary their bookreading linguistic interchanges and found subsequent significant increases in the children's expressive language usage. Similar studies were done by Hockenberger, Goldstein, and Haas (1999) and Baker, Sonnenshein, and Serpell (1999). Pellegrini and his colleagues (Pellegrini, Brody, & Sigel, 1985; Pellegrini, Perlmutter, Galda, & Brody, 1990) have found that most parents of even language-delayed children or low-income African American children make some accommodation for the abilities of their children during reading interactions. (See also Kaderavek & Sulzby, 1997, 2000.) They found that African American Head Start mothers in Georgia (with higher literacy levels than Edwards' sample) used a more interactive style with expository texts than with narratives. They showed sensitivity also to the level of their children's familiarity with the text. Bus and IJzendoorn (1988), studying emotional development in relation to emergent literacy, found different patterns of interaction depending on the text type. In studying parent–child dyads in The Netherlands, they found that children who were judged to be securely attached to their mothers responded more actively than children judged to be insecurely attached and also required less control strategies by the parents.

These studies of storybook reading were typically conducted within a Vygotskiian (Vygotsky, 1978, 1981) framework. It was assumed that children internalize patterns from social interaction and that a facilitative framework in which parents raise expectations only in relation to children's increasing abilities would be beneficial. Indeed, most of the findings appear to be consistent with this outlook.

A question that continues to be explored is how emergent storybook reading eventuates in conventional reading. The finding that reading to children is associated with higher subsequent achievement scores has been replicated many times with different methodologies (see Teale, 1984; Wells, 1985; Otto, 1993). (See also Senechal, LeFevre, Daley, & Thomas, 1996, and Barclay & Benelli, 1997.) Sulzby (1985a, 1988, 1991) has classified children's emergent storybook reading behavior into an 11-point classification scheme with developmental properties. The final point on that scale is reading conventionally from print and the subcategories just preceding conventional reading indicate that children are beginning to coordinate knowledge about letter-sound relationships, about word stability, and about comprehension of written language just prior to the time they begin to read conventionally, moving strategically across these bodies of knowledge. We need much more research into the topic of the transition into conventional literacy, both as it is seen in reading and in writing, the next topic for review.

## WRITING AS AN EMERGENT PHENOMENON

As with storybook reading, research in emergent writing has been heavily influenced by studies of home literacy. Refer to Sulzby (1992) for a review of the literature. Read's (1970, 1975) influential study of invented spelling was based on hypotheses that arose from retrospective reports and naturalistically gathered writing samples from parents of preschoolers. Clay (1975) also used voluntary compositions by young children. Teale (1986), Taylor (1983) and Taylor and Dorsey-Gaines (1988) observed children writing at home with their parents. Taylor reported that parents treated scribbling and other forms of writing as writing and called it writing.

Rowe (1987, 1988) and Dyson (1982a, 1982b, 1983, 1984, 1985, 1987, 1988) used naturalistic techniques to "hang out" where children in preschools, kindergartens, and first grades write. Rowe used a technique of writing in front of children while they write and observing their social interaction. Dyson observed how children negotiate or change a teacher's assigned task as they also negotiate their various social worlds with peers in the classroom.

Sulzby (1983) and Harste, Woodward, and Burke (1984) elicited story compositions by young children by encouraging and accepting any form of writing produced by the child. They used techniques derived from observations of home literacy studies, particularly the technique of asking children to write without any apology or acceptance of the idea that children cannot write. Sulzby (1983, 1988) reported the use of the prompt, "It doesn't have to be like grown-up writing, just write it your own way," as an effective means of eliciting children's emergent writing.

Other researchers (Ferreiro, 1978, 1985; Ferreiro & Gomez Palacio, 1982; Ferreiro & Teberosky, 1982; Tolchinsky-Landsmann & Levin, 1985, 1987) have asked children to write dictated words or sentences composed by adults. While the initial elicitation for the child to write words, phrases, or sentences from lists is similar to that used by researchers of invented spelling (Gentry, 1980; Henderson & Beers, 1980; Morris, 1980, 1981), the follow-up interviews and analyses are quite different. The Piagetian-based researchers typically conduct clinical interviews in order to infer children's concepts about what writing is, how it gets done, and how it can be read from. They tend to interpret children's responses along lines of epistemological distinctions about children's underlying concepts of representation (see the following); the invented spelling researchers tend to be more concerned with the exact orthographic patterns that children are acquiring and their sequence. Recent research in invented spelling (e.g., Chi, 1988; Ferroli & Shanahan, 1987; Richgels, 1986a, 1986b; Richgels, McGee, Hernandez, & Williams, 1988; Poole-Hayes & Dionne, 1996) has begun using tasks in which invented spelling has been elicited in sentential contexts and across compositional tasks, rather than simply from lists of isolated words.

Children have been observed to write in emergent forms from infancy onward. Researchers of home literacy (Taylor, 1983; also see Teale, 1986) have noted that parents use the simple terms "write" and "read" when describing their toddlers'

and preschoolers' emergent literacy behaviors, rather independently of how close to conventional the forms are. Parents occasionally may refer to the child's writing as scribbling, but often they just use the unhedged term "writing" to refer to emergent forms and functions. In homes where adults encourage children's interaction with print, children are typically included in "literacy events" in which writing is used functionally. However, children themselves often write spontaneously, just as they spontaneously do independent emergent storybook readings.

From naturalistic observations of this spontaneous writing behavior, as well as from more manipulative studies, we can begin to build a picture of when children begin to write and the forms that such writing takes. Sulzby (1989; Sulzby & Teale, 1985) has offered one sequence for when mainstream children from the U.S. typically begin to write with different writing forms such as scribbling, drawing, nonphonetic letterstrings, invented spelling, and conventional orthography. This sequence is generally comparable to some of the reports from Harste, Woodward, and Burke (1984; Harste & Woodward, 1989; also see Bissex, 1980 for the latter end of this development). Both sets of researchers refer primarily to the forms of writing used in connected discourse.

Tolchinsky-Landsmann and Levin (1985, 1987), drawing from the work of Ferreiro (1978; Ferreiro & Teberosky, 1982), offer a somewhat different sequence; the Spanish-speaking children are depicted as showing writing forms at a somewhat older age than Sulzby reports, but only efforts in which a quantitative match between written units and the requested terms were treated as analyzable. In other words, the researchers looked for matches between spoken and written words (thus holistic relationships between intended text and forms of writing such as continuous scribble or drawing would not be analyzed). This age difference runs counter to expectations because the Ferreiro methods tend to use requests for or observation of children writing isolated words or phrases and sentences suggested by an adult. Children in U.S. English-speaking samples tend to use more "advanced" writing forms with smaller linguistic units, such as words or phrases, and less advanced appearing forms for their own compositions of connected discourse. Bearing these differences in mind, let us examine the two sequences.

Tolchinsky-Landsmann and Levin (1987) suggest that the aspect of linearity is typically shown by Ferreiro's Spanish-speaking children between the ages of 3 and 4. The child will have neither sufficient marks to represent syllabic or phonemic elements nor a stereotypical estimate of how long a "word" should be; instead, the child may use one or two elements per sentence, representing only the nouns or may use a long string with no indication of a systematic relationship between marks and speech stimulus. However, 4- to 5-year-olds begin to try to use hypotheses about length of word and referential characteristics and come into conflicts that eventually lead, about a year later, to beginning explorations of phonetically based writing. In applying Ferreiro's analytic scheme, Tolchinsky-Landsmann and Levin (1987) noted that forms such as drawing and "long series of characters, often ligated, that could not be counted precisely" (p. 135) were treated as unanalyzable.

Using children's free attempts to compose stories, letters, or notes, Sulzby (1989) suggests that nonletter forms such as early scribbling or drawing frequently function as writing for the young child. Undifferentiated scribble begins at about age 12 to 18 months. This becomes differentiated into drawing and writinglike scribble between ages 2 and 3, for most U.S. mainstream children. Drawing may be used by the child either as drawing itself or as writing; children continue an ambivalence about whether drawing can or cannot be writing from this age well into kindergarten and sometimes first grade. Children typically begin to write with letters during the third, but sometimes as late as the fourth year. Most of this writing is comprised of nonphonetic letterstrings, but the child may also produce some conventional-appearing items (particularly the child's name) but not hold a conventional concept for them. Also, with any given writing form, children can use a range of compositional and reading systems (Sulzby, 1989). While it can appear earlier or later for a few children, invented spelling typically makes its appearance during kindergarten or first grade. Nurss (1988) made a useful compilation of various reports of age of acquisition of writing forms from 1936 to the present time and then used these in examining writing by Norwegian kindergarten (ages 3 to 6) children. The Norwegian children followed a similar sequence from those proposed by Sulzby and Ferreiro, but more in line with the time of acquisition suggested by Ferreiro. Unfortunately, the task used was to ask children to draw and then write; drawing was excluded from being considered a writing form.

It has become clear that it is insufficient simply to look at the forms of writing that children use. Clay (1975), Ferreiro (1986) and Sulzby (1983, 1989) warn that researchers and practitioners alike must examine children's underlying conceptions. Clay (1975) looked beyond the forms to underlying principles such as linearity and recurrence and resisted treating the appearance of forms of writing as alone being indicative of development. When Galda, Pellegrini, and Cox (1989) treated a logical analysis of the forms of writing as a developmental scheme and then correlated preschoolers' use of these forms with emergent reading, they found a low correlation and concluded an independent line of development for reading and writing. Unfortunately, such a conclusion cannot be drawn from such a design. However, the question of the relationships between emergent reading and writing is an important and complex one, perhaps changing over time as suggested by the theory of Stanovich (1986) and by Shanahan's (1984) research with school-age children. Much more research is needed before strong conclusions can be drawn about the relationships between reading and writing during the emergent period.

Ferreiro (1978, 1985, 1986; Ferreiro & Gomez Palacio, 1982; Ferreiro & Teberosky, 1982) has also investigated children's interpretations of how different pieces of writing can be read and has asked children to produce writing. She also interviewed the children about the relationship between the forms of their writing, their rereading, and the symbolic relationships involved, using clinical interviews. Ferreiro's work does not furnish an inventory of writing forms, as such.

Sulzby (1983, 1985b; Sulzby, Barnhart, & Hieshima, 1989) also claims that looking at the appearance of forms of writing alone is misleading. In a study of kindergarten children, Sulzby (1981) analyzed children's rereading from dictated and handwritten stories and devised a seven-point categorization of

emergent writing. That categorization system glossed over the forms of writing and focused almost entirely on rereading. It furnished useful rankings of children and correlations with other measures, but she has cautioned (Sulzby, 1988; Sulzby, Barnhart, & Hieshima, 1989) that it lacked the precision needed to understand the relationship between writing and rereading.

Sulzby (1989) designed a study of five classrooms in which children were invited to write "your own way" after a discussion and modeling of ways in which kindergarteners often write. Over kindergarten and first grade, teachers and researchers did not overtly push children to shift writing forms. Scribble, drawing, nonphonetic letter strings, invented spelling, and conventional orthography were the major writing forms used by children throughout the study, although other forms such as rebus, abbreviation, or idiosyncratic forms showed up on rare occasions, usually in first grade.

Children only gradually began to produce conventionally readable writing (writing in full invented spelling and or conventional orthography). Children did not immediately read conventionally themselves from this readable writing that had been phonetically encoded (Kamberelis & Sulzby, 1988). Throughout kindergarten and first grade children continued to move back and forth across forms as writing, even as they approached the ability to write conventionally. Change was found, not so much in the forms of writing, but in the language that surrounded the writing–compositional and rereading. By the end of first grade, however, all the children were writing conventionally. Similar patterns of development have been reported by Allen et al. (1989; Allen & Carr, 1989), and by Fang (1999). Vukelich and Edwards (1988) found similar patterns when they collected weekly writing samples from children in a university-run kindergarten. Gutman and Sulzby (2000) also explored the notion of motivation during writing tasks with African-American kindergarten children, when they explored the conditions under which the children demonstrated interest in the writing task.

In summary, it can be seen that emergent reading and writing are robust behaviors with young children; children show them freely in conducive settings. Additionally, while the patterns are not *simple*, researchers are making good progress in describing the paths of development for certain parts of reading and writing. However, the picture is far from being complete.

In the studies of home literacy, storybook reading, and writing, the role of talking was often observed and analyzed by the researchers. The section that follows recounts recent shifts in concepts about how oral and written language are related and the roles they may play in emergent literacy.

## ORAL LANGUAGE AND WRITTEN LANGUAGE

During the 1970s we saw an explosion of research in child language acquisition, which almost universally meant oral language acquisition. Instead of being viewed as faulty imitators of adult language, children were viewed as being active in the construction of language, creating hypotheses about how language operates, and testing these hypotheses in communicative contexts— texts that were primarily face-to-face and dependent on oral speech. Oral language was viewed as being relatively easy to acquire and somewhat consistent across cultures. While views of oral language acquisition have changed and become more complex—adults are viewed as being more active in the process that is viewed as being interactive, the speed and ease of acquisition without teaching has been questioned, and cross-cultural differences are viewed as greater and more important—the basic idea that oral language is actively constructed by the children in interaction with the environment has been maintained. Children's concepts about oral language are different from those of adults and change predictably as children grow older.

Similarly, written language has come to be viewed as a developmental phenomenon and children have come to be viewed as active constructors of concepts about written language. Coinciding in time with this view has been a resurgence in interest in oral and written language relationships by linguists, literacy critics, historians, psychologists, and anthropologists (Chafe, 1982; Goody, 1977, 1982; Heath, 1982a; Ong, 1982; Rubin, 1978; Shatz, 1984; Tannen, 1982, 1984). A number of researchers (e.g., Harste, Woodward, & Burke, 1984; King & Rentel, 1981; Martlew, 1988; Scollon & Scollon, 1981; Sulzby, 1981; Pellegrini, Galda, Dresden, & Cox, 1991; Pellegrini & Galda, 1996) posited that we need to think about the child as acquiring both oral language and written language from within a given cultural background. They conducted studies that focused on signs that the child is learning about both oral and written language during the preschool years. These early studies led to a number of conclusions.

First, speech and oral language are not synonymous; children's speech can contains signs that they are acquiring knowledge about the ability to use written language patterns or registers long before they are reading and writing conventionally. Children's ability to speak with oral and written language registers has been used as an important way to investigate emergent literacy. Purcell-Gates (1988) found that children who have been read to extensively before schooling used features of a written language register when they were asked to create a story to fit a wordless picturebook. Sulzby (1985a, 1988) found that when children "read" from favorite storybooks, some children use language that sounds conversational, others use a storytelling structure and intonation, and others use written language patterns. Pappas' (1986, 1988; Pappas & Brown, 1987, 1988; see also Purcell-Gates, 1988) research on protoreading (using a term adapted from Halliday, 1975) concluded that children often use a written language register in response to both narrative and expository texts.

Second, written language is not synonymous with print. Writers have to learn not only the conventions of encoding in print but also what it is that gets written and how it is expressed. King and Rentel's (1981) research with conventional writers showed that children in grades 1 to 4 still use patterns more appropriate to an oral, face-to-face context when they write.

The notions of *contextualization*, *decontextualization*, and *recontextualization* have been important in emergent literacy research. The reader is viewed as having needs for a text to provide sufficient context for it to be able to be read when the author is not present (Olson, 1977). It is relatively well established that young children often use features more appropriate to an oral, interactive context when writing; one measure of growth in writing is the ability to provide sufficient contextual cues within the text itself (Cox, Shanahan, & Sulzby,

1990). Conversely, children often use a written language register when composing with unreadable forms of writing (Sulzby, Barnhart, & Hieshima, 1989). In a somewhat different vein, researchers in metalinguistic awareness (Papapdropoulou & Sinclair, 1974) and emergent literacy (Ferreiro, 1986; Ferreiro & Teberosky, 1982; Tolchinsky-Landsmann & Levin, 1987; see also Barnhart, 1986) have shown that children do not necessarily expect that everything they say or that someone else says needs to be represented graphically: the 3-year-old may think that only nouns are "parts" of a spoken sentence or need to be written.

The research just summarized and much of the other research in this chapter provides some evidence that the young child is acquiring both oral and written language prior to conventional reading and writing. It seems likely that sorting out oral and written language relationships across different tasks, texts, and situations may be important learning for young children. Research in this area has begun to provide evidence for children's development in all of the "language arts"—listening and speaking as well as reading and writing. As can be seen from the following, literacy itself can be broadened to encompass other forms of symbolizing in addition to traditional reading and writing.

## OTHER FORMS OF SYMBOLIZING

In the research previously reviewed, we dealt with the child's emerging concepts for storybooks as defined both by the conventional printed text, as defined through parent–child interaction, and as defined by the child's reenactment of books. We dealt with writing as the child's use of forms in order to compose a message and dealt with drawing as a form of writing. Here, we discuss a brief bit of research and much speculation about how writing and other forms operate as symbol systems for the young child. Children appear to learn about the symbols used in writing and how to read them in a complex of symbols; part of their task is learning to sort out the symbol systems. Additionally, however, communicating in writing and reading from texts appears to involve interpreting alternative forms. Highly proficient reading and writing, which we assume should be an attainable outcome as children grow older, involves varying degrees of interpreting various symbol systems of which alphabetic writing is only part, although a crucial part.

We know, for example, that children often confuse the metalinguistic labels and their referents (word and sound, letter and number, drawing and writing). On the surface, these problems often appear to be simply an issue of getting a term properly connected (e.g., Mickish, 1974; Papandropoulou & Sinclair, 1974; Pontecorvo, Orsolini, Zucchermaglio, & Rossi, 1987). However, the issues appear to be far more complex. There are at least three possibilities whenever a child makes a "confusion," any one of and any combination of which might be in operation. The first possibility, that of confusing label and referent, may indeed be the case, but does not account for the persistence of the naming/referring problem that we see over the early childhood years. Second, the child may be seeing a connection between the forms of symbolizing that we no longer consciously think about. Third, the environment may be offering examples that lead the child to see relationships that we are no longer unaware of.

Let us consider drawing and writing, for example. At around age 2, many children begin to distinguish between scribble that they use as drawing and scribble that they use as writing. They may request an adult to "write Grandma" or "draw Grandma" and protest if the adult misinterprets their request, even if they reversed the labels. If confusion about labels were the only issue, simple feedback should correct this problem.

A number of children appear to be ambivalent about whether drawing can be a form of writing well into kindergarten age. They seem to use drawing appropriately when asked to draw, yet they may also use drawing when asked to write. Additionally, they "read" back from the drawing, sometimes even agreeing to "point while you are reading." Only gradually do children reach a point of articulating the differences in a stable fashion (Sulzby, 1983). At this point, children typically show a clear distinction between written text and drawing used as illustration. At this point in development, children begin to use rebus, rather than using rebus as a lower point in development to aid the understanding of letter–sound based symbolism. Another theoretical speculation (Sulzby, 1989) is that some children begin to deal with the "text" or "composition" as being both the entirety of the orthographically encoded passage and any also surrounding illustrations, similarly to the way in which many publishing authors do. Thus, drawing for the child becomes reorganized in a different manner into writing and representation systems in general.

We must, however, consider how children experience drawing in acts of reading and writing. Astorga (1999) for example, describes how illustrations faciliate the reading process for second-language learners. Illustrations are a key, if not primary, part of texts for young children (Smolkin, Conlon, & Yaden, 1988). Illustrations so dominate many labeling and concept books that the child may have difficulty noticing the print on the page. Additionally, children's illustrators often mix media by inserting dialogue balloons, labels, or expletives into the drawings (Sulzby, 1988). Thus, from children's books it is not often immediately evident which form of symbol is being read from. Again, if we invite children to "write a story" or "write a book" we may be inviting the mixing of the media. An issue for research is keeping the task definitions straight in our own designs and being alert for child redefinitions.

As seen in the work from Project Zero (Gardner & Wolfe, 1983; Gardner, Wolfe, & Smith, 1975; Wolfe & Gardner, 1981), children's use of drawing has its own developmental track as does writing. We need additional research that examines drawing used for drawing purposes and writing used for writing purposes, as well as the substitution of one for the other, both overtly at the graphic level and covertly through the means with which children compose and talk about their creations.

Ferreiro (1986; Ferreiro & Teberosky, 1982; see also Pontecorvo, 1984) has addressed some attention to numbers as a form of symbolization, contrasting them with letters. Numbers have a different relationship to pronunciation and to referential meaning than do letters. Numbers may name a set, serve as a counting unit, or indicate ordinal value; thus they are ambiguous within their canonical symbol system (Fuson, 1988). They have no assigned sound value and the Arabic numerals, for example, are pronounced in different ways in different languages (Ferreiro & Teberosky, 1982). Letters name only themselves. Yet letters also indicate sounds as they occur in words. Letters "name themselves" and stand for sounds. If a child does not yet understand these complexities, the two forms may appear to be highly similar. They are formed within the same units of physical space, through the same media, and in acts of accounting or inventorying.

Another tool for writing as well as reading is the computer, which is a machine with multifaceted potential, depending both on the hardware configuration and software used with it (Papert, 1980). It appears that young children can use the computer as an emergent literacy tool (Murphy & Appel, 1984; Sulzby, Olson, & Johnston, 1989; Shilling, 1997) and as a tool for writing collaboration in the early conventional period (Dickinson, 1986; Heap, 1989; Escobedo & Allen, 1996). Emergent writers move across representation systems, depending on what the software will allow, in many unpredicted manners. Exploring children's emergent writing with different kinds of computer capabilities is an area of research that is just in its infancy but offers important avenues to study children's development (Sulzby, Olson, & Johnston, 1989; Kelly & O'Kelly, 1993; Shilling, 1997; Eisenwine & Hunt, 2000). For example, children explore notation systems for music without the computer (Bamberger, 1986), but computer programs now allow the child to pick out a tune on an onscreen piano keyboard and see the notation for staves, notes, and timing created on the screen immediately. We have little idea of the effects of such representational possibilities on children's growing sense of what it means to be literate and how they can create, using such evolving tools.

We should not forget, in all of this speculation, that the child is working out relationships that may not have immediate resolution or may be resolved differently as children grow older or gain experience than we currently might think possible (see Stanovich, 1986). Harste, Woodward, and Burke (1984) have alerted researchers to the importance of considering a broad range of semiotic functions when studying children's literacy development.

## References

Allen, J. B., & Carr, E. (1989). Collaborative learning among kindergarten writers: James learns how to learn at school. In J. B. Allen & J. M. Mason (Eds.), *Risk makers, risk takers, risk breakers: Reducing the risks for young literacy learners* (pp. 30–47). Portsmouth, NH: Heinemann.

Allen, J. B., Clark, W., Cook, M., Crane, P., Fallon, I., Hoffman, L., Jennings, K. S., & Sours, M. A. (1989). Reading and writing development in whole language kindergartens. In J. Mason (Ed.), *Reading and writing connections* (pp. 121–146). Needham Heights, MA: Allyn & Bacon.

Allen, J. B., & Mason, J. M. (Eds.) (1989). *Risk makers, risk takers, risk breakers: Reducing the risks for young literacy learners.* Portsmouth, NH: Heinemann.

Anderson, A. B., & Stokes, S. J. (1984). Social and institutional influences on the development and practice of literacy. In H. Goelman, A. Oberg, & F. Smith (Eds.), *Awakening to literacy* (pp. 24–37). Exeter, NH: Heinemann.

Anderson, A. B., Teale, W. H., & Estrada, E. (1980). Low-income children's preschool literacy experiences: Some naturalistic observations. *The Quarterly Newsletter of the Laboratory of Comparative Human Cognition, 2,* 59–65.

Astorga, M. (1999). The text-image interaction and second language learning. *Australian Journal of Language and Learning, 22*(3), 213–233.

Baker, L., Sonnenschein, S., & Serpell, R. (1999). A five-year comparison of actual and recommended parental practices for promoting children's literacy development. (Report No. PS 028 034). Baltimore: National Reading Research Center. (ERIC Document Reproduction Service No. ED 435 466)

Bamberger, J. (1986). Cognitive issues in the development of musically gifted children. In R. J. Sternberg & J. Davidson, *Conceptions of giftedness.* New York: Cambridge University Press.

Barclay, K., & Benelli, C. (1997, Fall). Opening the world of literacy with infants and toddlers. Research Highlights. *Dimensions of Early Childhood 1997, 25*(4), 9–16.

Barnhart, J. E. (1986). *Written language concepts and cognitive development in kindergarten children.* Unpublished doctoral dissertation, Northwestern University, Evanston, IL.

Betts, E. A. (1946). *Foundations of reading instruction.* New York: American Book.

Bissex, G. (1980). *GNYS at work: A child learns to write and read.* Cambridge, MA: Harvard University Press.

Bus, A. G., & van IJzendoorn, M. H. (1988). Mother-child interactions, attachment and emergent literacy. A cross-sectional study. *Child Development, 59,* 1262–1272.

Bus, A. G., & van IJzendoorn, M. H. (1997). Affective dimension of mother-infant picturebook reading. *Journal of School Psychology 1997, 35*(1), 47–60.

Chafe, W. A. (1982). Integration and involvement in speaking, writing, and oral literature. In D. Tannen (Ed.), *Spoken and written language: Exploring orality and literacy* (pp. 35–54). Norwood, NJ: Ablex.

Chi, M. M.-Y. (1988). Invented spelling/writing in Chinese-speaking children: The developmental patterns. *National Reading Conference Yearbook, 37,* 385–296.

Clark, E. V. (1978). Awareness of language: Some evidence from what children say and do. In A. Sinclair, R. J. Jarvella, & W. M. Levelt (Eds.), *The child's conception of language.* New York: Springer-Verlag.

Clark, M. M. (1976). *Young fluent readers: What can they teach us?* London: Heinemann.

Clay, M. M. (1975). *What did I write?* Auckland, New Zealand: Heinemann.

Clay, M. M. (1993). *An observation survey of early literacy achievement.* Portsmouth, NH: Heinemann.

Clay, M. M. (1998). Literacy awareness: From acts to awareness. In M. M. Clay, *By different paths to common outcomes.* Portland, ME: Stenhouse.

Cox, B. E., Shanahan, T., & Sulzby, E. (1990). Good and poor elementary readers' use of cohesion in writing. *Reading Research Quarterly, 25,* 47–65.

De Temple, J. M., & Tabors, P. O. (1996, August). *Children's story retelling as a predictor of early reading achievement.* Paper presented at the biennial meeting of the International Society for the Study of Behavioral Development, Quebec City, Quebec, Canada. (ERIC Document Reproduction Service No. ED 403 543)

Dickinson, D. K. (1986). Cooperation, collaboration and a computer: Integrating a computer into a first-second grade writing program. *Research in the Teaching of English, 20*(4), 357–378.

Dickinson, D. (1989). Effects of a shared reading program on one Head Start language and literacy environment. In J. B. Allen & J. M. Mason (Eds.), *Risk makers, risk takers, risk breakers* (pp. 125–153). Portsmouth, NH: Heinemann.

Doake, D. (1985). Reading-like behavior: Its role in learning to read. In A. Jagger & M. T. Smith-Burke (Eds.), *Observing the language learner* (pp. 82–98). Newark, DE: International Reading Association.

Downing, J. (1979). *Reading and reasoning.* New York: Springer-Verlag.

Downing, J., & Oliver, P. (1973–1974). The child's conception of a word. *Reading Research Quarterly, 9,* 568–582.

Durkin, D. (1966). *Children who read early.* New York: Teachers College Press.

Dyson, A. H. (1982a). Reading, writing and language: Young children solving the written language puzzle. *Language Arts, 59,* 829–839.

Dyson, A. H. (1982b). The emergence of visible language: Interrelationships between drawing and early writing. *Visible Language, 16,* 360–381.

Dyson, A. H. (1983). The role of oral language in early writing. *Research in the Teaching of English, 17,* 1–30.

Dyson, A. H. (1984). Learning to write/learning to do school: Emergent writers' interpretations of school literacy tasks. *Research in the Teaching of English, 18,* 233–264.

Dyson, A. H. (1985). Individual differences in emergent writing. In M. Farr (Ed.), *Advances in writing research, Vol. 1: Children's early writing development* (pp. 59–126). Norwood, NJ: Ablex.

Dyson, A. H. (1987). Individual differences in beginning composing: An orchestral vision of learning to compose. *Written Communication, 4,* 411–422.

Dyson, A. H. (1988). Negotiating among multiple worlds: The space/time dimensions of young children's composing. *Research in the Teaching of English, 22*(4), 355–390.

Edwards, L. H. (1994). Kid's eye view of reading: Kindergartners talk about learning how to read. *Childhood Education, 70*(3), 137–141.

Edwards, P. A. (1989). Supporting lower SES mothers' attempts to provide scaffolding for bookreading. In J. B. Allen & J. Mason (Eds.), *Reading the risks for young learners: Literacy practices and policies.* Portsmouth, NH: Heinemann.

Eisenwine, M. J., & Hunt, D. A. (2000, March). Using a computer in literacy groups with emergent readers. *Reading Teacher 2000, 53*(6), 456–458.

Escobedo, T. H., & Allen, M. (1996, April). *Preschoolers' emergent writing at the computer.* Paper presented at the annual meeting of the American Educational Research Association, New York, NY. (ERIC Document Reproduction Service No. ED 402 342)

Ezell, H. K., Gonzales, M. D., & Randolph, E. (2000). Emergent literacy skills of migrant Mexican American preschoolers. *Communication Disorders Quarterly, 21*(3), 147–153.

Fang, Z. (1999). Expanding the vista of emergent writing research: Implications for early childhood educators. *Early Childhood Journal, 26*(3), 179–182.

Ferreiro, E. (1978). What is written in a written sentence? A developmental answer. *Journal of Education, 160,* 25–39.

Ferreiro, E. (1985). Literacy development: A psychogenetic perspective. In D. Olson, N. Torrance, & A. Hildyard (Eds.), *Literacy, language, and learning* (pp. 217–228). Cambridge, England: Cambridge University Press.

Ferreiro, E. (1986). The interplay between information and assimilation in beginning literacy. In W. H. Teale & E. Sulzby (Eds.), *Emergent literacy: Writing and reading* (pp. 15-49). Norwood, NJ: Ablex.

Ferreiro, E., & Gómez Palacio, M. (1982). *Análisis de las pertubaciones en el proceso aprendizaje de la lectoescritura* [Analysis of variations in the process of literacy development]. (5 vols.) Mexico City: Office of the Director General of Special Education.

Ferreiro, E., & Teberosky, A. (1982). *Literacy before schooling.* Exeter, NH: Heinemann.

Ferroli, L., & Shanahan, T. (1987). Kindergarten spelling: Explaining its relationship to first-grade reading. *National Reading Conference Yearbook, 36,* 93-99.

Fuson, K. (1988). *Children's counting and concepts of number.* New York: Springer-Verlag.

Galda, L., Pellegrini, A. D., & Cox, S. (1989). A short-term longitudinal study of preschoolers' emergent literacy. *Research in the Teaching of English, 23,* 292-309.

Gardner, H., & Wolf, D. (1983). Waves and streams of symbolization: Notes on the development of symbolic capacities in young children. In D. Rogers & J. Sloboda (Eds.), *The acquisition of symbolic skills* (pp. 1-37). New York: Plenum.

Gardner, H., Wolfe, D., & Smith, A. (1975). Artistic symbols in early childhood. *NYU Education Quarterly, 6,* 13-21.

Gates, A. I. (1937). The necessary mental age for beginning reading. *Elementary School Journal, 37,* 497-508.

Gates, A. I., & Bond, G. L. (1936). Reading readiness: A study of factors determining success and failure in beginning reading. *Teachers College Record, 37,* 679-685.

Gates, A. I., Bond, G. L., & Russell, D. H. (1939). *Methods of determining reading readiness.* New York: Bureau of Publications, Teachers College, Columbia University.

Gentry, J. R. (1980). Early spelling strategies. *Elementary School Journal, 79,* 88-92.

Goodman, Y. (1980). The roots of literacy. In M. P. Douglass (Ed.), *Claremont reading conference 44th yearbook.* Claremont, CA: Claremont Graduate School.

Goodman, Y. (1984). The development of initial literacy. In H. Goelman, A. Oberg, & F. Smith (Eds.), *Awakening to literacy* (pp. 102-109). Exeter, NH: Heinemann.

Goodman, Y., & Altweger, B. (1981). *Print awareness in preschool children: A study of the development of literacy in preschool children.* (Occasional Paper No. 4). Tucson, AZ: University of Arizona, Program in Language and Literacy, Arizona Center for Research and Development, College of Education.

Goody, J. (1977). *The domestication of the savage mind.* Cambridge, England: Cambridge University Press.

Goody, J. (1982). Alternative paths to knowledge in oral and literature cultures. In D. Tannen (Ed.), *Spoken and written language: Exploring orality and literacy* (pp. 201-215). Norwood, NJ: Ablex.

Gutman, L. M., & Sulzby, E. (2000). The role of autonomy-support versus control in the emergent writing behaviors of African-American kindergarten children. *Reading Research and Instruction, 39*(2), 170-184.

Haden, C. A., Reese, E., & Fivush, R. (1996). Mothers' extratextual comments during storybook reading: Stylistic differences over time and across texts. *Discourse Processes, 21*(2), 135-169.

Halliday, M. A. K. (1975). *Learning how to mean: Explorations in the development of language.* New York: Elsevier.

Harste, J. C., & Woodward, V. A. (1989). Fostering needed change in early literacy programs. In D. S. Strickland & L. M. Morrow (Eds.), *Emerging literacy: Young children learn to read and write* (pp. 147-159). Newark, DE: International Reading Association.

Harste, J. C., Woodward, V. A., & Burke, C. L. (1984). *Language stories and literacy lessons.* Portsmouth, NH: Heinemann.

Heap, J. L. (1989). Sociality and cognition in collaborative computer writing. In D. Bloome (Ed.), *Classrooms and literacy* (pp. 135-157). Norwood, NJ: Ablex.

Heath, S. B. (1982a). Protean shapes in literacy events: Ever-shifting oral and literate traditions. In D. Tannen (Ed.), *Spoken and written language: Exploring orality and literacy* (pp. 91-117). Norwood, NJ: Ablex.

Heath, S. B. (1982b). What no bedtime story means: Narrative skills at home and school. *Language in Society, 11,* 49-76.

Heath, S. B. (1983). *Ways with words: Language, life and work in communities and classrooms.* Cambridge, MA: Harvard University Press.

Heath, S. B. (1986). Separating "things of the imagination" from life: Learning to read and write. In W. H. Teale & E. Sulzby (Eds.), *Emergent literacy: Writing and reading* (pp. 156-172). Norwood, NJ: Ablex.

Heath, S. B. with Thomas, C. (1984). The achievement of preschool literacy for mother and child. In H. Goelman, A. Oberg, & F. Smith (Eds.), *Awakening to literacy* (pp. 51-72). Exeter, NH: Heinemann.

Henderson, E. H., & Beers, J. W. (Eds.). (1980). *Developmental and cognitive aspects of learning to spell.* Newark, DE: International Reading Association.

Hiebert, E. H. (1978). Preschool children's understanding of written language. *Child Development, 49,* 1231-1238.

Hiebert, E. H. (1980). The relationship of logical reasoning ability, oral language comprehension, and home experiences to preschool children's print awareness. *Journal of Reading Behavior, 12*(4), 313-324.

Hiebert, E. H. (1981). Developmental patterns and interrelationships of preschool children's print awareness. *Reading Research Quarterly, 16*(2), 236-260.

Hiebert, E. H. (1986). Issues related to home influences on young children's print-related development. In D. Yaden & S. Templeton (Eds.), *Metalinguistic awareness and beginning literacy: Conceptualizing what it means to read and write* (pp. 145-158). Portsmouth, NH: Heinemann.

Hildreth, G. (1932). Developmental sequences in name writing. *Child Development, 3,* 1-14.

Hockenberger, E. H., Goldstein, H., & Haas, L. S. (1999). Effects of commenting during joint book reading by mothers with low SES. *Topics in Early Childhood Special Education, 19*(1), 15-27.

Huey, E. B. (1908). *The psychology and pedagogy of reading.* New York: Macmillan.

Iredell, H. (1989). Eleanor learns to read. *Education, 19,* 233-248.

Kaderavek, J. N., & Sulzby, E. (1997, December). Oral narratives and emergent bookreadings of typically developing and language impaired children. Paper presented at the annual meeting of the National Reading Conference, Scottsdale, AZ. (ERIC Document Reproduction Service No. ED 420 850)

Kaderavek, J. N., & Sulzby, E. (2000). Narrative production by children with and without specific language impairment: Oral narratives and emergent readings. *Journal of Speech, Language, and Hearing Research, 43*(1), 34-49.

Kamberelis, G., & Sulzby, E. (1988). Transitional knowledge in emergent literacy. *National Reading Conference Yearbook, 37,* 95-106.

Kelly, A., & O'Kelly, J. (1993). Emergent literacy: Implications for the design of computer writing applications for children. *Journal of Computing in Childhood Education, 4*(1), 3-14.

King, M., & Rentel, V. (1981). *How children learn to write: A longitudinal study.* (Final report to the National Institute of Education, RF Project 761861/712383 and 765512/711748). Columbus, OH: Ohio State University Research Foundation.

Kirkland, L. (1991). Environmental print and the kindergarten classroom. *Reading Improvement, 28*(4), 219-222.

Kuby, P., Aldridge, J., & Snyder, S. (1994). Developmental progression of environmental print recognition in kindergarten children. *Reading Psychology, 15*(1), 1-9.

Martlew, M. (1988). Children's oral and written language. In A. D. Pellegrini (Ed.), *Psychological bases for early education* (pp. 77-122). Chichester, West Sussex, England: Wiley.

Mathews, M. M. (1966). *Teaching to read: Historically considered.* Chicago: University of Chicago Press.

Mason, J. M. (1980). When do children begin to read: An exploration of four year old children's letter and word reading competencies. *Reading Research Quarterly, 15,* 203-227.

Mason, J. M. (1986). Prereading: A developmental perspective. In P. D. Pearson (Ed.), *Handbook of research in reading, Vol. 1* (pp. 505-543). New York: Longman.

Mason, J. M., & Allen, J. B. (1986). A review of emergent literacy with implications for research and practice in reading. *Review of Research in Education, 13,* 3-47.

McCormick, C. E., & Mason, J. M. (1986). Intervention procedures for increasing preschool children's interest in and knowledge about reading. In W. H. Teale & E. Sulzby (Eds.), *Emergent literacy: Writing and reading* (pp. 90-115). Norwood, NJ: Ablex.

McGee, L., Lomax, R., & Head, M. (1988). Young children's written language knowledge: What environmental and functional print reading reveals. *Journal of Reading Behavior, 20,* 99-118.

McGill-Franzen, A., & Lanford, C. (1994). Exposing the edge of the preschool curriculum: Teachers' talk about text and children's literary understandings. *Language Arts, 71*(4), 264-273.

McMahon, R., & Others. (1996, April). The effect of a literacy-rich environment on children's concepts about print. Paper presented at the Annual International Study Conference of the Association of Childhood Education International, Minneapolis, MN. (ERIC Document Reproduction Service No. ED 399 043)

McNaughton, S. (1995). *Patterns of emergent literacy: Processes of development and transition.* Melbourne, Australia: Oxford University Press.

Meltzer, N. H., & Herse, R. (1969). The boundaries of written words as seen by first graders. *Journal of Reading Behavior, 1,* 3-14.

Mickish, V. (1974). Children's perception of written word boundaries. *Journal of Reading Behavior, 6,* 19-22.

Miller, P., Nemoianu, A., & DeJong, J. (1986). Early reading at home: Its practice and meanings in a working class community. In B. Schieffelin & P. Gilmore (Eds.), *The acquisition of literacy: Ethnographic perspectives* (pp. 3-15). Norwood, NJ: Ablex.

Morphett, M. V., & Washburne, C. (1931). When should children begin to read? *Elementary School Journal, 31,* 496-508.

Morris, D. (1980). Beginning readers' concept of word. In E. H. Henderson & J. W. Beers (Eds.), *Developmental and cognitive aspects of learning to spell* (pp. 97-111). Newark, DE: International Reading Association.

Morris, D. (1981). Concept of word: A developmental phenomenon in the beginning reading and writing program. *Language Arts, 58,* 659-668.

Morrow, L. M., & Smith, J. (Eds.). (1989). *The role of assessment and measurement in early literacy research.* Englewood Cliffs, NJ: Prentice-Hall.

Moschovaki, E. (1999). Home background and young children's literacy development. *Early Child Development and Care 1999, 158,* 11-19.

Murphy, R. T., & Appel, L. R. (1984). *Evaluation of the Writing to Read Instructional System, 1982-1984: Second year report.* Princeton, NJ: Educational Testing Service.

Nagy, W. E., & Anderson, R. C. (1995). *Metalinguistic awareness and literacy acquisition in different languages.* (Technical Report No. 618). Urbana, IL: Center for the Study of Reading.

Neuman, S. B. (1996). Children engaging in storybook reading: The influence of access to print resources, opportunity, and parental interaction. *Early Childhood Research Quarterly, 11*(4), 495-513.

Ninio, A. (1980). Picture-book reading in mother-infant dyads belonging to two subgroups in Israel. *Child Development, 51,* 587-590.

Nurss, J. R. (1988). Development of written communication in Norwegian kindergarten children. *Scandinavian Journal of Educational Research, 32,* 33-48.

Olson, D. R. (1977). From utterance to text: The bias of language in speech and writing. *Harvard Educational Review, 47*(3), 257-281.

Ong, W. J. (1982). *Orality and literacy: The technologizing of the words.* New York: Methuen.

Otto, B. W. (1993). Signs of emergent literacy among inner-city kindergartners in a storybook reading program. *Reading and Writing Quarterly: Overcoming Learning Difficulties, 9*(2), 151-162.

Papandropoulou, L., & Sinclair, H. (1974). What is a word? Experimental study of children's ideas on grammar. *Human Development, 17,* 241-258.

Papert, S. (1980). *Mindstorms: Children, computers, and powerful ideas.* New York: Basic Books.

Pappas, C. C. (1986). *Learning to ready by reading: Exploring text indices for understanding the process.* (Final report to the Research Committee for the Research Foundation of the National Council of Teachers of English No. R85:21). Lexington, KY: University of Kentucky.

Pappas, C. C. (1987). Exploring the textual properties of "protoreading." In R. Steele & T. Threadgold (Eds.), *Language topics: Essays in honour of Michael Halliday* (Vol. 1, pp. 137-162). Amsterdam, Netherlands John Benjamins.

Pappas, C. C. (1988, December). *Exploring the ontogenesis of the registers of written language: Young children tackling the "book language" of information books.* Paper presented at the 38th annual meeting of the National Reading Conference, Tucson, AZ.

Pappas, C. C., & Brown, E. (1987). Learning to read by reading: Learning how to extend the functional potential of language. *Research in the Teaching of English, 21,* 160-184.

Pappas, C. C., & Brown, E. (1988). The development of children's sense of the written story language register: An analysis of the texture of "pretend reading." *Linguistics and Education, 1,* 45-79.

Pellegrini, A. D., Brody, G. H., & Sigel, I. E. (1985). Parents' book-reading habits with their children. *Journal of Educational Psychology, 77*(3), 332-340.

Pellegrini, A. D., & Galda, L. (1996). Oral language and literacy learning in context: The role of social relationships (Reading Research Report No. 57). Athens, GA & College Park, MD: National Reading Research Center.

Pellegrini, A. D., Perlmutter, J. C., Galda, L., & Brody, G. H. (1990). Joint book reading between black Head Start children and their mothers. *Child Development, 61,* 443-453.

Pellegrini, A. D., Galda, L., Dresden, J., & Cox, S. (1991). A longitudinal study of the predictive relations among symbolic play, linguistic verbs and early literacy. *Research in the Teaching of English, 25*(2), 219-235.

Phillips, G., & McNaughton, S. (1990). The practice of storybook reading to preschool children in mainstream New Zealand families. *Reading Research Quarterly, 25*(3), 196-212.

Piaget, J. (1959). *The language and thought of the child* (3rd ed.). London, England: Routledge & Kegan Paul.

Poole-Hayes, U., & Dionne, J. (1996, April). *Invented spelling: An indicator of differential problem-solving strategies of good spellers and poor spellers at kindergarten and grade one.* Paper presented at the annual meeting of the American Educational Research Association, New York, NY. (ERIC Document Reproduction Service No. ED 394 128)

Pontecorvo, C. (1984). Figure, parole, numeri: Un problema di simbolizzazione. *Età evolutiva, 18,* 5-33.

Pontecorvo, C., Orsolini, M., Zucchermaglio, C., & Rossi, F. (1987, December). *Metalinguistic skills in children: What develops?* Paper presented at the National Reading Conference, St. Petersburg, FL.

Purcell-Gates, V. (1988). Lexical and syntactic knowledge of written narrative held by well-to-read kindergarteners and second graders. *Research in the Teaching of English, 22*(2), 128-160.

Read, C. (1970). *Children's perceptions of the sound of English.* Unpublished doctoral dissertation, Harvard University, Cambridge, MA.

Read, C. (1975). *Children's categorization of speech sounds in English.* (NCTE Res. Rep. No. 17). Urbana, IL: National Council of Teachers of English.

Reid, J. (1966). Learning to think about reading. *Educational Research, 9,* 56-62.

Richgels, D. J. (1986a). An investigation of preschool and kindergarten children's spelling and reading abilities. *Journal of Research and Development in Education, 19,* 41-47.

Richgels, D. J. (1986b). Beginning first graders' "invented spelling" ability and their performance in functional classroom writing activities. *Early Childhood Research Quarterly, 1,* 85-97.

Richgels, D. J., McGee, L. M., Hernandez, S., & Williams, N. (1988). Kindergarteners' attention to graphic detail in functional print: Letter name knowledge and invented spelling ability. *National Reading Conference Yearbook, 37,* 77-84.

Rodriguez, M. V. (1999). Home literacy experiences of three young Dominican children in New York City: Implications for teaching in urban settings. *Educators for Urban Minorities, 1*(1), 19-30.

Rowe, D. W. (1987). Literacy learning as an intertextual process. *National Reading Conference Yearbook, 36,* 101-112.

Rowe, D. W. (1988, April). *The impact of author/audience interaction on preschoolers' literacy learning.* Paper presented at the annual meeting of the American Educational Research Association, New Orleans, LA.

Rubin, A. D. (1978). A theoretical taxonomy of the differences between oral and written language (Tech. Rep. No. 35). Urbana/Champaign, IL: University of Illinois, Center for the Study of Reading.

Scollon, R., & Scollon, S. B. K. (1981). *Narrative, literacy, and face in interethnic communication.* Norwood, NJ: Ablex.

Senechal, M., LeFevre, J., Daley, K. E., & Thomas, E. (1996, August). Early exposure to storybooks as a predictor of reading in grade 1. Paper presented at the biennial meeting of the International Society for the Study of Behavioral Development, Quebec City, Quebec, Canada. (ERIC Document Reproduction Service No. ED 415 486)

Shanahan, T. (1984). The nature of reading-writing relations: An exploratory multivariate analysis. *Journal of Educational Psychology, 76,* 357-363.

Shatz, M. (1984). A song without music and other stories: How cognitive process constraints influence children's oral and written narratives. In D. Schiffrin (Ed.), *Meaning, form, and use in context: Linguistic applications.* Washington, DC: Georgetown University Press.

Shilling, W. A. (1997). Young children using computers to make discoveries about written language. *Early Childhood Education Journal, 24*(4), 253-259.

Sinclair, A., Jarvella, R. J., & Levelt, W. J. M. (Eds.) (1978). *The child's conception of language.* New York: Springer-Verlag.

Smolkin, L. B., Conlon, A., & Yaden, D. B. (1988). Print salient illustrations in children's picture books: The emergence of written language awareness. *National Reading Conference Yearbook, 37,* 59-68.

Snow, C. E. (1983). Literacy and language: Relationships during the preschool years. *Harvard Educational Review, 53*(2), 165-189.

Snow, C. E., & Goldfield, B. A. (1983). Turn the page, please: Situation-specific language acquisition. *Journal of Child Language, 10,* 535-549.

Snow, C. E., & Ninio, A. (1986). The contracts of literacy: What children learn from learning to read books. In W. H. Teale & E. Sulzby (Eds.), *Emergent literacy: Writing and reading* (pp. 116-138). Norwood, NJ: Ablex.

Stainthorp, R., & Hughes, D. (1999). *Learning from children who read at an early age.* New York: Routledge.

Stanovich, K. (1986). Matthew effects in reading: Some consequences of individual differences in the acquisition of literacy. *Reading Research Quarterly, 21,* 360-407.

Strickland, D. S., & Morrow, L. M. (Eds.) (1989). *Emerging literacy: Young children learn to read and write.* Newark, DE: International Reading Association.

Sulzby, E. (1981, August). *Kindergartners begin to read their own compositions: Beginning readers' developing knowledges about written language project.* (Final report to the Research Foundation of the National Council of Teachers of English). Evanston, IL: Northwestern University.

Sulzby, E. (1983, September). *Beginning readers' developing knowledges about written language.* (Final report to the National Institute of Education NIE-G-80-0176). Evanston, IL: Northwestern University.

Sulzby, E. (1985a). Children's emergent reading of favorite storybooks: A developmental study. *Reading Research Quarterly, 20,* 458-481.

Sulzby, E. (1985b). Kindergartners as writers and readers. In M. Farr (Ed.), *Advances in writing research, Vol. 1: Children's early writing development* (pp. 127-199). Norwood, NJ: Ablex.

Sulzby, E. (1988). A study of children's early reading development. In A. D. Pellegrini (Ed.), *Psychological bases for early education* (pp. 39-75). Chichester, ENG: Wiley.

Sulzby, E. (1989). Assessment of writing and of children's language while writing. In L. Morrow & J. Smith (Eds.), *The role of assessment and measurement in early literacy instruction* (pp. 83-109). Englewood Cliffs, NJ: Prentice-Hall.

Sulzby, E. (1991). Assessment of emergent literacy: Storybook reading (assessment). *Reading Teacher, 44*(7), 498-500.

Sulzby, E. (1991). Roles of oral and written language in children approaching conventional literacy. In M. Orsolini & C. Pontecorvo (Eds.), *La costruzione del primi testi scritti nel bambino* (pp. 57-75). Rome, Italy: La Nuova Italia.

Sulzby, E. (1992). Transitions from emergent to conventional writing (research directions). *Language Arts, 69*(4), 290-297.

Sulzby, E., Barnhart, J., & Hieshima, J. (1989). *Forms of writing and rereading from writing: A preliminary report.* In J. Mason (Ed.), *Reading and writing connections* (pp. 31-63). Needham Heights, MA: Allyn & Bacon. Also (1989) Tech. Rep. No. 20, Center for the Study of Writing, University of California, Berkeley, CA.

Sulzby, E., Olson, K. A., & Johnston, J. (1989). *The computer and young children: An emergent literacy perspective.* Working paper No. 1, Computers in Early Literacy (CIEL) Research Project. Institute for Social Research, The University of Michigan, Ann Arbor, MI.

Sulzby, E., & Teale, W. H. (1985). Writing development in early childhood. *Educational Horizons, 64,* 8-12.

Sulzby, E., & Teale, W. H. (1987, November). *Young children's storybook reading: Longitudinal study of parent-child interaction and children's independent functioning.* (Final report to The Spencer Foundation). Ann Arbor, MI: The University of Michigan.

Sulzby, E., & Teale, W. H. (1991). Emergent literacy. In R. Barr, M. L. Kamil, P. Mosenthal, & P. D. Pearson (Eds.), *Handbook of reading research, Vol. 2* (pp. 727-757). New York: Longman.

Tannen, D. (1982). The oral/literate continuum in discourse. In D. Tannen (Ed.), *Spoken and written language: Exploring orality and literacy* (pp. 1-16). Norwood, NJ: Ablex.

Tannen, D. (1984). Spoken and written narrative in English and Greek. In D. Tannen (Ed.), *Coherence in spoken and written discourse* (pp. 21-44). Norwood, NJ: Ablex.

Taylor, D. (1983). *Family literacy*. Exeter, NH: Heinemann.

Taylor, D., & Dorsey-Gaines, C. (1988). *Growing up literate: Learning from inner-city families*. Portsmouth, NH: Heinemann.

Teale, W. H. (1978). Positive environments for learning to read: What studies of early readers tell us. *Language Arts, 55*, 922–932.

Teale, W. H. (1984). Reading to young children: Its significance in the process of literacy development. In H. Goelman, A. Oberg, & F. Smith (Eds.), *Awakening to literacy* (pp. 110–121). Exeter, NH: Heinemann.

Teale, W. H. (1986). Home background and young children's literacy development. In W. H. Teale & E. Sulzby (Eds.), *Emergent literacy: Writing and reading* (pp. 173–206). Norwood, NJ: Ablex.

Teale, W. H. (1987). Emergent literacy: Reading and writing development in early childhood. *National Reading Conference Yearbook, 36*, 45–74.

Teale, W. H., Martinez, M. G., & Glass, W. L. (1989). Describing classroom storybook reading. In D. Bloome (Ed.), *Classrooms and literacy* (pp. 158–188). Norwood, NJ: Ablex.

Teale, W. H., & Sulzby, E. (Eds.). (1986). *Emergent literacy: Writing and reading*. Norwood, NJ: Ablex.

Teale, W. H., & Sulzby, E. (1987). Literacy acquisition in early childhood: The roles of access and meditation in storybook reading. In D. A. Wagner (Ed.), *The future of literacy in a changing world* (pp. 111–130). New York: Pergamon Press.

Tobin, A. W. (1981). *A multiple discriminant cross-validation of the factors associated with the development of precocious reading achievement*. Unpublished doctoral dissertation, University of Delaware, Newark, DE.

Tobin, A. W., & Pikulski, J. J. (1988). A longitudinal study of the reading achievement of early and nonearly readers through sixth grade. *National Reading Conference Yearbook, 37*, 49–58.

Tolchinsky-Landsmann, L., & Levin, I. (1985). Writing in preschoolers: An age related analysis. *Applied Psycholinguistics, 6*, 319–339.

Tolchinsky-Landsmann, L., & Levin, I. (1987). Writing in four- to six-year-olds: Representation of semantic and phonetic similarities and differences. *Journal of Child Language, 14*, 127–144.

van Kleeck, A., Alexander, E. I., Vigil, A., & Templeton, K. E. (1996). Verbally modeling thinking for infants: Middle-class mothers' presentation of information structures during book sharing. *Journal of Research in Childhood Education, 10*(2), 101–113.

Vukelich, C., & Edwards, N. (1988). The role of context and as-written orthography in kindergarteners' word recognition. *National Reading Conference Yearbook, 37*, 85–93.

Vygotsky, L. S. (1978). *Mind in society: The development of higher psychological processes*. Cambridge, MA: Harvard University Press.

Vygotsky, L. S. (1981). The genesis of higher mental functions. In J. V. Wertsch (Ed.), *The concept of activity in Soviety psychology* (pp. 144–188). White Plains, NY: M. E. Sharpe.

Wade, B., & Moore, M. (1996). Children's early book behavior. *Educational Review, 48*(3), 283–288.

Walter, E. L. (1994). A longitudinal study of literacy acquisition in a Native American community: Observation of the 4-year-old classes at Lummi Headstart. (Report submitted to the Lummi Tribal Council, State of Washington). (ERIC Document Reproduction Service No. ED 366 479)

Wan, G. (2000). A Chinese girl's storybook experience at home. *Language Arts, 77*(5), 398–405.

Wells, C. G. (1985). Pre-school literacy related activities and success in school. In D. Olson, N. Torrance, & A. Hildyard (Eds.), *Literacy, language and learning: The nature and consequence of literacy* (pp. 229–255). Cambridge, England: Cambridge University Press.

Whitehurst, G. J., Falco, F. L., Lonigan, C. J., Fischel, J. E., DeBaryshe, B. D., Valdez-Menchaca, M. C., & Caulfield, M. (1988). Accelerating language development through picture book reading. *Developmental psychology, 24*, 552–559.

Wolfe, D., & Gardner, H. (1981). On the structure of early symbolization. In R. L. Schiefelsbusch (Ed.), *Early language: Acquisition and intervention* (pp. 287–327). Baltimore, MD: University Park Press.

Yaden, D. B., & Templeton, S. (Eds.). (1986). *Metalinguistic awareness and beginning literacy*. Portsmouth, NH: Heinemann.

# STUDENT ACHIEVEMENT AND CLASSROOM CASE STUDIES OF PHONICS IN WHOLE LANGUAGE FIRST GRADES

*Karin L. Dahl, Patricia L. Scharer, and Lora L. Lawson*
*The Ohio State University*

*Patricia R. Grogan*
*University of Dayton*

The debate about phonics and whole language is about the ways skill instruction is addressed and whether whole language provides sufficiently rigorous skill teaching for beginning readers (Edelsky, 1990; Juel, 1994; Krashen, 1998; Lyon, 1998; Routman, 1996; Strickland, 1998a). Proponents of phonics-centered programs emphasize that explicit systematic phonics lessons are necessary for learning to read and write (Adams & Bruck, 1995; Beck & Juel, 1995; Chall, 1967; Ehri, 1991; Foorman, Francis, Fletcher, Schatschneider, & Mehta, 1998). The phonics-centered approach involves direct instruction (often in teacher-scripted whole class lessons) and learner practice in materials crafted to emphasize specific phonics concepts (Stahl, 1998).

In contrast, whole language advocates view phonics as one of the cueing systems that children use, along with syntactic, semantic, and pragmatic information, during reading and writing (Goodman, 1986, 1993; Strickland, 1998b; Weaver, 1990, 1998). Phonics instruction in whole language classrooms, they assert, is embedded in ongoing reading and writing activities. Instruction in whole language classrooms is shaped by the teacher's understanding of each individual child's development in written language and supports his or her individual language learning processes (Goodman, 1993).

Challenges to each of these positions have led to a heated and prolonged debate conducted not only in the popular press and

professional journals, but also in state legislatures throughout the United States. The whole language concept of embedded phonics instruction has been characterized as ad hoc teaching focusing on a random selection of word elements (Flanagan, 1997). Conversely, critics of phonics-centered instruction question the efficacy of predetermined sequences of phonics lessons isolated from actual reading and writing, arguing that transfer to these processes is unlikely from worksheets and drills (Weaver, 1991). These latter critics also claim that some children are taught phonics concepts they already know while others receive phonics instruction before they acquire the foundational concepts that make the lessons comprehensible (Moustafa, 1997).

The difficulty for educators, for parents, and for those concerned with policy making and curricular decisions is that this debate rests on rhetoric more than research (Cunningham, 1992). The body of research on whole language is relatively scant and has focused on issues other than the phonics question in whole language classrooms (Edelsky, 1990; McKenna, Robinson, & Miller, 1990, 1992; Stahl & Miller, 1989; Stephens, 1991). There are scholarly references that describe guidelines for phonics instruction in whole language classrooms (Strickland, 1998b; Weaver, 1994; Wilde, 1997), but little information is available about actual phonics instruction within whole language classroom practice.

## REVIEW OF RELATED RESEARCH

This chapter draws on the current body of studies on phonemic awareness, phonics research, and investigations of whole language in curricular studies. A growing body of research suggests a strong relationship between phonemic awareness and reading achievement (Adams & Bruck, 1995; Beck & Juel, 1995; Foorman et al., 1998). Phonics research indicates that readers and writers use letter/sound relationships as one of the cueing systems of written language (Adams, 1991; Ehri, 1987, 1991; Ehri & Wilce, 1987; Juel, 1994; McGuinnes, McGuinnes, & Donohue, 1995). The debate about phonics knowledge is concerned with effective instruction as well as how and when phonics is learned (Cunningham, 1992; Goodman, 1993; Juel, 1994; Wilde, 1997). Recent research indicates that children seek patterns, use analogies, and consider context in encoding and decoding words (Goswami, 1986, 1990, 1993; Goswami & Bryant, 1990; Goswami & Mead, 1992; Moustafa, 1990, 1995, 1997). Researchers exploring inventive spelling note that children often learn about phonics through early writing (Clay, 1991; Tierney & Leys, 1986; Treiman, 1993) and that experimentation with letter/sound relations has led to better spelling and improved reading (Clarke, 1988; Lomax & McGee, 1987). Thus, current information indicates that learners actively construct phonics knowledge and draw from both instruction and independent experimentation in order to understand phonics concepts.

The curriculum debate is about the ways skills instruction is provided and the extent to which whole language provides appropriate skills teaching for beginning readers (Adams, 1991; Chall, 1967; Edelsky, 1990; Foorman et al., 1998; McKenna, Robinson, & Miller, 1990, 1992; Stahl & Miller, 1989). Scholarly efforts to document the translation of whole language perspectives into actual classroom practice are few (Stephens, 1991; Weaver, 1998). Of these, Mills and Clyde (1990) and Vacca and Rasinski (1992) provide general descriptions of instruction through case studies and discuss various whole language issues, but do not analyze phonics instruction explicitly. Mills, O'Keefe, and Stephens (1992) described phonics instruction in one whole language first grade and examined curricular elements that support phonics learning. Their study traced phonics across the school day and described learner progress. Gunderson and Shapiro (1987) described whole language instruction in two first grades and examined children's writing. In this year-long study, the researchers assessed students' development of phonic skills and basic vocabulary. Dahl and Freppon (1995) documented children's interpretations of beginning reading and writing instruction in four kindergartens (two whole language and two skills-based classrooms) and four first grades (two whole language and two skills-based classrooms). Their work compared children's written language knowledge, including phonics concepts, across curricula. The focus, however, was primarily on children's interpretations of reading and writing instruction as well as learning outcomes in terms of achievement measures. As a comparative study, their investigation found cross-curricular differences in children's

applications of phonics knowledge. Their findings indicated the need for multisite documentation that would focus more closely on both phonics teaching and learning in whole language classrooms.

Other comparative studies (Stahl, Pagnucco, & Suttles, 1996; Freppon, McIntyre, & Dahl, 1995; Varble, 1990) looked at contrasts across curricula, but did not address phonics teaching and learning specifically. The Stahl et al. (1996) investigation found that the pacing in instruction was a significant variable favoring traditional programs. The other investigations focused on analysis of writing samples and found in each case that there were differences across whole language and traditional programs. Varble found that second graders in whole language classrooms produced better writing samples in terms of meaning and content, but their writing did not differ from the writing in traditional classrooms on mechanics. Freppon et al. (1995) found that the whole language writers used a wider range of text structures in their writing and that individual development in both curricula affected children's writing products.

While these investigations provide useful curricular information, their analyses do not include situated accounts depicting a range of classroom programs in whole language. The field still does not know what whole language teachers do when they teach embedded phonics nor what outcomes are realized in these classrooms in terms of phonics knowledge among first-grade learners. This study fills the need to understand the role of phonics in whole language curricula by providing a description across sites that samples the range of instruction.

## RATIONALE

The current debate about the nature of primary grade literacy curricula reflects our societal and cultural concerns about producing a literate citizenry. The common ground across various curricular positions is a shared commitment to sound teaching and learning experiences for children that lay the foundation for proficient reading and writing.

This study provides trustworthy research documentation that will inform teachers, parents, and members of the research community about the nature and efficacy of phonics teaching and learning within whole language classrooms. This piece has been missing from the whole language side of the research base and will allow the discussion to draw on classroom documentation. Currently, whole language is well established in many school systems and affects the literacy experiences of countless children. Whole language advocates include both beginning teachers and teachers with substantial experience in literacy instruction. When such teachers evaluate their own practice in light of current local and national pressures influencing their school systems, they need to draw on rigorous research evidence about phonics instruction conducted within a whole language perspective (Gunnison & Lucas, 1996; Thomas, 1996; Walmsley & Adams, 1993). Similarly, educators and policy makers debating systematic phonics and influencing curricular decisions about phonics instruction need to draw on research evidence on both sides of the current debate.

Given these purposes, there were two guiding research questions for this investigation. The first addressed what phonics teaching looked like in whole language first grade classrooms. It focused on what concepts were taught, where the phonics instruction occurred, and what teachers were doing. The second question addressed the patterns of phonics learning that were evident in pre and post comparisons of student achievement.

Since the current investigation was conducted within the context of the current phonics debate, it included specific provisions to address the concerns of advocates from opposing positions. Among the design considerations, the following four issues related to the debate about phonics: (a) how to determine what was to be counted as whole language, (b) whether to focus on how whole language teachers teach phonics or investigate whether they teach phonics, (c) how to measure phonics achievement in ways that would be credible to both sides of the debate, and (d) how to make provisions for evenhandedness and credibility.

## Defining Whole Language

Whole language definitions in this research were drawn from current scholarly literature about whole language to establish criteria for site selection. Three kinds of whole language writings were consulted as we searched for convergence: theory, descriptions of classroom programs, and research. From theory, definitions appearing in well-known whole language works were compared (Edelsky, Altwerger, & Flores, 1991; Goodman, 1992, 1993; Weaver, 1990, 1994). From classroom descriptions, documentations of practice were incorporated. These included descriptions gathered by Mills and Clyde (1990) and case studies by Vacca and Rasinski (1992). Finally, from research, the content analysis of whole language definitions (Bergeron, 1990) was used to list the characteristics commonly included in studies investigating whole language. Generally, these references supported the position that whole language is a "research-based theory of learning and teaching, which gives rise to certain kinds of practices in helping children develop literacy" (Weaver, 1998, p. 5). References indicate that whole language classroom teachers make theory-driven decisions that are translated into curricular actions and teaching practices.

Based on the concurrence of ideas and practices across these sources, we created a criteria sheet that defined whole language for site selection using observable outcomes from whole language theory and beliefs. The whole language selection criteria included the following:

1. *Child-centered curriculum.* The curriculum focuses on the learner and provides instruction that addresses the learner's processes of reading and writing. Learner patterns of development and learner interests are central to the curriculum.
2. *Teaching approach.* Reading and writing are taught as meaning-centered processes through experiences with connected text. Instruction includes skills and strategies for reading and writing along with process demonstrations. Embedded skill instruction is planned within meaning-centered, functional reading and writing experiences. Teachers encourage risk-taking. Learning proceeds from whole-to-part rather than from part-to-whole.
3. *Materials.* A wide selection of children's literature is used as well as a variety of print sources including children's writing. Children select trade books for reading and generate their own topics for writing.
4. *Classroom environment.* The classroom is a literate environment where reading and writing are viewed as tools for learning. There is sustained time for children to read self-selected books and write about topics of their choice.
5. *Collaborative peer contexts.* Collaborative peer contexts are provided that encourage children to exchange information and work together. Cooperative interactions among students are valued as crucial to language learning.

In general, these criteria support the goals of engaging students in activities with a genuine purpose and emphasizing inquiry. These defining dimensions are similar to the agreement on central whole language concepts that Barshinger (1995) established in his work with whole language experts. They also concur with the whole language instructional principles described by Traw (1996) as most germane to the learning of skills.

These defining criteria describe the continuum of classroom programs and practices that are regarded as falling within a whole language perspective. They include programs espousing the literacy goal of emancipation and programs that integrate the disciplines. We recognize that a considerable range of classroom programs are included within these general specifications.

## Focusing the Phonics Inquiry

Scholarly whole language references were also used to make the decision that the research focus would be to investigate *how* phonics was taught instead of *whether* it was taught. This literature on whole language described phonics as integral to the reading and writing processes. The consensus was that the whole language perspective recognizes the importance of phonics knowledge and the need to address strategies and skills that children use as they engage in reading and writing (Freppon & Headings, 1996; McIntyre, 1996; Mills, O'Keefe, & Stephens, 1992; Weaver, 1990, 1994). A number of references also described essential phonics concepts and cited the research base undergirding phonics instruction (Goodman, 1993; Moustafa, 1997; Weaver, 1996; Wilde, 1997). Others described the notion of no phonics in whole language as a myth used by critics who describe whole language as deficient in phonics (Church, 1994; Newman & Church, 1990; Weaver, 1990, 1994). Given this inclusion of phonics instruction as an expected feature of instruction described in the scholarly literature on whole language, the methodological descision was to address *how* phonics was taught—namely, the nature of that phonics instruction in actual classroom practice.

## Measurement of Phonics Achievement

The assessment of phonics knowledge is an ongoing feature of whole language classrooms. Children's acquisition of phonics knowledge is found in the day-by-day use of letter/sound relations in reading/writing experiences.

The selection of instruments to measure phonics achievement for this study took into account (a) the kinds of evidence that proponents on each side of the phonics debate were likely to value, and (b) measures that could appropriately assess phonics instruction in the context of whole language classroom instruction. Reviews of decoding and encoding instrumentation across a range of phonics-centered studies revealed that tests usually isolated phonics concepts at the word or letter level and focused on a specific aspect of phonics knowledge. Among these measures were tasks addressing the decoding of monosyllabic words and nonwords (Ehri & Wilce, 1980, 1987), tests of initial consonant knowledge (Stanovich, Cunningham, & Cramer, 1984), and assessments of phonemic segmentation (Yopp, 1988). Encoding research usually addressed dictated words that tapped knowledge of specific letter/sound relationships and focused on developmental spelling patterns (Henderson & Beers, 1980; Invernizzi, 1992; Morris & Perney, 1984; Schlagal, 1992; Zutell, 1979).

In contrast, the critical measurement dimensions for whole language studies were the inclusion of context (reading and writing using multiple cueing systems) and the concern about meaningful text. In these studies children were assessed not by a separate test or task but, rather, through analysis of their classroom writing and reading. For example, Mills et al. (1992) analyzed the daily reading/writing work of children in their case study of phonics teaching and learning. Other researchers, focusing specifically on encoding, analyzed students' invented spellings occurring in routine writing events within whole language classrooms (Clarke, 1988; Gunderson & Shaprio, 1987; Wilde, 1988).

With these studies in mind, and with the goal of describing achievement in terms of what children learn about letter/sound relations in whole language first grades, the assessment of student phonics achievement was conceptualized as including two significant dimensions: whether the task was presented in isolation or in context, and whether the task focused on decoding or encoding. The combination of these two important characteristics produced the need for four instruments.

On the phonics-centered side of the debate we included decoding in isolation using words on flash cards and encoding in isolation by writing dictated words with various letter/sound relations. Instrumentation with a whole language perspective included decoding words in the context of increasingly difficult stories with support of other cueing systems and encoding in context by writing dictated sentences.

The goal was to test children individually to ensure the accuracy of data. Individual assessment would allow testers to pace the administration according to children's needs and make notes about individual children's responses to particular tasks. The search was for tests with minimal ceiling effects that would be age-appropriate, credible, efficient, and not involved special student test training. Assessments were rejected that involved nonsense syllables (in decoding or encoding) because they lacked concurrence with whole language classroom programs.

## Provisions for Evenhandedness and Credibility

In order to monitor for bias and provide a credibility check on research procedures, two outside auditors reviewed and monitored site selection, data collection, and data analysis procedures. One auditor was a prominent phonics researcher, the other and equally prominent whole language researcher. The auditors reviewed site selection and achievement instrumentation through telephone interviews with the researchers. In October and February, the auditors met in day-long sessions with the research team to review the progress of the study and provide feedback on procedures.

## METHOD

### Site Selection

Two critical dimensions guided the selection of prospective teachers and classrooms for this study. The sites needed to be representative of whole language and to include a range of locations and student populations.

We asked whole language community members to nominate prospective sites. The research team visited several literacy groups (such as Teachers Applying Whole Language [TAWL] and the Literacy Connection) to present a broad overview of the study and request nominations. A total of 38 nominations was received. Using the whole language criteria developed for this study, the team screened nominations to ensure consistency with whole language descriptors. In addition, the researchers used classroom visits and telephone interviews to determine whether the 38 nominated teachers and their classrooms met the following six additional requirements for participation. These specific concerns were:

1. The prospective site had to be a first-grade classroom (not a multiage classroom).
2. The teacher was not to be trained in Reading Recovery, since Reading Recovery tutoring contains a very specific set of procedures and routines for letter/sound instruction.
3. The teacher was not to use a commercially prepared phonics program.
4. There were no student teachers in the classroom who would be conducting instruction.
5. The classroom had less than five students receiving Reading Recovery services.
6. The teacher was willing to invite researchers into the classroom while conducting the regular ongoing program of literacy instruction.

Sites were eliminated if they were not within the broad working definition of whole language, did not satisfy all of the classroom requirements for inclusion, or the teachers did not wish to participate. The researchers prepared summaries of each site addressing the five criteria in the whole language definition and organized demographic information.

The final procedure for site selection considered the range of site characteristics for the remaining nominees. The goal was to represent as wide a variety of locations and populations as possible. Thus, district and school demographic information about socioeconomic levels, ethnicity, and race guided the final selection. At the auditors' request, the eliminated schools and the reasons for nonparticipation were reviewed for compliance with the established selection criteria. The eight sites that were

TABLE 24.1. Characteristics of Selected Research Sites

| School | Teacher(s) | Teaching Experience | Class Population (As of Pretest) | % Free Or Reduced Lunch By School | Location & Description |
|---|---|---|---|---|---|
| Clifford | Mrs. Adams | 12 years | 2 African American 18 Caucasian 1 Asian | 19% | Suburban public |
| St. Paul | Mrs. Parker | 24 years | 28 Caucasian | 0% | Suburban/rural Catholic school |
| Cottage | Mrs. Olson | 24 years | 25 Caucasian 1 Asian | 0% | Suburban public Whole Language magnet school |
| Oak Park | Mrs. Evans | 23 years | 19 African American 5 Caucasian | 40% | Urban public Literature magnet school |
| Eastland | Mrs. Dean | 17 years | 1 African American 24 Caucasian 1 Latino | 4% | Suburban public Language Arts magnet school |
| Oldfield | Mrs. Lyon | 18 years | 2 African American 22 Caucasian | 10% | Suburban public |
| Garfield | Mrs. Miller | 23 years | 10 African American 9 Caucasian | 84% | Urban public Inner city |
| Hedgewood Park | Mrs. Spencer Mrs. Hillson | 8 years 7 years | 48 Caucasian | 28% | Urban public Whole language school Coteaching |

selected represented seven school districts (public and parochial) from five counties in central Ohio. A summary of site characteristics is displayed in Table 24.1. Fictional names for all teachers and schools are used in this table.

## Informants

The informants in this study were nine whole language teachers (one site was a coteaching situation) and the students in their eight classrooms. Observations, audiotape transcripts, and field notes were inclusive of all students present during a research visit. A pattern of student mobility affected the number of children included in the pre/post testing. Subject attrition occurred as students moved away or moved and later returned. Testing included all students who had parental permission, were not receiving Reading Recovery instruction, were not identified as special education students, and were full-time class members from the time of pretesting (October) through posttesting (May). Of the initial 191 children with permission slips signed, 13 students were not included, for a total of 178 subjects.

## Data Collection

Altogether, the research team visited classrooms for half-day observations at the eight sites 117 times from Novemeber through May and documented 364 extended teaching/learning events including phonics instruction in whole language classrooms. The testing team completed pre/post testing using four instruments with 178 first-grade children.

***Documentation of phonics instruction.*** Documentation of phonics instruction at each site included general field note

accounts of classroom teaching and learning to describe the whole program and specific documentation of phonics instruction. It also described materials, teaching approaches, collaborative peer contexts, and classroom environments. The researchers served as participant-observers with relatively low involvement, their role being to watch and write about teaching and learning in these classrooms.

Observation of phonics instruction focused primarily on the reading/writing instructional period, usually half of the school day. Initial observations included a sampling of the full school day, since whole language classrooms integrate reading and writing instruction across curricular areas. Once a sense was gained about where the primary phonics instruction occurred and a description was developed of the full program, the researchers began generating field note accounts of instruction and generally documented a half day in the classroom during each observation. As instruction changed across the span of the school year, data collection efforts shifted to capture evolving programs.

During research visits, the researcher produced field notes with detailed accounts of instruction, including those teacher and student interactions in which letter–sound relationships were addressed. Each teacher wore a remote microphone interfaced with a receiver and tape recorder. Transcripts of phonics activities and student interactions with the teacher were integrated into field note accounts to document letter–sound instruction. Copies of some student work were also collected along with these accounts during research visits. Interviews at two points in the study addressed the teacher's whole language program and individual history as a teacher. Researchers were interested in each teacher's philosophy of whole language and approach to teaching phonics.

Each member of the research team had primary responsibility for data collection and data analysis in two specific classroom sites. Researchers met in weekly research sessions to consider issues, refine coding, develop uniform procedures, monitor the quality of data collection, and share theoretical ideas.

***Instrumentation to document phonics achievement.*** The pre/post test battery of four quantitative measures of phonics learning dealt with two significant dimensions: whether the task was performed in context or in isolation, and whether the task focused on encoding or decoding. The combination of these two variables required four tools:

1. *Encoding in context.* Clay's Hearing and Recording Sounds in Words (1993) documented the child's developing phonemic awareness and knowledge of 37 specific letter–sound relationships. The child wrote two dictated sentences and was given credit for every sound (phoneme) written correctly, even if the whole word was not spelled correctly. The scores indicated the child's ability to anlayze and record the sounds in words. Clay's Form A sentence was dictated during the pretest: "I have a big dog at home. Today I am going to take him to school." The posttest sentence (Form E) was, "The boy is riding his bike. He can go very fast on it."

2. *Decoding in context.* The Text Reading Level assessment (Clay, 1993) provided a running record, word by word, of a student's attempt at reading leveled texts. Grade equivalents were established by Clay for each text. Students continued reading increasingly more difficult texts until their instructional level was established (up to Level 34, equivalent to Grade 8). Analysis of reading behaviors at this level provided insight into the decoding that the student employed while reading unfamiliar texts.

3. *Encoding in isolation.* The Developmental Spelling Analysis (Ganske, 1993) assessed children's encoding knowledge using four levels of spelling lists: Letter-Name, Within-Word Patterns, Syllable Juncture, and Derivational Constancy. Each list of 25 words focused on five different spelling features. Students progressed to the next level by spelling 12 words correctly from the previous list. Students' written attempts were analyzed within each stage for specific feature knowledge. Each correctly spelled word counted as two points. Incorrect spellings were further analyzed, and one point was awarded for correct representation of targeted features.

4. *Decoding in isolation.* The Qualitative Reading Inventory-II Word List (Leslie & Caldwell, 1995) used successive lists of 20 words ranging in difficulty of list from pre-primer to junior high levels. Following the authors' recommended procedures, words were presented on individual cards for students to read orally. One point was awarded for each word identified correctly (whether automatically, on inspection, or self-corrected). Students read increasingly more difficult lists until reaching their frustration level by accurately reading less than 14 (70%) words on a single list.

***Assessment procedures.*** The assessment team was comprised of trained former classroom teachers with previous experience administering the dictation and text reading level tasks and who were trained on the other two measures (DSA and QRI-II Word List) prior to pre/post testing. Testing occurred in a quiet, print-free location outside the child's classroom. Three of the assessments were individually administered (Hearing and Recording Sounds in Words, Text Reading Level, and the QRI-II word list); the Developmental Spelling Analysis was administered either individually or in small groups of four or fewer students. Audiotapes of the decoding measures (TRL and QRI-II Word List) enabled testers to recheck their scoring accuracy.

***Development of an assessment database.*** Using Microsoft Access, a database was designed to accommodate data specific to each of the four assessments. For each child, the instructional level for Text Reading Level, the accurate phonemes represented during the Hearing and Recording Sounds in Words assessment, words and features correctly identified through the instructional level of the DSA, and words correctly identified either automatically or on inspection at instructional level on the QRI-II Word Test were entered. Proofing sheets were generated, compared with the original data, and discrepancies resolved.

## Data Analysis

***Analysis of phonics instruction.*** The researchers reviewed data from all eight sites focusing on teacher behaviors, context, and content. Each researcher generated a list of examples of instructional events that included phonics teaching and learning. The teaching/learning events were defined as broad activity contexts within which specific phonics instruction occurred. Often, these extended events spanned 45 minutes or more. Descriptions for each broad teaching/learning events were compiled for all eight sites. They included the nature of the event in general terms, the various kinds of activities that were included, and whether they involved small groups or individual instruction. Documentation for extended teaching/learning events were compiled for all eight sites.

Participating teachers reviewed and verified the list as accurate and representative. The teaching/learning events list was organized into coding categories including information about whether the event was for whole group, small group, or individual students. Table 24.2 presents these categories.

Within these more lengthy teaching/learning events, specific phonics concepts, skills, and strategies were taught. Because teachers and students worked together during instruction, co-constructing knowledge, the unit of analysis was the phonics transaction, defined as teacher actions and teacher/student interactions imparting knowledge about specific phonics concepts, skills, and/or strategies. These phonics transactions were instances of instruction, with instruction being conceived of from a conservative definition for the purposes of this investigation. We included in the definition both teaching actions where information was presented by the teacher and the scaffolding instances where a series of interactions addressed a concept. We did not include simply mentioning something about a letter/sound relation within the definition of a phonics transaction. An example of mentioning would be the teacher commenting as the child reads in a guided reading lesson that the next word begins with an *S* and the child continuing with reading. Rather, we focused on instructional explanations in the definition of

TABLE 24.2. Coding for Teaching/Learning Events With Phonics

| Phonics Events & Examples | Descriptions |
|---|---|
| Language Exploration | • The teacher selected high quality children's literature to read aloud to the class to notice language and discuss specific qualities of the author's words. Language features discussed included letter–sound relationships such as initial consonants found in alphabet books and rhyming words in poetic texts.<br>• Children created word collections and discussed patterns they observed as they grouped words with the same letter/sound features. |
| Reading Instruction—Small Group, Large Group | • In small group guided reading lessons, instruction emphasized oral fluency and strategies for decoding unknown words in teacher-selected texts. After initial independent reading, teachers listened to individuals read and provided skill and strategy instruction supporting each student's efforts to decode unknown words.<br>• In shared reading lessons, the teacher read aloud from an enlarged text. Teachers often pointed to individual words while leading the group in choral reading of the text followed by phonics lessons emphasizing some skill (beginning and ending sounds, vowel patterns, word families, and/or voice/print matching). |
| Reading Instruction Individual | • Teachers listened to the student read a text, providing instruction when needed to support decoding of unknown words. Teachers questioned the learner after reading about specific difficulties with the text and emphasized needed phonics skills and strategies for reading unknown texts. |
| Shared Writing | • The teacher and students collaboratively generated sentences and the teacher served as scribe to write the text on large sheets of paper. Individual sentences were then read chorally and changes made as decided by the group. Phonics instruction occurred as the teacher and students discussed how individual words should be written. |
| Writing Demonstrations | • The teacher's demonstration was an enactment of what writers do when they write. It was a staged event, jointly managed by the teacher and her children, that included explicit actions and decisions to guide students' development, as well as implicit communication of the writing process (Grogan, 1998). |
| Interactive Writing | • Interactive writing involved the students and teacher in jointly creating text to be written on large chart paper. Student participation increased as the teacher shared the pen with students by inviting them to write some of the letters and words during composing. The final text was a combination of words written by the teacher and individual students. Phonics instruction addressed students' efforts to encode unfamiliar words. |
| Individual Writing Instruction | • While other students were writing independently, teachers conferenced with individual children. Students read their writing to the teacher. Instruction focused on questions students posed and the teacher provided focused instruction on writing skills including the letter/sound patterns in words written by the student. |
| Word Analysis and Pattern Instruction | • Inductive lessons focused on selected word features such as initial or final sounds, vowel patterns, or rhyming words.<br>— During "I Spy" students looked for specific words in previously generated texts (Our Daily News) or other enlarged texts.<br>— During other word analysis lessons, students wrote on chalk slates and discussed patterns in dictated words.<br>— They sorted word cards to determine letter/sound patterns. |

phonics transactions. For example, we counted as one phonics transaction the following (phonics transaction evidence is underlined):

During a writing conference where a child was attempting to write the word SISTER, the child said that the word began with S and ended with R. The teacher then tried to extend that representation by talking about the first vowel sound in the word.

Mrs. Evans: It's the letter I. Like Indian, ih. [She gestured to the short vowel chart with an Indian depicted for short I.] s-I-s-ter [She elongated the sounds and emphasized the short i].

[Oak Park 12/3/96]

***Establishing patterns of phonics instruction.*** Field notes were coded for broad teaching/learning events and then for specific phonics transactions as teachers and students dealt with phonics concepts, skills, and strategies. The purpose of coding the phonics transactions was not to count how many times a specific skill appeared in the single event, or to conduct a frequency count of instruction, but rather to determine what was being taught, where, and how. Thus, if the strategy "elongate to produce sounds in order" occurred four times in a row during a broad teaching/learning event, it was only coded once. Often the coding for a lengthy event included 2 or more different skills and 1 or 2 strategies. The purpose was to determine the range of what was being taught during these extended

TABLE 24.3. Coding Definitions for Concepts and Skills

| Focus | Code and Definition |
|---|---|
| Foundation concept | Phonological awareness: Instruction focused on developing the ability to hear and manipulate the sound units of language including syllables, onsets and rimes, and phonemes. |
| Foundation concept | Phonemic awareness: Instruction focused on an understanding that spoken words are made up of a sequence of separate phonemes. This includes the ability to subdivide words into phonemes and rearrange or substitute them one for another. |
| Foundation concept | Phonemic segmentation: Instruction focused on the ability to recognize and separate the sounds of each of the individual phonemes in sequential order from beginning to end and represent them with appropriate letters. |
| Phonics skills | Vowel instruction: Instruction about long vowels, short vowels, vowel digraphs, r-controlled vowels, word patterns in which a vowel was silent, and vowels in medial positions. |
| Phonics skills | Consonant instruction: Instruction about consonant sounds in the beginning, medial, and/or final positions in words. It also included instruction about consonants labeled as hard and soft sounds (c, g), consonant blends, consonant digraphs, and word patterns in which a consonant was silent. |
| Word analysis | Structural/morphemic analysis: Word analysis instruction about root words, affixes (prefixes and suffixes), compound words, contractions, and homonyms. |

teaching/learning events. The resulting patterns were determined across all eight sites to discover global teaching patterns for the study.

***Skill and concept analysis.*** Analysis focused on coding the phonics transactions and categorizing them. Because foundational concepts such as phonological awareness, phonemic awareness, and phonemic segmentation have been defined in various ways across references and often disputed, the researchers developed definitions for coding that took into account wordings mostly from three sources (Adams, 1991; Snow, Burns, & Griffin, 1998; Weaver, 1996, 1998). In addition, Salinger's (1996) listing of word analysis skills was used to identify instruction in phonetic, structural, and morphemic analysis. These coding definitions are presented in Table 24.3.

***Strategy analysis.*** Successive examination of the data across phonics transactions also revealed that instruction focused on phonics strategies across these sites. Strategies were defined as "conscious, instantiated, and flexible plans readers apply and adapt to a variety of texts and tasks" (Dole, Duffy, Roehler, & Pearson, 1991, p. 242). Researchers generated a report of the phonics strategies observed at each site including a representative vignette for each strategy. Analysis of these strategy accounts yielded the strategy codes in Table 24.4. Also included were three additional strategies that interlocked phonics with other cueing systems and classroom resources, drawing on the learner's language knowledge, involvement, and use of classroom resources.

***Instructional analysis.*** A further round of data analysis was conducted to investigate two researcher hypotheses emerging from successive readings of data: (a) that teachers were differentiating instruction to meet the needs of a range of learners, and (b) that teachers differentiated instruction within both individual and group contexts. The round of analysis on differentiation of instruction involved identifying instructional events where teachers delivered instruction that met a variety of differing individual needs. We looked within these specific instructional events to determine and list the range of concepts that were addressed and to look for ways that teachers gathered and used assessment data. For example, within a series of individual writing conferences on a given day, the instructional focus of each conference was noted. It was clear that teachers used their observations of specific learners and their knowledge of each child's particular areas of skill development and confusions to select a specific focus for each conference. Similarly, we looked at events involving group instruction where specific instruction for particular individuals was provided within the context of the ongoing whole group event. The range of skills and strategies provided was tabulated within and across sites.

***Procedures for accurate coding and auditing.*** Because the accuracy of coding was a critical concern for this study, three procedures were used to assure consistency. First, the research team met in weekly day-long coding sessions throughout a 6-month period. The work was to refine codes and coding procedures in light of each researcher's questions and site data. Team members discussed coding problems using their own field notes and classroom transcripts as examples. These team sessions often included coding the same passage, resolving differences through discussion, and revision of procedures and codes. When the coding scheme was finalized, the researchers completed their independent coding of site data. An interrater reliability of .90 was present when the team used the final set of procedures and codes.

The second procedure for ensuring accuracy was member checking of the final site analyses. The summarized patterns from data analyses across sites as well as the findings for the study as a whole were shared with participating teachers. Teachers' suggestions and questions were used in revising the written draft of the study. Generally, this member check provided an opportunity to verify the credibility of instructional patterns and discuss the specific achievement results.

Third, an auditing procedure addressing the quality of data analysis involved a session with outside research consultants. The auditors examined the legitimacy of analysis procedures and made suggestions about possible strategies. Since the analysis

TABLE 24.4. Phonics Strategy and Interlocking
Strategy Codes

| Phonics Strategies | Definition |
|---|---|
| Use of onset and meaning | Simultaneously using the onset of the word and sense of the sentence or phrase to rapidly decode an unknown word. |
| Elongate to produce sounds in order | In reading, using the sequence of letters to sound out a word by stretching out the sounds. In writing, segmenting phonemes across the word and matching sounds to appropriate letters. |
| Recheck writing by rereading | Self-monitoring during writing involves rereading to see if every sound is represented, checking spelling to see whether the word looks right. |
| Using graphophonemic information to rethink a miscue | Self correcting or confirming the accuracy of reading attempts using graphophonemic information in combination with language knowledge. |
| Using patterns or relatively consistent orthographic features | Working from the known to the unknown using word patterns, relatively consistent letter/sound relations, and morphemic patterns to read or write a word. |
| Working with complex orthographic features | Using orthographic information that is ambiguous or complex (vowel digraphs, vowel diphthongs, soft and hard sounds of c and g) to read or write a needed word. |
| Kinesthetic information | Focusing on body feedback, such as how the mouth is shaped in producing sounds for certain letter cues (/sh/, /wh/, etc.). |
| Voice print matching | Using finger pointing and voice emphasis to align the oral reading of a word with the word in print. |
| Phonics patterns have exceptions | Recognizing that some words do not fit simple or consistent rules or patterns requiring multiple attempts during decoding or encoding. |

| Interlocking Strategies | Definitions |
|---|---|
| Language knowledge | During encoding or decoding learners think of other words they know which fit syntactically in the sentence or make sense. |
| Expectation of student involvement and independence | Actively working at reading or writing a word by employing a sequence of strategies. |
| Multiple resources | Supporting and confirming attempts to read or write a word using a variety of resources in the classroom (word lists on the wall, dictionaries, other students). |

was ongoing at the time of this day-long session, it was not a traditional audit trail review. The session, nevertheless, was a critical discussion of data analysis procedures from varying perspectives and strongly influenced the final procedures.

***Analysis of achievement measures.*** Descriptive statistics for all students completing pre- and posttesting on all four measures were generated to establish general patterns of achievement. Scores on each instrument were determined following the specified procedures as described under instrumentation.

Pretest and posttest scores from three of the assessments (QRI-II Word List, Developmental Spelling Analysis, and Text Reading Level) were scaled together using the Rasch model, providing linear, test-free estimates of ability and person-free estimates of item difficulty (Wright & Masters, 1982). The Rasch measurement model has found application in a wide range of disciplines, such as medicine, education, psychology, archeology, and sociology. It is one of the latent-trait, or item response models, in which discrete responses are modeled by a person parameter of ability and one item parameter specifying location or difficulty. Analyzing test data with the Rasch model had several advantages over traditional methods. It provided a single linear, equal-interval scale for both persons and items, statistics for precision (reliability) and validity of each measure, and an easy procedure to equate forms. Scaling the multiple measures together provided a single composite score for each child for both pretesting and posttesting and yielded two benefits over the use of a single instrument: (a) greater statistical precision and (b) the opportunity to describe student gains across the three measures simultaneously.

The Rasch model for scaling the three instruments together involved concatenating horizontally the response data for the three assessments, producing a single record for each student. All items were then calibrated together as if they were from a single test. Examination of the item fit statistics showed no systematic pattern of misfit, indicating that the three assessments could be considered a single test. Composite scores from this analysis represented the students' overall ability on an equal-interval scale. Individual gains were calculated by subtracting the pretest composite score from the posttest composite score. Since the pre- and posttest data were calibrated simultaneously in this way (putting all sets of measures on the same scale), direct pre–post comparisons were nonproblematic.

In addition, pretest scores on Hearing and Recording Sounds in Words (the Dictation task) were used to create a histogram to determine naturally occurring groupings of students as a basis for further analysis. Scores on the Hearing and Recording Sounds in Words task represent a student's ability to hear and write up to 37 sounds from two dictated sentences. The correlation between pretest HRSW scores and pretest composite scores was .86. Analysis of the histogram revealed dividing points that defined relatively homogeneous groupings of students with similar HRSW scores. Scores on HRSW clustered in three categories of similar width (2–14, 15–26, 27–37) resulting in three groups with scores statistically different from adjacent groups. Composite pretest and posttest scores of students within the three groups were analyzed to determine gains between October and May.

# RESULTS

The instructional findings addressed what was taught during phonics instruction, where that instruction was situated in first-grade programs, and how phonics instruction was conducted. Each of these instructional findings is presented by providing a data narrative including representative vignettes. Subsequently, achievement outcomes are presented, reporting pre- and posttest gains in phonics skills and concepts across measures of decoding and encoding and descriptions of achievement groups.

Each of the classroom examples contain fictional names for the school, teacher, and students. The conventions used in presenting classroom transcriptions for examples in the instructional findings were:

1. *Written text*—Text being written or text already printed and being read was printed in capitals (e.g., The teacher read, JACK AND JILL WENT UP THE HILL).
2. *Elongation of sound*—The letters of the word were separated by dashes to show elongation (e.g., c-a-t).
3. *Emphasis*—A sound produced louder for emphasis was shown in upper case letters (e.g., c-A-t).
4. *Description of action*—Brackets enclosed the explanation of an action (e.g., [The teacher pauses.]).
5. *Naming a letter*—A letter identified by its name was capitalized and underlined (e.g., "That word is spelled *C A T*").

## Instructional Finding #1: What Was Taught

### *Overview*

1. The foundation concepts of phonological awareness, phonemic awareness, and phonemic segmentation constituted more than a third of the instruction that was coded.
2. Instruction addressed consonant and vowel patterns in the context of reading and writing activities.
3. Phonics skills were taught in tandem with phonics strategies. Phonics strategy lessons provided procedural explanations for using phonics skills and concepts.

***Foundation concepts.*** In 844 documented phonics transactions, 39% developed the foundation concepts of phonological awareness, phonemic awareness, and phonemic segmentation. Phonological awareness instruction occurred frequently as children listened to storybooks in whole group sessions. After reading and talking about a book or poem, the teacher would invite children to look at the written text and listen closely as she read in order to find rhyming pairs, or words with particular patterns. The sound of the rhyme or the word patterns formed the heart of the interactions that followed. An example from St. Paul Elementary, a Catholic whole language site, was representative of this foundation work. The children were working with a poem *Five Fat Turkeys* (Peek, 1985) and looking at the written text.

FIVE FAT TURKEYS
SITTING ON A GATE,
THE FIRST ONE SAID
"OH, MY, IT'S GETTING LATE!"
THE SECOND ONE SAID,
"THANKS GIVING IS NEAR."
"THE THIRD ONE SAID,
"THAT MAKES ME SHAKE WITH FEAR.". . .

They read the poem together; then Mrs. Parker asked children to listen as she alone read the poem from the chart. The children noticed rhymes.

| | |
|---|---|
| Mrs. Parker: | Yes, there's a rhyming pattern in this poem. Who will come up and frame two words that rhyme? |
| Charles: | [Walked up to the chart and framed GATE and LATE.] |
| Mrs. Parker: | Charles, say the two words you framed. |
| Charles: | GATE, LATE. |
| Mrs. Parker: | What do these two words do? |
| Charles: | Sound the same. |
| Mrs. Parker: | Where do they sound the same? At the beginning or the ending? |
| Charles: | The ending. |

[St. Paul, 11/2/96]

The lesson continued as other rhyming pairs were framed with children's hands on each side of the word and read aloud. The teacher reinforced the concept of seeing and hearing rhyming patterns at the ends of words.

Instruction in phonemic segmentation often took place in shared writing activities as first graders talked about the spellings of words to be written. These group lessons focused on hearing and representing sounds in sequence as a piece of writing was generated. An illustration of instruction from Garfield, an inner city, urban whole language classroom, shows a representative activity. Students worked each day on Our Daily News, a report of classroom events. The instructional activity, written with the teacher as scribe, emphasized phonemic segmentation and included a running teacher commentary about specific letter/sound relations within dictated words.

On one particular day the daily news included as its third sentence, TODAY LAUREN AND MACKENZIE READ A BOOK. The students were ready to work on the word BOOK.

| | |
|---|---|
| Mrs. Miller: | BOOK. Get us started, b-oo-k. |
| Lauren: | *B* |
| Mrs. Miller: | [Writes *B*]. Who can tell me some other letters? Don't give me the ending. We need something in between, b-OO-k. |
| Ann: | *O* |
| MacKenzie: | *C* |
| Mrs. Miller: | No *C* in it. |
| Rashana: | *K* |
| Mrs. Miller: | It has two *O*s in it, then the *K*. [Writes O O K.] These two *O*s say o-o [She makes the short *O* sound and points to the two *O*s.] Can you say it? |
| Children: | o-o |
| Mrs. Miller: | Good. |

[Garfield, 11/13/96]

The lesson continued as other words were written sound by sound and then the class read the text. Often these lessons were followed by I Spy, a game in which Mrs. Miller asked children to spy words with consonant blends or a particular vowel pattern. This game reinforced the letter/sound relations that were part of the day's shared writing.

***Consonants and vowels.*** Ongoing instruction on initial consonants, consonant blends, and various vowel patterns was conducted through various kinds of phonics instruction across the school year. Across the 844 phonics transactions documented in field notes, 28% addressed vowel skills, and 33% provided instruction about consonants. Specific letter/sound patterns were frequently highlighted in big book reading lessons where teachers covered specific words or word parts with sticky notes. Children predicted the covered word and talked about the letter/sound pattern that would be there. The sticky note was then removed and children sounded out the word, confirming or disconfirming their prediction.

For example, at Eastland, a language arts magnet school, the whole group lesson was about the nursery rhyme, *Jack and Jill* (Lobel, 1986). The teacher covered up each of the vowels in a chart version of the rhyme and explained that she wanted children to identify the missing vowels. The lesson began as the teacher pointed to each word. The children each had five index cards with a different vowel on each card.

Mrs. Dean: Find the vowel that goes in the middle of JACK and hold it up for me.
Children: [All raise their cards to show their answers.]
Mrs. Dean: Remember, *a* [She makes the short *A* sound]. Which one of these goes *a* [short *A* sound] as in Jack. [She asks a child to uncover the letter and nods her approval as children's cards agree with the uncovered vowel *A*.]
[Eastland, 12/2/96]

The lesson continued as the teacher checked each of the attempts by the students and repeated the vowel sounds for each word (for example, WENT, UP, and TUMBLING).

In other instruction, knowledge of consonants and vowels was developed as children brainstormed words having a specific beginning sound or certain vowel pattern. Chart paper lists from these ongoing lessons were accumulated on classroom walls documenting ongoing consonant and vowel insturction. They served as resources for children during their independent writing.

Specific letter/sound patterns were also the focus of instruction with children writing dictated words on individual chalk slates in word pattern lessons. During these events, teachers dictated words with a particular pattern and children wrote and talked about that letter/sound relationship.

A representative teaching event with individual chalk slates occurred at Oldfield Elementary, a suburban whole language site, as the teacher dictated words beginning with Y. Her lesson reviewed the sound by asking children to pronounce some words with initial Y. Children wrote the beginning and ending

sounds of several dictated words and subsequently wrote the whole word for YAK, YIP, YAM, and YARN. Later, with words copied by children onto the front chalkboard, they talked about student spellings and focused on one student's spelling (YORN for YARN).

Mrs. Lyon: Anyone spell it differently?
Chelsea: *Y A R N*
Mrs. Lyon: We've got two choices. What do you think?
Tony: *Y O R N*
Mrs. Lyon: What does *O R* Say?
Children: or
Mrs. Lyon: Let's put the or [sound] in there, what does it say?
Children: yorn?
Mrs. Lyon: [Pointed to the chart children had generated of word families with *A R* pattern words from an earlier lesson.]
[Oldfield, 1/29/97]

Chalkboard lessons such as this occurred frequently and presented phonics concepts that children struggled with in their writing.

***Strategies and skills.*** Phonics instruction also addressed knowing how to use skill knowledge strategically rather than merely knowing about particular skills. Often skills and strategies were integrated in single teaching/learning events. Most of the main instructional activities developed more than one phonics skill and presented multiple strategies. Analysis of 364 phonics teaching/learning events, the extended activity contexts for instruction, indicated 844 phonics transactions addressing skills and 714 phonics transactions focused on strategies.

Strategy instruction provided procedural explanations about how to work with letter/sound concepts and often included brief teacher demonstrations of strategy use while reading and writing. Many lessons worked with children's explanations, since teachers routinely asked children to explain their strategies, accounting for the way they figured out a word or worked through an unfamiliar spelling. The emphasis was on children's strategy explanations (in their own words) and on phonics strategy awareness.

The following five strategies were most likely to be included in a phonics teaching/learning event:

1. Using known letter/sound relations or relatively consistent orthographic patterns to work from known words to unknown.
2. Elongating the word to produce the sounds in order.
3. Using voice/print matching to align the word being read with the word in print.
4. Using graphophonemic information to rethink a miscue in reading.
5. Rechecking writing by rereading and monitoring letter/sound relations in the words written and read.

In the first strategy, learners were shown how to use what they already knew in decoding or encoding unknown words.

Working from known to unknown, children used patterns to create an analogy.

At St. Paul's Elementary, for example, the teacher asked children just before a writing project to explain the ways to figure out words they didn't know how to spell.

Mrs. Parker: What else can we do when we're writing?
Howard: You could find a word you know to help with another one.
Mrs. Parker: You can use words that you know to help you spell words you don't know.
[St. Paul, 3/5/98]

The interactions continued as children used this strategy and talked about how they figured out each word.

In the second strategy children were shown how to stretch out the sounds of a word. They maintained the left to right order and elongated the sounds. An example of this sounding out strategy occurred during a teacher/student writing conference at Oak Park Elementary, an urban literature magnet school. Michael was reading the end to his story, " . . . AND THEY LIVED HAPPILY EVER AFTER." He had written LVOAR. The teacher helped Michael rewrite his sentence elongating the words and representing the sounds. They worked together on THEY and LIVED stretching out the sounds and identifying needed letters.

Mrs. Evans: They lived happily [pointing to the place for the next word, HAPPLY, to be written].
Michael: Happily, hap-hap-pah-uh.
Mrs. Evans: Say it again. See if you hear any more sounds.
Michael: Hap-uh [pause]
Mrs. Evans: lee
Michael: L lee E
Mrs. Evans: Look how many sounds you heard in happily. That's really all the ones we hear.
Michael: [Begins to write the letters for HAPPILY].
[Oak Park, 1/8/97]

In this conference Mrs. Evans supported the stretching out strategy, Michael attempted it, and Mrs. Evans reinforced the strategy before he began to write.

The third strategy, voice/print matching, helped learners focus on the word that was actually being read. Teachers reading big books to groups or reading with individual learners emphasized voice/print matching by pointing to each word or asking children to do their own pointing when they were confused.

The two other most frequent strategies focused on working with miscues. In reading, learners were taught to rethink a miscue by looking again at the word and considering the letters and sounds. In writing, learners were taught to reread their text, remembering their intended meaning, and checking spellings to represent every sound. Both involved going back to use letter/sound knowledge to monitor what was produced.

Phonics skill and strategy instruction also took place as children read individually and wrote independently in workshop or project settings. The individual and small group

instruction provided by teachers on a daily basis reinforced vowel and consonant knowledge and guided students in the use of particular strategies. A representative segment from an individual reading conference at Cottage Elementary, a whole language magnet school, showed this reinforcement. Daniel was midway through *At the Zoo* (1979) and was reading the sentence, FIVE TIGERS CLAWING, to his teacher.

Daniel: Four tigers scratch.
Mrs. Olson: That's what the picture shows. [She then points to the word CLAWING and keeps her finger there.]
Daniel: *C, L,* c-1 [pauses].
Mrs. Olson: What does *A W* say? Aw.
Daniel: Cl- aw, four tigers clawing.
Mrs. Olson: Look at the picture.
Daniel: [Looked at the illustration of five tigers and then back at the word FIVE.]
[Cottage, 1/28/97]

In this conference the teacher emphasized the orchestration of information from multiple cueing systems. The letter/sound information was emphasized along with meaning as represented in the illustration and the text. Working across several pages, the teacher helped Daniel self-correct.

Interlocking strategies, a separate category of reading writing strategies related to phonics, were embedded in the instructions for learner independent work. These strategies, not included in the tallies for strictly phonics strategies, linked letter/sound relations with other kinds of information. For example, Mrs. Hillson at Hedgewood Park Elementary, the urban coteaching classroom, reviewed the resources that children could use in spelling a word. The teacher and students together had read the nursery rhyme "Hey Diddle Diddle" (dePaola, 1985) and were discussing how to write specific words as labels for their illustrations when they weren't sure of the spelling. The word being discussed was FIDDLE.

Mrs. Hillson: You can say, "Oh! I hear an '*F*' at the beginning of that," and just write the letters that you hear. You could ask a friend. You can look up here at the chart and try to find FIDDLE. You could look at the book. So there are lots of different things you can do to try to figure that out.
[Hedgewood Park, 2/25/97]

These interlocking strategies were indicative of the emphasis on multiple resources that learners could use independently.

***Summary of instructional finding #1.*** The essential characteristic of this finding about the content of phonics instruction in whole language classrooms was that phonics skills were taught with an emphasis on their application strategically. Instruction addressed not only the foundation skills essential to literacy achievement and the essential letter/sound relations, but also the connections with other cueing systems and language resources that children needed in their work as readers and writers.

## Instructional Finding #2: Where Phonics Instruction Occurred

### Overview

1. Phonics instruction was spread across a variety of standard whole language activities.
2. Writing experiences served as an essential context for developing phonics knowledge.
3. Phonics was taught at the point of use as teachers and children engaged in reading and writing.

**Location.** Phonics instruction was consistently documented within a variety of reading and writing activities typically found in whole language classrooms. Rankings of teaching/learning events with phonics showed four categories as occurring most frequently. Categories in reading were: reading instruction in small and large groups (33%) and reading instruction in individual conferences (14%). Categories in writing were: individual writing conferences (17%) and word analysis and pattern lessons (15%).

During reading group events teachers emphasized voice/print matching, talked about rhymes and word families, and pointed out words with particular letter/sound patterns for children to notice. Guided reading lessons, another kind of group reading instruction, focused on reading aloud, monitoring comprehension, decoding words in the text, and discussing children's phonics strategy explanations. For example, at Hedgewood Park, an instructional group of three children read *The Biggest Cake in the World* (Compton, 1988) aloud. They talked with the teacher about particular words written in the story. Because the teacher consistently asked the children to verbalize their thinking, the children were ready with their explanations.

| | |
|---|---|
| Mrs. Spencer: | On this page you read, "MR. D. MADE AND MADE." You then went back and changed it and looked at me. What did you change it to? |
| Kevin: | MIXED |
| George: | [explaining his reasons] MIX has *I* after it [after the *M*]. |
| Tim: | MIX has *X* in it. |
| Mrs. Spencer: | [nodded in agreement] |

[Hedgewood, 2/12/97]

In this lesson children responded to the teacher's question by demonstrating that they knew what the teacher wanted them to explain. They used the cognitive structures of these guided reading lessons to focus their decoding work. The teacher's scaffold (her question and monitoring of the children's explanation) constituted the phonics transaction.

Shared reading events often involved extended discussions and led to writing experiences. At Clifford Elementary on the first snowy day of winter, for example, instruction began with students dictating sentences about what they liked to do on a snowy day. The teacher emphasized hearing the sounds in particular words in the story (for example, SLEDDING) and represented each phoneme as she wrote the sentences. Mrs. Adams then introduced a big book version of *The Snowy Day*

by Ezra Jack Keats (1962) and invited children to find out if their snow activities were in the story. As she read the story, Mrs. Adams emphasized the words that contributed sounds to the story (CRUNCH, CRUNCH, CRUNCH) and she asked children about certain story moments. The reading continued, and they talked about what happened to the snowball that was hidden.

| | |
|---|---|
| Mrs. Adams: | [reading] BEFORE HE GOT INTO BED, HE LOOKED IN HIS POCKET. HIS POCKET WAS [turning to the class] what? |
| Children: | wet |
| Mrs. Adams: | It was wet! It sure was. There it is. Right there. [She points to the illustration]. It was wet. [Begins to read again] HIS POCKET WAS . . . but this can't be wet, because it doesn't start with a *W*. |
| Michael: | empty |
| Mrs. Adams: | EMPTY. [Nods in confirmation] THE SNOWBALL WASN'T THERE. |

[Clifford, 1/13/97]

The reading continued and finally the lesson connected back to the dictated sentences. Mrs. Adams asked, "Can you think of anything that we didn't write down here?" They added a new sentence, HE MADE A SNOW ANGEL, with the teacher again emphasizing the representation of sounds in each word.

The phonics transaction in this instance was a demonstration of using letter/sound knowledge in connection with meaning in order to identify a word. The instance of instruction was played out in the teacher's statement.

In addition, individual reading conferences occurred as teachers worked with children engaged in reading books of their choice or books selected by the teacher. Children also chose books related to the current project or theme. These conferences provided instruction focused on the reader's individual decoding skills and strategies. They were also used to monitor individual progress and to assist teachers in planning instruction that foregrounded the developmental patterns of the learner.

***The role of the writing program.*** A substantial portion of the phonics events coded in this study occurred in the writing program. Of the 364 broad teaching/learning events with phonics 45% were writing-centered activities. Lengthy uninterrupted writing periods where children wrote on topics of their choice or where a writing project was linked to literature provided sustained opportunities for children to grapple with phonics concepts. When children wrote in sustained writing periods where they chose their topic, they frequently received help from the teacher and other writers. For example, in Cottage Elementary, the interactions during one sustained writing session addressed words that children were trying to spell. At this site, children presented spelling attempts on small pieces of paper to the teacher as she circulated around the room during writing time. Teacher/student interactions addressing these spelling attempts focused on the learner's written word and provided the encoding information that the child requested.

| Julie: | Is this how you spell THROUGH? (Points to THOUGH on the spelling scrap of paper). |
| Mrs. Olson: | Almost. You are missing a letter. Add an *R* thRough and a *G*. |
| Mrs. Olson: | [Wrote the new letters in the student's word]. |
| Julie: | [Returned to her writing, copying the spelling from her scrap of paper]. |

[Cottage, 3/5/97]

The phonics transaction was simply the teacher sounding out the word emphasizing the medial sound, telling the letter to represent that sound and writing it. In this classroom there were 15 to 20 such interactions within the context of nearly every sustained writing period. Learners attempted the needed word on their paper, copied it onto the scrap of paper, asked for help, and wrote the conventional spelling in their draft. At the end of the year many of the spelling attempts served as confirmations that the learner had figured out the word. Across the year, the question that children asked their teacher shifted from "How do you spell . . . ?" to "Is this how you spell . . . ?"

Writing demonstrations by teachers provided contextualized explanations of a writer's work. They showed the decisions writers make as they consider what to say, encode needed words, monitor their message, and attend to print conventions. Mrs. Adams at Clifford Elementary routinely provided detailed writing demonstrations for her class. For example, in one event she wrote a piece about her cat. She talked about her thoughts on the topic and settled on a sentence to write.

| Mrs. Adams: | I'm going to write about my pet, Fluffy. She's a cat and we call her Fluffy because she is big and furry. So I'm going to begin my story with the sentence, MY CAT IS BIG AND FURRY. |
| Mrs. Adams: | [Talked about each word as she wrote it, involving children in decisions about letter choices and elongating the sounds as she wrote and said the words B-I-G, A-N-D]. |
| Mrs. Adams: | FURRY. What sounds do you hear in FURRY? |
| Timmy: | *E* |
| Mrs. Adams: | Yes, I hear *E* too. Where do you hear it? |
| Timmy: | At the end. |
| Mrs. Adams: | What other sounds do you hear in FURRY? I'm going to write FURRY. [She stretches out the sounds as she writes the word FURRY.] |
| Mrs. Adams: | [running her finger under the word, left-to-right] FURRY. I hear *E* but there's not an *E* in furry. What letter is making the *E* sound? |
| Children: | *Y* |

[Clifford, 11/12/96]

Mrs. Adams continued to talk about the *Y* sound in the final position, emphasizing her point by talking about the *Y* in three of the children's names: Ashley, Bethany, and Jimmy.

The demonstration as a whole event showed the production of the full message and included interactions about specific letter/sound patterns. It also integrated some strategies that writers use: stretching out sounds for particular words, using words that had known spellings, and segmenting the sounds

in a particularly difficult word to represent the sounds in order. The event closed with suggestions about ways to use the teacher's demonstration during individual writing.

Teachers planned inductive word analysis and pattern lessons that placed children in the role of discovering and discussing words that fit specific letter/sound patterns. Teachers asked questions and helped children talk about the evidence they gathered. At Oldfield, a suburban whole language site, the class was in the midst of a literature unit on bears, and the children's homework involved finding words that rhymed with bear. In this word study and pattern lesson the children generated a list on the board (HAIR, LAIR, DELAWARE, PEAR, PAIR, PARE, BARE, FARE, FAIR, WHERE, WEAR, STAIR, SCARE, MARE, CHAIR, SHARE, AIR, DARE, CARE, UNDERWEAR, TEAR, STARE, THERE, THEIR). The students and teacher developed categories and posted the words on a large chart with the headings (-ear, -air, -ere, -are and an empty column). Children talked about the groupings and patterns when the chart was complete. The teacher connected this categorization to poems students could write and to strategies for spelling. [Oldfield, 1/29/97]

The phonics transaction in this lesson was embedded in the interactions as children categorized the words and the teacher/student interactions emphasized the many ways the same sound was represented.

***Phonics at the point of personal use.*** As children read their chosen books and worked in daily writing sessions, teachers circulated and helped with individual decoding and encoding problems. Analysis of teaching/learning events showed that this phonics instruction addressed what children were working on at the moment; it focused on the particular reading and writing in which children were engaged. While each interaction was a quick exchange, the ongoing pattern of embedded instruction for individuals during their reading and writing amounted to a prominent strand of instruction day after day that helped children progress developmentally.

For example, at Garfield the teacher helped individuals who were writing about imaginary presents on pages to be assembled into a book about Christmas dreams. Kevin struggled with the word BIKE.

| Mrs. Miller: | How does BIKE begin? B-ike [emphasizing the initial sound]. |
| William: | *P* |
| Mrs. Miller: | No, BIKE. |
| William: | *B* [writes B on his paper.] |
| Mrs. Miller: | Listen. b-II-k |
| William: | *I* [writes I, Mrs. Miller nods in approval.] |
| Mrs. Miller: | Listen. What do you hear? bi-KK. |
| William: | Key [Looks at alphabet strip over chalkboard with a key depicted for *K*]. |
| Mrs. Miller: | No, you need a letter. What does key start with? |
| William: | *Y* |
| Mrs. Miller: | [points to a name plate on the neighbor's desk, whose name starts with K] Point to *K*. |
| William: | [Writes the K.] |
| Mrs. Miller: | You need an *E* on the end. |

[Garfield, 12/4/96]

TABLE 24.5. Distribution of Teaching/Learning Events
With Phonics

| Teaching/Learning Events With Phonics | Percentage of Total |
|---|---|
| Reading | |
| Reading instruction—small group, large group | 33% |
| Reading instruction individual | 14% |
| Language exploration | 8% |
| Writing | |
| Writing instruction individual | 17% |
| Word analysis and pattern events | 15% |
| Writing demonstrations | 6% |
| Shared writing | 6% |
| Interactive writing | 1% |
| Totals | |
| Total reading events with phonics instruction | 55% |
| Total writing events with phonics instruction | 45% |

Note. $N = 364$.

***Summary of instructional finding #2.*** Across these teaching/learning events, instruction in phonics was not a separate curriculum; instead, phonics skills and concepts were woven into daily whole language activities. Table 24.5 documents the range and distribution of these events.

In general, the writing program focused children's attention on encoding as first graders learned to write meaningful text. Children also engaged in ongoing reading and writing of their own chosen texts. Within the context of these self-sponsored events, they applied phonics skills and strategies at the point of personal use. Phonics concepts were discussed in the context of children's individual reading and writing.

## Instructional Finding #3: How Teachers Conducted Instruction

### *Overview*

1. Teachers kept track of the skill progress of individual children and used ongoing assessments to inform the instruction of individual children.
2. Instruction was tailor-made developmentally for learners in individual reading and writing conferences and a substantial portion of phonics instruction was conducted one-at-a-time.
3. Teachers conducted differentiated instruction across various reading and writing conferences on the same day, working on different skills with individual children.
4. Differentiated teacher actions supported individual children's participation in whole group reading and writing activities.

***Ongoing assessments.*** Across the eight sites, patterns of one-on-one instruction were documented nearly every day. Teachers organized classroom activities to provide extended periods of reading and writing that enabled students to work independently or with others as the teacher met with individual students.

Teachers used individual conferences to document student progress. Across the eight sites, literacy assessment tools included writing samples, checklists, student reading logs, running records on books used as specific achievement benchmarks, and observations during large and small group instruction. Of the 364 phonics teaching/learning events identified in this study, 128 (35%) were coded as one-on-one instruction within reading or writing conferences. Each of the 128 events included several conferences between teachers and children. Conferences provided in-depth documentation of student progress and enabled teachers to note changes in student understanding and respond with needed instruction.

A representative reading conference began when Mrs. Lyon at Oldfield, a suburban school, asked Sally to join her at the library table to read an unfamiliar text the teacher had selected. Mrs. Lyon's purpose was to assess Sally's reading processes on new text, identify the skills and strategies Sally used to read unfamiliar words, and support Sally's use of new skills and strategies. During the conference, Mrs. Lyon documented Sally's decoding strategies including: using onset and meaning in combination, elongating sounds, and rechecking by rereading. Mrs. Lyon provided time for Sally to identify, employ, and practice skills and strategies independently and taught her to strategically apply the hard and soft sounds of G in the text that was read. [Oldfield, 1/22/97]

***Tailor-made instruction.*** Teachers planned their sequence of phonics lessons based on individual reading and writing conferences like Sally's. This instruction was designed to match the student's development and provide information that would move the student along. Mrs. Spencer, for example, a team teacher at Hedgewood Park School, noted that Evie struggled with consistency in representing beginning and ending consonants and often added extraneous letters to words. In the following writing conference, Mrs. Spencer had listened to Evie read her writing, then began the instructional conversation with a specific instructional goal.

| | |
|---|---|
| Mrs. Spencer: | I want to look at two words with you. I've been noticing in your writing [that] you write lots of extra letters. [She points to KOBVK] |
| Evie: | [Reading] CAN. |
| Mrs. Spencer: | You said that CAN starts with a *K* sound and that's close. That is a good sound. It actually starts with a *C*, but *K* is a good guess. But, I want to think about the last letters. When you say can, do you hear a *V* in that? Say CAN. |
| Evie: | CAN |
| Mrs. Spencer: | Do you hear a *K* at the end of that? Let's cover up the extra letters that you put in. [Uses correction tape.] What do you hear at the end of CAN? |
| Evie: | *N* |
| Mrs. Spencer: | *N*. [She nods in confirmation.] Let's put it down here. |
| Evie: | [Writes it.] |

[Hedgewood Park, 2/6/97]

TABLE 24.6. Writing Instruction During
Individual Conferences

| Conference Number | Teaching That Occurred |
|---|---|
| Conference #1 | Editing final draft |
| | Period at end of sentence |
| | Using environmental print |
| Conference #2 | Phonemic segmentation |
| | Elongating to produce sounds in order |
| | Marking a long vowel with final silent E |
| Conference #3 | Teacher notes improvement in representing sounds, noting the word family (play, day, slay) |
| Conference #4 | Developing an ending for the story |
| Conference #5 | Phonemic segmentation |
| | Elongating to produce sounds in order |
| | Encouraging independence |
| Conference #6 | Phonemic segmentation |
| | Elongating to produce sounds in order |
| Conference #7 | Adding ideas to a story |
| | Marking a long vowel with final silent E |
| | Phonemic segmentation |
| | Elongating to produce sounds in order |
| | Use of upper and lower case letters |
| Conference #8 | Recheck writing by rereading |
| | Elongating to produce sounds in order |

The conference continued, focusing on the word, STORE, which Erin had written as SVRXYW. Based on Erin's writing, Mrs. Spencer carefully selected her teaching points to support Erin's developing knowledge of letter/sound relationships and encouraged her to listen carefully for the sequence of sounds in words and represent them with letters.

**Differentiated instruction.** Teachers met specific individual needs in conferences. These one-on-one events enabled teachers to tailor their instruction to meet the differing needs of students. During one conferencing period of about 45 minutes in an urban classroom, Mrs. Evans met with eight students separately for extended writing conferences. During the member checking meeting about the study, she explained her work in these conferences as, "listening to kids and knowing what they need at that moment."

Students began these conferences by reading their current piece of writing. The teacher's response was based on her extensive understanding of the literacy development of each child and the immediate opportunities posed by that particular piece of writing. Table 24.6 illustrates the range of teaching that occurred within a single series of conferences with students at a variety of levels of expertise [Oak Park, 1/8/97].

**Differentiation across group lessons.** The pattern of differentiated instruction, however, was not limited to one-on-one settings. Teachers' growing understanding of students' individual needs also influenced teacher actions during large and small group activities. Mrs. Dean at Eastland School regularly asked a small group of students to join her on the carpet during a writing project. The purpose was to provide extra support for children's writing efforts. Within such close proximity she could quickly respond, encourage, and suport individual efforts ensuring successful completion of the project. Evidence of teachers responding to individual needs was also documented during large group shared reading, shared writing, and interactive writing.

During interactive writing with the whole class at Clifford School, Mrs. Adams helped Bethany work on voice/print matching by finding the boundaries of two words that the student had written without a space between them. During the same lesson, she helped Doug hear the sounds in words by saying the word WE slowly as he wrote on the chart [11/5/96]. In these cases and others, teachers involved students in reading and writing activities aimed at their current developmental level to support continuous growth.

**Summary of instructional finding #3.** These findings document teachers' efforts to differentiate phonics instruction developmentally, based on the individual progress of their students. Instruction one-at-a-time began with assessment so teachers could hold an in-depth understanding of students' developing knowledge. Individual conferences contributed to that understanding and also provided opportunities for developmentally appropriate individual instruction according to the immediate needs of each student. Similarly, differentiated instruction was documented in small and large group lessons as teachers purposely involved students in reading and writing activities according to their abilities.

## Achievement Findings

Achievement findings reflected two kinds of analyses: (a) whole group gains reported for each of the four assessments of phonics knowledge, and (b) achievement group gains for the measures scaled together.

**Gain scores for each measure.** Table 24.7 depicts descriptive statistics for the 178 first grade students completing both pre- and posttest assessments. Pretest dictation scores revealed a wide range in students' ability to hear and record sounds in words (Scores 2–37) with a mean of 28.5 of a possible 37 points. Scores at posttesting increased to 34.6/37 indicating strong control of the dictation task. Mean pretest Text Reading Level scores were equivalent to the third preprimer; the posttest mean was Level 20, equivalent to basal texts used at the end of Grade 2.

Employing Ganske's scoring system, the DSA scores were calculated by awarding two points for each word spelled correctly and one point if the word was misspelled but the targeted feature was represented correctly. The DSA mean score rose from 15.0 during pretesting to 39.6 at posttesting revealing students' ability to accurately represent most of the words and sounds on the letter name test by the end of the school year. QRI-II scores reflect the number of words students correctly identified either automatically, upon inspection, or following self-correction. The pretest mean score (21.4) indicates control

TABLE 24.7. Descriptive Statistics for Whole Group (N = 178)

| Test | M | SD | Maximum | Top Quartile | Median | Low Quartile | Minimum |
|---|---|---|---|---|---|---|---|
| Pretest Dictation | 28.5 | 8.0 | 37 | 35 | 31 | 23 | 2 |
| Posttest Dictation | 34.6* | 3.8 | 37 | 37 | 36 | 34 | 7 |
| Pretest TRL | 8.3 | 8.3 | 30 | 10 | 5 | 3 | −1 |
| Posttest TRL | 20.0* | 9.9 | 34 | 30 | 22 | 14 | 2 |
| Pretest DSA | 15.0 | 16.5 | 131 | 21 | 12 | 2 | 0 |
| Posttest DSA | 39.6* | 25.3 | 163 | 53 | 39 | 21 | 0 |
| Pretest QRI-II | 21.4 | 23.3 | 98 | 21 | 12 | 7 | 1 |
| Posttest QRI-II | 63.9* | 41.1 | 160 | 87 | 67 | 28 | 2 |

Note. *$p < .0001$.

of preprimer words; the posttest mean (63.9) is equivalent to the beginning of Grade 2.

***Achievement clusters for documenting gains.*** The second analysis focused on three groups of students determined by clustering scores on the phonemic awareness task (Hearing and Recording Sounds in Words) as a pretest. These HRSW scores demonstrated the students' ability to hear sounds in words and demonstrate their knowledge of letter–sound relationships at the beginning of the study. They showed a strong ceiling effect for two of the three groups on the posttest. However, grouping students according to this measure as a pretest provided an opportunity to analyze gains for contrasting clusters of students based on their incoming knowledge of phonemic awareness. Students within each of the resulting groups had similar scores on Hearing and Recording Sounds in Words yet were statistically different from adjacent groups.

This second analysis presented the measures scaled together to create a composite score. These composite scores represented mean performance across measures, enabling a description of learners' proficiency in each condition (decoding in isolation, decoding in context, and encoding in isolation) when the difficulty level of items for each measures were aligned. The Rasch scaling put the composite scores for each learner and the level of difficulty for each test item on the same continuous, linear, content-referenced scale. Since all items were on the same scale, the difficulty of each word on the Developmental Spelling Analysis (DSA) and the Qualitative Reading Inventory (QRI-II) Word List and each level of the Text Reading Level (TRL) could be compared to all the other words or text levels. Composite scores for each group formed benchmarks enabling descriptions of specific words, features, and text reading levels scaled at or below pre/post composite scores. This analysis provided group descriptions of mean performance.

***Composite gain scores by group.*** Achievement documentation for each group included composite gain scores and descriptions of gains across the three scaled assessments for each of the three groupings. The clustering of scores initially on the HRSW task (measuring phonemic awareness) showed three groups of varying size. Group 1 consisted of 70% of the tested population while Groups 2 and 3 were much smaller (21% and 9% respectively). The Rasch scaling across instruments yielded equal interval scores for each student; means were

calculated for composite pretest and posttest scores for children in each group and gains determined (see Table 24.8).

Similar gains for Groups 1 and 3 were not statistically different from each other. This comparison indicated that students with the lowest HRSW scores in October made gains similar to students with the highest scores. Students in the middle grouping scoring 15–26 ($n = 42$) on the pretest HRSW task, however, achieved higher gain scores than either of the other two groups. Figure 24.1 presents these relative gain scores by group and provides the Text Reading Levels as benchmarks for interpreting pre- and posttest achievement levels.

These groupings of students each presented achievement patterns that were distinctive. The descriptions that follow present these achievement patterns by describing the group's performance in terms of means and sample items on each measure.

***Group 1 pre/post means across instruments.*** The largest number of students (70% of tested population) was identified within this first group. These students correctly represented 27 or more phonemes during the HRSW task in October. These scores indicated a strong ability to hear, segment, and represent sounds early in the year.

Figure 24.2 presents their mean performance across measures for pre- and posttests. It depicts learner achievement in terms of mean performance on each task.

TABLE 24.8. Achievement Gains of Comparison Groups

| Group | N | Composite Mean | SD |
|---|---|---|---|
| Group 1 (Dictation Score 27–37) | 123 | | |
| Pretest | | 43.33 | 4.46 |
| Posttest | | 50.47 | 4.45 |
| Gain | | 7.15* | 2.66 |
| Group 2 (Dictation Score 15–26) | 42 | | |
| Pretest | | 34.44 | 3.13 |
| Posttest | | 43.06 | 3.39 |
| Gain | | 8.61* | 3.03 |
| Group 3 (Dictation Score 2–14) | 13 | | |
| Pretest | | 31.68 | 3.63 |
| Posttest | | 37.76 | 4.84 |
| Gain | | 6.08* | 2.93 |

Note. *$p < .0001$.

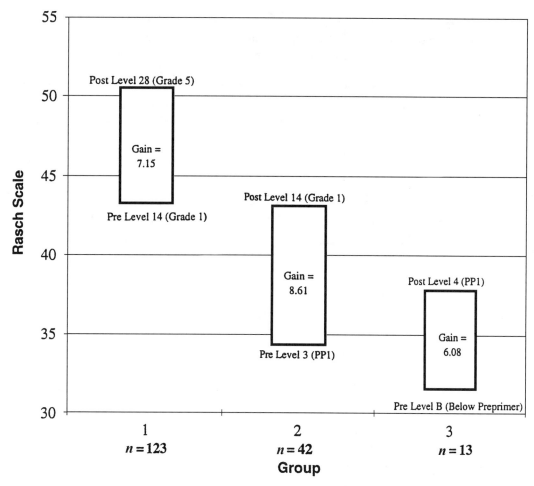

FIGURE 24.1. Relative pretest and posttest mean gains by group with text reading level means.

The gains for this group on the QRI-II Word List measuring decoding in isolation showed an expansion in automatic identification. At the beginning of the study, students, in Group 1 automatically read words largely from the preprimer and primer word lists and a few words from the lists for Grades 1, 2, and 3 (such as *bear, eat, room,* and *lunch*). By May, however, the average student in this group quickly decoded words on lists through Grade 3 and additional words on the Grade 4 and Grade 5 lists. Examples of these words include, for Grade 4: *body, pond, fame crop, ocean* and for Grade 5, *giant, creature, movement, sailor, route.*

The pre–post comparison of Text Reading Level scores revealed a substantial increase in this group's ability to decode words in unfamiliar text. During pretesting, the average student in this group accurately decoded 90% or more of the words from passages equivalent to a Grade 1 reader. The average posttest Text Reading Level was Level 28, demonstrating students' ability to accurately decode words in stories equivalent to Grade 5 readers.

Students demonstrated considerable gains on the Developmental Spelling Analysis. During pretesting the average learner

in this group spelled only two of the Letter-name words correctly but represented nearly all the features on this list including initial and final single consonants, blends, and digraphs as well as short vowels and affricates. Posttest scores revealed a shift to accurate spelling for nearly all of the 25 words on the Letter Name list. Students also demonstrated strong knowledge of several features on the Within Word list including marking long vowels with a final *E,* representing long vowel patterns, and accurately spelling more complex consonant units such as scr-, qu-, and ch-. They also showed beginning knowledge of r-controlled vowels and ambiguous vowel digraphs and diphthongs.

***Group 2 pre-post means across instruments.*** Students in this group constituted 21% of the tested population and had pretest HRSW scores of 15–26. Their gains across the school year can be seen in Fig. 24.3 depicting mean performance across each of the areas that were assessed.

The QRI-II Word List results (where word recognition was timed) indicated that students at the pretest quickly and automatically read only two words on the preprimer list (*the* and *I* ).

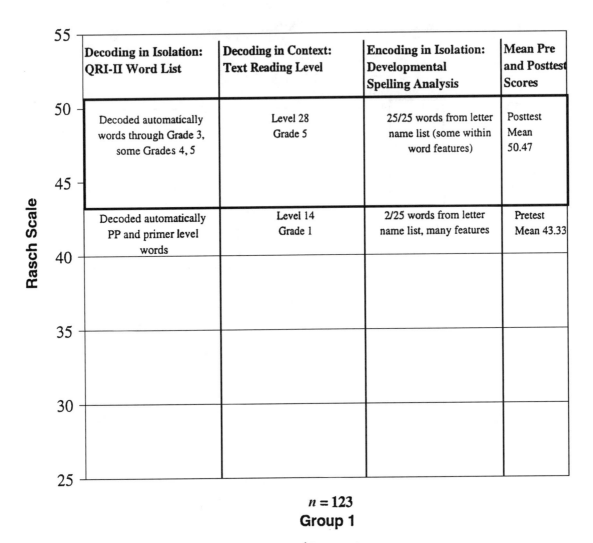

**Rasch Scale**

| | Decoding in Isolation: QRI-II Word List | Decoding in Context: Text Reading Level | Encoding in Isolation: Developmental Spelling Analysis | Mean Pre and Posttest Scores |
|---|---|---|---|---|
| 50 | Decoded automatically words through Grade 3, some Grades 4, 5 | Level 28 Grade 5 | 25/25 words from letter name list (some within word features) | Posttest Mean 50.47 |
| 45 | | | | |
| | Decoded automatically PP and primer level words | Level 14 Grade 1 | 2/25 words from letter name list, many features | Pretest Mean 43.33 |
| 40 | | | | |
| 35 | | | | |
| 30 | | | | |
| 25 | | | | |

*n* = 123
**Group 1**

FIGURE 24.2. Group 1 mean achievement across measures.

Upon inspection of the words, they were able to decode most of the preprimer list and a limited number of words from the Grade 1 and Grade 2 lists (*have, food, room*). At posttest, their ability to rapidly decode words extended beyond the preprimer and primer lists to include additional words from the lists of Grades 1, 2, and 3.

The Text Reading Level gains moved learners from a low preprimer level to a Grade 1 reader level. This posttest level is considered by sites in this study to be an end-of-the-year successful benchmark for reading achievement.

Clear gains in phonics knowledge were demonstrated through Developmental Spelling Analysis (DSA) scores. During pretesting, the average student in this group was unable to spell any of the words, on the first DSA list (Letter-name) or represent any of the targeted features. By posttesting, students demonstrated strong knowledge of each of the Letter Name features including initial and final single consonants, consonant blends and digraphs, short vowels, and affricates.

***Group 3 pre–post means across instruments.*** Students in this group represented 9% of the total number of students tested. Their gains were most clearly demonstrated through achievement on the HRSW task. The average pretest Dictations score of 10 rose to 27 during posttesting indicating gains in phonemic awareness and knowledge of letter-sound relationships. Gains on the other three instruments are represented on Fig. 24.4 depicting student mean performance across measures.

Performance on the QRI-II word list for these students on the pretest was limited. Students in this group were unable to quickly decode words on the preprimer list with the exception of the word *I*. Upon further inspection, additional words from the preprimer list were decoded, such as *go, my, too, in, to,* and *the*. During posttesting, the average student in this group was able to automatically read the preprimer words previously listed, and upon inspection, decode a range of words on lists from preprimer to Grade 3.

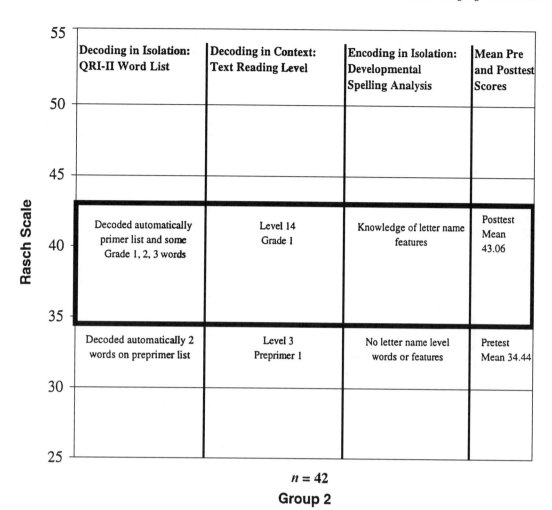

FIGURE 24.3. Group 2 mean achievement across measures.

The Text Reading Level for the pretest was at Level B, a level preliminary to the beginning preprimer. Students participated by responding to a predictable text and identifying the repeated word that had been used throughout the story. On the posttest children were identifying words with 90% accuracy in texts at the preprimer level.

The Developmental Spelling Analysis means showed that the average student in Group 3 was unable to correctly spell any of the Letter Name words or represent any of the focus features on this initial list. In May, however, a stronger understanding of letter/sound relationships was demonstrated by students. They correctly represented features on the Letter name list such as initial and final consonants and short vowel sounds.

***Summary of achievement findings.*** First graders in this study had diverse abilities typical of many classrooms; yet all learners made impressive gains in encoding and decoding as demonstrated on tasks in and out of context. During pottesting, the vast majority of students successfully decoded words in connected text and in isolation at grade 1 or beyond. This finding

demonstrated students' achievement in phonics knowledge by the end of the year.

## DISCUSSION

Literacy scholars from differing perspectives agree that phonemic awareness and understandings of letter–sound relationships support children's development as readers and writers (Adams, 1991; Juel, 1994; Moustafa, 1990, 1995, 1997; Weaver, 1998). The area of disagreement arises out of the question, "How should phonics concepts be taught in the early grades?"

The results of this study support our initial methodological decision to study how phonics was taught rather than whether there was phonics instruction in whole language first grade classrooms. This distinction is critical to debates that characterize whole language and phonics as diametrically opposed. Often, a deficit argument is used by those claiming that phonics is not taught in whole language classrooms. Critics who concede that phonics is taught in whole language classrooms

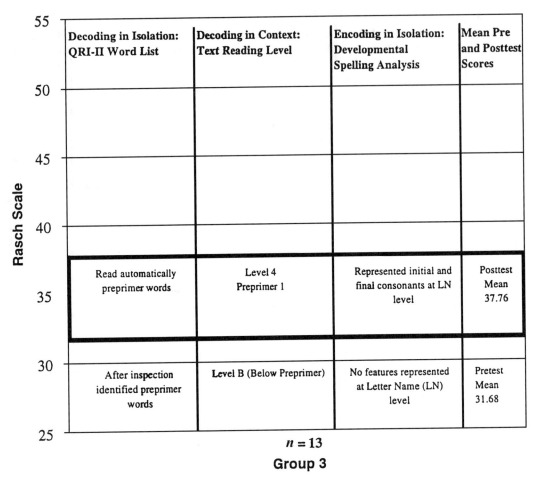

FIGURE 24.4. Group 3 mean achievement across measures.

describe such instruction as informal, ad hoc, or a minor, peripheral component—concluding that whole language instruction denies children the opportunity to learn phonics skills and, consequently, is insufficient.

This current study provided substantial documentation that phonics was taught in whole language first grade classrooms and that an extensive pattern of phonics achievement was present across decoding and encoding measures. Stahl, Duffy-Hester, and Stahl (1998) reviewed recent accounts of phonics instruction and concluded that phonics teaching in whole language settings may be limited to consonant skills and "indicative of whole language teachers' reticence to challenge their students" (p. 350). Data from this study, however, contrast sharply with this conclusion through extensive documentation of phonics skills instruction in vowels and consonants, foundational concepts such as phonological awareness, phonemic awareness, and phonemic segmentation, and word analysis instruction about root words, affixes, compound words, contractions, and homonyms. In fact, every set of field notes from this study documented that phonics instruction occurred within multiple contexts; children at various levels of initial understanding of phonics in October demonstrated substantial gains.

Pre- and posttests in this study documented a wide range of abilities across every measure within every classroom. This range of student knowledge about phonics challenges the efficacy argument of systematic phonics defined as a predetermined sequence of skills administered to the whole class with limited regard to the variety of achievement levels represented within a single class. Strickland (1998b) offered an alternative definition arguing that "instruction is systematic when it is planned, deliberate in application, and proceeds in an orderly manner. This does not mean a rigid progression of 'one-size-fits-all' instruction. Rather, it means a thoughtfully planned program that takes into account learner variability" (p. 51).

When analyzed using Strickland's definition of systematic phonics instruction, data from this study confirms that phonics instruction in each of these classrooms was, indeed, systematic, in that it was deliberate, planned, and intensive in at least two ways. First, phonics teaching was intensive in its frequency of occurrence, amount of attention from the teacher, and inclusion across a variety of instructional events during every day of observed instruction. Intensity was also demonstrated as teachers provided individual instruction to students based on their current reading and writing projects and children's specific patterns of development. Through differentiated activities and lessons, teachers provided thoughtfully planned (systematic) phonics instruction within the settings of inductive lessons, teacher/student conferences, and instruction supporting children engaged in self-selected reading and writing. Within both individual and group contexts, teachers based phonics lessons on the developmental patterns of students rather than the next skill in the teacher's manual. Data from this study support Strickland's second, related point that the "intensity of instruction on any particular skill or strategy should be based on need. Thus, intensity will vary both with individuals and groups" (1998b, p. 51).

Data analysis revealed that phonics instruction was not limited to skills, but almost equally emphasized strategies, and the multiple ways to flexibly use phonics skills during reading and writing. Strategy codes emerging from the data closely paralleled literacy researchers' strategy recommendations such as using analogies to read and write unfamiliar words (Adams, 1991; Cunningham, 1992) and slowly segmenting words to encode or decode (Yopp, 1988). The combination of both skills and strategies is particularly important in light of evidence that phonics skills may be insufficient support for young readers and writers without an understanding of how to apply such information to decode and encode unfamiliar words. Significantly, the current study documented a range of strategies taught in whole language classrooms that encouraged children to self-monitor during reading and writing and to work independently while flexibly employing a variety of strategies to read and write unknown words.

Finally, the achievement outcomes for this study support the efficacy of the kind of phonics instruction that children received in these whole language classroom programs. Children across the range made considerable gains on measures of decoding and encoding knowledge. The largest group of students in this study (70%) demonstrated strong phonics knowledge at the beginning of this study. Their teachers built on this knowledge and did not confine their learning activities to a predetermined grade 1 curriculum or set of materials. Students had extended work times to read books at their instructional level and compose their own books and stories. Through these opportunities students gained the ability to decode words in texts considerably beyond their grade level. This finding challenges recommendations for lengthy scripted phonics lessons in whole group settings.

Students in Groups 2 and 3 (30% of the first grade population) demonstrated limited understanding of phonics skills and concepts during pretesting. The superior achievement of Group 2 may be related to teachers' efforts to differentiate instruction providing phonics lessons based on student need rather than a set curriculum. Students in both groups were supported by one-on-one instruction, scaffolded by their peers, encouraged to read interesting books and write personal stories, and accomplished impressive gains across all four instruments. Although the small group of students in Group 3 were not reading grade 1 materials at the end of this study, the fact that their gains were similar to Group 1 is an indicator of significant learning during the year.

This documentation of phonics teaching and learning contrasted sharply with the previous study by Foorman et al. (1998) in the dimension of what constituted whole language

phonics instruction. Within the current investigation, findings demonstrated that whole language classrooms included a more complex and varied mix of phonics instructional events encompassing direct instruction, individualized instruction, and instruction embedded in ongoing reading and writing activities.

The results of this study contribute to a deeper, more inclusive definition of effective phonics instruction. Phonics skills and strategies were taught during instructional events typically found in whole language classrooms without prepackaged phonics materials. This was accomplished by teachers making informed instructional decisions based on the literacy development and progress of each student.

## LIMITATIONS AND RECOMMENDATIONS FOR FURTHER RESEARCH

The sites chosen for this study varied across demographic and socioeconomic criteria and were located in a range of school districts, yet the study was limited in scope to eight whole language classrooms and to first-grade classrooms. Research is needed with larger samples to facilitate cross-case analyses within a variety of contexts, including analyses with low-SES populations.

This study operationally defined whole language using the concurrence of core concepts across standard whole language references. The sites represented first-grade classrooms where teachers espoused whole language beliefs and structured their programs and practices accordingly. The participating teachers generally represented the whole language continuum when such concepts and practices are the core of the classroom program. The results of this study, however, cannot be taken as representative of all first-grade classroom programs with the label of whole language. Within that larger range are teachers who carry the banner of whole language but whose programs may vary considerably from the central concepts established in the literature. A limitation of this study is that it does not represent these classrooms. Further research is recommended to describe the varying practices within this wider range.

Pre- and posttest data from this study create a portrait of student achievement limited to a single school year. Multiyear studies documenting student achievement over time might focus on low-progress children to determine shifts in achievement beyond first grade. Multiage classrooms are potential sites for such longitudinal work allowing for documentation of student achievement over time with the same teacher.

The four student achievement instruments assessed encoding and decoding in and out of context. Documentation did not include comprehension data, so the decoding measures could not be referred to as reading. Similarly, the writing task did not include the generation and representation of original meaning, so the encoding measure could not be called writing. While these limitations in instrumentation represent the researchers' focus on the phonics issue exclusively and on measures used in arguments on student achievement, the documentation in future research could expand significantly on the kinds of information available by using measures of actual reading and writing performance. In addition, analysis of miscue information would explain how children were working with all cueing systems.

Generally, the major contribution of phonics instruction to reading is that automatic word recognition facilitates comprehension (Adams, 1991; Stanovich, 1991). During posttesting many students in this study accurately decoded 90% or more of the words in the upper levels of Text Reading Level assessments taken from readers for grades 6, 7, and 8. None of the instruments in this study, however, assessed comprehension; thus, this relationship was not explored.

The whole language classrooms in this study provided a wide variety of literacy events that did not involve phonics instruction. Many literature lessons, author studies, computer laboratory experiences, and dramatizations were outside the realm of

this analysis but were observed during research visits. Thus, the description of literacy teaching and learning across these sites represents a focus on one element of these complex classroom programs. The researchers' attention was directed to the teachers' actions and to the teaching/learning interactions that could be observed. It did not focus on what learners were teaching each other nor did it look at learner-initiated instructional events (such as spontaneous groups discussing a concept) that did not involve the teacher. The research questions were about what instruction the teacher was providing and did not encompass these additional items.

## ACKNOWLEDGMENT

This project was funded by the Office of Educational Research and Improvement, the U.S. Department of Education.

## References

Adams, M. (1991). *Beginning to read: Thinking and learning about print*. Cambridge, MA: MIT Press.

Adams, M., & Bruck, M. (1995). Resolving the "great debate." *American Educator, 19*(2), 7, 10–20.

*At the zoo.* (1979). Glenview, IL: Scott, Foresman.

Barshinger, J. (1995). *A national Delphi study of desired factors for whole-language classroom environments.* Unpublished doctoral dissertation. Northern Illinois University, DeKalb.

Beck, I., & Juel, C. (1995). The role of decoding in learning to read. *American Educator, 19*(2), 8, 21–25, 39–42.

Bergeron, B. (1990). What does the term whole language mean? Constructing a definition from the literature. *Journal of Reading Behavior, 22,* 301–323.

Chall, J. (1967). *Learning to read: The great debate.* New York: McGraw-Hill.

Church, S. M. (1994). Is whole language really warm and fuzzy? *The Reading Teacher, 47,* 362–369.

Clarke, L. (1988). Invented versus traditional spelling in first graders' writings: Effects on learning to spell and read. *Research in the Teaching of English, 22,* 281–309.

Clay, M. (1991). *Becoming literate: The construction of inner control.* Portsmouth, NH: Heinemann.

Clay, M. (1993). *An observation survey of early literacy achievement.* Portsmouth, NH: Heinemann.

Compton, J. (1988). *The biggest cake in the world.* New York: Scholastic.

Cunningham, P. M. (1992). What kind of phonics instruction will we have? In C. K. Kinzer & D. K. Leu (Eds.), *Literacy research, theory and practice: Views from many perspectives.* Forty-first Yearbook of the National Reading Conference (pp. 17–31). Chicago, IL: National Reading Conference.

Dahl, K., & Freppon, P. (1995). A comparison of inner-city children's interpretations of reading and writing instruction in the early grades in skills-based and whole language settings. *Reading Research Quarterly, 30,* 50–74.

dePaola, T. (1985). *Tomie dePaola's Mother Goose.* New York: Putnam.

Dole, J. A., Duffy, G. G., Roehler, L. R., & Pearson, P. D. (1991). Moving from the old to the new: Research on reading comprehension instruction. *Review of Educational Research, 61,* 239–264.

Edelsky, C. (1990). Whose agenda is this anyway? A response to McKenna, Robinson, & Miller. *Educational Researcher, 19*(8), 7–11.

Edelsky, C., Altwerger, B., & Flores, B. (1991). *Whole language: What's the difference?* Portsmouth, NH: Heinemann.

Ehri, L. C. (1987). Learning to read and spell words. *Jouranal of Reading Behavior, 19,* 5–30.

Ehri, L. (1991). The development of the ability to read words. In R. Barr, M. Kamil, P. Mosenthal, & P. D. Pearson (Eds.), *Handbook of reading research* (Vol. II, pp. 383–417). New York: Longman.

Ehri, L. C., & Wilce, L. S. (1980). The influence of orthography on readers' conceptualization of the phonemic structure of words. *Applied Psycholinguistics, 1,* 371–385.

Ehri, L. C., & Wilce, L. S. (1987). Cipher versus cue reading: An experiment in decoding acquisition. *Journal of Educational Psychology, 79,* 3–13.

Flanagan, A. (1997). Reading bill full of flaws. *The Council Chronicle, 7*(2), 1.

Foorman, B. R., Francis, D. J., Fletcher, J. M., Schatschneider, C., & Mehta, P. (1998). The role of instruction in learning to read: Preventing reading failure in at-risk children. *Journal of Educational Psychology, 90,* 1–15.

Freppon, P., & Headings, L. (1996). Keeping it whole in whole language: A first grade teacher's phonics instruction in an urban whole language classroom. In E. McIntyre & M. Pressley (Eds.), *Balanced instruction: Strategies and skills in whole language* (pp. 65–82). Norwood, MA: Christopher-Gordon.

Freppon, P., McIntyre, E., & Dahl, K. (1995). A comparison of young children's writing products in skills-based and whole language classrooms. *Reading Horizons, 36,* 151–165.

Ganske, K. (1993). *Developmental spelling analysis: A qualitative measure for assessment and instructional planning.* Charlottesville: University of Virginia.

Goodman, K. (1986). *What's whole in whole language?* Portsmouth, NH: Heinemann.

Goodman, K. (1992). Why whole language is today's agenda in education. *Language Arts, 69,* 354–363.

Goodman, K. (1993). *Phonics phacts.* Portsmouth, NH: Heinemann.

Goswami, U. (1986). Children's use of analogy in learning to read. *Journal of Experimental Child Psychology, 42,* 73–83.

Goswami, U. (1990). Phonological priming and orthographic analogies in reading. *Journal of Experimental Child Psychology, 49,* 323-340.

Goswami, U. (1993). Toward an interactive analogy model of reading development: Decoding vowel graphemes in beginning reading. *Journal of Experimental Child Psychology, 56,* 152-163.

Goswami, U., & Bryant, P. (1990). *Phonological skills and learning to read.* Hillsdale, NJ: Lawrence Erlbaum Associates.

Goswami, U., & Mead, F. (1992). Onset and rime awareness and analogies in reading. *Reading Research Quarterly, 27,* 152-163.

Grogan, P. (1998). *A descriptive analysis of composing demonstrations in a whole language first grade classroom.* Unpublished doctoral dissertation, Ohio State University, Columbus.

Gunderson, L., & Shapiro, J. (1987). Some findings on whole language instruction. *Reading-Canada-Lecture, 5*(1), 22-26.

Gunnison, R. B., & Lucas, G. (1996, May 6). Plan to boost reading scores: Wilson calls for $100 million in new books, teacher training. *San Francisco Chronicle,* p. A1.

Henderson, E. H., & Beers, J. W. (Eds.). (1980). *Developmental and cognitive aspects of learning to spell: A reflection of word knowledge.* Newark, DE: International Reading Association.

Invernizzi, M. A. (1992). The vowel and what follows: A phonological frame of orthographic analysis. In S. Templeton & D. Bear (Eds.), *Development of orthographic knowledge and the foundations of literacy: A memorial festschrift for Edmund H. Henderson* (pp. 105-136). Hillsdale, NJ: Lawrence Erlbaum Associates.

Juel, C. (1994). Teaching phonics in the context of the integrated language arts. In L. Morrow, J. Smith, & L. Wilkinson (Eds.), *Intergrated language arts: Controversy to consensus* (pp. 133-154). Boston, MA: Allyn & Bacon.

Keats, E. J. (1962). *The snowy day.* New York: Viking.

Krashen, S. (1998). Every person a reader: An alternative to the California Task Force report on reading. In C. Weaver (Ed.), *Reconsidering a balanced approach to reading* (pp. 425-452). Urbana, IL: National Council of Teachers of English.

Leslie, L., & Caldwell, J. (1995). *Qualitative reading inventory II.* New York: HarperCollins.

Lobel, A. (Ed.). (1986). *The Random House book of Mother Goose.* New York: Random House.

Lomax, R., & McGee, L. (1987). Young children's concepts about print and reading: Toward a model of word-reading acquisition. *Reading Research Quarterly, 22,* 237-256.

Lyon, G. R. (1998). Why reading is not a natural process. *Educational Leadership, 55*(6), 14-18.

McGuinnes, D., McGuinnes, C., & Donahue, J. (1995). Phonological training and the alphabet principle: Evidence for reciprocal causality. *Reading Research Quarterly, 30,* 830-852.

McIntyre. E. (1996). Strategies and skills in whole language: An introduction to balanced teaching. In E. McIntyre & M. Pressley (Eds.), *Balanced instruction: Strategies and skills in whole language* (pp. 1-20). Norwood, MA: Christopher-Gordon.

McKenna, M., Robinson, R., & Miller, J. (1990). Whole language: A research agenda for the nineties. *Educational Researcher, 19*(8), 3-6.

McKenna, M., Robinson, R., & Miller, J. (1992, December). *Whole language and research: The case for caution.* Paper presented at the meeting of the National Reading Conference, San Antonion, TX.

Mills, H., & Clyde, J. (1990). *Portraits of whole language classrooms.* Portsmouth, NH: Heinemann.

Mills, H., O'Keefe, T., & Stephens, D. (1992). *Looking closely: Exploring the role of phonics in one whole language classroom.* Urbana, IL: National Council of Teachers of English.

Morris, D., & Perney, J. (1984). Developmental spelling as a predictor of first grade reading achievement. *Elementary School Journal, 84,* 441-457.

Moustafa, M. (1990). *An interactive/cognitive model of the acquisition of a graphophonemic system by young children.* Unpublished doctoral dissertation, University of Southern California, Los Angeles.

Moustafa, M. (1995). Children's productive phonological recording. *Reading Research Quarterly, 30,* 464-476.

Moustafa, M. (1997). *Beyond traditional phonics.* Portsmouth, NH: Heinemann.

Newman, J., & Church, S. (1990). Myths of whole language. *The Reading Teacher, 44,* 20-26.

Peek, D. (1985). *Hoppity toad's fun time finger play book.* Minneapolis, MN: T. S. Denison.

Routman, R. (1996). *Literacy at the crossroads: Crucial talk about reading, writing, and other teaching dilemmas.* Portsmouth, NH: Heinemann.

Salinger, T. (1996). *Literacy for young children.* Columbus, OH: Merrill.

Schlagal, R. C. (1992). Patterns of orthographic development into the intermediate grades. In S. Templeton & D. Bear (Eds.), *Development of orthographic knowledge and the foundations of literacy: A memorial festschrift for Edmund H. Henderson* (pp. 31-52). Hillsdale, NJ: Lawrence Erlbaum Associates.

Snow, C., Burns, M., & Griffin, P. (Eds.). (1998). *Preventing reading difficulties in young children.* Washington, DC: National Academy Press.

Stahl, S. A. (1998). Teaching children with reading problems to decode: Phonics and "not-phonics" instruction. *Reading & Writing Quarterly, 14,* 165-188.

Stahl, S. A., Duffy-Hester, A. M., & Stahl, K. A. D. (1998). Everything you wanted to know about phonics (but were afraid to ask). *Reading Research Quarterly, 33,* 338-355.

Stahl, S. A., & Miller, P. (1989). Whole language and language experience approaches for beginning reading: A quantitative research synthesis. *Review of Educational Reserach, 59,* 88-116.

Stahl, S. A., Pagnucco, J. R., & Suttles, C. W. (1996). First graders' reading and writing instruction in traditional and process-oriented classes. *The Journal of Educational Research, 89,* 131-144.

Stanovich, K. E. (1991). Word recognition: Changing perspectives. In R. Barr, M. Kamil, P. Mosenthal, & P. D. Pearson (Eds.), *Handbook of reading research* (Vol. II, pp. 418-452). New York: Longman.

Stanovich, K. E., Cunningham, A., & Cramer, B. (1984). Assessing phonological awareness in kindergarten children: Issues of task comparability. *Journal of Experimental Child Psychology, 38,* 175-190.

Stephens, D. (1991). *Research on whole language: Support for a new curriculum.* Katonah, NY: Richard C. Owen.

Strickland, D. (1998a). What's basic in beginning reading? Finding common ground. *Educational Leadership, 55*(6), 6-10.

Strickland, D. (1998b). *Teaching phonics today: A primer for educators.* Newark, DE: International Reading Association.

Thomas, S. (1996, April 12). Pushing a finger into an international pie: A phonics scheme perfected over two decades in a Suffolk primary has found favour in Canada. *The Times Educational Supplement,* p. B5.

Tierney, R., & Leys, M. (1986). What is the value of connecting reading and writing? In B. Peterson (Ed.), *Convergences: Transactions in reading and writing* (pp. 15-29). Urbana, IL: National Council of Teachers of English.

Traw, R. (1996). Large-scale assessment of skills in a whole language curriculum: Two districts' experiences. *The Journal of Educational Research, 89,* 323-338.

Treiman, R. (1993). *Beginning to spell: A study of first grade children.* New York: Oxford University Press.

Vacca, R., & Rasinski, T. (1992). *Case studies in whole language*. Fort Worth, TX: Harcourt Brace Jovanovich.

Varble, M. E. (1990). Analysis of writing samples of students taught by teachers using whole language and traditional approaches. *The Journal of Educational Research, 83,* 245-251.

Walmsley, S. A., & Adams, E. L. (1993). Realities of "whole language." *Language Arts, 70,* 272-280.

Weaver, C. (1990). *Understanding whole language*. Portsmouth, NH: Heinemann.

Weaver, C. (1991). Weighing the claims about "phonics first." *Education Digest, 56,* 19-22.

Weaver, C. (1994). *Reading process and practice: From socio-psycholinguistics to whole language*. Portsmouth, NH: Heinemann.

Weaver, C. (1996). Phonics and the teaching of phonics. In C. Weaver, L. Fillmeister-Krause, & G. Vento-Zogby (Eds.), *Creating support for effective literacy education* (pp. 94-114). Portsmouth, NH: Heinemann.

Weaver, C. (Ed.). (1998). *Reconsidering a balanced approach to reading*. Urbana, IL: National Council of Teachers of English.

Wilde, S. (1988). Learning to spell and punctuate: A study of eight- and nine-year-old children. *Language and Education: An International Journal, 2,* 35-59.

Wilde, S. (1997). *What's a schwa sound anyway?* Portsmouth, NH: Heinemann.

Wright, B. D., & Masters, G. N. (1982). *Rating scale analysis*. Chicago, IL: MESA Press.

Yopp, H. (1988). The validity and reliability of phonemic awareness tests. *Reading Research Quarterly, 23,* 159-177.

Zutell, J. (1979). Spelling strategies of primary school children and their relationship to Piaget's concept of decentration. *Research in the Teaching of English, 13,* 69-80.

# · 25 ·

# DEVELOPMENT IN THE ELEMENTARY
# SCHOOL YEARS

*Dorothy S. Strickland*
Rutgers University

*Joan T. Feeley*
The William Paterson College of New Jersey

The acquisition of language, one of the most remarkable achievements of childhood, is also one of the most commonplace (Rice, 1996). Very early in life young children become adept at using oral language to address their needs and carry on social interactions. Though most of the research on children's language development has focused on these early years, the processes involved in achieving communicative competence continue throughout the elementary school years and beyond. This chapter is designed to inform educators and others about oral and written language development in the elementary years. It is grounded in the premise that what we believe both informs and influences how we teach.

We can never escape our fundamental beliefs and understandings. What we believe or think we know about our world affects everything we do. As teachers, we accumulate a set of beliefs about how children learn and develop. These understandings begin with our experiences as family members and participants in society. They are expanded and refined through the courses we take as preservice and inservice teachers, through our interactions with other professionals, and through our everyday dealings with children in the classroom. The belief systems we develop play a large part in determining the decisions we make about what we teach, how it will be taught, and how we view the effectiveness of our instruction. They are a powerful influence on determining what new methods and approaches we take into our classrooms, and they guide the way we implement them.

Our belief systems are extremely powerful. Yet, despite their power, they are often taken for granted. Methods and materials, and not understanding about children's learning, consume most teachers' time and energy. It is rare to hear teachers ask, "What theories of language and literacy development underlay these new materials or this new approach?" or "How can I implement this new program so that it is consistent with what I know about how children learn?"

We believe that teachers' knowledge about language learning is a major source of empowerment. It enables them to take control over methods and materials and to make informed curricular decisions. It was with these thoughts in mind, that we set out to write this chapter on language development during the elementary school years. It is our belief that a better understanding of children as language learners will lead to improved classroom instructional practices.

## THE LEARNER DEVELOPS: AN OVERVIEW

Elementary school-age children have been described as "being everywhere." They are on the playground, at the local store, at the pizza shop, traveling on the school bus, in the movies, and many other places. They are the most visible of all age groups. Yet, adults appear to pay less attention to this age group than they do to children during infancy, early childhood, and adolescence (Collins, 1984). One reason for this might be because school and friends take up much of children's time during the elementary years. Another might be that the physical and psychological changes that children undergo during the middle childhood period do not attract adult attention because they are not as obvious as the changes that occur at other stages of development (Shonkoff, 1984).

Many changes do occur during this developmental period, however. In addition to the shift to more formalized instruction, children are challenged to expand their world to include new acquaintances and experiences outside their immediate neighborhood. They are introduced to new social rules and expectations, and they are likely to be exposed to people from diverse cultural and linguistic backgrounds. All of these factors require children to make important changes in their ability to think about their world and to relate their own life experiences to the life experiences of others. These changes are of great significance to each child and to those interested in the language-arts education of children.

In order to provide a holistic framework for our discussion of children's oral and written language and their literary development, we begin with an outline of children's physical, cognitive, and social-emotional development during the elementary school years.

*Physical development* during the elementary years is generally slower than that during early childhood, but it is steady and sustained. Coordination becomes increasingly developed and control is attained on motor tasks of increasing complexity and difficulty. In relating children's motor development to appropriate toys, Bee (1985) suggests that children 7- and 8-years-old can usually ride a bicycle easily, skip rope, and play most games that require hitting, kicking, or throwing a ball. Previous practice with small-muscle coordination makes the elementary school-age child much more skillful with model building, arts and crafts, and even sewing.

*Cognitive development* during the middle childhood years has been characterized by Piaget (1970) as the period of concrete operations. This refers to children's ability to operate on the basis of rules when they examine and interact with phenomena. Reversibility and conservation are two key mental operations that children grasp during this period. Reversibility refers to the child's understanding that a basic property of any action is that it can be undone or reversed—either physically or mentally—and returned to the original position. Thus, the clay can once again be formed into a ball and the milk can be poured back into a taller, thinner glass.

Classification and seriation are important cognitive operations that flourish during this period. According to Zigler and Finn-Stevenson (1987):

During the middle childhood years, children begin to have an understanding that there is a hierarchical relationship between subordinate and superordinate classes—German Shepherds, Collies, and Great Danes belong to subordinate class of dogs and a super ordinate class of animals (p. 490).

The ability to arrange objects in an orderly series demonstrates systematic, planful thinking on the part of the school-age child (p. 491).

One way in which this planful behavior is demonstrated is they way that 6-year-olds begin to assign roles to individuals during dramatic play. Another is the increased interest in games with rules and creation of rules in play activities as children move through the grades.

*Social and emotional development* during the elementary years is generally characterized by excitement and joy. Children experience a growing sense of personal awareness as they interact with peers and adults outside the family. They become increasingly aware of how other people will react to their actions and ideas. Selman (1976) suggests that during these years, children evidence ability to infer accurately other people's thoughts and feelings, and they realize that because other people can do the same, their own thoughts and feelings are the object of other people's thinking.

Having the ability to take the perspective of others, the child becomes better able to communicate, since effective communication depends on the assessment of what other people already know and what they need to know. The ability to understand and vicariously feel what another person is feeling (Zigler & Finn-Stevenson, 1987, pp. 530–531).

Other important changes that occur during the elementary years involve the child's moral development and behavior. As children grow, they develop greater understanding of rules and appropriate behavior, and they increase in their ability to reason about moral issues. Self-concept, whether negative or positive, is greatly influenced during this period by children's relationships with parents, peers, and teachers.

The aspects of children's physical, cognitive, and social-emotional development, which we have highlighted, should be kept in mind as the research on children's language and literacy is discussed. It is the interdependence of all aspects of the child's life and learning that helps provide us with a profile of what these children are like and how we can best support them as they learn to read, write, and enjoy literature.

## ORAL LANGUAGE DEVELOPMENT

By the time most children enter kindergarten, they know a great deal about language. They have a vocabulary of several thousand words, and they have internalized the phonology and linguistic structures of their language (Berko Gleason, 1985; Brown, 1973; Fletcher & Garman, 1986; McNeil, 1970; Menyuk, 1969; Templin, 1987). They know that language is functional, and they use it to share ideas and facilitate their own purposes. Children continue to grow in language competence throughout the elementary school years. Their increasing language ability reflects a growing understanding of the physical and social world around them. As the range of their experiences increases, new concepts are formed and expressed through language. Their growing cognitive abilities also affect language development.

One of the most comprehensive studies of language development in school-age children was done by Walter Loban (1963). Loban followed children from kindergarten through grade 12. He started with 338 kindergartners, 30 of whom were rated exceptionally high in language development and 24 rated exceptionally low. Tracking these children over several years revealed that all of them increased the number of words spoken each year and increased their effectiveness in speaking. The high language-ability group maintained its superiority, increased complexity of sentence structure, and added vocabulary until it was about double that of the low language-ability group. Although recent change in the way we view nonstandard dialects may alter the way we construe these findings, the differences remain impressive. The high-ability group children used a greater number of less common words and were more fluent in language use than the low group or the remaining randomly chosen subjects. In addition, the high group continuously used a greater variety of sentence structures and were distinguished by greater effectiveness in their use of language.

Several instructional implications may be drawn from Loban's work. Once considered less fluent or linguistically disadvantaged, children in a regular school situation seem to be increasingly less able in other language areas when compared with more capable children. The difference could be the result of teaching practices, since the children who speak well and fluently are the ones who get the most opportunities to talk, while those less ready with words and assurance are sometimes ignored. Loban recommended less teacher reliance on workbook drill and more emphasis on encouraging speech to express ideas, attitudes, and values of concern to the learners. Rather than drill in usage, he suggested that teachers work with the individual to achieve coherence and organization in talking.

We believe these findings have implications relevant to teacher attitudes about children's language. Teachers who feel that the language of a particular student or group of students is deficient may indeed give those students fewer opportunities to speak in the belief that they are incapable of communicating well. Such teachers may be intolerant of language differences or they may act out of genuine concern for putting children in situations where they may not be as successful as others. In either case, they deny children the opportunity to demonstrate and build on what they do know about language in an atmosphere that is risk free and encouraging.

Another extensive study of elementary school children (Chomsky, 1969, 1972) involved their understanding of certain sentence structures. Chomsky found several sentence structures that school-age children consistently misinterpreted prior to a certain stage of development. Five of these proved to be acquired in a sequence, revealing developmental stages. Although the order of acquisition was constant, children varied greatly in their rate of acquisition.

First of these misinterpretations concerned the word *see*. A doll, whose eyes closed when lying down, was laid on a table. The children were asked, "Is the doll hard to see or easy to see?" Later, the doll was placed out of sight and the children were asked the same question. Children under $5\frac{1}{2}$ years old said the doll as hard to see in both instances. Beyond that age some children began to interpret the question correctly. By age 9 all children did.

The words *asked* and *promised* presented a second problem as used in the following sequences: (a) John asked Bill to leave. (b) John promised Bill to leave. Although all the children understood the meaning of *promised* in other types of sentences, children younger than $5\frac{1}{2}$ years old interpreted *promised* the same as *asked*. By age 9 all interpreted it correctly.

A third problem also involved the word *ask*. When children were told, "Ask Bruce what to feed the dog," the most frequent responses were, "What do you want to feed the dog?" or "What are you going to feed the dog?" Only one third of the group gave the correct response, "What should I feed the dog?"

A fourth problem involved referents of words in certain syntactic structures. When told, "Mother scolded Gloria for answering the phone and I would have done the same," many children thought "the same" meant "I would have answered the phone" rather than "I would have scolded Gloria."

When *although* was substituted for *and* in the same sentence, only 4 children of 36, the most advanced, made the correct distinction. When the less familiar concept of *although* was added to the uncertainty of the referent for same, difficulties increased.

Chomsky's study reminds us that children's language development is ongoing throughout the school-age years. The need to probe and explore their understandings and interpretations of language is a necessary part of classroom practice.

Numerous other researchers have examined the continued evolution of language during this period (Bormouth, Carr, Manning, & Pearson, 1970; Strickland, 1962). Their research has confirmed the fact that semantic and syntactic acquisition of language continues at least until age 9 or 10. This research is of vital importance to classroom teachers, as it relates to the cognitive and linguistic demands of the typical elementary classroom. It suggests that teachers need to be aware of the conditions under which the remarkable accomplishments of children's first language learning occurs and that teachers need to provide experiences that are open ended and flexible enough to accommodate a range of language backgrounds and competencies.

Strickland and Taylor (1989) observed that home language learning conditions are characterized by an atmosphere of success and child centeredness. They suggest that the home learning environment is a generally positive one, where adults use language with children rather than at them. They also contend that at home, children acquire spoken language in a meaningful context. Language learning and concept development are related to meaningful activities, objects, and situations in the child's environment. In addition, in language learning situations at home, the child is presented with the whole system to be learned. It is neither sequenced by some external force nor is it put into a skills array or management system. Finally, they remind us that none of these features, so characteristic of first language learning at home, requires standard forms. What *is* required is adult–child interaction where the focus is on whole language used in a meaningful context. We believe that these understandings, based on observation of children in natural settings outside of school, can serve as basic principles on which to build the language curriculum in school.

Language experiences that accommodate a range of linguistic backgrounds and competencies help support children's ongoing language development. The value of open-ended, multilevel language activities was demonstrated by Strickland (1973), who participated in a study to examine the possibility of expanding the speech of lower socioeconomic African American kindergarten children to include some standard dialect forms. Children in an experimental group listened daily to selected children's literature and took part in oral language activities such as creative dramatics, choral speaking, puppetry, and role playing. They participated in the imitation and repetition of language patterns used in the literature. All activities involved the children in active dialogue. The control group experienced the same daily oral reading of children's literature, but their follow-up activities did not include oral language participation by the children.

The procedures with the experimental group proved a successful way to expand the language repertoire of these linguistically different 5-year-olds without attempting to expunge or discredit their home language. Children began to include more standard dialect in their normal speech, an expansion of language rather than a substitution. An extension of the study to primary grades (Cullinan, Jaggar, & Strickland, 1974) yielded similar results. Kindergartners made the most dramatic gains, however, as demonstrated by their ability to repeat standard English sentences, an indication of growth in language proficiency. We believe that the dramatic effects of these kinds of activities on the language development of children, who are generally thought to be at a linguistic disadvantage in the schools, offers direction for working with *all* children to increase their communicative competence.

While other researchers studied children's developing ability to understand and use various grammatical structures, Halliday (1975) analyzed children's speech in terms of the functions to which children put it. This view of language involves focusing on how people use language in their everyday lives to communicate, to present themselves, to find out about things, to give information, to negotiate, and to interact. Halliday suggests a system of development that begins with the words "I want_____," representing the instrumental use of language. In the order they evolve, the seven functions, and examples of each use of speech, are as follows:

| | |
|---|---|
| Instrumental | I want |
| Regulatory | Do as I tell you |
| Interactional | Me and you |
| Personal | Here I come |
| Heuristic | Tell me why |
| Imaginative | Let's pretend |
| Informative | I've got something to tell you |

Informative use of language is generally the last to develop in children. The child uses it least and is least able to understand its use by others. Teachers of young children are generally aware of the danger of the overuse of telling as a means of transmitting information. They know the importance of involving children in firsthand experiences that require experimentation, demonstration, and manipulation of real objects. We believe that this kind of direct involvement is equally important throughout the elementary grades. In the process of developing a concept through first-hand experience, children begin to acquire the appropriate representational speech to describe and refer to that experience. They develop conceptual frameworks that help them internalize the ideas so that they are better able to think and talk about what they know and extend their ideas to new situations. Teachers who rely too heavily on merely telling children the information they want them to acquire risk promoting mindless regurgitation of that information without depth of understanding or ability to extend it to new learnings.

While most of the research on children's language development has focused on speech, the development of listening is also of critical importance. Listening is the primary source of language. It is the foundation on which all the other communication processes develop. The very young child is channeled to speech, reading, and writing through listening. Studies of physical disabilities (Brown, as cited in Lundsteen, 1976), such as hearing disorders and brain damage, have pointed to the interdependence among the various language processes with listening at the base. As language is expanded and developed, listening remains the primary mode for acquiring linguistic knowledge and skill. Because evidence of listening is indirect, researchers have been unable to learn a great deal about its development. Thus, no developmental stages of listening have been determined.

Some attention has been given to the amount of time children spend listening in school. Wilt (1950) found that out of a 5-hour school day, elementary school children spent $2\frac{1}{2}$ hours listening to others—primarily the teacher. Lundsteen (1971) reports that children may hear at least 20 times as many oral contributions from classmates as they themselves give. The need to nurture children's listening development is well established in the literature (Funk & Funk, 1989; Templeton, 1991). Children need planned, consistent help in learning to think about, react, and respond to what they hear.

Bromley (1988) gives two reasons for teaching children how to listen: children and adults spend enormous amounts of time each day listening, and the ability to be an effective listener is of major importance not only for learning in the classroom but also for survival in the everyday world where listening to news reports and political and consumer messages is a daily occurrence. In addition, the ability to listen for appreciation and enjoyment makes life fuller and more satisfying. Reviews by Devine (1978) and Pearson and Fielding (1982) cite numerous studies indicating that students who receive systematic instruction in listening improve in their abilities to process the information received and understand and remember it better.

## Language and Thought

To be born human is to be born with a potential for thinking, for knowing, for understanding, for interacting, for communicating, and for developing language (Goodman, 1996). Language and thought are so interconnected that it is impossible to discuss one without the other. Meaningful communication would be unattainable in the absence of thought. The construction of meaning, whether it be through listening, speaking, reading, or writing, is rooted in thought. Piaget (1955) and Vygotsky (1962) are two researchers who have greatly influenced our knowledge of the development of thinking in children. Piaget stressed the idea that young children learn by acting on their environment. They learn as they manipulate, explore, experiment, invent, and discover. He suggested that by imposing adult language on children's cognitive structures, we may actually impede their development rather than promote it. Piaget conceded that adults do act as language models for children; however, he believed that adult language could not expand the thinking of the child beyond the limits of the child's own cognitive development.

Recent researchers have turned to Vygotsky in order to better understand the role of the adult in children's language development. According to Vygotsky, the social context in which children learn to speak is extremely important. Vygotsky emphasized the interaction between the child and the language of the environment. Thus the role of the adult becomes crucial in language development. He believed that the dialogue between children and their parents or teachers played a major role in the creation of thought.

Research examining the dynamics of family storybook reading (Taylor & Strickland, 1986) confirm Vygotsky's notions about the critical role of parents in the development of children's language and thought. Audio recordings of 20 families of varied backgrounds and family structures were collected as they engaged in shared book experiences. Parents were interviewed as they listened to the tapes and reflected on their experiences. Although each family established its own unique routines and style of book sharing, certain aspects of the experience seemed to prevail. The talk between parent and child was critical to furthering children's understanding of the content of the books as well as their understanding about stories and concepts about print. For example, regardless of socioeconomic status, ethnic or educational background, parents instinctively relate new concepts to something the child already knows. They expand on vocabulary by using synonyms or brief explanations where needed. They augment the text in places where a problem is anticipated, and they listen and respond to their child's questions and comments about storyline, characters, pictures, words, and letters. It is no wonder that children fortunate enough to have had such experiences are likely to acquire literacy with ease (Clark, 1976; Durkin, 1966; Torrey, 1969). Family storybook reading also helps to underscore the role the child's environment plays on cognitive development. Gardner (1996) puts it well in his retelling of a metaphor offered by Guy Cellerier.

Cellerier proposed a metaphor that he felt described the growth of intellect: he compared the development of the mind to climbing a hill. Extending that metaphor, we can assume that the broad steps of the journey are preordained but that the steps that one will actually take—the footholds gained, the heights one will ultimately reach, one's perspective at the end of the journey cannot be anticipated (p. 35).

The theories of both Piaget and Vygotsky have implications for the classroom. Teachers should avoid confusing children by presenting them with abstract ideas in adult language before they have the background of concrete experiences to act as a framework for understanding. The importance of adult–child dialogue, however, cannot be overestimated. Interactive language between child and adult is a significant part of every stage of the child's language development. Teachers need to be aware of their important role in the language and cognitive development of children.

In summary, although children have acquired most of the basic structures of English by the time they enter school, their language development continues throughout the elementary school years. During the elementary years, children not only expand their use of syntactic structures, they acquire new ones. Children improve in effectiveness and control of language by building and expanding on already learned patterns. Children who are proficient in oral language tend to be higher achievers on measures of vocabulary and other aspects of language and literacy development.

Teachers need to be aware what is known about children's language development, including what has been learned about the conditions under which children are successful language learners outside of school. This information can help provide the basics for planning school experiences. The language curriculum should provide a wide variety of experiences that accommodate a range of language backgrounds and competencies. Following is a discussion of studies about language in the classroom. Suggestions are offered for improving the language learning that takes place there.

## Oral Language in the Classroom

Studies of classroom discourse reveal a great deal about whether or not oral language is being fostered at school. Cazden (1988), Dillon and Searle (1981), and Mehan (1979) indicate that the basic interactional pattern in classrooms is characterized by teacher initiation, student response, and teacher evaluation. Mehan's investigation of a combined first-, second-, and third-grade class further revealed that 81.1% of the instructional sequences were teacher-initiated, while only 17.9% were student-initiated.

Nearly 4 decades ago, Flanders' (1962) research on classroom interaction indicated that in a 5-hour day, most teachers talked nearly 2 hours and 20 minutes. Dividing the remaining 67 minutes among 30 children, Flanders suggested that each child was permitted only 2 minutes of talking time throughout the day. Flanders developed the Rule of Two Thirds: Two thirds of classroom time is devoted to talk, two thirds of the talk is teacher talk, and two thirds of what the teacher says is merely giving factual information or directions for assignments.

Researchers agree that if schools are to foster children's language development, children need opportunities to use their language resources and to build on them. Yet, studies suggest that the restrictive environment of the school is not conducive to language development. According to Dillon and Searle (1981), the classroom language code of students they studied was restricted while the home language was elaborated. The restricted or limited code seen in the classroom failed to make use of the children's full range of language and learning abilities. Several researchers have offered suggestions for change.

Pinnell (1996) suggests that teachers use the system developed by Halliday in order to observe how children use language. Whatever the system, Pinnell asserts that sensitive observation can help a teacher determine children's competence in using language that relates to real life situations. According to Pinnell, what children reveal about their use of language has implications for what is worth assessing and teaching in the classroom. Furniss and Green (1991) offer a system for analyzing anecdotal records of classroom discourse. Their system includes a series of points for teachers to ponder, such as the structure of the lesson, the teacher/student talk ratio, and the student reactions.

Michaels and Foster (1985) reported on the use of student-run sharing time in an ethnically mixed first- and second-grade classroom. Students successfully altered their style of communication according to whether they were speaking in a narrative or reportorial mode. Because these sessions were student controlled, pupils were in a better position to demonstrate their discourse skills and improve them.

Conferences with peers and teachers during the writing process is another important way to extend language development (Graves, 1983). During writing conferences, students exchange ideas with others in order to improve writing in progress or simply to respond to a completed work. During the exchange, students must talk and listen to the talk of others as they explain, clarify, and extend their ideas. Opportunities to engage in literature response groups is another way to expand children's language use. These share sessions are generally student directed and involve a student's presentation of a book he or she has read, followed by student reactions.

Strickland in collaboration with a group of teacher researchers (Strickland, Dillon, Funkhouser, Glick, & Rogers, 1989), examined the nature and quality of the classroom dialogue during literature response groups. Children in grades 1, 2, 4, and 6 were involved. Specifically, the following questions were asked: What was the content of the talk during literature response groups? What functions of language were in use by the students? What evidence of students' reading comprehension was demonstrated? Data were collected by the classroom teachers through observations using field notes and audiotape and videotape recordings. The findings supported the teachers' intuitive sense and informal observation that literature response groups provide an excellent resource for student learning through talk and support for literacy development. One of the most significant outcomes of this research was the opportunity it gave teachers to examine systematically the language learning environment in their classrooms and to make adjustments based on their observations and reflections regarding children's language behavior and growth.

Two other methods that effectively promote learning in and through oral language are reciprocal teaching and cooperative learning. These strategies are useful across the curriculum, and they may be used by both young and older students. In reciprocal teaching (Palinscar & Brown, 1985) students are involved in summarizing, question-generating, clarifying, and predicting as they read texts or observe phenomena. As with literature response groups, both teacher and students share responsibility for the conduct of the discussion. While the discussion is cognitively focused on a particular content, the talk is complex and multidimensional and avoids the restrictive question–answer pattern of recitation.

Cooperative learning strategies offer another valuable means of promoting students' communication skills as they use language for learning. When children engage in cooperative learning tasks, they must work together to complete a particular objective. The functions of language required as they work are multifaceted. They must make their ideas clear to others and extend themselves a bit to appreciate another's perspective on a problem. Johnson and Pearson (1984) suggests that this kind of guided classroom interaction has both social, value-shaping outcomes and cognitive meaning-making benefits.

Instructional scaffolding and inquiry teaching are strategies that may be infused into the many opportunities for class discussion throughout the day. Lehr (1985) describes instructional scaffolding as a widely applicable technique in which the teacher initially provides a relatively high degree of verbal structure—a "scaffold" that assures a firm grounding for student discourse—then gradually withdraws the structure as students become increasingly capable of building conceptual edifices on their own.

Inquiry teaching, a strategy frequently used in social studies and science, is an interactive method that has been expanded and refined in recent years. Hillocks (1986) reports that inquiry methods—teacher and student question/discussion-generating techniques—underlie numerous studies in which students show writing improvement. The trend toward encouraging students to generate questions for each other and share responsibility for determining topics and the course of group discussion are major breakthroughs in promoting competence and confidence in oral language. Collins (1986) describes how teachers use inquiry strategies during class discussion. Teachers help guide the course of the talk by helping students become aware of misconceptions, highlighting what is known and not known, and setting future directions for class activities.

Other opportunities for students to expand their oral language in school include dramatics, storytelling and retelling; activities involving brainstorming, planning and problem solving; and hands-on activities associated with content areas such as mathematics, social studies, and science. Activities of this type allow students to expand their oral language abilities by applying and refining what they already know. Equally important, they offer teachers excellent opportunities to make informed curricular decisions as they bring what they know about children's language development together with observations of children's language in use.

The Education Department of Western Australia has produced the *Oral Language Developmental Continuum* (1994), which outlines the stages of oral language development, teaching strategies, and indicators for assessment. This is arguably one of the most comprehensive documents available for informing the oral language curriculum.

## WRITTEN LANGUAGE DEVELOPMENT

Shanahan (1984) describes reading and writing as related processes, Tierney and Pearson (1984) see them as similar composing processes, and Harste, Woodward, and Burke (1984) characterize them as processes of context-driven meaning making and communication. Langer (1986) agrees with, but goes beyond, these explanations. Even for young children, she sees reading and writing as being both purposeful and cognitive activities that are used to help one conceptualize personal experience and world knowledge. Calling reading and writing the "interplay of mind and text" that brings about new learning, Langer says that they must be considered as they change over time.

However one tries to explain the connection between reading and writing, it is evident that the two processes depend on one's exposure to and uses of written language. The following section reports what the research says about how children in the elementary school years develop as readers and writers and what it all means for classroom teachers.

## PRIMARY YEARS (K–2)

When Don Graves (1983) asked children just beginning school if they could read and write, only 15% answered that they could read while 85% said they could write. Accordingly, we will begin with writing because of young children's perception of themselves as writers and the tremendous body of research on this area produced during the past 2 decades or so (e.g., Baghban, 1984; Bissex, 1980; Calkins, 1983, 1986, 1994; Clay, 1975; Dahl & Farnan, l998; De Ford & Hartse, 1982; Dyson, 1983; Ferreiro & Teberosky, 1983; Graves, 1981, 1994; Hansen, 1987; Hartse, Woodward, & Burke, 1984; King & Rentel, 1979).

### Writing

Attention to writing in kindergarten and grade 1, except for the literal meaning of forming letters, is a relatively recent phenomenon. Traditionally, children have not been expected to write/compose until the latter half of grade 1, and the major focus was put on learning to read. Writing was thought to begin through group and individual dictation that the teacher would write and the children would copy (Burrows, 1968). But, according to the vast amount of literature cited above, school beginners know much more about producing written language than we had expected.

Most kindergartens begin to write by drawing and scribbling (Sulzby, 1985a; Temple, Nathan, Burris, & Temple, 1988). They will write such things as messages, grocery lists, stories and notes, and "pretend read" them to you. As soon as they can write a few letters (e.g., those in their name), they begin to add these and other letter-like marks to their drawings/scribbles, showing that they know writing is not completely arbitrary but that it involves certain kinds of special marks (Clay, 1975). Temple et al. (1988) call this the prephonemic stage. Gentry (1981) notes that the scribbling stage parallels the babbling stage in oral language development.

When their informal exposure to written language through environmental print is augmented by more direct experiences with print such as group reading of a "big book" (Holdaway, 1979) and group composing of text via the language experience approach (Hall, 1981; Stauffer, 1980), children begin to internalize the alphabetic principle. They may use one or two letters, usually consonants, to stand for whole words. Temple et al. (1988) call this the early phonemic stage and give the following example: RCRBKDN = Our car broke down. With the accompanying illustration, the message is perfectly understandable. Forester (1980) compares this writing with the holophrases children begin to utter around the age of 2.

With daily meaningful reading/writing experiences, children move into the letter-name stage in which vowels begin to appear along with prominent consonants (Chomsky, 1979; Read, 1986; Temple et al., 1988). By now they know the names of the letters but not necessarily which letters represent which sounds. As active learners, they invent spellings according to their own phonemic rules, for example, "chran" for "train," "yet/yent" for "went," and "pan" for "pen." Soon standard spellings are mixed with invented spellings, and children are said to be in a transitional stage. Throughout the elementary school years, spelling tends to become more standard, but invented spellings can be found at all levels.

Taking a more global perspective of beginning spellers, Harste et al. (1984) suggest that children may be using three strategies: spelling the way it sounds ("jress" = "dress"); spelling the way it looks ("fro" = "for"); spelling the way it means ("wasapanataem" = the conceptual unit, "once upon a time"). They caution against attention to spelling in early years, since spelling is the biggest constraint that 5s and 6s see in writing. Some children realizing that there is a "right way" to write may temporarily refuse to "spell it like it sounds" or even to write much at all (Bissex, 1980). The public nature of writing also makes it risky business.

However, children do not move through these suggested phases evenly. Some may skip and appear to go from drawing directly to invented spelling. In her year-long study of 183 children in Whole Language kindergartens, Allen (1989) has found that growth patterns were very individual, with children often adding to their repertoire of writing behaviors without abandoning their old behaviors. For example, although prephonemic writing was the highest category observed during the first quarter and remained high through the second and third quarters, children were attempting more and more phonemic writing as the year unfolded. By the fourth quarter, 72% of the children were using some invented spelling. The numbers of children operating in three or more categories moved from 38% in the first quarter to 73% in the fourth.

Another very important finding of the Allen study was that growth was not limited by the level of literacy sophistication that the children brought with them to kindergarten. While children who came in with advanced skills continued their growth, those who entered with very little observable knowledge of reading and writing also made great gains. Instruction that continued exploration and invention of language made the difference.

Children will develop this control over written language if they are encouraged to write frequently in a workshop atmosphere in which they draw/write about real events in their own lives and read their work to peers in all-group share time (Graves, 1983; Hansen, 1987; Hansen & Graves, 1983).

Graves (1983) says that when 5s and 6s first start writing, they think their writing is good, and their self-centeredness protects them from their audiences. It is only toward the end of first grade that they begin to realize that others may not agree with them. By grade 2, children become much more concerned about their product and audience acceptance. They want their work to look like the basals and trade books they can now read. Share time can become risky business.

Besides being risky business, writing is noisy business. Dyson (1983) found that kindergartners talk to themselves as they draw and write, with oral language investing the graphics with meaning. Allen and Carr (1992) learned that they talk to each other to generate topics and develop them, to match print to pictures and letters to sounds, and to learn how "to do school."

Calkins (1986) believes that talk helps young children to hold onto their thoughts while pencils and markers are selected to get them down on paper. She says that both talking and drawing are necessary adjuncts to writing in kindergarten and grade 1. By grade 2, drawing becomes less necessary, but talking with others, as rehearsal for writing and for feedback on drafts, become even more important. Seven-year olds find emotional support in peer review. It appears that writing can be very social business, too.

Young children demonstrate their egocentricity in the writings. Manning, Manning, and Hughes (1987) found that personal content dominated the journals of first graders who wrote about themselves and their feelings and their families and pets. Demonstrating the effect of leaving home for wider vistas, they also wrote information pieces about school, holidays, and seasons.

Calkins (1986) says that first graders' early "published" pieces can be characterized as "all-about" or attribute books in which they tell everything they know about the topic. Toward the end of the year, many move toward writing narratives, that is, stories in which events are chronologically ordered. The main revision strategy for this age is adding on more information as it occurs to them. As second graders move away from "all-about" books, they begin to write "bed-to-bed" stories that are chronologically written but include everything that is remembered, with all events being given equal weight. Calkins characterized this time as a period of growth in writing.

Writers in the primary years are active, noisy, risk takers, internalizing the rules of written language as they use it to construct meaning in social situations.

## Reading

Smith (1985) describes reading as an active, constructive process in which one applies different kinds of knowledge (knowledge of the world, the language system, and the content) to make meaning from written language. While only 15% of school beginners *believe* they can read (Graves, 1983), almost all have some control over this process, but the range is wide. While most can read varying amounts of environmental print, such as stop signs, McDonald's signs A&P signs and food labels, some who have been read to frequently can "pretend-read" familiar picture books, and a few can read notes, signs, and picture books that they have not encountered before (Hartse et al., 1984; Taylor, 1983).

Over the past decade, the term "reading readiness" has given way to the new concept of "emergent literacy." Lapp and Flood (1978) define reading readiness as the necessary level of preparation children should attain before beginning formal reading instruction. Alphabet and word recognition, vocabulary knowledge, and visual discrimination are cited as possible predictors of reading readiness. In traditional readiness programs, prescribed skills in these areas are directly taught to get children "ready" to read.

On the other hand, emergent literacy looks at both reading and writing (literacy) as they are in the process of emerging in the everyday lives of children from their earliest years (Teale & Sulzby, 1986). Morrow (1989) says that the concept assumes that children acquire knowledge about oral and written language before coming to school. In their review of emergent literacy, Mason and Allen (1986) describe the social and linguistic contexts (community and parental priorities) and the special demands of written language that can affect how children develop as readers and writers. Children who have had many meaningful experiences with print such as being read to often and experimenting with writing, are more ready for school reading programs than those who had not had such exposures.

Children lacking these experiences, come to school in a state of "cognitive confusion" about the functions of print and the terms we use in formal reading instruction (Downing, 1970). Adults take it for granted that children know what they mean when they talk about a "word," a "letter," a "sound," but simple experiments with preschoolers proved otherwise (Feeley, 1984). In early seminal research, Downing and Oliver (1973–1974) found that many beginners lack concepts about these terms and other prints conventions. Clay (1979, 1985) has developed a simple test for assessing this metalinguistic knowledge. Called Concepts About Print (CAP), the test consists of a story book, with text on one side and pictures on the other, which is read to the child who is asked to help the tester. It explores concepts such as whether the child knows that print, not pictures, tells the story, what letters and words are, what some punctuation marks mean. Clay (1989) describes how educators from many parts of the world had adapted and used this instrument. Goodman & Altwerger (1981) recommend informal book handling tasks to assess this kind of knowledge.

Children come to school able to understand and respond to thousands of spoken words, but their ability to recognize words in print relates again to their preschool activities with written language. Most will be able to recognize their names and can quickly learn to read the names of their classmates, signs and labels in their classroom, and a basic vocabulary of common words from language experience and shared book activities (Johnson & Pearson, 1984; Mason & Au, 1986). Writing, too, adds to children's stock of sight words. When they compared the vocabulary produced by children in a writing-focused first grade with the vocabulary they would have encountered in a basal reading series, Gunderson and Shapiro (1988) found that the young writers produced 18 times the number of words found in the basals! (Studies like this need to be conducted on a regular basis to see what changes may occur as teachers begin to integrate literature and writing activities into their basal programs and use the most current editions of basals that are more likely to contain a wide variety of selections from the best of children's literature).

Chall (1983) has proposed a six-stage model of reading acquisition that no longer seems to fit with the current concept of emergent literacy. Her stages are: prereading (birth to 6), decoding (6 to 7), fluency (7 to 8), reading to learn (any age), multiple viewpoints (high school), and reconstruction (college and beyond). We now know that young children bring a wide range of literacy skills to their early school experiences (Teale & Sulzby, 1986) and that readers at all levels reconstruct text according to their background knowledge (Anderson & Pearson, 1984; Smith, 1985).

Bussis, Chittenden, Amarel, and Klausner (1985), who documented the development of reading ability in 26 children from K-2, posit that, from the outset, reading is the act of orchestrating diverse knowledge bases to construct meaning from text. They found that all their subjects began school with some knowledge of letter–sound correspondences, a small "sight word" vocabulary, a belief that reading had to make sense, and their own preferred learning styles. How they grew into able readers makes fascinating reading. Although exposed to an array of diverse reading programs (phonics, language experience, various basals), all had teachers who read to them every day, provided a large selection of trade books with time to read, and encouraged written composition frequently.

Admitting that it might be dangerous to try to talk about stages in learning to read because the process is so idiosyncratic, Weaver (1988) has suggested phases that children may go through, similar to those noted in spelling development. In the schema emphasis phase stage, which is compared with the pre-phonemic stage in spelling, children exhibit reading-like behavior, turning pages and "reading" from prior knowledge of story and picture clues. In the semantic/syntactic emphasis phase, which is like the phonemic or invented spelling stage in writing, they continue to use schematic knowledge and picture clues but begin to read some words in context. Miscues at this stage are likely to fit the context semantically and syntactically but may not reflect the actual words on the page, for example "bird" for "canary."

Bussis et al. (1985) noted "quasi-reading" among their kindergarteners and cited the work of Neisser (1967) to try to explain this phenomenon. Young readers probably have not "memorized" the 200 or so words in a story that they "pretend-read," but rather, they remember the phrase structures, chunking the meaning units and rehearsing them as adults do to remember telephone numbers. Bussis et al. wrote, "What Jenny and other quasi-readers committed to memory were not individual words but the phrase structures of a story. The individual words flowed from the structures" (p. 87).

When Sulzby (1985b) studied the emergent storybook reading attempts of preschoolers and children at the beginning and end of kindergarten, she found a developmental progression across age levels. When asked to read or "pretend-read" a story, they went from "reading" no real stories to stories in which they used oral language-like structures at first and finally written language-like structures. Bussis et al. (1985) also report that their quasi readers read in a "book voice."

According to Weaver (1988), in the grapho-phonemic emphasis phase children tend to read exactly what is on the page, with "sounding out" strategies producing "cainery" for "canary" even when they know it stands for a type of bird. This over-reliance on the grapho-phonemic cueing system may be a reflection of children's attempts to master this cue system in addition to the others; this phase corresponds to the transitional stage in writing when invented forms appear along with standard spellings.

Describing this early reading stage that occurred anywhere from the end of kindergarten to grade 2, Bussis et al. (1985) found that half of their subjects (Cluster B) revealed learning styles that caused them to value accuracy and linearity (getting the words right in order of appearance) over momentum (fluency). These readers would skip words and would frequently stop to sound out (even though blending sounds proved difficult for all the children). On the other hand, the other half (Cluster A) exhibited a penchant for momentum, forging ahead with word approximations or substitutions to produce a text that sounded like language.

Further supporting a development trend, in her storybook reading study, Sulzby (1985b) noted that independent reading seemed to begin when children started to attend more closely to the print on the page. Also Allen (1989) found the relationships between reading measures (letter/sound/word recognition and simple text reading) and the use of letters in spelling were very strong by the end of kindergarten.

Bussis et al. (1985) believe that, within their holistic (Cluster A) or linear (Cluster B) learning styles, children gradually orchestrate what they know about books, grammatical structures, literary styles, information encoded in writing, and the conventions of print to negotiate text. The one common characteristic of all their subjects that was observed around this time was mobility. During the time of physical development when they have begun to play active, organized games and have gained control over small muscle coordination through drawing, model building, and arts and crafts, children need to be able to move around in their interactions with written language. Although Bussis et al. (1985) found relationships between more sophisticated uses of invented spelling and reading skill, they found no relationship between reading and the mechanical aspects of writing. Often children whose handwriting was classified as "poor" or "messy" were very able readers.

Weaver (1988) says that when children are able to use all language cue systems (semantic and grapho-phonemic) to sample and predict text, they are in the simultaneous use phase and are likely to be using mostly conventional spelling when they write.

In looking at what primary children like to read, we again note egocentricity. They like to listen to/read stories about children their own age and about families and animals. They also enjoy fairy tales, folk literature, humor, and modern fantasy (Feeley, 1981). Studying kindergarten children's use of a classroom library, Martinez and Teale (1988) found that familiar books with predictable texts, reflecting the described genres, were most likely to be selected. Bussis et al. (1985) also found that young children read informational materials that meet their specialized interests or school assignment needs. During the course of their longitudinal study, every child elected to read some nonfiction texts on such far-ranging topics as care of animals, space exploration, and making puppets.

## Written Language in the Classroom: The Primary Years

Given the profile of the primary school child as an active, social, mobile, inductive thinker who goes from whole to part in learning the uses and conventions of written language, we suggest the following implications, based on those offered by Hartse et al. (1984), Mason and Au (1986), and Schwartz (1988):

1. There should be a rich print environment: a class library filled with appropriate literature; language experience stories on charts; songs, poems, chants, and notices in bold manuscript around the room; and prominent reading and writing centers (Feeley, 1982).

2. Children should be given many opportunities to test out their hypotheses about print in a risk-free atmosphere. In the primary years, Smith, Goodman, and Meredith (1976) say that children are between the stages Piaget calls "intuitive" (4 to 7) and concrete operations (7 to 11) and need interactive experiences with written language. Tunmer, Herriman, and Nesdale (1988) found that children's ability to acquire metalinguistic skills depends on their operativity or level of concrete operational thought. "Big books" that are read together several times before children read them to themselves and each other are one example of an activity that encourages hypothesis testing (Holdaway, 1979). Language experience activities (Hall, 1981; Stauffer, 1980) and uninterrupted reading and writing time (Hansen, 1987) are others.

3. Ellermeyer (1988) says that literacy programs for young children should focus on broadening each child's experiential background; as the conceptual base grows, so will the vocabulary for reading and writing. Reading and writing should not be isolated from each other or from other curricular areas. They are tools for getting things done and should be presented in realistic contexts.

4. Choice should be an integral part of the language program: children should be able to write about topics they know and read books of their own choosing.

5. Meaning should be at the center of all language activities: skills should be taught within the context of real reading and writing situations rather than in isolated workbook and worksheet activities.

6. Teachers should read to children daily and write with them, modeling the dynamic processes of reading and writing.

## MIDDLE ELEMENTARY YEARS

About the age of 8 or 9, most children can integrate the three cue systems (semantic, syntactic, and grapho-phonemic) as they gain more and more control over written language. The middle elementary years mark the period in which reading and writing become increasingly more important in the everyday lives of children.

### Writing

Our views about the teaching and learning of writing in the middle grades have undergone some changes in recent years. In their classic longitudinal study of writing in the elementary school first reported in 1939, Burrows, Jackson, and Saunders (1984) theorized that children produced mainly two kinds of writing (practical and personal) and to help them develop as writers, we should handle each differently. Practical or utilitarian writing of such things as reports, letters, and records should be more directly guided by teachers with mechanics directly taught through group compositions and editing conferences. On the other hand, personal writing of stories and poems develops when children are exposed to good literature and encouraged to write by themselves. For example, after hearing about the antics of five bears, the 9 and 10 year olds in their study began to write their own original bear stories, with one boy producing more than 25! While practical writing is "corrected" before a final copy is written, personal writing, which is done for enjoyment, is usually just read to the teacher or group.

Burrows et al. (1984) found that the fifth and sixth graders in their study grew in both composing techniques and mechanics through their approach. While they observed a gradual increase in the ability to handle mechanics in personal writing, they also found that the spontaneity and freedom enjoyed in imaginative, personal writing carried over to the reporting of information in practical writing situations.

The new view of teaching writing as a process (Calkins, 1986; Graves, 1983; Hansen, 1987) suggests continuing in the middle grades the workshop approach begun in primary years. As children engage in writing personal narrative and specialty reports, and move toward genre writing with feedback from teachers and peers, they will gain further control over written language.

Perhaps because of their new-found control over the mechanics of written language, third-graders in writing process classrooms seem to be preoccupied with correctness ad conventions (Calkins, 1986). Selecting giant topics and writing events in a chain-like manner, they like to demonstrate their new knowledge. For instance, once a convention like dialogue or exclamation is learned, it tends to appear in great abundance.

Reflecting typical Piagetian concrete operational thinking, 8-year-olds do not consider things in their mind's eye but write everything out completely. They may draft three leads or endings to select from and revise by copying a draft over with a few changes. Bereiter and Scardamalia (1982) say young children lack a central executive function to enable them to reflect on their writing, to shuttle back and forth between talking, listening, writing, and reading. They like to write short pieces that are technically correct but often lack "voice."

Studying children in grades 3 to 7 who were trying to write suspense stories, Bereiter and Scardamalia (1984) found that they were only moderately successful, even when revising after instruction and exposure to a model. They hypothesize that children may not be able to do the high level of planning that this type of narrative requires.

To promote planning and more reflective revisions, Graves (1983) suggests encouraging peer and teacher conferences about works in progress. The listener provides the needed executive structure to help writers "resee" their drafts. Scardamalia and Bereiter (1983) conducted a series of studies in which executive support was offered as children wrote. These "simulation by intervention" studies encouraged revision mainly at a local level; according to these researchers, children may need formal operational thought for reprocessing or revising texts in more global ways.

However, Calkins (1983; 1986) says that children begin to be able to reread to revise in grades 4 to 6, especially if they are in workshop situations in which they read their pieces to others for reaction and response. Soon they will be able to hold their own internal conferences; she quotes Vygotsky who said that what children can do today in cooperation with others, they can do alone tomorrow. Shifting from the concrete approach taken by younger children who write everything out, middle-graders write out only portions of alternative leads, endings, and titles, and "just think about" others as they move toward more representational thought. Writing becomes a means of thinking and rethinking.

By the age of 10, children can view their writing through the eyes of a reader. As they do more writing in their minds, they can begin to experiment, going back and forth from writing to reading. As they gain control over time and content, their writings become more multidimensional: They can shift between narrative and description and narrative and dialogue in one piece.

Although younger children want their writing to be correct, reflecting exactly what happened in real life, older children begin to weave together truth and fiction, learning to shape language to please an audience. Instead of telling everything from the beginning, they will start with the event to be highlighted. Writers in the middle elementary grades can take on the voice of a third person as they write genre and expository pieces as well as personal narrative. As they grow in competence and confidence, they find new ways to integrate writing into their lives (Calkins, 1986).

## Reading

Because of wide difference in abilities and experiences and the idiosyncratic nature of literacy development itself, describing readers in the middle grades is a difficult task. Third graders exhibit a growing independence in reading. Relying heavily on cues in the text, they can figure things out for themselves. They see print as literal truth and think that what the book says is right. Although they can read orally with meaning and expression, they like to read to themselves both for pleasure and information. By this time, most have internalized several print grammars, both narrative and simple expository, to help them make sense of written language appropriate to their experiential background (Cochrane, Cochrane, Scalena, & Buchanan, 1984).

Although narrative is the mainstay of the learning-to-read materials found in the primary grades, 8-year-olds have a clear, consistent knowledge of exposition (Langer, 1986). They can talk about the differences between stories and reports and know that they are used in different ways. Langer (1986), who studied 8- to 14-year olds, found that the younger children were less likely to set goals as they read and showed little concern with author or audience. However, the older children in her study were more able to temper their interpretations in light of the author's intentions.

As they move through the elementary school, children's ability to comprehend written language is limited only by their prior knowledge in general and their knowledge of text structures and topics specifically (Mason & Au, 1986). Schema theory posits that reading is the interaction between a reader and a text (Anderson & Pearson, 1984). Readers are actively constructing text, based on what they already know (schemata) and what the author has written. Serving many purposes, schemata help the reader make inferences, summarize, remember, add new knowledge, and make decisions about what is important (McNeil, 1970).

Lipson (1983) had middle-grade children who were either Catholic or Jewish in religious affiliation read passages about receiving first communion and making a bar mitzvah. Each group recalled more from and read faster their culturally familiar passage. Marr & Gromley (1982) reported that fourth graders had significantly better recall on passages about familiar rather than unfamiliar topics.

Smith (1985) says that reading comprehension is raising questions about a text and getting answers. Middle-grade children are active readers who can ask questions raised by others (Palinscar & Brown, 1984; Singer, 1978; Stauffer, 1975; Wong, 1985).

Besides being active readers, children in the middle grades are strategic readers. Meyers and Paris (1978) found that these children are aware of a variety of reading strategies and know how to use them, acquiring metacognitive capabilities as they go through the grades. Babbs and Moe (1983) define metacognition as the ability to monitor one's own thinking. Garner (1987) proposes that teachers actively promote metacognition by modeling comprehension strategies, having children practice them in a variety of situations and content areas, and encouraging students to teach each other about the reading process.

Vocabulary is another adjunct to comprehension (Davis, 1944). Although children build their meaning vocabulary from direct experiences, they add thousands of words each year from their reading of trade books and content area texts. Nagy and Anderson (1984) found that books for reading in the elementary grades contain approximately 90,000 different words. While children learn some words through direct instruction, they pick up many more within the context of their in-school and out-of-school reading.

Middle graders are exposed to written language in a variety of forms. Besides their school texts, trade books, and own writing, they read magazines, comics, newspapers, baseball and bubble gum cards, hobby books, directions, TV listings, video games, directories, scout manuals, computer manuals, and a host of other print materials that may be a part of their environments.

As for choice in trade books, from fourth grade on, strong sex differences emerge. Girls seek fiction more than do boys, especially stories with mystery-adventure, social empathy, and fantasy themes. Boys, while expressing interest in some fictional works like mysteries and science fiction, show more preference for nonfiction categories like sports, history, biography, and science (Feeley, 1981; Graham, 1986; Wolfson, Manning & Manning, 1984).

In the much publicized ChildRead survey, Burgess (1985) found that children in grades 4 to 7 selected books on the basis of appearance, author, and recommendations of peers and adults, especially parents and librarians. (Unfortunately, teachers were not viewed as resources for recreational reading). While most showed a preference for one kind of reading, supporting the interests research cited, all children read a variety of materials. A new area of general interest was the nonfiction category, "technology," which Burgess attributes to the current focus on computers. Interestingly, some are using nonfiction collections heavily for recreational reading. All children claimed to have at least one favorite book that they have reread as many as four or five times.

Toward the end of the elementary school years, as they move from concrete thinking toward formal operational thought, able readers can easily make inferences from print, discuss several aspects of a piece, and challenge its validity. They can process materials further and further removed from their own experiences, with reading providing a major source for continued schema development and refinement (Cochrane, et al., 1984).

## Written Language in the Classroom: The Middle Grades

For the 8- to 14-year-olds that she studied, Langer (1986) found the dominant concern was with the meanings they were developing while reading and writing. She wrote:

> Though children's behavior was always dominated by the content of the text-worlds being created, the differing purposes underlying reading and writing led to different problems and emphases in the reasoning operations. . . . Reading, while with the author's text to channel the reader's ideas, led to more focusing on specific content, and to validating of the text world that was being developed. Writing, on the other hand, forces the writer to take more overt control of the process, and this led to a greater focus on the strategies that could be used to create their meanings. In each case, the children relied upon operations that helped them to make sense—either of their own or someone else's ideas (p. 139).

Accordingly, for reading and writing programs in the middle elementary school, the focus should always be on meaning making, and the following recommendations are offered:

1. Reading and writing should be taught through a process approach (Calkins, 1986; Graves, 1983; Hansen, 1987). The conference aspect, in which listeners provide the external executive function needed by children still in the concrete operational thinking stage, works well for both reading and writing. While teaching writing as a process has been rapidly gaining acceptance over the past decade, a new thrust toward teaching reading as process is just emerging. While Hornsby, Sukarna, and Parry (1988) suggest a conference approach, Hancock and Hill (1988) and Routman (1988) offer models for literature-based reading programs, and Five (1988) describes her own transition from a structured basal reader program to a reading process approach. In order to teach reading through books and to encourage recreational reading, teachers must immerse themselves in appropriate children's literature. The ChildRead survey (Burgess, 1985) found that

middle graders welcomed and appreciated book talks by their teachers.

2. Before reading and writing, children should be encouraged to engage in schema activation activities so that they can make use of what they know about topics to aid in meaning making. Langer (1984) used a Pre Reading Plan (PReP) to assess children's text-specific background knowledge before they read. She found that the measure was a reliable and significant predictor of comprehension; also, the activity significantly raised background knowledge and thus improved comprehension.

McNeil (1987) suggests that webbing, semantic mapping, structured overviews, and other background-generating techniques such as the Directed Reading-Thinking Activity (Stauffer, 1975) and Au's Experience-Text-Relationship (Mason & Au, 1986) should be taught and modeled.

3. There should be increasing attention to expanding children's knowledge about text structures. Langer (1986) found that even 8-year-olds understood exposition, but they tended to use mainly description/collections, dominated by the title, when they wrote reports. She suggests starting with the known approach and moving to other rhetorical structures; for example, after a child wrote a report on English horseback riding and another on western riding, she could be encouraged to compare the two in a new piece.

Armbruster, Anderson, and Ostertag (1987) taught fifth graders to recognize and summarize a conventional text structure, problem/solution. As measured by responses to a main idea essay question and written summaries, the student's ability to abstract the macrostructure of a problem/solution text was significantly improved.

4. Vocabulary should be expanded through constructing networks of ideas; it is best developed in meaningful contexts (McNeil, 1987). While Mezynski's literature review (1983) concluded that vocabulary training had little effect on reading comprehension, Gipe (1978–79) found an interactive context method superior to other methods, including the time honored dictionary approach, for developing vocabulary and comprehension among third and fifth graders.

5. Children in the middle grades can begin to be reflective about their reading and writing. They can learn to step back and monitor their attempts at meaning making. Stevens, Madden, Slavin, and Farnish (1987), who taught third and fourth graders comprehension and meta-comprehension activities in a cooperative learning approach to reading and writing instruction, found significant effects on several measures of literacy achievement.

Paris, Cross, and Lipson (1984) successfully taught third and fifth graders to monitor their reading through a program called Informed Strategies for Learning (ISL). The students learn to plan, evaluate, and regulate their own comprehension, becoming significantly more aware of reading strategies and improving their performance on comprehension measures.

6. Writing across the curriculum holds much promise as a way to enhance learning in the content areas. Langer (1986) found that children were more able to talk about what strategies they used and how their knowledge changed after writing

than after reading. She says that writing seems to be useful in helping children focus on developing an understanding of subject matter and recommends writing to learn in the content areas.

## LITERARY DEVELOPMENT

Researchers studying children's concept of story have noted certain developmental trends. As in the learning of any concept, young children formulate a general sense or idea of what stories are all about, focusing on beginnings, endings, and obvious attempts. For example, McNeil (1987, p. 25) reports a kindergarten child's retelling of "The Lion and the Mouse" as follows: "A lion got trapped in a net and mighty mouse came and saved him." These early notions of story are gradually modified and refined as children continue to encounter new stories in a variety of situations.

Perhaps the first evidence of the developing sense of story in children is their use of language to create a special or private world. This is thought to be the forerunner to the child's use of language to create a world of make-believe, involving dramatic play and leading dramatic play and the gradual acquisition of the specific conventions that constitute a sense of story. As children mature, their stories increase in length and complexity. The characters, settings, and actions become further removed from the here and now of the immediate environment. Children gradually gain greater control over the events in their stories, moving from a loose collection of related events to tightly structured narratives that link a set of events to each other and to a common theme (Applebee, 1978). A fifth grader produced a much more detailed retelling of the "The Lion and the Mouse" than did the kindergartner previously quoted, including all attempts and reactions and even the theme or moral, " . . . sometimes little can help big" (McNeil, 1987, p. 29). According to McConaughy (1980), this older child is approaching an adult concept of story because of the attention to cause and effect and inferencing beyond the text.

Whaley (1981) found that when reading stories, older children were better at predicting events than younger children. She concluded that the expansion of a story sense in older students enabled them to predict more of the story structures. Mandler (1978) found that children seem to organize their recall according to an ideal story structure. They tap into their existing concept of a story as they attempt to remember new stories. Younger children tend to emphasize the outcomes of specific action sequences rather than the specific events and their causes. As children mature, their story retellings appear to move away from a simple, ideal concept of story toward a more complex adult model.

Analyses of children's written stories reveals the same developmental patterns. Sutton-Smith (1981) reports that young children organize their stories around basic pairs of actions such as chase and escape and that they tend to repeat these actions in their written stories. For example, three first graders who had made doughnuts with their class that morning were composing a follow-up written piece (Long & Bulgarella, 1985). Instead of

recording how doughnuts were made, they decided to write about a man who made doughnuts that came alive, " . . . kinda like Raggedy Ann and Andy" (p. 167). To avoid being eaten up, the doughnuts run away. Because one child in the group wanted a happy ending, both the doughnuts and the man go to a "cellabrashun" where they had " . . . wine and cake . . . and they both had a good time" (p. 171).

Sipe (1996) created a typology of children's literary understandings based on their oral responses to picture books. He describes three dimensions through which children's understandings can be seen:

1. Stance: How children situate themselves in relation to texts.
2. Action: What children do with texts.
3. Function: How texts function.

This typology suggests that even first and second graders analyze stories and consider the characteristics of books. They talk about plots and story endings, link stories to other literary works, and describe connections across authors or genres.

As children mature in written expression, multiple pairs of actions with supporting elements become apparent, suggesting a movement toward the elaboration of event structures. For instance, two fourth-grade boys we observed in a local elementary school had developed a super hero named "Machine Gun Joe," a tough army sergeant who saved Americans around the world, from Olympic athletes in Korea to kidnapped ambassadors in Italy. Each episode was connected by a staccato reprise: "It was a mean job, but somebody had to do it!"

Langer (1986) found that story forms used by 8-year-olds were similar in basic structure to those used by the 14-year-olds, even though the older children's stories had more detail. She hypothesized that although children enter school with a firm knowledge of story structure, limited opportunities to use more complex and varied story forms as they go through the grades may account for lack of growth in this genre. While elementary school teachers generally encourage the writing of narratives, upper grade and high school curricula focus mainly on expository writing.

In summary, the research focusing on the development of story in children suggests that virtually all children are exposed to story to some degree; that they begin to develop a concept of story and other literary understandings at an early age; and that as they mature these concepts expand.

### Linking Literary Development to Reading and Writing

Researchers studying the development of story in children have linked their findings to children's development of reading and writing. The role of prior knowledge and experience in reading and writing suggests that learners who have had many experiences with stories and who have developed a strong schema for stories make use of that framework as they read and write. Listeners and readers are said to use their knowledge of story structure to guide them in anticipating the events in a story. They make predictions about what will occur next in a story, a process believed to be essential to reading comprehension. Prior knowledge of what a story is helps facilitate recall of a text (Mandler & Johnson, 1977; Stein, 1979). Story schema actually acts as a guide or road map for retrieving story information. It may help a student to decide when a portion of a story is complete or incomplete and serve to assist in filling in or inferring information that may have been forgotten.

The learner's preexisting concept of story is equally as important in producing stories as it is in comprehending them. Several researchers who have analyzed children's written stories found story narratives to be the most prevalent structure (Applebee, 1978; Britton, Burgess, Martin, McLeod, & Rosen, 1975; Sutton-Smith, 1981). Story schema may be activated during the first stage of the writing process when ideas are being conceived (Britton et al., 1975). The author draws on the story elements of setting, character, and plot during the writing of the story and these may serve as a framework for revision as well.

Hancock (1993) investigated sixth graders' literary journal responses to four award-winning, realistic fiction books. Results from analyzing the responses revealed three categories of response: (a) immersion, which includes understanding, predicting, questioning, and character introspection; (b) self-involvement, which includes identifying with characters, assessing characters, and being involved in the story; and (c) detachment, which includes literary evaluation and reader–writer digressions. These studies connecting writing and literary development affirm the idea that writing can serve as a reflective device and as a way of personally connecting to literature.

## Literary Development in the Classroom

Researchers and curriculum specialists have sought to apply what has been learned about the relationship between children's knowledge of story and the development of literacy. These efforts have produced a variety of strategies for using story structure. Although there is some disagreement as to whether the direct teaching of story structure is either necessary or helpful, there is universal agreement about the need to expose students to an abundance of stories in a variety of ways and to expand that exposure to include activities that strengthen their concept of story (Strickland, 1984). Actually, explicit knowledge about story grammar may be most important for teachers as they plan literature experiences for their students.

Vacca, Vacca, and Gove (1987) do not advocate the direct teaching of the technical terms of story elements. Rather, they say that children will develop story schema informally through varied experiences with well-structured stories. For example, because Moldofsky (1983) noted that most fiction found in the elementary grades develops around a problem, it is important for children to recognize the central part played by this element. An appropriate strategy is to have children relate problems in their own lives to those in stories they read and write.

The popular practice of reading familiar stories over and over again for young children appears to promote their sense of story structure. Morrow (1988) found that the responses of children who were exposed to repeated readings of three selected stories over a 10-week period focused significantly more on story structure than did those of a group who were read different stories or a control group who were not exposed to storybook reading.

It is important to select books with predictable plots for young readers and to introduce stories with complicated plots or unexpected twists only after children have the cognitive base and literary experiences to deal with them. Stein and Tabasso (1982) found that readers and listeners tend to retell story events in time order even when an author has altered the order or special effects such as in mysteries and suspense stories. Brewer and Lichtenstein (1981) explain that different schemata may be operating. "Event schemas" represent readers' or listeners' knowledge about cause/effect and time relationships in a story, whereas "story schemas" represent their knowledge about constructing narratives. Younger children will have more difficulty reading stories that are not temporally ordered. Older children who have had more experience with stories of various genres and who are beginning to move toward more formal operational thought can deal with event and story schemas simultaneously.

Whole group and small group discussions about books allow children to share and reflect on their interpretations of literary experiences. Sloan (1984) offers teachers a series of questions for use in helping students strengthen their understanding of stories in relationship to various aspects of story structure. Galda (1982) used creative dramatics to help young children develop their reading comprehension and sense of story. According to Galda, when players discuss things such as roles, props, and story settings, they become more aware of aspects of the story that they individually might not have noticed (p. 53). Storytelling and retelling, as suggested in the oral language section of this chapter, are excellent means of deepening children's understandings of how narratives work, both for reading and writing. Cambourne (1984) developed a retelling strategy that makes use of children's story schema as they make and confirm their own predictions and retellings and compare them with the predictions and retellings of others.

Strickland and Feeley (1985) offer a model for improving story reading and writing that draws on a variety of modes of language. In this model, students focus on a particular genre of literature over an extended time. They listen to selections read aloud by the teacher and respond to literature through activities such as discussion, dramatics, and art. Book talks and displays related to the genre help to stimulate children's desire to read similar works on their own. As interest in the genre increases, children discuss its features and are encouraged to include the type of story under study in their writing repertoires. Immersing students in the study of a particular genre helps them to internalize the structure and strengthens their sensitivity and appreciation of literary form as readers and writers.

## CONCLUSION

Children bring their growing mastery over oral language and a wonderful sense of industry to their elementary school experience. Once in school, they begin to internalize in a formal way the rules of written language as they experiment with reading and writing in realistic social settings. With further exposure to the literature of the school-age years, they flesh out their emerging concept of story and learn to control expository as well as narrative text. Schematic knowledge grows in leaps and bounds as reading and writing extend what is learned through direct and vicarious experiences.

As for thinking processes, language learners in elementary school go from nonconservers who have difficulty dealing with print simultaneously as letters, sounds, and meanings to strategic readers who can understand a passage at several levels and reflective writers who can plan, draft, and reprocess text to achieve specific goals. Also, metacognition develops as children are encouraged to reflect on the reading, writing, listening, and speaking they and others do. The sense of industry and experimentation that characterizes middle childhood produces great growth in language, thinking, and knowledge during the elementary school years.

## References

Allen, J. (1989). Reading and writing development. In J. Mason (Ed.), *Reading and writing connections*. Needham Heights, MA: Allyn & Bacon.

Allen, J., & Carr, E. (1992). Collaborative learning among kindergarten writers: James learns how to learn at school. In J. Allen & J. Mason (Eds.), *Risk makers, risk takers, risk breakers: Reducing the risks for young literacy learners*. Portsmouth, NH: Heinemann.

Anderson, R. C., & Pearson, P. D. (1984). A schema-theoretic view of basic processes in reading. In P. D. Pearson (Ed.), *Handbook of reading research* (pp. 255-291). New York: Longman.

Applebee, A. N. (1978). *The child's concept of story*. Chicago: The University of Chicago Press.

Armbruster, B. B., Anderson, T. H., & Ostertag, J. (1987). Does text structure/summarization instruction facilitate learning from expository text? *Reading Research Quarterly, 22,* 331-346.

Babbs, P. J., & Moe, A. J. (1983). Metacognition: A key for independent learning from text. *The Reading Teacher, 32,* 422-426.

Baghban, M. (1984). *Our daughter learns to read and write: A case study from birth to three*. Newark, DE: International Reading Association.

Bee, H. (1985). *The developing child*. New York: Harper & Row.

Bereiter, C., & Scardamalia, M. (1982). From conversation to composition: The role of instruction in a developmental process. In R. Glaser (Ed.), *Advances in instructional psychology* (Vol. 2, pp. 1-64). Hillsdale, NJ: Lawrence Erlbaum Associates.

Bereiter, C., & Scardamalia, M. (1984). Learning about writing from reading. *Written Communication, 1,* 163-188.

Berko Gleason, J. B. (1985). *The development of language*. Columbus, OH: Merrill.

Bissex, G. L. (1980). *GYNS at WRK: A child learns to read and write*. Cambridge, MA: Harvard University Press.

Bormouth, J. R., Carr, J., Manning, J., & Pearson, D. (1970). Children's comprehension of between-and within-sentence syntactic structures. *Journal of Educational Psychology, 61,* 349-357.

Brewer, W. R., & Lichtenstein, E. H. (1981). Event schemas, story schemas, and story grammars. In A. D. Buddely & J. D. Lang (Eds.), *Attention and performance IX* (pp. 160-189). Hillsdale, NJ: Lawrence Erlbaum Associates.

Britton, J., Burgess, T., Martin, N., McLeod, A., & Rosen, H. (1975). *The development of writing abilities*. London: Macmillan Education Ltd.

Bromley, K. (1988). *Language arts: Exploring connections*. Boston: Allyn & Bacon.

Brown, R. (1973). *A first language: The early stages*. Cambridge, MA: Harvard University Press.

Burgess, S. A. (1985). Reading but not literate: The ChildRead survey. *School Library Journal, 31,* 27-30.

Burrows, A. (1968). *What research says to the teacher: Teaching composition*. Washington, DC: National Education Association.

Burrows, A., Jackson, D. C., & Saunders, D. O. (1984). *They all want to write* (4th ed.). New York: Library Professional Publications.

Bussis, A. M., Chittenden, E. A., Amarel, M., & Klausner, E. (1985). *Inquiry into meaning: An investigation of learning to read*. Hillsdale, NJ: Lawrence Erlbaum Associates.

Calkins, L. M. (1983). *Lessons from a child*. Exeter, NH: Heinemann.

Calkins, L. M. (1986). *The art of teaching writing*. Portsmouth, NH: Heinemann.

Calkins, L. (1994). *The art of teaching writing*. (Rev. ed.) Portsmouth, NH: Heinemann.

Cambourne, B. (1984). *Retelling a pedagogical strategy: Summary thoughts*. Paper presented at Miscue Update Conference, Detroit, MI.

Cazden, C. (1988). *Classroom discourse*. Portsmouth, NH: Heinemann.

Chall, J. (1983). *Stages of reading development*. New York: McGraw-Hill.

Chomsky, C. (1969). *The acquisition of syntax in children from 5 to 10* (Research Monograph No. 57). Cambridge, MA: MIT Press.

Chomsky, C. (1972). Stages in language development and reading exposure. *Harvard Educational Review, 42,* 1-33.

Chomsky, C. (1979). Approaching reading through invented spelling. In L. B. Resnick & P. A. Weaver (Eds.), *Theory and practice of early reading* (pp. 43-65). Hillsdale, NJ: Lawrence Erlbaum Associates.

Clark, M. M. (1976). *Young fluent readers*. London: Heinemann Educational Books.

Clay, M. (1975). *What did I write?* Exeter, NH: Heinemann.

Clay, M. (1979). *Concepts about print tests*. Exeter, NH: Heinemann.

Clay, M. (1985). *The early detection of reading difficulties*. Portsmouth, NH: Heinemann.

Clay, M. (1989). Concepts about print in English and other languages. The *Reading Teacher, 42,* 268-276.

Cochrane, O., Cochrane, D., Scalena, S., & Buchanan, E. (1984). *Reading, writing, and caring*. New York: Richard C. Owens.

Collins, W. A. (1984). Conclusion: The status of basic research on middle childhood. In W. A. Collins (Ed.), *Development during middle childhood: The years from six to twelve* (pp. 94-109). Washington, DC: National Academic Press.

Collins, A. (1986). *A sample dialogue based on a theory of inquiry reading*. (Tech. Rep. No. 367). Urbana, IL: Center for the Study of Reading.

Cullinan, B., Jaggar, A., & Strickland, D. (1974). Language expansion for black children in the primary grades: A research report. *Young Children, 29,* 98-112.

Dahl, K. L., & Farnan, N. (1998). *Children's writing: Perspectives from research*. Newark, DE: International Reading Association.

Davis, F. B. (1944). Fundamental factors of comprehension in reading. *Psychometrika, 9,* 185-197.

Deford, D., & Hartse, J. (1982). Child language research and curriculum. *Language Arts, 59,* 590–600.

Devine, T. (1978). Listening: What do we know after 50 years of research and theorizing? *Journal of Reading, 21,* 296–303.

Dillon, D., & Searle, D. (1981). The role of language in one first grade classroom. *Research in the Teaching of English, 15,* 311–328.

Downing, J. (1970). Children's concepts of language in learning to read. *Educational Research, 12,* 106–112.

Downing, J., & Oliver, P. (1973–1974). The child's conception of a word. *Reading Research Quarterly, 9,* 468–482.

Durkin, D. (1966). *Children who read early.* New York: Teachers College Press.

Dyson, A. H. (1983). The role of oral language in early writing processes. *Research in the Teaching of English, 17*(1), 1–30.

Ellermeyer, D. (1988). Kindergarten reading program to grow on. *The Reading Teacher, 41,* 402–405.

Feeley, J. T. (1981). What do our children like to read? *NJEA Review, 54*(8), 26–27.

Feeley, J. T. (1982). A print environment for beginning readers. *Reading, 16,* 23–50.

Feeley, J. T. (1984). Print and reading: What do preschoolers know? *Day Care and Early Education, 11,* 26–28.

Ferreiro, E., & Teberosky, A. (1983). *Writing before schooling.* Exeter, NH: Heinemann.

Five, C. L. (1988). From workbook to workshop: Increasing children's involvement in the reading process. *The New Advocate, 1,* 103–113.

Flanders, N. A. (1962). Using interaction analysis in the inservice training of teachers. *Journal of Experimental Education, 30,* 313–316.

Fletcher, P., & Garman, M. (Eds.). (1986). *Language acquisition: Studies in first language development.* London: Cambridge University Press.

Forester, A. D. (1980). Learning to spell by spelling. *Theory Into Practice, 19,* 186–193.

Funk, H. D., & Funk, G. D. (1989). Guidelines for developing listening skills. *The Reading Teacher, 42,* 660–663.

Furniss, E., & Green, P. (1991). *The literacy agenda.* Portsmouth, NH: Heinemann.

Galda, L. (1982). Playing about a story: Its impact on comprehension. *The Reading Teacher, 36,* 52–55.

Gardner, H. (1996). Encounter at Royaumont: The debate between Jean Piaget and Noam Chomsky. In B. M. Power & R. S. Hubbard (Eds.), *Language development: A reader for teachers.* Englewood, NJ: Prentice-Hall.

Garner, R. (1987). *Metacognition and reading comprehension.* Norwood, NJ: Ablex.

Gentry, J. R. (1981). Learning to spell developmentally. *The Reading Teacher, 34,* 378–381.

Gipe, J. P. (1978–1979). Investigating techniques for teaching word meanings. *Reading Research Quarterly, 14,* 624–644.

Goodman, K. S. (1996). Language development: Issues, insights, and implementation. In B. M. Power & R. S. Hubbard (Eds.), *Language development: A reader for teachers.* Englewood, NJ: Prentice-Hall.

Goodman, Y. M., & Altwerger, B. (1981). *Print awareness in preschool children: A working paper.* Tucson, AZ: Program in Languages and Literacy, University of Arizona.

Graham, S. (1986). Assessing reading preferences: A new approach. *New England Reading Association Journal, 21*(1), 8–11.

Graves, D. H. (1981). *A case study observing the development of primary children's composing, spelling, and motor behaviors during writing process.* Durham, NH: University of New Hampshire. (ERIC Document Reproduction Service No. ED 218 653).

Graves, D. H. (1983). *Writing: Teachers and children at work.* Exeter, NH: Heinemann.

Graves, D. H. (1994). *A fresh look at writing.* Portsmouth, NH: Heinemann.

Gunderson, L., & Shapiro, J. (1988). Whole language instruction: Writing in 1st grade. *The Reading Teacher, 41,* 430–437.

Hall, M. A. (1981). *Teaching reading as a language experience.* Columbus, OH: Merrill.

Halliday, M. A. K. (1975). *Explorations in the functions of language.* London: Edward Arnold.

Hancock, M. (1993). Exploring the meaning-making process through the content of literature response journals: A case study investigation. *Research in the Teaching of English, 27,* 335–368.

Hancock, J., & Hill, S. (1988). *Literature-based reading programs that work.* Portsmouth, NH: Heinemann.

Hansen, J. (1987). *When writers read.* Portsmouth, NH: Heinemann.

Hansen, J., & Graves, D. L. (1983). The author's chair. *Language Arts, 60,* 176–183.

Harste, J. C., Woodward, V. A., & Burke, C. L. (1984). *Language stories and literacy lessons.* Portsmouth, NH: Heinemann.

Hillocks, G. (1986). *Research on written composition: New directions for teaching.* Urbana, IL: ERIC Clearinghouse on Reading and Communication Skills and the National Conference on Research in English.

Holdaway, D. (1979). *Foundations of literacy.* Exeter, NH: Heinemann.

Hornsby, D., Sukarna, D., & Parry, J. (1988). *Read on: A conference approach to reading.* Portsmouth, NH: Heinemann.

Johnson, D. D., & Pearson, P. D. (1984). *Teaching reading vocabulary.* New York: Holt, Rinehart, & Winston.

King, M. L., & Rentel, V. (1979). Towards a theory of early writing development. *Research in Teaching English, 13,* 243–253.

Lapp, D. & Flood, J. (1978). *Teaching reading to every child.* New York: Macmillan.

Langer, J. A. (1984). Examining background knowledge and text comprehension. *Reading Research Quarterly, 19,* 468–481.

Langer, J. A. (1986). *Children reading and writing.* Norwood, NJ: Ablex.

Lehr, F. (1985). Instructional scaffolding. *Language Arts, 62,* 667–672.

Lipson, M. Y. (1983). The influence of religious affiliation on children's memory for text information. *Reading Research Quarterly, 18,* 448–457.

Loban, W. (1963). *Language development: Kindergarten through grade 12.* Urbana, IL: National Council of Teachers of English.

Long, R., & Bulgarella, L. K. (1985). Social interaction and the writing process. *Language Arts, 62,* 166–172.

Lundsteen, S. (1971). *Listening: Its impact on reading and the other language arts.* Urbana, IL: National Council of Teachers of English.

Lundsteen, S. (1976). *Children learn to communicate.* Englewood Cliffs, NJ: Prentice-Hall.

Mandler, J. (1978). A code in the node: The use of story schema in retrieval. *Discourse Processes, 1,* 1–13.

Mandler, J. M., & Johnson, N. S. (1977). Remembrance of things parsed: Story structure and recall. *Cognitive Psychology, 9*(1), 111–151.

Manning, M., Manning, G., & Hughes, J. (1987). Journals in first grade: What children write. *The Reading Teacher, 41,* 311–315.

Marr, M., & Gromley, K. (1982). Children's recall of familiar and unfamiliar text. *Reading Research Quarterly, 18,* 89–104.

Martinez, M., & Teale, W. (1988). Reading in the kindergarten classroom library. *The Reading Teacher, 41,* 568–573.

Mason, J. M., & Allen, J. (1986). A review of emergent literacy with implications for research and practice in reading. In E. Rothkopf (Ed.), *Review of research in education* (pp. 3–47). Washington, DC: American Educational Research Association.

Mason, J. M., & Au, K. H. (1986). *Reading instruction for today.* Glenview, IL: Scott, Foresman.

McConaughy, S. H. (1980). Using story structure in the classroom. *Language Arts, 57,* 157-165.

McNeil, J. (1970). *The acquisition of language: The study of development psycholinguistics.* New York: Harper & Row.

McNeil, J. D. (1987). *Reading comprehension: New directions for classroom practice* (3rd ed.). Glenview, IL: Scott, Foresman.

Mehan, H. (1979). *Learning lessons.* Cambridge, MA: Harvard University Press.

Menyuk, P. (1969). Syntactic structures in the language of children. *Child Development, 34,* 407-422.

Meyers, M., & Paris, S. G. (1978). Children's metacognitive knowledge about reading. *Journal of Educational Psychology, 70,* 680-690.

Mezynski, K. (1983). Issues concerning the acquisition of knowledge: Effect of vocabulary training on reading comprehension. *Review of Educational Research, 53,* 253-279.

Michaels, S., & Foster, M. (1985). Peer-peer learning: Evidence from a student-run sharing time. In A. Jaggar & M. Smith-Burke (Eds.), *Observing the Language Learner* (pp. 143-158). Newark, DE: International Reading Association.

Moldofsky, P. B. (1983). Teaching children to determine the central story problem: A practical application of schema theory. *The Reading Teacher, 36,* 745-749.

Morrow, L. M. (1988). Young children's responses to one-to-one story readings in school settings. *Reading Research Quarterly, 23,* 89-107.

Morrow, L. M. (1989). New perspectives in early literacy. *The Reading Instruction Journal, 32,* 8-15.

Nagy, W. E., & Anderson, R. C. (1984). How many words are there in printed school English? *Reading Research Quarterly, 19,* 304-330.

Neisser, U. (1967). *Cognitive psychology.* New York: Appleton-Century-Crofts.

Oral language developmental continuum. (1994). Education Department of Western Australia. Melbourne, Australia: Addison Wesley.

Palinscar, A. M., & Brown, A. (1984). Reciprocal teaching of comprehension. *Cognition and Instruction, 1,* 117-175.

Palinscar, A. M., & Brown, A. L. (1985). Reciprocal teaching: Activities to promote "reading with your mind." In T. L. Harris & E. J. Cooper (Eds.), *Reading, thinking, and concept development* (pp. 147-159). New York: The College Board.

Paris, S. G., Cross, D. R., & Lipson, M. Y. (1984). Informed strategies for learning: A program to improve children's reading awareness and comprehension. *Journal of Educational Psychology, 76,* 239-242.

Pearson, P. D., & Fielding, L. (1982). Research update: Listening comprehension. *Language Arts, 59,* 617-629.

Piaget, J. (1955). *The language and thought of the child.* New York: Meridian Books.

Piaget, J. (1970). Piaget's theory. In P. H. Mussen (Ed.), *Carmichael's manual of child psychology* (pp. 116-129). New York: Wiley.

Pinnell, G. S. (1996). Ways to look at the functions of children's language. In B. M. Power & R. S. Hubbard (Eds.), *Language development: A reader for teachers.* Englewood, NJ: Prentice-Hall.

Read, C. (1986). *Children's creative spelling.* Boston, MA: Routledge & Kegan Paul.

Rice, M. L. (1996). Children's language acquisition. In B. M. Power & R. S. Hubbard (Eds.), *Language development: A reader for teachers.* Englewood, NJ: Prentice-Hall.

Routman, R. (1988). *Transitions: From literature to literacy.* Portsmouth, NH: Heinemann.

Scardamalia, M., & Bereiter, C. (1983). The development of evaluative, diagnostic, and remedial capabilities in children's composing. In M. Martlew (Ed.), *The psychology of written language: Developmental and educational perspectives* (pp. 67-95). London: Wiley.

Schwartz, J. L. (1988). *Encouraging early literacy: An integral approach to reading and writing in N-3.* Portsmouth, NH: Heinemann.

Selman, R. L. (1976). Social cognitive understanding: A guide to educational and clinical practice. In T. Lickona (Ed.), *Moral development and behavior* (pp. 299-316). New York: Holt, Rinehart & Winston.

Shanahan, T. (1984). The nature of the reading–writing relation: An exploratory multivariate analysis. *Journal of Educational Psychology, 76,* 466-477.

Shonkoff, J. P. (1984). The biological substrate and physical health in middle childhood. In W. A. Collins (Ed.), *Development during middle childhood: The years from six to twelve* (pp. 213-254). Washington, DC: National Academy Press.

Singer, H. (1978). Active comprehension. *The Reading Teacher, 31,* 901-908.

Sipe, L. (1996). *The construction of literary understandings by first and second graders in response to picture storybook readalouds.* Unpublished doctoral dissertation, The Ohio State University, Columbus.

Sloan, G. (1984). *The child as critic.* New York: Teachers College Press.

Smith, E. B., Goodman, K. S., & Meredith, R. (1976). *Language and thinking in school.* New York: Holt, Rinehart & Winston.

Smith, F. (1985). *Reading without nonsense.* New York: Teachers College Press.

Stauffer, R. G. (1975). *Directing the reading-thinking process.* New York: Harper & Row.

Stauffer, R. (1980). *The language experience approach to teaching reading.* New York: Harper & Row.

Stein, N. (1979). How children understand stories: A developmental analysis. In *Current topics in early childhood education* (Vol. 11, pp. 261-290). Norwood, NJ: Ablex.

Stein, N. L., & Tabasso, T. (1982). What's in a story? Critical issues in comprehension and instruction. In R. Glaser (Ed.), *Advances in instructional psychology* (Vol. 2, pp. 213-254). Hillsdale, NJ: Lawrence Erlbaum Associates.

Stevens, R. J., Madden, N. A., Slavin, R. E., & Farnish, A. M. (1987). Cooperative integrated reading and composition. *Reading Research Quarterly, 22,* 433-454.

Strickland, D. (1973). A program for the linguistically different black children. *Research in the Teaching of English, 7,* 79-86.

Strickland, D. (1984). Building children's knowledge of stories. In J. Osborn, P. Wilson, & R. Anderson (Eds.), *Reading education: Foundations for a literate America.* Lexington, MA: Lexington Press.

Strickland, D., Dillon, R., Funkhouser, L., Glick, M., & Rogers, C. (1989). Research currents: Classroom dialogue during literature response groups. *Language Arts, 66,* 192-200.

Strickland, D. S., & Feeley, J. T. (1985). Using children's concept of story to improve reading and writing. In T. Harris & E. Cooper (Eds.), *Reading, thinking, and concept development* (pp. 163-175). New York: The College Board.

Strickland, D., & Taylor, D. (1989). Family storybook reading: Implications for children, families, and curriculum. In D. Strickland & L. Morrow (Eds.), *Emerging literacy: Young children learn to read and write.* Newark, DE: International Reading Association.

Strickland, R. (1962). The language of elementary school children: Its relationship to the language of reading textbooks and the quality of reading of selected children. *Bulletin of the School of Education, 38*(4). Bloomington, IN: Indiana University.

Sulzby, E. (1985a). Kindergartens as writers and readers. In M. Farr (Ed.), *Advances in writing research: Vol. 1. Children's early writing development* (pp. 127-199). Norwood, NJ: Ablex.

Sulzby, E. (1985b). Children's emergent reading of favorite story-books: A development study. *Reading Research Quarterly, 20,* 458–481.

Sutton-Smith, B. (1981). *The folkstories of children.* Philadelphia: University of Pennsylvania Press.

Taylor, D. (1983). *Family literacy: Young children learning to read and write.* Exeter, NH: Heinemann.

Taylor, D., & Strickland, D. (1986). *Family storybook reading.* Portsmouth, NH: Heinemann.

Teale, W., & Sulzby, E. (Eds.). (1986). *Emergent literacy: Writing and reading.* Norwood, NJ: Ablex.

Temple, C. A., Nathan, R. G., Burris, N. A., & Temple, F. (1988). *The beginnings of writing.* Boston, MA: Allyn & Bacon.

Templeton, S. (1991). *Teaching the integrated language arts.* Boston: Houghton Mifflin.

Templin, M. (1987). *Certain language skills in children: Their development and interrelationships.* Minneapolis: University of Minnesota Press.

Tierney, R. J., & Pearson, P. D. (1984). Toward a composing model of reading. In J. Jensen (Ed.), *Composing and comprehending* (pp. 33–46). Urbana, IL: National Conference on Research in English.

Torrey, J. W. (1969). Learning to read without a teacher: A case study. *Elementary English, 46,* 550–556.

Tunmer, W. E., Herriman, M. L., & Nesdale, A. R. (1988). Metalinguistic abilities and beginning reading. *Reading Research Quarterly, 23,* 134–158.

Vacca, J. L., Vacca, R. T., & Gove, M. (1987). *Reading and learning to read.* Boston, MA: Little, Brown.

Vygotsky, L. S. (1962). *Thought and language.* Cambridge, MA: MIT Press.

Weaver, C. (1988). *Reading process and practice.* Portsmouth, NH: Heinemann.

Whaley, J. F. (1981). Story grammar and reading instruction. *The Reading Teacher, 34,* 762–771.

Wilt, M. (1950, April). Study of teacher awareness of listening as a factor in elementary education. *Journal of Educational Research, 43,* 626–636.

Wolfson, B. J., Manning, G., & Manning, M. (1984). Revisiting what children say their reading interests are. *Reading World, 24*(2), 4–10.

Wong, B. Y. (1985). Self-questioning instructional research. *Review of Educational Research, 55,* 227–268.

Zigler, E. F., & Finn-Stevenson, M. (1987). *Children: Development and social issues.* Lexington, MA: D. C. Heath.

# TODAY'S MIDDLE GRADES: DIFFERENT STRUCTURES, STUDENTS, AND CLASSROOMS

## John Simmons and Pamela S. Carroll
### Florida State University

## INTRODUCTION

Although the philosophy and practices that define the modern middle school have become clearly articulated only during the past 30 years or so, American educators have called for attention to the particular needs of the young adolescents for over a century. In his 1920 text, *The Junior High School*, Leonard V. Koos, a Professor of Education at the University of Minnesota, noted that the impetus for the creation of junior high schools actually began with the Committee of Ten on Secondary School Studies, which began its work toward reorganizing the structure of American education in 1893. As Koos points out, a 1899 report for the Committee of Ten, the Committee on College Entrance and Requirements recommended a "'unified, six-year high school course of study beginning with the seventh grade,'" characterized by work that would be " 'enriched by eliminating nonessentials and adding new subjects formerly taught only in the high school' " (p. 6). The Committee was interested in finding ways to avoid what Bennett, in a 1926 text, *The Junior High*, revised edition, called "leakage"; that is, dropping out of school during the middle years. According to Koos, the Committee, "expressed the opinion that the transition from one to the other 'might be made more natural and easy by changing gradually from the one-teacher regimen to the system of special teachers, thus avoiding the shock now commonly felt on entering the high school' " (p. 6). They argued for specialized curricula and instructional practices for the middle grades, and acknowledged that young adolescents are different from children and from older adolescents: "'the seventh grade, rather than the ninth, is the natural turning point in the child's life, as the age of adolescence demands new methods and wiser direction'" (p. 6).

Koos was able to write that in 1920, the number of junior high and intermediate schools had increased to almost 1,000

since the publication of the Report of the Committee of Ten (p. 9). School leaders began to recognize that differences in young adolescents' prior experiences, their scholastic achievement, or their apparent capacity to learn, should be taken into consideration by school organizations, administrators, teachers, and the students themselves. As further evidence that the movement toward junior high schools was gaining momentum, Koos cites facts that are similar to ones we would draw on as evidence of the growth of a middle grades movement today:

Hardly an educational convention meets which does not give the discussion of the problems of this new school a prominent place on its programs. Educational periodicals devote much space to articles on the junior high school. Departments of education in colleges and universities are offering courses concerned exclusively with its problems and these and other training institutions claim to be preparing teachers for it. State legislatures are enacting laws to authorize its establishment or to regulate its operation (p. 10).

Forty-six years after Koos celebrated the development of junior high schools, Donald Eichhorn saw the publication of *The Middle School* (1966), one of the first texts that focus specifically on a conceptualization of middle grade schooling that departs from the junior high school. Eichhorn commends the junior high, which used curricular programs and pedagogy that were characteristic of high schools as its model, for providing "a transitional organization between the elementary and the high school levels, one which helps meet the physical, mental, and social needs of youngsters" (p. 2). He adds, though, that "significant trends in human growth and development and changes in American culture have produced deep implications as to what the nature of this transitional school should be" (p. 2). He uses the term "transescent" to refer to the students in the middle grades, and "transescence" to describe their stage of development (p. 3).

Today, the term "transescent" is usually replaced with the more palatable terms, "early adolescent" (Lipsitz, Jackson, & Austin, 1977; Manning, 1993; Maxwell & Meiser, 1997) or "young adolescent" (Glatthorn & Spencer, 1986; Ames & Miller, 1994; Wavering, 1995, for example). Other terms, including "pubescent," "prepubescent," "preteen," "pre-adolescent," "young person," and "youth," have been used by researchers, theorists, and teachers in reference to the period that follows childhood and precedes adolescence. The trouble with finding an appropriate label for this phase in the life span denotes a larger problem: Young adolescents defy easy description or classification. Teachers of middle and junior high school students can rely on knowledge of the typical physical, psychosocial, and cognitive development that characterize early adolescence in order make and implement appropriate decisions about curricula, instructional strategies, learning activities, and assessment and evaluation. However, they must also rely on observation of each student whom they teach for specific indications of development, because of the substantial variations in growth and maturity from one adolescent to the other, and even from one day to the next within an individual adolescent.

The teacher of English language arts in the middle and junior high school finds himself and herself in a challenging environment of swirling energy and constant change. In what is one of the most popular texts for teachers of English published during the second half of the 20th century, eighth-grade teacher Nancie Atwell articulates the challenge: "Surviving adolescence is no small matter; neither is surviving adolescents" (1987, p. 25). Those of us who teach or have taught middle school and junior high students understand; students in the middle grades are unique.

In this chapter, we summarize recent research and theories related to the organization of schools for the middle grades and the nature of young adolescents, and the specific challenges that face young adolescent students as language learners and users. Our goal is to provide a brief overview of research that informs teachers about the distinguishing characteristics of early adolescence, and research that is related to the implications of those characteristics for instruction in today's middle-level language arts classes.

The chapter is divided into two broad sections: The first section, "Middle Grade Schools and Young Adolescents," focuses on the history and organization of middle grades schools. Included are research-based recommendations for use of interdisciplinary teaming, cooperative learning, and technology in the classroom, and attention to the physical, psychosocial, and intellectual developmental characteristics of young adolescents. The second section, "Language Arts in the Middle Grades," focuses on specific instructional strategies and curricular choices that are proving to be appropriate and successful for teaching and learning language arts in middle grades classrooms. Primary attention is given to research related to reading, written composition, and young adult literature, as each is implemented in middle school language arts classes. A discussion of the whole language, or integrated instruction, movement, and its impact on current junior/middle school language arts instruction is central to this section. Specific attention is also given to censorship issues, because they have become inextricably linked to the classroom study of contemporary literature, and to assignments that encourage students to use written and oral language in order to express their own opinions and perspectives.

## THE MIDDLE GRADES AND YOUNG ADOLESCENTS

### Status of Today's Middle Schools and Junior High Schools

The structure of junior high schools is modeled on the structure of high schools; thus, the philosophies regarding learning environments, strategies for teaching and learning, and uses of time and space are similar in high schools and junior high schools. Middle schools are not modeled after high schools. Instead, they have a philosophy that is centered on the developmental needs of the young adolescent. As Alexander, Williams, Compton, Hines, and Prescott (1968) contend, the "emergent" middle school is a school "providing a program planned for a range of older children, preadolescents, and early adolescents that builds upon the elementary school program for earlier childhood and in turn is built upon by the high school's program for adolescence" (p. 5). The middle school philosophy has given rise to organizational, physical, and pedagogic changes that have increased in popularity and that have created a concurrent decrease in popularity of the junior high.

William M. Alexander and C. Kenneth McEwin (1989) have tracked national trends that demonstrate a strong move away from junior high schools, with the seventh through ninth-grade organization as most typical, to middle schools, with sixth through eighth-grade organization as most predominant. The latter increased 160% between 1971 and 1987, to account for approximately 40% of all middle grade schools in the United States. During this time, there was a 53% decrease in schools organized with a seventh through ninth-grade structure (p. 2). Alexander and McEwin report a "great acceleration in the establishment of middle schools after 1962" (p. 11). By 1993, public middle schools outnumbered public junior high schools by a margin of approximately three to one (National Council on Education Statistics, 1995). In their 25-year review of the development of middle schools in the United States, McEwin, Dickinson, and Jenkins (1996) note the following trend in organization of middle grade schools (while acknowledging that atypical patterns such as single-grade "centers" make absolute accuracy difficult to obtain):

| Percent of Schools Nationally | Grade Organization |
| --- | --- |
| 11 | 5–8 |
| 55 | 6–8 |
| 22 | 7–8 |
| 13 | 7–9 |

Clearly, the organizational frame that includes grades 6 to 8 in a middle school is currently the most popular in the United States.

In middle grades, students typically complete language arts, mathematics, science, and social studies as core academic courses. They also choose from either traditional exploratory courses, such as foreign language and music, or from newer exploratory courses, such as computers and sex education. Reading is the only exploratory course that became widely required in grades 6, 7, and 8 between 1968 and 1988 (p. 18). This development is interesting in light of the questions raised by Simmons (1991) regarding the paucity of required reading classes in the junior high schools since the 1950s (p. 320). More than 1,000 teachers and administrators who responded during Alexander and McEwin's 1989 study noted that they were particularly pleased with two aspects of middle schools: the creation of schools that provide specifically for the needs of young adolescents, and middle schools eliminated crowding in elementary and high schools (p. 11). Nevertheless, the shift toward middle schools has not been without drawbacks. The same respondents produced this list of concerns: "teacher adjustment, facilities, finances, and excessive pupil populations" (p. 44). Other reported concerns included staff opposition or resistance, lack of special training of teachers, middle schools being considered elementary, establishment of a teacher advisory plan, too little staff development, unfamiliar scheduling, lack of middle level supervisor, and confusion among schools that are middle in name and junior high in concept (p. 45).

These concerns, which grew out of teachers' and administrators' experiences during the early years of the shift toward middle schools, are addressed in the first report of the Carnegie Council on Adolescent Development, *Turning Points: Preparing American Youth for the 21st Century* (1989). This report, which promotes schools that "vastly improve the educational experiences of all middle grade students, but will most benefit those at risk of being left behind" (p. 9) has been influential in defining current middle school philosophy. D. B. Strahan (1992) explains the importance of the report:

As studies [of middle schools] have proliferated, patterns of results have emerged to such a degree that we are nearing a consensus about what middle level schools should be and about what needs to be done to improve middle level schools. I see the publication of *Turning Points: Preparing American Youth for the 21st Century* . . . as a milestone in focusing this emerging consensus" (p. 381).

(See also, Combs, 1997; Siu-Runyan & Faircloth, 1995; Wavering, 1995; Davies, 1995; Stevenson, 1998; *Great Transitions*, 1996).

In *Turning Points*, eight "transformations" are recommended in order to create schools at the middle level that best reflect the physical, emotional, psychosocial, cognitive, and moral development of young adolescents:

1. *Create small communities for learning* where stable, close, mutually respectful relationships with adults and peers are considered fundamental for intellectual development and personal growth . . . ;
2. *Teach a core academic program* that results in students who are literate, including in the sciences, and who know how to think critically, lead a healthy life, behave ethically, and assume the responsibilities of citizenship in a pluralistic society . . . ;
3. *Ensure success for all students* through elimination of tracking by achievement level and promotion of cooperative learning, flexibility in arranging instructional time, and adequate resources (time, space, equipment, and materials) for teachers;
4. *Empower teachers and administrators to make decisions about the experiences of middle grade students* through creative control by teachers over the instructional program linked to greater responsibilities for students' performance, governance committees that assist the principal in designing and coordinating school-wide programs, and autonomy and leadership within sub-schools or houses to create environments tailored to enhance the intellectual and emotional development of all youth;
5. *Staff middle grade schools with teachers who are expert at teaching young adolescents* and who have been specially prepared for assignments to the middle grades;
6. *Improve academic performance through fostering the health and fitness of young adolescents* . . . ;
7. *Reengage families in the education of young adolescents* by giving families meaningful roles in school governance, communicating with the families about the school program and students' progress, and offering families opportunities to support the learning process at home and at the school;
8. *Connect schools with communities,* which together share responsibility for each middle grade student's success, through identifying service opportunities in the community, establishing partnerships and collaborations to ensure students' access to health and social services, and using community resources to enrich the instructional program and opportunities for constructive after-school activities. (Carnegie Council, pp. 9-10).

Recommendations proposed by the Carnegie Council on Adolescent Development, some of which sound familiar to readers of Koos' 1920 text, and many of which reemphasize points made by Eichhorn (1966), reflect an interest in community involvement within the schools. Recommendations that focus almost exclusively on what should happen within schools themselves are outlined in *This We Believe: Developmentally Responsive Middle Level Schools* (1995), the revised position statement of the National Middle School Association (NMSA). In this statement, the NMSA outlines expectations that middle grade schools recognize the needs of young adolescents and use the following to address within the school: interdisciplinary teams, flexible organization, advisor/advisee groups, and varied teaching approaches, including heterogeneous and cooperative group learning.

The recommended transformations offered by the Carnegie Council, and the position statement presented by the NMSA, have guided the development of middle grade schools during the final decade of the 20th century, and are likely to continue to influence the way teachers, school administrators, parents, students, and others define and conceive of middle grade schools in the early 21st century. The job of teachers of language arts has changed its shape wherever the transformations are implemented. In transformed middle schools, teachers of language arts now find themselves making decisions about instructional focus as members of interdisciplinary teams instead of forging through the academic year making decisions that have an impact only on their own classes; they rely on cooperative learning activities instead of their single authority as the classroom source of information; they monitor the progress of individual students during carefully planned reading and writing workshops, and present mini-lessons more often than they engage in whole-class lecture and discussion.

In transformed middle schools, the perceptions of middle grade language arts teachers concerning appropriate curricula have also changed shape. Evidence includes the increasing popularity of required reading classes in middle grade schools, the implementation of young adult literature, and composition assignments that require students to communicate with members of the community, so that they may gain a sense of the power of language. These examples will be reviewed in the second section of this chapter.

## Interdisciplinary Instruction

Language arts teachers are not making and implementing teaching decisions independently as much as they have in the past; interdisciplinary teaming, which reflects an epistemology that is grounded in integrative learning (Brazee, as cited in Siu-Runyan & Faircloth, 1995, p. 27), is gaining popularity. In *Turning Points* (Carnegie Council, 1989), teaming is promoted for the affective and academic benefits it offers students and teachers:

Most middle grade schools are organized by academic department. Teachers' relationships with students are fragmented; math teachers see math students, history teachers see history students, and so on. Rarely, if ever, do teachers have the opportunity to develop an understanding of students as individuals, a prerequisite to teaching them well. . . . Teaming provides an environment conducive to learning by reducing the stress of anonymity and isolation on students. Common planning by teachers of different subjects enables students to sense consistent expectations of them and to strive to meet clearly understood standards of achievement. Teaming creates the kind of environment that encourages students to grapple with ideas that may span several disciplines, and to create solutions to problems that reflect understanding, not memorization (pp. 39–40).

Stevenson (1998) defines interdisciplinary team organization (ITO) as a design in which a group of 100 to 125 students and four or five core teachers spend most of their school time together, with a goal of promoting students' "academic and social welfare" in an environment that reciprocates the "belonging and healthy interdependence of an extended family" (p. 127). He notes that "ITO is widely employed to organize middle level schools" and recommends the following research reports and accounts of exemplary practice as excellent sources that describe use for middle grade schools: Erb and Doda, 1989; George and Stevenson, 1989; Arnold and Stevenson (1998) (p. 127). He further notes that a derivative of ITO that is gaining popularity is "partner teaming" organization, which is usually comprised of 40 to 70 students from the same grade level who work with 2 to 3 teachers of core curricular courses.

Stevenson notes that the "overarching emphasis" of partner teaming is, "matching curriculum and pedagogy to students in a context that ensures safety, mutual support, and success" (p. 127). In both organizational structures, there is strong focus on team membership and identification; team colors, names, mascots, logos, pledges, and T-shirts are common in middle schools. This team focus is a departure from the departmental structure of junior high schools, in which teachers align themselves primarily with their subject specialty and attend only to the academic matters that are directly related to their own curricula. (See also J. L. Epstein & D. J. MacIver, 1990.)

Alexander and McEwin (1989) report that during the 20-year span of 1968 to 1988, there was an increase from 6% to 26% of eighth grades utilizing interdisciplinary plans for instruction in language arts. Increases in seventh grade from 5% to 31%, and in sixth grade, from 8% to 40%, are also reported (p. 29). They also report that, although the four-core-subject scheme is the most widely used, it is not unusual for reading to be added as a fifth core subject, and a fifth teacher to be added to the team (p. 28).

Lounsbury (1992) has edited a useful collection of articles about interdisciplinary instruction that addresses both research on the effectiveness of interdisciplinary teaming and practices that take advantage of the format.

## Collaborative Group Learning

Noden and Vacca (1994) claim that "Teaching as we know it today will die a gradual death in the next century," when "All the classroom symbols of information giving, which have endured for over two hundred years—teachers up front, rows of seats, blackboards, chalk, large-class lectures—will fall victim to the dynamic appeal of modern technology" (p. 43). They suggest, however, that the one essential tool that teachers will be left with is "the interaction variable," an ingredient of collaborative learning. They then draw on research by Johnson, Johnson, and Holubec, 1988, to promote collaborative learning as a format that will result in "'higher levels of achievement, greater use of high-level reasoning, increased intrinsic motivation, better attitudes toward school and teachers, higher self-esteem, and more positive heterogeneous relationships'" (p. 43). Stevenson (1998) describes group investigation (Sharan & Sharan 1990), Student Teams Achievement Division (STAD), Teams Games Tournaments (TGT), and Cooperative Integrated Reading and Composition (CIRC) (Madden, Slavin, & Stevens, 1986) as popular formats for cooperative learning (pp. 234–237). Noden and Vacca describe the following formats: inquiry groups (Kagan, 1990), performance groups (Slavin, 1990), gaming groups (Bloom & Sosnik, 1981); they also suggest ways that teachers of language arts can incorporate each of these into their instruction. Both sources stress that, regardless of particular design, effective collaborative or cooperative group learning require students to fulfil specific group and individual responsibilities. The following is a brief description of research and theories that inform the way we have grown to think about the students who populate middle grade schools.

Atwell (1998) relieves fears that many teachers hold concerning collaboration. To those who believe that sharing responsibility for learning with students requires abdicating adult authority in the classroom, she explains that the teacher can—should—use his or her personal experience as a reader and writer, general knowledge of adolescents and the subject matter, and specific knowledge of individual students, in order to provide what students need (p. 20). In a departure from her earlier stance, in which she suggested that teachers encourage students by withholding their adult judgment in order to encourage adolescents to develop and articulate their own ideas, she now explains that:

Just as there are times when kids need a mirror, someone to reflect back their writing to them, there are times when they need an adult who will tell them what to do next or how to do it. Bottom line, what they need is a Teacher. Today, I'm striving for the fluid, subtle, *exhilarating* balance that allows me to function in my classroom as a listener, *and* a teller, an observer *and* an actor, a collaborator *and* a critic *and* a cheerleader (p. 21).

Using collaborative learning activities—whether formal formats such as Student Teams Achievement Division (STAD) or Cooperative Integrated Reading and Composition (CIRC) (Stevenson, 1998), or activities that teachers design for their own students—does not mean that the teacher gives away his or her role in the language arts classroom. Instead, incorporating collaborative learning requires changes in the role of the teacher, and also is likely to lead to changes in the physical layout of the classroom, the way learning time is spent, and the way learning is assessed and evaluated.

## Technology in Language Arts Classes

It may be worth noting that, in their chapters appearing in the 1991 edition of the *Handbook of Research on Teaching the English Language Arts*, neither J. Pikulsi, in "The Transition Years: Middle School" nor J. Simmons, in "The Junior High School Years," mentions technology as a specific area of research that is related to the language arts classrooms he describes. Of course, neither mentions that the teachers who engage in literature, composition, and language instruction are likely to rely on the technologies available to them; in the past, these technologies have included the reliable overhead projector, the film projector, the mimeograph machine, and the audio tape player/recorder, to name a few. The reason that technology is not treated as an individual feature of the language arts classroom is simple: Within those classrooms, technology has traditionally been used by the teacher to support and enhance instruction and recordkeeping. However, in the last decade of the 20th century, teachers, administrators, parents, and politicians began to expect *students* to engage actively in the use of computers and other modern technologies. A popular assumption is that middle school students are adept at using word processing, exploring the Internet and the World Wide Web, and finding images and voices in CD-Rom disks that would, in previous generations, be available only through the one-dimensional, silent medium of textbooks. A related assumption is that the use of these electronic tools necessarily improves students' reports and papers and helps them develop more sophisticated critical thinking skills.

Despite these popular assumptions, and calls for the use of technology in documents such as the annual *Education Week* publication, *Quality Counts* (*Education Week*, 1997, 1998), and *Great Transitions* (Carnegie Council, 1995), there is little evidence that the books devoted to the preparation of teachers of language arts, in particular, or the books devoted to the preparation of teachers in the middle grades, in general, give attention to theories, research, or best practices related to the place of technology in language arts classrooms. Few address the shift to the public's expectations that technology will be incorporated into classrooms. For example, none of the following "methods" textbooks specifically isolate the terms "technology," "Internet," "World Wide Web," or "computer(s)," in its index: Siu-Runyan and Faircloth (1995), Alexander and McEwin (1988) (general methods); and Combs (1997), Noden and Vacca (1994) (language arts methods). This omission indicates that each book either contains no references to technology, computers, and so on, or that the terms are embedded within discussion of other topics. This is not to imply that there are no methods texts and other books intended for practicing and prospective teachers of middle and junior high school language arts in which ways to implement available technologies are recommended. Examples of books that help teachers take advantage of technologies include these: Tchudi and Mitchell (1999); Stevenson (1998); Atwell (1998); Gere, Fairbanks, Howes, Roop, and Schaafsma (1992); Wresch (ed.) (1991). In addition, there are several texts that focus on individual aspects of the entire language arts rubric, such as literature study, which include attention to the implementation of technology to enhance teaching and learning. Examples include: Brown and Stephens (1998); Simmons and Baines (1998); Kaywell (ed.), (1993, 1995, 1997, 2000), and Beers and Samuels (1998).

The balance of teacher preparation texts, with some that do and others that do not include direct attention to implementation of technology into language arts lessons in middle and junior high schools, can be seen as a positive sign. At this point, our understanding of the impact of technology on learning and thinking is in its early development. Research in the field is increasing. Following are examples of research in technology and secondary education published in 1995 to 1997; the examples are listed as a means of emphasizing the range of technology-related topics that are currently being studied, and which are likely to have an impact on teaching and learning in language arts classrooms in the future:

- Land (1997), which presents ideas for incorporating technology into middle schools, with emphasis on typical pitfalls, such as initiation of programs and censorship.

- Eastman and Hollingsworth (1997), which considers that results of a survey that distinguishes between home and school computer use among middle school students to reveal that computer use is more prevalent in homes than in classrooms.

- Albaugh (1997), which describes the researcher's observations of a sixth-grade class as students used CD-Rom Encyclopedias as resources when gathering data for science reports.

- Carlson and Messier (1997), which describes a project in which middle school students produced a Shakespearean comedy as a part of an interdisciplinary unit that combined language arts, social studies, mathematics, music, art, home economics, technical education, and the learning center.

- Blanchard (1995), which discusses the ways that a middle school reading program can be transformed with the use of telecommunications, desktop publishing, and other electronic technologies.

- Baines (1997), which warns educators to develop a critical attitude when contemplating the use of technologies in classroom instruction.

Despite the increase in research that focuses on the potential for use of technology in classrooms, Baines (1997) reminds teachers, administrators, and the public of the need to carefully assess the actual impact of technology on classroom teaching and learning, and to scrutinize claims made by those who are not actually working in classrooms about the value of computers and other electronic tools:

Fabrication 1: Technology is a moral imperative that will increase student achievement and make American students globally competitive.

Reality: Technology can make learning more fun, easier, and cleaner. But no data support the conclusion that technology causes gains in student achievement (pp. 494–495).

Teachers must understand the complex interplay of adolescent development in order to work alongside today's adolescents in English language arts classes, where students' personal backgrounds, values, opinions, and ability to make sense of information and experiences are central to successful engagement in reading, writing, and thinking activities. Knowledge of innovative and promising practices that invigorate individual middle school language arts classes—including the use of interdisciplinary teaming, cooperative learning, and enhancement through technology—must be situated within the context of an understanding of young adolescents themselves in order to transform language arts education into the 21st century.

## CHARACTERISTICS OF YOUNG ADOLESCENTS

### Physical Characteristics of Young Adolescents

Hans Sebald (1992) explains that, while "adolescence refers to the period of social maturation, pubescence refers to the physiological development during which the reproductive system matures" (p. 103). For girls, a major growth spurt that marks puberty normally occurs between the ages of 10 and 14; adult size is usually reached between ages 15 to 18 (Wolman, 1998, p. 9). Besides an increase in height, this growth spurt is usually outwardly apparent in the softening and rounding of hips and development of breasts; girls also see the growth of body hair under the arms and in the pubic area, and at an average age of just over 12 years of age, they begin to menstruate. These changes are stimulated by hormonal changes, and can thus influence the young female's emotional condition as potently as her physical one. Today, girls are 4 inches taller and 22 pounds heavier than they were in the late 19th century; they also begin menstruation 5 years earlier than females did in the late 1800s (Sebald, 1992, p. 106).

Boys usually have their major growth spurt between the ages of 12 and 17; adult size is reached between 17 to 20 years of age (Wolman, 1998, p. 9). For young adolescent males, the growth spurt is outwardly apparent in increased height and weight and in muscular definition. Underarm and public hair growth is followed by the emergence of upper lip hair and a lowering of the voice. Between the ages of 13 to 14, the testes grow rapidly; between ages 14 to 17, the penis typically doubles in size.

Another indicator of puberty for males is the beginning of nocturnal emissions that accompany the development of the sex organs. On average, boys today are 5 inches taller and 24 pounds heavier than they were 100 years ago (Sebald, 1992, p. 106).

Nutritional advances and universal health care account for earlier maturation among American youth in the late 20th century. Sebald notes another interesting contributor: "Rate and quality of growth correlate positively with socioeconomic status.... Children of professionals are on the average taller and heavier than those from middle-class homes, who, in turn, exceed in all aspects of growth the children from the lowest socioeconomic class" (p. 107).

In most respects, early physical maturation is negative for females and positive for males. A. Caspi (1995) found that girls who mature early have more problems in school than do their later-maturing counterparts, particularly in mixed-sex schools. Problems including body image disturbance, lower academic success, and conduct problems in school are more prominent in early-maturing females than in their classmates (p. 63). On the other hand, males who become physically mature early are more popular among male and female peers; they are perceived to be leaders even by teachers, regardless of their emotional, social, or intellectual maturity when they have the physical appearance of an adult (Elkind, 1998, p. 66).

Changes in the biological indicators of puberty have been outpaced by changes in the societal indicators of adolescence. The "disjunction between biological and social development" that Hamburg (1994) identifies means that young people who are physically mature may be granted admission into adult activities for which they are not emotionally, socially, intellectually, or spiritually ready. For example, the Carnegie Council on Adolescent Development, in its final report, *Great Transitions: Preparing Adolescents for a New Century* (1995), cites evidence that sexual activity among young adolescent girls is initiated earlier than in previous generations, and that sexual intercourse involving girls 13 or younger is usually forced (p. 42). In *The Body Project: An Intimate History of American Girls* (1997), Joan Jacobs Brumberg insists that the consequences of the "mismatch between biology and culture" that results in treatment of adolescent females as if they are fully grown and intellectually mature women include teen pregnancy, females' dissatisfaction with their bodies; easy manipulation by media and advertisers (p. 197).

### Psychosocial Characteristics of Young Adolescents

It is crucial that teachers of middle grades students learn that physical maturity is no indicator of emotional, psychosocial, intellectual, or moral maturity. However, as John J. Pikulski states (1991), teachers need to recognize "well established relationship that these physical changes have on the self-concept and behavior of the early adolescent, which can certainly influence classroom behavior and learning, including language development" (p. 303). For many teachers, an understandings of the young adolescent's psychosocial development is reliant on the theories of Anna Freud, who views adolescence as necessarily a time of stress and storm. Others draw on the more encouraging interpretations of adolescent behavior that are provided by Erik Erickson. Erickson's theories about normative crises of adolescence allow adults to view challenges of authority, dramatic changes in behavior as a part of a process of self-identity. For Erikson, the most important identity crisis of adolescence involves the resolution of role identity versus role confusion; only those adolescents who develop an accurate self-identity are able to recognize and choose appropriate personal, social, and professional roles for themselves. Erickson's work has been influential in encouraging preservice and inservice teachers of English to consider the social and emotional growth of young adolescents at the same time that academic growth is planned, prompted, and evaluated. Today's teachers of students in the middle grades, with the support of current emphases on teaching the language arts in an integrated way, and within the context of an interdisciplinary instruction, are likely to take into account the psychosocial needs of students when they consider those students' academic and educational needs.

Teachers of language arts rely on understanding of human nature in order to make generalizations about the significance of literature. Literature study, which involves consideration of human values, therefore leads teachers of language arts to consideration of the psychology of adolescents. Whereas the theories of Robert Havighurst, as interpreted by G. Robert Carlsen (1968) provided a frame of reference for several decades, changes in adolescents and in society at the turn of the 21st century necessitate an updated theory of the stages of development that adolescents must navigate. One such explanation is provided by Newman and Newman (1987, as cited by Newton, 1994), for example, who concentrate on areas that are crucial to the individual's social and psychological growth that they believe are relevant for modern Western society and suggest that the following are tasks that youth aged 12 to 18 go through:

• Physical maturation (ability to adjust to changing body image)
• Formal operations (ability to reason and think abstractly)
• Emotional development (ability to accept volatile emotions and mood swings)
• Peer groups (ability to engage in psychological development)
• Heterosexual relations (ability to recognize importance of opposite sex friendships and to consider own sexual identity)

Newman and Newman explain that it is not until late adolescence, which they identify as ages eighteen to twenty-two, that following tasks become primary concerns: autonomy from parents, sex role identity, internalized morality, career choice (Newman & Newman, pp. 320–351).

Heaven (1994) compares the similarities of Havighurst's and Newman and Newman's descriptions of the developmental tasks of adolescence and finds that both give attention to the following: relationships with peers, emotional independence, preparation for career, sense of morality (or ethical system), and development of a sex-role identity (p. 5). It appears that today's teens must engage in developmental tasks that are similar to those which teens of the past generation dealt.

There are, of course, many varied perspectives through which one can examine adolescence; a more comprehensive examination of the issue than is possible herein might begin with inquiry into perspectives and leading proponents of those perspectives, including the following: David Ausubel, biological theories; Peter Blos and Louise Kaplan, psychodynamic theories; Harry Stack Sullivan, interpersonal theories; Erik Erickson and Arnold Gesell, developmental theories; Jean Piaget, cognitive theories; G. W. Rebok, information-processing orientation; Lawrence Kohlberg, moral development; Robert Selman and David Elkind, social learning theories; and Carol Gilligan, gender differences. Since adolescence, like all stages of life, is lived within the context of a culture and society, the problems of the culture and society must inform our study of adolescence. It is imperative that those of us who work with adolescents, especially perhaps those who will soon enter adult roles, look critically and realistically at that world.

According to Hamburg (1994), adolescents address these specific psychosocial developmental tasks: (1) Moving toward independence from parents, siblings, and childhood friends while retaining significant and enduring ties; (2) Developing increasing autonomy in making personal decisions, assuming responsibility for oneself, and regulating one's own behavior; (3) Establishing new friendships; (4) Moving toward greater personal intimacy and adult sexuality; (5) Dealing with more complex intellectual challenges (184). In addition to these tasks, many adolescents become involved in the following potential problems:

1. sexual activity and pregnancy, which are increasing among teens aged 15 and younger;
2. drug and alcohol abuse, with greatest increases in binge drinking among young adolescent females;
3. obesity, eating disorders, and poor physical fitness, with approximately 10% of today's adolescents suffering depression as either a cause or result of depression;
4. delinquency and violence, with adolescents twice as likely to be as victims of rape, robbery, or assault as those who are aged twenty and older;
5. serious injuries, which account for 57% of all deaths among 10–14 years olds, and risk factors identified as poverty, low status, propensity for high-risk behavior, quest for adult-like behavior, use of alcohol and drugs, easy availability of weapons and other dangerous objects, and lack of information about actual risks and consequences of behaviors;
6. suicide, with rates that have propelled it to the third leading cause of adolescent death, and correlations to access to guns and to alcohol intoxication. (According to a 1995 *Morbidity and Mortality Weekly Report* study cited in *Great Transitions*, page, there has been a 300% increase in suicide among Black males aged 10–14 between 1980 and 1992);
7. Single-parent families and stepfamilies, with poverty more closely associated with single-parent than with two-parent families, and with single parents less likely to be able to closely supervise adolescents' activities. (Hamburg, 188–195)

Many of the problems that young adolescents face today push them into adult roles sooner than in previous generations, despite the fact that they are not actually prepared to assume those roles. For example, Hamburg states that, "No problem in contemporary America is more serious than the plight of children and youth in our decaying cities. Almost a quarter of the nation's children grow up in poverty—and all too many of them are in smashed families and rotting communities" (p. xvi). He explains that children and adolescents who are poor come to school underprepared, and that their early problems begin a pattern of negative behaviors and unsuccessful school performance. For example, their attention spans are "relatively short, their verbal fluency is not well developed, and they lack basic skills. They frequently also lack social skills, are emotionally troubled, and may be listless, hyperactive, or aggressive. Very early on they are likely to be labeled slow learners and/or behavior problems" (p. 43). Poor children are also at higher risk of health problems than are their more advantaged counterparts. Although they may qualify for Medicaid, there is no continuity of care provided through Medicaid services—no family doctor who knows the child or adolescent and is personally familiar with his or her history. They are likely to have vision and hearing problems that go undiagnosed, and are more likely to become victims of accidents and physical abuse, and a "high degree of stress and violence in their social environment" (p. 46). He states, too, that children from very poor backgrounds also find a great discrepancy between what is allowed at school and what is expected at home; sometimes a student who seems aggressive at school is simply using the survival skills he has learned to rely on at home (p. 297).

Hamburg points out that in the early years of the 21st century, the majority of inner city secondary schools are populated by students from racial and ethnic minorities. These youth are, in large part, those who have not found a way out of the inner cities and have been left to "come of age on the streets, without dependable adult guidance and constructive support systems—and often, without parents" (p. 297). These adolescents are members of an American population that Hamburg says has been "relegated to marginal status in our society," those who are "the poorest and least educated Americans and are served by the least-adequate health care in the nation" (p. 297). Jonathan Kozol's *Amazing Grace: The Lives of Children and the Conscience of a Nation* (1995) provides anecdotal evidence of the impact of poverty on the lives of children and adolescents who grow up in the extreme poverty and violence of America's inner cities.

The number and kinds of studies that examine the relationship between the psychosocial development of young adolescents and the environment in which they live provide a strong indication that early adolescence is being viewed as a pivotal stage in life. Examples of research, which, taken together, indicate the diversity in this area, include these.

## HOW TEENS DEAL WITH THEIR WORLDS

Crockett and Crouter (1995), who examine the pathways of adolescence and the ways adults sabotage those paths; Winfield (1995), who explores resilience in African American adolescents; Rosenberg, Mercy, and Houk (1991) who report

that the odds of a depressed teen killing himself are increased 75 times if there is a gun kept in his home; Giroux (1997), who presents evidence that popular media, which is controlled by adults, prescribe troubling and detrimental roles for today's teens. Elkind (1998), who posits that the "growth markers"—such as appropriate clothing choices, extracurricular activities, and protection from unsupervised access to all news and other information—no longer exist and therefore adolescents are thrust, while still immature, into adult roles and situations; Brown, Lohr, Truhillo, and colleagues (1990), who conducted a study of teens' perceptions of stereotypes to gain understanding into how teens identify groups, and associate themselves with particular ones, at a time in their lives when age-mates take on a greater significance, and the influence of adults diminishes.

### Adolescent Sexual Activity and Adolescent Parenting

Scheier (1994), who reports on correlations between teen parenting and poverty; Portner (1998a), who provides statistics about sexual activity and pregnancy rates in the United States and compares them with lower rates of teen pregnancy in the rest of the industrialized world; Strasburger (1995), who states that the incidence of sex, rape, and premarital sex, as presented by television shows, is out of proportion with the lower incidence of these activities in real life; a 1996 *Youth Indicators* report that quotes a 1993 report of the United States Department of Health and Human Services, Centers for Disease Control and Prevention, and shows that during the decade between 1981 and 1991, between 1.1% and 1.4% of all births were to girls ages 10- to 14-years old. While during that same decade, pregnancies among 15- to 19-year olds increased from 53% of the total number in the United States to 62.1% of all pregnancies; Coles (1997), whose interviews with adolescent parents reveal, in anecdotal form, the frequent mismatch between adolescents' biological maturity and their psychosocial and intellectual maturity.

***Gender confusion among adolescents.*** Elkind (1998), who points out that 30% of all teen suicides involve gay and lesbian adolescents; Due (1995), who chronicles the lives of several gay and lesbian adolescents so that, through the anecdotes, readers can understand the world from the perspective of teens who feel at least doubly alienated, due to their age and their sexual preference.

***Violence, crime, and other high-risk behaviors among adolescents.*** Strasburger (1995), who notes that the United States leads the Western world in both handgun availability and handgun deaths (p. 33); Portner (1998b), who presents a federal report that indicates that almost 6,100 students were expelled for at least 1 year for bringing firearms, including hand guns, rifles, bombs, grenades, and starter pistols to campus during the 1996–1997 school year (p. 3); Giroux (1997) who notes that the number of schools that reported using some sort of weapon detection system in 1997 was 3,000 (p. 69) (a number that is sure to increase in response to the four incidents in the 1997–1998 school year in which middle and high school students, using guns on their classmates and teachers and, in two cases, also on their parents, became killers; Hamburg (1994), who indicates that out of every 1,000 youth who are 12 to 15 years old, 52 become victims of robbery, rape, or assault each year, and that the number of victims climbs to 68 out of every 1,000 for youth who are 17 to 18 years old, making the chances that adolescents will become victims of crime, according to Hamburg's statistics, "about twice as high as the rate for people aged 20 and over" (p. 191); Hamburg (1994) also points out that homicide, which is five times as common among Black as whites, is the leading cause of death for Black males between the ages of 14 and 44, and that nearly one-half of all adolescent homicides involve alcohol use (p. 193), and that growing up in extreme poverty, without a father present, and with little hope for the future are strong predictors of delinquent behavior; a 1997 *Digest of Education Statistics* report, which indicates that, according to a United States Department of Health and Human Services study:

only 3–6 percent of high school students reported feeling too unsafe to go to school, but that between 6.5–9.5 percent were threatened or injured with a weapon on school property; between 10.5 percent (in the 12th grade) and 21.6 percent (in the 9th grade) were in a physical fight on school property; between 7.6 percent and 10.7 percent of the high school students reported bringing a weapon onto school property.

(The report is available on-line at http://nces.ed.gov/pubs/d96/D96T145.html.)

Huizinga (1995), who reports on the kinds of criminal activity in which young and older adolescents frequently become involved, the sequential development of delinquency, and insights into how to help adolescents break the patterns that predict delinquency; Grinder (1990), who considers the correlation of high-risk behaviors, including illegal and life-threatening ones, adolescents' lack of regard for moral and social authority, and the effect these have on the vulnerability of adolescents to become involved in high-risk behaviors, and who urges adults to implement Friere's "emanicipatory education" in order to help adolescents understand the value of participating in life; Giroux (1997), who refuses to allow teens to take the blame for society's ills.

## Intellectual Characteristics of Young Adolescents

As was true in the 1991 edition of this volume, "discussions of cognitive development in early adolescence are almost always dominated by a Piagetian framework" (Pikulski, 1991, p. 306). Teachers of middle and junior high school English/language arts find Piaget's description of the stages of cognitive development particularly helpful, because it provides an outline for the cognitive changes that teachers can expect among students in middle grades. Students typically begin middle and junior high school using the concrete operational thought of 7- to 11-year-olds, but they begin the transition into formal operational thought from approximately 11 to 14 years of age. Preadolescent thinking involves the ability to think in terms of concrete objects instead of hypotheses and is characterized by trial and error problem

solving instead of the testing of various possible solutions. In contrast, adolescent thinking involves a more complete logic that includes formal reasoning that allows for "the subordination of the real to the realm of the possible, and consequently the linking of all possibilities to one another by necessary implications that encompass the real, but at the same time go beyond it" (Piaget, 1990, p. 62). Of special significance to teachers of English language arts is the fact that this new kind of thinking in hypotheses, with attention to possibilities, allows students to play with language more fully. They can begin to interpret the second symbol system of metaphors and similes; they enjoy puns; they write involved narratives about fantastic people and places. (See the following, recommended by Pikulski, for further discussion of Piaget's theories: Flavell, 1963, 1985; Ginsburg & Opper, 1979; Inhelder & Piaget, 1958.)

Moral development typically accompanies cognitive development (although the ability to use moral reasoning does not necessarily translate into the choice to take moral actions during adolescence). Lawrence Kohlberg is well known for his contributions to the understanding of moral development as a component of cognitive development. Kohlberg (1990) posits that people work through hierarchical stages, always moving forward, not backward, except in the case of extreme trauma, and in the context of the environment and social structures in which they live (p. 95). Kohlberg's former collaborator, Carol Gilligan (1990), who is well known for her work on gender differences in moral judgment, poses a major challenge to Kohlberg's theory by introducing a feminist perspective to moral development. She contends that neither males nor females are genetically more moral, but that they approach moral dilemmas in different ways. The tests of moral development that Kohlberg designed recognize only male ways of thinking as legitimate; Gilligan finds that males' and females' use of different kinds of logic are not contradictory, but are complementary (p. 105).

The kind of thinking that is new during adolescence is significant because of its psychosocial impact, as well as its implications for presenting cognitive challenges in the classroom. Adolescents are able to think about themselves and their problems in ways that children do not. Elkind (1998) notes that this new thinking includes what he calls the "imaginary audience" and "personal fable." The imaginary audience is manifested in the "assumption that everyone around them is preoccupied with the same subject that engrosses them: namely, themselves" and it is this notion that everyone is watching every move they make that accounts for teens' heightened self-consciousness (p. 40). The personal fable rests on adolescents' assumption that they are "special, different from other people," (p. 43) and that laws of nature and other forces that apply to other people do not apply to them. Adolescents who refuse to make oral presentations in class because they are convinced that everyone in the class will see each of their pimples are probably demonstrating the imaginary audience. Teens who smoke "under the belief that they are invulnerable to any harm from this habit," demonstrate the personal fable (p. 44). This new way of thinking leads to a change in the nature of adolescents' participation in classroom discussions. Conversations can be expected to grow in depth and creativity, because adolescents can look at issues from a variety of stances, and they can suspend judgment until they have heard ideas other than their own. Unlike most children, adolescents can agree to disagree and can even accept ambiguity when no definite answer is possible.

Other potent influences on adolescents' cognitive and psychosocial development involve popular media, music, and technology. Henry Giroux (1997) and Victor C. Strasburger (1995) point out the pervasive influence on adolescents' thinking by television, movies, other media, and advertising. Giroux convincingly argues, "Young people today live in an electronically mediated culture for which channel surfing, moving quickly from one mode of communication to another, becomes the primary method through which they are educated" (p. 5). Language arts teachers cannot ignore the power of television, movies, and popular music to determine what adolescents view as normal and desirable behavior. Neither can they ignore the potential impact of advertisers who attempt to convince adolescents that they need to participate in particular activities, dress in certain ways, and display certain attitudes.

## ADOLESCENT AND YOUNG ADULT LITERATURE (YAL)

One source of information about the world of today's youth that is readily available to middle school students and the adults who work with them is adolescent (young adult) literature (YAL).

G. Stanley Hall (1905) argues for the place of young adult literature and personal writing in *Adolescence*, the first American textbook on adolescent psychology:

It is, I believe, high time that ephebic literature should be recognized as a class by itself, and have a place of its own in the history of letters and in criticism. Much of it should be individually prescribed for the reading of the young, for whom it has a singular zest and is a true stimulus and corrective. This stage of life now has what might almost be called a school of its own. Here the young appeal to and listen to each other as they do not to adults, and in a way the latter have failed to appreciate. Again, no biography, and especially no autobiography, should henceforth be complete if it does not describe this period of transformation so all-determining for future life to which it alone can often give the key. To rightly draw the lessons of this age not only saves us from waste ineffable of this rich but crude area of experience, but makes maturity saner and more complete. Lastly, many if not most young people should be encouraged to enough of the confessional private journalism to teach them self-knowledge, for the art of self-expression usually begins now if ever, when it has a wealth of subjective material and needs forms of expression peculiar to itself (Vol. I, p. 589).

Hall noted that books written about adolescents appeal to young readers in ways that books for children, books for adults, and even conversations about growing up cannot. These are the books that are popularly called "young adult literature" or "adolescent literature." Books in this genre include fiction that can be categorized as "new realism," historic, science fiction and fantasy, adventure, and romance; it also includes nonfiction books such as autobiography and biography, how-to and self-help books, history, science, poetry, and drama (Nilsen & Donelson, 2001). Some teachers and researchers have begun to use the term "young adult literature" to refer to those books that

have widest appeal among older adolescents, and reserve the term "adolescent literature" for books that have the strongest appeal to middle and junior high students; however, this tendency is not yet a trend, and the terms are used synonymously herein.

Research in adolescent literature has contributed to the acceptance of the genre by many teachers and the public. Carroll (1994) reports on categories into which studies of adolescent literature typically fall. Included are the following categories, listed with updated examples of research:

- Literary quality/artistic merit: Moore, 1997; Peck, 1993; Dimmitt, 1993.
- Variety within selections (in terms of sophistication and demands on readers, depiction of multicultural populations and settings, and so on): Brown and Stephens, 1998; Mattson, 1997; Munde, 1997; Kaplan, 1993; Banker, 1995; Erickson, 1995; St. Clair, 1995; Harris, 1993.
- Books that are appropriate for special student populations, such as at-risk or gifted readers: Baines, 1997; Carroll and Corder, 1997; Pearlman, 1995.
- Place of adolescent literature in preservice and inservice teacher education courses: Chevalier and Houser, 1997; Abrahamson, 1997; Carroll, Gregg, and Watts, 1995.
- Incorporation of adolescent literature into curricula: Kaywell, 1993, 1995, 1997, 2000; Herz and Gallo, 1996; Bushman and Bushman, 1996; Reed, 1994a, 1994b; West and Galda, 1998; McAlpine, Putney, and Warren, 1997; Brown and Stephens, 1998.
- Evidence of growth of the significance of genre: Cart, 1996; Poe, Samuels, and Carter, 1993.
- In addition to these areas of concentration, recent research has revealed the appropriate use of adolescent literature across the middle school curriculum (see, for example, Kaywell & Oropallo, 1998; Davis, 1997).

Since 1982, the Assembly on Literature for Adolescents of the National Council of Teachers of English (ALAN) has supported research in young adult literature through its annual Foundation Research Award. The ALAN Foundation grant has recently funded many research projects, including these between 1996 and 1999:

- An anthology of poetry written by adolescents (James Brewbaker, Columbus State University).
- An exploration of young adult literature that addresses the Civil Rights Movement (Jean Brown and Elaine Stephens, Sagninaw Valley State University).
- A study of the literate behaviors of young adults (Kathleen Carico, Virginia Tech University).
- A content analysis of the literary elements of young adult books (Rosemary Chance, Texas Women's University).
- A study of the design and techniques of college young adult literature courses (Melissa Comer, Cumberland College).
- A longitudinal study of reading interests of high school students (Chris Crowe, Brigham Young University).

- A study of young adult books on audiotape (Melinda Franklin, Nashville, Tennessee).
- A study of folklore and young adult literature (F. Todd Goodson, East Carolina State University).
- A national survey of adolescent readers' preferences and reading habits (P. S. Carroll, Florida State University, and Gail P. Gregg, Florida International University).

Further evidence of the ascent of young adult literature as a valuable part of the secondary curriculum is provided by specialists within the profession of English education. In recent years, several journals for teachers have designated young adult literature as a theme for an entire issue. Notable among these journals are the following:

- *English Journal*, January, 2001 (*90*, 3)
- *English Journal*, March, 1997 (*86*, 3)
- *Voices from the Middle*, April, 1998 (*5*, 2)
- *Virginia English Bulletin*, fall, 1994 (*44*, 2)
- *Arizona English Bulletin*, fall, 1993 (*36*, 1)
- *Connecticut English Journal*, fall, 1993 (*22*, 1)

Other examples of the growing popularity of young adult literature include large projects that are supported by educational publishing houses. Patricia Kelly and Robert C. Small are co-editors of *Two Decades of the ALAN Review*, published by the National Council of Teachers of English (1999). The Twayne Publishers Young Adult Authors Series, under the guidance of series editor Patricia J. Campbell, was developed during the 1990s in order to offer adolescent readers and their teachers information about the life and work of popular writers for adolescents. Scarecrow Press initated its Scarecrow Studies in Young Adult Literature Series in 1998, under the editorship of Patricia J. Campbell. Charles Scribner's published the three-volume collection, *Writers for Young Adults*, under the direction of editor Ted Hipple, in 1997, and a supplement volume in 2000. The series is a collection of biographical and critical essays that introduces to adolescents the writers who are their favorites. Scott Foresman has published a classroom textbook selection, *Crossroads: Classical Themes in Young Adult Literature* (1995), with a foreword by acclaimed author Robert Cormier. Heinemann has a series of texts for practicing and preservice teachers that center on young adult literature; the series editor is Virginia Monseau. Included in this collection is a CD-ROM edition of 1,000 reviews of young adult books, *Complete Guide to Young Adult Literature* (1997), edited by Monseau and Salvner.

Despite its acceptance in many venues, there are still obstacles, such as potential censorship issues, that keep young adult literature out of the hands of teachers and students in middle and junior high classrooms. Simmons (1998) considers the reasons that one popular text is often the target of censors. Joseph (1998), presents a case for incorporating African American adolescent literature into the curriculum of a middle school language arts class, and the process that she developed in order to acquire parental permission for use of potentially controversial texts, for making interdisciplinary connections, and so on.

## CENSORSHIP

From its beginnings in the early 1970s, the Assembly on Literature for Adolescents, National (ALAN) has grown rapidly in size and prestige. It stands today as one of the largest subgroups in NCTE, and its annual postconvention workshop each November is heavily subscribed. This increase in interest/participation would seem natural; the growth of Young Adult Literature as a teachable genre has become one of the significant facts of life for teachers, supervisors, and indeed all professionals who are involved in teaching English in the middle grades.

One obvious reason for the increases noted is the rise in literary quality of texts for young people in the latter half of the 20th century. Research done in the 1940s, 50s, and 60s revealed the consistent preference of early adolescents for a picture of *reality* in the imaginative works they chose to read. (The fact that definitions of *reality* differ widely among young readers would pose another research endeavor.) Clearly, the popular "junior novels" of prewar America—Zane Grey's adventure novels, Edgar Rice Burroughs' Tarzan series, the Nancy Drew novels of Grace L. L. Hill, and the Sue Barton episodes of Emily Loring—did in no way meet that criterion, redolent as they were with contrivances, stereotypic characters, sentimentality, melodrama, and shallow didacticism. The concurrent rise in both literary quality and realism of Young Adult (YA) texts has been well documented earlier in this chapter. One highly pertinent characteristic of the new YA fiction needs identification at this point, however: The increasing preponderance of fictional texts focusing on contemporary (rather than historical) milieu has been evident over the past 30 to 35 years. Also noteworthy is the rapid growth in texts by authors of various racial/ethnic backgrounds who feature multicultural themes, communities, and groups of inhabitants in their texts.

For many years, researchers in the evolving YA genre decried the orthodox, distorted, and invalid pictures of the novels of their era. Alm (1954), Dunning (1959), Petitt (1960), Tingle (1958), Evans (1961), Blount (1963), Davis (1967), and Muller (1973) all complained about the lack of correspondence between the picture of life drawn by these texts and contemporary reality. Dunning labeled them consistently "wholesome and rigidly didactic." Petitt concluded that the *weltanschauungs* of too many YA novels both distorted and carefully selected aspects of life to portray. Davis echoed these conclusions. Ken Donelson often used the label "squeaky-clean" in his critical appraisals. The virtually simultaneous publication of three YA novels in the late 1960s changed all that.

From summer 1967 to early spring 1968, the world of YA fiction witnessed the publication of *The Outsiders* by Susan E. Hinton, *The Contender* by Robert Lipsyte, and *The Pigman* by Paul Zindel. Taken as a whole, these three texts, all with contemporary urban settings, flew in the face of the conventional wisdom of the day—that to be acceptable to school administrators, classroom teachers and librarians, books about kids needed to remain squeaky clean. Treated in this fictional trio were substance abuse, violence, racial hatred, police brutality, criminal behavior, gang conflict, anti-Semitism, teenage sexual activity, absent/indifferent parents, and young adult selfishness/insensitivity, to name the more prominent taboos violated by the three authors.

Since that watershed year, the YA publishing industry has seen an enormous increase in texts that depict, often with graphic realism, the life of teenagers in the latter years of the 20th century. Concurrently, the rise in popularity of these novels with both middle grade students and teachers shot up to the point where in today's middle grade classrooms, the works of such authors as Judy Blume, Robert Newton Peck, Paul Danziger, Gary Paulsen, Katherine Paterson, Robert Cormier, Norma Fox Mazur, Walter Dean Myers, Lawrence Yep, Sandra Cisneros, Zore Neale Hurston, Chris Crutcher, and many others are commonplace.

We all learned in our chemistry courses, however, that for every action, there is a reaction (or something like that). Consequently, the higher the levels of quality and (more so) realism evident in YA texts, the greater the questioning of them. The complaints and challenges came from an unhappy minority of community watchdogs. For many years, these complaints/ challenges came, for the most part, from individuals with their private, sometimes idiosyncratic gripes. The John Birch Society might attack authors such as John Steinbeck or Norman Mailer as writing "un-American trash," or the formidable Texas couple, Mel and Norma Gabler might comb the state adoption lists for examples of communist, antiChristian, antifree enterprise themes as well as profane language, but the concerted, organized opposition to school materials and YA novels in particular did not really evolve until the late 1970s.

In 1978, Senator Orrin Hatch (R-Utah) slipped in an amendment to the *Omnibus Education Bill* that made mandatory the granting of requests from any parent to examine—and possibly challenge—"all instructional materials used in any research or experimental program supported by federal funds." While the intent of this rider was to allow examinations of those materials used in public school testing, it was quickly seized on by a number of groups, mostly newly formed and mostly representing the fundamentalist Christian right. Some of the more prominent ones:

• The Family Research Council (Gary Bauer)
• The Christian Coalition (formerly Ralph Reid, now Donald Hodel)
• The Eagle Forum (Phyllis Schlafly)
• Concerned Women of America (Beverly LaHaye)
• Focus on the Family (Dr. James Dobson)
• The American Family Association (Donald Wildmon)
• The American Christian Educators Association with its strike force, Citizens for Excellence in Education (Robert L.Simonds)

Over the past two decades, these and other smaller groups have maintained an ongoing opposition to materials and teaching strategies at all levels of the curriculum, in most subject matter areas—most prominently English, Social Studies, Health, Art/ Music Appreciation, Basal Reading Series, as well as Guidance/ Counseling Services. While these challenges/complaints have been directed at explicit sexual descriptions and "inappropriate" language, the scope has recently broadened to include several levels of societal orthodoxy: antiChristian, family values, parental authority, criticism of institutions (police, Boy Scouts, etc.), sexual preferences, capitalistic satire, occult preoccupation, to name a few. In the decade of the 1990s, the buzzwords most often used by these groups have changed from "secular humanism" to "New Age" and have largely replaced the "communist" label of yore. The addition to this army of proponents of Political Correctness has expanded even further the scope of attacks. Thus, the much maligned Steinbeck novel, *Of Mice and Men*, has taken yet another shot, this time from those who oppose depiction of the mentally challenged; *The Adventures of Huckleberry Finn* has risen to third place in the most challenged list; and authors of *Webster's Dictionary* have, in 1998, beaten back the demand that certain racial, ethnic, and religious slur words be expunged from their most recent revision.

Chemistry scholars also inform us that for many reactions, there are counter reactions. In the early 80s, several agencies, both educational and otherwise, presented the case for the students' right to read, the teachers' right to teach, all citizens' right to study reflections of intellectual freedom, etc. The American Library Association put in place many years ago its Intellectual Freedom Committee, which, among other initiatives, publishes a bimonthly *Newsletter on Intellectual Freedom*. Its annual *Banned Books Week* is enthusiastically celebrated by public school media centers/libraries coast to coast. With the publication of *Dealing with Censorship* (Davis, 1979), NCTE began to weigh in with its response to what it considered unreasonable censorship demands. Its Standing Committee Against Censorship (SCAC), which published the useful pamphlet *The Students' Right to Read* (1972), has been increasingly active over the past 15 years, and certain of its major periodicals— *English Journal*, The *ALAN Review*, and *Language Arts*—have dedicated thematic issues to the censorship movement. In 1991, NCTE's SCAC joined forces with IRA's Committee on Intellectual Freedom to produce the pamphlet, *Common Ground* to reflect their combined opposition to unreasonable restriction of the right to reading and learning activities so central to American public education.

In the mid 1980s, the activist Normal Lear formed the nonprofit agency, People for the American Way (PFAW), whose main purpose was, and is, to oppose attempts to restrict intellectual freedom, especially in the classrooms and libraries of the nation's schools. In 1988, the organization first published *Attacks on the Freedom To Learn*, an annual summary, state-by-state of the incidences of challenges to materials either available or taught in public schools. Since these years of publication parallel the scope of this research, a summary/update will follow.

By analyzing the censorship episodes chronicled in the PFAW annual reports, some revealing—and discouraging—trends in the nature and incidence of complaints and challenges lodged against materials used in classrooms and placed in school libraries in grades 5 through 9, during the period 1988-97[1] can be discovered. First in importance  is the number of episodes

---

[1]It needs to be noted that, according to both ALA and PFAW sources, only about 20% of censorship cases are actually reported for publication.

recorded: 17 in 1988-89; 35 in 1989-90; 28 in 1990-91; 8- in 1991-92; 80 in 1992-93; 94 in 1993-94; 107 in 1994-95; 113 in 1995-96; and 120 in 1996-97. A quantitative analysis of the nature of complaints/challenges over that period also proved informative. First, the ratio of library complaints to those of the classroom was 60% to 40%. The incidence of complaints of works containing objectionable material was as follows:

Language—204
Explicit Sex—194
New Age; Anti-Religion—61
Patriotism, Established Authority—23
Violence, Brutality (including rape)—110
Satanism, Occult, Witchcraft—67
Family Values—68
Handicapped—4
Racism—39
Substance Abuse—31
Anti-Feminist; Sexism—11
Depressing; Morbid Topic—24

It is clear from this compilation that inappropriate language and explicitly described sex, the two "old standbys" of the would-be censors, still represent the most objectionable contents of materials used or shelved in grades 5 through 9. Violence, brutality, rape, etc., has also been a consistent target. The three features that follow: New Age/Religion, Satanism, etc., and Family Values have made a move upward on the hit lists, especially since 1992. They are prime targets of certain of the crusading groups mentioned earlier. Racism, another slow starter in the PFAW decade's review, picked up an increased number of citations in the years from 1994 to 1997.

One further item gleaned from this summary could easily be considered disturbing by teachers and librarians: The number of challenges reported as defeated was 293. The number of those that caused removal, restriction, or other modification was 201—too close for comfort. A further, chilling fact for the two groups of professions to think over lies in the fact that from 1988-91, the ratio of retentions to removals, etc., was about 2 to 1. From 1991 on, it was closer to 50-50, a finding that led the compilers of *Attacks on the Freedom To Learn* to warn all school personnel who choose texts, films, video, or audio tapes for classroom or media center to review them with great care.

A number of pertinent findings and conclusions gleaned from this study that provide food for thought among those connected with middle grade curricula are as follows:

• While the number of complaints/challenges to certain elements of middle grade programs of study have significantly escalated over the period reported by PFAW, the most targeted component of the K-12 spectrum remains elementary school libraries, and by a considerable margin.

• Literary works were often challenged, but materials related to health and safety, especially those including segments on sexually related issues were attacked even more widely, as were materials on developing self-esteem and facing diversity factors in the schools of the 90s.

• The geometric increase in censorship incidents across the curricular board has already been noted. Sad to say, PFAW has discontinued publication of this valuable yearly record. In fall 1997, it published a greatly reduced text, on a wide variety of intellectual freedom issues, titled *Coming in on a Right Wing and a Prayer*. Gone are the useful state summaries. School personnel wishing to stay abreast of challenges and their dispositions will need to consult ALA's *Newsletter* and/or the quarterly *Censorship News* produced by the National Coalition Against Censorship. Both these publications are quite limited in coverage when compared to *Attacks on the Freedom To Learn*.

• In reviewing the origins of complaints/challenges, it became most evidence that the organizations mentioned earlier in this discussion (Christian Coalition, Family Research Council, Eagle Forum, etc.) have provided and are providing a large amount of support to the challengers, usually in the form of legal advice, propaganda materials, guest speakers/consultants, etc. Local chapters of these groups, especially Citizens for Excellence in Education, have sprung up in communities large and small, coast to coast, during the decade of the 1990s.

• A source of disappointment and frustration lies in the imposing number of building principals and district superintendents who cave in when complaints and challenges are lodged. This record points to the great need for administrators' organizations, such as the American Association of School Administrators and the National Association of Secondary School Principals, as well as the U.S. Department of Education, to provide leadership in the overall area of defending students' right to read and teachers' right to teach.

• Since we seem to be a nation immersed in a Top-Ten mentality, the following young adult novels are those most frequently challenged since 1988. In no particular order, they are:

— Judy Blume, *Forever*
— Robert Cormier, *The Chocolate War*
— Anonymous, *Go Ask Alice*
— Robert Newton Peck, *A Day No Pigs Would Die*
— Katherine Paterson, *A Bridge to Terabithia*
— Lois Lowry, *The Giver*
— Chris Crutcher, *Running Loose*
— Lois Duncan, *Killing Mr. Griffin*
— Madeleine L'Engle, *A Wrinkle in Time*
— Judy Blume, *Blubber*

Added to these YA texts, the titles of five novels, widely read by teenage individuals (often outside of school), which challengers most frequently claim are too mature for children in the middle grades, are:

John Steinbeck, *Of Mice and Men*
Maya Angelou, *I Know Why the Caged Bird Sings*
Mark Twain, *The Adventures of Huckleberry Finn*
J. D. Salinger, *The Catcher in the Rye*
William Golding, *Lord of the Flies*

Certain other scholarly, research-based texts on the issue of school censorship have appeared over the past decade. In this review, only those that pertain substantially to middle grade examples will be mentioned. In 1988, James Moffett completed *Storm in the Mountains* (1988), a case study of the fundamentalist uprising that took place in Kanawha County,

West Virginia, with particular emphasis on its personal impact—Moffett's spouse was a native West Virginian, and he had done considerable consulting work with West Virginia language arts teachers just before the violent conflict took place. He states in his preface:

The constraints on the publication of textbooks exceed by far those just described for general trade books. The stakes are much higher, because textbooks are usually produced in series and in hard\cover, most often entail huge outlays of capital for development, and must conform to local school adoption requirements that make for a lose-all or win-all game. The content of textbooks has been very limited ever since 1974, when the most tumultuous and significant schoolbook controversy ever to occur in North American broke out in Kanawha County, West Virginia. The book you are holding is a case study of that dispute and its import (pp. ix–x).

Readers need not believe this themselves to appreciate perhaps that my believing it makes it possible for me to treat the protesters' religiosity as more than poppycock and to play on their theme in ways that may make this case study more interesting than it might have been if I merely scoffed at or ignored what, in their eyes, was the basis of all their objections. Textbooks, schools, and indeed the society itself do suffer terribly for want of a spiritual framework, it is true. Although such a framework cannot come into being the way the book banners tried—and continue to try—it would be best for all if a way *were* found, in keeping with the universalist spirituality of the founding fathers themselves (pp. xi–xii).

While this text/memoir was published almost 20 years after the fact, it does offer a clear representation of the intensity and singularity of purpose usually exhibited by members of the Christian Fundamentalist right in their approach to opposing students' right to read and teachers' right to teach.

Nicholas Karolides, John Kean, and the late Lee Burress completed a lengthy analysis of most censored books in U.S. Schools in 1990. They then identified those most frequently attacked and recruited a cadre of scholars/authors/researchers to compose essays in defense of these texts as used in middle and high school classrooms. The anthology produced by these three veteran Wisconsin English Educators, *Censored Books: Critical Viewpoints* (1993) features a series of essays by various authors that support the case for teaching some 45 texts in both public and private schools. Of particular interest is the fact that of the total defended, some 18 were Young Adult novels, all written since 1968. Furthermore, five of those that received similar apologies were among those mentioned earlier, which are generally considered "adult" novels, but which have found places in a considerable number of classrooms and libraries, grades 5 through 9. In their *Introduction*, the anthologists state:

The central charge to these reviewers was direct and simple: Why should anyone read this book? Why should it be recommended? They were asked to express their impressions of the text, of the concepts and emotions that readers might experience, of the personal and social understandings that might be achieved. A second concern addressed the question, Why is this book under attack? The reviewers were asked to consider the censorial challenges to the text in relation to its perceived merits. Another consideration suggested to reviewers was pedagogic, that is, classroom application.

The essays included in *Censored Books: Critical Viewpoints* provide, in effect, a defense of these frequently challenged books, a rationale for ensuring access to them for readers and support for teaching them. This collection does not, however, propose a curriculum for the English language arts classroom nor is it a cultural literacy list. The editors are not arguing that everyone must read all of these books. Rather, we strongly advocate the right of readers to select materials in an open marketplace of ideas and of teachers to select classroom materials in keeping with appropriate teaching objectives (Karolides, Burress, & Kean, 199, p. xx).

For any middle grade teacher or librarian who decides to introduce any of these works to classroom or bookshelf, the essays in the Karolidas/Burress/Kean anthology can provide valuable support.

While the 6th edition of Nilsen and Donelson's comprehensive *Literature for Today's Young Adults* (2001) provides its traditional wide coverage of YA topics, its treatment of the censorship issue is extensive and helpfully pragmatic. Aileen Nilsen was, for many years, a professor of Library Science at Arizona State University. Ken Donelson, a longtime English educator, has been in the forefront of the fight against unreasonable and mindless censorship for well over a quarter of a century.[2] Together, these researchers cover both major venues of censorship confrontations.

The anthology, *Censorship: A Threat to Reading Learning, Thinking* (Simmons, 1994) also represents a broad view of school censorship, including three primary subdivisions:

1. Some Dimensions of the Problem (7 essays)
2. Complaints and Challenges in the Classroom (8 essays)
3. Some Plans of Action (7 essays)

The essays cover K-12 and deal with several content areas. Given the fact that an extremely large number of middle school curricula now feature an integrated, team approach to subject matter, the anthology includes essays on content areas other than language arts. On the whole, there are a significant number of discussions in this text that would be of interest to teachers, grades 5 through 9. In his preface, editor John Simmons states:

It is easy—but dangerous—to underestimate the universal but idiosyncratic nature of censorship challenges: they can occur in virtually any community, at any time, in any classroom, and over any selection. Who would have thought, for instance, that

• School dictionaries would be barred from secondary school classrooms because they contained "dirty and suggestive" words?

• References to Ralph Bunch—an African American civil rights leader—in a high school history text would be challenged, and citizens would demand that his name be removed?

• Clergy of a community would lead an assault on a language arts program that had recently introduced instruction in U.S. regional and social dialects?

• Harper Lee's *To Kill a Mockingbird*, along with many other classics, would be challenged in numerous secondary schools for containing "racist language"?

---

[2]Donelson, it should be remembered, is the author of the popular NCTE pamphlet, *The Students' Right To Read* (1992).

- A beginning reading series would be challenged by several districts in California because its contents were "satanic and un-Christian" in nature?

- A big-city superintendent and widely respected educator would lose his job over his support of a contemporary, multicultural program of studies?

- *All* paperback books would be prohibited from use in the classrooms of several communities because of their "potentially obscene" nature?

- Children's fairy tales, including *Snow White* and *Sleeping Beauty*, would be challenged in elementary schools because of their "negative stereotyping of women"?

- A public library would be accused of taking the lead in promoting homosexuality because its collection included two children's books—*Heather Has Two Mommies* and *Daddy's Roommate*—about tolerance for families where parents are gay or lesbian couples?

- The Holocaust would be excluded from history courses in several communities because of its "mythological basis"?

- *The Diary of a Young Girl* by Anne Frank would be removed from an entire school district because the protagonist meditates briefly on her first menstrual period?

These examples of extremely varied and widespread censorship represent only a few of the vast number of incidents. Moreover, as this anthology is being readied for publication, many more notorious challenges to school material and courses will be recorded.

The purpose of this collection is to provide a comprehensive view of the current censorship scene. It is only as comprehensive as the essays included will permit and only as current as was the situation when the authors sat down to compose. That it is either is debatable; that it is germane to the real world of today's curriculum conflicts is undeniable (pp. ix–xi).

Four full years have passed since the Simmons text was made available. A review of the editions of the ALA *Newsletter on Intellectual Freedom* and PFAW's *Attacks on the Freedom To Learn* since that year offer eloquent testimony of the ongoing relevance of that warning.

---

## LANGUAGE

---

Of the major content components of the language arts curriculum, none saw a more radical change in the past 10 years than did linguistics. The long-standing dominance of Latinate grammar and the Doctrine of Correctness in usage finally relinquished its stranglehold on language study offered to American students in the middle grades. From the emergence of the Grammar Schools in the late 18th century, through the Latinate grammar text omnipresence to the decline of teaching absolute linguistic standards (largely through memorization) in the decade of the 90s, the shift to pluralism, relativism, and pragmatism has become the hallmark of current-day language pedagogy. The change was a long time coming.

The 1968 review of English Language Arts programs of study conducted by Squire and Applebee (1968) produced the following percentages for grades 7 through 12:

Language—43%
Literature—40%
Composition—17%

When the three junior high grades were isolated, language rose to above 50%, literature diminished to below 35%, and composition dropped to around 10%. Scores of teachers nationwide claimed that they were teaching writing and, to a lesser degree, speaking skills when they were teaching grammar—a contention that flew in the face of published research. Those data collected throughout the century repeated the distinct lack of correlation between formal grammar/usage/mechanics study and enhancement of language performance of any kind. The research summaries of Braddock, Lloyd-Jones, and Schoer (1963) and Hillocks (1986) provide consistent summaries to that effect:

The fierce adherence of U.S. junior high teachers (and to a slightly lesser degree, senior high teachers) to traditional grammar teaching in general and the Warriner's series (*English Grammar and Composition* Series, grades 7–12, by John Warriner) in particular remains somewhat of a phenomenon. As was stated earlier, it has withstood the accumulation of data generated by 85 years of research pointing unequivocally to the lack of transfer between grammar knowledge and language development of young people—this despite the fact that these data have been emphasized by linguistic scholars and English educators for a very long time. It has prevailed despite the work of Otto Jespersen (1956), Charles E. Fries (1940), and other historical linguists whose scholarship provides a thorough review of the inconsistencies and inadequacies of the Latinate grammatical system. The usage component has continued to embrace a doctrine of correctness in the face of all the research evidence produced by S. A. Leonard (1935), Albert Marckwardt and Fred G. Wolcott (1938), and Robert Pooley (1974), (to name only the most prominent researchers), all of whom have concluded that a relativistic position toward the teaching of English usage is the only tenable one (Finegan, 1980).

It has also survived the challenges of "new" grammars—structural/descriptive of the 1940s and 1950s, and transformational/generative of the 1960s and 1970s. Although these modern grammatical systems have become the source of intense scholarly concern among university-based linguists, they have never made a lasting impression on the secondary school English curriculum, especially on its junior high component.

Why this near-fanatical loyalty has persisted is truly hard to state with any degree of assurance. Some psycholinguists feel that grammar study has left the position of mere knowledge among secondary school English teachers and entered the realm of values. The theory goes that in the minds of the teachers it is as fundamentally important to teach grammar as it is to teach patriotism, sound health habits, and the Protestant work ethic. Whatever the nature of the influence, it is undeniably a visceral issue for an amazingly large number of teachers. When you attack their grammar program, you attack them; and when this happens, reasoned argument ceases to function in any persuasive sense.

Thus, despite the introduction of any competing linguistic systems, it is traditional grammar and prescriptive, "right-wrong" usage that continues to hold sway today in junior high English curricula. For a brief moment, in the now fabled 1960s, some other text materials found their way into print and even into use here and there. These texts, for the most part, presented linguistics in cultural, sociological, and psychological frameworks (Postman, Morine, & Morine, 1963; Allen, 1966; *Language of Man*, 1968; Summerfield, 1968; Glatthorn, 1971). They described the language learning process and how various aspects of linguistics—dialectology, relativistic usage, syntactic variety, semantics, and history—related to that process. Probably because of such political and social factors as school integration, Anglo-American professional dialogues, federally sponsored teacher institutes and curriculum study centers, student activism, and the quest for relevance, broader perspectives on language study did have some impact on junior high English curricula. Urban rioting, the Vietnam protest movement, the collapse of the Great Society domestic programs, and the rise of accountability in school systems (the latter culminating in the Great Testing Movement of the 1970s) all provided for an early departure for the linguistic adventurism of the previous decade. (NCTE/IRA, p. 327)

The Warriner's *Grammar and Composition* Series, first published by Harcourt Brace in 1946, represented to many middle school English teachers the trusted vehicle for dispensing language lore and processes for a 40+ year span. The year 1987, however, saw the publication switch the positions of the words *Grammar* and *Composition* in the title, including the new text for sixth graders. Nancie Atwell's *In the Middle: Writing, Reading and Learning with Adolescents* (1987) provided a persuasive reading/writing, student-centered approach to teachers of early adolescents. It became extremely popular with teachers, supervisors, district curriculum developers, and middle grade teachers from coast to coast. In 1998, a revised edition of the text has appeared—to be discussed later.

The editors of the 1987 Warriner's revision tried to update the series' content. The series mentioned, albeit sketchily, a relativistic dimension of usage, and it described a fairly conservative writing process paradigm. In its syntax sections, it offered a version of sentence combining as an optional teaching approach. It was universally clear, however, that by the late 80s, the days of prescriptive, rule-driven, absolutist language study were numbered. At the 1990 NCTE convention in Atlanta, the Warriner's series was not to be found on display. There is no reason to believe that a new, revised edition will be published as this monograph is written.

Thus, the past decade has witnessed a significant diminution of traditional grammar-usage-mechanics direct classroom activity redolent of language texts (as courses of study) and workbooks (for "skills" reinforcement). Concurrently, there has been no discernible resumption of the personal/social dimensions of language as practiced by earlier adolescents. E. D. Hirsch, Jr.'s best-selling treatise on cultural literacy (1987) offers a desultory attempt to link language study, *very* traditional in nature, to young people's introduction to the (Hirsch's) "Great Books." The connection is shaky at best, and there is nothing sociolinguistic in evidence. A more recent treatment of this approach is found in Simmons and Baines (1998) *Language Study in Middle School, High School, and Beyond*. In this collection of essays are some outstanding contemporary linguists, e.g., Hal Foster, Walt Wolfram, John Mayher, Kyoko Sato, among others. On the whole, the essays propose language as the central focus for study in the reading and related language arts in the classroom. Included are ideas for studying language through literature, the arts, writing, and speaking, and in different academic settings. The collection was, in actuality, the outgrowth of a Conference on Whole Language, held on the Florida State University campus in the spring of 1994.

A 1993 text, *Language Exploration and Awareness: A Resource Book for Teachers* by Larry Andrews offered a broadbrush overview of the place of linguistics, language learning, and sociological elements of language study that would enhance and bring vitality to the middle and high school classrooms. It included learning theory, communication processes, lexicology, syntax, dialectology, and general semantics components woven together to form a coherent curricular paradigm. Most germane to this discussion is the fact that it poses language study as its main thrust. In his *Preface*, the author states:

What are some of the more vivid memories of your English language lessons in school? Grammar drills? Usage worksheets? Memorizing 25 spelling words for Friday's final test? Writing "S," "V," "IO" and "DO" above the subject, verb, indirect, and direct objects in sentences?

These activities represent what many students remember, with little affection for the memories. For them, these drills and worksheets asked them to analyze language aspects they thought were unnecessarily "picky," primarily because the activities are so far removed from their sense of the world around them or one they might face.

Ironically, these same students laugh uproariously at the language play in poems, novels, and comic strips, and in the jokes of television comedians. They are emotionally touched by some lyrics. They become angry when their friends are the butt of namecalling, and are disillusioned when politicians, teachers, parents, or advertisements do not live up to their words. They knowingly smile at the seeming naivete of the words to songs from previous generations, music they call "oldies." In each of these cases the students are making significant language observations (p. ix).

The record reflects, however, the sad and symbolic fact that the Andrews monograph did not go into a second edition.

More popular in recent professional thinking has been what, in all honesty, must be considered a resurrection of the time-honored grammar-learning-will-improve-writing-theory. A series that has made a nationwide impact was published in 1992:

Peter Elbow and Sheridan Blau, two highly capable teacher/researchers, with the help of Arthur Applebee and Judith Langer, produced a secondary level English series titled *Writer's Craft* (MacDougal-Littell) which represents the embodiment of the reading–writing connection for students in upper grades (grades 9-12). Beginning each instruction unit with a high-interest reading selection, they moved students into the implementation of the writing process and added a grammar/usage/mechanics component for assistance in revision of drafted compositions. The initial popularity of this series provides some evidence of the impact student-centered, integrated instruction in literacy is having on adolescents and their teachers at this time (J. Simmons, 1996, p. 37).

Another prominent English educator, Constance Weaver, has made a continuing effort, through a number of publications, to provide a pragmatic approach to grammar/usage/mechanics as enablers of better writing. Her 1979 text, *Grammar for Teachers: Perspectives and Definitions*, examined the question of how teachers, kindergarten through college, can use grammar without intimidating young people. She also laid out ways in which different grammar systems can enhance the language performance of students. A more recent text, and one more closely focused on the grammar-writing link, is her 1996 publication, *Teaching Grammar in Context*. In this book, she provides an historical look at the value of teaching grammar to earlier and later adolescents as well as (more importantly) a closer look at those aspects of grammatical content that can assist students in revising and editing their writing. As in *Writer's*

*Craft*, grammar study is posed as an adjunct to instilling the writing process in young composers.

A text by Eleanor Kutz, *Language and Literacy* (1996), probes the ways in which language study can be used to enhance students' authentic discourse, both written and oral. Kutz presents a model for teachers in the process of selecting active, exploratory approaches to language study. In this process, she draws on studies from all walks of life.

The pragmatist approaches discussed do require the tests of time and rigorous research episodes of the experimental, case study, and/or the correlational variety to indicate whether they are something more than old wine in new bottles. It may be, however, more than coincidence that James Moffett's *Teaching the Universe of Discourse* (1968) is currently enjoying a resurgence of interest, among both theorists and practitioners. It may also be relevant to note that several contemporary linguistic pragmatists, e.g., Mayher, Blau, Weaver, Andrews, and others are to some degree Moffett aficionados.

The central battleground in *l'affair* language study for kids, however, has resided in the "to be or not to be" debate about the nature, place, and value of Whole Language study in the contemporary U.S. language arts curriculum, K–12. As will be seen, this debate is directly linked to a number of statewide testing efforts and will be considered again later in this chapter. The debate is of relatively recent vintage and includes all of the language skills that teachers of language arts seek to enhance. It is often acrimonious and, in a number of venues, especially the State of California, has deep-seated political overtones.

It would seem, on the surface, that there would be a natural marriage between current middle school/early adolescent curricular goals and Whole Language study. The student-centered direction of the former would seem to legislate Whole Language rather than traditional, prescriptive approaches. As the old ballad claims, however, "It ain't necessarily so."

Robert Shafer has provided a helpful historical outline of Whole Language. In a paper delivered at the 1990 NCTE Spring Conference in Colorado Springs, he traces the movement from the "Progressive Education" era, which began in the 1920s and "has never completely disappeared." He notes allusions to student-centered learning in the 1960s (Strickland, 1960; Cremin, 1961; McDonald, 1961; Whitehead, 1961; Holbrook, 1961; Dixon, 1967), and in linguistic scholarship produced in the 1970s (Britton, 1970; Wilkinson, 1971; Halliday, 1973, 1975; Barnes, 1976). While most of the researchers cited above are United Kingdom educators, Shafer also notes the work of U.S. scholars (Postman, 1963; DeMott, 1968; Elbow, 1973, 1990) and especially in the writing of James Moffett. His *Teaching the Universe of Discourse* (1968) proposes a student-centered linguistic construct as the basis for the total English Language Arts curriculum. His collaborative text with Betty Jane Wagner, *Student Centered Language Arts and Reading* (1976) provides a programmatic fleshing out of the *Universe of Discourse* theory.

Shafer also cites the 1970s work of Frank Smith and Kenneth Goodman in their psycholinguistic approaches to reading instruction (Smith, *Understanding Reading*, 1986; Smith & Goodman, *Psycholinguistics and Reading*, 1976) as further evidence of the growing emphasis on student-centered language learning in the latter half of the century. In sum, his historical review points to the conclusion that the Whole Language paradigms of the past 15 years are neither totally unprepared for nor wholly inspired by British educators.

Since the mid 1980s, however, a great deal of descriptive literature and curriculum overview has borne the name of Whole Language. The bulk of these writings relate to early childhood and elementary grades curricula. The number of theories that bear the label Whole Language, moreover, are quite large, often quite variant, and sometimes in conflict with one another. And, as is so often the case, the gap between professional understanding of this approach and perceptions of parents and "concerned citizens" is often wide indeed. The latter discrepancy has been fueled, in the past 2 decades, by the strident pronouncements of certain right-wing fundamentalist groups; e.g., the Christian Coalition, Eagle Forum, Concerned Women of American, Citizens for Excellence in Education, etc., who have on occasion associated Whole Language strategies with everything from witchcraft to secular humanism. The most common sobriquet of the moment is "New Age" thinking which, these self-righteous apostles claim presages the downfall of our civilization.

In 1987, Nancie Atwell's *In the Middle* sounded a keynote in the reading/writing collaborative learning model that has emerged as one of the staples of the Whole Language curricular thrust. The second edition of her influential text was published in 1998. Not surprisingly, Atwell's classroom experience is almost entirely in middle school. Her theories inspired a fellow New England middle school teacher, Linda Rief, whose text, *Seeking Diversity: Language Arts with Adolescents* (1996) reinforces much of Atwell's philosophical base and extends into classroom engagement with early adolescents whose skills with the mother tongue are significantly limited. In the 1990s, Whole Language monographs, most directed to students below senior high school age, have appeared in quantity. *Uncovering the Curriculum—Whole Language in Secondary and Post-Secondary Classrooms*, by Kathleen and James Strickland (1993), underscores the beliefs of many English educators that the Whole Language philosophy is applicable to *all* learners and *all* teachers rather than being one that relates only to the early grades. Harold Foster's *Crossing Over: Whole Language for Secondary Teachers* (1994) expresses essentially the same precepts but extends them to the high-tech, wired world of teenagers and offers potentially effective ways to integrate contemporary media with meaningful language activity in the classroom.

Julia DeCarlo produced a meta-analysis of the Whole Language philosophical tenets from 24 scholarly journals in a compilation titled *Perspectives in Whole Language* (1995). These essays represent the findings, opinions, and learning strategies as offered by leading researchers and practitioners in reading and language arts across the country. They speak to all curricular levels and reflect the diversity of thinking about the Whole Language issue. In the same year, Kathleen Strickland completed a monograph, *Literacy, Not Labels* (1995) that speaks to middle and high school teachers, especially those who are assigned classes that include "basic," "disabled," "handicapped," "limited," etc., students. Strickland's thesis is that these students will profit significantly from an atmosphere in which literacy instruction is "real, meaningful and individualized." This atmosphere will be enhanced by the Whole Language approach as introduced by her and her husband in their 1993 text.

The most comprehensive research analysis of Whole Language philosophy was published in the fall 1994 issue of *Reading Research Quarterly*. Gary Moorman, William Blanton, and Thomas McLaughlin, all of Appalachian State University (North Carolina), have examined the rhetoric of Whole Language. Their purpose was to reveal both the explicit and implicit assumptions that undergird the Whole Language movement. The researchers made an extensive search through all available professional literature on the topic. They then selected 18 essays from peer-reviewed journals for in-depth analyses. These were chosen as representative statements of the Whole Language position. Their first analysis was of the statements that explicitly defined elements of the position. These statements were then arranged in a framework that identified three themes that were recurrent in the essays:

1. General definitions
2. Learning and teaching
3. The reading process and reading instruction

The essays were then analyzed using deconstruction, a research method that is typically used in literary and historical criticism. Exponents of this approach claim that metaphor and other figures of language used on constructing texts usually reveal underlying assumptions that often exist beyond the conscious awareness of their authors. The deconstruction analysis focused on two oppositional metaphors found consistently throughout the essays; namely, natural versus artificial and personal ownership versus external control. Both explicit and implicit assumptions found by the three researchers are discussed at length as they relate specifically to literacy teaching and learning. The essays of some of the best known proponents of the Whole Language strategy are reviewed in this meta-analysis: Carol Edelsky, Ken and Yetta Goodman, Jerome Hapste, P. J. Farris, and Michael McKenna, to name a representative few.

Criticisms of the extended meta-analysis, presented by Brian Cambourne (Australia), John Willinsky (University of British Columbia) and Arizona's Kennth Goodman take issue with a number of reflections found therein. All three of these critical appraisals are found in the same issue of *Reading Research Quarterly*. A careful review of the entire periodical will provide invaluable data about the ways in which current scholars express their understanding of this hotly debated pedagogical issue.

That language study in the middle grades has moved in a dramatically new direction is most evident as our culture enters the next millenium. Given the heated debates of educational policy and practice now going on, it is not clear, at least to *this* observer where the linguistic trail will lead. It is indisputable, however, that the debate, as joined by federal, and state/local agencies; by politicians with varied agendas; by organizations both educational and noneducational in nature; and by the struggling middle grade teachers from Maine to California, will rage long into this new millenium. Those of us who have been in the trenches for awhile can only hope that those directions are in the best interests of our early adolescents.

## READING

Quite apart from the pedagogical dimensions of reading instruction to be presented to early adolescents is the political position that this most basic of literacy abilities has occupied over the past 30 years. In the heyday of the Great Society, with its high tone academic curricular offerings, reading was often to be presumed a *given*, especially in the proposals related to literature study. Otherwise, it was classified as a basic limitation among the "disadvantaged," the operant metaphor for underprivileged youth, many of whom were to be found within racial and ethnic minorities and who lived, more often than not, in the inner cities coast to coast. Much of the professional thinking about middle grade students who were not academically successful—or even involved—was condescending, mean spirited, and naïve. Consider this statement found in *Freedom and Discipline in English*, composed by the Commission on English of the College Entrance Examination Board in 1965 (p. 49):

Claims are frequently advanced for the use of so-called "junior books", a "literature of adolescence", on the ground that they ease the young reader into a frame of mind in which he will tackle something stronger, harder, and more adult. The Commission has serious doubts that it does anything of the sort. For classes in remedial reading a resort to such books may be necessary, but to make them a considerable part of the curriculum for most students is to subvert the purposes for which literature is included in the first place.

In the decade that followed, "accountability" became the watchword of public education. To the leaders in the (then) U.S. Office of Education, as well as state departments of education gurus from Maine to California, reading ability, or lack thereof, was the educational capacity most in need of scrutiny and remediation. By the early 70s, the National Assessment of Educational Progress, a creation of the Education Commission of the States, had already administered and reported results of nine academic tests given to students in Grades 3, 6, 9, and 12, randomly chosen from all geographic regions. Low reading ability was one of the not-so-surprising findings from those tests, and it engendered a public outcry seized on by opportunistic politicians and bureaucrats everywhere. In state after state, accountability legislation was hastily enacted, and reading teaching and testing was at or near the top of each mandate. Probably, it is more accurate to say that reading testing and teaching were reflected by the statewide "minimum competency tests" that became an integral part of the laws passed. By 1980, all 50 states had put in place mandatory testing programs, all of which placed reading at a place of central importance. These criterion-referenced tests were tied to high school graduation in a number of states. The state of Georgia was probably the most zealous, instituting tests in grades 2, 4, 6, 8, 10, and 12. These tests were almost without exception multiple choice in nature and leaned heavily on fact-and-detail items, largely eschewing components that dealt with higher order thinking skills and/or critical reading. Most reading researchers and scholars of the day, among them Frank Smith, Kenneth Goodman, Harold Herber, Robert Ruddell, and Richard Vacca (to name a representative few) raised protest against this isolated, fragmentary, limited assessment approach to where U.S. early adolescents stood on the literacy totem pole. Simmons summarizes the movement in this manner:

As the basic skills, competency-based, IPI movement enveloped the land, a new literacy label emerged: functional literacy. This umbrella term included the teaching of reading (mostly non-literary), traditional Latinate grammar (the cornerstone of writing "correctly"), study skills, writing about the contemporary environment (especially the world of *work*), and a few "useful" oral activities, such as the staged job interview. Literature, imaginative writing, and creative oral activity became back-burner enterprises (Marum, 1996, p. 20).

As the 70s gave way to the 80s, reading philosophy took a very different direction. The landslide victory of Ronald Reagan in the presidential elections of 1980 and 1984, followed by the convincing election of his erstwhile vice president, George Bush, in 1988, all led to a new elitism in education literature coming out of the (soon-to-be-phased-out) U.S. Office of Education and the National Endowment for the Humanities. Demands for increasing the substance of literacy programs increased. Spokespersons such as Chester Finn, Diane Ravitch, William Bennett, John Silber, Lynn Cheney, and E. D. Hirsch, Jr., theorized that the reading competencies of *all* American youth could and must be elevated. The label that replaced "functional literacy" was "cultural literacy" and this new direction was given voice toward the end of the decade in Hirsch's best selling *Cultural Literacy: What Every American Needs To Know* (1987). In his *Preface*, Hirsch pronounces the urgent need for *his* brand of literacy:

To be culturally literate is to possess the basic information needed to thrive in the modern world. The breadth of that information is great, extending over the major domains of human activity from sports to science. It is by no means confined to "culture" narrowly understood as an acquaintance with the arts. Nor is it confined to one social class. Quite the contrary, cultural literacy constitutes the only sure avenue of opportunity for disadvantaged children, the only reliable way of combating the social determinism that now condemns them to remain in the same social and educational condition as their parents. That children from poor and illiterate homes tend to remain poor and illiterate is an unacceptable failure of our schools, one which has occurred not because our teachers are inept but chiefly because they are compelled to teach a fragmented curriculum based on faulty educational theories. Some say that our schools by themselves are powerless to change the cycle of poverty and illiteracy. I do not agree. They can break the cycle, but only if they themselves break fundamentally with some of the theories and practices that education professors and school administrators have followed over the past fifty years (p. xiii).

Legislation passed in state after state to upgrade curricular and student performance criteria reflected the Reagan/Bennett/Cheney/Hirsch sentiments. The demand for "Core Knowledge" was the watchword of the next 5 years, but by 1992, its surge had diminished visibly.

In November 1992, with the election of William Jefferson Clinton, a return to a less academicized and more functional tone to literacy instruction began to emerge. The President and his U.S. Department of Education secretary, Richard Riley, were both influenced by Clinton's fellow Oxford student Robert Reich, a Harvard economist whose widely touted text, *The Work*

*of Nations* (1991) called for the improvement of reading capacities on a broad scale. In Reich's eyes, *belles lettres* must take its place with printed content that dealt with pragmatic sociology, core economics/consumerism, health and safety awareness, environmental warnings, and other such "real world" matters. In a very real sense, this position restored to reading curricular priorities for middle and secondary students one of the oldest cliches in the profession: that "every teacher is a teacher of reading."

Were the early adolescent middle grade students circa 1990s ready and willing to buy into this shift in curricular direction? In his chapter of the 1991 edition of his research review, "The Transition Years: Middle School," Pikulski states:

Some more specific empirical information about the reading development of early adolescents is obtainable from the *National Assessment of Educational Progress Examinations* (NAEP), which are administered in reading approximately every five years. These results are reviewed here both for their general interest and because they fit into the developmental framework suggested by Chall and the conclusions drawn by Early. The results reported in 1985 offer some information about the trends in the development of reading skills for students aged 13, who would fall into the age range of early adolescence, as well for students aged 9 and 17. Data from comparable NAEP examinations are available since 1971. In terms of trends of achievement, the overall picture for 13-year-olds is mildly encouraging. They showed statistically significant improvement during the 1970s, though their achievement remained steady between the 1980 and 1985 assessment.

The NAEP study reported the 1985 results according to five levels of reading attainment. It may be somewhat informative to look at the percentage of 13-year-old students who were able to meet the criteria for these various levels of proficiency.

The lowest level of proficiency, labeled "rudimentary," was defined as the level of proficiency needed to follow simple directions or to read a few simple sentences and to then answer factual questions. "Performance at this level suggests the ability to carry out simple, discrete reading tasks" (p. 15). Obviously, this level of proficiency also requires the mastery of basic decoding skills. In the 1984 assessment, 99.8 percent of the 13-year-olds were able to meet the criteria for mastering rudimentary skills, up very slightly from the first testing that was done in 1970. These results are in line with Chall's expectation that students at this age would be beyond the decoding stage of learning to read and offer confirmation for Early's conclusion that basic word identification skills have been mastered.

The second level of proficiency, termed "basic," requires application of comprehension strategies to simple stories and relatively noncomplex expository passages. "Proficiency at this level suggests the ability to understand specific and sequentially related information" (p. 15). Ninety four point five percent of the 13-year-olds achieved this level of proficiency in 1985, up from 92.3 percent in 1970, a statistically significant increase.

The third level, "intermediate" level skills, also showed improvement for 13-year-olds (60.0 percent, up from 57.0 percent) but this change was not statistically significant. Intermediate level reading requires application of comprehension strategies to relatively lengthy stories and informational passages. "Proficiency at this level suggests the ability to search for specific information, interrelate ideas, and make generalization" (p. 17).

Thirteen-year-olds did not fare very well in dealing with the two highest levels of complexity. "Adept" level items required students to understand, summarize, and explain a broad range of passages, including stories, poems, and information and graphic forms. "Performance at this level suggests the ability to find, understand, summarize and explain relatively complicated information" (p. 15). Only about 11 percent of the 13-year-olds could succeed at this level of proficiency, up insignificantly from about 9 percent in 1970. Finally, 13-year-olds showed no discernable improvement in achieving the "advanced" level of proficiency; less than 1 percent passed at any assessment point. Items at this level entailed restructuring and synthesizing ideas presented in passages using specialized content, difficult vocabulary, sophisticated syntax and specialized genres. "Performance at this level suggests the ability to synthesize and learn from specialized materials" (Pikulski, 1991, p. 15).

Pikulski goes on to generalize from the 1987 findings:

In general, the results were disappointing for all groups 3rd, 7th, 11th graders. For the seventh graders, more than a third failed to read a simple story and draw a reasonable conclusion, even at a minimally satisfactory level. On the expository material, more than 36 percent drew one comparison between information in the short article and their own experiences, and more than 60 percent made unsatisfactory comparisons. Only slightly more than 3 percent made minimal comparisons and virtually none made satisfactory or elaborated comparisons. The authors of the report conclude: "These findings are disturbing, but not surprising. They parallel the findings of earlier NAEP reading and writing assessments, which indicated that students in American schools can read with surface understanding, but have difficulty when asked to think more deeply about what they have read, to defend or elaborate upon their ideas, and to communicate them in writing." (Applebee, Langer, Mullis, *Who Reads Best? Factors Related to Reading Achievement in Grades 3, 7, and 11.* Princeton Education Testing Service, 1988, p. 25.)

From his review, Pikulski offered three significant conclusions to the research gathered to the moment:

• While middle schoolers have mastered basic vocabulary and comprehension skills, they encounter considerable difficulty in responding to more demanding critical and creative aspects of reading comprehension.
• There is a disturbing downturn in the amount of reading done by early adolescents and their choices of reading materials in terms of quality and sophistication.
• There is an enormous *range* of reading abilities among young people at this level, ranging from virtual non-readers to those whose abilities are not fully appraised by extant instruments. (Pikulski, 1991, p. 312)

Pikulski's first conclusion, a lack of critical reading ability among young people, has been echoed by results of the Florida Statewide Minimum Competency Testing Program, the first of its kind among the fifty states, and one that enjoyed a 15-year period of implementation among Florida public school students, Grades 3, 5, 8, and 11. These tests included a substantial number of reading comprehension items that reflected the following objectives:

1. To infer an idea from a selection.
2. To infer a cause or effect of an action.
3. To distinguish between fact and opinion.
4. To identify an unstated opinion (*Guide to Statewide Assessment*, Florida Department of Education, 1987).

These reading activities all can be placed under the rubric of critical reading. At this writing, 15 years of testing in Florida

have consistently reflected the same weaknesses throughout that period among eighth graders.

One explanation for all of these disturbing revelations could well be the current society's obsessive preoccupation with television, a reality eloquently expressed in Neil Postman's National Book Award winning *Amusing Ourselves to Death* (1985). Postman develops an image of American life in the 1980s, which is virtually dominated by television offerings. He states:

Television has become, so to speak, the background radiation of the social and intellectual universe, the all-but-imperceptible residue of the electronic big bang of a century past, so familiar and so thoroughly integrated with American culture that we no longer hear its faint hissing in the background or see the flickering gray light. This, in turn, means that its epistemology goes largely unknown. And the peek-a-boo world it has constructed around us no longer seems even strange.

There is no more disturbing consequence of the electronic and graphic revolution than this: that the world as given to us through television seems natural, not bizarre. For the loss of the sense of the strange is a sign of adjustment, and the extent to which we have adjusted is a measure of the extent to which we have been changed. Our culture's adjustment to the epistemology of television is by now all but complete; we have so thoroughly accepted its definitions of truth, knowledge and reality that irrelevance seems to us to be filled with import, and incoherence seems eminently sane. And if some of our institutions seem not to fit the template of the times, why is it they and not the template, that seems to us disordered and strange? (pp. 79–80)

Postman devotes a separate chapter, "Teaching As An Amusing Activity," to a pronouncement on *Sesame Street, The Electric Company*, and other televised productions whose goal was to enhance literacy. His basic premises are:

1. TV programs do not promote reading; they promote watching TV.
2. The methods of TV and silent reading are vastly different from each other; e.g., meaning through images versus meaning through language.
3. While reading demands concentration, sometimes intense concentration, over extended periods of time, TV exists in brief segments and is user friendly i.e., you can turn it off or switch channels at will.

This book's prophetic significance has not diminished; on the contrary, its warning has been borne out to thoughtful Americans throughout the 1990s. Lawrence Baines' essay, "The Future of the Written Word," (anthology by Simmons and Baines, *Language Study in the Middle School, High School, and Beyond*, 1998), places several of Postman's prophetic contentions about the effect of electronic media on the literacy capacities of today's youth in contemporary relief.

This rather dour outlook of the very existence of reading done by young people in future years has been re-emphasized in a text titled *Fostering the Love of Reading: The Affective Domain in Reading Instruction* (1994) by Eugene H. Cramer and Marietta Castle. The authors explore the role of affect, attitude, and motivation in reading, citing a number of discouraging incidences of regression in those areas among young people. The review of these data is followed by some persuasive suggestions for curricula and classrooms to help teachers at all levels lead their students into meaningful reading experiences.

A broader perspective on the motivational dimension of the process can be found in Gerald Duffy's text, *Reading in Middle School* (1990). Duffy describes ways in which evolving middle school reading programs reflect needed collaboration between teachers and university reading instruction toward the improvement and broadening of reading instruction.

A continuing direction followed by reading scholars/ researchers in recent years has been to analyze and theorize about the need for expanding the nature and scope of middle grades beyond the narrow confines of traditional content area study. In *What Research Has to Say About Reading Instruction*, Samuels and Farstrup (1992) cite studies that deal with how text structure, meta-cognition and home background affect reading achievement. The work of 25 noted authorities is cited in this review. One of the prominent facets of this research is that cultural, economic, social, and psychological factors all play a role in shaping early adolescents' reading capacity.

The 1987 text by Atwell, *In the Middle*, lays out a model for integrating language skill development activities, of recognizing backgrounds of students in planning instruction, and in developing close linkage between reading and writing strategies for middle grade students. A New England middle school associate, Linda Rief, has extended some of Atwell's suggestions in *Seeking Diversity: Language Arts with Adolescents* (1996). Rief adds theoretical frameworks found in the work of Tom Romano, Donald Graves, Lucy Calkins, and Yetta Goodman in her instructional paradigm for students in middle grades. She expands on establishing the reading/writing connection and insists on teachers leading students to lean heavily on their own life experiences in choosing content for their written work. Judith Irvin's *Reading and the Middle School Student* (1998) examines the effects that varied life experiences have on both middle grade students and teachers. She ties them to literacy instruction for early adolescents. In her revised edition, she cites new, pertinent research on the nature of early adolescence, additions to her list of well-written Young Adult novels, and practical views of assessment procedures, especially portfolio review. She also considers ways in which new technologies can assist all readers, particularly disabled ones. This second edition extends its author's belief that reading instruction for middle grades must go far beyond "skills and drills" techniques of the past.

A 1995 text, *Strategies for Guiding Content Reading* by Sharon Crawley and Lee Mountain provides further ideas for establishing the reading–writing connection. Their emphasis is on processes in three phases of classroom activity: reading comprehension, written composition, and study skills. While their suggestions have general application, they are aimed most directly at the middle years. Another text, *Content Reading and Learning: Instructional Strategies* (Flood et al., eds., 1996) offers ways to engage students in continuous learning activities before, during, and after their reading of a text. Practical applications and reading activities, research-based, provide an excellent teaching model for those dealing with middle grade students.

The issue of limitations in the critical reading capacities of early adolescents has also received research-based scrutiny in the 1990s. The third edition of Herber and Nelson's (1995) scholarly text, *Teaching Reading and Reasoning in Content Areas* has expanded significantly the authors' treatment of those factors that contribute to adolescents' critical reading capacities and predilections, or lack thereof. Using a series of research conclusions from recent studies in cognitive and culture-bound abilities, the authors describe a number of practical strategies for upgrading critical reading among young people. An interesting study by Robert Gaskins (1996), "That's Just How It Is" reveals a significant factor in critical reading skills-judgmental in specific—of eighth grade students. Three groups composed of this age level, both male and female, were asked to read a newspaper account of an NBA games between the Boston Celtics and the Philadelphia 76'ers, a game which ended in a bench-clearing brawl. One group of eight students was from the Boston area, a second from Philadelphia, and a third from a New York state community. The students recalled the details from the account and answered three questions based on their beliefs on who was culpable in the incident. The Boston and Philadelphia groups recorded distinct bias in their answers, while the answers of the third group were more neutral. These findings support the thesis that strong, previously developed emotions play an important role in the interpretation of text. They also contain implications for text processing, critical thinking, and self-reflection strategies in classroom settings.

A text by Fran Claggett, Louann Reid, and Ruth Vinz, *Learning the Landscape* (1996) explores some of the powerful learning experiences which can result from combining reading and writing activities in meaningful, interactive ways. The nature of these proposed experiences is further evidence of the degree to which affective experience and identifying crucial background elements can elicit both critical reading gains and creative writing products from students at all ability levels.

Evaluation of students' reading abilities continues to be of interest to teacher educators, supervisors, classroom teachers, researchers, and parents. Joel Brown, Kenneth Goodman, and Ann Marek (1996) have compiled an annotated bibliography, *Studies in Miscue Analysis*. This document contains an updated summary of research, authoritative statements, and teacher appraisals, both published and unpublished, on the topic. Brief but substantive annotations subtend each entry.

In the decade of the 1990s, an approach to individual assessment of children's reading capacities known as "Reading Rescue" came into prominence among reading educators and classroom teachers, especially those working with students in the middle grades. An adaptation of a model created by Marie Clay (1985) for first graders, the "Reading Rescue" instrument features a prescribed procedure: daily one-on-one tutorials, of roughly 30 minutes' duration, composed of oral reading of familiar materials; record-keeping of student behavior; vocabulary identification and knowledge; the writing of a brief, related story, followed by the disassembling of it; and the reading of new material. A comparison of the Clay model and the Reading Rescue counterpart is as follows:

---

**Marie Clay's model**
**Intended grade level: 1**
**Instructional components:**

1. Reading familiar material. (Pupil selects from previously mastered books.)
2. Taking a running record on a book introduced in the previous session.

3. Developing letter identification knowledge. (Use of magnetic board, plastic letters.)
4. Writing a story (Composing 1-2 sentences; then cutting up the sentence(s) and rearranging words in correct order.)
5. Reading new material.

**Materials**: Primary level books.

## Reading Rescue model
### Intended grade levels: 6-8
### Instructional components:

1. Reading familiar material. (Pupil selects from chapter book excerpts and LEA stories.)
2. Reading aloud to the student. (Teacher continues reading from chapter book.)
3. Taking a running record on a portion of new material introduced in the previous session.
4. Working with words and letters. (Use of magnetic board, plastic letters.)
5. Writing through language experience. (Use of computer and word processing software.)
6. Reading new material.

**Materials**: Chapter books in Scholastic Action Series.

(Lee & Neal, 1993, January, p. 279)

Lee and Neal reported gratifying results from several case studies using the instrument with middle grade (6-8) students. The guidelines they deduced from their studies were:

1. Emphasis on students' strengths.
2. Use of several indicators of literacy development to assess students' learning needs.
3. Incorporation of oral reading as a regular feature of classroom instruction.
4. Planning of opportunities for students to reread familiar, favorite material.
5. Planning of instruction that will reinforce the reading/writing connection (Lee & Neal, 1993, pp. 280-281).

The popularity of this approach has grown dramatically with middle grade teachers in succeeding years. In 1995, Wong, Groth, and O'Flahaven described an application of the instrument with students in the vicinity of College Park, Maryland, and characterized discourse of students and teachers. They found that "scaffolding" comments, i.e., methods teachers used to assist students with problem solving, were helpful, and that teachers constantly revised and updated their scaffolding comments. In general, the researchers reported great popularity of *Reading Rescue*, both with students and teachers. In a comparable summary, Susan O'Leary, in *Five Kids: Stories in Children's Learning to Read* (1998) reports similar success. In an unpublished doctoral study, Elizabeth Watts (1997) found that the *Reading Rescue* model enjoyed significant success with readers at the middle school level in predominantly multicultural groups. A problem often raised by classroom teachers regarding an all-out commitment to this diagnostic approach centers on its one-on-one nature, an issue which has beset reading educators who

have supported Informal Reading Inventories over the years. The question remains: What do I do with the other 29 seventh graders while I work with my client of the moment?

Finally, the politics of reading remain an issue which all involved in the educational process must confront, and on which most will take sides. Throughout the 90s, the controversy arising from the *Phonics-Versus-Whole Language Beginning Reading Approach* has been the subject of heated, widespread debate, especially in the State of California. It even seeped into the 1996 Presidential campaign. Also, there have been reactions by the profession to what many believe to be meddling, especially by Federal bureaucrats in areas in which they have little or no true expertise. The following two resolutions were passed by overwhelming majorities at the NCTE meeting in Detroit, November 1997. They are guaranteed to keep the pot boiling:

## Resolution 2
### On Phonics as a Part of Reading Instructions

**Resolved**, that the NCTE of Teachers of English declare that reading is a complex process of constructing meaning;
That phonics for beginning as well as experienced readers is only one part of the complex, socially constructed, and cognitively demanding process called reading;
That all readers need to learn a range of reading strategies, including phonics;
That it is the professional responsibility of teachers to develop extensive knowledge of reading and a repertoire of teaching strategies to adapt to the needs of individual children in order to ensure success;
That NCTE urge policymakers and legislators to affirm that decisions about reading instruction are primarily the responsibility of professional educators; and
That NCTE establish a continuous dialogue with other professional literacy organizations on reading and reading instruction.

## Resolution 3
### On Government Intrusion into Professional Decision Making

**Resolved**, that NCTE assert that any legislation that concerns reading needs to be acceptable to a wide spectrum of educators, reading researchers, teachers, administrators, and others concerned with literacy education. The Reading Excellence Act in its current form does not enjoy this support or acceptance;
That NCTE declare that neither Congress nor any federal agency should bypass traditional standards and procedures for peer review of research, nor should they centralize authority for decision making and review by putting these vital functions in the hands of a single individual or extraordinary authorities;
That NCTE proclaim that no federal law or program should be framed in such a way that its effect would be to provide substantial advantage to any commercial reading program. No person who could personally profit from any legislation or regulation should hold a staff position or be a paid consultant with the government agency that creates or monitors the legislation or regulation;
That NCTE immediately distribute this resolution to members of education committees and the full bodies of the U.S. Senate and House of Representatives, as well as to state legislators, and
That NCTE distribute this resolution to state education agencies, professional education associations, teacher unions, the media, parent groups, and the appropriate organizations, and urge them to voice their support of this resolution. (NCTE, Resolutions, Annual Business Meeting, Detroit, Nov. 1997)

Obviously, the long-range effects of these and similar resolutions will become more clear in the future.

In his eloquent and succinct review of research on reading, *What Really Matters for Struggling Readers*, Richard L. Allington takes to task the most recent national reading initiative: the Reading Excellence Act of 1998. He argues that the REA is biased by the narrow definition of research that was used by the National Reading Panel. He predicts that schools will feel the impact of the work of that group when funding for reading initiatives in schools are restricted to the kinds of programs supported by the National Reading Panel and its insistence on empirical research methods that, Allington argues, ignore realities of actual classrooms, instruction, and students. He suggests that researchers and teachers attend to the following needs of students, especially those who are not beginning readers: the need to read a lot, the need for books they can and will read, the need to develop fluency, and the need to develop thoughtful literacy (2001). These recommendations move teachers and researchers in a direction that is not suggested in the foci of the National Reading Panel, which include phonemic awareness and phonics skills instruction, guided oral reading, silent reading (but not necessarily on a sustained basis), direct teaching of comprehension strategies, and (possibly) the use of technology to enhance reading teaching and learning (Allington, 2).

## WRITING

It is in written composition that the teaching of English in the middle grades has made its greatest strides. In the early (1940s) days of middle school curricula, "real" composition instruction was almost totally absent. Drills and skills, which centered around isolated elements of language structure, were the rule of the day. Literature instruction was both restricted and stultified, but at least there was *something* going on. Extended encounters with spelling lists, often culminated by oral contests, were found to be in widespread use. And, in some "progressively" oriented districts, a loosely organized core curriculum in English featured a potpourri of simplistic language activities, group projects, reviews of current events, life management skills, considerations of community activities, and so on, all in the name of language development. Largely invisible in all of this was any semblance of effective, systematic, research-based instruction in writing.

All that changed dramatically in the early 1970s. First and foremost among the new directions established during that decade was the establishment in 1973 of the Bay Area Writing Project. As Mary Ann Smith recalls:

The dream child of former high school teacher James Gray, the project started in 1973 as an antidote to a pesky and embarrassing situation on the UC Berkeley campus. Nearly half of the entering freshmen, selected from among the top graduates in the nation, were landing in remedial writing classes. Clearly, writing was the short straw in teacher preparation courses, because most teachers had no idea, beyond the red-penciled papers of their past, how to teach writing. Something had to be done.

Something had to be done, too, about the teachers whose students were successful writers. Whatever these teachers were doing behind the closed doors of their classrooms was certainly worth a public hearing. It seemed a shame—no, a tragedy—that outstanding teachers went unheralded and unobserved by the very people who could benefit from their teaching approaches: other teachers. It also seemed wasteful that good teachers were not consistently and visibly active in the profession. Indeed, the profession could hardly be called a profession if its members met only on occasion and depended almost solely on outside consultants for nourishment (1996, June, pp. 122-123).

The Berkeley workshop became the National Writing Project (NWP), a growing network of local projects sponsored by, and to a small degree supported by, the National Endowment for the Humanities. In 1992, funding from federal sources were significantly increased and by 1997, some 160 projects received several thousand dollars for their summer institutes, the centerpiece of NWP activity. A number of other member programs sustained themselves through local, state, and private contributions. As of 1999 close to 200 projects following the Berkeley model were functioning in 45 states, Washington, D.C., and Puerto Rico. In March 1985, at an international meeting on the teaching of writing in the English speaking world and held at the University of East Anglia in Norwich, England, James Gray officially initiated the first writing projects in the United Kingdom.

The NWP has never been the stepchild of scholarly university-based professional types. It relies primarily on a close examination of successful, innovative classroom practices as found across the curricular spectrum, grades K through 12. Smith went on to enumerate and expand on the NWP goals:

- *Presenting writing as a process*: encouraging and teaching students to behave like writers by creating their own topics, planning or prewriting, consulting peers and other resources, drafting and revising, editing for publication.

- *Having students write for different purposes and audiences*: encouraging and teaching students to write in a wide range of situations, to tackle many different kinds of writing, and to think about readers (especially readers other than the teacher) as well as about their own intentions as writers.

- *Promoting writing as a way to learn*: encouraging and teaching students to write in every class, to use writing as a tool for thinking, solving problems, and understanding complicated concepts.

- *Creating a culture of learners and writers*: giving students permission to take risks, make mistakes, help one another, and engage actively in writing, reading, speaking and listening.

- *Being a practicing writer as part of being a teacher of writing*: becoming a full-fledged member of the learner/writer culture, both to improve the teaching of writing (who would take lessons from a driving teacher who doesn't drive?) and to improve as writers (Smith, 1996, June, pp. 127-128).

In recent years, NWP has received substantial praise from such prestigious organizations as the Carnegie Corporation of New York, the National Council of Teachers of English, the Council for Basic Education, the National Conference on Research in English, and the National Endowment for the Humanities. The 1996-97 *National Writing Project Annual Report* lists the following kinds of programs developed over the years by NWP chapters:

1. Advanced Institutes
2. Seminars and Study Groups
3. Young Writers' Programs
4. Assessment Workshops
5. Bilingual and ESL Programs
6. Emergent Literacy Programs
7. Writing Across the Curriculum Series
8. Writing/Reading Conferences
9. Teacher Research Groups
10. Parent Workshops

In 1988, Dipardo and Freedman completed a study titled *Peer Response Groups in Writing Classrooms: Theoretical Foundations and New Directions* at the site of the original NWP, the Berkeley area. In this research summary, they found two distinct kinds of peer response emerging: teacher controlled and those featuring true peer interaction in larger learning constructs. They noted trends toward (a) increasing incorporation of Vigotskyan and Piagetian learning theory in peer group activities, and (b) less teacher control and more spontaneous peer talk in the groups. They concluded that the more peer interaction was spontaneous and less teacher directed, the better the outcomes in the writing progress.

In the 1996-97 *National Writing Project Annual Report*, St. John of Iverness Research Associates states:

A concept that has grown in status and teacher appeal and which has become one of the main areas of study and application in NWP institutes is that of the writing process. The fundamental belief that the process of writing needs to be taught deliberately, systematically, and extensively in the classroom has deeply affected writing instruction at all levels during the decade of the 1980s. Whether its stages are identified as prewriting, drafting, sharing, revising, and editing (one common model) or by another set of labels is not terribly important. The fact is that this new concentration on how a piece of writing evolves has made significant changes in what goes on in English classes, across the middle grades and indeed across the curriculum (p. 19).

The text series by Sheridan Blau and Peter Elbow, *Writer's Craft* (1993), embodies both the writing process and the manner in which it can be made central to the English Language Arts—and quite possibly other curricular areas. In terms of the latter potential, its approach would seem to be ideal for middle grades curricula, with their student-centered, collaborative learning philosophies. The texts are divided into three sections. Section One provides a series of prompts that emanate from mass print media, student writing on personal issues, excerpts from literary selections, summaries of prominent citizens' biographies, and even short passages from content area texts (civics, natural science, health, and safety, etc.). Various oral activities, group and all-class, are included in order to clarify issues, peak interests, relate to readers' backgrounds, even generate controversy. Once these prompts have been extensively treated in the classroom, the teacher/user of the series moves into Section Two, the Writing Process. It is in this section that practice is presented in terms of *relevant* (to the work in Section One) pre-writing, arranging, drafting, sharing, utilizing peer and teacher input, revising, editing, and publishing. When the students reach the final three phases, as noted above, they find Section Three with its glossary of grammar, usage, diction, and writing mechanics

elements. By cross referencing their evolving written products with appropriate Section Three components, the students are able to improve the micro-rhetoric within their papers.

In the Winter 1989 issue of *Review of Educational Research*, Durst and Newell present the findings from their study of ways in which James Britton's categories-of-writing paradigm has been implemented in a selected sample of middle and high schools in the United States. They discovered uses of the Britton system and its heuristics in a wide range of classrooms dominated heretofore by emphasis on grammatical and usage rule adherence along with strict adherence to mechanical dicta. The teachers in the study were interviewed about their knowledge of Britton's model. The researchers were particularly interested in (a) the nature of school writing, (b) the writing process as offered in classes, (c) connections that were established between writing and learning, and (d) student/teacher critiques of the value of this model. They concluded that Britton's work has had a significant liberalizing effect on a large number of U.S. middle and high school language arts classrooms.

More recently, Melanie Sperling (1996) investigated "Revisiting the Writing–Speaking Connection: Challenges for Writing and Writing Instruction". In this ambitious meta-analysis, the researcher looked at the use of writing process techniques as implemented in some middle school classrooms as contrasted with traditional, prescriptive, grammar-focused approaches in others. She looked at a number of factors found within the strategies, namely: Basil Bernstein's restrictive code, cultural influences identified by William Labov and Courtney Cazden; the writing–speaking similarities theories of Anne R. Gere, Andrea Lunsford, and Richard Beach and attendant problems students face in addressing specific audiences, especially in writing. She also examined the presence of teacher–student conferencing strategies as described by Jerome Bruner, Arthur Applebee, Susan Langer, Roger Farr, and Donald Graves. She found generally mixed results as to the relative success of such conferencing, although there were more positive than negatives reported. In summarizing her findings, Sperling suggested that the teacher control–manipulation factor was the single most consistent inhibitor to the increase in use of modern rhetorical thinking in writing instruction at the middle school level.

Eileen Oliver (1995, December) looked at the relationship between quality of writing and rhetorical specificity in writing prompts. Using three grade levels, all college bound, she presented writing tasks in which three composing variables—topic, purpose, and audience—were deliberately manipulated. The grade levels in question were 7, 9, and 11. A class of college freshmen was also used in the study. Eight assignments were created by the researcher and administered to all four groups, and papers were evaluated holistically by a group of trained, experienced English teachers using a 6-point criterion measure. She found that students of different grade levels used different types of rhetorical information: seventh graders responded more positively to simpler, more limited topic specifications; ninth graders related more positively to more complex ones, as did those at the eleventh grade and college freshman levels. She recommended that teachers use relative complexity in the writing prompts they create and assign at the various grade levels and that they follow such guidelines both in their writing instruction and assessment procedures. She was particularly specific about the length and diction used in prompts at each level.

Peyton and Seymour (1989, October) at the Center of Applied Linguistics, looked at several approaches to journal writing. In a case study approach, the researchers had one teacher work with 12 limited English proficient (LEP) students in leading them to write journal entries in several different ways. They found that the teacher interacted more effectively with the students when the topics chosen were student initiated rather than ones she proposed. The teacher also created more dialogue with the students by making statements and offering opinions of her own rather than asking students questions. As a result, the researchers concluded that when students and teachers developed topics of mutual interest, the amount of student writing increased and the quality improved.

In *Writing Across the Curriculum for Middle and High Schools*, Rhoda J. Maxwell (1996) presents a multitude of ways to incorporate writing into programs of study for both early and later adolescents. Her emphasis is on strategies that lead students to become active learners. Her core intent is for teachers to use writing, in workshop style, as a tool for learning information, for understanding concepts both expressed and implied, and to retain knowledge. The length of retention that results from her strategies in the latter area, however, has not yet been vigorously assessed.

The National Council of Teachers of English, in 1996, produced a monograph titled *Motivating Writing in Middle School*. The text enumerates a variety of inducements for stimulation of student writing, which include the use of artifacts (provided by teachers, student, and guest speakers), experiences from students and their friends, memories from personal backgrounds as well as those found in literary selections, history texts, and media products, both print and nonprint. The experiences shared do not invade the privacy of the contributors, but should, according to the authors, be more frequently based in reality than fantasy.

A collection of essays by teachers, supervisors, and teacher educators, *Programs and Practices—Writing Across the Secondary School Curriculum* by Pamela Farrell-Childers, Anne Ruggles Gere, and Art Young (1994) describes and critiques various means by which Writing Across the Curriculum (WAC) has been incorporated into middle and high school classrooms. The ideas found in the anthology range from individual/teacher contributions to paradigms created by teams and instituted as statewide programs. In addition to including statements of philosophical foundations for WAC programs, the anthology offers numerous specific applications to be introduced into the classroom. The essays have been critiqued and expanded upon before they were included in the collection.

Linking reading and writing as an integrated classroom activity was the focus of teacher educators, researchers, and classroom teachers at all curricular levels for much of the 20th century. In *Time for Meaning: Crafting Literate Lives in Middle and High Schools* Randy Bomer (1995) structured an ambitious curricular model that joins literary theory and practice to the writing workshop. Using her own development of increasingly effective classroom strategies, the author describes a series of down-to-earth activities that integrate correlative experience, critical thinking, and the writing process.

Kirby and Liner (1997) produced a second edition of their popular *Inside Out*. In this edition, the authors, with the added input of Ruth Vinz, Teachers' College, Columbia, have probed deeply into the needs, concerns, fears, and aspirations of early adolescents, especially those who have been classified "nonacademic." The authors then propose a series of persuasive motivating activities that will lead such students into the development of coherent written prose implementing the writing process as they go. A realistic assessment of what real problems face young writers as they move through that process carries a number of implications for teacher interventions during the evolution of student writing. In general, this text offers more realistic and detailed ideas for all teachers but particularly for those who are relative newcomers to the classroom.

A highly informative and practically valuable summary of writing instruction over the past 30 years can be found in *Taking Stock: The Writing Process Movement in the 90s* by Lad Tobin and Thomas Newkirk (1994). The creators of this anthology have included an outstanding series of essays on the evolution of process writing by some of the major rhetoric-composition authorities of the second half of the 20th century. Contributions by Donald Murray, James Moffett, Ken Macrorie, James Marshall, Wendy Bishop, James Britton, and Peter Elbow are among those featured in this text. Several of these essays emanated from the 1992 University of New Hampshire historic writing conference. They offer a range of illustrative programs and practices all reflecting the growing presence of writing process strategies across the curriculum.

To culminate this review of writing pedagogy, the issue of assessment/evaluation seems appropriate. The problem of valid, communicable, consistent, and, above all, positive approaches to the judgment of student writing is one that has bedeviled honest, thoughtful teachers since the Lyceum. The publication of meaningful research and scholarly insight in this area of student writing in the middle grades has kept pace with such production in all other phases of writing pedagogy; indeed, the attention paid to the teaching of writing in classes of elementary, middle, high school, and college levels has enabled the most significant advance of English Language Arts scholarship over the past quarter century. A teacher educator, curriculum theorist, supervisor, or classroom teacher just emerging from a Rip Van Winkle hibernation would be awe-struck by the new composition landscape.

Karen Spear (1993) has highlighted the work of 11 public school English teachers, grades 7 through 12, and their efforts to create communities of writers in *Peer Response Groups in Action: Writing Together in Secondary Schools*. Their major stratagem was the establishment of peer response groups as an ongoing activity throughout an entire school year. As an outgrowth of their initial involvement in a National Writing Project summer institute, these teachers developed a collaborative model that placed writing, especially drafting-sharing-revising, at the center of their courses of studies.

The distinguished English educator, Stephen Tchudi (1997) produced *Alternatives to Grading Student Writing*, a comprehensive review of recent research on grading papers. The bulk of this research argues against traditional "A through F" paper grading, and in summarizing it, Tchudi advocates a shift in the whole evaluation-of-writing paradigm. Subsequent essays describe workshop activity, peer response, revising, and portfolio alternatives, with a heavy emphasis on formative rather than summative practices. Plans of action appear in these essays—for individual classrooms, whole schools (middle and high), and total district reorganization of evaluation approaches.

The most visible advance in evaluation and assessment of student writing, however, has occurred in the literature describing portfolio development. Space limits prohibit a truly adequate review of the documents on portfolio use that have appeared in the decade of the 1990s; however, here are a representative few.

A 1995 edition of the *Iowa English Bulletin* was dedicated entirely to literacy portfolios and what makes them distinctive. In *Assessing Portfolios: A Portfolio*, Bonnie Sunstein and Julie Cheville (1998) gathered sundry descriptions of portfolio strategies created by classroom teachers and research from all over the country. Divided into five sections, the collection of statements explores important questions; e.g., "What is a reflective state of mind?" "How can portfolios foster such a mind set?" "What is the characteristic appearance of a portfolio-keeping classroom?" and others. Several of the responses to such questions are both ingenious and practical.

*Situating Portfolios: Functional Perspectives* by Kathleen Yancy and Irwin Weiser (1998) provides another collection of insights into the portfolio issue. In this text, the contributions of 31 writing teachers from diverse levels of instruction offer up-to-date thinking on the portfolio approach. Some important perspectives considered are the status of portfolios as hyper-text, the Web, and other electronic issues. Much of the discussion in these essays speaks to the need for all-department, all-school, and all-district conversion to the portfolio means of writing evaluation.

Kent Gill (1993) and other members of NCTE's Committee on Classroom Practices produced still another anthology of professional essays in *Process and Portfolios in Writing Instruction*. The classroom teachers contributing to this collection discuss ways in which portfolio establishment and peer involvement in assessment of student writing enhance student writers' self-confidence and develop sensitivity as to what is good writing among these young people. These teacher-authors also stress the need for student initiated topical choices as well as students' freedom in reworking their own drafts.

Geoff Hewitt, chair of Vermont's Writing Assessment Leadership Committee, has authored a significant monograph, *A Portfolio Primer: Teaching, Collecting, and Assessing Student Writing* (1994). He explores a broad range of uses for portfolios that can complement formal assessment of writing in all school subjects. In a step-by-step review of the writing process, Hewitt explains ways of guiding students in development of their *own* processes and contends that "the process" be reserved for only those products to which students feel substantial commitment. This text provides a considerable number of exemplary student writings as well as two portfolios reproduced in their entirety. The text also includes a variety of tools for formal and informal assessment. The student ownership factor is stressed throughout in relation to their writing.

Two classroom teachers from Mundelein, Illinois, Carol Porter and Janel Cleland, published *The Portfolio as a Learning Strategy* in 1994 the result of a collaborative effort which had

a duration of 6 years. Their school, a 7 through 12 institution, allowed them to implement portfolios at both the junior and senior high levels. Their text is a report of a trial-and-error experience with this approach. Their six chapters speak to the following issues:

- The reason for needing portfolios in the learning process.
- How portfolios can be used to support learning.
- The appropriate contents of a portfolio.
- The assembling of a portfolio.
- Uses of a completed portfolio.
- Related concerns teachers may harbor about portfolios.

The text provides an in-depth look at the instructional framework of a student-centered classroom. The authors support several generalizations with concrete examples from student portfolios they have supervised and reviewed.

Easily one of the most lucid and persuasive texts on the whole assessment issue is Fran Claggett's *A Measure of Success: From Assignment to Assessment in English Language Arts* (1996). Chapters include lengthy discussions assigning/assessing reading and writing as well as one structuring and assessing integrated projects. Her treatment of portfolios, however, is arguably the high point in the entire text. She summarizes the several facets of portfolios assessment, contrasting *Formative* and *Showcase* portfolios (pp. 132–133):

---

Formative Portfolios for classroom or personal use

**Purpose:** to show student growth or progress in a given area(s); purpose established by student and/or teacher

**Audience:** most often known to the portfolio creator, often consisting of peers, teacher, parents, and/or others whom the student may choose

**Artifacts:** may include pieces of work that the student may not choose to display publicly—pieces that are appropriate to this portfolio because they offer benchmarks from which growth can be measured or because they represent a turning point in a student's learning, though they may not show a pinnacle of achievement

**Structure:** arranged according to student/teacher purposes; contains a cover, a table of contents, a preface or introductory letter, selected artifacts, and a final reflective piece; may include artifacts other than written documents, e.g., tapes, graphics, photographs

**Reflection:** focuses on processes in which students engaged as they completed each work and examines their new perceptions as they re-vision it for inclusion in this particular portfolio; helps establish and maintain focus by explaining how each slection adds to the pictures students are building of their growth and learning; includes self-assessment, exploring the degree of participation and the quality of performance represented by each selection; often exploratory in tone, reflective piece may consider how entries show patterns of learning and speculate on direction of future growth

**Assessment:** external assessment is largely holistic and response-based; focuses on the extent to which students fulfill their stated purpose; may include, in addition to the final reflective piece, a measure of self-assessment threaded throughout; self-assessment is taken into account by those assessing the portfolio as a whole; generally assessment is performed by people known to the portfolio creator

Showcase Portfolios for classroom or large-scale assessment

**Purpose:** to show student accomplishment in a pre-determined area(s); provides a showcase of work; purpose established externally (by district, state, national assessor, employer, etc.)

**Audience:** a wider, more public audience than that of the classroom portfolio; audience may consist of people unknown to the portfolio creator

**Artifacts:** will most likely showcase only the student's best works of required types or evidence of required performances

**Structure:** arranged according to specifications set up by the assessment body

**Reflections:** focuses on the importance of the required artifacts and/or how each selection shows evidence of accomplishment; may show how each entry adds to the picture students are creating of themselves; may include some discussion of the processes that went into the final construction of each selection or into the selection process itself

**Assessment:** external assessment is largely analytical; portfolios are measured against pre-established purposes and externally imposed standards; may be assigned several different scores reflecting degree of achievement in specific areas (e.g., reading, writing, scientific method, etc.) as well as effectiveness of portfolio as a whole; often assessment is performed by people unknown to the portfolio creator

---

In the middle grades, as well as at higher levels throughout the U.S., portfolio assessment in English language arts classrooms has come to the fore. This expansion of paper evaluation is possibly the most prominent of the several progressive practices cited in this summary. To wax metaphoric, the past quarter century has seen the teaching and evaluation of writing in middle grades classrooms move from a position of under the rug to the front burner of pedagogical considerations.

## ASSESSMENT/EVALUATION

The following discussion of assessment/evaluation (A/E) events of the past decade will be somewhat abbreviated. In actuality, this topic has permeated virtually all previous segments of this chapter. The descriptions of such important topics as Reading Rescue and Portfolio Assessment need not be discussed further. In a certain sense, even the consideration of censorship has a direct connection with A/E. When citizens raise questions and/or complaints about the appropriateness of materials in classrooms or school libraries, they are offering assessments of vital factors in teachers' teaching and students' learning.

The review of professional literature/research on portfolio introduction into middle grade (and other level) writing classes serves as an effective transition to the A/E consideration; it represents a recent, growing, and much discussed alternative to narrow, quantitative, analytic approaches to grading the papers of student writers. The status of that writing assessment in U.S. schools, in terms of cumulative research, was compiled by Brian Hurst (1998, Summer) in "The Literature of Direct Writing Assessment: Major Problems and Prevailing Trends". Hurst reflected on current data as they define important issues and reveal trends useful to classroom teachers and teacher educators. In this follow-up to the influential research-in-writing reviews

of Braddock et al. (1963), and Hillocks (1986), the author has included studies on middle/junior high populations with his total coverage of kindergarten through college. He generally supported the contentions of Braddock et al.: "Today's research in composition, taken as a whole, may be compared with chemical research as it emerged from the alchemy era." (p. 237) He confirms that practice runs far ahead of theory; that models differ greatly and tend to be situational, arbitrary, and highly subjective across the curricular spectrum.

In a more recent analysis, *Reflections on Assessment: Its Purposes, Methods, and Effects on Learning*, Strickland and Strickland (1998) have presented middle grade and high school teachers with a comprehensive picture of student-centered A/E. The authors examined practical strategies that have yielded generally positive results and thus offer teachers several practical ideas for implementing student-centered assessment work that is nevertheless based on behavioristic principles.

James Moffett's *Detecting Growth in Language* (1992) zeroes in on encouraging teachers to assess for themselves their students' improvement in several areas of linguistic capacity instead of submitting to the often politicized results of standardized testing. Moffett describes a wide panoply of language behaviors of young people and suggests a series of lucid, persuasive strategies teachers can use to measure growth in those behaviors, e.g., portfolios, projects, peer responses, and publication.

The two major organizations sponsoring this compendium have produced three major documents during the decade of the 1990s that feature significant aspects of A/E. In 1992, IRA published *Standards for Reading Professionals*, a result of efforts made by the Professional Standards and Ethics Committee of the National Council for Accreditation in Teacher Education (NCATE) Joint Task Force. It produced a set of guidelines and evaluation standards for reading professionals, private and state agencies, policymakers at all levels, and the general public.

NCTE and IRA co-published *Standards for Assessment in Reading and Writing* (1994). This document sets out guidelines based on the work of the Joint Task Force on Assessment. It describes sound decisions about assessing the teaching and learning of reading and writing, all of which have been based on the accumulation and analysis of research and scholarship gathered to date on best classroom practices and A/E instruments in the overall area of young peoples' language growth.

In a three-book series, *Assessing Student Performance: Grades K–5, 6–8, and 9–12*, editors Miles Myers and Elizabeth Spalding (1995) have illustrated the several ways in which the NCTE–IRA standards for the English language arts have become, and are, embodied in student work throughout the U.S. The series also includes descriptions of learning tasks, samples of students' work, rubrics for describing a range of varying achievement levels of middle grade students, and commentaries that consider the relationship of each student sample produced to its pertinent rubric.

No review of recent research on A/E in North American schools would be complete without some coverage of work in progress of the National Assessment of Educational Progress (NAEP). During the decades of the 1970s and 1980s, the NAEP assessors tested representative groups of U.S. third, sixth, ninth, and twelfth grade students, plus a cohort of volunteer adults, on a series of educational topics: civics, natural science, history, mathematics, and the like. Needless to say, two of the areas assessed were those of reading and writing. In the 1990s, four assessments were completed. In the Introduction to *Reading Framework for the 1992 and 1994 NAEP*, the directors state:

Reading is the most important, fundamental ability taught in the nation's schools. It is vital to society and to the people within it. It is the door to knowledge and a capability that can liberate people both intellectually and personally.

For more than 20 years, the National Assessment of Educational Progress (NAEP) has been reporting the reading achievement of students in the United States. Known in recent years as "The Nation's Report Card," NAEP reports provide descriptive information about student strengths and weaknesses in reading and a number of other subjects. They provide data that compare groups of students by race and ethnicity, gender, type of community, and region, as well as data that chart trends in achievement over time. Relationships between student achievement and school-related experiences such as homework and instruction are also reported.

Beginning in 1990, a significant change occurred in how and for whom NAEP results are reported. On a trial basis, the 1990 NAEP Mathematics assessment collected information to provide "state report cards" that allow state-to-nation and state-to-state comparisons. In 1992, the NAEP Reading assessment included state-level reporting, on a trial basis, of fourth grade results. For 1994, reading will be assessed again at the national and state levels (National Reading Consensus Project, 1994).

In a report issued 2 years later, NAEP issued the following table of results: (See Table 1, *Report in Brief: NAEP 1996 Trends in Academic Progress, August 1997—Percentages of Students Performing At or Above Reading Performance Levels, Ages 9, 13, 17, 1971 and 1996*)

And, in relation to writing profiles, NAEP has collected these data: (See Table 2, *Report in Brief: NAEP 1996 Trends in Academic Progress, August 1997—Percentages of Students Performing At or Above Writing Performance Levels, Grades 4, 8, and 11, 1971 and 1996*)

Clearly, students in the middle grades, age 13 in reading and grade 8 in writing, have made some progress from 1994 to 1996 although the increases in both areas cannot truly be considered dramatic.

Statewide testing remains a significant fact of American educational life. While the nature of the tests has changed considerably over the past 20 years, the nationwide concern about the basic skills of reading, writing, and computation remains strong. Rather than attempt to review statewide assessment programs in their current forms, the authors of this chapter have chosen to illustrate these newer protocols with two of those now in use in the state of Florida. Two reasons for this choice are: it was Florida that started the statewide basic skills ball rolling in the fall of 1977; and the authors are both state of Florida university system employees, both of whom teach at an institution that is located in the state capital. Thus, they have the advantage of "being where the action is" in all state-initiated education programs.

In 1992, *Florida Writes!*, a statewide product writing test was introduced. Previous attempts to institute such an apparatus had been cancelled in 1979 and 1985. State legislators, however, were eventually persuaded that a writing test that actually contained student writing was of vital importance in the total testing paradigm. In the introduction to the current edition of *Florida Writes! A Report on the 1998 Assessment* (1998), the following descriptive statement can be found:

Florida's direct writing assessment can best be described as demand writing. Demand writing assessments are completed within a designated time period (e.g., 45 minutes) and involve the scoring of student responses to assigned topics. This kind of assessment has been used in classrooms (e.g., essay questions on a social studies test), in several large-scale assessments (e.g., National Assessment of Educational Progress [NAEP], the Scholastic Aptitude Test [SAT], and the American College Testing Program [ACT], and by many employers during the job interview process. For a statewide assessment, demand writing involves limited preparation time for students and teachers and less time and money to score than project or portfolio assessments. (See Appendix B for definitions of project and portfolio assessments.)

The Florida Writing Assessment Program has adopted demand writing as an efficient and effective method of assessing Florida's eighth graders. For this program, students are expected to produce within a 45-minute time period a focused, organized, supported *draft* response to an assigned topic.

Students' success in writing can be enhanced by giving them frequent opportunities to express themselves through writing, beginning in kindergarten. The skill of effective writing cannot be taught in several easy lessons. A curriculum that consistently emphasizes reading and the use of spoken and written language in all subject areas and all grade levels will increase students' ability to write effectively for a variety of purposes.

Appendix C contains suggestions for how district- and school-level administrators, teachers, and parents or guardians can help prepare students for the assessment (p. 2).

For a number of years, critics of the testing program, especially those groups representing specific, vested interests, had raised numerous complaints about the nature and implications of writing prompts developed by test makers. Concerns with privacy invasion, racial/ethnic/religious, regional biases, exceeding the background limits of writers found voice in these complaints. These dissenting feelings were frequently leveled at the eighth-grade component, given (the dissidents' claim) the low correlation between the sophistication of the students and the abstruse nature of the prompts. To answer these concerns, the *Florida Writes!* authors provided this descriptive statement:

The prompts for the 1998 assessment were carefully selected to ensure that the subject matter was interesting and appropriate for eighth grade students. In addition, prompts were reviewed for offensive or biased language relating to religion, gender, and racial or ethnic background.

All prompts were written with the assistance of members of the Eighth Grade Writing Assessment Advisory Committee and were pilot tested on a small group of students and then field tested on 1,000 students across the state. The development of the prompts is a continuing process. The Department will continue to write, review, pilot test, and field test additional prompts for measuring writing proficiency. See Appendix E for more information on the procedures used by the advisory committee to write and review prompts.

Prompts are written to elicit writing for specific purposes. For instance, expository prompts ask students to explain why or how, and persuasive prompts require students to convince a person to accept a point of view or to take a particular action.

Prompts have two basic components: the writing situation and the directions for writing. The writing situation orients students to the subject about which they are to write. The directions for writing set the parameters for writing, and in the case of persuasive prompts, identify the audience to whom the writing is to be directed.

Below is an example of an expository prompt. The first component orients the student to the topic: jobs or chores. The second component suggests that the student think about various jobs or chores and then explain why a particular job or chore is done.

<u>Writing Situation:</u>

*Everyone has jobs or chores.*

<u>Directions for Writing:</u>

*Think about why you do one of your jobs or chores.*
*Now explain why you do your job or chore. (Florida Writes!, p. 30)*

As this chapter is written, *Florida Writes!* has gained the general support of teachers, district officials, bureaucrats, and legislators throughout the Sunshine State.

Soon after the publication of *Florida Writes!*, the A/E section of the Florida Department of Education created, at the behest of the Florida Legislature, a new Basic Skills test battery to replace the statewide minimum competency/functional literacy apparatus that had been administered to all Florida public school students, grades 3, 5, 8, and 11, from 1977 through 1991. All of these earlier instruments were multiple choice in nature and the difficulty levels of their reading components were carefully controlled. The replacement battery, which focuses on reading, writing, and mathematical computation, was called the *Florida Comprehensive Assessment Test* (FCAT) and was directed at students in grades 4, 8, and 10.

In the reading section of the eighth-grade test, the psychometricians introduced two significant departures from the earlier one: (a) the reading difficulty levels were raised significantly, and (b) ten of the items demand that students write short responses, all reflecting critical reading skill. The test was piloted statewide in the fall of 1997 and was administered to fourth, eighth, and twelfth graders in the fall of 1998.

In the preamble found in the *Sample Reading Book, Grade 8* the following statements appear:

FCAT contains test items and performance tasks that are challenging for all students. The FCAT Reading Test contains passages from informational and literary texts. Some of these selections come from other content areas such as mathematics, science, social studies, foreign language, the arts, health education, and physical education.

Many of the test questions on FCAT are like those on other tests. FCAT includes multiple-choice questions and questions called "performance tasks." These performance tasks require using problem-solving strategies and thinking the questions through carefully.

Performance tasks ask you to think about an answer to a question and then write the answer. Some questions require short responses; however, others require longer, more detailed answers. Performance tasks are called "Read, Think, and Explain" questions in reading and "Think, Solve, and Explain" questions in math.

Recently, what students in Florida are expected to learn and be able to do has increased a great deal. The job market of today requires people who can read difficult and technical texts. FCAT is being given to measure achievement of the higher standards that are being taught to and learned by Florida students (*Florida Writes!*, pp. 1–4).

The issue of assessing the literacy of American middle graders, basic, functional, cultural, and—coming soon—computer,

will be high on the agendas of federal, state, and local officials. Moreover, through the miracle of contemporary media, the issue will be flashed to U.S. citizens from coast to coast, in perpetuity. Where it all will lead is anybody's guess; that it will continue to resonate is virtually an inevitability.

The degree to which politics affects testing programs can be found in the rejection of the California Learning Assessment System, Language Arts Component. In late 1994, funds requested for the continuation of this 9-year-long test development were vetoed by Republican Governor Pete Wilson. Dr. Sheridan Blau, the senior advisor of the Language Arts Test Development Team, reports in an essay on the demise of this reseach-based instrument. Following the work of the renowned English educator James Moffett, the test reflected contemporary thinking on the pedagogy of literacy. Its inclusion of reader response elements, the reading–writing connection, Moffett's discourse topology, holistic scoring, and open prompts about literary test, which allowed for personal reflection and critical thinking, reflected a connection among effective teaching strategies, recent research findings, and "real world" aspects of literary texts and student writing. It also followed the widely respected *California English Language Arts Frameworks* (1987). It was exhaustively field tested, revised, and validated over the 9-year process.

As the nature of the test became better known to California's citizenry, vocal opposition to its use grew:

In many cases . . . we discovered (much to our surprise—a measure of our naiveté) that for a significant segment of the public, any action represented in a literary work printed on a test was assumed to be endorsed not only by the author but by the authority of the testmaker—no matter how the act might be treated within the text, no matter what context might qualify it or moral judgment might implicitly or explicitly frame it. Similarly, all language uses represented in reading selections on the test were seen by many parents and public officials as exemplars for student use, including all passages of dialogue which might include speech in various non-standard dialects. Thus many parents seeing test forms with literary text that included realistic representations of the speech of speakers of non-standard dialects (including immigrant speakers speaking fractured English) objected to the fact that the tests (or any books that included such stories) were teaching their children to use improper English (Blau, 1998, p. 14).

While much of the opposition came from some of the right-wing, Fundamentalist Christian groups described earlier in this chapter, much greater opposition was raised by citizens with no such affiliations. The fact that this test did *not* conform to the traditional multiple choice, one right answer, orthodox linguistic tenets that had represented testing as *they* understood it, confused, rankled, and evoked hostility in large numbers of middle-of-the-road Californians. Their responses were widespread and usually vituperative. This was not lost on their state legislators who rose to attack the test with increasing vigor. The reaction caused Governor Wilson to kill it with his veto.

A stunned Sheridan Blau has analyzed the outcomes of this educational catastrophe in his essay:

Perhaps the most important lesson to be learned from the defeat of California's progressive reading assessment is one I have already alluded to about how wide the gap is between the way reading—particularly literary reading—is construed by well-informed professionals in the language arts and the way it is construed by the wider lay public, including most parents . . . We see other dimensions of the gap in the fact that what

The Professional View

1. *Reading is a transactional and experiential process.* Readers may be seen as engaged in a transaction with a text—a transaction to which they bring their own background knowledge, values, and prior experience (their culture) and, guided by the language and structure of the text, undergo a new experience out of which they construct a meaning for the text and a sense of its value to them (Rosenblatt, 1938, 1978).

2. *Meaning is negotiated and subject to change.* The meaning of a text is seen as something a reader arrives at through a problem-solving process, working with a text, asking questions, obtaining contextual and background information, and consulting other readers, including readers who may perceive the same text differently. Each construction of a sense of the meaning of a text is tentative because it is subject to change with subsequent and better informed and increasingly mature readings.

3. *Interpretations of texts are subject to evaluation by the criterion of plausibility.* Interpretations are always subject to challenge, and the process of adjudicating between competing interpretations is a process of weighing textual and contextual evidence.

4. *Critical reading (which is built on or follows from interpretive reading) may entail resistant reading* or reading against the ideological or ethical grain of a text. Strong readers often talk back to texts, challenging their ideology or values. Texts selected for study, including classic or canonical texts, command our attention, but not necessarily our belief or endorsement.

The Public's View

1. *Reading is essentially a process of information retrieval.* Texts give information. Readers may be said to understand a text when they can show that they have received the information given.

2. *The meaning of a text (especially canonical literary texts) is not negotiable or tentative*; it is known and fixed by authorities (who have usually discerned the intentions of authors). Teachers and other authorized sources (e.g., Cliff's Notes are responsible for transmitting these meanings to students and students are responsible for knowing them. That (and technical terms and description of technical elements about texts) is what constitutes literary knowledge and it is testable through multiple choice tests.

3. *Interpretations may be evaluated by the criterion of correctness.* Correct interpretations are those that represent (usually) the intentions of authors and that are known and transmitted by authorities.

4. *Critical reading means appreciating* the artistry of a work and its moral vision. All texts worthy enough to be taught are to be revered. And, (for a smaller yet still sizable segment of the public), whatever is textually represented is thereby endorsed. Furthermore, students may be said to be encouraged to imitate any action represented in an assigned or recommended text, because every action, thought, or event represented, even in a work of fiction, is at least tacitly recommended by the author and by the teacher or school that approves or requires the reading of the text (Blau, 1998, pp. 24-26).

the public found most suspect or objectionable in the CLAS reading test were the very features of the test that language arts professionals most valued.

We can characterize the difference between professional and public or popular conceptions of reading as representing two different and oppositional paradigms which apply to reading both as a private activity and as an academic discipline to be taught and evaluated. The oppositional character of these paradigms may be quickly and perhaps not reductively apprehended by the following chart, showing contrasting sets of assumptions or postulates.

The CLAS experience is one that all who are affiliated with the teaching and testing of the English Language Arts, *fin de siecle*, need to consider with careful scrutiny. Clearly, the matter of what should be tested—and how—is one on which the profession and the community-at-large are not in agreement. To conclude the A/E segment of this chapter, a summary of a study done by Simmons and Shafer (1994) on the attitudes of education and noneducation organizations toward such teaching. The data for this unfunded research were collected in the fall of 1992, at the height of the presidential campaign pitting Bill Clinton, then-President George Bush, and Ross Perot against each other. These results were gathered from a four-phase inventory instrument

that implemented the Likert Scale on questions based on the teaching of language, literature, and composition, as well as the English curriculum broadly conceived.

The "Professional Education" list contained 20 organizations such as Pi Lambda Theta, Phi Delta Kappa, National Education Association, National School Board Association, as well as NCTE and IRA. The "Noneducation" group included 20 organizations, among which were the National Organization of Women, Eagle Forum, Chamber of Commerce (USA), People for the American Way, and the John Birch Society. The "Noneducation" group was subdivided, arbitrarily (and admittedly subjectively and unscientifically), into two groups labeled *liberal* and *conservative*. Given the rudimentary procedures used and the ultramodest expenditures made, the researchers were gratified at the 77% return they could report. Briefly, what follows are the results of comparisons between aggregate response of the "Noneducation" (NE) and "Professional Education" (PE) groups, as well as those drawn between the *liberal* and *conservative* designees in the NE organizations:

1. The NE and PE groups held remarkably similar attitudes toward the teaching of literature. Their differences were more

pronounced on composition issues and even more pronounced on general English language arts matters. Their most notable differences could be seen in their attitudes toward the teaching of the English language with the NE group, much more traditionally oriented, as a whole, than the PE group.

2. Within the NE ranks, there were discernible differences between the sub group labeled *conservative* and the one identified as *liberal*. The former group was visibly committed to teaching of Latinate grammar and largely skeptical of sociolinguistic topics for the classroom. They favored formal, scholarly writing over more personal choices, and they were somewhat more ambivalent on students and teachers being granted freedom of choice in their reading. Moreover, they manifested a certain wariness of the inclusion of multicultural texts (being widely introduced to the young people of the decade) in the literature bill of fare. In general, the NE group as a whole, and the *conservative* cluster in particular favored a Eurocentric approach to cultural literacy and showed a greater commitment to time-honored texts and teaching practices as compared to the PE group. Those organizations taken together, however, were somewhat leery of a significant number of innovative practices and contemporary text offerings.

3. All groups demonstrated a lack of awareness of recent research on the teaching/learning practices in the discipline, particularly as they relate to traditional approaches. This lack of knowledge was most evident in the linguistic component and was only somewhat less so in the teaching and evaluating of writing. This finding certainly corroborated the concerns expressed by numerous English and reading educators since World War II—that dissemination and acceptance of significant published research is badly lacking within the profession, especially among classroom teachers.

The summary of conclusions presented represents the thinking of those who are concerned about the education (specifically, *English* education) of tomorrow's citizens of the U.S.—both leaders and followers. With all the standards created in the 1990s by so many education agencies (among them NCTE, IRA, and NCATE), there promises to be a wealth of English/reading research to sift through before the 21st century gets very far down the road.

## CONCLUSION

While puberty is a specific period of physical change, adolescence is much more difficult to define and delimit. Sebald (1992) states, "Adolescence is an invention of modern civilization. It lacks the universality and naturalness that are innate to such stauses as childhood and adulthood" (p. 1). He points out that adolescence, in American society, has become an indeterminate span of time during which society expects to see "poorly defined expectations and corresponding behavior" (p. 2). He further points out that in the United States, "there are no rituals signifying the termination of childhood and entry into adulthood" that in some societies, "provide guidance to the individual and serve as an integrative function for society" (p. 3). This point is echoed by child and adolescent development expert David Elkind, who provides evidence in *All Grown Up and No Place to Go: Teenagers in Crisis* (1998), that the markers that once signaled the beginning of adolescence, such as when it is appropriate to wear sophisticated clothing, and that marked the end of adolescence, such as graduating from postsecondary school, are now missing from American society. These stances correspond with the findings of J. Schulenberg and A. T. Ebata (1994) who, in a comparison of adolescence in the United States with adolescence in other countries, conclude that, "the period of adolescence in the United States has been getting longer, because it is starting earlier and, for most, ending later"; the result is that "our young people are spending more years in a period of semi-independence, where they have many adulthood freedoms without many of the traditional adulthood commitments and responsibilities" (p. 428). Wolman (1998) refers to earlier entry into adolescence during the 20th century as the "secular trend" (p. 11). For teachers, ambiguity about the time that adolescence begins and ends is translated into confusion in terms of appropriate curricula, activities, and even expectations for the youth in classes.

Hamburg (1994) envisions middle schools as those in which "The physical, social, and emotional changes of adolescence intersect with the new intellectual tasks and organizational structure" (p. 184). Teachers of language arts in the middle grades have a challenging responsibility; they must work with parents and administrators to create schools that encourage the growth of young adolescents; they must understand and recognize the physical, psychosocial, intellectual, and moral traits that are characteristic of early adolescence, and attend to the individual differences in life situations of their students. They must continually update their knowledge of research and practices in the teaching of written composition, literature, reading, oral language, media, and critical thinking, as well as teaching strategies including interdisciplinary instruction, collaborative learning, and technology-enhanced instruction. They must integrate each of these aspects of teaching in order to make curricular, instructional, and evaluative decisions based not only on their subject expertise and pedagogical knowledge, but also on their understanding of how young adolescents think, and how environments and instruction are best organized to promote the development of young adolescents.

## *References*

Abrahamson, R. F. (1997). Collected wisdom: The best articles ever written on young adult literature and teen reading. *English Journal, 86*(7), 50–54.

Albaugh, P. R. (1997). Using a CD-ROM encyclopedia: Interaction of teachers, middle school students, and library media specialists. *Research in Middle Level Education Quarterly, 20*(3), 43–55.

Alexander, W., & McEwin, C. K. (1988). *Preparing to teach at the middle level.* Columbus, OH: National Middle School Association.

Alexander, W., & McEwin, C. K. (1989). *Schools in the middle: Status and progress.* Columbus, OH: National Middle School Association.

Alexander, W. M., Williams, E. L., Compton, M., Hines, V. A., & Prescott, D. (1968). *The emergent middle school.* New York: Holt, Rinehart & Winston.

Allington, R. L. (2001). What really matters for struggling readers: Designing research-based programs. New York: Addison Wesley Longman.

Alm, R. S. (1954). *A study of assumptions concerning human experience underlying certain works of fiction written for and about adolescence.* Unpublished Ph.D. dissertation: University of Minnesota.

Ames, N. L., & Miller, E. (1994). *Changing middle schools: How to make schools work for young adolescents.* San Francisco: Jossey-Bass.

Arnold, J., & Stevenson, C. (1998). *Teacher's handbook on teaming.* Fort Worth: Harcourt Brace.

*Attacks on the Freedom To Learn.* (1988–1996). Washington, DC: People for the American Way.

Atwell, N. (1998). *In the middle: New understandings about writing, reading, and learning* (2nd ed.). Portsmouth, NH: Boynton/Cook and Heinemann.

Atwell, N. (1987). *In the middle: Writing, reading, and learning with adolescents.* Portsmouth, NH: Boynton/Cook.

Atwell, N. (1998). *In the middle: Writing, reading, and learning with adolescents* (2nd ed.). Westport, CT: Heinemann-Boynton/Cook.

Baines, L. (1994). Cool books for tough guys. *The ALAN Review, 22*(1), 43–46.

Baines, L. (1997, March). "Future schlock." *Phi Delta Kappan, 28*(7), 492–498.

Baines, L. (1998). The future of the written word. In J. Simmons & L. Baines (Eds.), *Language study in middle school, high school, and beyond: Views on enhancing the study of language* (pp. 190–214). Newark, DE: International Reading Association.

Banker, D. C. (1995). Too real for fiction: Abortion themes in YA literature. *The ALAN Review, 23*(1), 19–23.

*Banned books* (1998). Chicago: American Library Association.

Beane, J. A. (1993). *Middle school curriculum: From rhetoric to reform* (2nd ed.). Columbus, OH: NMSA.

Beers, K., & Samuels, B. G. (1998). *Into focus: Understanding and creating middle school readers.* Norwood, MA: Christopher-Gordon.

Belanoff, P., & Dickson, M. (1991). *Portfolios: Process and product.* Westport, CT: Heinemann-Boynton/Cook.

Bennett, G. V. (1926). *The junior high school* (Rev. ed.). Baltimore: Warick & York.

Bishop, W. (Ed.) (1993). *The subject is writing: Essays by teachers and students.* Westport, CT: Heinemann-Boynton/Cook.

Black, L., Daiker, D., Sommers, J., & Stygall, G. (Eds.) (1994). *New directions in portfolio assessment: Reflective practice, critical theory, and large-scale scoring.* Westport, CT: Heinemann-Boynton/Cook.

Blanchard, J. (1995). Technology in middle school reading education: Opportunities to transform the classroom. *Computers in the Schools, 11*(3), 79–91.

Blau, S. (1998). *Politics and the English language arts.* Unpublished essay. Santa Barbara: University of California.

Blau, S., & Elbow, P. (1992). *Writer's craft.* Chicago: McDougal Little.

Blau, S., Elbow, P., & Killgallon, D. (1993). *The Writer's craft: Idea to expression.* Evanston, IL: MacDougall Littell.

Blount, Nathan S. (1963). *The effects of certain junior novels and selected adult novels on student attitudes toward the "ideal" novel.* Unpublished Ph.D. dissertation. Florida State University.

Bomer, R. (1995). *Time for meaning: Crafting literate lives in middle and high school.* Westport, CT: Heinemann-Boynton/Cook.

Braddock, R., Lloyd-Jones, R., & Schoer, L. (1963). *Research in written composition.* Urbana, IL: National Council of Teachers of English.

Brand, A. G., & Graves, R. L. (1994). *Presence of mind: Writing and the domain beyond the cognitive.* Westport, CT: Heinemann-Boynton/Cook.

Britton, J., Shafer, R. E., & Watson, K. (Eds.) (1990). *Teaching and learning English worldwide.* Clevedon, England: Multilingual Matters.

Brown, Bradford B., Lohr, Mary Jane, Trujillo, & Carla (1990). "Multiple Crowds and Multiple Life Styles: Adolescents' Perceptions of Peer-Group Stereotypes," in Rolf E. Muuss (Ed.), *Adolescent behavior and society: A book of readings* (4th ed.), (pp. 30–36). NY: McGraw-Hill.

Brown, J. E., & Stephens, E. C. (Eds.) (1998). *United in diversity: Using multicultural young adult literature in the classroom.* Urbana, IL: NCTE.

Brown, J., Goodman, K. S., & Marek, A. M. (Eds.) (1996). *Studies in miscue analysis: An annotated bibliography.* Westport, CT: Heinemann-Boynton/Cook.

Brumberg, J. J. (1997). *The body project: An intimate history of American girls.* New York: Random House.

Burress, L., & Jenkins, E. (1983). *The students' right to know.* Urbana, IL: National Council of Teachers of English.

Burress, L. (1989). *The battle of the books: Literary censorship in the public schools.* Metuchen, NJ: Scarecrow Press.

Bushman, J. H., & Bushman, K. P. (1996). *Using young adult literature in the English classroom* (2nd ed.). New York: Prentice Hall.

California Department of Education (1987). *California English Language Arts Framework.* Sacramento: California Department of Education.

Carlsen, G. R. (1968). *Books and the teen-age reader: A guide for teachers, librarians, and parents.* New York: Bantam.

Carlson, S., & Messier, A. (1997). Where there's a will, there's a play. *Voices From the Middle, 4*(2), 11–15.

Carnegie Council on Adolescent Development (1989). *Turning points: Preparing American youth for the 21st century.* New York: Carnegie Corporation.

Carnegie Council on Adolescent Development (1996). *Great transitions: Preparing adolescents for a new century.* New York: Carnegie Corporation of New York.

Carroll, P. S. (1994). Dancing with YA lit: Review of a year's work. *The ALAN Review, 22*(1), 56–65.

Carroll, P. S., Gregg, G. P., & Watts, E. (1995). Seeking our students in literature: Teachers' perspectives. *The ALAN Review, 23*(1), 48–54.

Cart, M. (1996). *From romance to realism: 50 Years of growth and change in young adult literature.* New York: HarperCollins.

Caspi, A. (1995). Puberty and the gender organization of schools: How biology and social context shape the adolescent experience. In L. Crockett & A. C. Crouter (Eds.), *Pathways Through Adolescence: Individual development in relation to social contexts* (pp. 57–74). Mahwah, NJ: Lawrence Erlbaum Associates.

*Censorship news* (1990–1998). New York: National Coalition Against Censorship.

*Censorship: Managing the controversy* (1990). Washington, DC: National School Board Association.

Chevalier, M., & Houser, N. O. (1997). Preservice teachers' multicultural self-development through adolescent fiction. *Journal of Adolescent and Adult Literacy, 40*(6), 426–436.

Claggett, F. (1996). *A measure of success: From assignment to assessment in the English language arts.* Westport, CT: Heinemann-Boynton/Cook.

Claggett, F., Reid, L., & Vinz, R. (1996). *Learning the landscape: Inquiry-based activities for comprehending and composing.* Westport, CT: Heinemann-Boynton/Cook.

Coles, R. E. (1997). *The youngest parents: Teenage pregnancy as it shapes lives.* Durham, NC: Center for Documentary Studies, in association with New York: W. W. Norton.

Combs, M. (1997). *Developing competent readers and writers in the middle grades.* Upper Saddle River, NJ: Merrill.

Commission on English of the College Entrance Examination Board (1965). *Freedom and discipline in English.* Princeton, NJ: College Entrance Examination Board.

*Common ground* [pamphlet] (1992). Newark, DE: International Reading Association.

*Content reading and learning strategies* (1996). Boston: Allyn-Bacon.

Cramer, E. H., & Castle, M. (1994). *Fostering the love of reading: The affective domain in reading education.* Newark, DE: International Reading Association.

Crawley, S. C., & Mountain, L. (1995). *Strategies for guiding content reading.* Newark, DE: International Reading Association.

Cremin, L. A. (1969). *American education: From servitude to service.* Pondview Books.

Crockett, L. J., & Crouter, A. C. (Eds.) (1995). *Pathways through adolescence: Individual development in relation to social contexts.* Mahwah, NJ: Lawrence Erlbaum Associates.

Crouter, A. C. (1995). *Pathways through adolescence: Individual development in relation to social contexts.* Mahwah, NJ: Lawrence Erlbaum Associates.

Davies, M. A. (1995). The ideal middle level teacher. In M. Wavering (Ed.), *Educating young adolescents: Life in the middle* (pp. 95-101). New York: Garland.

Davis, J. E. (1967). "The Junior Novel: 1960-1965: More of the Same." Unpublished graduate paper. Florida State University.

Davis, J. E. (1967). *The well written junior novel,* 1959-1966. Unpublished manuscript, Florida State University, Tallahassee.

Davis, J. E. (Ed.) (1979). *Dealing with censorship.* Urbana, IL: National Council of Teachers of English.

Davis, T. (1997). On the question of integrating young adult literature into the mainstream. *The ALAN Review, 24*(3), 5-8.

DeCarlo, J. (1995). "Precepts in Whole Language: Review and Analysis." J. de Carlo (Ed.), *Perspectives in whole language* (pp. 109-116). Boston, MA: Allyn-Bacon.

Dimmitt, J. P. (1993). More on model writers in adolescent literature. *The ALAN Review, 21*(1), 26-29.

DiPardo, A., & Freedman, S. W. (1988, Summer). Peer response groups in writing classrooms: Theoretical foundations and new directions. *Review of Educational Research,* 119.

Dixon, J. (1967). *Growth through English: A report based on the Dartmouth seminar 1966.* National Association for Teaching English.

Dole, J., Duffy, G., Roehler, L., & Pearson, P. D. (1991, Summer). Moving from the old to the new: Research in written comprehension instruction. *Review of Educational Research,* 239-243.

Donelson, K. L., & Nilsen, A. P. (1993). *Literature for today's young adults* (4th ed.). Glenview, IL: Scott, Foresman.

Donelson, K. L. (1972). *The students' right to read.* Urbana, IL: National Council of Teachers of English.

Due, L. (1995). *Joining the tribe: Growing up gay and lesbian in the 90s.* New York: Anchor.

Duffy, G. R. (Ed.) (1990). *Reading in middle school* (2nd ed.). Newark, DE: International Reading Association.

Dunning, S. A. (1959). *A definition of the role of the junior novel based on analyses of 30 selected junior novels.* Unpublished Ph.D. dissertation, Florida State University.

Durst, K., & Newell, T. (1989, Winter). Uses of fiction: James Britton's category system and research on writing. *Review of Educational Research,* 375.

Eastman, S. T., & Hollingsworth, H. L. (1997). Homes more high tech than schools? *Educational Technology, 37*(6), 46-51.

Eichhorn, D. (1966). *The middle school.* New York: Center for Applied Research in Education.

Elbow, P. (1990). *What is English?* New York: Modern Language Association and National Council of Teachers of English.

Elkind, D. (1998). *All grown up and no place to go: Teenagers in crisis* (Rev. Ed.). Reading, MA: Addison-Wesley.

Epstein, J. L., & Maciver, D. J. (1990). *Education in the middle grades: Overview of national policies and trends.* Columbus, OH: National Middle School Association.

Epstein, J. L., & Maciver, D. J. (1992). *Opportunities to learn: Effects on eighth-graders of curriculum offerings and instructional approaches. Report# 34.* Baltimore: Johns Hopkins University, Center for Research on Effective Schooling for Disadvantaged Students.

Erb, T. O., & Doda, N. M. (1989). *Team organization—practices and possibilities.* Washington, DC: National Education Association. (Analysis and Action Series)

Erickson, B. O. (1995). At home with multicultural adolescent literature. *The ALAN Review, 23*(1), 44-46.

Evans, W. R. (1961). *Superior junior novels versus* Silas Marner. Unpublished Ph.D. dissertation. Florida State University.

Farrell-Childers, P., Gere, A. R., & Young, A. (1994). *Programs and practices: Writing across the secondary school curriculum.* Westport, CT: Heinemann-Boynton/Cook.

*FCAT sample reading book, Grade 8* (1997). Tallahassee, FL: Florida Dept. of Education.

Finegan, E. T. (1980). *Attitudes toward English usage: The war of words.* New York: Teachers College Press.

Flavell, J. (1963/1985). *The developmental psychology of Jean Piaget.* New York, NY: Van Nostrand Reinhold.

Flood, J. et al. (Eds.) (1996). *Content reading and learning: Instructional strategies.* Boston, MA: Allyn Bacon.

Florida Department of Education (1987). A guide to statewide assessment. Tallhassee, FL: Florida Department of Education, 21.

*Florida writes! Report on the 1998 assessment* (1998). Tallahassee, FL: Florida Dept. of Education.

Fogarty, R. (Ed.) (1996). *Student portfolios: A collection of articles.* Palatine, IL: IRF/Skyline Training and Publishing.

Foster, H. M. (1998). Reading and writing in the shadow of film and television. In J. Simmons & L. Baines (Eds.), *Language study in middle school, high school, and beyond: Views on enhancing the study of language* (pp. 167-189). Newark, DE: International Reading Association.

Foster, H. (1994). *Crossing over: Whole language for secondary English teachers.* Ft. Worth, TX: Harcourt Brace.

*Freedom and discipline in English.* (196: Princeton, NJ: Commission on English of the College Entrance Examination Board.

Fulwiler, T. (1994). *The journal book.* Westport, CT: Heinemann-Boynton/Cook.

Gaskins, R. (1996, Fall). That's just how it is: The effect of issue-related emotional involvement in reading comprehension. *Reading Research Quarterly,* 386-405.

George, P. S., & Alexander, W. M. (1993). *The exemplary middle school* (2nd ed.). New York: Harcourt Brace.

George, P. S., & Stevenson C. (1989). The "Very Best Teams" in the Very Best Schools as Described by Middle School Principals. *TEAM, 3*(5), 6-14.

Gere, A. R., Fairbanks, C., Howes, A., Roop, L., & Schaafsma, D. (1992). *Language and reflection: An integrated approach to teaching English.* New York: Macmillan.

Gere, A. R., & Smith, E. (1972). *Attitudes, language and change.* Urbana, IL: National Council of Teachers of English.

Gill, K. (Ed.) (1993). *Process and portfolios in writing instruction.* Urbana, IL: National Council of Teachers of English.

Gilligan, C. (1990). New maps of development: New visions of maturity. In R. E. Muuss (Ed.), *Adolescent behavior and society: A book of readings* (4th ed.) (pp. 101-111). New York: McGraw-Hill.

Ginsberg, H., & Opper, S. (1969). *Piaget's theory of intellectual development: An introduction.* Engelwood Cliffs, NJ: Prentice-Hall.

Giroux, H. A. (1997). *Channel surfing: Race talk and the destruction of today's youth.* New York: St. Martin's.

Giroux, H. A. (1996). *Fugitive cultures: Race, violence, and youth.* New York: Routledge.

Glatthorn, A. (1971). *Dynamics of language.* Boston: D. C. Heath.

Glatthorn, A. A., & Spencer, N. K. (1986). *Middle school/junior high principal's handbook.* Englewood Cliffs, NJ: Prentice-Hall.

Grinder, R. E. (1990). "The Promise of Critical Literacy for Irrelevant Adolescents," in R. Muuss (Ed.), *Adolescent behavior and society: Book of readings* (4th Ed.). New York: McGraw-Hill, 1990.

Hall, G. S. (1969). Adolescence. [Originally Published (1905) as Adolescence: Its psychology and its relations to physiology, anthropology, sociology, sex, crime, religion, and education.] New York: Arno Press and *The NY Times.*

Hamburg, D. (1994). *Today's children: Creating a future for a generation in crisis.* New York: Times Books of Random House.

Harris, V. J. (Ed.) (1993). *Teaching multicultural literature in grades K-8.* Norwood, MA: Christopher Gordon.

Hayakawa, S. I., & Hayakawa, A. (1990). *Language in thought and action* (5th ed.). New York: Harcourt Brace Jovanovich.

Heaven, P. (1994). *Contemporary adolescence: A social psychological approach.* South Melbourne, Australia: Macmillan.

Herber, H., & Nelson, J. (1995). *Teaching reading and reasoning in the content areas.* Englewood Cliffs, NJ: Prentice-Hall.

Herz, S. K., & Gallo, D. P. (1996). *From Hinton to Hamlet: Building Bridges between Young Adult literature and the classics.* Westport, CT: Greenwood.

Hewitt, G. (1994). *A portfolio primer: Teaching, collecting, and assessing student writing.* Westport, CT: Heinemann-Boynton/Cook.

Hillocks, G. S. (1986). *Research on written composition: New directions for teaching.* Urbana, IL: ERIC Clearinghouse on Reading and Communication Skills and the National Conference on Research in English.

Hipple, T., & Goza, E. (1998). It ain't only in books any more. In *Into focus: understanding and creating middle school readers* (pp. 363-373). Norwood, MA: Christopher-Gordon.

Hirsch, Jr., E. D. (1987). *Cultural literacy: What every American needs to know.* Boston: Houghton Mifflin.

Huizinga, D. (1995). Developmental sequences in delinquency: Dynamic typologies. In L. J. Crockett & A. C. Crouter (Eds.), *Pathways through adolescence: Individual development in relation to social contexts* (pp. 15-34). Mahwah, NJ: Lawrence Erlbaum Associates.

Hunter, S., & Wallace, R. (Eds.) (1995). *The place of grammar in writing instruction.* Westport, CT: Heinemann-Boynton/Cook.

Hurst, B. (1998, Summer). The literature of direct writing assessment: Major problems and prevailing trends. *Review of English Journal Research, 237.*

Irvin, J. L. (Ed.) (1992). *Transforming middle level education.* Needham Heights, MA: Allyn & Bacon.

Irvin, J. L. (1998). *Reading and the middle school student* (2nd ed.). Boston: Allyn & Bacon.

Jenkins, E., Matlock, J., & Slocum, T. (1995). Two approaches to vocabulary instruction: Teaching word meaning and practice in deriving word meaning from context. *Reading Research Quarterly,* 215-235.

Joseph, R. J. (1998). Is this really English?: Using young adult literature in an urban middle school. *Voices from the Middle, 5*(2), 21-25.

Kaplan, J. S. (1993). Merry Christmas Jeffrey Kaplan: A review of adolescent literature about contemporary judaism. *The ALAN Review, 21*(1), 18-25.

Karolides, N., Burress, L., & Kean, J. (1993). *Censored books: Critical viewpoints.* Metuchen, NJ: Scarecrow Press.

Kaywell, J. (Ed.) (1993). *Adolescent literature as a complement to the classics* (Vol. 1). Norwood, MA: Christopher-Gordon.

Kaywell, J. (Ed.) (1995). *Adolescent literature as a complement to the classics* (Vol. 2). Norwood, MA: Christopher-Gordon.

Kaywell, J. (Ed.) (1997). *Adolescent literature as a complement to the classics* (Vol. 3). Norwood, MA: Christopher-Gordon.

Kaywell, J., & Oropallo, K. (1998). Modernizing the study of history using young adult literature. *English Journal, 87*(5), 102-107.

Kaywell, J. (2000). *Adolescent literature as a complement to the classics* (Vol. 4). Norwood, MA: Christopher-Gordon.

Kent, R. (1995). *Room 109: The promise of a portfolio classroom.* Westport, CT: Heinemann-Boynton/Cook.

Killgallon, D. (1997). *Sentence composing for middle school: A worktext on sentence variety and maturity.* Westport, CT: Heinemann-Boynton/Cook.

Kirby, D., & Liner, T. (1998). *Inside out* (2nd ed.). Westport, CT: Heinemann-Boynton/Cook.

Kohlberg, L. (1990). The cognitive-developmental approach to education. In R. E. Muuss (Ed.), *Adolescent behavior and society: A book of readings* (4th ed.), (pp. 91-101). New York: McGraw-Hill.

Koos, L. V. (1920). *The junior high school.* New York: Harcourt, Brace & Howe.

Kozol, J. (1995). *Amazing grace: The lives of children and the conscience of a nation.* New York: HarperCollins.

Krug, J. (Ed.) (1988-1998). *Newsletter on intellectual freedom.* Chicago: American Library Association.

Kutz, E. (1996). *Language and literacy: Studying discourse in communities and classrooms.* Westport, CT: Heinemann-Boynton/Cook.

Land, M. (1997). Helping teachers integrate internet resources into the curriculum. *NASSP Bulletin, 81*(592), 59-65.

Lapp, D., Flood, J., & Farman, N. (1996). *Content area reading and learning: Instructional strategies* (2nd ed.). Boston: Allyn & Bacon.

Lee, N. G., & Neal, J. C. (1993, January). Reading rescue: Intervention for a student 'at promise.' *Journal of Reading,* 276-282.

Lipsitz, J., Jackson, A. W., & Austin, L. M. (1997). What works in middle-grades school reform. *Phi Delta Kappan, 78*(7), 517-556.

Lounsbury, J. H. (1992). *Connecting the curriculum through interdisciplinary instruction.* Columbus, OH: National Middle School Association.

MacCrorie, K. (1996). *Uptaught* (2nd ed.). Westport, CT: Heinemann-Boynton/Cook.

Madden, N. A., Slaven, R. E., & Stevens, R. J. (1986). *Cooperative integrated reading and composition: teacher's manual.* Baltimore, MD: Center for Research on Elementary and Middle Schools, Johns Hopkins University.

Manning, M. L. (1993). *Developmentally appropriate middle level schools.* Wheaton, MD: Association for Childhood Education International.

Marum, E. (Ed.) (1996). *Children and books in the modern world.* London: The Falmer Press.

Mattson, D. P. (1997). Finding your way home: Orphan stories in young adult literature. *The ALAN Review, 24*(3), 17-21.

Maxwell, R. J., & Meiser, M. J. (1997). *Teaching english in middle and secondary schools* (2nd ed.). Upper Saddle River, NJ: Merrill.

Maxwell, J. (1996). *Writing across the curriculum for middle and high schools.* Boston: Allyn & Bacon.

Mayher, J. (1990). *Uncommon sense: Theoretical practice in language education.* Portsmouth, NH: Heinemann-Boynton/Cook.

McAlpine, G., Putney, D., & Warren, J. (1997). Opening texts: Student writing based on *Priscilla and the Wimps. The ALAN Review, 24*(3), 40-41.

McCann, T. (1989, February). Student argumentative writing knowledge and ability at three grade levels. In *Research in the Teaching of English* (p. 62). Urbana, IL: National Council of Teachers of English.

McEwin, C. K., Dickinson, T. C., & Jenkins, D. M. (1996). *America's middle schools: Practices and progress: A 25 year perspective.* Columbus, OH: NMSA.

Moffett, J. (1968). *Teaching the universe of discourse.* Boston, MA: Houghton Mifflin.

Moffett, J. (1988). *Storm in the mountains.* Carbondale, IL: Southern Illinois Press.

Moffett, J. (1992). *Detecting growth in language.* Westport, CT: Heinemann-Boynton/Cook.

Moffett, J., & Wagner, B. J. (1976). *Student centered language arts and reading.* Boston: Houghton Mifflin.

Moore, J. N. (1997). *Interpreting young adult literature: Literary theory in the secondary classroom.* Portsmouth, NH: Heinemann-Boynton/Cook.

Moorman, G., Blanton, W. B., & McLaughlin, T. (1994, Fall). The rhetoric of whole language. *Reading Research Quarterly,* 308–346.

*Motivating writing in middle school* (1996). Urbana, IL: National Council of Teachers of English.

Muller, A. P. (1973). *The current popular adolescent novel as transitional literature.* Unpublished Ph.D. dissertation. Florida State University.

Munde, G. (1997). Into the woods again: Three recent young adult novels of parental abandonment. *The ALAN Review, 24*(3), 22–26.

Muth, K. D., & Alvermann, D. E. (1992). *Teaching and learning in the middle grades.* Boston: Allyn & Bacon.

Myers, M., & Spalding, E. (Eds.) (1995). *Assessing student performances, Grades K–5, 6–8, and 9–12.* Urbana, IL: National Council of Teachers of English, Washington, DC: U.S. Dept. of Education.

National Board for Professional Teaching Standards (1993). *The early adolescence/generalist standards.* San Antonio, TX: Author.

National Council of Teachers of English (1997). "On Government Intrusion into Professional Decision Making." Resolution, annual business meeting, Detroit, IL, November, 1997.

National Council on Education Statistics (1995). *Digest of education statistics.* Washington, D.C: National Council on Education Statistics.

National Middle School Association (1995). *This we believe: Developmentally responsive middle level schools.* Columbus, OH: Author.

National Reading Consensus Project (1994). National Assessment of Educational Progress 1994: Trends in Academic Progress. Report in Brief. Washington, DC: U.S. Government Printing Office.

*National writing project annual report, 1996–97* (1997). Berkeley, CA: University of California.

Nilsen, A. P., & Donelson, K. L. (2001). *Literature for today's young adults* (6th ed.). New York: Addison Wesley Longman.

Noden, H. R., & Vacca, R. T. (1994). *Whole language in middle and secondary classrooms.* NY: HarperCollins.

O'Leary, S. (1998). *Five kids: Stories in children's learning to read.* New York: The Wright Group.

Oliver, E. (1995, December). The writing quality of 7th, 9th, and 11th graders and college freshmen: Does rhetorical specification in writing prompts make a difference? In *Research in the Teaching of English* (p. 215). Urbana, IL: National Council of Teachers of English.

Pearlman, M. (1995). The role of socioeconomic status in adolescent literature. *Adolescence, 30,* 223–231.

Peck, R. (1993). The silver anniversary of young adult books. *Journal of Youth Services in Libraries, 7*(1), 19–23.

Petitt, D. J. (1960). *A study of the qualities of literary excellence which characterize selected fiction for younger adolescents.* Unpublished doctoral dissertation, University of Minnesota, Minneapolis.

Petitt, D. J. (1961). *A study of the qualities of literary experience which characterize selected fiction for younger adolescents.* Unpublished Ph.D. dissertation. University of Minnesota.

Peyton, J. K., & Seymour, M. (1989, October). The effect of teachers' strategies on students' interactive journal writing. In *Research in the Teaching of English* (p. 310). Urbana, IL: National Council of Teachers of English.

Piaget, J., Inhelder, B., & Szeminksa, A. (1960). *The child's conception of geometry.* New York, NY: Basic Books.

Piaget, J. (1990). Intellectual evolution from adolescence to adulthood. In R. E. Muuss (Ed.), *Adolescent behavior and society: A book of readings* (4th ed.), (pp. 61–67). New York: McGraw-Hill.

Pikulski, J. J. (1991). The transition years: Middle school. In J. Flood, J. Jensen, D. Lapp, & J. Squire (Eds.), *Handbook of research on teaching the English language arts* (pp. 303–319). New York: Macmillan.

Poe, E., Samuels, B., & Carter, B. (1993). Twenty-five years of research in young adult literature: Past perspectives and future directions. *Journal of Youth Services in Libraries, 7*(1), 65–73.

Porter, C., & Cleland, J. (1994). *The portfolio as a learning strategy.* Westport, CT: Heinemann-Boynton/Cook.

Portner, J. (1998a, May 20). "U.S. Teenage birthrate Tops Industrial Nations," in *Education Week,* 5.

Portner, J. (1998b, May 20). "Officials Call Gun Report Proof of Crackdown," in *Education Week,* 3.

Postman, N. (1985). *Amusing ourselves to death.* New York: Penguin Books.

Postman, N., Morine, J., & Morine, L. (1963). *Postman language series.* New York: Holt, Rinehart, & Winston.

Rapp-Ruddell, M. (1997). *Teaching content reading and writing* (2nd ed.). Boston: Allyn & Bacon.

Reed, A. (1994a). *Comics to classics: A guide to books for teens and preteens.* New York: Penguin.

Reed, A. (1994b). *Reaching adolescents: The young adult book and the school.* New York: MacMillan.

Reich, R. B. (1991). *The work of nations.* New York: Vintage Books.

Resolution 2 (1998, July). *Florida Council of Teachers of English Newsletter,* 8.

Rief, L. (1996). *Seeking diversity—Language arts with adolescents.* Westport, CT: Heinemann-Boynton/Cook.

Romano, T. (1987). *Clearing the way: Working with teen age writers.* Westport, CT: Heinemann-Boynton/Cook.

Rosenzweig, S. (1997, March). The five-foot bookshelf: Readings on middle-level education and reform. *PDK, 87*(7), 551–556.

Samuels, J. S., & Farstrup, A. E. (Eds.) (1992). *What research says about reading instruction* (2nd ed.). Westport, CT: Heinemann-Boynton/Cook.

Scheier, R. (1994). "Clinton, Gingrich Take Aim at Teen Pregnancy," in *Christian Science Monitor,* 01/23/94. Cover and page 11.

Schulenberg, J., & Ebata, A. T. (1994). The United States. In K. Hurrelmann (Ed.), *International handbook of adolescence* (pp. 414–440). Westport, CT: Greenwood.

Sebald, H. (1992). *Adolescence: A social psychological analysis.* Englewood Cliffs, NJ: Prentice-Hall.

Shafer, R. E. (1990, March). Where did whole language come from? Paper presented at NCTE Spring Conference, Colorado Springs, Co.

Sharan, Y., & Sharan, S. (1989/1990). "Group Investigation Expands Cooperative Learning." *Educational Leadership, 47,* 17–21.

Simmons, J. S. (1981, December). Proactive censorship: The new wave. *English Journal, 70*(8), 18–20.

Simmons, J. S. (1991). The junior high school years. In J. Flood, J. Jensen, D. Lapp, & J. Squire (Eds.), *Handbook of research on teaching the English language arts* (pp. 320–330). New York: Macmillan.

Simmons, J. S. (Ed.) (1993, Winter). *Censored issue of ALAN Review*. Urbana, IL: National Council of Teachers of English.

Simmons, J. S. (Ed.) (1994). *Censorship: A threat to reading, learning, thinking*. Newark, DE: International Reading Association.

Simmons, J. S. (1996). Literacy: Its roller coaster ride through U.S. education. In E. Marum (Ed.), *Children and books in the modern world: Contemporary perspectives on literacy* (pp. 7–41). London: Falmer Press.

Simmons, J. S., & Baines, L. (Eds.) (1998). *Language study in middle school, high school, and beyond: Views on enhancing the study of language*. Newark, DE: International Reading Association.

Simmons, J. S., & Baines, L. (Eds.) (1998). *Language study in middle school, high school, and beyond*. Newark, DE: International Reading Association.

Simmons, J. S., & Deluzain, E. (1992). *Teaching literature in middle and secondary grades*. Boston: Allyn & Bacon.

Simmons, J. S., & Shafer, R. E. (1994, March). A survey of attitudes towards certain aspects of English curriculum held by educational and non-educational groups. Washington, DC: ERIC.

Siu-Runyan, Y., & Faircloth, V. (1995). *Beyond separate subjects: Integrative learning at the middle level*. Norwood, MA: Christopher-Gordon.

Smith, F., & Goodman, K. (1976). *Psycholinguistics and reading*. New York: Holt, Rinehart, & Winston.

Smith, F. (1986). *Understanding reading* (3rd ed.). Hillsdale, NJ: Lawrence Erlbaum Associates.

Smith, M. A. (1996, June). The national writing project after 22 years. *Phi Delta Kappan*, 688–692.

Snyder, T. D., & Shafer, L. L. (1996). *Youth indicators 1996: Trends in the well-being of American youth*. Washington, DC: U.S. Department of Education, Office of Educational Research and Improvement.

Spear, K. (1993). *Peer response groups in action: Writing together in secondary schools*. Westport, CT: Heinemann-Boynton/Cook.

Sperling, M. (1996, Spring). Revisiting the writing–spelling connection: Challenges for writing and writing instruction. *Review of Educational Research*, 53.

Squire, J., & Applebee, R. (1968). *High school English instruction today*. New York: Appleton-Century-Crofts.

St. Clair, N. (1995). Outside looking in: Representations of gay and lesbian experiences in the young adult novel. *The ALAN Review*, 23(1), 38–43.

*Standards for reading professionals* (1992). Newark, DE: International Reading Association and National Council of Teachers of English Joint Task Force.

*Standards for reading and writing* (1994). Newark, DE: International Reading Association and National Council of Teachers of English Joint Task Force.

*Standards for the assessment of reading and writing* (1994). Newark, DE: International Reading Association and National Council of Teachers of English Joint Task Force on Assessment.

Stephens, E. (1998). The genie in the computer. In K. Beers & B. G. Samuels (Eds.), *Into focus: Understanding and creating middle school readers* (pp. 375–393). Norwood, MA: Christopher-Gordon.

Stevenson, Chris (1998). *Teaching ten to fourteen year olds* (2nd ed.). New York: Addison Wesley Longman.

Stevenson, C. (1999). *Teaching ten to fourteen year olds* (2nd ed.). New York: Longman.

Strasburger, V. C. (1995). Adolescents and the media: Medical and psychological impact. (Volume 33 in A. E. Kazdin (Ed.)), *Developmental Clinical Pychology and Psychiatry*. Thousand Oaks, CA: Sage Publications.

Strathan, D. B. Turning points and beyond: Coming of age in middle level research. In J. L. Irvin (Ed.), *Transforming middle level education* (pp. 381–399). Needham Heights, MA: Allyn & Bacon.

Strickland, K. (1995). *Literacy, not labels: Celebrating students' strengths through whole language*. Westport, CT: Heinemann-Boynton/Cook.

Strickland, K., & Strickland, J. (Eds.) (1993). *Uncovering the curriculum*. Portsmouth, NH: Heinemann.

Strickland, K., & Strickland, J. (1998). *Reflections on assessment: Its purposes, methods, and effects on learning*. Westport, CT: Heinemann-Boynton/Cook.

Sunstein, B., & Cheville, J. (1998). *Assessing portfolios: A portfolio*. Urbana, IL: National Council of Teachers of English.

Tchudi, S. (1997). *Alternatives to grading student writing*. Urbana, IL: National Council of Teachers of English.

Tchudi, S., & Mitchell, D. (1999). *Exploring and teaching the English language arts* (4th ed.). New York: Longman.

Tingle, M. (1958). *The image of the family in selected junior novels*. Unpublished Ph.D. dissertation, University of Minnesota.

Tobin, L., & Newkirk, T. (1994). *Taking stock: The writing process movement in the 90's*. Westport, CT: Heinemann-Boynton/Cook.

Tobin, L. (1993). *Writing relationships: What really happens in the composition class*. Westport, CT: Heinemann-Boynton/Cook.

Totten, S. (1996). *Middle level education: An annotated bibliography*. Westport, CT: Greenwood.

Van Allen, L. (1993). Poll Taken at the JH/MS Assembly Session. *The ALAN Review*, 21(1), 49–50.

Warriner, J. (1987). *English composition and grammar*. Orlando, FL: Harcourt, Brace, & Jovanovich.

Warriner, J. (1946). *English grammar and composition*. New York: Harcourt Brace.

Watts, E. (1997). Reading Rescue: Case studies of English language learners in a middle school. Unpublished doctoral dissertation, Florida State University, Tallahassee.

Wavering, M. (Ed.) (1995). *Educating young adolescents: Life in the middle*. New York: Garland.

Weaver, C. (1979). *Grammar for teachers*: Perspectives and definitions. Westport, CT: Heinemann-Boynton/Cook.

Weaver, C. (1996). *Teaching grammar in context*. Westport, CT: Heinemann-Boynton/Cook.

West, J., & Galda, L. (1998). Young adult literature in the English classroom. *Voices From the Middle*, 11(3), 187–191.

Wilkinson, A. M. (1971). *The foundations of language: Talking and reading in young children*. Oxford University Press.

Willinsky, J. (1988). *The well tempered tongue: The politics of standard English in the high school*. New York: Teachers College Press.

Wilson, D. E. (1994). *Attempting change: Teachers moving from writing project to classroom practice*. Westport, CT: Heinemann-Boynton/Cook.

Winfield, L. F. (1995). The knowledge base on resilience in African-American adolescents. In L. J. Crockett & A. C. Crouter (Eds.), *Pathways through adolescence: Individual development in relation to social contexts*. Mahwah, NJ: Lawrence Erlbaum Associates.

Wolman, B. B. (1998). *Adolescence: Biological and psychosocial perspectives*. Westport, CT: Greenwood.

Wong, S., Groth, L., & O'Flahaven, J. (1995-96, December–January). Classroom implications of reading recovery. *Reading Today*, 12.

Wood, K., Lapp, D., & Flood, J. (1992). *Guiding readers through text: A review of study guides*. Newark, DE: International Reading Association.

Wresch, W. (Ed.) (1991). *The English classroom in the computer age: Thirty lesson plans*. Urbana, IL: NCTE.

Yancy, K., & Weiser, I. (1998). *Situating portfolios: Functional perspectives*. Urbana, IL: National Council of Teachers of English.

# · 27 ·

# THE LEARNER DEVELOPS:
# THE HIGH SCHOOL YEARS

## Thomas Newkirk
### University of New Hampshire

This chapter focuses on development, and for that reason it begins with a problem of definition—development *toward what*. It is perhaps possible to view development as a purely neurophysiological event, the unfolding of innate intellectual abilities that occurs along a predetermined path. But recent studies of language development have rejected this biological view in favor of one that gives more importance to culture (e.g., Dyson, 1997; Harste, Woodward, & Burke, 1984; Heath, 1983) and views development as an interaction between biological potential and cultural patterns. This dialectical view of development is grounded in the work of Lev Vygotsky (1978) who viewed the learner as gradually appropriating thought patterns that are first manifest in interactions with others. According to Vygotsky, all thought is social (or interpersonal) before it is internalized (or intrapersonal). Put another way, his major work *Mind in Society* might just as well be entitled *Society in Mind*.

This view of development forecloses any possibility of reducing language development to universal stages or patterns, appealing as that possibility might be. In order to understand the high school learner, it is therefore necessary to consider the institution where that learner spends 180 days a year, and to understand the often conflicting demands placed on that institution. This chapter's thesis is that studies of intellectual development, measured through language performance, indicate a "low ceiling" for most high school students and that this impeded development is related to the diffuse structure and mission of the high school.

The charter for the modern comprehensive high school was written by James Conant in *The American High School Today* (1959). There he asked the fundamentally important question:

Can a school at one and the same time provide a good general education for all the pupils as future citizens of a democracy, provide elective programs for the majority to develop useful skills, and educate adequately those with a talent for handling advanced academic subjects—particularly foreign languages and mathematics (p. 15)?

Conant describes this challenge more expansively in *The Comprehensive High School* (1967):

The comprehensive high school is a particularly American phenomenon because it offers, under one administration and under one roof (or series of roofs), secondary education for almost all high school age children of one town or neighborhood. It is responsible for educating the boy who will become an atomic scientist and the girl who will marry at eighteen; the prospective captain of a ship and the future captain of industry. It is responsible for educating the bright and the not bright children with different vocational and professional ambitions and various motivations. It is responsible, in sum, for providing good and appropriate education, both academic and vocational, for all young children within a democratic environment which the American people believe serves the principles they cherish (p. 3).

If anything, this charter has expanded in recent years: High schools have become the front line for combating social problems such as alcoholism, AIDS, and drug addiction. They are expected to provide special support for students with learning difficulties as well as those with emotional and physical handicaps. School administrators are evaluated on their ability to raise academic standards, invariably measured in standardized test scores, and at the same time to retain potential dropouts, often weaker students who will pull those scores down. Parents want their adolescents to receive individual attention from teachers, yet will often resist the elimination of options or electives that fragment the school day and make this attention impossible. Schools claim that critical thinking is a primary goal, yet the high school schedule works against the individual attention implicit in that goal; typically, teachers are expected to meet up to 175 students per day in periods as short as 40 minutes, though often shorter because of interruptions. As Goodlad observes in *A Place Called School*, "We want it all" (1984, p. 33).

Often the calls for higher standards or for a greater emphasis on writing as a mode of thinking ignore the complexity of the high schools' mandate. Some of the calls for reform (e.g., *A Nation at Risk*, 1983) suggest that these intellectual goals are paramount, if unrealized, in high schools and that by exhortation or by relatively straightforward measures like lengthening the school day or requiring more courses for graduation, schools can be recalled to their true mission. In the 1990s virtually every state initiated some form of proficiency testing—with results printed in the newspaper—in the belief that testing can drive reform.

Powell, Farrar, and Cohen (1985) provide a more provocative reason for the apparent neglect of critical thinking in high schools. They compare the high school to a shopping mall:

Both types of institutions are profoundly consumer-oriented. Both try to hold customers by offering something for everyone. Individual stores or departments, and salespeople or teachers, try their best to attract customers by advertisements of various sorts, yet in the end the customer has the final word (p. 3).

In this mall, one of the "specialty shops" is the honors program where critical thinking and in-depth engagement has a "clientele." But for the general student, the unspecial student, the pattern is one of accommodation, or what Powell, Farrar, and Cohen call "treaties"; the unspecial student may willingly work at essentially uninteresting worksheets if that means he or she can get a good grade without having to go beyond fill-in-the-blank work. One teacher described the treaty process this way:

We have all compromised on our values. Inside the classroom, students will work for me or I see to it that they don't stay there. But I don't give them nearly as much homework as I would like because I have been beaten down: too many simply will not do it (Boyer, 1983, p. 144).

The shopping mall school can best be viewed as an adaptable and enduring democratic institution; it is doing "what comes naturally in a popular democracy; paying attention to their constituents" (p. 239). One of the greatest virtues of the shopping mall school is its adaptability, its ability to deal with the contrary visions of education that were explicit in Conant's charter. As a result we have:

institutions that are remarkably flexible, ambitious, and tolerant, capable of making room for many different sorts of students and teachers and many different wishes for education. They are institutions nicely suited to cope with America's fickle and political educational sensibilities. All are important strengths, but they have had crippling effects. They have stunted the high schools' capacity to take all students seriously. They have blocked teachers' capacity to cultivate those qualities long valued in educated men and women—the ability to read well and critically, to write plainly and persuasively, and to reason clearly (Powell, Farrar, & Cohen, 1985, p. 309).

It is the general student who suffers most. James Squire and Roger Applebee in their 1968 survey of high school English instruction, noted that the better students were expected to do close reading of texts, whereas weaker students were asked to learn historical facts. "The honors student thinks, while his less gifted peers regurgitate" (1968, p. 174).

Assessment of student performance reinforces these observations. The chapter begins by examining status studies that provide a picture of instructional practices and student achievement. The review then shifts to sections on language development, response to literature, and the teaching of writing. These divisions are, of course, convenient fictions; they do not indicate support for the tripod model of the English curriculum with three clear components (literature, composition, and language). Ultimately any discussion of how English is taught cannot, finally, be divorced from an examination of the high school itself. The structure of the high school—the bell schedule, the size of the classes, the politics of curriculum development—all contribute directly to the development of the high school learner.

## STATUS STUDIES

The most extensive of these surveys has been Goodlad's (1984) examination of 38 schools, a project involving 20 trained data collectors that gathered data from 8,624 parents, 1,350 teachers, and 17,163 student. The researchers made detailed observations in over 1,000 classrooms, making it the largest observational study ever conducted in this country. His conclusions make for painful reading. In these classes students "made scarcely any decisions about their learning" (p. 229). Over 75% of class time was spent on instruction and nearly 70% of this was usually teacher to student. Only 5% of instruction was designed to elicit any student response and *not even 1% required some kind of open response involving perhaps an opinion from the student* (p. 229). Boyer, in his Carnegie Foundation study of high schools, found the same pattern:

Most discussion in classrooms, when it occurs, calls for simple recall (What were the provisions of the Treaty of 1763) or the application of in idea (Use the periodic table to find an atomic number). Occasionally students are asked to develop explanations (If we release ammonia in one corner of the room why is it possible to smell it in the opposite corner?) But serious intellectual discussion is rare (Boyer, 1983, p. 146).

Written work resembles this oral recitation method. Goodlad found that English language arts classes emphasized a "kind of repetitive reinforcement of basic skills of language usage throughout the twelve grades—a heavy emphasis on mechanics in the topics covered by teachers, textbooks stressing these topics, and workbooks, worksheets, and quizzes emphasizing short answers and the recall of specific information (p. 207)."

Goodlad's conclusions are supported by a smaller survey conducted by Applebee (1981). Applebee's study involved 259 observations of ninth- and tenth-grade classes at two schools. He found that 44% of class time was spent on some form of writing, broadly defined, but most of this writing was very brief (short answer or fill-in-the-blank) or note taking. Writing a paragraph or longer occurred about 3% of the time. Even some of the writing that seemed to call for analytic thought actually called for a summary of class notes. Applebee gives these examples:

(a) Western Europe on the eve of the Reformation was a civilization going through great changes. In a well-written essay describe the political, economic, social, and cultural changes Europe was going through at the time of the Reformation.
(b) Select some phase of twentieth century American literature and discuss it in a theme of 300–500 words. Turn in polished draft only (p. 74).

Applebee concludes that these assignments "become reasonable tasks only when they are interpreted by students as requests to summarize material previously presented in lessons or texts" (p. 74). Surveys conducted by the National Assessment of Educational Progress indicate that when students are expected to write at length, 82% of their writing is in the form of essays or reports; formal academic writing, then, is stressed almost to the exclusion of personal or creative writing (Applebee, Langer, & Mullis, 1987a), a result similar to that found by British researchers in the 1970s (Britton, Burgess, Martin, McLeod, & Rosen, 1975).

Another barrier to analytic thinking may be the textbooks themselves. Analysis, if it is to occur, must begin with a response—outrage, delight, disagreement, approval, puzzlement—and the potential for response is enhanced if the text has a strong point of view. Fitzgerald (1979) in her survey of U.S. history texts notes a significant change in textbooks that occurred in the 1890s. Up until that time, textbooks would often openly reveal the opinions of the author, but in the 1890s history texts began to assume the tone of objectivity and impersonality. From the 1890s on, Fitzgerald concludes, "what textbooks said about American history would appear to children to be the truth" (p. 52). Fitzgerald particularly deplores the evasiveness of contemporary books: frequently "problems" (e.g., "the race problem") seem to arise through a kind of historical spontaneous generation: They occur without human agency. They happen. Fitzgerald criticizes many of these books as irresponsible history, but this evasiveness, this lack of any point of view that students can identify, also reduces the range of options a reader might assume. These books, mainly committee documents, seem to demand not response, but acceptance. They suggest what Friere (1970) has called a "banking" concept of education where information is passed on (deposited) in students, rather than a curriculum that fosters critical consciousness.

Since Fitzgerald's critique, there has been an even more evident "dumbing down," with some texts obviously written to accommodate readability formula. Stille (1998) quotes this passage from Harcourt Brace's *America's Story*:

Abraham Lincoln ran as a member of the Republican party. He spoke out strongly against the spread of slavery. He promised not to stop slavery in the South, where it was already practiced. But he said that he hoped it would end there, too.

Many white Southerners worried about what would happen if Lincoln became President. They thought the problem was far greater than the question of slavery. They believed that their whole way of life was being attacked (Quoted in Stille, 1998, p. 18).

Textbooks from major publishers are scanned by computers to ensure that sentences are simple enough and "exotic" words are kept to a minimum. The result is often so numbingly simplistic that the text does not invite interpretation.

The results of the various National Assessment of Educational Progress (NAEP) reports suggest students have learned what they have been taught: They are generally strong on factual recall of information, and on the mechanics of writing, but they lack the ability to critically explore their ideas or responses (Applebee, Langer, & Mullis, 1987b). These results indicate that a focus on achieving rudimentary or minimal competence, going back to the basics, is misdirected. The vast majority of students achieve competence on this minimal level. The problems lie with the more complex tasks, hardly a surprising conclusion in the light of the surveys of teaching methods already cited.

One of the major innovations of NAEP was a redefinition of reading competence. Traditionally reading comprehension has been tested through multiple-choice questions that were either literal, inferential, or interpretive. NAEP developed a more exacting definition:

In school and in society, we expect a reader to be able to analyze, evaluate, and extend the ideas that are being presented, just as we expect a writer to elaborate upon and defend judgments that are expressed. We expect people to know how to get information and how to use it and shape it to suit their needs (Applebee, Langer, & Mullis, 1987b, p. 9).

This definition necessitates a form of assessment that links reading and writing (or speaking) because it is through writing and speaking that we elaborate and shape understandings.

The 1979–1980 assessment of 39,000 student was the first to link reading and writing. The authors state:

When reading is divorced from the process of discussing the meaning of a work (as it often is in teaching and testing), comprehension can be misunderstood to be a sudden "click" of meaning measurable only through short answer and multiple choice questions that require little struggle for full understanding (*Reading, Writing, and Thinking*, 1981, p. ix).

The 1979–1980 assessment used a four-stage model of response that began with

1. Initial comprehension leading to
2. Preliminary interpretations followed by
3. Reexamination of the text in light of these interpretations, leading to
4. Extended and documented interpretation.

In the 1979–1980 assessment, students seemed able to handle the first two steps of this process but were unable to move to steps three and four. The students also seemed able to handle inferential multiple-choice questions, but they had far more difficulty on open-ended questions. When asked to write, students were often unable to do more than summarize. The authors concluded that students lacked experience with reading/writing tasks that involve critical thinking or problem-solving. (It should be noted that students had only 9 minutes to complete the reading/writing task on the 1979–80 assessment. This time limitation may have precluded some of the more elaborated responses the authors were hoping for.)

This theme is echoed in two NAEP publications. *The Writing Report Card* (Applebee, Langer, & Mullis, 1986b) and *The Reading Report Card* (Applebee, Langer, & Mullis, 1986a) that report on the 1984 writing and reading assessment. Both assessment reports contain some good news: Reading scores and writing scores are up from the previous assessment, and students report that they are doing more writing than had been reported 5 years earlier. But again the percentage of students who can go beyond minimally adequate written responses or intermediate comprehension was found to be disturbingly low. For example, on the persuasive writing task only 23% of the 11th graders wrote better than a minimal response and only 2% were classified as "elaborated." Though the reading results were more positive, with 44% of 17-year-olds reading at the "adept" or "advanced" level, the authors conclude that:

by and large 17-year-olds do not have consistent control of the reading skills or strategies needed to comprehend material such as primary source historical documents, scientific documents, or financial and technical documents—those often needed to achieve excellence in academic, business, or government environments (1986b, p. 28).

The NAEP assessments conducted in the 1990s show small, but consistent declines in both writing and reading performance (Campbell, Voelkl, & Donahue, 1996). The 1994 reading assessment shows a discouraging decline in student-reported activities that require interpretation (NAEP, 1994). These declines, however, were not evenly spread among the population being tested. In the 1994 Reading Assessment, there was no decline among the better students, those in the 75th to 90th percentiles. The decline was limited to those in the 10th, 25th, or 50th percentiles. In other words, changes in performance may mirror the the increasing income gap between the upper and lower income levels.

The NAEP studies also show significant differences in male and female performance on literacy tasks. In the 1996 writing assessment, males scored 18 points lower than females (350-point scale); this difference is equivalent to the difference between Whites and Hispanics, and approaches the gap between Whites and Blacks. The gender gap is even bigger in eighth grade where females outperformed males by a margin of 25 points (Campbell, Voelkl, & Donohue, 1996, p. 21). Put another way, males perform in much the same way as economically disadvantaged ethnic or racial groups in our society. The implications of this gap are significant, given the shift in the economy away from manufacturing jobs to those which place a premium on communication skills (see Wilson, 1996, for a description of the effect of this shift on Black males).

The New Hampshire statewide writing assessment provides some insight into the reasons why students fail to score in the higher levels. Typically, the 1996 state assessment placed only 2% of students in the Advanced Level and 8% on the Proficient Level. In the analysis of the 40,000 comments made by the raters on the 12,469 writing samples, the most frequent category was "details," followed by "topic development" (New Hampshire Educational Improvement and Assessment Program, 1997). Approximately 25,000 of the comments dealt with elaboration.

The study divided these comments into commendations and needs: It reports that 12,868 "needs" comments dealt with elaboration while there were 3,703 needs comments, combined, in "organization," "sentence structure," "wording," and "mechanics." These results suggest that high school students need more work with pre-writing or invention strategies, and with reflective moves—shifts from rendering to analysis—that would help a writer develop a thoughtful piece of work.

Whatever their limitations, these surveys of instruction and performance are painfully consistent. There is a repetitive attention to basic facts and skills and a corresponding lack of attention to intellectual development: the ability to think rationally, the ability to use, evaluate, and interrelate knowledge. "Coverage" becomes the goal of teaching, or perhaps the rationale for not spending time on more in-depth learning.

One response to this continuing crisis in secondary education has been a shift from low-stakes testing (i.e., tests designed to provide a sense of how schools are doing) to high-stakes tests that will require a passing grade in order for students to graduate. While these new tests tend to have more writing and open-ended responses than the standard multiple choice tests, it remains to be seen if this external pressure will focus instruction productively on reading, writing, and reasoning. Or, as Moffett (1992) argues, these new tests may work to disempower teachers and administrators:

What evidence exists that the threat of being beaten will spur and cure schools? The fact is that as much as anything, this very authoritarian approach has demoralized teachers and principals, who simply never have had decision-making power commensurate with responsibility for results, because tests and texts—the major determinants of curriculum—are usually selected over their heads, if not behind their backs (p. 2).

Moffett is profoundly skeptical of these attempts to "embarrass schools into improvement" (p. 2).

## RESEARCH ON LANGUAGE DEVELOPMENT

This section examines research studies that contribute to an understanding of language development. The critical issue in this research is whether instruction should focus on the sentence level, or whether growth in syntactic competence is the result of the writer's attempts to deal with more global rhetorical issues. Polanyi's (1958) distinction between focal and subsidiary awareness can clarify this issue. In his famous example, Polanyi claims that when we pound a nail, we are attending to the head of the hammer hitting the nail; we are focally aware of the impact, the straightness of the nail, and its progress into the board. We are aware in a *subsidiary* way of our grip on the handle and the movements we make in hitting the nail. Should we shift our focal attention to the grip or to the mechanics of moving the hammer, we would be unable to pound the nail. Rhetoricians would argue that writers develop not by shifting their focal awareness to the level of sentence structure, but by using language in a variety of situations, for a variety of purposes and audiences.

Perhaps the most regularly researched question in the area of composition concerns the effect of formal grammar instruction on writing. Braddock, Lloyd-Jones, and Schoer (1963) in their survey of research concluded that this one issue had been resolved: Formal grammar instruction had been shown to be an ineffective way of teaching writing and, because such instruction often took away time from actual writing practice, it probably had a negative effect on writing development. Although some have questioned this sweeping dismissal (e.g., Kolnn, 1981), clearly there is no reason to believe that formal, traditional grammar instruction should occupy the prominent position it holds in many English curricula. Hartwell (1985) has suggested that while experimentation may not be able to resolve the issue, grammar instruction can be abandoned on theoretical grounds. He argues that any claim for the effectiveness of grammar instruction rests on premises that, when made explicit, can be immediately recognized as implausible.

Ten years before the Braddock, Lloyd-Jones, and Schoer survey, Walter Loban had begun his 13-year longitudinal study of oral and written language development. In 1953 Loban selected 338 kindergarten pupils and twice each year for the next 13 years collected oral samples and (beginning in fourth grade) written samples of discourse in order to (a) determine changes in syntactic development over this 13-year period and (b) to determine which features of this development contribute to what teachers considered proficiency. Loban (1976) found that in both oral and written language, the key index of growth, and the key difference between stronger and weaker language users, was elaboration or modification within the main clause. Older (and better) language users tended to use longer communication units because they used greater elaboration of subject and predicate, used more embedding, and used more dependent clauses of all kinds.

Hunt (1965), whose research paralleled Loban's, helped to consolidate Loban's conclusions by introducing the concept of a T-unit that he used to designate the main clause and all modification or elaboration of that clause. A major index of language growth became words/T-unit. Since young children tend to connect short main clauses with "and," they tend to use relatively few words/T-unit. But as they mature, they begin to use a range of appositives, prepositional phrases, and dependent clauses that increase the number of words/T-unit. In subsequent work, Hunt (1977) demonstrated that there is a developmental order in which students develop the capacity to perform types of embedding. Other researchers (e.g., O'Donnell, Griffin, & Norris, 1967) used Hunt's unit of measurement to conclusively show that the words/T-unit ratio went up in both oral and written discourse as writers matured.

The T-unit became an important unit of measurement in sentence-combining research in the late 1960s and 1970s. This research shifted from the normative question (How do writers develop?) to one of experimental intervention (How can we speed up this development?). Mellon (1969), in a large and carefully designed study, tried to determine the effects of cued sentence-combining practice where students are given the sentence components and "cues" for combining. Interestingly, at the time of his study, Mellon did not view sentence-combining as a way of teaching writing, but as a form of linguistic play that

could increase student's awareness of various language forms. His position seems somewhat different in the epilogue of his study, written 2 years later, which emphasizes the linguistic growth that sentence combining can enhance.

Other researchers did not share Mellon's ambivalence. O'Hare (1973) simplified the sentence-combining practice and in a much smaller study reported extraordinary differences between control and experimental groups. O'Hare also found that the writing quality of work done by the experimental groups was ranked higher than that of the control groups. Subsequent researchers were unable to reproduce the magnitude of difference found by O'Hare, but they generally found fairly strong evidence of differences in syntactic fluency (later called "syntactic maturity") with less conclusive results on improvement in writing quality (Combs, 1976; Stewart, 1978). The most thorough study, conducted with college freshmen at Miami University (Morenberg, Daiker, & Kerek, 1978), showed superior results on both syntactic maturity and writing quality for the sentence-combining group.

The Miami study was the last major one on sentence-combining. In part, the point had been proven, sentence-combining could accelerate writing development. But a follow-up of the Miami study showed that students in the control groups caught up with the experimental groups (1980), raising questions about the permanence of the gains. If the method only temporarily accelerates development that would occur through reading, writing, and speaking experiences, is it really such an advance? Finally, rhetorically based models of development seemed to offer more productive explanations of development. Moffett's *Teaching the Universe of Discourse* (1968) remains the most innovative and profound attempt to base the English curriculum on principles of development. Too often, Moffett claims, curricula are set up around divisions in the subject matter (e.g., American Lit—10th grade; British Lit—11th grade) rather than on an understanding of ways learners develop. Moffett writes:

The sequence of psychological development should be the backbone of curriculum continuity, and the logical formulations of the subject should serve only as an aid in describing this natural growth. Meshing learner and learned, in the case of a native language, is a matter of translating inner reality in to the public realm of the subject (1968, pp. 14-15).

Drawing on the work of Piaget, Moffett suggests that abstraction or de-centering is a central principle in growth; as the learner develops, he or she is more capable of moving beyond an immediate experience and audience. The learner, for example, may begin by recounting an experience, but the more mature learner can abstract from it, can generalize or theorize, can treat the experience as an instance of a more general concept. The child can also begin to frame discourse to meet the demands of increasingly unfamiliar audiences that demand greater explicitness. Syntactic development, the various forms of embedding and conjoining, is a by-product of the learner's attempt to deal with increasingly more demanding rhetorical and intellectual tasks.

Moffett's last and most comprehensive outline of growth in language is *Detecting Growth in Language* (1992). There he briefly describe 24 growth sequences, many of them echoing his earlier work: For example, the first was growth toward "generalizing more broadly while elaborating more finely" (p. 14). Another sequence is "[t]oward discourse increasingly expanded across time and space as indicated by overall organization and dominance of tense" (p. 59). Some of the sequences Moffett notes recall the work of William Perry (1970) on intellectual development: for example, "toward increasing awareness that people create what they know and that this knowledge is partial" (p. 16). Moffett's later work on development, influenced by his interest in meditation and Eastern religion, also reflects an attempt to respect both analytic and holistic modes of thought, the left and right brain hemispheres. While he at times reduces his model of growth to various schema, his conception is never one of unidirectional movement; rather his goal is development toward the ability to play among a range of discursive possibilities.

The other major attempt to ground a model of language development on principles of intellectual development was that of James Britton and his colleagues who collaborated on *The Development of Writing Abilities: 11–18* (1975), perhaps the most influential piece of research in the past 30 years. Like Moffett, the Britton team viewed the young language learner as working within an intimate context where the language is largely "expressive"—highly contextualized where the speaker or writer assumes that the listener or reader shares common background knowledge and interests. As the language learner matures, he or she can move beyond this expressive matrix in one of two directions: toward the transactional (informing and persuading) where the speaker/writer must provide contextual information, anticipate the audience's position, and answer possible objections. Or the speaker/writer moves toward the poetic that Britton et al. define broadly to include jokes, anecdotes, stories, as well as poetry, plays, and novels. What all poetic discourse has in common is its attention to form, the way we shape inchoate experience into a structure that allows us to take what Britton calls a spectator role.

Britton and his colleagues validated their discourse model by applying it to over 2,000 pieces, written by British secondary students in all subject areas. This categorization clearly revealed ways that students were stifled by the demands placed on them. Virtually all the writing students did was transactional, and the potential of writing in the spectator mode was largely unrealized; the only exception was in English, but once students began to prepare for exams (around the fifth year), that writing, too, became almost exclusively transactional. Similarly, students rarely wrote expressive discourse; the only examples of expressive discourse were in English and religious education, and this category accounted for only 5.5% of the sample. Finally, teachers generally took on the role of "examiner," particularly in nonEnglish subjects; by the time students reached their seventh year, the teacher acted as "examiner" 61% of the time. Writing, by this point, was essentially a means of testing the student.

Britton viewed the student as occupying an impossible rhetorical position, writing on a given topic to someone who knew more about the topic, not for any purpose of communication, but simply to demonstrate if certain material had been mastered. Even more limiting, the student was cut off from the resources of speech (or as the British would prefer "talk") or expressive language that, according to his model, is the "matrix," the starting point, for more formalized expression. The alternative, implicit in *The Development of Writing Abilities*, became explicit of subsequent work by the Language Across the Curriculum team under the direction of Nancy Martin (Martin, D'Arcy, Newton, & Parker, 1976). This team began to publish a series of pamphlets illustrating ways that informal, speech-like writing (writing that assumed the teacher was engaged in a dialogue, not acting as examiner) could be used in a variety of subject areas. This work had a major influence on the Writing Across the Curriculum movement in the United States (e.g., Fulwiler, 1988).

While these discourse-based models of development represented a clear advance over more atomistic word counts, they too are open to criticism. Typically, models of discourse development claim that some kinds of discourse are more advanced than others. In Bloom's (1959) widely used taxonomy of the cognitive domain, evaluation occupies a higher plane than summarizing or analyzing. And the NAEP reports regularly equate "higher order thinking" with analysis. There is a tendency, then, in many of these models to claim a natural progression from "lower" level cognitive processes, those that are empathetic, affective, situated, narrative, and strongly dependent on memory, to "higher" levels that are distanced, "autonomous," "dependent on abstraction, analysis, and reflection."

A major problem with these hierarchies is their hidden ideological bias. No model of development is natural or neutral. Most developmental models reflect a preference for the theoretical over the practical, for the abstract over the particular, for objectivity over subjectivity. Those capabilities at the top of the hierarchies are typically ones valued in the educational institutions where the hierarchies are developed. The university, which values analytic reasoning above storytelling, is likely to place it at a higher level. A novelist would draw the map a different way.

There is nothing inappropriate in constructing these hierarchies. The problem comes when a particular order is perceived as natural, as the neutral mapping of a domain, as an objective reading of nature. Feminists like Gilligan (1982) have made this objection to Kohlberg's (1981) model of moral development; she has argued that women's moral decision making is more contextual, less tied to abstract principles of good and bad (Kohlberg's highest level). Kohlberg's model, she argues, is not neutral, but reflects a male bias. Similarly, Belenky, Clinchy, Goldberger, and Tarule (1986) argue that models of academic achievement may discriminate against women because women's personal, empathetic, connected styles of engagement are viewed as less rigorous, less developed, than the more distanced, argumentative styles of men. No developmental scheme is innocent of ideology.

## THE DEVELOPMENT OF LITERARY RESPONSE

'Virtually' all studies of literary response trace back to one source: I. A. Richards' *Practical Criticism* (1929). Richards presented a group of Cambridge students with 13 poems (with the names of the poets removed) and asked them to analyze the poems. Most of *Practical Criticism* is taken up with a discussion of the inadequacies of the responses that include: stock responses, irrelevant personal associations, inappropriate critical predispositions, sentimentality, and the inhibition of emotional response. Richards viewed these protocols as signs of the breakdown of literary education.

Researchers in this country who drew from Richards' study took a less pathological approach toward reader response. One of the most painstaking projects was James Squire's (1964) study of 52 ninth and tenth graders who were reading four short stories. Each student was asked to comment aloud at six carefully chosen spots in each story, and these oral commentaries were then classified into six categories: literary judgment, interpretational responses, narrational reactions (retellings), associational responses, self-involvement responses, and prescriptive judgments. In addition to some of the same difficulties found by Richards, Squire found that students were often limited by a search for certainty and a "happiness binding," a resistance to conclusions that were not upbeat. Purves and Rippere (1968) developed a more systematic and comprehensive taxonomy of responses grouped around four major categories: involvement engagement, perception, interpretation, and evaluation. This category system proved capable of reliable coding of responses and was used in a number of subsequent studies (summarized by Applebee, 1977).

Virtually all of the literary response studies were short-term studies (usually dissertations) that examined a single age group and therefore provided little information about the development of literary response. Unfortunately, the profession lacks longitudinal data of the type that Loban has provided on the development of syntax. Research on the development of literary responses has focused on asking students of differing ages to respond to texts and, on the basis of these responses, to suggest a developmental model. Svennson (1985) has made a useful distinction between "cognitive-developmental" and "cultural-developmental" studies of literary response.

Svennson cites Applebee's (1978a) study as cognitive-developmental. According to Applebee, the individual's capacity to respond is tightly linked to Piagetian stages of development. The capacity to analyze literature, for example, is dependent on the emergence of the formal operations stage that occurs between ages 12 and 19. Up until that time the child's response is one of "exacting literalism." With the emergence of formal operations, the adolescent can begin to examine character motives, the structure of a work, and the reasons for personal reactions of pleasure or distaste.

Applebee's linking of formal operations' with the capacity for analysis is common among language educators who attempt to "apply Piaget" (see also Lindemann, 1982). Yet, models like this one are open to challenge. Even if one accepts Piaget's stage theory of development (see Boden, 1980 for a skeptical review), it does not follow that all analysis is dependent on the emergence of formal operations. The analytic writing of students may change as they begin to perform formal operations, but much younger children can, for example discuss why a character did what he did or they can articulate reasons why they like or dislike a piece of literature (Calkins, 1983; Hemming, 1985). It is a serious misreading of Piaget to equate the capacity to analyze with "formal operations." The central question should be not when students begin analyzing but how

their ability to analyze changes as they mature. Svennson, drawing on the work of Fish (1980), argues for the superiority of cultural-developmental models that view development in literary response as a form of socialization. Students in high school enter an "interpretive community" with its own particular strategies for reading. In other words, changes in reading behavior are not viewed as the inevitable outcome of neurophysiological development but as the acquisition of accepted ways of reading. In her own study, Svennson found that older students tended to read symbolic meaning into poems whereas younger students stayed closer to the literal meaning. She also found that the older students were more able to justify and explain their symbolic strategies. In many cases the older students could apply conventional symbolic motifs (light = good; darkness = evil) where younger students did not apply them.

The developmental work of Beach and Wendler (1987) parallels that of Svennson. It examines the responses of students at four levels (8th, 11th, college freshmen, and college juniors) to two short stories. The authors note three shifts across this age span:

1. While younger students conceived of characters' actions as autonomous physical behaviors, older students viewed characters' actions as embedded within socially or psychologically defined contexts.
2. While younger students understood characters' perceptions in terms of immediate feelings, older students conceived of them in terms of characters' social–psychological beliefs.
3. While younger students conceived of characters' goals in terms of characters' immediate or short-term needs, older students saw characters' goals in terms of long-term plans or strategies.

In general, older students viewed characters in a wider context whereas younger readers reacted more to the immediate action rather than its wider implications. Unlike Svennson, Beach and Wendler attribute this change to the capacity of older students to operate at the level of "formal operations." Yet, the work of Nancie Atwell (1987) with dialogue journals at least raises the possibility that eighth graders are capable of the more theoretical responses given by older students; the performance of younger students in the Beach and Wendler study may reflect the instruction they receive (e.g., a focus on summarizing books and literal questions) rather than any inherent developmental limitations.

In fact, the cognitive-developmental models of response may foster a type of fatalism. If a student's difficulty with analysis is due to the lack of formal operational thinking, and if this stage of thinking occurs on a biological timetable, a teacher naturally may attribute the difficulty to the student's lack of development and not to inadequate instruction. These models, by suggesting biological ceilings for students at particular ages, may actually have the effect of lowering expectations. By contrast, the cultural developmental model, although not ignoring the biological component of development, assigns a far greater role to culture to the ways talking, reading, and writing function in the students' environment. While biology cannot be changed, culture can.

The high point in work on literary response may have been the Winter 1976 issue of *Research in the Teaching of English*, which was entirely devoted to response to literature. But there was a significant decrease in empirical work on reader response in the late 1970s. In part, attention seemed to shift from empirical studies to more speculative work in literary theory. It is also possible that the elements of response approach, so dominant in this wave of research, may have failed to elucidate or explain the complex ways that texts and readers transact. This failure may have been due to the breadth of the elements; simply classifying responses as "evaluative" or "interpretive" misses the more central question of the *nature* of the evaluation or interpretation going on. Finally, there was a clear shift of interest away from literary response and toward the study of the writing process, a shift initiated by Janet Emig's *The Composing Processes of Twelfth Graders* (1971).

## THE WRITING PROCESS

Shifting attention to the writing process in the 1970s represents both a scholarly and a political redirection. On the one hand, it was comprised of a set of investigations into the nature of the composing process; but it was also an attack on traditional instruction. And fittingly, both of these elements were present in the research study that is widely acknowledged as the starting point for this movement, Janet Emig's (1971) monograph, *The Composing Process of Twelfth Graders*.

For her case studies, Emig collected background information on the subjects, carefully observed their writing behavior, elicited oral composing protocols, and interviewed the subjects about their processes; in effect, she employed the means of data gathering that would be refined and used by subsequent researchers of the writing process. Most of her report is taken up with one of her subjects, Lynn, a good student who, despite her verbal facility, seems to consistently avoid risks in her writing, particularly when it comes to revealing feelings.

Emig goes well beyond her data in her conclusions where she blames Lynn's schools, and by extension school writing instruction in general, for inhibiting student development:

This inquiry strongly suggests that, for a number of reasons, school-sponsored writing experienced by older secondary students is a limited, and limiting experience. The teaching of composition at this level is essentially unimodal, with only extensive [what Britton called "transactional"] writing given sanction in many schools. Almost by definition, this mode is other-directed—in fact it is other-centered. The concern is with sending a message, a communication out into the world for the edification, the enlightenment, and ultimately the evaluation of another. Too often the other is a teacher, interested chiefly in a product he can criticize rather than in a process he can help initiate through empathy and support (p. 97).

This statement might serve as the political manifesto of the writing process movement, whatever its merits as a research conclusion.

Research on writing processes drew on Emig's research methods. Flower and Hayes (1980, 1981) refined oral composing as a method for uncovering the cognitive dimensions of the writing process, and particularly the differences between skilled and novice writers. Sommers (1980) and Bridwell (1980) focused on revision processes and demonstrated that students rarely made major changes in their writing after a first draft. Matsuhashi (1981) refined Emig's mode of observation, and using a double camera, she was able to monitor pauses in composing; she found students had different pause patterns when they shifted from narrative to expository writing, indicating that the cognitive processes for composing in these models might be different. Perl (1979) combined oral composing protocols and observations of writing behavior to illustrate how basic writers seemed to fixate on surface features.

Emig's political attack may have been even more influential than her research innovations. At the time of her study, composition was almost subsumed under literature; Squire and Applebee (1968) found that two thirds of composition topics were tied to literature. Moreover, students were asked to write about literature in a distanced way; the structure for papers was typically thesis-support and the tone impersonal (the first-person often prohibited). What Louise Rosenblatt (1978) called the "transaction" of reading, the narrative moment-by-moment activity of interpretation, seemed incompatible with the rigid requirements of the formal argumentative essays students were asked to write. One guide for students even stated: "When your professor reads a paper, he is less interested in the actual process by which you arrived at the thesis than by the *result* of the process, the thesis itself, supported by a clear, lively, organized argument."

One solution to this undue restriction on writing possibilities was to allow students freedom in choosing topics. Elbow (1973) and Macrorie (1968) demonstrated ways that free writing could help writers discover ideas, insights, and topics; the activity of nonstop writing could act as a heuristic to allow these submerged possibilities to take shape. Murray (1968) similarly claimed that if students are to be treated as writers, they should be allowed to choose topics they know and care about. In this way they could write from a position of authority rather than write to an authority.

Other means of responding were also proposed. Elbow (1973), Moffett (1968), and Macrorie (1968) proposed student writing groups, where response would come from peers rather than the teacher acting as evaluator. Garrison (1974), Carnicelli (1980), and Murray (1968) demonstrated ways in which one-on-one writing conferences could also remove the teacher from the limiting role of evaluator and could help provide the empathy and support Emig claimed was lacking in traditional instruction.

Like most challenges to the status quo, this one at times was taken to extremes. Brannon and Knoblauch (1982) invoked the metaphor of "Ownership" to describe the students' relationship to their own texts; it follows that the expectations of teachers, schools, or communities could be viewed as infringements on the expressive rights of students. If students are given almost complete freedom in choosing what they want to write, they might stay close to the narrative forms that are most familiar to them and avoid forms of analytic writing that are less familiar. Unless one takes the extreme position, arguing that discourse forms are somehow innate in the learners mind, like the basic grammar of the language, it not clear how students will learn new forms in a classroom where they receive no structured assistance in their writing.

Equally troublesome was the polarizing of process and product, as if teachers and researchers had to choose between the two. The focus on process was primarily intended to redirect attention to teaching writing. Christensen commented, at about the time of Emig's study, that students were not "taught" to write, they were "expected" to write (1967, p. 3). And, as Murray repeatedly reminded his readers, written products do not reveal the process of their production—"you can't infer the pig from the sausage" (1980, p. 3). Yet, successful employment of writing processes is, to a considerable extent, dependent on an awareness of the type of product or text to be produced. Correlational studies consistently show that writing ability is strongly related to reading ability and to the availability of reading material in the home (Applebee, Langer, & Mullis, 1987a); students inevitably draw on the knowledge of language conventions and discourse structures they gain through reading when they write. By polarizing process and product, these reformers may have obscured their dynamic interdependence and unwisely minimized the ways that reading exemplary texts provides goals and cultural landmarks, which writers use to guide their processes.

The sharpest critique of some writing process approaches came in George Hillocks' (1986) encyclopedic review of over 2,000 studies in composition. The centerpiece of Hillocks' critique is a meta-analysis of experimental studies that he compares to four broadly defined approaches to composition teaching: the presentational, the individual, the natural process, and the environmental. The presentational mode includes methods that emphasize teacher lecture or teacher-led discussions, use of models, specific objectives, and teacher feedback only when papers are returned. The natural process mode includes general objectives (e.g., fluency, voice), free writing, extensive peer interaction, generally positive feedback, and opportunities for revision. The environmental mode shares some elements with the natural process mode; it avoids teacher lecture and it engages the student in a process of planning, drafting, and revision. It also encourages group interaction. It differs from natural process in that the goals are more specific (e.g., to increase the use of details and specific language), and the student is guided through a structured process designed around the more specific goals. The final mode, the individualized mode includes one-on-one instruction including tutorial and programmed learning approaches.

In his meta-analysis, Hillocks grouped 29 treatments (4 presentational, 9 natural process, 9 environmental, 6 individualized), and for each mode he compared the average difference in improvement between the experimental and control groups. He concluded that the environmental approach was statistically superior and demonstrably more effective than the other three modes. Hillocks speculates that the natural process approaches are less effective because of the generalized nature of the tasks students are asked to perform.

Applebee, while challenging Hillocks' natural process/environmental distinction, credits Hillocks' study with shifting the emphasis away from global generalized processes to processes that are specifically linked with various writing tasks, an approach he calls "structured process." Even educators sympathetic to expanding reading and writing possibilities for students, have been critical of "whole language" and "writing

process" as they are often enacted in schools. Delpit (1994) raised important questions about the possible negative effects of inexplicit instruction for African American students who might not be familiar with some mainstream literate practices (a concern echoed by Purcell-Gates [1995] in reference to Appalachian students). Nancie Atwell (1998) described her own evolution in her sense of authority:

I have become a teacher with a capital T. This does not mean I've reverted to playing God and making all the writing decisions from behind my big desk. But it does mean I'm no longer willing to withhold suggestions and directions from kids when I can help them solve a problem, do something they've never done before, produce stunning writing, and ultimately, become more independent of me (p. 21).

Applebee also notes that process approaches, particularly those that adhere to what Bizzell calls a "pedagogy of personal style" (1986), are mismatched with traditional subject-centered notions of instruction in secondary schools. English teachers, for example, continue to view themselves primarily as literature teachers; over 70% of students surveyed in the 1986 literature assessment reported that over half of their class time was spent on literature (Applebee, Langer, & Mullis, 1987a). A process pedagogy stressing free choice of topics will naturally be viewed by these teachers as taking time and effort away from their primary mission. Applebee concludes that, "put simply, process-oriented approaches may be, by definition, impossible to implement successfully, given traditional notions of instruction" (1986, p. 108).

Attempts to relate process techniques with the more traditional aims of English classes—the analysis of literary texts—may be met with less resistance. Researchers like Marshall (1987) and Durst (1984) claim that the traditional, thesis-driven critical analysis paper, may actually preclude the kind of analysis it is intended to foster. Marshall quotes one student:

In a limited essay, it's already written. I mean there's an opening paragraph where you tell what it's about. This is always very technical. Automatic. The first sentence is always "In blank's novel" and there's the title. It's all by formula, it's just to what degree. And then you have the example for one character and then an example for another and then you compare the two people and then you conclude. And that's it. It's totally set (pp. 38–39).

Statements like this one lend support to Bartholomae's indictment of this form of school writing:

When, for example, we ask students to write about texts, the tyranny of the thesis often invalidates the very act of analysis we hope to invoke. Hence in assignment after assignment, we find students asked to reduce a novel, a poem, or their own experience into a single sentence, and then to use the act of writing in order to defend or "support" that single sentence. Writing is used to close a subject down rather than open it up, to put an end to discourse, rather than to open up a project (1983, p. 311).

Zeiger (1985) has similarly argued that the *closed* thesis-driven essay dominates academic writing at the expense of more *open* forms, suggesting to students that "the ability to support an assertion is more important than the ability to examine an issue" (p. 458). The school essay has come to bear little resemblance to the essay as it was originally defined by Montaigne, an "essai" or attempt, a trial to see what one knows and thinks about a subject. Contemporary essayists, Montaigne's heirs, also view that form as fluid and exploratory. Edward Hoagland (1976) writes:

A personal essay is like a human voice talking, its order, the mind's natural flow, instead of a systemized outline of ideas. Though more wayward or informal than an article or treatise, somewhere it contains a point which is its real center, even if the point couldn't be uttered in fewer words than the essayist has used. Essays don't usually boil down to a summary, as articles do (in Smart, 1985, p. 223).

## SCHOOL REFORM—REEXAMINING CONANT'S WAGER

This chapter began with the claim that student's language development is not a natural biological unfolding but rather reflects and gains direction from the culture of the school: as Vygotsy claimed 50 years ago, reversing Piagetian logic, instruction precedes development. Studies of high school instruction and student achievement in U.S. schools provide a clear illustration of Vygotsky's contention. Instruction emphasizes the acquisition of factual information and repetitive exercises dealing with the mechanics of language, to the neglect of objectives dealing with critical thinking and intellectual development. Similarly, students seem to attain a basic competence on reading and writing, but they have difficulty in the extension and elaboration of their ideas. They have learned what they have been taught.

It is unlikely that this problem identified in virtually all of the high school reports can be remedied through exhortation or accountability schemes, tougher graduation requirements, or career ladders, all of which would leave the basic structure of the high school and the working conditions of teachers unchanged. The first article to appear in the *English Journal*, which began publication in 1912, identified the workload of the high school teacher as the major obstacle to effective writing instruction. Entitled, "Can Good Composition Teaching Be Done Under Present Conditions?" it began:

No.
This is a small and apparently unprotected word, occupying a somewhat exposed position; but it is upborne by indisputable truth (Hopkins, 1912, p. 1).

Hopkins' essay recounts the attempts to assign the responsibility for teaching writing to English teachers without any reduction in teacher–pupil ratio. Writing, Hopkins contends, can only be learned through writing; in the terminology of the day it was a "laboratory subject." Yet, the demands of responding to student writing were causing teachers to "resign, break down, perhaps become permanent invalids, having sacrificed ambition, health, and in not a few instances even life, in the struggle to do all the work" (p. 1).

A 1977 survey of teaching conditions in English suggest that the teacher-student ratio has actually worsened in the time since Hopkins wrote. The typical load is five classes per day, and in randomly selected schools 28.7% of classes had 26 to 30 students, and 30.2% had more than 31 students (Applebee, 1978b). And so long as English teachers meet five classes a day, they must engage with well over a hundred students a day—even

if class size is kept down. It is hardly surprising that instruction is largely presentational, that it focuses on information and mechanical skills that can be efficiently tested. Given this teaching load, it is also understandable why teachers rely on formulaic essay writing and the factual testing of reading.

Reformers like Sizer (1984) argue that high schools could be organized in different ways; that this pattern of requiring a teacher to meet a large number of students for a short time each day is an accommodation schools make to the "shopping mall" concept. The fragmented day is a necessary compromise if students are to have an array of options to choose from. Sizer's recommendation is to renegotiate the compromises schools make: academic subjects, rather than imitating the divisions of the university, could be consolidated into four areas: inquiry and expression, mathematics and science, literature and arts, and philosophy and history. In exchange for teaching more broadly defined subjects, teachers would teach fewer students and therefore be able to break out of the presentational mode and provide more individualized attention. Block scheduling— where students meet for longer periods of time, but not every day—also works to reduce the number of students taught in a day.

One of the best-known reform efforts inspired by Sizer is Central Park East (Meier, 1995). The faculty rethought the curriculum from the bottom up, even challenging the sacrosanct place of subjects like algebra and calculus; they began basing evaluation on presentations of learning, and instituted flexible scheduling in longer time segments. According to Meier, the key and indispensable element in these changes was the small size of the school:

Small autonomous schools, are, when all is said and done, a way to reestablish for us all, adults and children, the experience of community, of conversation, of the stuff of public as well as academic life. They expose us, young and old, to the workings of our political arrangements as we see how the politics of a school, the decisions made by kids and teachers, actually happen and how we can affect them (p. 118).

Meier and Sizer are making the case for revisualizing what high schools should be like; they are challenging Conant's model of the comprehensive high school that *had to be large* in order to offer the needed array of opportunities—the physics *and* chemistry labs, the elaborate set of tracks for students, and so much more. As smaller regional schools consolidated into larger schools in the 1960s, there was a trade of intimacy for supposed choice. Conant underestimated the price to be paid for comprehensiveness, the alienation of both teachers and students, in educational structures that seemed less and less able to respond to them: "Large schools neither nourish the spirit nor educate the mind" (Meier, p. 107).

Yet there is an image of high school that is embedded in the minds of all who went through them: It has a particular architecture, a system of bells, seating charts, wall posters, subjects, tests, grades, proms, athletic events, that is both maddeningly and reassuringly familiar. For all the criticism of schools, the public is quite resistant to major tampering with this picture (e.g., the suggestion that trigonometry may have undeserved prominence). Yet, it is a system where a majority of students fail to develop the habits of mind central to reflective thought.

# References

Applebee, A. N. (1977). ERIC/RCS report: The elements of response to a literary work: What have we learned. *Research in the Teaching of English, 11,* 255-271.

Applebee, A. N. (1978a). *The child's concept of story: Ages two to seventeen.* Chicago: University of Chicago Press.

Applebee, A. N. (1978b). *A survey of teaching conditions in English, 1977.* Urbana, IL: ERIC/National Council of Teachers of English.

Applebee, A. N. (1981). *Writing in the secondary school: English and the content areas* (Research Report 21). Urbana, IL: National Council of Teachers of English.

Applebee, A. N., Langer, J. A., & Mullis, I. V. S. (1986a). *The reading report card. Progress toward excellence in our schools.* Princeton, NJ: Educational Testing Service.

Applebee, A. N., Langer, J. A., & Mullis, I. V. S. (1986b). *The writing report card: Writing achievement in American schools.* Princeton, NJ: Educational Testing Service.

Applebee, A. N., Langer, J. A., & Mullis, I. V. S. (1987a). *Literature and U.S. history: The instructional experience and factual knowledge of high school juniors.* Princeton, NJ: Educational Testing Service.

Applebee, A. N., Langer. J. A., & Mullis, I. V. S. (1987b). *Learning to be literate in America: Reading, writing, and reasoning* Princeton, NJ: Educational Testing Service.

Atwell, N. (1998). *In the middle: New understandings about writing, reading, and learning.* Portsmouth: Heinemann.

Bartholomae, D. (1983). Writing assignments: Where writing begins. In P. Stock (Ed.), *Forum: Essays on theory and practice in the teaching of writing.* Portsmouth, NH: Heinemann/Boynton Cook.

Beach, R., & Wendler, L. (1987). Development differences in response to a story. *Research in the Teaching of English, 21,* 286-297.

Belenky, M. F., Clinchy, B. M., Goldberger, N., & Tarule, J. M. (1986). *Women's ways of knowing: The development of self, voice, and mind.* New York: Basic Books.

Bizzell, P. (1986). Composing processes: An overview. In A. Petrosky & D. Bartholomae (Eds.), *The teaching of writing: Eighty-fifth yearbook of the national society for the study of education, part II.* Chicago: National Society for the Study of Education.

Bloom. B. (Ed.). (1959). *Taxonomy of educational objectives: The classification of goals by a committee of college and university examiners.* New York: Longman.

Boden, M. (1980). *Jean Piaget.* New York: Viking.

Boyer, E. (1983). *High school: A report on secondary education in America.* New York: Harper & Row.

Braddock, J, Lloyd-Jones, R., & Schoer, L. (1963). *Research in written composition.* Urbana, IL: National Council of Teachers of English.

Brannon, L., & Knoblauch, C. H. (1982). On students' rights to their own texts: A model of teacher response. *College Composition and Communication, 33,* 157-166.

Bridwell, L. (1980). Revising strategies in twelfth grade students' transactional writing. *Research in the Teaching of English, 14,* 197-222.

Britton, J., Burgess, T., Martin, N., McLeod, A., & Rosen, H. (1975). *The development of writing abilities: 11-18.* London: Macmillan Education.

Calkins, L. (1983). *Lessons from a child.* Exeter, NH: Heinemann.

Campbell, J., Voelkl, K., & Donahue, P. (1996). *Report in Brief: NAEP 1996 Trends in Academic Progress.* Washington, DC: U.S. Office of Education.

Carnicelli, T. (1980). The writing conference: A one-to-one conversation. In T. Donovan & B. McClelland (Eds.), *Eight approaches to teaching composition.* Urbana, IL: National Council of Teachers of English.

Christensen, F. (1967). *Notes toward a new rhetoric.* New York: Harper & Row.

Combs, W. (1976). Further effects of sentence-combining on writing ability. *Research in the Teaching of English, 10,* 137-149.

Conant, J. B. (1959). *The American high school today.* New York: McGraw-Hill.

Conant, J. B. (1967). *The comprehensive high school.* New York: McGraw-Hill.

Delpit, L. (1994). *Other people's children: Cultural conflict in the classroom.* New York: New Press.

Durst, R. (1984). The development of analytic writing. In A. Applebee, *Contexts for Learning to Write: Studies of Secondary School Instruction.* Norwood, NJ: Ablex.

Dyson, A. (1997). *Writing superheroes: Contemporary childhood, popular culture, and classroom literacy.* New York: Teachers College Press.

Elbow, P. (1973). *Writing without teachers.* New York: Oxford University Press.

Emig, J. (1971). *The composing process of twelfth graders.* (Research Report 13). Urbana, IL: National Council of Teachers of English.

Fish, S. (1980). *Is there a text in this class?: The authority of interpretive communities.* Cambridge, MA: Harvard University Press.

Fitzgerald, F. (1979). *America revised.* New York: Vintage Books.

Flower, L., & Hayes, J. R. (1981). A cognitive process theory of writing. *College Composition and Communication, 32,* 365-387.

Flower, L., & Hayes, J. R. (1980). The dynamics of composing: Making plans and juggling constraints. In L. W. Gregg & E. R. Steinberg, (Eds.), *Cognitive Processes in Writing* (pp. 00-00). Hillsdale, NJ: Lawrence Earlbaum Associates.

Friere, P. (1970). *Pedagogy of the oppressed.* New York: Herder & Herder.

Fulwiler, T. (1988). *The journal book.* Portsmouth, NH: Boynton/Cook and Heinemann.

Garrison, R. (1974). One-to-one: Tutorial instruction in freshman English. *New Directions for Community Colleges, 2*(1), 55-84.

Gilligan, C. (1982). *In a different voice: Psychological theory and women's development.* Cambridge, MA: Harvard University Press.

Goodlad, J. (1984). *A place called school: Prospects for the future.* New York: McGraw-Hill.

Harste, J., Woodward, V., & Burke, C. (1984). *Language stories and literacy lessons.* Portsmouth, NH: Heinemann.

Hartwell, P. (1985). Grammar, grammars, and the teaching of grammar. *College English, 47,* 105-127.

Heath, S. B. (1983). *Ways with words: Language, life, and work in communities and classrooms.* Cambridge, England: Cambridge University Press.

Hemming, H. (1985). Reading: A monitor for writing. In J. Hansen, T. Newkirk, & D. Graves (Eds.), *Breaking ground: Teachers relate reading and writing in the elementary school.* Portsmouth, NH: Heinemann.

Hillocks, G. (1986). *Research on written composition: New directions for teaching.* Urbana, IL: National Conference on Research in English.

Hopkins, E. M. (1912). Can good composition teaching be done under present conditions. *English Journal, 1,* 1-7.

Hunt, K. (1977). Early blooming and late blooming syntactic structures. In C. Cooper & L. Odell (Eds.), *Evaluating writing: Describing, measuring, judging.* Urbana, IL: National Council of Teachers of English.

Hunt, K. (1965). *Grammatical structures written at three grade levels* (Research Report 3). Urbana, IL: National Council of Teachers of English.

Kohlberg, L. (1981). *The philosophy of moral development.* New York: Harper & Row.

Kolnn, M. (1981). Closing the books on alchemy. *College Composition and Communication, 32,* 139-151.

Lindemann, E. (1982). *A rhetoric for writers.* New York: Oxford University Press.

Loban, W. (1976). *Language development: Kindergarten through grade twelve.* (Research Report 18). Urbana, IL: National Council of Teachers of English.

Macrorie, K. (1968). *Writing to be read.* Rochelle Park, NJ: Hayden.

Marshall, J. (1987). The effects of writing on students' understanding of literary texts. *Research in the Teaching of English, 21,* 30-63.

Martin, N., D'Arcy, P., Newton, B., & Parker, R. (1976). *Writing and learning across the curriculum, 11-16.* Portsmouth, NH: Boynton/Cook.

Matsuhashi, A. (1981). Pausing and planning: The tempo of written discourse production. *Research in the Teaching of English, 15,* 113-134.

Meier, D. (1995). *The power of their ideas: Lessons for America from a small school in Harlem.* Boston: Beacon Press.

Mellon, J. (1969). *Transformational sentence combining.* (Research Report 10). Urbana, IL: National Council of Teachers of English.

Moffett, J. (1992). *Detecting growth in language.* Portsmouth, NH: Heinemann.

Moffett, J. (1968). *Teaching the universe of discourse.* Boston: Houghton Mifflin.

Morenberg, M., Daiker, D., & Kerek, A. (1978). Sentence combining at the college level: An experimental study. *Research in the Teaching of English, 12,* 245-256.

Morenberg, M., Daiker, D., & Kerek, A. (1980). Sentence-combining over a three-year period: A case study. Paper, annual meeting of the CCC. (ERIC Document Reproduction Service No. ED 186 921)

Murray, D. (1968). *A writer teaches writing.* Boston: Houghton Miffin.

Murray, D. (1980). Writing as process: How writing finds it's own meaning. In T. Donovan & B. McClelland (Eds.), *Eight approaches to teaching composition.* Urbana, IL: National Council of Teachers of English.

*A Nation At Risk.* (1983). (Report by the National Commission on Excellence). Washington, DC: U.S. Government Printing Office.

National Assessment of Educational Progress. (1994). *NAEP 1994 reading assessment—at a glance.* Washington, DC: U.S. Office of Education.

New Hampshire Educational Improvement and Assessment Program. (1997). *Educational assessment report—End of grade 10.* Concord, NH: State Department of Education.

O'Donnell, R., Griffin, W., & Norris, R. (1967). *Syntax of kindergarten and elementary school children: A transformational analysis.* (Research Report 8). Urbana, IL: National Council of Teachers of English.

O'Hare, F. (1973). *Sentence combining: Improving student writing without formal grammar instruction.* (Research Report 15). Urbana, IL: National Council of Teachers of English.

Odell, L., & Cooper, C. (1976). Describing responses to works of fiction. *Research in the Teaching of English, 10,* 203-225.

Perl, S. (1979). The composing process of unskilled college writers. *Research in the Teaching of English, 13,* 317-336.

Perry, W. (1970). *Forms of intellectual and ethical development in the college years: A scheme.* New York: Holt, Rinehart, & Winston.

Polanyi, M. (1958). *Personal knowledge: Toward a post-critical philosophy.* Chicago: University of Chicago Press.

Powell, A., Farrar, E., & Cohen, D. (1985). *The shopping mall high school.* Boston: Houghton Muffin.

Purcell-Gates, V. (1995). *Other people's words: The cycle of low literacy.* Cambridge, MA: Harvard University Press.

Purves, A., & Rippere, V. (1968). *Elements of writing about a literary work: A study of response to literature.* (Research Report 9). Urbana, IL: National Council of Teachers of English.

*Reading, writing, and thinking:* Results from the 1979-1980 assessment of reading and literature. (1981). Denver, CO: National Assessment of Educational Progress.

Richards, I. A. (1929). *Practical Criticism.* New York: Harcourt, Brace, & World.

Rosenblatt, L. (1978). *The reader, the text, and the poem: The transactional theory of the literacy work.* Carbondale, IL: Southern Illinois University Press.

Sizer, T. (1984). *Horace's compromise: The dilemma of the American high school.* Boston: Houghton Mifflin.

Smart, W. (1985). *Eight modern essays.* (4th ed.). New York: St. Martins.

Sommers, N. (1980). Revision strategies of student writers and experienced writers. *College Composition and Communication, 31,* 378-388.

Stewart, M. (1978). Freshman sentence combining: A Canadian project. *Research in the Teaching of English, 12,* 257-268.

Stille, A. (1998, June 11). The betrayal of history. *The New York Review of Books, 44*(10), 15-20.

Squire, J. (1964). *The responses of adolescents while reading four short stories.* (Research Report 2). Urbana, IL: National Council of Teachers.

Squire, J., & Applebee, R. (1968). *High school English instruction today.* New York: Appleton-Century-Crofts.

Svennson, C. (1985). *The construction of poetic meaning: A cultural developmental study of symbolic and non-symbolic strategies in the interpretation of contemporary poetry.* Malmo, Sweden: Liber Forlag.

Vygotsky, L. (1978). *Mind in society.* Cambridge, MA: Harvard University Press.

Wilson, W. (1996). *When work disappears: The world of the new urban poor.* New York: Vintage.

Zeiger, W. (1985). The exploratory essay: Enfranchising the spirit of inquiry in college composition. *College English, 47,* 454-466.

# LITERACY LEARNING AFTER HIGH SCHOOL

## Richard L. Venezky
### University of Delaware

The earliest studies ever recorded on reading, performed in France at the end of the 18th century, assessed the ability of adults to read different type fonts. From that time until the present, adults have been the primary subjects of psychological studies of reading, yet the improvement of literacy abilities beyond childhood, and especially beyond high school, has an impoverished empirical base, anchored primarily in research on reading in children. Darkenwald (1986), for example, in surveying 236 journal articles published between 1975 and 1980 on adult literacy education, found fewer than 12 that qualified as research. Although we know with great certainty the average number of milliseconds a skilled adult will fixate during silent reading and the distance in letter spaces from the center of the fovea to where single letters can no longer be recognized, we have almost no data on how decoding ability develops for those who acquire it after their teens, or even on how different instructional approaches influence reading strategies for this same population. On one hand, assumptions made for children are often extended without question to adults; on the other, lessons acquired in the investigation of child learning are ignored in the study of adults.

The review of adult literacy learning that follows is organized around three issues: What literacy skills develop after high school; what limits development for those with further literacy needs; and what types of training are most helpful at these levels. Cutting across these issues will be two further concerns. One is the nature of literacy research, especially at the postsecondary level. At present many literacy practices derive more from personal opinions than they do from empirical results. Problems are seldom pursued to satisfactory closure and no well-defined cutting edge for research exists. The healthy competition among researchers that is evidenced in low temperature fusion, genetics, and superconductivity, for example, has no counterparts in the field of adult literacy. Critical response to experiments is almost nonexistent, thus allowing some poorly designed and poorly executed studies to be touted as gospel, and some excellent

ones to remain in cluttered obscurity. The quality of research on reading and the haphazard connection between research and practice have been concerns for more than a half century (e.g., Vernon, 1931; Robinson, 1968; Singer, 1970; Gibson & Levin, 1975; Kamil, 1995).

By research is meant true empirical studies, with appropriate experimental designs. However, the finding from 40 years ago that the definitions of research for adult education were "exceedingly liberal" remains true today (Brunner, Wilder, Kirschner, & Newberry, 1959, cited in Weber, 1975, p. 156). For gauging what has changed in research and practice on adult literacy between the 1950s and now, the reader is encouraged to consult the overview of adult education research by Venezky, Oney, Sabatini, and Jain (1998). French (1987) presents an extensive overview and bibliography on the entire field of adult literacy up to the mid 1980s, including literacy research, while Cook (1977) reviews the 20th-century history of adult literacy education. A brief review of both research and practice can be found in Sticht (1988).

The second concern is the possibility that the K-12 language arts curriculum is a major contributor to the problems of the postsecondary literacy learner. By focusing so narrowing on "good" literature as a basis for literacy learning, the schools are denying to many, and especially those who drop out early, the essential skills they need for coping with everyday literacy demands (Venezky, 1982).

Although the interest of this chapter is in literacy in the broadest terms, that is, the utilization of reading, writing, numeracy, and document processing for social ends, studies on adult literacy are, with a few exceptions, studies of adult reading. Therefore, reading will be the focus here although "literacy" will occasionally be used, mostly as a reminder that the empirical base required for principled literacy instruction includes more than a knowledge of how reading is acquired. Because adult reading interests and basic processing habits have been reviewed extensively elsewhere (e.g., Gibson & Levin, 1975;

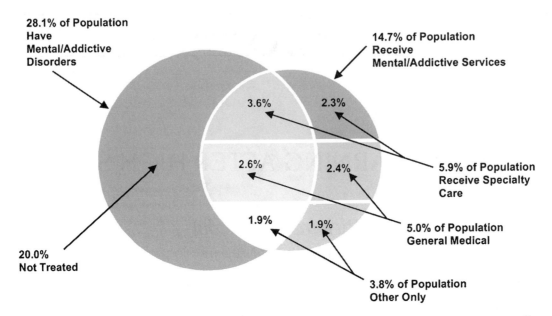

FIGURE 28.1. Annual prevalence of mental/addictive disorders and services.

Gray & Munroe, 1929; Buswell, 1937; Murphy, 1975; Pearson, Barr, Kamil, & Mosenthal, 1984; Sharon, 1973–74), little mention will be made of these topics. Instead, attention is focused on those areas of research that illuminate the questions previously stated. Many other important topics are not covered due to space limitations, including bilingualism and the social context of literacy learning.

## WHAT DEVELOPS AFTER HIGH SCHOOL

The nature of cognitive development and the adaptation of individual development to the demands of society, particularly after high school, leads to a practical classification of readers and reading development in the postsecondary years. In one category are those who failed to learn to read adequately—those who typically enter or are in need of adult basic education courses or the equivalent. Although many of these people hold certificates of graduation from high school, many do not. At the bottom of this group are students who read well below the fourth-grade level and for whom tutoring is usually recommended.

In the second group are students admitted to 2- and 4-year colleges but who lack essential reading skills and therefore typically are placed in skills courses or in other types of remedial instruction. And finally there are those who fall within the normal range or above for reading ability, whether they are in postsecondary education, work, the home, or the military.

Some insights into the nature of postsecondary development for these three groups can be gained from an analysis of the results of the National Adult Literacy Survey (NALS), carried out with over 26,000 adults (ages 16 and above) in the U.S. in 1992 (Kirsch, Jungeblut, Jenkins, & Kolstad, 1993). Figure 28.1 shows the percentages of the adult population, based on a projected total of 191,289,000 persons in the five proficiency levels for the prose scale, one of three scales on the survey. Level 1, which represents marginal reading ability, involves short texts and generally the location of a single, well-specified piece of information. Level 2 involves similar tasks, but, for example, with distractors present or low-level inferences required. A typical Level 3 task might require integration of information from a lengthy text without organizational aids, while levels 4 and 5 require corresponding more complex processing with more complex texts.

From Fig. 28.1 it can be seen that 21% of the projected population performed at Level 1, a level below what is required for most remunerative jobs today. Of this group 62% did not finish high school and 33% were age 65 or older. Only 29% reported that they did not read well (English) and only 34% claimed that they did not write (English) well. On the high end of the literacy scale, represented by Level 5 in the NALS survey, are only 3% of the adult population. Although conclusions based on a single examination, unanchored to any established criteria, and given without practice, could be debated, it is doubtful that extremely large improvements in outcomes would occur with other thoughtful approaches to assessment.

A second important outcome of NALS was the finding that across the sample tested, scores on the prose scale improved with increasing age until around age 45, and then began to decline steeply. Even though NALS was not a longitudinal study, re-analyses of the data, holding education and occupation constant, still found an increase in performance into the 40–50 age range. Thus, one could conclude that performance on NALS-like tests, which tap reading for problem solving, increases from the end of high school until mid-life, on the average. The two most common approaches for accounting for such changes have been stage models, which focus on the development of reading from an instructional perspective, and component skills models, which focus on mental processing from a psychological perspective.

## Stages Models for Reading Development

The earliest approximation to a stage model for reading development was published by Horace Mann (1839), in which mechanical and mental parts for reading were defined. Mann did not present these parts as a developmental sequence, but that could be inferred from his presentation. In the 20th century several developmental models for reading development were proposed, based on observations of children's reading habits. The two most elaborate of these are Gray (1937), which includes five stages, and Chall (1983), which posits six stages. Other influential models have been proposed by Gates (1947) and by Russell (1961) (see Chall, 1999, for a review). Chall (1994) has suggested a modification for adults of her model, collapsing the six stages into three: basic literacy, functional literacy, and advanced literacy. She also posits three broad components, based on Carroll (1977): language, cognition, and reading skills, that have different levels of importance at each of the proficiency levels.

A different form of developmental model for reading is implied by a reading maturity scaling developed by Gray and Rogers (1956). From studies of adult reading interests, attitudes, and abilities, a scaling procedure was devised and built around interest in reading, purposes for reading, recognition and construction of meaning, reaction to and use of ideas apprehended, and kinds of material read. Within each category three or four topics were defined, with a 5-point scale for evaluating subjects on each of these. Thus, interest in reading was evaluated for (a) enthusiasm for reading, (b) amount of time spent reading, (c) breadth of interest, and (d) depth of interest. What is important about this scheme is that it defines the mature adult reader in terms not only of latent skill, as measured on a reading test, but also in terms of interests, breadth and depth of actual reading practices, willingness to relate ideas read to other information, concepts, and kinds of materials read.

The school's responsibility in literacy training is not only to engender the skills required for competent reading, but also to encourage the full application of these abilities for personal and social ends. Studies done over the last 60 years indicate that many adults have little interest in reading beyond the more shallow components of newspapers and magazines, and that book reading for all but the highly educated is minimal at best (Gray & Munroe, 1929; Gray, 1956; Gray & Rogers, 1956; Kirsch & Jungeblut, 1986; Sharon, 1973–74, Zill & Winglee, 1990).

The validity and utility of any of these models for adult learners, however, remains to be demonstrated. Although children tend to follow similar paths from total unawareness of letters and words to fully mature reading, adults who are in need of literacy instruction (the first category defined above) are a far more diverse group, both in reading ability and in background knowledge. Some low literate adults, either for reasons of health or opportunity, have had limited exposure to reading instruction, while others have passed through 8 or more years of instruction, acquiring, in some cases, faulty strategies for coping with the demands of print.

In reviewing studies and opinions on stages of reading, furthermore, it is difficult to ignore the paucity of empirical data to support any stage-by-stage model for adult learners. Nevertheless, if stages that characterize literacy development in adults can be verified, then attention could shift to the instructional implications of each stage and especially to the instructional strategies that most effectively assist progression from stage to stage.

## Component Skills Models

Most psychological models for reading, whether linear, interactive, or networked, focus on one or more components of the reading process (see Samuels & Kamil, 1984 for a review). The more complete models usually have separable components for word recognition and for language comprehension while the less complete may focus on one or the other of these two basic processes. These models tend to differ from the stage models just discussed in that processing variables such as the size of the units operated on and the speed of processing play critical roles. Most of the research on adult reading tends to derive from component models rather than developmental models, although the relationship of much of the work to any theoretical underpinnings is tenuous at best.

Malicky and Norman (1982), for example, analyzed the reading strategies of 16 adults who were full-time students in an adult basic education program. The subjects ranged in age from 18 to 35 years, and in reading levels from readiness to sixth grade, based on a reading inventory. From an analysis of oral reading errors obtained at different times during the course, different patterns of processing changes were detected. For example, for one group of readers who on entry over-relied on graphemic cues, a shift was made toward a more balanced reliance on both graphemic and grammatical cues. This group, however, made no gains in reading ability. Another group that did make gains in reading ability showed slightly less ability than the no gain group to use semantic cues.

In a related study, Leibert (1983) compared the oral reading errors of adult basic education students to elementary-level students with comparable reading levels. For children, rate of reading as well as accuracy of recall declined with passage difficulty, while for the adults only rate of reading declined over the same set of passages. Given the vastly different knowledge and experience bases that adults and children bring to a reading task, plus the superior experience that most adults have had with language communication, differences in processing strategies should be expected, even for those who produce similar scores on reading tests. Even the approaches to taking tests may differ. Adults, according to Karlsen (1970), take fewer risks than children and therefore tend to omit items they are not sure of rather than guessing at them. Sticht (1982) has also found from a series of comparisons of adult and children in reading and reading-related tasks that processing strategies often differ for those who appear to be at the same reading level.

One difficulty in evaluating any of these models is that adult readers vary across the entire range of this ability, and among those on the lowest end are many with disabilities. Some college-level students read on grade level and can continue to improve their reading speeds and their vocabularies through increased reading. Other college students have incomplete or dysfunctional comprehension strategies, especially for nonnarrative texts, and need specific attention to these needs, while many adults who fit into the lowest level on the NALS need a wide range of assistance and will probably never reach the average level for their ages. Just what limits adults from reaching higher reading levels is the topic of the next section.

## BARRIERS TO IMPROVED READING

Among the many suggestions for exploring barriers to improved adult reading, one of the most interesting involves general language comprehension, especially as marked by listening comprehension. The relationship of listening comprehension to reading comprehension is a theme that threads its way through the last 50 years or so of reading research. It has been argued that because reading is language based and language is acquired first by most people through listening, a comparison of listening to reading ability might reveal capacity to learn to read (e.g., Goldstein, 1940). Several dissertations have been done on the topic, a few standardized tests developed, and at least two monographs published (Goldstein, 1940; Sticht, Beck, Hauke, Kleiman, & James, 1974). One hypothesis drawn from this work is that listening (i.e., auding) ability represents an upper bound on reading ability, particularly after eighth grade, and that mature reading can be defined as the quality of reading where comprehension is at least equivalent to listening comprehension.

The problems with this notion are first that we know less about the development of listening comprehension than we do about reading comprehension, and second, that the relationship of listening comprehension to reading comprehension is more complex than most recent studies admit, depending on, among other variables, the difficulty level of the text and the intelligence of the reader/listener. Goldstein (1940), whose work in this area remains as the most thorough, found from studies of adults (ages 18 to 65) the following:

1. Superiority of listening over reading decreases with increasing difficulty of the text. For easy texts, listening is superior to reading regardless of intelligence.
2. Difference between listening and reading ability increases with decreasing intelligence.
3. Passages that are equivalent for reading may not be equivalent for listening.

The use of a listening/reading ratio as an indicator of learning capacity engenders a number of risks, based on the findings of Goldstein (1940). Persons who measure low in listening comprehension may do so for a variety of reasons, none of which are well understood. Then, persons with low listening ability might be helped best by extensive reading training, especially because beyond the initial levels of learning, self-instruction becomes more practicable with reading training than listening training. The claim that listening ability for adults represents an upper bound for reading ability has no empirical support. The differences between the two might provide useful diagnostic information, particularly about the mechanics of reading, but even this awaits more careful analysis.

### Specific Processing Problems

Studies in a number of different languages suggest that adults who cannot read an alphabetic orthography have difficulty in manipulating phonemes. A series of studies that investigated metalinguistic abilities in adult illiterates in rural Portugal (Morais, Cary, Alegria, & Bertelson, 1979; Morais, Bertelson, Cary, & Alegria, 1986; Morais, Content, Bertelson, & Cary, 1988) showed that illiterates performed very poorly on tasks such as phoneme deletion or phoneme substitution, which both require phonemic awareness. Lukatela, Carello, Shankweiler, and Liberman (1995) also found minimal phonemic awareness among truly illiterate adults in Serbo-Croatia. The impairment in phonemic segmentation skills of low-literacy adults have been demonstrated among English-speakers as well (Liberman, Rubin, Duques, & Carlisle, 1985). A group of quasi-literate adults who had serious difficulties in spelling were able to achieve only a 58% success rate in phoneme segmentation tested by phoneme deletion. (That is, they had difficulties with tasks such as orally deleting the /l/ in *slip* and determining that the resulting word was *sip*). Similarly, a group of low-literacy adults performing at or below fifth-grade level have been shown to perform poorly on phonemic awareness tasks (Read & Ruyter, 1985). As with children, the difficulties low-literacy adults demonstrated were greater at the phoneme than syllable level.

Byrne and Ledez (1983) also investigated phonological awareness skills in adult poor readers and found unusually low performances on tasks related to this skill, as did Liberman, Rubin, Duques, and Carlisle (1985) with adults seeking literacy instruction. Comparing the decoding and phoneme awareness skills of adult dyslexics to those in normal adults, Kitz and Tarver (1989) showed that adult dyslexics performed worse on phoneme reversal and decoding tasks than average reading adults.

A second major area of processing weakness with low-literate adults is in word recognition, which is a function of both vocabulary size and familiarity with print. Not only is word recognition ability correlated with reading ability in adults, but it is also an independent predictor of it (Stanovich, 1991). Since a major portion of vocabulary growth during and after high school derives from reading, adults who read poorly or who seldom read tend to fall further behind in vocabulary development.

In contrast to these studies, which show a core phonological deficit and vocabulary problems in many low-literate adults, related studies have generally found that low-literate adults have an appreciation for comprehension and often try to apply appropriate comprehension strategies to different types of print (Forlizzi, 1992). Good and poor adult readers also tend to vary little in some metacognitive skills (Cull & Zechmeister, 1994). However, at a more detailed level, at least one study found that poor adult readers lacked appropriate sensitivity to the structure of paragraphs and stories (Gambrell & Heathington, 1981).

## HOW DO WE IMPROVE ADULT READING ABILITY?

### Processing Modes

From studies done early in the 20th century that appeared to show that eye movements varied according to text content (e.g., Judd & Buswell, 1922), suggestions were made for remedial reading programs built around different types of reading for different subject areas. McCaul (1944), for example, proposed that literature be used to increase reading speed, social studies for improving organization ability, and science for precision and accuracy. Dixon (1951), in criticizing the studies done up to that time, pointed out that Judd and Buswell (1922) based their results on only four college students, made no tests for significance of differences, and did not equate passages for conceptual load, vocabulary, or any other internal variable. (Judd & Buswell, 1922, report fixations per line for reading fiction, geography, rhetoric, easy verse, French grammar, blank verse, and algebra.) Studies by Terry (1922), Tinker (1928), Stone (1941), and others were found to suffer from similar problems.

Dixon (1951) replicated these studies, using reading speed and various eye movement variables as dependent measures, but equated passages for objective difficulty, using the Flesch and Lorge readability formulas. Passages were selected from the fields of education, history, and physics, and the subjects were university professors and graduate students from these same areas. Subjects read a single practice passage in each area and then the test passage, answering five general yes–no questions after each reading. The results showed no intrinsic subject matter differences. Each group of subjects read fastest from its own field, and no group was significantly better than any other. As would be expected from modern data, individual variation within fields was as wide if not wider than differences across fields.

Although Dixon (1951) has rejected the idea of subject-based differences in reading habits, at least as assayed by reading speed and eye movements, this study is limited to a single type of reading task, albeit, the one most commonly encountered in schooling (i.e., read the passage for general meaning and answer questions on it afterwards). Other investigators have pursued the notion of reading differences by attending to task differences in reading (and occasionally writing).

### Reading Tasks

Most researchers agree that school and adult reading requirements differ, but exactly how to characterize this difference is not settled. Caylor and Sticht (1973), Diehl and Mikulecky (1980), and others have made a distinction between reading-to-learn and reading-to-do. The former, which applies to reading tasks in which new information is obtained for nonimmediate purposes, characterizes most in-school reading requirements, while the latter is typical of reading tasks faced by adults, particularly job-related reading tasks. Mikulecky (1982) analyzed the reading tasks of 48 high school juniors, 51 adult technical

school students, and 150 workers drawn from a cross section of occupations, using interviews and a variety of reading assessment procedures. High school students differed significantly from middle-level workers in reading demands encountered, in literacy competencies, and in reading strategies employed. The workers, for example, had significantly higher percentage of reading-to-do tasks (generally with learning occurring in the process), and used problem solving techniques, note taking, and underlining more often. The students, on the other hand, employed rereading as their primary strategy for getting meaning from a text. Blue-collar workers rated accurate reading as more important than technical school students did, while professionals had a significantly broader scope of reading materials than all the other groups and tended to strive more to relate what they read to what they already knew.

Although the reading-to-learn versus reading-to-do contrast captures a portion of the difference between school-based reading and job reading, it does not give a complete characterization of these differences. First, schooling by definition has a high reading-to-learn component. Without it, much of our mass educational system would be ineffective. But some reading-to-learn can and does require reading-to-do. Instructions, such as for laboratory experiments and for assignments in general fit this class, and many math word problems do also. But even within the pure reading-to-learn class, reading strategies may differ according to purpose for reading (Bond & Bond, 1941). How a student reads a history passage, for example, might depend on whether the goal is passing a short-answer test, answering an essay test, developing a poster representation of the content, or finding a topic for a report.

Elementary school reading differs dramatically from adult reading both in types of materials used for reading instruction and in reading tasks. Within the context of the basal reader, the central goals of reading are defined around the characteristics of narrative fiction: getting the main point of the story, understanding the author's purpose, following the plot, and building character representations. Nonfiction is underrepresented relative to its importance in the school curriculum and is often taught as if it were a flawed form of fiction (Venezky, 1982). Fiction tends to have a total text focus, a high aesthetic component, subtlety by intention, and an emphasis more on general than particular understanding. Most expository writing, in contrast, is information focused, low on aesthetic aspirations, direct, and requiring attention to details. In elementary school reading classes the primary reading task remains constant and is seldom made overt: read and understand the entire passage, with emphasis at the higher grades on plot, character, and the author's intentions. For adult reading (other than fiction), tasks vary considerably, but usually have a problem solving flavor: Find how much sugar we need to make four quarts of blackberry jam; determine which foods I can eat on my diet; find what time the movie starts. These differences apply not only to the tasks involved but also to the strategies that readers need to be successful in the tasks (Gutherie & Kirsch, 1987).

Everyday reading tasks can be characterized by three phases: locate information, operate on what is found, and respond. All three phases can vary in difficulty, although the first two tend to have the greatest range of complexity. How difficult any one will be depends first on the task and then on the text. Finding from *Lincoln's Gettysburg Address*, for example, who brought forth a new nation is a significantly easier task than deciding how in the *Address* Lincoln resolves the paradox in the *Declaration of Independence* of equality being both a natural right and a right that could be altered by popular consent. Assessing text difficulty by readability measures ignores the role of reading task in directing reading strategy. Readability measures have some (limited) utility for elementary school reading so long as reading is based primarily on narrative fiction and the reading task is to read and digest the entire text. When realistic reading tasks are required, readability indexes fail.

In the items on the NALS survey previously discussed, the processing demands rather than the document forms were the primary determinants of task difficulty. Furthermore, the traditional division of comprehension tasks into literal and inferential categories did not predict task difficulty. Some literal tasks, for example, were more difficult than some inferential tasks. In some cases the vocabulary differences between the task specification and the matching text information created the difficulty; in other cases it was the presence of redundant information; and in others, it was the number of features or items of information that had to be attended for successful completion of the task. Furthermore, the factors that created difficulties in these tasks were similar to the factors that determine difficulty of math word problems (Carpenter, Corbitt, Kepner, Linquist, & Reys, 1980).

Problem solving appears to be poorly taught in American schools, if by problem solving we mean the types of tasks reflected in the NAEP science and math assessments. In the Third International Survey of Mathematics and Science Skills (TIMSS), for example, U.S. students in fourth grade were near the top of the performance scale but by eighth grade were around the middle and by the twelfth grade, close to the bottom (NCES, 1999). Since a large component of adult literacy demands require problem-solving skills, adults with low reading skills and poor problem solving abilities suffer a double disadvantage. The root of this problem is centered in two time-honored school practices. The first is basing reading instruction primarily on narrative fiction; the second is isolating reading practice from the content areas. Learning to read legal arguments, editorials, repair manuals, and the like is at least as important for success in school and later life as learning to read and enjoy "good" fiction, yet the latter is favored disproportionately over the former for reading instruction.

### Other Instructional Issues

Missing from adult studies are attempts to relate reading strategies to reading instruction. Barr (1972), for example, found a strong influence of instruction on the types of oral reading errors made by children in first grade. There is every reason to assume that similar influence occurs with adult learners. Also missing is a serious consideration of the role of automaticity in fluent reading behavior. In executing complex skills, the ability to do lower order skills rapidly and without overt attention has been shown to be critical for successful performance

(Anderson, 1985). For reading this appears to be especially true (Perfetti, 1985). Word recognition, whether acquired through intensive phonics or through any other means, needs to be done rapidly if processing attention is to be available for higher level comprehension. Where adult literacy educators now debate whether or not to teach phonics, they should be debating how to build up rapid word recognition.

The role of vocabulary in literacy acquisition is yet another area where further instructional research is needed at the adult level. Through the school years reading vocabulary increases on the average at the rate of approximately 5,000 words per year, assuming a conservative definition of the term word (Miller & Gildea, 1987). For the poorer readers, for the dropouts, and for those especially from limited English environments, English vocabulary acquisition is significantly below this figure. Among those adults most in need of literacy training, vocabulary learning is problematic, due in part to the low level of literacy use in the environments in which many of them exist (Taylor, Wade, Jackson, Blum, & Goold, 1980). Improved vocabulary training may be as important for adult literacy as any of the abilities currently driving literacy instruction.

A final issue to consider is that of situated versus decontextualized knowledge. Opinion among adult educators appears to favor strongly the placing of literacy training within the contexts that adults are most familiar with and which most clearly distinguish the adult world from that of the child (French, 1987). Yet there should be reservations about the extent to which effective literacy learning can be divorced from a classroom, intellectual setting. Scribner and Cole (1981), for example, found among the Vai that the cognitive consequences of literacy learning from a natural setting were inferior to those from a schooling environment. Other researchers have found that years of completion of formal schooling is a better predictor of Wechsler Adult Intelligence scores than age (Birren & Morrison, 1961), although this may reflect subject selectivity as much as schooling consequences. At a minimum, the current debate over situated learning should be observed closely by adult reading researchers, and perhaps used as a guide for research planning.

## CONCLUSIONS

Research on adult literacy learning, if it is to inform adult instruction, must become more focused on serious problems, become more sensitive to the major issues emerging from cognitive studies within and without reading, and must be subjected to the same intensive peer review that sustains and drives research in other fields. Whether there are five or six stages to adult literacy development is a far less important issue than whether or not self-sustained literacy learning can take place before automaticity in word recognition is achieved. For building adult reading instruction, a problem-solving perspective appears to be superior to a traditional reading comprehension perspective. Although the evidence for assessing literacy needs in adults is not as extensive as we would like it to be, a pattern can be discerned wherein the best readers are able to transfer their school-based skills to adult reading tasks, the average ones do so with difficulty, and the poorer ones hardly at all. Elementary and high school reading instruction has, for at least the past century, been constructed around "good literature," leaving most students to acquire information processing skills on their own. What is needed is an expanded view of literacy instruction, wherein locating and operating on information can share stage center with reading and enjoying fiction. The schools in general are not doing an adequate job in teaching problem solving, and adult literacy failures are a special case of this. So long as reading instruction and reading assessment are mired in grade level equivalents, readability indexes, and other oversimplifications of a narrative fiction orientation, literacy in America will continue to be a problem. Nevertheless, enough good research on adult literacy learning exists to foster the hope that with sufficient funding and a more focused research orientation, major contributions could be made toward the improvement of adult literacy learning.

# References

Anderson, J. R. (1985). *Cognitive psychology and its implications* (2nd ed.). New York: W. H. Freeman.

Barr, R. (1972). The influence of instructional conditions on word recognition errors. *Reading Research Quarterly, 7,* 509-579.

Birren, J. E., & Morrison, D. F. (1961). Analysis of the WAIS subtests in relation to age and education. *Journal of Gerontology, 16,* 363-369.

Bond, G. L., & Bond, E. (1941). *Developmental reading in high school.* New York: Macmillan.

Brunner, E. de S., Wilder, D. S., Kirschner, C., & Newbery, J. S. (1959). *An overview of adult education research.* Chicago: Adult Education Association of the U.S.A.

Buswell, G. T. (1937). *How adults read.* Chicago: University of Chicago Press.

Byrne, B., & Ledez, J. (1983). Phonological awareness in reading-disabled adults. *Australian Journal of Psychology, 35*(2), 185-197.

Carpenter, T. P., Corbitt, M. K., Kepner, H. S., Jr., Linquist, M. M., & Reys, R. E. (1980). National Assessment: A perspective of students' mastery of basic mathematics skills. In M. M. Linquist (Ed.), *Selected issues in mathematics education.* Berkeley, CA: McCutchan.

Carroll, J. B. (1977). Developmental parameters of reading comprehension. In J. T. Guthrie (Ed.), *Cognition, curriculum, and comprehension* (pp. 1-15). Newark, DE: International Reading Association.

Caylor, J. S., & Sticht, T. G. (1973). *Development of a simple readability index for job reading material.* Alexandria, VA: Human Resources Research Organization.

Chall, J. S. (1983). *Stages of reading development.* New York: McGraw-Hill.

Chall, J. S. (1994). Patterns of adult reading. *Learning Disabilities: A Multidisciplinary Journal, 5*(1), 29-33.

Chall, J. S. (1999). Models of reading. In D. A. Wagner, R. L. Venezky, & B. V. Street (Eds.), *Literacy: An international handbook* (pp. 163-166). Boulder, CO: Westview Press.

Cook, W. D. (1977). *Adult literacy education in the United States.* Newark, DE: International Reading Association.

Cull, W. L., & Zechmeister, E. B. (1994). The learning ability paradox in adult metamemory research: Where are the metamemory differences between good and poor learners? *Memory and Cognition, 22*(2), 249-257.

Darkenwald, G. G. (1986). *Adult literacy education: A review of the research and priorities for future inquiry.* New York: Literacy Assistance Center, Inc.

Diehl, W. A., & Mikulecky, L. (1980). The nature of reading at work. *Journal of Reading, 24,* 221-227.

Dixon, W. R. (1951). Studies of the eye movements in reading of university professors and graduate students. In W. C. Morse, F. A. Ballantine, & W. R. Dixon (Eds.), *Studies in the psychology of reading.* Ann Arbor: University of Michigan Press.

Forlizzi, L. (1992). *Exploring the comprehension skills and strategies of ABE students.* University Park: Pennsylvania State University, Institute for the Study of Adult Literacy.

French, J. (1987). *Adult literacy: A source book and guide.* New York: Garland.

Gambrell, L. B., & Heathington, B. S. (1981). Adult disabled readers' metacognitive awareness about reading tasks and strategies. *Journal of Reading Behaviour, 13*(3), 215-222.

Gates, A. I. (1947). *The improvement of reading.* New York: McGraw-Hill.

Gibson, E. J., & Levin, H. (1975). *The psychology of reading.* Cambridge, MA: MIT Press.

Goldstein, H. (1940). *Reading and listening comprehension at various controlled rates.* New York: Bureau of Publications, Teachers College, Columbia University.

Gray, W. S. (1937). The teaching of reading: A second report. In W. S. Gray (Ed.), *The teaching of reading [Thirty-sixth yearbook of the National Society for the Study of Education, Part 1].* Bloomington, IL: Public School Publishing Co.

Gray, W. S. (1939). Reading. In C. Washburne (Ed.), *Child development and the curriculum [Thirty-eighth yearbook of the National Society for the Study of Education, Part I]* (pp. 185-209). Bloomington, IL: Public School Publishing Co.

Gray, W. S. (1956). How well do adults read? In N. B. Henry (Ed.), *Adult Reading [Fifty-fifth Yearbook of the NSSE, Part II].* Chicago: National Society for the Study of Education.

Gray, W. S., & Munroe, R. (1929). *The reading interests and habits of adults.* New York: Macmillan.

Gray, W. S., & Rogers, B. (1956). *Maturity in reading: Its nature and appraisal.* Chicago: University of Chicago Press.

Guthrie, J. T., & Kirsch, I. S. (1987). Distinctions between reading comprehension and locating information in text. *Journal of Educational Psychology, 79,* 212-219.

Judd, C. H., & Buswell, G. T. (1922). *Silent reading: A study of the various types* (Supplementary Educational Monographs No. 23). Chicago: University of Chicago Press.

Kamil, M. L. (1995). Some alternatives to paradigm wars in literacy research. *Journal of Reading Behavior, 27*(2), 243-261.

Karlsen, B. (1970). Educational achievement testing with adults—Some research findings. In W. S. Griffith & A. P. Hayes (Eds.), *Adult basic education: The state of the art* (pp. 99-103). Washington, DC: U.S. Government Printing Office.

Kirsch, I. S., & Jungeblut, A. (1986). *Literacy: Profiles of America's young adults* (NAEP Report No. 16-PL-02). Princeton, NJ: Educational Testing Service.

Kirsch, I. S., Jungeblut, A., Jenkins, L., & Kolstad, A. (1993). *Adult literacy in America: A first look at the results of the National Adult Literacy Survey.* Washington, DC: National Center for Education Statistics, U.S. Department of Education.

Kitz, W. R., & Tarver, S. G. (1989). Comparison of dyslexic and nondyslexic adults on decoding and phonemic awareness tasks. *Annals of Dyslexia, 39,* 196-205.

Leibert, R. E. (1983). Performance of ABE students and children on an informal reading inventory. *Reading Psychology: An International Quarterly, 4,* 141-150.

Liberman, I. Y., Rubin, H., Duques, S., & Carlisle, J. (1985). Linguistic abilities and spelling proficiency in kindergartners and adult poor spellers. In J. Kavanagh & D. Gray (Eds.), *Biobehavioral measures of dyslexia* (pp. 163-176). Parkton, MD: York Press.

Lukatela, K., Carello, C., Shankweiler, D., & Liberman, I. Y. (1995). Phonological awareness in illiterates: Observations from Serbo-Croatia. *Applied Psycholinguistics, 16*(4), 463-487.

Malicky, G., & Norman, C. A. (1982). Reading strategies of adult illiterates. *Journal of Reading, 25,* 731-735.

Mann, H. (1839). Mechanical, mental stages in reading. *American Annals of Education,* 289-299.

McCaul, R. L. (1944). The effect of attitude upon reading interpretation. *Journal of Educational Research, 37,* 451-458.

Mikulecky, L. (1982). Job literacy: The relationship between school preparation and workplace actuality. *Reading Research Quarterly, 7*(3), 400-419.

Miller, G. A., & Gildea, P. M. (1987). How children learn words. *Scientific American, 257*(3), 94-99.

Morais, J., Bertelson, P., Cary, L., & Alegria, J. (1986). Literacy training and speech segmentation. *Cognition, 24*(1-2), 45-64.

Morais, J., Cary, L., Alegria, J., & Bertelson, P. (1979). Does awareness of speech as a sequence of phones arise spontaneously? *Cognition, 7*(4), 323-331.

Morais, J., Content, A., Bertelson, P., & Cary, L. (1988). Is there a critical period for the acquisition of segmental analysis? *Cognitive Neuropsychology, 5*(3), 347-352.

Murphy, R. T. (1975). Assessment of adult reading competence. In A. H. Nielson (Eds.), *Reading and career education* (pp. 50-61). Newark, DE: International Reading Association.

National Center for Education Statistics (NCES) (1999). *Highlights from TIMSS: Overview and key findings across grade levels.* (Report No. 1999-081). Washington, DC: Author.

Pearson, P. D., Barr, R., Kamil, M. L., & Mosenthal, P. B. (Eds.) (1984). *Handbook of reading research.* New York: Longman.

Perfetti, C. A. (1985). *Reading ability.* New York: Oxford University Press.

Read, C., & Ruyter, L. (1985). Reading and spelling skills in adults of low literacy. *Reading and Special Education, 6,* 43-52.

Robinson, H. M. (1968). The next decade. In H. M. Robinson (Ed.), *Innovation and change in reading instruction* [*The Sixty-seventh Yearbook of the National Society for the Study of Education, Part II*] (pp. 397-430). Chicago: Distributed by the University of Chicago Press.

Russell, D. H. (1961). *Children learn to read* (2nd ed.). Boston: Ginn.

Samuels, S. J., & Kamil, M. L. (1984). Models of the reading process. In P. D. Pearson (Ed.), *Handbook of reading research* (pp. 185-224). New York: Longman.

Scribner, S., & Cole, M. (1981). *The psychology of literacy.* Cambridge, MA: Harvard University Press.

Sharon, A. T. (1973-74). What do adults read? *Reading Research Quarterly, 9,* 148-169.

Singer, H. (1970). Research that should have made a difference. *Elementary English, 47,* 27-34.

Stanovich, K. E. (1991). Discrepancy definitions of reading disability: Has intelligence led us astray? *Reading Research Quarterly, 26*(1), 7-29.

Sticht, T. G., Beck, Hauke, Kleiman, & James (1974). *Auding and reading: A developmental model.* Alexandria, VA: Human Resources Research Organization.

Sticht, T. G. (1982). *Basic skills in defense.* Alexandria, VA: Human Resources Research Organization.

Sticht, T. G. (1988). Adult literacy education. In E. Rothkopf (Ed.), *Review of research in education* (pp. 59-96). Washington, DC: American Educational Research Association.

Stone, L. G. (1941). Reading reactions for various types of subject matter. *Journal of Experimental Education, 10,* 64-77.

Taylor, N., Wade, P., Jackson, S., Blum, I., & Goold, L. (1980). A study of low-literate adults: Personal, environmental and program considerations. *The Urban Review, 12*(2), 69-77.

Terry, P. W. (1922). How numerals are read. *Supplementary Educational Monographs, 18.* Chicago: University of Chicago Press.

Tinker, M. A. (1928). A photographic study of eye-movements in reading formulas. *Genetic Psychology Monographs, 3,* 68-182.

Venezky, R. L. (1982). The origins of the present-day chasm between adult literacy needs and school literacy instruction. *Visible Language, 16,* 113-127.

Venezky, R. L., Oney, B., Sabatini, J., & Jain, R. (1998). *Teaching adults to read and write: A research synthesis.* Washington, DC: U.S. Department of Education, Planning and Evaluation Services.

Vernon, M. D. (1931). *The experimental study of reading.* Cambridge, England: Cambridge University Press.

Weber, R.-M. (1975). Adult illiteracy in the United States. In J. B. Carroll & J. S. Chall (Eds.), *Toward a literate society.* New York: McGraw-Hill.

Zill, N., & Winglee, M. (1990). *Who reads literature? The future of the United States as a nation of readers.* Cabin John, MD: Seven Locks Press.

# · 29 ·

# CHILDREN WITH READING DIFFICULTIES

Jeanne S. Chall
*Harvard University*

Mary E. Curtis
*Boys' Town Reading Center*

Our concern in this chapter is with those children who encounter school difficulties because of a reading or related language problem.

From the earliest scientific studies of education, success in learning to read has been linked to school achievement. Among school subjects, problems in reading constitute the majority of referrals for learning difficulties. Moreover, as it is becoming increasingly apparent, poor reading is a common factor underlying high school dropout, delinquency, teenage pregnancy, unemployment, and criminal behavior (Davidson & Koppenhaver, 1993; Kellerman, Fuqua-Whitley, & Rivara, 1996). In other words, difficulty in reading and related language skills places students at risk not only for success in school, but for personal, social, and civic well being as well.

Although important differences exist among the millions of children in this country who encounter difficulties in school because of a reading problem, many share at least one of the following characteristics: they come from families of low socioeconomic status, and/or they have been classified as children with reading or related language disabilities. In this chapter we focus on some of the theories and research related to how these characteristics affect reading development, and we describe some of the instructional approaches that have been found to be effective in overcoming these factors.

## LOW-INCOME CHILDREN

Almost every study that relates socioeconomic status (SES) to achievement in school finds that middle-class children are more advanced, age for age, than low SES children (Coleman et al., 1966; McLoyd, 1998; NAEP, 1993). This is so not only in this country, but in other countries as well (Thorndike, 1973).

In the United States, the relationship between SES and reading achievement is most clearly demonstrated by the results of the National Assessment of Educational Progress (NAEP). On each of its assessments in reading, NAEP's results have shown a large gap between the achievement of disadvantaged urban children and their more advantaged age peers. And, while the longer students are in school, the smaller this gap becomes, by age 17, disadvantaged urban youth are still reading below the level achieved by advantaged 13-year-olds (NAEP, 1993).

NAEP's results are consistent with the conclusion drawn earlier by Coleman and his associates that differences in family background are the best predictor of verbal achievement. But why is it that so many children from low-income families are at risk for reading failure, and why do they fail to catch up as they proceed through school?

Because a large proportion of low SES children are members of minority groups, considerable debate has taken place about whether it is their minority group membership that places them at risk. Increasingly, however, there is consensus that their socioeconomic status is the significant factor in their academic difficulties (McLoyd, 1998; Wilson, 1987). More specifically, the educational attainment of their parents seems to be among the most critical factors (Binkley & Williams, 1996).

Again, why this is so has been much discussed. During the 1970s, and on and off again up to the present day, questions have been raised about how dialect differences, particularly among low SES African American children, relate to difficulties in acquiring literacy (Labov, 1995). Efforts have been made to teach these children to read from special dialect readers (rather than traditional reading textbooks), or from stories dictated by the children and written down in dialect by the teacher (Baratz & Shuy, 1969). Such approaches are always short lived, however, in part because dialect readers are not acceptable to parents

413

(Labov, 1995), but also because a considerable number of studies have found that dialect has little effect on reading comprehension (e.g., see Simons, 1979).

Another perspective on the problem stems from differences that have been identified in the ways that various social and ethnic groups use oral and written language. Low-income children come from a variety of cultures in which expectations and uses of language can differ from those practiced in school. As a consequence, low reading achievement in low-income children has been linked to a mismatch between the style of language used in school and the various styles of language used in these children's homes and communities.

Heath (1983a, 1983b, 1986) is among those who have espoused this view, based on her study of the language and culture in different working class communities. From her observational work, Heath concluded that the differences in academic achievement of these three groups were related to differences in the language in the three communities, differences such as the ways in which questions and narrative structures were used. This led Heath to suggest that teachers of low SES children should modify their instruction so that the children are surrounded with many different kinds of talk that will lead them to academic success. (See also Delpit, 1995 and Garcia, 1992.)

For example, Heath (1983a) described a first-grade teacher of a class of 19 African-American students who were, according to readiness test results, "potential failures" (p. 284). Heath noted that the teacher used activities such as: teaching the shapes of letters as structured symbols that appeared in the children's communities; teaching the sounds of letters; teaching symbol–sound correspondences (i.e., phonics); teaching the configuration of certain function words; teaching sight words; reading to the children, along with choral reading and repeated readings; asking children to predict what will happen next in a story; and inviting them to make up other endings to stories.

At the end of the year, all but one child (who went to a class for emotionally impaired children) were reading on or above grade level. In other words, low SES first graders whose language was judged at the beginning of first grade to be different from that required in school were able, with proper instruction, to succeed in learning to read. Although Heath stressed the importance of the kinds of oral language underlying these instructional activities, it should be noted that most of the activities have long been recognized as effective techniques for teaching reading to children at all social levels (e.g., see Adams, 1990; Chall, 1967/1983/1996; Harris & Sipay, 1985; Spear-Swerling & Sternberg, 1996).

In addition to Heath's work, The Kamehameha Early Education Project (KEEP) is often cited as an example of the success of using linguistically and culturally appropriate styles of instruction (Tharp, 1989). KEEP, which is targeted at low-achieving, native Hawaiian children, resulted in improved reading skills through use of more oral participation and opportunities for children to help each other—practices designed to match an Hawaiian–Polynesian style of learning (Au & Mason, 1981). What is interesting, however, is that the program also incorporates activation of prior knowledge, active participation by the students, and numerous opportunities for them to engage in informed practice before they are asked to work independently—all techniques that have also been used successfully in teaching students with reading difficulties (Blanton & Blanton, 1994; Chall & Curtis, 1992; Palinscar & Brown, 1984; Roswell & Chall, 1994). Thus, it may be that future research will reveal that the success of KEEP stemmed more from the nature of the instructional techniques it incorporated than from its emphasis on the importance of "cultural matching". It may even be that techniques like these will prove to be helpful in promoting success in learning to read for all children, regardless of their language, culture, or economic status (e.g., see Snow, Burns, & Griffin, 1998).

Still another view why low SES children are at risk is that the kind of oral language environment that stimulates literacy development is found less often in their homes than in those of middle-class children (e.g., see Snow, 1983; Snow, Barnes, Chandler, Goodman, & Hemphill, 1991). In particular, practices such as paraphrasing, expanding on children's utterances, and adult–child book sharing—practices that provide links between oral language development and literacy skills—are less prevalent in low income homes (Rice, 1989). Hence, according to this view, it is not low SES per se that places a child at risk as much as the need for certain kinds of linguistic and educational stimulation (e.g., see Bloom, 1976).

Early intervention programs such as Head Start, Sesame Street, and The Electric Company were, in fact, designed to provide these kinds of stimulation, and evidence suggests their success in doing so (e.g., see Chall, 1983/1996; Woodhead, 1988). However, initial gains in the language and literacy achievement of low SES children are not always maintained as the children grow older (e.g., see Caldwell, 1987; Chall, Jacobs, & Baldwin, 1990; Lazer, Darlington, Murray, & Snipper, 1982), suggesting that a good start, in and of itself, is not enough.

Why early intervention effects dissipate with age can be understood when acquisition of language and literacy are viewed as developmental processes, ones that go through various stages.

Menyuk (1988) has described the following sequence in language development. From ages 1 to 3 the average child acquires from 2,000 to 3,000 lexical items (words). From ages 3 to 5, they can rhyme words, reconstruct segmented words familiar to them, and they have command of basic morphological rules. From 5 to 8, children learn more complex phonological aspects of language—segmenting words into sounds, blending separate sounds into words—and they learn more elaborate syntactic structures. From age 8 on up, they develop further in aspects of language such as pragmatics, semantics, and phonology.

Beyond these more general developmental changes in language, the nature of reading also changes with development, from global, meaning-oriented tasks, to ones requiring mastery and fluency with print, to use of reading for the purposes of learning new information and perspectives (Chall, 1979, 1983/1996). As the task of reading changes, so too do the demands for cognition, language, and skills for dealing with print.

For children from low-income families, the stages of literacy development are probably much the same as they are for more advantaged children. Print skills are more essential for success in the early grades, language and cognition more essential later on. However, if growth in some aspect of low-income children's language or literacy development becomes delayed by conditions at home or experiences in school, these delays will have a negative effect on their later development (Stanovich, 1986).

A study of children from low-income families in grades 2 to 7 provides support for this explanation (Chall & Jacobs, 1983; Chall, Jacobs, & Baldwin, 1990; Chall & Snow, 1982). When children were tested at the end of the second grade, they scored, as a group, at grade level on all reading and vocabulary tests. A year later, at the end of third grade, they were still at, or very close to, grade level. By the end of fourth grade, however, average scores for the children on three of the tests—word meaning, word recognition, and spelling—had slipped below grade level. By grade 7, most of the children were substantially below grade level.

The writing development of these children followed the same pattern as their reading, with decelerating gains from grades 4 to 7. Overall, the students were strong in ideas but weak in organization, structure, and form. Interestingly, similar trends were reported by Shaughnessy (1977) in the writing of at-risk college students: difficulty with syntax and structural forms rather than with ideas.

A longitudinal study of low-income children in grades 1 through 4 conducted by Juel (1988) helps to specify further trends in these children's literacy development. Juel found that children who entered grade 1 with little awareness about the relationships among words, letters, and sounds were children who experienced problems in learning to read. And, when children experienced reading failure in grade 1, the probability was quite high that they were still having problems in grade 4.

In contrast to the reading results, Juel found that poor writers in grade 1 were not always poor writers by grade 4. However, early poor readers tended to become poor writers. Poor readers also experienced less growth in their ability to tell a story than did good readers.

These findings from studies of low-income children's language and literacy development support the view that language is related to literacy differently at different points of development. When children first learn to read, at ages 5 or 6, most native speakers have sufficient lexical and syntactic development to cope with the materials they are expected to read. Those children who experience difficulty usually have difficulty with the phonological aspects of language (e.g., phonemic awareness). That is, their problems become apparent when they are asked to hear rhymes, hear the separate sounds in words, blend sounds to form words, and relate sounds to print. Research also suggests that when given good instruction in print and phonemic skills, low-income children can progress as expected in the primary grades because reading tasks deal with words that are already in their oral language vocabularies (Foorman, Francis, Fletcher, Schatschneider, & Mehta, 1998).

When reading tasks become more complex (requiring fluency as well as knowledge of less familiar words and language patterns), congnitive and linguistic demands become greater. The materials to be read are no longer familiar, and knowledge of word meanings and problem-solving skills have a stronger role to play in reading. And, if instruction does not meet their needs

in these areas, low SES children who were successful initially may begin to falter (Chall, Jacobs, & Baldwin, 1990).

Before going more into the kinds of instructional approaches that research has shown to be effective for children with reading problems, let us first discuss another group of these children, those who experience difficulties in school because of reading and related language disabilities.

## CHILDREN WITH LEARNING DISABILITIES

Over the years, children whose learning disability involves reading have been referred to by a variety of labels—poor readers, remedial readers, disabled readers, or as children with specific or developmental language disabilities. More recently, the term dyslexia has had wider use. A specific learning disability is defined as:

a disorder in one or more of basic psychological processes involved in using language, spoken or written, which may manifest itself in an imperfect ability to listen, think, speak, read, write, spell, or do mathematical calculations. The term includes such conditions as perceptual handicaps, brain injury, minimal brain dysfunction, dyslexia, and developmental aphasia. The term does not include children who have learning problems which are primarily the result of visual, hearing, or motor handicaps, of mental retardation, of emotional disturbance, or of environmental, cultural, or economic disadvantage. (From the Individuals with Disabilities Education Act of 1990, P.L. 101-476).

Reading disability, or dyslexia, is by far the most prevalent among the learning disabilities, and by far the most studied. Current estimates are that dyslexia affects anywhere from 5% to 17.5% of children (Shaywitz, 1998). Based on research conducted over several decades, though, we also know that about half of American children experience difficulty in learning to read, and among those who have not learned to read by age 9, approximately 75% continue to experience severe reading difficulties throughout high school and adulthood (Lyon, 1997/1998).

During the 1940s and 1950s, psychiatrists interested in reading disability proposed various theories of the unconscious as the cause of reading failure. One impetus for such theories came from Robinson's (1946) landmark study of reading disability in which she concluded that the most frequent characteristics of her population were social and emotional difficulties. Recognition of social and emotional disturbances in reading disabled children led many to assume that individual or family therapy was needed before a child could benefit from remediation in reading. As Roswell and Natchez (1989) point out, however, this assumption has some serious flaws:

A diagnostician may discover that a student with learning disabilities has personality disturbances and needs psychotherapy. If this choice alone is instituted and the student still does not learn to read within a reasonable length of time, he or she will fall further and further behind. Even worse, whatever emotional problems were present will be exacerbated through daily academic failure. This does not discredit the psychodynamic stance. It simply states that when other factors continue undetected or ignored, the individual can try, even try *hard*, only to flounder, fumble, and finally despair (p. 52).

Consider, for example, students who come to Boys Town with the most severe reading problems (i.e., they are reading several years below their grade level in school). Difficulty in reading is typically noted in their educational records 2 years after emotional and/or behavior problems were first noticed. We also find that the younger students were when someone first recognized a reading problem, the greater the severity of their emotional/behavior problems at the time of their admission to Boys Town (Curtis & Longo, 1998).

During the 1960s and 1970s, neurological theories of reading disability—which place the major cause on differences in the development and organization of the brain—became increasingly popular. Although first proposed in the United States by Orton (1937), the neurological view became more prevalent as scientific knowledge and technology advanced. Neurological factors such as premature birth, perceptual–motor development, and difficulty with sequencing and blending of sounds were identified as significant to reading failure in young children (de Hirsch, Jansky, & Langford, 1966; Jansky & de Hirsch, 1972). Brain study following the accidental death of a young man who had suffered from severe reading disability since childhood revealed abnormalities in those areas known to deal with language (Galuburda & Kemper, 1979). And several types of reading disability began to be associated with different language difficulties (e.g., see Doehring, Trites, Patel, & Fiedorowicz, 1981).

The instructional implications of a neurological view of reading disability have not been straightforward (Chall & Peterson, 1986). However, Orton's recommendation for a highly structured, multisensory, direct phonics procedure to help severely disabled students with difficulties in dealing with printed symbols is still the one that is followed by most programs (see Clark & Uhry, 1995). In addition, treatment of deficits associated with reading difficulties (e.g., memory, attention, auditory discrimination, visual tracking, perception, and so on) has also been recommended. Deficit training is based on the assumption that reading difficulties are only symptoms—symptoms that will go away as deficits in more basic processing improve. Deficit training has become less prevalent, however, due to research that questions its effectiveness (see Arter & Jenkins, 1979; Chall, 1978). Instead, specific focus has shifted to the oral language development of those preschool children who lag significantly behind their peers (Rice, 1989), with particular emphasis being placed on promoting neural efficiency in perceiving the sounds that make up words (Lyon, 1997/1998).

In contrast to single factor explanations of reading and related language disabilities, such as the social-emotional or neuropsychological, the treatment followed today in most schools and university clinics is based on a multifactor view (see Chall & Curtis, 1987). Prevalent since the 1920s, beginning with the work of Gray (1922) and Gates (1922), a multifactor view assumes that any of several factors can "cause" difficulties in learning, including: inadequate methods of teaching; insufficient time spent practicing; home and family circumstances; differences in brain functioning; and so on. Instead of trying to identify the underlying causes, though, a multifactor approach assumes that the academic difficulties of children should be treated directly, using methods and materials based on their academic strengths and weaknesses (see also Brown & Campione, 1986). In reading, a multifactor approach entails focusing on components such as: accuracy and fluency in word identification; breadth and depth of knowledge of word meanings; success in literal and inferential understanding of what has been read; application of strategies for monitoring and improving understanding and learning (see Roswell & Chall, 1994; Spear-Swerling & Sternberg, 1996).

Up to this point, we have described some of the theories and research related to why two different groups of children—those from low-income families and those with reading and related language and learning disabilities—are at risk for academic success because of their reading difficulties. In the sections that follow, we would like to give a brief overview of the instructional approaches that researchers have examined for use with both of these groups.

## INSTRUCTIONAL APPROACHES

### Early Intervention

The quest to prevent reading failure even before formal instruction begins goes back 70 years. The early studies, called studies of reading readiness, were influenced by child development research that found that there was an optimal time for learning various tasks.

The first readiness study in reading (Morphett & Washburne, 1931) found that mental age was the best predictor of beginning reading success, and recommended a mental age of $6\frac{1}{2}$ as the optimal time for beginning reading instruction. Gates (1937), on the other hand, found that the minimum mental age for beginning reading varied with the instructional program, the teacher, and the learning environment. With easy methods and materials and well organized teaching, even a mental age of 5 was sufficient for learning to read.

Gates notwithstanding, from the 1930s to the early 1960s, schools tended to delay formal reading instruction for those children who were presumed to lack readiness, even though there seemed to be no controlled studies that supported such an approach. Research in the 1960s and 1970s, however, suggested that early intervention was more effective than delay. Studies of children taught to read early (Durkin, 1974-1975), along with studies on the effectiveness of Head Start (Zigler & Valentine, 1979) and the improved reading scores on the National Assessment of the 1980 cohort of 9-year-olds, who had an earlier, more systematic start in reading instruction than the 1970 cohort (NAEP, 1985), all pointed to the value of early intervention.

More recently, work in the area of "emergent literacy" has reminded us that very young children can know much about language and literacy without being directly taught, particularly children who come from linguistically rich environments (e.g., see Teale & Sulzby, 1986). However, researchers in the area of emergent literacy have been reluctant to specify what kinds of knowledge and skills are missing in children who do not "naturally" acquire readiness skills, and what kinds of interventions will be helpful for them (see McGee & Purcell-Gates, 1997). A number of other studies suggest, though, that if one waits for readiness skills to emerge, and does not intervene, the child at risk will not make it (e.g., see Juel, 1988; Lyon, 1997/1998). The nature of the intervention has also been shown to make a difference (Adams, 1990; Slavin, Karweit, & Madden, 1989; Slavin & Madden, 1989). In particular, those programs that combine oral language activities with letter–sound associations seem to be the most successful in preparing students to learn to read (Blachman, Ball, Black, & Tangel, 1994; Hatcher, Hulme, & Ellis, 1994; Vandervelden & Siegel, 1997).

## Direct and Explicit Instruction

Research comparing the effectiveness of specific kinds of approaches to teaching reading has been limited (Bond & Dystra, 1967/1997; Chall, 1967/1983/1996). Overall, though, studies of instructional effectiveness (Rosenshine, 1997; Slavin et al., 1989) and of teacher influences on student achievement (Brophy, 1986) suggest that the following factors are important: (a) well-defined instructional objectives through which teachers help students to relate new information and skills to what they already know and already can do, and (b) opportunities to apply new knowledge and skills, along with feedback about the effectiveness of those applications (see also Wasik & Slavin, 1993.)

To be more specific, consider how the results from the study by Chall and her associates of children from low-income families relate to these factors. For students in the intermediate grades who made at least the expected year's growth from one school year to the next, classroom observations and teacher interviews revealed the following: (a) reading instruction was provided on or above the child's current reading level (not below); (b) instruction was given in comprehension of texts in reading, social studies, science, health, and other content areas; (c) meaning vocabulary was stressed during content-area reading instruction as well as during reading and language arts; (d) diverse materials were provided on a wide variety of reading levels, some of which challenged even the best readers; (e) frequent field trips and other activities were conducted to expose students to new experiences and new vocabulary and to help build up background knowledge for reading about the unfamiliar; (f) homework was assigned in reading that included workbooks in the earlier grades, and reading of trade books and content area materials in the later grades; and (g) the children's parents were in direct personal contact with their teachers (see Chall & Snow, 1982; Chall et al., 1990; Snow et al., 1991).

In other words, the factors that were related to greater gains and to higher levels of achievement among these low-income students were similar to the factors that have been shown to contribute to the success of all children: a good, strong start in the primary grades, followed in the intermediate and upper grades by structured and challenging instruction in reading, along with multiple and varied opportunities to practice and apply literacy skills. Even when stimulation for language and literacy development was not prevalent in their homes, instruction in school was able to meet their needs. When neither home or school provided that stimulation, the children were unable to progress at expected levels.

Intervention studies have shown that direct and explicit instruction in identifying words (Adams, 1990; Chall, 1967/1983/1996, Foorman et al., 1998), in word meanings and background knowledge (Curtis, 1996; Curtis & Longo, 1998; Snider, 1989; Stahl, in press), and in strategies such as paraphrasing, summarizing, and generating questions (Deschler, Warner, Schumaker, & Alley, 1983; Palinscar, Winn, David, Snyder, & Stevens, 1993; Rosenshine, Meister, & Chapman, 1996) all can improve the reading achievement of students with reading difficulties.

## Matching Instruction to Students' Needs

The issue of whether methods of teaching reading can be matched to learning styles for more effective learning is a perennial one. Currently, concerns are being raised once again over whether visual methods (sight, whole words) work better for children who are visual learners, while phonics works better for children who are auditory learners. However, little previous research has demonstrated success in matching methods to learning styles (see Cronbach & Snow, 1977). In the area of reading in particular, a review of available studies suggests that basing methods of reading instruction on styles of learning is a questionable practice (Stahl, 1988).

What research has revealed as important for students with reading difficulties is instruction that is matched to their academic needs (e.g., see Curtis & Longo, 1998). As Slavin and Madden (1989) summarized it: "Virtually all of the programs found to be instructionally effective for students at risk assess student progress frequently and use the results to modify groupings or instructional content to meet students' individual needs" (p. 11).

This means that when students are not accurate or fluent in dealing with print, then these skills must be addressed in order for their reading to improve. When students are proficient with print but deficient in reading comprehension, then instruction in word meanings, background knowledge, text structures, or strategies for comprehension may be necessary for improvement. Only through assessment of students' strengths and needs in language and literacy, viewed in the context of their literacy development, can appropriate instructional decisions be made (Curtis & Longo, 1998; Roswell & Chall, 1994).

## Technology and Children with Reading Difficulties

Computers have been shown to enhance the learning of students with reading difficulties both through their use as tutors and as tools (Balajthy, 1996).

As tutors, computer-assisted instruction has proven to be effective in providing training and practice in phonological awareness, word analysis and word recognition skills, vocabulary knowledge, comprehension of connected text, and use of reading and writing to solve problems (e.g., see Hyland, 1998; Torgesen & Barker, 1995).

As tools, computers have been used to facilitate diagnosis of reading problems (McEneaney, 1996), to monitor progress in reading (e.g., the *Accelerated Reader* program), to provide structure for classroom discussions, and as part of larger interactive technology systems.

The reasons why technology is so powerful with these students are many. In their comprehensive review of the uses of computers with children who have reading difficulties, Meyer and Rose (in press) relate the effectiveness of computers to recent neurological theory and research, as well as to reading development and research.

## CONCLUDING REMARKS

The search for the causes, the cures, and preventative measures for failure in language and literacy has been a long one. And the lessons learned so far, if implemented, can help children with reading difficulties to learn to achieve well.

What we need to remember is that the vast majority of children who lag behind in reading can be helped, whether they are behind because of a less academically stimulating home or school environment, or because of a learning difficulty that may or may not be neurologically based. As our review has indicated, the research on both groups of children points to the benefits of instruction that is designed to raise their level of reading development. For those not at risk, a facilitative, noninterventionist approach to literacy instruction may be effective. But, for children who are at risk for reading failure, a more formal, direct kind of instruction—aimed at building on their strengths while addressing their needs—has been shown to be the most beneficial.

## *References*

Adams, M. J. (1990). *Beginning to read: Thinking and learning about print*. Cambridge, MA: The MIT Press.

Arter, J. A., & Jenkins, J. R. (1979). Differential diagnosis—prescriptive teaching: A critical appraisal. *Review of Educational Research, 49*, 517-555.

Au, K. H., & Mason, J. M. (1981). School organizational factors in learning to read: The balance of rights hypothesis. *Reading Research Quarterly, 17*, 115-151.

Balajthy, E. (1996). Using computer technology to aid the disabled reader. In L. R. Putnam (Ed.), *How to become a better reading teacher* (pp. 331-343). Englewood Cliffs, NJ: Prentice-Hall.

Baratz, J. C., & Shuy, R. (Eds.). (1969). *Teaching black children to read*. Washington, DC: Center for Applied Linguistics.

Binkley, M., & Willams, T. (1996). *Reading literacy in the United States: Findings from the IEA Reading Literacy Study*. (ERIC Document Reproduction Service No. ED 396 245)

Blachman, B. A., Ball, E. W., Black, R. S., & Tangel, D. M. (1994). Kindergarten teachers develop phonemic awareness in low-income, inner-city classrooms: Does it make a difference? *Reading and Writing: An Interdisciplinary Journal, 6*, 1-18.

Blanton, L. P., & Blanton, W. E. (1994). Providing reading instruction to mildly disabled students: Research into practice. In K. D. Wood & B. Algozzine (Eds.), *Teaching reading to high-risk learners* (pp. 9-48). Boston: Allyn & Bacon.

Bloom, B. S. (1976). *Human characteristics and school learning*. New York: McGraw-Hill.

Bond, G. L., & Dystra, R. (1997). The cooperative research program in first-grade reading instruction. *Reading Research Quarterly, 32*, 348-427. (Reprinted from *Reading Research Quarterly*, 1967, *2*, 1-142.)

Brophy, J. (1986). Teacher influences on student achievement. *American Psychologist, 41*, 1069-1077.

Brown, A. L., & Campione, J. C. (1986). Psychological theory and the study of learning disabilities. *American Psychologist, 41*, 1059-1068.

Caldwell, B. (1987). Staying ahead: The challenge of third-grade slump. *Principal, 66*, 10-14.

Chall, J. S. (1967/1983/1996). *Learning to read: The great debate*. New York: Harcourt Brace.

Chall, J. S. (1978). A decade of research on reading and learning disabilities. In S. J. Samuels (Ed.), *What research has to say about reading instruction* (pp. 31-42). Newark, DE: IRA.

Chall, J. S. (1979). The great debate: Ten years later, with a modest proposal for reading stages. In L. B. Resnick & P. A. Weaver (Eds.),

*Theory and practice of early reading* (Vol. 1, pp. 29-55). Hillsdale, NJ: Lawrence Erlbaum Associates.

Chall, J. S. (1983/1996). *Stages of reading development*. New York: Harcourt Brace.

Chall, J. S., & Curtis, M. E. (1987). What clinical diagnosis tells us about children's reading. *The Reading Teacher, 40*, 784-788.

Chall, J. S., & Curtis, M. E. (1992). Teaching the disabled or below average reader. In A. E. Farstrup & S. J. Samuels (Eds.), *What research has to say about reading instruction* (2nd ed., pp. 253-276). Newark, DE: IRA.

Chall, J. S., & Jacobs, V. A. (1983). Writing and reading in the elementary grades: Developmental trends among low SES children. *Language Arts, 60*, 617-626.

Chall, J. S., Jacobs, V. A., & Baldwin, L. E. (1990). *The reading crisis: Why poor children fall behind*. Cambridge, MA: Harvard University Press.

Chall, J. S., & Peterson, R. W. (1986). The influence of neuroscience on educational practice. In S. L. Friedman, K. A. Klivington, & R. W. Peterson (Eds.), *The brain, cognition, and education* (pp. 287-318). New York: Academic Press.

Chall, J. S., & Snow, C. (1982). *Families and literacy*. Washington, DC: National Institute of Education.

Clark, D. B., & Uhry, J. K. (1995). *Dyslexia: Theory and practice of remedial instruction*. Baltimore: York Press.

Coleman, J. S., Campbell, E. Q., Hobson, C. J., McPartland, J., Mood, A. M., Weenfeld, F. D., & York, R. L. (1966). *Equality of educational opportunity*. Washington, DC: U.S. Government Printing Office.

Cronbach, L. J., & Snow, R. E. (1977). *Aptitude and instructional methods: A handbook for research on interactions*. New York: Halstead.

Curtis, M. E. (1996). Intervention for adolescents "at risk". In L. R. Putnam (Ed.), *How to become a better reading teacher* (pp. 231-239). Englewood Cliffs, NJ: Prentice-Hall.

Curtis, M. E., & Longo, A. M. (1998). *When adolescents can't read: methods and materials that work*. Cambridge, MA: Brookline Books.

Davidson, J., & Koppenhaver, D. (1993). *Adolescent literacy: What works and why* (2nd ed.). New York: Garland.

de Hirsch, K., Jansky, J. J., & Langford, W. S. (1966). *Predicting reading failure*. New York: Harper & Row.

Delpit, L. (1995). *Other people's children: Cultural conflict in the classroom*. New York: The New Press.

Deschler, D. D., Warner, M. M., Schumaker, J. B., & Alley, G. R. (1983). The learning strategies intervention model: Key components and current status. In J. D. McKinney & L. Feagans (Eds.), *Current topics in learning disabilities*. Norwood, NJ: Ablex.

Doehring, D. G., Trites, R. L., Patel, P. G., & Fiedorowicz, C. A. M. (1981). *Reading disabilities: The interaction of reading, language, and neuropsychological deficits*. New York: Academic Press.

Durkin, D. (1974-1975). A six year study of children who learned to read in school at the age of four. *Reading Research Quarterly, 10,* 9-61.

Foorman, B. R., Francis, D. J., Fletcher, J. M., Schatschneider, C., & Mehta, P. (1998). The role of reading instruction in learning to read: Preventing reading failure in at-risk children. *Journal of Educational Psychology, 90,* 37-55.

Galuburda, A. M., & Kemper, L. (1979). Cytoarchitectonic abnormalities in developmental dyslexia: A case study. *Annals of Neurology, 6,* 94-100.

Garcia, E. E. (1992). Linguistically and culturally diverse children: Effective instructional practices and related policy issues. In H. C. Waxman, J. W. deFelix, J. E. Anderson, & H. P. Baptiste, Jr. (Eds.), *Students at risk in at-risk schools* (pp. 65-86). Newbury Park, CA: Corwin Press.

Gates, A. I. (1922). *Psychology of reading and spelling with special reference to disability* (Contributions to Education No. 129). New York: Bureau of Publications, Columbia University, Teachers College.

Gates, A. I. (1937). The necessary mental age for beginning reading. *Elementary School Journal, 37,* 497-508.

Gray, W. S. (1922). *Remedial cases in reading: Their diagnosis and treatment* (Supplementary Educational Monograph No 22). Chicago: University of Chicago Press.

Harris, A. J., & Sipay, E. R. (1985). *How to increase reading ability* (8th ed.) New York: Longman.

Hatcher, P. J., Hulme, C., & Ellis, A. W. (1994). Ameliorating early reading failure by integrating the teaching of reading and phonological skills: The phonological linkage hypothesis. *Child Development, 65,* 41-57.

Heath, S. B. (1983a). *Ways with words: Language, life, and work in communities and classrooms*. Cambridge, England: Cambridge University Press.

Heath, S. B. (1983b). Research currents: A lot of talk about nothing. *Language Arts, 60,* 999-1007.

Heath, S. B. (1986). Taking a cross-cultural look at narratives. *Topics in Language Disorders, 7,* 220-227.

Hyland, T. (1998). Readers play catch up—and win. *Technos, 7,* 23-26.

Jansky, J., & de Hirsch, K. (1972). *Preventing reading failure*. New York: Harper & Row.

Juel, C. (1988). Learning to read and write: A longitudinal study of 54 children from first through fourth grades. *Journal of Educational Psychology, 80,* 437-447.

Kellerman, A. L., Fuqua-Whitley, D. S., & Rivara, F. P. (1996). *Preventing youth violence. A summary of program evaluation.* (Available from America's Promise, 7900 E. Greenlake Drive N., Suite 302, Seattle, WA, 98103-4850).

Labov, W. (1995). Can reading failure be reversed: A linguistic approach to the question. In V. L. Gadsen & D. A. Wagner (Eds.), *Literacy among African-American youth* (pp. 39-68). Cresskill, NJ: Hampton Press.

Lazar, I., Darlington, R. B., Murray, H. W., & Snipper, A. S. (1982). Lasting effects of early education: A report from the Consortium for Longitudinal Studies. *Monograph of Society for Research in Child Development, 47.*

Lyon, G. R. (1997/1998). Learning to read: A call from research to action. *Their World,* 16-25. (Available from the National Center for Learning Disabilities, 381 Park Avenue South, New York, NY 10016).

McEneaney, J. E. (1996). The role of technology in reading diagnosis and remediation. In L. R. Putnam (Ed.), *How to become a better reading teacher* (pp. 75-84). Englewood Cliffs, NJ: Prentice-Hall.

McGee, L. M., & Purcell-Gates, V. (1997). "So what's going on in research on emergent literacy?" *Reading Research Quarterly, 32,* 310-318.

McLoyd, V. C. (1998). Socioeconomic disadvantage and child development. *American Psychologist, 53,* 185-204.

Menyuk, P. (1988). *Language development*. Glenview, IL: Scott, Foresman.

Meyer, A., & Rose, D. (in press). *Run chip run*. Cambridge, MA: Brookline Books.

Morphett, M. J., & Washburne, C. (1931). When should children begin to read? *Elementary School Journal, 31,* 496-503.

National Assessment of Educational Progress (1985). *The reading report card: Progress toward excellence in our schools*. Princeton, NJ: ETS.

National Assessment of Educational Progress (1993). *NAEP 1992 reading report card for the nation and the states*. Princeton, NJ: ETS.

Orton, S. T. (1937). *Reading, writing, and speech problems in children*. London: Chapman and Hall.

Palinscar, A. S., & Brown, A. L. (1984). Reciprocal teaching of comprehension-fostering and monitoring activities. *Cognition and Instruction, 1,* 177-195.

Palinscar, A. S., Winn, J., David, Y., Snyder, B., & Stevens, D. (1993). Approaches to strategic reading instruction reflecting different assumptions regarding teaching and learning. In L. Meltzer (Ed.), *Strategy assessment and instruction for students with learning disabilities* (pp. 247-270). Austin, TX: Pro-Ed.

Rice, M. L. (1989). Children's language acquisition. *American Psychologist, 44,* 149-156.

Robinson, H. M. (1946). *Why pupils fail in reading*. Chicago: University of Chicago Press.

Rosenshine, B. (1997, March). *The case for explicit, teacher-led, cognitive strategy instruction*. Paper presented at the annual meeting of the American Educational Research Association, Chicago, IL.

Rosenshine, B., Meister, C., & Chapman, S. (1996). Teaching students to generate questions: A review of the intervention studies. *Review of Educational Research, 66,* 181-221.

Roswell, F. G., & Chall, J. S. (1994). *Creating successful readers: A practical guide to testing and teaching at all levels*. Chicago: Riverside.

Roswell, F. G., & Natchez, G. (1989). *Reading disability: A human approach to learning* (4th ed.). New York: Basic Books.

Shaughnessy, M. (1977). *Errors and expectations*. New York: Oxford University Press.

Shaywitz, S. E. (1998). Dyslexia. *New England Journal of Medicine, 338,* 307-312.

Simons, H. D. (1979). Black dialect, reading interference, and classroom interaction. In L. B. Resnick & P. A. Weaver (Eds.), *Theory and practice of early reading* (Vol. 3, pp. 111-129). Hillsdale, NJ: Lawrence Erlbaum Associates.

Slavin, R. E., Karweit, N. L., & Madden, N. A. (1989). *Effective programs for students at risk*. Needham Heights, MA: Allyn & Bacon.

Slavin, R. E., & Madden, N. A. (1989). What works for students at risk: A research synthesis. *Educational Leadership, 64,* 4-13.

Snider, V. E. (1989). Reading comprehension performance of adolescents with learning disabilities. *Learning Disability Quarterly, 12,* 87-96.

Snow, C. E. (1983). Literacy and language: Relationships during the preschool years. *Harvard Educational Review, 53,* 165-189.

Snow, C. E., Barnes, W. S., Chandler, J., Goodman, I. F., & Hemphill, L. (1991). *Unfulfilled expectations: Home and school influences on literacy*. Cambridge, MA: Harvard University Press.

Snow, C. E., Burns, M. M., & Griffin, P. (Eds.). (1998). *Preventing reading difficulties in young children*. Washington, DC: National Academy Press.

Spear-Swerling, L., & Sternberg, R. J. (1996). *Off track: When poor readers become "learning disabled"*. Boulder, CO: Westview Press.

Stahl, S. A. (1988). Is there evidence to support matching reading styles and initial reading methods? A reply to Carbo. *Phi Delta Kappan, 70,* 317-322.

Stahl, S. A. (in press). Vocabulary development. Cambridge, MA: Brookline Books.

Stanovich, K. E. (1986). Matthew effects in reading: Some consequences of individual differences in the acquisition of reading. *Reading Research Quarterly, 21,* 360-407.

Teale, W., & Sulzby, E. (Eds.). (1986). *Emergent literacy*. Norwood, NJ: Ablex.

Tharp, R. (1989). Psychocultural variables and constants: Effects on teaching and learning in schools. *American Psychologist, 44,* 1-11.

Thorndike, R. L. (1973). *Reading comprehension education in fifteen countries: An empirical study*. New York: Wiley.

Torgesen, J. K., & Barker, T. A. (1995). Computers as aids in the prevention and remediation of reading disabilities. *Learning Disability Quarterly, 18,* 76-87.

Vandervelden, M. D., & Siegel, L. S. (1997). Teaching phonological processing skills in early literacy: A developmental approach. *Learning Disabilities Quarterly, 20,* 63-81.

Wasik, B. A., & Slavin, B. A. (1993). Preventing early reading failure with one-to-one tutoring: A review of five programs. *Reading Research Quarterly, 28,* 178-200.

Wilson, W. J. (1987). *The truly disadvantaged: The inner city, the underclass, and public policy*. Chicago: University of Chicago Press.

Woodhead, M. (1988). When psychology informs public policy: The case of early childhood intervention. *American Psychologist, 43,* 443-454.

Zigler, E. F., & Valentine, J. (Eds.). (1979). *Project Head Start: A legacy of the war on poverty*. New York: Free Press.

# · 30 ·

# TEACHING BILINGUAL AND ESL CHILDREN AND ADOLESCENTS

*Sarah Hudelson and Leslie Poynor*
Arizona State University

*Paula Wolfe*
New Mexico State University

In the first edition of this volume, Virginia Allen wrote about bilingual and second language learners (Allen, 1991). Allen described the increase in the numbers of children in our schools whose native language is other than English and reviewed the existing literature on children's second language acquisition and development, including in her discussion both spoken and written language learning. By 1990 we had learned that, as with children acquiring their first language, children are active constructors of their second language. Second language learning, of both the oral and the written language, involves learners in generating and testing out hypotheses about how the new language works, gradually refining those hypotheses, and over time more and more closely approximating adult conventional language. Second language learning is also social, in that learners learn the new language as they interact with others who provide both language data and authentic contexts for using the language.

Allen also reported on research carried out to examine nonnative English speaking learners' English language achievement in bilingual classrooms, in which both the learners' native language and English are used for instruction, as compared to English as a second language settings, in which the language of instruction is exclusively English. Allen concluded that existing research supported the position that well designed bilingual education programs facilitated rather than retarded children's English language development.

Finally, Allen summarized work done to identify and describe features of classroom environments that support learners' second language acquisition. These features were: input understandable to the learners from both peers and adults; multiple opportunities to use the new language (in both spoken and written forms) with others for a variety of reasons; and integration of all the language processes in the classroom and integration of content into themes.

Now, at the beginning of the new millenium, the numbers of nonnative English speaking learners in the schools are still increasing (America's Children, 1998). More and more classrooms include children and adolescents whose first language is other than English. These learners have been labeled in different ways—as Limited English Proficient (LEP), as English as a Second Language (ESL) speakers, as English Language Learners (ELL), as Potentially English Proficient (PEP), as Readers and Writers of English as an Additional Language (REAL), as English as a New Language (ENL) learners, as English Speakers of Other Languages (ESOL), and as second language learners (Faltis & Hudelson, 1998). All these labels point to educators' concerns for the English language learning and achievement of these students. In this chapter, then, we focus on the current knowledge base (from 1990 on) with regard to English learners' attainment of high levels of proficiency in spoken and written English and school achievement through English in both elementary and secondary education settings. We begin with global, large sample studies, which examine nonnative English speaking learners' English language achievement in bilingual and ESL settings. Then we will move to smaller, more qualitative studies that identify and describe features of classroom environments and instructional practices that support learners' second language acquisition.

## LARGE SCALE STUDIES
## OF BILINGUAL EDUCATION

Given current antibilingual education rhetoric, as well as antibilingual education political initiatives (for example, Proposition 227 in California), it seems appropriate to begin by examining the effectiveness of bilingual education programs with respect to program participants' English language achievement. That is, how effective are bilingual education programs in promoting English language development?

Prior to 1990, several large-scale studies of bilingual education programs had been carried out, some of them concluding that dual language instruction was no more effective than English-only instruction in terms of learners' acquisition of English (AIR, 1975; Baker & deKanter, 1983). However, detailed meta-analyses of these studies concluded that bilingual education programs were at least as effective as English-only programs in promoting English language development and sometimes more effective (Willig, 1981, 1985). In the early 1990s another large-scale federally funded study of bilingual education was carried out to study the effectiveness of bilingual instruction. Ramirez and his colleagues (Ramirez, Yuen, Ramsay, & Pasta, 1991; Ramirez, 1992) compared the English language, English reading, and mathematics achievement scores of English language learners enrolled in three different kinds of instructional programs: transitional bilingual education (in which learners transfer out of dual language instruction no later than third grade), late exit bilingual education (in which learners continue to use their native language, along with English, through sixth grade), and structured immersion (no use of the native language). The researchers found no significant differences between these three groups in terms of achievement. Regardless of instructional program, children achieved in English equally well, suggesting that substantial use of the native language does not impede English language acquisition.

Later, Ramirez and his colleagues collected English language, reading, and mathematics achievement data from students enrolled in fourth, fifth, and sixth grades late exit bilingual education (BLE) classrooms. They compared the achievement of these learners to children of similar socioeconomic status and language background not enrolled in BLE programs. The children enrolled in late exit BLE programs achieved better in English than did their counterparts who had been schooled only in English, a finding that offered support for the contention that time spent in the native language may actually contribute to later achievement in English.

Ramirez's work began to address the length of time English language learners need to spend in bilingual instruction in order to become proficient enough in English to compete academically with native speakers of English. To examine this question further, Thomas and Collier (1997) collaborated with five school districts representing different regions of the United States. All of these districts had (and have) substantial numbers of second language learners and all had (and have) well-established instructional programs for these learners. Thomas and Collier analyzed ESL student performance from kindergarten through 12th grade according to the type of program in which the learners were enrolled. The program types ranged from traditional and content-based ESL through transitional and maintenance BLE programs to two-way developmental BLE in which English speakers and English language learners received academic content taught through two languages.

Thomas and Collier found that the most effective program in terms of English language achievement was the two-way bilingual program. ESL learners who participated in well-designed two-way programs for 4 to 7 years were most likely to attain grade level achievement each year in the native language and achieve in English as well as native speakers of English. Following the developmental bilingual model in terms of effectiveness were: maintenance BLE, transitional BLE with content ESL, transitional BLE with traditional ESL, content ESL, traditional ESL (Collier, 1995; Thomas & Collier, 1997). In the transitional and ESL models, the ESL learners were never able to compete academically with native English speaking students. In spite of the common sense notion that the fastest route to English proficiency is through instruction exclusively in English, Collier's and Thomas's work supports previous research that utilization of students' native languages in classroom settings for extended periods of time benefits their eventual academic achievement in English.

But questions about the effectiveness of bilingual education are still being raised. In a 1996 analysis of bilingual education research, Rossell and Baker (1996) concluded that there was no evidence that transitional bilingual programs were superior to English-only options in terms of the English language achievement of English language learners. However, Greene (1997, 1998) critiqued the 75 studies that Rossell and Baker found to be methodologically acceptable, applying what he termed clear standards to the criteria they had used to select their studies. He then performed a meta-analysis on the 11 studies remaining, from which he concluded that some use of the native language is more likely to help students' English achievement (as measured by standardized tests) than utilization of English exclusively.

Greene and others (for example, Hakuta & August, 1997) readily acknowledge that much of the research conducted has not been high quality, and they have called for more and higher quality research. However, in a recent reanalysis and critique of Greene, Rossell and Baker, and Hakuta and August, Cummins (1999) has asserted that "research shows clearly that successful bilingual education programs have been implemented in countries around the world for both linguistic minority and majority students and exactly the same patterns are observed in well-implemented programs: Students do not lose out in their development of academic skills in the majority language despite spending a considerable amount of instructional time learning through the minority language" (p. 31).

Cummins' conclusion leads logically to the questions: What is meant by well-implemented programs? What do these programs look like? What are their instructional features? Questions such as these prompted researchers to examine work that has described educationally effective practices in use with linguistically and culturally diverse learners in schools across the United States. In one such report, Garcia (1991) analyzed findings from studies done in California and Arizona that described schools and classrooms where Latino, American Indian, Asian and Southeast Asian students were successful academically (with academic success defined as student achievement at or above national norms). Garcia concluded that these sites exhibited five effective instructional practices:

1. The instruction of basic skills and academic content was organized around thematic units, and learners often contributed to the selection of some of the units.
2. Classrooms exhibited high levels of communicating, in terms both of students working together in small groups and teachers interacting and communicating with students individually and in small group settings.
3. Collaborative learning involved students asking each other hard questions and challenging each others' learning. Students sought assistance from other students.
4. Latino students were allowed and often encouraged to use their native language, including developing literacy in the native language, and those students who were proficient readers and writers in Spanish made the transition to English themselves.
5. Educators exhibited high levels of commitment to their students and their families and held high expectations for student achievement.

More recently, Tharp (1997) examined literature reviews subsequent to Garcia's and concluded that five generic principles of instruction contribute to high levels of academic achievement for language minority learners. They are:

1. Facilitate learning through joint productive activity among teachers and students. Learning is most effective when novices and experts work together for a common product or goal, and when they have opportunities to converse about what they are doing.
2. Develop competence in the language and literacy of instruction throughout all instructional activities. Language and literacy development should be fostered through use and through purposive conversation not through drills and decontextualized rules.
3. Contextualize teaching and curriculum in the experiences and skills of home and community. Schools need to provide experiences that show how rules are drawn from and apply to the everyday world. Patterns of participation and speech from family and community life should be utilized in schools and used to bridge to school patterns of participation.
4. Challenge students with cognitively complex, intellectually engaging curricula.
5. Engage students through dialogue, especially the instructional conversation, which is a way of engaging students and teachers in a process of questioning and sharing ideas and knowledge.

These two sets of general effective instructional practices share several features. Both emphasize high expectations for learners accompanied by engaging content. Both advocate that learners and teachers collaborate and that engaging in dialogue is central to language development and to academic achievement. Both speak to the centrality of literacy in learners' academic development. Both suggest a social constructivist view of learning, that is, that knowledge (including literacy and academic discourse) is constructed through interactions among individuals within a specific social and cultural environment, and that more knowledgeable members of the social and cultural group assist others in knowledge construction (Raphael & Brock, 1993). These generic practices lead naturally to interest in how the details would play themselves in specific classrooms. Therefore, from these broad guidelines we now turn to examples of qualitative studies that identify and describe specific classroom environments and instructional practices that support learners' second language acquisition. We have divided this part of our review into studies that examine English learning and learners in elementary settings and studies that examine English learning and learners in secondary classrooms.

## ELEMENTARY LEARNERS

In this section on elementary learners we have loosely grouped the studies into those that examine instructional practices in ESL classrooms (both self-contained and resource classrooms) and those that examine instructional practices in bilingual classrooms. Despite evidence that second language learners achieve better in bilingual classrooms (both two-way and late exit), the majority of second language learners are still enrolled in ESL classes, both self-contained and pull-out. Furthermore, the majority of classroom-based research on instructional practices for second language learners has been conducted in ESL classrooms. In this section, therefore, we begin with a review of ESL studies, and we follow with a review of studies carried out in bilingual classrooms.

### Primary Children Learning English in Mainstream Classroom Settings

Several studies have looked at what happens to young non-English-speaking children immersed in English language school settings, both in terms of children's developing abilities to use language forms and to participate appropriately in classroom activities in English. Researchers also have been interested in teachers' and peers' roles in children's language learning and classroom acculturation. Tabors (1997) for example, studied the ESL development of several 3- and 4-year-old children (from Spanish, Chinese, and Korean speaking homes) in a preschool setting over the course of a school year. Tabors looked both at what the teachers did to promote the children's understanding and use of English and what the children's language learning strategies were. Tabors discovered that the teachers made multiple behavioral and verbal adjustments to accommodate the non-English speakers. Nonlinguistically, the teachers provided extralinguistic support for their speech in the form of gestures, acting out, facial expressions, and the use of visual aids. Teachers consciously maintained highly predictable classroom routines so that the non-English-speaking children were able to anticipate occurrences and participate more fully. Teachers also made deliberate attempts to incorporate beginning English language learners into classroom routines.

Linguistically, adults adjusted their speech when they were speaking to non-English speakers, talking about concrete realities and working to make themselves understood by slowing down and exaggerating speech. As the children began to verbalize in English, one teacher in particular made sure to include the ESL learners in activities with other children; she encouraged the children to talk by engaging in direct interactions with them, and she provided language samples for them to use with other children. Adults also joined independent play and activity groups on a regular basis and provided what Tabors termed running commentary, ongoing explanations of their actions and the actions of other children during an activity. This language input connected directly to classroom activity was an important source of data for English language learners.

Tabors also discerned an overall progression in the young children's classroom use of English. The earliest attempts at communication were nonverbal in nature. The children used gestures and actions to catch the attention of or insert themselves into the action of others. This was followed by children's falling back on speaking their native language while acting as though their interlocutors could understand them. Children's earliest English productions were utterances that they had memorized and used as formulae, followed gradually by the generation of English forms that indicated that the children were trying to figure out the rules of English and that they were using their English to involve themselves in classroom life.

Tabors' work suggests that teachers play a crucial role in children's ESL development, both in the environment they set up and in their language interactions with children. A related study suggests that teachers may also play an important role by influencing the behavior of English speaking children toward their ESL peers. Hirschler (1994) discovered that a preschool teacher could model strategies for her native speakers to use as they interacted with ESL peers. This modeling led to decreased instances of English speaking children ignoring or walking away from ESL learners and more instances of efforts to include the ESL learners in classroom activities.

In the investigations just reviewed the focus was on oral language and social interactions. We turn now to studies that examine literacy as well as oral language development. In a yearlong case study of a young Filipino, Tagalog speaking child, Xu (1996) described Emily's evolving patterns of and strategies for interactions with peers and teachers during a variety of literacy events and her teachers' support of her emerging literacy learning. Emily's earliest strategy was to observe others. This was followed by the strategy of observing and imitating what others did prior to making any verbal response within an activity. An active response strategy developed next, which meant that, in conjunction with observing and imitating, Emily began to respond either verbally or with gestures to questions or comments made by her peers during independent reading or journal time. Later Emily actively initiated conversations with her peers, using the language that she was learning within the context of the literacy activities. Over time, as Emily became more actively engaged in interactions, she expanded her repertoire of appropriate ways of interacting with others across literacy events.

Xu (1996) also made careful observations of the teachers' interactions with Emily. Very importantly, her teachers spent time observing Emily as she played with other children. During literacy activities such as journal writing, they then grouped Emily with children with whom she enjoyed playing, and they used these children and their work as models for Emily to follow. However, the teachers did not rely on peers as teachers; they also sat with Emily more frequently than with many other children so that they could support her learning, with both verbal and nonverbal feedback and encouragement. These actions enabled Emily to become a participant in daily literacy events. And, while encouraging Emily to participate and to talk, the teachers respected Emily's early needs to be silent and to observe before becoming a more active participant and talking. Thus, the teachers' sensitivity to Emily's gradual development facilitated her language use and her ability to become a contributing member of the class.

Fitzgerald and Noblit (1999) also report on a yearlong examination of emerging second language literacy, in this case of two Spanish speaking boys enrolled in a first-grade classroom described as using "a balanced approach to emerging reading instruction, which would emphasize both word getting and comprehension, but which would make word getting central" (p. 141). The detailed descriptions of the two children's struggles to become readers and writers of English highlight the reality of individual rates of literacy development among children, as well as differential responses to instruction. The descriptions also parallel the paths to literacy revealed in studies of emerging literacy in native speakers of English.

Other researchers have approached the question of the relationship between ESL emerging literacy and spoken language development by focusing on children's interactions with picture books. Carger (1993) discovered that when kindergarten ESL learners engaged in repeated pretend readings of the same book, the repetition led to increases in the amount and choice of vocabulary used in the children's story renditions. Ferguson and Young (1996) found that a kindergarten teacher who used familiar picture books with second language (L2) learners to initiate dialogue and to offer patterned conversations, provided the children with low-risk, meaningful opportunities to use and to learn English. In a similar vein, Fassler (1998) looked at how kindergarten ESL students made use of previously read-aloud picture books in informal interactions with peers. She found that the children engaged in picture-governed emergent reading, labeling and commenting on pictures and including some present tense descriptions of some of the action. She also discovered that the children carrying out the reading often incorporated the responses/comments of the listeners into their story tellings, and that both listeners and readers utilized drama in some of their responses. These opportunities to use English contributed to the children's second language speaking abilities as well as to their emerging reading.

Studies of young second language learners in mainstream classrooms suggest that ESL children must learn to accommodate to classroom settings and classroom settings must accommodate somewhat to learners. A crucial aspect of language learning in school is figuring out how to act appropriately in mainstream classroom settings. In a phonics-based first-grade classroom, Willett (1996) has detailed how three ESL girls, seated together, learned how to negotiate the demands of seatwork and language arts recitation. By observing and imitating, by using assistance from adults, and by relying on each other, they became adept at accomplishing the phonics recitation lessons and workbook activities.

Learning appropriate ways of interacting may sometimes be more challenging than learning the linguistic forms. In an observational study of the interactions of two ethnic-minority children (one from Southeast Asia and one from India) in a mainstream, suburban kindergarten, Schmidt (1993) discovered that while Peley and Raji experienced some successes in emerging as readers and writers in their kindergarten classroom, they also experienced ongoing academic difficulties in following oral directions, in understanding the vocabulary in stories, and in processing idiomatic expressions in English. However, more serious than their academic challenges were their social ones. Neither child developed close friendships during the school year. When Peley and Raji attempted to play with their classmates or engage in social interactions at learning centers, they were openly rejected by others because of what mainstream children considered inappropriate behavior. Because they left the room for ESL lessons during part of reading time, they did not become an integral part of the literacy learning community. Additionally, the children's home cultural experiences did not find their way into classroom literacy or community building activities. During classroom celebrations and holiday festivities, the children appeared confused and did not carry out special activities appropriately. The kindergarten teacher repeatedly expressed concern about the two children's lack of social progress. Additionally, she found it difficult to communicate with these children's families, and the families did not understand how to communicate effectively with the school.

Schmidt's findings contrast starkly with those of Abbott and Grose (1998) who examined a first-grade classroom that included several ESL learners. In this setting, the classroom teacher deliberately made extensive use of the parents of the second language learners so that the children's native languages and cultural features such as celebrations and folk stories became an integral part of the experiences of all the children in the classroom. She created a place for the ESL children's experiences within the classroom community. Abbott and Grose also discovered that multiple opportunities for talk (in circle time, in response to read-aloud, during Share Time after writing) gave all children, but especially the ESL children, opportunities to hear English and later to incorporate what they had heard into what they were writing. Thus, opportunities to hear and speak English contributed to the children's written English.

Finally, Townsend and Fu (1998) carried out a yearlong case study of one Chinese boy's entry into a community of second-grade writers and readers where the children participated daily in reading and writing workshops. Xiaodi had been to school in China in first grade, where he had been developing his literacy in Chinese. Through observations, collections of Xiaodi's work, and interviews with them, Townsend and Fu came to understand that Xiaodi's literacy journey in English was facilitated by his native language literacy. He used his prior knowledge of Chinese and of literacy to contribute to his literacy in English. He began the school year writing in Chinese and gradually began to write in English, using English spellings that reflected his accent and the English structures he knew (for example, I like). An early strategy was to write a sentence in Chinese and then translate it into English. When he could not express himself well in words, Xiaodi used drawing to make his meanings clear. As he learned more English, especially the English of story books that he attended to during read-aloud and paired reading time, this was reflected in his writing. He used his knowledge of both cultures in his creation of stories. He also participated in 45-minute a day ESL classes, and in those classes he received more explicit instruction in English sentence structure, vocabulary, phonics, and so on. In both the ESL and the mainstream classes talk was valued, and he had multiple opportunities to work in paired and small group settings with other children. All of this contributed to Xiaodi's rapid progress in English reading and writing.

## Upper Elementary School Children in Mainstream Classrooms

Older elementary school learners new to English also face challenges as they confront a new language, a new culture, and a new education system. Clayton (1996) studied the acculturation of four elementary school children ages 9 to 11, newly arrived in the U.S. from Brazil, Norway, Russia, and Bulgaria, students in mainstream fourth- to sixth-grade classrooms. Clayton's research asked: Is there some kind of underlying pattern of acculturation that the four students share? and What is the role of the school and the classroom teacher in the process? Clayton followed these students through their first 3 months of school, observing them, interviewing school personnel, interviewing (through a translator) the children and their parents, and analyzing journals the students kept (translated for her). Through the children's individual stories, certain patterns appeared. All of the children initially were lost in a sea of English that, by the end of the third month of school, began to become somewhat comprehensible. But full participation in all class events was difficult. All wanted desperately not only to do their schoolwork in English but to make friends and use English socially. All experienced dissonance between the textbook curriculum experienced in their home schools and the experiential, group work and project-based learning of their U.S. classrooms. Early on PE, music, and art classes were the easiest for the learners, the ones where they could participate most successfully, probably because the English was contextualized so that what was expected was more transparent. The children found their ESL resource room classes enjoyable and helpful to them in learning language forms used in their regular classrooms.

Clayton also found that the classroom teachers' approaches to the learners varied from choosing to treat them exactly as any other student to trying to ensure that they were included in class activities. No teacher had a clear understanding of second language acquisition or of the cross-cultural issues in education. Especially when students first arrived, the teachers commented that they did not know what to do with them.

With older ESL learners, too, questions have been raised about engagement with literature, about what they are able to do and what they learn, and about what the most effective ways to use literature are. In work done by Samway, Whang, Cade, Gamil, Lubandina, and Phommachanh (1991), ESL and native English speaking fifth- and sixth-grade students participated in literature study (Peterson & Eeds, 1990) of self-selected novels. After reading a novel, small groups of students met with a teacher for several 20- to 30-minute sessions to discuss the book. Initial discussions focused on personal responses to the book, but subsequent discussions focused on literary elements and the craft of writing. At the beginning of the year students could read only for about 20 minutes, but by the end of the year they could sustain the reading for an hour or more. Students initially were drawn to books with more pictures and fewer words, but as their confidence grew, they began to look for books that interested them regardless of illustrations and length. As a result of engaging in literature study, students "naturally and spontaneously compared books and authors; initiated and sustained discussion topics as they arose; built their literary repertoires (e.g., about books, authors and literary terms); and made associations between events and characters in books and their own lives" (p. 205).

While Samway's work focuses on literature study groups where the teacher is a group member, a literature-based instructional strategy called Book Club features student-led discussion groups. Book Club configurations that included Mei, a Vietnamese fourth and fifth grader, were the focus of work that examined how the participation of this ESL child changed over time in small discussion groups (Raphael & Brock, 1993; Goatley, Brock, & Raphael, 1995). Mei's general participation increased over time, and her confidence in speaking up within the group also increased. She initiated more topics, reintroduced topics, persisted in her comments, and asked more questions in discussions in fifth grade as compared to fourth grade. Her comments also became longer and more substantive as she became more able to use academic discourse in English to discuss the texts. The authors argue that it was through participation in reading a novel and discussing it with often more knowledgeable and more fluent peers (as well as through written reflections and teacher-fronted whole-class sharing) that Mei became a more able and confident user of the academic English expected for discussing literature.

In a related examination, Brock and Raphael (1994) contrasted Mei's literacy engagement in Book Club to her work with a sixth-grade social studies text. As Mei came to understand that the agenda in social studies was producing correct answers to specific questions, she developed specific strategies (such as using the questions at the end of each chapter and answering with as little detail as necessary) to accomplish the task.

Older ESL children's writing also has received researchers' attention. The utilization of dialogue journals by second language writers in a sixth-grade classroom was the focus of investigations led by and reported in Peyton and Staton (1993). A set of interrelated studies documented the effectiveness of this instructional strategy for L2 learners of whatever proficiency level. Dialogue journals became a place to try out English, to experiment with the new language. The journals played an important role in students' language and social development. Through her dialogue responses, the classroom teacher was able to provide clear and comprehensible input to the learners and also to expand and elaborate on learners' comments. As the children's writing became more complex and complete, the teacher's responses became more sophisticated as well. Thus, the written conversations resembled adult–child interactions documented in the characteristic of first language (L1) spoken language acquisition. Teachers and children used the journals for a variety of functions, for example, sharing and reporting facts, requesting information, complaining, apologizing, and so on. When dialogue journal entries were compared to assigned writings such as letters and essays, the journal entries were found to be both longer and syntactically more complex than the other kinds of writing. In the context of this particular classroom, the dialogue journals were a powerful language learning tool.

Another classroom study focusing on second language learners' writing considered the ability of ESL fourth graders to engage in student-to-student conferences as part of writing workshop. Blake (1992) analyzed the talk in peer writing conferences, focusing on the talk of ESL learners (either their talk with another ESL child or with a native speaker). She found that these children were able to engage in substantive talk around a piece of writing, and that they gradually became able to offer both supportive and critical comments to peers. Important to the development of this ability was teacher modelling and multiple opportunities to engage in talk about writing. Blake also found that the talk about writing was important for helping the students begin their revisions. An examination of student pieces revealed that those revised after talking were longer, clearer, and more coherent than others.

A suggestion frequently made to teachers whose older elementary students include second language learners is that they adopt collaborative or cooperative learning, so that students will learn both academic language and content from each other. Evelyn Jacob and colleagues (Jacob, Rottenberg, Patrick, & Wheeler, 1996) looked closely at cooperative learning in a sixth-grade social studies classroom where one third of the students were ESL learners. In their analyses of videotaped lessons, they discovered that carefully structured cooperative learning groups *did* provide ESL learners with more positive opportunities to use and learn academic English than occurred in a typical teacher-fronted class. These opportunities included: receiving and giving help with academic terms, concepts, and task directions; linking familiar words to unfamiliar ones; figuring out the meanings of homonyms; and receiving help in spelling words correctly and in producing a particular academic register in written English. However, the cooperative groups did *not* provide as rich an environment as might have been possible. The researchers found multiple instances of missed opportunities and negative input, which they identified as related to student understanding of and engagement with learning tasks, the substance and difficulty of some tasks, and student ability to enact the participant structures the teacher organized. The researchers concluded that the mixed results they found substantiated findings of other researchers. They concluded that for ESL students to receive maximum benefit from cooperative learning groups, teachers need a broad understanding not only of second language acquisition but also of academic language. This fine tuned understanding needs to be used to consider instructional goals and "structure classroom tasks to support the desired opportunities for L2 learners, monitor what is happening in groups and fine tune their implementation if they are not getting what they want" (pp. 275–76). It is not enough simply to "do" cooperative learning.

Classroom researchers also have begun to investigate culturally congruent communication patterns between teachers and students as intermediate-age students use English to learn school content. Science learning received attention in studies where interactions between teachers and students from the same cultural-linguistic groups (Spanish speaking, Haitian Creole, and monolingual English speaking) were analyzed during science lessons (Lee & Fradd, 1996, 1998). Within each language group, consistent patterns of interaction were identified, but each group's patterns were different from the others, suggesting that teachers of linguistically diverse students may need to attend to ways of interacting with students that are culturally appropriate as an important part of what the researchers term instructional congruence in science teaching. Instructional congruence means not only that teachers are knowledgeable about specific science content, but also that they are able both to relate their students' life experiences to science content and utilize their ways of participating in lessons as vehicles for developing students' science knowledge and scientific discourse.

## ESL Learning in Resource (Pullout) Classrooms

In addition to mainstream classroom membership, children learning ESL often spend part of their school days in ESL resource rooms, where they work exclusively with other second language learners and a teacher. Ernst (1994) conducted a study of how the use of a particular ESL resource room classroom strategy called the talking circle provided opportunities for English language learners to practice their L2 by engaging in meaningful interaction with both the teacher and other children. Talking circle involved the participants (ESL children in first through fourth grades with an ESL volunteer) in conversations on topics of personal interest and relevance (for example, going swimming, playing Nintendo games, getting a tan, getting a haircut). In her analysis of teacher and student talk, Ernst divided the talking circle into five distinct phases. In Phase 1 (Getting Ready) and Phase 2 (Entry), participants negotiated the creation of a circle, sat down and began to talk. Phase 3 (Core) began when one child was able to get the group's attention and thus control the topic. Phases 4 (Teacher's Agenda) and 5 (Moving On) signaled the teacher's moving the group away from conversation and into their assigned work at centers. Ernst found that in all 5 circle phases the teacher promoted language learning either by encouraging student participation in an ongoing conversation or by providing L2 input through her explanations and descriptions of activities. Similarly, in all 5 phases the students had opportunities to talk and listen. However in Phase 3 the children took more and longer turns, their roles were more active, and their talk was richest. In Phase 3, the teacher's role

was very much like that of the students': to be a talker and a listener as well as to provide support for the L2 speakers. In Phases 4 and 5, however, the teacher took on a more dominant role, the learners' turns were fewer, shorter, and more recitation-based. Ernst concluded that, in order to practice the L2 and negotiate meaning, ESL students need to engage in conversation that is encouraged, orchestrated, supported, and monitored by the teacher; and have some control over the topic of conversation.

In a study of process writing in ESL pullout contexts, Peyton, Jones, Vincent, and Greenblatt (1994) investigated how ESL resource teachers in a study group on writers workshop utilized what they learned in study group in their own teaching. There were significant differences between the ideal writing workshop described in the literature and what the teachers were able to put into practice. Lack of time was a significant issue in the pullout ESL setting. Additionally, many of the ESL learners had such limited proficiency in English that they were reluctant to write anything. Nevertheless, most teachers did put some of the writing workshop into practice. Classroom adjustments commonly made included spending significant time talking and building vocabulary prior to writing, focusing extensively on developing writing fluency, engaging in extensive modelling of sharing and conferencing, and setting out reasonable expectations for revising and creating multiple drafts of pieces.

In another look at writing in the context of an ESL pullout class, Samway (1993) asked whether second-through sixth-grade children could learn to comment on each others' pieces during sharing and conferencing. She found that, with a great deal of teacher modelling over time in mini-lessons, teacher-student conferences, and whole group discussions that children could learn to talk critically about each other's work.

Another influence on ESL students' writing can be their reading. Samway and Taylor (1993) examined the writing done in an ESL resource room by three nonnative-English speaking middle school children and interviewed them about ways that their reading influenced their writing. An important influence on writing was the writing techniques children attended to in stories they read (for example, O Henry's use of unexpected endings, or the use of a powerful lead-in to a story). Reading fiction and reading multiple genres also influenced these writers to think about what was plausible in their own stories, as well as to use the conventions of particular genres (for example, the convention of writing a moral at the end of a fable). These ESL learners made substantive changes in their pieces based not only on conferences, but also on their experiences as readers.

## Bilingual Classroom Studies

While the work has not been as extensive, within bilingual classrooms (most often Spanish–English speakers) researchers also have examined children's spoken and written English language abilities, use, and development. Given claims that bilingual classrooms do *not* foster English language development, a recurring school and classroom issue has been the status of English or the importance of English in relation to the native language.

In a special double issue of the *Bilingual Research Journal* (Leone & Cisneros, 1995), detailed descriptions of the ESL component in specific bilingual schools and classrooms around the U.S. and Canada make it clear that English language instruction and learning is a central feature of well-designed programs. Additionally, school- and classroom-based research has demonstrated that English permeates bilingual school settings, as well as the community beyond the school (Escamilla, 1994), making it the prestige language and impelling children into using it. Case studies of bilingual classrooms have documented that teachers must make concerted, even heroic, efforts to retain the Spanish language and Spanish literacy in the face of learners choosing to use English (Shannon, 1995).

The power of English also becomes evident in bilingual classroom research that has looked at primary children's emerging biliteracy. Some might assume that Spanish–English bilingual children who have learned to write and read in Spanish would need organized structures and procedures to lead them into English (this assumption stands behind persistent questions about when and how to transition or move learners into English). However, several studies have demonstrated that learners, once they develop confidence in themselves as writers and readers in Spanish, will often choose, of their own accord, to experiment with or to add on English reading and writing (Garcia & Colon, 1995; Hudelson & Serna, 1994; Serna & Hudelson, 1993). Bilingual children often choose to use one language instead of another for writing based on the person to whom they are writing, the topic they are writing about, or enjoyment of a particular language (Garcia & Colon, 1995; Hudelson & Serna, 1994). Initially the learners' English writing is not conventional (taking spelling, segmentation, punctuation into account), but it is recognizable as English (Hudelson & Serna, 1994).

Another recurring issue with regard to literacy instruction in bilingual classrooms has been whether progressive pedagogies (for example, process, writing workshop, literature study) should be utilized without modification in classrooms for linguistically and culturally diverse learners. Delpit (1988), for example, has questioned whether all learners benefit equally from writing process approaches that advocate minimizing the teaching of specific writing skills, as she maintains that some children, especially nonmiddle-class minority children, may need explicit instruction of conventions and skills. Applying this questioning to bilingual settings, Reyes (1991) examined the English language literature journals of bilingual fourth graders over the course of several months. The teacher responded to the children's literature log entries with conventionally written entries of her own, but did not directly correct the children's spelling or mechanics. Reyes discovered that the children's spelling did not improve significantly over time, a finding that led her to question and critique the utilization of writing process pedagogy with second language learners who need to use conventional forms in their writing.

Within bilingual classrooms, pedagogical labels such as literature study or writing process are beginning to be examined to learn more about what actually occurs during instruction. Gutierrez (1992), for example, conducted a 2-year observational study in five second- and third-grade Spanish–English transitional bilingual classrooms designated by the school principal as writing process classrooms taught by exemplary teachers. Analysis of videotapes and field notes, child and teacher interviews, and child products revealed tremendous variation in writing process instruction and its impact on the children in the classrooms. Some teachers organized writing process instruction as a series of activities to be carried out in a unidirectional fashion, allowing almost no time for talk, generation of ideas, experimentation and meaning-making. The teachers' role was transmitter of knowledge, and there were few opportunities for student interaction or even writing.

Other writing process classrooms were open to student talk and interaction, and to students assuming multiple roles as writing contexts tasks varied. In these responsive/collaborative classrooms, writing was truly a social process. Writing time included time for talking, for working with and helping others, and for receiving appropriate assistance from teachers. When written products were compared, Gutierrez found that the children in the truly responsive/collaborative settings created written pieces that were elaborated, that created and sustained ideas and arguments, and that utilized both children's personal experiences and texts that they had read. In later work with bilingual children's journal writing in English, Gutierrez (1994) found again that when children shared journal entries in groups structured by the teacher to be responsive/collaborative, more possibilities existed for children to make revisions to what they had written.

Another example of looking closely at writing instruction comes from work in a third-grade Spanish–English bilingual classroom where children engaged in story writing as the culmination of a unit of study on space (Tuyay, Jennings, & Dixon, 1995, Tuyay, 1999). A close look at the child–child and adult–child discourse revealed that collaborative interaction with peers, with the teacher, and with other more knowledgeable adults was vital to the children's generation and revisioning of possible texts. Talk and collaboration were essential to writing. Children needed significant amounts of time to construct text, and accomplishment of writing tasks varied among the children. Child choice of topic and content, along with scaffolding from the teacher, were also important as children worked to construct meaning both through talk and through writing (Tuyay et al., 1995). An examination of the resulting written products indicated that children did successfully combine elements of fantasy and reality into their stories (Tuyay, 1999).

In other bilingual classroom work, Floriani (1994) examined collaboration among pairs of sixth graders as the children constructed social science reports at the conclusion of a project in which they worked as social scientists, observing, collecting data, interpreting evidence, drawing conclusions, and writing up their findings. Over time, through collaborative work, the children's writing shifted from a more personal style to a more social science writing style, to writing that was more academic in nature.

Collaboration in literature response and in the construction of story meaning was examined by Battle (1993, 1995) who studied a Spanish–English bilingual kindergarten. She focused on teacher and child behaviors and interactions during daily read-aloud time of high quality children's books in English. Battle discovered that the teacher consistently: encouraged children to participate orally in the reading, but did not require it; allowed and encouraged children to ask questions, make observations, relate the story to personal experience, and give opinions, thus engaging in a joint construction of meaning of the text; allowed children to use their native language, Spanish, as they asked questions and made statements; and used Spanish herself, sometimes summarizing a book in Spanish before reading it in English, at other times using Spanish when questions came up and when the children switched into Spanish. Battle concluded that the teacher's supportive role in encouraging the children to talk, and her allowing the children to use their native language as well as English, contributed to the children's willingness to respond to the literature she read and to the group's collaborative meaning making.

Another view of teacher–child collaborative interaction around literature is that proposed by the developers of a strategy designed specifically for linguistically diverse learners, the instructional conversation or IC (Goldenberg, 1992/93). In ICs teacher and students discuss literature, but the teacher has identified themes and concepts that he or she wants to focus on during talk. Thus, the teacher guides the conversation to create an "excellent discussion by a teacher and a group of students . . . teachers and students are responsive to what others say, so that each statement or contribution builds upon, challenges, or extends a previous one" (Goldenberg, 1992/93, p. 318). Saunders and Goldenberg (1999) designed a study to examine the use of instructional conversations around an English language piece of literature with fourth- and fifth-grade transitional bilingual education LEP (school designation) students. Learners were part of one of four treatments: read and study the story, utilize literature logs to reflect on the story, participate in instructional conversation about the story, participate in instructional conversation and utilize literature logs. The most effective treatment for developing story comprehension and interpreting the story theme for LEP learners was the combination of instructional conversations and written reflection in a literature log. In related work, Patthey-Chavez and Clare (1996) found that fourth-grade Spanish–English bilingual learners making the transition to English instruction benefited as users of English from the guided exploration of literature provided by instructional conversations. The children's reading comprehension benefited in that their conversations provided opportunities for collaborative construction of meaning. The children's writing benefited in that ideas, interpretations, and language forms raised in discussions later appeared in children's writing. And the children's writing itself also improved on a number of linguistic variables.

## Implications

From these smaller qualitative case studies at the elementary level, we note first and foremost that the teacher plays a crucial role in children's second language development by:

1. Creating an environment that both acknowledges and respects the language and literacy development of the child's home and community;

2. Providing multiple opportunities for language interactions that include oral and written experiences with both the teacher and the classmates;
3. Observing children's language interactions and planning instructional activities that reflect the reality of the idiosyncratic nature of literacy development in children; and
4. Allowing and valuing the use of the L1 in the language and literacy development of the L2.

Teachers in successful classrooms for second language learners also demonstrate an understanding of and appreciation for language and literacy development as a social process that involves talking, sharing, and collaborating through instructional activities such as literature studies, book clubs, dialogue journals, writing workshops, and carefully orchestrated cooperative learning groups. Furthermore, they recognize that language and literacy development is a time consuming task that requires repeated opportunities for authentic use.

In one final note, we point out again that most of the classroom-based research has been conducted in ESL classrooms. Thus, more research on bilingual, both two-way and late exit, classrooms is needed to more fully understand the successful practices used with children in true bilingual settings.

## SECONDARY LEARNERS

The most encompassing statement that can be made regarding secondary school ESL learners is that they have long been neglected by researchers and practitioners alike. Fortunately, in the decade of the 1990s this situation started to change. This section of our chapter reviews several aspects of bilingual secondary students in the high school level ranging from who the students are and how they are being currently being served in schools, to research on effective classroom practice and school-wide design considerations.

### Who Are Bilingual Secondary Students?

According to recent U.S. census reports, while the population of the United States increased by 10%, the population speaking languages other than English at home increased by 38% between 1980 and 1990 (Waggoner, 1999). Furthermore, one in six of all youth in the United States, aged 14 to 19, either speaks a language other than English at home, was born in a foreign country, or both. As more and more high school students come from homes where English is not the primary language, it is equally clear that most American schools are unprepared to meet the needs of these students. As Waggoner (1999) shows, one in five speakers from nonEnglish homes drop out of high schools. Clearly, as Valdes (1999) argues, "Schools, especially those that until recently served mainstream English-speaking populations, are unprepared to work with large numbers of very different students who often have had little access to quality education in their own countries" (p. 318).

Currently, many English learners in secondary schools have had limited or sporadic schooling in their native countries (Garcia, 1999; Minicucci & Olsen, 1992), and so, most are years behind in terms of preparation for the academic demands of high school. For this reason, many of the students stay in ESL programs throughout their school careers and are labeled "ESL lifers" (Minicucci & Olsen, 1992). Also, students in these ESL programs often have limited access to school social events such as extracurricular events and activities (Necochea & Romero, 1989).

Students who are not isolated in ESL programs often are thrust into mainstream classrooms with teachers little prepared to accommodate them. As Castro and Ingle (1993) argue, most teachers who work with secondary English learners are not trained in second language instruction theory or methodology and correspondingly feel unprepared to work with ESL students. This means that mainstream teachers may unwittingly limit the ESL students' opportunities to interact verbally. For example, in a 1998 study of secondary science teachers working to assist ESL learners in their science classes, Verplaeste discovered that by increasing their use of directives and decreasing their use of questions, the secondary science teachers she studied actually closed out English learners from participation in classroom talk. The science teachers, lacking confidence in English learners' abilities to express themselves about science content, were trying to make the science content more accessible to the English learners. Furthermore, those things that are the mainstays of traditional classrooms, such as an abundance of initiation-response-evaluation (IRE) (Mehan, 1979) teacher talk, makes classrooms difficult for English learners (Harklau, 1994).

## What Works in Secondary ESL/Bilingual Classrooms?

It *is* possible for teachers to include English learners in mainstream classrooms in ways that prove academically rich not only for the ESL student but for native English speakers as well. Schlater (1997) and Wolfe (2000) have shown how English learners can be academic assets to mainstream classrooms by, for example, offering unique information and text interpretations. Other studies of teaching practices have shown that teachers who emphasize authentic, meaningful language use over drill and practice activities promote success for ESL students (Constantino & Lavadenz, 1993). For example, secondary ESL students involved in a sustained silent reading program showed gains in reading comprehension and reported that they read more often and from a wider variety of books (Pilgreen & Krashen, 1993). Similarly, Hornberger and Micheau (1993) argue for the necessity of student involvement in highly communicative activities and social interaction. Wheelock (1992) argues for the necessity of combining language and content learning through the use of hands-on activities involving collaborative teacher teams. Having students "do" does not seem to be enough, however. In order to truly grasp content, students must also be exposed to a teacher who models content area knowledge and language (Cone, 1991). This is demonstrated by Valdes (1999) whose study of writing

contexts for immigrant ESL students shows that what was most helpful in the writing development of adolescent incipient bilinguals was a process-oriented teacher who had students participate in academic writing (e.g., reports) while deliberately pointing out many features that undergird well-written texts in English.

Other research has supported the importance of authentic language in the classroom: using life experiences, writing for real purposes, and moving away from isolated skill and drill exercises (Fu, 1995; Perez, 1995; Trueba & Goldman, 1987). Langer (1997) has documented the value of personal book writing projects done bilingually in the fostering of literacy acquisition for adolescent language learners. It is important to note that "skills" were not ignored in successful classrooms, rather, as Olsen and Mullen (1990) argue, students were encouraged to "use their own experiences as the content for their work and learn the skills in the process" (p. 17). Unfortunately, meaningful language use in high school ESL classrooms seems to be in short supply (Walker de Felix, Waxman, Paige, & Huang, 1993). Beyond literacy activities, Tikunoff et al. (1991) document that student talk is a central feature of effective second language learning. Not all talk is created equal, however. As Faltis (1993) argues, talk in secondary classrooms must find a way to connect complex content with the lives of the bilingual students.

For secondary school English learners to be successful, it is necessary for them to learn content at the same time they are learning English (not after they have mastered the language) (Wu, 1996). One way for this to happen is to allow native language use that facilitates content learning as students are developing their English. Hewlett-Gomez and Solis (1995) have shown the value of using both Spanish and English integrated with content to promote the English language literacy development of immigrant Spanish speaking adolescents. They argue that accomodating varying levels of Spanish and English through the implementation of literacy strategies similar to those used in elementary schools has a positive effect on language learners' success in secondary school. Furthermore, creating new curriculum materials, doing staff development, involving parents, and employing Mexican teachers as aides proved to be important factors in student success.

Researchers also have constructed ways of enabling bilingual students to acquire discipline-specific language that is academically challenging at different classroom levels and that incorporates varied subject matter contents and classroom tasks (Short, 1994; Solomon & Rhodes, 1995). A major challenge with this focus on adapting content and teaching strategies has been training mainstream teachers to work with English language learners. In order to improve the sparse coverage of content that is currently being offered by sheltered content classes (Minicucci & Olsen, 1992), researchers have suggested the necessity of greater contact between ESL and subject area teachers. In this scenario, ESL teachers offer their expertise on inviting language learners participation in classrooms while the content teachers offer insights into the development of academically rigorous sheltered content classes (Lucas, Henze, & Donato, 1990). In other words, it is essential that schools offer a systemic integration of content and language

(Harklau, 1994) to ESL students. One option for greater access to content is to offer classes in the students' native language.

## Bilingual Classrooms at the High School

One aspect of support for English learners that has received little attention at the high school level is the inclusion of bilingual area content area classes. Although the importance of the use of students' first language in ESL classrooms is documented in the development of English language skills (Lucas & Katz, 1994), first language usage is also connected to the acquisition of subject area knowledge (Garcia, 1999). Medina and Mishra (1994), for example, have shown a significant association between Spanish reading achievement and Mexican American students' performance in mathematics, social studies, and science. Furthermore, Rosebery, Warren, and Conant have done extensive work showing the value of using the students' native language, specifically Haitian Creole, in the teaching of science (Rosebery, Warren, & Conant, 1992; Warren & Rosebery, 1995) Although research seems to show that secondary students in well-designed bilingual programs can match and even outperform grade level norms (Medina, 1991), these programs remain rare. Furthermore, when Spanish for native speakers programs (Colombi & Alarcon, 1997) are available in secondary schools, they are more often than not fragmented, isolated, and administered from the top down (Faltis & Wolfe, 1999). While they may offer academic support to English learners, they also create social isolation to such a degree that some researchers have argued that ESL/bilingual programs may constitute a case of segregation (Donato & Garcia, 1992).

## Schoolwide Efforts in Secondary Schools

Several recent studies have focused on the elements of effective secondary schools for English language learners. Lucas, Henze, and Donato (1990) studied six high schools in California and Arizona that were nominated as being exemplary in serving the needs of language minority students. From this study, the researchers identified several features of schools that promote success. When schools offered a variety of courses and programs of instruction and teachers who were trained in secondary bilingual and ESL-related methodology, language minority students were more successful. These researchers also found that English learners were most successful when they were provided ample and appropriate opportunities to develop both their native language and English proficiency. Furthermore, students needed access to a range of academic courses and content.

Lucas, Henze, and Donato's study suggests two main points that distinguish secondary schools that are successful in serving language learners from those that are not. First, successful schools are characterized by a schoolwide commitment to valuing and encouraging the success of English learners. Huerta-Macias and Gonzalez (1997) argue for the importance of staff development and a schoolwide effort in order to serve language minority students effectively. This schoolwide effort includes the creation of awareness among staff members that language

development and academic competence on the part of the student are often assumed to be one and the same thing on the part of the (untrained) teacher (Hornberger, 1989). This confusion often leads secondary schools to place English language learners on low academic tracks and, as Harklau (1999) argues, "Language minority students are adversely affected by ability grouping practices in American schools" (p. 55). Fu's study (1995) of four Vietnamese students assigned to Basic English tracks substantiates Harklau's findings and demonstrates the differences in student performance in the skills worksheets, Basic English context as contrasted with assignments that challenged the students to write extended discourse from their own experiences. Schools' negative evaluations of students often leads to the student rejection of the school system (Page, 1990, 1991).

Along with a schoolwide commitment to serving the needs of language learners, another solution appears to be for schools to invite local minority communities to participate in deciding the shape and direction of their children's schools (Corson, 1992). Several options for improvement of school response to language learners in the secondary school have been offered, including: team teaching to improve access to content areas; use of interactive technology to support native language instruction; temporary teaching certificates for bilingual adults with content area knowledge; allowing ESL secondary students extra time to attain credits for graduation, and more local responsibility for inservice teacher training.

Walsh (1991) also argues for a reexamination of the structure of secondary schooling in terms of its effectiveness in serving language learners, and more specifically, immigrant students. Correspondingly, Walsh offers several suggestions for a well-designed program for immigrant adolescents including:

1. Individual learning plans set up by the teacher and student leading to an alternative high school diploma.
2. Flexible scheduling allowing for work study programs.
3. Student access to counselors and mentors who speak the student's native language.
4. An ungraded course structure.
5. Small classes.
6. Literacy and content courses taught in the student's native language.
7. Double period ESL classes that offer support for subject-matter content and skill development.
8. Common planning periods for bilingual content-area and ESL teachers.
9. A well-defined exit criteria to measure student readiness for bilingual or mainstream content classes.

## Implications

What seems to be clear from the literature emerging on bilingual students in the secondary school is that in order to create opportunities for success, high schools must give serious consideration to a restructuring of their entire design (Wanko, 1997). Secondary schools and secondary teachers must make a serious and comprehensive commitment to the success of all students and especially those most at risk, English language learners. Furthermore, the apparent success of bilingual programs at the secondary level cannot go unnoticed. In the future, it may be inevitable that schools offer classes in more than one language and that researchers do more large-scale studies of these bilingual programs.

## CONCLUSION

From our review of the current literature on both elementary and secondary second language learners, we conclude that all children (K-12) need classrooms that view ESL/bilingual learners as smart, capable assets to the mainstream classroom. Furthermore, all second language learners need opportunities for authentic language use that they can connect with their own lives through oral and written interactions. Finally, our review makes it clear to us that a research agenda that focuses on bilingual classrooms at both the elementary and secondary level must be put into place. This agenda should include more classroom-based research conducted by university researchers, by classroom teachers as researchers of their own practice, by administrators as researchers of practices in their schools, and perhaps even by the students themselves as researchers of their own experience.

## References

Abbott, S., & Grose, C. (1998). "I know Englishes so many, Mrs. Abbott": Reciprocal discoveries in a linguistically diverse classroom. *Language Arts, 75,* 175-184.

AIR (American Institute for Research) (1975). *Identification and description of exemplary bilingual education programs.* Palo Alto, CA: AIR.

Allen, V. (1991). Teaching bilingual and ESL children. In J. Flood, J. Jensen, D. Lapp, & J. Squires (Eds.), *Research in the teaching of the English language arts* (pp. 356-364). New York: Macmillan.

America's children (1998). *Key indicators of well-being.* Washington, DC: Federal Interagency Forum on Child and Family Statistics.

Baker, K., & deKanter, A. (1983). Federal policy and the effectiveness of bilingual education. In K. Baker & A. deKanter (Eds.), *Bilingual education.* Lexington, MA: DC Heath.

Battle, J. (1993). Mexican-American bilingual kindergartners' collaborations in meaning making. In D. Leu & C. J. Kinzer (Eds.), *Examining central issues in literacy research, theory and practice* (pp. 163-169). Chicago: National Reading Conference.

Battle, J. (1995). Collaborative story talk in a bilingual classroom. In N. Roser & M. Martinez (Eds.), *Book talk and beyond: Children and teachers respond to literature* (pp. 157-167). Newark, DE: International Reading Association.

Blake, B. (1992). Talk in non-native and native English speakers' peer writing conferences: What's the difference? *Language Arts, 69,* 604-610.

Brock, C., & Raphael, T. (1994). Mei: Constructing meaning during a sixth-grade social studies unit. In D. Leu & C. J. Kinzer (Eds.), *Multidimensional aspects of literacy research, theory and practice* (pp. 89-100). Chicago: National Reading Conference.

Carger, C. (1993). Louis comes to life: Pretend reading with second language emergent readers. *Language Arts, 70,* 542-547.

Castro, R., & Ingle, Y. (1993). A proposal to reshape teacher education in the Southwest. In R. Castro & Y. Ingle (Eds.), *Reshaping teacher education in the Southwest: A response to the needs of Latino students and teachers* (pp. 1-12). Claremont, CA: Tomas Rivera Policy Institute.

Clayton, J. (1996). *Your land, my land: Children in the process of acculturation.* Portsmouth, NH: Heinemann.

Collier, V. (1995). *Promoting academic success for ESL students.* Jersey City, NJ: New Jersey Teachers of English to Speakers of Other Languages—Bilingual Educators.

Colombi, C., & Alarcon, F. (Eds.) (1997). *La enseñanza del español a hispanohablantes* [English translation]. Boston: Houghton Mifflin.

Cone, J. R. (1991). Untracking advanced placement English: Creating opportunity is not enough. *Phi Delta Kappan,* 712-717.

Constantino, R., & Lavadenz, M. (1993). Newcomer schools: First impressions. *Peabody Journal of Education, 69,* 82-101.

Corson, D. (1992). Bilingual education policy and social justice. *Journal of Education Policy, 7,* 45-69.

Cummins, J. (1999). Alternative paradigms in bilingual education research: Does theory have a place? *Educational Researcher, 28,* 26-34.

Delpit, L. (1988). The silenced dialogue: Power and pedagogy in educating other people's children. *Harvard Educational Review, 58,* 280-298.

Donato, R., & Garcia, H. (1992). Language segregation in desegregated schools: A question of equity. *Equity and Excellence, 25,* 94-99.

Ernst, G. (1994). "Talking circle": Conversation and negotiation in the ESL classroom. *TESOL Quarterly, 28,* 293-322.

Escamilla, K. (1994). The sociolinguistic environment of a bilingual school: A case study introduction. *Bilingual Research Journal, 18,* 21-48.

Faltis, C. (1993). Critical issues in the use of sheltered content teaching in high school bilingual programs. *Peabody Journal of Education, 69,* 136-151.

Faltis, C., & Hudelson, S. (1998). *Bilingual education in elementary and secondary school communities.* Boston: Allyn & Bacon.

Faltis, C., & Wolfe, P. (1999). Conclusion. In C. Faltis & P. Wolfe (Eds.), *So much to say: Adolescents, bilingualism, and ESL in the secondary school* (pp. 267-272). New York: Teacher's College Press.

Fassler, R. (1998). "Let's do it again": Peer collaboration in an ESL kindergarten. *Language Arts, 75,* 202-210.

Ferguson, P. M., & Young, T. A. (1996). Literature talk: dialogue improvisation and patterned conversations with second language learners. *Language Arts, 73,* 597-600.

Fitzgerald, J., & Noblit, G. (1999). About hopes, aspirations, and uncertainty: First-grade English-language learners' emergent reading. *Journal of Literacy Research, 31,* 133-181.

Floriani, A. (1994). Negotiating what counts: Roles and relationships, texts and contexts, content and meaning. *Linguistics and Education, 5,* 241-274.

Fu, D. (1995) "*My trouble is my English.*" Portsmouth, NH: Heinemann and Boynton-Cook.

Garcia, E. (1991). *Education of linguistically and culturally diverse students: Effective instructional practices.* Washington, DC and Santa Cruz, CA: National Center for Research on Cultural Diversity and Second Language Learning.

Garcia, E., & Colon, M. (1995). Interactive journals in bilingual classrooms: An analysis of language "transition." *Discourse Processes, 19,* 39-56.

Garcia, O. (1999). Educating Latino high school students with little formal schooling. In C. Faltis & P. Wolfe (Eds.), *So much to say: Adolescents, bilingualism, and ESL* (pp. 267-272). New York: Teacher's College Press.

Goatley, V., Brock, C., & Raphael, T. (1995). Diverse learners participating in regular education "Book clubs." *Reading Research Quarterly, 30,* 352-381.

Goldenberg, C. (1992/1993). Instructional conversations: Promoting comprehension through discussion. *The Reading Teacher, 46,* 316-326.

Greene, J. (1997). A meta-analysis of the Rossell and Baker review of bilingual education. *Bilingual Research Journal, 21,* 103-122.

Greene, J. (1998). *A meta-analysis of the effectiveness of bilingual education.* Claremont, CA: Tomas Rivera Policy Institute.

Gutierrez, K. (1992). A comparison of instructional contexts in writing process classrooms with Latino children. *Education and Urban Society, 24,* 244-262.

Gutierrez, K. (1994). How talk, context and script share contexts for learning: A cross-case comparison of journal sharing. *Linguistics and Education, 5,* 335-365.

Hakuta, K., & August, D. (1997). *Improving schooling for language minority children: A research agenda.* Washington, DC: National Academy Press.

Harklau, L. (1994). ESL versus mainstream classes: Contrasting L2 learning environments. *TESOL Quarterly, 28,* 241-272.

Harklau, L. (1999). The ESL learning environment in secondary school. In C. Faltis & P. Wolfe (Eds.), *So much to say: Adolescents, bilingualism, and ESL* (pp. 267-272). New York: Teacher's College Press.

Hewlett-Gomez, M. R., & Solis, A. (1995). Dual language instructional design for educating recent immigrant secondary students on the Texas-Mexican border. *Bilingual Research Journal, 19,* 429-452.

Hirschler, J. (1994). Preschool children's help to second language learners. *Journal of Educational Issues of Language Minority Students, 14,* 112-126.

Hornberger, N. H. (1989). Continua of biliteracy. Review of Educational Research, 59, 271-296.

Hornberger, N. H., & Micheau, C. (1993). "Getting far enough to like it": Biliteracy in the middle school. *Peabody Journal of Education, 69,* 30-53.

Hudelson, S., & Serna, I. (1994). Beginning literacy in English in a whole language bilingual program. In A. Flurkey & R. Meyer (Eds.), *Under the whole language umbrella: Many cultures, many languages* (pp. 278-294). Urbana, IL: NCTE.

Huerta-Macias, A., & Gonzalez, M. L. (1997). Beyond ESL instruction: Creating structures that promote achievement for all secondary students. *TESOL Journal, 6,* 16-19.

Jacob, E., Rottenberg, L., Patrick, S., & Wheeler, E. (1996). Cooperative learning: Context and opportunities for acquiring academic English. *TESOL Quarterly, 30,* 253-280.

Langer, J. (1997). Literacy acquisition through literacy. *Journal of Adolescent & Adult Literacy, 40,* 606-614.

Lee, O., & Fradd, S. (1996). Interactional patterns of linguistically diverse students and teachers: Insights for promoting science learning. *Linguistics and Education, 8,* 269-297.

Lee, O., & Fradd, S. (1998). Science for all, including students from non-English-language backgrounds. *Educational Researcher, 27,* 12-21.

Leone, E., & Cisneros, R. (Eds.) (1995). The ESL component of bilingual education in practice. *Bilingual Research Journal, 19.*

Lucas, T., Henze, R., & Donato, R. (1990). Promoting the success of Latino language minority students: An exploratory study of six high schools. *Harvard Educational Review, 60,* 315-340.

Lucas, T., & Katz, A. (1994). Reframing the debate. The roles of native languages in English-only programs and language minority students. *TESOL Quarterly, 28,* 537-556.

Medina, M. (1991). Native and Spanish language proficiency in a bilingual education program. *Journal of Educational Research, 84,* 100-106.

Medina, M., & Mishra, S. P. (1994). Relationships among Spanish reading achievement and selected content areas for fluent and limited Spanish proficient Mexican-Americans. *Bilingual Review/Revista Bilingue, 19,* 134-141.

Mehan, H. (1979). *Learning lessons.* Cambridge, MA: Harvard University Press.

Minicucci, C., & Olsen, L. (1992). *Programs for secondary limited English proficient students: A California study (Occasional Papers in Bilingual Education (No. 5)).* Washington, DC: National Clearinghouse for Bilingual Education.

Necochea, J., & Romero, M. (1989). *High school experiences of limited English proficient students: A cross case analysis of interviews with Hispanic, American Indian, and Vietnamese students in Arizona. Executive Summary of the High School Educational Program for Language Minority Students: The Arizona Picture* (pp. 21-22). Los Alamitos, CA: The Southwest Regional Educational Laboratory.

Olsen, L., & Mullen, N. A. (1990). *Embracing diversity: Teacher's voices from California's classrooms.* San Francisco: California Tomorrow.

Page, R. N. (1990). Games of chance: The lower-track curriculum in a college-preparatory high school. *Curriculum Inquiry, 20,* 249-281.

Page, R. N. (1991). *Lower-track classrooms: A curricular and cultural perspective.* New York: Teachers College Press.

Patthey-Chavez, G., & Clare, L. (1996). Task, talk and text: The influence of instructional conversation on transitional bilingual writers. *Written Communication, 13,* 515-563.

Perez, B. (1995). Language and literacy issues related to Mexican-American secondary students. *High School Journal, 78,* 236-243.

Peterson, R., & Eeds, M. (1990). *Grand conversations: Literature groups in action.* Richmond Hill, ON: Scholastic-Tab.

Peyton, J., & Staton, J. (1993). *Dialogue journals in the multicultural classroom: Building language fluency and writing skills through written interactions.* Norwood, NJ: Ablex.

Peyton, J., Jones, C., Vincent, A., & Greenblatt, L. (1994). Implementing writing workshop with ESOL students: Visions and realities. *TESOL Quarterly, 28,* 469-487.

Pilgreen, J., & Krashen, S. (1993). Sustained silent reading with English as a second language high school students: Impact on reading comprehension, reading frequency, and reading enjoyment. *School Library Media Quarterly, 22,* 21-23.

Ramirez, D. (1992). Executive summary. *Bilingual Research Journal, 16,* 1-62.

Ramirez, D., Yuen, S., Ramsay, D., & Pasta, D. (1991). *Final report: Longitudinal study of structured English immersion strategy, early-exit, and late-exit bilingual education programs for language minority children.* San Mateo, CA: Aguirre International.

Raphael, T., & Brock, C. (1993). Mei: Learning the literacy culture in an urban elementary school. In D. Leu & C. J. Kinzer (Eds.), *Examining central issues in literacy research, theory and practice* (pp. 179-188). Chicago: National Reading Conference.

Reyes, M. (1991). A process approach to literacy using dialogue journals and literature with second language learners. *Research in the Teaching of English, 25,* 291-313.

Rosebery, A., Warren, B., & Conant, F. (1992). *Appropriating scientific discourse: Findings from language minority classrooms.* Santa Cruz, CA: The National Center for Research on Cultural Diversity and Second Language Learning.

Rossell, C., & Baker, K. (1996). The educational effectiveness of bilingual education. *Research in the Teaching of English, 30,* 7-74.

Samway, K. (1993). "This is hard, isn't it?": Children evaluating writing. *TESOL Quarterly, 27,* 233-258.

Samway, K., & Taylor, D. (1993). Inviting children to make connections between reading and writing. *TESOL Journal, 3,* 7-11.

Samway, K., Whang, G., Cade, C., Gamil, M., Lubandina, M., & Phommachanh, K. (1991). Reading the skeleton, the heart, and the brain of a book: Students' perspectives on literature study circles. *The Reading Teacher, 45,* 196-205.

Saunders, W., & Goldenberg, C. (1999). *The effects of instructional conversations and literature logs on the story comprehension and thematic understanding of English proficient and limited English proficient students.* Washington, DC: Center for Research on Education, Diversity and Excellence.

Schlater, S. (1997). Assets to reading instruction: Second language learners in our classrooms. *Ohio Reading Teacher, 31,* 7-10.

Schmidt, P. (1993). Literacy development of two bilingual, ethnic-minority children in a kindergarten program. In D. Leu & C. J. Kinzer (Eds.), *Examining central issues in literacy research, theory and practice* (pp. 189-196). Chicago: National Reading Conference.

Serna, I., & Hudelson, S. (1993). Becoming a writer of Spanish and English. *The Quarterly of the National Writing Project and the Center for the Study of Writing and Literacy, 15,* 1-5.

Shannon, S. (1995). The hegemony of English: A case study of one bilingual classroom as a site of resistance. *Linguistics and Education, 7,* 175-200.

Short, D. (1994). Expanding middle school horizons: Integrating language, culture, and social studies. *TESOL Quarterly, 28,* 589-608.

Solomon, J., & Rhodes, N. (1995). *Conceptualizing academic language.* Santa Cruz, CA: University of California, National Center for Research on Cultural Diversity and Second Language Learning.

Tabors, P. (1997). *One child, two languages.* Baltimore, MD: Paul Brookes.

Tharp, R. (1997). *From at-risk to excellence: Research, theory and principles for practice.* Santa Cruz, CA: Center for Research on Education, Diversity, & Excellence.

Thomas, W., & Collier, V. (1997). *School effectiveness for language-minority students.* Washington, DC: National Clearinghouse for Bilingual Education.

Tikunoff, W. J., Ward, B. A., van Broekhuizen, L. D., Romero, M., Vega Castaneda, L., Lucas, T., & Katz, A. (1991). *A descriptive study of significant features of exemplary special alternative instructional programs.* Los Alamitos, CA: The Southwest Regional Educational Laboratory.

Townsend, J., & Fu, D. (1998). A Chinese boy's joyful initiation into American literacy. *Language Arts, 75,* 193-201.

Trueba, H., & Goldman, S. (1987). Organizing classroom instruction in a sociocultural context: Teaching Mexican youth to write in English. In S. Goldman & H. Trueba (Eds.), *Becoming literate in English as a second language: Advanced in research and theory* (pp. 235-252). Norwood, NJ: Ablex.

Tuyay, S. (1999). Exploring the relationship between literate practices and opportunities for learning. *Primary voices, 7,* 17-24.

Tuyay, S., Jennings, L., & Dixon, C. (1995). Classroom discourse and opportunities to learn: An ethnographic study of knowledge construction in a bilingual third-grade classroom. *Discourse Processes, 19,* 75-110.

Valdes, G. (1999). Incipient bilingualism and the development of English language writing abilities in the secondary school. In C. Faltis & P. Wolfe (Eds.), *So much to say: Adolescents, bilingualism and ESL in the secondary school* (pp.138-175). New York: Teacher's College Press.

Verplaeste, L. S. (1998). How content teachers interact with English language learners. *TESOL Journal, 7,* 24-28.

Waggoner, D. (1999). Who are secondary newcomer and linguistically different youth? In C. Faltis & P. Wolfe (Eds.), *So much to say: Adolescents, bilingualism, and ESL in the secondary school* (pp. 13-41). New York: Teachers College Press.

Walker de Felix, J., Waxman, H. C., Paige, S., & Huang, S. L. (1993). A comparison of classroom instruction in bilingual and monolingual secondary school classrooms. Peabody *Journal of Education, 69,* 102-116.

Walsh, C. (1991). Literacy and school success: Considerations for programming and instruction. In C. Walsh & H. Prashker (Eds.), *Literacy development for bilingual students.* Boston: New England Multifunctional Resource Center for Language and Culture Education.

Wanko, M. (1997). Managing diversity at a large urban high school. *High School Magazine, 5,* 26-29.

Warren, B., & Rosebery, A. (1995). *"This question is just too, too easy!": Perspectives from the classroom on accountability in science.* Santa Cruz, CA: The National Center for Research on Cultural Diversity and Second Language Learning.

Wheelock, A. (1992). *Crossing the tracks: How "untracking" can save America's schools.* New York: New Press.

Willett, J. (1995). Becoming first graders in an L2: An ethnographic study of L2 socialization. *TESOL Quarterly, 29,* 473-504.

Willig, A. (1981). The effectiveness of bilingual education: Review of a report. *NABE Journal, 6,* 1-19.

Willig, A. (1985). A meta-analysis of selected studies on the effectiveness of bilingual education. *Review of Educational Research, 55,* 269-317.

Wolfe, P. (2000). Official versions: Encouraging students' first language writing in ESL classrooms. In R. DeVillar & J. Tinajero (Eds.), *The power of two languages: Effective dual language use across the curriculum for academic success* (2nd ed.). New York: McGraw-Hill.

Wu, S. (1996). Content-based ESL at the high school level: A case study. *Prospect, 11,* 1-18.

Xu, H. (1996). A Filipino ESL kindergartner's successful beginning literacy learning experiences in a mainstream classroom. In D. Leu, C. J. Kinzer, & K. Hinchman (Eds.), *Literacies for the 21st century* (pp.219-231). Chicago: National Reading Conference.

# ·31·

# LANGUAGE VARIETIES, CULTURE AND TEACHING THE ENGLISH LANGUAGE ARTS

*Arnetha F. Ball*
Stanford University

*Marcia Farr*
University of Illinois, Chicago

The United States is a country of great cultural and linguistic diversity. Recognition of the nature and extent of that diversity is increasing as Americans acknowledge the human resources that come together to position them as leaders within today's global society. The recognition and acknowledgement of that diversity comes none too soon, as individuals who have traditionally been considered "minorities" in this country are now becoming the majority population in many of the nation's largest cities (Banks, 1991). According to Garcia (1993), this trend toward ethnic and linguistic diversity is most apparent among the nation's young and school-age children. For example, by 1991 in states like California, 52% of the students came from what had previously been considered "minority" populations, and these figures are expected to increase to 70% by the year 2005 (Garcia, 1993). Nationwide, White, non-Hispanic student enrollments decreased by 13% between 1976 and 1986 and by an additional 5.6% between 1986 and 1995, while "minority" enrollment as a proportion of total enrollment in elementary schools rose by 6% between 1976 and 1986 and by an additional 5.4% between 1986 and 1995 (National Center for Educational Statistics, 1991, 1998). Garcia (1993) and others have predicted that by the year 2030, White, non-Hispanic students will be a minority in every category of public education as we now know it, while culturally and linguistically diverse students will continue to be the nation's "emerging majority." As this emerging majority enters the English language arts classroom, they bring with them the rich linguistic resources that are generally spoken and written in their home and community settings. In earlier decades, the varieties of language spoken and written by "minorities" were considered inappropriate for use in formal, institutional settings like schools. Although linguists agree that the many varieties of English spoken by diverse groups in our society are cohesive, logical, highly structured linguistic systems in their own right, negative values have often been associated with many varieties of English used by diverse members of our society at large. In most cases, nonacademic varieties of English are seen as inferior to their mainstream academic English counterparts. Clearly, with the demographic changes that are occurring in our country, Americans will need to realign their attitudes concerning language use with the realities of the changing population.

Educators who are interested in successfully teaching the English language arts to all students are concerned about the fact that the "emerging majority" of culturally and linguistically diverse students are placed at risk of educational failure. This reality is highlighted by statistics that show drop out rates for White, non-Hispanic students at 7.3% in 1996 but at 13% for African American students and 29.4% for Hispanics. These figures illustrate the need for a growing concern about the educational plight of the "emerging majority." This chapter will address the significance of our nation's growing diversity for the classroom, focusing on the teaching of the English language arts (i.e., reading, writing, and speaking "standard" English). In particular, this chapter will review research on culturally and linguistically diverse populations and discuss how this research can inform effective language arts teaching.

Before synthesizing what research has documented regarding the cultural and linguistic characteristics of various groups, a few definitions are in order. The terms language, dialect, and varieties of English are sometimes used interchangeably in discussions that focus on cultural and linguistic diversity in classrooms. Linguists, however, use these terms to make specific distinctions. The term *language* is used to refer to the abstract system underlying the collective totality of the speech and writing behavior of a community; the term *dialect* is used to refer to a regional or socially distinctive variety of a language, identified by a particular set of words and grammatical structures. Any language with a reasonably large number of speakers will develop dialects, especially if there are geographic or social barriers separating groups of people from one another. Although dialects are generally considered to be subdivisions of languages, the distinction between these two notions is much more complex. It is usually said that people speak different languages when they do not understand each other; however, many of the so-called dialects of Chinese (Mandarin, Cantonese, Pekingese) are mutually unintelligible in their spoken form while Swedes, Norwegians, and Danes are generally able to understand each other but are considered to be speakers of different languages. In reality, the distinction between a language and a dialect is often determined by matters of social practice; it has much more to do with issues of power and politics than it has with any inherent characteristics or qualities of the linguistic system itself. The term *variety* is used in sociolinguistics to refer to any system of linguistic expression whose use is governed by situational variables (Crystal, 1990, p. 324). Within each community, there is a variety of language codes and ways of speaking available to its members that vary at the levels of different languages, regional and social dialects, registers, and channels of communication. The nature and extent of this diversity is related to the social organization of the group, which is likely to include differences in age, gender, social status, ethnicity, etc. In the U.S., as in other societies, distinctive features may be maintained and cultivated by groups as linguistic markers of regional and ethnic identities. One of the best described examples of ethnically marked speech in the United States has been African American Vernacular English (AAVE). As is the case of classical and colloquial varieties of Arabic, Katharevousa and Demotike varieties of Greek, and Standard German and Swiss German, AAVE in the U.S. is in a diglossic relationship with mainstream English. Diglossia exists when a high-status variety is used along with a low-status variety in the same society and the use of each is generally correlated with domain (e.g., within the home) and channel (e.g., written literature).

In discussions concerning varieties of English throughout the world, the terms nonstandard and standard are also often used. In the U.S., the term nonstandard English is often used to refer to any variety of English that does not conform in pronunciation, grammatical structure, idiomatic usage, or choice of words generally characteristic of educated native speakers of American English. Standard English is itself a variety of American English and is often referred to as mainstream or academic English. Specifically, it is that variant that is taught in schools and is regarded as the "prestigious" dialect in this society. Nonstandard English, on the other hand, is often spoken by groups of people who have been isolated from the standard dialect, who have not had the opportunity to acquire the dialect of the social elites, or who see value in preserving their own group dialect or variety of English. Some varieties of nonstandard English include, but are not limited to, Appalachian Mountain speech, African American vernacular English, Chicano English, Hawaiian Creole, Native American English, Puerto Rican English, and Southern White speech. In general, these varieties do not differ greatly from standard English, but instead are closely related to it with different versions of the same rules that govern all varieties of English. As we realign our attitudes concerning language use with the realities of our changing population, these varieties will no longer be viewed as low-status or nonstandard varieties; they will rather be recognized as part of the repertoire of linguistic resources that contribute to the communicative competence of the diverse members of our English speaking community.

## CULTURAL AND LINGUISTIC DIFFERENCES

"Culture" is an equally important term to define for the purposes of this chapter, but it is an elusive one. Numerous definitions have been offered by anthropologists through the years, although in recent decades two schools of thought have predominated. Geertz and other symbolic anthropologists view culture as publicly enacted systems of symbols (Geertz, 1973, chap. 1). That is, culture does not reside within individuals, but in the public sphere, where behavior is enacted and understood according to shared understandings. The other predominant definition of culture is a cognitive one: Culture exists within the minds of people and is a (cognitive) system of knowledge that both gives rise to behavior and is used to interpret experience. Spradley, for example, in his methodological text, *Participant Observation* (1980), refers to three fundamental aspects of human experience with which ethnographers, or those who study culture, must deal: what people do, what people know, and the things people make and use (1980, p. 5). Of these three aspects, Spradley puts primary emphasis on what people know, or on cultural knowledge. He thus essentially defines culture as "*the acquired knowledge people use to interpret experience and generate behavior*" (1980, p. 6) [italics in original]. Although it would seem that these two schools of thought would be incompatible, some theorists recently have attempted to bring them together under the rubric of "practice theory" in which knowledge and action are interdependent. For example, Foley (1997) suggests that cultural practices, including linguistic practices, enact shared understandings within a particular group, and that these practices are constrained but not determined by structural factors (e.g., social class or status), so change is possible within the general process of cultural reproduction. Most importantly, however, these practices and understandings are not uniformly shared by all members; that is, variation in both knowledge and practices exists within every cultural group, no matter how small. Keesing's (1974) review of theories of culture anticipated this emphasis on variation within culture.

In spite of this variation, however, all human beings who have been enculturated into one group or another possess enough shared linguistic and cultural competence both to communicate in the language of their group and to behave in ways generally appropriate to that group. This is true for all normal human beings, regardless of the language variety they speak. Because most schools in Western societies are controlled by the dominant "mainstream culture," the linguistic and cultural competence expected within them closely resembles the language and culture of (dominant members of) the dominant mainstream group. Heath (1983), for example, has discussed how members of the "mainstream" in the community that she studied used "expository talk" that was similar to school-taught expository prose on the job (in her study of mill executives and teachers) and at home as parents. Children who came to school with rich linguistic resources that did not, however, conform to the form and structure of the language used by the mainstreamers, were referred to as nonmainstream (Heath, 1983). Nonmainstream groups, in contrast to mainstreamers, enter school with a set of linguistic and cultural resources that are in some respects different from, and may even conflict with, those of the school culture. As has been repeatedly argued, such children do not possess linguistic or cultural deficits (although that is a widespread misconception that is held by many mainstreamers); rather, some of their cognitive and linguistic skills are simply different from those of their mainstream counterparts.

A substantial body of sociolinguistic research has documented some of the linguistic characteristics of these nonmainstream, low-prestige varieties of American English, including African American Vernacular English (Ball, 1992; Baugh, 1990, 1992; Edwards, 1992; Fasold, 1972; Labov, 1972a; Kochman, 1972; Poplack & Tagliamonte, 1994; Wolfram, 1969); Puerto Rican English (Wolfram, 1974; Zentella, 1981); Appalachian English (Wolfram & Christian, 1976); varieties of American Indian English (Wolfram, Christian, Potter, & Leap, 1979; Leap, 1993); Vietnamese English (Wolfram & Hatfield, 1984); and others (Amastae & Elias-Olivares, 1982; Ferguson & Heath, 1981; Labov, 1980). The primary findings of all this work is that nonmainstream varieties of English, in fact of any language, are as complex and as regularly patterned as are mainstream varieties. That is, speakers of these nonmainstrean varieties often have different linguistic rules that govern their grammars or use of lexical items; again, contrary to conventional "wisdom" among mainstreamers, they do not have linguistic deficits.

Other sociolinguistic research has focused on culturally embedded aspects of language use (both oral and written), rather than on grammatical characteristics of nonstandard dialects. Much of this work has been carried out within the conceptual framework developed by Hymes (1972, 1974) for what he termed "the ethnography of communication" (Saville-Troike, 1982). These studies have taken place both within classrooms (Ball, 1995a; Cazden, John, & Hymes, 1972; Charrow, 1981; Cook-Gumperz, 1986; Gilmore & Glatthorn, 1982; Green & Wallat, 1981; Saravia-Shore & Arvizu, 1992) and within home and community contexts (Ball, 1995b; Cintron, 1997; Delgado-Gaitan, 1990, 1996; Delgado-Gaitan & Trueba, 1991; Farr, 1993, 1994a, 1994b, 1994c, 2000; Gumperz, 1982; Heath, 1983; Kochman, 1981; Mahiri, 1994; Moss, 1994; Scollon & Scollon, 1981, 1995; Tannen, 1982, 1984; Valdés, 1996; Zentella, 1997). This work has found that ways of using language can vary extensively from one cultural group to another and that such

difference can cause miscommunication between speakers from different groups. School classrooms are particularly significant arenas for such cross-cultural communication, and the learning of literacy, in particular, is often a context in which communicative systems not only differ, but conflict. That is, when learning to read and to write, many students from nonmainstream groups are faced with a conflict between their own cultural and linguistic systems (and their own sense of identity) and those of the standard academic written language. The difficulties inherent in resolving such conflicts provide one explanation for low literacy levels among diverse populations.

A few other studies have focused on the writing of culturally and linguistically diverse students (Balester, 1993; Ball, 1992, 1995c, 1997; Farr Whiteman, 1981; Reed, 1981; Smitherman, 1994; Valadez, 1981) or on literacy in homes and other nonschool community settings (Ball, 1995b; Fishman, 1988; Heath, 1983; Mahiri, 1994; Moll & Diaz, 1987; Scribner & Cole, 1981b; Schieffelin & Cochran-Smith, 1984; Street, 1984, 1993; Taylor & Dorsey-Gaines, 1988; Teale, 1986).

The research on language variation and writing has identified particular linguistic features characteristic of the "home language" of various groups that speak nonmainstream varieties of English that occur in the writing of children, adolescents, and adults from these groups. For example, when an AAVE speaker writes "Doug be trying to tell . . . ," she is using what is referred to as the "habitual be" in her writing. In the mainstream academic English variety, only adverbs are used to distinguish something that happens on an ongoing basis from something that does not. In AAVE, however, the distinction can be made by using the "habitual be." Thus, an AAVE speaker might write, "Doug be trying to tell . . ." while a mainstream academic English speaker might write, "Doug is often trying to tell . . ." The "habitual be" is most often used in instances where a speaker of mainstream academic English might use adverbs like sometimes, often, always, and whenever (Ball, 1998). Work in this area has identified similar characteristics in the writing of African American Vernacular English speakers, Latino and Indian bilinguals, and deaf users of American Sign Language. A particular challenge to teachers in the English language arts is the assessment of writing by students from diverse linguistic backgrounds. Ball (1998) discusses issues of assessment with AAVE-speaking students and provides examples of instances in which characteristic features of spoken AAVE appear in a student's written text at the phonological, syntactic, semantic, and discourse levels. Ball (1997) discusses how the voices of teachers from diverse backgrounds can be helpful for broadening debates about the reform of writing assessment in general, and the assessment of writing for culturally and linguistically diverse students in particular.

Most of the work on the relation of home language to literacy learning explicitly advocates what Baugh (1981) terms "ethnosensitivity," rather than ethnocentricity, on the part of those teaching such students. In this view, an emphasis is placed on understanding and building on the cultural values and linguistic patterns of diverse student populations.

The work on literacy in community settings has found that literacy is not a single entity that occurs in different contexts, but a social practice that varies according to the particular use to which it is put in each context. Likewise, the cognitive demands of writing and reading, and the cognitive effects of learning to do so, also vary according to particular uses. Thus, as uses of language and literacy may differ between school and nonschool context, so apparently do the cognitive styles that underlie these uses.

For a more detailed review of sociolinguistic research on AAVE that explores the relation between social dialects, language learning, and the teaching of reading, see Rickford and Rickford (1997). For a more detailed review of sociolinguistic research and its relevance to the teaching and learning of writing, see Farr (1986). These reviews synthesize research on culturally and linguistically diverse cultural groups and provide specific examples, drawn from the research, of particular conflicts between mainstream and nonmainstream communicative systems. Farr (1986) provides examples of conflicts at the phonological, syntactic, semantic, pragmatic, and discourse levels of language, as well as the broader cultural level of language use.

## POLITICAL ISSUES

Recognition of the differences between the linguistic and cultural resources of diverse students and those that are needed for success in academic settings lead to decisions that are essentially political in nature. Such decisions constitute a language policy regarding what language arts should be taught to a multicultural student population. As Fasold and Shuy pointed out years ago, there are essentially three positions that can be assumed in this situation: eradication, biloquialism, and valuing of dialect differences (Fasold & Shuy, 1970, p. xi). Eradication, the traditional policy "long nourished in the English profession" (Fasold & Shuy, 1970, p. x), assumes the undesirability of speech patterns associated with culturally and linguistically diverse groups and attempts to rid students of these features, replacing them with more desirable "standard" ones. This, in fact, describes the status quo in most schools, and, without a concerted effort to develop a different language policy, this position will probably prevail. Whether it succeeds or not, is a separate question.

Biloquialism calls for the learning of new, standard patterns without eliminating the old nonstandard ones. Often called bidialectalism or biculturalism (as parallel to bilingualism), this position attempts to provide academic linguistic and cultural resources to students who speak nonprestige varieties of English, while respecting nonmainstream cultures and dialects. The goal of this kind of instruction is to enable students to switch from one linguistic style to another, guided by a sense of appropriateness to the context in which the language is used. Since all speakers, mainstream and nonmainstream alike, shift among more or less formal styles, depending on context, to some degree, this position is a relatively natural one. It also has the advantage of being currently the most pragmatic position, given the deep-seated negative attitudes of most members of the public toward nonstandard varieties of English.

Valuing linguistic differences is the logical opposite of eradicationism. This position holds that, since research has clearly shown nonprestige varieties of English to be the linguistic equals of mainstream academic or standard English, it is wrong to insist on replacing such varieties with the national standard. Moreover, as many have argued (see, for example, Sledd, 1988), the time and effort spent on eradication, with remarkably unsuccessful results, would be better spent on enlightening mainstreamers about the naturalness of variation in language and eliminating their prejudices against culturally and linguistically diverse groups. Whether or not such efforts could prevail is a matter of some debate.

Although these three positions were described almost 3 decades ago, the situation remains almost the same today. There is as yet no widespread consensus on which to base a new language policy. Three decades ago, however, the discussion revolved primarily around oral language, with some attention to reading (Baratz & Shuy, 1969; Fasold & Shuy, 1970; Feigenbaum, 1970; Shuy, 1980). As writing has gained in prominence as an educational and research issue, however, the situation has shifted somewhat (Hillocks, 1995; Odell, 1993; Severino, Guerra, & Butler, 1997). Researchers recently have begun to address the concerns of reading and writing together, joining the emerging field of literacy studies (Alvermann, Hinchman, Moore, Phelps, & Waff, 1998; Ferdman, Weber, & Ramirez, 1994; Gee, 1996; Langer, 1988; Lunsford, Moglen, & Slevin, 1990; Mitchell & Weiler, 1991; Street, 1984, 1993).

Some studies of literacy have emphasized its importance in modernization and all the processes (e.g., urbanization, industrialization) that go along with it (Goody, 1977, 1986, 1987; Goody & Watt, 1963; Ong, 1982). This view holds that literacy brings with it cognitive changes that are necessary for coping in a modern industrial society. A number of researchers have critiqued this view as being ethnocentrically biased in favor of Western culture and have provided counter evidence, from anthropological studies, of supposedly literate cognitive processes in nonliterate cultures (Finnegan, 1988; Scribner & Cole, 1981a; Street, 1984, 1993). Moreover, Levine (1986) has questioned the necessity of standard English literacy for many kinds of employment, while acknowledging the continued use by employers of literacy tests to select workers apparently for other reasons. Other kinds of employment do involve literacy, although the kinds of writing and reading (and learning) required vary widely according to workers and contexts (Hull, 1997).

The most pragmatic position may continue to be that of biloquialism, the teaching of mainstream patterns as an expansion of students' linguistic repertoires, not as a replacement for indigenous dialects or local ways of using language and literacy. Although this position seems to avoid the injustice of eradicationism, as well as the not-very-practical idealism, some would say, of valuing indigenous varieties without imposing a standard variety, one must question whether it is as attainable as it appears to be. It is certainly true that both bilingualism and bidialectalism exist in societies around the world, indicating that, in themselves, these phenomena are natural and attainable. It then must be asked why that has not happened in, for example, the United States, to a greater extent than it has. The work of two researchers in particular, Fred Erickson and John Ogbu, has suggested some explanations for this.

Ogbu (1987) argues that some minorities in modern urban industrial societies form "a collective oppositional identity" for support and survival that makes "intercultural learning or crossing cultural/language boundaries... problematic" (p. 164). In other words, Ogbu argues that a vernacular dialect is one set of symbols supporting an identity opposed to the forces that denigrate the vernacular culture. To learn mainstream language and cultural patterns, then, is tantamount to denying one's identity and joining forces with those who are rejecting one's group. Ogbu's argument, however, lacks explanatory power for those vernacular speaking minorities in modern urban industrial societies with strong, supportive, and collective ethnic identities who excel academically and who have no difficulty crossing cultural/language boundaries.

Erickson (1984) offers explanations drawn from the micropolitical processes in communicative interactions between individuals. In discussing the miscommunication, in the classroom and elsewhere, that can result from cultural differences in language form and use, he cites studies (Giles & Powesland, 1975; Labov, 1972b; Piestrup, 1973) that show such differences seem to increase in contexts where there is conflict (for example, if such differences lead to negative perceptions of a student by a teacher). When there is no conflict (for example, when instruction is congruent with the culture of the students), such differences can be "sidestepped." The implication here is that these micropolitical processes, reflecting more macro ones from the larger society, may be partially responsible for so many students not learning, or not choosing to use, standard English.

Clearly, the problem of teaching standard English and literacy is more complicated than was thought by many 3 decades ago. Part of that complexity resides in the attitudes that individuals hold about language and its use by others. Smitherman (1997, personal communication) has said, "what we did not realize 20 years ago is that negative attitudes concerning language are very deep seated. We therefore did not realize how difficult it would be to have an impact on those attitudes and to change them." For example, during the summer of 1996, the Oakland Public School District formed a task force that concluded that the primary deterrent to school success for the predominately African American population of the Oakland Public School District was language. Following the recommendations of the task force, the school board adopted a resolution to officially recognize the primary language of the students and to devise and implement the best possible academic program for imparting instruction to African American students in their primary language for the combined purposes of maintaining the legitimacy and richness of the students' language, and to facilitate their acquisition and mastery of English language skills. Nationwide, the response to the Oakland School Board's decision was a media frenzy that dismissed and ultimately trivialized the effort on the part of the Oakland Public Schools to respond to the growing crisis in the academic achievement of African American students. One reason for the negative response was the negative values that many mainstreamers associate with having diverse varieties of English recognized or used by students in the classroom (see Ball, Williams, & Cooks, 1997), even when the ultimate goal is to use the students' home language resources to facilitate the students' acquisition and mastery of standard English language skills.

In the current climate, bidialectalism/bilingualism may be the most realistically attainable position in discussions concerning the sociolinguistic resources of diverse students and those needed for academic success. But, if it is to be a truly effective policy for language and literacy learning, it will have to be supported by a reality that makes oppositional identity formation unnecessary and a reality that provides the social and economic support needed to develop and implement effective teaching approaches. Such a reality, of course, will require social and economic change beyond the scope of language arts teaching. Language arts teaching, however, can contribute to broader, more long-term change if efforts are made within society and within teacher education programs to negate the use of cultural and linguistic differences as resources for conflict. Instead, as will be discussed in the next section, such differences can be viewed as positive resources that can be used to make instruction more effective with culturally and linguistically diverse students.

## EDUCATIONAL ISSUES

Ethnographic studies of local uses of language and literacy have been used to improve instruction in two ways: by modifying instruction to be congruent with what research has shown to be local ways of using language, and by involving students themselves in doing and writing up the results of ethnographic research in their own communities. Heath (1983) provides a model for both uses. Her ethnographic research on language acquisition in one African American and one White southern, rural, working class community was used in the local school to modify instruction to students from these communities. Moreover, in a science classroom, students were involved in ethnographic research in their communities on such topics as ways of growing foodstuffs; they then compared these local ways with scientific approaches in an effort to determine "whether or not science could explain why the local folk methods either worked or did not work" (Heath, 1983, p. 317).

Researchers in Hawaii and in San Diego, California, also have applied the results of ethnographic research to instruction. Au (1980) reports on the successful results obtained by modifying reading instruction to be more congruent with the Hawaiian "talk story," a local speech event identified and described by ethnographers (Watson, 1975; Watson-Gegeo, & Boggs, 1977). Diaz, Moll, and Mehan (1986) and Moll and Diaz (1987) report on another use of ethnographic research results in the classroom. In this project, "social content: the substance of... discourse, parents' educational values, life history, and condition of... sample families" (Diaz, Moll, & Mehan, 1986, p. 223) is used to reorganize instruction in ways that increased student participation in the lessons and, consequently, improved student performance.

Other researchers that introduce improved instruction that is congruent with students' local ways of using language include Lee (1993) and Ball and Cooks (1998). Lee's (1993) work builds on the practice of cultural scaffolding. Scaffolding is a process that enables students to use resources they have already mastered through cultural experiences in order to understand and undertake new and more advanced academic tasks. Many AAVE-speaking students who are struggling with the task of interpreting new literary texts or providing rich detail in their writing assignments are already competent in the verbal skills of signifying. Signifying is an African American discourse style that requires, in most cases, the encoding of messages that involve an element of indirection, speaking in innuendoes, and using double meanings. According to Lee (1993), this discourse form can also serve as a medium for the internal organization of experience and, as such, can provide a heuristic for problem solving in the English language arts classroom because it requires analytical reasoning and a strong ability to use higher order thinking skills that are useful to students who are attempting to master skills in text interpretation and elaboration. As demonstrated in Lee's research, African American students are capable of using the verbal art form of signifying as a scaffold in interpreting and elaborating on different texts.

Drawing on popular literary texts by Zora Neal Hurston, Alice Walker, and Toni Morrison, Lee demonstrates how, after becoming cognitively aware of the skills and resources they use on a daily basis when signifying, students were able to draw on similar conventions to interpret and elaborate on the subtleties in texts that were introduced to them within the classroom setting. Lee offers this study as an example of the value of using an African American discourse genre as a scaffold for academic success and explains how the act of signifying—a social discourse practice primarily used and rooted in the AAVE-speaking community—can have positive cognitive consequences in the form of support for the development of critical strategies for interpreting literature.

Building on Ball's (1992) earlier work that revealed African American adolescents' preferred ways of organizing oral and written expository texts in formal and informal settings, Ball and Cooks (1998) report on research designed to implement a literacy training program that uses interactive technology to link at-risk high school students and preservice teachers together to teach expository writing skills by building bridges between the students' home and community-based communicative skills and the academic literacy skills needed in today's schools. Drawing on such models, English language arts educators can help students to see similarities between their preferred home-based language patterns and academic tasks, thus aiding the students in developing competencies in new and diverse areas of literacy. Using these models, teachers draw on what students already know from their own home and community practices in order to teach them how to master various aspects of classroom culture.

Other studies have provided an understanding of other principles underlying effective language arts instruction. Before summarizing two such studies that have focused on teaching students from culturally and linguistically diverse groups, it is important to emphasize that it is not so much the pedagogical technique itself that promotes learning, as it is the principles underlying successful techniques. Even the most successful and innovative technique can be misapplied, or can be inappropriate for a particular classroom, teacher, or cultural group. An actual incident (reported in Zemelman & Daniels, 1988) may be helpful as an example here.

A sixth-grade student in a highly regarded middle school in a suburb of Chicago was observed going over her well-written essay, erasing more sophisticated words and replacing them with simpler ones. Then she crossed out the simpler words, and drew arrows from them toward the more sophisticated ones written in the margins of the paper. When asked what she was doing, she replied, "I'm doing the writing process. We have to do it this way; it's what the teacher wants." The point of this story, of course, is that, although an emphasis on writing process is in general a welcome improvement to the traditional focus only on written products, replacing one rigid program of instruction with another doesn't really improve instruction at all. In short, the principles (e.g., the teacher turning over much of the responsibility for writing to the student) underlying the studies of writing process instruction (see, for example, Calkins, 1983; Graves, 1983; Perl & Wilson, 1986; Zemelman & Daniels, 1988) are equally as important as the focus on process itself.

For culturally and linguistically diverse students, misapplications of instructional improvements such as the one just described add insult to injury. Most of the schools these students attend, in the United States at least, are already burdened with problems that have little to do with instruction itself. Consequently, any instructional changes made in such schools not only should reflect the underlying principles of successful techniques, but also should be congruent with the realities of such schools. Three essential principles will be discussed; for a more detailed synthesis of such research, see Farr and Daniels (1986), which presents 15 principles of effective writing instruction for culturally and linguistically diverse (and other) students. See also Langer and Applebee (1986), which describes five components for effective literacy instruction for all students, and Ball (1998), which describes five key principles that underlie the creation of successful writing and assessment contexts for all students and important points that should remain foremost in teachers' minds when facilitating, supporting, and evaluating the writing of diverse students.

The most important principle of effective instruction for culturally and linguistically diverse student is that of ethnosensitivity (Baugh, 1981). It is crucial that teachers understand that their own views of the world, or ways of using language in that world, are not necessarily shared by others. A deep understanding of cultural and linguistic differences, either through living in another culture or through preservice or inservice coursework, can help reduce the ethnocentrism that is widespread in Western societies. Teachers, like most other members of society, are generally unaware of the extent to which they believe that their own cultural and linguistic patterns are natural or logical, nor do they generally realize how they tend to interpret other behavior according to their own cultural norms. For example, indirectness in language or nonverbal behavior can signify respect in one culture and dishonesty in another. If a teacher and a student are from different cultures, or subcultures, the very same behavior can be interpreted quite differently by each of them. Because communication between teacher and student is crucial to effective teaching and learning, it should be clear why ethnosensitivity is so important.

A second principle involves structuring activities that promote functional and interactive communication and allows students to feel "ownership" of their own writing. That is, writing that is intended as actual communication is much more effective in engaging students in literacy learning. Staton, Shuy, Kreeft Paton, and Reed (1988) provide an example of this. Staton et al. studied the use of dialogue journals in a sixth-grade classroom in a multicultural section of Los Angeles (the students in the particular classroom, for example, spoke 13 different languages). Their teacher, who had been using dialogue journals for 17 years, asked her students to write, in English, daily entries in the journal, to which she wrote short responses. Even those students who had minimal literacy skills in English were asked to write, as best they could, at least three sentences per day. The teacher did not evaluate this writing, but, instead, responded to it as a natural form of communication between two people who were writing and reading rather than talking.

Analysis of the journals over the course of a year showed substantial growth in writing, including an increase in quantity, elaboration of student-initiated topic, fluency, and control of English syntax (Kreeft & Shuy, 1985; Staton et al., 1988). Moreover, these students experienced, some for the first time, writing and reading for a purpose of their own. They eagerly read the teacher's responses to their own entries and wrote copiously, some even ending the year with several filled notebooks composing their year-long dialogue journal.

Heath & Branscombe (1985) also show that structuring activities that promote functional and interactive communication helps students learn how to write and read in mainstream academic ways. In this study, ninth-grade, remedial track, English students (primarily nonmainstream African Americans and a few nonmainstream Whites in a southern city) being taught by Branscombe, wrote and read long letters to and from Heath and her family, whom the students did not know; they also corresponded with Branscombe's regular eleventh-grade students.

As in the journals of the Staton study, the letters emphasized "real" communication, i.e., an interaction between writers and readers about thoughts, ideas, and other information. Branscombe's students, over the course of the year, became comfortable operating as writers and readers and learned much about school literacy in the process. They learned, for example, that (mainstream) expository writing requires "linguistic" devices and background information in explicated form if the addressee is to understand the [writer]" (Heath & Branscombe, 1985, p. 26).

A third principle is also illustrated by both the Staton et al. and the Heath and Branscombe studies: the need for abundant experience with written academic text. Such texts are replete with the linguistic resources of Western "essayist" literacy (Farr, 1993; Scollon & Scollon, 1981) such as standard grammar, explicit connectives (e.g., therefore, consequently, although), Latinate vocabulary, a clear sequencing of "points," allusions to other written texts, and so on. The more experience students have with such texts, the more easily they will acquire the particular linguistic devices and cultural orientation that they contain. This means that extensive reading and writing of extended discourse is necessary, not the reading and writing of multiple choice or fill-in-the-blank forms. Unfortunately, it is the

latter that now prevails in most U.S. schools, and particularly in schools serving culturally and linguistically diverse populations (Goodlad, 1984).

In the Staton study, students daily read the teacher-written responses to their dialogue journal entries. These responses, although not correcting student entries, modeled standard academic literate prose; for example, often the teacher would use a word, spelled correctly, that the student had misspelled. Moreover, the teacher's responses provided a framework (which she referred to as "scaffolding" according to Bruner's extension of Vygotskian theory) for the students to use in learning new reasoning processes. As students wrote back to the teacher, they too began to model standard academic literacy and mainstream reasoning processes. In the Heath and Branscombe study, the students read, and attempted to write, the kind of expository prose to or from an unknown audience that school literacy so often requires.

It is important to stress that in both of these studies, the emphasis in the activities was on actual communication through reading and writing, not on the linguistic forms of mainstream literacy. That is, these activities did not involve rote drills and exercises in which students practiced academic literate forms. In contrast, the students, while actually writing and reading with another real writer/reader, were abundantly exposed to such literate forms. These students had multiple and redundant opportunities to become familiar with literate academic language resources in dialogue with the teacher and others, and through the journals, letters, and books, but resources were less emphasized than the interaction itself.

One final area of research that is critical in improving the teaching of the English language arts to culturally and linguistically diverse students is teacher preparation. Although the term multicultural education began to appear in the literature in the early 1970s, only a few reviews have looked at multicultural teacher education (Baptiste & Baptiste, 1980; Commission on Multicultural Education, 1978; Grant & Secada, 1990). Ladson-Billings (1995) provides a summary of these reviews as well as a discussion of the nature of other studies that have been generated on multicultural teacher education since the Grant and Secada (1990) review. Ladson-Billings concludes that of the 39 ERIC research entries located between 1988 and 1992, 18 were position or opinion papers, 11 were descriptive studies, 2 were evaluative studies, and only 4 were empirical studies. She further notes that, "One of the 'cutting-edge' trends in multicultural teacher education . . . is the examination of classroom practice of successful teachers in diverse classrooms . . ." While most of this literature has focused on effective practice with African American students, a parallel literature exists in uncovering the effective practices of teachers of linguistically diverse students (see Bountress, 1994; Garcia, 1991; Hornberger, 1990; Moll, 1988).

Lucas and Borders' (1994) review of the information made available to developing teachers in the teacher education materials in the late 1980s and early 1990s revealed that these texts pay varying amounts of attention to the issue of linguistic diversity in schools. While many of the materials show an awareness of the issue, some provide more details than others on the nature of the linguistic diversity that teachers can expect to encounter in their future classrooms. According to Lucas and Borders (1994), two things seem to be lacking in these materials: information on exactly when and how dialect features are used in the classroom (which their research addresses) and discussions of the overall role of language in education. They conclude that a great deal more information is needed to help teachers understand what it means to have cultural and linguistically diverse students in the classroom. In response to that need, Ball (1998, 2000) provides specific information geared toward raising teachers' levels of linguistic sensitivity, increasing their knowledge base concerning the nature of the linguistic characteristics students bring into the classroom, and research on teachers' changing perspectives on their students' literacy practices. Ball, Williams, and Cooks (1997) provide specific applications of the research to the classroom setting. Clearly, more research is needed that focuses on teacher preparation programs that enable teachers to work effectively with students who are culturally and linguistically diverse (Carnegie Council on Adolescent Development, 1989; Darling-Hammond, 1986; Quality Education for Minority Project, 1990). In particular, studies are needed that better conceptualize the processes by which preservice teachers develop the reflection and commitment needed to transform the theory that they encounter in teacher education programs into practical curriculum and pedagogy that better serve the educational needs of diverse students (Ball, 2000). As Grant and Secada (1990) point out, empirical research is needed to give direction and focus to current debates on classroom practice, curriculum development, policy, and on finding solutions to problems of teaching and learning with culturally and linguistically diverse students (Darling-Hammond, 1994).

## CONCLUSION

At the beginning of this chapter, it was noted that culturally and linguistically diverse groups, taken together, are increasingly no longer the minority in many United States settings. Within 40 years, in fact, such groups will outnumber non-Hispanic European-origin Whites in many contexts. The primary argument of this chapter has been that this reality must be addressed within our educational system, or that system will be doomed to repeat its current failures with culturally and linguistically diverse populations. In addition to more widespread social change, especially in mainstream attitudes and values, and economic support for needed research and the implementation of effective programs, a number of improvements in the current educational system can be made. These include:

- Improving literacy instruction for all students, mainstream and nonmainstream alike, in ways that are consonant with the principles underlying successful techniques that have been documented by research.

- Requiring all current and future teachers to take coursework that presents the results of sociolinguistic research on culturally and linguistically diverse groups in order to explode the myths of ethnocentrism and develop ethnosensitivity and a clearer understanding of the resources that diverse students bring into the classroom.

- Using research to identify community uses of language and literacy to modify instruction so that it connects such community practices with practices in the classroom.

## *References*

Alvermann, D. E., Hinchman, K. A., Moore, D. W., Phelps, S. F., & Waff, D. R. (1998). *Reconceptualizing the literacies in adolescent lives.* Mahwah, NJ: Lawrence Erlbaum Associates.

Amastae, J., & Elias-Olivares, L. (Eds.). (1982). *Spanish in the United States: Sociolinguistic aspects.* Cambridge, England: Cambridge University Press.

Au, K. (1980). Participation structures in a reading lesson with Hawaiian children. *Anthropology and Education Quarterly, 11,* 91–115.

Balester, V. M. (1993). *Cultural divide: A study of African-American college-level writers.* Portsmouth, NH: Boynton/Cook.

Ball, A. F. (1992). Cultural preference and the expository writing of African-American adolescents. *Written Communication, 9*(4), 501–532.

Ball, A. F. (1995a). Investigating language, learning, and linguistic competence of African-American children: Torrey revisited. *Linguistics and Education, 7*(1), 23–46.

Ball, A. F. (1995b). Community-based learning in urban settings as a model for educational reform. *Applied Behavioral Science Review, 3*(2), 127–146.

Ball, A. F. (1995c). Text design patterns in the writing of urban African-American students: Teaching to the strengths of students in multicultural settings. *Urban Education, 30*(3), 253–289.

Ball, A. F. (1997). Expanding the dialogue on culture as a critical component when assessing writing. *Assessing Writing, 4*(2), 169–202.

Ball, A. F. (1998). Evaluating the writing of culturally and linguistically diverse students: The case of the African American English speaker. In C. R. Cooper & L. Odell (Eds.), *Evaluating writing* (2nd ed., pp. 225–23). Urbana, IL: National Council of Teachers of English.

Ball, A. F. (2000). Preservice teachers' perspectives on literacy and its use in urban schools: A Vygotskian perspective on internal activity and teacher change. In C. Lee & P. Smagorinsky (Eds.), *Worlds of meaning: Vygotskian perspectives on literacy research.* Cambridge, MA: Cambridge University Press.

Ball, A. F., & Cooks, J. (1998, February 20). *Literacies unleashed through technology: Expanding community-based discourse practices and instilling a passion to write in urban at-risk youth.* Paper presented at the National Council of Teachers of English, Research Assembly Midwinter Conference, UCLA.

Ball, A. F., Williams, J., & Cooks, J. (1997). An Ebonics-based curriculum: The educational value. *Thought & Action: The NEA Higher Education Journal, 13*(2), 39–50.

Banks, J. A. (1991). Multicultural literacy and curriculum reform. *Educational Horizons, 69,* 135–140.

Baptiste, H. P., & Baptiste, M. (1980). Competencies toward multiculturalism. In H. P. Baptiste, M. Baptiste, & D. Gollnick (Eds.), *Multicultural teacher education: Preparing educators to provide educational equity* (Vol. 1, pp. 44–72). Washington, DC: American Association of Colleges for Teacher Education.

Baratz, J., & Shuy, R. (Eds.). (1969). *Teaching black children to read.* Washington, DC: Center for Applied Linguistics.

Baugh, J. (1981). Design and implementation of writing instruction for speakers of non-standard English: Perspectives for a national neighborhood literacy program. In B. Cronnell (Ed.), *The writing needs of linguistically different students.* Los Alamitos, CA: SWRL Research and Development.

Baugh, J. (1990). A survey of the suffix /-s/ analyses in Black English. In J. A. Edmondson, C. Feagin, & P. Mühlhäusler (Eds.), *Development and diversity: Language variation across time and space.* Arlington: University of Texas and Summer Institute of Linguistics.

Baugh, J. (1992). Hypercorrection: Mistakes in production of vernacular African American English as a second dialect. *Language and Education, 6,* 47–61.

Bountress, N. G. (1994, Summer). The classroom teacher and the language-different student: Why, when, and how of intervention. *Preventing School Failure, 38*(10), 10–15.

Calkins, L. (1983). Lessons from a child: On the teaching and learning of writing. Exeter, NH: Heinemann.

Carnegie Council on Adolescent Development. (1989). *Turning point: Preparing American youth for the 21st century.* New York: Carnegie Corporation.

Cazden, C., John, V., & Hymes, D. (1972). *Functions of language in the classroom.* New York: Teachers College Press.

Charrow, V. (1981). The written English of deaf adolescents. In M. Farr Whiteman (Ed.), *Variation in writing: Functional and linguistic-cultural differences.* Hillsdale, NJ: Lawrence Erlbaum Associates.

Cintron, R. (1997). *Angels town: 'Chero ways, gang life, and rhetorics of the everyday.'* Boston: Beacon.

Commission on Multicultural Education. (1978). *Directory: Multicultural education programs in teacher education institutions in the United States.* Washington, DC: American Association of Colleges for Teacher Education.

Cook-Gumperz, J. (Ed.). (1986). *The social construction of literacy.* Cambridge, England: Cambridge University Press.

Crystal, D. (1990). *A dictionary of linguistics and phonetics.* Cambridge, MA: Basil Blackwell.

Darling-Hammond, L. (1986). A proposal for evaluation in the teaching profession. *Elementary School Journal, 86,* 531–551.

Darling-Hammond, L. (1994, September). Who will speak for the children? How "Teach for America" hurts urban schools and students. *Phi Delta Kappan,* 21–34.

Delgado-Gaitan, C. (1990). Literacy for empowerment: The role of parents in children's education. New York: Falmer.

Delgado-Gaitan, C. (1996). *Protean literacy: Extending the discourse on empowerment.* New York: Falmer Press.

Delgado-Gaitan, C., & Trueba, H. (1991). *Crossing cultural borders: Education for immigrant families in America.* New York: Falmer Press.

Diaz, S., Moll, L., & Mehan, H. (1986). Sociocultural resources in instruction: A context-specific approach. In *Beyond language: Social and cultural factors in schooling language minority students.* Los Angeles: Evaluation, Dissemination and Assessment Center, California State University.

Edwards, W. (1992). Sociolinguistic behavior in a Detroit inner-city black neighborhood. *Language in Society, 21,* 93–116.

Erickson, F. (1984). School literacy, reasoning and civility: An anthropologist's perspective. *Review of Educational Research, 54,* 525–46. Washington, DC: American Educational Research Association.

Farr, M. (1986). Language, culture, and writing: Sociolinguistic foundations of research on writing. In E. Rothkopf (Ed.), *Review of Research in Education, 13,* 195–223. Washington, DC: American Educational Research Association.

Farr, M. (1993). Essayist literacy and other verbal performances. *Written Communication, 10*(1), 4–38.

Farr, M. (1994a). Biliteracy in the home: Practices among Mexicano families in Chicago. In D. Spener (Ed.), *Adult biliteracy in the United States.* McHenry, IL and Washington, D.C.: Delta Systems and Center for Applied Linguistics.

Farr, M. (1994b). En los dos idiomas: Literacy practices among Chicago Mexicanos. In B. J. Moss (Ed.), *Literacy across communities.* Cresskill, NJ: Hampton Press.

Farr, M. (1994c). Echando relajo: Verbal art and gender among Mexicanas in Chicago. *Proceedings of the 1994 Berkeley Conference on Women and Language.* Berkeley, CA: Department of Linguistics, University of California, Berkeley.

Farr, M. (2000). Literacy and religion: Reading, writing, and gender among Mexican women in Chicago. In P. Griffin, J. K. Peyton, W. Wolfram, & R. Fasold (Eds.), *Language in action: New studies of language in society.* Cresskill, NJ: Hampton Press.

Farr Whiteman, M. (1981). Dialect influence in writing. In M. Farr Whiteman (Ed.). *Variations in writing: Functional and linguistic-cultural differences.* Hillsdale, NJ: Lawrence Erlbaum Associates.

Farr, M., & Daniels, H. (1986). *Language diversity and writing instruction.* Urbana, IL: NCTE.

Fasold, R. (1972). *Tense marking in Black English.* Washington, DC: Center for Applied Linguistics.

Fasold, R., & Shuy, R. (1970). Preface. In *Teaching standard English in the inner city.* Washington, DC: Center for Applied Linguistics.

Feigenbaum, I. (1970). *English now.* New York: New Century.

Ferdman, B., Weber, R., & Ramirez, A. (Eds.). (1994). *Literacy across languages and cultures.* Albany: State University of New York Press.

Ferguson, C., & Heath, S. B. (Eds.). (1981). *Language in the USA.* Cambridge, England: Cambridge University Press.

Finnegan, R. (1988). *Literacy and orality: Studies in the technology of communications.* Oxford and New York: Oxford University Press.

Fishman, A. (1988). *Amish literacy: What and how it means.* Portsmouth, NH: Heinemann.

Foley, W. (1997). *Anthropological linguistics.* Oxford, England: Blackwell.

Garcia, E. (1991). Effective instruction for language minority students: The teacher. *Journal of Education, 173*(2), 130–141.

Garcia, E. E. (1993). Language, culture, and education. In L. Darling-Hammond (Ed.), *Review of research in education* (Vol. 19, pp. 51–98). Washington, DC: American Educational Research Association.

Gee, J. (1996). *Social linguistics and literacies: Ideology in discourses.* Bristol, PA: Falmer Press.

Geertz, C. (1973). *The interpretation of cultures.* New York: Basic Books.

Giles, H., & Powesland, P. F. (1975). *Speech style and social evaluation.* London: Academic Press.

Gilmore, P., & Glatthorn, A. (Eds.). (1982). *Children in and out of school: Ethnography and education.* Washington, DC: Center for Applied Linguistics.

Goodlad, J. (1984). *A place called school.* New York: McGraw-Hill.

Goody, J., & Watt, I. (1963). The consequences of literacy. *Comparative Studies in History and Society, 5,* 304–345.

Goody, J. (1977). *The domestication of the savage mind.* Cambridge, England: Cambridge University Press.

Goody, J. (1986). *The logic of writing and the organization of society.* Cambridge, England: Cambridge University Press.

Goody, J. (1987). *The interface between the written and the oral.* Cambridge, England: Cambridge University Press.

Grant, C. A., & Secada, W. G. (1990). Preparing teachers for diversity: In W. R. Houston (Ed.), *Handbook of research on teacher education* (pp. 403–422). New York: Macmillan.

Graves, D. (1983). *Writing: Children and teachers at work*. Exeter, NH: Heinemann.

Green, J., & Wallat, C. (Eds.). (1981). *Ethnography and language in educational settings*. Norwood, NJ: Ablex.

Gumperz, J. J. (1982). *Discourse strategies*. Cambridge, England: Cambridge University Press.

Heath, S. B. (1983). *Ways with words: Language, life and work in communities and classrooms*. Cambridge, England: Cambridge University Press.

Heath, S. B. (1986). Critical factors in literacy development. In S. de Castell, A. Luke, & K. Egan (Eds.), *Literacy, society, & schooling: A reader*. Cambridge, England: Cambridge University Press.

Heath, S. B., & Branscombe, A. (1985). "Intelligent writing" in an audience community: Teachers, students, and researcher. In S. Freedman (Ed.), *The acquisition of written language: Response and revision*. Norwood, NJ: Ablex.

Hillocks, G., Jr. (1995). *Teaching writing as reflective practice*. New York: Teachers College Press, Columbia University.

Hornberger, N. (1990). Creating successful learning contexts for bilingual literacy. *Teachers Colleges Record, 92*, 212–229.

Hull, G. (Ed.). (1997). *Changing work, changing workers: Critical perspectives on language, literacy, and skills*. Albany: State University of New York Press.

Hymes, D. (1972). Models of the interaction of language and social life. In J. Gumperz & D. Hymes (Eds.), *Directions in sociolinguistics: The ethnography of communication*. New York: Holt, Rinehart, & Winston.

Hymes, D. (1974). *Foundations in sociolinguistics*. Philadelphia: University of Pennsylvania Press.

Keesing, R. (1974). Theories of culture. *The Annual Review of Anthropology, 73–97*.

Kochman, T. (Ed.). (1972). *Rappin' and stylin' out: Communication in urban black America*. Urbana, IL: University of Illinois Press.

Kochman, T. (1981). *Black and white styles in conflict*. Chicago: University of Chicago Press.

Kreeft, J. P., & Shuy, R. W. (1985). *Dialogue writing: Analysis of student-teacher interactive writing in the learning of English as a second language*. (Final Rep. to the National Institute of Education, NIE-G-83-0030). Washington, DC: Center for Applied Linguistics.

Labov, W. (1972a). *Language in the inner city: Studies in the Black English Vernacular*. Philadelphia: University of Pennsylvania Press.

Labov, W. (1972b). *Sociolinguistic patterns*. Philadelphia: University of Pennsylvania Press.

Labov, W. (Ed.). (1980). *Locating language in time and space*. New York: Academic Press.

Ladson-Billings, G. (1995). Multicultural teacher education: Research, practice, and policy. In J. A. Banks & C. A. Banks (Eds.), *Handbook of research on multicultural education* (pp. 747–759). NY: Macmillan.

Langer, J. (1988). The state of research on literacy. *Educational Researcher, 17*(3), 42–46.

Langer, J., & Applebee, A. (1986). Reading and writing instruction: Toward a theory of teaching and learning. In E. Rothkopf (Ed.), *Review of research in education* (p. 13). Washington, DC: American Educational Research Association.

Leap, W. (1993). *American Indian English*. Salt Lake City: University of Utah Press.

Lee, C. (1993). *Signifying as a scaffold for literary interpretation: The pedagogical implications of an African American discourse genre*. Urbana, IL: National Council of Teachers of English.

Levine, K. (1986). *The social context of literacy*. London: Routledge & Kegan Paul.

Lucas, C., & Borders, D. G. (1994). *Language diversity and classroom discourse*. Norwood, NJ: Ablex.

Lunsford, A. A., Moglen, H, & Slevin, J. (Eds.). (1990). *The right to literacy*. New York: The Modern Language Association of America.

Mahiri, J. (1994). African American males and learning: What discourse in sports offers schooling. *Anthropology and Education, 25*, 364–375.

Mitchell, C., & Weiler, K. (1991). *Rewriting literacy: Culture and the discourse of the other*. Westport, CT: Bergin & Garvey.

Moll (1988). Some key issues in teaching Latino students. *Language Arts, 65*, 465–472.

Moll, L., & Diaz, R. (1987). Teaching writing as communication: The use of ethnographic findings in classroom practice. In D. Bloome (Ed.), *Literacy, language and schooling*. Norwood, NJ: Ablex.

Moss, B. (ed.). (1994). *Literacy across communities*. Cresskill, NJ: Hampton Press.

National Center for Educational Statistics. (1991). Washington, DC: Author.

National Center for Educational Statistics. (1998). Washington, DC: Author.

Odell, L. (Ed.). (1993). *Theory and practice in the teaching of writing: Re-thinking the discipline*. Carbondale: Southern Illinois University Press.

Ogbu, J. (1987). Opportunity structure, cultural boundaries, and literacy. In J. Langer (Ed.), *Language, literacy, & culture*. Norwood, NJ: Ablex.

Ong, W. J. (1982). *Orality and literacy: The technologizing of the word*. New York: Methuen.

Perl, S., & Wilson, N. (1986). *Through teachers' eyes: Portraits of writing teachers at work*. Portsmouth, NH: Heinemann.

Piestrup, A. (1973). *Black dialect interference and accommodation of reading instructions in first grade*. (Monograph No. 4). Berkeley, CA: Language-Behavior Research Laboratory.

Poplack, S., & Tagliamonte, S. (1994). -S or nothing: Marking the plural in the African-American diaspora. American Speech, 69, 227–59.

Quality Education for Minority Project. (1990). *Education that works: An action plan for the education of minorities*. Cambridge: Massachusetts Institute of Technology.

Reed, C. (1981). Teaching teachers about teaching writing to students from varied linguistic social and cultural groups. In M. Farr Whiteman (Ed.), *Variation of writing: Functional and linguistic-cultural differences*. Hillsdale, NJ: Lawrence Erlbaum Associates.

Rickford, J. R., & Rickford, A. E. (1995). Dialect readers revisited. *Linguistics and Education, 7*, 107–128.

Saravia-Shore, M., & Arvizu, S. (1992). *Cross-cultural literacy: Ethnographies of communication in multi-ethnic classrooms*. New York: Garland.

Saville-Troike, M. (1982). *The ethnography of communication: An introduction*. Oxford, England: Basil Blackwell.

Scollon, R., & Scollon, S. B. K. (1981). *Narrative, literacy, & face in interethnic communication*. Norwood, NJ: Ablex.

Scollon, R., & Scollon, S. W. (1995). *Intercultural communication*. Oxford, England: Blackwell.

Scribner, S., & Cole, M. (1981a). Unpacking literacy. In M. Farr Whiteman (Ed.), *Writing: The nature, development, and teaching of written communication*. Hillsdale, NJ: Lawrence Erlbaum Associates.

Scribner, S., & Cole, M. (1981b). *The psychology of literacy*. Cambridge, MA: Harvard University Press.

Severino, C., Guerra, J. C., & Butler, J. E. (Eds.). (1997). *Writing in multicultural settings*. New York: The Modern Language Association of America.

Shuy, R. (1980). Vernacular Black English: Setting the issues in time. In M. Farr Whiteman (Ed.), *Reactions to Ann Arbor: Vernacular*

*Black English and education*. Washington, DC: Center for Applied Linguistics.

Sledd, J. (1988). Product in process: From ambiguities of Standard English to issues that divide us. *College English, 50*(2), 168–76.

Smitherman, G. (1994). "The blacker the berry, the sweeter the juice": African-American student writers and the National Assessment of Educational Progress. In A. H. Dyson & C. Genishi (Eds.), *The need for story: Cultural diversity in classroom and community* (pp. 80–101). Urbana, IL: National Council of Teachers of English.

Spradley, J. (1980). *Participant observation*. New York: Holt, Rinehart, & Wilson.

Staton, J., Shuy, R., Kreeft Payton, J., & Reed, L. (1988). *Dialogue journal communication: Classroom, linguistic, social, and cognitive views*. Norwood, NJ: Ablex.

Street, B. (1984). *Literacy in theory and practice*. Cambridge, England: Cambridge University Press.

Street, B. (Ed.). (1993). *Cross cultural approaches to literacy*. Cambridge, England: Cambridge University Press.

Tannen, D. (Ed.). (1982). *Spoken and written language: Exploring orality and literacy*. Norwood, NJ: Ablex.

Tannen, D. (Ed.). (1984). *Coherence in spoken and written discourse*. Norwood, NJ: Ablex.

Taylor, D., & Dorsey-Gaines, C. (1988). *Growing up literate: Learning from inner-city families*. Portsmouth, NH: Heinemann.

Teale, W. (1986). Home background and young children's literacy development. In W. Teale & E. Sulzby (Eds.), *Emerging literacy: Writing and reading*. Norwood, NJ: Ablex.

Valdés, G. (1996). *Con respeto: Bridging the distances between culturally diverse families and schools*. New York: Teachers College Press.

Valadez, C. (1981). Identity, power and writing skills: The case of the Hispanic bilingual student. In M. Farr Whiteman (Ed.), *Variations in writing: Functional and linguistic-cultural differences*. Hillsdale, NJ: Lawrence Erlbaum Associates.

Watson, K. (1975). Transferable communicative routines: Strategies and group identity in two speech events. *Language in Society, 4*, 53–72.

Watson-Gegeo, K., & Boggs, S. (1977). From verbal play to talk-story: The role of routines in speech events among Hawaiian children. In S. Ervin-Tripp & C. Mitchell-Kernan (Eds.), *Child discourse*. New York: Academic Press.

Wolfram, W. (1969). *A sociolinguistic description of Detroit Negro speech*. Washington, DC: Center for Applied Linguistics.

Wolfram, W. (1974). *Sociolinguistic aspects of assimilation: Puerto Rican English in New York City*. Washington, DC: Center for Applied Linguistics.

Wolfram, W., & Christian, D. (1976). *Appalachian speech*. Washington, DC: Center for Applied Linguistics.

Wolfram, W., Christian, D., Potter, L., & Leap, W. (1979). *Variability in the English of two Indian communities and its effects on reading and writing*. (Final rep. to the National Institute of Education, NIE-G-77-0006). Washington, DC: Center for Applied Linguistics.

Wolfram, W., & Hatfield, D. (1984). *The tense marking in second language learning: Patterns of spoken and written English in a Vietnamese community*. Washington, DC: Center for Applied Linguistics.

Zemelman, S., & Daniels, H. (1988). *A community of writers: Teaching writing in the junior and senior high school*. Portsmouth, NH: Heinemann.

Zentella, A. C. (1981). "Hablamos los Dos. We speak both": Growing up bilingual in El Barrio. Unpublished doctoral dissertation, University of Pennsylvania.

Zentella, A. C. (1997). *Growing up bilingual: Puerto Rican children in New York*. Oxford, England: Blackwell.

# VARIATION IN LANGUAGE AND THE USE

# OF LANGUAGE ACROSS CONTEXTS:

# IMPLICATIONS FOR LITERACY LEARNING

Cynthia H. Brock
*The University of Nevada Reno*

Fenice B. Boyd
*University at Buffalo, Suny*

Juel A. Moore
*San Diego Unified School District*

This chapter explores how variation in spoken and written language, as well as variation in the use of language across contexts, impacts children's literacy learning. In the first part of this chapter we explore conceptions of language, literacy, and learning. This background frames our later discussion of empirical work. Next, we articulate the data sources and procedures we drew on for this chapter. Finally, we introduce and discuss pertinent empirical studies that were conducted in the past decade since the previous handbook chapter was written on a related topic (Farr, 1991).

## SETTING THE CONTEXT: ARTICULATING OUR BELIEFS ABOUT LITERACY, LEARNING, AND LANGUAGE VARIATION

We begin our exploration of language variation and literacy learning by articulating our beliefs about language, literacy, and learning that served as a framework for selecting and interpreting the studies in this chapter. According to Gee

(1996) we, as literacy educators, have a moral obligation to make explicit theories about language, literacy, and learning because theories drive our actions, and our actions have the potential to be harmful to those we serve—namely children. By making our theories explicit, we articulate our biases and beliefs and leave them open for question, debate, and discussion.

Our goals in this section are twofold. One goal is to explicate our beliefs about key concepts discussed in the chapter. A second goal is to situate our beliefs and definitions historically in the field. The three broad areas we explore include literacy learning and language variation, variation in language use within and across communicative contexts, and a working definition of literacy.

### Literacy Learning, Language, and Language Variation

Human learning in general, and literacy learning, in particular, is facilitated through effectively mediated social interactions (Cole, 1996; Wertsch, 1998). Vygotsky (1978) argued that higher psychological processes, such as those involved in literacy learning, occur first in interactions with others. Then, over time, they are appropriated within an individual. That is, learning does not happen merely "in the head" of the learner. Rather, interactions with others shape the very nature of the unique knowledge and ideas about the world that learners are able to construct. These interactions occur through language. Whereby, language plays a central role in shaping the literacy learning opportunities that are constructed in social interactions.

Halliday suggests that "learning is **learning to mean**, and to expand one's meaning potential" (1993, p. 113, emphasis in original). Learners "learn to mean" about any given phenomenon through language. Since language plays a central role in learning, we explore some of the many complexities of language. However, because we are interested in factors that impact the language that children speak and write as well as the ways that children's language backgrounds impact their literacy learning, we draw on the work of scholars (e.g., Gee, 1996; Halliday, 1993; Wardhaugh, 1998) who stress the importance of studying how language is used in society.

Effective language use requires competence between and among language users. Communicative competence refers to the ability to "read" different contexts, and to use speech and gestures to convey and construct meanings with others (Gumperz, 1982). Competent users of language are aware of how and when to use language in different situations to act successfully on and in the world. However, questions arise about competence in light of the ambiguous or nonuniform manner in which language actually functions within and across contexts (Crawford, 1993; Fillmore, 1997). That is, language varies in many complex ways in different contexts.

Over twenty years ago, Hymes (1974) articulated some of the many complexities of language use and variation. He argued that speakers of English do not speak in some idealized or pure form of English, but vary their use of English according to the following: (a) manner of speaking, (b) choice of speech genres, and (c) roles assumed and enacted between speakers and listeners in conversational encounters. Additionally, conversations occur in communities that are situated culturally, socially, politically, and historically (Hymes, 1974). The conversational norms established in communities, and the variations of those norms, impact what is said, heard, and, perhaps most importantly, interpreted, in conversational encounters.

Like Hymes (1974) more than a quarter of a century before them, other scholars maintain that language variation refers to the nonuniform nature of language (Wardhaugh, 1998; Wolfram, Adger, & Christian, 1999). Language varies with respect to "sociocultural characteristics of groups of people such as their cultural background, geographical location, social class, gender, or age" (Wolfram et al., 1999, p. 1). Moreover, language variation may refer to the different ways in which language is used in different contexts and situations. For example, language is used differently when speaking at a research conference than when speaking in an informal conversation at dinner with family members.

## Exploring Variation in Language Use Within and Across Communicative Contexts

We look historically at work done in the field in order to explore conceptions of variation in language use within and across contexts. Language is complex, and dynamic, socially and culturally situated and tool used to mediate thinking. Because of the dynamic and situated nature of language, norms for speaking and writing can vary significantly between different communities and cultures (Heath, 1983; Scollon & Scollon, 1995). Oftentimes norms for speaking and writing are invisible to the members within cultures and incomprehensible to members of different cultures. Articulating these norms and making them explicit can facilitate communication between people within and across different communities and cultures. Important scholarly work (e.g., Heath, 1983) conducted in the last few decades has shed light on the different uses of language in home, community, and school contexts. Other important work conducted in the last few decades (e.g., Au, 1980; Cazden, 1988) has helped to make classroom conversational norms explicit and has explored ways to help students gain access to classroom conversational norms.

Scholars have highlighted crucial differences between home and school language and literacy practices, as well as mismatches between teachers' and children's language practices. For example, Heath (1983) studied differences in language and literacy practices in the two different communities of Roadville and Trackton. Her work illustrated the impact that different home language and literacy practices can have on children's school-based literacy learning opportunities. Studying patterns of interactions among Native Americans in Warm Springs, Philips (1983) examined the misunderstandings and lack of student learning that can occur in classrooms when teachers are not aware of different cultural groups' ways of interacting and communicating.

Au (1980) explored reading lessons conducted by European American teachers with Hawaiian children. She discovered that Hawaiian children typically interacted in a "talk-story" manner whereby conversants created a story by randomly contributing to a conversation using overlapping speech. When working with teachers who had significantly different expectations for interactions, such as individually taking turns when called upon by the teachers, Hawaiian children experienced less success in reading lessons.

Exploring different ways in which children construct stories during sharing time, Michaels (1981), noted that African American children tended to tell stories in a topic-associating style that literally chained related topics together until a story was completed. European American children, on the other hand, tended to create stories using a topic-centered style that was developed throughout the story. Although different, both approaches are linguistically sound (Gee, 1996); however, only the topic-centered approach was sanctioned by the teacher in the classroom.

Scholars such as Cazden (1988) and John-Steiner (1985) argue that studies such as these just discussed help to shed light on relationships between home and school discourse, the subtleties of classroom social organization, and the role that classroom discourse can play in fostering, or not fostering, learning opportunities for children. That is, understanding variation in ways that language is used can lead to powerful means for educating effectively all children. This is especially true for children who use language in ways that vary from mainstream language use because variation in language use does not simply express the social structure. Rather, "context plays a role in determining what we say, and what we say plays a role in determining the context" (Halliday, 1978, p. 3). Educators who understand the reciprocal relationship between language and social context can thoughtfully and carefully craft their use of language in the classroom to shape the ways in which learning communities are constructed, thereby constructing communities that serve all children in the classroom.

## Defining Literacy

While we believe that literacy involves complex relationships between spoken and written language, conventions of print, fluency, knowledge of letters, sounds, and words, comprehension, and so forth, (Clay, 1991; Hiebert & Raphael, 1996; Kaestle, 1985; Pinnell & Fountas, 1998), in presenting our working definition of literacy, we foreground the work of scholars who stress the complex, dynamic, and socially and culturally situated nature of literacy. Ferdman (1990) argues that conceptions of literacy that take into account social and cultural contexts significantly influence the ways in which literacy is defined and interpreted. For example, when membership in cultural groups is taken into account, students' literacy behaviors would be interpreted in light of group patterns rather than solely as attributes of an individual. While it can be "easy to think of literacy simply in terms of specific skills and activities," doing so makes literacy appear to be a characteristic inherent in an individual (Ferdman, 1990, p. 186). This approach can blind us to the fact that literacy "involves facility in manipulating the symbols that codify and represent the values, beliefs, and norms of the culture—the same symbols that incorporate the culture's representations of reality" (Ferdman, 1990, p. 187).

Like Ferdman, Freire (1990) believes that literacy consists of much more than decoding the written word; "rather, it is preceded by and intertwined with knowledge of the world" (p. 21), and is always embedded within some context. For Freire, reading the world and the word are recursive processes. Freire does see the need for explicit instruction in order to help students understand literacy. However, his idea of instruction is not reductionist. He argues:

Mechanically memorizing the description of an object does not constitute knowing the object. That is why reading a text as pure description of an object (like a syntactical rule), and undertaking to memorize the description, is neither real reading nor does it result in knowledge of the object to which the text refers (Freire, 1987, p. 24).

Freire believes that helping students understand literacy involves helping them to think about the underlying significance of the word and its relationship to the world. Moreover, reading, for Freire, involves attending to specific contexts and being open for critique and analysis, for "reading always involves critical perception, interpretation, and rewriting of what is read" (p. 26).

Gee (1996) examined the discourse, acquisition, and learning aspects of language use in order to arrive at a definition of literacy beyond the component skills involved in reading and writing. Gee defines literacy as the control of language use in various contexts and situations in order to function in given roles. Children from mainstream middle-class backgrounds, according to Gee, acquire literacy through experiences in the home—both before and during their schooling careers—that relates to the nature of literacy required in schools. Children from nonmainstream homes, on the other hand, often acquire different forms of literacy that are not typically sanctioned in school contexts, such as a topic-associating style of telling stories rather than a topic-centered style of telling stories (Michaels, 1981). Situations such as this present "playing fields" that are not level for all children within the educational arena.

Using three metaphors to explore definitions of literacy, Scribner (1984) suggested that literacy could be conceptualized as adaptation, power, or a state of grace. Literacy as adaptation stresses the pragmatic or survival value of literacy for the individual. The literacy as power metaphor emphasizes relationships between the literate development of the individual and the communities in which the individual operates. Historically, for example, literacy has been used as an exclusionary tool such as when slaves in the United States were prohibited from learning to read and write in order to maintain the status quo of political, economic, and social control. Literacy as power might be viewed as a tool for expansion where the poor and politically powerless acquire access to equal opportunities to claim status in society. Literacy as a state of grace suggests a religious connotation; however, Scribner depicts this metaphor of literacy as one that typically endows the literate person with special qualities such as intellectual prowess and spirituality. While Scribner argues that all three metaphors are problematic with respect to the boundaries they evoke, careful critique and analysis of each metaphor could raise important questions about facts, values, purposes, and objectives relating to literacy teaching and learning.

We draw on the work of these scholars to frame our conception of literacy and its relationship to language use. Literacy learning is situated culturally, socially, and historically. It is a complex endeavor that extends beyond childhood and classroom experiences, into adulthood and multiple life experiences. While understanding specific literacy skills is undeniably necessary for the journey to becoming a literate and functional being, as acknowledged by Ferdman (1990), Freire (1987), Gee (1996), and Scribner (1984), knowledge of specific literacy skills is not enough. Thus, we believe that literacy and language use encompasses multiple purposes, requires knowledge of skills and strategies to be strategic readers in order to make interpretations, and requires the ability and disposition to be able to critique and analyze our own cultural and linguistic contexts as well as the cultural and linguistic context of others. Such aspects of literacy and language use are necessary for all people in a multicultural, pluralistic society.

## DATA SOURCES FOR THIS CHAPTER

Our work focuses on studies that were published in the past decade because we choose to review relatively recent work pertaining to language variation. We conducted large-scale database searches using the key words "language variation and literacy" and "dialect and literacy." Additionally, since our focus is language variation and its varied use in communicative contexts as related to children's literacy learning, we targeted select journals that publish work pertaining to literacy research including: *Anthropology and Education Quarterly, American Educational Research Journal, College English, Discourse Processes, Elementary School Journal, Journal of Literacy Research, Linguistics and Education, Reading Research Quarterly, and Written Communication.*

Our search yielded very few studies pertaining specifically to language variation as it relates directly to literacy learning; however, we did find studies pertaining to language variation in language use across communicative contexts. Because linguists attribute variation in people's language and ways of communicating to socioeconomic status, social/cultural background, gender, geographical location, and ethnicity (Wardhaugh, 1998; Wolfram & Schilling-Estes, 1998; Wolfram, Adger, & Christian, 1999), we collected and analyzed studies that related to those categories. Even though most studies within these categories related indirectly to specific features of language variation, we sought to explore possible links between the categories important to linguists and research that has been conducted in the field of literacy. This approach is consistent with the views of scholars who argue for exploring broad social, cultural, and historical dimensions of language and learning rather than focusing primarily on features of language (Foster, 1995). Finally, we narrowed our focus to empirical studies involving the language use and literacy learning of students in kindergarten through 12th grades.

Our search of the literature revealed literacy-related studies pertaining to socioeconomic status, gender, ethnicity, and cultural background. We did not find any studies that focused solely on geographical location with respect to language and literacy learning. We did, however, find interesting work that deals with the complexity of geographical location in conjunction with other dimensions of language variation. For example, in a case study involving Donny and his mother, Purcell-Gates (1995) discussed the impact of her informants' rural Appalachian background on their present lives and experiences in an urban context. In a compelling observation about how different cultural groups of people can live in the same urban neighborhood yet engage in no interactions, Hornberger (1992) suggests that, in some cases, the importance of social networks may transcend the importance of geographical location. People can, she argues, live in the same communities but be a part of such different social networks that barriers to potential interactions may be as great as actual physical location and distance.

## RESULTS

Our literature search also shed light on the many complex interconnections between socioeconomic status, gender, ethnicity, and cultural background. For the purposes of this chapter, we grouped the studies we reviewed into the following categories: socioeconomic status, gender, and ethnicity and cultural background.

### Socioeconomic Dimensions of Language Use: Implications for Literacy Learning

The literacy and language-related studies from the 1990s that we explore in this section focus primarily on children of low socioeconomic status (SES) and their knowledge of and interactions around forms of written English. Empirical studies conducted in the past decade challenge several widely held misconceptions about children from low SES backgrounds. The first misconception is that children from low SES backgrounds come to school unprepared with the appropriate language and literacy backgrounds to begin to engage in school literacy. A second misconception about the literacy and language-related preparation of children from low SES backgrounds follows from the first and states that because children from low SES backgrounds are not prepared for school, they need to focus on isolated language and literacy skills before they can engage in critical and creative aspects of literacy learning. This deficit-driven, reductionist approach assumes that the child must be ready for the school rather than the school ready for the child (Connell, 1994).

***First misconception: Children from low SES backgrounds come to school unprepared to effectively engage in school literacy.*** Purcell-Gates (1996) explored the ways in which 20 families from low socioeconomic backgrounds used print with young children in their home, and how print use impacted the written language knowledge that children brought with them to school. She found that children who had more interactions with their parents around print developed a clearer "big picture" of the functions and uses of print. Additionally, the more complex the interactions that children had with their parents (e.g., extended storybook reading as opposed to interactions that focused primarily on individual words, for example) the more sophisticated were the children's understandings of print. Purcell-Gates' work emphasizes that children from low SES backgrounds come to school with very different literate backgrounds and experiences. Moreover, it is not the socioeconomic backgrounds of families that determines whether or not children will be successful in school, but rather the quality and quantity of interactions around print prior to entering school that better prepare some children for school success.

A related study by Purcell-Gates, McIntyre, and Freppon (1995) explored whether children from low SES backgrounds who enter school with little written narrative knowledge can actually acquire that knowledge in school. Purcell-Gates and her colleagues studied 36 randomly selected children from low SES backgrounds (two thirds of the children were African American and one third of the children were European American urban Appalachian) in three different schools. Some of the children were enrolled in skills-based classrooms while others were en-rolled in classrooms that practiced whole-language philoso-phy. Purcell-Gates et al. found that "children who begin school knowing relatively little about the vocabulary and syntax of written stories can acquire this knowledge through experiences with books in school" (p. 677). Moreover, children acquired this knowledge more effectively in classrooms that emphasized more holistic uses and functions of language where students had more opportunities to listen and respond to stories in a variety of different ways.

The studies reported by Purcell-Gates and her colleagues re-late to the work of scholars such as Moll (1997) who explored the rich *funds of knowledge* that make up the lives and experi-ences of children and their families from diverse cultural and lin-guistic backgrounds. Moll asserts that "common lore in the field of education would have these households (i.e., the households of children and their families from diverse cultural, linguistic, and economic backgrounds) . . . devoid of practices and knowl-edge of relevance for the children's schooling" (1997, p. 192). Moll and his colleagues found that when educators seek first hand to understand about the lives of children and their fam-ilies who come from diverse cultures and backgrounds, they come to understand the rich linguistic and cultural resources that these bring to classrooms. This line of scholarship illustrates that when educators and researchers strive to "gain access to the conceptual worlds" (Geertz, 1973, p. 24) in which others live—including the worlds of children from low SES backgrounds as well as diverse cultural and linguistic backgrounds—they can come to understand, value, and build on difference rather than view difference as deficient and in need of remediation.

***Second misconception: Instruction for children from low SES backgrounds should focus first and primarily on skills-based instruction.*** Freppon (1995) explored the impact of different types of instruction on second-grade children from low SES backgrounds. All of the children in her study had been in holistic classroom contexts for kindergarten and first grade where the functional nature of language and print was foregrounded. In second grade some of the children were placed in a skills-based classroom and some of the children were placed in a holistic classroom context. While children in both contexts showed improvement overall in their literacy learning, similar to the results in the Purcell-Gates et al. (1995) study, the children in a more holistic context fared better in terms of viewing themselves as readers and writers. Moreover, the children in the holistic setting tended to be less passive learners than the children in the skills-based classroom. Freppon's work confirms and extends earlier findings by Purcell-Gates and Dahl (1991). If children do not enter school understanding the functions and uses of print in a broad conceptual sense

(referred to by Purcell-Gates & Dahl, as "the bigger picture" of literacy) they are less able to understand how the different pieces of literacy that tend to be emphasized in skills-based instruction actually fit together (p. 26).

The authors of the studies reported in this section employed methodological rigor and careful interpretation of data based on specific contexts in their work to avoid simplistic dichotomous overgeneralizations about holistic versus skills-oriented con-texts that are sometimes touted by those with particular political agendas (see Routman, 1996, and Taylor, 1998 for discussions of this issue). While acknowledging the rich literacy learning opportunities that can be present in holistic classrooms, a study by McIntyre (1995) problematizes potential misconceptions of holistic classroom contexts as panaceas for literacy learning.

McIntyre (1995) examined closely the writing skills of a group of low SES children in one primary holistic classroom context. While she documented that the writing skills of the focus children in her study improved across the year, the chil-dren did not consistently apply the school writing skills they were exposed to across all writing contexts in the classroom. McIntyre contended that while children should be immersed in meaningful literacy learning contexts, they also need quality explicit instruction, and guidance to develop the skills of good writers. This finding is consistent with the work of scholars such as Delpit (1995) and De la Luz Reyes (1992) who study the literacy learning of children from diverse cultural and linguistic backgrounds. When children from diverse economic, cultural, and/or linguistic backgrounds enter schools with backgrounds different from those that schools are prepared to serve, chil-dren need explicit guidance, albeit in meaningful contexts, to understand the ways that oral and written language function in school-based literacy practices.

Exploring the learning of children from low SES backgrounds in a much broader research context, Battistich, Solomon, Kim, Watson, and Schaps (1995) designed a survey study of over 4,500 students in 24 different schools to examine the "impact of the sense of the school as a community on elementary school students" in general (p. 632). Their primary interest and focus, however, was students from disadvantaged backgrounds in these school communities. Battistich et al. found that, overall, school is not as positive and rewarding an experience for chil-dren from low SES backgrounds as compared with students from middle and upper SES backgrounds. Not surprisingly, Battistich and colleagues discovered that the schools most successful with children of poverty are those schools that can create caring communities for students. Moreover, the instructional practices typically afforded students from disadvantaged backgrounds—including a greater focus on teaching rote skills and providing students with less autonomy with respect to instructional de-cisions and choices during instruction—often mitigate against the success of children of poverty. Consistent with the find-ings from McIntyre (1995), learning environments that provide for autonomy and active student involvement, with appropriate teacher guidance and direction, are more effective for students from low SES backgrounds labeled "at risk" for school failure.

***Relationships between SES, literacy, and variation within language and communicative contexts.*** The studies in this section investigated the varieties of ways that children from low SES backgrounds are prepared at home for school-based literacy as well as variation in the ways that classroom communicative contexts impact children's literacy learning. Exploring variation in the ways that parents interacted with their preschool children around print, Purcell-Gates (1996) noted that those parents who engaged in multiple and extended interactions around print with their children helped them to understand relationships between oral and written language as well as functions of print. Several researchers explored the role that different classroom contexts have on children's learning. While some children do not enter school with well-developed understandings of relationships between oral and written language and the functions of print, they can learn these aspects of literacy if they are in classrooms where teachers provide positive, explicit, caring, and meaning-centered instruction (Battistich et al., 1995; McIntyre, 1995; Purcell-Gates et al., 1995).

Connell (1994) directs the educational and policy making communities on a useful path with respect to instructional practices and research programs that may actually make a difference in the lives and learning opportunities of children from low SES backgrounds. Rather than looking through a window to view children of poverty as deficient and in need of remediation, Connell suggests that policymakers, educators, and scholars look in a mirror to remediate deficient instructional practices and programs that do not meet the needs of children entering U.S. public schools. Connell's suggestions include both large-scale programs, such as Title I, as well as small-scale "teacher-proof" programs that seek quick fixes by displacing and devaluing the central role that knowledgeable, professional educators must play in striving to meet the unique language and literacy learning needs of individual children in their classrooms (Duffy & Hoffman, 1999).

## Gender: Implications for Language Use and Literacy Learning

Our search for studies conducted in the past decade related to literacy, variation within language and communicative contexts, and gender revealed two broad categories of work. One set of gender-related studies focuses on commonalities in written and spoken discourse within gender roles and differences between gender roles. Another group of gender-related studies explores the complexities of differences within gender roles.

***Commonalities within gender roles and differences between gender roles.*** Several groups of researchers designed studies to compare the nature of oral and/or written discourse in interactions between groups of boys and groups of girls. Goodwin (1990) explored ways that boys and girls used storytelling to construct their social identities during disputes. Boys used storytelling to reinforce their use of insults during disputes. Girls, on the other hand, typically strove to avoid direct conflict and often told stories behind others' backs rather than confront them directly. Even though Goodwin noted differences between gender roles, she cautions against overinterpreting

gender differences across all contexts. She argues that behaviors "must be interpreted as situated presentations of self, sensitive to the contexts in which they occur" (Goodwin, 1990, p. 55).

Like Goodwin, Tannen (1990) examined the discourse of boys and girls and studied conversational coherence between groups of boys and groups of girls in grades 2, 6, and 10. While acknowledging that there were some interactional variations between all-male or all-female groups of conversants in establishing and displaying conversational competence, Tannen found surprising uniformity in the ways that girls and boys interacted within same-gender groups. In general, across all grade levels, girls found more topics to discuss and elaborated on those topics in much greater detail than the boys. Tannen maintains that boys and girls have different ways of signaling intentions and meaning in conversations. She argues that "ways of constituting the context of communication" are not universal, but socially and culturally contingent and vary in gendered interactions (p. 88).

Focusing solely on girls, Eckert (1990) and Phinney (1994) studied girls of different ages to investigate their uses for oral and written language in interactive social settings. Phinney's yearlong study focused on the written discourse of a group of kindergarten girls and illustrated how they used writing to maintain cohesion in their peer social interactions. Working with high school girls and focusing on their oral discourse, Eckert (1990) found that her study participants engaged in a painstaking process of negotiation and consensus building in their conversations. Eckert posits that the preponderance of work on the nature of females' roles as consensus builders reflects differences between gender roles in society. Women, Eckert argues, have long been relegated to less dominant positions in society and have had to negotiate to "create freedom to function in the world" (p. 122).

***Exploring differences within gender roles.*** Several researchers explored the many unique differences within gender roles. Moore (1997), for example, studied closely the discussions of a high school boy and a high school girl in a variety of classroom contexts. Moore's work showed that the two case study students both enacted and contested traditional female/male role expectations. Individuals display multilayered identities and educators must be aware of the fine distinctions within and across gendered classroom interactions. Moore argues that "presenting singular unified characterizations of a group misses exceptions within the group" (p. 524).

Other social markers (e.g., SES) work in conjunction with gender to impact the varieties of ways in which boys and girls use language to act and interact (Evans, 1996). Studying the manner in which a small group of fifth-grade boys and girls negotiated understandings during peer-led discussions of the text *The Perilous Road* (Steele, 1958), Evans noted that a complex array of factors such as group members' different social statuses as well as their gender impacted the manner in which they assumed and enacted roles in their ongoing conversations over a period of several weeks. For example, one group member, Vivianne, assumed a leadership position in the group during the first few meetings until the boys in the group challenged her and said that she was being bossy. She countered that she was not bossy, and subsequently remained silent during most of the rest of the discussions of the text. Evans argued that Vivianne's low status in the group influenced her decision to acquiesce to the boys' assertion to prove that she was not bossy.

Socioeconomic status also coalesces with gender to influence the varieties of ways in which girls interact (Lowrey, 1989). Examining interactions within groups of European American high school girls, Lowrey revealed the many complexities of interactions within gender roles by studying the construction of topic development by two different groups of European American high school girls. One group of girls represented a lower SES class and another group represented middle class. His findings revealed that the middle-class group of girls tended to hold the conversational floor longer than those from a lower SES class. Additionally, the middle-class girls tended to interact in a manner whereby they contrasted their ideas from one another. The working-class girls, on the other hand, tended to build on one another's ideas and yield turns to one another more frequently. However, while Lowrey noted that different sorts of speaker–listener relations were created in each conversational style, both groups of girls were interested in maintaining positive social relationships.

Rather than exploring the nuanced characteristics of individuals as they assume gendered roles (Evans, 1996; Lowrey, 1989; Moore, 1997), several researchers explored the complex process of constructing gendered identities (Finders, 1996; Henry, 1998). Identity refers to the "multiple and shifting roles" that individuals assume and enact as well as their perceptions of who they are as literate individuals (Finders, 1996, p. 109). In a yearlong study, Finders documented the evolving literacy lives at home and school of two different groups of junior high girls. Her work explored the many complexities of the girls' literate identities within and across the two groups. For example, group membership impacted the ways that the girls in the study complied with and resisted school expectations. Both groups of girls in the study were considered to be good girls by their teachers and parents. Nonetheless, girls in each group "negotiated how far out of bounds they might go and remain in good standing at school and home" (p. 109). For example, one group of girls developed an elaborate system of note writing that they engaged in during school. Sometimes their engagement occurred at appropriate times (e.g., between classes) and in appropriate ways (e.g., on paper). Other times, however, engagement occurred at inappropriate times (e.g., during class) or in inappropriate ways (e.g., on restroom walls).

While Finders' work illustrates that peers can significantly impact the development of adolescents' identities, adults can also provide this influence. Finders argues for the need to determine ways to work effectively with children to guide them through the process of developing their literate identities. Drawing on the work of Pratt (1991), she advocates for the notion of a contact zone where class participants can use literacy to sort out and sort through issues of real concern in their lives. That is, adults can help adolescents to use literacy as a tool in meaningful ways to address the real life issues and concerns with which adolescents grapple.

Henry (1998) conducted a long-term ethnography with a group of African Caribbean teenage girls who participated in a reading, writing, and discussion group with the author. Like Finders, Henry engaged in the complicated process of exploring the construction of the girls' literate identities. Henry explicated the struggles of working with this marginalized group of girls to seek ways to help the girls construct their individual voices and points of view through talk and writing. The process of grappling with tough, but real, issues in the lives of the girls was a transforming experience for Henry as well as for the girls in the group. Henry argues that in order to effectively engage in such a process, researchers and educators must be willing to question their own aims, objectives, and ideologies and allow them to be shaped and reshaped in the ongoing process of our literacy work with children.

***Relationships between gender, literacy, and variation within language and within and across communicative contexts.*** The literacy and language-related studies from the past 10 years that focus on gender and variations within language and communicative contexts revealed that much has been learned about how boys and girls use language to act and interact in the world. The studies in the first section offer considerable evidence that girls tend to use language to build consensus and negotiate meanings. Boys, on the other hand, tend to use language in more competitive and individualistic ways. However, caution is warranted so that we do not overgeneralize gender roles. While there may be some commonalities within gender roles, individual boys and girls use language in unique ways to construct their individual identities. Moreover, gendered literate identities are not monolithic entities. Rather, individuals' identities are constantly in the process of evolving.

Exploring the complex nature of the varieties of ways that boys and girls use language in a variety of school-related contexts is important work. The oral and written language that boys and girls use and the ways in which they use it with others impacts the literacy learning that occurs in classrooms (Barnes, 1992; Evans, 1996). Evans (1996) argues that we need to learn more about how various social markers like gender, race, and social status influence the nature of classroom discourse and subsequently the literacy learning that occurs in classrooms.

## Ethnicity and Cultural Background: Implications for Language Use and Literacy Learning

Scholars (e.g., Cole, 1996; Wertsch, 1998) argue that conceptions of ethnicity and culture are socially constructed, intricately intertwined, and historically contingent. Consequently, we explore studies pertaining to ways that these dimensions transact and impact different ways that people use language within and across contexts. Taken together, the studies in this section explore relationships between language use, ethnicity, and cultural background. We discerned three broad categories of work including (a) the complexities of language use across contexts and cultures, (b) variation in engaging with written language, and (c) the role of teachers' understanding of cultural and linguistic variation across contexts.

***Complexities of language use across contexts and cultures.*** People of different cultural groups use language as a tool in a variety of different and complex ways to accomplish a variety of intentions, meanings, and tasks (Cole, 1996; Scribner, 1984; Vygotsky, 1978). In some cases, language is used by groups of people to serve different conversational purposes (Camilleri, 1996). In other cases, language is used to transform cultural practices in ways that align them more closely with the educational expectations of a dominant culture (Crago, Annahatak, & Ningiuruvik, 1993; Levin, 1992).

Studying language practices in secondary classrooms in Malta, Camilleri (1996) learned that teachers and students employed code switching between Maltese and English as a communicative resource. Use of English in the classroom created academic distance between speakers and was oftentimes perceived as being "snobbish." Speaking Maltese, however, was seen as being friendly and warm. Thus, conversants carefully chose to use the code that best served their conversational purposes.

Language can also serve as a tool for transforming cultural practices, and this process often involves tension. Levin (1992) engaged in a 2-year ethnographic investigation to study interactions between low-income native Hawaiian preschool children and their parents to explore how sending a child to preschool affects teaching and learning in the families. She learned that "typical" household interactions involve children learning through observation and asking questions. Hawaiian parents have learned, however, that direct instruction from adults is a typical means of interacting at school. Consequently, parents often use "direct instruction" when teaching their children school-related literacy tasks, such as the alphabet, at home. This approach is different from the ways in which parents interact with their children and teach them about tasks not related to school. Consequently, children and their parents often experience frustration when they engage in literacy-related activities at home.

Crago, Annahatak, and Ningiuruvik (1993) explored the impact of cultural change in the form of schooling, on the communicative interactions between Inuit children and their families. A variety of differences were found in communicative interactions between an older and younger generation of mothers. The older generation of mothers believed that children should not participate in adult conversation. In contrast, knowing that children were expected to interact in particular ways in school, second generation Inuit mothers allowed their children to not only participate in adult conversation, but to question adults and other children. These changes in linguistic practices sometimes created discord in families. The work of Crago et al. demonstrates that school-related language practices may impact home language practices. Moreover, in the context under investigation, economic, sociocultural, and political aspects of the majority culture have prevailed over those of the Inuit. That is, the actions of the younger Inuit mothers involved in this study revealed that they felt the need to assimilate to the interactional patterns of the dominant culture (Ferdman, 1990).

***Cultural and linguistic variation when engaging with oral and written text.*** Moving from a broader look at some of the complexities of cultural and linguistic variation within and between groups of people, we explore ways that ethnic and cultural backgrounds influence students' engagement with oral and written texts. The studies reviewed here illustrate the need for educators to take seriously relationships between children's backgrounds and the nature of the texts they are asked to read in school. The kinds of texts that students are asked to read and write, and the match between texts used and the children's cultural and linguistic backgrounds, play an important role in determining whether or not children become competent readers and writers.

Ball (1992; 1995) engaged in two studies that focused on African American students' use of, and preference for, particular text design features including mainstream expository-based text structures or vernacular-based text structures. Ball's (1992) study involved 102 students from Grades 5 through high school who represented a wide range of ethnicities. She sought to discern which oral and written text structures children of different ethnicities preferred. Results revealed that while elementary-level African American children did not show a clear preference for either type of text structure, African American high school students preferred using vernacular-based organizational patterns, including narrative interspersion and circumlocution, for both written academic work as well as conversations. Ball argues that children's discourse preferences are influenced by social and cultural experiences and should be taken into account when educators are working with children from diverse backgrounds.

In her 1995 work, Ball engaged in a yearlong study to analyze the written discourse of four successful African American high school students. Ball found that the children in her study were effective code switchers; they could communicate well when speaking or writing African American Vernacular English (AAVE) and Standard English depending on the nature of the writing task in which they were engaged. Ball asserts that all too often, however, children's unique linguistic abilities are unrecognized and underappreciated by teachers. She calls for educators to acknowledge "the value in diverse voices" and to cultivate "a desire to actually hear those voices" (p. 283).

Rickford and Rickford (1995) reopened the empirical issue of studying reading materials written alternatively in African American Vernacular English (AAVE) and Standard English (SE). Working with small groups of elementary school teachers and students in San Francisco, the researchers tested the students' responses to dialect readers. Considering the lessons learned about dialect readers from prior research conducted in the 1960s and 1970s, as well as the current study, Rickford and Rickford conclude that while more research needs to be done relative to this issue, using dialect readers merits consideration. Using culturally and linguistically familiar texts may enhance opportunities for African American children who speak AAVE to learn to read and write.

The above premise has been echoed in the work of other scholars, noting that connections to culture also plays an important role in students' literacy learning. Pritchard (1990) worked with 11th-grade proficient American and Palauan readers to explore the strategies that proficient readers use to read culturally familiar and unfamiliar texts. Additionally, he explored relationships between the strategies students use, the cultural backgrounds of the readers, and cultural perspectives of the reading materials. Two passages describing a "typical" funeral were written in the appropriate language for each group of the students. One passage described a "typical" funeral for Palauan culture and the other passage described a "typical" funeral for American culture. Students read the passages and thought aloud during their reading about what they were thinking and doing as they read.

Results of Pritchard's work indicated that readers employed the same strategies when reading both culturally familiar and unfamiliar texts; however, there were differences in the frequencies with which individual strategies were used. Readers from both cultures tended to use the strategies of establishing ties between sentences and drawing on background knowledge more when they were reading culturally familiar text. Readers from both cultures tended to use the strategies of developing awareness, accepting ambiguity, and establishing understanding about particular sentences more when reading culturally unfamiliar texts. Results of this study illustrate that readers engage in the reading process in different ways depending on the cultural familiarity of the materials they are reading and their own cultural backgrounds.

The Rickfords' work relates in interesting ways to the work of Pritchard (1990) and Ball (1992; 1995). Pritchard found that high school students comprehend texts better when the texts relate to their own cultural and linguistic backgrounds. The African American high school students in Ball's studies indicated a clear preference for vernacular-based text structures. Given that cultural and linguistic backgrounds do make a difference in terms of comprehension (Pritchard, 1990) and given that some children prefer text structures related to their own linguistic backgrounds (Ball, 1992; 1995) the use of dialect readers merits consideration. An important difference between the work of Pritchard and Ball, and the Rickfords' work, however, is that the work of Pritchard and Ball is based on findings pertaining to high-achieving high school children. Also, Ball (1992) did not find a preferential text structure difference for elementary-level African American children in her work. These findings suggest that further research with dialect speakers and readers is warranted.

***The impact of teachers' understanding of cultural and linguistic variation.*** We found several studies that examined the role that African American Vernacular English (AAVE) plays in school success (Adams & Singh, 1998; Washington & Miller-Jones, 1989). Washington and Miller-Jones (1989) were interested in how teachers' knowledge of African American Vernacular English (AAVE) impacted children's learning opportunities in school. In an effort to study teachers' responses to students who demonstrated higher and lower uses of AAVE during reading instruction, the researchers examined the classroom interactions of two second-grade teachers who had different knowledge and understanding about AAVE. The researchers found that the teacher who knew more about AAVE exhibited more positive behaviors in response to children's use of AAVE during reading instruction. The researchers suggest that it is essential for teachers to recognize dialectical influences on speech and reading and monitor the ways in which they respond to these dialectical differences.

This study relates to research conducted by Moll (1997) discussed earlier in this chapter. Moll argued that all children bring important linguistic and cultural *funds of knowledge* to classroom contexts that can be drawn on by educators to help children enter into school-based literacy practices. When educators understand the different linguistic and cultural backgrounds that children bring to school contexts, they are more likely to see difference as a strength that would inform instructional decisions rather than as a weakness in need of correcting (Moore, 1997). Thus, these studies suggest that further consideration needs to be given to mainstream teachers' beliefs, knowledge, and attitude in working with children who come from nonmainstream linguistic and cultural backgrounds to develop workable ways to assist these students.

In a 6-month ethnographic study designed to explore the process of transitioning from Spanish to English instruction for two groups of Puerto Rican children, Shannon (1990) followed 6 case study students transitioning from Grade 3 to Grade 4 at one site, and seven children transitioning from fifth grade to a local middle school at another site. Findings suggest that, in general, all of the case study students needed more support as they transitioned from Spanish to English instruction; however, the teachers' attitudes in the English transition classes played a central role in the success of the children's transition. Language transitioning students were more successful when they were placed in English language classrooms with caring teachers who valued the children and provided the necessary scaffolding and support to help the children become academically successful in their classrooms. The researchers concluded that monolingual English speaking teachers must monitor carefully the nature of the emotional and academic support that they provide to children transitioning into English in order for these students to be successful in their classrooms.

Not only are teachers' attitudes about linguistic and cultural variation important, but students' perceptions of their teachers' attitudes impacts their school success. Adams and Singh (1998) analyzed data from African American students who participated in the National Educational Longitudinal Study of 1988. Their goal was to discover the factors that contributed to the academic success of African American students. Results showed that while factors such as students' prior level of achievement, their SES, and their gender were related to student achievement, one of the most significant factors to influence student achievement was students' perceptions of their teachers' attitudes. When instructors are perceived in a positive light by their students, the learners are most likely to be successful.

***Relationships between ethnicity and cultural background, literacy, and variation within language and across communicative contexts.*** The ways in which individuals in particular ethnic and cultural groups use language varies considerably in a host of complex ways. For example, the study of language use and variation and its impact on school literacy learning is not confined solely to the use of language in classrooms. The language practices of communities in which schools are situated play a role in the language used in schools. School-based language practices can influence the ways in which children and parents interact around school-related work (Crago et al., 1993; Levin, 1992), and can result in frustrating interactions within families when adopting school-related language practices.

An issue worth pondering in the educational community is whether language can be used and taught in schools in ways that honor differences in language practices between home and school (Ferdman, 1990). This perspective is considerably different from the perspective that leads culturally and linguistically marginalized groups of people to feel as if they have to adopt school-based language practices in their homes in order for their children to be successful in school. An important caveat to this issue, however, is that understanding children's cultural and linguistic backgrounds is a complex undertaking. Cultural backgrounds and linguistic systems are not monolithic entities that all users of a language system or members of a culture use in similar ways (McAlpine, Eriks-Brophy, & Crago, 1996). When striving to understand cultural and linguistic differences, it is also important to consider cultural and linguistic identity at the level of the individual to avoid inappropriate stereotyping when working with children (Ferdman, 1990).

Children from different cultural and linguistic backgrounds engage with oral and written texts in different ways. For example, Pritchard's (1990) work explored the ways that students in two different cultures engaged with culturally familiar and unfamiliar texts noting that readers use reading strategies in different ways depending on the cultural familiarity of the texts they are reading. Ball (1992; 1995) looked at African American students' preferences for engaging with different oral and written text structures and found that African American students at the high school level indicated a clear preference for vernacular-based text structures. Finally, Rickford and Rickford (1995) studied how using particular types of texts (i.e., dialect readers) with African American children impacts their engagement with text. Taken together, these studies indicate that literacy educators should attend to the educational needs of children from different cultural and linguistic backgrounds. The nature of text structures used in classrooms can impact children's transactions with texts and their subsequent understanding of what they read and write. Moreover, the ways in which educators interact with children around the materials they use in class impacts children's literacy learning. When teachers understand the cultural and linguistic backgrounds of the children they serve, they are more likely to provide effective learning communities for them (Adams & Singh, 1998; Washington & Miller-Jones, 1989).

## DISCUSSION

This chapter explored how variation in spoken and written language, as well as variation in the use of language across contexts, impacts children's literacy learning. We structured our review of the literature for this project using the categories of socioeconomic status, gender, and ethnicity and cultural background. We caste a wide net across a variety of different data sources, including databases and peer-reviewed journals, to explore studies within these categories that pertained to literacy and variation in language use. Our work has led us to identify a central theme that merits consideration in education and research. Educators and researchers need to simultaneously employ two lenses when exploring issues pertaining to literacy and language variation. One lens should be focused on the individual and her unique and situated use of language. The other lens should be focused on the group(s) of which the individual is a part and group norms for language use and interactions. Each lens offers different affordances and constraints, and each lens offers a perspective on the individual that the other does not.

### Focusing on Group Norms: Implications for Language Use and Literacy Learning

Taking group membership into account is important because many differences among people are rooted in their group membership (Ferdman, 1990; Noll, 1998). With respect to gender, for example, there are many differences in the ways in which boys and girls interact. Boys use storytelling to confront others during disputes; whereas, girls use storytelling to avoid direct confrontation with others (Goodwin, 1990). Across a variety of different grade levels from elementary to high school, girls tend to discuss and elaborate on topics in more detail than boys (Tannen, 1990). Moreover, differences in the ways in which boys and girls interact begin well before they enter school (Sheldon, 1990). If membership in groups is not taken into account, then characteristics such as motivation and intelligence may be attributed solely to the individual with little or no attention given to such factors as ethnicity, gender, and culture, "and therefore with little or no thought to the differential meaning, expression, or incidence of these factors across groups" (Ferdman, 1990, p. 185).

The work of Moll (1997) illustrates the importance of studying the unique cultural and linguistic backgrounds that children bring to school contexts. When educators understand, value, and draw on the cultural, linguistic, and experiential differences of children and their families, everyone—including children, families, and schools—benefits. On the other hand, when educators and researchers fail to study and understand the richness of the different linguistic, cultural, and experiential backgrounds of the students served in U.S. schools, they can engage in practices that are harmful to children.

Perhaps nowhere is this latter point more prevalent than in the research done with African Americans. When educators do not understand and appreciate the value and complexity of African American Vernacular English (AAVE), students suffer. Unfortunately, the general public, and many educators, have had a history of misunderstanding AAVE and the cognitive abilities of children who speak AAVE. Linguists (e.g., Labov, 1972) have long informed us that AAVE is a viable and rule-governed symbol system. But, unstudied perceptions and beliefs rooted in ignorance and prejudice seem difficult to dispel in education and at the societal level. Writing over a quarter century ago, Torrey posits:

My thesis is that the main impact of Afro-American dialect on education has not been its structural differences from standard English, nor its relative intrinsic usefulness as a medium of thought, but its function as a low-status stigma and its association with a rejected culture. The attitudes of teachers toward this dialect and of dialect speakers towards the teachers' language have affected the social relationships of children with the schools in such a way as to make education of many children almost impossible. Black children of rural southern background have entered the urban schools to find that nearly everything they said was branded as "wrong." In order to be "right" they had to adopt forms that seemed alien even when they were able to learn how to use them. Their own spontaneous products were punished and treated as worthless, including the only language they knew really well. Because of this, they were almost forced to regard themselves and their society as bad, ugly, or even sinful (1970, p. 257).

The work reported in this chapter and elsewhere (see, for example, Perry & Delpit, 1998) illustrates that a lack of understanding of, and appreciation for, the cultural and linguistic backgrounds of many African American children still persists more than a quarter of a century later. Students are still taught by teachers who provide inappropriate instruction based on misperceptions that language difference represents cognitive and linguistic deficit in need of remediation (Washington & Miller-Jones, 1989). As another example, students are still incorrectly placed in speech and language programs designed to "remediate" their language based on evaluators' lack of understanding of AAVE (Cole & Taylor, 1990).

While there are many important reasons to consider group membership when working with children, there are many cautions that must be considered relative to interpreting children's words and actions due to the groups of which they are a part. First, students are not merely members of one group. Group membership occurs in a host of complex and interconnected ways. For example, individuals can simultaneously be members of many different types of groups including: socioeconomic groups, cultural groups, ethnic groups, language groups, and gendered groups. Interpretations in work with children must be carefully rendered based on the understanding that children are simultaneously members of many different groups.

Second, the nature of norms and interactions within groups can vary across time and according to different circumstances. In an effort to more closely match their perceptions of adult–child interactions at school, for example, some Hawaiian parents, have changed typical cultural patterns of interacting with their children as they assist their children to do literacy homework at home (Levin, 1992). This change has introduced discord to adult–child family interactions in addition to shifting traditional cultural interactions in the families. Clearly, if membership within various groups is viewed in a static and monolithic manner, educators run the risk of stereotyping children and not recognizing the diversity of individuals within groups.

## Focusing on the Individual: Implications for Language Use and Literacy Learning

Whereas membership in groups shapes and impacts the language and actions of individuals, people in groups vary considerably both "in the extent of their identification with the group and in the degree to which their behavior is based on the groups' norms" (Ferdman, 1990, p. 191). Viewing people solely as members of particular groups with similar attributes risks stereotyping. If children are incorrectly stereotyped because of their membership in particular groups, they may be treated inappropriately in classrooms and schools. For example, although schools overwhelmingly fail to serve children from low SES backgrounds, it is not because all, or even most, children from low SES backgrounds, come to schools unprepared, or underprepared, to engage in school-based literacy (Connell, 1994). The work of Purcell-Gates (1996) illustrates that educators must look carefully at individual children and their specific learning strengths and needs because children from low SES backgrounds come to school with a wide variety of different literacy and language-related backgrounds and experiences.

Several studies relating to gender illustrate the nuanced, complex, and nonuniform nature of individual identity development (Finders, 1996; Henry, 1998). Literate identities are "dynamic in that they are built and rebuilt as people interact within and across social and institutional contexts" (Egan-Robertson, 1998, p. 454). The process of working with children to help them to develop rich literate identities requires a great deal of effort, a willingness to take risks, and is best facilitated with the thoughtful guidance and assistance of an adult who understands language and literacy (Finders, 1996; Henry, 1998). Educators should take care that classroom interactions between teachers and their students from a variety of different backgrounds do not foster the "discourses of deficit" that negatively impact the development of children's literate identities that, in turn, negatively impact their literacy learning opportunities (Egan-Robertson, 1998, p. 455).

## CONCLUDING COMMENT

Different lenses, such as focusing on the individual or focusing on the groups of which the individual is a member, can yield different information about children; however, the knowledge gleaned from attending to both lenses undoubtedly creates a more informed approach for working with children in schools. The more complex our understandings of children, the more knowledge we have available to make informed decisions about our work with them. Acquiring more informed conceptions of children is, according to Gee (1996), an ethical and moral obligation for those who serve them—including educators and policymakers. Also worth noting, however, is that our beliefs or understandings about others are based on our ideological stances toward their languages, cultures, and backgrounds. A question worth continuously pondering, both individually and collectively, is whether our interpretations—and the ideological stances behind them—are based on scholarly research and evidence as well as a desire to honor and serve effectively all children in American public schools.

## ACKNOWLEDGMENTS

We are deeply indebted to the following reviewers for their outstanding feedback on earlier drafts of this work: Carolyn Temple Adger, Diane Barone, Betsy Rhymes, Mary Rozendal, and Rose-Marie Weber. We are responsible for the contents of the final text.

# References

Adams, C. R., & Singh, K. (1998). Direct and indirect effects of school learning variables on the academic achievement of African American 10th graders. *Journal of Negro Education, 67*(1), 48-66.

Au, K. (1980). Participation structures in a reading lesson with Hawaiian children: Analysis of a culturally appropriate instructional event. *Anthropology and Education Quarterly, 11*(2), 91-115.

Ball, A. (1992). Cultural preference and the expository writing of African-American adolescents. *Written Communication, 9*(4), 501-532.

Ball, A. (1995). Text design patterns in the writing of urban African American students: Teaching to the cultural strengths of students in multicultural settings. *Urban Education, 30*(3), 253-289.

Barnes, D. (1992). *From communication to curriculum*. Harmondsworth, UK: Penguin.

Battistich, V., Solomon, D., Kim, D., Watson, M., & Schaps, E. (1995). Schools as communities, poverty levels of student populations, and students' attitudes, motives, and performance: A multilevel analysis. *American Educational Research Journal, 32*(3), 627-658.

Camilleri, A. (1996). Language values and identities: Code switching in secondary classrooms in Malta. *Linguistics and Education, 8*, 85-103.

Cazden, C. (1988). *Classroom discourse: The language of teaching and learning*. Portsmouth, NH: Heinemann.

Clay, M. (1991). *Becoming literate: The construction of inner control*. Portsmouth, NH: Heinemann.

Cole, M. (1996). *Cultural Psychology; A once and future discipline*. Cambridge, MA: Harvard University Press.

Cole, P. A., & Taylor, O. L. (1990). Performance of working class African-American children on three tests of articulation. *American Speech-Language-Hearing Association, 21*, 171-176.

Connell, R. W. (1994). Poverty and education. *Harvard Educational Review, 64*(2), 125-129.

Crago, M., Annahatak, B., & Ningiuruvik, L. (1993). Changing patterns of language socialization in Inuit homes. *Anthropology & Education Quarterly, 24*, 205-223.

Crawford, L. W. (1993). *Language and literacy learning in multicultural classrooms*. Boston: Allyn and Bacon.

De la Luz Reyes, M. (1992). Challenging venerable assumptions: Literacy instruction for linguistically different students. *Harvard Educational Review, 62*, 427-447.

Delpit, L. (1995). *Other people's children; Cultural conflict in the classroom*. New York: The New Press.

Duffy, G., & Hoffman, J. (1999). In pursuit of an illusion: The flawed search for a perfect method. *The Reading Teacher, 53*(1), 10-16.

Eckert, P. (1990). Cooperative competition in adolescent "girl" talk. *Discourse Processes, 13*, 91-122.

Egan-Robertson, A. (1998). Learning about culture, language, and power: Understanding relationships among personhood, literacy practices, and intertextuality. *Journal of Literacy Research, 30*(4), 449-488.

Evans, K. (1996). Creating spaces for equity? The role of positioning in peer-led literature discussions. *Language Arts, 73*, 194-202.

Farr, M. (1991). Dialects, culture, and teaching the English language arts. In J. Flood, J. M. Jensen, D. Lapp, & J. R. Squire (Eds.), *Handbook of Research on Teaching the English Language Arts* (pp. 365-371). New York: Macmillan.

Ferdman, B. (1990). Literacy and cultural identity. *Harvard Educational Review, 60*(2), 181-204.

Fillmore, L. (1986). Language and Education, Pittsburgh: A paper presented at the Third Eastern States Conference on Linguistics. (ERIC Document Reproduction Services No. ED 308 705).

Finders, M. J. (1996). "Just girls": Literacy and allegiance in junior high school. *Written Communication, 13*(1), 93-129.

Flood, J., Jensen, J. M., Lapp, D., Squire, J. R. (Eds.) (1991). *Handbook of research on teaching the English language arts*. New York: Macmillan.

Foster, M. (1995). Talking that talk: The language of curriculum and critique. *Linguistics and Education, 7*, 129-150.

Freire, P. (1987). The importance of the act of reading. In B. M. Power & R. Hubbard (Eds.), *Literacy in Process* (pp. 21-26). Portsmouth, NH: Heinemann.

Freppon, P. (1995). Low income children's literacy interpretations in a skills-based and a whole-language classroom. *Journal of Reading Behavior, 27*(4), 505-533.

Galda, L. (1998). Mirrors and windows: Reading as transformation. In T. Raphael & K. Au (Eds.), *Literature-based instruction: Reshaping the curriculum* (pp. 1-12). Norwood, MA: Christophere-Gordon.

Gee, J. P. (1996). *Social linguistics and literacies: Ideology in discourses*. Bristol, PA: Taylor & Francis.

Geertz, C. (1973). *The interpretation of cultures: Selected essays*. New York: Basic Books.

Goodwin, M. H. (1990). Tactical uses of stories: Participation frameworks within girls' and boys' disputes. *Discourse Processes, 13*, 33-71.

Gumperz, J. J. (1982). *Discourse strategies*. Cambridge, England: Cambridge University Press.

Halliday, M. A. K. (1978). *Language as social semiotic: The social interpretation of language and meaning*. London: Arnold.

Halliday, M. A. K. (1993). Towards a language-based theory of learning. *Linguistics and Education, 5*, 93-116.

Heath, S. B. (1983). *Ways with words: Language, life, and work in communities and classrooms*. Cambridge, England: Cambridge University Press.

Henry, A. (1998). "Speaking up" and "speaking out": Examining "Voice" in a reading/writing program with adolescent African Caribbean girls. *Journal of Literacy Research, 30*(2), 233-252.

Hiebert, E., & Raphael, T. (1996). Perspectives from educational psychology on literacy and literacy learning and their extensions to school practices. In R. Calfee & D. Berliner (Eds.), *Handbook of educational psychology* (pp. 550-602). New York: Macmillan.

Hornberger, N. (1992). Presenting a holistic and an emic view: The literacy in two languages project. *Anthropology and Education Quarterly, 23*(2), 160-165.

Hymes, D. (1974). *Foundations in sociolinguistics*. Philadelphia: University of Pennsylvania Press.

John-Steiner, V. (1985). The road to competence in an alien land: A Vygotskian perspective on bilingualism. In J. V. Wertsch (Ed.), *Culture, communication, and cognition: Vygotskian perspectives* (pp. 348-372). New York: Cambridge University Press.

Kaestle, C. F. (1985). The history of literacy and the history of readers. *Review of Research in Education, 12*, 11-53.

Labov, W. (1972). *Language in the inner city: Studies in Black English vernacular*. Philadelphia: University of Pennsylvania Press.

Levin, P. (1992). The impact of preschool on teaching and learning in Hawaiian families. *Anthropology & Education Quarterly, 23*, 59-72.

Lowrey, B. (1989). School site selection and approval guide. California State Dept. of Education. Sacramento, CA.

McAlpine, L., Eriks-Brophy, A., & Crago, M. (1996). Teaching beliefs in Mohawk classrooms: Issues of language and culture. *Anthropology & Education Quarterly, 27*(3), 390–413.

McIntyre, E. (1995). Teaching and learning writing skills in a low-SES, urban primary classroom. *Journal of Reading Behavior, 27*(2), 213–242.

McLaughlin, D. (1989). The sociolinguistics of Navajo literacy. *Anthropology & Education Quarterly, 20,* 275–290.

Michaels, S. (1981). Sharing time: Children's narrative styles and differential access to literacy. *Language in Society, 10,* 423–442.

Moll, L. (1997). The creation of mediating settings. *Mind, Culture, and Activity, 4*(3), 191–200.

Moore, D. W. (1997). Some complexities of gendered talk about texts. *Journal of Literacy Research, 29*(4), 507–530.

Moore, J. A. (1998). *Black English speakers: An examination of language registers of high and low achieving Black elementary school students.* Unpublished doctoral dissertation, San Diego State University/Claremont Graduate School, San Diego, California.

Noll, E. (1998). Experiencing literacy in and out of school: Case studies of two American Indian youths. *Journal of Literacy Research, 30,* 205–232.

Perry, T., & Delpit, L. (Eds.) (1998). *The real Ebonics debate: Power, language, and the education of African American children.* Boston: Beacon Press.

Philips, S. (1983). *The invisible culture: Communication in classroom and community on the Warm Springs Indian Reservation.* New York: Longman.

Phinney, M. Y. (1994). Gender, status, writing, and the resolution of kindergarten girls' social tensions. *Linguistics and Education, 6,* 311–330.

Pinnell, G. S., & Fountas, I. C. (1998). *Word matters: Teaching phonics and spelling in the reading/writing classroom.* Portsmouth, NH: Heinemann.

Postman, N. (1970). The politics of reading. *Harvard Educational Review, 40*(2), 244–252.

Pratt, M. (1991). *Arts of the contact zone in profession.* New York: Modern Language Association.

Pritchard, R. (1990). The effects of cultural schemata on reading processing strategies. *Research Quarterly, 25,* 273–295.

Purcell-Gates, V. (1995). *Other people's worlds: The cycle of low literacy.* Cambridge, MA: Harvard University Press.

Purcell-Gates, V. (1996). Stories, coupons, and the TV Guide: Relationships between home literacy experiences and emergent literacy knowledge. *Reading Research Quarterly, 31*(4), 406–428.

Purcell-Gates, V., & Dahl, K. L. (1991). Low-SES children's successes and failure at early literacy learning in skills-based classrooms. *Journal of Reading Behavior, 23*(1), 1–34.

Purcell-Gates, V., McIntyre, E., & Freppon, P. (1995). Learning written storybook language in school: A comparison of low-SES children in skills-based and whole language classrooms. *American Educational Research Journal, 32*(3), 659–685.

Rickford, J. R., & Rickford, A. E. (1995). Dialect readers revisited. *Linguistics and Education, 7,* 107–128.

Routman, R. (1996). *Literacy at the crossroads.* Portsmouth, NH: Heinemann.

Sawyer, R. K. (1996). Role voicing, gender, and age in preschool play discourse. *Discourse Processes, 22,* 289–307.

Scollon, R., & Scollon, S. W. (1995). *Intercultural communication: A discourse approach.* Cambridge, MA: Blackwell.

Scribner, S. (1984). Literacy in three metaphors. *American Journal of Education, 93,* 6–21.

Shannon, S. (1990). Transition from bilingual programs to all-English programs: Issues about and beyond language. *Linguistics and Education, 2,* 323–343.

Sheldon, A. (1990). Pickle fights: Gendered talk in preschool disputes. *Discourse Processes, 13,* 5–31.

Steele, W. (1958). *The perilous road.* New York: Harcourt Brace.

Tannen, D. (1990). Gender difference in topical coherence: Creating involvement in best friends' talk. *Discourse Processes, 13,* 73–90.

Taylor, D. (1998). *Beginning to read and the spin doctors of science: The political campaign to change America's mind about how children learn to read.* Urbana, IL: National Council of Teachers of English.

Torrey, J. W. (1970). Illiteracy in the ghetto. *Harvard Educational Review, 40,* 253–259.

Vygotsky, L. (1978). *Mind in society: The development of higher psychological processes.* Cambridge, MA: Harvard University Press.

Wardhaugh, R. (1998). *An introduction to sociolinguistics.* Malden, MA: Blackwell Publishers.

Washington, V., & Miller-Jones, D. (1989). Teacher interaction with nonstandard English speakers during reading instruction. *Contemporary Educational Psychology, 14,* 280–312.

Wertsch, J. (1998). *Mind as action.* New York: Oxford University Press.

Wolfram, W., Adger, C., & Christian, D. (1999). *Dialectics in school and communities.* Mahwah, NJ: Lawrence Erlbaum Associates.

Wolfram, W., & Schilling-Estes, N. (1998). *American English.* Malden, MA: Blackwell.

# ·33·

# ISSUES IN TEACHER PREPARATION AND STAFF DEVELOPMENT IN ENGLISH LANGUAGE ARTS

## Miles Myers
### National Council of Teachers of English

Since *A Nation at Risk* (Gardner, 1983) and the subsequent nationwide debate about school reform (Boyer, 1983; Powell, Farrar, & Cohen, 1985; Sarason, 1983; Sizer, 1984), two sets of reforms have been advanced for teacher education, one set focusing on the content of teacher education—what courses and topics should be included—and the other set focusing on the structure—where and when should teacher education take place and who should manage it. Concerns about content and structure have a long history in teacher preparation (Mattingly, 1975), and have until recently involved a structural struggle over control—Should teacher preparation be reserved for teachers colleges?—and content struggle between those emphasizing teaching and management strategies (for instance, the psychological processes of learning) and those emphasizing subject matter knowledge (the content of literature, grammar, and rhetoric).

Some parts of these old struggles seem to have subsided as teachers' colleges have become increasingly academic in their orientation and as organizations like the Holmes Group, the National Council for the Accreditation of Teacher Education (NCATE), National Commission on Teaching and America's Future and many state agencies have called for teachers to complete an undergraduate academic major before entering a teacher preparation program (Hammond & Berry, 1988). In addition, many of these groups have argued that teacher development cannot stop after the fifth year, and, therefore, staff development programs continuing throughout the career of teachers have become permanent fixtures in state policy (Little, Gerritz, Stern, Gutherie, Kirst, & Marsh, 1987). Not everyone, of course, has endorsed these changes; many colleges still keep their budgets balanced by enrolling 4-year education majors, and market pressures for warm bodies to reduce the growing shortage of teachers have conspired to set aside many, if not most, of the implementation of high quality preparation. The endorsements

are still there; the practices have not been sustained. For example, although in 1987, Shulman called teacher knowledge the foundation of the New Reform (Shulman, 1987), by 1999, nearly 25% of the nation's English teachers had "neither a major or minor in English or related subjects such as literature, communications, speech, journalism, English education, or reading education" (Ingersoll, 1999, p. 27). Now, let us review the issues surrounding the content of teacher knowledge and the structure of teacher preparation and staff development.

## THE CONTENT OF TEACHER KNOWLEDGE

What knowledge must teachers learn in teacher preparation programs? One of the first major disputes in this century over what English teachers should know erupted around the Uniform Book List, adopted in 1907 by the College Entrance Examination Board and various Eastern accreditation agencies as the content that teachers must know and that students must master in secondary English. Arguing that the List's definition of teacher knowledge focused only on students going to college and ignored the more democratic ideas of John Dewey, high school English teachers revolted against the College Board's high school programs and organized in 1911 the National Council of Teachers of English. However, the revolt left unanswered which high school programs were the most effective—the traditional programs featuring the Uniform Book List or the progressive programs suggested by Dewey? To answer this question, the Progressive Education Association, the General Education Board, and several foundations sponsored the one-million-dollar Eight Year Study (1933–1941), which involved over 200 colleges and 29 high schools selected from a nominated pool of 200. Led by Ralph Tyler, this study examined whether students attending a "progressive" high school would achieve college grades equivalent to those of students attending "traditional" high schools. The 29 experimental schools were small, organized around common goals developed at the site, had substantial involvement of students in school decision making, and had academic courses and courses that crossed departmental boundaries and included community service. Linda Darling Hammond observed that these schools were "like the highly successful schools of today's reform initiatives" (Hammond, 1997, p. 10).

The high schools in this study, by agreement with 200 colleges, were freed from the requirement of Carnegie units in specific courses, thereby allowing the high schools to experiment with many different curriculum structures, especially inquiry-oriented teaching and interdisciplinary courses. The college grades of the graduates from the high schools with the most intense programs of progressive education were then compared with the grades of a matched set of 1,475 peers from traditional high schools, and the findings showed that the graduates from the progressive high schools did better in academic achievement in college and were consistently more active in collegiate social, artistic, and political life. Calling the results "carefully proved," Linda Darling Hammond reported that the study "painstakingly documented how students from progressive schools were more academically successful, practically resourceful, and socially responsible" (Hammond, 1997, p. 10). However, in a follow-up review in 1950, most of the 29 progressive high schools had dropped most of their reforms, returning to practices that were more traditional. Why? One reason, argued Tyack and Cuban (Tyack & Cuban, 1995), is that the grammar of schooling is very difficult to change, no matter what the results on achievement measures. Another reason is the absence of well-prepared teachers. Lawrence Cremin argued that "progressive education . . . demanded infinitely skilled teachers, and it failed because such teachers could not be recruited in sufficient numbers" (Cremin, 1965a, p. 56). Still another reason, according to Linda Darling Hammond, is that "reformers rarely engaged the political system in considering the implications of their work" (Hammond, 1997, p. 10), often believing that changing the preparation of teachers could substitute for the social and political movements needed to reform schools (Cuban, 1987). The message is simple: Alone, a strong teacher preparation program is not enough, and without a strong preparation program, nothing else will work. Despite the limited impact of its findings, the Eight Year Study did promote a closer look at K–12 classrooms, especially what teachers should know. Today, teacher preparation studies emphasize nine areas of teacher knowledge: subject matter, teaching strategies, time management, student variations, models of cognitive variation, technology, subject and literacy history, school structure and culture, and reflective practices.

## Teacher Knowledge of Subject Matter: The Structure of the Discipline

The study of subject matter in K–12 classrooms was launched in 1959 at a Woods Hole Conference sponsored by the National Academy of Sciences and chaired by Jerome Bruner. The assumption of the conference was that K–12 students could not learn solid subject matter if solid subject matter was not taught in good teaching materials. Teacher and student motivations, for instance, were not on the agenda. Bruner's Conference Report *The Process of Education* introduced a structuralist view of K–12 subject matter, using three questions to guide the organization of K–12 curriculum (What is the organizational structure of the discipline? What kinds of questions are asked in the discipline? and How is data collected and tested in the discipline?) (J. Bruner, 1960). In a somewhat different approach, Professors Lynch and Evans, both from the English Department of the University of California, Berkeley, published a widely read critique of high school literature anthologies and outlined the intellectual failures of professional schools of education (Lynch & Evans, 1963). Numerous curriculum reorganization projects were initiated: *Man: A Course of Study* (J. Bruner, 1970), a reorganization of social studies; New Math from the School Mathematics Study Group (SMSG) and the University of Illinois Committee on School Mathematics (UICSM), emphasizing discovery methods for understanding the structure of mathematics (Beberman, 1958); the Biological Sciences Curriculum Study (BSCS) (Schwab, 1965); the New Physics from the Physical Science Study Committee (Zacharias & White, 1964); and the NDEA (National Defense Education Act) Project English Institutes. Project English established 20 curriculum study centers to translate disciplinary knowledge from the liberal arts (literature, linguistics, rhetoric) into curriculum guides for K–12 English/English language arts teachers. For example, the Nebraska Center, led by Paul Olson and Frank Rice, translated Northrup Frye's archetypal patterns in literature into a K–12 curriculum (Frye, 1957); the Northern Illinois Project translated the history of the English language into materials for Grades 11–12; and the Northwestern Center at Northwestern University, led by Wallace Douglas, translated composition studies into secondary writing assignments highlighting the interaction of audience and situation with text. In addition, as a follow-up to these projects, many local curriculum efforts developed materials based on Moffett's structural analysis of composition (Moffett, 1968), Mellon's analysis of transformational grammar (Mellon, 1969), Christensen's analysis of sentence and paragraph structure (Christensen, 1967), Booth's analysis of fiction (Booth, 1961); and Brooks and Warren's *Understanding Poetry* (Brooks & Warren, 1951).

The subject matter analysis in these curriculum projects left deep imprints on the content of teacher preparation programs, but the teaching assumptions of these materials received "scathing criticism" for "both their underlying conceptions and their outcomes"—especially for ignoring such questions as Who is ready to learn what? and Who mandates what teachers teach? (Ausubel, 1967; Epstein, 1964; S. B. Sarason, 1971). These criticisms alleged that many of the university leaders of the NDEA Institutes knew little or nothing about day-to-day teaching in K–12 classrooms, and, as a result, these programs was too often unconnected to what students needed to learn next. Linda Darling Hammond reports, "The top-down curriculum reform worked in those schools that were directly involved in bottom-up work on the ideas and practices embodied in the curriculum" (Hammond, 1997, p. 216). However, when teachers were not involved in the bottom-up work necessary for a solid subject matter curriculum and a coherent evaluation, reform leaders were left on their own to explain why programs were not working. Zacharias, a leader in the New Physics, decided that the impact of the New Math was overall negative because it, like other subject matter reforms, was too concerned with pure subject matter (McNeil, 1985). Zacharis called for mathematics courses that taught students how to bake a cake, to leave a tip, and to estimate the amount of paint needed to paint a room (McNeil, 1985, p. 248). Bruner, too, changed his emphasis, calling for subject matter related to the social needs and problems of the American people (J. S. Bruner, 1971). Indeed, by the end of the 1960s, a reaction against the formalisms of academic subject matter was pervasive in English education (Squire & Applebee, 1968). As Grossman reported in another study many years later, "When the beginning teachers without teacher education . . . tried to teach what they knew about Shakespeare to high school students, they discovered the limitations of untransformed disciplinary knowledge" (Grossman & Shulman, 1994).

## Teacher Knowledge of Teaching Strategies: Indirect and Direct Psychological Process

Transformed how? Through teaching strategies? In 1954, Marsh and Wilder, after reviewing the research on teaching from 1900 to 1952, reported, "no single, specific, observable teacher act has yet been found whose frequency or percentage of occurrence has invariably and significantly correlated with student achievement" (N. Bennett, 1976, p. 13; Marsh & Wilder, 1954). They could have also said that until the 1950s many researchers of teaching did not even attempt to describe the relationships between teacher behaviors and student achievement.

During the late 1960s, to avoid the storms of subject matter knowledge and to build on recent studies of teacher behavior, The National Institute of Education (N.I.E.) shifted its budget to basic and applied research on what teachers needed to know about the psychological processes of teaching, at least as reflected in the relationship between teacher behaviors and student achievement (Schaffarzick & Sykes, 1978). In the middle of the civil rights movement, the Coleman Report gave the N.I.E. the perfect question: Did schools matter at all? Coleman suggested that "schools bring little influence to bear on a child's achievement that is independent of his background and general social context" (J. S. Coleman, Campbell, Hobson, McPartland, Mood, Weinfeld, & York, 1966, p. 335). To test Coleman's 1966 findings, which had not examined teacher knowledge and pedagogy in detail, the Office of Education and later the National Institute of Education (NIE) funded several large scale correlational studies of basic skill instruction, beginning with the Project Follow Through experiment in 1968. Project Follow Through began as a response to President Johnson's call for a program to "follow through after Head Start," but after budget reductions, Project Follow Through became a planned variation study to determine whether particular teaching approaches in the early grades might produce significant achievement in three areas—basic skills (word knowledge,

spelling, math computation), cognitive skills (comprehension, math problem solving), and affective attitudes. Test results from all three areas were collected from K–3 children who were attending schools with nine different teaching approaches: The Open Classroom, based on British Infant Schools; Cognitively Oriented High Scope Program, based on Piagetian theory; The Response Education Model from the Far West Laboratory; The Direct Instruction Model from the University of Oregon; The Bank Street Early Childhood Model; A Bilingual Model from the Southwest Laboratory; The Tucson (University of Arizona) Early Education Model, based on a language experience approach; The Behavior Analysis Model (B-Mod) from the University of Kansas; and a Parent Education Model.

To some degree, the Follow-Through Study was a return to the psychological orientation of the 1950s (Gage, 1963), focusing on how teacher behavior in the classroom correlated with student achievement on nationally published tests. However, the Follow-Through Study was also focusing on a more detailed question: do successful programs emphasize indirect or direct psychological processes. For example, researchers using the Flanders Interaction instrument, a 10-category scale for observing classrooms and training teachers, suggested that to improve pupil achievement and attitudes, teachers must have knowledge of such strategies of indirect teaching as accepting, praising, encouraging, and questioning (Flanders, 1970). Many teacher preparation and staff development programs began to teach Flanders' strategies to teachers, but some researchers insisted that the more effective strategies were direct and explicit.

The evaluation of Follow Through, which continued as a service program from 1976 to 1995, was inconclusive, with one study suggesting that models like Direct Instruction showed some effectiveness (Bock, Stebbins, & Proper, 1977) and another study concluding that there were no significant differences in achievement (House, Glass, McLean, & Walker, 1978). Incidentally, the Direct Instruction Model, published under the trade name DISTAR, was described as "small group, face-to-face instruction by teachers and aides using carefully sequenced lessons in reading, arithmetic, and language" (Becker & Carnine, 1981; Becker & Engelmann, 1995–1996). Although the evaluation of Follow Through was inconclusive, primarily because of defects in experimental design, other studies without these design flaws were also making strong claims for "direct" teaching. For example, the Bennett report (N. Bennett, 1976) from England claimed that in a survey-observational study of over 800 primary classrooms (Years 3 and 4) "indirect" or "progressive" methods did not work as well as "traditional," "explicit" methods. Brophy also reported that "recent research from the primary grades seems to flatly contradict" the achievement claims of Flanders' "indirect teaching" (Brophy, 1979, p. 737), and in an analysis of this contradiction, Barr and Dreeben (Barr & Dreeben, 1978) suggested that the contradiction resulted from the way Flanders calculated an "indirect teaching" score, which was the ratio of "indirect teaching" to "direct teaching." As a result, those with high "indirect teaching" scores had also displayed the largest amount of teaching overall, which, of course, could have included "direct" teaching (L. S. Shulman, 1986a, p. 12).

In any case, by 1974, Dunkin and Biddle in *The Study of Teaching* were including only those studies with quantifiable measures of process-product relationships, including both direct and indirect processes (Dunkin & Biddle, 1974). To sort out the pedagogical details left somewhat ill-defined in the large scale Follow Through study, NIE began to fund many quantifiable measures of process-product relationships in elementary (J. A. Stallings & Kaskowitz, 1974) (Brophy & Evertson, 1974) (Good & Grouws, 1979) and secondary classrooms (Evertson, Anderson, & Brophy, 1978) (Good & Grouws, 1981). In these process-product studies, the researchers developed classifications of teaching processes, measured the frequency of these processes (teacher directions, teacher praise, peer group editing, explicit drills, and so forth), and then correlated these processes with results on tests of basic skills.

In general, direct instruction became the favored model, Rosenshine (B. Rosenshine, 1979) concluding that the findings of most studies confirmed the effectiveness of "direct instruction." Rosenshine's description of direct instruction differed only a little from the Direct Instruction Model in the Follow Through program (Becker & Carnine, 1981) and paralleled very closely other models of effective teaching—for instance, Gagne's "key components of instruction (Gagne, 1970) and Good and Grouws's "key instructional behaviors" (Good & Grouws, 1979):

large groups, decision making by the teacher, limited choice of materials and activities by the students, orderliness, factual questions, limited exploration of ideas, drill, and high percentages of correct answers (B. V. Rosenshine, 1979, p. 47).

## Teacher Knowledge of Time Management

Although teacher preparation programs began giving considerable emphasis to teaching strategies, especially direct instruction, many researchers began raising the question of whether correlating teaching strategies and test scores told the whole story. Most important of all, the Beginning Teacher Evaluation Study (B.T.E.S.) focused on the teacher's management of time in the classroom. John B. Carroll in a highly influential article argued that because schools allocated limited time for learning and because student aptitude is an index of learning rate, many students who needed more time to learn were being denied an education by being denied the time to learn (Carroll, 1963). From 1972 to 1977, led by David Berliner, Charles Fisher, and Leonard Cahen and funded largely by the California Credential Commission, the Beginning Teacher Evaluation Study (BTES) tested some of Carroll's claims about time in a three, large studies in second and fifth grade classrooms (Fisher, Berliner, Filby, Marliave, Cahen, Dishaw, & Moore, 1978). Unlike the other process-product studies in the previous section, the Beginning Teacher Evaluation Study did not correlate all of the separate processes with achievement, reporting on only a few processes that seemed to improve achievement. Using an analysis of time of student engagement, BTES found that many kinds of instruction worked if students had more Academic Learning Time (ALT), a formula combining the amount of time teachers assigned to such

tasks (*allocated time*) and the amount of time students actually focused on the task (*engaged time*) (Rosenshine & Berliner, 1978). *Engaged time* was dependent on *success rate*, which required continuing teacher diagnosis of the learning rate of individual students. B.T.E.S. found that only about 58% of the day in second and fifth grade classrooms was allocated to academics. These B.T.E.S. findings were almost immediately translated into a Time-on-Task Teaching Model that was widely disseminated to teacher preparation programs by the California Commission on Teacher Credentialing (CTC) and the California State Department of Education (CDE) (CDE, 1980). In addition, the CTC and the CDE gave grants to teacher preparation programs to develop new variations of the Time-on-Task Teaching Model, all designed to train new and experienced teachers to measure and to increase *engaged time*.

Another generic teaching model widely used in teacher preparation programs to increase *allocated* time was the Madeline Hunter "Lesson Model" (Hunter & Russell, 1981) developed at the elementary lab school at UCLA. This model was a four-or-five-step lesson format including anticipatory set, objectives, modeling, and guided practice. Yet another teaching model designed to increase time allocated to academics was The Stallings Teaching Model, organized around the "The Stallings Observation Strategy," developed by the Stallings' Teaching and Learning Institute of La Honda, California (J. Stallings, 1980; J. Stallings, Corey, Fairweather, & Needels, 1978). This teaching model provided a list of activities and a recommended percentage of time for each activity. An accompanying teacher evaluation instrument told teachers when to increase/decrease the time allocated to particular activities.

Another generic teaching model suggesting a time sequence was Rosenshine's and Robert Stevens' model of the "major components of systematic teaching" (Rosenshine & Stevens, 1986, p. 377):

Begin a lesson with a short statement of goals.
Present new material in small steps with student practice after each step.
Give clear and detailed instructions and explanations.
Provide a high level of active practice for all students.
Ask a large number of questions, check for student understanding, and obtain responses from all students.
Guide students during initial practice.
Provide systematic feedback and corrections.
Provide explicit instruction and practice for seatwork exercises and, where necessary, monitor students during seatwork.

By focusing on how time was allocated, researchers were able to report what steps or what subject matter was present or missing from instruction. For example, Applebee reported that "the typical writing assignment in American schools is a page or less, first and final draft, completed within a day (either in class or taken home to finish up), and serving an examining function" (A. N. Applebee, 1986) Applebee also reported that writing assignments typically focus on informational writing, and personal and imaginative writing "have little place in most classrooms" in secondary schools. In addition, Applebee found that overall, 78 percent of time in English classes was allocated to literature-related activities (A. N. Applebee, 1989b). Teacher preparation programs for elementary teachers especially have struggled with how to allocate time for literature, composition, language, and, in recent years, media, and some researchers have provided excellent guidance for allocating time in an integrated English language arts curriculum (Fountas & Pinnell, 2001).

## Teacher Knowledge of Management of Student Variations

Some researchers have insisted that student differences are not an important variable in some subjects. For instance, in reading instruction, Becker and Engelmann have claimed, "The popular belief that it is necessary to teach different students in different ways is, for the most part, a fiction . . . In the DISTAR programs used by the Direct Instruction Model, each child faces the same sequence of tasks and the same teaching strategies" (Becker & Engelmann, 1995–1996, p. 10). However, in Cuban's review of the research on Lesson Design, Cuban adds two features to Rosenshine's model of direct instruction: (1) Teacher's management abilities prevent disturbances by encouraging cooperation, and (2) Teacher paces instruction to fit students (Cuban, 1984). Both of these additions focus on varying lesson design to fit student variations. The first focuses on discipline procedures, and the second focuses on pace. The B.T.E.S., like most studies of teaching, gave almost no attention to the first feature—the development of knowledge about handing student disciplinary problems in the classroom. This area of K–12 teacher knowledge remains the most understudied and ignored in teacher preparation programs throughout the country, and, at the same time, is the knowledge most sought-after by new teachers. Among new teachers, one of the most popular, current texts on managing student disciplinary problems is *The First Days of School* by Harry K. and Rosemary T. Wong (Wong & Wong, 1998). Experienced teachers urge new teachers to select from this text only a few devices for trials runs before adopting any devices as permanent classroom procedures.

Although the B.T.E.S. did ignore student discipline problems in the classroom, the B.T.E.S. did not ignore the problem of the level of difficulty in instructional materials, giving considerable attention to the fit between what students can learn next and what the teaching materials demand. One of the most popular frameworks for analyzing level of difficulty was Benjamin Bloom's mastery learning taxonomy (Benjamin S. Bloom, 1976; B. S. Bloom, Engelhart, Furst, Hill, & Krathwohl, 1956). Bloom, like John B. Carroll, had claimed that students could learn if they were given enough time and if they were introduced to instructional material at an appropriate level (Benjamin S. Bloom, Hastings, & Madaus, 1971; Carroll, 1963). Bloom's taxonomy of six levels of cognitive structure in the classroom provided a guide for diagnosing a lesson's level of difficulty. To determine what cognitive level students had attained and to trace movement from one cognitive level to another—say, from Knowledge and Comprehension at a lower level to Synthesis and Evaluation at a higher level—frequent testing and/or monitoring had to be added to instruction. A major popularizer

of Bloom's ideas was Thomas R. Guskey (Guskey, 1985), whose Mastery Learning teaching model was adopted by school districts and teacher preparation programs throughout the country. But mastery learning, although very popular in teacher preparation programs, did not enjoy great success as an institutionalized program in school districts. For example, Chicago, which at one time mandated Mastery Learning in all of its schools, dropped Mastery Learning after scores on external tests declined. Teachers argued that Chicago's Mastery Learning became an accumulation of small bits and frequent skill testing and did not translate into real skills (Hammond, 1997, p. 53). Another problem was that Bloom's taxonomy, along with most hierarchies of knowledge, did not in practice always adequately distinguish between lower and higher levels of cognitive complexity (R. Wood, 1977). Many teacher preparation programs took other approaches to cognitive complexity in instructional materials, using either developmental theories (Case, 1985; Chall, 1983; Piaget & Inhelder, 1969) or metacognitive theories (Resnick, 1987) to sketch out different levels in a student's learning. An integrated approach to matching materials to students is represented by the work of Pinnell, Bridges and Fountas (Pinnell, Bridges, & Fountas, 1999), and Purves suggests that level of difficulty in literature can be understood as different ways of reading (Purves, 1991).

Another important area of teacher knowledge about student variation is multicultural awareness. In 1965, a black family became a part of the all white suburban world of the Dick and Jane reading series, and many teacher preparation programs for English teachers began to include minority authors and minority themes in recommended book lists emphasizing cultural pluralism and a curriculum of inclusion. In a few cases, teachers were encouraged to plan special literature courses emphasizing one group or another (Black Literature, Asian Literature, Hispanic Literature), causing some observers to suggest that schools programs were beginning to drop traditional literary content from the K–12 curriculum (A. Bloom, 1987) and creating, they claimed, a curriculum of cultural exclusion. However, Applebee, comparing the results of his 1963 study of literature books assigned in high school to the results of his 1988 survey, reported, "In all settings which we examined, the lists of most frequently required books and authors were dominated by white males, with little change in overall balance from similar lists 25 or 80 years ago" (A. N. Applebee, 1989a, p. 18). However, Applebee also reports a few changes: in 30 percent or more of the public schools, Harper Lee's *To Kill a Mockingbird* increased from 8% of the schools in 1963 to 74% in 1988. Applebee also reports, "In the public schools, the highest ranked minority authors in 1988 were Lorraine Hansbury and Richard Wright, who ranked 42nd and 53rd, respectively. In the urban schools . . . they move up to ranks 25 and 37; in schools with 50 percent or more minority students, they rank 14th and 17th" (A. N. Applebee, 1989a, p. 16). Applebee concludes, "The shifting ranks for Wright and Hansberry suggest that teachers are making some changes in the curriculum in response to the perceived backgrounds and interests of their students" (A. N. Applebee, 1989a, p. 16).

But, as Rudine Sims has noted (Sims, 1982), teacher preparation issues in multiculturalism go well beyond book lists.

One issue has been the language used to describe minority students—for instance, replacing "culturally disadvantaged" and "culturally deprived" with "disadvantaged" (Weiner, 1993), and another issue has been the teaching method itself. Basil Bernstein warned some time ago that some teaching methods had a class bias, favoring the work and home experience of some social classes and not others (Bernstein, 1990). Lisa Delpit has pointed to writing process approaches and peer response groups in writing classes as potentially undermining the education of some poor and minority students. She quotes one student's criticism of one writing class: "I didn't feel she was teaching us anything. She wanted us to correct each other's papers, and we were there to learn from her. She didn't teach us anything" (Delpit, 1995, p. 31) Delpit suggests that the progressive methods of immersion, process, and implicit knowledge may work for advantaged students who get explicit academic instruction as part of home life, but may not work for students who depend upon school for academic knowledge. She says, "In fact, DISTAR was 'successful' because it *taught* new information to children who had not already acquired it at home. Although the more progressive system was ideal for some children, for others it was a disaster" (Delpit, 1995, p. 30).

These cultural conflicts in the classroom are intensified by the fact that K–12 classrooms often have a "steering group" that teachers use as an informal reference point for deciding what material to select and what pacing is appropriate for whole class instruction. For example, in Michaels' analysis of the show-and-tell episodes in elementary classrooms, discourse that works at home for one student does not work in the dominant discourse of the classroom (Michaels, 1981). The problem here is not usage or grammar. The problem is the dominant form of discourse in the classroom is a mismatch with the dominant discourse or "ways with words" from home (Heath, 1983). Some researchers have suggested that if teachers knew more about the discourse of minority children, they could help provide a scaffold between school discourse and home discourse (Delain, Pearson, & Anderson, 1985; Lee, 1993). In general, these discourse issues are ignored in most teacher preparation programs.

In another important study of student variation, Uri Treisman examined the mathematics performance of black students at the University of California in the late 1970s and early 1980s (Treisman, 1985). Treisman was "struck by the sharp separation that most black students maintained—regardless of class or educational background—between their school lives and their social lives" and by the contrast of black students with Asian students who "sought peers with whom to collaborate" (Treisman, 1985, p. 12). To teach students how to collaborate, Treisman started a new seminar called Merit Workshop, a teaching model that continues at the universities of California (Berkeley), Texas (Austin), and Illinois (Urbana).

Critics have charged that attempts to honor these student differences in student learning—pace, cognitive level, diverse books, learning patterns, and discourse patterns—have created wildly differentiated ability groups within classes, tracking across classes, and a smorgasbord curriculum leading to the shopping mall high school (Powell, Farrar, & Cohen, 1985; Ravitch, 1985). Although Applebee, for instance, has shown that the books in secondary English classes have not changed

much (A. N. Applebee, 1989a), E. D. Hirsch and others have insisted that a common core curriculum is not being taught to all students and that minority students, especially, are being denied the explicit knowledge they need to succeed (Hirsch, 1987). The challenge for teacher preparation has been how to balance the need for solid subject matter with the need for the recognition of student variations.

## Teacher Knowledge of Learning Systems at the Intersection of Cognitive, Subject, and Student Variations

Schulman has suggested that the teacher's knowledge of the intersection of subject matter, cognition, and students has been too often overlooked in teacher preparation programs: "Where the teacher cognition program has clearly fallen short is in the elucidation of teacher cognitive understanding of the subject matter content and the relationships between such understanding and the instruction teachers provide for students" (L. S. Shulman, 1986a). Although the finding of BTES produced a number of Generic Teaching Models used in teacher preparation programs (Guskey's Mastery Learning, Rosenshine's Direct Instruction, and Hunter's Lesson Model), there was substantial evidence that generic teaching models did not work well with all students and in all subjects. Process alone, said Lynn Cheney, was "the culprit," resulting in no subject "worth thinking about" (Cheney, 1987). Generalzing-beyond-evidence was the problem, argued Arthur Wise, head of NCATE:

... the effort to rationalize beyond the bounds of knowledge ... imposing means which do not result in the attainment of ends or the setting of ends which cannot be attained, given the available means—imposing unproven techniques, on the one hand, and setting unrealistic expectations on the other (Wise, 1979, p. 65).

Ignoring purpose was the problem, said Bruce Joyce and Marsha Weil, who as early as 1972 had argued that different models of teaching were effective because they had different purposes:

We begin by challenging the idea that there is any such thing as a perfect model. We should not limit our methods to any single model, however attractive it may seem at first glance, because no model of teaching is designed to accomplish all types of learning or to work for all learning styles (Joyce & Weil, 1972, p. 1).

Ignoring-subject-matter-variations was the problem, said Soar and Soar (Soar & Soar, 1972), who reported that the generic models of direct instruction did not produce good results in all subject matter. After gathering pupil achievement and observational data (teacher behavior, curricular emphasis) from 70 kindergarten and first-grade classrooms, Soar and Soar reported that pupil growth in "simple-concrete" subject matter increased as "directive" teaching increased and that pupil growth in "complex-abstract" subject matter reached its maximum with a moderate amount of "directiveness" but fell off dramatically when "directiveness" was further increased.

Many studies began to analyze the specific areas of subject matter taught in the classroom. For instance, Dolores Durkin (1978–1979), instead of asking about reading in general, asked whether 24 fourth grade reading teachers were providing explicit instruction in the cognitive strategies of reading comprehension. She observed these 24 teachers for 5,000 minutes and found that explicit comprehension instruction occurred less than 1% of the time. She also found an absence of explicit comprehension instruction in the reading textbooks themselves (Durkin, 1981). Earlier, Dunkin and Biddle had warned that given the variations of cognitive challenge within different parts of subject matter and the differences of subject matter from one test to another, test results from one test alone could be seriously misleading about subject matter achievement:

"Consider the finding that teacher use of higher cognitive demand leads to lower pupil achievement. It seems possible to us that lower cognitive demand is more efficient for putting across facts, while higher cognitive demand encourages independence of thought. The latter, of course, is not measured by standardized achievement tests. Hypothesis of this sort cannot be tested until more sensitive criteria are developed and used in research on teaching" (Dunkin & Biddle, 1974, p. 409).

In another study of subject matter variation, Peterson found that students who received direct instruction in problem-solving classes tended to do worse on problem-solving tests than students who received what she calls more "open teaching" (Peterson, 1981, p. 63).

Thus, the contradictory findings of studies appear to result from subject matter variations. For example, in some of the Stallings' studies, the variables negatively associated with achievement were written assignments in class, many choices for the students, and conferencing with one student at a time (J. Stallings, 1980), and yet these same variables were found by many researchers to be part of a good model for writing instruction: Sarah Freedman pointed to the value of thoughtfully conceived one-to-one conferencing in the teaching of writing (Freedman, 1987), and Charles Cooper emphasized the importance of working individually with students on their writing, increasing the writing of pieces of at least paragraph length, decreasing short answer quizzes, and devoting much of class time to writing so that teachers can be available to give help and guidance (Cooper, 1981). Freedman and Cooper, it appears, were not talking about teaching the same subject matter as Stalling.

Similarly, Evertson, Anderson, and Brophy found little support for generic direct instruction models in their study of seventh and eighth grade English classes, and they suggested that the reason might be that seventh and eighth grade English classes have instructional objectives more variable than those found in the math or the basic skill classes in the early grades (basic reading skills, grammar, spelling) usually used as the data base for direct instruction studies (Evertson, Anderson, & Brophy, 1978).

By 1986, Rosenshine and Stevens were acknowledging that their general model of effective instruction is not well suited for all students and all subjects:

It would be a mistake to claim that the teaching procedures which have emerged from this research apply to all subjects and all learners, all the time. Rather, these procedures are most applicable for the 'well structured' parts of any content area, and are the least applicable to the 'ill structured' parts of any content area (Rosenshine & Stevens, 1986, p. 377).

Rosenshine and Stevens then itemized the subjects covered and not covered by the findings:

These explicit teaching procedures are most applicable in . . . arithmetic facts, decoding procedures, vocabulary, musical notation, English grammar, the factual parts of science and history, the vocabulary and grammar of foreign languages, and the factual and explicit parts of electronics, cooking, and accounting . . . mathematical computation, blending sounds in decoding, map reading, the mechanics of writing personal and business letters, English grammar, applying scientific laws, solving algebraic equations, or tuning an automobile engine. . . . The findings are least applicable for teaching composition and writing of term papers, analysis of literature, problem solving in specific content areas, discussion of social issues, or the development of unique or creative responses . . . teaching students to appreciate the story, evaluate the ideas, or critique the style of writing (Rosenshine & Stevens, 1986, p. 377).

Other studies have also suggested that direct instruction may not work for all students.

A number of researchers undertook the task of developing teaching models at the intersection of subject matter, student variations, and teaching strategies. These teaching models, whether small scale teaching units or large scale classroom structures or communities, were often designed as learning systems featuring interaction among knowledge structures, the classroom's developmental inclinations, and the cognition of the teacher and the individual student. One example was the Interaction Series developed by James Moffett and published by the Houghton Mifflin Company (Moffett, 1973). In its general outlines, this project was inspired by the 1965 Dartmouth Conference where Americans discovered that the British, proponents of a personal growth model of instruction, were putting dramatic activities and writing at the center of the English language arts program. Beginning with the essay *The Structural Curriculum in English* (Moffett, 1966) and the monograph *Drama: what is happening?* (Moffett, 1967), Moffett proposed that the structure of discourse in writing and literature should be organized around a set of I-You-It relationships representing the student's cognitive development from close personal relationships and experiences to more distant audience relationships and experiences. Said Moffett, "Or perhaps it is more accurate to say that the self enlarges, assimilating the world to itself and accommodating itself to the world . . . In moving outward from himself, the child becomes more himself. The teacher's art is to move with this movement, a subtle act possible only if he shifts his gaze from the subject to the learner, for the subject is in the learner" (Moffett, 1968, p. 59). At the center of Moffett's program was the student, embedded in various projects emphasizing writing, oral and dramatic activities. The program took hold for a time in some schools, and it was the center of some teacher preparation programs, but it suffered first from the absence of a management and assessment system to help teachers keep track of what was going on and second from the inability of many teachers to manage timely, explicit instruction. The Whole Language movement, primarily inspired by the work of Kenneth and Yetta Goodman, was a similar effort to bring together the parts of English language arts into teaching models focused on the student. While the Moffett program was especially influential in the secondary schools, the Whole Language movement was especially influential in elementary schools, taking aim at basal-reader reading programs and testing in elementary schools (K. S. Goodman, Goodman, & Hood, 1989; K. S. Goodman, Smith, Meredith, & Goodman, 1987; Y. Goodman, 1978).

In a quite different approach to model development, George Hillocks used meta-analysis to identify patterns of effectiveness in various approaches to teaching composition. After summing results across nearly a dozen studies of writing classes in grades 6–13, Hillocks recommended that the Environmental Mode of instruction as the most effective in the teaching of written composition (Hillocks, 1986). In what Applebee called "some of the most carefully worked out illustrations of . . . structure in the teaching of writing" (Arthur N. Applebee, 1991, p. 555), Hillocks describes the features of the Environmental Mode as embedded in actual or simulated "real life" situations—such things as preparing a tour package or preparing an investment report. It is important to note that Hillocks' Environmental Mode of Instruction includes numerous writing process techniques, leading Applebee to suggest, "Indeed, 'environmental' instruction in Hillocks terminology might be better labeled 'structured process'" (A. N. Applebee, 1986). Hillocks' Environmental Mode was also a form of the Dewey Project Method, and, in fact, Hillocks acknowledges that the Environmental Mode has intellectual antecedents in Dewey (Hillocks, 1986, p. 248). Hillocks attributes the effectiveness of the Environmental Mode to its capacity to bring "teacher, student, and materials into balance" (Hillocks, 1986, p. 247), a claim that Dewey made for the Project Method.

To develop effective teaching models in literature, a number of researchers combined literary theory with cognitive and metacognitive strategies. Smith used Booth's *Rhetoric of Fiction* (Booth, 1961) to describe and explain how students learn to understand unreliable narrators (M. W. Smith, 1991); Appleman (Appleman, 2000) described how various theories of literary criticism could be used to shape the reading of literature in the secondary classroom; Probst (Probst, 1992) described the five ways of knowing a literary work (self, others, text, content, process); Rabinowitz and Smith described the differences between resistance and acceptance of a text and between being an authorized reader (the kind of reader the author intended) and an unauthorized reader (Rabinowitz & Smith, 1997); and Langer described in some detail how the process of envisionment, the building of text-worlds in the mind, functions in literature classes. Langer makes clear that envisionment as a cognitive process depends upon an understanding of literary concepts and a community framework in the class: "Thus, the development of literary language and concepts goes hand in hand with the material read, the focus of the class as a literary discussion community, and the student's desire to participate in that community" (Langer, 1995, p. 129).

Some researchers developed teaching models organized around collaboration and cognitive apprenticeships. In these collaborative learning models, students had two parallel lines of development, one being what learners know independently—for example, the things students get right on tests—and the other being what learners can only know with help from peers, adults, or other instructional scaffolds (Cazden, 1983; Rogoff &

Gardner, 1984; Vygotsky, 1981, 1986; D. J. Wood, Bruner, & Ross, 1976). This latter type of learning, at the very frontier of the student's development, is called the zone of proximal development (Griffin & Cole, 1984). The Langer/Applebee model of collaboration had five criteria for effective instructional scaffolding: ownership, appropriateness, support, collaboration, and internalization (Arthur N. Applebee, 1991; Arthur N. Applebee & Langer, 1983). In another model of collaboration, the Reciprocal Teaching Model, Palincsar and Brown had four carefully developed collaborative-cognitive strategies in reading (generating questions, summarizing, clarifying word or test meaning, and predicting) and a carefully developed rotation of roles in a small group dialogue about a reading passage (one asks questions, another answers, a third comments on answers; or one summarizes, another comments, and another identifies a difficult word or passage) (Palincsar & Brown, 1984). Slavin's Success-for-All Reading Program is another collaborative teaching model, using teams, peer tutoring, and "cooperative learning" as critical features in learning to read (Slavin, 1980).

These collaborative models were very consistent with proposals that English classrooms, in order to hold the parts of English instruction together, should adopt a larger organizing principle of community—Stock suggesting a dialogic curriculum (Stock, 1995), Frank Smith suggesting initiation into a literacy club (F. Smith, 1988), Graff suggesting "entering into a disciplinary or cultural conversation, a process not unlike an initiation into a social club" (Graff, 1992), Bartholomae suggesting initiation into a community or a university invented for class purposes (Bartholomae, 1985), and Applebee calling for classrooms as "cultural conversations" in which literary traditions are placed in contemporary contexts (Arthur N. Applebee, 1994). In general, the components of classroom-as-club (or community) have not been spelled out with enough detail to be useful in most teacher preparation programs, although Applebee has sketched out the principles on which a teaching model like "community" could be built. There are, however, several very useful proposals for how to organize teaching units—for example, Harvey Daniels' literature circles (Daniels, 1994) and Bartholome and Petrotsky's Reading and Writing Course (Bartholomae & Petrotsky, 1986).

Are these collaborative models successful? In specific subjects and grade levels, yes. For example, in a review of 23 studies of Reciprocal Teaching, Rosenshine and Meister (Rosenshine & Meister, 1994) found that 2 of 13 studies had significant results on standardized tests and 8 of 10 studies had significant results on "experimenter-developed" comprehension tests. In a comparison of a standardized test and an experimenter-developed test, Rosenshine and Meister found that passages in the experimenter-developed test were longer, had more topic sentences, and had other differences. The point is that Reciprocal Teaching is especially effective in classrooms focusing on subject matter in texts that are longer and have more topic sentences.

It is important to recall again that there is an underlying student steering group in all of these studies. As noted earlier, the grade level of the students matters because, for one thing, the structure of the subject matter changes from the early grades to the later. For example, the original study of the Palincsar/Brown

Reciprocal Teaching Model selected only students who were near grade level in decoding and below grade level in comprehension (Rosenshine & Meister, 1994), and the Hillocks' environmental teaching model was based on studies of student effects from sixth grade through the college freshman year. Kindergarten through fifth grade, where, incidentally, over half of the nation's K–12 children go to school, are not included in Hillocks' study (Hillocks, 1986).

The Hillocks' Environmental Teaching Model, the Palincar/Brown Reciprocal Reading Model, Harvey Daniels' Literature Circles, Moffett's Interaction Series, Applebee's Cultural Conversations, and many other models mentioned above are attempting to find a coherent balance among disciplinary knowledge, student variations, and the teacher's cognitive strategies in both overall curriculum and daily lesson design. Applebee describes this struggle as an effort to bring together constructivism and tradition: "The book [*Curriculum as Cultural Conversation*] seeks to rehabilitate 'tradition' as an important component of a constructivist pedagogy—in fact, my original title was *Transforming Traditions* in a deliberate echoing of Elizabeth Minnich's (Minnich, 1990) *Transforming Knowledge*—and to situate curriculum within traditions in which we want students to participate" (A. N. Applebee, 1999). Underlying many of these efforts to bring together subject matter traditions and constructivist psychology was an inclination toward Dewey's Project Method and pragmatism (Orrill, 1995).

The general disenchantment with generic teaching skills covering all students and subjects has been reflected in the dramatic increase in specialized credentials for teachers. For example, Nebraska has now established 20, Montana 44, Massachusettts 52, Michigan 60 or more, and South Dakota 20 (Hammond and Berry, 1988, pp. 18–19). In addition, many states—for example, California, North Carolina, and Washington—have all passed laws providing some kind of penalty for giving teachers assignments outside the specialty of their credential. In summary, teacher decisions about how to teach are a complicated intersection of knowledge from cognitive psychology, subject disciplines, and the social-historical trends in student development. To understand what teachers must know to construct these intersections in class, many researchers interested in teacher preparation have turned their attention to four specialized areas of emerging interest: (1) the impact of technology and computerized lesson design, (2) the impact of subject theory and literacy policies on lesson design, (3) the impact of the structure of school and school-as-a-culture on lesson design, and (4) the emerging models of reflective practice.

## Emerging Teacher Knowledge of Technology and Computerized Lesson Design

Some of the initial opposition to computers in the classroom has disappeared—the conversion of former Secretary of Education Bennett being one example (Steinberg, 2000). It is now understood that electronic tools (computers, calculators, the internet) significantly interact with English language arts in primarily three areas: the student's computer literacy in English

Language, the methods of instruction used by the teachers, and the methods of assessment used by teachers, districts, and the state. First, student literacy. Electronic tools and technology have modified our society's definition of the minimum literacy needed for work, civic participation, and personal growth (M. Myers, 1996; Purves, 1990), and, as a result, many teacher credential programs have added teacher knowledge of technology as part of what teachers should know and be able to teach. Second, instruction. Electronic tools have been particularly effective in creating easy access to distant audiences in composition instruction and in solving the problems of the Project Method in the teaching of reading, writing, and literature. The Project Method, illustrated above with the Hillocks' Environmental Mode for composition instruction and Moffett's Interaction series for instruction in reading and composition, has been extensively criticized for its so-called failure to provide for explicit instruction. Diane Ravitch, for one, argues that the Project Method fails to transmit necessary knowledge and hails the early criticisms of the Project Method by William C. Bagley (Ravitch, 2000). Bagley, calling the Project Method "a constructive achievement of the first magnitude," observed in 1921 that the purpose-driven organization of the Project Method had a tendency to ignore the learner's need for explicit instruction in the knowledge necessary to achieve the purpose:

I should like to dwell a little longer on this tendency of the immediate purpose to overshadow the instruments used in its realization. The failure to recognize this tendency has, I think, been cause of the failure of the project method generally to secure the results that formal and systematic teaching, with all of its evils and all of the wastage involved in divided attention, often succeeded in securing. Good teachers who have used the project method and testified to its virtues have often added the reservation that, as they expressed it, "You must still have some drill." Now to say that you "must still have some drill" is only another way of saying that that you must take a procedure out of its purpose-context and give it a little time and attention in its own right, as an abstract entity if you please. Until further evidence is at hand, I should strongly recommend . . . facts and principles as such rather than as instruments for solving impelling problems (Bagley, 1921, p. 4).

In Moffett's paper-based Interaction Series (Moffett, 1973), for example, teachers found that projects often lost their direction when teachers stopped the projects in order to link students to explicit knowledge through drills or lectures or whatever. In addition, students involved in the processes of the project often lost track of the structure of the subject they were learning. Finally, the Moffett Interaction Series did not have a management system enabling teachers to keep track of what was happening. To solve these problems of Links, Explicit Structure, and Management, Robert Romano, with assistance from James Moffett and Tom Gage, translated some of Moffett's ideas into computer software using Links, Virtual Toys, and Digital Portfolios (M. A. Myers, in process). Through Optional and Required Links in the computer's project sequence, the student using the computer to engage in project work could be linked at various points to sites where the student could learn the explicit knowledge he/she needed for project work. In addition, the student could be returned to the exact point where he/she had left the project and could consult at any time an available map of the project's work showing where the student is located. The computer makes it possible for a student to link to explicit knowledge in the middle of a project and not to lose a sense of either current location or the overall structure of the project. In addition, the computer's digital portfolios for each student could automatically store the work the student produces and prepare reports showing how long the student spent on one task or another, the student's scores on short tests of explicit knowledge, and so forth.

Next, using Virtual Toys, the computer enables students to bridge from the abstract ideas of a subject to a concrete model of the subject's structure. Alan Kay, vice-president of research and development at the Walt Disney Company and one of the original architects of the personal pc, has called Virtual Toys one of the key capabilities of the computer in educational settings. When he looked at Seymour Papert's Logo, Kay realized that computer-created Virtual Toys could be a computerized bridge from the abstract to the concrete Says Kay, "He (Papert) realized that computers turn abstraction in math into concrete toys for students. He allowed them to make things that were mathematical, but his program, Logo, failed because elementary teachers were unable to understand what this was all about" (Kay, 2000, p. 22). The point is that teachers need to understand how computers make possible a much more flexible use of Links and Virtual Toys in Lesson Design and how the flexible use of Links and Virtual Toys can solve some of the teaching problems of the Project Method.

Finally, using digital portfolios for each student, computers and the internet can help teachers solve the enormous problems of managing the records of student work in the Project Method—or any method, for that matter. In addition, the computers and the internet appear to be ready to "revolutionize the business and substance of large scale assessment," attacking, for one thing, the mismatch between testing and the curriculum and creating more efficient ways to communicate to students, the public, and educators the indicators of student achievement (Randy Elliot Bennett, 2001, p. 3). In August 2000, 42% of the homes in the U.S. were connected to the internet (U.S. Dept of Commerce, 2000 #242)—potentially, a direct connection between the classroom and the home—and the connections are becoming increasingly broadband with more information and more types of information (video, audio) (R. E. Bennett, Goodman, Hessinger, Ligget, Marshall, Kahn, & Zack, 1999). In general, most summaries of teacher knowledge have recognized that teachers, as managers and disseminators of information about students, will need to understand how to use the new technology in their teaching (NCTE, 1996).

## Emerging Teacher Knowledge of the History of Subjects and of Literacy Policies

One of Shulman's seven categories of essential teacher knowledge is "knowledge of educational ends, purposes, and values" (L. S. Shulman, 1987), and in this review, I have narrowed this area to teacher knowledge of the history of English as a school subject and the history of U.S. literacy policies, especially the impact of these literacy policies on the subject itself. First subject history. Simon has argued that one way "to solve a problem is to reduce it to a problem previously solved—to show what steps lead from the earlier solution to a solution of the new problem" (Simon, 1981), and in professional education, knowledge of old knowledge is essential: " . . . curriculum revisions that rid us of accumulations of the past are infrequent and painful. Nor are they always desirable—partial recapitulation may, in many instances, provide the most expeditious route to advanced knowledge" (Simon, 1981). The shifting paradigms within the subject field of English language arts have often produced a wide range of K–12 textbooks with different theoretical frameworks, and many of these different approaches are available in the school textbook room and in the syllabus used for one course or another. In English grammar, for example, teachers will often find textbooks from traditional grammar, generative grammar, structural grammar, and transformational grammar. Each of these frameworks, although quite different, can offer some insight into a student's misunderstanding of the grammar taught in school. High school literature textbooks, like grammar textbooks, have their own conflicting frameworks for what constitutes evidence of understanding of literature. For instance, the understanding of literature could be defined within a reader response theory of literature (Rosenblatt, 1996) or within a cognitive theory of reading (Anderson & Pearson, 1984).

Writing, too, has changed. It is no longer simply a five paragraph written product and a list of right conventions and samples of wrong efforts. It is now also a process, from pre-writing to writing and revising, and it is also a social context in which a set of social relationships are negotiated between reader and writer. Learning how to establish these social relationships in writing often takes the form of genre study in some writing classes, but some researchers have suggested that learning to write in a disciplinary area is much more like learning how to be initiated into a specialized community.

Teachers with a subject matter background often reflect their different assumptions about the structure of subject matter in their various departmental interactions (M. Myers & Thomas, 1982). In Grossman's study of how teachers proposed to teach Randall Jarrell's *Death of a Ball Turret Gunner*, Grossman found marked differences in approach—one promoting individual responses from students, another stressing the identification of patterns in the text (not a prose summary of overall meaning), and yet another focusing on intertextual discussions (comparing the themes in one or more texts with the Jarrell's poem) (Grossman, 1990). Clearly, an understanding of the many paradigms in the history of a subject helps a teacher understand differences in the field.

Shifts in the structure and priorities of subject matter cannot be understood and productively evaluated without an understanding of the history of literacy in the United States (Purves, 1990). For example, new forms of literacy used in the workplace and civic life in U.S. have already started to shape the subjects taught in school in four areas: sign shifting, context shifting, collaboration or cognitive apprenticeships, and the use of technology in schools (M. Myers, 1996). Sign shifting refers to the importance of experimenting in school with recoding information, say, from words to graphs and maps, from print to sounds, from graphs to numbers, from still-visuals to action sequences, from lists to narrative; and content shifting refers, among other things, to an understanding of how the academic report can be translated into the personal narrative and how conversational language can be translated into report language. These new forms of literacy are at the heart of the standards discussions that have occupied states and districts for the past ten years (Myers, 1996).

## Emerging Teacher Knowledge of School Structure and Culture

In 1974 Dunkin and Biddle excluded Phillip Jackson's *Life in Classrooms* from their *The Study of Teaching* because, according to Shulman (L. S. Shulman, 1986a), Jackson, like many other researchers of school culture, did not use quantifiable measures of process-product relationships (Jackson, 1968). However, as Shulman notes, Jackson's work "is one of the most frequently cited references in their conceptual analysis of teaching" (L. S. Shulman, 1986a, p. 5). Shulman himself names "knowledge of educational contents" as one of his seven essential categories of teacher knowledge (L. S. Shulman, 1987). The structure of schools and districts is one part of educational contexts. For example, a school's attendance and tardy patterns, for instance, can have a devastating influence on the school, and the absence of clear school goals, other than "getting along," can turn a school into a shopping mall with a set of hidden treaties and compromises undermining any common set of standards for all students (Powell, et al., 1985). Another part of educational contexts is the culture of schools and districts. For example, in his design of the English Language Arts assessment for the National Board of Professional Teaching Standards, Petrosky named teacher knowledge of professional organizations and community groups as one of his six essential areas (Petrosky, 1994). In the area of community groups, Coleman (J. Coleman & Hoffer, 1987a) reported that private religious schools, not public schools, have the better success rate because of "social capital," peer and family interactions in the school as a social, supportive network. Coleman de-emphasized teacher knowledge about subjects and pedagogy and emphasized school size, parent attendance at school events, parent volunteer work for the school, parent expectations and support of school program. In summary, to understand effective classrooms, teachers need some knowledge about school structure and school culture, including the impact of school size and financing on teaching (Hammond, 1998, p. 10), the impact of race, social class, and tracking on teaching (Oakes, 1985), the importance of social capital and parent involvement in school success (J. Coleman, 1987(b)), and the role of professional organizations and community groups (Petrosky, 1994).

## Emerging Teacher Knowledge of Reflective Practice

In general, teacher knowledge of procedures for reflective practice is now recognized as necessary teacher knowledge.

In practice, very few teacher preparation programs actually include teacher research and reflection as a part of their programs. Finally, there is very little agreement in English language arts about the purposes or the structure of teacher research and reflection, although Cochran-Smith and Lytle have done an admirable job of sketching out the issues and a typoloy of teacher research projects (Cochran-Smith & Lytle, 1993). The arguments about the purposes and forms of teacher research range from arguments that conceptualize teacher research as folk lore, separate from University research, to arguments that conceptualize teacher research as part of the University research community. Fenstermacher observes that the efforts of Shulman and others to clarify the claims of teacher research is bedeviled by discourse problems (Fenstermacher, 1994, p. 16). Some of these problems originate in the differing sources for the U.S. teacher researcher movement: the efforts of teacher organizations and schools in England, represented by Lawrence Stenhouse (Stenhouse, 1975, 1985); the work of Vito Perrone's North Dakota Study Group on Evaluation, represented by the work of Pat Carini at Prospect Center and Prospect School (P. Carini, 1975, 1979; P. F. Carini, 2001); the work of national networks of teachers, represented by the work of the Bread Loaf group (Goswami & Stillman, 1987) and the many teacher research projects of the National Writing Project (Buchanan, 1993; Cone, 1990; Hahn, 1991; Mohr & Maclean, 1987; M. Myers, 1985); the writing assessment work of Paul Diederch and Evans Alloway at the Education Testing Service during the 1960s; the University-based course work of (1) Glenda Bissex (Bissex & Bullock, 1987), (2) Marilyn Cochran-Smith and Susan L. Lytle in Project START (Student Teachers as Researching Teachers) in Philadelphia (Cochran-Smith & Lytle, 1993), and (3) Eleanor Duckworth (Duckworth, 1972) and Jeanne Bamberger in the Teacher Project at Harvard. Drawing on the records of the Teacher Project at Harvard, Donald Schon applied to K–12 teachers the ideas in his *The Reflective Practiner* and *Educating the Reflective Practiner* (D. Schon, 1988), suggesting that practitioner inquiry had its own unique form.

In his *The Reflective Practiner*, Schon uses evidence from his studies of architects, psychotherapists, and engineers to object to many of the rule-based applications of social science research to professional practices—what he calls Technical Rationality. Schon argues that the knowledge of professional practitioners often involves "confusing 'messes' incapable of technical solutions" (D. A. Schon, 1983, p. 43). To solve these problems, among others, Shulman proposes three approaches to teacher reflection: case knowledge, proposition knowledge (technical rationality), and strategic knowledge, the latter being "a strategy for transforming more propositional knowledge into narratives that motivate and educate," especially in instances when principles of propositional knowledge appear to conflict in practice (L. S. Shulman, 1992). Many teacher research projects have characterized teacher research strategies as criss-crossing (Spiro, Coulson, Feltovish, & Anderson, 1988), satisfying (Simon, 1981), giving reasons to classroom events and student behavior (Duckworth, 1972), shaping images and narratives (Connelly & Clandinin, 1990), developing a Descriptive Review of the Child (Kanevsky, 1993), and pretending an argument, the latter serving "as a kind of analytical device for understanding how teachers think about what they do" (Fenstermacher, 1988, p. 41; Green, 1976).

The evidence from law (Redlich, 1914) and from medical programs (Williams, 1992) is that cases can become a strong foundation for reflection and research by K–12 teachers as long as cases and rules interact with each other. Schwab (Schwab, 1983), among others, has argued that pedagogical knowledge must be an artistic combination of rules and cases:

Art arises as the knower of the rule learns to apply them appropriately to the particular case. Application, in turn, requires acute awareness of the particularities of the case and ways in which the rule can be modified to fit the case without complete abrogation of the rule (Schwab, 1983, p. 265).

In Schwab's view, technical rules do not have a one-to-one correspondence with an all-purpose definition of good teaching, but instead are like maxims that must be tested and illustrated by cases. As a result, it is the catalogue of cases, not the rules themselves, which define the central tendency or limits of a rule. Shulman describes the relationship as follows: "Both our scientific knowledge of rules and principles (properly construed as grounds, not prescriptions) and our knowledge of richly described and critically analyzed cases combine to define the knowledge base of teaching" (L. S. Shulman, 1986a). He also says, " . . . from an epistemological perspective, cases may be more congruent with the forms of practical knowledge" (L. S. Shulman, 1992). This makes teaching like other subject matter communities in which exemplars "are far more effective determinants of community substructure than are symbolic generalizations" (Kuhn, 1977):

Acquiring an arsenal of exemplars, just as much as learning symbolic generalizations, is integral to the process by which a student gains access to the achievements of a disciplinary group. Without exemplars he would never learn much of what the group knows about such fundamental concepts as field and force, element and compound, or nucleus and cell (Kuhn, 1977).

Exemplars and cases allow for fuzzy boundaries and areas of uncertainty that, according to David Schon, are typical of teaching situations. Schon says that in teaching we find many indeterminate zones of practice—matters of "uncertainty, uniqueness, and value conflict" (D. Schon, 1987). In teaching, tightly structured procedures and feature lists are relatively less helpful than they are in many technologically-dominate activities (McLaughlin & Marsh, 1978).

Paul Diederich suggested many years ago that the Bay Area Writing Project's major contribution to teacher preparation was its introduction of a way to do case-based staff development. The BAWP Summer Institutes, he said, are simply ways for organizing outstanding cases of teaching for later publication as presentations in follow-up programs in school districts and as actual written documents published by BAWP Thus, Rebecca Caplan's case begins as a summer institute presentation, then becomes a presentation in a school district workshop, and then evolves into a written document published by BAWP (Caplan, 1982). According to Diederich, BAWP's contribution was equivalent to Christopher Langdell's introduction of the case study method

in law (BAWP, 1978; Redlich, 1914). Another example of the use of case studies in staff development is Judith Shulman's training program for mentor teachers (J. Shulman & Colbert, 1987). Although there is considerable agreement in English language arts about the value of teacher research and reflective practices, there is almost no agreement about the three components discussed here—propositional knowledge (technical rationality), cases, and strategies (rules of thumb and genres of inquiry).

## Summary of Teacher Content

There is not any doubt that the content of teacher preparation matters. Coleman was right about the importance of peers and networks of parental and community support, but he was wrong about school effects, including teacher knowledge. Teacher knowledge matters, and more and more studies in recent years have provided the evidence for that claim. In a recent review of 60 production function studies, Greenwald, Hedges, and Laine found that teacher education, ability, and experience, along with small schools and lower teacher-pupil ratios, are associated with significant increases in student achievement (Greenwald, Hedges, & Laine, 1996). In addition, Ronald Ferguson found that in 900 Texas school districts, teacher scores on licensing exams, masters degrees, and experience accounted for almost 40% of measured variance in students' reading and mathematics gains at grades one though 11 (Ferguson, 1991). In other words, teacher expertise, in a database larger than that in the Coleman study, accounted for more gains in student achievement than any other factor. Says Linda Darling Hammond, "The effects were so strong, and the variations in teacher expertise so great that, after controlling for SES, the large disparities in achievement between Black and White students were almost entirely accounted for by differences in the qualifications of their teachers" (Hammond, 1998, p. 7). In a study of Alabama schools, Ferguson and Ladd found sizable influences of teacher qualifications on student achievement gains in reading and mathematics (Ferguson & Ladd, 1996). In a summary of many studies, Linda Darling Hammond concludes:

Using increasingly fine-grained measures of teacher knowledge and disaggregated analysis of large-scale data sets, a number of recent studies suggest that teacher expertise is one of the most important factors in determining student achievement, followed by the smaller but consistently positive influences of small schools and small class sizes. That is, teachers who know a lot about teaching and learning and who work in environments that allow them to know students well are the critical elements of successful learning (Hammond, 1998 p. ).

## THE STRUCTURE OF TEACHER PREPARATION

The problems of structure in teacher preparation (who controls teacher preparation?) begin with the bargain made many years by Thorstein Veblen: "the professional school as a 'lower school' wholly devoted to applying fundamental research from the 'higher school' of the disciplines" (D. Schon, 1987).

Notice that the structural issue here is whether the disciplinary departments of the university will control teacher education. To avoid this bargain in which professional schools grant all leadership to the disciplines, Herbert Simon proposed a solution: "A full solution . . . hinges on the prospect of developing an explicit, abstract, intellectual theory of the processes of synthesis and design, a theory that can be analyzed and taught in the same way that the laws of chemistry, physiology, and economics can be analyzed and taught" (Simon, 1969). In *The Sciences of the Artificial (Simon, 1981)*, Simon proposed the general outlines of a science of professional practice, what he called the science of design. Among teacher preparation studies in English language arts, the Lesson Design project of James Stigler, Ron Galimore, and others at UCLA comes the closest to answering Simon's call for a science of design. Says Stigler and Hiebert, "In our opinion, lesson study is an ideal process for gradually working through new recommendations and giving them life in the classroom" (Stigler & Hiebert, 1999).

With the exception of the Lesson Design group at UCLA and a few other programs, professional programs of teacher preparation did not answer Simon's challenge to develop their own theories of design. Commenting on one teaching model, Rosenshine and Meister report " . . . not enough has been written on implementation" (Rosenshine & Meister, 1994), and Smargorinsky and Whiting report that there is "little formal knowledge of how preservice teachers are educated" (Smagorinsky & Whiting, 1995), although their study of English preparation is a promising beginning. The general failure to respond to Simon's challenge is not limited to English language arts. Dinham and Stritter report, "Research on teaching and learning processes in professional education's clinical component—the apprenticeship—is virtually nonexistent in all but the health professions" (Dinham & Sritter, 1986). Of course, some things were known about teacher preparation—for instance, the "dirty little secret" that university teacher preparation had become a welfare program for graduate students who needed employment to pay tuitions to stay enrolled in disciplinary programs (Sykes, 1983). It is these graduate students, not the professors, who observed the teaching of student teachers and who taught the methods classes.

Reform of teacher preparation took a big step forward with the publication of Harry Judge's study describing how U.S. research universities had systematically distanced themselves from the study of teaching and teacher education (Judge, 1982). It was Judge's study that "nearly single handedly led to the formation of the Holmes Group" (L. S. Shulman, 1988). Fifteen years ago, the reform of university-based teacher preparation seemed to be just around the corner, led by the Holmes Group proposal that professional schools of education assume leadership for new, substantive programs (Group, 1986). Ernest Boyer and John Goodland, for example, called for university teacher preparation courses in learning theory, the teaching of writing, the use of technology, the history of schooling in the United States, and examination of inquiry methods (Boyer, 1983; Goodlad, 1984). These calls for intellectual rigor seemed to work against the claims that teachers needed to be taught routine sequences of instruction or the claim of some university teacher educators that the role of the teacher is "analogous to the builder" who takes directions from the university researcher

or specialist who is analogous to the architect or creator of blue prints (Eggen, Kauchak, & Harder, 1979).

After an initial ten-year interest in the Holmes Group's efforts, the influence of the Holmes Group itself began a slow decline. It has now all but disappeared. With a few exceptions, teacher preparation has returned to its old ways, and the question in teacher preparation appears to be not how to get more intellectual rigor but how to get enough teachers to fill the empty slots in K-12 classrooms.

As class sizes are reduced, as teachers retire, as salary disparities increase, the number of teachers without credentials and with inadequate educational backgrounds begins to increase. In the past, to produce a pool of bright, capable teachers, the teaching pool for K-12 has depended upon major dislocations in jobs and upon workplace discrimination against ethnic minorities and women. When women and minorities were discriminated against in placements for commercial jobs, they could still turn to public education for employment. When returning veterans created a glut on the employment market at the end of World War II, the Korean War, and the Vietnam War, many unemployed males with college degrees, often earned with the G. I. Bill, turned to K-12 teaching for employment. If there is no economic recession and if the economic rewards for teachers do not improve, then there is likely to be an increasing shortage of K-12 teachers. The results of this shortage are already being felt.

One result of the decreasing labor pool of teachers has been that structural questions have changed. Dissatisfied with the university and college certification in teacher preparation, districts and states have moved teacher preparation away from colleges and universities and passed the responsibility to school districts, off-campus centers, teachers unions, and, now and then, professional development schools at school sites. Many states and districts have contracted for K-12 staff development from an increasing number of commercial companies, many allied with book publishers. In addition, states have re-written the teacher preparation curriculum by mandating more hours of field experience for teacher candidates. Colorado has legislated 100 hours of field experience for teacher candidates, Kentucky 150 hours, Ohio 300 hours, North Carolina ten weeks, North Dakota 10 weeks, and so forth across more than thirty states (Hammond & Berry, 1988, p. 16). Next, states have introduced their own exams for the certification of teachers, arguing that college and university certification was not enough. By 1999, 44 states had some kind of licensing exam for a secondary teaching credential, and only 29 of those states required exams in subject matter knowledge. The content of these secondary subject matter exams, according to one review, is "about the same as in high-level high school courses" (Mitchell & Barth, 1999, p. 3), and the same review reported that tests for elementary credentials "assess verbal and mathematical literacy at about the tenth grade level" (Mitchell & Barth, 1999, p. 3).

At the same time, states have established their own teacher preparation networks. California and Vermont, for example, have established state-supported teacher networks (California Subject Matter Projects and Vermont Portfolio Projects) to continue teacher preparation throughout the teaching career, giving special emphasis to the subject matter itself (Pennell &

Firestone, 1998). In addition, California has established a network of training sites (Beginning Teacher Support Assistance-BTSA) for unlicensed teachers, often turning teacher preparation over to school districts. Next, states have eliminated life credentials, requiring that teachers be re-licensed every 3 to 5 years, and by granting districts the authority to issue units for re-licensing, the states have again transferred new teacher preparation responsibilities to school districts. In addition, some states have written into law the curriculum for reading and writing courses for teachers, California going so far as to outlaw the mention of "invented spelling" in state funded staff development programs on writing (M. A. Myers & Spain, 2001).

Next, states have begun to embed teacher preparation programs in district teacher mentoring and evaluation programs. In programs of Peer Assistance Review (PAR), mentor teachers work with beginning or experienced teachers in a coaching relationship that often involves evaluation and recommendations for employment. PAR, first initiated by Dal Lawrence in Toledo, Ohio in 1981, and usually managed by a partnership of the school district and the teachers' union, has been adopted in Poway and Lompac, California; Columbus and Cicinnati, Ohio; Rochester, New York; and elsewhere (Koppich, 2000). Finally, many states and districts have added salary incentives for teachers who are certified by the private, independent National Board for Professional Teaching Standards, a certification based on tests developed and administered by the Education Testing Service. As a result, preparation for NBPTS testing and certification has become an on-going staff development program throughout the country, sometimes sponsored by districts, teachers unions, private companies, regional networks.

The structural debates in teacher preparation have turned to issues of purposes and situated learning. The central purpose question is: Are these programs socializing well-educated teacher candidates into a teaching profession in which candidates will become effective teachers and school decision makers or are these programs simply providing some technical skills to marginally educated candidates who are filling slots on an emergency credential? The Bay Area Writing Project, for example, sees itself as first a professionalization project that identifies examples of best practice among practicing teachers. These teachers present cases of their practice to other teachers, establishing the legitimacy of teacher knowledge and, at the same time, building a community of teacher leaders. In addition, BAWP will invite a few outside experts with special subject knowledge to share what they know with teachers. William Strong, who has studied many different types of teacher preparation , concluded, "I came to see anew how NWP (the National Writing Project) is as much about teacher empowerment as it is about the teaching and learning of writing" (Strong, 1988).

BAWP's emphasis on expertise, teacher empowerment, and high standards of teacher preparation is not just frosting-on-the-cake. It turns out that de-professionalized, marginally educated teachers have a disastrous impact on the education of minority and poor children. Katti Haycock, Director of The Education Trust, has observed that if we took the a simple step of assuring that poor and minority children had teachers of good quality, about half the achievement gap between minority and white children would disappear (Haycock, 1998). For example,

Sanders and Rivers have reported that their data suggest that well-prepared teachers post gains for low achieving students averaging 53 percentile points during a school year, and marginally qualified teachers post gains for low achieving students averaging 14 percentile points during a school year (Sanders & Rivers, 1998). Despite the evidence of the negative effects, marginally prepared teachers are still being hired in large numbers.

The second major issue in the structure of teacher preparation is where teacher preparation is situated? Is it, for instance, embedded in instruction, reform, and teacher leadership at school sites—sometimes called Professional Development Schools. For example, Cochran-Smith and Lytle have argued that "Reflective Practice" modifies the question of both content and role: "the question here is not whether we need a knowledge base for teaching but rather what kind of knowledge base is needed, who constructs it, and what roles teachers play in its formation" (Cochran-Smith & Lytle, 1993). For example, David Cohen found that teachers who worked directly on teaching materials associated with the new frameworks in mathematics had higher student scores on state assessments in mathematics (Cohen & Hill, 1997). In addition, a large study of 820 secondary schools nationwide found that those who had undertaken greater levels of restructuring aimed at "personalization, higher order learning for all students, teacher learning and collaboration, and parent and student involvement produced significantly greater achievement gains for students of all achievement levels" (Hammond, 1998, p. 11).

These findings suggest that teacher preparation should be embedded in the actual on-site problems of student achievement and school structure, thereby helping "teachers improve instruction from the inside out instead of decreeing change by remote control" (Tyack & Cuban, 1995). Of course, one of the reasons for not situating teacher preparation at school sites is that school sites themselves often inhibit learning, as Peter Senge has observed: "making continual learning a way of organizational life . . . can only be achieved by breaking with the traditional authoritarian command and control hierarchy, where the top thinks and the local acts, to merge thinking and acting at all levels" (Senge, 1992). Creating excellent programs of teacher preparation at school sites is a very difficult task. Because the school has immediate instructional goals for its students, it often does not have the time or the resources for attending to the learning needs of teachers. School site teacher preparation often becomes merely another form of peer coaching to-get-the-day's-work-done. Hargraves and Dawe have criticized peer coaching in these circumstances for skill reductionism: "what is to be coached in teaching cannot be reduced solely to matters of technical skills and competence, but involves choices of a personal, moral, and sociopolitical nature" (Hargraves & Dawe, 1989). They are arguing that teacher preparation must develop a framework larger than the next lesson plan and must focus on topics of subject structure and sociopolitical influences in depth. To have an extended conversation on these topics, one obviously needs Time, away from students. Hargraves and Dawe have questioned whether these time problems have been solved: " . . . it seems to us that the implications of implementing peer coaching are being treated a little too dismissively here" (Hargraves & Dawe, 1989).

In summary, the old control debate in teacher preparation between professional schools and the disciplinary departments has been replaced by debates about the features of teacher preparation and staff development in a wide range of setting. The question of "who runs teacher preparation programs?" has been answered in many places with "Everybody!" At one time, I thought teachers' unions would pressure schools of education to improve teacher preparation. Instead, teachers' unions are one of the many groups taking over teacher preparation (Higuchi, 2001). It is the program features that are now the areas of intense interest and debate. Professional Development Schools, organized like medical internships around on-going school programs, sound very promising. In practice, they are less impressive, even disappointing. The agenda of the Lesson Design Group at UCLA, however, appears very promising next step, and my visit to the UCLA Lesson Lab, watching a careful analysis of videotaped lessons, gives me hope. In conclusion, whatever the knowledge of teachers or the structure of preparation programs, teachers should have a passion for teaching and an enjoyment of the company of young people. When these qualities cannot be taught, recruit people who already have them.

# References

Anderson, R. C., & Pearson, P. D. (1984). A schematic-theoretic view of basic processes in reading comprehension. In P. D. Pearson (Ed.), *Handbook of reading research*. New York: Longman.

Applebee, A. N. (1986). Problems in process approaches: Reconceptualization of process instruction. In D. Bartholomae & A. R. Petrotsky (Eds.), *The teaching of writing: Eighty-fifth yearbook of the national society for the study of education* (Vol. 85, pp. 95–113). Chicago, IL: The National Society for the Study of Education.

Applebee, A. N. (1989a). *A study of book-length works taught in high school English courses*. Albany, New York: Center for the Learning and Teaching of Literature, University at Albany, State University of New York.

Applebee, A. N. (1989b). *The teaching of literature in programs with reputations for excellence in English courses* (Vol. Report Series 1.2). Albany, NY: Center for the Learning and Teaching of Literature, SUNY at Albany.

Applebee, A. N. (1991). Environments for language teaching and learning: Contemporary issues and future directions. In J. Flood, J. M. Jensen, D. Lapp, & J. R. Squire (Eds.), *Handbook of Research on Teaching the English Language Arts*. New York: MacMillan.

Applebee, A. N. (1994). *Toward thoughtful curriculum: Fostering discipline-based conversation in the English classroom*. Albany, NY: National Research Center on Literature Teaching and Learning.

Applebee, A. N. (1999). Building a foundation for effective teaching and learning of English: A personal perspective on thirty years of research. *Research in the Teaching of English, 33*(May), 352–366.

Applebee, A. N., & Langer, J. (1983). Instructional scaffolding: Reading and writing as natural language activities. *Language Arts, 60*(2), 168–175.

Appleman, D. (2000). *Critical encounters in high school English: Teaching literary theory to adolescents*. New York: Teachers College Press; and Urbana, IL: NCTE.

Ausubel, D. P. (1967). Crucial psychological issues in the objectives, organization, and evaluation of curriculum reform movements. *Psychology in the Schools, IV*, 111–120.

Bagley, W. (1921). Dangers and difficulties of the project method and how to overcome them: Projects and purposes in teaching and learning. *Teachers College Record, 22*(4), 288–297.

Barr, R., & Dreeben, R. (1978). Instruction in classrooms. In L. S. Shulman (Ed.), *Review of Research in Education* (Vol. 5). Itasca, Ill: F. E. Peacock.

Bartholomae, D. (1985). Inventing the university when a writer can't write. In M. Rose (Ed.), *When a Writer Can't Write: Studies in Writer's Block and Other Composing Process Problems*. New York, New York: Guilford.

Bartholomae, D., & Petrotsky, A. R. (1986). *Facts, artifacts, and counterfacts: Theory and method for a reading and writing course*. Porstmouth, NH: Boyton/Cook Publishers.

BAWP (1978). *Report of the Bay Area Writing Project*. Berkeley, CA: University of California.

Beberman, M. (1958). *An emerging program of secondary school mathematics*. Cambridge, MA: Harvard University Press.

Becker, W. C., & Carnine, D. (1981). Direct Instruction: A behavior theory model for comprehensive educational intervention with the disadvantaged. In S. W. Bijou & R. Ruiz (Eds.), *Behavior Modification: Contributions to Education* (pp. 145–210). Hillsdale, New Jersey: Lawrence Erlbaum Associates.

Becker, W. C., & Engelmann, S. (1995-1996). Sponsor findings from Project Follow Through. *Effective School Practices, 15*(1, Winter).

Bennett, N. (1976). *Teaching styles and pupil progress*. London: Open Books.

Bennett, R. E. (2001). How the internet will help large scale assessment reinvent itself. *Educational Policy Analysis, 9*(5), 1–26.

Bennett, R. E., Goodman, M., Hessinger, J., Ligget, J., Marshall, G., Kahn, H., & Zack, J. (1999). Using multimedia in large-scale computer-based testing programs. *Computers in Human Behavior, 15*, 283–294.

Bernstein, B. (1990). *The structuring of pedagogic discourse* (Vol. 4). London: Routledge and Kegan Paul.

Bissex, G., & Bullock, R. (1987). *Seeing for ourselves: Case study research by teachers of writing*. Portsmouth, New Hampshire: Heinemann.

Bloom, A. (1987). *The closing of the American mind*. New York: Simon and Schuster.

Bloom, B. S. (1976). *Human characteristics and school learning*. New York: McGraw-Hill.

Bloom, B. S., Engelhart, M. D., Furst, E. J., Hill, W. H., & Krathwohl, D. R. (1956). *Taxonomy of educational objectives: The classification of educational goals*. New York: David McKay.

Bloom, B. S., Hastings, T., & Madaus, G. (1971). Learning for mastery. In B. S. B. et al. (Ed.), *Handbook on Formative and Sumative Evaluation of Student Learning*. New York: McGraw-Hill.

Bock, G., Stebbins, L., & Proper, E. (1977). *Education as experimentation: A planned variation model* (Vol. IV-A&B). Washington, DC: Abt Associates.

Booth, W. (1961). *Rhetoric of fiction*. Chicago: University of Chicago Press.

Boyer, E. L. (1983). *High school: A report on secondary education*. New York: Harper and Row.

Brooks, C., & Warren, R. P. (1951). *Understanding poetry*. New York: Henry Holt and Company.

Brophy, J. (1979). Teacher behavior and Its effects. *Journal of Educational Psychology, 71*, 733-750.

Brophy, J., & Evertson, C. (1974). *The Texas teacher effectiveness project: Presentation of non-linear relationships and discussion.* Austin, Texas: R&D Center for Teacher Education, University of Texas.

Bruner, J. (1960). *The process of education.* Cambridge, MA: Harvard University Press.

Bruner, J. (1970). *Man: A course of study.* Washington, DC: Curriculum Development Associates.

Bruner, J. S. (1971). *The relevance of education.* New York: Norton.

Buchanan, J. (1993). Listening to the voices. In M. Cochran-Smith & S. L. Lytle (Eds.), *Inside outside: Teacher research and knowledge.* New York: Teachers College Press.

Caplan, R. (1982). Showing writing: A training program to help students be specific. In G. Camp (Ed.), *Teaching Writing.* Montclair, New Jersey: Boynton Cook.

Carini, P. (1975). *Observation and description: An alternative methodology for the investigation of human phenomena.* Grand Forks, North Dakota: University of North Dakota Press.

Carini, P. (1979). *The art of seeing and the visibility of the person.* Grand Forks, North Dakota: University of North Dakota.

Carini, P. F. (2001). *Starting strong.* New York: Teachers College Press.

Carroll, J. B. (1963). A model for school learning. *Teachers College Record, 64*(8), 723-733.

Case, R. (1985). *Intellectual development, birth to adulthood.* New York: Academic Press.

Cazden, C. B. (1983). Peekaboo as an instructional model: Discourse development at school and at home. In B. Bain (Ed.), *The Sociogenesis of Language and Human Conduct: A Multi-Disciplinary Book of Readings* (Revision of 1979 article by Cazden ed., pp. 330-358). New York, New York: Plenum.

CDE (1980). *Inservice Packet.* Sacramento, California: California State Department of Education.

Chall, J. S. (1983). *Stages of reading development.* New York: McGraw-Hill.

Cheney, L. V. (1987). *The American memory: A report on the humanities in the nation's public schools.* Washington, DC: National Endowment for the Humanities.

Christensen, F. (1967). *Notes toward a new rhetoric.* New York: Harper and Row.

Cochran-Smith, M., & Lytle, S. (1993). *Inside/outside: Teacher research and knowledge.* New York and London: Teachers College Press, Teachers College, Columbia University.

Cohen, D. K., & Hill, H. (1997, March 1997). *Policy, practice, and performance: Teaching and learning mathematics in California.* Paper presented at the American Educational Research Association Conference, Chicago.

Coleman, J. (1987(b)). Families and schools. *Educational Researcher* (August-September), 32-38.

Coleman, J., & Hoffer, T. (1987a). *Public and private high schools.* New YorK: Basic Books.

Coleman, J. S., Campbell, E. Q., Hobson, C. J., McPartland, C. J., Mood, A. M., Weinfeld, F. D., & York, R. L. (1966). *Equality of educational opportunity.* Washington, DC: U.S. Government Printing Office.

Cone, J. (1990). Untracking advanced placement English: Creating opportunity is not enough, *Research in writing: Working papers of teacher researchers.* Berkeley, California: Bay Area Writing Project, University of California.

Connelly, F. M., & Clandinin, D. J. (1990). Stories of experience and narrative inquiry. *Educational Researcher, 19*(5), 2-14.

Cooper, C. (1981). Forward. In A. N. Applebee (Ed.), *Writing in the secondary schools.* Urbana, Illinois: National Council of Teachers of English.

Cremin, L. A. (1965a). *The genius of American education.* New York: Vintage Books.

Cuban, L. (1984). *How teachers taught: Constancy and change in American classrooms.* New York: Longman.

Cuban, L. (1987). The Holmes group: Why reach exceeds grasp. *Teachers College Record, 88*(Spring, 1987), 348-353.

Daniels, H. (1994). Literature circles: Voice and choice in the student-centered classroom. York, Maine: Stenhouse.

Delain, M., Pearson, P., & Anderson, R. (1985). Reading comprehension and creativity in Black English use: You stand to gain by playing the sounding game. *American Educational Research Journal, 22*(2), 155-173.

Delpit, L. (1995). *Other people's children: Cultural conflict in the classroom.* New York: New Press.

Dinham, S., & Sritter, F. T. (1986). Research on profesional education. In M. C. Wittrock (Ed.), *Handbook of research on teaching.*

Duckworth, E. (1972). The having of wonderful ideas. *Harvard Educational Review, 42*(2), 217-231.

Dunkin, M. J., & Biddle, B. J. (1974). *The study of teaching.* New York: Holt, Rinehart, and Winston.

Durkin, D. (1981). Reading comprehension instruction in five basal reading series. *Reading Research Quarterly, 16*(4), 515-544.

Eggen, P. D., Kauchak, D. P., & Harder, R. J. (1979). *Strategies for teachers.* Englewood, New Jersey: Prentice-Hall.

Epstein, J. (1964). Book review. *New York Review of Books, 3*(December).

Evertson, C., Anderson, L., & Brophy, J. (1978). *Texas junior high school study: Final report of process-outcome relationships.* Austin, Texas: R&D Center for Teacher Education, University of Texas.

Fenstermacher, G. D. (1988). The place of science and epistemology in Schoen's conception of reflective practice. In P. P. Gimmett & G. L. Erikson (Eds.), *Reflection in teacher education* (pp. 39-46). New York: Teachers College Press.

Fenstermacher, G. D. (1994). The knower and the known: The nature of knowledge in research on teaching. In L. D. Hammond (Ed.), *Review of Research in Education* (Vol. 20, pp. 3-56). Washington, DC: AERA.

Ferguson, R. (1991). Paying for public education: New evidence on how and why money matters. *Harvard Journal of Legislation, 28*, 465-498.

Ferguson, R., & Ladd, H. F. (1996). How and why money matters: An analysis of Alabama schools. In H. Ladd (Ed.), *Holding Schools Accountable* (pp. 265-298). Washington, DC: Brookings Institute.

Fisher, C. W., Berliner, D., Filby, N. N., Marliave, R., Cahen, L. S., Dishaw, M. M., & Moore, J. E. (1978). *Beginning teacher evaluation study. Technical Report Series.* San Francisco: Far West Laboratory.

Flanders, N. (1970). *Analyzing teacher behavior.* Reading, MA: Addison-Wesley.

Fountas, I. C., & Pinnell, G. S. (2001). *Guiding readers and writers (grades 3-6): teaching content, genre, and content literacy.* Portsmouth, New Hampshire: Heinemann.

Freedman, S. (1987). *Peer response groups in two ninth-grade classrooms* (Technical Report No. 12). Berkeley, California: Center for the Study of Writing, University of California.

Frye, N. (1957). *Anatomy of criticism: four essays.* Princeton, New Jersey: Princeton University Press.

Gage, N. L. (1963). Paradigms for research on teaching. In N. L. E. Gage (Ed.), *Handbook of research on teaching* (pp. 94-141). Chicaco: Rand McNally.

Gagne, R. M. (1970). *The conditions of learning* (Second ed.). New York: Holt, Rinehard, and Winston.

Gardner, D. (1983). *A nation at risk: The imperative for educational reform*. Washington, DC: U.S. Department of Education.

Good, T. L., & Grouws, D. (1981). *Experimental research in secondary mathematics (Final Report of NIE Grant G-79-0103)*. Columbia, Missouri: Center for the Study of Human Behavior, University of Missouri.

Good, T. L., & Grouws, D. A. (1979). The Missouri mathematics effectiveness project: An experimental study in fourth-grade classrooms. *Journal of Educational Psychology, 71*(3), 355–362.

Goodlad, J. (1984). *A place called school*. New York, New York: McGraw-Hill.

Goodman, K. S., Goodman, Y. M., & Hood, W. J. (Eds.) (1989). *The whole language evaluation book*. Concord, Ontario: Irwin Publishing.

Goodman, K. S., Smith, E. B., Meredith, R., & Goodman, Y. (1987). *Language and thinking in school: A whole language curriculum*. New York: Richard C. Owen.

Goodman, Y. (1978). Kidwatching: An alternative to testing. *The National Elementary Principal* (June), 41–45.

Goswami, D., & Stillman, P. (1987). *Reclaiming the classroom: Teacher research as a agency for change*. Upper Montclair, New Jersey: Boynton/Cook.

Graff, G. (1992). *Beyond the culture wars*. New York: W. W. Norton.

Green, T. F. (1976). Teacher competence as practical rationality. *Educational Theory, 26*, 249–258.

Greenwald, R., Hedges, L. V., & Laine, R. D. (1996). The effect of school resources on student achievement. *Review of Educational Research, 66*, 361–396.

Griffin, P., & Cole, M. (1984). Current activity for the future: The zo-ped. In B. Rogoff & J. Wertsch (Eds.), *Children's learning in the zone of proximal development* (pp. 45–64). San Francisco: Jossey-Bass.

Grossman, P. L. (1990). *The making of a teacher: Teacher knowledge and teacher education*. New York City: Teachers College Press.

Grossman, P. L., & Shulman, L. S. (1994). Knowing, believing, and the teaching of English. In T. Shanahan (Ed.), *Teacher thinking, teachers knowing* (pp. 3–22). Urbana, Illinois: National Council of Teachers of English and the National Conference on Research in English.

Guskey, T. R. (1985). *Implementing mastery learning*. Belmont, California: Wadsworth Pubishing Co.

Hahn, J. (1991). *Teacher research as a catalyst for teacher change*. Paper presented at the Ethnography in Education Forum, Philadelphia.

Hammond, L. D. (1997). *The right to learn*. San Francisco: Jossey-Bass Publishers.

Hammond, L. D. (1998). Teachers and teaching: Testing hypotheses from a national commission report. *Educational Researcher, 27* (1, January–February), 5–15.

Hammond, L. D., & Berry, B. (1988). *The evolution of teacher policy*. Santa Monica, California: Rand Center for the Study of the Teaching Profession.

Hargraves, A., & Dawe, R. (1989). *Coaching as unreflective practice: Contrived collegiality or collaborative culture*. Paper presented at the American Educational Research Annual Convention, San Francisco.

Haycock, K. (1998). Good teaching matters: How well-qualified teachers can close the gap. *Thinking K-16, 3*(Summer 1998), 1–16.

Heath, S. B. (1983). *Ways with words*. Cambridge: Cambridge University Press.

Higuchi, Charlotte (2001). Lesson study: Language arts handbook integrating standards, curricula, and assessment. Vol. 2. Los Angeles, CA: United Teachers of Los Angeles.

Hillocks, G. (1986). *Research on written composition*. Urbana, Ill: National Council of Teachers of English.

Hirsch, E. D., Jr. (1987). *Cultural literacy: What every American needs to know*. Boston: Houghton Mifflin Company.

Holmes Group (1986). *Tomorrow's teachers: A report of the Holmes Group*. East Lansing, Michigan: The Holmes Group, Inc.

House, E., Glass, G., McLean, L., & Walker, D. (1978). No simple answer: Critique of the Follow Through evaluation. *Harvard Educational Review, 48*(2), 128–160.

Hunter, M., & Russell, D. (1981). *Planning for effective instruction: Lesson design in increasing your teaching effectiveness*. Palo Alto, California: The Learning Institute.

Ingersoll, R. M. (1999). The problem of underqualified teachers in American secondary schools. *Educational Researcher, 28*(2), 26–37.

Jackson, P. W. (1968). *Life in Classrooms*. New York, New York: Holt, Rinehart, and Winston.

Joyce, B., & Weil, M. (1972). *Models of Teaching*. Englewood Cliffs, New Jersey: Prentice-Hall.

Judge, H. G. (1982). *American graduate schools of education: A view from abroad (A report to the Ford Foundation)*. New York: The Ford Foundation.

Kanevsky, R. D. (1993). Descriptive review of a child: A way of knowing about teaching and learning. In M. Cochran-Smith & S. L. Lytle (Eds.), *Inside/outside: Teacher research and knowledge*. New York: Teachers College Press.

Kay, A. (2000, October 23-25, 2000). *Keynote*. Paper presented at the New Directions in Student Testing and Technology, APEC 2000 International Conference, UCLA, Los Angeles, California.

Koppich, J. (2000). Enhancing what teachers know and can do. In G. Bloom & J. Goldstein (Eds.), *The peer assistance and review reader* (pp. 19–31). Santa Cruz, California: New Teacher Center, University of California, Santa Cruz.

Kuhn, T. (1977). Second thoughts on paradigms. In F. Suppe (Ed.), *The Structure of Scientific Theories*. Chicago, Ill: University of Chicago Press.

Langer, J. (1995). *Envisioning literature: Literary understanding and literature instruction*. New York: Teachers College Press and Newark, Del: IRA.

Lee, C. (1993). *Signifying as a scaffold for literarey interpretation*. Urbana, Ill: NCTE.

Little, J. W., Gerritz, W. H., Stern, D. S., Gutherie, J. W., Kirst, M. W., & Marsh, D. D. (1987). *Staff development in California: Public and personal Investments, program patterns, and policy choices*. Berkeley and San Francisco, California: Far West Laboratory for Educational Research PACE: Policy Analysis for California Education.

Lynch, J., & Evans, B. (1963). *High school English textbooks: A critical examination*. Boston: Little, Brown, and Company.

Marsh, J. E., & Wilder, E. W. (1954). Identifying the effective instructor: A review of the quantitative studies 1900-52. *Research Bulletin of the U.S.A.F. Personnel Training Research Center, San Antonio, Texas, 13*(No. AFPTRC-TR-54-44).

Mattingly, P. H. (1975). *The classless profession*. New York: New York University Press.

McLaughlin, M., & Marsh, D. (1978). Staff development and school change. *Teachers College Record, 80*(1), 69–94.

McNeil, J. D. (1985). *Curriculum: A comprehensive introduction*. Boston: Little, Brown, and Company.

Mellon, J. (1969). *Transformational sentence combining: A method for enhancing the development of syntactic fluency in English composition*. Urbana, IL: National Council of Teachers of English.

Michaels, S. (1981). Sharing time: Children's narrative styles and differential access to literacy. *Language in Society, 10*, 423–442.

Minnich, E. K. (1990). *Transforming knowledge*. Philadelphia, PA: Temple University Press.

Mitchell, R., & Barth, P. (1999). How teacher licensing tests fall short. *Thinking K-16, The Education Trust, 3*(Spring), 3-24.

Moffett, J. (1966). A structural curriculum in English. *Harvard Educational Review, 36*(Winter), 17-28.

Moffett, J. (1967). *Drama: what is happening*. Urbana, Illinois: National Council of Teachers of English.

Moffett, J. (1968). *Teaching the universe of discourse*. Boston, MA: Houghton.

Moffett, J. (Ed.) (1973). *Interaction: A student-centered language arts and reading program*. Boston: Houghton Mifflin Company.

Mohr, M., & Maclean, M. (1987). *Working together: A guide for teacher researchers*. Urbana, Ill: National Council of Teachers of English.

Myers, M. (1985). *How to do teacher research in the classroom*. Urbana, Ill: National Council of Teachers of English.

Myers, M. (1996). *Changing our minds: Negotiating English and literacy*. Urbana, Ill: National Council of Teachers of English.

Myers, M., & Thomas, S. C. (1982). *The interaction of teacher roles in the teaching of writing in inner city secondary schools* (N.I.E. Contract Number 400-80-0024). Washington, DC: National Institute of Education.

Myers, M. A. (in process). What can computers contribute to the K-12 writing program. In M. D. Shermis & J. Burstein (Eds.), *Automated Essay Scoring: A Cross-disciplinary Perspective*. New York: Erlbaum.

Myers, M., A., & Spain, A. (2001). *Report of the conference chairs on the Asilomar conference on testing and accountability*. Berkeley, California: Curriculum Study Commission of the Central California Council of Teachers of English.

NCTE (1996). *Guidelines for the preparation of teachers of English language arts*. Urbana, Illinois: National Council of Teachers of English.

National Commission on Teaching and America's Future (1996). *What matters most: Teaching and America's future*. New York, New York: Teachers College Press, Columbia University.

Nebraska Curriculum Center (1966). *A curriculum for English language explorations for the elementary grades*. Lincoln, NE: University of Nebraska Press.

Oakes, J. (1985). *Keeping track: How schools structure inequality*. New Haven, CT: Yale University Press.

Orrill, R. (1995). An end to mourning: Liberal education in contemporary America. In R. Orille (Ed.), *The condition of American liberal education* (pp. ix-xx). New York City: College Entrance Examination Board.

Palincsar, A. S., & Brown, A. L. (1984). Reciprocal teaching of comprehension-fostering and monitoring activities. *Cognition and Instruction, 1*, 117-175.

Pennell, J. R., & Firestone, W. A. (1998). Teacher-to-teacher professional development through state-sponsored networks. *Phi Delta Kappan* (January), 354-357.

Peterson, P. (1981). Direct instruction reconsidered. In P. Peterson & H. Walbert (Eds.), *Research on Teaching* (Vol. 79, pp. 57-69). Berkeley: McCutchan Publishing Company.

Petrosky, A. (1994). Producing and assessing knowledge: Beginning to understand teachers' knowledge through the work of four theorists. In T. Shanahan (Ed.), *Teachers thinking, teachers knowing* (pp. 23-38). Urbana, Illinois: National Council of Teachers of English.

Piaget, J., & Inhelder, B. (1969). *The psychology of the child*. New York: Basic Books.

Pinnell, G. S., Bridges, L., & Fountas, I. C. (1999). *Matching books to readers: Using leveled books in guided reading, K-3*. Portsmouth, New Hampshire: Heinemann.

Powell, A. G., Farrar, E., & Cohen, D. K. (1985). *The shopping mall high school*. Boston: Houghton Mifflin Company.

Probst, R. (1992). Five kinds of literary knowing. In J. Langer (Ed.), *Literature Instruction: A Focus on Student Response*. Urbana, Ill: NCTE.

Purves, A. C. (1990). *The scribal society*. New York: Longman.

Purves, A. C. (1991). *The idea of difficulty in literature*. Albany, New York: State University of New York Press.

Rabinowitz, P. J., & Smith, M. W. (1997). *Authorizing readers: resistance and respect in the teaching of literature*. New York: Teachers College Press.

Ravitch, D. (1985). From history to social studies: Delimmas and problems. In D. Ravitch (Ed.), *The Schools We Deserve* (pp. 112-132). New York: Basic Book.

Ravitch, D. (2000). *Left back: A century of failed school reforms*. New York: Simon and Shuster.

Redlich, J. (1914). *The case method in American law schools: A report to the Carnegie Foundation for the Advancement of Teaching*. New York, New York: Updike.

Resnick, L. B. (1987). *Education and learning to think*. Washington, DC: National Academy Press.

Rogoff, B., & Gardner, W. P. (1984). Adult guidance of cognitive development. In B. Rogoff & J. Lave (Eds.), *Everyday Cognition: Its Development in Social Context*. Cambridge, Mass.: Harvard University Press.

Rosenblatt, L. (1996). *Literature as exploration*. New York: Modern Language Association.

Rosenshine, B. (1979). Content, time, and Direct Instruction. In P. Peterson & H. J. Walbert (Eds.), *Research on teaching: Concepts, findings, and implications* (pp. 28-56). Berkeley, California: McCutchan.

Rosenshine, B., & Berliner, D. (1978). Academic engaged time. *British Journal of Teacher Education, 4*, 3-16.

Rosenshine, B., & Meister, C. (1994). Reciprocal teaching: A review of the research. *Review of Educational Research, 64*(4), 479-530.

Rosenshine, B., & Stevens, R. (1986). Teaching functions. In M. Wittrock (Ed.), *Handbook of Research on Teaching* (pp. 376-391). New York, New York: MacMillan Publishing Company.

Rosenshine, B. V. (1979). Content, time, and Direct Instruction. In P. Peterson & H. Walberg (Eds.), *Research on teaching: Concepts, findings, and implications*. Berkeley, California: McCutchen Publishing Corporation.

Sanders, W. I., & Rivers, J. C. (1998). *Cumulative and residual effects of teachers on future students academic achievement*. Knoxville: Value Added Research and Assessment Center, University of Tennesse.

Sarason, S. (1983). *Schooling in America*. New York: Free Press.

Sarason, S. B. (1971). *The culture of the school and the problem of change*. Boston: Allyn and Bacon.

Schaffarzick, J., & Sykes, G. (1978). A changing NIE: New leadership, a new climate. *Educational Leadership, 35*(5) (February 1978), 367-372.

Schon, D. (1987). *Educating the reflective practitioner*. San Francisco: Jossey-Bass.

Schon, D. (1988). Coaching reflective practice. In P. P. Grimmett & G. L. Erickson (Eds.), *Reflection in Teacher Education* (pp. 19-29). New York: Teachers College Press.

Schon, D. A. (1983). *The reflective practitioner: How professionals think in practice*. New York: Basic Books.

Schwab, J. J. (1965). *Biological sciences curriculum study: Biology teachers' handbook*. New York: John Wiley and Sons.

Schwab, J. J. (1983). The practical: Something for curriculum professors to do. *Curriculum Inquiry, 13*(3), 239-265.

Senge, P. (1992). Building learning organizations. *Journal for Quality and Participation, 15*(2), 30-38.

Shulman, J., & Colbert, J. (1987). *The mentor teacher case book.* San Francisco: Far West Laboratory for Educational Research and Development.

Shulman, L. S. (1986a). Paradigms and research programs in the study of teaching: A contemporary perspective. In M. Wittrock (Ed.), *Handbook of Research on Teaching* (pp. 3-36). New York, New York: MacMillan Publishing Company.

Shulman, L. S. (1987). Knowledge and teaching: Foundations of the new reform. *Harvard Educational Review, 57,* 1-220.

Shulman, L. S. (1988). The dangers of dichotomous thinking in education. In P. P. Gimmett & G. L. Erickson (Eds.), *Reflection in teacher education.* New York: Teachers College Press.

Shulman, L. S. (1992). Toward a pedagogy of cases. In J. Shulman (Ed.), *Case Studies in Teacher Education* (pp. 1-29). New York, New York: Teachers College Press.

Simon, H. (1969). *Administrative Behavior* (Second ed.). New York: Macmillan.

Simon, H. (1981). *The Sciences of the Artifical.* Cambridge, MA: MIT Press.

Sims, R. (1982). *Shadow and substance: Afro-American experience in contemporary children's literature.* Urbana, Illinois: National Council of Teachers of English.

Sizer, T. (1984). *Horace's compromise: The dilemma of the American high school.* Boston: Houghton Mifflin.

Slavin, R. E. (1980). Effects of student teams and peer tutoring on academic achievement and time on task. *Journal of Experimental Education, 48,* 252-257.

Smagorinsky, P., & Whiting, M. (1995). *How English teachers get taught.* Urbana, Illinois: National Council of Teachers of English.

Smith, F. (1988). Misleading metaphors in education. In F. Smith (Ed.), *Joining the literacy club* (pp. 93-108). Portsmouth, New Hampshire: Heinemann.

Smith, M. W. (1991). *Understanding unreliable narrators: Reading between the lines in the literature classroom.* Urbana, Ill: NCTE.

Soar, R. S., & Soar, R. M. (1972). An empirical analysis of selected Follow Through programs: An example of a process approach to evaluation. In I. Gordon (Ed.), *Early Childhood Education.* Chicago: National Society for the Study of Education.

Spiro, R. J., Coulson, R. L., Feltovish, P. J., & Anderson, D. K. (1988). *Cognitive flexibility theory: Advanced knowledge acquisition in ill-structured domains* (Technical Report No. 441). Urbana, Illinois: Center for the Study of Reading.

Squire, J. R., & Applebee, R. K. (1968). *High school English instruction today: The national study of high school English programs.* New York: Appleton-Century-Crofts.

Stallings, J. (1980). Allocated academic learning time revisisted or beyond time on task. *Educational Researcher, 8*(11), 11-16.

Stallings, J., Corey, R., Fairweather, J., & Needels, M. (1978). *Early childhood education classroom evaluation.* Menlo Park, California: SRI International.

Stallings, J. A., & Kaskowitz, D. (1974). *Follow Through classroom observation evaluation (1972-1973).* Menlo, Park, California: Stanford Research Institute.

Steinberg, J. (2000, December 28, 2000). Skeptic now sees the virtue in teaching children online: Ex-education chief founds K-12 e-school. *The New York Times,* pp. page A10.

Stenhouse, L. A. (1975). *An introduction to curriculum research and development.* London: Heinemann.

Stenhouse, L. A. (1985). *Research as a basis for teaching.* London: Heinemann.

Stigler, J., & Hiebert, J. (1999). *The teaching gap.* New York: The Free Press.

Stock, P. (1995). *The dialogic curriculum.* Portsmouth, New Hampshire: Heinemann.

Strong, W. (1988). Report inside the New Hampshire Writing Project. *The Quarterly of the National Writing Project and the Center for the Study of Writing, 10*(4).

Sykes, G. (1983). Contradictions, ironies, and promises unfilled: A contemporary account of the status of teaching. *Phi Delta Kappan, 65*(2).

Treisman, P. M. U. (1985). *A study of the mathematics performance of black students at the University of California, Berkeley.* Berkeley, CA: University of California.

Tyack, D., & Cuban, L. (1995). *Tinkering toward utopia.* Cambridge, Massachusetts: Harvard University Press.

United States Department of Commerce (2000). *Falling through the net: Toward digital inclusion.* Washington, DC: Available: www.esa.doc.gov/fttn00.pdf.

Vygotsky, L. S. (1981). *Mind and society: The development of higher psychological processes.* Cambridge, Mass.: Harvard University Press.

Vygotsky, L. S. (1986). *Thought and language.* Boston: MIT Press.

Weiner, L. (1993). *Preparing teachers for urban schools.* New York: Teachers College Press.

Williams, S. M. (1992). Putting case-based instruction into context: Examples from the legal and medical profession. *The Journal of the Learning Sciences, 2*(4), 367-427.

Wise, A. (1979). *Legislated learning.* Berkeley, California: University of California Press.

Wong, H. K., & Wong, R. T. (1998). *The first days of school.* Mountain View, California: Harry K. Wong Publications, Inc.

Wood, D. J., Bruner, J. S., & Ross, G. (1976). The role of tutoring in problem solving. *Journal of Child Psychology and Psychiatry, 17,* 89-100.

Wood, R. (1977). Multiple choice: A state of the art report. *Evaluation in Education, 1,* 191-280.

Zacharias, J. R., & White, S. (1964). The requirements for major curriculum revision. In R. W. Health (Ed.), *New Curricula.* New York: Harper and Row.

# TEACHER EVALUATION

## Sheila Fitzgerald
### Michigan State University

The General Assembly of the state of North Carolina provides nearly 65% of the school budget for the 140 school districts in the state. It expects to have some say about the teachers working in North Carolina Schools—and it does. Along with 47 other states, North Carolina is evaluating the competencies of its teachers.

In 1979, the North Carolina General Assembly enacted a law requiring local boards of education to evaluate the performance of teachers annually following criteria established by the State Board of Education. It identified 28 generic teaching practices applicable across school subjects. Each school year since 1979, all first-year teachers in North Carolina and teachers whose certificates have expired are observed three times, at least once when the visit is unannounced. The observer, usually the principal, then prepares a narrative that becomes the basis for a conference with the teacher. Near the end of the school year when all three observations are completed, the principal rates the teacher numerically on eight subsets of the criteria, and the teacher and the principal formulate a Professional Development Plan to guide the teacher's efforts the following school year. (Holdzkom, 1987)

North Carolina is one of only seven states conducting performance tests of beginning teachers in their classrooms; most states test teachers earlier in their careers. These assessments are designed primarily to protect the public from incompetent and unethical educational practices, but they also attempt to improve teacher performance.

Why has there been a meteoric rise in legislature-mandated teacher evaluations in the last 10 years? What are the forms that preservice and inservice teacher tests take? How are teacher's language arts skills tested, and how are their skills in teaching language arts measured? What impact will tests of teachers have on the goals for language arts teachers? A few answers and many questions arise out of an examination of the current literature on state teacher-assessment efforts.

## DEFINING TERMS

The terms testing, measuring, assessing, and evaluating are often used interchangeably, causing some of the confusion that abounds in the literature on teacher evaluation. Purves (1977) says that testing refers to formal means used to get people to perform so that their behavior can be measured, while measurement properly refers to any attempt to describe human behavior, usually in mathematical rather than verbal terms. He contrasts evaluation with measurement by noting that evaluation is the assignment of worth to human behavior (p. 245). The dictionary defines assessment as judging worth or importance, appearing to make it synonymous with evaluation, yet assessment is often used to refer to testing. In this chapter, testing will refer to the use made of standardized, largely computer-scored instruments. Measurement will refer to the accumulation of data, often from test results. Assessment and evaluation will both be used in describing judgments made about the worth of teachers.

Also, because the terms certification and licensure are often used interchangeably in publications, in this chapter the term certification will refer to both the licensing of teachers by the state and the endorsement of teachers proposed by independent agencies and professional associations. However, due to recent developments in teacher evaluation, some authorities are now making a clear distinction between licensure and certification:

Licensure is a legal process by which individual states set minimum standards for entry into a profession. These standards are designed to ensure that the individual is competent to practice, and, therefore, the standards protect the public . . . Certification is a process which relies on high standards set by members of a profession through their own independent organizations for entry into the profession. Certification is a professional rather than a legal process, and it tends more toward knowledge-based assessments for processional entry (Shive, 1988, p. 2).

In evaluating teachers, however, defining *good teaching* is a more central issue. Some authorities define teaching expertise in ways that seem to defy measurement. Rubin (1985) states:

There is a striking quality to fine classrooms. Students are caught up in the learning; excitement abounds; and playfulness and seriousness blend easily because the purposes are clear, the goals sensible, and an unmistakable feeling of well-being prevails.

Artist teachers achieve these qualities by knowing both their subject matter and their students; by guiding the learning with deft control—a control that itself is born out of perception, intuition, and creative impulse. (p. v)

In contrast, Berliner says:

We have identified a whole host of teacher behaviors and skills that are clearly related to achievement, pacing, structure, monitoring, feedback, certain kinds of questioning behavior. We have research on all sorts of academic climate variables. We know, in other words, what observable teacher characteristics are related to effective teaching. Now we want to go inside teachers' heads and ask them why they do the things they do (Brandt, 1986, p. 9).

In 1974, a committee of the National Conference on Research in English (NCRE) produced a document defining teacher effectiveness in elementary school language arts. Its expressed purpose was "to guide the adaptation and/or creation of instruments for identifying and studying teachers' behaviors," (Robinson & Burrows, 1974, p. 89) and it said, "it could be argued that many behaviors of the mature-person-competent-professional are basic to all teaching, not limited to the language arts, and that particulars of teaching behaviors included in this concept come dangerously close to being personality factors" (p. 70). The committee identified five categories of criteria for excellence in teaching language arts in elementary schools:

*Category I:* Interactions with Pupils Applying Knowledge of Child Development and Individual Differences
Seeks to understand each learner's background—social, cultural, linguistic—in relation to established sequences of child development.
*Category II:* Interactions with Pupils Applying Knowledge of Teaching and Learning
Seeks to unify cognitive and affective learnings through action and reflection.
*Category III:* Interactions with Pupils Showing Awareness of Societal Needs and Values
Acts upon knowledge that communication springs from, is supported by, and contributes to social interaction; utilizes children's language to capitalize on such interaction.
*Category IV:* Interactions with Pupils Showing Maturity as a Person and as a Professional
Sees self as a guide, listener, questioner, reactor, and in general, as facilitator of language.
*Category V:* Interaction with Pupils Demonstrating Knowledge of the Language Arts
Builds language on experience and experience on language; fosters genuine, purposeful, enjoyable communication

among pupils and with others; shows appreciation for pupils' uniqueness and growth in the use of language (pp. 71-75).

The NCRE document demonstrates a commitment to process as central for learning. For the last 20 years, English language arts teaching at both the elementary and secondary levels has focused on process approaches in instruction, on helping students use language for a variety of purposes, on helping them interact with peers and adults in written and oral forms, on helping them respond to their experiences in ways that enlighten themselves and others.

In a 1986 International Reading Association (IRA) publication, *Effective Teaching of Reading: Research and Practice* (Hoffman, 1986) the history of research on elementary and secondary teaching is examined by Rupley, Wise, and Logan. They explain that teacher effectiveness research in the 1980s has taken on new dimensions due to concerns for process:

With the increased interest in cognitive psychology and cognitive information processing, many teacher effectiveness researchers are looking beyond direct instruction, management, and psychological conditions to determine goals, intentions, judgments, decisions, and information processing. Teacher effectiveness researchers have begun to examine the nature of teacher rationales (pp. 31-32).

The National Council of Teachers of English (NCTE) published *Guidelines for the Preparation of Teachers of English Language Arts* in 1986. In defining the roles of elementary and secondary teachers of English language arts, its authors recognized three categories: knowledge, pedagogy, and attitudes. They were careful to delineate *process* focused goals for each category but also recognized *mastery* modes in their use of performance based concepts, and *heritage* models: the "traditions, history, the time-honored values of civilized thought and feeling (including the time-honored resistance to these values) and the skills that make it possible to share in one's culture and to pass it on." (Mandel, 1980, p. 8):

*Knowledge:* Teachers of English language arts need to know the following:

1. That growth in language maturity is a developmental process.
2. How students develop in understanding and using language.
3. How speaking, listening, writing, reading, and thinking are interrelated.
4. How social, cultural, and economic environments influence language learning.
5. The processes and elements involved in the acts of composing in oral and written forms (e.g., considerations of subject, purpose, audience, point-of-view, mode, tone, and style).
6. Major developments in language history.
7. Major grammatical theories of English.
8. How people use language and visual images to influence the thinking and actions of others.
9. How students respond to their reading and how they interpret it.
10. How readers create and discover meaning from print, as well as monitor their comprehension.
11. An extensive body of literature and literary types in English and its translation.

12. Literature as a source for exploring and interpreting human experience—its achievements, frustrations, foibles, values, and conflicts.
13. How nonprint and nonverbal media differ from print and verbal media.
14. How to evaluate, select, and use an array of instructional materials and equipment that can help students perform instructional tasks, as well as understand and respond to what they are studying.
15. Evaluative techniques for describing students' progress in English.
16. The uses and abuses of testing instruments and procedures.
17. Major historical and current research findings in the content of the English curriculum.

*Pedagogy:* Teachers of English language arts must be able to do the following:

1. Select, design, and organize objectives, strategies, and materials for teaching English language arts.
2. Organize students for effective whole-class, small-group, and individual work in English language arts.
3. Use a variety of effective instructional strategies appropriate to diverse cultural groups and individual learning styles.
4. Employ a variety of stimulating instructional strategies that aid students in their development of speaking, listening, reading, and writing abilities.
5. Ask questions at varying levels of abstraction that elicit personal responses, as well as facts and inferences.
6. Respond constructively and promptly to students work.
7. Assess student progress and interpret it to students, parents, and administrators.
8. Help students develop the ability to recognize and use oral and written language appropriate in different social and cultural settings.
9. Guide students in experiencing and improving their processes of speaking, listening, and writing for satisfying their personal, social, and academic needs and intentions.
10. Guide students in developing an appreciation for the history, structure, and dynamic quality of the English language.
11. Guide students in experiencing and improving their processes of reading for personal growth, information, understanding, and enjoyment.
12. Guide students toward enjoyment, aesthetic appreciation, and critical understanding of literary types, styles, themes, and history.
13. Guide students toward enjoyment and critical understanding of nonprint forms.
14. Help students make appropriate use of computers and other emerging technologies to improve their learning and performance.
15. Help students use oral and written language to improve their learning.

*Attitudes:* Teachers of English language arts need to develop the following attitudes:

1. A recognition that all students are worthy of a teachers' sympathetic attention in the English language arts classroom.
2. A desire to use the English language arts curriculum for helping students become familiar with diverse peoples and cultures.
3. A respect for the individual language and dialect of each student.
4. A conviction that teachers help students grow by encouraging creative and responsible uses of language.

5. A willingness to seek a match between students' needs and teachers' objectives, methods, and materials for instruction in English language arts.
6. A willingness to respond critically to all the different media of communication and a willingness to encourage students to respond critically.
7. A commitment to continued professional growth in the teaching of English language arts.
8. A pride in the teaching of English language arts and a willingness to take informed stands on current issues of professional concern.
9. A sensitivity to the impact that events and developments in the world outside the school may have on teachers, their colleagues, their students, and the English language arts curriculum.*

It is evident from NCTE's *Guidelines for the Preparation of Teachers of English Language Arts* and from IRA's *Guidelines for the Specialized Preparation of Reading Professionals* (Professional Standards and Ethics Committee, 1986) that the roles of teachers of English language arts are very complex, that knowledge of language and literature are hardly sufficient for meeting the needs of students, that teaching skills without knowledge are also inadequate. Personality, insight, knowledge, pedagogy, and attitudes of teachers intertwine with those same qualities in students in each language arts classroom.

## HISTORICAL ROOTS OF TEACHER EVALUATION

In the United States, the control of teacher behavior has been the goal of supervision since the 18th century, and it has been accompanied "by a well-entrenced view that schools would be run according to the business management canons of efficiency, effectiveness, inspection, and quality control." (Gitlin & Smyth, 1988, p. 240) Furthermore, early 20th century authorities claimed that using new, scientific perspectives on teaching would allow superintendents to remove teaching from the control of school boards who used teaching positions as patronage. Cubberley, author of the 1922 text *Public School Administration* "saw in testing the opportunity for the supervisor to change school supervision from guesswork to scientific accuracy, and (to) . . . establish . . . standards of work by which he may defend what he is doing" (Gitlin & Symth, 1988, p. 241).

As the number of schools in districts increased, supervision of teachers became the responsibility of the principal, a policy that continues in most school districts today. "Teachers anticipate that annual brief visit from the principal who, according to the stereotype, stands stone-faced at the back of the classroom filling out a form . . . judgments typically rest on assessment of generic teaching skills, which means that the evaluator need not have in-depth knowledge of the subject matter and grade-level pedagogical demands" (Wise & Darling-Hammond, 1985, p. 28, 30). Continuing dissatisfaction with administrators' evaluation of teachers, increasing calls for accountability in schooling, and the growing influence of federal and state governments in education prompted new approaches to controlling teacher behavior.

---

*From Wolfe, D. (1986). *Guidelines for the preparation of teachers of English Language Arts.* Urbana, IL: National Council of Teachers of English. Copyright © 1986 by the National Council of Teachers of English. Reprinted with permission.

The profession of English language arts teachers gained some measure of influence over the direction of teaching in 1988 with *The Basic Issues in the Teaching of English*, a publication resulting from four national conferences designed to reexamine the teaching of English from the elementary grades through graduate school. Influenced in strong measure by this document, the U.S. Office of Education (USOE) funded several Curriculum Study Centers at major research universities under the title Project English and funded conferences, research projects, and demonstration centers. As a result, Shugrue (1968) states, "The exhilaration of the profession late in 1963 can scarcely by overestimated" (p. 37).

Among the influential reports coming out of Project English was *A Study of English Programs in Selected High Schools Which Consistently Educate Outstanding Students in English* (Squire & Appleby, 1966). This case study examination of 158 high schools in 45 states prompted Squire to comment, "if the quality of instruction which we have seen seems sometimes not quite good enough, one has only to imagine what may be characteristic of many practices in unselected high school English programs" (Squire, 1966, p. 614). Another striking example of the influence of Project English was the Illinois Statewide Curriculum Study Center in the Preparation of Secondary English Teachers (ISCPET) directed by J. N. Hook. Although designed as a statewide program involving 20 colleges and universities in Illinois, over 40,000 copies of its report were distributed nationally to assist teacher preparation institutions in measuring the quality of their programs for teacher education in English. The document listed minimal, good, and superior qualifications of teachers in five areas: knowledge of language, knowledge and skill in written composition, literature, oral communication, and the teaching of English (Shugrue, 1968, p. 105–106).

Project English studies were addressing the needs of English teaching for model curricula and teaching units, yet nagging concerns about the quality of teacher preparation and measures of competency prevailed. State departments of education had emerged as powers in education in the 1940s and 1950s when the number of school districts expanded and inefficiency was suspected. In addition, an increasing need for more teachers in the early 1960s prompted state legislatures to authorize state departments of education to set guidelines for teacher preparation and certification. In the middle 1960s, USOE funded the *English Teacher Preparation Study: Guidelines for the Preparation of Teachers of English*, a joint effort of the National Association of State Directors of Teacher Education and Certification (NASDTEC), the Modern Language Association (MLA), and NCTE. The guidelines, "intended to suggest desirable competencies for teachers of English" (Viall, 1967, p. 885) emphasized not only the reading and appreciation of literature that characterized English studies in American colleges and universities but declared that

the preparation of the elementary school teacher and of the secondary school teacher of English must include work in the English language, in composition, and in listening, speaking, reading, and writing, both to extend the teacher's own background and to prepare him to meet the full range of his obligations as a teacher of English (Viall, 1967, p. 886).

Brown vs. Board of Education of Topeka, however, escalated equity issues across the nation. Equity and the implications for American schooling of Russia's Sputnik launching shifted additional aspects of educational governance to the federal level. Yet, it was this federal involvement that was soon responsible for increasing influence of state departments of education. Title V of the Elementary and Secondary Act of 1965 strengthened state departments to ensure that federal mandates would be implemented at the local level. Local control of education had eroded beginning in the 1950s, and when national reports critical of education appeared in the 1980s, catapulting states into renewed action, "cries of infringement on local control [of education] barely slowed the waves of reform and change" (Frazier, 1987, p. 107).

Over the years, principals and parents had quietly judged the abilities of school teachers, but in the late 1980s, the formal assessment of teacher competencies became a central educational issue in state reform packages. The previous decade, the 1970s, had demonstrated that the testing of students and the widespread publication of student test results fueled concerns over quality of schooling, and that the increasing sophistication of technology offered new possibilities for statistical analyses of large bodies of test data.

Standardized, computer-scored tests of students' learning, rising out of Skinnerian stimulus-response psychology and prompted by America's perceived loss of world stature following the Russians' successful launching of Sputnik, promoted science-based instruction as a cure-all for problems in American education, and legitimized numerical representations of education's results. Parents, students, administrators, legislators, and teachers themselves came to rely on test data to tell them about the quality of their school programs.

In the early 1970s, most standardized tests given to students were produced by commercial companies and selected by individual school districts to supplement teachers' evaluations of students' progress. Comparisons of test results among schools and school districts were not made in any formal way. Local school districts maintained control of the content of the curriculum for the most part, and the control of their test results.

The political potential of standardized tests, however, reached national attention with the creation of the National Assessment of Educational Progress (NAEP) in 1967. Designed by the National Commission of the States to obtain statistical evidence about school performance for use in federal policy formation, NAEP evaluated student learning on a yearly rotating cycle using a national matrix sampling of students, ages 9, 13, 17 and young adults ages 26 to 35. Although in later years NAEP expanded to include 10 subject areas, test results in reading, writing, and math continued to receive the most press.

The NAEP student test scores and other computer-scored test results accumulated between the late 1960s and the middle 1980s did little to inspire public confidence in teachers, those perceived by the society to be primarily responsible for the learning of children from age 5 to 17. Inadequacies in teaching—not the limitations of the tests, the testing circumstances, or the backgrounds of the children—were blamed for low test scores. Increasing doubts about competitiveness of United States products in the world market, worries about the potential of workers educated in American schools, and fears about the growing power of teacher unions led Americans to seek reassurances about the education they were financing:

Evaluation is a form of reassurance. When living standards are rising, economic factors stable or expanding, and when there is optimism about national and world circumstances, the public mood is buoyant and confident and educational climate is secure and enterprising. But when forebodings arise about trading conditions, when money gets short and insularity prevails, activities like education which depend for their success on trust and optimism are particularly vulnerable to the climate of doubt and fear (Holt, 1981, p. 26–7).

Individual teachers and school districts, however, could not be held accountable for NAEP scores that only projected national conditions based on a statistical sampling of students. The rise of student testing by individual state departments of education brought accountability closer to home. Starting in the 1960s and accelerated by the Back to the Basics movement of the 1970s, state departments of education began to develop basic skills tests, usually in reading and math, that were similar to the NAEP tests or adaptations of NAEP. By 1980, 37 of the 50 states had basic skills tests for students, and many were committed to testing every pupil, allowing the comparison of school districts, schools, and sometimes individual classrooms.

Up to the mid 1980s, the state tests, as well as most commercial tests, assessed student performance primarily in reading and math; for writing, only the ability to identify errors in usage, punctuation, or spelling were included. As a result, many elementary and secondary teachers neglected to teach composition in favor of writing's more readily testable subskills. The oral skills of listening and speaking, which were not amenable to paper and pencil measures, continued to be neglected in testing and in teaching, even after they were declared basic skills by Title II of the 1978 Elementary and Secondary Education Act.

If many students tested poorly, and if teachers were responsible for the learning of school children, then it seemed to follow that too many of those certified to teach in the nations' schools lacked needed skills. Therefore, authorization to teach granted with a degree from an approved teacher training college or university no longer seemed sufficient proof of competency. Tests of teachers, mandated by state legislatures and controlled by state departments of education, contributed to what some were calling the *evaluating eighties* (Holt, 1981, p. 174).

## TYPES OF STATE MANDATED TESTING OF TEACHERS

### Admission Tests

The testing of applicants for admission to teacher education programs is a common form of teacher testing. Currently, 27 states are testing or planning to test applicants desiring majors in education. A few states have developed their own tests or required the colleges to design admission tests for in-coming education students. Some states require application to achieve a certain minimum percentile or a stated score on such tests

as the Scholastic Aptitude Test, the American College Test, the California Test of Basic Skills, or the Pre-Professional Skills Test.

All state teacher tests include some measures of teacher's language competencies, particularly reading, but usually these measures take the form of multiple choice items. Some states, like Arizona, include essay testing or writing samples as well as multiple choice questions. Only Colorado requires applicants in teacher education to demonstrate oral English competency "by either completing a college level public speaking course with a B minus or better, or by passing an oral English competency assessment conducted by a panel of three judges" (Rudner, 1987, p. 55).

Currently, an average of 72% of applicants to teacher education programs in states requiring admissions tests reach or surpass the minimum passing grade.

### Certification Tests

Certification tests given to the graduates of teacher education programs are the most common form of teacher assessment required by the states. Currently, 44 states have mandated or are in the process of initiating certification test requirements. The National Teacher Examination (NTE), developed originally in 1940 by the American Council on Education and now part of the Educational Testing Service (ETS), was the most used instrument for certification assessment until it was discontinued by ETS in October 1988 (Fiske, 1988). The complete battery of the NTE took $5\frac{1}{2}$ hours to complete and contained 340 multiple choice items and one essay question (Rudner, 1987, p. 33).

General and professional knowledge and communication skills, using a multiple choice formate, are tested in most certification tests. For example, the communications skills measured by NTE included reading, writing, and listening—but not speaking, the language skill teachers seem to use most. The communications content of the NTE included the following:

*Reading:* Understanding the explicit content of a written message; clarifying a written message; judging the nature and merits of a written message.
*Writing:* Grammar and syntax; sentence correction.
*Listening:* Message comprehension; analysis of a message; evaluation of a message; feedback and response.

Under the General Knowledge category of the NTE, literature was tested along with fine arts:

*Literature and Fine Arts:* Recognizing basic elements and works of literature and fine arts; analyzing and interpreting works of literature and art to one another.

States have set different minimum passing scores even on the same tests. For the NTE, scores ranged from 630 to 657; most states took into account the error of measurement by lowering the NTE minimum by an average of eight points. Even with passing scores set relatively low, passing rates for the states that required the NTE reached only 87% (Rudner, 1987, p. 37).

The NTE was strongly criticized over the years. The National Education Association (NEA) charged that it was racially biased. Teachers also argued that "the multiple choice format is gallingly simplistic because it implies that complex classroom management problems have predetermined answers" (Fiske, 1988, p. 6). In deciding to scrap NTE, the Educational Testing Service announced that it would be replaced by 1992 with a "multiple choice test of general knowledge to be taken after the sophomore year in college; a test of pedagogical knowledge using video and other new formats just before certification; and classroom observations once a new teacher is on the job" (Fiske, 1988, p. 6).

## Performance Tests

Seven states currently have internship programs using observation instruments, and 17 additional states are considering using them in the future. Proponents of performance tests claim that classroom observation evaluations help beginning teachers in their first year, as well as determine if they will be eligible for regular certification (Rudner, 1987, p. 39).

Typically, the observation scales in use evaluate the following six phases of instruction:

Daily use of previous work.
Presentation of subject matter with an emphasis on the efficient use of time and materials.
Guided student practice, including (a) frequent questioning to practice learned knowledge and skills and checking for comprehension, (b) cuing to maintain academic focus, and (c) instructing the whole group; feedback and correction, where the teacher either praises superior academic performance or corrects or clarifies incorrect student performance.
Independent practice, either seatwork or homework which is designed to reinforce the content being studied.
Regular review to maintain the currency of the material that has been studied over the year (Rudner, 1987, p. 40).

The evaluation of the beginning teacher or intern is usually conducted during nine classroom visits by the principal, a teacher educator, and the supervisory teacher who is assigned to work with the beginning teacher throughout the school year. Instrument validity and the results of observation assessments are insufficient at this time for judging the effects of this form of teacher testing (Rudner, 1987, p. 42).

## Recertification Tests

Three states currently include a test in their recertification requirements for practicing teachers: Arkansas, Georgia, and Texas. Each uses a custom-made test.

Between 1985 and 1987, 35,000 Arkansas teachers took the Arkansas Educational Skills Assessment Test (AESAT), which measured reading, mathematics, writing and subject matter knowledge. To retain certification, all teachers were required to pass the AESAT by June 1987. Passing rates are not available (Rudner, 1987, p. 52).

The Teacher Certification Test (TCT) was first required of Georgia teachers seeking initial certification after September 1, 1978. In 1986 it was expanded to require the test for all teachers seeking renewal of certificates after July 1, 1986. The 28 criterion-referenced tests that composed the TCT measured subject matter content. Nearly 4,500 teachers were tested in Georgia in 1986, and no one was denied certification renewal that year (Rudner, 1987, p. 65).

The State of Georgia declares two major purposes for its process of teacher certification: First, it claims to provide a formal method whereby an educator may be officially recognized as a professional person. Secondly, through certification, citizens may be assured that their state constitutional guarantee of an adequate educational opportunity for children and youth is being fulfilled in part through the employment of qualified teachers and other professional school personnel.

The Texas Examination for Current Administrators and Teachers (TECAT) was first administered in March 1986 to all persons certified to teach in Texas prior to May 1, 1986. Nearly 250,000 took the test of reading and writing skill that year. For reading, a minimum of 75% was expected on a multiple-choice test of 55 items; for writing, a "clearly acceptable essay" (Rudner, 1987, p. 118). The 150-word essay caused problems for the greatest number of Texas teachers, yet on the first try, 96.7% of the 202,000 teachers who first took the test passed, and 99% had passed after two tries. Shop teachers, special education teachers, and coaches were most likely to be among the failures.

Shepard and Kreitzer (1987) determined that $35.5 million in tax-supported funds were spent to develop, administer, and score TECAT, as well as to assign regular Texas Education Agency staff to the assessment task and provide inservice days so that teachers could take the test. These authors also state:

Politicians had expected the failure rates to be on order of 10,000 *after remediation*, not 1,200. Legislators had wanted to weed out social studies teachers who were deficient in American history and elementary teachers who didn't know the location of Alaska. The TECAT standard was too low to touch these teachers...

At the same time that some incompetent social studies and English teachers surely passed, some teachers with badly needed skills were removed. More than half of those eliminated by TECAT were in vocational studies, special education, P.E. (physical education), kindergarten, health, and counseling. They were also disproportionately minority teachers in districts with high concentrations of minority children (Shepard & Kreitzer, 1987, p. 30).

In summary, all states but Alaska and Iowa currently require some form of teacher assessment. Most are standardized, computer-scored instruments measuring reading, mechanical skills in writing and math, but a few require written essays, and one has a measure of oral language competencies. Subject matter knowledge is tested by some states, but general and professional knowledge is more frequently measured. Preservice candidates and beginning teachers are the targets of most assessments, but veteran teachers have been tested in three states. Because the goals of the state mandated tests are not only to protect society from incompetent teachers but also to improve instruction, seven states currently assess beginning teachers' performance in their classrooms, and seventeen additional states have performance assessments under study.

## EVALUATION OF TEACHERS FOR MERIT PAY AND CAREER LADDER PROMOTIONS

School reform procedures have sometimes taken the form of incentives for teachers to improve their performance so they can earn higher wages or qualify for somewhat different responsibilities. Merit pay plans reward teachers monetarily for doing their jobs in ways judged to be superior by systematic appraisal of their teaching in the classroom or by improvement in their students' test scores. Merit pay is in addition to base pay and increments for years of service and graduate degrees that have been established by collective bargaining. Career ladder promotions differ from merit pay schemes by qualifying teachers who are judged meritorious to participate in supervisory or research responsibilities as part of their assignments. Like merit pay, however, rising on the career ladder probably means an advance in pay as well. Career ladder plans assume that teachers desire advancement opportunities that give them job responsibilities outside of their classrooms in addition to teaching. Merit pay schemes assume that the primary concern of teachers is low pay, and that they would prefer to be paid on the quality of their teaching over and above their position on a specified pay scale. Both types of programs also assume that competition among teachers will motivate those teachers who are disinterested or unchallenged.

In 1983, 200 of 240 teachers in Niskayuna Central School district in Schenectady, New York, received from $1,000 to $2,000 in merit pay based on individual observations conducted by school principals. In this case and in the majority of merit pay programs, classroom performance is used as the basis of evaluation, assessing such matters as lesson preparation, knowledge of subject matter, and relationships with students (Johnson, 1984, pp. 13-14).

Teachers in the Weber School District in Ogden, Utah, qualify for $1,300 in merit pay on the basis of their student test scores. Dallas, Texas, uses a group incentive plan: all teachers in schools achieving "exceptional progress" on student test scores receive bonus pay (Johnson, 1984, p. 13, 15). Yet, school districts using students' competency test scores as evaluations of teachers are being challenged in the courts. The American Federation of Teachers charged the St. Louis Public Schools with violations of constitutional equal protection and due process provisions for requiring at least half of teachers' students to perform at or above the national norm on the California Achievement Test ("Current Developments," 1987).

However, James Popham (1987) argues that measurement-driven instruction is the most cost-effective way of improving the quality of public education:

Whether they are concerned about their own self-esteem or their students' well-being, teachers clearly want students to perform well on such tests. Accordingly, teachers tend to focus a significant portion of their instructional activities on the knowledge and skills assessed by such tests. A high stakes test of educational achievement, then, services

as a powerful "curricular magnet." Those who deny the instructional influence of high-stakes tests have not spent much time in public school classrooms recently (p. 680).

Although she claims that "the money, time, and spirit spent trying to make merit pay work would be better spent elsewhere," Johnson (1984) assumes that merit pay will be adopted by many school districts. There is continuing public pressure for accountability and less opposition to merit pay from teachers and union leaders. Career ladders, on the other hand, require considerable funds to support substantially higher salaries, and they are administratively complex, Johnson says, so they are unlikely to replace merit pay proposals in school reform packages (p. 37).

## RECENT INITIATIVES IN TEACHER EDUCATION

In 1988, *The Personnel Evaluation Standards* was published by the Joint Committee on Standards for Educational Evaluation, an incorporated organization of fourteen associations: American Association of School Administrators, American Association of School Personnel Administrators, American Educational Research Association, American Evaluation Association, American Federation of Teachers, American Psychological Association, Association for Measurement and Evaluation in Counseling and Development, Association for Supervision and Curriculum Development, Education Commission of the States, National Association of Secondary School Principals, National Council on Measurement in Education, National Education Association, and National School Boards Association. Beyond developing standards for teachers and other school personnel, the group also promotes the use of its standards through articles in the newsletters and journals of member associations and presentations at its conventions.

In addition to the assessment procedure ETS plans as a replacement for the National Teacher exam, teacher performance is the subject of another initiative for assessment. The National Board of Professional Teaching Standards (NBPTS), funded by the Carnegie Foundation in 1987 as a result of its report, *A Nation Prepared: Teachers for the 21st Century* (1986), is a joint effort of business leaders, government officials, and teacher union representatives. It was created with a $5 million grant from the foundation's Forum on Education and the Economy "to project an image of the (teaching) profession," said board president James Kelly, "by setting up tough, voluntary certification standards" in any of 20 teaching specialties (1988, p. B:4).

Sykes (1987) notes that this effort is an attempt to change the control of teaching to an agency other than one directed by government, to an association similar to those that govern entrance to the medical and legal professions:

A profession agrees to develop and enforce standards of good practice in exchange for the right to practice free of bureaucratic supervision and external regulation. At the policy level, this contract applies to standards for licensure, certification, and program accreditation. The state delegates substantial responsibility for such standards to the organizations that represent the occupation. At the practice level, this contract applies to the organization and management of work. Collegial norms and peer evaluation direct work that is amenable neither to administrative oversight nor to routinization (p. 19).

Sykes goes on to establish NEA and the American Federation of Teachers (AFT) as the organizations that represent the occupation of teaching:

Now emerges in both teacher organizations a leadership vanguard at national, state, and local levels committed to change. In my opinion, their appearance is the most promising development in education in the last decade. The unadulterated industrial model is losing its hold on the imagination of teacher leaders, and this opens real possibilities for the future. Without a willingness on the part of organized teachers to take risks, to experiment with new forms of agreement and cooperation, there will be no genuine reform. Teacher organizations (NEA and AFT) are the key because they wield two forms of power. They can effectively veto top-down mandates at the implementation stage or, by genuinely supporting change, can help make it happen (p. 20).

Marc Tucker, Carnegie Forum executive director, said that the NBPTS planning group is made up of members, half of whom "are themselves teachers or have been selected by teachers to represent teachers" ("Planning Group," 1987, p. 5). Most board members are NEA and AFT representatives; some also are associated with IRA and NCTE, but these organizations do not have official representation.

NBPTS is seeking federal government support and funding for its program. In February 1989, Senator Christopher Dodd of Connecticut introduced a bill in Congress to grant NBPTS up to $25 million over 3 years for targeting standards in mathematics, foreign languages, English literacy, and the sciences, particularly citing standards for teachers who work with special classifications of students: handicapped, gifted and talented, students with limited English language skills, and economically and educationally deprived.

Certification of teachers on a national level by NBPTS is not intended to replace state licensure, but will certify nationally teachers who exceed certain evaluation standards set by the board, claiming to give those teachers recognition as among the best in their field. Lee Shulman and a team of researchers at Stanford University have set a target date of 1992 for the assessments they are developing for the NBPTS; they envision assessing provisionally certified teachers during a required 1- or 2-year internship to determine their capacities and performance. Several sources of data are apt to be accumulated, only one of which would be a conventional test, before a decision on permanent certification or tenure is made; this is now referred to as portfolio assessment. Shulman argues that generic checklists usually used to evaluate teachers in any discipline, such as those mandated in some state assessment programs, misinterpret current research on effective teaching. The assessments his team are working on will "call upon candidates to demonstrate both an understanding of the content of teaching, and [of the] pedagogy, but probably most important of all, the mutual adaptation of the content and the pedagogy to one another" ("Teacher Assessments," 1988, p. 1). Cost of certification by NBPTS for the individual applicant has yet to be determined.

## THE RESPONSE OF PROFESSIONAL ENGLISH LANGUAGE ARTS TEACHER ORGANIZATIONS TO TEACHER EVALUATION PROGRAMS

Both the IRA and NCTE have been studying the issues of teacher testing in the field of language arts. In 1986, the National Council of Teachers of English established a Taskforce on Teacher Competency Issues (Mertz, 1987). The committee's report expressed concern over efforts to assess and regulate entry and continuance in the profession—and asserted NCTE's authority as "the organization which is best qualified to define competency for English Language Arts teachers" (p. 188):

However well-intentioned many teacher evaluation efforts may be, we believe they could easily backfire. In particular and more strongly, we oppose any teacher assessment/testing/evaluation program that does not conform to guidelines established by NCTE committees for general test use, teacher certification and program accreditation. These guidelines have been spelled out in numerous council publications over the years. Of primary importance are the following considerations:

- The program must not focus on minimums; it must address comprehensively the skills and knowledge central to success in teaching reading, writing, literature, and other English-language related subjects.

- The program must be more than a "test," though a good examination might well be part of it. Candidate data should include observational materials, written work, interviews, and other indicators necessary for making reasonable and fair judgments.

- One dimension of the program must address instructional and individual improvement. Feedback from evaluation must be useful for those evaluated.

- The program must be developed by responsible faculty in each institution, working with teachers who are active in the classroom.

- The program should not be standardized across institutions. Complicated as that may make decisions, it is a necessary safeguard to protect diversity in higher education (Mertz, 1987, p. 182).

Over the years, the Board of Directors of the National Council of Teachers of English has passed several resolutions related to testing of students and assessment of teachers (NCTE, 1987): In 1977:

RESOLVED that NCTE oppose legislatively mandated competency-based testing until such time as it is determined to be socially and educationally beneficial. RESOLVED that NCTE work with legislators and other policy makers to determine how language competence can be best assured; RESOLVED that appropriate NCTE standing committees and commissions examine alternative ways of assuring competence while determining through practice, theory, and research if competency-based education is in the best interest of all members of the educational community. (#77.6)

In 1978:

RESOLVED, that the NCTE Executive Committee or headquarters staff prepare a statement urging that state departments of education, when contemplating changes in requirements for certification, recertification, or licensure for English language arts teachers or for accreditation of English language arts teachers or for accreditation of English language arts teacher education programs, include on the committee as members or advisors a specialist in English Education, a classroom teacher of English language arts, and one or more representatives of National Council of Teachers of English affiliates. (#78.4)

In 1979:

RESOLVED that the National Council of Teachers of English (1) encourage the assignment to the teaching of English only those persons who have been prepared in accordance with the goals and emphases in the "Statement on the Preparation of Teachers of English"; (2) call upon its individual members and affiliate organizations to increase their support of the goals and emphases of the "Statement on the Preparation of Teachers of English"; and (3) urge the National Council of Teachers of English Executive Committee to intensify its efforts in cooperation with other Professional organizations to implement items (1) and (2) of this resolution. (#79.3)

In 1985 the essence of the 1979 resolution on teacher preparation was reaffirmed in a new resolution. (#85.2)

In July 1987, representatives of several professional organizations concerned with the teaching of English met for 3 weeks to address issues affecting language arts instruction, kindergarten through college, into the 21st century: the Modern Language Association (MLA), the Association of Departments of English (ADE), the Conference on English Education (CEE), the Conference of Secondary School Department Chairs (CSSEDC), the College English Association (CEA), the College Language Association (CLA), the Conference on College Composition and Communication (CCCC), and NCTE. In one of their resolutions, "Rights and Responsibilities for Students and Teachers," three statements refer to the rights of teachers in evaluation:

Evaluation [should be conducted] only by persons with current knowledge about the learning and teaching of English;
Evaluation [should be] aimed at improving instruction rather than at judging the person;
[There should be] reciprocal evaluation: teachers evaluate all those who evaluate them (Lloyd-Jones & Lunsford, 1989, p. 48).

A 1988 resolution approved by IRA considered teacher qualifications in relation to emergency certificates sometimes granted to relieve teacher shortages, a practice the organization asserts "jeopardizes effective teaching and learning in the language arts":

Resolved, that all personnel responsible for teaching reading and language arts at both elementary and secondary levels be appropriately prepared, qualified and certificated (i.e., licensed); and that IRA urge local, state and national school board officials, accrediting agencies and teacher education institutions to adhere to the IRA guidelines for preparing appropriately qualified and certificated teachers ("Resolutions Passed," p. 12).

## ISSUES IN THE EVALUATION OF LANGUAGE ARTS TEACHERS

Who should evaluate teachers? Should those who evaluate teachers also be subject to evaluation? Who should make decisions about what constitutes quality language arts teaching? Will teachers and teacher educators limit curricula to what tests measure? Are there more profitable uses for the time, energy, and money that currently goes into evaluating teachers?

Remarkably little is written about the cost of producing the various forms of teacher evaluations now in use, costs that go beyond important monetary considerations to include the intangibles of time and effort that are very costly to school and college programs and to government. Rudner (1987) gives some figures on the money states spend to develop test instruments:

Costs to the state depend upon the tests selected, the complexity of the policy, the system on monitoring and reporting, and the charges to the examinee. The most expensive route is for the state to have a custom-made test developed and then to pay for its administration. Teacher tests cost approximately $50,000–$100,000 to develop and $5,000–$50,000 to validate. A test program consisting of a basic skills test and 25 subject matter tests can cost close to $1,000,000 to develop and over $100 per examinee to administer and score. These costs do not include the costs for a state department of education to manage and evaluate the program.

The least expensive route is to use a ready-made, nationally recognized instrument and have the candidates pay administration costs. A testing program using an off-the-shelf basic skills test and 25 subject matter tests would cost approximately $100,000 to validate. Scoring and administration costs would be the same, approximately $100 per examinee (p. 6).

Setting priorities for the use of education funds will always be in debate. Few will claim that passing a test makes any preservice or inservice teachers better at the art or craft of teaching, although many claim that there are long-term benefits on teacher education programs and on the respect accorded teaching as a profession when teacher evaluation measures are expected. Yet there is ample evidence that current needs in instruction and money, time, and effort are sorely needed to improve teachers' competencies in many areas. In writing, for example, the latest NAEP assessment results indicate that fewer than one third of participating students report their teachers discussing the quality of their ideas with them and helping them rewrite unclear passages, yet these were precisely the skills on which many students failed in the NAEP writing test.

In addition to concern over misplaced money and effort, many fear that tests disqualify teachers who are competent to teach but ill-prepared for the tests. Some individuals whose academic preparation is weak may be screened out of education by certification tests. Approximately 72% of current applicants pass the admissions tests to teacher education programs, and approximately 83% of college graduates pass certification tests in states requiring the exam (Rudner, 1987, p. 6). A high percentage of those who fail, however, are minorities. G. P. Smith estimates that 12.5% of the current national teaching force are minorities, but the percentage may be reduced to 5% or less by 1990 if current passing rates on tests, enrollment declines, and attrition rates for minorities in teaching continue (Rudner, 1987, p. 5).

Chaplin (1986) states that many minority students applying for teacher certification came to college as a result of equal access legislation, during a time of great upheaval in the English profession, yet:

English departments in many institutions are just beginning to adjust curricula to reflect new advancements; others continue to resist. Therefore, the incompetencies that the tests are revealing in minority applicants may more accurately show the failure of the traditional English curriculum to meet the needs of a diverse student population than they indicate that minorities are inherently inferior prospects for teaching careers. Of course, it is also disturbing to realize that teacher competency testing, regardless of the underlying reason, is reducing the number of minority teachers at a time when minority student populations continue to increase. Since the reduction will lead to fewer role models for students, there may be a resurgence of the self-image problems experienced by minority student a decade ago (p. 119).

One could readily claim that the current practice of denying many minorities access to the teaching profession parallels the undemocratic ways used in the early intelligence and achievement tests to limit professional and managerial positions to those born into the middle classes or to those who could easily acquire the middle-class standards of language and speech (Purves, 1977, p. 234).

English language arts teachers are concerned not only about who will teach but also what will be taught in college preparatory classes and school classrooms as teacher evaluation programs have increasing impact on the content of teacher education curricula. Most tests of teachers currently in use, and most observation designs that measure competencies in classrooms, are poor reflections of the precise standards set by English teachers described in documents such as *Guidelines for the Preparation of Teachers of English Language Arts* (Wolfe, 1986). Knowledge of English must be an important consideration in evaluating all teachers, because it is through the English language that teaching and learning in all school subject areas will take place. In addition, the tests that measure teachers' knowledge of English and its pedagogy must be updated frequently as new understandings about language learning and literacy are gleaned from research and practice. Support for these views are coming not just from the organizations directly concerned for the English language arts but from other subject matter organizations. Fortunately, organizations of school administrators also are upholding the importance of teachers' current subject matter knowledge in their publication *Teacher Evaluation: Five Keys to Growth*, a joint effort of the American Association of School Administrators, National Association of Elementary School Principals, National Association of Secondary School Principals, and NEA (Duke & Stiggens, 1986):

Technical knowledge of instruction is one thing; content knowledge is quite another. Content knowledge consists of two elements: knowledge of the subject matter to be taught and knowledge of the district's reflection of that content in the curriculum plan. How much a teacher knows about his or her subject can greatly influence the effect of the evaluation process. Teachers who are teaching a subject for the first time may be much more concerned about what they are teaching than how they are teaching it. The situation may be reversed for teachers with years of experience teaching the same content. Even so, these individuals may need to examine their content knowledge and be open to improving it (p. 20).

This group also identifies six areas of credibility necessary for those who observe and evaluate teaching:

• Knowledge of technical aspects of teaching.
• Knowledge of subject area.
• Years of classroom teaching experience.
• Years of experience in the school and school district.
• Recency of teaching experience.
• Familiarity with the teacher's classroom and students (p. 22).

Classroom observation evaluations are of particular concern for all teachers, including English teachers. Many aspects of classroom life affect instruction, but teachers have little or no control over them: the size and make-up of the classes, the students' home environments, students' attitudes, student absenteeism, and students' jobs outside of school. Teachers wonder if observers will take into account the time of day and year when the observation takes place, and if time will be given to preobservation and postobservation sessions with the teacher. Will they consider the effects on students of having an observer in the classroom? (Schlatter, 1985). English teachers are concerned, also, that observers, most often principals, have documented evidence that they are competent to judge the English teaching they observe at the grade level in which the observation occurs.

English teachers are concerned that all the documentation on teaching in tests and observations may direct evaluators and the teachers themselves from the heart of the matter, that it may make language arts teaching a set of prescriptions. Is mechanical precision in English teaching a desirable goal anyway? Probably not, according to James Moffett (1968):

Untidy and amorphous as it is, "English" seems like a very unattractive candidate for a structural curriculum, which undoubtedly is a main reason for its being the caboose on the train of educational renovation ... Although [the particle approach] pays lip service to the interrelations of elements, it cannot escape its own format. To cash in on current slogans like "sequential development," publishers often arrange these particles in an order of smaller to larger—from the word to the sentence to the paragraph to the whole composition. I do not know what development this corresponds to—certainly not to the functioning of either the language or the student ... Atomizing a subject into analytical categories, inherent only in the subject, necessarily slights the internal processes of the student or language-user, who in any given instance of an authentic discourse is employing all the sub-structures, working in all the categories, at once (p. 3, 5, 13).

Evaluators of English language arts teachers, those who develop formal tests and those who observe in classrooms, need to be well-schooled in the broad field of English language arts and well experienced in classroom teaching. This is rarely the case, but there is evidence that state departments of education are increasing attention to the training of classroom observers, if not to improve their insight into subject matter teaching, at least to coach observers in general instructional methods. Florida, for example, gives principals and supervisors charged with observing teachers a 3-day training session "followed by a criterion test of observation competence, an examination on teacher effectiveness research, a coding quiz, and periodic update sessions. Approximately 700 principals and supervisors and 3,000 teachers have qualified as observers" (Smith, Peterson, & Micceri, 1987, p. 19). Is this the most needed training for principals and supervisors in Florida school districts or might knowledge of subject matter and pedagogy be more productive? Will the additional time spent observing in classrooms and filling in the required forms improve the quality of teaching in their schools?

## LEGAL IMPLICATIONS OF TEACHER TESTING

Of prime concern in a legalistic society is whether teacher competency tests of any kind will continue to stand up under challenge. In concluding his study of legal cases, Hammes (1985) determines that teacher testing is not apt to be challenged in the courts:

- The State has the power and the right to use any means it chooses to fulfill its compelling interest, which in this case is maintaining the quality of education in the state, as long as those means are consistent with the Federal and State Constitution and Federal Law . . .

- The use of a test constructed by teaching peers and validated appropriately has been upheld by the courts, but the case has limited generalization due to the fact that the plaintiffs were probationary teachers who had signed a contract with renewal conditional on their passing the test.

- The State cannot use means that are arbitrary, capricious, or discriminatory. Thus, when a State uses competency testing, it must be rationally related not only to a legal and acceptable state goal, but also to the job, or job-related (business necessity). This will rebut a Title VII challenge of adverse impact.

- If a use of a competency test can be proven to be intentionally discriminatory, its use will not be upheld by the courts.

- To prove a Constitutional violation, it is necessary for the plaintiff to prove that the purpose of a competency test by a board is to discriminate. Title VII disparate impact discrimination charges, however, do not require proof of a discriminatory motive; there does, however, appear to be a trend for the courts to place a heavier burden on the plaintiff to show that the state, in fact, did have discriminatory purpose (pp. 18–19).

Hammes ends by saying:

Thus, it appears that with all of the problems of competency testing for teachers—legal, measurement, and educational—the phenomenon is not only here to stay, but gives all indications of increased use throughout the United States. Under the correct conditions, it has and will pass legal muster (p. 19).

## Summary

*A Nation at Risk* (Gardner, 1983), the report of the National Commission on Excellence in Education, electrified the country when it appeared early in the 1980s. Among its recommendations for teaching were the following:

Persons preparing to teach should be required to meet high educational standards, to demonstrate an aptitude for teaching, and to demonstrate competence in an academic discipline. Colleges and universities offering teacher preparation programs should be judged by how well their graduates meet these criteria;
 School boards, administrators, and teachers should cooperate to develop career ladders for teachers that distinguish among the beginning instructor, the experienced teacher, and the master teacher (pp. 30–31).

In the few years since the publication of *A Nation at Risk*, most states have rushed to put in place some type of teacher evaluation as one response to public pressure for better teaching in the nation's elementary and secondary schools. The 19th Annual Gallup Poll of the Public's Attitudes Toward the Public Schools (Gallup & Clark, 1987) seems to support the need for action to improve schooling: Only 26% of those surveyed rate the nation's schools A or B and 56% grade them C or D, yet 69% give their own child's school an A or B and only 25% rate that school C or D. In addition, American teachers, at least those surveyed in The Metropolitan Life Survey of the American Teacher (1984), seem to give support to measures that evaluate their teaching performance:

90% were willing to have their overall performance evaluated by their administrator;
72% were willing to have their overall performance evaluated by a committee of teachers in their school, chosen by fellow teachers;
70% were willing to have the improvements their students make on standardized tests used to measure them as teachers;
60% were willing to use standardized tests to measure teachers' skills.

Yet, a May 1988 study of teachers by the Carnegie Foundation, "Report Card on School Reform: The Teachers Speak," indicates that 7 to 10 teachers give school reform efforts a "C" or less, and half of the 13,500 public school teachers surveyed feel that teacher morale is down in spite of gains on student test scores. A majority of teachers reported no improvement or a worsening of working conditions, study space for teachers, assigned teaching load, preparation time, class size, freedom from nonteaching duties, teacher awards, and money to support innovative ideas (Mitgang, 1988).

 There is little indication that the professional organizations of English language arts teachers have had much impact on the designs for teacher evaluation so far, yet English teachers use language well, and as Dixon (1985) asserts "democratic power depends crucially on language" (p. 135). Elementary and secondary English language arts teachers need to have a strong voice in the programs that determine quality instruction and quality teaching, and they are capable of exerting that influence.

Holt (1981) substantiates the need for an alliance between teachers and evaluation if instruction and learning are to improve.

Evaluation is an activity which cannot be meaningfully separated from curriculum action, and which is best left to those committing the action and therefore privileged to judge it. Formal evaluation is a needlessly elaborated search for inaccessible truths, and one which substitutes the drab routines of assessment and categorization for creative pleasures of planning, teaching, and learning. If instead we can promote the concept of the teacher as an autonomous professional, accountable to himself as a reasoning person, then curriculum will be a natural expression of the teacher's self understanding (p. 175).

The National Governors' Association may be recognizing some of what Holt suggests. In *Time for Results: The Governors' 1991 Report on Education* ("Governors Propose," 1986) the state leaders call for fewer legislated requirements on school districts, allowing teachers and administrators a greater say in how money and time are spent and how staff and teaching materials are chosen. They state that greater employee involvement will raise morale and increase productivity. The report supports, however, the development of a national board on teaching standards and the governors' plan to reward schools for raising student achievement on mandated tests. "Educationally

bankrupt schools," presumably those whose students do not reach stated minimums on tests, would be taken over by the state and reorganized (p. 1).

In describing the growing power of state legislators, departments of education and governors' offices, Frazier (1987) states, "the educational train has returned from the nation's capitol, and for the foreseeable future the driving force for educational change is going to be the state" (p. 108). He warns:

If this country is to emerge from the present focus on education with a markedly stronger, self-correcting program in each of its elementary and secondary schools, then the first step in each state must be to reestablish the credibility of educators and thereby extend the focus of reform more strenuously to the schools and school district level. Otherwise there will be no real and lasting change (p. 109).

Do current teacher evaluation schemes add to the credibility of language arts educators? There is no evidence that they do. Is it reasonable to use evaluation instruments that make little use of the research and accumulated wisdom of the language arts field? Certainly not. Would language arts teachers support new initiatives in teacher evaluation that are based on what is known about good language arts instruction? Probably they would, although many would despair over massive expenditures for any type of teacher evaluation when there are critical instructional needs that go unattended year after year.

## References

*Basic Issues in the Teaching of English* (1988). New York: Modern Language Association and National Council of Teachers of English.

Brandt, R. (1986). On the expert teacher: A conversation with David Berliner. *Educational Leadership, 44*(2), 4-9.

Carnegie Forum on Education and the Economy (1986). *A Nation Prepared: Teachers for the 21st Century.* Washington, DC: Author.

Certification project to lure top teachers. (1988, April 30). *Lansing (MI) State Journal,* B-4.

Chaplin, M. (1986). The political issues since 1960. In M. Farmer (Ed.). *Consensus and Dissent* (pp. 113-125). Urbana, IL: National Council of Teachers of English.

Current developments in testing: Southern states compare SATs. (1987, January) NCTE *Council-Grams,* 6.

Dixon, J. (1985). Study group 1: Language, politics, and public affairs. In S. Tchudi (Ed.), *Language, schooling, and society* (pp. 135-144). Upper Montclair, NJ: Boynton/Cook.

Duke, D., & Stiggins, R. (1986). *Teacher evaluation: Five keys to growth.* Washington, DC: National Education Association.

Fiske, E. B. (1988, November 2). Lessons: A test for teachers dies as concern about professionalism rises. *New York Times,* pp. 2, 6.

Frazier, C. (1987). The 1980's: States assume educational leadership. *The ecology of school renewal.* Chicago, IL: National Society for the Study of Education.

Gallup, A., & Clark, D. (1987). The 19th annual Gallup poll of the public's attitudes toward the public school. *Phi Delta Kappan, 69*(1), 17-30.

Gardner, D. (1983). *A nation at risk.* Washington, DC: U.S. Department of Education.

Gitlin, A., & Smyth, J. (1988). 'Dominant' view of teacher evaluation and appraisal: An international perspective. *Journal of Education for Teaching, 14,* 237-257.

Governors propose new roles, responsibilities for teachers. (1986, November). NCTE *Council-Grams,* 1.

Hammes, R. R. (1985). Testing the teacher: A legal prospective. *Action in Teacher Education, 7*(3), 13-19.

Hoffman, J. V. (Ed.) (1986). *Effective teaching of reading: Research and practice.* Newark, DE: International Reading Association.

Holdzkom, D. (1987). Appraising teacher performance in North Carolina. *Educational Leadership, 44*(7), 40-44.

Holt, M. (1981). *Evaluating the evaluators.* London: Hodder and Stoughton.

Johnson, S. M. (1984). *Pros and cons of merit pay* (Fastback No. 203). Bloomington, IN: Phi Delta Kappa Educational Foundation.

Joint Committee on Standards for Education Evaluation. (1988). *The Personnel Education Standards.* Beverly Hills, CA: Sage.

Lloyd-Jones, R., & Lunsford, A. (Eds.) (1989). *The English coalition conference; Democracy through language.* Urbana, IL: National Council of Teachers of English.

Mandel, B. J. (Ed.) (1980). *Three language arts curriculum models: Pre-kindergarten through college.* Urbana, IL: National Council of Teachers of English.

Mertz, M. P. (1987). Report of the NCTE task force on teacher competency issues. *English Education, 19,* 181-192.

*Metropolitan Life survey of the American teacher.* (1984). New York: Metropolitan Life Insurance Co.

Mitgang, L. (1988, May 22). Teachers work with spirits low, survey says. *Lansing (MI) State Journal,* p. A:3.

Moffett, James. (1968). *Teaching the universe of discourse*. Boston: Houghton Mifflin.

National Council of Teachers of English. (1987). *Handbook on Public Communication*. Urbana, IL: Author.

Planning group for certification board includes English teachers. (1987, January). NCTE *Council-Grams*, 5.

Popham, W. J. (1987). The merits of measurement-driven instruction. *Phi Delta Kappan, 68,* 679-682.

Professional Standards and Ethics Committee. (1986). *Guidelines for the specialized preparation of reading professionals*. Newark, DE: IRA.

Purves, A. (1977). Evaluating growth in English. In J. R. Squire (Ed.), *The teaching of English* (pp. 230-259). Chicago, IL: National Society for the Study of Education.

Resolutions passed at delegates assembly. (1988, June/July). IRA, *Reading Today, V*(6), 12-13.

Robinson, H. A., & Burrows, A. T. (1974). *Teacher effectiveness in elementary language arts: A progress report*. Urbana, IL: National Conference on Research in English.

Rubin, L. (1985). *Artistry in teaching*. New York: Random House.

Rudner, L. (1987). *What's happening in teacher testing*. Washington, DC: U.S. Department of Education.

Schlatter, F. (1985, March). Questions about merit pay and teacher evaluation that proponents must answer. NCTE *Slate*, 1.

Shepard, L. A., & Kreitzer, A. E. (1987). The Texas teacher test. *Educational Researcher, 16*(6), 22-31.

Shive, J. J. (1988). Professional practices boards for teachers. *Journal of Teacher Education, 39*(6), 1-7.

Shugrue, M. F. (1968). *English in a decade of change*. New York: Western.

Smith, B. O., Peterson, D., & Micceri, T. (1987). Evaluation and professional improvement aspects of the Florida performance measurement system. *Educational Leadership, 44*(7), 16-19.

Squire, J. R., & Applebee, R. K. (1966). *A study of English programs in selected high schools which consistently educate outstanding students in English*. Urbana, IL: University of Illinois.

Sykes, G. (1987). Reckoning with the spectre. *Educational Researcher, 16*(6), 19-21.

Teacher assessments too simplistic, Shulman contends. (1988, May). ASCD *Update*, 1.

Viall, W. P. (1967). English teacher preparation study. *English Journal, 56,* 884-895.

Wise, A. E., & Darling-Hammond, L. (1985). Teacher evaluation and teacher professionalism. *Educational Leadership, 42*(4), 28-35.

Wolfe, D. (1986). *Guidelines for the preparation of teachers of English language arts*. Urbana, IL: National Council of Teachers of English.

# ·35·

# PURSUING DIVERSITY

## Jerome C. Harste
### Indiana University

## Robert F. Carey
### Rhode Island College

For our parents, those lucky enough to finish high school, a good education was a knowledge of the classics, a course in Latin, or at least Latin derivatives, the ability to spin a good phrase in clear, grammatically correct English (with the cost of giving up one's mother tongue thought to be necessary), and the ability to give a good, clear, persuasive public speech. Citizenship was seen as a convoluted version of the Protestant Ethic: "Work 6 full days, play hard on Saturday night, but go to church on Sunday." Technologically, our parents had the same basic writing equipment as did Socrates and Confucius.

By the time I and the other author of this paper went to school the world had gone through two world wars. Our homes and schools had hot and cold running water, electricity, central heating, radios, and movies. While we were in school we saw the smoky tail of the first jet airplane fly overhead and heard the first sonic boom of that plane breaking the sound barrier. By the time we entered sixth grade our parents had purchased their first television set. The year before we graduated from high school Sputnik first orbited the earth and, because of the Conant Report (1958), seniors identified by school officials as "academically talented" had to forgo their free periods and study halls to take advanced courses in physics, mathematics, and English.

In school we read the classics and studied Cliff Notes to make sure we understood the official meaning, but got away with not taking Latin. We still were expected to spin a clever phrase, but neither of us remember having to have a course in public speaking. Citizenship was equated with patriotism and xenophobia, a deep fear of others, particularly communists. The Protestant Ethic was still alive and well, though we did start "dropping out," "dropping acid," and "dropping our drawers" more blatantly than did previous generations. We still think our best legacy is our liberalization of the dress code.

By the time our children started school, microcomputers were a part of daily life. The majority of the children in our country were spending more time watching television than attending school or reading. The classics were no longer part of schooling. Children were expected to be able to fill in the blanks in worksheets and multiple choice tests, and multinational corporations had become more significant political and economic entities than many nations on the earth. Women demanded equality, African Americans gained an identity through "Black Power," and the gay, lesbian, and bisexual community were shouting "We're queer. We're here. Get used to it!!"

It is safe to say that no one can predict what kind of world our grandchildren will find upon graduation. In three generations the world experienced greater change than at any other time in history. The cultural and technological gulf between Socrates and our parents is much less than the gulf between the world our parents knew and the world our grandchildren will enter.

As we watch this gulf continue to widen, we rightfully need to be concerned. What is an appropriate education for our children? How can we prepare them for an unknown world? What are the possibilities?

In the 5 decades since World War II we have tried to make adjustments to curriculum by adding things here and dropping things there. Our personal assessment is that mostly we have been "tinkering." Further, we have been doing more adding than subtracting. The result is that we have lost a philosophical sense of curriculum.

We define curriculum as a metaphor for the lives we want to live and the people we want to be (Harste, 1990). Carolyn Burke notes that curriculum exists "to give us perspective" (as cited in Short & Burke, 1991). Eisner (1982) says curriculum should be thought of as a program of "activities and opportunities" based on selected perception (p. 61).

Building from the papers in this volume, we explore a number of movements and theoretical perspectives that call for a re-thinking of curriculum. We review the work of several scholars to support our claim that together these perspectives provide a much needed conceptual frame on which we prepare for the future. The analysis we offer suggests a series of needed changes, imposing challenges, and possible choices that could redefine our profession and the roles we play in education in the new millennium.

## CURRICULUM AS DIVERSITY

Let's suppose for a moment that our countries were really democratic and that teachers of the language arts really cared that this were so. One of the first changes that would have to be made is that our conformity and consensus model of education would have to be thrown out and replaced with a new model that advocates and appreciates diversity and difference. Conformity and consensus are about standards, standardized testing, common knowledge, and common objectives. Diversity and difference are about culture and community, uncommon knowledge, culturally responsive schools and multiple literacies. We hope that by unpacking the phrase "multiple literacies" we will explicate several key notions that undergird a model of difference.

The notion of multiple literacies is not a metaphor. It represents the strength of a curriculum that celebrates diversity in all its forms. We argue that it provides a framework from which we can grow and within which we can celebrate differences that make a difference. It also positions us as inquirers, learners who acknowledge that they still have lots to learn about the cultures and communities in which we teach.

Gloria Ladson-Billings (1999) says we don't know the first thing about building an educational system based on diversity. While we think this is somewhat of an overstatement and we sort of agree, we believe some progress has been made on some fronts. We'll share some specific instances of what we see as progress later on.

For the moment, we wish to argue that if we are to make the kind of educational progress we envision we need to make, it is going to have to begin in the language arts classroom. Where better place to begin!?! We language teachers, after all, understand the importance of voice. Further, we know how to use literature to support critical conversations about social justice (see, for example, Harste et al., 2000), how to use reading and writing as tools for thinking, and how to support children interrogate text—politically and ideologically—for purposes of developing an awareness of how texts are and can be used to position people and ideas (see, for example Comber, 1997; Edelsky, 1994). We could even help children understand that they haven't really finished reading until they have taken some form of social action by mentally and physically repositioning themselves in the world. It is not enough, for example, to read about women's rights. You have to act and talk differently too.

We see multiple literacies as a composite of three elements: multiple discourses, multiple sign systems, and multiple realities. Let us consider each of these in turn and discuss their implications for learning and curriculum in the schools of tomorrow.

## MULTIPLE DISCOURSES

We started this paper with a recent history of what literacy has meant to the four generations of European Americans who are currently alive on this planet. For most of the 19th century, literacy was defined as the ability to read and write. The crucible was the ability to sign one's name.

For most of our history literacy has been seen as a monolithic skill, one which first is acquired and then applied. Literacy was seen as a tool—let's envision it as a pen knife—one carried in one's back pocket: When the need arose, you simply brought out the tool, applied it to the problem at hand, and returned it to the pocket. In elementary school, it was thought, one learned to read; in secondary school, one reads to learn.

Lately, of course, we've come to realize that literacy has more in common with a bulky and expensive Swiss army knife than it does with the simple pen knife of earlier times. We purposefully use the analogy of literacy and knives. Literacy cuts. It cuts people in. It cuts people out. It positions us by reflecting dominant values that are taken as "givens" in our societies.

Let's consider how conventional views of literacy are still reflected in educational practice:

- For the most part, reading and writing are still considered subjects that need their own time slots during the school day.
- As subjects, reading and writing are still mainly seen as the responsibility of elementary school teachers.
- For the most part, it is still believed that students entering secondary school should already be able to read and write.

The goal of teachers at these levels is to ensure that students apply these skills in their classes.

Embedded in these conventional statements of wisdom is the belief that literacy, once acquired, can be universally applied to all subject areas and disciplines.

The last 25 years of inquiry in education have demonstrated quite convincingly that such assumptions and beliefs are no longer valid. Language theorists such as Gee (1996, 1997) and Street (1995) have helped us understand that language is never neutral, but rather reflects particular ways of thinking, acting, interacting, and knowing. Gee describes discourse as "an identity kit" that comes complete with the appropriate costume and instructions on how to act and talk so as to take on a particular role that others will recognize (p. 21). Street sees "literacy practices as culturally constructed," leaving behind models in our minds of how to behave (p. 133).

As an extension of this notion, Gee and Street would argue that if you want to think, act, talk, identify, and solve problems like a scientist or mathematician or a computer analyst, then you need to have internalized the forms of language that such groups use in order to participate in the activities that go with these affiliations. The same is true for out-of-school contexts. When we return to our childhood homes, for example, we participate in the local cultures rather than the culture of "professorhood." One could get seriously hurt if one didn't.

"Common sense," says Mary Douglas, "is cultural sense" (as cited in Hertsfelt, 1990a). "Culture," Hertsfelt says (1990b), "is when you sound like your mother and you never meant to."

Ludwig Fleck (1935) sees various groups as forming "thought collectives," each with its own terms and particular ways of thinking with those terms. To be literate in terms of these groups (scientists, educators, circus performers, Nova Scotia fishermen, Minnesota farmers), one must be inducted into the thought collective.

We can extend this logic to the subjects we teach in school. Each discipline builds on and utilizes a discourse that identifies it and marks it off as a special domain of knowledge and expertise. If one wants to "do science," or "do math," or "do art," then one must internalize the patterns of discourse that enable one to think, learn, know, behave, and act like a scientist, mathematician, or artist. It enables what Eisner calls the "utility of antecedent knowledge" (1989, p. 64).

When taken to practice, these ideas call for new ways of doing school. Lipka (as cited in Lipka & McCarty, 1994) tells how Alaskan educators are videotaping summer indigenous fishing activities, studying these tapes with community elders and mathematicians to identify what mathematical concepts are employed, and beginning instruction for Yup'ik children from that base.

Such thinking and such practices represent a quantum change in the meaning of the terms "literacy" and "literacy instruction." Instead of one literacy, there are multiple literacies tempered by knowledge domains and contexts of use. While it may be helpful to think in terms of "scientific literacy," "mathematical literacy," "musical literacy," "computer literacy," and "visual literacy," we need to be mindful that these categories are still glosses that need the specifics of context to constitute culturally responsive practice.

Cambourne (1998) warns us that it is also critical that we do not debase these ways of thinking about literacy by confusing them with "skills." Computer literacy must mean more than the limited "skills" one needs to work with a computer. Scientific literacy means more than a nodding familiarity with the jargon of test tubes, or even a passing familiarity with empiricism. Mathematical literacy clearly has more to do with exploring patterns than the ability to perform rudimentary computations. Bishop (1988) sees mathematics as "the search for unsuspected harmonies" (p. 103).

What are the implications of this thoughtful shift from "literacy" to authentic "multiple literacies?" There are many:

- Community members and subject matter specialists need to join hands in an effort successfully to induct children into the discourse of schooling.
- Primary school teachers cannot be expected to produce accomplished students who have acquired the multiple literacies necessary for success in secondary schools.
- English faculty should not be expected to sharpen and refine discourse in a discipline if students have not had authentic opportunity to learn that discourse through use.

- Only a real student of discourse or a practicing discourse user can recognize neophyte forms and support their development in others.

## MULTIPLE SIGN SYSTEMS

The study of sign systems is called semiotics. Semioticians arise in virtually every field of endeavor: philosophers, linguists, anthropologists, educators, literary critics—all can lay claim to the study of how signs come to mean what they do. When applied to the study of literacy, semiotics brings insights on a regular basis.

Among the earliest generalizations derived from the semiotic study of sign systems was the notion that various cultures induct their children into literacy quite differently. What is literacy to us may not be literacy for the parents of the children we teach.

Various cultures have various ways of knowing and as such various ways of thinking and making sense of the world. This insight has led cultural anthropologists, sociologists, psychologists, and educators to investigate the manner in which boys and girls, as well as various racial and ethnic groups—not to mention genders—position themselves with regard to literacy.

Another popular outgrowth of this position has been the theory of multiple intelligences. Gardner (1993) argues that different cultures have different ways of knowing. He initially posited seven intelligences based on his study of cultures and of children and adults who had various brain dysfunctions.

Gardner's intelligences include verbal intelligence, logico-mathematical intelligence, bodily-kinesthetic intelligence, visual-spatial intelligence, musical-rhythmic intelligence, interpersonal intelligence, and intrapersonal intelligence. Lately, Gardner has posited a naturalistic intelligence characterized by an extreme interest in and sensitivity to the natural environment and ritualistic intelligence characterized by a deep understanding of connectedness and community that comes from participation in rituals.

These intelligences are interesting, perhaps more so to many of us who noticed their correlation with the "core arts" much praised in ancient China: writing, arithmetic, horsemanship, archery, and the rites and ceremonies of public and private life. Gardner says that the lack of interpersonal and intrapersonal intelligence is the reason why so many children commit suicide, react with fists and guns rather than reason, and in other ways demonstrate self-destructive and antisocial behavior. He thinks schools should help children learn to read their internal mental states and know how to position themselves with regard to those states in more positive ways.

Gardner argues that while members of each culture have all of these intelligences, each culture puts a different emphasis on some over others. European culture, for example, puts a great deal of emphasis on verbal and logico-mathematical intelligence. Alaskan educators see indigenous cultures as putting less emphasis on verbal intelligence and more on naturalistic intelligence. At the Center for Inquiry in Indiana we are exploring how the use of rituals might strengthen interpersonal and intrapersonal intelligence.

Parallel to this work has been research in literacy. Semioticians—those who study how individuals and groups signify and interpret meaning—have suggested that any instance of language always involves more than just language (Halliday, 1975; Harste, Woodward, & Burke, 1984; Johns Steiner, 1981). Predictable picture books, a topic about which we know something, for example, involve visual as well as verbal literacy. Some even involve aspects of musical literacy in their reliance on rhyme and cadence. As another example, computer literacy seems both verbal and logico-mathematical, not to mention spatial and interpersonal. Flexibility in the use of sign systems to create texts that work successfully in a specific context is clearly one aspect of what it means to "be literate" in the millennium.

Semioticians argue that literacy is an ability to create a multimodal text that is successful (that is communicative in its fullest sense) in a given context using all the ways we have at our disposal to mean. Language alone doesn't make one a successful communicator. In order to be successful, a children's author must use art, language, and a sense of music to create a successful text. It is also nice if the author has something to say or the ability to make the familiar strange. Writing, like other expressions of literacy, begins with inquiry and observation. Similarly, scientists need to know when to use a physical model, a sketch, or an analogy to communicate their ideas. It is also nice if they know to make the print on their overheads large enough for people in the audience to see.

Literacy, then, from a semiotic point of view, is the ability to use a variety of sign systems in appropriate contexts to mean. The multimodal nature of literacy and the notion of multiple intelligences offer a variety of ways to approach literacy instruction. We can employ the notion of multiple intelligences in curriculum planning, for example, to give greater access to education to more children.

Students can begin to value other peoples' differences and begin to gain proficiency in areas in which they are less comfortable. Learning theory would suggest that working in sign systems that are less comfortable for us is at least as important, in a developmental sense, as working in those areas in which we are more comfortable. At the very least, such experiences develop empathy within us for those who are decidedly not verbal, not mathematical, not technological. The goal, as we see it, is not to hone talent so much as it is to expand the communication potential of everyone.

## MULTIPLE REALITIES

Viewing language as discourse explains a great deal. Luke and Freebody (1997), for example, say that all discourses are ideological—another way of saying that embedded within each discourse is a particular belief structure and way of viewing the world.

They argue that language is best seen as social practice. Historically, they say reading has been seen as decoding and the function of reading instruction was the development of the child's ability to break the code. During the 1970s and '80s, psycholinguists and schema-theorists emphasized reader–text interactions and drew attention to "text-meaning practices," or, more specifically, the development of a reader who understands how to use the textual and personal resources at hand to coproduce a meaningful reading.

In the late 1980s and early '90s, sociolinguistic and sociosemiotic theorists focused our attention on language in use. During this period, reading was viewed in terms of what it did, or could accomplish pragmatically in the real world. More recently, Luke and Freebody (in press) have suggested that reading should be seen as a non-neutral form of cultural practice, one that positions readers and obliterates as much as it illuminates. Readers for the 21st century, they argue, need to be able to interrogate the assumptions that are embedded in text as well as the assumptions that they, as culturally indoctrinated beings, bring to the text. Questions such as "Whose story is this?" "Who benefits?" and "What voices are not being heard?" invite children to interrogate the systems of meaning that operate both consciously and unconsciously in text as well as in society.

In some ways, of course, history is repeating itself. Researchers with limited vision and institutional backing, such as those affiliated with the National Institute for Child Health and Human Development, are attempting to bring back a new version of "decoding" as reading (see Goodman, 1999, for a critique and a look at who is behind this movement). All this as we stand as literate beings on the edge of a new millennium in which it will behoove us not only to know how to decode and make meaning, but also to understand how language works and to what ends, so that we can better position ourselves in light of the kind of world we wish to create and the kind of people we wish to become.

## UNDERSTANDING THE SIGNIFICANCE OF MULTIPLE DISCOURSES, SIGN SYSTEMS, AND REALITIES

The complementary notions of multiple discourses, multiple sign systems, and multiple realities represent a quantum leap in our understanding of language. When language was seen as meaning making, we spent our time making personal connections and accepting alternate interpretations. Often we treated these interpretations as innocent, inevitable, and logical.

To see language as discourse is to see "texts" as representing particular ways of thinking and knowing and readers as capable of becoming consciously aware of how they are positioned by literacy. When literacy is reconceived in terms of discourse, literacy instruction must actively involve students in interrogating how they have been self-implicated in the thesis of the author by the meaning-making process in which they have engaged and in taking personal and social responsibility for the interpretations they make. While such a stance raises instructional stakes, it also creates tension that propels learning and makes engagement in literacy events an emotionally charged problem situation of personal and communal importance.

This architectonic change in our view of learning has been vastly aided by breakthroughs in cognitive science. Recent advances in brain research using tools like magnetic resonance imaging (MRI) are providing us with new information unprecedented in its scope. Symeonides (1999) writes:

Biologically, our brains weigh about 1 kg, are the size of a cantaloupe and are roughly the texture of a ripe avocado. After the age of five there is no new growth and the average brain contains 100 billion neurons at that point. The brain is basically a web of neurons and we do not produce new neuron cells, the brain "grows" smarter by making connections between neurons. Neurons makes these connections by growing dendrites. Dendrites are formed when the brain is actively engaged.

We also know that the brain has evolved to accommodate rapid thinking and to react to dramatic changes in its environment, like predatory danger. In fact, it is indifferent to situations that do not involve immediate survival. Our brain has evolved and survived over the ages because it is so adept at adaptation. The brain views each problem and adapts its understanding to accommodate challenges. The brain thrives on novelty and seeks to find patterns and multiple solutions. Such an organ, then, is well equipped to deal with sudden emotionally charged problem situations, but is uninspired when dealing with rote, sustained attention activities. (p. 3)

Still quoting Symeonides:

Another brain factor that has implications for the classroom is emotion. It has become increasingly apparent that emotion has a far greater role in our lives than we often care to admit. It is emotion that prompts attention, which is necessary for learning to take place and impacts on memory and behavior. By loading our educational practices in favor of mastery of skills and content and by ignoring the emotional aspect, our schools have become recipes of misbehavior (p. 3).

In all our enthusiasm for cognitive science, though, one caution: mind is not brain. No amount of research into the biological or physiological bases for social and intellectual behavior is likely to replace careful, sustained observation and inquiry into the actual processes that occur in situated instances of teaching and learning.

## IMPLICATIONS FOR TEACHING

How, then, do we teach? What are our roles and responsibilities as teachers in light of these new frameworks? How can multiple discourses, multiple sign systems, and multiple realities inform what we do in this millennium?

Consider these translations of principle into authentic school reform in venues as apparently unrelated as Indianapolis, Indiana; Providence, Rhode Island; Tucson, Arizona; and Juneau, Alaska. These are just some of the ways that we and other educators are seeking reform in our classrooms and in our instruction:

• Instead of falling prey to a "banking theory of education" in which knowledge is transmitted from the knowing adult to the unknowing child, we attempt to create multiple opportunities for our students to be exposed to and to use the language of various knowledge domains in authentic and realistic ways. In selected classrooms in Arizona and in all of the classrooms at The Center for Inquiry in Indianapolis—a public school we created to see if curriculum could be organized around the personal

and social inquiry questions of learners rather than around the disciplines—we do this through focused studies. Focused studies begin by immersing students in the language of the study through readings, videotapes, guest lectures, and hands-on activities. In preparing for focused studies we think in terms of the conversations, both those raging in the field and in which we want children to engage. The result is that students are positioned at the forefront of the debate (Applebee, 1996). As students become ready, they are invited to find topics of interest to them, which they pursue using the inquiry cycle as their guide.

• In each class session we make time for students to be immersed in talk, reading, writing, and demonstration. The process of writing is highlighted as a tool for thinking rather than as a process of publication (Harste, Short, & Burke, 1988; Short, Harste, & Burke, 1996). We believe, after Vygotsky (1978), that the social becomes the psychological; that is, what students can do first with others orally they later internalize and can do mentally with themselves. It is important that students see teachers who are absorbed in the problems and questions of curriculum. We want teachers who are conducting their own focused studies at the side of the students they teach. (This is, by the way, a good way to get teachers to eliminate from curriculum things they think others think they should teach but which they don't really care about and hence teach rather badly in the first place.) Students who see teachers absorbed in curriculum become absorbed as well. Theodore Roethke, the poet, once said, "A teacher is one who carries on his [sic] education in public." By placing the focus of our curricula on learning, we have merged the teacher, the students, and the guest experts—be they community elders or academicians—into a collaborative learning team. For this collaboration to work effectively, the teachers must be able to demonstrate collectively through talk and action how people interested in this topic think and act. Everyone becomes both a teacher and a learner engaged in the joint tasks of observation, experimentation, analysis, reflection, and action. Like all good learning, the essence of inquiry, Scollon and Scollon (1986) say, "consists of listening much and speaking little, of observing much but manipulating little, of remaining open to new information and avoiding premature conclusions" (p. 93). Collaboration and inquiry-based instruction are not only the best means of teaching and learning, they are also the best ways to evaluate student learning and education more generally.

• Instead of desks arranged in rows facing the front of the room, we arrange the furniture so as to encourage students to interact with each other. We do not assign seats, but rather have tables numbered so that we can make sure all students interact with the diversity that our classrooms offer in terms of ways of knowing and thinking. Further, we have found having unclaimed space allows students to form work groups on a need-to basis. Schools have always "othered" some groups of students. This is why we have cliques of African American students all sitting together in the lunch room while would-be-Yuppies "hang" together in another part of the same room, and "nerds" in still another part. The Colorado school shootings, teenage suicides, and the startling jump in the number of children in foster homes demand we do better. While we don't have the answer, we believe there is no better place than the

English language arts classroom for creating space for these much needed critical conversations.

• This does not mean that we do not ever do more conventional paper and pencil activities. But, instead of students working independently from textbooks and worksheets, we encourage students to work collaboratively in completing charts that summarize, recap, explain, extend, as well as transform the meanings, concepts, and connections they have made. Ideally this work is publically displayed so that it can be revisited, re-read, and re-discussed frequently. Importantly, we focus as much on tension—surprises, oddities, anomalies, differences—as we do on patterns and connections. The mind we know naturally gravitates to the new (Bateson, 1972, 1979). I must confess we also teach to the test; i.e., when skills are encountered that we know are on the test, we teach them directly and try to use the natural context in which they came up as justification. Teachers simply feel too vulnerable given the focus on raising test scores in our district not to be mindful of this constraint. By the way, last year, children at The Center for Inquiry in Indianapolis performed 40 points higher than other children in the district matched on race, IQ, and socioeconomic status. In all too many modern day contexts, Susan Ohanian (1999) reminds us that literacy is still defined in terms of "the schwa." We need to fight such nonsense proposed by what Ohanian dubs "standardistos," while facing the political realities of our times. Ohanian charges that some school districts have co-mingled "the schwa" and Shakespeare. The new battle cry in these districts is: "The schwa. The schwa. My kingdom for the schwa" (p. 35).

• In addition to flooding our classrooms with books and writing materials, we have art and musical instruments readily available. Students are encouraged to create multimodal texts as well as re-represent what they make of reading in art, music, or drama. Asking students to take what they made of something into an alternate form often re-opens discussions and captures aspects of meaning not attended to earlier. Further, the arts seem to encourage attention to the emotional aspects of learning. Porter (1999) recently finished her dissertation studying Sam, a Mexican American student who did poorly in English but brilliantly in art. Her inquiry transformed her notions of learning and of teaching. Multicultural literature is being used to support critical conversation in monocultural and bicultural classrooms. After using several titles of children's books that support critical conversations about literacy—pulled together by NCTE (Mitchell-Pierce, 2000)—Lee Hamilton, a second-grade teacher in a high SES school in Bloomington, Indiana, reported, "I can tell you one thing about these books. You can hear a pin drop as you are reading them" (Leland, Harste, Oceipka, Lewison, & Vasquez, 1999).

• Instead of rushing out the door at the end of the day, students are encouraged to spend the last 5 minutes reflecting on their learning by writing at least one observation, one surprise, one connection, and one question in a personal learning log. How people learn alone and in groups is a topic of constant inquiry in our classroom and made explicit through various charts and banners. Becoming conscious of the range of strategies people use as learners opens up options. To be literate in the 21st century students need to see stance as an option and understand the consequences of how they position themselves as individuals and as part of a group. "How people learn" is a year-long, every year, focused study. While we try to create ourselves into a community of learners by beginning and ending each week with rituals, we also want "the differences that make a difference" between us to expand our horizons and re-engage our imaginations.

• Literature is used to raise critical issues. We try to select books that explore what differences make a difference, that enrich our understanding of history and life by giving voice to those who have traditionally been silenced or marginalized (we call them "the indignant ones"), that show how people can begin to take action on important social issues, that explore dominant systems of meaning that operate in our society to position people and groups of people, and that help us question why certain groups are positioned as "others." In as many ways as we can, we try to connect schooling to the personal and communal lives that our students know. We record key ideas from these conversations on what the children in Vasquez' classroom (1999) called "a learning wall" and decide what social action to take based on core values and explicit discussions about what we think constitutes a "better community." In inner city Indianapolis, where a second Center for Inquiry is being located, we did manage to get a numbers house closed down. School officials have promised to turn the area into a school parking lot and the current parking lot into a school playground appropriate for all age groups. Can you imagine a school without a playground!?! They don't understand that play is inquiry not even once removed.

• We'd like to do more with computers and technology, but unfortunately we work in inner city environments where the inequities of a property tax as a way of funding schools are all too blatant. Probably the National Council of Teachers of English, the International Reading Association, and other literacy groups need to start a class action suit against some large school district. For better or for worse, computers are a way of life. Students who do not have access, even to all the silly stuff you can waste your time with on them, are disadvantaged when compared to their computer literate, suburban age-mates.

• We have tried to bring the community into the school by inviting parents to run discovery clubs that feature their ways of knowing: bricklaying, karate, gardening, or karaoke. We have begun to invite parents to inquire with us into their student's learning. The culturally responsive school movement in Alaska has much, we believe, to teach us (Oleska, 1992).

• Taking Eisner's wit and insight to heart (1989), we've stopped educating "by litter." All of our classrooms are multiaged. Experience is a bigger factor than age when it comes to learning (Harste, Woodward, & Burke, 1984), and social learning theory has taught us that most of what we know we have learned from being in the presence of others (Wells, 1986). Who ever came up with the idea of herding all 6-year-olds together for purposes of instruction doesn't understand how learning works in real life situations. Bateson (1972, 1979) says a theory of difference is a theory of learning. We have yet to explore this fundamental insight or use it as a argument to support inclusionary classrooms.

• As teachers, we form ourselves into study groups to share what worked and what it is we are having trouble doing given our vision of the world we want to create and the people we want to be. Like Lipka and McCarty (1994), we see the function of teacher study groups as creating zones of safety. Here is what they say on this topic:

The notion of safety implies risk, boundaries, and even danger. These are not "comfort zones"; they are sites of great personal and collective discomfort as teachers revisit their own educational histories and as they challenge their pedagogical assumptions and those of the institutions in which they work. Schooling occurs within contested space . . . [Study groups] created room within that space for opposition—for critically examining their roles and the context of schooling itself. The study group process has been one of self-revelation and group identification. . . . The process is equally one of contention and trepidation. . . . [While] powerful institutional forces can and do suppress and marginalize the work of such groups . . . the most appropriate way to conceptualize the success of these teacher groups may be to consider the situation without them. The historical record, unfortunately, all too clearly documents the latter alternative [by which the authors mean a state of schooling as usual] (pp. 250–251).

This is what makes NCTE's Reading Initiative (Smith & Crafton, 1998) such a powerful project as it invites university and school partnerships, long-term commitments, inquiry-based learning, and situated knowing. Further, it confirms what we all know: The key to school change is a knowledgeable professional in every classroom. That is why school districts need to reinvest in professional development and support teachers in attending conferences.

## ENGAGING THE FUTURE: SOME FINAL THOUGHTS

Nearly everyone would say that the purpose of education is to prepare students for the world they will enter after graduation. Wouldn't it be wonderful if as part of marketability we could guarantee that they had the inquiry skills to continue to learn as the world continues to change? If they knew how to use reading, writing, speaking, and listening actively to support them as lifelong learners? Wouldn't it be wonderful if we knew how to create spaces so that all voices could be heard in the creation

of a more just, a more thoughtful, and a more democratic way of living out the imagination of our elders?

We maintain it will only happen if we prepare. We further maintain that it will only happen if English language arts teachers seize the opportunities that have been given them through the way that their discipline has positioned them for leadership. This begins with mental preparation rather than rock-solid plans.

Scollon and Scollon (1986) say:

Planning is our most frequent defense against the unknown future. With a plan we seek to control outcomes, to eliminate change, to eliminate the random and the wild. . . . Preparing is different. In preparing we always expect diversity of outcomes. In preparing we enlarge the future in our imagination . . . [and] we seek to make ourselves ready (p. 94).

We know that, given the way schools are structured and resources distributed, the barriers to teaching in new ways may seem overwhelming. In most middle school and high school classrooms, teachers are faced with 40- to 55-minute periods, large numbers of learners, itinerant classrooms with no place to call "home," and an examination system that emphasizes and tests knowledge of content. Such policies and barriers almost force all teachers to adopt a "transmission of knowledge game plan."

This does not, however, mean that we should give up. More than ever, we need as many highly literate students graduating from our schools as possible if we are going to survive as democratic nations in this millennium.

How will educators at the end of this millennium describe their grandparents, their parents, and their own education? Let's hope they can say, "Wow, there was a radical shift in education at the turn of the 21st century. All of a sudden, being different was valued and diversity was seen as knowing twice as much."

In preparation, together, we need to forge a discourse for education that sees diversity and difference, not as problems, but as new possibilities for the revitalization of both teaching, learning, and the societies in which we live. Like good literature, we English language arts teachers need to begin by re-awakening the imagination. What can be imagined can be done. What cannot be imagined has no hope of ever being done. We English teachers know this. Let us teach the world.

## *References*

Applebee, A. N. (1996). *Curriculum as conversation: Transforming traditions of teaching and learning.* Chicago: University of Chicago Press.

Bateson, G. (1972). *Steps towards an ecology of mind.* New York: Ballantine.

Bateson, G. (1979). *Mind and nature: A necessary unity.* New York: Bantam.

Bishop, A. J. (1988). *Mathematical enculturation: A cultural perspective on mathematics education.* Boston: Kluwer Academic Publishers.

Cambourne, B. (1998). Research-based changes for the teaching of reading. In J. Tucker (Ed.), *The Gander-Lewisport Curriculum Guide in the Language Arts.* Gander, Newfoundland: Gander-Lewisport School Board.

*Conant Report* (1958). Washington, DC: Government Printing Office.

Comber, B. (1997). Literacy, poverty, and schooling: Working against deficit equations. *English in Australia, 119*(20), 22–34.

Edelsky, C. (1994). Education for democracy. *Language Arts, 71*(4), 252–257.

Eisner, E. (1989, September). *Educational reform: Some priorities.* Speech given at the British Columbia Teachers Union annual meeting, Vancouver, British Columbia.

Eisner, E. W. (1982). *Cognition and curriculum.* New York: Longman.

Fleck, L. (1935) (1979). *Genesis and development of a scientific fact.* Chicago: University of Chicago Press.

Freire, P. (1985). *The politics of education.* South Hadley, MA: Bergin & Garvey.

Gardner, H. (1993). *Multiple intelligences: The theory into practice.* New York: Basic Books.

Gee, J. P. (1996). *Social linguistics and literacies: Ideology in discourses* (2nd ed.). London: Taylor & Francis.

Gee, J. P. (1997). Meaning in discourses: Coordinating and being coordinated. In S. Muspratt, A. Luke, & P. Freebody (Eds.), *Constructing critical literacies: Teaching and learning textual practice.* Cresskill, NJ: Hampton Press.

Goodman, K. S. (1999). In the meantime (Ken's Kolumn). *Talking Points, 10*(2), 20-21.

Halliday, M. A. K. (1975). *Learning to mean: Explorations in the development of language.* London: Edward Arnold.

Harste, J. C. (1990). Inquiry-based instruction. *Primary Voices, 1*(1), 7-8.

Harste, J. C. (1993). Literacy as curricular conversations about knowledge, inquiry, and morality. In M. Ruddell & R. Ruddell, *Theoretical models and process of reading* (4th ed.). Newark, DE: International Reading Association.

Harste, J. C., Short, K. G., with Burke, C. L. (1988). *Creating classrooms for authors.* Portsmouth, NH: Heinemann.

Harste, J. C., Vasquez, V., Lewison, M., Leland, C., Oceipka, A., & Brea, A. (2000). Supporting critical conversations in classrooms. In K. Mitchell-Pierce, *Adventuring with books* (4th ed.). Urbana, IL: National Council of Teachers of English.

Harste, J. C., Woodward, V. A., & Burke, C. L. (1984). *Language stories and literacy lessons.* Portsmouth, NH: Heinemann.

Hertsfelt, M. (1990a). *The poetics of manhood.* Bloomington, IN: Indiana University Press.

Hertsfelt, M. (1990b). *The semiotics of culture.* Class lecture given at Indiana University in doctoral seminar on women's ways of knowing, Bloomington, IN.

Johns Steiner, V. (1981). *Notebooks of the mind.* Albuquerque, NM: University of New Mexico Press.

Ladson-Billings, G. (1999, April). *Teacher education: Directions for the future.* Panel presentation given at the annual meeting of the American Educational Research Association. Montreal, Quebec, Canada.

Leland, C., Harste, J. C., Oceipka, A., Lewison, M., & Vasquez, V. (1999). Exploring critical literacy: You can hear a pin drop. *Language Arts, 77*(1), 70-78.

Lipka, J., & McCarty, T. L. (1994). Changing the culture of schooling: Navajo and Yup'ik cases. *Anthropology & Education Quarterly, 25*(3), 265-284.

Luke, A., & Freebody, P. (1997). Shaping the school practices of reading. In S. Muspratt, A. Luke, & P. Freebody (Eds.), *Constructing critical literacies.* Cresskill, NJ: Hampton Press.

Luke, A., & Freebody, P. (in press). *Future notes on the four resources model.* Practically Primary.

Mitchell-Pierce, K. (Ed.) (2000). *Adventuring with books* (4th ed.). Urbana, IL: National Council of Teachers of English.

Oleksa, M. (1992). Conflicting worldviews. In M. Oleksa (ed.), *Orthodox Alaska: A theology of mission.* Juneau, Alaska: St. Vladimir's Seminar Press.

Ohanian, S. (1999). *One size fits few.* Portsmouth, NH: Heinemann.

Porter, C. (1999). *Multiple ways of knowing: Expanding our notions of literacy.* Unpublished doctoral thesis, National-Lewis University, Chicago.

Scollon, R., & Scollon, S. (1986). The axe handle academy: A proposal for a bioregional, thematic, humanities education (Commissioned Paper). Juneau, Alaska: Sealaska Heritage Foundation.

Short, K. G., & Burke, C. L. (1991). *Creating curriculum: Teachers and students as a community of learners.* Portsmouth, NH: Heinemann.

Short, K. G., Harste, J. C., with Burke, C. (1996). *Creating classrooms for authors and inquirers.* Portsmouth, NH: Heinemann.

Smith, F. (1981). Demonstrations, engagement, and sensitivity: A revised approach to the language arts. *Language Arts, 52*(1), 103-112.

Smith, K., & Crafton, L. (1998). *NCTE's reading initiative guidelines.* Urbana, IL: National Council of Teachers of English.

Street, B. (1995). *Multiple literacies.* Portsmouth, NH: Heinemann.

Symeonides, D. (1999). Bilingual education: Changes, challenges, and choices for the new millennium. *Reflexions: The Journal of the Canadian Association of Second Language Teachers, 99*(1), 8-10.

Vasquez, V. (1999). *Negotiating critical literacies with young children.* Unpublished doctoral dissertation, Indiana University, Bloomington.

Vygotsky, L. S. (1978). *Mind in society: The development of higher psychological processes* (M. Cole, V. John-Steiner, S. Scribner, & E. Souberman, Trans. & Eds.). Cambridge, MA: Harvard University Press.

Wells, G. (1986). *The meaning makers: Children learning language and using language to learn.* Portsmouth, NH: Heinemann.

# Part
## ·IV·

# ENVIRONMENTS FOR ENGLISH LANGUAGE ARTS TEACHING

# ·36·

# THE ELEMENTARY SCHOOL CLASSROOM

## Gail E. Tompkins
### California State University, Fresno

## Eileen Tway
### Miami University

More than 30 years ago Philip W. Jackson (1968) took a close look at "life in classrooms" to find what it was really like in the daily course of events that make up school life. Jackson spent considerable time observing what went on in elementary classrooms, and his close-look research showed the unpredictable and sometimes chaotic nature of everyday classroom life. He pointed out that researchers who do not work in actual classroom environments (and most did not at that time) were missing the social realities of classroom life. Jackson's observational research was one of the pioneer studies, and he predicted then that future researchers would work inside classrooms.

Jackson's predictions have been fulfilled. Donald Graves (1975, 1983, 1994) made case-study observational research respectable as good research design and gave new direction to writing research in his shift from examining students' written products to studying their writing processes in a classroom context. More recently, Goodman and Wilde (1992) used ethnographic techniques to study third- and fourth-grade Native American writers in a reservation community, and Anne Haas Dyson (1993) used similar methods to examine urban primary grade writers in their classroom community.

As researchers have moved into the classroom to observe what actually goes on there, they have had to give up prior assumptions, or what Jackson (1968) called "comfortable beliefs" about what classroom life is like. The classroom is different from a laboratory where outside distractions can be largely controlled. Researchers have become more open to the social realities of the classroom; they began to look at social interaction between teacher and students and among students. Researchers began to paint descriptive pictures of classroom life. This new descriptive research brought together several disciplines, including sociology and anthropology, to aid in taking a

closer look at classroom interactions. Wilkinson (1982) referred to a "new wave" of multidisciplinary research on the functions of language in the classroom.

The roles of "teacher" and "researcher" are changing, too, as teachers become teacher researchers (Burton, 1986; Cochran-Smith & Lytle, 1993; Hubbard & Power, 1993; MacLean & Mohr, 1999). Teachers are redefining what it means to be a teacher as they become participant observers in the classroom to gain insights and understandings about classroom life. During the 1990s, the Santa Barbara Classroom Discourse Group, a group of teacher researchers, university faculty, and graduate students, has developed a new way of looking in classrooms to make the often invisible patterns and practices of classroom life more visible (Santa Barbara Classroom Discourse Group, 1992a, 1992b). This group, founded by Carol Dixon and Judith Green, has used ethnography to observe life in elementary classrooms and to record, analyze, and represent classroom culture (Dixon, Frank, & Green, 1999).

## A COMMUNITY OF LEARNERS

Elementary classrooms are increasingly being viewed as communities of learners, and researchers are interested in how teachers and students develop the classroom culture and how the social context affects learning. The concept of "community" is not new. John Dewey (1938/1974) argued for the education of students within a community of learners, and Brazilian Paolo Freire (1970) wrote that literacy is best taught in social contexts. The Carnegie Foundation for the Advancement of Teaching encouraged teachers to build classroom communities to enhance learning (Boyer, 1995).

Yetta Goodman (1987) said, "The classroom is greater than the sum of its parts. The classroom is more than one child plus one child plus one child. It is a community." (p. xiii). Lucy McCormick Calkins (1994) challenged teachers to create writing classrooms that are learning communities, with everyone serving as both teacher and student, and Frank Smith (1988) described learning to read as "joining the literacy club."

At the heart of this view of classrooms as social learning environments is Lev Vygotsky's (1978, 1986) theory of the social nature of learning. According to Vygotsky's concept of internalization, learning transfers from external social interaction to internal thought processes. His concept of a Zone of Proximal Development suggests that more knowledgeable classmates and the teacher scaffold students' learning through instructional conversations, modeling, and collaborative activities (Dixon-Krauss, 1996; Moll, 1990). These types of instruction are not only possible but actively encouraged in a community of learners.

## Creating the Community

A classroom community of learners is a group of students who feel a sense of belonging, show care for their classmates, and are responsible for their own learning. The teacher and students develop their community spirit together as they learn to respect each other and learn ways to collaborate with others. Ralph Peterson identified eight components of learning communities in his book *Life in a Crowded Place* (1992):

1. *Ceremonies*. Class meetings give shape and life to the community and to foster group identity. Students and the teacher use class meetings to begin and end the school day, and other meetings may be called during the day.

2. *Rituals*. Students and the teacher use symbolic acts to express value and commitment in the classroom.

3. *Rites*. Students and the teacher develop their own rites of accomplishment, initiation of new students into the class, and year-end closure to signify the value of the classroom community.

4. *Celebrations*. Festive activities are used to highlight special days, students' achievements, and birthdays. They also have spur-of-the-moment celebrations, for example, when students see a rainbow after a storm. These activities strengthen the bonds of the community.

5. *Talk*. Talk is an essential part of community life and an important learning tool. Students and teachers use conversation to develop social relationships and to interact with one another, story talk to recount events in their lives, and discussion to gain knowledge.

6. *Play*. Students engage in play as they create projects and work collaboratively on activities that encourage students' imaginative responses. Play is a spirit or attitude that students exhibit as they work on projects. Teachers, too, need to have playful spirits.

7. *Routines and Jobs*. Students learn procedures for keeping the physical space of the classroom orderly and then assume responsibility for completing the tasks regularly.

8. *Residency*. Students gain membership in the classroom community as they develop confidence and feel accepted by classmates and the teacher. This sense of belonging is residency.

Peterson believed that the classroom community is a more important factor in students' academic success than any particular instructional method.

Graves (1991) echoed many of Peterson's components as he urged teachers to build "literate classrooms." He, too, viewed classrooms as communities of learners where teachers and students work cooperatively to design and structure the classroom to meet their needs. He suggested that teachers create a studio-like atmosphere where they can demonstrate reading and writing, conduct conferences, and convene small groups of students. In order for classroom life to operate while teachers work with small groups, Graves recommended that teachers delegate many room maintenance tasks to students, such as taking care of the classroom library and preparing and posting bulletin board displays. He explained that

classrooms need careful structuring so that children can function more independently. Structure also helps to integrate the enormous range of differences among children in any classroom. Structure and responsibility must be carefully developed throughout the school year: What is possible in January may not be possible in September. (pp. 44–45)

Seiler, Schuelke, and Lieb-Brilhart (1984) believed that every classroom "generates an atmosphere, which is often not articulated explicitly, but which leaves a distinct impression of the interrelationships of the educators and the students" (p. 19). The manner in which these interrelationships are conducted affects the classroom climate. Research on school climate shows that some climates promote learning while others may even hinder the learning process. According to Seiler, Schuelke, and Lieb-Brilhart,

evidence shows that effective and ineffective schools differ in the climates that they have established in a number of characteristics: openness vs. defensiveness, confidence vs. fear, acceptance vs. rejection, belonging vs. alienation, trust vs. suspicion, high expectations vs. low expectations, order vs. chaos, and control vs. frustration. (p. 19)

These differences have strong implications for the quality of communication in a classroom. One that seems especially pertinent for success in language learning and that has a lot to do with influencing the other factors is the difference made by high expectations versus low expectations.

Teachers also think of their classroom communities as "families." Teachers at Gardendale Elementary School, an urban, multicultural school in San Antonio, Texas created the Gardendale Family with vertically aligned teams (Martinez, Perez, & Cook, 1998). Teachers from each grade level in the school come together to form closely connected communities or family units. These units function as schools within a school, and students stay in the same family unit through the elementary grades. The teachers and administrators planned this arrangement because they believed in the power of classroom communities. They believed that when students and teachers know each other well there is a greater likelihood that students will become more involved in their own learning.

The goals of the Gardendale Family were to:

- Develop a sense of community within the school.
- Promote family involvement.
- Develop a curriculum that was cognitively engaging and personally relevant.
- Engage students in authentic learning experiences.
- Develop programs that would take into account each individual student and encourage students to take responsibility for their own learning. (Martinez et al., 1998, p. 4)

Students have a classroom family as well as a larger vertically aligned team family. Students in the vertically aligned teams met together regularly, and older and younger students have opportunities to interact and work collaboratively (Gorman, Tschoepe, & Martinez, 1998). The students participate in a reading buddies program, work collaboratively on research projects, present poetry performances, and participate in a conflict-resolution program. Through these activities, the younger students become active members of the "family," and the older students offer feedback and validation to younger students.

## Democratic Classrooms

Other researchers have recommended and described democratic classrooms that foster democratic practices because the mission of public education is students' preparation for the role of citizen. Wood (1998) explained that "it is only through the experience of democratic community that students will learn what it means to live a democratic life" (p. 6). In democratic classrooms, according to Paul (1998), students and teachers build a community in which all members are valued, respected, and bonded to the community and make decisions about the learning that goes on in the classroom. Wolk (1998) explained that "for a classroom to be a community, there must be spontaneous social interaction. Students must be free to interact and communicate, not all of the time but as a regular and important part of the classroom life" (p. 59). Democratic classrooms seem to embody all the qualities of a classroom community in addition to the focus on democratic ideals.

A fundamental characteristic of democratic classrooms is collaboration for the good of everyone in the classroom (Wood, 1998, 1992). Students meet in class meetings to plan activities, make decisions, and discuss group issues. They work collaboratively, too, on projects and provide assistance and support for classmates as they read and write.

Students learn tolerance and respect for each other in democratic classrooms (Siller, 1998). Teachers teach students to be tolerant of those who have different opinions, and students learn to talk out differences. Siller recommends that teachers set up peace chairs—two white chairs facing each other—in the classroom. To resolve conflicts, students who are having difficulties getting along sit in the chairs and talk out their problem. In democratic classrooms, teachers help students to view diversity and multiculturalism as strengths.

## The Physical Arrangement of the Classroom

The arrangements of furniture, materials, and centers in a classroom shape the behaviors of students and teachers by "giving very strong messages, encouraging them to act in particular ways," according to Loughlin and Martin (1987, p. 7). As researchers have moved from the laboratory to the real world of the classroom, they have discovered the efficacy of the classroom environment as instructional tool. The classroom can be set up in such a way that it issues an invitation to learning.

Teachers arrange furniture to facilitate the creation of a community of learners and support students' learning (Ross, 1996). Open areas are arranged for group meetings, sharing literature, presentations, and dramatizations; and individual spaces are created for reading and writing. In addition, the classroom library is organized and stocked with books. Teachers cluster desks in small groups, not in straight rows and arrange learning centers and computer areas with space for needed supplies. Loughlin and Martin explained that "The arranged environment functions as an instructional tool, complementing and reinforcing other strategies the teacher uses to support children's learning" (1987, p. 6).

Students are less likely to make connections between materials or to combine them or use them effectively when materials are widely scattered, according to Loughlin and Suina (1982). Much more direct teacher instruction is needed if scattered materials are to be combined in learning activities. When materials are arranged so that connections are easily inferred, teacher assignments are not required, and the teacher is freed to work with individual students or to "float" around the classroom as a facilitator wherever needed. Loughlin and Martin (1987) advocated the placement of materials where possibilities for their use exist. This is not a "scattering" of materials, but carefully placed combinations that encourage effective use. Loughlin and Martin described these careful placements as "decentralizing literacy materials" (p. 38), and they found that decentralizing literacy materials for better accessibility minimizes crowding or traffic congestion in classrooms and has a positive influence on the use of the materials.

Teachers' ability to place materials strategically in the environment is evidently crucial to the productivity of a language arts classroom. Smith (1978) argued that immersion in the language environment is essential for language acquisition. Teachers who provide classroom libraries and comfortable pillows or chairs for reading, computers near writing centers, and puppets for retelling stories, are giving the kind of help that Cazden (1972) called "environmental assistance" and aiding students in continued language acquisition.

***Computers.*** "Teaching occurs as children use materials, work with each other, see demonstrations, and talk with the teacher" according to Genishi, McCarrier, and Nussbaum (1988, p. 184). Computers are an increasingly important part of the materials in elementary classrooms, and students use computers to word process, create multimedia programs, read electronic texts, practice reading skills, and conduct research on the Internet. Genishi, McCollom, and Strand (1985) reported that the research suggests that computers do support students' learning:

"Our observations lead us to conclude that computer activity can be highly sociable" (p. 531). They reported, for example, how children helped each other solve problems as they worked at the computer. And Reid (1985) conducted an ethnographic study of computer use in a fourth-grade classroom, and found that the computer created a new writing environment, transforming writing from a private to a public activity.

It is difficult, however, to quantify the efficacy of computer use in teaching reading (Meyer & Rose, 1998). Some studies do show that computers contribute to improved reading achievement (e.g., Greenlee-Moore & Smith, 1996), and others show that students having the most difficulty learning to read benefit the most by using computers (e.g., Niemec, Samson, Weinstein, & Walberg, 1987). Interestingly, Reinking, Labbo, and McKenna (1997) found that the teacher's philosophy influenced the effectiveness of computers in teaching reading because teachers used computers in ways that reflected their views of reading. Cochran-Smith, Kahn, and Paris (1990) reached similar conclusions. They concluded that teachers' beliefs influenced the ways that computers were integrated into the writing program.

El-Hindi (1998) researched how teachers use technology to support literacy learning and found, not surprisingly, that the Internet has quickly become an important teaching tool. Elementary students use the Internet to research language arts and content area topics, to access current events, to chat online about a favorite book, to exchange messages with pen pals, to publish a bulletin board on a school Web site, and to create multimedia presentations. These activities foster communities of learners and collaboration.

One of the most important benefits of computer use, according to Leu and Leu (1997), is that the computer is changing how students and teachers interact and how they think. Newman, Vibert, Freeman, and Scharp (1988) pointed out that computers encourage collaborative learning, even when students play story games. Contrary to adult assumptions that using the computer is a solitary activity, students almost always use computers and play games in groups. Newman et al. concluded that when students are encouraged to experiment with computer programs and create their own literacy events, computers support the development of a classroom community because the activities are interactive and collaborative.

***Learning centers.*** Teachers arrange learning centers in their classrooms to provide students with opportunities to read, write, practice skills they are learning, and explore realia. Some centers, such as library and listening centers, are part of the physical arrangement of the classroom, and other centers are set up on tables, in corners, or anywhere in the classroom that there is available space. Leslie Morrow (1989, 1997) studied library centers in primary-grade classrooms, and made these recommendations:

- Make the library center inviting.
- Define the library center with shelves, carpets, benches, sofas, or other partitions.
- Make the center large enough to accommodate five or six students comfortably at one time.

- Use two kinds of bookshelves. Most of the collection should be shelved with the spines facing outward, but some books should be set so that the front covers are displayed.
- Shelve books by category, and color-code books by type.
- Display books written by one author or related to a theme being studied, and change the displays regularly.
- Cover the floor with a rug and furnish the area with pillows, beanbag chairs, or comfortable furniture.
- Stock the center with at least four times as many books as there are students in the classroom.
- Include a variety of types of reading materials, including books, newspapers, magazines, posters, and charts, in the center.
- Display posters that encourage reading in the library center.

These recommendations are based on research in primary-grade classrooms, but they are equally appropriate for older students.

Staab (1991) studied how centers were used in a multiage primary classroom. Eight centers—library, language, math, science, writing, home, construction, and art—were set up in the classroom and the teacher coordinated center activities with thematic units. Most of the instruction in the classroom was whole-class, and students worked independently at the centers to practice concepts that were first presented to the whole class and to work collaboratively with classmates on projects. Students chose which centers to work at and the teacher monitored students' activities with a pocket chart management system. Students' names were written on the pockets and students placed color-coded strips of paper in their pockets on the chart to indicate the center they were working at. From her classroom observations, Staab identified 10 characteristics of these centers:

1. The centers evolve from children's ideas and interests.
2. The centers provide opportunities for purposeful, meaningful follow-up to whole group instruction.
3. Students choose the centers they will work at and make choices about the activities they will pursue at the centers.
4. The centers provide teachers with opportunities to monitor students' progress and work with individuals and small groups.
5. Learning is individualized at centers.
6. Reading, writing, and talk are integrated with the content area unit in the center activities.
7. The centers provide many opportunities for students to talk and interact.
8. Students develop responsibility for their own learning through the center activities.
9. Teachers assess students' ability to work with classmates at centers and the work that students produce.
10. Students have opportunities to play and socialize at the centers.

Staab concluded that thematic centers are more than opportunities to practice skills; instead they can be an integral part of a thematic unit. She wrote that "dependent upon their purpose, organization, and content, centers can foster a child's natural curiosity to learn as materials and resources are gathered and assembled to held a child discover what is known and to push beyond to what is unknown" (p. 113).

## SOCIAL INTERACTION IN THE CLASSROOM

Studies of early (or first) language learning of preschool children have shown that an immersion-in-language environment is essential for language acquisition. Brian Cambourne (1984) identified seven conditions that facilitate young children's acquisition of oral language:

1. *Immersion*. From the time children are born, they are immersed in a "language flood" within their home and neighborhood communities as children and adults use speech around them.
2. *Demonstration*. Adults and other children provide models and examples of purposeful and meaningful language use.
3. *Expectation*. Adults expect children to learn to talk successfully, and they transmit this expectation to children as they interact with them.
4. *Responsibility*. Adults allow children to be responsible for learning to talk, and they accept individual differences in children's learning rates. Parents don't closely monitor and continually assess children's progress.
5. *Approximation*. Adults understand that children will approximate adult speech patterns, and they reward children's attempts even though the speech may not be correct by adult standards.
6. *Employment*. Children learn to talk by talking, and they have many opportunities to talk every day.
7. *Feedback*. Children receive supportive feedback from adults and other children as they learn to talk.

Cambourne's seven conditions for language learning have important implications for learning to read and write, and they greatly influenced the whole language movement (Butler & Turbill, 1984). The condition of employment, for example, is applied in reading and writing workshop, and the condition of approximation is reflected in teachers' acceptance of invented or temporary spellings.

Teachers create a classroom environment to provide similar language-rich experiences. Courtney Cazden (1972) called this kind of manipulation, or influence, "environmental assistance." Loughlin and Martin (1987) called it an "arranged environment." They wrote, "The arranged environment functions as an instructional tool, complementing and reinforcing other strategies the teacher uses to support children's learning" (p. 6). Loughlin and Suina (1982) reported that the provision and arrangement of materials, such as trade books, influence their potential in encouraging student learning.

Janet Emig (1983) described the classroom as an "enabling environment" and Karelitz (1993) applied Emig's guidelines as she created her first-grade classroom that included independent learning, talk, and instruction. Karelitz explained:

I think the key idea here is that students and teacher are all practitioners, teaching and learning from one another. If this is true, the place in which children learn needs to be supplied with resources and organized in ways that will encourage independent learning ... Making my classroom an enabling environment is a constant challenge. I must find ways to present new information and skills and to allow my students to experiment and make their own discoveries, to teach me what they can do and what they need to know. Writing—their own and that which they read and discuss—is the glue that binds the activities and ideas together. The trick is to set up the classroom to support this kind of written expression from day one. (p. 25)

Language learning depends on social interaction (Johnson & Johnson, 1975). It follows that language learning in school is inextricably bound up with the classroom environment as the scene for interaction. Instead of dispensing knowledge, teachers engage students with experiences that require them to modify their cognitive structures and construct their own knowledge, as they interact with and adapt to their environment. Teaching becomes a linguistic process in which individuals in a classroom interact with language and each other as they move toward collaborative constructions of meaning (Cazden, 1988; Erickson, 1986; Genishi, McCarrier, & Nussbaum, 1988).

Loughlin and Martin (1987) emphasized the social nature of the classroom community by saying, "After a number of decades of research focusing on individual learners as if they were isolated from others, concern is once again turned to issues related to the classroom community as a social entity" (p. xiii). Certainly language learning, while the creative activity of each learner, is not something that happens in isolation. It is a function of communication, and communication implies, even requires, two or more participants. These participants form a language community.

### Talk and Collaboration

Students use talk as they actively construct meaning. Barnes (1992) called this kind of talk exploratory talk. Students use talk to formulate and sort out ideas and to think aloud. He contrasted exploratory talk with a second, more formal type of talk—presentational talk. It's used in classrooms for communicating information and correct answers. Too often, Barnes, lamented, "schooling is often dominated by presentational talk, whereas it would benefit the students to have more opportunities for 'working on understanding,' that is, more opportunities for exploratory talk" (1993, p. 30). Teachers create a supportive environment when they provide a range of talking activities, encourage students to work in small groups, and value exploratory talk.

In a 2-year study of third- and fourth-grade Native American students' writing at their reservation school, Goodman and Wilde (1992) documented the role of talk and collaboration in writing. They concluded that literacy learning is strongly influenced by social interaction in the classroom community. Three broad categories of influences on writing are the writer, the writing, and the community. Writing takes place in the social context of the classroom—the community, and the classroom community is a force to enhance everyone's learning, according to Goodman (1992). As students write, they interact with teachers and classmates. They listen to classmates read their writing aloud, and conference with the teacher and classmates. The classroom community provides an audience for students' writing—both the rough drafts and the final copies. Students share information, provide words, suggest ways of phrasing ideas, and provide correct spellings and conventions of print.

As part of the Goodman and Wilde's (1992) study, Kasten (1992) examined the third graders' oral language and found that their talk was purposeful and related to their writing. Thirty-one percent of the talk occurred during prewriting, 27% during drafting, and 18% during revision. Another 22% of the talk was related to writing but was not scored according to writing activity. Only 2% of the talk was unrelated to writing.

Kasten also examined the third graders' talk using Halliday's seven functions of language (1977). His language functions are:

1. *Instrumental*. Language used to obtain something from the speaker, such as "Can I use your eraser ?"
2. *Regulatory*. Language used to control the behavior of others, such as "Give me my paper back."
3. *Interactional*. The "me and you" function of language, such as "Can I read your story?"
4. *Personal*. Language used to express the child's uniqueness or awareness of self, such as "This is hard," or "I think I'll name her Tiffany."
5. *Heuristic*. Language used to explore the environment, ask questions, or find things out, such as "Does mother need a capital letter?"
6. *Imaginative*. Language through which the child creates an environment of his or her own, such as "Let's pretend."
7. *Informative*. Language with the "I've got something to tell you" function, such as "I wrote *food* but it looks like *lood*." (Kasten, 1992, p. 94)

Kasten found that 31% of students' talk was interactional, serving the "me and you" social function of language. Nineteen percent of the utterances were heuristic talk, and 17% was informative. None of the other categories included more than 7% of the talk. Kasten recorded two types of talk that could not be classified using Halliday's functions. They were subvocablizations—when students talked to themselves and reading aloud—when students reread their writing. Kasten concluded that these two activities represented Vygotsky's (1978) intrapersonal function of language and were used as problem-solving tools.

Elementary students use collaborative activities to learn in the classroom community. Barr and Dreeben (1983) stressed that learning is a function of groups in a classroom. Wood (1984) said that in group work "students are more intensely involved in learning because their chances of oral participation are increased" (p. 117).

Fourth-grade teacher Jean Dickinson (1993) studied how she and her students used talk to develop their classroom learning community. She identified these beliefs about the role of talk in a classroom community:

1. It is through talk that we build our learning community in the classroom.

2. When the community is established, students participate in curriculum planning and assume ownership of their learning.
3. By talking with each other, we support the telling and writing of stories in our community.
4. Given guidance and direction, students develop methods that enable them to identify their own best learning strategies. The students participate in evaluating and planning curriculums.
5. It is through talk that children learn. (pp. 101–102)

Dickinson concluded that a classroom community was necessary to support the kinds of talk her fourth graders used to learn. Her students felt safe and secure so that they could be risk-takers, and they respected each other.

## Classroom Discourse Analysis

Interaction analysis of oral participation in the classroom enables researchers to determine who gets the talking time and what kinds of talk occur (Flanders, 1970). The results of interaction analysis are often surprising, especially the ratio of teacher talk to student talk.

Cazden (1988) has used interaction analysis and other techniques to study classroom discourse. She pointed out, "Just as all speech has an accent, even though we are not made aware of our own until we travel somewhere where there is a different norm, so patterns of teacher–student interactions in typical classroom lessons are cultural phenomena" (p. 67). Some children are culturally equipped to adapt better to the language life of the classroom than others are. Studies, such as those by Heath (1983), show the need for adjustments on the part of teacher and students to make the classroom a rich language environment for all students.

To do well in classrooms children must understand the communication context of the classroom and how to operate socially within that context (Wilkinson, 1982). Courtney Cazden's studies of classroom discourse analysis show the complexities involved, even in everyday talk. Cazden (1988) said that the study of classroom discourse is the study of situated language use in a social setting. She pointed out the special features of spoken language in the classroom setting. "First," Cazden wrote that "spoken language is the medium by which much teaching takes place, and in which students demonstrate to teachers much of what they have learned" (p. 2). Second, she observed that in classrooms, unlike other social situations, such as restaurants or buses, "one person, the teacher, is responsible for controlling all the talk that occurs" and third, she noted, "spoken language is an important part of the identities of all the participants" (p. 3).

Early research on analyzing classroom talk proved enlightening to researchers and teachers alike. Flanders' (1970) work on interaction analysis was a foundation on which Cazden and many researchers built as they studied oral communication in the classroom. Flanders' system of interaction analysis, enabled researchers and teachers to determine the kinds of interaction going on in the classroom and the proportion of time devoted to the various kinds. It was often a revelation to teachers and observers to see the ratio of teacher talk to student talk and especially the ratio of teacher-initiated talk to student-initiated talk (initiation as opposed to response).

Flanders and his colleagues did not prioritize one kind of interaction over another; rather, they focused on the variety of kinds, the flexibility in the range of spoken language, the ratio of controlling kinds of teacher talk to freeing, encouraging kinds, and other ratios. It is a numerical, tally-taking kind of system that leaves interpretation to the teachers involved or to other observers.

Flanders classified the categories of teacher talk according to initiation (direct influence) and response (indirect influence). Most interpreters, including Flanders, agree that when the teacher is direct, it minimizes children's freedom to respond and when the teacher is indirect, it maximizes the freedom of children in their oral expression. However, these interpretations or beliefs are not meant to be judgmental in the absolute sense, because there are times when the teacher's role calls for direct influence. What is gained from the analysis of direct versus indirect categories is an awareness of freeing and directing behaviors and whether or not there is some kind of balance in these behaviors, that is, approximately as much indirect as direct behavior. Both kinds of teacher-talk have their place, but teacher-response and indirect influence should not be neglected or relegated to second place, most interpreters stress (Seiler, Schuelke, & Lieb-Brilhart, 1984).

## Cultural Conflict in the Classroom

Cultural differences among students have been found to affect the way they use language in the classroom, language growth, and freedom of expression. Cazden (1988) reported that the patterns of teacher–student interactions in typical classroom lessons are cultural phenomena. She discussed possible culturally–related disadvantages for some children in their classroom language use as follows:

In some of its aspects, the demands of classroom discourse are new to all children. In the classroom, the group is larger than even the largest family gathered at meals, and so getting a turn to talk is much harder. When one does get a turn, acceptable topics for talk are more restricted and more predetermined by someone else … But beyond these commonalities, some children may be at a special disadvantage. For some children there will be greater cultural discontinuity, greater sociolinguistic interference, between home and school. (pp. 67-68)

Teachers are usually aware of individual differences among students and attempt to adapt the classroom situation accordingly, but the way in which the adaptation is done is a crucial consideration if all children are to benefit. In some cases, such as the one where one boy exhibited a definitely nonstandard dialect, the teacher may adapt expectations and not expect as much in the way of language learning. This, in turn, may well keep some children from meeting their growth potential.

Other researchers have examined the compatibility of home and school communities. In a groundbreaking study, Heath (1983) compared African American and White communities in the Piedmont area of the Carolinas. The central question for the study was: "For each of these groups, what were the effects of the preschool home and community environment on the learning of those language structures and uses which were needed in classrooms and job settings?" (p. 4). Since Heath was also connected to a local institution of higher education and involved in teacher education at the time, she was able to work with teachers in the area in a research–partner relationship. She worked with teachers specifically to try new methods, materials, and motivations to help the working class African American and White children of the area learn more effectively than they had in the past. She reported that teachers "constructed curricula from the world of the home to enable students to move to the curricular content of the school" (p. 340). In constructing such curricula, teachers' goals were:

1. To provide a foundation of familiar knowledge to serve as context for classroom information.
2. To engage students in collecting and analyzing familiar ways of knowing and translating these into scientific or school-accepted labels, concepts, and generalizations.
3. To provide students with meaningful opportunities to learn ways of talking about using language to organize and express information. (p. 340)

The central focus was the promotion of ethnographic methods for students to look at their own language use at home and at school. With the new curricula, students improved their textbook unit test scores, standardized test results, attendance records, and attitudes toward school.

In an ambitious 10-year study to determine the relationship between language and school achievement, Gordon Wells (1985) tracked the day-to-day language experiences of high to low socioeconomic status (SES) English-speaking children at home and at school. He found that students' language interactions at home were similar across SES levels, but that their apparent oral language differences at school were due to differences in teachers' conversation styles. When teachers tried to elicit information from low SES students, the students appeared to lack competence, but when teachers used conversation styles more similar to the meaning-making ones used by their parents, low SES students were as competent as high SES students.

Barnes' (1992) categories of exploratory and presentational talk may help to explain the difference between low-SES and high-SES students' school success. Low-SES students were successful in exploratory talk activities but not in presentational talk. When teachers required students to use presentational talk, low-SES students often responded with single words or not at all in contrast to high-SES students who could handle both exploratory and presentational talk. Low-SES students' inability to use presentational talk seemed to lead teachers to conclude that these students lacked oral language ability.

Different cultures and dialects do not have to interfere with language learning, but rather can enhance it, if teachers adjust the classroom environment to reflect some of the home culture. Lucas and Borders (1987) found that some children show a much wider range of functional language competence in situations in which their dialect features are considered acceptable. Teachers who capitalize on the already-existing functional language competence of their students will use this foundation to help students develop sociolinguistic skills for a variety of settings, according to Lucas and Borders.

Lisa Delpit's articles "Skills and Other Dilemmas of a Progressive Black Educator" (1986) and "The Silenced Dialogue: Power and Pedagogy in Educating Other People's Children" (1988) brought to the forefront the issue of the culture of power in the elementary classroom. Delpit argued that African American children are oppressed by holistic process-oriented approaches to writing instruction, and she viewed the teaching of skills to be essential to African American students' ability to compete in mainstream society. More than an argument of which instructional approach is better for a group of students, Delpit concluded that the issue is communicating across cultures—listening to the voices of African American children, parents, and teachers. Mainstream and African American teachers must start a dialogue and carefully listen to perspectives that are very different than their own.

Research points to the need for adaptive action that would make classrooms more culturally compatible places, where the transition between the home and school culture is positively supported. There should be mutual adaptation, so that children are not required to do all of the adjusting to a new situation, but the situation is also adapted to their cultural differences.

## Gender Issues in the Classroom

Gender issues are often invisible and naturalized in the elementary school classroom. Books in many classroom libraries contain stereotypical messages about gender roles and expected cultural behaviors. Jett-Simpson and Masland (1993) recommended that teachers choose books for literature circles that present nonstereotypical main characters and remove books from classroom libraries that are offensive unless teachers use the books to help students recognize harmful stereotypes.

Gender issues also affect writing workshop and other writing activities. Topics that students choose to write about reflect the classroom culture and gender issues (Fishman, 1996; Kamler, 1993). Henkin (1998) observed in a first-grade writing workshop classroom for 2 years to see which children were invited to share in conversations and activities and which children were not chosen to participate. She found gender discrimination. Boys and girls worked together when required, but they chose most of the time to work in same sex groupings. Through interviews she found that there was a "boys' club" and a "girls' club," much like Dyson's (1993) "unofficial classroom worlds." The boys told her that they didn't consider girls to be adequate partners, and the girls told her they were aware that boys did not want to work with them. Henkin concluded that writing workshop served an important function in the classroom and the discrimination reflected society. She emphasized the need for more democratic classrooms. Henkin recommended these guidelines for promoting equity in classrooms:

1. Teachers should use gender neutral terms such as "students" or "fourth graders" instead of gender terms such as "boys" and "girls."

2. Teachers should take care to alternate between boys and girls when calling on students.
3. Teachers should line students up together in one line rather than line children up in boys' and girls' lines.
4. Teachers should group students into mixed gender groups and not allow them to segregate into single-gender groups.
5. Teachers should model equity in the classroom.

## The Role of the Teacher

Teachers play a crucial role in creating the social context in which literacy flourishes in a classroom community of learners. Barnes (1992) identified five ways teachers support collaboration and learning communities. These five ways are:

1. To ensure that students feel confident that they can learn and that they are valued in the classroom community.
2. To create opportunities for shared experiences.
3. To assist students in posing questions and assuming responsibility for learning.
4. To monitor time use and pacing of activities to allow for students to construct new knowledge.
5. To provide audiences for students to showcase their learning.

Ruddell (1995) studied influential teachers who had made a vital difference in the academic and personal lives of their students to identify the unique characteristics of these teachers, and he found that the teacher's knowledge and beliefs about instruction and control during instruction were crucial. He defined an influential teacher as "an instructional decision maker who develops clear goals and purposes and conducts daily learning through well formed plans and teaching strategies" (p. 455). Ruddell identified these characteristics of influential teachers:

1. *Personal characteristics.* These teachers show commitment and passion; they are caring, flexible, and have high expectations for themselves.
2. *Understanding of learner potential.* These teachers are sensitive to individual students' needs, motivations, and aptitudes; they place high demands on learners, and they understand that students are developmental learners.
3. *Attitude toward subject.* These teachers are enthusiastic and create intellectual excitement in their students. They also consider alternative viewpoints.
4. *Life adjustment.* These teachers show concern for their students as persons, and they are attentive to their students' academic and personal problems.
5. *Quality of instruction.* These teachers make instruction personally relevant to students, stress basic literacy competencies, develop strategy-oriented instruction, and involve students in the process of intellectual discovery.

Ruddell concluded that influential teachers create opportunities for literacy learning to be "an active, exciting, collaborative, and learner-centered process of discovery" (p. 462).

Nurturing students' interest in reading and writing is crucial. Gambrell (1996) identified six research-based factors related to increased motivation for reading:

1. Teachers model a love of reading.
2. The classroom library is stocked with a wide variety of appealing books.
3. Students have daily opportunities to self-select books to read.
4. Students have daily opportunities to talk with classmates about books.
5. Students are familiar with lots of books.
6. Teachers provide incentives for reading.

From the research she conducted and other studies that she reviewed, Gambrell concluded that teachers can motivate students when they "serve as reading models and motivators and create classroom cultures that are book-rich, provide opportunities for choice, encourage social interactions about books, build on the familiar, and reflect on the view that books are the best reward" (p. 23).

Effective teachers are learners, too. Cullinan and Strickland's (1986) experiences in working with teachers as researchers show that these teachers see themselves as learners in the classroom, along with their students. They are continually seeking better opportunities for nurturing reading and writing, for creating important literacy events in the classroom. They are not afraid to question traditional assumptions and to encourage their students to be questioners. Teaching becomes, for them, a matter of designing situations and events for inquiry and learning.

## COMPARING CLASSROOM ENVIRONMENTS

Researchers have begun to consider the influence of the instructional setting. Often they compare the effectiveness of instruction in traditional and holistic classrooms and the impact of the classroom environment on learning. Scharer (1992) documented the changes in five elementary teachers' classrooms as they transitioned from basal reading programs to literature-based programs. The teachers changed the reading materials that they used and the instructional activities they used, but what was important for this discussion, is that the roles of teachers and students changed. Teachers changed from be providers of knowledge to facilitators of learning. Scharer concluded that change is slow, and that districts should avoid rapid, large-scale, mandated changes and attempt implementation slowly, beginning with a few interested teachers to pilot the innovation.

In a 2-year naturalistic case study, McIntyre and Freppon (1994) studied how six young low-income children developed as readers and writers in two different instructional settings. One classroom was described as "skills-based" and the other as "whole language." All six children in the 2-year period in both classrooms learned alphabetic concepts and skills necessary for reading and writing. The researchers concluded that phonics instruction was necessary for learning to read and write but that alphabetic knowledge could be developed successfully in both instructional contexts.

Dahl and Freppon (1995) compared two studies investigating inner-city first graders' reading and writing instruction in skills-based and whole language classrooms. They found that students in both classrooms learned phonics, but the students in whole language classrooms were better able to read and self-correct while reading. The students in both classrooms enjoyed literature, but they differed in how they responded to books. Children in whole language classrooms were better able to assume a critical stance toward the books, and the researchers concluded that this effect was because children in whole language classrooms were more actively involved while listening to books read aloud.

The children in the two types of classrooms also varied in how they used coping strategies when they ran into difficulty. Students in skills-based classrooms appeared to become passive. They sat quietly and randomly marked worksheets just to finish. They also copied classmates' work and tried to bluff their way through the reading lesson. In contrast, students in whole language classrooms interacted with their classmates when they didn't know what to do. They established their own support system and attempted to carry on the activity meaningfully.

Next, students in the two types of classrooms varied in their sense of what it means to be a reader and writer. Whole language students viewed themselves as readers and writers rather than focusing on the acts of reading and writing. In contrast, only the most capable readers and writers in skills-based classrooms showed the same awareness of being readers and writers. Dahl and Freppon (1995) concluded that students in the skills classrooms did not get personally involved in reading and writing. In contrast, students in whole language classrooms engaged in literate behaviors in addition to learning literacy skills.

The classroom context became an important aspect when Barone (1994) examined the literacy development of young children who were prenatally exposed to crack/cocaine. She found that students' literacy development was consistent with the development of children who had not been exposed to crack/cocaine. Some students were placed in whole language classrooms and others in traditional classrooms, and their reading and writing achievement was similar. The main difference, she concluded, was that students in holistic classrooms could also make intertextual connections between books they had read.

While these studies do not show tremendous differences that are due to varying classroom environments, researchers have noted subtle differences and validated child-centered and holistic classrooms. It seems likely that research will continue to examine the influence of the classroom community—especially literature-based and balanced classroom environments—on learning.

## CONCLUSION

Classrooms are complex settings, and through careful observation and analysis, researchers are attempting to describe the communities that teachers and students create in elementary classrooms (Cambourne, 2000). Researchers use ethnographic methodologies to examine these learning communities and the social interaction and learning that takes place in the classrooms. Elementary school teachers increasingly see themselves as learners, and they conduct teacher researcher studies in their own classrooms to better understand their students and their learning processes. This view of the classroom as a community of learners represents a change in how learning and teaching are viewed, and researchers have also compared students' learning in these holistic, child-centered classrooms with students' learning in traditional classrooms.

It is important to point out, however, that not all elementary classrooms function as they have been described in this chapter. Schmuck & Schmuck (1992) studied 119 elementary teachers in 80 small town schools and found that two thirds of classroom talk was teachers' talk. In addition, they found that most of these classrooms were teacher-centered. Most surprisingly, however, was that the researchers saw student-to-student talk that was planned by the teacher in only 10 of the classrooms. The communities of learners that researchers are now studying represent a new direction for elementary classrooms.

# References

Barnes, D. (1992). *From communication to curriculum* (2nd ed.). Portsmouth, NH: Boynton/Cook.

Barnes, D. (1993). Supporting exploratory talk for learning. In K. M. Pierce & C. J. Gilles (Eds.), *Cycles of meaning: Exploring the potential of talk in learning communities* (pp. 17–34). Portsmouth, NH: Heinemann.

Barone, D. (1994). The importance of classroom context: Literacy development of children prenatally exposed to crack/cocaine—year two. *Research in the Teaching of English, 28,* 286–312.

Barr, R., & Dreeben, R. (1983). *How schools work.* Chicago: The University of Chicago Press.

Boyer, E. (1995). *The basic school: A community for learning.* Princeton, NJ: Carnegie Foundation for the Advancement of Teaching.

Burton, F. R. (1986). Research currents: A teacher's conception of the action research process. *Language Arts, 63,* 718–723.

Butler, A., & Turbill, J. (1984). *Towards a reading-writing classroom.* Portsmouth, NH: Heinemann.

Calkins, L. M. (1994). *The art of teaching writing* (Rev. ed.). Portsmouth, NH: Heinemann.

Cambourne, B. (1984). Language, learning, and literacy. In A. Butler & J. Turbill (Eds.), *Towards a reading-writing classroom* (pp. 5–10). Portsmouth, NH: Heinemann.

Cambourne, B. (2000). Conditions for literacy learning—Observing literacy learning in elementary classrooms: Nine years of classroom anthropology. *The Reading Teacher, 53,* 512–515.

Cazden, C. B. (1972). *Child language and education.* New York: Holt, Rinehart & Winston.

Cazden, C. B. (1988). *Classroom discourse.* Portsmouth, NH: Heinemann.

Cochran-Smith, M., & Lytle, S. L. (1993). *Inside/outside: Teacher research and knowledge.* New York: Teachers College Press.

Cochran-Smith, M., Kahn, J., & Paris, C. L. (1990). When word processors come into the classroom. In J. L. Hoot & S. B. Silver (Eds.), *Writing with computers in the early grades* (pp. 43–74). New York: Teachers College Press.

Cullinan, B. E., & Strickland, D. S. (1986). The early years: Language, literature, and literacy in classroom research. *The Reading Teacher, 39,* 788–806.

Dahl, K. L., & Freppon, P. A. (1995). A comparison of inner city children's interpretations of reading and writing instruction in the early grades in skills-based and whole language classrooms. *Reading Research Quarterly, 30,* 50–74.

Delpit, L. (1986). Skills and other dilemmas of a progressive black educator. *Harvard Educational Review, 56,* 85–111.

Delpit, L. (1988). The silenced dialogue: Power and pedagogy in educating other people's children. *Harvard Educational Review, 58,* 280–298.

Dewey, J. (1938/1974). *Experience and education.* New York: Macmillan.

Dickinson, J. (1993). Children's perspectives on talk: Building a learning community. In K. M. Pierce & C. J. Gilles (Eds.), *Cycles of meaning: Exploring the potential of talk in learning communities* (pp. 99–116). Portsmouth, NH: Heinemann.

Dixon, C. N., Frank, C. R., & Green, J. L. (1999). Classrooms as cultures: Understanding the constructed nature of life in classrooms. *Primary Voices, 7*(3), 4–8.

Dixon-Krauss, L. (1996). *Vygotsky in the classroom: Mediated literacy instruction and assessment.* White Plains, NY: Longman.

Dyson, A. H. (1993). *Social worlds of children learning to write in an urban primary school.* New York: Teachers College Press.

El-Hindi, A. E. (1998). Beyond classroom boundaries: Constructivist teaching with the Internet. *The Reading Teacher, 51,* 694–700.

Emig, J. (1983). Non-magical thinking: Presenting writing developmentally in schools. In D. Goswami & M. Butler (Eds.), *The web of meaning* (pp. 135–144). Portsmouth, NH: Heinemann & Boynton/Cook.

Erickson, F. (1986). Qualitative methods in research on teaching. In M. C. Wittrock (Ed.), *Handbook of research on teaching* (3rd ed.) (pp. 119–161). New York: Macmillan.

Fishman, A. R. (1996). Getting what they deserve: Eighth-grade girls, culture, and empowerment. *Voices from the Middle, 3*(1), 25–32.

Flanders, N. (1970). *Analyzing teacher behavior.* Reading, MA: Addison-Wesley.

Friere, P. (1970). *Pedagogy of the oppressed.* New York: Continuum.

Gambrell, L. B. (1996). Creating classroom cultures that foster reading motivation. *The Reading Teacher, 50,* 14–25.

Genishi, C., McCarrier, A., & Nussbaum, N. R. (1988). Research currents: Dialogue as a context for teaching and learning. *Language Arts, 65,* 182–191.

Genishi, C., McCollom, P., & Strand, E. (1985). Research currents: The international richness of children's computer use. *Language Arts, 62,* 526–532.

Goodman, Y. M. (1987). Forward. In C. E. Loughlin & M. D. Martin, *Supporting literacy* (pp. xii–xiv). New York: Teachers College Press.

Goodman, Y. M. (1992). The writing process: The making of meaning. In Y. M. Goodman & S. Wilde (Eds.), *Literacy events in a community of young writers* (pp. 1–16). New York: Teachers College Press.

Goodman, Y. M., & Wilde, S. (Eds.) (1992). *Literacy events in a community of young writers.* New York: Teachers College Press.

Gorman, A., Tschoepe, M., & Martinez, M. (1998). Language and literacy. *Primary Voices K-6, 6*(1), 10–23.

Graves, D. H. (1975). An examination of the writing processes of seven-year-old children. *Research in the Teaching of English, 9,* 225–241.

Graves, D. H. (1983). *Writing: Teachers and children at work.* Exeter, NH: Heinemann.

Graves, D. H. (1991). *Build a literate classroom.* Portsmouth, NH: Heinemann.

Graves, D. H. (1994). *A fresh look at writing.* Portsmouth, NH: Heinemann.

Greenlee-Moore, M. E., & Smith, L. L. (1996). Interactive computer software: The effects on young children's reading achievement. *Reading Psychology, 17,* 43–64.

Halliday, M. A. K. (1977). *Learning how to mean: Explorations in the development of language*. New York: Elsevier.

Heath, S. B. (1983). *Ways with words*. New York: Cambridge University Press.

Henkin, R. (1998). *Who's invited to share? Using literacy to teach for equity and social justice*. Portsmouth, NH: Heinemann.

Hubbard, R., & Power, B. M. (1993). *The art of classroom inquiry: A handbook for teacher researchers*. Portsmouth, NH: Heinemann.

Jackson, P. W. (1968). *Life in classrooms*. New York: Holt, Rinehart, & Winston.

Jett-Simpson, M., & Masland, S. (1993). Girls are not dodo birds? Exploring gender equity issues in the language arts classroom. *Language Arts, 70,* 104-107.

Johnson, D. W., & Johnson, R. T. (1975). *Learning together and alone: Cooperation, competition and individualization*. Englewood Cliffs, NJ: Prentice-Hall.

Kamler, B. (1993). Constructing gender in the process writing classroom. *Language Arts, 70,* 95-103.

Karelitz, E. B. (1993). *The author's chair and beyond: Language and literacy in a primary classroom*. Portsmouth, NH: Heinemann.

Kasten, W. C. (1992). Speaking, searching and sharing in the community of writers. In Y. M. Goodman & S. Wilde (Eds.), Literacy events in a community of young writers (pp. 87-103). New York: Teachers College Press.

Leu, D. J., & Leu, D. D. (1997). *Teaching with the Internet: Lessons from the classroom*. Norwood, MA: Christopher-Gordon.

Loughlin, C. E., & Martin, M. S. (1987). *Supporting literacy: Developing effective learning environments*. New York: Teachers College Press.

Loughlin, C. E., & Suina, J. H. (1982). *The learning environment: An instructional strategy*. New York: Teachers College Press.

Lucas, C., & Borders, D. (1987). Language diversity and classroom discourse. *American Educational Research Journal, 24,* 119-141.

MacLean, M. S., & Mohr, M. M. (1999). *Teacher-researchers at work*. Berkeley, CA: National Writing Project.

Martinez, M., Perez, B., & Cook, G. (1998). Key dimensions of school life. *Primary Voices K-6, 6*(1), 3-9.

McIntyre, E., & Freppon, P. A. (1994). A comparison of children's development of alphabetic knowledge in a skills-based and a whole language classroom. *Research in the Teaching of English, 28,* 391-417.

Meyer, A., & Rose, D. H. (1998). *Learning to read in the computer age*. Cambridge, MA: Brookline Books.

Moll, L. C. (Ed.) (1990). *Vygotsky and education: Instructional implications and applications of sociohistorical psychology*. Cambridge, UK: Cambridge University Press.

Morrow, L. M. (1989). Designing the classroom to promote literacy development. In D. S. Strickland & L. M. Morrow (Eds.), *Emerging literacy: Young children learn to read and write*. Newark, DE: International Reading Association.

Morrow, L. M. (1997). *The literacy center: Contexts for reading and writing*. York, ME: Stenhouse.

Newman, J. M., Vibert, A., Freeman, L. M., & Scharp, P. L. (1988). Online: Learning collaboratively. *Language Arts, 65,* 74-79.

Niemec, R., Samson, G., Weinstein, T., & Walberg, J. (1987). The effects of computer-based instruction in elementary schools: A quantitative synthesis. *Journal of Research on Computing in Education, 20,* 85-103.

Paul, K. C. (1998). Democracy in room 122. *Primary Voices K-6, 7*(2), 7-12.

Peterson, R. (1992). *Life in a crowded place: Making a learning community*. Portsmouth, NH: Heinemann.

Reid, T. R. A. (1985). Writing with micro-computers in a fourth grade classroom: An ethnographic study. *Dissertation Abstracts International, 47,* 03A.

Reinking, D., Labbo, L., & McKenna, M. (1997). Navigating the changing landscape of literacy: Current theory and research in computer-based reading and writing. In J. Flood, S. B. Heath, & D. Lapp (Eds.), *Handbook of research on teaching literacy through the communicative and visual arts* (pp. 77-92). New York: Macmillan.

Ross, E. P. (1996). *The workshop approach: A framework for literacy*. Norwood, MA: Christopher-Gordon.

Ruddell, R. B. (1995). Those influential literacy teachers: Meaning negotiators and motivation builders. *The Reading Teacher, 48,* 454-463.

Santa Barbara Classroom Discourse Group (1992a). Constructing literacy in classrooms: Literate action as social accomplishment. In H. Marshall (Ed.), *Redefining student learning: Roots of educational change* (pp. 119-150). Norwood, NJ: Ablex.

Santa Barbara Classroom Discourse Group (1992b). Do you see what we see? The referential and intertextual nature of classroom life. *Journal of Classroom Interaction, 27*(2), 29-36.

Scharer, P. L. (1992). Teachers in transition: An exploration of changes in teachers and classrooms during implementation of literature-based reading instruction. *Research in the Teaching of English, 26,* 408-445.

Schmuck, R. A., & Schmuck, P. A. (1992). Group processes in the classroom (6th ed.). Dubuque, IA: William C. Brown.

Seiler, W. J., Schuelke, L. D., & Lieb-Brilhart, B. (1984). *Communication for the contemporary classroom*. New York: Holt, Rinehart, & Winston.

Siller, D. (1998). A student teacher's perspective on a democratic classroom. *Primary Voices K-6, 7*(2), 20-25.

Smith, F. (1978). *Reading without nonsense*. New York: Teachers College Press.

Smith, F. (1988). *Joining the literacy club: Further essays into education*. Portsmouth, NH: Heinemann.

Staab, C. (1991). Classroom organization: Thematic centers revisited. *Language Arts, 68,* 108-113.

Vygotsky, L. S. (1931/1986). *Thought and language*. Cambridge, MA: MIT Press.

Vygotsky, L. S. (1978). *Mind in society: The development of higher psychological processes*. Cambridge, MA: Harvard University Press.

Wells, G. (1985). Preschool literacy related activities and success in school. In D. Olson, N. Torrance, & A. Hildyard (Eds.), *Literacy, language, and learning: The nature and consequences of reading and writing*. Cambridge, UK: Cambridge University Press.

Wilkinson, L. C. (Ed.) (1982). *Communicating in the classroom*. New York: Academic Press.

Wolk, S. (1998). *A democratic classroom*. Portsmouth, NH: Heinemann.

Wood, B. S. (1984). Oral communication in the elementary school. In C. Thaiss & C. Suhor (Eds.), *Speaking and writing K-12* (pp. 104-125). Urbana, IL: National Council of Teachers of English.

Wood, G. (1992). *Schools that work: America's most innovative public education programs*. New York: Dutton.

Wood, G. (1998). Educating for democracy in the elementary school classroom. *Primary Voices K-6, 7*(2), 3-6.

# SECONDARY ENGLISH CLASSROOM ENVIRONMENTS

## Allan A. Glatthorn and Daniel L. Shouse
### East Carolina University

This chapter reviews and synthesizes the research on the learning environment of secondary English classrooms. It begins by presenting a conceptualization of that environment that is based on four key components: the physical environment; the group environment; the work environment; and the psychosocial environment. That conceptualization provides an organizing system for the rest of the chapter.

The review of the literature was conducted by first locating sources that related to the topic addressed here; the author conducted a comprehensive examination of the ERIC database, using these descriptors: *learning environment; classroom environment; English classroom environment; learning climate; school environment*. The same descriptors were used in reviewing *Dissertation Abstracts* and *Subject Guide to Books in Print*. Those publications that met generally accepted standards for research design were identified and examined.

## The English Classroom Environment: An Alternative Conceptualization

In most of the related research, *classroom environment* has been conceptualized somewhat narrowly, focusing essentially on what is termed here the psychosocial environment. The best way to understand this narrowness is to examine the two most widely used scales for measuring secondary classroom learning environments—the Classroom Environment Scale (CES) (Moos & Trickett, 1974) and the Learning Environment Inventory (LEI) (Fraser, Anderson, & Walberg, 1982). The CES measures students' perceptions across three broad dimensions: relationship, the nature and intensity of personal relationships within the environment; personal development, the basic directions along which personal growth happens; and system

maintenance and system change, the extent to which the environment is orderly, clear in expectations, control-oriented, and responsive to change. These 3 broad dimensions subsume 9 subscales; the dimensions and subscales are identified and defined briefly in Fig. 37.1. (The subscale definitions are paraphrased from Moos, 1980.)

The LEI (Secondary Level) includes 105 items descriptive of secondary school classes; these items are related to 15 scales. The scales and their definitions (paraphrased from Fraser, Anderson, & Walberg, 1982) are shown in Fig. 37.2.

These two instruments seem to be both sound in their design and productive in their use. First, both have achieved a satisfactory degree of reliability and validity. As Fraser (1986) notes, the alpha reliability coefficents (a measure of internal consistency reliability) for the nine subscales of the CES range from 0.51 to 0.75; and those of the LEI, from 0.54 to 0.85. The mean correlations of one scale with other scales (a measure of discriminant validity) for the CES range from 0.09 to 0.40; those for the LEI, from 0.08 to 0.40. The two inventories have also produced a significant body of research. (For a review of that research, see the section on "Psychosocial Environment.")

However, both instruments seem somewhat narrow in their conceptualization of classroom environment. Except for the "Difficulty" and "Material Environment" scales of the LEI, both inventories address elements of only the psychosocial environment—the patterns of relationships and interactions between students and students and teacher and students. For the purposes of this review, a more inclusive conceptualization seems needed.

Such a conceptualization would begin by placing the classroom environment in a broader context. Here a synthesis of the research on educational productivity by Fraser, Walberg, Welch, and Hattie (1987) seems useful. On the basis of their review

## Relationship Dimensions

1. **Involvement.** The extent to which students are attentive and interested.
2. **Affiliation.** Student friendship; the extent to which students cooperate and enjoy working together.
3. **Teacher support.** The help, trust, and friendship demonstrated by the teacher.

## Personal Growth or Goal Orientation Dimensions

4. **Task orientation.** The importance of completing activities and sticking to the subject matter.
5. **Competition.** The emphasis placed on competition and grades and the difficulty of achieving good grades.

## System Maintenance and Change Dimensions

6. **Order and organization.** The emphasis on students behaving in an orderly manner and on the organization of assignments and class activities.
7. **Rule clarity.** The emphasis on establishing and following clear rules and on students knowing the consequences of not following them.
8. **Teacher control.** How strict the teacher is in enforcing rules and punishing rule infractions.
9. **Innovation.** How much students are involved in planning classroom activities and the number of innovative activities planned by the teacher.

FIGURE 37.1. Dimensions and subscales of the classroom environment scale.

of about 3,000 studies of educational research, they identified 9 factors (falling into 3 groups) that increase student learning. Three of the factors related to student aptitude: ability or prior achievement; development, as indexed by age or maturation; and motivation, or self-concept. Two of the factors related to instruction: the amount of time students were engaged in learning; and the quality of the learning experience, including both psychological and curricular aspects. Four of the factors related to what they term the "psychological environments": the home; the peer group outside school; the amount of leisure-time television viewing; and the classroom environment.

Thus, by a process of elimination, "classroom environment" seems to be used to mean all those classroom elements other than student aptitude and instruction (including the curriculum and time allocations). By excluding these elements and by reviewing the research on secondary English classrooms, one can analyze the construct *classroom environment* into four related elements. (See Fig. 37.3 for a schematic representation of these elements.)

1. Physical environment. The physical environment of the classroom includes such elements as the presence or absence of walls, classroom design and furniture, and classroom density and crowding.
2. Group environment. The group environment (as the term is used here) involves the way students are grouped for

1. **Cohesiveness.** Extent to which students help and are friendly with each other.
2. **Diversity.** Extent to which students' differences are provided for.
3. **Formality.** Extent to which behavior is guided by formal rules.
4. **Speed.** Extent to which class work is covered rapidly.
5. **Material Environment.** Availability of adequate books, equipment, and space.
6. **Friction.** Amount of tension among students.
7. **Goal direction.** Degree of goal clarity.
8. **Favoritism.** Extent to which teacher treats some students more favorably than others.
9. **Difficulty.** Extent to which students find class work difficult.
10. **Apathy.** Extent to which the class feels no affinity with class activities.
11. **Democracy.** Extent to which students share equally in decision-making.
12. **Cliqueness.** Extent to which students refuse to mix with rest of class.
13. **Satisfaction.** Extent of enjoyment of class work.
14. **Disorganization.** Extent to which class activities are confusing and disorganized.
15. **Competitiveness.** Emphasis placed on students competing with each other.

FIGURE 37.2. Scales of the learning environment inventory.

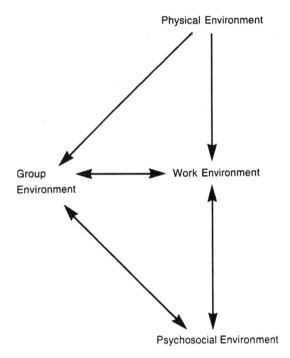

(Note: The lines and arrows are intended to suggest general relationship, not casual influences and directions.)

FIGURE 37.3. Elements of classroom learning environment.

learning—the size of the class and the tracking and grouping systems used to assign students to a class.

3. Work environment. The work environment is the nature of the academic work and its related activities, as construed by the teacher and the students.

4. Psychosocial environment. The psychosocial environment is the shared perceptions of the people in an environment about the nature of the psychosocial interactions of that environment.

These four elements are used as the organizing bases for the reviews that follow.

## THE PHYSICAL ENVIRONMENT

The *physical environment of the classroom* is a comprehensive concept that includes the following elements: the presence or absence of walls ("open space" or "traditional" classrooms); classroom design and furniture; seating arrangements; the density and crowding of classrooms; and the amount of noise in the classroom. Surprisingly, perhaps, there have been only a handful of research studies that have specifically examined the relationship of the physical environment of the secondary English classroom to student achievement and student attitude.

The only major publication dealing with the issue of the physical nature of the English classroom was Whalen's (1972) report for the National Council of Teachers of English Committee on English Learning Environment. Since the committee

functioned during the years when flexible grouping schemes were popular with many educators, they predictably concluded that varied spatial arrangements were needed. They proposed a set of recommendations that from this vantage point seem somewhat unrealistic: a large auditorium for the presentation of plays and other artistic performances; several regular classrooms designed to accommodate up to 30 students; smallgroup seminar rooms; conference spaces for 1 to 2 students; and numerous spaces for individual study. The committee provided little research support for their recommendations, relying solely on the recommendations of experts and their own experience. Somewhat similar recommendations were made by Krovetz (1977), although again without much research support.

Since there is thus a rather narrow research base on the specific issue of the physical environment of secondary English classrooms, the following review will examine the research on the general issue of the relationship of the physical environment of classrooms to student achievement and attitude. Those studies that used achievement as the dependent variable equated achievement with performance on either a subject-based test or a standardized test; those using attitude as the variable relied on scores on some attitudinal measure. The review concludes by discussing the implications of that research of the secondary English classroom.

### The Presence or Absence of Classroom Walls

During the school building boom of late 1960s and early 1970s, many school boards followed the recommendations of architects who advocated the construction of "open space" schools. In fact, a 1975 study by George reported that more than half of the schools built between 1967 and 1970 were open space schools. While there was much variation in how this concept was understood and implemented, most open space schools were characterized by the presence of several large general teaching and learning areas (often called "pods") that could accommodate up to 150 students and 5 teachers. In some open space schools, pods were assigned to grade levels; thus, an English teacher would share this open space with teachers of social studies and mathematics. In other open space schools, pods were assigned to departments; thus, five English teachers might share one pod.

Because most open Space schools were built in earlier decades, most of the research dates from that era. Several studies examined the nature of student activity in open space schools. An early study by Burnham (1970) of open space and traditional schools determined that in the open environment, students were more often observed initiating activities, engaging in cooperative learning with teachers and each other, assuming personal responsibility, and in general demonstrating a "spirit of inquiry." Gump (1974) found that life in open space schools seemed more active: students entered more sites and spent more time in transitions from space to space. However, as Durlak, Beardsley, and Murray (1972) note, it would be unwise to equate type of space and type of program: they discovered that some traditional schools supported rather open patterns of activity, while some open environments housed traditional programs.

One major study (Gump & Ross, 1977) examined the nature of teacher behavior in open space settings over a 2-year period. As the school year progressed, teacher tended to close off and define space with the use of furniture. Tall furniture was used to create visual barriers, and low furniture to mark off territorial boundaries.

What are the effects of open space schools on teachers and students? In general open space seems to have a positive effect on teachers, although Weinstein (1979) notes that the problem of self-selection may be a confounding factor: teachers who prefer an open environment would be more likely to volunteer for assignment to open space schools. Given that limitation, teachers in open space schools, when compared with their counter parts in traditional buildings, tend to show the following characteristics: have increased interaction with peers (Meyer, 1971); have greater feelings of autonomy (Brunetti, 1971); express greater satisfaction (Meyer, 1971); spend less time on routine activities (Ellison, Gibert, & Ratsoy, 1969); and more often use variable group activities (Warner, 1971).

What is the effect of open space on student attitudes and learning? In general the evidence suggests that students in open space schools tend to have more positive attitudes than their counterparts in traditional schools: they have greater feelings of autonomy (Meyer, 1971); are more willing to take risks (Anifant, 1972); and show greater task persistence (Reiss & Dyhaldo, 1975). There also seem to be some important behavioral differences. Students in open space schools tend to interact with a greater number of teachers during the day (Gump, 1974) and engage in a greater variety of activities (Clem, Ahern, Dailey, Gary & Scantlebury, undated).

The evidence on the effects of open space schools on student achievement is somewhat conflicting. The only two studies that attempted to control curricular and other variables yielded different results. The study by Traub, Weiss, Fisher, and Khan (1976) of 30 schools found no consistent relationship between space and achievement. However, the researchers did discover that students in open space schools displayed more positive attitudes toward school, their teachers, and themselves; they also scored higher on independence. Teachers in open space schools also seemed more positive toward their work and demonstrated more interactions with peers and administrators. However, Beck (1979) found in a study of 120 schools that students in traditional schools achieved at significantly higher rates in mathematics and reading than did students in open space schools; there were no significant differences in such noncognitive outcomes as attitude toward school and locus of control. On the basis of his review of the evidence, George (1975) concluded that "neither the open space schools or the conventional schools have demonstrated a clear superiority" (p. 63).

## Classroom Design and Furniture

If classrooms are separated by walls, then the next issue to examine is whether variations in classroom design and classroom furniture make any significant difference.

First, how do teachers place themselves in classrooms? There is some evidence that teachers place themselves "front and center" regardless of whether the classroom is perceived as open or traditional. In Rivlin and Rothenberg's (1976) study of two schools using open classroom approaches, teachers tended to remain in the front center of the room, near the blackboard and the classroom door. The students in those classrooms tended to spend most of their time close to the teacher, even though more space was available in other portions of the room. When teachers varied from that standard pattern by placing their desks in the corner of the room, Zifferblatt (1972) determined that teachers moved around the room more and seemed more involved with students.

The general attractiveness of the classroom and the type and placement of classroom furniture seem to affect student attitudes and behavior, although there is no demonstrable relationship between these elements of the physical environment and student achievement. Early laboratory studies by Mintz (1956) concluded that there was a relationship between an "ugly" environment and feelings of discontent and fatigue. In the Zifferblatt study, the clustering of 2 or 3 student desks together seemed to be more satisfactory than clustering 10 or 12 desks together. An "alternative learning facility" for college students that made use of much color, movable panels, and comfortable sets seemed to result in better attendance, greater student participation, and increased group cohesiveness (Horowitz & Otto, 1973). And Santrock (1976) concluded that the affective quality of the environment seemed to influence student task persistence: students worked longer in a "happy" setting than in a "sad" or neutral one.

Although the conventional wisdom suggests that placing student desks in circles, squares or horseshoes should facilitate student participation, the available evidence does not support this belief. Johnson's (1973) study of the effect of furniture arrangement on student participation showed no significant differences in the patterns of verbal interaction. One study suggested that traditional rows are academically useful: Bennett and Blundell (1983) found that having students work independently in rows before they did group work resulted in an increased quantity of work with a similar level of quality. Despite this finding, the issue of furniture placement and student achievement seems unresolved. As Weinstein (1979) notes, it may be that the differences between rows, horseshoes, and circles are not powerful enough to affect achievement and verbal interaction.

High school teachers report clear preferences about classroom equipment and furniture, according to Foster-Harrison and Adams-Bullock (1998). They ranked student desks as the most important furniture item; they also wanted a clean classroom, with attractive murals and colorful walls. In the same study they also reported that having their own desk in the classroom and having their name on the door were critical professional prerequisites.

## Seating Arrangements

As noted, the placement of furniture in general seems not be an important environmental factor. However, where students sit in the classroom does seem to be important. When desks are arranged in traditional rows, students sitting in the front and center seem to get more than their share of teacher attention. Early studies by Adams (1969) and Adams and Biddle (1970) established that students who sat in the "action zone" (in the front and center of the room) interacted most frequently with the teacher. Later studies did not consistently support these early findings. The Koneya (1976) study substantiated the existence of the action zone; the Delefes and Jackson (1972) study did not.

Additional studies have analyzed seating arrangements with different constructs. Brooks, Silvern, and Wooten (1978) identified the front and center as the "social-consultive" zone, finding that students who sat in that zone received a more permissive and interactive type of communication from the teacher; students in the public zone (middle and back of the room) received more lecturing and one-way communication.

Several studies have tried to establish the causal direction of seating patterns and positions: do verbally active students choose front and center positions? or do front and center positions seem to increase student participation? The results are generally inconclusive. A study by Schwebel and Cherlin (1972) indicated that moving students to the action zone tended to increase students' on-task behavior and increased the number of favorable teacher ratings. Stires (1978) discovered that, whether or not students chose their own seats or were randomly assigned, those in the middle received higher grades and liked both the course and the instructor better than those on the side. However, Koneya (1976) discovered that highly verbal college students chose front-center seats when asked to indicate their preference on a seating chart. In the same study, the participation by highly and moderately verbal students was affected by seat placement; these students participated more frequently when they sat in the action zone, whereas the participation of low verbalizers was not affected by seat placement.

In her review of the research, Weinstein (1979) suggests that the better achievement, attitudes, and participation of students sitting in the action zone result from their greater proximity to the teacher, resulting in increased eye contact and greater opportunities for other kinds of nonverbal communication.

## Density and Crowding

In analyzing the effects of the number of students in a given space, Stokols (1972) makes a useful distinction between density and crowding: density is a mathematical measure of the number of people in a given space; crowding is the perceived judgment of excessive density. Perceptions of crowding seem to depend on several factors, including personal preferences and the kind of activity. According to Epstein and Karlin (1975), individuals have certain expectations about appropriate space for given kinds of interactions and feel that they are crowded when they are not provided with what they believe is appropriate distance.

Crowding would seem to be the more important measure in studying achievement. Yet when achievement of a complex task is the criterion, crowding does not seem to be a significant variable. Weinstein (1979) offers three explanations for this somewhat surprising conclusion: Some studies examined only density, ignoring the more important phenomenon of crowding; in many of the studies, the tasks were not sufficiently complex, and even more complex tasks that do not require interaction are not impaired by high density.

However, density does seem to affect behavior. In general, high density classrooms have been found to be associated with increased aggression (Loo & Kennelly, 1979), decreased social interaction (Hutt & Hutt, 1970), and noninvolvement with lesson activities (Shapiro, 1975). And in a major study that systematically varied density and the resources available in a day-care classroom, Rohe and Patterson (1974) discovered that as density was increased, aggressive, destructive, and uninvolved behavior increased. Finally, a study of college students by Schettino and Borden (1976) determined that increased density was associated with increased feelings of nervousness and crowdedness for women and increased feelings of aggressiveness for men.

## Noise

Researchers investigating the effects of noise on learning usually make a distinction between short-term exposure to moderate within-school or within-classroom noise and long-term exposure to external noise, such as that from an airport or highway. In general within-classroom noise does not seem to have a deleterious effect on learning. A (1979) study by Weinstein and Weinstein on the effect of noise in an open space school on reading comprehension found no significant differences in performance under conditions of quiet and normal background noise.

However, studies of schools located near airports, busy highways, or elevated trains indicated that there may be effects from long-term exposure to increased noise levels. Children on the noisy side of a school near an elevated train had reading scores significantly lower than those on the less noisy side (Bronzaft & McCarthy, 1975). In classrooms facing a major traffic artery, almost 17 minutes were lost from teaching time on the noisy side of the building, whereas only 7.5 minutes were lost on the quiet side (Kyzar, 1977). Similar results were obtained in a study of schools close to the Heathrow Airport in London (Crook & Langdon, 1974).

## Students' Individual Preferences

Some educators who advocate the importance of assessing student learning styles and adjusting instructional conditions accordingly view environmental factors as critical aspects of style preference. Thus, the Learning Style Profile published by the National Association of Secondary School Principals (Keefe, 1988) includes items on sound preference, lighting preference, and temperature preference; and the Learning Style Inventory (Dunn, Dunn, & Price, 1985) assesses learner preferences for sound, light, temperature, and need for either a formal or informal design.

Dunn and Dunn (1987) cite several studies supporting their belief that responding to such preferences will result in improved learning. Shea (1983) determined that when students who preferred sitting informally on cushions, couches, and carpeting were permitted to work that way, they performed significantly better on an English comprehension test than when they were required to sit in conventional seats. Some adolescents, according to Price's (1980) study, seemed to think and remember best when studying with music. Some students performed better in low rather than bright light (Krimsky, 1982). Middle school students achieved better when they were tested in a thermal setting that matched their preferences (Murrain, 1983). On the basis of this review, the Dunns recommend that teachers provide environmental options in classrooms and let students learn in the kind of environment they prefer.

Others are not persuaded either by this limited body of evidence or the assumptions that undergird it. David Kolb, who has done extensive research on the conceptual dimensions of learning styles, expresses this caution in his commentary on a 1981 article by Dunn and De Bello:

I feel there are great dangers in the misuse of learning style concepts. Specifically, we must avoid turning these ideas into stereotypes used to pigeon hole individuals. Furthermore, we should not deny students the opportunity to develop themselves fully by only exposing them to educational environments that match their strengths (p. 373).

Other criticisms of learning style accommodation have been offered by Curry (1990), who argues that the research supporting the use of learning style approaches suffers from several flaws: There is a bewildering array of definitions of the concept; the instruments used lack sufficient reliability and validity; the reports do not discriminate between the effectiveness of several types of adaptations; there are several unacknowledged external threats to validity.

These problems do not seem to be associated with the use of *4MAT*, developed by McCarthy (1980). This instructional model systematically varies for all students the learning strategies, according to the brain hemispheres. Wilkerson and White (1988) determined that the use of 4MAT was associated with higher achievement on a test that measured knowledge, comprehension, application, and analysis—but no difference on a performance test that measured synthesis and evaluation. In an anecdotal report, Blair and Judah (1990) reported its successful use in high school English.

## Implications for the Secondary English Classroom

The assumption here is that school administrators and English teachers want learning environments that reflect these characteristics: Students are engaged in a variety of learning tasks; much of the teaching–learning transactions involve group discussion; students seem to be achieving a broad range of outcomes; students are developing positive attitudes about themselves, the teacher, and the study of English.

What kind of physical environment would best reflect those characteristics? The first point to make is that the physical environment does not matter, if student achievement is the sole

criterion. Weinstein's review of the research leads her to this conclusion:

Despite the objections voiced by many of these humanist educators to the hard "tight spaces" ... characteristic of our schools ..., it would seem that the physical environment of the conventional classroom has little impact on achievement (1979, p. 598).

However, the physical environment does seem to make a difference in relation to student attitudes and behavior. In determining which of those characteristics would be important for the secondary English classroom, only tentative recommendations can be offered, since the research base is somewhat limited.

1. Open space schools would seem to provide a hospitable environment for teaching English.
2. English classrooms should be attractive and uncrowded places.
3. English teachers should vary the seating arrangements to accommodate the instructional activity. They should feel free to experiment with circles and horseshoes when discussion is important. They should have students sit in rows when independent work is desired.
4. English teachers should be sensitive to the effects of seating arrangements on student participation. If they wish to encourage particular students to become more actively involved in activities, they should seat those students in the action zone.
5. English teachers should learn to tolerate the moderate noise levels produced by active learning and discussion, without worrying that that noise is distracting.

## GROUP ENVIRONMENT

As the term is used in this work, *group environment* refers to those aspects of the classroom learning environment that derive from administrative decisions about how many and which students are assigned to a class and teacher decisions about how that class is organized once those decisions have been implemented. Two aspects of the group environment seem important: class size; and tracking and ability grouping.

### Class Size

Teachers have always wanted smaller classes. Over the years, they have been uniformly insistent in their claims that smaller classes create a more desirable learning environment, result in better student achievement, and make their own professional lives more rewarding. (See, for example, Millard, 1977; Haddad, 1978; and Cotton & Savard, 1980.) And, as Suhor (1986) notes, the National Council of Teachers of English has for several years undertaken numerous efforts to persuade the public and school administrators that smaller classes are especially important for English teachers. As he points out, as far back as the 1950s, the NCTE recommended maximum class loads of

100 students for each English teacher; during the 1960s it recognized schools that had made significant efforts in reducing class size and teacher workload by designating them "Honor Roll" schools. And during the past 3 decades, it has appointed several committees to study the issue, has published bibliographies, and has disseminated kits to its members to help them achieve the goal of smaller classes.

To what extent are these beliefs and their resulting actions supported by the research? As Smith (1986) indicates, there is little research on the effects of class size and the teaching of English. It therefore seems useful here to review the large body of research on class size in general and then draw some tentative inferences about its implications for English classes.

### Class size and achievement.

Although the issue continues to be debated by both researchers and practitioners, it now seems reasonably safe to conclude that greater achievement occurs in smaller classes than in larger ones. This finding was first firmly established by Glass and Smith (1978) in their meta-analysis of 76 studies of the issue. They summarized their findings in this manner:

As class size increased, achievement decreased. A pupil who would score at about the 63rd percentile on a national test when taught individually would score about the 37th percentile in a class of 40 pupils. The difference is being taught in a class of 20 versus a class of 40 is an advantage of ten percentile ranks (p._).

They further noted that the greatest gains occurred in classes of 15 pupils or fewer; in classes of 20 to 40 students, gains were not as pronounced.

The Glass and Smith conclusions were strongly attacked by the authors of the Educational Research Service (1980) critique. They faulted the Glass and Smith meta-analysis on several grounds: A substantial number of the studies involved extremely small groups of 1 to 5 pupils; Glass and Smith relied on too few studies; they over-generalized from their results; and they ignored the political and fiscal realities that make the goal of very small classes almost impossible to achieve. However, a reanalysis of the Glass and Smith data by Hedges and Stock (1983) generally supports the Glass and Smith findings. They conclude that the "suboptimal statistical methods" used by Glass and Smith did not greatly affect the results of their meta-analysis.

One relatively recent study does bear out the value of reduction of English class size, as reported by the San Juan Unified School District (1992). Reducing freshman English classes from 30 to 20 resulted in significant gains in reading comprehension; students were also more engaged in the instructional process.

It should also be noted here that interest in class size has been reinvigorated by the longitudinal study of class size reduction in Tennessee. Terming that study "one of the great experiments in education in U.S. history," Mosteller, Light, and Sachs (1996, p. 814) note that the multiphase study concluded that students in primary classes of 15 experienced substantial improvement in reading and mathematics (when compared with those in classes of 30). The same effects persisted in grades 4, 5, 6, and 7, even though they returned to the larger classes.

### Class size and the nature of classroom interactions.

These generally positive effects of smaller classes can be understood by examining the research on the nature of classroom interactions in smaller and larger classes.

First, discipline is better in smaller classes. Several studies have concluded that in smaller classes, students are more likely to remain on task, the teacher is better able to manage disruptive behavior, and students seem to demonstrate greater self-control. (See, for example, Filby, 1980; Smith & Glass, 1979; and Noli, 1980.) Second, as determined in those same studies, student participation and involvement tends to increase when classes are small. This finding is perhaps predictable: Students who are not so aggressive in their responding behaviors are more likely to gain the floor in smaller classes.

Third, teachers in smaller classes tend to give more and better feedback than those in larger classes (Noli, 1980: McDonald, 1980; Smith & Glass, 1979). Finally, students show general improvement in a range of attitudinal responses. Smith and Glass's 1979 meta-analysis indicated that students in smaller classes had stronger motivation, better self-concept, and less anxiety.

Surprisingly, perhaps, teachers do not seem to vary their teaching methods when they teach smaller classes. Although there are some conflicting findings here, two major studies found that giving teachers smaller classes did not result in different teaching practices. In a 2-year study in Ontario, Shapson, Wright, Eason, and Fitzgerald (1978) determined that smaller classes did not result in greater individualization of instruction, even though the teachers involved were sure that greater individualization would occur. Field studies conducted by the Far West Regional Laboratory of two urban schools and two rural schools reached the same conclusion. As Filby (1980) noted in reviewing the results of these studies, the teachers were not likely to try dramatically different methods of instruction even though they had smaller classes, perhaps because they were not trained in such approaches.

### Class size and the teaching of English.

As noted, there have been relatively few studies that examined class size in teaching English. In a study of college instructional practices, Cheatham and Jordan (1976) determined that smaller classes of 20 were more desirable for what they termed "performance oriented" courses—and they included in this group English composition and speech communication. And McDonald (1980) concluded that classes of 15 or fewer were associated with improved student writing, because they made it possible for students to receive more feedback and do more revising under supervision. This relative lack of research seemed to place the NCTE Task Force on Class Size and Workload in Secondary English Instruction in a somewhat awkward position. After reviewing the research, the task force seemed to be able to make only weak claims about the advantages of smaller classes. Here is one example of their tentativeness:

if the goal is for students to analyze the theme and structure of any novel, common sense suggests that students will, at some point, have to engage in such analyses under the guidance of a teacher. In such cases, classes of thirty to forty may very well be too large (Smith, 1986, p. 3).

After noting the value of such teaching/learning activities as mastery learning, peer group problem solving, and homework with feedback, they offer this observation.

All of these and other powerful instructional variables are quite time-consuming, however, *Class size, therefore, may determine whether or not they are ever put into practice, for class size influences the extent to which they can be successfully employed.* Yet there is no research on the relationship of these variables to class size [Italics in original.] (Smith, 1986, p. 4).

Yet a later chapter in the same report concludes, that teachers with smaller classes did not vary their instructional techniques.

The body of research on class size in general would seem to warrant stronger claims. Smaller classes are also associated with better achievement. Smaller classes are also associated with other indicators of quality, such as better student discipline and increased student participation. And if English teachers are expected to respond to student writing and to involve students in discussion, then the argument about the need for smaller English classes would seem to be ended. Despite this evidence, school administrators seem relatively indifferent to the matter. The Applebee (1977) study of teaching conditions in English indicated that the typical secondary school English teacher taught five classes a day, with 26 to 30 students per class. There is no recent evidence to suggest that those conditions have changed substantially.

## Curriculum Tracking and Ability Grouping

The second aspect of the group environment is the way in which students are grouped for instruction. In general three grouping practices are widely used in American secondary schools: curriculum tracking; ability grouping; and within-class grouping. Curriculum tracking is a practice of assigning secondary students to a particular curricular sequence (such as college preparatory, general, or vocational) and scheduling them as curricular groups for their instruction. Thus, a student would take college preparatory English, college preparatory mathematics, and so on. Ability grouping is a practice of assigning students to classes on the basis of their ability in that particular subject. Thus, a student might be in a high ability English class and a middle ability class in mathematics. Within-class grouping is a practice by which a teacher, once having been assigned a class, divides that class into instructional groups on the basis of their ability. In this instance, an English teacher might have in the same class one group of excellent writers, one group of average writers, and one group of weaker writers.

Rather than organizing this discussion in relation to the type of grouping practice, it seems to make more sense to analyze the impact of ability grouping in general. After examining the evidence about the various processes by which students are assigned to instructional groups, Bolvin (1982) concluded that "there is little difference between curriculum grouping and ability-achievement grouping" (p. 266). Although elementary teachers seem to make extensive use of within-class grouping (especially for reading), secondary English teachers are less likely to use within-class ability grouping. Therefore, the discussion that follows examines the evidence relative to ability grouping in general, noting distinctions between the types only when that seems important.

***How students are assigned to groups.*** In examining how group assignments are determined, the distinction between curriculum tracking and ability grouping is important. In general, students (and their parents) choose the curriculum track; teachers and counselors usually determine ability group placement.

The research on how students choose curriculum tracks suggests a rather complex process. (The description that follows is a synthesis of three major sources: Alexander & Cook, 1982; Oakes, 1985; and Rosenbaum, 1980.) Early in the secondary years, the student begins to think about post-high school plans (influenced by school experience, parent expectations, and peer norms) and begins to make some early choices about curriculum. For example, early in the middle school years, one student may decide to take foreign language; another decides (or is told) to take a reading course. Those early choices begin the process of curriculum stratification. At the end of eighth or ninth grade, when the student is asked to make a definite commitment, the student talks with a guidance counselor, who gives the student advice, based on the counselor's perceptions of the student's interests and strengths. Rosenbaum points out several related problems here: Counselors tend to spend more time with college preparatory students; counselors seem to give different advice depending on students' social characteristics; and counselors tend to give information that is consonant with their advice. The result is that many students make choices on the basis of incomplete or inaccurate information and find themselves in a curriculum track not related to their career plans. Thus, as Rosenbaum notes, the supposedly "free" choice made by students and their parents is not really free at all, since it is made on the basis of incomplete and inaccurate information.

To what extent does social class bias affect this process? While there is clear evidence that poor and minority students are overrepresented in noncollege preparatory programs, the research is somewhat conflicting as to whether social class operates as a major and direct factor in curriculum tracking. While some earlier studies suggested that social class influenced track assignments, a study by Alexander and Cook (1982) found little evidence of SES background, race, or gender bias.

Ability group placement operates somewhat differently. In secondary schools the decision to place a student in a particular ability group for the coming school year is usually made by the student's teacher at the end of the school year when administrators begin to determine scheduling parameters. In making this critical decision, the teacher tends to place greatest reliance on achievement and aptitude test scores, student motivation, and classroom performance (Finley, 1984; Heyns, 1974; Metz, 1978; Rehberg & Rosenthal, 1978; Schafer & Olexa, 1971). If the teacher is uncertain about placement, he or she usually consults with the department chair. The final decision is often influenced by the department head's assessment of several scheduling factors. How many teachers are available for low-ability classes? How many teachers want to teach honors sections? How many students should there be in low-ability classes?

The process by which these scheduling factors are analyzed and assessed is illuminated in Finley's (1984) study of how English teachers and the English department chair in a comprehensive high school made decisions about teacher assignments. As Finley described the process, it seemed to be a highly political one, fraught with sensitive issues of power and influence. All teachers wanted to avoid the "lemon" classes the remedial sections designed for students in the lowest 25% in English achievement. At the end of each school year, English teachers filled out preference sheets listing courses they wanted to teach. The department chairperson and the vice-principal assigned classes based on those requests, giving teachers some of the classes they preferred and filling out with the leftovers no one wanted. In this process, however, there were certain tacit assumptions operating about priorities in responding to preferences. Electives and advanced courses were seen as the property of those currently teaching them. Part-time English teachers (who taught part time in some other department) were usually assigned remedial sections. Teachers new to the school were assigned only low-track classes at first, until they had proven themselves.

What effect do social class and ethnic identity play in the process of assigning students to certain ability groups? Here again there is some ambiguity about the effect of student's social class and race on the decision-making process. In one study of 49 elementary schools. Haller (1985) discovered that in making decisions about reading groups, teachers most frequently discussed students' reading skills, with general academic competence, behavior and personality traits, work habits, and home background also mentioned frequently. While he discovered that African American students were overrepresented in lower ability groups, he concluded that "these results do not suggest that teachers are illegitimately influenced by pupils' race in making group decisions . . . the association of race with reading group assignments is primarily an artifact of its association with achievement" (p. 480). And Finley discovered that the English teachers in her study were primarily influenced by their assessments of student motivation. However, Oakes (1985) notes that most standardized tests are culturally biased. She also points out that the personal characteristics (such as speech patterns, dress, and ways of interacting with adults) that affect teachers' decisions about grouping are factors often influenced by race and class. Thus, she argues that race and class play an indirect but influential role in grouping decisions.

There is, however, some evidence that teachers vary a great deal in how they would sort students (Low, 1988). Three factors seem to affect teachers' decision about grouping: the teacher's views of the curriculum; the teacher's perspective about grouping; and the teacher's attitudes about student characteristics.

### Major differences between low- and high-ability classes.

Once students are placed in a particular section, they experience some important differences in curriculum, instruction, and classroom climate. And those differences would seem to argue for a more equitable heterogeneous grouping.

First, the curriculum for low-ability classes is significantly different. In her study of 25 of the secondary schools included in John Goodlad's major project (A Place Called School, 1984). Oakes discovered some key differences in the English curriculum of the 299 English classes examined. Students in high-ability English classes were exposed to what she calls "high status" knowledge: standard works of literature; historical development of literature; characteristics of literary genres; literary elements; the writing of expository essays; College Board vocabulary and reading skills. On the other hand, students in low-ability English classes were exposed to "low prestige" knowledge: they read young-adult fiction, used workbooks and reading kits, wrote short simple paragraphs, studied English usage, and learned how to complete application forms.

Instructional practices also vary widely between the two extremes, as Gamoran and Berends' (1987) review indicates. First, teachers of low-ability classes spend less time on instruction than those in high-ability classes. The most comprehensive study of this aspect is Oakes' analysis. By examining teachers' perceptions of time spent on instruction, direct observation of time spent on instruction, teachers' expectations of homework time, and observations of on-task and off-task behavior, she determined "that, without question, low-track classes have considerably less of both the necessary and the sufficient elements of classroom time for student learning" (p. 104). She also found significant differences in what she termed the "quality of instruction." In comparison with students in low-ability classes, students in high-ability classes reported that their teachers were more enthusiastic, were clearer about learning expectations, and were less punitive in their approach to discipline. The Finley study tends to supports Oakes' findings. While teachers of high-ability sections typically used large-group discussion and small-group projects, teachers of the low sections used lesson plans based on individual worksheets dealing with grammar and mechanics.

Finally, there are some important differences in the classroom climate. The research suggests in general that the climate in high-ability classes is a more desirable one than that in low-ability classes. Students in high-ability classes seem to get to the learning task more quickly (Evertson & Hickman, 1981). Observers of high-ability classes report better work habits, higher levels of participation, and more dependable behavior (Veldman & Sanford, 1984). Also reported are more trust, cooperation, and good will among students in higher-track classes (Oakes, 1985). One problem in using heterogeneous grouping in junior high English classes was noted by Evertson, Sanford, and Emmer (1981). In their study of 27 junior high school English classes in a large metropolitan school district, they found that extreme heterogeneity limited teachers' ability to respond to individual students' needs, made it less possible for them to respond to students' affective concerns, and resulted in lower task engagement and cooperation.

One caveat should be noted in assessing the evidence for these perceived differences. Page (1991) argues that "tracking is easily a red herring" (p. 236). She notes that the meaning of tracking varies with the context: low-track classes can be caring, with a rigorous curriculum; regular-track classes can be "mindlessly controlling" (p. 236).

***Outcome differences in heterogeneous and homogeneous classes.*** The key question, of course, is whether heterogeneous or homogeneous classes achieve better outcomes. The discussion that follows reviews first the research on achievement outcomes and then that on noncognitive ones.

Recent reviews of the research on achievement outcomes suggest that there are no significant differences between heterogeneous classes and homogeneous classes in terms of school achievement, although the evidence is far from conclusive. A 1982 meta-analysis by Kulik and Kulik of 52 studies of grouping at the secondary level concluded that, in general, students in grouped classes outperformed nongrouped students only slightly; however, students in gifted and talented programs performed better than they would have in heterogeneous classes.

A 1988 review by Slavin reached similar conclusions. As he put it, "Overall, the effects of ability grouping cluster closely around zero for students of all ability levels" (p. 69). He adds, however, that ability grouping may produce psychological drawbacks, especially for less able learners.

However, there are some important findings from individual studies that usefully supplement the conclusions from the meta-analyses. Veldman and Sanford's (1984) study of 135 junior high school mathematics and English classes indicated that both higher ability students and lower ability students achieved better in high-ability classes and that the differences in classroom environment had a greater impact on lower ability students. The researchers infer that these students are more reactive to or dependent on class norms than are their higher ability counterparts. Becker's (1987) analysis of state reading achievement test scores of 8,000 Pennsylvania sixth graders suggested that the effects of tracking varied in relation to students' socio-economic class. Among students of "low" background, test scores in reading were negatively associated with tracking. However, he also notes that tracking for English was associated with higher English test scores for both the low- and high-background groups.

A (1986) study of grouping conducted by Dar and Resh of Israeli middle schools yielded some differential effects in relation to student ability. They found that "high resource" students in homogeneous classes did not do significantly better than similar students in heterogeneous ones; however, "low resource" students found the heterogeneous classes more advantageous. They summarized their findings in this manner. "In separation (into homogeneous classes), the low-resource students' loss is greater than the high-resource students' profit, and in mixing (in heterogeneous classes), the high resource students' loss is smaller than the low-resource students' gain" (p. 357).

The same inconclusiveness characterizes the research on the noncognitive outcomes of grouping practices. The Kulik and Kulik meta-analysis concluded that students in grouped classes developed more positive attitudes toward the subject being studied; but grouping practices did not seem to influence students' attitudes toward themselves and their schools. However, in his (1980) review of the related studies, Rosenbaum reaches a different conclusion: "the majority of studies find that ability grouping hurts the self-evaluations of average and low-ability students" (p. 372). The Newfield and McElyea (1983) study of ability grouping in English classes concluded that high

achieving sophomores and seniors in homogeneous classes (in comparison with high achievers in heterogeneous classes) rated their school higher on academic instruction, expressed more interest in school, had more positive attitudes toward themselves, and perceived English as more useful. The researchers found no significant differences among low achievers in heterogeneous and homogeneous classes in attitudes toward self and school.

The research on the impact of heterogeneous grouping on the gifted seems inconclusive. Allan (1991) argues from her review of the research that gifted students achieve better results in "honors" classes; in the same issue, Slavin (1991) responds that he finds that homogeneous grouping does not benefit gifted students—the differences were not statistically significant. Robinson (1990) cautions that using cooperative learning in heterogeneous classes often exploits the gifted, since in such arrangements they are often required to tutor slower learners.

The inconclusiveness of all these findings is probably attributable to the difficulties noted by Good and Marshall (1984): Many of the studies have been narrowly designed, focusing only on one variable when a complex set are operating; the concepts of *heterogeneous* and *homogeneous* have been poorly defined and operationalized; and direct observations of classrooms have too often not been made.

## Implications of Practitioners

The findings presented yield no simple answer to English teachers, supervisors, and school administrators trying to find the best grouping arrangements for secondary English. Taken together, however, the research would suggest a compromise strategy of the following sort.

1. Separate gifted students into honors and advanced placement classes. There seems to be consistent evidence that such grouping results in better achievement for more able students.
2. Group the rest of the students heterogeneously. The dangers of tracking and the resulting stratification probably outweigh any slight advantage that might accrue with homogeneous grouping.
3. Provide teachers with the training needed to teach heterogeneous groups, giving special emphasis to the use of cooperative learning groups.

A special note might be made about this last suggestion. A substantial body of research suggests that cooperative learning approaches are very effective in achieving cognitive and noncognitive outcomes with heterogeneous classes. (See, for example, Slavin 1983). One form of cooperative learning, Cooperative Integrated Reading and Composition (CIRC), has been shown to be especially effective in English classes. As Slavin (1987) explains, students in the CIRC program work in mixed ability teams on a series of reading activities (reading aloud to each other and completing several kinds of reading-related activities) and engage in peer response groups in a writing process model. He notes that in one 24-week study, students using the CIRC approach gained 64% of a grade equivalent more than control students in reading comprehension, language expression, and language mechanics.

## THE WORK ENVIRONMENT

The work environment, as conceptualized here, is the nature of the academic work and its related activities, as construed by both the teacher and the students. The concept of *academic work* was initially developed by Doyle as a means of analyzing and understanding the nature of teaching–learning transactions as they occur in the classroom. (See Doyle & Carter's 1984 publication for a detailed explication of the concept and its applications.) The discussion that follows represents this author's attempts to integrate Doyle's theory and research with that of other scholars who analyze the concept somewhat differently. (See, for example, Blumenfeld & Meece, 1988; and Anderson, Stevens, Prawat, & Nickerson, 1988.) It should be noted, of course, that other metaphors and constructs might be used in examining the teaching–learning transactions and would obviously yield different findings. However, the concept of *academic work* is so widely accepted by scholars in the field and seems so potentially useful that it is accepted here as the operative construct.

Figure 37.4 presents a schematic representation of the major elements in academic work. Each is treated briefly here and explicated more fully in the discussion that follows. First, the teacher makes plans for what might be termed the intended work. Those plans are influenced by several sources—chiefly, the curriculum guides, the textbooks, the tests, and the teacher's knowledge and previous experience. As the teacher attempts to structure the intended work, those intentions are mediated by both external occurrences (such as a fire drill) and by internal events (such as students' questions or behaviors). Those internal events are themselves influenced by the students' goals for that classroom session and the pressures students exert to achieve those goals. Those external and internal events operating on the teacher's plans result in what might be termed the actual work—what finally occurs in the classroom.

### Teachers' Plans for Academic Work

The processes by which teachers plan for academic work are complex, not yet fully understood either by researchers or teachers themselves. The general picture of those complex processes that is presented here must therefore be seen as a preliminary sketch, subject to further revision as additional research findings are generated. The difficulty of delineating a general process is complicated by the fact that, as both Favor-Lydecker (1981) and Sardo (1982) noted, teachers have different planning styles that cannot be completely captured in a general portrait.

Teachers consider unit planning as the most important type of planning; they view daily lesson planning as much less important. As Clark and Yinger (1979) discovered, unit planning is a cyclical and an incremental process that begins with a general idea and moves through phases of successive elaboration. In making those unit plans, teachers seem to respond differentially to several pressures. For most teachers, standardized and curriculum-based tests exercise a powerful influence. For others the textbook is the primary determiner of what is taught. For most secondary teachers, their own knowledge and experience is dominant, with the district's curriculum guide exerting only a modest influence on their decisions. (For the research on factors influencing teachers' planning, see Clark & Elmore, 1981; Floden, Porter, Schmidt, Freeman & Schwille, 1980; Leithwood, Ross, & Montgomery, 1982.)

At a time when the use of external "high-stakes tests" as an accountability measure seems to be increasing, concerns

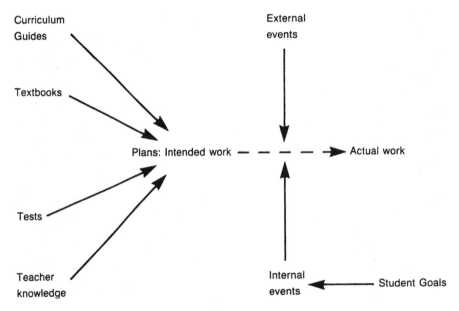

FIGURE 37.4. The academic work environment.

about this practice should be noted. Smith's (1991) study concluded that such testing programs reduced instructional time, narrowed the curriculum, and limited the teacher's mode of instruction.

In making their plans, teachers seem to focus either on content ("It's time to start *Julius Caesar*), activities ("I'll begin class with a quiz"), or tasks ("They should start writing their personal essay"). Although the research is not uniform on this issue of focus, most studies indicate that teachers do not use the rational planning approach of first identifying objectives and then selecting activities to achieve those objections. (See Zahorik, 1975; and Sardo, 1982.)

Although these plans for work are usually not implemented with a high degree of fidelity, the evidence suggests that long-term and short-term planning is important. First, the teacher's yearly, semester, and unit plans are the chief means by which the teacher makes decisions about content selection and time allocation. The research on teacher effectiveness suggests that student achievement is higher when teachers deal with the prescribed content of the curriculum and allocate time consistent with district priorities. (See the Brophy & Good, 1986, review.) Second, well-organized instruction pays off, as Rosenshine and Stevens (1986) point out. While there is no direct relationship between the quality of the written lesson plans and the organization of the taught lesson, it seems safe to conclude, as Clark and Peterson (1986) do, that teacher planning does influence opportunity to learn, content coverage, grouping for instruction, and the general focus of classroom processes, all important elements of effective teaching.

## External and Internal Events

As noted, those plans are not always delivered as intended. First, there are external factors that require changes in the plans. As McCutcheon (1980) learned, many teachers view long-range planning as counterproductive because of unpredictable changes in the schedule and interruptions of class. An assembly scheduled at the last minute, an early dismissal because of threatening weather, an unannounced guest speaker who must be accommodated—such interruptions and intrusions require the teacher to make last-minute changes in the carefully planned unit.

Internal events also play an important role. Clark and Peterson (1986) observe that, once class begins, the plan moves to the background and interactive decision making becomes more important. In this sense then the teacher's interactive decision making is the process by which the intended work is transformed into the actual work. Teachers' reports of their interactive thoughts suggest that those thoughts are concerned primarily with the students and their responses ("they're starting to lose interest in the story"); instructional processes ("this would be a good time for a small-group discussion") are second in importance. (See the Clark & Peterson, 1986, review.) Those thoughts about the students and the activities lead them to make numerous interaction decisions—one every 2 minutes, according to the Clark and Peterson review.

## Student Pressures

As noted, student behavior tends to play a major role in teachers' interactive decision making. The research suggests that often this behavior is intended to reduce the complexity of classroom work, to make classroom life less demanding. Doyle and Carter's (1984) study of an English teacher teaching writing is instructive here. In this 2-month observational study, the researchers noted significant changes from the time the task was introduced by the teacher to the time it was accomplished by the students: the writing task became less ambiguous and more explicit; the teacher did an increasing amount of work for the students by specifying the features of an acceptable product; and the accountability system was softened. These changes were brought about largely by the students: students influenced task demands by asking questions about content and procedures and by offering guesses to teacher questions in order to elicit clarifying instructions from the teachers. They also exerted indirect pressure on the task system by slowing down the pace of classroom events, frequently punctuating work periods with questions.

## The Actual Work

All these factors interact to produce the actual work of the classroom—work that, as Doyle (1986) notes, acts as the substance of classroom events, directs students' information processing, and affects their attitudes about participation and cooperation. This actual work can perhaps best be conceptualized as a series of academic tasks. Those tasks involve several components: content, resources, procedures, activities, goals or products, and an accountability system.

To understand the nature and interrelationships of these components of the academic task, consider the English teacher planning and teaching a unit on the persuasive essay. The content—the substantive focus—is the persuasive essay as a type of writing. The resources include models of persuasive essays, textbook explanations of how to write a persuasive essay, teacher presentations and questions, and the ideas and responses of other students. The procedures, the operations that the student brings to bear to transform the resources into the product, would include such processes as analyzing the audience, prioritizing arguments, selecting evidence, and organizing the essay. The activities, the specific teaching–learning transactions orchestrated by the teacher to help the student complete the product, might involve such things as reading a model essay, discussing the essay in small groups, and writing a brief response to the essay. The product, of course, is the essay the student submits; and the accountability system involves both the monitoring of the activities and the grading of the final product.

## Activities in the English Class

In the foregoing analysis, the activity is seen as a component of the task, although some researchers focus on either activity or task, to the exclusion of the other. Several researchers have examined the nature and function of activities, which Doyle (1983) defines as "a bounded segment of classroom time characterized by an identifiable (a) focal content or concern and (b) pattern or program of action" (p. 2).

Doyle's (1983) study of seven junior high English teachers yielded useful insights about the importance of activities as a means of achieving order. First, he discovered that the school schedule acted as a major constraint for teachers; they often had problems fitting activities into the 55-minute period provided for English. In some cases, activities ran short and students had nothing to do for several minutes; in other cases the bell interrupted the last activity. He noted that more effective teachers were consistently able to fit activities to periods. Second, he discovered much mixing of activity types: teachers often inserted questions into lectures or made announcements during seatwork. However, the more effective teachers in his study made sure that these activity mixes had a clear sense of purpose, working jointly toward a single theme.

Next, the successful managers had developed and used distinct patterns for opening the class session, for marking transitions, and for ending the period. They also demonstrated what Doyle called "situational awareness," frequently scanning the class for signs of confusion and inattention, making brief contacts with individual students, and making brief comments on events occurring in the room. They also protected activities by blocking any event or incident that might interrupt activity flow: "We can take care of that later." And they pushed students through the curriculum, focusing on content even when misbehavior seemed prevalent.

## The Tasks of English Classes

The special nature of tasks in the English classroom has been the focus of several other studies. First, some studies have examined the intellectual or cognitive nature of tasks in the English class, in comparison with other subjects. Steele, Walberg, and House (1974) determined that there were some important differences in the cognitive press of secondary English language arts classes when compared with secondary mathematics, science, and social studies classes: English language arts classes were most divergent in their cognitive press (there is no right answer) and were most concerned with syntax over substance (focused more on having students synthesize, translate, and apply, rather than summarize and memorize). Their study was replicated by Kuert (1977) with essentially the same findings. However, Randhawa and Hunt (1982) in their study of the perceptions of 10th grade Canadian students found that English and mathematics were quite similar in their intellectual climate.

An analysis of tasks in middle school English, science, and social studies classes by Korth and Cornbleth (1982) concluded that the English curriculum was more diverse than the social studies and involved less seat work than social studies. However, in all three classes the dominant whole-class task involved what the researchers called "QATE," teacher question, student answer, and teacher elaboration.

One major study by Applebee (1984) examined the special nature of writing tasks in the English classroom, yielding some important findings. On the average the students in the study completed an average of approximately 14 papers in the course of the school year. For two thirds of those papers, the audience was the "teacher-as-examiner." Informational writing accounted for close to 85% of the English papers written, with analysis and summary accounting for almost all of the informational tasks. The information for these writing tasks was drawn chiefly from the teacher or the text. For those advocating a diversified writing program emphasizing real problems and real audiences, the findings must seem rather discouraging.

Finally, a study by Doyle and Sanford (1982) of secondary English classes focused on managing student work in secondary classrooms, concluding with several "practical lessons" for English teachers for managing classroom work more effectively. First, they recommend that teachers should take special pains to communicate the task clearly to students, noting that students often misinterpret assigned tasks. In this explanation, they should clarify the assignment, identify the steps and strategies to be used, analyze a model response, call attention to the goal, and identify the criteria to be used for grading.

Second, they should carefully monitor students' understanding of the work and the strategies for accomplishing it. In making long-term assignments, like reading a novel or writing an essay, the teacher should confer with individual students at the start of the task, to be sure that they understand both task and strategies. They should ask students "strategic questions" that probe for understanding and ask students to explain their answers. They should also monitor student group work and observe student–student interactions.

Third, they should encourage students to engage in novel tasks that involve more risk for the student. Since students will exert pressure for the teacher to do their work for them, teachers should determine which aspects of the task should be carried out completely by the students and insist that students carry out those aspects, regardless of student questions and requests. They should also provide "safety nets" for students doing novel work: let them revise and resubmit without penalty, provide for cooperative learning, and adjust the grading system.

Finally, and perhaps most important, teachers should help students find meaning in the tasks they are doing. The researchers noted that they seldom saw students doing tasks in which they were required to struggle with meaning. Grammar consisted of multiple-choice exercises that asked students to select the word that sounded right, instead of sentence combining and sentence writing. Literature consisted of memorizing the facts of a story or learning the standard interpretation of a passage, rather than struggling with what the work meant to the student. To help students find meaning in their classroom tasks, the authors recommend several strategies: When assignments are introduced, make explicit statements about the relationship between the current work and previous work; build a meaningful system of related tasks, instead of fragmented and disjointed ones; culminate units by assigning tasks that require students to review and integrate previous work.

## Implications for Administrators and Supervisors

The research reviewed here suggests that administrators and supervisors concerned about making the English classroom a better work environment should provide English teachers with systematic staff development focusing on the following skills.

- Developing long-term plans that reflect curricular priorities and make appropriate time allocations.
- Making effective interactive decisions in the classroom—knowing when to adhere to and when to deviate from the intended work, knowing when to respond and when to ignore student pressures to simplify the task.
- Communicating the task clearly and monitoring student behavior to ensure that students understand both the task and the needed strategies.
- Conducting activities effectively: marking activity boundaries, showing situational awareness, protecting the activity flow.
- Presenting novel tasks when appropriate and providing students with the support needed to complete those tasks effectively.
- Helping students find meaning in classroom tasks by showing them relationships and assisting them in making connections.

## PSYCHOSOCIAL ENVIRONMENT

The psychosocial environment is defined here as the shared perceptions of the people in an environment about the nature of the psychosocial interactions of that environment. The following discussion examines its nature more specifically, reviews the findings on the psychosocial environment in general, discusses the research on secondary English classroom environments, reviews the research on person–environment interactions, and concludes by discussing the implications of that complex body of research.

### The Nature of the Psychosocial Environment

In analyzing the special nature of the psychosocial environment, the subscales of the Classroom Environment Scale (Moos & Trickett, 1974) seem to be especially useful. Although the Learning Environment Inventory (Fraser, Anderson, & Walberg, 1982) has been more widely used in research on the classroom environment, the LEI includes one subscale ("material environment") that in this chapter is considered as the "physical environment" and includes three subscales ("diversity," "speed," and "difficulty") that are here considered aspects of the work environment.

In the following discussion, therefore, the concept of the psychosocial environment will be considered as embodying the nine elements reflected in the CES: involvement, affiliation, teacher support, task orientation, competition, order and organization, role clarity, teacher control, and innovation. However, research findings from the LEI, as well as those

from other measures, will be included in the review wherever appropriate.

### The Importance of the Psychosocial Environment

This section will review the research on the relationship between these environmental factors and student outcomes, first clarifying the general nature of that relationship, then examining broad environmental types, and finally considering specific environmental factors. Before reviewing that research, it would be useful to keep in mind Fraser's (1986) cautionary note: all the research up to this point has been correlational in nature; there are no experimental studies providing support for a casual relationship.

The research suggests rather clearly that the psychosocial environment is strongly associated with both achievement and attitudinal outcomes. Two major reviews of studies related to the psychosocial environment suggest that student perception of the classroom environment accounted for between 13 and 46% of the variance in cognitive, affective, and behavioral outcomes (Anderson & Walberg, 1974; Haertel, Walberg, & Haertel, 1981).

Supporting the general importance of the psychosocial environment is Moos' (1980) analysis of the major types of classroom environment. By using cluster analysis of data from 200 classes that had been assessed with the Classroom Environment Scale (CES), Moos was able to identify six basic types of classrooms. From his review of this large body of research, he was able to arrive at four conclusions concerning the relationship of these general types to student outcomes. First, those classes oriented toward relationships and innovation enhance social growth and personal growth, but do less well in improving achievement scores. Second, classes that emphasize goal accomplishment and classroom maintenance can bring about high achievement but are associated with lower student interest, morale, and creativity. Third, control-oriented classrooms lead to dissatisfaction and alienation and at the same time are not related to personal, social, or academic growth. Finally—and most importantly—classrooms that combine warm and supportive relationships, an emphasis on academic tasks and accomplishments, and an orderly and well-structured milieu are associated with achievements gains, creativity, and personal growth.

Moos (1987) summarizes the general import of these findings in this manner:

Overall, these findings imply that basic skills programs will have more positive effects if they are supportive as well as task-oriented, whereas alternative school programs need more task focus, though not at the expense of engagement and support (p. 4).

Several specific psychosocial factors seem to be important in relation to student outcomes. The meta-analysis by Haertel, Walberg, and Haertel (1981) concluded that the following psychosocial factors were positively associated with gains in learning in several subject areas: cohesiveness, satisfaction, formality, goal direction, and democracy. Adjusted gains in learning were negatively associated with these factors: friction, cliqueness, apathy, and disorganization.

## The Psychosocial Environment of the Secondary English Classroom

A comprehensive search of the ERIC database and *Dissertation Abstracts International* failed to identify any study that focused on the psychosocial environment of the secondary English class alone; however, several studies have examined the differences between the environments of English classes and those of other secondary subjects. Anderson (1971) found several interesting differences and similarities between humanities classes (English literature and history) and science, mathematics, and French classes in Montreal: compared with mathematics classes, English classes were lower on friction, favoritism, disorganization, and cliqueness and higher on formality and goal direction; compared with science classes; humanities classes were seen as less formal and slower moving, with more friction, favoritism, cliqueness, and disorganization; compared with French classes, humanities classes were seen as lower on goal direction and higher on friction and disorganization.

Although Randhawa and Michayluk (1975) determined that subject content did not significantly affect the learning environment of the classroom, they concluded that mathematics and social studies classrooms seemed to the students to be more cohesive than English classrooms.

Hearn and Moos (1978) used a conceptualization of personalities and environments developed by Holland (1973) to classify school subjects as one of the following five types: realistic (vocational–technical shops); investigative (mathematics and science); artistic (English, music, foreign language and art); social (social studies); and conventional (business subjects). In a study of 209 classes, they found that students in the artistic classes had a high emphasis on task orientation and teacher control, with a lack of emphasis on involvement, affiliation, and innovation. Realistic classes were high on several factors (competition, rule clarity, teacher control, involvement, affiliation, and innovation) and low on task orientation. Conventional classes were high on involvement, affiliation, task orientation, competition, and rule clarity and low only on innovation. Social classes were low on several dimensions: task orientation, rule clarity, teacher control, involvement, and affiliation.

Although not specifically concerned with classroom envionment as such, Evertson's (1979) study examined the affective behaviors of 39 junior high English teachers and 29 mathematics teachers over the course of 1 year. In both subjects, high-achieving classes were characterized as having good classroom management, effective teaching, a large proportion of time spent in teaching, and a positive student attitude. In focusing on English teachers, Evertson pointed out that the more effective teachers had an overall sense of purpose; less effective teachers seemed on the other hand to have a day-to-day attitude of survival, without a clear sense of instructional purpose. As she put it, less effective teachers were "either marking time or filling it with activities whose functions appear to be 'making it through the period'" (p. 24).

Finally, Costello (1987) determined that students in high-ability track mathematics and English classes both assessed the learning environment more favorably than students in middle- and lower-ability tracks. He also concluded that the relationship between Classroom Environment Scale scores and student achievement on the Stanford Test of Academic Skills varied somewhat in relation to the ability level of the English classes. He found that English achievement on this standardized test was positively associated with these subscales of the CES: in low-track classes, with Task Orientation, Order and Organization, and Teacher Control; in middle-track classes, with Teacher Support and Order and Organization. Although there were no significant relationships between standardized test scores and CES subscales for the high-ability track students, he discovered that semester grades for these students were positively associated with Affiliation, Teacher Support, Order and Organization, and Innovation.

These studies are so few in number, so different in their methodologies, and so varied in their findings that it would seem unwise to generalize about the special nature of English classroom environments.

## The Person–Environment Fit

In general a relatively small body of research suggests that students will achieve more and have better attitudes when there is congruence between the actual learning environment and the preferred learning environment.

Several studies have provided general support for Hunt's (1975) theory about conceptual level and environment. Students with a higher conceptual level are able to organize their environments, whereas those at a lower conceptual level learn better when the teacher provides a more structured environment. Harpin and Sandler (1979) found that junior high boys who were more comfortable with teacher-provided structure adjusted better in a classroom with high teacher control. In a later (1985) study they discovered that student perception of the relevance of the classroom environment was an important factor: internally-oriented students who viewed classroom control as relevant adapted better in low-control classrooms, whereas such congruence was not a factor with students who saw the environment as less relevant. Moos (1987) reaches this general conclusion about the importance of conceptual level: "In general, externally oriented students tend to adjust better in more flexibly organized settings. Similarly, students who want to explore and shape their environments and who exhibit a strong need for independence profit more from less structured learning environments" (p. 6).

Studies making use of other inventories have also provided tentative support for the importance of person–environment fit. Nielsen and Moos (1978) explored the relationship of students' preference for social exploration (the willingness to explore or change relationships) and the actual extent of classroom social exploration. Students high in exploration preference achieved better in classrooms high in actual exploration; there was no difference for students low in exploration preference. A study by Rich and Bush (1978) examined the effect of congruence between teacher style (direct or indirect verbal behavior) and student social–emotional development. Ten congruent groups were obtained by matching teachers with a natural direct style with students high in social–emotional development;

10 incongruent groups matched 5 direct teachers with students low in social-emotional development and 5 indirect teachers with students high in social-emotional development. The congruent groups performed better than the incongruent groups on reading achievement, time on task, and affective perception. Fraser (1986) observes, on the basis of this and other related studies, that person-environment fit is at least as important as actual environment in predicting learning outcomes.

Since these studies have used the class as the level of analysis, Fraser's caution here seems appropriate. He points out that, although class achievement of certain outcomes might be enhanced by attempting to change the environment to make it more congruent with class preferences, it cannot be inferred that an individual's achievement will be improved by moving that student from an incongruent to a congruent environment. He reports three case studies he conducted in which a teacher was able to bring about such change through a problem-solving process: the teacher administered one of the learning environment surveys to students; the data were analyzed and presented to the teacher as profiles showing class means of actual and preferred environmental scores; after private reflection and informal discussion with the researchers, the teacher used several strategies to change the environment to achieve greater congruence.

Moos (1980) notes other cautions about trying to match the environment with individual student preferences. He points out first that students' preferences change over time, as they experience different settings. He also observes that students may prefer environments that are not sufficiently challenging. One final argument could be presented against matching individuals' preferences with the environment provided: One important outcome of schooling should be the ability to adjust to and learn in a variety of environments. Adults need to work in a variety of environments—many of which are not congruent with their preferences. Those arguing for the person-environment fit should also note the reservations previously expressed concerning learning style accommodation.

### The Implications for Practice

What are the implications of the research on psychosocial environments for school administrators and English language arts supervisors? Since relatively little research has addressed the specific issue of secondary English environments, the following recommendations for practice are offered rather tentatively:

1. English teachers should be provided with the staff development that would enable them to examine and discuss the characteristics that seem to define an effective psychosocial environment. Those characteristics would seem to be the following:
   - There are supportive relationships between the teacher and the students and among the students.
   - There is an emphasis on accomplishing the academic tasks important in English language arts: writing effectively, reading intelligently, communicating clearly.
   - There is an orderly and well-structured classroom environment.
   - The English teacher has a clear sense of purpose and direction; there is a sense of intentionality about classroom events.

2. English teachers should receive constructive feedback about the type of environment they are providing. This feedback can come from two chief sources: observations by a trained observer (an administrator, supervisor, or colleague); and feedback from students.

3. Administrators, supervisors, and teachers should collaborate in organizing and implementing staff development sessions that would enable teachers to make needed modifications in the environment.

## A CONCLUDING NOTE

Each of the sections of this chapter has concluded with an analysis of the implications of the research on the four chief components of the classroom learning environment: the physical environment; the group environment; the work environment; and the psychosocial environment. These analyses are not intended to offer a set of prescriptions for all secondary English classrooms; there is not yet sufficient knowledge about these crucial and sensitive issues to warrant prescriptive advice. Rather they are presented as tentative suggestions that need additional study and analysis.

An analysis of the literature suggests the need for three kinds of research here. First, there is clearly a need for carefully designed empirical studies that would focus on the learning environment of secondary English classrooms examining the relationship between certain environmental factors and student affective and cognitive outcomes. Second, there is a need for additional ethnographic studies of secondary English classrooms that would provide the rich detail that is so important in understanding learning environments. Finally, there is a need for action research of the collaborative sort recommended by Lieberman and Miller (1986) that would enable practitioners to diagnose and modify these environments for both teachers and students.

## References

Adams, R. S. (1969). Location as a factor of instructional interaction. *Merrill Palmer Quarterly, 15,* 309–322.

Adams, R. S., & Biddle, B. J. (1970). *Realities of teaching: Explorations with video tape.* New York: Holt, Rinehart, & Winston.

Allan, S. D. (1991). Ability-grouping research reviews: What do they say about grouping and the gifted? *Educational Leadership, 48*(6), 60–65.

Alexander, K. L., & Cook, M. A. (1982). Curricula and course work: A surprise ending to a familiar story. *American Sociological Review, 47,* 626–640.

Anderson, G. J. (1971). Effects of course content and teacher sex on the social climate of learning. *American Educational Research Journal, 8,* 649-663.

Anderson, G. J., & Walberg, H. J. (1974). Learning environments. In H. J. Walberg (Ed.), *Evaluating educational performance: A sourcebook of methods, instruments, and examples* (pp. 81-98). Berkeley, CA: McCutchan.

Anderson, L. M., Stevens, D. D., Prawat, R. S., & Nickerson, J. (1988). Classroom task environments and students' task-related beliefs. *Elementary School Journal, 88,* 281-295.

Anifant, D. C. (1972). Risk-taking behavior in children experiencing open space and traditional school environments. (Doctoral dissertation, University of Maryland, College Park, MD, 1971.) *Disseratation Abstracts International, 33,* 2491A.

Applebee, A. N. (1977). *A survey of teaching conditions in English, 1972.* Urbana, IL: ERIC Clearinghouse on Reading and Communication Skills, National Council of Teachers of English.

Applebee, A. N. (1984). *Contexts for learning to write: Studies of secondary school instruction.* Norwood, NJ: Ablex.

Beck, T. M. (1979, April). *An Australian study of school environments.* Paper presented at the annual meeting of the American Educational Research Association, San Francisco. (ERIC Document Reproduction Service No. ED 172 357.)

Becker, H. J. (1987). *Addressing the needs of different groups of early adolescents: Effects of varying school and classroom organization practices on students from different social backgrounds and abilities.* Baltimore, MD: Center for Research on Elementary and Middle Schools, Johns Hopkins University.

Bennett, N., & Blundell, D. (1983). Quantity and quality of work in rows and classroom groups. *Educational Psychology, 3,* 93-105.

Blair, D., & Judah, S. S. (1990). Need a strong foundation for an interdisciplinary program? Try 4MAT! *Educational Leadership, 48*(2), 37-38.

Blumenfeld, P. C., & Meece, J. L. (1988). Task factors, teacher behavior, and students' involvement and use of learning strategies in science. *Elementary School Journal, 88,* 235-250.

Bolvin, J. O. (1982). Classroom organization. In H. E. Mitzell (Ed.), *Encyclopedia of educational research* (5th ed.) (pp. 265-274). New York: Free Press.

Bronzaft, A. L., & McCarthy, D. P. (1975). The effect of elevated train noise on reading ability. *Environment and Behavior, 7,* 51-527.

Brooks, D. M., Silvern, S. B., & Wooten, M. (1978). The ecology of teacher-pupil verbal interaction. *Journal of Classroom Interaction, 14,* 39-45.

Brophy, J. E., & Good, T. L. (1986). Teacher behavior and student achievement. In M. C. Wittrock (Ed.), *Handbook of research on teaching* (3rd ed.) (pp. 328-375). New York: Macmillan.

Brunetti, F. A. (1971). The teacher in the authority structure of the elementary school: A study of open space and self-contained classroom schools. (Doctoral dissertation, Stanford University, Stanford, CA, 1970.) *Dissertation Abstracts International, 31,* 4405A.

Burnham, B. (1970). *A day in the life: Case studies of pupils in open plan schools.* Toronto, Canada: York County Board of Education.

Cheatham, R., & Jordan, W. (1976). Cognitive and affective implications of class size in a lecture-practicum speech communication course. *Improving College and University Teaching, 24,* 251-254.

Clark, C. M., & Elmore, J. L. (1981). *Transforming curriculum in mathematics, science, and writing. A case study of teachers' yearly planning.* East Lansing, MI: Institute for Research in Teaching, Michigan State University.

Clark, C. M., & Peterson, P. L. (1986). Teachers' thought processes. In M. C. Wittrock (Ed.), *Handbook of research on teaching* (3rd ed.) (pp. 255-296). New York: Macmillan.

Clark, C. M., & Yinger, R. J. (1979). *Three studies of teacher planning.* East Lansing, MI: Institute for Research in Teaching, Michigan State University.

Clem, P., Ahern, K., Dailey, N., Gary, M., & Scantlebury, M. (n.d.). *A comparison of interaction patterns in an open space and a fixed paln school.* Blacksburg, VA: Virginia Polytechnical Institute and State University.

Costello, R. W. (1987). Relationships among ability grouping, classroom climate, and academic achievement in mathematics and English classes. In B. J. Fraser (Ed.), *The study of learning environments, Vol. 3* (pp. 60-67). Baton Rouge, LA: Louisiana State University College of Education.

Cotton, K., & Savard, W. G. (1980). *Class size research on school effectiveness project.* Portland, OR: Northwest Regional Laboratory.

Crook, M. A., & Langdon, F. J. (1974). The effects of aircraft noise in schools around London airport. *Journal of Sound and Vibration, 34,* 221-232.

Curry, L. (1990). A critique of the research on learning styles. *Educational Leadership, 48*(2), 50-56.

Dar, Y., & Resh, N. (1986). Classroom intellectual composition and academic achievement. *American Educational Research Journal, 23,* 357-374.

Delefes, P., & Jackson, B. (1972). Teacher–pupil interaction as a function of location in the classroom. *Psychology in the Schools, 9,* 119-123.

Doyle, W. (1983). *Managing classroom activities in junior high English classes: An interim report.* Austin, TX: Research and Development Center for Teacher Education, University of Texas.

Doyle, W. (1986). Classroom management. In M. C. Wittrock (Ed.), *Handbook of research on teaching* (3rd ed.) (pp. 392-431). New York: Free Press.

Doyle, W., & Carter, K. (1984). Academic tasks in classrooms. *Curriculum Inquiry, 14,* 129-147.

Doyle, W., & Sanford, J. P. (1982). *Managing student work in secondary classrooms: Practical lessons from a study of classroom tasks.* Austin, TX: Research and Development Center for Teacher Education, University of Texas.

Dunn, K., & Dunn, R. (1987, March). Dispelling outmoded beliefs about student learning. *Educational Leadership, 44*(5), 55-62.

Dunn, R., Dunn, K., & Price, G. (1985). *Learning style inventory.* Lawrence, KS: Price Systems.

Durlak, J., Beardsley, B., & Murray, J. (1972). Observations of user activity patterns in open and traditional plan school environments. *Proceedings of the Environmental Design and Research Association Conference.* Los Angeles: University of California.

Educational Research Service (1980). Class size research: A critique of recent meta-analyses. *Phi Delta Kappan, 62,* 239-241.

Ellison, M., Gilbert, L. L., & Ratsoy, E. W. (1969). Teacher behavior in openarea classrooms. *Canadian Administration Quarterly, 8,* 17-21.

Epstein, Y. M., & Karlin, R. A. (1975). Effects of acute experimental crowding. *Journal of Applied Psychology, 5,* 34-53.

Evertson, C. M. (1979). *Teacher behavior, student achievement, and student attitudes: Description of selected classrooms.* Austin, TX: Research and Development Center for Teacher Education.

Evertson, C. M., & Hickman, R. C. (1981). *The tasks of teaching classes of varied group composition.* Austin, TX: Research and Development Center for Teacher Education.

Evertson, C. M., Sanford, J. P., & Emmer, E. T. (1981). Effects of class heterogeneity in junior high school. *American Educational Research Journal, 18,* 219-232.

Favor-Lydecker, A. (1981, April). *Teacher planning of social studies units.* Paper presented at annual conference of the American Educational Research Association, Los Angeles.

Filby, N. A. (1980, February). *Evidence of class-size effects*. Paper presented at annual conference of the American Educational Research Association, Anaheim, CA.

Finley, M. K. (1984). Teachers and tracking in a comprehensive high school. *Sociology of Teaching, 57*, 233-243.

Floden, R. E., Porter, A. C., Schmidt, W. J., Freeman, D. J., & Schwille, J. R. (1980). *Responses to curriculum pressures: A policy capturing study of teacher decisions about content*. East Lansing, MI: Institute for Research on Teaching, Michigan State University.

Foster-Harrison, E. S., & Adams-Bullock, A. (1998). *Creating an inviting classroom environment*. Bloomington, IN: Phi Delta Kappa.

Fraser, B. J. (1986). *Classroom environment*. Dover, NH: Croom Helm.

Fraser, B. J., Anderson, G. J., & Walberg, H. J. (1982). *Assessment of learning environments: Manual for Learning Environment Inventory (LEI) and My Class Inventory (MCI)* (3rd ed.). Perth: Western Australian Institute of Technology.

Fraser, B. J., Walberg, H. J., Welch, W. W., & Hattie, J. A. (1987). Syntheses of educational productivity research. *International Journal of Educational Research, 11*, 145-252.

Gamoran, A., & Berends, M. (1987). The effects of stratification in secondary schools: Synthesis of survey and ethnographic research. *Review of Educational Research, 57*, 415-435.

George, P. S. (1975). *Ten years of open space schools: A review of the research*. Gainesville, FL: Florida Educational Research and Development Council, University of Florida.

Glass, G. V., & Smith, M. L. (1978). *Meta-analysis of research on the relationship of class size and achievement*. San Francisco: Far West Laboratory for Educational Research and Development.

Good, T. L., & Marshall, S. (1984). Do students learn more in heterogeneous or homogeneous groups? In P. L. Peterson, L. C. Wilkinson, & M. Hallman (Eds.), *The social context of instruction: Group organization and group processes* (pp. 15-38). Orlando, FL: Academic Press.

Goodlad, J. (1984). *A place called school: Prospects for the future*. New York: McGraw-Hill.

Gump, P. V. (1974). Operating environments in schools of open and traditional design. *School Review, 82*, 575-593.

Gump, P. V., & Ross, R. (1977). The fit of milieu and programme in school environments. In H. McGurk (Ed.), *Ecological factors in human design*. New York: North-Holland.

Haddad, W. D. (1978). *Educational effects of class size*. World Bank Staff Working Paper #280. (ERIC Document Reproduction Service No. ED 179 003)

Haertel, G. D., Walberg, H. J., & Haertel, E. H. (1981). Sociopsychological environments and learning: A quantitative synthesis. *British Educational Research Journal, 7*, 27-36.

Haller, E. J. (1985). Pupil race and elementary school ability grouping: Are teachers biased against black children? *American Educational Research Journal, 22*, 465-483.

Harpin, P., & Sandler, I. (1979). Interaction of sex, locus of control, and teacher control: Toward a student–classroom match. *American Journal of Community Psychology, 7*, 621-632.

Harpin, P., & Sandler, I. (1985). Relevance of social climate: An improved approach to assessing persons by environment interactions in the classroom. *American Journal of Community Psychology, 13*, 381-392.

Hearn, J. C., & Moos, R. H. (1978). Subject matter and classroom climate: A test of Holland's environmental propositions. *American Educational Research Journal, 15*, 111-124.

Hedges, L. V., & Stock, W. (1983). The effects of class size: An examination of rival hypotheses. *American Educational Research Journal, 20*, 63-85.

Heyns, B. (1974). Social selection and stratification within schools. *American Journal of Sociology, 79*, 1434-1451.

Holland, J. L. (1973). *Making vocational choices: A theory of careers*. Englewood Cliffs, NJ: Prentice-Hall.

Horowitz, P., & Otto, P. (1973). *The teaching effectiveness of an alternative teaching facility*. (ERIC Document Reproduction Service No. ED 083 242). Alberta, Canada: University of Alberta.

Hunt, D. (1975). Person–environment interaction: A challenge found wanting before it was tried. *Review of Educational Research, 45*, 209-230.

Hutt, S. J., & Hutt, C. (1970). *Direct observation and measurement of behavior*. Springfield, IL: Thomas.

Johnson, R. H. (1973). The effects of four modified elements of a classroom's physical environment on the social-psychological environment of a class. (Doctoral dissertation, Oregon State University, Corvallis, OR, 1973.) *Dissertation Abstracts International, 1973, 34*, 1002A.

Keefe, J. W. (Ed.) (1988). *Profiling and utilizing learning style*. Reston, VA: National Association of Secondary School Principals.

Kolb, D. (1981). Commentary on Dunn and De Bello article. *Educational Leadership, 38*, 372-375.

Koneya, M. (1976). Location and interaction in row and column seating arrangements. *Environment and Behavior, 8*, 265-270.

Korth, W., & Cornbleth, C. (1982, March). *Classroom activities as settings for cognitive learning opportunity and instruction*. Paper presented at annual meeting of the American Educational Research Association, New York.

Krimsky, J. S. (1982). *A comparative analysis of the effects of matching and mismatching fourth grade students with their learning style preferences for the environmental element of light and their subsequent reading speed and accuracy*. Doctoral dissertation, St. John's University, Jamaica, New York.

Krovetz, M. L. (1977). Who needs what when: Design of pluralistic learning environments. In D. Stokols (Ed.), *Perspectives on environment and behavior: Theory, research, and applications*. New York: Plenum Press.

Kuert, W. P. (1977). *Differences in course content at the high school level characterized by multivariate measures of cognitive and sociopsychological climate*. Doctoral dissertation, University of Tulsa, Tulsa, Oklahoma.

Kulik, C. L., & Kulik, J. A. (1982). Effects of ability grouping on secondary school students: A meta-analysis of evaluation findings. *American Educational Research Journal, 19*, 415-428.

Kyzar, B. L. (1977). Noise pollution and schools: How much is too much? *CEFP Journal, 4*, 10-11.

Leithwood, K. A., Ross, J. A., & Montgomery, D. J. (1982). An investigation of teachers' curriculum decision-making. In K. A. Leithwood (Ed.), *Studies in curriculum decision-making* (pp. 14-46). Toronto: Ontario Institute for Studies in Education.

Lieberman, A., & Miller, L. (1986). School improvement: Themes and variations. In A. Lieberman (Ed.), *Rethinking school improvement: Research, craft, and concept* (pp. 96-114). New York: Teachers College Press.

Loo, C., & Kennelly, D. (1979). Social density: Its effects on behavior and perceptions of preschoolers. *Environmental Psychology and Nonverbal Behavior, 3*, 131-146.

Low, D. (1988, April). *Ability grouping: Decision-making at the secondary level*. Paper presented at the annual meeting of the American Educational Research Association, New Orleans.

McCarthy, B. (1980). *The 4MAT system*. Oakbrook, IL: Excel.

McCutcheon, G. (1980). How do elementary school teachers plan? The nature of planning and influences on it. *Elementary School Journal, 81*, 4-23.

McDonald, S. P. (1980). Interpreting growth in writing. *College Composition and Communication, 31,* 301-310.

Metz, M. H. (1978). *Classrooms and corridors: The crisis of authority in desegregated schools.* Berkeley, CA: University of California Press.

Meyer, J. (1971). *The impact of the open space school upon teacher influence and autonomy: The effects of an organizational innovation.* Stanford, CA: Stanford University. (ERIC Document Reproduction Service No. 062 291)

Millard, J. E. (1977). *Small classes? What research says about the effects of class size and possible alternatives to small classes.* Aukeny, IA: Heartland Educational Association. (ERIC Document Reproduction Service No. 133 897)

Mintz, N. L. (1956). Effects of esthetic surroundings, II: Prolonged and repeated experiences in a "beautiful" and "ugly" room. *Journal of Psychology, 41,* 459-466.

Moos, R. H. (1980). Evaluating classroom learning environments. *Studies in Educational Evaluation, 6,* 239-252.

Moos, R. H. (1987). Learning environments in contexts: Links between school, work, and family settings. In B. J. Fraser (Ed.), *The study of learning environments* (Vol. 2) (pp. 1-16). Baton Rouge, LA: Louisiana State University College of Education.

Moos, R. H., & Trickett, E. J. (1974). *Classroom environment scale manual.* Palo Alto, CA: Consulting Psychologists Press.

Mosteller, F., Light, R. J., & Sachs, J. A. (1996). Sustained inquiry in education: Lessons from skill grouping and class size. *Harvard Educational Review, 66*(4), 797-842.

Murrain, P. G. (1983). *Administrative determinations concerning facilities utilization and instructional grouping: An analysis of the relationship(s) between selected thermal environments and preferences for temperature, an element of learning style, as they affect word recognition scores of secondary students.* Doctoral dissertation, St. John's University, Jamaica, New York.

Newfield, J., & McElyea, V. B. (1983). Achievement and attitudinal differences among students in regular, remedial, and advanced classes. *Journal of Experimental Education, 52,* 47-56.

Nielsen, H. D., & Moos, R. H. (1978). Exploration and adjustment in high school classrooms: A study of person-environment fit. *Journal of Educational Research, 72,* 52-57.

Noli, P. M. (1980, February). *Implications of class size research.* Paper presented at annual meeting of American Association of School Administrators, Anaheim, California. (ERIC Document Reproduction Service No. 184 237)

Oakes, J. (1985). *Keeping track: How schools structure inequality.* New Haven, CT: Yale University Press.

Page, R. N. (1991). *Lower track classrooms: A curricular and cultural perspective.* New York: Teachers College Press.

Price, G. (1980). Which learning style elements are stable and which tend to change? *Learning Styles Network Newsletter, 4*(2), 38-40.

Randhawa, B. S., & Hunt, D. (1982, September). *Structure of learning environment variables in mathematics and English courses.* Paper presented at annual meeting of the British Educational Research Association, St. Andrews, Scotland. (ERIC Document Reproduction Service No. 223 667)

Randhawa, B. S., & Michayluk, J. O. (1975). Learning environments in rural and urban classrooms. *American Educational Research Journal, 12,* 265-285.

Rehberg, R. A., & Rosenthal, E. R. (1978). *Class and merit in the American high school,* New York: Longman.

Reiss, S., & Dyhaldo, N. (1975). Persistence, achievement, and open space environments. *Journal of Educational Psychology, 67,* 506-513.

Rich, H. L., & Bush, A. J. (1978). The effects of congruent teacher-student characteristics on instructional outcomes. *American Educational Research Journal, 15,* 451-457.

Rivlin, L. G., & Rothenberg, M. (1976). The use of space in open classrooms. In H. M. Proshansky, W. H. Ittelson, & L. G. Rivlin (Eds.), *Environmental psychology: People and their physical settings* (2nd ed.). New York: Holt, Rinehart, & Winston.

Robinson, A. (1990). Cooperation or exploitation? The argument against cooperative learning for talented students. *Journal for the Education of the Gifted, 14*(1), 9-27.

Rohe, W., & Patterson, A. J. (1974). The effects of varied levels of resources and density on behavior in a day care center: In D. H. Carson (Ed.), *Man-environment interaction: The evaluations and applications* (Part III). Stroudsburg, PA: Dowden, Hutchinson, & Ross.

Rosenbaum, J. E. (1980). Social implications of educational groupings. In D. C. Berliner (Ed.), *Review of research in education (Vol. 8)* (pp. 361-404.) Washington, DC: American Educational Research Association.

Rosenshine, B., & Stevens, R. (1986). Teaching functions. In M. C. Wittrock (Ed.), *Handbook of Research on Teaching* (3rd ed.) (pp. 376-391).

San Juan Unified School District. (1992). *Class size reduction evaluation: Freshman English, Spring 1991.* Carmichael, CA: Author. (ERIC Document Reproduction Service No. ED 344 239)

Santrock, J. W. (1976). Affect and facilitative self-control: Influence of ecological setting, cognition, and social agent. *Journal of Educational Psychology, 68,* 529-535.

Sardo, D. (1982, October). *Teacher planning styles in the middle school.* Paper presented to the Eastern Educational Research Association, Ellenville, New York.

Schettino, A. P., & Borden, R. J. (1976). Sex differences in response to naturalistic crowding: Affective reactions to group size and group density. *Personality and Social Psychology Bulletin, 2,* 67-70.

Schwebel, A. I., & Cherlin, D. L. (1972). Physical and social distancing in teacher-pupil relationships. *Journal of Educational Psychology, 63,* 543-550.

Schafer, W. E., & Olexa, C. (1971). *Tracking and opportunity.* Scranton, PA: Chandler.

Shapiro, S. (1975). Preschool ecology: A study of three environmental variables. *Reading Improvement, 12,* 236-241.

Shapson, S. M., Wright, E. N., Eason, G., & Fitzgeral, J. (1978, March). *Results of an experimental study of the effects of class size.* Paper presented at the annual meeting of the American Educational Research Association, Toronto. (ERIC Document Reproduction Service No. 151 985)

Shea, T. C. (1983). *An investigation of the relationship among preferences for the learning style element of design, selected instructional environments, and reading achievement of 9th grade students to improve administrative determinations concerning effective educational facilities.* Doctoral dissertation, St. John's University, Jamaica, New York.

Slavin, R. E. (1983). *Cooperative learning.* New York: Longman.

Slavin, R. E. (1987). *Grouping for instruction: Equity and effectiveness.* Baltimore, MD: Center for Research on Elementary and Middle Schools, Johns Hopkins University.

Slavin, R. E. (1988). Synthesis of research on grouping in elementary and secondary schools. *Educational Leadership, 45*(1), 67-77.

Slavin, R. E. (1991). Are cooperative learning and "untracking" harmful to the gifted? *Educational Leadership, 48*(6), 68-71.

Smith, M. L. (1991). Put to the test: The effects of external testing on teachers. *Educational Researcher, 20*(5), 8-11.

Smith, M. L., & Glass, G. V. (1979). *Relationship of class size to classroom processes, teacher satisfaction, and pupil affect: A meta-analysis*. San Francisco: Far West Laboratory for Educational Research and Development.

Smith, W. L. (Chair) and the NCTE Task Force on Class Size and Workload in Secondary English Instruction (1986). *Class size and English in the secondary school*. Urbana, IL: National Council of Teachers of English.

Steele, J. M., Walberg, H. J., & House, E. R. (1974). Subject areas and cognitive press. *Journal of Educational Psychology, 66,* 363-366.

Stires, L. (1978, March). *The effect of classroom seating location on student grades and attitudes: Environment or self-selection?* Paper presented at the annual meeting of the Eastern Psychological Association, Washington, DC.

Stokols, D. (1972). On the distinction between density and crowding: Some implications for future research. *Psychological Review, 79,* 275-277.

Suhor, C. (1986). Introduction. In W. L. Smith (Chair), *Class size and English in the secondary school* (pp. ix-xii.) Urbana. IL: National Council of Teachers of English.

Traub, R., Weiss, J., Fisher, C., & Khan, Y. (1976). *Openness in schools: An evaluation study*. Toronto, Canada: Ontario Institute for Studies in Education.

Veldman, D. J., & Sanford, J. P. (1984). The influence of class ability level on student achievement and classroom behavior. *American Educational Research Journal, 21,* 629-644.

Warner, J. B. (1971). A comparison of students' and teachers' performance in an open space facility and in self-contained classrooms. (Doctoral dissertation, University of Houston, Houston, TX, 1970.) *Dissertation Abstracts International, 31,* 3851A.

Weinstein, C. S. (1979). The physical environment of the school: A review of the research. *Review of Educational Research, 49,* 577-610.

Weinstein, C. S., & Weinstein, N. D. (1979). Noise and reading performance in an open space school. *Journal of Educational Research, 72,* 210-213.

Whalen, H. L. (1972). *English Learning Environment. Urbana*, IL: National Council of Teachers of English.

Wilkerson, R. M., & White, K. P. (1988). Effects of the 4MAT system of instruction on students' achievement, retention, and attitudes. *Elementary School Journal, 88,* 357-368.

Zahorik, J. A. (1975). Teachers' planning models. *Educational Leadership, 33,* 134-139.

Zifferblatt, S. M. (1972). Architecture and human behavior. Toward increased understanding of a functional relationship. *Educational Technology, 12,* 54-57.

# ·38·

# FAMILY LITERACY AT THE TURN
# OF THE MILLENNIUM: THE COSTLY FUTURE
# OF MAINTAINING THE STATUS QUO

## David B. Yaden, Jr.
### University of Southern California

## Jeanne R. Paratore
### Boston University

The year 2000 saw the publication of two comprehensive descriptions and critical reviews of family literacy research (Gadsden, 2000; Purcell-Gates, 2000). In addition, researchers published numerous reports of individual family literacy initiatives and programs (e.g., Auerbach, 1992; Brooks, 1996, 1997; Cairney, 1995; Cairney & Munsie, 1995; Delgado-Gaitan, 1991, 1994, 1996; Delgado-Gaitan & Trueba, 1991; Edwards, 1991, 1995; Handel, 1999; Paratore, 1993, 2001; Paratore, Melzi, & Krol-Sinclair, 1999; Shanahan, Mulhern, & Rodriguez-Brown, 1995; Rodriguez-Brown, & Mulhern, 1993; Rodriguez-Brown, Li, & Albom, 1999) as well as several publications in which collections of family literacy programs were described, evaluated, or critiqued (e.g., Auerbach, 1995a, 1995b, 1995c; Benjamin & Lord, 1996; Harrison, 1995; Lancy, 1994; Morrow, 1995; Morrow, Tracey, & Maxwell, 1995; Paratore, 1994; Taylor, 1997; Tao, Khan, Gamse, St. Pierre, & Tarr, 1998; Yaden, 2001). Together, these works provided a broad, summary corpus of family literacy research and practice leading up to this new millennium.

Rather than restate, reword, or summarize the many conceptual issues and programs that have already been effectively reported, we have chosen to set out some extant conditions or "realities," if you will, that are mentioned less in the research literature but that, nonetheless, circumscribe and perhaps even constitute some of the major stumbling blocks in reaching full, or even adequate, understanding of family and intergenerational literacies in the United States and abroad.

Our discussion is laid out in the following manner. In the first major section, as a point of departure for our own comments, we present a brief summary of major findings, conclusions, and recommendations for future directions in family literacy as they have been reported in existing literature. To accomplish this, we rely primarily on the two most recent research reviews (Gadsden, 2000; Purcell-Gates, 2000). Although we acknowledge that there is a large community of researchers outside the literacy research community who study families (e.g., physicians, sociologists, anthropologists) and recognize that as literacy educators there is much for us to learn from these other areas of research, for the purposes of this chapter, we have limited our examination to the domain of literacy research.

In the second section, we briefly examine evidence that challenges many beliefs and assumptions about families who are most often targeted for family literacy interventions. We then put forth two critical realities, as it were, concerning difficulties with the academic language used to describe family literacy participants as well as some theoretical and methodological shortcomings that both quantitative and qualitative researchers face when confronted with understanding complex literacy interactions within families. Subsequently, in the fourth section, we describe an approach to research inquiry that in itself is not new but that has yet to be applied in family literacy studies. This approach, we believe, offers promise in overcoming many of the difficulties we discuss in section three. Finally, we conclude with an exhortation for all researchers in this field to embrace more fully the notion that an understanding of the complex socio-cultural and sociopolitical nature of literacy imbues us all with additional responsibilities in research reporting and equitable program design and implementation.

## FAMILY LITERACY: A RESEARCH DIASPORA

### Major Tensions in Research

Perhaps the most defining feature of the state of knowledge in family literacy is the lack of consensus about the most elemental issues that surround it. These include: (a) a suitable definition for family literacy and even literacy itself; (b) whether services are best directed at children, their parents and caregivers, or both together; (c) what measures effectively document both short- and long-term effectiveness; and (d) even whether or not the achievement gains made in any program are any sure hedge against such social conditions such as widespread poverty, lack of career opportunities, or the continuing attrition in the gradua-tion rates of the populations that family literacy programs aim to provide services (see St. Pierre, Gamse, Alamprese, Rimdzius, & Tao, 1998, p. 48).

The task of untangling these issues is complex. Not only do theoreticians, researchers, and practitioners disagree on defi-nitions, purposes, appropriate practices, and evaluation mea-sures; they also disagree on the fundamental issue of how to do research. The two most recent research reviews of family and intergenerational literacy effectively illustrate the dilemma that family literacy researchers face. In the first review, Purcell-Gates (2000) reported on approximately a dozen investiga-tions distributed across the United States, Canada, Australia, and the United Kingdom, having delimited the literature to be reviewed to those studies that included a discussion of the choice of design, description of the participants, procedures, analysis procedures, results, and interpretation. Following the typology established by Nickse (1991), which divides programs into three types, depending on whether children, adults or both are the focus, Purcell-Gates (2000) arrived at the following conclusions:

1. Although increasing numbers of large-scale, as well as small single-program, evaluations are being conducted, the cen-tral difficulty of eliminating competing explanations for results remains and weakens virtually all attempts at establishing pro-gram effectiveness. Therefore, all reports that claim to "show" that programs "work" must be read and interpreted with ex-treme caution. (p. 860)

2. Children of parents involved in some form of family literacy program did improve in areas relevant to school suc-cess. Most of the studies, however, lacked appropriate controls and must be taken as suggestive only. (p. 860)

3. Although parent–child interactions around print are at the heart of most family literacy programs, documentation of program impact on the frequency and nature of these

interactions is difficult and thus insufficient at the present time. (p. 866)

Throughout the review, Purcell-Gates (2000) repeatedly de-scribed the extant studies in the field as "lacking appropriate controls" (p. 860), representing at best a "relative paucity of data" (p. 864) and even, in the final analysis, constituting "no em-pirical research" (p. 859) with which to confidently judge and evaluate outcomes or direct future policy. Even in the few places where she noted that research is increasingly "documenting clear benefits to children of family programs of all types," she concluded that this trend is nullified because there is no way to tell if the growth would not have happened anyway in the normal course of children's schooling (p. 863).

Although the conclusions Purcell-Gates (2000) drew are clearly consistent with long and widely held standards of aca-demic scholarship and evaluation of educational research, some in the research community (e.g., Cummins, 1999; Fitzgerald & Cummins, 1999), and even the very authors whose writing re-mains the classic texts from which experimental methodology is learned (Cook & Campbell, 1979; Popper, 1935/1965), have suggested that achieving true experimental control with any exactness within any social science discipline is very nearly impossible.

In the second review, Gadsden (2000) focused less on the ef-fects and outcomes of family literacy interventions and more on the adequacy of existing investigations in helping researchers and practitioners to understand the ways research in intergen-erational literacy

pushes the discourse . . . toward a deepening of knowledge and under-standing of social, cultural, and gender factors that influence literacy within and across different generations the extent to which it utilizes in-terdisciplinary knowledge about intergenerational learning within fami-lies; and the ways in which it can advance the construction of integrative frameworks that capture the nature and mode of literacy's transmission within diverse populations. (p. 872)

Although driven by a different purpose than Purcell-Gates (2000), Gadsden (2000) reached a similar conclusion: Existing research evidence is largely inadequate. Unlike Purcell-Gates, however, whose review appears to be based on an assump-tion that family literacy researchers and practitioners share the same set of purposes and expectations for outcomes and ef-fects, Gadsden argued that a fundamental weakness in existing studies is the lack of awareness and understanding of the wide diversity of social, cultural, and family experiences that charac-terize the populations that are typically targeted by family lit-eracy researchers and practitioners. Gadsden joins a growing group of scholars (cf. Auerbach, 1989, 1995b; Lankshear & McClaren, 1993; Lankshear, Gee, Knobel, & Searle, 1997; Taylor, 1997) critical of programs whose aims are to raise the level of low-income, minority families' parenting behaviors and home activities involving literacy to the putative levels required by our current educational system. Gadsden suggested that research maturity in this field will only be reached when views of family literacy take into consideration the social, cultural, and familial experiences and beliefs that undergird the living and learning routines of the most frequent target of literacy programs—that of marginalized populations. She argued that maturity in methodological approaches needs to reach beyond the pursuit of the "significant difference." She concluded:

1. Depending upon how processes of reading and writing and family values about literacy are conceptualized, framed, studied or understood, they can enable us to move past the inherent constrictions of focusing on consequences and singular outcomes alone; rather they can help us to investigate more deeply what constitutes important knowledge within social and cultural contexts and with what implications for learners over the short and long term. (p. 872)

2. Despite increasing attention to questions about children's learning in families, familial beliefs and values related to literacy learning and families, however, there is still relatively little work that connects intergenerational learning or life-course family development, kinship and kin ties, or community relationships. (p. 873)

3. Within families, attention to intergenerational literacy should be expanded to capture the range of relationships, contributions, and contributors to literacy across ages. In addition, intergenerational literacy may be considered a tool or means to investigating and understanding individual learning, family influences to individual learning, or family learning and the effects of social change.... The issue facing the field is how to confront the complexity of conceptual issues that weaken possibilities for the field to project an agenda of rigorous research and practice that provides for intensive instruction and support to families, and to incorporate what has been learned about families to coordinate efforts for literacy learners across the life span and multiple generations. (p. 884)

In contrast to Purcell-Gates (2000) who stressed the need for experimental control and procedures to eliminate unwanted and extraneous factors which cloud the emergence of clear outcomes, Gadsden (2000) urged the opening up of researchers' horizons to those very variables which account for the incredible diversity in human learning. In addition to encouraging intergenerational researchers to accept as part of their paradigm "neurological and biological predispositions to learning" (p. 873), they should also be examining the influences of relevant social and cultural constructs, transfers of learning between peers as well as between generations, and the impact of various social spaces on learning. Implicit in Gadsden's remarks is the suggestion that family literacy researchers are unwise to overlook anything that is a relevant part of life-course development.

## The Research Ouroboros[1]

Although it might seem on the surface that the views expressed in these two chapters are diametrically opposed, both researchers use similar language to describe the state of knowledge and to suggest future directions. For example, in outlining the parameters of a truly "integrative research framework," Gadsden (2000) noted that "lacking in most analysis that link families, literacy, and intergenerationality is an examination of the variations in families" (p. 875). Similarly, Purcell-Gates (2000) stated that the issues of "compatibility among cultures of schools, homes, and family literacy programs" are "virtually unexplored" (p. 866). Gadsden observed that "there is generally little research that makes any pronouncements about sustained effects of intergenerational literacy" (p. 877), and both authors stressed the need for "rigorous research" (Gadsden, 2000, p. 884), which is "data-based" (Purcell-Gates, 2000, p. 853), "empirical" (Gadsden, 2000, p. 872), "longitudinal" (Purcell-Gates, 2000, p. 866; Gadsden, 2000, p. 884) and representative of important issues across "class, race and ethnicity" (Purcell-Gates, 2000, p. 867).

Although there may be differences in the meanings ascribed by each author to such terms as "rigorous," "data-based," and "empirical," both authors, despite beginning from different stances, lead the reader to similar conclusions:

1. Despite the corpus of studies, which exist in family and intergenerational literacy, there exists "little research" in the areas deemed most important.
2. The research done to date across all methodological designs has been flawed in such ways that no conclusive evidence about effectiveness exists.
3. Most, if not all, of the research done in family and intergenerational literacy to date is not longitudinal and, therefore, cannot be reliably used to plan programs.
4. All family literacy programs and research agendas fail to encompass what is needed to adequately represent the diversity in populations served.

Taken together, these reviews underscore the dilemma facing those whose interests and efforts lie in the area of family literacy. Scholars are faced with the prospect that "more" needs to be done, but how? can studies be designed, at once, that meet the design characteristics of experimental research and recognize and account for variability in individuals and families studied? In one research paradigm, one might control for factors such as income, language proficiency, years of residency in the country of study, parents' level of education, intensity of the program of study, attendance, quality of instruction, or cognitive ability. In another paradigm, variables change—to, for example, attitudes and beliefs, family routines, social needs and desires. As well, outcome measures change. In one case, researchers might seek evidence that children and adults perform better on widely used school-based measures; in the other, researchers seek evidence that parents and children advance their ability to negotiate and accomplish tasks in their daily lives. Is there a research design that is robust enough to accommodate all of the factors that influence how different family members acquire and use literacy in the course of their daily lives? Is it possible to pull off a "descriptive, ethnographic and experimental investigation" as

---

[1] From E. R. Eddison's (1926/1962) *The Worm Ouroboros*—a mythical dragon who swallows his tail, thus creating a circle and symbolizing a closed world, impervious to any outside change.

Purcell-Gates (2000) recommended (p. 867)? Or is this another methodological chimera to chase?

There are no immediate answers to these questions, only the feeling that we as a community of educators are in that place where John-Paul Sartre (1963) has said that there is "no exit." In an age when policymakers are increasingly choosing to support only what is "reliable" or "replicable," researchers wonder if the consequences of suggesting a research paradigm that may in fact be unattainable may lead to the design of studies that may be judged to be methodologically rigorous but that hold little truthfulness for the families they represent.

## MISTAKEN ASSUMPTIONS

Many of the foundational assumptions that have undergirded early national efforts to launch family literacy programs, and even some of late (e.g., Darling & Hayes, 1988–89; Potts & Paull, 1995; Tao et al., 1998), have been questioned for nearly 20 years in the research literature as being inaccurate and unrepresentative of nonmainstream families and an obstacle to working with families of all types (see Delgado-Gaitan, 1990, 1996; Heath, 1983; Moll, Amanti, Neff, & Gonzalez, 1992; Purcell-Gates, 1996; Taylor, 1983, 1997). There are three particular assumptions that have significant influence on the ways many family literacy programs are designed and implemented. One is an assumption that in families in which parents are undereducated or have low levels of English literacy, there is an absence of any form of literacy interaction. A second assumption is that in homes in which parents are undereducated, have low levels of literacy, or have low levels of English language proficiency, these parents are uninterested in or unable to support their children's success in school. A third assumption is that parents who are uneducated or have low levels of English literacy also lack effective parenting skills. In the next section, evidence underlying each of these assumptions is presented.

### Absence of Literacy Practices

What does the absence of home storybook reading really mean? The assumption that in families where parents are undereducated or have low levels of English literacy there is a general absence of literacy practice is based largely on evidence from studies of storybook reading. Several researchers, perhaps most notably among them, Heath (1983) and Teale (1986), have reported that in some families, storybook reading virtually never occurs. These early ethnographic findings have found wide support in the research literature (e.g., see the review by Scarborough & Dobrich, 1994) and most recently in survey data from the U.S. Department of Education (National Center for Educational Statistics, 1999), which indicated that in African American and Hispanic households parents are substantially less likely to read aloud to their children. Although the importance of storybook reading as preparation for eventual success in literacy acquisition has been well documented over the years (Bus, van Ijzendoorn, & Pellegrini, 1995; Clark, 1976; Durkin, 1966; Morrow, 1983; Teale, 1984; Wells, 1986), interpreting the finding of the absence of storybook reading in particular as an absence of literacy interactions in general is based on an incomplete understanding of the data. Heath (1983), for example, reported that although the adults in one of the communities she studied rarely engaged their children in storybook reading, they did immerse their children in a wide range of literacy events, almost all of which were integrally interwoven within the fabric of everyday life. She observed, for example, children reading price tags at the food store so that they would not spend too much and names and addresses on mail so that they could distribute to family members. She also observed them telling stories, answering challenging questions, and using language to entertain and hold the attention of adults. Similarly, Teale (1986) observed little or no storybook reading in some households, but he too noted the presence of some form of literacy in most households, a finding that led to the oft-quoted statement that "virtually all children in a literate society like ours have numerous experiences with written language before they ever get to school" (p. 192).

In the years since these investigations, several other studies have verified that although storybook reading may not be a staple in every household, in almost all cases, literacy mediates daily household and community routines (e.g., Delgado-Gaitan, 1996; Gadsden, 1995; Melzi, Paratore, & Krol-Sinclair, 2000; Paratore et al., 1999, 2001; Purcell-Gates, 1995, 1996). Such evidence, however, has had little influence on the rhetoric that surrounds what has come to be known as the family literacy movement, and a commonly held belief is that family literacy "means changing attitudes, values, and in some cases, cultures" (National Center for Family Literacy, 1991, p. 7).

The tendency of many to ignore the evidence that in families in which parents are undereducated and linguistically different adults and children are not illiterate but rather "differently literate" (Purcell-Gates, 1995) has led Taylor (1993, 1997) and Auerbach (1995a, 1995b) to argue that too often family literacy intervention programs are based on a deficit perspective that focuses only on the development of the literacy event that is thought to be absent (storybook reading) and fully ignores the literacies that are present. By so doing, Taylor and Auerbach argue, educators fail to recognize and acknowledge a rich foundation on which to build new literacies. The argument, then, is not that storybook reading is unimportant or unnecessary in the literacy development of the children in these families but rather that exclusive focus on storybook reading results in a misrepresentation of the literacy knowledge of both parents and adults in linguistically and culturally different families.

Furthermore, we might also ask why the evidence that linguistically and culturally different families are in fact not illiterate but rather differently literate is so often ignored, not only by family literacy teachers and researchers but also by early childhood and elementary grade teachers and researchers. It is our view that the educational community within which we are members largely doesn't have a theory for how "nonnarrative" literacy knowledge (cf. Bruner, 1987) can form the basis for instruction in literacy as it is currently conceptualized. We know a good deal about how storybook reading "maps on" to early literacy acquisition, but we are less able to make the connection between, for example, nonnarrative text structure (cf. Duke, 2000; Pappas,

1993; Tufte, 1983, 1997) and orality itself (see, e.g., Egan, 1988; Havelock, 1963, 1991; Levi-Strauss, 1966; Olson, 1994; Olson & Torrance, 1991; Ong, 1982) and literacy learning as related to both (Cushman, 1998). Although such enlightened concepts as "household funds of knowledge" (Moll, 1992; Moll et al., 1992; Moll & Greenberg, 1991) provide a promising direction for helping educators to become more knowledgeable about children's learning resources at home and in the community, these findings speak more to the ways parents and teachers may learn to interact with each other across the curriculum than to a theoretical model of the ways teachers might build on children's home and community resources in the teaching of emergent and beginning literacy.

In other words, it appears that we are restricted to only one way to work with families, and that way does not recognize the importance of reciprocity in learning between parents and teachers. That is, as educators, we know that it is important to teach parents about schools and classroom literacies (Corno, 1989) and how to suggest ways for them to add these literacies to their family literacy repertoires, but we know little of the importance of learning from parents about family literacies and of developing ways to add family literacies to our classroom literacy repertoires.

## Lack of Interest in Their Children's Education

When one reads the accounts of the hazards of border crossings, overland trips of several hundred miles, inhuman living conditions, and discriminatory treatment on arrival in the United States (see, e.g., Carger, 1996; Donato, 1999; Fuentes, 1997; Guerra, 1998; Gutíerrez, 1995; Hellman, 1994; Ruiz, 2000; Sánchez, 1993, for numerous examples), one finds it hard to reconcile the motivation and stamina needed by families to endure these situations with the oft-heard complaint of many teachers that immigrant parents, particularly Hispanic parents, show little motivation to assist their children in school activities. Indeed, it is the search for "a life of dignity" for the family as a whole that is one of the many driving forces behind the emigrant journey itself. As Yberra (1999) has written in the volume *Americanos*, "Despite our diversity, we are nonetheless bound together by a common search for a better life for ourselves and our children. Thus, our destiny has brought us to this country, whether it was generations ago or merely this morning" (p. 84). That many immigrant families perceive formal schooling as the vehicle for improving their own and their children's opportunities is attested to by several studies (e.g., Delgado-Gaitan, 1992; Delgado-Gaitan & Trueba, 1991; Valdés, 1996; Yaden et al., 2000; Yaden, Madrigal, & Tam, in press).

Despite evidence to the contrary, however, the belief that immigrant parents (and perhaps nonmainstream parents in general) have little interest in their children's education is persistent and widespread. For example, in a survey of 1,000 public school teachers conducted by the organization Public Agenda most teachers (83%) indicated that they believe that many parents are failing to meet obligations such as creating structure and setting limits, monitoring TV viewing and video games, and holding their children accountable for behavior and academic performance (Farkas, Johnson, Duffett, Aulicino, & McHugh, 1999). Majorities of both suburban (67%) and urban (82%) teachers reported that too many parents have little sense of what is going on with their children's education. Nearly 7 in 10 teachers indicated that "the most serious problem they face is with students who try to get by doing as little work as possible" (p. 25) and they blame parents for this behavior.

However, when polled by this same survey, parents directly contradicted teachers' beliefs. Over half (51%) said they worry more about the quality of their children's education than they do about other contemporary social pressures such as the threat of crime or drugs or economic security. Furthermore, 73% reported that their concern about their child's education determined the community in which they chose to live, and 56% said they spoke with the principal or teachers before their child enrolled in their current school. Additionally, 33% of those surveyed indicated that they checked with other parents to see which teachers would be best. Finally, three quarters of respondents believed that they are more involved in their children's education than their own parents were.

The apparent contradictions in teachers' and parents' beliefs about the latter's interest and involvement in their children's education may be explained by evidence that the ways parents perceive their roles and responsibilities in relation to their children's schooling varies by ethnic and socioeconomic groups (Delgado-Gaitan, 1990; Galindo & Escamilla, 1995; Goldenberg, 1987; Lareau, 1987, 1989; Lynch & Stein, 1987; Orellana, 1996; Orellana, Monkman, & MacGillivray, 1998; Parra & Henderson, 1982; Valdés, 1996). Unlike middle-class parents who understand their role to be one of helping children learn and study, many working-class parents believe that their roles involve getting children ready for school, making certain that they are courteous, respectful, and prompt but do not believe that their roles include helping children learn. Rather, they see directing and supporting children's learning as the province of the teacher and even interpret intrusion into the realm of learning and study as disrespectful to the teacher. Although there are certainly studies in which nonmainstream families take a view of their roles in relation to their children's learning that is closely aligned with that of middle-class parents (e.g., Clark, 1983; Segal, 1985), it is difficult to deny the presence of dissonance between parents' and teachers' expectations for parental actions in at least some households. The consequence of the misunderstanding is that parents fail to perform the tasks that teachers perceive as an essential part of school success, and teachers conclude that parents are uninterested and uninvolved in their children's education.

However, the ability to participate in school activities is more than just a matter of intent or a shared understanding of roles and responsibilities. In her study of parents and their roles in their children's schooling, Lareau (1987, 1989) observed that low-income parents lack the social and cultural capital necessary to participate in the same ways as high-income parents:

[S]ocial class offered parents, and ultimately children, an advantage in discovering and complying with [institutional] standards. It facilitated— or impeded—parents' educational involvement in terms of the amount of work they did with children at home, the kind of work they did at home, and the interpretation they made of why they attended school events. Most importantly, social class position largely excluded working-class parents from taking a leadership role in education.... Overall, there are signs that higher social class provides resources which parents can draw on to help their children excel in school. Social class gave children a home advantage. (p. 176)

Similarly, Sosa (1997) identified considerable logistical (time, money, safety, child care) and attitudinal barriers (uncertainty, communication problems) that discourage poor, linguistic and cultural minority parents from visiting and participating in their children's schools.

Thus, differing views of the roles of the parent–school partnership and differences in the availability of important resources explain why some families have less contact with their children's school and teachers. Also contributing to lower levels of engagement in school activities by some parents is the failure of many educators to look beyond the school doors at the actual life circumstances that define daily and weekly family routines and, particularly, to understand the ways certain family routines may differ from those that are familiar to and expected by mainstream teachers.

### Poor Parenting

Finally, implicit in many family literacy program models, particularly those advanced by the National Center for Family Literacy (Darling & Hayes, 1988–89) and by the Even Start Family Literacy Initiative (McKee & Rhett, 1995), is an assumption that parents who have low levels of education, English literacy, or English language proficiency also lack knowledge and strategies related to effective parenting practices. Descriptions of these models cite parenting education as an essential program component (McKee & Rhett, 1995; Potts & Paull, 1995). Tao, Swartz, St. Pierre, & Tarr (1997) reported that of 476 Even Start projects included in its National Even Start Evaluation Project, 82% included parenting education and 88% of these sites taught "most families how to provide for their children's safety and well-being" (p. 68). Further, Tao et al. reported that "an important aspect of parenting education is to strengthen the parents' personal skills and capabilities; in essence, to empower them to be self-reliant in all aspects of their lives" (p. 68). They found that 97% of projects "touched on self-esteem with at least some of their families" (p. 68) and 93% did so with "most of their families" (p. 68).

The amount of time dedicated to these program goals is substantial. Tao et al. (1997) reported an average of 99 hours a year (2–264 = hour range) with parents alone and an additional 96 hours a year (2–240 = hour range) with parents and children together. In the case of parents who are described as beginning literacy learners parenting education accounts for and average of 36% of their instructional time. In the case of parents who are described as English language learners, the time spent in parenting education accounts for an average of 47% of their instructional time.

Of importance, however, is the fact that despite the substantial amount of time dedicated to the development of parenting strategies, little attention has been paid to testing or

documenting the assumption that parents who participate in family literacy programs as a group are ineffective parents and, further, that parents who are English language learners require even greater emphasis on parenting education than their native English-speaking counterparts.

The cost of accepting this assumption without some evidentiary basis is high. With one third to nearly one half of instructional time allocated to parenting as a curricular focus, time to develop English literacy and language abilities and to help parents acquire knowledge about ways to support their children's literacy and school success is substantially, and, at least in some cases, perhaps unnecessarily, diminished. This is an assumption in need of careful and thoughtful investigation.

## ADVANCING RESEARCH IN FAMILY LITERACY: CONFRONTING CRITICAL REALITIES

In this section, we examine two conditions or extant realities that we believe to be critical to the advancement of research and practice in family literacy: (a) that the language that often characterizes both oral and written texts common to family literacy creates a barrier to understanding the very people we seek to come to know; and (b) that family literacy interactions are influenced by a complex system of individual and group behaviors that can be more fully understood within the context of complexity theory.

### Reality One: The Disfiguring Mirror of Academic Language

At a particular fund-raising event attended by one of the authors, a mother and her two children were being used as an example of the type of family that benefited from the donors' gifts. The mother was described as coming home exhausted from working long hours in the downtown factory area, alone without help, the house as having no furniture, and the children, although bright, facing an uphill struggle to become "successful" as the audience would understand that word. The following reflection was derived from field notes taken at the event.

As I sat there listening to this description, I felt this unsettling in my stomach because I knew this family, had even recently been in their home; and the description I was hearing didn't match the circumstances that I observed. In actuality at this particular time, the mother felt incredibly hopeful about their future. They had moved to a much better part of town into a new apartment, and to celebrate they invited family members, several friends, and acquaintances.

True, there weren't enough chairs for all of us to sit, but no one seemed to mind as we scattered ourselves around the house, in the kitchen, in the living room, and bedrooms in small groups engaged in lively conversation. As the smell of Mexican cuisine drifted out of the kitchen and filled the apartment in the most appetizing way, the mother proudly led groups of guests through each room describing their plans for furnishings, whose room would be like what, and showing off the library of children's books which they had amassed over the last few years.

As I listened to her, watched her face, catching those few phrases which my paucity of Spanish allowed me, I was struck and humbled at this woman standing before me who had already worked her early morning shift in the factory that morning and now had gladly opened her home to not only family but to someone like me who only understood a fraction of what she said and who represented the very segment of society whose own privilege left little room for hers. Perhaps there was exhaustion, but this was extinguished by the exuberance of her spirit. If she felt embarrassment about her house, I didn't see it. And if there was any gloom because of the portent of a future life of deprivation, nobody could have detected it in the happy chorus of voices which filled the air (D. B. Yaden, March 3, 2000).

In sharing this story, we do not mean to suggest that the economic situation of this family could not or even should not be improved, nor that this mother was content with her present situation. There were and are plenty of worries, some of which were evident, others perhaps less so. But to portray her as being unable to help herself or her children without the assistance of the fund-raising audience of primarily White business and corporate executives and concerned benefactors from the ranks of the wealthy is a clear misrepresentation.

*How language shapes perception.* The problems involved with representation of other persons, particularly by people in privileged positions, have been insightfully discussed by a number of writers (e.g., Guha, 1997; Heath & McLaughlin, 1993; Hitchcock, 1993; Said, 1978). As Said (1994) pointed out in *Culture and Imperialism*, words matter: Certain terms create impressions that block our understanding of the real condition or value of those who are represented. For family literacy educators, the words and phrases that obscure rather than clarify are many: high-poverty environments, depressed neighborhood conditions, low-income learners, low-income homes, low-income families, nonmainstream homes, urban children, at-risk learners, inner-city youths, disadvantaged youths, minority children, English language learners, immigrant families, and inner-city families. From the point of view of the classifiers, primarily those of us in the research community, the terms we choose seem innocent enough. However, as Freire (1970/2000) pointed out, these "codified" descriptions, left in their initial form, and without the benefit of critical reflection, fail to focus one's view on the actual elements of experience as perceived by those in the situation to which the categories refer. In other words, the "deep structure" of the codified representation remains masked. Thus, potentially, unexamined or insufficiently understood terminology may lead us to inadequate or, worse, inaccurate conclusions and recommendations.

*The misrepresented represent themselves.* One of the authors, being curious about what terms or phrases persons in commonly researched environments by family literacy workers would use to describe themselves, informally queried several people about whether or not they would agree with written statements characterizing them as "poor" or "disadvantaged." One person who eventually obtained a teaching certificate from a major university said that she was surprised to see herself and family represented in the literature assigned for class reading as "poverty stricken." She said that she had never thought of herself as poor because, in her circle of acquaintances, that description was only used to refer to the situation of family and friends back in their home countries in which conditions were far worse than those endured here. Compared with them, she said, she felt fortunate. Another mother, when asked if she would describe herself as "needy," declared that while there certainly were things her family needed, more often it was opportunity that was lacking. She said her family was fully capable of capitalizing on opportunities when they arose and had been bothered by recent media attention to her own living conditions. Weren't these conditions or experiences (e.g., sometimes working long hours, lacking important material resources, sacrificing personal goals for the sake of her children) that all families went through in the course of daily or weekly living? Why should her family be looked on as different from others?

To document that such misrepresentations are keenly felt by the persons they are intended to describe, we point beyond these particular anecdotes to literature that has represented the experiences of marginalized peoples throughout this century. In the work of Achebe (1987), Chatwin (1977, 1987), Du Bois (1903/1996), Fanon (1963), Guha and Spivak (1998), James (1938/1989), Martí (1871/1999), and Ngugi (1965), we find evidence that the language of the business community, property owners, government officials, educators, and scientists is often perceived by those it describes as deeply degrading, dehumanizing, and lacking insight into the realities with which they live.

The consequences of using inaccurate and imprecise language to represent the families we seek to learn about and to teach are of import not only to the individuals who are misrepresented but also to the community of researchers and practitioners as a whole, for our ill-formed assumptions limit our ability to study and to understand who the families are, how they use literacy to mediate their daily activities, and how they might be effectively served.

## Reality Two: Nature and Human Behavior as Primarily Nonlinear

In the decade of the 90s, in particular, the principles and workings of complexity theory have been advanced by scientists and scholars from several disciplines within the natural sciences, mathematics, and medicine (e.g., Bak, 1996; Capra, 1996; Cohen & Stewart, 1994; Edelman, 1992; Freeman, 1991; Goldberger, Rigney, & West, 1990; Holland, 1998; Kauffman, 1995; Kellert, 1993; Lipsitz & Goldberger, 1992; Lorenz, 1993; Penrose, 1989; Prigogine, 1996; Ruelle, 1991; Stewart, 1989). As well, concepts related to complexity and systems theory have been popularized for the general public in several books, including *Chaos* (Gleick, 1987), *The Cosmic Blueprint* (Davies, 1988), *The Turbulent Mirror* (Briggs & Peat, 1989), *Complexity* (Waldrop, 1992; Lewin, 1992), *Artificial Life* (Levy, 1992), *Out of Control* (Kelly, 1994), and *Strange Beauty* (Johnson, 2000). Perhaps the best evidence of the appeal of these ideas to a widespread audience are the movies *Jurassic Park* and *The Lost World*, both based on a book of the same name by Michael Crichton (1990, 1995) in which a mathematician, Malcolm, predicts the unraveling of a live dinosaur theme park through chaos theory. Even on prime time television (Bruckheimer, 2001) a popular crime drama series recently aired an episode entitled "chaos theory."

In addition, the notion of complexity theory has found wide application to a number of problems in cognitive science (see Maturana & Varela, 1998; Varela, Thompson, & Rosch, 1997) as well as within the social sciences and education. For example, complexity theory has been applied effectively to the study of organizational behavior and theory (Goldstein, 1994; Guastello, 1995), psychology (Abraham, Abraham, Shaw, & Garfinkel, 1990; Abraham & Gilgen, 1995; Barton, 1994), sociology (Baker, 1993), counseling (Torres-Rivera, 1996), social psychology (Vallacher & Nowak, 1994), literary criticism (Hayles, 1990, 1991, 1999), composition studies (Greening, 1993; Kahn, 1996; Syverson, 1999), curriculum theory (Doll, 1989, 1993), special education (Guess & Sailor, 1993), second language acquisition (Larsen-Freeman, 1997), learning theory (Ennis, 1992; Greeley, 1995, 1996; Lindsay, 1989, 1991), reading (Plaut, McClelland, Seidenberg, & Patterson, 1996; Robinson & Yaden, 1996; Seidenberg & McClelland, 1989; Sumara, 2000; Weaver, 1989; Yaden, 1995, 1999; Yaden & Greeley, 1997), and teacher education (Patterson, 1995; Patterson, Cotton, Kimball-Lopez, Pavonetti, L., & VanHorn, 1998).

These applications share an understanding that in most areas of human endeavor, the forces or factors that determine patterns of behavior are dynamical, nonlinear, and, as a whole, not amenable to standard research design and statistical evaluation. In the next few paragraphs, we provide a brief explanation of this point by citing the work of computer scientist John Holland, perhaps better known as the creator of genetic algorithms.

***Principles of complexity.*** According to Holland (1994) complexity theory can be fairly represented by seven general principles: (a) All complex adaptive systems (CASs) consist of large numbers of components or agents that incessantly interact with each other; (b) it is the concerted behavior of these agents—the aggregate behavior—that researchers must understand; (c) in all CASs, the interactions that generate this aggregate behavior are nonlinear, so that the aggregate behavior cannot be derived by summing up the behavior of isolated elements; (d) CAS agents are not only numerous, but also diverse and melded in a complex web of interactions; (e) the persistence of any given part (agent) depends directly on the context provided by the rest or aggregate; (f) aggregate behavior, instead of settling down, exhibits a perpetual novelty, an aspect which bodes ill for standard mathematical approaches; and (g) all CAS agents employ internal models or schema to direct their behavior and anticipate the consequences of their actions (pp. 310-311).

To sum up, all complex systems are driven by both directed individual behavior and also by the direct or indirect influences of larger groups. Individuals are in a continual process of interaction with each other, and the resulting behavior is, for the most part, nonlinear in that the consequences of behavior cannot be attributed reliably to any one large or small initial influence. Furthermore, the diversity in individual and group behavior is always evolving. Individuals reorganize themselves according to changes in the overall system, which, in turn, create more diversity and new webs of interaction; finally, individual actions,

even less insightful ones, may substantially alter the behavior of the whole.

***Applications of systems theory to family literacy studies.*** Systems theory as applied to families has long been discussed within psychology (cf. von Bertalanffy, 1968), particularly within group and family psychotherapy (Burlingame, Fuhriman, & Barnum, 1995), and we believe that there may be a similar application to the study of family literacy. As Gadsden (2000) suggested, to begin to understand the factors that influence both children's and parents' experiences with literacy materials and activities, families must be studied in context. To do so, research investigations must dramatically increase in complexity. However, within a systems approach, the large number of interacting variables need not be viewed as overwhelming. Several techniques have been developed to identify the most likely of interacting variables that drive the system under study such that the dynamic system is preserved, but the number of variables needing to be analyzed is considerably reduced (see Guastello, 1995, for a number of applications applied to human behavior). Examples of some of these techniques as applied to literacy research include examinations of parent–child storybook reading and reading difficulties (Yaden, 1999; in press), classroom literature discussions (Patterson et al., 1998), and reader-response theory (Sumara, 2000).

Moreover, if the behaviors of families over a broad range of literacy interactions are viewed as a dynamical system (in the technical sense of the word), then even though it is a rule-bound system, these principles may be beyond the scope of any standard experimental paradigm due to their nonlinearity and immanent causes of variability. With systems theory as the theoretical underpinning for research design, it is virtually impossible to conceive a study in which precise control could be maintained and, relatedly, unlikely that any resulting conclusions could be viewed as anything more than "suggestive." However, this assessment need not be a uniformly pejorative condition, as implied by Purcell-Gates (2000). Rather, given the complexity in family systems, even suggestive findings may be expected to lead us toward a deeper understanding of the families involved. These nascent attempts to apply systems principles to complex situations in education must be viewed as just that—beginnings. However, we believe it to be imperative that educational researchers acknowledge that the study of literacy development within the complex context of family life demands an equally complex theoretical and methodological framework. It is our view that we as a research community cannot continue to apply our standard designs and methods without fully understanding in an epistemological sense that they will almost certainly fall short of producing any definitive explanatory power.

## LOOKING TOWARD THE FUTURE

In 1979, Bronfenbrenner (as cited in Valdés, 1996) commented on the state of research knowledge about families:

I shall presume to speak for the profession in pointing out what we do know and what we don't. We know a great deal about children's behavior and development, and quite a bit about what can and does happen inside of families—parent child interaction, family dynamics, and all that. But we know precious little about the circumstances under which families live, how these circumstances affect their lives, and what might happen if the circumstances were altered.... Before we can engage in parent education of the kinds here proposed, we have to learn a good deal more than we know at present about the actual experience of families in different segments of our society. (p. 220)

We believe that the state of uncertainty and near confusion in the research knowledge that surrounds family literacy suggests that 2 decades later the field still lacks adequate understanding of the literate traditions, values, and practices of families outside the American mainstream. We also believe that attempts at investigation have been limited in large part by the methodological procedures employed which, as Purcell-Gates (1996) noted, too often cause us to "fool ourselves into believing that we are looking through a window when instead we are looking into a mirror" (p. 6).

It is not our intent to further polarize those in the research community by suggesting that either quantitative or qualitative methodologies are fully adequate to understand the complex dynamics of human interaction—for we believe they are not. However, it is less a matter of striking a compromise between the two methodologies than achieving the realization that the very phenomenon under study—family interaction—will always exceed exact or definitive description, regardless of how it is measured. We suggest that the primary problem is that both approaches are mistakenly using "induction" as a criterion for research quality. Although this approach is still believed by many to be the hallmark of the scientific method, Karl Popper (1934/1965), in his classic book, *The Logic of Scientific Discovery*, as well as other philosophers of science (Lakatos, 1970/1999; Lakatos & Feyerabend, 1999) long ago showed that the possibility of inferring universal statements or conclusions from the results of single experiments or clusters of experiments was implausible (see also Gould, 1981; Popper, 1996). In his recent biography of Nobel laureate Murray Gell-Mann, George Johnson (2000) related that the renowned physicist expressed a similar point of view:

This idea of breaking the world into pieces and then explaining the pieces in terms of smaller pieces is called reductionism. It would be perfectly justified to consider Gell-Mann, the father of the quark, to be the century's arch-reductionist, but very early on, long before the mushy notions of holism became trendy, Gell-Mann appreciated an important truth: While you can reduce downward, that doesn't automatically mean that you can explain upward. People can be divided into cells, cells into molecules, molecules into atoms, atoms into electrons and nuclei, nuclei into subatomic particles, and those into still tinier things called quarks. But, true as that may be, there is nothing written in the laws of subatomic physics that can be used to explain higher level phenomena like human behavior. There is no way that one can start with quarks and predict that cellular life would emerge and evolve over the eons to produce physicists. Reducing downward is vastly easier than explaining upward—a truth that bears repeating. (p. 9)

We believe that the hallmarks—and associated risks—of reductionist approaches are evident in many areas of family literacy research and practice, perhaps most fundamentally in

the ways that literacy, is defined and measured. To the extent that researchers, both quantitative and qualitative alike, insist on tying the effectiveness of family literacy programs to achievement of higher levels of performance on school-based measures of literacy, we will likely fail to understand and recognize the diverse ways in which families use, embed, extend, and learn from literacy in their daily lives. In the absence of such understanding and recognition, we believe the field will be paralyzed in its ability to move forward.

As an alternative to a reductionist approach, Cummins (1999; see also Fitzgerald & Cummins, 1999), posed a "research-theory-policy" approach to evaluating research studies in which

knowledge is generated not by evaluating the effects of particular treatments under strictly controlled conditions, but by observing phenomena, forming hypotheses to account for the observed phenomena, testing these hypotheses against additional data, and gradually refining the hypotheses into more comprehensive theories that have broader explanatory and predictive power. (p. 30)

In this approach, hypotheses would be evaluated by examining whether or not behaviors predicted by a particular theory are in fact observed and confirmed in the practical applications. Notably, Cummins' (1999) proposal for educational research and evaluation reflects the same epistemological parameters for the "corroboration" or "falsification" of theories suggested by Popper (1934/1965) nearly 70 years earlier in that it is a "deductive" approach to science which is able to reveal the existence of theories which have the capability to "prove their mettle" (p. 33).

Our conclusion is that the field of family literacy research would profit from evaluations that first uncover the theoretical underpinnings of particular practices and then examine or verify the outcomes of those theoretically based practices. This approach to research and evaluation not only increases the explanatory power of family literacy research but, more important, places responsibility on program designers and researchers to ensure that particular efforts to deliver family literacy services are undergirded by clear, and explicable theoretical frameworks.

## CONCLUSION

Literacy is a complex phenomenon, and its complexity confounds its instruction. In 1991, Alan Purves cautioned those who teach literacy to be aware of the social responsibility they bear: "The activity of being literate ... is a deliberate and social activity, one that takes place in the world; it should not be seen as an abstracted mental state or condition. Those who are involved in literacy education should, therefore, be aware of their social responsibility" (p. 51). More recently, Gee (1999) challenged the conclusions of a national panel on effective approaches to literacy instruction, and in doing so, echoed Purves' comments: "One cannot coherently debate ways of improving reading and leave out social, cultural, institutional, and political issues and interventions as if they were 'separate' from literacy (mere 'background noise' as it were)" (p. 360).

The statements of Purves (1991) and Gee (1999) remind us that advancing the state of family literacy research and practice will not be accomplished by addressing methodological considerations alone; we must also recognize and address the social and political nature of literacy, in general, and of literacy research, in particular. Although this may seem far afield from our purposes in this review, nonetheless we believe that it is possible for the academic community in the field of family literacy studies to have a substantial impact in determining what types of programs will meet the substantial challenges ahead. In Edward Said's (1994) conclusion to *Culture and Imperialism*, he suggested that those in places of privilege and having the power to speak should use those abilities in "first distilling, then articulating the predicaments that disfigure modernity—mass

deportation, imprisonment, population transfer, collective dispossession, and forced immigrations" (pp. 332–333). For us this means that as a community of educators we must use our considerable, collective energies in ways that help us to identify the hallmarks of equitable family literacy programs and to speak out against those that are not.

What this doesn't mean for family literacy advocates is striving for the elimination of many diverse programs in favor of only one kind. It is rather, as Said (1994) continues, evidenced in "not trying to rule others, not trying to classify them or put them into hierarchies, and above all, not constantly reiterating how 'our' culture or country is number one" (p. 336). From these basic values we believe that the best hopes for family literacy research and programs will be realized.

# References

Abraham, F. D., & Gilgen, A. R. (Eds.) (1995). *Chaos theory in psychology*. Westport, CT: Praeger.

Abraham, F. D., Abraham, R. H., Shaw, C. D., & Garfinkel, A. (1990). *A visual introduction to dynamical systems theory for psychology*. Santa Cruz, CA: Aerial Press.

Achebe, C. (1987). *Anthills of the savannah*. New York: Doubleday.

Auerbach, E. R. (1989). Toward a socio-cultural approach to family literacy. *Harvard Educational Review, 59*, 165–181.

Auerbach, E. R. (1992). *Making meaning, making change: Participatory curriculum development for adult ESL literacy*. Washington, DC: Center for Applied Linguistics; McHenry, IL: Delta Systems.

Auerbach, E. R. (1995a). Deconstructing the discourse of strengths in family literacy. *Journal of Reading Behavior, 27*, 643–661.

Auerbach, E. R. (1995b). From deficit to strength: Changing perspectives on family literacy. In G. Weinstein-Shur & E. Quintero (Eds.), *Immigrant learners and their families: Literacy to connect the generations* (pp. 63–76). Washington, DC: Center for Applied Linguistics.

Auerbach, E. R. (1995c). Which way for family literacy: Intervention or empowerment. In L. M. Morrow (Ed.), *Family literacy: Connections in schools and communities* (pp. 11–28). Newark, DE: International Reading Association.

Bak, P. (1996). *How nature works: the science of self-organized criticality*. New York: Springer-Verlag.

Baker, P. L. (1993). Chaos, order and sociological theory. *Sociological Inquiry, 63*(2), 123–149.

Barton, S. (1994). Chaos, self-organization, and psychology. *American Psychologist, 49*(1), 5–14.

Benjamin, L. A., & Lord, J. (Eds.) (1996). *Family literacy: Directions in research and implications for practice*. Washington, DC: U.S. Department of Education, Office of Educational Research and Improvement.

Briggs, J., & Peat, F. D. (1989). *Turbulent mirror: An illustrated guide to chaos theory and the science of wholeness*. NY: Harper Row.

Brooks, G., Gorman, T., Harman, J., Hutchison, D., Kinder, K., Moor, H., & Wilkin, A. (1997). *Family literacy lasts: The NFER follow-up study of the Basic Skills Agency's Demonstration Programmes*. London: Basic Skills Agency. (ERIC Document Reproduction Service No. ED 419 159)

Brooks, G., Gorman, T., Harman, J., Hutchison, D., & Wilkin, A. (1996). *Family literacy works*. London: Basic Skills Agency.

Bruckheimer, J. (Producer) (2001). *Las Vegas Crime Scene Investigation*. New York: CBS Worldwide Inc.

Bruner, J. (1987). *Actual minds, possible worlds*. Cambridge, MA: Harvard University Press.

Burlingame, G. M., Fuhriman, A., & Barnum, K. R. (1995). Group therapy as a nonlinear, dynamical system: Analysis of therapeutic communication for chaotic patterns. In F. D. Abraham & A. R. Gilgen (Eds.), *Chaos theory in psychology* (pp. 87–106). Westport, CT: Praeger.

Bus, A. G., van Ijzendoorn, M. H., & Pellegrini, A. D. (1995). Joint book reading makes for success in learning to read: A meta-analysis in intergenerational transmission of literacy. *Review of Educational Research, 65*, 1–21.

Cairney, T. H. (1995). Developing parent partnerships in secondary literacy learning. *Journal of Reading, 38*, 520–526.

Cairney, T. H., & Munsie, L. (1995). *Beyond tokenism: Parents as partners in literacy*. Portsmouth, NH: Heinemann.

Capra, F. (1996). *The web of life: A new scientific understanding of living systems*. New York: Doubleday.

Carger, C. L. (1996). *Of borders and dreams*. New York: Teachers College Press.

Chatwin, B. (1977). *In Patagonia*. New York: Penguin.

Chatwin, B. (1987). *The songlines*. New York: Penguin.

Clark, M. (1976). *Young fluent readers: What they can teach us*. London: Heinemann.

Clark, R. (1983). *Family life and school achievement*. Chicago: University of Chicago Press.

Cohen, J., & Stewart, I. (1994). *The collapse of chaos: Discovering simplicity in a complex world*. New York: Viking Penguin.

Cook, T. D., & Campbell, D. T. (1979). *Quasi-experimentation: Design and analysis for field settings*. Boston: Houghton Mifflin Company.

Corno, L. (1989). What it means to be literate about classrooms. In D. Bloome (Ed.), *Classrooms and literacy* (pp. 29–52). Norwood, NJ: Ablex.

Crichton, M. (1990). *Jurassic park*. New York: Alfred A. Knopf.

Crichton, M. (1995). *The lost world*. New York: Alfred A. Knopf.

Cummins, J. (1999). Alternative paradigms in bilingual education research: Does theory have a place? *Educational Researcher, 28*, 26–32.

Cushman, E. (1998). *The struggle and the tools*. Albany: State University of New York Press.

Darling, S., & Hayes, A. (1988–89). *Family literacy project final project report*. Louisville, KY: National Center for Family Literacy.

Davies, P. (1988). *The cosmic blueprint: New discoveries in nature's creative ability to order the universe*. New York: Simon & Shuster.

Delgado-Gaitan, C. (1990). *Literacy for empowerment: The role of parents in children's education*. New York: Falmer Press.

Delgado-Gaitan, C. (1991). Involving parents in the schools: A process of empowerment. *American Journal of Education, 100*, 20–46.

Delgado-Gaitan, C. (1992). School matters in the Mexican American home: Socializing children to education. *American Educational Research Journal, 29*, 495–513.

Delgado-Gaitan, C. (1994). Socio-cultural change through literacy: Toward the empowerment of families. In B. M. Ferdman, R. M. Weber & A. G. Ramírez (Eds.), *Literacy across languages and cultures* (143–169). Albany: State University of New York Press.

Delgado-Gaitan, C. (1996). *Protean literacy: Extending the discourse on empowerment*. New York: Falmer Press.

Delgado-Gaitan, C., & Trueba, H. (1991). *Crossing cultural borders: Education for immigrant families in America*. New York: The Falmer Press.

Doll, W. E. (1989). Complexity in the classroom. *Educational Leadership, 47*(1), 65–70.

Doll, W. E., Jr. (1993). *A post-modern perspective on curriculum*. New York: Teachers College Press.

Donato, R. (1999). Hispano education and the implications of autonomy: Four school systems in southern Colorado. *Harvard Educational Review, 69*, 117–149.

Du Bois, W. E. B. (1996). *The souls of black folks*. New York: Penguin. (Original work published 1903)

Duke, N. K. (2000). 3.6 minutes per day: The scarcity of informational texts in first grade. *Reading Research Quarterly, 35*, 202–225.

Durkin, D. (1966). *Children who read early*. New York: Teachers College Press.

Eddison, E. R. (1962). *The worm Ouroboros*. New York: Ballantine Books. (Original work published 1926)

Edelman, G. M. (1992). *Bright air, brilliant fire: On the matter of mind*. New York: Basic Books.

Edwards, P. A. (1991). Fostering early literacy through parent coaching. In E. Hiebert (Ed.), *Literacy for a diverse society* (pp. 199–213). New York: Teachers College Press.

Edwards, P. A. (1995). Empowering low-income mothers and fathers to share books with young children. *The Reading Teacher, 48*, 558–565.

Egan, K. (1988). *Primary understanding: Education in early childhood*. New York: Routledge.

Ennis, C. D. (1992). Reconceptualizing learning as a dynamical system. *Journal of Curriculum and Supervision, 7*(2), 115–1130.

Fanon, F. (1963). *The wretched of the earth* (C. Farrington, Trans.). New York: Grove Press. (Original work published 1961)

Farkas, S., Johnson, J., Duffett, A., Aulicino, C., & McHugh, J. (1999). *Playing their parts: Parents and teachers talk about parental involvement in public schools*. New York: Public Agenda.

Fitzgerald, J., & Cummins, J. (1999). Bridging disciplines to critique a national research agenda for language-minority children's schooling. *Reading Research Quarterly, 34*(3), 378–390.

Freeman, W. J. (1991). The physiology of perception. *Scientific American, 264*(2), 78–85.

Freire, P. (2000). The adult literacy process as cultural action for freedom. *Harvard Educational Review Monograph Series No. 1* (rev. ed.), 13–37. Cambridge, MA: (Original work published 1970)

Fuentes, C. (1997). *A new time for Mexico*. Berkeley and Los Angeles: University of California Press.

Gadsden, V. L. (1995). Representations of literacy: Parents images in two communities. In L. M. Morrow (Ed.), *Family literacy: Connections in schools and communities*. Newark, DE: International Reading Association.

Gadsden, V. L. (2000). Intergenerational literacy within families. In M. L. Kamil, P. B. Mosenthal, P. David Pearson, & R. Barr (Eds.), *Handbook of reading research* (Vol. III, pp. 871–888). Mahwah, NJ: Lawrence Erlbaum Associates, Inc.

Galindo, R., & Escamilla, K. (1995). A biographical perspective on Chicano educational success. *Urban Review, 27*, 1–29.

Gee, J. P. (1999). Critical issues: Reading and the new literacy studies: Reframing the National Academy of Sciences report on reading. *Journal of Literacy Research, 31*, 355–374.

Gleick, J. (1987). *Chaos: Making new science*. New York: Viking.

Goldenberg, C. N. (1987). Low income Hispanic parents' contributions to their first-grade children's word-recognition skills. *Anthropology and Education Quarterly, 18*, 149–179.

Goldberger, A. L., Rigney, D. R., & West, B. J. (1990). Chaos and fractals in human physiology. *Scientific American, 262*(2), 43–49.

Goldstein, J. (1994). *The unshackled organization: Facing the challenge of unpredictability through spontaneous reorganization*. Portland, OR: Productivity Press.

Gould, S. J. (1981). *The mismeasure of man*. New York: Norton.

Greeley, L. (1990). *Philosophical spacing: Key to the nonlinear complex dynamics of the attentional system of the cognitive learning process in the philosophical dialectic method*. Unpublished doctoral dissertation, Harvard University, Cambridge, MA.

Greeley, L. (1995). Complexity in the attention system of the cognitive generative learning process. In A. Albert (Ed.), *Chaos and society* (pp. 373–386). Canada and Amsterdam: Presses de L'Universite du Quebec and IOS Press.

Greeley, L. (1996). The attractor of the intentional learning system. In K. H. Pribam & J. Kings (Eds.), *Learning as self-organization* (pp. 173–179). Mahwah, NJ: Lawrence Erlbaum Associates, Inc.

Greening, M. M. (1993). *The sense of chaos: A dynamical theory of narrative*. Unpublished dissertation, University of California, Santa Cruz.

Guastello, S. J. (1995). *Chaos, catastrophe, and human affairs: Applications of nonlinear dynamics to work, organizations, and social evolution*. Hillsdale, NJ: Lawrence Erlbaum Associates.

Guerra, J. C. (1998). *Close to home*. New York: Teachers College Press.

Guess, D., & Sailor, W. (1993). Chaos theory and the study of human behavior: Implications for special education and developmental disabilities. *The Journal of Special Education, 27*(1), 16–34.

Guha, R. (Ed.) (1997). *A subaltern studies reader, 1986–1995*. Minneapolis, MN: University of Minnesota Press.

Guha, R., & Spivak, G. C. (Eds.) (1988). *Selected subaltern studies*. New York: Oxford University Press.

Gutiérrez, D. G. (1995). *Walls and mirrors: Mexican Americans, Mexican immigrants and the politics of ethnicity*. Berkeley: University of California Press.

Handel, R. (1999). *Building family literacy in an urban community*. New York: Teachers College Press.

Harrison, C. (1995). Family literacy practice in the United Kingdom: An international perspective. In L. Morrow (Ed.), *Family literacy connections in schools and communities* (pp. 223–235). Newark, DE: International Reading Association.

Havelock, E. (1963). *Preface to Plato*. Cambridge, MA: Harvard University Press.

Havelock, E. (1991). The oral-literate equation: A formula for the modern mind. In D. Olson & N. Torrance (Eds.), *Orality and literacy* (pp. 11–27). Cambridge, England: Cambridge University Press.

Hayles, N. K. (1990). *Chaos bound: Orderly disorder in contemporary literature and science*. Ithaca, NY: Cornell University Press.

Hayles, N. K. (Ed.) (1991). *Chaos and order: Complex dynamics in literature and science*. Chicago: University of Chicago Press.

Hayles, N. K. (1999). *How we became posthuman: Virtual bodies in cybernetics, literature, and informatics*. Chicago: University of Chicago Press.

Heath, S. B. (1983). *Ways with words: Language, life, and work in communities and classrooms*. Cambridge, England: Cambridge University Press.

Heath, S. B., & McLaughlin, M. W. (1993). *Identity & inner-city youth: Beyond ethnicity and gender*. New York: Teachers College Press.

Hellman, J. A. (1994). *Mexican lives*. New York: The New Press.

Hitchcock, P. ( 1993). *Dialogics of the oppressed*. Minneapolis, MN: University of Minnesota Press.

Holland, J. H. (1994). Echoing emergence: Objectives, rough definitions, and speculations for ECHO-Class models. In G. Cowan, D. Pines, & D. Meltzer (Eds.), *Complexity: Metaphors, models, and reality* (pp. 309–342). Reading, MA: Addison-Wesley.

Holland, J. H. (1998). *Emergence: From chaos to order*. Reading, MA: Addison-Wesley.

James, C. L. R. (1989). *The black jacobins*. New York: Vintage. (Original work published 1938)

Johnson, G. (2000). *Strange beauty: Murry Gell-Mann and the revolution in twentieth-century physics*. New York: Vintage.

Kahn, B. E. (1996, June). *Attitudes as attractors: Reading, writing and phase space*. Paper presented at the Sixth Annual Conference for Chaos Theory in Psychology and the Life Sciences, Berkeley.

Kauffman, S. (1995). *At home in the universe: The search for the laws of self-organization and complexity*. New York: Oxford University Press.

Kellert, S. H. (1993). *In the wake of chaos*. Chicago: University of Chicago Press.

Kelly, K. (1994). *Out of control: The rise of neo-biological civilization*. Reading, MA: Addison-Wesley.

Lakatos, I. (1999). Falsification and the methodology of scientific research programs. In I. Lakatos, & A. Musgrave (Eds.), *Criticism and the growth of knowledge* (pp. 91–196). Cambridge, England: Cambridge University Press.

Lakatos, I., & Feyerabend, P. (1999). *For and against method*. Chicago: University of Chicago Press.

Lancy, D. (1994). *Children's emergent literacy: From research to practice*. Westport, CT: Praeger.

Lankshear, C. (1987). *Literacy, schooling and revolution*. East Sussex, UK: Falmer Press.

Lankshear, C., & McClaren, P. (Eds.) (1993). *Critical literacy: Politics, praxis, and the postmodern*. New York: State University of New York Press.

Lankshear, C., Gee, J. P., Knobel, M., & Searle, C. (1997). *Changing literacies*. Buckingham, England: Open University Press.

Lareau, A. (1987). Social class differences in family–school relationships: The importance of cultural capital. *Sociology of Education, 60,* 73–85.

Lareau, A. (1989). *Home advantage: Social class and parental intervention*. New York: Falmer Press.

Larsen-Freeman, D. (1997). Chaos/complexity science and second language acquisition. *Applied Linguistics, 18*(7), 141–165.

Levi-Strauss, C. (1966). *The savage mind*. Chicago: University of Chicago Press.

Levy, S. (1992). *Artificial life: A report from the frontier where computers meet biology*. New York: Vintage.

Lewin, R. (1992). *Complexity: Life at the edge of chaos*. New York: Collier.

Lindsay, J. S. (1989, February). *Chaos theory: implications for educational research*. Paper presented at the Twelfth Annual Meeting of the Eastern Educational Research Association, Savannah, GA.

Lindsay, J. S. (1991). *The chaos pattern in Piaget's theory of cognitive development*. Unpublished manuscript, University of Virginia, Charlottesville, VA.

Lipsitz, L. A., & Goldberger, A. L. (1992). Loss of 'complexity' and aging: Potential applications of fractals and chaos theory to senescence. *JAMA, 267*(13), 1806–1809.

Lorenz, E. N. (1993). *The essence of chaos*. Seattle: University of Washington Press.

Lynch, E. W., & Stein, R. C. (1987). Parent participation by ethnicity. *Exceptional Children, 54,* 105–111.

Martí, J. (1999). Political prison in Cuba. In D. Shnookal & M. Muñiz (Eds.), *José Martí reader: Writings on the Americas* (pp. 25–31). New York: Ocean Press. (Original work published 1871)

Maturana, H. R., & Varela, F. J. (1998). *The tree of knowledge: The biological roots of human understanding* (rev. ed.). Boston: Shambhala Publications, Inc.

McKee, P. A., & Rhett, N. (1995). The Even Start Family Literacy Program. In L. M. Morrow (Ed.), *Family literacy: Connections in schools and communities* (pp. 155–166). Newark, DE: International Reading Association.

Melzi, G., Paratore, J. R., & Krol-Sinclair, B. (2000). Reading and writing in the daily lives of Latino mothers who participate in a family literacy program. *National Reading Conference Yearbook, 49,* 178–193.

Moll, L. C. (1992). Literacy research in community and classrooms: A sociocultural approach. In R. Beach, J. L. Green, M. L. Kamil, & T. Shanahan (Eds.), *Multidisciplinary perspectives in literacy research* (pp. 211–244). Urbana, IL: National Council of Teachers of English.

Moll, L. C., Amanti, C., Neff, D., & Gonzalez, N. (1992). Funds of knowledge for teaching: Using a qualitative approach to connect homes and classrooms. *Theory Into Practice, 31,* 132–141.

Moll, L., & Greenberg, J. B. (1991). Creating zones of possibilities: Combining social contexts for instruction. In L. C. Moll (Ed.), *Vygotsky in education* (pp. 319–348). Cambridge, England: Cambridge University Press.

Morrow, L. M. (1983). Home and school correlates of early interest in literature. *Journal of Educational Research, 76,* 221–230.

Morrow, L. M. (Ed.) (1995). *Family literacy: Connections in schools and communities*. Newark, DE: International Reading Association.

Morrow, L. M., Tracey, D. H., & Maxwell, C. M. (Eds.) (1995). *A survey of familiy literacy in the United States*. Newark, DE: International Reading Association.

Mulhern, M., Rodriguez-Brown, F. V., & Shanahan, T. (1995). *Family literacy for language minority families: Issues for program implementation*. Washington, DC: National Clearinghouse for Bilingual Education.

National Center for Education Statistics (1999). *Parental involvement in children's education: Efforts by public elementary schools*. Washington, DC: U.S. Department of Education, National Center for Education Statistics.

National Center for Family Literacy (1991). *Spreading the word and spreading the seed*. Louisville, KY: Author.

Ngg, W. T. (1965). *The river between*. Oxford: William Heinemann.

Nickse, R. S. (1991, April). *A typology of family and intergenerational literacy programs: Implications for evaluation*. Paper presented at the Annual Meeting of the American Educational Research Association, Chicago.

Olson, D. R. (1994). *The world on paper: The conceptual and cognitive implications of writing and reading*. Cambridge, England: Cambridge University Press.

Olson, D. R., & Torrance, N. (1991). *Orality and literacy*. Cambridge, England: Cambridge University Press.

Ong, W. (1982). *Orality and literacy: The technologizing of the word*. London: Methuen.

Orellana, M. F. (1996). Aquí Vivimos! Voices of Central American and Mexican participants in a family literacy project. *The Journal of Educational Issues of Language Minority Students, 16*, 115-130.

Orellana, M. F., Monkman, K., & MacGillivray, L. (1998, December). *Parents and teachers talk about literacy and success*. Paper presented at the National Reading Conference, Austin, TX.

Pappas, C. C. (1993). Is narrative "primary"? Some insights from kindergartners' pretend readings of stories and information books. *Journal of Reading Behavior, 25*(1), 97-130.

Paratore, J. R. (1993). Influence of an intergenerational approach to literacy on the practice of literacy of parents and their children. In C. Kinzer & D. Leu (Eds.), *Examining central issues in literacy, research, theory, and practice: Forty-second yearbook of the National Reading Conference* (Vol. 42, pp. 83-91). Chicago: National Reading Conference.

Paratore, J. R. (1994). Parents and children sharing literacy. In D. Lancy (Ed.), *Children's emergent literacy* (pp. 193-216). Westport, CT: Praeger.

Paratore, J. R. (2001). *Opening doors, opening opportunities: Family literacy in an urban community*. Needham Heights, MA: Allyn & Bacon.

Paratore, J. R., Melzi, G., & Krol-Sinclair, B. (1999). *What should we expect of family literacy? Experiences of Latino children whose parents participate in an intergenerational literacy program*. Newark, DE: International Reading Association.

Paratore, J. R., Hindin, A., Krol-Sinclair, B., & Durán, P. (1999). Discourse between teachers and Latino parents during conferences based upon home literacy portfolios. *Education and Urban Society, 32*, 58-82.

Parra, E., & Henderson, R. W. (1982). Mexican-American perceptions of parent and teacher roles in child development. In J. A. Fishman & G. D. Keller (Eds.), *Bilingual education for Hispanic students in the US* (pp. 289-302). New York: Teachers College Press.

Patterson, L. (1995, December). Teacher research as a dynamical variable: Applications of chaos theory to case study methods at the high school level. In D. Yaden (Chair), *Applications of complexity theory to reading, writing, and teacher research: A discussion of metaphors and methodologies in dynamical systems analysis*. Symposium conducted at the 45th Annual meeting of the National Reading Conference, New Orleans.

Patterson, L., Cotton, C., Kimball-Lopez, K., Pavonetti, L, & VanHorn, L. (1998). The shared "AH-HA experience": Literature conversations and self-organizing complex adaptive systems. In T. Shanahan & F. V. Rodriguez-Brown (Eds.), *National Reading Conference Yearbook* (Vol. 47, pp. 143-156). Chicago: National Reading Conference, Inc.

Plaut, D. C., McClelland, J. L., Seidenberg, J. S., & Patterson, K. (1996). Understanding normal and impaired word reading: Computational principles in quasi-regular domains. *Psychological Review, 103*, 56-115.

Popper, K. R. (1965). *The logic of scientific discovery*. NY: Harper & Row. (Original work published 1935)

Popper, K. R. (1996). *The myth of the framework: In defence of science and rationality*. London and New York: Routledge.

Potts, M. W., & Paull, S. (1995). A comprehensive approach to family-focused services. In L. M. Morrow (Ed.), *Family literacy: Connections in schools and communities* (pp. 167-183). Newark, DE: International Reading Association.

Prigogine, I. (1996). *The end of certainty: Time, chaos and the new laws of nature*. New York: The Free Press.

Purcell-Gates, V. (1995). *Other people's words: The cycle of illiteracy*. Cambridge, MA: Harvard University Press.

Purcell-Gates, V. (1996). Stories, coupons, and the TV Guide: Relationships between home literacy experiences and emergent literacy knowledge. *Reading Research Quarterly, 31*, 406-428.

Purcell-Gates, V. (2000). Family literacy. In M. L. Kamil, P. B. Mosenthal, P. David Pearson, & R. Barr (Eds.), *Handbook of reading research* (Vol. III, pp. 853-870). Mahwah, NJ: Lawrence Erlbaum Associates, Inc.

Purves, A. C. (1991). The textual contract: Literacy as common knowledge and conventional wisdom. In E. M. Jennings & A. C. Purves (Eds.), *Literate systems and individual lives* (pp. 51-72). Albany, NY: State University of New York Press.

Robinson, R., & Yaden, D. B. (1993). Chaos or nonlinear dynamics: Implications for reading research. *Reading Research and Instruction, 32*(3), 10-14.

Rodriguez-Brown, F. V., Li, R. F., & Albom, J. A. (1999). Hispanic parents' awareness and use of literacy-rich environments at home and in the community. *Education and Urban Society, 32*, 41-57.

Rodriguez-Brown, F. V., & Mulhern, M. (1993). Fostering critical literacy through family literacy. *Bilingual Research Journal, 17*, 1-15.

Ruelle, D. (1991). *Chance and chaos*. Princeton, NJ: Princeton University Press.

Ruiz, E. R. (2000). *On the rim of Mexico*. Boulder, CO: Westview Press.

Said, E. W. (1978). *Orientalism*. New York: Vintage.

Said, E. W. (1994). *Culture and imperialism*. New York: Vintage.

Sánchez, G. J. (1993). *Becoming Mexican American: Ethnicity, culture and identity in Chicano Los Angeles, 1900-1945*. New York: Oxford University Press.

Sartre, J. (1989). *No exit and three other plays*. New York: Vintage. (Original work published 1947)

Scarborough, H. S., & Dobrich, W. (1994). On the efficacy of reading to preschoolers. *Developmental Review, 14*, 245-302.

Segal, M. (1985). A study of maternal beliefs and values within the context of an intervention program. In I. E. Sigel (Ed.), *Parental belief systems: The psychological consequences for children* (pp. 271-286). Hillsdale, NJ: Lawrence Erllbaum Associates.

Seidenberg, M. S., & McClelland, J. L. (1989). A distributed developmental model of word recognition and naming. *Psychological Review, 96*, 523-568.

Shanahan, T., Mulhern, M., & Rodriguez-Brown, F. (1995). Project FLAME: Lessons learned from a family literacy program for minority families. *The Reading Teacher, 48*, 586.

Sosa, A. S. (1997). Involving Hispanic parents in educational activities through collaborative relationships. *Bilingual Research Journal, 21*, 285-293.

Stewart, I. (1989). *Does God play dice? The mathematics of chaos*. Cambridge, MA: Basil Blackwell.

St. Pierre, R., Gamse, B., Alamprese, J., Rimdzius, T., & Tao, F. (1998). *Even Start: Evidence from the past and a look to the future. National evaluation of the Even Start family literacy program*. Washington, DC: U.S. Department of Education, Planning and Evaluation Service. (ERIC Document Reproduction Service No. ED 427 890)

Sumara, D. J. (2000). Critical issues: Researching complexity. *Journal of Literacy Research, 32*, 267-281.

Syverson, M. A. (1999). *The wealth of reality: An ecology of composition*. Carbondale and Edwardsville, IL: Southern Illinois University Press.

Tao, F., Swartz, J., St. Pierre, R., & Tarr, H. (1997). *National evaluation of the Even Start family literacy program: 1995 interim report*. Alexandria, VA: Fu Associates, Ltd.

Tao, F., Khan, S., Gamse, B., St. Pierre, R., & Tarr, H. (1998). *National evaluation of the Even Start family literacy program* (1996 Interim Report ED 418 815). Bethesda, MD: Abt.

Taylor, D. (1983). *Family literacy*. Exeter, NH: Heinemann Educational Books.

Taylor, D. (1993). Family literacy: Resisting the deficit hypothesis. *TESOL Quarterly, 27,* 550-553.

Taylor, D. (1997). *Many families, many literacies*. Portsmouth, NH: Heinemann.

Teale, W. H. (1984). Reading to young children: Its significance for literacy development. In H. Goelman, A. Oberg, & F. Smith (Eds.), *Awakening to literacy* (pp. 110-121). Exeter, NH: Heinemann Educational Books.

Teale, W. H. (1986). Home background and young children's literacy development. In W. H. Teale & E. Sulzby (Eds.), *Emergent literacy: Writing and reading* (pp. 173-206). Norwood, NJ: Ablex.

Torres-Rivera, E. (1996, June). *Chaos theory, minority belief systems and multicultural counseling*. Paper presented at the Sixth Annual International Conference of the Society for Chaos Theory in Psychology and the Life Sciences, Berkeley.

Tufte, E. R. (1983). *The visual display of quantitative information*. Cheshire, CT: Graphics Press.

Tufte, E. R. (1997). *Visual explanations: Images and quantities, evidence and narrative*. Cheshire, CT: Graphics Press.

Valdés, G. (1996). *Con respeto: Bridging the differences between culturally diverse families and schools*. New York: Teachers College Press.

Vallacher, R. R., & Nowak, A. (Eds.) (1994). *Dynamical systems in social psychology*. San Diego, CA: Academic Press.

Varela, F. J., Thompson, E., & Rosch, E. (1997). *The embodied mind: Cognitive science and human experience*. Cambridge, MA: MIT Press.

von Bertalanffy, L. (1968). *General systems theory: Foundations, development, applications*. New York: Braziller.

Waldrop, M. M. (1992). *Complexity: The emerging science at the edge of order and chaos*. New York: Simon & Schuster.

Weaver, C. (1985). Parallels between new paradigms in science and in reading and literacy theories: An essay review. *Research in the Teaching of English, 19*(3), 298-316.

Wells, G. (1986). *The meaning makers: Children learning language and using language to learn*. Portsmouth, NH: Heinemann.

Yaden, D. B., Jr. (1995, December). *Complexity theory and parent-child storybook reading: Exploring the topology of conversation*. Paper presented at the 45th Annual Meeting of the National Reading Conference, New Orleans.

Yaden, D. B., Jr. (1999). Reading disability and dynamical systems: When predictability implies pathology. In P. Mosenthal & D. Evenson (Eds.), *The role of the reading clinic in the 21st century: Advances in reading/language research* (Vol. 6, pp. 293-323). Stamford, CT: JAI Press.

Yaden, D. B., Jr. (2001). *Enhancing emergent literacy with Spanish-speaking preschoolers in the inner-city: Overcoming the odds*. Manuscript submitted for publication.

Yaden, D. B., Jr. (in press). Parent-child storybook reading as a complex adaptive system: Or "An Igloo is a House for Bears." In A. van Kleeck, S. Stahl, & E. Bauer (Eds.), *On reading books to children: Parents and teachers*. Mahwah, NJ: Lawrence Erlbaum Associates.

Yaden, D. B., Jr., & Greeley, L. (1997). Reconstructing the state space of parent-child storybook reading conversations: A synopsis. In D. Kirshner (Chair), *Chaos and complexity as methodological tools*. Paper presented at the Annual Meeting of the American Educational Research Association, March 24-28, Chicago.

Yaden, D. B., Jr., & Tam, A. (2000). *Enhancing emergent literacy in a preschool program through teacher-researcher collaboration* (CIERA Report # 2-011). Ann Arbor: University of Michigan, Graduate School of Education, Center for the Improvement of Early Reading Achievement.

Yaden, D. B., Jr., Madrigal, P., & Tam, A. (in press). Access to books and beyond: Creating and learning from a book lending program for Latino families in the inner-city. In G. Garcia (Ed.), *English learners: Reaching the highest level of English Literacy*. Newark, DE: International Reading Association.

Yaden, D. B. Jr., Tam, A., Madrigal, P., Massa, J., Brassell, D., Altamirano, L. S., & Armendariz, J. (2000). Early literacy for inner-city children: The effects of reading and writing interventions in English and Spanish during the preschool years. *The Reading Teacher, 54*(2), 186-189.

Yberra, L. (1999). The family/la familia. In E. J. Olmos, L. Yberra, & M. Monterrey (Eds.), *Americanos: Latino life in the United States/La vida Latina en los Estados Unidos* (p. 84). New York: Little, Brown & Company.

# TECHNOLOGY AND THE LANGUAGE ARTS:
# IMPLICATIONS OF AN EXPANDED DEFINITION
# OF LITERACY

*Charles K. Kinzer and Kevin Leander*
Vanderbilt University

> Figuratively speaking, it is as difficult for those who have become fully literate within a world dominated by print to see how their own literacy has been shaped—indeed limited—by the technology used to produce and disseminate printed materials as it is for a fish to think about the water in which it swims.
>
> —Reinking (1998, p. xvii)

Reinking's (1998) insight provides the starting point for this chapter because most discussions about literacy are grounded implicitly or explicitly in print, even though, on reflection, this presupposition may no longer be appropriate. The children who have entered school since at least 1990 are being shaped within a world that is not dominated by print in the way that their teachers' and parents' world was. Since Bruce (1991) wrote about computer technology in the first edition of this *Handbook*, it is undisputable that technology is making an increasingly large impact in our lives, in society as a whole, in the nation's schools, and in teaching the language arts. If anything, Bruce underestimated the impact and potential of technology in the decade that has passed as we write this chapter. In the intervening time, much has happened to indicate a growing recognition and use of technology in today's language arts classrooms. Computers are a growing fact of life in schools. In 1993, approximately 32% of school-age children had access to a computer in the home, and 60.6% reported using a computer at school. According to U.S. census statistics, in 1997 approximately 50% of school-age children had access to a computer at home, and 71% used a computer at school (Neuberger, 1999).

The research and practice communities in language and literacy education reflect this growth in computer availability. Almost every issue of professional journals now has at least one article related to technology or computer use; every journal intended for a teacher or practitioner audience has a technology or computer column, major professional associations have online journals dedicated to reading and language arts, professional meetings and conferences include significant representation in their program sessions dedicated to technology; and methodology and research textbooks have incorporated chapters about technology, with additional texts integrating technology throughout their pages. (Labbo & Reinking, 1999, noted that the appearance of technology in literacy textbooks is almost "obligatory.")

Technology is a clear presence in our schools and in our nation. Reinking (1998) called the era in which we now teach a "post-typographic world" (p. xi), and public policy related to education not only takes into account technology's presence in our schools but also often uses technology as a driving force to compel needed changes. In a State of the Union address, for example, former president Bill Clinton (2000) linked vital repairs to school buildings to technology rather than to an argument that decaying buildings are not conducive to learning, pointing out that "a third of all our schools are in serious disrepair. . . . I propose to help 5,000 schools a year make immediate and urgent repairs; and again, to help build or modernize 6,000 more, to get students out of trailers and into high-tech classrooms." Clearly, as a matter of public perception, business leaders, parents, policymakers, and students themselves view technology as important to the future and vital to include in schooling. However, questions about how text types, literacies, assessment, curriculum, and teacher education are impacted by present and emerging technologies must be addressed in order for literacy educators are shape theories and pedagogies of literacy that dynamically respond to social and technological change.

Perhaps more than most forms of practice and research in literacy education, technology polarizes and shapes constituencies around gut-level response and desire. Deliberations about schools installing networked computer labs and universities developing online courses and technology degree programs create sites of emotional, polemical struggle that evoke heated claims about what technologies will do for or against social relations, learning, and literacy. The hopeful side to these debates is that they appear to index an important anxiety that technological change has significant social meaning, even while technologies are paradoxically debated as relatively isolated "tools." Still, such debate also perpetuates an "autonomy myth" (Bruce, 1997b, p. 293) of the relations between technology and literacy practices as embedded within social relations. Essentially, the autonomy myth suggests that technology and literacy can be considered separately. A corollary to the myth is that a course of reasonable action and inquiry can be charted for educational practice and research by combining and studying otherwise distinct realms, exemplified in these questions: How can technology be best used to teach story reading? How do computers help writers improve essays? How might we invent a computer program to help students think critically?

Leu (2000) and Leu and Kinzer (2000) stated that *literacy* has become a deictic term. Bruce (1997a) similarly noted that the concept of literacy "never seems to stand still" (p. 875). Literacy, and what it means to be literate, takes into account various societal aspects related to money, power, and human relationships. Literacy, therefore, may be thought of as a moving target, continually changing its meaning depending on what society expects literate individuals to do. As societal expectations for literacy change, and as the demands on literate functions in a society change, so too must definitions of literacy change to reflect this moving target.

Current definitions of literacy have moved well beyond defining literacy as the ability to sound out words and/or copy accurately what is dictated. Definitions of reading, for example, have moved far beyond Flesch's (1955, 1981) views that "[we should teach the child] letter-by-letter and sound-by-sound until he knows it—and when he knows it he knows how to read" (1955, p. 121) and "[L]earning to read is like learning to drive a car. . . . The child learns the mechanics of reading, and when he's through, he can read" (1981, p. 3). Definitions by Dechant (1982), Goodman (1976), Rumelhart (1994), and others include

one's interaction between the text and the reader and include comprehension of the message in addition to decoding the printed page. Definitions of literacy now acknowledge the interaction between reader and text. They recognize that the ability to communicate, to present one's message, to understand and evaluate another's message is part of reading, and that an interaction and transaction into one's experiences as well as personal response and meaning making is part of the goal for literacy instruction (Harste, 1990; Rosenblatt, 1994; Shanahan, 1990). However, all these definitions come from a perspective of print, and all are reminiscent of Reinking's quotation used to open this chapter. We argue that as the medium of the message changes, comprehension processes and decoding process must be learned and taught so that these changes can be reflected in readers' and authors' strategies for comprehension and response. Thus, the language arts curriculum must adjust to incorporate evolving definitions of literacy.

Clearly, definitions of literacy are changing to include electronic environments. Clearly, the answers to the questions posed at the beginning of this section point us to the need to acknowledge and incorporate electronic environments into definitions of literacy. However, beyond the general argument of the instability and evolution of "literacy" in relation to developing technologies, what is driving changes in our conceptions of literacy? What movements or forces are language arts educators responding to in the development of new practices and curricula? We posit that three powerful social developments offer at least partial explanation for the development of the meanings of literacy in relation to technology while also making a presumed literacy/technology divide increasingly untenable. First, the increasing availability of technology, and the closely related notion that technology signifies literacy, power, and knowledge, are shaping the meanings of literacy within, and often well beyond, school contexts. Second, the multimedia nature of the Internet has pushed educators toward an expansionist view of the "text" and associated literate practices, in which meaning making includes symbolic systems extending well beyond traditional print texts. Third, theoretic developments have pushed toward an understanding of both literacy and technology as social practices; recent perspectives allow us to conceive of their significant historical and developing coevolution.

## THE AVAILABILITY AND SIGNIFICATION OF NEW TECHNOLOGIES

In part, conceptions and definitions of literacy have been influenced by the increasing availability of technology and the increasing expertise with technology in society at large. Computers have become increasingly available and inexpensive. As we write this, $500 will purchase a package including a 750 megahertz computer with a monitor, a CD-ROM drive, a 57 K modem, a 60 megabyte hard drive and a basic printer. The used computer market provides usable hardware for even lower cost. These lowered price points have affected the growth in computer use and availability for K–12 children noted earlier and have also resulted in Internet connectivity being a reality in schools (in 1998, 89% of U.S. public schools had Internet access, as did 51% of instructional classrooms, with 100% connectivity as a stated goal in the president's 1999 State of the Union address; National Center for Educational Statistics, 1999). Increased availability of computers and Internet connectivity has resulted in a concomitant increase in literacy-related uses and, because software has incorporated the computer's capability for graphics, moving video, audio, and hyperlinks, teachers are being forced to rethink definitions of literacy to incorporate the authoring and communicative functions that have become widely used and available (discussed later).

The increase in availability and use of hardware has moved hand in hand with increased use and availability of literacy-related software. Sales of audio books (e.g., on CD-ROM and audiotape) are booming, which prompts us to reconsider the importance of listening to texts as a current literacy practice (Cunningham, 2000). Electronic books can reproduce accurately the print, fonts, and illustrations found in paper books, and many include music to reflect mood and setting, hyperlinks to read, define and segment each word or phrase in the book, and background material on the author or Web-based links to a space where other readers of the book can share thoughts or express feelings about what was read—and this can be done in different languages and at the choice of the reader or the teacher. Further, consider the differences in just 3 years since Venezky (1997) wrote, "Portable (i.e., laptop) computers of the power required for sustained reading by students are still too expensive, too heavy, and too limited in screen quality to be considered as replacements for printed books" (p. 531). Laptop computers are not nearly as expensive as they were, and screen quality (and size) allows extended periods of reading with high-quality reproduction of pages.

But perceptions of the importance of technology to children's futures are equally important to changing definitions and conceptions of literacy and to the integration of technology into the language arts. The explosion of technology and Internet use in society at large has placed enormous pressure on schools and teachers to include and integrate technology into their lessons. Whether or not teachers feel that use of computers and the Internet in schools is important, societal demands and perceptions of workforce needs are driving calls for technology in schools, and these calls are too powerful to be ignored for several reasons. If schools are to be seen as current and relevant in the eyes of policymakers and the general public, they cannot run the danger of being viewed as out of date, irrelevant, or not preparing children for demands of an increasingly technologically oriented workforce.

In some ways, incorporating technology into definitions of literacy, and by extension into the language arts curriculum, thus becomes less an argument about whether or not such changes are needed or are effective, and more a recognition that schools must incorporate technology or be viewed as out of touch or even irrelevant. Even research about technology's educational usefulness has, in some ways, become less important in terms of deciding whether or not to place computers in schools, as acknowledged by a preeminent group of educational researchers and theorists in the closing sentence from the report of the President's Committee of Advisors on Science and Technology, which stated, "The Panel does *not*, however, recommend that the deployment of technology within America's schools be deferred pending the completion of [a major program of experimental] research" (Panel on Educational Technology, PCAST, 1997, p. 131). Even though many are calling for more research on the efficacy of technology in learning, there is increasing recognition that technology is here to stay and that the demand from businesses, parents, and society at large is such that technology will continue to appear in schools even before research outcomes are known.

In sum, the significance of the increasing availability of technology within and beyond schools relates to their situated use in literacy practice, and perhaps just as much to the symbolic capital (Bourdieu, 1991) of the technologies in relation to the social spaces of schooling (Bromley & Apple, 1998; Bruce, 1997b). Technology availability in schools both changes literate signifying practices and signifies in and of itself. The material and ideological meanings of the computer, as with any tool (Cole, 1996), are deeply intertwined. Although this double relation of meaning is true across the subject areas of schooling, it may be particularly true for language arts given the significant construction of a discourse on *technological* knowledge as a form of literacy. In this sense, "literacy" might index a very broad range of knowledge and practice with developing technologies (e.g., technical skill across programs and platforms, how to install and upgrade software, etc.).

Within such a web of practice and representation, schools and districts lacking technology could well be imagined as only "partially literate" spaces. This, of course, is not an argument for the proliferation of technology in schooling. Rather, it is an argument that, in many ways, the meaning of schooled literacy has already been (and will continue to be) articulated with the availability and meaning of technology.

## MULTIPLE LITERACIES AND HYPERMEDIA

Definitions of literacy must move beyond being located in only paper-printed media. Children's literature cannot be limited only to the pages in a paper-based book of printed pages but must include books in electronic formats as well. The added information and capabilities that electronic formats provide for authors and readers necessitate an expanded view of literacy, what it means to be literate, and what it means to be a teacher (and learner) in the language arts (see, e.g., Reinking, 1994).

Consider, for example, that "decoding" in a print context involves decoding the alphabetic characters as well as any pictures, charts, maps, and graphs that are included on the page. In this sense, the decoding and interpretation of graphics and other forms of media as literacy practice is certainly not a new development, and over the last decade or so researchers are giving increasing attention to the significance of images, television, drama, and other forms of media and signification in the literate lives of children (Alvermann, Hinchman, Moore, Phelps, & Waff, 1998; Dyson, 1999; Flood & Lapp, 1995; Rowe, 1998).

Such work provides an important research base from which to analyze literacy practices in the multimedia environment of the Internet. At the same time, the nature and relationships of Internet multimedia also pose unique problems that the study of offline multimedia forms cannot adequately address. For example, forms of decoding are developing that were either relatively minor or simply not possible offline. In an electronic environment, decoding for comprehension includes decoding the strategic use of color; decoding various clues that indicate hyperlinked texts and graphics; decoding the possible actions of meaning-bearing icons and animations; and decoding pictures, maps, charts, and graphs that are not static but that can change to address questions that an interactive reader can pose to informational text during the reading act. Although definitions of literacy must still include concepts of composition, decoding, comprehension, and response, to understand how each of these definitional factors play out in electronic environments, language arts educators must take into account current uses and thus current definitions of literacy.

After the advent of Mosaic in 1993, the Internet's first graphical interface, it is no longer possible to position the print text as the focal text, with images serving a supporting role in meaning construction. As many web pages are overwhelmingly an assemblage of images, understanding reading across these images significantly decenters print-based reading (Flood & Lapp, 1995). Hypermedia reading practices have at least as much to do with the multiple relations between images as they do with the paths among segments of print text. Significantly, the nature of images also permits writers and readers to link them in ways other than paper-based texts. For instance, although typically a term or phrase of text is linked in linear sequence, an image may be divided up into an "image map," in which diverse topological parts of the image are linked to other various images, text, video, or media objects. Running a mouse pointer over an image, for example, often "pops up" text without the mouse's being clicked or causes expansion of an image or graphic. Part of a pie chart might expand with new information when the pointer is moved over its slices, yet no overt clue exists that this would occur, presenting a serendipitous and differential experience across readers who might or might not have moved the mouse pointer over the image.

Research is needed that will lead to a better understanding of literate practices and rhetorical conventions (Bolter, 1998) used in reading images. More important for the study of hypermedia, ongoing research must be directed toward understanding the relations among multiple symbolic systems. How do images—simple PICT files, Quicktime movies, three-dimensional graphics—modify the meanings with other symbolic forms with which they come into contact? As the presence of multimedia has greatly expanded, new combinations of authoring (e.g., voice-annotated Web sites, video clips with hypertextual analysis, etc.) are proliferating. Jay Lemke (1998), from a semiotic perspective, argued convincingly that a central problem is that meanings are not fixed and additive but multiplicative

(p. 283). That is, in the electronic environment what must be interpreted is not a complementary relation of separately developed texts but the expansive signification of a an entire sign system. The literacies necessary to understand multiple, interdependent meanings index the need for complex understandings of literacy "tool kits" (Gee, 1990; Wertsch, 1991) for interpreting and producing meaning in hypermedia that includes but extends traditional texts. Such tool kits—bringing together strategies for meaning construction, material practices, social relations, and symbolic systems—would permit students to navigate, author, and construct complex and resistant readings of hypermedia.[1]

## THEORETICAL RAPPROCHEMENT OF LITERACY AND TECHNOLOGY AS SOCIAL PRACTICES

Currently, perspectives that are based on an assumed separation between technology and literacy are being challenged by the convergence of several areas of research and theory across disciplines, including perspectives on multiple literacies as social practice (Gee, 1990; New London Group, 1996; Street, 1984); an emphasis on intertextuality across literate practices and texts (Bloome & Egan-Robertson, 1993; Lemke, 1995); the prominence of the screen and the image as semiotic "text" in classroom studies (Baker & Kinzer, 1999; Labbo, 1996); relations of human and nonhuman "actors" in science and technology studies (Latour, 1996; Latour & Woolgar, 1988; Star & Griesemer, 1989); and "ecosocial" (Lemke, 1998), critical (Bromley & Apple, 1998) and situated (Bruce & Rubin, 1993) perspectives on technology. Additionally, the way in which the Internet has created a forum for the creation of multimedia and has provided a metaphor for the distribution and interdependence of social mind has been a catalyst across broad streams of research on articulations of sociocultural practice and technology.

Rather than beginning with an assumption of the relative separation of technology and literacy, recent work has begun to conceive of their interdependence in complex ways. Rather than deciding what positive or negative "effects" that new technologies might have, researchers have turned to analyze the complex relations of literacy and technology, as they codevelop as social practice in unpredictable ways with unpredictable effects (Bruce & Rubin, 1993; Gruber, Peyton, & Bruce, 1995; Hawisher & Sullivan, 1999; Neilsen, 1998). Furthermore, rather than focusing on only the production of new tools, researchers are also studying technologies with long histories (e.g., the pencil, Baron, 1999; and the file folder, Yates & Orlinkowski, 1992). As new technologies develop, former literacy technologies do not disappear, and studying these relations has become increasingly important. As Sharples (1999) noted, "The computer has flourished until now by imitating and then swallowing up other tools and media: the calculator, the typewriter, the spreadsheet. Soon it will devour the television" (p. 2). Understanding how former

---

[1]As with print texts, students must be taught not only to comprehend online texts but to critique them as situated, perspectival constructions.

technologies shape and are shaped by new ones is necessary for unpacking the multiple literacies of emerging synergistic systems that incorporate multiple technologies, of which the primary example is the Internet.

An expanded definition of technology-as-practice (rather than simply material "tool"), along with an expanded view of literacy as social practice, has affirmed that literacy itself may be considered a type of technology. From a critical perspective, literacies and other technologies, in linking "people, media objects, and strategies for meaning making" (Lemke, 1998, p. 283) index and appropriate social relations of power (Bruce, 1996). Analyzing the relations of power as the articulation of technology education is the focus of a growing body of critical work on technology (e.g., Bromley & Apple, 1998), including work by several scholars whose earlier analyses were primarily celebratory of the advent of new technologies for the improvement of literacy practice.

Although hope in the improvement and effective employment of students' literacy practices through learning with new technologies (Beach & Lundell, 1998; Garner & Gillingham, 1996; Myers, Hammett, & McKillop, 1998) is still strongly present among many educators, the dynamic relations of literacy, technology, and society, particularly with global flows of information and economy, have made identifying "improvement" or "effective employment" more problematic and contested. Additionally, developing methods to understand what develops within complex social–technical relations is a central problem. New methodologies for the formative (Baker & O'Neil, 1994) and situated (Bruce & Rubin, 1993) evaluation of literacy technologies are needed; methodologies that reach beyond current qualitative and experimental designs. How might we study online communities and their relation to offline communities with respect to literacy development? How does the production and consumption of online images differ from that of the typographic text? How do screen and paper textual "settings" differently shape literate activities?

Not only are new methodologies needed for the study of such difficult questions, but new recognition about change is needed as well. As technologies and literacies are situated in complex social relations, shifting our expectations about change involves understanding the scales of time across which forms of change might occur (Lemke, 2000). It has been said that we expect both too little and too much change with the development of technologies in their social relations. An understanding of the relative timescales for different forms of change—the differences and boundaries between changes that take minutes to observe within a single classroom and those that take decades or centuries to shape institutional, cultural, and global forms of activity—will assist us in understanding development and stability within literacy practices. Further, new expectations for change must be supported by deeper analyses of how stability is maintained within schools and across social settings beyond them (Hodas, 1994). Although stability is sometimes (appropriately or inappropriately) associated with teacher and student resistance, we need deeper and broader understandings of how the agency to resist (and support) change is widely distributed— across more or less stubborn technical tools and their corporate origins, across literacy practices and their histories, and across

teaching practices as they are worked out in relation to institutional support and control.

## Literacy Definitions and Positioning

We have discussed some of the dynamics that shape a definition of literacy in relation to technology at length because we believe that a clearer vision of language arts curriculum, pedagogy, and educational research is dependent on such definitional work. In this sense, we consider this work not as a foundational stable "text" but instead as a partial analysis of the developing articulations of literacy and technology. Moreover, definitional work is important in that the relations between literacy and technology also serve to construct available positions for educators within these discourses. As noted earlier, issues of technology and schooling often spur polemical debates; educators sometimes divide themselves along the lines of technology advocates versus technology adversaries, cyberspace enthusiasts versus Luddites (cf. Bromley & Shutkin, 1999).

Bruce (1997b) discussed several available positions or stances vis-à-vis technology and literacy, including neutrality, opposition, utilitarianism, skepticism, aestheticism, and transformationalism. A difficulty posed by available positions is that divided subjectivies, such as the "engaged critic," are currently not well-developed positions within educational practice and scholarship (Bromley & Shutkin, 1999). Moreover, although we anticipate significant developments, we believe it is important that both stability and change be anticipated and understood; we must look not simply to future possibilities (as in the transformationalist perspective) but also to the history of literacy practices and their current sociocultural meanings. Such a perspective considers literacy and technology in continual transaction (Bruce, 1997b), grounded in the shifting realities of dynamic social systems. To us, it means engaging ourselves in understanding the expansion (cf. Engestrom, 1987) of literacies and their adherent sociotechnical systems. To consider this expansion of literacy, we take a divided position that at once projects possible realizations of new literacy curricula and also problematizes social, political, and economic effects of the gap between the technologically priviliged and the technologically poor.

## LITERACY PRACTICE IN HYPERMEDIA ENVIRONMENTS

Our argument about the need for expanded definitions of literacy can be illustrated through a discussion of hypermedia on the Internet as used in language arts classroom settings. In our discussion we focus on the Internet because of its pervasive nature and its potential for being used in schools. The Internet is the fastest-growing communication tool ever (Brown & Jolly, 1999). It took 36 years before personal computers reached a base of 50 million users worldwide and 13 years for television to gain such a user base. It took only 4 years from inception for the Internet to gain a user base of 50 million (*Economist*, 1998).

We therefore focus our discussion on the Internet because it appears to be the vehicle that is most likely to impact literacy use and practice in our technological world; we focus, too, on hypermedia because it is pervasive on the Internet and in presentation (e.g., PowerPoint, Hyperstudio) and educational software (including CD-ROM books) that are commonly found in school settings. Recognizing and acknowledging the demands of authorship and readership in hypermedia are necessary steps to understanding the shifting requirements of an expanded language arts curriculum responsive to expanding meanings of literacy.

## Hypermedia Reading as Authorship

How might we understand the practices of reading hypermedia documents? Various scholars have pointed out that hypermedia reading practices have been supported by material technologies with long histories. Dictionaries, encyclopedias, phone books, and other reference materials are often given as examples of print media that encourage hypermedia reading. Such examples emphasize the nonlinearity of hypertextual reading, and less so, the centrality of the image in hypermedia. Alan Purves (1998) posited that comics support an important historical form of hypermedia reading. Comics, in their panel-based design, break up a "cross-linear" pattern of reading; the text can be traversed in many different ways and various links can be constructed by readers through both (spatial) images and (temporal) text. Significantly, Purves focused in his analysis on the space between panels, the gutter or white space that creates an openness and unpredictability to reading practice.

Discussions of hypermedia have often focused upon the potential openness of the text as supporting coauthorship between the reader and author, the sense that hypertext (as a form of hypermedia) is a set of potential texts waiting to be realized by the reader (Bolter, 1991; Landow, 1992), which in some fashion "erodes" the authority of the text (Bolter, 1998, p. 6). New writing genres have also been imagined in hypertextual form, genres more open to shared power and meaning relations between reader and writer. For example, Bolter imagined a hypertextual model for the persuasive essay, in which "writers lay out possible points without attempting to adjudicate" (p. 7). Although the potential for hypermedia technologies to fundamentally change reading practices and relationships seems clear, and though the lived experience of the constructive reading of hypertext may support such notions, much less clear from research are the developing relations, in practice, among hypermedia technologies, reading practices, and educational settings. If we begin with the idea of authorship, we might ask, for example, the extent to which the reader is indeed the coauthor of the text.

Because authorship on the Internet or of a hypermedia text is quite different from authorship of a paper-based text, the relation between author and reader differs significantly as well. In a paper-based text we may assume a type of coengagement along a single sequence of language or other signs, a relation described collaboratively and with positive affect by Howerton (1999):

I think there is something to be said for the passionate dedication to an idea that compels an author to lay it out with unalterable precision, and something to be said also for the respect inherent when a reader willingly subjects herself to another's world view for the time it takes to get from one cover to the next. . . . I happen to enjoy immensely the act of submitting myself to another person's psyche for a short time, allowing them to walk me through an argument that they are passionate about, an argument in which they are so invested that they felt the need to document it in writing. Every word, every sentence, in a written message has its designated place, and alterations to that structure do serious violence to the message. I can assume that such authors choose their words, and the sequence of those words, carefully—choose those particular words in that particular sequence over all the other possibilities, because it's those words in that order that best express the contents of their minds.

Even if a reader of a paper-based text is engaged in resistant or divergent readings, the sequential sequencing of a text affords a closer alignment to *a text* between author and reader. Howerton acknowledged that it would be inappropriate to say that hypertext authors are "any less skilled or less passionate about their ideas. Authors of hypertext may very well choose that medium precisely because they feel their topic can best be addressed in an associative and interactive manner." However, Howerton argued that authors of hypertext must have to "relinquish some control over the text that a reader receives." This seems a reasonable stance to take, given the multiple nature of the medium.

Reinking (1996; see also McEneaney, 1999) made the point that an author is "idolized" in print, that print has consequence and that to be published places an author on an elevated platform. The Internet provides an environment where anyone can be published, and to use hypermedia on the Internet means that authors cannot assume that readers will take a given path through an intended message. Thus, even though each reader in any text has a different "lived experience," this is not the same as saying that readers have different actual, physical paths through a hypertext environment, where the document that is read is physically different across readers. This results, theoretically, in an infinite number of paths through a document or domain, especially if an author provides links that can take a reader outside the actual document being "written"—perhaps by jumping to a search engine or to a list of related Web sites.

At the same time, the nature of the textual form only suggests so much about the nature of the relationship between author and reader (e.g., Brandt, 1990). How, as a form of involvement with singular or plural audiences, are hypermedia documents composed? The openness of hypermedia on the Internet seems broad enough to support an unlimited number of readings, yet at the same time, as a produced artifact, the text is also a selection of links and thus only offers selected potential readings. Limited study of the authorial relation in early, stand-alone constructions of hypertext (e.g., StorySpace; Hocks, 1997) has suggested that the hypertextual author, while offering choices to the reader and backgrounded in the text, may in this diminished visibility and construction of possible links actually be constructing a more insidious form of power. The seeming production of unlimited readings of hypertexts may, in practice, be the *re*production of strategically designed multiple readings.

Although Internet-based hypertexts may appear to loosen this form of authorial control, a much better understanding is needed of the work of diverse authors that can appear on the Internet (e.g., kindergartners, corporations, governments, hate groups), their symbolic and material resources, and the literate and discursive nature of diverse coauthorships. Clearly, a consideration of authorial control must consider hypertextual readings in practice, and not merely in potential. For example, it has been argued that hypertext is not nonlinear but rather "multilinear" (Bolter, 1998, p. 5), offering multiple spatial connections among text and images while at the same time relying on linear reading strategies within pages and linear movements between them. In sum, the relative roles, relationships, and responsibilities of authors and readers must be reconsidered in relation to expanding textual forms, contexts, and literacy practices.

## Critical Literacy and Hypertext: What's in a Link?

Although hypermedia reading is often distanced from the official literacy curriculum, a hidden literacy (Finders, 1997) with respect to many school settings, it already constitutes a major form of literacy practice in students' homes, after-school clubs and community organization. Landow (1992) argued for a "rhetoric of departures and arrivals," a rhetoric robust enough to allow us to forge rhetorical and critical meanings of our movements across hyperlinked media. A limited amount of such work has begun. Drawing from Peirce for their analytical framework, Myers et al. (1998) researched the hypertextual authoring strategies of a group of undergraduate students as well as a group of seventh-graders. The principal concern of the researchers was to trace the development of oppositional readings and writings within this authoring. From Eco and Sebeok (1983), the researchers evoked three sign functions: (a) *icon*, a sign that resembles another sign; (b) *index*, a sign that points to some meaning but needs additional interpretants to be meaningful; and (c) *symbol*, a sign that arbitrarily stands for another sign. An important distinction the researchers make is between student-authored links that make meanings problematic and links that simply define or illustrate text meanings.

Although students needed a similar level of technological knowledge to link texts in critical and relatively acritical ways, a semiotic analysis of these links revealed significantly different levels of critical engagement by the students. Significantly, the researchers' critiqued claims that the inherent "linked" nature of hypertext leads to critical engagement (e.g., Bolter, 1991; Landow, 1992), and argued that hypermedia must be strongly articulated with critical pedagogy. However, this work also prompts many questions about critical literacy practices in hypertextual environments. For instance, although the analysis gives a clear sense of the authors' categorizations of more or less oppositional readings to student texts, much less clear are the students' own readings of hypertexts. How might these readings differ from those of the researchers? Moreover, how might oppositional readings of various symbolic relations be developed within practice?

## A Literacy Task in an Electronic Environment

As another means of discussing the expansion of literacy practice in hypermedia environments, we shift from argument to an extended narrative of a student working in a language arts classroom. Imagine "Tara," a middle school student working on a classroom assignment in which she is to create a presentation for the class on "some aspect of science in everyday life." Imagine further that this assignment is integrated across science, social studies and language arts, where demands of what have been historically categorized as content area reading and writing occur in all three areas, though the language arts teacher is additionally asking for a story based on Tara's thoughts about her search process on the Web. For her research, Tara is to make use of the Web as much as possible (given the limitations of sharing access with other students). For her final presentation, Tara is to create a set of PowerPoint slides.

Tara's teachers have given her guidance on how to get started, including some focal web addresses that might be promising for the assignment. One of those in the list is the Exploratorium in San Francisco, and she selects it. As luck would have it, early in her search of the Exploratorium pages she comes across a link to Skateboard Science, which looks promising for her presentation. She clicks on the link and it brings up the home page for Skateboard Science (Fig. 39.1).

The page has a large graphic of a skateboarder and a background street scene. The skateboarder is circled by the stylized *O* in the word *explOratorium*. Why did the designer of this page circle the skateboarder? What is the relation between the Exploratorium and skateboarders? Is it just a nice background scene? There are other graphics, a tiny photo, and different fonts on the page. What catches Tara's eye, however, is the brand name *Thrasher*—a bold, stylized red logo. She's seen *Thrasher* magazine before. Could she read it on the Web? She tries clicking on the black words *Thrasher Magazine*, above the red logo, because she'd most like to see the magazine. Nothing happens. Next, a bit of experience has taught her to try clicking on different words and pictures, so she clicks the large red Thrasher logo. That works, and now she is transported to a page that includes a picture of the magazine cover and several bold, capitalized words to the side of the cover (SCENE, TRICK, TRASH). She decides she would like to see the magazine better. Will the cover graphic get bigger if she clicks on it, like some graphics do? Not this time. Clicking on the cover actually takes her to the following page (Fig. 39.2). Could she order the magazine here, in class? She tries clicking on one of the boxes that offers a one-year subscription magazine for $8.95, but nothing happens. (To properly purchase online, she'll need to learn about filling in the quantity (abbreviated "Qty") box next to her item and to recognize the common parlance of "Add to Cart" for online shopping.) However, her main problem now is not ordering but that the teacher is circulating in the room and helping students with their science projects. She knows that being at the *Thrasher* magazine Web site won't go over very well with the teacher. Plus, class time is about up, and she isn't sure how to get back to the Skateboarding Science page. But, scanning the top of the screen her eye catches the "Back" icon. Remembering that she

FIGURE 39.1. From http://www.exploratorium.edu/skateboarding/

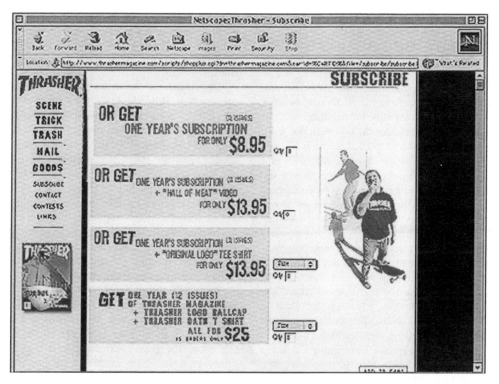

FIGURE 39.2. From http://www.thrashermagazine.com/scripts/shopplus.
cgi?dn=thrashermagazine.com&cartid=%CARTID%&file=/subscribe/
subscribe.html

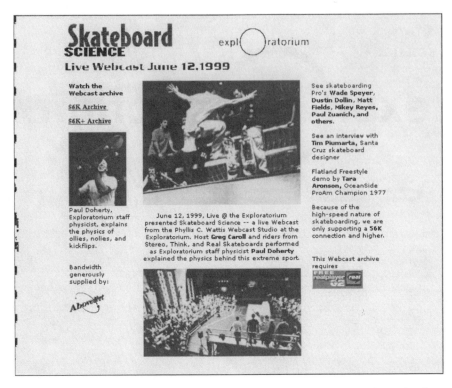

FIGURE 39.3. From <u>http://www.exploratorium.edu/skateboarding/webcast.html</u>

was only one click away from where she started, she tries that button and returns to the Skateboard Science home page. How will she find this page tomorrow, if she gets more computer time?

Tara remembers the next day to start from Exploratorium again, and she makes her way back to the Skateboard Science home page. What catches Tara's eye this time are the four ovals in the middle of the page, in particular the one with the word *webcast*. She clicks on it and is transported to the web page depicted in Fig. 39.3. The top image shows a side shot of a young man in air jumping off of a ramp with his skateboard; the bottom photo is a high-angle, distant shot of the same young man coming off of the ramp. Why did the web page's designer choose these two pictures? How do they relate to the web cast? Some text separates the two photos. Text to the left side of the images proclaims what the observer can "see": "See skateboarding Pro's Wade Speyer, Dustin Dollin, Matt Fields, Mikey Reyes. . . . See an interview with Tim Piumarta." If this web cast was "live" on June 12, does that mean she missed it? In case it's still there, she clicks on the bottom picture. Nothing happens. She clicks on the top picture. Fortunately, the media specialist at the school had recently downloaded a later version of RealPlayer, a program that allows her web browser to receive a streaming video and audio signal. Thus, shortly after she clicks on the top photograph a video starts playing in a tiny screen within a new window. The video is a little confusing at the beginning: a head shot of a man who is walking while a different off-camera voice narrates. The camera zooms out and a few skateboarders can be seen

in the background. Finally, the camera moves to another man, seated, who is giving the narration: "These kids right here are defying gravity. Know what that means? Gravity? Gravity rules."

Tara wonders if she could use the video for her PowerPoint presentation. How would she get it off the web? She has never developed a set of PowerPoint slides before, but she has seen her social studies teacher present some lessons with Power-Point. Her teacher's slides had small segments of text and some images in them—much like overhead transparencies. As Tara searches, therefore, she tries to imagine what pieces of media could readily be made into a slide. Right now, this work feels more like creating a collection—looking for material that fits a page—than writing a report or other paper for school. How much does she have to change the information to use it in her PowerPoint presentation and in the story assignment from her language arts teacher? Can she just paste it in? If she does change it, how can she change the graphics?

Tara remembers one of the other icons on the Skateboard Science page, "trick science," and thinks that might be a good match for her assignment. She returns to the home page and clicks that button. This takes her to the page depicted in Fig. 39.4. The page looks fairly standard by most measures. However, it does have a different background color (burnt orange in her browser) than the Skateboard Science page. Is it part of the same Web site? The authors are listed at the top of the page as Pearl Tesler and Paul Doherty. She doesn't recall their names on the other parts of the site—who are they?

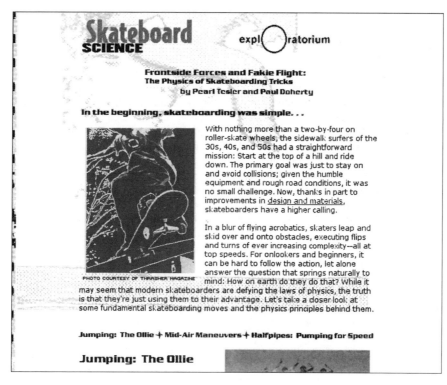

FIGURE 39.4. From http://www.exploratorium.edu/skateboarding/trick/html

Do they work at the Exploratorium? Tara tries clicking on their names, but nothing happens. Next, she notices that the pictures in the articles are courtesy of *Thrasher* magazine. (Maybe the authors work for *Thrasher*?) As she reads the short article, her focus is pulled to the pictures that the article wraps around. In particular, she is interested in the time-lapsed action shot of a skateboarder jumping across some stairs. It would make a good slide for her presentation. Does it get any bigger?

Tara clicks on the image but nothing happens, and so her eyes just fix on it for a while. How do they take time-lapsed photos like that? What does that writing say on the concrete wall? After a few minutes, Tara reads part of the article, and her eyes stop on the word *ollie*, which is underlined, and the text appears white. She infers that "ollie" must be a link, and clicking on the word indeed takes her to a different page full of text. It's hard for Tara to understand exactly why she is on this particular page. There is a bold white heading in the middle that reads "Types of Skateboarding." "Street skating" and "vert skating," along with other terms, are defined underneath this heading, but she cannot find "ollie," not realizing that the link was created so that the term would appear at the very top of the page, listed as one of many terms in the glossary below a main heading invisible on this page (because of the size of her monitor, only a part of each page is on the screen—to see the rest the scroll bar must be used). However, she does find a link to a "Quicktime 3 movie 450k." Another movie—this time the "50–50 Grind by Diego Bucchierii." She clicks on the link. After a

pause, a large *Q* logo appears on her screen. Next, a small movie screen appears and a short movie begins of a skateboarder going up a ramp. Why can't she hear the movie? Why is this movie in a different format than the last one?

During the course of the following week, as Tara identifies key media segments—including images, text, and a video file from the Skateboard Science Web site—she learns how to copy and save these media segments. To have one holding place for the text and images, Tara pastes them all into a word processing file, leaving the video saved file on her desktop. Some notes she has taken from a physical science textbook also appear in this file, as do notes from a few other sources (including a hard copy of *Thrasher* that a friend loaned to her). From this word processing file, Tara begins to select, cut, and paste segments of other authors' texts; other artists' images; and other photographers' photos into a developing PowerPoint presentation. How much of the text can she borrow without getting in trouble for plagiarism? Tara selects a photo of a skateboarder and a scientific graphic representing motion and force that seem to fit together very well as she assembles and composes her multimedia presentation. However, she decides that these bits of media need some explanation. Tara begins to write out this explanation on a PowerPoint slide, but it quickly gets too long, and she remembers that she needs to make the font larger anyway, so the whole class could read it off of the screen when she presents. Wait—maybe she should make a list instead of writing in sentences? A list with bullets? Her teacher did that sometimes.

## EXPANDING THE LANGUAGE ARTS CURRICULUM

The imagined scenario, just described, which necessarily simplifies the hypertextual movements of an actual student and his or her interpretive processes, suggests the enormous complexity of such activity. If we were to imagine a language arts curriculum that was responsive to the literacy activities suggested by this reading and to the more traditionally valued importance of students gathering information and learning from content-based texts (Armbruster & Armstrong, 1993; Armbruster et al., 1991), what would this curriculum include? What forms of learning and development would it attempt to facilitate? As a starting point, we suggest that the scenario offers three broad types of closely interrelated activity in need of curricular support: information searching, interpretation, and evaluation. These categories of information bear a close relationship to a model of the "life cycle" of information in academic research and the workplace (Borgman, 1996). The information life cycle depicts three broad phases of information use and life in a social system: creation, searching, and utilization. Within a school context, "searching" may begin the information life cycle, and interpretation and evaluation provide means to both utilize and create information.

### Information Searching as Curriculum

In February 1999, Lawrence and Giles noted that the publicly indexable World Wide Web contained approximately 800 million pages (see also Lawrence & Giles, 1998). Because, as Dahn (2000) pointed out, one must be careful to distinguish between "publicly indexable" and "publicly accessible," it is likely that the publicly accessible web pages in February 1999 was on the order of 1.6 billion pages, and Dahn projected a conservative growth rate of approximately 4.25% *per month* since that time. Clearly, the Web contains a vast array of information. However, growth rates and estimates of size are also misleading, because the Web is an evolving entity that is in a state of constant flux. Even while growing, many pages and links either change or are deleted (meaning that a user who expects to see certain things at a Web site and who has expectations about how to navigate within the site finds those expectations violated and must learn new strategies "on the fly"). For example, Lawrence and Giles (1999) found that approximately 9.6% of the pages indexed by Northern Light (reportedly the largest search engine at that time), consisted of bad links—links that were no longer active or were otherwise inaccessible.

The sheer size, rapid growth, and unstable nature of the Internet provide important arguments for developing information-searching curricula. However, curricula for teaching students information searching strategies within digital environments must be clearly different than available resources developed for academics and adults in the workplace (Bruce & Leander, 1997). Analyses are only beginning to reflect how such a curriculum might be constructed (e.g., McEneaney, 2000). The earlier illustration about the student, Tara, indexed some of the questions that must be addressed. For example, how

might students be guided at the outset of a search? Suggesting possible opening sites is one option, but this process can be both overly limiting and poses other types of problems as well (e.g., students approaching such sites less critically). Consider, for example, that students usually receive an orientation to searching for information in a library—usually consisting of the use of a card catalog (either in paper or electronic form) and of various indexes that access encyclopedias and other reference sources. Learning about indexes is also important to searching on the Web, because users need to know what kind of information is available and how to find it and because searching the Web is somewhat specialized.

Often, students are not taught that the Web employs two types of tools: The first type is a hierarchical subject guide called an information index made up of lists of subjects with each subject divided into subdirectories containing lists of Web sites with their abstracts and addresses. In addition to general indexes that attempt to cover the entire Web, there are specialized lists including lists designed especially for children, for example, Kid's Web, a service at Syracuse University. Information indexes have advantages for children. First, the items retrieved are likely to be relevant, a plus for students who have difficulty reading. Second, an index can serve as a prompt; that is, the user doesn't need to know all synonyms of a term to search a topic.

A second type of search tool is called a search engine. These computer tools locate and list Web resources according to key words and Boolean operators entered by the user. When set up properly, search engines return only sites that are relevant. Unfortunately, there are no standards for search engines. No two function in the same way and their differences are not obvious. Sherman (2000) asked three search services three identical questions and found that each of the three services "had strengths and weaknesses and aren't directly comparable to one another. The choice of which to use should be driven by user need." (p. 56). Different search engines produce different results, and require different skills to use them—from asking questions in real language to understanding Boolean operators. Moreover, search engines are not benign; certain kind of information may be given privileged position through commercial arrangements. Advanced Internet authors are also very skilled about having their sites given higher priority by search engines. While practical guides to Internet searching abound, research is needed that empirically documents differences in search strategies across students of varying ability levels and how search strategies relate to understanding of task demands and implicit and explicit goals on the part of the learner. Incorporating the new demands of electronic search strategies into the language arts curriculum will become increasingly important as the Internet becomes more pervasive in classrooms.

Knowing starting points for information searching, however, is only the first curve in a complex literacy practice. Information searching is often most disorienting once this beginning process is already under way. An information curriculum for the beginning of this century must assist students in developing strategies that will help them "mine" information while avoiding overload and unnecessary distractions. Part of this curriculum would involve technical and rhetorical knowledge of hypermedia: How are links signaled? How are text and images linked differently? What are generic conventions used in hypermedia documents (e.g., the interactive glossary that caused Tara to become lost)? What does page color, image color, and font color signify, and *when* does it signify? Moreover, how might pedagogies for teaching searching and navigation be developed that scaffold student learning of the multiple forms of media, bits of technical information, and social processes in play within a given search. Such pedagogies are beginning to be developed that begin to focus on at least part of these questions. For example, John McEneaney (2000) began to illustrate how prescriptive hypertextual "paths" can help students learn to navigate within hypertextual environments and suggestively scaffold the steep learning curve of search processes.

Furthermore, educators' goals may well include the "mining" and "retention" of resources, but they also want children to share, manipulate, play with, imitate, critique, oppose, and become increasingly curious about resources that they encounter. Many educators value children's learning certain intertextual connections between resources, but they also want them to develop their own categories, relationships, and understandings. In teaching students processes of searching, how can the goals of searching to facilitate true inquiry be left intact? How might some degree of scaffolding or simplification of processes for the sake of learning be achieved while nurturing students' desires to inquire about the world around them? This will perhaps be one of the greatest challenges for an information searching curriculum in language arts.

Many of the above issues, when translated into classroom environments, must consider concerns about child safety and are juxtaposed with issues of censorship and power relationships in classrooms (see Bloome & Kinzer, 1999; Leu & Kinzer, 2000, for a discussion of these and related issues). Although the Internet provides rich venues for sharing information as well resources for gathering information and publishing one's work, it also contains sites that many feel are inappropriate for children's use (indeed, some policymakers are advocating regulation of what can appear on the Internet in general, although these views have not yet gained significant momentum). At present, teachers rely on "filtering" software to close out certain categories of Internet sites, restrict students' searches to predetermined Web sites, or restrict students' use of the Internet to sites that have prescreened all links and deemed them appropriate for children's use (sites such as Yahooligans at http://www.yahooligans.com/, and Berit's Best Sites for Children at http://www.cochran.com/theodore/beritsbest/, are examples). Although prescreening and censorship issues are often determined by advantaged groups who use their own views to decide what is appropriate for others, we simply note here that issues of child safety, censorship, and control are also expanded in expanded definitions of literacy.

## Multimedia Interpretation as Curriculum

Tara must not only know how to access and navigate information, she must also know how to interpret the multiple forms of media she encounters. As previously discussed, a major area of curriculum development in this respect is not simply knowing how to interpret multiple semiotic systems, as in film study, but rather interpreting such systems in their complex relation to one another. As an illustration, what sense should Tara make of the film clip of skateboarding, which is linked to a still photo (a selected frame from it), which itself is surrounded by print texts of different types? How should she interpret both within these forms of media and across them? What forms of interpretation are more meaningful for navigation, and what forms are more meaningful for understanding and critique? How might she interpret the forms of navigation that this set of web pages indexes? Of course, an important part of this interpretive knowledge will include a base of technical knowledge as well, suggesting once again the nonseparation of technology and literacy. For example, Tara must know something of how different media are being downloaded to her (e.g., video formats) and options she has for retrieving and saving this information for her own use. Equally important, she should have some sense of what different forms of media leave out—what limited perspectives and gaps are apparent within text excerpts, images, and film? This level of interpretive activity, of course, reflects the degree to which interpretation and evaluation are closely interwoven.

## Information Evaluation as Curriculum

The problem of source evaluation is an issue with a long history in the domain of language arts education. At the same time, the evaluation of sources has traditionally been seriously underemphasized in language arts education and has been replaced by source knowledge and use. We may think back on our own histories in schooling:

> In retrospect, I needed to be critically conscious of what was presented as factual information in the state-approved textbooks I read about Columbus. Questioning assumptions, beliefs, and values underlying newspaper articles, television shows, and journal articles was necessary when I was a student and will be in the future. I believe that what will be different in the new millennium is the accepted view of what basic literacy entails. (Cunningham, 2000, p. 66)

New media and literacy practices are pushing us to expand the relatively insignificant role that information evaluation has had within the language arts curriculum. However, as networked computers are placed in classrooms in increasing quantities, curriculum and pedagogies for web-based source evaluation have been slow to develop. Although there is a large degree of publication on web site evaluation, primarily in library and information science sources (cf. the online bibliography at Virginia Tech University Libraries at http://www.lib.vt.edu/research/libinst/evalbiblio.html), and although various educational tools for evaluation have been developed (e.g., checklists at http://school.discovery.com/schrockguide/eval.html), a significant amount of work on curriculum and pedagogy needs to be done to translate these preliminary resources into effective educational practice.

It is likely that students currently develop their means of evaluating information tacitly rather than through school-based curriculum and instruction. The tacit nature of this learning is suggested by the very limited role that information evaluation has had in most language arts curricula. As a medium, the Internet greatly increases problems of information authorship and credibility. What are the particular problems of information evaluation presented by the Internet?

Moreover, what are some of the problems of relying on students' tacit knowledge of print media for the evaluation of online sources? December (1994, p. 9) posited three large problems that web-based media present for such tacit knowledge. First, the "surface cues" in online sources are gone or have been significantly altered. The material authority of a book jacket or journal cover is one important (albeit sometimes misleading) source of text-based authority that is transformed within web-based media. Other surface cues may be less obvious, and include the material presence of the source in relation to other trustworthy sources, as well as sophisticated layout, fonts, and graphics.

Related to surface cues is the important notion that the scarcity of space in traditional presentation media has limited many resources from being published. Although these limitations are certainly not eliminated on the Internet, they are rapidly being reconfigured. Today, for example, through free public access to a computer located in a community center or library, it is at least theoretically feasible that any individual in the United States could develop his or her own Web site and publish that site, without cost, through one of several services in exchange for sharing his or her web space with commercial advertising. Thus, although web space may need to be understood, within a literacy curriculum, as a site of knowledge and power struggle among various interests, students also need to shift from tacit, traditional understandings of how information is socially "authorized" simply through its presence in print.

Third, December (1994) noted that web-based media have different patterns of peer review than do print-based sources. Understanding these patterns as they develop today is critically important. Students and teachers need to avoid the essentialist critique that the Web is simply lawless, and without review, while at the same time avoiding the belief that traditional review procedures are active in web-based sources, whether or not these sources appear otherwise to be authoritative.

Within the language arts curriculum, web-based information poses special challenges to the traditional evaluation categories of source purpose, authorship, and credibility. How might a rhetoric of Web site purpose appear, and how might it lead to curriculum and pedagogy development? Once again, traditional approaches to the purpose of texts fall short of addressing this need. Although some resources for Web site evaluation have encouraged users to check for statements of purpose, interpreting the purpose of a Web site must extend well beyond this and be constructed as an intertextual act. Rather than simply studying a single text's content and form, to read critically students will need to understand a site's explicit and implicit positioning with respect to other sites. Part of this curriculum will involve technical knowledge, such as interpreting domain names and other parts of uniform resource locators, or URLs—the addresses by which we access Web sites. Another intertextual aspect must be interpreting hyperlinks toward other sites and from them to a site in question. Given this type of activity, explicit statements of purpose will be read rhetorically; the Web

provides a uniquely complex medium to understand the purpose of texts as intertextually and intercontextually developed.

Authorship on the Web also provides unique opportunities and challenges for the development of a literacy curriculum. The authors of web pages and sites are often not nearly so apparent as in print texts, and students need to be taught to interpret the multiple forms of authorship and sponsorship that may be evident through graphics, domain of the site, links to other sites, and textual segments directly or indirectly borrowed from other locations. For example, the only authors explicitly noted in the Skateboard Science pages are Pearl Tesler and Paul Doherty. Other implicit authors that Tara must consider in her interpretation and use of the site are the Exploratorium as an institution, *Thrasher* magazine as a commercial interest, and the unidentified speaker in the video clip, from a San Francisco-based skateboarding company.

As in the case of purpose, questions of authorship in cyberspace become intertextual questions. The importance of interpreting a text in relation to its "authorial audience"—a social world in which it is situated (Rabinowitz & Smith, 1998) heightens the importance of considering multiple authors and multiple readerships. In addition to decoding particular hypermedia documents for authorial presence, students need to be taught strategies for meta-analysis of the Web with respect to authorship, including using search engines to trace an author's or group's work, and comparing web-based and print-based resources. Moreover, the increasingly powerful commercial presence on the Web shapes questions of authorship into questions about the commodification of knowledge and identity, significant as part of a critically oriented literacy for the Internet. Tara, for instance, needs not simply to recognize the authorial presence of *Thrasher* magazine in the Exploratorium site but also to consider its interests, the way in which it develops a relationship with her, and the way in which it situates or constructs her as a reader. The immense body of information on the Web poses significant problems for assessing credibility. In addition to information scale, authorship, the web-based presence of hate sites, misinformation, commercial interests, and pornography make questions of information credibility increasingly complex. Issues of plagiarism, as students are able to cut-and-paste text, pictures, and video from other documents into their own, also become complex, and the changing nature of plagiarism and how to address this issue is becoming an increasing concern (Austin & Brown, 1999).

How might a literacy curriculum respond to issues of information credibility? Purpose and authorship, as discussed above, are closely interwoven with issues of credibility. As in these discussions, issues of credibility must be understood with respect to a single web page or site and, equally important, as an intertextual act through the manner in which a site has linked and server-based relations to other sites. Site credibility can also be partially interpreted from technical and structural issues in a site. For example, students need to be able to identify when a site was last updated and to understand the potential meaning of broken links, slow servers, and nonfunctioning graphics.

Beyond assessing credibility of web-based information as such, a broad issue for considering information-based literacy practices is how the Web as a source shifts the timeliness of authoritative information. Although information timeliness has traditionally been limited by print-based media within schools, what expectations do literacy educators have for information timeliness once students have real-time access to breaking news across disciplinary fields? Is the Web as up-to-date as it appears? What formats of student (re)presentation would best capture the time scales of web-based information? Finally, although questionable credibility is often thought of as a defect of web-based information, it may be one of its greatest assets for literacy educators invested in developing students' critical tool kits. Beyond having students critique and shore up the credibility of a resource used, curriculum can be designed in which students compare contradictory accounts of the same social event, contradictory readings of the same text, and opposing interpretations of so-called scientific facts. Literacy curricula for web-based information evaluation should respond to the need to gather, sort, and synthesize information, on the one hand, as discussed in standards documents (e.g., National Council of Teachers of English and the International Reading Association, 1996) and, on the other hand, to juxtapose contradictory texts and explore divergent readings. Although the Web poses special problems for the former goal, it is a uniquely rich resource for the latter.

## Assessment of Literacy in Hypermedia Environments

As we develop classroom practices within hypermedia environments, we must also question the role and value of traditional practices in assessment. If what counts as text and literacy practice moves beyond print to include all of the items discussed previously, then assessment practices, and also the actual items assessed, will need to change. On the one hand, assessment questions might be conceptualized as "How would standardized (or holistic) assessments of writing evaluate a hypermedia document in ways that students, parents, and future employers would find useful in judging an emerging author's progress?" Similarly, one could ask, "How would comprehension of a hypertext or hypermedia document be assessed when different readers link to different parts of such documents and so actually read different documents within a possible domain?" Would assessment take into account exactly what was read (and, if so, how would a comparison test across students be carried out, if this was a goal), or would only core concepts, however defined, be part of a comprehension assessment? Would the actual linking process be a part of the assessment? How would one assess the comprehension of particular components within and across hypermedia documents (comprehension of an embedded video, for example, and its relationship to the entire document)?

New assessment tools will need to be developed to encompass the multiple new uses of literacy practices in school and community settings, yet little work has been done in this area. When considering assessment of reading and writing in hypermedia, both skills development and high-level problem-solving processes will need to be considered, and both will need to be done in ways that reflect the multiple aspects of hypermedia. Putting the above assessment questions into perspective, how would Tara's comprehension be assessed during her reading of

the Skateboarding Science hypermedia text, and how would (or should) her comprehension of information on the Skateboarding Science site be compared to other students' comprehension of the same site? Assessment of Tara's actions could, for example, include aspects of decoding of print but also decoding of icons and other information that appear in a hypertext document, as could her choice of path through the document in light of her goal and task. Moreover, how might we assess Tara's production of a multimedia composition? What dimensions and qualities of other more traditional textual genres apply to to this assessment? What do we already value in hypermedia genres, and what do these values themselves suggest about the hypermedia genres as a form of social practice? (e.g., Prior, 1998; Russell, 1997). Although the questions that we just posed cannot, at present, be answered, we believe strongly that current measures are not adequate to assess reading and writing when viewed from a perspective of expanded definitions of literacy.

## Expanded Definitions of Literacy, Classroom Practice, and Teacher Education

As children in language arts classes become used to fluid movement among writing on paper, publishing their original paper products on the Web, reading a book, posting messages, and chatting about the book with others around the world, and so on, a more seamless definition of literacy emerges—one that includes both paper-based and electronic environments and that requires that teachers be both familiar with possibilities and facile with technology. Still, we are mindful of a recent survey in the United States in which only one in five full-time public school teachers reported feeling very well prepared to integrate educational technology into classroom instruction (U.S. Department of Education, 1999). Even among 1st-year teachers, Strudler, McKinney and Jones (1999) found that beginning teachers are not well prepared to integrate technology into their subject area or to teach using technology. In fact, the 1st-year teachers that they studied reported that "their preparation to teach with technology lagged behind their preparation for other instructional strategies and [that] student teaching had a minimal impact on their preparation to teach with computers." (p. 115).

These findings, coupled with calls for better subject-specific technology education for children in schools by a wide variety of influential business, community, and educational leaders, have provided an impetus for school districts nationally to require inservice experiences for practicing teachers. Inservice programs are occurring on-site in school districts, on university campuses, and through online and distance learning delivery systems.

However, much of the future, in terms of teacher education that takes into account expanded definitions of literacy, rests on preservice teacher education programs. A recent CEO Forum report (CEO Forum, 1999) noted that one half of the states in the United States already require computer education for teacher licensure, and the report calls for more comprehensive course offerings in all states for future teachers. Of the states now requiring computer education for licensure, at present two (North Carolina and Vermont) require students to demonstrate their ability with technologies within a portfolio. More states will do so in short order, partly because of NCATE guidelines that are requiring teacher licensure programs to show that graduates meet increasingly stringent competencies related to use of technology in K–12 instruction (National Council for Accreditation of Teacher Education [NCATE], 1997). Other recent, influential reports and white papers are also calling for inservice and preservice programs to ensure that teachers can fully and meaningfully integrate technology into their subject areas and that they do so using the best knowledge available about how teachers teach and how learners learn (see, e.g., the PCAST, 1997; also see Bransford, Brown, & Cocking, 2000). Increasingly, we are seeing calls that outline specific competencies with technology for K–12 teachers (see, e.g., Coughlin, 1999; Coughlin & Lemke, 1999).

However, challenges in preservice education remain. The recent report from NCATE (1997) noted, "Not using technology much in their own research and teaching, teacher education faculty have insufficient understanding of the demands on classroom teachers to incorporate technology into their teaching." Although many schools of education do a good job at using technology to teach their courses (the use of multimedia case studies are becoming more prevalent; Baker, 1999; Kinzer & Risko, 1998; Hughes, Packard, & Pearson, 2000) and often model uses of technology for presentation, more emphasis will need to be placed on teaching preservice students how to integrate technology in their future language arts curriculum. Preservice field experiences, for example, will need to require preservice students to use technology with children in practicum or student teaching settings so that "hands-on" expertise with strategies such as Internet Activity, Internet Project, Internet Inquiry, and Internet Workshop (Leu & Leu, 2000) and Web Quests (Dodge, 1995) can be developed, as can movement toward more student-centered classrooms (Sandholtz, Ringstaff, & Dwyer, 1997).

## Technology, Language Arts, and Issues of Access

One often hears arguments that the Internet allows free and open access and communication across many groups and all countries, and statistics about Internet use and access in U.S. schools can sometimes leave the impression that Internet use is a way of life for all. Issues of access have been linked to rhetoric around what has come to be known as the "digital divide" (Hoffman & Novak, 1998; National Telecommunications and Information Association [NTIA], 1999). Issues of access, across the diverse groups in our global society, need to be seriously considered with respect to the literacy practices we have discussed above.

The 1999 *Human Development Report* from the United Nations (Brown & Jolly, 1999) presented worldwide statistics about access to technology and to the Internet. Perhaps its summary statement best encapsulates the issues of access as seen on a global basis: "Current access to the Internet runs along the fault lines of national societies, dividing educated from illiterate, men from women, rich from poor, young from old, urban from rural" (p. 62). The report discussed issues of access from the perspective that 15% of the world's population accounts for

88% of Internet users and noted that this is largely due to issues of access. The report observed that in many countries, where English is not a primary language, access to the Internet must be considered not based on connectivity but on utility. Because 80% of Internet sites in 1998 were in English, 90% of the world's population (the percentage of the world's population who do not speak English by United Nations estimates; Brown & Jolly, 1999) would have difficulty using much of what the Internet offers even if connectivity were not an issue.

Connectivity, however, remains an issue worldwide. When many developing countries have only 1 telephone per 100 people, access to Internet technology must first wait for infrastructure before issues of use can be considered. However, governments worldwide, from both developed and developing nations, have already begun to take steps to mitigate issues of access to compete in markets where technology is not only a product in itself but influences sales of nontechnology goods as well (Leu & Kinzer, 2000, presented several initiatives by governments aimed at increasing technology access and argued that this is an important factor in the convergence of literacy and technology). Issues of access in a global economy will be continually addressed as public policy initiatives support technology as necessary to compete in a global economy.

In the United States, the digital divide has come to embody statistics showing that access to the Internet is differentiated by socioeconomic status, race, gender, and cultural groups. The NTIA (1999) executive summary highlighted these statistics:

- Those with a college degree are more than 8 times as likely to have a computer at home and nearly 16 times as likely to have home Internet access, as those with an elementary school education.
- A high-income household in an urban area is more than 20 times as likely as a rural, low-income household to have Internet access.
- A child in a low-income White family is three times as likely to have Internet access as a child in a comparable Black family and four times as likely to have access as children in a comparable Hispanic household.
- A wealthy household of Asian/Pacific Islander descent is nearly 13 times as likely to own a computer as a poor Black household, and nearly 34 times as likely to have Internet access.
- A child in a dual-parent White household is nearly twice as likely to have Internet access as a child in a White single-parent household, whereas a child in a dual-parent Black family is almost four times as likely to have access as a child in a single-parent Black household.

However, the NTIA (1999) report also stated that although some evidence shows that the divide noted above has widened, from 1997 to 1998, other statistics are cause for cautious optimism, noting that for comparable income levels Internet access and computer use across households has narrowed. This might result in a converging trend line in which even though growth rates in certain groups are moving more slowly, they are in fact moving in an upward direction.

Access in language arts classrooms is also complex and must be considered both from connectivity and other perspectives. In terms of connectivity potential, access to the Internet seems common in U.S. classrooms. In 1998, 51% of instructional classrooms had Internet connections, and this number is projected to reach 80% soon. Programs such as the E-rate program created under the Telecommunications Act of 1996 (Federal Communications Commission, 1996) will continue to address issues related to access in terms of connectivity. However, access also involves issues of teacher support and expertise (discussed in an earlier section); issues related to differential access in classrooms because of such factors as gender, reading ability, overall expertise with technology, and so on; and issues related to ongoing availability of funds for maintenance, upgrades, and supplies. Leu and Kinzer (2000) pointed out that hardware availability will not be the most important consideration for school budgets. Rather, already insufficient instructional supplies budgets that now pay for paper, pencils, manipulatives, art supplies, crayons, and so on will additionally be forced to pay for computer paper, ink cartridges, Internet service providers, telephone line charges, maintenance contracts, diskettes for students, and other budgetary needs. If additional funds are not made available to cover such costs, available computers may well sit idle and thus deny access even where connectivity exists. On the one hand, classroom access issues must consider connectivity; on the other hand, issues of who the teacher privileges with computer time (perhaps faster workers as opposed to those who have not finished other assignments) must also be considered.

Of course, within social relations, technologies both create greater access and limit our access depending on who or what we wish to approach; technologies enable and disable. Although e-mail communication allows us the freedom to collaborate with friends, colleagues, and pen pals at spatial distance, it also disables our temporal worlds and prohibits us from spending as much face-to-face time with the colleague in the office next door or with classmates in face-to-face discussions. Technologies can also have effects in sorting those who know how to gain access from those who do not. Bruce and Hogan (1998) proposed a stage theory of how technologies contribute to the creation of "perceived" disabilities in individuals when tools do not work as intended. They observed:

In the early stages of use, disability is counted as a flaw in the tool: We say that poor design of the technology makes it difficult to use. Later, the disability becomes an attribute of the user, not the tool. We say that the user needs more training, or worse, is incapable of using the tool. Once that status of the tool as a technology has fully emerged into daily practice, the disability to use it becomes an essential attribute of certain people. (p. 270)

Just as less able readers can quickly be stereotyped and have difficulty breaking out of "poor reader" labels, so can children be stereotyped as "illiterate" computer or Internet users.

Finally, we consider issues related to the provision of access to further agendas that may diverge from educational goals and endeavors. Here, we note the entwining of schooling and business interests, with computer technology as a pivotal artifact in this relationship. Education social critics, for example, have addressed how Channel One has exchanged "free" satellite educational programming for students who become a captive audience to commercial advertisement targeted at students during what would otherwise be instructional time (Apple, 1992, 2000). Any Internet access already embeds within it a commercial presence that in most ways is more pernicious than that of Channel One, as this presence is ubiquitous and woven into the fabric of other information (rather than marked with clear boundaries from educational content). As schools enable student literacies with online technologies, at the same time they participate in the commodification of those students to business interests by permitting businesses access to them. Thus, among many other issues, within literacy curriculum and practice we must consider how students are positioned and how they might learn to actively position themselves through new Internet-based literacies. Consider the following offer through ZapMe! Corporation:

When ZapMe! provides your school with the latest computer hardware, it's complete, ready-to-use and absolutely free of charge. That means ZapMe! and its technology partners install a network of 15 state-of-the-art multimedia desktop computer systems, a high speed "broadband" rooftop satellite for Internet connectivity, a high-performance Internet server, and a laser printer. (ZapMe!.com)

In addition to setting up a state-of-the-art computer lab within selected schools for free, ZapMe! will offer training for teachers and students. Essentially, the school only needs to allow ZapMe! access to its students and their time in school. The price of this service is that students using the computers will be continuously exposed to advertisements on the "free" workstations of key companies supporting the effort. Moreover, ZapMe! will also collect aggregate data on student web use and viewing preferences.[2]

Although ZapMe! ultimately failed, the ideological argument of whether or not students ought to be positioned as active consumers in the moment-by-moment flow of technology-based work during school hours and in school space may hold less force than the socially constructed need to place Internet-ready technology into schools combined with the expense of doing so. It has been estimated by Gibbs that businesses spend $13,000 per workstation per annum to cover depreciation in software and hardware, support, training, and the start-up time for the productive use of equipment (as cited in Moran & Selfe, 1999). It has also been argued that schools should not assume that their costs would be much different (Moran & Selfe, 1999) and that when cut-backs are made on needed costs, they are typically made on the side of support and professional development (Moran & Selfe, 1999; Zehr, 1997).

---

[2]Collection of data for demographic and targeted advertising use, and attendant invasion of privacy issues are just coming to the fore. When online, many companies collect data on computer use through "cookies" that are placed on a user's machine and that transmit information about the machine and Web sites viewed back to various agencies.

The underfunded categories of support and development raise a thorny meaning of access in schools. Even if schools are completely "wired," with up-to-date equipment, what meaning does this have if teachers and students are not supported with technological and pedagogical support? To what would they have access? For whom would access be possible under such conditions? One possible meaning is that students and teachers who gain access to computer training and support from sources beyond school will be increasingly distanced, in terms of access, from those who rely upon in-school support. That is, it is not enough to talk about divisions between schools; we need also to consider how intraschool divisions are facilitated in terms of knowledge, technology, and literacy relations. From a technology literacies perspective, the "haves" and the "have-nots" are not predicated on the supplying and wiring of schools alone but, as always, on the particular relations of tools, pedagogies, material support, and teacher development.

## CONCLUDING COMMENTS

In this chapter, we have argued that definitions of literacy must be expanded to include literacy as practiced in electronic environments; we have also argued that discussing literacy and literacy practices in print-based and electronic environments as dichotomous is inappropriate. We have presented what we believe with regard to the possibilities and potentials of technology, noting that almost all schools have Internet connections, that almost all classrooms will have such connection soon, that computer availability and use has increased dramatically, and that computer use among school-age children has now topped the 70% level in classrooms (Neuberger, 1999). In addition, we have presented a view that expanded definitions of literacy have ramifications for curriculum, what counts as text, the nature of reading and writing practices, how literacy is assessed, and the meaning of literacy expansion alongside inequities of access.

However, even though teacher education is increasingly incorporating technology into preservice and inservice education programs, existing classroom practices must also reflect technology integration into language arts classrooms. Although more information about technology integration is becoming known (see, e.g., Colburn, 2000), there are still relatively few replicable systems being proposed for integrating technology into language arts curriculum. Some exceptions are the procedures for implementing Internet Activity, Internet Project, Internet Inquiry, and Internet Workshop, presented by Leu and Leu (2000) and the Web Quest strategy advocated by Dodge (1995). As in all such strategies, of course, it is the teacher's

knowledge, guidance, and expectations for the activity that move it beyond simply finding facts to actualizing higher level stated instructional goals.

Others have used technology to enhance instructional offerings by incorporating what is known about literacy and learning to develop programs from the ground up that use technology's potential. Examples include Schwartz et al.'s (1999) Star Legacy environment, in which learning occurs in a generative and constructivist learning cycle of setting a challenge and responding to it, generating ideas, examining problems from multiple perspectives, doing research and revising questions, testing findings and presenting results to others, and to reflecting on one's work and progress. Other examples include Scardamalia and Bereiter's (1991, 1993, 1996) CSILE environment and work by the Cognition and Technology Group at Vanderbilt (CTGV, 1993, 2000). CSILE facilitates group communication and extends the notion of learning communities (and concepts such as author circles and peer response) in ways not possible in traditional print media, whereas the CTGV examines literacy-related teaching and learning from the framework of anchored instruction and situated cognition (Brown, Collins, & Duguid, 1989; CTGV, 1993). These programs contain examples of expanded definitions of literacy teaching and learning in electronic environments by using the value-added aspects of technology (see also Lin, Hmelo, Kinzer, & Secules, 2000, for design principles that faciliatate technology's ability to aid learner's reflective processes).

Often beyond the domain of print-based published research, teachers are shaping future visions and current practices as they implement the realities of electronic literacies in their own classrooms. These teachers are providing their students with opportunities to immerse themselves in a literacy environment that moves well beyond traditional, print-based language arts education (Kinzer & Leu, 1997; Leu, Karchmer, & Leu, 1999). Some examples include Ted Nellen's Cyber English (http://199.233.193.1/cybereng/), Room 100 at Buckman Elementary School (http://buckman.pps.k12.or.us/room100/room100.html) and Mrs. Silverman's second-grade classroom at (http://kids-learn.org/). Visiting these sites shows how students from primary grades through high school use scanners, Quicktime VR video, audio files, text, digital cameras, Internet research skills, and so on in their literacy development. Such sites of promise and vision—working out the complexities of electronic literacies within situated classrooms—are a clear indication that realizing the expansive meanings of literacy is feasible in today's schools and provide indications of directions for the continued evolution of literacy as practiced in language arts classrooms.

## *References*

Alvermann, D. E., Hinchman, K. A., Moore, D. W., Phelps, S. F., & Waff, D. R. (Eds.) (1998). *Reconceptualizing the literacies in adolescents' lives*. Mahwah, NJ: Lawrence Erlbaum Associates.

Apple, M. (1992). Constructing the captive audience: Channel One and the political economy of the text. *International Studies in Sociology of Education, 2*(2), 107–131.

Apple, M. (2000, January). *Markets, standards, and inequality*. Paper presented at the Spring Lecture Series on Issues of Cultural Diversity and Equity in Evaluation, Nashville, TN.

Armbruster, B. B., Anderson, T. H., Armstrong, J. O., Wise, M. A., Janish, C., & Meyer, L. A. (1991). Reading and questionning content area lessons. *Journal of Reading Behavior, 23*, 35–59.

Armbruster, B. B., & Armstrong, J. O. (1993). Locating information in text: A focus on children in the elementary grades. *Contemporary Educational Psychology, 18,* 139–161.

Austin, M. J., & Brown, L. D. (1999). Internet plagiarism: Developing strategies to curb students academic dishonesty. *The Internet and Higher Education, 2*(1), 21–33.

Baker, E. (1999, December). *Case-based learning theories: Not just for learners any more.* Paper presented at the 49th meeting of the National Reading Conference, Orlando, FL.

Baker, E., & Kinzer, C. K. (1999). Effects of technology on process writing: Are they all good? In T. Shannahan & F. Rodriguez-Brown (Eds.), *Forty-eighth yearbook of the National Reading Conference* (Vol. 48, pp. 428–440). Chicago: National Reading Conference.

Baker, E. L., & O'Neil, H. F. (Eds.) (1994). *Technology assessment in education and training.* Hillsdale, NJ: Lawrence Erlbaum Associates.

Baron, D. (1999). From pencils to pixels: The stages of literacy technologies. In G. E. Hawisher & C. L. Selfe (Eds.), *Passions, pedagogies, and 21st century technologies* (pp. 268–291). Logan: Utah State University Press.

Beach, R., & Lundell, D. (1998). Early adolescents' use of computer-mediated communication in writing and reading. In D. Reinking, M. C. McKenna, L. D. Labbo, & R. D. Kieffer (Eds.), *Handbook of literacy and technology: Transformations in a post-typographic world* (pp. 93–112). Mahwah, NJ: Lawrence Erlbaum Associates.

Bloome, D., & Egan-Robertson, A. (1993). The social construction of intertextuality and classroom reading and writing. *Reading Research Quarterly, 28*(4), 303–333.

Bloome, D., & Kinzer, C. K. (1999). Hard times or cosmetics? Changes in literacy. *Peabody Journal of Education,* 341–375.

Bolter, J. D. (1991). *Writing space: The computer, hypertext, and the history of writing.* Hillsdale, NJ: Lawrence Erlbaum Associates.

Bolter, J. D. (1998). Hypertext and the question of visual literacy. In D. Reinking, M. C. McKenna, L. D. Labbo, & R. D. Kieffer (Eds.), *Handbook of literacy and technology: Transformations in a post-typographic world* (pp. 3–14). Mahwah, NJ: Lawrence Erlbaum Associates.

Borgman, C. (1996). *Social aspects of digital libraries workshop: Preliminary workshop report.* Retrieved January 17, 1997, from http://www.gslis/ucla/edu/DL/

Bourdieu, P. (1991). *Language and symbolic power* (G. Raymond & M. Adamson, Trans.). Cambridge, MA: Harvard University Press.

Brandt, D. (1990). *Literacy as involvement: The acts of writers, readers, and texts.* Carbondale: Southern Illinois University Press.

Bransford, J. D., Brown, A., & Cocking, R. P. (Eds.) (1999). *How people learn: Brain, mind, experience, and school* (Expanded Edition). Washington, DC: National Academy Press.

Bromley, H., & Apple, M. W. (1998). *Education, technology, power: Educational computing as a social practice.* Albany: State University of New York Press.

Bromley, H., & Shutkin, D. (1999, April). *Refusing to choose: Dilemmas of dissenting technology educators.* Paper presented at the annual meeting of the American Educational Research Association, Montreal, Canada.

Brown, J. S., Collins, A., & Duguid, A. (1989). Situated cognition and the culture of learning. *Educational Researcher, 18*(1), 32–42.

Brown, M. M., & Jolly, R. (1999). *UNDP human development report.* New York: United Nations Publications.

Bruce, B. (1991). Roles for computers in teaching the English language arts. In J. Flood, J. M. Jensen, D. Lapp, & J. R. Squire (Eds.), *Handbook of research on teaching the English language arts* (pp. 536–541). New York: Macmillan.

Bruce, B. (1997a). Current and future directions. In J. Flood, S. B. Heath, & D. Lapp (Eds.), *Handbook of research on teaching literacy through the communicative and visual arts* (pp. 875–884). New York: Simon & Schuster Macmillan.

Bruce, B. (1997b). Literacy technologies: What stance should we take? *Journal of Literacy Research, 29*(2), 289–309.

Bruce, B. C., & Hogan, M. P. (1998). The disappearance of technology: Toward an ecological model of literacy. In D. Reinking, M. C. McKenna, L. D. Labbo, & R. D. Kieffer (Eds.), *Handbook of literacy and technology: Transformations in a post-typographic world* (pp. 269–282). Mahwah, NJ: Lawrence Erlbaum Associates.

Bruce, B. C., & Leander, K. (1997). Searching for digital libraries in education: Why computers cannot tell the story. *Library Trends, 45*(4), 746–770.

Bruce, B. C., & Rubin, A. (1993). *Electronic quills: A situated evaluation of using computers for writing in classrooms.* Hillsdale, NJ: Lawrence Erlbaum Associates.

CEO Forum (1999). *Professional development: A link to better learning.* Retrieved March 1, 1999, from http://www.ceoforum.org/report99/99report.pdf

Clinton, W. J. (2000, January 27). *State of the union address: Community, opportunity, responsibility.* Retrieved from http://www2.whitehouse.gov/WH/SOTU00/sotu-text.html

Colburn, L. (2000). *An analysis of teacher change and required supports as technology is integrated into the classroom curriculum.* Unpublished doctoral dissertation, Vanderbilt University, Nashville, TN.

Cole, M. (1996). *Cultural psychology: A once and future discipline.* Cambridge, MA: Belknap Press of Harvard University Press.

Coughlin, E. (1999, November 30). *Professional competencies for the digital age classroom.* Retrieved from http://www.iste.org//L&L/archive/vol27/no3/features/coughlin/index.html

Coughlin, E., & Lemke, C. (1999). *Professional competency continuum: Professional skills for the digital age classroom.* Retrieved from www.milkenexchange.org/project/pcc/ME159.pdf

Cunningham, J. W. (2000). How will literacy be defined in the new millenium? *Reading Research Quarterly, 35*(1), 64–65.

Dahn, M. (2000, January). Counting angels on a pinhead: Critically interpreting web size estimates. *Online,* 35–40. Retrieved from http://www.onlineinc.com/onlinemag/OL2000/dahn1.html

December, J. (1994). Challenges for web information providers. *Computer-Mediated Communication Magazine, 1,* 13–17.

Dechant, E. (1982). *Improving the teaching of reading* (3rd ed.). Englewood Cliffs, NJ: Prentice-Hall.

Dodge, B. (1995). http://edweb.sdsu.edu/courses/edtec596/about_webquests.html

Dyson, A. H. (1999). Coach Bombay's kids learn to write: Children's appropriation of media material for school literacy. *Research in the Teaching of English, 33*(4), 367–402.

*Economist* (1998). The World in figures: Industries. *The world in 1999.*

Engestrom, Y. (1987). *Learning by expanding: An activity-theoretical approach to developmental research.* Helsinki, Finland: Orienta-Konsultit Oy.

Federal Communications Commission (1996). *Telecommunications Act of 1996, Section 254.* Retrieved from http://www.fcc.gov/learnnet/254.html

Finders, M. J. (1997). *Just girls: Hidden literacies and life in jr. high.* New York: Teachers College Press.

Flesch, R. (1955). *Why Johnny can't read.* New York: Harper & Brothers.

Flesch, R. (1981). *Why Johnny still can't read.* New York: Harper & Row.

Flood, J., & Lapp, D. (1995). Broadening the lens: Toward an expanded conception of literacy. In K. A. Hinchman, D. J. Leu, & K. C. Kinzer (Eds.), *Perspectives on literacy research and practice: Forty-fourth yearbook of the National Reading Conference* (Vol. 44, pp. 1-16). Chicago: National Reading Conference.

Garner, R., & Gillingham, M. G. (1996). *Internet communication in six classrooms: Conversations across time, space, and culture.* Mahwah, NJ: Lawrence Erlbaum Associates.

Gee, J. (1990). *Social linguistics and literacies: Ideology in discourses.* New York: Falmer Press.

Goodman, K. S. (1976). Reading: A psycholinguistic guessing game. In H. Singer & R. Ruddell (Eds.), *Theoretical models and processes of reading* (2nd ed., pp. 497-508). Newark, DE: International Reading Association.

Gruber, S., Peyton, J. K., & Bruce, B. C. (1995). Collaborative writing in multiple discourse contexts. *Computer Supported Cooperative Work: An International Journal, 3*(3-4), 247-269.

Harste, J. C. (1990). Jerry Harste speaks on reading and writing. *The Reading Teacher, 43,* 316-318.

Hawisher, G. E., & Sullivan, P. A. (1999). Fleeting images: Women visually writing the web. In G. E. Hawisher & C. L. Selfe (Eds.), *Passions, pedagogies, and 21st century technologies* (pp. 268-291). Logan: Utah State University Press.

Hocks, M. (1995). Technotropes of liberation: Utopian discourse in theories of hypertext. *Pre/Text, 16*(1-2), 98-108.

Hodas, S. (1994). *Technology refusal and the organizational culture of schools.* Paper presented at Cyberspace Superhighways: Access, Ethics, and Control, the Fourth Conference on Computers, Freedom, and Privacy, Chicago.

Hoffman, D. L., & Novak, T. P. (1998, February). *Bridging the digital divide: The impact of race on computer access and Internet use* [Electronic version]. Nashville, TN: Vanderbilt University Project 2000. Retrieved from http://www.ed.gov/Technology/digdiv.html

Howerton, A. (1999). *Discussant's comments of "Me and my hypertext: A multiple digression analysis of technology and literacy (sic)."* Retrieved from http://www.oakland.edu/~mceneane/nrc/conf99/mceneane/paper1/mandywrd.doc

Hughes, J. E., Packard, B. W., & Pearson, P. D. (2000). Preservice teachers' experiences using hypermedia and video to learn about literacy instruction. *Journal of Literacy Research, 32*(4), 599-629.

Kinzer, C. K., & Leu, D. J. (1997). The challenge of change: Exploring literacy and learning in electronic environments. *Language Arts,* (74)2, 126-136.

Kinzer, C. K., & Risko, V. J. (1998). Multimedia and Enhanced Learning: Transforming Preservice Education. In D. Reinking, M. McKenna, L. Labbo, & R. Kieffer (Eds.), *Handbook of technology and literacy: Transformations in a post-typographic world* (pp. 185-202). Mahwah, NJ: Lawrence Erlbaum Associates.

Labbo, L. (1996). A semiotic analysis of young children's symbol making in a classroom computer center. *Reading Research Quarterly, 31*(4), 356-385.

Labbo, L. (1999). *Toward a vision of the future role of technology in literacy education.* Athens: University of Georgia, College of Education.

Labbo, L., & Reinking, D. (1999). Negotiating the multiple realities of technology in literacy research and instruction. *Reading Research Quarterly, 34,* 478-492.

Landow, G. P. (1992). *Hypertext: The convergence of contemporary critical theory and technology.* Baltimore: Johns Hopkins University Press.

Latour, B. (1996). *Aramis or the love of technology.* Cambridge, MA: Harvard University Press.

Latour, B., & Woolgar, S. (1986). *Laboratory life: The construction of scientific facts.* Princeton, NJ: Princeton University Press.

Lawrence, S., & Giles, C. L. (1998). Searching the world wide web [Electronic version]. *Science, 280*(5360), 98-100. Retrieved from http://www.neci.nj.nec.com/~lawrence/science98.html

Lawrence, S., & Giles, C. L. (1999, July). Accessibility of Information on the Web. *Nature, 400*(6740), 107-109.

Lemke, J. (1995). *Textual politics: Discourse and social dynamics.* London: Taylor & Francis.

Lemke, J. L. (1998). Metamedia literacy: Transforming meanings and media. In D. Reinking, M. C. McKenna, L. D. Labbo, & R. D. Kieffer (Eds.), *Literacy and technology: Transformations in a post-typographic world.* Mahwah, NJ: Lawrence Erlbaum Associates.

Lemke, J. L. (2000). Across the scales of time: Artifacts, activities, and meanings in ecosocial systems. *Mind, Culture, and Activity, 7*(4), 273-290.

Leu, D. J. (2000). Literacy and technology: Deictic consequences for literacy education in an information age. In R. Barr, M. L. Kamil, P. Mosenthal, & P. P. Pearson (Eds.), *Handbook of reading research* (Vol. 3). White Plains, NY: Longman.

Leu, D. J., Karchmer, R., & Leu, D. D. (2000). Exploring literacy on the Internet. *The Reading Teacher, 52*(6), 636-642.

Leu, D. J., & Kinzer, C. K. (2000). The convergence of literacy instruction with networked technologies for information, communication, and education. *Reading Research Quarterly, 35*(1), 108-127.

Leu, D. J., & Leu, D. D. (2000). *Teaching with the Internet: Lessons from the classroom* (3rd ed.). Norwood, MA: Christopher-Gordon.

Lin, X., Hmelo, C., Kinzer, C. K., & Secules, T. (1999). Designing technology to support reflection. *Educational Technology Research and Development, 47*(3), 43-62.

McEneaney, J. E. (1999, December). *Visualizing and assessing reader navigation in hypertext.* Paper presented at the 49th meeting of the National Reading Conference, Orlando, FL.

McEneaney, J. E. (2000, January). Learning on the Web: A content literacy perepective. *Reading Online.* Retrieved from http://www.readingonline.org/articles/mceneaney/

Moran, C., & Selfe, C. (1999). Teaching English across the Technology/Wealth Gap. *English Journal, 88*(6), 48-54.

Myers, J., Hammett, R., & McKillop, A. M. (1998). Opportunities for critical literacy and pedagogy in student-authored hypermedia. In D. Reinking, M. C. McKenna, L. D. Labbo, & R. D. Kieffer (Eds.), *Handbook of literacy and technology: Transformations in a post-typographic world* (pp. 63-78). Mahwah, NJ: Lawrence Erlbaum Associates.

National Center for Educational Statistics (1999, February). *Internet access in public schools and classrooms: 1994-98* [Issue Brief]. Retrieved from http://nces.ed.gov/pubs99/1999017.html

National Council for Accreditation of Teacher Education (1997). *Technology and the new professional teacher: Preparing for the 21st century classroom.* Retrieved March 1, 1999, from http://www.ncate.org/projects/tech/TECH.HTM

National Council of Teachers of English and the International Reading Association (1996). *Standards for the English language arts.* Urbana, IL: National Council of Teachers of English.

National Telecommunications and Information Association (1999). *Falling through the Net: Defining the digital divide.* Retrieved from http://www.ntia.doc.gov/ntiahome/fttn99/contents.html

Neilsen, L. (1998). Coding the light: Rethinking generational authority in a rural high school telecommunications project. In D. Reinking, M. C. McKenna, L. D. Labbo, & R. D. Kieffer (Eds.), *Handbook of literacy and technology: Transformations in a post-typographic world* (pp. 129-144). Mahwah, NJ: Lawrence Erlbaum Associates.

Neuberger, E. C. (1999). Computer use in the United States: Population characteristics October, 1997. Washington, DC: U.S. Census Bureau.

New London Group. (1996). A pedagogy of multiliteracies: Designing social futures. *Harvard Educational Review, 66*(1), 60-92.

President's Committee of Advisors on Science and Technology, Panel on Educational Technology (1997). *Report to the President on the use of technology to strengthen K-12 education in the United States* [Electronic version]. Washington, DC: Executive Office of the President of the United States. Retrieved January 1, 1999, from http://www.whitehouse.gov/WH/EOP/OSTP/NSTC/PCAST/k-12ed.html

Prior, P. (1998). *Writing/disciplinarity: A sociohistoric account of literate activity in the academy.* Mahwah, NJ: Lawrence Erlbaum Associates.

Purves, A. (1998). Flies in the web of hypertext. In D. Reinking, M. C. McKenna, L. D. Labbo, & R. D. Kieffer (Eds.), *Handbook of literacy and technology: Transformations in a post-typographic world* (pp. 235-252). Mahwah, NJ: Lawrence Erlbaum Associates.

Rabinowitz, P. J., & Smith, M. W. (1998). *Authorizing readers: Resistance and respect in the teaching of literature.* New York: Teachers College Press.

Reinking, D. (1994). *Elkectronic literacy* (Perspectives in Reading Research No. 4). Athens, GA: National Reading Research Center. (ERIC Document Reproduction Service No. ED 371 324)

Reinking, D. (1998). Introduction: Synthesizing technological transformations of literacy in a post-typographic world. In D. Reinking, M. McKenna, L. Labbo, & R. Kieffer (Eds.), *Handbook of technology and literacy: Transformations in a post-typographic world* (pp. xi-xxx). Mahwah, NJ: Lawrence Erlbaum Associates.

Reinking, D. (1999, December). *Me and my hypertext revisited: A multiple digression analysis of technology and linearity (sic).* Paper presented at the 49th meeting of the National Reading Conference, Orlando, FL. Retrieved from http://www.oakland.edu/~mceneane/nrc/conf99/mceneane/paper1/

Rosenblatt, L. M. (1994). The transactional theory of reading and writing. In R. B. Ruddell, M. R. Ruddell, & H. Singer (Eds.), *Theoretical models and processes of reading* (4th ed., pp. 1057-1092). Urbana, IL: Center for the Study of Reading.

Rowe, D. W. (1998). The literate potentials of book-related dramatic play. *Reading Research Quarterly, 33*(1), 10-35.

Rumelhart, D. (1994). In H. Singer & R. Ruddell (Eds.), *Theoretical models and processes of reading* (4th ed., pp. 864-894). Newark, DE: International Reading Association.

Russell, D. R. (1997). Rethinking genre in school and society: An activity theory analysis. *Written Communication, 14*(4), 504-554.

Sandholtz, J. H., Ringstaff, C., & Dwyer, D. C. (1997). *Teaching with technology: Creating student-centered classrooms.* New York: Teachers College Press.

Scardamalia, M., & Bereiter, C. (1991). Higher levels of agency for children in knowledge building: A challenge for the design of new knowledge media. *Journal of the Learning Sciences, 1,* 37-68.

Scardamalia, M., & Bereiter, C. (1993). The CSILE Project: Trying to bring the classroom into World 3. In K. McGilly (Ed.), *Classroom lessons: Integrating cognitive theory and classroom proactice* (pp. 201-228). Cambridge, MA: MIT Press/Bradford Press.

Scardamalia, M., & Bereiter, C. (1996). Adaptation and understanding: A case for new cultures of schooling. In S. Vosniadou, E. De Corte, R. Glaser, & H. Mandl (Eds.). *International perspectives on the Psychological foundations of technology-based learning environments* (pp. 149-165). Hillsdale, NJ: Lawrence Erlbaum Associates.

Shanahan, T. (1990). Reading and writing together: What does it really mean? In T. Shanahan (Ed.), *Reading and writing together: New perspectives for the classroom* (pp. 1-18). Norwood, MA: Christopher-Gordon.

Sharples, M. (1999). Electronic publication writing for the screen. *Journal of Adolescent and Adult Learning, 43*(2), 156-159.

Sherman, C. (2000, January-February). Reference resources on the Web. *Online, 24*(1), 52-56.

Star, L., & Griesemer, R. J. (1989). Institutional ecology, "translations" and boundary objects: Amateurs and professionals in Berkeley's Museum of Vertebrate Zoology, 1907-39. *Social Studies of Science, 19,* 387-420.

Street, B. V. (1984). *Literacy in theory and practice.* Cambridge, England: Cambridge University Press.

Strudler, N. B., McKinney, M. O., & Jones, W. P. (1999). First-year teachers' use of technology: Preparation, expectations and realities. *Journal of Technology and Teacher Education, 7*(2), 115-129.

Schwartz, D. L., Lin, X. D., Brophy, S., & Bransford, J. D. (1999). Toward the development of flexibly adaptive instructional designs. In C. M. Reigeluth (Ed.), *Instructional design theories and models,* vol. II. (pp. 183-213). Mahwah, NJ: Erlbaum.

U.S. Department of Education (1999). *Teacher quality: A report on the preparation and qualifications of public school teachers* [Electronic version] (USDE Publication No. NCES 1999-080). Washington, DC: U.S. Government Printing Office. Retrieved on January 30, 1999, from http://nces.ed.gov/pubs99/1999080.htm

Venezky, R. (1997). The literacy text: Its future in the classroom. In J. Flood, S. B. Heath, & D. Lapp (Eds.), *Handbook of research on teaching literacy through the communicative and visual arts* (pp. 528-535). New York: Simon & Schuster Macmillan.

Wertsch, J. V. (1991). *Voices of the mind: A sociocultural approach to mediated action.* Cambridge, MA: Harvard University Press.

Williams, S. M., Kinzer, C. K., & Leander, K. M. (2000). *Untangling the Web: What makes inquiry and the Internet work for elementary students?* (Proposal to Office of Educational Research and Imporovement). Nashville, TN: Peabody College of Vanderbilt University.

Yates, J., & Orlinkowski, W. J. (1992). Genres of organizational communication: A structurational approach to studying communication and media. *Academy of Management Review, 17*(2), 299-326.

Zehr, M. A. (1997). Teaching the teachers. *Education Week, 17*(11), 24-29.

# GROUPING FOR INSTRUCTION IN LITERACY

## Jeanne R. Paratore and Roselmina Indrisano
### Boston University

Throughout the history of reading research, attention has been paid to the effects of grouping practices on children's performance in reading. Particularly during the decades of the 1960s, 1970s, and 1980s, the practices of ability grouping, cooperative learning, and peer tutoring were widely investigated. Since the conduct of those studies, several syntheses and meta-analyses have been completed (e.g., Cohen, Kulik, & Kulik, 1982; Good & Marshall, 1984; Johnson, Maruyama, Johnson, & Nelson, 1981; Kulik & Kulik, 1984; Lou et al., 1996; Slavin, 1980, 1987, 1990). These have been beneficial in making sense of what Jeannie Oakes (1985) referred to as "mountains of research evidence" (p. 7) about instructional grouping practices.

To understand the evidence related to ability grouping, the work of Good and Marshall (1984) is especially instructive. In their review, they controlled for the various differences in published studies limiting their analysis to observational studies in which researchers were explicit in all aspects of their research design and in which they tracked classrooms across a number of different process variables, including peer effects, teacher behavior and attitudes, and instructional content. Focusing on studies that examined between-class grouping, Good and Marshall concluded that the evidence showed "a consistent pattern of deprivation for low students in schools that practice tracking" (p. 25). This conclusion received strong support in the work of other researchers who have systematically and carefully examined heterogeneous versus homogeneous small group instruction.

In summary, the evidence indicates several findings. First, when children are grouped according to their reading ability, they do not achieve the intended academic gains. Specifically, low-performing students have been found consistently to maintain low levels of performance (Good & Marshall, 1984; Oakes, 1985; Slavin, 1987). Second, ability grouping does not affect the achievement of different levels of learners differentially. That is, despite the widely held belief that high-ability

learners are more successful when they work with students like themselves, the evidence does not support the contention (Slavin, 1990). The exception to this is when high-achieving learners are provided accelerated content that essentially allows them to be instructed in the curriculum of a higher grade level and complete elementary or secondary schooling in fewer years than the average learner (Kulik & Kulik, 1984). Third, the curriculum offered to students in different levels of ability groups is qualitatively different, providing high-achieving students access to more cognitively challenging, interesting, and motivating material than that given to their lower achieving peers (Allington, 1984; Hiebert, 1983). Fourth, students in different levels of ability groups are provided qualitatively different teaching practices, with students in high ability groups more consistently exposed to teaching behaviors that are associated with effective instruction (Allington, 1984; Hiebert, 1983). Fifth, students placed in low-achieving groups often experience low self-esteem and negative attitudes toward reading and learning (Barr & Dreeben, 1991; Dweck, 1986; Eder, 1983; Swanson, 1985). Finally, students who are poor and members of racial and ethnic minority groups are substantially overrepresented in low-achieving groups (Braddock & Dawkins, 1993; Oakes, 1985).

It should also be noted that many studies have examined the effects of ability grouping versus no grouping at all, or whole-class instruction. A meta-analysis conducted by Lou et al. (1996) found conclusive results favoring ability grouping over no grouping at all, with positive findings related to achievement, attitude, and self-concept.

In contrast to the negative findings of research on ability grouping and whole-class instruction, investigations of cooperative learning and peer tutoring suggest promising learning effects. In the area of cooperative learning, studies (Johnson et al., 1981; Sharan, 1980; Slavin, 1980) indicate that (a) students of all ability levels who work in cooperative learning groups do better than their peers who work in traditional groups,

(b) students who work in cooperative learning groups have an opportunity to develop strong interpersonal ties and a better understanding of how to develop social relationships, and (c) students who work in cooperative learning groups may develop a stronger sense of self-efficacy.

Studies related to peer tutoring (e.g., Cohen et al., 1982) support a conclusion that this grouping strategy can lead to higher levels of achievement for both members of tutoring dyads but that such effects are likely to be documented only when the learning task is highly structured and explicit in nature and measured with an instrument highly congruent with the learning activity.

In the late 1980s and early 1990s, teachers in many classrooms responded to the evidence related to various grouping practices by rethinking the ways students are grouped for literacy instruction and by implementing various forms of heterogeneous grouping in place of rigid ability groups. Some tried whole-class instruction, a plan that seemed to fit well with the then popular movement toward whole language. Others tried different forms of multiability grouping, teaching students within large or small heterogeneous groups that changed from day to day and lesson to lesson. Still others attempted to combine the different grouping options, using large heterogeneous groups for part of the time and smaller homogeneous groups for part of the time.

As is the case with any educational innovation, not everyone has embraced the change in grouping patterns. Many teachers, administrators, and researchers have voiced concerns about the appropriateness of heterogeneous grouping, especially for learners who are in the early stages of learning to read. Some have particular concerns about the use of a single text for all students. They cite findings from studies of researchers such as Juel (1990) who found that first-grade children's learning of basal words needs to be carefully monitored and remain at high levels of accuracy in order to achieve reading success as evidence that children learn best when the text is carefully matched to their individual reading levels. Others argue that often the lowest performing children within heterogeneous reading groups are not actually learning to read; they are instead learning to listen to text that is read to them. Yet other teachers and researchers (e.g., Allan, 1991; Renzulli & Reis, 1991) question the learning opportunities offered to the highest performing students and wonder if they are sufficiently challenging to advance the learning of already able readers.

Although the evidence to respond to these questions and concerns is yet slight, recent empirical studies have examined how well children are learning to read when their instruction occurs within various forms of heterogeneous grouping models. In this chapter we present the evidence from such studies. We have limited our examination to studies of elementary-grade students. We have organized studies within three sections: (a) those that examined how well students learn to read when taught within heterogeneous grouping frameworks, (b) those that examined students' discussion and interaction strategies within heterogeneous grouping contexts, and (c) those that examined students' perceptions of different grouping formats.

## STUDIES OF READING ACHIEVEMENT

Among the earliest efforts to empirically investigate alternatives to ability grouping for the teaching of reading were those of Stevens, Madden, Slavin, and Farnish (1987). They conducted two studies to examine the effects of a comprehensive cooperative learning approach to elementary reading and writing instruction. Cooperative integrated reading and composition (CIRC) includes three main elements: basal-related activities, direct instruction in reading comprehension, and integrated language arts and writing. As explained by the researchers, CIRC was developed to focus simultaneously on state-of-the-art curricular practices derived from research in reading and writing and on the use of cooperative learning as a vehicle for teaching. The cycle of instruction included teacher introduction of new skills, vocabulary, and story concepts in reading groups to which children were assigned by reading level. These teacher-led, small-group lessons were followed by student practice in heterogeneous learning teams. Direct instruction of comprehension strategies was provided once a week and was followed by practice with team members. A process approach to writing instruction guided by a project-developed language arts and writing curriculum was implemented during daily language arts periods. All language arts and writing activities involved cooperative practice and feedback within learning teams. Children were asked to read a trade book of their choice at home for at least 20 minutes every evening. Parents were asked to monitor this process by initialing a form, and students submitted a book report at least once every 2 weeks.

The effectiveness of CIRC was investigated in two separate studies. The first was conducted in third- and fourth-grade classrooms within a suburban school district and examined the performance of 11 experimental classes where CIRC was implemented and 10 control classes where teachers continued using their traditional methods and curriculum materials. In both experimental and control classes, special education and remedial reading students were included. Teachers in each grade were allocated the same amounts of time for reading and language arts instruction. The treatment was implemented over a 12-week period. Experimental and control classes were initially matched on the basis of standardized test scores. Statistical analyses found no significant differences on the Total Reading score, whereas differences on Total Language favored the control group at the start of the study. In reading, posttesting found statistically significant differences favoring the experimental group on four of the five standardized tests, including Reading Comprehension, Reading Vocabulary, Language Expression, and Spelling. In writing, posttesting found statistically significant differences in ratings for Organization, favoring the experimental group. No significant difference was found on ratings for Mechanics, paralleling the results of the standardized Language Mechanics posttest. There were no significant ability by treatment interactions on any posttest measures.

The second study also examined the performance of third- and fourth-grade students within a suburban school district, maintaining essentially the same study design but this time extending the intervention period from 12 to 24 weeks. Pretest measures again established equivalence of the experimental and control groups at the start of the study. Posttests found significant differences favoring the experimental group on standardized tests of Reading Comprehension; in Reading Vocabulary, means favored the experimental group but did not reach significance. Analysis of scores from an informal reading inventory found significant effects favoring the experimental group on measures of word recognition, word analysis, reading rate, and grade-level achievement. The effect sizes on these oral reading measures were moderate (.44–.64). Posttests also revealed significant differences favoring the experimental group on standardized tests of Language Expression and Language Mechanics. Analyses of the writing samples found a significant main effect on Ideas, but no significant differences on Organization or Mechanics. As in the first study, there were no significant ability by treatment interactions on any posttest measure.

In a later study, Stevens and Slavin (1995) continued their examination of CIRC, this time by studying its implementation over a 2-year period in Grades 2 through 6. Subjects were 1,299 students in 63 classrooms (31 experimental; 32 nonexperimental) in a suburban, working-class school district. Experimental and nonexperimental schools were matched on socioeconomic and ethnic characteristics. Because pretests revealed significant differences in reading and language arts achievement, students' Total Reading and Language pretest scores were used as covariates in the data analyses. In both the 1st and 2nd year, posttests indicated significant effects favoring the experimental group on measures of Reading Vocabulary and Reading Comprehension. There were mixed results over the 2-year period on measures of Language Mechanics and Language Expression.

The data for students who received special education or remedial services were analyzed separately. These analyses found significant differences favoring the experimental group on measures of Reading Vocabulary and Reading Comprehension after both the 1st and 2nd years.

CIRC maintains the practice of placing children in ability-based reading materials while providing them practice in heterogeneous, cooperative learning practice groups. In an effort to eliminate the practice of ability grouping altogether, Jenkins et al. (1994) experimented with an adapted version of CIRC. Their nonability grouped approach used the CIRC instructional model with an important adaptation. They eliminated instructional groups that were divided according to reading ability and used the same instructional materials for all students. To accommodate the difficulty that less skilled students would encounter in the grade-level text, they included three practices designed to help low-achieving students succeed in their classroom assignments: cross-age and peer tutoring, specialized decoding instruction, administered within a limited pullout program 12 to 20 minutes daily, and in-class instructional support from specialists. During the yearlong study, the researchers collected data from two schools, one in which the experimental package was implemented and a second that served as a comparison school. Each school had at least two classrooms at each grade level and all students (regular education and special education) in Grades 1 through 6 in both schools participated. Pretest measures established equivalence of treatment and comparison schools at the start of the study. Results from a series of posttest measures were mixed. Findings indicated that students in the experimental school demonstrated significantly superior gains on several scales of the Metropolitan Achievement Test, including Reading Vocabulary, Total Reading, and Language and a marginally significant effect on Reading Comprehension. However, on three other measures (Gates MacGinitie Reading Test, the Reading subtest of Basic Academic Skills Samples, and Passage Reading Tests), no significant differences were found between experimental and control schools, although the direction of the gains favored the experimental schools.

In 1989, Patricia Cunningham and her colleagues began their examination of what they initially described as "non-ability-grouped, multi-level instruction" (Cunningham, Hall, & Defee, 1991, p. 571). In a first-grade classroom, they implemented an instructional model in which the instructional time was equally divided among four instructional blocks that included time for instruction in a basal reader, self-selected reading, writing, and working with words. Unlike the studies previously cited, these researchers did not compare children's performance to that of a control group but rather judged the effectiveness of the program by comparing the children's achievement of grade level standards against levels that children taught within traditional ability groups are generally expected to achieve. At the end of the 1st year, they found that half of the children who would otherwise have been placed in a bottom, below-grade-level reading group were reading at or above grade level. All children who would have been in a middle group read at or above grade level. All children who would have been in the top group read above grade level, achieving reading levels from third to sixth grade.

This early study was the first in what was to become a series of studies conducted over a 6-year period examining the achievement of children in first- and second-grade classrooms who participated in what Hall and Cunningham (1996) eventually called "multi-level, multi-method" (p. 197) literacy instruction. This work was implemented within regular education classrooms in a large suburban school with a diverse student population. In a summary article, Hall and Cunningham (1996) reported that the findings collected across 5 years and five groups of 100 to 140 children were remarkably stable. At the end of first grade, 58% to 64% of the children read above grade level, 22% to 28% read on grade level, and 10% to 17% read below grade level. At the end of second grade, 68% to 76% of children read above grade level, 14% to 25% read at grade level, and 2% to 9% read below grade level. Hall and Cunningham noted that this study was limited by the lack of a control group but suggested that the consistency of results across years and classrooms offset the limitation.

To examine the influence of heterogeneous grouping on the reading achievement of the lowest performing students in a first-grade classroom, Turpie and Paratore (1995) examined the reading performance of four children who had performed below the 48th percentile on a standardized readiness test and who were identified as "at risk" for reading failure by their classroom teacher. The children were members of a first-grade classroom of 25 children where the teacher used a flexible grouping model based on heterogeneous whole-class instruction and needs-based, small-group instruction (Paratore, 1991). Reading materials included a combination of first-grade texts of a basal reading program and trade book literature. Literacy instruction was organized within four components: (a) reading, rereading, and responding to shared text; (b) sustained silent reading of easy text; (c) phonemic awareness training; and (d) spelling-sound instruction. Using a single case, multiple baseline design, Turpie and Paratore (1995) maintained the general practices offered to all children in the flexible grouping model and examined the effects of repeated readings on children's word reading accuracy, fluency, self-correction behaviors, and reading comprehension. Results indicated that students made substantial increases in reading accuracy, improving from an average of 75% word accuracy during baseline to 97% word accuracy during the intervention. In fluency, all students were able to read three times as many words per minute during the intervention as they did at baseline. The children increased their self-correction rate from an average of 9% in baseline to an average of 50% in intervention, an indication that increases in accuracy and fluency were not due to memorization but rather to attention to graphemic–phonemic cues. Students also improved their reading comprehension, including an average of 62% of major story structure elements in retellings in baseline and 95% of minor story structure elements in their retellings during intervention.

Although the number of studies investigating alternative forms of grouping for literacy instruction is small, and the differences among the instructional frameworks are many, the results are largely consistent: When students are grouped for reading within grouping structures that abandon the traditional static ability grouping framework, students at all levels of ability achieve at higher levels on measures of reading vocabulary, reading comprehension, and reading fluency. In addition, the studies of Hall and Cunningham (1996) and Turpie and Paratore (1995) provided evidence that when children are taught within heterogeneous grouping contexts that are rich in opportunities for reading, rereading, writing, and word practice low-performing learners acquire the word identification skills necessary to read grade-appropriate text.

## STUDIES OF STUDENTS' INTERACTIONS WITHIN HETEROGENEOUS GROUPS

In some cases, researchers have argued that traditional methods of measuring students' reading achievement fail to assess the full range of outcomes related to alternative grouping practices (e.g., Hiebert, 1993, 1997). In an effort to broaden the ways we define literacy achievement and more accurately examine changes in students' literacy learning, some studies have examined the ways students of varying reading abilities talk about books when they meet in heterogeneous groups.

In an ongoing series of studies related to the Book Club program, Taffy Raphael and her colleagues have examined the effects of a literature-based reading program implemented within flexibly grouped classrooms (Goatley, Brock, & Raphael, 1995; McMahon & Goatley, 1995; Raphael & Brock, 1993; Raphael, Brock, & Wallace, 1996). At the heart of the project are heterogeneously formed, student-led discussion groups. Students are prepared to participate in these groups through

reading activities that occur in silent, paired, and choral reading contexts; writing activities that support preparation for and reflection on the book club discussions; and whole-class, "community share" discussions that lead to and follow the book club discussions. Much of the research related to the Book Club project has focused particularly on the performance of students with diverse learning needs within peer-led groups.

Using data from three book club discussions, Raphael and Brock (1993) examined the use of language and social interactions by a Vietnamese English bilingual student, Mei. During her fourth-grade year Mei spent half her time in a bilingual classroom and half her time in the Book Club program in the regular education classroom. In fifth grade she was fully mainstreamed in the regular education classroom. The conversations selected for analysis occurred over the 2-year period, the first in the winter of fourth grade (when she was in the bilingual program), the second in the fall of fifth grade, and the third in the winter of fifth grade. Data analysis indicated that Mei's participation changed in important ways. She substantially increased her general participation over time, from 21 to 94 individual exchanges over the period the three discussions. In addition, the researchers found an increase in the number of new topics initiated by Mei and in her persistence in getting her topics discussed by her peers. They interpreted her ability to get the floor as evidence of increased self-confidence. They also observed changes in features of Mei's discourse. In the first book club discussion, Mei's comments were limited to simple statements of affirmation or state of knowledge ("Yeah"; "I don't know"). In the second discussion, when Mei was challenged by peers to elaborate, she read what she had written in her reading log and summarized parts of the story to support her point of view. By the third discussion, Mei offered a counterargument with supporting details and issued a challenge to her peers to provide more information.

In another study, Goatley, Brock, and Raphael (1995) continued their examination of the ways students who typically received literacy instruction outside the regular classroom setting performed in the Book Club program in the general education classroom. They observed a group of five fifth-grade students, three of whom in previous years had received reading instruction in Chapter 1, English as a Second Language, and Special Education resource room programs. One of these three students was Mei, the subject of the earlier case study. The researchers examined students' participation in small-group literature discussions and students' strategies for drawing on their own knowledge and the knowledge of their peers as they worked to understand the texts they were reading. Data were collected over a 3-week period and included interviews and written questionnaires that elicited students' understanding of their roles within their book clubs, audiotaped discussions and transcripts of both the book club and whole-class activities, videotapes of book clubs, students' written work samples, and researchers' field notes.

Analysis of the data indicated that the modes of participation varied widely and did not correlate with students' ability levels, experience within American schools or regular education classrooms, or English language proficiency. Furthermore, the investigators reported that although they did so in diverse ways and with differing degrees of frequency, all members of the group succeeded in getting the floor and contributing to the discussion. The analysis also indicated that students' strategies for text comprehension deviated from what is typically expected of students labeled as poor or struggling readers. They found, for example, that it was a regular education student in the group who attributed his confusion with the story details to the text being boring; with the help of his peers, he resolved his comprehension difficulties and regained his enthusiasm for reading. Throughout the series of book club discussions, the investigators observed group members relying on a number of strategies to construct meaning. They relied on knowledgeable others, both peers and the teacher; they consulted the cover, title, and book jacket; they used their knowledge of text structure to organize their thinking; they related events and ideas from earlier readings; they consulted reference materials; and they recalled earlier book club discussions. The researchers interpreted the data as evidence that the heterogeneous, regular-education-based learning context afforded this group of diverse students important learning opportunities.

In a later analysis, Raphael, Brock, and Wallace (1996) examined data from three cases, all again representing students who participated in the Book Club project. Two cases were drawn from the fifth-grade classroom that provided the context for the previous two studies and one was drawn from a fourth-grade classroom. Again, the focus was on how the children used discourse to construct text comprehension. Across all three cases, they found evidence to support the following findings:

1. Students demonstrated that they were not only able to make contributions to the topics at hand but that they were also able to challenge the thinking of their peers identified as more competent literacy users.
2. Students assumed leadership and supported and extended the learning of others during peer discussion groups.
3. Students were not reluctant to seek assistance and clarification from their peers when they were confused and were often more likely to save their questions and comments for the peer discussion groups than pose them during the teacher-led segment of the lesson.

As in the previous work, the researchers interpreted the data as evidence that the diverse learners benefited from the opportunities to participate in heterogeneous, regular-education-based instruction in literacy.

The studies that examine the Book Club program as an approach to improving reading instruction for diverse learners are limited by the small number of subjects and by overlap in the data sources. In some cases, as was noted, individual case studies provided the data source for two or more of the analyses. At the same time, however, the findings are strengthened by the consistency in the results across two different classroom settings, across learners with very diverse learning needs, and across the reading of varied instructional texts.

## STUDIES OF STUDENTS' PERCEPTIONS OF GROUPING FORMATS

Among the criticisms of ability grouping has been the evidence that the practice of sorting children by ability has resulted in serious instructional limitations for many students, most

particularly low-performing students, resulting in low self-esteem, low teacher expectations, and inferior curriculum (Braddock & Dawkins, 1993; Oakes, 1985). In our search for evidence of the effectiveness of alternatives to ability grouping, we found one recent study that examined perceptions that students have of different grouping formats. Elbaum, Schumm, and Vaughn (1997) conducted a study in which the participants were third, fourth, and fifth grade students from three schools in a large, urban school district. A questionnaire that included both closed and open-ended questions was administered in students' classrooms during regular class time with two researchers present during the administration.

Results related to two analyses are included here: the students' liking of different grouping formats and their views of the advantages and disadvantages of the various formats. Using a significance level of $p < .001$, mean scores indicated that students rated mixed-ability groups and pairs significantly higher than whole-group instruction, whole-group instruction significantly higher than same-ability pairs, and same-ability pairs significantly higher than either same-ability groups or working alone. Students also reported that they preferred having all students use the same book to having students use different books and that they preferred changing group assignments to stable group assignments. There were no significant grade or gender differences in the findings.

A second analysis examined students' perceptions of various characteristics of the different grouping formats. Almost all students (96%) described mixed-ability groups as more cooperative in nature and a large majority (85%) believed them to be more effective in promoting learning. In response to questions, students justified their response by commenting on advantages afforded to poor readers in mixed-ability groups, explaining that they would benefit from being with more able readers and that they could receive help from better readers. Approximately two-thirds judged mixed-ability groups to be more fair than same-ability groups. Again, students' comments suggested that they judged fairness on the basis of consequences of the various grouping practices for poor readers. On questions related to pacing, 100% of students favored same-ability groups, noting that better readers may be frustrated by the slowness of poorer readers. In the category of enjoyment of the different grouping practices, student responses were equally split between mixed- and same-ability groups.

In presenting these findings, the authors acknowledged that in some cases, students had very little experience with some of the grouping formats and their perceptions may have been based on expectations rather than experience. In addition, even in those cases where students experienced various grouping practices, no attempt was made to define the types of activities that actually occurred within the groups.

## CONCLUSIONS

At the start of this chapter, we made the claim that when carefully controlled studies are conducted, the use of traditional forms of ability grouping for the teaching of reading are not found to serve students well. Particularly, there is little evidence that high-performing students are advantaged by traditional ability grouping and substantial evidence that low-performing learners are disadvantaged by traditional ability groups. Furthermore, although other practices such as cooperative learning and peer tutoring have been proven to be advantageous for learning in general, few studies prior to the late 1980s and early 1990s had examined these practices in relation to the teaching of beginning reading. As a result, despite the compelling nature of grouping research, the existing evidence provided elementary teachers of reading little guidance in improving the instruction of reading by changing the ways children are grouped. How, then, were teachers to reconcile their students' diverse word recognition and language needs with the need to create a heterogeneous learning climate? How could children be taught to read text that was quite simply out of their reading range? How could able readers be challenged with text that they could read prior to ever entering the classroom door?

Although the evidence to answer these questions is yet limited to studies by a few teams of researchers, it is nonetheless evidence worthy of attention. Preliminarily, at least, some conclusions can be drawn. First, when looking at studies that measured reading achievement in traditional ways, that is, through the administration of either achievement tests or informal reading inventories, across all of the studies, the results are largely consistent: When students are grouped for reading within grouping structures that abandon the traditional, static, ability grouping framework, students at all levels of ability achieve at higher levels on measures of reading vocabulary, reading comprehension, and reading fluency. Second, when nontraditional measures of reading achievement are considered, such as the ways children demonstrate understanding through group discussions and the ways they assume leadership during the discussions, evidence again supports the effectiveness of heterogeneous grouping in the teaching of reading.

Of critical importance in reviewing these findings, however, is the comprehensive, varied, and flexible nature of the instructional framework within each of the examined studies. In addition to varying the grouping practices used in the classroom, each of the studies provided students intensive instruction in word study, many opportunities to read and reread text individually and with others, many opportunities to write both in response to text and in contexts unrelated to their reading texts, and many opportunities to engage in oral discussions with their peers.

Furthermore, the nature of the various instructional opportunities is important. In no case, for example, were children who were struggling readers expected to contend with difficult text on their own. Instead, each of the studies utilized a variety of strategies to help children negotiate difficult text. Included were teacher read-alouds, opportunities for individual and paired rereadings, intensive instruction and practice in word study, and practice reading easy text. In addition, in some of the classrooms, students who were struggling were provided pull-out instruction in direct support of the classroom activities and in some cases they were provided in-class support directly related to regular education tasks. In some studies, children who were advanced readers were provided daily opportunities to read text at more challenging levels and, in some cases, opportunities to serve as peer or cross-age tutors. In short, in no case did the instructional model represent a one-size-fits-all framework.

The comprehensive and flexible nature of the grouping models certainly represents their instructional strength but likely also represents a methodological weakness. Can we attribute the success of any of the models investigated specifically to the nature of flexible and heterogeneous grouping practices? Probably not. Can we say with a degree of confidence that at least in this small collection of studies, students who were taught within flexible, heterogeneously grouped classrooms had effective and successful opportunities to read and write? It would seem so.

## FUTURE RESEARCH DIRECTIONS

Existing studies on alternative grouping practices offer encouraging directions to teachers as they explore alternatives to ability grouping, but they provide just a hint of the evidence that is necessary to derive strong and firm conclusions. We need to continue to explore and document in trustworthy ways the various grouping practices that are effective in meeting both the particular needs of individual children and also the general needs of classrooms full of children.

## *References*

Allan, S. D. (1991). Ability-grouping research reviews: What do they say about grouping and the gifted? *Educational Leadership, 48,* 60–65.

Allington, R. L. (1984). Content coverage and contextual reading in reading groups. *Journal of Reading Behavior, 16,* 85–96.

Barr, R., & Dreeben, R. (1983). *How schools work.* Chicago: University of Chicago Press.

Braddock, J. H., II, & Dawkins, M. P. (1993). Ability grouping, aspirations, and attainments: Evidence from the National Educational Longitudinal Study of 1988. *Journal of Negro Education, 62,* 324–336.

Cohen, P. A., Kulik, J. A., & Kulik, C. L. C. (1982). Educational outcomes of tutoring: A meta-analysis of findings. *American Educational Research Journal, 19,* 237–248.

Cunningham, P. M., Hall, D. P., & Defee, M. (1991). Non-ability grouped, multilevel instruction: A year in a first-grade classroom. *The Reading Teacher, 44,* 566–571.

Dweck, C. S. (1986). Motivational processes affecting learning. *American Psychologist, 41,* 1040–1048.

Eder, D. (1983). Ability grouping and students' academic self-concepts: A case study. *The Elementary School Journal, 84,* 149–161.

Elbaum, B. E., Schumm, J. S., & Vaughn, S. (1997). Urban middle-elementary students' perceptions of grouping formats for reading instruction. *The Elementary School Journal, 97,* 475–500.

Goatley, V. J., Brock, C. H., & Raphael, T. E. (1995). Diverse learners participating in regular education "Book Clubs." *Reading Research Quarterly, 30,* 332–380.

Good, T. L., & Marshall, S. (1984). Do students learn more in heterogeneous or homogeneous groups? In P. L. Peterson, L. C. Wilkinson, & M. Hallinan (Eds.), *The social context of instruction: Group organization and group processes* (pp. 15–38). New York: Academic Press.

Hall, D. P., & Cunningham, P. M. (1996). Becoming literate in first and second grades: Six years of multimethod, multilevel instruction. In D. J. Leu, C. K. Kinzer, & K. H. Hinchman (Eds.), *Literacies for the twenty-first century: Research and practice: Forty-fifth yearbook of National Reading Confrence* (pp. 295–204). Chicago: National Reading Conference.

Hiebert, E. H. (1983). An examination of ability grouping for reading instruction. *Reading Research Quarterly, 18,* 231–255.

Hiebert, E. H. (1993). Lesson from a Chapter 1 project. In I. C. Rotberg (Ed.), *Federal policy options for improving the education of low-income students* (pp. 48–53). Santa Monica, CA: Rand.

Hiebert, E. H. (1997). Commentary: Assessment research in the Book Club program. In S. I. McMahon & T. E. Raphael (Eds.) *The book club connection* (pp. 205–207). Newark, DE: International Reading Association.

Jenkins, J. R., Jewell, M., Leicester, N., O'Connor, R., Jenkins, L. M., Troutner, N. M. (1994). Accommodations for individual differences without classroom ability groups: An experiment in school restructuring. *Exceptional Children, 60,* 344–358.

Johnson, D. W., Maruyama, G., Johnson, R., & Nelson, D. (1981). Effects of cooperative, competitive, and individualistic goal structures on achievement: A meta-analysis. *Psychological Bulletin, 89,* 47–62.

Juel, C. (1990). Effects of reading group assignment on reading development I first and second grade. *Journal of Reading Behavior, 22,* 233–254.

Kulik, J. A., & Kulik, C. L. C. (1984). *Effects of accelerated instruction on students. Review of Educational Research, 54,* 409–425.

Lou, Y., Abrami, P. C., Spence, C., Poulsen, C., Chambers, B., d'Apollonia, S. (1996). Within-class grouping: A meta-analysis. *Review of Educational Research, 66,* 423–458.

McMahon, S. I., & Goatley, V. J. (1995). Fifth graders help peers discuss texts in student-led groups. *J of Ed Research, 89,* 23–35.

Oakes, J. (1985). *Keeping track: How schools structure inequality.* New Haven, CT: Yale University Press.

Paratore, J. R. (1991). *Flexible grouping: Why and how?* Morristown, NJ: Silver Burdett & Ginn.

Raphael, T. E., & Brock, C. H. (1993). Mei: Learning the literacy culture in an urban elementary school. In D. J. Leu & C. K. Kinzer (Eds.), *Examining central issues in literacy research, theory, and practice: Forty-second year book of the National Reading Conference* (Vol. 42, pp. 179–188).

Raphael, T. E., Brock, C. H., & Wallace, S. M. (1996). Encouraging quality peer talk with diverse students in mainstream classrooms: Learning from and with teachers. In J. R. Paratore & R. L. McCormack (Eds.), *Peer talk in the classroom: Learning from research* (pp. 176–206). Newark, DE: International Reading Association.

Renzulli, J. S., & Reis, S. M. (1991). The reform movement and the quiet crisis in gifted education. *Gifted Child Quarterly, 35,* 26–35.

Sharan, S. (1980). Cooperative learning in small groups: Recent methods and effects on achievement, attitudes, and ethnic relations. *Review of Educational Research, 50,* 241–271.

Slavin, R. E. (1980). Cooperative learning. *Review of Educational Research, 50,* 315–342.

Slavin, R. E. (1987). *Ability grouping and student achievement in elementary school: A best evidence synthesis.* Baltimore: Johns Hopkins University, Center for Research on Elementary and Secondary Schools.

Slavin, R. E. (1990). Ability grouping in the middle grades: Achievement effects and alternatives. *Review of Educational Research, 60,* 471–499.

Stevens, R. J., Madden, N. A., Slavin, R. E., & Farnish, A. M. (1987). Cooperative integrated reading and composition: Two field experiments. *Reading Research Quarterly, 22,* 433–454.

Stevens, R. J., & Slavin, R. E. (1995). Effects of a cooperatie learning approach to reading and writing on academically handicapped and nonhandicapped students. *The Elementary School Journal, 95,* 241–262.

Swanson, B. B. (1985). Listening to students about reading. *Reading Horizons, 25,* 123–128.

Turpie, J., & Paratore, J. R. (1995). Using repeated readings to promote reading success in a heterogeneously grouped first grade. In K. A. Hinchman, D. J. Leu, & C. K. Kinzer (Eds.), *Perspectives on literacy research and practice: Forty-fourth yearbook of the National Reading Conference* (Vol. 44, pp. 255–264). Chicago: National Reading Conference.

# ·41·

# UNIFYING THE DOMAIN OF K–12 ENGLISH LANGUAGE ARTS CURRICULUM

*Charles W. Peters and Karen K. Wixson*
University of Michigan

During the late 1990s, the quality of the school curriculum has come under close scrutiny by both the general public and the educational community. A front page story in *The New York Times* proclaimed, "A large majority of New York City eighth graders have failed to meet tough new state standards on tests in mathematics and English, raising questions about the quality and content of the curriculum in middle school" (Hirsch, 1999, p. 27). Many, like Gross (1999), share the belief that the educational establishment has nurtured a conspiracy of ignorance that can be linked to low standards perpetuated by ineffective curriculum. Others, however, note that trying to resolve curricular questions "is like trying to make a sculpture out of ice. We often begin thinking that we are dealing with an object we can mold in our hands, but we quickly find the ice beginning to melt" (Hatcher, 1999, p. 2).

As Kliebard (1998) noted, the controversy over the state and nature of the curriculum is not new. In fact, it has not changed much in the last 2,000 years. Aristotle (trans. 1945) observed that a wide disagreement existed as to what was an appropriate course of study:

At present opinion is divided about the subjects of education. All do not take the same view about what should be learned by the young, either with a view to plain goodness or with a view to the best life possible; nor is opinion clear whether education should be directed mainly to the understanding, or mainly to moral character. If we look at actual practice, the result is sadly confusing; it throws no light on the problem whether the proper studies to be followed are those which are useful in life, or those which make for goodness, or those which advance the bounds of knowledge. Each sort of study receives some votes in its favor. (p. 159)

That the debate about the curriculum is ongoing does not diminish the fact that there are serious problems. For some the problem is that the curriculum is hopelessly ill defined or ambiguous at best (McDonald, 1999). They warn that students cannot afford to wait until their senior year in high school to discover what they should have learned, teachers cannot afford to spend an entire year inventing their own curriculum, and the public cannot afford to support schools that are unclear about what they are teaching. A major consequence of the ill-designed curriculum is that it raises serious questions about equal opportunity. Despite improvements, minorities still lag behind the general population averages in academic achievement (Jencks & Phillips, 1998). As a result, large numbers of children are prevented from getting jobs, gaining admission to elite academic institutions, or from participating in civic events. For this group, access to an adequate curriculum is a civil right established by the courts. For example, in 1993 a state court in Alabama ruled that the K–12 school system is unconstitutional, because it does not provide students with an opportunity to attain skills necessary to compete in the world outside the classroom. Those who believe that curricular equity is the issue look around and see a multitiered system in which "excellence" in relationship to the curriculum is defined differently depending on where one goes to school. This increases the pressure to have a clearly articulated curriculum that shares common features with other districts (Myers, 1996).

For others the problem is that the curriculum is influenced by ideological extremists. It is a war over the issue of what knowledge is most worth knowing. At one end of the curricular continuum are those who are concerned about our cultural heritage. They believe that the curriculum does not transmit many of the important values that unite us as a nation and underpin the western views of democracy. They want the school curriculum to be a broader conception of experience, rooted perhaps in constitutional principles and in an exposure to a variety of values, attitudes, and knowledge that might otherwise not be gained by the students (Bloom, 1994; Delbanco, 1997; Ellis, 1997; Hirsch, 1987; Ravitch & Finn, 1987). At the other end of the ideological spectrum are the postmodernists who believe that to standardize the curriculum is to reify one version of "truth" to the exclusion of multiple and conflicting perspectives on any given subject or topic (Beyer & Apple, 1998; Beyer & Liston, 1996; Pinar, 1996). In other words, they are curricular relativists. For many who hold this view, curriculum is viewed as political and therefore should include a focus on issues of gender, race, and class (Apple, 1990; Atwell-Vasey, 1998; de Castell & Bryson, 1998; Pinar, 1996).

Finally, there are those who view the problem with curriculum as the lack of alignment between what is taught and how it is assessed. This group believes that there is a major disconnect between what qualifies as evidence of learning in the classroom and what a district or state uses to document student understanding. For teachers, it seems like the wrong tests are driving the curriculum, because the content of the curriculum is not adequately reflected in the types of assessments that carry weight with the district, state, and the public (Hirsch, 2000; Scholes, 1999; Wiggins, 1989a, 1993). In cases like this, some believe that alignment contributes to poor student performance. They point out that although educational research has contributed to advances in our understanding of teaching and learning, there has been little improvement in student performance (Applebee, 1999). Others believe poor student performance is the result of the failure to articulate a clear pathway through the curriculum. In other words, there is no K–12 sequence and without a clear and consistent curricular road map, it is impossible to design assessments that are aligned with the curriculum (Smagorinsky & Smith, 1992).

## HOW DO PROBLEMS MANIFEST THEMSELVES IN ENGLISH LANGUAGE ARTS?

In many ways the English language arts (ELA) curriculum is a microcosm of the larger curricular issues of content, ideological extremism, and alignment. Differences along these dimensions are apparent in the three models used to characterize ELA curricula over the past 20 years—mastery, cultural heritage, and process (Farrell, 1991; Mandel, 1980).

The mastery model is closely associated with competency assessment, instructional objectives, and basic skills learning (Farrell, 1991). This model advocates specifying the behaviors to be achieved as a means of giving teaching precision. In the form described by scholars such as B. Bloom (1968, 1981), students' experience carefully controlled, sequenced learning activities until mastery of the skill and knowledge is exhibited and they are allowed to proceed to other skills. The curricula planned with this model in mind often consist of lists of activities and objectives. Although the model itself says little about the content of the ELA curriculum, it has become closely identified with skills-based content characteristic of the scope and sequence charts for commercial reading and language arts programs during the 1970s (Gehrke, Knapp, & Sirotnik, 1992). Consistent with this tradition, more attention is paid to skills and processes than to literature and its content. As a result, it does not have a K–12 scope and sequence or is it connected to the other ELA processes—writing, listening, speaking, and

viewing. Many would also suggest that this model reflects an idelogical extreme with regard to its conceptual stance toward teaching and learning.

The cultural heritage model looks to the traditionally accepted literary canon as the basis for the ELA curriculum, that is, literature of enduring worth that embodies the values and great ideas of the larger culture. Alter (1989), A. Bloom (1987), H. Bloom (1994), Cheney (1987), Hirsch (1996), Ravitch and Finn (1987), and Ravitch and Viteritte (1999) are among the more prominent advocates of the heritage model and Hirsch (1987) is one of the most outspoken and best-known proponents of an ELA content-based curriculum. Hirsch argued that curricula ought to emphasize a literacy of culture, a shared set of facts and ideas that educators define as "important," rather than making basic literacy skills the exclusive focus of our educational efforts. He believes that children ought to receive "core information," which he defined as those things that "American readers are assumed to have a general knowledge of" (p. 29). If we systematically begin imparting cultural literacy to children from the first grade forward, we will, Hirsch suggested, "ensure that everyone commands enough shared background knowledge to be able to communicate effectively with everyone else" (p. 32). This model represents another ideological extreme. It also emphasizes a particular aspect of the ELA domain, literature, at the expense of other dimensions such as skills and processes. In addition, it fails to address issues of scope and sequence, alignment, or both.

The process model is considered the most student centered and is especially concerned with the way each individual constructs knowledge from experience. Scholars working from this model see language use as developmental, encourage creativity and writing from an early age, and focus on students' understanding of the relationship between the writer's intent and the reader's response. Rosenblatt (1938), Britton (1972), and Moffett and Wagner (1983) are considered among the primary spokespersons for the process model, which provides much of the basis for integrated, literature-based instruction. Firmly grounded in a constructivist framework, process-oriented approaches draw from research on the process of writing, reader response theories, and social theories of reading comprehension. These conceptualizations are currently more ideologically mainstream than the conceptualizations underlying the previous models. However, this model still suffers from problems of content. Although it makes clear students' role as active participants in their own learning, it provides little guidance about what it is students should be processing and it fails to place curriculum in a K–12 sequences.

Since 1980, when Mandel categorized language arts curricula into these three models, there has been a steady stream of debate and conflict over which of these models will win the battle for the soul of language arts curriculum. Witness the proliferation of books dealing with the content issue alone— *What Is English?* (Elbow, 1990), *Redrawing the Boundaries: The Transformation of English and American Literacy Studies* (Greenblatt & Gunn, 1992), *English as a Discipline or Is There a Plot in This Play?* (Raymond, 1996); and *The Rise and Fall of English: Restructuring English as a Discipline* (Scholes, 1998). And, to be sure, new models continue to arise. For example, some have moved into a realm of curriculum as inquiry and conversation (e.g., Applebee, 1996; Harste, 1994; Short et al., 1996). The controversies about ELA curricula led Peter Elbow (1993) to conclude that ELA "seems to be more divided or disunified across levels than other disciplines" (p. 114). They have also led some, like Hawisher (1990), to call for an end to the false dichotomy between content and process and a move toward a balanced emphasis on the writer, the text, and the reader.

For those who are struggling with the state of the ELA curriculum, it is truly our winter of discontent. The challenge confronting us is how to bring order out of what appears to be chaos. E. O. Wilson (1998a) in "Back From Chaos" believes there is an ongoing fragmentation of knowledge and the resulting chaos is reflected in how we think about our own world. He believes that the key to unification is "consilience." The term comes from William Whewell who defined it as literally the "jumping together" of knowledge as a result of the linking of facts and fact-based theory across disciplines to create a common groundwork of explanation (Wilson, 1998b). Educators need to think about the unification of ELA into a K–12 curriculum. There is a curricular labyrinthine to conquer as they deal with issues of ideology, content, alignment, and equity, and if they are not careful they will wander hopelessly in the curricular maze searching for a way out. The first step is to determine the properties of an effective ELA curriculum, a concern that has been avoided far too long (Applebee, 1996).

## WHAT IS AN EFFECTIVE ELA CURRICULUM?

Curriculum development is not a neutral activity. The way the ELA curriculum is conceptualized has a critical impact on the way courses of study are designed; the types of materials selected; the types of assessments used; the forms of writing taught; and the learning strategies, techniques, or methods employed in the classrooms. The task is to conceptualize a useful, indeed a compelling, basis for the construction of an ELA curriculum. Careful thought and deliberation must be given to theoretical, as well as practical considerations, in putting together K–12 ELA curricula. We propose here a set of principles to guide the design and development of K–12 ELA curricula. As suggested by Applebee (1996), we draw these principles from research and practice, including our work with teachers, local districts, regional institutions, and state agencies. The four principles we believe provide the foundation for effective ELA curricula are (a) the use of a comprehensive conceptual framework, (b) the explicit identification of content, (c) a clear K–12 sequence of study, and (d) an aligned assessment system.

## A COMPREHENSIVE CONCEPTUAL FRAMEWORK: THE SOCIOCOGNITIVE PERSPECTIVE

Whether explicit or implicit, curricula represent different views of learning and knowing. A first step in curriculum development is establishing the perspective on learning and knowing that will provide the basis for future decision making. We have chosen what has become known as the "situative perspective" (Greeno,

1997; Greeno, Collins, & Resnick, 1996), which holds that learning is situated in particular physical and social contexts, social in nature, and distributed across the individual, other persons, and tools (Putnam & Borko, 2000). Traditional cognitive perspectives treat knowing as within the mind of the individual and learning as the acquisition of knowledge and skills thought to be applicable to a variety of settings. In contrast, "situative perspectives focus on interactive systems that include individuals as participants, interacting with each other as well as materials and representational systems" (Cobb & Bowers, 1999; see also Putnam & Borko, 2000, p. 4).

Using a situative perspective as a foundation, we then looked to perspectives on literacy and literacy learning that embody this view of learning and knowing. Given our sense of the need to rethink the content-process issue, we also looked for a view of literacy that deals directly with the relations between the situated nature of learning and disciplinary knowledge. At present, the sociocognitive view of literacy described by Langer (1987, 1991), comes closest to embodying the perspectives on learning, literacy, and knowing we want to advance in a K–12 ELA curriculum. Langer's sociocognitive perspective grows out of theory and research on language, literacy, and learning conducted in the areas of psychology, anthropology, and sociolinguistics (Langer, 1987, 1991). According to this view, literacy is the ability to think and reason like a literate person within a particular society. Literacy learning is socially based and cognition grows out of one's socially based experiences. Within social settings, both at home and in school, students learn how literacy is used, what literacy behaviors entail, and what literacy habits are to be cultivated. As children learn to engage in literate behaviors to serve the functions and reach the ends they see modeled around them, they become part of a community and what that community considers literate.

Langer's sociocognitive perspective has implications for the way that literacy learning and issues of schooling are addressed. It forces us to look at ways in which literacy is used, what is valued as knowing, how it is demonstrated and communicated, and the kind of thinking as well as content knowledge that result. This view makes prominent the role of language in the social context of learning, especially learning in a school context. As studies of language demonstrate there is a difference between language learning at home and at school (Gee, 1989; Heath, 1982, 1983). Both Heath and Gee support the notion that for children to be fully successful, they must be able to communicate in the language of school and the disciplines they are learning about. Children who fail at school often do not have access to the discourse communities necessary for school success (Cope & Kalantzis, 1993).

This sociocognitive perspective on literacy suggests three elements that are important to curriculum development: (a) the social context in which learning occurs, (b) the nature and structure of the content to be learned, and (c) the inclusion of cognitive skills that help students think more deeply about subject matter. Research and practice based on this perspective must be used to decide about the nature and structure of ELA curriculum and instruction. As Langer (1991) stated, "A sociocognitive view means . . . more attention is paid to the social purposes to which the literacy skills are being put—students learn best when they are trying to accomplish something that is personally and socially meaningful [and] to the structure as well as content of tasks that we ask students to undertake" (p. 18).

School-based literacy needs to help students think more deeply and more broadly about language and content and their use in socially purposeful activities. These activities must provide a pathway through the curriculum if the fragmentation and disconnected nature of learning that pervades K–12 education are to be avoided. This occurs when students are engaged in tasks that involve interpretation, evaluation, synthesis, or organization of information that gets applied to authentic contexts (Hillocks, 1999; Newmann, 1990; Onosko & Newmann, 1994). This approach to curriculum creates "minds on" learning where students use their creative power in thoughtful and reflective ways as they seek answers to authentic issues raised by the powerful ideas in the curriculum.

## Explicit Content

A second guiding principle in the creation and design of an effective K–12 ELA curriculum and one that is consistent with the tenets of a sociocognitive perspective is the identification of explicit content. As a subject area, ELA needs to be clear about what students need to know and be able to do. To accomplish this goal content must be explicit enough so that teachers clearly understand what it is students must learn, it cannot be amorphous or relative to what each individual teacher thinks it should be. Teachers play a vital and critical role in its development, however, no one teacher is the curriculum. In other words, to share content knowledge that is derived from a common curriculum, we need to decide what it is. This means carefully delineating the core concepts and principles targeted in the curriculum (Alexander, 1998; Hynd & Stahl, 1998; Matthews, 1994; West & Pines, 1985).

An example of this type of content is knowledge about the role and function of genre. Genre knowledge can be broken down into two broad categories, narrative and informational text. In turn, these two general categories can be subdivided into forms of narrative text (e.g., myth, historical fiction, and mystery) or forms of informational text (e.g., essay, report, and critique; Peters & Carlsen, 1989; Slater & Graves, 1989). It is also important to know how writers and speakers use the features of narrative and informational text to craft language in artful ways, features such as metaphors, similes, imagery, marginal notes, and subheadings. When writers or speakers create text, they also use conventions such as commas, periods, and organizational techniques. All of these elements help writers and speakers more effectively communicate with their intended audience.

The types of knowledge and skills we are describing here cannot be achieved purely from everyday experience but rather must be acquired, in some measure, through continuous and systematic instruction. Expertise must be developed and schemas expanded so students can acquire the foundational knowledge to formulate requisite generalizations and abstractions (Gagnon, 1989; VanSledright, 1996). Although the curriculum development process must explicitly formalize the agreed on body of knowledge, it is also important to keep in mind that domains like ELA are in the process of perpetual evolvement; they are not fixed or static bodies of knowledge. For curriculum development this means continual adjustments and revisions. In the end, curriculum must provide a sense of the content of ELA, which means it must be explicit enough to develop the internal skills, structures of knowledge, and routines to accomplish purposeful and thoughtful activities that are reflective of the educational context in which it is learned. Explicit content identified in the ELA curriculum must help students think more deeply and more broadly about language and content in purposeful ways (Alexander, 1998).

## Scope and Sequence

Teachers continually deplore the fact it is not always clear what they are responsible for teaching. They are often handed an anthology, basal, or list of novels, short stories, plays, poems, and essays to choose from, without being given a clear idea as to what content they are supposed to teach or to align with other grade levels. This leads to inefficient teaching. Teachers find themselves trying to teach students how to write an organized paragraph in ninth grade when students have been writing in paragraphs since early elementary school. We seem to teach some concepts over and over, where others are rarely addressed. The problem is not the teachers or materials; it is a lack of a road map through the curriculum.

A scope and sequence provides a developmental continuum as content knowledge progresses from simple to complex. In a review by Smagorinsky and Smith (1992) on the nature of content knowledge related to composition and literary understanding, they indicate that a continuum reflecting a "curricular pathway" is essential for curricular planning. This systematic approach ensures that concepts are learned over time. In fact, the more a student considers a given concept, adds to the concept, reorganizes the concept, or discusses the concept with others, the more highly connected to other concepts it becomes (Hynd & Stahl, 1998). To illustrate this point, consider the concept of metaphor, which is recursive in literary texts. In children's literature, simple comparisons are made to highlight key ideas in stories and novels. For example, Joan Blos (1990) uses metaphors in *Old Henry* to emphasize his eccentric nature. By the time students reach high school they encounter authors who use extended and more complex metaphors. *A Tale of Two Cities* by Charles Dickens (1859/1981) uses extended metaphors including an approaching storm or footsteps that progressively become louder to reinforce the theme of the impending French Revolution.

To ensure that students learn the language of the discipline that is called for in the sociocognitive perspective, content knowledge must be delineated by grade levels, developmental level, or both. Scope and sequence brings order and structure to the curriculum. We are not talking about a lockestep, mindless, inflexible structure prescribed by mastery learning in the 1970s and 1980s but rather a more flexible approach, one that involves conversations about the curriculum (Applebee, 1996; Myers, 1996). Teachers work within and across grade levels to determine their pathway through the curriculum. Decisions are not arbitrary and capricious but instead are focused and direct. Questions like "What should exemplary fourth-grade writing look like?" and "What content knowledge do students need to get them to this point?" are explored.

A central theme of research on cognition and learning is that conceptual power derives from taking a complex cognitive phenomenon and analyzing it into its underlying components (Anderson, Reder, & Simon, 1998). Wiggins and McTighe (1998) referred to this as designing down. In part, teacher conversations about the K-12 scope and sequence help ensure that content knowledge can be transferred from level to level. When there is no scope and sequence, the ELA curriculum is loosely organized and frequently becomes fragmented and disconnected; teachers only have a vague notion of what others are doing. When this occurs, there is nothing that ties learning expectations together other than a set of activities, a list of books, projects, writing assignments, or a common philosophy or methodology. There are no common expectations for learners except those that may be very board and overly general. Therefore, the sequencing of the explicit content to be learned and used is a critical element in the curriculum (Pirie, 1997).

## Alignment

With the increased demands for curricular accountability, there are accompanying demands for more direct alignment between curriculum and assessment (Bennett, Cribb, & Finn, 1999; Gross, 1999; Hirsch, 1999; Wiggins, 1991, 1993). Although the principle of alignment is one that many educators support, there are significant differences in how it is defined and operationalized (Johnston, 1999; Newmann & Associates, 1998; *Standards for the Assessment of Reading and Writing*, 1994; Wiggins, 1998). There are those who advocate a relativistic approach to alignment (Harp, 1994; Johnston, 1998, 1999; Murphy, 1998). In their view both the curriculum and the accompanying assessment tasks are whatever each individual teacher believes they should be. Those who maintain this perspective are often opposed to establishing districtwide parameters to guide the decision making about what types of assessments should be used as evidence of student learning. When this perspective prevails, there are no common assessment tasks or yardsticks for judging the quality of student work.

Others believe that alignment exists when, in fact, only a portion of the curriculum is assessed. This is often the situation when alignment is attributed to the administration of large-scale, paper-and-pencil tests that favor multiple-choice formats. Unlike good curricula, many of these tests deal primarily with lower order thinking skills and focus on trivial or insignificant information. There is minimal attempt to capture more complex cognitive performances and issues of authentic assesssment are almost never addressed with these types of tests. Often these tests are selected for their relatively low cost and high levels of reliability and not the extent to which they adequately evaluate the curriculum or capture authentic performances that represent what goes on in the world beyond the classroom.

A view of alignment that is consistent with the principles of explicit content and scope and sequence is one that requires a direct and systematic link between the content of the curriculum and the assessment tasks used to document student learning. With this approach, authentic content leads to authentic assessment (Peters, 1991). As Newmann et al. (1998) pointed out, authentic assessment is a consequence of a number of factors but especially curriculum that emphasizes the development of deep understanding of significant concepts, principles, and theories that are applied to significant and worthwhile problems and issues that have value beyond the school. What is particularly important about this view is that authentic assessment begins with a vision of intellectual achievement rather than a set of assessment procedures.

Documentation of student learning requires evidence of the construction of knowledge through disciplined inquiry to produce discourse, products, or performances that have meaning or value beyond success in the classroom. Because of the complex nature of the curriculum, assessment cannot be based on a unidimensional measure such as state assessments or commercial tests, but rather it requires a multilevel, multidimensional assessment system. The curriculum leads to specific parameters that provide guidelines for the development of common assessment tasks that share a common definition of quality. This approach to alignmnet is consistent with others advocating authenticity in assessment (Darling-Hammond, Ancess, & Falk, 1995; Glatthorn, 1999; Wiggins, 1989a, 1989b, 1991, 1993, 1998). Educators have a moral obligation to provide students, teachers, parents, policymakers, and community members with evidence of student learning that is based on common standards. When the parameters of the assessment are derived from a sound curriculum, there is less chance that the assessment will be trivialized and fragmented.

## A SOCIOCOGNITIVE K–12 ENGLISH LANGUAGE ARTS CURRICULUM

The purpose of this section is to provide an overview of a sociocognitive K–12 English language arts curriculum that is consistent with the four principles just described. The curriculum we present here represents a detailed and explicit way to capture the essence of ELA. This curriculum is derived from two primary sources, the Michigan Department of Education's ELA content standards and benchmarks and the work we have done with local districts in modifying these standards and benchmarks (*Michigan Curriculum Framework*, 1996; *Oakland Schools K-12 Model English Language Arts Curriculum*, 1999; Wixson, Peters, & Potter, 1997).[1]

The curriculum we describe comprises of four strands, 16 content standards, and 54 benchmarks (Table 41.1). The four

---

[1]All examples used in this chapter are from a model K–12 ELA curriculam developed at Oakland Intermediate School District, Waterford, MI, by Charles W. Peters and Julie Casteel.

TABLE 41.1. English Language Arts K–12 Curriculum: Strands and Content Standards

| Strands | | | |
|---|---|---|---|
| 1 | 2 | 3 | 4 |
| Genre, Craft, and the Conventions of Language | Literature and Understanding | Elements of Effective Communication | Skills, Strategies, Processes, and Dispositions |
| 1.1 Narrative Text<br>  1.1.1 Genre Characteristics<br>  1.1.2 Literacy Devices<br>  1.1.3 Core Genre<br>1.2 Informational Text<br>  1.2.1 Organizational Patterns<br>  1.2.2 Textual Features<br>  1.2.3 Core Genre<br>1.3 Author's Craft<br>  1.3.1 Written Narrative<br>  1.3.2 Written Expository<br>  1.3.3 Oral Narrative<br>  1.3.4 Oral Expository<br>1.4 Language Conventions<br>  1.4.1 Oral Language<br>  1.4.2 Written Language<br>  1.4.3 Spelling | 2.1 Key Concepts and Beliefs<br>  2.1.1 Key Concepts<br>  2.1.2 Beliefs and Values<br>2.2 Various Perspectives<br>  2.2.1 Cultural Perspectives<br>  2.2.2 Personal Perspective<br>  2.2.3 Author's Perspective | 3.1 Form, Purpose, and Audience Within the Classroom<br>  3.1.1 Written Narrative<br>  3.1.2 Written Expository<br>  3.1.3 Spoken Narrative<br>  3.1.4 Spoken Expository<br>3.2 Form, Purpose, and Audience Beyond the Classroom<br>  3.2.1 Written Narrative<br>  3.2.2 Written Expository<br>  3.2.3 Spoken Narrative<br>  3.2.4 Spoken Expository<br>3.3 Vocabulary<br>  3.3.1 Key Concepts, Values and Beliefs<br>  3.3.2 ELA Vocabulary<br>  3.3.3 General Vocabulary | 4.1 Word Recognition<br>  4.1.1 Concepts About Print<br>  4.1.2 Phonemic Knowledge<br>  4.1.3 Strategic Knowledge<br>  4.1.4 Fluency<br>4.2 Comprehension Strategies<br>  4.2.1 Text Structure Strategies<br>  4.2.2 General Comprehension Strategies<br>  4.2.3 Specific Comprehension Strategies<br>4.3 Writing Process<br>  4.3.1 Prewriting<br>  4.3.2 Drafting<br>  4.3.3 Revising<br>  4.3.4 Editing<br>  4.3.5 Fluency<br>4.4 Inquiry and Research<br>  4.4.1 Question Generation<br>  4.4.2 Use of Resources<br>  4.4.3 Analyzing and Organizing Information<br>  4.4.4 Written and Spoken Forms of Research<br>4.5 Monitoring<br>  4.5.1 Planning<br>  4.5.2 Regulating<br>  4.5.3 Evaluating<br>4.6 Critical Standards<br>  4.6.1 Individual<br>  4.6.2 Shared<br>4.7 Dispositions<br>  4.7.1 Reflectiveness<br>  4.7.2 Curiosity<br>  4.7.3 Flexibility<br>  4.7.4 Rationality |

strands are Genre, Craft, and the Conventions of Language; Literature and Understanding; Elements of Effective Communication; and Skills, Strategies, Processes, and Dispositions. Recognizing that every parsing of the domain of ELA is arbitrary in some way, these four strands do provide a systematic way to organize the curriculum because they represent the interrelationships among the basic components of the domain. Strand 1 identifies specific genres to be read or listened to, which also serve as models for writing and speaking; Strand 2 provides the ideas, problems, and issues that engage students; Strand 3 identifies the forms, audiences, and purposes for writing and speaking; and Strand 4 describes the skills, strategies, processes, and dispositions required to use and apply the content within the other strands. Each strand describes content at two levels: a general content level, which defines the focus of the content

standards, and a specific content level, which defines the focus of the benchmarks.

The strands, content standards, and benchmarks provide a detailed outline for the curriculum. Further elaboration is required at the local level, however, for the curriculum to become fully specified. Teachers engage in thoughtful conversation about what the emphasis should be at each particular level. They examine their own teaching practices and materials and determine what the specific content for each benchmark should be. In addition, they consider how it fits with the grade level before and after their own. For example, one of the benchmarks in our model requires attention to specific genres, their characteristics and features for each grade level. It is the responsibility of the district to determine which genres they wish to teach and how they fit with other components of the curriculum.

Because the content standards and benchmarks also call for the integration of reading and writing, teachers must also discuss which forms of writing they want students to produce at each grade level and how they will help make a connection between reading and writing. The example we present here is complete with illustrations of what the curriculum might include after such local conversations have taken place.

The content standards and benchmarks are designed to provide enough detail for the district to make specific content decisions without the frustration of trying to figure out what vague and overly general content standards mean or, conversely, trying to identify a long list of skills or procedures that become so numerous they are impossible to teach well. They provide an entry point for a series of conversations about the curriculum that focus on issues such as the big ideas or concepts to be covered within the context of specific literature, along with discussions about how the connections within and across grade levels are maintained, and how the integrated nature of the ELA curriculum is sustained across the strands. The section that follows provides a rationale for each of the four strands and accompanying content standards and benchmarks along with examples of the content standards and benchmarks aligned with each of the strands. This and the final section of this chapter also address the relations between the four principles of curriculum development outlined here and this sociocognitive K–12 ELA curriculum.

## Strand I: Genre, Craft, and the Conventions of Language

The first strand is Genre, Craft, and the Conventions of Language. Within this strand there are four content standards: Narrative Text (Content Standard 1.1), Informational Text (Content Standard 1.2), Author's Craft (Content Standard 1.3), and Language Convention (Content Standard 1.4). Narrative and informational text standards each focus on three types of content: specific genre characteristics, textual features and literary devices associated with the genre, and a list of genre explored at each particular grade level. The elements of craft standard identifies those textual features and literary devices students use in their writing and speaking. Although narrative and informational texts and elements of craft content standards all identify textual features and literary devices, there is an important difference between them. The textual features and literary devices in the narrative and informational text standards are introduced as features of text students should know; in the elements of craft standard these are the textual features and literary devices students are expected to use in their own writing. In other words, they are first introduced in the context of narrative and informational texts and from this list of textual features and literary devices, teachers identify the particular ones they believe students should be using in their own writing and speaking.[2]

Literary scholars and educational researchers have long recognized the influence that knowledge of the characteristics and structural features of different genres, and language and literary conventions have on learning. The findings are very clear and convincing, knowing how texts are structured helps students to better understand what texts do and how they do it (Anderson & Armbruster, 1984; Berkenkotter & Huckin, 1993; Kintsch & van Dijk, 1978; Kress, 1987; Mandler, 1984; Meyer, 1975; Peters & Carlsen, 1989; Rabinowitz, 1987; Rabinowitz & Smith, 1998; Scholes, 1985; Stein & Glenn, 1979). With respect to narrative texts, this means understanding the various narrative elements such as problem, conflict, and resolution and how the knowledge of their organization impacts understanding. For expository texts, it means understanding how the various organizational patterns such as cause and effect, theory and evidence, and compare and contrast are different from narrative text and how understanding these differences influences learning.

In a practical sense it means understanding that literary and expository texts are not read in the same way. Students orient themselves differently depending on the type of text they are reading. For example, in literary texts, authors create different audiences that provide different perspectives. Two of these are the *authorial audience*, the audience the author targets outside the text, and the *narrative audience*, the audience authors create within the text (Rabinowitz, 1987; Rabinowitz & Smith, 1998). When interpreting the text from the authorial perspective, students seek information about what the author means by interpreting certain signals or cues the author is sending about the characters in the story. For instance, in Elizabeth George Speare's novel, *The Sign of the Beaver* (1994), what message is she conveying about tolerating those who are culturally different, because the two main characters, Matt and Attean, come from different cultural groups? How does the reader feel about the treatment of Native Americans as they are depicted in the novel?

The narrative audience provides another perspective and what students must understand is that the narrative audience is a hypothetical, an audience created by the author in order to present different perspectives within the text. In John Steinbeck's (1945) *The Pearl* most of the novel is told through the eyes of the main character, Kino, and the narrator that speaks primarily to the audience outside the text. At strategic points the author lets other voices emerge; they come through some of the other characters in the book. In *The Pearl* this means certain events unfold through the eyes of Kino and the narrator, and others through the dialogue of other characters that are aimed at the audience within the text. This is the narrative audience and through these conversations and actions, the reader sees other perspectives, ones that are different from the authorial audience. Students need to understand the various voices created within narrative text and how they shape or influence meaning. By being aware of the difference, students gain additional insight by understanding how the narrator manipulates other characters and situations.

In contrast, organizational patterns are a feature that is important for understanding expository texts. For example, Slater and Graves (1989) listed description, sequence explanation,

---

[2] Craft as a concept in the curriculum is discussed in the next section.

compare–contrast, definition–examples, and problem–solution as typical organizational patterns. However, it is important to note that typically a single informational text may have many organizational patterns. For example, a chapter on plate tectonics within a science textbook could go from definitional and example to theory and evidence or a social studies chapter on the American Civil War could embed cause and effect within problem and solution. Still, what it important to keep in mind is that knowledge of how an informational text is organized and structured is critical to comprehension and writing. It is not merely that expository texts have distinct organizational patterns but that they are used differently in disparate subject areas and that this can impact student learning (Hynd, 1998). As Wineburg (1991) pointed out, differences in how subject areas present information in expository text influence the extent to which students understand the author's message. These differences can cause students to miss the nuances of the subtext which impacts meaning that is embedded in the types of materials subject area specialists such as historians use (e.g., documents, letters, speeches, diaries).

Scholars are urging educators to attend more systematically to the differences between narrative and expository texts, because these structural differences impact student performance. Research has pointed out that for many studetns, expository texts are more difficult to read than narrative text (Hiebert & Fisher, 1990; Langer, Applebee, Mullis, & Foertsch, 1990; Olson, 1985). This is especially important at the early grades where there seems to be a dearth of well-developed informational material in the ELA curriculum (Duke, 2000).

The content standards and benchmarks in this strand provide the general parameters for what students are to know and be able to do; however, the specific grade level content and the sequence in which it must be taught are determined at the local level. For example, Content Standard 1.2, Informational Text, provides has three identifiable components, which are articulated as benchmarks: Organizational Patterns (Benchmark 1.2.1), Textual Features (Benchmark 1.2.2), and Core Genre (Benchmark 1.2.3). The specific content for each of these benchmarks is identified at the local level. Table 41.2 provides an example of how teachers in one district defined the content for these benchmarks. As the examples in Table 41.2 reveal, the content for Grades 2 to 4 is clear and explicit. Specific organizational patterns, textual features, and genre are identified at each grade level.

Grammar, mechanics, and usage have always played a role in the ELA curricula. In fact, for 2 millennia grammar has been central to school curricula. It was the subject of one of the earliest textbooks, antedated only by Euclid's text about geometry (Hillocks, 1986b; Hillocks & Smith, 1991). As a result, a great deal of research in the past nine decades has been devoted to investigating the validity of studying grammar. The findings seem to indicate that the teaching of grammar in isolation has little impact on student writing (Hillocks, 1986a; Hunter & Wallace, 1995; Weaver, 1979, 1997). Typical of the research is a study

**TABLE 41.2. Benchmarks for Content Standard 1.2: Informational Text**

Benchmark 1.2.1: Organizational Patterns

| | |
|---|---|
| Second grade: | Knows simple compare and contrast, cause and effect, and sequence (chronology) patterns |
| Third grade: | Knows simple problem and solution and sequence (enumeration) patterns |
| Fourth grade: | Knows hierarchical levels (three levels of subordination: central ideas, key ideas, and supporting ideas), definition, description, example, and classification |

Benchmark 1.2.2: Textual Features

| | |
|---|---|
| Second grade: | Knows simple graphs, maps, diagrams, charts, and captions |
| Third grade: | Knows simple bold face, italics, table of contents, titles, marginal notes, time lines glossaries, and prefaces |
| Fourth grade: | Knows simple appendices, subheading (three levels), keys, legends, figures, bibliographies, and footnotes |

Benchmark 1.2.3: Core Genre

| | |
|---|---|
| Second grade: | Knows science and social studies magazines, social studies, science, and math textbooks |
| Third grade: | Knows simple how-to-books, simple reports, newspapers, science and social studies magazines, social studies, science, and math textbooks |
| Fourth grade: | Knows simple personal essay, biographies, simple descriptive essay, science and social studies magazines, social studies, science, and math textbooks |

conducted by Shaughnessy (1977) who found that to be useful a student's knowledge of grammatical terms must go well beyond the ability to state definitions. To be effective grammar, mechanics, and usage must be presented in an integrated manner within the context of writing. However, what must not be lost in the debate is that it is important for student writers to know a number of grammatical terms and their functions (Schuster, 1999). To this end, the focus of language conventions in the curriculum must be to help students understand how language works in relationship to the writing process.

## Strand 2: Literature and Understanding

The second strand, Literature and Understanding, is related to content presented in Strand 1.[3] Although it is essential to know the internal workings of texts, it is equally important to identify content that engages students in interpreting, analyzing, critiquing, applying, and responding personally to the big ideas or key concepts authors write about in literature and other texts. Strand 2, Literature and Understanding, is divided into two content standards: One emphasizes key concepts, and beliefs in literature (Content Standard 2.1), and the other emphasizes various interpretative perspectives, that is, cultural, personal, and

---

[3]When literature is used in conjunction with this strand it refers to narrative as well as informational material directly connected to the ELA curriculum.

authorial, associated with the understanding standing of the key concepts, and beliefs embedded within literature (Content Standard 2.2).

Historically, literature assumes an important place in the ELA curriculum but its role has never been without strife. Ever since Plato banned the poets from his ideal society, literature has been in trouble, and it is certainly no different in our present politically contentious climate (Probst, 1988). Despite historical or contemporary diffidence, literature remains a critical part of the ELA curriculum. Literature is important for several reasons. It explores a rich collection of ideas, issues, and problems that are central to the human condition; it provides the source of much of the best knowledge that humanity possesses; and it allows individuals to engage in ongoing dialogue or experience intellectual encounters with varying cultural beliefs. It provides the enduring ideas that raise questions about life that can be applied to the world outside the classroom (Applebee, 1991; Applebee, Burroughs, & Stevens, 2000; Burke, 1999; Langer, 1993; Purves, 1991; Purves, Rogers, & Soter, 1995; Rabinowitz & Smith, 1998).

We are not talking here about literature as either a body of knowledge to be imparted as either a narrow notion of literary heritage or of cultural or political perspectives guided by race, gender, or class. If either of these perspectives dominate the literature strand of the curriculum, one of two things will occur, an overemphasis on the past or an overemphasis on the present. Our approach takes a broader view, which encompasses both classic and contemporary literature. When a more balanced perspective prevails, the lives and values of all students are represented in the material they listen to, read, or view. As Applebee (1991) pointed out, when literature is thought of in this manner, it ensures that all students will find both a common culture and the unique voice that assures them that they too come from a tradition that gives them roots and offers a future.

The Literature and Understanding strand also incorporates the view that great literature is inspired in part by great ideas and that these great ideas raise issues and problems that recur and persist across time. An important part of this strand is to explore these ideas at times in students' development when they are likely to be invested in them (Applebee et al., 2000; H. Bloom, 1994; Delbanco, 1997; Ellis, 1997; Purves, 1991; Purves, Rogers, & Soter, 1995; Scholes, 1998). With this as a focus, an important function of this strand of the curriculum is to identify key concepts linked to issues and problems that can be used to raise engaging questions that can be analyzed from a variety of perspectives—political, ethical, cultural, social, or ideological.

Another equally important curricular component in this strand is building toward a more complex understanding of the various key concepts, values, beliefs, and perspectives in literature. Students must move through a cognitive sequence that takes into account not only the increasing complexity of the key concepts, beliefs, values, and diverse perspectives presented in various text but also the increasing complexity of the text. More specifically, students must be able to deal with the increasing complexity of vocabulary, sentence structure, text structures, text features such as literary devices and levels of subheadings, the embeddedness of the ideas, and the artistic conventions used by authors to highlight or reinforce the meaning of key concepts.

The recurrence of literary devices and other adjunct aids in this strand is an example of how strands are interrelated. In Strand 1 elements of the author's craft are identified in the Content Standard 1.3. The literary devices and textual features identified here are those students are expected to use in their own writing and come from content identified in Content Standards 1.1 and 1.2. In this strand, under the benchmark on author's perspective (Benchmark 2.2.3), literary devices and textual features are once again identified. However, the emphasis has changed from what the student is expected to do with them to how an author uses them to craft their ideas. Because most students do not pay attention to issues of craft, it is incumbent on the curriculum to make them explicit. When students understand how they function, they can make use of them in their own writing (L. Z. Bloom, 1995; Fletcher & Portalupi, 1998; Hillocks, 1995; Smagorinsky, 1993). In the content standard on various perspectives (2.2) students are expected to study both how an author uses literary devices and textual features to reinforce key concepts, values, and beliefs, and how they use them as elements of craft. In this sense they become both a tool for more depth of understanding as well as model for understanding how authors craft their texts.

Content Standard 2.1, Key Concepts and Beliefs, indicates that students should use contemporary and classic literature and other texts to identify, synthesize, compare, evaluate, and critique the key ideas, beliefs, and values found in them. This content standard has two benchmarks, Key Concepts (Benchmark 2.1.1) and Beliefs (Benchmark 2.1.2). Table 41.3 presents an example of the content represented for Benchmarks 2.1.1 and 2.1.2. The key concepts for Benchmark 2.1.1 and beliefs associated with those key concepts (Benchmark 2.1.2) that are central to their curriculum at each particular grade level must be identified at the local level. In our example three key concepts are identified for each grade level. For each of the three key concepts there is a focus question. The purpose of the focus question is to provide a context for studying the key concepts, one that is engaging to students (Newmann, 1992; Peters & Wixson, 1998; Wiggins & McTighe, 1998; for a detailed explanation of the role of focus questions in unit development, see Peters & Wixson, 1998).

Key beliefs for each of the three key concepts are also identified. The beliefs are connected to the key concepts and often become the basis for exploring different interpretative perspectives, such as how region, time, age, gender, and race influence its understanding (see Table 41.3). Focus questions connect the beliefs to the key concepts. For example, in one district, fourth-grade teachers identified cultural diversity as one of their three key concepts. Their focus question was "What is cultural diversity?" and their accompanying beliefs for cultural diversity were "self-reliance," "flexibility," and "acceptance." The focus question linking these beliefs to cultural diversity was "How have people from different cultures adapted to new cultures?" Focus questions such as these provide teachers with a specific direction.

It is the general structure of the curriculum that establishes the importance of studying classic and contemporary literature, the accompanying ideas, problems, and issues embedded within these text that become the catalyst for engaging

TABLE 41.3. Benchmarks for Content Standard 2.1: Understanding Key Concepts, and Beliefs

**Benchmark 2.1.1: Key Concepts**

Fourth grade: Compares themes, central ideas, key ideas, and supporting ideas from multiple text that represent various perspectives on problems and/or issues raised by focus questions

| *Key Concepts* | *Focus Questions* |
| --- | --- |
| Environmental preservation | What are some problems and issues related to the of the environment? |
| Courage | What is courage? |
| Cultural diversity | What is cultural diversity? |

Fifth grade: Analyzes themes, central ideas, key ideas, and supporting ideas from multiple text that represent various perspectives on problems and/or issues raised by focus questions

| *Key Concepts* | *Focus Questions* |
| --- | --- |
| Exploration | What does it mean to be an explorer? |
| Diversity | How has our understanding of diversity changed over time? |
| Adversity | What types of adversity do people face? |

Sixth grade: Evaluates themes, central ideas, key ideas, and supporting ideas from multiple text that represent various perspectives on problems and/or issues raised by focus questions

| *Key Concepts* | *Focus Questions* |
| --- | --- |
| Leadership | How do people demonstrate leadership? |
| Aspirations/goals | What barriers do people face when attempting to reach their goals? |
| Promise keeping | What kinds of promises are difficult to keep? |

**Benchmark 2.1.2: Beliefs and Values**

Fourth grade: Compares the beliefs and values that underlie our common heritage through focus questions

| *Beliefs and Values* | *Focus Questions* |
| --- | --- |
| Duty, cooperation, preservation | What principles are important to preserving the environment? |
| Bravery, hope, perseverance | How do people respond when faced with adversity? |
| Self-reliance, flexibility, shared acceptance | What common values are by different groups of people? |

Fifth grade: Analyzes the beliefs and values that underlie our common heritage through focus questions

| *Beliefs and Values* | *Focus Questions* |
| --- | --- |
| Prudent, courageous, adventurous | What qualities are needed to be an explorer? |
| Tolerant, empathetic, open-mindedness | Why is it important to consider different points of view? |
| Courageous, hopeful, respond optimistic | How do different people respond to adversity? |

Sixth grade: Evaluates the beliefs and values that underlie our common heritage through focus questions

| *Beliefs and Values* | *Focus Questions* |
| --- | --- |
| Dedication, integrity, thrustworthiness | What values underlie leadership? |
| Resolve, hopefulness, deliberation | What values and believes help one achieve their goals? |
| Fidelity, loyality, duty | What qualities would you look for within a person with whom you would share a personal secret? |

students as well as the focus on different interpretative perspectives. However, the literature and specific ideas, issues, and problems that will be studied are identified at the local level. When it is the expectation that the curriculum should produce greater depth of understanding, it is essential to clarify what students are acquiring depth about and this is what this strand does.

## Strand 3: Elements of Effective Communication

The Elements of Effective Communication strand identifies the forms, audiences, purposes for writing and speaking, and the vocabulary required for effective communication. It is in this strand that teachers identify the specific spoken and written products that students should be able to produce at designated grade levels. The identification and selection of these products are related to the content of the other two strands. In other words, the spoken and written products in this strand are aligned with the specific content of the other strands. A

student does not produce a written or spoken product unless it is modeled in Strand 1. For example, if persuasive speaking and writing are included at the eighth grade level as part of Strand 3, then they must also appear as an informational genre in Strand 1. In our model of the ELA curriculum reading, writing, listening, speaking, and viewing are inextricably linked which means that students need to read, view or listen to persuasive text in order to produce it. This ensures the necessary alignment between Strands 1 and 3. The specific ideas, problems, and issues emphasized in spoken and written products come from Strand 2.

Strand 3 is broken down into three content standards. Content Standard 3.1 is Form, Purpose, and Audience Within the Classroom. The audience for these products is the students and teacher(s) within the classroom. Content Standard 3.2 is Form, Purpose, and Audience Beyond the Classroom. The audience for these products is people outside the classroom. This is where authentic connections to the world outside the classroom are made. Content Standard 3.3, Vocabulary, focuses on expanding and using vocabulary that is essential for effective communication.

Research suggests that an important part of learning how the writing process works involves exploring exemplary models of writing, analyzing their characteristic elements, and then reproducing them. This type of knowledge allows writers to see the relations among content, form, and function. As the knowledge of content, form, and function increases, so does writing ability. Students must learn that each form of writing possesses a distinct set of traits and that as the form becomes more complex so must the knowledge of those forms (Applebee, 1986; Hillocks, 1982, 1984, 1986a, 1986b; Johannessen, Kahn, & Walter, 1982; Smagorinsky, 1986, 1991, 1992; Smith, 1984).

As Hillocks (1995) contended, the more complex the writing form the greater the demands for specialized types of knowledge. For example, writing a fable requires writers to develop strategies for producing personification, narration, and exaggeration. These considerations are different from other forms of writing such as the persuasive essay. As L. Z. Bloom (1999) suggested, examination of the persuasive essay suggests, argumentative writing requires a very different set of considerations when it comes to form, technique, and audience. However, both forms require different declarative and procedural knowledge of content and form. In other words, one does not write poems and memos in the same way.

These findings are consistent with genre theorists who maintain that the explicit teaching of text structures in writing is an essential component of learning how to write (Martin, Christie, & Rothery, 1987; Martin & Rothery, 1993). In fact, they call for the explicit breaking down of texts and the naming of formal structures so there is an emphasis on the explicit modeling of text and children's subsequent practice in the construction of specific kinds of texts. Martin and Rothery (1993) advocate a sequential process of learning rhetorical forms that engenders greater success with writing, and with school learning more generally. The curricular implications are important. Reading and writng must be connected so that learning a discipline also means learning its associated powerful genres.

An example of the more specific content associated with each standard is provided for Content Standard 3.2, Form, Purpose, and Audience Beyond the Classroom. The four benchmarks delineated in this content standard each focus on a different form, purpose, and audience. They are Written Narrative (3.2.1), Written Expository (3.2.2), Narrative Spoken (3.2.3), and Spoken Expository (3.2.4). Table 41.4 presents an example of the content represented for Benchmarks 3.2.1 and 3.2.3 that was identified by one local district.

Benchmark 3.2.1 identifies the specific narrative forms for purposes and audiences beyond the classroom at the seventh-, eighth-, and ninth-grade levels. One of the forms of narrative writing at the seventh grade is the myth. The decisions about what forms to include are guided by the content delineated in other standards. The rationale is that students should not be asked to use a particular form of writing unless they have seen exemplary models. In addition to identifying the form, Benchmark 3.2.1 also specifies possible themes for the myth, ones that come from the key concepts identified in Strand 2, Benchmark 2.1.1. Benchmark 3.2.1 also suggests a potential authentic audience, the school library. Students are also asked to

**TABLE 41.4. Benchmarks for Content Standard 3.2: Form Purpose and Audience Beyond the Classroom**

Benchmark 3.2.1: Written Narrative

Seventh grade: Writes a myth for the school library collection of student works. The theme of the myth should focus on tests of conscience individual face in their lives and how they are resolved. The myth should contain the following textual features: exaggeration; understatement; anthropomorphism; dialogue between characters; and connection among theme, setting, and selected literary devices.

Eighth grade: Writes a fictional diary entry for a children's magazine that describes a real historical event from American history. The event should center on dangerous circumstances that describe how characters responded them. The diary should contain the following textual features: character monologue, rising action, and internal conflicts connected to the theme of survival.

Ninth grade: Writes a piece of realistic fiction for a student publication that describes how two characters react differently to opportunities. The story should include the following textual features: complex theme, problem, conflict, metaphors, and similes.

Benchmark 3.2.3: Spoken Narrative

Eighth grade: Reads previously written poetry for a Parent–Teacher Association reflection contest. The poem should address conflicts that are an outgrowth of discovering one's identity. The presentation should contain the following elements of speaker's craft: visual cues to enhance imagery, facial expressions, and phrasing to emphasize key ideas.

Ninth grade: Performs an imaginative skit for a ninth-grade talent show that depicts individual who have difficulty facing reality (e.g., one who wants to be a professional athlete but lacks the physical prowess or one who wants to be a rock star but lacks musical ability). The imaginative skit should include the following elements of speaker's craft: inflection, rhythm, flow, simple irony, and mood.

use a variety of textual features or literary devices, all of which are specified in the curriculum (Benchmark 1.3.1). This means that students not only read myths (Benchmark 1.1.3) but also analyze aesthetic elements (Benchmark 2.2.3), learning how authors use literary devices to reinforce key ideas before they begin writing a myth. However, what makes this strand unique it that this is where students apply what they have learned in the other strands. Strand 3 places the emphasis on creating products or participating in a performance that are guided by content that has been explicitly identified in other strands. It is in this strand where the true integrated nature of the ELA curriculum is realized.

## Strand 4: Skills, Strategies, Process, and Dispositions

Our curriculum model includes a separate strand for skills, strategies, processes, and dispositions, because there is a tendency to let them fall through the cracks when they are not explicitly identified. The specific skills, strategies, processes, and dispositions are identified in relation to decisions about such things as the specific types of material students are expected to read, the complexity of the ideas they are expected to understand, and the forms of writing and speaking they are expected to produce. It is also recognized that some skills assume a more prominent position in the curriculum in the primary grades. Although at times the primary-grade curriculum may be more skills driven than content driven, it is also expected that skills are related to the other elements of the curriculum as much as possible. With this approach skills are not isolated elements of the curriculum. Instead, they are recursive in nature and designed to interact with all elements of the curriculum.

The general content of this strand has been known for many years and described in various syntheses of research, some focused on early literacy (Adams, 1990) and others on the entire developmental spectrum (Anderson, Hiebert, Scott, Wilkinson, & Silkinson, 1985). For example, *Becoming a Nation of Readers* (Anderson et al., 1985) simply stated that early literacy instruction should focus on oral language, concepts about the functions of printed language and communicating through writing, knowledge about letters and words, phonics strategies, oral and silent reading, and strategies for understanding and appreciating the content of what they are reading or listening to. It is no different at the secondary level where skills and strategies have been integrated within the teaching of literature and other texts (Burke, 1999; Harker, 1989; Hawisher, 1990; Langer, 1995; Probst, 1988; Purves et al., 1995; Smagorinsky & Smith, 1992). This general content is reflected in the seven content standards for Strand 4: Word Recognition (Content Strandard 4.1), Comprehension Strategies (Content Standard 4.2), Writing Process (Content Standard 4.3), Inquiry and Research (Content Standard 4.4), Monitoring (Content Standard 4.5), Critical Standards (Content Standard 4.6), and Dispositions (Content Standard 4.7).

The specific content of the benchmarks in this strand is related to the specific content of the benchmarks in this other three strands. Content Standard 4.3, the Writing Process, provides an example of specific content defined by a group of teachers that is consistent with the examples provided for the other three strands. There are five benchmarks delineated in this content standard, each of which focuses on a different part of the writing process. Benchmarks 4.3.2, Drafting, and 4.3.3, Revising, identify specific skills needed for the specific forms of writing that are identified in the curriculum. For example, in third grade one suggestion is for using foreshadowing. The suggestion is targeted at creating suspense in the context of a mystery, because it is one of the narrative forms of writing at the third-grade level. Another recommendation suggests using subheadings to designate three levels of subordination. Subheadings are used because they are specified as one of the crafting elements for expository text at this level and should therefore be something students are watching for as they revise particular forms of writing. In other words, skills and strategies for drafting and revising are contextualized by the curriculum and are not checklists or generic statements that tend to be decontextualized.

Content Standard 4.1, Word Recognition, provides an example of specific content defined by a group of teachers that is focused on foundational skills. There are four benchmarks delineated in this content standard, each of which focuses on an aspect of word recognition. They are Concepts About Print (Benchmark 4.1.1), Phonemic Knowledge (Benchmark 4.1.2), Strategic Knowledge (Benchmark 4.1.3), and Fluency (Benchmark 4.1.4).[4] Table 41.5 presents an example of the

TABLE 41.5. Benchmarks for Content Standard 4.1:
Word Recognition (First Grade)

Benchmark 4.1.1: Concepts About Print

- Understands that text is written by other people
- Recognizes different forms of texts (e.g., signs, comics, books, newspapers)

Benchmark 4.1.2: Phonemic Knowledge

- Decodes phonetically regular one-syllable words in texts (phonemic segmentation)
- Matches known clusters of letters in unknown words
- Knows initial and final sounds
- Knows consonants, consonant blends, and consonant digraphs
- Knows word families (phonograms)

Benchmark 4.1.3: Strategic Knowledge

- Self-corrects when incorrectly identified word does not fit with clues provided by the letters in the word or the context surrounding the word
- Uses picture clues to get meaning from text
- Asks others for help with unknown words
- Notices when difficulties are encountered in understanding text
- Draws on knowledge of letter-sound relationships when trying to identify unknown words (sounds out, attempts to break words into syllables)
- Asks others for help with meaning and pronunciation of words

Benchmark 4.1.4: Fluency

- Reads aloud independently unfamiliar books appropriate for the grade level with 95% word recognition accuracy
- Knows grade level specific sight words
- Uses the cues of punctuation, including commas, periods, question marks, and quotation marks, as a guide in getting meaning
- Recognizes 150 common, irregularly spelled words by sight (e.g., have, said, where, two)

---

[4]Content Standard 4.1, Word Recognition, only applies to Grades K through 5. By the end of Grade 5 all students are expected to have all the requisite knowledge to be successful at word recognition. Benchmark 4.1, Concepts About Print, applies only to Grades K through 1 and Benchmark 4.4 applies only to Grades K through 3.

content represented by Content Standard 4.1, Benchmarks 4.1.1 through 4.1.4, for the first grade. For example, in first grade there is a great deal to learn about word recognition (see Table 41.5). At this level, it is likely to be important to identify other elements of the curriculum (e.g., genre, forms of writing, key concepts, etc.) that provide the best vehicle for teaching word recognition content. For example, predictable books may be a genre that provides the opportunity for students to learn about using picture clues, whereas alphabet books may be better for reinforcing learning about sound–letter relations.

The role of the curriculum is to ensure that skills, strategies, processes, and dispositions are not decontextualized. This means that all ELA teachers, irrespective of their level, have an obligation to teach skills in relation to the other strands of the ELA curriculum.

## DISCUSSION

In the previous section we described a sociocognitive model of a K–12 ELA curriculum that is based on principles that are essential for the development of comprehensive, unified curricula. It is also important to recognize that curriculum development of this nature requires a variety of resources including time, money, and access to knowledgeable teachers with the disposition to engage in this type of activity.

Developing curricula in the manner described here is not an easy process; it takes both money and time. Financial resources are needed to support released time for teachers to develop the curriculum, conduct professional development that ensures all teachers understand and can implement the curriculum, identify any new materials that may be required to teach the curriculum, and develop a districtwide assessment system that documents student learning. These activities are also very time consuming.

Typically, the first phase of the curriculum development process, clarifying the meaning of the strands, standards, and benchmarks takes approximately a year. During the first year, K–12 teachers meet at least 1 day a month to work through the standards and benchmarks identifying the content for each grade level. The goal is not to produce lists of skills, books, or forms of writing but rather a coherent, systematic flow of content. In other words, a curricular road map is developed that allows teachers and students to navigate their way through it. This provides teachers, students, parents, policymakers, and community members a clear and concrete idea of what students are expected to learn at each leave of schooling. In the subsequent phases teachers share the curriculum with their colleagues, write common units based on the benchmarks, develop common assessment tasks aligned with the benchmarks, acquire needed materials and other instructional resources, and revisit and revise the curriculum when necessary.

Perhaps most important, the type of curriculum development described here requires teachers to possess a collective knowledge of the content identified by each of the benchmarks so they can translate abstract concepts into concrete examples of explicit grade-level content. In addition, teachers must be knowledgeable about their own practice and have the ability to communicate with others about what best practice looks like relative to the benchmarks in the curriculum. Because an important part of the curriculum development process is the conversations that occur among teachers, they must also possess certain dispositions (e.g., flexibility, curiosity, reflectivity, and perseverance) that will ensure the conversation moves forward in a productive manner. Such conversation also requires a commitment to a common vision and perseverance to see the process through to the end. Although the process is not easy, the alternative likely means returning to the status quo, a curriculum that is perceived by many as woefully inadequate.

## THE IMPORTANCE OF THE GUIDING PRINCIPLES

As Applebee (1996) maintained, an effective curriculum is guided by principles based on research and practice. The curriculum described in the previous section is guided by four principles: (a) the use of a comprehensive conceptual framework, (b) the explicit identification of content, (c) a clear K–12 sequence of study, and (d) an assessment system aligned with the curriculum. These principles are important because they have an impact on the design of courses of study; the type of materials selected; the type of assessments used; the forms of writing taught; and the learning strategies, techniques, or methods employed in the classrooms.

The influece of the sociocognitive conceptual framework used in this curriculum development effort can be seen in several ways. For example, this conceptual framework calls for attention to both the content of ELA and the skills, strategies, processes, and dispositions essential to successful performance in this domain. This conceptual framework also points to curricula that promote engagement in authentic activities which help students think more deeply about subject matter. Almost by definition, the tenet of this conceptual framework dealing with the social nature of learning is more likely to be apparent in instruction than in curriculum. However, the process of identifying specific content at the local level does reflect the need to consider the social context as a factor in fully instantiating the curriculum.

Similarly, the principles of explicitness and sequence are used to guide decisions about the way grade level specific content is identified. Because of the need for a coherent progression of content, careful thought is given to how concepts are linked together so that students form an interconnected body of knowledge. The curriculum is scaffolded so that students see the connections among its various components. The interconnection among concepts allows students to formulate principles and generalizations that deepen their knowledge of the domain as they traverse the curriculum and makes the content more overt. Adherence to the principles of explicitness and sequence helps guide the decision making process in a very direct way; it requires teachers to be clear and explicit about what the content is so students can progress successfully through the curriculum.

The principle of alignment means that the assessment tasks come from the curriculum. This calls for an examination of the benchmarks to determine what they suggest about the various types of assessments that should be used. Written and spoken products that define exemplary performance at each grade are identified (i.e., Strand 3, Content Standards 3.1 and 3.2). The alignment principle is also useful in the selection of rubrics, which need to be directly linked to the benchmarks in the curriculum. With this principle, local districts gain control over the assessment process.

In conclusion, we believe that adherence to the four guiding principles described in this chapter will go a long way toward addressing the problems associated with current and past ELA curricular models. Current and past ELA curricular models often address some, but not all, of the principles outlined here. They often suffer from overemphasis on a particular area within the language arts, or a particular developmental level, or an ideology that is ill suited for the development of a full, rich curriculum. When all four principles are addressed by a given model, the chances are greatly increased that it will not suffer from the problems of content, ideological extremism, or alignment.

# References

Adams, M. J. (1990). *Beginning to read: Thinking and learning about print.* Cambridge, MA: MIT Press.

Alexander, P. A. (1998). The nature of disciplinary and domain learning: The knowledge, interest, and strategic dimensions of learning from subject matter text. In C. R. Hynd (Ed.), *Learning from text across conceptual domains* (pp. 263–287). Mahwah, NJ: Lawrence Erlbaum Associates.

Alter, R. (1989). *The pleasures of reading in an ideological age.* New York: Simon & Schuster.

Anderson, J. R., Reder, L. M., & Simon, H. A. (1998). Radical constructivism and cognitive psychology. In D. Ravitch (Ed.), *Brookings papers on educational policy* (pp. 227–278). Washington, DC: Brookings Institute Press.

Anderson, R. C., Hiebert, E., Scott, J. A., & Silkinson, A. G. (1985). *Becoming a nation of readers: The report of the commission on reading.* Washington, DC: National Institute of Education.

Anderson, T. H., & Armbruster, B. B. (1984). Content area textbooks. In R. C. Anderson, J. Osborne, & R. J. Tierney (Eds.), *Learning to read in American schools: Basal readers and content texts* (pp. 193–226). Hillsdale, NJ: Lawrence Erlbaum Associates.

Apple, M. W. (1990). *Ideology and curriculum* (2nd ed.). New York: Routledge.

Applebee, A. N. (1986). Problems in process approaches: Toward a reconceptualization of process instruction. In A. R. Petrosky & D. Bartholmae (Eds.), *The teaching of writing: Eighty-Fifth yearbook of the National Society for the Study of Education* (Vol. 85, pp. 95–113). Chicago: National Society for the Study of Education.

Applebee, A. N. (1991). Literature: Whose heritage? In E. H. Hiebert (Ed.), *Literacy for a diverse society: Perspectives, practices, and policies* (pp. 228–236). New York: Teachers College Press.

Applebee, A. N. (1996). *Curriculum as conversation: Transforming traditions of teaching and learning.* Chicago: University of Chicago Press.

Applebee, A. N. (1999). Building a foundation for effective teaching and learning of English: A personal perspective on thirty years of research. *Research in the Teaching of English, 33*(4), 352–366.

Applebee, A. N., Burroughs, R., & Stevens, A. S. (2000). Creating continuity and coherence in high school literature curricula. *Research in the Teaching of English, 34*(3), 369–428.

Aristotle (1945). *Politics* (Ernest Baker, Translator). New York: Oxford University Press.

Atwell-Vasey, W. (1998). Psychoanalytic-feminism and the powerful teacher. In W. F. Pinar (Ed.), *Curriculum: Toward new identities* (Vol. 12, pp. 143–156). New York: Garland.

Bennett, W. J., Cribb, J. T. G., Jr., & Finn, C. E., Jr. (1999). *The educated child: A parent's guide preschool through eighth grade.* New York: Free Press.

Berkenkotter, C., & Huckin, T. N. (1993). Rethinking genre from a sociocognitive perspective. *Written Communication, 10*(4), 475–509.

Beyer, L. E., & Apple, M. W. (1998). Values and politics in the curriculum. In L. E. Beyer & M. W. Apple (Eds.), *The curriculum: Problems, politics, and possibilities* (2nd ed., pp. 3–20). Albany: State University of New York Press.

Beyer, L. E., & Liston, D. P. (1996). *Curriculum in conflict: Social visions, educational agendas, and progressive school reform.* New York: Teachers College Press.

Bloom, A. (1987). *The closing of the American mind.* New York: Simon & Schuster.

Bloom, B. (1968). Learning for mastery. *Evaluation Comment, 1,* 1–22. University of California at Los Angeles: Center for the Study of Evaluation of Instructional Programs.

Bloom, B. (1981). *All our children learning.* New York: Macmillan.

Bloom, H. (1994). *The Western canon: The books and school of the ages.* New York: Harcourt Brace.

Bloom, L. Z. (1995). Textual terror, textual power: Teaching literature through writing literature. In A. Young & T. Fulwiler (Eds.), *When writing teachers teach literature: Bringing writing to reading* (pp. 77–86). Portsmouth, NH: Boynton/Cook.

Bloom, L. Z. (1999). The essay canon. *College English, 61*(4), 401–430. Braddock, R., Lloyd-Jones, R., & Schoer, L. (1963). *Research on written composition.* Champaign, IL: National Council of Teachers of English.

Blos, J. W. (1990). *Old Henry.* New York: Morrow, Williams.

Britton, J. (1972). *Language and learning.* Harmondsworth, Middlesex, England: Penguin.

Burke, J. (1999). *The English teacher's companion: A complete guide to classroom, curriculum, and the profession.* Portsmouth, NH: Boynton/Cook.

Cheney, L. V. (1987). *American memory: A report on the humanities in the nation's public schools.* Washington, DC: U.S. Government Printing Office.

Cobb, P., & Bowers, J. S. (1999). Cognitive and situated learning perspectives in theory and practice. *Educational Researcher, 28,* 4–15.

Cope, B., & Kalantzis, M. (Eds.) (1993). *The powers of literacy: A genre approach to teaching writing.* Pittsburg: Falmer Press.

Darling-Hammond, L., Ancess, J., & Falk, B. (1995). *Authentic assessment in action.* New York: Teachers College Press.

de Castell, S., & Bryson, M. (1998). Don't ask; don't tell: "Sniffing out queers" in education. In W. F. Pinar (Ed.), *Curriculum: Toward new identities* (Vol. 12, pp. 233–252). New York: Garland.

Delbanco, A. (1997). *Required reading: Why our American classics matter now.* New York: Farrar, Straus & Giroux.

Dickens, C. (1981). *A tale of two cities*. New York: Bantam Doubleday. (Original work published 1859)

Duke, N. K. (2000). 3.6 minutes per day: The scarcity of informational texts in first grade. *Reading Research Quarterly, 35*(2), 202-224.

Elbow, P. (1990). *What is English?* New York: Modern Language Association of America.

Elbow, P. (1993). The war between reading and writing—And how to end it. *Rhetoric, 12*(1), 5-24.

Ellis, J. M. (1997). *Literature lost: Social agendas and the corruption of the humanities*. New Haven, CT: Yale University Press.

Farrell, E. J. (1991). Instructional models for English language arts, K–12. In J. Flood, J. M. Jensen, D. Lapp, & J. R. Squire (Eds.), *Handbook of research on teaching the English language arts* (pp. 63-84). New York: Macmillan.

Fletcher, R., & Portalupi, J. (1998). *Craft lessons: Teaching writing K–8*. York, ME: Stenhouse.

Gagnon, P. (Ed.) (1989). *Historical literacy: The case for history in American education*. New York: Macmillan.

Gee, J. P. (1989). What is literacy? *Journal of Education, 171*(1), 18-25.

Gehrke, N. J., Knapp, M. S., & Sirotnik, K. A. (1992). In search of the school curriculum. In G. Grant (Ed.), *Review of research in education* (Vol. 18, pp. 51-110). Washington, DC: American Educational Research Association.

Glatthorn, A. A. (1999). *Performance standards and authentic learning*. Larchmont, NY: Eye on Education.

Greenblatt, S., & Gunn, G. (Eds.). (1992). *Redrawing the boundaries: The transformation of English and American literary studies*. New York: Modern Language Association of America.

Greeno, J. G. (1997). On claims that answer the wrong questions. *Educational Researcher, 26,* 5-17.

Greeno, J. G., Collins, A. M., & Resnick, L. B. (1996). Cognition and learning. In D. Berlinger & R. Calfee (Eds.), *Handbook of educational psychology* (pp. 15-46). New York: Macmillan.

Gross, M. L. (1999). *The conspiracy of ignorance: The failure of American public schools*. New York: HarperCollins.

Harker, W. J. (1989). Information processing and the reading of literary texts. *New Literary History, 20*(2), 465-481.

Harp, B. (Ed.) (1994). *Assessment and evaluation for student centered learning* (2nd ed.). Norwood, MA: Christopher-Gordon.

Harste, J. C. (1994). Literacy as curricular conversation about knowledge, inquiry, and morality. In R. B. Ruddell, M. R. Ruddell, & H. Singer (Eds.), *Theoretical models and processes of reading* (4th ed., pp. 1220-1244). Newark, DE: International Reading Association.

Hatcher, T. (1999). Dilemmas of theory, design, and practice in school improvement: Editor's introduction. *Peabody Journal of Education, 74*(1), 1-11.

Hawisher, G. E. (1990). Content knowledge versus process knowledge: A false dichotomy. In G. E. Hawisher & A. O. Soter (Eds.), *On literacy and teaching: Issues in English education* (pp. 1-18). Albany: State University of New York Press.

Heath, S. B. (1982). What no bedtime story means: Narrative skills at home and at school. *Language in Society, 11,* 49-76.

Heath, S. B. (1983). *Ways with words: Language, life, and work in communities and classroom*. New York: Cambridge University Press.

Hiebert, E. H., & Fisher, C. W. (1990). Whole language: Three themes for the future. *Educational Leadership, 47*(6), 62-64.

Hillocks, G. J. (1982). The interaction of instruction, teacher comment, and revision in teaching the composing process. *Research in the Teaching of English, 17,* 261-278.

Hillocks, G. J. (1984). What works in teaching composition: A meta-analysis of experimental treatment studies. *American Journal of Education, 92,* 133-170.

Hillocks, G. J. (1986a). *Research on written composition: New directions for teaching*. Urbana, IL: National Conference on Research in the Teaching of English and ERIC Clearinghouse on Reading and Communication Skills.

Hillocks, G. J. (1986b). The writer's knowledge: Theory, research, and implications for practice. In A. Petrosky & D. Bartholomae (Eds.), *The teaching of writing: Eighty-Fifth yearbook of the National Society for the Study of Education* (Vol. 85, pp. 71-94). Chicago: National Society for the Study of Education.

Hillocks, G. J. (Ed.) (1995). *Teaching writing as reflective practice*. New York: Teachers College Press.

Hillocks, G. J. (1999). *Ways of thinking, ways of teaching*. New York: Teachers College Press.

Hillocks, G. J., & Smith, M. W. (1991). Grammar and usage. In J. Flood, J. M. Jensen, D. Lapp, & J. R. Squire (Eds.), *Handbook of research on teaching the English language arts* (pp. 591-603). New York: Macmillan.

Hirsch, E. D. (1987). *Cultural literacy*. New York: Doubleday.

Hirsch, E. D. (1996). *The schools we need: Why we don't have them*. New York: Doubleday.

Hirsch, E. D. (1999, November 4). One curriculum for New York. *The New York Times,* p. A27.

Hirsch, E. D., Jr. (2000). The tests we need. *Educational Week, 19*(21), 64, 39-41.

Hunter, S., & Wallace, R. (Eds.) (1995). *The place of grammar in writing instruction*. Portsmouth, NH: Boynton/Cook.

Hynd, C. R. (Ed.) (1998). *Learning from text across conceptual*. Mahwah, NJ: Lawrence Erlbaum Associates.

Hynd, C. R., & Stahl, S. A. (1998). What do we mean by knowledge and learning? In C. R. Hynd (Ed.), *Learning from text across conceptual domains* (pp. 15-44). Mahwah, NJ: Lawrence Erlbaum Associates.

Jencks, C., & Phillips, M. (Eds.) (1998). *The black-white test score gap*. Washington, DC: Brookings Institute Press.

Johannessen, L. R., Kahn, E. A., & Walter, C. C. (1982). *Designing and sequencing prewriting activities*. Urbana, IL: National Council of Teachers of English and ERIC Clearinghouse on Reading and Communication Skills.

Johnston, P. (1998). The consequences of the use of standardized tests. In S. Murphy (Ed.), *Fragile evidence: A critique of reading assessment* (pp. 89-101). Mahwah, NJ: Lawrence Erlbaum Associates.

Johnston, P. (1999). *Unpacking literate "achievement"* (Report Series 12007). Albany, NY: National Research Center on English Learning & Achievement.

Kintch, W., & van Dijk, T. A. (1978). Toward a model of discourse comprehension and production. *Psychological Review, 85,* 363-394.

Kliebard, H. M. (1998). The effort to reconstruct the modern American curriculum. In L. E. Beyer & M. W. Apple (Eds.), *The curriculum: Problems, politics, and possibilities* (2nd ed., pp. 21-33). Albany: State University of New Press.

Kress, G. (1987). Genre in a social theory of language: A reply to John Dixon. In I. Reid (Ed.), *The place of genre in learning* (pp. 35-45). Geelong, Australia: Deakin University Press.

Langer, J. A. (1987). A sociocognitive perspective on literacy. In J. Langer (Ed.), *Language, literacy, and culture: Issues of society and schooling* (pp. 1-20). Norwood, NJ: Ablex.

Langer, J. A. (1991). Literacy and schooling: A sociocognitive perspective. In E. A. Hiebert (Ed.), *Literacy for a diverse society: Perspectives, practices, and policies* (pp. 9-27). New York: Teachers College Press.

Langer, J. A. (1993). Discussion as exploration: Literature and the horizon of possibilities. In G. E. Newell & R. K. Durst (Eds.), *Exploring* texts: The role of discussion and writing in the teaching and learning of literature (pp. 23–44). Norwood, MA: Christopher-Gordon.

Langer, J. A., (1995). *Envisioning literature: Literary understanding and literature instruction.* New York: Teachers College Press.

Langer, J. A., Applebee, A. N., Mullis, I. V. S., & Foertsch, M. A. (1990). *Learning to read in our nation's schools: Instruction and achievement in 1988 at Grades 4, 8, and 12.* Princeton, NJ: Educational Testing Service.

Mandel, B. J. (Ed.) (1980). *Three language arts curriculum models: Prekindergarten through college.* Urbana, IL: National Council of Teachers of English.

Mandler, J. M. (1984). *Stories, scripts, and scenes: Aspects of schema theory.* Hillsdale, NJ: Lawrence Erlbaum Associates.

Martin, J. R., Christie, F., & Rothery, J. (1987). Social processes in education: A reply to Sawyer & Watson (and others). In I. Reid (Ed.), *The place of genre in learning: Current debates* (pp. 58–82). Geelong, Australia: Deakin University Press.

Martin, J. R., & Rothery, J. (1993). Grammar: Making meaning in writing. In B. Cope & M. Kalantzis (Eds.), *The powers of literacy: A genre approach to teaching writing* (pp. 137–153). New York: Falmer Press.

Matthews, M. R. (1994). *Science teaching: The role of history and philosophy of science.* New York: Routledge.

McDonald, J. P. (1999). Redesigning curriculum: New conceptions and tools. *Peabody Journal of Education, 74*(1), 12–28.

Meyer, B. J. F. (1975). *The organization of prose and its effects on memory.* Amsterdam: North-Holland.

*Michigan curriculum framework* (1996). Michigan Department of Education, Lansing, MI.

Moffett, J., & Wagner, B. J. (1983). *Student-centered language arts and reading, K-13: A handbook for teachers* (3rd ed.). Boston: Houghton Mifflin.

Murphy, S. (Ed.) (1998). *Fragile evidence: A critique of reading assessment.* Mahwah, NJ: Lawrence Erlbaum Associates.

Myers, M. (1996). *Changing our minds: Negotiating English and literacy.* Urbana, IL: National Council of Teachers of English.

Newmann, F. M. (1990). A test of higher order thinking in social studies: Persuasive writing on constitutional issues using the NAEP approach. *Social Education, 18,* 369–373.

Newmann, F. M. (1992). Higher order thinking and prospects for classroom thoughtfulness. In F. M. Newmann (Ed.), *Student engagement and achievement in American secondary schools.* New York: Teachers College Press.

Newmann, F. M., & Associates (Eds.) (1998). *Authentic achievement: Restructuring schools for intellectual quality.* San Francisco: Jossey-Bass.

*Oakland Schools K-12 model English language arts curriculum* (1999). Oakland Intermediate School District, Waterford, MI.

Olson, M. W. (1985). Text type and reader ability: The effects of paraphrase and text-based inference questions. *Journal of Reading Behavior, 65,* 109–117.

Onosko, J. J., & Newmann, F. M. (1994). Creating more thoughtful learning environments. In J. N. Mangieri & C. C. Block (Eds.), *Creating powerful thinking teachers and students: Diverse perspectives.* New York: Harcourt Brace.

Peters, C. W. (1991). You can't have authentic assessment without authentic content. *The Reading Teacher, 44*(8), 590–592.

Peters, C. W., & Carlsen, M. (1989). Using a literary framework to teach mysteries. In K. D. Muth (Ed.), *Children's comprehension of text: Research into practice* (103–139). Newark, DE: International Reading Association.

Peters, C. W., & Wixson, K. K. (1998). Aligning curriculum, instruction, and assessment in literature-based approaches. In T. E. Raphael &

K. H. Au (Eds.), *Literature-based instruction: Reshaping the curriculum* (pp. 261–284). Norwood, MA: Christopher-Gordon.

Pinar, W. F. (1996). *Understanding curriculum: An introduction to the study of historical and contemporary curricular discourses* (Vol. 17). New York: Lang.

Pirie, B. (1997). *Reshaping high school English.* Urbana, IL: National Council of Teachers of English.

Probst, R. E. (1988). *Response and analysis: Teaching litreature in junior and senior high school.* Portsmouth, NH: Boynton/Cook.

Purves, A. C. (1991). The school subject literature. In J. Flood, J. M. Jensen, D. Lapp, & J. R. Squire (Eds.), *Handbook of research on teaching the English language arts* (pp. 674–680). New York: Macmillan.

Purves, A. C., Rogers, T., & Soter, A. O. (1995). *How porchpines make love: Vol. III. Readers, texts, cultures, in the response-based literature classroom.* White Plains, NY: Longman.

Putnam, R. T., & Borko, H. (2000). What do new view of knowledge and thinking have to say about research on teacher learning? *Educational Researcher, 29,* 4–15.

Rabinowitz, P. J. (1987). *Before reading: Narrative conventions and the politics of interpretation.* Ithaca, NY: Cornell University Press.

Rabinowitz, P. J., & Smith, M. W. (1998). *Authorizing readers: Resistance and respect in the teaching of literature.* New York: Teachers College Press.

Ravitch, D., & Finn, C. E. (1987). *What do our 17-year-olds know? A report on the first national assessment of history and literature.* New York: Harper & Row.

Ravitch, D., & Viteritti, J. R. (Eds.) (1999). *New schools for a new century: The redesign of urban education.* New Haven, CT: Yale University Press.

Raymond, J. C. (Ed.) (1996). *English as a discipline or is there a plot in this play?* Tuscaloosa: University of Alabama Press.

Rosenblatt, L. M. (1938). *Literature as exploration.* New York: Appleton-Century (New York: Noble & Noble, Modern Language Association, 1983 [4th ed.]).

Scholes, R. (1985). *Textual power: Literary theory and the teaching of English.* New Haven, CT: Yale University Press.

Scholes, R. (1998). *The rise and fall of English: Restructuring English as a discipline.* New Haven, CT: Yale University.

Scholes, R. (1999). Mission impossible. *English Journal, 68*(6), 28–35.

Schuster, E. H. (1999). Reforming English language arts: Let's trash the tradition. *Phi Delta Kappan, 80,* 518–524.

Shaughnessy, M. P. (1977). *Errors and expectations: A guide for the teacher of basic writing.* New York: Oxford University Press.

Short, K. G., Schroeder, J., Laird, J., Kauffman, G., Ferguson, M. J., & Crawford, K. M. (1996). *Learning together through inquiry: From Columbus to integrated curriculum.* York, ME: Stenhouse.

Slater, W. H., & Graves, M. F. (1989). Research on expository text: Implications for teachers. In K. D. Muth (Ed.), *Children's comprehension of text: Research into practice* (pp. 103–139). Newark, DE: International Reading Association.

Smagorinsky, P. (1986). An apology for structured composition instruction. *Written Communication, 3,* 105–121.

Smagorinsky, P. (1991). The writer's knowledge and the writing process: A protocol analysis. *Research in the Teaching of English, 25,* 339–364.

Smagorinsky, P. (1992). How reading model essays affects writers. In J. W. Irwin & M. A. E. Doyle, *Reading writing connections: Learning from research* (pp. 35–44). Newark, DE: International Reading Association.

Smagorinsky, P. (1993). Preparing students for enriched reading. In G. E. Newell & R. K. Durst (Eds.), *Exploring texts: The role of discussion and writing in the teaching and learning of literature* (pp. 153-174). Norwood, MA: Christopher-Gordon.

Smagorinsky, P., & Smith, M. W. (1992). The nature of knowledge in composition and literacy understanding: The question of specificity. *Review of Educational Research, 62*(3), 279-305.

Smith, M. (1984). *Reducing writing apprehension.* Urbana, IL: National Council of Teachers of English and ERIC Clearinghouse on Reading and Communication.

Speare, E. G. (1994). *The sign of the beaver.* New York: Yearling.

*Standards for the assessment of reading and writing* (1994). Newark, DE: International Reading Association and National Council of Teachers of English.

Stein, N. L., & Glenn, C. G. (1979). An analysis of story comprehension in elementary school children. In R. O. Freedle (Ed.), *New directions in discourse processing* (pp. 53-120). Norwood, NJ: Ablex.

Steinbeck, J. (1945). *The pearl.* New York: Penguin.

VanSledright, B. A. (1996). Closing the gap between school and disciplinary hostory? Historian as high school history teacher. In J. Brophy (Ed.), *Advances in research on teaching* (Vol. 6, pp. 257-289). Greenwich, CT: JAI.

Weaver, C. (1979). *Grammar for teachers: Perspectives and definitions.* Urbana, IL: National Council of Teachers of English.

Weaver, C. (1997). *Teaching grammar in context.* Portsmouth, NH: Boynton/Cook.

West, L. H. T., & Pines, A. L. (1985). *Cognitive structures and conceptual change.* New York: Academic Press.

Wiggins, G. P. (1989a). Teaching to the (authentic) test. *Educational Leadership, 46,* 41-47.

Wiggins, G. P. (1989b). A true test: Toward more authentic and equitable assessment. *Phi Delta Kappan, 70,* 703-713.

Wiggins, G. P. (1991). Standards, not standarization: Evoking quality student work. *Educational Leadership, 48,* 18-25.

Wiggins, G. P. (1993). *Assessing student performance: Exploring the purpose and limits of testing.* San Francisco: Jossey-Bass.

Wiggins, G. P. (1998). *Educative assessment: Designing assessments to inform and improve student performance.* San Francisco: Jossey-Bass Publishers.

Wiggins, G. P., & McTighe, J. (1998). *Understanding by design.* Alexandria, VA: Association for Supervision & Curriculum Development.

Wilson, E. O. (1998a). Back from chaos. *The Atlantic Monthly, 281*(3), 41-62.

Wilson, E. O. (1998b). *Consilience: The unity of knowledge.* New York: Knopf.

Winebrug, S. (1991). On the reading of historical texts: Notes on the breach between school and academy. *American Journal of Education, 28*(3), 495-519.

Wixson, K. K., Peters, C. W., & Potter, S. A. (1997). Developing state standards in English language arts: A case study. In J. Flood, S. B. Heath, & D. Lapp (Eds.), *Handbook of research on teaching literacy through the communication and visual arts* (pp. 776-785). New York: Macmillan.

# EVALUATING LANGUAGE DEVELOPMENT

## Roger Farr
### Indiana University

## Michael D. Beck
### BETA, Inc.

Formal methods of assessing language development usually have as their goal the determination of how well students are able to read, write, listen, or speak. Knowing how well students can use language skills is important to administrators, teachers, researchers, evaluators—and the public. However, the narrow focus on test scores and the predominant use of multiple-choice tests rather than forms of assessment with more construct validity seriously limits the usefulness of formal assessments. Despite these critical problems, the formal assessment of students' language development is both necessary and useful.

Assessment is of fundamental concern to language arts teachers and curriculum leaders for providing information necessary to plan instruction. Some form of assessment is essential if educators are to understand what is working. Information concerning student growth and development in language performance is needed to evaluate the effectiveness of various teaching strategies, and the study of experimental programs must indicate whether intended results are being achieved. In addition, the focus on assessment forces language educators to define operationally what they mean by reading and writing, and what evidence they will accept as indicators of progress.

However, formal assessment is only one part of a total evaluation program and, as such, provides only a limited view of how well students use language skills (cf., Guba & Lincoln, 1981). To provide a more complete understanding of a student's literacy abilities, more comprehensive evaluations are needed (Guba, 1969; McClellan, 1988). The issues in conducting a comprehensive evaluation are more extensive than can be treated in this chapter that focuses only on the formal assessment of students' language development (see Guba, 1978; Popham, 1974; Stake, 1975; Tyler, 1969; Wolf, 1977).

Although evaluation should be much more than a simple assessment of student achievement, there is no question that assessing student achievement should generally be a significant component of a complete evaluation program. Even though new forms of assessment are regularly called for, formal assessment of some kind is always included in the pronouncements of the need for curriculum revision (R. C. Anderson, E. G. Hiebert, J. A. Scott, & J. A. G. Wilkinson, 1985; English Language Arts Curriculum Framework and Criteria Committee, 1987; National Commission on Excellence in Education, 1983). Indeed, many new (or perhaps rediscovered) types of tests and assessment techniques have been developed for reading, and to some extent writing, although few formal methods are available for assessing listening and speaking (B. Anderson, 1982; Bock & Bock, 1981; Carlisle, 1991; Farr & Carey, 1986; Resnick, 1982; Rubin & Mead, 1984). Regardless of the type of assessment, the issues are the same. Assessment must produce information in a timely and efficient manner and the information that is rendered must be both valid and reliable.

## FORMAL AND INFORMAL ASSESSMENT: CONTRASTS AND SIMILARITIES

Comparing and contrasting formal and informal assessment may bring into clearer focus some of the relevant issues that concern both. Formal assessment is conducted to determine *how much* students have learned. Most often, formal assessment takes place at the end of some phase of instruction, such as the end of a school year or the completion of a unit of work or level of an instructional program. Formal assessment of this type is usually clearly identifiable. Students are told they are going to take a test, and the tests are presented in recognizable test format. There is no pretext that formal assessment is an integral part of instruction, and sometimes (though not often enough) students are told the use to which the test results will be put.

Informal assessment is an attempt to determine *why* students perform as they do rather than *how well* they perform. Informal assessment is exemplified by a teacher at a student's side looking over the student's shoulder and commenting that what the student has written might be organized more effectively. In these situations, students are often not even aware that they are being assessed. Indeed, they might view this assessment as the teacher simply commenting on their work rather than as testing.

Formal assessment is an attempt to determine *whether a student can do something*; in informal assessment the aim is to determine *how a student does something*. Although this suggests that informal and formal assessments differ, the distinctions are often blurred or nonexistent. The timing of formal assessment, for example, need not be only at the end of an instructional period. Periodic assessments prior to and throughout an instructional period would provide better information about a student's language development than would a single test used at the end of instruction.

The distinction that formal assessment is concerned with product (how well) and informal assessment is concerned with process (how) is often one of degree. All assessment must rely on student performance. That performance can be used to infer *how well* a student might perform on similar tasks. However, if the same exhibited behavior is used to infer *how* students performed as they did, it then becomes a process measure. For example, a student's writing can be compared to some standard of good writing (criterion referencing) or to other student essays (norm referencing). In either case, the writing sample is used to infer *how well* the student writes. The same writing sample can also be used to understand *how* the student writes by discussing the writing with the student and asking about the source of the ideas, how he or she wanted to make his points, as well as revisions that would make the ideas in the writing more compelling.

Even the typical distinction that formal tests are published and informal tests are unpublished is obscured when one considers the many tests published with the label of "Informal Assessment of . . ." as part of the title. A plethora of observation checklists, interview guides, and similar assessments are also readily available from publishers.

Perhaps the major element that distinguishes formal from informal assessments is the existence of performance indicators or scales. Formal assessment usually includes some predetermined scale against which a student's performance can be interpreted. Sometimes these are norm-referenced scales that relate test results to those students who are comparable in some way—sex, age, or grade most typically. These scales, however, can be scientifically challenged (Beck, 1981). Other times, these are criterion-referenced scales, which are comparisons of performance to acceptable levels as determined by some type of judgment or expectation. Informal evaluations, with the exception of some that are published, seldom include predetermined scales of interpretation. Teachers interpret the results according to their individual expectations of performance for a class or individual student, or in comparison to what has been taught.

Although formal and informal assessment may differ enough to be discussed in separate chapters, such a separation incorrectly suggests that formal and informal assessment involve different issues. It would be unfortunate if the division separates formal and informal assessments in the thinking of language arts specialists. Assessment is best thought of as gathering a variety of information, at diverse times, and under differing conditions. Too many educators now see assessment as being of two types—that which teachers do to help students (informal assessment) and that which is forced on teachers and students by the administration (formal assessment).

Such differences should not exist. Formal assessment could be strengthened considerably through the addition of information gathered informally. On the other hand, the informal assessment conducted by teachers could be enhanced with greater attention to reliability and validity and with an eye toward using the information to communicate students' achievement to administrators and to the public.

Although accepting the notion that formal and informal assessment have more similarities than differences, this chapter focuses on formal assessment used to evaluate students' language development. Formal assessment, for purposes of this chapter, includes published tests that generally provide product rather than process information and that provide either norm-referenced or criterion-referenced scales for interpretation.

## ISSUES IN LANGUAGE ARTS ASSESSMENT

### Purposes for Assessment: The Test User's Perspective

If language arts educators are to foster the development of better tests, then they must clearly and explicitly define the purposes for which they need information. They also need to describe the language behaviors they want to test, which is a concern relating to the test's validity. It is not enough to know what performance one wants to know about. The first question to be answered is why the information is needed.

Improved test usage, as well as the development of better tests, is hampered by the expectations of some language arts specialists that eventually the best test will be developed. That "best test" is viewed as one that would provide exactly what one needs to know to summarize status and to guide instruction and would be quick and easy to administer and interpret. The problem is that the expectation for such a test is unrealistic. The answer lies not in the search for the elusive best test, but rather in setting clear and specific purposes for testing and then choosing or building an instrument to fit that purpose. Almost always the need will be for a variety of assessments collected concomitantly with instruction.

The ultimate goal in evaluating any language-arts program should be the improvement of instruction. Information is needed to plan instruction, but the purposes of evaluation must be more specific than merely the improvement of instruction. For example, the information a curriculum director needs to determine which students are making adequate progress differs from the information a teacher needs for planning tomorrow's lesson. There is a broad range of legitimate purposes for language assessments, and there is a broad range of formal and informal tests. Good assessment is possible only when information needs are matched with appropriate assessment types. Poor assessment results when a test is used for a purpose for which it was never intended. The purposes for which assessments are needed in language education are those that are responsive to program decision making (Guba & Lincoln, 1981).

Tests in the area of language arts are sometimes administered when there is no clearly stated purpose for administering them. This leads to such questions as "Now that we have given the tests, what do the results mean, and what do we do with them?" When there are clearly defined purposes for the test information, the use of the results will be obvious. Kaplan (1964) succinctly stated the importance of testing purposes:

Too often, we ask how to measure something without raising the question of what we would do with the measurement if we had it. We want to know *how* without thinking of *why*. I hope I may say without impiety seek ye first what is right for your needs, and all these things shall be added to you as well. (p. 214)

In essence, the overriding purpose for assessment in language arts is to promote a broad understanding of students' language skills that can lead to constructive change. To create this change, information must be collected about students' language behaviors. The assessment must be conducted in a timely and efficient manner, and the information produced by the assessment must be valid and reliable. Above all, the information must be focused on *the purpose to which the information will be put*.

## Purposes for Assessment: The Test Taker's Perspective

Any assessment should pose a clear and realistic purpose to examinees. When students face a set of questions to answer with no purpose-setting question for their work, the test does not represent normal reading or writing activities; nor does it represent sound classroom instruction that emphasizes helping readers establish purposes for reading and helping writers focus on an audience and a purpose for their writing.

How an examinee interprets and internalizes a test task can significantly affect the response. For example, researchers in the area of writing assessment have suggested that the framing of the writing task may have an important influence on what students write (Odell, Cooper, & Courts, 1978). The issue goes beyond concern with the framing of the test task. Those who develop and interpret tests must realize that the task may be interpreted differently by different examinees (Greenberg, Weiner, & Donovan, 1986).

Research suggests that better readers establish their own purposes for reading, and these purposes facilitate comprehension (O'Shea & O'Shea, 1994; H. K. Smith, 1967). One attempt by test makers to incorporate what we now know about the importance of identifying a purpose for reading in text comprehension was the inclusion of a "purpose question" at the beginning of each reading comprehension passage on the Metropolitan Achievement Tests (Prescott, Balow, Hogan, & Farr, 1985). Test takers were asked to read the purpose question before reading the passage and then to try to answer the question as they read. One reason for including such purpose questions was to give the test taker a concrete reason for reading, thus providing a more realistic reading situation.

Rowe and Rayford (1987) investigated whether setting a purpose for reading a test passage prior to reading helped students establish a schema for reading the passage. The types of purposes they examined were those that related reading purposes and passage content. For example, "Why did the neighbors plant trees?" "How good were Jules Verne's predictions?" and "How are these scientists trying to read your mind?" Rowe and Rayford found that readers were able to make valid predictions about the content and type of passages from reading these purpose-setting questions. In brief, the purposes did help the students develop a schema for reading. However, data as to whether such purposes actually produced better reading comprehension, and thus a better reading assessment, were inconclusive. There is, however, no question that establishing a purpose for reading a selection makes the reading task more closely resemble typical reading.

Of equal importance to providing test takers with a purpose for reading, is providing them with a clear purpose for writing. Traditionally writing prompts on tests too seldom have specified either an audience or the reason for the writing task. Primary trait writing assessment clearly addresses the issue of providing a purpose for the test taker. In primary trait assessment, the writing task specifies the audience, the purpose to be served by the writing, and oftentimes the writing format. Writing a letter to school board members to persuade them to keep the school library open on Saturday mornings is an example of one such writing task. In primary trait scoring, the writing is evaluated in terms of whether the goal for the writing has been achieved. It is a more difficult task to evaluate an essay by determining whether it accomplished the writer's rhetorical goal than it is merely to judge whether the writing is of reasonable quality without regard to writing purpose (Brown, 1986). It is clear that primary trait writing assessment attempts to set task purposes that not only guide the examinee's response, but also make the task seem more realistic to the examinees.

It is becoming more and more common to develop tests with specific examinee purposes. This practice may result in there being less concern with test wiseness (Carter, 1986). Rather than studying whether students can "psyche out" the test task and answer questions based on cues that are part of the test format, such tests more closely reflect realistic tasks.

## Validity and Reliability

Reliability and validity are characteristic of all sound measurement procedures, whether formal or informal, commercial or teacher developed. Opponents of standardized measures often object to such tests on the basis of (generally undocumented) claims that such assessments lack these qualities. The less ingenuous of these attacks may simply result from a lack of clear understanding of the meaning of the terms.

***Validity.*** The validity of a test relates to what the test assesses and how well it does so. As with reliability, validity is inherent not in the instrument but in its application: A test has (or lacks) validity for a particular use or in a particular situation, not in general.

A valid test is one that yields results that can be interpreted in light of the purposes for which the test was created. For example, a valid test of students' language skills would yield results that would allow interpretations to be made about those students reading, writing, listening, and speaking abilities. However, for many language specialists, the traditional tests do not match the tasks they have set as goals for their students. Kaplan (1964) made this very point when he wrote in his discussion of validity:

> If you can measure it, that ain't it! For the student of human behavior at any rate—so the view goes—measurement is pointless at best, and at worst, a hopeless distortion of what is really important. The exact sciences belong to the study of nature, not of man. (p. 207)

Kaplan (1964) explained that we can assess many aspects of human behavior, but we must emphasize the limitations of the measurement. For Kaplan, validity resides in part in an analysis of the use that will be made of the measurement.

Kaplan (1964) alluded to an area of validity that has received much attention over recent years—that of consequential validity (Messick, 1989; Moss, 1995; Yen, 1998). Consequential validity refers to whether the decisions that are made based on students' test scores are warranted. Consequential validity is a particularly popular issue in light of those decisions made based on high-stakes tests. For example, is it justifiable to use test scores to make such decisions as whether a student should be allowed to take an advanced placement course, be considered for the college one chooses, or even graduate from high school? In other words, are the consequences of test scores always legitimate?

According to Kaplan (1964), validity of a test depends in part on the purpose established for the test task. Wiggins (1993) contended that valid tests are those that provide reasonable testing purposes. According to Wiggins, those purposes must appear to both examinees and test users to assess what is relevant. The test task should pose an activity and a purpose for engaging in that activity that correspond with everyday language activities. Such tests are often called "authentic assessments" because they ask that students engage in tasks that occur in real-life, authentic situations (Callison, 1998; Wiggins, 1989). As such, assessments considered to be authentic assessments do not consist of traditional test items such as multiple-choice and short-answer questions, but instead ask that students construct unique solutions to unique problems, using information and situations set up by the test task.

According to Linn, Baker, and Dunbar (1991), an authentic assessment is thus described because the behavior assessed by the test is valued in its own right, whereas discrete-item tests acquire their value primarily as indicators of other valued skills or performances. Authentic performance assessments look like what they are supposed to be assessing, and they are actual samples (or even the behaviors themselves) of what they are supposed to be assessing. As a result, these assessments are often

considered to be valid assessors of "higher order" skills such as problem solving. On the other hand, discrete-item tests are considered to be limited in what they assess and are rarely thought of as valid assessors of anything more than "lower order" skills—certainly not of problem solving. However, studies suggest that multiple-choice tests can in fact assess problem solving and critical thinking (Farr, Pritchard, & Smitten, 1990; Thissen, Wainer, & Wang, 1994). Moreover, no research to date suggests that multiple-choice tests do not assess higher order skills. Surprisingly, with regard to authentic performance assessments, there is very little research to support that they do in fact assess higher order skills. These assessments are often deemed to be valid assessors of problem solving and critical thinking based on face and content validity alone. Few studies have sought to systematically determine the construct validity of problem-solving performance assessments. However, see Conner (1999) Baxter and Glaser (1998) as exceptions to this generalization.

***Reliability.*** Reliability is defined as the consistency of scores obtained when persons are reexamined with the same test on different occasions or with tests composed of parallel sets of items. Simply speaking, a test's reliability is an expression of the amount of error present in a set of scores. As such, it is important to note that reliability is a property not of the test per se but rather of a particular set of scores resulting from the test. Thus, a test does not possess high or low reliability in general; a particular set of scores obtained from the test has this quality. It is possible, indeed quite common, for a test with sound technical characteristics for most populations and uses to have poor reliability when applied to particular groups. This occurs most frequently when the group tested is small or atypical in performance (e.g., compensatory education samples or classroom-sized groups scoring very high or low on the test). For prospective users of a particular test, it is important to review reliability data collected on the group for which the test will be used or on groups comparable in ability and variability to those to whom the test will be given.

One situation in which cautious interpretation is called for with regard to reliability is in essay exams. Reliability for essay scoring is typically defined as the correlation between two independently determined scores on the same set of papers, two scorers or one rater who rescores the papers after some period of time. The reliability of scores derived from a single essay scored by a pair of professionally trained readers using carefully selected orientation or scale-point selection papers and using a well-conceived scoring scheme is generally on a level of $.75 \pm .05$. If a single reader is used, if training is less-than-comprehensive, if score points are not clearly defined and described, and if the essay topics have not been pretested, such figures drop dramatically. The upper practical limit of the reliability of such essay scores is the low .80s, below the rule-of-thumb guideline for interpreting an individual's score. In most practical situations in which important test-based decisions are to be made (e.g., state-assessment graduation or promotion tests), essay scores must be combined in some way with the results of objectively scored items to increase the reliability of the total score.

A final point to this discussion of validity and reliability concerns an often expressed perception of formal testing. That perception generally translates into such statements as "This test was a waste of time—it told me what I already knew." This confirmation that test results generally provide is one of their great strengths, *not* a weakness. Indeed, this confirmation is what reliability and validity mean. That is, the tests—without observing and by using procedures and questions and approaches far different from those used by a sensitive, involved teacher—are validating that teacher's judgment. It is, of course, the exceptions to this confirmation that generally receive and deserve the bulk of the interpretive attention; however, the confirmations evidence their greatest strength.

Furthermore, extensive research has clearly shown (Kellaghan, Madaus, & Airasian, 1981; Rudman et al., 1980; Salmon-Cox, 1981; Stetz & Beck, 1979) that when test scores and teacher judgments of pupil abilities differ, teachers are inclined to change their views to the benefits of children. That is, when a child's test scores are higher than the teacher would predict, the teacher tends to inflate his or her view of the child's ability; when scores are lower than teacher judgment would predict, the test scores are dismissed.

## TRENDS IN LANGUAGE ARTS ASSESSMENT

### Curriculum-Driven Assessment

One of the important issues facing language educators is whether tests should lead or follow the curriculum. The debate over the influence of tests on what is taught in classrooms is a long-standing one. The issue is actually one of the influence of test results on curriculum, not whether tests lead or follow the curriculum. Moreover, the issue has long been decided: Tests *do* determine, at least to some extent, what is taught, Therefore, the issue is really a concern with whether what is tested is what ought to be taught, or whether the tests reflect important curriculum goals.

Commentators on the political use of high-stakes tests promote the merits of (Popham, 1987, 1993; Popham, Cruse, Rankin, Sandifer, & Williams, 1985) or lament the narrowness or other evils of "teaching to the test" (Bracey, 1987; Madaus, 1985). Even in its most acceptable form of teaching the skills underlying the test, rather than the test content per se, the thought of tests leading, rather than following, the curriculum is embraced by few measurement specialists. However, as more states have aligned their state-designed tests to the curriculum, teaching to the test has become less of a stigmatized practice. When tests resemble good instruction, having more performance components that reflect the types of activities that state curricula embrace, teaching the test may become a by-product of teaching to the curriculum.

The natural extension of the phenomenon of teaching to the test is that there can be no question that student scores on these high-stakes tests have improved (Stake, Bettridge, Metzer, & Switzer, 1987). The critical question that remains unanswered is whether the underlying, broader skills assessed on such tests have improved or whether the change has been test, or

even test-item specific. Although measurement philosophers disagree on the advisability of such a phenomenon (Airasian, 1988), pragmatists argue that we should take pedagogical advantage of the situation, not lament it or turn ostrich. Because tests *do* drive instruction, and what is stressed in instruction is learned (Popham et al., 1985), the joint task of language arts curriculum developers and language arts test developers is to ensure that what is tested on such high stakes is what *should* be taught.

Curriculum-driven assessment would not be a major concern to language arts educators if they believed the tests adequately assessed all-important aspects of the language arts curriculum. Witty (1949) recognized the problem that can result from a lack of curriculum–assessment congruence many years ago:

> It is necessary to supplement the knowledge of a child's reading status derived from standard tests by an estimate of his success in comprehending whole episodes or stories. In addition, understanding of each child's reading can be enhanced by examining a record of the books he has read in and out of school. (p. 215)

Some 35 years later, Purves (1984), commented on the influence of minimum competency tests on the language arts curriculum, made the same point when he presented the criticisms of those who opposed minimum competency assessment in language arts: "Statements of competence produced a circumscribing of the curriculum to a point where it merely prepared students for the test rather than being concerned with broad educative functions"(p. 6).

The impact of testing on instruction is viewed as a positive influence by a growing number of curriculum leaders or at least as a lever they can use to change curriculum. Airasian (1988) described measurement-driven instruction (MDI) as a change from measurement that takes its direction from curriculum to one in which curriculum takes its direction from testing. MDI is not a new phenomenon; tests have always driven instruction to a lesser or greater extent, but earlier tests were usually written after the curriculum was developed. In MDI, the tests are written as, or even before, the curriculum is developed. In effect, MDI proponents are saying, "Here is the goal for instruction (performance on this test), now you curriculum people do what needs to be done in instruction to produce good scores."

There are those who applaud the MDI movement as one that will lead to a clarification of instructional goals and increased academic achievement (cf., Popham, 1987). On the other hand, many educators, including a number of measurement specialists, are concerned that MDI narrows the curriculum and removes the last vestiges of decision making from the teacher (Madaus, 1985). Airasian (1988) viewed MDI as more complex than it appears on the surface. He suggested three factors that determine the impact of assessment on instruction: the nature of the content being measured, the standards established for satisfactory test performance, and the test stakes (the decision to be made from the test results, e.g., promotion, graduation, and teacher salaries).

The issues of MDI are those of curriculum control and decision making in regard to what will be taught and how it will be taught. Language arts curriculum leaders have always been concerned about these issues. Indeed, one of the strongest fears when the National Assessment of Educational Progress (NAEP) was first being established was its potential for dictating a national curriculum. Because of these concerns, NAEP was set up so that state comparisons and individual school districts comparisons were not possible. The goal of NAEP was to find out, in general and on a national basis, how students were achieving in various areas of the curriculum. Results were not to be used to determine curriculum or to foster specific course content. Recent reports, however, have called for a change in NAEP to provide more definite information about more precisely defined groups so the results of NAEP may be used to foster curriculum change. The recent reporting of NAEP summary data on a state-by-state basis is one sign of this movement. See Linn (1998) for a review of issues with regard to NAEP data.

Other educators and education reviewers have noted the impact of assessment on the control of education. Salganik (1985) believed that the reliance on test scores has weakened the authority of professional judgment and pushed schools toward more centralized governance. Moreover, she rightly predicted that this trend would continue.

Language education seems to be one area where the emphasis on test scores is growing concurrently with the development of new approaches to assessment and the use of a greater variety of assessments. Many language arts curriculum leaders, who may in the past have paid little attention to assessment or merely been critics of assessment, now see assessment as a way to induce schools to incorporate into the curriculum what the leaders believe is important. Measurement-driven instruction is a fact of life, and many curriculum battles in language arts revolve around the control of assessment.

This trend is almost sure to produce increased criticisms of tests regardless of their content because tests by themselves are too narrow and too insensitive to measure all those things schools are trying to achieve. The concern with the limits of test scores to assess the quality of education was emphasized by Sizer (1984), who declared that test scores cause educators and policymakers to focus on the wrong problems and, more important, on the wrong solutions to those problems:

I have little confidence in the educational significance of the use of standardized achievement test scores. It's not that the scores have no meaning, it's simply that they tap much too slender a slice of what I believe is important in education. (p. 49)

The now pervasive assessment of written language achievement based on student writing samples is a clear attempt to more closely align curriculum and assessment in language arts or at least what language arts curriculum leaders would like to see emphasized in schools. The desire to induce more schools to teach writing as a process and to prod teachers to provide students with more writing opportunities has had a significant impact on assessment over the past decade. As well, the establishment of writing assessment programs has resulted in increased classroom writing activities. Writing samples are now used in over half of the states as part of their statewide testing programs, and numerous school districts include writing samples as part of

their annual school assessments. In addition, most commercial standardized tests now include writing sample tests as part of their test batteries.

The concern with higher order thinking skills in the language arts is another curriculum movement that has found its way into the assessment area. Although some educators have argued that thinking skills cannot be taught through the typical state the objectives, teach the skills, and provide practice used for other skills (Sternberg, 1987), and others have argued that it is absurd to assume that thinking can be taught at all (F. Smith, 1989), the teaching and assessment of higher order thinking skills continues to flourish (Norris, 1985; Paul, 1985).

This phenomenon may have originated with earlier reviews of the NAEP reading data, and the same conclusion has been reinforced in the most recent NAEP results. The general conclusion was that students were doing quite well with literal (lower order) reading comprehension, but they were not doing well with inferential, critical, and evaluative (higher order) reading comprehension. This gave rise to a school curriculum and testing emphasis on higher order thinking skills. Rather than attempting to look for ways to emphasize and teach these skills within the existing curriculum, and to assess the skills within already existing testing areas, separate curriculum and assessment areas have developed. (For a well-developed review of research on the teaching of thinking skills, see Nickerson, 1988.)

Higher order thinking skills are now commonly listed in the curriculum of many state and school district curriculum guides, and those who select tests insist that such skills be included on the tests. Regardless of the lack of evidence for the validity of such assessment, because it is in the curriculum, it must be tested; and if it is on the tests, then teachers will attempt to teach the skills.

The examples of changes in language arts assessment surveyed in this section have as their goal the closer tie of curriculum and assessment. It is not a matter of whether or not MDI is a reality in the language arts—it *is*.

## Testing at the Early Elementary School Grade Levels

Kindergarten and first-grade students are no longer strangers to test taking. Children are being tested at a younger than ever before. Many educators condemn the practice, arguing that testing children at such a young age unnecessarily results in a loss of learning time and frustrates teachers, parents (to whom scores are often not adequately explained), and most of all, children (Andersen, 1993, 1998).

Shepard (1994) contended that the growing trend of testing in the early elementary school grades is due in great part to the abuse of readiness testing that occurred in the 1980s. During that decade there were a number of curricular changes at the kindergarten level due to a variety of indirect pressures, such as parental demands that reading be taught in kindergarten and accountability testing at the higher grades. As a result, what was once being expected of first-grade students was now expected of kindergarten children. According to Shepard, "The result of these changes was an aversive learning environment inconsistent with the learning needs of young children" (p. 206). Kindergarten children were being expected to engage in extended periods of seat work. This type of instruction requires children to have longer attention spans, a higher threshold for stress, and a greater level of social maturity than was previously expected of kindergarten children. In response to this change in curriculum, reading readiness screening became common in many school districts across the country.

To make matters worse, the validity of the tests that have been used as readiness tests over the last 3 decades is questionable (Shepard, 1994). For one thing, they were not originally created for the purposes for which they are being used and therefore were never validated for those purposes. An additional variable that causes the validity of young children's tests results to be questionable is the fact that many young children have little experience in answering test questions. Therefore, misunderstandings easily arise when they are subjected to tests (Elbers & Kelderman, 1994).

One wonders what the effects of testing young children will be if the current trend continues. The reality of test anxiety is well documented. Secondary school students, who are also being tested more than ever before, understand how important the tests they take can be to their futures. They have learned that in school it is the test that counts. The more young children are tested, the more quickly they will realize the significant role that tests will play in their lives as students and the more susceptible they will be to the anxieties of testing at an early age.

## Evolving Issues

Farr and Carey (1986) described the limited change in the structure and content of standardized reading tests over the past 50 years. The same summary applies to the other areas of language arts testing as well. The only possible exception to this is the area of writing assessment, where the use (though not the structure) of essay examinations has increased markedly. With regard to formal assessment, changes in language arts testing have been evolutionary rather than revolutionary. We identify two significant trends: holistic reading comprehension measures and the teacher scoring of large-scale assessments.

***Holistic reading comprehension measures.*** Although it is likely that the soundness of traditional measures of reading comprehension has been questioned since the first day such tests were used, the current direction for comprehension assessment seems to have begun with Simons (1971). He attacked the several approaches to comprehension assessment used at that time and proposed that new measures be more attentive to reading processes than to the product of these processes.

With some differences in focus, wording, and item format, newer assessments often have all or most of four interrelated parts:

1. Comprehension/constructing meaning.
2. Metacognition/reading strategies.
3. Topic familiarity/background knowledge.
4. Attitudes/self-perceptions/literary experiences.

Most traditional tests have focused almost exclusively on only the constructing meaning portion of the above group of factors, although commercial reading surveys and attitude scales have long been available, albeit seldom linked to comprehension measures.

Although proponents of these new measures may argue that the constructing meaning and attitude components differ in substance from those in traditional tests, clearly the most unique elements of the new measures are the portions assessing metacognition and background knowledge. It remains to be seen empirically whether these new assessments add significant and sound information and, if so, what contribution they make to future large-scale reading assessments and, more important, to instruction. However, at the very least, such developments have raised the consciousness of a broad range of developers and users of reading assessment instruments.

Perhaps the most significant potential for failure of these instruments is the mismatch between their structure and the tests' purpose. The majority of these instruments are developed, interpreted, and used almost exclusively for ranking and sorting (accountability) purposes. Such instruments, regardless of how faithful they are to current reading theory, will be used or misused no less often or seriously than is predictable from their purpose. The Stanford–Binet is an excellent psychometric instrument, built to be consistent with a well-explicated theory of ability. However, it would not be the instrument of choice for planning tomorrow's instruction for a group of children. The instrumentation and the purpose for its use simply would not be well matched. So it is with the use of instructionally oriented reading tests built for state accountability purposes. We can only hope that the instruments will be used by insightful, caring educators in ways consistent with their development.

***Teacher scoring of large-scale assessments.*** One of the greatest challenges resulting from two educational assessments trends—assessing students more frequently and adding a writing component to many large-scale assessments—is scoring. When large-scale assessments consisted of only multiple-choice items, scoring these assessments was not a challenge. A machine did all of the work. However, with the addition of student-generated responses to many large-scale assessments, scoring has become a problematic issue. States are encountering difficulties related not only to the high cost of scoring these assessments, but also to scoring reliability (Caudell, 1996; Engelhard, 1994).

More teachers are being asked to score their students' assessments. There have been both benefits and drawbacks to this practice. Clearly, having teachers score their students' assessments is more cost effective than sending the assessments off to be scored by testing centers. Furthermore, when teachers score their students' work they gain insights into their students' abilities that one cannot gain from test scores alone. New York State, which has a long tradition of involving teachers in developing, evaluating, and scoring state examinations, recently relied on teachers to score exams for the Goals 2000 New Assessments Project. Teacher reaction to participating in the scoring process was overwhelmingly positive. They felt that doing so helped clarify for them the goals and expectations of the assessments, deepen disciplinary knowledge, as well as develop instructional insights (Falk & Ort, 1998). Likewise, Maryland teachers identified several advantages to administering and scoring the Maryland School Performance Assessment Program tests, including being able to familiarize themselves with the test and its objectives, as well as providing an opportunity for professional development (Goldberg & Roswell, 1998).

There are some problems inherent in having teachers score statewide assessments, however. For one thing, scoring openended responses is time consuming. Teachers are being asked to devote even more of their already scarce time to grading student work, resulting in less instructional planning time. In addition to the time teachers actually spend reviewing students' work is the time spent learning how to use the scoring guides to be followed. Another serious concern is that of reliability. When students' work is scored by machine, the results are very reliable; when human judgment plays a role in assigning student scores, there will be some errors in scoring. However, both operational and psychometric efforts are being made to detect and control for those errors. Engelhard (1994) proposed a method for detecting rater errors with a many-faceted Rasch model. The use of procedures to detect rater errors, as well as providing raters with thorough training can minimize rater errors, thus increasing the reliability of scoring.

## CONTINUING ISSUES

One of the most dominant themes in current discussions of language arts assessment is process. The call has been for instruments more attentive to the processes of language development rather than the products. The argument underlying this theme is that the processes of, say, reading, are more important than the product. Such an argument is specious in isolation. Clearly, both process and product are important, both for "formative" and "summative" assessment. The key element missing in such discussions is the *purpose* for which the information is being collected. Teachers, administrators, boards of education, and parents are all interested in both process and product, though in generally different ways. Teachers are obviously concerned primarily with process as they help a child move toward increased language proficiency; however, they are also by necessity concerned with the product of all the processes. Process assessment is critical in planning and guiding instruction, but product measurement is essential in gauging the success of a program or intervention. Similarly, administrators are primarily concerned with product, but cannot neglect the processes that lead to it.

To a significant extent, the process–product distinction is an illusion in that, by definition, all assessments must be of a product. Even with brilliantly conceived and developed assessment instruments, we can only observe a product and infer the intervening or enabling processes that led to it.

It is certain from the trends of the past few years, that the next several years will witness increased use of writing, continued development of and evolution in the concept of performance assessment, and a push for more approaches to the assessment of metacognitive skills in both reading and writing. If these approaches are to provide meaningful (valid) and useful (reliable) results for teachers and administrators, much work needs to be done. Moreover, the issue of teacher time to engage in these additional tasks needs to be addressed. Even if teachers find these new forms of assessment to be especially useful, time will need to be found in an already overloaded schedule for reviewing and using the information derived from these assessments. The efficiency of assessment will always be an issue in determining new directions.

Formal assessments were developed and have maintained their dominant position in the measurement armamentarium primarily because of their financial and temporal efficiency. Compared with "better" (read "less formal") techniques, the unchanging multiple-choice product measures are cheap and quick. In the efforts by instructional leaders and creative measurement specialists to evolve instrumentation that is more attentive to what we are coming to understand about the language development process (i.e., tests that are more valid), the efficiency is sacrificed. We must wonder whether the increase in fidelity or validity is proportionate with the increased cost in time and money. Our general conclusion is that it is easier, faster, and cheaper, and more valid, to approach the measurement of process indicators via informal procedures applied in a timely, as-needed way by the teacher in the privacy of his or her classroom. While there is undeniably a need to continue to progress in making formal product assessments more faithful to what we know and are learning about reading or other language constructs, efforts to assess process through such tests are bound to lead to less than satisfying results.

This conclusion leads necessarily to a call to train, retrain, and otherwise assist classroom teachers in designing and conducting valid informal and semiformal assessments. Current indications (Carter, 1984; Gullickson & Ellwein, 1985; Rudman et al., 1980; Stiggins & Bridgeford, 1985; Stiggins, Conklin, & Bridgeford, 1986) are that most teachers do not have a high degree of knowledge about the development, analysis, and interpretation of assessment instruments, formal or informal. The challenges to teacher-training institutions and forward-looking school districts and state departments of education are obvious.

## References

Afflerbach, P. (1985). *Statewide assessment of writing*. Princeton, NJ: ERIC Clearinghouse on Tests, Measurement, and Evaluation.

Airasian, P. W. (1988). Measurement driven instruction: A closer look. *Educational Measurement: Issues and Practice, 7*(4), 6–11.

Andersen, S. R. (1993). Trouble with testing. *American School Board Journal, 180*(6), 24–26.

Andersen, S. R. (1998). The trouble with testing. *Young children, 53*(4), 25–29.

Anderson, B. (1982). Test use today in elementary and secondary schools. In A. K. Wigdor & W. R. Garner (Eds.), *Ability testing: Uses; consequences, and controversies* (Pt. 2). Washington, DC: National Academy Press.

Anderson, R. C. (1984). *Becoming a nation of readers: The report of the commission on reading.* Washington, DC: U.S. Department of Education, National Institute of Education.

Beck, M. D. (1981). Critique of *Does "nationally" normed really mean nationally?* Unpublished manuscript, Psychological Corporation, New York.

Berk, R. A. (Ed.) (1980). *Criterion-referenced measurement: The state of the art.* Baltimore: Johns Hopkins University Press.

Bock, D. C., & Bock, E. H. (1981). *Evaluating classroom speaking.* Annandale, VA: Speech Communication Association.

Bracy, G. W. (1987). Measurement-driven instruction: Catchy phrase, dangerous practice. *Phi Delta Kappan, 68,* 683–686.

Brown, R. (1986). Evaluation and teaming. In A. R. Petrosky & D. Bartholomae (Eds.), *The teaching of writing; Eighty-fifth yearbook of the National Society for the Study of Education.* Chicago: University of Chicago Press.

Callison, D. (1998). Authentic assessment. *School Library Media Activities Monthly, 14*(5), 42–43.

Carlisle, J. F. (1991). Planning an assessment of listening and reading comprehension. *Topics in Language Disorders, 12*(1), 17–31.

Carter, K. (1984). Do teachers understand the principles for writing tests? *Journal of Teacher Education, 35*(6), 57–60.

Carter, K. (1986). Test wiseness for teachers and students. *Educational Measurement: Issues and Practice, 5*(4), 20–23.

Caudell, L. S. (1996). High stakes: Innovation meets backlash as states struggle with large-scale assessment. *Northwest Education, 2*(1), 26–28, 35.

Conner, J. M. (1999). *Determining the construct validity of a problem-solving performance assessment through the use of verbal protocols.* Unpublished doctoral dissertation, Indiana University, Bloomington.

Elbers, E., & Kelderman, A. (1994). Ground Rules for Testing: Expectations and Misunderstandings in Test Situations. *European Journal of Psychology of Education, 9*(2), 111–120.

Engelhard, G. (1994). Examining rater errors in the assessment of written composition with a many-faceted Rasch model. *Journal of Educational Measurement, 31,* 93–122.

English Language Arts Curriculum Framework and Criteria Committee (1987). *English-language arts framework.* Sacramento: California State Department of Education.

Falk, B., & Ort, S. (1998). Sitting down to score: Teacher learning through assessment. *Phi Delta Kappan, 80*(1), 59–64.

Farr, R., & Carey, R. F. (1986). *Reading: What can be measured?* Newark, DE: International Reading Association.

Farr, R., Pritchard, R., & Smitten, B. (1990). A description of what happens when an examinee takes a multiple-choice reading comprehension test. *Journal of Educational Measurement, 27*(3), 209–226.

Frisbie, D. A. (1988). NCME instructional module on reliability of scores from teacher-made tests. *Educational Measurement: Issues and Practice, 7*(1), 25–35.

Goldberg, G. L., & Roswell, B. S. (1998, April). *Perception and practice: The impact of teachers' scoring experience on performance-based instruction and classroom assessment.* Paper presented at the annual meeting of the American Educational Research Association, San Diego, CA. (ERIC Document Reproduction Service No. ED 420 670)

Greenberg, K., Weiner, H., & Donovan, R. (Eds.) (1986). *Wilting assessment: Issues and strategies.* New York: Longman.

Guba, E. (1969). The failure of educational evaluation. *Educational Technology, 9,* 29–33.

Guba, E., & Lincoln, Y. (1981). *Effective evaluation.* San Francisco: Jossey-Bass.

Guba, E. G. (1978). *Toward a methodology of naturalistic inquiry in educational evaluation* (Monograph Series No. 8). Los Angeles: University of California, Center for the Study of Evaluation.

Gullickson, A. R., & Ellwein, M. C. (1985). Post hoc analysis of teacher-made tests: The goodness-of-fit between prescription and practice. *Educational Measurement: Issues and Practice, 4*(1), 15–18.

James, H. T. (1987). *The nation's report card: Improving the assessment of student achievement.* Cambridge, MA: National Academy of Education.

Kaplan, S. (1964). *The conduct of inquiry.* San Francisco: Chandler.

Kellaghan, T., Madaus, G. F., & Airasian, P. W. (1981). *The effects of standardized testing.* Boston: Kluwer-Nijhoff.

Linn, R. L., Baker, E. L., & Dunbar, S. B. (1991). Complex, performance-based assessment: Expectations and validation criteria. *Educational Researcher, 20*(8), 15–21.

Madaus, G. F. (1985). Public policy and the testing profession: You've never had it so good? *Educational Measurement: Issues and Practice, 4,* 5–11.

McClellan, M. C. (1988). Testing and reform. *Phi Delta Kappan, 69,* 766–771.

Messick, S. (1989). Meaning and values in test validation: The science and ethics of assessment. *Educational Researcher, 18*(2), 5–11.

National Commission on Excellence in Education (1983). *A nation at risk.* Washington, DC: U.S. Department of Education.

Nickerson, R. S. (1988). On improving thinking through instruction. In E. Z. Rodikopf (Ed.), *Review of research in education* (Vol. 15, pp. 3–57). Washington, DC: American Educational Research Association.

Norris, S. P. (1985). Synthesis of research on critical thinking. *Educational Leadership, 42*(8), 40–45.

Odell, L., Cooper, C. R., & Courts, C. (1978). Discourse theory: Implications for research in composing. In C. R. Cooper & L. Odell (Eds.), *Research on composing: Points of departure.* Urbana, IL: National Council of Teachers of English.

O'Shea, L. J., & O'Shea, D. J. (1994). A component analysis of metacognition in reading comprehension: The contributions of awareness and self-regulation. *International Journal of Disability, Development, and Education, 41*(1), 15–32.

Paul, R. W. (1985). Bloom's taxonomy and critical thinking instruction. *Educational Leadership, 42*(8), 36–39.

Popham, W. J. (1971). *Criterion-referenced measurement.* Englewood Cliffs, NJ: Educational Technology Publications.

Popham, W. J. (1974). *Evaluation in education.* Berkeley, CA: McCutchan Publishing Corp.

Popham, W. J. (1987). The merits of measurement-driven instruction. *Phi Delta Kappan, 68,* 679–682.

Popham, W. J. (1993). Measurement-driven instruction as a "quick-fix" reform strategy. *Measurement and Evaluation in Counseling and Development, 26*(1), 31–34.

Popham, W. J., Cruse, K. L., Rankin, S. L., Sandifer, P. D., & Williams, P. L. (1985). Measurement driven instruction: It's on the road. *Phi Delta Kappan, 66,* 628–634.

Prescott, G. A., Balow, I. H., Hogan, T. P., & Farr, R. C. (1984). *Metropolitan achievement tests.* San Antonio, TX: Psychological Corporation.

Purves, A. (1984). The challenge to education to produce literate citizens. In A. Purves & O. Niles (Eds.), *Becoming readers in a complex society: Eighty-third yearbook of the National Society for the Study of Education.* Chicago: University of Chicago Press.

Resnick, D. (1982). History of educational testing. In A. K. Wigdor & W. R. Garner (Eds.), *Ability testing: Uses, consequences, and controversies* (Pt. 2). Washington, DC: National Academy Press.

Rowe, D. W., & Rayford, L. (1987). Activating background knowledge in reading comprehension assessment. *Reading Research Quarterly 2,* 160-176.

Rubin, D., & Mead, N. (1984). *Large-scale assessment of oral communication skills: Kindergarten through Grade 12.* Annandale, VA: Speech Communication Association.

Rudman, H. C., Kelly, J. L., Wanous, D. S., Mehrens, W. A., Clark, C. M., & Porter, A. C. (1980). *Integrating assessment with instruction: A review.* East Lansing: Michigan State University, Institute for Research on Teaching.

Salganik, L. H. (1985). Why testing reforms are so popular and how they are changing education. *Phi Delta Kappan, 66,* 628-634.

Salmon-Cox, L. (1981). Teachers and tests: What's really happening? *Phi Delta Kappan, 62,* 631-634.

Scriven, M. (1973). Goal free evaluation. In E. R. House (Ed.), *School evaluation: The politics and process.* Berkeley, CA: McCutchan Publishing.

Scriven, M. (1994). Evaluation as a discipline. *Studies in Educational Evaluation, 20*(1), 147-166.

Shepard, L. A. (1994). The challenges of assessing young children appropriately. *Phi Delta Kappan, 76*(3), 206-212.

Simons, H. D. (1971). Reading comprehension: The need for a new perspective. *Reading Research Quarterly, 6,* 338-363.

Sizer, T. R. (1984). *Horace's compromise.* Boston: Houghton Mifflin.

Smith, F. (1989). Overselling literacy. *Phi Delta Kappan, 70,* 353-359.

Smith, H. K. (1967). The responses of good and poor readers when asked to read for different purposes. *Reading Research Quarterly, 3,* 56-83.

Stake, R. E. (1975). *Preordinate vs. responsive evaluation* [Mimeograph]. Urbana: University of Illinois.

Stake, R. E., Bettridge, J., Metzer, D., & Switzer, D. (1987). *Review of literature on effects of achievement testing.* Champaign, IL: University of Illinois Center for Instructional Research.

Sternberg, R. (1987). Teaching critical thinking: Eight easy ways to fail before you begin. *Phi Delta Kappan, 68,* 456-459.

Stetz, F. P., & Beck, M. D. (1981). Attitudes toward standardized tests: Students, teachers, and measurement specialists. *Measurement in Education, 12*(l),

Stiggins, R. J., & Bridgeford, N. J. (1985). The ecology of classroom assessment. *Journal of Educational Measurement, 22,* 271-286.

Stiggins, R. J., Conklin, N. F., & Bridgeford, N. J. (1986). Classroom assessment: A key to effective education. *Educational Measurement: Issues and Practice, 5*(2), 5-17.

Subkoviak, M. J. (1988). A practitioner's guide to computation and interpretation of reliability indices for mastery tests. *Journal of Educational Measurement, 25,* 47-55.

Tyler, R. W. (Ed.) (1969). *Educational evaluation: New roles, new means: Sixty-eighth yearbook of the National Society for the Study of Education* (Pt. 2). Chicago: University of Chicago Press.

Wiggins, G. (1989). A true test: Toward more authentic and equitable assessment. *Phi Delta Kappan, 70,* 703-713.

Wiggins, G. (1993). *Assessing student performance: Exploring the purpose and limits of testing.* San Francisco: Jossey-Boss.

Witty, P. (1949). *Reading in modern education.* Boston: Heath.

Wolf, R. L. (1977). Toward more natural inquiry in education. *CEDR Quarterly, 10,* 7-9.

Yen, W. M. (1998). Investigating the consequential aspects of validity: What is responsible and what should they do? *Educational Measurement: Issues and Practice, 17*(2), 5.

# INFORMAL METHODS OF EVALUATION

## Yetta M. Goodman
### University of Arizona

Mary K. finishes talking to a small group of fifth-graders about a story they are writing. She stands, moves over to the side of the room, looks around the class, and notes to herself that Chris and Isaac have their heads together over Isaac's radio play. Hopefully they are going to tape-record both of their plays with the help of a Halloween sound effects record. Chris has written Isaac in as a major character in his play and has shared it with Isaac and a few other classmates from beginning draft through two revisions. Isaac has read his draft to Chris but does not seem to be seeking more than approval. The class members worked on their radio plays on Tuesday and Wednesday. They revised Tuesday's "sloppy copy" into another "sloppy copy" on Wednesday. Some merely recopied the first draft, but a few incorporated a little more detail. Mary had typed some of the more cohesive plays as best she could. Chris and Isaac are both working from typed versions, filling in what she couldn't make out from their invented spelling and making changes they now desire (Marek et al., 1984).

Don H. is reading a story to his second-graders and the text refers to somebody being horsewhipped. Kalman interrupts and reminds the class that being horsewhipped is like being hit with a whip made out of horses. "That's like the book we read a long time before about that king who reigned [rained]" he calls out excitedly. Don was struck by the fact that only 4 weeks earlier he had relegated a plan to have the children make books about homonyms to a good idea gone bad since the kids at that time hadn't responded to his suggestion. Now the children themselves had related this story to the previous one and from Kalman's suggestions the class made a set of books similar to Fred Gwynne's (1998). *The King Who Rained*.

Corol A. is having a writing conference with Marlene, one of her first-graders (Fig. 43.1). Carol describes her responses: "I asked Marlene to read her writing to me. 'I am outside, under a rainbow and beside a tree,' she read as she moved her finger under the letters in a very precise, deliberate fashion."

"Tell me about these O's," I responded. Marlene looked at me and giggled that I didn't see what was so obvious.

"Those aren't O's," she said. "They're circles."

"Circles?" I was still puzzled. "Well, why did you decide to put circles in the middle of your writing?"

"Because. See, I couldn't tell what letters make those sounds so I just put circles for what goes there because something goes there only I don't know what. I can't tell what letter makes that sound, so I just put circles."

Marlene read and pointed her way through the line again. "I am—oops, I forgot to write *I*." Her finger lands under the first circle as she says "am". She continues on, and I can see that Marlene has correctly written *S* for "side," *RB* for "rainbow," *BS* for "beside," and *T* for "tree." The sounds she was unable to identify are vowel sounds, but Marlene was able to develop a strategy to deal with this.

When I looked again at Marlene's writing and listened to her explanation, I understood that she could distinguish vowel sounds in words but could not identify them with a corresponding letter (Avery, unpublished paper).

Nancie Atwell (1987) transcribed an evaluation conference she had with one of her adolescent students in *In the Middle:*

*Atwell*: Okay, Mike your goals for this past quarter were to try some new kinds of writing, going beyond personal experience narrative, and to work on proofreading finals so you don't end up making a lot of new mistakes on the published copy.

*Mike*: I really spent a lot of time on that.

*A*: So, that's a goal you've conquered. . . . What about the other goal, trying something new?

*M*: I really didn't do much on that. . . . But I'm going to try fiction this quarter.

Mary, Don, Carol, and Nancie are professionals. They know their students well. They use observations, questioning techniques, individual and small-group interactions, conferences,

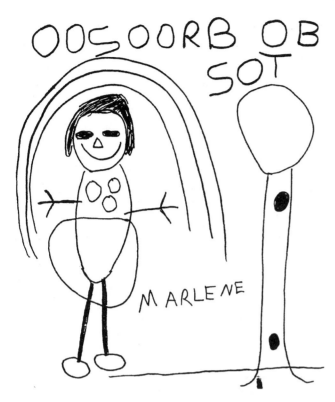

FIGURE 43.1. Marlene's writing sample.

and in-depth analysis of their students' oral and written productions to engage in daily evaluation of development. They understand what they are observing because they are knowledgeable about learning, language, and language learning. They are interested in both the process of their students' learning as well as the products that result in order to: (a) share their professional insights with their students and their parents, (b) use their insights reflectively for purposes of continuous curriculum planning and professional growth, and (c) provide permanent records as a history of their students experiences in school. They are involved in ongoing interpretive evaluation. Over the years such evaluation has often been called informal, but I prefer to avoid that term because it reflects a view of evaluation that assumes that only controlled and quantifiable evaluation is worthy of being considered formal, Chapter 42.

Fred Erickson (1987) used the term *interpretive* in a relevant and significant article titled "Qualitative Methods in Research on Teaching" in relation to classroom research because of a "central research interest (among a range of qualitative researchers) in human meaning in social life and in its elucidation and exposition by the researcher" (p. 119). In a similar way, the term *interpretive evaluation* can be used to suggest evaluation that is integral to the ongoing daily experiences that teachers use to elucidate and explicate the nature of learning and teaching at the same time that they are building meanings about the social life of the classroom. The questions researchers and teachers who use interpretive evaluation ask and the uses they make of the information gathered in classroom settings are often different, but the methodology each uses to collect

and analyze the information are similar. Teachers who are consciously aware of the significance of their role in interpretive evaluation have similar views about the nature of human beings as do researchers who engage in interpretive research.

## CALL FOR RESEARCH ON INTERPRETIVE EVALUATION

Ongoing interpretive evaluation has been little researched. In 1967 the Association for Supervision and Curriculum Development published *Evaluation as Feedback and Guide* (Wilhelms, 1967) with the purpose of "understanding the role of evaluation in education." In a section of the book focusing on alternative views of evaluation, the authors explored the answers to questions such as:

How does a learner's ceaseless evaluation shape a lifetime of becoming? How does the teacher handle precise and clear evaluation in response to the learner so it leads to challenge rather than threat; to encouragement rather than defeat; to a richer more valid self-image rather than need-distortion: and to the involvement of the learner in a cooperative, ongoing inquiry rather than to imposition by the teacher? (p. 47)

The ASCD Yearbook Committee called for research to understand the role of evaluation in education. In the past decades, although there has been abundant research on the use of testing in response to the committee's recommendation, there has been little research that would address the issues related to alternative views of education including those of interpretive evaluation. In a special issue of *The Reading Teacher* (Squire, 1987) on the state of reading assessment, there were a number of articles that address issues of teacher evaluation in the classroom; however, there is no documentation of research on such evaluation.

What I hope to accomplish in this article is:

1. Explore why there is a paucity of research on interpretive evaluation.
2. Provide a theoretical rationale for the use of interpretive evaluation.
3. Explore why professionals must find ways to legitimatize research on the use of such evaluation techniques.
4. Suggest some specific activities that might be included in doing such research.

## THE PAUCITY OF RESEARCH ON INTERPRETIVE EVALUATION

Although classroom research has been gaining respectability in the field of educational research (Erickson, 1987), there are agencies that still will not fund research that does not have an experimental design, and there are institutions that still restrict graduate students from designing research to evaluate their own classroom practices and from applying ethnographic research techniques to classroom settings.

Classroom research has provided teachers researchers with knowledge about classroom interactions and about the meanings being generated by students and teachers in classroom settings. At the present time there is still limited knowledge, however, that documents:

1. Continuous interpretive evaluation teachers do.
2. Responses and understandings of students that result from ongoing interpretive evaluation.
3. Degree to which teachers are consciously aware of the evaluative processes they are engaged in.
4. Effectiveness of interpretive evaluation on teachers' professional development and the growth of students.
5. Role such evaluation plays for parents, subsequent teachers, administrators, and other interested members of the school community.

The lack of research in this area is due, in part, to the belief that interpretive evaluation is informal and subjective and therefore not to be valued or taken seriously. At the same time it is not uncommon to hear people say that such evaluation is too difficult and time consuming. Research on such evaluation calls for longitudinal studies for which there is little financial or institutional support. In addition, because such research is often not valued, researchers are reluctant to expend a great deal of energy on research that does not yield much recognition from the reward system within academic institutions.

Other issues that limit research on interpretive evaluation are related to the knowledge and time needed to analyze, interpret, and discuss the information collected. Research, especially when the focus is the English or language arts classroom, involves careful analysis of language experiences and products, often after school hours, as well as the continuous observation and interaction with students within the classroom setting. It takes a good deal of knowledge and understanding about language processes—reading, composition, oral discourse, and text analysis—and about curriculum and evaluation in order to do research on interpretive evaluation. Such research is not easy nor can it be done quickly or neatly.

However, from the point of view of scholars who support a constructionist point of view of learning knowledgeable evaluative interpretation of what students are doing is precisely the kind of evaluation that ultimately has the most impact on students' growth in all language areas, on the professional development of teachers, and on the potential for significant changes for teaching and curriculum development. Research is necessary to document this impact.

## RATIONALE FOR RESEARCH ON ONGOING INTERPRETIVE EVALUATION

All teachers are constantly involved in evaluation whether they are consciously aware of doing so or not. This ongoing evaluation reflects their beliefs about schooling, their theories and knowledge about language, about humans, about development and learning. Teachers are involved in evaluating individual students, groups of students, and whole classrooms. They make decisions about instruction based on these evaluations and in so doing are reflecting on themselves as professionals. In other words, as they evaluate their students, they are not only involved in curriculum development but in the process of self-evaluation as well.

Teachers' comments and behaviors in classrooms and teachers' lunchrooms and at conferences and social gatherings indicate the wide range of evaluative judgments they make about their students. Researchers have documented that teachers respond differently to different kinds of students in classrooms. They may correct the oral reading miscues of their slower students, yet when their better readers make the same miscues, they seem to overlook or not be aware of their productions. Students with different language backgrounds get more or less wait time from teachers when they are asked questions. Teachers ask certain students more difficult questions than others based on their often unexamined views of the students' abilities (Allington, 1980; Hoffman, 1987; McDermott, 1974). Teachers frequently comment that one class is more difficult than another, that one group of children is working more independently than another. These responses indicate the degree to which teachers are continuously involved in evaluation and suggest that their evaluative judgments are the basis for instructional decisions that teachers make daily about the lives of their students. It is interesting to note that in reviews on teachers' decision making, although there is discussion about teacher judgment, there is no obvious link expected between teachers' ongoing decision making and the evaluation of students (Shavelson & Stern, 1981). I believe this is related to viewing evaluation as an end product of teaching and not as an ongoing and continuous process. Unfortunately, if the field of education does not consider continuous evaluation significant to the teaching–learning process and does not develop ways to study such evaluation, then we allow the subtle unstated actions in classrooms to impact students' lives without any consideration whatsoever.

If we accept the assumption that teachers are indeed evaluating at all times, then it is necessary to call for serious research into such activities. Such research will help teachers who are not yet consciously aware of their tacit evaluation to become more reflective about their responses to students. For informed teachers such as Mary, Don, Carol, and Nancie, who talk and write about the power of such evaluation on their own teaching and the growth of their students, research will legitimatize their professional inquiry into their teaching and their evaluation of students (K. Goodman, Y. Goodman, & Hood, 1989, Hubbard & Powers, 1993).

Research that is to have any important impact on interpretive evaluation must include the teachers being studied, either as principal investigators or as collaborators. Interpretive research (Erickson, 1987) is one of the best methodologies to use to study interpretive evaluation in classroom settings. In this way the meanings that teachers have about the impact of ongoing interpretive evaluation in classroom settings will be well understood. Through such understandings, professional educators will become more consciously tuned into the power of interpretive evaluation on teacher change, learning, and the development of students.

Teachers who observe students with a perspective based on the latest knowledge and theories about language and learning, who question students in ways that support their development, who know the significance of the nature of error, and who organize the kinds of environments in which students are willing to take risks in their language use promote language development in their classrooms and are reflective about their teaching. John Dewey argued for the importance of reflective thinking on the part of teachers. As Archambault (1964), writing on Dewey, observed:

It (reflective thinking) emancipates us from merely impulsive and merely routine activity.... (It) enables us to direct our activities with foresight and to plan according to ... purposes of which we are aware. It enables us to act in deliberate and intentional fashion to ... come into command of what is now distant and lacking. By putting the consequences of different ways and lines of action before the mind, it enables us to know what we are about when we act. It converts action that is merely appetitive, blind, and impulsive into intelligent action. (p. 212)

Professionals who understand their power and their ability to observe development in students make use of inquiry for their own purposes. They begin to realize that they are developing professional responses to their students' language activities. They know how to ask questions that reflect their own theoretical view of teaching, learning, and language. They find ways to answer their own questions and to solve their own problems through reading, involvement with other professionals, careful evaluation of the oral and written language of their students, and continuous evaluation of their English or language arts curriculum. They confidently question educational theory, the results of the research, and new innovations in curriculum and material development (Moll, 1988). They are learners and inquirers of their own professional activities.

There are growing numbers of teachers seriously taking on the role of learner and inquirer. Many have begun writing about their experiences. Some call themselves writing process teachers, others whole-language teachers, teachers who believe in language across the curriculum, integrated curriculum, or curriculum devoted to serious problem solving on the part of their students. Nancie Atwell (1988) described such teachers, reflecting on herself as a teacher researcher.

## LEGITIMIZING ONGOING INTERPRETIVE EVALUATIVE RESEARCH IN THE CLASSROOM

Erickson (1987) stated that fieldwork for purposes of interpretive research involves:

(a) intensive, long-term participation in a field setting;
(b) careful recording of what happens in the setting by writing field notes and collecting other kinds of documentary evidence;
(c) analytic reflection on the ... record obtained and reporting by means of detailed description. (p. 118)

In ongoing interpretive evaluation, the teacher has an intensive and long-term relationship with those being evaluated (the teacher and the students); the teacher keeps careful notes and collects other kinds of documentary evidence, reflecting continuously on the nature of what the records and other related evidence mean in terms of student growth and professional self-evaluation.

Teachers may not be able to be as thorough as the researcher in analyzing all the data, but they may be even more reflective. Teachers are not studying the activities of outsiders but trying to understand the meanings of what they are doing, what the students are doing, and how these activities relate to each other and influence development and growth in students.

Evaluation like research is also based on asking questions, although many of the questions teachers ask about evaluation will be different than the questions researchers ask.

Teachers' questions might include: How does what I do influence what students are doing? What do the students' productions reveal about their linguistic and conceptual knowledge and their intellectual functioning? In what ways do classroom experiences with reading, writing, speaking, and listening influence the students' products? To what degree are students consciously aware of their own processes? How does this conscious awareness or lack of it influence students' compositions and comprehension?

At the same time that teachers use the answers to their questions to continuously plan instructional experiences for students, researchers will ask a different set of questions in order to explore the nature of interpretive evaluation. Their questions might include: What are the interaction patterns that influence evaluation by the teacher and self-evaluation on the part of students? What kinds of questions do teachers ask of themeselves and of students in order to evaluate? How do teachers learn to ask different types of questions? What devices do teachers use to answer their own questions about students' development, about curriculum, and about their own professional development? In what ways do outside-of-school language experiences influence students' compositions and comprehension? Answers to these kinds of questions among many others will inform the profession in general about the nature of ongoing interpretive evaluation. If researchers are working collaboratively with teachers, answers to these questions will provide teachres with information about the growth of individual students, about how various groups of students work together in classroom settings, and about how the community outside of the classroom influences teaching and learning.

Erickson (1987) listed reasons for interpretive research on teaching. One is the "need for specific understanding through documentation of concrete details of practice" (p. _). As has been stated, teachers are involved in ongoing evaluation in all phases of teaching. They make judgments constantly about students that may support or hinder student growth. Although classroom research has focused on many aspects of classroom practice, it needs to more specifically focus on the kinds of influences that ongoing interpretive evaluation has on teaching and learning English or language arts.

## SUGGESTIONS FOR RESEARCH ON INTERPRETIVE EVALUATION

We need to examine various aspects of ongoing interpretive evaluation through the use of interpretive research methodology using participant-observation fieldwork for researchers and for classroom teachers as well. Erickson (1987) argued:

The results of interpretive research are of special interest to teachers, who share similar concerns with the interpretive researcher. Teachers too are concerned with specifics of local meaning and local action; that is the stuff of life in daily classroom practice. (p. 156)

Collaboration between teachers and researchers is important because teachers working alone in the classroom may not always have the time or the opportunity to observe carefully enough. Together with a researcher, however, the teacher has another informed person's perspective on the meanings being expressed in the classroom setting. The researcher on the other hand gains a view of the classroom from someone who is extremely knowledgeable about daily life in that contextual setting and who can explain meanings that might take a researcher as a participant observer months and years to understand. When teacher and researcher collaborate by reading each other's field notes and deliberate carefully about their respective meanings they build a stronger case for their understandings and conclusions (Matlin & Wortman, 1989).

Whether researchers or teachers are working collaboratively or alone, there are a number of techniques especially relevant to English or language arts to help gather the kinds of information that would result in answering questions and developing important insights. Many instruments that can be used to collect such information are documented in the second volume of *Measures for Research and Evaluation in the English Language Arts* (Fagan, Jensen, & Cooper, 1985). Others can be found in recent publications that feature writing process and whole language teachers' descriptions of their own classrooms (K. Goodman et al., 1989; Hanson, Newkirk, & Graves, 1985; Meek, Armstrong, Austerfield, Graham, & Pakcett, 1983).

## Checklists, Inventories, and Interviews

Checklists, inventories, and interviews allow teachers to see change in their students and in their teaching. Answers to questions that focus on students' attitudes about language, the kinds of materials they read, and the range of topics they write about provide insight into students' beliefs about the power of language and its influence on their lives. Changes in such beliefs and attitudes can be traced across time and to specific curricular activities. Students can also be involved in recording their own work with a focus on self-evaluation. Research can document the use of such record keeping, its impact on students and reveal what understanding students and teachers have regarding the meanings of record keeping, its uses, and its purposes.

## Portfolios and Samples of Work

In programs where students write regularly and participate in literature-based reading programs, teachers keep portfolios of students' written work, which may include tapes of oral reading, lists of readings, reading responses, results of reading conferences between the teacher and the student, and selections of oral and written compositions. It would be important to document:

1. Ways that teachers collect, store, and analyze students' speech acts and literacy events.
2. Students' behaviors as they participate in reading, writing, and oral language activities.
3. Ways teachers respond to students during such activities.
4. How students respond to teacher's comments, interactions, and questions.
5. Kinds of information teachers want to know in order to make the best use of the student's work portfolio.
6. Ways that the analysis of such work influences teachers' views about language processes and instruction.

Other questions that research can detail include: Do teachers make use of special trait scoring, holistic scoring, miscue analysis, or other ways of analyzing students' work? How do such ways of evaluating become internalized? Do teachers use them in informal and incidental situations or only in carefully planned and formal ways? In what ways do teachers believe such knowledge helps them in working with students? In what ways do teachers use such knowledge to help students develop techniques of self-evaluation?

Teacher educators and researchers who have examined the use of miscue analysis by teachers (Long, 1985) report that teachers discuss the reading process in more sophisticated ways and often indicate that they will never be able to listen to students read in the same way that they did prior to learning miscue analysis procedures (Y. Goodman, Watson, & Burke, 1987). Teachers who involve their students in writing on a regular basis often question the use of holistic scoring when they realize that it masks specific growth over time. They begin to ask insightful questions about linguistic systems, cohesive analysis, voice, sense of story, and genre variations in order to be able to analyze and understand more about their students' development. I am more aware of this growth from working with teachers in inservice courses and professional development workshops. It would be important to know how these changes that teachers are able to talk about manifested in their actual daily interactions with their students.

## Dialogue Journals and Learning Logs

For those teachers who use dialogue journals (Staton, 1984) or learning logs with their students on a regular basis, it would be helpful to document teachers' responses to journals or logs to discover what this reveals about teacher evaluation, how teachers help students reflect on their own learning, and how teachers reflect in their curriculum planning what they've learned from such experiences. Analysis of teachers' responses to classroom experiences kept regularly in logs or as field notes would also yield important information about interpretive evaluation. Questions that researchers and teachers could explore include: In what ways do teachers respond to students' journals to allow students to become more reflective about their own processes?

In what ways are different kinds of responses from the teacher reflected in what the students write or think about? In what ways do journals and logs reveal the meanings students and teachers have about classroom contexts, especially as it relates to evaluation? In what ways do journals and logs reveal self-evaluation on the part of teachers and students?

In Japan there are teachers who analyze carefully the impact their written responses to students' writing have on the writing development of students (Kitagawa & Kitagawa, 1987). Similar insights gained from the analysis of teachers' responses to dialogue journals and learning logs would provide important information about the impact journals and logs have on student growth, teacher evaluation of students, self-evaluation on the part of both teachers and students, and teacher change.

## Anecdotal Records

Discussions about anecdotal records are usually found in sections labeled informal assessment techniques in professional languages arts textbooks. However, a carefully documented record of the setting of a particular significant event accompanied by information about time, persons involved, and other important aspects of the social context is one of the most useful pieces of evaluative information a teacher can have. It provides a record that a number of interested parties can review independently or discuss together to interpret its possible meanings. It provides opportunities for students to verify the teacher's perceptions. In many ways, anecdotal records are akin to the anthroplogist's field notes.

Discussions about anecdotal records often assume that the records are kept in the same way, at exact specified intervals, and in the same form throughout a school year. However, my experiences verified by others who also use anecdotal records suggest that such records change over time depending on the time of the year, the knowledge the teacher has accumulated about the student, and the particular kinds of information the teacher is trying to gather. Early in the year teachers may make very regular and detailed entries about many aspects of reading, writing, speaking, and listening, but as teachers get to know their students, the type of entries change focusing more specifically and are recorded only when a relevant activity occurs. The dynamic nature of whole language classrooms suggests that teachers who take responsibility for their own evaluation change the kinds of use they make of their evaluative instruments as well as the form of the instrument and the kinds of information they decide to document (Y. Goodman et al., 1989). The ways that teachers change their documentation of student growth, why and when they change the instruments they use are all kinds of understandings that need to be carefully researched to understand how anecdotal records help teachers in the evaluation of their students and at the same time help both teachers and students in self-evaluation.

## Observation Techniques: Kidwatching

As teachers are working directly with the students, they often step back to observe students and, in such moments of professional observation, make evaluative judgments about the students that inform instructional planning. Research questions that can provide needed documentation about professional observations include: How do teachers build a professional sense across time that helps them understand what they are looking at, what they are looking for, and what their observations mean in terms of student evaluation and curriculum planning? Why are some teachers more confident about their abilities in professional decision making about student evaluation than others? How do teachers' interpretive evaluations match the preceptions of students?

I call this kind of observation "kidwatching" (Y. Goodman, 1978, 1985) to highlight its ongoing and interpretive nature within the classroom setting in the hands of a professional. Kidwatching may be one of the major forces that influences teachers' reflective thinking about evaluation of students and the planning of instructional activities in the classroom. Kidwatching is not as conscious as it probably needs to be for teachers to gain the greatest insights from it. The ways teachers react to these observational moments in the classroom deserve serious study in order to understand the nature and the influences of kidwatching on curriculum development and instruction. Indeed, such study will provide understandings about the nature of teaching itself. It will reveal the development of a professional sense: the ability of teachers to understand how to respond to students in order to enhance their growth. This relates significantly to the concept of the zone of proximal development (Vygotsky, 1986).

## Questioning and Interactions

There is a wide range of issues concerning the nature of questions and interactions between teachers and students relating to ongoing interpretive evaluation in the classroom that can be addressed through research. How do the kinds of questions teachers ask of students reflect what teachers understand about language and language learning? When do teacher questions and interactions and what types of questions and interactions move students toward greater intuitive leaps in thinking and conceptual development? What kinds of teachers' questions focus students' attention on aspects of language learning that help them learn about language in appropriate ways? What is the nature of teachers' questions and interactions that enhance learning or interiere with learning? How do interactions and questions by teachers and students differ in large-group settings, small-group settings and in one-on-one relationships? How do students' questions reflect the use of questions by teachers?

## Conferences

A major aspect of the writing process curriculum that has become popular in recent years includes the use of different kinds of conferences between the teacher and the students in response to their writing. Teacher–student conferences have also focused on students' reading and other language activities and provide important avenues to both student and teacher evaluation. Although a good deal has been written about such conferences, there has been a lack of in-depth research detailing different kinds of conferences, their various procedures and purposes, the language structures that occur during such conferences, the meanings students and teachers have about such conferences, and its impact on student growth.

## Collaborative Learning

There is growing insight into the nature of collaborative learning in classrooms (Pontecorvo, 1987; Pontecorvo & Zucchermaglio, 1990; Teberosky, 1982). This includes not only peer interactions but also the collaborations between students and the teacher. Ongoing interpretive research would be helpful to gain in-depth understandings of how these learnings influence interpretive evaluation.

## Student Self-Evaluation

Self-evaluation and record keeping by students and how parents are involved in the evaluation are also an important aspect of the kind of evaluation that has been under discussion. The analysis of how students develop self-evaluation techniques, how teachers support such a process, and how parents are involved in a student's evaluation would be most informative.

## IN ANTICIPATION

The purpose here is not to be exhaustive concerning the potential research within the classroom that will result in significant and necessary information to help educational professionals understand constant and ongoing interpretive evaluation. Rather, I have suggested possibilities for research that will result in greater legitimacy for the kind of evaluation that I have been advocating. Once interpretive evaluation is taken seriously, valued in an appropriate manner, and understood better, the ways that such techniques can be used and studied in classroom settings will grow dynamically.

It is fitting therefore to conclude by quoting from a parent's evaluative response to a teacher's evaluation system that results in the kind of interpretive evaluation that has been explored in this article. It reflects the issue that the total school community is an integral part of ongoing interpretive evaluation and would benefit from the research on such evaluation.

Dear Ms. D.,

I just finished reading R.'s self evaluation form and I had to sit down and tell you about how I feel. With teachers of three children to see, a parent often has to stop and see teachers in trouble areas first and catch the others later or miss them totally. Unfortunately, I put your class in that trouble free category. After talking with you at open house and talking with R., I felt quite comfortable with skipping you at conference time.

R.'s dad and I know that R. is quite capable in doing her schoolwork and if problems arise they are probably in social areas as she is approaching her teen age years.

Back to the evaluation. Your developing this tool was an excellent idea in my estimation. Of course I know it's a pleasure to read that your child is doing well and is able to express it and why in writing. But I also think that if my child were having problems, reading this form would help to point them out.

As a parent involved for the past twelve years in this school, I have never received a form that dealt so clearly with communicating to parents the child's progress and ability and reason for the grade. I appreciate your effort in developing and using this form of communication. Keep talking to kids and parents and you will have reached us all.

Thanks so much for all your efforts.

F. D.

## References

Allington, R. (1980). Teacher interruption behaviors during primary-grade oral reading. *Journal of Educational Psychology, 72,* 371–377.

Archambault, R. (Ed.) (1964). *John Dewey on education.* Chicago: University of Chicago Press.

Atwell, N. (1987). *In the middle.* Portsmouth, NH: Boynton/Cook.

Artwell, N. (1988). *"Wonderings to pursue": The writing teacher as researcher.* Paper presented at the conference of the National Council of Teachers of English, Boston.

Erickson, F. (1987). Qualitative methods in research on teaching. *Handbook on research in teaching* (pp. 119–160). In V. K. Richardson (Ed.), American Educational Research Association.

Fagan, J., Jensen, J., & Cooper, C. (1985). *Measures for research and evaluation in the English language arts* (Vol. 2) Urbana, IL: ERIC and National Council of Teachers of English.

Goodman, K., Goodman, Y., & Hood, W. (Eds.) (1989). *The whole language evaluation book.* Postmouth, NH: Heinemann Educational Books.

Goodman, Y. (1978, June). Kidwatching: An alternative to testing. *The National Elementary Principal,* 41–45.

Goodman, Y. (1985). Kidwatching: Observing children in the classroom. In A. Jaggar & M. T. Smith-Burke (Eds.). *Observing the language learner* (pp. 9–18). Urbana, IL: National Council of Teachers of English; Newark, DE: International Reading Association.

Goodman, Y., Watson, D., & Burke, C. (1987). *Reading miscue inventory: Alternative procedures.* New York: Owen.

Gwynne, F. (1988). *The king who rained.* Englewood Cliffs, NJ: Prentice-Hall.

Hanson, J., Newkirk, T., & Graves, D. (Eds.) (1985). *Breaking ground.* Portsmouth, NH: Heinemann.

Hoffman, J. (1987). Rethinking the role of oral reading in basal instruction. *The Elementary School Journal, 87*(3), 367–374.

Hubbard, R., & Powers, B. (1993). *The art of classroom inquiry.* Portsmouth, NH: Heinemann.

Kitagawa, M. M., & Kitagawa, C. (1987). *Making connections with writing.* Portsmouth, NH: Heinemann.

Long, P. (1985). *The effectiveness of reading miscue instruments.* (Occasional Paper No. 13). Program in Language and Literacy. Tucson: University of Arizona.

Marek, A., Howard, D., Disinger, J., Jacobson, D., Earle, N., Goodman, Y., Hood, W., Woodley, C., Wortman, J., & Wortman, R. (1984). *The kidwatchers's guide: A whole language guide to assessment.* (Occasional Paper No. 9). Program in Language and Literacy. Tucson: University of Arizona.

Matlin, M., & Wortman, R. (1989). Observing readers and writers: A teacher and a researcher learn together. In G. S. Pinell & M. L. Matlin (Eds.), *Teachers and research: Language learning in the classroom.* Newark, DE: International Reading Association.

McDermott, R. (1974). Achieving school failure: An anthropological approach to illiteracy and social stratification. In G. D. Spindler (Ed.), *Education and cultural processes* (pp. 82–118). New York: Holt, Rinehart & Winston.

Meek, M., Armstrong, S., Austerfield, V., Graham, J., & Pakcett, E. (1983). *Achieving literacy: Longitudinal studies of adolescents learning to read.* London: Routledge & Kegan Paul.

Moll, L. (1988). Some key issues in teaching Latino students. *Language Arts, 65*(5), 465–473.

Pontecorvo, V. (1987). Discussing for reasoning: The role of argument in knowledge construction. In E. De Corte, J. G. L. C. Lodewjks, R. Parmentier, & P. Span (Eds.), *Learning and instruction.* Oxford, England: Pergamon Press; Louvain, Belgium: Louvain University Press.

Pontecorvo C., & Zucchermaglio, C. (1990). A passage to literacy: Learning in a social context. In Y. Goodman (Ed.), *How children construct literacy: Piagetian perspectives.* Newark DE: International Reading Association.

Shavelson, R. J., & Stern, P. (1981). Research on teachers' pedagogical thoughts, judgments, decisions, and behavior. *Review of Educational Research, 51*(4), 455–499.

Squire, J. (Ed.) (1987, April). A special themed issue: The state of assessment in reading. *The Reading Teacher, 40*(8).

Staton, J. (1984. November). Research ideas: Using school records. *Dialogue 2,* 3. p. 6. Washington, DC: Center For Applied Linguistics.

Teberosky, A. (1982). Construccion de escritura atraves de la interaccion grupal. In E. Ferriero & M. Gomez Palacio (Eds.). *Nuevas perspectivas sobres los procesos de lectura y escritura.* Mexico City, Mexico: Siglo Veintiuno Editores.

Vygotsky, L. (1986). *Thought and language* (Kozulin, Ed.). Cambridge, MA: MIT Press.

Wilhelms, F. (Ed.) (1967). *Evaluation as feedback and guide.* Washington, DC: Association for Supervision and Curriculum Development.

# TEACHER-BASED ASSESSMENT
# OF LITERACY LEARNING

## Nancy Frey
San Diego State University

## Elfrieda H. Hiebert
University of Colorado

Teachers have an abundance of information about their students' literacy accomplishments and their classrooms as literate environments. As teachers examine students' writing, they can see the influence of books read by the class. As teachers listen to students in a social studies lesson, they can detect whether a critical perspective toward point of view taught in reading extends to discussion about expository content. Wise practitioners recognize the value of these observations as a rich source of assessment data (R. C. Anderson, Hiebert, Scott, & Wilkinson, 1985; Church, 1994; Dorr-Bremme & Herman, 1986; K. Goodman, 1997; Salmon-Cox, 1981; West, 1998).

Policymakers, parents, and the public are also interested in the information gained through assessment. Critical literacy goals like students' ability to select literature or to detect bias in writing cannot be assessed adequately through multiple-choice tests. If students' progress toward such goals is to be measured, data from children's participation in classroom literacy events must be considered with data from other forms of measurement (Valencia, 1997; Winograd & Arrington, 1999).

Assessment methods and purposes often appear confusing to parents and practitioners. Although most recognize the need to sample student performance for the purpose of accountability, standardized test results reveal little about the individual student because these samples are gained in an atypical situation and with limited response modes. This is particularly problematic because the data yielded are decontextualized and fail to reflect the experiences of many students (Madaus, 1994). Fortunately, the increased emphasis on assessment and testing in the past decade has led to a growing knowledge base, and evaluation

researchers have differentiated the purposes of assessment (Lipson & Wixson, 1997; Winograd & Arrington, 1999; Wixson & Pearson, 1998). Lapp, Fisher, Flood, and Cabello (2000) categorized the purposes of assessment as follows:

1. Diagnosis of individual student needs.
2. Provision of accountability information.
3. Evaluation of programs.
4. Assessment to inform instruction.

It is this last purpose that serves as the focus for this discussion of assessment. In an era where test scores are being used to make far-reaching educational decisions about students, it is vital that teacher-based assessments be recognized for their contribution of information about an individual student. This balanced use of broad-based measures to evaluate programs and provide accountability information with other measures that gauge the individual learner is referred to as "system validity" (Wixson & Pearson, 1998).

In this chapter, the existing literature on teacher-based assessment is reviewed with the aims of creating a unified perspective and suggesting next steps to align current practice with available knowledge on teacher-based assessment. Assessment of literacy skills and practices will be the focus in this review. Since the publication of the first edition of this *Handbook* in 1991, the number of studies of teacher-based assessment practices has increased significantly, and a growing body of scholarship is available. This chapter presents current work in the field, emanating both from research and exemplary practice.

## A MODEL OF TEACHER-BASED ASSESSMENT

Some elements of teacher-based assessment have a long history, such as informal reading inventories (Gray, 1920), sight word tests (Dolch, 1926), and measures of silent reading ability (Dearborn & Westbrook, 1921). The role of assessment has been expanded from these early measures of skills. Teacher-based assessments are now valued as a necessary element in determining future instruction. This concept was illustrated in the work of Vygotsky (1962) and was extended by Brown and Reeve (1985). Vygotsky's concept of the zone of proximal development suggests that students may perform at one level when working independently but, with guidance, may be capable of higher levels of performance. This "bandwidth" (Brown & Reeve, 1985) between students' independent work and their performance with guidance is termed the zone of proximal development. Assessment is critical because teachers construct a framework or scaffold within the individual's zone of proximal development, facilitating acquisition of skills and strategies.

The principles of sound assessment and the practices of effective instruction merge in teacher-based assessment. Cronbach (1960) identified three principles of assessment: careful observations, a variety of methods and measures, and integration of information. Expanding this definition, Calfee and Hiebert (1988, 1991) proposed that teachers participate in several practices that reflect Cronbach's elements of assessment. These practices, discussed later, are planning goals and purposes, collecting data, and interpretation. These activities are also synonymous with the processes of effective instruction (Bereiter & Scardamalia, 1996). As with instruction, these dimensions are recursive rather than linear, but at times each phase becomes the center of attention. How this occurs is described next.

### Planning Goals and Purposes

The basis of teacher assessment is necessarily linked to the teacher's vision of literacy. The questions that guide teachers' assessment and their interpretations of children's products and processes are determined by the view of literacy the individual teacher holds. Consequently, visions of literacy require some clarification on the part of the teacher as to how a literate individual appears at different points of development (Farnan, Flood, & Lapp, 1994). For example, fundamental processes such as decoding and self-monitoring for meaning underlie comprehension and composition at all stages. Teachers look for behaviors that serve as evidence of these processes based on their view of literacy development. Thus, the goals of a teacher's assessment practice begin with his or her beliefs about literacy.

The purpose for gathering information also plays a role in determining what is assessed. Teachers use information for a variety of purposes, foremost to plan instructional experiences for children. Information on students' existing strategies and knowledge is necessary for choosing materials and activities forming groups (Flood, Lapp, Flood, & Nagel, 1992), and determining the appropriate amount of teacher direction (Bauer, 1999). In

each case, the teacher chooses methods and instruments that will best capture the specific data needed to make informed instructional decisions. For this reason, a variety of procedures for data collection in teacher-based assessment are necessary.

### Collecting Data

A review of the literature reveals a variety of informal assessment measures: performance samples, conferences, questioning, observations, checklists, portfolios, inventories, surveys, and interviews. These techniques can be collapsed into three basic activities on the part of the teacher: observing, dialogue with students, and sampling student work. A description of the methods involved in observing, talking with students, and sampling work follows.

***Observing.*** As students work in classrooms, teachers observe and gain information about their knowledge and strategies. Sometimes these observations occur in unlikely settings, such as an informal exchange on the playground. More often, they are carefully planned and carried out by the teacher, using checklists and inventories. The wealth of information gained from observations makes it understandable that teachers identify these as their most important source of information (Church, 1994; Dorr-Bremme & Herman, 1986; Salmon-Cox, 1981; West, 1998). Observations have a benefit because information about students' behaviors can be acquired in everyday settings. Evaluative contexts like tests can produce less than optimal performances for many students (Hill, 1984; Moore, 1996; Mosenthal & Na, 1980); while observations, however, permit teachers to gain information about students without the constraints of tests. When this information is combined with analyses of student work samples, a comprehensive view of students' processes and products within particular domains emerges (Rupley et al., 1999). Although teachers cannot possibly begin to document all their observations, documentation on some occasions can assist reflective practice and provide information to share with students, parents, administrators, and other teachers (Hole & McEntree, 1999).

Checklists and inventories can be helpful because they specify particular dimensions for observation and provide a means for summarizing those observations (Martin, 1999). Ruddell's (1991) Developmental Inventory is an example of a simple instrument for capturing students' evolving listening, reading, speaking, and writing skills. Like many inventories, the Developmental Inventory is a log for a broad range of literacy behaviors observed by the teacher over a period of days or weeks. In contrast, checklists are most frequently used to record a specific behavior performed in a single session. Table 44.1 illustrates a checklist based on the work of Sulzby (1991) and notes the developmental progress of early readers as they make meaning of text. These and other checklists and inventories assist teachers is determining what strategies are being used, as well as those that require reteaching (Valencia, 1997).

Many other teacher-based assessments are not commercially prepared but rather are created by the teacher in an effort to capture specific details about a student (K. P. Wolf, 1993).

TABLE 44.1. Checklist of Storybook Reading

| Broad Categories | Date | Book Title |
|---|---|---|
| 1. Attending to pictures, not forming stories. | ——— | ——— |
| 2. Attending to pictures, forming *oral* stories. | ——— | ——— |
| 3. Attending to pictures, reading, and storytelling mixed. | ——— | ——— |
| 4. Attending to pictures, forming *written* stories. | ——— | ——— |
| 5. Attending to print. | ——— | ——— |

*Note.* Adapted from "Assessing Young Children's Literacy: Documenting Growth and Informing Practice," by C. Vukelich, 1997, *The Reading Teacher, 50,* p. 432. Adapted with permission.

These anecdotal records are notes and observations written by the teacher to record events and behaviors about a student (Winograd & Arrington, 1999). Anecdotal records also serve to refine future instruction (Y. Goodman, 1985) because they promote reflective practice. In fact, experienced teachers report that the true value of anecdotal records occurs when a series of notes is analyzed for patterns (Winograd & Arrington, 1999).

Observations in teacher-based assessments are not limited to a child's performance. They are also used to consider the nature of literacy experiences. A child's failure to progress may reflect a lack of opportunities to participate in activities rather than any deficiency in capability, as when a student's morning is frequently disrupted by pull-out services (Vaughn, Moody, & Schumm, 1998). Assessing the instructional experiences that are available to children provides another critical source of information for teachers.

***Dialogue with students.*** The second dimension in data collection for teacher-based assessment is dialogue with students. Questioning, conferencing, and surveys are the major activities involving teacher-student interaction Questioning refers to the interaction between students and teachers that occurs in typical classroom contexts (e.g., Fisette, 1993). Conferencing is a more structured interaction than questioning because it typically involves an individual student and is organized around a specific task or set of questions (Ediger, 1999). However, teachers may find it impractical to conference with children as often as they would like. Another technique for gathering data is surveying. Teachers may choose to administer questionnaires or surveys that involve written responses. Such surveys yield a different data set than questioning and conferencing. Thus, the three types of interaction—questioning, conferencing, and surveys—are treated separately.

The most frequent type of classroom interaction is for teachers to question students (Cazden, 1986). In turn, students also pose questions. The use of questioning strategies increases student engagement and provides the teacher with an opportunity to gauge understanding and inform practice (Alvermann & Guthrie, 1993). This dual purpose of questioning—to gauge understanding and inform instruction—is a primary illustration of the recursive relationship between assessment and practice. Although many studies have analyzed the quality of teacher questioning techniques (e.g., Alvermann & Hayes, 1989; Armbruster, 1991; Carlsen, 1991; Guzack, 1969), the relationship of questioning to teacher-based assessment requires a further extension.

Questioning frameworks like K-W-L, which stands for Know, Want to Know, and Learned (Ogle, 1986), and Question the Author (Beck, McKeown, Worthy, Sandora, & Kucan, 1993) provide guidance for teachers in both the content and process of questioning and instruction. These teacher-based assessment strategies embed assessment with instruction because they are used within the delivery of content. At the same time, these procedures are taught to students to increase their comprehension of content. The K-W-L framework is a graphic organizer for brainstorming and information gathering (Ogle, 1986). This technique furnishes the teacher with vital information on the prior knowledge of the group (McAllister, 1994) by displaying the collective knowledge and curiosity of the class regarding a particular topic. Like K-W-L, Question the Author serves the dual purpose of assessment and instruction. As a strategy for student use, it encourages learners to focus on the intent of the author. The teacher first models the reader's questions by "thinking aloud." The teacher reads a passage and interjects queries about the author's message (Beck, McKeown, Hamilton, & Kucan, 1997). Question the Author becomes an assessment tool when the teacher uses the questions generated by students to clarify, reteach, and extend. The use of Question the Author has been shown to promote the reflective teaching practices necessary for teacher-based assessment (Almasi, McKeown, & Beck, 1996).

Raphael (1986) also discussed a framework for teaching students about the relationship between questions and answers through the use of "Right There," "Putting It Together," and "On My Own" questions. In the case of Right There questions, students look to the text for answers. Putting It Together questions require the student to connect information across texts using multiple sources. Students apply their unique background knowledge to On My Own questions (Raphael, 1986). When students are made aware of different structures in expository text, their writing and comprehension can improve (Raphael, Engler, & Kirschner, 1986). Similarly, the use of questioning techniques like questions and answers focuses teachers' assessment efforts in ascertaining their students' comprehension of the text (Leu & Kinzer, 1999). Determining this relationship between the text and the background knowledge of students is at the heart of effective questioning in the English language arts.

Conferencing, like questioning, is another strategy used by teachers to assess their students. Much of the guidance for conferencing as a classroom interaction and assessment tool comes from work in writing process and writer's workshop (e.g., Atwell, 1998; Calkins, 1986; Dahl & Farnan, 1998; Graves, 1983). In writer's workshop, the teacher and student meet to discuss aspects of the student's current work. The teacher–student conference occurs primarily as a short (5 minutes) individual exchange to discuss a composition (Johnston, 1987). These

TABLE 44.2. Planning Questions of the Index of Reading Awareness

1. If you could only read some of the sentences in the story because you were in a hurry, which ones would you read?

0  a. Read the sentences in the middle of the story.
2  b. Read the sentences that tell you the most about the story.
1  c. Read the interesting, exciting sentences.

2. When you tell other people about what you read, what do you tell them?

2  a. What happened in the story.
0  b. The number of pages in the book.
1  c. Who the characters are.

3. If the teacher told you to read a story to remember the general meaning, what would you do?

2  a. Skim through the story to find the main parts.
1  b. Read all of the story and try to remember everything.
0  c. Read the story and remember all of the words.

4. Before you start to read, what kind of plans do you make to help you read better?

0  a. You don't make any plans. You just start reading.
1  b. You choose a comfortable place.
2  c. You think about why you are reading.

5. If you had to read very fast and could only read some words, which ones would you try to read?

1  a. Read the new vocabulary words because they are important.
0  b. Read the words that you could pronounce.
2  c. Read the words that tell the most about the story.

Note. A score of 2 indicates a strategic response that is planful and exhibits awareness of reading goals and strategies; a score of 1 indicates a response that describes a general cognitive act including an understanding that some extra effort and special thinking will be required to remember the material; a score of 0 indicates an inappropriate response. From "Children's Metacognition About Reading: Issues in Definition, Measurement and Instruction," by J. E. Jacobs and S. G. Paris, 1987, *Educational Psychologist, 22*, p. 269. Copyright 1987 by Educational Psychologist.

writing conferences are frequently used for editing and revision of a work in progress and allow the teacher to gauge current skills and gain insight into the individual's problem-solving strategies (Graves, 1983).

Surveys are another form of data collection in teacher-based assessment and are an alternative response to the time constraints faced by classroom teachers. Surveys are typically administered to groups of students, and their responses are in written form. Jacobs and Paris' (1987) Index of Reading Awareness can give teachers information about the repertoire of strategies used by students in planning, and regulating and evaluating their reading. The questions for planning one's reading (Table 44.2) could be used in an interview, but Jacobs and Paris' categorization of typical responses assists teachers who wish to get information quickly from many students. Numerous measures can also be found to survey children about their reading habits and attitudes (e.g., Allen, Cipielewski, & Stanovich, 1992; Estes, 1971; McKenna & Kear, 1990), motivation for reading (Constantino, Lee, Cho, & Krashen, 1997; Heathington, 1979), and literature preferences (Bushman, 1997). Because children's interests can change frequently, surveys also aid teachers in making choices about topics for demonstration lessons in writing, and in selecting books for instruction, read alouds, and the classroom library.

***Sampling student work.*** The third method for collecting data for the purposes of teacher-based assessment is student work samples. Work samples, also called performance samples, refer to student work that remains as an artifact for teachers to analyze

to determine progress. Writing and reading samples are often selected by teachers to evaluate progress and determine future teaching points. Portfolios are used in many classrooms to represent the body of work completed by the student, as well as a method for a student and teacher to have focused conversations about the work (Winograd & Arrington, 1999). Each of these is discussed separately.

***Writing samples.*** Student writing samples are collected by teachers to gauge progress in both the mechanics and craft of writing. Teachers are guided by a long tradition of evaluation in the field of writing (Dahl & Farnan, 1998) that differentiates between quantitative and qualitative aspects of writing. As stated earlier in the chapter, the teacher's vision of literacy dictates what will be assessed. Simple counts of elements like adjectives, T units, words, or sentences can be used as gross indicators of progress. In a classroom in which writing is taught in this manner, measurements of story structure have little status. Conversely, writing assessments focused on character, plot, setting, and audience will fail to capture the evidence of writing as a measure of output (S. A. Wolf & Gearhart, 1997). As with all teacher-based assessments, planning for the goals of purposes of assessment is essential to capture the information needed to inform future writing instruction.

Single global ratings of students' compositions (like a letter grade or numerical score) may be helpful for accountability purposes but usually will not provide sufficient information for the classroom teacher in planning instructional experiences. For classroom purposes, schemes that focus on specific

TABLE 44.3. Criteria for Evaluating Writing

| Trait | Level | Criteria |
|---|---|---|
| Message quality | 1–2 | Focus is unclear; there is no elaboration of ideas; there is no evidence of awareness of intended reader. |
| | 3–4 | Message is communicated, although focus may change; elaboration occurs through additional evidence or details; ideas, information, genre, register are not consistent. |
| | 5–6 | Message is tightly; ideas and details create a mood, tone; ideas, information, genre, register are chosen to communicate message. |
| Coherence | 1–2 | There is no relationship among ideas; clear organizational design is lacking; no transitions are used. |
| | 3–4 | Organizational design, differentiation of important from less important ideas, and some transitions linking ideas beginning to appear. |
| | 5–6 | Relationships among ideas are established through order or subordination; organizational design is compatible with purpose. |
| Language | 1–2 | Flat, unimaginative language is used; incomplete, run-on, or simple sentences are used. |
| | 3–4 | Simple sentences are used effectively and attempts are made in variety of imaginative language, word order, and type and length of sentences. |
| | 5–6 | Fresh, imaginative language is used to create an image and capture reader's interest such as leads, strong verbs, vivid descriptions, figures of speech; word order and type and length of sentences are varied for emphasis or effect. |
| Language conventions | 1–2 | Many spelling, grammatical, punctuation, capitalization, and format errors make message difficult to understand. |
| | 3–4 | Some errors are made in spelling, grammar, capitalization, punctuation, and format. |
| | 5–6 | Conventions of spelling, grammar, capitalization, punctuation, and format are observed at developmental level. |

Note. Adapted from *Criteria for Evaluating Writing* (*Grades 2–6*), by Adams County (CO) School District 12, 1989, Thornton, CO: Author.

dimensions are more helpful. The compositions of children who have been working on mysteries, for example, might be rated for creation of setting and maintenance of suspense. Reports can be rated for coherence of the organization and elaboration of ideas within paragraphs.

Rubrics are a useful tool for focusing on specific dimensions of student writing samples, and can be designed to incorporate both the quantitative and qualitative aspects of writing. Rubrics are a framework for measurement that contains descriptors of the essential elements of a piece of work (Winograd & Arrington, 1999). Many rubrics use a holistic scoring approach (Cooper, 1977). Holistic scoring techniques allow teachers to consider students' writing in depth because ratings are given to a number of different dimensions in a composition, frequently referred to as features or primary traits (Winograd & Arrington, 1999). Table 44.3 is an example of a holistic rubric used to assist teachers in their assessment and instruction of writing in Adams County (CO) School District 12 (1989). This scheme illustrates the manner in which criteria for scores related to both writing conventions and message quality can be addressed.

***Reading samples.*** Like writing, the evaluation of reading in teacher-based assessment has a long history (Venezky, 1984). One of the earliest teacher-based assessments used in the United States were the informal reading inventories developed by Gray (1915, 1920). In informal reading inventories (IRIs), students read passages aloud. Errors, identified as deviations from the text, are counted. Responses to comprehension questions about the reading passage are also analyzed (Swearingen & Allen, 2000). Many of the informal reading inventories available today (e.g., Burns & Roe, 1999; Swearingen & Allen, 2000) go beyond the simple counting of errors and include an analysis component for the teacher in classifying errors by type (e.g., omissions, insertions). Comprehension error patterns are also used

to ascertain areas of needed work such as context clues or main idea. Despite this emphasis on patterns of errors, the use of informal reading inventories has remained largely quantitative in that numbers of oral reading errors or incorrect comprehension responses are used to establish students' frustration, instruction, and independent reading levels. The reading passages in IRIs are often assigned a grade level designation to assist the teacher in determining whether the student is reading at the expected level for age (Burns & Roe, 1999).

Miscue analysis is a teacher-based assessment for reading that extends the quantified data yielded from informal reading inventories. K. S. Goodman (1968) used students' miscues (deviations from texts) to determine the reader's underlying understanding of semantic, syntactic, and graphophonic systems of written language. Children's miscues are viewed as windows into their knowledge of those systems. Thus, the concern in miscue analysis is not with determining the student's grade level but in sampling students' reading performances so that their control of reading strategies become apparent (Y. M. Goodman & K. S. Goodman, 1996). When teachers view children's attempts as evidence of their underlying strategies and knowledge, they can obtain valuable information about future instruction. Miscue analysis calls for teachers to view children's deviations from the text as clues about what they do know (Leslie & Jett-Simpson, 1997) rather than as mistakes to be corrected.

Marie M. Clay (1979) developed a popular form of teacher-based assessment in reading by creating a recording system for applying the principles of miscue analysis in the classroom. This procedure, called running records, uses a coding system to record the reading behaviors exhibited by an emergent reader. Errors of omission, substitution, and deletion, as well as self-corrections, are then analyzed at a later time by the teacher (Clay, 1993). The running record is scored both quantitatively and qualitatively. Errors are first counted to determine the proper instructional text level for the reader. In Clay's model, the instructional text level is identified by a score of 90% to 94% accuracy. A score of 95% or above is termed an independent reading level, and a score of 89% or lower is considered too difficult for the reader (Fountas & Pinnell, 1996). Each error and self-correction is then evaluated to determine what cueing systems where being applied by the reader at the time. As with miscue analysis, the teacher hypothesizes whether the reader was using meaning, structural, and visual information to problem solve (Fountas & Pinnell, 1996). Future instruction for the reader centers on assisting the reader in integrating all three cueing systems to read with improved accuracy and fluency (Clay, 1993).

*Portfolios.* Sampling student work is not a new idea, however, the use of portfolio assessments has redefined what constitutes performance assessment because of the involvement of the student in selecting entries. Tierney (1998) reminded us that "this entails a shift from something you *do to* students to something you *do with* them" (p. 378). The original use of the term *portfolio* comes from the collections of the best work of artists and architects. In education, portfolios more typically consist of samples that represent particular genres of tasks over a period of time rather than just the students' best work (Tierney et al., 1998). The idea of examining samples of work that come from everyday settings rather than from test settings is restructuring assessment in many classrooms, school districts, and even state departments of education (Brewer, 1989; Calfee & Gearhart, 1998; Flood & Lapp, 1989; Kentucky Department of Education, 2000).

Teachers use various structures to organize and store their portfolios. Many use binders or expanding files to store student work, and some use baskets or bins (Vukelich, 1997). It is the organizational structures for portfolios that continue to challenge teachers beyond the logistical issues of storage. Teachers are advised to begin with targeting one aspect of literacy at a time (writing, for instance) in order to refine criteria and teach students about the portfolios (Vukelvich, 1997; Winograd & Arrington, 1999). Once a target has been established, criteria for portfolio entries should be established and taught (Courtney & Abodeeb, 1999; Potter, 1999; Winograd & Arrington, 1999). These criteria commonly center on pieces to be proud of, work that demonstrates growth and change, and goals developed by the teacher and student (Vukelvich, 1997). Wilcox (1997) suggested organizing portfolios around the types of artifacts themselves:

*Reading artifacts* that make connections through reading, such as diagrams, outlines, and summaries.
*Thinking artifacts* that construct our knowledge base, such as mind maps, steps to problem solving, and responses to prompts.
*Writing artifacts* that make meaning through writing, such as self-evaluations, a publication piece, and reflections on a learning experience.
*Interacting artifacts* that share and scaffold ideas, such as peer assessments, brainstorming charts, and a problem and solution.

*Demonstrating artifacts* that show application and transfer of new learning, such as a project or exhibition. (p. 35)

Many teachers use portfolios as a dynamic teacher-based assessment to advise instructional and curricular decisions (Tierney et al., 1998). To accomplish this, portfolios require clearly defined goals and purposes, data collection that traverses time and task, and a system of interpretation. This "portfolio pedagogy" (Yancey, 1992) can guarantee meaningful effort for both student and teacher and prevent the creation of portfolios that simply serve as collection bins of random student work (Wilcox, 1997).

## Interpretation

Once goals and purposes for teacher-based assessment have been planned, and data have been collected on a student's literacy experiences, the final task is to interpret and act on the information gathered. Accurate interpretation and meaningful response depend on three practices: the recursive nature of assessment and instruction, attention to process as well as product, and sensitivity to the needs of diverse learners.

In practice, skilled teachers interpret and act on information as they gather it, illustrating how assessment is embedded in instruction, rather than competing with it. As teachers listen to students respond to a reading, they are assessing students' content knowledge and literacy processes. These on-the-spot interpretations may lead to changes in the questions that a teacher asks or in the activities themselves. For example, when a teacher realizes that students are unfamiliar with a topic, semantic mapping may be added to the lesson. A teacher's line of questioning may change quickly when a student offers an opinion that demands further discussion.

Useful interpretations of teacher-based assessments mean that teachers also attend to the processes in which students are engaged, not just the final products they produce. Products are not disregarded; however, the way readers and writers plan, monitor, and revise their interpretations as they read and write becomes of interest as well. As teachers delve into students' thinking processes rather than simply examine products, they will uncover surprises (Harste, Burke, & Woodward, 1994).

Understanding the influence of their students' cultural and linguistic experiences on classroom performances is especially critical in interpreting and acting on teacher-based assessment data (Schmidt, 1995). Even children's willingness to express themselves in classroom contexts may be a function of different cultural norms or facility with English. This discontinuity between interaction patterns of children's culture and that of the school has been well illustrated (e.g., Au & Mason, 1981; Heath, 1982; Ogbu, 1999; Philips, 1983; see also Chapter 32, this volume). Sometimes, children's use of Black Vernacular English is incorrectly interpreted as evidence of decoding problems (Burke, Pflaum, & Krafle, 1982; Washington & Miller-Jones, 1989). Misjudgments based on fluency are also made with children for whom English is a second language. This contributes to the overrepresentation of students from other cultures in special education (MacMillan & Reschly, 1998; Patton, 1998). Because children from nonmainstream cultures are often placed in programs that emphasize skill and drill (Delpit, 1995; Godina, 1999; Moll, Estrada, Diaz, & Lopes, 1980), teachers should think about previous learning experiences before they make generalizations about children's capabilities.

A more equitable response to the needs of diverse learners is to establish practices in assessment and instruction that encourage their participation. Studies have shown that classroom environments can be created that allow the communicative patterns of children from nonmainstream cultures to be recognized (Au & Jordan, 1981; Heath, 1982; Heath & Mangiola, 1991; Pang & Cheng, 1998). Some general shifts in classrooms participation structures can create interactions that are more amenable for all children. For example, formats where children are encouraged to contribute questions and comments create more student participation and increase learning (Alfassi, 1998; Palincsar & Brown, 1984; Rosenshine & Meister, 1994; Tower, 2000). The use of questioning frames like K-W-L (Ogle, 1986), Question the Author (Beck et al., 1993), and questions and answers (Raphael, 1986) honor the needs of diverse learners because there are deliberately structured opportunities for students to contribute their questions and insights. By extension, the quality of the assessment information is increased because the interactions are constructed to elicit the background knowledge and experiences of students (Bachman, 1992).

Even though information may be shared with parents or administrators, the primary reason for teachers to engage in teacher-based assessments is to assist student learning. At one point or another, teachers use information to adapt, initiate, or eliminate learning experiences in their classrooms. It would be assumed that teachers trained in literacy would respond more to the quality of the message, and not to the conventions alone. There can be no doubt that a view toward alternative interpretations of students' efforts only serve to create a deeper understanding of students' capabilities and needs.

## FUTURE DIRECTIONS

Action on three fronts will forward the alignment of practice with the existing knowledge base on teacher-based assessment. The first is preservice experiences in university programs; the second is continued staff development for inservice teachers, and the third is a solid research base that verifies the nature and effects of teacher-based assessment practices.

### Preservice Experiences

Since the first edition of this book was published in 1991, there has been an increased interest in teacher-based assessment and its importance in preservice teacher preparation programs (e.g., N. A. Anderson, 1999; Briggs, Tully, & Stiefer, 1998; Hedrick, 1999). Preservice field experiences today are more likely to involve assessment, tutoring, and small group instruction in reading and language arts. This may be in response to former president Bill Clinton's "America's Reading Challenge," a program that emphasized tutoring for struggling readers (U.S.

Department of Education, 1996). However, even those who advocate teachers as evaluation experts (e.g., Y. Goodman, 1985; Johnston, 1987) provide little indication of the manner in which teachers gain this expertise. Teaching has been a profession very different than a field like clinical psychology, which also relies on expertise in assessment. Clinical psychologists have internships in the hundreds of hours. In some teacher preparation programs, teachers have only one course on evaluation and assessment, and that one course most likely emphasizes test development. A growing body of work suggests a necessary shift to explicit teacher-based assessment training in university teacher preparation programs (Briggs, Tully, & Stiefer, 1998; Education Commission of the States, 1999; Popham, 1999) in order to provide all students with meaningful instruction (Spinelli, 1998).

Laboratory experiences, such as those proposed by Berliner (1985) and supported by Metcalf and Kahlich (1998) are critical to teacher education programs. Student teachers participating in this model can gain expertise in observing children, analyzing samples of their work, and interpreting and acting on results (Berliner, 1985). Berliner described university-based laboratories in addition to field-based ones. Field-based situations give prospective teachers the opportunity to apply knowledge as they interview youngsters and observe them in daily classroom life. In laboratory contexts, prospective teachers can reflect on students' processes and products as they mull over videotapes of classroom events, analyze transcripts of class discussions, and study samples of student work. Support of Berliner's proposal can be found in a study by Metcalf and Kahlich (1998) that reported that student teachers that participated in clinical experiences developed effective teaching skills at a faster rate than those who did not.

### Staff Development for Inservice Teachers

Once in the teaching field, teachers need ongoing experiences to refine their assessment practice. To date, little research has been concerned with verifying the features of staff development that are successful in creating teacher expertise in assessing students. However, some informed predictions can be made about the form such expertise would take, based on the authors' experiences with a variety of innovative school districts in several states. A composite has been developed from these school districts.

In this composite school district, teams of teachers identified goals of their literacy programs. These goals, based on state content and performance standards, were large enough in scope to be significant but not so large that it would be unclear if a student had accomplished the goal. For example, one goal was for students to understand the themes of different kinds of texts. The evidence of these goals at different developmental levels were identified. First-grade students were expected to understand that there are problems in stories that characters need to resolve. The ability to extract themes from stories and to develop these themes in their own writing served as evidence at the third-grade level. Evidence of goals were articulated in recognition that students utilize a continuum of strategies across grade levels (Hiebert, 1994).

Once goals had been identified, ways of assessing student acquisition of goals within and beyond instructional activities were established. The school district then offered inservice sessions in which teachers at school sites worked on implementing instructional and assessment activities for particular goals. Part of this inservice consisted of teachers observing one another in implementing instructional and assessment strategies in their classrooms. This use of such a peer coaching model has been shown to positively effect both teacher and student outcomes (Kohler, 1997). When teachers are guided in evaluation theory and then supported in classroom application, the outcomes are positive. Staff development in classroom assessment can increase considerably the consistency of teachers' evaluation of information (Borko, 1997; Gil, Polin, Vinsonhaler, & Van Roekel, 1980). Calfee (1994) observed that teachers "need well-designed and adequately supported staff development to acquire skill and confidence. Without skill, classroom assessment is likely to be misguided and invalid. Without confidence, it simply will not happen" (p. 347).

Several characteristics of this program should be noted. The first is that the changes emanated from teachers' concerns. As state mandates have increased the focus on test scores, teachers have protested that standardized tests do not capture the goals of their classroom programs. The district responded by supporting ways to supplement standardized test data.

A second characteristic is the school site as the unit of change. A very different sense of collegiality exists among teachers when, performance samples in hand, they interact about their students' progress than when teachers meet with ill-defined goals. In fact, time for reflection and collegial interaction in decision making are a primary goal of many school restructuring efforts (e.g., Hiebert & Calfee, 1989; Schaefer, 1967; Yopp & Guillaume, 1999; Zederayko & Ward, 1999), This school-wide action research (Allen & Calhoun, 1998) relies on the very same tenets of effective teacher-based assessment: planning for goals and purposes, collecting data, and interpreting information. This recursive process (Stringer, 1999) serves a school in much the same manner as teacher-based assessment, because its results can inform future decisions regarding staff development.

### Research

On the basis of scholarship and good practice, a rather coherent argument can be made that classroom environments are more conductive to learning when students and teachers are involved in planning, monitoring, and assessing as part of daily classroom tasks. Data confirming the nature and effects of teacher-based assessments are warranted in order to refine our knowledge of how effective assessment is defined and implemented and how to interpret the evidence it yields. Evidence supporting the use of teacher-based assessment is unlikely to be found in standard evaluations of classroom practice that measure effectiveness solely by student test performances. A broader view of what constitutes evidence for wise practice is required. Two lines of research illustrate the form that this evidence could take.

The first line of research to pursue might involve documenting the effects of teacher-based assessments on teacher practice. Capable teachers actively engage in refining their practice, and they do so in part by analyzing the information they gather from their students in order to make instructional decisions. Reflective practice has been identified as a trait of master teachers, and research that examines the role of teacher-based assessment can further our understanding of effective practices for preservice and inservice teacher development.

A second line of research would describe changes in classroom environments when assessment is an integral part of teachers' instructional practices. This research would document changes in teacher–student interaction, student tasks, and student outcomes as teachers become more facile at observing, questioning, and sampling student work. A critical part of this work would be the documentation of changes in students' perceptions and performances, as their self-assessments are integrated into classroom decision making.

## CONCLUSION

The conversation about assessment now includes teacher-based assessment, as evidenced by reports from policy centers (e.g., International Reading Association, 2000; National Association of Secondary School Principals, 2000), journals (e.g., *Theory Into Practice* [Borko, 1997]) and state policies (Valencia & Wixson, 1999). If critical goals of literacy are to be captured and if teachers are to become more adept in creating optimal instructional environments, teacher-based assessment must be a critical dimension of this conversation. Calfee (1994) stated:

The classroom teacher is in a unique position to apply the experimental method. When the connection between assessment and instruction is close, then initial observations lead to intervention, followed by the next round of observation. In this situation, the purpose of assessment is not only to determine student performance but equally to guide the teacher's instruction. (p. 347)

Clearly articulated policy that values teacher-based assessment as a critical component of a responsive pedagogy will deliver what it has promised—high standards and achievement for all.

## *References*

Adams County (CO) School District 12 (1989). *Criteria for evaluating writing (Grades 2-6)*. Thornton, CO: Author.

Alfassi, M. (1998). Reading for meaning: The efficacy of reciprocal teaching in fostering reading comprehension in high school students in remedial reading classes. *American Educational Research Journal, 35*, 309-332.

Allen, L., & Calhoun, E. F. (1998). Schoolwide action research: Findings from six years of study. *Phi Delta Kappan, 79*, 706-710.

Allen, L., Cipielewski, J., & Stanovich, K. E. (1992). Multiple indicators of children's reading habits and attitudes: Construct validity and cognitive correlates. *Journal of Educational Psychology, 84,* 489–503.

Almasi, J. F., McKeown, M. G., & Beck, I. L. (1996). The nature of engaged reading in classroom discussions of literature. *Journal of Literacy Research, 28,* 97–146.

Alvermann, D. E., & Guthrie, J. T. (1993). *Themes and directions of the National Reading Research Center* (Perspectives in Reading Research No. 1). Athens, GA: National Reading Research Center.

Alvermann, D. E., & Hayes, D. A. (1989). Classroom discussion of content area reading assignments: An intervention study. *Reading Research Quarterly, 24,* 305–335.

Anderson, N. A. (1999). Providing feedback to preservice teachers of reading in field settings. *Reading Research and Instruction, 37,* 123–136.

Anderson, R. C., Hiebert, E. H., Scott, J. A., & Wilkinson, I. A. (1985). *Becoming a nation of readers.* Urbana, IL: University of Illinois, Center for the Study of Reading.

Armbruster, B. E. (1991). Reading and questioning in content area lessons. *Journal of Reading Behavior, 23*(1), 35–59.

Atwell, N. (1998). *In the middle: New understandings about writing, reading, and learning* (2nd ed.). Portsmouth, NH: Boynton/Cook.

Au, K. H., & Jordan, C. (1981). Teaching reading to Hawaiian children: Finding a culturally appropriate solution. In H. T. Treuba, G. P. Guthrie, & K. H. Au (Eds.), *Culture and the bilingual classroom: Studies in classroom ethnography* (pp. 139–152). Rowley, MA: Newbury House.

Au, K. H., & Mason, J. M. (1981). Social organizational factors in learning to read: The balance of rights hypothesis. *Reading Research Quarterly, 17,* 115–152.

Bachman, L. F. (1992). What does language testing have to offer? *TESOL Quarterly, 25,* 671–704.

Bauer, E. B. (1999). The promise of alternative literacy assessments in the classroom: A review of empirical studies. *Reading Research and Instruction, 38,* 153–168.

Beck, I. L., McKeown, M. G., Hamilton, R. L., & Kucan, L. L. (1997). *Questioning the Author: An approach for enhancing student engagement with text.* Newark, DE: International Reading Association.

Beck, I. L., McKeown, M. G., Worthy, J., Sandora, C. A., & Kucan, L. L. (1993). *Questioning the Author: A year-long classroom implementation to engage students with text* (Technical Report). Pittsburgh, PA: University of Pittsburgh, Learning Research and Development Center.

Bereiter, C., & Scardamalia, M. (1996). Cognition and curriculum. In P. W. Jackson (Ed.), *Handbook of research on curriculum* (pp. 517–542). New York: Macmillan.

Berliner, D. C. (1985). Laboratory settings and the study of teacher education. *Journal of Teacher Education, 36,* 2–8.

Borko, H. (1997). New forms of classroom assessment: Implications for staff development. *Theory Into Practice, 36,* 231–238.

Brewer, R. (1989, June). *State assessments of student performance.* Paper presented at the 19th Annual Assessment Conference of the Education Commission of the States, Colorado Department of Education, Boulder.

Briggs, C., Tully, B., & Stiefer, T. (1998). Direct informed assessment: Frequency of use in preservice teacher education programs within a five-state region. *Action in Teacher Education, 20*(3), 30–38.

Brown, A. L., & Reeve, R. A. (1985). *Bandwidths of competence: The role of supportive contexts in learning and development* (Tech. Rep. No. 336). Urbana: University of Illinois, Center for the Study of Reading.

Burke, S. M., Pflaum, W., & Krafle, J. D. (1982). The influence of Black English on diagnosis of reading in learning-disabled and normal readers. *Journal of Learning Disabilities, 15,* 19–22.

Burns, P. C., & Roe, B. D. (1999). *Informal reading inventory: Preprimer to twelfth grade* (5th ed.). Boston: Houghton Mifflin.

Bushman, J. H. (1997). Young adult literature in the classroom—Or is it? *English Journal, 86*(3), 35–40.

Calfee, R. C. (1994). Cognitive assessment of classroom learning. *Education and Urban Society, 26,* 340–351.

Calfee, R. C., & Gearhart, M. (1998). Introduction: Portfolios and large-scale assessment. *Educational Assessment, 5,* 1–3.

Calfee, R. C., & Hiebert, E. H. (1988). The teacher's role in using assessment to improve literacy. In C. U. Bunderson (Ed.), *Assessment in the service of learning* (pp. 45–61). Princeton, NJ: Educational Testing Service.

Calfee, R. C., & Hiebert, E. H. (1991). Classroom assessment in reading. In R. Barr, M. Kamil, P. Rosenthal, & P. D. Pearson (Eds.), *Handbook of research on reading* (2nd ed., pp. 281–309). New York: Longman.

Calkins, L. M. (1986). *The art of teaching writing.* Portsmouth, NH: Heinemann.

Carlsen, W. S. (1991). Questioning in classrooms: A sociolinguistic perspective. *Review of Educational Research, 61,* 157–178.

Cazden, C. B. (1986). Classroom discourse. In M. C. Wittrock (Ed.), *Handbook of research on teaching* (3rd ed., pp. 432–463). New York: Macmillan.

Church, J. (1994). Record keeping in whole language classrooms. In B. Harp (Ed.), *Assessment and evaluation for student centered learning* (pp. 231–266). Portsmouth, NH: Heinemann.

Clay, M. M. (1979). *The early detection of reading difficulties: A diagnostic survey with recovery procedures* (2nd ed.). Portsmouth, NH: Heinemann.

Clay, M. M. (1993). *An observation survey of early literacy achievement.* Portsmouth, NH: Heinemann.

Constantino, R., Lee, S. Y., Cho, K. S., & Krashen, S. (1997). Free voluntary reading as a predictor of TOEFL scores. *Applied Language Learning, 8*(1), 111–118.

Cooper, C. R. (1977). Holistic evaluation of writing. In C. R. Cooper & L. Odell (Eds.), *Evaluating writing: Describing, measuring, judging* (pp. 3–31). Urbana, IL: National Council of Teachers of English.

Courtney, A. M., & Abodeeb, T. L. (1999). Diagnostic-reflective portfolios. *The Reading Teacher, 52,* 708–714.

Cronbach, L. J. (1960). *Essentials of psychological testing* (3rd ed.). New York: Harper & Row.

Dahl, K. L., & Farnan, N. (1998). *Children's writing: Perspectives from research.* Newark, DE: International Reading Association.

Dearborn, W. F., & Westbrook, C. H. (1921). *A silent reading test.* Cambridge, MA: Dearborn & Westbrook.

Delpit, L. D. (1995). *Other people's children: Cultural conflict in the classroom.* New York: New Press.

Dolch, E. W. (1926). *Basic sight vocabulary cards test.* Champaign, IL: Garrard.

Dorr-Bremme, D. W., & Herman, J. L. (1986). *Assessing student achievement: A profile of classroom practices* (Center for the Study of Evaluation Monograph No. 11). UCLA: Center for the Study of Evaluation.

Ediger, M. (1999). Evaluation of reading progress. *Reading Improvement, 36*(2), 50–56.

Education Commission of the States (1999). *Quality teachers for the 21st century.* Denver, CO: Author.

Estes, T. H. (1971). A scale to measure attitudes toward reading. *Journal of Reading, 15,* 135–138.

Farnan, N., Flood, J., & Lapp, D. (1994). Comprehending through reading and writing: Six research-based instructional strategies. In K. Spangenberg-Urbschat & R. Pritchard (Eds.), *Kids come in all languages: Reading instruction for ESL students* (pp. 135-157). Newark: DE: International Reading Association.

Fisette, D. (1993). Practical authentic assessment: Good kidwatchers know what to teach next. *The California Reader, 26*(4), 4-7.

Flood, J., & Lapp, D. (1989). Reporting reading progress: A comparison portfolio for parents. *The Reading Teacher, 42*, 508-514.

Flood, J., Lapp, D., Flood, S., & Nagel, G. (1992). Am I allowed to group? Using flexible patterns for effective instruction. *The Reading Teacher, 45*, 608-616.

Fountas, I. C., & Pinnell, G. S. (1996). *Guided reading: Good first teaching for all children*. Portsmouth, NH: Heinemann.

Gil, D., Polin, R. M., Vinsonhaler, J. F., & Van Roekel, J. (1980). *The impact of training on diagnostic consistency* (Tech. Rep. No. 67). East Lansing, MI: Institute for Research on Teaching.

Godina, H. (1999). High school students of Mexican background in the Midwest: Cultural differences as a constraint to effective literacy instruction. *National Reading Conference Yearbook, 48*, 266-279.

Goodman, K. (1997). Putting theory and research in the context of history. *Language Arts, 74*, 595-599.

Goodman, K. S. (1968). The psycholinguistic nature of the reading process. In K. S. Goodman (Ed.), The *psycholinguistic nature of the reading process* (pp. 13-26). Detroit, MI: Wayne State University Press.

Goodman, Y. (1985). Kidwatching: Observing children in the classroom. In A. Jaggar & M. T. Smith-Burke (Eds.), *Observing the language learner*. Newark, DE: International Reading Association.

Goodman, Y. M., & Goodman, K. S. (1996). To err is human: Learning about language processes by analyzing miscues. In R. B. Ruddell, M. R. Ruddell, & H. Singer (Eds.), *Theoretical models and processes of reading* (4th ed., pp. 104-123). Newark, DE: International Reading Association.

Graves, D. (1983). *Writing: Teachers and children at work*. Portsmouth, NH: Heinemann.

Gray, W. S. (1915). Methods of testing reading I. *The Elementary School Journal, 1*, 231-246.

Gray, W. S. (1920). The value of informal tests of reading achievement. *Journal of Educational Research*, 103-111.

Guzack, F. J. (1969). Questioning strategies of elementary teachers in relation to comprehension. *International Reading Association Conference, 1*(13), 110-116.

Harste, J. C., Burke, C. L., & Woodward, V. A. (1994). Children's language and world: Initial encounters with print. In R. B. Ruddell, M. R. Ruddell, & H. Singer (Eds.), *Theoretical models and processes of reading* (4th ed., pp. 48-69). Newark, DE: International Reading Association.

Heath, S. B. (1982). Questioning at home and at school: A comparative study. In G. Spindler (Ed.), *Doing the ethnography of schooling: Educational anthropology in action* (pp. 102-131). New York: Holt, Rinehart & Winston.

Heath, S. B., & Mangiola, L. (1991). *Children of promise: Literate activity in linguistically and culturally diverse classrooms*. Washington, DC: National Education Association.

Heathington, B. S. (1979). What to do about reading motivation in the middle school. *Journal of Reading, 22*, 709-713.

Hedrick, W. B. (1999). Preservice teachers tutoring 3rd, 4th, and 5th graders one-on-one within the school setting. *Reading Research and Instruction, 38*, 211-219.

Hiebert, E. H. (1980). Peers as reading teachers. *Language Arts, 57*, 877-881.

Hiebert, E. H. (1994). Becoming literate through authentic tasks: Evidence and adaptations. In R. B. Ruddell, M. R. Ruddell, & H. Singer (Eds.), *Theoretical models and processes of reading* (4th ed., pp. 391-413). Newark, DE: International Reading Association.

Hiebert, E. H., & Calfee, R. C. (1989). Advancing academic literacy through teachers' assessments. *Educational Leadership, 46*(7), 50-54.

Hill, K. T. (1984). Debilitating motivation and testing: A major educational problem—Possible solutions and policy. In R. Ames & C. Ames (Eds.), *Research on motivation in education: Student motivation* (Vol. 1). New York: Academic Press.

Hole, S., & McEntree, G. H. (1999). *Reflection is at the heart of practice*. *Educational Leadership, 56*(8), 34-37.

International Reading Association (2000). *Making a difference means making it different: Honoring childrens' rights to excellence in reading education* [Position statement]. Newark, DE: International Reading Association.

Jacobs, J. E., & Paris, S. G. (1987). Children's metacognition about reading: Issues in definition, measurement, and instruction. *Educational Psychologist, 22*, 255-278.

Johnston, P. H. (1987). Teachers as evaluation experts. *The Reading Teacher, 40*, 744-748.

Kentucky Department of Education (2000). *Writing portfolio assessments*. Retrieved form http://www.kde.state.ky.us/oapd/curric/portfolios/

Kohler, F. W. (1997). Effects of peer coaching on teacher and student outcomes. *Journal of Educational Research, 90*, 240-250.

Lapp, D., Fisher, D., Flood, J., & Cabello, A. (2000). An integrated approach to the teaching and assessment of language arts. In S. Hurley & J. Tinajero (Eds.), *Assessing literacy for English language learners*. Boston: Allyn & Bacon.

Leslie, L., & Jett-Simpson, M. (1997). *Authentic literacy assessment: An ecological approach*. New York: Longman.

Leu, D. J., Jr., & Kinzer, C. K. (1999). *Effective literacy instruction: K-8* (4th ed.). Upper Saddle Englewood Cliffs, NJ: Prentice-Hall.

Lipson, M. Y., & Wixson, K. K. (1997). *Assessment and instruction of reading and writing disability*. New York: Longman.

MacMillan, D. L., & Reschly, D. J. (1998). Overrepresentation of minority students: The case for greater specificity or reconsideration of the variables examined. *Journal of Special Education, 32*, 15-24.

Madaus, G. (1994). A technological and historical consideration of equity issues associated with proposals to change the nation's testing policy. *Harvard Educational Review, 64*, 76-95.

Martin, S. (1999). *Take a look: Observation and portfolio assessment in early childhood* (2nd ed.). Reading, MA: Addison-Wesley.

McAllister, P. J. (1994). Using K-W-L as an informal assessment. *The Reading Teacher, 47*, 510-511.

McKenna, M. C., & Kear, D. J. (1990). Measuring attitude towards reading: A new tool for teachers. *The Reading Teacher, 43*, 626-639.

Metcalf, K. K., & Kahlich, P. A. (1998). Nontraditional preservice teacher development: The value of clinical experience. *Journal of Research and Development in Education, 31*(2), 69-82.

Moll, L. C., Estrada, E., Diaz, E., & Lopes, L. M. (1980). The organization of bilingual lessons: Implications for schooling. *The Quarterly Newsletter of the Laboratory of Comparative Human Cognition, 2*, 53-58.

Moore, A. (1996). Assessing young readers: Questions of culture and ability. *Language Arts, 73*, 306-316.

Mosenthal, P., & Na, T. J. (1980). Quality of children's recall under two classroom testing tasks: Towards a socio-psycholinguistic model of reading comprehension. *Reading Research Quarterly, 15*, 504-528.

National Association of Secondary School Principals (2000). *NASSP board of directors position statement on standards and assessment*. Retrieved from http://www.nassp.org/hot_topics/ps_stand_assess.html

Ogbu, J. U. (1999). Beyond language: Ebonics, proper English, and identity in a Black-American speech community. *American Educational Research Journal, 36,* 147-184.

Ogle, D. M. (1986). K-W-L: A teaching model that develops active reading of expository text. *The Reading Teacher, 39,* 564-570.

Palincsar, A. S., & Brown, A. L. (1984). Reciprocal teaching of comprehension-fostering and comprehension-monitoring activities. *Cognition and Instruction, 1,* 117-175.

Pang, V. O., & Cheng, L. L. (Eds.) (1998). *Struggling to be heard: The unmet needs of Asian Pacific American children*. Albany: State University of New York.

Patton, J. M. (1998). The Disproportionate representation of African-Americans in special education: Looking behind the curtain for understanding and solutions. *Journal of Special Education, 32,* 25-31.

Pearson, P. D., & Tierney, R. J. (1984). *On becoming a thoughtful reader: Learning to read like a writer* (Reading Ed. Rep. No. 50). Urbana, IL: University of Illinois, Center for the Study of Reading.

Philips, S. U. (1983). *The invisible culture: Communication in the classroom and community on the Warm Springs Indian Reservation*. New York: Longman.

Popham, W. J. (1999). *Classroom assessment: What teachers need to know* (2nd ed.). Boston: Allyn & Bacon.

Potter, E. F. (1999). What should I put in my portfolio? Supporting young children's goals and evaluations. *Childhood Education, 75,* 210-214.

Raphael, T. E. (1986). Teaching question–answer relationships, revisited. *The Reading Teacher, 39,* 516-523.

Raphael, T. E., Engler, C. S., & Kirschner, B. W. (1986). *The impact of text structure instruction and social context on students' comprehension and production of expository text*. (Research Series No. 177). East Lansing: Michigan State University, Institute for Research on Teaching.

Rosenshine, B., & Meister, C. (1994). Reciprocal teaching: A review of the research. *Review of Educational Research, 64,* 479-530.

Ruddell, M. R. H. (1991). Authentic assessment: Focused observation as a means for evaluating language and literacy development. *The California Reader, 24*(2), 2-7.

Rupley, W. H., Willson, V. L., Mergen, S. L., Rodriguez, M., Nichols, W. D., & Logan, J. W. (1999). Teachers' use of informal assessment and students' reading performance. *National Reading Conference Yearbook, 48,* 201-208.

Salmon-Cox, L. (1981). Teachers and standardized achievement tests: What's really happening? *Phi Delta Kappan, 62,* 631-634.

Schaefer, R. J. (1967). *The school as a center of inquiry*. New York: Harper & Row.

Schmidt, P. R. (1995). Working and playing with others: Cultural conflict in a kindergarten literacy program. *The Reading Teacher, 48,* 404-412.

Spinelli, C. G. (1998). *Teacher education reform: Promoting interactive teaching strategies and authentic assessment for instructing an increasingly diverse population of students*. (ED 418076)

Stringer, E. T. (1999). *Action research* (2nd ed.). Thousand Oaks, CA: Sage.

Sulzby, E. (1991). Assessment of emergent literacy: Storybook reading. *The Reading Teacher, 44,* 498-500.

Swearingen, R., & Allen, D. (2000). *Classroom assessment of reading processes* (2nd ed.). Boston, MA: Houghton Mifflin.

Tierney, R. J. (1998). Literacy assessment reform: Shifting beliefs, principled possibilities, and emerging practices. *Reading Teacher, 51,* 374-390.

Tierney, R. J., Clark, C., Wiser, B., Simpson, C. S., Herter, R. J., & Fenner, L. (1998). Portfolios: Assumptions, tensions, and possibilities. *Reading Research Quarterly, 33,* 474-486.

Tower, C. (2000). Questions that matter: Preparing elementary students for the inquiry process. *The Reading Teacher, 53,* 550-563.

U.S. Department of Education (1996). *President Clinton's America's Reading Challenge: Helping every child read well by the end of third grade*. Retrieved from http://www.ed.gov/updates/reading/read-1.html

Valencia, S. W. (1997). Authentic classroom assessment of early reading: Alternatives to standardized tests. *Preventing School Failure, 41*(2), 63-70.

Valencia, S. W., Wixson, K. K. (1999). *Policy-oriented research on literacy standards and assessment*. Ann Arbor, MI: Center for the Improvement of Early Reading Achievement.

Vaughn, S., Moody, S. W., & Schumm, J. S. (1998). Broken promises: Reading instruction in the resource room. *Exceptional Children, 64,* 211-225.

Venezky, R. L. (1984). The history of reading research. In P. D. Pearson, R. Barr, M. L. Kamil, & P. Mosenthal (Eds.), *Handbook of reading research* (pp. 3-38). New York: Longman.

Vukelich, C. (1997). Assessing young children's literacy: Documenting growth and informing practice. *The Reading Teacher, 50,* 430-434.

Vygotsky, L. (1962). *Thought and language*. Cambridge, MA: MIT Press.

Washington, V. M., & Miller-Jones, D. (1989). Teacher interactions with nonstandard English speakers during reading. *Instruction Contemporary Educational Psychology, 14,* 280-312.

West, K. R. (1998). Noticing and responding to learners: Literacy evaluation and instruction in the primary grades. *The Reading Teacher, 51,* 550-559.

Wilcox, B. L. (1997). Writing portfolios: Active vs. passive. *English Journal, 86*(6), 34-37.

Winograd, P., & Arrington, H. J. (1999). Best practices in literacy assessment. In L. B. Gambrell, L. M. Morrow, S. B. Neumann, & M. Pressley (Eds.), *Best Practices in Literacy Instruction* (pp. 210-241). New York: Guilford.

Wixson, K. K., & Pearson, P. D. (1998). Policy and assessment strategies to support literacy instruction for a new century. *Peabody Journal of Education, 73,* 202-227.

Wolf, K. P. (1993). From informal to informed assessment: Recognizing the role of the classroom Teacher. *Journal of Reading, 36,* 518-523.

Wolf, S. A., & Gearhart, M. (1997). New writing assessments: The challenge of changing teachers' beliefs about students as writers. *Theory into Practice, 36,* 220-230.

Yancey, K. B. (1992). *Portfolios in the writing classroom*. Urbana, IL: National Council of Teachers of English.

Yopp, H. K., & Guillaume, A. M. (1999). Preparing preservice teachers for collaboration. *Teacher Education Quarterly, 26,* 5-19.

Zederayko, G. E., & Ward, K. (1999). Schools as learning organizations: How can the work of teachers be both learning and teaching? *NASSP Bulletin, 83*(604), 35-45.

# HIGH-STAKES ASSESSMENT IN THE LANGUAGE ARTS: THE PIPER PLAYS, THE PLAYERS DANCE, BUT WHO PAYS THE PRICE?

*James V. Hoffman*
University of Texas, Austin

*Scott G. Paris*
University of Michigan/CIERA

*Rachel Salas*
Texas A&M University, Corpus Christi

*Elizabeth Patterson and Lori Assaf*
University of Texas, Austin

> It seems when you put things in the accountability system, schools pay attention to it.
>
> —Moses (1998)

One of the most dramatic changes in American education in the past 50 years has been the expanding role of standardized tests. Madaus and Tan (1993) noted the changes over the past 5 decades. Standardized tests were innocuous in the 1940s but emerged as tools to shape policies in the 1950s. Standardized achievement tests were used to evaluate programs in the 1960s; they were used to evaluate student retention, graduation, and placement in the 1970s; and they became instruments of evaluation for teachers and school programs in the 1980s. In the 1990s, standardized tests have been linked with proscribed educational standards, political agenda, and systemic school reform. Within

these rapidly changing roles of testing, states began to create, not just purchase, statewide tests of achievement in specific academic subject areas such as reading, writing, math, science, and social studies. Evidence for the rapidly changing testing environment can be seen in the fact that prior to 1970 no state used criterion-referenced testing, and today every state mandates the use of some standardized test.

Accompanying this expanding role for testing, we have seen the broader application of consequences associated with student performance on tests. More and more states are imposing "high-stakes" consequences for performance on their testing plans. Our goal in this chapter is to explore the high-stakes testing movement with a focus on the intersection of policy, research, and practice in the areas of reading and writing. We begin with a description of high stakes assessments and their history. We explore the contexts and influences on the use of high stakes testing. Next, we consider some of the areas of concern regarding this movement with particular attention to the negative consequences on teaching, the curriculum, students, and assessment itself. Finally, we suggest some of the ways in which we might exercise professional responsibility and reestablish reasonable connections among assessment, policy, and practice.

## HIGH-STAKES ASSESSMENTS: WHAT ARE THEY?

High-stakes assessment is the term used to describe assessments that involve substantial consequences for good (high) or poor (low) performance. (International Reading Association, 1999.)

High-stakes testing is not new in the United States. The Regents exam has been used in New York since the 1870s as a condition of graduation; group-administered, multiple-choice tests of intelligence have been used since 1917 to classify individuals for service and treatment; and the SAT was revised to a multiple-choice format in 1937 so that it could be used more effectively in determining college admissions and awards. There is also a tradition of high-stakes examinations in the United States for entry programs of study in some professional areas such as medicine and law.

What is new to the scene within the United States is the broad application of high-stakes assessments across all levels of public education with the stakes rising continually. The stakes may be for the student (e.g., retention or denial of graduation), the teacher (e.g., pay raises, reprimands), the school (e.g., disaccreditation, front-page headlines), or the campus administrator (e.g., transfer, reassignment). The stakes may have positive outcomes as well (e.g., bonus money for principals in high-achieving schools or merit pay compensation for teachers). These are not hypothetical outcomes. These are the daily realities in schools across the United States. Educators may never come to exact agreement on what makes an assessment high stakes because the judgment of severity of consequences will always be a relative term. However, for the purposes of this chapter, we assume that the severity of consequences in high-stakes assessment involves a denial of access to something desired (e.g., passing on to the next grade level for students, a job for the following year for a teacher), or a denial of the reward/recognition given to others who perform at a higher level (e.g., no merit pay for administrators). We offer this as an illustrative, not restrictive, definition of the term. No doubt there are other possibilities.

### The Form of High-Stakes Assessments

It is important to separate the form of the assessment itself from the high-stakes context in which assessments may occur. Almost any form of assessment can involve high stakes. It is conceivable, for example, to use student performance on a running record as the basis for decisions about promotion to the next grade level. The stakes are high for the student and therefore this would qualify under our definition of a high-stakes assessment. The fact is, though, that most of the high-stakes assessments are part of large-scale, standardized testing. Indeed, the term *high-stakes assessment* is often used interchangeably with the term *high-stakes testing*. There are important differences. Assessment encompasses a broad array of strategies by which data are systematically collected to inform stakeholders. Testing involves the sampling of behaviors under highly controlled conditions. It is just one form of assessment. The confusion between the terms is not surprising given the fact that most high-stakes assessments take the form of standardized, paper-and-pencil kinds of tests. We wish to be clear in asserting that not all standardized tests are high stakes (e.g., a reading test used as a diagnostic tool for a reading improvement course). Further, it is possible for alternate forms of assessment to become high stakes (e.g., college admission interviews).

In the area of reading, most of the tests that are used in a high-stakes context are of the paper-and-pencil, multiple-choice variety. In the area of writing, standardized tests that use a multiple-choice format (e.g., for judging spelling accuracy, grammatical acceptability, correct punctuation) are still popular, but there has been a trend toward tests that require students to produce stories, essays, or other genre of written products. These written products are then subjected to holistic scoring procedures with clear criteria for passing or failing.

## HIGH-STAKES ASSESSMENTS: WHAT DRIVES THEIR DEVELOPMENT?

No single factor can be used to explain the rapid expansion of standardized testing and the application of consequences linked to performance. We would suggest a combination of seven factors that have been at work. To understand these is to begin to understand the complexity of the movement itself and the momentum it has achieved.

### Federal Program Initiatives

Some have suggested that the rise in interest and use of standardized tests coupled with a high-stakes mentality had its seeds sown in the increase in educational funding by the federal government that began in the mid-1960s with President Johnson's Great Society initiative (e.g., Madaus & Tan, 1993; Resnick & Resnick, 1985). The Elementary and Secondary Education Act brought substantial resources into state and local programs with "evaluation" strings attached. The conditions for continued funding were not stringent, but demonstrations of positive results were expected for continuation.

The increase in high-stakes assessment has been most apparent, however, at the state level. During the mid- to late 1970s a number of states initiated basic skills testing programs in many subject areas and multiple grade levels. These tests were initiated in response to public concerns over the quality of education in the basic skill areas and the capacity of students to read, write, and compute. Most of these tests were rationalized as a means of getting some "hard" data on student performance levels (i.e., a "report card" on the performance of schools). The high-stakes aspect of these assessments was absent initially, but as the term *educational accountability* began to creep in to the jargon of policymakers the tone began to change. The testing movement at the state level expanded during the 1980s and 1990s as test scores were used to evaluate and compare students, schools, and districts.

## The Crisis Mentality for Reading and Writing

It is nearly impossible to pick up a magazine or newspaper today and not be bombarded with reports on the reading crisis in America. The headlines send out alarm signals to the public suggesting a severe decline in literacy levels. It is often claimed that the United States ranks far below other industrialized nations in literacy levels and below our own historical standards (Stevenson & Stigler, 1992). Few of the claims regarding a "crisis" in learning to read and write hold up under scrutiny (Berliner & Biddle, 1997). Indeed, most serious analyses of achievement in the areas of reading and writing suggest that students are learning to read and write at least as well, if not better, than they have in the past. Nonetheless, the repeated claims in the media that there is a crisis and that schools are failing to meet the needs of students creates a public image of educational failure.

The perceived failure of schools rests largely on the evidence of standardized tests yet few media report the characteristics of the tests accurately and completely. Murphy, Shannon, Johnston, and Hansen (1998) refer to performance on standardized tests as "fragile evidence" because it represents such a narrow and limited part of students' accomplishments and it is used to make high stakes decisions. They argued that few educators or public reports examine the fragility of this evidence, and thus a false sense of validity and trust is created for test results. Large-scale assessments are viewed by the public as valuable mechanisms for monitoring school quality and student literacy levels. Highly visible assessments that promise accountability are appealing to a public who is uncertain or irate. The media often play to the public's dissatisfaction with education by using test results to foment the crisis mentality. It is clearly more newsworthy than tepid accounts of progress or the status quo.

## Competition for Resources

Clearly, standardized testing in general and high-stakes tests in particular have been used to leverage resource allocations and public priorities. Madaus (1985) claims that advocates for various racial and ethnic groups have used the discrepancy in achievement levels to argue for increased resource commitments. Echoing this position, Gregory Anrig (1985), president of the Educational Testing Service, wrote:

I know the concerns that minority parents, students, and organizations have about testing. I share many of those concerns. The commitments to civil rights and educational justice that I felt during my 25 years of public service have not changed, now that I am in the private sector. . . . I also recognize that testing is important for improving education—including the education of black children. Test data provide information that can be used for a number of worthwhile purposes. . . . Tests provide the data that enable parents and others to keep the pressure on communities, schools, and educators to "close the gap" between the performance of black students and that of whites. (p. 624)

Test scores are a dilemma for minorities because, on the one hand, the lower scores perpetuate stereotypical beliefs about their lower academic ability while, on the other hand, simultaneously providing the rationale for greater resource allocation to students of color. Lost in the arguments are issues about poverty, parental income and resources, conditions of the schools and neighborhoods, and other factors that influence the quality of education and levels of academic achievement among minorities.

## The State Frameworks and Standards Movement

Much of the initial work in state assessments during the late 1960s and 1970s was targeted toward the measurement of minimum competencies. The public wanted assurance that students in schools were learning the basics. The criteria for these tests were based on some fairly simple notions of what it meant to be minimally competent in such basic skill areas as reading, writing, and mathematics. As concerns over the notion that the curriculum was being "dumbed down" to focus just on the basics (with the dangers of the minimum becoming the maximum), a different reference point for the criterion referenced testing emerged. Many states formulated curricular frameworks that would specify what students would be taught at each grade level in each subject area. State testing programs evolved from a minimum competency test to a test over the mastery of the essential elements of the curriculum.

The most recent iterations of these frameworks, spurred by the Goals 2000 initiative and the national standards movement, have yielded a new generation of curricular frameworks. This new generation of curricula is being represented as performance standards and not opportunity standards. These performance standards specify in detail what readers and writers are expected do as well as the criterion levels for each grade. These standards provide a convenient basis for the construction of state assessments and a criterion referenced perspective (Johnston, 1997; Sabers & Sabers, 1996). The net result of these changes at the state level is increased testing for students. Why? Because states introduce new curricular tests without deleting old tests, or, if they replace old tests, local districts often add the new tests to their own testing agenda without eliminating their traditional standardized tests.

## Advances in Holistic Assessment

Holistic assessment, in particular as it has been applied in the areas of reading and writing, has changed the face of large-scale testing. The old notions and lines of demarcation between objective and subjective testing have been blurred with the introduction of performance assessments, portfolios, on-demand assessments, constructed response items, and prompted writing. Rubrics, benchmarks, and analytic scales have become routine tools in the assessment of reading and writing. Many states have scoring teams or companies that evaluate open-ended responses items or written work. These new ways to evaluate reading and writing can be subjected to the same psychometric criteria as traditional, standardized forms of testing such as content validity, construct validity, and criterion-related validity although some suggest that they may have greater validity than traditional standardized tests. In particular, advocates of holistic assessment suggest that the "consequential validity" of authentic assessments is higher and thus the benefits to teachers and students of the new assessments are greater than traditional standardized tests. However, the new tests may cost more to administer and score and the public may not attribute the same value to holistic assessments as traditional test scores. The public apprehension over holistic assessment may be due to novelty, unfamiliarity, or perceived subjectivity of scores and only time will tell if the skepticism subsides.

## Economic Forces

There is money to be made in assessment—a lot of money. Resnick (1981) cited data reflecting growth in sales of standardized tests from just under $8 million in 1946 to over $40 million in 1976. Morison (1992, p. 5) cited statistics from the U.S. Department of Education noting revenues from sales of commercial published standardized K–12 tests have more than doubled in the last 3 decades from about $40 million to over $80 million. Madaus and Tan (1993) estimated that sales of tests were over $100 million by the late 1980s. The development, administration, scoring, interpretation, and results management carry an enormous price tag.

This is to say nothing of the hundreds of cottage businesses that have boomed with services ranging from practice materials to workshops for teachers and administrators. Madaus and Tan (1993) argued that the services affiliated with increased testing actually multiply the costs four to five times, so they estimated that income generated from the testing industry by 1990 exceeded a half billion dollars! These trends have continued to increase through the 1990s. One should not overlook as well the enormous bureaucracies that have developed within states to manage the testing programs and associated accountability systems. Testing has clearly been a growth industry for education in the past 40 years, and it is responsible for a huge increase in educational budgets. Registered lobbyists who are promoting the use of tests are a sure sign that there is a profit to be made.

Finally, it is worth noting the hidden costs of increased testing on teaching. The more time spent testing and getting students prepared to take tests, the less time there is for teaching the regular curriculum. Paris, Lawton, and Turner (1991) suggested that test preparation, administration, interpretation, and reporting may take as much as 5% to 10% of teachers' time during a year. That is the equivalent of 9 to 18 days during the year devoted to testing and lost from the curriculum. Alternatively, school districts might estimate the costs of testing by adding 5% to 10% of teachers' salaries to the costs of testing. The hidden cost in time that teachers and students spend in testing is even greater than the costs of the test themselves.

## Models for Change

The spread of educational innovations often reflects a kind of "snowball" effect. They start slowly but gain momentum after the initial wave of "risk takers" and "early adopters" have broken into new territory. These innovators become the models for others to follow. There are several states that have taken the lead in the high-stakes assessment and accountability movement. These states are reporting changes in teaching practices and changes in student achievement (i.e., improvement in test scores) and both are attributed directly to the effects of high-stakes assessments. What the remaining states have discovered is that the development of new standards documents that specify new curricula are relatively ineffective in promoting change in the absence of a strong accountability system. When the accountability system is tied to the curriculum with high stakes, then change occurs. The fact that "exemplary" models exist for other states to emulate is no doubt a factor in the rapid spread of high-stakes assessment. *Education Week's* "Quality Counts '99" cited Texas for having one of the most comprehensive school accountability systems in the country. North Carolina was the only other state named for having a similarly comprehensive system of ranking school districts and student performance.

The case of each state is unique, although there are some common themes across contexts. To illustrate the issues involved, we will focus on two states in particular: Texas and Michigan. We have chosen these states because they have a substantial history of involvement in high-stakes assessments, have been the focal point for research on high-stakes assessment, and have been at the forefront in terms of expansion and innovation in high stakes assessments.

## HIGH-STAKES ASSESSMENT IN TEXAS

Texas, with the nation's second-largest school enrollment, serves over 3.9 million schoolchildren. The schools of Texas serve an ethnically and economically diverse population. According to a recent Texas Education Agency (TEA) Division of Performance Reporting 1997–1998 (available at http://tea.state.tx.us./perfreport/pocked/), during the 1997 to 1998 school year, the number of minority students in Texas public schools made up 55% of the 3.89 million Texas public school students. Hispanic students accounted for 38% of all Texas public school students in 1997 to 1998, with African Americans comprising 14% and other minorities making up 3%. White students, meanwhile, accounted for 45% of the population and had by far the slowest growth rate of all students, increasing by just 5% since 1987 to 1988. By comparison, the growth rate for Hispanic students during the 10-year period was 45% and 19% for African American students. Other minority groups, most of which are of Asian ancestry, had the highest growth rate—63%—over the period.

Interestingly, the growth of economically disadvantaged students grew by a staggering 65%, outpacing any other population group. Students who are classified as economically disadvantaged are eligible for the U.S. Department of Agriculture's free or reduced-price meal program, which makes free or low-cost breakfast and lunch meals available to children of low-income families. These economically disadvantaged students now account for 48% of all Texas public school students, compared with 35% in 1987 to 1988 (TEA, 1998; Funkhouser, 2000).

Accompanying the rise in minority and low-income students in Texas schools have come increased public concerns over achievement in the basic skill areas of reading, writing, and mathematics. Schools were perceived as soft and ineffective in meeting the challenges these students present. The current assessment system in Texas began with "get-tough, centralized reforms of the 1980's" (Johnston, 1998). The first wave of tests came in 1980 when Texas implemented the Texas Assessment of Basic Skills (TABS), the first statewide assessment to measure fifth- and ninth-grade student achievement in reading, writing, and math. Over 400,000 students completed the TABS during the first administration. Although there were no direct consequences imposed on students or schools for performance, for the first time school and district results were made public. In 1983, the Texas legislature passed House Bill 723, which introduced the notion of consequences for poor performance by requiring ninth-graders who did not pass the TABS to retake the test each year until they demonstrated competency (Cruise, 1985).

Texas raised the ante in 1985 when they replaced TABS with the Texas Educational Assessment of Minimum Skills (TEAMS). With TEAMS all students in Grades 1, 3, 5, 7, 9, and 11 were tested with on-grade-level basic skills texts in reading, writing, and mathematics. Between 1986 and 1989, 1,400,000 students were tested annually on grade-level basic skills in reading, writing, and math. Texas students were required to pass the exit-level test to earn a high school diploma (TEA, 1997; Office of Technology Assessment, 1987).

As Texas lawmakers attempted to bestow more authority on individual schools they also bolstered school accountability by creating a more rigorous testing program. In 1990 the TEA created the Texas Assessment of Academic Skills (TAAS), a criterion-referenced test that is designed to link the test items to specific learning objectives of the statewide curriculum (the Essential Elements). Currently, the TAAS tests assess a broad range of content. All students in Grades 3 through 8 are tested in reading and mathematics. Students in Grades 4, 8, and 10 are tested in writing. Grade 8 students also take tests in science and social studies. Spanish-version TAAS tests in reading and mathematics at Grades 3 through 6 and in writing at Grade 4 are also administered. Students are required to pass the exit-level test to receive a high school diploma (Funkhouser, 2000). Future assessments being developed are reading proficiency tests in English to be administered to limited English proficient students in Grades 3 through 8 as well as end of course tests in English II and U.S. History. At the same time, a sample of Texas students are biannually tested against a national comparative criterion-referenced test which measures student performance in relation to the performance of a norm group (Funkhouser, 2000).

Test performance is reported to students, campuses, school districts, education service centers, and, most important, to the public. Test results can often be found in newspapers and on television. The scores for each school are then combined with dropout and attendance data and given ratings of exemplary, recognized, acceptable, or low performing. Within each rating category, the percentage of passing grades are allocated by total student population as well as individual student groups African American, Hispanic, Asian. When a school has less than 40% subject area passing in its total student population or each student group, it is given 5 years to improve its scores. This information is tracked on a statewide education data system that is available to the public on the World Wide Web. Texas Education Agency Division of Performance Reporting (available at http://tea.state.tx.us/perfreport/pocked/ ).

The general pattern of performance on these tests has been to show increases from year to year. On occasion the minimum passing levels have been raised with the goal of raising standards. These years are marked with a drop in performance followed by years of rising scores. Drops have also occurred as the state raised standards and moved from TABS (clearly a minimum-skills test) to TEAMS to TAAS. Current TAAS results show that the proportion of students passing the Texas test has improved from 55% in 1994 to 74% in 1997. Specifically, 32% of African American students passed the tests in 1994. This jumped to 56% in 1997. The passing rate for Hispanics rose from 41% to 62% in the same time period. The state's rating system for its 6,665 schools and 1,061 districts has also seen a shift (TEA). In 1994, 34 districts and 267 schools were characterized as low performing when only four districts and 59 schools earned that designation last year (TEA; Funkhouser, 2000).

Future plans for TAAS include raising standards (by raising the passing scores and the test difficulty), expanding the numbers of grade levels at which the tests are administered, and increasing the consequences for passing and failing. Proposals for ending social promotion and imposing strict guidelines for passing TAAS in order to advance are clearly in the works. The raising of accountability and stakes are all part of a general political agenda within the state that offers districts great latitude in terms of making decisions related to curriculum, instruction, and resource allocation linked to the idea that the state will monitor who is and is not achieving goals.

Concerns over the expansion of testing appear in professional settings (state education journals, conferences, etc.) as well as in the public media. Challenges focus on numerous areas. Many of these areas of concern have been documented through a recent statewide survey of TAAS (Hoffman, Assaf, & Paris, 1999). The following issues are being discussed:

• *Costs.* Recent proposals for expanding TAAS would carry a price tag of over $102 million per year (Brooks, 1998). These are direct costs only. These do not consider the costs that is incurred within school districts, service centers, and in the TEA. It does not include costs associated with all of the training programs, training materials, and consulting services that have mushroomed in the state.

• *Expansion.* The commissioner of education for the state of Texas has proposed expanding the annual testing to include

600,000 additional students. Basically, all students between Grades 3 and 11 would take the TAAS. The TAAS exams would be created and required at certain grade levels in the areas of social studies and science. The commissioner has also proposed raising the passing standards.

• *Cheating.* Concerns over cheating on the TAAS have grown along with the stakes. The TEA conducts ongoing evaluations of school districts and teachers suspected of unethical practices. These cases are receiving prominent attention in the media (e.g., Jayson, 1998). There is the likelihood that one Texas school district will be charged with criminal action in relation to test score tampering. Judicial scholars regard this as the first instance of a state indicting a school district for criminal actions.

• *Curriculum Narrowing.* The axiom of "what is tested is what is taught" is amplified in a high-stakes context. Time is scarce and prime time is reserved for the areas that count. The rest of the curriculum, even though it may exist in the curriculum frameworks, is marginalized.

• *Teacher Morale and Motivation.* Results from several teacher surveys (Gordon & Reese, 1997; Hoffman et al., 1999) make clear that teacher morale related to TAAS and the accountability system is mostly negative. In his extensive review on the testing in Texas, Haney states that "emphasis on TAAS is hurting more than helping teaching and learning in Texas schools." (Haney, 2000, p. 110). The 2001 *Education Weekly* (Education Weekly, 2001) report that rated the Texas school system with an B for its accountability and testing scheme, awarded C ratings for school climate and a grade of D for its efforts to raise teacher quality. Most teacher surveys suggest that teacher morale related to TAAS and the accountability system is mostly negative. (Hoffman et al., 1999; Gordon & Resse, 1997).

• *Equity Issues.* Challenges that the TAAS and the associated accountability system unfairly discriminate against minority students are currently under consideration in the courts. Both Mexican American and African American groups have challenged the use of TAAS when used in such areas as student promotion and graduation.

Despite these growing concerns, there is a prevailing view in the state that student performance is rising and that TAAS has been a direct cause of the increases. Mike Moses, commissioner of education in Texas, stated: "We believe our strong system of holding schools accountable is helping to drive student performance up in this state" (as cited in Brooks, 1998).

## HIGH-STAKES ASSESSMENTS IN MICHIGAN

The Michigan Educational Assessment Program (MEAP) began with a program of commercial, norm-referenced tests in 1969 to 1973 for reading and mathematics. The tests were given to all Michigan fourth- and seventh-graders in the fall. It was intended initially to provide diagnostic information for teachers rather than comparative information about students. With the advent of criterion-referenced testing in the 1960s, the MEAP was redesigned by teachers and curriculum specialists according to specific performance objectives. The objectives-referenced

version of the MEAP was used first in 1973 to 1974 and was one of the first state-level tests based on objectives. The test was given to all fourth- and seventh-graders in the state, and in 1979 to 1980 it was also given to 10th-graders. The tests were revised again in 1980 to 1981 but continued to focus on isolated skills in the objectives. Although other subject areas were periodically tested, the MEAP science tests for fifth- and eighth-graders were introduced in 1986 to 1987. These tests were still given in the fall, after approximately 2 months of school.

By the mid-1980s, several problems with the MEAP tests became evident. First, the scores were rising each year and nearly 90% of all students passed the tests. The MEAP was viewed by some as too easy and not discriminating enough by other. Part of the reason for increasing test scores may have been due to the fact that the tests were unsecured and most Michigan teachers kept a copy in their desks. In the weeks preceding MEAP testing, teachers used the tests to familiarize students with the format and types of items to expect. There have been no studies about the degree to which teachers taught the exact same information on the MEAP test to students but anecdotal reports indicate that the practice was widespread.

A second problem with the objective-referenced MEAP tests was that the scores were misunderstood by many teachers and by most parents. The test actually had several items for a specific objective and students could "pass" that objective if they correctly answered, three of four items on that objective. The score reported for the test was actually the percent of objectives passed and, in order to pass the test, students had to pass 85% of the objectives. Actually, a student could pass the test by answering just over half the items correctly but nearly all students passed more than 85% of the objectives. In a study of parents' understanding of the MEAP scores, it was found that the vast majority of parents thought that the percentage of objectives passed indicated the child's percentile rank among all test takers (Barber, Paris, Evans, & Gadsden, 1992). This means that a student who passed 85% of the objectives, the minimum required, may actually have been near the bottom of the distribution of test takers but parents thought the child was in the top 15% of all students who took the test. Given this fundamental misunderstanding, it is ironic that most parents thought the MEAP test was useful and wanted the accountability it provided.

A third problem with the MEAP tests was their focus on isolated skills that were not congruent with the reading and mathematics curricula of the 1980s. Thus, the Michigan Department of Education adopted a new definition of reading in 1986 and created a test of essential reading skills that was introduced to students in Grades 4, 7, and 10 in 1989. The essential-skills MEAP test in mathematics for students in Grades 4, 7, and 10 was introduced in 1991. The reading test consisted of two long passages, one narrative and one informational text, followed by comprehension questions, "knowledge about reading" questions (assessments of metacognition and strategies), and attitude and self-perception questions. These tests were very different from traditional standardized tests and were specifically designed to support changes in reading and mathematics instruction. Despite little statistical support for the separate factors in the Michigan model of reading, the MEAP office approved the

| Grade Level | 1994 | 1995 | 1996 | 1997 |
|---|---|---|---|---|
| 3 | 77% | 79% | 80% | 81% |
| 4 | 75% | 79% | 78% | 82% |
| 5 | 77% | 79% | 82% | 84% |
| 6 | 73% | 78% | 78% | 84% |
| 7 | 75% | 78% | 82% | 84% |
| 8 | 76% | 75% | 77% | 83% |
| 10 | 76% | 76% | 81% | 86% |

FIGURE 45.1. Percent of students meeting TAAS minimum expectations in Reading (source, Texas Education Agency, Student Performance Results Report 1996–1997; p. 6).

| Grade Level | 1993 | 1994 | 1995 | 1996 |
|---|---|---|---|---|
| 3 | 50.4 | 50.6 | 48.9 | 49.9 |
| 4 | 51.8 | 51.8 | 47.2 | 49.3 |
| 5 | 49.7 | 49.7 | 48.4 | 50.2 |
| 6 | 49.7 | 50.2 | 47.3 | 48.2 |
| 7 | 49.7 | 49.9 | 48.4 | 47.7 |
| 8 | 48.4 | 49.9 | 46.3 | 47.2 |
| 10 | 48.4 | 47.7 | 43.1 | 44.5 |

FIGURE 45.2. Texas National Comparative Data Study Results: Mean Normal Curve Equivalent (NCE) scores (source, Texas Education Agency, Student Performance Results Report 1995–1996; p. 221).

new test. The state sponsored many workshops and presentations describing the pedagogical shifts in both assessment and instruction that were intended by the new MEAP tests. The new MEAP tests were now given in the winter, midyear, in order to assess achievement better.

The MEAP tests were modified throughout the 1990s. Science and writing MEAP tests for students in Grades 5 and 8 were created based on performance assessment tasks. It is interesting to note that all MEAP tests of 10th-graders were suspended in 1994 because of legislative actions that had required passing scores on the MEAP tests for high school graduation. This policy resulted in several challenges through the courts, so the MDE created a new series of High School Proficiency Tests (HSPTs), first administered in 1996, that were required in order for high school students to graduate with an endorsed diploma. These tests continue to be challenged in courts and many students are excused from taking the tests. It is ironic that both low-scoring minorities and high-scoring college-bound students have objected to the HSPTs as unnecessary and potentially harmful to their future academic opportunities. (Additional information about the MEAP tests can be found on the Web site http://www.mde.state.mi.us.)

## THE IMPACT OF HIGH-STAKES ASSESSMENT

We consider the impact of high-stakes assessment in several areas. In each area, we begin with the "illusion" of a positive impact. We follow this up with a description of the reality that

focuses on the potential for negative consequences. In illustrating our points we will draw on the data from the states of Texas and Michigan, but we argue that the underlying themes can be generalized across other states.

## The Impact on Students

*Illusion:* Because of high stakes assessments, students are learning to read and write better today than they have in the past.

In practically every state analysis we could uncover, the pattern is clear: Student performance on high-stakes assessments rises year after year. For example, the chart in Fig. 45.1 presents the data for student performance in reading on the TAAS test for the years 1994 to 1997. These data create the illusion that there is significant growth at practically every grade level and across reading and writing abilities. But do these data mean that students are reading and reading better than they were in the past? The answer to this question is not as simple as it may appear.

Consider first that these data reflect performance on a criterion-referenced measure. The tests are designed to assess whether students can demonstrate certain skills or understandings up to a "passing" level of performance. The data collected by the state of Texas over this period on a norm-referenced test suggest that there has been little change in the relative levels of Texas students as compared with national norms (Fig. 45.2). These conflicting results in Texas have been reported in other settings as well (e.g., Koretz, 1991). The recently reported state-by-state comparison scores on the National Assessment of Educational Progress also suggest that growth in reading achievement has been flat over the same period that the TAAS scores have been rising dramatically (Weisman, 2000).

Could it be that the increases in performance on the state tests are the result of teachers "teaching to the test"? Here we refer to practices that go beyond just orienting the students to the formatting of the tests to a range of decisions that involve everything from organizing the curriculum exclusively around those elements that are tested to daily practice tests that involve the application of the same scoring rubrics (e.g., in writing) that are used on the test itself. A recent survey conducted among educators in the State of Texas suggests these strategies for preparing students are widespread. It is not just the case that the teachers are preparing students for the test, the test has become the curriculum.

Could it be that the increases in performance on the state tests are the result of cheating on the test? The issue of cheating on tests is one that most educators are reluctant to address, but in the context of high-stakes assessments the issues are real. The illusion is that these high-stakes assessments are "objective" and what you see in students' scores reflects their true abilities. The fact is that all tests are simply estimates of students' true abilities. Further, all tests are subject to what Haladyna, Nolen, and Haas (1991) called "test pollution." Test pollution occurs when factors other than those targeted on the assessment (e.g., a student's reading or writing abilities) influence performance. Haladyna et al. (1991) reported a variety of teacher practices that may not be appropriate. For example, they conducted a survey of 2,500 Arizona teachers and administrators and found that there was great variability in the ways that the teachers helped children prepare for standardized achievement testing. For example, some teachers spent several hours a week helping children learn how to take multiple-choice, timed tests, whereas other teachers spent only 1 or 2 hours of preparation for the test. Some teachers taught test-taking skills and provided repeated practice with test facsimiles, whereas other teachers simply taught their regular curriculum. About 40% of teachers used commercial test preparation materials; 60% provided practice with sample questions; 13% gave students tests used in previous years as practice; 26% taught vocabulary on the *current* test; and 10% actually instructed students on items from the *current* test. Are these instances of cheating? The issues are complex.

Often lost in all of the analyses of high stakes assessments is the impact of the tests on students themselves. Reported data on the impact of such tests on student motivation, self-concept, or physical well-being are rare. Teachers assume that students take the test, try hard, and then resume with schoolwork as if there has been no effect on them directly. This is not the case (Nolen et al., 1992; Smith, Edelsky, Draper, Rottenberg, & Cherland, 1991). When high test-scores become the goal rather than self-regulated learning, students invest disproportionate value and effort in high-stakes tests. For many students, the consequences of testing are neutral or negative, ranging from the innocuous lack of feedback to negative feedback about one's competence. The ones who suffer most from repeated testing are the students who score poorly each year and are told annually that they do not measure up. Low achievers are left with few choices. If they believe that the tests are good measures of ability, then they may only try halfheartedly so that they can claim their poor test scores reflect low effort rather than low ability. Their other choices are to discount the importance of the test entirely, cheat, or sabotage the test. All these options make the scores meaningless indicators of the students' ability (which is the students' intention) and thus invalidate the test data for those most at risk. With age and practice, these counterproductive strategies become more prevalent and more creative (Paris, Lawton, Turner, & Roth, 1991).

## The Impact on Teachers

*Illusion:* With the introduction of high-stakes testing, teachers will teach better because they are held directly accountable for student learning.

The more visible the accountability, the more policymakers can leverage the level and focus of effort. Those teachers who do not, will not, or cannot get their students to perform at satisfactory levels will be "revealed" by the test and can then be directed to careers elsewhere. Teacher bonuses, teacher evaluations, teacher advancement, and so on are becoming a common part of the high-stakes formula.

The pressure on teachers to improve test scores has a profound impact on teaching practices. One direct consequence is a narrowed curriculum because teachers focus on information covered by the test. Moore (1994) investigated how teachers in one district responded to a new testing program and found that 97% of the teachers had increased their instructional emphasis on the material in the program, 75% had eliminated topics from the local curriculum to make time for test-related instruction, and 88% had aligned their instruction with the test skills and objectives. Charlesworth, Fleege, and Weitman (1994) concluded that the effects of standardized testing included "narrowing and fragmenting of the curriculum, limiting the nature of thinking, or forcing teachers to rush too much for students to learn well" (p. 198). Thus, teachers respond to pressure from administrators and parents to raise test scores at the expense of the curriculum. Who is the better teacher—one who provides frequent and rigorous test preparation activities or one who provides minimal test preparation but provides a rich and integrated curriculum?

The reality is that tests are affecting teaching but perhaps not in the ways intended or with the goals articulated. The pressure is great. For example, Shepard and Dougherty (1991) found that 92% of the teachers working in a high-stakes testing context reported sensing pressure to raise scores from administration and the media. What we are seeing is an increase in test score pollution. As the pressure to increase test scores rises, teachers are more likely to employ such practices as teaching to the test, using test preparation materials, and even cheating. These practices have the effect of altering levels of performance without having a direct, positive impact on the skill being assessed. Some of the practices reach into the arena of unethical (Haladyna et al., 1991; Mehrens & Kaminski, 1989).

Another reality is that high-stakes assessment is having a negative impact on teacher's motivations. Studies suggest that classroom teachers are almost unanimous in their opposition to the rise of high-stakes assessments. They believe that these assessments are impeding good instructional decision making and are not in the long-range interests of students. High-stakes assessments are driving teachers out of teaching as a career. Teaching is being deskilled by tests (Smith, 1991). Is this a case of sour grapes or teachers not willing to work hard or teachers who do not have the right learning priorities in mind? Perhaps it is the case that those who work most closely with students on a daily basis experience firsthand how such high-stakes assessments can distort fundamental educational goals, purposes, and processes. Madaus (1988) argued that high-stakes assessments have made teaching easier. It is, he argued, a "comfortable" form of pedagogy with students' becoming proficient at passing tests by mastering the tradition of past tests. But good teachers don't want teaching made easy because it is not in the nature of the work of teaching. Good teachers are frustrated by the push to make it easy and are particularly concerned with the fact that the schools in need of the best teachers are the schools that are becoming the least desirable contexts in which to work.

## The Impact on Curriculum

*Illusion:* High-stakes assessments are bringing coherence and order to the reading/language arts curriculum.

As educators adapt to the diverse students and competing agenda in schools, the public has become concerned that the basic educational mission has been lost (Green, 1987). A carefully defined curriculum with an assessment plan that is tied closely to each element will yield a standardized curriculum across education. The alignment of goals, objectives, resource materials, and testing will lead to the same coherent educational plan for all students. In this case, we agree that the illusion is the reality. What is tested will be taught—in particular under high-stakes conditions. What is not tested will not be taught. We question the reality, however, as a reasonable goal for education. There is no evidence that a highly centralized and controlled curriculum leads to better teaching or learning. In states with high-stakes assessments, the centralized control has moved from the district level to the state levels. One can easily foresee a future when the centralized control over the curriculum passes on to the federal level using the same basic arguments. The fact is that centralized control and the distancing of decision making from the classroom level leads to ineffective teaching. The research on teaching is clear on the finding that effective teachers are responsive to curriculum and instructional decision making. As the "degrees of freedom" to make responsive decisions are removed, the effectiveness of the teacher is diminished. This is indeed the effect of high-stakes assessment. Teachers are robbed of the opportunity and the responsibility for shaping the curriculum (Green & Stager, 1986). Educators can achieve conformity, but do they want to sacrifice quality in the process?

The curriculum of the future, if high-stakes assessments prevail, is the content and format of the tests. Everything else is left out. Darling-Hammond and Wise (1985) found that tested content was taught at the expense of untested content and the teachers taught the specific content and formats used on the test rather than the underlying concepts or principles. Smith,

Edelsky, Draper, Rotenberg, and Charleand (1990) found that high-stakes testing reduces time for ordinary instruction and content, leads schools and teachers to neglect content that is not tested, and encourages instruction that resembles the testing. Johnston (1997) lamented that just at the time when the field of language arts has come to embrace a complex, social-constructivist view of language learning, teachers are compelled by the limitations of standardized tests and the pressure of high-stakes contexts to reduce the curriculum back to a simple behaviorist reference point.

## The Impact on Assessment

*Illusion:* High-stakes testing fills a critical void, because teachers are not capable of conducting assessments that are trustworthy, valid, and useful to those responsible for educational decisions.

Objecting to high-stakes assessments is seen as a sign of professional weakness or incompetence. The reality is that effective teachers thrive on assessment and hold themselves accountable (almost to a fault) for student progress. Effective teachers are invested in assessment in the classroom. Their assessments are the basis for the decisions they make on a daily basis. These assessments are systematic, reliable, and valid. A strong performance assessment plan in a classroom is far more informative to a teacher regarding student abilities than any standardized measure. Research has demonstrated that teachers who have implemented a strong assessment plan in their classroom can, if asked, rank their students in terms of abilities with greater reliability than a standardized test. This is not suprising. What is more important is that data they gather on students is rich in qualitative information as well. This is the basis for good instructional decision making.

The implementation of such performance assessment plans in classrooms is far from widespread. This is an area where much staff development work is needed. Our fear is that in the context of a high-stakes assessments movement, performance assessment will be shunned aside as unnecessary and irrelevant. What is needed is a strengthening of internal assessments in the classroom and demonstrations that these assessments can be used for both instructional decision-making and accountability purposes.

Tests are designed to measure certain properties. The degree to which tests measure the properties that have been targeted is an index of test validity. This notion of validity has been a part of test design for a long time. Recently, assessment experts have come to focus on an extension of this basic idea of validity to include consideration of the uses of the test itself (intended or unintended). In other words, implicit in the development of a test is, not only a conception of the property to be measured, but also an intention as to how the results of the test might be used to guide decisions. As an example, a writing test might be developed to measure a student's skills and abilities in producing persuasive writing. The scoring procedures might focus on both control over mechanics as well as control over the content and rhetorical structure. The test may be designed for use in assessing strengths and weaknesses and lead to an instructional plan for improvement. The consequential validity of the test would be judged in terms of the degree to which the diagnosis and the instructional plan lead to improvement. Now consider that the same test is selected by a college to be used in the screening of applicants. Those who are using the test see it as a tool to eliminate potential candidates who are not prepared to meet the writing demands of their program. On implementation of this test as a screening device, large numbers of students are rejected. The test may be a valid measure of the writing ability that has been targeted, but the use of the test as a screening device is inconsiderate of its purpose. The test would be unproven, unsupported, and invalid under these conditions.

## HOW CAN EDUCATORS CHART A NEW COURSE FOR POLICY AND PRACTICE IN ASSESSMENT?

As described earlier, the forces that gave life to and sustain the high-stakes assessment movement are strong. The professional responsibility of educators is to redirect this movement, and recognize that it is perfectly appropriate for the public to be informed about the progress and learning of students. This is not just a reasonable idea; it is fundamental requirement for any public service. Educators have failed in this responsibility in the past, and it is now up to them to demonstrate ways that they can fulfill their responsibility to the public without compromising the quality of teaching and schooling.

### Teachers

Teachers must construct more systematic and rigorous plans for assessment in their classrooms. They must assume responsibility for educating parents and the public on the quality of these assessments and their utility in guiding educational decision making.

### Researchers

Researchers must conduct ongoing investigations of high-stakes assessments that examine issues of consequential validity. These studies should include but not be limited to: teacher use of results, impact on curriculum focus, time spent in testing and test preparation, the costs of the tests (both direct and hidden), parent and community communication, and effects on teacher; and student; motivations. Researchers must also explore better ways to link the performance assessments used by teachers in classroom settings to the kinds of questions that the educators outside the classroom must address in making planning decisions.

### Parents and Community Members

The data regarding the public at large and parents in particular with respect to standardized testing are disturbing. The vast majority of citizens perceive standardized testing, high-stakes assessments, and "comparisons" as highly valuable. A 1987 Gallup poll revealed that 74% of the public at large endorsed a national testing program from public school students, although only 31% of professional educators endorsed such a testing program (Elam, 1987). What the public is unaware of are the real costs and impacts of such tests on the quality of teaching and learning in schools. The public must be vigilant regarding the costs of high-stakes testing—not just the economic costs but also the costs on students' learning and teachers' instruction. The public must be prepared to ask tough, direct questions regarding the assessments being used and not simply accept the "we're just holding schools accountable" rhetoric. At what costs and with what benefits are these data being collected? Are there alternatives? The public and the educational community are clearly out of alignment with respect to this issue.

### Policymakers

We encourage policymakers to consider the following recommendations of the International Reading Association in their response to the high-stakes assessments movement:

- Design an assessment plan that is considerate of the complexity of reading, learning to read, and the teaching of reading.
- When decisions about students must be made that involve high-stakes outcomes (e.g., graduation, matriculation, awards), rely on multiple measures rather than just the performance on a single test.
- When assessments do not involve decisions related to the performance of individual students (e.g., program evaluation), use sampling strategies.
- Do not resort to a reward–punish mentality for schools, teachers, and systems.
- Do not attempt to manipulate instruction through assessments.

## CONCLUSIONS

American education has a long history of scrutiny and reform. At the turn of the 21st century the primary issues stimulating reform involve standards, accountability, and assessment. More fundamentally, though, the battle is over control of the curriculum and agenda. The main issue is whether they should be centralized and controlled by state and federal policymakers or left in the hands of local schools and districts. When educators use high-stakes tests to guide their curricula, evaluate students, and make decisions about which students, teachers, and schools are successful, they succumb to centralized authority and narrow criteria. When multiple assessments are administered and interpreted by teachers, local control increases the variety of criteria that are applied to evaluate students and programs and decreases the uniform comparisons of students, teachers, and schools. The issue was similar at the turn of the 20th century according to H. G. Wells (1892) who said:

"The examiner pipes and the teacher must dance—and the examiner sticks to the old tune. If the educational reformers really wish the dance altered, they must turn their attention from the dancers to the musicians" (cited in Madaus, 1985).

In this metaphor, teachers dance to the music established by policymakers who choose the standards and tests used for accountability, so the key to reform is to change the music. Wells argued over 100 years ago to establish policies in order to make teachers adhere to a uniform curriculum and set of standards, a theme that is echoed today. So the issue of control becomes focused on policies external to the classroom, but the impact is clearly on the curriculum. External control through high-stakes tests does establish uniformity among teachers in their objectives but part of the cost is a narrowed curriculum. This seems like a high price to pay for increases in test scores that may be modest, illusory, or short-lived.

If there is a solution to the struggle over control of education through testing and accountability, it will have to be achieved through negotiation and a pluralistic approach to student achievement. Bob Chase, the President of the National Education Association, said,

"Together, I believe that parents and educators can restore sanity and common sense to student assessment. Testing is an indispensable tool of our teacher's trade. However, to tie education reform to the single goal of raising test scores may seem like a good idea atop Mount Olympus, where no children live, but in the real world, it has produced a rash of negative and unintended consequences.

There is mounting evidence, for instance, that high-stakes tests in states such as Texas are spurring a dramatic rise in dropout rates, especially among black and Hispanic students. In addition, high-stakes tests are driving good teachers right out of the profession. One teacher e-mailed me last spring:' "It's not the lousy pay that making me leave teaching. It's the unrelenting pressure to raise scores on a single, multiple-choice test. I didn't become a teacher to become a test preparation drill sergeant." Unfortunately, I have received all too many letters over the past year (Chase, 2001, p. 5).

Educators know and understand the virtues and pitfalls of high-stakes tests and assessment of student learning better than policymakers, commercial publishers, and the public. Educators need to inform the public about the consequences of such accountability systems before the price paid by students and teachers becomes exorbitant. This discussion must move beyond the academy, beyond scholarly journals, and into the public domain where policies are formed. There, the wisdom of experienced educators can shape more beneficial approaches to student assessment.

# References

Anrig, G. R. (1985). Educational standards, testing, and equity. *Phi Delta Kappan,* 623–626.

Barber, B. L., Paris, S. G., Evans, M., & Gadsden, V. (1992). Policies for reporting test results to parents. *Educational Measurement: Issues and Practices, 11,* 15–20.

Berliner, D. C., & Biddle, B. J. (1997). *The manufactured crisis: Myths, frauds, and the attack on America's public schools.* White Plains, NY: Longman.

Brooks, A. P. (1998, December 16). Lawmaker proposes more-frequent TAAS testing. *Austin American-Statesman,* p. B5.

Charlesworth, R., Fleege, P. O., & Weitman, C. J. (1994). Research on the effects of group standardized testing on instruction, pupils, and teachers: New directions for policy. *Early Education and Development, 5,* 195–212.

Chase, B. (2001). Challenging the almighty test. *NEA today.* Washington, D.C.: National Education Association, October, p. 15.

Cruise, K. L. (1985). Test scores rise in Texas. *Phi Delta Kappa, 66,* no. 9, pp. 629–631.

Darling-Hammond, L., & Wise, A. E. (1985). Beyond standardization: State standards and school improvement. *The Elementary School Journal, 85,* 315–336.

Education Weekly (2001). Quality Counts. *Editorial Projects in Education,* Vol. 20, Number 17.

Elam, S. (1987). Differences between educators and the public on questions of education policy. *Phi Delta Kappan, 69*(4), 294–296.

Funkhouser, C. W. (2000). Education in Texas. Policies, Practices, and Perspectives (9th Edition). Upper Saddle River, NJ: Prentice-Hall, Inc.

Gordon, S. P., & Resse, M. (1997). High Stakes Testing: Worth the Price? Journal of School Leadership. Vol. 7 (July), pp. 3435–368.)

Green, K. E., & Staiger, S. F. (1986). Measuring attitudes of teachers towards testing. *Measurement and Evaluation in Counseling and Development, 9,* 141–150.

Green, K. E. (1987, October). *Quality in teacher education.* Paper presented at the Northeast Holmes Group Conference, Boston.

Greenberger, S. (1998, December 5). Moses aims to beef up TAAS exams. *Austin American-Statesman,* pp. 1, 16.

Haladyna, T., Nolan, S. B., & Haas, N. S. (1991). Raising standardized achievement test scores and the origins of test score pollution, *Educational Researcher, 20*(5), 2–7.

Haney, W. (2000). The Myth of the Texas Miracle in Education. Paper presented at the Annual Meeting of the American Educational Research Association. New Orleans. April 2000.

Hoffman, J. V., Assaf, L. C., & Paris, S. G. (2001). High-stakes testing in reading: today in Texas, tomorrow? *Reading Teacher,* Vol. 54, No. 5, pp. 482–492.

International Reading Association (1999). High Stakes Assessments in Reading. A Position Statement of the International reading association. Newark, Del.: International Reading Association.

Jayson, S. (1998a). Education chief seeks higher TAAS standard. *Austin American Statesman.* November 25, p. A11.

Jayson, S. (1998b). State: 3 Austin school ratings rigged. *Austin American-Statesman,* September 15, pp. A1, A6.

Johnston, P. (1997). Performance assessment and the English language arts standards. *The Language and Literacy Spectrum, 7,* 2326.

Johnston, R. C. (1998). In Texas, the arrival of spring means the focus is on Testing. *Education Week on the Web,* Vol. 17, Issue 42.

Koretz, D. (1991). *The effects of high stakes testing on achievement: Findings about generalization across tests.* Paper presented at the annual meeting of the American Educational Research Council and the National Council on Measurement in Education, Chicago III. April 4–6, 1991.

Madaus, G. F., & Tan, A. G. A. (1993). The growth of assessment. In G. Cawelti (Ed.), *Challenges and achievements of American education* (pp. 53–79). Alexandria, VA: Association for Supervision and Curriculum Development.

Madaus, G. (1988). The distortion of teaching and testing. *Peabody Journal of Education,* Vol. 65, No. 3, pp. 29–46.

Madaus, G. (1985). Test Scores as administrative mechanisms in educational policy. *Phi Delta Kappan,* May, 1985, pp. 611–617.

Mehrens, W. A., & Kaminski, J. (1989). Methods for improving standardized test scores: Fruitful, fruitless, or fraudulent? *Educational Measurement: Issues and Practice, 8,* 14–22.

Moore, W. P. (1994). The devaluation of standardized testing: One district's response to a mandated assessment. *Applied Measurement in Education, 7,* 343–367.

Morison, P. (1992). Testing in American Schools: Issues for research and policy. *Social Policy Report, 6*(2), 1–24.

Murphy, S., Shannon, P., Johnston, P., & Hansen, J. (1998). *Fragile evidence: A critique of reading assessment.* Mahwah, NJ: Lawrence Erlbaum Associates.

Nolen, S. B., Haladyna, T. M., & Haas, N. S. (1992). Uses and abuses of achievement test scores. *Educational Measurement: Issues and Practice, 11*(2), 9–15.

Paris, S. G., Lawton, T. A., & Turner, J. C. (1991). Reforming achievement testing to promote students' learning. In C. Collins & J. Mangieri (Eds.), *Teaching thinking: An agenda for the twenty-first century* (pp. 223–241). Hillsdale, NJ: Lawrence Erlbaum Associates.

Paris, S. G., Lawton, T. A., Turner, J. C., & Roth, J. L. (1991). A developmental perspective on standardized achievement testing. *Educational Researcher, 20*(5), 12–20.

Resnick, D. P. (1981). Testing in America: A supportive environment. *Phi Delta Kappan,* May, 1981, pp. 625–628.

Resnick, D. P., & Resnick, L. B. (1985). Standards, curricula, and performance: A historical and comparative perspective. *Educational Researcher, 14*(4), 5–20.

Sabers, D., & Sabers, D. (1996). Conceptualizing, measuring, and implementing higher (high or hire) standards. *Educational Researcher, 25,* 19–21.

Shepard, L. A., & Doughterty, K. C. (1991, April). *Effects of high stakes testing on instruction and achievement.* Paper presented at the annual meeting of the National Council on Measurement in Education, Chicago.

Smith, M. (1991). Put to the test: The effects of external testing on teachers. *Educational Researcher, 20*(5), 8–11.

Smith, M. L., Edelsky, C., Draper, K., Rottenberg, C., & Cherland, M. (1991). *The role of testing in elementary schools.* CSE technical Report #321. Los Angeles Center for the study of education.

State Educational Testing Practices. (Background Paper, December, 1987). Washington, D.C.: Office of Technology Assessment.

Stevenson, H. W., & Stigler, J. W. (1992). *The learning gap: Why our schools are failing and what we can learn from Japanese and Chinese education.* New York: Summit.

Texas Education Agency Division of Performance Reporting 1997–1998 (available at http://tea.state.tx.us/perfreport/pocked/)

Weisman, J. (2000). School testing put to the test, Texas miracle doesn't reflect highler level of learning, researchers say. *The Baltimore Sun,* March 30, p. A3.

Wells, H. G. (1892). On the true lever of education. *Educational Review, 4,* 382.

# ·46·

# ELEMENTARY LANGUAGE ARTS TEXTBOOKS:
# A DECADE OF CHANGE

## Janice A. Dole
### University of Utah

## Jean Osborn
### University of Illinois, Urbana-Champaign

About 10 years ago we reviewed a body of research on the selection and use of language arts textbooks in American schools (Dole & Osborn, 1991). In that review, we made the argument that up to and including that time, textbooks were a ubiquitous part of language arts and English instruction in this country. We reported the results of various surveys conducted between 1960 and 1990 about the use of language arts textbooks. These surveys reported that up to 95% of instructional time allocated to the language arts was devoted to textbook use (see, e.g., Austin & Morrison, 1963; Duffy & McIntyre, 1982; Durkin, 1978–79). Because of the heavy use of language arts textbooks, we addressed the following two questions: What do we know about how these textbooks are *selected* for use in American schools today, and how are these textbooks actually *used* by teachers in their classrooms?

To answer the first question, we examined the small but robust body of research on language arts textbook selection that had been conducted during the 1980s. We found two sets of selection procedures in use across the country, one for textbook adoption states and one for school and district level adoptions. We documented the complex set of pedagogical, social, and political influences affecting the selection of reading and language arts textbooks at the state and local levels (Dole & Osborn, 1991; see also Chall & Squire, 1991). To answer the second question, we discussed reasons teachers gave for using these textbooks in their classrooms, and we described how teachers used them.

As we prepared for an updated chapter on English language arts textbook selection and use, we found very little primary research on these topics during the 1990s. Nevertheless, we realized that many changes had taken place in the reading field and in educators' views about how to teach reading and the other language arts. Certain changes can be inferred from research, for example, a study of how basal publishers reacted to changes called for in basal reading programs (Hoffman et al., 1994). Other changes can be inferred from assessment documents of the 1990s, that is, the decline of certain reading scores during the early 1990s followed by some gains in the late 1990s. Still other changes can be inferred from philosophical changes in the nature of reading and reading instruction as documented by state proclamations such as those from California and Texas.

Our focus in this chapter, then, is on discussing the changes that we think have taken place over the last 10 years and to present the available evidence we have for these changes. The chapter is divided into three major sections. In the first section, we examine major criticisms of basal reading programs from cognitive theorists, whole-language advocates, and literature-based instruction advocates. We focus specifically on the content of basal reading programs, both the stories selected for the student textbooks and the instruction in the teachers' manuals that accompanies those stories. We also address key state initiatives to changing views about the reading process. In the next section, we discuss how publishers responded to these criticisms through changes in basal reading programs in the early 1990s. We then consider two significant events occurring in the mid-1990s that appeared to influence the reading field yet again. In the final section, we point out the need for additional research on the quality and content of new basal reading programs.

Before we begin our discussion, we must define what we mean by "language arts textbooks." We rely on Warren's (1981) definition of a textbook as "printed instructional material in bound form, the contents of which are properly organized and intended for use in elementary and high school curricula" (p. 43). Note that this definition includes other programs, in addition to reading, used to teach language arts, such as spelling, composition, grammar and handwriting textbooks. Although we found some research on these textbooks for the earlier edition of this volume (Dole & Osborn, 1991), we found almost no new research conducted since 1991. Therefore, these texts and their use by teachers are not reviewed here.

Note also in Warren's (1981) definition of a textbook that he included both "elementary and high school curricula." In our 1991 review (Dole & Osborn, 1991), we discussed basal reading programs and middle and secondary English anthologies. Here we focus on elementary basal reading programs only. We were unable to find primary research on secondary language arts textbooks or their use. Therefore, we chose to limit our discussion to elementary textbooks only.

We begin with a discussion of some of the major criticisms leveled against the basal reading programs in the late 1980s and early 1990s.

## CRITICISMS OF BASAL READING PROGRAMS

As we reported in 1991 (Dole & Osborn, 1991), American classroom reading instruction has been dominated by the use of basal reading programs throughout most of the 20th century. Basal reading programs and the instruction in them defined a national curriculum in reading for many years. Up to the early 1990s, it can be said that most American children learned how to read through the instruction suggested in basal reading programs. During the late 1980s, however, changes began to take place in the reading field that were to affect reading instruction in the 1990s. We reported some of these changes in the 1991 chapter, but more changes were to come.

### Criticisms of Basal Reading Programs by Cognitive Research

As we reported in 1991 (Dole & Osborn, 1991), several lines of cognitive research carried out during the 1970s and 1980s led reading researchers to rethink prevailing notions about the reading process and about reading instruction (Kintsch & van dijk, 1978; Rumelhart, 1977). We do not discuss cognitive theory and research here as it is reviewed extensively elsewhere, including in seminal works by Bransford (1979) and Anderson and Pearson (1984), as well as in a chapter by Schallert (1991), and a chapter by Marzano (Chapter 52, this volume). However, we do discuss several ways in which cognitive theory was applied to the instruction and stories in basal textbooks.

In the late 1980s, one seminal study proved to have an enormous impact on basal reading programs. Durkin (1978–79) published an observational study in which she found that

teachers following the instructional directives of basal reading programs did not in fact teach comprehension. She recorded, described, and analyzed the instructional tasks of teachers and students. She also noted the high number of questions that were asked during and after students read the basal stories. Durkin concluded that teachers *tested* rather than *taught* comprehension.

Following Durkin's (1978–79) lead, research evaluating basal reading programs continued and expanded during the 1980s. Researchers questioned not only the questions asked as part of comprehension instruction but also the comprehension skills included as part of the instruction. Cognitive research proposed that reading was a complex process that could not be reduced to the hierarchy of skills that were typically found in basal programs (Anderson, Hiebert, Scott, & Wilkinson, 1985). Cognitive research about the reading process called into question the whole framework of comprehension skill development that had been so central to basal reading programs instruction.

One line of cognitive research lead educational researchers to a different conceptualization of comprehension "skills." Cognitive research indicated that good readers used various "strategies," as opposed to "skills," as they read (for reviews, see Dole, Duffy, Roehler, & Pearson, 1991; Pressley, Johnson, Symons, McGoldrick, & Kurita, 1989). These strategies, like predicting, summarizing, determining importance, and monitoring comprehension, were not rotelike skills that readers could learn simply by practice on workbook pages. Instead, these strategies were conscious plans made by good readers to help them comprehend what they read. Researchers found that good readers summarized text as they read, they monitored their understanding as they read, and they changed strategies when they realized that they did not understand what they read. Furthermore, in research studies in which poor readers were taught strategies that good readers used, poor readers' comprehension improved significantly.

In another early seminal study, Beck, McKeown, McCaslin, and Burkes (1979) also used cognitive research as a framework for evaluating basal reading programs. Beck and her colleagues found that the instructions suggested in the teachers' manuals often fell short of high-quality reading instruction based on cognitive research. For example, many before-reading activities focused on information not central to the upcoming story. As such, these activities might lead students off track in their comprehension. They also evaluated the quality of the questions proposed during and after reading and found those questions to be in need of improvement. Beck and her colleagues suggested ways in which basal instructions could be changed to improve their overall quality.

Another line of research conducted during the 1980s criticized the selections found in the student editions of the basals. Researchers criticized the difficulty level of these texts (Davison, 1984). The publishers had adapted many selections from children's trade books. However, since most of these trade books were too difficult for elementary students to read even with teacher assistance, the editors rewrote the texts to make them easier to read. In doing so, they applied "readability formulas" that were based on the difficulty of the vocabulary and on word and sentence length (for a review, see Klare, 1984). The thinking was that shorter words and shorter sentences reduced the difficulty of a given text (Hiebert & Raphael, 1998). Thus, publishers rewrote much of the children's literature they included in the basal texts by replacing less frequent with more frequent words and by reducing sentence length. Linguists analyzed some of these rewritten texts and compared them to the originals. They found that the rewritten texts were often more, rather than less, difficult to read and understand (Davison, 1984; Davison & Kantor, 1982).

Thus, when educational researchers applied knowledge gleaned from cognitive research to basal reading programs, they found that many of the text selections were not of high quality. Moreover, they found that the instruction suggested in the teachers' manuals was problematic in a number of ways.

At the same time that cognitive researchers were evaluating the selections and instructional quality of basal programs, there was a parallel development in the reading field. It is to this development that we now turn

## Criticisms of Basal Reading Programs by Advocates of Whole Language

One significant change taking place in the reading field in the early 1990s was the continued growth of what has come to be known as the whole language movement. Some understanding of this movement is necessary to understand how the movement affected the content and use of basal reading programs.

Whole language is a philosophy of teaching based on classic tenets of Dewey (Dewey & Dewey, 1915) about child-centered instruction and writings by Smith (1971) and Goodman (see, e.g., Goodman, 1986; Goodman & Goodman, 1979). One basic tenet of whole language was that children learn to read just as they learn to speak and listen and that just as oral language development is a natural process, literacy development is a natural process (Goodman & Goodman, 1979). Whole-language advocates believed that the conditions that allow oral language to flourish will also allow written language to flourish (Goodman, 1986). Because children's oral language learning occurs in rich contexts, written language should occur in rich contexts. Just as there are multiple opportunities for young children to hear oral language in many different contexts, so should there be multiple opportunities for them to see and use written language in its many different contexts. These contexts should be "authentic," ones in which there are real purposes for reading, as, for example, with cereal boxes, signs, posters, letters, TV ads, magazines, newspapers, and books (Garcia & Pearson, 1990; Goodman, 1986).

A second major tenet of whole language was that phonics was overemphasized in the learning to read process. Early on, Goodman (1967) made the argument that reading was "a psycholinguistic guessing game" that relied more on context than on automatic decoding skills (but see Nicholson, 1991). Smith (1973) also argued that good readers primarily used context clues to figure out unknown words; they did not "sound out" unknown words. Furthermore, Smith (1973) applied this belief to beginning readers by stating that, "decoding skills are used [by beginning readers] only to a very limited extent" (p. 71).

These two basic tenets of whole language have been definitely debunked within the last decade. Research reviewed and summarized by Adams and Bruck (1995) suggested that written language acquisition is a qualitatively different process from oral language acquisition. In short, the process of learning to read is clearly not like the process of learning to speak and listen. Furthermore, a large body of research has suggested that even good readers rely on the alphabetic principle, albeit in an automated rather than deliberate and conscious way. Thus, the important foundation on which whole language rested has been rebuked over the last decade. We discuss more about this issue later in this chapter.

Nevertheless, in the early 1990s, beliefs about the reading process based on whole language affected how many educators viewed basal reading programs. Whole-language advocates believed that basal reading programs and the instruction built into them did all the wrong things to teach reading to children (Goodman, 1989; Shannon, 1989). For example, proponents of whole language found many problems with the watered-down and rewritten excerpts from literature placed in basal reading programs. They believed that the written language children read should be "natural." Because we do not say "Sally, cookie" to ask a child if she would like a cookie, we should not give children stilted and unnatural prose to read, such as the famous "See Dick run." Instead, we should write for children just as we talk to them. This writing should come from high-quality children's literature available in trade books.

One of the problematic outcomes arising from this particular argument was that many first- and second-grade teachers took the old beginning reader stories (similar to what is now called "leveled" books) *out* of the hands of their students. Instead, these teachers provided students with trade books with no vocabulary control at all as well as patterned or predictable books with repetitive rhymes (e.g., "Run, run as fast as you can"). Although we have no data on just how many teachers made these changes, we do know that such a practice flies in the face of over 20 years of research on beginning reading (Adams, 1990; Anderson et al., 1985).

Advocates of whole language not only opposed the content of the student textbooks, but they also opposed much of the instruction suggested in basal programs. They said that learning the skills of written language should mirror learning the skills of oral language. This meant that phonics skills—such as recognizing beginning consonant and medial vowel sounds—should not be taught in isolation and often need not be taught at all. It also meant that teaching other reading skills, including comprehension skills, was counterproductive. The belief was that reading skills will develop naturally and informally as children engage in the reading of authentic literature under the guidance of a skilled teacher.

## Criticisms of Basal Reading Programs by Literary Response Theorists and Literature-Based Instruction

Although cognitive theory and research and whole-language advocates criticized many aspects of basal reading programs, an alternative movement was developing among some educators.

These educators drew their theoretical underpinnings from "reader response" or "literary response" (Beach, 1993; Beach & Hynds, 1991). This theory arose from the rhetoric tradition, often translated into practice in secondary, rather than elementary, English language arts programs.

Literary response theory was consistent with many cognitive views about the reading process. Both viewed meaning not as residing in the text but instead as arising from an interaction (Rumelhart, 1977) or transaction (Rosenblatt, 1978) between the reader and the text. Both highlighted the importance of the reader in comprehension. Both put different weights at different times on the reader and the text, and both allowed alternative, but plausible, interpretations of a text.

The focus of much of the literary response research has been on readers and the different social, personal, cultural and idiosyncratic responses they make to texts. Reader response researchers have looked at how readers respond emotionally to texts, connect texts to their own experiences, attitudes and beliefs, and interpret and evaluate texts (see Beach & Hynds, 1991, for a review). They have also focused on particular stances that readers take and how those stances affect responses (Langer, 1992; Rosenblatt, 1978).

In our view, literary response theory was translated into practice in the form of literature-based instruction. Those who supported literature-based instruction argued that students should not be reading adapted and excerpted stories in basal anthologies. Instead, students should read the original stories—high-quality children's literature or trade books (Karolides, 1997). The advantage of these books was that they are engaging, inspiring, and well written, unlike basal stories. Moreover, proponents of literature-based instruction argued that high-quality literature was far more likely to lead readers to become motivated to read. (The disadvantage of these books, of course, is that they are often too difficult for young readers to read on their own).

As students read these trade books, proponents of literature-based instruction believed that teachers need not teach specific reading skills—finding the main idea, predicting, or inferring—suggested in the instructions of basal reading programs. The belief was that teachers also need not ask students convergent questions to which they themselves already know the answer. Instead, literature-based proponents believed teachers and students should conduct discussions about the meaning of the literature and its connections to their own lives and experiences (Hill, Johnson, & Schlick Noe, 1995; Karnowski,1997; Karolides, 1997). In addition, teachers should focus on students' personal and social reactions to the texts.

Literature-based instruction advocates espoused discussion groups or literature circles rather than the traditional "round robin reading groups" practiced with basal reading programs. Literature discussions were held informally in literature circles or study groups (Eeds & Wells, 1989; Pederson & Eeds, 1990). Students worked in small groups based on their common interest in a particular picture or chapter book. They developed questions about a story. They related the stories to themselves or those they knew. They related the stories and characters to other stories and characters, much like adults do in more formal book clubs. Teachers participated in the literature groups,

but they did so without the assumption that they carried the "right" interpretation or understanding of a story. Teachers did not direct literature circles the way they directed round robin reading groups.

It must be noted that both reader response theory and literature-based instruction arose from a model of reading based on expert readers, not beginning readers. The extrapolation from what might be good practice for experienced readers to beginning readers was based on neither theory nor research.

## State Level Criticisms of Basal Reading Programs

As basal reading programs and the instruction in them continued to be criticized from many different sources, key adoption states listened to these criticisms and began requiring changes in the basal programs they would consider for state adoption.

In our earlier review (Dole & Osborn, 1991), and also in Chall and Squire's (1991) review of textbooks, the importance of state level adoptions in the development of basal reading programs was documented. Because some states adopted basal textbooks for every one of their students, key states like California, Texas, and Florida could make demands on the content and quality of basal programs. Publishers listened to these demands and made appropriate changes because they wanted to sell their textbooks in these states. Therefore, what states asked for and demanded in basal reading programs heavily impacted the development of those programs.

A significant development occurred in the late 1980s when California adopted the California Reading Initiative, or CRI (California English Language Arts Curriculum Framework Committee, 1987). Responding to the many criticisms of basal reading programs, the CRI was developed to raise the overall quality of reading instruction in California's schools. This framework was then used to evaluate and select reading programs for the state (Honig, 1988).

The CRI incorporated many of the components of whole language and literature-based instruction into its new curricular framework. In general, the CRI promoted student-centered learning and an integration of reading and the other language arts. In addition, the CRI endorsed children's trade books in place of the anthologies or basal readers. Third, the CRI proposed the elimination of workbooks and a focus on developing positive attitudes toward reading (Harris, 1993). Most important, though, the CRI included almost no attention to beginning reading. This was a critically important omission, but one that was consistent with whole language and literature-based instruction where the focus was on reading practice with high-quality literature and authentic texts.

In 1990, Texas also developed a document, the Texas Proclamation. This document also made significant changes in its curricular framework based on current criticisms of basal reading programs. The 1990 Texas Proclamation espoused an interactive and constructive model of reading (Hoffman et al., 1994) and therefore had a focus different from the CRI. Like the California document, though, the Texas Proclamation included the use of high-quality literature that was whole and original rather than adapted and excerpted (Cullinan, 1991). Unlike California, however, the Texas Proclamation also included attention to beginning reading skills.

## Summary

Beginning in the mid-1980s, basal reading programs came under attack from a number of different sources. Cognitive researchers criticized many aspects of basal reading programs based on an extensive body of research on the reading process. As a matter of fact, based on this body of research, we argued in 1991 that "[c]urrent theory and research about reading and writing are not reflected in the reading and writing practices of current textbooks" (Dole & Osborn, 1991, p. 526). In addition, during the 1970s and 1980s whole-language proponents viewed reading from a very different perspective from the then current basal reading programs. They cited many problems with existing reading instruction in American schools and blamed these problems directly on basal reading programs. Shannon (1989) even argued that the programs "deskilled" teachers because they prescribed instruction so directly and were followed so faithfully by many teachers. Finally, literature-based instruction proponents used literary response theory as a framework for understanding why basal programs should be replaced by high-quality children's trade books. Proponents of literature-based instruction rejected the use of basal readers and their instructional suggestions in the teachers' manuals. They wanted to see reading taught as literature groups and book clubs, not as formal lessons in reading skills.

## PUBLISHERS' RESPONSES TO CRITICISMS: FOUR BASAL PROGRAMS

As we completed the 1991 chapter on language arts textbook selection and use (Dole & Osborn, 1991), we wondered whether and how publishers would respond to the many demands for changes in basal reading programs. One study from the mid-1990s shed some light on the specific changes made by basal programs in response to pressures, criticisms from the field, and state initiatives.

Hoffman et al. (1994) compared new (1993) and older (1986–87) versions of four major reading programs at the first-grade level. The findings from this study showed that, over the last 5 years, publishers made significant changes in the content of these four programs. First, stories for beginning readers were written to more closely match the "authentic" literature of children's trade books espoused by whole-language and literature-based instruction proponents. The new basals included overall fewer words in the beginning readers yet a greater number of unique words. Hoffman and his colleagues concluded that publishers had reduced the vocabulary control and the repetition of words. Relatedly, the researachers found that early readers included more predictable text, over 50% in the new series, and less decodable text than in the older series.

Next, Hoffman et al. (1994) examined the quality of the literature included in the student textbooks. They observed that while 80% of the first-grade stories in the older series were written "on order" for the series, most of the first-grade stories in the newer series were the original stories in children's trade books. In general, they found that publishers had made only a few adaptations in the language and content of the stories in the newer series. In addition, they found that the new series contained a broader range of types of literature, including poetry.

To further evaluate the quality of the literature, Hoffman et al. (1994) used a 5-point scoring rubric to examine the content, language, design, predictability and decodability of the stories included in the old 1986 to 1987 and 1993 basal programs. Raters were trained to examine these dimensions according to a detailed scoring rubric. Findings from this analysis indicated that the 1993 basals seemed to contain more complex plots and character development, more metaphors and imagery, and aesthetic design features like color, form and design. The researchers concluded that the newer basals were more engaging than the old ones, although even the new ones averaged only a 3 on the 1- to 5-point scale.

An additional noticeable change between old and new programs related to their instructional design. The researchers found a significant reduction in the accompanying worksheet activities for students in the new series. They also found that the new teachers' manuals made a number of changes in their instructional suggestions. These suggestions included using more vocabulary in context; asking fewer questions; offering less isolated skill work; and, in general, offering less prescription about how to instruct.

In their analyses, Hoffman et al. (1994) demonstrated that these four basal reading programs had, in fact, responded to criticisms about the content of the basal student text and to the design of the program of instruction. They observed, "Innovations were being offered on a scale unparalleled in the history of basals. Notable was the fact that the differences between the old and the new versions were far greater than the variations between publishers" (p. 65).

What happened to these new versions of basal reading programs? Were they used by teachers? Did teachers put them aside and use children's trade books instead? Did they continue using the older versions? Did teachers use the newer versions and adapt them to meet their needs, or did they use the newer versions as they were written? We have been unable to find data to provide any answers to these critical questions.

## THE READING FIELD IN THE MID-1990S

By the mid-1990s, the differences among factions in the reading field resulted in fragmentation, disarray and division. The field was polarized along a number of dimensions, for example, phonics versus whole language, explicit versus implicit instruction, skills versus strategies, textbooks versus trade books, predictable versus decodable books, and reading groups versus literature circles (Graves, 1998). Although publishers of basal reading programs responded to at least some of these divisions, basal programs and their use were themselves a source of contention and division.

It is beyond the scope of this chapter to discuss the serious divisions within the field. Some of these have been documented in professional publications (see, e.g., Edelsky, 1990; McKenna, Robinson, & Miller, 1990), and they have been discussed regularly in local and national newspapers and magazines.

We see at least two important events occurring during the mid-1990s, though, that were to affect the reading field significantly. We discuss these events next.

## Declining Reading Scores in California

In 1994, important new data were released from the National Assessment of Educational Progress that showed that although reading achievement scores across the nation remained relatively stable, scores in the state of California significantly dropped, making California students among the lowest scoring in the nation. This decline was consistent across ethnic and socioeconomic groups (Loveless, 1998).

These declining test scores were received with alarm in California and across the nation. Educators and the public asked many questions. Was the decline in reading achievement due to the adoption of the CRI framework? Was it due to the diminished use of basal reading programs? Was it due to recent changes in the basals, such as the uncontrolled vocabulary of early readers? Was it due to the diminished teaching of phonics and other word identification skills? Was it due to both preservice and inservice teacher development programs that focused more on whole language than on more explicit methods of teaching reading? Was it due to the whole-language approach? Was it due to the division and fragmentation in the reading field itself? Was it due to the mixed messages reading educators gave teachers? Was it due to teachers' resulting confusions about how to teach reading?

We know of no primary research that can help us answer these questions. We do know, however, that beginning in the mid-1990s, there appeared to be a backlash from educators and the public against whole language. This backlash could be seen in the popular press as well as in professional documents (Loveless, 1998). One of the prevailing popular beliefs, especially among the public, was that whole language was responsible for the decline in reading test scores, especially in California (see, e.g., Colvin, 1995; Jones, 1995; Stewart, 1996).

We, along with many of our reading educator colleagues, argue that one critical issue affecting reading instruction in America in general, and probably California, too, was the fragmentation and division of the reading field in the early 1990s. At this point in time, reading educators had mixed and confusing messages for teachers. We believe many teachers got the message that their use of basal reading programs was "bad," and their use of children's trade books was "good." Beyond that, however, many teachers did not seem to know what to do.

## Putting to Rest the Debate About Phonics

Although educators were divided over reasons behind California's declining test scores, a critical mass of research was rapidly accumulating from the large and robust body of research on the importance of phonics and phonics instruction in beginning reading. We have already discussed the seminal review of the research on beginning reading (Adams, 1990) that highlighted the importance of phonics and word identification skills in beginning reading instruction. However, even though Adams reviewed research conducted during the 1970s and 1980s, additional research was conducted during the 1990s, and the results of that research were unequivocal (for excellent discussions, see Adams & Bruck, 1995; Stanovich, 1998).

Studies conducted after 1990 confirmed the significant role that phonological processes play in learning to read (see, e.g., Stanovich, 1992; Vellutino, 1991; Wagner, Torgesen, Laughon, Simmons, & Rashotte, 1993). Phonological processes enable young children to hear the sounds in words. Researchers have consistently found that improving children's phonological abilities improved their chances of learning how to read, particularly for at-risk readers and students with reading disabilities (Foorman, Francis, Fletcher, Schatschneider, & Mehta, 1998; Spector, 1992; Torgesen & Burgess, 1998).

Research conducted on phonemic awareness (and its relationship to phonics instruction) during the 1990s had an impact on researchers' and educators' understandings about the role of phonics in early reading. Remember, though, as Hoffman et al. (1994) documented, this new knowledge was not reflected in the teachers' guides of most of the 1990s basal reading programs. Our own examination of the programs from 1995 to 1997 suggested that publishers had not yet received the message about the essential role of both phonemic awareness and phonics in early reading instruction. They were responding more to an early 1990 market, a market that devalued phonics.

## California and Texas Revisit Their Standards for Reading Instruction

Although basal reading programs had not yet responded to the critical mass of research on the importance of phonics, at least some states did respond. For example, in 1997, the California Department of Education adopted a set of standards called *English-Language Arts Content Standards for California Public Schools*. A year later, these standards were followed by another document, *The Reading/Language Arts Framework for California Public Schools* (California Department of Education, 1998). Together, these documents replaced the CRI adopted in 1987.

In contrast to the 1987 CRI, these two new documents devote a great deal of attention to beginning reading instruction. They called for direct and explicit instruction in concepts about print, phonemic awareness, decoding and word recognition, fluency and systematic vocabulary, and concept development. They included such details as matching consonant and vowel sounds to appropriate letters, blending practice, and applying knowledge of word families to decode unfamiliar words. The framework emphasized the need for some students to practice their developing word identification skills first in decodable texts, then in more freely written texts.

Although each of these documents devoted considerable attention to the development of skills associated with beginning reading, they each also emphasized the importance of wide reading in a variety of texts, both in and out of school. The comprehension instruction described in each document focused on comprehension strategies rather than comprehension skills, and also called for students to learn how to analyze the text structures of narrative and expository texts. At every grade level these documents emphasized the importance of extensive reading.

*The Texas Essential Knowledge and Skills for the English Language Arts and Reading* was approved by the state board of education in July 1997. Accompanying this document were separate documents developed for both bilingual and English-language learners. *The Proclamation for Reading and Language Arts Programs*, intended for publishers of instructional materials, was also approved by the state board in November 1997. Like the California standards and framework, the Texas documents devoted a great deal of attention to beginning reading. The specifications in the Texas Proclamation dealt with print awareness, phonological awareness, letter–sound relationships, and reading fluency. First-grade specifications also included instruction that would help students "decode by using all letter–sound correspondences within regularly spelled words, "use letter-sound knowledge to read decodable texts," and "blend initial letter-sounds with common vowel spelling patterns to read words."

In addition, the Texas documents, like the California documents, included a great deal of attention to vocabulary development, to the strategies associated with reading comprehension, and to students' response to literature. Furthermore, students were expected to learn how to analyze text structures and understand literary forms and concepts.

As we complete this chapter, the publishers of basal reading programs have now completed their changes for the new 2000 programs. These changes have been made to meet the changing needs of publishers' constituencies around the country, and especially key states like California and Texas. Over the next few years, readers of this chapter will be able to examine the programs that basal publishers have produced and perhaps observe them in use in classrooms—or, as teachers, use them in classrooms.

## RESEARCH BEYOND THE YEAR 2000

As we view the reading field in 2001, some say that the well-known "reading wars" have diminished; others say that they are still with us. What we see in the professional and popular press and what we hear at conferences is the frequent call for "balanced literacy instruction."

We believe that many educators envision balanced instruction, at least in the primary grades, as a combination of extremes, for example, phonics and other word identification instruction combined with the wide reading and lots of writing advocated by the whole language approach. We, along with other researchers (see, e.g., Baumann, Hoffman, Moon, & Duffy-Hester, 1998; Baumann & Ivey, 1997; Warton-McDonald et al., 1997) believe that best practice in reading instruction is more complicated than a simple mixing of extremes. Graves (1998) pointed out that we cannot conceive of balanced instruction as "a little of this and a little of that" (p. 16). Reutzel (1999) also cautioned that an oversimplified definition of balance may end up costing us dearly. He pointed out that balanced literacy instruction is a complex collage of modeling, interacting, guiding, assessing, practicing, and motivating readers and writers.

Having now entered the 21st century, we look forward to a renewed interest in instructional research in reading. This research should guide publishers as they develop new reading programs. We believe that research is essential to the significant improvement of reading instruction.

However, the fact is that we have a disturbingly limited amount of empirical knowledge about reading instruction in American classrooms during the 1990s. We consider this a serious problem that must be changed over the next decade. Texas and California standards in the late 1980s and throughout the 1990s managed to wield enormous power in the textbook development and adoption process (Chall & Squire, 1991), yet we know little about how changes in textbook development impacted teachers and instruction. We believe that during the early 1990s many teachers changed their teaching of reading, yet we lack a coherent description and explanation of just what happened. We also have little research examining the effect of changing basal programs on student achievement in reading. We know reading scores declined in California in the early 1990s, but we do not know exactly why. We know they are beginning to go back up again, but we lack systematic gathering of data as to why. We need to know what happens when the next set of revised basal reading programs come into the classrooms. Will they be used? If so, how?

Two large, glaring questions remain: Have publishers made the needed changes in basal reading programs based on theory and research about the beginning reading process, and if so, will these changes result in improved student achievement in reading, especially for our young readers? Unfortunately, we are no closer to answering these questions than we were 10 years ago.

## *References*

Adams, M. (1990). *Beginning to read.* Cambridge, MA: Harvard University Press.

Adams, M. J., & Bruck, M. (1995). Resolving the "Great Debate." *American Educator, 19,* 7.

Anderson, R. C., Hiebert, E. H., Scott, J. A., & Wilkinson, I. A. G. (1985). *Becoming a nation of readers.* Washington, DC: National Institute of Education.

Anderson, R. C., & Pearson, P. (1984). A schema-theoretic view of basic processes in reading comprehension. In P. D. Pearson, R. Barr,

M. L. Kamil, & P. Mosenthal (Eds.), *Handbook of reading research* (pp. 255–291). New York: Longman.

Austin, M., & Morrison, C. (1963). *The first R: The Harvard report on reading in elementary schools.* New York: Macmillan.

Baumann, J. F., Hoffman, J. V., Moon, J., & Duffy-Hester, A. M. (1998). Where are teachers' voices in the phonics/whole language debate? Results from a survey of U.S. elementary teachers. *The Reading Teacher, 50,* 636–650.

Baumann, J. F., & Ivey, G. (1997). Delicate balances: Striving for curricular and instructional equilibrium in a second-grade, literature/strategy-based classroom. *Reading Research Quarterly, 32,* 244–275.

Beach, R. (1993). *A teacher's introduction to reader-response theories.* Urbana, IL: National Council of Teachers of English.

Beach, R., & Hynds, S. (1991). Research on response to literature. In R. Barr, M. L. Kamil, P. Mosenthal, & P. D. Pearson (Eds.), *Handbook of reading research* (Vol. 2, pp. 453–489). White Plains, NY: Longman.

Beck, I. L., McKeown, M. G., McCaslin, E. S., & Burkes, A. M. (1979). *Instructional dimensions that may affect reading comprehension: Examples from two commercial reading programs.* Pittsburgh, PA: University of Pittsburgh, Learning Research and Development Center.

Bransford, J. D. (1979). *Learning, understanding and remembering.* Belmont, CA: Wadsworth.

California Department of Education (1997). *English-language arts content standards for California public schools.* Sacramento: California Department of Education.

California Department of Education (1998). *The reading/language arts framework for California public schools.* Sacramento: California Department of Education.

California English Language Arts Curriculum Framework Committee. (1987). *California Reading Initiative.* Sacramento: California Department of Education.

Chall, J. S., & Squire, J. R. (1991). The publishing industry and textbooks. In R. Barr, M. L. Kamil, P. Mosenthal, & P. D. Pearson (Eds.), *Handbook of reading research* (Vol. 2, pp. 120–146). White Plains, NY: Longman.

Colvin, R. L. (1995, March 23). State's reading, math reforms under review as scores fall. *Los Angeles Times.*

Cullinan, B. (1991). These turbulent times. *Publishing Research Quarterly, 7* (3), 15–22.

Davison, A. (1984). Readability—Appraising text difficulty. In R. C. Anderson, J. Osborn, & R. J. Tierney (Eds.), *Learning to read in American schools: Basal readers and content texts* (pp. 121–139). Hillsdale, NJ: Lawrence Erlbaum Associates.

Davison, A., & Kantor, R. N. (1982). On the failure of readability formulas to define readable texts: A case study from adaptations. *Reading Research Quarterly, 17,* 187–209.

Dewey, J., & Dewey, K. (1915). *Schools of tomorrow.* New York: Liveright.

Dole, J. A., Duffy, G. G., Roehler, L. R., & Pearson, P. D. (1991). Moving from the old to the new: Research on reading comprehension instruction. *Review of Educational Research, 61,* 239–264.

Dole, J. A., & Osborn, J. (1991). The selection and use of language arts textbooks. In J. Flood, J. M. Jensen, D. Lapp, & J. R. Squire (Eds.), *Handbook for research on teaching the English language arts* (pp. 521–528). New York: Macmillan.

Duffy, G., & McIntyre, L. (1982). A naturalistic study of instructional assistance in primary-grade reading. *Elementary School Journal, 83,* 15–23.

Durkin, D. (1978–79). What classroom observations reveal about reading comprehension instruction. *Reading Research Quarterly, 14,* 481–533.

Edelsky, C. (1990). Whose agenda is this anyway? A response to McKenna, Robinson, and Miller. *Educational Researcher, 19*(8), 7–11.

Eeds, M., & Wells, D. (1989). Grand conversations: An explanation of meaning construction in literature study groups. *Research in the Teaching of English, 23,* 4–29.

Foorman, B. R., Francis, D. J., Fletcher, J. M., Schatschneider, C., & Mehta, P. (1998). The role of instruction in learning to read: Preventing reading failure in at-risk children. *Journal of Educational Psychology, 90,* 37–55.

Garcia, G. E., & Pearson, P. D. (1990). *Modifying reading instruction to maximize its effectiveness for all students.* (Tech. Rep. No. 489). Urbana, IL: Center for the Study of Reading.

Goodman, K. S. (1967). Reading: A psycholinguistic guessing game. *Journal of the Reading Specialist, 4,* 126–135.

Goodman, K. S. (1986). *What's whole in whole language?* Portsmouth, NH: Heinemann.

Goodman, K. S. (1989). Access to literacy: Basals and other barriers. *Theory Into Practice, 28,* 300–306.

Goodman, K., & Goodman, Y. (1979). Learning to read is natural. In L. Resnick & P. Weaver (Eds.), *Theory and practice in early reading* (Vol. 1, pp. 137–154). Hillsdale, NJ: Lawrence Erlbaum Associates.

Graves, M. F. (1998). Beyond balance. *Reading Today,* October/November, 16.

Harris, V. J. (1993). Literature-based approaches to reading instruction. In L. D. Hammond (Ed.), *Review of research in education* (pp. 269–297). Washington, DC: American Educational Research Association.

Hiebert, E. H., & Raphael, T. E. (1998). Psychological perspectives on literacy and extensions to educational practice. In D. C. Berliner & R. C. Calfee (Eds.), *Handbook of educational psychology* (pp. 550–602). New York: Macmillan.

Hill, B. C., Johnson, N. J., & Schlick Noe, K. L. (1995). *Literature circles and response.* Norwood, MA: Christopher-Gordon.

Hoffman, J. V., McCarthey, S. J., Abbott, J., Christian, C., Corman, L., Curry, C., Dressman, M., Elliott, B., Matherne, D., & Sable, D. (1994). So what's new in the new basals? A focus on first grade. *Journal of Reading Behavior, 26,* 47–73.

Honig, B. (1988). The California Reading Initiative. *The New Advocate, 1,* 235–240.

Jones, S. L. (1995, August 21). Reading approach may turn new leaf: Task force will urge teaching basic skills. *The San Diego Union-Tribune.*

Karnowski, L. (1997). Reconsidering teachers' roles and procedures: Developing dialoguing skills. In N. J. Karolides (Ed.), *Reader response in elementary classrooms* (pp. 301–313). Mahwah, NJ: Lawrence Erlbaum Associates.

Karolides, N. J. (Ed.). (1997). *Reader response in elementary classrooms.* Mahwah, NJ: Lawrence Erlbaum Associates.

Kintsch, W., & van Dijk, T. A. (1978). Toward a model of discourse comprehension and production. *Psychological Review, 85,* 363–394.

Klare, G. R. (1984). Readability. In P. D. Pearson (Ed.), *Handbook of reading research* (pp. 681–744). New York: Longman.

Langer, J. A. (1992). *Literature instruction: A focus on student response.* Urbana, IL: National Council of Teachers of English.

Loveless, T. (1998). The use and misuse of research in educational reform. In D. Ravitch (Ed.), *Brookings papers on educational policy* (pp. 279–318). Washington, DC: Brookings Institution Press.

McKenna, M. C., Robinson, R. D., & Miller, J. W. (1990). Whole language: A research agenda for the nineties. *Educational Researcher, 19*(8), 3–6.

Nicholson, T. (1991). Do children read words better in context or in lists? A classic study revisited. *Journal of Educational Psychology, 83,* 444–450.

Pederson, R., & Eeds, M. (1990). *Grand conversations: Literature groups in action.* New York: Scholastic.

Pressley, M., Johnson, C., Symons, S., McGoldrick, J., & Kurita, J. (1989). Strategies that improve children's memory and comprehension of text. *Elementary School Journal, 90,* 3–32.

Reutzel, R. D. (1999). On balanced reading. *The Reading Teacher, 52,* 322–324.

Rosenblatt, L. M. (1978). *The reader, the text, the poem.* Carbondale: Southern Illinois University Press.

Rumelhart, D. E. (1977). Toward an interactive model of reading. In S. Dornic (Ed.), Attention and performance (Vol. 6, pp. 573–603). Hillsdale, NJ: Lawrence Erlbaum Associates.

Schallert, D. L. (1991). The contributions of psychology to teaching the language arts. In J. Flood, J. M. Jensen, D. Lapp, & J. R. Squire (Eds.), *Handbook of research on teaching the English language arts* (pp. 30–39). New York: Macmillan.

Shannon, P. (1989). *Broken promises: Reading instruction in twentieth century America.* New York: Bergin & Garvey.

Smith, F. (1971). *Understanding reading.* New York: Holt, Rinehart & Winston.

Smith, F. (1973). *Psycholinguistics and reading.* New York: Holt, Rinehart & Winston.

Spector, J. E. (1992). Predicting progess in beginning reading: Dynamic assessment of phonemic awareness. *Journal of Educational Psychology, 84,* 353–363.

Stanovich, K. (1992). Speculations on the causes and consequences of individual differences in early reading acquisition. In P. B. Gough, L. C. Ehri, & R. Treiman (Eds.), *Reading acquisition* (pp. 307–342). Hillsdale, NJ: Lawrence Erlbaum Associates.

Stanovich, K. (1998). Twenty-five years of research on the reading process: The grand synthesis and what it means for our field. In *Forty-seventh yearbook of the National Reading Conference Yearbook* (Vol. 47, pp. 45–58). Chicago: National Reading Conference.

Stewart, J. (1996, March). Why California kids can't read. *Sacramento Bee,* pp. F1, F2.

Torgesen, J. K., & Burgess, S. R. (1998). Consistency of reading-related phonological processes throughout early childhood: Evidence from longitudinal-correlational and instructional studies. In J. Metsala & L. Ehri (Eds.), *Word recognition in beginning reading.* Mahwah, NJ: Lawrence Erlbaum Associates.

Vellutino, F. R. (1991). Introduction to three studies on reading acquisition: Convergent findings on theoretical foundations of code-oriented versus whole language approaches to reading instruction. *Journal of Educational Psychology, 83,* 437–443.

Wagner, R. K., Torgesen, J. K., Laughon, P., Simmons, K., & Rashotte, C. A. (1993). The development of young readers' phonological processing abilities. *Journal of Educational Psychology, 85,* 1–20.

Warren, C. C. (1981). Adopting textbooks. In J. Y. Cole & T. G. Sticht (Eds.), *The textbook in American society* (pp. 43–45). Washington, DC: Library of Congress.

Warton-McDonald, R., Pressley, M., Rankin, J., Mistretta, J., Yokoi, L., & Ettenberger, S. (1997). Effective primary-grades literacy instruction = balanced literacy instruction. *The Reading Teacher, 50,* 518–521.

# ·47·

# LITERATURE FOR LITERACY: WHAT RESEARCH SAYS ABOUT THE BENEFITS OF USING TRADE BOOKS IN THE CLASSROOM

## Lee Galda
### University of Georgia

## Bernice E. Cullinan
### New York University

Children's and young adult literature—trade books—are good for children. Parents spend millions of dollars each year, publishers produce thousands of books each year, librarians purchase hundreds of books each year, and teachers make countless instructional decisions based on this premise. What is the research evidence for this claim and how powerful is it? Why are some teachers, schools, school districts, and states committed to using literature in their classrooms? This chapter explores reasons for using trade books as an integral part of an instructional program, presenting what current research tells us about the effectiveness of such a practice.

Theorists have long argued that reading to children will help prepare them for literacy and develop their literacy skills (Cullinan & Galda, 1998; Huey, 1908; Snow, 1983). Noted authorities in the field of children's and young adult literature stress the importance of reading to and with students of all ages and of providing them with ample opportunity to read and respond to a variety of excellent trade books in the classroom as well as the library media center (Cullinan & Galda, 1998; Donelson & Nilsen, 1989; Huck, Hepler, & Hickman, 1987). These authorities note that being surrounded by trade books and supportive adults helps children in their active acquisition of literacy much as being surrounded by oral language is a necessary factor in learning to talk. Furthermore, they reason, frequent and positive contact with trade books engenders interest in reading, increased interest results in reading more, reading more results in reading better. It also is widely held that vocabulary and syntax are developed by extensive use of trade books. Others argue that listening to trade books helps children build a schema for stories that is crucial for comprehending text presented in story form. Writing is also said to be affected by reading trade books, as the lexical choices, style, and content of what children read becomes a part of their reading and writing repertoire. Despite these widely held claims for the efficacy of using trade books for literacy development, however, many teachers are frustrated in their attempts to incorporate literature into their daily schedule because there is not time. Too often, literature is not given its place as a central part of the curriculum. A look at research in the use of trade books demonstrates the importance of literature in building literacy, and argues for the planned inclusion of trade books in all classrooms.

## THE PRESCHOOL YEARS

Children's educational achievement is related to early experiences listening to stories both at home and school.

### The Home

Researchers who examine the beginnings of literacy in the preschool years find that interactions between adults and children around books at home promote literacy (Baghban, 1984; Clark, 1984; Durkin, 1974; Holdaway, 1979; Moon & Wells, 1979; Teale, 1978, 1981). Relationships between learning to read at an early age and being read to have been documented time and again. An early study by Durkin (1966) showed that children who learned to read before entering first grade were ones who were read to by siblings, parents, or another caring adult. Neither race, ethnicity, and socioeconomic level nor IQ distinguished between readers and nonreaders; access to print, being read to, parents valuing education, and early writing did. Durkin called these early readers "paper and pencil kids," kids who liked to make marks on paper. Wells (1986) spent 15 years in a longitudinal study of 32 children from shortly after their first birthdays until the last year of their elementary schooling. In *The Meaning Makers*, Wells presented case studies of six of those children to identify the major linguistic influences on their later educational achievement. Wells found that stories are the way that children make sense of their lives; they give meaning to observable events by making connections between them and the real world, and the number of stories children heard before schooling had a lasting effect. Experience with books at age 5 was directly related to reading comprehension at age 7 and again at 11. Primarily case and correlational, these studies of early literacy show that children who are read to at home come to school reading or ready to learn to read.

Many researchers have looked closely at what children who are read to come to know about books. They point out several positive outcomes of involvement with storybooks in the home. Children who are read to develop highly positive associations for books (Holdaway, 1979). Reading books is a pleasurable activity, one that children seek and value. This pleasure is true not only for the child listener but also for the reader, thus providing a positive social model (Hiebert, 1981). How children perceive their parents' attitudes toward reading is an important influence on their own attitudes (Ransbury, 1973). Research also indicates a positive relationship between the number of books in the home and children's reading ability (Durkin, 1966; Lamme, 1985, Sheldon & Carrillo, 1952). A greater number of books was associated with high reading achievement and fewer books with low reading achievement.

Being read to helps children develop familiarity with the conventions of print (Clay, 1979; Doake, 1981; Taylor, 1983) as well as metalinguistic awareness about print (Schickedanz, 1986). Hearing books read aloud helps develop children's vocabulary (Ninio, 1980; Ninio & Bruner, 1978) and other language skills. Early exposure to books in the home helps children come to know two essential things. They learn how print works and that reading is worth the effort it takes.

Listening to storybooks also acquaints a child with the special use of language found in storybooks, not language to get something done but language to represent experience, language that encourages the contemplation and evaluation of experience (Britton, 1970). Being read to also helps children understand the differences between oral and written language (Clark, 1976; Smith, 1978). Moreover, because storybook language is often the language of narrative, knowledge about narrative structure is yet another benefit for those children who are read to (Meyer & Rice, 1984). Finally, being read to increases

young children's knowledge of the world, helping to provide a broad base of experience from which to comprehend and interpret other texts (Steffensen, Joag-Dev, & Anderson, 1979). Anderson, Hiebert, Scott, and Wilkinson (1985) noted in *Becoming a Nation of Readers* that independent reading is a major source of building background knowledge. Research on emergent literacy clearly demonstrates that trade books play a significant role in helping preschool children become literate. Simply put, children who spend time interacting with adults around books develop understandings about the functions and the processes of reading that help them develop literacy skills when they enter traditional classrooms. There is a strong body of research that documents the importance of reading trade books in the home. What of books in the classroom?

## The Classroom

Reading to children in preschool classrooms positively affects their literacy development. Research that examines the use of literature in preschool classrooms provides an excellent base from which we can extrapolate to elementary school classrooms. Morrow (1988) attempted to replicate one-to-one storybook reading at home in a low socioeconomic strata day-care center. The 4-year-olds in her study who were read to for 10 weeks became better and more frequent question askers, gave more interpretive responses to the stories they read, and responded more often to the print and the story structure. Cochran-Smith (1984) described in *The Making of a Reader* how story reading happened in one middle class preschool class and what the consequences were of the literacy events that occurred in that classroom. Although the children she studied were not being taught to read, their interactions with adults around books did result in the growth of important knowledge about books and print. The children learned, among other things, that reading and writing were important parts of their world and could help them accomplish many purposes. They learned how to interpret and use contextualized and decontextualized print, and how they could use their real-world experiences to understand texts and their experiences with texts to understand the real world. This ethnographic study of one preschool classroom has increased our knowledge of the effect of reading trade books with preschoolers.

## THE SCHOOL YEARS

Experiences with literature during the school years promote interest in reading, language development, reading achievement, and growth in writing ability. A number of recent studies have described both classroom contexts and teacher behaviors which surround the use of trade books.

### Interest

Reading and listening to a variety of good books increases interest in reading. Both elementary (Mendoza, 1985) and high school (Bruckerhoff, 1977) students affirm that they like to be read to and that being read to is an important factor in their positive attitude toward books. Positive associations with trade books encourage school-age children to practice the skill of reading until they become good at it. Being read to increases reading interest (Porter, 1969).

The level of reading comprehension, the amount of reading done, and the attitude toward reading are all affected by the student's interest in the materials. Students understand materials best when they are interested, they read more when they find materials that interest them, and they have a more positive attitude toward reading when they can choose materials of interest. For example, Asher (1980), Asher and Markell (1974), and Mathewson (1985) found that the interest level of the material was a determining factor in reading comprehension. Asher assessed fifth-grade students' interests and later gave them three reading passages corresponding to their highest rated topics and three passages corresponding to their lowest rated topics. All children comprehended the high interest materials better than they did the low interest materials.

## Language Development

Being read to from trade books also positively affects children's general language development. Chomsky (1972) found a strong positive relationship between the stages of children's development and their exposure to literature; the greater the exposure to literature the more advanced the stage of linguistic development. Harste, Woodward, and Burke (1984) described children feeding their "linguistic data pool" from encounters with stories and using those experiences with stories to help make sense of subsequent language encounters. Language skills such as vocabulary and syntax are positively influenced by listening to trade books read aloud (Cohen, 1968; Feitelson, 1988). Anderson et al. (1985) reported that independent reading is probably a major source of vocabulary growth. Nagy, Herman, and Anderson (1984) found that children in Grades 3 through 12 learn the meanings of about 3,000 new words a year. Although some of these words are taught in school, direct instruction could only account for a modest proportion of the total since learning 3,000 words a year would require learning about 15 words every school day. Nagy et al. believed that beyond the third grade children incidentally acquire the majority of the new words they learn while reading books and other material. Furthermore, Stanovich (1988) described how extensive reading and vocabulary development reinforce each other in a "rich get richer" cycle.

Children's oral language also reflects the literary register they hear in trade books. Pappas and Brown (1987) described the development of the literary register in the retellings of a kindergarten student. Hade (1988) also described how children who heard stories read aloud adopted syntactic, and some semantic structures that they heard when producing their own retellings. The results of these studies and others strongly suggest that reading trade books to children benefits their general language development.

## Reading Achievement

Reading literature develops readers' schemata for narrative form and life experiences. Many trade books read aloud or on classroom bookshelves are narratives. Listening to these books helps children develop a narrative schema that aids in their ability to comprehend the stories they encounter in their reading (Rumelhart & Ortony, 1977; Spiro, 1977). Schema theory, as set forth by Anderson (1977), and Rumelhart and Ortony (1977), and others stresses that readers bring their own knowledge, in conjunction with the signals or clues that the text provides, which guides comprehension. Thus, more knowledge leads to better comprehension. Exposure to trade books is one way to provide this knowledge.

Exposure to narrative patterns through extensive use of trade books increases knowledge about story structure, which in turn improves comprehension of narrative texts (Adams & Collins, 1979; Stein & Glenn, 1979). Further, as one would expect, these schema begin to develop in young children as the result of exposure to stories (usually gained through interaction with adults around trade books) and continue to develop in complexity throughout the school years and into adulthood (Stein & Glenn, 1979).

In like manner, trade books provide windows (Cullinan & Galda, 1998) on other worlds and other experiences, windows that become virtual experience as we read. These virtual experiences are then added to children's knowledge of the world. This increase in knowledge, in turn, increases the possibilities for responding to the world. Reading extensively in trade books not only increases children's sense of narrative patterns but also their storehouse of experiences. This aids in the comprehension of texts, especially narratives, and in the composition of texts.

There is a relationship between the amount of reading done and reading achievement. Reading widely from real books that bring enjoyment and information makes fluent readers. The research evidence on how much time children spend reading independently in school or out of school, however, is discouraging. Anderson et al. (1985) reported that the amount of independent, silent reading children do is significantly related to gains in reading achievement. They also reported that the amount of time children spend reading in the average classroom is small. Children in primary grade classrooms average 7 or 8 minutes a day reading silently—less than 10% of the total time devoted to reading. Students in the middle grades average 15 minutes per school day reading silently. Obviously, children do not get much reading practice in school.

What is the picture outside of school? Anderson et al. (1985) also reported that the amount of reading students do out of school is consistently related to gains in reading achievement. In a study by Fielding, Wilson, and Anderson (1986), fifth-graders completed a daily log of after-school activities for periods ranging from 2 to 6 months. They found that 50% of the children read books for an average of 4 minutes or less a day, 30% read 2 minutes or less per day, and fully 10% never reported reading any book on any day. For the majority of children, reading from books occupied less than 1% of their free time. In contrast, the children averaged 130 minutes of television viewing per day.

The avid readers in this study did as much as 20 times more independent reading than did the children who chose to read less often. As a result, these avid readers got a great deal more practice in reading, a factor that helps to explain why children who read a lot make more progress in reading. Independent reading is undoubtedly a major source of reading fluency. In a study of the leisure reading habits of Irish fifth-grade students Greaney (1980) found that even reading the comics was positively related to reading achievement and that those students who spent little time reading for pleasure tended to score low on the achievement measure.

Studies conducted by the National Assessment of Educational Progress have also shown that students who read most read best. In the recent report, *Who Reads Best? Factors Related to Reading Achievement in Grades 3, 7, and 11*, Applebee, Langer, and Mullis (1988) reported similar findings. There were dramatic differences between the amount of independent reading reported by the better and poorer students, particularly in school. In the third grade, 75% of the readers in the highest quartile reported reading daily in school, compared with 57% of the readers in the lowest quartile. The same discrepancy appeared in the results for reading independently outside of school: Fifty-six percent of the better readers read at home every day, whereas only 48% of the poorer readers did. For Grades 7 and 11, student reports were combined into a composite variable reflecting both frequency and variety of materials read. At both grade levels, the greater the breadth of materials the students reported reading, the better the student's reading performance was likely to be. There were also differences between how better and poorer seventh-graders reported using the library. Students in the highest quartile reported using the library to read on their own, look up facts for school, and take out books. Students in the lowest quartile reported using the library as a quiet place to study and to find books about their hobbies. Similarly, the 11th-grade better readers used the library more frequently for academic purposes and the poorer readers used it more frequently to find out about their hobbies (pp. 37–43). Others have also noted the relationship between reading achievement and the amount of time spent reading (Taylor, Frye, & Maruyama, 1990; West, Stanovich, & Mitchell, 1993), concluding that the amount of time spent reading books contributes of gains in reading achievement.

## Composing

Reading literature is linked to success in becoming a proficient writer. Many similarities have been noted between the acts of comprehending and composing (Goodman & Goodman, 1983; Squire, 1983; Tierney & Pearson, 1983; Wittrock, Marks, & Doctorow, 1975), and it seems that doing one affects one's ability to do the other (Smith, 1983). Contact with literature exposes writers to a variety of lexical and syntactic choices as well as to a variety of narrative patterns that they then may call on in their own production of written text (Chomsky, 1972).

There is evidence that success in writing is predicted by reading scores (Loban, 1963). But what kind of reading is important? Eckhoff (1983) studied second-grade children's writing

and their basal reading texts. She found that those children who worked in a reading text that "more closely matched the style and complexity of literary prose" (p. 608) used more elaborate linguistic structures in their own writing than did those children who used a more traditional basal containing simplified sentence structures. DeFord's (1981) work documented the same phenomenon with first-grade children. These benefits extend to other grades as well. Lancia (1997) found that reading children's literature positively affected the language second grade children used in their writing, and Dressel (1990) found that children exposed to quality literature were more likely to reflect literary elements in their own writing than were children exposed to writing of lesser quality. Thus, it seems that the language of the trade books that children read significantly affects the language they use in composition.

The narrative structures found in trade books also help children become better writers. King, Rentel, Pappas, Pettigrew, and Zutell (1981) argued that children have a basic understanding of folktale structure by the time they enter school, as evidenced by their oral stories (Applebee, 1978; Leondar, 1977). The findings in their longitudinal study of first- and second-grade children indicated that the folktales that children encounter in their contacts with trade books serve as "rhetorical models" for beginning writers. Comprehending and remembering familiar folktales seemed to result in a rudimentary rhetorical scheme from which young children could draw during their written production of folktalelike narratives. One child borrowed freely from "The Ugly Duckling," "Frog and Toad," "The Gingerbread Boy," and "Little Red Riding Hood" as he created his own original story. The literature children hear is reflected in the content and form of their language and their stories. Blackburn (1985) described children's use of the stories they heard in the stories they wrote as "borrowings" in a cycle of never-ending story. Reading and discussing both trade books and their own compositions can also help children become aware of the choices authors make, make them more critical consumers of texts, and increase their sense of authorship (Graves, 1983; Hansen, 1987).

Other investigations have confirmed the relation between literature and composition. Children exposed to quality literature reflected that quality in their own narrative writing (Dressel, 1990; Lancia, 1997). Thus, reading achievement, oral language development, and composition are related to the amount of reading students do, and this, in turn, depends on the availability of reading materials (Krashen, 1993; McQuillan, 1998; Morrow, 1992), most notably trade books.

## LITERATURE-RICH CLASSROOMS

Theorists agree that language learning is social and collaborative (Jaggar & Smith-Burke, 1985; Vygotsky, 1962, 1978). Children acquire language in meaningful interactions with others who provide models and support their learning by responding to what they are trying to say and do, rather than to the form. Interactive social experiences are also at the heart of literacy learning. Such experiences involve children as active learners in cooperative social environments in which an adult serves as a model, structures the environment, or offers direct instruction that helps learners complete tasks they could not have completed alone (Langer, 1987). Children learn to think about and approach literacy tasks by seeing adults, classmates, and teachers engage in those activities. Eventually, they internalize the rules needed to complete the tasks alone.

Books, time to spend with books, and a supportive, enthusiastic teacher are essential elements in the creation of readers. Kiefer (1988) spent many hours observing children responding to picture books in literature-rich settings from grades kindergarten through Grade 4. She recorded their reactions during read-aloud sessions with their teachers, in small-group peer interaction, and in interviews. She demonstrated that children can and do respond in profound ways to the meaning making choices of artists, but their insights do not develop by chance. Such insights grow best in very special classrooms which develop the potential for communication of meaning between the child and the picture book. The context for communication and for learning was found in classrooms in which teachers and students pursued thematic units involving numerous experiences. One of the prime features of the classroom context was time—time to look at books, to think about the experience, to listen to books read aloud, to respond to books, and to read independently. Another feature was availability. There were numerous books in the classrooms and children had easy access to them. Most important, teachers played the key role in creating rich classroom contexts, providing children with the opportunities to develop literacy and to deepen aesthetic and literary response. In one of the classrooms Kiefer described, the teacher's knowledge and enthusiasm about literature, her invitations to find "secrets" in books, and her encouragement to notice and appreciate details were all factors in creating an effective context for literacy.

Hickman (1981) studied the responses of 90 children in three classrooms spanning kindergarten through Grade 5 by serving as a participant observer for 4 months. She found that the responses to the literature children read were closely tied to the settings in which they occurred and were influenced by the teachers who created those settings. Her work underscores the importance of a rich literacy environment and the teacher's enthusiasm for literature.

Patterns of response to literature were the focus of Hepler's (1982) yearlong study of a combined fifth- and sixth-grade classroom. Among other things, she learned that response is social—that children use the classroom community to "pick their way to literacy." Hepler and Hickman (1982) referred to "a community of readers" to describe what they observed happening in middle grade classrooms. Comments such as "Everyone in the class read it, so I figured I ought to, too" and "I usually read what Tammy reads" showed the effect of belonging to a community of readers. Hepler (1982) also found that students read more books when they were in a literature-rich environment. Students read from 24 to 122 books over the year. In this class, book discussions occurred daily during the last 15 minutes of an hour-long period for sustained silent reading. The children supported each other in their selections of books and in their evaluations as a community of readers.

Talk helps children negotiate meanings (Hepler & Hickman, 1982). Talk in the literature-rich classrooms was made easier by having others who shared the same context. Clusters, pairs, and small groups shared comments about books that were based on mutual understanding from having read the same books. Hepler and Hickman stated, "Perhaps the single most important function of the community of readers is to provide a model set of reader behaviors which tell children how readers act. Readers enjoy books, thinks the child, and I do, too." Furthermore, once children discern that the teacher values reading, they are most anxious to let the teacher know that they are reading (p. 282).

Books are discussed within the social world of the classroom, and what these discussions consist of makes a difference in the responses of young readers. Eeds and Wells (1989) documented how children were able to connect stories to their own lives, make and evaluate their predictions about story outcomes, and evaluate what they read. They were also able to consider the ideas of others as they constructed their own meaning. McGee (1992) looked at young children's discussions, determining that children made more interpretive comments after they had been asked an interpretive question.

What is being discussed also affects talk. Leal (1992) found that discussion of an informational storybook allowed first-, third-, and fifth-grade students to stay on task, make predictions and inferences, use peer input, and discuss related topics than did discussion of a storybook or an informational book. Whatever the book, students' engagement is strengthened when teachers ask authentic questions and incorporate students' responses into the discussion. The quality of the literary text, deliberate instruction, and the ability to engage in real conversations shape students' engagement in reading (Almasi & McKeown, 1996).

In a study of the effects of a literature-based classroom on the achievement, use of literature, and attitudes of children, Morrow (1992) found that students involved in the literature program did better at retelling stories, as well as identifying and using story elements than did students in a basal and workbook oriented program. Children who are given the opportunity to approach texts from an aesthetic stance also are able to identify and use literary elements (Many, 1991; Many & Wiseman, 1992).

The Book Club project (McMahon & Raphael, 1997) developed and examined a model for practice that focuses on the exploration of children's literature. The model includes community share, reading, writing, and book clubs, in which small groups of students discuss the book they are reading. They might share personal responses, clarify potentially confusing aspects of their reading, discuss an author's intent, create interpretations, or critique a text. They found that in this model students were more likely to lead their own discussions, engage in more exploratory talk, and assume ownership for their conversations because they were pursuing their own questions. Students were able to critically analyze their work, set criteria for grading, and come to consensus (Wixson, 1997). Book clubs extended the social nature of the classroom by providing opportunities for students to interact in a structured manner. It also provided abundant opportunities for demonstrations of fluent reading behaviors, as well as for linking the language arts (Scherer, 1997).

Teachers of children spend a great deal of time behind the scenes, playing the role of community planner. At any grade level, the teacher is also the person who functions to hold the group history in memory and to ask questions that allow children to range back over what they have read. By asking students to relate their current reading to other things they have read, they help them see reading as a part of a wider literary framework. Behind one child lost in a good work stands a community of other children and interested adults who help the reader choose, respond, and enjoy (Hepler & Hickman, 1982, p. 283). Books, time, and interactions with interested others create avid readers.

## TEACHER BEHAVIORS

How teachers read books affects their students' understanding of how to listen and respond to books. A number of researchers interested in the use of trade books in the classroom have noted that in many studies of the use of trade books in the classroom one important variable has often been ignored. Quite often, trade books are read aloud by a teacher to a class. Thus, teacher behaviors become an important factor in examining the effective use of trade books. Green and Harker (1982) argued that how teachers present trade books to their students makes the difference between effective and ineffective story reading situations. The manner in which teachers present stories is influenced by "factors such as developmental differences, teacher's goals, the nature of the text, as well as skills and abilities of students, all [of which] influence the instructional process and potentially influence the effectiveness of a given set of strategies" (p. 197). Reading to children involves at least three components—children, teachers, and texts—and these factors must be considered when planning lessons involving trade books. However, Green and Harker pointed out that it is the implementation of these plans in the highly interactive context of a classroom that holds the key to effective teaching. Their research shows how two teachers with similar goals had very different ways of "orchestrating" the interactions of children around the same trade book. It was suggested that these differences in orchestration influenced student performance on a story retelling measure of comprehension.

Using a similar analytic strategy, Cochran-Smith (1984) looked closely at the use of trade books in a preschool classroom. She closely examined the literacy events she observed and described in detail three ways in which the storybook reader mediated the text for her audience. The reader initiated or guided three main interactions during storybook reading. Type I interactions (readiness for reading) involved appropriate behaviors when listening and responding to a story. Type II interactions (life to text) involved making sense of the books read aloud by bringing life knowledge to bear on the text. This included but was not limited to "knowledge of lexical labels, literary and cultural heritage, narrative structures, human nature, and literary conventions" (p. 173). Type III interactions (text to life) involved "helping children discover the meaning that a book's message, theme or information might have in their own lives" (p. 173). These interactions were crucial to the development of literacy in this preschool classroom. One of the important contributions Cochran-Smith made is that she, also, shows how important it is for researchers to examine what actually occurs during a storybook reading session rather than simply assuming that all such sessions share the same characteristics.

The importance of knowing how books are presented to children as well as knowing how often they are presented is amply documented in these studies as well as other studies of book reading with preschoolers at home (e.g., Ninio & Bruner, 1978) and at school (e.g., Morrow, 1988). Mason, Peterman, Powell, and Kerr (1989) have shown how kindergarten children's story recall was best when teachers read a story and then followed with a thorough discussion of story events. Furthermore, what teachers stressed during book-reading episodes influenced children's comprehension. Another group of researchers has looked closely at story-reading interaction patterns in elementary classrooms.

Studies such as Green and Harker's (1982) and Cochran-Smith's (1984) as well as studies of home storybook reading events (Heath, 1982; Teale, 1978, 1981) described the great variability in interactional patterns during book reading. Martinez and Teale (1993) proposed that storybook reading style varies according to the focus of teacher talk, the information shared during the reading, and the strategies used by the teacher. How these variations affect students' developing literacy is still unknown.

Group configuration also can make a difference in the effects of reading aloud. Morrow (1988, 1990) and Morrow and Smith (1990) explored the effects of group size during read-alouds on children's comprehension and response. They found that although both one-on-one and small-group read-alouds resulted in more questions and comments than whole class readings, a small-group setting led to better comprehension. Their results were replicated by Klesius and Griffith (1996).

The type of book read can also make a difference in effects. Rosenhouse, Feitelson, Kita, and Goldstein (1997) found that series books increased first graders' reading for pleasure as well as producing positive effects in decoding, comprehension, and story retelling. Interactive reading of nonfiction texts also benefit children's reading (Oyler & Barry, 1996), as does repeated reading. Children who hear a book repeatedly seem to respond more deeply, with greater interpretation (Martinez & Roser, 1985; Morrow, 1988).

It seems clear that not only is reading aloud important for children's literacy development, but how and what teachers read also affects the benefits that children accrue from listening to good books.

## FUTURE RESEARCH

By considering closely both the texts being read and teacher behavior, researchers now can measure more accurately the effects of reading aloud on children's interest, language development, reading achievement, and writing ability. Moreover, researchers should be able to describe the most effective ways to read and discuss trade books by attending closely to teacher behaviors.

At the present time, in addition to the research discussed above, there are literally hundreds of articles by K-12 teachers that describe effective uses of trade books in their classrooms. These articles testify to increased interest in reading, increased enjoyment of reading, and increased ability in reading and writing. Although these articles represent a different type of research, the sheer number of teachers saying the same thing, regardless of differences in demographics, student ability, grade level, and teacher styles, should at least be considered a strong indicator of the central place of literature in the development of literacy.

It may also be that the essential nature of the importance of literature in literacy learning cannot be measured fully. Literature in most of its guises appears in a narrative form and, as Hardy (1978) so aptly put it, narrative is a "primary act of mind." Beyond its use as a pedagogical tool, literature seems to speak to our elemental need for story. Bruner (1984) called for using literature as a way into literacy because it is most constitutive of human experience. Literature, he says, is an "instrument for entering possible worlds of human experience" (p. 200) that is the driving force in language learning.

Young children learn to talk by engaging in talk with supportive others. Smith has said that we "learn to read by actually reading," both independently and within a supportive social context in the classroom. Child language researchers have demonstrated that children learn to talk in part because it is a meaningful, indeed essential, part of life. Meaningfulness in reading, rarely captured in textbooks, is surely present in literature that readers can make their own, creating as they read stories that speak to their own needs, desires, and expectations. This is the literature found in the thousands of trade books readily available in school and public libraries. Why read trade books to children and encourage them to read for themselves? Because reading literature is a most effective way into literacy. Being able to read literature is one basic reason for becoming literate and for making reading a lifelong habit.

## References

Adams, M. J., & Collins, A. (1979). A schema-theoretic view of reading. In R. Freedle (Ed.), *New directions in discourse processing*. Norwood, NJ: Ablex.

Almasi, J. F., & McKeown, M. G. (1996). The nature of engaged reading in classroom discussions of literature. *Journal of Literacy Research, 28,* 107-146.

Anderson, R. C. (1977). *Schema-directed process in language comprehension* (Tech. Rep. No. 50). Cambridge, MA: Bolt, Beranek & Newman; Urbana, IL: Center for the Study of Reading.

Anderson, R. C., Hiebert, E. H., Scott, J. A., & Wilkinson, I. A. G. (1985). *Becoming a nation of readers: The report of the Commission on Reading*. Washington, DC: National Institute of Education.

Applebee, A. N. (1978). *The child's concept of story: Ages two to seventeen*. Chicago: University of Chicago Press.

Applebee, A. N., Langer, J. A., & Mullis, V. S. (1988). *Who reads best? Factors related to reading achievement in grades 3, 7, and 11* (Report No. 17-R-01). Princeton, NJ: Educational Testing Service.

Asher, S. R. (1980). Topic interest and children's reading comprehension. In R. J. Spiro, B. Bruce, & W. Brewer (Eds.), *Theoretical issues in reading comprehension*. Hillsdale, NJ: Lawrence Erlbaum Associates.

Asher, S. R., & Markell, R. A. (1974). Sex differences in comprehension of high- and low-interest reading material. *Journal of Educational Psychology, 66,* 680-687.

Baghban, M. J. M. (1984). *Our daughter learns to read and write: A case study from birth to three*. Newark, DE: International Reading Association.

Blackburn, E. (1985). Stories never end. In J. Hansen, T. Newkirk, & D. Graves (Eds.), *Breaking ground: Teachers relate reading and writing in the elementary school* (pp. 3-13). Portsmouth, NH: Heinemann.

Britton, J. (1970). *Language and learning*. London: Penguin.

Bruckerhoff, C. (1977). What do students say about reading instruction? *The Clearing House, 51,* 104-107.

Bruner, J. (1984). Language, mind, and reading. In H. Goelman, A. Oberg, & F. Smith (Eds.), *Awakening to literacy* (pp. 193-200). Portsmouth, NH: Heinemann.

Chomsky, C. (1972). Stages in language development and reading exposure. *Harvard Educational Review, 42,* 1-33.

Clark, M. M. (1976). *Young fluent readers*. London: Heinemann.

Clark, M. M. (1984). Literacy at home and at school: Insights from a study of young fluent readers. In J. Goelman, A. Oberg, & F. Smith (Eds.), *Awakening to Literacy* (pp. 122-130). Portsmouth, NH: Heinemann.

Clay, M. M. (1979). *Reading: The patterning of complex behavior* (2nd ed.). Auckland, New Zealand: Heinemann.

Cochran-Smith, M. (1984). *The making of a reader*. Norwood, NJ: Ablex.

Cohen, D. (1968). The effect of literature on vocabulary and reading. *Elementary English, 45,* 209-213.

Cullinan, B. E., & Galda, L. (1998). *Literature and the child* (4th ed.). San Diego, CA: Harcourt Brace Jovanovich.

DeFord, D. E. (1981). Literacy: Reading, writing and other essentials. *Language Arts, 58,* 652-658.

Doake, D. (1981). *Book experience and emergent reading in preschool children*. Unpublished doctoral dissertation, University of Alberta, Alberta, Canada.

Donelson, K. L., & Nilsen, A. P. (1989). *Literature for today's young adults* (3rd ed.). Glenview, IL: Scott, Foresman.

Dressel, J. H. (1990). The effects of listening to and discussing different qualities of children's literature on the narrative writing of fifth graders. *Research in the Teaching of English, 24*(11), 397-444.

Durkin, D. (1966). *Children who read early*. New York: Teachers College Press.

Durkin, D. (1974). A six-year study of children who learned to read in school at the age of four. *Reading Research Quarterly, 10,* 9-61.

Eckhoff, B. (1983). How reading affects children's writing. *Language Arts, 60,* 607-616.

Eeds, M., & Wells, D. (1989). Grand conversations: An exploration of meaning construction in literature study groups. *Research in the Teaching of English, 23*(10), 4-29.

Feitelson, D. (1988). *Facts and fads in beginning reading: A cross-language perspective*. Norwood, NJ: Ablex.

Fielding, L., Wilson, P. T., & Anderson, R. (1986). A new focus on free reading: The role of trade books in reading instruction. In T. E. Raphael (Ed.), *The contexts of school-based literacy* (pp. 149-160). New York: Random House.

Goodman, K., & Goodman, Y. (1983). Reading and writing relationships: Pragmatic functions. *Language Arts, 69,* 590-599.

Graves, D. H. (1983). *Writing: Teachers and children at work.* Portsmouth, NH: Heinemann.

Greaney, V. (1980). Factors related to amount and type of leisure time reading. *Reading Research Quarterly, 15,* 337-357.

Green, J. L., & Harker, J. O. (1982). Reading to children: A communicative process. In J. A. Langer & M. T. Smith-Burke (Eds.), *Reader meets author: Bridging the gap* (pp. 196-122). Newark, DE: International Reading Association.

Hade, D. D. (1988). Children, stories, and narrative transformations. *Research in the Teaching of English, 22,* 310-325.

Hansen, J. (1987). *When writers read.* Portsmouth, NH: Heinemann.

Hardy, B. (1978). Towards a poetics of fiction: An approach through narrative. In M. Meek, A. Warlow, & G. Barton (Eds.), *The cool web* (pp. 12-23). New York: Atheneum.

Harste, J., Woodward, V., & Burke, C. (1984). *Language stories and literacy lessons.* Portsmouth, NH: Heinemann.

Heath, S. B. (1982). What no bedtime story means: Narrative skills at home and school. *Language in Society, 11,* 49-76.

Hepler, S. (1982). *Patterns of response to literature: A one-year study of fifth- and sixth-grade classrooms.* Unpublished doctoral dissertation, Ohio State University, Columbus.

Hepler, S. I., & Hickman, J. (1982). "The book was okay, I love you"— Social aspects of response to literature. *Theory Into Practice, 21,* 278-283.

Hickman, J. (1981). A new perspective on response to literature: Research in an elementary school setting. *Research in the Teaching of English, 15*(4), 343-354.

Hiebert, E. H. (1981). Developmental patterns and interrelationships of preschool children's print awareness. *Reading Research Quarterly, 16,* 236-260.

Holdaway, D. (1979). *The foundations of literacy.* Sydney, Australia: Ashton Scholastic.

Huck, C., Hepler, S., & Hickman, J. (1987). *Children's literature in the elementary school* (4th ed.). New York: Holt, Rinehart & Winston.

Huey, E. B. (1908). *The psychology and pedagogy of reading.* New York: Macmillan.

Jaggar, A., & Smith-Burke, M. T. (1985). *Observing the language learner.* Newark, DE: International Reading Association and National Council of Teachers of English.

Kiefer, B. (1988). Picture books as contexts for literary, aesthetic, and real world understandings. *Language Arts, 65*(3), 260-271.

King, M., Rentel, V., Pappas, C., Pettigrew, B., & Zutell, J. (1981). *How children learn to write: A longitudinal study* (ERIC Document No. 213 050). Columbus, OH: National Institute of Education Grant G-79-0137.

Klesius, J. P., & Griffith, P. L. (1996). Interactive storybook reading for at-risk learners. *The Reading Teacher, 49,* 552-560.

Krashen, S. (1993). *The power of reading: Insights from the research.* Englewood, CA: Libraries Unlimited.

Lamme, L. (1985). *Growing up reading.* Washington, DC: Acropolis.

Lancia, P. J. (1997). Literary borrowing: The effects of literature on children's writing. *The Reading Teacher, 50,* 470-475.

Langer, J. (1987). Book review: The contexts of school-based literacy. *Journal of Reading Behavior, 19*(4), 437-440.

Leal, D. J. (1992). The nature of talk about three types of text during peer group discussions. *Journal of Reading Behavior, 24,* 313-338.

Leondar, B. (1977). Hatching plots: Genesis of storymaking. In D. Perkins & B. Leondar (Eds.), *The arts and cognition* (pp. 172-191). Baltimore, MD: Johns Hopkins University Press.

Loban, W. (1963). *The language of elementary school children* (Research Report No. 1). Urbana, IL: National Council of Teachers of English.

Many, J. E. (1991). The effects of stance and age level on children's literary responses. *Journal of Reading Behavior, 23,* 61-85.

Many, J. E., & Wiseman, D. L. (1992). The effect of teaching approach on third grade students' response to literature. *Journal of Reading Behavior, 24,* 265-287.

Martinez, M., & Roser, N. (1985). Read it again: The value of repeated readings during storytime. *The Reading Teacher, 38,* 782-786.

Martinez, M., & Teale, W. H. (1993). Teacher storybook reading style: A comparison of six teachers. *Research in the Teaching of English, 27,* 175-199.

Mason, J. M., Peterman, C. L., Powell, B. M., & Kerr, B. M. (1989). Reading and writing attempts by kindergartners after book reading by teachers. In J. M. Mason (Ed.), *Reading and writing connections.* Boston: Allyn & Bacon.

Mathewson, G. C. (1985). Toward a comprehensive model of affect in the reading process. In H. Singer & R. B. Ruddell (Eds.), *Theoretical models and processes of reading* (3rd ed., pp. 841-856). Newark, DE: International Reading Association.

McGee, L. (1992). An exploration of meaning construction in first graders' grand conversations. In C. K. Kinzer & D. J. Leu (Eds.), *Literacy research, theory, and practice: Views from many perspectives: Forty-first yearbook of the National Reading Conference* (Vol. 41, pp. 177-186). Chicago: National Reading Conference.

McMahon, S. I., & Raphael, T. E. (1997). *The book club connection: Literacy learning and classroom talk.* New York: Teachers College Press.

McQuillan, J. (1988). *The literacy crisis: False claims, real solutions.* Portsmouth, NH: Heinemann.

Mendoza, A. (1985). Reading to children: Their preferences. *The Reading Teacher, 38,* 522-527.

Meyer, B. J., & Rice, G. E. (1984). The structure of text. In P. D. Pearson (Ed.), *Handbook of reading research* (pp. 319-351). New York: Longman.

Moon, C., & Wells, C. (1979). The influence of the home on learning to read. *Journal of Research in Reading, 2,* 53-62.

Morrow, L. M. (1988). Young children's responses to one-to-one story readings in school settings. *Reading Research Quarterly, 23,* 89-107.

Morrow, L. M. (1990). Small group story readings: The effects of children's comprehension and responses to literature. *Reading Research and Instruction, 29*(4), 1-17.

Morrow, L. M. (1992). The impact of a literature-based program on the literacy achievement, use of literature, and attitudes of children from minority backgrounds. *Reading Research Quarterly, 27,* 251-275.

Morrow, L. M., & Smith, J. K. (1990). The effects of group size on interactive storybook reading. *Reading Research Quarterly, 25,* 213-231.

Nagy, W. E., Herman, P. A., & Anderson, R. C. (1985). Learning words in context. *Reading Research Quarterly, 20,* 233-253.

Ninio, A. (1980). Picture-book reading in mother-infant dyads belonging to two sub-groups in Israel. *Child Development, 51,* 587-590.

Ninio, A., & Bruner, J. (1978). The achievement and antecedents of labeling. *Journal of Child Language, 5,* 5-15.

Oyler, C., & Barry, A. (1996). Intertextual connections in read-alouds of information books. *Language Arts, 73,* 324-329.

Pappas, C. C., & Brown, E. (1987). Learning to read by reading: Learning how to extend the functional potential of language. *Research in the Teaching of English, 21,* 160-177.

Ransbury, M. K. (1973). An assessment of reading attitudes. *Journal of Reading, 17,* 25-28.

Rosenhouse, J., Feitelson, D., Kita, B., & Goldstein, Z. (1997). Interactive reading aloud to Israeli first graders: Its contribution to literacy development. *Reading Research Quarterly, 32,* 169-183.

Rumelhart, D. E., & Ortony, A. (1977). Representation of knowledge. In R. C. Anderson, R. J. Spiro, & W. E. Montague (Eds.), *Schooling and the acquisition of knowledge* (pp. 99-135). Hillsdale, NJ: Erlbaum.

Scherer, P. (1997). Book Club through a fishbowl: Extensions to early elementary classrooms. In S. I. McMahon & T. E. Raphael (Eds.), *The book club connection: Literacy learning and classroom talk* (pp. 250-263). New York: Teachers College Press.

Sheldon, W., & Carrillo, R. (1952). Relation of parent, home and certain development characteristics to children's reading ability. *Elementary School Journal, 52,* 262-270.

Smith, F. (1978). *Understanding reading* (2nd ed.). New York: Holt, Rinehart & Winston.

Smith, F. (1983). Reading like a writer. *Language Arts, 60,* 558-567.

Snow, C. E. (1983). Literacy and language: Relationships during the preschool years. *Harvard Educational Review, 55,* 165-189.

Spiro, R. J. (1977). Remembering information from text: The state of schema approach. In R. C. Anderson, R. J. Spiro, & W. E. Montague (Eds.), *Schooling and the acquisition of knowledge* (pp. 137-165). Hillsdale, NJ: Erlbaum.

Squire, J. R. (1983). Composing and comprehending: Two sides of the same basic process. *Language Arts, 60,* 581-589.

Steffensen, M. W., Joag-Dev, C., & Anderson, R. C. (1979). A cross-cultural perspective on reading comprehension. *Reading Research Quarterly, 15,* 10-29.

Stein, N. L., & Glenn, C. G. (1979). An analysis of story comprehension in elementary school children. In R. O. Freedle (Ed.), *Advances in discourse process*: Vol. 2. *New directions in discourse processing* (pp. 53-120). Norwood, NJ: Ablex.

Taylor, D. (1983). *Family literacy: Young children learning to read and write*. Portsmouth, NH: Heinemann.

Taylor, B. M., Frye, B., & Maruyama, G. (1990). Time spent reading and reading growth. *American Educational Research Journal, 27,* 351-362.

Teale, W. H. (1978). Positive environments for learning to read: What studies of early readers tell us. *Language Arts, 55,* 922-932.

Teale, W. H. (1981). Parents reading to their children: What we know and need to know. *Language Arts, 58,* 902-911.

Tierney, R. J., & Pearson, P. D. (1983). Toward a composing model of reading. *Language Arts, 60,* 568-580.

Vygotsky, L. S. (1962). *Thought and language*. Cambridge, MA: MIT Press.

Vygotsky, L. S. (1978). *Mind in society*. Cambridge, MA: Harvard University Press.

Wells, G. (1986). *The meaning makers*. Portsmouth, NH: Heinemann.

West, R., Stanovich, K., & Mitchell, H. (1993). Reading in the real world and its correlates. *Reading Research Quarterly, 28,* 34-50.

Wittrock, M. C., Marks, C. B., & Doctorow, M. J. (1975). Reading as a generative process. *Journal of Educational Psychology, 67,* 484-489.

Wixson, K. K. (1997). Commentary. In S. I. McMahon & T. E. Raphael (Eds.), *The book club connection: Literacy learning and classroom talk* (pp. 299-300). New York: Teachers College Press.

# ·48·

# ROLES FOR NEW TECHNOLOGIES IN LANGUAGE ARTS: INQUIRY, COMMUNICATION, CONSTRUCTION, AND EXPRESSION

*Bertram Bruce and James Levin*
*University of Illinois, Champaign*

About a decade ago, about the time work began on the precursor of this chapter (Bruce, 1991), televisions around the world displayed scenes of confrontation between students and soldiers in Tiananmen Square. Thousands of people died in the streets of Beijing that June in 1989. No one can forget the words of Ling Chai, then a student at Beijing Normal University, "We, the children, are ready to die. We, the children, are ready to use our lives to pursue the truth. We, the children, are willing to sacrifice ourselves" (Buruma, 1999). These words initiated the hunger strike that eventually led to the forcible entry of the army into Beijing and ultimately Tiananmen Square itself.

The events of that time were later seen to be much more complex than they first appeared. The students had conflicting strategies and goals, and many were more aligned with the central government than with the ordinary citizens who suffered most when the tanks rolled in (Long Bow Group, 1995; Schell, 1994). Nevertheless, the word *Tiananmen* has come to symbolize the struggle for freedom and the courage of young people to challenge powerful civil and military authority.

Today, Ling Chai lives in Cambridge, Massachusetts, and is chief executive officer of Jenzabar, a company that develops web-based intranets for schools and colleges. According to the web site http://jenzabar.com/, the company provides communication tools (e-mail, chat rooms, instant messaging, course bulletin board discussions, customized posting to a user group's front page, "personal profiles" to browse and customize), learning tools (custom course web pages; a handout section

for text, audio, video, or multimedia resources; syllabus posting with daily reminders for students), organizational tools (a calendar with course schedules and personal events, a résumé builder and portfolio center), and fun tools (games, contests, and a social area, guides to build web pages, web shopping, and travel centers with discounts and deals).

Few people can claim to have experienced a decade of changes as dramatic as Ling Chai's. But a decade is a long time for any of us, and for an area of study as well. Although the first author (Bruce, 1991) endeavored to write about issues, not simply the latest technological devices, his chapter from a decade ago now seems quaint rather than prescient. The tools offered by Ling Chai's company are now commonplace, and although early versions of each of these existed more than a decade ago, forecasts of their widespread adoption and incorporation into the World Wide Web cannot be seen in that earlier work. It is all too clear that its description of *what is* has become a record of *what was*. Although this must be true of any area in the language arts, the use of new information and communication technologies unquestionably challenges our abilities to reflect in useful ways.

As we set out once again to consider the interactions between new technologies and the language arts, we wonder what massive changes may be lurking about, ready to apply a harsh time stamp to our words. Looking back, we see that many of the specific applications described in the previous version of this chapter are irrelevant or have been superseded by technological developments. Still, some of the general conceptions of the computer's role stands up well.

## IS IT POSSIBLE TO WRITE THIS CHAPTER?

In 1991, the first author wrote:

The time is near when computers, and other new information technologies, such as video, telecommunications, and speech synthesis, will play such important roles in English and language arts classrooms that it will not be possible to write a chapter like this one. (Bruce, 1991, p. 536)

The point was that new information and communication technologies were beginning to show up in every one of the traditional topics, methods, and goals of teaching. Thus, research on the use of computers in teaching would become in effect research on every aspect of pedagogy. Moreover, one could not sensibly pull out computers as an object of study when they were becoming so thoroughly integrated with other media and approaches.

The process of digitization, of incorporating new information and communication technologies into our social practices has not merely continued but has accelerated over the last decade. Thus, although we began with the idea of revising the earlier work, we find that few of the words there can remain untouched by the changes in the society in which our schools are situated. Nevertheless, the recommendation of that earlier work to consider critically the roles that new technologies can play in education still stands.

A narrow conception of the computer's use within English language arts teaching would see the computer as a device with some well-defined function, such as drill on basic skills. Under this conception, it would make sense to examine critically the research that has been done specifically on computer use, with the aim of identifying the programs that are most effective and the populations of students who could be most helped. One would look for evidence of the effectiveness of this technique across curricular goals in comparison to other technologies. Thus, one might compare a multimedia presentation to a lecture, or the use of film strips to learn about famous authors; or one might compare playing word games on the computer versus a board game as a way to build vocabulary.

We can learn from studies such as these, but it is important to be cautious in interpreting the results. Some might be tempted to dismiss the new technologies, to resist their use because results are conflicting or yield too little benefit for the costs involved. Others are tempted to embrace the very same technologies and see them as the secret to educational reform, based on studies that all too often confound the effects of new tools with issues of pedagogical approach or teacher enthusiasm. Both of these interpretations suffer from inadequacies in the research base about the use of new technologies. More important, they both miss what may be more profound changes, for better or worse, in the whole educational enterprise.

Stepping back, we can see a need to reconceive technologies for language arts, and perhaps, to reconceive language arts. Such a reconception would envision the emergence of a set of flexible media, which can be employed in such diverse ways that the basic question shifts from "How effective are these new technologies in teaching the language arts?" to "How are they being used to accomplish pedagogical goals?" The latter question in turn leads us to consider the shift in practices as people find out new things, communicate with one another, make meaning, and express themselves. Thus, rather than looking at technologies as simply a new method to be assessed, we must understand more about how pedagogical goals are realized in new media.

New technologies such as computers and networks now find their way into instruction in composition, literature, decoding, reading comprehension, spelling, vocabulary, grammar, usage, punctuation, capitalization, brainstorming, planning, reasoning, outlining, reference use, study skills, rhetoric, handwriting, drama—in short, they are evident in every area of language arts. There are also programs specifically designed for learners in preschool, primary, upper elementary, middle school, high school, and college grades, as well as in such programs as adult education, English as a Second Language, foreign language classes, bilingual education, special needs classes, home schools, and organizations such as libraries and museums.

These wide-ranging applications of technology raise the question, "What role should the computer, the Web, and other new communication and information technologies play in language arts teaching and learning?" The research in this area overlaps considerably with that of other research on technology in education. It has been a process of discovery, and at times, of contention between rival camps. There are divergent conceptions regarding whether, why, and how these new media are to be used for instruction.

This is not surprising given that there is no clearly identifiable thing to be evaluated. Turkle (1984) suggested that the computer acts like a Rorschach ink blot test in the way it evokes diverse responses from people. She argued that these responses tell more about people than about the computer. Similarly, the ways that computers are used in schools reveals more about conceptions of learning than they do about what computers can or cannot do.

This poses a challenge for even initiating a discussion on the topic of the use of new technologies in language arts. We need to analyze three complex, diverse, and evolving arenas. First, we need to consider how new communication and information technologies are developing and to examine their various features. Second, we need a way to characterize the diverse and rapidly evolving integration of these new technologies into daily life and literacy practices. Third, we need a way to conceptualize the diverse goals of language arts instruction so that we may productively consider how the new media are being used to address those goals.

How then can we simultaneously make sense of three such dynamic enterprises? A promising approach comes, not from looking ahead to a science fiction world, but rather from looking backward, to some of Dewey's (1902, 1915/1956) writings on curriculum. Dewey saw that any curriculum could be specified only in part by cultural resources and societal needs. In addition, the enacted curriculum must derive in large part from the interests, or impulses, of the child. Although these interests themselves cannot be conceived independent of their sociohistorical circumstances, it is nevertheless the case that they constitute an alternative framework for shaping the curriculum.

Dewey (1902, 1915/1956) saw that the greatest educational resource were these "natural impulses": to inquire or find out things, to use language and thereby to enter into the social world, to build or make things, and to express one's feelings and ideas. These were the foundation for the curriculum; the pedagogical challenge is to nurture them for lifelong learning. Dewey's four categories, developed long before the electronic age, have turned out to be quite useful for analyzing applications of educational technology (see Bruce & Levin, 1997, for its application to learning technologies for science and mathematics). Rather than building a taxonomy on formal instructional models or on hardware and software features, one can begin with these "impulses" to learn and grow.

If we apply this four-part taxonomy to the use of new media in language arts, we see a broad array of applications:

1. *Media for Communication.* New media establish social realms that permit new forms of meaningful communication and reconfigure the relationships between students and teachers and between the school and the world outside the school. They provide automatic translations between language and hyperlinked definitions of new words.

2. *Media for expression.* New media make possible new modes of self-representation. Hypermedia allows the intermixing of photos, drawings, sounds, video, tables, charts, graphs, and text.

3. *Media for inquiry.* New media expand the definition of reading to include hypertexts and multimedia; they represent in easily accessible forms all sorts of information that learners need about books and authors; about history, science, and the arts; and about how to inquire in different domains. They make the regularities, the beauties, and the difficulties of language something that students can examine and interact with in new ways.

4. *Media for construction.* New media allow students to produce and format texts easily; they facilitate revision of texts, check for spelling and grammar; provide interactive style sheets; they assist in the construction of tables, charts, and graphs.

Rather than attempting a comprehensive survey of computer use within each of these roles, this chapter presents some representative uses as a way of suggesting possible directions for future teaching and research. Our goal is to see how typical applications of new technologies in language arts can be understood in terms of the four-part taxonomy and how uses in language arts relate to those in other curricular areas. This examination can test and extend the taxonomy, as well as reveal directions for future work. For this purpose, we selected a popular catalog (Sunburst Communications, 1998) of educational software representing a range of widely used applications.[1]

## Media for Communication

Increasingly, computer-based writing never appears as words on a printed page. E-mail, online documentation, and electronic encyclopedias are read directly from a video screen. The computer has thus become a new communications medium, one that facilitates traditional paper-based writing but allows other forms of writing as well. There are now multimedia messaging and conferencing systems that allow users to send not just text but also images, graphics, spread sheets, voice, and video. These systems are being equipped with a variety of fonts to permit writing in languages such as Arabic, Russian, and Chinese; they can also display text in appropriate orientations, such as right to left, or down a column.

In the original version of our taxonomy (Bruce & Levin, 1997), we proposed four subcategories of media for communication: (a) document preparation, (b) communication, (c) collaborative media, and (d) teaching media. Document preparation includes word processing, outlining, spelling, grammar, usage, and style aids, desktop publishing, and presentation system. In the catalog we examined, there are seven different programs available for document preparation, including word processing (Sunbuddy Writer), outlining (Expression, Author's Toolkit), graphic organizers of writing (Visual Planner), multimedia word processors (Kid's Media Magic, Media Weaver, multimedia dictionaries (Bubble Land Word Discovery), and book and newspaper publishing programs (Easybook). The main difference among these different programs is the age level of the users, ranging from prekindergarten–Grade 4 to Grades 5–12.

Another major subcategory is direct communication with other students, teachers, experts in various fields, and people around the world. Examples are direct communication via e-mail, asynchronous and synchronous computer conferencing, distributed information servers (the Web), and student-created hypermedia environments. This is an increasingly common use of technologies for language arts learning and teaching. The only program in this category in the catalog is a web editor for students (Web Workshop).

A third subcategory is collaborative media. These include collaborative remote environments for sharing data, graphics, and text, group decision support systems, shared document preparation, and other ways that people can remotely work on common text and graphic objects. This is a category not represented in the catalog, probably because many of these are relatively new and still cutting-edge applications. This is likely to be a real growth area for language arts uses of new technologies.

The last subcategory, teaching media, includes tutoring systems, instructional simulations, drill-and-practice systems, telementoring, and educational games. This subcategory is well-represented in the catalog. There are applications for teaching at all ages. At the prekindergarten end are classic tutoring systems (Type to Learn, Every Child a Reader, Learning to Read on the Promenade, Reading Who? Reading You!) and educational games (Type for Fun, First Phonics). Note that some of these teaching media include several different approaches in one package. The catalog also contains numerous teaching media for older students as well: Reader's Quest, Write On! Plus, Read On! Plus.

---

[1] Sunburst Communications, http://www.sunburst.com offers catalogs and a web site that list products from a variety of developers. There is software for language arts as well as social studies, mathematics, and science.

Individual software applications such as those represented in the catalog were the dominant form of new digital tools 10 years ago. However, at the time the first version of this chapter was being written (Bruce, 1991), Tim Berners-Lee and Robert Cailliau (1990) were proposing a computer system that would significantly alter the literacy practices of a generation. They wanted to implement in a major way the hypertext ideas that Ted Nelson, Doug Engelbart, Vannevar Bush and others had written about earlier. Their idea was to implement simple browsers for finding "large classes of information (reports, notes, databases, computer documentation and on-line help)" (p. 1) and also allow users to add new material.

Computers can now be used to create webs of related information. Explicit connections between texts allow readers to travel from one document to another, or from one place within a document to another. The computer can help a reader to follow trails of cross-reference without losing the original context. Electronic document systems also facilitate coauthoring of text. A group of children can create a common electronic notebook, by making their own contributions, viewing and editing one another's items, and then linking the items together.

Authors and readers can now be given the same set of integrated tools to create, browse, and develop text. They can move through material created by other people, add their own links and annotations, and merge the material with their own writings. In consequence, the boundaries between author and reader may begin to disappear. Research is needed to understand these changes and the consequences they have for reading and writing instruction.

The development of the Web over the last decade has been changing our concepts of texts, documents, and media. Educators are only now coming to recognize the significance of these new practices and to understand the full possibilities for enhancing communication and exploring language (see Reinking, McKenna, Labbo, & Kieffer, 1999). Electronic networks are being used increasingly for communication among students. Research in underway (see Riel, 1988) to explore different ways of organizing such networks. Some networks are focused on specific tasks; others have a looser conference structure. Some have centralized direction and others do not.

Research has been conducted on using real-time communication networks to teach English language skills or composition, as in the ENFI consortium (Bruce, Peyton, & Batson, 1993). In these systems, students engage in a written form of conversation. Their typed messages are transmitted immediately to others in the group. Such an environment requires students to formulate their ideas as written text but allows faster response than traditional writing or even electronic mail. Many students find these environments more conducive to writing than traditional writing classes.

Word processing has become such a commonplace fixture within English and language arts classrooms that some students now take it for granted, saying, "We only do word processing; when will we start real computer use?" Of course, word processing is real computer use and serves an important function, even if it only helps with the practical details of creating and sharing texts within a classroom. Moreover, there is increasing evidence that in making it easier to compose and revise, to

see problems with a text, and to share texts, students learn to be better writers and readers (Bruce & Rubin, 1993; Bruce & Michaels, 1988; Daiute, 1985; Levin, Boruta, & Vasconcellos, 1982; Rubin & Bruce, 1985, 1986; Wresch, 1984).

There are now hundreds of word processing programs, all of which allow writers to enter and revise text. Some present menus of functions from which the author chooses, thus making them easy to learn and to use, but with some sacrifice of flexibility. More complex programs allow writers to control details of text format, permit access to indexed notes, and have capabilities for tables of contents, lists, footnotes and end notes, bibliographies, and indexes.

It is in the area of writing that we find the widest range of tool-like uses of computers. Many programs and Web sites have been designed to help with the tasks of planning and generating ideas. Several word processing programs have an option to turn off the screen, when text is being entered, so that the student is not distracted by the visual image of what is written. This technique of "invisible writing" (Marcus & Blau, 1983) is a way to facilitate "free writing" (Elbow, 1973) and encourages students not to focus on editing prematurely. Idea generation activities are included in many other programs. Outline generating programs can create empty, numbered outline structures within a word processing program. These programs have become known as "idea processors."

Finally, of course, the web offers unlimited opportunities for communication. For example, the TeenLit site (www.teenlit.com), which is administered entirely by secondary teachers, provides "a forum for teen writers to publish and discuss their writing, review and discuss books they read." Young writers anywhere can submit their creative works to share with others around the world. Now that any student with web access can set up a web page, personal pages have become another important medium for communication (Bruce, 1998–99). Young people throughout the world now routinely build sites with their own stories, photos, music, and graphics.

## Media for Expression

Another major use of technologies in language arts learning and teaching is as media for expression. Uses of media for expression have as a major goal for a person to express his or her own thoughts for their own future comprehension; uses of media for communication have as a major goal the expression of thoughts for the comprehension of others. Technologies that are used for expression include drawing and painting programs, music making and accompaniment, music composing and editing, interactive video and hypermedia creation and editing, animation software, and multimedia composition more generally.

Many of the same programs in the catalog listed under media for communication can also be considered as media for. Thus, the use of multimedia word processors (Kid's Media Magic, Media Weaver) could be used for expression to create personal diaries or documents primarily to be viewed later by the author. Many of the uses of the writing tools in the catalog (Sunbuddy Writer, Write On! Plus) include language arts activities that are typically self-expression, such as poetry writing (even though poetry writing can then be shared in communication with others). In addition, almost all the other technologies described previously as uses as media for communication can also be used as media for expression.

## Media for Inquiry

A third major category of new technologies for learning and teaching is as media for inquiry. In our original description of the taxonomy (Bruce & Levin 1997), we found a large number of uses of technologies for inquiry when looking at software developed for science, mathematics, and technology education. However, when looking at the language arts software described in the catalog, there are only a few programs that serve as media for inquiry. For younger students, a program called M-SS-NG L-NKS is a language puzzle generator. In each puzzle, learners use their knowledge of context and language to make educated guesses to fill in blanks in the puzzle. For older students, there are Write On! Plus modules that focus on the analysis of settings, characters, plot, and themes focusing on "great literature."

Word processing is only one of the ways computers serve as tools for writing and reading (see Wresch, 1988). Programs with speech synthesizers or digitized speech now assist readers who encounter unfamiliar words. Online dictionaries help with word meanings. Hypertext systems, which allow the storage of multiple linked texts, can provide further explanations, additional examples, or commentaries on the text at hand.

Databases of information make it possible for students to browse text as a method of stimulating their reading and writing. There are now large data bases available on CD-ROMs as well as on the web. These include the *Oxford English Dictionary*, the *Encyclopedia Britannica*, and complete statistics from recent Olympics games. Many computers now come with "bundled software" that includes thesauruses, dictionaries, or even the *Complete Works of Shakespeare*. There are also many computer-based databases that allow students to explore new worlds of information.

Despite extensive research on writing (Graves, 1982; Hillocks, 1986), there is still much to be learned about how writers generate ideas, how they revise, how they use what they have read in writing, or how their writing changes over time. One reason is that such processes occur in the writers' heads, and external manifestations, such as pauses, backtracking, use of resources, oral interactions with others, and so on are difficult to record and interpret. The use of technology to support inquiry into these language arts processes is another promising domain.

## Media for Construction

The fourth major use of technologies is as media for construction. These are uses of technologies to affect the world. In the area of language arts, this would include uses of technologies to create text and multimedia. For example, in the catalog, there is software that provides environments for students to create animated stories (Storybook Theatre Bundle). There have been several such "storymaker" programs developed over the recent past, but this remains yet another domain that may be open to substantial opportunities for development of innovative approaches in the future.

For example, computer-based microworlds have been developed in various areas of science and mathematics to allow students to explore new domains, test hypotheses, construct models, and discover new phenomena. The same technology can be used to create microworlds for language. Investigations within these microworlds can be highly motivating for students; moreover, they lead students to think deeply about language patterns, conceptual relationships, and the structure of ideas. We are only at the beginning of this potentially powerful role for computers in language instruction.

There are also an increasing number of tools that allow the construction of web pages, building from pre-existing templates under the guidance of software "wizard" agents. These tools, even when the ultimate goal is the construction of a web site for communication or expression, can also be used for just for pure construction goals as well. The use of technology to support construction in language arts is another promising domain for developing powerful new media for learning and teaching.

## Summary of the Catalog Analysis

Our analysis of the catalog shows a variety of uses of technology in language arts being marketed today. Table 48.1 shows our placement of these programs within our four main categories and their subcategories. It is evident that although there are a variety of uses of new technologies represented, certain of the subcategories predominate, notably document preparation, teaching media, and media for expression.

In Table 48.2, we summarize this analysis in terms of the four main categories and contrast those numbers with previous results derived from an analysis of science education projects (Bruce & Levin, 1997). What we see here is that communication plays an important role in both science and language arts software. On the other hand, the science projects emphasize software that fits within inquiry uses whereas the language arts software includes more examples of Expression uses.

## USING THE TAXONOMY TO LOOK AHEAD

One of the uses of a taxonomy is to help us better understand a diverse set of objects. Another use is to predict new cases suggested by gaps in instances of categories defined by the taxonomy. We can take that approach here with the language arts software represented in the catalog. A majority of the uses of technologies we see there fit in the categories of expression and communication. In contrast, the majority of uses of technologies for science, mathematics and technology classified in an earlier article (Bruce & Levin, 1997) were in the category of inquiry. Neither of these domains included many examples of construction. Are there powerful uses of technologies for language arts that fall within inquiry or construction?

TABLE 48.1. Catalog Software in the Taxonomy

| | | |
|---|---|---|
| **A. Media for inquiry** | • Theory building—technology as media for thinking.<br>• Data access—connecting to the world of texts, video, data<br>• Data collection—using technology to extend the senses<br>• Data analysis | M-SS-NG L-NKS, Write On! Plus modules |
| **B. Media for communication** | • Document preparation | Sunbuddy Writer, Expression, Author's Toolkit, Visual Planner, Kid's Media Magic, Media Weaver, Bubble Land Word Discovery, Easybook |
| | • Communication—with other students, teachers, experts in various fields, and people around the world | Web Workshop |
| | • Collaborative media | |
| | • Teaching media | Type to Learn, Every Child a Reader, Learning to Read on the Promenade, Reading Who? Reading You!, Type for Fun, First Phonics, Reader's Quest, Write On! Plus, Read On! Plus |
| **C. Media for construction** | | Storybook Theatre Bundle |
| **D. Media for expression** | | Kid's Media Magic, Media Weaver, Sunbuddy Writer, Write On! Plus, Expression, Author's Toolkit, Visual Planner, Bubble Land Word Discovery, Easybook, Web Workshop |

Source: Bruce & Levin (1997).

## Potential Inquiry Uses of Technology

Let us look at the subcategories of media for inquiry: (a) theory building, (b) data access, (c) data collection, and (d) data analysis. Certainly language can be used as a theory-building tool. Most of our scientific, political and other theories are expressed in words (in addition to other media like mathematics, graphics, or computer models). The taxonomy points to a need for technologies for writing that support this kind of theory-building language uses.

Language is used to store and retrieve data. Some trace the origins of written language to its use for recording business transactions and inventories, a specific kind of data storage and retrieval. Something as simple as a shopping list is a kind of data storage (recording what needs to be bought) and retrieval

TABLE 48.2. Examples of Software Organized by the Taxonomy

| Category | Language Arts Software in the Sunburst Catalog | National Science Foundation Science Education Projects |
|---|---|---|
| Inquiry | 2 | 43 |
| Communication | 17 | 27 |
| Construction | 1 | 3 |
| Expression | 10 | 0 |

Source: Bruce & Levin (1997).

(its use in the store to remember what to buy). Now with palm-top devices (and soon, wearable computers), uses of technologies of language arts for data access (calendars, to-do lists, address books, etc.) will become very common. Teaching students effective uses of these language arts uses, however, remains a largely neglected domain.

Language is used to record data. In its broadest sense, any history or other written notes describing the world (meeting notes, newspaper reports, personal diaries, etc.) is a sort of data collection. New technologies have an impact on these recording and reporting functions—reporters are using laptops and wireless networks to create news stories on the site of the news and immediately send them to their editors. Web cams allow new multimedia "diaries" of personal life to be recorded and widely shared. In Japan, written personal diaries are common on the Web (Sugimoto & Levin, 1999), turning a use of language for the self-expression of recorded personal events into a use for communication of that data to others.

Language is used in the analysis of text that has recorded data. Reflections or analyses of reports of the world are common both in society generally and also in intellectual work. We are just starting to see technologies that aid in that analysis process. Thus this is another area in which language arts uses of technology presents opportunities for innovation.

Now, these subcategories are not the usual ways that we think about language uses and technology. However, the fact that they are unusual for language uses (but common for number uses) may generate more powerful ways of thinking about how to use the new technologies for more effective language arts learning and teaching.

Let us look briefly at how biologists have recently started using new computational and communication technologies for their work, and then extend that notion into the language arts. Computational biology has become increasingly important for making progress in the biological sciences. A new tool for conducting computational biology is the Biology Workbench (Lathrop, Jakobsson, & Bourne, 1999). This tools allows both professional biologists and students of biology to access web-based databases of protein and DNA sequences and to compare and contrast the sequences of different organism.

Let us imagine a "Language Workbench," analogous to the Biology Workbench, with which scholars and students could do a variety of analyses of literature texts. This would be a web-based interface to distributed texts, with a set of tools for analyzing those texts, allowing a user to compare and contrast patterns in the texts. With this hypothetical Language Workbench, both scholars and students could participate in debates about whether Shakespeare wrote Shakespeare's plays, how much was Writer A influenced by Writer B, and so forth. This Language Workbench could span the range of inquiry uses, and could involve students in joint activities with literature scholars as well as their use of it in more self-contained ways.

## Potential Construction Uses of Technology

An example of the construction category is the use of the programming language Logo to construct models of language structure and use (Goldenberg & Feurzeig, 1987). Students work within any genre, or mode of discourse, to build up their theories about meaning and form. For instance, they can write programs that "gossip." In this case, gossip is viewed as comprising descriptions of actions that someone else has allegedly taken, actions that are newsworthy because they involve surprising revelations about the other's character. Thus, there is a predication about a subject. In Logo, this might be expressed by the following procedure:

```
TO GOSSIP
    OUTPUT (SENTENCE PERSON DOESWHAT)
END
```

This procedure is a small computer program that, when executed, produces a sentence composed of a first part, which is the name of a person, and a second part, which is a description of some action that person did. This only works if the procedures PERSON and DOESWHAT are appropriately defined. For example:

```
TO PERSON
    OUTPUT PICK [SANDY DALE DANA CHRIS]
END
TO DOESWHAT
    OUTPUT PICK [CHEATS. [LOVES TO WALK.]
                [TALKS A MILE A MINUTE.] YELLS.]
END
```

The first procedure, PERSON, selects one person from a list. The second procedure, DOESWHAT, selects a predicate to apply to that person. In this case, the predicate is expressed by an unanalyzed verb phrase. With these procedures, a student can then ask the computer to print out any number of gossip statements. At first, the interest for students comes from the fact that they can be playful, making the computer print out funny, and sometimes, surprising statements, even though they provided it with all its data. As they continue to explore the gossip domain, though, the interest comes from something deeper, a developing appreciation of the complexities, beauties, and regularities of language.

For example, students can revise the original procedures to produce more versatile Gossip programs. They can break apart the predication into transitive verbs with objects, or expand the range of possible subjects. They can add conditional actions to the procedures, for instance, that only certain people can do particular actions. As they construct their Gossip programs, they are forced to confront fundamental questions about language, such as "What is the relationship between syntax and semantics?," "What is a word?," or "What makes a sentence interesting?" Although the program has no means for answering such questions, it provides an environment in which students can seek answers themselves; it allows them to see the consequences of their own hypotheses about language.

This approach is but one example drawn from a family of programs and activities designed to encourage students to explore language. Phrasebooks and Boxes (Sharples, 1985) are two extensions of Logo that allow children to classify words, create their own dictionaries and phrasebooks, devise a quiz, write a program that will converse in natural language, or build their own "adventure games," in which other students explore a student-created fantasy world. It would be interesting to develop a general purpose Language Construction Set, which students of language could use. Imagine an environment, in which students could be given a set of words, phrases, or other language elements, displayed visually on the screen. Then they could build language construction machines, that combine those language elements and then display the "output" of the construction. There is still little research regarding classroom use of these constructive approaches to language understanding.

## CONCLUSION

Technology can be used to change writing instruction in a variety of ways. Computers can aid at places where teacher time and attention are insufficient. They can facilitate the processes of generating ideas and organizing text. Unlike teachers, they can give feedback at any convenient moment. They can comment on features of written texts. With the aid of a text editor, revision of text is more efficient and rewarding. Computers can help students spend more time actually using language. They can thus create opportunities for teacher involvement with essential aspects of writing processes that are beyond the reach of the computer.

As we consider the various uses of new technologies, it is important to balance the fascination in the power of new tools with reflection on pedagogical goals. This chapter has outlined only one such approach, by highlighting the learner's needs to inquiry, communicate, construct, and express. The lens of learner needs emphasizes how new technologies can help realize a more functional way of teaching writing. By means of computer networking, communities of student writers can be established. Real audiences and meaningful goals can stimulate the development of competency in written communication as well as enhance motivation.

But the potential value of computers is far from full realization. Many of the uses described here require a rethinking of student and teacher roles, of curricula, and of school activities. Moreover, current programs and models for computer-based activities are often clumsy to use or difficult to integrate with other learning. Costs are still high, especially when viewed as only a portion of the meager resources available for instructional materials. And too often, the best computer resources are inequitably distributed. Despite these problems, the use of computers for English language arts instruction is in fact growing and promises to be an increasingly important aspect of learning in the future.

## References

Alessi, S. M., & Trollip, S. R. (1991). *Computer-based instruction: Methods and development*. Englewood Cliffs, NJ: Prentice-Hall.

Barker, T. T., & Kemp, F. O. (1990). Network theory: A postmodern pedagogy for the writing classroom. In C. Handa (Ed.), *Computers and community* (pp. 1–27). Portsmouth, NH: Boynton/Cook.

Bates, M., & Wilson, K. (1982). *ILIAD: Interactive language instruction assistance for the deaf* (BBN Report No. 4771). Cambridge, MA: Bolt Beranek & Newman.

Batson, T. (1988). The ENFI Project: A networked classroom approach to writing instruction. *Academic Computing, 2*(5), 32–33, 55–56.

Beeman, W. O. (1988). *Intermedia: A case study of innovation in higher education* [Final report to the Annenberg/CPB Project]. Providence, RI: Brown University, IRIS.

Berners-Lee, T., & Cailliau, R. (1990). *World-Wide Web: Proposal for hypertext*. Geneva: Conseil Européen pour la Recherche Nucleaire Memo.

Bruce, B. (1991). Roles for computers in teaching the English language arts. In J. Flood, J. M. Jensen, D. Lapp, & J. R. Squire (Eds.), *Handbook of research on teaching the English language arts* (pp. 536–541). New York: Macmillan.

Bruce, B. C. (1998-99). Learning through expression. *Journal of Adolescent and Adult Literacy, 42*(4), 306–310.

Bruce, B. C., & Levin, J. A. (1997). Educational technology: Media for inquiry, communication, construction, and expression. [Electronic version]. *Journal of Educational Computing Research, 17*(1), 79–102. http://www.ed.uiuc.edu/facstaff/chip/taxonomy/

Bruce, B. C., Peyton, J. K., & Batson, T. W. (Eds.) (1993). *Network-based classrooms: Promises and realities*. New York: Cambridge University Press.

Bruce, B. C., & Rubin, A. D. (1993). *Electronic Quills: A situated evaluation of using computers for writing in classrooms*. Hillsdale, NJ: Lawrence Erlbaum Associates.

Buruma, I. (1999). Tiananmen, Inc. *The New Yorker, 75*(13), 45–52.

Daiute, C. (1985). *Writing and computers*. Reading, MA: Addison-Wesley.

Dewey, J. (1956). *The child and the curriculum and The school and society*. Chicago: University of Chicago Press. (Original works published 1902 and 1915)

Elbow, P. (1973). *Writing without teachers*. London: Oxford University Press.

Goldenberg, E. P., & Feurzeig, W. (1987). *Exploring language with Logo*. Cambridge, MA: MIT Press.

Graves, D. H. (1982). *Writing: Teachers and children at work*. Portsmouth, NH: Heinemann.

Hawisher, G. E. (1994). Blinding insights: Classification schemes and software for literacy instruction. In C. Selfe & S. Hilligoss (Eds.), *Literacy and computers: The complications of teaching and learning with technology* (pp. 37–55). New York: Modern Language Association.

Hillocks, G. (1986). *Research on written composition: New directions for teaching*. Urbana, IL: National Conference on Research in English.

Knapp, L. R. (1986). *The word processor and the writing teacher*. Englewood Cliffs, NJ: Prentice-Hall.

Lathrop, S., Jakobsson, E., & Bourne, P. (1999). Educational enhancements prepare Biology Workbench for the classroom [Electronic version]. In G. Moses, R. Giles, & R. Tapia (Eds.), *Touch the future*. Champaign, IL: Education, Outreach, and Training Partnership for Advanced Computational Infrastructure. http://www.eot.org/TTF/Learn/lrn05-bio.html

Levin, J. A. (1982). Microcomputers as interactive communication media: An interactive text interpreter. *The Quarterly Newsletter of the Laboratory of Comparative Human Cognition, 4*, 34–36.

Levin, J. A., Boruta, M. J., & Vasconcellos, M. T. (1982). Microcomputer-based environments for writing: A writer's assistant. In A. C. Wilkinson (Ed.), *Classroom computers and cognitive science* (pp. 219–232). New York: Academic Press.

Long Bow Group (1995). *The gate of heavenly peace* [Film transcript]. from http://www.nmis.org/gate/

Marcus, S. (1982). Compupoem: CAI for writing and studying poetry. *The Computing Teacher*, 28–31.

Marcus, S., & Blau, S. (1983). Not seeing is relieving: Invisible writing with computers. *Educational Technology*, 12–15.

Means, B. (1994). Introduction: Using technology to advance educational goals. In B. Means (Ed.), *Technology and education reform: The reality behind the promise* (pp. 1–21). San Francisco: Jossey-Bass.

Michaels, S., & Bruce, B. (1988). *Classroom contexts and literacy development: How writing systems shape the teaching and learning of composition* (Technical Report). Urbana, IL: University of Illinois at Urbana-Champaign, Center for the Study of Reading .

Olds, H. F. (1985). A new generation of word processors. *Classroom Computer Learning*, pp. 22–25.

Olds, H. F., Schwartz, J. L., & Willie, N. A. (1980). *People and computers: Who teaches whom?* Newton, MA: Education Development Center.

Pea, R. D., & Kurland, D. M. (1986). Cognitive technologies for writing. *Review of Research in Education, 13*, —.

Reinking, D., McKenna, M., Labbo, L., & Kieffer, R. (Eds.) (1999). *Literacy for the 21st Century: Technological transformations in a post-typographic world*. Mahwah, NJ: Lawrence Erlbaum Associates.

Riel, M. (1988). *Telecommunication: Connections to the future*. California State Educational Technology Committee.

Roblyer, M. D., Castine, W. H., & King, F. J. (1988). *Assessing the impact of computer-based instruction: A review of the literature*. New York: Haworth.

Rubin, A. D., & Bruce, B. C. (1985). QUILL: Reading and writing with a microcomputer. In B. A. Hutson (Ed.), *Advances in reading and language research*. Greenwich, CT: JAI.

Rubin, A. D., & Bruce, B. C. (1986). Learning with QUILL: Lessons for students, teachers and software designers. In T. E. Raphael (Ed.), *Contexts of school based literacy* (pp. 217-230). New York: Random House.

Schell, O. (1994). *Mandate of heaven*. New York: Simon & Schuster.

Schiebinger, L. (1996). The loves of the plants. *Scientific American*.

Schwartz, H. (1982). Monsters and mentors: Computer applications for humanistic education. *College English, 44*, 141-152.

Sharples, M. (1985). *Phrasebooks and boxes: Microworlds for language*. Paper presented at the World Conference of Computers and Education, Norfolk, VA.

Sirc, G. (1988). Learning to write on a LAN. *T.H.E. Journal, 15*(8), 99-104.

Sirc, G. (1989). Response in the electronic medium. In Chris Anson (Ed.), *Writing and response* (pp. __). Urbana, IL: National Council of Teachers of English.

Sugimoto, T., & Levin, J. A. (1999). Multiple literacies and multimedia: A comparison of Japanese and American uses of the Internet. In C. Self & G. Hawisher (Eds.), *Global literacies and the World-Wide Web* (pp. 133-153). London: Routledge.

Sunburst Communications. (1998). *Sunburst 1998 educational software catalog*. Pleasantville, NY: 1998.

Taylor, R. P. (1980). *The computer in the school: Tutor, tool, tutee*. New York: Teachers College Press.

Thomas, R. H., Forsdick, H. C., Crowley, T. R., Robertson, G. G., Schaaf, R. W., Tomlinson, R. S., & Travers, V. M. (1985). Diamond: A multimedia message system built upon a distributed architecture. *IEEE Computer*.

Thompson, D. (1987). Teaching writing on a local area network. *T.H.E. Journal, 15*(2), 92-97.

Turkle, S. (1984). *The second self: Computers and the human spirit*. New York: Simon & Schuster.

Warren, B., & Rosebery, A. S. (1988). Theory and practice: Uses of the computer in reading. *Remedial and Special Education, 9*(2), 29-38.

Wresch, W. (Ed.) (1984). *The computer in composition instruction*. Urbana, IL: National Council of Teachers of English.

Wresch, W. (1988). Six directions for computer analysis of student writing. *Computers and the Language Arts*, 13-16.

# ·49·

# THE MEDIA ARTS

## Carole Cox
### California State University

Although there have been many film and media arts advocates among English language arts educators over the years, the research on the media arts in relation to English language arts learning and teaching is limited. Media studies focused primarily on direct effects of the mass media on children (Luke, 1985), generally using a behaviorally grounded cause-and-effect model for hypothesis generating (Meadowcroft & McDonald, 1986) that was largely atheoretical (Salomon, 1979). These studies were situated in social contexts outside the classroom, frequently showing a causal relationship between television viewing and violence (e.g., Cantor & Hoffner, 1990; Chu & Schramm, 1967; Crosser, 1995; Hepburn, 1997; Himmelweit, Oppenheim, & Vince, 1958; Javier, Herron, & Primavera, 1998; Kirman, 1997; Molitor & Hirsch, 1994; Pezdek, Lehrer, & Simon, 1984; Schramm, Lyle, & Parker, 1961; Wartella, Alexander, & Lemish, 1997), although Primavera, Herron, and Jauier (1996) concluded that there is no evidence that television violence increases aggression in children or adults but viewing it can trigger aggression in some.

Another research trend related to the large number of studies of mass media use and effects on children was the effects of students' exposure to nonprint media on reading (Allen, 1960; Dillingofski, 1979; Wartella & Reeves, 1985). Books like Winn's (1977) *The Plug-In Drug* articulated a generally accepted popular view that increased exposure to media has had a negative effect on reading among school-age children. In contrast, Neumann (1991) reviewed research on reading and nonprint media, demythologizing the notion that media is a deterrent to literacy. In a review of reading ability in America between 1840 and 1990 Kibby (1993) showed that, contrary to popular belief about the decline of reading due to multiple factors including effects of the mass media, today's students read better than in previous periods in history. In an exploration of reading behavior in Israel between 1970 and 1990, however, Adoni (1995) found that although electronic media had not displaced print media and the majority of the population uses all available print

media, traditional illiteracy is making a comeback due to the prevalent high use of audiovisual media, although other possible influences are not addressed. Reinking and Wu (1988) also summarized the research on the relationship between television viewing and reading using the history of this research as a case study to highlight the difficulties inherent in generating research-based responses to complex educational issues. They recommended that teachers shape and exploit the television viewing habits of their students.

A frequent recommendation of studies on mass media effects, including the effects on print literacy, has been to develop school curricula in critical viewing skills. Such curricula and related research on the media arts, media literacy or media education has not been forthcoming to any great extent, although media advocacy has grown via independent grass roots organizations and subgroups of professional organizations such as the National Council of Teachers of English that realize the impact of mass media on students' lives. These advocates and organizations have concentrated efforts on bonding with each other, defining terms (Avgerinou & Ericson, 1997), and articulating the media education and information literacy movement (Alvermann, Moon, & Hagood, 1999; Considine & Haley, 1999; Duncan, 1997; Hobbs, 1997; Luke, 1999; Masterman, 1990; Phillips, 1998; Thoman, 1999; Tyner, 1998; Watts Pailliotet et al., 2000).

Media education advocacy is not new, however, and some of these same positions argued today date back almost to the advent of mass media in American culture (Dorris, 1930/1995), and, interestingly enough, the arguments remain remarkably similar today. The media education movement in Canada (Brandeis, 1992) and the United Kingdom (Hart & Benson, 1996) is more fully realized than in the United States. Leaders in this country have made efforts to forge relationships and learn from the examples of success in other countries (Clark, 1990; Forsslund, 1991; Ishigaki, 1996; von Feilitzen & Carlsson, 1999).

## TRENDS IN RESEARCH ON THE MEDIA ARTS

This chapter focuses on media research trends most relevant to understanding film and other media arts in learning environments for teaching the English language arts. These fall primarily into four categories: comparative effects of the media arts on learning from narrative, preference and response studies in the media arts, creating and communicating through the media arts, and media arts education.

### Comparative Effects of the Media Arts on Learning From Narrative

This research has compared the effects of film and other nonprint media and print on learning, cognitive skills, attitudes, and behaviors relevant to teaching the English language arts, particularly learning from narrative. Modes of narrative presentation such as storytelling, picture books read aloud, film, video, television, filmstrip, audiocassettes, and recording of a storyteller have been analyzed and compared for either a generalized or isolatable effect on specific learning from narrative such as story vocabulary, comprehension, identification with characters, enjoyment, or listening skills (e.g., Beentjes & van der Voor, 1991; Ruch & Levin, 1977; Small & Ferreira, 1994; Spencer, 1991). Large (1995), for example, compared the effects of animation to still imagery in enhancing sixth-graders learning from text. Results indicated that animation did not help recall but may have helped comprehension. These studies have not demonstrated that one medium was consistently more effective than another for any general effects on learning from narrative.

Other studies, however, showed that media arts differ in their effectiveness for conveying different types of information from narrative (Alwitt, Anderson, Lorch, & Levin, 1980; Greenfield, 1984; Huston & Wright, 1983; Salomon, 1983). There is some evidence that aural renditions of stories enhance verbal comprehension (Beagles-Roos & Gat, 1983); that radio is more stimulating to the imagination but television leads to greater overall recall of information (Greenfield & Beagle-Roos, 1988); and that young children remember more visual than auditory information, especially as it pertained to the central characteristics of a story when presented in media form (Pezdek & Stevens, 1984). For example, in a study typical of this trend, Meringoff (1980) compared children's understanding of an unfamiliar story either read to them from an illustrated book or presented as a televised film, measuring recall of story content and inferences about characters and events. She found that children who saw the film remembered more story actions and relied more on visual content as a basis for inferences, and those who were read the story in picture-book form remembered more vocabulary and relied more on textual content as a basis for inferences, providing support for Salomon's (1979) notion that differences in the symbol systems used by media to represent content, rather than media per se, influence learning: "[I]f their unique symbolic capabilities are capitalized upon, each medium addresses itself to different . . . mental skills, thus benefits learners of

different aptitudes and serves different educational ends" (p. 144). Others have offered theoretical perspectives sensitive to these media differences with regard to the nature of symbolization (Kelly & Gardner, 1981). Gardner, Howard, and Perkins (1974) pointed out that the same medium (television) may be a vehicle for different symbol systems (language, visual imagery), and the same symbol system (language) may occur in different media (book, television).

A shift in research focus from simply looking at how media effected learning from narrative in general, especially as it pertained to understanding print narrative, to studies that compared how students understanding varied across media is reviewed by Spencer (1991), who discusses the instructional effectiveness of various educational media, including illustrations, visual-based instructional media, including films, filmstrips, and television, and programmed learning as well as research methodologies, meta-analysis, and effect size. For example, researchers explored the relationships among cognitive, affective, and social factors of understanding of various forms of media (Buckingham, 1993, 1999; Greenfield & Beagles-Roos, 1988; Korac, 1988; Kozma, 1991; Plowman, 1994; Wilson, 1991), comparison of visual and auditory information (Magliano, 1996), and understanding of visual and nonvisual media codes (Zindovic-Vukadinovic, 1998). One conclusion to be drawn from this type of research is that the extent to which students are exposed to certain media may result in the cultivation of the unique cognitive skills necessary to gain meaning from the particular symbol system used by each different media. Hobbs et al. (1988), however, found that the skill suggested by the concept "media literacy" may not be strictly a result of experience and familiarity with the medium, and that at least some media-specific codes are analogs of perceptual processes. In a phenomenological twist, Haynes (1988) suggested that literate biases may hinder the mastery of oral and video media.

### Preference and Response Studies in the Media Arts

Numerous studies have analyzed media preferences since the turn of the century, and television in particular through the 1980s (Comstock, Chaffee, Katzman, McCombs, & Roberts, 1978; Wartella & Reeves, 1985). In contrast to the numerous studies on students' literature and print preferences (Purves & Beach, 1972), however, there has been little research on preferences for the media arts other than for television despite strong interest in film among school-age children and adolescents. The National Assessment of Educational Progress (1981) during this period found that given a choice of watching television, going to a movie, reading a book, or reading a magazine, one half of the 9-year-olds and nearly two thirds of the 17-year-olds sampled at that time chose film first.

A few studies have looked at children's film preferences and responses. Cox (1978, 1982) examined fourth-grade students' film preferences. These students preferred live-action realistic, narrative, storylike films to animated, abstract, nonnarrative films; focused their responses on film content rather than form; and were more likely to explain and interpret their responses to the realistic narrative films they liked most, findings that paralleled childrens' responses to other nonprint and print media, such as television and literature. In a study which analyzed fifth-grade students' responses to both film and literature from the perspective of Rosenblatt's (1986) transactional theory of a literary work, Cox and Many (1992) found that although students tended to respond more aesthetically, or personally, to books than to films, there were no differences between books and film with regard to understanding. Students' more efferent, analytical responses to film were more complex and may have led to higher levels of interpretation because they have become mature film viewers and critics as a result of their years of experiences viewing and talking about films with adults and their peers outside the classroom.

Other studies have examined 5- to 7- and 9- to 11-year-old childrens' responses to frightening film sequences, finding that knowledge of happy outcomes reduced enjoyment, as do unresolved endings, and that ability to enjoy fear-reducing media increases with age (Hoffner, 1997; Hoffner & Cantor, 1991). Wilson (1989a, 1989b) assessed the impact of two strategies for reducing children's emotional response to mass media: passive exposure, modeled exposure, or no exposure to lizards before watching a horror movie involving lizards, finding that modeled exposure decreased emotional reactions and negative interpretations. Moss (1993) investigated children's discussion of television horror shows recommending that more attention be paid to the importance of social contexts in which both reading and responding to television occur. Probes of adolescents' interest and response to horror film found that motivations for watching these films (gore watching, thrill watching, independent watching, and problem watching) were related to viewers' cognitive and affective responses and a tendency to identify with the killer or victims (Johnston, 1995) and that more permissive sexual attitudes, lower levels of punitiveness, and traditional attitude towards females' sexuality were positively associated with gore-watching motivations and with great enjoyment of "slasher films" (Oliver, 1993). These studies echo the research trend of examining expected negative emotional effects of mass media rather than exploring responses to films more broadly.

Other preference and response studies in the media arts include those focused on ethnographic analysis of adolescent's television viewing (Fisherkeller, 1998), and students' preferences for various media in school library collections (Callison, 1991). A study that provides support for film study in schools showed that the higher amounts of information student subjects read about a film, such as film reviews, the more interest they had in a film and the more critically they viewed it (Wyatt & Badger, 1990).

## Creating and Communicating Through the Media Arts

A few studies have focused exclusively on film as a constructed object, looking for links between the film form and possibly other mass media forms, such as television, with the interpretive, creative, or cognitive skills of audiences. This type of research has analyzed films made by children, hoping to gain insights about both the development of learning processes in general, and, more specifically, the communication of meaning in the context of the development of literacy, particularly as a cultural phenomenon (Chalfen, 1981; Durkin, 1970; Larson & Meade, 1969; Sutton-Smith, Eadie, & Griffin, 1983; Sutton-Smith, Eadie, Griffin, & Zarem, 1979; Worth & Adair, 1972).

Griffin (1985) has observed students becoming more intelligent and skillful filmmakers and became interested in both the topics and events that were most important to them in the creation of their own fims. He identified patterns of editing and narrative structure, and the variance among these patterns. Although age was a factor in the development of filmmaking abilities, even more important was familiarity with television content and a desire to incorporate it into films, and technical competence was more related to experience in filmmaking than age. The most consistent finding underlying developmental differences as students became more proficient filmmakers was their increased use of television as a model for narrative form, theme, camera work, and editing style. These findings suggest the great extent to which television as a cultural model may be shaping the unique symbolic patterns children draw on to organize and represent the world to others. In ethnographic studies of childrens' writing development, Dyson (1997, 1999) similarly showed the ways in which children appropriate popular culture and media material in their language and literacy development, revealing the hybrid nature of even the earliest of children's written texts. In England, examination of a pilot project by the Center for Research on Literacy and the Media in which primary school pupils adapted a print text to an animated film suggests that constructing media texts can benefit literacy development (Parker, 1999).

Other studies of students' composing processes through audiovisual symbol systems have found that the experience of transforming ideas and images from one medium to another, such as words to pictures (Hubbard, 1990) stimulate a challenge to children's intellectual powers and a desire to be analytical and through and provide specific concrete examples of abstract ideas as they communicated through media creation (Weiss, 1982), and that the experience of active communication in cinematic codes through filmmaking significantly affected mental skills, especially the effect of editing activity on children's ability to form logical inferences (Tidhar, 1984).

Findings such as these on the relationship of skills requisite to creating and communicating through media and cognitive development lend support to the notion that the mastery of such skills represents a high level of literacy involving top-down elaboration processes that are not specific to any symbol system but can be transferred across mediums.

## Film and Media Arts Education

Earlier research on film and media arts education was limited to surveys (Barry, 1979; Lynch, 1986; Pryluck & Hemenway, 1982; Squire & Applebee, 1968) showing that film and media arts were not used with any consistency in English education. Film was the most frequently used media art, primarily in secondary classrooms and most often tied to the teaching of literature. Little attention was paid to the teaching of film as an art form. In high schools, for example, there was no real consensus of what even constituted an introductory course on film. The less teachers used film, the more likely they were to use an instructional film or a filmed version of a book to support literature study. More frequent film users were more likely to use film to encourage students to think, as a common topic for discussion, as an alternative medium for less able students, or in lieu of literature. Overall, decisions about how much to use film, which films to use, and how to approach film in the classroom (e.g., film study, mass media study, filmmaking and TV production, interdisciplinary courses using film, or film as literature), was highly idiosyncratic. Film was taught even less at the elementary than the secondary level. Elementary teachers tended to use film to support the curriculum of films of childrens' books. Reasons cited by teachers for not using film were lack of access to equipment and films, and lack of familiarity with films or media arts education as reasons they did not use film. Film education in general has not been well defined in the United States.

In contrast, British media study has been well articulated. In the 1980s a model to test the efficacy of a classroom-taught course on television, including televised films, was piloted in Great Britain in response not only to the broad goal of learning about the media but, more specifically, because the study of television and film became part of the study of English literature. The television film *Flying Into the Wind* became the first film to be studied as a "set text" in an English literature "O"-level examination (Kelley, Gunter, & Buckle, 1987). The 6-week course for 14- and 15-year-olds included study and production of video programs and critical evaluation of television drama, documentary, and news programming. Test results indicated that students were better able to understand and evaluate the medium and plans were made to implement the study of media in schools in Britain as part of the Media Studies and English Literature GSCE examinations. Recent research on media arts education in the United Kingdom has focused on improving visual media and television literacy and understanding effects on learning (Buckle & Kelley, 1990; Kelley, 1991) and as an outgrowth of the Models of Media Education research projects (Hart & Benson, 1996).

In an American study, Frost and Hobbs (1998) investigated the impact of instructional practices involving media literacy education across the curriculum by examining the work of four different teams of ninth-grade teachers, showing that students' media literacy skills were highest where media education activities were integrated across all subject areas, in which both analysis and production activities and explicit instruction in various genres were included. This important study confirms the implications of many previous studies that have underscored the need for a well-articulated integrated curriculum model of media literacy education. A successful example of such an integrated curriculum model was the subject of a 5-year study by Bristor and Drake (1994) in which a science–reading strategy replaced traditional reading–writing instruction through exploiting the links between print and visual literacy.

The relationship among teacher training, beliefs, and media use in classrooms has also been examined in recent studies (Cropp, 1990; Lowther & Sullivan, 1994) finding that new teachers had a preference for less complex media formats (e.g., bulletin boards, posters, and pictures) (Descy, 1992); that experience with media facilitated teachers' use of it in classrooms,

and that teachers supported the idea of media education but were concerned about interference with more traditional instruction, indicating that formulating a sound, integrated mass media curriculum would increase the likelihood of media use by teachers in the classroom (Koziol, 1991).

## PICTURING THE FUTURE OF MEDIA ARTS RESEARCH AND PRACTICE

A crucial question for future research in the media arts will most certainly be to continue to explore issues of intertextuality (Lemke, 1991) and, more fundamentally, definitions of text in the context of media literacy. In the *Encyclopedia of English Studies and Language Arts* (Purves, 1994) media literacy was defined as follows:

Media literacy refers to composing, comprehending, interpreting, analyzing, and appreciating the language and texts of multiple symbol systems of both print and nonprint media. The use of media presupposes an expanded definition of "text" in the English language arts classroom. Print media texts include books, magazines, and newspapers. Non-print media include photography, recordings, radio, film, televisions, videotape, videogames, computers, the performing arts, and virtual reality. On the full range of media channels, all these types of texts constantly interact. They are all texts to be experienced, appreciated, and analyzed and created by students. (Cox, 1994, p. 791)

The *Standards for the English Language Arts* (1996) acknowledged this expanded definition of literacy and what students should learn in the English language arts as "reading, writing, listening, speaking, viewing, and visually representing" (p. 1). Other terms have been redefined in the standards: Text includes spoken language, graphics, and technological communications; language encompasses visual communication; and reading refers to listening and viewing.

In a review of the psychological research on semiotics and multiple intelligences, Smagorinsky (1995) analyzed the appropriateness of textual media in the construction of meaning. This broadened notion of text was supported with the findings from research on the construction of nonprint texts in disciplines other than English, suggesting that exclusively focusing on written texts limits students' development of conceptual knowledge. Suhor and Little (1988) and others (e.g., Allan, 1992; Buckland, 1991; Korac, 1988) explored this territory by mapping a semiotic model onto current and recommended practices in media arts education.

Reader response criticism (Beach, 1993), which has grounded much research on teaching with literature (Many & Cox, 1992), offers a framework for exploring media arts in education as well. Louise Rosenblatt's (1978) transactional model of reader response took an eclectic view of what constitutes a "work" or "text." She used the term *poem* to stand for an literary work of art that she described as "not an object but an event, a lived-through process or experience" (p. 35). The formal differences between stories, poems, and plays, which she classified together as literary events, are no less great than the differences between literature and film. Indeed, she suggested that the transactional theory, which seeks to account for the question of "'literariness' or 'poeticity'—i.e., of 'the aesthetic' in 'literature'—has implications for aesthetic education in general" (Rosenblatt, 1986, p. 122). An aesthetic transaction, in which the focus of attention is on the lived-through experience and the accompanying ideas, sensations, feelings, and images, can occur between any perceiver and any artifact, as between any reader and any text, including film and other media texts. In his psychoanalytic model of the literary process, Holland (1968, 1990) saw little difference between the two from the point of view of audience response.

Much of what we know about media can be traced to a research tradition that has focused on questions of media effectiveness but the meaningfulness of this tradition has been questioned. Clark (1990) and others (Luke, 1997; Reinking & Wu, 1988) maintained that this work has not produced meaningful results because such studies have simply not asked the right questions. Nor have they used useful methods, for by controlling for everything other than medium, including method, it is not reasonable to expect that differences would be found. The argument is that simple medium differences do not make a difference and that the learning context and methods that are used should center work in the field.

Research on the media arts in education has also been relatively unfettered by theory. Needed is a more complex theoretical basis for media education (Buckingham, 1993). Efforts to develop theories and models of use of media have emerged primarily from the work of cognitive psychologists, mass media researchers, and visual arts and communication theorists who have explored the complex relationship of the symbol system of television to childrens' learning in social contexts other than school (Jacobson, 1994). For example, cognitive psychologist Gavriel Salomon (1983, 1997) suggested that media's role in cognition is determined by students' perceptions that affect the amount of mental effort they are willing to invest in learning from media. Essential differences among media are the unique ways in which their symbol systems structure and convey content. He described an interactive model of the visual media experience that draws from work in schema theory as explanation for the processing of text discourse. Within this model, the meaning of a communication is what is attributed to it by the viewer, not an intrinsic and immutable proper of the message itself. This model acknowledges the viewer's prior knowledge, considers viewing as active communication, and emphasizes the need for critical and literate viewing instruction in schools.

One of Salomon's research hypotheses in his efforts to theoretically ground research in media, is that early exposure to a medium's symbol system in the context of interactions with adults who support the learner's efforts to address themselves to symbolic modes they might not explore otherwise, will make a difference in their learning from these systems. When *Sesame Street* was first introduced in Israel, Salomon showed that co-observing mothers caused children to invest more effort in the viewing experience and, as a result, gain more knowledge.

There is certainly a research base for such a perspective in studies of media, which rejected the traditional cause-and-effect model and replaced it with one that considers students as active, schema-guided viewers. Rather than simply comparing the effects of one presentation mode with another, the comparative effects of unmediated and mediated with adult interaction or instructional intervention have been examined (Anderson, Lorch, Field, & Sanders, 1981; Buerkel-Rothfuss, Greenberg, Atkin, & Neuendorff, 1982; Collins, 1981; Desmond & Jeffries-Fox, 1983; Dorr, 1981; Liebes, 1992; Lorch, Bellack, & Augsback, 1987; Moss, 1993). Others have investigated the nature of siblings' verbal interaction during television viewing and found that children play an active role in interpreting the television world for each other. Other studies have shown the positive influence of adults and caretakers on childrens' critical viewing during media use (Cohen & Salomon, 1979; Collins, Sobol, & Westby, 1981; Corder-Bolz, 1980).

Findings that active engagement in viewing experiences increased learning with media echo constructivist (Piaget, 1969) and social interactionist perspectives on learning (Vygotsky, 1986) that currently guide much research and practice in curriculum and instruction in elementary and secondary education. Visual media are eclectic symbol systems merging characteristics of photography, music, cultural codes, and speech. The mental effort required by a viewer to interpret these symbol systems directly corresponds to the amount of prior experience and knowledge of the viewer, and the optimum learning from a media experience depends on the amount of social interaction that takes place, as when young children talk with other children or adults while watching a children's television show like *Sesame Street*.

It is most probable that media arts literacy and education will not gain a foothold in classrooms in the United States or become widely accepted in the American educational community without a body of educational research on its effectiveness or impact on stated national goals (Reck, 1991), content standards, performance objectives, or reform movements (Zancanella, 1994); relationship to already identified priorities, such as higher success rates on standardized tests and increased print literacy; or alignment with prevailing political educational agendas that demand research to bolster arguments for policies driving one approach or another. Witness the current reading wars and ongoing debates over whose research is worthy. It is paradoxical that there is so little research on the media arts in education in the most mass-mediated country in the world.

## References

Adoni, H. (1995). Literacy and reading in a multimedia environment. *Journal of Communication, 45*(2), 152–174.

Allan, D. W. (1992). A phenomenological perspective on motion media: The iconic phenomena communication model. *International Journal of Instructional Media, 19*(2), 149–155.

Allen, W. H. (1960). Audio-visual communication. In C. W. Harris (Ed.), *Encyclopedia of educational research* (3rd ed., pp. 115–137). New York: Macmillan.

Alvermann, D. E., Moon, J. S., & Hagood, M. C. (1999). *Popular culture in the classroom: Teaching and researching critical media literacy*. Newark, DE: International Reading Association.

Alwitt, L. F., Anderson, D. R., Lorch, E. P., & Levin, S. R. (1980). Preschool children's visual attention to attributes of television. *Human Communication Research, 7,* 52-67.

Anderson, D., Lorch, E., Field, D., & Sanders, J. (1981). The effects of television comprehensibility on preschool children's visual attention to television. *Child Development, 52,* 151-157.

Avgerinou, M., & Ericson, J. (1997). A review of the concept of visual literacy. *British Journal of Educational Technology, 28*(4), 280-291.

Barry, R. V. (1979). Using media in the classroom: A selected replication of the Squire-Applebee survey. *English Education, 11,* 48-52.

Beach, R. (1993). *A teacher's introduction to reader-response theories.* Urbana, IL: National Council of Teachers of English.

Beagles-Roos, J., & Gat, I. (1983). The specific impact of radio and television on children's story comprehension. *Journal of Educational Psychology, 75,* 128-137.

Beentjes, J. W. J., & van der Voort, T. H. A. (1991). Children's written accounts of televised and printed stories. *Educational Technology, Research and Development, 39*(3), 15-26.

Brandeis, J. (1992). Media education: Initiatives across Canada. *English Quarterly, 25*(2-3), 45-57.

Bristor, V. J., & Drake, S. V. (1994). Linking the language arts and content areas through visual technology. *T.H.E. Journal, 22*(2), 74-77.

Buckingham, D. (1993). Going critical: The limits of media literacy. *Australian Journal of Education, 37*(2), 42-52.

Buckingham, D. (1999). Superhighway or road to nowhere? Children's relationship with digital technology. *English in Education, 33*(1), 3-12.

Buckland, W. (1991). The structural linguistic foundation of film semiology. *Language and Communication, 11*(3), 197-216.

Buckle, L., & Kelley, P. (1990). Understanding images: Educating the viewer. *Journal of Educational Television, 16*(1), 23-30.

Buerkel-Rothfuss, N. L., Greenberg, B. S., Atkin, C. K., & Neuendorff, K. (1982). Learning about the family from television. *Journal of Communication, 32,* 191-201.

Callison, D. (1991). A review of the research related to school library media collections. *School Library Media Quarterly, 19*(2), 117-121.

Cantor, J., & Hoffner, C. (1990). Children's fear reactions to a televised film as a function of perceived immediacy of depicted threat. *Journal of Broadcasting and Electronic Media, 34,* 421-442.

Chalfen, R. (1981). A sociovidistic approach to children's filmmaking: The Philadelphia Project. *Studies in Visual Communication, 7,* 2-32.

Chu, G. C., & Schramm, W. (1967). *Learning from television: What the research says.* Stanford, CA: Institute for Communication Research.

Clark, R. E. (1990). Instructional media and technology research. *International Journal of Educational Research, 14*(6), 485-579.

Cohen, A., & Salomon, G. (1979). Children's literate TV viewing: Surprises and possible exceptions. *Journal of Communication, 29,* 156-163.

Collins, W. A. (1981). Recent advances in research on cognitive processing during television viewing. *Journal of Broadcasting, 25,* 327-334.

Collins, W. A., Sobol, B. L., & Westby, S. (1981). Effects of adult commentary on children's comprehension and inferences about a televised aggressive portrayal. *Child Development, 52,* 158-163.

Comstock, G., Chaffee, S., Katzman, N., McCombs, M., & Roberts, D. (1978). *Television and human behavior.* New York: Columbia University Press.

Considine, D., & Haley, G. E. (1999). *Visual messages: Integrating imagery into instruction* (2nd ed.). Englewood, CO: Teacher Ideas Press.

Corder-Bolz, C. R. (1980). Mediation: The role of significant others. *Journal of Communication, 30,* 106-108.

Cox, C. (1978). Films children like—And dislike. *Language Arts, 55,* 334-338, 345.

Cox, C. (1982). Children's preferences for film form and technique. *Language Arts, 59,* 231-238.

Cox, C. (1994). Media literacy. In A. C. Purves (Ed.), *Encyclopedia of English Studies and Language Arts* (pp. 791-795). Urbana, IL: National Council of Teachers of English and Scholastic.

Cox, C., & Many, J. E. (1992). Beyond choosing: Emergent categories of efferent and aesthetic stances. In J. Many & C. Cox (Eds.), *Reader stance and literary understanding: Exploring the theories, research, and practice* (pp. 103-126). Norwood, NJ: Ablex.

Cropp, D. (1990). Are media needs being met for the beginning teacher? *Journal of Educational Technology Systems, 18*(3), 215-234.

Crosser, S. (1995). Mighty morphin power ranger play: Research and reality. *Early Childhood News, 7*(3), 25-27.

Descy, D. E. (1992). First year elementary schoolteachers' utilization of instructional media. *International Journal of Instructional Media, 19*(1), 15-21.

Desmond, J. D., & Jeffries-Fox, A. (1983). Elevating children's awareness of television advertising: The effects of a critical viewing program. *Communication Education, 32,* 107-115.

Dillingofski, M. S. (1979). *Nonprint media and reading.* Newark, DE: International Reading Association.

Dorr, A. (1981). Television and affective development and functioning: Maybe this decade. *Journal of Broadcasting, 25,* 335-345.

Dorris, A. V. (1995). Educating the twentieth-century youth. *Clearing House, 69*(2), 77-79. (Original work published 1930)

Duncan, B. (1997). Media education and information literacy: Are we missing most of the real lessons? *School Libraries in Canada, 17*(2), 3-5.

Durkin, R. (1970). *Involvement and making movies: A study of the introductions of movie making to poverty boys: Final report.* New York: Columbia University. (ERIC Document Reproduction Service No. ED 045 648)

Dyson, A. H. (1997). *Writing superheroes: Contemporary childhood, popular culture and classroom literacy.* New York: Teachers College Press.

Dyson, A. H. (1999). Coach Bombay's kids learn to write: Children's appropriation of media materials for school literacy. *Research in the Teaching of English, 33*(4), 367-402.

Fisherkeller, J. (1998). Learning from young adolescent television viewers. *New Jersey Journal of Communication, 6*(2), 149-169.

Forsslund, T. (1991). Factors that influence the use and impact of educational television in school. *Journal of Educational Television, 17*(1), 15-30.

Frost, R., & Hobbs, R. (1998). Instructional practices in media literacy education and their impact on students' learning. *New Jersey Journal of Communication, 6*(2), 123-148.

Gardner, H., Howard, V., & Perkins, D. (1974). Symbol systems: A philosophical, psychological, and educational investigation. In D. R. Olson (Ed.), *Media and symbols: The forms of expression, communication, and education* (pp. 27-55). Chicago: University of Chicago Press.

Greenfield, P. M. (1984). *Mind and media: The effects of television, video games, and computers.* Cambridge, MA: Harvard University Press.

Greenfield, P., & Beagles-Roos, J. (1988). Radio vs. Television: Their cognitive impact on children of different socioeconomic and ethnic groups. *Journal of Communication, 38*(2), 71-92.

Griffin, M. (1985). What young filmmakers learn from television: A study of structure in films made by children. *Journal of Broadcasting and Electronic Media, 29,* 79-92.

Hart, A., & Benson, A. (1996). Researching media education in English classrooms in the UK. *Journal of Educational Media, 22*(1), 7-21.

Haynes, W. L. (1988). Of that which we cannot write: Some notes on the phenomenology of media. *Quarterly Journal of Speech, 74*(1), 71-101.

Hepburn, M. A. (1997). TV violence: A medium effects under scrutiny. *Social Education, 61*(5), 244-249.

Himmelweit, H. T., Oppenheim, A. N., & Vince, P. (1958). *Television and the child*. London: Oxford University Press.

Hobbs, R. (1988). How first-time viewers comprehend editing conventions. *Journal of Communication, 38*(4), 50-6.

Hobbs, R. (1997). Expanding the concept of literacy. In R. Kubey (Ed.), *Media literacy in the information age* (pp. 163-183). New Brunswick, NJ: Transaction.

Hoffner, C. (1997). Children's emotional reactions to a scary film: The role of prior outcome information and coping style. *Human Communication Research, 23*(3), 323-341.

Hoffner, C., & Cantor, J. (1991). Factors affecting children's enjoyment of a frightening film sequence. *Communication Monographs, 58*(1), 41-62.

Holland, N. (1968). *The dynamics of literary response*. New York: Oxford University Press.

Holland, N. (1990). *Holland's guide to psychoanalytic psychology and literature and psychology*. New York: Oxford University Press.

Hubbard, R. (1990). There's more than black and white in literacy's palette: Children's use of color. *Language Arts, 67*(5), 492-500.

Huston, A. C., & Wright, J. C. (1983). Children's processing of television: The informative functions of formal features. In J. Bryant & D. R. Anderson (Eds.), *Children's understanding of television: Research on attention and comprehension* (pp. 35-58). New York: Academic Press.

Ishigaki, E. H. (1996). Young children's communication and self expression in the technological era. *Early Child Development and Care, 119*, 101-117.

Jacobson, M. J. (1994). Issues in hypertext and hypermedia research: Toward a framework for linking theory-to-design. *Journal of Educational Multimedia and Hypermedia, 3*(2), 141-154.

Javier, F. A., Herron, W. G., & Primavera, L. (1998). Violence and the media: A psychological analysis. *International Journal of Instructional Media, 25*(4), 339-356.

Johnston, D. D. (1995). Adolescent's motivations for viewing graphic horror. *Human Communication Research, 21*(4), 522-552.

Kelley, P. (1991). Failing our children? The comprehension of younger viewers. *Journal of Educational Television, 17*(3), 149-158.

Kelley, P., Gunter, B., & Buckle, L. (1987). 'Reading' television in the classroom: More results from the Television Literacy Project. *Journal of Educational Television, 13*, 7-19.

Kelly, H., & Gardner, H. (1981). *Viewing children through television*. San Francisco: Jossey-Bass.

Kibby, M. W. (1993). What reading teachers should know about reading proficiency in the U.S. *Journal of Reading, 37*(1), 28-40.

Kirman, J. M. (1997). Murder and media: What elementary teachers can do about video violence. *McGill Journal of Education, 32*(3), 231-147.

Korac, N. (1988). Functional, cognitive and semiotic factors in the development of audiovisual comprehension. *Educational Communication and Technology Journal, 37*(2), 67-91.

Koziol, R. V. (1991). Mass media consumption education. *Communication: Journalism Education Today, 24*(3), 21-23.

Kozma, R. B. (1991). Learning with media. *Review of Educational Research, 61*(2), 179-211.

Large, A. (1995). Multimedia in primary education: How effective is it? *School Library Media Quarterly, 24*(1), 19-25.

Larson, R., & Meade, E. (1969). *Young filmmakers*. New York: Dutton.

Lemke, J. L. (1991). Intertextuality and educational research. *Linguistics Education, 4*(3-4), 257-267.

Liebes, T. (1992). Television, parents, and the political socialization of children. *Teachers College Record, 94*(1), 73-86.

Lorch, E. P., Bellack, D. R., & Augsback, L. H. (1987). Young children's memory for televised stories: Effects of importance. *Child Development, 58*, 453-463.

Lowther, D. L., & Sullivan, H. J. (1994). Teacher and technologist beliefs about educational technology. *Educational Technology Research and Development, 42*(4), 73-87.

Luke, C. (1985). Television discourse processing: A schema theoretic approach. *Communication Education, 34*, 91-105.

Luke, C. (1997). Media and cultural studies. In S. Muspratt, A. Luke, & P. Freebody (Eds.), *Constructing critical literacies: Teaching and learning textual practice* (pp. 19-49). Cresskill, NJ: Hampton Press.

Lyle, J., & Hoffman, H. (1972). Children's use of television and other media. In E. Rubenstein, D. Comstock, & J. Murray (Eds.), *Television and Social Behavior,* Vol. 4 (pp. 129-256). Washington, DC: U.S. Government Printing Office.

Lynch, J. (1986). Film education research: An overview. *Teaching English in the Two-Year College, 13*, 245-253.

Magliano, J. P. (1996). Generating predictive inferences while viewing a movie. *Discourse Processes, 22*(3), 199-224.

Many, J., & Cox, C. (1992). *Reader stance and literary understanding: Exploring the theories, research, and practice*. Norwood, NJ: Ablex.

Masterman, L. (1990). *Teaching the media*. New York: Routlege.

Meadowcroft, J. M., & McDonald, D. G. (1986). Meta-analysis of research on children and the media: Atypical development? *Journalism Quarterly, 63*, 474-480.

Meringoff, L. K. (1980). Influence of the medium on children's story apprehension. *Journal of Educational Psychology, 72*, 240-249.

Molitor, F., & Hirsch, K. W. (1994). Children's toleration of real-life aggression after exposure to media violence: A replication of the Drabman and Thomas studies. *Child Study Journal, 24*(3), 191-207.

Moss, G. (1993). Children talk horror videos: Reading as a social performance. *Australian Journal of Education, 37*(2), 169-181.

National Assessment of Educational Progress (1981). *Reading, thinking, and writing: Results from the 1979-1989 National Assessment of Reading and Literature*. Denver, CO: Education Commission of the States.

Neumann, S. B. (1991). *Literacy in the television age: The myth of the TV effect*. Norwood, NJ: Ablex.

Oliver, M. B. (1993). Adolescent's enjoyment of graphic horror: Effects of viewer's attitudes and portrayals of victim. *Communication Research, 20*(1), 30-50.

Parker, D. (1999). You've read the book, now make the film: Moving image media, print literacy and narrative. *English in Education, 33*(1), 24-35.

Pezdek, K., Lehrer, A., & Simon, S. (1984). The relationship between reading and cognitive processing of television and radio. *Child Development, 55*, 2072-2082.

Pezdek, K., & Stevens, E. (1984). Children's memory for auditory and visual information on television. *Developmental Psychology, 20*, 212-218.

Phillips, M. (1998). Media education on the United States: A check under the "Gestalt" hood. *New Jersey Journal of Communication, 6*(2), 109-122.

Piaget, J. (1969). *The language and thought of the child*. London: Routledge & Kegan Paul.

Plowman, L. (1994). The "Primitive Mode of Representation" and the evolution of interactive multimedia. *Journal of Educational Multimedia and Hypermedia, 3*(3-4), 275-293.

Primavera, L. H., Herron, W. G., & Jauier, R. A. (1996). The effects of viewing television violence on aggression. *International Journal of Instructional Media, 23*(1), 91-104.

Pryluck, C., & Hemenway, P. T. M. (1982). *The American Film Institute second survey of higher education.* Los Angeles, CA: American Film Institute.

Purves, A. C. (Ed.) (1994). *Encyclopedia of English Studies and Language Arts.* Urbana, IL: National Council of Teachers of English and Scholastic.

Purves, A. C., & Beach, R. (1972). *Literature and the reader: Research in response to literature, reading interests, and the teaching of literature.* Urbana, IL: National Council of Teachers of English.

Reck, L. (1991). Technology: What and when? *Contemporary Education, 63*(1), 42-46.

Reinking, D., & Wu, J. (1988). Research into practice: Reading vs. Television: Will we ever have the answer? *Georgia Journal of Reading, 13*(2), 34-41.

Rosenblatt, L. M. (1978). *The reader, the text, the poem: The transactional theory of the literary work.* Carbondale: Southern Illinois University Press.

Rosenblatt, L. M. (1986). The aesthetic transaction. *Journal of Aesthetic Education, 20,* 122-128.

Ruch, M., & Levin, J. (1977). Pictorial organization versus verbal repetition of children's prose: Evidence for processing differences. *Audio Visual Communication Review, 25,* 269-280.

Salomon, G. (1979). *Interaction of media, cognition, and learning.* San Francisco, CA: Jossey-Bass.

Salomon, G. (1983). Television watching and mental effort: A social psychological view. In J. Bryant & D. R. Anderson (Eds.), *Children's understanding of television: Research on attention and comprehension* (pp. 265-296). New York: Academic Press.

Salomon, G. (Ed.) (1997). *Distributed cognitions: Psychological and educational considerations.* New York: Cambridge University Press.

Schramm, W., Lyle, J., & Parker, E. B. (1961). *Television and the lives of children.* Palo Alto, CA: Stanford University Press.

Smagorinsky, P. (1995). Constructing meaning in the disciplines: Reconceptualizing writing across the curriculum as composing across the curriculum. *American Journal of Education, 103*(2), 160-184.

Small, R. V., & Ferreira, S. M. (1994). Information location and use, motivation, and learning patterns when using print or multimedia information resources. *Journal of Educational Multimedia and Hypermedia, 3*(3-4), 251-273.

Spencer, K. (1991). Models, media, and methods: The search for educational effectiveness. *British Journal of Educational Technology, 22*(1), 12-22.

Squire, J. R., & Applebee, R. K. (1968). *High school English instruction today.* New York: Appleton-Century-Crofts.

*Standards for the English Language Arts* (1996). Urbana, IL: National Council of Teachers of English/International Reading Association.

Suhor, C., & Little, D. (1988). Visual literacy and print literacy—theoretical considerations and points of contact. *Reading Psychology, 9*(4), 469-481.

Sutton-Smith, B., Eadie, F., Griffin, M. (1983). Filmmaking by young filmmakers. *Studies in Visual Communication, 9,* 65-75.

Sutton-Smith, B., Eadie, F., Griffin, M., & Zarem, S. (1979). *A developmental psychology of childrens' filmmaking.* New York: Ford Foundation. (ERIC Document Reproduction Service No. ED 148 330)

Thoman, E. (1999). Skills and strategies for media education. *Educational Leadership, 56*(5), 50-54.

Tidhar, C. (1984). Children communicate in cinematic codes: Effects on cognitive skills. *Journal of Educational Psychology, 76,* 957-965.

Tyner, K. (1998). *Literacy in a digital world: Teaching and learning in the age of information.* Mahwah, NJ: Lawrence Erlbaum Associates.

von Feilitzen, C., & Carlsson, U. (Eds.) (1999). *Children and media: Image, education, participation.* Yearbook from the UNESCO International Clearinghouse on Children and Violence on the Screen, Götenborg, Sweden.

Vygotsky, L. S. (1986). *Thought and language.* Cambridge, MA: MIT Press.

Wartella, E. Alexander, A., & Lemish, D. (1979). The mass media environment of children. *American Behavioral Scientist, 23,* 33-52.

Wartella, E., & Reeves, B. (1985). Historical trends in research on children and the media: 1900-1960. *Journal of Communication, 35,* 118-133.

Watts Pailliotet, A., Semali, L., Rodenberg, R. K., Giles, J. K., & Macaul, S. L. (2000). Intermediality: Bridge to critical media literacy. *The Reading Teacher, 54*(2), 208-219.

Weiss, M. (1982). Children using audiovisual media for communication: A new language? *Journal of Educational Television, 8,* 109-112.

Wilson, B. J. (1989a). Desensitizing children's emotional reactions to mass media. *Communication Research, 16*(6), 723-745.

Wilson, B. J. (1989b). The effects of two control strategies on children's emotional reactions to a frightening movie scene. *Journal of Broadcasting and Electronic Media, 33*(4), 397-418.

Wilson, B. J. (1991). Children's reactions to dreams conveyed in mass media programming. *Communication Research, 18*(3), 283-305.

Winn, M. (1977). *The plug-in drug.* New York: Viking.

Worth, S., & Adair, J. (1972). *Through Navajo eyes: An exploration in film communication and anthropology.* Bloomington: Indiana University Press.

Wyatt, R. O., & Badger, D. P. (1990). Effects of information and evaluation in film criticism. *Journalism Quarterly, 67*(2), 359-368.

Zancanella, D. (1994). Local conversations, national standards, and the future of English. *English Journal, 83*(3), 23-29.

Zindovic-Vukadinovic, G. (1998). Media literacy for children in the compulsory school system. *Educational Media International, 35*(2) 133-137.

# ·50·

# READING MATTERS: HOW READING ENGAGEMENT INFLUENCES COGNITION

## Anne E. Cunningham
### University of California, Berkeley

## Keith E. Stanovich
### University of Toronto

Over the past 20 years researchers have made many important discoveries in our understanding of how children learn to read. They have learned, for example, that several factors such as phonemic awareness and letter knowledge are key predictors of reading success or failure (see Adams, 1990). This view of reading development has focused largely on the *predictors* of reading development, but there is growing concern among educators that the *reciprocal* influence of reading success or failure might also be a contributing factor to the academic experiences of some children (Chall, Jacobs, & Baldwin, 1990; Stanovich, 1986, 1993). That is, reading activity itself serves to increase the achievement differences between children.

It is becoming increasingly evident that rich-get-richer and poor-get-poorer mechanisms are embedded in the social and cognitive contexts of schooling. These rich-get-richer effects in academic achievement have been termed "Matthew effects" (Stanovich, 1986; Walberg & Tsai, 1983). A model of such effects has been emerging in recent years (Adams, 1990; Chall et al., 1990; Cunningham & Stanovich, 1997; Juel, 1994; Stanovich, 1986). Very early in the reading process, poor readers who experience greater difficulty in breaking the spelling-to-sound code begin to be exposed to much less text than their more skilled peers (Allington, 1984; Biemiller, 1977–78). Further exacerbating the problem of differential exposure is that less skilled readers often find themselves in materials that are too difficult for them (Allington, 1977, 1983, 1984; Gambrell, Wilson, & Gantt, 1981). The combination of deficient decoding skills, lack of practice, and difficult materials results in unrewarding early reading experiences that lead to less involvement in

reading-related activities. Lack of exposure and practice on the part of the less skilled reader delays the development of automaticity and speed at the word recognition level. Slow, capacity-draining word recognition processes require cognitive resources that should be allocated to higher level processes of text integration and comprehension (LaBerge & Samuels, 1974; Perfetti, 1985; Stanovich, 1980). Thus, reading for meaning is hindered, unrewarding reading experiences multiply, and practice is avoided or merely tolerated without real cognitive involvement.

There are, however, even further effects on processes whose domains extend outside the reading process itself. As skill develops and word recognition becomes less resource-demanding by taking place via relatively automatic processes, more general language skills become the limiting factor on reading ability (Chall, 1983; Sticht, 1979). However, the reading *experience* of the better reader has the potential to provide an advantage here if—as our research (Cunningham & Stanovich, 1997; Echols, West, Stanovich, & Zehr, 1996; Stanovich & Cunningham, 1992, 1993) suggests—extensive reading serves to develop processes and knowledge bases that facilitate reading comprehension (vocabulary, familiarity with complex syntactic structures, etc.). From the standpoint of a reciprocal model of reading development, such effects imply that many cognitive differences observed between readers of differing skill may in fact be consequences of *differential practice* that itself resulted from early differences in the *speed* of initial reading acquisition. The increased reading experiences of children who master the spelling-to-sound code early (see Adams, 1990) thus might have important positive feedback effects that are denied the slowly progressing reader. In our research, we have begun to explore these reciprocal effects by examining the role that reading volume plays in influencing cognition and will share many of our findings in this paper.

A common educational practice has been to immerse children in literature and to increase their amount of free reading time. Despite this common practice, we must ask whether research has demonstrated that reading has positive cognitive consequences. Here, it must be admitted that we have often been building policy more on assumptions and theory than on demonstrated fact. Still, it is difficult to tease apart the unique contribution of independent reading. One of the difficulties is that levels of reading volume are correlated with too many other cognitive and behavioral characteristics. Avid readers tend to be different from nonreaders on a wide variety of cognitive skills, behavioral habits, and background variables (Guthrie, Schafer, & Hutchinson, 1991; Kaestle, 1991; Zill & Winglee, 1990). Attributing any particular outcome to reading volume is thus extremely difficult.

## THE LEXICAL RICHNESS OF TEXT: READING AND VOCABULARY GROWTH

Print seems to be a uniquely rich source of vocabulary information. Many researchers are convinced that differences in reading volume are a critical source of individual differences in children's vocabularies (Miller & Gildea, 1987; Nagy & Anderson, 1984; Nagy, Herman, & Anderson, 1985; Sternberg, 1985, 1987). Microanalyses of the effects of print on vocabulary development are developing rapidly using connectionist technologies. For example, Landauer's (1998; Landauer & Dumais, 1996, 1997) latent semantic analysis provided a refined way of measuring the density and complexity of semantic relationships in texts. Landauer's (1998) work with latent semantic analysis drives home the importance of print exposure, because this work demonstrated how substantial amounts of vocabulary growth can be explained by the effects of concentrated exposure. Specifically, when a word is encountered in the context of other known words, it is not just the representation of the unknown word that is sharpened but rather that of all related words in the lexicon (which in the abstract includes *all* words in the lexicon, although at some lexical distance the effect becomes vanishingly small). Landauer (1998) emphasized that "we believe that central human cognitive abilities often depend on immense amounts of experience" (p. 163). Thus, print exposure appears to be a critical mechanism for vocabulary growth in school-age populations and beyond.

Additionally, the structured experience of both classroom vocabulary exposure and practice would, of course, be even more effective. We know that increased generalizability of learning occurs when explicit instruction rather than implicit or incidental learning experiences are provided to students (e.g., Cunningham, 1990). This should be the case in vocabulary development as well. With more explicit instruction in word structure and morphology, for example, word meanings would be generalized as a result of knowing a corpus of root words, prefixes, and suffixes. The combination of classroom-based vocabulary instruction and print exposure should thus create the ideal environment for maximizing the exposure that Landauer (1998) delineated.

It is extremely important for teachers to recognize the unique lexical richness of print and the implications that this richness has for vocabulary development. The vocabulary density of print (relative to oral language) can be illustrated with the help of some simple statistics from the work of Hayes and Ahrens (1988) who analyzed the distributions of words used in various contexts. Some of the differences between print and oral language are illustrated in Table 50.1. The table illustrates the three different categories of language that were analyzed: written language sampled from genres as difficult as scientific articles and as simple as preschool books; words spoken on television shows of various types; and adult speech in two contexts varying in formality. The words used in the different contexts were analyzed according to a standard frequency count of English (Carroll, Davies, & Richman, 1971). This frequency count ranks the 86,741 different words in English according to their frequency of occurrence in a large corpus of written English. For example, the word *the* is ranked 1st in frequency, the word is *it* is ranked 10th, the word *know* is ranked 100th, the word *pass* is ranked 1,000th, the word *vibrate* is 5,000th, the word *shrimp* is 9000th, and the word *amplifier* is 16,000th.

The column in Table 50.1 labeled Rank of Median Word, is simply the frequency rank of the average word (after a small correction) in each of categories. For example, the average word in children's books was ranked 627th most frequent in the Carroll et al.'s (1971) word count, the average word in popular magazines was ranked 1,399th most frequent, and the average word in the abstracts of scientific articles had, not surprisingly, a very low rank (4,389).

What becomes immediately apparent is how lexically impoverished is most speech when compared with written language. With the exception of the special situation of courtroom testimony, the average frequency of the words in all of the samples of oral speech is quite low, hovering in the 400 to 600 range of ranks. The relative rarity of the words in children's books is in fact greater than that in all of the adult conversation, except for the courtroom testimony. Indeed, the words used in children's books are considerably rarer than those in the speech on prime-time adult television (which of course has been intentionally stripped of low-frequency words so as not to scare off the audience). The categories of adult reading matter contain words that are considerably rarer than those heard on television. These relative differences in word rarity have direct implications for vocabulary development. The only opportunities to acquire new words occur when an individual is exposed to a word in written or oral language that is outside their current vocabulary. That this will happen vastly more often while reading than while talking or watching television is illustrated in the second column of Table 50.1. The column lists how many rare words per 1,000 are contained in each of the categories. A rare word is defined as one with a rank lower than 10,000—roughly a word that is outside the vocabulary of fourth- through sixth-graders. For vocabulary growth to occur after the middle grades, children

TABLE 50.1. Selected Statistics for Major Sources of Spoken and Written Language (Sample Means)

| | Rank of Median Word | Rare Words per 1,000 |
|---|---|---|
| I. Printed texts | | |
| Abstracts of scientific articles | 4,389 | 128.0 |
| Newspapers | 1,690 | 68.3 |
| Popular magazines | 1,399 | 65.7 |
| Adult books | 1,058 | 52.7 |
| Comic books | 867 | 53.5 |
| Children's books | 627 | 30.9 |
| Preschool books | 578 | 16.3 |
| II. Television texts | | |
| Popular prime-time adult shows | 490 | 22.7 |
| Popular prime-time children's shows | 543 | 20.2 |
| Cartoon shows | 598 | 30.8 |
| Mr. Rogers and Sesame Street | 413 | 2.0 |
| III. Adult speech | | |
| Expert witness testimony | 1,008 | 28.4 |
| College graduates to friends, spouses | 496 | 17.3 |

Note. Adapted from "Vocabulary Simplification for Children: A Special Case of 'Motherese'?," by D. P. Hayes and M. Ahrens, 1988, *Journal of Child Language, 15*, pp. 395–410. Copyright 1988 by Academic Press. Adapted with permission.

must be exposed to words that are rare by this definition. Again, it is print that provides many more such word-learning opportunities. Children's books have 50% more rare words in them than does adult prime-time television and the conversation of college graduates. Popular magazines have roughly three times as many opportunities for new word learning than does prime-time television and adult conversation. Assurances that "what they read and write may make people smarter, but so will any activity that engages the mind, including interesting conversation" (Smith, 1989, p. 354) by some educators are overstated, at least when applied to the domain of vocabulary learning. The data in Table 50.1 indicate that conversation is not a substitute for reading. An oral culture plus visual images (increasingly the environment of children) is no substitute for print.

Baines (1996) conducted an interesting analysis of the lexical consequences of the transition from the written to the oral. He analyzed the vocabulary differences between books and the movies that had been made of those books. For example, Table 50.2 provides an analysis of the words in *To Kill a Mockingbird*, both the script (Fook, 1962) and book (Lee, 1960) versions.

In the left column are all the words beginning with the letter *u* that appear in the script of the movie. In the right column are all the words beginning with the letter *u* that appear in the book.

Table 50.3 illustrates a similar analysis of *Wuthering Heights*. (Brontë, 1847; 1939). In the left column are all the words beginning with the letter *i* that appear in the script of the movie. In the right column are all the words beginning with the letter *i* that appear in the book. Immediately apparent is the severe "lexical pruning" that occurs when a story goes from book to screen.

It is sometimes argued or implied that the type of words present in print but not represented in speech are unnecessary words—jargon, academic doublespeak, elitist terms of social advantage, or words used to maintain the status of the users but that serve no real functional purpose. A consideration of the frequency distributions of written and spoken words reveals

this argument to be patently false as is readily apparent from a perusal of some words that do not occur at all in two large corpora of oral language (Berger, 1977; Brown, 1984) but that have appreciable frequencies in a written frequency count (Francis & Kucera, 1982). An example is the following list of words: participation, luxury, maneuver, provoke, reluctantly, relinquish, portray, equate, hormone, exposure, display, invariably, dominance, literal, legitimate, and infinite. These words are not unnecessary appendages, concocted by the ruling class to oppress those who are unfamiliar with them. They are words that are

TABLE 50.2. Comparison of Words in Script and Book Versions of *To Kill a Mockingbird*

| Script | Book |
|---|---|
| ugly | up |
| under | us |
| until | use |
| up | used |
| upstairs | upon |
| us | until |
| used | upstairs |
| | unceiled |
| | unpainted |
| | uncontrollable |
| | uncrossed |
| | under |
| | undress |
| | unhitched |
| | unique |
| | unless |
| | unlighted |

Note. From "From Page to Screen: When a Novel Is Interpreted for Film, What Gets Lost in Translation?," by L. Baines, 1996, *Journal of Adolescent and Adult Literacy, 39*, p. __. Copyright__by__. Reprinted with permission.

TABLE 50.3. Comparison of Words in Script and Book
Versions of *Wuthering Heights*

| Script | | Book | |
|---|---|---|---|
| I'd | is | I'd | I'll |
| I'll | isn't | I've | idea |
| I'm | It | ideas | ideal |
| I've | it's | idleness | idiot |
| icy | | if | ill |
| If | | in | is |
| ill | | into | it's |
| ills | | illusions | imagined |
| imp | | impressed | impulse |
| improved | | incoherent | irks |
| in | | indefinite | indoors |
| indeed | | indignant | induced |
| injured | | inexquisite | instant |
| inside | | inquiring | instead |
| insolent | | inscribed | instinct |
| into | | inscription | invalid |
| introduce | | interesting | interposed |
| irony | | interrogatively | introduction |

Note. From "From Page to Screen: When a Novel Is Interpreted for Film, What Gets Lost in Translation?," by L. Baines, 1996, *Journal of Adolescent and Adult Literacy, 39*, pp. 612–622. Copyright 1996 by International Reading Association. Reprinted with permission.

TABLE 50.4. Variation in Amount of Independent Reading

| % | Minutes of Reading per Day | | | Words Read per Year | |
|---|---|---|---|---|---|
| | Books | Text | All Reading | Books | Text |
| 98 | 65.0 | 67.3 | 90.7 | 4,358,000 | 4,733,000 |
| 90 | 21.1 | 33.4 | 40.4 | 1,823,000 | 2,357,000 |
| 80 | 14.2 | 24.6 | 31.1 | 1,146,000 | 1,697,000 |
| 70 | 9.6 | 16.9 | 21.7 | 622,000 | 1,168,000 |
| 60 | 6.5 | 13.1 | 18.1 | 432,000 | 722,000 |
| 50 | 4.6 | 9.2 | 12.9 | 282,000 | 601,000 |
| 40 | 3.2 | 6.2 | 8.6 | 200,000 | 421,000 |
| 30 | 1.3 | 4.3 | 5.8 | 106,000 | 251,000 |
| 20 | 0.7 | 2.4 | 3.1 | 21,000 | 134,000 |
| 10 | 0.1 | 1.0 | 1.6 | 8,000 | 51,000 |
| 2 | 0.0 | 0.0 | 0.2 | 0 | 8,000 |

Note. Adapted from "Growth in Reading and How Children Spend Their Time Outside of School," by R. C. Anderson, P. T. Wilson, and L. G. Fielding, 1988, *Reading Research Quarterly, 23*, pp. 285–303. Copyright 1988 by International Reading Association. Adapted with permission.

necessary to make critical distinctions in the physical and social world in which we live. Without such lexical tools, one will be severely disadvantaged in attaining one's goals in a technological society. In response to arguments that these words are unnecessary, D. R. Olson (1986) argued:

[T]he distinctions on which such questions are based are extremely important to many forms of intellectual activity in a literate society. It is easy to show that sensitivity to the subtleties of language are crucial to some undertakings. A person who does not clearly see the difference between an expression of intention and a promise or between a mistake and an accident, or between a falsehood and a lie, should avoid a legal career or, for that matter, a theological one. (p. 341)

D. R. Olson's (1986) statement reflects a stark fact about modern technological societies—they are providing lucrative employment only for those who acquire increasingly complex verbal skills and vocabulary (Bronfenbrenner, McClelland, Wethington, Moen, & Ceci, 1996; Frank & Cook, 1995; Gottfredson, 1997; Hunt, 1995, 1999). The large differences in lexical richness between speech and print are a major source of individual differences in those complex verbal skills. These differences are created by the large variability among children in exposure to literacy. Table 50.4 presents the data from a study of the out-of-school time use by fifth-graders conducted by Anderson, Wilson, and Fielding (1988). From diaries that the children filled out daily over several month's time, the investigators estimated how many minutes per day that individuals were engaged in reading and other activities while not in school. The table indicates that the child at the 50th percentile in amount of book reading was reading approximately 4.6 minutes per day, over six times as much as the child at the 20th percentile in amount of reading time (less than a minute daily). To take another example, the child at the 80th percentile in amount of

book reading time (14.2 minutes) was reading over 20 times as much as the child at the 20th percentile.

Anderson et al. (1988) estimated the children's reading rates and used these, in conjunction with the amount of reading in minutes per day, to extrapolate a figure for the number of words that the children at various percentiles were reading. These figures (see Table 50.4) illustrate the enormous differences in word exposure that are generated by children's differential proclivities toward reading. For example, the average child at the 90th percentile in reading volume reads almost 2.5 million words per year outside of school, over 46 times more words than the child at the 10th percentile, who is exposed to just 51,000 words outside of school during a year. To put it another way, the entire year's out-of-school exposure for the child at the 10th percentile amounts to just 8 days of reading for the child at the 90th percentile. These are the differences that, combined with the lexical richness of print, act to create large vocabulary differences among children.

## LINKING READING VOLUME TO COGNITIVE OUTCOMES

In our research, we have sought empirical evidence for the specific facilitative effects of reading volume, effects that do not simply result from the higher cognitive abilities and skills of the more avid reader. We have attempted to examine the unique contribution that independent or out-of-school reading makes toward reading ability, aspects of verbal intelligence, and general knowledge about the world. As part of this research program, our research group has pioneered the use of a measure of reading volume that has some unique advantages in investigations of this kind (for detailed discussions of these methods, see Cunningham & Stanovich, 1997; Stanovich, 2000; Stanovich, Cunningham, & West, 1998). In our technical reports on this work, we have used a statistical technique, hierarchical multiple regression to solve the interpretive problem that avid readers excel in most domains of verbal learning and therefore our measures of reading volume might be spuriously correlated to a host of abilities. We have found that even when performance is statistically equated for reading comprehension and general ability, reading volume is still a very powerful predictor of vocabulary and knowledge differences. Thus, we believe that reading volume is not simply an indirect indicator of ability. It is actually a potentially separable, independent source of cognitive differences.

In a study of fourth-, fifth-, and sixth-grade children (Cunningham & Stanovich, 1991), we examined whether reading volume accounts for differences in vocabulary development once controls for both general and specific (i.e., vocabulary relevant) abilities were invoked. We employed multiple measures of vocabulary and controlled for the effects of age and intelligence. We also controlled for the effect of another ability that may be more closely linked to vocabulary acquisition mechanisms: decoding ability. Decoding skill might mediate a relationship between reading volume and a variable like vocabulary size in numerous ways. High levels of decoding skill, certainly a contributor to greater reading volume, might provide relatively complete verbal contexts for the induction of word meanings during reading. Thus, reading volume and vocabulary might be spuriously linked via their connection with decoding ability: Good decoders read a lot and have the best context available for inferring new words. This spurious linkage was controlled by statistically controlling for decoding ability prior to investigating reading volume. However, we found that even after accounting for general intelligence and decoding ability, reading volume contributed significantly and independently to vocabulary knowledge in fourth-, fifth-, and sixth-grade children. These findings demonstrate that reading volume, although clearly a consequence of developed reading ability, is a significant contributor to the development of other aspects of verbal intelligence. Such rich-get-richer (and, of course, their converse, poor-get-poorer) effects are becoming of increasing concern in the educational community (Adams, 1990; Chall, 1989) and are playing an increasingly prominent role in theories of individual differences in reading ability and growth (Chall et al., 1990; Cunningham & Stanovich, 1997; Juel, 1988, 1994; Stanovich, 2000).

An additional way to illustrate the importance of reading volume is to examine the consequences of a mismatch between general cognitive ability and print exposure. Can, for example, high reading volume compensate for modest levels of reading comprehension abilities? The strong and independent effects of reading volume can be illustrated in our studies (see Stanovich & Cunningham, 1992, 1993) in which we examined the data from two subgroups, one that was high in reading volume but low in reading comprehension (HiPrint/LoComp) and one that was low in reading volume but high on measures of reading comprehension (LoPrint/HiComp). We then compared the two groups on measures of vocabulary and declarative knowledge. Of course, there were large differences on the variables that had defined the groups: reading volume and reading comprehension. However, on our other measures of vocabulary and knowledge about the world, the HiPrint/LoComp group was superior. In short, as regards the acquisition of cultural knowledge and vocabulary, we find that reading volume seems to compensate for lack of general ability, even for the lack of reading

comprehension ability itself. Declarative knowledge and vocabulary will be built by reading—even for those low in subcomponent skills. In contrast, the LoPrint/HiComp group in our study demonstrate that a high level of cognitive ability is no substitute for reading volume when it comes to vocabulary and declarative knowledge. This group is perhaps representative of what has been termed "aliteracy": the failure to engage in the act of reading even though the requisite reading abilities are developed.

Across a variety of our studies, we have shown that exposure to print is efficacious regardless of the level of the student's cognitive and reading abilities. That is, we do not have to wait for certain skills to be in place before promoting independent reading. Even the student with limited reading skills will build vocabulary and cognitive structures through immersion in literacy activities.

In another test of our theory, we conducted an even more stringent test of whether reading volume is a unique predictor of verbal skill in a study of college subjects (Stanovich & Cunningham, 1992). We found a significant contribution of reading volume to *multiple* measures of vocabulary, general knowledge, spelling, and verbal fluency even after reading comprehension ability had been partialed along with nonverbal ability, which attests to the potency and strength of reading volume. In this and in other of our studies (see Stanovich, 2000; Stanovich et al., 1998), we have often stacked the deck against reading volume by sometimes partialing even variables that are affected by print exposure themselves, such as reading comprehension ability. By structuring the analyses in this way, we did not mean to imply that reading volume is not a determinant of reading comprehension ability. Indeed, we argue that there *are* grounds for believing that reading volume facilitates growth in comprehension ability. However, we wanted to construct the most conservative analysis possible by deliberately allowing the comprehension measure to steal some variance that is rightfully attributed to the measure of reading volume.

One way of demonstrating the conservative nature of these analyses is illustrated in a longitudinal study that we have conducted (Cipielewski & Stanovich, 1992). We addressed the question of whether reading volume can predict individual differences in *growth* in reading comprehension from third grade to fifth grade. We found that reading volume predicted variance in fifth-grade reading comprehension ability after third-grade reading comprehension scores had been removed. Thus, in removing the contribution of reading comprehension as in our adult studies, we are undoubtedly removing some of the variance in variables such as vocabulary and general knowledge that is rightfully attributed to reading volume.

Since beginning this research program on the contribution of print exposure to a model of reading development, the methodology and measures we developed have been widely adopted and the basic data patterns that we have briefly described here have been replicated using variants of our methodology. These patterns have been found in Canada (Chateau & Jared, 2000; Senechal, LeFevre, Hudson, & Lawson, 1996), the United States (Barker, Torgesen, & Wagner, 1992; Hall, Chiarello, & Edmondson, 1996; Lewellen, Goldinger, Pisoni, & Greene,

1993), Great Britain (Stainthorp, 1997), The Netherlands (de Groot & Bus, 1995), China (McBride-Chang & Chang, 1995), Norway (Braten, Lie, Andreassen, & Olaussen, 1999), and Taiwan (Lee, 1996). Populations such as second-language learners (Jackson, Ju, & Lu, 1994), Spanish speakers (Rodrigo, McQuillan, & Krashen, 1996), and learning disabled individuals (McBride-Chang, Manis, Seidenberg, Custodio, & Doi, 1993) have also been examined using variants of our methodology. Sticht, Hofstetter, and Hofstetter (1996) studied a sample by telephone that was representative of the demographics in the United States census. It has even been tested on a prison population (Rice, Howes, & Connell, 1998). We have been pleased to see that the methodology and tasks have been adapted by other investigators and used for disparate purposes—for example, in twin studies of genetic and environmental determinants of reading subprocesses (Castles, Datta, Gayan, & Olson, 1999; R. K. Olson, Forsberg, & Wise, 1994). They have also been used to examine the effects of parents' knowledge of children's literature (Senechal et al., 1996).

## THE DEVELOPMENT OF READING ENGAGEMENT AND VOLUME: THE IMPORTANCE OF AN EARLY START

Given that lifelong reading habits are such strong predictors of verbal cognitive growth, one must ask, what is it that predicts these habits? We have been looking at reading volume as a predictor of reading comprehension and cognitive ability—but what predicts reading volume or avid reading?

It is well accepted that comprehension ability and reading volume are in a reciprocal relationship. In an attempt to tease apart this reciprocal relationship, we explored the linkages between children's 1st-grade reading and cognitive abilities and 11th-grade outcomes in a unique 10-year longitudinal study (Cunningham & Stanovich, 1997). Most of our earlier studies involved assessing contemporaneous relations, but in this study we examined the performance of a sample of students who had been tested as first-graders (see Stanovich, Cunningham, & Feeman, 1984). About one half of these students were available 10 years later for testing as 11th-graders. At this time, we administered a set of reading comprehension, cognitive ability, vocabulary, and general knowledge tasks, as well as several measures of reading volume. Additionally, some standardized test scores from the intervening period were available. We were therefore able to examine what variables in the 1st grade predicted these cognitive outcomes in the 11th grade. We interpreted the reading volume measures administered in the 11th grade as cumulative indicators of variance in reading volume that had taken place many years earlier. Thus, we viewed the measures as in some sense retrospective indicators tapping the cumulative experiences and habits of the students some distance in time before actual assessment. As a result, we were able to examine how far this retrospective feature could be stretched.

In this study, we examined whether the *speed* of initial reading acquisition in the first grade could predict later tendencies to engage in reading activities even after differences in general cognitive abilities were controlled, as some models of Matthew effects in educational achievement would predict (Chall et al., 1990; Juel, 1994; Stanovich, 1986). We statistically removed the contribution of 11th-grade reading comprehension ability, in order to remove the direct association between reading volume and contemporaneous reading ability. Then we examined the contribution of three standardized measures of 1st-grade reading ability and observed that *all three* measures predicted 11th-grade reading volume even after *11th-grade* reading *comprehension* ability had been partialed out! We also observed that 1st-grade intelligence measures do *not* uniquely predict 11th-grade reading volume in the same way. Thus, this study showed us that an early start in reading is important in predicting a lifetime of literacy experience—and this is true *regardless* of the level of reading comprehension ability that the individual eventually attains. This is a stunning finding because it indicates that if students get off to a fast start in reading (as indicated by their 1st-grade decoding, word recognition, and comprehension), then they are more likely to engage in more reading activity as adults.

## THE IMPORTANCE OF PHONOLOGICAL PROCESSING IN EARLY READING ACQUISITION: HOW TO GET THE FAST START THAT LEADS TO THE LIFETIME READING HABIT

Research is converging on an increasingly explicit model of the determinants of early reading success (see Adams, 1990; Share, 1995; Share & Stanovich, 1995; Stanovich, 2000). The speed of early reading acquisition is closely tied to the development of word recognition skills and these skills require facility at grapheme-to-phoneme decoding. The underpinning skill of decoding is in turn phonological awareness, which in turn is reliant on the quality of phonological representations. Much research has converged on this general model of early reading acquisition (see Adams, 1990; Adams & Bruck, 1993; Byrne, 1998; Byrne & Liberman, 1999; Liberman, 1999; Liberman & Liberman, 1990; Perfetti, 1991, 1994; Shankweiler, 1999; Share & Stanovich, 1995; Stanovich, 2000). Research has also converged on the conclusion that skill at decoding can be developed by instruction and that children lacking such skill will fall behind in reading acquisition if not given specific and structured instruction in decoding (Adams, 1990; Bradley & Bryant, 1985; Byrne, 1998; Chall, 1983, 1989; Evans & Carr, 1985; Felton, 1993; Foorman, Francis, Fletcher, Schatschneider, & Mehta, 1998; Hatcher, Hulme, & Ellis, 1994; Iversen & Tunmer, 1993; Scanlon & Vellutino, 1997; Share, 1995; Stanovich, 2000; Tunmer & Nesdale, 1985).

Early success at reading acquisition is one of the keys that unlocks a lifetime of reading habits. The subsequent *exercise* of this habit serves to further develop reading comprehension ability in an interlocking positive feedback logic (Juel, 1988; Juel, Griffith, & Gough, 1986; Snow, Barnes, Chandler, Goodman, & Hemphill, 1991; Stanovich, 1986, 1993). Although it is difficult to tease apart, in our research program we have attempted to trace the increasing divergence in children's reading ability as well as other cognitive outcomes, by examining both sides of the important role of reciprocal causation. Our longitudinal study, for example, has permitted us to observe these effects, whereby children who get out of the gate quickly—who crack the spelling-to-sound code early on, appear to enter into a positive feedback loop. One of the benefits of these reciprocating effects may be a level of participation in literacy activities that leads to a lifetime habit of reading and thus sets the stage for future opportunities—opportunities not enjoyed by children who enter into this feedback loop more slowly.

Our studies may be seen as instances of Matthew effects in literacy development. We observe educational sequences in which early and efficient acquisition of reading skill yields faster rates of growth in reading achievement and other cognitive skills, which illustrate these rich-get-richer and poor-get-poorer effects (see Stanovich, 1986; Walberg & Tsai, 1983). Independent reading may explain part of the puzzle, and the pressing social problem, of widening achievement disparities between the educational haves and the have-nots (Chall et al., 1990; Dreeben & Gamoran, 1986; Snow et al., 1991; Stanovich, 1993; van Keulen, Weddington, & DeBose, 1998). A positive dimension of this research is that all of our studies have demonstrated that reading a lot is efficacious regardless of the level of a child's cognitive and reading ability. We do not have to wait for "prerequisite" abilities to be in place before encouraging free reading. Even the child with limited reading and comprehension skills will build vocabulary and cognitive structures through immersion in literacy activities. An encouraging message for teachers of low achieving students is implicit here. We often despair of changing our students' "abilities," but there is at least one partially malleable habit that will itself develop "abilities"— reading!

If reading influences cognition, then it becomes doubly imperative that we do not deny reading experiences to precisely those children whose verbal abilities are most in need of bolstering. Allowing the reading activities of those already low in ability to decline further sets up a particularly perverse poor-get-poorer effect whereby we attribute negative habits ("This child doesn't like to read") to abilities ("No wonder, he has low ability"). It is the very act of reading, however, that could foster precisely the verbal abilities that are employed as an explanation for lack of reading. The causal model we have portrayed in this chapter is thus more complex than that usually assumed. Although it is true that verbal skills and reading efficiency are dependent on developed abilities, those same developed abilities are fostered by the reading act itself.

Consider a further implication: The research reported here supports the increasing concern voiced by reading educators on the habits and acts that surround literacy itself. These habits foster important verbal skills. Although it is fine to focus on the notion of reading comprehension viewed as a developed ability, it is equally important to focus on the exercise of that ability. Simply put, there are increasing indications that we are producing children who can read but simply choose not to. Thus, we are producing what might be called a second-level disability—aliteracy. As far as unlocking the world's storehouse of knowledge, many people might as well be having basic ability problems—they appear to be so little better off for having the skills. In short, we are teaching the basic skills of reading as well as we ever did (Berliner & Biddle, 1995; Campbell, Voelkl, & Donahue, 1997; Stedman, 1996)—the "crisis" of low literacy levels results because of rising *demands* for literacy, not because absolute levels of literacy are falling. However, our performance in the domain of fostering positive reading habits and attitudes falls short. The importance of treating the latter as an indicator variable is reinforced by the data presented above showing that the positive consequences of print exposure can occur independently of ability.

Finally, from the standpoint of teacher morale, a focus on fostering reading habits seems motivated. Reading education has been dogged by indicators that are minimally sensitive to instructional effects (Cross & Paris, 1987). Reading comprehension tests constructed in the typical manner are a case in point. Conceiving reading as a stable cognitive ability, they are not designed to track more malleable instructional effects (Cross & Paris, 1987). Treating reading habits as an indicator variable would give teacher efforts a fairer chance to be reflected in assessment.

In summary, the push to immerse children in literature and to increase their amount of free reading is an educational practice that is supported by empirical evidence. If reading makes you smarter (Stanovich, 1993, 2000) and if it is important to get off to a successful early start for future reading ability and engagement (Cunningham & Stanovich, 1997; Stanovich, 1986), then we are not overestimating the importance of early reading engagement and volume.

## ACKNOWLEDGMENT

This research was supported by a University of California, Berkeley Faculty Research Grant to Anne Cunningham and a grant from the Social Sciences and Humanities Research Council of Canada to Keith Stanovich.

## *References*

Adams, M. J. (1990). *Beginning to read: Thinking and learning about print*. Cambridge, MA: MIT Press.

Adams, M. J., & Bruck, M. (1993). Word recognition: The interface of educational policies and scientific research. *Reading and Writing: An Interdisciplinary Journal, 5,* 113–139.

Allington, R. L. (1977). If they don't read much, how they ever gonna get good? *Journal of Reading, 21,* 57–61.

Allington, R. L. (1983). The reading instruction provided readers of differing reading abilities. *The Elementary School Journal, 83,* 548–559.

Allington, R. L. (1984). Content coverage and contextual reading in reading groups. *Journal of Reading Behavior, 16,* 85-96.

Anderson, R. C., Wilson, P. T., & Fielding, L. G. (1988). Growth in reading and how children spend their time outside of school. *Reading Research Quarterly, 23,* 285-303.

Baines, L. (1996). From page to screen: When a novel is interpreted for film, what gets lost in translation. *Journal of Adolescent & Adult Literacy, 39,* 612-622.

Barker, K., Torgesen, J. K., & Wagner, R. K. (1992). The role of orthographic processing skills on five different reading tasks. *Reading Research Quarterly, 27,* 334-345.

Berger, K. W. (1977). *The most common 100,000 words used in conversations.* Kent, OH: Herald.

Berliner, D. C., & Biddle, B. (1995). *The manufactured crisis: Myths, fraud, and the attack on America's public schools.* Reading, MA: Addison-Wesley.

Biemiller, A. (1977-78). Relationships between oral reading rates for letters, words, and simple text in the development of reading achievement. *Reading Research Quarterly, 13,* 223-253.

Bradley, L., & Bryant, P. (1985). *Rhyme and reason in reading and spelling.* Ann Arbor: University of Michigan Press.

Braten, I., Lie, R., Andreassen, R., & Olaussen, B. S. (1999). Leisure time reading and orthographic processes in word recognition among Norwegian third- and fourth-grade students. *Reading and Writing: An Interdisciplinary Journal, 11,* 65-88.

Bronfenbrenner, U., McClelland, P., Wethington, E., Moen, P., & Ceci, S. J. (1996). *The state of Americans.* New York: Free Press.

Brown, G. D. (1984). A frequency count of 190,000 word in the London-Lund Corpus of English Conversation. *Behavior Research Methods, Instruments, & Computers, 16,* 502-532.

Byrne, B. (1998). *The foundation of literacy: The child's acquisition of the alphabetic principle.* Hove, England: Psychology Press.

Byrne, B., & Liberman, A. M. (1999). Meaninglessness, productivity and reading: Some observations about the relation between the alphabet and speech. In J. Oakhill & R. Beard (Eds.), *Reading development and the teaching of reading* (pp. 157-173). Oxford: Blackwell.

Campbell, J., Voelkl, K., & Donahue, P. (1997). *NAEP 1996 trends in academic progress.* Washington, DC: National Center for Education Statistics.

Carroll, J. B., Davies, P., & Richman, B. (1971). *Word frequency book.* Boston: Houghton Mifflin.

Castles, A., Datta, H., Gayan, J., & Olson, R. K. (1999). Varieties of developmental reading disorder: Genetic and environmental influences. *Journal of Experimental Child Psychology, 72,* 73-94.

Chall, J. S. (1983). *Stages of reading development.* New York: McGraw-Hill.

Chall, J. S. (1989). Learning to read: The great debate twenty years later. A response to "Debunking the great phonics myth." *Phi Delta Kappan, 71,* 521-538.

Chall, J. S., Jacobs, V., & Baldwin, L. (1990). *The reading crisis: Why poor children fall behind.* Cambridge, MA: Harvard University Press.

Chateau, D., & Jared, D. (2000). Exposure to print and word recognition Processes. *Memory & Cognition, 28,* 143-153.

Cipielewski, J., & Stanovich, K. E. (1992). Predicting growth in reading ability from children's exposure to print. *Journal of Experimental Child Psychology, 54,* 74-89.

Cross, D. R., & Paris, S. G. (1987). Assessment of reading comprehension: Matching test purposes and test properties. *Educational Psychologist, 22,* 313-332.

Cunningham, A. E. (1990). Explicit versus implicit instruction in phonemic awareness. *Journal of Experimental Child Psychology, 50,* 429-444.

Cunningham, A. E., & Stanovich, K. E. (1991). Tracking the unique effects of print exposure in children: Associations with vocabulary, general knowledge, and spelling. *Journal of Educational Psychology, 83,* 264-274.

Cunningham, A. E., & Stanovich, K. E. (1997). Early reading acquisition and its relation to reading experience and ability 10 years later. *Developmental Psychology, 33*(6), 934-945.

de Groot, I., & Bus, A. (1995). *Boekenpret voor baby's.* Leiden, The Netherlands: Boekenpret.

Dreeben, R., & Gamoran, A. (1986). Race, instruction, and learning. *American Sociological Review, 51,* 660-669.

Echols, L. D., West, R. F., Stanovich, K. E., & Zehr, K. S. (1996). Using children's literacy activities to predict growth in verbal cognitive skills: A longitudinal investigation. *Journal of Educational Psychology, 88,* 296-304.

Evans, M. A., & Carr, T. H. (1985). Cognitive abilities, conditions of learning, and the early development of reading skill. *Reading Research Quarterly, 20,* 327-350.

Felton, R. H. (1993). Effects of instruction on the decoding skills of children with phonological-processing problems. *Journal of Learning Disabilities, 26,* 583-589.

Foorman, B. R., Francis, D. J., Fletcher, J. M., Schatschneider, C., & Mehta, P. (1998). The role of instruction in learning to read: Preventing reading failure in at-risk children. *Journal of Educational Psychology, 90,* 37-55.

Francis, W. N., & Kucera, H. (1982). *Frequency analysis of English usage: Lexicon and grammar.* Boston: Houghton Mifflin.

Frank, R. H., & Cook, P. J. (1995). *The winner-take-all society.* New York: Free Press.

Gambrell, L. B., Wilson, R. M., & Gantt, W. N. (1981). Classroom observations of task-attending behaviors of good and poor readers. *Journal of Educational Research, 74,* 400-404.

Gottfredson, L. S. (1997). Why g matters: The complexity of everyday life. *Intelligence, 24,* 79-132.

Guthrie, J. T., Schafer, W. D., & Hutchinson, S. R. (1991). Relation of document literacy and prose literacy to occupational and societal characteristics of young black and white adults. *Reading Research Quarterly, 26,* 30-48.

Hall, V. C., Chiarello, K., & Edmondson, B. (1996). Deciding where knowledge comes from depends on where you look. *Journal of Educational Psychology, 88,* 305-313.

Hatcher, P., Hulme, C., & Ellis, A. W. (1994). Ameliorating early reading failure by integrating the teaching of reading and phonological skills: The phonological linkage hypothesis. *Child Development, 65,* 41-57.

Hayes, D. P., & Ahrens, M. (1988). Vocabulary simplification for children: A special case of "motherese"? *Journal of Child Language, 15,* 395-410.

Hunt, E. (1995). *Will we be smart enough? A cognitive analysis of the coming workforce.* New York: Russell Sage Foundation.

Hunt, E. (1999). Intelligence and human resources: Past, present, and future. In P. Ackerman, P. Kyllonen, & R. Richards (Eds.), *Learning and individual differences: Process, trait, and content determinants* (pp. 3-28). Washington, DC: American Psychological Association.

Iversen, S., & Tunmer, W. E. (1993). Phonological processing skills and the Reading Recovery Program. *Journal of Educational Psychology, 85,* 112-126.

Jackson, N. E., Ju, D., & Lu, W. (1994). Chinese readers of English: Orthographic and phonological processing, word identification, and exposure to print. In V. Berninger (Ed.), *Varieties of orthographic knowledge: Theoretical and developmental issues* (Vol. 1, pp. 73-109). Dordrecht, The Netherlands: Kluwer.

Juel, C. (1988). Learning to read and write: A longitudinal study of fifty-four children from first through fourth grade. *Journal of Educational Psychology, 80,* 437-447.

Juel, C. (1994). *Learning to read and write in one elementary school.* New York: Springer-Verlag.

Juel, C., Griffith, P. L., & Gough, P. B. (1986). Acquisition of literacy: A longitudinal study of children in first and second grade. *Journal of Educational Psychology, 78,* 243-255.

Kaestle, C. F. (1991). *Literacy in the United States.* New Haven, CT: Yale University Press.

LaBerge, D., & Samuels, S. (1974). Toward a theory of automatic information processing in reading. *Cognitive Psychology, 6,* 293-323.

Landauer, T. K. (1998). Learning and representing verbal meaning: The latent semantic analysis theory. *Current Directions in Psychological Science, 7,* 161-164.

Landauer, T. K., & Dumais, S. (1996). How come you know so much? In D. Herrmann, C. Hertzog, C. McEvoy, P. Hertel, & M. Johnson (Eds.), *Basic and applied memory: Memory in context* (pp. 105-126). Mahwah, NJ: Lawrence Erlbaum Associates.

Landauer, T. K., & Dumais, S. (1997). A solution to Plato's problem: The latent semantic analysis theory of acquisition, induction, and representation of knowledge. *Psychological Review, 104,* 211-240.

Lee, S. (1996). Free voluntary reading and writing competence in Taiwanese high school students. *Perceptual and Motor Skills, 83,* 687-690.

Lewellen, M. J., Goldinger, S., Pisoni, D. B., & Greene, B. (1993). Lexical familiarity and processing efficiency: Individual differences in naming, lexical decision, and semantic categorization. *Journal of Experimental Psychology: General, 122,* 316-330.

Liberman, A. M. (1999). The reading researcher and the reading teacher need the right theory of speech. *Scientific Studies of Reading, 3,* 95-111.

Liberman, I. Y., & Liberman, A. M. (1990). Whole language vs. code emphasis: Underlying assumptions and their implications for reading instruction. *Annals of Dyslexia, 40,* 51-77.

McBride-Chang, C., & Chang, L. (1995). Memory, print exposure, and metacognition: Components of reading in Chinese children. *International Journal of Psychology, 30,* 607-616.

McBride-Chang, C., Manis, F. R., Seidenberg, M. S., Custodio, R., & Doi, L. (1993). Print exposure as a predictor of word reading and reading comprehension in disabled and nondisabled readers. *Journal of Educational Psychology, 85,* 230-238.

Miller, G. A., & Gildea, P. M. (1987). How children learn words. *Scientific American, 257*(3), 94-99.

Nagy, W. E., & Anderson, R. C. (1984). How many words are there in printed school English? *Reading Research Quarterly, 19,* 304-330.

Nagy, W. E., Herman, P. A., & Anderson, R. C. (1985). Learning words from context. *Reading Research Quarterly, 20,* 233-253.

Olson, D. R. (1986). Intelligence and literacy: The relationships between intelligence and the technologies of representation and communication. In R. J. Sternberg & R. K. Wagner (Eds.), *Practical intelligence* (pp. 338-360). Cambridge: Cambridge University Press.

Olson, R. K., Forsberg, H., & Wise, B. (1994). Genes, environment, and the development of orthographic skills. In V. Berninger (Ed.), *Varieties of orthographic knowledge: Theoretical and developmental issues* (pp. _). Dordrecht, The Netherlands: Kluwer.

Perfetti, C. A. (1985). *Reading ability.* New York: Oxford University Press.

Perfetti, C. A. (1991). The psychology, pedagogy, and politics of reading. *Psychological Science, 2,* 70-76.

Perfetti, C. A. (1994). Psycholinguistics and reading ability. In M. Gernsbacher (Ed.), *Handbook of psycholinguistics* (pp. 849-894). San Diego, CA: Academic Press.

Rice, M., Howes, M., & Connell, P. (1998). *The Prison Reading Survey: A report to HM Prison Service Planning Group. No.* Cambridge.

Rodrigo, V., McQuillan, J., & Krashen, S. (1996). Free voluntary reading and vocabulary knowledge in native speakers of Spanish. *Perceptual and Motor Skills, 83,* 648-650.

Scanlon, D. M., & Vellutino, F. R. (1997). A comparison of the instructional backgrounds and cognitive profiles of poor, average, and good readers who were initially identified as at risk for reading failure. *Scientific Studies of Reading, 1,* 191-215.

Senechal, M., LeFevre, J., Hudson, E., & Lawson, E. P. (1996). Knowledge of storybooks as a predictor of young children's vocabulary. *Journal of Educational Psychology, 88,* 520-536.

Shankweiler, D. (1999). Words to meaning. *Scientific Studies of Reading, 3,* 113-127.

Share, D. L. (1995). Phonological recoding and self-teaching: Sine qua non of reading acquisition. *Cognition, 55,* 151-218.

Share, D. L., & Stanovich, K. E. (1995). Cognitive processes in early reading development: Accommodating individual differences into a model of acquisition. *Issues in Education: Contributions from Educational Psychology, 1,* 1-57.

Smith, F. (1989). Overselling literacy. *Phi Delta Kappan, 70*(5), 354.

Snow, C. E., Barnes, W. S., Chandler, J., Goodman, I., & Hemphill, L. (1991). *Unfulfilled expectations: Home and school influences on literacy.* Cambridge, MA: Harvard University Press.

Stainthorp, R. (1997). A children's Author Recognition Test: A useful tool in reading research. *Journal of Research in Reading, 20,* 148-158.

Stanovich, K. E. (1980). Toward an interactive-compensatory model of individual differences in the development of reading fluency. *Reading Research Quarterly, 16,* 32-71.

Stanovich, K. E. (1986). Matthew effects in reading: Some consequences of individual differences in the acquisition of literacy. *Reading Research Quarterly, 21,* 360-407.

Stanovich, K. E. (1993). Does reading make you smarter? Literacy and the development of verbal intelligence. In H. Reese (Ed.), *Advances in child development and behavior, 24,* 133-180. San Diego, CA: Academic Press.

Stanovich, K. E. (2000). Progress in understanding reading: Scientific foundations and new frontiers. New York: Guilford Press.

Stanovich, K. E., & Cunningham, A. E. (1992). Studying the consequences of literacy within a literate society: The cognitive correlates of print exposure. *Memory and Cognition, 20,* 51-68.

Stanovich, K. E., & Cunningham, A. E. (1993). Where does knowledge come from? Specific associations between print exposure and information acquisition. *Journal of Educational Psychology, 85,* 211-229.

Stanovich, K. E., Cunningham, A. E., & Feeman, D. J. (1984). Intelligence, cognitive skills, and early reading progress. *Reading Research Quarterly, 19,* 278-303.

Stanovich, K. E., Cunningham, A. E., & West, R. F. (1998). Literacy experiences and the shaping of cognition. In S. Paris & H. Wellman (Eds.), *Global prospects for education: Development, culture, and schooling* (pp. 253-288). Washington, DC: American Psychological Association.

Stedman, L. (1996). As assessment of literacy trends, past and present. *Research in the Teaching of English, 30,* 283-302.

Sternberg, R. J. (1985). *Beyond IQ: A triarchic theory of human intelligence.* Cambridge, England: Cambridge University Press.

Sternberg, R. J. (1987). Most vocabulary is learned from context. In M. G. McKeown & M. E. Curtis (Eds.), *The nature of vocabulary acquisition* (pp. 89-105). Hillsdale, NJ: Lawrence Erlbaum Associates.

Sticht, T. (1979). Applications of the audread model to reading evaluation and instruction. In L. B. Resnick & P. Weaver (Eds.), *Theory and practice of early reading* (pp. 209–226). Hillsdale, NJ: Lawrence Erlbaum Associates.

Sticht, T. G., Hofstetter, C. R., & Hofstetter, C. H. (1996). Assessing adult literacy by telephone. *Journal of Literacy Research, 28,* 525–559.

Tunmer, W. E., & Nesdale, A. R. (1985). Phonemic segmentation skill and beginning reading. *Journal of Educational Psychology, 77,* 417–427.

van Keulen, J. E., Weddington, G. T., & DeBose, C. E. (1998). *Speech, language, learning and the African American child*. Boston: Allyn & Bacon.

Walberg, H. J., & Tsai, S. (1983). Matthew effects in education. *American Educational Research Journal, 20,* 359–373.

Zill, N., & Winglee, W. (1990). *Who reads literature?* Cabin John, MD: Seven Locks Press.

# ·51·

# BALANCING THE CURRICULUM IN THE ENGLISH LANGUAGE ARTS: EXPLORING THE COMPONENTS OF EFFECTIVE TEACHING AND LEARNING

*Arthur N. Applebee*
*State University of New York, Albany*

The past several decades have been a period of sharp debate about the nature of effective curriculum and instruction, for the curriculum as a whole as well as for the teaching of the English language arts. Calls for a return to the "basics," to a traditional liberal arts curriculum, to the classical works of Western civilization, and to direct instruction have echoed against calls for contemporary relevance, content reflecting the contributions of minorities and of women, process-oriented approaches, and student-centered classrooms. These calls have been intertwined with a national movement toward more rigorous, and more uniform, standards for curriculum, assessment, and teacher preparation. These debates are far from over, but this chapter describes the dimensions of an emerging consensus about many of the most important components of effective curriculum and instruction. The discussion is organized around changing perceptions of three components of effective contexts for teaching and learning—the teacher, the student, and the curriculum—and of the metaphors that govern how these components interact in teaching and learning.

## THE TEACHER

The teacher plays an obvious and central role in effective language teaching and learning, and some of the most important developments in the language arts during the past decades have focused directly on the teacher. One recurring theme has been the need for the teacher to be regarded, and to act, as a professional within the larger context of the school. The image of teacher as professional carries with it a clear set of responsibilities for planning and decision making, as well as a clear set of obligations in terms of knowledge and competence in structuring teaching and learning in the language arts classroom.

The emphasis on professionalism has come from a variety of directions, some essentially "top down" and others "bottom up." The growing strength of teacher unions, with their insistence that their collective voice be included in dialogues about school reform, has certainly played an important role. So, too, has the influence of the National Writing Project, which has stressed both the classroom knowledge that successful, experienced teachers possess, and the importance of teacher research as a vehicle for self-reflection and analysis of what is happening within the classroom. At a more academic level, the movement has gained momentum from a reexamination of the nature of pedagogical knowledge in general and that of subject-specific pedagogical knowledge in particular. This reexamination has challenged the notion that effective teaching can be described in terms of a limited set of generic teaching skills and has led to an exploration of the knowledge of the subject area teacher, including the teacher of English (Agee, 1998; Shulman, 1987; Siskin, 1994; Grossman, 1990). The most practical, and potentially the most far-reaching, of the outcomes of this movement have been the prototype examination questions developed for the teacher certification project of the Carnegie Foundation by Shulman and his colleagues and their institutionalization through the National Board for Professional Teaching Standards.

The professionalism of successful teachers manifests itself in a number of ways. Schools and districts that are outperforming schools serving similar populations of students support teachers' participation in a wide range of activities through which the teachers contribute to the profession as a whole as well as to their own continuing development as teachers (Langer, 1999). Activities may range from involvement in school based management to participation in local, state, and national professional associations, to involvement in design and implementation of new curriculum and assessments. Such involvement gives teachers a sense of agency, a belief that each student can succeed, and that each teacher and school can make (and indeed has an obligation to make) a significant contribution to that success. And when teachers have that sense of agency, national assessment results indicate that their students are indeed more successful (Applebee et al., 1994, pp. 164–165).

The role of the teacher, however, is only one part of the configuration of factors that shapes the nature of effective teaching and learning. The decisions the teacher makes are shaped in part by perceptions of the students—who they are and what they need to know.

## CONCEPTIONS OF THE STUDENT

The second component shaping effective language teaching and learning is the underlying conception of the student. Such conceptions begin with perceptions of who the students are and what they know and proceed from there to assumptions about the learning objectives that are most appropriate for them. Our understandings about both of these dimensions have altered considerably during the past decades.

One of the long-standing findings in research on student language skills is that achievement is influenced by the resources that students have available in the home. Students are likely to do better in all aspects of literacy if they come from supportive home environments, with abundant literacy material in the home, and with care givers who are themselves well educated (Applebee, Langer, & Mullis, 1988; Elley, 1994; Heath, 1983). Such students often do well whatever the characteristics of the educational program at their schools. Conversely, students who come from poor families unable to provide rich environments for literacy pose a particular challenge to schools.

During much of the 1980s, the education of such "at-risk" students received relatively little attention. The situation began to change late in the decade, in the face of a continuing pattern of unacceptably low performance for at-risk groups (Applebee, Langer, & Mullis, 1987) and of the recognition that minority students are becoming the majority in many school districts, and already have done so in some. Although there has been some narrowing of the gap in performance between historically at-risk and historically successful groups of students, the gap remains unacceptably large. In 1996, for example, Black and Hispanic 17-year-olds averaged approximately 4 years behind their White peers in reading and writing achievement (Wirt et al., 1998, pp. 5, 13). On equity grounds alone, such imbalances require special attention.

At the same time that educators have begun to turn their attention to at-risk students, the demands for literacy skills have been increasing. The same assessment studies that have suggested some narrowing of the performance gap have also indicated that this narrowing has occurred almost entirely through improvements in lower level or "basic" skills. These skills for the most part reflect rote or routine performance, rather than the ability to use literacy skills in broader contexts. Indeed, national assessment results suggest that very few students in any group—historically at risk or historically high achieving—do well on tasks that require them to justify conclusions or elaborate on particular points of view.

Rising expectations for all students have been coupled with demands for new standards of achievement that all students should be expected to meet. These demands have become quite widespread, strengthened by two quite different lines of argument. One argument says that it is time to stop rewarding poor performance with passing grades and graduation certificates that bear no relationship to the competence of the students. Rigorous standards of achievement should be put in place for all grade levels, and all students should be held to these standards so that school achievement will once again be meaningful when students apply for jobs or institutions of higher education. The other line of argument claims that allowing some students to proceed through school meeting lowered standards has resulted in denying the benefits of a good education to many students, particularly the children of the poor and of marginalized groups within our culture. Practices such as social promotion and grading based on effort rather than accomplishment, however well intentioned they may have been, have proven to be discriminatory, perpetuating deeply ingrained racial and class separations within American society. Both lines of argument have had a powerful effect on state and national efforts to specify appropriate goals and standards for performance in the core academic subjects. The result has been a broad consensus about the importance of uniform, and uniformly high, standards of performance in the core academic disciplines.

## THE CURRICULUM

The curriculum is the third component of effective language learning; it represents a translation of teachers' goals and perceptions of students' needs into specific content and activities. Some of the major changes in language teaching and learning during the past several decades have involved the curriculum. Over time, there has been a shift in emphasis from knowledge and skills taught out of context, to an emphasis on strategies and processes, to an emerging consensus on the need for a balanced curriculum in which important knowledge and skills are taught and learned in conjunction with language activities that require meaningful, extended engagement with interesting issues or ideas (Spiegel, 1998; Weaver, 1998).

The recent history of the teaching of writing can serve to illustrate trends that have also occurred in the teaching of reading and of literature. Traditional approaches to the teaching of writing treated the subject as a body of knowledge concerned with the characteristics of effective text. To write well, the argument went, students would have to learn the "rules" or formulae governing sentences, paragraphs, and larger units. The curriculum that resulted usually ended up specifying a variety of rules, and providing various exercises in which the rules could be applied and practiced. The amount of practice varied inversely with the level at which the rule applied: The greater part of the curriculum usually focused on sentence-level rules, the next largest segment on paragraph-level structures, and the least on how to put these components together into larger texts.

During the 1970s and 1980s, this traditional approach to the writing curriculum faced a number of challenges, some internal and some external. Internal challenges questioned the validity of the rules themselves: Braddock (1974), for example, found that textbook prescriptions for the use of topic sentences in paragraphs bore little relationship to topic-sentence usage in published articles; Meade and Ellis (1970) posed similar questions about textbook prescriptions for paragraph organization. The adequacy of grammar rules received an even greater challenge, as the field of linguistics passed successively through structural, transformational, and posttransformational approaches to syntactic description. The effect of such internal challenges was to weaken traditional approaches to writing instruction, leaving the profession open, even eager, for an alternative approach.

The alternative that was widely advocated shifted the focus of the curriculum away from the final written text toward the various cognitive and linguistic skills that effective writers draw upon in the process of shaping that text. Such process-oriented approaches to the curriculum had a number of appeals: They paralleled attention in cognitive psychology to processes of problem solving, they seemed to support a student-centered rather than a content-centered pedagogy, and they led to a variety of specific teaching suggestions. The characteristics of process-oriented instruction varied from classroom to classroom, but as a group they shared an emphasis on prewriting and revision activities, multiple drafts, small group instruction, peer response, the provision of audiences for student work, and the postponement of evaluation until late in the process.

As process-oriented approaches became more widespread, however, they generated their own reaction from commentators who worried that students were not learning accepted conventions of grammar, spelling, and usage—and that children from groups historically at risk for school failure were being denied the very skills that could ensure their success in the broader culture (Delpit, 1995; Hirsch, 1987; Villanueva, 1993). These fears were reinforced by increasing scholarly attention to genre study, including the specification of the components of genres important to success in a variety of school subjects (cf. Cope & Kalantzis, 1993). These components in turn have been offered as essential features of curriculum designed to ensure the success of all students.

These conflicting trends have recently begun to resolve themselves into calls for "balanced" curriculum (Spiegel, 1998; Weaver, 1998). The central argument in such calls is that the long-standing debates between skills-centered and student-centered instruction have been unproductive and misleading: There are strengths on both sides, and in spite of the prevailing rhetoric they do not have to be seen as contradictory (Langer, 1997). Rather than simply emphasizing language processes and assuming skills will be unconsciously assimilated, or simply emphasizing skills and assuming students will understand how to put them to use, balanced instruction links systematic instruction with language activities that students find meaningful and interesting. Students can be taught the central characteristics of a genre, for example, while they are reading and writing within that genre—whether the genre be that of a lab report or a haiku. In drawing on insights from conflicting traditions of curriculum and instruction, advocates of balanced approaches have the opportunity to develop principled practices that move beyond teachers long-standing tendency to draw whatever they consider useful from a variety of different sources, sources that may base their recommendations on inherently contradictory premises (Applebee, 1993; Applebee, Langer, Mullis, Latham, & Gentile, 1994). The challenge, in fact, is to develop approaches that integrate these different facets of curriculum and instruction rather than segregating them as inherently unrelated strands of activity. The critical issue in achieving balance, then, is not *how much* of one approach or the other but *how* they are interrelated.

The forces that have transformed the teaching of writing have also transformed other aspects of the teaching of English and the language arts. The traditional literature lesson, for example, utilized a lecture-and-discussion format designed to lead students toward a canonical interpretation of standard texts (Applebee, 1993). As in writing, these traditional approaches were seen as being in opposition to more process-oriented approaches, which were variously described as reader response based or student centered. The most extreme reader response methods emphasized the student's individual process of understanding at the expense of the development of commonalities (and differences) with other readers, all without much attention to the author's context and purposes (Bleich, 1978). As response-centered approaches became more widespread, more balanced versions have sought to build students' knowledge about ways to read and interpret literature in the context of developing their own understandings, as well as understanding the differing interpretations that other readers may construct (Langer, 1995) and the influences and assumptions within which an author may have been working (Rabinowitz & Smith, 1998).

## FINDING NEW METAPHORS FOR TEACHING AND LEARNING

Assumptions about the most effective approaches to curriculum and instruction have evolved more rapidly than our metaphors for thinking about what and how we teach. Such metaphors are important, because they provide teachers with an overarching framework for thinking about issues of teaching and learning. These frameworks, in turn, shape the curriculum that students experience and the learning that results.

In looking for metaphors to replace the traditional model of teaching and learning, there is considerable consensus on the conceptual underpinnings that will give those metaphors depth and power. Educators and scholars have turned increasingly during the past several decades toward constructivist theories of language and learning, initially as a way to explain processes of child language development, and more recently as a framework for understanding school learning as well.

Constructivist approaches have a variety of roots, with related frameworks emerging in fields as seemingly diverse as linguistics (Halliday, 1977), psychology (Bruner, 1996; Vygotsky, 1962), history of science (Kuhn, 1970), and philosophy (Polanyi, 1958). What these various scholars share is a view of knowledge, and of mind, as an active construction built up by the individual's acting within a social context that shapes and constrains that knowledge but does not determine it in an absolute sense.

Constructivist approaches have in turn provoked their own critique, from a variety of different directions. One line of argument accuses constructivists as being too conservative, accepting the established, shaping social contexts rather than challenging them directly. Another line of argument attacks constructivists for emphasizing the development of student values and opinions, rather than upholding the traditional values of home and community. Both critiques seem to conflate a theory of knowing with (contradictory) concerns about social change, forgetting that (as Kuhn, 1970, argued in discussing the norms of science) revolutions in ways of knowing grow out of, rather than outside of, prevailing systems of understanding.

Constructivist orientations have become popular in education in part because they provide a powerful framework for thinking about teaching and learning (Britton, 1970). Rather than focusing either on specific content to be learned or on the nature of the learner, they lead to a consideration of learning in context—to how knowledge develops within a particular classroom. Such a framework provides a way to approach the problem of defining broad underlying principles that govern effective effective teaching and learning. In the language arts, a number of scholars have built on this framework to move research on teaching away from previous process–product or treatment-group studies, looking in more detail at the ways the structure of interaction within a particular context for learning shapes the knowledge and skills that students develop, including their understanding of and ability to function within the social context itself (e.g., Dyson, 1993, 1994; Griffin & Cole, 1984; Heath, 1983; Langer & Applebee, 1987; McMahon, Raphael, & Goatley, 1997; Palincsar & Brown, 1984).

Langer and Applebee (1986), building on work by Bruner (e.g., Wood, Bruner, & Ross, 1976), Cazden (1979), and others, have used the metaphor of "instructional scaffolding" as one alternative to traditional models of teaching and learning. In this metaphor, children learn to do new things with language in contexts that provide scaffolding or support for tasks they could not do on their own. In studies of early language development, the parent or caregiver provided the scaffolds (Wood et al., 1976). In classrooms, as students attempt new tasks, the instructional scaffolding is broader and more social, stemming from a wide variety of sources, including the teacher, other students in group or whole class contexts, and the instructional materials that are available. These various resources provide the necessary support (including necessary new knowledge)—and at the same time model or lead the student through effective strategies for completing that task. Over time and with repetition, the knowledge and strategies become internalized, and the student becomes capable of deploying them in addressing other tasks and negotiating other social contexts.

Basing their work on studies of process-oriented approaches to instruction, Langer and Applebee (1986) suggested five criteria for effective instructional scaffolding. These criteria are not meant as a complete model of teaching and learning, but focus instead on problems that occur in both traditional and process-oriented classrooms. They represent one attempt to describe the dimensions of effective teaching and learning of the English language arts.

## Ownership

Effective teaching and learning must allow room for students to make their own contribution to ongoing tasks. They must establish their own purposes for what they are doing with language, for it is these purposes that integrate and give point to the specific skills and strategies they may draw on as a task is carried out.

The need for ownership militates against traditional demands for recitation of previous learning and demonstration of skills, where the purposes are simply to display information that is already better known by the teacher. Instead, it requires tasks where specific answers are less certain, depending not only on what the teacher or textbook has presented but also on how the student makes use of that new information. In writing, opportunities for ownership occur when topics call for students to explore their own experiences and opinions, to elaborate on a point of view, and to develop their own positioning within a social group. In reading and literature, similar opportunities for ownership occur when students are encouraged to develop—and defend—their own interpretations, in a context that assumes that there will be multiple perspectives and contrasting points of view.

When activities are structured to encourage students to take ownership, students must take responsibility for the conclusions they reach, and be able to justify and defend them in the light of what others may say or do. Thus, classrooms that provide opportunities for students to take ownership for their work are not abandoning standards of excellence; on the contrary, they lead to the development of rigorous standards of argument and evidence in defense of the positions that students adopt. As an important by-product, classrooms that stress ownership are also likely to be classrooms that lead to the develop of more effective reasoning and thinking skills.

The notion of ownership is related to a variety of other recent suggestions for educational reform. Graves (1983) used the term to argue for the importance of writing about self-selected, rather than teacher-provided, topics. Britton, Burgess, Martin, McLeod, and Rosen (1975) pointed out the emptiness of "dry runs" in school writing and pointed to the motivating effect of "real" writing tasks. Moffett (1981) argued for the importance of writers finding their own voice in the assignments they undertake and noted the deadlines of the "Engfish" that results when students write without vesting themselves and their own opinions and experiences in the task. In literature, Rosenblatt (1978) and others observed the importance of the individual transaction between reader and work—a transaction without which the work does not in any real sense exist for the reader.

Langer (1995), in turn, argued that the exploration of multiple possibilities is a defining characteristic of engaging in literary experiences, in contrast with other kinds of text in which possibilities are narrowed in the process of more fully exploring a topic or idea.

## Appropriateness

Effective instructional tasks will build on literacy and thinking skills that students already have, helping them to accomplish tasks that they could not otherwise complete on their own. In Vygotsky's (1962) terms, teaching and learning will be aimed "not so much at the ripe, but at the ripening functions."

This is a commonsense principle, often phrased in terms of "starting where the students are," but it is a principle that is easily violated in practice. Curriculum that is built around scope-and-sequence charts targeted at particular grade levels almost inevitably means that many of the activities that take place will be inappropriate for many of the children present. The activities either will involve repetition of things that many students already know how to do, or will lead to unsuccessful struggles with tasks that are too difficult for many students to complete.

The ways around this problem have to do with the types of tasks that are embedded within the curriculum. When tasks become more open ended, rather than focused on achieving a particular correct solution, students have more chance of working at the appropriate level. Their interpretations of literature will be more or less abstract, more or less complex, for example; their writing will move further along a continuum from narrative commentary to tight argument. In turn, the responses that the student receives, whether from the teacher or from other students working on related problems within the same classroom, will adjust to the appropriate level.

## Support

To be an effective vehicle for learning, instructional tasks must make the structure of the activity clear and must guide the student through in a way that will provide the knowledge and skills necessary for successful performance. Put another way, the task must support a natural sequence of thought and language within which productive learning will take place.

This criterion lies at the heart of the notion of instructional scaffolding; it focuses on the interaction between the student and the supporting context that provides the structure and knowledge that makes it possible for learning to occur. The implications of this criterion for the shape of instruction are dramatic, for it implies that the teaching of skills unconnected to their contexts for use will not be effective.

At the same time, this criterion places the attention at the heart of the teaching and learning process—for students need help and support if they are to continue to grow as language learners and language users. The teacher must understand the kinds of knowledge and skill that need to be drawn on in particular tasks and, accordingly, must structure the classroom so

that students will be introduced to appropriate knowledge and skills at the point at which this information is needed. In writing, for example, this may take the form of suggesting appropriate prewriting activities to help students gather and organize pertinent information, ways to segment the task to make it easier to accomplish, or the provision of constructive critical response (either from teacher the or from other students) to help shape initial ideas into a more effective draft. In reading and literature, it may include prereading activities to provide a context for the work to be read, carefully constructed guide questions to lead the student through difficult sections of the text itself, or mutual exploration of first interpretations as students first work their way into and then back out of a text (Langer, 1995).

Traditional critical apparatus and technical terminology may play an important role in these processes. They will do so by being introduced in contexts where they can be connected to what students are reading or writing, as tools that help students elaborate on and make sense of what they are doing.

Hillocks' (1979; Hillocks, Kahn, & Johannessen, 1983) examples of "environmental learning" offer some carefully worked out illustrations of such structure in the teaching of writing. In his approach, writing activities involve real problems to be solved, with appropriate problem-solving strategies introduced as they are needed in the course of the task. The problems and the tasks are both highlighted, so that the students understand the instrumental nature of the activities they are asked to do. In a metaanalysis of experimental studies since 1962, Hillocks (1986) concluded that such environmental teaching was some three times as effective in developing writing skills as were more traditional approaches.

These examples also highlight another important feature of the notion of instructional scaffolding as a way to think about teaching and learning: It works by providing a way to think about and organize familiar activities and approaches, rather than by asking teachers to abandon what they already know. Instructional scaffolding is a beginning at the complex problem of codifying principles of effective teaching and learning.

## Collaboration

In effective classrooms, the teacher's role needs to be one of collaboration, setting consistent high standards but postponing evaluation of the final product. Evaluation has an important role in most classrooms, but it is a role that needs to be separated from feedback on work in progress. Only in this way can the teacher offer support that allows tentative explorations of new learning, with the inevitable false starts and initial misapprehensions that such explorations entail. If evaluation intrudes too soon, students will retreat to safer, and in many ways simpler, routines of recitation and display of previous learning.

## Internalization

As students, peers, and teachers tackle new problems and carry their language activities through to completion, the young learners internalize the strategies and skills that were involved in solving those problems and negotiating these social contexts. These skills and strategies become resources to be drawn upon in new contexts; the socially embedded and transmitted knowledge that they represent becomes part of the individual student's repertoire. It is this process that leads to the astonishingly rapid emergence of language skills in the infant, and it is this same process that lies at the heart of language learning during childhood, adolescence, and adulthood.

Effective classrooms learning will be structured to welcome this process, providing opportunities for young learners to take greater control of their language activities as they develop new skills. They must have room to initiate as well as respond, to explore the strengths as well as the limitations of their new knowledge and strategies. For this to happen, the teacher must be ready to step back as well as forward, providing room for students to use the skills they have as well as providing support for new skills that students are still in the process of developing.

Palincsar and Brown's (1984) notion of "reciprocal teaching" emphasizes this process of internalization, as well as the stepping back that is essential to success. In their approach, developed in the context of reading instruction, students' understanding is supported initially through a series of questions that the teachers ask about difficult passages. Gradually, students learn to take over these questions, using them overtly as they enter reciprocally into the teaching practice within small groups of their peers, and covertly as they read new passages on their own.

Griffin and Cole (1984) similarly stressed the importance of interaction in the process of completing new tasks as a mechanism for the internalization of new knowledge and skills.

## ENSURING SEQUENCE AND CONTINUITY

When the language arts curriculum was defined in terms of particular content knowledge, the task of imposing structure and sequence on the curriculum was straightforward (if somewhat imposing, given the large number of items of content that remained to be put into coherent order). The usual approach was to develop a detailed curriculum guide or a scope-and-sequence chart. When the curriculum was defined in terms of process-related cognitive and linguistic skills, however, the task of laying out an orderly, sequential curriculum became quite different. Rather than an external order based on the subject matter, the curriculum had to be structured to foster the growth of problem-solving skills that may develop quite differently from student to student, depending upon background and previous experiences. The issue for curriculum theory became one of providing an orderly, coherent set of experiences, each of which is flexible enough to provide the appropriate degrees of challenge and support to students whose knowledge and skills may differ widely from each other.

In practice, this usually meant that the external curriculum was highly indeterminate, with few constraints on school-level decisions about materials and activities assigned to various grades and classes. The critical curriculum decisions, those that shaped the teaching and learning that took place within these broad frameworks, were made by the individual teacher for the individual class. These included decisions about the individual assignments and the nature of the teaching that surrounded the assignments. Thus, for the most part, implementation of process-oriented curricula depended on the day-to-day judgment of the teacher, rather than on the prescriptions of an external curriculum. There has never been much consensus, however, about what such ordering principles should look like.

Such implicit indeterminancy contributed to the discontent that many expressed about process-oriented curricula in all subject areas. The lack of a clear sense of what was being taught led many to assume that the curriculum had lost focus and that little was being taught at all (Ravitch & Finn, 1987). In an effort to refocus the discussion about teaching and learning around a more balanced metaphor, I proposed (Applebee, 1994, 1996) that curriculum can be more profitably thought of in terms of the conversations that it supports, in which conversations are broadly construed to include speech and writing as well as other media, the voices of contemporary as well as canonical authors, and the talk and writing of students and their teachers. The problem for curriculum, then, becomes one of selecting conversations that we want our students to be able to engage in; the problem for instruction becomes how to help students enter into the conversations that we value.

In arguing for this view of curriculum, I am building on an old notion that subject areas and the disciplines they incorporate represent conversations about things that matter, conversations that extend over time and space and involve the contributions of many different people. As a metaphor for curriculum and instruction, it is important to recognize that conversations can evolve in many different ways: They can be one-sided and monologic, as traditional lecture-oriented teaching used to be; they can be disorganized and wander off track; they can lead to consensus or disagreement; or they can reinforce conformity or invite diversity and multiple points of view. From studies of how experienced teachers achieve coherent and cohesive curricular conversations that stretch over units or semesters, my colleagues and I have described a number of features of an effective curriculum that have to do with the quantity and quality of material included in the curriculum, the relatedness among its parts, and the manner in which it is delivered (cf. Grice, 1975).

### Quality

At the simplest level, the demand for quality means that contributions to a curricular conversation need to be clear and accurate. Though obvious enough, this can sometimes be difficult to achieve. Much of the curriculum in American schools is based on textbooks, though a variety of studies of textbooks have indicted them for being difficult to comprehend, out of date, and sometimes even factually incorrect. Although textbooks are the usual target for complaints, there is nothing to suggest that the individual collections of materials that busy teachers are able to put together for themselves are any more comprehensive, accurate, or up to date.

Complicating matters further, judgments of the quality of curricular materials are likely to shift as the conversation changes. Thus the excerpts and catalog of minor works by great Americans that were appropriate to an American literature course in which the conversation dealt with patriotism and civic virtues became inappropriate when the conversation shifted to new critical discussions of the structure and integrity of individual works. Similarly, popular fiction by authors such as Stephen King and Jackie Collins may be rejected as low quality in a course on literary masterworks but may be considered highly appropriate for a conversation about gender stereotypes, formula fiction, and popular culture. Quality is always relative to the conversation in which the material is embedded—a point that is worth remembering in book selection controversies, in which the underlying agenda may have more to do with disagreements about the conversations in which we want our students to engage then in divergent assessments about particular titles and authors.

## Quantity

A curriculum must provide students with enough materials to sustain substantive conversation but not so many as to overwhelm the conversation that might be engendered. Both problems occur fairly regularly in American classrooms, as the result of good intentions gone astray. Discussions of curriculum have long pointed out the superficial nature of the learning that results when too much emphasis is placed on "coverage," a problem that may only get worse as schools try to adapt to the demands of the various new sets of national curriculum standards being issued by various subject organizations. Rather than adopting a comprehensive view of the curriculum, each special interest group has seemed intent on justifying its importance by presenting an expansive range of content that must be covered. Too much breadth in the curriculum usually results in superficial coverage emphasizing surface understandings, which, in turn, are assessed through multiple-choice or short-answer tests.

For underachieving students, on the other hand, the curriculum is sometimes watered down in an attempt to make it more comprehensible. The result all too often is to leave them with nothing to sustain interest or promote conversation at all.

## Relatedness

Interrelatedness within the curricular domain makes cumulative conversation possible, providing a sense of direction to what has been covered and what is to come. English language arts, however, has a predisposition to come unglued, absorbing everything that involves the use of language. Thus, although students may learn to make introductions, analyze rap lyrics, write thank-you letters, use the library catalog, use the spell-checker, criticize advertisements, interpret myths and legends, or write reports for math and science, such catalogs of language activities reflect no sense of the peripheral and the central; they do not define a coherent curricular domain.

Integrated language arts, in the sense of instruction that unifies the teaching of reading, writing, and language, is a necessary, but not sufficient, condition for relatedness among contributions to a curricular conversation. Relatedness in this sense refers instead to a web of interconnections among previous and ongoing experiences that allows understandings to continue to grow and develop over time. Rather than a linear learning and moving on to new topics, integrated curricular structures lead to a gradual deepening and expansion of understanding. Cecila Milanes (1992), describing the advantages of such integration in a course that presented students with a wide variety of unfamiliar texts, explained how their understanding "came, not suddenly, but as a result of dealing with the issue [of institutionalized racism] (and other related issues) over the semester: reading works treating it, writing about it, and talking about it with others" (p. 253). In such a course, students and teacher gradually build a shared representation of the curricular domain, construing and reconstruing individual works, ideas, and positions within it.

## Manner

It is here, in the concern with manner of instruction, that the previous decades of work on effective instruction comes together with the present focus on curriculum. Constructivist notions that treat knowledge as the result of meaning making processes in which each learner must engage led in turn to new ways of thinking about the role of the teacher, and generated such now familiar terms as scaffolding, reciprocal teaching, apprenticeship, and mentoring. From our present perspective, this previous work on instruction provides new and more powerful ways of thinking about how students can best be helped to enter into important domains for conversation. Only in conversation guided by others will students develop the tacit knowledge necessary to participate on their own.

## CONCLUSION

Historically, in the United States, standards of performance have been locally set and have varied greatly from one community to another (and even from one group of students to another within the same school). Against this background, the movements toward higher standards that must be reached by all students pose a significant challenge, one that will require rethinking of accepted approaches to curriculum and instruction. In the classrooms of the past, interaction has been one-sided, emphasizing the teacher as custodian of the past and deliverer of knowledge or the student as the independent discoverer or creator of knowledge. Although both approaches have worked well for some students, neither has worked very well in promoting academic achievement among traditionally at-risk students, or in developing reasoned and disciplined thinking among any groups.

In the successful classroom of the future, curriculum and instruction will need to be better balanced, recognizing the need for a new synthesis that emphasizes the importance both of the content to be learned and of the active involvement of the learner in effective curriculum and instruction (cf. Prawat, 1995). The teacher will play a central role, choosing the material that will be introduced, providing the structure that ensures learning can take place, introducing new knowledge and skills in relationship to the ongoing conversations, ensuring students get the support they need to complete new and difficult tasks, and mediating between the classroom conversations and the larger cultural conversations to which they are related. In doing so, the teacher will be encouraging the students to take a more active role: advancing their own interpretations and opinions, defending them against alternatives raised by their teachers and peers, and checking them against their own experience and the logic and rigor of the texts with which they deal. In such classrooms, students will find their own voices as they develop the knowledge and skills to become participants in the "great conversations" that they must both learn to work within and, eventually, to revitalize and carry forward (Applebee, 1996).

## ACKNOWLEDGMENT

Preparation of this chapter was supported in part under the Research and Development Centers Program (Award No. R305A60005) as administered by the National Institute on Student Achievement, Curriculum, and Assessment, Office of Educational Research and Improvement, U.S. Department of Education. However, the contents do not necessarily represent the positions or policies of the sponsoring agencies.

Sections of this chapter were drawn in part from "Toward Thoughtful Curriculum: Fostering Discipline-Based Conversation," by A. N. Applebee, 1994, *English Journal, 83*(3).

## *References*

Agee, J. (1998). Negotiating different conceptions about reading and teaching literature in a preservice literature class. *Research in the Teaching of English, 33*(1), 85-120.

Applebee, A. N. (1993). *Literature in the secondary school: Studies of curriculum and instruction in the United States.* Urbana, IL: National Council of Teachers of English.

Applebee, A. N. (1994). Toward thoughtful curriculum: Fostering discipline-based conversation. *English Journal, 83*(3), 45-52.

Applebee, A. N. (1996). *Curriculum as conversation: Transforming traditions of teaching and learning.* Chicago: University of Chicago Press.

Applebee, A. N., Langer, J. A., & Mullis, I. V. S. (1987). *Learning to be literate in America.* Princeton, NJ: National Assessment of Educational Progress.

Applebee, A. N., Langer, J. A., & Mullis, I. V. S. (1988). *Who reads best? Factors related to reading achievement in grades 3, 7, and 11.* Princeton, NJ: Educational Testing Service.

Applebee, A. N., Langer, J. A., Mullis, I. V. S., Latham, A. S., & Gentile, C. A. (1994). *NAEP 1992 writing report card.* Washington, DC: U.S. Government Printing Office.

Bleich, D. (1978). *Subjective criticism.* Baltimore, MD: Johns Hopkins University Press.

Braddock, R. (1974). The frequency and placement of topic sentences in expository prose. *Research in the Teaching of English, 8,* 287-302.

Britton, J. N. (1970). *Language and learning.* London: Penguin.

Britton, J. N., Burgess, T., Martin, N., McLeod, A., & Rosen, H. (1975). *The development of writing abilities* (pp. 11-18). London: Macmillan.

Bruner, J. (1996). *The culture of education.* Cambridge, MA: Harvard University Press.

Cazden, C. (1979). Peekaboo as an instructional model: Discourse development at home and at school. *Papers and Reports on Child Language Development, 17,* 1-19.

Cope, B., & Kalantzis, M. (Eds.) (1993). *The powers of literacy: A genre approach to teaching writing.* Pittsburgh, PA: University of Pittsburgh Press.

Delpit, L. (1995). *Other people's children: Cultural conflict in the classroom.* New York: New Press.

Dyson, A. H. (1993). *Social worlds of children learning to write in an urban primary school.* New York: Teachers College Press.

Dyson, A. H. (1994). Confronting the split between "the child" and children: Toward new curricular visions of the child writer. *English Education, 26*(1), 12-28.

Elley, W. B. (Ed.) (1994). *The IEA study of reading literacy: Achievement and instruction in thirty-two school systems.* Exeter, UK: Pergamon.

Graves, D. (1983). *Writing: Teachers and children a work.* Exeter, NH: Heinemann.

Grice, H. P. (1975). Logic and conversation. In P. Cole & J. L. Morgan (Eds.), *Syntax and semantics,* Vol. 3 (pp. 41-58). New York: Seminar Press.

Griffin, P., & Cole, M. (1984). Current activity for the future: The zo-ped. In B. Rogoff & J. Wertsch (Eds.), *Children's learning in the zone of proximal development* (New Directions for Child Development, No. 23). San Francisco: Jossey-Bass.

Grossman, P. (1990). *The making of a teacher: Teacher knowledge and teacher education.* New York: Teachers College Press.

Halliday, M. A. K. (1977). *Learning how to mean.* New York: Elsevier.

Heath, S. B. (1983). *Ways with words.* New York: Cambridge University Press.

Hillocks, G., Jr. (1979). The effects of observational activities on student writing. *Research in the Teaching of English, 13,* 23-35.

Hillocks, G., Jr. (1986). *Research on written composition.* Urbana, IL: National Conference on Research in English.

Hillocks, G., Jr., Kahn, E., & Johannessen, L. (1983). Teaching defining strategies as a mode of inquiry. *Research in the Teaching of English, 17*(3), 275-284.

Hirsch, E. D., Jr. (1987). *Cultural literacy: What every American needs to know.* Boston: Houghton Mifflin.

Kuhn, T. S. (1970). *The structure of scientific revolutions* (2nd ed.). Chicago: University of Chicago Press.

Langer, J. A. (1995). *Envisioning literature: Literary understanding and literature instruction.* New York: Teachers College Press.

Langer, J. A. (1997). Beyond winners and losers. *English Update* (Fall), 1.

Langer, J. A. (1999). *Excellence in English in middle and high school: How teachers' professional lives support student achievement.* Albany, NY: Center on English Learning and Achievement, State University of New York at Albany.

Langer, J. A., & Applebee, A. N. (1986). Reading and writing instruction: Toward a theory of teaching and learning. *Review of research in education, 13,* 171-194.

Langer, J. A., & Applebee, A. N. (1987). *How writing shapes thinking: A study of teaching and learning.* Urbana, IL: National Council of Teachers of English.

McMahon, S. I., Raphael, T. E., & Goatley, V. J. (Eds.) (1997). *The book club connection: Literacy learning and classroom talk.* New York: Teachers College Press.

Meade, R. A., & Ellis, W. G. (1970). Paragraph development in the modern age of rhetoric. *English Journal, 59,* 219-226.

Milanes, C. R. (1992). Racism and the marvelous real. In C. M. Hurlbert & S. Totten (Eds.), *Social issues in the English classroom* (pp. 246-257). Urbana, IL: National Council of Teachers of English.

Moffett, J. (1981). *Active voice: A Writing Program Across The Curriculum.* Portsmouth, NH: Boynton-Cook.

Palincsar, A. S., & Brown, A. L. (1984). Reciprocal teaching of comprehension-fostering and monitoring activities. *Cognition and Instruction, 1*(2), 117-175.

Polanyi, M. (1958). *Personal knowledge.* London: Routledge & Kegan Paul.

Prawat, R. S. (1995). Misreading Dewey: Reform, projects, and the language game. *Educational Researcher, 24*(7), 13-22.

Rabinowitz, P. J., & Smith, M. W. (1998). *Authorizing readers: Resistance and respect in the teaching of literature.* New York: Teachers College Press; and Urbana, IL: National Council of Teachers of English.

Ravitch, D., & Finn, C. E. (1987). *What do our 17-year-olds know?* New York: Harper & Row.

Rosenblatt, L. M. (1978). *The reader, the text, the poem: The transactional theory of the literary work.* Carbondale: Southern Illinois University Press.

Shulman, L. (1987). Knowledge and teaching: Foundations of the new reform. *Harvard Educational Review, 57,* 1-22.

Siskin, L. S. (1994). *Realms of knowledge: Academic departments in secondary schools.* Washington, DC: Falmer Press.

Spiegel, D. L. (1998). Silver bullets, babies, and bath water: Literature response groups in a balanced literacy program. *Reading Teacher, 52*(2), 114-124.

Villanueva, V., Jr. (1993). *Bootstraps: From an American academic of color.* Urbana, IL: National Council of Teachers of English.

Vygotsky, L. S. (1962). *Thought and language.* Cambridge, MA: M.I.T. Press.

Weaver, C. (Ed.) (1998). *Reconsidering a balanced approach to reading.* Urbana, IL: National Council of Teachers of English.

Wirt, J., Snyder, T., Sable, J., Choy, S. P., Bae, Y., Stennett, J., Gruner, A., & Perie, M. (1998). *The condition of education 1998* (NCES 98-013). Washington, DC: U.S. Department of Education, National Center for Education Statistics.

Wood, D., Bruner, J. S., & Ross, G. (1976). The role of tutoring in problem solving. *Journal of Child Psychology and Psychiatry, 17,* 89-100.

# Part

## ·V·

# RESEARCH ON TEACHING SPECIFIC ASPECTS OF THE ENGLISH LANGUAGE ARTS CURRICULUM

# ·52·

# LANGUAGE, THE LANGUAGE ARTS, AND THINKING

## Robert J. Marzano
### Mid-Continent Regional Educational Laboratory

The last two decades have seen an explicit recognition of the need to foster thinking and reasoning in K–12 classrooms. Calls for improved instructional techniques to enhance thinking arose in congressional hearings in the early 1980s as demands for graduates better able to engage in work that requires responsibility and judgment (L. B. Resnick, 1987). Evidence that U.S. students do not reason well has been reported from many quarters, the most public of which is arguably the National Assessment of Educational Progress (NAEP). For example, the results of the 1996 NAEP assessment of reading and writing show that only 39% of 17-year-old Americans can understand relatively complex reading material and only 2% can write effective essays that contain supportive details and discussions (National Center for Education Statistics, 1999).

Perhaps the teaching of thinking received its strongest endorsement at the first education summit in 1989 in Charlottesville, Virginia. At the summit, President George Bush and the nation's governors, including then governor Bill Clinton, agreed on six broad goals for education to be reached by the year 2000. These goals and the rationale for them were published under the title *The National Education Goals Report: Building a Nation of Learners* (National Education Goals Panel, 1991). One of those goals explicitly mentioned teaching thinking: "[E]very school in America will ensure that all students learn to use their minds well so that they may be prepared for responsible citizenship, further learning, and productive employment in our modern economy" (p. ix).

As novel as it might appear, the current emphasis on thinking is not new. According to Baron and Brown (1991b), enhancing the thinking of students was a topic of interest centuries before Plato and Aristotle. The Port Royal Logic was used extensively in upper class education in France and England in the late 1600s. It was designed to enhance reasoning and logical

choice. D. P. Resnick and L. B. Resnick (1977) noted that since there have been books and writing there have also been schools (mostly private and religious) established to train students in reasoning, rhetoric, mathematics, and scientific thought. What is new about the current emphasis on thinking is that it is recommended for all students: "Although it is not new to include thinking, problem solving and reasoning in *someone's* school curriculum, it is new to include it in *everyone's* curriculum" (L. B. Resnick, 1987, p. 7). Within the last century, one can trace the call for an emphasis on teaching thinking back to Dewey (1916, 1933).

In response to the perceived need to enhance students' thinking and reasoning skills, a plethora of programs have been developed. Although many of the practices within these programs are drawn from fields traditionally not considered cognate to the language arts, much of what is currently being proposed to enhance thinking has its roots in language and many practices are direct applications of language arts strategies. To highlight these relationships, this chapter is organized around three principles:

1. Language and thinking are inextricably linked.
2. Many of the current practices designed to enhance thinking have strong roots or corollaries within the language arts.
3. Some of the theory and practice which has been developed to enhance thinking can be used to augment current conceptions of language arts.

To expand on these principles, the chapter is organized into three sections. The first section describes the interrelationship of thought and language. The second describes current approaches to the teaching of thinking and discusses the relationship of these approaches to the language arts. Finally, the third section describes ways in which current theory and practice in the teaching of thinking can expand on traditional views of the language arts.

## THE PRIMACY OF LANGUAGE IN COGNITION

Language and thought are related in a number of ways. In this section three relationships are discussed: language as a form of thought, language as a mediator of thought, and language as a tool for enhancing thought.

### Language as a Form of Thought

Language is fundamentally linked to thought by the manner in which information is represented in memory—specifically, permanent memory. Before discussing language as a representational format in memory, it is important to consider the basic nature and function of memory itself. J. R. Anderson (1995) explained that the long-held conception of two types of memory—short term and long term—has been replaced with the theory that there is only one type of memory with different functions: sensory memory, permanent memory, and working memory. Sensory memory deals with the temporary storage of data from the senses. Permanent memory contains all information and skills that constitute one explicit and tacit knowledge. Working memory utilizes data from both sensory memory and from permanent memory. As its name implies, working memory is where data is actively processed. To this extent, it is the venue in which consciousness occurs (Dennett, 1969, 1991). Language has a role in each of these aspects of memory.

Researchers in the neural aspects of cognition (e.g., M. S. Gazzaniga, 1985; M. S. Gazzaniga & LeDoux, 1978; M. S. Gazzaniga & Sperry, 1967; Luria, 1961, 1969; Sperry, 1965) assert that language is the manifestation of a unique form of coding which augments and, over time, synthesizes the other nonlinguistic codes. For example, M. S. Gazzaniga and LeDoux stated that "the behaviors that these separate (nonlinguistic) systems are monitored by the one system we come to use more and more, namely, the verbal natural language system" (1978, p. 150). Tulving (1972), in his landmark work, described the integrative nature of language in his discussion of semantic versus episodic memory structures, which he refers to as episodic memory and semantic memory. Episodic memory, according to Tulving, comprises records of experienced events stored as perceptual (e.g., auditory, olfactory, tactile, kinesthetic, etc.) features. Semantic memory contains decontextualized information that is fundamentally linguistic in nature. Input to semantic memory comes directly from episodic memory and from the cognitive products of semantic memory. In other words, the semantic information in permanent memory is derived from translating and synthesizing the information stored as episodes and information induced or deduced from semantic memory.

Language philosophers go a step further in their assertions about the relationship of language to human thought. Some argue that language is at the root of the type of thinking that ultimately separates human thought from that of other animal forms (for a discussion, see Pinker, 1994). Where higher animal forms have episodic representations, they do not have semantic representations. Some language philosophers (e.g., Fodor, 1975) postulate the existence of a deep level, linguistically based abstract code that is certainly more abstract than surface structure language and even more abstract than deep structure language as described by Chomsky in *Syntactic Structures* (1957) and elaborated on in his later works (see Chomsky, 1965, 1980, 1988). Similarly, Schlesinger (1971) posited the existence of abstract linguistic "intention markers" that form the basis of thought, and Schank and Reiger (1974) identified 12 primitive actions that form the basis for the linguistic coding of human perception. In effect, then, the writings of theorists such as Fodor, Schlesinger, Schank, and Rieger, point to a form of thought that is prelinguistic in nature and uniquely human. Some evidence for this prelinguistic form of thought can be found in the research on how writers generate sentences (see Hayes, 1996; Kaufer, Hayes, & Flower, 1986). Specifically, this body of research strongly suggests that while composing, a person retrieves ideas from permanent memory that are not formed as language. Rather, a "language generation" mechanism translates these prelinguistic thoughts into surface language. It is important to note, however, that arguments have been articulated against the existence of a prelinguistic form of thought (see Bishop, 1983).

Another characteristic sometimes associated with language is its power to shape human thought. For example, drawing from the work of case grammarians (Chafe, 1970; Fillmore, 1968), D. McNeil (1975) noted that language is organized around such conceptual entities as objects, agents, states and events. Even abstract content where there may or may not be real objects, actions, states or events must be organized into these structures. Thus, the semantic structure of language is a frame or matrix around which the somewhat random array of data initially received in sensory memory is organized (Lindsay & Norman, 1977). Whorf's (1956) concept of linguistic relativity is commonly thought to epitomize the principle that language shapes perception. Specifically, building on the teaching of Sapir (1921), Whorf proposed dissecting nature along the lines laid down by native languages. The thoughts we isolate from the world of sensory stimuli are not there because they stare every observer in the face: "On the contrary, the world is presented in a kaleidoscopic flux of impressions which has to be organized by our mind—and this means largely by the linguistic system in our minds" (p. 213). In recent years, the principle of linguistic relativity has been severely criticized. For example, Pinker (1994) noted that "the more you examine Whorf's arguments, the less sense they make" (p. 60). Pinker argued that Whorf's claims about the influence of language on human perception far surpasses the empirical evidence. Pinker went so far as to say that some of Whorf's assertions were "hoaxes" (p. 64). Other criticisms of Whorf's theories have been summarized by Clarke, Losoff, and Rood (1982). In his defense, Whorfian scholars explain that Whorf's concept of linguistic relativity has been misunderstood. For example, Lee (1997) explained that Whorf hypothesized that language shapes one's interpretation and analysis of information, but it certainly does not alter the raw perceptual data loaded into working memory from sensory memory. According to Lee, Whorf saw language as a filter through which sensory data are interpreted as opposed to an a priori determiner of perceptions.

The role of language as a form of thought has been further described by the discipline of semiotics or the study of signs. Semiotic theorists such as Deely (1982) and Eco (1976, 1984) described human cognition as an interactive triad composed of objects, signs and an interpretant. Objects are those physical entities and events external to the individual. Signs are abstract mental representations commonly expressed in linguistic form. The interpretant is a parallel representation that helps one place meaning on, or interpret, the abstract code. From this perspective, language is the mediator between objective reality and personal interpretation of that reality. Individuals within a society have subjective interpretations of reality but through language can share commonalities within these experiences. There is a growing interest in analyzing domain-specific knowledge from the semiotic perspective as language-based sign systems (Cunningham & Luk, 1985; Dickson, 1985; Suhor, 1984).

Even if language does not organize thought, the study of language has greatly enhanced our understanding of thought. Specifically, much of the research in cognitive science is linguistically based (Graesser, Millis, & Long, 1986; J. R. Anderson, 1995). For example, Schank and Abelson (1977) identified scripts, plans, and goals as fundamental cognitive structures in permanent memory that account for much of human behavior. Similarly, de Beaugrande (1980) identified frames, scripts, and schemata. All these structures are presumably comprised of nonlinguistic information organized by a linguistic code.

The work in cognitive science on different types of cognitive structure has been greatly enabled by the research on discourse structures. In fact, some discourse structures directly parallel cognitive structures in permanent memory (van Dijk, 1980). Harris (1952) is commonly credited as being among the first to propose a serious model for linguistic analysis that extended beyond the sentence. Since then, there have been a number of models developed to describe intersentential and intrasentential semantic links, the most influential of which were Young, Becker, and Pike's (Pike, 1964; R. E. Young & Becker, 1965; R. W. Young, Becker, & Pike, 1970) work on tagmemics and Halliday and Hasan's (1976) *Cohesion in English*. (For a review of semantically based surface structure models, see C. R. Cooper, 1983.) These models of surface-level discourse characteristics formed the basis for models that could be used not only to describe surface-level, textual characteristics but also the mental representation of those textual characteristics. A number of such systems have been proposed (C. H. Frederiksen, 1977; Marzano, 1987; Meyer, 1975; Nold & Davis, 1980; Stein & Glenn, 1979; Turner & Greene, 1977). From these systems came theories of the process by which surface-level, textual characteristics are translated into permanent memory cognitive structures. To illustrate, one theory asserts that the process is one of translating or transforming a microstructure to a

macrostructure (Kintsch & van Dijk, 1978; van Dijk, 1977, 1980). The microstructure of discourse is the "local structure," the literal meaning of the words, phrases, sentences, and the relationships among them within discourse. The macrostructure is the global meaning extracted and inferred from the microstructure via such macrorules as deletion, construction and generalization. It is the macrostructure rather than the microstructure of text that is stored in permanent memory. This explains why an individual will tend to recall the "gist," or general theme, rather than the detail of information read or heard (C. H. Frederiksen, 1977; Meyer, 1975; van Dijk & Kintsch, 1983). Analogous structures to microstructures and macrostructures along with accompanying transformational processes have also been proposed (Crothers, 1979).

## Language as a Mediator of Thought

A second relationship language has to thought is that of mediator of cognition. As mediator, language allows one cognitive system to interact with, and sometimes control, another system. This aspect of language is perhaps most evident in the functioning of the phonological loop. The phonological loop and the visual-spatial sketch pad (discussed in a subsequent section) are the mechanisms that allow one to retain data in working memory so that it might be further analyzed (J. R. Anderson, 1995). Specifically, the data in sensory memory last for about a second before they decay. The phonological loop and the visual-spatial sketch pad are automatic rehearsal mechanisms that keep data active in working memory. By definition, then, language mediates thought via the phonological loop.

The mediational function of language is also evident in the development of complex skills. Specifically, complex skills are often mediated by language until they have been developed to the level of automaticity (Sokolov, 1972). For example, a learner will commonly rehearse via inner speech the various components of a complex skill at the early stages of skill development (Fitts, 1964). In short, we learn complex skills with the aid of words that we articulate to ourselves (Meichenbaum, 1977; Sokolov, 1972). The use and development of inner speech as a mediational tool for learning complex cognitive skills can be traced to the late 1960s and the early 1970s (Meichenbaum, 1985). Many of the current programs and practices that use inner speech evolved partially from laboratory-based investigations of children's self-mediated cognitive strategies in social situations (Kanfer & Goldfoot, 1966; Kanfer & Phillips, 1970). This research demonstrated that young children quite naturally use inner or covert speech to enhance their understanding and use of the rules and principles of social behavior within peer groups. Russian psychologist Luria (1961, 1969) proposed three stages by which the initiation and inhibition of voluntary behaviors come under verbal control. In the first stage, the speech of others controls and directs a child's behavior. In the second stage, the child's own overt speech becomes an effective regulator. Finally, in the third stage, a child's covert or inner speech is used to regulate behavior and cognition. (See Meichenbaum, 1975, and Wozniak, 1972, for reviews.) Inner speech has also been linked to learning tasks such as reading and problem solving (Bem, 1971; Flavell, Beach, & Chinsky, 1966; Reese, 1962). One model for teaching the use of inner speech as a mediational tool for enhancing learning includes:

1. Cognitive modeling—An adult model performs the task while talking to himself out loud.
2. Overt, external guidance—The child performs the same task under the direction of model.
3. Overt self-guidance—The child performs the task while instructing himself out loud.
4. Faded, overt, self-guidance—The child whispers the instructions to himself as he progresses through the task.
5. Covert self-instruction—The child performs the task while guiding his performance via inaudible or private speech. (Meichenbaum, 1985)

The process of going from external to internal speech is key to the instructional sequence and should not be considered, warned Meichenbaum (1985), a simple matter of faded overt speech. Rather, covert speech is a unique form of language with properties distinct from overt speech. Similarly, Vygotsky (1962) noted that the transfer from overt to covert speech is a change to a distinctly different form of cognition both in purpose and content.

Using the instructional model described above or variations of it, programs and practices have been constructed that purport to successfully develop varying levels of control over the disruptive behavior of hyperactive children (Douglas, Parry, Martin, & Garson, 1976), the overt negative behaviors of aggressive children (Camp, Blom, Herbert, & van Dournick, 1977), and the impulsivity of children (Bender, 1976; Meichenbaum & Goodman, 1971).

## Language as a Tool for Enhancing Thought

A third type of relationship language has to thought is as a tool to enhance one's own thinking and that of others. Used in this way, language does not mediate thought; rather, it is used as a somewhat artificial tool for eliciting certain types of thinking and as a tool for making more salient the type of thinking occurring at any given time so that it can be analyzed and subsequently improved. Language used to enhance thinking is always overt. This section considers both overt speech and writing as tools for enhancing thinking.

***Overt speech as a tool for enhancing thinking.*** The importance of overt speech as a tool for enhancing thinking was evidenced in 1974 when the National Institute of Education identified overt speech in the classroom as one aspect of its research agenda. Green (1983) provided a summary of the research funded at that time. Cazden (1986) explained that much of that research focused on identifying the linguistic rules which govern speech in specific classroom situations. A broader perspective for studying overt speech in classrooms, asserted Cazden (1988), is to view it as the vehicle that creates classroom context. Building on the work of Bateson (1972) and

Erickson (1975), Cazden (1979, 1988) showed that the use of oral language by both teachers and students serves to establish a classroom atmosphere that either elicits or discourages certain types of thinking. Cuing and questioning are two primary ways that teachers use overt speech to elicit specific types of thought.

Cuing involves teachers' use of overt speech to signal specific learning episodes. That is, teachers verbally signal the type of learning expected within a given period of time. Ideally students then retrieve appropriate mental scripts to match the learning episode. Elaborate coding schemes have been developed to describe the different forms of teacher language used as cues for various episodes (Mehan, 1979; Sinclair & Coulthard, 1975). Cues such as verbal advanced organizers that signal the structure of content are among the most powerful. That is, when students learn new content, the structure that information takes in permanent memory is greatly influenced by how the teacher talks about the content (Moore, 1977). A number of studies have shown that structure of content as stored in students' permanent memory corresponds more closely to the a priori structure of the content after verbal instruction (P. E. Johnson, 1967, 1969; P. E. Johnson, Cox, & Curran, 1970; Shavelson & Geeslin, 1973).

One of the primary ways that teachers signal the cognitive structure of content is through staging (Cazden, 1988; Clements, 1979). Staging refers to a set of decisions that a teacher (or any speaker or writer) makes to communicate information in the most efficient manner. Based on the work of Clark and Haviland (1977), C. H. Frederiksen (1977), and Grimes (1975), Clements identified staging rules such as (a) identification of topic, (b) determination of what is known and unknown, and (c) coordination with other topics.

The research on staging has illuminated the effects of cuing on students' understanding of textual information; the research on scaffolding has provided evidence for the importance of teachers' use of language to signal the structure of nontextual information. The distinguishing feature of scaffolded instruction is the prominent role of dialogue between teacher and students to provide the learner with enough support and guidance to comprehend information and perform tasks in a manner that would be beyond unassisted efforts (Wertsch, 1984; P. Wood, Bruner, & Ross, 1976). Scaffolded instruction involves reducing a task to a somewhat hierarchic, well-structured format. The teacher then keeps the learner in pursuit of the task, demonstrates an idealized version of the task, and marks the critical features of the task for the learner. Scaffolding derives its theoretical base from theorists such as Vygotsky (1978) and Wertsch (1984) who assert that an individual's learning of higher order cognitive processes is enhanced by shaping those processes via verbal interaction with expert models. This assertion is also supported by many of the current pedagogical models (Davies, 1980; Marzano, 1998; Pask, 1975; Reigeluth & Stein, 1983).

Questioning is a third way that teachers use overt speech to elicit specific types of thought. Christenbury and Kelly (1983) and Hunkins (1995) described and critiqued many of the taxonomic and classification systems used to study teacher questioning. In general, teachers ask far more questions than they are aware of. For example, elementary teachers who thought they were asking 12 to 20 questions every half hour were actually asking 45 to 150 (Nash & Shiman, 1974). There is some evidence that asking questions improves students' comprehension and retention of content (Yost, Avila, & Vexler, 1977). When questions are given after content has been presented and students are required to construct answers rather than select from among alternatives, the benefits tend to be strongest (Christenbury & Kelly, 1983). Higher level questions also appear to be instrumental in enhancing student thinking (Redfield & Rousseau, 1981), although there is considerable disagreement as to what constitutes higher-level questions (Fairbrother, 1975; R. Wood, 1977). One powerful distinction is that between recitation questions (those requiring students to simply retrieve information previously learned) and construction questions (those requiring students to construct new ideas or conclusions relative to information in permanent memory). Christenbury and Kelly (1983) described a system of questioning that is neither sequential nor hierarchic yet allows a teacher to systematically ask construction questions that stimulate various types and levels of thought.

A subset of the research on teacher questioning is the research on teacher use of "wait time." Expanding on M. Rowe's (1974) original definition of wait time as pausing for several seconds after asking a question to give students time to think before being called on to answer, Tobin (1987) identified a number of different types of wait time including the pause following any teacher utterance and any student utterance and the pause following any student utterance and preceding any teacher utterance. He concluded that extended teacher wait time after asking questions should be viewed as a necessary but insufficient condition for higher, cognitive-level achievement. Results obtained by Granato (1983) and Knickerbocker (1984) suggest that a longer wait time after questions provides students with opportunities to get involved in verbal interactions. Similarly, extended wait time has been associated with more student discourse (Swift & Gooding, 1983), more student-to-student interactions (T. W. Fowler, 1975; Honea, 1982), decrease in student confusion (DeTure & Miller, 1985), higher achievement (Riley, 1986; Tobin, 1986), and increase in complexity and cognitive level of student responses (DeTure & Miller, 1985; Fagan, Hassler, & Szabo, 1981).

Just as teachers use overt speech to enhance learning, so, too, do students. This assertion is supported by much of the research on small-group interactions within the cooperative learning literature (see D. Johnson, Maruyama, R. Johnson, Nelson, & Skon, 1981). It is a basic assumption of many cooperative learning strategies that student-to-student verbal interactions about content improve learning and increase the level of thinking: "It is through the medium of this interaction and communication within small groups cooperating on academic tasks that these team-learning methods strive to influence pupils' cognitive learning" (Sharan, 1980, p. 242).

A number of studies on the relationship between small-group interaction and achievement have highlighted the importance of helping behavior in improving student learning (Hanelin, 1978; J. A. Johnson, 1979; Slavin, 1978a, 1978b; for a review of the research on the effects of small-group interaction on student learning, see Webb, 1982). Further studies differentiated the effects for the individual providing the help from those obtained by the individual receiving the help. A majority of studies that analyzed the effects of providing help to peers in the form of verbal explanations (Peterson & Janicki, 1979; Peterson, Janicki, & Swing, 1981; Webb, 1980a, 1980c, 1980d) found that it increased achievement. However, the effects of receiving help are much less robust. Specifically, receiving help positively affects achievement when it is elicited by the individual receiving help rather than volunteered by the help giver (Webb, 1980a, 1980b). In fact, it has been found that terminal feedback—providing a correct answer in the absence of an explanation of why the error is incorrect—is negatively related to achievement (L. M. Anderson, Evertson, & Brophy, 1979). The explanation for the powerful effect of verbalization when helping a peer is that it forces the help giver to critically analyze and sometimes restructure known information (Bargh & Schul, 1980).

***Writing as a tool for enhancing thinking.*** In terms of the relationship of writing to thinking, Nickerson (1984) stated: "Writing is viewed not only as a medium of thought but also as a vehicle for developing it" (p. 33). It is the robust and complex nature of the writing task that renders it a powerful tool for enhancing thinking. By definition, the composing process is highly difficult. For example, in a study of writing performance within a number of disciplines, Perkins (1981) found that the ability to produce final copy easily and on the first draft is rare, even among professionals.

In a series of articles, Flower and Hayes (1980a, 1980b, 1981) developed a model for the writing process. Although it was criticized (Cooper & Holzman, 1983), it was widely used and highly influential in terms of shaping research in writing. As Applebee (1984) noted, it was "the most thoroughly formalized model of the writing process" (p. 582). That model was later revised (see Hayes, 1996). Flower and Hayes initially characterized writing as a set of iterative, recursive, phases which include planning, translating, and reviewing, all of which are under the control of an executive monitor. Within each phase the writer is continually weighing the effects of current decisions on those previously made. The longer the process continues and the more the quantity of written discourse increases, the more interdependency is effected. Over time the process becomes one of making decisions based on increasingly more numerous and complex conditions. The updated model (Hayes, 1996) outlined the writing process in even more complex terms by adding a number of components.

From these accounts, writing can be considered one of the most taxing of cognitive acts because it maximizes the load of data that must be maintained in working memory during its execution. The complexity of the writing process is easily seen from the perspective of J. Anderson's (1983; see also J. R. Anderson, 1995) production model of cognition. That model postulates that the more branch decisions involved in a cognitive act, the more difficult its execution. The numbers of decisions, then, that must be made during writing, and the interdependence of these decisions makes it one of the most difficult of cognitive processes. As writers become more skilled, their ability to monitor and control the many variables involved increases. It is this control that is hypothesized to generalize to other tasks (de Beaugrande, 1984).

Presumably, practice in writing should enhance performance in any cognitive process in which executive control over a number of variables is a factor (e.g., some forms of problem solving); however, not all forms of writing instruction will enhance such executive control. Specifically, in his meta-analysis of writing research, Hillocks (1986) concluded that it is only when teachers plan instructional activities that result in a high level of student autonomy and interaction about the problems faced in composing that writing instruction has a powerful effect on student thinking. Hillocks referred to this as the environmental mode of instruction.

In summary, language and thought are inextricably linked. Language can be viewed as a separate form of thinking that is at the root of human cognition. It can also be viewed as a mediator to thought, using covert speech to control and orchestrate one's own thinking. Finally, it can be viewed as a tool used by both teacher and student for enhancing thought, using spoken and written language to elicit and improve specific types of cognition.

## APPROACHES TO THE TEACHING OF THINKING AND THEIR BASES IN THE LANGUAGE ARTS

The recent interest in thinking has spawned the development of myriad programs and practices designed to enhance thinking. (For reviews of these programs and practices, see Baron & Brown, 1991; Chance, 1986; Costa, 1985a; Halpern, 1996; Nickerson, Perkins, & Smith, 1985.) Although there are many ways to categorize the different approaches to teaching thinking (e.g., L. B. Resnick, 1987; Segal, Chipman, & Glaser, 1985), the following four categories are useful in highlighting the role of the language arts in the teaching of thinking: metacognitive approaches, componential approaches, heuristic approaches, and critical- and creative-thinking approaches. In this section, programs and practices within those four categories are discussed along with the related language arts research within each category.

### Metacognitive Approaches

Metacognition as defined by Flavell (1976, 1977, 1978) refers to one's knowledge concerning one's own cognitive processes and products or anything related to them. Brown (1978) broke metacognition into two components: awareness and control of the factual or declarative knowledge necessary to complete a specific task and awareness and control over the processes or procedural knowledge to complete a task. Awareness and control refer to the executive monitoring of knowledge. (Declarative and procedural knowledge are discussed in depth in a subsequent section.) Others, such as Paris and Lindauer (1982) and Paris, Lipson, and Wixson (1983), broadened the notion of metacognition beyond the awareness and control of declarative and procedural knowledge to include the executive monitoring of one's self-system and how that self-system interacts with the task. In this section programs and practices that emphasize executive control of the self-system are first described.

Next are described programs and practices that emphasize executive control over task-related declarative and procedural knowledge.

***Control of the self-system.*** In a series of studies, McCombs (1984, 1986, 1987), building on the work of others (Baird & White, 1984; Connell & Ryan, 1984; Harter, 1982; Shavelson & Bolus, 1982), established that an individual's motivation for and efficiency at a given task are, at least, partially a function of a set of perceptions, goals, and beliefs referred to as the self-system. Programs and practices that attempt to improve students' knowledge and control of self usually employ some form of verbal mediation (use of covert speech) to generate positive affect and enhance efficacy. (For reviews of programs, see McCombs, 1984; W. Reynolds & Stark, 1983.) For example, drawing on the work of Ellis (1962), Luria (1961), and Vygotsky (1962), Meichenbaum (1977) developed verbal mediation strategies that provide the learner with an awareness of the effect (both negative and positive) of specific self-statements on task performance. Meichenbaum's strategies are based on the assumption that negative self-statements reflect the structure of the self-system through which a given task is processed. He asserted that by rehearsing positive self-statements in specific task situations one gradually changes the structure of the self-system relative to the task. To illustrate the relationship between self-statements and performance on creativity, Henshaw (1978) studied the verbalizations of high-creative versus low-creative college students and found that the high-creative students differed significantly from low-creative students in the frequency with which they emitted self-statements that were supportive and in the amount of positive affect they experienced for the task. Low-creative students produced significantly more negative self-statements and experienced more negative affect for the task. Working with army recruits, McCombs (1984, 1986) found that training in techniques to monitor and control the self-system improved subjects' perceptions of control and their ability to perform specific tasks. Allen (1972), however, warned that strategies aimed at mediating the self-system have long-term effects only when coupled with counseling.

***Control of task.*** Programs and practices emphasizing metacognitive control over task-related declarative and procedural knowledge are growing in number. In fact, over the last decade scores of "learning strategies" for increasing students' control over the processing of a task have been developed and tested. (For a review, see Derry & Murphy, 1986; Hattie, Biggs, & Purdie, 1996.) Snowman and McCown (1984) made a distinction between learning strategies and learning tactics. A learning strategy is an overall plan one makes for performing a task, whereas a tactic is a more specific skill one uses in the service of a strategy. Strategies are metacognitive. In fact, they are sometimes referred to as metastrategies or metacognitive strategies (Dansereau, 1978; Pressley, Borkowski, & O'Sullivan, 1984). Pressley, Levin, and Ghatala (1984) coined the acronym MAPS, for Metamemory Acquisition Procedures, to stand for instruction that enhances students' abilities to evaluate the tactics they are using to complete a specific task. For example, a strategy that teaches students a particular method for taking notes and then asks the student to evaluate the effectiveness of that strategy would be considered a MAPS technique. In general, MAPS techniques have been found to improve students' use of the specific tactics used in the task and their general metacognitive control over the task (Brown, 1978; Flavell, 1981). Metacognitive programs that are considered part of the mainstream emphasis to enhance thinking include the Productive Thinking Program and paired problem solving.

The Productive Thinking Program (Covington, 1985) is designed for upper elementary schoolchildren and reinforces a variety of metacognitive strategies such as setting goals, planning and monitoring progress toward goals. The program also emphasizes monitoring such self-system variables as resisting immobilization caused by failure anxiety. Compared with other programs, the Productive Thinking Program has been evaluated rather extensively (Covington, 1983, 1985). Subjects who have gone through the program exhibit more efficient use of the metacognitive strategies presented and, more important, stated L. B. Resnick (1987), they tend to use the strategies in tasks not covered in the program such as writing a report, studying for a test, or approaching a problem.

Whimbey and Lochhead (1982, 1984) described a paired problem-solving process in which students alternate the roles of problem solver and listener-critic. Its intent is to improve student abilities in such metacognitive strategies as analyzing tasks, formulating plans, and evaluating outcomes. According to Lochhead (1985), few formal evaluations have been conducted to assess the effectiveness of paired problem solving. The most carefully designed studies have involved courses that used paired problem solving in conjunction with other approaches with advanced secondary or post-secondary students. For example, Lochhead cited a 1979 summer program for 34 prefreshmen students who had scored below the 12th-grade level on a standardized reading achievement test. These students were subjected to a multiapproach course that included use of the text *Problem Solving and Comprehension* (Whimbey & Lochhead, 1982). Before and after results indicated that subjects increased their use of metacognitive strategies and exhibited significant grade-level gains in reading comprehension.

***Metacognition and the language arts.*** Although metacognition as it relates to a knowledge and control of the self-system has received little attention from the English language arts, metacognition as it relates to a knowledge and control of task has received a great deal of attention particularly within the research and theory on writing and reading. For example, a key component of the Hayes and Flower (1980; Hayes, 1996) model of writing is the monitor that exerts executive or metacognitive control over the component processes. Key to this metacognitive control of the task is goal setting. Specifically, writers translate high-level goals into subgoals. The result is that subgoals tend to pile up creating a potential overload on working memory (Flower & Hayes, 1981). The writer, in turn, develops strategies for handling this "memory overload" condition taking advantage of situations where the creation of one subgoal generates an opportunity for the completion of another (Hayes-Roth & Hayes-Roth, 1979). Thus, the generation of subgoals in the writing process is dynamic rather than a priori (Matsuhashi, 1982).

The result is that high-level goals are sometimes replaced by subgoals generated relatively late in the writing process. Thus, the end product of the composing process is often a surprise to the writer (Murray, 1978).

It is the metacognitive ability to monitor this highly complex process of juggling goals and subgoals that separates the writing of skilled versus novice writers and the writing of adults from that of children (Scardamalia, Bereiter, & Steinbach, 1984). However, it has been shown that children's metacognitive control over goals can be improved by giving them verbal prompts about possible next steps in the writing process as they "think aloud" while engaged in the task (Bereiter & Scardamalia, 1982; Scardamalia & Bereiter, 1983, 1985).

The influence of the research and theory on metacognition in the language arts is also evidenced in the literature on reading (Cox, 1994; Garner, 1994; Paris, Lipson, & Wixson, 1983). Parallels have been drawn between metacognition in reading and metacognitive behavior in other disciplines such as mathematics, memory, and problem solving (Brown, 1975; Kail & Hagen, 1982; L. B. Resnick & Ford, 1981; Siegler, 1983). The strategic reader, like the strategic mathematician or problem solver, juggles goals and subgoals relative to the purpose of reading, the changing nature of the text, and the extent to which information is new or old (Clark & Haviland, 1977). In fact, one of the more powerful reading interventions is Palincsar and Brown's (1984) reciprocal teaching, which is fundamentally metacognitive in nature. Reciprocal teaching employs a process of cooperative question asking between teacher and students to highlight many of the metacognitive demands of reading. The teacher models the overt summarizing, questioning, clarifying, and predicting processes, which are assumed to be internal processes executed during reading, while students comment on the quality of questions and summaries, and try to construct better ones. A meta-analysis of the research on reciprocal teaching by Rosenshine and Meister (1994) reported that it has an average effect size of .88.

## Componental Approaches

Componential approaches to teaching thinking are those that attempt to develop specific cognitive operations. Although many componential approaches also enhance metacognition, it is not a necessary by-product of such approaches. That is, specific cognitive operations can be enhanced without enhancing a general knowledge and control of self and task. Using the terminology of Snowman and McCown (1984), componential approaches stress learning tactics rather than learning strategies. Componential approaches can be organized into three categories: (a) model-based approaches, (b) eclectic approaches, and (c) single-tactic approaches.

***Model-based approaches.*** Some componential approaches attempt to operationalize a complete model of intelligence or learning. For example, the Structure of Intelligence (SOI) program (Meeker, 1969) is based on Guilford's model of intelligence (Guilford, 1967; Guilford & Hoepfner, 1971), which proposes 120 intellectual abilities that are combinations of *operations* (e.g., comprehending, remembering and analyzing), *content* (e.g., words, forms and symbols), and *products* (e.g., single words, groups and relationships). The SOI program reportedly reinforces 90 of Guilford's 120 components using materials that range from primary through high school grades. Evaluations of SOI are based on tasks specifically designed to measure Guilford's components and generally show an increase in subjects' abilities to perform these tasks as a result of using the materials. However, its transfer to non-SOI tasks has not been established (Nickerson, Perkins, & Smith, 1985). However, this same criticism can be leveled at many of the programs that purport to enhance thinking (L. B. Resnick, 1987).

Instrumental Enrichment (IE; Feuerstein, Rand, Hoffman, & Miller, 1980) is a program composed of a series of problem-solving tasks and exercises that are grouped in 14 areas. Exercises are called instruments rather than lessons because their intent is to be content free (Link, 1985). The goal of each instrument is to reinforce the cognitive operations relative to the *input phase* (e.g., gathering relevant information relative to a problem), the *elaboration phase* (e.g., operating on input information), and the *output phase* (e.g., reporting the desired result) of problem solving.

Feuerstein et al.'s (1980) model assumes that cognitive deficits occur when processing breaks down relative to the operations within any of the three phases (Messerer, Hunt, Meyers, & Lerner, 1984). The initial 2-year evaluation of IE in Israeli schools with students aged 12 to 15 (Feuerstein et al., 1980) indicated that IE produced substantial gains in performance in a variety of intellectual tasks including general cognitive tasks, as measured by Thurstone's Primary Mental Abilities test, and content-specific cognitive abilities, as measured by standardized achievement tests. In a replication of the original Feuerstein study, Ruiz and Castaneda (as cited in Savell, Twohig, & Rachford, 1986) administered IE to experimental and control Venezuelan children aged 10 to 14 over a 2-year period. The results indicated that subjects in the experimental group scored significantly higher than control subjects in all measures, which included intelligence tests, math tests, and language achievement tests. Similar studies have been conducted in Nashville, Toronto, and other cities. (For a review see Savell, Twohig, & Rachford, 1986.) Relative to the effectiveness of IE, Campione, Brown, and Ferrara (1982) suggested that the materials themselves have less to do with the program's success than the reinforcement of the specific cognitive components (input, elaboration, output) that are emphasized.

***Eclectic approaches.*** There are many componential approaches to teaching thinking that can be classified as eclectic; they employ multiple tactics but draw their components from various models of learning and intelligence as opposed to a single model. Included in such programs are Project Intelligence, BASICS, and Dimensions of Learning.

Begun in 1979, Project Intelligence was a joint effort by researchers at Harvard University, Bolt, Beranek and Newman, Inc., and the Venezuelan Ministry of Education to develop methods and materials that enhance the ability of students to perform a wide variety of cognitive operations including inferential use of information in long-term memory, hypothesis generation, predicting, classifying, problem solving, and decision making (Nickerson, Perkins, & Smith, 1985). The backbone of the program is approximately 100 lessons aimed at teaching and reinforcing these tactics.

The materials were initially tested using 12 experimental and 12 control classes. A variety of tests were administered to both groups including a number of general abilities tests and some special abilities tests developed by the researchers to measure specific skills within the program. A detailed discussion of the results appears in the project's final report (Harvard University, 1983). As summarized by Nickerson, Perkins, and Smith (1985), in the large majority of cases the gains shown by students in the experimental group were greater than those shown by the control. The differences were both statistically significant and substantial in size especially for the special abilities tests.

BASICS is an acronym for building and applying strategies for intellectual competencies in students (Ehrenberg, Ehrenberg, & Durfee, 1979). It is designed to enhance thinking in 18 thinking or learning tactics, which include such cognitive operations as noting differences and similarities, grouping, classifying, generalizing, and inferring causes and effects. Detailed, almost algorithmic processes are presented for each of the thinking tactics.

Although no formal evaluation of the BASICS program has been published, Nickerson et al. (1985) critiqued the program relative to its construct validity. They noted that the program appears conceptually sound in that the tactics are sequenced so that later ones build on earlier ones. "Also, all of the strategies (tactics) repeat certain characteristics that seem designed to foster a sound cognitive style. There is emphasis throughout on systematizing, thoroughness, checking judgments, storing or communicating results, justifying conclusions, and producing overt 'thought products'" (p. 180). However, they also noted that the program has some conceptual flaws in that some of the tactics are based on conceptions of thinking that do not reflect the latest research and theory in psychology. They stated that the effectiveness of the BASICS program "must remain an open question until the necessary evaluation studies are undertaken" (p. 181).

Dimensions of Learning (Marzano, 1992; Marzano et al., 1997) is an eclectic approach that is based on the Association for Supervision and Curriculum Development publication *Dimensions of Thinking* (Marzano et al., 1988). The program organizes thinking into five basic categories, or dimensions. Dimension 1 addresses the attitudes and perceptions students bring to a learning situation. Dimension 2 involves the acquisition and integration of new information and skill. Dimension 3 deals with the refinement and extension of knowledge via such processes as comparison, classification, induction and deduction. Dimension 4 addresses the use of knowledge within processes such as problem solving, decision making, and investigation. Finally, Dimension 5 includes mental dispositions such as controlling impulsivity and monitoring accuracy. Within each dimension are a variety of instructional techniques. For example, an adaptation of Ogle's (1986) K-W-L strategy (discussed in a subsequent section) is classified as a Dimension 2 strategy. Thus, the model can be thought of as an organizational framework for a wide variety of instructional strategies. Research on the model has demonstrated that it enhances students' ability to (a) engage in complex tasks and the metacognitive control of such tasks (Fisher, Horton, & Marzano, 1993; Tarleton, 1992), (b) establish strategies in problem-solving situations (Fahara, 1997; Thompson, 1999), and (c) acquire and integrate subject-specific knowledge (Dujari, 1994; Scanlon, 1997; M. K. Simon, Bornstein, & Snyder, 1992; Tarleton, 1992; Thompson, 1999).

***Single-tactic approaches.*** A number of componential approaches emphasize a single cognitive operation that is directly or indirectly related to some model of cognition or learning. Within such approaches subjects are usually presented with tactics rather than strategies for enhancing the underlying cognitive operation. Below five general categories of such tactics are described: encoding, matching, analyzing, representing, and extending.

***Encoding tactics.*** Encoding involves representing selected information in such a way as to make it more easily retrieved from permanent memory. Encoding tactics include rehearsal and mnemonics. In their review of a wide variety of tactics of which rehearsal is one type, Weinstein and Mayer (1986) reported that rehearsal includes verbatim rehearsal and generative rehearsal. Verbatim rehearsal involves the repetition of information to be remembered, either overtly or covertly, using words or mental pictures. Generative rehearsal involves the selection of information from a text via copying, underlining or highlighting and then subsequently repeating this selected information either covertly or overtly. Flavell, Friedrichs, and Hoyt (1970) found that students' spontaneous use of rehearsal tactics increases in frequency and effectiveness with age. In addition, it has been shown that students can be overtly taught to effectively use both verbatim rehearsal tactics (Kenney, Cannizzo, & Flavell, 1967) and generative rehearsal tactics (Rickards & August, 1975), but younger students (e.g., below the age of 7) are not adept at selecting appropriate rehearsal tactics across different tasks (Appel et al., 1972), nor are students below a certain age (e.g., sixth grade) adept at identifying important information on which to use rehearsal tactics (Brown & Smiley, 1977).

Mnemonic devices are learning tactics that enhance the recall of information (Belleza, 1981). A number of studies have shown rather dramatic effects on recall performance when using such mnemonic devices as the method of loci (Ross & Lawrence, 1968), the peg-word mnemonic (Bugelski, 1968), the link mnemonic (Delin, 1969), and the story mnemonic (Bower, 1972; Bower & Clark, 1969). Belleza (1981) explained that mnemonic devices have often been considered "artificial memory devices" because they use cognitive structures that, "somewhat disturbingly, have little or no relationship to the conceptual content of the material being learned" (p. 247). Belleza noted that much of the past research has, unfortunately, focused on the visual imagery aspects of mnemonics creating the inaccurate perception that mnemonics and visual imagery mediation are synonymous. In fact, mnemonics operate by the creation and use of a variety of types of *cognitive cuing structures*, which include selection of important information, organization of that

information, and creation of salient cues that are nonlinguistic and linguistic in nature.

***Matching tactics.*** A number of componentially based approaches fall under the general rubric of what J. Anderson (1983) referred to as matching, determining how one or more entities are alike and/or different on one or more characteristics, and then using those distinctions to reorganize the information. Research indicates that this is one of the most basic of cognitive operations (see Genter & Markman, 1994; Markman & Genter, 1993a, 1993b). Matching tactics include comparing, categorizing, and ordering.

Comparing is identifying and articulating the similarities and differences between elements. Although the difficulty of a comparison task is partially a function of the individual's knowledge of the content being compared (G. Mandler, 1983), skill at comparing can be improved. For example, Raphael and Kirschner (1985) found that students' comprehension, and their production of comparative written summaries, improved when they were taught specific types of comparison structures (e.g., whole/whole, part/part, and mixed).

Classifying also is a central component of many theories of cognition and learning (Mervis, 1980; Smith & Medin, 1981). To classify, individuals must be able to identify the common features or attributes of various entities that form a group or groups. There is evidence that young children can categorize information with which they are very familiar but have difficulty using categorization as a tool for processing unfamiliar content unless they receive explicit instruction to do so (Moely, 1977). Jones, Amiran, and Katims (1985) found that students' ability at categorizing can be improved with explicit instruction, yet extended practice and feedback is needed for transfer to occur.

Closely related to classifying is ordering, which is sequencing or ordering entities on selected characteristics or attributes. Although Piaget and Szeminska (1941) concluded that children do not usually master ordering until the concrete operational stage, generally at about age 7 or 8, Feuerstein et al. (1980) found that low-achieving and very young children can develop competence in ordering tasks when specific tactics are reinforced. Similarly, matrix outlining strategies (discussed in conjunction with representing components) have proven to be effective tools for enhancing the ability to order.

***Analyzing tactics.*** Analyzing tactics are those that help the learner identify component parts of information and articulate the subordinate and superordinate relationships among those parts. From this perspective analyzing tactics are fairly direct applications of Kintsch and van Dijk's (1978) theory of macrostructures and microstructures, J. Anderson's (1982, 1983) principle of generalization, and Bransford and Frank's (1976) concept of decontextualizing. Tactics in this category include summarizing, note taking, and finding main idea.

Brown, Campione, and Day (1981) use a rule-based approach to summarizing that includes deleting trivial and redundant material, substituting superordinate terms for lists, and selecting or inventing a topic. Their research suggests that younger and low-achieving students have difficulty using these rules, especially the last one, which requires them to select or invent a topic.

Often, they will select what interests them rather than what is a good organizer for the information that is to be summarized.

Note taking is another tactic that can be classified as analyzing. DiVesta and Gray (1972) found that note taking provides both encoding and storage functions. It aids the learner in creating a macrostructure for information and provides a form of external storage for later review. In general, results of note taking have shown better recall of information at a time proximal to the presentation of the information, but there have been mixed results at distal points (Barnett, DiVesta, & Rogozinski, 1981; Peper & Mayer, 1978).

Finding the main idea is another cognitive process that includes the properties of analysis. However, main idea as a construct is not well defined. For example, Cunningham and Moore (1986) listed 10 different ways of conceptualizing main idea and the task of finding it. From an instructional perspective, main idea is commonly approached as the topic sentence within textual information (Braddock, 1974). Ashton, O'Hear, and Pherson (1985) found that many of the linguistic cues for identifying topic sentences taught in study skill texts apply quite well to sociology textbooks. However, studies of other types of textbooks indicate that topic sentence is not a reliable cue for main ideas (Alexander, 1976; Axelrod, 1975). Another perspective of main idea is that it is the most salient discourse structure within the text (T. H. Anderson & Armbruster, 1985). From this perspective, much of the work on superordinate discourse structures (Meyer, 1975, 1985; van Dijk & Kintsch, 1983) supports the viability of instruction in main idea. For example, it has been found that informal oral summarizing can be effectively elicited from students before, during, and after reading text segments via teacher- and student-directed questions that focus attention on the subordinate and superordinate structure of discourse (Jones, Palincsar, Ogle, & Carr, 1987).

***Representing tactics.*** Representing tactics are those used to change the form of information to improve understanding and ease of recall. A key characteristic of representation is that the learner encodes the information in a new form or new modality. That is, the learner transforms linguistic information into some form that uses symbols and diagrams to represent semantic relationships among concepts. In a series of studies, Mayer (1989) showed that representation is a key aspect of understanding text-based information. Within this category fall graphic organizing tactics (e.g., webs and maps). Graphic organizers have been shown to enhance both comprehension and recall of information (Holley & Dansereau, 1984; Jones, Tinzmann, Friedman, & Walker, 1987; Van Patten, Chao, & Reigeluth, 1986). Also included in this category are the matrix outlining tactics that have been used to help students classify, identify, and articulate main ideas (Jones et al., 1985). Presumably, these tactics aid recall because they increase the number of association points with which information can be retrieved (J. R. Anderson, 1995). Similarly, they aid understanding because they increase the variety of information representation allowing for information linkages not possible in a strictly linguistic mode.

***Extending tactics.*** Extending tactics are those that enable the learner to go beyond what is explicitly stated in textual informa-

tion. Bartlett (1932) is usually credited as being the first psychologist to document the fact that individuals' recall of information read or heard is inaccurate; elements are distorted to conform to prior knowledge. He interpreted these results as an indication that information in permanent memory shapes and extends incoming information. In recent years, a number of types of information-shaping and extending tactics have been identified, most of them falling within the general rubric of inference. (For a review of extending tactics, see Reder, 1980.) For example, many typologies and thinking skills programs have defined various types of inductive and deductive tactics (Nickerson, Perkins, & Smith, 1985; Costa, 1985b). Many of these are based on inductive and deductive rules from syllogistic models. Some theorists have criticized the traditional definitions of induction and deduction (Deely, 1982; Eco, 1976, 1979, 1984) asserting that the normal process of inference is nonlinear and far more "messy" than that described within the inductive–deductive models.

Instructionally, extending is commonly reinforced by presenting students with tactics for creating analogies and metaphors. They have been shown to be powerful cognitive tools in developing ideas in oral discourse, composing, and creative thinking (Bransford, Sherwood, Rieser, & Vye, 1986; Mayer, 1984; Weinstein & Mayer, 1986). In addition, Koch (1970, 1974) developed tactics for eliciting strikingly original metaphoric language from children of all ages.

***Componential approaches and language arts.*** Many of the single-tactic componential approaches described above have roots or corollaries in the language arts. For example, a significant proportion of the previously described matching tactics for comparison and contrast were initially field-tested and evaluated in language arts settings (Jones et al., 1987; Raphael & Kirschner, 1985). Similarly, summarizing tactics have been used extensively within reading. For example, Day (as cited in Raphael, 1987) developed a series of six summarization rules designed for use with poor readers and writers. Working with average and above-average 11th-grade students, Bean, Singer, Sorter, and Frazee (1983) found that instruction in summarization rules increased students' ability to retrieve information from memory and express it in a succinct way, although it did not increase their ability to select key ideas. Similarly, McNeil and Donant (1982) found that sixth-graders could be taught to use summarization rules that significantly affected their comprehension scores (see Hidi & Anderson, 1986, for a review of research on summarization).

Note taking is an analyzing tactic that also has been studied within the context of the language arts. For example, note taking traditionally has been taught within language-arts-based study skills courses or as a part of composition courses (Weinstein & Mayer, 1986). A number of studies have demonstrated its effect on recall for information in notes, although instruction in note taking does not ensure that students will identify important information on which to take notes (Einstein, Morris, & Smith, 1985).

Main idea also is traditionally based in the language arts. For example, the International Reading Association published an edited work (Bauman, 1986) in teaching main idea as an aid to comprehension. Strategies covered include generating hypotheses before reading and then testing the accuracy of these hypotheses during and after reading, looking for superordinate structures, looking for linguistic cues, and looking for topic sentences (see Cunningham & Moore, 1986, and Winograd & Bridge, 1986, for reviews of the different conceptions of main idea and the different tactics for teaching it).

Representing tactics are relatively new in the language arts, although incidents of their use are rapidly increasing. Such tactics have been effectively used as tools for enhancing reading comprehension (Miccinati, 1988). For example, Singer and Bean (1984) found that students who created a graphic organizer for information read recalled more information than those who outlined. Similarly, Slater, Graves, and Piche (1985) found that representing in visual form produced better recall of information than taking notes. Representational techniques have also been used with the language arts as tools for improving vocabulary development (Marzano, Hagerty, Valencia, & DiStefano, 1987), taking notes (Dansereau, 1985), and developing content-area schemata (Freedman & Reynolds, 1980).

Extending tactics have received language arts attention primarily in the area of inferences made while reading. For example, Warren, Nicholas, and Trabasso (1979) developed a hierarchy of the types of reading inferences commonly made. The taxonomy includes logical inferences (e.g., motivation, psychological causation, physical causation), informational inferences (e.g., spatiotemporal, world frame), and value inferences (e.g., evaluative). Similarly, Crothers (1979) identified two major categories of text inferences (implicational and referential). Instructionally, within the language arts, a number of tactics have been developed that aid students in making and checking elaborative inferences. For example, Pearson and Johnson (1978) proposed a three-way relationship among questions, the text, and prior knowledge of the content being read. Using this basic framework, Raphael (1982, 1984) developed a QARS tactic (Question–Answer Relationships) in which students differentiate between questions for which the answers are "right there" in the text and are cued directly by the question stem versus questions that are in the text but must be found via a "think and search" process, versus questions for which the student will have to generate the answers "on their own."

## Heuristic Approaches

A number of approaches to teaching thinking are heuristically based. Heuristics are general rules that when followed increase the likelihood of success at a given task. At their core, heuristic approaches provide the learner with actions that when followed increase the likelihood of successful completing specific cognitive operations. Heuristic approaches differ from componential approaches in that they are more "macro" in nature; they deal with more global cognitive operations. Arguably, the techniques presented within heuristic approach are quite similar to the tactics presented within componential programs.

Although heuristics have been developed for a number of cognitive operations (e.g., Beyer, 1988), problem solving and decision making are commonly the focus of heuristically based

approaches. Both problem solving and decision making have been identified as central to a variety of situations (J. Anderson, 1982, 1983; Baron & Brown, 1991b; H. Rowe, 1985). Studies on expert versus novice approaches to problem solving indicate that experts differ from novice problem solvers in their knowledge and use of general problem-solving heuristics such as devising a plan, representing the problem, carrying out a plan, and checking results (Gick & Holyoak, 1980; Schoenfeld, 1980; H. A. Simon, 1980). Schoenfeld (1983a, 1983b) noted that expert problem solvers are better than novice problem solvers even when dealing with problems outside of their domain of expertise, because they use their general problem-solving heuristics better.

Most programs that attempt to foster thinking use a problem-solving orientation even though they might purport to emphasize decision making (see Baron & Brown, 1991b). For example, the Productive Thinking Program by Covington, Crutchfield, Davies, and Olton (1974) and IE by Feuerstein, Hoffman, and Miller (1980) use problem solving as the primary instructional vehicle. Wales and Stager (1977; see also Nardi & Wales, 1985) developed a heuristically based approach to enhancing problem solving and decision making that they refer to as Guided Design. Guided Design has been offered in high schools and colleges as a course to accompany a wide variety of disciplines (e.g., the humanities, the social sciences, the physical sciences and engineering). Using freshmen in engineering at West Virginia University, Wales (1979) found increases in grade point averages after 4 years even after controlling for grade inflation. As described by Resnick (1987):

Before the introduction of Guided Design, engineering students' average freshman GPAs were well below the university average; after Guided Design, their GPAs were well above the average. Students who had participated in the Guided Design program as freshmen also had higher four-year GPAs than (transfer) students who had not participated. (p. 21)

Many of the processes within the CoRT Thinking Program (de Bono, 1976, 1983, 1985) also can be classified as decision-making and problem-solving heuristics. The materials are as content free as possible, reflecting de Bono's desire to develop heuristics for real-life thinking versus artificial, academic situations. This position is echoed by N. Frederiksen (1984), who noted that most of the problems presented to students in academic situations are well structured with straightforward paths to a solution, whereas problems faced in life are not.

Although it is probably the most widely used program for teaching thinking on an international scale, CoRT has not been extensively evaluated (L. B. Resnick, 1987). De Bono (1976) reported several experiments involving idea counts contrasting students who had received CoRT instruction with control groups. Results indicated that CoRT instruction leads to the production of more ideas and a more balanced and less egocentric view of problems. Edwards and Baldauf (1983) reported a study in which 10th-grade students in a science course were exposed to the CoRT materials. The researchers found a statistically significant relationship between gain scores on items testing CoRT heuristics and science exam scores after controlling for IQ. "This says that those who learned CoRT better also learned science better, discounting IQ, suggesting that CoRT addresses some aspect of ability in science other than IQ" (Nickerson, Perkins, & Smith, 1985, p. 218).

***Heuristic approaches and the language arts.*** Again, given their close connections, many of the language arts tactics discussed previously also might be described as heuristics (e.g., Brown, Campione, & Day, 1981; Raphael, 1982, 1984). Within the language arts, many of the approaches to processing textual information are heuristically based. For example, Ogle's (1986) K-W-L is a heuristically based approach for improving student comprehension of textual material. It involves having students identify what they know (K), what they would like to know (W), and what they have learned (L) within the process of reading. Similarly, PReP, which is an acronym for Pre-Reading Plan, is a three-step procedure intended to help students access and use prior knowledge while reading (Langer, 1982). Closely related is Anticipation, Realization, and Contemplation, or ARC, developed by Estes (in Marzano et al., 1987), which helps students articulate what they think they know in a text, note what they would like to know, and then summarize their findings after reading.

One text-processing heuristic is Dansereau's (1985) MURDER, which is an acronym for:

1. Setting the *mood* to study.
2. Reading for *understanding*.
3. *Recalling* the material without referring to the text.
4. *Digesting* the material by recalling and amplifying it.
5. *Expanding* knowledge by self-inquiry.
6. *Reviewing* mistakes.

The research on MURDER indicates that it is a highly generalizable technique that can be learned with relative ease and produces positive effects on student understanding and recall of information (Chance, 1986; Dansereau, 1985).

## Critical- and Creative-Thinking Approaches

The approaches to teaching thinking described thus far spring from a psychological tradition. However, it was not until the mid-19th century that scholars viewed the human mind as a working mechanism with underlying operations that could be studied from a psychological perspective (H. Rowe, 1985). In contrast, the roots to the philosophical interest in thinking reach back to the classical past. Greene (1984) noted that in the Western World, philosophy preceded by at least 2,000 years the growth of what we now call psychology. At the heart of the philosophic perspective of thinking is the use of reason to guide behavior (Paul, 1990). For example, Aristotle described the process of discerning truth through rational thought as grasping the design or *telos* of reality.

Most critical-thinking approaches to enhancing thinking are rooted in philosophy. Although once defined in a narrow sense as assessing the accuracy of statements, critical thinking is now defined in a more robust manner as "reasonable reflective thinking that is focused on deciding what to do or believe" (Ennis, 1985, p. 54). This broader conception of critical thinking is consistent with the adopted educational goals of most states and school systems (Goodlad, 1984) primarily because critical thinking is considered essential for democratic citizenship (Dewey, 1916; Remy, 1980).

As opposed to componential and heuristic approaches, which focus on fairly specific cognitive operations, critical-thinking approaches attempt to enhance use of informal logic and dispositions of thought neither of which is easily reduced to a series of steps. Teaching informal logic as a means of enhancing thinking presupposes the existence of a mental logic. Johnson-Laird (1983) explained that in an attempt to describe how humans can draw conclusions that must be true given that the premises are true, some have postulated the existence of a mental logic (e.g., Gentzen, 1964; Lakoff, 1970). An extreme form of this idea is that "reasoning is nothing more than the propositional calculus itself" (Inhelder & Piaget, 1958, p. 305). It is well known that many 19th-century logicians (e.g., Boole, 1854; Mill, 1874) regarded logic as providing the basis of everyday reasoning. That is, they assumed that one is always using logic to make decisions, solve problems, and complete tasks. However, in recent years a number of studies have shown that, in everyday thinking, highly intelligent individuals often fall prey to a variety of errors in logic (Perkins, Allen, & Hafner, 1983; Staudenmayer, 1975). It is now more commonly assumed that people have the power to use mental logic within their daily endeavors but frequently misunderstand or forget premises and infuse additional and unwarranted assumptions into their reasoning (Henle, 1978).

Until recently, many theorists (e.g., Chapman & Chapman, 1959; Henle, 1962) assumed that mental logic was akin to Aristotelian logic. However, a number of researchers (e.g., Braine, 1978; Johnson-Laird, 1983) have demonstrated that pure Aristotelian logic does not account for many common inferences. Consequently, modern theories conceptualize mental logic in a way that incorporates many of the principles of schema-driven models of inference (e.g., Warren, Nicholas, & Trabasso, 1979).

Some critical-thinking programs have attempted to develop mental logic through the teaching of syllogistic rules of reasoning. For example, IE (Feuerstein, Hoffman, & Miller, 1980) contains instruments that deal with syllogisms. Similarly, Philosophy for Children (Lipman, Sharp, & Oscanyan, 1980) includes exercises in syllogistic reasoning. More commonly, though, critical-thinking programs include practice in recognizing informal fallacies (e.g., the gambler's fallacy, equivocation) that purportedly introduce error into one's normally error-free system of mental logic (e.g., Beyth-Marom & Dekel, 1985; Negin, 1987; Toulmin, Rieke, & Janik, 1981).

Although there has been research on the ability of both children and adults to reason in ways consistent with principles of logic (e.g., Johnson-Laird, 1975; Johnson-Laird & Steedman, 1978), studies linking the teaching of formal or informal logic with achievement are inconclusive (Halpern, 1996). Bransford (1979) noted that it is generally assumed that practice in performing logic problems and recognizing informal fallacies will increase the accessibility of these skills in everyday reasoning situations. However, there is evidence that students who receive only formal reasoning exercises such as these may have a very limited idea of the purpose of the exercises; they might, therefore, be able to activate appropriate logic-related skills when presented with familiar problems yet not be able to transfer these skills to other situations (Bransford, Arbitman-Smith, Stein, & Vye, 1985; Brown, Bransford, Ferrera, & Campione, 1986; Maratsos, 1977). Outside of the classroom there is, however, a growing interest in using informal logic as a clinical tool for increasing patients' ability to control dysfunctional emotions through increased emphasis on rational thought. For example, based on the work of Ellis (1977), Cohen (1987) described how therapy patients can be taught to use an adaptation of Aristotle's practical syllogisms to gain insight into and control over their irrational behaviors.

A second approach to teaching critical thinking is dispositional in nature. Dispositions, as described here, are habits of thought, cognitive "mental sets" for specific situations (L. B. Resnick, 1987). There have been a number of attempts to identify the dispositions of effective reasoning. For example, building on the work of Dewey (1916), Baron (1985) identified a number of dispositions for "good thinking." These include such mental habits as recognizing a sense of disequilibrium or doubt, identifying goals, searching for evidence, and revising one's plans when appropriate. Similarly, Ennis (1985) identified a set of critical-thinking dispositions that include many of Baron's along with seeking precision, looking for alternatives, and seeing others' points of view.

Reinforcing critical-thinking dispositions is a far less straightforward process than reinforcing the skills of informal logic. Here the tools are discussion (commonly Socratic) and modeling of dispositions around issues gleaned from literature or current events (Paul, 1990). One model for enhancing critical-thinking dispositions is Philosophy for Children (Lipman, Sharp, & Oscanyan, 1980). Although, as mentioned previously, the program does contain activities designed to enhance informal logic, it also attempts to enhance critical-thinking dispositions by developing a community of inquiry in the classroom (Chance, 1986). This is accomplished by teacher and students' interactions around a set of booklets (Lippman 1974, 1978, 1980) specially designed to highlight issues that elicit specific critical-thinking dispositions.

Relative to other programs, Philosophy for Children is one of the most thoroughly evaluated. (For reviews, see Chance, 1986; Lipman, 1985.) For example, Haas (in Chance, 1986) studied the effects of Philosophy for Children on 200 fifth- and sixth-graders over a 6-month period while 200 students from other schools acted as controls. A comparison of reading scores on the Metropolitan Achievement Test revealed that those who had studied Philosophy for Children gained an average of 8 months in reading ability; the comparison subjects advanced 5 months in the same time. In the initial evaluation of the program, 40 fifth-grade students were randomly assigned to experimental and control groups. The experimental group received 18 40-minute sessions on Philosophy for Children over a period of 9 weeks. Both groups were initially tested in the California Test of Mental Maturity. The groups were not significantly different in pretesting, but in posttesting the experimental group's mental age scores were 27 months higher than those of the control group. Two years after the study, the experimental group had significantly higher reading scores in the Iowa Achievement Test even though the two groups were not significantly different at pretesting. The program also has produced positive effects on student participation in class, social behavior and motivation (Chance, 1986).

Closely related to critical thinking is creative thinking. Both require a certain precision and rigor of thought, yet creative thinking is geared more toward the production of information whereas critical thinking is geared more toward the analysis of information. Halpern (1984) stated that "creativity can be thought of as the ability to form new combinations of ideas to fulfill a need" (p. 344). Perkins (1984) also stressed the notion of new and unique combinations of ideas as a defining characteristic of creative thinking but emphasized the importance of generating a product (mental or physical) that fulfills a specific function in an appropriate, yet unique, way. A number of approaches to creative thinking are highly dispositional in nature (e.g., Amabile, 1983; Marzano et al., 1988) stressing the fact that creative products spring from a set of high-level operating principles (dispositions) engaged in by an individual.

In spite of its highly dispositional nature, the teaching of creativity is commonly approached from a heuristics or tactics perspective and is usually practiced on gifted populations (Mitchell, 1980, 1984). Many approaches to enhancing creativity focus on solving novel and sometimes unstructured problems in new and unusual ways. For example, two international, interscholastic competitions, the Future Problem Solving Program (Crabbe, 1982; Torrance, 1980) and Olympics of the Mind (Gourley, 1981) use a problem-solving format to enhance creative thinking. It is estimated that over 150,000 gifted students participate each year in each of these programs (Torrance, 1986). Both programs use a game format in which teams compete with one another in solving specially selected problems. Team responses are scored on a number of criteria including originality and divergence of thinking.

In a review of 166 experimental studies of teaching creativity skills at elementary and secondary levels since 1972, Torrance (1986) found that 17% used some type of creative problem-solving process similar to those used in Olympics of the Mind and Future Problem Solving. Torrance reported that other approaches included the use of media and reading, the creative arts, training in affective components, tactics to effect altered awareness, and packaged materials. Of these, the creative problem-solving approaches had a 77% success rate.

***Critical and creative thinking and the language arts.*** Critical and creative thinking is grounded in the English language arts in a variety of ways. For example, language arts teachers have traditionally used oral and written language as tools for enhancing critical and creative thought. Similarly Socratic questions that induce thoughtful student response, large- and small-group discussions, in-depth analysis of texts, the study of language in relation to nonprint media, propaganda, and persuasion, among others, have been means to this end. Indeed, critical and creative thought can be considered the very core of literacy (L. M. Rosenblatt, 1994).

Defined in the "low" sense, literacy is the ability to read and write in a manner consistent with the adult norms in a society (L. B. Resnick, 1987). However, defined in the "high" sense, literacy includes many of the critical- and creative-thinking skills and dispositions (L. B. Resnick, 1987). For example, Tuman (1987) described the low model of literacy as the ability to read with understanding anything that one could understand if it had been spoken and the ability to write so that it could be read, anything that one can say. The high model of literacy, asserted Tuman, includes all characteristics of the low model but also involves the cultivation of the habits of critical and creative thinking.

Although the high-literacy tradition is less popular (with many of the national reports being concerned with functional and normal literacy for adults), there are a growing number of examples of attempts to frame literacy in the high fashion. For example, the College Board (1983) in its description of the necessary skills for success in postsecondary education explicitly, listed reasoning and a number of critical and creative thinking dispositions as fundamental literacy requirements. Similarly, in 1986, the Massachusetts Department of Education made critical and creative thinking an integral part of their assessment of the reading ability of third-, seventh-, and eighth-grade students (Swartz, 1987).

The high-literacy tradition has emphasized critical and creative thinking under the general rubric of rhetorical invention (Clanchy, 1983; Clifford, 1984). Kinneavy's (1980) work on the invention process is of particular importance here. Also included in the high-literacy tradition are new theories of the nature and process of reading. Specifically, L. Rosenblatt's (1978; see also L. M. Rosenblatt, 1994) work on the transactional nature of literacy has helped define reading and writing as processes that, by definition, include critical and creative thought. Perhaps the most comprehensive attempt to incorporate the high-literacy tradition within the framework of the language arts is Moffett's (1968; see also Moffett & Wagner, 1983) "interaction" approach. Moffett conceptualized the "universe of discourse" to encompass the linguistic modes of listening, speaking, reading, and writing; the different forms of audience; and the egocentricity versus the exocentricity (decentration) of the thought being experienced. The ultimate goal of a language arts program in Moffett's scheme is to create flexible language users and thinkers, those capable of using different modes of discourse for different audiences at differing levels of decentration. Instructionally, Moffett's model calls for a classroom laid out for simultaneous group and individual activities (e.g., games, the arts, drama) with no set curriculum. Rather, students progress through self-selected and teacher-directed activities. Interaction among peers and teachers and students is the key to the curriculum. The high-literacy nature of Moffett's approach is evident in its emphasis on student's creation of new products (e.g., essays, plays, poems), which implicitly demand attention to invention, arrangement, style, delivery, synthesis, extension, and other activities associated with critical and creative thought. Although Moffett's approach has received some criticism for its lack of empirical testing (Nickerson, Perkins, & Smith, 1985), it has for years served as a model for those curricular and instructional

changes that can, and perhaps should, occur when one tries to operationalize high literacy.

In summary, the various approaches to teaching can be described as metacognitive, componential, heuristic, and critical and creative. Metacognitive approaches emphasize strategies that help the learner control the general processing of a task and components of the self system as they relate to the task. Componential approaches attempt to reinforce single, or sets of, cognitive operations by presenting the learner with tactics designed to enhance performance in specific cognitive operations. Heuristically based approaches focus on slightly more global cognitive operations and provide the learner with rules which facilitate the execution of these operations. Finally, critical and creative approaches are geared toward enhancing use of informal logic as well as various dispositions toward critical and creative thought.

Many of the current practices designed to enhance thinking have their roots or strong corollaries in the language arts. Metacognition, especially as it relates to control of task, is emphasized in the research and practice on both writing and reading. Some of the componential approaches (e.g., comparing, summarizing, note taking, finding main idea, representing, and tactics) have explicit tactics developed and used within the language arts. Similarly, many techniques designed to improve comprehension are heuristically based. Finally, critical and creative thinking are reinforced in the language arts through various approaches to reinforcing high literacy.

## ADVANCES IN THINKING AND THE LANGUAGE ARTS

Just as the teaching of thinking owes much to the language arts, the language arts can benefit from the advances in the teaching of thinking. Specifically, the scope of the language arts can be considerably broadened by incorporating some of the current work on thinking. Shuell (1986) asserted that the stage is set for the development of a comprehensive theory of learning, one that would illustrate the interrelationship of the various types of thinking within a successful learning experience.

There have been a number of attempts to describe fairly robust frameworks of intelligence and learning (e.g., Baron, 1982; Sternberg, 1985). In spite of the breadth of these efforts, no single model exists that is readily translatable into classroom pedagogy. However, from the models and frameworks that do exist, a number of principles can be identified that have significant implications for language arts instruction. Below, five such principles are described.

### Principle 1: Affect Influences Thought

The relationship of affect to thought has been recognized for years (Bearison & Zimiles, 1986; Combs, 1982; Ellis, 1977; G. Mandler, 1983; Meichenbaum, 1977). Piaget (1962) proposed a metaphor likening affect to the gasoline that fuels the engine of the intellect. Any discussion of affect requires some consideration of the physical workings of the brain because affect, by definition, is inherently physiological.

There are a number of different perspectives on the nature of affect. In fact, even the term *affect* is commonly misunderstood (Stuss & Benson, 1983). Affect is the broadest term subsuming the terms feeling, emotion, and mood. The term *feeling* refers to one's internal physiological state at any given point in time. *Emotions* refer to the combination of feelings and the thoughts that are associated with the feelings. Finally, the term *mood* refers to a long-term emotion or the most representative emotion over a long period of time. From these definitions, one might conclude that internal physiological states are the primary elements of feelings, emotions, and moods.

Many researchers agree that the limbic system is the part of the brain responsible for internal physiological states (M. Gazzaniga, 1992; LeDoux, 1994; Restak, 1994; Sylwester, 1995). The limbic system consists of a number of specific organs and elements that include the pituitary gland, the thalamus, the hippocampus, and the amygdala. It is generally believed that the amygdala, an almond-shaped organ buried in each temporal lobe, "houses the main circuits that color our experiences with emotions" (Pinker, 1997, p. 371)—that is, internal physiological states. Relative to the discussion in this chapter, it is important to note that the limbic system affects virtually every part of the brain (Damasio & Van Hoesen, 1983). To illustrate, Sylwester (1995) explained that the limbic system is central to the execution of such rudimentary processes as how we categorize memories and what we choose to pay attention to. Pinker (1997) noted that the amygdala even effects the decision-making circuiting of the cortex (p. 372). All of this implies that affective representations permeate human memory.

The influence affect exerts over thought is further highlighted when one considers its chemistry. It appears that one type of neurotransmitter—peptides—plays a vital role in the determination of internal physiological states (M. Gazzaniga, 1992; LeDoux, 1994, 1996). The important aspect of peptides, in terms of understanding the nature of affect, is that they modulate one's experience of pleasure and pain. Additionally, peptides transmit data not only through the nervous system but also via the circulatory system and air passages, again proving evidence for the robust influence of affect.

Some researchers have identified basic emotions. For example, Tomkins (1962) proposed the existence of eight basic emotions: surprise, interest, joy, rage, fear, disgust, shame, and anguish. Ekman (1992) had a shorter list of basic emotions: surprise, happiness, anger, fear, disgust, and sadness. Plutchik (1980, 1993) had one of the more well-developed theories of emotions, positing a circle of emotions analogous to a circle of colors in which the mixing of elementary colors results in new colors.

Pinker (1997) argued that sociologists have erroneously concluded that certain cultures experience some emotions whereas others do not:

cultures surely differ in how often their members express, talk about, and act on various emotions. But that says nothing about what their people feel. The evidence suggests that the emotions of all normal members of our species are played on the same keyboard. (p. 365)

The keyboard Pinker referred to is the internal physiological states produced by the limbic system. Stated differently, all cultures experience the same range of physiological states or feelings. However, the extent to which they have names for these states or openly discuss these states differs dramatically from culture to culture.

Affect, then, can be described as a continuum of internal physiological states that are interpreted as feelings, emotions, and ultimately, moods. The endpoints of the physiological continuum are pleasure and pain. Different cultures make different distinctions regarding specific types of internal states in terms of the labels they employ and the extent to which they publicly acknowledge their feelings. However, the experience of feelings is probably identical from culture to culture.

As mentioned previously, some psychologists believe that, over time, language or the linguistic system becomes the dominant mode of processing (see J. M. Mandler & Ritchey, 1977). Conversely, arguments are also made that the emotional system is the primary representational modality. Specifically, a good case can be made for the assertion affective exerts the most influence over human thought and experience. This case is well articulated in LeDoux's (1996) *The Emotional Brain: The Mysterious Underpinnings of Emotional Life*.

Among other things, as a result of his analysis of the research on emotions, LeDoux (1996) concluded that human beings have little direct control over their emotional reactions, and once emotions occur, they become powerful motivators of future behavior. For LeDoux, emotions are primary motivators that often outstrip an individual's system of values and beliefs relative to their influence on human behavior. This was demonstrated in a study by Nisbett and Wilson (1977) who found that people are often mistaken about internal causes of their actions and feelings. The researchers noted that individuals always provide reasons for their actions. However, when reasoned and plausible reasons are not available, people make up reasons and believe them. As described by LeDoux, this illustrates that the forces that drive human behavior cannot be attributed to the rational conclusions generated by our linguistic mind but are functions of the inner workings of our emotional mind.

***Implications for the language arts.*** The role of affect in human thought has powerful implications for the language arts. In fact, affect is commonly considered in current models of reading and writing (see Hayes, 1996). However, the area of the language arts where the new research and theory in affect has the potential of making the biggest impact is probably reader response.

As described by Probst (1988), theories of literary response can be placed on a continuum. At one end is the New Criticism. According to the New Criticism, true literary response should be bounded by the meaning conveyed within the text without any elaboration or speculation by the reader. Probst notes that the pedagogy inspired by the New Criticism subordinates the reader to the text. Scholes (1982) characterized the type of instructional practices inspired by the New Criticism as devoid of any reference to the context in which a literary work was created:

Students were given poems to interpret with their titles removed, their author's names concealed, and their dates ignored. Anthologies were produced with the works ordered not by chronology but by the alphabet, with biographical information omitted or hidden in appendices, with no visible clues as to country or date or origin. (p. 15)

At the other end of the continuum are theories that locate the source of meaning in the reader. For example, Bleich (1978) insisted that knowledge is made rather than found. For Bleich, all but the simplest acts of perception are in fact intellectual acts of making symbols and then interpreting them.

In the middle of the continuum is the approach represented by L. Rosenblatt (1978; see also L. M. Rosenblatt, 1994) and Iser (1978), commonly referred to as the transactional approach. In very rough terms, the transactional approach posits an interaction, or "transaction," between the reader and the text. Although the reader's unique perspective will greatly influence the shape the literary work takes in his mind, the work itself has the power to affect his responses, guiding him in some directions and steering him away from others. It is the transactional approach to reader response and that articulated by Bleich (1978) that might benefit from an in-depth understanding of affect. Specifically, Marzano (1991) described how readers can use their emotional response as an entry point to ascertain their attitudes and beliefs about the content of the passage. This information, in turn, can lead readers to an awareness of specific incidents in their lives that were the foundations for the identified attitudes and beliefs. One's emotional response, then, can be the pivotal point for analysis of reader response. Squire (1994) implied that this perspective is a useful and potentially beneficial one for future research in reader response.

## Principle 2: Learning Occurs in an Attitudinal Context

Learning of any type takes place in an attitudinal environment that either enables or inhibits learning (Weiner, 1972, 1983). Simply stated, one is or is not "mentally set" for learning at any given time. Technically stated, one's thinking at any time can be mathemagenic (i.e., conducive to learning) or mathemathanic (i.e., detrimental to learning) (Loman, 1986; Rothkopf, 1970). Marzano (1998; Marzano & Marzano, 1987) identified five categories of attitudes that determine one's mental set for learning:

1. *Attitudes About Self-Attributes.* A great deal of research attests to the importance of one's beliefs about his or her personal attributes (see Bandura, 1982, 1991, 1993, 1996, 1997; Connell & Ryan, 1984; Markus & Ruvulo, 1990; Markus & Wurf, 1987). These beliefs are commonly thought of as existing in categories such as beliefs about physical appearance, intellectual ability, athletic ability, social ability, and so on (Harter, 1990). It is the combined effect of these beliefs that constitutes one's overall self-concept or "sense of self."

2. *Attitudes About Self and Others.* Some psychologists assert that human beings have an innate drive for acceptance within one or more groups (see Combs, 1962, 1982; Maslow, 1968). The extent to which an individual perceives that he or she has high status within groups that he or she values determines the individual's overall sense of acceptance.

3. *Attitudes About the Nature of the World.* Beliefs about the nature of the world form one's worldview or epistemology (Bagwell-Reese & Brack, 1997; Mau & Pope-Davis, 1993). As Kluckhohn and Strodtbeck (1961) noted, it is this system that addresses fundamental perceptions such as the relationship of human beings to nature, the temporal focus of human nature, and whether the world is generally a hostile versus friendly environment.

4. *Attitudes About Efficacy.* Efficacy deals with the extent to which one believes he or she is in control of what happens to them. This striving for control of one's life has been described as an inborn drive (Deci & Ryan, 1985; White, 1959), an "intrinsic necessity of life" (Adler, 1956), "a primary motivational propensity" (DeCharms, 1968), a motive system that impels the organisms, and a universal "inborn desire" for competence (Skinner, 1995). Research indicates that self-efficacy is not a generalizable construct. Rather, an individual might have a strong sense of efficacy in one situation yet feel relatively powerless in another (see Bandura, 1997; Seligman, 1990, 1994).

5. *Attitudes About Purpose.* Perhaps the most overarching category of attitudes and beliefs addresses life purpose or perceptions about the purpose, or lack thereof, of life. Philosophers such as Frankl (1967) and Buber (1958) asserted that beliefs about one's ultimate purpose are a central feature of one's psychological makeup. A case can be made that this set of beliefs ultimately exerts control over all other elements in the self-system because the purpose or purposes identified for one's life dictate what the individual considers important (see Marzano, 1998).

*Implications for the language arts.* The principle that learning occurs within an attitudinal context has fairly clear implications for the language arts. Specifically, language arts instruction should attend to the mental context or attitudinal environment of the learner and perhaps provide students with specific strategies for establishing an awareness and control of their mental set. Instructional techniques that indirectly address students' attitudes were introduced in the late 1970s with the "effective schools" research (see Brophy & Good, 1986; Emmer, Evertson & Anderson, 1980). However, more direct interventions have been developed that are intended to make learners more aware of their attitudes as expressed in their self-talk and then dampen the effects of the negative attitudes and perceptions by altering self-talk (Ellis, 1962; Meichenbaum, 1977). In reading, Mathewson (1985) detailed the influence attitude has on the process. Additionally, Mathewson (1994) identified specific instructional implications of his model that include: fostering foundational attitudes in students about reading, and identifying and addressing negative attitudes in students prior to engaging in the reading process.

## Principle 3: Knowledge Comes in Two Basic Types

A fundamental distinction in psychology is that between declarative and procedural knowledge. Snow and Lohman (1989) noted that this distinction is one of the most basic in terms of guiding educational practice.

***Declarative knowledge.*** Declarative knowledge is factual in nature and can be subdivided into at least four basic types: concepts, facts, principles, and schemata. Concepts are abstract structures usually represented by a word within a society (Klausmeier, 1985). Relative to classroom learning, concepts can be organized into four broad categories: animate entities (e.g., animals, plants), inanimate objects (e.g., weapons, tools), locations (e.g., North America, Denver), and events (e.g., festivals, carnivals) (Marzano, 1987).

Facts are statements of relationships between or among concepts. Linguistically, facts are commonly communicated as propositions—"conceptual structures that are the minimal bearers of truth" (van Dijk, 1980, p. 107). For example, *Columbus*, *discovery*, and *America* are concepts but are not information that can be examined for truth or falsity. However, "Columbus discovered America" is a proposition, because one can ask and answer whether it is true or false. Facts, then, are propositions important to a given content area.

Like facts, principles are propositional in form. However, principles assert information that can be exemplified whereas facts do not. Moreover, principles tend to be used as major organizers of domain specific content whereas facts do not (Klausmeier, 1985). Katz (1976) identified four types of principle important to various content areas:

1. Cause and effect (e.g., "Tuberculosis is caused by the organism microbacterium tuberculosis").
2. Correlational (e.g., "The increase in lung cancer among women is directly proportional to the increase in the number of women who smoke").
3. Probability (e.g., "The chances of giving birth to a boy during any one pregnancy is 52").
4. Axiomatic (e.g., "All people are created equal").

Schemata represent the broadest and perhaps loosest category of declarative knowledge. Rumelhart (1980) described schemata as "packages" of information stored in permanent memory. A commonly used example of a schema is that knowledge associated with going to a restaurant. That is, people in our culture have an internalized restaurant schema that includes knowledge about reading a menu, ordering food, waiting for it to come, eating with an array of utensils, and paying the bill. Theorists and researchers in artificial intelligence (e.g., Schank & Abelson, 1977) subdivide the broad notion of schemata into a number of distinct types, whereas psycholinguists commonly do not make fine distinctions as to different categories or types of schemata.

Once initially learned, declarative knowledge undergoes changes. Theories of change in declarative knowledge have been extensively reviewed by Reynolds, Sinatra, and Jetton (1996). Rumelhart and Norman (1981) identified three ways in which declarative knowledge (schemata) can be modified: accretion, tuning, and restructuring. Accretion refers to the changes in knowledge in permanent memory over time due to the gradual accumulation of information. It involves additive components. Tuning refers to the creation of generalizations about existing schema and the identification of default values. Finally, restructuring refers to the creation of new structures either to reinterpret old information or create new information. Vosniadou and Brewer (1987) distinguished between global restructuring and domain-specific restructuring. Global restructuring refers to changes in cognitive operations that work on knowledge in permanent memory. In contrast to global restructuring is domain-specific restructuring, which is not a change in cognitive operations but a change in the knowledge within a domain. Vosniadou and Brewer identified three categories of domain-specific restructuring: weak restructuring, strong restructuring, and paradigm shift.

Much of the basis for the descriptions of weak and strong restructuring is derived from the research on experts and novices within various domains (e.g., di Sessa, 1982; Larkin, 1979, 1981). Weak restructuring involves the creation of new and more numerous links among conceptual nodes for information in permanent memory. It also involves the use of more abstract schemata to link conceptual nodes. Radical restructuring involves the development of totally new theories to explain and organize information. That is, where weak restructuring makes a knowledge base more complex and abstract, radical restructuring changes the theory base or exploratory system that guides the organization of information. For example, di Sessa (1982) and B. Y. White (1983) found that novices in physics use explanatory theories that resemble those of Aristotle more than those of Newton. Finally, paradigm shifts are major reorganizations of assumptions underlying a domain. Kuhn (1962) described paradigm shift as a radical reorganization of the beliefs within a domain such that new insights are possible. Sawada and Caley (1985) explained that new paradigms do not emerge in a linear fashion as a natural outgrowth of existing paradigms. Rather, new paradigms emerge via a radical restructuring of old paradigms, which occurs when a system maintains a state "far from equilibrium" for a prolonged period of time. When systems approach a far-from-equilibrium state, which Sawada and Caley referred to as the "threshold of becoming," they are subject to spontaneous reorganization or "bifurcation."

***Procedural knowledge.*** Procedural knowledge is sometimes characterized as knowledge of *how* (Paris & Lindauer, 1982; Paris, Lipson, & Wixson, 1983). For example, knowing how to read a bar graph or how to perform long division is procedural. Anderson (1983) described the basic nature of procedural networks as "if-then" structures called productions. A complex procedure consists of a series of interrelated productions. Below are the first two productions of a procedure for comparing two figures:

P1: If the goal is to compare Object 1 to Object 2, then set as the subgoal to create an image of Object 2 that is congruent to Object 1.

P2: If the goal is to create an image of Object 2 that is congruent to Object 1 and Part 1 is a part of Object 1, then set as a subgoal to create an image of a part of Object 2 corresponding to Part 1.

As described by J. Anderson (1983), this procedure contains 24 productions in all. Procedural knowledge can be mental or physical in nature. The example above is mental. An example of a physical procedural network would be the series of steps involved in hitting a baseball.

Although declarative and procedural knowledge have been discussed separately here, they are not independent. To illustrate, consider the following production that deals with combining sentences:

IF: 1. two short sentences are adjacent in an essay, and
2. both have a subject–linking verb–adjective structure, and
3. both have the same subject,
THEN: embed the adjective from one sentence in the other.

The conditional knowledge is represented in Statements 1, 2, and 3. Together the process and conditional knowledge make up the procedure. However, contained within the procedure are such declarative components as the concepts *sentence, subject* and the fact that subject–linking verb–adjective represents a particular syntactic structure. Hence, this production contains both declarative and procedural knowledge integrated in a unified whole.

Procedural knowledge progresses through various stages as it is being learned. These stages are the cognitive, associated, and autonomous stages (J. Anderson, 1983; Fitts, 1964). During the cognitive stage, learners deal with procedural knowledge just as they would declarative knowledge, attempting to understand its component parts. During the associate stage, learners begin to smooth out the process, adding to and deleting from the information understood at the associated stage. Finally, during the autonomous stage, learners store the information as abstract production units that can be accessed and executed with little conscious thought.

***Implications for the language arts.*** The fact that declarative and procedural knowledge have distinct features, both in terms of their structure and how they are learned, implies that language arts content should be partitioned accordingly. For example, as a result of analyzing a number of national- and state-level documents, all of which purport to identify language arts standards (i.e., what students should know and be able to do in the language arts), Kendall and Marzano (1997) found that 90% of the content was procedural in nature. This indicates an emphasis in these documents on the *processes* inherent in the language arts, specifically, reading, writing, listening, and speaking, as opposed to the *information* inherent in the language arts such as specific literary works and their historical content. Although this is a legitimate emphasis, educators who design language arts curricula should be cognizant of values held by the general public that might dictate more of a balance between declarative and procedural knowledge. If language arts specialists desire a curriculum that emphasizes procedural knowledge, they should at least provide a well-articulated rationale for this emphasis.

An implication of the manner in which declarative knowledge is learned is that the scope of activities within the language arts curriculum should be expanded to enhance the restructuring of information. Here the programs and practices designed to enhance thinking have much to offer the language arts. For example, Gubbins (in Sternberg, 1985) lists over 30 types of tasks which engage the learner in shaping and sharpening forms of cognition. Similarly, Marzano et al. (1988) identified a number of cognitive tasks that require the learner to rethink and reorganize information. These practices are supported by the meta-analysis conducted by Guzzetti, Snyder, and Glass (1993) who found that students must engage with content in a "refutational" manner for significant conceptual change to occur. Work by Dole and Sinatra has significantly added to our knowledge of what must occur in the classroom to effect substantive knowledge change. They noted that the information (i.e, "message") with which students are interacting must be exceptionally well formed. Additionally, students must perceive the message to be coherent, comprehensible, plausible, and rhetorically compelling. Finally, students must be motivated to interact with the message at the highest end of the engagement continuum. This model implies an attention to language arts curricula that is not commonly found (N. Frederiksen, 1984).

An implication of the way procedural knowledge is learned is that the processes in the language arts should be thought of developmentally—progressing through a series of stages in which learners gradually shape the process to conform to their own styles while still meeting certain accepted standards. Here great strides are being made. Specifically, Scardamalia and Bereiter (1985) documented differences between the writing of children and unskilled writers that emphasized the developing complexity of the writing tasks. (For a review of writing development, see Stein, 1986.) Children and unskilled writers view the process as simply recording what they know. This is referred to as "associative writing" (Bereiter, 1980). The writer records on paper whatever comes to mind, searches for another thought, and then transcribes that. Bereiter and Scardamalia (1982) referred to this strategy as "knowledge telling"—telling what one knows in the simplest possible way. Additional stages of writing include "performative writing"—similar to the associative stage but adding control of grammar, spelling, and other mechanics; "communicative writing"—writing which includes control of mechanics and is shaped by the needs of different audiences; "unified writing"—writing in which the writer uses herself as a critical reader and editor; and, finally, "epistemic writing"—writing which functions as a tool for developing knowledge within a discipline (Bereiter, 1980). Similarly, Gentry (1982, 1987), building on the work of others (Hanna, Hanna, Hodges, & Rudorf, 1966), characterized the various phases within the acquisition of spelling strategies. Finally, at a very general level the entire emergent literacy field has begun to identify developmental components of all language-arts-related cognitive processes (Clifford, 1984; Sulzby, 1985, 1986; Teale, 1987). For example, Mason and Allen (1986) characterized the development of reading and writing ability as an integrated complex process of the learner gradually identifying and then developing their own strategies and rules for particular situations.

## Principle 4: Knowledge Involves Nonlinguistic Representations

Paivio (1969, 1971, 1990) and Bower (1972) asserted that knowledge is stored in long-term memory in two primary forms: linguistic and nonlinguistic. This has been referred to as the "dual-coding theory". The linguistic encoding of knowledge is commonly manifested as inner speech (Sokolov, 1972; Vygotsky, 1962). As discussed previously, it is a misconception to think that linguistic thought is represented only as words. Linguistic thought is probably represented in its most basic form as highly abstract semantic units (Kintsch, 1974; van Dijk, 1980). Consequently, storage of declarative knowledge can also occur as symbolic representations.

When information is represented nonlinguistically, it can contain visual, auditory, kinesthetic, tactile, and olfactory components (M. S. Gazzaniga, 1985; M. S. Gazzaniga & LeDoux, 1978; Underwood, 1969). Perhaps the most powerful form of nonlinguistic coding for learning purposes is visual. Most models of working memory address the visual encoding of information via the functioning of the visual-spatial sketch pad (see J. R. Anderson, 1995). The sketch pad is the mechanism by which an individual keeps visual data active so that it might be analyzed.

Visual representations fall in a continuum that runs from episodic to symbolic. Episodic visual representations are those mental pictures that come from "true-to-life" episodes or fabricated episodes. Symbolic, visual, mental representations are not true to life. That is, they are not composed of pictures of real people, places, and things organized as events. Instead, they are made up of abstract shapes and forms that convey meaning to the learner about the information being represented. Symbolic mental representations are quite common within the domains of mathematics and science (Tweney, Doherty, & Mynatt, 1981). Johnson-Laird (1983, 1999) found that they are fundamental to formal and informal syllogistic reasoning.

***Implications for the language arts.*** One of the main implications of the fact that information is encoded in both linguistic and nonlinguistic modes is that language arts instruction should involve a variety of nonlinguistic modes of processing information. It is safe to say that this is occurring in the language arts. For example, in their meta-analysis, Stahl and Fairbanks (1986) found that visually based techniques had an impact on learning vocabulary. McCarthy's (1980) 4MAT system provides for ways of enhancing the visual, auditory, olfactory, tactile, and kinetic aspects of processing information within reading, writing, and oral language. Similarly, Carbo, Dunn, and Dunn (1986) described ways of utilizing multisensory approaches

to language-arts instruction. Fernald (1988) has popularized a multisensory approach to language arts instruction that dates back to 1921. Finally, current models of the writing process quite commonly include a visual processing component. For example, Hayes' (1996) model includes the visual-spatial sketch pad which encodes ideas visually prior to being encoded linguistically. Similarly, Kellogg (1996) included the visual-spatial sketch pad in his model of writing noting that it is crucial to planning within the writing process.

## Principle 5: Higher Order Thinking Involves Mindfulness

There have been many attempts to distinguish higher order versus lower order types of thought. Most attempts have focused on hierarchies of information processing skills. In education, Bloom, Englehart, Furst, Hill, and Krathwohl's (1956) taxonomy of cognitive objectives is certainly the most well known. Unfortunately, Bloom et al.'s taxonomy suffers from an indeterminacy at the higher levels (as do most taxonomies). Specifically, tasks that are at higher levels cannot be differentiated from tasks supposedly at lower levels (Fairbrother, 1975; Wood, 1977), although some evidence for hierarchic structures similar to Bloom et al.'s has been found for questions pertaining to different discourse types (Hillocks & Ludlow, 1984). Similarly, hierarchies of cognitive operations based on complexity have been articulated and validated from developmental perspectives (Case, 1985; Gagne, 1975). For example, Fischer (1980) noted that complex tasks are built on substructures of less complex cognitive operations performed at an automatic level. However, J. Anderson (1982, 1983) and Fitts (1964) noted that the learner inevitably progresses to a stage where a cognitive process can be executed automatically without much conscious thought. From this perspective, a definition of higher order thinking that relies on the complexity of cognitive operations will invariably break down.

L. B. Resnick (1987) took another perspective. She asserted that higher order thinking is not so much the use of one set of cognitive processes versus another but rather the extent to which an individual is aware of the manner in which he or she is approaching a task. This goes beyond metacognition to include awareness of such elements as attitudes and affect. Finally, the conception of higher order thinking was developed even further with the idea of "mindfulness." Mindfulness involves awareness of not only the perceptual parameters imposed by the individual but also those parameters imposed by one's culture.

***Implications for the language arts.*** The major implication of the fact that higher order thinking involves mindfulness is that ultimately the language arts (or any other discipline) cannot be reduced to a set of processes and algorithms. Although such content is important (see discussion of procedural knowledge in Principle 3), language arts instruction must include a balance between the acquisition and development of knowledge and a mindfulness about that knowledge. Although mindfulness is not a common topic with the psychological literature, it is at the center of philosophic discussions of thought. For example, Heidegger (1968) noted that what is commonly called thinking is fundamentally a reactive process—the automatic execution of what modern psychologists would call productions. True thought is observing and controlling one's own cognition. Similar assertions have been made by Searle (1984) objected to what he called "bloodless reason" or cognition without deliberation.

Operationally mindfulness is difficult to describe because by definition it does not lend itself to a set of heuristics or algorithms that can be taught. Rather, Csikszentmihalyi (1975) noted that mindfulness is most common within "flow experiences"—those actions selected by individuals as expressions of their individuality and self-actualization. Key to flow experiences are the freedom of selection of task and establishment of criteria for success. This would imply that language arts instruction should involve many more tasks that are selected, planned, developed, and evaluated by students. Unfortunately, more often than not language arts instruction is characterized by tasks that are teacher directed, controlled, and evaluated (Fisher & Hiebert, 1988).

In summary, five principles can be drawn from the current research and theory in the teaching of thinking. These principles imply the following:

1. Language arts instruction should address the attitudinal context of the learner.
2. Language arts instruction should address the learner's emotions.
3. The language arts should attend to the inherent differences between declarative and procedural knowledge.
4. Language arts instruction should include the development of nonlinguistic representations of knowledge.
5. Language arts instruction should attempt to enhance the mindfulness of students.

## SUMMARY

Language, the language arts, and thinking are inextricably linked. First, language itself represents a type of thinking. It also is a vehicle by which thought is mediated and enhanced. Recently, a number of programs and practices have been developed that are designed to teach thinking. Many of the strategies and tactics employed within these programs are based in the language arts. Finally, the current research and theory on the teaching of thinking suggests a number of principles that can significantly affect language arts instruction.

## References

Adler, A. (1956). *The individual psychology of Alfred Adler* (H. C. Ansbacher & R. R. Ansbacher, Eds.). New York: Harper & Row.

Alexander, G. P. (1976). Strategies for finding the main idea. *Journal of Reading, 19,* 299-301.

Allen, G. J. (1972). The behavioral treatment of test anxiety. *Behavior Therapy, 3,* 253-262.

Amabile, T. M. (1983). *The social psychology of creativity.* New York: Springer-Verlag.

Anderson, J. (1982). Acquisition of cognitive skills. *Psychological Review, 89,* 369-406.

Anderson, J. (1983). *The architecture of cognition.* Cambridge, MA: Harvard University Press.

Anderson, J. R. (1995). *Learning and memory: An integrated approach.* New York: Wiley.

Anderson, R. C., Hiebert, E. H., Scott, J. A., & Wilkinsen, I. A. (1985). *Becoming a nation of readers.* Washington, DC: National Institute of Education.

Anderson, T. H., & Armbruster, B. B. (1985). Studying. In P. D. Pearson (Ed.), *Handbook of reading research.* New York: Longman.

Appel, L. F., Cooper, R. G., McCarrell, N., Sims-Knight, J., Yussen, S. R., & Flavell, J. H. (1972). The development of the distinction between perceiving and memorizing. *Child Development, 43,* 1365-1381.

Applebee, A. N. (1984). Writing and reasoning. *Review of Educational Research, 54,* 577-596.

Ashton, P. J., O'Hear, M. F., & Pherson, V. E. (1985). The presence of main idea clues in college textbooks. *Journal of College Reading and Learning, 18,* 59-67.

Axelrod, J. (1975). Getting the main idea is still the main idea. *Journal of Reading, 18,* 383-387.

Bagwell-Reese, M. K., & Brack, G. (1997). The therapeutic use of reframing and world view in mental health counseling. *Journal of Mental Health Counseling, 19*(1), 78-85.

Baird, J. R., & White, R. T. (1984). *Improving learning through enhanced metacognition: A classroom study.* Paper presented at the annual meeting of the American Educational Research Association, New Orleans, LA.

Bandura, A. (1982). Self-efficacy mechanism in human agency. *American Psychologist, 37,* 122-147.

Bandura, A. (1991). Social cognitive theory of self-regulation. *Organizational Behavior and Human Decision Processes, 50,* 248-287.

Bandura, A. (1993). Perceived self-efficacy in cognitive development and functioning. *Educational Psychologist, 28,* 117-148.

Bandura, A. (1996). Ontological and epistemological terrains revisited. *Journal of Behavior Therapy and Experimental Psychiatry, 27,* 323-345.

Bandura, A. (1997). *Self-efficacy: The exercise of control.* New York: Freeman.

Bargh, J. A., & Schul, Y. (1980). On the cognitive benefits of teaching. *Journal of Educational Psychology, 72,* 593-604.

Barnett, J. E., DiVesta, F. J., & Rogozinski, J. T. (1981). What is learned in note-taking? *Journal of Educational Psychology, 73,* 181-191.

Baron, J. (1982). Personality and intelligence. In R. J. Sternberg (Ed.), *Handbook of human intelligence* (pp. 308-351). London: Cambridge University Press.

Baron, J. (1985). *Rationality and intelligence.* New York: Cambridge University Press.

Baron, J., & Brown, R. V. (1991). Why Americans can't think straight. In J. Baron & R. V. Brown (Eds.), *Teaching decision making to adolescents* (pp. 1-18). Hillsdale, NJ: Lawrence Erlbaum Associates.

Bartlett, F. C. (1932). *Remembering: A study in experimental and social psychology*. Cambridge, England: Cambridge University Press.

Bateson, G. (1972). *Steps to an ecology of mind*. New York: Ballantine.

Bauman, J. F. (Ed.) (1986). *Teaching main idea comprehension*. Newark, DE: International Reading Association.

Bean, T. W., Singer, H., Sorter, J., & Frazee, C. (1983). Acquisition of summarization rules as a basis for question generation in learning from expository text at the high school level. In J. A. Niles & L. A. Harris (Eds.), *Searching for meaning in reading/language processing and instruction: Thirty-second yearbook of the National Reading Conference* (pp. 43-49). Rochester, NY: National Reading Conference.

Bearison, D. J., & Zimiles, H. (1986). Developmental perspectives on thought and emotion: An introduction. In D. J. Bearison & H. Zimiles, *Thought and emotion: Developmental perspectives* (pp. 1-10). Hillsdale, NJ: Lawrence Erlbaum Associates.

Belleza, F. (1981). Mnemonic devices: Classification characteristics and criteria. *Review of Educational Research, 51,* 247-275.

Bem, S. (1971). The role of comprehension in children's problem solving. *Developmental Psychology, 2,* 351-354.

Bender, N. (1976). Self-verbalization versus tutor verbalization in modifying impulsivity. *Journal of Educational Psychology, 68,* 347-354.

Bereiter, C. (1980). Development in writing. In L. W. Gregg & E. R. Steinberg (Eds.), *Cognitive processes in writing*. Hillsdale, NJ: Lawrence Erlbaum Associates.

Bereiter, C., & Scardamalia, M. (1982). From conversation to composition: The role of instruction in a developmental process. In R. Glaser (Ed.), *Advances in instructional psychology* (Vol. 2, pp. 1-64). Hillsdale, NJ: Lawrence Erlbaum Associates.

Beyer, B. E. (1988). *Developing a thinking skills program*. Boston: Allyn & Bacon.

Beyth-Marom, R., & Dekel, S. (1985). *An elementary approach to thinking under uncertainty*. Hillsdale, NJ: Lawrence Erlbaum Associates.

Bishop, J. C. (1983). Can there be thought without language? In W. Maxwell (Ed.), *Thinking, the expanding frontier* (pp. 13-24). Philadelphia: Franklin Institute Press.

Bleich, D. (1978). *Subjective criticism*. Baltimore, MD: Johns Hopkins University Press.

Bloom, B. S., Englehart, M. D., Furst, E. J., Hill, W. H., & Krathwohl, D. R. (Eds.) (1956). *Taxonomy of educational objectives: The classification of educational goals. Handbook I: Cognitive domain*. New York: McKay.

Boole, G. (1854). *An investigation of the laws of thought*. London: Walton & Manerly.

Bower, G. (1972). Analysis of a mnemonic device. In M. Coltheart (Ed.), *Readings in cognitive psychology* (pp. 399-426). Toronto: Holt, Rinehart & Winston.

Bower, G. H., & Clark, M. C. (1969). Narrative stories as mediators for serial learning. *Psychonomic Science, 14,* 181-182.

Braddock, R. (1974). Frequency and placement of topic sentences in expository prose. *Research in Teaching English, 8,* 287-302.

Braine, M. D. S. (1978). On the relation between the natural logic of reasoning and standard logic. *Psychological Review, 85,* 1-21.

Bransford, J. D. (1979). *Human cognition: Learning, understanding and remembering*. Belmont, CA: Wadsworth.

Bransford, J. D., Arbitman-Smith, R., Stein, B. S., & Vye, N. J. (1985). Improving thinking and learning skills: An analysis of three approaches. In J. W. Segal, S. F. Chipman, & R. Glaser (Eds.), *Thinking and Learning skills: Vol. 1. Relating instruction to research* (pp. 133-206). Hillsdale, NJ: Lawrence Erlbaum Associates.

Bransford, J. D., & Franks, J. J. (1976). Toward a framework for understanding learning. In G. H. Bower (Ed.), *Psychology of learning and motivation* (Vol. 10, pp. 93-127). New York: Academic Press.

Bransford, J. D., Sherwood, R., Rieser, J., & Vye, N. (1986). Teaching thinking and problem solving: Research foundations. *American Psychologist, 41,* 1078-1089.

Brophy, J., & Good, T. L. (1986). Teacher behavior and student achievement. In M. C. Wittrock (Ed.), *Handbook of research on teaching* (3rd ed., pp. 328-375). New York: Macmillan.

Brown, A. L. (1975). The development of memory: Knowing knowing about knowing, and knowing how to know. In H. W. Reese (Ed.), *Advances in child development and behavior* (Vol. 10). New York: Academic Press.

Brown, A. L. (1978). Knowing when, where and how to remember: A problem of metacognition. In R. Glaser (Ed.), *Advances in instructional psychology* (Vol. 1, pp. 77-165). Hillsdale, NJ: Lawrence Erlbaum Associates.

Brown, A. L., Bransford, J. D., Ferrara, R., & Campione, J. (1986). Learning, understanding and remembering. In J. H. Flavell & E. Markman (Eds.), *Mussen handbook of child psychology: Vol. 1. Cognitive development* (4th ed.). New York: Wiley.

Brown, A. L., Campione, J. C., & Day, J. (1981). Learning to learn: On training students to learn from texts. *Educational Researcher, 10,* 14-24.

Brown, A. L., & Smiley, S. S. (1977). Rating the importance of structural units of prose passages: A problem of metacognitive development. *Child Development, 48,* 1-8.

Buber, M. (1958). *I and thou*. New York: Scribner's.

Bugelski, B. R. (1968). Images as mediators in one-trial paired-associate learning. II: Self-timing in successive lists. *Journal of Experimental Psychology, 77,* 328-334.

Camp, E., Blom, G., Herbert, P., & Van Dournick, W. (1977). Think aloud: A program for developing self-control in young aggressive boys. *Journal of Abnormal Child Psychology, 8,* 157-169.

Campione, J. C., Brown, A. L., & Ferrara, R. A. (1982). Mental retardation and intelligence. In R. J. Sternberg (Ed.), *Handbook of human intelligence* (pp. 392-490). New York: Cambridge University Press.

Carbo, M., Dunn, R., & Dunn, K. (1986). *Teaching students to read through their individual styles*. Englewood Cliffs, NJ: Prentice-Hall.

Case, R. (1985). *Intellectual development, birth to adulthood*. New York: Academic Press.

Cazden, C. B. (1979). Language in education: Variation in the teacher-talk register. In J. Alatis & R. Rucker (Eds.), *Language in public life* (pp. 120-147). Washington, DC: Georgetown University Round Table in Language and Linguistics.

Cazden, C. B. (1986). Classroom discourse. In M. C. Wittrock (Ed.), *Handbook of research on teaching* (3rd ed., pp. 432-463). New York: Macmillan.

Cazden, C. B. (1988). *Classroom discourse: The language of teaching and learning*. Portsmouth, NH: Heinemann.

Chafe, W. L. (1970). *Meaning and structure of language*. Chicago: University of Chicago Press.

Chance, P. (1986). *Thinking in the classroom*. New York: Teacher's College Press.

Chomsky, N. (1957). *Syntactic structures*. The Hague, Netherlands: Mouton.

Chomsky, N. (1965). *Aspects of a theory of syntax*. Cambridge, MA: MIT Press.

Chomsky, N. (1980). Rules and representations. *Behavioral and Brain Science, 3,* 1-61.

Chomsky, N. (1988). *Language and the problems of knowledge: The Managua lectures*. Cambridge, MA: MIT Press.

Christenbury, L., & Kelly, P. P. (1983). *Questioning: A path to critical thinking*. Urbana, IL: Clearinghouse on Reading and Communication Skills, National Council of Teachers of English.

Clanchy, M. T. (1983). Looking back from the invention of printing. In D. P. Resnick (Ed.), *Literacy in historical perspective* (pp. 7-22). Washington, DC: Library of Congress.

Clark, H. H., & Haviland, S. E. (1977). Comprehension and the given-new contract. In R. O. Freedle (Ed.), *Discourse production and comprehension* (Vol. 1, pp. 1-40). Norwood, NJ: Ablex.

Clarke, M., Losoff, A., & Rood, D. S. (1982). Untangling referent and reference in linguistic relativity studies: A response from Clark et al. *Language learning, 32,* 209-217.

Clements, P. (1979). The effects of staging on recall from prose. In R. O. Freedle (Ed.), *New directions in discourse processing* (Vol. 2, pp. 287-330). Norwood, NJ: Ablex.

Clifford, G. J. (1984). Buch and lesen: Historical perspectives on literacy and schooling. *Review of Educational Research, 54,* 472-500.

Cohen, E. D. (1987). The use of syllogism in rational-emotive therapy. *Journal of Counseling and Development, 66,* 37-39.

College Board (1983). *Academic preparation for college: What students need to know and be able to do.* New York: Author.

Combs, A. W. (1962). A perceptual view of the adequate personality. In A. W. Combs (Ed.), *Perceiving, behaving, becoming: A new focus for education.* Alexandria, VA: Association for Supervision and Curriculum Development.

Combs, A. W. (1982). *A personal approach to teaching: Beliefs that make a difference.* Boston: Allyn & Bacon.

Connell, J. P., & Ryan, R. M. (1984). A developmental theory of motivation in the classroom. *Teacher Education Quality, 11*(4), 64-77.

Cooper, C. R. (1983). Procedures for describing written texts. In P. Mosenthal, L. Tamor, & S. A. Walmsley (Eds.), *Research on writing* (pp. 287-313). New York: Longman.

Cooper, M., & Holzman, M. (1983). Talking about protocols. *College Composition and Communication, 34,* 284-293.

Costa, A. L. (Ed.) (1985a). *Developing minds: A resource book for teaching thinking.* Alexandria, VA: Association for Supervision and Curriculum Development.

Costa, A. L. (1985b). Toward a model of human intellectual functioning. In A. L. Costa (Ed.), *Developing minds: A resource book for teaching thinking* (pp. 62-65). Alexandria, VA: Association for Supervision and Curriculum Development.

Covington, M. V. (1983). Motivated cognitions. In S. G. Paris, G. M. Olson, & H. W. Stevenson (Eds.), *Learning and motivation in the classroom* (pp. 139-164). Hillsdale, NJ: Lawrence Erlbaum Associates.

Covington, M. V. (1985). Strategic thinking and the fear of failure. In J. W. Segal, S. F. Chipman, & R. Glaser (Eds.), *Thinking and learning skills: Vol. 1. Relating instruction to research* (pp. 389-416). Hillsdale, NJ: Lawrence Erlbaum Associates.

Covington, M. V., Crutchfield, R. S., Davies, L., & Olton, R. M. (1974). *The productive thinking program: A course in learning to think.* Columbus, OH: Merrill.

Cox, B. G. (1994). Young children's regulatory self-talk: Evidence of emerging metacognitive control over literacy products and processes. In R. B. Ruddell, M. R. Ruddell, & H. Singer (Eds.), *Theoretical models and processes of reading* (4th ed., pp. 733-756). Newark, DE: International Reading Association.

Crabbe, A. B. (1982). Creating a brighter future: An update on the Future Problem Solving Program. *Journal for the Education of the Gifted, 5,* 2-11.

Crothers, E. J. (1979). *Paragraph structure inferences.* Norwood, NJ: Ablex.

Csikszentmihalyi, M. (1975). *Beyond boredom and anxiety.* San Francisco: Jossey-Bass.

Cunningham, D., & Luk, H. (1985, March). *Student as semiotician.* Paper presented at the annual meeting of American Educational Research Association, Chicago.

Cunningham, J. W., & Moore, D. W. (1986). The confused world of main idea. In J. F. Bauman (Ed.), *Teaching main idea comprehension* (pp. 1-17). Newark, DE: International Reading Association.

Damasio, A. R., & Van Hoesen, G. W. (1983). Emotional disturbances associated with focal lesions of the limbic frontal lobe. In K. M. Heilman & P. Satz (Eds.), *Neuropsychology of human emotion* (pp. 85-110). New York: Guilford Press.

Dansereau, D. F. (1978). The development of a learning strategy curriculum. In H. F. O'Neill, Jr. (Ed.), *Learning strategies* (pp. 1-29). New York: Academic Press.

Dansereau, D. F. (1985). Learning strategy research. In J. W. Segal, S. F. Chipman, & R. Glaser (Eds.), *Thinking and learning skills: Vol. 1. Relating instruction to research* (pp. 209-240). Hillsdale, NJ: Lawrence Erlbaum Associates.

Davies, I. K. (1980). *Instructional technique.* New York: McGraw-Hill.

de Beaugrande, R. (1980). *Text, discourse and process: Toward a multi-disciplinary science of text.* Norwood, NJ: Ablex.

de Beaugrande, R. (1984). *Text production: Toward a science of composition.* Norwood, NJ: Ablex.

de Bono, E. (1976). *Teaching thinking.* London: Temple Smith.

de Bono, E. (1983). The cognitive research trust (CoRT) thinking program. In W. Maxwell (Ed.), *Thinking: The expanding frontier.* Philadelphia: Franklin Institute Press.

de Bono, E. (1985). The CoRT thinking program. In J. W. Segal, S. F. Chipman, & R. Glaser (Eds.), *Thinking and learning skills: Vol. 1. Relating instruction to research* (pp. 363-388). Hillsdale, NJ: Lawrence Erlbaum Associates.

DeCharms, R. (1968). *Personal causation: The internal affective determinants of behavior.* New York: Academic Press.

Deci, E. L., & Ryan, R. M. (1985). *Intrinsic motivation and self-determination in human behavior.* New York: Plenum.

Deely, J. (1982). *Semiotics: Its history and doctrine.* Bloomington: Indiana University Press.

Delin, P. S. (1969). The learning to criterion of a serial list with and without mnemonic instructions. *Psychonomic Science, 16,* 169-170.

Dennett, D. C. (1969). *Content and consciousness.* London: Routledge & Kegan Paul.

Dennett, D. C. (1991). *Consciousness explained.* Boston: Little, Brown.

Derry, S., & Murphy, D. (1986). Designing systems that train learning ability. *Review of Educational Research, 56,* 1-39.

DeTure, L. R., & Miller, A. P. (1985). *The effects of a written protocol model on teacher acquisition of extended wait-time.* Paper presented at the annual meeting of the National Science Teachers Association, Cincinnati, OH.

Dewey, J. (1916). *Democracy and education.* New York: Macmillan.

Dewey, J. (1933). *How we think: A restatement of the relation of subjective thinking to the educative process.* Boston: Heath.

di Sessa, A. (1982). Unlearning Aristotelian physics: A study of knowledge-based learning. *Cognitive Science, 6,* 37-75.

Dickson, W. P. (1985). Thought-provoking software: Juxtaposing symbol systems. *Educational Research, 14,* 30-38.

DiVesta, F. J., & Gray, G. S. (1972). Listening and note-taking. *Journal of Educational Psychology, 63,* 8-14.

Douglas, V., Parry, P., Martin, P., & Garson, C. (1976). Assessment of a cognitive training program for hyperactive children. *Journal of Abnormal Child Psychology, 4,* 389-410.

Eco, U. (1976). *A theory of semiotics.* Bloomington: Indiana University Press.

Eco, U. (1979). *The role of the reader.* Bloomington: Indiana University Press.

Eco, U. (1984). *Semiotics and the philosophy of language.* Bloomington: Indiana University Press.

Edwards, J., & Baldauf, R. B. (1983). Teaching thinking in secondary science. In W. Maxwell (Ed.), *Thinking: The expanding frontier.* Philadelphia: Franklin Institute Press.

Ehrenberg, S. D., Ehrenberg, L. M., & Durfee, D. (1979). *BASICS: Teaching/learning strategies.* Miami Beach, FL: Institute for Curriculum and Instruction.

Einstein, G. C., Morris, J., & Smith, S. (1985). Note-taking, individual differences, and memory for lecture information. *Journal of Educational Psychology, 77,* 522-532.

Ekman, P. (1992). An argument for basic emotions. *Cognition and Emotion, 6,* 169-200.

Ellis, A. (1962). *Reason and emotion in psychotherapy.* New York: Lyle Stuart.

Ellis, A. (1977). The basic clinical theory of rational-emotive therapy. In A. Ellis & R. Grieger (Eds.), *Handbook of rationale-emotive therapy.* New York: Springer.

Emmer, E. T., Evertson, C. M., & Anderson, L. (1980). Effective management at the beginning of the school year. *Elementary School Journal, 80,* 219-231.

Ennis, R. H. (1985). Goals for a critical thinking curriculum. In A. Costa (Ed.), *Developing minds: A resource book for teaching thinking* (pp. 54-57). Alexandria, VA: Association for Supervision and Curriculum Development.

Erickson, F. (1975). Gate-keeping and the melting pot: Interaction in counseling interviews. *Harvard Educational Review, 45,* 44-70.

Fagan, E. R., Hassler, D. M., & Szabo, M. (1981). Evaluation of questioning strategies in language arts instruction. *Research in the Teaching of English, 15,* 267-273.

Fahara, M. S. (1997). *University students' problem-solving and decision-making responses using the Dimensions of Learning model.* Unpublished doctoral dissertation, University of Texas, Austin.

Fairbrother, R. (1975). The reliability of teachers' judgments of the abilities being tested by multiple choice items. *Educational Researcher, 17,* 202-210.

Fernald, G. M. (1988). *Remedial techniques in basic school subjects* (L. Idol, Ed.). Austin, TX: Pro-ed.

Feuerstein, R., Rand, Y., Hoffman, M. B., & Miller, R. (1980). *Instrumental enrichment: An intervention program for cognitive modifiability.* Baltimore, MD: University Park Press.

Fillmore, C. J. (1968). The case for case. In E. Beck & R. T. Harms (Eds.), *Universals in linguistic theory* (pp. 1-210). New York: Holt, Rinehart & Winston.

Fischer, K. W. (1980). A theory of cognitive development: The control and construction of hierarchies of skills. *Psychological Review, 87*(6), 477-531.

Fisher, C., Horton, A., & Marzano, R. J. (1993, April). *Acquiring science content and thinking processes in different task and talk structures.* Paper presented at the annual meeting of the American Educational Research Association, Atlanta, GA.

Fisher, C. W., & Hiebert, E. F. (1988). *Characteristics of literacy learning activities in elementary schools.* Paper presented at the annual meeting of the National Reading Conference, Tucson, AZ.

Fitts, P. M. (1964). Perceptual-motor skill learning. In A. W. Melton (Ed.), *Categories of human learning.* New York: Wiley.

Flavell, J. H. (1976). Metacognitive aspects of problem solving. In L. B. Resnick (Ed.), *The nature of intelligence.* Hillsdale, NJ: Lawrence Erlbaum Associates.

Flavell, J. H. (1977). *Cognitive development.* Englewood Cliffs, NJ: Prentice-Hall.

Flavell, J. H. (1978). Metacognitive development. In J. M. Scandura & C. J. Brainerd (Eds.), *Structural/process theories of complex human behavior* (pp. 213-245). Netherlands: Sijthoff & Noordoff.

Flavell, J. H. (1981). Cognitive monitoring. In W. P. Dickson (Ed.), *Children's oral communication skill* (pp. 35-60). New York: Academic Press.

Flavell, J. H., Beach, D., & Chinsky, J. (1966). Spontaneous verbal rehearsal in a memory task as a function of age. *Child Development, 37,* 283-299.

Flavell, J. H., Friedrichs, A. H., & Hogt, J. D. (1970). Developmental changes in memorization processes. *Cognitive Psychology, 1,* 324-340.

Flower, L. A., & Hayes, J. R. (1980a). The cognition of discovery, defining a rhetorical problem. *College Composition and Communication, 13,* 21-32.

Flower, L. A., & Hayes, J. R. (1980b). The dynamics of composing: Making plans and juggling constraints. In L. W. Gregg & E. R. Steinberg (Eds.), *Cognitive processing in writing.* Hillsdale, NJ: Lawrence Erlbaum Associates.

Flower, L. A., & Hayes, J. R. (1981). A cognitive process theory of writing. *College Composition and Communication, 32,* 365-387.

Fodor, J. (1975). *The language of thought.* New York: Crowell.

Fowler, T. W. (1975, March). *An investigation of the teacher behavior of wait-time during an inquiry science lesson.* Paper presented at the annual meeting of the National Association for Research in Science Teaching, Los Angeles. (ERIC Document Reproduction Service No. ED 108 872)

Frankl, V. E. (1967). *Psychotherapy and existentialism.* New York: Pocket Books.

Frederiksen, C. H. (1977). Semantic processing units in understanding text. In R. O. Freedle (Ed.), *Discourse production and comprehension* (Vol. 1, pp. 57-88). Norwood, NJ: Ablex.

Frederiksen, N. (1984). Implications of cognitive theory for instruction in problem solving. *Review of Educational Research, 54,* 363-407.

Freedman, G., & Reynolds, E. G. (1980). Enriched basic reader lessons with semantic webbing. *Reading Teacher, 33,* 677-683.

Gagne, R. M. (1975). *The conditions of learning* (3rd ed.). New York: Holt, Rinehart & Winston.

Garner, R. (1994). Metacognition and executive control. In R. B. Ruddell, M. R. Ruddell, & H. Singer (Eds.), *Theoretical models and processes of reading* (4th ed., pp. 715-732). Newark, DE: International Reading Association.

Gazzaniga, M. (1992). *Nature's mind: The biological roots of thinking, emotions, sexuality, language and intelligence.* New York: Basic Books.

Gazzaniga, M. S. (1985). *The social brain.* New York: Basic Books.

Gazzaniga, M. S., & LeDoux, J. E. (1978). *The integrated mind.* New York: Plenum Press.

Gazzaniga, M. S., & Sperry, R. W. (1967). Language after section of the cerebral commissures. *Brain, 90,* 131-148.

Gentner, D., & Markman, A. B. (1994). Structural alignment in comparison: No difference without similarity. *Psychological Science, 5*(3), 152-158.

Gentry, J. R. (1982). An analysis of developmental spelling in GYNS AT WRK. *Reading Teacher, 36,* 192-200.

Gentry, J. R. (1987). *Spel . . . is a four-letter word.* Portsmouth, NH: Heinemann.

Gentzen, G. (1964). Investigations into logical deduction. *American Psychological Quarterly, 1,* 288-306.

Gick, M. L., & Holyoak, K. J. (1980). Analogical problem solving. *Cognitive Psychology, 12,* 306-355.

Goodlad, J. L. (1984). *A place called school.* New York: McGraw-Hill.

Goodman, K. (1986). *What's whole in whole language.* Portsmouth, NH: Heinemann.

Gourley, T. J. (1981). Adapting the varsity sports model of non-psychomotor gifted students. *Gifted Child Quarterly, 25,* 164–166.

Graesser, A. C., Millis, K. K., & Long, D. L. (1986). The construction of knowledge structures and inferences during text comprehension. In N. E. Sharkey (Ed.), *Advances in cognitive science* (pp. 125–157). New York: Ellis Horwood.

Granato, J. M. (1983, April). *The effects of wait time on the verbal behavior of kindergarten children.* Paper presented at the annual conference of the New England Educational Research Organization, Rockport, ME.

Greene, M. (1984). Philosophy, reason and literacy. *Review of Educational Research, 54*(4), 547–559.

Grimes, J. E. (1975). *The thread of discourse.* The Hague, Netherlands: Mouton.

Guilford, J. P. (1967). *The nature of human intelligence.* New York: McGraw-Hill.

Guilford, J. P., & Hoepfner, R. (1971). *The analysis of intelligence.* New York: McGraw-Hill.

Guzzetti, B. J., Snyder, T. E., & Glass, G. V. (1993). Promoting conceptual change in science: A comparative meta-analysis of instructional interventions from reading education and science education. *Reading Research Quarterly, 28*(2), 117–155.

Halpern, D. F. (1984). *Thought and knowledge: An introduction to critical thinking.* Hillsdale, NJ: Lawrence Erlbaum Associates.

Halpern, D. F. (1996). *Thought and knowledge: An introduction to critical thinking* (3rd ed.). Mahwah, NJ: Lawrence Erlbaum Associates.

Hanelin, S. J. (1978). *Learning, behavior and attitudes under individual and group contingencies.* Unpublished doctoral dissertation, University of California, Los Angeles.

Hanna, P., Hanna, J., Hodges, R., & Rudorf, E. (1966). *Phoneme grapheme correspondence as cues to spelling improvement.* Washington, DC: U.S. Government Printing Office.

Harris, Z. S. (1952). Discourse analysis. *Language, 28,* 1–30.

Harter, S. (1982). A developmental perspective on some parameters of self-regulation in children. In P. Karoly & F. H. Kanfer (Eds.), *Self-management and behavior change: From theory to practice* (pp. 165–204). New York: Pergamon Press.

Harter, S. (1990). Causes, correlates, and the functional role of global self-worth: A life-span perspective. In R. J. Sternberg & J. Kolligian, Jr. (Eds.), *Competence considered* (pp. 67–97). New Haven, CT: Yale University Press.

Harvard University (1983). *Project intelligence: The development of procedures to enhance thinking skills* [Final report, submitted to the Minister of the Development of Human Intelligence, Republic of Venezuela].

Hattie, J., Biggs, J., & Purdie, N. (1996). Effects of learning skills interventions on student learning: A meta-analysis. *Review of Educational Research, 66*(2), 99–136.

Hayes, J. R. (1996). A new framework for understanding cognition and affect in writing. In C. M. Levy & S. Ransdell (Eds.), *The science of writing: Theories, methods, individual differences, and applications* (pp. 1–27). Mahwah, NJ: Lawrence Erlbaum Associates.

Hayes-Roth, B., & Hayes-Roth, F. (1979). A cognitive model of planning. *Cognitive Science, 3,* 275–310.

Heidegger, M. (1968). *What is called thinking?* (J. G. Gray, Trans.). New York: Harper & Row. (Original work published 1954)

Henle, M. O. (1978). Foreword. In R. Revlin & R. E. Mayer (Eds.), *Human reasoning.* Washington, DC: Winston.

Henshaw, D. (1978). *A cognitive analysis of creative problem-solving.* Unpublished doctoral dissertation, University of Waterloo, Waterloo, Ontario, Canada.

Hidi, S., & Anderson, V. (1986). Producing written summaries: Task demands, cognitive operations, and implications for instruction. *Review of Educational Research, 56,* 473–494.

Hillocks, G., Jr. (1986). *Research on written composition.* Urbana, IL: ERIC Clearinghouse on Reading and Communication Skills.

Hillocks, G., Jr., & Ludlow, L. H. (1984). A taxonomy of skills in reading and interpreting fiction. *American Educational Research Journal, 21*(1), 7–24.

Holley, C. D., & Dansereau, D. F. (1984). *Spatial learning strategies: Techniques, applications, and related issues.* New York: Academic Press.

Honea, M. J. (1982). Wait time as an instructional variable: An influence on teacher and student. *Clearinghouse, 56*(4),167–170.

Hunkins, F. P. (1995). *Teaching thinking through effective questioning* (2nd ed.). Norwood, MA: Christopher-Gordon.

Inhelder, B., & Piaget, J. (1958). *The growth of logical thinking from childhood to adolescence.* London: Routledge & Kegan Paul.

Iser, W. (1978). *The act of reading: A theory of aesthetic response.* Baltimore: Johns Hopkins University Press.

Johnson, D., Maruyama, G., Johnson, R., Nelson, D., & Skon, L. (1981). Effects of cooperative, competitive, and individualistic goal structures on achievement: A meta-analysis. *Psychological Bulletin, 89*(1), 47–62.

Johnson, J. A. (1979). Learning in peer tutoring interactions: The influence of status, role change, time-on-task, feedback and verbalization. *Dissertation Abstracts International, 39,* 5469A–5470A. (University Microfilms No. 79-06, 175)

Johnson, P. E. (1967). Some psychological aspects of subject-matter structure. *Journal of Educational Psychology, 58,* 75–83.

Johnson, P. E. (1969). On the communication of concepts in science. *Journal of Educational Psychology, 60,* 32–40.

Johnson, P. E., Cox, D. L., & Curran, T. E. (1970). Psychological reality of physical concepts. *Psychonomic Science, 19,* 245–247.

Johnson-Laird, P. N. (1975). Models of deduction. In R. J. Falmagne (Ed.), *Reasoning: Representation and process in children and adults.* Hillsdale, NJ: Lawrence Erlbaum Associates.

Johnson-Laird, P. N. (1983). *Mental models.* Cambridge, MA: Harvard University Press.

Johnson-Laird, P. N. (1999). Strategies in syllogistic reasoning. *Cognitive Science, 23*(3), 247–303.

Johnson-Laird, P. N., & Steedman, M. J. (1978). The psychology of syllogisms. *Cognitive Psychology, 10,* 64–99.

Jones, B. F., Amiran, M., & Katims, M. (1985). Teaching cognitive strategies and text structures within language arts programs. In J. W. Segal, S. F. Chipman, & R. Glaser (Eds.), *Thinking and learning skills: Vol. 1. Relating instruction to research* (pp. 259–295). Hillsdale, NJ: Lawrence Erlbaum Associates.

Jones, B. F., Palincsar, A. S., Ogle, D. S., & Carr, E. G. (1987). *Strategic teaching: Cognitive instruction in the content areas.* Alexandria, VA: Association of Supervision and Curriculum Development.

Jones, B. F., Tinzmann, M., Friedman, L. B., & Walker, B. J. (1987). *Teaching thinking skills in English/Language Arts.* Washington, DC: National Education Association.

Kail, R. V., & Hagen, J. W. (1982). Memory in childhood. In B. Wolman (Ed.), *Handbook of developmental psychology.* Englewood Cliffs, NJ: Prentice-Hall.

Kanfer, F., & Goldfoot, D. (1966). Self-control and tolerance of noxious stimulation. *Psychological Reports, 18,* 79–85.

Kanfer, F., & Phillips, J. (1970). *Learning foundations of behavior therapy.* New York: Wiley.

Katz, S. E. (1976). *The effect of each of four instructional treatments on the learning of principles by children.* Madison: University of

Wisconsin, Wisconsin Research and Development Center for Cognitive Learning.

Kaufer, D. S., Hayes, J. R., & Flower, L. S. (1986). Composing written sentences. *Research in the Teaching of English, 20*(2), 121–140.

Kellogg, R. T. (1996). A model of working memory in writing. In C. M. Levy & S. Ransdell (Eds.), *The science of writing: Theories, methods, individual differences, and applications* (pp. 57–72). Mahwah, NJ: Lawrence Erlbaum Associates.

Kendall, J. S., & Marzano, R. J. (1997). *Content knowledge: A compendium of standards and benchmarks for K-12 education* (2nd ed.). Alexandria, VA: Association for Supervision and Curriculum Development.

Kenney, T. J., Cannizzo, S. R., & Flavell, J. H. (1967). Spontaneous and induced verbal rehearsal in a recall task. *Child Development, 38,* 953–966.

Kinneavy, J. (1980). *A theory of discourse.* New York: Norton.

Kintsch, W. (1974). *The representation of meaning in memory.* Hillsdale, NJ: Lawrence Erlbaum Associates.

Kintsch, W., & van Dijk, T. A. (1978). Toward a model of text comprehension and production. *Psychological Review, 85,* 363–394.

Klausmeier, H. J. (1985). *Educational psychology* (5th ed.). New York: Harper & Row.

Kluckhohn, F. R., & Strodtbeck, F. L. (1961). *Variation in value orientations.* Evanston, IL: Row, Patterson.

Knickerbocker, M. E. (1984). *The effects of wait time on verbal behavior of kindergarten children: A replication.* Unpublished master's thesis, University of New York, Oswego.

Koch, K. (1970). *Wishes, lies, and dreams.* New York: Chelsea.

Koch, K. (1974). *Rose, where did you get that red?* New York: Random House.

Kuhn, T. (1962). *The structure of scientific revolutions.* Chicago: University of Chicago Press.

Lakoff, G. (1970). Linguistics and natural logic. *Syntheses, 22,* 151–271.

Langer, J. A. (1982). Facilitating text processing: The elaboration of prior knowledge. In M. Trika Burke-Smith (Eds.), *Reader meets author: Bridging the gap.* Newark, DE: International Reading Association.

Larkin, J. H. (1979). Information processing models and science instruction. In J. Lochhead & J. Clement (Eds.), *Cognitive process instruction* (pp. 109–118). Philadelphia: Franklin Institute Press.

Larkin, J. H. (1981). Enriching formal knowledge: A model of learning to solve textbook physics problems. In J. Anderson (Ed.), *Cognitive skills and their acquisition* (pp. 311–334). Hillsdale, NJ: Lawrence Erlbaum Associates.

LeDoux, J. E. (1994, June). Emotion, memory, and brain. *Scientific American, 270*(6), 50–57.

LeDoux, J. E. (1996). *The emotional brain: The mysterious underpinnings of emotional life.* New York: Simon & Schuster.

Lee, P. (1997). Language in thinking and learning: Pedagogy and the new Whorfian framework. *Harvard Educational Review, 67*(3), 430–471.

Lindsay, P. H., & Norman, D. A. (1977). *Human information processing.* New York: Academic Press.

Link, F. (1985). Instrumental enrichment. In A. Costa (Ed.), *Developing minds: A resource book for teaching thinking* (pp. 193–195). Alexandria, VA: Associates for Supervision and Curriculum Development.

Lipman, M. (1974). *Harry.* Upper Montclair, NJ: Institute for the Advancement of Philosophy for Children.

Lipman, M. (1978). *Suki.* Upper Montclair, NJ: Institute for the Advancement of Philosophy for Children.

Lipman, M. (1980). *Mark.* Upper Montclair, NJ: Institute for the Advancement of Philosophy for Children.

Lipman, M. (1985). Thinking skills fostered by philosophy for children. In J. W. Segal, S. F. Chipman, & R. Glaser (Eds.), *Thinking and learning skills: Vol. 1. Relating instruction to research* (pp. 83–108). Hillsdale, NJ: Lawrence Erlbaum Associates.

Lipman, M., Sharp, A. M., & Oscanyan, F. S. (1980). *Philosophy in the classroom* (2nd ed.). Philadelphia: Temple University Press.

Lochhead, J. (1985). Teaching analytic reasoning skills through pair problem solving. In J. W. Segal, S. F. Chipman, & R. Glaser (Eds.), *Thinking and learning skills: Vol. 1. Relating instruction to research* (pp. 109–131). Hillsdale, NJ: Lawrence Erlbaum Associates.

Loman, D. F. (1986). *Predicting mathemathanic effects in the teaching of higher order thinking skills.* Unpublished manuscript, University of Iowa, School of Education, Iowa City, IA.

Luria, A. (1961). *The role of speech in the regulation of normal and abnormal behaviors.* New York: Liveright.

Luria, A. (1969). Speech and formation of mental processes. In M. Cole & I. Maltzman (Eds.), *A handbook of contemporary Soviet psychology* (pp. 519–541). New York: Basic Books.

Mandler, G. (1983). The nature of emotions. In J. Miller (Ed.), *States of mind* (pp. 136–153). New York: Pantheon.

Mandler, J. M., & Ritchey, G. H. (1977). Long-term memory for pictures. *Journal of Experimental Psychology: Human Learning and Memory, 3,* 386–396.

Maratsos, M. P. (1977). Disorganization in thought and word. In R. Shaw & J. Bransford (Eds.), *Perceiving, acting and knowing* (pp. 171–189). Hillsdale, NJ: Lawrence Erlbaum Associates.

Markman, A. B., & Gentner, D. (1993a). Splitting the differences: A structural alignment view of similarity. *Journal of Memory and Learning, 32,* 517–535.

Markman, A. B., & Gentner, D. (1993b). Structural alignment during similarity comparisons. *Cognitive Psychology, 25,* 431–467.

Markus, H., & Ruvulo, A. (1990). Possible selves. Personalized representations of goals. In L. Pervin (Ed.), *Goal concepts in psychology* (pp. 211–241). Hillsdale, NJ: Lawrence Erlbaum Associates.

Markus, H., & Wurf, E. (1987). The dynamic self-concept. A social psychological perspective. *Annual Review of Psychology, 38,* 299–337.

Marzano, R. J. (1987). *Decomposing curricular objectives for specivity of instruction* (Technical Report). Aurora, CO: Mid-Continent Regional Educational Laboratory. (ERIC Document Reproduction Service No. ED 290 220)

Marzano, R. J. (1991). *Cultivating thinking in English and the language arts.* Urbana, IL: National Council of Teachers of English.

Marzano, R. J. (1992). *A different kind of classroom: Teaching with Dimensions of Learning.* Alexandria, VA: Association for Supervision and Curriculum Development.

Marzano, R. J. (1998). *A theory-based meta-analysis of research on instruction.* Aurora, CO: Mid-Continent Research for Education and Learning. (ERIC Document Reproduction No. ED 427 087)

Marzano, R. J., & Marzano, J. S. (1987). *Contextual thinking: The most basic of the cognitive skills* (Technical Report). Aurora, CO: Mid-Continent Regional Educational Laboratory. (ERIC Document Reproduction Service No. ED 286 634)

Marzano, R. J., Brandt, R. S., Hughes, C. S., Jones, B. F., Presseisen, B. Z., Rankin, S. C., & Suhor, C. (1988). *Dimensions of thinking: A framework for curriculum and instruction.* Alexandria, VA: Association for Supervision and Curriculum Development.

Marzano, R. J., Hagerty, P. J., Valencia, S. W., & DiStefano, P. P. (1987). *Reading diagnosis and instruction: Theory into practice.* Englewood Cliffs, NJ: Prentice-Hall.

Marzano, R. J., Pickering, D. J., Arredondo, D. E., Blackburn, G. J., Brandt, R. S., Moffett, C. A., Paynter, D. E., Pollock, J. E., & Whisler, J. S. (1997). *Dimensions of learning: Teacher's manual* (2nd ed.).

Alexandria, VA: Association for Supervision and Curriculum Development.

Maslow, A. H. (1968). *Toward a psychology of being.* New York: Van Nostrand Reinhold.

Mathewson, G. C. (1985). Toward a comprehensive model of affect in the reading process. In H. Singer & R. B. Ruddell (Eds.), *Theoretical models and processes of reading* (3rd ed., pp. 841–856). Newark, DE: International Reading Association.

Mathewson, G. C. (1994). Model of attitude influence upon reading and learning to read. In R. B. Ruddell, M. R. Ruddell, & H. Singer (Eds.), *Theoretical models and processes of reading* (4th ed., pp. 1131–1161). Newark, DE: International Reading Association.

Matsuhashi, A. (1982). Explorations in the real-time production of written discourse. In M. Nystrand (Ed.), *What writers know: The language, process, and structure of written discourse* (pp. 269–290). New York: Academic Press.

Mau, W., & Pope-Davis, D. B. (1993). Worldview differences between college students and graduate counseling trainees. *Counseling and Values, 38,* 42–50.

Mayer, R. E. (1984). Aids to text comprehension. *Educational Psychologist, 19,* 30–42.

Mayer, R. E. (1989). Models of understanding. *Review of Educational Research, 59*(1), 43–64.

McCarthy, B. (1980). *The 4MAT system.* Oak Harbor, IL: Excel.

McCombs, B. (1984). Processes and skills underlying continuing intrinsic motivation to learn: Toward a definition of motivational skills training intervention. *Educational Psychologist, 19,* 197–218.

McCombs, B. (1986). The role of the self system in self-regulated learning. *Contemporary Educational Psychology, 11,* 314–332.

McCombs, B. (1987, April). *Issues in the measurement by standardized tests of primary motivation variables related to self-regulated learning.* Paper presented at the annual meeting of the American Educational Research Association, Washington, DC.

McNeil, D. (1975). Semiotic extension. In R. L. Solso (Ed.), *Information processing and cognition: The Loyola symposium.* Hillsdale, NJ: Lawrence Erlbaum Associates.

McNeil, J., & Donant, L. (1982). Summarization strategy for improving reading comprehension. In J. A. Niles & L. A. Harris (Eds.), *New inquiries in reading research and instruction: Thirty-first yearbook of the National Reading Conference* (Vol. 31, pp. 215–219). Rochester, NY: National Reading Conference.

McNeil, J. D. (1984). *Reading comprehension. New directions for classroom practice.* Glenview, IL: Scott, Foresman.

Meeker, M. N. (1969). *The structure of intelligence: Its interpretation and uses.* Columbus, OH: Charles E. Merrill.

Mehan, H. (1979). *Learning lessons.* Cambridge, MA: Harvard University Press.

Meichenbaum, D. (1975). Theoretical and treatment implications of developmental research on verbal control of behavior. *Canadian Psychological Review, 16,* 22–27.

Meichenbaum, D. (1977). *Cognitive behavior modification.* New York: Plenum Press.

Meichenbaum, D. (1985). Teaching thinking: A cognitive behavioral perspective. In S. F. Chipman, J. W. Segal, & R. Glaser (Eds.), *Thinking and learning skills: Vol. 2. Research and open questions* (pp. 407–426). Hillsdale, NJ: Lawrence Erlbaum Associates.

Meichenbaum, D., & Goodman, S. (1971). Training impulsive children to talk to themselves: A means of developing self-control. *Journal of Abnormal Psychology, 77,* 115–126.

Mervis, C. B. (1980). Category structure and the development of categorization. In R. J. Spiro, B. C. Bruce, & W. F. Brewer (Eds.), *Theoretical issues in reading comprehension* (pp. 279–307). Hillsdale, NJ: Lawrence Erlbaum Associates.

Messerer, J., Hunt, E., Meyers, G., & Lerner, J. (1984). Feuerstein's instrumental enrichment: A new approach for activating intellectual potential in learning disabled youth. *Journal of Learning Disabilities, 17,* 322–325.

Meyer, B. J. F. (1975). *The organization of prose and its effects on memory.* New York: American Elsevier.

Meyer, B. J. F. (1985). The structure of text. In P. D. Pearson (Ed.), *Handbook of reading research.* New York: Longman.

Miccinati, J. L. (1988). Mapping the terrain: Connecting reading with academic writing. *Journal of Reading, 31,* 542–552.

Mill, J. S. (1874). *A system of logic* (8th ed.). New York: Harper.

Mitchell, B. M. (1980). What's happening to gifted education in the U.S. today? *Roeper Review, 2,* 7–10.

Mitchell, B. M. (1984). An update on gifted/talented education in the U.S. *Roeper Review, 6,* 161–163.

Moely, B. E. (1977). Organization factors in the development of memory. In R. V. Kail & J. W. Hagen (Eds.), *Perspectives on the development of memory and cognition* (pp. 314–352). Hillsdale, NJ: Lawrence Erlbaum Associates.

Moffett, J. (1968). *Teaching the universe of discourse.* Boston: Houghton Mifflin.

Moffett, J., & Wagner, B. J. (1983). *Student-centered language arts and reading, K–13: A handbook for teachers* (3rd ed.). Boston: Houghton Mifflin.

Moore, C. A. (1977). Verbal teaching patterns under simulated teaching conditions. In R. O. Freedle (Ed.), *Discourse production in comprehension* (Vol. 1, pp. 271–305). Norwood, NJ: Ablex.

Murray, D. M. (1978). International revision: A process of discovery. In C. R. Cooper & L. Odell (Eds.), *Research on composing* (pp. 85–103). Urbana, IL: National Council of Teachers of English.

Nardi, A. H., & Wales, C. E. (1985). Teaching decision-making with guided design. In A. L. Costa (Ed.), *Developing minds: A resource book for teaching thinking* (pp. 220–225). Alexandria, VA: Association for Supervision and Curriculum Development.

Nash, R. J., & Shiman, D. A. (1974). The English teacher as questioner. *English Journal, 63,* 42–45.

National Center for Education Statistics (1999). *National assessment of educational progress (NAEP), 1996 Long-term trend assessment.* From http://nces.ed.gov/naep/index.html

National Education Goals Panel (1991). *The national education goals report: Building a nation of learners.* Washington, DC: Author.

Negin, G. (1987). *Inferential reasoning for teachers.* Dubuque, IA: Kendall/Hunt.

Nickerson, R. S. (1984). Kinds of thinking taught in current programs. *Educational Leadership, 42,* 26–37.

Nickerson, R. S., Perkins, D. N., & Smith, E. E. (1985). *The teaching of thinking.* Hillsdale, NJ: Lawrence Erlbaum Associates.

Nisbett, R. E., & Wilson, T. D. (1977). Telling more than we can know: Verbal reports on mental processes. *Psychological Review, 84,* 231–259.

Nold, E. W., & Davis, B. E. (1980). The discourse matrix. *College Composition and Communication, 31,* 141–147.

Ogle, D. (1986). The K-W-L: A teaching model that develops active reading of expository text. *The Reading Teacher, 39,* 564–576.

Paivio, A. (1969). Mental imagery in associative learning and memory. *Psychological Review, 76,* 241–263.

Paivio, A. (1971). *Imagery and verbal processing.* New York: Holt, Rinehart & Winston.

Paivio, A. (1990). *Mental representations: A dual coding approach.* New York: Oxford University Press.

Palincsar, A. S., & Brown, A. L. (1984). Reciprocal teaching of comprehension-fostering and comprehension-monitoring activities. *Cognition and Instruction, 1,* 117–175.

Paris, S. G., & Lindauer, B. K. (1982). The development of cognitive skills during childhood. In B. W. Wolman (Ed.), *Handbook of developmental psychology*. Englewood Cliffs, NJ: Prentice-Hall.

Paris, S. G., Lipson, M. Y., & Wixson, K. K. (1983). Becoming a strategic reader. *Contemporary Educational Psychology, 8,* 293–316.

Pask, G. (1975). *Conversations, cognition and learning*. Amsterdam: Elsevier.

Paul, R. (1990). *Critical thinking: What every person needs to survive in a rapidly changing world*. Rohnert Park, CA: Sonoma State University, Center for Critical Thinking and Moral Critique.

Pearson, P. D., & Johnson, D. D. (1978). *Teaching reading comprehension*. New York: Holt, Rinehart & Winston.

Peper, R. J., & Mayer, R. E. (1978). Note-taking as generative activity. *Journal of Educational Psychology, 70,* 514–522.

Perkins, D. N. (1981). *The mind's best work*. Cambridge, MA: Harvard University Press.

Perkins, D. N. (1984). Creativity by design. *Educational Leadership, 42,* 18–25.

Perkins, D. N., Allen, R., & Hafner, J. (1983). Difficulties in everyday reasoning. In W. Maxwell (Ed.), *Thinking: The expanding frontier*. Philadelphia: Franklin Institute Press.

Peterson, P. L., & Janicki, T. C. (1979). Individual characteristics and children's learning in large-group and small-group approaches. *Journal of Educational Psychology, 71,* 677–687.

Peterson, P. L., Janicki, T. C., & Swing, S. R. (1981). Ability × Treatment interaction effects on children's learning in large-group and small-group approaches. *American Educational Research Journal, 18,* 453–473.

Piaget, J. (1962). The relationship of affectivity to intelligence in the mental development of the child. *Bulletin of the Menninger Clinic, 26,* 129–137.

Piaget, J., & Szeminska, A. (1941). *The child's conception of number*. Atlantic Highlands, NJ: Humanities Press.

Pike, K. L. (1964). A linguistic contribution to composition: A hypothesis. *College Composition and Communication, 15,* 82–88.

Pinker, S. (1994). *The language instinct: How the mind creates language*. New York: Harper Perennial.

Pinker, S. (1997). *How the mind works*. New York: Norton.

Plutchik, R. (1980). *Emotion: A psychoevolutionary synthesis*. New York: Harper & Row.

Plutchik, R. (1993). Emotions and their vicissitudes: Emotions and psychopathology. In M. Lewis & J. Mitoviland (Eds.), *Handbook of emotions* (pp. 53–65). New York: Guilford.

Pressley, M., Borkowski, J. G., & O'Sullivan, J. T. (1984). Memory strategy instruction is made of this: Meta-memory and durable strategy use. *Educational Psychologist, 19,* 94–107.

Pressley, M., Levin, J. R., & Ghatala, E. S. (1984). Memory strategy monitoring in adults and children. *Journal of Verbal Learning and Verbal Behavior, 23,* 270–288.

Probst, R. E. (1988). *Response and analysis: Teaching literature in junior and senior high school*. Portsmouth, NH: Heinemann.

Raphael, T. E. (1982). Question-answering strategies for children. *Reading Teacher, 36,* 186–190.

Raphael, T. E. (1984). Teaching learners about sources of information for answering comprehension questions. *Journal of Reading, 27,* 303–311.

Raphael, T. E. (1987). Research on reading: But what can I teach on Monday? In V. Richardson-Koehler (Ed.), *Educator's handbook: A research perspective* (pp. 26–49). New York: Longman.

Raphael, T. E., & Kirschner, B. M. (1985). *The effects of instruction in compare/contrast text structure on sixth-grade students' reading comprehension and writing products* (Research Series 161).

East Lansing: Michigan State University, Institute for Research on Teaching.

Reder, L. M. (1980). The role of elaboration in the comprehension of prose: A critical review. *Review of Educational Research, 50,* 5–53.

Redfield, D. L., & Rousseau, E. W. (1981). A meta-analysis of experimental research on teacher questioning behavior. *Review of Educational Research, 51,* 237–245.

Reese, H. (1962). Verbal mediation as a function of age. *Psychological Bulletin, 59,* 502–509.

Reigeluth, C. M., & Stein, F. S. (1983). The elaboration theory of instruction. In. C. M. Reigeluth (Ed.), *Instructional design theories and models: An overview of their current status* (pp. 335–381). Hillsdale, NJ: Lawrence Erlbaum Associates.

Remy, R. C. (1980). *Handbook of basic citizenship competencies: Guidelines for comparing materials, assessing instruction, and setting goals*. Alexandria, VA: Association for Supervision and Curriculum Development.

Resnick, D. P., & Resnick L. B. (1977). The nature of literacy: An historical exploration. *Harvard Educational Review, 47,* 370–385.

Resnick, L. B. (1987). *Educational and learning to think*. Washington, DC: National Academy Press.

Resnick, L. B., & Ford, W. W. (1981). *The psychology of mathematics for instruction*. Hillsdale, NJ: Lawrence Erlbaum Associates.

Restak, R. M. (1994). *The modular brain*. New York: Touchstone.

Reynolds, R. E., Sinatra, G. M., & Jetton, T. L. (1996). Views of knowledge acquisition and representation: A continuum from experience centered to mind centered. *Educational Psychologist, 31*(2), 93–104.

Reynolds, W., & Stark, F. (1983). Cognitive behavior modifications: The clinical application of cognitive strategies. In M. Pressley & J. Levin (Eds.), *Cognitive strategy research: Psychological foundations* (pp. 221–266). New York: Springer-Verlag.

Rickards, J., & August, G. J. (1975). Generative underlining strategies in prose recall. *Journal of Educational Psychology, 67,* 860–865.

Riley, J. P., II (1986). The effects of teachers' wait-time and knowledge comprehension questioning on pupil science achievement. *Journal of Research in Science Teaching, 23*(4), 335–342.

Rosenblatt, L. (1978). *The reader, the text, the poem*. Carbondale: Southern Illinois University Press.

Rosenblatt, L. M. (1994). The transactional theory of reading and writing. In R. B. Ruddell, M. K. Ruddell, & H. Singer (Eds.), *Theoretical models of reading* (4th ed., pp. 1057–1092). Newark, DE: International Reading Association.

Rosenshine, B., & Meister, C. C. (1994). Reciprocal teaching: A review of the research. *Review of Educational Research, 64*(4), 479–530.

Ross, J., & Lawrence, K. A. (1968). Some observations on memory artifice. *Psychonomic Science, 13,* 107–108.

Rothkopf, E. Z. (1970). The concept of mathemagenic activities. *Review of Educational Research, 40,* 325–336.

Rowe, H. (1985). *Problem solving and intelligence*. Hillsdale, NJ: Lawrence Erlbaum Associates.

Rowe, M. (1974). Wait-time and rewards as instructional variables, their influence on language, logic and fate control: Part 1. Wait-time. *Journal of Research in Science Teaching, 11,* 81–94.

Rumelhart, D. E. (1980). Schemata: The building blocks of cognition. In R. J. Spiro, B. C. Bruce, & W. F. Brewer (Eds.), *Theoretical issues in reading comprehension* (pp. 33–58). Hillsdale, NJ: Lawrence Erlbaum Associates.

Rumelhart, D. E., & Norman, D. A. (1981). Accretion, tuning and restructuring: Three modes of learning. In J. W. Colton & R. Klatzky (Eds.), *Semantic factors in cognition*. Hillsdale, NJ: Lawrence Erlbaum Associates.

Sapir, E. (1921). *Language: An introduction to the study of speech.* New York: Harcourt Brace Jovanovich.

Savell, J. M., Twohig, P. T., & Rachford, D. L. (1986). Empirical status of "Feuerstein's instrumental enrichment" technique as a method of teaching thinking skills. *Review of Educational Research, 56,* 38-410.

Sawada, D., & Caley, M. T. (1985). Dissipative structures: New metaphors for becoming in education. *Educational Researcher, 14,* 3-19.

Scanlon, J. R. (1997). *The Dimensions of Learning staff development model and its impact on teacher attitudes and student achievement for fourth grade students in the Neshaminy school district.* Unpublished doctoral dissertation, Temple University, Philadelphia.

Scardamalia, M., & Bereiter, C. (1983). Child as co-investigator: Helping children gain insight into their own mental processes. In S. Paris, G. Olson, & H. Stevenson (Eds.), *Learning and motivation in the classroom* (pp. 61-82). Hillsdale, NJ: Lawrence Erlbaum Associates.

Scardamalia, M., & Bereiter, C. (1985). Fostering the development of self-regulation in children's knowledge processing. In S. F. Chipman, J. W. Segal, & R. Glaser (Eds.), *Thinking and learning skills: Vol. 2. Research and open questions* (pp. 563-578). Hillsdale, NJ: Lawrence Erlbaum Associates.

Scardamalia, M., Bereiter, C., & Steinbach, R. (1984). Teachability of reflective processes in written composition. *Cognitive Science, 8*(2), 173-190.

Schank, R. C., & Abelson, R. (1977). *Scripts, plans, goals and understanding.* Hillsdale, NJ: Lawrence Erlbaum Associates.

Schank, R. C., & Rieger, C. J. (1974). Inference and the computer understanding of natural language. *Artificial Intelligence, 5,* 373-412.

Schlesinger, M. (1971). Production of utterances in language acquisition. In D. I. Slobin (Ed.), *The ontogenesis of grammar* (pp. 63-101). New York: Academic Press.

Schoenfeld, A. H. (1980). Teaching problem-solving skills. *American Mathematical Monthly, 87*(10), 794-805.

Schoenfeld, A. H. (1983a). Episodes and executive decisions in mathematical problem solving. In R. Lesh & M. Landau (Eds.), *Acquisition of mathematical concepts and processes.* New York: Academic Press.

Schoenfeld, A. H. (1983b, April). *Theoretical and pragmatic issues in the design of mathematical "problem solving" instruction.* Paper presented at the annual meeting of the American Educational Research Association, Montreal, Canada.

Scholes, R. (1982). *Semiotics and interpretation.* New Haven, CT: Yale University Press.

Searle, J. (1984). *Minds, brains, and science.* Cambridge, MA: Harvard University Press.

Segal, J. W., Chipman, S. F., & Glaser, R. (Eds.) (1985). *Thinking and learning skills: Vol. 1. Relating instruction to research.* Hillsdale, NJ: Lawrence Erlbaum Associates.

Seligman, M. E. P. (1990). *Learned optimism.* New York: Pocket Books.

Seligman, M. E. P. (1994). *What you can change and what you can't.* New York: Knopf.

Sharan, S. (1980). Cooperative learning in small groups: Recent methods and effects on achievement, attitudes and ethnic relations. *Review of Educational Research, 50,* 241-272.

Shavelson, R. J., & Bolus, R. (1982). Self-concept: The interplay of theory and methods. *Journal of Educational Psychology, 74,* 3-17.

Shavelson, R. J., & Geeslin, W. E. (1973). A method for examining subject matter structure in written material. *Journal of Structural Learning, 4,* 101-111.

Shuell, T. J. (1986). Cognitive conceptions of learning. *Review of Educational Research, 56,* 411-436.

Siegler, R. S. (1983). Information processing approaches to development. In W. Kessen (Ed.), *Manual of child psychology: History, theories, and methods* (pp. 420-442). New York: Wiley.

Simon, H. A. (1980). Problem solving and education. In D. T. Tuma & F. Reif (Eds.), *Problem solving and education: Issues in teaching and research* (pp. 81-96). Hillsdale, NJ: Lawrence Erlbaum Associates.

Simon, M. K., Bornstein, S. J., & Snyder, S. (1992). *A case study of transition in achievment, interest and attitudes accompanying an immersion program using the Dimensions of Learning framework in a fifth grade curriculum at Palmdale, California.* Unpublished manuscript.

Sinclair, J. M., & Coulthard, R. M. (1975). *Towards an analysis of discourse: The English used by teachers and pupils.* London: Oxford University Press.

Singer, H., & Bean, T. (Eds.) (1984). Learning from texts: Selection of friendly texts. *Proceedings of the Lake Arrowhead Conference on learning from text.* Arlington, VA. (ERIC Document Reproduction Service No. ED 251 512)

Skinner, E. A. (1995). *Perceived control, motivation, & coping.* Thousand Oaks, CA: Sage.

Slater, W., Graves, M., & Piche, G. (1985). Effects of structural organizers on ninth-grade students' comprehension and recall of four patterns of expository text. *Reading Research Quarterly, 20,* 189-202.

Slavin, R. E. (1978a). Effects of student teams and peer tutoring on academic achievement and time-on-task. *Journal of Experimental Education, 48,* 252-257.

Slavin, R. E. (1978b). Student teams and comparison among equals: Effects on academic performance and student attitudes. *Journal of Educational Psychology, 70,* 532-538.

Smith, E. E., & Medin, D. L. (1981). *Categories and concepts.* Cambridge, MA: Harvard University Press.

Snow, R. E., & Lohman, D. F. (1989). Implications of cognitive psychology for educational measurement. In R. L. Linn (Ed.), *Educational measurement* (3rd ed., pp. 263-331). New York: American Council on Education and Macmillan.

Snowman, J., & McCown, R. (1984, April). *Cognitive processes in learning: A model for investigating strategies and tactics.* Paper presented at the annual meeting of the American Educational Research Association, New Orleans, LA.

Sokolov, A. N. (1972). *Inner speech and thought* (G. T. Onischenko, Trans). New York: Plenum Press.

Sperry, R. W. (1985). Brain bisection and mechanisms of consciousness. In J. C. Eccles (Ed.), *Brain mechanisms and conscious experience.* New York: Springer-Verlag.

Squire, J. R. (1994). The research in reader response: Naturally interdisciplinary. In R. B. Ruddell, M. R. Ruddell, & H. Singer (Eds.), *Theoretical models and processes of reading* (4th ed., pp. 637-652). Newark, DE: International Reading Association.

Stahl, S. A., & Fairbanks, M. M. (1986). The effects of vocabulary instruction: A model-based meta-analysis. *Review of Educational Research, 56*(1), 72-110.

Staudenmayer, H. (1975). Understanding conditional reasoning with meaningful propositions. In R. Falmagne (Ed.), *Reasoning: Representation a process in children and adults.* Hillsdale, NJ: Lawrence Erlbaum Associates.

Stein, N. L. (1986). Knowledge and process in the acquisition of writing skills. In E. Z. Rothkopf (Ed.), *Review of research in education* (Vol. 10, pp. 255-258). Washington, DC: American Educational Research Association.

Stein, N. L., & Glenn, C. G. (1979). An analysis of story comprehension in elementary school children. In R. O. Freedle (Ed.), *New directions in discourse processing* (Vol. 1, pp. 53-120). Norwood, NJ: Ablex.

Sternberg, R. J. (1985). *Beyond IQ.* Cambridge University Press.

Stuss, D. T., & Benson, F. D. (1983). Emotional concomitants of psychosurgery. In K. M. Heilman & P. Satz (Eds.), *Neuropsychology of human emotion* (pp. 111-140). New York: Guilford.

Suhor, C. (1984). Toward a semiotics-based curriculum. *Journal of Curriculum Studies, 16,* 247-257.

Sulzby, E. (1985). Kindergartners as writers and readers. In M. Farr (Ed.), *Advances in writing research: Vol. 1. Children's early writing development* (pp. 127-199). Norwood, NJ: Ablex.

Sulzby, E. (1986). Writing and reading: Signs of oral and written language organization in the young child. In W. H. Teale & E. Sulzby (Eds.), *Emergent literacy: Writing and reading* (pp. 50-89). Norwood, NJ: Ablex.

Swartz, R. J. (1987). *Reading and thinking: A new framework for comprehension.* Boston: Massachusetts Department of Education.

Swift, J. N., & Gooding, C. T. (1983). Interaction of wait time feedback and questioning instruction on middle school science teaching. *Journal of Research in Science Teaching, 20*(8), 721-730.

Sylwester, R. (1995). *A celebration of neurons: An educator's guide to the human brain.* Alexandria, VA: Association for Supervision and Curriculum Development.

Tarleton, D. (1992). *Dimensions of learning: A model for enhanced student thinking and learning.* Unpublished doctoral dissertation, Nova University, Colorado Cluster.

Teale, W. H. (1987). Emergent literacy: Reading and writing development in early childhood. In J. E. Readence & R. S. Baldwin (Eds.), *Research in literacy: Merging perspectives: Thirty-sixth yearbook of the National Reading Conference.* Rochester, NJ: The National Reading Conference.

Thompson, M. (1999). *An evaluation of the implementation of the Dimensions of Learning program in an Australian independent boy's school.* Unpublished doctoral dissertation, Flinders University of South Australia.

Tobin, K. (1986). Effects of teacher wait time on discourse characteristics in mathematics and language arts classes. *American Educational Research Journal, 23,* 191-200.

Tobin, K. (1987). The role of wait time in higher cognitive level learning. *Review of Educational Research, 57,* 69-95.

Tomkins, S. S. (1962). *Affect, imagery, consciousness.* New York: Springer.

Torrance, E. P. (1980). More than the ten rational processes. *Creative Child and Adult Quarterly, 5,* 9-19.

Torrance, E. P. (1986). Teaching creative and gifted learners. In M. C. Wittrock (Ed.), *Handbook of research on teaching* (3rd ed., pp. 630-647). New York: Macmillan.

Toulmin, S., Rieke, R., & Janik, A. (1981). *An introduction to reasoning.* New York: Macmillan.

Tulving, E. (1972). Episodic and semantic memory. In E. Tulving & W. Donaldson (Eds.), *Organization of memory* (pp. 185-191). New York: Academic Press.

Tuman, M. C. (1987). *A preface to literacy: An inquiry into pedagogy, practice, and progress.* Tuscaloosa: University of Alabama Press.

Turner, A., & Greene, E. (1977). *The construction of a propositional text base.* Boulder: University of Colorado at Boulder, Institute for the Study of Intellectual Behavior.

Tweney, R. D., Doherty, M. E., & Mynatt, C. R. (1981). *On scientific thinking.* New York: Columbia University Press.

Underwood, B. J. (1969). Attributes of memory. *Psychological Review, 76,* 559-573.

van Dijk, T. A. (1977). *Text and context.* London: Longman.

van Dijk, T. A. (1980). *Macrostructures.* Hillsdale, NJ: Lawrence Erlbaum Associates.

van Dijk, T. A., & Kintsch, W. (1983). *Strategies of discourse comprehension.* Hillsdale, NJ: Lawrence Erlbaum Associates.

Van Patten, J. R., Chao, C. I., & Reigeluth, C. M. (1986). A review of strategies for sequencing and synthesizing information. *Review of Educational Research, 56,* 437-472.

Vosniadou, S., & Brewer, W. F. (1987). Theories of knowledge restructuring in development. *Review of Educational Research, 51*(1), 51-67.

Vygotsky, L. (1962). *Thought and language.* New York: Wiley.

Vygotsky, L. (1978). *Mind in society.* Cambridge, MA: Harvard University Press.

Wales, C. E. (1979). Does how you teach make a difference? *Engineering Education, 69,* 394-398.

Wales, C. E., & Stager, R. A. (1977). *Guided design.* Morgantown: West Virginia University Center for Guided Design.

Warren, W. H., Nicholas, D. W., & Trabasso, T. (1979). Event chains and inferences in understanding narratives. In R. O. Freedle (Ed.), *New directions in discourse processing* (Vol. 2, pp. 23-52). Norwood, NJ: Ablex.

Webb, N. M. (1980a). An analysis of group interaction and mathematical errors in heterogeneous ability groups. *British Journal of Educational Psychology, 50,* 1-11.

Webb, N. M. (1980b). Group process and learning in an interacting group. *The Quarterly Newsletter of the Laboratory of Comparative Human Cognition, 2,* 10-15.

Webb, N. M. (1980c). Group process: The key to learning in groups. *New Directions for Methodology of Social and Behavioral Science: Issues in Aggregation, 6,* 77-87.

Webb, N. M. (1980d). A process-outcome analysis of learning in group and individual settings. *Educational Psychologist, 15,* 69-83.

Webb, N. M. (1982). Student interaction and learning in small groups. *Review of Educational Research, 52,* 421-445.

Weiner, B. (1972). Attribution theory, achievement motivation and the educational process. *Review of Educational Research, 42,* 203-215.

Weiner, B. (1983). Speculations regarding the role of affect in achievement-change programs guided by attributional principles. In J. M. Levine & M. C. Wang (Eds.), *Teaching and student perceptions: Implications for learning* (pp. 57-73). Hillsdale, NJ: Lawrence Erlbaum Associates.

Weinstein, C. E., & Mayer, R. E. (1986). The teaching of learning strategies. In M. C. Wittrock (Ed.), *Handbook of research on teaching* (3rd ed., pp. 315-327). New York: Macmillan.

Wertsch, J. V. (1984). The zone of proximal development: Some conceptual issues. In B. Rogoff & J. Wertsch (Eds.), *Children's learning in the zone of proximal development* (pp. 7-18). San Francisco: Jossey-Bass.

Whimbey, A., & Lochhead, J. (1982). *Problem solving and comprehension.* Philadelphia: Franklin Institute Press.

Whimbey, A., & Lochhead, J. (1984). *Beyond problem solving and comprehension.* Philadelphia: Franklin Institute Press.

White, B. Y. (1983). Sources of difficulty in understanding Newtonian dynamics. *Cognitive Science, 7,* 41-65.

White, R. W. (1959). Motivation reconsidered: The concept of competence. *Psychological Review, 66,* 297-333.

Whorf, B. L. (1956). *Language, thought and reality.* Cambridge, MA: MIT Press.

Winograd, P. N., & Bridge, C. A. (1986). The comprehension of important information in written prose. In J. F. Bauman (Ed.), *Teaching main idea comprehension* (pp. 18-48). Newark DE: International Reading Association.

Wood, P., Bruner, J., & Ross, G. (1976). The role of tutoring in problem solving. *Journal of Child Psychology and Psychiatry, 17,* 89-100.

Wood, R. (1977). Multiple choice: A state of the art report. *Evaluation in Education, 1,* 191–280.

Wozniak, R. (1972). Verbal regulation of motor behavior: Soviet research and non-Soviet replications. *Human Development, 15,* 13–57.

Yost, M., Avila, L., & Vexler, E. B. (1977). Effects of learning of post-instructional responses to questions of differing degrees of complexity. *Journal of Educational Psychology, 69,* 398–401.

Young, R. E., & Becker, A. L. (1965). Toward a modern theory of rhetoric: A tagmemic contribution. *Harvard Educational Review, 35,* 450–468.

Young, R. W., Becker, A. L., & Pike, K. L. (1970). *Rhetoric: Discovery and change.* New York: Harcourt Brace.

# TEACHING THE ROOTS OF MODERN ENGLISH: THE HISTORY OF THE LANGUAGE IN THE LANGUAGE ARTS CLASS

James W. Ney

Arizona State University

Any chapter on the teaching of the history of the English language at the elementary or high school level must start with a caveat. As Marckwardt (1963, p. 3) pointed out at the Allerton Park Conference, there is a vacuum on research on how to teach *any* linguistics in the schools, including the teaching of the history of the language.

It is interesting to note that language arts texts seem to follow the emphasis set by Savage (1977, pp. 72–78) for treating aspects of the history of the English language by concentrating largely on etymology. As a result, very little on the history of the English language is taught in the schools unless it is taught in relationship to brief etymological excerpts. Quandt (1983) actually rationalized the current situation by stating:

One implication of linguistic discoveries is that children learn to communicate by experimenting with language and practicing it in meaningful ways. It would seem to be a contradiction to the work of linguists if we made linguistics a major part of the language arts content. (p. 30)

With this observation, however, he neglects the intermediate position, the teaching of *some* linguistics, and appears to advocate the teaching of *none*. In fairness to Quandt, he did recommend the study of synonyms, dialects and "a few historical aspects of English" (p. 30). He also stated that "individuals who become interested in language study should be encouraged and supported by the teacher." Moreover, he noted that when children are regularly forced to memorize the facts of language, they do not develop an interest in language, but if some young students do develop an interest in language, then "the teacher can also provide resources on language histories" (p. 31). He closed his discussion, reiterating his previous sentiments—"Linguistic content...should not become a major component in the language arts curriculum"—thereby consigning a generation of students to ignorance of the history and the structure of the language that they speak. All this is reminiscent of the remark made by one participant of the Dartmouth conference who is reported to have said: "English has no content; there are virtually no facts to transmit" (Muller, 1967, p. 12).

During the 1950s and 1960s, the members of the Commission on the English Curriculum of the National Council of Teachers of English seemed to feel that the history of the English language had no real place in the English curriculum except on the graduate level where they recommended two courses for doctoral students. (Commission on the English Curriculum, 1952, 1954, 1963, p. 553). Members of the Commission had no trouble in recommending "social studies and science and all learning experiences of the school" as "occasions and materials for developing power in...outlining for a purpose, and various other types of speech and writing" (Commission on the English Curriculum of the National Council of Teachers of English, 1963, p. 390). However, they seem to have overlooked the fact that such activities could be planned around studies in the history of the English language in the schools.

The position of the Commission and Quandt is not necessarily typical, however. In the 1960s, there were a number of ambitious projects aimed at including work on the history of the English language in school curricula. Some of these probably owed their impetus to the 1961 Woods Curriculum Workshop and, later, to the 1966 Dartmouth conference. In the latter, participants such as Kitzhaber, Gleason, and Britton helped form a consensus producing statements about language becoming the "'integrating centre, about which a new curriculum'" was to be built. (Kitzhaber, as cited in Allen, 1980, p. 30) As a result, ambitious elementary and high school curriculum guides were produced that dealt with all aspects of language including the history of the English language (see Atlanta Regional Curriculum Project, 1968; Kitzhaber, 1968; Minnesota Center for Curriculum Development in English, 1968a, 1968b, 1968c; Muinzer, 1960; Nebraska Curriculum Development Center, 1966; North Carolina State Board of Education, 1968; Northern Illinois Project English Curriculum Center, 1966; Oregon Elementary English Project, 1971). One of these, that of the Minnesota Center for Curriculum Development in English (1968a), followed the procedure of Savage (1977) by approaching the teaching of the history of the English language through etymology. Milosh (1972, pp. 49–50) made drudgery of the study of the history of the English language.

Some of these curricula were quite ambitious. For instance, the Atlanta Regional Curriculum Project (1968) was summarized in the following statement:

This curriculum guide, developed for pre-kindergartners through grade 12 as part of the total English curriculum, is concerned with the English language as it is now known and as it evolved from its Indo-European roots. Materials include (1) an overview of the origin and development of the English language from Old English through Middle English to Modern English, (2) a design for teaching sequentially the underlying principle that the English language has changed drastically from its beginnings and is being changed now, (3) 23 items of selected knowledge to be grasped during the course of study, from the simplest concept of English as a member of a language family to the more complex concept, the historical and cultural influences contributing to language changes, and (4) recommended learning experiences, which at an elementary level provide such activities as hearing and discussing a recording and improvising a meeting between a Viking and an Englishman; on the junior high level, charting family trees and researching the Teutonic Conquest; on the high school level, examining an example of modern English for its syntax and tracing word origins in *The Oxford English Dictionary*.

Some suggestions for introducing the study of the history of the English language into the schools tried to do so in a novel manner. For instance, Harder (1967), attempted to introduce the history of the English language through a study of place names. Ali (1969) attempted the same through the use of slang, jargon, colloquialisms, and regional dialects; Peterson (1987) through the study of Appalachian English; and Lesiak (1978) and Tompkins and Yaden (1986) through the study of etymology.

It is difficult, however, to assess the impact of these suggested curricula on the schools. One study (Cleaver, 1976) seemed to indicate that the extent of the teaching of the history of the English language is spotty and mixed. According to Cleaver, most of the "teaching" of this subject is done in conjunction with discussions about usage. Similarly, a survey of language arts texts would seem to indicate the same haphazard treatment on the history of the English language. For instance, in the popular Laidlaw Language Experience for Grades 3 through 8 (Hand, Harsh, Ney, & Shane, 1972b), only the sixth-grade book, *Progress in English*, had material that overtly discussed history of the English language. Of the 375 pages in this text, it devoted only 16 pages on the history of the language out of 60 pages devoted to linguistic matters. References to the history of the English language also occurred in treatments on spelling, naming, and dictionary exercises in this and other books in the series. Even in the trendsetting *Roberts English Series* (Roberts, 1966) very little space was devoted to matters pertaining to the history of the English language, and most of this dealt with dictionaries and etymologies. Perhaps the most that can be expected of the commercial texts under review is enshrined in the American Book Company series with Conlin, Herman, and Martin (1966) in which the sixth-, seventh-, and eighth-grade books each have a single-page section at the beginning of each chapter titled "The English Language and How It Grew," for a total of 14 pages out of about 375 pages, or the Laidlaw Language Experience Program's eighth-grade book in which there are 36 pages out of 413 devoted to the history of the English language (Ney, Harsh, Lapp, Myerson, & Armstead, 1979). Of the texts under review, only the supplementary work by Horn (1967) devoted a reasonable amount of space to the topic, fully one third of the work.

Perhaps, the views of Quandt (1983) and the silence of other methodologists on the issue of the teaching of the history of the English language is a result of the focus of contemporary linguistics. For the last 2 decades, linguistics has focused on transformational generative grammar. As a result, educator-statesmen-linguists such as A. H. Marckwardt and H. B. Allen have not been on the scene or center stage to focus attention on other types of linguistics and the history of the English language. This is evident from a perusal of the proceedings of the Fourth International Conference of English teachers (Tchudi et al., 1986) under the auspices of the International Federation for the Teaching of English. Hardly a word is printed there in favor of teaching language as a content area even though such linguists as Fries and Ney were present during the proceedings. Another sign of the same problem can be found in the fact that works such as Crystal's (1981) book on applied linguistics have nothing to say on the history of the English language; evidently, linguists working in this area have nothing worthy of application to classroom settings. Besides this, King (1986, p. 161), although finding a few positive things to say about transformational linguistics and its impact on the attitudes of language educators, admitted that findings from this school of linguistics are too complex for teachers to introduce into the classroom as content. It is no wonder, then, that methodology books published in the 1980s show little concern for the teaching of the history of the English language (Anderson, 1988; Chenfield, 1987; Cushenbery, 1986; Glatthorn, 1980; Hadley, 1985; Mangieri, Staley, & Wilhide, 1984; Moffett & Wagner, 1983; Myers, 1984; Staub, 1986). As far as more recent methods texts, such as those of Collins (1992) and MacKenthun and Thoresen (1994), were concerned, no suggestions are made for teaching the history of the language. A similar statement could be made about articles such as those by Guttierez and Baquedano-Lopez (1997), which advocated more language in the language arts. There is no mention of teaching the history of English.

If the teaching of one part of cultural heritage—the history of the English language—is in such a state of neglect, then, realistically, what can be done to strengthen the teaching of this subject matter in the schools? It is strange that educators do not raise the specter of boredom when the history of colonial America is the topic to be presented in the social studies class when that very specter *is* raised when linguistic studies, in particular studies on the history of the English language, are mentioned (Quandt, 1983, p. 30). There are, however, a number of suggestions for making the study of the history of the English language more interesting.

Peterson (1987) suggested that a study into the history of the English language can be made more interesting by relating that history to the current scene through the study of a dialect of English. The Minnesota Center for Curriculum Development (1968b) suggested the use of Old English to Modern English versions of the Prodigal Son and the Lord's Prayer to lighten the study in the history of the language. Kitzhaber (1968) suggested the teaching of the history of the English language through the literature of Old English, Middle English, and Early Modern English. The Oregon curriculum (Oregan Elementary English Project, 1971) would have fifth- and sixth-graders study the history of the various periods assigned to the English language and correlate that with the study of the history of the English language. Muinzer (1960) tried to lighten his approach to the teaching of the history of the English language for high school students by presenting "two major ingredients of linguistic history [which] are illustrated with plans for short classroom discussions on four aspects of linguistic change: error, intentional innovations, semantic change, and the linguistic impact of history" Another publication suggested that interest can be added to the study of the history of the language by the reading of actual texts (National Council of Teachers of English, 1967). Milosh (1972, p. 20) suggested that the subject matter itself can set students aglow with interest.

Certainly, with state, local, and federally mandated requirements focusing on skills such as reading and writing, little time can be spent on subject matter that is perceived as being a "frill" in spite of arguments to the contrary (Moss, 1987). One method, frequently exploited, for avoiding the appearance of frivolity in the study of linguistic history is to link that study to the development of dictionary skills, which are considered a necessity. This technique, apparent in the materials of the Center for Curriculum Development in English is suggested by Corcoran (1970, pp. 160-162), the Minnesota Center for Curriculum Development (1968c), and Chenfield (1987) and is used by Hand, Harsh, Ney, and Shane (1972b, pp. 106-107). Thus, it would appear that there is no shortage of ideas for the implementation of the study of the history of the English language in the schools. What is lacking is the will to implement the studies and the research showing that such implementation is not only feasible but also beneficial for the students.

# References

Ali, F. (1969). Do you know where I come from? *Use of English, 21*(1), 35-37.

Allen, D. (1980). *English teaching since 1965: How much growth?* London: Heinemann.

Anderson, P. S. (1988). *Language skills in elementary education.* New York: Macmillan.

Atlanta Regional Curriculum Project (1968). *History of the English language.* Atlanta, GA: Author. (ERIC Document Reproduction Service No. ED 042 743)

Chenfield, M. B. (1987). *Teaching language arts creatively.* San Diego, CA: Harcourt Brace Jovanovich.

Cleaver, B. P. (1976). Teaching the history of the English language: A study of English programs in North Carolina Schools, 1974-1975. *Dissertation Abstracts International, 77,* 3573A. (University Microfilms No. 76-27,960)

Collins, C. (1992). *126 strategies to build language arts abilities: A month-by-month resource.* Boston: Allyn & Bacon.

Commission on the English Curriculum of the National Council of Teachers of English (1952). *The English language arts.* New York: Appleton-Century-Crofts.

Commission on the English Curriculum of the National Council of Teachers of English (1954). *Language arts for today's children.* New York: Appleton-Century-Crofts.

Commission on the English Curriculum of the National Council of Teachers of English (1963). *The education of teachers of English.* New York: Appleton-Century-Crofts.

Conlin, D. A., Herman, G. R., & Martin, J. (1966). *Our language today.* New York: American Book.

Corcoran, G. B. (1970). *Language arts in the elementary school: A moder linguistic approach.* New York: Ronald Press.

Crystal, D. (1981). *Directions in applied linguistics.* New York: Academic Press.

Cushenbery, D. C. (1986). *Directing an effective language arts program for your students.* Springfield, IL: Thomas.

Donahue, M. R. (1985). *The child and the English language arts.* Dubuque, IA: Brown.

Glatthorn, A. A. (1980). *A guide for developing an English curriculum for the eighties.* Urbana, IL: National Council of Teachers of English.

Gutierrez, K. D., & Baquedano-Lopez, P. (1997). Putting language back into language arts: When the radical middle meets the third space. *Language Arts, 74,* 368-376.

Hadley, E. (1985). *English in the middle years.* London: Edward Arnold.

Hand, J. S., Harsh, W., Ney, J. W., & Shane, H. G. (1972a). *Exploring in English: Experiences in language.* River Forest, IL: Laidlaw Brothers.

Hand, J. S., Harsh, W., Ney, J. W., & Shane, H. G. (1972b). *Progress in English: Experiences in language.* River Forest, IL: Laidlaw Brothers.

Harder, K. B. (1967). *Place names in the classroom.* (ERIC Document Reproduction Service No. ED 017 500.)

Horn, R. E. (1967). *A programmed course in language change and communication.* Chicago: Science Research Associates.

King, M. (1986). What is Language for? A functional view of the language arts. In P. Demers (Ed.), *The creating word* (pp. 158-177). London: Macmillan.

Kitzhaber, A. R. (1968). *History of English, Parts 3 and 4—Old English to early modern—Language Curriculum V and VI, teacher and student versions.* Eugene: University of Oregon Press. (ERIC Document Reproduction Service No. ED 015 920)

Lesiak, J. (1978). The origin of words: A unit of study: Briefs. *Language Arts, 55*(3), 317-319.

MacKenthun, C., & Thoresen, K. (1994). *100 best ideas for primary language arts.* Carthage, IL: Teaching and Learning.

Mangieri, J. N., Staley, N. K., & Wilhide, J. A. (1984). *Teaching language arts: Classroom applications.* New York: McGraw Hill.

Marckwardt, A. H. (1963). Research in the teaching of English language and linguistics (A summary). In R. W. Rogers (Ed.), *Proceedings of the Allerton Park Conference on Research in the teaching of English.* Unpublished report of a USOE Project No. G-1006, Urbana, IL.

Milosh, J. E., Jr. (1972). *Teaching the history of the English language in the secondary classroom.* Urbana, IL: ERIC Clearinghouse on the Teaching of English of the National Council of Teachers of English.

Minnesota Center for Curriculum Development in English (1968a). *The dictionary: Describer or prescriber?* Minneapolis: University of Minnesota, Center for Curriculum Development in English. (ERIC Document Reproduction Service No. ED 041 881)

Minnesota Center for Curriculum Development in English (1968b). *A historical study of English phonology, morphology, and syntax.* Minneapolis: University of Minnesota, Center for Curriculum Development in English. (ERIC Document Reproduction Service No. ED 028 182)

Minnesota Center for Curriculum Development in English (1968c). *A historical study of the English lexicon.* Minneapolis: University of Minnesota, Center for Curriculum Development in English. (ERIC Document Reproduction Service No. ED 027 326)

Moffett, J., & Wagner, B. J. (1983). *Student-centered language arts and reading K-13: A handbook for teachers.* Boston: Houghton Mifflin.

Moss, R. F. (1987). Plumbing the surfaces: The value of frivolous subjects in developmental English, *The English Record, 38,* 18-21.

Muinzer, L. A. (1960). History: The life in language; and historical linguistics in the classroom. (Reprinted from *The Illinois English Bulletin, 47*(8), and 48(1), (ERIC Document Reproduction Service No. ED 041 894)

Muller, H. J. (1967). *The uses of English: Guidelines for the teaching of English from the Anglo-American Conference at Dartmouth College.* New York: Holt, Rinehart & Winston.

Myers, D. T. (1984). *Understanding language.* Upper Montclair, NJ: Boynton/Cook.

National Council of Teachers of English (1967). *Comments and exercises on historical linguistics.* Urbana, IL: National Council of Teachers of English. (ERIC Document Reproduction Service No. ED 144 086)

Nebraska Curriculum Development Center (1966). *A curriculum for English: Language explorations for the elementary grades.* Lincoln: University of Nebraska Press.

Ney, J. W., Harsh, W., Lapp, D., Myerson, M. L., & Armstead, M. (1979). *Good English: Blue book.* River Forest, IL: Laidlaw Brothers.

North Carolina State Board of Education (1968). *We speak with the tongue of men and of angels: Essays in the history of the English language.* Raleigh: North Carolina State Board of Education, Department of Public Instruction. (ERIC Document Reproduction Service No. ED 029 886)

Northern Illinois Project English Curriculum Center (1966). *History of the language, material for incorporation in curricula of Grades 11 and 12.* De Kalb: Northern Illinois University, Project English Curriculum Center (ERIC Document Reproduction Service No. ED 019 259)

Oregon Elementary English Project (1971). *History of the English language: Language V-VI (Grades Five and Six); Teacher's guide.* Eugene: University of Oregon, Oregon Elementary English Project. (ERIC Document Reproduction Service No. ED 075 838)

Peterson, B. (1987). Why they talk that talk: Language in Appalachian studies." *English Journal, 76*(6), 53-56.

Quandt, I. J. (1983). *Language arts for the child.* Englewood Cliffs, NJ: Prentice-Hall.

Roberts, P. (1966). *The Roberts English Series: A linguistics program.* New York: Harcourt, Brace & World.

Savage, J. F. (1977). *Effective communication: Language arts instruction in the elementary school.* Chicago: Science Research Associates.

Staub, M. (1986). *Educational linguistics.* Oxford, England: Basil Blackwell.

Tchudi, S., Boomer, G., Maguire, M., Creber, J. W. P., D'Arcy, P., & Johnson, F. (Eds.) (1986). *English teachers at work.* Upper Montclair, NJ: Boynton/Cook.

Tompkins, G. E., & Yaden, D. B., Jr. (1986). *Answering students' questions about words.* Urbana, IL: ERIC Clearinghouse on Reading and Communication Skills, National Council of Teachers of English. (ERIC Document Reproduction Service No. ED 268 548)

# GRAMMARS AND LITERACY LEARNING

*George Hillocks, Jr.*
University of Chicago

*Michael W. Smith*
Rutgers University

For 2 millennia, grammar has been central to school curricula. It was the subject of one of the earliest textbooks, antedated only by Euclid's text about geometry (Casson, 1985). Though grammar is ancient, conflicting views of what it is and what it is worth continue to haunt teachers. Research over a period of 100 years has consistently shown that the teaching of traditional school grammar (TSG) has little or no effect on students, particularly on their writing. Still it seems to usurp a major portion of time available for the English curricula of today's schools, and in certain states, such as Texas, many teachers see it as mandated by the state because of tests of usage and mechanics that are part of the state's writing assessment. This chapter may not be able to explain that paradox but it will examine the questions surrounding it:

1. What meanings do we attach to the word grammar?
2. How did grammar develop as a school subject?
3. What grammars are there other than school grammar?
4. What is the evidence for the effects of teaching grammar on learning it, on thinking, on correctness, and on writing?

The first three of these questions are addressed in the first section of this chapter, Grammars and Language Study. The fourth question is addressed in the chapter's second section, Grammar: Knowledge and Learning in Schools.

## GRAMMARS AND LANGUAGE STUDY

In classical Greek and Latin, the Oxford English Dictionary (*OED*, explains, the word for grammar "denoted the methodical study of literature . . . including textual and aesthetic criticism, investigation of literary history and antiquities, explanation of allusions," and so forth. Postclassically, *gramrnatica* came to apply largely to the linguistic rather. than literary portion of this ancient discipline. The *OED* explains that in the Middle Ages, the word *grammar* meant Latin grammar and was "often used as synonymous with learning in general, the knowledge peculiar to the learned class." Because the knowledge of the learned class was popularly supposed to include magic and astrology, grammar came to include these meanings that survive in what the *OED* calls corrupt forms: French, *grimoire* (book of spells or black book) and English, *glamour* (magic, enchantment; a magical or fictitious beauty attaching to any person or object). Interestingly, the latter has appeared in English as a verb: to cast a spell on someone or something. We might say, then, that grammar has glamoured English teachers.

Hartwell (1985), building on an important article by Francis (1954), enumerates five "meanings" of grammar. The first such meaning may be conceived as the set of formal patterns that speakers of a language use automatically to construct and construe larger meanings. These patterns are shared by all speakers though few may be able to explain what they are and how they work. Hartwell provides several examples of such internalized rules: e.g., the rule for the distribution of plural morphemes /s, iz, z/ in speech).

Second, grammar may refer to the scientific study (description, analysis, and articulation) of the formal patterns of a language, the primary definition in the *OED*. Such scientific study, however, has not produced a single body of knowledge on which all linguists agree. Rather, it has produced different grammars that are each dependent on different underlying assumptions and different methods of analysis and, accordingly, have different results. These grammars include structural linguistics, generative, and functional grammar or systemic functional linguistics.

Third, grammar is a set of rules governing how one ought to speak or write. In this sense, grammar is prescriptive rather than simply descriptive as is the case above. This is the third meaning offered by the *OED*.

Fourth, grammar may refer to the grammar traditionally taught in schools. This is somewhat misleading, suggesting, as it does, that school grammar is a distinct variety. It is not, however, for it combines all three of Francis' (1954) types. It assumes the existence of Type I grammar in students. It provides what many teachers see as a "description" of language, although that "description" has little to do with the reality of the English language, and it certainly provides Type III grammar, prescriptions for usage.

The fifth concept of grammar harks back to the uses of grammar in classical times when grammar was closely connected to literary study. This is a textual, or genre, grammar. Several writers have recently called for such a reintegration of grammar and textual study. For example, Glenn (1995), writing on grammar as a language art, cites classical and modern authorities to argue that grammar and grammatical exercises need to be included in a writing program in order to ensure the achievement of style and grace. One of the chief means of accomplishing this is the use of "grammatical exercises" that emphasize copying 500-word passages from established writers. She cites Corbett's (1990) recommendation that students "read through slowly a five-hundred word passage and then copy it out by hand and word-for-word" (p. 22). Beyond such copying, which she sometimes refers to as imitation, Glenn makes no further specific recommendation for the use of grammatical exercises. We have no empirical evidence that such copying has the hypothesized effects.

However, proponents of what is sometimes referred to as the genre movement argue that particular genres of writing entail the use of certain grammatical structures and conventions. Thus, for example, Halliday (1993a), in an essay "On the Language of Physical Sciences," outlines certain features of writing in the physical sciences, including the structure and uses of nominal groups to form technical taxonomies and to "summarize and package representations of processes" and verbal elements to relate and present the nominalized processes (p. 64). He argues that these nominalizations permit the presentation of the processes as the theme (old information) of sentences and passages and to use them in the rheme (new information) position as commentary on the theme. He argues that passives become part of this effort to organize themes for clearer presentation. Other writers point out even more basic tendencies in scientific writing such as the requirement to use simple present and generic references in writing reports, for example, "Tigers attack their prey" rather than "A tiger attacked its prey" (Schleppegrell, 1998). Advocates of the textual or genre grammar suggest that students must be taught these specialized structures as they undertake to write in a particular genre (Kamberelis, 1999).

## The Development of Grammar as a School Subject

In the ancient world grammar developed largely as a result of two needs. One was the philosophical desire "to understand nature in order to live a harmonious and therefore virtuous life" (Huntsman, 1983, p. 61). This tradition emanated from Aristotle and the Stoics who saw language as imposing order on reality and grammar as a means of understanding language. However, they believed that grammar could not provide a complete understanding of language because, as a product of man's nature, language is "subject to anomalies inexplicable within any strict system of grammar" (Huntsman, 1983, p. 61). The Alexandrian grammarians, on the other hand, worked in the world's first great library with texts several hundred years old. These they found to be filled with language they could no longer understand. They assumed, unlike the Stoics, that language had once reflected reality. They attempted to find as many regularities as possible in order "to explain unusual or archaic forms by analogy" (Huntsman, 1983, p. 61). This practical need gave rise to dictionaries and to the first grammar text, published by Dionysios of Thrace late in the 2nd century B.C.

This grammar became the standard grammar for Greek schoolboys up until the 12th century A.D. and the model on which Latin grammars were based (Casson, 1985). Moreover, it has had a continuing impact on school grammars. Its assumptions that language forms can be explicated by analogy and that "right" forms are discoverable determined from the outset both the paradigmatic character of school grammars and their emphasis on correctness. More than 2,000 years later these are still with us.

That first grammar by Dionysios of Thrace was short, treating only the phonological values of the alphabet and eight parts of speech: nouns, verbs, participles, articles, pronouns, prepositions, adverbs, and conjunctions. The parts of speech were defined primarily by their formal attributes although semantic definitions crept in. Later grammars, especially that by Appolonios Dyskolos, provided a description of Greek syntax and a model for describing syntax. The ideas of these Greek grammarians passed directly into their Roman successors' texts and from there into the works of two premedieval grammarians, Donatus and Priscian, whose works dominated school grammar study throughout the Middle Ages to the Renaissance. Donatus (4th century) preserved the eight parts of speech of Dionysios' work, even though Latin had no article. He simply substituted the interjection. His parts of speech were defined by a mixture of formal and semantic features. Priscian (6th century) defined the parts of speech primarily through semantic as opposed to formal characteristics. Thus, a verb is defined as signifying action or being, and an adverb as qualifying a verb. Even when the works of these two men were no longer in actual circulation, their ideas and procedures continued to influence school grammars.

School grammars for English first developed late in the 18th century. English was not a highly inflected language, although it once had been, and was therefore not suitable to the same paradigmatic treatment afforded Latin and Greek. Nonetheless, these grammars present nouns in paradigms that include nominative and objective cases. They treat other parts of speech and aspects of syntax much as had the medieval Latin grammars preceding them.

Although in the library of Alexandria, grammar had to be invented as a tool to help in the decoding of archaic forms in ancient texts, by the Middle Ages it had gone far beyond the status of mere tool. It had become the foundation of all knowledge. The beginning point of education in the seven liberal arts was the word. Grammar became, for most of the Middle Ages, the chief subject of the trivium (grammar, rhetoric, and logic), which was key to the quadrivium. Grammar was the "gateway" to all of knowledge, particularly sacred knowledge. "Grammar was thought to discipline the mind and the soul at the same time, honing the intellectual and spiritual abilities that the future cleric would need to read and speak with discernment" (Huntsman, 1983, p. 59). The major task of the cleric, according to Morrison (1983), was to use the arts, chief of which was grammar, first "to disclose the hidden mysteries of Scripture; and, second, to express esoteric doctrine for the wise, while disguising it from the simple without falsifying it" (p. 38). When Christians turned from Scripture to the arts themselves, they once again trusted to the power of grammar: "Their object was to examine . . . valid processes of reasoning, the operations of the mind itself. God had established these in the order of nature, but they too were hidden . . . by the fallacious content and methods of instruction in the arts" (p. 39). The object of education then involved the near paradox of revealing the hidden truth of Scripture by means of arts which are themselves cloaked in error. In the Middle Ages grammar was the key to the entire enterprise.

Early English school grammar evolved from a direct application of Latin grammars to the English language. As Applebee (1974) explains, "Grammatical studies in the classical languages had traditionally emphasized two elements: the learning of rules, and their 'use' or practical application. An extensive methodology had grown up around both aspects, and this was transferred more or less intact to studies of English grammar" (p. 6). Indeed, school grammars commonly treated English as though it were a highly inflected language. One text, for example, by T. S. Pinneo (1850) presents nouns as having four cases: nominative, possessive, objective and independent. 'Case,' the author claims, "is that property of a noun which denotes its *relation to other words*" (p. 35). The case endings of Latin nouns did indeed denote the relationships among words. Indeed, they did in Old English. But they do not for modern English. These Latinate grammars taught that nouns are the names of things, that verbs denote actions or being, that sentences are complete thoughts. These grammars require that students parse sentences by attending to each word in turn and naming its part of speech, its properties (for nouns these include person, gender, number, and case), and its relationships to other words in the sentence.

For the most part, current grammar texts are direct descendants of the late-18th-century Latinate grammars and present what we will call traditional school grammer (TSG), Hartwell's Type 3. Except for less emphasis on the case and gender of nouns and mode of verbs, the declarations about the grammar of English found in most contemporary texts are essentially the same as those in their counterparts of nearly 200 years ago. However, since the 1950s, two more modern kinds of grammar, structural and generative, have had some impact on curricular thinking and instructional practice. For the last decade, functional grammar has begun to have some impact as well.

## Attacks on Traditional School Grammar (TSG)

Textbooks on grammar have remained largely impervious to direct criticisms of what they offer as knowledge worth having and to developments in the field of grammar. The strongest and most typical criticism appears in C. C. Fries' *The Structure of English* (1952). First, Fries argues that TSG ignores many crucial features of English (e.g., phonology, morphology, pitch, stress, juncture), features that make differences in meaning. Second, he demonstrates that the categories of language that TSG attempts to establish are hopelessly ambiguous. Traditional school grammar presents definitions that cannot function with desired results unless the person using them has more information about language than the definition provides. For example, traditional grammars tell us that a noun is the name of a person, place, or thing—and some add idea to the list. *Blue, red*, and *yellow* are the names of colors but would not be considered nouns in the phrase *the blue shirt*. *Up, down*, and *across* are the names of directions but would not pass as nouns to most traditional grammarians. Fries points out that a large part of this difficulty arises because the definitions are not parallel. That is, a word like *blue* is the name of a color but, at the same time, can be used to modify a noun. It fits two definitions. The definition for nouns attempts to classify words according to the lexical meanings, whereas that for adjectives classifies words by function (cf. Fries, 1952, pp. 65–86). In chapter after chapter Fries enumerates the ambiguities and unexplained paradoxes of TSG.

## Structural Grammar

Structural grammarians believe that to avoid the difficulties of earlier grammars, they would have to examine a body of real language and describe it by means of its structural features rather than by semantic content. Gleason (1965) assigns the origins of such grammar to the work of 19th-century cultural anthropologists and philologists who wished to describe languages previously unknown to European and American scholarship and for which there was often no written version. Indeed, the purpose in describing the spoken language was often to devise a system of writing for the language.

The basic technique involves finding native speakers of the language and recording what they say. When a sufficient sample of the spoken language has been collected in its phonetic form (including all sounds, meaningful or not), linguists analyze it into three levels: the phonemic (significant sounds or alphabet), the morphological (words and parts of words that carry distinctive meaning), and the syntactic (sentence structures and substructures such as clauses and phrases). The grammar of a language is a description of all the elements in each of these levels.

Structural linguists identify the elements of these levels through structural features. At the phonemic level, for example, they show that voicing was a structural contrastive feature of consonants, such that certain pairs of consonants differ only in that vocal cords vibrate for one but not the other. That is, the lips, teeth, and tongue are in the same positions for each member of a given pair. But the members of the pair contrast because one is voiced whereas the other is not: /b/ and /p/; /d/ and /t/; and /g/ and /k/, for instance.

In a similar way structural grammarians analyze parts of speech through structural features. Nouns, for example, take plural and possessive inflections; use certain derivational affixes as -er, -ism, and -tion; and fit in frames of the following kind: One _____ is here. A complete analysis of any form class in English is quite complex (see, e.g., Francis, 1958, pp. 237-288).

Structural grammar examines syntax most commonly through immediate constituent analysis, a technique based on the assumption that linguistic structures may be analyzed by dichotomous cuts to the level of individual words and sometimes meaningful segments of words (morphemes). Although this analysis helps to show certain relationships among the words and phrases which constitute sentences, the rules for making the cuts were never clearly laid out. Structural grammar does not provide much insight into syntax.

The purpose of structural linguistics is to describe the structures in the language as it is used by native speakers. In doing that, the discipline had profound effects in the study of language. It provided a scientific basis for the study of language, allowed for far greater accuracy and detail in description, and avoided the prescriptivism of TSG that was often based on uninformed personal bias (J. M. Williams, 1981).

However, certain basic assumptions of structural linguistics were to come under sharp criticism. One was its rejection of meaning as a criterion for the analysis of language. Some critics argued that the structuralists' own techniques contradicted this belief. That is, although a linguist may not know the meaning of a language, the native informant's identification of contrastive features depends on the informant's knowledge of meaning. A second important assumption inherent in descriptive procedures, also came under attack: the philosophical view that language is what comes out of the mouth of a speaker. Assuming that to be true, then no matter how large a sample of language is collected, it will remain a tiny proportion of what may be spoken. The experience of any speaker with a particular language is likely to be limited to a very small proportion of that language. Her experience is likely to be accidental rather than systematic. Yet she will be able to produce an infinite number of utterances she has not heard before but that will be recognized by other native speakers as "grammatical"—that is, recognizable as an English utterance. ("Grammatical" here has nothing to do with correctness in the usual TSG sense.) Structural grammar provides no explanation of how that is possible.

In a sense, generative grammar developed as a response to these problems in structural linguistics. One of the first questions Chomsky (1957) raises in *Syntactic Structures* is that of how a speaker whose experience with language is finite and essentially accidental "can produce or understand an indefinite number of new sentences" (p. 15). No matter how accurate a description of language structural linguistics might provide, the description cannot explain how sentences are formed or predict what might be formed. Beyond that, descriptive techniques, because they are limited to observations, can never explain structures that cannot occur in a language. For example,

no English speaker would produce the following utterance even though each word is an English word: Blinking drinks of into boxes fleas.

Descriptive techniques commonly used by structuralists for generalizing about rules for clusters within sentences are limited as well. For example, the test frame for adjective presented by Francis (1958) is as follows: The _____ noun is very _____. True adjectives are said to fit in both slots. If we fill the noun slot with the word *woman*, the adjectives *old*, *young*, *decrepit*, and *happy* fit both slots. If we change, the noun to *plate*, however, we find that although *old*, and possibly *decrepit*, fit both slots, *happy* and *young* fit only as metaphor. (*Young* cannot fit literally because the semantically appropriate contrast for *old* with inanimate nouns is *new*.) The structuralist attempt to reject meaning as a basis for analysis of relationships results in the failure to produce rules that account for such relationships.

## Generative Grammar

Generative grammars reject the view that the whole of language is contained in actually observed utterances. On the contrary, they argue that language is an abstract entity and that utterances actually spoken represent epiphenomenal evidence of the existence of the abstract language. Many believe that Saussure's (1959) dichotomy of *langue* and *parole* is the source of this idea.

Chomsky (1957, 1965) and many others view grammar as theory of the language. Native speakers intuit the grammar of their languages. The task of grammarians is to make explicit the rules of the grammar operating the language. (It is important to note that the use of the term *rule* here has nothing to do with rules for correctness found in TSG.) In generative grammar rules account for the production of sentences. Early generative grammars comparable to those used in a variety of studies (e.g., Elley, Barham, Lamb, & Wyllie, 1976; Mellon, 1969) regard a sentence as a "deep structure" containing elements of semantic content such as *boy play. The rules of the grammar act on this deep structure and result in the "surface structure" that actually occurs: "The boy is playing." This sentence is only one of many possible surface structures that the grammar might generate: A boy plays; a boy does play; a boy was playing; was a boy playing; where is the boy playing; and so on.

The purpose of studying grammar, then, is to develop the rules that will explain how surface structures are generated from deep structures and to state these rules so that they have the widest possible generality in their application (Hillocks, McCabe, McCampbell, 1971, p. 427).

Chomsky was very careful to warn enthusiasts that his theoretic model did not represent the psychological processes of speakers. In 1965, he wrote:

To avoid what has been a continuing misunderstanding, it is perhaps worthwhile to reiterate that a generative grammar is not a model for a speaker or a hearer. It attempts to characterize in the most neutral possible terms the knowledge of the language that provides the basis for actual use of language by a speaker-hearer. When we speak of a grammar as generating a sentence with a certain structural description, we mean simply that the grammar assigns this structural description to the sentence. (p. 9)

## Systemic Functional Linguistics

Systemic functional linguistics (SFL) is a system of language analysis developed by M. A. K. Halliday and his colleagues, which is, in some ways, an extension of structural grammar. However, in others, it moves into territory never explored by the older structural grammars. While structural grammar rejected meaning as a means of analysis, SFL and its grammar make meaning one of its chief means of analysis. The systematic elucidation of how language provides a resource for meaning is its chief goal. The concern for meaning is what the term *functional* conveys. Further, while generative grammar treats sentences, SFL is primarily concerned with texts as the basic units through which meanings develop and while the other grammars discussed are concerned with the structures of individual sentences with little or no regard to context, SFL is deeply engaged in examining how texts convey meaning and how they relate to their social contexts. In the words of Halliday and Martin (1993), "SFL focuses on solidary . . . (mutually predictive) relationships between texts and the social practices they realize" (p. 22).

Halliday and Martin (1993) refer to their analytical model as extravagant rather than parsimonious. While previous linguists have aimed at parsimonious models of language, models that delineate the fewest rules and/or descriptors to maximum effect, SFL aims at extravagant description, an elaborate model in which "language, life, the universe and everything can be viewed in communicative (i.e., semiotic) terms" (p. 23). Because we believe this model may help us reach new understandings about students and their literacy learning, we include a brief outline of what seem to us to be some of its most important concepts.

In the grammar of SFL, Halliday (1985), although recognizing the phonemic and morphemic levels of language, moves directly to the analysis of sentences. This analysis is based on contrasts of minimal changes in linguistic sequences that reveal differences in meaning, a technique comparable to that used in determining the meaningful sounds in a language. Halliday uses the following three sentences, among others, to demonstrate some of the basic functions of word order in sentences:

1. The duke gave my aunt this teapot. (p. 32).
2. This teapot my aunt was given by the duke. (p. 35).
3. My aunt was given this teapot by the duke. (p. 35).

Halliday argues that the position of "the duke" at the beginning of Sentence 1 has the effect of announcing, "I am going to tell you something about the duke. He gave my aunt this teapot." This position results in what he calls the psychological subject or theme, a notion of subject that has been included in TSG as when a teacher explains, "The subject tells you what the sentence is about."

The "duke" is also the subject in that he is the doer of the act in question, as when teachers explain that the subject is the actor in the sentence. Halliday (1985) calls this the logical

subject or actor. However, the "duke" is also the term in the sentence in which the truth is invested. That is, Sentence 1 is a predication or proposition about the duke; the question that it generates is "Did the duke give my aunt this teapot?" Halliday calls this function the grammatical subject. In Sentence 1 all three senses of the traditional concept of subject are fulfilled by a single term. In idealized sentences, the kind we find in TSG books, one term frequently fulfills all three functions. The question arises whether that is a necessary condition.

Sentence 2 ("This teapot my aunt was given by the duke") demonstrates that it is not. In this sentence the three functions are split among three separate terms. The shift of "this teapot" to the beginning of the sentence announces, "I am going to tell you something about this teapot." It also adds a new semantic dimension, indicating the idea of exclusivity with two possibilities of meaning depending on the tonal pattern of the noun phrase. With primary stress on the word *this*, it indicates that this particular and no other teapot was given my aunt by the duke. With primary stress on *teapot*, it indicates that the duke gave my aunt the teapot and no other item. Sentence 1, on the other hand, indicates that while the duke gave my aunt a teapot, he may have given her other things as well.

In short, the word *teapot* fulfills the role of theme in the sentence, while the word *duke* remains the actor and *aunt* becomes the grammatical subject, that about which something is predicated. In this case, then, the three functions are split among three separate terms. Halliday (1985) extends the discussion to make the case stronger. We let this brief discussion stand as an illustration of the principles involved. However, a key insight of SFL is this demonstration of the multiple coding of language.

In further examining the role of theme, Halliday (1985) shows how clauses are organized as messages, with the theme standing as the indication of topic and the remainder of the clause as commentary on the topic, what Halliday has termed *rheme*. Thus, if the theme in Sentence 2 is "this teapot," the rheme is the remainder of the sentence. This analysis of clause Halliday refers to as clause as message. The analysis of themes and rhemes provide a major means of examining the ways in which texts are conceptualized and organized and has been widely used by those interested in teaching clearer sentence structure and stronger passage flow (e.g., J. M. Williams, 1999).

Using the idea of grammatical subject, clauses may also be analyzed as exchanges between speaker and listener or between writer and reader. Halliday (1985) argues that "the most fundamental types of speech role, which lie behind all the more specific types that we may be able to recognize, are just two: (i) giving, and (ii) demanding" (p. 68). Cutting across this basic distinction is another fundamental one involving the commodity exchanged: either goods and services or information. When we say something with the aim of getting a person to do something for us, "the exchange commodity is strictly non-verbal" (p. 68), as in "Hand me the scissors" or "Will you pick up potatoes at the store?" What is being demanded is an object in the first and an action in the second. Taken together, these "define the four primary speech functions of offer, command, statement, and question" (p. 68). Each of these is paired with a desired response: accepting an offer, following a command, accepting a statement, and answering a question. Only the last of these is essentially verbal. The others may all be nonverbal.

In the exchange of information, clauses take the form of propositions, statements that may be affirmed or denied, about which we may argue. In exchanges of goods and services, Halliday (1985) sees clauses as proposals that may be consented to or refused but that may not be affirmed or denied. That is, one can refuse to pass the salt upon a request, but one cannot affirm or deny the truth of the command "Pass the salt."

Halliday (1985) also treats the clause as representation,

its role as a means of representing patterns of experience. A fundamental property of language is that it enables human beings to build a mental picture of reality, to make sense of their experience of what goes on around them and inside them. Here again the clause is the most significant grammatical unit, in this case because it is the clause that functions as the representation of processes. (p. 101)

Halliday argues that a process consists essentially of three components: the process itself, the participants in it, and, optionally, the circumstances associated with it. Halliday argues that there are few processes that our language does not analyze into these components. Statements such as "It's raining" or "It's snowing" do not, but most representations of processes in English do. Many of these may be analyzed into the categories of actor, process, and goal, as in Table 54.1.

TABLE 54.1. Halliday's Process Analysis

| Actor | Process | Goal |
| --- | --- | --- |
| Geoffrey | flew | the kite. |
| The kite | hit | the tree. |

Halliday designates clauses that may be analyzed in this way as material processes, which may be analyzed as clauses of doing. They express the "notion that some entity 'does' something—which may be done 'to' some other entity" (p. 103). These clauses may be probed by questions such as the following: What did Geoffrey do? What did the kite do? We cannot ask what the tree did; rather, we ask what happened to the tree. In short, material processes are processes of doing and happening. Furthermore, every participant is a thing, a "phenomenon of our experience, including of course our inner experience or imagination" (p. 108).

However, many clauses may not be analyzed in this way. If we pose the sentence "Geoffrey liked the kite," we cannot probe with either *do* or *happen*. In this sentence, we cannot say that *Geoffrey* is an actor, that he is doing something to the kite. At the risk of oversimplifying, but for the sake of brevity, we can say that on this basis, Halliday (1985) posits the category of mental processes. In mental process clauses, there is always one participant who is human or, alternatively, one who is endowed with consciousness, as in "The tree liked the kite, too." In addition, in mental processes the participants may be things or facts. That is, we can also say "The tree was pleased that the kite nestled in its branches." In this case, Halliday says that what is being sensed is not a thing, but a fact. The typical way to express a fact is with a *that* clause. (Obviously they can also be

expressed in verbal structures such as "to have the kite nestled in its branches" as well as in other structures.) Facts cannot participate in material process clauses. "Grammatically speaking, facts can be sensed—seen, felt, or thought; but they cannot do anything, nor can they have anything done to them" (p. 109).

Because mental processes are not processes of doing or happening as are the material processes, the terms *actor, process, goal* do not apply. Halliday (1985) makes use of different terminology for these mental processes: *senser, process, phenomenon* (thing or fact). He makes other distinctions between these two types of processes as well, but which we cannot examine here. Halliday identifies four other types of processes: (a) relational, which involve identification and attribution, as in "He is the flyer" or "The kite is red"; (b) behavioral, which have to do with physiological and psychological behavior such as breathing, coughing, and so forth; (c) verbal, which have to do with symbolic exchanges of meaning (e.g., saying); and (d) existential, which assert that something exists (e.g., "There is a skunk in the drive"). Each of these, like material and mental processes may be discriminated from the others and shown to be systematically different in their requirements and functioning. These categories above and their extensions and elaborations permit the analysis of how genres of discourse differ from one another. As indicated earlier, these analyses suggest what features students may have to learn to participate in the discourse of various fields.

Using these concepts, for example, Halliday (1993) demonstrates how scientific discourse over the course of several centuries as scientists strove to develop a step by step discourse, with each step building on what had preceded it. To do this, scientists made use of resources that were latent in English, transforming material and mental process clauses into nominalizations that could be used as themes in other material, mental, and relational clauses. In this way, facts can be treated grammatically as things and, in this transformed state, can act on other things. Additionally, the nominalization of previously stated clauses allows for the logical progression of theme-rheme arrangements so that the discourse moves forward in a logical and clear fashion.

Halliday (1993b) puts it this way:

Newton and his successors were creating a new variety of English for a new kind of knowledge; a kind of knowledge in which experiments were carried out; general principles [were] derived by reasoning from these experiments, with the aid of mathematics; and these principles in turn tested by further experiments. The discourse had to proceed step by step, with a constant movement from 'this is what we have established so far' to 'this is what follows from it next'; and each of these two parts, both the 'taken for granted' part and the new information, had to be presented in a way that would make its status in the argument clear. The most effective way to do this, in English grammar, is to constrict the whole step as a single clause, with the two parts turned into nouns, one at the beginning and one at the end, and a verb in between saying how the second follows from the first (p. 81).

As the current work in SFL demonstrates, research in linguistics has continued to generate new insights and theories about how language works. However, school curricula in grammar have generally ignored these developments. Fortunately, scholars interested in SFL are considering the instructional implication of that model. Thus far, the majority of the work in SFL has been devoted to elaborating the theoretical perspective, work of the sort that we have outlined here, and to demonstrating that that perspective is useful for analyzing both model texts (cf. Ravelli, 1996) and student texts (cf. Schlepegrell, 1998). However, some recent research has begun to document how teachers make use of SFL in their classrooms and what effect their teaching has on their students. Unlike the studies on TSG (we review these studies later), which have, for the most part, examined the effect of TSG in quasi-experimental designs, research on SFL has been more descriptive in nature. G. Williams (1998), for example, draws on an analysis of classroom transcripts to argue that a diverse classroom of upper elementary students (Year 6 in the New South Wales primary school system) was able to learn and apply important constructs from SFL to become more critically aware readers of a children's storybook. Although this may seem to be a modest claim, it is striking when compared to the wealth of research that has documented no, or even negative, effects for teaching TSG.

## Dialect Study

The focus of descriptive linguists on the variation of actual utterances led quite naturally to the study of dialect. Dialecticians, working within the traditions of structural linguistics, have shown that most differences in usage among speakers cannot be considered aberrations from some standard preferred speech with its origins in a distant Edenic past when all things were perfect. Rather, most variations in usage derive from different language communities that develop their own varying norms. Labov (1972) argues forcefully, for example, that what he calls Black Vernacular English (BVE) is not simply a mass of error as was thought by earlier researchers. On the contrary, Labov shows clearly that BVE is "a distinct subsystem within the larger grammar of English" (pp. 63–64) with its own regular conventions and a few clearly different rules for the production of utterances.

One such rule, for example, allows for what Labov (1972) calls a remote present perfect in the use of *been* in an expression such as "I been know your name" (pp. 53–55), in which *been know* means "have known for a long time and still know." Heath (1983) explains that such forms cause difficulty in classrooms when teachers do not know BVE usage, for they often interpret them as incorrect Standard English as in the following revealing incident related by Heath:

A teacher asked one day: "Where is Susan? Isn't she here today?" Lem answered, "She ain't ride de bus." The teacher responded: "She *doesn't* ride the bus, Lem." Lem answered: "She do be ridin' de bus." The teacher frowned at Lem and turned away. Within the system of Black English Lem used, *ain't* was used as equivalent to *didn't*, the negative of the past tense of auxiliary *do*; thus his answer had to be interpreted as "She didn't ride the bus." The teacher heard the ain't as equivalent to *doesn't* and corrected Lem accordingly; he rejected this shift of meaning and asserted through his use of *do be ridin'* that Susan did indeed regularly ride the bus. (pp. 277–278)

In addition to demonstrating the internal regularities of BVE and how failures to comprehend it lead to serious misunderstandings by educators, linguists have also demonstrated that speakers of BVE develop a finely honed sense of logic and argument within their own language conventions (Labov, 1972, pp. 201–240). Further, Heath (1983) showed in rich detail how conflicting language conventions of people living and working in the same community lead to misunderstandings on the part of teachers and students, to inappropriate judgments of the students, and hence to failure to learn on both sides of the desk. Heath has also provided accounts of how teachers in one community found ways to overcome such problems.

## GRAMMAR: KNOWLEDGE AND LEARNING IN SCHOOLS

Knowledge about language has been systematized in various ways and taught for over 2,000 years. Reasons for such study have varied: in the ancient world to recover the meaning of old texts and in the middle ages to provide the foundation for art and knowledge. In general, modern proponents of grammar instruction cite three reasons for teaching it: the insight it offers' into the way the language works, its usefulness in mastering standard forms of English, and its usefulness in improving composition skill.

A great deal of research in the past 9 decades has been devoted to investigating the validity of these and other reasons for studying grammar. At the same time, it has become clear that native speakers intuit a grammar of greater complexity than has so far been described by linguists. Moreover, it is doubtful that this complexity can be taught. What follows briefly reviews studies of tacit knowledge and then turns to studies that investigate effectiveness of teaching grammar in order to understand language as a supreme human achievement, improve composition, improve usage. Finally, the chapter examines the use of tacit grammatical concepts to enhance students' syntactic versatility—sentence combining and sentence construction.

### Students' Tacit Knowledge of Grammar

If knowledge of grammar is defined as the ability to produce and understand a wide range of grammatical structures, then students have a substantial knowledge of grammar before they receive any formal instruction. In her extensive study of the language of elementary-schoolchildren in Grades 1 through 6, Strickland (1962) concludes that "children learn fairly thoroughly at an early age the basic structures of their language" (p. 106). Strickland's finding has been corroborated by a variety of researchers. Hunt (1965) notes that "the average child in the fourth grade produces virtually all the grammatical structures ever described in a course in school grammar" (p. 156). O'Donnell, Griffin, and Norris (1967) in their study of kindergarten and elementary-school children state that kindergartners produced essentially the same sentence patterns as seventh graders. Labov (1970) argues on the basis of his study of speakers of nonstandard dialects that "the child who comes to school is already in possession of an extremely complex set of linguistic rules—more complex than any linguist is now able to describe" (p. 48). He explains that "most linguistic rules . . . are not consciously recognized and are never violated" (p. 29).

One example of such an "automatic rule" is the rule for contracting the word *is* to, '*s*. Labov (1970) explains that even though no one is taught the complex conditions under which one can make the contraction, native speakers would say "He's here" but would never say "Here he's." Hartwell (1985) offers another example. He reports asking a variety of people, from sixth graders to high school teachers, to cite the rule for combining adjectives of age, nationality, and number in English. No one is able to do so. However, when he asked these same people to arrange the words *French the young girls four* in a natural order, all native speakers immediately produce "the four young French girls." Interestingly, when he provided the rule for using the definite article, the indefinite article, or no article and asked native speakers to apply it in a passage in which the articles were deleted, he found that most native speakers reported "a great deal of frustration." He concludes that "the rule . . . is, for the most part, simply unusable for native speakers of the language" (p. 116). Shaughnessy (1977), in her study of basic writers in college composition, explains that "despite their difficulties with common errors, their intuition about English are the intuitions of native speakers. Most of what they need to know has already been learned—without teachers" (p. 129). McCutcheon, Hull, and Smith's (1987) empirical work resonates with the arguments of Hartwell and Shaughnessy. They note that basic writing students have two very different editing strategies: a consulting strategy, in which grammatical rules are consulted, and an intuiting strategy, in which the text is assessed for goodness by how it sounded. The basic writing students consistently used their intuiting strategy more effectively. Quite clearly, students have an immense amount of tacit grammatical knowledge without any formal instruction, and attempts to formalize that knowledge may actually interfere with applying it.

The fact that students enter school with this knowledge already in place does not imply that they do not develop during their years of formal schooling. Hunt (1965) notes that the younger student

does not produce as many [grammatical structures] at the same time—as many inside each other, or on top of each other—as older students do. He does subordinate some clauses to others, but not as many. He does reduce some coordinate clauses to coordinations inside a single clause, but not enough. . . . He does write some complicated nominals, but his are never most highly complicated. It is what the older student does *in extremis* that especially distinguishes him. (p. 156)

Hunt's (1965) findings that more mature writers produce longer T units with more embeddings were supported by O'Donnell, Griffin, and Norris (1967) who especially note an increase in making structures more compact through deletion transformations. Loban (1976) noted that these two characteristics together with increased elaboration and a reduction in mazes (confused patterns) most clearly distinguished the language of proficient subjects as compared with those who use

language ineffectively. Each of the groups (high, random, and low) in his longitudinal study of children's language from kindergarten through 12th grade was characterized by "steady nondramatic chronological development" (p. 84) in most of the language behavior he studied.

## Grammar for Appreciation of Human Language

Since the 1960s, one of the most frequently cited reasons for studying grammar is its humanistic value. Weaver (1979) lists it first among various reasons offered for teaching grammar: "The study of grammar is important simply because language is a supreme (and perhaps unique) human achievement which deserves to be studied as such" (p. 3). This, of course, is not an empirically arguable claim, but it has an empirical dimension. That is, researchers could ask whether students are successful in learning the system of grammar taught in order to understand the working of language.

Generally speaking, as indicated above, linguists regard TSG as an inadequate description and explanation of how the English language works. If educators wish to teach grammar for humanistic reasons, it seems to follow that the curriculum should make use of relatively current knowledge about grammar. Structural grammar had some currency during the 1960s. Alva (1960), for example, reports that structural grammar was generally taught in California schools in 1960 and seemed to be increasing in popularity. Also in the 1960s, structural and generative grammars were incorporated into the curricula developed by the Project English Curriculum Centers at Nebraska and Oregon and by the Euclid (Ohio) Western Reserve Project English Demonstration Center.

Some researchers have considered the effects of newer grammars. For example, Bateman and Zidonis (1966) contrast the effects on ninth-graders of 2 years of instruction in a generative grammar as compared with a control group that studied no grammar. They report a statistically significant difference in the number of well-formed sentences written by the experimental group. Working with classes from 21 schools, H. L. Smith and Sustakowski (1968) compare the effects of a structural grammar to the effects of traditional grammar. They report large gains on the Modern Language Aptitude Test (MLAT) by the group that studied structural grammar. The MLAT measures sensitivity to phonological, morphological, and syntactic structures, something the structural group studied but the traditional group did not. (However, the researchers did not find significant differences on a variety of measures of correctness.)

In 1966, the Dartmouth Conference of British and American scholars and teachers concerned with the teaching of English agreed in principle that "language study may be justified simply as a humanistic study, valuable in itself" (Muller, 1967, p. 72). However, when they considered a curricular document purporting to teach a newer grammar, in Muller's words, "Disaster struck. . . . It looked just as dreary as the old exercises in grammar. The British were appalled by it; they wanted to know how these ghastly exercises could be considered 'humanistic'" (p. 72). Muller himself states that "the clearest contribution of linguistics to the teaching of English remains its studies of usage, not the new modes in grammatical exercises" (p. 73). The Dartmouth Conference may have sounded the death knell of newer grammars in the schools. This review includes a brief description of functional grammar. However, we know of only a few attempts to teach it in Australian schools.

The value of studying grammar for humanistic reasons is dependent on the extent to which students learn it and on how they feel about learning it. Some studies examine the extent to which students learn the grammar they are taught. Briggs (1913) reports that groups with considerable training in TSG did less well on a test of formal grammar than students with no such instruction. The test included items examining the ability to parse and to identify types of clauses and complete sentences. One item included parsing a predicate attribute of the object which "represents the effect of the act expressed in the predicate on that which the object represents" (p. 294).

Macauley (1947) examines knowledge of grammar using a seemingly simpler test. He presented Scottish students at various levels sets of sentences and asked that they identify the nouns, verbs, adjectives, and adverbs. He administered the test to 131 students who had completed primary school with 30 minutes of grammar instruction daily for 4 years. With passing set at 50%, only one student passed. Thirty-seven percent passed on nouns, 21% on verbs, and only 5% and 4% passed on adjectives and adverbs, respectively. He administered the same test to students completing the elite senior secondary school which, in Scotland, admitted only the top 20% of junior secondary school graduates. These students had studied grammar for 9 years. Of these top students only 42% were able to identify 50% of the items correctly. In other words, in Macaulay's study, a majority of even the most capable students failed to learn what teachers think of as fundamental concepts of TSG. It may be that the inherent ambiguities of TSG identified by Fries (1952) make learning parts of speech extremely difficult even for the best students, or it may be that the subject of grammar is so abstract that it is difficult to learn. Whatever the reason, if students cannot or do not learn the fundamental concepts, the class time spent on the study of grammar in order to appreciate language as a human achievement is wasted.

A few studies inquire into student attitudes toward the study of language. Hillocks (1971) surveyed attitudes toward English of over 3,000 high school students in three predominantly blue-collar suburban communities. He reports that students rated the study of TSG and mechanics as the least interesting part of their English programs. Elley et al. (1976), whose study included two different grammar treatments (TSG and generative), reports that both groups found English less "interesting" than the no-grammar group. In regard to feelings about sentence study and language textbooks the generative grammar group showed predominantly negative attitudes, especially on such dimensions as "useless," "unimaginative," "repetitive," "passive," "complicated," and "unpleasant." Clearly, the [generative grammar] strand of the Oregon Curriculum "was not popular" (p. 16).

In short, there is little to suggest that students either learn grammar or enjoy it. Such findings seem to weaken the case for promoting formal grammar study in the schools in the hope that students will appreciate language as "a supreme (and perhaps unique) human achievement" (Weaver, 1979, p. 3).

## Grammar and Composition

In their 1963 review of research in written composition, Braddock, Lloyd-Jones, and Schoer make this now famous pronouncement: "The teaching of formal grammar has a negligible or, because it usually displaces some instruction and practice in actual composition, even a harmful effect on the improvement of writing" (pp. 37–38). Hillocks (1986) in his review of research in written composition done from 1963 to 1982 makes an equally strong statement:

School boards, administrators, and teachers who impose the systematic study of traditional school grammar on their students over lengthy periods of time in the name of teaching writing do them a gross disservice which should not be tolerated by anyone concerned with the effective teaching of good writing. (p. 248)

Hillocks bases his conclusion both on his narrative review (Hillocks & Smith, 1986) of studies and his meta-analysis of composition studies (Hillocks, 1986), 14 of which involved grammar as either the experimental or control treatment.

Of all of the studies Hillocks and Smith (1986) reviewed, by far the most impressive is by Elley et al. (1976). Meckel (1963) comments that the training periods in many studies "have been comparatively short, and the amount of grammar instruction has frequently been small" (p. 981). In contrast, Elley et al. consider the achievement of New Zealand high school students as they moved through the third, fourth, and fifth forms and in a follow-up 1 year after the completion of instruction. The time period is notable. The sample is large (248 students at the outset and 166 after 3 years) and carefully controlled. Students were divided into eight classes matched on the basis of four test scores, sex, ethnicity, contributing school, and subject option. Three of these classes studied the Oregon curriculum, which included generative (transformational) grammar. Three other classes studied the same curriculum, replacing the study of transformational grammar with extra literature and creative writing. The final two classes studied TSG. The instruction in literature for these classes was centered on the study of six to eight sets of popular fiction. During each year of the study, teachers taught a different treatment so that no one method was taught by the same teacher for more than 1 year. The researchers used a variety of measures after each year of the study: tests of reading, listening, English usage, spelling, English literature, and sentence combining; criterion referenced scales on essays the students had written; and attitude surveys.

The findings are notable not for the differences that emerged but rather for the lack of differences. At the end of the 1st year, no significant differences among groups existed on any of the measures. At the end of the 2nd year, the traditional grammar group's essay content was significantly better than the no-grammar group, and the generative grammar group's attitude toward writing and literature was significantly worse than the other two groups. At the end of the 3rd year the generative grammar group and the no-grammar group performed significantly better on the sentence combining test. Both grammar groups performed significantly better on the English usage test. However, there were no significant differences in the quality or correctness of students' actual writing. The fact that the differences among groups was small is clear. Indeed, even the superiority of the grammar groups on the test of English usage is questionable because it "was dispersed over a wide range of mechanical conventions, and was not clearly associated with sentence structure" (Elley et al., 1976, p. 15). This advantage must be weighed against the negative effect of studying grammar on students' attitudes toward English.

A variety of studies corroborate the most important finding of Elley et al. (1976): Teaching grammar does not have a beneficial effect on students' writing. White (1965), Whitehead (1966), J. L. Sullivan (1969), Bowden (1979), and S. R. Morrow (1984) all compared the effects of teaching traditional school grammar with the effects of teaching no grammar and found no significant differences.

Perhaps the strongest support for the conclusion of Elley et al. (1976) is Hillocks' (1986) meta-analysis of composition studies. To be included in the meta-analysis a study had to meet several criteria, among them consideration of students' actual writing and not standardized measures of writing quality, appropriate scoring procedures, at least minimal teacher controls, and reporting of data which allowed the computation of effect size.

Meta-analysis has several important advantages as an analytic tool. In the first place, it focuses on the size of gains (effect size), and not simply on statistical significance, which depends in part on the number of subjects in a study. Second, because it pools data from several sources and tests the similarity of findings through a homogeneity statistic, it can determine whether or not a study's findings are merely idiosyncratic.

For the purposes of the meta-analysis, Hillocks (1986) groups treatments that focus on grammar with those that focus on mechanics and those that combine instruction in grammar and mechanics. Of all of the studies on grammar and mechanics only three, Elley et al. (1976), A. E. Thibodeau (1964), and A. L. Thibodeau (1964) met the criteria for inclusion and, in addition, compare the study of grammar and/or mechanics to some other instruction. These three studies include a total of five treatments. Hillocks (1986) reports that students in the grammar and/or mechanics treatments score .29 standard deviations lower than students in the control no-grammar and/or mechanics treatments. Furthermore, this is a highly homogeneous effect.

Hillocks (1986) also examines the pre- to post effect sizes of all treatments focusing on grammar in studies qualifying for the meta-analysis. This allows inclusion of nine control treatments that appear in other categories when experimental/control effects are examined. The resulting 14 treatments of grammar and/or mechanics produce a mean pregain to postgain of .06 standard deviations. In contrast, the mean pre-to-post gain for the 75 treatments that include no instruction in grammar and/or mechanics is .44 of a standard deviation. This difference is quite large and highly significant ($p < .0001$). Apparently any focus of instruction is more effective in improving the quality of writing than grammar and mechanics.

Even studies purporting to support the teaching of grammar offer findings consistent with this argument. Noyce and Christie (1983) compare the impact of teaching third-grade students six complex syntactic structures through three different treatments: an integrated approach that offered listening, speaking, writing, and reading activities; a writing-only approach, and a traditional approach that focused on the study of parts of speech. They report that the integrated approach resulted in statistically significant differences among the groups' improvement in reading comprehension as measured by a standardized test and in the difference in the length of pretreatment and posttreatment timed writing samples. Although the authors claim that a strategy for teaching grammar can be extrapolated from their research, their integrated approach did not involve the teaching of grammar in any of Hartwell's five definitions. What their research seems to suggest instead is that targeted listening, speaking, writing, and reading activities that build students' tacit knowledge of the language are more effective than are attempts to develop that knowledge through explicit grammar instruction. Consequently, their research is consistent with Hillocks' (1986) finding.

Despite all the evidence of the failure of grammar instruction to have an effect on the quality of writing, many classroom teachers reject the finding and are suspicious of those who offer it. Taylor (1986) explains that "teachers working with student writing know that their students need some knowledge of language and its conventions" (p. 95). She furthermore notes: "When 'experts' tell teachers that the research says that grammar should not be taught at all, teachers are suspicious of the research and inclined to reject it" (p. 95). This is especially true when teachers equate the recommendation not to teach grammar with a lack of concern with "correctness."

## Grammar and Usage

Supporters of grammar instruction argue that the study of grammar is essential in improving writing quality because grammar instruction will reduce error rates in mechanics and usage. Such reduction is clearly important, at least for success in the academy. In fact, Rafoth and Rubin (1984) found that mechanics had a greater influence on college instructors' judgments than either content or rating instructions. The influence of mechanics was so great in their study that Raforth and Rubin question evaluators' ability to disregard mechanics when they assess other aspects of students' work. Connors (1985) offers an interesting historical analysis of where the emphasis on mechanics comes from. But whatever its source, its power in undeniable.

However, the study of error is complex. In the first place, research suggests that teachers differ dramatically in their assessment of what counts as error. Connors and Lundsford (1988), in fact, argue that an historical analysis demonstrates that "teachers' ideas about errors and error classification have always been absolute products of their times and cultures" (p. 399). Moreover, as we have seen, many items that teachers regard as errors (e.g., "He don't") are not. Such items simply follow the rules of the dialect spoken by the person using them. Even if teachers could agree on a definition of error, there is no clear evidence that the study of grammar would have a significant impact on their reduction. As noted earlier, Elley et al. (1976) found no significant difference between the grammar and no-grammar groups on the mechanics rating of students' actual writing.

Supporters of grammar instruction also argue that students must learn grammar so that teachers and students have a common vocabulary to discuss writing. The question of the importance of grammatical terminology is one the research has not fully answered. As we noted above, research does make it clear that students have difficulty applying their knowledge of grammatical terms. Students tend not to learn even the fundamental concepts of grammar (Macauley, 1947). Teaching grammatical terms to provide teachers a quick way to grade papers does not seem justified. Hartwell (1985) explains, with an acronym, that the rules of traditional grammar are COIK, or clear only if known. Hillocks, McCabe, and McCampbell (1971) came to a similar conclusion: "If the student understands the error he has made, the problem is not grammar but proofreading and should consequently be treated differently. If he does not understand the error, the teacher's reference to it will be futile" (p. 411).

Some proponents of instruction in grammar argue that it is not the grammar that is the problem but rather the way that grammar is taught. Shaughnessy (1977), for example, explains that to be useful a student's knowledge of grammatical terms must go well beyond the ability to state definitions. She advocates teaching four key concepts: the sentence, inflection, tense, and agreement. She makes it clear that learning something as complex as the third-person singular inflections requires far more detailed knowledge than provided by most traditional instruction in grammar. Noguchi (1991) begins his book on grammar and the teaching of writing by examining some of the studies we have reviewed here and analyzing possible causes for the failure of grammar to improve writing. Noguchi argues that although grammar instruction cannot affect crucial aspects of writing such as content and organization, it has the potential to affect a writer's style (he includes nonstandard usages as part of style). Noguchi advocates less and more focused grammar instruction, a recommendation also made by Weaver (1996). At present, however, research does not suggest how much or what kinds of instruction in grammar writers must have to achieve the effects these proponents of grammar seek.

As Shaughnessy (1977) and Hillocks (1986) argue, a more focused approach to teaching grammar to reduce error depends on an analysis of the causes of error. Shaughnessy's book is a powerful argument that errors are not random but rather happen for a reason. One of the causes Shaughnessy examines is dialect interference. However, research done since her groundbreaking effort has complicated that analysis. Reading across studies by Armstrong (1982), Cheesboro (1982), Cronnell (1984), Epes (1985), Farr and Janda (1985), Graham (1983), D. H. Morrow (1988), and Williamson (1990) suggests that the impact of dialect interference on students' writing is at best problematic. Other research suggests causes for error that seem beyond the reach of instruction. Connors and Lundsford (1998) argue, for example, that the error patterns they observed suggest a "declining familiarity with the written page" (p. 406), a cause deeply woven into the fabric of an increasingly electronic culture. Belanger (1986) argues that the causes of error are so idiosyncratic that no one set of rules could be applied to all of the students in his study, a finding that suggests the difficulty that an individual classroom teacher might encounter in addressing error.

Other studies paint a more optimistic portrait. For example, Kagan (1980) presented two tests to 202 remedial college freshmen. One test consists of 15 different syntactic structures together with five complete sentences randomly ordered. She asks students to identify which are sentences and which are parts of sentences. She reports that students most often mistake a verb plus a subordinate clause, a verb plus a direct object and a prepositional phrase, and two prepositional phrases for sentences. Her analysis of a similar test on run-on sentences reveals that the most common errors relate to combinations of long and short sentences. This study suggested that learning to identify basic sentence patterns and expand them in a variety of ways might help students identify sentence boundaries more consistently. Wofford (1986) suggests that daily written and oral practice in targeted structures has a greater impact on correctly using those targeted structure than does traditional grammar instruction.

Taylor (1986) argues that teachers cling to traditional grammar because they have not developed alternative approaches. Unfortunately, ways to improve students' "correctness," an issue important to teachers, has been largely neglected by researchers.

## Sentence Combining

In his preface to Hunt's 1965 study, G. Robert Carlsen states that "the school's program should facilitate the student's moving in the direction of mature writing patterns" (p. vi). Mellon's 1969 study was the first consideration of instruction designed to do just that. Mellon theorized that applying a knowledge of transformational grammar to concrete sentence combining problems would result in greater syntactic fluency. (Other researchers use the term *syntactic maturity*.) That is, he believed that the experimental treatment would result in students' writing longer T units that would display enhanced growth in the use of the types of transformations that Hunt (1965) found characterized mature syntax. He was right, and this "pioneering experiment . . . laid the foundations for subsequent experimental research in sentence combining" (Kerek, Daiker, & Morenberg, 1980, p. 1061).

However, sentence combining did not become an important focus of instruction until O'Hare's 1973 study. O'Hare hypothesized that the gains in Mellon's (1969) experimental group were the result of sentence combining practice rather than knowledge of transformational grammar. To test his hypothesis, O'Hare's experimental group worked with combining sets of sentences into increasingly complex structures. The combinations were cued by connecting words rather than by grammatical terminology. O'Hare reports significant increases in syntactic fluency on a variety of measures as well as an overall growth in quality. Since O'Hare's study, sentence combining has been enormously popular. Cooper (1975) argues that "no other single teaching approach has ever consistently been shown to have a beneficial effect on syntactic maturity and writing quality" (p. 72). Mellon (1979) concurs: "The best advice I can give teachers today, relative to sentence combining, is—Do it!" (p. 35).

***Sentence combining and syntactic fluency.*** Kerek et al. (1980) report that sentence combining "has been proven again and again to be an effective means of fostering growth in syntactic maturity" (p. 1067). In a later review Hillocks and Mavrogenes (1986) consider the "host" of sentence-combining studies done from 1973 to 1982. They report that "the overwhelming majority of these studies have been positive, with about 60 percent of them reporting that work in sentence combining, from as low as grade 2 through the adult level, results in significant advances (at least $p < .05$) on measures of syntactic maturity" (pp. 142–143). Furthermore, they reported that an additional 30% of the studies found some improvement at a nonsignificant level. Only 10% of the studies that Hillocks and Mavrogenes review are negative, showing no differences or mixed results.

In addition to working with all ages of subjects, sentence combining appears to increase syntactic fluency in all types of students. Hunt and O'Donnell (1970), Ross (1971), Perron (1975), Schuster (1976, 1977), and Waterfall (1978) report that remedial or disadvantaged students especially benefit from sentence-combining instruction. Stoddard and Renzulli (1983) indicate that sentence combining is effective for above-average students.

Research, however, does not provide unqualified support for using sentence combining. Perhaps the most important question is whether longer T units, the most common measure of syntactic fluency, are desirable. Hake and Williams (1979 and 1985) argue that when students who were initially judged to be incompetent writers become competent writers, their T-unit length decreases.

A variety of correlational studies also question whether syntactic fluency as it is commonly measured is an important curricular goal. Faigley (1979) examines the correlations between measures for a set of pretest and posttest narratives by college freshmen. He reports that measures related to elaboration (words in final free modifiers, percentage of T units with final free modifiers, and overall length) were significantly related to the quality of writing. Syntactic measures unrelated to elaboration, however, are not significant.

Other studies have also shown a very low correlation between mean T-unit length and quality ratings: Belanger (1978), Nold and Freedman (1977), Stewart and Grobe (1979), and Wille (1982). The only significant correlation between T-unit length and writing quality was for Stewart and Grobe's fifth-graders, and their other results strongly suggest that the significance of this relationship decreases as students continue in school. These findings question whether the overwhelming evidence that sentence combining increases syntactic fluency is sufficient justification for recommending its use.

Other studies question the reliability of T-unit length as a measure of syntactic fluency. Martinez San Jose (1973), Perron (1977), and Crowhurst and Piche (1979) all strongly suggest that different modes of discourse produce different syntactic structures as well as different mean T-unit lengths. It may be that mean T-unit length is a function of the writer's purpose in a specific piece of writing. If so, mean T-unit length cannot be an effective measure of syntactic fluency, unless there is some control for writer's purpose.

Even if one accepts the importance of syntactic fluency measures, however, questions about sentence combining remain. A variety of studies have considered whether gains in syntactic fluency are maintained. Several studies (Combs, 1977; Maimon & Nodine, 1978; 1979; Morenberg, Daiker, & Kerek, 1978; Pederson, 1978) suggest that gains are maintained for a period of several months. Other studies, however, offer clearly negative (Callaghan, 1978; Green, 1973) or somewhat negative (Combs, 1976; Ofsa, 1975; M. A. Sullivan, 1978, 1979) answers to this question.

Strong (1986) labels the Morenberg et al. (1978) study "probably the best designed, best funded, and most carefully executed [sentence combining] study to date" (p. 7). In their study of 290 college freshmen, Morenberg et al. report that the experimental group, whose instruction focused on whole-discourse, open sentence-combining problems scored significantly higher on holistic and analytic measures than the control group, whose instruction focused on modes of discourse. They also report that these gains were maintained for several months. However, 28 months after the instruction Kerek et al. (1980) gave their subjects a delayed posttest and found that while the experimental group's scores did not decline, the control group gained significantly without specific instruction. These results suggest that syntactic fluency may be, in part, the result of maturity, and they raise a question of the ultimate benefits of accelerating what may be natural development.

A related question is whether sentence combining actually increases students' skill in manipulating syntax or rather simply cues them to make use of resources they already have. Smith and Combs (1980) study this question. They presented three assignment conditions to college freshmen: the assignment with no cue about structure; the assignment plus a cue indicating that the audience would be impressed with long, complex sentences; and a covert cue of 2 days of sentence combining. Their results indicate that a combination of the overt and covert cues over 1 week produced mean gains in words per clause comparable to those gains produced by a semester of sentence-combining practice in other studies. Smith and Hull (1985) also consider the power of sentence combining as a cue. Their study targets three syntactic structures: relative clauses, appositives, and infinitive nominals. They selected students who used these three structures significantly more or less than average on the basis of a pretest writing sample. They explained to these high-use and low-use students that because the students had an idiosyncratic problem, they were to do sentence-combining exercises. The results indicate that the high-use groups reduced their use of each of the targeted structures, whereas the low-use group increased their use of the structures on a posttest. The authors theorize that the sentence-combining exercises act as a cue to increase or decrease the structures. Furthermore, they report that the cue retained its strength for the low-use group when they revised both the pretest and the posttest. However, they report that the strength of the cue diminished for the high-use group who increased their use of the targeted structures on their revisions of the pretest and the posttest.

On balance, the evidence strongly suggests that sentence combining increases syntactic maturity, but by itself this evidence does not stand as an unqualified endorsement of sentence combining. A far more important question is, What are the effects of sentence combining on writing quality?

***Sentence combining and writing quality.*** A variety of studies (Combs, 1976, 1977; Howie 1979; Morenberg et al., 1978; Obenchain, 1979; Ofsa, 1975; O'Hare, 1973; Pederson, 1978; Schuster, 1976, 1977; Stewart, 1978; Stoddard & Renzulli, 1983; Waterfall, 1978) explore the effect of sentence combining on writing quality. Hillocks (1986) examines each of these studies in his meta-analysis of composition studies, with the exception of Stoddard and Renzulli (1983), which was published after Hillocks had collected his data. He includes four in his meta-analysis (Howie, 1979; Morenberg et al., 1978; Pederson, 1978; Waterfall, 1978), grouping them with Faigley's 1979 study of sentence construction, one of the few studies that considers an experimental treatment derived from Christensen's (1967) generative rhetoric.

Hillocks' (1986) meta-analysis reports a highly homogeneous effect size of .35 standard deviations. This effect is significantly greater than the average effect of grammar ($-.29$), free writing (.16), and the study of models (.22). The mean effect size of sentence combining is approximately the same as the effect size of treatments using rating scales (.36). Only the inquiry focus (.56) has a significantly greater effect size than sentence combining. A subsequent meta-analysis by William Asher (1988) includes the studies Hillocks uses as well as several that failed to meet Hillocks' criteria, and found the same effect size without the homogeneity.

What could explain the apparent impact of sentence combining on the quality of writing? Research by Bereiter and Scardamalia (1982) provide one possible explanation. They found that when children revise, they avoid changing basic sentence plans. Shaughnessy's (1977) analysis of sentence consolidation errors suggests that basic writers are plagued by the same tendency. Perhaps sentence combining provides students with a more systematic repertoire of syntactic choices and helps them avoid this difficulty. Crowhurst (1983) offers three possible explanations. She notes that the increase in writing quality may be the result of increased practice in writing sentences, greater facility in constructing sentences, and an increased attention to other aspects of composing as a consequence of students' facility in constructing sentences. Strong (1986) supports Crowhurst's third alternative. He believes that "sentence combining may help with automaticity in syntax, freeing up mental energy so that learners can concentrate on planning and composing" (p. 3). He also argues that revising and editing are the main skills affected by sentence combining practice. Freedman (1985) believes that sentence combining promotes skill in perceiving relationships on the T-unit level and that this skill transfers to the whole-text level. She contends that because sentence combining causes students to search for these relationships, they develop a habit of mind that, in turn, extends conceptual knowledge.

Why does sentence combining improve students' writing? Experimental research has raised an important question that can best be answered by descriptive studies, for example, case studies of why writers make certain syntactic choices or how concern for syntax assists or interferes with planning and composing. A consideration of questions like these would be a fruitful direction for future research.

***Sentence combining and error.*** Another area of concern for researchers is the effect of sentence combining on error. Ross (1971) finds that her experimental group had fewer inaccurate sentences in their posttest essays than did her control group, but the results were not statistically significant. Schuster's (1976, 1977) experimental groups also exhibit fewer errors on their posttest essays, both in usage and mechanics. Obenchain (1979) finds substantial decreases in errors of emphasis, punctuation, and spelling. Argall (1982) reports her success in reducing a variety of errors in her developmental students' writing through the use of sentence combining. On the other hand, Maimon and Nodine (1978, 1979) find that sentence-combining practice results in more errors on a rewriting passage, though this is not true for free writing. Hake and Williams (1979, 1985) report a higher "flaw count" with increased T-unit length. In their study, flaws include problems of content and organization as well as usage and punctuation. Strong (1986) cites Guttry (1982) who finds that sentence combining is no more effective in reducing errors of community college freshmen, Jackson (1982) who finds that sentence-combining practice does not reduce the errors of basic writers, and Hayes (1984) who finds that sentence combining instruction is no more effective than regular instruction in reducing error.

Clearly, these findings produce mixed results. Perhaps that is to be expected. If instruction results in students' experimenting with more complex structures, errors are bound to result. On the other hand, if sentence-combining practice focuses on producing specific structures and learning how to punctuate those structures, it is likely to prove effective.

This raises another set of questions that researchers could profitably pursue, for example, How do teachers use sentence combining? What instructional techniques promote what sort of changes? Researchers might profitably sharpen their focus in their consideration of sentence combining. Strong (1986) notes that only Henderson (1980) considers the relative effects of different sentence-combining treatments. (She finds that signaled exercises promote a greater gain in clauses per T unit but that open exercises produce more nonclausal embeddings and a greater improvement in quality.)

***Sentence combining and reading.*** Kerek et al. (1980) state that "after 10 years of prolific research and in spite of some promising results, Mellon's early remark that sentence combining practice 'may contribute to the development of reading ability' (1969, p. 75) still remains more a reasonable possibility than an unassailable fact" (p. 1072). Not only the inconsistent results of this body of research, but also the variety of measures and control groups employed make generalization extremely difficult. For example, Straw and Schreiner (1982) compare the results of 25 lessons of sentence combining to the results of labeling and identifying sentence parts for fourth-graders. They found a significant difference favoring sentence combining on a cloze test but no significant difference on a standardized test of reading comprehension. On the other hand, Levine (1977) compares the results of 96 lessons combining sentence-combining exercises with instruction from a basal text to instruction from the basal text without sentence combining for third-graders. She reports a significant difference on a standardized test favoring the sentence-combining group but no significant difference between the groups on a cloze test. Several studies report significant results on one set of measures but no significant results on others. Until researchers can agree on effective measures of reading comprehension that would be sensitive to changes that might come as a result of lessons in sentence combining, it is unlikely that any clear conclusions in this area will emerge.

## IMPLICATIONS FOR TEACHING AND RESEARCH

From all accounts, despite the huge body of research over the past 90 years, TSG remains a potent force in the curriculum of today's schools. Curriculum outlines and guides in many schools demand that great blocks of time be spent on grammar. Publishers say privately that composition texts lacking the usual thorough (and lengthy) grammar section will lose sales to texts that have it. State guidelines (e.g., Texas) insist on extensive treatments of grammar in textbooks. Why does grammar retain such glamour when research over the past 100 years reveals not only that students do not learn it and are hostile toward it but also that the study of grammar has no impact on writing quality and little, if any, on editing?

Many explanations have been adduced, some not so flattering: It is easy to teach by simply assigning page and exercise numbers; it is easy to grade; it provides security in having "right" answers, a luxury not so readily available in teaching writing or literature; it helps to demarcate social distinctions, at the same time raising the teacher to higher status by virtue of at least seeming to possess a prestige dialect; and it is an instrument of power by which one may hold those unable to learn in thrall. The more

generous explanations for the persistence of grammar have to do with the lingering legacy of the middle ages—the belief that grammar is the key to something else. At the very least, teachers say, grammar provides the basis for correctness in writing, for putting commas and periods in the conventional places.

Unfortunately, the research provides no evidence to suggest that the study of TSG helps students become more proficient at placing punctuation in the spots designated by the style sheets. We assume that to proofread with any care, some knowledge of grammar must be necessary. What knowledge that is and how it is acquired are questions that have not been explored. It may be that a less ambiguous grammar that proceeded from basic sentence patterns (cf. Roberts, 1962) to increasingly complex expansions would help students learn to identify clause, phrase, and sentence boundaries. It may be that SFL grammar will provide insights into the reasons so many students have difficulty with the conventions of writing. Perhaps more research of the kind conducted by Kagan (1980) and Schleppegrell (1998) will provide insight into student conceptions of sentences. Research in these areas may provide some solutions to the nagging problems of correctness. However, at present, the research in our field focuses almost exclusively on richly contextualized, descriptive studies. Solving the problems of teaching conventions, however, we believe will entail both descriptive and interventional studies.

Until we have far more knowledge, the grammar sections of a textbook should be treated as a reference tool that might provide some insight into conventions of mechanics and usage. It should not be treated as a course of study to improve the quality of writing. Several far more successful paths to improving writing are available (Hillocks, 1986). If grammar is to be treated as a humanistic study, TSG alone is inadequate. It must be supplemented with more accurate, less ambiguous grammars with greater explanatory power.

## References

Alva, C. A. (1960). Structural grammar in California high schools. *English Journal, 49,* 606–611.

Applebee, A. N. (1974). *Tradition and reform in the teaching of English: A history.* Urbana, IL: National Council of Teachers of English.

Argall, R. (1982). *Sentence combining: An incisive tool for proofreading.* Paper presented at the annual meeting of the Conference on College Composition and Communication, San Francisco. (ERIC Document Reproduction Service No. ED 214 186)

Armstrong, B. E. (1982). A study of dialect and its interference with learning to write. *Dissertation Abstracts International, 43*(07), 2335.

Asher, W. (1988). *The effects of sentence-combining interventions on children's and adolescents' written language development and some data on methodological concerns in writing research.* Paper presented at the annual meeting of the American Educational Research Association, New Orleans, LA.

Bateman, D. R., & Zidonis, F. J. (1966). *The effect of a study of transformational grammar on the writing of ninth and tenth graders.* Champaign, IL: National Council of Teachers of English.

Belanger, J. F. (1978). *Reading skill as an influence on writing skill.*

Unpublished doctoral dissertation, University of Alberta, Alberta, Saskatchewan, Canada. (ERIC Document Reproduction Service No. ED 163 409)

Belanger, J. F. (1986). *Student written errors and teacher marking: A search for patterns.* Vancouver: Educational Research Institute of British Columbia. (ERIC Document Reproduction Service No. ED 273 960)

Bereiter, C., & Scardamalia, M. (1982). From conversation to composition: The role of instruction in a developmental process. In *Advances in instructional psychology, Vol. 2.* Edited by R. Glaser, 1–64. Hillsdale, NJ: Lawrence Erlbaum Associates.

Bowden, S. P. (1979). The effects of formal, traditional grammar study on the writing ability of secondary school students. *Dissertation Abstracts International, 40,* 1389A. (University Microfilms No. 790025)

Braddock, R., Lloyd-Jones, R., & Schoer, L. (1963). *Research in written composition.* Champaign, IL: National Council of Teachers of English.

Briggs, T. H. (1913). Formal English grammar as a discipline. *Teachers College Record, 14,* 251–343.

Callaghan, T. F. (1978). The effects of sentence-combining exercises on the syntactic maturity, quality of writing, reading ability, and attitudes of ninth grade students. *Dissertation Abstracts International, 39,* 637A. (University Microfilms No. 7813980)

Casson, L. (1985). Breakthrough at the first think tank. *Smithsonian, 16*(3), 158–168.

Cheesboro, M. E. (1982). A study of the relationship between the oral and written narrative and expository compositions of ninth grade students. *Dissertation Abstracts International, 43*(05), 206.

Chomsky, N. (1957). *Syntactic structures.* The Hague, The Netherlands: Mouton.

Chomsky, N. (1965). *Aspects of the theory of syntax.* Cambridge, MA: MIT Press.

Christensen, F. (1967). *Notes toward a new rhetoric: Six essays for teachers.* New York: Harper & Row.

Combs, W. E. (1976). Further effects of sentence-combining practice on writing ability. *Research in the Teaching of English, 10,* 137–149.

Combs, W. E. (1977). Sentence-combining practice: Do gains in judgments of writing "quality" persist? *Journal of Educational Research, 70,* 318–321.

Connors, R. J. (1985). Mechanical correctness as a focus in composition instruction. *College Composition and Communication, 36,* 61–72.

Connors, R. J., & Lunsford, A. A. (1988). Frequency of formal errors in current college writing, or Ma and Pa Kettle do research. *College Composition and Communication, 39,* 395–409.

Cooper, C. (1975). Research roundup: Oral and written composition. *English Journal, 64*(9), 72–74.

Corbett, E. P. J. (1990). *Classical rhetoric for the modern student* (3rd ed.). New York: Oxford University Press.

Cronnell, B. (1984). Black-English influences in the writing of third- and sixth-grade Black students. *Journal of Educational Research, 77,* 233–236.

Crowhurst, M. (1983). Sentence combining: Maintaining realistic expectations. *College Composition and Communication, 34,* 62–72.

Crowhurst, M., & Piche, G. L. (1979). Audience and mode of discourse effects on syntactic complexity in writing at two grade levels. *Research in the Teaching of English, 13,* 101–109.

Elley, W. B., Barham, I. H., Lamb, H., & Wyllie, M. (1976). The role of grammar in a secondary school English curriculum. *Research in the Teaching of English, 10,* 5–21.

Epes, M. (1985). Tracing errors to their sources: A study of the encoding processes of adult basic writers. *Journal of Basic Writing, 4,* 4–33.

Faigley, L. (1979). The influence of generative rhetoric on the syntactic maturity and writing effectiveness of college freshmen. *Research in the Teaching of English, 13,* 197–206.

Farr, M., & Janda, M. A. (1985). Basic writing students: Investigating oral and written language. *Research in the Teaching of English, 19,* 62–83.

Francis, W. N. (1954). Revolution in grammar. *Quarterly Journal of Speech, 40,* 299–312.

Francis, W. N. (1958). *The structure of American English.* New York: Ronald Press.

Freedman, A. (1985). Sentence combining: Some questions. In A. Freedman (Ed.), *Carleton Papers in Applied Language Studies,* (Vol. 2, pp. 17–32). (ERIC Document Reproduction Service No. ED 267 602)

Fries, C. C. (1952). *The structure of English.* New York: Harcourt, Brace, & World.

Gleason, H. A., Jr. (1965). *Linguistics and English grammar.* New York: Holt, Rinehart, & Winston.

Glenn, C. (1995). When grammar was a language art. In S. Hunter & R. Wallace (Eds.), *The place of grammar in writing instruction.* Portsmouth, NH: Boynton/Cook Heinemann.

Graham, M. S. (1983). The effect of teacher feedback on the reduction of usage errors in junior college freshmen's writing. *Dissertation Abstracts International, 45*(04), 91.

Green, E. A. (1973). An experimental study of sentence-combining to improve written syntactic fluency in fifth-grade children. *Dissertation Abstracts International, 33,* 4057A. (University Microfilms No. 73-4169)

Guttry, L. L. (1982). The effects of sentence-combining exercises on syntactic fluency, quality of writing, and usage in the writing of community college freshman. Unpublished doctoral dissertation. East Texas State University.

Hake, R. L., & Williams, J. M. (1979). Sentence expanding: Not can, or how, but when. In D. A. Daiker, A. Kerek, & M. Morenberg (Eds.), *Sentence combining and the teaching of writing* (pp. 134–146). Conway, AK: University of Akron and University of Central Arkansas.

Hake, R. L., & Williams, J. M. (1985). Some cognitive issues in sentence combining: On the theory that smaller is better. In D. A. Daiker, A. Kerek, & M. Morenberg (Eds.), *Sentence combining: A rhetorical perspective* (pp. 86–106). Carbondale: Southern Illinois University Press.

Halliday, M. A. K. (1985). *An introduction to functional grammar.* London: Edward Arnold.

Halliday, M. A. K. (1993a). On the language of physical science. In M. A. K. Halliday & J. R. Martin (Eds.), *Writing science: Literacy and discursive power.* (pp. 54–68). Pittsburgh, PA: University of Pittsburgh Press.

Halliday, M. A. K. (1993b). Some grammatical problems in scientific English. In M. A. K. Halliday & J. R. Martin (Eds.), *Writing science: Literacy and discursive power* (pp. 69–85). Pittsburgh, PA: University of Pittsburgh Press.

Halliday, M. A. K., & Martin, J. R. (1993). *Writing science: Literacy and discursive power.* Pittsburgh, PA: University of Pittsburgh Press.

Hartwell, P. (1985). Grammar, grammars, and the teaching of grammar. *College English, 47,* 105–127.

Hayes, I. (1984). An experimental study of sentence combining as a means of improving syntactic maturity, writing quality and grammatical fluency in the compositions of remedial high school students. Unpublished doctoral dissertation. Columbia University: Teachers College.

Heath, S. B. (1983). *Ways with words: Language, life, and work in communities and classrooms.* New York: Cambridge University Press.

Henderson, H. K. (1980). A comparison of the effects of practice with signaled or open sentence-combining with varying instructional time frames. Unpublished doctoral dissertation. University of Houston.

Hillocks, G., Jr. (1971). *An evaluation of Project Apex, a non-graded phase-elective English program.* Trenton, MI: Trenton Public Schools.

Hillocks, G., Jr. (1986). *Research on written composition: New directions for teaching.* Urbana, IL: Educational Resource Information Center and National Conference on Research in English.

Hillocks, G., Jr., & Mavrogenes, N. (1986). Sentence combining. In *Research on written composition: New directions for teaching* (pp. 142–146). Urbana, IL: ERIC and National Council of Teachers of English.

Hillocks, G., Jr., McCabe, B. J., & McCampbell, J. F. (1971). *The dynamics of English instruction: Grades 7–12.* New York: Random House.

Hillocks, G., Jr., & Smith, M. J. (1986). Grammar. In *Research on written composition: New directions for teaching* (pp. 134–141). Urbana, IL: ERIC and National Council of Teachers of English.

Howie, S. M. H. (1979). A study: The effects of sentence combining practice on the writing ability and reading level of ninth grade students.

*Dissertation Abstracts International, 40,* 1980-A. (University Microfilms No. 7923248)

Hunt, K. (1965). *Grammatical structures written at three grade levels.* Champaign, IL: National Council of Teachers of English.

Hunt, K. W., & O'Donnell, R. C. (1970). *An elementary school curriculum to develop better writing skills.* Tallahassee: Florida State University. (ERIC Document Reproduction Service No. ED 050 108)

Huntsman, J. F. (1983). Grammar. In D. L. Wagner (Ed.), *The seven liberal arts in the Middle Ages* (pp. 58-95). Bloomington: Indiana University Press.

Jackson, K. D. (1982). The effects of sentence combining practice on the reduction of syntactic errors in basic writing. Unpublished doctoral dissertation. Auburn University.

Kagan, D. M. (1980). Run-on and fragment sentences: An error analysis. *Research in the Teaching of English, 14,* 127-138.

Kamberelis, G. (1999). Genre development and learning: Children writing stories, science reports, and poems. *Research in the Teaching of English, 33,* 403-460.

Kerek, A., Daiker, D., & Morenberg, M. (1980). Sentence combining and college composition. *Perceptual and Motor Skills, 51,* 1059-1157.

Labov, W. (1970). *The study of nonstandard English.* Urbana, IL: National Council of Teachers of English.

Labov, W. (1972). *Language in the inner city: Studies in the black English vernacular.* Philadelphia: University of Pennsylvania Press.

Levine, S. S. (1977). The effect of transformational sentence-combining exercises on the reading comprehension and written composition of third-grade children. *Dissertation Abstracts International, 37,* 6431A. (University Microfilms No. 77-7653)

Loban, W. (1976). *Language development: Kindergarten through grade twelve.* Urbana, IL: National Council of Teachers of English.

Macauley, W. J. (1947). The difficulty of grammar. *British Journal of Educational Psychology, 17,* 153-162.

Maimon, E. P., & Nodine, B. F. (1979). Words enough and time: Syntax and error one year after. In D. A. Daiker, A. Kerek, & M. Morenberg (eds.), *Sentence combining and the teaching of writing* (pp. 101-108). Conway, AK: University of Akron and University of Central Arkansas.

Maimon, E. P., & Nodine, B. F. (1978). Measuring syntactic growth: Errors and expectations in sentence-combining practice with college freshmen. *Research in the Teaching of English, 12,* 233-244.

Martinez San Jose, C. P. (1973). Grammatical structures in four modes of writing at fourth grade level. *Dissertation Abstracts International, 33,* 5411A. (University Microfilms No. 73-9563)

McCutchen, D., Hull, G. A., & Smith, W. L. Editing strategies and error correction in basic writing. *Written Communication, 4,* 139-154.

Meckel, H. C. (1963). Research on teaching composition and literature. In N. L. Gage (Ed.), *Handbook of research on teaching* (pp. 966-1006). Chicago: Rand McNally.

Mellon, J. C. (1969). *Transformational sentence-combining: A method for enhancing the development of syntactic fluency in English composition.* Urbana, IL: National Council of Teachers of English.

Mellon, J. C. (1979). Issues in the theory and practice of sentence combining: A twenty-year perspective. In D. A. Daiker, A. Kerek, & M. Morenberg (Eds.), *Sentence combining and the teaching of writing* (pp. 1-38). Conway, AK: University of Akron and University of Central Arkansas.

Morenberg, M., Daiker, D., & Kerek, A. (1978). Sentence combining at the college level: An experimental study. *Research in the Teaching of English, 12,* 245-256.

Morrison, K. F. (1983). Incentives for studying the liberal arts. In D. L. Wagner (Ed.), *The seven liberal arts in the Middle Ages* (pp. 32-57). Bloomington: Indiana University Press.

Morrow, D. H. (1988). Black American English style shifting and writing error. *Research in the Teaching of English, 22,* 326-340.

Morrow, S. R. (1984). A model for grammar instruction using error analysis in a college freshman composition course. *Dissertation Abstracts International, 46*(09), 246.

Muller, H. J. (1967). *The uses of English: Guidelines for the teaching of English from the Anglo-American conference at Dartmouth College.* New York: Holt, Rinehart & Winston.

Noguchi, R. R. (1991). *Grammar and the teaching of writing: Limits and possibilities.* Urbana, IL: National Council of Teachers of English.

Nold, E. W., & Freedman, S. W. (1977). An analysis of readers' responses to essays. *Research in the Teaching of English, 11,* 164-174.

Noyce, R. M., & Christie, J. F. (1983). Effects of an integrated approach to grammar instruction on third graders' reading and writing. *Elementary School Journal, 81,* 63-69.

Obenchain, A. (1979). Developing paragraph power through sentence combining. In D. A. Daiker, A. Kerek, & M. Morenberg (Eds.), *Sentence combining and the teaching of writing* (pp. 123-133). Conway, AK: University of Akron and University of Central Arkansas.

O'Donnell, R. C., Griffin, W. J., & Norris, R. C. (1967). *Syntax of kindergarten and elementary school children: A transformational analysis.* Champaign, IL: National Council of Teachers of English.

Ofsa, W. J. (1975). An experiment in using research in composition in the training of teachers of English. *Dissertation Abstracts International, 35,* 7174A. (University Microfilms No. 75-11,711)

O'Hare, F. (1973). *Sentence combining: Improving student writing without formal grammar instruction.* Urbana, IL: National Council of Teachers of English.

*Oxford English Dictionary* (1971). New York: Oxford University Press.

Pederson, E. L. (1978). Improving syntactic and semantic fluency in the writing of language arts students through extended practice in sentence-combining. *Dissertation Abstracts International, 38,* 5892A. (University Microfilms No. 7802703)

Perron, J. D. (1975). An exploratory approach to extending the syntactic development of fourth-grade students through the use of sentence-combining methods. *Dissertation Abstracts International, 35,* 4316A. (University Microfilms No. 75-1744)

Perron, J. D. (1977). *Written syntactic complexity and the modes of discourse.* Paper presented at the annual meeting of the American Educational Research Association, New York. (ERIC Document Reproduction Service No. ED 139 009)

Pinneo, T. S. (1850). *Analytical grammar of the English language.* Cincinnati, OH: W. B. Smith.

Rafoth, B. A., & Rubin, D. L. (1984). The impact of content and mechanics on judgments of writing quality. *Written Communication, 1,* 446-458.

Ravelli, L. (1996). Making language accessible: Successful text writing for museum visitors. *Linguistics and Education, 8,* 367-388.

Roberts, P. (1962). *English sentences.* New York: Harcourt, Brace & World.

Ross, J. (1971). A transformational approach to teaching composition. *College Composition and Communication, 22,* 179-184.

Saussure, F., de. (1959). *Course in general linguistics* (W. Baskin, Trans.). New York: Philosophical Library.

Schleppegrell, M. P. (1998). Grammar as a resource: Writing a description. *Research in the Teaching of English, 32*(2), 184-211.

Schuster, E. H. (1976). *Forward to basics through sentence combining.* Paper presented at the annual meeting of the Pennsylvania Council of Teachers of English, Harrisburg, PA. (ERIC Document Reproduction Service No. ED 133 774)

Schuster, E. H. (1977). *Using sentence combining to teach writing to inner-city students.* Paper presented at the annual meeting of

National Council of Teachers of English. New York. (ERIC Document Reproduction Service No. ED 150 614).

Shaughnessy, M. P. (1977). *Errors and expectations: A guide for the teacher of basic writing.* New York: Oxford University Press.

Smith, H. L., Jr., & Sustakowski, H. J. (1968). *The application of descriptive linguistics to the teaching of English and a statistically-measured comparison of the relative effectiveness of the linguistically-oriented and traditional methods of instruction.* Buffalo: State University of New York. (ERIC Document Reproduction Service No. ED 021 216)

Smith, W. L., & Combs, W. E. (1980). The effects of overt and covert cues on written syntax. *Research in the Teaching of English, 14,* 19-38.

Smith, W. L., & Hull, G. A. (1985). Differential effects of sentence combining on college students who use particular structures with high and low frequencies. In D. A. Daiker, A. Kerek, & M. Morenberg (Eds.), *Sentence combining: A rhetorical perspective* (pp. 17-32). Carbondale: Southern Illinois University Press.

Stewart, M. F., & Grobe, C. H. (1979). Syntactic maturity, mechanics of writing, and teachers' quality ratings. *Research in the Teaching of English, 13,* 207-215.

Stoddard, E. P., & Renzulli, J. S. (1983). Improving the writing skills of talent pool students. *Gifted Child Quarterly, 27,* 21-27.

Straw, S. B., & Schreiner, R. (1982). The effect of sentence manipulation on subsequent measures of reading and listening comprehension. *Reading Research Quarterly, 17,* 339-352.

Strickland, R. G. (1962). The language of elementary school children: Its relationship to the language of reading textbooks and the quality of reading of selected children. *Bulletin of the School of Education, Indiana University, 38*(4),

Strong, W. (1986). *Creative approaches to sentence combining.* Urbana, IL: Educational Resource Information Center (ERIC) and National Council of Teachers of English.

Sullivan, J. L. (1969). A study of the relative merits of traditional grammar) generative-transformational grammar, or no grammar in an approach to writing in Communication One at Colorado State College. *Dissertation Abstracts, 29,* 2686A.

Sullivan, M. A. (1978). The effects of sentence-combining exercises on syntactic maturity, quality of writing, reading ability, and attitudes of students in grade eleven. *Dissertation Abstracts International, 39,* 1197A. (University Microfilms No. 7814240)

Sullivan, M. A. (1979). Parallel sentence-combining activities in grades nine and eleven. In D. A. Daiker, A. Kerek, & M. Morenberg (Eds.), *Sentence combining and the teaching of writing* (pp. 79-93). Conway, AK: University of Akron and University of Central Arkansas.

Taylor, S. J. (1986). Grammar curriculum—back to square one. *English Journal, 75*(1), 94-98.

Thibodeau, A. E. (1964). Improving composition writing with grammar and organization exercises utilizing differentiated group patterns. *Dissertation Abstracts, 25,* 2389. (University Microfilms No. 64-4048)

Thibodeau, A. L. (1964). A study of the effects of elaborative thinking and vocabulary enrichment exercises on written composition. *Dissertation Abstracts, 25,* 2388. (University Microfilms No. 64-4041)

Waterfall, C. M. (1978). An experimental study of sentence-combining as a means of increasing syntactic maturity and writing quality in the compositions of college-age students enrolled in remedial English classes. *Dissertation Abstracts International, 38,* 7131-A. (University Microfilms No. 7808144)

Weaver, C. (1979). *Grammar for teachers: Perspectives and definitions.* Urbana, IL: National Council of Teachers of English.

Weaver, C. (1996). *Teaching grammar in context.* Portsmouth, NH: Boynton/Cook.

White, R. H. (1965). The effect of structural linguistics on improving English composition compared to that of prescriptive grammar or the absence of grammar instruction. *Dissertation Abstracts, 25,* 5032.

Whitehead, C. E., Jr. (1966). The effect of grammar-diagraming on student writing skills. *Dissertation Abstracts, 26,* 3710. (University Microfilms No. 66-508)

Wille, S. C. (1982). The effect of prewriting observational activities on syntactic structures. Unpublished master's thesis. University of Chicago.

Williams, G. (1998). Grammar as a metasemiotic tool in child literacy development. *Proceedings of the Regional Language Centre Conference,* Singapore.

Williams, J. M. (1981). The phenomenology of error. *College Composition and Communication, 32,* 152-168.

Williams, J. M. (1999). *Style: Ten lessons in clarity and grace* (6th ed.). New York: Addison-Wesley.

Williamson, J. (1990). "Divven't write that, man": The influence of Tyneside dialect forms on children's free writing. *Educational Studies, 16,* 251-260.

Wofford, F. E. B. (1986). The effects of daily oral and written language drill on the proofreading of eighth grade language arts students. *Dissertation Abstracts International, 47*(07), 152.

# ·55·

# SPELLING

## Shane Templeton
### University of Nevada, Reno

In the last quarter of the 20th century spelling emerged as one of the most critical areas of interest and concern not only among English language arts educators but among other scholars and professionals as well. *Language Arts*, the elementary journal of the National Council of Teachers of English, published themed issues on spelling in 1992 and 2000. *Reading Teacher*, the elementary journal of the International Reading Association, published significantly many more articles on the topic throughout this period than in previous years. During the last few years of the 20th century, there were a number of educational books published addressing issues of spelling (e.g., Bear, Invernizzi, Templeton, & Johnston, 2000; Fountas & Pinnell, 1998, 1999; Ganske, 2000; Gentry & Gillet, 1993; Wilde, 1997). Interest and research in spelling soared among psychologists investigating processes of literacy and language; the number of scholarly books dedicated to the topic of spelling soared as well (e.g., Berninger, 1994, 1995; Brown & Ellis, 1994; Cummings, 1988; Perfetti, Rieben, & Fayol, 1997; S. Templeton & Bear, 1992; Venezky, 1999). Speech and language professionals were similarly engaged, as evidenced by a special themed issue on spelling (Apel & Masterson, 2000).

It has not, of course, always been this way. Traditionally viewed as a convention of writing, spelling has been acknowledged as an important skill while reviled as a subject, most probably because of its legacy of persistent pedagogical drudgery (S. Templeton, 1992). Spelling has long been a stepchild of the language arts, an unwelcome though obligatory guest lingering on the fringes of the party. As a topic within reading and language arts it has been almost nonexistent in teacher education programs. Why, then, such interest now?

The interest among educators stems from real and perceived weaknesses in students' spelling ability as well as from a dawning awareness that more engaging and effective approaches to the teaching of spelling exist. The renewed interest among researchers reflects recent psychological investigations of the reading process that situate word recognition as the precipitating event in this process, and many cognitive

psychologists believe spelling, or orthographic, knowledge is at the core of the reading process: "Spelling and reading use the same lexical representation. In fact, spelling is a good test of the quality of representation" (Perfetti, 1993, p. 170). For both educators and researchers, the examination of an individual's spellings may provide the most direct insight into that individual's word knowledge, knowledge that is applied in both the encoding and decoding of words.

Thus, spelling is enjoying a renaissance both in its traditional role as an important skill in the writing process and in its newer role as a critical component in the reading process as well. This chapter attempts to sketch the gestation and continued nurturing of this renaissance and to update the review of recent research and theoretical perspectives presented in S. Templeton and Morris (2000). The chapter is organized according to the following sections: the nature of the English spelling system; three perspectives on spelling theory, research, and pedagogy in the 20th century; and implications of research for classroom instruction.

## THE NATURE OF THE ENGLISH SPELLING SYSTEM

Most classroom teachers may not be explicitly aware of the nature of English spelling and the different types of information that the system represents; nor may they be comfortable with how best to facilitate the development of this knowledge in students (Barone, 1992; Fresch, 2000; Ganske, 1999; Gill & Scharer, 1996; Hughes & Searle, 1997; Moats, 2000). Hughes and Searle (1997) observed:

[M]any teachers themselves see spelling as more arbitrary than systematic; at least, they give that impression to their students. Even when that is not the case, it is likely that their own knowledge of the spelling system is largely implicit or relatively poorly understood. For example, they may teach spelling as a solely sound-based system long after than it useful . . . If we teachers do not believe that spelling has logical, negotiable patterns, how can we hope to help children develop that insight? (p. 133)

The description of English spelling presented here is intended to address the main features of the system and the underlying logic according to which it is governed. More extensive treatments are offered in Bear et al. (2000), Ganske (2000), Moats (2000) and especially Venezky (1999).

Most literate native speakers of English today would probably concur with Zachrisson's observation that "everyone . . . has to admit that of all languages . . . English has the most antiquated, inconsistent, and illogical spelling" (as cited in Venezky, 1999, p. vii). A common belief is that the primary purpose of the spelling system should be to represent sound and to do so much more consistently than English spelling does at present. In explaining the history of English spelling, or orthography, however, Venezky offered the insight that "the fact is that the present orthography is not merely a letter-to-sound system riddled with imperfections. Instead, it is a more complex and more regular relationship, wherein phonemes [units of sounds] and morphemes [units of meaning] share leading roles" (1999, p. ix). Cummings (1988) described this "sharing" in terms of a balance that is struck between the need to spell units of sounds consistently from word to word with the need to spell units of meaning consistently from word to word.

In the case of a large segment of English vocabulary, "Visual identity of word parts takes precedence over letter-sound simplicity" (Venezky, 1999, p. 197). In other words, what is lost in the simplicity of a system in which a single letter predictably and always corresponds to one and only one sound is gained in a system in which a group of letters predictably and consistently corresponds to a particular meaning. For example, the words *senile* and *senility* are not spelled *seenile* and *suniluty*, as they might be if we tried to represent more directly the sounds in each word; instead, they retain the common spelling *senil*, thus preserving the semantic or meaning relationship shared by the base and its derivative (both words come from the Latin root *sen* [*senilis*], meaning "old"). Similarly, the common spelling of the base *defin* is retained in the words *define*, *definition*, and *definitive*, despite a different pronunciation of the base in each word.

Learning to spell English is a developmental exploration of this balance between sound and meaning in which learners move from the expectation that spelling represents sound to the understanding that spelling also represents meaning. Along the way, learners may discern the regularity that operates within the system. This regularity may be described in terms of three types, or layers, of information in the system: alphabetic, pattern, and meaning. These layers are often described as principles of spelling:

The alphabetic layer represents the most straightforward representation of sound, matching letters in a left-to-right manner as in the words *top*, *grip*, and *me*. As discussed later, this type of sequential representation corresponds to the way in which young children expect the spelling system to work.

The pattern layer represents regular sound–spelling correspondences within and between syllables. This regularity is one step removed from the alphabetic level: Within syllables, in contrast to the expectation that words should be spelled according to a sequential one letter–one sound matchup, learners develop the understanding that a group or pattern of letters functions as a unit that corresponds in a predictable way to sound. For example, in the word *scrape* the vowel–consonant–"silent" *e* (VCe) spelling pattern represents a long vowel pronunciation; the silent *e* in this spelling pattern distinguishes this "long" *a* pronunciation from the "short" *a* pronunciation in the word *scrap*. Within syllables, the pattern layer reflects the role of position on spelling: How a sound is spelled very often depends on its position within a syllable and its relation to other sounds within the syllable. For example, the /k/ following a short vowel pattern at the end of a syllable will usually be spelled *ck*; on the other hand, this spelling will never represent /k/ at the beginning of a syllable. The /ch/ at the end of a syllable will usually be spelled *tch* if it follows a short vowel (*batch*, *snitch*); when /ch/ follows a long vowel it is usually spelled *ch* (*poach*, *beach*).

In addition to governing the spelling of vowels and consonants within syllables, the pattern principle often determines the spelling between syllables, at their junctures. Learners' understanding of these syllable juncture patterns builds on their understanding of long and short vowel spelling patterns within single syllables. Understanding juncture patterns begins when students examine the effects of adding inflectional endings such as -*ed* and -*ing* to simple base words. For example, tap + ing = tapping; tape + ing = taping. The final consonant in the word *tap* must be doubled because of the short vowel, thus differentiating *tapping* from *taping*. This knowledge of when to double and when not to double, developed through examining the spelling of base words plus inflectional suffixes, is later applied within base words: Because the vowel in the first syllable of *hammer* is short, the *m* is doubled; because the vowel in the first syllable of *razor* is long, the following consonant is not doubled. The patterns represented by these spellings are referred to, respectively, as VCCV and VCV syllable juncture patterns. This doubling feature is widely applicable in English; vowel sounds that are not long are often followed by doubled consonants whereas long vowel sounds are usually followed by a single consonant.

In those cases when a word's spelling appears to be an exception to these regular sound-based principles, it is most often because the *meaning* layer has taken precedence. For example, in the word *finish* the *n* is not doubled after the short *i* as would be predicted by the VCCV syllable pattern generalization. This is because the spelling *fin* preserves the meaning relationship with the related word *final*. Similarly, in the spelling of *punish* the *n* is not doubled after the short *u* because the spelling *pun* preserves the meaning relationship with the related word *punitive*. As will be explored below, an individual's awareness of the role meaning plays in spelling will be an important tool for vocabulary development. Students may reinforce their memory for the spelling of *punish* by learning the related word *punitive*, thus expanding their vocabulary as well. The morphological or meaning core is also preserved across words that at first glance may not appear related but that in fact share a common word history or etymology and thus some relationship in meaning; for example, the words *humble*, *humiliate*, and *humility* are all from the Latin *humus*, meaning "earth". This type of understanding also supports vocabulary development and expansion.

This emphasis on the visual preservation of meaning relationships among words arose during the Renaissance, when many scholars viewed the Classical languages as "purer" than English (S. Templeton, 1980). Coupled with the advent of the printing press in the 15th century and the consequent explosion in the availability and use of print, "The connotations of the written as opposed to the spoken word grew . . . it was inevitable that writers should try to extend the associations of English words by giving them *visual connections* [italics added] with related Latin ones" (Scragg, 1974, p. 56). The word *indict* is an illustrative case study of this phenomenon (*Oxford English Dictionary*, 1994). Between 1300 and 1700 the word evolved orthographically from *endyte* to *endite*, *indyte*, *endight*, *indight*, and *indite*; moreover, at any one time it could be spelled differently depending on the writer, the typesetter, or both. The spelling *indict*, which established a visual connection with the related Latin word *dictare* (meaning "to say, declare") was first documented in 1640. Alternative sound-based spellings continued, however, and it was not until the 18th century that *indict* was established as the standard spelling. By that time, though, *indict* also shared a visual orthographic connection with other words that were at root derived or thought to be derived from the common Latin form *dictare*—*dictate*, *dictionary*, *predict*, and so forth.

In summary, linguistic analyses have demonstrated that the spelling system of English is considerably more logical when one breaks through the "sound barrier," as it were—the failed expectation that spelling should always and consistently represent sounds at the alphabetic level—and sees beyond to the consistency with which sound is represented at the pattern layer and, more important, the consistency with which meaning relationships among words are visually preserved. This spelling/meaning relationship among words has important implications for vocabulary instruction as well as for spelling; vocabulary and spelling instruction can become two sides of the same instructional coin (S. Templeton, 1991). As discussed in the next section, learning English spelling follows a developmental course in which the alphabetic, pattern, and meaning layers, respectively, are explored. As each new layer is explored it incorporates and reorganizes the layer that preceded it, so a reader or writer may implicitly as well as explicitly access this underlying knowledge when encoding words in writing and decoding words in reading.

## THREE PERSPECTIVES ON SPELLING THEORY, RESEARCH, AND PEDAGOGY IN THE 20TH CENTURY

As is the case today, spelling research and pedagogy over the years has unavoidably been based on assumptions about learners and the system to be learned. Although a few linguists have noted the semantic function of English spelling, most educators and educational researchers worked from an assumption that learners were passive recipients of information and that the spelling system did not make sense.

In describing spelling research throughout the 20th century, S. Templeton and Morris (2000) suggested three successive periods, each reflecting a distinct theoretical and pedagogical perspective: spelling as a process of rote memorization, spelling as a process of abstracting regular sound–spelling patterns, and spelling as a developmental process. A summary of each period follows.

### Spelling as a Process of Rote Memorization

The earliest psychological and educational research in the 20th century was guided by the view that English spelling is irregular and that learning is a behavioral, stimulus–response phenomenon: Learning to spell, therefore, is essentially a process of rote memorization and instruction should emphasize the development of visual memory for the spelling of words (E. Horn, 1960; T. Horn, 1969). Horn (1969) presented a comprehensive discussion of this research. Most notably, the emphasis was on identifying the most appropriate words for instruction, tabulating students' spelling errors across the grades, and determining effective instructional practices.

Words were selected for study based primarily on frequency counts of English (E. Horn, 1926; Thorndike, 1921) and instruction focused on the most frequently occurring words. Because of the "irregular" sound–symbol correspondences manifest in so many of these words, this emphasis reinforced a pedagogical notion that nothing less than strict memorization would suffice. Gates (1937) conducted the first large-scale error analysis research in which common spelling errors were arrayed across the grades. Notably, the errors schoolchildren were committing in the 1930s are a distant mirror of the errors committed by students in recent years. At the time, Gates explained these errors in terms of their correspondence to sound; failure to double a consonant, for example, constituted a single error category. (More recently, researchers have made developmental distinctions among such errors. The case of consonant doubling is of particular interest because, though it is a constant source of error across the grades, for example, the conditions that determine doubling become conceptually more complex. Thus, most 8- and 9-year-olds can master a simpler doubling convention in which inflectional suffixes are added to base words: fit + ed = fitting vs. bake + ing = baking. On the other hand, it may be years before the more complex doubling condition of *assimilated* or *absorbed* prefixes is understood, requiring the type of word knowledge characteristic of more advanced readers and spellers: ad + count = account; ad + sign = assign.)

Research that examined effective instructional practice concluded that words selected for spelling study should be presented in lists rather than in context (McKee, 1924), self-corrected pretests followed by study is more effective than study followed by a posttest (Gates, 1931; E. Horn, 1960; T. Horn, 1946); 60 to 75 minutes per week should be spent on spelling instruction (E. Horn, 1960).

## Spelling as a Process of Abstracting Regular Sound–Spelling Patterns

As noted in the previous discussion concerning consonant doubling, early research into spelling had proceeded without a prior analysis or consideration of the nature of the orthographic system to be learned. The second half of the 20th century witnessed more comprehensive analyses of the alphabetic, syllabic, and morphological aspects of English spelling (Chomsky & Halle, 1968; Cummings, 1988; Hanna, Hanna, Hodges, & Rudorf, 1966; Venezky, 1970, 1999). The landmark research by Hanna et al. demonstrated how English spelling quite reliably represents the sounds of English when patterns of letters within syllables are the units of analysis as opposed to an exclusive focus on the phoneme. In addition, the research demonstrated the "learnability" of the spelling system. Programming a computer to detect and learn regularities, Hanna et al. demonstrated the regularity of the system by noting the effect of position within a syllable on the spelling of a particular sound—in so doing, refuting a classic indictment of English spelling attributed to George Bernard Shaw. Shaw allegedly contended the spelling system was so illogical that the word *fish* could theoretically be spelled *ghoti* because *gh* represents the sound /f/, *ti* the sound /sh/, and *o* the short *i* sound in *women*. Hanna et al.'s computer generated no such spelling; it "learned" that *gh* represents an /f/ sound only at the end of syllables, never at the beginning, and that *ti* only represents /sh/ at the juncture of syllables, never at the end of a word. Notably, Hanna et al. also observed that had morphological information been available to the computer, it would have been able to generate correct spelling of an even higher percentage of words.

In large part because of Hanna et al.'s (1966) study, the selection of words for spelling instruction came to include the patterns of letters in addition to simple frequency. Designers of spelling curricula determined which words students were likely to have encountered a number of times in their reading and which included most frequently occurring spelling patterns. These criteria still play a significant role in guiding the selection and sequencing of patterns in most spelling and word study curricula.

It was during this period that a number of researchers and educators recognized the role that morphology plays in English spelling and emphasized in particular the desirability of integrating instruction in spelling and morphology (Dale, O'Rourke, & Bamman, 1971; Hanna, Hodges, & Hanna, 1971). As we will see below, this emphasis has in recent years been extended and expanded.

## Spelling as a Developmental Process

Spurred by the Chomskian revolution in linguistics and psychology (e.g., N. Chomsky, 1957, 1959; Lenneberg, 1967), research investigating young children's language revealed a complexity to the task that belied the simplicity of the behavioristic paradigm of language learning (Read & Hodges, 1982). Notably, it was Read's (1971) attempt to test the psychological reality of the phonological component of Chomsky's theory of tranformational generative grammar that revealed the impressive logic of young children's spellings. Read discovered that without explicit instruction, young children tacitly applied the articulatory and acoustic features of letter names to represent the spoken messages they wished to write. His work provided significant explanatory support for other studies that investigated children's errors in spelling as a developmental process incorporating cognitive as well as linguistic aspects. Another impetus came from stage models of development, spurred primarily by the work of Piaget (Piaget & Inhelder, 1969), the preeminent developmental theorist at the time; stage models of language acquisition were similarly influential (e.g., Brown, 1973).

Based on error analyses of spelling in both spontaneous writing and spelling dictation assessments, a number of researchers have suggested stages of orthographic knowledge, each characterized by the predominance of a particular type of orthographic information—alphabetic, orthographic/ pattern, structural/morphological—in the learner's spelling and reading of words (e.g., Ehri, 1997; Henderson, 1985, 1990; S. Templeton & Bear, 1992). In general, the types of children's errors have been found to more or less consistent. "Spelling has always afforded a privileged window into the mind," Frith (1994) observed, "and spelling errors are a magnifying glass in that window" (p. xiii). Most of the studies that have mapped the developmental nature of spelling have investigated the early stages or phases of learning to spell (e.g., J. W. Beers & Henderson, 1977; Ehri, 1993; Ellis & Cataldo, 1990; Frith, 1985; Hughes & Searle, 1997; Marsh, Friedman, Welch, & Desberg, 1980; Nunes, Bryant, & Bindman, 1997; Seymour, 1992; Stage & Wagner, 1992; Treiman, 1993). A few studies have explored word knowledge as manifested through spelling at later phases of literacy development (e.g., Derwing, Smith, & Wiebe, 1995; Fischer, Shankweiler, & Liberman, 1985; Hughes & Searle, 1997; Marsh et al., 1980; Fowler & Liberman, 1995; S. Templeton, 1979; S. Templeton & Scarborough-Franks, 1985).

The significant finding from the developmental research has been that most learners share a common developmental sequence in their acquisition of orthographic knowledge, despite natural variation in their attention to printed language and their understanding of the relationships between print and speech. Studies undertaken by Henderson and his students at the University of Virginia (Henderson & J. Beers, 1980; S. Templeton & Bear, 1992) explored and refined developmental stages or phases of orthographic knowledge that Henderson labeled preliterate, letter name, within-word pattern, *syllable juncture*, and *derivational constancy* (Barnes, 1982; Bear, 1982; C. Beers, 1980; J. W. Beers, 1974; J. W. Beers & Henderson, 1977; Gentry, 1977; C. E. Gill, 1980; J. T. Gill, 1992; Invernizzi, 1985; Morris, 1983, 1993; R. C. Schlagal, 1992; Temple, 1978; S. Templeton, 1979; W. S. Templeton, 1976; Zutell, 1975). The labels were chosen to reflect the most salient orthographic features learners explore in both spelling and reading at each developmental phase. Over the years, as learners move from the letter name to the derivational phase, their underlying word knowledge reflects a growth in sophistication of knowledge about letters and sounds, letters patterns and syllable patterns, and how meaning is directly represented through spelling:

> The developmental stages of word knowledge, like the evolutionary periods of the language itself, are somewhat arbitrary divisions. Language change is continuous, and continuous, too, is the learner's progress as he or she gradually masters English spelling. Still, there are periods of more rapid change and then longer periods when a new understanding is tested and refined. Our decision has been to divide English word knowledge into . . . such periods, or stages. . . . The age ranges given for each stage are, of course, quite broad. (Henderson, 1990, p. 43)

Subsequent to the Virginia studies, a number of investigations explored further the invented spellings of young children (e.g., Ellis & Cataldo, 1990; Huxford, Terrell, & Bradley, 1992; Mann, Tobin, & Wilson, 1987; Nunes, Bryant, & Bindman, 1997; Stage & Wagner, 1992; Treiman, 1993; Viise, 1995). As discussed below, researchers' interpretations of these error types and what they mean differ with respect to the types of knowledge that children are applying as they engage in spelling.

Developmental research has explored the logic underlying the writing of emergent readers and writers. Knowledge of the names of the letters of the alphabet becomes a critical feature guiding their written attempts. In English, the representation of the beginning sounds of syllables usually emerges first. These early spelling attempts are a strong facilitator of the development of a concept of word in print (Morris, 1983, 1992, 1993) and of phonemic awareness, which in turn support beginning reading (Ehri & L. Wilce, 1987; Ellis & Cataldo, 1990; Mann, Tobin, & Wilson, 1987). In time, children's invented spellings subsequently reflect the fact that they are attending consciously to each consonant and vowel sound within single syllables. The early developmental studies (Henderson & J. Beers, 1980; S. Templeton & Bear, 1992) suggested that these spellings, such as *bop* (*bump*) and *jriv* (*drive*) reflected children's tacit theory of how the spelling system works; sounds are represented in a linear left-to-right encoding (or decoding) of letters. The primary strategy for representing a particular sound is the selection of a letter whose name shares common articulatory and acoustic features with that sound (Read, 1971, 1975). This strategy was the rationale for Henderson labeling this phase letter name; Ehri (1997) referred to this as the full alphabetic level.

As beginning readers or letter name spellers are engaged with printed texts, however, it is not long before this "linear" theory is challenged, that is, learners encounter an increasing number of words that represent pattern or orthographic features that cannot be explained simply by a left-to-right matchup of sounds and letters. As learners pay more explicit attention to these types of words, these pattern features are increasingly apparent in their writing. Errors include, for example, *roap* (*rope*) and *backe* (*bake*). According to the Virginia researchers, such errors indicate that children's theory of how the spelling system works has moved beyond a one-to-one linear matchup to include the understanding that groups of letters, specifically the vowel and what follows, function as a unit to represent sound (Ehri, 1997). These orthographic patterns include letters that themselves do not represent sounds directly—the silent *e* in *cake* and the *i* in *rain*, for example—but provide information about the pronunciation of other letters within the pattern. Henderson (1985) referred to this level of spelling knowledge as the within-word pattern phase; Ehri (1997) applied the term *consolidated alphabetic* (she also considered the further development of word knowledge as falling within the consolidated alphabetic phase as well).

As learners encounter more polysyllabic words in their reading and examine the structure of these words, errors in their spellings reveal (a) that they apply what they know about vowel patterns in single-syllable words to the spelling of vowel sounds in the syllables of polysyllabic words (e.g., *paraiding* for *parading*); (b) though aware of doubled consonants at the juncture of syllables, they inconsistently apply this knowledge (*hapen* for *happen*; *stripped* for *striped*; Bear, S. Templeton, & Warner, 1991; Ganske, 1994; R. Schlagal, 1992); and (c) there are frequent errors in spelling the schwa or reduced vowel in unstressed syllables, for example, *mentle* (*mental*) and *pilat* (*pilot*). Henderson labeled this phase the syllable juncture phase.

As students move through the intermediate grades and beyond, the words they encounter in their reading increasingly reflect morphological processes that reflect the meaning relationships among words (Derwing et al., 1995; Fischer et al., 1985; Fowler & Liberman, 1995; Hughes & Searle, 1997; Smith, 1998; S. Templeton, 1979; S. Templeton & Scarborough-Franks, 1985). Spelling errors in students' spontaneous writing are few, but they reflect students' readiness to explore at length how spelling visually preserves the semantic relationships across derivationally related words, for example, *prohabition* (*prohibition*), *compisition* (*composition*), *critacize* (*criticize*), and *ammusement* (*amusement*). Henderson labeled this phase derivational constancy, reflecting the constancy of spelling that links bases, roots, and their derivatives. Interestingly, the application of a knowledge of more advanced derivational processes appears to be more secure in students' spelling than in their pronunciation (S. Templeton, 1979; S. Templeton & Scarborough-Franks, 1985), lending empirical support to C. Chomsky's (1970) observation:

> This process of internalization . . . is no doubt facilitated in many cases by an awareness of how words are spelled. . . . Thus the underlying system which the child has constructed from evidence provided by the spoken language . . . may itself be improved by his increased familiarity with the written language. (p. 298)

Shankweiler and Lundquist (1992) noted, "The evidence supports the expectation that both phonologic and morphologic aspects of linguistic awareness are relevant to success in spelling and reading" (p. 182). This level of awareness can facilitate the development of vocabulary knowledge as well (Fowler & Liberman, 1995). As with the development of alphabetic and orthographic knowledge at earlier developmental levels, some older learners may abstract these morphological consistencies implicitly through reading and writing. Most, however, do not and need explicit instruction (Henry, 1989; Wysocki & Jenkins, 1987). Henry (1989) found that intermediate students who had received explicit instruction in Greek and Latin word roots became significantly more proficient at both reading and spelling.

Henderson (1981) proposed that the ability to spell words and read words draws on the same foundation of underlying word knowledge; research by his students in the 1970s and 1980s explored and supported this contention (Invernizzi, 1985; J. T. Gill, 1992). Interestingly, research by Ehri (1997; Ehri & L. S. Wilce, 1997) has also converged on this conclusion. In the mid-1970s Ehri (1975; Ehri & L. S. Wilce, 1997) undertook a line of research exploring the development of children's ability to read words; a natural outgrowth of this research was the investigation of children's spellings as a means of determining the types of knowledge they might use when reading words. Several cognitive psychologists adopted this notion as well (e.g., Perfetti, 1993, 1997). Spelling became a critical area of investigation in psychological research, offering researchers their most direct glimpse into the developing lexicon and the knowledge that individuals apply in reading and spelling. Thus, children's invented spellings could indeed be, as Frith characterized them, a "magnifying glass" on the "window into the mind."

Increasingly, research is exploring the metalinguistic reflection and verbal reports that accompany students' spelling attempts (e.g., Fresch, 2000; Hughes & Searle, 1997, 2000; Sabey, 1999; Steffler, Varnhagen, Friesen, & Treiman, 1998). This research also provides insights into the nature of how knowledge about spelling is socially constructed. In investigations of students' metalinguistic reflections, it is striking how infrequently their explicit awareness mirrors their performance capability. The phonocentric perspective (S. Templeton & Morris, 2000) appears to be the "default" option for most students, perhaps reflecting the stance assumed by their teachers, many of whom "teach spelling as if it were a solely sound-based phenomenon long after that is useful" (Hughes & Searle, 1997). Elementary students are not explicitly aware of all the types of information on which they implicitly draw in order to think about the spelling of words; most students explain their reasoning in terms of "sounding out" spellings. Fresch (2000) and Sabey (1997, 1999) observed that students' verbal reports most often reflect the use of information that is at least one developmental level below their current level. Their research engaged students in word-sort activities in which students attempted to categorize groups of words according to different criteria. Sabey's informants, determined to be at the syllable juncture phase of development, evidenced the reflective use primarily of alphabetic and orthographic information; less use was made of syllable pattern knowledge—evidence that Sabey suggested reflected the fact that this developing knowledge was in flux. Significantly, however, Fresch (2000) found that, with prompting, students were able to discuss orthographic principles commensurate with their developmental level.

In interviewing middle school students whose word knowledge was advanced (the morphological or derivational constancy level), S. Templeton (1985) found that their implicit command of derivational morphological principles was not matched by an explicit, reflective awareness of these principles. When engaged in a discussion about the possible morphological/meaning relationships, however, most of the subjects were able to understand these connections. There is in fact a substantial body of research that supports the finding that by the intermediate school years most students have at least a dawning awareness of the morphological aspects of English spelling and its implications for learning vocabulary and spelling (Derwing et al., 1995; Freyd & Baron, 1983; Leong, 1998; Marsh et al., 1980; Shankweiler & Lundquist, 1992; Smith, 1998; S. Templeton, 1979, 1985; S. Templeton & Scarborough-Franks, 1985; Tyler & Nagy, 1989; Wysocki & Jenkins, 1987). For students at the intermediate level and above, however, growing beyond the phonocentric perspective requires a sustained experience with teacher-guided direct exploration before it begins to yield; Hughes and Searle (2000) cited the example of a student who spelled *responsible* and *responsibility* correctly but spelled *irresponsibility* as *irrisponsibility*. She acknowledged that *irresponsibility* means the opposite of *responsibility* but explained her spelling in terms of sound: She heard "more of an 'i' than an 'e'" in the second syllable of *irresponsibility* (p. 207). Though most students are developmentally ready to explore and develop morphological knowledge more systematically, it is ironic that it is precisely during these school years that such instruction is withheld (Hughes & Searle, 1997; S. Templeton, 1992).

***Conflicting models of development.*** Although Henderson (1992) observed that "[d]evelopmental stages on any dimension of human behavior are always proximate statements with gray areas between them" (p. 24), for many researchers the use of the term *stage* in conceptualizing development has become problematic, connoting rigidity and abrupt passage from one particular stage to the next (e.g., Baker, 1999; Snowling, 1994; Steffler, Varnhagen, Friesen, & Treiman, 1998; Treiman, 1993; Varnhagen, 1995). Some researchers have instead used the terms *phase* or *level* to capture more appropriately the nature of development. For example Ehri (1997), in emphasizing use of the term *phase*, described the rationale underlying her designation of each developmental phase of word knowledge as reflecting the "key capability that *distinguishes among the levels* [italics added] and underlies development. Each level characterizes *the approach that predominates at that level* [italics added]" (p. 253). Similarly, Reiben and Saada-Robert (1997) described a phases of dominance developmental model. In addressing this issue, Nunes, Bryant, and Bindman (1997) observed: "We do not think that children abandon letter-sound correspondences in spelling... [sound-based errors occurred] to a decreasing extent as the children ascended our developmental ladder" (p. 163).

In contrast to a developmental stagelike, or phaselike, progression, several researchers have postulated an interactive process or model in which multiple sources of information interact in complex ways as learners advance in their spelling knowledge and that they may develop a larger array of strategies for problem solving (Varnhagen, 1995). For example, Treiman and Cassar (1997) offered as an example young children who, in addition to applying knowledge of letter names exclusively in their spelling, "also have *some budding knowledge* [italics added] about the orthographic regularities... and about the role of morphology in spelling" (p. 64). Brown and Ellis (1994) also noted that recent research challenges the notion that learners progress through a "clear sequence of separate stages" but argue instead for "a more interactive approach where several different knowledge sources interact in parallel to constrain the operation of the spelling output mechanisms" (p. 7). These knowledge sources or strategies include alphabetic, orthographic, and morphological information.

In addition to developmental and interaction models, connectionist models have been of considerable influence in explaining the neuropsychological processes involved in learning to read and spell words (e.g., Brown & Loosemore, 1994; Rumelhart & McClelland, 1986; Seidenberg & McClelland, 1989). Connectionist models work on the assumption that it is possible to model closely on computers the development of the neuronal networking and functioning in the human brain. In contrast to stage or phase models or the interactive models that posit cognitive explanations for learning to spell, connectionist models suggest that learning to read and spell words involves a lower level process, which Brown and Loosemore (1994) described as one of "mastering the statistical associations between a set of patterns representing the phonological forms of words and a set of patterns representing the orthographic forms" (p. 333). Based on the words to which the learner is exposed, therefore, the brain's task is to compute the likelihood of the occurrence of particular letter sequences in spelling and the strength or magnitude of their correspondence to particular phonological sequences—for example, how often the letter sequence *ead* occurs in words and, when it does, the likelihood of it corresponding to /ēd/ or /ĕd/. Connectionist models provide a promising means of accounting for and conceptualizing spelling development at the alphabetic level and, to a certain degree, the within-word pattern level, but appear to need structural or morphological information to "learn" regularities in orthographically more complex words (e.g., Olson & Caramazza, 1994; Reuckl & Raveh, 1999). Without such information, such models would spell *syntax*, for example, as *sintax* (Zesiger & dePartz, 1997).

Although research still explores the issue of the degree to which learners use different types of information and how they use it at different points along a developmental continuum; the stage, or phase, model; the interactive model; and the connectionist model have offered solid insights from which effective instructional practice may be derived. It is important to understand that these models are in fundamental agreement that learners' application of word knowledge grows from the simple to the more complex. The models agree that the complexity of the incoming information to the learner—the orthographic structure of words—should be presented in a manner that facilitates the brain's processing and organizing of this information so that it can most productively be applied in spelling and reading words. Stage theorists acknowledge that learners draw from multiple sources of information but emphasize that the degree to which these different sources are used varies as learning progresses. The models differ in their emphasis on the degree to which different mechanisms within the learner's brain account for and nurture this growth.

Research in instruction and in students' metalinguistic reflections on their strategies for spelling allows for at least two fundamental and important conclusions to be drawn: First, at any point along a developmental continuum of literacy, there is a common core of word knowledge that underlies the processes of spelling words and reading words; "the reading and writing of words are complementary activities based on the same orthographical and phonological knowledge that is stored in a single system" (Reiben & Saada-Robert, 1997, p. 295). Second, the type of model that at present better explains the development of this common core of word knowledge is flexible rather than rigid. Although particular sources of information may predominate at different points along a developmental continuum—for example, alphabetic for beginning spellers and readers and syllabic and morphemic for more skilled and proficient readers and spellers—there may also be subtle influences of or interaction with other sources of information.

## IMPLICATIONS OF RESEARCH FOR CLASSROOM INSTRUCTION

Although sustained reading and writing are absolutely necessary for the development of spelling knowledge, for most students reading and writing alone are not sufficient; some combination of meaningful reading and writing with focused and sustained word study is necessary (e.g., Allal, 1997; Brooks, Begay, Curtin, Byrd, & Graham, 2000; Graham, 2000; S. Templeton & Morris, 1999; Zutell, 1994). Bosman and Van Orden (1997) noted that reading "is not the most effective way to learn to spell" (p. 188); rather, spelling benefits from instruction in specific spelling strategies. Perfetti (1997) underscored the more critical role of spelling knowledge when he concluded, "Practice at spelling should help reading more than practice at reading helps spelling" (p. 31). For most normally developing students, and even for most learning disabled or special needs students, therefore, ongoing examination of words and their structure is necessary throughout the school years.

It should be noted that this conclusion is not universal (e.g., Krashen, 1989; Wilde, 1997). Krashen offered the most compelling argument in support of the position that spelling knowledge develops primarily through reading and writing without studying words out of context. It is important to acknowledge that at the time Krashen reviewed the research most of the studies involved narrower, more constrained approaches to spelling study in which all students in a classroom usually studied the same spelling words. A number of more recent studies have examined different instructional contexts and methodologies, specifically differentiated or developmentally based instruction in which students examine words out of running text, from a variety of perspectives.

The challenge for teachers, then, is how to sustain and nurture students' spelling and word knowledge in the most efficient, effective, and engaging manner. The challenge can be addressed through effective assessment of students' spelling knowledge, an understanding of what features should then be studied based on each student's developmental spelling level, and an understanding of how these features should be studied.

### Assessment

Ganske (1994) noted that for "the many educators with more limited experience in [recognizing and intepreting students' spelling] . . . despite their best intentions, the act of translating invented spellings into child-centered classroom strategies can turn into hit and miss courses of action" (p. 141). In recent years a number of well-constructed assessment inventories have been developed. In addition, materials published for word study, including basal programs, usually include assessments that will help teachers determine the instructional and developmental range of the students in their classrooms and effectively match instruction to these levels. Grade-specific assessments may be used to determine students' spelling instructional level (R. Shlagal, 1992) whereas developmental-level assessments identify the stage within which students are primarily functioning (Bear, Invernizzi, Templeton, & Johnston, 2000). Bear et al. (2000) and Ganske (1999, 2000) have refined developmental-level assessments so that they may be more efficiently administered and more clearly identify the features within phases that students have acquired as well as those they are ready to explore.

## The Spelling Curriculum

Because of the importance of orthographic knowledge in writing and reading and the importance of discerning orthographic patterns, the general content and sequence of a spelling and word study curriculum should present important features and patterns arrayed in a manner that reflects this developmental continuum.

Instructional programs that emphasize only "most frequently misspelled" words or words that each individual student is having difficulty learning to spell do not provide opportunities to discern logical and negotiable patterns but lead instead to a word-by-word, rote memory-dependent approach. Note that the features and patterns grow from simpler alphabetic understandings (single consonant spellings, short vowel patterns, consonant digraphs and blends) to more abstract orthographic understandings (long vowel patterns and position-dependent spellings such as *ck* for terminal /k/) to syllable juncture patterns, simpler and then more advanced morphological combinatorial features. Beginning with the syllables and affixes phase, as Dale, O'Rourke, and Bamman (1971) observed, "Organizing spelling lessons to coincide with the study of morphology gives the students a contextual structure for the study of spelling" (p. 172). This is reflected in the emphasis on the relationship between spelling and meaning through the exploration of affixes and base words and, later, affixes and Greek and Latin word roots.

This emphasis on spelling and meaning or morphological relationships suggests a stronger integration of spelling and vocabulary instruction at the intermediate grades and beyond (Aronoff, 1994) than has traditionally occurred: Research in developmental word knowledge at the upper levels suggests guidelines for organizing and sequencing this instruction (S. Templeton, 1992). At these upper levels, students may be shown how the spelling/morphological relationships they are exploring can also be tools for vocabulary expansion. The most productive exercise of this knowledge is through analysis of unfamiliar words encountered in reading. Beginning in the intermediate grades, students' reading presents them with an increasing number of polysyllabic words. When these words

are unfamiliar, in most instances they are morphological derivatives of known words (Aronoff, 1994) and it is very often possible to determine the meaning of such words because of their visual similarity to more familiar words. Aronoff observed, "Unfortunately, very little time is spent in school on systematic learning of morphology" (pp. 820–821). One possible explanation for spending little time on such systematic learning, as noted in the first section of this chapter, is the lack of a substantial teacher knowledge base in this area (Moats & Smith, 1992). It has not been until the last 20 years or so that spelling–meaning relationships have been emphasized in the instructional literature and in curriculum design (Henderson & S. Templeton, 1986; Moats & Smith, 1992; Templeton, 1983, 1991).

Beginning at the consolidated alphabetic–within-word pattern phase, the words that students explore for purposes of learning conventional spelling should be words that they know how to read; in that sense, reading is the pacemaker for their spelling (Frith, 1985). At all developmental levels, however, the ability to read words is supported by the spelling of words (Ellis, 1994; Perfetti, 1997). This may occur in two ways: First, the memory for each specific word and its structure is reinforced; second, common patterns across words are discerned and abstracted. For example, consider what happens for older students who examine a pair of words such as *sign* and *signature*. Although they can read these words and understand their meaning, they usually have not explicitly noted the spelling/meaning or morphological relationships among the words unless they explore the words through activities that include writing the words while attending to these types of relationships. At this level, of course, spelling of the words is reinforced—including alphabetic memory for the silent *g* in *sign*. This focused attention, however, facilitates as well two operations that are critical for reading. First, these words are bonded more tightly in the lexicon (Bybee, 1985); when each is accessed in reading, then, there may be a more elaborate and interconnected conceptual domain that each will tap. Second, awareness of the consistent spelling of morphemes, despite changes in their pronunciation, is developed and reinforced. This awareness of the common visual identity may guide students' identification of unfamiliar words they encounter in their reading.

It is important to note that the reconceptualization of spelling as a reflection of word knowledge more generally shifts the instructional emphasis from the traditional concern with numbers of words studied to the search for patterns across words. When spelling is considered only as a skill for writing, the focus of instruction is more narrowly conceived and the number of words to be studied becomes an issue, as does the fact that students may already know how to spell correctly a fair number of the words they are expected to study (Manolakes, 1975). Research on appropriate spelling instructional level reveals that learners make better progress toward conventional spelling if they spell between 50% and 90% of the words on a pretest correctly (Morris et al., 1995). This is because students have enough underlying or implicit knowledge of the patterns to be explored to support memory for the words they have misspelled. This fact is related to a larger issue, however. This level may be more comfortable and appropriate for students because the emphasis is not on number of words spelled correctly but rather on using words as a means of becoming aware of and reinforcing patterns.

## Spelling Instruction

Several recent studies emphasize the importance of pacing instruction to developmental level and engaging learners in the active search for "logical, negotiable patterns" (Hughes & Searle, 1997, p. 133). At all developmental levels, an effective means of facilitating active search for patterns is through word categorization, or word-sort activities (e.g., Bear et al., 2000; Brooks et al., 2000; Fountas & Pinnell, 1998; Fresch & Wheaton, 1997; Graham, 2000; Henderson, 1985, 1990; Hughes & Searle, 1997; Morris, 1983; S. Templeton, 1991; Zutell, 1996, 1998). This type of active exploration of words encourages the examination of words from multiple perspectives, noting common sound, spelling, and meaning patterns within words. This exploration is conducted primarily by reading and writing words while comparing, contrasting, and classifying them in this search for pattern. An important benefit of this exploration and active engagement is the strengthening of connections within and between orthographic and phonological knowledge, contributing to the automatic identification of words during reading and the automatic access of words during writing.

In a recent review of spelling research Templeton and Morris (2000) concluded, "There is now the potential for an engaging blend of traditional and contemporary aspects of instruction that promotes an appropriate synthesis of meaningful reading and writing experiences with developmentally-paced word study" (p. 539). For example, most educators have long realized that words experienced in reading need to be examined out of running text and that a practice such as "pretest study" is effective and that (since at least the middle of the 20th century) arranging words for study according to increasing patterns of orthographic complexity is effective. Contemporary research builds on these insights in the following ways:

1. Because spelling is not a rote memory task but instead a process of abstracting patterns, this process of abstraction is facilitated by ensuring that students are examining words at their appropriate spelling instructional and developmental levels.

2. Examining words at the appropriate spelling instructional and developmental levels in turn ensures that techniques such as administering a self-corrected pretest will be more effective because students will not be attempting merely to memorize individual words; their search for pattern will be directed to all of the words, not just the ones that were incorrect on the pretest.

3. Although most researchers and curriculum designers have long concurred as to the sequence of words and patterns for study at the primary level, the sequence at the intermediate grade levels and beyond has been less certain. Recently, however, the evidence more strongly suggests support for a more logical scope and sequence of these elements, focusing now more directly on morphology—on the interrelationships between spelling and vocabulary knowledge.

4. The ways in which students explore words out of the context of running text should be more active and engaging; this in turn leads to the more explicit understanding of the logic underlying written words and may help replace a phonocentric, rote-memory-based stance with a more inquisitive one.

5. It is helpful to consider the application of word knowledge in reading and writing as also exercising that knowledge. Given that writing words exercises and develops specific word knowledge more effectively than solely reading words, students should be doing a lot of writing in school. The continual application of word knowledge in writing, in the service of conveying thought, is powerful exercise. It is most effective if students like to write and write frequently.

6. Given that phonics and spelling and word study more generally compose an area about which many teachers feel less prepared to teach, there are more resources available to provide the knowledge base and the specific curriculum.

## Implications for Learners of English as a New Language

For most of the world's languages that have writing systems, each system or orthography matches its spoken language fairly well (Jaffre, 1997). In addition, very few spelling systems or orthographies are pure in the sense that they represent sound or meaning exclusively. Rather, most orthographies include to varying degrees aspects of both sound and meaning. As we have seen, English orthography, though reflecting more consistency than often believed at the level of sound, also reflects a very significant degree of morphological information. Among alphabetic orthographies, for example, Spanish is more phonemic and French, like English, is more morphological. Even Chinese, for example, has evolved such that each character comprises both a meaning element and a radical, or cue to the pronunciation.

Educators who know the native language spoken by their students acquiring English, of course, have an advantage, as they understand the features of English that are likely to be most problematic—as for example the greater number of vowels in English in comparison to Spanish and the differences between the languages in pronunciation of certain consonant letters. Unless educators are also familiar with the types of information represented in English orthography, however, they may still be uncertain about how best to facilitate their English-learning students' development in this area. Teachers who do not know the language of their students may work to become more familiar with it, focusing on those general features of the language that are most at variance with English, such as aspects of syntactic structure and tonality of vowels.

Over the last few decades, a number of studies have addressed the issue of spelling acquisition and instruction for students who are learning English as a new language (e.g., Fashola, Drum, & Mayer, 1996; Holm & Dodd, 1996; Nathenson-Mejia, 1989; Zutell & Allen, 1988). As with all aspects of literacy, if students acquiring English are literate to some degree in their first language, this will support their developing knowledge of English orthography (Holm & Dodd, 1996; Tyler, 1997). A significant body of research supports the observation that for students who are literate in their first language and who are acquiring a new language, the lens through which they first examine the new orthography is determined by the nature and characteristics of their first orthography (Chikamatsu, 1996; Holm & Dodd, 1997). In the case of learning English spelling, if the first language has an alphabetically based orthography, this will afford students an advantage. Letter–sound correspondences are first attempted through the patterns learned in the first language; as orthographic patterns in English are noted and explored, however, these patterns can facilitate the perception and acquisition of aspects of English phonology (Dickerson, 1985, 1990; Fashola, Drum, & Mayer, 1996). Significantly, the knowledgeable interpretation of errors can be as insightful for the English Language Learning teacher as they can be for regular classroom teachers. In this regard, Tyler (1997) commented that "when teachers examine the spelling problems of their learners, they are observing the visible signs of a *reading process* [italics added] which has been only partially absorbed" (p. 194).

In addition to facilitating students' acquisition of English spelling, two areas of ongoing spelling research should better inform our efforts to facilitate the acquisition of English as a new language. First, the developmental spelling research being conducted in other countries and with other languages (e.g., Bear & Shen, 2000; Perfetti, Rieben, & Fayol, 1997); this research is clarifying those cognitive and linguistic universals with which all learners approach the task of literacy learning, regardless of the orthography they are learning. Second, the research investigating English language learners' acquisition of English spelling; educators are just beginning to understand how the nature and structure of English orthography can facilitate these learners' acquisition of English phonology as well as their acquisition of literacy in English (not to mention the acquisition of other languages by native speakers of English). Moreover, insights gained from this research may complement another important area of research—how better to facilitate native English speakers' acquisition of the spoken and written forms of other languages.

## CONCLUSION

Although educators are not entirely in accord as to the degree to which words should be examined outside of connected text in order to develop spelling knowledge, to date the weight of most recent research supports the need for most learners to experience words through reading, writing, and focused examination. Such examination may facilitate the explicit awareness

and application of the logical spelling patterns that exist at the alphabetic level, the within- and between-syllable level, and the meaning or morphological level. In the past, debates about systematic and sequenced spelling apart from actual reading and writing were cast in terms of a trade-off: More time spent in isolated spelling instruction meant less time spent actually reading and writing; moreover, the nature of the actual spelling instruction and activities was often questionable. The field is now at a point at which this either-or perspective may be replaced.

Word knowledge drives efficient reading and writing. Although the processes of writing words and reading words are not identical, they are nevertheless integrally related in that they both draw on the same underlying foundation of spelling or orthographic knowledge. In writing, the higher level aspects of intended meaning, audience, word choice, and so forth cannot be effectively exercised if a significant amount of attention must be allocated to spelling the words. Words and the alphabetic, pattern, and meaning elements must be accessed efficiently and automatically. This access is the first step toward making the task demands of writing easier thus allocating attention to the more substantive aspects of writing. The manner in which this automaticity is developed includes instruction that links the traditional curricular components of word study—phonics, spelling, and vocabulary—in an articulated sequence grounded in development.

The English language arts field is beginning to move beyond the narrow conceptualization of spelling as the obligatory, though unexciting, guest on the fringes of the language arts. Such a view has led in the past to narrower and more constraining instructional questions, such as "How many words should students study?," "How can we get students to memorize these words?," "Can't we just teach spelling rules?," and "Why should students study words they already know how to spell?" Instead, emerging from the field is a newer conceptualization of spelling, one that acknowledges the role of spelling knowledge in the decoding of words in reading as well as in the encoding of words in writing—and that also is directly related to the expansion and elaboration of vocabulary knowledge. Cummings (1988) succinctly expressed the potential of this conceptualization: "It seems probable that a better understanding of the American English orthographic system *would lead us toward a better teaching of literacy*" [italics added] (p. 463). This broader conceptualization of spelling can significantly inform if not revolutionize the efforts of teachers at all grade levels, teacher educators, and designers of curriculum.

## *References*

Allal, L. (1997). Learning to spell in the classroom. In C. A. Perfetti & L. Reiben (Eds.), *Learning to spell: Research, theory, and practice across languages* (pp. 129–150). Mahwah, NJ: Lawrence Erlbaum Associates.

Apel, K., & Masterson, J. (Eds.) (2000). The ABCs of spelling: Development, assessment, and intervention [Special issue]. *Topics in Language Disorders, 20.*

Aronoff, M. (1994). Morphology. In A. C. Purves, L. Papa, & S. Jordan (Eds.), *Encyclopedia of English studies and language arts* (Vol. 2, pp. 820–821). New York: Scholastic.

Baker, B. (1999). The dangerous and the good? Developmentalism, progress, and public schooling. *American Educational Research Journal, 36*(4), 797.

Barnes, W. (1982). *The developmental acquisition of silent letters and orthographic images in English spelling.* Unpublished doctoral dissertation, University of Virginia, Charlottesville.

Barone, D. (1992). Whatever happened to spelling? The role of spelling instruction in process-centered classrooms. *Reading Psychology, 13*(1), 1-18.

Bear, D. R. (1982). *Patterns of oral reading across stages of word knowledge.* Unpublished doctoral dissertation, University of Virginia, Charlottesville, Virginia.

Bear, D. R., Invernizzi, M., Templeton, S., & Johnston, F. (2000). *Words their way: Word study for phonics, vocabulary, and spelling instruction* (2nd ed.). Upper Saddle River, NJ: Merrill/Prentice-Hall.

Bear, D. R., & Shen, H. H. (2000). Development of orthographic skills in Chinese children. *Reading and Writing: An Interdisciplinary Journal, 13,* 197-236.

Bear, D. R., Templeton, S., & Warner, M. (1991). The development of a qualitative inventory of higher levels of orthographic knowledge. In J. Zutell & S. McCormick (Eds.), *Learner factors/teacher factors: Issues in literacy research and instruction: Fortieth yearbook of the National Reading Conference.* Chicago: National Reading Conference.

Beers, C. (1980). The relationship of cognitive development to spelling and reading abilities. In E. H. Henderson & J. W. Beers (Eds.), *Developmental and cognitive aspects of learning to spell* (pp. 74-84). Newark, DE: International Reading Association.

Beers, J. W., & Henderson, E. H. (1977). A study of developing orthographic concepts among first graders. *Research in the Teaching of English, 11,* 133-148.

Berninger, V. W. (Ed.) (1994). *The varieties of orthographic knowledge I: Theoretical and developmental issues.* Dordrecht, The Netherlands: Kluwer.

Berninger, V. W. (Ed.) (1995). *The varieties of orthographic knowledge II: Relationships to phonology, reading, and writing.* Dordrecht, The Netherlands: Kluwer.

Bosman, A. T., & Van Orden, G. C. (1997). Why spelling is more difficult than reading. In C. A. Perfetti & L. Rieben (Eds.), *Learning to spell: Research, theory, and practice across languages* (pp. 173-194). Mahwah, NJ: Lawrence Erlbaum Associates.

Brooks, A., Begay, K., Curtin, G., Byrd, K., & Graham, S. (2000). Language-based spelling instruction: Teaching children to make multiple connections between spoken and written words. *Learning Disability Quarterly, 2,* 117-135.

Brown, G. D. A., & Ellis, N. C. (Eds.) (1994). *Handbook of spelling: Theory, process and intervention.* Chichester, England: Wiley.

Brown, G. D. A., & Loosemore, R. P. W. (1994). Computational approaches to normal and impaired spelling. In G. D. A. Brown & N. C. Ellis (Eds.), *Handbook of spelling: Theory, process and intervention* (pp. 319-335). Chichester, England: Wiley.

Brown, R. (1973). *A first language.* Cambridge, MA: Harvard University Press.

Bybee, J. L. (1985). *Morphology: A study of the relation between meaning and form.* Amsterdam: John Benjamins.

Chikamatsu, N. (1996). The effects of L1 orthography on L2 word recognition: A study of American and Chinese learners of Japanese. *Studies in Second Language Acquisition, 18,* 403-432.

Chomsky, C. (1970). Reading, writing, and phonology. *Harvard Educational Review, 40,* 287-309.

Chomsky, N. (1957). *Syntactic structures.* The Hague, The Netherlands: Mouton.

Chomsky, N. (1959). A review of B. F. Skinner's "Verbal behavior." *Language, 35*(1), 25-58.

Chomsky, N., & Halle, M. (1968). *The sound pattern of English.* New York: Harper & Row.

Cummings, D. W. (1988). *American English spelling.* Baltimore, MD: Johns Hopkins University Press.

Dale, E., O'Rourke, J., & Bamman, H. (1971). *Techniques of teaching vocabulary.* Palo Alto, CA: Field Education Enterprises.

Derwing, B. L., Smith, M. L., & Wiebe, G. E. (1995). On the role of spelling in morpheme recognition: Experimental studies with children and adults. In L. B. Feldman (Ed.), *Morphological aspects of language processing* (pp. 3-27). Hillsdale, NJ: Lawrence Erlbaum Associates.

Dickerson, W. B. (1985). The invisible Y: A case for spelling in pronunciation learning. *TESOL Quarterly, 19,* 303-316.

Dickerson, W. B. (1990). Morphology via orthography: A visual approach to oral decisions. *Applied Linguistics, 11,* 238-252.

Ehri, L. C. (1975). Word consciousness in readers and prereaders. *Journal of Educational Psychology, 67,* 204-212.

Ehri, L. C. (1993). How English orthography influences phonological knowledge as children learn to read and spell. In R. J. Scales (Ed.), *Literacy and language analysis* (pp. 21-43). Hillsdale, NJ: Lawrence Erlbaum Associates.

Ehri, L. C. (1997). Learning to read and learning to spell are one and the same, almost. In C. A. Perfetti, L. Rieben, & M. Fayol (Eds.), *Learning to spell: Research, theory, and practice across languages* (pp. 237-269). Mahwah, NJ: Lawrence Erlbaum Associates.

Ehri, L. C., & Wilce, L. (1987). Does learning to spell help beginners learn to read words? *Reading Research Quarterly, 22,* 47-65.

Ellis, N. (1994). Longitudinal studies of spelling development. In G. D. Brown & N. C. Ellis (Eds.) (1994). *Handbook of spelling: Theory, process and intervention* (pp. 155-177). Chichester, England: Wiley.

Ellis, N., & Cataldo, S. (1990). The role of spelling in learning to read. *Language and Education, 4,* 1-28.

Fashola, O., Drum, P. A., & Mayer, R. E. (1996). A cognitive theory of orthographic transitioning: Predictable errors in how Spanish-speaking children spell English words. *American Educational Research Journal, 33,* 825-843.

Fischer, F., Shankweiler, D., & Liberman, I. Y. (1985). Spelling proficiency and sensitivity to word structure. *Journal of Memory and Language, 24,* 423-441.

Fountas, I., & Pinnell, G. (1998). *Word matters.* Portsmouth, NH: Heinemann.

Fountas, I., & Pinnell, G. (Eds.) (1999). *Voices on word matters.* Portsmouth, NH: Heinemann.

Fowler, A. E., & Liberman, I. Y. (1995). The role of phonology and orthography in morphological awareness. In L. B. Feldman (Ed.), *Morphological aspects of language processing* (pp. 157-188). Hillsdale, NJ: Lawrence Erlbaum Associates.

Fresch, M. (2000). What we learned from Josh: A visual approach to oral decisions. *Language Arts, 77,* 232-240.

Fresch, M., & Wheaton, A. (1997). Sort, search, and discover: Spelling in the child-centered classroom. *Reading Teacher, 51,* 20-31.

Freyd, P., & Baron, J. (1983). Individual differences in acquisition of derivational morphology. *Journal of Verbal Learning & Verbal Behavior, 21,* 282-295.

Frith, U. (1985). Beneath the surface of developmental dyslexia. In K. Patterson, J. Marshall, & M. Coltheart (Eds.), London: Lawrence Erlbaum Associates.

Frith, U. (1994). Foreward. In G. D. Brown & N. C. Ellis (Eds.) (1994). *Handbook of spelling: Theory, process and intervention* (pp. xi-xiv). Chichester, England: Wiley.

Ganske, K. (1994). *Developmental spelling analysis: A diagnostic measure for instruction and research.* Unpublished doctoral dissertation, University of Virginia, Charlottesville.

Ganske, K. (1999). The Developmental Spelling Analysis: A measure of orthographic knowledge. *Educational Assessment, 6,* 41-70.

Ganske, K. (2000). *Word journeys.* New York: Guilford Press.

Gates, A. I. (1931). An experimental comparison of the study-test and test-study methods in spelling. *Journal of Educational Psychology, 22.*

Gates, A. I. (1937). *A list of spelling difficulties in 3876 words.* New York: Teachers College Press.

Gentry, J. R. (1977). *A study of the orthographic strategies of beginning readers. Dissertation Abstracts International, 39*(07A), 4017. (University Microfilms No. AAG7901152)

Gentry, J. R., & Gillet, J. W. (1993). *Teaching kids to spell.* Portsmouth, NH: Heinemann.

Gill, C. E. (1980). An analysis of spelling errors in French. *Dissertation Abstracts International, 41*(09A), 3924. (University Microfilms No. AAG8026641)

Gill, C. H., & Scharer, P. L. (1996). "Why do they get it on Friday and misspell it on Monday?" Teachers inquiring about their students as spellers. *Language Arts, 73,* 89–96.

Gill, J. T. (1992). The relationship between word recognition and spelling. In S. Templeton & D. R. Bear (Eds.), *Development of orthographic knowledge and the foundations of literacy: A memorial Festschrift for Edmund H. Henderson* (pp. 79–104). Hillsdale, NJ: Lawrence Erlbaum Associates.

Graham, S. (2000). Should the natural learning approach replace spelling instruction? *Journal of Educational Psychology, 92,* 235–247.

Hanna, P. R., Hanna, J. S., Hodges, R. E., & Rudorf, H. (1966). Phoneme-grapheme correspondences as cues to spelling improvement. Washington, DC: United States Office of Education Cooperative Research.

Hanna, P., Hodges, R., & Hanna, J. (1971). *Spelling: Structure and strategies.* Boston: Houghton Mifflin.

Henderson, E. H. (1981). *Learning to read and spell: The child's knowledge of words.* DeKalb, IL: Northern Illinois Press.

Henderson, E. H. (1985). *Teaching spelling.* Boston: Houghton Mifflin.

Henderson, E. H. (1990). *Teaching spelling* (2nd ed.). Boston: Houghton Mifflin.

Henderson, E. H. (1992). The interface of lexical competence and knowledge of written words. In S. Templeton & D. R. Bear (Eds.), *Development of orthographic knowledge and the foundations of literacy: A memorial Festschrift for Edmund H. Henderson* (pp. 1–30). Hillsdale, NJ: Lawrence Erlbaum Associates.

Henderson, E. H., & Beers, J. (Eds.) (1980). *Developmental and cognitive aspects of learning to spell: A reflection of word knowledge.* Newark, DE: International Reading Association.

Henderson, E. H., & Templeton, S. (1986). A developmental perspective of formal spelling instruction through alphabet, pattern, and meaning. *Elementary School Journal, 86,* 305–316.

Henry, M. K. (1989). Children's word structure knowledge: Implications for decoding and spelling instruction. *Reading and Writing, 1,* 135–152.

Henry, M. K. (1993). Morphological structure: Latin and Greek roots and affixes as upper grade code strategies. *Reading and Writing, 5,* 227–241.

Holm, A., & Dodd, B. (1996). The effect of first written language on the acquisition of English literacy. *Cognition, 59,* 119–147.

Horn, E. (1926). *A basic vocabulary of 10,000 words most commonly used in writing.* Iowa City: University of Iowa.

Horn, E. (1960). Spelling. In C. W. Harris (Ed.), *Encyclopedia of Educational Research* (3rd ed., pp. 1337–1354). New York: Macmillan.

Horn, T. (1946). *The effect of the corrected test on learning to spell.* Unpublished Master's thesis, University of Iowa, Iowa City.

Horn, T. (1969). Spelling. In R. L. Ebel (Ed.), *Encyclopedia of educational research* (4th ed., pp. 1282–1299). New York: Macmillan.

Hughes, M., & Searle, D. (1997). *The violent e and other tricky sounds: Learning to spell from kindergarten through grade 6.* York, ME: Stenhouse.

Hughes, M., & Searle, D. (2000). Spelling and "the second 'R.'" *Language Arts, 77,* 203–208.

Huxford, L., Terrell, C., & Bradley, L. (1992). 'Invented' spelling and learning to read. In C. Sterling & C. Robson (Eds.), *Psychology, spelling, and education* (pp. 159–167). Clevedon, UK: Multilingual Matters.

Invernizzi, M. (1985). A cross-sectional analysis of children's recognition and recall of word elements. *Dissertation Abstracts International, 47*(02A), 483. (University Microfilms No. AAG8526886)

Jaffre, J. (1997). From writing to orthography: The functions and limits of the notion of system. In C. A. Perfetti, L. Rieben, & M. Fayol (Eds.), *Learning to spell: Research, theory, and practice across languages* (pp. 3–20). Mahwah, NJ: Lawrence Erlbaum Associates.

Krashen, S. (1989). We acquire vocabulary and spelling by reading: additional evidence for the input hypothesis. *The Modern Language Journal, 73,* 440–464.

Lenneberg, E. (1967). *The biological foundations of language.* New York: Wiley.

Leong, C. K. (1998). Strategies used by 9- to 12-year-old children in written spelling. In C. Hulme & R. M. Joshi (Eds.), *Reading and spelling: Development and disorders* (pp. 421–432). Mahwah, NJ: Lawrence Erlbaum Associates.

Mann, V. A., Tobin, P., & Wilson, R. (1987). Measuring phonological awareness through the invented spellings of kindergarten children. *Merrill-Palmer Quarterly, 33,* 365–391.

Manolakes, G. (1975). The teaching of spelling: A pilot study. *Elementary English, 52,* 243–247.

Marsh, G., Friedman, M., Welch, V., & Desberg, P. (1980). The development of strategies in spelling. In U. Frith (Ed.), *Cognitive strategies in spelling* (pp. 339–353). New York: Academic Press.

McKee, P. (1924). *Teaching and testing spelling by column and context forms.* Unpublished doctoral dissertation, University of Iowa, Iowa City.

Moats, L. (2000). *Speech to print: Language essentials for teachers.* Baltimore, MD: Brookes.

Moats, L., & Smith, C. (1992). Derivational morphology: Why it should be included in assessment and instruction. *Language, Speech, and Hearing in the Schools, 23,* 312–319.

Morris, D. (1983). Concept of word and phoneme awareness in the beginning reader. *Research in the Teaching of English, 17,* 359–373.

Morris, D. (1992). Concept of word: A pivotal understanding in the learning-to-read process. In S. Templeton & D. R. Bear (Eds.), *Development of orthographic knowledge and the foundations of literacy: A Memorial Festschrift for Edmund H. Henderson* (pp. 53–77). Hillsdale, NJ: Lawrence Erlbaum Associates.

Morris, D. (1993). The relationship between children's concept of word in text and phoneme awareness in learning to read: A longitudinal study. *Research in the Teaching of English, 27,* 133–154.

Nathenson-Mejia, S. (1989). Writing in a second language: Negotiating meaning through invented spelling. *Language Arts,* 516–526.

Nunes, S., Bryant, P., & Bindman, M. (1997). Spelling and grammar: The necsed move. In C. A. Perfetti, L. Rieben, & M. Fayol (Eds.), *Learning to spell: Research, theory, and practice across languages* (pp. 151–170). Mahwah, NJ: Lawrence Erlbaum Associates.

Olson, A., & Caramazza, A. (1994). Representation and connectionist models: The NETspell experience. In G. D. A. Brown & N. C. Ellis (Eds.), *Handbook of spelling: Theory, process and intervention* (pp. 337–363).

*Oxford English Dictionary* (2nd ed.) [CD-ROM]. Oxford, England: Oxford University Press.

Perfetti, C. A. (1993). The representation problem in reading acquisition. In P. B. Gough, L. C. Ehri, & R. Treiman (Eds.), *Reading acquisition* (pp. 145–174). Hillsdale, NJ: Lawrence Erlbaum Associates.

Perfetti, C. A. (1997). The psycholinguistics of spelling and reading. In C. A. Perfetti, L. Rieben, & M. Fayol (Eds.), *Learning to spell: Research, theory, and practice across languages* (pp. 21-38). Mahwah, NJ: Lawrence Erlbaum Associates.

Perfetti, C. A., Rieben, L., & Fayol, M. (Eds.) (1997). *Learning to spell: Research, theory, and practice across languages*. Mahwah, NJ: Lawrence Erlbaum Associates.

Piaget, J., & Inhelder, B. (1969). *The psychology of the child*. New York: Basic Books.

Read, C. (1971). Preschool children's knowledge of English phonology. *Harvard Educational Review, 41*, 1-34.

Read, C. (1975). *Children's categorizations of speech sounds in English* (Research Report No. 17). Urbana, IL: National Council of Teachers of English.

Read, C., & Hodges, R. (1982). Spelling. In H. Mitzel (Ed.), *Encyclopedia of Educational Research* (5th ed., pp. 1758-1767). New York: Macmillan.

Reiben, L., & Saada-Robert, M. (1997). Relation between word-search strategies and word-copying strategies in children aged 5-6 years old. In C. A. Perfetti, L. Rieben, & M. Fayol (Eds.), *Learning to spell: Research, theory, and practice across languages* (pp. 295-318). Mahwah, NJ: Lawrence Erlbaum Associates.

Reuckl, J. G., & Raveh, M. (1999). The influence of morphological regularities on the dynamics of a connectionist model. *Brain and Language, 68*, 110-117.

Rumelhart, D. E., & McClelland, J. L. (Eds.) (1986). *Parallel distributed processing: Explorations in the microstructure of cognition* (Vol. 2). Cambridge, MA: MIT Press/Bradford.

Sabey, B. L. (1997). *Metacognitive responses of syllable juncture spellers while performing three literacy tasks. Dissertation Abstracts International, 58*(8-A), 3066. (University Microfilms No. AAM9804622)

Sabey, B. L. (1999). Metacognitive responses of an intermediate speller while performing three literacy tasks. *Journal of Literacy Research, 31*, 415-455.

Schlagal, R. (1992). Patterns of orthographic development into the intermediate grades. In S. Templeton & D. R. Bear (Eds.), *Development of orthographic knowledge and the foundations of literacy: A memorial Festschrift for Edmund H. Henderson* (pp. 31-52). Hillsdale, NJ: Lawrence Erlbaum Associates.

Schlagal, R. C. (1982). *A qualitative inventory of word knowledge: A developmental study of spelling, grades one through six. Dissertation Abstracts International, 47*(03A), 915. (University Microfilms No. AAG8611798)

Scott, C. M. (2000). Principles and methods of spelling instruction: Applications for poor spellers. *Topics in Language Disorders, 20*, 66-82.

Scragg, D. G. (1974). *A history of English spelling*. New York: Barnes & Noble.

Seidenberg, M., & McClelland, J. (1989). A distributed developmental model for word recognition and naming. *Psychological Review, 96*, 523-568.

Seymour, P. (1992). Cognitive theories of spelling and implications for instruction. In C. M. Sterling & C. Robson (Eds.), *Psychology, spelling, and education* (pp. 50-70). Clevedon, UK: Multilingual Matters.

Shankweiler, D., & Lundquist, E. (1992). On the relations between learning to spell and learning to read. In R. Frost & L. Katz (Eds.), *Orthography, phonology, morphology, and meaning* (pp. 179-192). Amsterdam: North-Holland.

Smith, M. L. (1998). *Sense and sensitivity: An investigation into fifth-grade children's knowledge of English derivational morphology and its relationship to vocabulary and reading ability. Dissertation Abstracts International, 59*(4-A), 1111. (University Microfilms No. AAM9830072)

Snowling, M. (1994). Towards a model of spelling acquisition: The development of some component skills. In G. D. A. Brown & N. C. Ellis (Eds.) (1994). *Handbook of spelling: Theory, process, and intervention* (pp. 111-128). Chichester, England: Wiley.

Stage, S. C., & Wagner, R. K. (1992). Development of young children's phonological and orthographic knowledge as revealed by their spellings. *Developmental Psychology, 28*, 287-296.

Steffler, D. J., Varnhagen, C. K., Friesen, C. K., & Treiman, R. (1998). There's more to children's spelling than the errors they make: Strategic and automatic processes for one-syllable words. *Journal of Educational Psychology, 90*, 492-505.

Temple, C. A. (1978). An analysis of spelling errors in Spanish. *Dissertation Abstracts International, 40*(02A), 721. (University Microfilms No. AAG7916258)

Templeton, S. (1979). Spelling first, sound later: The relationship between orthography and higher order phonological knowledge in older students. *Research in the Teaching of English, 13*, 255-264.

Templeton, S. (1980). Logic and mnemonics for demons and curiosities: Spelling awareness for middle- and secondary-level students. *Reading World, 20*, 123-130.

Templeton, S. (1983). Using the spelling/meaning connection to develop word knowledge in older students. *Journal of Reading, 27*(1), 8-14.

Templeton, S. (1985, June). *Awareness of the relationship between structural and semantic features in English orthography among 12-, 13-, and 14-year-old American students*. Paper presented at the First International Congress on Applied Psycholinguistics, Barcelona, Spain.

Templeton, S. (1991). Teaching and learning the English spelling system: Reconceptualizing method and purpose. *Elementary School Journal, 92*, 183-199.

Templeton, S. (1992). Theory, nature, and pedagogy of higher-order orthographic development in older students. In S. Templeton & D. R. Bear (Eds.), *Development of orthographic knowledge and the foundations of literacy: A memorial Festschrift for Edmund H. Henderson* (pp. 253-277). Hillsdale, NJ: Lawrence Erlbaum Associates.

Templeton, S., & Bear, D. R. (Eds.) (1992). *Development of orthographic knowledge and the foundations of literacy: A memorial Festschrift for Edmund H. Henderson*. Hillsdale, NJ: Lawrence Erlbaum Associates.

Templeton, S., & Morris, D. (2000). Spelling. In M. Kamil, P. Mosenthal, P. D. Pearson, & R. Barr (Eds.). *Handbook of reading research* (Vol. 3, pp. 525-543). Mahwah, NJ: Lawrence Erlbaum Associates.

Templeton, S., & Scarborough-Franks, L. (1985). The spelling's the thing: Older students' knowledge of derivational morphology in phonology and orthography. *Applied Psycholinguistics, 6*, 371-389.

Templeton, W. S. (1976). An awareness of certain aspects of derivational morphology in phonology and orthography among sixth-, eighth-, and tenth-graders. *Dissertation Abstracts International, 37*(07A), 4190. (University Microfilms No. AAG7700209)

Thorndike, E. L. (1921). *The teacher's word book*. New York: Teachers College Press.

Treiman, R. (1993). *Beginning to spell*. New York: Oxford University Press.

Treiman, R., & Cassar, M. (1997). Spelling acquisition in English. In C. A. Perfetti, L. Rieben, & M. Fayol (Eds.), *Learning to spell: Research, theory, and practice across languages* (pp. 61-80). Mahwah, NJ: Lawrence Erlbaum Associates.

Tyler, A. (1997). Learning the orthographic form of L2 vocabulary—A receptive and a productive process. In N. Schmitt & M. McCarthy (Eds.). *Vocabulary: Description, acquisition, and pedagogy* (pp. 182-195). Cambridge, England: Cambridge University Press.

Varnhagen, V. W. (1995). Children's spelling strategies. In V. W. Berninger (Ed.). *The varieties of orthographic knowledge: Volume 2. Relationships to phonology, reading and writing* (pp. 251-290). The Netherlands: Kluwer.

Venezky, R. L. (1970). *The structure of English orthography*. The Hague, Netherlands: Mouton.

Venezky, R. L. (1999). *The American way of spelling: The structure and origins of American English orthography*. New York: Guilford Press.

Viise, N. M. (1995). A study of the spelling development of adult literacy learners compared with that of classroom children. *Journal of Literacy Research, 28,* 561-587.

Wilde, S. (1997). *What's a schwa sound anyway?: A holistic guide to phonetics, phonics, and spelling*. Portsmouth, NH: Heinemann.

Wysocki, K., & Jenkins, J. R. (1987). Deriving word meanings through morphological generalization. *Reading Research Quarterly, 22,* 66-81.

Zesiger, P. & dePartz, M. (1997). The cognitive neuropsychology of spelling. In C. A. Perfetti, L. Rieben, & M. Fayol (Eds.), *Learning to spell: Research, theory, and practice across languages* (pp. 39-57). Mahwah, NJ: Lawrence Erlbaum Associates.

Zutell, J. (1975). Spelling strategies of primary school children and their relationship to the Piagetian concept of decentration. *Dissertation Abstracts International, 36*(08A), 5030. (University Microfilms No. AAG7600018)

Zutell, J. (1994). Spelling instruction. In A. C. Purves, L. Papa, & S. Jordan (Eds.), *Encyclopedia of English studies and language arts* (Vol. 2, pp. 1098-1100). New York: Scholastic.

Zutell, J. (1996). The Directed Spelling Thinking Activity (DSTA): Providing an effective balance in word study instruction. *Reading Teacher, 50,* 98-108.

Zutell, J. (1998). Word sorting: A developmental spelling approach to word study for delayed readers. *Reading and Writing Quarterly: Overcoming Learning Difficulties, 14,* 219-238.

Zutell, J., & Allen, V. (1988). The English spelling strategies of Spanish-speaking bilingual children. *TESOL Quarterly, 22,* 333-340.

# RESEARCH ON VOCABULARY INSTRUCTION:
# VOLTAIRE REDUX

## James F. Baumann
### University of Georgia

## Edward J. Kame'enui
### University of Oregon

## Gwynne E. Ash
### University of Delaware

> Language is very difficult to put into words.
> —Voltaire

It seems only fitting in the research on vocabulary learning and instruction that we recall the wistful admonition by a poet-writer-philosopher who knew intimately the beguiling charm and character of words. As we initially wrote this chapter for publication in this volume's first edition (Baumann & Kame'enui, 1991), and as we revised it for this second edition, we quickly came to appreciate the veracity of Voltaire's seemingly glib statement—it was indeed challenging to find the proper words to describe what we know (and do not know) about word meanings and how to teach them.

Words. According to one estimate, printed school English, as represented by the materials in Grades 3 to 9, contains 88,533 distinct word families (Nagy & Anderson, 1984). This results in a total volume of nearly one-half million graphically distinct word types when one includes all proper names. Interestingly, roughly half of these 500,000 or so words occurs once or less in a billion words of text. Some of these words are encountered fairly often, and others appear quite infrequently. The challenge facing language users, learners, and teachers is literally and figuratively immense.

When preparing this updated chapter, we were again tempted to follow the literary precedent set by François Marie Arouet (alias Voltaire) and adopt pen names to conceal our real identities. We were convinced we did not have much that was new to say about vocabulary instruction that had not already been said and repeated (e.g., see extensive reviews by Anderson & Nagy, 1991; Baker, Simmons, & Kame'enui, 1998b; Beck & McKeown, 1991; Blachowicz & Fisher, 1996, 2000; Calfee & Drum, 1986; Graves, 1986; Herman & Dole, 1988; McKeown & Curtis, 1987; Mezynski, 1983; Miller & Gildea, 1987; Nagy & Scott, 2000; Stahl & Fairbanks, 1986). Our dilemma, we came to recognize, was in sharp contrast to the conclusion reached by Petty, Herold, and Stoll (1967) more than 3 decades ago after reviewing vocabulary instruction research: "The teaching profession seems to know little of substance about the teaching of vocabulary" (p. 85). Thus, we cannot take cover behind Petty et al.'s conclusion. Instead, we find ourselves facing just the opposite dilemma: We know too much to say we know too little, and we know too little to say that we know enough. Indeed, language is difficult to put into words.

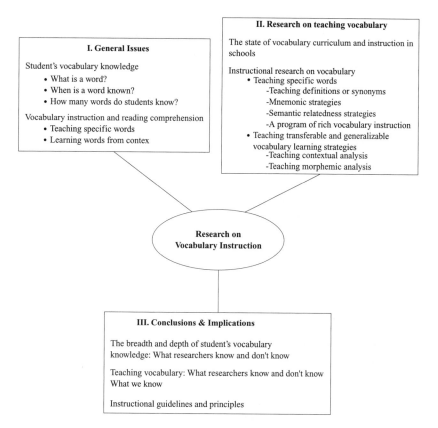

**I. General Issues**

Student's vocabulary knowledge
- What is a word?
- When is a word known?
- How many words do students know?

Vocabulary instruction and reading comprehension
- Teaching specific words
- Learning words from contex

**II. Research on teaching vocabulary**

The state of vocabulary curriculum and instruction in schools

Instructional research on vocabulary
- Teaching specific words
  - Teaching definitions or synonyms
  - Mnemonic strategies
  - Semantic relatedness strategies
  - A program of rich vocabulary instruction
- Teaching transferable and generalizable vocabulary learning strategies
  - Teaching contextual analysis
  - Teaching morphemic analysis

**Research on Vocabulary Instruction**

**III. Conclusions & Implications**

The breadth and depth of student's vocabulary knowledge: What researchers know and don't know

Teaching vocabulary: What researchers know and don't know What we know

Instructional guidelines and principles

Within the last 3 decades, there has been a great deal of ambitious, rigorous, and focused research on all aspects of vocabulary learning and instruction; hence, we are in a position to be clearer about what we know and do not know about this topic. We are hopeful that this updated chapter will provide educators substance and guidance in the quest to provide students with a sensible, pedagogically sound, and empirically based program of vocabulary instruction.

Because this is a language arts handbook, our charge is to present research on both expressive vocabulary (speaking, writing) and receptive vocabulary (listening, reading). However, given the limited space we have to address this broad topic, and in light of the limited research on teaching speaking and writing vocabularies (Duin & Graves, 1987), we have devoted our greatest efforts to presenting and evaluating the research on reading vocabulary instruction and its relationship to text comprehension. We have also focused our review on the learning of vocabulary in a student's native language, almost exclusively English. The nature of vocabulary learning in nonnative languages is also precluded from review by our limited space.

We have organized the content of this chapter into three major sections which, in the spirit of our topic, we have depicted in a semantic map. First, we address several theoretical and pedagogical issues that continue to haunt the research on vocabulary instruction. Second, we examine the research on vocabulary instruction. Here we review and highlight selected studies from the voluminous body of research that attempts to answer the question, "How can we best teach school-age students vocabulary?" Finally, we sum up our review by discussing what we

know and do not know about teaching vocabulary and extend it by considering what this knowledge might mean for practice.

## ISSUES RELATED TO VOCABULARY KNOWLEDGE AND INSTRUCTION

It is difficult to have a sensible discussion about vocabulary knowledge, learning, and instruction without first examining several important theoretical and pedagogical issues. These issues are not new to the research on vocabulary knowledge (cf. Anderson & Freebody, 1981; Nagy & Scott, 2000; Russell & Fea, 1963), but they must be addressed in order to appreciate the nature of the task facing teachers and researchers concerned with vocabulary instruction. In this section, we examine two general sets of issues related to the development of an empirically based program of vocabulary learning. First, we examine the quality and quantity of children's vocabulary knowledge. Second, we attempt to determine what this information says about the importance of vocabulary instruction and its influence on reading comprehension.

### The Quality and Quantity of Students' Vocabulary Knowledge

We first attempt to answer two questions about vocabulary knowledge: What does it mean to know a word, and how many words do students know? We then address the question of when a word is known.

***What does it mean to know a word?*** The study of vocabulary knowledge is as much a study about *knowing* and how we as researchers and practitioners decide when a student really knows something as it is a study about words and students. Determining what a student knows, how much is known, when it is known, and how the depth and breadth of that knowing changes developmentally have been issues at the heart of vocabulary inquiry for at least a century. For example, in the first *Handbook of Research on Teaching* (Gage, 1963), Russell and Fea (1963) pointed out that attempts to measure "children's vocabularies have been numerous during the past 75 years" and that "investigators cannot agree as to what evidence indicates that the word is 'known' by the child" (p. 889).

Our historical and logical sensibilities tell us that it simply does not make sense to discuss the number of words a child knows or must know without first defining what it means to know a word. In his extensive review of vocabulary learning and instruction, Graves (1986) stated twice "there has been little research on depth of word knowledge in school-age children" (pp. 54–55), and unfortunately this assertion remains true today. If we ponder Graves' iterative assessment of this issue today and Russell and Fea's (1963) similar observation many years ago, it is fairly clear that we have advanced very little, if at all, in addressing the question, "What does it mean to know a word?"

If our assessment of this situation is correct, we must ascertain why it is that we know little about what it means to know a word. This task obviously hides more than it reveals. Were it an easy, straightforward task, it would have been settled many years ago. Nagy and Scott (2000) argued that there are five aspects of words and their meanings that affect this complexity of word knowledge: incrementality, multidimensionality, polysemy, interrelatedness, and heterogeneity. That is, we learn words in degrees, understand words through different types of knowledge, come to recognize multiple meanings for words, learn words in relation to our knowledge of other words, and learn different types of words differently. This complex nature of word knowledge could be seen as related to two factors: (a) the difficulty of delimiting the boundaries of a word, especially when a word can be defined in numerous ways, and (b) the inherent difficulty in deciding when something is known (or not known). In the next two sections, we examine each of these issues.

***What is a word?*** The concept word can be defined along various dimensions: semantic, graphic, psychological, sociological, linguistic, historical, or philosophical. Each dimension is likely to reflect a particular theory or ideology that gives primacy to one feature or another (Mezynski, 1983; Mosenthal, 1984). For example, according to Vygotsky (1962) a word is a unit of "verbal thought" that is "already a generalization" (p. 5). Vygotsky viewed word meanings as "dynamic rather than static formations. They change as the child develops; they change with the various ways in which thought functions" (p. 124). Vygotsky noted in the final sentence of *Thought and Language*, "A word is a microcosm of human consciousness" (p. 153). Vygotsky's definition appears to reify the concept of word as a psychological state that ultimately shapes human behavior and action.

On the other hand, Serra (1953; as cited in Russell & Fea, 1963) spoke of words as "verbalized concepts." These concepts represent "through general agreement certain sounds, symbolized in writing by certain combinations of letters . . . and certain meanings attached to certain words" (p. 888). Knowing a word, according to Serra, is simply a matter of determining "whether a child is aware of, and in accord with, the common agreement concerning each word" (p. 888).

If we were to appreciate fully Vygotsky's (1962) insights about words, we would be saddled with the Sisyphean task of having to continuously uncover or disentangle an intricate and complex psychological network of meanings, intentions, affective tendencies, emotions, and so on. The Vygotskian standard of using words as a psychological tool for measuring students' consciousness reveals the potential drama of words. However, Serra's (1953) definition of word knowledge leaves little of the complexity and charm of words. To appreciate this definition, we need only to assess if a student's awareness of a word as a graphically distinct sequence of letters matches the meaning of the word agreed on at the time.

In contrast to the definitions offered by Vygotsky (1962) and Serra (1953), Nagy and Anderson (1984) defined the concept word in terms of the semantic relatedness of words to each other.

We analyzed relatedness among words, not in terms of their historical derivations, but in terms of similarity of their current meanings. For example, the relationship of a derivative word to its base (e.g., business to busy or darkness to dark) was viewed in terms of the relative ease or difficulty with which an individual who knew the meaning of only one of the words could guess or infer the meaning of the other when encountering it in context while reading. (p. 307)

Using this definition, Nagy and Anderson (1984) identified 15 different types of relationships (e.g., regular inflections: walks and walk; suffixation: frustration and frustrate) between a target word and an "immediate ancestor" (p. 309), that is, a word that was most closely related to the target word. In addition, they identified six different levels of semantic relatedness between a target word and its immediate ancestor. These relationships ranged from "semantically transparent" (e.g., *cleverness* and *clever*), words that could be comprehended without assistance from the context, to "semantically opaque" (e.g., *dash* and *dashboard*), words that were not connected semantically.

So, what is a word? Well, it depends. It depends on your purpose for asking the question and your view of thought and language. Word may be defined in a very pragmatic way (Serra, 1953); it may be defined in order to answer a specific question (e.g., "How many words are there?"; Nagy & Anderson, 1984); or it may be defined in a psychological or philosophical manner (Vygotsky, 1962). For us, like Nagy and Anderson, word will be defined operationally according to the questions we ask about their various dimensions, that is, questions that help us evaluate students' abilities to know and be taught word meanings.

This pragmatic stance seems to mirror children's own concept of word which appears to evolve developmentally, with older students able to define what a word is, as well as able to use individual words appropriately (Roberts, 1992). The developing conception, however, is just as difficult for children to articulate as it is for adults. Nevertheless, according to

Roberts (1992), "children continue to be able to use their knowledge of concept of word to perform the tasks but are less able to explain what they know" (p. 132). We likewise continue to perform our tasks, even when there is some difficulty in precisely expressing our definition which creates those tasks, separate from the tasks themselves.

***When is a word known?*** When we speak of vocabulary knowledge, we implicitly recognize four different vocabularies that can be thought of as either expressive (i.e., speaking and writing) or receptive (i.e., reading and listening). *Expressive vocabulary* requires the speaker or writer *to produce* a specific label (e.g., *dope*) for a particular meaning (e.g., a thick, pasty liquid used as a lubricant or absorbent). In contrast, *receptive vocabulary* requires the reader or listener *to associate* a specific meaning with a given label as in reading or listening (Kame'enui, Dixon, & Carnine, 1987).

For a word to be used in expressive vocabulary, the word must be adequately learned or acquired, retained in memory, and retrieved either "out of the blue" (Crowder, 1976, p. 4) or as part of a common expression. In short, the word and its attendant meanings must be fairly well-known and established in memory. Hence, if a student is unable to produce a specific vocabulary word in attempting to express a particular meaning during the acts of writing or speaking, we could say with confidence that the child simply does not know the word. However, as Crowder insightfully noted, unpacking the "fundamental ambiguity" (p. 4) as to exactly why something is not known is a most intricate undertaking.

In receptive vocabulary, however, a student need not know a word in the same way a word is known in expressive vocabulary in order to appreciate its meaning. In fact, in some instances, a word does not need to be known at all, and the reader or listener can still derive a meaning for the unknown label or word. For example, in the following sentence, it is not imperative for the reader or listener to know the meaning of *altercation*: "The altercation left Rocky smiling at his powerful fists and Herbert holding his broken jaw with one band and his broken ribs with the other." The reader or listener can rely on the unknown word's immediate environment (i.e., the verbal context surrounding the word) for assistance. The unknown word does not just appear from "out of the blue" but in the context of other words that will determine how much prior knowledge the child must possess to understand it.

However, as Freebody and Anderson (1983) suggested, an unknown word's immediate environment may need to be fairly obvious and helpful (as in the *altercation* example), or "readers, upon encountering a word they do not known, [may] simply skip it, avoiding a drain on resources" (p. 286). This is not to suggest that difficult words will be skipped automatically or that readers and listeners are instantly paralyzed by such words. Comprehension performance usually suffers when the text contains difficult vocabulary (Carver, 1994; Kame'enui, Carnine, & Freschi, 1982; Stahl, Jacobson, Davis, & Davis, 1989), but the suffering is not akin to comprehension death, as Freebody and Anderson have argued.

If a word does appear from "out of the blue," either in isolation or in a hostile context surrounded by unknown words, the learner might infer the word's meaning from individual parts of the unknown word itself. As Wysocki and Jenkins (1987) noted, this process is called morphological generalization. For example, knowledge of the base word *altercate* may allow a learner to decipher the meanings of *altercation* or *altercative*. It appears that children's ability to utilize morphological clues is influenced significantly by learning and reading experience (Nagy & Anderson, 1984; Wysocki & Jenkins, 1987). Specifically, adults and adolescents tend to use the internal clues more successfully than younger children. These findings suggest that word meanings must be fairly well known in order for morphological generalization to occur. The reliance on morphology as a strategy may also depend upon motivated and word-wise readers or listeners. Therefore, an unknown word can be known in degrees, depending on the internal clues of the word itself or the accompanying verbal context that influences the degree of prior knowledge the learner must have about the word.

In summary, expressive vocabulary requires a learner to know a word rather well before using it; not knowing a word is likely to result in the learner not using the word at all. On the other hand, the standards for knowing a word in receptive vocabulary are not as stringent. In fact, a word need not be known prior to its use in a receptive task, and the learner may still be able to discern its meaning. As Freebody and Anderson (1983) stated, "[I]t takes a surprisingly high proportion of difficult vocabulary to produce reliable decrements in comprehension measures" (p. 293).

If a word in a receptive task is known in degrees, then it is important that we examine the research on degrees of vocabulary knowledge, a topic we now address.

***Degrees of word knowledge.*** It has been argued that vocabulary knowledge is often more than merely the sum of its parts. As Kame'enui et al. (1987) pointed out, "[I]t is conceivable that two students might know the same number of words, and possibly, even roughly the same words, but . . . have 'different vocabularies,' due to differences in the quality or extensiveness of their knowledge of particular words" (p. 133). McKeown and Beck (1988) succinctly captured the issue by noting that "word knowledge is not an all-or-nothing proposition. Words may be known at different levels" (p. 42).

Reviews and analyses on the degrees of word knowledge (Anderson & Freebody, 1981; Dixon & Jenkins, 1984; Durso & Shore, 1991; Graves, 1986; Kame'enui et al., 1987; Shore & Durso, 1990) have, for all practical purposes, relied on the concept learning and development research. For example, Graves (1986) analyzed the developmental concept learning models of Clark (1973), Carey (1978), and Anglin (1977, 1993), all of whom relied on a features analysis of word meanings. For young children, acquiring word meanings is a gradual process based on the experiences a child has with words. Initial learning of word meanings tends to be useful but incomplete. A child's awareness of critical features of words (i.e., those common to *all* instances of a concept) and variable features of words (i.e., those common to *some* concepts) appears to be highly stipulated by the use of words in limited contexts. Naturally, the more experiences a child has, the more mature and complete the word knowledge becomes (Miller & Gildea, 1987). However, as Graves (1986) noted, "Such findings . . . do not say much about the development of the meanings of individual words or suggest specific ways of characterizing the richness of the word knowledge children of various ages have developed" (p. 54).

Dixon and Jenkins (1984) and Kame'enui et al. (1987) also relied on a concept analysis of word learning. However, their analyses were not derived from the results of descriptive studies documenting children's developmental acquisition of word meanings. Instead, these researchers argued that determining the qualities of receptive vocabulary knowledge requires not only a logical analysis of the features of word meanings but also an analysis of the attributes of the vocabulary tasks and contexts in which those words are found. Knowing the meaning of a word, they reasoned, also requires knowing the conditions of the task in which the word is nested because words rarely occur in isolation. Vocabulary knowledge involves determining more than what is known about a word per se; it also involves assessing the dimensions of the immediate task environment in which the word is embedded.

Furthermore, words that seem to be unknown to readers are often known to the degree that readers can discern between correct and incorrect uses in context, even when readers indicate that they do not know the word. These degrees of partial word knowledge seem to be keyed to implicit prior knowledge of the words and language system cues (Durso & Shore, 1991; Shore & Durso, 1990). These systems (implicit prior knowledge and language cues) appear to be more significant than the availability of dictionary definitions for words that are not entirely foreign to the reader.

The notion that a word can be known at different levels is well accepted (Graves, 1984; McKeown & Beck, 1988; Nagy & Anderson, 1984). However, less accepted are the various approaches that have been offered to characterize these levels and to capture the salient features that differentiate one level from another. For example, Beck, McCaslin, and McKeown (1980) suggested scaling the qualities of word knowledge according to three different levels of lexical access: unknown, acquainted, and established word knowledge. A word, according to this scale, would be judged broadly as either well known (i.e., easily and rapidly accessed in memory), known but not well known, or unknown.

Stahl (1985, 1986) suggested an intuitive scale consisting of three successively deeper levels of processing word meanings during reading: association, comprehension, and generation. Generative processing requires the child to produce the target word in a novel context, which is considered to reflect a deeper level of cognitive processing than the association and comprehension of the word. According to Beck et al. (1980) and Stahl, a word is really known when a child is able to retrieve that word from memory rapidly and use it correctly in an uninstructed context. This standard of knowing word meanings is akin to the standard we discussed earlier for expressive vocabulary.

Like Beck et al. (1980) and Stahl (1985, 1986), Kame'enui et al. (1987) proposed three continuous levels of word knowledge: full concept knowledge, partial concept knowledge, and verbal association knowledge. In addition, they propose a framework for thinking about the influence contexts have on words. For example, when a word is embedded in a rich context of supportive and redundant information, the learner might be more likely to acquire its meaning than when the same word

is found in a lean context (i.e., it is surrounded by other equally difficult words). In the former context, knowledge of a word is said to be derived, prompted, or assisted by the verbal context (reading or listening). In the latter situation, word knowledge is considered to be unprompted and therefore unassisted by the immediate context. According to this analysis, knowing the meaning of a word also requires scrutinizing the word's immediate environment and understanding the task conditions under which the word is being assessed.

***Assessing vocabulary knowledge.*** Determining when a word is known also depends to a great extent on how knowledge of that word is assessed. Graves (1986), like Russell (1954) before him, pointed out that word knowledge typically is assessed through the use of a multiple-choice format that measures vocabulary knowledge by the recognition of a synonym or definitional phrase. Although this form of assessing vocabulary knowledge is widely used, convenient, and differentiates between "those who have no knowledge of a word and those who have some knowledge" (Graves, 1986, p. 56), some argue that multiple-choice vocabulary tasks "are useless at best and dangerous at worst" (Kame'enui et al., 1987, p. 138) because they are not sensitive to the various dimensions of vocabulary knowledge (see Anderson & Freebody, 1981; Curtis, 1987).

Attempts have been made to modify the traditional multiple-choice test format (Graves, 1989; Nagy, Herman, & Anderson, 1985). Noting the insensitivity of vocabulary measures to the incremental and partial learning of word meanings from context, Nagy et al. (1985) designed a set of multiple-choice questions to explicitly measure degrees of word knowledge. Instead of relying on one multiple-choice test item per word, they developed test items that assessed three different levels of difficulty for each word. Test items in which the distractors were the most semantically and syntactically similar to the target word were considered the most difficult. The least difficult test items included distractors that were very dissimilar in meaning and speech part to the target word. Nagy et al. also utilized an interview test that called for students to produce the meanings of target words.

Graves (1989) studied a similar dichotomy in a mixed-methods study. Students were assessed either using a group multiple-choice assessment or an individual free-response interview. While the multiple-choice task differentiated performance according to grade, ability, mode (reading or listening), and word difficulty, having to give multiple meanings for isolated words in the free-response interview setting most differentiated the performance of good and poor readers. Although these modifications of the multiple-choice test represent a significant improvement of the traditional format, it also implicitly acknowledges the importance of matching assessment task conditions to the dimensions of vocabulary knowledge one is interested in assessing, especially if the objective involves acquisition of partial word knowledge.

Kame'enui et al. (1987) argued that the focus on assessing knowledge of specific word meanings has resulted in researchers and practitioners neglecting other equally important dimensions of vocabulary learning. Specifically, they call attention to the relationship between vocabulary instruction and assessment. Such a focus, they argued, "holds that the relationship between vocabulary learning and reading comprehension is dependent on consistencies of objectives, instructional tasks, and assessment tasks within an intricate set of requirements that vary" (p. 139).

In summary, what does it mean to know a word? Well, again it depends. It depends on how you define *word* (cf., Nagy & Herman, 1984; Serra, 1953, as cited in Russell & Fea, 1963; Vygotsky, 1962), and it depends on how you measure it. For us, how you measure words depends on the kinds of questions one asks about a student's word knowledge. These might include questions such as: Can a student identify a synonym for a word? Can a student generate an oral definition? Can a student place a word within a semantic category? Can a student discriminate a word's denotative and connotative meanings? Can a student express the obvious and subtle differences in meanings among a set of synonyms? Can a student use a word sensibly in an oral or written context?

Our lack of clarity and closure on the question "What does it mean to know a word?" may not be very satisfying—it isn't for us—but for now our best response to what it means to know a word is captured by the exchange between Humpty Dumpty and Alice in Lewis Carroll's *Through the Looking Glass*:

"When I use a word," Humpty Dumpty said in a rather scornful tone, "It means just what I choose it to mean—neither more nor less."

"The question is," said Alice, "whether you *can* make words mean so many different things."

"The question is," said Humpty Dumpty, "which is to be master—that's all."

***How many words do students know?*** According to Graves' (1986) review, estimating vocabulary size is not a new endeavor. In citing Dale, Razik, and Petty's (1973) *Bibliography of Vocabulary Studies*, he noted that 35 studies investigating vocabulary size were published between 1891 and 1960. Graves and Nagy and Anderson (1984) pointed out that research on vocabulary size prior to the 1980s suffered from numerous methodological problems (e.g., poor sampling procedures, imprecise definition of *word*). As a result, estimates of vocabulary size for first graders ranged from 2,562 to 26,000 words, and for university graduate students from 19,000 to 200,000 (Graves, 1986, p. 50).

For a long time, estimates of vocabulary size were viewed primarily as numerical and theoretical artifacts with little real pedagogical significance. However, Becker (1977) added a sharp edge to this issue by linking estimated vocabulary size to the academic achievement of disadvantaged children. Becker asserted that deficiencies in vocabulary knowledge were primary in accounting for the academic failure of disadvantaged students in grades 3 through 12. His call for teaching these students a core vocabulary of basic 8,000 words (Becker, Dixon, & Anderson-Inman, 1980) served in part to prompt a closer scrutiny of vocabulary size (Graves, 1980, 1986).

However, as Nagy and Anderson (1984) suggested, if only a handful of words is required to be known, then a "ruthlessly systematically direct instruction" (p. 304) program could perhaps muscle its way into making a significant difference. On the other hand, if the number of words was much, much greater, then a different kind of instructional program would be required.

The real number appears to be 10 times greater than what Becker (1977) proposed. Nagy and Anderson (1984) estimated

that printed school English contains 88,533 word families. There appears to be wide agreement with this estimate and its accuracy (e.g., Graves, 1986; Kame'enui et al., 1987). However, as Graves (1986) cautioned, this figure does not represent the "number of different word families that any one 3rd through 9th grader will ever deal with," nor is it the "number of words known by any one student" (p. 52). Instead, this figure is based on a sample of words taken from school materials (e.g., textbooks, workbooks, novels, magazines, encyclopedias) used in Grades 3 through 9. Furthermore, this figure does not represent the total number of word families that Nagy and Anderson identified. Instead, approximately 180,000, semantically related words were identified. The 88,533 distinct word families represent only the morphological basic words they identified that they defined as "a group of morphologically related words such that if a person knows one member of the family, he or she will probably be able to figure out the meaning of any other member upon encountering it in text" (p. 315).

Nagy and Anderson's (1984) analysis also offered some interesting insights into the number of words students would actually encounter in Grades 3 through 9, as well as the distribution of words by frequency. For example, they note that approximately half of the words in printed school English occur "roughly once in a billion words of text or less" (p. 320). However, these frequencies betray the real utility of some of these words. Specifically, words such as *seagull, deform, billfold,* and *inflate* were counted as occurring less than three times in a billion words of text (p. 321).

Nagy and Anderson (1984) also estimated that a student in Grades 6 through 9 is likely to encounter approximately 3,000 or 4,000 new vocabulary words each year, assuming he or she reads between 500,000 and a million running words of text in a school year, which is not an unrealistic range (see Anderson, Wilson, & Fielding, 1986). Nagy and Herman's (1987) recalibration of this extrapolation suggests a similar finding in which an average student in Grades 3 through 12 is likely to learn approximately 3,000 new vocabulary words each year.

However, more recent studies of vocabulary size have indicated that past estimates are perhaps inflated, and the number of words known by competent adults is much smaller than had been anticipated earlier. These studies suggest a renewed role for the direct instruction of specific words. Goulden, Nation, and Read (1990) evaluated methods of selecting and counting words in a vocabulary and concluded that when these factors were controlled across studies, conservative estimates of adult vocabulary were most consistent; that is, they concluded that an average adult vocabulary contains about 17,000 base words, results that were supported by D'Anna, Zechmeister, and Hall (1991). When studying the growth of a functionally important lexicon from junior high to adulthood, words that students would need to be able to read their texts in contrast to all words that they might encounter, Zechmeister, Chronis, Cull, D'Anna, and Healy (1995) concluded:

When vocabulary size is expressed in terms of functionally important words, the typical rate of lexicon growth may not be so fast, nor the number of words at a particular stage of development so large that attempts to affect this process through direct instruction will be of little consequence to normal vocabulary development. (p. 211)

So the size of both vocabularies and words to be learned remains unsettled and controversial.

White, Graves, and Slater (1990) evaluated reading vocabulary knowledge for middle-class and disadvantaged children in Grades 1 through 4. Although minority students' vocabularies were generally one half to two thirds that of middle-class students, White et al. reported estimated yearly increases of vocabulary in excess of Nagy and Herman's (1987) recalibrations. For example, White et al. estimated that between Grades 1 and 3, minority students' vocabularies increased by about 3,500 words a year and middle-class students' vocabularies increased by about 5,000 words a year.

Likewise social class can also affect the size of vocabulary and the quality and rate of vocabulary growth. Corson (1989), in his study of British and Australian adolescents, found that students who belonged to a lower social class were much less likely to know the specialized words on which they were tested. He argued, however, that these adolescents' overall lexicon might be different and *not* smaller, with an awareness of words that would not be tested by standard school instruments. Furthermore, not only did the students of lower social classes know fewer school words, but also the words that they knew were known less well, or at least differently than they were known by members of the middle and upper classes. These conclusions further support the existence of a gap between students who are acquiring the vocabulary necessary to be successful in schools and those who are not.

The task facing school-age children and teachers is an enormous one, if we accept Nagy and Anderson's (1984) appraisal of the number of word families in printed school English. However, as Beck, McKeown, and Omanson (1984) noted in the face of Nagy and Anderson's (1984; see also Nagy & Herman, 1984) appraisal, there is much debate over the role of instruction in vocabulary learning (see also D'Anna et al., 1991; Zechmeister et al., 1995). In the following section, we examine the implications of the research on the quality and quantity of vocabulary knowledge for designing a program of vocabulary instruction.

## Dimensions of Vocabulary Instruction and Their Effects on Reading Comprehension

Factor analytic studies document that vocabulary knowledge is an important predictor of reading comprehension (Davis, 1944, 1968; Singer, 1965; Spearitt, 1972; Thurstone, 1946). However, the evidence of a causal link between vocabulary and comprehension is historically long but empirically soft (Kame'enui et al., 1982; McKeown, Beck, Omanson, & Pople, 1985), although its intuitive appeal is as solid as granite (Kame'enui et al., 1987). It is probably because of this sleight-of-hand intuition that practitioners have insisted on teaching vocabulary words as a way to influence comprehension (Cole, 1946).

Educators now know that the relationship between vocabulary instruction and comprehension is more complex than simply teaching students more words (Nagy & Anderson, 1984; Stahl & Fairbanks, 1986) and that the causal association between vocabulary and comprehension is tricky and elusive, as Beck, McKeown, and Omanson (1987) noted:

The causal links between vocabulary knowledge and reading comprehension are not well understood. For instance, are people good comprehenders because they know a lot of words, or do people know a lot of words because they are good comprehenders and in the course of comprehending text, learn a lot of words, or is there some combination of directionality? (p. 147).

In this section, we explore some of the issues related to the connection between vocabulary and comprehension. Specifically, we present what has been referred to as the fertility–futility debate; then we review what we know about learning words incidentally from context.

***To teach or not to teach words: that is not the question.*** The sheer volume of printed school English appears to defy direct systematic instruction. It is also obvious from the nature of receptive tasks that children learn new words, albeit incompletely and gradually, through reading and hearing unknown words read or spoken in context (Anderson, 1996; Krashen, 1989; Nagy et al., 1985; Nagy, Anderson, & Herman, 1987). What has not been obvious until recently is the nature and degree of vocabulary learning from context and its effects on reading comprehension (Anderson, Wilson, & Fielding, 1988; Jenkins, Stein, & Wysocki, 1984).

Researchers know that children's vocabulary increases at a rate of approximately 3,000 new words per year (Nagy & Anderson, 1984; Nagy & Herman, 1987). They also know that children's vocabulary size, regardless of the method used to count specific vocabulary words, approximately doubles between Grades 3 and 7 (Jenkins & Dixon, 1983). It is also evident, as Nagy et al. (1985) pointed out, that this "massive vocabulary growth seems to occur without much help from teachers" (p. 235), as systematic, intensive vocabulary instruction may not be a prominent feature of basal reading programs (Jenkins & Dixon, 1983), and we have little evidence that teachers demonstrate significant amounts of direct instruction in vocabulary (Durkin, 1978-79; Ryder & Graves, 1994). To reconcile the massive growth in children's vocabulary with the lack of vocabulary instruction in schools, Nagy et al. argued that "[t]he only plausible explanation seems to be some type of incidental learning from context" (p. 234).

The plausibility of this explanation was greeted skeptically by Beck, McKeown, and McCaslin (1983) in an article titled cleverly "All Contexts Are Not Created Equal." Beck et al. distinguished between natural contexts, those in which words reside in honestly written materials, and pedagogical contexts, those that are contrived for teaching or testing contextual analysis ability. Beck et al. pointed out that natural contexts do not necessarily provide strong clues to word meanings. In fact, they argued that some natural contexts might be *nondirective*, those "which seem to be of no assistance in directing the reader toward any particular meaning for a word," or even *misdirective*, "those that seem to direct the student to an incorrect meaning for a target word" (p. 178). Baldwin and Schatz (1985; Schatz & Baldwin, 1986) also argued that many contexts are misdirective, and they have provided additional empirical support for this assertion. In short, it has been argued that natural contexts at best may be insufficient to help readers infer word meanings and at worst may be misleading to readers.

The contrasting positions represented by Nagy and his colleagues and Beck and her colleagues characterized what has been called the "fertility versus futility" debate (cf., Beck et al., 1984; Nagy & Herman, 1984). The debate captures the dilemma facing practitioners and researchers in determining the role of instruction in learning and using vocabulary (Glaser, 1984). Those who argue for *fertile* vocabulary instruction point to the unreliability of natural contexts to assist readers in understanding an unknown word (Beck et al., 1983; Kame'enui et al., 1982). They also argue that learning word meanings from natural contexts is less efficient than direct instruction (Miller & Gildea, 1987; Stahl & Fairbanks, 1986).

In contrast, those who see direct instruction as *futile* note that there are just too many words to be taught directly and too little instructional time to do it for direct instruction to be an effective means of sustained vocabulary development (Anderson, 1996; Krashen, 1989; Nagy & Herman, 1987; Sternberg, 1987). They also point out that vocabulary development is a gradual process that takes place within a broader learning context of acquiring other knowledge structures or schemata (Nagy & Herman, 1987). Finally, it is argued that experimental evidence supporting the relationship between vocabulary instruction and reading comprehension is less than robust (Freebody & Anderson, 1981).

As in the case of most debates, the fertility versus futility debate tends to accentuate contrasting views, while it masks subtle, more complex issues that need to be addressed. For example, those who argue of the futility of vocabulary instruction do not call for direct instruction to cease altogether: "We would not care to maintain that no direct instruction in vocabulary should ever be undertaken (Nagy et al., 1985, p. 252). Similarly, those who argue for fertility of direct vocabulary instruction do not call for direct instruction alone but for "carefully crafted, multifaceted instruction" (Beck et al., 1984, p. 8). As Stahl (1988) suggested, the real issue is that of striking a balance between direct instruction and learning from context. We address the specifics of a balanced vocabulary program at the conclusion of this chapter.

We now turn to the topic of incidental word learning, information germane to our later discussion of instruction in contextual analysis.

***Incidental learning of word meanings from context.*** We noted earlier that receptive language processes—reading and listening—provide learners with a context for discerning the meanings of unknown words. These contexts can be generous or parsimonious, helpful or hostile in the amount of assistance they provide the reader or listener (Beck et al., 1983). Studies that have investigated the effects of these contexts on students' ability to learn uninstructed words have relied on either experimenter-contrived texts or natural, ecologically valid texts selected from basal reading programs or content textbooks.

In general, these studies suggest that children of varying ages (8-year-olds to college students) and abilities (lowability versus highability) are able to derive the meanings of unknown words from context (Carnine, Kame'enui, & Coyle, 1984; Daalen-Kapteijns & Elshout-Mohr, 1981; McKeown, 1985; Sternberg, Powell, & Kaye, 1983; Werner & Kaplan, 1952). As Herman,

Anderson, Pearson, and Nagy (1987) pointed out, in most of these studies, readers were directed to figure out the meanings of specific words that were highlighted in some fashion. They also noted that "few studies have investigated the *incidental* learning of word meanings from written context. That is, few studies have examined how much word learning occurs when students are reading selections for a purpose, such as to understand and remember information in a text or to enjoy a story" (p. 265). To date, seven studies have examined incidental learning from context.

Jenkins et al. (1984) required average and above-average fifth-grade students to read experimenter-contrived texts in which difficult vocabulary words were embedded 0, 2, 6, or 10 times. The unknown words were contained in passages that were fairly generous with redundant information about the targeted words. Results showed that 6 or 10 encounters with a word resulted in greater word learning than 2 encounters; 2 encounters did not promote word learning; and the above-average students learned more word meanings than the average ability students.

Herman et al. (1987) noted, however, that in the Jenkins et al. (1984) study, "students may have been alerted to the nature of the study because they read aloud the target words beforehand. Thus, learning may not have been entirely incidental" (p. 265). Also, Nagy et al. (1985) noted that the contexts Jenkins et al. constructed were most likely richer than natural ones. To address these concerns, Nagy and his colleagues conducted several experiments.

In their first study, Nagy et al. (1985) required eighth-grade average and above-average students to read 1,000-word narrative and expository basal reader excerpts containing 15 difficult words. On several dependent measures sensitive to complete and partial word knowledge (see earlier discussion), students demonstrated a context effect that was "small in absolute terms" but "statistically robust and very consistent across types of text, methods of measurement, and level of scoring." (p. 245). Nagy et al. concluded, "There can be no doubt that the effect was real" (p. 245).

In an extended replication of this experiment, Nagy et al. (1987) found a similar effect with a larger sample of students in Grades 3, 5, and 7. Again, "small but reliable gains in knowledge of words from the passages read were found at all grade and ability levels" (p. 237) for both narrative and expository passages.

In another study, Herman et al. (1987) investigated the extent to which variations in text features influenced incidental word learning. Eighth-grade students read either an original, unedited science textbook excerpt or one of three revised versions each designed to enhance text comprehension. Results indicated that both able and less able students who read a revised version that thoroughly explains key concepts and the relations between them acquired more word meanings incidentally than those who read either the original version or the other two revised versions.

Shefelbine (1990) studied individual differences in incidental word learning from context, examining the various contributions of familiarity of concepts, vocabulary knowledge, and analytical reasoning. Sixth-graders read narrative and expository texts taken from the sixth-grade basal series. All students regardless of vocabulary knowledge learned some meanings from context, but those with higher initial levels of vocabulary knowledge were more able to learn words that represented unfamiliar concepts than were those with lower initial levels, a finding supporting Nagy et al. (1987). Although general analytic reasoning did not seem to influence incidental word learning from context, preexisting vocabulary knowledge had a significant impact, sometimes preventing students from learning meanings from context because they could not understand the explanatory words. Stanvovich (1986) termed the condition of reading acquisition in which those readers who are more proficient readers grow more quickly in their proficiency than less proficient readers, that is the rich get richer and the poor get poorer, the Matthew effect. This Matthew effect, in which students with larger vocabularies are more likely to increase their vocabularies from context, although specifically named and identified in some of the following studies, is not, however, a consistent trend across all studies.

In the first cross-cultural and cross-linguistic study of incidental word learning from context, Shu, Anderson, and Zhang (1995) studied third- and fifth-graders in the United States and China. Students read two selections at each grade level, one a story written in their native language, the other a story translated to their native language (the same two stories were used for this purpose). Examining factors such as grade, verbal ability, prior vocabulary knowledge, characteristics of the words themselves, conceptual difficulty of the word, and the strength of conceptual support for the word, the authors found that both groups of students learned vocabulary from their reading at a similar rate. Three major factors influenced vocabulary acquisition: conceptual difficulty of the word, strength of contextual support, and morphological transparency (for the Chinese children). Additionally, although only measured in the Chinese children, amount of out-of-school reading appeared to influence positively the ability to learn new words implicitly from context. Shu et al. did not find a Matthew effect in the amount of word learning, but they did find that the type of words learned differed between the groups. Nevertheless both high and low ability children learned vocabulary, leading the authors to conclude, "It seems that incidental learning from context may be a universal in the written vocabulary development of children" (p. 88).

Higgins and Cocks (1999) investigated incidental word learning with CD-ROM storybooks. Using a CD-ROM of Jack Prelutsky's *The New Kid on the Block,* they charted students' learning of six target words through the animation which was designed to illustrate words as students clicked on them. The mean gain was 3.43 words from pretest to posttest, and 40% of the students were able to define all six target words correctly after their reading of it in hypermedia. This study further supports the effect of incidental word learning from text, in this case the format of electronic text.

Incidental learning from context has also been found in studies of both discussion and teachers' storybook reading. Elley (1989) found that storybook reading resulted in vocabulary gains of words in the stories for 7- and 8-year-olds, for readers of all ability and vocabulary levels, and even when the teachers did not give explicit explanations of the words in addition to the reading. Likewise, Leung (1992), Leung and Pikulski (1990),

Robbins and Ehri (1994), and Sénéchal, Thomas, and Monker (1995) found that the pattern was supported in younger students (preschool, kindergarten, and primary grades) and that the probability of learning a word was keyed to how often it was used in a text as well as how often a text was read. Robbins and Ehri (1994) and Sénéchal et al. (1995) found a Matthew effect (Stanovich, 1986), with students with larger vocabularies learning more new words, a finding confirmed by Nicholson and Whyte (1992) in their replication of Elley (1989). However, Stahl, Richek, and Vandevier's (1991) replication with sixth-grade students indicated no Matthew effect with all students learning new words from the read-aloud context, a finding that would seem to recommend the continuance of read-aloud experiences through middle school for, among other things, vocabulary growth. So although it seems clear that students' vocabularies benefit from read-aloud experiences, the extent to which students of varying ability levels benefit remains unclear.

The type of talk that occurs around the text in the storybook reading experience as well as classroom talk experiences can affect how many words are learned incidentally in aural context. Dickinson and Smith (1994) and Sénéchal and Cornell (1993) both investigated the influence on vocabulary learning of teacher–student or parent–child talk before, during, and after the reading experience. Results indicated that active discussion during reading did not improve vocabulary learning, while extensive postreading discussion where the students and the teachers both used the vocabulary was influential. Likewise, teachers' use of unfamiliar vocabulary in preschool classroom discussions appears to contribute positively to students' vocabulary growth (Dickinson, Cote, & Smith, 1993).

The results of the research on incidental word learning from context are perhaps still best summarized by Jenkins et al. (1984) who noted that learning word meanings incidentally during reading "apparently does not come easily or in large quantities" (p. 782). However, the evidence that incidental word learning does occur is unequivocal as Nagy et al. concluded from their 1987 experiment: "Our results demonstrate beyond a reasonable doubt that incidental learning of word meanings does take place during normal reading" (p. 261). Nagy et al. stated further that "[t]he results of this study support our earlier contention (Nagy, Herman, & Anderson, 1985) that regular, wide reading must be seen as the major avenue of large-scale, long-term vocabulary growth" (p. 266).

Cunningham and Stanovich (1998) concurred with Nagy et al. (1987), arguing that wide reading, as measured through reading volume, "is the prime contributor to individual differences in children's vocabularies" (p. 9). Drawing on the work of Hayes and Ahrens (1988), Cunningham and Stanovich further argued that spoken language has proportionally only a relatively minor impact on overall vocabulary growth, particularly after the middle grades. Hayes and Ahrens's research suggests that there is a wide gap between the lexical richness, that is richness of use of low frequency words, in oral language and that in print, even print written for children, in favor of print. That greater lexical richness, when applied to the reading volume of children at varying levels of proficiency in reading, seems to account for the great differences in the amount of incidental word learning between proficient and less proficient readers. However, when reading similar amounts of text, word learning seems to be equivalent. There is some suggestion that students of different proficiencies reading the same text learn a similar amount of words, but learn different words. The individual differences in reading volume, both in and out of school, often related to students' reading proficiency seem to affect differentially children's vocabulary learning, particularly in amount and possibly in types of words learned (Cunningham & Stanovich, 1991).

We certainly agree with Nagy et al. (1987) and Cunningham and Stanovich (1998) that word learning does occur during normal reading and that wide reading is a necessary and probably a causal factor for large levels of vocabulary growth. However, we also believe that instruction has a distinct role in vocabulary development, as will be demonstrated in the remaining sections of this chapter.

## RESEARCH ON TEACHING VOCABULARY

In this section, we examine the research on vocabulary instruction. We begin with a description of the state of vocabulary instruction in schools. We then examine those intervention studies that have compared and contrasted the effectiveness of various kinds of curriculum and instruction in vocabulary. This includes a brief discussion of classic research on teaching vocabulary, followed by a detailed review of studies conducted in the past 30 years, studies that are representative of the resurgent interest in researching vocabulary that began in the 1970s.

### The State of Vocabulary Curriculum and Instruction in Schools

***Vocabulary curriculum.*** Because basal readers are the pervasive curricular vehicle of reading instruction in schools (a 95% usage estimate in elementary grades, Chall & Squire, 1991), we have restricted our discussion here to basal materials. Criticisms of basal readers have included many dimensions (cf., Goodman, Shannon, Freeman, & Murphy, 1988; Squire, 1987), but the quantity and quality of vocabulary instruction has come under especially careful scrutiny (Beck, 1984; Beck & McKeown, 1987; Beck, McKeown, McCaslin, & Burkes, 1979; Jenkins & Dixon, 1983; Ryder & Graves, 1994; Sorenson, 1985).

For example, Jenkins and Dixon (1983) reported that at best no more than 300 words per year were taught in three basal programs they examined, and at worst virtually no words were taught. Further, they stated that "program developers seem not to rely much on direct teaching to produce growth in vocabulary knowledge" (p. 247). In short, they noted that few words were taught and even fewer were taught well.

Beck et al. (1979) examined two basal series and found vocabulary instruction in each lacking in both intensity and scope. To illustrate the range of quality in basal reader vocabulary instruction, Beck (1984) described the best and worst instances of vocabulary instruction:

Let us now for a moment consider the best case of vocabulary instruction that we found in the programs we studied. A new vocabulary word is presented in a sentence that elucidates the meaning of the new word; the word is encountered in the text selection, and the student looks it up in the glossary if she/he does not remember its meaning; the word appears a third time in an independently completed, after-reading activity. The word does not appear again in subsequent selections or in vocabulary work. Remember, this is the best instance of new word experience that we encountered. It does not necessarily occur with any regularity.

At worst, a new word appers solely in a selection and the student skips over it because she/he either does not recognize it as an unknown word or does not want to be bothered with the disruptive glossary step. (pp. 11–12)

Durkin (1981a) evaluated the suggestions for comprehension instruction found in the teachers' manuals (kindergarten through grade six) for five basal reading series. One of her categories of analysis involved prereading activities that she called "preparation" and included "attention to new vocabulary, word meanings, background knowledge, and prereading questions" (p. 520). Durkin reported finding 1,929 total instances of preparation suggestions across the five series, an average of 386 per series (i.e., across the K–6 manuals) and interpreted these values as indicative of "limited attention given new vocabulary, especially in the middle-and upper-grade manuals" (p. 525). She concluded her analysis of the preparation suggestions as follows: "That manuals and teachers may need to do much more with new words before children attempt to read a selection is something that merits serious consideration" (p. 526).

There is some evidence that more contemporary basal reading programs provide teachers more useful vocabulary instructional guidance. Ryder and Graves (1994) analyzed vocabulary instruction in the fourth- and sixth-grade textbooks of one 1989 and one 1991 basal program. They reported that one series provided a rationale for vocabulary instruction consistent with theory and research whereas the other did not, but they noted that "both series do a relatively good job of focusing on words that are important to understanding the selections in which they occur" (p. 148). The numbers of words taught directly at Grades 4 and 6 were 174 and 165, respectively, for one series and 215 and 239, respectively, for the other, which shows more explicit instruction in vocabulary compared to earlier basal programs (Jenkins & Dixon, 1983).

Ryder and Graves (1994) also assessed which of the words targeted for instruction were already known by fourth- and sixth-grade students, reporting that approximately three fourths of the words were known by the students prior to the implementation of the lessons. These findings replicate classic studies by Gates (1961, 1962) and a similar study by Stallman et al. (1990), who found that second- and fifth-grade students already knew at least 70% of targeted vocabulary prior to instruction. Ryder and Graves concluded that even though, "the vocabulary instruction that students receive prior to reading basal selections has improved from what it once was" (p. 151), "over the last quarter of a century, basal readers have continued to target large numbers of words that students know for instruction" (p. 149).

In conclusion, even though there is some indication that more recent basal programs are providing more theoretically based and intensive vocabulary instruction, Ryder and Graves (1994) are correct in stating that such instruction "could be improved further" (p. 151).

***Vocabulary instruction.*** What do researchers know about the quantity and quality of vocabulary instruction that teachers actually administer in schools? Several studies and have addressed this question.

Durkin (1978–79) reported that not much attention was given to vocabulary instruction in fourth-grade classrooms. Of the 4,469 minutes of reading instruction she and her assistants observed in 24 different classrooms, 19 minutes were devoted to what she labeled "word meanings: instruction," 4 minutes were devoted to "word meanings: review," and 94 minutes were devoted to "word meanings: application." These three categories accounted for 2.6% of the *total* observed time. Even if one includes whatever attention was given to vocabulary during prereading activities (what she called "comprehension: preparation for reading"), this encompassed only an additional 247 minutes, and it is undetermined what proportion of the prereading activities actually involved vocabulary. At one extreme, all four of these categories account for about 8% of the total observed time; however, if one includes only the "word meaning: instruction" and "word meaning: review"—what we consider to be explicit vocabulary instructional activities—then only about *one half of 1%* of the observed time involved vocabulary instruction.

Durkin's (1978–79) data were corroborated by findings of a similar observational study briefly noted by Roser and Juel (1982). They observed reading lessons in 12 Grade 1 through 5 classrooms. Of approximately 1,200 minutes of observation, only 65 minutes, about 5%, were devoted to vocabulary instruction, a mean of 1.67 minutes per lesson. Word meaning instruction per lesson ranged from 0 to 12 minutes, but the modal value was 0.

However, as Durkin's (1981 a) evaluation of basal reader manuals indicated, teachers may not be provided much guidance in how to teach vocabulary, so the lack of attention to vocabulary should come as no surprise. To pursue this issue further, Durkin (1984) returned to elementary classrooms to find out if there was a match between what basal manuals recommended and what teachers actually did. She found little match.

Durkin (1984) observed 16 first-, third-, and fifth-grade teachers for 1,920 minutes as they taught reading using basal readers. She compared what they did to the recommendations present in the basal manuals they were using. Regarding vocabulary, there were suggestions in the basal manuals to present new vocabulary in context for 13 of the 16 teachers. However, only three teachers presented the words in context as the manual directed: the other 10 simply wrote the words in lists on the board or on charts, and the explanation they gave for doing this according to Durkin was "writing the context sentences took too much time" (p. 737). One might interpret these data to suggest that even if publishers do provide good, strong prereading vocabulary activities in basal materials, some teachers will still choose not to use them.

Johnson, Levin, and Pittelman (1984) surveyed 228 teachers in Grades 1 through 5 in seven different geographic regions in the United State about their beliefs and practices regarding vocabulary instruction. When asked if they teach vocabulary to prepare students to read a basal selection, the majority of teachers responded affirmatively. Approximately 75% of the primary grade teachers and 85% of the intermediate grade teachers reported that they "almost always" introduced new vocabulary before students read a basal selection. However, less than one third of those surveyed indicated that they related new vocabulary to past experiences. Ninety-six percent responded that they teach vocabulary as part of content instruction, and about three fourths of the teachers said they spend more than 15 minutes each week on vocabulary in content subjects. Whether the teachers' perceptions of their behaviors were accurate representations of what they actually did cannot be determined, of course, but it is clear that the respondents indicated that much more vocabulary instruction was occurring than prior observational studies had indicated (Durkin 1978–79; Roser & Juel, 1982).

A recent observational study suggested that contemporary teachers may provide more attention to vocabulary. Replicating Durkin's (1978–79) techniques, Scott, Jamieson, and Asselin (1998) spent 3 full days in 23 sixth-grade classrooms (several were fifth- and sixth- or sixth- and seventh-grade splits) in British Columbia recording all instructional and noninstructional classroom events. Results revealed that there were 39 incidents of vocabulary activities involving all 23 teachers, and that this attention to vocabulary totaled 1, 106 minutes. This accounted for 6% of the total possible instructional time and 12% of the time on activities involving some use of the language arts. Scott et al. classified the time dedicated to vocabulary into three categories: isolated vocabulary activities (24% of total time on vocabulary), vocabulary within language arts (52%), and vocabulary within subject areas (24%). Although Scott et al. reported greater attention to vocabulary than prior research had suggested, they did not find much depth to vocabulary activities. Instead, teachers tended to mention vocabulary and assign activities rather than engaging students in activities that promoted the development of rich word concepts and relationships.

Blachowicz (1987) reported the results of a study in which she observed six fourth-grade reading groups as they each completed three basal reader selections (10–15 observation days per teacher, 20–40 minutes per observation). Results revealed that time spent on vocabulary ranged from 14% of the reading instructional time (according to a strict definition of vocabulary instruction) to 19% of instructional time (according to a lenient definition). When asked how much time they thought they spent on vocabulary instruction, the teachers estimated about 15% of the time was spent on vocabulary. Almost all of the time devoted to vocabulary (1,075 total minutes) involved prereading activities. Forty-five percent of this time involved determining the meanings of words in context, and 28% was spent on defining or pronouncing specific words. Activities such as categorizing words, reminders to use context clues, and teaching word structure clues consumed the balance of vocabulary instructional time.

The teachers Blachowicz (1987) observed spent more time on vocabulary than those observed by other researchers (cf. Durkin 1978–79; Roser & Juel, 1982). One possible explanation for this difference is that because the basal materials used by the teachers Blachowicz observed were more recent (1982 editions of the Ginn and Houghton Mifflin reading programs), they provided more guidance in how to each vocabulary. In fact, Blachowicz noted that one basal series had a "high vocabulary load (the Ginn Reading Program, 1982), one that emphasized preparation of vocabulary and routinely introduced 10–15 words per lesson" (p. 136). Durkin's (1984) findings would seem to refute the hypothesis that more emphasis on vocabulary in the basal materials would result in greater attention to vocabulary, because she reported that teachers often did not adhere to basal manual suggestions. However, Blachowicz noted that teachers followed the manuals very closely and "teachers of the high load series [Ginn Reading Program] spent more time on vocabulary instruction and introduced more words" (p. 136).

Two other studies support the notion that the adopted reading program appears to influence the nature of vocabulary instruction. Barr and Sadow (1989) observed fourth-grade teachers' use of basal readers in two school districts, each of which used a different basal program. Although Barr and Sadow acknowledged that there was considerable variation among teachers in their vocabulary instruction, they found that the instructional emphases in the basal programs generally paralleled teachers' instructional actions. In the basal program that identified new vocabulary and provided practice using those words in the prereading phase of the basal lesson, teachers "not only focused on the words identified as vocabulary words (usually without omitting any), but also followed through by assigning the practice exercises" (p. 63). In contrast, there was generally less attention to vocabulary by teachers using the other series which deemphasized vocabulary.

Watts (1995) observed vocabulary instruction in three fifth- and three sixth-grade classrooms and, like Barr and Sadow (1989), found that most vocabulary instruction occurred during prereading activities. Teachers most often employed definitional and contextual information for presenting words and tended not to link words to prior experiences or teach independent word learning strategies. Watts also reported that "teachers' stated purposes for vocabulary instruction were congruent with the requirements of the basal reading series" (p. 399).

In conclusion, the research on the quantity and quality of vocabulary instruction in schools paints a somewhat opaque picture. Whereas Durkin (1978–79) and Roser and Juel (1982) reported little time spent on vocabulary instruction, Blachowicz (1987) observed greater amounts of instruction on vocabulary, a finding supported by the Johnson, Levin, et al. (1984) survey data. There also appears to be a connection between the nature of vocabulary instruction and the basal reading programs (Barr & Sadow, 1989; Watts, 1995). It may be that as the instructional guidance for teaching vocabulary provided teachers has evolved over more recent basal editions (cf. Beck et al., 1979; Ryder & Graves, 1994), teachers have begun to direct more instructional time and effort toward teaching vocabulary.

## Instructional Research on Vocabulary: Pre-1970

Research on vocabulary instruction is hardly a recent phenomenon. In 1963, Dale and Razik published a bibliography of vocabulary research that included 3,125 entries. However, the interest in vocabulary instruction and the volume of research it produced failed to advance the state of knowledge significantly; much of the research was inconclusive, at least with respect to the persistently asked question about the comparative effectiveness of one approach to vocabulary teaching versus another. McKeown and Curtis (1987) commented on the equivocal

results of much of the extant vocabulary research when they noted that "Clearly, missing answers have not resulted from a reluctance to search for them" (p. 1).

What, if anything, was learned about vocabulary instruction prior to about 1970? The conclusions drawn by Petty et al. from their 1967 literature review of 80 instructional studies typify the state of the art of vocabulary instruction research in the late 1960s:

The studies investigated show that vocabulary can be taught: they do not show that a "direct" method is better than an "indirect" one, that teaching words in isolation is better than teaching them in context, that an inductive approach is better than a deductive one. That is, it is not clear that these or any other dichotomies—other than that of teaching vocabulary versus not teaching it—have been resolved as a consequence of the designing, executing, and reporting of these many studies. (p. 25)

In other words, they acknowledged that some kind of instruction was better than no instruction in vocabulary, but the superiority of one strategy over another could not be established. The authors admitted that they initially conducted their review on the assumption that "there is some best way to teach vocabulary" but concluded, "This simply is not the case" (p. 25).

Chall (1987) found it interesting that the results of the Petty et al. (1967) review have often been interpreted pessimistically by researchers and practitioners. Rather than recognizing that direct teaching of vocabulary works (i.e., some kind of instruction was better than no instruction), the results of the review were often interpreted as a lack of support for direct teaching because there was no clearly superior method. We agree with Chall that as unsatisfying as the early research on vocabulary may have been, it was valuable in that it answered affirmatively at least one important research question: Can vocabulary be taught? It would be left to the next generation of vocabulary researchers, however, to tease out the discriminating features of the various instructional methods and to evaluate their relative effectiveness.

## Instructional Research on Vocabulary: Post-1970

There are several ways that a discussion of research and practice in vocabulary instruction can be structured (cf. Beck & McKeown, 1991; Herman & Dole, 1988; Mezynski, 1983; Stahl & Fairbanks, 1986). We have organized our review of recent instructional research according to a scheme similar to one used by Graves (1986) that places studies within one of two categories: (a) research on strategies designed to teach the meanings of specific words or (b) research on generalizable and transferable strategies designed to promote the acquisition of new word meanings. We acknowledge that this dichotomy is not perfect (e.g., some research includes or compares both specific word and generalizable and transferable instructional methods), but it does enable us to organize our review in a manner that brings some structure to an otherwise diverse and expansive body of literature.

***Teaching specific words.*** Many strategies have been recommended for teaching students the meanings of specific words (see collections of techniques in Blachowicz & Fisher, 1996; Carnine, Silbert, & Kame'enui, 1990; Dale, O'Rourke,

& Bamman, 1971; Johnson, 1986; Johnson & Pearson, 1984; Klein, 1988; McNeil, 1987; Nagy, 1988; Tierney, Readence, & Dishner, 1985; Wilson & Gambrell, 1988). Until recently, strategy selection could be based only on intuition, face validity, or testimony regarding the efficacy of a particular instructional approach. However, there now exists empirical evidence on which strategy selection can be based.

In this section, we review research on various strategies for teaching specific words. Again, we draw upon Graves' (1986) organizational scheme. He identified two specific word-learning instructional tasks: "learning new labels" and "learning new concepts." The former involves teaching alternate names (synonyms) or definitions for known concepts (e.g., a learner is taught that *irate* means about the same as *very angry*); the latter involves teaching words that represent difficult or entirely new concepts (e.g., a learner is taught words and corresponding concepts such as *spectroscope, democracy,* or *photosynthesis*). First, we present research on teaching students new labels for known concepts, which is achieved primarily through instruction in definitions or synonyms. Second, we present research on teaching students new concepts, which is achieved primarily through the use of semantic relatedness and prior knowledge strategies.

***Learning new labels: research on strategies designed to teach word definitions or synonyms.*** Learning labels for words involves associative learning, which is pairing or associating two ideas—a concept and a label (learning definitions for words) or a known label with a new label (learning synonyms). Two different types of associative vocabulary learning approaches will be discussed: rote learning and mnemonic learning. Rote associative vocabulary learning involves drill and practice so that students learn or memorize definitions or synonyms. Mnemonic associative vocabulary learning involves use of specific strategies to help students remember concepts and their accompanying labels.

***Rote vocabulary learning: research on teaching definitions or synonyms.*** Historically, the most common approach to teaching vocabulary was through a rote method; students learned definitions or synonyms through the use of a dictionary, glossary, or selected list of words and their definitions (Manzo & Sherk, 1972; Petty et al., 1967). Typically, vocabulary learning was self-directed. Students looked up words, wrote their definitions, used them in sentences, found synonyms or antonyms, and engaged in oral or written drill by way of worksheets or workbooks.

Indeed, students can be taught definitions or synonyms for specific words as Petty et al. (1967) noted in their review of early studies on vocabulary. This finding was replicated in later experiments (e.g., Kame'enui et al., 1982; McKeown et al., 1985; Pany & Jenkins, 1978; Pany, Jenkins, & Schreck, 1982; Parker, 1984; Stahl, 1983). For example, Stahl (1983) reported that fifth-grade students who looked up words in a dictionary, wrote their definitions, and discussed their meanings (definitional treatment) learned more word meanings than controls who worked in a comprehension skills book. Similarly, McKeown et al. (1985) found that students who were given "traditional" vocabulary

instruction (drill, practice, and games designed to teach definitions or synonyms for target words) learned the meanings of more words, as measured by a multiple-choice test, than students in an uninstructed control group.

Furthermore, the more intense or direct definitional vocabulary instruction is, the greater the gains in word knowledge. For example, like Stahl (1983) and McKeown et al. (1985). Pany et al. (1982) found that students who were provided simple definitional information (meanings given condition) learned more word meanings than control subjects. However, students who were provided intensive, teacher-led drill and practice on target words (meanings practiced condition) outperformed students in the meanings given group. Therefore, there is evidence that intensive, teacher-led definitional instruction (McKeown et al.'s traditional group being a prime example) is superior to independent, student-directed vocabulary study.

Memory (1990) found that *when* definitional instruction is provided does not affect vocabulary learning, for high school students learned technical vocabulary from science and social science textbooks equally well when instruction was before, during, or after reading the textbook selections. Memory did report, however, a strong teacher effect, suggesting the manner in which the definitional instruction was implemented was more critical than when it occurred.

The effectiveness of instructing students in word definitions is supported by Stahl and Fairbanks' (1986) meta-analysis. For the 29 vocabulary training studies that compared a "definitional only" or a "definitional emphasis" treatment to a no-exposure control group, the average effect size for dependent measures that assessed word knowledge was significantly different from zero (effect size of 1.37 for definitional only and 1.62 for definitional emphasis). In other words, students who were taught definitions consistently outperformed control group subjects on tests of word knowledge. However, simple definitional instruction did not enhance passage comprehension.

Although teaching definitions or synonyms does work, it may not be the most effective vocabulary teaching method. In studies that compared a definition or synonym approach (usually involving dictionary look-up), other strategies typically surpassed definition instruction. Specifically, students who were trained according to a semantic feature analysis approach (Anders, Bos, & Filip, 1984), a context method (Gipe, 1978–79), a semantic relatedness approach (McKeown et al., 1985), a vocabulary with writing approach (Duin & Graves, 1987), and a definition-plus-context approach (Stahl, 1983) all exceeded students who received rote definitional/synonym instruction only. In summary, definition instruction works; however, as Beck et al. (1987) noted, definitional training is effective only when the instructional objective is limited knowledge of new vocabulary items.

Additionally, results of several studies have questioned the efficiency of using dictionary definitions for teaching the meanings of new words. McKeown (1993) reported that, when relying on traditional dictionary definitions, fifth-graders could write acceptable sentences using the defined words only 25% of the time, and this increased to only 50% when the dictionary definitions were revised to be more child-friendly. McKeown commented that "simply learning definitions is not a potent route to vocabulary development" (p. 29). Similarly, Scott and Nagy

(1997) found that definitions were not particularly helpful for upper elementary students to learn the meanings of unfamiliar verbs, concluding that "our results should be seen as a caution—a warning against sending upper elementary students to dictionaries with the expectation that they will be able to use this important resource independently to understand the meaning of a new word" (p. 198).

When one examines the impact learning definitions or synonyms has on comprehension of text that contains taught words, the limitation of rote vocabulary instruction becomes apparent. With the exception of only a few experiments (e.g., Kame'enui et al., 1982), training in definitions or synonyms *only* has not improved students' understanding of texts that contain those words (e.g., Ahlfors, 1979; Jackson & Dizney, 1963; McKeown et al., 1985; Pany & Jenkins, 1978; Pany et al., 1982; Tuinman & Brady, 1974).

For example, in the McKeown et al. (1985) experiment, students in the traditional treatment learned word meanings (as measured by a multiple-choice test) as well as students in a rich or an extended rich treatment (intensive instruction on sets of semantically related words), and all groups outperformed uninstructed controls. However, only subjects in the rich and extended rich groups demonstrated improved passage comprehension. Similarly, Stahl (1983) reported that his definitional treatment did not promote comprehension, whereas a mixed treatment (students provided both definitional and contextual information) did enhance passage comprehension.

The power of a combination of definitional and contextual information appears to be robust across instructional modalities. Kolich (1991) found that 11th-grade students learned word meanings more effectively in a computer-assisted instructional environment when the program included contextual and definitional clues in tandem rather than alone. Brett, Rothlein, and Hurley (1996) assessed fourth-graders' learning of words presented in trade books read aloud to them. They found that students' learning and retention were enhanced when the teacher provided a simple explanation (i.e., a definition) for the target words when they occurred in the story (i.e., in context), as compared to children who simply heard the words when they appeared in the story (i.e., context only). On the basis of their meta-analysis, Stahl and Fairbanks (1986) reached the following conclusion regarding the issue of what type of vocabulary instruction affects comprehension:

> Methods that provided only definitional information about each to-be-learned word did not produce a reliable effect on comprehension.... Also, drill-and-practice methods, which involve multiple repetitions of the same type of information about a target word using only associative processing, did not appear to have reliable effects on comprehension. (p. 101)

Therefore, definitional instruction alone is not likely to promote comprehension of passages that contain taught words. Additional instructional dimensions–contextual information or semantic relatedness, for example—must support or extend definition instruction.

In conclusion, students can learn word meanings according to rote vocabulary learning methods. However, other approaches may be more effective and efficient, especially if the objective is a richer, deeper understanding of words. Furthermore, if passage comprehension is the objective of vocabulary instruction, then it is unlikely that rote definition/synonym strategies alone will achieve this goal.

***Mnemonic vocabulary learning: research on the keyword method.*** The word *mnemonic* refers to memory and strategies intended to improve memory or memorizing (Harris & Hodges, 1981). Nonacademic mnemonics include the use of phrases such as "Thirty days has September..." to remember the number of days in each month or "*Every good boy does fine*" to remember the notes represented by the lines on the treble clef.

One specific form of academic mnemonic strategy designed to teach definitions for words is the keyword method (Pressley, Levin, & McDaniel, 1987). Like rote learning of definitions or synonyms, the keyword method involves associative learning, but associative learning that includes a mental crutch. In its most common version, the keyword method requires the learner to construct an interactive visual image between the definition of the to-be-learned word and a familiar, concrete word that shares some common features. For example, to teach the English word *carlin*, which means "old woman," the keyword *car* could be used to have the learner generate the image of an old woman driving a car (example from Pressley et al., 1987). When later asked to recall the definition of *carlin*, the learner would retrieve *car*, because of its acoustic similarity and then recall the visual image and hence the meaning of *carlin*. An alternate version of the keyword method is a verbal-only one (Atkinson, 1975; Rohwer, 1973) that uses a sentence containing the keyword and definition to retrieve the target word, for example, "The *car* was driven by an *old woman*" (also from Pressley et al., 1987).

The keyword method has been heavily researched, and results favoring its efficacy as a definition-remembering technique have been consistent and robust (see reviews by Pressley, Levin, & Delaney, 1982; Pressley et al., 1987). Furthermore, the keyword method has been shown to be effective for learning a variety of vocabulary item types (Levin, 1985) and across many diverse populations of learners that include normally achieving students (Levin et al., 1984; Levin, McCormick, Miller, Berry, & Pressley, 1982; Pressley, Ross, Levin, & Ghatala, 1984), learning-disabled children (Mastropieri, Scruggs, & Levin, 1985), university students (McDaniel & Pressley, 1984), and mentally handicapped students (Scruggs, Mastropieri, & Levin, 1985).

However, as Stahl and Fairbanks (1986) noted, because the purpose of such keyword research has been to establish its validity as a viable strategy for vocabulary learning, it often has been compared only to no-strategy control groups, in which subjects typically were directed to read and study words and their definitions but without the aid of any specific strategy or training (Levin & Pressley, 1985; Pressley et al., 1982). Hence, those studies are not helpful in evaluating the comparative effectiveness of keyword learning with other vocabulary learning approaches. However, in several recent experiments with children, the keyword method has been compared to other ecologically valid approaches for learning word meanings. For example, Levin et al. (1984) reported that the keyboard method was superior to semantic mapping and a contextual analysis strategy for teaching high-achieving fourth- and low-achieving fifth-grade students the definitions of 12 low-frequency target words, although the keyword group's advantage was not evident one week later on a definition-matching test.

The keyword method has also been compared to a contextual analysis method. Working with 10- to 13-year-old students, Pressley et al. (1984) compared the keyword method to a context approach in which students constructed sentence contexts for 22 low-frequency English nouns. Results revealed that students recalled definitions for 51% of the words presented according to the keyword method versus only 8.5% presented through the use of the context items. In two experiments with fourth-graders, Levin et al. (1982) compared the keyword method to a study method that presented subjects with the same low-frequency words in a meaningful sentence or paragraph context. Again, the keyword method resulted in significantly greater recall of definitions for target words. Similar experiments with adult subjects (e.g., McDaniel, Pressley, & Dunay, 1987; McDaniel & Tillman, 1987), normally achieving elementary and middle school students (Levin, Levin, Glasman, & Nordwall, 1992), and middle school special education students (King-Sears, Mercer, & Sindelar, 1992) support the conclusion that the keyword method is more effective than passage context alone for learning the meanings of specific words. There is also some indication that the keyword method positively affected students' reading comprehension of passages that contained taught vocabulary items (Levin et al., 1992; McDaniel & Pressley, 1989).

To summarize, the results of these and other studies with children and adult learners (Pressley et al., 1987) indicate that the keyword method is more effective in promoting recall of definitions of words when compared to a contextual presentation of the same target words (e.g., Levin et al., 1982, 1984; Pressley et al., 1984). Also, there is some indication that it is superior to a semantic mapping procedure (Levin et al., 1984) when training individual students and the criterion measure is definition recall.

### Learning new concepts: research on semantic relatedness and prior knowledge strategies.

Semantic relatedness and prior knowledge strategies involve presenting new words in relation to words of similar meaning and/or relating new words or concepts to those that lie within the learner's realm of experience. Unlike rote and mnemonic associative approaches for learning new labels, semantic relatedness and prior knowledge approaches involve organizational processing and learning (Just & Carpenter, 1987, p. 402). In organizational learning, the emphasis is on acquiring new concepts rather than learning labels for known concepts.

Theoretical support for semantic relatedness and prior knowledge strategies comes from the *knowledge hypothesis*, which Anderson and Freebody (1981, 1983) have posed to explain the relationship between vocabulary and comprehension. The knowledge hypothesis is founded on a schema-theoretic view of comprehension (Adams & Collins, 1979; Anderson & Pearson, 1984), which asserts that understanding involves an integration of textual information and a comprehender's prior knowledge, or schemata. Thus, understanding is relational and

occurs within the context of what the learner already knows or believes. As a result, semantic relatedness strategies, which present new words and concepts in relation to known words and concepts, are viewed as the pedagogical extension of the knowledge hypothesis.

Many strategies for teaching vocabulary fall under the rubric of semantic relatedness or prior knowledge. These include (a) semantic mapping (Hagen-Heimlich & Pittelman, 1984; Hanf, 1971; Heimlich & Pittelman, 1986; Johnson, 1984; Johnson & Pearson, 1984; Johnson, Pittelman, & Heimlich, 1986) and semantic feature analysis (Anders & Bos, 1986; Johnson, 1984; Johnson & Pearson, 1984); (b) other clustering and labeling strategies such as the List-Group-Label procedure (Taba, 1967), word or concept maps (Schwartz, 1988; Schwartz & Raphael, 1985a), webbing (Calfee & Drum, 1986; Cooper, 1986), and hierarchical classification (Calfee & Drum, 1986); (c) a comprehensive semantic relatedness program involving cognitive, physical, and affective dimensions (Beck & McKeown, 1983; Beck et al., 1980); and (d) other semantic relatedness, prior knowledge, experiential, or personalized approaches that purport to capitalize on learners' schemata (Bean, Singer, & Cowan, 1985; Carr, 1985; Cunningham, 1987; Duffelmeyer, 1985; Duin & Graves, 1988; Haggard, 1982, 1985, 1986; Ignoffo, 1980; Johnson & Johnson, 1986; Manzo, 1983; Marzano, 1984; Marzano & Marzano, 1988; Powell, 1986; Thelen, 1986). Because of the great volume of research on semantic relatedness and prior knowledge strategies, we have organized this research into four categories, each of which is discussed in a separate section.

### Research on semantic mapping and semantic feature analysis.

Semantic mapping is a categorization procedure that organizes words related to a core concept into meaningful clusters. The steps of semantic mapping (see Heimlich & Pittelman, 1986, pp. 5-6; Johnson & Pearson, 1984, pp. 37-38) typically include:

1. Selecting a key or central word from a reading selection about which the teacher can assume that the students have some familiarity.
2. Having the students free associate on the core word and generate a list of related words.
3. Organizing the words into categories (and perhaps labeling them).
4. Discussing alternate ways of categorizing the words, adding new words, and forming new categories.

Semantic feature analysis also draws on a learner's prior knowledge, but unlike semantic mapping in which a group of words is organized according to common features (i.e., placed into categories), students examine how a group of related words differs—that is, how they can be discriminated from one another according to their features. Typical procedures for semantic feature analysis (see Johnson, 1984, pp. 32-33; Johnson & Pearson, 1984, p. 42) include:

1. Selecting a key or central word from a reading selection about which the teacher can assume that the students have some familiarity.
2. Listing, in a column on a matrix, several words that fall within the category.

3. Listing, in a row on the matrix, characteristics or attributes (i.e., semantic features) of some but not all of the words.
4. Determining which words do or do not possess those features, for example, using plus (+) and minus (−).
5. Adding additional words and features and completing the matrix.
6. Discussing how words that are semantically related are alike and different.

Several investigations have examined the effectiveness of semantic mapping and semantic feature analysis for teaching the meanings of specific sets of related words. Johnson, Toms-Bronowski, and Pittelman (1982) and Toms-Bronowski (1983) reported that intermediate grade students who were taught target words according to semantic mapping and semantic feature analysis procedures outperformed students (on immediate and delayed measures) who learned the words through contextual analysis. Pittelman, Levin, and Johnson (1985) reported that semantic mapping was also an effective vocabulary building strategy when used with poor readers, and that it was equally effective when the poor readers were organized in small groups or in a whole class setting.

Johnson, Pittelman, Toms-Bronowski, and Levin (1984) used either semantic mapping, semantic feature analysis, or a modification of a traditional basal approach for prereading instruction with fourth-grade students. The two semantic-based strategies proved to be equally effective and, in some cases, more effective than the modified basal technique for general vocabulary development. All three treatments resulted in improved passage comprehension with a tendency for the comprehension scores for students in both semantic groups to be higher than scores for students who received the modified basal instruction.

Hagen (1980) also experimented with semantic mapping as a prereading strategy with fourth- and fifth-grade students. She found that in addition to enhancing vocabulary knowledge and comprehension, semantic mapping was a valuable diagnostic tool for assessing prior knowledge. The strategy also encouraged divergent thinking, and it was an effective motivator.

As noted in the prior section on mnemonic strategies, Levin et al. (1984) compared the effectiveness of semantic mapping, a contextual analysis method, and the keyword method for teaching high-achieving fourth- and low-achieving fifth-grade students the definitions of words. Keyword subjects outperformed semantic mapping students on an immediate definition recall test, but not on a delayed definition matching test. Also, the keyword and semantic mapping groups did not differ on two measures of sentence comprehension. Levin et al. interpreted their results as support for the use of the keyword method as the preferred method to teach immediate definition recall.

Stahl and Vancil (1986) sought to isolate the effect of the visual map itself from the effect of an accompanying class discussion of the semantic map. Sixth-grade students received one of three approaches to semantic mapping instruction: (a) full treatment, in which students generated and discussed semantic maps; (b) discussion-only treatment, in which students only discussed the relationships among a cluster of words but saw no visual semantic map; or (c) map-only treatment, in which a semantic map was provided for the students, but no discussion occurred. Results revealed that both the full treatment and discussion-only treatments were superior to the map-only treatment as documented by students' ability to identify synonyms for taught words and to insert them in sentences, although neither discussion group differed on these measures. Stahl and Vancil concluded that discussion is a critical element in semantic mapping. Their finding perhaps explains the somewhat poor performance of the semantic mapping group in the Levin et al. (1984) study, since all instruction in their experiment was conducted individually, thus precluding the opportunity for discussion.

There also is evidence that semantic mapping and semantic feature analysis are effective strategies when used with disabled readers, learning-disabled students, and culturally diverse populations. Margosein, Pascarella, and Pflaum (1982) compared semantic mapping to contextual analysis and found that semantic mapping was superior for teaching vocabulary to reading disabled seventh- and eight-graders of Hispanic background. Karbon (1984) investigated the use of semantic mapping with rural Native American, inner city African Americans, and suburban sixth-grade students. She found that semantic mapping enabled students to rely on their prior knowledge and experiences as a means to expand their vocabulary. Jones (1984) replicated the Johnson, Pittelman, et al. (1984) study with African American inner city fifth-graders. In addition, there is evidence that semantic mapping and semantic feature analysis are effective when used with an ideographic language such as Chinese (Johnson, Pittelman, et al., 1982).

Anders et al. (1984) used semantic feature analysis as a prereading and postreading strategy to teach high school learning-disabled students information covered in a social studies chapter. Students who received this instruction outperformed comparable control group subjects (who looked up difficult words from the chapter in a dictionary and wrote out their definitions) on both a vocabulary test of the words that were covered as well as a general comprehension test over the material. Bos, Anders, Filip, and Jaffe (1985) readministered the identical posttests to the same subjects six months later and found the same pattern of results: experimental subjects outperformed controls on both vocabulary and comprehension.

In conclusion, in the majority of studies (Levin et al., 1984, being somewhat the exception), semantic mapping and semantic feature analysis appear to be effective strategies for teaching students the meanings of new words that lie within a semantically related category of which students are familiar. In addition, there is evidence that these techniques also promote passage comprehension and are effective with learners of diverse ages, ethnic backgrounds, and reading abilities.

***Research on other clustering and labeling strategies.*** The effectiveness of several other procedures that involve clustering semantically related words and labeling them have also been researched. One such procedure is Taba's (1967) List-Group-Label (LGL), which involves selecting a topic, brainstorming terms that relate to the topic, and grouping and labeling clusters of related terms. This is similar to semantic mapping except that a visual representation of the relationships among the words is typically not included. Bean, Inabinette, and Ryan (1983) evaluated the effectiveness of LGL for teaching 10th- through 12th-grade students a series of literary terms (e.g., *allusion*). The LGL treatment group read an essay that discussed a particular literary element, were presented with an explanation of the element by the teacher, read a story that exemplified the element, and then completed an LGL lesson on the literary element. Results revealed that LGL group students were more successful in learning literary terms than students who received the same sequence of instruction but without the LGL component.

Thames and Readence (1988) examined the effects of three forms of prereading vocabulary instruction used in conjunction with basal reader stories on second-grade students vocabulary learning and comprehension. Students engaged in one of three approaches for dealing with preselected vocabulary: (a) use of the List-Group-Label (Taba, 1967) procedure; (b) use of the Reconciled Reading Lesson (RRL; Reutzel, 1985), in which enrichment or extension activities commonly found at the end of the basal reader lesson are used before the story is read; or (c) use of a traditional directed reading activity (DRA) as prescribed in the basal manual (i.e., words are presented in context and discussed). Students read three basal stories using one of these procedures and after each responded to objective-item posttests that evaluated pretaught vocabulary and story comprehension. Results across all stories revealed that the RRL group outperformed both other groups, but the LGL and basal DRA groups did not differ. The authors suggested that the active, energetic responses promoted by the RRL approach might account for its superior performance and that the LGL might be a more appropriate postreading, rather than prereading, activity (i.e., how LGL was used by Bean et al., 1983).

Schwartz and Raphael (1985a; see also Schwartz, 1988) proposed a "concept of definition" approach to vocabulary learning that teaches students what types of information make up a definition and how they can use context and their own knowledge to learn word meanings. The strategy includes the use of a modified semantic map, which they call a word or concept map and context clues. Using the word map, students are taught to answer three questions that specify a word's definition: what it is, what is it like, and what are some examples? The concept of definition procedure involves high levels of teacher direction at the onset of the instructional sequence, but students are taught to use the procedure independently by gradually assuming more responsibility for applying it in later lessons.

The efficacy of the concept of definition approach has been tested in two experiments involving fourth- and fifth-grade students (Schwartz & Raphael, 1985b). In both experiments, students taught the concept of definition strategy outperformed students in a practice-control group (subjects worked independently to define the same words) or a no-treatment-control group (subjects only participated in pretesting and posttesting) on posttests that required them to write definitions for words presented with and without supporting context. Schwartz and Raphael concluded from their work that the concept of definition procedure has promise, especially in content area instruction, for teaching students an independent strategy to help them understand new concepts and associated texts.

To summarize, there is some indication that the use of other clustering and labeling strategies, such as List-Group-Label and the concept of definition, may be effective in teaching vocabulary that is central to the understanding of basal reader and content area selections. However, the equivocal findings of research on LGL (cf. Bean et al., 1983; Thames & Readence, 1988) and the limited research on concept of definition suggest that additional studies are needed before strong claims regarding their efficacy as vocabulary instruction or comprehension-enhancing techniques can be justified.

***Research on the Beck and McKeown program of rich vocabulary instruction.*** A comprehensive program of vocabulary research and development using a semantic relatedness perspective was initiated by Beck, McKeown, and colleagues. Their instructional program (see Beck & McKeown, 1983; Beck et al., 1980) presented words to students in semantic categories, not unlike a semantic mapping exercise, but instruction also included multimodal tasks such as definition, sentence generation, and oral production. Gamelike activities to promote response speed, interest in vocabulary and word play, and the use of learned words in new contexts beyond the classroom are additional components of their program. Also, instruction is intensive (30-minute lessons) and long term (up to 6 months in duration).

In their first two experiments involving fourth-graders, Beck and her colleagues (Beck, Perfetti, & McKeown, 1982; McKeown, Beck, Omanson, and Perfetti, 1983) evaluated the effectiveness of their instructional program compared to control subjects who participated in regular reading and language arts activities. Results demonstrated that the rich vocabulary instruction received by experimental subjects was superior in three ways: (a) instructed students learned the meanings of more of the words that were taught; (b) they demonstrated greater speed of lexical access (as measured by reaction time on a word categorization task); and (c) comprehension of stories that contained taught words was superior for instructed students.

In a third study, McKeown et al. (1985) systematically examined the effects of the nature of vocabulary instruction and the frequency of instructional encounters of taught words. Fourth-grade students received one of three kinds of instruction: Traditional instruction (learning definitions for words), rich instruction, or extended rich instruction. The latter two treatments involved variations of their intensive program of vocabulary instruction (i.e., Beck et al., 1982; McKeown et al., 1983); what discriminated them was that extended rich instruction encouraged students to be aware of and use the taught words outside of class, whereas the rich instruction did not include this component. An uninstructed control group was also included in the experiment. Frequency was manipulated by providing either 4 or 12 encounters with each word. Dependent variables were measures of definition knowledge, fluency of access to word meanings, context interpretation, and story comprehension. Results indicated that the three instructional groups did not differ on simple definitional word knowledge, although any instruction was superior to no instruction (control group). Extended rich instruction was superior to rich instruction in fluency of access and story comprehension, and rich instruction was superior to Traditional instruction in context interpretation and story comprehension. High frequency resulted in better performance on all measures. In a review of their work, Beck et al. (1987) drew the following conclusions from this experiment:

First of all, even a few, in this case four, encounters with a word within rather narrow instructional activities [traditional treatment] will produce some, albeit limited, results. Second, a greater number of encounters with words is generally more helpful toward a variety of vocabulary learning goals. One exception to this was that even a higher number of encounters with traditional instruction did not enhance reading comprehension. Only rich instruction, and only in the high encounter condition, was powerful enough to affect comprehension. Finally, extending instruction beyond the classroom held advantage in making knowledge about the words more readily available for processing. (p. 154)

Stahl, Burdge, Machuga, and Steryk (1992) assessed the effects of semantic groupings on vocabulary learning within a modified version of the Beck et al. (1982) program. They found that fourth-graders were equally successful in learning word meanings, using them in context, and classifying them regardless of whether the words were taught in semantic groups or simply in random lists. The authors argued that it was the rich, intensive nature of the Beck et al. program that led to its efficacy in vocabulary learning rather than to the presentation of words in semantic groups.

In conclusion, in spite of the caveats noted by Stahl et al. (1992), the work of Beck, McKeown, and their colleagues has demonstrated that an intensive, long-term program of vocabulary instruction can have positive effects not only on students' word learning but also on their comprehension of texts that contain taught words. They also have clarified somewhat the conditions of vocabulary instruction that influence passage comprehension. It appears that only frequent, rich instruction on words critical to story understanding, particulary when instruction extends beyond the confines of the classroom, affects comprehension. In contrast, traditional, definitional training in word meanings, even when such instruction is frequent, does not enhance passage comprehension. However, definitional training is effective and efficient when the instructional goal is only limited facility with new vocabulary.

***Research on other semantic relatedness or prior knowledge approaches.*** Additional experiments have investigated the effectiveness of various other semantic relatedness or prior knowledge strategies for teaching word meanings. For example, Bean et al. (1985) developed a procedure for using analogical study guides for use in content area subjects as a means to relate familiar words and concepts to unfamiliar ones. In an experiment with high school biology students (Bean, Singer, & Cowan, 1984), an analogical study guide that compared cell anatomy to a factory (e.g., cell wall = factory wall; cytoplasm = work area; lysosomes = cleanup crew) was used to teach cell structure–cell function associations. Results revealed that the analogical study guide was more effective in teaching structure–function associations than a traditional study method (cell parts related to their function but no analogy used) for students who were weak in comprehension abilities; however, neither method was superior for students who were above average in comprehension ability.

Duin and Graves (1987) explored the impact instruction in a set of semantically related words has on essay writing. Seventh-grade students were taught 13 target words over 6 days according to one of three methods: (a) intensive vocabulary and writing instruction (similar to the McKeown et al., 1985, extended rich

instruction, but it included many writing activities), (b) intensive vocabulary alone (same as intensive vocabulary and writing, but no writing activities were included), or (c) traditional vocabulary instruction (worksheet/definition activities). As measured by a multiple-choice vocabulary knowledge test, an analysis of the students' use of target words in essays, and holistic analyses of the essays, the vocabulary and writing group consistently outperformed the other two groups, and the vocabulary alone group outperformed the traditional vocabulary group. The authors concluded that teaching a set of related words to students before they write not only results in students learning the meanings of those words but also improves the quality of their essays.

Wixson (1986) contrasted the effectiveness of two approaches to preteaching vocabulary for basal reader selections: (a) a traditional dictionary word look-up method and (b) a concept method using the Frayer model (Frayer, Frederick, & Klausmeir, 1969), in which students list attributes for target words and generate examples and nonexamples for each. Results indicated that preteaching unfamiliar central story words enhanced understanding of the selection, but both methods were equally effective in achieving this effect. Wixson stated that the comparison of methods was equivocal due to an interaction with instructional texts and that future research was needed to explore the relative effectiveness of a dictionary method versus the Frayer model.

Carr (1985) developed the Vocabulary Overview Guide (VOG), a procedure that requires students to draw from their prior knowledge in order to learn the meanings of semantically related groups of words contained in a selection they must read. The words along with synonyms and personal clues to their meanings are displayed in a graphic organizer. The VOG also has a metacognitive component that enables students to quiz themselves on words they are learning and employ review or corrective strategies as needed. To test this procedure, Carr and Mazur-Stewart (1988) taught developmental college readers to use the VOG and compared its effectiveness to a list treatment, in which comparable students read the same passages but simply underlined and listed unknown vocabulary and ascertained their meanings from context. Results indicated that the VOG students demonstrated superior performance on a vocabulary test that evaluated their knowledge of the 100 words dealt with during intervention; this was true at the conclusion of training and 4 weeks later when the same test was readministered. The VOG students also demonstrated greater awareness and control of vocabulary learning strategies as measured by a metacognitive awareness posttest.

Medo and Ryder (1993) implemented a program that included discussion of word relationships and semantic mapping for teaching text-specific vocabulary in expository selections. When compared to instructed controls who received instruction in question generation, students in the experimental group demonstrated higher levels of comprehension and ability to make causal connections.

Duffelmeyer (1980) tested the effectiveness of an "experiential" approach to vocabulary learning. Students in a college reading/study skills course were taught low frequency words according to one of two methods: (a) an experiential method, in which students enacted brief skits that involved the use of a target word and then related personal experiences that also exemplified the target word; or (b) a traditional approach, in which the same words were taught through contextual analysis, structural analysis, and dictionary usage. As measured by "paragraph-to-word" posttests that required students to match target words to paragraphs that described them, subjects in the experiential group consistently outperformed students in the traditional group.

Dole, Sloan, and Trathen (1995) developed a program of rich, varied vocabulary instruction that included teaching procedural and conditional knowledge for learning words contained in novels read by students in tenth-grade English classes. The program for experimental condition students involved modeling, guided practice, and independent practice in how to select story-critical words, how to use context and a dictionary to learn word meanings, and how to use discussion to obtain a deeper understanding of words in a story context. When compared to students who received a traditional, didactic approach to vocabulary instruction, experimentals demonstrated greater comprehension of taught vocabulary and overall comprehension of the novels themselves. Additional, descriptive studies indicate that student choice in identifying difficult or interesting words in literature enhances both motivation and vocabulary learning for elementary (Fisher, Blachowicz, & Smith, 1991) and high school (Chase & Duffelmeyer, 1990) students.

Eeds and Cockrum (1985) experimented with a teacher prior knowledge/teacher interaction approach for teaching fifth-grade students the meanings of unknown words that appeared in a novel students were reading. Four target words contained in each day's segment of the novel were presented by having the students respond to questions that tapped their prior knowledge and experiences related to each target word. Students also generated examples and nonexamples of each target word and composed a definition for each. Compared to a dictionary look-up group and a control group that only read the novel, prior knowledge/interaction group students' performance on immediate and delayed multiple-choice posttests of target words exceeded the performance of both other groups.

Finally, in an experiment with third-grade students, Reutzel and Hollingsworth (1988) compared two strategies for teaching inferential comprehension: (a) a strategy that taught students to highlight vocabulary critical for the understanding of specific inference types (Johnson & Johnson, 1986) and (b) regular basal reader inferential comprehension instruction. Students receiving strategy instruction outperformed the basal group and controls on a series of near and far measures of inferential comprehension. Although the Reutzel and Hollingsworth strategy did not directly include a semantic relatedness dimension (rather, it involved a combination of text generation activities and aspects of reciprocal teaching), their experiment is noteworthy because it demonstrates further that a rich, elaborated form of vocabulary instruction does promote comprehension abilities.

In conclusion, research on a potpourri of other instructional strategies suggests that iterations of semantic relatedness and prior knowledge procedures are effective in teaching students word meanings. Specifically, an analogical study guide, intensive vocabulary and writing instruction, the Frayer concept model, the vocabulary overview guide, and experiential or interaction procedures have all been shown to enhance students' understanding of word meanings. Future research is required to evaluate the effectiveness and efficiency of these procedures relative to one another and to other semantic relatedness instructional techniques.

***Summary of research on strategies for teaching specific words.*** The following statements summarize what we have learned from our review of research on teaching specific words:

1. Students can learn word meanings by rote vocabulary learning methods, such as definition or synonym instruction, and these procedures are sensible if the instructional objective is limited or partial knowledge of fairly large numbers of words. However, other approaches may be more effective if a deeper and fuller understanding of word meanings is desired. If passage comprehension is the objective of vocabulary instruction, then it is unlikely that rote definition/synonym strategies will achieve this goal.

2. The mnemonic keyword method is effective in teaching diverse groups of students definitions or synonyms, and there is some indirect evidence of enhanced comprehension of passages that contain words learned through the keyword approach.

3. Various semantic relatedness and prior knowledge approaches, such as semantic mapping and semantic feature analysis, are effective techniques for teaching new concepts to students of varied abilities and different cultural and ethnic backgrounds. Further, there is some evidence that these methods also enhance passage comprehension.

4. The Beck and McKeown comprehensive program of rich vocabulary instruction has been shown to be effective in teaching fourth-grade students word meanings, and there is strong evidence that such instruction positively affects the comprehension of texts that contain taught words.

***Teaching transferable and generalizable vocabulary learning strategies.*** In this section, we present research on teaching students transferable and generalizable vocabulary learning strategies. Unlike procedures designed to teach *specific* words (e.g., definition or mnemonic keyword instruction) or concepts (e.g., semantic relatedness techniques), the objective of strategies discussed here is to teach students skills and abilities that will enable them to acquire the meanings of *many* words. Research on two sets of strategies will be reviewed: research on teaching contextual analysis and research on teaching morphemic analysis.

***Research on teaching contextual analysis.*** Contextual analysis is a strategy readers or listeners use to infer or predict the meaning of a word by scrutinizing the semantic and syntactic cues present in the preceding and following words, phrases, and sentences. As we noted earlier in this review, descriptive research provides evidence that extensive reading promotes word learning. This is true of students in Grades 3, 5, 7, and 8 who read narrative and expository texts (Nagy et al., 1985, 1987) as well as kindergarten children who listened to picture books (Eller, Pappas, & Brown, 1988). There are a number of factors that affect learning from context such as frequency of occurrence (Jenkins et al., 1984), proximity of a clue to an unknown word (Carroll & Drum, 1982; Kame'enui, Simmons, & Darch, 1987; Madison, Carroll, & Drum, 1982), the explicitness of a clue (Carnine, Kame'enui, & Woolfson, 1982; Carroll & Drum, 1983), the proportion of difficult words (Nagy et al., 1985, 1987), the students' preexisting general vocabulary knowledge (Shefelbine, 1990), the ability level of the student (Jenkins et al., 1984; McKeown, 1985), the degree to which words are abstract or concrete (Schwanenflugel & Akin, 1994), and the considerateness or clarity of the text (Gordon, Schumm, Offland, & Doucette, 1992; Herman et al., 1987; Konopak, 1988). Furthermore, not all contexts are equally rich (Beck et al., 1983; Nist & Olejnik, 1995) and some may be ineffective or unreliable in providing meaning clues (Baldwin & Schatz, 1985; Schatz & Baldwin, 1986). Nevertheless, the accumulated evidence indicates that words are learned incidentally by reading or listening (Drum & Konopak, 1987; Nagy & Herman, 1987; Sternberg, 1987).

Although it is clear that words are learned incidentally through context, what does the research say about the effectiveness and efficiency of *teaching* students contextual analysis as a vocabulary acquisition strategy? To answer this question, results of two different sets of experiments on instruction in contextual analysis are reviewed.

***Research comparing the effectiveness of contexual analysis and specific word learning strategies.*** Several studies have compared contextual analysis to strategies designed to teach the meanings of specific words. In most instances, contextual analysis has not fared very well in these experments. As indicated by studies reviewed in preceding sections of this chapter, contextual analysis was found to be less effective than semantic mapping (Johnson et al., 1982; Margosein et al., 1982; Toms-Bronowski, 1983) and the keyword method (Levin et al., 1982, 1984; Levin, Levin, Glasman, & Nordwall, 1992; Pressley et al., 1984) for teaching students definitions or synonyms. These findings are supported by Stahl and Fairbank's (1986) meta-analysis which demonstrated that strategies representing a balanced mixture of definitional and contextual information were superior to strategies emphasizing only definitional or only contextual information.

In contrast, results of a few studies suggest that contextual analysis may be an effective method for teaching specific word meanings. Most notably, Gipe (1978–79) reported that what she called a context method was superior to an association method (an associative labeling task), a category method (a semantic relatedness approach), and a dictionary look-up method for teaching word meanings. Somewhat similarly, Kame'enui et al. (1982) found that when vocabulary definition training was integrated with passage reading (i.e., students were required to recall the meanings of previously taught words as they read them in context), it resulted in greater word learning and passage comprehension than when definition instruction was not integrated with passage reading.

However, as Kame'enui et al. (1982) pointed out, neither Gipe's (1978–79) experiment nor their own exclusively involved context clues. Rather, contextual and definitional information were combined to produce the positive effects. In fact,

Stahl and Fairbanks (1986) labeled both Gipe's context method and Kame'enui et al.'s passage integration method as being "balanced" approaches, which they defined as providing "a balance or near balance between definitional and contextual information" (p. 75). Therefore, it is safe to say that *purely* contextual approaches are not as effective in teaching new labels or concepts for specific words as are other direct, associative approaches, most notably the mnemonic keyword method (Pressley et al., 1987).

Does this mean that instruction in contextual analysis is never justified? Not at all. The experiments noted above (e.g., Johnson et al., 1982; Levin et al., 1984) suffer from an apples and oranges limitation: Specific-word methods (e.g., semantic mapping, keyword) were contrasted to a generalizable strategy (contextual analysis) that is not bound to specific words. It is true that strategies such as the keyword method are more effective than context for teaching synonyms or definitions for specific words, but they are not easily generalizable and transferable. In contrast, instruction in the *process* of contextual analysis has the potential to help students acquire the meanings of many words they encounter, not just those they are taught directly. Sternberg (1987) made this point very well as he elaborated on his claim that most vocabulary is learned from context:

What the claim does imply is that teaching people to learn better from context can be a highly effective way of enhancing vocabulary development. What the claim does not imply is that teaching specific vocabulary using context is the most effective, or even a relatively effective, way of teaching that vocabulary. Unfortunately, many believers in learning from context, as well as their detractors, have drawn the second inference rather than the first. As a result, they are on the verge of throwing out a perfectly clean and healthy baby with its, admittedly, less than sparkling bath water. (p. 89)

An analog to this situation is instruction in word pronunciation. We can teach students to pronounce specific words through a look-say or sight word method, or we can teach them transferable and generalizable word pronunciation rules through instruction in phonic analysis. The former teaches the pronunciations of specific words; the latter teaches a process to pronounce many words. No doubt, a sight word method is more effective for teaching students to pronounce *specific* words, but one is limited in the number of specific words that can be taught. Each approach is justifiable and useful, but the objectives and outcomes differ significantly. So, too, teaching contextual analysis and the meanings of specific words, though both justifiable and useful, have very different objectives and outcomes. In the following section, we examine research on teaching contextual analysis as an independent word learning strategy.

***Research on teaching contextual analysis as an independent word learning strategy.*** What research has been conducted on teaching the process of contextual analysis as a transferable and generalizable strategy to acquire vocabulary? Unfortunately, the volume of research is fairly limited. As noted in an earlier section, Jenkins et al. (1984) reported that high ability fifth-grade students were able to supply definitions for words presented in contrived passages after 6 or 10 exposures, but not with only 2 exposures. However, when students were provided informal instruction for target words, preexposure to synonyms prior to reading the selection, they were much more efficient in using the context. Thus, even minimal instruction may enhance the effect context has on acquiring word meanings.

Sampson, Valmont, and Allen (1982) provided indirect instruction in contextual analysis to third-grade children by training them in the use of instructional cloze. They reported that cloze-trained students outperformed controls on an experimenter-conducted cloze test as well as on a standardized reading comprehension test; however, experimentals and controls did not differ on a standardized vocabulary measure. This latter finding requires some qualification, however, for the standardized vocabulary test used (*Gates–MacGinite Reading Tests*, MacGinite, 1978) employed a synonym matching format that presented the target word in isolation. Therefore, students were unable to rely on context clues when completing this test.

Instruction in contextual analysis is also a part of the VOG proposed by Carr (1985) as well as the "concept of definition" strategy proposed by Schwartz and Raphael (1985a), and each procedure was designed to enable students to achieve independence in acquiring word meanings from context as they read content area selections. However, the strategies involve a combination of semantic relatedness procedures and instruction in contextual analysis, and research on the efficacy of these approaches is limited (Carr & Mazur-Stewart, 1988; Schwartz & Raphael, 1985b). Therefore, more research on these procedures is required, particularly experiments that contrast these approaches to others intended to teach independent word learning, before conclusions can be drawn regarding the relative effectiveness of these promising instructional strategies.

Several other experiments have been conducted in which more systematic and intensive instruction in contextual analysis has occurred. Hafner (1965) conducted a monthlong experiment in which fifth-grade students were taught to use context clues; however, experimentals did not outperform controls. Askov and Kamm (1976) trained third-, fourth-, and fifth-grade students to use cause/effect and description context clues. After 4 hours of training, experimentals outperformed controls on a criterion-referenced test specifically designed to measures use of context.

Sternberg and Powell (1983) and Sternberg et al. (1983) described a set of context clue types and an accompanying theory for their use by readers. They provided evidence in support of their theory (Sternberg & Powell, 1983) and conducted two experiments to see if students could be taught to improve their use of context clues (see descriptions of both experiments in Sternberg, 1987). In their first training study, 10th- and 11th-grade students were taught to use six types of context clues. Instruction spanned six class periods. Experimentals outperformed controls on a test that included neologisms (invented, newly coined words) and cloze blanks, although the pretest–posttest gains were modest. In a second experiment, adult subjects who received 45 minutes of training according to one of three different procedures based upon the Sternberg theory outperformed controls who either memorized words or who practiced using context clues. Although the results of these studies are promising, few conclusions can be drawn because Sternberg (1987) only presented summaries of these studies, not complete research reports.

Building on the work of Carnine et al. (1984), Patberg, Graves, and Stibbe (1984) taught fifth-grade students synonym and contrast context clues according to an "active teaching" procedure based on teacher effectiveness principles. Comparison groups consisted of students who practiced contextual analysis on worksheets and an uninstructed control group. Results indicated that the active teaching group outperformed both the practice and control groups in ability to determine the meanings of low-frequency, novel words that were presented in short texts that contained synonym and contrast context clues.

In a somewhat similar study, Jenkins, Matlock, and Slocum (1989) taught fifth-grade students a general strategy for deriving the meanings of words from context. The strategy required students to scrutinize the context, supply a plausible synonym, evaluate the sensibility of the substitution, and generate another synonym if necessary. Results indicated that when the context strategy was provided in medium or high intensities (i.e., over 11 or 20 sessions, respectively), as opposed to low intensity (9 sessions), experimentals demonstrated small but reliable gains in ability to use context to infer the meanings of untaught words when compared to students who received word definition instruction.

Buikema and Graves (1993) taught seventh and eighth grade students to use descriptive context clues through a week-long instructional unit. Experimental group students outperformed controls who followed the normal English curriculum on several measures that assessed students' ability to infer the meanings of novel words from context. The authors argued that the effects of their program were the results of the combination of direct instruction in the use of descriptive context clues and considerable practice.

Kuhn and Stahl (1998) picked up on the issue of effects of instruction versus practice in their review of instructional research on contextual analysis. Noting that in four studies that included a practice-only comparison treatment, the direct instruction treatment group did not outperform these students who just practiced figuring out word meanings from context. They concluded from their review that "students taught to use context to derive word meanings generally do better on measures that assess that skill," but they argued further that "it is likely that students benefit as much from practice in deriving words from context as they would from instruction in either a specific set of strategies or a list of clues" (p. 129).

In summary, research on teaching the process of contextual analysis as a transferable and generalizable skill is somewhat limited and at times equivocal (cf. Askov & Kamn, 1976; Hafner, 1965). However, experiments by Buikema and Graves (1993), Jenkins et al. (1989), Patberg et al. (1984), and Sternberg (1987) provide some evidence that instruction in contextual analysis may enable students to infer the meanings of words that have not been taught directly. In conclusion, we see promise in this line of inquiry, but we agree with Kuhn and Stahl (1998) that "the paucity of research evidence is disappointing" (p. 129). Unfortunately, the situation today remains about the same it was in 1984 when Johnson and Baumann reviewed the instructional research on contextual analysis and reached the following conclusion:

So, while there is little doubt that contextual clues are potentially powerful aids in identifying unknown words, much additional educational research is warranted in order to determine what specific pedagogical procedures will be most effective in teaching children to learn and apply this skill. (p. 602)

***Research on teaching morphemic analysis.*** Morphemic analysis is a word identification strategy in which the meanings of words can be determined or inferred by examining their meaningful parts. A *morpheme,* the smallest unit of meaning in language, can occur in two forms: free and bound. Free morphemes function independently and are often referred to as base words or roots words (e.g., *walk, girl, happy*). Bound morphemes (*ing, s, un, ness*) also convey meaning, but they cannot stand alone; they must be attached to free morphemes. By combining free and bound morphemes, many different words can be formed (e.g., *walking, girls, unhappiness*). Morphemic analysis, which is also called structural analysis, typically includes four components:

(a) affixes—how the addition of various prefixes and suffixes affects word meaning, (b) inflections—how plurals, comparatives, verb tenses, and possessives alter word meanings, (c) compound words—how the conjoining of two free morphemes can result in a new word that is different in meaning but still retains some kernel of meaning of each of the base words, and (d) contractions—the merging and condensing of two free morphemes through usage. (Baumann, 1988, p. 202)

The rationale that underlies instruction in morphemic analysis is that if students can be taught basic and recurring free and bound morphemes, knowledge of many semantically related words can be acquired. For example, knowing the base word *add* and the meanings of various bound morphemes could enable students to understand *adds, added, adding, addend, addition, additional, additive,* and *additives* (example from Nagy & Anderson, 1984, p. 309).

Nagy and Anderson (1984) estimated that about 230,000 words, 170,000 inflections, and another 100,000 proper names are to be found in printed school English (reading materials for students in Grades 3 through 9). However, they estimate that this volume reduces to 88,533 words families, which are defined as follows:

A word family consists of the set of words for which there is a transparent, predictable relationship in both form and meaning. For example, *persecute, persecution,* and *persecutor* would all be considered as constituting a single word family, along with regular inflections such as *persecuted* and *persecutions.* (Nagy & Herman, 1987, p. 20)

Nagy and Anderson stated that "for every word a child learns, we estimate that there are an average of one to three additional words that should also be understandable to the child, the exact number depending on how well the child is able to utilize context and morphology to induce meanings" (p. 304). Therefore, instruction in morphemic analysis is potentially a powerful and fruitful means for students to acquire new vocabulary.

Nagy, Diakidoy, and Anderson (1993) evaluated the knowledge of 10 common English suffixes by students in Grade 4, Grade 7, and high school. They found significant growth, particularly between Grades 4 and 7, concluding that "knowledge

of suffixes constitutes a distinct component of skilled reading" (p. 168).

White, Power, and White (1989) analyzed words with prefixes and estimated that about 80% of words with affixes can be inferred from their morphological root words. They also reported that the number of words morphologically analyzable increased significantly from Grades 3 to 7, although they recommend deferring intensive instruction in morphological analysis until Grade 4 when the texts students read begin to offer them a much broader diet of words whose meanings can be inferred by analyzing constituent parts. White Power, et al. concluded by saying that "our data support the practice of direct morphological instruction in Grades 4 and above, provided that the instruction is (a) based on knowledge of frequently occurring affixes, and (b) strategic and contextualized" (p. 303).

Many strategies for teaching morphemic analysis have been proposed (e.g., Becker, 1977; Durkin, 1981b; Johnson & Pearson, 1984), and reading experts suggest that structural or morphemic analysis be a part of developmental (Duffy & Roehler, 1986; Mason & Au, 1986) and corrective/remedial (e.g., Carnine et al., 1990; Taylor, Harris, & Pearson, 1988) reading instruction. Furthermore, all basal reading programs contain instruction in structural elements such as base words, inflections, contractions, and compound words. In spite of the conventional wisdom that instruction in morphemic analysis is an appropriate transferable and generalizable vocabulary strategy, research on the efficacy of such instruction is fairly limited.

Otterman (1955) taught seventh-grade students various morphological elements. Results revealed that although experimentals outperformed controls on tests of spelling and the instructed morphemic elements, they did not demonstrate superior performance on tests of new words, general vocabulary, or comprehension. Similarly, Freyd and Baron (1982) taught fifth-grade students specific suffixes but found that they were no more adept than controls at using this knowledge to understand untaught derived words. Freyd and Baron attributed this finding to the limited amount of time the experimental subjects were provided for instruction and practice. Hanson (1966) reported success in teaching first-grade students inflected endings but that this knowledge was not manifest on measures of general reading ability. In contrast, Thompson (1958) reported success in teaching college students 20 prefixes and 14 roots. Students not only learned the prefixes and roots and were able to identify them in words, but they also improved their ability to recognize words that possessed the prefixes.

One of the more technically sound morphemic analysis training studies was conducted by Graves and Hammond (1980). They taught seventh-grade students the meanings of nine commonly occurring prefixes (prefix group) and how to use them to discover the meanings of unfamiliar words that contained the prefixes. A second group of students (whole word group) was taught definitions for the same set of words as the prefix group (each of which contained one of the nine prefixes), but no mention was made of the prefixes. Results indicated that the prefix group learned the prefixes that they were taught when compared to the whole word group and an uninstructed control group; both treatments outperformed the controls on the set of taught words; but the prefix group outperformed both the whole word and control group on a set of transfer words, difficult vocabulary words that contained taught prefixes. Graves and Hammond concluded that "students can use their knowledge of the prefixes they are taught as a generative tool that will help them unlock the meaning of novel words" (p. 187).

In several more recent, small-scale studies, elementary children have been taught the meanings of prefixes as a generative tool. White, Sowell, and Yanagihara (1989) taught high-ability third-grade children selected prefixes and reported that those students outperformed uninstructured controls on two transfers tests involving unfamiliar prefixed words. Nicol and Graves (1990) reported similar findings for high-, middle-, and low-ability fourth-, fifth-, and sixth-grade students; further, the instructed students maintained their advantage over uninstructed controls on a delayed measure administered 3 weeks after instruction.

Wysocki and Jenkins (1987) examined the effect of instructing 135 fourth-, sixth-, and eight-grade students in derivational morphemes. Students were taught definitions or synonyms of six words for which there was a paired morphological derivative. Each set consisted of a stimulus word in which the students were instructed (e.g., *melancholic*) and a transfer word that was not taught (e.g., *melancholia*). Posttesting required the students to provide a definition for (a) transfer words in weak context, (b) transfer words in strong context, and (c) stimulus words in weak context. Results indicated that all students demonstrated morphological generalization ability (i.e., ability to define *melancholia* after have been taught *melancholic*), although this finding was much more robust under a lenient, as opposed to strict, scoring criteria. Stronger context also enhanced students' ability to make morphological generalizations, although unexpectedly, the effects of morphological generalization and context did not appear to be additive. In other words, unlike Nagy and Anderson's (1984) suggestion that morphology and rich context should enhance vocabulary acquisition, Wysocki and Jenkins found no evidence that their subjects combined these two sources of information. In contrast, data by White et al. (1989) suggest that context is important in identifying the appropriate root meaning for an affixed words.

In conclusion, similar to the research on teaching contextual analysis, research on teaching morphological analysis is both limited and sometimes equivocal. Although several studies suggest that instruction in morphological elements may not be fruitful (e.g., Freyd & Baron, 1982; Otterman, 1955), other, perhaps more methodologically and pedagogically sound, experiments suggest that such training may be effective. Specifically, it appears as though elementary and middle grade students can be taught specific morphemic elements (e.g., Graves & Hammond, 1980) and that they are able to spontaneously generalize (infer) the meaning of one word from a morphologically similar derivative (Wysocki & Jenkins, 1987).

***Summary of research on teaching transferable and generalizable vocabulary learning strategies.*** The following statements summarize what we have learned from our review of research on contextual analysis and morphological analysis.

1. Use of context clues is a relatively ineffective means for inferring the meanings of specific words; rather, semantic relatedness procedures and mnemonic methods are preferred approaches for teaching the meanings of specific words.

2. When definitional information is combined with contextual cues, students are more apt to learn specific new vocabulary than when contextual analysis is used in isolation.

3. Research on teaching contextual analysis as a transferable and generalizable strategy for word learning suggests that instruction does facilitate students' ability to infer word meanings from surrounding context, although the relative efficacy of instruction in specific context clues versus simple practice in inferring meanings from context remains in question.

4. Research on teaching morphological analysis as a transferable and generalizable strategy for word learning is limited. There is some indication that students can be taught specific morphemes (e.g., prefixes) that may enable them to unlock the meanings of unknown words containing these elements; also, there is some evidence that teaching students the meanings of unfamiliar words enables them to infer the meanings of morphologically related words. However, additional research is required in this area.

## WHAT RESEARCHERS KNOW AND DON'T KNOW ABOUT VOCABULARY INSTRUCTION

In the final section of this chapter, we sum up what we have learned from our review of the literature on vocabulary acquisition and instruction and what we believe we have yet to learn. We have organized this section into three parts: (a) what researchers know and do not know about the breadth and depth of students' vocabulary knowledge, (b) what researchers know and don't know about teaching vocabulary, and (c) several conclusions about vocabulary teaching and learning.

### The Breadth and Depth of Students' Vocabulary Knowledge: What Researchers Know and Don't Know

***What researchers know.*** Researchers know that students are faced with many words in the oral language they hear (Hayes & Ahrens, 1988) and the written language they read. Nagy and Anderson (1984) estimated that there are over 88,500 distinct word families in printed school English for students in Grades 3 to 9. With an average family size of about 4.5 words, this means that there are nearly 400,000 graphically distinct word types in books used in schools, and this does not even include an estimated 100,000 proper names. Of course not all students will encounter all these word types, but clearly the printed vocabulary presented to students is immense, and there is evidence to suggest that print provides greater breadth of novel words than oral language (Hayes & Ahrens, 1988; see discussion in Cunningham & Stanovich, 1998).

Interestingly, in contrast to the printed vocabulary of 500,000 words that students might encounter in school that Nagy and Anderson (1984) proposed originally, recent estimates of the number of words known by competent adults (D'Anna et al., 1991; Goulden et al., 1990; Zechmeister et al., 1995) suggest a more manageable number. The average adult vocabulary appears to contain approximately 17,000 base words, but these words are considered "functionally important words," or words that students would need to know to read their junior high and high school texts. These more recent estimates suggest a more viable role for the direct instruction of words; it would not be "futile" to directly teach a manageable number of highly functional words important to adulthood.

Researchers know that students do learn the meanings of many words. Nagy and Herman (1987) estimated that students learn approximately 3,000 new words per year during the school years, and that a high school senior's vocabulary measures approximately 40,000 words. Data by White et al. (1990) suggest that these estimates may even be conservative. There are individual differences, of course (e.g., disadvantaged students know about 50% to 70% of the words known by middle class students; White et al.), but vocabulary learning does proceed at a fairly high rate throughout the school years.

Researchers know that students encounter many unknown words as they read. Based on work by Nagy and Anderson (1984) and Anderson and Freebody (1983), Nagy and Herman (1987) estimated that an average fifth-grade student who does only a modest amount of reading (3,000 words per school day) is likely to encounter almost 10,000 different unknown words a year. So, in spite of the vocabulary growth that occurs by way of instruction, incidental learning, or natural development, students are faced with many unknown words.

For students who are disadvantaged by virtue of their socioeconomic status and have fewer daily opportunities to be exposed to rich and sustained oral and written vocabularies (Corson, 1989; Hart & Risley, 1992), the Matthew effect (Stanovich, 1986) is real; students with large and rich vocabularies appear to be more successful in school than students with small and relatively poor vocabularies. Moreover, the differences in the trajectories of vocabulary growth appear to start early in life and become more discrepant and resistant to instruction than previously thought (Hart & Risley, 1992).

Researchers know that students learn word meanings incidentally through oral and written context. Estimates of word learning from oral context (e.g., conversation, television, films) are unavailable; however, it is clear that students learn vocabulary from context while reading (Durso & Shore, 1991; Nagy et al., 1985, 1987; Shore & Durso, 1990). Such gains are modest but nonetheless real. However, the cumulative effect of years of wide reading appears to be large (Cunningham & Stanovich, 1991). Although the probability of learning the meaning of a word from a single encounter of it in text is low (about 1 in 20), if students read regularly for even modest amounts of time (e.g., 25 minutes per day for 200 days a year), they will learn from 750 to 1,500 words a year (all estimates from Nagy & Herman, 1987). Thus, from 20% to 50% of the estimated annual growth of vocabulary can be attributed to incidental learning from context while reading. However, if only "functionally important words" are considered in this growth (D'Anna et al., 1991; Goulden et al., 1990; Zechmeister et al., 1995), perhaps this annual growth is more significant than previously thought.

Researchers know that vocabulary knowledge is related to and affects comprehension. The relationship between word knowledge and comprehension is unequivocal (e.g., Davis, 1944, 1968). Furthermore, instruction in vocabulary, if done in systematic, intense, and rich ways and if aligned with clear and specific vocabulary goals, does positively affect comprehension (Beck et al., 1987; Mezynski, 1983; Stahl & Fairbanks, 1986).

***What researchers don't know.*** What don't researchers know about the breadth and depth of student's vocabulary knowledge? They are still not in agreement on several basic issues and questions such as, What is a word, and when is a word known? Such issues may never be resolved completely, but more attention must be given to specifying the basic concept of word and when one is known (Anderson, 1990; Roberts, 1992). In addition, establishing clear vocabulary goals and objectives that align with well-developed vocabulary measures and vocabulary tasks, as called for by Kame'enui et al. (1987) more than a decade ago, should assist in clarifying and avoiding some of the knotty definitional issues that have haunted vocabulary learning for a long time.

More needs to be learned about incidental vocabulary learning. Although we reviewed seven studies that examined incidental learning from context, we have yet to explore fully the effects of school and recreational reading on word learning. Carefully designed studies must still unpack the intricate interactions between factors such as type of material read, the volume of reading students do, the number of incidental encounters with a given unknown word, and a reader's skill level and motivation. What might be the effects of electronic texts such as hypermedia on incidental word learning? An investigation into the effects of supportive text on students' incidental word learning might reveal information about the differences between incidental and instructional word learning through the blurring of the two.

Despite some of the more recent findings on the importance of oral language to the development of vocabulary knowledge (e.g., Dickinson & Smith, 1994; Hart & Risley, 1992; Sénéchal & Cornell, 1993), many questions remain unanswered. How does the volume and quality of language that students are exposed to affect vocabulary learning? What are the individual and combined effects of oral and written context? What can be done to enhance the environment to optimize learning words from oral contexts? Longitudinal and developmental research is needed to address these questions.

Finally, much remains to be learned about the relationship between vocabulary and comprehension. Researchers know there is one and that it probably is causal. However, their power to predict what words will influence comprehension is weak, and the subtleties of the relationship between depth of word knowledge and the type and level of understanding remain elusive.

## Teaching Vocabulary: What Researchers Know and Don't Know

***What researchers know.*** What do researchers know about teaching vocabulary? First, they know that vocabulary instructional materials, basal reading series with 1970s' copyrights in particular, were criticized for a lack of breadth and depth of vocabulary instruction (Beck et al., 1979; Durkin, 1981a; Jenkins & Dixon, 1983). However, more recent basal reading series (with copyrights of 1989 and 1991) appear to provide teachers with more useful vocabulary instructional guidelines (Ryder &

Graves, 1994). Second, apparently elementary and secondary teachers do not teach vocabulary very often or very intensively (Durkin, 1978-79, 1984; Graves, 1987; Roser & Juel, 1982), and when they do teach vocabulary, they teach words that students already appear to know (Ryder & Graves, 1994). Nevertheless, there is some indication that this situation is improving (Blachowicz, 1987; Johnson, Levin, & Pittelman, 1984; Ryder & Graves, 1994). Third, the adopted reading program does appear to influence the nature of vocabulary instruction in classrooms (Barr & Sadow, 1989; Watts, 1995).

Researchers know that early vocabulary research (before 1970) was not particularly illuminating. They learned that some form of vocabulary instruction was better than no instruction, an important but oftentimes ignored fact (Chall, 1987), but little could be stated about the relative effectiveness of one approach versus another (Petty et al., 1967).

Researchers know that since 1970 there has been increased interest in vocabulary research, with many experiments comparing the effectiveness of different approaches to teaching vocabulary. A brief summary of the results of those comparative studies follows:

1. Students can be taught labels (definitions, synonyms) for specific words through associative teacher-led definitional methods (e.g., Blachowicz & Fisher, 1996; Kame'enui et al., 1982; Pany et al., 1982; Stahl, 1983). However, definitional instruction alone is not likely to result in enhanced comprehension of text that contains taught words (e.g., McKeown, 1993; McKeown et al., 1983; Pany & Jenkins, 1978; Scott & Nagy, 1997; Stahl & Fairbanks, 1986).

2. Students also can be taught labels for specific words very effectively through the associative mnemonic approach known as the keyword method (e.g., Levin et al., 1982, 1992; McDaniel & Pressley, 1989). Furthermore, the keyword method has been shown to be more effective than semantic relatedness methods (Levin et al., 1984) and simple use of context (Pressley et al., 1987) for learning specific word labels. Recent evidence also appears to support the keyword method for improving students' comprehension of passages (Levin et al., 1992; McDaniel & Pressley, 1989).

3. Various semantic relatedness approaches such as semantic mapping (e.g., Johnson, Pittelman et al., 1984), semantic feature analysis (e.g., Anders et al., 1984), and other similar approaches (e.g., Bean et al., 1983; Dole et al., 1995; Medo & Ryder, 1993; Schwartz & Raphael, 1985b) have been shown to be effective for teaching students new concepts and labels for them. In addition, there is evidence that such approaches positively affect the comprehension of texts that contain taught words (e.g., Anders et al., 1984; Johnson, Pittelman et al., 1984).

4. The intensive program of rich vocabulary instruction devised and tested by Beck and McKeown (e.g., Beck et al., 1982; McKeown et al., 1983, 1985) has been shown to be effective in teaching concepts and improving the comprehension of texts that contain such concepts. Stahl et al. (1992) recently confirmed the power of the rich, intensive nature of the Beck et al. vocabulary program.

5. Compared to associative tasks (e.g., keyword) or semantic relatedness approaches (e.g., semantic mapping), context clues are relatively inefficient for inferring the meanings of specific words (e.g., Johnson et al., 1982; Levin et al., 1984).

6. Recent research appears to suggest that contextual analysis may help students infer meanings of words that have not been taught. However, simple practice appears to play an important role in learning unknown words from context (Buikema & Graves, 1993; Kuhn & Stahl, 1998).

7. When definitional information is combined with contextual cues, students are more likely to learn new vocabulary than when contextual analysis is used in isolation (e.g., Brett et al., 1996; Kolich, 1991; Stahl, 1983).

8. There is some evidence that teaching contextual analysis (e.g., Jenkins et al., 1989; Sternberg, 1987) and morphemic analysis (e.g., Graves & Hammond, 1980; Nagy et al., 1993; White, Power, & White, 1989) as transferable and generalizable strategies are effective means for students to learn word meanings independently.

***What researchers don't know.*** What is still unknown about vocabulary instruction? What are areas in need of further inquiry? Researchers do not know if current commercial materials, basal reading series in particular, provide teachers stronger, richer, more comprehensive programs of instruction than previous programs that have been extensively analyzed and found lacking. Furthermore, they still know little about the quantity and quality of (a) vocabulary instructional materials in literature-based versus basal-oriented classrooms; (b) vocabulary instructional methods, suggestions, and procedures found in supplemental vocabulary programs; and (c) vocabulary instruction that might be incorporated into content textbooks. In sum, much descriptive materials evaluation and analysis needs to be done to determine if current instructional materials provide sufficient attention to vocabulary instruction and if such instruction reflects our current knowledge base.

Researchers do not know if classroom instructional practices in vocabulary have improved or are improving in a systematically and sustained manner. Evidence reported by Barr and Sadow (1989), Blachowicz (1987), Johnson, Pittelman, and Levin (1984), and Watts (1995) suggests that this may be happening, but more data are needed to document this apparent trend. Large-scale, long-term classroom observational studies of elementary and secondary teachers and students are required to establish what attention is given to vocabulary within reading/language arts and content instruction.

There are things researchers do not know about specific vocabulary instructional approaches, strategies, and programs. For example, regarding rote vocabulary learning, they do not know what the most effective and efficient means are to provide students initial, limited definitional knowledge of vocabulary such that it will serve as the foundation for subsequent deeper, richer instruction or the acquisition of meanings from context.

Researchers know that it takes more than definitional knowledge of words to affect comprehension, but they still do not know what the optimal ratio of definitional knowledge to contextual/semantic relatedness information might be. How much emphasis on definitions relative to the use of new words in context or in semantically related ways is required to positively affect comprehension of texts containing taught words?

There is modest but compelling new evidence that the key word method positively affects the comprehension of text containing taught words (Levin et al., 1992; McDaniel & Pressley, 1989). However, much more evidence is needed. Also, one must still question the efficiency of keyword instruction (cf., Beck et al., 1984; Nagy & Herman, 1984): Will students be able to retain mnemonic keys for large numbers of words taught across time according to the keyword method? Will long-term instruction in keyword become tiring as Graves (1986) suggested? What about polysemous words? Can the keyword method be used to teach multiple meanings?

What are the critical features of semantic relatedness instruction? Researchers know that many different strategies work, but what are the underlying general principles? What is the relative power of focusing on word *similarities* (e.g., semantic mapping) versus focusing on *differences* in meaning (e.g., semantic feature analysis)? What are the individual and interactive effects of discussion and visual displays that appear to be central to semantic relatedness procedures?

Researchers do not know if students can be taught to use contextual and morphemic analysis independently and systematically to learn the meanings of unknown words. If so, for which ages and grades of learners is this instruction effective? What role do students' individual differences play in contextual and morphemic analysis instruction? What types of context clues and morphemic elements are the most efficient to teach students? Might it be possible to define a scope and sequence of instruction in generalizable word learning skills? How efficient is instruction in generalizable vocabulary strategies? Do students who are taught to use contextual or morphemic clues learn significantly more words than what they might acquire incidentally through reading or listening? The promise of providing students transferable and generalizable tools for independent word learning through contextual and morphemic analysis is great, but the promise currently outstrips the evidence we possess on the efficacy of such instruction.

## What Does It All Mean?

In the original version of this chapter (Baumann & Kame'enui, 1991), we posed the following questions: Can the knowledge researchers have of vocabulary instruction be reduced or synthesized? Are there any general, global principles that teachers, teacher trainers, supervisors, curriculum developers, or educational publishers might adhere to as they develop or administer vocabulary curriculum and instruction? Although several writers proposed guidelines for teaching vocabulary (e.g., Blachowicz, 1985, pp. 879–880; Blachowicz, 1986, p. 644; Carr & Wixson, 1986, pp. 589–592; Marzano & Marzano, 1988, pp. 11–12; Mezynski, 1983, p. 273; Stahl, 1985, pp. 19–20; Stahl & Fairbanks, 1986, p. 101), we found Stahl's (1986) three principles for effective vocabulary instruction representative of many of the guidelines: (a) "Principle 1: Give both context and definitions," (b) "Principle 2: Encourage 'deep' processing" and (c) "Principle 3: Give multiple exposures" (663–665).

For the most part, principles or guidelines like Stahl's (1986) are sensible, empirically based, and practical. However, we

typically find them to be linked to a specific vocabulary instructional objective, usually one involving teaching specific words. For example, Stahl's suggestions are appropriate if one's objective is to promote students' comprehension of texts. In order to achieve this goal, research suggests that it makes sense to provide deep instruction with multiple exposures with words for which both context and definitional information is provided. However, if one's objective were different, for example, to make students skillful in independent word learning strategies (e.g., ability to use contextual analysis), then Stahl's three principles would not be applicable.

More recent guidelines for teaching vocabulary (e.g., Baker, Simmons, & Kame'enui, 1998a; Blachowicz & Fisher, 1996; Nagy, 1998; Thomas, 1998) have strengthened our belief that there needs to be an alignment between instructional objectives and the instructional means to achieve them. Actually, we see the need for two related sets of decision-making guidelines: a global set and a specific set. At the global level, we see the need for a set of decision-making principles that must be superordinate to, but complementary with, specific instructional principles like Stahl's (1986), which were drafted more than a decade ago. These principles would guide the design of a comprehensive program of vocabulary instruction. What would we recommend? Here are our suggestions for making *global* instructional decisions regarding vocabulary instruction:

1. Establish vocabulary learning goals for your students.
2. Include goals that provide for teacher-initiated vocabulary learning as well as ones that strive for student independence in vocabulary learning (Fisher et al., 1991).
3. Include instruction in both specific-word and transferable and generalizable strategies.
4. Select instructional strategies and procedures that are carefully aligned with each of your goals (Baker et al., 1998a).
5. Provide struggling readers a systematic and sustained program of vocabulary instruction that teaches them more important words and efficient strategies in less time (Baker et al., 1998a; Kame'enui & Simmons, 1990; Stanovich, 1986).
6. Select assessment tasks and formats that are consistent with your instructional strategies and desired outcomes.
7. Consider the costs and benefits of instruction (Graves & Prenn, 1986) in terms of student and teacher time and effort when matching instructional methods to goals.
8. Select the most effective and efficient strategy or strategies for each instructional objective.
9. Do not limit yourself to a narrow set of vocabulary instructional techniques. Select suitable strategies from a range of empirically validated instructional procedures that are compatible with your instructional objectives.
10. Continually evaluate your vocabulary learning objectives and the procedures and techniques you have chosen to address each.

At the *specific* level would come guidelines like those Stahl (1986) has recommended. For example, given a decision to provide vocabulary instruction that will enhance text comprehension, then a procedure that employs Stahl's three principles could be selected (e.g., the Beck & McKeown, 1983, program or rich instruction).

What help can be provided when deciding which specific strategy to select? We agree with McKeown and Beck (1988) that "the choice of the kind of instruction to use in specific instances depends on the goal of the instruction, the kinds of words being presented, and the characteristics of the learners" (p. 44). In other words, the method you select for teaching vocabulary depends on the instructional objective you have.

Graves and Prenn (1986) have elaborated on the relational nature of vocabulary instruction. They argued, quite convincingly, we believe, that methods must be selected by weighing their costs and benefits:

Different methods of teaching words are appropriate in difference circumstances.... Our purpose is to make the point that there is no one best method of teaching words—that various methods have both their costs and their benefits and will be very appropriate and effective in some circumstances and less appropriate and effective in others. (pp. 596–597)

For example, if one's objective were to teach the meanings of a relatively few specific words in a content subject like science, the least costly approach might be to use a definitional method. However, if one wished to teach meanings for many words, or if the goal were to enhance passage comprehension, another method, perhaps a semantic relatedness procedure, would be preferred. If one's goal were long-term, expansive, independent vocabulary learning, regular independent reading combined with instruction in use of contextual and morphemic analysis would be the logical approach. In short, the simplicity of Graves and Prenn's statement, "[T]here is no one best method of teaching words," should not mask its importance.

What about a comprehensive program of vocabulary instruction? We have outlined 10 principles above that might be used to guide decision making in vocabulary instruction, but what about the substance or content of such a comprehensive program? What would be the objectives of it, and what would be the means to reach those objectives? Relatively few writers have addressed this issue directly (Beck et al., 1987; Kame'enui et al., 1987; McKeown & Beck, 1988; being the exceptions). We conclude our review with three instructional objectives and corresponding means to achieve each. In doing this, we draw from the empirical evidence on vocabulary teaching and learning; a similar plan outlined by Graves (1987) and more recently by Baker et al., (1998a); and our own intuition, common sense, biases, and beliefs. We have organized the components according to an objective/means format.

### Objective 1: Teach students to learn words independently

### Means to achieve objective 1.

1. Have students listen to live and recorded oral discourse. Read to them and have them listen to stories, books, plays, songs, poems, fiction and nonfiction prose, and simple conversation. It would be very unwise to underestimate the power of simple oral exposure to vocabulary.

2. Promote wide independent reading at home and school. Make independent reading a regular, significant part of the language arts curriculum. We believe in the power of incidental learning of vocabulary, but incidental word learning cannot rely on accidental reading.

3. Engage students in oral and written composition on a regular and sustained basis. Have students express themselves in writing and speech daily. Generative processes must be used and exercised if receptive vocabulary is to become expressive.

4. Teach students formally and directly the transferable and generalizable vocabulary learning strategies of morphemic and contextual analysis. It is likely that this instruction will enhance students' ability to acquire word meanings incidentally from written and oral texts.

5. Teach students to use regular and specialized dictionaries and the thesaurus. This instruction may be mundane, but skilled and timely use of these tools is essential for later sustained and independent vocabulary growth.

6. Provide students with activities that allow them to explore the richness and subtlties of word meanings in natural contexts (Scott, Butler, Asselin, & Henry, 1996), and provide them opportunities to make choices about and to assume responsibility for which vocabulary to learn (Fisher et al., 1996).

### Objective 2: Teach students the meanings of specific words

### Means to achieve objective 2.

1. Teach synonyms or definitions for specific words through rote or mnemonic strategies. There will be times when students must learn labels for limited numbers of words; in those situations, select the most efficient and cost effective approaches.

2. Provide students partial knowledge of many unknown words. Simple definitional strategies or preexposure prior to reading or listening will provide students a foot-in-the-door level of knowledge for words that they may learn more deeply and fully over time with additional subsequent exposures.

3. Preteach critical vocabulary necessary to comprehend selections students read in basal readers and in content area textbooks. Deep, rich levels of word knowledge are needed in order to affect text comprehension, and costly strategies such as semantic relatedness or definitional/context methods must be employed in order to achieve this objective.

### Objective 3: Help students to develop an appreciation for words and to experience enjoyment and satisfaction in their use

### Means to achieve objective 3.

1. Set a positive model. Demonstrate how word play can be interesting and enjoyable by expressing the value in possessing a versatile vocabulary and by demonstrating how word learning can be interesting and fun.

2. Have fun with words. Play word games linked to content topics and ones that may be done purely for entertainment and enjoyment.

3. Promote student use of vocabulary learned at school in nonschool contexts (e.g., Beck & McKeown's, 1983, "Word Wizard").

We acknowledge that several of the preceding objectives and means are based as much upon our intuition and beliefs as on hard data. We do not apologize for this, for we offer them more to challenge researchers and developers than to present them as truth. We await eagerly the generation of data that will affirm or refute what we now conceive to be an appropriately balanced vocabulary instructional program. Stated alternatively, time will tell whether we should have selected pseudonyms when we wrote and revised this chapter.

In closing, having completed this revision, we still recognize that it was relatively easy to express what we know and don't know about vocabulary acquisition and what works and does not work in vocabulary instruction. It was quite another matter to translate this knowledge into sound pedagogy. In short, the bridge from theory to practice is shrouded in mist and haunted by all sorts of insalubrious creatures. Therefore, we agree with Voltaire that "[L]anguage is very difficult to put into words." However, as educators, we find the reciprocal of Voltaire's statement even more challenging: Words are indeed very difficult to put into language (instruction).

---

## ACKNOWLEDGMENTS

The authors thank Camille Blachowicz, Margaret McKeown, and Judith Scott for their most helpful comments on earlier versions of this revised chapter.

---

## *References*

Adams, M., & Collins, A. (1979). A schema-theoretic view of reading. In R. Freedle (Ed.), *New directions in discourse processing,* Norwood, NJ: Ablex.

Ahlfors, G. (1979). *Learning word meanings: A comparison of three instructional procedures.* Unpublished doctoral dissertation, University of Minnesota, Minneapolis.

Anders, P. L., & Bos, C. S. (1986). Semantic feature analysis: An interactive strategy for vocabulary development and text comprehension. *Journal of Reading, 39,* 610-616.

Anders, P. L., Bos, C. S., & Filip, D. (1984). The effect of semantic feature analysis on the reading comprehension of learning-disabled students. In J. A. Niles & L. A. Harris (Eds.). *Changing perspectives on research in reading/language processing and instruction: Thirty-third yearbook of the National Reading Conference* (Vol. 33, pp. 162-166). Rochester, NY: National Reading Conferece.

Anderson, R. C. (1990). Inferences about word meanings. In A. C. Graesser, & G. H. Bowen (Eds.), *The psychology of learning and motivation* (Vol. 25, pp. 1-15). San Diego: Academic Press.

Anderson, R. C. (1996). Research foundations to support wide reading. In V. Greaney (Ed.), *Promoting reading in developing countries* (pp. 55-77). Newark, DE: International Reading Association.

Anderson, R. C., & Freebody, P. (1981). Vocabulary knowledge. In J. T. Guthrie (Ed.), *Comprehension and teaching* (pp. 77-117). Newark, DE: International Reading Association.

Anderson, R. C., & Freebody, P. (1983). Reading comprehension and the assessment and acquisition of word knowledge. In B. Hutson (Ed.), *Advances in reading/language research: A research annual* (pp. 231-256). Greenwich, CT: JAI Press.

Anderson, R. C., & Nagy, W. (1991). Word meanings. In R. Barr, M. Kamil, P. Mosenthal, & P. D. Pearson (Eds.), *Handbook of reading research* (Vol. 2, pp. 690-724). New York: Longman.

Anderson, R. C., & Pearson, P. D. (1984). A schema-theoretic view of basic processes in reading comprehension. In P. D. Pearson (Ed.), *Handbook of reading research* (pp. 255-291). New York: Longman.

Anderson, R. C., Wilson, P. T., & Fielding, L. G. (1986). *Growth in reading and how children spend their time outside of school* (Tech. Rep. No. 389). Urbana: University of Illinois, Center for the Study of Reading.

Anderson, R. C., Wilson, P. T., & Fielding, L. G. (1988). Growth in reading and how children spend their time outside of school. *Reading Research Quarterly, 23*(3), 285-303.

Anglin, J. M. (1977). *Word, object, and conceptual development.* New York: Norton.

Anglin, J. M. (1993). Vocabulary development: A morphological analysis. *Monographs of the Society for Research in Child Development, 58* (10, Serial No. 238).

Askov, E. N., & Kamm, K. (1976). Context clues: Should we teach children to use a classification system in reading? *Journal of Educational Research, 69,* 341-344.

Atkinson, R. C. (1975). Mnemotechnics in second-language learning. *American Psychologist, 30,* 821-828.

Baker, S. K., Simmons, D. C., Kame'enui, E. J. (1998a). Vocabulary acquisition: Instructional and curricular basics and implications. In D. C. Simmons & E. J. Kame'enui (Eds.), *What reading research tells us about children with diverse learning needs* (pp. 219-238). Mahwah, NJ: Lawrence Erlbaum Associates.

Baker, S. K., Simmons, D. C., Kame'enui, E. J. (1998b). Vocabulary acquisition: Research bases. In D. C. Simmons & E. J. Kame'enui (Eds.), *What reading research tells us about children with diverse learning needs* (pp. 183-217). Mahwah, NJ: Lawrence Erlbaum Associates.

Baldwin, R. S., & Schatz, E. L. (1985). Context clues are ineffective with low frequency words in naturally occurring prose. In J. A. Niles & R. V. Lalik (Eds.), *Issues in literacy: A research perspective: Thirty-fourth yearbook of the National Reading Conference* (Vol. 34, pp. 132-135). Rochester, NY: National Reading Conference.

Barr, R., & Sadow, M. W. (1989). Influence of basal programs on fourth grade reading instruction. *Reading Research Quarterly, 24*(1), 44-71.

Baumann, J. F. (1988). *Reading assessment: An instructional decision-making perspective.* Columbus, OH: Merrill.

Baumann, J. F., & Kame'enui, E. J. (1991). Research on vocabulary instruction: Ode to Voltaire. In J. Flood, J. M. Jensen, D. Lapp, & J. R. Squire (Eds.), *Handbook of research on teaching the English language arts* (pp. 604-632). New York: macMillan.

Bean, T. W., Inabinette, N. B., & Ryan, R. (1983). The effect of a categorization strategy on secondary students' retention of literary vocabulary. *Reading Psychology, 4,* 247-252.

Bean, T. W., Singer, H., & Cowan, S. (1984, December). *Acquisition of a topic schema in high school biology through an analogical study guide.* Paper presented at the meeting of the National Reading Conference, St. Petersburg, FL.

Bean, T. W., Singer, H., & Cowan, S. (1985). Analogical study guides: Improving comprehension in science. *Journal of Reading, 29,* 246-250.

Beck, I. L. (1984). Developing comprehension: The impact of the directed reading lesson. In R. C. Anderson, J. Osborn, & R. J. Tierney (Eds.), *Learning to read in American schools* (pp. 3–20). Hillsdale, NJ: Lawrence Erlbaum Associates.

Beck, I. L., McCaslin, E. S., & McKeown, M. G. (1980). *The rationale and design of a program to teach vocabulary to fourth-grade students* (LRDC Publication 1980/25). Pittsburgh, PA: University of Pittsburgh, Learning Research and Development Center.

Beck, I. L., & McKeown, M. G. (1983). Learning words well—A program to enhance vocabulary and comprehension. *The Reading Teacher, 36,* 622–625.

Beck, I. L., & McKeown, M. G. (1987). Getting the most from basal reading selections. *Elementary School Journal, 87,* 343–356.

Beck, I. L., & McKeown, M. G. (1991). Conditions of vocabulary acquisition. In R. Barr, M. Kamil, P. Mosenthal, & P. D. Pearson (Eds.), *Handbook of reading research* (Vol. 2, pp. 789–814). New York: Longman.

Beck, I. L., McKeown, M. G., & McCaslin, E. S. (1983). Vocabulary development: All contexts are not created equal. *Elementary School Journal, 83,* 177–181.

Beck, I. L., McKeown, M. G., McCaslin, E. S., & Burkes, A. M. (1979). *Instructional dimensions that may affect reading comprehension: Examples from two commercial reading programs* (LRDC Publication 1979/20). Pittsburgh, PA: University of Pittsburgh, Learning Research and Development Center.

Beck, I. L., McKeown, M. G., & Omanson, R. C. (1984, April). *The fertility of some types of vocabulary instruction.* Paper presented at the meeting of the American Educational Research Association, New Orleans.

Beck, I. L., McKeown, M. G., & Omanson, R. C. (1987). The effects and uses of diverse vocabulary instructional techniques. In M. G. McKeown & M. E. Curtis (Eds.), *The nature of vocabulary acquisition* (pp. 147–163). Hillsdale, NJ: Lawrence Erlbaum Associates.

Beck, I. L., Perfetti, C. A., & McKeown, M. G. (1982). Effects of long-term vocabulary instruction on lexical access and reading comprehension. *Journal of Educational Psychology, 74,* 506–521.

Becker, W. C. (1977). Teaching reading and language to the disadvantaged—What we have learned from field research. *Harvard Educational Review, 47,* 518–543.

Becker, W. C., Dixon, R., & Anderson-Inman, L. (1980). *Morphographic and root word analysis of 26,000 high frequency words* (Tech. Rep. No. 1980-1). Eugene: University of Oregon Follow Through Project, College of Education.

Blachowicz, C. L. Z. (1985). Vocabulary development and reading: From research to instruction. *The Reading Teacher, 38,* 876–881.

Blachowlcz, C. L. Z. (1986). Making connections: Alternatives to the vocabulary notebook. *Journal of Reading, 29,* 643–649.

Blachowicz, C. L. Z. (1987). Vocabulary instruction: What goes on in the classroom? *The Reading Teacher, 41,* 132–137.

Blachowicz, C. L. Z., & Fisher, P. (1996). *Teaching vocabulary in all classrooms.* Englewood Cliffs, NJ: Merrill/Prentice-Hall.

Blachowicz, C. L. Z., & Fisher, P. (2000). Vocabulary instruction. In R. Barr, P. Mosenthal, P. D. Pearson, & M. Kamil (Eds.), *Handbook of Reading Research* (Vol. 3, pp. 503–523). Hillsdale, NJ: Lawrence Erlbaum Associates.

Bos, C. S., Anders, P. L., Filip, D., & Jaffe, L. E. (1985). Semantic feature analysis and long-term learning. In J. A. Niles & R. V. Lalik (Eds.), *Issues in literacy: A research perspective: Thirty-fourth yearbook of the National Reading Conference* (Vol. 34, pp. 42–47). Rochester, NY: National Reading Conference.

Brett, A., Rothlein, L., & Hurley, M. (1996). Vocabulary acquisition from listening to stories and explanations of target words. *Elementary School Journal, 96,* 415–421.

Buikema, J. L., & Graves, M. F. (1993). Teaching students to use context cues to infer word meanings. *Journal of Reading, 36*(6), 450–457.

Calfee, R., & Drum, P. (1986). Research on teaching reading. In M. C. Wittrock (Ed.), *Handbook of research on teaching* (3rd ed. pp. 804–849). New York: Macmillan.

Carey, S. (1978). Child as word learner. In M. Halle, J. Bresnam, & G. Miller (Eds.), *Linguistic theory and psychological reality* (pp. 264–293). Cambridge, MA: MIT Press.

Carnine, D. W., Kame'enui, E. J., & Coyle, G. (1984). Utilization of contextual information in determining the meaning of unfamiliar words. *Reading Research Quarterly, 19,* 188–204.

Carnine, D. W., Kame'enui, E. J., & Woolfson, N. (1982). Training textual dimensions related to text-based inferences. *Journal of Reading Behavior, 14,* 331–340.

Carnine, D. W., Silbert, J., & Kame'enui, E. J. (1990). *Direct instruction reading* (2nd ed.). Columbus, OH: Merrill.

Carr, E. M. (1985). The vocabulary overview guide: A metacognitive strategy to improve vocabulary comprehension and retention. *Journal of Reading, 28,* 648–689.

Carr, E. M., & Mazur-Stewart, M. (1988). The effects of the vocabulary overview guide on vocabulary comprehension and retention. *Journal of Reading Behavior, 20*(1), 43–62.

Carr, E. M., & Wixson, K. K. (1986). Guidelines for evaluating vocabulary instruction. *Journal of Reading, 29,* 588–595.

Carroll, B. A., & Drum, P. A. (1982). The effects of context clue type and variations in content on the comprehension of unknown words. In J. A. Niles & L. A. Harris (Eds.), *New inquiries in reading research and instruction: Thirty-first yearbook of the National Reading Conference* (Vol. 31, pp. 89–93). Rochester, NY: National Reading Conference.

Carroll, B. A., & Drum, P. A. (1983). Definitional gains for explicit and implicit context clues. In J. A. Niles & L. A. Harris (Eds.), *Searches for meaning in reading/language processing & instruction: Thirty-second yearbook of the National Reading Conference* (Vol. 32, pp. 158–162). Rochester, NY: National Reading Conference.

Carver, R. P. (1994). Percentage of unknown vocabulary words in text as a function of the relative difficulty of the text: Implications for instruction. *Journal of Reading Behavior, 26*(4), 413–437.

Chall, J. S. (1987). Two vocabularies for reading: Recognition and meaning. In M. G. McKeown & M. E. Curtis (Eds.), *The nature of vocabulary acquisition* (pp. 7–17). Hillsdale, NJ: Lawrence Erlbaum Associates.

Chall, J. S. & Squire, J. R. (1991). The publishing industry and textbooks. In R. Barr, M. Kamil, P. Mosenthal, & P. D. Pearson (Eds.), *Handbook of reading research* (Vol. 2, pp. 120–146). New York: Longman.

Chase, A. C., & Duffelmeyer, F. A. (1990). VOCAB-LIT: Integrating vocabulary study and literature study. *Journal of Reading, 34*(3), 188–193.

Clark, E. V. (1973). What's in a word? On the child's acquisition of semantics in his first language. In T. E. Moore (Ed.), *Cognitive development and the acquisition of language* (pp. 65–110). New York: Academic Press.

Cole, L. (1946). *The elementary school subjects.* New York: Rinehart.

Cooper, J. D. (1986). *Improving reading comprehension.* Boston: Houghton Mifflin.

Corson, D. (1989). Adolescent lexical differences in Australia and England by social group. *Journal of Educational Research, 82*(3), 146–157.

Crowder, R. G. (1976). *Principles of learning and memory.* Hillsdale, NJ: Lawrence Erlbaum Associates.

Cunningham, A., & Stanovich, K. E. (1991). Tracking unique effects of print exposure in children: Associations with vocabulary, general knowledge, and spelling. *Journal of Educational Psychology, 83,* 264-274.

Cunningham, A., & Stanovich, K. E. (Spring/Summer 1998). What reading does for the mind. *American Educator,* 8-15.

Cunningham, P. M. (1987). Are your vocabulary words lunules or lupulins? *Journal of Reading, 30,* 344-348.

Curtis, M. E. (1987). Vocabulary testing and instruction. In M. G. McKeown & M. E. Curtis (Eds.), *The nature of vocabulary acquisition* (pp. 37-51), Hillsdale, NJ: Lawrence Erlbaum Associates.

Daalen-Kapteijns, M. M. van, & Elshout-Mohr, M. (1981). The acquisition of word meanings as a cognitive verbal process. *Journal of Verbal Learning and Verbal Behavior, 20,* 386-399.

Dale, E., O'Rourke, J., & Bamman, H. A. (1971). *Techniques of teaching vocabulary.* Palo Alto, CA: Field Educational Publications.

Dale, E., & Razik, T. (1963). *Bibliography of vocabulary studies.* Columbus: Ohio State University Bureau of Educational Research and Service.

Dale, E., Razik, T., & Petty, W. (1973). *Bibliography of vocabulary studies.* Columbus: Ohio State University.

D'Anna, C. A., Zechmeister, E. B., & Hall, J. W. (1991). Toward a meaningful definition of vocabulary size. *Journal of Reading Behavior, 23*(1), 109-122.

Davis, F. B. (1944). Fundamental factors in reading comprehension. *Psychometrika, 9,* 185-197.

Davis, F. B. (1968). Research in comprehension in reading. *Reading Research Quarterly, 3,* 499-545.

Dickinson, D. K., Cote, L., & Smith, M. W. (1993). Learning vocabulary in preschool: Social and discourse contexts affecting vocabulary growth. In C. Daiute (Ed.), *The development of literacy through social interaction* (New Directions for Child Development, No. 61, pp. 67-78). San Francisco, CA: Jossey-Bass.

Dickinson, D. K., & Smith, M. W. (1994). Long-term effects of preschool teachers' book readings on low-income children's vocabulary and story comprehension. *Reading Research Quarterly, 29*(2), 104-122.

Dixon, R. C., & Jenkins, J. R. (1984). *An outcome analysis of receptive vocabulary knowledge.* Unpublished manuscript, University of Illinois, Champaign-Urbana.

Dole, J. A., Sloan, C., & Trathen, W. (1995). Teaching vocabulary within the context of literature. *Journal of Reading, 38*(6), 452-460.

Drum, P. A., & Konopak, B. C. (1987). Learning word meanings from written context. In M. G. McKeown & M. E. Curtis (Eds.), *The nature of vocabulary acquisition* (pp. 73-87). Hillsdale, NJ: Lawrence Erlbaum Associates.

Duffelmeyer, F. A. (1980). The influence of experience-based vocabulary instruction on learning word meanings. *Journal of Reading, 24,* 35-40.

Duffelmeyer, F. A. (1985). Teaching word meaning from an experience base. *The Reading Teacher, 39,* 6-9.

Duffy, G. G., & Roehler, L. R. (1986). *Improving classroom reading instruction: A decision-making approach.* New York: Random House.

Duin, A. H., & Graves, M. F. (1987). Intensive vocabulary instruction as a prewriting technique. *Reading Research Quarterly, 22,* 311-330.

Duin, A. H., & Graves, M. F. (1988). Teaching vocabulary as a writing prompt. *Journal of Reading, 32,* 204-212.

Durkin, D. D. (1978-79). What classroom observations reveal about reading comprehension instruction. *Reading Research Quarterly, 14,* 481-533.

Durkin, D. D. (1981a). Reading comprehension instruction in five basal reader series. *Reading Research Quarterly, 16,* 515-544.

Durkin, D. D. (1981b). *Strategies for identifying words* (2nd ed.), Boston: Allyna & Bacon.

Durkin, D. D. (1984). Is there a match between what elementary teachers do and what basal reader manuals recommend? *The Reading Teacher, 37,* 734-744.

Durso, F. T., & Shore, W. J. (1991). Partial knowledge of word meanings. *Journal of Experimental Psychology: General, 120*(2), 190-202.

Eeds, M., & Cockrum, W. A. (1985). Teaching word meanings by expanding schemata vs. dictionary work vs. reading in context. *Journal of Reading, 28,* 492-497.

Eller, R. G., Pappas, C. C., & Brown, E. (1988). The lexical development of kindergarteners: Learning from written context. *Journal of Reading Behavior, 20*(1), 5-24.

Elley, W. B. (1989). Vocabulary acquisition from listening to stories. *Reading Research Quarterly, 24*(2), 174-187.

Fisher, P. J. L., Blachowicz, C. L. Z., & Smith, J. C. (1991). Vocabulary learning in literature discussion groups. In J. Zuttell & S. McCormick (Eds.), *Learner factors/teacher factors: Issues in literacy research and instruction: Fortieth yearbook of the National Reading Conference* (pp. 201-217). Chicago: National Reading Conference.

Frayer, D. A., Frederick, W. C., & Klausmeir, H. J. (1969). *A schema for testing the level of concept mastery* (Working Paper No. 16). Madison: University of Wisconsin, Wisconsin Research and Development Center for Cognitive Learning.

Freebody, P., & Anderson, R. C. (1981). *Effects of differing proportions and locations of difficult vocabulary on text comprehension.* (Tech. Rep. No. 202). Champaign: University of Illinois, Center for the Study of Reading.

Freebody, P., & Anderson, R. C. (1983). Effects of vocabulary difficulty, text cohesion, and schema availability, on reading comprehension. *Reading Research Quarterly, 18,* 277-294.

Freyd, P., & Baron, J. (1982). Individual differences in acquisition of derivational morphology. *Journal of Verbal Learning and Verbal Behavior, 21,* 282-295.

Gage, N. L. (Ed.) (1963). *Handbook of research on teaching.* Chicago: Rand McNally.

Gates, A. I. (1961). Vocabulary control in basal reading material. *The Reading Teacher, 15,* 81.

Gates, A. I. (1962). The word recognition ability and the reading vocabulary of second and third grade children. *The Reading Teacher, 15,* 443-448.

Gipe, J. P. (1978-79). Investigating techniques for teaching word meanings. *Reading Research Quarterly, 14,* 624-645.

Glaser, R. (Chair). (1984, April). *What is the role of instruction in learning and using vocabulary?* Symposium conducted at the meeting of the American Educational Research Association, New Orleans.

Goodman, K. S., Shannon, P., Freeman, Y. S., & Murphy, S. (1988). *Report card on basal readers.* Katonah, NY: Owen.

Gordon, J., Schumm, J. S., Offland, C., & Doucette, M. (1992). Effects of inconsiderate versus considerate text on elementary students' vocabulary learning. *Reading Psychology, 13,* 157-169.

Goulden, R., Nation, P., & Read, J. (1990). How large can a receptive vocabulary be? *Applied Linguistics, 11,* 341-363.

Graves, M. F. (1980, April). *A quantitative and qualitative study of students' reading vocabularies.* Paper presented at the meeting of the American Educational Research Association, Boston.

Graves, M. F. (1984). Selecting vocabulary to teach in the intermediate and secondary grades. In J. Flood (Ed.), *Promoting reading comprehension* (pp. 245-260). Newark, DE: International Reading Association.

Graves, M. F. (1986). Vocabulary learning and instruction. In E. Z. Rothkopf (Ed.), *Review of research in education* (Vol. 13, pp. 49-89). Washington, DC: American Educational Research Association.

Graves, M. F. (1987). The roles of instruction in fostering vocabulary development. In M. G. McKeown & M. E. Curtis (Eds.), *The nature of vocabulary acquisition* (pp. 165–184). Hillsdale, NJ: Lawrence Erlbaum Associates.

Graves, M. F. (1989). A quantitative and qualitative study of elementary school children's vocabularies. *Journal of Educational Research, 82*(4), 203–209.

Graves, M. F., & Hammond, H. K. (1980). A validated procedure for teaching prefixes and its effect on students' ability to assign meaning to novel words. In M. L., Kamil & A. J. Moe (Eds), *Perspectives on reading research and instruction: Twenty-ninth yearbook of the National Reading Conference* (Vol. 29, pp. 184–188). Washington, DC: National Reading Conference.

Graves, M. F., & Prenn, M. C. (1986). Costs and benefits at various methods of teaching vocabulary. *Journal of Reading, 29,* 596–602.

Hafner, L. E. (1965). A one-month experiment in teaching context aids in fifth grade. *Journal of Educational Research, 58,* 471–474.

Hagen, J. E. (1980). The effects of selected prereading vocabulary building activities on literal comprehension, vocabulary understanding, and attitudes of fourth and fifth grade students with reading problems (Doctoral dissertation, University of Wisconsin, Madison, 1980). *Dissertation Abstracts International, 40,* 6216A. (University Microfilms No. 80-07, 553)

Hagen-Heimlich, J. E., & Pittelman, S. D. (1984). *Classroom application of the semantic mapping procedure in reading and writing* (Program Report No. 84-4). Madison: University of Wisconsin, Wisconsin Center for Education Research.

Haggard, M. R. (1982). The vocabulary self-collection strategy: An active approach to word learning. *Journal of Reading, 26,* 203–207.

Haggard, M. R. (1985). An interactive strategies approach to content reading. *Journal of Reading, 29,* 204–210.

Haggard, M. R. (1986). The vocabulary self-collection strategy: Using student interest and word knowledge to enhance vocabulary growth. *Journal of Reading, 29,* 634–612.

Hanf, M. B. (1971). Mapping: A technique for translating reading into thinking. *Journal of Reading, 14,* 225–230.

Hanson, I. W. (1966). First grade children work with variant word endings. *The Reading Teacher, 19,* 505–507, 511.

Hart, B., & Risley, T. R. (1995). *Meaningful differences in the everyday experience of young American children.* Baltimore, MD: Brookes.

Hayes, D. P., & Ahrens, M. (1988). Vocabulary simplification for children: A special case of "motherese." *Journal of Child Language, 15,* 395–410.

Harris, T. L., & Hodges, R. C. (Eds.) (1981). *A dictionary of reading and related terms.* Newark, DE: International Reading Association.

Heimlich, J. E., & Pittelman, S. D. (1986). *Semantic mapping: Classroom applications.* Newark, DE: International Reading Association.

Herman, P. A., Anderson, R. C., Pearson, P. D., & Nagy, W. E. (1987). Incidental acquisition of word meaning from expositions with varied text features. *Reading Research Quarterly, 22,* 263–284.

Herman, P. A., & Dole, J. (1988). Theory and practice in vocabulary learning and instruction. *Elementary School Journal, 89,* 43–54.

Higgins, N. C., & Cocks, P. (1999). The effects of animation cues on vocabulary development. *Reading Psychology, 20*(1), 1–10.

Ignoffo, M. F. (1980). The thread of thought: Analogies as a vocabulary building method. *Journal of Reading, 23,* 519–521.

Jackson, J. R., & Dizney, H. (1963). Intensive vocabulary training. *Journal of Developmental Reading, 6,* 221–229.

Jenkins, J. R., & Dixon, R. (1983). Learning vocabulary. *Contemporary Educational Psychology, 8,* 237–260.

Jenkins, J. R., Matlock, B., & Slocum, T. A. (1989). Approaches to vocabulary instruction: The teaching of individual word meanings and practice in deriving word "meaning from context. *Reading research Quarterly, 24,* 215–235.

Jenkins, J. R., Stein, M. L., & Wysocki, K. (1984). Learning vocabulary

through reading. *American Educational Research Journal, 21,* 767–787.

Johnson, D. D. (1984). Expanding vocabulary through classification. In J. F. Baumann & D. D. Johnson (Eds.), *Reading instruction and the beginning teacher: A practical guide* (pp. 28–38). Minneapolis, MN: Burgess.

Johnson, D. D. (Ed.) (1986). Vocabulary [Special issue]. *Journal of Reading, 29*(7).

Johnson, D. D., & Baumann, J. F. (1984). Word identification. In P. D. Pearson (Ed.), *Handbook of reading research* (pp. 583–608). New York: Longman.

Johnson, D. D., & Johnson, B. V. (1986). Highlighting vocabulary in inferential comprehension instruction. *Journal of Reading, 29,* 622–625.

Johnson, D. D., Levin, K. M., & Pittelman, S. D. (1984). *A field assessment of vocabulary instruction in the elementary school classroom* (Program Rep. No. 84-3). Madison: University of Wisconsin, Wisconsin Center for Education Research.

Johnson, D. D., & Pearson, P. D. (1984). *Teaching reading vocabulary* (2nd ed.), New York: Holt, Rinehart, and Winston.

Johnson, D. D., Pittelman, S. D., & Helmlich, J. E. (1986). Semantic mapping. *The Reading Teacher, 39,* 778–783.

Johnson, D. D., Pittelman, S. D., Toms-Bronowski, S., Chu-Chang, M., Tsul, G., Yin., M. C., Chien, C. Y., & Chin, P. (1982). *Studies of vocabulary development techniques in the United States of America and the Republic of China* (Program Rep. No. 83-4). Madison: University of Wisconsin, Wisconsin Centre for Education Research.

Johnson, D. D., Pittelman, S. D., Toms-Bronowski, S., & Levin, K. M. (1984). *An investigation of the effects of prior knowledge and vocabulary acquistion on passage comprehension* (Program Rep. No. 84-5). Madison: University of Wisconsin, Wisconsin Center for Education Research.

Johnson, D. D., Toms-Bronowski, S., & Pittelman, S. D. (1982). *An investigation of the effectiveness of semantic mapping and semantic feature analysis with intermediate grade level students* (Program Rep. No. 83-3). Madison: University of Wisconsin, Wisconsin Center for Education Research.

Jones, S. T. (1984). *The effects of semantic mapping on vocabulary acquisition and reading comprehension of innercity black students.* Unpublished doctoral dissertation, University of Wisconsin, Madison.

Just, M. A., & Carpenter, P. A. (1987). *The psychology of reading and language comprehension.* Newton, MA: Allyn & Bacon.

Kame'enui, E. J., Carnine, D. W., & Freschi, R. (1982). Effects of text construction and instructional procedures for teaching word meanings on comprehension and recall. *Reading Research Quarterly, 17,* 367–388.

Kame'enui, E. J., Dixon, D. W., & Carnine, R. C. (1987). Issues in the design of vocabulary instruction. In M. G. McKeown & M. E. Curtis (Eds.), *The nature of vocabulary acquisition* (pp. 129–145). Hillsdale, NJ: Lawrence Erlbaum Associates.

Kame'enui, E. J., & Simmons, D. (1990). *Designing instructional strategies for the prevention of academic learning problems.* Columbus, OH: Merrill.

Kame'enui, E. J., Simmons, D., & Darch, C. (1987). Learning disabled children's comprehension of selected textual characteristics: Proximity of critical information. *Learning Disabilities Quarterly, 10,* 237–248.

Karbon, J. C. (1984). *An investigation of the relationships between prior knowledge and vocabulary development using semantic mapping with culturally diverse students.* Unpublished doctoral dissertation, University of Wisconsin, Madison.

King-Sears, M. E., Mercer, C. D., Sindelar, P. T. (1992). Toward independence with keyword mnemonics: A strategy for science vocabulary instruction. *Remedial and Special Education, 13*(5), 22–33.

Klein, M. L. (1988). *Teaching reading comprehension and vocabulary: A guide for teachers.* Englewood Cliffs, NJ: Prentice-Hall.

Kolich, E. M. (1991). Effects of computer-assisted vocabulary training on word knowledge. *Journal of Educational Research, 84*(1), 177-182.

Konopak, B. C. (1988a). Effects of inconsiderate vs. considerate text on secondary students' vocabulary learning. *Journal of Reading Behavior, 20*(1), 25-41.

Konopak, B. C. (1988b). Eighth graders' vocabulary learning from inconsiderate and considerate text. *Reading Research and instruction, 27,* 1-14.

Krashen, S. (1989). We acquire vocabulary and spelling by reading: Additional evidence for the input hypothesis. *The Modern Language Journal, 73*(4), 440-464.

Kuhn, M. R., & Stahl, S. A. (1998). Teaching children to learn word meanings from context: A synthesis and some questions. *Journal of Literacy Research, 30*(1), 119-138.

Leung, C. B. (1992). Effects of word-related variables on vocabulary growth through repeated read-aloud events. In C. K. Kinzer & D. J. Leu (Eds.), *Literacy research, theory, and practice: Views from many perspectives: Forty-first yearbook of the National Reading Conference* (pp. 491-498). Chicago: National Reading Conference.

Leung, C. B., & Pikulski, J. J. (1990). Incidental learning of word meanings by kindergarten and first grade children through repeated read aloud events. In J. Zuttell & S. McCormick (Eds.), *Literacy theory and research: Analyses from multiple paradigms: Thirty-ninth yearbook of the National Reading Conference* (pp. 231-239). Chicago: National Reading Conference.

Levin, J. R. (1985). Educational applications of mnemonic pictures: Possibilities beyond your wildest imagination. In A. A. Sheikh (Ed.), *Imagery in the educational process* (pp. 63-87). Farmingdale, NY: Baywood.

Levin, J. R., Johnson, D. D., Pittelman, S. D., Levin, K. M., Shriberg, L. K., Toms-Bronowski, S., & Hayes, B. L. (1984). A comparison of semantic- and mnemonic-based vocabulary learning strategies. *Reading Psychology, 5,* 1-15.

Levin, J. R., Levin, M. E., Glasman, L. D., & Nordwall, M. B. (1992). Mnemonic vocabulary instruction: Additional effectiveness evidence. *Contemporary Educational Psychology, 17,* 156-174.

Levin, J. R., McCormick, C. B., Miller, G. E., Berry, J. K., & Pressley, M. (1982). Mnemonic versus nonmnemonic vocabulary-learning strategies for children. *American Educational Research Journal, 19,* 121-136.

Levin, J. R., & Pressley, M. (1985). Mnemonic vocabulary instruction: What's fact, what's fiction. In R. F. Dillon (Ed.), *Individual differences in cognition* (Vol. 2, pp. 145-172). New York: Academic Press.

MacGinite, W. H. (1978). *Gates-MacGinite reading tests.* Boston: Houghton Mifflin.

Madison, J. Y., Carroll, B. A., & Drum, P. A. (1982). The effects of directionality and proximity of context clues on the comprehension of unknown words. In J. A. Niles & L. A. Harris (Eds.), *New inquiries in reading research and instruction; Thirty-first yearbook of the National Reading Conference* (Vol. 31, pp. 105-109). Rochester, NY: National Reading Conference.

Manzo, A. V. (1983). "Subjective approach to vocabulary" acquisition ("or...I think my brother is arboreall"). *Reading Psychology, 3,* 155-160.

Manzo, A., & Sherk, J. (1972). Some generalizations and strategies to guide vocabulary acquisition. *Journal of Reading Behavior, 4,* 78-89.

Margosein, C. M., Pascarella, E. T., & Pflaum, S. W. (1982, April). *The effects of instruction using semantic mapping on vocabulary and comprehension.* Paper presented at the annual meeting of the American Educational Research Association, New York.

Marzano, R. J. (1984). A cluster approach to vocabulary instruction. *The Reading Teacher, 38,* 168-173.

Marzano, R. J., & Marzano, J. S. (1988). *A cluster approach to elementary vocabulary instruction.* Newark, DE: International Reading Association.

Mason, J. M., & Au, K. H. (1986). *Reading instruction for today.* Glenview, IL: Scott, Foresman.

Mastropleri, M. A., Scruggs, T. E., & Levin, J. R. (1985). Maximizing what exceptional children can learn: A review of research on the keyword method and related mnemonic techniques. *Remedial and Special Education, 6,* 39-45.

McDaniel, M. A., & Pressley, M. (1984). Putting the keyword method in context. *Journal of Educational Psychology, 76,* 598-609.

McDaniel, M. A., & Pressley, M. (1989). Keyword and context instruction of new vocabulary meanings: Effect on text comprehension and memory. *Journal of Educational Psychology, 81*(2), 204-213.

McDaniel, M. A., & Pressley, M., & Dunay, P. K. (1987). Long-term retention of vocabulary learning after keyword and context learning. *Journal of Educational Psychology, 79,* 87-89.

McDaniel, M. A., & Tillman, V. P. (1987). Discovering a meaning versus applying the keyword method: Effects on recall. *Contemporary Educational Psychology, 12,* 156-175.

McKeown, M. G. (1985). The acquisition of word meaning from context by children of high and low ability. *Reading Research Quarterly, 20,* 482-496.

McKeown, M. G. (1993). Creating effective definitions for young word learners. *Reading Research Quarterly, 28*(1), 16-31.

McKeown, M. G., & Beck, I. L. (1988). Learning vocabulary: Different ways for different goals. *Remedial and Special Education, 9,* 42-46.

McKeown, M. G., Beck, I. L., Omanson, R., & Perfetti, C. A. (1983). The effects of long-term vocabulary instruction on reading comprehension: A replication. *Journal of Reading Behavior, 15,* 3-18.

McKeown, M. G., Beck, I. L., Omanson, R., & Pople, M. T. (1985). Some effects of the nature and frequency of vocabulary instruction on the knowledge and use of words. *Reading Research Quarterly, 20,* 522-535.

McKeown, M. G., & Curtis, M. E. (Eds.) (1987). *The nature of vocabulary acquisition.* Hillsdale, NJ: Lawrence Erlbaum Associates.

McNeil, J. D. (1987). *Reading comprehension: New directions for classroom practice* (2nd ed.). Glenview, IL: Scott, Foresman.

Medo, M. A., & Ryder, R. J. (1993). The effects of vocabulary instruction on reader's ability to make causal connections. *Reading Research and Instruction, 33*(2), 119-134.

Memory, D. M. (1990). Teaching technical vocabulary: Before, during, or after the reading assignment? *Journal of Reading Behavior, 22*(1), 39-53.

Mezynski, K. (1983). Issues concerning the acquisition of knowledge: Effects of vocabulary training on reading comprehension. *Review of Research in Education, 53,* 253-279.

Miller, G. A., & Gildea, P. M. (1987). How children learn words. *Scientific American, 257,* 94-99.

Mosenthal, P. (1984). The problem of partial specification in translating reading research into practice. *Elementary School Journal, 85,* 1-28.

Nagy, W. E. (1988). *Teaching vocabulary to improve reading comprehension.* Newark, DE: International Reading Association.

Nagy, W. E. (1998, February). *Address.* Paper presented at the Commissioner's Reading Day Challenge, Austin, TX.

Nagy, W. E., & Anderson, R. C. (1984). How many words are there in printed school English? *Reading Research Quarterly, 19,* 303-330.

Nagy, W. E., Anderson, R. C., & Herman, P. A. (1987). Learning word meanings from context during normal reading. *American Educational Research Journal, 24,* 237-270.

Nagy, W. E., Diakidoy, I. N., & Anderson, R. C. (1993). The acquisition of morphology: Learning the contribution of suffixes to the meanings of derivatives. *Journal of Reading Behavior, 25*(2), 155-170.

Nagy, W. E., & Herman, P. A. (1984). *Limitations of vocabulary instruction.* (Tech. Rep. No. 326). Urbana: University of Illinois. Center for the Study of Reading. (ERIC Document Reproduction Service No. ED 248 498).

Nagy, W. E., & Herman, P. A. (1987). Breadth and depth of vocabulary knowledge: Implications for acquisition and instruction. In M. G. McKeown & M. E. Curtis (Eds.), *The nature of vocabulary acquisition* (pp. 19-35). Hillsdale, NJ: Lawrence Erlbaum Associates.

Nagy, W. E., Herman, P. A., & Anderson, R. C. (1985). Learning words from context. *Reading Research Quarterly, 20,* 233-253.

Nagy, W., & Scott, J. (2000). Vocabulary Processing. In R. Barr, P. Mosenthal, P. D. Pearson, & M. Kamil (Eds.), *Handbook of Reading Research* (Vol. 3, pp. 269-284). Hillsdale, NJ: Lawrence Erlbaum Associates.

Nicol, J. E., & Graves, M. F. (1990). *Building vocabulary through prefix instruction.* Unpublished manuscript, University of Minnesota.

Nicholson, T., & Whyte, B. (1992). Matthew effects in learning new words while listening to stories. In C. K. Kinzer & D. J. Leu (Eds.), *Literacy research, theory, and practice: Views from many perspectives: Forty-first yearbook of the National Reading Conference* (pp. 499-503). Chicago: National Reading Conference.

Nist, S. L., & Olejnik, S. (1995). The role of context and dictionary definitions on varying levels of word knowledge. *Reading Research Quarterly, 30*(2), 172-193.

Otterman, L. M. (1995). The value of teaching prefixes and word-roots. *Journal of Educational Research, 48,* 611-616.

Pany, D., & Jenkins, J. R. (1978). Learning word meanings: A comparison of instructional procedures and effects on measures of reading comprehension with learning disabled students. *Learning Disability Quarterly, 1,* 21-32.

Pany, D., Jenkins, J. R., & Schreck, J. (1982). Vocabulary Instruction: Effects on word knowledge and reading comprehension. *Learning Disability Quarterly, 5,* 202-215.

Parker, S. I. (1984). *A comparison of four types of initial vocabulary instruction.* Unpublished master's thesis, University of Minnesota, Minneapolis.

Patberg, J. P., Graves, M. F., & Stibbe, M. A. (1984). Effects of active teaching and practice in facilitating students' use of context clues. *Changing perspectives on research in reading language processing and instruction. Thirty-third yearbook of the National Reading Conference* (Vol. 33, pp. 146-151). Rochester, NY: National Reading Conference.

Petty, W., Herold, C., & Stohl, E. (1967). *The state of the knowledge about the teaching of vocabulary* (Cooperative Research Project No. 3128). Urbana, IL: National Council of Teachers of English. (ERIC Document Reproduction Service No. ED 012 395)

Pittelman, S. D., Levin, K. M., & Johnson, D. D. (1985). *An investigation of two instructional settings in the use of semantic mapping with poor readers* (Program Rep. No. 85-4). Madison, WI: University of Wisconsin Center for Education Research.

Powell, W. R. (1986). Teaching vocabulary through opposition. *Journal of Reading, 29,* 617-621.

Pressley, M., Levin, J. R., & DeLaney, H. D. (1982). The mnemonic keyword method. *Review of Educational Research, 52,* 61-92.

Pressley, M., Levin, J. R., & McDaniel, M. A. (1987). Remembering versus inferring what a word means: Mnemonic and contextual approaches. In M. G. McKeown & M. E. Curtis (Eds.), *The nature of vocabulary acquisition* (pp. 107-127). Hillsdale, NJ: Lawrence Erlbaum Associates.

Pressley, M., Ross, K. A., Levin, J. R., & Ghatala, E. S. (1984). The role of strategy utility knowledge in children's strategy decision making. *Journal of Experimental Child Psychology, 38,* 491-504.

Reutzel, D. R. (1985). Reconciling schema, theory and the basal reading lesson. *The Reading Teacher, 39,* 194-197.

Reutzel, D. R., & Hollingsworth, P. M. (1988). Highlighting key vocabulary: A generative-reciprocal procedure for teaching selected inference types. *Reading Research Quarterly, 23,* 358-378.

Robbins, C., & Ehri, L. C. (1994). Reading storybooks to kindergartners helps them learn new vocabulary words. *Journal of Educational Psychology, 86*(1), 54-64.

Roberts, B. (1992). The evolution of the young child's concepts of *word* as a unit of spoken and written language. *Reading Research Quarterly, 27*(2), 124-138.

Rohwer, W. D. (1973). Elaboration and learning in childhood and adolescence. In H. W. Reese (Ed.), *Advances in child development and behavior* (Vol. 8, pp. 1-57). New York: Academic Press.

Roser, N., & Juel, C. (1982). Effect of vocabulary instruction on reading comprehension. In J. A. Niles & L. A. Harris (Eds.), *New inquiries in reading: Research and instruction: Thirty-first yearbook of the National Reading Converence* (Vol. 31, pp. 110-118). Rochester, NY: National Reading Conference.

Russell, D. H. (1954). The dimensions of children's meaning vocabulary in grades four through twelve. *University of California Publications in Education, 11,* 315-414.

Russell, D. H., & Fea, H. R. (1963). Research on teaching reading. In N. L. Gage (Ed.), *Handbook of research on teaching* (pp. 865-928). Chicago: Rand McNally.

Ryder, R. J., & Graves, M. F. (1994). Vocabulary instruction presented prior to reading in two basal readers. *Elementary School Journal, 95*(2), 139-153.

Sampson, M. R., Valmont, W. J., & Allen, R. V. (1982). The effects of instructional cloze on the comprehension, vocabulary, and divergent production of third-grade students. *Reading Research Quarterly, 17,* 389-399.

Schatz, E. K., & Baldwin, R. S. (1986). Context clues area unreliable predictors of word meanings. *Reading Research Quarterly, 21,* 439-453.

Schwanenflugel, P. J., & Akin, C. E. (1994). Developmental trends in lexical decisions for abstract and concrete words. *Reading Research Quarterly, 29*(3), 250-264.

Schwartz, R. M. (1988). Learning to learn vocabulary in content area textbooks. *Journal of Reading, 32,* 108-118.

Schwartz, R. M., & Raphael, T. E. (1985a). Concept of definition: A key to improving students' vocabulary. *The Reading Teacher, 39,* 198-205.

Schwartz, R. M., & Raphael, T. E. (1985b). Instruction in the concept of definition as a basic for vocabulary acquisition. In J. A. Niles & R. V. Lalik (Eds.), *Issues in literacy: A research perspective: Thirty-fourth yearbook of the National Reading Conference* (Vol. 34, pp. 116-123). Rochester, NY: National Reading Conference.

Scott, J. A., Butler, C. E., Asselin, M. M., & Henry, S. K. (1996, December). *The effect of mediated assistance in word learning.* Paper presented at the annual meeting of the National Reading Conference, Charleston, SC.

Scott, J. A., Jamieson, D., & Asselin, M. (1998, April). *Learning words: Findings from 69 days in 23 intermediate classrooms.* Paper presented at the annual meeting of the American Educational Research Association, San Diego, CA.

Scott, J. A., & Nagy, W. E. (1997). Understanding the definitions of unfamiliar verbs. *Reading Research Quarterly, 32*(2), 184-200.

Scruggs, T. E., Mastropleri, M. A., & Levin, J. R. (1985). Vocabulary acquisition of retarded students under direct mnemonic instruction. *American Journal of Mental Deficiency, 89,* 546-551.

Sénéchal, M., & Cornell, E. H. (1993). Vocabulary acquisition through shared reading experiences. *Reading Research Quarterly, 28*(4), 360–374.

Sénéchal, M., Thomas, E., & Monker J. (1995). Individual differences in 4-year-old children's acquisition of vocabulary during storybook reading. *Journal of Educational Psychology, 87*(2), 218–229.

Serra, M. C. (1953). How to develop concepts and their verbal representations. *Elementary School Journal, 53,* 275–285.

Shefelbine, J. L. (1990). Student factors related to variability in learning word meanings from context. *Journal of Reading Behavior, 22*(1), 71–97.

Shore, W. J., & Durso, F. T. (1990). Partial knowledge in vocabulary acquisition: General constraints and specific detail. *Journal of Educational Psychology, 82*(2), 315–318.

Shu, H., Anderson, R. C., Zhang, H. (1995). Incidental learning of word meanings while reading: A Chinese and American cross-cultural study. *Reading Research Quarterly, 30*(1), 76–95.

Singer, H. A. (1965). A developmental model of speed of reading in grades 3 through 6. *Reading Research Quarterly, 1,* 29–49.

Sorenson, N. L. (1985). Basal reading vocabulary instructions: A critique and suggestions. *The Reading Teacher, 39,* 80–85.

Spearitt, D. (1972). Identification of subskills of reading comprehension by maximum likelihood factor analysis. *Reading Research Quarterly, 8,* 92–111.

Squire, J. R. (1987, November). *A publisher responds to that basal reader report card.* Paper presented at the meeting of the National Council of Teachers of English, Los Angeles.

Stahl, S. A. (1983). Differential word knowledge and reading comprehension. *Journal of Reading Behavior, 15*(4), 33–50.

Stahl, S. A. (1985). To teach a word well: A framework for vocabulary instruction. *Reading World, 24*(3), 16–27.

Stahl, S. A. (1986). Three principles of effective vocabulary instruction. *Journal of Reading, 29,* 662–668.

Stahl, S. A. (1988). [Review of *The nature of vocabulary acquisition*]. *Journal of Reading Behavior, 20*(1), 89–95.

Stahl, S. A., Burdge, J. L., Machuga, M. B., & Stecyk, S. (1992). The effects of semantic grouping on learning word meaning. *Reading Psychology, 13*(1), 19–35.

Stahl, S. A., & Fairbanks, M. M. (1986). The effects of vocabulary instruction: A model-based meta-analysis. *Review of Educational Research, 56,* 72–110.

Stahl, S. A., Jacobson, M. G., Davis, C. E., & Davis, R. L. (1989). Prior knowledge and difficult vocabulary in the comprehension of unfamiliar text. *Reading Research Quarterly, 24*(1), 27–43.

Stahl, S. A., Richeck, M. A., & Vandevier, R. J. (1991). Learning meaning vocabulary through listening: A sixth grade replication. In J. Zuttell & S. McCormick (Eds.), *Learner factors/teacher factors: Issues in literacy research and instruction: Fortieth yearbook of the National Reading Conference* (Vol. 40, pp. 185–192). Chicago: National Reading Conference.

Stahl, S. A., & Vancil, S. J. (1986). Discussion is what makes semantic maps work in vocabulary instruction. *The Reading Teacher, 40,* 62–67.

Stallman, A. C., Commeyras, M., Kerr, B., Jimenez, R., Hartman, D. K., & Person, P. D. (1990). Are "new" words really new? *Reading Research and Instruction, 29*(2), 12–29.

Stanovich, K. E. (1986). Matthew effects in reading: Some consequences of individual differences in the acquisition of literacy. *Reading Research Quarterly, 21,* 360–407.

Sternberg, R. B. (1987). Most vocabulary is learned from context. In M. G. McKeown & M. E. Curtis (Eds.). *The nature of vocabulary acquisition* (pp. 89–105). Hillsdale, NJ: Lawrence Erlbaum Associates.

Sternberg, R., & Powell, J. S. (1983). Comprehending verbal comprehension. *American Psychologist, 38,* 878–893.

Sternberg, R., & Powell, J. S., & Kaye, D. B. (1983). The nature of verbal comprehension. In A. C. Wilkinson (Ed.), *Communicating with computers in classrooms: Prospects for applied cognitive science* (pp. 121–143). New York: Academic Press.

Taba, H. (1967). *Teacher's handbook for elementary social studies.* Reading, MA: Addison-Wesley.

Taylor, B., Harri., L. A., & Pearson, P. D. (1988). *Reading difficulties: Instruction and assessment.* New York: Random House.

Thames, D. G., & Readence, J. E. (1988). Effects of differential vocabulary instruction and lesson frameworks on the reading comprehension of primary grade children. *Reading Research and Instruction, 27,* 1–12.

Thelen, J. N. (1986). Vocabulary instruction and meaningful learning. *Journal of Reading, 29,* 603–609.

Thomas, C. L. (1998). *The effects of three levels of curricular modifications on the vocabulary knowledge and comprehension of regular education students and students with learning disabilities in content-area classrooms.* Unpublished doctoral dissertation, University of Oregon, Eugene.

Thompson, E. (1958). The "master word" approach to vocabulary training. *Journal of Developmental Reading, 2,* 62–66.

Thurstone, L. L. (1946). A note on a reanalysis of Davis' reading tests. *Psychometrika, 11,* 185–188.

Tierney, R. J., Readence, J. E., & Dishner, E. K. (1985). *Reading strategies and practices: A compendium* (2nd ed.). Newton, MA: Allyn & Bacon.

Toms-Bronowski, S. (1983). An investigation of the effectiveness of selected vocabulary teaching strategies with intermediate grade level students (Doctoral dissertation, University of Wisconsin, Madison, 1983). *Dissertation Abstracts International, 44,* 1405A. (University Microfilms, No. 83-16, 238)

Tuinman, J. J., & Brady, M. E. (1974). How does vocabulary account for varlance on reading comprehension tests: A preliminary instructinal analysis. In P. Nack (Ed.), *Twenty-third national reading conference yearbook* (Vol. 23, pp. 176–184). Clemson, SC: National Reading Conference.

Vygotsky, F. (1962). *Thought and language.* Cambridge, MA: MIT Press.

Watts, S. M. (1995). Vocabulary instruction during reading lessons in six classrooms. *Journal of Reading Behavior, 27*(3), 399–424.

Werner, H., & Kaplan, B. (1952). The acquisition of word meanings: A developmental study. *Monographs of the Society for Research in Child Development, 15* (Serial No. 51, No. 1).

White, T. G., Graves, M. F., & Slater, W. H. (1990). Growth of reading vocabulary in diverse elementary schools. *Journal of Educational Psychology, 82*(2), 281–290.

White, T. G., Power, M. A., & White, S. (1989). Morphological analysis: Implications for teaching and understanding vocabulary growth. *Reading Research Quarterly, 24*(3), 283–304.

White, T. G., Sowell, J., & Yanagihara, A. (1989). Teaching elementary students to use word-part clues. *The Reading Teacher, 42,* 302–308.

Wilson, R. M., & Gambrell, L. B. (1988). *Reading comprehension in the elementary school: A teacher's practical guide.* Newton, MA: Allyn & Bacon.

Wixson, K. K. (1986). Vocabulary instruction and children's comprehension of basal stories. *Reading Research Quarterly, 21,* 317–329.

Wysocki, K., & Jenkins, J. R. (1987). Deriving word meanings through morphological generalization. *Reading Research Quarterly, 22,* 66–81.

Zechmeister, E. B., Chronis, A., Cull, W. L., D'Anna, C. A., & Healy, N. A. (1995). Growth of a functionally important lexicon. *Journal of Reading Behavior, 27*(2), 201–212.

# ·57·

# RHETORIC

## Nancy Nelson
### Louisiana State University

## James L. Kinneavy
### University of Texas at Austin

Throughout history, the term *rhetoric* has referred to the uses of language in social contexts. The traditional realm of rhetoric in classical times was persuasive discourse, especially as it was used in law courts and in politics, and later in sermons. That definition persisted for centuries, but the term eventually broadened to include other uses of language. As such, it includes the more specific meaning of persuasion, but it also includes informative uses, expressive uses, and the belletristic uses of language to produce literature. These uses are called by some the functions of language (Britton, Burgess, Martin, McLeod, & Rosen, 1975) and by others the aims of discourse (Kinneavy, 1969, 1971, 1980; Morris, 1955). In such phrases as "the rhetoric of architecture," "the rhetoric of fashion," "the rhetoric of confrontation," and the "rhetoric of feminism," the term signals the specialized language and communicative practices that are associated with a particular group.

Particularly relevant to English studies is the use of the word *rhetoric* also to refer to *the study* of language use, usually with the aim of ensuring that students learn how to communicate more effectively. Rhetoric was a major subject of study in antiquity, both in Greece and Rome, and it has played a role in the educational curriculum throughout history to the present time. Students take courses in rhetoric to learn how to produce their own effective texts and sometimes also to analyze and critique the texts of others. Because the term can signify both the productive and receptive aspects of language, both oral and written, rhetoric becomes almost a synonym for the study of writing, speaking, reading, and listening—the language arts.

Rhetorical concerns often relate to four major components of an act of communication: author, audience, subject matter, and text. The four components of rhetoric can be positioned on the rhetorical triangle, shown in Fig. 57.1, because all are factors to be taken into account in an act of communication (cf. Bühler, 1933; Jakobson, 1967; Shannon & Weaver, 1949). Concerns related to author might have to do, for instance, with the voice or the persona being projected; concerns related to audience might be manifested in audience analysis and audience adaptation; concerns related to subject matter might deal with emphasis and elaboration; and concerns related to text might encompass organization, word choice, and style. In a "rhetorical situation," to use Lloyd Bitzer's (1968) term, a person faces an exigence (a need, something to be done) and considers various constraints, including those related to the context and the nature of audience, when producing a text. Rhetorical education typically gives much attention to the process of creating and presenting a text, including such matters as generating and ordering material.

After a brief introduction to classical rhetoric, this chapter provides an historical overview of rhetorical education through the years. Then the discussion focuses on some major rhetorical concepts, summarizing their various transformations over time. These concepts include the canons, the modes, the appeals, and the aims of discourse. The chapter concludes with a consideration of the relation between rhetoric and the current conception of English language arts.

## CLASSICAL RHETORIC

Rhetoric arose in the transition of the city-states of Greece and Sicily from monarchies to oligarchies to democracies from the 6th to the 5th century B.C. The division of land among commoners occasioned many legal disputes, and techniques to persuade in court were codified. At the same time, the new commoners had a say in the political decisions of the city-state and needed to learn how to persuade their fellow citizens. Thus, the legal

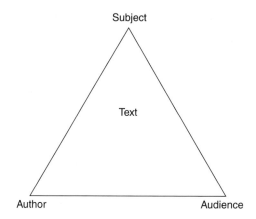

FIGURE 57.1. The rhetorical triangle.

and political rhetoric of persuasion arose at the same time, and these remained for centuries the two main forms of rhetoric. In addition, there were also epideictic, or display, speeches intended to demonstrate the orator's virtuosity, cleverness, or technique. Teachers of rhetoric often composed and delivered such speeches to attract students.

There are many rhetorical treatises from both Greece and Rome teaching students how to write these legal, political, and display speeches. Some early conributions to rhetorical theory were made by the Greek Sophists and by Plato, but the major works in the rhetorical tradition of persuasion are from Aristotle, Cicero, Quintilian, and also an anonymous Roman author, whose conceptions dominated not only antiquity but also the Middle Ages and the Renaissance. It was the Greeks, mainly Aristotle, who provided the conceptual framework.

However, it was the Romans, particularly Cicero and Quintilian, who developed an approach to the teaching of rhetoric based on Aristotelian theory. Important contributions were also made by the anonymous author of *Ad C. Herennium*, a rhetorical treatise sometimes attributed to Cicero ([Cicero], trans. 1954). As a result of the appropriation by the Romans, the Aristotelian conception had widespread influence as educators in other parts of Europe followed the Roman model. The classic conception, which Aristotle (trans. 1926) articulated in *The "Art" of Rhetoric*, has been widely adopted as a beginning system for teaching rhetoric as persuasion, even at the present time. For basic texts and translations, see Aristotle (trans. 1926), Cicero (trans. 1942a, 1942b, 1949), [Cicero], trans. 1954, and Quintilian (trans. 1920-22); for modern treatments, see Corbett (1971), and Horner (1988).

## RHETORIC AND EDUCATION

### Rhetorical Education in Ancient Greece and Rome

In ancient Greece and Rome, rhetoric played a central role in education designed to prepare students for lives that would involve much oral discourse. Because the Greek conception formed the basis for education in Rome, one can speak of Greco–Roman education. In the education of young men,

rhetoric was one of the advanced subjects, which also included grammar (the study of texts and the language itself) and logic (the study of proof in language). Rhetoric was the culminating art of language to be studied, and it built on much that had been learned through grammar and logic, which tended to precede but also to overlap with it. Little is known about the actual places *where* education took place, but there was probably much variety in the types of settings. Some individuals, no doubt, had their own tutors and studied at home or in apprentice situations, and others studied in groups in schools run by a single teacher. However, through the writings left by the Romans, much is known about *what* was taught, and there seemed to be much commonality in the language curriculum. Treatments of the Roman rhetorical education are provided by Kennedy (1972) and Murphy (1983, 1998).

The major classical sources on rhetorical education are Cicero's (trans. 1949) *De Inventione* and *De Oratore* (trans. 1942a, 1942b), the *Ad C. Herennium* ([Cicero], trans. 1954) by the unknown author, and by Quintilian's *Institutio Oratoria* (trans. 1920-22). When studying rhetoric, students engaged in much practice through writing, reading, listening, and speaking. They wrote persuasive texts, delivered them orally, listened to others' speeches, and read persuasive texts written by others. They studied the five parts, or canons, of rhetoric: invention, arrangement, style, memory, and delivery. Through studying invention, they learned methods of self-questioning to generate subject matter; through studying arrangement, they learned some general methods of organizing their speeches; through studying style, they learned how to embellish or simplify their speeches and adjust them into high, low, or medium styles; through studying memory, they learned mnemonic strategies for remembering their speeches; and through studying delivery, they learned about such matters as voice modulation and gestures. Exercises often involved imitation of models, in part, to add to a student's "bank" of expressions and words, which was called a *copia*. Quintilian, in particular, gave much attention to the notion of *copia*.

Rhetoric included two main types of persuasive discourse: the *suasoria* and the *controversia*. The first was a persuasive piece of advice, for instance, to Alexander about whether he should cross the ocean after he had conquered everything on land. The subjects were often drawn from history (or fictional history) and were supposed to train the student for the courtroom. The other type, which centered on a disputed topic, was intended to prepare the student for political speeches. The topics usually revolved around issues of morality or laws, and, like the legal topic, were often given an imaginary situational context.

In addition to these two kinds of declamations, there was also the epideictic speech intended to display the orator's character and skill. Often these speeches too were based on history or fictional history. Frequently, the speaker presented himself as the spokesman for a whole culture and the embodiment of the aspirations and ideals of the culture. Pericles' speech to the Athenians on the occasion of the funeral for the first dead in the Peloponnesian War, which is available in reconstructed form in Thucydides (trans. 1998), is often cited as the exemplar for such a topic.

In preparation for their rhetorical studies, students performed early composition exercises, called the *progymnasmata*. These early exercises seemed to draw heavily from mythology and fables and to be embodied in initiation of models of description, narration, and other types of discourse drawn from canonical writers. An example can be seen in Nadeau's (1952) translation of Aphthonius' *Progymnasmata*.

## Rhetoric: Diminished, Recovered, Truncated

Classical rhetoric, as the study of persuasive discourse, continued in the Middle Ages as one of the three subjects studied in the *trivium*—the first three of the seven liberal arts. The other two subjects of the *trivium* were grammar and logic. Possibly the most thorough treatment of the three strands in education associated with the *trivium* has been that of Kenneth Burke (1941, 1945, 1953, 1955), who wrote major books on rhetorical persuasion, on literature, and on science and dialectic.

In the Middle Ages, the major rhetorical text was Cicero's *De Inventione* (trans. 1949), the primary concern of which was the modes, which were methods of approaching a subject. Also still surviving was the anonymous *Ad C. Herennium* ([Cicero], trans. 1954), which provided a similar system. With the advent of Christianity, rhetoric was turned to the service of religion, which became the dominant topic of rhetoric for centuries, displacing both law and politics in importance. The major text in this displacement appeared in the 5th century as Book IV of *De Doctrina Christiana,* in which St. Augustine channeled classical rhetoric into the study of the Bible. (For one translation, see Augustine, trans. 1958; for the history of medieval rhetoric, see Murphy, 1978, 1981). During the Middle Ages, rhetoric diminished somewhat in importance in the curriculum as some of its traditional parts, such as attention to figures of speech and metric patterns, went to grammar, and other parts, such as proofs and techniques of argumentation, went to logic.

In the Renaissance, rhetoric experienced some reawakening. During the 14th century, Petrarch, who promoted the study of "humane letters," had made a major contribution by starting a search for, and recovering, some of the classical sources, including some speeches, letters, and texts of Cicero and some writings of Quintilian. In the next century, Erasmus, the "wandering" Dutch scholar who lectured for a number of years at Cambridge University, redirected attention to the classical concerns of rhetoric. He did so with his educational treatises, collected in Erasmus (trans. 1978), in which he drew from the Roman rhetoricians, and with his applications of rhetorical theory to the preparation of sermons. He is well known for his emphasis on *copia*, following Quintilian, and his compilations of material from sources, intended to serve as additions to a rhetorical repertoire. A major educational practice for students too was the keeping of their own "commonplace books," in which they recorded material they read or heard. These entries were organized by topic so that students could retrieve information on a given subject when needed. The modes continued to be important throughout the Renaissance, mainly through the work of Hermogenes, the most read Greek rhetorician during those times (cf. Nadeau, 1964).

For much of the 16th century, which saw the invention of the printing press as well as major developments in economics, religion, and social structure, the *trivium* of grammar, rhetoric, and logic still prevailed, but the ordering of the subjects had been changed. Rhetoric, which now typically preceded instead of following logic, still included the five parts, or canons. However, by the end of the century the classical conception of what belonged in rhetoric and what belonged in logic was being questioned by some people, in particular, the French educator Peter Ramus. Ramus (1555), with the assistance of his colleague, Omar Talon, attempted to restructure the language curriculum. Although rhetoric still preceded logic, the Ramist curriculum took invention and arrangement out of rhetoric and assigned them to logic, and also collapsed memory with arrangement. These changes left rhetoric with only style and delivery and left the rhetorician with the tasks of embellishing material and delivering material but not inventing or arranging it. (See Ong, 1979, for a description of the educational changes associated with Ramism.) This modification, which gave rhetoric only the surface features and removed from rhetoric the classical emphasis on thought processes, had some influence in the new American colleges as they were formed by the colonists (Morison, 1936).

During the 17th and 18th centuries, with the rise of science and journalism, there was some questioning of the techniques and style of classical rhetoric to handle the presentation of the new sciences and the beginning reportorial writing of journalistic media. New topics from the many new sciences and current events of all types invaded the hitherto sequestered domain of legal, political, and religious discourse. A classic presentation of this movement can be seen in Williamson's (1951) *The Senecan Amble.* However, these new concerns did not make the transformations one might expect in the teaching of rhetoric. Although commerce and trade and the beginning of modern advertising added new subjects to the range of writing topics, the rhetoric textbooks of the times did not reflect this universality.

Toward the end of the 18th century and into the 19th century, when the focus of rhetoric shifted from oral to written language, two Scottish rhetoricians, George Campbell and Hugh Blair, provided rhetoric textbooks that were influential in America as well as Europe. Campbell's *The Philosophy of Rhetoric* was first published in 1776 and Blair's *Lectures on Rhetoric and Belles Lettres* in 1783, but both books went through several editions (cf. Blair, 1867; Campbell, 1846). Despite different approaches, both of these texts gave much of their attention to arrangement and style. Campbell, who retained many concepts of classical rhetoric, is known for his interesting treatments of arrangement and of audience analysis, which he accomplished by applying the psychology of his day, associationism, to rhetorical matters. Blair is known for extending rhetorical concepts to the analysis and criticism of texts. Both scholars overlapped the concerns of rhetoric with those of belles lettres, such as poetry, essays, and novels, and used examples from these sources. The models that the students were to imitate were largely drawn from the literary canon, not from science or advertising or politics. The trends of emphasizing style and arrangement continued in two major treatments of rhetoric that were introduced in the 19th century: Richard Whately's (1867), which drew attention to reasoning, and Alexander Bain's

(1887), which focused to a great extent on paragraph structure and development. Although religious topics retained some importance in the textbooks that were produced then, literary topics were increasingly being used.

The 19th century brought some major changes in the curriculum—and a decline in the importance of rhetorical study as English became a department in higher education and a subject in the schools. The liberal arts colleges, dissatisfied with their entering students' writing skills, instituted composition courses, which were considered remedial. These often became amalgamated with rhetoric, focusing on arrangement and style, and sometimes even the hyphenated label *composition–rhetoric* was used. After the Civil War, when the universities were established and the disciplinary departments were formed, English became a discipline comprising a collection of subjects—philology, literary studies, composition (or composition–rhetoric), rhetoric, and, for a while, elocution. Of the collection, one member, literature, became increasingly important, and, as it gained importance, rhetoric (often linked to composition or conceived as oratory) lost much of its scholarly importance. Right before the turn of the century, the Committee of Ten established English in the secondary schools as a major school subject with two parts, the first more important than the second. They were the study of literature and the development of expression, mainly written composition (National Education Association, 1894). The concerns of classical rhetoric received little attention in the school subject known as English.

There were more struggles over the English curriculum. In the early decades of the 20th century, secondary teachers began to resist the control that colleges and universities had over the high school curriculum, particularly with respect to the rigidly prescribed literature and the heavy emphasis on the writing of literary essays. (See N. Nelson & Calfee, 1998, for a more detailed historical account.) In accordance with the progressivist focus on experience and expression, influenced by the ideas of Dewey (1902), they wanted more choice for students in terms of works for reading and topics for writing. This was one reason for forming the National Council of Teachers of English in 1911. The progressivist movement also had some impact at the college level mainly with respect to integration across areas of learning. Composition teachers, who attempted to implement correlated instruction in written and oral communication, established in 1949 the organization known as the Conference on College Composition and Communication (CCCC). Although the initiative to reconnect oral and written language was short-lived, the organization thrived and grew into the torchbearer for composition studies in this country and, indeed, the world at large.

With the onset of the Cold War and launching of *Sputnik*, public attention was directed to public education, and there were concerns about nontraditional approaches. Composition instruction at all levels became what Dan Fogarty (1959) called "the current traditional" approach (p. 118), which meant focusing instruction on arrangement and style, emphasizing mechanical correctness instead of rhetorical effectiveness, assigning topics for writing, stressing paragraph development, and teaching students about some abstract qualities of writing, such as unity and coherence.

## The New Rhetoric

Beginning in the 1950s there was talk of a *new* rhetoric (Burke, 1951; Fogarty, 1959), and the "new" label continues to be used for developments today. No consensus has been reached about what the new rhetoric is (or should be); instead, there are multiple versions. What these all have in common, though, is the new life that they have brought back to the liberal art of rhetoric.

For some rhetoricians, the course to be taken by the new rhetoric is to return to the issues of classical rhetoric and develop them theoretically. Three major contributors are Kenneth Burke, James Kinneavy, and Chaim Perelman. Burke (1951, 1955) extended Aristotelian rhetoric psychologically, sociologically, and biologically in his version, which he himself called a "new" rhetoric. It is based on a conception of a human as a symbol user relating to, and identifying with, the ways of other people through communication and seeking to induce cooperation, not only with respect to action but also with respect to attitude. Aristotle also looms large in Kinneavy's (1971, 1980) *Theory of Discourse*, to be discussed in more detail later, which argues for a focus on the aims of discourse implicit in the liberal arts tradition of grammar, rhetoric, and logic. In their *New Rhetoric*, first published in French in 1958, the Belgian scholar, Perelman, and his coauthor, Lucie Olbrechts-Tyteca (1969) addressed the rhetorical relation between author and audience that was so central to classical rhetoric. Perelman and Olbrechts-Tyteca pointed to the situated and interactive nature of that relationship. In this theoretical treatment, the audience is central, since it is the audience who determines "the quality of argument and the behavior of orators" (p. 24).

Concurrent with the theoretical rhetorics of Burke (1951, 1955), Kinneavy (1971, 1980), and Perelman and Olbrechts-Tyteca (1969), there have been other important developments in composition studies and rhetoric. The second major form of new rhetoric is what is now being called expressivist. The slogan, articulated by Don Murray (1972) and echoed repeatedly by others, is to "teach process not product"—a response to the rigidity and sterility of the pervasive "current-traditional" instruction. Lou Kelley (1972), in *From Dialogue to Discourse*, Ken Macrorie (1970), in *Uptaught*, and Peter Elbow (1973), in *Writing Without Teachers*, have all emphasized expressive discourse and have had a major influence on the American educational scene. Much attention is given to individual students' processes of composing, particularly the generative aspects. The student, who "owns" the writing, decides what to write, uses his or her own knowledge in writing it, and determines when it is completed. Although the focus is on individual's composing processes, instruction also incorporates social aspects of writing as well, such as conferences with the teacher and response from one's peers, and the classroom may be called a writing workshop. Critics, such as James Berlin (1982), pointed to an overemphasis on the individual and a lack of attention to large-scale sociocultural concerns, but the movement continues to be strong. Its influence can be seen especially at the elementary (Graves, 1983) and secondary levels (Atwell, 1998).

A third form of new rhetoric comes from empirical research, which was called for by Richard Braddock, Richard Lloyd-Jones, and Lowell Schoer in 1963 and which became a major source of knowledge about composition beginning in the 1970s. Janet Emig's (1971) groundbreaking study of the composing processes of 12th-graders was followed by studies that focused on the composing processes of other groups of writers and examined other rhetorical concerns as well. Studies have provided detailed analyses of individuals' cognitive processes, viewed through such means as think-aloud protocols (Hayes & Flower, 1980), and have also examined other issues relevant to the writer, the task, the audience, and the text. Today there is much interest in context and social processes, such as those manifested in collaboration, and even the knowledge-making processes associated with large groups.

The fourth—and final—major source of new life for rhetoric to be discussed here is what might be called disciplinary rhetoric, or the rhetoric of the disciplines. This movement has some connections with the earlier Writing Across the Curriculum initiative, or WAC, which was started by Britton et al. (1975) in England and which spread rapidly throughout colleges and universities in the United States (Fulwiler & Young, 1982; Gere, 1985; Kinneavy, McCleary, & Nakadate, 1983; Maimon, Belcher, Hearn, Nodine, & O'Connor, 1981). Writing Across the Curriculum programs on campuses today can be divided into two general types, the program that insists on a writing component in the traditional content courses in chemistry, art education, sociology, civil engineering, philosophy, and so on, and the program that has the students write about their specific subject matter in a centralized writing department (usually English). The major justification for WAC is that writing has unique properties for enhancing learning—a point made in influential essays by Janet Emig (1977) and Anne Herrington (1981).

Today many rhetoricians are studying the specialized discourses of the disciplines and are examining the features and uses of language associated with such disciplines as psychology, economics, or physics. The underlying assumption in this relatively new line of work is that there is an important connection between the ways of writing (or speaking) and the ways of knowing associated with the various academic fields (cf. Becher, 1989) or, as Herbert Simons (1990) said, "the influence of discursive forms on thought and expression" (p. 3). The more specific term *rhetoric of inquiry* is sometimes used for the discourse of the sciences and social sciences (J. S. Nelson, Megill, & McCloskey, 1981). Some scholars (e.g., Bazerman, 1987; D. R. Russell, 1991) have taken an historical approach, showing changes and developments over time. Through these studies of disciplinary discourse, rhetorical scholarship overlaps with other lines of scholarly work, in particular, the philosophy of science and the sociology of knowledge.

## CONCERNS OF RHETORIC

### The Canons

As already noted, the five parts of rhetoric—invention, arrangement, style, memory, and delivery—remained in rhetorical studies through the Middle Ages, even though the medieval form was somewhat truncated, and into the Renaissance, when they experienced some new vitality as ancient manuscripts were discovered. The parts were modified dramatically in the 16th century by Ramus, who removed invention, arrangement, and memory from rhetoric, leaving only style and delivery. However, those three elements were not totally abandoned; the fuller classical version had something of a comeback in the 17th and 18th centuries. More changes occurred in the 19th century as writing became educationally more important than speaking. There seemed to be no need to teach memory and delivery if instruction focused on writing, and so those two parts dropped out. Later, invention diminished in importance too, as attention was put on arranging material but not generating it. The two parts left in the "current traditional" rhetoric of the 20th century were arrangement and style.

One accomplishment of the various forms of new rhetoric is the reclamation of invention. When rhetoric lost invention, it lost its emphasis on generative thought. Now invention and thought processes have been reclaimed for rhetoric in the various innovations that together make up the new rhetoric. Some rhetoricians have revived the systematic self-examination associated with the topics of classical rhetoric, and others have developed their own systems. Now speakers or writers can also use Burke's (1945, 1975) pentad of act, scene, agent, agency, and purpose to think in a "rounded" way about an issue, or Richard Young, Alton Becker, and Kenneth Pike's (1970) tagmemics to view a subject from multiple perspectives (particle, wave, field). They can also apply an expressivist approach called "prewriting" (Rohman & Wlecke, 1964) to generate material through analogic thinking. The reclamation of invention has come from other "new" rhetoricians too: the composition researchers, who have studied the nature of planning and have shown the importance of thinking about a topic, and the disciplinary rhetoricians, who have pointed to the creative aspects of science.

Another important development has been a critique of the ordering of the canons and its implicit linear model: that first one invents, then arranges, then adds stylistic embellishment, then memorizes, and finally delivers. The empirical studies of composing have shown how recursive the process is—how writers often return to earlier processes. Invention can occur throughout the process, beginning before a person writes a word and continuing up to the last change that he or she makes and perhaps even after the final version is completed. Even delivery (the fifth canon) relates to invention (the first) now that hyperlinked texts are possible with electronic technologies. David Bolter (1993), who reclaimed delivery for rhetoric, argued that electronic communication blurs the conventional distinctions between the parts even further than they were blurred in the process studies and that the text is "defined" in its delivery.

### The Modes

Throughout much of history the modes of discourse were tied to the *status,* from the Latin term that Cicero and others used for the place for starting an argument. The Greek term was *stasis.* At least one third of the extant Greek rhetorics, as well as many of the Latin rhetorics, focus on the modes. In Cicero's

*De Inventione* (trans. 1949) modes were the primary concern, and they were also important throughout the Renaissance (cf. Nadeau, 1964) and into the 18th and 19th centuries.

Cicero considered the *status* mainly from a lawyer's point of view. What aspect of the case should the lawyer emphasize in his speech? One option would be staying with the facts of the case: Did Brutus actually stab Caesar? Did the event happen as the prosecution alleged? Another option would be to define the action: Should the lawyer concede the fact that Brutus did stab Caesar but attempt to prove that it was not really a murder, but rather a case of self-defense? In this second instance, the issue becomes a matter of definition. A third option would be to evaluate the event: Should the lawyer concede the fact of the stabbing, concede also the classification of the case as a murder, but argue that this factual murder was justified by the circumstances because Caesar was threatening the Roman republic? This third defense turns the case into an evaluation of an event in the light of a possibly unjust law. These three perspectives of fact, definition, and value were summarized by Cicero in a classic rule: *Sitne? Quid sit? Quale sit?* (Is it? What is it? What value does it have?), which occurs in his most famous treatise, *De Oratore* (Cicero, trans. 1942a, 1942b). These were also adopted by Quintilian, Hermogenes, and other rhetoricians, although sometimes other approaches were added. Each *status* is given a lengthy treatment, and they were taught throughout history from antiquity through the Renaissance.

Through the years there has continued to be much concern with the way in which the subject matter is approached. When writing or speaking about a political figure, for example, one can select among several different approaches: giving a biographical account, analyzing the person's character, considering the individual's contributions, or using the person's current ideological position to define some facet of the political situation. The resulting texts would differ. The first would be a narrative, the second a description, the third an evaluation, and the fourth a definition, which would be a type of classification. These methods of organization are called the modes of discourse, although there has been some disagreement on the various categories. Sometimes exposition, persuasion, argumentation, and even poetry have been included.

Beginning in the 17th century and becoming stronger in the 18th and 19th centuries, there was a movement to link the modes with the faculties of the mind: to enlighten the understanding, to please the imagination, to move the passions, and to influence the will. Boswell (1987) wrote an article chronicling this development. Bain (1887), for example, said that description, narration, and exposition enlightened the understanding; that persuasion moved the will; and that poetry gave pleasure to the feelings. Later, poetry was dropped as a major kind of discourse for pedagogical purposes, and persuasion was changed to argumentation. These four—description, narration, exposition, and argumentation—structured composition books for over a century, at all levels of schooling. The modes dominated composition practice in America from the middle of the 19th century until the 1970s, owing to Bain's influence.

The hegemony of the modes was challenged by Kinneavy (1969, 1971, 1980) and Britton et al. (1975), who maintained that the modes are really only means to achieve the aims or functions of language. Despite Robert J. Connors' (1981) influential essay on "The Rise and Fall of the Modes of Discourse," which almost dismissed the baby with the bath, assigning no importance to the modes at all, the modes remained important though not preeminent. They appeared as "kinds of discourse" in James Moffett's (1968) still influential text, *Teaching the Universe of Discourse*. They were used as an exploratory heuristic in the tagmemic approach of Young et al. (1970) in *Rhetoric: Discovery and Change*. They were treated historically through the classical topics and parallel figurative language in Frank J. D'Angelo's (1975) *A Conceptual Theory of Rhetoric*, and they provided the basis for a Jeanne Fahnstock and Marie Secor's (1990) *Rhetoric of Argument*, a college textbook that has gone through several editions. In fact, Kinneavy, whom Connors (1981) invoked to dethrone the modes, retained them in his theory and in his textbooks (e.g., Kinneavy, McCleary, & Nakadate, 1985). These texts and programs are not atypical: The modes still continue to be an integral part of nearly all writing texts from elementary school through college, as well as technical writing manuals.

When speaking of arrangement, the matter of genre is relevant, too. Genres are typically thought of as recurring types of discourse, which employ particular modes and have particular kinds of ordering to their parts. In classical times, for instance, a speech would include an introduction, a statement of the case, a preview specifying the sections of the discussion to follow, the arguments for the speaker's position, a refutation of the arguments against it, and a conclusion. Today there is some questioning of the concept of genre as a static text type chosen rather arbitrarily by a writer or speaker. A major contribution to this reconceptualization was made by Carolyn Miller (1984) in her article, "Genre as Social Action," in which she questioned the notion of genre as arbitrary forms used to accomplish goals. She posited that genres are social *actions*—typified actions of members of a group or society in response to recurrent situations. For her, genre "acquires meaning from situation and from the social context in which that situation arose. . . . A genre is a rhetorical means for mediating private intentions and social exigence; it motivates by connecting the private with the public, the singular with the recurrent" (p. 163). Along the same line, Anis Bawarshi (2000) pointed to the constitutive function of genres point, saying that genres contribute to our social realities—"how we recognize and enact these realities" (p. 337).

## The Appeals

The classical presentation of persuasion taught students to use four main types of appeals to persuade their audiences. These include persuading their audience through projecting personalities that engender credibility; appealing to the emotions, interests, and biases of the readers; employing the more intellectual means of logical arguments; and, finally, using an effective style. Most of the time, of course, a speaker uses all or at least several of these appeals in a given text, and a given slogan, for instance, will embody a rational argument, an appeal to the audience's emotions, and a clever wording. The four appeals are often represented graphically by grouping them around the rhetorical triangle shown in Fig. 57. 1. The four appeals have been the core of the persuasion teaching throughout history. See Cope (1867) for a thorough commentary on Aristotle on these issues, and see Corbett (1971), Horner (1988), and Kinneavy (1980) for more recent treatments.

***Ethos, pathos, and logos.*** Appeals to the author, audience, and subject matter can be associated with particular points of the triangle in Fig. 57. 1. *Ethos* is associated with author, *pathos* with audience, and *logos* with subject matter.

The author's (speaker's or writer's) personal credibility was called in classical rhetoric the "ethical argument," or *ethos,* which meant the conviction carried by the author's sincerity, sympathy for the audience, knowledge, and decisiveness. A major study of these appeals based on character, or charisma, deals with the author's trustworthiness, intentions, and expertness as the main dimensions of "ethical appeal" (Hovland, Janis, & Kelly, 1953), paralleling Aristotle's factors. As Aristotle himself said, the most efficient means of persuasion may well be the character of the speaker (cf. Aristotle, trans. 1960). Of course, the image of the speaker or writer is also indirectly reinforced by the three other appeals—by the manner of appealing to the audience's interests and emotions, by the subject matter arguments, and by the style. Directly or indirectly, the establishment of credibility is paramount; if the writer is not believed, the rest of the speech is wasted on the audience.

The second rhetorical appeal is based on incentives grounded in the interests and emotions of the audience. These emotions and interests may even change with different cultures or subcultures, but this "pathetic" appeal, or *pathos,* as it was traditionally called, has been a staple of rhetoric in all cultures. The history of political propaganda, religious sermons, commercial advertising, and legal rhetoric attests to the importance of appealing to the audience's emotions and self-interest. Aristotle in the 4th century devoted more attention to this appeal than to any other—and this is true of many rhetoricians through the years. It is the basis for most of the marketing research carried on by advertising agencies, by political pollsters, and public relation firms. This is even more true when attempts are made to persuade people from other cultures (cf. discussion by Brown, 1963).

The third appeal consists of rational appeals grounded in the subject matter under consideration. Aristotle called this the logical argument, or *logos.* It can be based on deductive reasoning—beginning with principles or axioms that the writer and readers share and drawing from them inferences that apply to the issue at hand. Alternatively, it can be based on inductive reasoning—moving from particulars to a generalization. The patterns, which are called *topics,* or places, can vary in accordance with particular subcultures. For example, in his society, Aristotle found that an argument with an a fortiori base like the following would be convincing to a Greek audience: If even the gods are not omniscient, certainly human beings are not. He also gave examples of topics used in special areas like politics and law. With today's emphasis on specialized audiences, the study of topics has received considerable attention, especially in legal, political, literary, and ethical discourse (e.g., Bornscheuer, 1976; Curtius, 1973; Perelman & Obrechts-Tyteca, 1969).

***Appeal based on style.*** In addition to the appeals of *ethos, pathos,* and *logos,* there is a fourth based on style, which relates to features of the text itself (in center of the triangle). Most of the major rhetoricians have treated style under the headings of the four virtues, which were dignity, propriety, clarity, and correctness.

The four virtues of style correspond in emphasis to the four elements of the rhetorical triangle in Fig. 57. 1. Dignity enhances the credibility of the author, propriety realizes the adaptability of the style to the audience, clarity ensures an accurate transmission of the subject matter, and correctness takes care of the conventions of the language. Dignity of style was usually looked upon as being secured by figures of speech, such as metaphor, synecdoche, hyperbole, and irony, intended to clarify the meaning of concepts and to embellish the speech. Just as important as the figures of speech were the figures of sound, based on rhythm, rhyme, alliteration, and assonance. Almost one third of the rhetorical manuals from Greek antiquity were limited to these and other stylistic considerations. For instance, three fourths of Cicero's *Orator* (trans. 1939) which paints the picture of the perfect speaker, goes to style (or *elocutio*), as pointed out by translator and editor, H. M. Hubbell, in the introduction to the Loeb edition.

With respect to the second virtue, propriety, the doctrine of the three styles established the appropriateness of the style primarily relative to the audience and secondarily to the other elements of the rhetorical situation. The three styles were usually referred to as the high (grand, Asian) style, the low (plain, Attic) style, and the middle (Rhodian) style. In the *Orator,* Cicero (trans. 1939) described the high style as highly ornamental in its use of figures of speech, often bombastic in diction, and characterized by striking and obvious sound structures; the low style as not emphasizing rhythm at all, as not adorned (except with a few metaphors), as elegant and neat, as humorous and witty, as purist in grammar, and especially as clear; and the middle style, which was the language of philosophers, as restrained and even, though using some figurative language. He described the best orator in a famous passage that dominated rhetorical history for 1,700 years: "He is in fact eloquent who can discuss commonplace matters simply, lofty matters impressively, and topics ranging in between in a tempered style" (Cicero, trans. 1949, p. 379).

The third virtue of style is the virtue of clarity. To achieve clarity, Aristotle (trans. 1926) insisted on the use of figurative language, the uses of both ordinary and extraordinary language, and especially on the use of lively and dynamic imagery. At some times in the rhetorical tradition, clarity almost preempted all other considerations. This is true of the period of Ramus and his influence from the 16th until the 19th century, and for some writers, Tolstoy, for example, clarity becomes a matter of ethics. An emphasis on clarity can be seen in the current "plain English" movement (cf. Cutts, 1996).

The final virtue of the rhetorical tradition was correctness. This element has often been given a chauvinistic interpretation, dignifying a prestige dialect and demeaning other (usually more provincial) dialects. This began with the Greeks and the Romans and has been true of nearly all treatments. In the 1960s, it began to be challenged in this country by modern linguistics, which demonstrated the complexity and the historical development of all dialects. In composition studies, this challenge was reflected in a position taken in 1974 by the CCCC called the "Students' Rights to Their Own Language," a position intended to honor African American, Hispanic, and other minority American dialects (CCCC Committee on Language Statement, 1974). The issue remains important today as there is increasing awareness of the complex relation of language to other aspects of identity (cf. Delpit, 1995). Gee (1989), for instance, used the term *identity kit* for the "*saying* (writing)-*doing-being-valuing-believing* combination" that marks a person as a member of a group (p. 6). Also, today there is more awareness of how different registers or dialects are "appropriate" in different contexts and how necessary code switching can often be.

***The rhetorical stance.*** In producing a text, a writer (or speaker) would likely use appeals of all these types—those related to the subject itself, to the characteristics of the audience, to his or her own character, and to the nature of the text itself. However, for a text to accomplish the desired effect, its author must have what Booth (1963) has called the rhetorical stance: "a stance which depends on discovering and maintaining in any writing situation a proper balance" among the elements (p. 141)—proper, that is, for a particular situation. There is no magic formula for balance; it must come from a "reading" of the context. Unbalanced stances, in which one element is overplayed and other elements are underplayed, include the "pedant's stance," which overemphasizes subject matter and neglects the human relation between author and audience; the "advertiser's stance," which overemphasizes the effect on audience and does not give enough attention to subject matter; and the "entertainer's stance," which overemphasizes one's own personality and charm and sacrifices substance.

***Use and abuse of the appeals.*** The four appeals of rhetoric can all be abused and used to manipulate audiences, rather than to attempt to lead them to a free and rational decision. And rhetoric has been under attack for these abuses, since its foundation. Plato (trans. 1925) led the attack against these abuses in the *Gorgias*, and many others have followed him through the centuries, criticizing, for instance, political propaganda, much commercial advertising, some religious proselytism, and some types of education (cf. Doob, 1971; Lasswell et al., 1965; Packard, 1958).

The manipulative use of rhetoric tends to change the nature of all the proofs. Persuasion by personal credibility can degenerate into projection of a false image; appeals can be made to base instincts and biases; logic can be only apparent logic or even deceptive fallacy; and style can sometimes take over as the main appeal, in the absence of any substantial argument. The latter is what is often meant by the pejorative phrase *mere rhetoric*.

Despite the abuses to which it has been put, rhetoric has had its champions from an ethical point of view. In antiquity, Tacitus in his *Dialogus* (trans. 1958) maintained that rhetoric only prospered in free societies and declined and languished under tyrants and emperors—a defense echoed in more recent times by Harris and Seldon (1962) and Brown (1963) with respect to advertising. Possibly the most significant defense of the ethical aspects of rhetoric came in the mid-1800s from Kierkegaard, who said that only rhetoric is "engaged"—to use a word much employed in existential philosophy—as he condemned both science and literature as being too neutral and noncommitted to issues. (See translations in Kierkegaard, 1962, 1992.) The relation between ethics and rhetoric continues to be discussed. For instance, James Porter (1993) argued that ethics, rather than being based on universal precepts, result from a writer's "complex negotiation of various principles, theories, and strategies to decide what is 'good or desirable' in a given situation" (p. 223).

## The Aims

The challenge to the modes, which dominated rhetorical education for centuries, came from Kinneavy (1969, 1971), who used authorities from Aristotle and Aquinas to Bertrand Russell (1945) and George Miller (1951) to make his case for the primacy of aims over modes. He argued that modes are simply approaches to accomplish goals. The four general aims that people have for their communication—persuasive, referential, literary, and expressive—emphasize different parts of the rhetorical triangle illustrated in Fig. 57. 1. The persuasive use is directed toward the audience, who might be listeners or readers; the referential aim, which includes informative and exploratory discourse, is directed toward subject matter; the expressive use is directed toward the author himself or herself; and literary use is directed toward the text or work, the writing itself. Although one aim is usually dominant in a given situation, a person usually has more than one of these aims. For instance, even if the major aim is to persuade an audience of something, another aim would likely be to provide information.

***The persuasive aim.*** Persuasion, as we have already seen, was the major province of rhetoric for centuries, and the classical conception gave considerable attention to persuasive appeals. For the last 2 centuries persuasion has retained its importance, but increasingly the focus went to the logical arrangement of persuasive arguments. Very recently, there have been some important new developments with respect to persuasion through argumentation.

A major contribution to the rethinking of persuasive argumentation has come from Perelman and Olbrechts-Tyteca (1969) in their book *The New Rhetoric*, mentioned earlier. These theorists emphasized rhetorical approaches that might be considered illogical according to Cartesian logic but nevertheless "induce or increase the mind's adherence to theses presented for its assent" (p. 4), and they maintained that "action on the mind and action on the will" are not distinct (p. 46). Audience is central to their conception, because the quality of an argument is determined by the audience's interpretation. Other rhetoricians, particularly those studying the rhetoric of the disciplines, have also distinguished between the claims made by professional logicians and the more informal logic used in such fields as law, ethics, aesthetics, politics, psychology, economics, and the like (e.g., Billig, 1993; Maimon, 1984; McClosky, 1985).

Stephen Toulmin (1964) also maintained that that reasoning is not limited to formal logic. His approach to persuasion, which has been largely adopted by many authorities in speech communication departments, discarded the customary methods of proof and analyzes arguments by their various claims and the levels of warrants that can be made for them (cf. McCleary, 1979). Toulmin's approach can be considered *functional*, because he dealt with the functions that statements fill in the reasoning process. Although he considered some standards to be universal, he acknowledged that there are standards that are field dependent in that they are limited to specific social groups and their discourses.

***The referential aim.*** Referential writing, often called expository, has been predominant in the teaching of composition in America for more than a century. Today it includes the traditional thesis type of writing based on a "logical" progression from generals to specifics or specifics to general, in which subtopics are presented and supporting material and logical connectives are provided. It also includes essays intended to inform that are created through other kinds of development, such as that offered by the functional rhetoric of Toulmin (1964). In English classes informative writing often takes the form of a literary essay, telling readers about a particular element of a literary text. Informative writing across the disciplines includes such genres (or social actions) as reports, proposals, summaries and abstracts, and reviews.

Referential discourse also includes the hypothesis type of writing that explores a topic without necessarily taking a stand or considering the issue settled. At the elementary and secondary level, this is sometimes presented as the problem-solving technique, following Dewey's (1938) methodology. At the college level it is frequently presented as an exploration following the scientific method. The most influential paradigm of this method in rhetorical studies has been that of Thomas Kuhn (1970), which has been adopted by Kinneavy (1980) and Zeiger (1985), among others. A different theoretical basis—that of the linguist Kenneth Pike—was used as the basis for Young et al.'s (1970) *Rhetoric: Discovery and Change.* Writing of both types issues in a question, not a definitive answer. Many students find this a healthy alternative to the thesis theme, since we actually live in an exploratory world rather than a world of definitive answers, and students reflect this reality.

***The expressive aim.*** There was no explicit provision for self-expression, as such, in the classical education, although there has always been an informal practice of such writing in Western culture. But, beginning explicitly in the Renaissance and reaching a full tide in the 19th century, the notion that students might write simply to express their own ideas, ideals, frustrations, gripes, and reactions to situations, without any prior persuasive, expository, or literary aim, began to emerge. The notion was linked to the Romantic idea of individualism, the Freudian idea of expression of the unconscious, and the Hegelian idea of full development of the individual, and was developed further philosophically by Heidegger, Sartre, Cassirer, and Gusdorf.

During the 1960s, when these theories hit the American scene, the practitioners mentioned earlier in this essay, such as Kelley (1972), Macrorie (1970), Elbow (1973), began emphasizing the psychological importance of expressive discourse. The emphasis on expressive discourse has had a strong influence on the American educational scene—some have felt too strong—and there have been pendulum swings away from and then back again to an emphasis on this kind of writing. Some educators see expressive discourse as a psychological beginning for all types of writing, and consequently they tend to place it at the beginning of syllabuses or textbooks and even to emphasize it more at the elementary and secondary levels and to ignore it at the college level. Others see its overlap with other aims of discourse at all levels of education.

The practice of expressive writing is quite varied at both the secondary school and college levels. The personal movie or book reaction (rather than a formal review) has proven very popular at the secondary and college level, and some teachers have tried music, to which the students then react in personal and imaginative ways. Expressive discourse is also used in personal letters and many descriptions of places or of persons. A systematic heuristic for self-expression has been developed by Cynthia Selfe and Sue Rodi (1980), based on the existential notion of self-expression found in Jean-Paul Sartre. It can be applied at any level.

In schools, possibly the most frequent format for expressive writing is the journal. For some, the journal is used almost as a private sanctuary of reactions to parents, teachers, fellow students, boyfriends, girlfriends, events, movies—almost anything. As such, it is frequently not graded, occasionally not even read except by the teacher. Sometimes a journal entry is later rewritten into a more polished paper. Occasionally, the journal as learning log has been used in writing across the curriculum programs (cf. Fulwiler, 1986).

***The literary aim.*** The term *creative writing* is today usually reserved for poetry, dramas, novels, and short stories. The unfortunate implication is that there is not much creativity involved in other types of writing. Sometimes in high school textbooks the term *imaginative writing* is used, but this suffers from the same objection. Throughout history, creative writing was taught with texts usually called poetics, which handled drama, epic, and lyric poetry. Historically, teaching students how to write belletristically often took place within the liberal art of grammar, understood as the study and writing of literature. The two dominant texts in this history have been *The Poetics* of Aristotle and the *Poetic Arts* of Horace (cf. Aristotle, trans. 1960; Horace, trans. 1940.) Aristotle argued that literature is intended to satisfy a craving for the perception of structures, of suspense in plot, of character juxtaposition, of thematic unity of scenic relevance, and of sound patterns; and Horace generally agreed, although he emphasized the local conventions of plot, character, and dialect more than did Aristotle. The major modern treatment taking a rhetorical approach to literary discourse is Booth's (1961) *Rhetoric of Fiction.*

The liberal arts tradition, emphasizing the influences of Aristotle and Horace, had kept the importance of creative writing in the forefront of academic education. In general, our forefathers in Western culture who went to school wrote more poetry than most of us ever attempt. And this emphasis continued throughout much of the 19th century. Even when the poetics and rhetorics of the liberal arts tradition no longer dominated the education scene, for instance, in Bain's (1887) approach, which was heavily influential in this country, in Great Britain, and in South America for over a century, most of the reading assignments and models continued to be the literary giants of British and American literature, and the models for exposition were the essayists of the same tradition, such as Irving, Newman, Ruskin, and Carlyle.

Beginning in the latter part of the 19th century and especially in the 20th century, this emphasis shifted to exposition, particularly in the secondary schools and in the colleges. Frequently, creative writing has been neglected in favor of expository writing, both in this country and in Great Britain. Britton et al.'s (1975) study of writing in England showed the heavy emphasis in that country on transactional writing to the exclusion of the other aims. In the United States, too, the emphasis has clearly been on informative discourse—especially since the scientific threat from Russia in the mid-1950s and the challenges of globalization and international competition that continue today.

For the better part of a century, one persuasive counterpart to this expository emphasis has come from the progressive school movement of the 1930s and 1940s, largely based on Dewey's educational philosophy, which culminated in self-expression. For Dewey (1934), self-expression ideally eventuated in the aesthetic experience. Consequently, it is not surprising that the pedagogical application of self-expression in the progressive schools heavily emphasized the aesthetic. Through neoprogressive initiatives, Dewey's massive influence on education both in America and in many other parts of the world continues to stem the tide of an exclusive emphasis on the expository.

Several decades ago, another healthy opposition to this movement came through *Wishes, Lies, and Dreams: Teaching Children to Write*, a popular book in which Kenneth Koch (1971) described his success in teaching poetry in Harlem, using repeated general sentence types calling for concrete images as structures on which to hang the poem. Thus, the imagery structure of "I wish I were with Charlie Brown in a blue shirt in France" is repeated multiple times, with each student supplying a similar line, like "I wish I was Blondie in the color sea green and the state of California."

Today at the elementary level, especially, there is much attention on children's writing their own stories and poems, publishing them as books, and seeing connections between themselves and other "authors." According to Donald Graves and Jane Hansen (1983), "Children's concept of author changes from a vague notion about some other person who writes books to the additional perception of themselves as authors to the realization that they have choices and decisions to make as authors" (p. 182). At the college level creative writing is almost always determined by the individual theories of the teacher, often a poet or a novelist or a dramatist who also teaches. Typically there is no composition textbook used; instead, most of the texts are anthologies of creative writing.

## RHETORIC AND THE LANGUAGE ARTS

When laying out his system, Aristotle (trans. 1926, 1960) presented rhetoric as an art (*technē*) through which complex thought (*theoria*) was applied (*praxis*) in situations. As an art of production, rhetoric emphasized the constructive aspects of language use, which included considering the nature of rhetorical situations (the persona of author, the nature of audience, the relation between author and audience, the exigence, the context), reasoning about the topic, generating relevant material, and making strategic choices about the kinds of appeals and presentation that would be most effective. Rhetoric was much more than simple rules or techniques. In a classical education rhetoric was an integrative subject, involving all modalities of language—reading, writing, speaking, and listening—and knowledge acquired through one modality, for example reading, would be applied and developed through others. The term *art* continues to be applicable today in speaking of rhetoric because it draws attention to dynamic, functional, performative, and pragmatic aspects.

At the present time, the term *language arts* is being used for reading, writing, listening, and speaking as they are taught and learned in elementary and secondary schools. The listing of the modalities is significant: Since the 1890s, when the emphasis in education went to written over oral language and when literature became preeminent in English studies, reading has been accorded a primary importance, with writing as secondary, and speaking and listening in distant third and fourth rankings. Also, since the end of the 19th century, the pedagogy of literature and the pedagogy of composition have tended to develop separately with different theoretical foundations and even different terminologies. Moreover, the commonalities and overlap among the modalities have not been as apparent in discussions of the language arts as they are in most treatments of rhetoric, and today there are numerous calls and initiatives to integrate the language arts. Rhetoric can provide some means of accomplishing that integration, not through becoming a subject of formal study in the elementary or secondary curriculum but by providing a knowledge base (*theoria*) as well as an emphasis on practice (*praxis*).

Rhetorical principles can do much to integrate the language arts. Particularly important to emphasize is the relation between author and audience, whether the communication is oral or written. Language use, whether one is writing, speaking, reading, or listening, is a means of connecting with others. This relation is at the center of the classic conception as well as of the new rhetorics of Kinneavy (1971, 1980), Burke (1955), Perleman and Olbrechts-Tyteca (1969), and others. Reading and listening, like writing and speaking, should involve an awareness of the human or humans at the other end of the rhetorical triangle (cf. Haas & Flower, 1988). Language use is situated and purposive. Whether reading, writing, speaking, or listening, students should analyze or "read" the rhetorical situation and should attend to purpose, considering not only their own intentions but also the possible aims of others.

Also, through reading and listening to others' texts, individuals can gain much knowledge to use in writing and speaking, and vice versa. This is particularly true when attention is drawn, as it is in much rhetorical pedagogy, to relevant aspects of discourse, such as the rhetorical effectiveness of various appeals or the nature of a speaker or writer's "rhetorical stance" (Booth, 1963). Individuals can also build *copia* of material and strategies to employ in their own texts—ideas drawn or generated from their reading or listening. Moreover, they can see that reading and writing are not always separable processes, because people often write from their reading; they transform others' texts in the act of producing their own, as in writing reports, critiques, summaries, and synthetic essays (N. Nelson, 1998; Spivey, 1990, 1997).

Rhetorical principles can do much also to invigorate the language arts. This can be accomplished by drawing more attention to the *artistic* (in Aristotle's sense of *technē*) aspects of language, whether reading, writing, listening, or speaking. Artistic knowledge is not a set of rules and techniques to be applied mechanically, though it does include principles, precepts, and approaches. Instead, it is flexible, dynamic knowledge to be applied strategically and creatively in specific situations, and it is gained from experience in other social situations. George Hillocks (1984) demonstrated the value of this emphasis on strategic knowledge and social exchanges in what he called the environmental approach to instruction. For the language arts to be *arts*, they must embrace the complex pragmatic (from *praxis*) aspects of language use.

## ACKNOWLEDGMENT

I (Nancy Nelson) consider it a great honor to publish this revision of the chapter on rhetoric that was first written by the late James Kinneavy for the previous edition of the Handbook. Since the first chapter was published in 1991, much has happened in the field of rhetoric that needed to be a part of its treatment here. For me as an author, though, it is somewhat daunting to submit a piece that has another person's name as coauthor when that person has not read and has not given approval to what I said. I can only take responsibility myself for the new treatment and hope that Professor Kinneavy, for whom I always had tremendous respect, would approve.

Appreciation goes to James Catano and Deborah Davis, who read previous versions of this updated chapter.

## *References*

Aristotle (1926). *The "art" of rhetoric* (J. H. Freese, Trans.). The Loeb Classical Library. Cambridge, MA: Harvard University Press.

Aristotle (1960). *The poetics. "Longinus" on the sublime* (W. H. Fyfe, Trans.). *Demetrius, on style* (W. R. Roberts, Trans.). The Loeb Classical Library. Cambridge, MA: Harvard University Press.

Atwell, N. (1998). *In the middle: New understandings about writing, reading, and learning*. Portsmouth, NH: Heinemann.

Augustine (1958). *On Christian doctrine* (D. W. Robertson, Trans.). Library of Liberal Arts, 80. New York: Bobbs-Merrill.

Bain, A. (1887). *English composition and rhetoric: A manual*. New York: Appleton.

Bawarshi, A. (2000). The genre function. *College English, 62*, 335-360.

Bazerman, C. (1987). Codifying the social-scientific style: The APA publication manual as a behaviorist rhetoric. In J. S. Nelson, A. Megill, & D. N. McCloskey (Eds.), *The rhetoric of the humanities* (pp. 125-144). Madison: University of Wisconsin Press.

Becher, T. (1989). *Academic tribes and territories: Intellectual enquiry and the cultures of the disciplines*. Milton Keynes, England: Open University Press.

Berlin, J. (1982). Contemporary composition: The major pedagogical theories. *College English, 44*, 756-777.

Billig, M. (1993). Psychology, rhetoric, and cognition. In R. H. Roberts & J. M. M. Good (Eds.), *The recovery of rhetoric* (pp. 119-136). Charlottesville: University Press of Virginia.

Bitzer, L. F. (1968). The rhetorical situation. *Philosophy and Rhetoric, 1*, 1-14.

Blair, H. (1867). *Lectures on rhetoric and belles lettres*. Philadelphia: Robert Aitken.

Bolter, D. (1993). Hypertext and the rhetorical canons. In J. F. Reynolds (Ed.), *Rhetorical memory and delivery: Classical concepts for contemporary composition and communication* (pp. 97-111). Hillsdale, NJ: Lawrence Erlbaum Associates.

Booth, W. (1961). *The rhetoric of fiction*. Chicago: University of Chicago Press.

Booth, W. (1963). The rhetorical stance. *College Composition and Communication, 14*, 139-145.

Bornscheuer, L. (1976). *Topik Zur struktur der gesellschaftlichen einbildungskraft*. Frankfurt am Main, Germany: Suhrkamp.

Boswell, G. (1988). The disfunction of rhetoric: Invention, imaginative excess, and the origin of the modes of discourse. *Rhetoric Society Quarterly, 18*(3-4), 237-248.

Braddock, R., Lloyd-Jones, R., & Schoer, L. (1963). *Research in written composition*. Urbana, IL: National Council of Teachers of English.

Britton, J. N., Burgess, T., Martin, N., McCleod, A., & Rosen, H. (1975). *The development of writing ability, 11-18*. London: Macmillan.

Brown, J. A. C. (1963). *Techniques of persuasion, from propaganda to brainwashing*. Baltimore: Penguin.

Bühler, K. (1933). Die Axionmatik der Sprachwisssenschaften. *Kant-Studien, 398*, 19-90.

Burke, K. (1941). *The philosophy of literary form*. Baton Rouge: Louisiana State University Press.

Burke, K. (1945). *A grammar of motives*. New York: Prentice-Hall.

Burke, K. (1951). Rhetoric old and new. *Journal of General Education, 5*, 203-209.

Burke, K. (1953). *Counter-statement*. Los Altos, CA: Hermes.

Burke, K. (1955). *A rhetoric of motives*. New York: Braziller.

Burke, K. (1975). The five key terms of dramatism. In W. R. Winterowd (Ed.), *Contemporary rhetoric: A conceptual background with readings* (pp. 155-162). New York: Harcourt Brace Jovanovich.

Campbell, G. (1846). *The philosophy of rhetoric*. New York: Harper & Brothers.

Conference on College Composition and Communication Committee on Language Statement (1974). Students' right to their own language. *College Composition and Communication, 25*, 1-18.

Cicero (1939). *Brutus* (G. L. Hendrickson, Trans.). *Orator* (H. M. Hubbell, Trans.). The Loeb Classical Library. Cambridge, MA: Harvard University Press.

Cicero (1942a). *De oratore, Books I-II* (E. W. Sutton & H. Rackham, Trans.). The Loeb Classical Library. Cambridge, MA: Harvard University Press.

Cicero (1942b). *De oratore, Book III. De fato. Paradoxa stoicorum. De partitione oratoria* (H. Rackham, Trans.). The Loeb Classical Library. Cambridge, MA: Harvard University Press.

Cicero (1949). *De inventione. De optimo genere oratorum. Topica* (H. M. Hubbell, Trans.). The Loeb Classical Library. Cambridge, MA: Harvard University Press.

Cicero (1954). *Ad C. Herennium. De ratione dicendi.* (H. Caplan, Trans.). The Loeb Classical Library. Cambridge, MA: Harvard University Press.

Connors, R. J. (1981). The rise and fall of the modes of discourse. *College Composition and Communication, 32,* 444-455.

Cope, E. M. (1867). *An introduction to Aristotle's rhetoric with analysis, notes.* London: Macmillan.

Corbett, E. P. J. (1971). *Classical rhetoric for the modern student.* New York: Oxford University Press.

Curtius, E. R. (1973). *European literature and the Latin middle ages* (W. R. Trask, Trans.). Princeton, NJ: Princeton University Press.

Cutts, M. (1996). *The plain English guide.* New York: Oxford University Press.

D'Angelo, F. J. (1975). *A conceptual theory of rhetoric.* Cambridge, MA: Winthrop.

Delpit, L. (1995). *Other people's children: Cultural conflict in the classroom.* New York: New Press.

Dewey, J. (1902). *The child and the curriculum.* Chicago: University of Chicago Press.

Dewey, J. (1934). *Art as experience.* New York: Minton, Balch.

Dewey, J. (1938). *Logic: The theory of inquiry.* New York: Henry Holt.

Doob, L. W. (1961). *Communication in Africa: A search for boundaries.* New Haven, CT: Yale University Press.

Elbow, P. (1973). *Writing without teachers.* New York: Oxford University Press.

Emig, J. (1971). *The composing processes of twelfth graders.* (Research Report No. 13). Urbana, IL: National Council of Teachers of English.

Emig, J. (1977). Writing as a mode of learning. *College Composition and Communication, 28,* 122-128.

Erasmus, D. (1978). *Collected works of Erasmus, Vols. 23-24: Literary and educational writings 1 and 2.* Toronto, Canada: University of Toronto Press.

Fahnstock, J., & Secor, M. (1990). *A rhetoric of argument.* New York: McGraw Hill.

Fogarty, D. J. (1959). *Notes for a new rhetoric.* New York: Teachers College Press.

Fulwiler, T. (1987). *The journal book.* Portsmouth, NH: Boynton/Cook.

Fulwiler, T., & Young, A. (1982). *Language connections: Writing and reading across the curriculum.* Urbana, IL: National Council of Teachers of English.

Gee, J. P. (1989). Literacy, discourse, and linguistics. *Journal of Education, 171,* 5-17.

Gere, A. R. (Ed.) (1985). *Roots in the sawdust: Writing to learn across the disciplines.* Urbana, IL: National Council of Teachers of English.

Graves, D. (1983). *Writing: Teachers and students at work.* Portsmouth, NH: Heinemann.

Graves, D., & Hansen, J. (1983). The author's chair. *Language Arts, 60,* 176-183.

Haas, C., & Flower, L. (1988). Rhetorical reading strategies and the construction of meaning. *College Composition and Communication, 39,* 167-183.

Harris, R., & Seldon, A. (1962). *Advertising and the public.* London: A. Deutsch.

Hayes, J. R., & Flower, L. S. (1980). Identifying the organization of writing processes. In L. W. Gregg & E. R. Steinberg (Eds.), *Cognitive processes in writing* (pp. 3-30). Hillsdale, NJ: Lawrence Erlbaum.

Herrington, A. J. (1981). Writing to learn: Writing across the disciplines. *College English, 43,* 379-387.

Hillocks, G. (1984). What works in teaching composition: A meta-analysis of experimental treatment studies. *American Journal of Education, 93,* 133-170.

Horace (1940). Ars poetica (E. Blakeney, Trans.). In A. H. Gilbert (Ed.), *Literary criticism from Plato to Dryden* (pp. 128-143). New York: American Book.

Horner, W. B. (1988). *Rhetoric in the classical tradition.* New York: St. Martin's Press.

Hovland, C. I., Janis, I. R., & Kelly, H. H. (1953). *Communication and persuasion.* New Haven, CT: Yale University Press.

Jakobson, R. (1967). Linguistics and poetics. In S. Chatman & S. R. Levin (Eds.), *Essays on the language of literature* (pp. 296-322). Boston: Houghton Mifflin.

Kelley, L. (1972). *From dialogue to discourse: An open approach to competence and creativity.* Glenview, IL: Scott, Foresman.

Kennedy, G. (1972). *The art of rhetoric in the Roman world, 300 BC-AD300.* Princeton, NJ: Princeton University Press.

Kierkegaard, S. (1962). *The point of view for my work as an author: A report to history and related writings* (B. Nelson, Ed., W. Lowrie, Trans.). New York: Harper & Row.

Kierkegaard, S. (1992). *Kierkegaard's writings: XII. Concluding unscientific postscript to philosophical fragments* (Vol. 1, H. V. Hong & E. H. Hong, Ed. and Trans.). Princeton, NJ: Princeton University Press.

Kinneavy, J. L. (1969). The basic aims of discourse. *College Composition and Communication, 20,* 297-304.

Kinneavy, J. L. (1971). *A theory of discourse.* Englewood Cliffs, NJ: Prentice-Hall.

Kinneavy, J. L. (1980). *A theory of discourse* (2nd ed). New York: Norton.

Kinneavy, J. L., McCleary, W., & Nakadate, N. (1983). Writing across the curriculum. *Profession, 83,* 13-20.

Kinneavy, J. L., McCleary, W., & Nakadate, N. (1985). *Writing in the liberal arts tradition.* New York: Harper & Row.

Koch, K. (1971). *Wishes, lies, and dreams: Teaching children to write poetry.* New York: Vantage.

Kuhn, T. (1970). *The structure of scientific revolutions* (2nd ed.). Chicago: University of Chicago Press.

Lasswell, H. D., Leites, N., Janis, I. L., Kaplan, A., Goldsen, J. M., Grey, A., Kaplan, D., Mintz, A., Yakobson, S., & de Sola Pool, I. (1965). *Language of politics.* Cambridge, MA: MIT Press.

Macrorie, K. (1970). *Uptaught.* Rochelle Park, NJ: Hayden.

Maimon, E. (1984). *Readings in arts and sciences.* Boston: Little, Brown.

Maimon, E., Belcher, G. L., Hearn, G. W., Nodine, B. F., & O'Connor, F. W. (1981). *Writing in the arts and sciences.* Cambridge, MA: Winthrop.

McCleary, W. J. (1979). *Teaching deductive logic: A test of the Toulmin and Aristotelian models for critical thinking and college composition.* Unpublished doctoral dissertation, University of Texas, Austin.

McClosky, D. N. (1985). *The rhetoric of economics.* Madison: University of Wisconsin Press.

Miller, C. R. (1984). Genre as social action. *Quarterly Journal of Speech, 70,* 151-167.

Miller, G. A. (1951). *Language and communications.* New York: McGraw Hill.

Moffett, J. (1968). *Teaching the universe of discourse*. Boston: Houghton Mifflin.

Morris, C. W. (1955). *Signs, language and behavior*. New York: Braziller.

Morison, S. E. (1936). *Harvard College in the seventeenth century*. Cambridge, MA: Harvard University Press.

Murphy, J. J. (Ed.) (1978). *Medieval eloquence: Studies in the theory and practice of medieval rhetoric*. Berkeley: University of California Press.

Murphy, J. J. (Ed.) (1981). *Rhetoric in the Middle Ages: A history of rhetorical theory from Saint Augustine to the Renaissance*. Berkeley: University of California Press.

Murphy, J. J. (1983). The origins and early development of rhetoric. In J. J. Murphy (Ed.), *A synoptic history of classical rhetoric* (pp. 13-18). Davis, CA: Hermagoras Press.

Murphy, J. J. (1998). What is rhetoric and what can it do for writers and readers? In N. Nelson & R. C. Calfee (Eds.), *The reading-writing connection: 97th yearbook of the National Society for the Study of Education* (Vol. 97, pp. 74-87). Chicago: University of Chicago Press.

Murray, D. (1972, November). Teach writing as process not product. *The Leaflet of the New England Association of Teachers of English*, 11-14.

Nadeau, R. (1952). The progymnasmata of Aphthonius in translation, *Speech Monographs, 19*, 264-285.

Nadeau, R. (1964). Hermogenes on stases: A translation with an introduction and notes. *Speech Monographs, 31*, 361-424.

National Education Association (1894). *Report of the Committee of Ten on secondary school studies*. New York: American Book.

Nelson, J. S., Megill, A., & McCloskey, D. N. (1987). Rhetoric of inquiry. In J. S. Nelson, A. Megill, & D. N. McCloskey (Eds.), *The rhetoric of the human sciences: Language and argument in scholarship and public affairs* (pp. 3-18). Madison: University of Wisconsin Press.

Nelson, N. (1998). Reading and writing contextualized. In N. Nelson & R. C. Calfee (Eds.), *The reading-writing connection: 97th yearbook of the National Society for the Study of Education* (pp. 266-287). Chicago: University of Chicago Press.

Nelson, N., & Calfee, R. C. (1998). The reading-writing connection viewed historically. In N. Nelson & R. C. Calfee (Eds.), *The reading-writing connection: 97th yearbook of the National Society for the Study of Education* (pp. 1-52). Chicago: University of Chicago Press.

Ong, W. J. (1979). *Ramus: Method and the decay of dialogue*. New York: McKay.

Packard, V. (1958). *The hidden persuaders*. New York: Pocket Books.

Perelman, C., & Olbrechts-Tyteca, L. (1969). *The new rhetoric: A treatise on argumentation* (J. Wilkinson & P. Weaver, Trans.).

Notre Dame, IN: University of Notre Dame Press. (Original work published 1958)

Plato (1925). *Lysis. Symposium. Gorgias* (W. R. M. Lamb, Trans.). The Loeb Classical Library. Cambridge, MA: Harvard University Press.

Porter, J. E. (1993). Developing a postmodern ethics of rhetoric and composition. In T. Enos & S. C. Brown (Eds.), *Defining the new rhetorics* (pp. 207-226). Newbury Park, CA: Sage.

Quintilian (1920-22). *The institutio oratoria of Quintilian* (Vols. 1-4, H. E. Butler, Trans.). The Loeb Classical Library. New York: G. P. Putnam's Sons.

Ramus, P. (1555). *Dialectique*. Geneva, Switzerland: Droz.

Rohman, D. G., & Wlecke, A. O. (1964). *Prewriting: The construction and application of models for concept formation in writing*. East Lansing: Michigan State University, US Office of Education Cooperative Research Project, No. 2174. (ERIC Document Reproduction Service ED 001 273)

Russell, B. (1948). *Human knowledge: Its scope and limits*. London: G. Allen & Unwin.

Russell, D. R. (1991). *Writing in the academic disciplines, 1870-1990: A curricular history*. Carbondale: Southern Illinois University Press.

Selfe, C. L., & Rodi, S. (1980). An invention heuristic for expressive writing. *College Composition and Communication, 31*, 169-174.

Shannon, C. E., & Weaver, W. (1949). *The mathematical theory of communication*. Urbana: University of Illinois Press.

Simons, H. W. (1990). Introduction: The rhetoric of inquiry as an intellectual movement. In H. W. Simons (Ed.), *The rhetorical turn: Invention and persuasion in the conduct of inquiry* (pp. 1-31). Chicago: University of Chicago Press.

Spivey, N. N. (1990). Transforming texts: Constructive processes in reading and writing. *Written Communication, 7*, 256-287.

Spivey, N. N. (1997). *The constructivist metaphor: Reading, writing, and the making of meaning*. San Diego, CA: Academic Press.

Tacitus, C. (1958). *Dialogus* (W. Peterson, Trans.). *Agricola. Germania* (M. Hutton, Trans.). The Loeb Classical Library. Cambridge, MA: Harvard University Press.

Thucydides (1998). *The Peloponnesian War* (W. Blanco, Trans.; W. Blanco & J. T. Roberts, Eds.). New York: W. W. Norton.

Toulmin, S. E. (1958). *The uses of argument*. Cambridge, England: Cambridge University Press.

Whately, R. (1867). *Elements of rhetoric*. New York: Sheldon.

Williamson, G. (1951). *The Senecan amble: A study in prose form from Bacon to Collier*. Chicago: University of Chicago Press.

Young, R. E., Becker, A. L., & Pike, K. L. (1970). *Rhetoric: Discovery and change*. New York: Harcourt, Brace.

Zeiger, W. (1985). The exploratory essay: Enfranchising the spirit of inquiry in college composition. *College English, 48*, 454-464.

# ·58·

# CHILDREN'S RESPONSES TO LITERATURE

*Miriam Martinez*
University of Texas at San Antonio

*Nancy L. Roser*
University of Texas, Austin

In the intervening years since the first edition of the *Handbook of Research on Teaching the English Language Arts* (Flood, Jensen, Lapp, & Squire, 1991), reader response has been examined, interpreted, and grappled with in a plethora of settings and from multiple vantage points. For decades, descriptions, comparisons, and analyses had been drawn from older students' written responses to prescribed text. However, in his report of the proceedings of the Dartmouth Seminar, Harding (1968) observed that young children's responses to literature may be qualitatively different from those of adolescents and adults. Following Squire (1964) and others' attention to older students' *oral* responses, the earliest studies of younger readers relied primarily on structured interviews to get at children's responses (e.g., Applebee, 1978; Cullinan, Harwood, & Galda, 1983). Later investigators, using ethnographic techniques, studied children's naturally occurring responses in homes and classrooms. Hickman (1979) became a participant–observer in three literature-rich, multiage classrooms (Grades K–1, 2–3, and 4–5). In this role, she was able to tap dimensions of response that had remained untouched by research approaches that relied on more structured techniques. Following Hickman's lead, other researchers attempted to observe and describe children's thinking about literature in more naturalistic contexts. For example, Lehr (1988) invited young children to draw pictures about books they thought had the same ideas. Lehr conducted subsequent interviews in a comfortable setting in which the target books were available for the children to handle if they so chose. Changes in methodology of this nature contributed to the changing view of the child as responder.

In their comprehensive review, Beach and Hynds' (1991) challenged the field to move research beyond merely describing responses toward "consider[ing] the purposes underlying various response types" (p. 480). Increasingly, researchers have worked with broader visions of what response is, as well as by attempting to understand how contexts and cultures nurture and support responses (Bloome & Bailey, 1992). Both in homes and classroom settings, investigators have attended to spontaneous and planned "literacy events" and the responses they evoke—learning about the nature and process of response.

As investigations have shifted in both their scope and nature, researchers such as McGinley and Kamberelis (1996) widened the lens by documenting ways children talk (as well as read and write) when encouraged to reflect on personally and socially relevant themes. Other recent studies have provided inspections of the responses of prereaders, of children learning English as their second language, of handicapped children, of struggling readers involved in the process of response, have looked at gender differences, and at the effects of culture on response (e.g., Enciso, 1994; Evans, 1997; Goatley, Brock, & Raphael, 1995; Liaw, 1995; McGill-Franzen & Lanford, 1994; E. B. Smith, 1995; Williams & McLean, 1997; Wollman-Bonilla, 1994).

Since our earlier review (Martinez & Roser, 1991) in the first edition of this volume, the number of published research studies has proliferated, reflecting increasingly diverse ways of investigating responses. As more researchers and teachers have focused on the nature of children's literary meaning making, they have chosen methodologies ranging from case studies for understanding individual children's capacity for response (McGill-Franzen & Lanford, 1994; McMahon, Pardo, & Raphael, 1991) to complex combinations of methodologies for understanding how groups undertake meaning making (e.g., Almasi, 1995). Furthermore, many more classification schemes of student response have been produced as researchers relied on inductive techniques for data analysis (e.g., Leal, 1992; Martinez, Roser,

Hoffman, & Battle, 1992; McGee, 1992). In classrooms, many more innovative strategies have been employed both to encourage and support responses (e.g., Hancock, 1993; Kelly, 1990; Raphael & McMahon, 1994; Wollman-Bonilla & Werchadlo, 1995).

There have also been changes, too, both in terms of the focus and content of the literacy curriculum. Teachers report the use of more authentic children's literature assuming an instructional place and value in classrooms. For example, in a survey of over 1,000 randomly selected teachers from across the United States, 97% of the prekindergarten through second-grade teachers reported regularly reading aloud, 83% reported engaging children in oral language activities, and 69% reported use of response activities. Seventy-nine percent of teachers in Grades 3 through 5 reported they provided literature response activities, and 67% said they used trade books instructionally (Baumann, Hoffman, Moon, & Duffy-Hester, 1998). Simultaneously, publishers have included more original and uncut selections from trade publications into reading texts (Kucan, 1994; Singleton, 1997).

When Purves and Beach (1972) produced their comprehensive review of research on responses to literature nearly 20 years ago, they noted in the foreword (p. vii) they faced two major problems in their effort: The first was finding some way of classifying the studies being examined; the second was weighing the merits of those studies. Based on the advice of an advisory board of eminent scholars, Purves and Beach decided that a classification system must grow from consideration of the studies themselves rather than from a preordained formulation; second, they decided the contribution of any study would be gauged from the importance of the question being considered—the conception of a worthwhile problem—rather than solely from the sophistication of its statistical properties. In this chapter, we continue to follow the lead provided by Purves and Beach in an attempt to take stock of the increasing number of investigations of children's responses to literature. We once again let the organization of the review grow from the studies themselves and were vigilant for the thoughtful question.

Intriguingly, because many of the studies summarized in this chapter were reported in the pages of journals intended for curriculum "implementers," the studies often moved quickly from the evidence to the findings so that the "analysis" of the data was often the least visible part of the report. We did not discount studies written for a teacher audience; nor did we permit only one or two such studies to shape a "category" of evidence. Rather, we stacked and restacked the classroom accounts, looking for the "preponderance of evidence" necessary to make summative claims.

We do not include in this chapter studies of classroom discourse that did not focus on children's literary responses—even if the study's materials included literary text. Nor do we include descriptions of classroom activities that did not claim or provide systematic data analysis. We also exclude reports that were only testimonies to the success of a particular organization or methodology and those that provided only isolated examples of a selected student's responsive insights while claiming (without showing) that the perspicacity was widespread.

We exclude studies of students' responses in seventh grade and above, and, finally, we focus primarily on research published since our review in the first edition of this *Handbook* (Flood et al., 1991).

## EXPLORING CHILDREN'S LITERARY MEANING MAKING

From its beginnings in the late 1970s, research on children's responses to literature addressed the question of *how* children respond—a question researchers have continued to address. Yet another factor contributing to the evolving view of the child as responder has been the increasing grounding of research in literary response theory. Louise Rosenblatt (1978) described the relationship between reader and text as a "transaction" in which the reader not only attends to "what the words point . . . to in the external world, to their referents . . . [but also] to the images, feelings, attitudes, associations and ideas that the words and their referents evoked in him" (p. 10). Rosenblatt argued that readers must attend *both* to the text and to the "poem" being evoked.

Much of the early research on children's responses to literature was defined by a developmental focus as researchers sought to describe differences in how children talk about literature at different age levels. The category systems these researchers developed to describe children's responses reflected this perspective. Applebee (1978), for example, rooted his category system for the careful delineation of children's developing sense of story in Piagetian theory. As literary response theory (Iser, 1980; Rosenblatt, 1938/1976, 1978) captured the forefront in educational circles in the last decade of the 20th century, researchers have increasingly drawn on their understanding of the literary response process in developing category systems to describe children's literary meaning making. For example, McGee (1992) relied on both Garrison and Hynds (1991) and Eeds and Wells (1989), as well as her own inspections of the responses of first graders, to derive a category system that represented "a continuum of responses from attention to evocation of readers' experiences and emotions to attention to the text" (p. 179). Similarly, the category system Hancock (1993) developed to describe the responses of her subjects emerged from the data but reflected theoretical beliefs about the nature of the literary transaction. This system identified three major categories of response—immersion, self-involvement, and detachment. The immersion subcategories reflected the reader's immersion in the text "as he or she attempts to make sense of the emerging plot and characters" (p. 343). Self-involvement subcategories reflected readers' personal involvement with characters or plot, and detachment subcategories indicated that the reader had stepped outside the story world in order to make evaluative statements about the literature or to contemplate his or her perspective on the process of reading or writing. Taken together, these changes in the ways children's responses have been evoked and inspected reveal an ever richer picture of children's transactions with literature.

## CURRENT UNDERSTANDINGS FROM RESEARCH ON CHILDREN'S LITERARY MEANING MAKING

From a review of over 100 studies of children's responses, several characterizations of children's responses to literature seemed to emerge: (a) children's responses are rich and varied, centering both on texts and on their transaction with the "evoked poem" (Rosenblatt, 1978, p. 48); (b) children exhibit distinct response profiles; (c) responses vary across age groups; and (c) responses change when the texts become familiar.

### Children Respond in Rich and Varied Ways

*Text-centered responses.* Early descriptions of children's responses to literature suggested that children's responses were primarily text-centered in nature. For example, Applebee (1978) found that his younger subjects (6- and 9-year-olds) focused on story action as they retold or summarized favorite stories. However, as researchers began to rely on more naturalistic methodology and to develop categorization systems based on increasingly diverse perspectives, the portrait of child as responder became more complex. Guided by a definition of a response event as any behavior revealing a connection between children and literature, Hickman (1981) found that children responded to literature in a variety of ways—through body movements such as dance and applause, by acting on the impulse to share discoveries in books, through actions and drama, by making representations based on literature, by writing about literature or using literary models in their writing, and through talk. Both researchers confirmed the importance of the story world to young respondents. Similarly, Martinez and Roser (1994) found that most of the participants in their study of kindergarten through fifth-graders' responses to a chapter book focused on the story world rather than on the messages or themes that emerge or on the story as a crafted object.

Other recent investigators have found this engagement with the story world to be active and dynamic. For example, Hancock's (1993) sixth-grade subjects attempted "to make sense of the emerging plot and characters" (p. 343) by questioning, making predictions, interpreting, and making discoveries as they read. In a similar fashion, Sipe (1998) found that almost a quarter of the responses contributed by first and second graders during story discussions were analytical responses in which the children worked to construct meaning through analysis of text and illustrations.

Early researchers also concluded that children comprehended stories at literal levels. Applebee, for example, argued that elementary-age children are developmentally unable to analyze and generalize about stories, and Cullinan et al. (1983) found that their younger elementary-age subjects did not readily interpret and evaluate literature. However, subsequent investigations countered these findings. Lehr's (1988) in-depth investigation of elementary-age children's ability to infer thematic meaning found that even the youngest children were able to successfully generate thematic statements for stories. Although

their statements often differed from constructions of text messages offered by adults, the children's thematic statements were, nonetheless, congruent with the text, leading Lehr to conclude that "young children process meaning in literature with perspectives that differ from those of adults" (p. 350). Subsequent research has confirmed that children can make interpretations about many facets of stories in addition to theme (Many, 1991; Martinez et al., 1992; McGee, 1992).

Children's text-focused responses also include attention to the author at work, as they step outside the story world to "objectify" their experience with text (Langer, 1995). Although children's response to features and qualities of texts appears to occur less frequently than other types of response (Hancock, 1993; Martinez et al., 1992; McGee, 1992; Sipe, 1998), a number of researchers have documented children's attention to the text as a crafted object (Kelly, 1990; Smolkin, 1995; Wollman-Bonilla, 1989). Children are especially likely to focus on the artistry of literature in contexts in which their attention is directed toward features of craft. Kiefer (1988) found that "as children communicate with and about picture books, they seem to develop a growing awareness of aesthetic factors and of the artist's role in choosing these factors to express meaning" (p. 264). Madura (1995) and Bloem and Manna (1999) engaged children in author study as one way to engage readers in thoughtful literary analysis. Bloem and Manna found that the second- and fourth-graders in their investigation followed both the artistry of the texts and the teacher models of response to engage aesthetically in the literature study. The children found pleasure in the nuances of texts and in querying how the authors and illustrators featured in their literature study crafted her work. Madura (1995) described an approach to the teaching of language arts through the "world of the picture book," documenting how her students came to understand themselves as readers and writers in a learning environment that valued "beauty, personal reflection, and the process of creating visual and written compositions" (p. 116).

*Reader-centered responses.* Although attention to text is significant as children respond to literature, researchers have also established the centrality of more reader-centered responses. Children build bridges between their personal experiences and the literature they read, making what Cochran-Smith (1984) has termed "life to text connections" (p. 34). Hickman (1979) described the personal associations children make when reading literature, and numerous researchers have subsequently confirmed her findings (e.g., Farest & Miller, 1993; Martinez et al., 1992; Raphael et al., 1992; Short, 1992; Sipe, 1998; Wollman-Bonilla, 1989; Wollman-Bonilla & Werchadlo, 1995).

The personal experiences children bring with them to literature study include experiences with other texts, and various researchers have found that children make intertextual connections when responding to literature (Farest & Miller, 1993; Short, 1992; Sipe, 1998). Elementary-age students also become personally involved with characters as they vicariously step into character roles and make judgments about how they would feel if they found themselves in a character's situation

(Hancock, 1993; McGee, 1992; Wollman-Bonilla & Werchadlo, 1995).

The very few investigations of children's responses framed by a cultural perspective indicate that cultural experience can be an important factor shaping response—with readers bringing their cultural experiences to literature. Sims (1983) conducted a case study of a 10-year-old African American girl's responses to literature and found that her subject strongly preferred books featuring strong female, African American protagonists. Although the child expressed a preference for reading about experiences similar to her own, she was also interested in reading about African Americans whose experiences differed from hers. Similarly, E. B. Smith's (1995) case studies of three African American fifth-graders showed that her subjects' responses to African American literature were different than their responses to other literature. Her subjects, one of whom she characterized as a reluctant reader and another as an academically struggling student, sought out and avidly read literature related to their culture. Smith concluded that the three students sought out African American literature because it mirrored their own frame of reference.

McGinley and Kamberelis (1996) found that literature served both a personal function and a social function for these third- and fourth-graders who were invited to use literature as a means of reflecting on personal experiences and as a means of imagining possibilities for their own futures. Response opportunities were also ways through which the children attempted to understand and negotiate social relationships and significant social problems. In effect, McGinley and Kamberelis found that children use literature as a lens through which they can better understand their own personal experiences and their world. Langer (1995) has described this as a process in which readers "step out" of stories to reflect on how the stories relate to their own lives or the lives of others.

## Individuals Have Distinct Response Profiles

Using case study methodology, which permitted rich characterizations of individual respondents, Galda (1982) collected the responses to two works of realistic fiction of three fifth-grade girls during one-on-one conversations, as well as during small group discussions. She found substantial differences in the responses of her three subjects—Emily, Ann, and Charlotte—concluding that individual readers have distinctive styles of response. Emily read stories primarily for the plot. She wanted to find out what happened in a story and was especially responsive to unusual twists in the plot. Evaluation was Emily's most frequent mode of response, and her evaluations employed general labels (e.g., "good," "nice style") that were rarely supported with references to the stories. Galda concluded that Emily was unable to assume what Britton (1970) has termed the "spectator stance" (p. 102) and thereby accept the world created by the author on its own terms. Rather, her responses were governed by her personal view of reality, and she criticized characters and events that did not conform to her reality. In contrast to Emily, Charlotte focused on the central conflict and the main characters' reactions to that conflict. However, she took deliberate steps to maintain a distance from the conflict to prevent personal involvement in the story. One way in which she did this was by assuming the role of the observer-critic. As an observer-critic, Charlotte, like Emily, criticized the story in terms of her own perceived reality, but she couched her criticism in objective terms by comparing characters' behavior with what she called "typical" behavior. Unlike Emily, Charlotte supported her evaluations with examples from the texts.

Galda (1982) characterized the third respondent, Ann, as a mature responder, one who analyzed both the text and her responses to it. Unlike her peers, Ann focused on characters' feelings, personalities, and motives rather than solely on story events. Galda described Ann as being able to assume a spectator stance as she "entered into the experience the text offered" (p. 16), accepting realities present in the story that were not her own. Through her analysis, Galda identified distinctive, styles of response that pointed to the individual nature of children's transactions with literature.

To examine individual response styles and meaning-making patterns, Hancock (1993) selected 4 of the 10 sixth-grade students in her investigation for more intensive case studies. Like Galda (1982), Hancock's case study methodology revealed that children may have distinctive styles of literary meaning making. Hancock characterized Erin, one of the case study subjects, as an "involved, immersed meaning-maker" (p. 348) who began her reading of realistic fiction through character introspection before moving on to character identification and story involvement. Michael, by contrast, was a "detached literary critic" (p. 352) who, from his earliest journal entries, consistently evaluated stories rather than writing responses reflecting story engagement. Ellen was the "unpredictable reader" (p. 357) whose response style varied dramatically from story to story. For example, in writing about *Hatchet* (Paulsen, 1987), her responses reflected a high degree of engagement but in reading *The Great Gilly Hopkins* (Paterson, 1978), character assessment was Ellen's most frequent mode of response. Finally, Courtney was the "uncertain seeker of meaning" (p. 361) in whose journal entries a thread of questioning consistently appeared. Though Hancock acknowledged limitations in capturing children's responses in written format, she nonetheless was confident in concluding that children exhibit diverse response profiles, underscoring the individual nature of the literary transaction.

Investigating the responses of first and second graders during story time discussions, Sipe (1998) described the distinctive response styles of four of his subjects. Sally's responses were marked by logical reasoning and close analysis and her use of intertextual references to substantiate the points she made during discussions. She was also repeatedly concerned with identifying relationships between fictional stories and reality. A final feature of Sally's response style was her sensitivity to the feelings of story characters and to issues of equity and justice. By contrast, Charles was a "performative responder" (p. 82) who would often use story worlds as springboards for his own flights of fancy. In addition, Charles liked to take on the roles of characters and create voices for them. He further engaged in the world of stories by frequently predicting upcoming story events. Krissy's response style was most distinctly defined by her tendency to suggest story-based creative activities that she and her classmates might engage in—art activities, drama activities, and so on. Krissy also relished inventing alternatives to the plot of stories and sharing her speculations about stories with her peers. She was especially interested in the artistic styles and techniques used by illustrators. The defining feature of Jim's response styles was his ability to take a broad perspective on stories; frequently during literature discussions Jim shared thematic and quasi-thematic statements with his classmates.

McGinley and Kamberelis (1996) also selected two case study subjects from the third and fourth-graders in their investigation. These children used reading and writing for distinctly different purposes. Jamar, one of the case study subjects, was a third grader living in a community which experienced a host of social problems, some of which had directly impacted his own life. Jamar frequently used books such as *Maniac Magee* (Spinelli, 1991) to help him better understand the greater community in which he lived and to explore possible solutions to the problems in his world. Literature typically functioned differently for Tanya, a fourth-grade case study subject. Often the literature Tanya read evoked personal memories and led her to reflect on important personal experiences. Tanya also used literature as a vehicle for exploring her future self. Especially when she read biographies about African American women, Tanya often reflected on her own life and imagined possibilities for the person she would one day become.

## Children Respond Differently Across Age Levels

In a pioneering effort to understand the developmental nature of children's literary responses, Applebee (1978) looked at responses across 6-, 9-, 13-, and 17-year-olds. He asked 6- and 9-year-olds to identify, tell about, and evaluate favorite stories, while older subjects were asked to write about stories. Applebee found differences in responses across age levels between children's objective responses (i.e., those responses concerned with a story's publicly verifiable characteristics) and their subjective or personal responses. Younger subjects' objective responses focused on story action rather than story characteristics such as point of view or theme. Only the forms of objective responses differed between 6 and 9-year-olds, with the younger children typically producing retellings and the 9-year-olds producing synopses or summaries. The subjective responses of 6-year-olds typically consisted of global evaluations (e.g., "It's good"), whereas 9-year-olds evaluated by placing stories in categories with clearly marked attributes (e.g., "dreary" or "interesting"). The objective responses of 13- and 17-year-olds changed dramatically with the adolescents being concerned with analyzing the structures of stories and forming generalizations about their meanings. Moreover, their objective and subjective responses were closely linked, as their evaluations emerged from their analyses of the structure of literary works. Applebee concluded that these more sophisticated avenues of response did not yet appear to be open to younger children for whom the story remained "primarily a patterning of events" (p. 115).

Extending the work of Applebee, Galda (1990) systematically examined evaluative responses by not only looking at the responses of children in different grade levels (fourth, sixth, and eighth grades) but also by providing a longitudinal view of a group of children across 4 years—from fourth through seventh grade. Galda was able to show that students' responses varied not only by grade but also with the genre of the text they read. Like Applebee's subjects, students' evaluative responses were largely categoric at fourth grade, while upper grade students were more analytic in their responses. Even so, Galda found grade level by genre interactions. That is, students responded to fantasy with more categoric evaluations and to realism with more analytic evaluations, regardless of grade level.

Hickman (1981) also looked at differences in children's responses across grade levels (Grades K-1, 2-3, and 4-5). As noted earlier, she defined response more broadly than earlier researchers and included in her analysis both verbal and physical modes of response. Although Hickman found instances of both modes of response in each of the three multigrade classrooms in which she collected data, she found that some modes were more characteristic of particular grade levels. For example, the younger subjects (kindergartners and first graders) were more likely to use their bodies to respond. These children often echoed the action in stories during reading and in teacher-led discussions; parts of stories also appeared frequently in their dramatic play. Hickman described the Grade 2 to Grade 3 level as a transitional one in which children seemed at different times more like the younger or older groups. The children in the Grade 4 to Grade 5 class were characterized as being intensely attentive to books. Only at this level did children become so engrossed in texts as to be described as "lost in a book."

In their oral responses, Hickman (1981) found that her younger subjects expressed more interest in stories than in the authors of stories. Although they were very much concerned with sorting out what was happening in stories, they could reduce stories to "lessons" when invited to interpret meaning. The personal statements these kindergartners and first graders made were only loosely tied to stories. Finally, these younger children expressed concern with the reality of stories by talking about whether stories were "true" or "possible." By contrast, the older children had less need to focus on story line in their verbal responses and instead often revealed connections between their own experiences and interpreted story meanings. They frequently relied on literary terminology in discussing the reality of stories and expressed understandings of meaning using disembedded thematic statements. The fourth- and fifth-graders in Hickman's study clearly recognized the role of author as the creator of a story.

Lehr (1988) found developmental trends in children's ability to identify and articulate story themes. Lehr asked her subjects—kindergartners, second-graders, and fourth-graders—to identify realistic books with related themes and folktales with related themes. Although all the children were more successful in identifying related themes of realistic stories, the second-grade and fourth-grade students made the same selections as adults more often than did the kindergartners. Older children were also more successful in making their own thematic statements for the stories. Additionally, Lehr found differences across grade levels in awareness of character motivation. The older children "identified with characters and expected characters to change, whereas kindergarten children typically did not want to change actions of characters" (p. 351).

Martinez and Roser (1994) examined the literature talk of classes of kindergartners and second-, fourth-, and fifth-graders responding to the turning-point chapter of the same chapter book. They found that the younger children were generally most concerned with following the immediate plot line, whereas the older children talked about "unsolved problems, about events that occurred prior to [the turning-point] chapter, or about global concerns that transcended particular events (e.g., characterization as revealed throughout the book rather than as revealed through a single story event)" (p. 320).

Although researchers have documented differences in children's literary responses across grade levels, it is not yet clear the extent to which differences may reflect the influence of factors such as instructional context rather than developmental constraints. For example, in examining children's responses, Lehr found that her subjects' previous experience with literature was a mitigating factor. Case studies, which have revealed distinctive differences in individual styles of response, also call into question a too rigid adherence to developmental constraints.

## Children Talk Differently When the Text Is Familiar

A number of investigators have examined children's responses across time to the same story (cf. Crago & Crago, 1976; Hickman, 1979; Kiefer, 1986; Yaden, 1988). Listening to stories repeatedly, an experience that frequently occurs in homes and classrooms, appears to impact children's responses. Martinez and Roser (1985) examined changes in children's naturally occurring responses as they listened to stories read aloud more than one time. Focusing on the story time interactions of a 4-year-old and her father and a group of 4-year-olds and their preschool teacher, the researchers described at least four changes that signaled the differences in children's responses as they listened to stories repeatedly. First, the children in both settings talked more about familiar than unfamiliar stories. Second, the form of the children's responses changed when listening to unfamiliar and familiar stories. The child reading with her father asked more questions when a story was read for the first time and made more comments when listening to familiar stories. In the preschool, the children also made more comments when stories were familiar. The focus of responses (i.e., talk centering on characters, events, details, titles, setting, story language, or theme) changed over repeated readings of stories. Although the pattern of change varied from story to story, the shifts in focus suggest that, as children gain control over particular aspects of stories, they are able to attend to other dimensions. Finally, when children chose to discuss a particular aspect of a story across multiple readings, the discussion indicated that the children were probing the story more deeply than they had initially. For these preschoolers, the increased opportunities to listen to a story resulted in more complex responses.

As part of an experimental study designed to increase the number and complexity of 4-year-olds' responses to literature, Morrow (1988) also investigated children's responses to stories read to them repeatedly. The children, all of low socioeco-

nomic status attending urban day-care centers, were assigned to two experimental groups and one control group. In the first experimental group, the children were read a different book each week for 10 weeks on a one-to-one basis. Children in the second experimental group heard repeated readings of only three different books, whereas those in the control group were involved in traditional reading readiness activities. Morrow found that participation in one-to-one read-aloud events increased the quantity and complexity of the children's responses. On the posttreatment measure, children in both experimental groups asked more questions and made more comments than those in the control group. Children in the different-book experimental group asked more questions, whereas those in the repeated-book experimental group made more comments about the stories they heard. In addition, repeated experiences with stories fostered a wider variety of response and more complex, interpretive comments than did single readings of stories.

## NURTURING RESPONSE IN CLASSROOMS

### Creating Literature-Rich Classrooms

Hickman (1981) first studied children's naturally occurring responses in a school setting, and she found that children's responses were tied to the context in which they occurred. Throughout the school in which Hickman observed, children's literature was a central part of the students' experience, and this was clearly apparent in the three focal classrooms in which she conducted her investigation. Although the classroom literature programs organized by the teachers were not identical, Hickman (1981) was able to identify some common strategies used by the teachers:

1. The teachers selected titles for classroom use with an emphasis on quality and relatedness. Hickman found that the presentation of related selections influenced the children's responses in at least two ways. First, these units of study appeared to encourage the children to make explicit connections among literature selections. In addition, she found that where related selections were less available, the children had less to say about the formal properties of a selection.

2. The teachers assured children of access to books by displaying the books attractively and by providing ample time for children to read. Hickman found that children more readily expressed their responses when they had the book in hand. Although they made brief comments about books not physically available, more reflective thinking (expressed through artwork, writing, or discussion) emerged when children had direct access to a book.

3. The teachers presented literature to the children daily, both by reading aloud and by introducing books to the children. Books read aloud or introduced by the teacher were the ones most often sought by the children. These were also the titles that generated the most talk and the greatest variety of response events (e.g., artwork, writing).

4. The teachers discussed books with the children, using critical terminology to support children who had an idea, but needed words to express that idea.

5. The teachers provided the space, time, materials, and suggestions for book related activities.

6. The teachers provided for the formal sharing and display of completed book extensions.

7. The teachers planned for cumulative experiences with literature. These experiences allowed the children to consider some selections and genre in depth, and in a variety of ways over time. This temporal dimension of response is of special note because Hickman found that the children's responses to particular books frequently changed over time. Hickman noted that "both the length involved (allowing reflection and repetition) and the cumulative effect of employing a variety of modes seems to be important in determining qualitative shifts in the content of response." (p. 349)

Many of Hickman's (1981) observations previewed characteristics of effective literacy centers identified by Morrow and Weinstein (1982). In addition, Kiefer (1983) extended one aspect of Hickman's study by focusing on children's naturally occurring responses to picture books in a classroom setting. The classroom was a multilevel first- and second-grade mix, in which picture books played a central role; in fact, picture books served as the basis for reading instruction. Like Hickman, Kiefer found that the teacher played a key role in influencing responses. In this classroom, the teacher chose to read and reread books, and Kiefer found a marked deepening and broadening of response as the children had repeated opportunities to interact with a book. The language the teacher chose to use in discussing books also influenced the children, who in turn frequently used specialized terminology such as "media," "collage," and "acrylics" in talking about illustrations in books. In addition, the teacher used open-ended discussion strategies to elicit a variety of responses, and Kiefer found that the children talked among themselves, expressing feelings, making predictions and inferences, asking questions, exchanging information, and connecting new books with others they had read.

Using a participant-observer stance, McClure (1985) studied a class of fifth- and sixth-grade children's responses to poetry over the course of a school year, focusing especially on the relationship of their responses to the context in which they occurred. She chose to look within a classroom in which poetry already held a significant place in order to describe the classroom factors that seemed to support the students' responses. She observed episodes related to sharing published poetry, writing poetry, and extending poetry through art. Students both shared and critiqued poetry with peers and teachers in large and small group settings. McClure noted that it was evident that the two teachers in whose classrooms she observed had "created a physical and emotional climate which supported children's emerging responses to poetry" (p. 274) by interweaving the context factors of time, space, materials, and the teachers' own convictions. Their nondirective teaching role appeared to nurture an active, exploratory learner role. McClure described the aspects of the classroom environment that seemed to be supportive of children's tentative, exploratory

poetic responses. These included sanctioning peer interaction, teachers' acknowledgement of the struggle required to create poetry, as well as their establishment of clear-cut expectations, from which children could operate comfortably and with much self-determination.

## THE SOCIAL NATURE OF RESPONSE

A major underpinning of research in recent decades has been on the social nature of learning. Stemming from the influence of Vygotsky (1978) and others who considered the vital role that social development plays in shaping and clarifying language and thought, teachers and researchers have seemed to provide increased opportunities for learners to work together to untangle complexities, problem solve, and hypothesize (i.e., to "construct" meanings). Researchers argue that the deepest levels of understanding are made possible though social interaction, or what Fish (1980) called "interpretive communities." Applied to literature study, students talk over their reactions and interpretations with other readers. Hepler and Hickman (1982) noted that the "literary transaction, the one-to-one conversation between author and audience, is frequently surrounded by other voices" (p. 279). Repeatedly, observers have argued that the conversations in which different ideas, conjectures, and backgrounds are shared allow for enriched understanding and experience (Bakhtin, 1986; Lindfors, 1999).

Almasi and Gambrell (1997) described literature discussion as speech events in which participants collaboratively produce meaning or consider alternative interpretations in adjusting or making new understandings. Because literature discussion involves "discussion" as well as "literature," there is necessity for the "communicative competence" (Bloome & Bailey, 1992) that skilled conversationalists display. Almasi and Gambrell include as indicators of competence the ability to initiate topics of conversation, to link information one wants to offer with what has already been discussed, to respond to others appropriately, and to speak so as to be understood.

Even so, the insertion of discussion groups into classrooms opens the possibility for the same sorts of negotiation of position and power that members of larger groups experience. Evans (1996) described, for example, a classroom in which the literature discussion took a far back seat to positioning and challenge. As in the larger classroom group, gender, background, and status played roles in whose ideas were expressed and listened to.

### The Role of Discussion in Promoting Response

Although there is testimony and allegiance to the need for children to work together in literature circles, book clubs, or discussion groups, there is not as much demonstrated evidence of "how" children work together or clear documentation of the effects of their thought and talk on one another. Nevertheless, some research on children's literature discussions has described what children actually do or accomplish collectively as they talk about literature. In their seminal study of "Grand Conversations" in fifth-grade classrooms, Eeds and Wells (1989) identified a number of ways in which children and adults worked as members of literature discussion groups: First, participants relied on one another as they constructed and articulated meanings, even changing as they encountered different perspectives. Second, children involved in literature discussion shared personal stories, and, in the process of sharing, both grappled with how the story was personally significant for them and shaped the significance of the text for others. Third, Eeds and Wells found that children in the midst of a text engaged in a "group inquiry process" (p. 21)—predicting, hypothesizing, confirming, and disconfirming. Finally, the participants engaged in group "critiquing" of stories, as they shared their insights about how the author crafted the text. In a similar fashion, Almasi (1995) found in her investigation of fourth-graders' discussions of literature that discussants work together to resolve their "cognitive conflicts" (p. 317)—the interpersonal conflicts, questions, and confusions that readers encounter when reading literature.

A more fully developed strand of the literature may be in cataloging what book talkers seem to be attempting—what they seem be trying to do with their book talk. After examining the book club talk of fourth- and fifth-graders, Raphael et al. (1992), found that children engaged in talk for nine purposes: (a) to share written responses from logs; (b) to clarify points of confusion; (c) to discuss main themes of stories; (d) to make connections across texts; (e) to critique the author's success; (f) to identify the author's purpose; (g) to relate ideas from texts to personal experience; (h) to relate prior knowledge to text; and (i) to discuss the procedures for responding within the group.

Frank, Dixon, and Brandts (1998) found that participation in book groups seemed to teach children that readers share books, engage in civil conversation, and even have apple juice as they talk. Their second-graders, who met once every 2 weeks in book clubs to talk about self-selected (but different) titles, talked about, for example, "the things authors do when they write books" (p. 110). In addition, the children entertained talk on characters with traits and problems similar to theirs and their friends.

## Organizing for the Study of Literature in Classrooms

Although numerous educators have shared recommendations for organizing literature study (e.g., Dugan, 1997; Keegan & Shrake, 1991; Waggoner, Chinn, Yi, & Anderson, 1995), only a few investigators have studied the way in which approach to literature study affects children's responses. Many and Wiseman (1992) compared the impact of three different approaches to literature instruction on third-graders' responses to literature. The first approach, the literary-analysis approach, emphasized identifying and critiquing literary elements. The literary-experience approach encouraged students to live through and react to the story line. In this approach, students were encouraged to share personal associations and feelings, to empathize with characters, and predict the way in which stories would proceed. In the final treatment, students listened to stories but were not invited to participate in literature discussion. After listening to each of three picture books read aloud, students in each approach were asked to write anything they wanted to about the story. Many and Wiseman found that teaching approach was related to the

children's written responses. Children in the literary-analysis approach typically assumed an efferent stance as they identified and discussed literary elements. By contrast, the children in the literary-experience approach were more likely to assume an aesthetic stance toward the stories. Their written responses revealed they were involved in story events and made connections between characters and real people. When asked to write anything they wanted about the stories, the children in the no discussion group typically retold the stories.

In a subsequent investigation, Wiseman, Many, and Altieri (1992) examined the impact of three somewhat different approaches to literature instruction on third-graders' literary responses. In the student-centered approach, students were engaged in free discussion of stories read aloud. Students in the teacher-guided aesthetic approach were invited to share their thoughts and reactions to stories read aloud. In the teacher-guided aesthetic/literary-analysis approach, students began with an aesthetic discussion and then "analyzed literary or artistic elements and reflected on their personal reaction to that aspect of the story" (p. 285). When invited to "write anything you want about the story we just heard," students in the student-centered discussion groups were more likely to focus on literary analysis in their written responses. Students in the teacher-guided aesthetic approach and the teacher-guided aesthetic/literary analysis approach wrote more aesthetic responses in which they "explained their feelings or described real life happenings or people or other literary characters that reminded them of story events" (p. 286). The researchers noted that the students who analyzed how the literary elements affected their responses were just as likely to assume an aesthetic stance as the students in the purely aesthetic discussion group.

Raphael and McMahon (1994) organized students into "book clubs" originally as an "alternative (literature-based) framework" to the students' traditional reading instruction. Early on, the intermediate-grade students in their investigation engaged in group tasks that focused more on comprehension than response. For example, they sequenced the events in *Sadako and the Thousand Paper Cranes* (Coerr, 1977) and kept track of occurrences and page numbers for important vocabulary words. In addition, because the students were learning a different organizational system—one that required self-directed activity—much effort had to be expended in getting students accustomed to the routines of book clubs. Even so, the researchers reported that book club conversations helped students discuss their personal responses in addition to the content of books under study (Raphael & McMahon, 1994). Further, the researchers' book club organization, which consists of reading, writing, community share, and instruction, also helped struggling readers frame responses (Goatley et al., 1995).

O'Flahavan (1989) designed an instructional framework that allows teachers to gradually relinquish their social and interpretive authority over discussions. The approach, called conversational discussion groups, divides a typical 30-minute group meeting into three phases: opening, discussion, and debriefing. Although the teacher has major responsibilities in the first and last phase, as children become accustomed to managing their own routines and discussions, the need for those organizing, guiding, and evaluating features lessens, and students come to manage their discussions largely on their own. Even so, the teacher may monitor the conversations from the sidelines to gauge the necessity for coaching or scaffolding some burgeoning understanding. In addition, Weincek and O'Flahavan (1994) offered strategies for rating children's social and reading skills as ways to ensure a range of strengths in the discussion group.

Almasi (1995) adapted O'Flahavan's (1989) discussion procedures in her study of the nature of sociocognitive conflicts during peer discussion. Almasi had clear instructional goals for students learning to operate in peer groups. These focused on (a) learning to interact with others in ways that allowed meaningful interpretation of literature; (b) becoming a support structure for one another, as the group worked collaboratively to "interpret literature and construct meaning"; and c) setting and following the agenda and procedures for conversing (p. 318).

The Language to Literacy frame offered by Roser, Hoffman, and Farest (1990) provided for group discussion of books by children whose first language was not English. Over a period of approximately 2 weeks, related books were read aloud, discussed, responded to, and inspected for the themes and threads that cross them. Children in the classrooms who experienced literature units outperformed matched classrooms on a standardized test. In a subsequent investigation of the effectiveness of the Language to Literacy plan for children in selected classrooms (Hoffman et al., 1991), the researchers reported positive effects for children's book knowledge and literary insights. Efforts to implement and extend Language to Literacy in other settings have shown positive effects on students' written responses (Martinez et al., 1992), as well as on children's language and insights when the plan was implemented in Belize (Winsor & Hansen, 1999).

Whether labeled literature circles, book clubs, or discussion groups, the organizational structures through which children talk about books seem to have some features in common: Probably most important, the students get to read (or are read) books in their entirety. Furthermore, children often get to choose what they read. The students are most frequently grouped heterogeneously for book talk. The membership of the groups is often flexible, with membership typically lasting as long as it takes to read and discuss a particular title or text set. Each of the organization schemes also seems to have similar cognitive and social goals for the individual readers or learners. Finally, each system recommends and provides for more teacher management at the initiation of change to literature groups from more traditional class organizations.

## Roles of Teachers and Peers in Evoking and Supporting Response

A burgeoning strand of the research literature describing book conversations focuses on the roles of the participants—both student and teacher—and, less frequently, on the differences in those roles. Roser and Martinez (1985) identified three roles that teachers and parents seemed to take as they read and talked about stories with preschoolers: coresponder, when the adult entered the conversation as a participant, informer, when the adult interpreted aspects of the story, and director, when the adult managed aspects of the storytime situation, including turn taking.

Current research has investigated teachers in a less dominant role in discussion, suggesting that both the quality and quantity of students' talk can be effected by carefully considered teacher roles. Eeds and Wells (1989) encouraged the inexperienced teachers in their study to serve as equal participants in discussions of literature. They asked whether preservice teachers engaged in literature discussion with fifth- and sixth-graders could refrain from imposing their own interpretations and engage instead in "dialogue" in which the literature discussion group would work together to "construct and disclose deeper meaning, enriching understanding for all participants" (p. 5). They compared "successful" and "less successful" conversations to determine some of the differences. Eeds and Wells hypothesized that the less successful teachers would be those who talked too much, took over the pauses in conversations, missed too many "literary teachable moments," and who had participated in conversations that did not move beyond the surface meanings (p. 7). Data analysis showed, however, that "too much teacher talk" was not necessarily a characteristic of the less successful conversations. Instead, teachers who had taken part in more successful conversations seemed to be highly encouraging of students' responses, appeared to curb their own questions, and seemed able to notice and take advantage of real literary dialogue—calling attention to and even labeling, for example, a literary element being discussed. Interestingly, even outside the presence of traditional teacher questions ("the gentle inquisition," p. 26), students in this study showed they were actively interpreting what they had read.

In her study of the "grand conversations" of first-graders, McGee (1992) compared the level of interpretive discourse before and after teachers inserted one interpretive question into the literary conversation. In each case, children had talked freely about one of three picture books, with the teacher initially following the children's conversational leads. After reading each story, the discussion leader simply asked, "What do you think?" They neither asked questions nor made comments while the children talked (other than to encourage or ask for clarification). When the discussion waned, the teacher leaders then posed one interpretive question intended to focus children on the significance of the story as a whole. The conversations were transcribed and analyzed on a continuum from text bound to reader-bound responses. Each discussion revealed interpretive thought both before and after the interpretive question was posed, yet students made more interpretive responses and focused responses after the question than before it. McGee concluded:

Although it seemed important for students to explore stories on their own terms, switching from topic to topic in an open-ended conversation prompted by their own responses and questions, it also seemed important to focus the conversation around a teacher-posed interpretive question which called for students to reflect on the work as a whole and to use inferential and critical thinking (p. 186).

Even so, McGee (1992) explained that the evocative question was not intended to elicit only one interpretation, and, like the neophyte teachers in Eeds and Wells' (1989) study, the discussion leaders in McGee's study were often surprised and impressed with the interpretations that emerged. In an analysis of teachers' roles in first-graders "grand conversations," McGee,

Courtney, and Lomax (1994) noted that teachers took on the roles of "facilitators" and "helpers/nudgers." As facilitators, they both helped to identify topics and helped children clarify and expand their responses. As nudgers, they urged children to take other perspectives and to support their thinking. The researchers noted that teachers rarely took on the role of "literary curator" except when posing the interpretive question.

In her study of bilingual kindergarten children responding to picture books, Battle (1993, 1995) found that the teacher contributed to children's collaborative meaning making in English and Spanish by encouraging her children's responses in three ways during storytime: First, during story discussion, the teacher focused on what the children had to say rather than the language forms they used; by withholding corrections, she made it "safe to talk" (Battle, 1995, p. 158). Second, the teacher encouraged questions, observations, and opinions *throughout* the read-aloud event. At times, she repeated, paraphrased, or added to the children's talk, sharing her own enthusiasms. Third, the teacher provided multiple invitations to speak, but did not demand or require response. Battle (1993) concluded that this teacher's participation supported and maintained thought and talk in book discussion: "The teacher's role seemed to be to highlight either the aspects of text or the children's comments and questions that might hold potential for... discussion, and then to allow the children to talk" (p. 166).

Farest, Miller, and Fewin (1997) focused on the role of the teacher in discussion of a selected nonfiction tradebook in an ongoing classroom investigation of bats. The researchers identified ways in which a fourth-grade teacher (skilled with guiding aesthetic discussions) supported and participated in talk about nonfiction. The researchers' qualitative analysis revealed five specific teacher strategies. The teacher (a) modeled ways to read and think about information books, (b) encouraged children to examine information critically, (c) provided background information that enriched understanding, (d) invited children to rethink their initial views or misconceptions, and (e) challenged them to go beyond the facts to connect with the issues and points of view the bat scientist faced.

Frank et al. (1998) investigated book club meetings in which the second-grade teacher was present but encouraged her students to take command of the conversation. The researchers' close inspection of one session of book club, in which the teacher left the group momentarily, revealed that even though three separate conversations occurred simultaneously (child to child), each conversation was related to the books being discussed.

After matching students for comprehension level and ability to solve cognitive conflicts, Almasi (1995) compared the nature of conversations led by groups of fourth-grade students with groups led by teachers. She found that when students were engaged in peer-led groups, their conflicts were most often resolved through the shared work of group members—including the person experiencing the conflict. (Almasi defined a "sociocognitive conflict" as the state of dissonance or unrest that occurs during social interactions rather than in isolation.) She found that students in peer-led groups offered more comments of medium and high complexity, and asked significantly more questions than students in teacher-led groups. She concluded that participants in peer-led discussion have opportunity to

both observe and take part in constructing meaningful interpretations, including the variety of ways that conflicts can be resolved. By contrast, teacher-led discussions tended to be dominated by the teacher who often focused on explicit questions. When students' responses seemed incongruous (in conflict) with the text, the teacher often sought resolution from others rather than from the students experiencing the conflict.

Kauffman, Short, Crawford, Kahn, and Kaser (1996) observed the talk that occurred in literature circles when the teacher was present and not present. They identified four roles that teachers assumed, including teachers as facilitators, as participants, as kid watchers, and as active listeners. The researchers observed that the roles were not discrete and that teachers moved among the positions throughout the discussion. Of the four roles, the primary role that teachers assumed was that of "facilitator," who posed questions ("What do you mean?" or "Why do you think that?") to encourage student talk. Within the role of facilitator, teachers also provided additional information, clarified misunderstandings, restated, and took charge of conversational maintenance—the kind of talk that ensures all participants can hear, that all potential speakers have adequate access to the floor, or that invites a topic switch. The researchers' interpretation of the "facilitator" role as "something teachers just do" corresponds with Evans' (1996) descriptions of the power and positioning within literature circles.

O'Flahavan (1994-95) and Wiencek and O'Flahavan (1994) advised that teachers can work before and after peer-led discussion groups both to prepare the conversational settings and to debrief with the students at their close—again, guiding children to the potential sources for talk and discovery. Even so, O'Flahavan (1994-95) cautioned:

No matter what role a teacher chooses, excessive teacher participation subverts the very norms that the teacher is trying to establish. Teachers must learn to listen to students' interpretive talk, fight the urge to control it, and provide support when the students demonstrate or request that they need help (p. 356)

Eeds and Peterson (1991) raised the issue that it is the teacher who is the most knowledgeable "curator" of the literary arts and the one who can often recognize and respond to a students' developing insight. Still, there is room for considering how soon, how often, and how explicitly curators guide and inform the "patrons" of the arts. The value of teacher-led (versus peer-led) discussions may depend on particular (and varying) goals for book discussion as well as the age and experience of the discussants. If an accepted goal of literary discussions is to honor the children's perspectives, providing them opportunity to resolve their conflicts with text and the varied interpretations of their peers, Almasi's (1995) peer-led groups have shown themselves effective. On the other hand, if the purpose of a particular literary discussion is to discover the text as crafted object, discussion may profit from the presence of a literary curator (Eeds & Peterson, 1991; K. Smith, 1990) or a knowing guide (Lindfors, 1999). The question may not be whether teacher should be present or absent in discussion groups, but rather what the target goals for the conversation are. As Kaufmann et al. (1996) contended, "Instead of arguing for or against teacher presence in literature circles, we believe that discussions with and without teachers offer different, but equally valuable, potentials for social interaction and the negotiation of meaning" (p. 373).

## Organizing Units or Text Sets to Evoke Response

In her study of children's literary responses in literature-rich classrooms, Hickman (1981) found that children were most likely to make explicit connections among pieces of literature when the selections were part of a literature unit. In addition, she found that where related selections were less available, the children had less to say about the formal properties of a selection. Hickman's findings set the stage for subsequent investigations focused on the impact of different ways of grouping texts for literature study. Many educators advocate a unit approach to the study of literature and provide anecdotal evidence of the effectiveness of such an approach (e.g., Madura, 1995; Moss, 1978). Author study, genre study, and thematic study have all been recommended as approaches that encourage students to engage in higher levels of thinking in response to literature. Moss's descriptions of "focus units," for example, recommend sharing sets of texts that reveal a genre, unveil character stereotypes, or explore the body of work of an author/illustrator. Her descriptions of focus units are accompanied by anecdotal evidence of children's insights, increasing willingness to support their judgments, and "growing store of literary ideas" (p. 485).

However, relatively few studies have documented the impact of unit approaches on children's thinking about literature. Roser et al. (1990) provided books organized into literature units (focusing on author-, theme-, topic-, or genre-related works) to primary aged children whose first language was Spanish. Teachers in 78 classrooms read the books aloud to approximately 2,500 children, modeling and encouraging children's thoughtful responses, as well as collecting those responses onto large wall charts (called language charts) designed either to highlight or cause children to discover the connections among the books. The researchers reported significant changes in language arts scores (compared with matched schools), as well as the range of literary connections that analysis of the language charts revealed (Roser, Hoffman, Farest & Labbo, 1992). Eventually, the researchers added a response framework and introduced response logs to the Language to Literacy plan for further encouraging and supporting thought and talk about literature (Martinez et al., 1992).

Bloem and Manna (1999) engaged second- and fourth-graders in a study of the works of Patricia Polacco. This author study was organized with the dual goals of respecting children's personal responses to Polacco stories and helping them discover what Polacco does as a writer and illustrator that gets them to think and feel the way they do. The researchers read Polacco stories aloud, modeled questions they had about Polacco's work, invited the children to share their own questions, and, finally, had the children conduct a telephone author interview. Bloem and Manna found that the students responded aesthetically in rich and diverse ways that defied a developmental progression. Both their comments and questions were varied in nature, depth, and type. Over the course of the unit, they found a shift in children's questions from being text based to revealing connections they

were making with Polacco and with her books. The latter type of question especially came to dominate once the children had viewed a videotape on Polacco's life and work and realized they would have an opportunity to interview the author. The children "delighted in the nuances of the texts, and found great pleasure, at the end of the project, in learning ways that the texts reflected Polacco's history and recorded her family stories" (p. 806).

Short (1992) introduced text sets to groups of third- and sixth-grade students who met to read and discuss the related books over a 4- to 5-week period. Although Short noted differences in the ways groups of children organized their book discussions and in the ways they made connections across the texts and their lives, she found that the intertextual links most frequently discussed included connections to the literary elements of the story, connections to the illustrations, connections to the lives of authors and illustrators, and connections with the children's own life experiences and other texts.

## Other Instructional Procedures and Tools for Evoking Response

Over the last decade, as authentic literature has come to play an increasingly integral role in classrooms, there has been a concomitant increase in research focused on strategies which might have the potential to mediate and sustain literary responses. Chief among the mediators that have been investigated are literary journals, response frameworks, and response prompts, with many investigators having combined the use of journal and frameworks or prompts into a single instructional strategy. Investigators have examined the influence of these mediators on children's written responses and on literature discussions.

***Impact of mediators on written response.*** The findings from a number of investigations of literature journals have converged to suggest that opportunities over time to write about literature in journals support growth in children's responses to literature. Wollman-Bonilla and Werchadlo (1995), examining first-graders' entries in literature journals over the course of a school year, found a shift in the children's responses from primarily text-centered responses to more reader-centered responses. These researchers concluded that the primary value of the journal was that it encouraged children to "take time to think about what had been read" (p. 566). They also observed that opportunities to share their written responses with their teacher was crucial for these first-graders. Farest and Miller (1993) examined the responses of fourth-graders in dialogue journals. They found a deepening of response in their subjects' entries as they engaged in written dialogues with the researchers. Wollman-Bonilla (1989) found that literature journals were especially supportive mediators for fourth grade, nonfluent readers who typically found it difficult to participate in literature discussions.

As a teacher-researcher, Kelly (1990) combined the use of written logs with response prompts. She invited her third-grade students to write in response to relatively open-ended prompts based on the work of Bleich (1978): What did you notice? How did you feel about the book? How is the book related to your experiences? In the early part of the school year, Kelly recorded the children's responses on butcher paper; then, in midyear, she invited the children to begin writing in response to the same prompts. Kelly found that across the school year the children's responses grew in length and began to move from initial retellings and summaries to more analytic responses and responses that reflected greater emotional involvement with stories. Kelly and Farnan (1991) compared the use of prompts that "emphasized and elicited readers' personal interpretations and interactions with text" (p. 278) with a nonreader response prompt ("Tell me about your book"). They found that the reader response prompts elicited more critical and analytic thinking from the fourth-graders in their study.

***Impact of mediators on literature discussion.*** Researchers have also found that literature journals and response frameworks nurture richer oral discussions of literature. After collecting baseline data during literature discussions in a second-grade classroom, Martinez et al. (1992) introduced response journals in which children wrote after listening to read alouds and prior to participating in literature discussion. In the next phase of the investigation, they introduced an open-ended discussion framework based on the work of Chambers (1985): What did you notice? What did you wonder about? What were you reminded of? The researchers found that the introduction of each intervention broadened the types of responses the children contributed during literature discussion. The introduction of the literature logs also appeared to impact the role the teacher assumed during discussion. Prior to the introduction of the journals, the teacher assumed a highly directive role; however, once the children began to write and share their own responses to literature as a way of initiating discussion, the teacher's strategies during discussion changed to more sharing and inviting. These researchers concluded that the introduction of logs appeared to transform the teacher's view of literature discussion and her role in that discussion.

Hubbard (1996) investigated the impact of visual response logs on children's literature discussions. They invited their primary-level subjects to draw their favorite section of a story or to draw what was going on in their minds as they read or heard a story. The researchers found that the resulting visual representations not only encouraged personal connections, which led to greater involvement in stories, but they also served as conversation starters when shared during literature circles. Visual representations were especially effective mediators for students learning English as their second language.

As part of their investigation of the nature of fourth- and fifth-graders' classroom book club talk, Raphael et al. (1992) examined the interrelationships between the writing and discussion components of the program. They found that during literature discussion students pulled on the ideas they had written about in their logs, and in a reciprocal manner, the topics the students explored during discussion impacted their subsequent journal entries.

## SUMMARIZING RESPONSE RESEARCH

Rosenblatt (1985) urged researchers to "reflect on the 'fit' of a problem into a broader perspective related to human development" (p. 51). By considering the research question in view of its broadest implications, investigations into responses to literature are likely to produce teaching effects "that foster the capacity for more and more rewarding transactions between readers and text" (p. 51). The researchers whose efforts are summarized in this review themselves have called for "more" of the many facets of research on response—more comparisons of children's oral and written responses, more investigations of the collaborative nature of response, more studies of responses of varying learner groups, more inspection of the contexts for response, and more study of the participants' and texts' contributions to response.

There may be many reasons why studies of children's book discussions are difficult to conduct and interpret: First, neophyte book talkers are often much more eager to "talk" than to listen, making genuine conversation less prevalent than assorted strings of observations and responses. At the beginning of children's book conversations, their attention to other speakers may be limited. Second, the collaborative nature of responses are neither easy to capture or account for. Third, so many factors influence responses (as with any complex literacy event), even seemingly slight variance in any one factor—whether text, participants' experience, presence or absence of the teacher, or the expectations/purposes for the book conversation—will affect responses. It is little wonder that the evidence to date is not definitive. Finally, the many separate systems for categorizing responses make it difficult to compare across studies. As researchers investigating different children, texts, communities, leader roles, and expectations analyze children's talk, they have let their categorization systems emerge from the data. The varied systems make it difficult to compare findings across studies.

What may be necessary for researchers in the future is to try more replications of their own systems across studies, to ground studies more thoroughly in both theoretical and practical ways, and to aim for understandings that allow for planning for the confluence of purposes and procedures that will elicit divergent and defensible responses to texts.

## *References*

Almasi, J. F. (1995). The nature of fourth graders' sociocognitive conflicts in peer-led and teacher-led discussions of literature. *Reading Research Quarterly, 30,* 314–351.

Almasi, J. F., & Gambrell, L. B. (1997). Conflict during classroom discussions can be a good thing. In J. R. Paratore & R. L. McCormack (Eds.), *Peer talk in the classroom: Learning from research* (pp. 130–155). Newark, DE: International Reading Association.

Applebee, A. (1978). *The child's concept of story.* Chicago: University of Chicago Press.

Bakhtin, M. M. (1986). *Speech genres and other late essays.* Austin: University of Texas Press.

Battle, J. (1993). Mexican-American bilingual kindergartners' collaborations in meaning making. In D. J. Leu & C. K. Kinzer (Eds.), *Examining central issues in literacy research, theory, and practice:*

*Forty-second yearbook of the National Reading Conference* (Vol. 42, pp. 163–169). Chicago: National Reading Conference.

Battle, J. (1995). Collaborative story talk in a bilingual kindergarten. In N. Roser & M. Martinez (Eds.), *Book talk and beyond: Children and teachers respond to literature* (pp. 157–167). Newark, DE: International Reading Association.

Baumann, J. F., Hoffman, J. V., Moon, J., & Duffy-Hester, A. M. (1998). Where are teachers' voices in the phonics/whole language debate? Results from a survey of U.S. elementary classroom teachers. *The Reading Teacher, 51,* 636–650.

Beach, R., & Hynds, S. (1991). Research on response to literature. In R. Barr, M. L. Kamil, P. Mosenthal, & P. D. Pearson (Eds.), *Handbook of reading research* (pp. 453–489). White Plains, NY: Longman.

Bleich, D. (1978). *Subjective criticism.* Baltimore: John Hopkins University Press.

Bloem, P. L., & Manna, A. L. (1999). A chorus of questions: Readers respond to Patricia Polacco. *The Reading Teacher, 52,* 802–808.

Bloome, D., & Bailey, F. M. (1992). Studying language and literacy through events, particularity, and intertextuality. In R. Beach, J. L. Green, M. L. Kamil, & T. Shanahan (Eds.), *Multidisciplinary perspectives on literacy research* (pp. 181–210). Urbana, IL: National Conference on Research in English and National Council of Teachers of English.

Britton, J. (1970). *Language and learning.* London: Penguin Books.

Chambers, A. (1985). *Booktalk: Occasional writing on literature and children.* New York: Harper & Row.

Cochran-Smith, M. (1984). *The making of a reader.* Norwood, NJ: Ablex.

Coerr, E. (1977). *Sadako and the thousand paper cranes.* New York: Dell Yearling.

Crago, H., & Crago, M. (1976). The untrained eye? A preschool child explores Felix Hoffman's "Rapunzel." *Children's Literature in Education, 22,* 135–151.

Cullinan, B., Harwood, K., & Galda, L. (1983). The reader and the story: Comprehension and response. *Journal of Research and Development in Education, 16,* 29–37.

Dugan, J. A. (1997). Transactional literature discussions: Engaging students in the appreciation and understanding of literature. *The Reading Teacher, 51,* 86–96.

Eeds, M., & Peterson, R. (1991). Teacher as curator: Learning to talk about literature. *The Reading Teacher, 45,* 118–126.

Eeds, M., & Wells, D. (1989). Grand conversations: An exploration of meaning construction in literature study groups. *Research in the Teaching of English, 23,* 4–29.

Enciso, P. (1994). Cultural identify and response to literature: Running lessons from *Maniac McGee. Language Arts, 71,* 524–533.

Evans, K. S. (1996). Creating spaces for equity? The role of positioning in peer-led literature discussions. *Language Arts, 73,* 194–202.

Evans, K. S. (1997). Exploring the complexities of peer-led literature discussion: The influence of gender. In J. R. Paratore & R. L. McCormack (Eds.), *Peer talk in the classroom: Learning from research* (pp. 156–173). Newark, DE: International Reading Association.

Farest, C., & Miller, C. (1993). Children's insights into literature: Using dialogue journals to invite literary response. In D. J. Leu & C. K. Kinzer (Eds.). *Examining central issues in literacy research, theory, and practice: Forty-second yearbook of the National Reading Conference* ( Vol. 42, pp. 271–278). Chicago: National Reading Conference.

Farest, C., Miller, C. J., & Fewin, S. (1997). Responding to information books: The role of the teacher. In C. K. Kinzer, K. A. Hinchman, & D. J. Leu (Eds.), *Inquiries in literacy: Theory and practice: Forty-sixth yearbook of the National Reading Conference* (Vol. 46, pp. 229–236). Chicago: National Reading Conference.

Fish, S. (1980). *Is there a text in this class? The authority of interpretive communities.* Cambridge, MA: Harvard University Press.

Flood, J., Jensen, J. M., Lapp, D., & Squire, J. R. (1991). *Handbook of research on teaching the English language arts.* New York: Macmillan.

Frank, C. R., Dixon, C. N., & Brandts, L. R. (1998). "Dear book club": A sociolinguistic and ethnographic analysis of literature discussion groups in second grade. In T. Shanahan & F. V. Rodriguez-Brown (Eds.), *Forty-seventh yearbook of the National Reading Conference* (pp. 103–115). Chicago: National Reading Conference.

Galda, L. (1982). Assuming the spectator stance: An examination of the responses of three young readers. *Research in the Teaching of English, 16,* 1–20.

Galda, L. (1990). A longitudinal study of the spectator stance as a function of age and genre. *Research in the Teaching of English, 24,* 261–277.

Garrison, B. M., & Hynds, S. (1991). Evocation and reflection in the reading transaction: A comparison of proficient and less proficient readers. *Journal of Reading Behavior, 23,* 259–280.

Goatley, V. J., Brock, C. H., & Raphael, T. (1995). Diverse learners participating in regular education "book clubs." *Reading Research Quarterly, 30,* 352–380.

Hancock, M. R. (1993). Exploring the meaning-making process through the content of literature response journals: A case study investigation. *Research in the Teaching of English, 27,* 335–368.

Harding, D. W. (1968). Response to literature: The report of the study group. In J. R. Squire (Ed.), *Response to literature* (pp. 11–27). Champaign, IL: National Council of Teachers of English.

Hepler, S., & Hickman, J. (1982). "The book was okay. I love you"— Social aspects of response to literature. *Theory Into Practice, 21,* 278–283.

Hickman, J. (1979). *Response to literature in a school environment, Grades K through 5.* Unpublished doctoral dissertation, Ohio State University, Columbus.

Hickman, J. (1981). A new perspective on response to literature: Research in an elementary school setting. *Research in the Teaching of English, 15,* 343–354.

Hoffman, J. V., Roser, N. L., Battle, J., Farest, C., Myers, P., & Labbo, L. (1991). Learner factors/teacher factors: Issues in literacy research and instruction. In J. Zutell & S. McCormick (Eds.), *Evaluating the effects of a read-aloud/response program: Fortieth yearbook of the National Reading Conference* (Vol. 40, pp. 297–303). Chicago: National Reading Conference.

Hubbard, R. S. (with Winterbourne, N., & Ostrow, J.). (1996). Visual responses to literature: Imagination through images. *The New Advocate, 9,* 309–323.

Iser, W. (1980). The reading process: A phenomenological approach. In J. P. Tompkins (Ed.), *Reader response criticisms: From formalism to poststructuralism* (pp. 50–60). Baltimore: Johns Hopkins University Press.

Kauffman, G., Short, K. G., Crawford, K. M., Kahn, L., & Kaser, S. (1996). Examining the roles of teachers and students in literature circles across classroom contexts. In D. J. Leu, C. K. Kinzer, & K. A. Hinchman (Eds.), *Literacies for the 21st century: Forty-fifth yearbook of the National Reading Conference* (Vol. 45, pp. 373–384). Chicago: National Reading Conference.

Keegan, S., & Shrake, K. (1991). Literature study groups: An alternative to ability grouping. *The Reading Teacher, 44,* 542–547.

Kelly, P. R. (1990). Guiding young students' response to literature. *The Reading Teacher, 43,* 464–470.

Kelly, P. R., & Farnan, N. (1991). Promoting critical thinking through response logs: A reader-response approach with fourth graders. In J. Zutell & S. McCormick (Eds.), *Learner factors/teacher factors:*

*Issues in literacy research and instruction: Fortieth yearbook of the National Reading Conference* (Vol. 40, pp. 277-284). Chicago: National Reading Conference.

Kiefer, B. (1983). The responses of children in a combination first/second grade classroom to picture books in a variety of artistic styles. *Journal of Research and Development in Education, 16,* 14-20.

Kiefer, B. (1986). The child and the picture book: Creating live circuits. *Children's Literature Association Quarterly, 11,* 63-68.

Kiefer, B. (1988). Picture books as contexts for literary, aesthetic, and real world understandings. *Language Arts, 65,* 260-271.

Kucan, L. (1994). The art of publishing illustrated tradebooks that have already been published. *Language Arts, 71,* 220-228.

Langer, J. A. (1995). *Envisioning literature: Literary understanding and literature instruction.* Newark, DE: International Reading Association and Teachers College Press.

Leal, D. J. (1992). The nature of talk about three types of text during peer group discussion. *Journal of Reading Behavior, 24,* 313-338.

Lehr, S. (1988). The child's developing sense of theme as a response to literature. *Reading Research Quarterly, 23,* 337-357.

Liaw, M. (1995). Looking into the mirror: Chinese children's responses to Chinese children's books. *Reading Horizons, 35,* 185-197.

Lindfors, J. (1999). *Children's inquiry: Using language to make sense of the world.* New York: Teachers College Press.

Madura, S. (1995). The line and texture of aesthetic response: Primary children study authors and illustrators. *The Reading Teacher, 49,* 110-118.

Many, J. E. (1991). The effects of stance and age level on children's literary responses. *Journal of Reading Behavior, 23,* 61-85.

Many, J. E., & Wiseman, D. L. (1992). The effects of teaching approach on third-grade students' response to literature. *Journal of Reading Behavior, 24,* 265-287.

Martinez, M., & Roser, N. L. (1985). Read it again: The value of repeated readings during storytime. *The Reading Teacher, 38,* 782-786.

Martinez, M., & Roser, N. L. (1991). Children's responses to literature. In J. Flood, Jensen, J. M., Lapp, D., & Squire, J. R. (Eds.), *Handbook of research on teaching the English language arts* (pp. 643-654). New York: Macmillan.

Martinez, M., & Roser, N. L. (1994). Children's responses to a chapter book across grade levels: Implications for sustained text. In C. K. Kinzer & D. J. Leu (Eds.), *Multidimensional aspects of literacy research, theory, and practice: Forty-third yearbook of the National Reading Conference* (Vol. 43, pp. 317-324). Chicago: National Reading Conference.

Martinez, M., Roser, N. L., Hoffman, J. V., & Battle, J. (1992). Fostering better book discussions through response logs and a response framework: A case description. In C. K. Kinzer & D. J. Leu (Eds.), *Literacy research, theory, and practice: Views from many perspectives: Forty-first yearbook of the National Reading Conference* (Vol. 41, pp. 303-311). Chicago: National Reading Conference.

McClure, A. A. (1985). *Children's responses to poetry in a supportive context.* Unpublished doctoral dissertation. Ohio State University, Columbus.

McGee, L. M. (1992). An exploration of meaning construction in first graders' grand conversations. In C. K. Kinzer & D. J. Leu (Eds.), *Literacy research, theory, and practice: Views from many perspectives: Forty-first yearbook of the National Reading Conference* (Vol. 41, pp. 177-186). Chicago: National Reading Conference.

McGill-Franzen, A., & Lanford, C. (1994). Exposing the edge of the preschool curriculum: Teachers' talk about text and children's literary understandings. *Language Arts, 71,* 264-273.

McGinley, W., & Kamberelis, G. (1996). *Maniac Magee* and *Ragtime Tumpie*: Children negotiating self and world through reading and writing. *Research in the Teaching of English, 30,* 75-113.

McMahon, S. I., Pardo, L. S., & Raphael, T. E. (1991). Bart: A case study in discourse about text. In S. McCormick & J. Zutell (Eds.), *Learner factors/teacher factors: Issues in literacy research and instruction: Fortieth yearbook of the National Reading Conference* (Vol. 40, pp. 285-296). Chicago: National Reading Conference.

Morrow, L. M. (1988). Young children's responses to one-to-one story readings in school settings. *Reading Research Quarterly, 23,* 89-107.

Morrow, L. M., & Weinstein, C. (1982). Increasing children's use of literature through program and physical design changes. *Elementary School Journal, 83,* 131-137.

Moss, J. (1978). Using the "focus unit" to enhance children's response to literature. *Language Arts, 55,* 482-488.

O'Flahavan, J. F. (1989). *An exploration of the effects of participant structure upon literacy development in reading group discussion.* Unpublished doctoral dissertation, University of Illinois, Urbana-Champaign.

O'Flahavan, J. F. (1994-95). Teacher role options in peer discussions about literature. *The Reading Teacher, 48,* 354-356.

Paterson, K. (1978). *The great Gilly Hopkins.* New York: HarperCollins.

Paulsen, G. (1987). *Hatchet.* New York: Bradbury.

Purves, A. C., & Beach, R. (1972). *Literature and the reader: Research in response to literature, reading interests, and the teaching of literature.* Urbana, IL: National Council of Teachers of English.

Raphael, T. E., & McMahon, S. I. (1994). Book club: An alternative framework for reading instruction. *The Reading Teacher, 48,* 102-116.

Raphael, T. E., McMahon, S. I., Goatley, V. J., Bentley, J. L., Boyd, F. B., Pardo, L. S. & Woodman, D. A. (1992). Research directions: Literature and discussion in the reading program. *Language Arts, 69,* 54-61.

Rosenblatt, L. M. (1976). *Literature as exploration.* New York: Noble & Noble. (Original work published 1938)

Rosenblatt, L. M. (1978). *The reader, the text, the poem: The transactional theory of the literary work.* Carbondale: Southern Illinois University Press.

Rosenblatt, L. M. (1985). The transactional theory of literary work: Implications for research. In C. Cooper (Ed.), *Researching response to literature and the teaching of literature. Point of departure* (pp. 33-53). Norwood, NJ: Ablex.

Roser, N., Hoffman, J., & Farest, C. (1990). Language, literature, and at-risk children. *The Reading Teacher, 43,* 554-559.

Roser, N., Hoffman, J., Farest, C., & Labbo, L. (1992). Language charts: A record of story time talk. *Language Arts, 69,* 44-52.

Roser, N., & Martinez, M. (1985). Roles adults play in preschoolers' response to literature. *Language Arts, 62,* 485-490.

Short, K. G. (1992). Intertextuality: Searching for patterns that connect. In C. K. Kinzer & D. J. Leu (Eds.), *Literacy research, theory, and practice: Views from many perspectives: Forty-first yearbook of the National Reading Conference* (Vol. 41, pp. 187-197). Chicago: National Reading Conference.

Sims, R. (1983). Strong black girls: A ten year old responds to fiction about Afro-Americans. *Journal of Research and Development in Education, 16,* 21-28.

Singleton, S. (1997). The creation of a basal program: A collaborative effort. In J. Flood, S. B. Heath, & D. Lapp (Eds.), *Handbook of research on teaching literacy through the communicative and visual arts* (pp. 869-871). New York: Macmillan.

Sipe, L. (1998). Individual literary response styles of first and second graders. In T. Shanahan and F. V. Rodriguez-Brown (Eds.), *Forty-seventh yearbook of the National Reading Conference* (Vol. 47, pp. 76-89). Chicago: National Reading Conference.

Smith, E. B. (1995). Anchored in our literature: Students responding to African American literature. *Language Arts, 72,* 571–574.

Smith, K. (1990). Entertaining a text: A reciprocal process. In K. G. Short & K. M. Pierce (Eds.), *Talking about books: Creating literate communities* (pp. 17–31). Portsmouth, NH: Heinemann.

Smolkin, L. B. (1995). The literature of the theatre and aesthetic response: Welcoming plays into the world of children's literature. *The New Advocate, 8,* 109–123.

Spinelli, J. (1991). *Maniac Magee.* Boston: Little, Brown.

Squire, J. R. (1964). *The responses of adolescents while reading four short stories* (Research Report No. 2). Urbana, IL: National Council of Teachers of English.

Vygotsky, L. (1978). *Mind in society: The development of higher psychological processes.* Cambridge, MA: MIT Press.

Waggoner, M., Chinn, C., Yi, H., & Anderson, R. C. (1995). Collaborative reasoning about stories. *Language Arts, 72,* 582–589.

Wiencek, J., & O'Flahavan, J. F. (1994). From teacher-led to peer discussions about literature: Suggestions for making the shift. *Language Arts, 71,* 488–498.

Williams, C. L., & McLean, M. M. (1997). Young deaf children's response to picture book reading in a preschool setting. *Research in the Teaching of English, 31,* 337–366.

Winsor, P., & Hansen, J. (1999). Coming to know as teachers: Learning together in Belize. *The Reading Teacher, 52,* 810–818.

Wiseman, D. L., Many, J. E., & Altieri, J. (1992). Enabling complex aesthetic responses: An examination of three literary discussion approaches. In C. K. Kinzer & d. J. Leu (Eds.), *Literacy research, theory, and practice: Views from many perspectives* (pp. 283–291). Forty-first yearbook of the National Reading Conference. Chicago: National Reading Conference.

Wollman-Bonilla, J. E. (1989). Reading journals: Invitations to participate in literature. *The Reading Teacher, 42,* 112–120.

Wollman-Bonilla, J. E. (1994). Why don't they "just speak?" Attempting literature discussion with more and less able readers. *Research in the Teaching of English, 28,* 231–258.

Wollman-Bonilla, J. E., & Werchadlo, B. (1995). Literature response journals in a first-grade classroom. *Language Arts, 72,* 562–570.

Yaden, D. (1988). Understanding stories through repeated read-alouds: How many does it take? *The Reading Teacher, 41,* 556–560.

# ·59·

# RESPONSE TO LITERATURE

## Robert E. Probst
### Georgia State University

Within the past 30 years or so, more and more teachers and researchers have begun to take serious interest in the concept of response to literature. That is not to say that the questions about the reader's role in making sense of literary texts are all new. They had been asked at least as early as the late 1920s.

In England, Richards (1929/1956) had raised many of them in *Practical Criticism*, one of the first experimental looks at response to literature. In the United States, Rosenblatt (1983) had raised the issue as long ago as 1938 with *Literature as Exploration*, another of the progenitory works in this area. In that text, she argued persuasively that the uniqueness of individual readers must shape their understandings of a text. Because readers differed, because they bring to texts different histories, beliefs, values, contexts, and purposes, their readings must inevitably differ. Meaning, she proposed, does not reside purely and simply within a text, to be extracted whole and complete; rather, it lies in the transaction between reader and text. It is the result of a meeting between reader and text. Thus, she argued, readers must look not only at the characteristics of texts if they wish to understand literary experience but also at people reading texts.

Harding (1937) was raising similar questions at about the same time. In one of many essays in *Scrutiny*, he examined in great detail the behavior of the onlooker, suggesting the importance of understanding his attitudes and practices if readers are to understand the nature of literary art. "The playwright, the novelist, the song-writer and the film-producing team," he noted, "are all doing the same thing as the gossip" (p. 257). That is to say, they are each inviting "the audience to agree that the experience he portrays is possible and interesting, and that his attitude to it, implicit in his portrayal, is fitting" (pp. 257–258). Harding suggested that literary experience involves an important social dimension and urged readers to examine it: "[I]s our taste in gossip the same kind of thing, or not, as our taste in films and trivial fiction? And is this latter continuous, or not, with our taste in literature?" (p. 258). Such questions clearly point toward investigation of the reader's role in literary experience.

Richards' (1929/1956) *Practical Criticism* had begun that investigation. He asked students to respond to poems offered them with no clues about authorship or source. "The attempt to read without this guidance puts a strain upon us that we are little accustomed to," he reported (p. 316). Lacking the provenance of that supporting information, students were, he found, virtually unable to function. They felt confused, desperate, unsure. Richards suggested that they had come to rely heavily on the established, accepted critical opinions, simply applying them as labels in accordance with the judgments they had learned but had not learned to make *by themselves*. When deprived of those approved opinions, they often succumbed to other temptations and their statements about the poems were characterized by reliance on stock responses, expressions of sentimentality, overindulgence in irrelevant memories, and the like. Richards found his students little able to make sense themselves of the texts and his final recommendation was to teach them self-reliance: "The lesson of all criticism is that we have nothing to rely upon in making our choices but ourselves. The lesson of good poetry seems to be that, when we have understood it, in the degree in which we can order ourselves, we need nothing more" (p. 351).

That lesson—and all that it has led to—has proved to be an exciting but problematic notion. Some teachers—respecting the uniqueness of their students, believing in the value of their students' idiosyncratic and personal readings of texts, and sensing perhaps that even the digressions, the departures from the text, the excursions into memories or personal narrative, may be legitimate responses to literary works—have tried to attend to response in their classrooms. The classroom, and the curricula in general, occasionally seem inhospitable. Students trained to produce answers to multiple-choice questions, taught to find out precisely what they need to know, expected to accumulate information and develop skills, and conditioned to regard the teacher as the source of knowledge and the voice of judgment may look askance at the teacher who invites them to respond. It does not look like school work, and they may not trust it.

814

It does not lend itself to grades, and if it does not clearly earn points then its value is likely to be suspect for any student who sees good grades as the achievement to be pursued and bad ones as the penalty to be avoided.

Furthermore, planning instruction to elicit and respect students' responses to texts seems difficult. Response may be unpredictable, diverse, digressive—it is hard to plan the craftsmanlike lesson, moving logically from objective to evaluation, its purpose always clearly evident, and still allow for the uncertainties of response. On a broader scale, the curriculum, too, looks more difficult to design. If teachers organize the literature program based on historical principles, then they arrange things chronologically, and if they choose to study formal elements, then they may arrange texts by genre, but what pattern do teachers have if they decide to focus on the unique readings of their students? No such pattern presented itself at first, and so teachers were often reluctant to consider such approaches to teaching. It is only the most recent generation of literature textbooks that has made an attempt to respect and encourage the readers' responses and accept their unique readings of text.

If the concept of response to literature has posed problems for teachers, it may have been even more unwieldy for researchers who have taken an interest in it. It is an elusive concept, hard to define and difficult to assess. Response takes place in the black box of the mind, and it has been difficult to look inside and see what is going on. All that researchers have had to work with is expressed response and it is likely that expressed response reveals only part of the transaction. Hansson (1973) observed in his studies that "the PASSIVE ability of the less educated readers to notice and judge linguistic, literary and experiential qualities is much more developed than their ACTIVE ability to verbalize their interpretations and experiences in a written statement" (p. 268). The connections between what is expressed and what has actually happened can only be hypothesized.

## THE ANALYSIS OF RESPONSES

Nonetheless, most of the early studies concentrated attention on expressed, recorded responses. Purves (1968) has provided, in *The Elements of Writing About a Literary Work*, a scheme for analyzing the content of responses, and researchers immediately put it to use. The Purves–Rippere system identified, in the writings of both critics and students, the kinds of statement that might be made about a literary work. The unwieldy list numbers more than a hundred, but the statements cluster more conveniently into four major categories:

1. Engagement-involvement: Statements indicating the writer's involvement in the work, the strength of its emotional impact on him or her or the degree of interest it has aroused within him or her.
2. Perception: Statements describing the work itself, which may include retellings of the story, summaries of the content, comments about formal elements or historical context, and the like.

3. Interpretation: Interpretive statements attempting to ascribe meaning to the text, to explain or generalize about it, perhaps to move beyond it to issues broader or more inclusive than those dealt with in the text itself.
4. Evaluation: Judgments about the quality of the work that may be, at one extreme, simplistic or unelaborated or, at the other, complex analyses based upon carefully articulated criteria.

The categories, derived as they were from written statements of response, gave researchers a tool for analyzing other written responses. Analyses using these categories (or adaptations of them, such as the expansion of the four original categories into nine subcategories proposed by Purves & Beach, 1972, and then modified slightly by Odell & Cooper, 1976) proliferated during the 10 or 15 years following the publication of *Elements* ( ). Summarizing the results of many of those studies, Applebee's (1977) ERIC/RCS Report noted several generalizations toward which the research was leading. The finding that he saw as most important was that "the approach to literature adopted by the individual teacher does affect the content of the response from that teacher's pupils" (p. 256). The patterns of response, in other words, are taught and learned. Students figure out the expectations of their teachers—or perhaps, more broadly, of their culture—and conform to them.

Data from the International Association for the Evaluation of Educational Achievement confirmed that observation dramatically, revealing some striking differences among the response patterns of students in the 10 countries participating. Purves (1973), in his report of the IEA, suggested:

Because the patterns differ not simply in degree but also in kind as one moves from population to population within a country, and because there exist national differences in patterns, one's best inference is that the differences result from education rather than from a general progress through adolescence....

Response to literature is a learned behavior. (pp. 314-315)

In light of that observation, some of the other findings are less than surprising. Studies that examined differences across grades or ages, such as the massive National Assessment of Educational Progress, found a clear tendency to shift with age toward more interpretive responses and fewer engagement-involvement responses. Considering the emphasis in secondary literature programs on interpretation and the New Criticism's disparaging of personal, especially emotional, responses, that seems an entirely predictable trend. Students learn that interpretive statements are valued and that expressions of involvement in the text are of less significance.

There are, of course, other influences on the choice of mode. Gender is one such variable, though Applebee's survey found that differences in response preferences (not in reading interests or in achievement) were minor, with girls slightly more willing than boys to express engagement with literary works. Work by Beach and Brunetti in the 1970s looked at both age and gender as variables influencing readers' perceptions of characters in short stories and observed that although there was marked difference in the way males and females judged themselves, there was little difference in the characteristics they attributed to male and female characters in the fiction they read.

The text itself is another variable shaping responses. Work by Angelotti in the 1970s, for example, compared responses to an adolescent novel with those to an adult novel and observed that students were more willing to attempt interpretive statements with the easier book, relying on description—statements of perception—with the more difficult text. He suggested the importance of identifying material within the students' grasp if teachers intend to give them practice in literary analysis. Student ability also played a role, though again a small one, with those students who scored higher on achievements tests indicating a stronger preference for the interpretive responses.

Cornaby (1975) concluded that differences between patterns of response to traditional and nontraditional novels, to poems and short stories, and to traditional novels and poems could be attributed to textual differences in the genre. W. T. Corcoran (1979) also found different response patterns resulting from differences in the genre, with poetry generally more problematic than stories and yielding fewer retellings. Zaharias (1986) looked at the effects of both tone and genre on response preferences, using adapted IEA Response Preference Measures, and discovered that lighter readings tended to evoke a descriptive response whereas a more serious tone resulted in personal, interpretive, and evaluative statements. Poetry tended to yield descriptive statements, and short stories led to expressions of personal response.

The research clearly indicates that selection of texts cannot be based solely on a conception of literary merit without taking into account the age, gender, interests, and abilities of the readers and that curriculum cannot be satisfactorily planned without considering the range of response we hope to encourage or allow.

## RESPONSE CATEGORIES AND READER CHARACTERISTICS

Efforts to sharpen the analysis of response led some researchers to look for relationships between the response categories and other aspects of psychology or of intellectual functioning. Odell and Cooper (1976), for instance, in their adaptation of the Purves-Beach categories, suggested that the concept of "intellectual strategies" borrowed from Young, Becker, and Pike (1970) might contribute some insight into the processes readers engaged in as they read. They argued that although the four categories (engagement-involvement, perception, interpretation, and evaluation), even in their expanded nine-subcategory version, may tell educators something about *what* the responses were, they did not tell us enough about *how* they came to be. They sought to sharpen their insight into the processes by combining those categories with the intellectual processes Young, et al. had deduced. Those processes, as Odell and Cooper adopted them, included (a) focus (the segmenting of experience so that particular aspects might be investigated); (b) contrast (the making of distinctions between items or events); (c) classification (the recognition of similarities or groupings among items); (d) change (the awareness of movement, evolution, or

development); and (e) reference to chronology, logical order, and context. The resulting categories were these:

Personal Statement

1. about the reader, an "auto biographical digression"
2. about the work, expressing personal engagement with it

Descriptive Statement

3. narrational, retelling part of the work
4. descriptive of aspects of the work: language, characters, setting, etc.

Interpretive Statement

5. of parts of the work
6. of the whole work

Evaluative Statement

7. about the evocativeness of the work
8. about the construction of the work
9. about the meaningfulness of the work (Odell & Cooper, 1976, pp. 205–206)

Odell and Cooper (1976) suggested that the refined analysis made possible by this slightly more complex scheme could tell us something about the strategies students actually employed to make meaning out of literary experience. They pointed out that Somers' study in the 1970s using the four Purves categories had failed to reveal differences among 7th-, 9th-, and 11th-graders' responses and speculated about the questions that raised:

In view of this rather surprising finding, we wonder if use of the nine categories of the Purves and Beach scheme would show that students in these different grades make different responses. Also: when seventh, ninth, and eleventh graders' make the same sort of response, are there differences in the sort of intellectual strategies they use? If so, can we (should we) help seventh graders use intellectual strategies in the same ways that eleventh graders do? (Odell & Cooper, 1976, p. 224)

Their parenthetical question implies, of course, the problem that this sort of research cannot fully answer. And that is the question of what we value in our teaching. The Purves categories are descriptive but not necessarily hierarchical. That is, not one of the categories is assumed to be better or higher or more desirable than the others. The schools have, of course, seemed to value the interpretive most highly, though this research does not speak to that issue at all. Whether they should place such emphasis on interpretation or not is another question, and it demands that teachers not only acquire information about what happens as students read in school but also pass some judgment on what happens and how teachers wish to affect it. It is, in other words, a philosophical question as much, or more, than it is a research problem.

In the effort to explain the meeting of reader and text, researchers began to draw on other psychological research for concepts or strategies useful in examining response to literature. Piaget's work on cognitive development, for example, and Kohlberg's on the development of moral reasoning were employed in work by Parnell in the 1980s, who loked into the matter of development by interviewing students at four grade levels. He concluded that response matured in ways predicted both by Kohlberg's levels of moral reasoning and by Piaget's levels of cognitive development. That conclusion may lead researchers to wonder if cognitive development and heightened moral reasoning might be encouraged or supported by attention to response in the literature classroom.

Construct theory (Kelly, 1955) has also offered a tool for these studies. Kelly suggested that people develop intellectual constructs, bipolar scales (e.g., good–bad, kind–cruel) with which they organize their social experience. Hynds (1985), arguing that "readers must often invoke social perceptual skills in interpreting the actions and motivations of literary characters" (p. 387), examined the relationship between the complexity of readers' constructs and their response preferences, their impressions of characters, their comprehension of texts, and their attitudes toward literature. She concluded that students with more complex constructs for interpersonal relationships tended also to have more complex understandings of characters in the stories they read. Moreover, she found that "interpersonal cognitive complexity is related to inferential comprehension, but not to literal comprehension of a literary work" (p. 398), thus calling into question the appropriateness of literal questions in judging students understanding of texts.

Hynds' (1985) study is especially interesting because it ties together our dealings with texts and our dealings with the world. "If," she noted, "there is a relationship between cognitive complexity in the social environment and complexity in the realm of literature, the teaching of literature takes on yet another dimension and offers another challenge" (p. 399), suggesting that literary experiences may have implications for the way readers deal with social experiences. "Literature provides a vehicle a for enlarging students' understanding of the people they are likely to encounter in the social world" (p. 399).

A subsequent study by Hynds (1989) looks further into the connection between social and literary understanding. In this project, Hynds was especially interested in how adolescent readers used their understandings of people as they read literary texts, and in the influence of other social and home experiences on attitudes toward reading. For a case study design, Hynds chose four students representing each of four prototypes. One tended to have high complexity ratings on interpersonal constructs for peers, less complex for literary characters. One showed the opposite pattern: less complex interpersonal constructs for peers and more complex for literary characters. The third had high complexity ratings on constructs for both peers and literary characters, and the fourth had lower ratings for both peers and literary characters (p. 33).

Hynds (1989) observed that students do use their social understandings "to predict what will happen next in the story or to speculate beyond it; to understand people around them; to reflect on their own personal lives; and to compare the world of the text with the everyday world in which they live" (p. 49). She pointed out, however, that how much they do so depends a great deal on such factors as the encouragement they find at home for reading, the strength of their motivation to perform in the classroom, and, of course, their competence.

The comments of the students themselves offered Hynds (1989) some insight into their conception of the literature classroom. They reported to her the "constraining

influence" (p. 57) of ceaseless evaluation and of having their interpretations rejected by teachers too strongly devoted to their own. They noted, too, the pleasure, rare though it was, of working with teachers "who were willing to act as 'co-learner' in the process of literary analysis" (p. 57). Their observations indicated to Hynds that they would see clearer connections between literature and their lives "when teachers model literature as a way of learning about and reflecting upon life, when they are willing to act as co-learner rather than expert in that process, and when they offer choices of response modes and assessment measures" (p. 58).

Beach and Wendler (1987) also examined cognitive complexity, looking particularly at the developmental differences in student ability to draw inferences about characters' acts, perceptions, and goals. They hypothesized that as readers matured from adolescence to adulthood they would begin to judge characters' acts less as "autonomous physical behaviors" (p. 288) and instead speak of their social or psychological significance. Similarly, they would see characters' perceptions less in terms of apparent emotions or feelings and more as evidence of the characters' beliefs or values. Furthermore, they would come to understand not just the immediacy of characters' goals but also their longer range implications. Examining 8th- and 11th-graders, and college freshmen and juniors, Beach and Wendler did observe the predicted development of their inferential abilities.

Such research may help us clarify our expectations of readers at different levels of schooling, and suggest directions for our teaching. Beach and Wendler (1987) noted, for example, that younger readers tended to discuss characters' acts in simpler terms of their feelings; older readers were more likely to consider "conflicting perceptions between characters" (p. 295). Understanding something of the pattern of development in ability to infer about literary works may help educators decide what issues are suitable for particular grades and what depth of thought they may expect of or encourage in students. Younger students' tendency to think about characters' acts as physical behaviors and to ignore their broader social or psychological implications may make it difficult for them to move from event to theme in literary works, requiring teachers to provide some sort of assistance with that process.

Most of these studies obtained their data through the analysis of written responses to texts, or in some cases, such as Zaharias' (1986) study, simply through response preference inventories that ask students to rate the relative importance of 20 or so questions representing the categories of personal, descriptive, interpretive, and evaluative response. Such methods enabled researchers to segment responses, to discriminate among them, and to correlate them with other variables, but it did not allow them to see the responses as living, changing processes. As Odell and Cooper (1976) remarked, "Purves (1968) suggests a number of ways of describing the kinds of responses students make. He is, however, much less helpful in providing ways to describe the *processes* by which students formulate their responses" (p. 204).

Just as composition research had at one time focused almost exclusively on the written product rather than on the act of writing, so much of the research on response to literature had concentrated on the written report of response rather than on the vital act of responding. It gave researchers, consequently, a still picture of response—response frozen, divided, counted—and it told them something about what they had after the reading but little about what happened as the reading progressed. Despite its limitation, the research had nonetheless begun to tell researchers something about the diversity of readings, the factors that shape them, and the potential influence of teachers on them. It had also suggested that there was an important social dimension to the process of reading literary texts and encouraged both researchers and teachers to consider the importance of the interactions among readers.

The fundamental question, of course, is, What does happen as a reader reads? Several studies had begun to explore this problem.

## THE ANALYSIS OF TRANSACTIONS

Squire's examination in the 1960s of responses to short stories, predating the Purves *Elements* by 4 years, may be one of the first that attempted to look at what happens *as* the reader reads. Squire thought that asking students to respond orally, rather than in writing, would elicit from them a clearer and more accurate picture of their responses to the works. Dividing the stories into several parts, he interviewed students after they had read each section and thus was able to view the reading as a sequence of events, a process, rather than as a static entity.

Squire's analysis suggested seven categories of response, similar to those that Purves (1968) would later identify: literary judgments, interpretational responses, narrational reactions, associational responses, self-involvement, prescriptive judgments, and miscellaneous. Tracking the responses through six divisions of each story revealed some interesting relationships among the categories of response, relationships that would have been obscured in a written record produced at the conclusion of the reading. He noted, for instance, that narrational and associational responses—that is, retellings of the story and departures from the text to talk about the reader's own experience—tended to remain constant throughout the reading, suggesting that readers might find their own history insinuating itself into the reading at almost any point. Students do not necessarily "comprehend" the work first and then extend into their own experiences; rather, it may well be that they call on their history throughout the reading of a literary text. Literary judgments, however, were concentrated in the first divisions of the story and in the last. Readers may, perhaps, pass a hasty judgment upon the story as they begin it, quickly assessing its potential for pain or pleasure, then gradually become absorbed in the story, withholding further evaluation until they have completed it.

Self-involvement responses—statements indicating that the reader associates himself with the actions or the feelings of the character—increase quickly after the first division and then hold fairly constant throughout the reading. Squire noted a curious relationship between the involvement and the judgmental responses, observing that during the time readers were deeply involved they made fewer judgments. Nonetheless, those students who were more emotionally involved tended ultimately to offer more literary judgments about the texts. Speculating about that observation, Squire suggested that this "calls into question the tendency to assume an unnecessary opposition between intellectual and emotional responses to literature" (p. 22). It is an assumption still held by many, unfortunately, for it encourages teaching likely to neglect one aspect of literary experience or the other. Teachers who value only the intellectual may demand rigorous analysis and lose the human significance of the texts; those who value only the emotional may encourage response without inviting the reflection and analysis that would sharpen understanding of the text, one's self, and other readers.

Squire's study followed the students through the process of reading and responding and thus was able to give us some picture of the movement. He showed a reader passing early judgment on the merits of a text, becoming absorbed in the narration, attending occasionally throughout the reading to memories and associations called to mind by the text, and, at the end, evaluating the text once again. If a reader becomes deeply involved in the story, he or she is also likely to evaluate it more extensively. With Squire's study researchers began to develop a picture not just of the categories of response but also of the active, responding reader.

Later studies filled out the picture. Mauro (1983), for instance, conducted case studies of five high school students in an effort to see how their construct system might shape the process of response. Drawing on suggestions in Applebee's (1978) study of the development of a sense of story, Mauro investigated three construct systems that she thought might shape response: constructs of experience or content, constructs of literary conventions and form, and constructs of process. Her strategy for investigating the readings was similar to Squire's (1964). She asked the individual students to read the items—stories and poems—and to interrupt their readings, whenever they thought appropriate, to respond. (She did not divide the stories or poems for the students, as Squire had done, relying instead on their felt need—with occasional prompting—to speak.) Mauro taped all of the sessions and was present for all but one, which she intentionally skipped so that she might assess the effect of reading and responding in solitude.

Mauro's (1983) analysis of the students' transactions with the texts suggested that the individual's construct systems would be likely to shape his responses (making unlikely a unanimity in interpretation). One of the students, for example, revealed such strong disapproval of suicide that it seemed difficult for her to address any other topic when discussing a text that dealt with that issue. Another student, for whom suicide was not an important construct, scarcely mentioned it.

Mauro (1983) noticed also that students had certain expectations of texts—constructs of form—that in some cases seemed to shape responses more powerfully than did constructs of content. Stories, for some, were expected to provide vivid, living characters. Stories that did not ("The Sniper" was one such story) were likely to be viewed by those students as defective and unsatisfactory.

Perhaps most interesting of all, however, were Mauro's observations about the construct of process. Students, she found, had developed a notion of what was appropriate and what was not in the reading of a literary work. Analyzing and generalizing were, as might be predicted, assumed by all of the students to be suitable behaviors. There was more variation on other matters. One student demonstrated a strong interest in sharing his thoughts with others; another showed no inclination whatsoever to do so. One indicated clearly that the sharing of personal response was not an academically responsible behavior, and regardless of how interesting it might be, was not relevant or important in the literature classroom. Another seemed to think that the appropriate behavior was to sit patiently and wait for the researcher to ask questions rather to initiate any discussion on his own.

Mauro (1983) noticed also that the "permeability"—that is, the openness to change—of the constructs was a significant factor. Students whose constructs were relatively impermeable—rigid and inflexible—tended to reject texts that did not confirm them. The student, for example, who was deeply offended by the concept of suicide found it extremely difficult to deal with such texts as "Richard Corey." More flexible readers, tolerating if not approving, could at least consider the texts and reflect on them without serious discomfort.

Langer's (1989) study focused not so much on what students bring to the text as on what they do with it. She attempted to describe the nature of literary experience in terms of changing "stances" toward the text as readings progress. Thirty-six students in Grades 7 through 11 were asked to think aloud while reading six texts—two short stories, two poems, one science text, and one social studies text. Her analysis of transcripts of the readings suggested that "readers were always actively engaged in creating meanings when they read. However, as they developed their meanings across time, their stance (the way in which they related to the text) changed, with each stance adding a somewhat different dimension to the reader's understanding of the entire piece" (p. 7). The stances she identified were these:

"Being Out and Stepping Into an Envisionment"—this is the reader's attempt, drawing upon prior knowledge and upon characteristics of the text, to begin to comprehend what is happening in the text.

"Being In and Moving Through an Envisionment"—the reader is involved in the text, has some understanding of what is transpiring, and is building more complex understandings.

"Stepping Back and Rethinking What One Knows"—here the reader reflects, using the envisionment offered by the text to reconsider knowledge, assumptions, attitudes brought to the reading.

"Stepping Out and Objectifying the Experience"—the reader moves away from the text, reflecting on it and the experience of reading it. (p. 7)

This study may offer educators some interesting implications for the classroom. It clearly suggests, for instance, a pattern for questioning and discussing in the literature classroom. Teachers might experiment with plans devised to assist the students to move through these four stances, and see if such designs yield more satisfying experiences.

Some researchers have begun to look at various patterns teachers have devised for their literature lessons to see what effects they have on the students' readings of texts. Farest and Miller (1994), for instance, observed the effects of inviting fourth-grade students to engage in "written conversations" about the works they were reading. These conversations, apparently between child and adult responder, were conducted in the form of dialogue journals and embedded in an instructional program that included reading aloud to the students and both large and small group discussions. The researchers observed that the dialogue provided the opportunity for students to (a) "ask questions and seek clarification"; (b) "think through writing," wondering about the text; (c) "express personal connections" with the story and speak about what they know; (d) analyze the literature and draw inferences about the author; (e) examine their own values; (f) engage in "extended conversations," revisiting an issue over several journal entries; and (g) provide support for their subsequent small group discussions. Their study looked at the written conversation between student and teacher and suggests the possibility that we might look, too, at the merits of such conversations between student and student.

Studies such as these remind us that response to literature is a complex phenomenon. It is not simply a matter of liking or disliking, feeling or not feeling. Nor can it simply be viewed as a transaction between a solitary reader and a single text. Rather, it is that transaction as it has been shaped by all the social and pedagogic experiences that precede it. The student comes to any text with ideas about its content, with expectations about what the text should offer, and with notions about his own responsibilities as a reader. The response is, in part at least, the consequence of all of those factors, and it may be the teacher's responsibility to consider all of those factors. Educators have occasionally been encouraged, by tests in teachers' handbooks, by the ominous specter of Scholastic Aptitude and Achievement Tests, and by other forces to view student accomplishment in simple terms. Teachers may look to see if students understand the text, judging them by their ability to produce, reproduce, or at least identify acceptable interpretations. The research into the nature of response suggests that educators should perhaps consider more. Mauro's (1983) study in particular suggested that teachers consider the complex set of expectations and intellectual habits students bring with them or develop in classes, and Langer's (1989) urged teachers to look carefully at the actual process of making sense of literary texts. Farest and Miller's (1994) research suggested increased attention to the social dimensions of the literature classes and signaled a gradual shift in the attention of researchers from the responses processes of individuals to those of groups.

## THE ANALYSIS OF DEVELOPMENT

Much of the research drawing on the Purves–Beach (1972) system of analyzing responses, in an effort to objectively describe readers and reading, intentionally avoided making value judgments about the categories of response. However, the efforts to describe the processes of response and to depict its "natural" development have revealed that there is no such thing as natural development. Response patterns mature within a cultural context that reinforces some patterns and discourages others. When New Criticism dominated—and it may dominate still—students learned to analyze and interpret literature, suppressing personal response and resisting, if they were good students, the desire to digress to their own stories or to other matters outside the text. As attention to response grows more and more respectable, it is likely that students will learn to respond and to express those responses in academically approved ways.

Thus, it is hard to speak of development without considering how we channel it, encourage it, interfere with it—the value judgments lurk close to the surface. Developmental models have consequently grown more sophisticated. The model Protherough (1983) proposed would analyze students responses on four dimensions: awareness of theme, ability to emphathize with characters, understanding of motivation, and ability to predict beyond the story. He argued that levels of response identified within each of these dimensions provide a model of development indicating "a shift away from reacting to isolated, particular details towards more perceptive responses to the total meaning of a text" (p. 45). It should be noted that in this model the text still dictates. Maturity in reading is a matter of more perceptive responses *to the text*.

Thomson, however, proposes a somewhat more comprehensive model by suggesting six stages:

1. Unreflective interest in action.
2. Empathising.
3. Analogising.
4. Reflecting on the significance of events (theme) and behaviour (distanced evaluation of characters).
5. Reviewing the whole work as the author's creation.
6. Consciously considered relationship with the author, recognition of textual ideology, and understanding of self (identity theme) and of one's own reading process. (pp. 360–361)

The fifth and sixth stages are most interesting, because it is here that Thomson most clearly indicates his attention to the investigations into response. Note the parallels with Mauro's (1983) study. She had observed the influence of construct systems related to the three points at issue in these stages. The construct of content is echoed in Thomson's idea of recognizing textual ideology—both have to do with understanding the values or ideas carried by both text and reader. Mauro's construct of process is Thomson's notion of understanding one's own reading process, and Mauro's construct of form is recalled by the fifth stage, seeing the work as an author's creation. Thomson broadened the picture to include not just attention to text but also to writer, to culture, to self, and to self-as-reader.

The extent of the change may be even more apparent in the "process strategies" that amplify each stage. At the third stage, Thomson (1987) suggested that the process is one of "drawing on the repertoire of personal experiences, making connections between characters and one's own life." Clearly he would have the student go beyond the text and he would consider reading to be more than simply comprehending what transpires within the text itself. At the fifth stage he saw students "drawing on literary and cultural repertoires," comparing the "author's representations with one's own," and recognizing the "implied author" behind the text. Here again response and comprehension consist of a great deal more than simple submission to text. Finally, in the sixth stage, he called for awareness of the expectations of the reader implicit within the text. Drawing on Iser (1978) and Booth (1961), he suggested that the process involves the recognition of the "implied reader in the text, and the relationship between implied author and implied reader" The last strategy in his list of thirteen is reflexiveness—"understanding of textual ideology, personal identity and one's own reading processes".

It is probably dangerous, however, to allow the seductiveness of such developmental models as this one to delude us into thinking that the student's ability to respond to and think about literary texts develops in a simple, linear pattern, moving from one level to the next in a predictable and unvarying progression, like climbing the steps. Such a view of the reader's development may tempt us to oversimplify instruction and perhaps to expect too little of readers. A number of studies suggest that students may be able to perform with texts in richer and more diverse ways than we might have expected (Cullinan, Harwood, & Galda, 1983; Lehr, 1988). Many (1991), in a study of the effects of stance and age level on the responses of children in Grades 4, 6, and 8, for instance, observed that "although students will increase in ability to apply story events to life and to make abstract generalizations, this ability is not beyond the capabilities of younger students" (p. 77). Her study, which looked in part at the interaction of the reader's stance—aesthetic or efferent—and level of understanding, concluded that stance did "significantly affect level of understanding, with higher levels of understanding associated with the aesthetic stance. . . . The subjects who focused in their responses on the lived-through experience of the story were significantly more likely to interpret story events, to apply the story to life, and to make abstract generalizations than were students who responded efferently. . . . The majority of the efferent responses focusing on the literary elements," on the other hand, "tended to be trite and superficial" (p. 77).

Such studies as Many's (1991) reconfirm the validity of Rosenblatt's conception of the literary transaction and argue strongly for instruction that respects the reader's vital experience in and with the text. They suggest that if teachers want students to understand the literature, much less to enjoy it, then teachers must focus less on what students can extract from it and remember for Friday's test and more on the aesthetic dimension—visualizing, imagining, responding, associating, questioning, predicting, and the like. Such studies challenge the tendency to reduce literature to what can be tested, to reduce the act of reading to the simple task of extracting information or identifying literary elements, and to reduce teaching to the simple task of leading students to see what the teachers has decided is there in the text to be seen.

## THE ANALYSIS OF INTERACTIONS

One critically important question for research on response has to do with the shaping effects of teachers and teaching. As the IEA study pointed out, response to literature is learned. To ask what natural, uncontaminated response would be is to ask an impossible question, because literary response is not a biological phenomenon but rather a cultural one; it occurs, that is to say, within a social context—the context of the school. Efforts to examine developmental stages in response may provide some indications about how the reader's mind, ability, and attitudes change over time, but whether those changes are attributable to natural processes or to the consequences of schooling or, more likely, to some infinitely complex combination of those and other factors is difficult to assess.

A number of studies have noted the narrowing of readers' range of responses, with the focus gradually, over the years of schooling, coming to bear on interpreting texts. Researchers had assumed that interpretation was what was needed, but the Purves–Beach (1972) categories suggested that there was more that can be done with literature. Rosenblatt's (1983) vision of the reader, first articulated at length in 1938 in *Literature as Exploration*, compelled educators to look more closely at the act of reading. She suggested that a formal, distanced interpretation, one that failed to take into account the uniqueness of the reader, would neglect essential elements in the literary experience. It would fail, in particular, to consider the aesthetic and emotional. On the one hand, instruction was having its effects; on the other hand, teachers were beginning to doubt that these were the *desired* effects.

Lucking (1976) attempted to assess the effects of different questioning strategies on the responses to short stories. Comparing no instruction, traditional instruction, and instruction arranged according to the hierarchy dictated by Bloom's taxonomy, Lucking noted several sharp differences in response patterns. Compared with no instruction, the traditional instruction yielded fewer engagement and evaluation responses, and more perception and miscellaneous. The major difference observable between traditional and experimental was a dramatic increase in interpretational responses after the hierarchically arranged questioning session. Although there is some uncertainty about what the traditional instruction consisted of, because Lucking seemed to be relying on the training and instincts of the teachers to mold them to some traditional patterns, and although patterns of questioning suggested by Bloom's taxonomy could hardly be said to respect individual response, it was fairly clear that differences in questioning did yield differences in response patterns, suggesting the importance of considering the shaping influence of classroom discourse on the thinking of the students.

A study by Marshall (1987) looked not at oral questioning but instead at the writing students were expected to undertake. He examined the effects of several conditions—no writing, restricted writing, personal analytical writing, and formal analytical writing—on the responses of 11th-grade students to each of four short stories. The restricted writing assignments consisted of eight short-answer questions, all of which seemed, from the examples provided, to focus on the text itself. Similarly, the formal writing assignments directed the students' attention to the text, asking them to interpret in somewhat more extensive form than was expected in the restricted assignments. The personal writing asked the students to "elaborate upon their responses to the story, drawing on their own values and personal experience to make sense of their reactions to the text" (p. 43).

Marshall (1987) observed that the three different writing tasks did in fact shape the responses of the students in fairly predictable ways. The short answers evoked predominantly interpretive statements, with some description offered, presumably as support for the interpretation. The formal analytical assignment, predictably, did the same—interpretive statements supported by description of the text. The personal analytical, however, also elicited interpretive statements, though not as high a percentage as the other two forms. Here, however, the interpretations were supported or developed with personal statements, connecting the reading with the students' other experiences as well as with descriptions of the text. Invitation to address personal reactions did not, as some have feared it might, lead the students into orgies of self-revelation or otherwise distract them entirely from the text. Instead, it allowed them to consider the text in the light of their own lives. As Marshall put it:

> Because the form was more flexible, the students could employ in their personal writing a language more clearly consonant with their initial experience of the stories. Because the tasks asked them to address that experience directly, their personal essays were less a report on shared knowledge than an opportunity to begin the process of independent analysis. (p. 59)

Work by Newell, Suszynski, and Weingart in the late 1980s looked at similar matters, examining the effects of writing in modes they labeled reader based and text based. The reader-based mode invited students to write in less formal, more personal, tentative, and exploratory ways about the story under consideration whereas the text-based mode called for interpretation drawing exclusively on the text for evidence. The study found that students writing the less formal, reader-based, essays wrote significantly more and better. In particular, they wrote a great many more statements that Newell et al. labeled reflexive, which was a category "developed to capture statements in which the students applied aspects of their personal knowledge and experience in their attempts to interpret the story" (p. 43). The other categories into which they sorted the statements were descriptive, personal, interpretive, and evaluative. The researchers thought that the category "personal" failed to distinguish between those comments that simply recounted personal associations and those that linked personal associations to the reading employing them to deepen the reader's understanding of the text. Newell et al. arrived at conclusions consistent with Marshall's (1987), that writing in the personal, expressive mode, tentatively exploring the significance of the text soon after reading, is likely to lead to more sophisticated literary responses. It is, they asserted, "a bridge to more public forms of written discourse" (p. 51).

The students' apparent preference for the reader-based, personal, or aesthetic approaches to literature observed in this study are echoed elsewhere. Many and Wiseman (1992), for instance, in a study with third-graders, came to very similar conclusions, finding that "the students' preferred choice when responding to literature is to focus on their aesthetic experience of the story," (p. 282) and suggesting that "an aesthetic approach which focuses on the associations, emotions, and ideas evoked needs to be employed" (p. 283).

Recently, studies have begun to attend more and more to the social setting in which these personally significant encounters with texts might be explored and enriched. Villaume and

Hopkins (1995), for example, focused on the text as a vehicle of communication among readers, as well as between author and solitary reader (p. 191). Villaume and Hopkins noted that the talk among students "stimulated and served as a scaffold for personal response," (p. 202), suggesting that much of response to literature takes place during the conversations, and not in the solitary meeting of child and book. Guice (1995) spoke of "creating communities of readers" echoing and explicitly referring to Fish's (1980) notion of interpretive communities. Pointing out that researchers "seem to know more about readers and texts than we do contexts for responding to books," she argued that researchers need "an investigation of the social construction of the contexts for reading" (p. 379). Guice was particularly interested in the perspective of the children themselves, so she attempted to understand their reactions to the contexts the classroom provided. She observed sixth-graders in one classroom, taping their discussions, reading what they wrote, and interviewing them. From the data, she concluded that there were four contexts in which the children talked about their reading: "silent reading," "book selection," "writing," and "aesthetic activity" (p. 387). Each of these contexts, she noted, shaped the talk differently. As the students selected books, for example, there was, as might be expected, sharing of titles, talk about reading interests, and trading of opinions; as they wrote, they shared drafts and offered editorial suggests. Possibly most interesting, however, is the students' compulsion to talk. Even in the context of silent reading Guice observed talk, much of it furtive, quiet, whispered. In the context of book selection, hushed conversations were conducted in the aisles of the library while students pretended only to be looking for books. Guice further noted:

The teacher often reprimanded children for talking, even though the talk was productive. Talk for the sake of selecting topics for writing, for discussing books and authors, for sharing texts, and for sharing process was not condoned. The children were aware of this rule, although most of them constantly broke it. . . .

Despite the teacher's rules concerning talk, the children talked constantly and enjoyed events, such as reading books in common, that promoted a feeling of togetherness, community. (p. 386)

Guice's (1995) study, following in the footsteps of Eeds and Wells (1989), reminded researchers that the reading of literature, though it is often a lonely event undertaken in the solitude of our living room or our airplane seat, is fundamentally a social event. Through the trading of stories and reactions to them, people come together in families, communities, and societies. In preliterate days, when stories were passed on orally, the literary event *had* to be social—individuals who could not read could not take the book that was not available off into a quiet corner. Rather, they had to sit with others and listen with them to a storyteller. It would be interesting to know how those ancient listeners reacted to those stories and talked about them. It is possible that their conversations around communal fires, though untutored and undirected, had something in common with the conversations Guice envisioned for our students when she concluded with the hope that we will encourage children to "talk about books in ways that are natural to them—to construct a community of readers." (p. 396)

That suggestion seems to capture much of the movement in research in response to literature over the last decade or so. These recent studies have focused more and more on the climate of the literature classroom and on the social dimensions of the act of reading literary works. When Hansson (1973), reporting on studies he had done in Sweden, suggested four possible effects of teaching, he said little about the community in the classroom. The consequences of teaching, he suggested, could be:

the intellectual understanding of a poem could often be enriched and diversified, while the emotional qualities of the experience remained more or less unchanged; shallow and impersonal experiences could be influenced if the reader was not wholly indifferent to the poem; strongly personal experiences were not open to outside influences except for details; well-founded and well-defined critical opinions were hard to change. (p. 263)

He did note several reservations. Students who were engaged in analysis and discussion of a short story "acquired a more uniform understanding of the text and reached more uniform interpretations" (p. 274) than did individuals who were allowed to study it on their own, but "at the same time the attitude of these students had grown more negative, and they felt less keen on reading more texts by the same author than did the students who had not been taught in class" (p. 274). He suggested that it might be appropriate, especially in the United States where New Critism's analyses of texts seemed to be the dominant approach, to examine the various effects, both academic and psychological, of the methods of the literature classroom. Were he writing now, he would very likely comment further on the effects that educators' methods have on the community of the classroom and persuade them to consider how they might encourage our students to engage in conversations about literature that would serve to strengthen and enrich those communities rather than divide and stratify them.

## FINAL COMMENTS

The impossibility of defining natural response processes in the reading of literature forces researchers to move at some point from empirical research to philosophy. The efforts to categorize response, to correlate it with features of texts, personality traits, and instructional methods may tell researchers something about what happens in the literature classroom, but ultimately they are left with the question of what should happen in literature teaching, a question that leads not to multivariate statistics, or even to ethnography, but instead to philosophy. Researchers' answers will depend on their vision of the good life, on their hopes for their children, as much as on the information, valuable as that is, that research itself provides.

Much of the current research in response to literature lends strength, however, to a democratic vision of the classroom. It suggests that significant and enjoyable learning can occur when the classroom respects the unique responses of readers, encouraging them to make meaning of texts in personally significant ways. The possibilities remain both exciting and problematic for teachers. On the one hand, they have the prospects for classroom exchanges in which the learning may take on a much more significant role in the lives of their students. Literary experience, in classes shaped by this body of research, may bring texts and lives to bear on one another in ways that enliven and enrich the discourse. On the other hand, teachers will face the problems of working within a tradition that discourages their efforts. The emphasis schools have always placed on correctness, on the gathering of information whether assimilated or not, and on measuring learning will likely prove discouraging to teachers hoping to work with the notions of literature instruction sustained by this research.

The research, however, provides arguments against this tradition. It has powerfully defended the notion that alternative readings of texts are both natural and desirable and thus has rejected the idea that literary experiences can be simply and easily judged as correct or incorrect. It has demonstrated the great importance of connecting the text with the other experiences, the prior knowledge of the reader, and thus rejected the notion that

simply acquiring information—facts, dates, memorized judgments, and the like—amounts to significant learning. Moreover, it has surely indicated the complexity of literary experience, suggesting that efforts to reduce it to discrete, isolable, measurable units will be either futile or immensely difficult.

Teachers—and schools—will have to respond to the notion, fundamental in the work on response, that literary experience is much more than the acquiring of information. It is in the literature classroom, and in other transactions with the stories of cultures, that students forge their sense of human possibilities and shape the families, communities, and, ultimately, the society in which we all will live. The sense that literature touches the individual and shapes his or her vision of human possibilities explains its enduring in the curriculum, despite this culture's seduction by the quantifying methods of empirical science. The vision of literature and literature instruction that informs much of the research on response accepts and sustains that notion of literature's place.

# References

Applebee, A. N. (1977). ERIC/RCS Report: The elements of response to a literary work: What we have learned. *Research in the Teaching of English, 11,* 255-271.

Applebee, A. N. (1978). *The child's concept of story.* Chicago: University of Chicago Press.

Beach, R. (1976). Differences between high school and university students in their conceptions of literary characters. *Research in the Teaching of English, 10,* 259-268.

Beach, R. (1983). Attitudes, social conventions, and response to literature. *Journal of Research and Development in Education, 16,* 47-54.

Beach, R. (1985). Discourse conventions and researching response to literary dialogue. In C. R. Cooper (Ed.), *Researching response to literature and the teaching of literature* (pp. 103-127). Norwood, NJ: Ablex.

Beach, R., & Wendler, L. (1987). Developmental differences in response to a story. *Research in the Teaching of English, 21,* 286-297.

Bleich, D. (1969). Emotional origins of literary meaning. *College English, 31,* 30-40.

Bleich, D. (1971). Psychological bases of learning from literature. *College English, 33,* 32-45.

Bleich, D. (1975a). *Readings and feelings: An introduction to subjective criticism.* Urbana, IL: National Council of Teachers of English.

Bleich, D. (1975b). The subjective character of critical interpretation. *College English, 36,* 739-755.

Bleich, D. (1976). The subjective paradigm in science, psychology, and criticism. *New Literary History, 7,* 313-334.

Bleich, D. (1978). *Subjective criticism.* Baltimore, MD: Johns Hopkins University Press.

Booth, W. (1961). *The rhetoric of fiction.* Chicago: University of Chicago Press.

Corcoran, W. T. (1979). *A study of the responses of superior and average students in grades eight, ten, and twelve to a short story and a poem.* University of Alberta, Edmonton, Alberta, Canada.

Cornaby, B. J. (1975). A study of the influence of form on responses of twelfth-grade students in college-preparatory classes to dissimilar novels, a short story, and a poem. *Dissertation Abstracts International, 35,* 4856-4857A. (University Microfilms)

Cullinan, B. E., Harwood, K. T., & Galda, L. (1983). The reader and the story: Comprehension and response. *Journal of Research and Development in Education, 16*(3), 20-38.

Education Department of South Australia (1983). *A single impulse: Developing responses to literature.* Adelaide, South Australia: Author.

Eeds, M., & Wells, D. (1989). Grand Conversations: An exploration of meaning construction in literature study groups. *Research in the Teaching of English, 23,* 4-29.

Farest, C. A., & Miller, C. J. (1994, March). *Having written conversations: Dialogues about literature.* Paper presented at the spring meeting of the National Council of Teachers of English, Portland, OR. ED 386 740.

Fish, S. (1980). *Is there a text in this class? The authority of interpretive communities.* Cambridge, MA: Harvard University Press.

Guice, S. L. (1995). Creating communities of readers: A study of children's information networks as multiple contexts for responding to texts. *Journal of Reading Behavior, 27*(3), 379-397.

Hansson, G. (1973). Some types of research on response to literature. *Research in the Teaching of English, 7,* 260-284.

Harding, D. W. (1937). The role of the on-looker. *Scrutiny, 6,* 247-258.

Holland, N. (1968). *The dynamics of literary response.* London: Oxford University Press.

Holland, N. (1973). *Poems in persons: An introduction to the psychoanalysis of literature.* New York: Norton.

Holland, N. (1975a). *5 readers reading.* New Haven, CT: Yale University Press.

Holland, N. (1975b). Unity identity text self. *PMLA, 9,* 813-822.

Holland, N. (1977). Transactive teaching: Cordelia's death. *College English, 39,* 276-285.

Holland, N., & Schwartz, M. (1975). The Delphi seminar. *College English, 36,* 789-800.

Hynds, S. D. (1985). Interpersonal cognitive complexity and the literary response processes of adolescent readers. *Research in the Teaching of English, 19,* 386-402.

Hynds, S. D. (1989). Bring life to literature and literature to life: Social constructs and contexts of four adolescent readers. *Research in the Teaching of English, 23,* 30-61.

Iser, W. (1978). *The act of reading: A theory of aesthetic response.* Baltimore, MD: Johns Hopkins University Press.

Kelly, G. A. (1955). *A theory of personality.* New York: Norton.

Langer, J. (1989). *The process of understanding literature* (Report Series 2.1). Albany: State University of New York, Center for the Learning and Teaching of Literature.

Lehr, S. (1988). The child's developing sense of theme as a response to literature. *Reading Research Quarterly, 23,* 337-357.

Lucking, R. A. (1976). A study of the effects of a hierarchically-ordered questioning technique on adolescents' responses to short stories. *Research in the Teaching of English, 1,* 269-276.

Many, J. E. (1991). The effects of stance and age level on children's literary responses. *Journal of Reading Behavior, 23*(1), 61-85.

Many, J. E., & Wiseman, D. L. (1992). The effect of teaching approach on third-grade students' response to literature. *Journal of Reading Behavior, 24*(3), 265-287.

Marshall, J. D. (1987). The effects of writing on students' understanding of literary texts. *Research in the teaching of English, 21,* 30-63.

Mauro, L. H. (1983). Personal constructs and response to literature: Case studies of adolescents reading about death (Doctoral dissertation, Rutgers University, 19__). *Dissertation Abstracts International, 44*/07A.

Odell, L., & Cooper, C. (1976). Describing responses to works of fiction. *Research in the Teaching of English, 10,* 203-225.

Petrosky, A. R. (1976). The effects of reality perception and fantasy on response to literature: Two case studies. *Research in the Teaching of English, 1,* 239-258.

Petrosky, A. R. (1982a). From story to essay: Reading and writing. *College Composition and Communication, 33,* 19-36.

Petersen, B. T. (1982b). Writing about responses: A unified model of reading, interpretation, and composition. *College English, 44,* 459-468.

Petrosky, A. R., & Cooper, C. (1978). Evaluating the results of classroom literary study. *English Journal, 67,* 96-99.

Protherough, R. (1983). *Developing response to fiction.* Milton Keynes: Open University Press.

Purves, A. C. (1968). *Elements of writing about a literary work: A study of response to literature.* Urbana, IL: National Council of Teachers of English.

Richards, I. A. (1956). *Practical criticism* (__ ed.). New York: Harcourt, Brace. (Original work published 1929)

Rosenblatt, L. M. (1983). *Literature as exploration* (4th ed.). New York: Modern Language Association.

Thomson, J. (1987). *Understanding teenagers reading: Reading processes and the teaching of literature.* New York: Nichols.

Villaume, S. K., & Hopkins, L. (1995). A transactional and sociocultural view of response in a fourth-grade literature discussion group. *Reading Research and Instruction, 34*(3), 190-203.

Young, R. E., Becker, A. L., & Pike, K. L. (1970). *Rhetoric: Discovery and change.* New York: Harcourt, Brace.

Zaharias, J. A. (1986). The effects of genre and tone on undergraduate students' preferred patterns of response to two short stories and two poems. *Research in the Teaching of English, 2,* 56-68.

# ·60·

# MULTICULTURALISM, LITERATURE, AND CURRICULUM ISSUES

## Violet J. Harris and Arlette I. Willis
### University of Illinois at Urbana-Champaign

The World War II era seems an unlikely time for selecting *multicultural* as the word symbolizing the year 1941. Multiculturalism was evoked as a political and ideological stance in a book review published in *The New York Herald* in 1941 as cited in (Barnhart & Metcalf, 1997). The reviewer conceived of the term as "a fervent sermon against nationalism, national prejudice and behavior in favor of a 'multicultural' way of life" (p. 236). Simply defined, it meant, respect for the ways of all nations and peoples (p. 236). Further, the term was adopted to counter other ideologies such as imperialism and colonialism (Barnhart & Metcalf, 1997).

The American Dialect Society chose multiculturalism as symbolic of the year. In other years, the society chose the words *jeep* (1940), *gizmo* (1942), *acronym* (1943), *snafu* (1944), *showbiz* (1945), and *Iron Curtain/Cold War* (1946) for the years identified. These words and phrases, with the exception of *Iron Curtain/Cold War*, contradict the political tenor of the period. In contrast, one could argue words such as *balkanization*, *Nazism*, and *Aryanism* should have emerged as likely candidates. The term *multicultural* does suggest an element of acceptance of difference. The political situation suggested another reality. Different languages, skin colors, religions, and cultural practices, for instance, were targets for laws that restricted and subjugated, triangles that signaled ethnic and racial identity, and behaviors and individuals that required eradication not celebration. That multiculturalism emerged as a symbol during World War II is all the more ironic.

In this chapter we discuss topics related to multiculturalism, literature, and curriculum. First, we begin with some of the philosophical and theoretical foundations because these are often omitted from debates. This discussion serves as a framework for the examination of related areas. Next, conceptions of multiculturalism are assessed to illustrate how shifting identities, ideology, and historical currents affect applications of multiculturalism to literacy and literature instruction. Arguments about multicultural literature are insufficient if the various conditions related to its creation, publication, and dissemination are not critiqued. Then we examine the types of research completed on multicultural literature and curriculum. Finally, we explore the intersection of multiculturalism, literature, and instruction.

## PHILOSOPHICAL AND IDEOLOGICAL FOUNDATIONS

Attempting to locate the philosophical and ideological foundations of multiculturalism is like looking for the proverbial needle in a haystack. Rarely do researchers look to intellectual histories and traditions to inform their understanding of multiculturalism. Those who do tend to begin with the Enlightenment period, drawing on ideas of the importance of the individual. For others, notions of multiculturalism are drawn from philosophies that center on ideas about difference and identity as well as liberation and emancipation.

Critical multiculturalism draws from articulations of critical theory by philosophers, social and educational theorists, and cultural workers. A comprehensive overview is beyond the scope of this chapter. Martin Jay's (1996) history of the Frankfurt school traces the evolution of the concept of critical theory, and in his words the "theoretical inspiration" (p. xii) it has inspired. There are a host of critical theorists whose work informs critical multiculturalism from the Frankfurt school's multiple generations (Wiggershaus, 1994). Mark Poster (1989) wrote that this form of critique was needed to account for the "ideological hegemony of capitalism and the cultural supremacy of mass society" (p. 2). Other philosophers, social theorists, and educators

(Freire, 1970; Giroux, 1988; and Gramsci, 1971) also held similar interests. An argument also can be made that scholars such as Alain Locke (1926, 1968) and W. E. B. Du Bois (1926) provided crucial foundational theories about identity, race, and power in the United States that preceded many of the aforementioned. One of the most important tenets of varying forms of critical theory is the critique of the cultural, social, and historical events of society; their impact on individuals and groups, especially oppressed groups; the struggle against social injustice; and the hope of emancipation.

Educational theorists Giroux (1988), Macedo (1994), McLaren (1988), Popkewitz (1984), and Shor (1987), among others, have drawn on critical theory as far as they found it helpful to articulate the forms of oppression within contemporary American society and education. Using the essay as their form of critique, these theorists have articulated and challenged the "commonsense" rhetoric that underpins much of education. They are joined by cultural workers who embrace the need for social change and actively engage in work towards that end. Our use of the term *cultural worker*, is captured in a definition offered by Leistyna, Woodrum, and Sherblom (1996) as "an educator who critically engages learning (wherever it may take place) with the goal of working pedagogically and politically to ensure the development of a socially responsible citizenry and a critical, multicultural, democracy" (p. 335). As such, cultural workers need not be theorists, researchers, or teachers in the traditional sense but must be committed educators in the ordinary sense. There have been and currently are countless cultural workers (e.g., Septima Clark, Concha Delgado-Gaitin, Myles Horton, Luis Moll, and Sonia Nieto, to name a few) to whom we are indebted. We draw on their work in framing our discussion of multiculturalism, literature, and curriculum.

Banks and Banks (1997) defined *multiculturalism* as "a philosophical position and movement that assumes that the gender, ethnic, racial, and cultural diversity of a pluralistic society should be reflected in all of the institutionalized structures of educational institutions, including the staff, the norms and values, the curriculum, and the student body" (p. 435). In addition, the editors of *The Encyclopedia of Multicultural Education* (Mitchell & Salsbury, 1999) defined the term as "a new kind of cultural pluralism which stresses the inclusion of multicultural perspectives and empowerment of members of minority groups in all aspects of public life" (p. 151). The past 4 decades have seen important changes in how the term is defined, used, defended, opposed, maligned, and appended for particular audiences and constituencies. What appears to be a semantic battle is a more pervasive struggle over the range of possible philosophical and ideological assumptions that support multiculturalism. The resulting discourse surrounding multiculturalism often sounds discordant, and proponents appear to fail to harmonize their beliefs and values into a single defensible definition, set of purposes, or goals for multiculturalism. Multiculturalism, like many educational ideas, does not stem from one singular source, nor has its history traveled a linear course. The power of the concept is drawn from its own multiplicity, but this, too, is its weakness, resulting in a matrix, the intersection and overlap of ideas, that will only become more complex.

In this chapter, we cannot possibly undertake an exhaustive review of the philosophical, ideological, social, or historical foundations of the many variants of multiculturalism. There are myriad intellectual currents and tenets that inform our understanding of multiculturalism and frame how multiculturalism is currently understood and applied to literacy. The foundations of multiculturalism much like its definition and application, have changed overtime and reflect the beliefs, values, and ideas of proponents as well as the historical and social contexts in which their ideas are espoused. A common assumption underlying all is the importance of the struggle against social injustice.

## CONCEPTIONS OF MULTICULTURALISM

The terms *multicultural education* and *multicultural literature* also exhibited a comparable tortuous development in the period from 1970 to 1999. Proponents viewed the concepts as helping to fulfill the ideals of educational equity, equal access, and expansion of the body of knowledge deemed important and worthy of institutionalization (Banks, 2001; Grant & Sleeter, 1999; Nieto, 2002; Sims Bishop, 1998; Spears-Bunton, 1999; Taxel, 1997). Opponents noted the denigration of the idea of an American identity, lowered educational standards, and political correctness (Bloom, 1998; D'Souza, 1996; Scheslinger, 1991; Stodsky, 1996). This thinking is "restricted by an ethnocentrism and a patriotism cognizant of the exclusion of peoples of color, certain immigrants and women yet fearful of the subversive demands these excluded people might make and enact" (West, 1989, p. 5). However, more informed views point to a wider array of philosophical schools of thought and social theories that inform present day manifestations of multiculturalism.

Conceptions and definitions of multicultural literature are fluid. Meanings change as a result of shifting political, cultural, and social contexts. Variants of multiculturalism included boutique and strong multiculturalism (Fish, 1997), cosmetic and discrete multiculturalism (Wiel, 1998); critical multiculturalism (Giroux, 1992; Kanpol and McLaren, 1995), particular and pluralistic multiculturalism (Ravitch, 1990), and radical multiculturalism, among others. As West (1993) observed, "race matters"; however, it never has mattered enough in American society to transform society to become more equal, just, and democratic. Thus, early notions of multiculturalism as ethnic study have given way to versions of multiculturalism that include gender, class, sexual orientation, ableism, age, religion, and geographical location.

The term gained some acceptance in the late 1980s. For example, *The Horn Book Guide* editors adopted the term in addition to other categories such as Afro-American and Black. Heightened acceptance occurred in the 1990s along with a spate of textbooks, journal articles, and presentations at conferences. Earlier definitions centered on race, ethnicity, gender, and, to a lesser extent, class (Bishop, 1992; Kruse et al., 1997; Taxel, 1997). As the distinct historic and contemporary conditions of other groups acquired greater prominence in the political realm, for instance, individuals with disabilities, the elderly, and religious groups, they, too, have been included in descriptions or listings of the groups placed under the multicul-tural umbrella (Harris, 1997; Lindgren, 1991; Muse, 1997). The inclusion of gays and lesbians (and later transgender individuals) sparked contentious debate among supporters and opponents of multiculturalism and multicultural literature (Harris, 1997). Still others advocated for the inclusion of Whites, especially eth-nic groups such as Irish-Americans (Shannon, 1994).

A few argued for the liberatory power of postcolonial theory and criticism as well as a radicalized feminist theory in addi-tion or in contrast to multiculturalism (Schwartz, 1995; Shome, 1996). Postcolonial theory examines the dominance of Eurocen-tric or Western thought and the ways in which cultural institu-tions, practices, and knowledge are shaped and institutionalized by this ideological stance. Central components of postcolonial theory are notions of cultural hybridity and diasporic identity.

Cai and Sims Bishop (1994) offered reconceptualizations and clarifications of multicultural literature that parallel postcolonial theory. They argued for a reconsideration of multicultural litera-ture in terms of three categories: world literature, cross-cultural literature, and parallel culture literature. World literature would encompass all literature. Cross-cultural literature categorizes the contentious body of work written about various cultural groups, often by those who are not members. Literature about African Americans, Latinos and Latinas, Native Americans, and Asian Pacific Americans and written by members of those groups was classified as parallel culture literature (Cai & Sims Bishop, 1994). In some ways, this typology lessens the possibility of argu-ments about inclusion–exclusion, authors as insiders–outsiders, and culturally authentic–inaccurate arguments, which have con-sumed recent discourse about multicultural literature (Aronson, 1995; Harris, 1997; Hearne, 1999; Lasky, 1996; Reese et al., 1999). The novel *Monster* (Myers, 1999) is constructed in such a manner that it invites analysis from a postmodern stance. The book jacket breaks with tradition in that its size is less than that of the book. The photograph on the cover, in the style of a mug shot, is of an African American male. The narrative struc-ture adopted is that of a film script, with close-ups, fades, and flashbacks. On one level, the novel reinforces traditional repre-sentations of Black males as violent and criminal. On the other hand, a far more complex narrative emerges than the one sug-gested by the book jacket because the author spent scores of hours interviewing youth in and out of jails and juvenile deten-tion centers and attending court cases (Campbell, 1999). Myers allowed the reader to engage with ideas about masculinity, class antagonism, racial and ethnic group hostility, violence, and the protagonist's guilt or innocence.

Debates such as the aforementioned highlight serious cul-tural, social, aesthetic, and economic realities. Critical scholar-ship on the roles played by publishing companies, librarians, and teachers in the acceptance or rejection of multicultural liter-ature has emerged. These issues assume magnified importance.

## STATUS OF MULTICULTURAL LITERATURE

Questions about authorship, publication, dissemination, and institutionalization continue to bedevil supporters and oppo-nents. Many of these questions result from shifts in power

relations within society. Prior to the 1970s, children's book and magazine publishing in the United States was perceived as a genteel profession and the domain of Eastern, elitist, edu-cated, upper-class individuals (Kelly, 1974). These "guardians of tradition" provided literature that reinforced certain cultural and ideological traditions (Kelly, 1974; Taxel, 1997). Part of that tra-dition included paternalistic, inaccurate, and stereotypic images of various groups, although some exceptions were apparent. As groups included under the multicultural rubric acquired greater power within society, a concurrent change in the literary depic-tions of the groups emerged. Clearly, the more complex images were a direct effect of both the efforts of many groups such as the Interracial Council on Books for Children, and changes within publishing companies (Harris, 1997; Hill, 1998; Taxel, 1997).

### Authorial Identity

Despite protests to the contrary, a grand conspiracy does not exist that prevents European Americans from writing about other groups (Lasky, 1996; Rochman, 1993). For example, most of the books written about Native Americans are written by non–Native Americans, especially European Americans (Reese et al., 1999). Many view the right of historically disenfranchised groups to write about themselves of paramount importance (Myers, 1986/1995; Seto, 1995; Sims Bishop, 1997). Although others would defend the right of authors to write about any topic, the lack of knowledge about the major and minor details that constitute a culture can entangle an author and her pub-lishing company in debates, calls for boycotts, and charges of cultural genocide.

A volume in Scholastic's *Dear America* series, *My Heart Is On the Ground* (Rinaldi, 1999) is a case in point. The novel detailed the "biography" of a fictional Sioux girl at the Carlisle Indian School in Pennsylvania. Critics of the novel published a manuscript in an issue of *Rethinking Schools* in which they provided an overview of the depiction of Native Americans in children's literature, the paucity of Native American authors, and a critical analysis of the novel (Reese et al., 1999). The analysis contained an examination of fundamental issues such as imaginative license versus historical accuracy, the appropriation and misappropriation of culture, and publishers' dismissal of the concerns of an informed group of readers.

Unquestionably, the ranks of publishing have opened and more diversity is evident. An increase in the number of multi-cultural titles; the launching of the Jump to the Sun imprint at Hyperion Books; the emergence of editors who are people of color at major publishing houses; and the continued existence of small independent publishers (e.g., Children's Book Press, Just Us Books, Lee & Low Books, and Polychrome) are examples of a continued pluralistic impulse in publishing.

Reminders exist among the anecdotes shared by writers about the responses of editors to their manuscripts (Hill, 1998). In one such anecdote authors are told that a market does not exist for a manuscript, especially if focused on people of color. Newbery Award–winning author Christopher Paul Curtis *The Watsons Go to Birmingham—1963* (Barrera & Harris, 2001).

Controversy about who has the power to publish books about the various groups will persist until multitextured literary depictions become more common. The immense changes taking place in publishing and shifts in cultural noblesse surely have the potential to influence the status of multicultural literature. Among the possible influences are decreased number of books published, fewer author appearances at major conferences and author tours, and less willingness to publish the "little books" that are not blockbusters (Britton, 2001; Hill, 1998). Most important, these potential consequences limit children's access to a multiplicity of texts.

## Availability to Children

Not surprisingly, the status of multicultural literature was enhanced during this time as teachers and librarians included the works in their collections. Unfortunately, the increased demand was not sustained each year. Most journals, *Booklist, Horn-Book Magazine, Language Arts, The New Advocate, The Reading Teacher*, and many others routinely or frequently include information about multicultural literature.

The inclusion of literature in basal readers also has had a positive effect on the inclusion of multicultural literature (Harris, 1997). Most of the major series published in the 1990s included significant amounts of multicultural literature. Whether or not this was due to the increased diversity among the authoring teams is a question to ponder. Such inclusion is important because it helps to canonize some of the literature. Strickland and et al. (1995/1996) illustrated another way in which the literature has been institutionalized through book clubs such as Trumpet and Scholastic (which are now owned by the same company).

## Obstacles to Inclusion of Multicultural Literature

Many of the books garner critical accolades, but misconceptions about intended audience hamper widespread acceptance. Typical excuses offered for omission of the literature range from classroom demographics to moral or religious stances. The following six reasons are typically offered:

1. There are no children of color in the classroom.
2. Religious values mandate personal opposition to gay and lesbian lifestyles.
3. The literary and artistic quality of the texts is mediocre.
4. Disagreement with ideological or worldviews evident in the works garners opposition especially if those views contradict long-held beliefs.
5. Dialect or other languages provide inappropriate language models.
6. Values evident in the text are too liberal or radical.

The opposition of cultural conservatives has begun to have a perceptible, negative impact on the inclusion of multicultural literature (Bloom, 1998; Stodsky, 1999). These obstacles are long-standing and represent a historical fact about the precarious existence of multicultural literature.

## CURRICULAR AND RESEARCH USES OF MULTICULTURAL LITERATURE

Several historic studies examining the status of various racial and ethnic groups provided the catalyst for much of the research in multicultural literature (Broderick, 1973; Brown, 1933; Du Bois, 1926; Schon, 1996; Sims, 1982; Slapin & Seale, 1992). Commentary in these works focused on publication figures, content and linguistic analyses, publishing conditions, and critiques about the social and cultural conditions that shaped the literature. Later studies assessed the impact of the literature on intercultural and cross-racial interactions (Dudley-Marling, 1997). Appearing less often are the studies in which the literature is examined solely on the basis of literary and artistic merit (Johnson, 1990). Many monographs include some combination of the aforementioned because of the assumption that the literature does not solely exist as a literary product. Rather, the literature is also a reflection of specific conditions in several realms including the political, economic, educational, and cultural (Taxel, 1997). These areas of inquiry remain popular today and can be grouped into five broad categories: (a) thought pieces about the meanings of multicultural literature and its role in multiple institutions, (b) publishing conditions, (c) uses of the literature in content area instruction, (d) response studies, and (e) the teacher self-reflection about the literature.

## Philosophical Musings

Cai (1998) critiqued ideas about the boundaries of multicultural literature and whether those boundaries are static or amorphous. For example, is all literature multicultural or only literature of specific groups? Cai tackled the matter and pointed out that unending inclusion can lead to the "deconstructing of its [multicultural literature] sociopolitical basis" or its "possible demise" (pp. 313–314). Further, he argued against the view that discussions about multicultural literature must seek a point of entry, especially for European Americans, that hinges on notions of universality or parallels to their personal experiences. To do so would continue the process of dismissing the unique conditions, created by racism, of those who have been "othered."

Another element that calls into question the level of inclusivity associated with multiculturalism is religious fundamentalism (Milligan, 1999). Ideally, religious diversity should constitute an element of multicultural literature given the increasing numbers of Muslims, Buddhists, and evangelical Christians. However, some essential elements of religious fundamentalism are antithetical to multiculturalism.

The arguments among writers, illustrators, critics, editors, and scholars about artistic freedom and who can tell multicultural stories or the stories of those who have been "othered" belie the image of children's literature as a genteel (Aronson, 1995; Hamanaka, 1994; Howard, 1991; Lasky, 1996; Seto, 1995; Sims, 1982). Miller (1998) argued that a central issue at the "heart of teaching and learning about cultural diversity" (p. 76) is who has permission to or appropriates the right to tell a story. He reaffirmed the idea that history, in particular, "is always about someone's interpretation of those events, a process of distillation, selection, inclusion, exclusion, reorganization, and prioritizing rather than one of merely unfolding—the partial truth, possibly, but never the whole truth" (p. 76). As a consequence, then, multiple documents, preferably original, from numerous perspectives is necessary in order to help unfold truth. His argument is particularly salient in the case of some groups, for instance Native Americans, because tradition has mandated that others tell their stories.

In a similar fashion, Hearne (1999) examined a genre, folktales, that often results in cultural border crossings and elucidates some of the problems that emerge "between cultural responsibility and artistic freedom" (p. 509). Attribution and interpretation are two of the critical problems that emerge. Hearne argued instead for a position that stories cannot be owned; instead, she posited, an individual storyteller possesses them. The storyteller is free to reinterpret or pass on the tale unaltered. In contrast, publishers, must decide whether the reinterpretation or nearly original variant warrants publication. Although the writer takes artistic risks, the publisher assumes artistic and financial risks.

## Publishing Context

Publishers cannot ignore questions about who creates multicultural literature (Madigan, 1993). For example, the Pleasant Company, creator of the *American Girl* series, encountered some initial opposition with the publication of the Addy volumes (Smith, 1996). The opposition decreased as editors referred critics to members of the advisory board that comprised African Americans with expertise in African American history, literature, culture, and education. In contrast, Scholastic garnered the ire of many with its *Dear America* series and the two volumes devoted to Native American characters (Reese et al., 1999). Publishers' responses, to some extent, shaped the acceptance of the books among book buyers.

In the 1960s and 1970s, the Council on Interracial Books for Children sponsored contests in which talented authors such as Walter Dean Myers, Virginia Driving Hawk Sneve, and Mildred Taylor were discovered. Independent publishers play a vital role as well (Madigan, 1993). Ginnie Moore Kruse (as cited in Madigan, 1993) identified the key purposes of independents as helping authors retain elements of creative and distributive control; meeting the needs of a niche audience; and keeping books in print that are published for specific audiences. Rohmer, the founder of Children's Book Press agreed with the previously cited roles and highlighted the grass roots nature of independent publishers and the transformative role they play in society for social change (Madigan, 1993).

The goal of keeping books in print is an essential problem facing multicultural literature (Cai & Bishop, 1994; Muse, 1997; Reimer, 1992). For instance, Oxford University Press has reprinted some of early works of Langston Hughes and Arna Bontemps, thereby saving a vital component of African American children's literature for future generations. Similarly, Boyds Mill Press reprinted the poetry of Effie Lee Newsome, one of the first African American poets for children. The volume

*Wonders: The Best Children's Poems of Effie Lee Newsone* (Sims Bishop, 1997) is notable because the original illustrations by Lois Mailou Jones have been retained and the publishers included an introduction by Rudine Sims Bishop that places the poetry in historic context (Sims Bishop, 1997).

Progress in publishing multicultural literature is evident. Cautious optimism is warranted given the changeable nature of book buyers' interests, shifting economic conditions, mergers among publishers, and the reluctance among some educational policymakers, teachers, and librarians to include the literature in curricula and libraries.

## TEACHER EDUCATION

During the last decade, a major focus of many teacher education programs has been the incorporation of multicultural literature into the curriculum. Across the nation teacher educators have diligently attempted to prepare future teachers for a diverse student body. Paramount among their concerns is equipping future teachers to understand their own lives and biases within a pluralistic society. One of the major focuses of these efforts has been the use of reader response theory with multicultural literature (Sims Bishop, 1998). This instructional focus is designed, in part, to enhance self-identity, multicultural awareness, and sensitivities to the needs of students from culturally diverse backgrounds. Sims Bishop (1998) articulated the phenomenon this way:

The professional writing on the role of multicultural literature in classrooms has primarily focused on the need to make visible underrepresented groups and to counter negative images and stereotypes.... For readers who are members of dominant groups the assumption has been that becoming acquainted with and finding their own connections to literature about people from non dominant groups would help them to value all peoples, accept differences as a natural aspect of human societies, and even celebrate cultural pluralism as a desirable feature of the world in which they live (pp. vii–viii).

We agree, and add that multicultural literature is important for all students, not just for Whites who need to be decentered in the curriculum and to learn about others but also for students of color who need to be added to the curriculum and have their cultures affirmed. Multicultural literature, especially the works that move individuals outside of their comfort zones, raise critical consciousness, and challenge the status quo is needed. Moreover, we argue that teachers, at all levels, need to be equipped to use multicultural literature to critique the past and present and conceive of a hopeful future.

Hankins (1999), a middle-class European American Title I teacher, passionately reflected on her evolving understanding of literacy connections made by the African American students in her class. She read extensively African American children's literature because as she acknowledged, "my limited ability to cross cultures keeps me from understanding half of the children I teach". Hankins is conducting a self-study of her teaching for her dissertation, and her recent conference presentation revolved around her reflection of one literacy event she recorded. In a moving anecdote she told of her attempts to read a storybook about an African American grandfather and his grandson to the five African American children in her class. As she read the story, the children talked among themselves about story, a behavior she found annoying. Reflecting on the literacy event, she painfully noted, "I was too busy *managing poor behavior*. I was too busy reading text *I* was creating instead of listening to the text they collaboratively wrote." In her analysis, she examined her own behavior and the children's response to her reading of the books. She noted her lack of support of the children's developing oral competence as well as their complex interactions with the text. Compellingly, she concluded, "[T]hat day I missed it. I just missed it! How many misses does it take to strike out, to fail a child?" (Hankins, 1999).

## Pedagogical and Curricular Considerations

The literacy wars that have been waged over the past 2 generations highlight the tenuous role of literature, especially multicultural literature in literacy curricula. Despite the increasingly conservative political and educational conditions, some researchers push forth and continue to argue for acknowledgment and incorporation of diversity in curricula. Gee (1999), for example, contended that "new literacy studies" offers a theoretical framework for understanding literacy as inextricably linked to "social, cultural, institutional, and political practices" (p. 356). Literacy in this paradigm must be understood in terms of culture, language, identities, ways of being and knowing, and other elements that make up the human condition. Research studies using the perspective on new literacy studies illustrate the complex and unpredictable responses that can result when literacy is viewed from a cultural and political filter.

## School Contexts

A young European American teacher in Brooklyn, New York, introduced the picture book *Nappy Hair* (Herron, 1997) to a third-grade classroom of predominately African American and Latino and Latina children (Clemetson, 1998). Parents objected to the book and expressed their views at school meetings. A national debate erupted when word of the events filtered to various media outlets. Immediately, the discourse surrounding the use of the book became polarized and racialized (Freedman, 1999; Nelson, 1998). The teacher's youth, blond hair, and missionary-like attitude toward her students were venerated in many media reports (*Newsweek*, 1999). In contrast, the parents were demonized as loud, scary, potentially violent, and disinterested in their children's academic experiences. Many pundits viewed the episode as political correctness run *amok*. Missing in the clamor was the responsibility of the teacher to review carefully any literature shared with children and her responsibility to understand the content of the literature and any background information needed for that process. Absent also was some acknowledgment that the teacher also lacked an understanding of the cultural nuances associated with beauty standards and the historic denigration of African American physical characteristics in popular culture. A different type of response may have been

evoked had the teacher possessed a greater amount of knowledge about the children's culture.

A local elementary teacher noticed that the latest version of the Illinois State Achievement Tests made a grave error. An excerpt from *More Stories Julian Tells*, a novel by Ann Cameron (1989) about two African American boys, was used in the test. However, the illustration accompanying the state test pictured two European American boys. Participants in online literature discussions debated the issue, including the author, Ann Cameron. One of our colleagues, Susan Noffke, approached a local school board demanding to know why the mistake occurred. The state testing board was contacted as well. Its response was that it was an error and there was no ill intent on the part of the board. Ann Cameron countered by calling the testing situation "racist" and demanding that a letter of apology be sent to every third-grade classroom that used the version of the exam containing the error. Noffke, in an interview with a local newspaper, argued that the intent of the state was not at question, but it was the "assumption of whiteness" on which they had made decisions that was most disturbing (Puch, 2000).

More typical are the less newsworthy responses in classrooms across the country. Martínez-Roldán and López-Robertson (1999, 1999–2000) provided excerpts from literature discussion groups held in a primary bilingual classroom. They determined that the multicultural literature shared with the children—for instance, *A Picture Book of Martin Luther King, Jr.* (Adler, 1989), and *Friends From the Other Side* (Anzaldua, 1993)—prompted the children to identify connections to their lives and discuss issues such as racism and discrimination. Equally important, the children were able to discuss elements of text and their responses in Spanish or English.

African American children in a fifth-grade classroom showed evidence of changed behavior toward literacy after a yearlong exposure to multicultural literature (Bauman, Hooten, & White, 1999). The children stated that they valued reading more. They were observed to have engaged in more free-choice reading during school and at other times. A greater appreciation for books and more definitive preferences for particular genres, authors, and styles of writing were evident. One notable aspect of the study was that the multicultural literature was integrated into other instruction in a purposeful manner.

Social studies offer many ways to introduce multicultural literature to children. Edgington (1998) argued that the research was inconclusive in terms of the effects on students mastery of content and attitudes toward the subject. In contrast, Elster & Zych (1998) found that multicultural literature could serve as a springboard for changed attitudes among a diverse group of fourth-graders toward individuals of different ethnicities when coupled with opportunities to communicate via technology.

Other content areas, art (Carger, 1998), and literature (E. B. Smith, 1995) were selected to determine the effects of including multicultural literature. Art offers numerous opportunities to examine culture, identity, and ways of knowing that is rooted in specific traditions (Greene, 1994). Carger drew on the writings of Maxine Greene for work with eighth-graders in Chicago public schools. She contended that the integration of art, art activities, and multicultural literature were powerful catalysts for imaginative possibilities as evidenced by the students' conversations and art projects. Mathematics was often perceived of as being culturally neutral, although some have argued for the influence of culture (Moses, 2001). Although multicultural literature was not the focus of the research, Friedman (1997) examined the use of literature to introduce young children to mathematical concepts such as commutative principles. Some of the texts used, however, were multicultural such as *Nine-in-One Grr! Grr!* (Xiong & Spagnoli, 1989).

More is known about the use of multicultural literature in literacy or language arts instruction (Enciso & Medina, 2001). The types of discussions around books vary depending on the participants, their background knowledge, personal experiences, and so forth. Raphael et al. (1994) assessed student participation in book clubs. They determined that the racially diverse participants displayed different levels of knowledge based on their cultural knowledge, mode of participation, and textual interpretations. Those who possessed an insider's knowledge were able to shape the conversations about books. Spears-Bunton (1990) determined similar patterns with secondary students with the distinction that some European American students were angered by the authority and knowledge exhibited by their African American peers. In a like vein, E. B. Smith (1995) presented case studies that indicated the empowering effect multicultural literature has for some children of color. Most of the sense of empowerment stemmed from reading books with characters that were like themselves.

The studies referenced here and others provide a foundation on which other types of studies can emerge about the effects of multicultural literature focus on cognitive and linguistic development as well as affective growth. Another shift in emphasis is the role of the teacher. Negative attitudes about racial, cultural, and linguistic difference are longstanding, and they provide painful reminders of how "reciprocal distancing" impacts negatively on students' literacy learning (Larson & Levine, 1999). Research by Ladson-Billings (1994) and Foster (1998), on the other hand, documents the beneficial consequences on students' learning when teachers are familiar with aspects of students' culture.

## Teacher Change and Multicultural Literature

Teacher change can occur in provisional and hesitant fashion or significant and enthusiastic ways. The tentative steps made by teachers toward the inclusion of multicultural literature have been noted. Rabinowitz & Smith (1998) identified a propensity of teachers to accept safe literature that allows Whites to feel comfortable and that does engender critical analysis of cultural issues. We have noted similar tendencies among our students as well. Other teachers engage more boldly in critical self-reflection while attempting to meet the needs of the children of color whom they teach (Paley, 1995). Sometimes the process of critical self-reflection evolves over decades as access to new knowledge is acquired.

Diller (1999) documented her growth from a traditional pedagogy toward one that was culturally centered. Part of the process entailed accepting the notion of multiple perspectives and

ways of knowing. This she acquired from reading an extensive body of African American literature. Another aspect included seeking the advice and support from cultural insiders. Still other elements of the process required extensive reading from educational research and theory created by African Americans as well as literary texts. The remaining components included lots of dialogue with children and parents. Diller is astute enough to understand that the process towards acquiring a culturally centered pedagogy is an ongoing one.

Other teachers form literature study groups and concentrate on the works of a single author or illustrator or a sampling. Zaleski (1997) captured the dynamics and interaction among a group of White teachers who decided to study the works of illustrator Jerry Pinkney, an African American. Pinkney was scheduled for a school visit and the teachers decided to form a reading group in preparation for his visit. Initial discussions revolved around the teachers' responses to the art and texts in several picture books. Only later did a more tentative discussion of the multicultural aspects of the text emerge. Zaleski's study highlights the need for a safe space in which to discuss ideas, texts, and issues that can be controversial.

An assumption might exist that only White teachers need to engage in self-examination about diverse student populations or multicultural literature. However, many teachers of color also show evidence of a need for similar reflection. Spears-Bunton (1999) clearly revealed the stereotypes and lack of knowledge some members of the African diaspora hold about each other. Furthermore, she demonstrated how such attitudes and behaviors could affect students' literacy experiences and academic achievement.

Faculty members in schools and colleges of education are increasingly aware of the need to offer preservice teachers chances to explore ideas about diversity and multiculturalism. Those who teach children's literature courses have a vested interest in the process of institutionalizing the use of multicultural literature (Enciso & Medina, 2001). Wolf, Ballentine, and Hill (1999) offered a view of how the process might occur in a yearlong methods course. Planning, study, and time are crucial elements if a tourist or a food-and-festival approach is to be avoided and genuine introspection is desired.

The body of research that exists about multicultural literature, curriculum, academic achievement, preparation of preservice and inservice, and children's responses to the literature is insufficient. Rigorous studies are needed that are longitudinal, expansive, and structured to acknowledge the complex nature of the topic.

## SUMMARY

We began this chapter by tracing the popularization of the term *multiculturalism* to its award-winning status in 1941, although we argued that the concept has been a part of social thought for much longer. The term *multiculturalism* has been marred since its inception over a half a century ago. There have been numerous changes in how the term is defined, used, defended, opposed, maligned, and appended for particular audiences and constituencies. Current uses are informed by critical theory, postmodernism, and poststructualism. These new currents have added the notion of critique to multiculturalism as they challenge dominant ideologies and assumptions that underpin education and forestall educational equity. Changes in its use and emphases reflect sociohistorical contexts and applications, however the basic premise of "respect for all nations and people" (Barnhart & Metcalf, 1997) remains the same.

Our research in schools; our university teaching; and our conversations with colleagues, librarians, teachers, students and parents have convinced us to include discussions of curriculum, literature, and instruction in this chapter. We believe that the importance of understanding the concept of multiculturalism should not be divorced from the actions that are needed to make it a reality as it relates to literacy. The interrelatedness of curriculum, literature, and instruction suggests that the idea of multiculturalism's influence on the curriculum through literature and instruction are important components of a quality education. This three-pronged approach also suggests improved decision making, quality, and delivery of literacy instruction for all students.

We are hopeful about the future as we look to innovative data-gathering methods and analysis to inform our thinking. We envision several future directions for the field: mixed methods studies of the effects of culturally responsive instruction in multiracial, multiethnic, multilingual school settings and longitudinal studies of literacy learners, multicultural literature, and interactions.

## References

Alder, D. (1989). *A picture book of Martin Luther King, Jr.* New York: Holiday House, Inc.

Anzaldúa, G. (1993). *Friends from the other side/Amigos del otro lado.* San Francisco: Children's Book Press.

Aronson, M. (1995, March/April). *The Horn Book Magazine, 61,* 163-168.

Banks, J., & Banks, C. (Eds.) (1997). *Multicultural education: Issues and perspectives* (3rd ed.). Boston: Allyn & Bacon.

Barnhart, D. K., & Metcalf, A. A. (1997). *America in so many words.* Boston: Houghton Mifflin.

Barrera, R. R., & Harris, V. J. (2001). A conversation with Christopher Paul Curtis. *The New Advocate, 14*(1), 1-10.

Bauman, J., Hooten, H., & White, P. (1999). Teaching comprehension through literature: A teacher-research project to develop fifth graders' reading strategies and motivation. *The Reading Teacher, 53*(1), 38-51.

Bloom, A. (1998). *The closing of the American mind: How higher education has failed democracy and impoverished the souls of today's students.* New York: Simon & Schuster.

Britton, J. (2001, February 12). Representing change. *Publishers Weekly, 248*(7), 96-99.

Broderick, D. (1973). *Image of the Black in children's literature.* New York: R. R. Bowker.

Brown, S. (1933). Negro character as seen by white authors. *The Journal of Negro Education, 2,* 179-203.

Cai, M. (1998). Multiple definitions of multicultural literature: Is the debate really just "Ivory Tower" bickering? *The New Advocate, 11*(4), 311-324.

Cai, M., & Sims Bishop, R. (1994). Multicultural literature for children: Towards a clarification of the concept. In A. H. Dyson & C. Genishi (Eds.), *The need for story: Cultural diversity in classroom and community* (pp. 57-71). Urbana, IL: National Council of Teachers of English.

Campbell, P. (1999). The sand in the oyster: Radical monster. *Horn Book Magazine,* 769-773.

Cameron, A. (1989). *More stories Julian tells.* New York: Alfred Knopf.

Carger, C. (1998). The Anansi Connection. *Educational Leadership, 56,* 76-80.

Diamond, B., & Moore, M. (1995). *Multicultural literacy: Mirroring the reality of the classroom.* New York: Longman.

Diller, D. (1999). Opening the dialogue: Using culture as a tool in teaching young African American children. *The Reading Teacher, 52*(8), 820-828.

D'Souza, D. (1996). *The end of racism: Principles for a multicultural society.* New York: Simon & Schuster.

Dudley-Marling, C. (1997). "I'm not from Pakistan": Multicultural literature and the problem of representation. *The New Advocate, 10*(2), 123-134.

Edgington, W. (1998). The use of children's literature in middle school social studies: What research does and does not show. *The Clearing House, 72,* 121-126.

Elster, C., & Zych, T. (1998). "I wish I could have been there dancing with you": Linking diverse communities through social studies and literature. *The Social Studies, 89,* 25-30.

Enciso, P., & Medina, C. L. (2001). 'Some words are messengers/Hay palabras mensajeras': Interpreting sociopolitical themes in Latino children's literature. *The New Advocate, 15*(1), 35-47.

Fish, S. (1997). Boutique multiculturalism, or why liberals are incapable of thinking about hate speech. *Critical Inquiry, 23*(2), 378-386.

Foster, M. (1998). *Black teachers on teaching.* New York: New Press.

Freire, P. (1970). *Pedagogy of the oppressed.* New York: Continuum.

Friedman, J. (1997). What is the math moral of the story. *Childhood Education, 74*(1), 33-35.

Gee, J. (1999). Critical issues: Reading and the new literacy studies: Reframing the National Academy of Sciences Report on Reading. *Journal of Literacy Research, 31*(3), 355-374.

Genishi, C. (Ed.) (1992). *Ways of assessing children and curriculum: Stories of early childhood practice.* New York: Teachers College Press.

Giroux, H. A. (1992). Curriculum, multiculturalism, and the politics of identity. *Nassp Bulletin, 76*(548), 1-11.

Giroux, H. (1988). *Teachers as intellectuals: Toward a critical pedagogy of learning.* South Hadley, MA: Bergin & Garvey.

Goatley, V. J., Brock, C. H., & Raphael, T. E. (1995). Diverse learners participating in regular education "book clubs." *Reading Research Quarterly, 30*(3), 352-380.

Gordon Kelly, R. (1974). *Mother was a lady: Self and society in selected American children's periodicals, 1865-1890.* Westport, CT: Greenwood Press.

Gramsci, A. (1971). *Selections from the Prison Notebooks.* New York: International Publishers.

Grant, C., & Sleeter, C. (1999). *Turning on learning: Five approaches for multicultural teaching plans for race, class, gender, and disability.* New York: Simon & Schuster.

Greene, M. (1994). Multiculturalism, community, and the arts. In A. H. Dyson & C. Genishi (Eds.), *The need for story: Cultural diversity in classroom and community* (pp. 11-27). Urbana, IL: National Council of Teachers of English.

Hamanaka, S. (1994). I hope their ears are burning: An author of color talks about racism in children's literature. *The New Advocate, 7*(4), 227-238.

Hankins, K. (1999, December). *The transformative power of narratives: Reshaping curriculum through response and reflection.* Paper presented at the annual conference of the National Reading Conference, Orlando, FL.

Harris, V. J. (Ed.) (1997). *Using multiethnic literature in the K-8 classroom.* Norwood, MA: Christopher_Gordon Publishers.

Harris, V. J. (1997). Why are you always giving us that Black, Latino, Gay, Asian (Fill in the blank) stuff? In D. Muse (Ed.), *The New Press guide to multicultural resources for young readers* (pp. 486-490). New York: The New Press.

Hearne, B. (1999, Winter). Swapping tales and stealing stories: The ethics and aesthetics of folklore in children's literature. *Library Trends, 47*(3), 509-528.

Herron, C. (1997). *Nappy Hair.* New York: Random House.

Hill, T. (1998). Multicultural children's books: An American fairy tale. *Publishing Research Quarterly, 14*(1), 36-45.

Howard, E. (1991). Authentic multicultural literature for children: An author's perspective. In M. Lindgren (Ed.). *The multicolored mirror: Cultural substabce in literature for children and young adults.* Fort Atkinson, WI: Highsmith Press.

Jay, M. (1996). *The dialectical imagination: A history of the Frankfurt school and the Institute of Social Research, 1923-1950.* Berkeley: University of California Press.

Johnson, D. (1990). *Telling tales: the pedagogy and promise of African American literature for youth.* New York: Greenwood.

Kanpol, B., and McLaren, P. (Eds.). (1995). *Critical multiculturalism.* New York: Bergin & Garvey.

Kruse, G. M. (1991). *Multicultural literature for children and young adults.* Atkinson, WI: CCBC/Highsmith Press.

Kruse, G. M., Horning, K. T., & Schliesman, M. (1997). *Multicultural literature for children and young adults* (Vol. 2). Atkinson, WI: CCBC/Highsmith Press.

Ladson Billings, G. (1994). *Dreamkeppers: Successful teachers of African American children.* San Francisco, CA: Jossey-Bass.

Larson, J., & Irvine, P. D. (1999). "We call him Dr. King": Reciprocal distancing in urban classrooms. *Language Arts, 76*(5), 393-400.

Lasky, K. (1996). To stingo with love: An author's perspective on writing outside one's culture. *New Advocate, 9*(1), 1-7.

Leistyna, P., Woodrum, A., & Sherblom, S. (Eds.) (1996). *Breaking Free: The transformative power of critical pedagogy.* Cambridge, MA: Harvard Educational Review.

Lester, J. (1988). The storyteller's voice: Reflections on the rewriting of Uncle Remus (the creative process). *New Advocate, 1*(3), 143-147.

Lindgren, M. V. (1991). *The multicolored mirror: Cultural substance in literature for children and young adults.* Fort Atkinson, WI: Highsmith Press.

Macedo, D. (1994). *Literacies of power: What Americans are not allowed to know.* Boulder, CO: Westiview.

Madigan, D. (1993). The politics of multicultural literature for children and adolescents: Combing perspectives and conversations. *Language Arts, 70,* 168-176.

Martínez-Roldán, C., & López-Robertson, J. (1999). "Stop, think, and listen to the heart": Literature discussions in a primary bilingual classroom. *The New Advocate, 12*(4), 377-379.

Martínez-Roldán, C., & López-Robertson, J. (1999-2000). Initiating literature circles in a first-grade bilingual classroom. *The Reading Teacher, 53*(4), 270-281.

McLaren, P. (1988). *Life in schools.* New York: Longman.

Meyers, W. D. (1986, November 9). I actually thought we would revolutionize the industry. *New York Times Book Review, 91,* 50.

Meyers, W. D. (1995). 1994 Margaret A. Edwards award acceptance speech. *Journal of Youth Services in Libaries, 8,* 129-133.

Meyers, W. D. (1997). *Monster.* New York: Harper Collins.

Miller, H. (1998). Who owns history? *The Reading Teacher, 52*(1), 76-78.

Milligan, J. A. (1999). Gender and the limits of inclusion: Should multiculturalism "include" fundamentalisms? *Religious Education, 94*(1), 75-83.

Muse, D. (Ed.) (1997). The new press guide to multicultural resources for young readers. New York: New Press.

Mitchell, B., & Salsbury, R. (Eds.) (1999). *Encyclopedia of multicultural education.* Westport, CT: Greenwood Press.

Nelson, J. (1998 November 28). Stumbling upon a race secret: What the uproar over a children's book says about blacks' self-esteem. *New York Times,* A10.

Newsome, E. L., & Sims Bishop, R. (Eds.) (1999). *Wonders: The Best Children's Poems of Effie Lee Newsome.* New York: Boyd Mills Press.

Nieto, S. (2002). *Language, culture, and teaching: Critical perspectives for a new century.* Mahwah, NJ: Lawrence Erlbaum Associates.

Paley, V. (1995). *Kwanzaa and me: A teacher's story.* Cambridge, MA: Harvard University Press.

Popkewitz, T. (1984). *Paradigm and ideology in education research: The social functions in intellectual.* Philadelphia: Falmer Press.

Poster, M. (1989) Critical theory and poststructuralism: In search of a context. Ithaca, NY: Cornell University Press.

Puch, D. (2000, February 17). Black characters depicted as white in tests. *The News-Gazette,* pp. A1, A8.

Rabinowitz, P., & Smith, M. (1998). *Authorizing readers: Resistance and respect in the teaching of literature.* New York: Teachers College Press.

Raphael, T. E. et al. (1994). Collaboration on the book club project: The multiple roles of researchers, teachers, and students. *Reading Horizons, 34*(5), 381-405.

Ravitch, D. (1990). Multiculturalism: E pluribus plures. *The American Scholar, 54,* 337-354.

Reese, D. (1999). Authenticity & sensitivity. *School Library Journal,* _, 36-37.

Reese, D. et al. (1999). Fiction posing as truth. *Rethinking Schools, 13*(4), 14-16.

Reimer, K. M. (1992). Multiethnic literature: Holding fast to dreams. *Language Arts, 69,* 14-21.

Rinaldi, A. (1999). *My heart is on the ground.* New York: Scholastic.

Rochman, H. (1993). *Against borders: Promoting books for a multicultural world.* Chicago: American Library Association.

Schlesinger, A. M. (1991). Multiculturalism or cultural separatism: The choice is ours. *New Perspectives Quarterly, 8,* 79.

Schon, I. (1988). *A Hispanic heritage: A guide to juvenile books about Hispanic people and culture.* White Plains, NY: Scarecrow.

Shor, I. (1987) (Ed.). *Freire for the classroom: A sourcebook for liberatory teaching.* Portsmouth, NH: Boynton.

Schwartz, E. G. (1995). Crossing borders/shifting paradigms: Multiculturalism and children's literature. *Harvard Educational Review, 65*(4), 634-650.

Shannon, P. (1994). I am the canon: Finding ourselves in multiculturalism. *Journal of Children's Literature, 20*(1), 1-5.

Shome, R. (1996). Postcolonial interventions in the rhetorical canon: An "Other" view. *Communication Theory, 61,* 40-59.

Sims, R. (1982). *Shadow and substance: Afro-American experience in contemporary children's fiction.* Urbana, IL: National Council of Teachers of English.

Sims Bishop, R. (1996). Letter to the editor. *The New Advocate, 9*(2), vii–viii.

Sims Bishop, R. (1997). Multicultural literature for children: Making informed choices (pp. 37–53). In V. J. Harris (Ed.) *Using multiethnic literature in the K-8 classroom.* Norwood, MA: Christopher–Gordon Publishers.

Sims Bishop, R. (1998, March/April). Following in their fathers' paths. *The Horn Book Magazine, 74*(2), 249–255.

Sims Bishop, R. (1998). Working together for Literacy: Faces of Hope. *Journal of Children's Literature, 24*(1), 90–97.

Slapin, B., & Searle, D. (Eds.) (1992). *Through Indian eyes: The native experience in books for children.* Philadelphia: New Society Publishers.

Smith, E. B. (1995). Anchored in our literature: Students responding to African American literature. *Language Arts, 72,* 571–574.

Smith, S. L. (1996). Changing face of girlhood in America. *Wisconsin State Journal.*

Spears-Bunton, L. A. (1990). Welcome to my house: African American and European American students' responses to Virginia Hamilton's "House of Dies Drear." *Journal of Negro Education. 59*(4), 566–576.

Spears-Bunton, L. (1999). Calypso, jazz, reggae, and salsa: Literature, response, and the African diaspora. In N. Karolides (Ed.), *Reader response in secondary and college classrooms* (2nd ed., pp. 311–326). Mahwah, NJ: Lawrence Erlbaum Associates.

Strickland, D. S., Walmsley, S., Wollner, W., et al. (1995/1996). What's in those boxes anyway? An analysis of school book club offerings. *Reading Teacher, 49*(4), 344–346.

Stotsky, S. (1995). Changes in American's secondary literature programs: Good news and bad. *Phi Delta Kappan, 76*(8), 605–613.

Stotsky, S. (1999). *Losing our language: How multicultural classroom instruction is undermining our children's ability to read, write, and reason.* New York: Simon & Schuster.

Taxel, J. (1997). Multicultural literature and the politics of reaction. *Teachers College Record, 98*(3), 417–448.

West, C. (1995) *Race matters.* New York: Random House.

West, C. (1993). The new cultural politics of difference. In C. McCarthey & W. Crichlow (Eds.), *Race identity and representation in education* (pp. 11–23). New York: Routlege.

Wiggershaus, R. (1994). *The Frankfurt School: Its history, theories, and political significance.* Cambridge, MA: MIT Press. (Trans., Michael Roberston)

Wolf, S. A., Ballentine, D., & Hill, L. (1999). The right to write: Preservice teachers' evolving understandings of authenticity and aesthetic heat in multicultural literature. *Research in the Teaching of English, 34*(1), 130–184.

Xiong, B., & Spagnoli, C. (1990). *Nine-in-one, grr! grr!: A folktale from the Hmong people of Laos.* San Francisco: Children's Book Press.

Zaleski, J. (1997). Teachers as readers: A look at one group's discoveries with the works of Jerry Pinkney. *Journal of Children's Literature, 23*(1), 26–35.

# ·61·

# READING PREFERENCES

## Sam L. Sebesta
### University of Washington

## Dianne L. Monson
### University of Minnesota

Given a choice of materials to be read, which do children and adolescents prefer? More broadly, do young people have interests that impel them to seek out reading materials to meet those interests? Getzels (1966) distinguished between the two stances: "[A] preference is relatively passive, while interest is inevitably dynamic" (p. 7).

To reveal the more powerful motivator, interest, has proved a difficult task. H. M. Robinson and Weintraub (1973) critiqued attempts to study young readers' interests; they included research using forced-choice instruments, interviews, written logs, and records of library books chosen. In most of these attempts, the results were at best a list of topics or titles indicating preferences. Furthermore, the authors observed, "Group studies only suggest the topic which about half the pupils prefer" (p. 89). Weintraub (1969) warned that research designed to reveal preferred topics may mislead: "Live animals may mean turtles to one child, dogs to a second youngster, and monkeys to a third" (p. 659).

Therefore, studies to identify children's reading interests more often reveal the weaker element, preferences. Moreover, the results may be overgeneralized or misinterpreted. They lack reliability; or inconsistent results from sample to sample, especially across generations, suggest that interests and preferences are idiosyncratic (Summers & Lukevich, 1983).

Still, for over 100 years researchers have pursued the elusive concepts of reading preferences and reading interests. The change, perhaps the evolution, in their reasons for those studies is as thought provoking as their results. Modern studies sometimes replicate earlier ones, using library book withdrawals (C. C. Robinson, Larsen, Haupt, & Mohlman, 1997), fictitious titles (Haynes & Richgels, 1992), and other devices of the past. However, there is a difference: The search for preferences merges with investigation of reader response. The question of

*what* young people prefer to read is now more likely to include the *why* of the preference and the nature of the response that accompanies choice.

In the sections that follow, we document these observations about reading preference research, past and present, and speculate on its future.

## READING PREFERENCES: HISTORICAL

### Early Studies and a Mission

Jordan (1921) prefaced a review of past studies with this observation: "If we could determine what the child's major interests are, be those interests good or bad, it would be possible to direct these forces along lines which are desirable" (p. 1). He cited the importance of guiding interests toward "socially desirable" books "recommended by teachers" (p. 1). Among sources of error in the studies, he noted "the reserve of children concerning their clandestine reading" (p. 2).

The forced-choice topics of the earliest study (*NEA Proceedings*, 1897) revealed boys' predominant choices to be war and adventure whereas girls preferred adventure, travel, love, and biographies of women. In a concurrent study (Shaw, 1897), 900 children with "access to thousands of books" gave preferences that resemble a list of family classics, headed by *Robinson Crusoe, Little Women, Little Lord Fauntleroy, Grimm's Fairy Tales,* and *Swiss Family Robinson*. Wissler's (1898) open questionnaire to fourth- and fifth-graders asked, "If you were taken to a book store and told you might select just one book of your own what would you take?" (p. 5). Girls' top choice was *Longfellow's Poems*; boys gave a slight edge to *Robinson Crusoe*. Fiction far outranked other genres, but from fourth to fifth grade there was a doubling of interest in poetry, which the author attributed to the study of *Evangeline*, "Thanatopsis," and *Snowbound* in the latter grade.

Jordan's (1921) own research models how to design a study based on one's critique of those that preceded. His simple questionnaire asked children to name their favorite books and magazines, requesting that they identify themselves by first name only and promising that "school authorities would not see the answers" (p. 43). In all, 3,598 students, aged 9 and older, responded. Jordan's curiosity about "underground reading" (p. 93) led to observations in eight libraries to find out which books were available and which, in multiple copies to meet demand, were worn out. For once, boys' top preferences did not show approved classics but instead books by Altsheler, Henty, and Barbour. Mainly from these, Jordan deduced "satisfiers" in boys' preferred literature: love of sensory life, rivalry, kindliness embedded in a "fighting instinct," and gregariousness. Girls' choices were more compatible with approved lists (Alcott and Burnett were the most popular authors) but also included authors with lesser reputation, such as Deland, Woolsey, Richards, and Taggart. These choices, wrote Jordan, indicated satisfiers for girls, aged 10 to 13: kindliness, well-tailored clothes, clean mind, and unselfishness, among other qualities. Whether such satisfiers might be obtained through an exclusive offering of books deemed more socially desirable is, surprisingly, not discussed in Jordan's report.

The studies in this section were done at the end of a period in American literacy that historian N. B. Smith (1934) called "Reading as a Cultural Asset" (p. 115). Their authors show an adult preference that young people *should* prefer established literature with high literary credentials. Indeed, to some extent this adult bias is reflected in the lists of youths' preferences. It appears that the researchers at first ignored and subsequently deplored reading material deemed less socially acceptable, especially adventure-romances like those so lovingly satirized in Chapter 2 of Tarkington's (1914) *Penrod*. The uneasy situation—what to do about undesirable preferences—permeates another study, that of Terman and Lima (1925), who acknowledged the importance of "the natural reading interests of children" (p. 8) and then decreed, "The child should be allowed to choose his own books, but only the best should be presented for his choice" (p. 8).

## Curriculum-Related Studies

The early preference studies contain no mention of turn-of-century children's writers such as Beatrix Potter, Kenneth Grahame, E. Nesbit, and L. Frank Baum—authors who may be said to have helped establish a domain of children's literature. There seem to be two reasons for such omission. First, the studies focused on older subjects, usually aged 10 and above. Second, results seem biased toward works that might appear in the school curriculum.

By the 1920s, however, attention had shifted to the younger child and to broadened objectives for reading (N. B. Smith, 1934, pp. 185–228). These changes were reflected in trade book and textbook publishing. In fact, preference studies of this period are aimed at publishing as well as school practice.

An investigation of poetry of this time is directed at placement through preference. Huber, Bruner, and Curry (1927) chose 100 poems per grade level, Grades 1 through 9, as provided by current textbooks and courses of study. Arranging each 100-poem group into sets of 15 and subsets of 5, the researchers requested that students identify best liked and least liked items. Each set was submitted not just to the grade level designated but to two levels above and two levels below the level indicated by publication. Through an intricate weighting system, Huber et al. were able to assign a grade level preference for each poem, observing "We find that present practice is only 39 per cent right" (p. 71).

Gates' (1930) study represents a departure in aim and method, although he acknowledged that it derived from an earlier study by Dunn (1921). The intent appears to be to help select and create high-interest material for basal readers and comprehension testing.

Gates (1930) devised a list of 14 literary characteristics drawn partly from the Dunn (1921) study. He hired "several persons highly familiar with children's materials and highly capable of judging such qualities" (p. 74) to estimate the weighting of each characteristic in each of 30 selections considered to be "representative of the range of children's literature" (p. 73). Selections were randomly paired and read to classes whose pupils indicated which of the paired selections was preferred. Gates estimated that about 15,000 individual votes were collected. Then, through partial correlations, the independent weighting of each literary characteristic across preferences was determined. The ranking, from highest preferred to lowest, is as follows: surprise, liveliness, animalness, conversation, humor, plot, narrativeness, poeticalness, familiarity, repetition, fancifulness, realism, verse form, moralness. Gates concluded that the first six characteristics are "the six main elements among those here studied to weave into a selection" (p. 89). Moralness appeared to decrease interest, as did what some adults appraise as humor: "We must conclude that we have much yet to learn about what is, fundamentally, funny to young children" (p. 90).

This study foreshadows attempts to pinpoint characteristics that describe appeal. It is probably among the earliest attempts at market research in young people's literature, attempting to discern preferences in order that new materials may conform to reader approval. Its effects are seen in N. B. Smith's (1934) history, which notes for this period the rise of new material in basals "written by authors of textbooks" (p. 268), presumably to mount "a type of instruction in which reading is taught largely as it enters into or flows out of children's interests and activities" (p. 265).

From the start, a majority of preference studies found distinct differences according to sex and age. To these factors Huber (1928) added intelligence, but she concluded that preference differences among "dull, average, and superior intelligence" are to be attributed to complexity of material rather than to topic or literary type: "It is necessary that materials be graded carefully to the pupils' level of intelligence" (p. 39). A rather different profile of students labeled "dull" in IQ (Stanford–Binet Scale, 90 and below) emerged from Lazar (1937): "There was a consistent gradation of responses for bright, average, and dull pupils in every item analyzed" (p. 104). Lower intelligence pupils avoided subjects that involved reading; they preferred literature consisting of "the simpler and less realistic types" (p. 102), including fairy tales. Lazar's conclusion that the "aim of the schools should be to reduce these differences between the various groups of pupils as far as possible" (p. 104) now seems, in context, a plea to help the challenged learner through a supportive curriculum!

## Interest Score Studies

Influenced by the psychometrics movement, Thorndike (1941) devised an "interest score" formula to show valence of a group or subgroup's regard for a title or topic. For each item, students were asked to mark yes, question mark, or no to indicate whether they would like to read it. Then Thorndike applied the following formula:

$$\frac{\text{number marking "yes"} + \frac{1}{2} \text{ number marking "?"}}{\text{Total number responding to the item}}$$

To prevent bias from prior experience with a specific title, Thorndike wrote a "fictitious annotated titles questionnaire" consisting of 88 items. Through various combinations of these items, the author was able to find interest scores for 14 fiction topics and 10 nonfiction topics, these scores representing reactions of 2,891 students in Grades 4 through 12.

The results enabled Thorndike (1941) to indicate by age, sex, and IQ the "maximum interest level" for each category. For instance, the topic "School Stories" was designated low to moderate interest for boys and moderate to high interest for girls, aged 11 to 12 for "bright group" and aged 13 to 15 for "slow group." Thorndike found that sex accounts for much greater difference in interests than do age and intelligence. Within the same sex, "bright" subjects have interests comparable to "mentally slower" subjects who are 2 to 3 years older (p. 35). Still, Thorndike urged caution: "No generalization about the reading interests of groups will take the place, for the teacher, of a knowledge of the personal pattern of choices for each individual" (p. 37).

Norvell (1950) used Thorndike's interest score concept to explore opinions of 50,000 secondary-level students regarding 1,700 selections identified by teachers as "studied or read by the class this school year" (p. 10). A typical class balloted 40 to 50 selections, rating each as very interesting, fairly interesting, or uninteresting—a total of 1.59 million ratings gathered from 200 New York schools. From these data, Norvell published indexes for each selection by sex, grade, and genre (novels, plays, poems, short stories, biographies, and essays). In this study, neither age nor intelligence appeared to bring major differences in choices at the secondary level, but "sex is a dominating factor which attains its maximum during the junior high school period" (p. 48). Norvell noted, however, that stories and poems dealing with adventure, obvious humor, animals, and patriotism appealed to both sexes, but neither group liked many selections about the supernatural or with didactic themes.

In a second study, Norvell (1958) obtained 960,000 opinions from 24,000 children in Grades 3 through 6, yielding interest scores on 1,576 selections studied in class, read independently or read by teachers with discussion. Compared with the earlier study, age was an important factor. Sex differences appeared to vary by genre and, at least in regard to poetry, by individual selections. The author began his report with an attack on "the ineptness of expert judgment on children's reading interests" (p. 4). He cited, as evidence, an assortment of authors and works praised or negatively reviewed by adults, noting in each instance that interest scores of children indicated an opposite opinion. Norvell's concluded, "That adult standards for literature are not children's standards has been emphasized through this report" (p. 149). He argued for "relinquishment" of adult selection "in favor of the acceptance of children's own choices" (p. 174).

The issue raised by Norvell (1958) is important because it pertains to the implications of all interest and preference studies. Should findings be used literally in selecting literature for young people and helping them select their own? Or, presuming that judgment of authorities differs from judgment of young readers, is the dual system of selection to be desired? Norvell adamantly rejected the latter. It should be noted, however, that his studies lack a basis for a final opinion. Titles in the two Norvell studies are drawn mainly from those provided in school; hence they do not represent "seeking out" behavior so much as preferences among literary examples in the curriculum. Furthermore, Norvell may have overestimated the gulf between adult and child literacy choice: He made no systematic survey to find out whether adult choices really contrast with what he identified as choices of children and adolescents.

The interest score idea persisted. Terry (1974) obtained interest scores on 113 poems found frequently in anthologies for children. The poems were audiotaped by an expert reader and played, in rotated order, to 422 pupils, Grades 4 through 6, in 42 classrooms in four regions of the United States. The resulting scores showed that interest in poetry was highest in Grade 4, steadily declining in Grades 5 and 6. Inner city subjects displayed highest interest, with metropolitan, rural, and suburban subjects evidencing, respectively, less favorable reactions. The 25 most popular poems in this study were characterized by narrative form, rhyme, rhythm, sound, humor, and pleasant familiar experience. The 25 most disliked poems included haiku, free verse, imagery that tended to obscure meaning, and "traditional" rather than modern authorship. On the basis of teacher questionnaires, Terry concluded that "poetry is sadly neglected in upper elementary school classrooms" (p. 47).

## Do These Studies Make a Difference?

Methods and purposes in literacy education changed vastly during the hundred years of the studies reviewed in this section. A curriculum emphasizing classics in literature was inevitably altered by the flood of new literature for children and young adults. Initial focus on literary choices for upper grades broadened to include lower grades; indeed, attention to reading material for the primary-age child overshadowed other preference concerns for a time. Now let us speculate on the role that these preference studies may have played in effecting change.

*A criterion for choice.* Preference studies accompanied a change from idealist to a more child-centered approach in education (Morris, 1961). Hence, literary preference of children emerged as a criterion for selection, although from the start there were warnings: "There may be excellent types of materials in which children should be interested but are not" (N. B. Smith, 1934, p. 271). A complication was the diversity in preferences attributed to sex and intelligence, although later studies seemed to downplay these differences. For instance, Wolfson, Manning, and Manning (1984) concluded: "It is important to avoid stereotyping one type of book for boys and another type for girls, or one type of book for minority children and another type for nonminority children" (p. 9).

*Recognition of "clandestine" reading.* It seems to have taken a long time for educators to view young folks' "underground" reading seriously. When they did, they were concerned about the harm that unwise preferences might bring. Such concern extended to the 1950s in regard to comic books (Witty & Keppel, 1959) and to the 1990s preferment for paperback-original series such as *Goosebumps*. In most cases, however, the negative concerns were modified, often with the suggestion that alternative choices might satisfy the perceived qualities that underlay preferences considered undesirable. Such substitution might not be desirable or feasible; Greenlee, Monson, and Taylor (1996) interviewed 11- and 12-year-olds to conclude that reading series books of alleged low quality did not "interfere with reader appreciation for literature of higher quality" (p. 224). Perhaps the result is a closer alliance between adult sanctioned literature and young people's preferences.

*Placement.* Beginning in the 1920s, there is an almost overwhelming concern with placing literary selections at the appropriate age level to maximize preference. Reading lists and graded basals and anthologies reflect the results of these studies. Norvell (1958), in particular, argued that without the evidence of preference surveys, adults misjudge selection and placement.

At the time, the psychometrics of placement ran counter to the psychometrics of readability formulas. A belief that children must acquire reading competence *before* they can be bothered to choose reading material is apparent in midcentury reading methodology, as indicated in Smith and Dechant's (1961) account: "Although in the primary grades the teacher's concern is fostering interest in developing basic reading skills, once children have acquired ability to read, the teacher's concern shifts to promoting reading development through a continuing interest in reading" (p. 275). The influence of preference studies from the 1920s onward has been to show that children of *all* ages can exhibit literary preferences, with the parallel argument that preference factors intertwine with readability. One recent study (Anderson, Shirey, Wilson, & Fielding, 1987) reinforced this observation by showing that "interestingness" accounted for 30 times as much variance in comprehension as did readability!

*Awareness of needs.* Johns (1973) asked inner city children to choose between trade book selections presenting "the stark, crowded conditions of urban or rural living" contrasted with selections displaying "more favorable living conditions in urban or in suburban areas" (p. 464). His results showed that "innercity children in the intermediate grades expressed reading preferences for stories or books which depicted middle class settings" (p. 466). Such a study may point to an often ignored reason behind preferences: children often indicate choices that coincide with literature that is already familiar to them. In this case, the middle-class content of basal texts may have influenced preference, and, if so, the results might be interpreted to indicate a need for wider scope in choices.

Likewise, the Terry (1974) study, finding a narrow range in poetry preferences, also noted that many teachers depended solely on basal readers for poetry selection and pedagogy. Shapiro (1985) used these results as a basis for exploring the need. She compared the teaching procedures recommended in basal texts to experts' "pedagogical procedures for effective poetry instruction" (p. 369). She documented the mismatch, concluding that the teacher manuals accompanying basals "emphasize learning in the cognitive rather than the affective domain" (p. 375). An informal analysis of subsequent editions of basals, undertaken by the authors of this chapter, indicated that basal publishers were influenced by Shapiro's study. For instance, basal instructions more frequently adhered to Shapiro's findings that "[p]oetry should be orally interpreted by the teacher" and should include "exploration of feelings, thoughts, and ideas" (p. 373). Kutiper and Wilson (1993), using library circulation figures, confirmed Terry's findings regarding the narrow characteristics of preferred poetry. By citing modern exemplary poets (e.g., Kuskin, Merriam, Adoff, Worth), they suggested ways to reduce the neglect found in Terry's study. These are instances in which preference studies have, we believe, influenced procedure beyond lists of topics, characteristics, and titles.

## READING PREFERENCES: CONTEMPORARY STUDIES

### Content Factors

How do recent studies add to or change beliefs about reading preferences? Researchers have continued to study reading preferences by identifying topics, subject matter, and genres that appear to have the greatest appeal. The results reveal some trends in subject matter appealing to students of a particular age level and support the notion that interests change with age. There are problems with the commonly used categories, however. So-called subject-matter categories (such as adventure, animal stories, realistic stories, make-believe, nature, science, biography, etc.) borrow from topic choice as well as from genre choice. Furthermore, these subject-matter categories are not mutually exclusive; that is, a child who chooses to read animal stories may choose those that are realistic, those that are make-believe, or a mixture of both. The common ground is simply a focus on animals as characters. There is also a problem with a category such as make-believe, because it does not give information about specific elements of the genre that appeal to the child. More specific descriptions such as fables, myths, or folk tales might be more revealing.

Several recent studies have categorized preferences according to topic or purpose for reading rather than genre or subject matter. For example, McGinley and Kamberlis (1996) classified books read by students in Grades 3 and 4 as fitting one of these purposes for reading: recreational interests, self and personal issues, social relationships, and social issues. The students in their sample most often chose books that fit recreational interests. Ley, Schaer, and Dismukes (1994) used the Teale–Lewis Reading Attitude Scale to examine reading attitudes and behaviors of students in Grades 6 through 8. Although this was not so much a study of reading interests as reading attitudes, students did also complete a reading behavior profile in which they reported their current levels of voluntary reading. Findings indicated that students at all three grade levels read most often for utilitarian purposes and less often for individual development or enjoyment. These studies may indicate school demands on students more than student interests through free choice of reading materials, but they do offer a different way of thinking about the choices students make in book selection.

Reading preferences of students may also be examined in terms of stages of schooling. Studies that cut across the elementary grades highlight the general interest in animals, mystery, science, history, make-believe, and people (Beta Upsilon Chapter, & Pi Lambda Theta, 1974; Chiu, 1984). Several studies suggest that animals, nature, fantasy and child characters are preferred by children in Grades 1 and 2 (Consuelo, 1967; Nelson, 1966; Witty, Coomer, & McBean, 1946). Primary-grade children have also indicated interest in reading general informational material, history, and science informational materials (Carter, 1976; Huus, 1979; Itzkowitz, 1982; Kirsch, 1975). Children in Grades 3 and 4 continue to be interested in reading about nature and animals and begin to develop interest in adventure and familiar experiences but show decreased interest in fables (Curley, 1929; Graham, 1986). There is evidence that at least by fourth grade the reading interests of boys and girls are beginning to diverge. Boys show stronger preference for nonfiction and girls for realistic fiction (Landy, 1977; Lynch-Brown, 1977; Wolfson, Manning, & Manning, 1984). Baraks, Hoffman, and Bauer (1997) asked children in Grades 4 and 5 to name their "most favorite book." Boys more often chose fantasy and girls realistic fiction; inner city children tended to select fantasy and suburban children realistic fiction. By fifth and sixth grades, interests begin to differ by sex with boys more interested in reading about war, travel, and mystery (Row, 1968) and girls interested in animal stories, westerns, and fairy tales (Shores, 1954). Several studies indicated that intermediate grade students are interested in history and science and that they also enjoy reading mystery and adventure (Bundy, 1983; Graham, 1986; Hawkins, 1983).

In junior high, reading interests continue to differ according to sex. Seventh- and eighth-Grade girls prefer mystery, romance, animals, religion, career stories, comedy, and biography. Boys prefer science fiction, mystery, adventure, biography, history, animals, and sports. Both boys and girls show increased interest in nonfiction, historical fiction, romantic fiction, and

books dealing with adolescence (Carlsen, 1967; Carter & Harris, 1982; Gallo, 1983; Leafe, 1951; McBroom, 1981; M. L. Smith & Eno, 1961; Strang, 1946). Contemporary realism is an important genre for this age group, too (Coomer & Tessmer, 1986). Diaz-Rubin (1996) found that preferences of students in Grades 10 through 12 were for movies, adventure, horror, mysteries, sports, murder, crime, humor, love, and fantasy. Benton's (1995) study of reading interests in the United Kingdom indicated that many 14- and 15-year-olds were reading adult titles. Teachers and librarians in the United States have also made this observation (Poe, Samuels, & Carter, 1995).

## Literary Forms and Devices

Historically, studies have tended to show that students preferred narrative material to informational material. Even as far back as 1898, Wissler pointed out that preferences went to plots with suspense and action and stories with humor. Studies by Dunn (1921) and Gates (1930) agreed. More recent studies have tended to support the liking for action and humor. Within the broad category of narrative, it is not really clear whether children prefer realistic stories or fantasy. Studies tend to suggest that fantasy is preferred more by primary-age children and realism more by those in the intermediate grades (Peltola, 1965).

Recent research does not show any clear trend toward greater liking for informational books. Wray and Lewis (1993), studying reading preferences of U.K. children aged 7 through 11, found a low level of interest in informational books. The students chose fiction books more than 70% of the time in this study that involved recording titles of books the children read. In contrast, Simpson's (1995) study of reading interests in Australia revealed that the boys in this aged 10 to 12 sample read nearly as much nonfiction (47%) as fiction (53%); the girls chose fiction 90% of the time. McGinley and Kamberelis (1996) reported strong interest in biography for U.S. children in the upper grades and high school. One reason for inconsistent findings regarding preference for nonfiction may be availability. Although more well-written informational books have been published in the past decade, Duke (2000) in a survey of 20 first-grade classrooms found that only 6% to 11% of the materials in classroom libraries were nonfiction; teachers utilized nonfiction text an average of only 3.6 minutes per day. In such cases, lack of preference for nonfiction might be attributed to lack of familiarity and accessibility.

There is some evidence that literary devices may influence reading interests. Humor is one factor that has emerged in a number of studies. Some forms of humor seem to have greatest appeal and perhaps are better understood by children in elementary and junior high school than others. The totally ridiculous situation and humorous characters are well liked, as is the humor associated with exaggeration, a surprising event, and play on words (McNamara, 1984; Monson, 1968; Wells, 1934). There is some evidence that readers in the middle grades also enjoy satirical literature, though they may not associate it with their own lives (McNamara, 1984).

Attention to literary characteristics as an influence on reading preferences is evident in responses of elementary-age schoolchildren, though relatively few studies have attempted to examine this dimension. It appears that elementary school students prefer books with happy endings (Mendoza, 1983) and episodic plots (Abrahamson, 1979; Abrahamson & Shannon, 1983). The development of characterization may also influence reader interest. Students prefer books in which characters are shown to have contrasting points of view (Abrahamson & Shannon, 1983). There is some evidence that boys and girls in fourth grade prefer books in which the main characters are of their own sex groups (Harkrader & Moore, 1997). Adolescents also seem to prefer characters they view as being like themselves and they pay attention to the age and sex of the protagonists in books they choose (Carter & Harris, 1982; J. Ingham, 1982; Johnson, Peer, & Baldwin, 1984; Yoder, 1978). Indeed, increased identification with characters appears to produce more suspense for readers (Jose & Brewer, 1984). M. L. Smith and Eno (1961) used a strategy of asking students what type of story they would want an author to write. They found students preferred characters between the ages of 15 and 19 who were attractive, intelligent, and physically strong. Malchow's (1937) study also revealed students' liking for characters who are clever, bright, and successful.

Abrahamson's (1980) analysis of responses to the International Reading Association (IRA) Children's Choices picture books suggests that students appreciate books with qualities of good literature (characters confronting a problem and seeking a solution, plots that focus on characters with different points of view or who experience the same thing in contrasting ways). Ingham (1982), however, found in her English subjects' responses to Enid Blyton's books a liking for books written to a formula that provided for predictability and security. Two studies, one looking at books in the IRA Children's Choices list (Greenlaw & Wielan, 1979) and the other a survey of library users aged 11 to 20 (Goodhope, 1982) reinforce the cross-age appeal of books that contain humor and adventure. In a 1969 review of reading interests, Squire noted that "scientific themes and such elements as humor, surprise, and a stirring plot appeal to most young readers" (p. 467). He also indicated that the research in reading interests published over a period of time tended to show that patterns of interest remain fairly constant over several generations of children.

Studies of poetry preferences generally indicate appreciation for rhythm, rhyme, and humor (Cullingford, 1979; Fisher & Natarella, 1982; R. O. Ingham, 1980; Terry, 1974). The research also suggests that students in the middle grades prefer to read poems rather than to listen to them (Cullingford, 1979; Kutiper, 1985). These studies add something to what we know from earlier work, indicating that the reasons for poetry preference may not have changed greatly over the years since Mackintosh published her study in 1924. Favorite poems may change for each generation according to what is available to them, but it is clear that today students use many of the criteria Mackintosh identified: funny, tells a good story, has adventure and excitement, has romantic and dramatic qualities, deals with material understandable and interesting, and has rhythm and rhyme.

Kutiper and Wilson (1993) used library circulation data as a basis for examining poetry interests of elementary school students. These students often chose books by Jack Prelutsky, Shel Silverstein, and Judith Viorst. Poetry by Paul Janeczko was also among the top group of selections, somewhat surprising because his poems do not usually meet the student criteria for popularity based on earlier studies. It is not clear from existing research whether instruction can move students to enjoy poems that do not fit the rhythm, rhyme, humor pattern seen in current choices but that may be a useful topic for further research in this area.

## Cross-National Comparisons

It is difficult to make valid cross-national comparisons because the research in this area is limited. Kirsch, Pehrsson, and Robinson (1976) examined interests of a large number of children from 10 countries and reported more similarities than differences among them. Other studies, though not all of them cross-national, tend to support the notion that reading interests do not vary greatly from country to country, yet they also enlarge our understanding of qualities that draw children to books. A study of Japanese 5-year-olds revealed an interest in books that contained unexpected developments and books in which main characters attempted to solve problems in order to attain a goal (Tokogi, 1980). A comparison of reading preferences of British and American children aged 7 to 10 showed similarities in favorite categories for boys and girls in both countries, with adventure, animals, fantasy, hobbies, and travel the most preferred categories. The group diverged in response to poetry: British children preferred to read poetry rather than read about people, but American children preferred to read about people (Schofer, 1981). A study of the reading interests of intermediate grade Canadian children indicated that both boys and girls preferred themes of mystery, adventure, and fantasy (Summers & Lukevich, 1983). The pattern is not unlike what is known of U.S. children's interests, although fantasy is not generally a favorite with this age group in most U.S. studies.

There is some evidence that interest in reading informational books may differ by country (McGinley & Kamberelis, 1996; Simpson, 1995; Wray & Lewis, 1993). So, although there are certainly some similarities among the reading preferences of students across countries, it seems clear that there are also some differences. Such differences may be influenced by gender, or by factors such as the school curriculum and the availability of quality nonfiction books in the school library media center.

## External Factors

As students progress through the middle grades and into adolescence, they rely less on teachers and parents for reading guidance and more on peers (Shore, 1968; Wendelin & Zinck, 1983). Response to questionnaires as well as observational studies suggest that children in this age group select books according to favorite authors and are influenced by the appearance of a book, including the cover and the content of the first page, the length, and the illustrations as well as the title (Burgess, 1985; Higgins & Elliott, 1982; Wendelin & Zinck, 1983). A study utilizing reading journals, essays, and interviews of eighth graders indicated that 75% accurately predicted whether they would like to read a book by studying the cover (Rinehart, Gerlach, Wisell, & Welker, 1998). They also reported that the BOB (back-of-book summary on a paperback) enhanced the self-selection process for recreational reading. When intermediate grade children in Australia were surveyed to determine factors that influence book choices (Hill, 1984), content and cover or title were reported as strong. Format of a book, title, cover, and size may also act as an influence on expressed interests and preferences. Several recent studies have examined factors related to format of books. For some lower achieving students, physical elements of a book such as print, illustration, and length join with the title to assist in determining book selection (Higgins & Elliott, 1982; White, 1973; Wilson, 1985).

A study by Reutzels and Gali (1997) examined book selection behaviors in a school library media center. They observed elementary-age schoolchildren to note the routines used in book selection and also to look for more specific differences in the selection process. Research procedures included video and audio tapes as well as verbatim transcripts of think-alouds. Findings suggested that the most sophisticated students seemed to scan or read books during the selection process. Motivation to choose or reject a book was most often based on a personal preference or an emotional response to the book or on the physical characteristics of the book. A rather surprising finding was that bookshelf level was important. Nearly two thirds of the books chosen were at eye level or below. An interesting observation was that students often ran out of time and failed to have chosen books when the period ended. This may suggest the need to teach the skill of book selection and to inform students well in advance of the end of the library period so they can use their time to better advantage.

## Means of Eliciting and Measuring Reading Interests and Preferences

Researchers have used a variety of strategies to attempt to gain access to information about reading interests. These include questionnaires, interviews, checklists of book titles assumed to be popular, checklists of fictitious titles, paired comparisons of fictitious story synopses, paired comparisons questionnaire with content categories, reading records kept by students or teachers, library withdrawal records, student ratings of samples from a text, free response measures, and semantic differential formats. Reading interests or preferences also have been examined by means of interest inventories, analysis of library selections (N. B. Smith, 1926), open-ended questionnaires (Shore, 1968), relating freely discussed topics to interests (Byers, 1964), and nonverbal evaluations (Ford & Koplyay, 1968).

It is immediately clear that some strategies are constructed from preconceived ideas of what students will be interested in reading. Others leave the matter open, relying on reader response to an open-ended interview or questionnaire. Clearly, the information resulting from a forced choice situation may be considerably different from information gained through open-ended response. On another dimension, there is a distinction between strategies that rely on fictitious titles and synopses (Thorndike,

1941; Zais, 1969) and those that draw from samples of actual texts. The use of fictitious titles and synopses can remove the interference of previous experience with a text but the strategy assumes that the titles and synopses actually represent those characteristics of literary genres or devices that are intended. Purves and Beach (1972) pointed out that samples from a text may fail to reflect key qualities of that book. In that way, the results can be misleading. On the other hand, this method can reveal interest in specific literary qualities or devices, response to writing style or to genre. A mechanism like the semantic differential allows for response to fairly specific qualities of a text, but it does not necessarily give an indication of a reader's preference for or interest in that genre as opposed to other genres. The semantic differential has been employed in a number of studies (Hansson, 1973; Klein, 1968). A Likert-type scale has also been used successfully to document response to excerpts from reading texts (Coleman & Jungeblut, 1961). The effectiveness of a strategy for eliciting information about reading interests comes down to the question of which strategy or strategies provide the most accurate assessment.

The search for appropriate strategy is exemplified in a survey by Worthy, Moorman, and Turner (1999), who compared reading preferences with availability. Questionnaires, interviews, and open (written) responses encouraged 419 sixth-graders to cite titles and topics that interested them, along with sources they used for obtaining such materials. Results showed preferences for scary books, cartoons and comics, and popular magazines, and for authors such as R. L. Stine, Stephen King, and Judy Blume. Subsequently, a survey of school library materials revealed relative absence of these preferred materials and, in fact, 56% of the students surveyed stated that they purchased what they wanted to read. Various reasons (e.g., "explicit sexual content," "graphic description of violence," p. 21) were offered for what the authors concluded to be "and ever-increasing gap between student preferences and materials that schools provide and recommend" (p. 23).

Although numerous instruments have been used in reading interest studies, rarely have the instruments been subjected to tests of reliability (Weintraub, 1969). Joels and Anderson (1983) used a Reading Interest Survey, Forms A and B, consisting of fictitious titles. Form A was administered initially and Form B was administered after 1 week and again after a 6-month interval. Correlation coefficients were computed for each of the six interest categories: fantasy, love and romance, mystery/adventure, religion, science, and sports. Coefficients ranged from .65 to .82 after 1 week and from .58 to .76 after 6 months. Although the interests did change, the change does not appear to be great.

The differences in assumptions underlying these strategies add to difficulties in comparing findings across studies. It is also important to take into account the accuracy and authenticity of the strategies used. The study of library/media center behavior as a means of determining reading choices appears to be increasing. The observational study by Reutzel and Gali (1997) has been described. Kutiper (1993) used circulation records in the study of poetry interests and that strategy was also employed by Isaacs (1992) in studying reading interests of middle school students. Reading records kept by students or teachers and library withdrawal records may be quite easily obtained and classified by genre, but such records do not necessarily mean that the student was interested enough in the book to complete it. Free-response measures are more likely to reveal factors related to interests but are complicated by the need to maintain reliability of judges in content analysis of those responses.

Longitudinal studies of reading interests and preferences are rare. Ley et al. (1994) used the Teale–Lewis Reading Attitudes Scale to study reading attitudes and behaviors of middle school students over a period of 3 school years, Grades 6 through 8. The scale records attitudes toward reading and values placed on reading for these purposes: Individual Development, Utilitarian Purposes, and Enjoyment. Their data indicated a decline in voluntary reading from grades six to eight and also in attitude toward reading. At all three grade levels, the scores for Utilitarian Reading were higher than for Individual Development or Enjoyment, and this was true for both sexes. Longitudinal studies that follow the same students through several grades might provide useful information about the changes in preference patterns over a period of time as well as changes in attitudes toward reading.

## READING PREFERENCES: FUTURE STUDIES

"Reading Interest" articles listed in *Current Index to Journals in Education* total 165 in 1970 to 1977, 273 in 1980 to 1987, and 99 in 1990 to 1997. Why the decrease? Do researchers infer that the topic has been adequately explored? Have warnings about limits in validity and reliability of preference or interest studies discouraged further investigations?

A more proactive view is that preference studies, formerly discrete, now merge with broader inquiry. Specifically, the concept of reading preference can be discerned in studies of attitude toward reading, the effects of teaching to broaden interests and tastes, the mission to expand selections to include diverse cultures (Au, 1995), and reader response.

### Attitudes Toward Reading

McKenna, Kear, and Ellsworth (1995), in a groundbreaking study, submitted a 20-item Elementary Reading Attitude Survey (McKenna & Kear, 1990) to 18,185 students, Grades 1 through 6, across the United States. The scale was designed to elicit "normative beliefs, beliefs about the outcomes of reading, and specific reading experiences" (p. 939). Results differed by gender and ability, though not by presence or absence of basal readers. The overall finding was that "attitude toward reading both as a pastime and as a school-related undertaking was observed to grow increasingly negative as students passed from first grade to sixth grade" (p. 945). The "relatively positive" attitude at grade 1 ended in "relative indifference" at Grade 6 (p. 952). The authors concluded that the "5-year negative pattern . . . is educationally significant and challenges reading education to understand its etiology" (p. 952).

McKenna and Kear's (1990) study noted "a parallel decline in the number of reading interests" (p. 937), raising once again the question of the distinction among attitudes, interests,

and preferences. Theorists have emphasized this distinction, asserting that interest in reading is not to be confused with reading interests or the passive concept of preferences. However, the distinction may becloud the relationship. Preferences are not necessarily interests, but a strong preference is more likely to lead to interest than is a nonpreference. Furthermore, the active nature of reading interest becomes an ingredient of global attitude toward reading, implicit in Dewey's (1913) observation: "The root idea of the term [interest] seems to be that of being engaged, engrossed, or entirely taken up with some activity because of its recognized worth" (p. 17).

The contribution of future preference studies will increase if their design includes assessment of interests and attitudes toward reading. Researchers will need to answer the question of when a reading preference can be determined a reading interest. Norvell (1958) attempted an answer by establishing an interest index of 86.0 and above to show the upper 10% (hence "best liked") selections tested (p. 17). Anderson, Wilson, and Fielding (1988) gave clues to finding reading interests by logs reporting free reading. For future studies to be useful, however, they will need to focus on works, topics, or characteristics that "impel" readers to "seek out" reading experiences, along with positive global attitudes toward reading.

### Effects of Teaching

Preferences are shaped by direct and vicarious experience, including the effects of teaching. Preference studies of the past seldom described this factor, with the result that it is overlooked when, in fact, the alleged idiosyncratic nature of preference might be ascribed to differences in training.

Such effects may be negative or insignificant. Quiocho (1984) instructed fifth-graders in intensive reading of three historical novels over a 6-month period. Although comprehension and response level showed expected gains, interest did not. Interest scores for the genre, historical fiction, dropped by 4.99 points. The decline should concern those who plan intensive literature units for teaching, and it might suggest a need for further study of the way to teach historical fiction. A different example is Morrow's (1992) attempt to add a parent training component to encourage second-graders' interest and response to books and the unexpected result: "The study did not demonstrate that the home-and-school program was superior to the school-only program" (p. 271). Because home influence is a positive factor in other studies (Palmer & Codling, 1994), the nonsignificant finding in the Morrow study suggests a need to identify procedures to make home programs effective in regard to reading preferences and interests.

The influence of teaching with positive effect on preferences and interests is to be found in a few studies, and these show wide variety in design. Thames and Reeves (1994) used a classic design: preassessment and postassessment of attitudes toward reading and reading achievement. Their 12-week program for 29 subjects, Grades 2 through 6, began with an interest inventory after which tutors matched interests with trade books and articles from newspapers and magazines. This procedure produced significant gains in both criteria, compared with a control group who received individualized basal-text instruction. Wray and Lewis (1993), by contrast, planned no treatment but instead surveyed 464 British children, aged 7 to 11, to find reading interests and habits, concurrently interviewing teachers about their presentation of literature. Vast differences in preference were found among schools and classrooms; the report explores "how differing practices and views seemed to influence the children's choice of books" (p. 256). For example, 20% of the students in one class "cited poetry books as the books they enjoyed reading most" (p. 257), a finding the authors attributed directly to the teacher's enthusiasm for poetry. In similar vein, Wolf (1996) studied the dynamics of literature-into-drama sessions, speculating on the "transformation" toward interest (p. 43).

In *Literature Circles and Response* (Hill, Johnson, & Noe, 1995), a group of teachers described in great detail the results of fostering daily small-group discussions of core books representing various fiction genres, with anecdotal evidence that these sessions increased students' preferences for similar works, with concomitant rise in interest. Qualitative instruments (Chapter 12) are included in the study, a boon to future investigation, especially for classroom teachers aspiring to assess the results of their efforts.

Despite these examples, few preference studies of the past have been designed to show effects of treatment. At times, the procedure to investigate preferences, though not designated as treatment, may actually be considered a form of brief instruction. For example, Pappas (1993) paired fiction and informational nonfiction books, presenting each pair to 20 kindergarteners to elicit preference. In each session, she read a pair to the children, responded to their questions, and then assisted them to "pretend read" each book. The results were counter to prior studies and to teachers' assumption that primary literature should be "made up mostly of fiction books" (p. 126): Children in this study chose information books over stories. In this case, the extended presentation of each selection may have influenced the outcome. Kirby's (1999) survey of 2,211 sixth-graders' preferences among Newbery Medal books indicated seven titles best liked by both genders (*Maniac Magee, Shiloh, The Giver, A Wrinkle in Time, Island of the Blue Dolphins, Mrs. Frisby and the Rats of NIMH*, and *Number the Stars*). Such results cannot be generalized if indeed they derive from "treatment" specifically involving Newbery items in the sampled classrooms.

## Preference Studies and Cultural Diversity

Au (1995) noted the movement to devise "a new (literary) cannon incorporating works by authors who represent different ethnic backgrounds" (p. 95) and to represent "ethnicity, social class, primary language, and gender" (p. 85) in children's reading. The history of this movement, including efforts by publishers, children's literature experts, and curriculum specialists to meet the need, is outside the purview of this chapter, but implications for future preference studies should be mentioned. First, a working hypothesis is that preferences are likely to expand as literature expands to include diverse cultures. However, it is likely that literary characteristics shown to be preferred in

the past will also be operative, so selection to include these characteristics insofar as possible will support the inclusion. Second, this is an area inviting training studies. How, for instance, might literature units exploring ethnic-specific literature (Hansen-Krening & Mizokawa, 1997) affect subsequent preference and interest?

## Reading Preferences and Reader Response

Reading preferences are identified *before* reading, as when subjects select a fictitious title or genre they might like to read, or *after* reading, as when subjects cite favorite books, poems, or authors. In most studies, the motives for preference, such as the appeal of a topic or a literary characteristic, have had to be inferred. As Jordan (1921) noted nearly a century ago, "It seems evident that children, even those of high school age, have not the ability to explain why they like certain books rather than others" (p. 43). In recent times, however, researchers seem to have found more direct ways to learn the reasons behind choices. Their efforts come under the heading of reader response, cited here because such studies appear to complement studies of reading preferences.

In a typical response study, students read one or more books, usually fiction selected by the researcher but with an assumption that the material will engage the readers. Through group discussions, interviews, or journals, students reveal their responses during and after the reading. Researchers organize these responses into categories frequently derived from reader response theory proposed by Purves and Rippere (1968) and Rosenblatt (1938/1995).

Relevant to preference research, these studies give a context for choices—that is, for evaluating the selections, the transaction itself, and whether to seek out similar literary experience. Such evaluation does not take place immediately. Eeds and Wells (1989) noted that students constructed simple meaning, personal involvement, and inquiry before critiquing a selection. Hancock (1993), using journals and interviews, identified immersion and self-involvement in responses mainly before students focused on "detachment," which included "literary evaluation." Sebesta, Monson, and Senn (1995) asked students, Grades 4 through 10, to "fill a page" of writing and drawing in response to a folktale read to them. The results appeared to support a response hierarchy progressing from evocation to considered alternatives to reflective thinking, and finally to evaluation.

As a result, response studies come closer to explaining the why of preference and interest. First, they report considered evaluation supported by earlier stages of transaction. Second, these considered evaluations are amplified by discourse that gives reasons for the judgment. Here is an area, then, for future study: What is the difference, if any, between off-the-cuff preferences and preferences that result from considered judgment that follows transaction? Do evaluation-level responses identify more clearly readers' preferences and interests? For example, response studies may provide information about interests that relate to literary elements, as when a student indicates strong interest in a story where the major character is successful in an athletic contest or rejects a book because the plot lacks an element of surprise. Reader response studies may also help to reveal mismatches between child and adult perception as, for example, a judgment about what is funny in a story (Munde, 1997). The information from such studies might advance preference research and inform teaching procedure to improve transaction, a result of merging preference research with reader response research.

If we assume that teachers influence through inquiry and modeling, future studies might profitably be done to reveal the preferences and responses of teachers themselves. The results might arouse concern, with implications for teacher training. Small (2000) found, in a questionnaire survey of 150 teachers, that the majority did not approach children's literature from an aesthetic stance; 34% approached it efferently, 25% for its instructional application.

## Implications for Teachers

To learn about student interests, teachers might seize the opportunity to observe closely book selection behavior in the library media center, as described by Reutzel and Gali (1997). A related option is to instruct students in means of selecting books by using more sophisticated techniques such as reading part of a first chapter or scanning sections of the story. Engaging children in conversation about what they would look for in making this appraisal can lead to information about content and/or stylistic elements that truly interest that child.

Over the century, the domain of reading preferences has changed. Early studies pointed to classics, with limited access to other reading materials. Modern studies often occur in the midst of plenty, with materials to meet almost any interest but now with competing media and competing demands for attention and time. A small percentage of young people are avid readers, voluntarily choosing reading over other activities (Anderson et al., 1988), but the mode, the pattern of highest frequency, is aliteracy—that is, choosing not to read voluntarily (McKenna et al., 1995). Teachers and other leaders, if they are to remedy aliteracy, must first be aware of preference. Through studies such as those we have cited and through inventories of their own, they can personalize reading, helping young people to match preference with reading fare.

The job does not end there. Preference must activate into interest if reading is to thrive. The young person's global attitude toward reading should, we believe, be assessed as attentively as reading achievement. In this way, teachers and other leaders can determine whether the effort to meet preferences is productive. Such effort may include teaching procedures specifically aimed to activate interest, for example, literature circles, oral interpretation, reading aloud, book talks, drama, and visual arts.

Adult attitudes toward young people's reading preferences have varied. Proponents of self-selection advise that readers be free to choose whatever they want to read. Other proponents, as we have seen, would assess preferences with a mission to change them. There is little doubt that criteria for selection held by children and by adults present disparity (Munde, 1997; Norvell, 1958; Worthy & Turner, 1999). For example, historical fiction, certain types of poetry, and nonnarrative genres are found in some studies to be unpopular. Presently, there is little information as to preference regarding the increased offerings of literature of diverse cultures and attractive new editions of classics. Teachers and other leaders should realize that preferences are shaped by prior experience; that such experience often is limited, that to guide selection includes the nourishing of preference and interest.

## References

Abrahamson, R. F. (1979). *Children's favorite picture storybooks: An analysis of structure and reading preferences.* (ERIC Documents Reproduction Service No. ED 174 977)

Abrahamson, R. F. (1980). An analysis of children's favorite picture storybooks. *The Reading Teacher, 34,* 167–170.

Abrahamson, R. F., & Shannon, P. (1983). A plot structure analysis of favorite picture books. *The Reading Teacher, 37,* 44–48.

Anderson, R. C., Shirey, L. L., Wilson, P. T., & Fielding, L. G. (1987). Interestingness of children's reading materials. In R. E. Snow & M. J. Farr (Eds.), Aptitude, learning, and instruction, 3, *Cognitive and Affective Process Analyses* (pp. 287–299).

Anderson, R. C., Wilson, P. T., & Fielding, L. G. (1988). Growth in reading and how children spend their time outside school. *Reading Research Quarterly, 23,* 285–303.

Au, K. H. (1995). Multicultural perspectives on literacy research. *Journal of Reading Behavior, 27,* 85–100.

Baraks, N., Hoffman, A., & Bauer, D. (1997). Children's books preferences: Patterns, particulars, and possible implications. *Reading Psychology, 18,* 309–341.

Benton, P. (1995). Conflicting cultures: Reflections on the reading and viewing of secondary-school pupils. *Oxford Review of Education, 21,* 457–470.

Beta Upsilon Chapter, & Pi Lambda Theta (1974). Children's reading interests classified by age level. *The Reading Teacher, 27,* 694–700.

Bundy, B. A. (1983). The development of a survey to ascertain the reading preferences of fourth, fifth and sixth graders. *Dissertation Abstracts International, 44,* 68A. (University Microfilms No. DA 8312392)

Burgess, S. A. (1985). Reading but not literate: The ChildRead Survey. *School Library Journal, 31,* 27–30.

Byers, L. (1964). Pupils interests in the content of primary reading texts. *The Reading Teacher, 17,* 227–233.

Carlsen, G. R. (1967). *Books and the teen-age reader.* New York: Harper & Row.

Carter, S. M. (1976). *Interpreting interests and reading interests of pupils in grades one through three.* Unpublished doctoral dissertation, University of Georgia, Athens.

Carter, B., & Harris, K. (1982). What junior high students like in books. *Journal of Reading, 26,* 42–46.

Chiu, L.-H. (1984). Children's attitudes toward reading and reading interests. *Perceptual and Motor Skills, 58,* 960–962.

Coleman, J. H., & Jungeblut, A. (1961). Children's likes and dislikes about what they read. *Journal of Educational Research, 54,* 221–228.

Consuelo, M., Sr. (1967). What do first graders like to read? *Catholic School Journal, 67,* 42–43.

Coomer, J. W., & Tessmer, K. M. (1986). 1986 books for young adults poll. *English Journal, 75.*

Cullingford, C. (1979). Children and poetry. *English in Education, 13,* 58–61.

Curley, A. M. (1929). An analysis of the textbooks used in investigating children's interests and a summary of the findings. In W. S. Gray & R. Munroe (Eds.), *The reading interests and habits of adults* (pp. 108–110). New York: Macmillan.

Dewey, J. (1913). *Interest and effort in education.* Boston: Houghton Mifflin.

Diaz-Rubin, C. (1996). Reading interests of high school students. *Reading Improvement, 33,* 169–175.

Duke, N. K. (2000). 3.6 minutes per day: The scarcity of informational texts in first grade. *Reading Research Quarterly, 35,* 202–224.

Dunn, F. W. (1921). Interest factors in primary reading material. *Teachers: College Contributions to Education, No. 113.* New York: Bureau of Publications, Teachers College, Columbia University.

Eeds, M., & Wells, D. (1989). Grand conversations: An exploration of meaning construction in literature study groups. *Research in the Teaching of English, 23,* 4–29.

Fisher, C., & Natarella, M. A. (1982). Young children's preferences in poetry: A national survey of first, second, and third graders. *Research in the Teaching of English, 16,* 339–354.

Ford, R. C., & Koplyay, J. (1968). Children's story preferences. *The Reading Teacher, 22,* 232–237.

Gallo, D. R. (1983). *Students' reading interests—A report of a Connecticut survey.* (ERIC Documents Reproduction Service No. ED 232 143)

Gates, A. (1930). *Interest and ability in reading.* New York: Macmillan.

Getzels, J. W. (1966). The problem of interests: A reconsideration. In H. A. Robinson (Ed.), *Reading: Seventy five years of progress* (pp. 97–106). (Supplementary Educational Monographs No. 96.) Chicago: University of Chicago Press.

Goodhope, J. (1982). Into the eighties: BAYA's fourth interest survey. *School Library Journal, 29,* 33.

Graham, S. A. (1986). Assessing reading preferences: A new approach. *New England Reading Association Journal, 21,* 811.

Greenlaw, M. J., & Wielan, O. P. (1979). Reading interests revisited. *Language Arts, 56,* 432–433.

Greenlee, A. A., Monson, D. L., & Taylor, B. M. (1966). The lure of series books: Does it affect appreciation for recommended literature? *The Reading Teacher, 50,* 216–225.

Hancock, M. R. (1993). Exploring the meaning-making process through the content of literature response journals: A case study investigation. *Research in the Teaching of English, 27,* 335–368.

Hansen-Krening, N., & Mizokawa, D. T. (1997). Exploring ethnic-specific literature: A unity of parents, families, and educators. *Journal of Adolescent & Adult Literacy, 41,* 180–189.

Hansson, G. (1973). Some types of research on response to literature. *Research in the Teaching of English, 7,* 260–284.

Harkrader, M. A., & Moore, R. (1997). Literature preferences of fourth graders. *Reading Research and Instruction, 36,* 325–339.

Hawkins, S. (1983). Reading interests of gifted children. *Reading Horizons, 24,* 18–22.

Haynes, C., & Richgels, D. J. (1992). Fourth graders' literature preferences. *Journal of Educational Research, 85,* 208–219.

Higgins, D., & Elliott, D. (1982). Shadowing kids in the library: Observational study of the free reading behavior and book selection process of lower achieving fourth grade students. *Arizona Reading Journal, 21,* 5–7.

Hill, B. C., Johnson, N. J., & Noe, K. L. S. (Eds.) (1995). *Literature circles and response.* Norwood, MA: Christopher-Gordon.

Hill, S. (1984). What are children reading? *Australia Journal of Reading, 7,* 196–199.

Huber, M. (1928). *The influence of intelligence upon children's reading interests.* New York: Bureau of Publications, Teachers College, Columbia University.

Huber, M., Bruner, H. B., & Curry, C. M. (1927). *Children's interests in poetry.* Chicago: Rand McNally.

Huus, H. (1979). A new look at children's interests. In J. E. Shapiro (Ed.), *Using literature and poetry affectively* (pp. 37–45). Newark, DE: International Reading Association.

Ingham, J. (1982). Middle school children's responses to E. Blyton in "The Bradford book flood experience." *Journal of Research in Reading, 5,* 43–56.

Ingham, R. O. (1980). The poetry preferences of fourth and fifth grade students in a suburban setting in 1980. (Doctoral dissertation, University of Houston.) *Dissertation Abstracts International, 42,* 984A, No. 8112331.

Isaacs, K. T. (1992). *Go ask Alice*: What middle schoolers choose to read. *The New Advocate, 5,* 129–143.

Itzkowitz, S. G. (1982). Reading interests of first grade students and basal story content. *The Reading Instruction Journal, 26,* 18–19.

Joels, R. W., & Anderson, B. (1983). Reliability of reading interest assessment: An applied study. *Reading Horizons, 23,* 230–234.

Johns, J. L. (1973). What do innercity children prefer to read? *The Reading Teacher, 26,* 462–467.

Johnson, D. M., Peer, G. R., & Baldwin, R. (1984). Protagonists preference among juvenile and adolescent readers. *Journal of Educational Research, 77,* 147–150.

Jordan, A. M. (1921). *Children's interests in reading.* New York: Bureau of Publications, Teachers College, Columbia University.

Jose, P. E., & Brewer, S. F. (1984). Development of story liking: Character identification, suspense, and outcome resolution. *Developmental Psychology, 20,* 911–924.

Kirby, R. N. (1999). Favorite Newbery books of sixth grade students, teachers, and library media specialists. *Reading Research and Instruction, 38,* 131–141.

Kirsch, D. (1975). From athletes to zebras—Young children want to read about them. *Elementary English, 52,* 73–78.

Kirsch, D., Pehrsson, R., & Robinson, H. A. (1976). Expressed reading interests of young children: An international study. In J. E. Merritt (Ed.), *New horizons in reading* (pp. 45–56). Newark, DE: International Reading Association.

Klein, H. A. (1968). *Interest and comprehension in sex-typed materials.* Unpublished doctoral dissertation, Syracuse University, Syracuse, NY.

Kutiper, K. S. (1985). A survey of the adolescent poetry preferences of seventh, eighth, and ninth graders. *Dissertation Abstracts International, 47,* 02A, No. 86-07, 020.

Kutiper, K., & Wilson, P. (1993). Updating poetry preferences: A look at the poetry children really like. *The Reading Teacher, 47,* 28–35.

Landy, S. (1977). Why Johnny can read...but doesn't. *Canadian Literary Journal, 34,* 379–387.

Lazar, M. (1937). *Reading interests, activities, and opportunities of bright, average, and dull children.* New York: Bureau of Publications, Teachers College, Columbia University.

Leafe, B. (1961). A survey of reading interests and habits of high school students in the Sacramento area. In H. A. Bammen, U. Hogan, & C. E. Greene (Eds.), *Reading instruction in the secondary school* (pp. 258–260). New York: McKay.

Ley, T. C., Schaer, B. B., & Dismukes, B. W. (1994). Longitudinal study of the reading attitudes and behaviors of middle school students. *Reading Psychology: An International Quarterly, 15*, 11–38.

Lynch-Brown, C. (1977). Procedures for determining children's book choices: Comparison and criticism. *Reading Horizons, 17*, 243–250.

Mackintosh, H. K. (1924). A study of children's choices in poetry. *The Elementary English Review, 1*, 85–89.

Malchow, E. C. (1937). Reading interests of junior high school pupils. *School Review, 45*, 175–185.

McBroom, G. (1981). Research: Our defense begins here. *English Journal, 70*, 75–77.

McGinley, W., & Kamberelis, G. (1996). Maniac Magee and Ragtime Tumpie: Children negotiating self and world through reading and writing. *Research in the Teaching of English, 30*, 75–113.

McKenna, M. C., & Kear, D. J. (1990). Measuring attitude toward reading: A new tool for teachers. *The Reading Teacher, 44*, 626–640.

McKenna, M. C., Kear, D. J., & Ellsworth, R. A. (1995). Children's attitudes toward reading: A national survey. *Reading Research Quarterly, 30*, 934–956.

McNamara, S. G. (1984). Children respond to satire in picture books. *Reading Improvement, 21*, 303–323.

Mendoza, A. (1983). Elementary school children's preference in literature. *Childhood Education, 59*, 193–197.

Monson, D. L. (1968). Children's test responses to seven humorous stories. *Elementary School Journal, 68*, 334–339.

Morris, V. C. (1961). *Philosophy and the American school*. Boston: Houghton Mifflin.

Morrow, L. M. (1992). The impact of a literature-based program on literacy achievement, use of literature, and attitudes of children from minority backgrounds. *Reading Research Quarterly, 27*, 250–275.

Munde, G. (1997). What are you laughing at? Differences in children's and adults' humorous book selections for children. *Children's Literature in Education, 28*, 219–233.

*NEA Proceedings*. (1897). Some observations of children's reading, 1015–1021.

Nelson, R. C. (1966). Children's poetry preferences. *Elementary English, 43*, 247–251.

Norvell, G. W. (1950). *The reading interests of young people*. Boston: Heath.

Norvell, G. W. (1958). *What boys and girls like to read*. Morristown, NJ: Silver Burdett & Ginn.

Palmer, B. M., & Codling, R. M. (1994). In their own words: What elementary students have to say about motivation to read. *The Reading Teacher, 48*, 176–178.

Pappas, C. C. (1993). Is narrative "primary"? Some insights from kindergartners' pretend readings of stories and information books. *Journal of Reading Behavior, 25*, 97–129.

Peltola, B. J. (1965). *A study of the indicated literary choices and measured literary knowledge of fourth and sixth grade boys and girls*. Unpublished doctoral dissertation, University of Minnesota.

Poe, E., Samuels, B. G., & Carter, B. (1995). Past perspectives and future directions: An interim analysis of twenty-five years of research on young adult literature. *The ALAN Review, 22*, 46–50.

Purves, A. C., & Beach, R. (1972). *Literature and the reader: Research in response to literature, reading interests, and the teaching of literature*. Urbana, IL: National Council of Teachers of English.

Purves, A., & Rippere, V. (1968). *Elements of writing about a literary work: A study of response to literature* (Research Report No. 9). Urbana, IL: National Council of Teachers of English.

Quiocho, A. M. L. L. (1984). *The effects of schema development strategies on fifth-graders' comprehension of responses to, and interest in historical fiction: A classroom study*. Unpublished doctoral dissertation, University of Washington, Seattle.

Reutzel, D. R., & Gali, K. (1997). The art of children's book selection: A labyrinth unexplored. *Reading Psychology: An International Quarterly, 18*, 131–171.

Rinehart, S., Gerlach, J. M., Wisell, D. L., & Walker, W. A. (1998). Would I like to read the book? Eighth graders' use of book cover clues to help choose recreational reading. *Reading Research and Instruction, 37*, 263–279.

Robinson, C. C., Larsen, J. M., Haupt, J. H., & Mohlman, J. (1997). Picture book selection behaviours of emergent readers: Influence of genre, familiarity, and book attributes. *Reading Research and Instruction, 36*, 287–304.

Robinson, H. M., & Weintraub, S. (1973). Research related to children's interests and to developmental values of reading. *Library Trends, 22*, 81–108.

Rosenblatt, L. M. (1995). *Literature as exploration* (5th ed.). New York: Modern Language Association of America.

Row, B. H. (1968). *Reading interests of elementary school pupils in selected schools in Muscogee County, Georgia*. Unpublished doctoral dissertation, Auburn University, Auburn, AL.

Sebesta, S. L., Monson, D. L., & Senn, H. D. (1995). A hierachy to assess reader response. *Journal of Reading, 38*, 444–450.

Shapiro, S. (1985). An analysis of poetry teaching procedures in sixth-grade basal manuals. *Reading Research Quarterly, 20*, 368–381.

Shaw, J. C. (1897, October). (Untitled). *West Virginia Journal*.

Schofer, G. (1981). Reading preferences of British and American elementary children. *Reading Improvement, 18*, 127–131.

Shore, R. B. (1968). Perceived influence of peers, parents, and teachers on fifth and ninth graders' preferences of reading material. *Dissertation Abstracts International, 47*, OSA, No. 86-16, 829.

Shores, J. H. (1954). Reading interests and informational needs of children in grades four to eight. *Elementary English, 31*, 493–500.

Simpson, A. (1995). Fictions and facts: An investigation of the reading practices of girls and boys. *English Education, 28*, 268–279.

Small, M. D. (2000). *Elementary teachers' resources for learning about, reasons for reading, and responses to children's literature*. Unpublished doctoral dissertation, University of Minnesota.

Smith, H. P., & Dechant, E. V. (1961). *Psychology in teaching reading*. Englewood Cliffs, NJ: Prentice-Hall.

Smith, M. L., & Eno, I. V. (1961). What do they really want to read? *English Journal, 50*, 343–345.

Smith, N. B. (1926). An investigation in children's interests in different types of stories. *Detroit Educational Bulletin, 9*, 3–4.

Smith, N. B. (1934). *American reading instruction*. New York: Silver Burdett & Ginn.

Spache, G. D. (1963). *Toward better reading*. Champaign, IL: Garrard.

Squire, J. R. (1969). English literature. In R. Ebel (Ed.), *Encyclopedia of educational Research* (4th ed.).

Strang, R. E. (1946). Reading interests. *English Journal, 35*, 477–482.

Summers, E. G., & Lukevich, A. (1983). Reading preferences of intermediate-grade children in relation to sex, community, and maturation (grade-level): A Canadian perspective. *Reading Research Quarterly, 18*, 347–360.

Tarkington, B. (1914). *Penrod*. New York: Grosset & Dunlap.

Terman, L. M., & Lima, M. (1925–26). *Children's reading: A guide for parents and teachers*. New York: Appleton.

Terry, A. (1974). *Children's poetry preferences: A national survey of upper elementary grades* (NCTE Research Report No. 16). Urbana, IL: National Council of Teachers of English.

Thames, D. G., & Reeves, C. K. (1994). Poor readers' attitudes: Effects of using interests and trade books in an integrated language arts approach. *Reading Research and Instruction, 33,* 293–308.

Thorndike, R. L. (1941). *A comparative study of children's reading interests.* New York: Bureau of Publications, Teachers College, Columbia University.

Tokogi, K. (1980). Interests in picture books of Japanese five-year-olds. *The Reading Teacher, 33,* 442–444.

Weintraub, S. (1969). Children's reading interests. *The Reading Teacher, 22,* 655–659.

Wells, R. E. (1934). A study of tastes in humorous literature among pupils of junior and senior high schools. *Journal of Educational Research, 28,* 81–91.

Wendelin, K., & Zinck, R. A. (1983). How students make book choices. *Reading Horizon, 23,* 84–88.

White, S. F. (1973). A study of the relationship between racial illustrations accompanying stories in basal readers and children's preferences for these stories. *Dissertation Abstracts International, 34,* 77A.

Wilson, R. J. (1985). Children's classics: A reading preference study of fifth and sixth graders. *Dissertation Abstracts International, 47,* 02A, No. 86-09, 031.

Witty, P., Coomer, A., & McBean, D. (1946). Children's choices of favorite books: A study conducted in ten elementary schools. *Journal of Educational Psychology, 37,* 266–278.

Witty, P., & Keppel, D. K. (1959). *Reading and the educative process.* Lexington, MA: Ginn.

Wolf, S. A. (1996). Learning to act/acting to learn: Children as actors, critics, and characters in classroom theatre. *Research in the Teaching of English, 28,* 7–44.

Wolfson, B. J., Manning, G., & Manning, M. (1984). Revisiting what children say their reading interests are. *Reading World, 24,* 4–10.

Worthy, J., Moorman, M., & Turner, M. (1999). What Johnny likes to read is hard to find in schools. *Reading Research Quarterly, 34,* 12–27.

Wray, D., & Lewis, M. (1993). The reading experiences and interests of junior school children. *Children's Literature in Education, 24,* 251–263.

Yoder, J. M. (1978). The relative importance of four narrative factors in the reading interests of male and female adolescents in grades ten through twelve. *Dissertation Abstracts International, 39,* 219A.

Zais, R. S. (1969). A scale to measure sophistication of reading interests. *Journal of Reading, 12,* 273–276.

# · 62 ·

# THE SCHOOL SUBJECT LITERATURE

## Alan C. Purves
### State University of New York, Albany

## Gordon M. Pradl
### New York University

Literature as a school subject has been variously defined over the last century, but through those definitions certain constants have remained (Applebee, 1974; Beach & Marshall, 1991; Burton, 1964; Purves, 1971, 1975; Squire & Applebee, 1968). Although the emphases of the subject may vary, with a corresponding effect on student learning, they generally exist within a framework of content and behavior. In short, the literature curriculum consists of literary texts and information surrounding those texts, on the one hand, and various transactions related to reading the texts, talking about the reading, and writing about the reading, on the other. What texts? What information? What focus in the reading? What sort of talk? What sort of writing? These questions continue to mark controversy in the profession. The focus of this discussion will be on the secondary school curriculum. This is not meant to slight the central importance of literature in the elementary school; however, the issues surrounding literature and the language arts and initial reading instruction require separate consideration.

Teachers have traditionally limited the content of literature instruction to four areas: the literary works themselves, background information, literary terminology and theory, and cultural information. Some curricula have made a point of introducing a fifth area, the responses of the students (Cooper & Purves, 1973; Corcoran, Hayhoe, & Pradl, 1995; Langer, 1992; Tompkins, 1980), and taking such responses seriously have led others to argue for a reinterpretation of the work as content, because all that can be known is the work as it is perceived and responded to (Fish, 1980; Rosenblatt, 1994). In terms of behavior, the foci of the literature curriculum range from rote recognition and recall through higher level thinking operations of interpretation and evaluation to the affective categories of personal preferences and the exploration of values.

The shifts of emphasis along these continua depend on the purposes of the curriculum makers and their particular philosophic biases. In his review of European curricula, Van de Ven (1987) showed how the various influences of nationalism, scientism, pragmatism, and moralism have exerted themselves on the literature curriculum, and these influences have been parallel across national boundaries. His review strikingly resembled Applebee's (1974) depiction of the U.S. curriculum and the analysis of international curricula by Purves (1973b, 1975).

All these reviews suggest that literature instruction addresses in some manner three crucial dimensions: the skills of "reading" literary texts (response, analysis, and interpretation), the body of knowledge and the social and moral values to be acquired, and the personal evocations and development of the learner. This triad of concerns, of course, typifies all literacy education and represents at its core the taxonomy outlined by Dixon (1967) in his report of the Anglo-American Conference held at Dartmouth in 1966: skills, cultural heritage, and personal growth. Each dimension addresses a separate question for the learner, but despite efforts to the contrary, no question can ever be free of the other two, just as all imply the potential for further modification and development: What can I do? (acting), With whom do I belong? (knowing), and Who am I? (being). How a student ends up reading in the presence of any given literary work very much relates to the patterns of meaning making that are modeled in the literature classroom. This in turn will shift depending on what reading selections are approved and how connections to the ongoing life of the reader are either encouraged or discouraged. Thus, as with other areas of the curriculum, literature instruction moves either closer to or farther from the student in relation to both how the purposes of reading literature are construed and who does the construing.

Curriculum approaches that emphasize skills and/or cultural heritage make reading selections from the canon, either focusing on the author or on the ostensible moral and social content of the text. Their major behavioral focus is compliant knowledge acquisition and valuation, rather than independent response, analysis, and interpretation. "Flow," enjoyment, and celebration are in short supply when the learning of literature ignores what the individual brings to each reading transaction (Rosenblatt, 1995), and simply serves as an occasion for assessing one's ability to recall information and perform scripted academic routines (whether they be New Critical, psychoanalytic, Marxist, deconstructive, or feminist) dictated by the teacher.

Because literary texts are "open" representations of what it means to be human, no other school subject has the capacity for exposing and consequently interrogating the values and beliefs of the society. Given our pluralistic democracy, this often makes the literature classroom a hotly contested arena, one in which all sorts of groups across the political spectrum argue for their view of truth and proper conduct. In an analysis of censorship attempts between 1965 and 1985, Burress (1989) found close to 900 titles under attack, and Jenkinson (1986) estimated that there are at least 2,000 organizations at all levels that in some way are seeking the banning of school texts. The continuing debate on "cultural literacy," for example, serves to highlight the dilemmas faced by every teacher of literature, for it raises sharply the conflicting positions concerning texts and activities surrounding texts, and because, perhaps more than any other phenomenon, it has served to turn the attention of the profession away from language and composition and back toward the neglected field of literature. Furthermore, as "educational standards" proliferate across the country the choice of text has become as much the crux of the curricular issue in literature education as the particular approach to meaning making that is being encouraged.

## CULTURAL LITERACY

Although the current embroilments surrounding cultural literacy stem from the article and book by E. D. Hirsch, Jr. (1983, 1987) and the measure of cultural knowledge in the National Assessment initiated by Diane Ravitch and Chester Finn, Jr. (1987), the idea is far from new. The call for a precisely circumscribed curriculum goes back to the work of Eliot and Erskine in the early 20th century, the Lynch and Evans (1963) report on secondary literature in the late 1950s, and, more recently, to Mortimer Adler's (1982) Paideia proposal. The concept of "culture" goes back at least as far as Vico and Herder and may best be defined by Edward Said (1983) as all that an individual possesses and that possesses an individual. As Said wrote:

[C]ulture is used to designate not merely something to which one belongs but something that one possesses, and along with that proprietary process, culture also designates a boundary by which the concepts of what is extrinsic or intrinsic to the culture comes into forceful play. (pp. 8–9)

Anthropologists tend to see culture somewhat differently from literary people, but this root definition of possession and being possessed seems to apply both to those societies that operate through what might be called natural filiation (a system of intergenerational and familial relationships), and those that operate through affiliation to some arbitrarily instituted set of relationships. Current "American" culture is a culture of affiliation, whether it be the culture of Nathaniel Hawthorne and Harriet Beecher Stowe, the culture of African American Studies, the culture of feminism, or the culture of punk.

Any culture serves to isolate its members from other cultures and any culture is elitist in some senses, as Said (1983) pointed out:

What is more important in culture is that it is a system of values saturating downward almost everything within its purview; yet paradoxically culture dominates from above without at the same time being available to everything and everyone that it dominates. (p. 9)

Cultures are exclusionary by definition; ensconced in their own culture, people tend to see others as *outsiders* and often as existing *lower* on what we perceive as some "natural" hierarchy. Certainly very few people transcend cultures or are full members of more than one culture, although they may be members of several subcultures, such as the subculture of reader response researchers in the United States, which has its body of shared knowledge, its sets of allegiances to I. A. Richards, Louise Rosenblatt, and James Squire, and its tendency to exclude those who, even though very well educated in other respects, fail to share certain knowledge and beliefs. The members of this subculture may also be members of such other subcultures as that of mycologists, joggers, or heavy-metal enthusiasts as well as of the broader culture of literate Americans. As social beings, humans are always searching for those with whom they feel they can belong, even as they seem to exclude others to make their "belonging" that much more precious.

With cultural membership comes a significant amount of knowledge, much of it tacit, concerning the culture: its rules, rituals, mores, heroes, gods, and demigods. Such knowledge sanctions individuals entering certain realms of experience and possibility, even while it simultaneously constrains them from realizing others. Dressed correctly might get one into a trendy club, just as the wrong dialect might spell some social disaster. Individuals explicitly make use of this cultural knowledge, which lies at the heart of cultural literacy, when they read and respond to a piece of literature that originates from their own culture. It is such knowledge that, in fact, enables people to read that literature, and it includes semantic knowledge, knowledge of text structures and models, and pragmatic knowledge or knowledge as to how to act before, during, and after reading a particular text in a given situation (Purves, 1987). Humans are wholly dependent on these forms of knowledge when they read and write as social beings. Indeed, it is the lack of such knowledge that keeps people *outside*, as witness the traveler who often suffers trifling embarrassments or serious misunderstandings when visiting another culture.

# LITERATURE AND THE STRUGGLE
## FOR CULTURAL COHESION

Kádár-Fülop (1988) wrote that there are three major functions of the language curriculum in school. Basing her argument on a survey of curriculum goals in 15 countries, she found that these three functions accord with the earlier definitions of language functions proposed by Weinreich (1963). The first of these functions is the promotion of cultural communication (skills) so as to enable the individual to communicate with a wider circle than the home, the peers, or the village. Such a function clearly calls for the individual to learn the cultural norms of semantics, morphology, syntax, text structures, and pragmatics and some of the common metaphors and allusions particularly to folklore and legend as well as procedural routines so as to operate within those norms and be understood.

The second function is the promotion of cultural loyalty (cultural heritage) or the acceptance and valuing of those norms and the inculcation of a desire to have them remain. A culturally loyal literate would have certain expectations about how texts are to be written or to be read, as well as what they should look like, and would expect others in the culture to follow those same norms. Thus, it would offend, if not surprise, culturally literate Americans to hear someone call for the banning of *The Adventures of Huckleberry Finn*, though this might in turn commit them to the trials and tribulations of cultural pluralism. Finally, the third function of literacy education focuses on the development of individuality (personal growth); after one has learned to communicate within the culture and developed a loyalty to it, then one is able to responsibly express independence. For as Lev Vygotsky (1956) concluded: "In reality a child's thought progresses from the social to the individual not from the individual to the socialized" The creativity involved in "rule breaking" only makes sense, from this perspective, when one has shown adequate command of the rules in the first place.

When critics such as Hirsch speak of cultural literacy they are echoing Eliot, Adler, among others, by advocating the first two goals set forth by Kádár-Fülop (1988); they restrict the sense of the term to *their* literacy, which exists in a particular domain of high culture, such as F. R. Leavis "Great Tradition" in the English novel or that aspect of general education that is defined as "the humanities" or "American classics." From this tautological perspective cultural literacy is viewed as the "common" denominator that enables readers to read certain kinds of texts—notably texts that are shared by their group as defining "highly literate Americans." These would be people, for example, who read *The New York Times* with understanding and also frequent journals and books such as *The Atlantic Monthly* or Katherine Paterson's *Jacob Have I Loved* (1990).

The chief argument for this standard of cultural literacy was earlier used to support the Chicago Great Books Program, Harvard's General Education proposal, and Columbia's humanities program: Such literacy brings together a disparate immigrant population and helps the melting pot do its job (Bell, 1966). Such proposals carried forward the reasoning of critics from Arnold to Leavis and Eliot that a common culture, namely the Judeo-Christian tradition, forged society into unity through affiliation—yet not without cost, as Said (1983) pointed out:

When our students are taught such things as "the humanities" they are almost always taught that these classic texts embody, express, represent what is best in our, that is, the only, tradition. Moreover, they are taught that such fields as the humanities and such subfields as "literature" exist in a relatively neutral political element, that they are to be appreciated and venerated, that they define the limits of what is acceptable, appropriate, and legitimate as far as culture is concerned. (p. 21)

Other critics such as Eagleton (1996) and Tompkins (1980) concluded that Arnold's conservative polemics for literary culture ended with literature forming a secular religion, with the study of literature parallelling seminary training. To a great extent, Arnold's project has simply been recast by such writers as Randall Jarrell in the 1950s or by William Bennett (1983), whose dogmatic tracts scorn any attempt to broaden the canon.

A corollary to this argument (Hirsch, 1987; Ravitch & Finn, 1987) appears in a more pragmatic political form: A mobile school population needs stability for common communication and the schools can best provide this stability through the choosing of common texts. The literature curriculum apparently witnessed this stability only in the eleventh grade where traditionally American literature has been taught, though even here few common threads might be secured. This desire for some certainty of reference and experience beyond a modern tower of Babel is not easily discredited; however, who selects the unifying texts remains an insurmountable political issue. Still, a prior question exists: how did the idea of a cultural heritage come to disappear in our educational system? Why should Hirsch and associates have come to decry the lack of a cultural center?

During the middle third of the century, a number of groups coalesced to drive literature, and the notion of cultural literacy, from its former central position in the curriculum. These groups existed not just in the United States but in most of the European nations as well (Ball, 1984). The first is the group that advocated comprehensive secondary schools, the second promoted the dominance of a linguistic and cognitive perspective, the third is the functionalists, and the fourth includes literature teachers themselves. The sources for these arguments are many and diverse, but they constitute much of the theme of such documents as those of the Anglo-American conference (Dixon, 1967), the writing surrounding the student-centered curriculum of James Moffett (1968), the various articles and editorial stands in *The English Journal* beginning at the end of the 1960s and such books as the 1973 edition of *How Porcupines Make Love* (Purves, 1973a). Additionally, these forces had the curious side effect of drawing the attention of researchers, curriculum makers, and teacher educators away from literature and toward language and composition.

The arguments of these groups against teaching a cultural heritage with a unified canon can be enumerated as follows:

1. With increasingly diverse groups passing through our comprehensive secondary school system, it is imperative to attend more directly to their cultural needs. The current canon

does not address these minority groups and it certainly does not address the concerns of women. This claim also acknowledged the world as multi-cultural and the need of students to learn a smattering about all cultures. A traditional cultural heritage strand appears to run counter to such concerns.

2. A mother-tongue education should be dominated by language study and the appropriate teaching of the functional and workplace uses of language, whether the focus is on a skills approach or on fostering the personal growth of the individual student; thus there is no time for the deliberate study of literature as such.

3. Many of the canonical works are simply too difficult for the "new" students and beyond their range of experience. Rather than bowdlerize them or present them in film, we should turn to the kinds of works that students can read, particularly adolescent and popular fiction. The curriculum in literature should echo Henry Ford's "History is bunk," and turn to immediate relevance as the only criterion for text selection. (Purves, 1973a)

The proponents of "cultural literacy," who advocate our need for unification within a diverse nation through the study of "common" cultural texts and information, have not addressed such counterarguments, some of which are dubious at best. Still, the argument is not *whether* cultural literacy, for all literature curricula imply some body of works that constitute a de facto canon and thus serve to acculturate youth as does television and other nonschool phenomena. The argument continues to be, *What* should serve to define the operable culture or cultures of our society and *who* then will be responsible for the choices of texts to be read in our schools? (Guillory, 1993). Whatever the temporary "solutions," it appears that those who have raised the "cultural literacy" issue have forced a whole generation of critics and educational researchers and planners to reconsider the importance of literature in the curriculum.

## CULTURAL LITERACY AND READING

Although the continuing "cultural literacy" debate often appears locked in the struggle of whose texts and facts will predominate, Hirsch also supported his view with current research in reading, which has demonstrated that prior knowledge is a key factor in reading comprehension. Most of that research has looked at substantive knowledge of the material in the text, such as knowledge about automobiles with reference to a text concerning automobiles. It has not dealt with more literary or metaphorical schemata. This argument begins with the assertion that texts within a culture, particularly literary texts, build on each other, so that contemporary texts employ a complex web of allusion or metaphor building upon previous texts. Such metaphors control how writers think about their material, and writers trade on the cumulative nature of literary texts as well as commentaries on texts. Katherine Paterson's *Jacob Have I Loved* alluded to the biblical story of Jacob and Esau, as she pointed out directly by quotation. But she also relies on the reader's knowing something of the whole story of Jacob and Esau and the foundation of the tribes of Israel. The use of allusion was one of the bases of the

Nebraska Curriculum of the 1960s (Olson, 1967, 1968). Most other contemporary novels, poems, and plays, not to mention cartoons and comic strips, build on other works in even more subtle ways.

Consider a typical piece in *The New York Times*:

Thirteen hundred years ago in Japan, three slender documents—letters? shopping lists? birth certificates?—were placed in a thin box which was then wrapped in brocade.

Over the centuries the box was put in three larger boxes each one of which was wrapped in cloth.

In 1660 the letter box was placed in yet another box and adorned with a covering note. Don't open this, it read, unless you don't mind being tossed out of the Horyuji, a temple in Nara containing the country's oldest Buddhist compound. Eight-five years later the fourth box was put into a fifth, and the warning was repeated.

This week art scholars who had found the package on the temple grounds opened the fifth, fourth, third, second and first boxes. But did they open the final box? Not on your life. Hadn't the letters said that was a no-no? Instead they X-rayed it, which is how the world knows that it holds three documents.

That, then, is all the world will ever know about that box—and all it needs to know. In putting Pandora to shame, the Japanese have turned what may be three ordinary missives into three extraordinary mysteries. ("Pandora Shamed," 1985)

Aside from the fact that the article dealt with a somewhat exotic topic, it is unexceptional to many readers. However, it used an allusion to Pandora and failed to provide any context to help the reader determine who Pandora is and why this action of Japanese scholars might put her (or possibly him or it) to shame. In articles on various topics, the pages of *The New York Times* frequently contain this sort of allusion to Greek and Old Testament mythology. The writers have a set of expectations about their readers, and the set clearly differs from that held by the editors of *People* or *Field and Stream*.

A study conducted by Broudy (1982) shed light on what he referred to as the uses of learning. Using several passages from *The New York Times*, as well as a poem, he asked 1st-year graduate students to read them, commenting as they read. Broudy selected students on the basis of their backgrounds, including an artist; a dancer; and a student each in the humanities, engineering, law, business, social studies, and physical sciences. The results showed that some of the students had trouble with passages like "Pandora Shamed"; they did not know how to respond and so shut themselves off from it, primarily because they did not have the specific piece of information that allowed them to understand the passage. In some cases the allusion was to mythology; in other cases it was to "general knowledge" from science, the arts, economics, or history.

Given the reading dynamics that Broudy documented, it is not surprising that writers of all sorts presume a certain fund of knowledge on the part of their prospective readers and that writers for a publication like *The New York Times* presume a level of general knowledge similar to that possessed by someone who has had an undergraduate program in general education—say, two semesters each in the humanities, the social sciences, and the natural sciences. In short, the editors assume, as does a critic like Hirsch, that their readers are culturally literate to the level of Mortimer Adler's Great Books. Such an assumption may be elitist—it may be seen as opposed to the liberation literacy of a Jonathan Kozol or a Richard Ohmann (both of whom possess exactly the sort of cultural literacy they decry, which makes it easy for them to decry it)—but it is simply a fact of the world of media in current times. *The New York Times* assumes a lesser body of knowledge than did Anne Bradstreet or Margaret Fuller, Edith Wharton or Emma Goldman, but it assumes more than is covered in the curriculum of many elementary and secondary schools in this country.

Broudy's four "uses of learning" (replicative, applicative, interpretive, and associative) provided one way of mapping the complexity of the activities and tasks that constitute the teaching of literature in secondary schools. The replicative and applicative uses are those he found to be most frequently addressed: that is, students are to give back what they learn or apply it directly to a new situation. The interpretive use, where the individual at some later point takes what has been learned in order to come to an understanding of a phenomenon that may or may not be directly related to the item learned, can be seen in the ways by which a reader is expected to use knowledge about the legend of Pandora in construing the brief article or the knowledge about Jacob and Esau in construing Paterson's novel. The associative use of learning occurs when something in the new phenomenon elicits an indirect connection with an item previously learned. This sort of learning is displayed in reading and response to literature, when a reader makes a connection between Shakespeare's story of *Hamlet* and Homer's *Oedipus Rex*. No explicit connection exists, but for a reader steeped in Greek drama, the implicit connections appear present.

The dividing line between explicit and implicit connections among texts is not a clear one. Some poets, such as Keats, Shelley, or T. S. Eliot, use a great deal of overt allusion to various earlier literatures, and in the case of the first two appear to have expected their readers to share the world of allusion, while the last often provided appropriate glosses, something that Ezra Pound did not. A writer like Faulkner tends to be somewhat less explicit in his use of allusion in a story such as "The Bear," (1942) and one like Carl Sandburg appears to have virtually no explicit literary allusions, so each reader infers whatever connections are adduced. Thus, there seems to be a continuum of texts based on their apparent dependency on prior texts and therefore the amount of shared cultural knowledge assumed by the writer. This dimension differs from the dimension of topicality, which distinguishes a writer like Swift, who continually referred to events of his day, from a writer like Emily Brontë, who, if not otherworldly, created a self-contained world outside of history.

Broudy's study, with its focus on prior knowledge, goes directly to the imaginative recreation that might be initiated in "open" acts of reading literature. Given the various sorts of allusions contained in texts, successful reading will be marked by a reader's ability to interconnect accumulating knowledge and experience, often in unpredictable ways. The reading transaction (Rosenblatt, 1994), in other words, never occurs in a vacuum; student readers are continually filling in gaps, moving from the given to the new, just as readers are expected to know the referents of metaphoric language as in a phrase such as "I stretched thy joints to make thee even feet, / Yet still thou run'st more hobbling than is meet." However, as Broudy confirmed, when readers find they haven't that knowledge, they "stop" reading or responding to the text. Thus, the challenge for the literature teacher, both in terms of content and process, is to find ways to encourage students to continue their reading journeys and conversations. How can students be helped to remain "hooked on books" and so accumulate the "information" that makes each subsequent reading encounter that much richer? Heeding the "interconnection" imperative, effective literature teachers do not consider works in isolation, but are forever concerned with chains, patterns, and sequences. This in turn will occasion varying combinations of pleasure and discipline—a major difficulty being to remember that the reading experience will not be the same for every student.

## STALKING THE ILLUSORY CANON

The various efforts to codify and enforce educational standards, whether at the state or national level, have often included lists of recommended literature readings. These lists, however, are eclectic at best and certainly in no way ensure that all students will have access to the common literary culture that the likes of Hirsch, Bennett, and Cheney have in mind. New York City's *Performance Standards* (Rizzo, 1997), for instance, stated that students should read at least 25 books each year, while including titles of 32 novels ranging from academic "classics" such as *The Scarlet Letter, For Whom the Bell Tolls, The Invisible Man*, and *1984* to the tried-and-true school novels *A Separate Peace* and *To Kill a Mocking Bird*. There is no rhyme or reason here except a good will attempt to be fair and representative. Thus, we find *The Bluest Eye, Down These Mean Streets*, and *Black Elk Speaks* alongside *Alice's Adventures in Wonderland*. Also, *El Bronx Remembered, The Joy Luck Club*, and *Woman Warrior*. One can of course compile any number of equally circumspect lists, but with completely different titles included. This suggests that such top-down efforts to influence what texts are actually read in high school English classrooms will continue to have little effect.

Nationally, it is difficult to determine finally what works are actually taught to how many students where. Educators do not know whether there is an adolescent literature canon, an anthology canon, or a Harlequin romance canon in the schools of the United States. Applebee's (1989) replication of a study completed 20 years earlier (Anderson, 1964) showed little change. Based on a questionnaire sent to several hundred secondary schools, it showed that the list of most frequently taught long works continues to be headed by Shakespeare; the only woman to make the top 10 is Harper Lee. No African Americans or other minorities are among the most read authors. This study only included "full-length works"—short stories, short plays, and poems were not mentioned. The schools say they are teaching the classics and have not admitted a multicultural and double-gendered culture, but one is unsure whether they have omitted the more popular works such as adolescent or young-adult fiction, because they do not "teach" it or because this appears more frequently in "reading programs."

Curriculua also appear dominated by anthologies, which thus can lay claims to being a more formidable influence than the College Entrance Examination Board or other educational governing organizations. The publishers who put together these collections, including those trade or reprint houses that cater to the schools and school libraries, seek in different ways to create a canon or canons so as to sell their merchandise. One group works at "watering down" the classics with bowdlerized versions, which raises the question as to whether these watered-down versions considered appropriate for high school students or nonreaders can provide the same experience as the original no matter how difficult. There have also been some attempts by publishers to make the classics available without watering them down; the most notable example is the series of "comic book" versions of Shakespeare done by distinguished British illustrators and using the uncut Quarto texts without footnotes.

Another group within publishing, abetted by such authors' lobbies as the Children's Book Council and the Adolescent Literature Assembly, touted the latest trade book and the latest writer and had virtually no interest in any culture but the culture of the present. This group helped expand the market for the adolescent novel in school classes as well as out of them and worked to have what was essentially spare-time reading incorporated into the new canon. Even *A Catcher in the Rye* is old hat to the adolescent literature lobby and who would want to read *The Adventures of Tom Sawyer*? Stocking the bookstores and school libraries does not provide sufficient sales, particulary when library budgets have to include computer software. The classroom book budget thus becomes a useful source of income.

This group vies with the anthology publishers, often from the text division of the same house. The latter are more than willing to have the older writers in their texts because, being dead, they do not request reprint fees. They are also less controversial than the living writers, and the publishers need to appeal to the large adoption states which attract the most censors. Anthologies are good moneymakers particularly if they seldom have authors who receive royalties. Even a cursory glance at current anthologies leads one to conclude see that the presence of contemporary literature and literature by minorities and women is hardly on the upswing.

## LITERATURE LEARNING: A PROCESS LEADING TO UNDERSTANDING

The domain of school literature is usually seen as one of the four language arts: reading, writing, speaking, and listening. Because literature involves text that people read or write, and because students often write about the literature they have read, literature is often seen as simply a subset of reading and writing, with an occasional nod to speaking and listening. However, those who take literature seriously as a way of thinking and knowing separate from the discursive parts of the curriculum (Langer, 1998) are uneasy with this subordinate status. They become more uneasy when they look at the world of tests and see that literature is simply a vehicle for measuring reading comprehension or writing proficiency. There must be something more than recall and recognition, for literature uses allusion and builds on itself at a "deeper" level than simply that of naming. Robbin's *West Side Story*, for example, is a complex retelling of Shakespeare's *Romeo and Juliet* and requires a knowledge not simply of names, but of character relationships, scenes, and images. To define the literature curriculum as merely a subset of reading and writing neglects a number of the acts that go on within the activity of a vital literature education.

Some would define literature as a school subject that has its own body of knowledge. Initially, this includes the information associated with a particular set of texts: authors, characters, plots, and themes. From there it expands to critical terms like metaphor and simile as well as genres, schools or styles of writing, and whole critical approaches. Others emphasize the uniqueness of literature according to *how* it is read. Rosenblatt (1994) called this kind of reading "aesthetic," as opposed to "efferent" reading, what one does with informational texts such as those of social studies and science. Britton (1982) labeled it "poetic," or the use of language in the *spectator* role, and contrasted it to our pragmatic uses of language in the *participant* role. From this perspective, literature education involves the development of what one might call preferences or imaginative judgments, which is to say habits of mind in reading and writing. In addition, literature education is intended to foster something called "taste" or appreciation (which most literature teachers hope will lead to the love of "good literature"). Thus, literature education goes well beyond the mechanics of reading and writing by inculcating specific habits of reading and patterns of critical response and valuation.

It is also important to recognize that the category "literature" itself remains in dispute, for its meaning has shifted over the past 200 years (Williams, 1985). Currently, it appears straightforward to fit poetry, drama, and fiction under its domain. However, even this last term sparks quarrels about the distinction between fiction and nonfiction, as genres evolve and all dogmatic theories purporting to set the boundaries of fantasy, reality, and history become less convincing. Similarly, the essay with its unique tradition of combining "fact" and "opinion" might be included under literature. Once the door is ajar, however, advocates of "critical literacy," who attack any privileged status for so-called literary artifacts, would widen the subject literature to include a range of cultural studies and thus not limit any text from potential examination in the English classroom (Eagleton, 1996).

Despite its contested nature, dividing the domain of school literature into three aspects—practice, knowledge/understanding, and preference—encourages educators to appreciate the complex interrelationships among them: Educators use and explore knowledge in the various acts that constitute their practice and preferences, and their practices and preferences serve to shape and extend our understanding of literature. At the same time one can separate them for the purposes of curriculum planning and assessment. These three subdomains may be schematized, as shown in Table 62.1, and each may be associated with its corollary dimension of each student's literary quest: What can I do? With whom do I belong? Who am I?

Unfortunately, as a comprehensive study by Brody, DeMilo, and Purves (1989) demonstrated, the current tests of literature available through the anthology series and the proprietary testing companies treat literature as little more than fodder for reading scores. Even the university entrance groups (except for the Advanced Placement Examination of the College Entrance

TABLE 62.1. School Literature

| Practice (What Can I Do?) | | Knowledge/Understanding (With Whom Do I Belong?) | | Preference (Who Am I?) | |
|---|---|---|---|---|---|
| Reading | Writing | Textual | Extratextual | Aesthetic | Habits |
| Decoding Envisioning | Retelling Criticizing single works | Specific text Cultural allusion | History Author | Evaluating Selecting | Reading Criticizing |
| Analyzing Personalizing | Generalizing across works | | Genre Styles | Valuing | |
| Interpreting | | | Critical Terms | | |

Examination Board) neglect the aesthetic dimension entirely. Literature testing thus appears to construe cultural literacy as knowledge of particulars and vocabulary in the style of a reading test. Knowledge of the canon is measured as superficial, trivial pursuit knowledge if at all. There is relatively little application or interpretation. Only where there are writing measures attached to the objective tests does there seem to be any tapping of generalizing or interpreting and occasionally evaluating.

This dismal picture of literature assessment contrasts starkly with the important investigations carried out by the National Research Center on Literature Teaching and Learning during its 8 years of funding beginning in 1987. Through their extensive case studies of individual literature classrooms, these researchers decisively established:

[L]iterature is a discipline like mathematics and science. It has a content to be learned but also a way of reasoning underlying it. It involves a way of thinking about things and solving problems that is useful not only in the understanding of literature but also in academic learning and daily living—when we are engaged in discourse with others and when we are thinking alone. Although literary reasoning is both creative and imaginative, it is also highly intellectual in a particular kind of way. (Langer, 1995, p. 158)

Clearly teachers are capable of moving literature learning beyond the narrow confines of transmitted information when they construe it as an opportunity for provoking thoughts rather than giving answers. By employing complete texts rather than anthologized fragments, by working through multiple perspectives and encouraging what (Langer) called "envisionment" or "horizons-of-possibilities thinking" (p. ), the literature classroom offers students a significant "contact zone" (Pratt, 1991). Here students might engage conflicting views of reality and explore the consequences of alternative value systems, even while experiencing the trust of a safe haven.

In those instances when literature teaching/learning broke through to "envisionment," Langer (1995) found four crucial principles to be operating. First, there is respect, continuity, and stability: Students are treated as lifelong envisionment builders. Second, the excitement of solving open-ended problems animates the social space: Questions are treated as part of the literary experience. Third, discussions are reciprocal and dynamic, providing a space to work through possible meanings: Class meetings are a time to develop understandings (which

are fluid and changing). Fourth, the literary quest is never for a single or final conclusion: Multiple perspectives are used to enrich interpretation (pp. 57–59). By convening rich social processes of reading, the literature classroom can be a spellbinding place where aesthetic response and puzzlement provide a way to deepen human insight and understanding.

## LITERATURE TEACHING AS A MIRROR ON SOCIETY

Regardless of what lens is finally used to view the school subject literature, two last considerations must not be overlooked. First, we must realize that *the teaching of literature is always embedded in a particular social system*, in our case democracy (Pradl, 1991, 1996). The social relationships within which literature is read inevitably inform teachers' practices. Desiring these relationships to be democratic commits educators to shaping conversational encounters in the classroom, not extended monologues. In an extensive study of classroom talk in 112 eighth- and ninth-grade English classes, Nystrand (1997) documented that students learn literature best when they are engaged in free response and dialogue. Through the use of "dialogism," literature teachers, as Nystrand showed, can encourage a rich, holistic context that serves as a way for students to connect to and make sense of literary texts.

By focusing on overarching correspondences rather than addressing the sea of fragmented trivia that confronts students in classrooms that are typically teacher centered, a democratic teacher brings reading into the realm of the authentic. Also, as Langer's (1998) research confirmed, knowledge of literature is not neglected when student understanding is of primary concern; instead, "literary concepts and language become part of the fabric of ongoing thought and communication" (p. 21). When teachers ensure that all students have the right to their own reading responses as part of a continuing social conversation, they help keep the democratic experience alive. What matters most about the reading of literature in a democracy is not *what* the text actually means, because this is a constantly fleeing chimera. Instead, the emphasis must be on *how*, together, teacher and student go about making it mean whatever it does. Inadequate meanings might be winnowed out when each individual a say in relation to the other.

Second, teachers must refuse to oversimplify *the profoundly paradoxical nature of teaching what in the end are value driven and indeterminate texts*. As Hynds' (1997) research confirmed, teachers own reading and learning styles affect their teaching, but often teachers are unaware of how their prejudices come into play, of how the literature lesson is often about struggles over control and authority. Although it may be easy to acknowledge the openness of any given work of literature, it is far more difficult to let go of being the expert, to risk not knowing the answer and thus reveal vulnerability and inadequacy.

Still, in the attempt to model democratic relationships, educators must listen attentively to the contradictions and confusions embedded in adolescent student questioning and not deny the many ways such questioning may correspond to that of the educators themselves. Even as students seek answers to what they *can do*, with whom they *belong*, and, ultimately, who they *are*, literature teachers must try to keep their perspectives permeable and charged with possibility. When teachers and curriculum makers take seriously the complex, and often perplexing, social roles embedded in the collaborative negotiation of knowledge and understanding that can take place in the literature classroom, they become witnesses for the importance to a democracy of sharing and learning from each other's interpretations. In this way, students add confidence to their developing competence as aesthetic readers of the world. Because of these efforts to fuel a renewed interest in the school subject literature, the profession of English teaching has an important dynamic and standard to offer educational policymakers in the classroom and at the state and national levels.

## References

Adler, M. (1982). *The Paideia proposal*. New York: Macmillan.

Anderson, S. (1964). *From the Grimms to the group*. Princeton, NJ: Educational Testing Service.

Applebee, A. (1974). *Tradition and reform in the teaching of English: A history*. Urbana, IL: National Council of Teachers of English.

Applebee, A. (1989). *A study of book-length works taught in high school English courses* (Report 1.2). Albany, NY: Center for the Learning and Teaching of Literature.

Ball, S. (1984). Conflict, panic and inertia: Mother tongue teaching in England 1970-1983. In W. Herrlitz, A. Kamer, S. Kroon, H. Peters, & J. Sturm (Eds.), *Mother tongue education in Europe: A survey of standard language teaching in nine European countries*. Enschede, The Netherlands: International Mother Tongue Education Network.

Beach, R., & Marshall, J. (1991). *Teaching literature in the secondary school*. New York: Harcourt Brace Jovanovich.

Bell, D. (1966). *The reforming of general education*. New York: Columbia University Press.

Bennett, W. (1983). *To reclaim a legacy*. Washington, DC: U.S. Government Printing Office.

Britton, J. (1982). Spectator role and the beginnings of writing. In G. Pradl (Ed.), *Prospect and retrospect: Selected essays of James Britton* (pp. 46-67). Portsmouth, NH: Boynton/Cook.

Brody, P., DeMilo, C., & Purves, A. (1989). *The current state of assessment in literature* (Report 3.1). Albany, NY: Center for the Learning and Teaching of Literature.

Broudy, H. (1982). *Report: On case studies on uses of knowledge*. Chicago: Spencer Foundation (ERIC Documents Reproduction Service No. ED 224016).

Burress, L. (1989). *Battle of the books: Literary censorship in the public schools, 1950-1985*. Metuchen, NJ: Scarecrow Press.

Burton, D. (1964). *Literature study in the high schools*. New York: Holt, Rinehart & Winston.

Cooper, C., & Purves, A. (1973). *Responding: Guide to evaluation*. Lexington, MA: Ginn.

Corcoran, B., Hayhoe, M., & Pradl, G. (Eds.) (1995). *Knowledge in the making: Challenging the text in the classroom*. Portsmouth, NH: Boynton/Cook Heinemann.

Dixon, J. (1967). *Growth through English*. Oxford, England: Oxford University Press.

Eagleton, T. (1996). *Literary theory: An introduction* (2nd ed.). Minneapolis: University of Minnesota Press.

Fish, S. (1980). *Is there a text in this class? The authority of interpretation communities*. Cambridge, MA: Harvard University Press.

Guillory, J. (1993). *Cultural capital: The problem of literary canon formation*. Chicago: University of Chicago Press.

Hirsch, E., Jr. (1983). Cultural literacy. *The American Scholar,* 159-169.

Hirsch, E., Jr. (1987). *Cultural literacy*. Boston: Houghton Mifflin.

Hynds, S. (1997). *On the brink: Negotiating literature and life with adolescents*. New York: Teachers College Press.

Jenkinson, E. (1986). *The schoolbook protest movement: 40 questions and answers*. Bloomington, IN: Phi Delta Kappa Educational Foundation.

Kádár-Fülop, J. (1988). Culture, writing, curriculum. In A. Purves (Ed.), *Writing across languages and cultures: Issues in contrastive rhetoric* (pp. 25-30). Newbury Park, CA: Sage, 25-50.

Langer, J. (Ed.) (1992). *Literature instruction: A focus on student response*. Urbana, IL: National Council of Teachers of English.

Langer, J. (1995). *Envisioning literature: Literary understanding and literature instruction*. New York: Teachers College Press.

Langer, J. (1998). Thinking and doing literature: An eight-year study. *English Journal, 87*(2), 16-23.

Lynch, J., & Evans, B. (1963). *High-school English textbooks: A critical examination*. Boston: Little, Brown.

Moffett, J. (1968). *Teaching the universe of discourse: A theory of discourse—A rationale for English teaching used in a student-centered language arts curriculum*. Boston: Houghton Mifflin.

Nystrand, M. (1997). *Opening dialogue: Understanding the dynamics of language and learning in the English classroom*. New York: Teachers College Press.

Olson, P. (1967). *A curriculum study center in English*. Lincoln: University of Nebraska.

Olson, P. (Ed.) (1968). *The uses of myth; papers relating to the Anglo-American seminar on the teaching of English at Dartmouth College, New Hampshire, 1966*. Urbana, IL: National Council of Teachers of English.

"Pandora Shamed." ( 1985, November 7). *The New York Times*, p. 25.

Pradl, G. (1991). Reading literature in a democracy: The challenge of Louise Rosenblatt. In J. Clifford (Ed.), *The experience of reading: Lousie Rosenblatt and reader-response theory* (pp. 23-46). Portsmouth, NH: Boynton/Cook.

Pradl, G. (1996). *Literature for democracy*. Portsmouth, NH: Boynton/Cook Heinemann.

Pratt, M. (1991). Arts of the contact zone. *Profession 91* (pp. 33–40). New York: Modern Language Association.

Purves, A. (1971). Evaluation of learning in literature. In B. Bloom, J. Hastings, & G. Madaus (Eds.), *Handbook of formative and summative evaluation of student learning*. New York: McGraw-Hill.

Purves, A. (1973a). *How porcupines make live*. Lexington, MA: Xerox College Publishing.

Purves, A. (1973b). *Literature education in ten countries: An empirical study: International studies in evaluation*. Stockholm: Almqvist & Wiksell.

Purves, A. (1975). Culture and deep structure in the literature curriculum. *Curriculum Theory Network, 2,* 139–150.

Purves, A. (1987). Literacy, culture and community. In D. Wagner (Ed.), *The future of literacy in a changing world* (pp. 216–232). Oxford, England: Pergamon Press.

Ravitch, D., & Finn, C., Jr. (1987). *What seventeen-year-olds know*. Boston: Houghton Mifflin.

Rizzo, J. (1997). *Performance standards: English language arts, English as a second language, Spanish language arts*. New York: Board of Education of the City of New York.

Rosenblatt, L. (1994). *The reader the text the poem: The transactional theory of the literary work*. Carbondale: Southern Illinois University Press.

Rosenblatt, L. (1995). *Literature as exploration* (5th ed.). New York: Modern Language Association.

Said, E. (1983). *The world, the text and the critic*. Cambridge, MA: Harvard University Press.

Squire, J., & Applebee, R. (1968). *High-school English instruction today*. New York: Appleton-Century Crofts.

Tompkins, J. (Ed.) (1980). *Reader response criticism: From formalism to post-structuralism*. Baltimore, MD: Johns Hopkins University Press.

Van de Ven, P. (1987). Some histories of mother tongue teaching in western Europe. *Mother Tongue Education Bulletin, 2,* 40–49.

Vygotsky, L. (1956). *Izbrannye psikhologicheskie isseldovaniia*. Moscow: RSFR Academy of Pedagogical Sciences.

Weinreich, U. (1963). *Languages in contact: Findings and problems*. The Hague, Netherlands: Mouton.

Williams, R. (1985). *Keywords: A vocabulary of culture and society* (rev. ed.). Oxford, England: Oxford University Press.

# ·63·

# MOTIVATING LIFELONG VOLUNTARY READERS

*Lesley Mandel Morrow*
*Rutgers University*

We must reignite our romance with the written word.
—Spielberg, 1987

Because a thoroughly democratic society depends on the cultivation and practice of literacy, the promotion of voluntary reading among children should rank high as a goal of parents and teachers. Both at home and in school, voluntary reading should be cultivated as a habit of personal choice beginning in a child's very earliest years. Through voluntary reading, children learn to associate reading with pleasure, especially while they are very young. If youngsters enjoy looking at books, then eventually reading them, they will tend to read more, which in turn can lead to improved reading ability. Voluntary, recreational independent reading must be an integral part of the total developmental reading program.

In this chapter, the terms *voluntary reading, recreational reading,* and *independent reading* are used to connote children's own decisions to spend portions of their time in reading or participating in reading-related activities, including listening to stories and looking at books in and out of school. The practice includes voluntary reading of newspapers, magazines, pamphlets, and brochures; listening to taped stories; and reading directions and other informational literature.

The problem of illiteracy in the United States has been a major concern. There are different estimates concerning the number of illiterate U.S. adults. The typical estimate seems to be that about one in five adults cannot read well enough to carry on activities that involve reading in their personal and working lives effectively. This accounts for about 20% of the population (Woiwode, 1992).

Although these statistics are staggering, they reflect only part of the problem. In a 1984 report to Congress entitled *Books in our Future*, Daniel Boorstin, Librarian of Congress, warned that *alliterates*—individuals who can read but choose not to do so—constitute a threat at least equal to that of *illiterates* in a democratic tradition built on books and reading. The practice or absence of voluntary reading, he wrote, "will determine the extent of self-improvement and enlightenment, the ability to share wisdom and the delights of our civilization, and our capacity for intelligent self-government" (p. iv). It is difficult to secure figures on the numbers of alliterates in the United States; however through surveys it has been found that about 20% of the adults who are able to read do so voluntarily on a regular basis. This means that of the four out of five Americans who can read only one chooses to do so for pleasure or for information. Other surveys have indicated that after Americans finish school about 60% never read a single book all the way through, and the rest read about one book a year (Woiwode, 1992).

Teaching people to read is certainly the most prevalent goal of American schooling. It is all but impossible to identify a goal more basic or more traditional. The same attention paid to create strategies for developing the ability to read should be given to developing voluntary readers, youngsters who will choose to read widely and often on their own.

History attests to the tremendous impact that common literacy has had on the development of societies and civilization. As early as 1647, American dedication to literacy was established in a belief that ability to read was necessary not only to a well-ordered society but to the moral welfare of the individual as well. That was the year the General Court of Massachusetts enacted legislation mandating universal reading instruction so

[t]hat learning might not be buried in the grave of our fathers in church and commonwealth.... It is therefore ordered that every township in this jurisdiction, after the Lord hath increased them to the number of fifty householders, shall then forthwith appoint one within their town to teach all such children as shall resort to him to write and read (E. W. Clews, as cited in N. B. Smith, 1934).

Little more than a century later, Thomas Jefferson spelled out three fundamental beliefs about literacy and education that remain fundamental in our national ethos. First, democratic functioning depends on every citizen's ability to read. Second, because of that fact, it is the general public's responsibility to support the teaching of reading to all youngsters. Third, reading should be taught during the earliest years of schooling. Among the reasons he cited, "[N]one is more important, none more legitimate, than that of rendering the people safe, as they are the ultimate guardians of their own liberty" (Koch & Peden, 1944).

Nineteenth-century America not only accepted those fundamental beliefs but also extended them into everyday practicality. Anyone who was to tame the wilderness, work the soil, and later fuel the factories of industrial society needed certain reading and writing skills to do so. In this present age of audio and video technology of all kinds, it is pervasive and clear that a democratic and productive society depends on citizens who can and do read.

The purpose of this chapter is to review the professional literature about motivating voluntary readers and to provide a statement of its significance and a rationale for its greater role in the reading instructional program, including research that describes successful programs in promoting voluntary reading. It is interesting to note that since the publication of an earlier version of this chapter (Morrow, 1991), the pendulum concerning literacy instruction has swung from the right to the left and now back to the right again. This chapter was first written, during the end of an era that placed great emphasis on explicit instruction of skills without much concern for creating motivated voluntary readers. Since that time, educators embraced the "Whole Language" philosophy, which put a great deal of emphasis on independent reading and strategies that emphasized the joy and motivation of reading. At this particular time, politicians and policymakers are suggesting the need to move back to the more explicit type of instruction and that issues of voluntary reading and motivation for wanting to read are not a major concern. The approach being advocated defines reading instruction almost entirely as an array of psychological and linguistic skills and subskills with infrequent use of literary activities that include immersion in stories and time for self-selected reading. Children would be taught to read but not to develop the habit of reading. On the occasions when literacy activities were introduced into the classroom, they would be considered supplementary or classroom extras rather than keys to the development of total readers or voluntary readers. Ironically, if schools spend a great deal of time teaching skills, then leave little room for children to practice those skills (Holdaway, 1979), it would not be surprising that substantial numbers of children choose not to read for pleasure or for information on their own. If schools evaluate their reading programs by "successful" scores on standardized reading tests only, and do not include personal reading habits of their students and their application of reading skills to personal use and benefit, children may be taught to read but not to develop the habit of reading (Irving, 1980; Speigel, 1981).

It would be unfortunate if we moved into another either–or era, that is, a period of total emphasis on explicit skill instruction or of a total constructivist approach to learning to read. There is a balance that can bring together instructional programs that can accommodate all issues surrounding the complexity of literacy development and creating a complete reader. In classrooms that utilize a balanced perspective in literacy instruction, skill development is taught explicitly and in the context of authentic literature, and literature immersion experiences exist as well. There is transmission and constructivism. On one hand, the explicit teaching of skills is a good start for constructivist activities and thinking; on the other, the constructivist activities permit consolidation and elaboration of skills and thought (Pressley, Rankin, & Yokoi, 1996).

Due to the changes in the climate in the country from one decade to the next, this chapter takes a historical, current, and thoughtful view concerning motivating voluntary reading as an integral part of reading instruction. In the review, the following areas are addressed: (a) the extent of voluntary reading, (b) benefits associated with motivating voluntary reading, (c) characteristics of motivated voluntary readers and their homes, (d) a theoretical framework for promoting voluntary reading at school, (e) strategies for promoting motivated voluntary readers in school, (f) use of literature to promote voluntary reading, and (g) the role of the classroom environment in promoting voluntary reading.

## THE EXTENT OF VOLUNTARY READING

Unfortunately, it is clear that substantial numbers of children and adults read neither for pleasure nor for information. Studies by Morrow and Weinstein (1982), for example, observed that few primary grade children choose to look at books during free-choice time in school. Greaney (1980) found that fifth-grade students spent only 5.4% of their leisure time engaged in reading, and 22% did not read at all. Similar results were found in studies by Anderson, Wilson and Fielding (1985), Greaney and Hegarty (1987), and Walberg and Tsai (1984).

It has been hypothesized that audio and visual forms of technology may divert the attention of children away from books. Electronic entertainment could be one reason for low levels of voluntary reading. However, studies that have compared television viewing and leisure reading have not substantiated this hypothesis. Researchers have found inconclusive data. There are apparently both heavy and light readers who watch a substantial amount of television and heavy and light readers who do not watch much television. These studies also confirm that television does not interfere with the reading of books (Flood & Lapp, 1994; Neuman, 1981). In a longitudinal survey from 1949 to 1965, Witty (1967) found that even though children increased in the amount of television they viewed, the number of books they read remained the same.

## BENEFITS ASSOCIATED WITH VOLUNTARY READING

Some studies that found that children do not spend a lot of time involved in voluntary reading also conversely revealed strong relationships between the amount of leisure reading and success in reading. Research has found a relationship between the amount of time that children leisure read (or read for fun on their own) and reading achievement (Greaney, 1980; National Assessment of Educational Progress, 1996; Taylor, Frye, & Marugama, 1990). In a study by Anderson, Fielding, and Wilson (1988), children recorded the number of minutes of their out-of-school reading. The number of minutes correlated positively with reading achievement. For example, children who score at the 90th percentile on a reading test spend five times as many minutes per day reading books as children at the 50th percentile and more than 200 times as many minutes per day reading books as the child at the 10th percentile. Children who do a substantial amount of voluntary reading also demonstrate positive attitudes toward reading as well as increased performance in reading (Calkins, 1996; Greaney, 1980; Krashen, 1994). Apparently, an element of personal motivation in voluntary reading leads to greater interest and skill development (Irving, 1980). In a study of kindergarten children (Morrow, 1983), it was found that those who demonstrated a voluntary interest in books were rated by their teachers as displaying high performance in fine motor control, social and emotional maturity, work habits and general school achievement. They also performed well on a standardized reading readiness test.

The cultural benefits of reading are taken for granted in every academic institution and in many U.S. corporate head-quarters. It is commonly recognized that reading enables, develops, or informs technological know-how, intellectual stimulation and growth, leisure, cultural identification, and transfer of information. From Jefferson's day forward, and even earlier, universal literacy has supported and informed our political, democratic processes. Americans' faith in literacy is established firmly in U.S. law through the doctrines of free speech and free press, both in development since before the War for Independence. Americans recognize that citizens need to read widely and deeply if they are to make informed decisions about their own self-government. That fact was recognized in Colonial America no less than it is now, in the depth and breadth of analysis, reflection, and perspective on political issues available only through the printed page.

Literacy also supports and informs morality, a fact evident in the central positions of liturgy, discourse, law, and commentary in all major Western religions. It is conversely evident in the attacks on specific books and instructional materials by various doctrinaire or sectarian groups in attempts at censorship within the schools.

One obvious assumption underlies all these benefits—cultural, political, moral, and educational: The well-educated person will choose to read because it is socially, individually, and educationally beneficial to do so. Youngsters are taught to read so they can participate fully in a civilized society. For such participation, they must become readers by choice, not by coercion. How else will they or our society realize all the benefits that ability to read brings with it?

The promotion of voluntary reading, then, is appropriate among children from their very earliest years. Educators must study and promote the techniques of developing voluntary readers at least to the same extent as they explore the process of training children to decipher the printed page (Morrow, 1986).

## CHARACTERISTICS OF VOLUNTARY READERS AND THEIR HOMES

Researchers have investigated the characteristics of home environments in which children have demonstrated early voluntary interest in books and established voluntary reading habits.

Children who show a voluntary interest in books tend to be from small families with parents having formal educations. These parents have been reported to offer a great deal of support for their children in literacy development (Greaney & Hegarty, 1985; Morrow, 1983). On the other hand, it has been found that a rich literary environment, not the education or socioeconomic backgrounds of families, was the most significant contribution of children's voluntary reading behavior (Purcell-Gates, 1996). In homes with low socioeconomic backgrounds, in which literate members of the family read and wrote for their own entertainment and leisure and parents were involved when children began formal literacy instruction in school, children became interested in reading and read on their own more. Across classes and cultures, literacy is used in a variety of ways. In families of extreme poverty there are many print materials at home and parents who engage in literacy activities of many kinds on a daily basis (Delgado-Gaitan, 1987; Taylor & Dorsey-Gaines, 1988). Voluntary readers have been found to come from homes where they were given a certain amount of independence and responsibility. They participated in diverse leisure activities, and, most of all, their parents encouraged reading, which proved to be the most significantly related factor to children's leisure reading behavior.

Many studies have also found that a rich literacy environment at home contributes to children's voluntary interest in literature. Results of many investigations (Clay, 1976; Morrow, 1983; Purcell-Gates, 1996) have demonstrated that parents with children who showed an early voluntary interest in books served as reading models for their children because in their leisure time they often read novels, magazine, newspapers, and work-related materials. Parents with children who were not interested in books tended to read only newspapers and work-related materials. A distinction emerges: Newspapers and work-related materials were read by all, but novels and magazines, which are linked more closely with recreation and voluntary choice, were read more often by parents of children who showed an early voluntary interest in books.

Other characteristics of homes in which children were voluntary readers became evident. There were more books found in these homes and the books were placed in many different rooms, including playrooms, kitchens, and children's bedrooms. Parents of voluntary readers took their children to the library often and read to them daily. They enforced television rules related to the amount of TV viewing allowed and selective viewing habits, and they were responsive to their children's questions about books and print (Neuman, 1986, 1991; Taylor, 1983; W. Teale, 1984). These children are in a natural setting that provides an interaction between adult and child that is socially, emotionally, and intellectually conducive to literacy growth (Holdaway, 1979).

Children who are voluntary readers demonstrate distinct characteristics. They tend to be girls who are high achievers in school and particularly successful in reading performance (Greaney, 1980). Young children who demonstrate a voluntary interest in books tend to spend their playtime at home writing and drawing with paper and crayons as well as looking at books, whereas children who show a low interest prefer playing outdoors and with toys. Children who demonstrate an interest in books watch less television daily than those who do not demonstrate an interest in books (Lomax, 1976; Morrow, 1983). Most of the research reviewed also indicates that voluntary readers and children with strong interest in books score well on reading tests at school.

In one investigation, however, some children were identified who had low interest in books but received mean percentile scores on a reading readiness test higher than the average of the total high-interest group. Conversely, there were children in the high-interest group who received mean percentile scores on the test similar to the average for the total low-interest group (Morrow, 1983). These findings present an interesting consideration. It has been generally accepted that school achievement and recreational reading are related, but according to the study, skilled readers are not always voluntary readers. Even though a child demonstrates academic ability, if a supportive literary environment is not present at home or in school, voluntary reading habits may not develop. On the other hand, a child exposed to literature at home and in school may develop a strong interest in books in spite of lower academic ability as indicated on scores from standardized tests. Anderson et al. (1988) found that children who were in classrooms that promoted voluntary reading did more reading at home than children from classrooms where there was little emphasis in this direction.

## A THEORETICAL FRAMEWORK FOR PROMOTING VOLUNTARY READING AT SCHOOL

The importance of promoting voluntary reading as an integral part of the reading program is based on the premise that educators are not interested in creating a reader who is just capable of reading but will be a lifelong engaged reader. The engaged reader, one who reaches his or her fullest potential as a reader, is a *strategic* reader, who has knowledge about print and the meaning of printed material. Engaged readers possess multiple skills that enable them to read independently and comprehend what they read. Engaged readers are *knowledgeable* and gain knowledge from information they learn through reading. They read to learn more and transfer and apply their knowledge into new contexts. Engaged readers are aware that reading

is sometimes a *social* endeavor to share with others and learn from others. Finally, engaged readers are *motivated* readers who read voluntarily for pleasure and for information as a lifelong endeavor (Guthrie et al., 1997). If success in reading is influenced by children's attitudes toward reading, by their association of reading with pleasure, by the opportunity to practice skills through actual reading, and by exposure to a rich literacy environments, then the development of voluntary reading must be a key component of efforts to foster literacy. Such a program integrates a voluntary reading program and more explicit instruction of skills to develop a complete engaged reader. The portion of the program that promotes voluntary reading would include (a) a variety of regularly scheduled literature activities that are first modeled by adults and then engaged in by children in social cooperative settings, (b) the creation of literacy centers in the classroom for housing books and related literature materials to be used and read in school and taken home, and (c) time set aside on a regular basis for recreational reading in school.

This proposed framework for reading instruction, with specific concern for the development of voluntary readers in this chapter, is guided by Holdaway's (1979) developmental literacy theory and W. H. Teale's (1982) discussion of natural literacy development. It is also influenced by theory concerning motivation. W. H. Teale argued that "the typical literacy curriculum with its progression from part to whole and its hierarchy of skills" does not reflect the way children learn to read:

The belief is that literacy development is a case of building competencies in certain cognitive operations with letters, words, sentences and texts, competencies which can be applied in a variety of situations. A critical mistake here is that the motives, goals, and conditions have been abstracted away from the activity in the belief that this enables the student to "get down to" working on the essential process of reading and writing. But . . . these features are critical aspects of the reading and writing themselves. By organizing instruction which omits them, the teacher ignores how literacy is practiced (and therefore learned) and thereby creates a situation in which the teaching is an inappropriate model for the learning. (p. 567)

In W. H. Teale's view, literacy learning is the result of children's involvement in reading and writing activities that are mediated by literate others. It is the interaction accompanying these activities that makes them so significant to the child's development. Not only do interactive literacy events teach children the societal functions and conventions of literature, they also link reading and writing with enjoyment and satisfaction, and thus increase children's desire to engage in literacy activities.

W. H. Teale's (1982) emphasis on the social aspects of literacy development reflects the influence of Vygotsky's (1981) more general theory of intellectual development. Vygotsky defined "all higher mental functions (as) internalized social relationships". This movement from interpsychological learning to intrapsychological learning is apparent as children become increasingly able to engage independently in literacy activities that previously required interaction with more literate others.

Holdaways's (1979) theory of literacy development is consistent with W. H. Teale's (1982) positions. According to Holdaway:

The way in which supportive adults are induced by affection and common sense to intervene in the development of their children proves upon close examination to embody the most sound principles of teaching. Rather than provide verbal instructions about how a skill should be carried out, the parent sets up an emulative model of the skill in operation and induces activity in the child which approximates towards use of the skill. The first attempts of the child are to do something that is like the skill he wishes to emulate. This activity is then "shaped" or refined by immediate rewards.... From this point of view, so-called "natural" learning is in fact supported by higher quality teaching intervention than is normally the case in the school setting. (p. 22)

Holdaway (1979) contended that this form of "developmental" teaching is appropriate for school-based literacy instruction. Characterized by self-regulated, individualized activities, frequent peer interaction, and an environment rich with materials, Holdaway's model is derived from observations of home environments where children have learned to read without direct instruction. Such supportive home literacy environments have a large supply of accessible reading and writing materials; moreover, parents read to children regularly, are responsive to their children's questions about books and print, view reading as a key to achievement, and read a great deal themselves (W. Teale, 1978).

Four processes are defined that enable children to acquire literacy abilities. The first is *observation* of literacy behaviors—being read to, for example, or seeing adults read and write. The second is *collaboration*, the interaction of another individual with the child, providing encouragement, motivation, and help. The third is *practice*, during which the learner tries out alone what has been learned, reading for pleasure or to others, for instance, without direction or adult observation. Practice gives children opportunities to evaluate their own performances, make corrections, and increase skills. In the fourth process, *performance*, the child shares what has been learned and seeks approval from adults who are supportive and interested (Holdaway, 1986; Snow, 1983).

Promoting voluntary reading suggests that we hope to motivate a child to want to read. Motivation is indicated by an individual's initiating and sustaining a particular activity, that is, the tendency to return to and continue working on a task with sustained engagement (Maehr, 1976; Wittrock, 1986). A motivated reader chooses to read on a regular basis and for many different reasons. Researchers have found that experiences that afford students the opportunity for *choice, challenge, social interaction, and success* are likely to promote motivation.

To foster success, a learning environment must enable a student to perceive the challenge in the activity at hand as one that he or she can accomplish. When the task has been completed, the student must perceive success (Ford, 1992; McCombs, 1989; Spaulding, 1992; Turner, 1992). Tasks are appropriate only if they are perceived to be challenging, that is, not too hard and not too easy. When children view a task as too easy, they become disinterested; if they view a task as too difficult they become frustrated. Intrinsic motivation is enhanced when individuals see themselves as competent or successful in challenging situations (Spaulding, 1992).

Letting children choose specific literacy activities in which to participate gives them a sense of responsibility and control over a situation. Like challenges and success, self-selection of tasks instills intrinsic motivation (Morrow, 1997; Turner, 1992). Finally, opportunities for social collaboration also nurture motivation. Give children the opportunity to engage in learning through collaboration with a teacher or with peers, and they are more intrinsically motivated and likely to get more done than if they work alone (Brandt, 1990; Oldfather, 1993). Investigations by Gambrell, Palmer, & Codling (1993) supported the findings of other research reviewed here—that choice, challenge, success, and social collaboration tend to motivate children to read and write.

Motivation theory and the theoretical perspectives of W. H. Teale (1982), Holdaway (1979), and Vygotsky (1981) are reflected in reading programs proposed from research investigations to help to create voluntary readers. These programs provide children with the opportunity to:

1. Observe and emulate the modeled behavior of literate adults who read to them and read themselves.
2. Enjoy the support of adults who collaborate or interact socially with them during literature activities and reward literacy behaviors.
3. Have the opportunity to practice skills learned by engaging in free self-selected reading during recreational reading periods that provide choice of activity, and the use of materials from classroom literacy centers that are challenging but can lead to success.
4. Perform or share literature experiences, demonstrating what has been learned, through pleasurable activities such as discussing books read, and experiencing success.

## GENERAL STRATEGIES FOR PROMOTING VOLUNTARY READING IN SCHOOL

There is widespread agreement among educators that encouraging students to develop lifelong, voluntary reading habits is important. The literature from the past has shed some light on strategies that promote voluntary readers. Researchers have found the following elements to be important toward motivating the desire to read: discussing story meaning, reading to children, using children's literature in content area teaching, scheduling recreational reading, doing art activities related to stories, maintaining a classroom library, asking children to record books read, asking children to write stories for the classroom library, encouraging children to read to each other, encouraging children to tell stories, using the school and public library, sharing books read at home and school, discussing authors and illustrators, and asking children to keep records of books they have read (Cullinan, 1987; Hall, 1971; Huck, 1976; Morrow, 1982, 1983, 1987; Morrow & Weinstein, 1982, 1986; Stewig & Sebesta, 1978).

The teacher plays a critical role in influencing children's attitudes toward reading. Children live what they learn. If children associate reading only with repetition of skill, drill, teach, and test, they will never reach for a book on their own initiative. As Niles wrote in the foreword to *Reading for Pleasure: Guidelines* (Speigel, 1981), "If we teach children to read, but do not instill the desire to read, what will we have accomplished?" (p. v). If, on the other hand, children live in an environment that associates reading with pleasure and enjoyment as well as with skill development, they are likely to become voluntary readers. How children live and learn in the classroom ultimately determines whether they will live their lives as literate or alliterate individuals. Irving (1980) contended:

One of the clear points to emerge from research into reading failure is that there was no association between reading and pleasure. . . . The role of teachers in stimulating voluntary reading among children and young people is . . . potentially the most powerful of all adult influences upon the young (p. 7).

## THE USE OF LITERATURE TO PROMOTE VOLUNTARY READING

Research that incorporates correlational data, experimental paradigms, and anecdotal observations have been carried out to describe programs designed to promote voluntary reading. These investigations for the most part make use of children's literature as a strong component in the program.

Early investigations on promoting interest in books and the use of literature in the classroom were mainly anecdotal in nature. Schools have emphasized the importance of literature by supplementing their regular reading programs with Spring Reading Campaigns, Reading Awareness Weeks, and Reading Celebrations (Irving, 1980; Manley & Simon, 1980; Manning & Manning, 1984; Rosler, 1979; Yatvin, 1977). These anecdotal reports suggested that such programs invariably enhance students' enthusiasm and foster positive attitudes toward books.

In three similar "Book Flood" studies, classrooms were filled with large numbers of trade books, and teachers were asked to encourage free reading. The results of these investigations reported improvement in children's reading achievement, gains in vocabulary and comprehension, increased reading, and better attitudes toward reading than exhibited by children in comparison schools who did not participate in such programs (Elley & Mangubhai, 1983; Fielding, Wilson, & Anderson, 1989; Ingham, 1981). Research by Morrow and Weinstein (1982, 1986) found that literature use increased dramatically when teachers incorporated enjoyable literature activities into the daily program, when library centers were created in the classrooms, and when recreational reading periods were regularly scheduled. Interestingly, there was no difference in the frequency with which high achievers and low achievers chose to use literature; the recreational reading program succeeded in attracting even poor readers to literature. In a similar study of inner city minority children in after-school and summer day-care centers for youngsters from 6 to 11 years of age, significant increase in book reading occurred from the beginning to the end of the program (Morrow, 1987).

Empirical research by Morrow (1982, 1992) and Morrow and Weinstein (1982, 1986) suggests specific activities in preschool through sixth grade classroom recreational reading programs that increased the use of literature by children. The results of their studies indicate that one practice of utmost importance

is to read to children daily. Storytelling by teachers and use of storytelling props, such as felt-board stories, puppets, filmstrips and taped stories, were all found to be valuable in creating interest in books. When props were used to tell stories, the teachers involved made sure that the actual storybooks were available for children to use later on. All story-related materials, such as felt boards and roll movies, were left for children to use. Discussions that focused on interpretive and critical issues within the stories also served to heighten interest in books. Authors and illustrators were discussed and compared. Children's books brought from home and those written by the children themselves were extremely popular. Using literature related to content area topics correlated positively with children's increased use of literature, as did time set aside specifically for voluntary reading. All these activities promoted voluntary reading when carried out regularly.

More recent studies have illustrated improved attitudes toward reading as a result of literature-based instruction and elements that motivate reading. Gambrell et al. (1993) confirmed motivation theory, discussed earlier, when they interviewed third- and fifth-grade students about elements that encourage them to read. They found children want to read more when they have the power of choice about what they will read, and they want to be able to socially interact with others to discuss what they read. Gambrell et al. also noted the importance of the feelings of competence and accomplishment that children experience. That is, children enjoy challenging books that they can read and feel successful about reading. Gambrell, Almasi, Xie, and Heland (1994) designed a project that included the elements of choice, challenge, and social collaboration in a Running Start program along with Reading Is Fundamental. The results of the investigation demonstrated that motivation to read was enhanced as a result incorporating choice, challenge, social interaction, and success experiences in the program.

Children's attitude is likely to determine whether students choose to read or not. There are mixed findings concerning the effects of literature-based instruction and children's attitude toward reading. Studies have found that there is no difference between basal reading instruction and the use of literature-based instruction and children's attitude toward reading (McKenna, Kear, & Ellsworth, 1995; McKenna, Stratton, Grindler, & Jenkins, 1995; Stahl, McKenna, & Pagnucco 1994). There were no studies found demonstrating that basal reading instruction improved attitude toward reading over literature-based reading. There are, however, a number of studies that used a range of quantitative and qualitative methodologies, in which literature-based programs positively affected children's attitudes toward reading (Gerla, 1996; Goatley, Brock, & Raphael, 1995; Goatley & Raphael, 1992; Oberlin & Shugarman, 1989; Richeck & McTague, 1988), and frequency of reading (Dahl & Freppon, 1995; Morrow, Pressley, Smith, & Smith, 1997; Stewart, Paradis, Ross, & Lewis, 1996).

Other studies have investigated the effect of literature based instruction on attitudes toward reading and content area learning. J. A. Smith (1993) explored the attitudes of fifth-graders using either historical fiction novels or a combination of basal readers and social studies textbooks. Students in the literature based group outperformed the comparison group on content knowledge, and survey responses revealed that students preferred using historical fiction novels rather than a basal reader and textbook to learn about history. In another study investigating sixth-grade students' attitudes toward literature and textbook instruction in social studies, Jones, Coombs, and McKinney (1994) found that students in the literature group outperformed the comparison group on achievement and desire to use literature in social studies.

Morrow et al. (1997) compared the reading and science achievement and the attitudes of students in three treatment conditions: (a) basal plus literature-based reading and literature-based science instruction, (b) basal plus literature based reading instruction and textbook based science instruction, and (c) basal reading instruction and textbook based science instruction. The achievement scores across several measures of reading performance favored the basal plus literature based reading and science group. Attitudes toward science were more positive for this group as compared with the other two groups.

It seems apparent that literature-based instruction in literacy development and in content areas can have a positive effect on achievement and also on attitude toward reading and subject areas. With this increased success and interest, more sustained reading should occur.

In the previous recent studies, we acknowledged both achievement gains and enhanced interest in reading using literature based instruction. Although discussed earlier, exposure to literature is beneficial to children in so many other ways that it seems important to mention some of them at this point. As voluntary reading is being promoted through the use of literature, other skills are also being acquired. Studies indicate that there is a strong relationship between use of literature at home and in classrooms and the development of oral and written language. Children exposed to books early and frequently become aware that printed words have sounds, and recognize that print carries meaning. Both decoding and comprehension are enhanced from frequent pleasurable experiences with literature (Clark, 1984; Clay, 1979; Cohen, 1969; Feitleson, Kita, & Goldstein, 1986).

Research has focused on trying to identify specific beneficial behaviors during story book readings. It has been found that kind and amount of verbal interaction between adult and child during such events can influence literacy development (Heath, 1982; Ninio, 1980; W. H. Teale & Sulzby, 1987). Teachers' reading styles were also found to affect children's comprehension (Dunning & Mason, 1984; Green & Harker, 1982). The social interaction between readers and listeners during read-aloud events seems to help participants actively construct meaning based on text (Bloom, 1985). Story reading also leads children to practice reading on their own by reenacting the story by reading and modeling the adult–child interaction. The nature of the interaction may even affect how much information the child learns as well as the child's skills and attitudes towards reading (W. H. Teale & Sulzby, 1987). The read-aloud event itself does not necessarily enhance literacy, but certain methods, environmental influences, attitudes, and interactive behaviors do contribute.

Experimental treatments in school settings have been studied in other attempts to define specific story reading elements

that enhance literacy skills (Morrow, 1985b; Pellegrini & Galda, 1982). Children were read stories, then asked to respond by role playing, retelling, or reconstructing the stories with pictures. Children in the experimental groups improved more than those in control groups. Eliciting children's responses to literature seemed to enable them to integrate information and see relationships among various parts of a story. Besides enticing them to books, storybook reading has been found to help children construct meaning about the text through the interaction between adult and child. During story reading, the adult helps the child understand and interpret text according to experiences, background, and beliefs (Altwerger, Diehl-Faxon, & Dockstader-Anderson, 1985).

## THE ROLE OF THE CLASSROOM ENVIRONMENT AND THE PROMOTION OF VOLUNTARY READING AT SCHOOL

Researchers have studied the effects of manipulating the physical environments of the classroom. Studies by Bumstead (1981), Morrow (1992), and Sutfin (1980), showed that changes in classroom environment can bring about desirable changes in the students' choices of activities and the ability to engage in social activities. The classroom environment is often overlooked in instructional planning. Energies are directed almost exclusively toward varying teaching strategies. When program and environment are not coordinated, they fail to support the activities and needs of the students.

The research on voluntary reading has demonstrated the important role that physical setting plays. It is an active and pervasive influence on children's attitudes and the ability to choose classroom activities during the school day. Appropriate physical arrangement of furniture, material selection, and the aesthetic quality of different parts of a classroom, in this case the literacy center, can provide a setting that contributes to teaching, learning, and the promotion of voluntary reading (Castle, 1987; Fracter, Woodruff, Martinez, & W. H. Teale, 1993; Hickman, 1983; Morrow, 1982, 1992).

Surveys found that library corners as they typically existed were among the least popular areas in early childhood classrooms during free play periods. In most rooms, library centers consisted simply of a bookshelf with books shelved in a disorderly fashion. Frequently, the area was difficult to find, little care was taken to make it attractive and physically accessible, and it did not contain interesting literature-related materials (Morrow, 1982, 1983). The effort of creating an inviting atmosphere for a classroom library is rewarded by children's increased interest in reading. The classroom library should be the focal area in the room since it is a principal source of knowledge. It has been found that when literature collections exist in classrooms students read 50% more books than children in classrooms without such collections. The more immediate the access to library materials, the greater the amount of recreational reading by pupils (Anderson et al., 1985; Morrow, 1983). Correlational and experimental studies have identified many positive relationships between the frequency with which young children use literature in the classroom and physical design characteristics of library centers. Studies also report increased use of literature during free-choice periods in classrooms where library corners featured specific design characteristics (Anderson, Wilson, & Fielding, 1985; Ingham, 1981; Morrow, 1982, 1983; Morrow & Weinstein, 1982, 1986). Library centers that promoted children's voluntary use of books:

- Were physically accessible and visually attractive.
- Were partitioned off from the rest of the room on at least two sides to give a feeling of privacy.
- Were large enough to hold about five children at a time.
- Offered comfortable seating, such as a rocking chair, pillows to lean on, and a rug.
- Provided five to eight books per child at varied reading levels.
- Held a variety of children's literature, including picture story books, novels, magazines, informational books, newspapers, poetry, fairy tales, fables, realistic literature and biographies.
- Categorized books for selection.
- Circulated new books regularly.
- Offered a simple procedure for checking books in and out.
- Had open-faced bookshelves to feature particular books.
- Had attractive posters and literature related bulletin boards
- Provided story props such as a felt board and cutout characters as well as puppets for storytelling.
- Offered taped stories with headsets.

Studies referred to earlier have illustrated that characteristics of the physical environment play an important role in promoting voluntary reading in the classroom. However, the very same studies indicate that without the support of the teacher who introduces the materials and features books in their daily routines, the physical factors alone will not succeed.

## DISCUSSION

*Becoming a Nation of Readers* (Anderson, Hiebert, Scott, & Wilkinson, 1985) referred to independent reading as a major source of reading fluency. Opportunities for recreational reading in school allow children to practice skills they are taught in typical reading instruction. Practice must be easy enough to give them a sense of success and enjoyable enough that they will continue to read by choice. The literature review reveals the benefits of voluntary reading and the characteristics of voluntary readers and provides documentation of the fact that children's voluntary reading habits can be increased when teachers carry out literature activities designed to create an interest in books, along with a supportive physical environment. Home studies identify characteristics that foster the development of voluntary readers. Teachers can share this information with parents about home environments and activities to help increase their children's voluntary reading.

Educators need to continue investigating the promotion of voluntary reading to demonstrate its importance. It is often the "forgotten goal" in reading instruction. If the promotion of vol-untary reading is to take its place as an integral part of reading programs, researchers must present data to confirm its importance. They need to continue to carry out longitudinal, experimental research on the promotion of voluntary reading with children from different socioeconomic levels, from both urban and suburban environments, and with different cultural backgrounds to identify the benefits of such programs on literacy development. The research should include parent involvement, which the literature review demonstrates is an important element in creating voluntary readers (Morrow, 1985a). Assuming that the results of these experimental data reinforce the positive findings already documented for voluntary reading, they will help to keep it as an integral part of reading instruction.

Shavelson and Borko (1979) have studied factors that affect teachers' decision making about classroom instruction. In addition to a teacher's personal attitudes, they found that institutional constraints, external pressure, and instructional materials shape beliefs and consequently affect classroom practice. Teachers perceive money, space, and time as institutional constraints that hinder the promotion of voluntary reading. The external pressures to improve standardized test scores are felt rather generally by teachers. Pressure from local and state officials as well as from parents are as apparent as ever now. Teachers feel pressured to use classroom time for the skill development that will help children achieve high scores on such tests. Skills-oriented programs are more easily measured on standardized tests, the results of which are in turn appreciated by the school boards, parents and taxpayers. Voluntary reading, by contrast, is a matter that requires qualitative evaluation as well as quantitative. The benefits of voluntary reading as intellectual stimulation and growth, acculturation, and general transfer of information are a matter of long-range development rather than of an immediate payoff.

After nearly a decade of promoting the use of children's literature as a major source for reading instruction, the pendulum is swinging once again toward the use of materials that strongly emphasize word recognition skill development, with a converse lack of attention to the promotion of recreational reading. Although it cannot be denied that skills are an important part of reading instruction, the climate is such that any focus toward the promotion of voluntary reading could be seen as detracting from the main goal of learning to read. As discussed in the beginning of this paper, there is adequate research to demonstrate that we need to balance literacy instruction with skill development and activities that help to create motivated voluntary readers. The aspects of literacy instruction that deal with promoting voluntary reading, however, cannot be the optional or supplementary activities.

Recent instructional mandates are defining reading as process somewhat at the expense of essence. Those in policymaking positions seem to be concerned with teaching children how to read, rather than paying attention to what they read or why they should want to read at all. There are more things to be read and more reasons to read them than at any other time in history. From the late 1980s to the mid-1990s, motivation was an element of literacy instruction that was getting some attention (Cramer & Castle, 1994). One of the main goals of the National Reading Research Center between (1992 and 1997 was to investigate the issues surrounding motivation and promoting lifelong readers (Guthrie & Wigfield, 1997). Now, however, recent priorities and debates about how best to teach reading could short-circuit fundamental motivation to read. Are youngsters being taught to read to raise reading test scores or to nurture individuals who will choose to read throughout their lives?

Educators need to look at achievement test performance and beyond to implement reading programs that include the development of voluntary reading as a major purpose. If educators believe fundamentally that they teach children to read because their own voluntary reading throughout life is necessary if they are to participate to their fullest in a democratic, civilized society, with all the benefits a literate society affords, then educators need to be certain that our approaches to reading instruction in the elementary school match these goals. Foremost in that remedy is a general commitment to systematic, programmatic development of voluntary reading. That development should be one of the primary objective of education, especially of early childhood and elementary education.

Such a developmental approach to literacy requires classroom environments rich in literary activities, classroom literacy centers bountifully stocked, frequent use of such areas by children of all ability levels and interests, children reading for their own purposes and practicing skills learned from direct instruction. As various research reports have found, incorporating recreational reading and pleasurable literary activities into instructional programs both enhances enthusiasm and fosters positive attitudes toward reading at the same time it improves vocabulary, comprehension, and language development.

To avoid a situation in which voluntary reading is not given priority in literacy instruction, educators must develop and regularly use appropriate instructional activities. They must allocate resources, direct the preservice and inservice preparation of teachers and encourage mutual support among all concerned, especially teachers, administrators, parents, and policymakers. As primary decision makers in curriculum and instruction, teachers must recognize that they not only influence instruction but also determine what children learn. They must be encouraged by administrators and colleagues to act on their beliefs in the value and importance of developing voluntary readers. It requires no great expenditure of time, effort, or money to achieve our ultimate goal in teaching children to read. Techniques and materials are readily available. Educators need only the will to put them to use in general practice.

We are aware that systematic and explicit skill development is important and necessary. By itself, it is simply incomplete. Systematically integrating direct instruction with the promotion of voluntary, recreational reading endows skill development with a reason for being and points the reader toward lifetime fulfillment and continued growth. Every classroom can and should become a literacy-rich environment in which children read not because they have to but because they want to.

# References

Altwerger, A., Diehl-Faxon, J., & Dockstader-Anderson, K. (1985). Read aloud events as meaning construction. *Language Arts, 62,* 476–484.

Anderson, R. C., Fielding, L. G., & Wilson, P. T. (1988). Growth in reading and how children spend their time outside of school. *Reading Research Quarterly, 23,* 285–304.

Anderson, R. C., Hiebert, E. H., Scott, J. A., & Wilkinson, I. A. G. (1985). *Becoming a nation of readers.* Washington, DC: National Institute of Education.

Anderson, R. C., Wilson, P. T., & Fielding, L. G. (1985). *A new focus on free-reading.* Symposium conducted at the National Reading Conference, San Diego, CA.

Bloom, D. (1985). Bedtime reading as a social process. In J. A. Niles & R. V. Lalik (Eds.), *Issues in literacy: A research perspective.* Rochester, NY: National Reading Conference.

Boorstin, D. (1984). Letter of transmittal. In *Books in our future: A report from the Librarian of Congress to the Congress* (p. iv). Washington, DC: U.S. Congress, Joint Committee on the Library.

Brandt, D. (1990). *Literacy as involvement: The acts of writers, readers, and texts.* Carbondale: Southern Illinois University Press.

Bumstead, L. A. (1981). *Influencing the frequency of children's cooperative and learning task-related behavior through change in the design and management of the classroom.* Unpublished master's thesis, Cornell University, Ithaca, NY.

Calkins, L. M. (1996). *Lessons from a child.* Portsmouth, NH: Heinemann.

Castle, M. (1987). Classroom libraries: Valuable resources for developing readers. *The Delta Kappa Gamma Bulletin, 54*(1), 18–20, 50.

Clark, M. M. (1984). Literacy at home and at school: Insights from a study of young fluent readers. In J. Goelman, A. A. Oberg, & F. Smith (Eds.), *Awakening to literacy.* London: Heinemann Educational Books.

Clay, M. M. (1976). *Reading: The patterning of complex behavior.* Auckland, Australia: Heinemann Educational Books.

Cohen, D. (1969). The effect of literature on vocabulary and reading achievement. *Elementary English, 45,* 209–213, 217.

Cramer, E. H., & Castle, M. (Eds.). (1994). *Fostering the love of reading: The affective domain.* Newark, DE: International Reading Association.

Cullinan, B. (Ed.). (1987). *Children's literature in the reading program.* Newark, DE: International Reading Association.

Dahl, K. L., & Freppon, P. A. (1995). A comparison of innercity children's interpretations of reading and writing instruction in the early grades in skills-based and whole language classrooms. *Reading Research Quarterly, 30*(1), 50–74.

Delgado-Guitan, C. (1987). Mexican adult literacy: New directions for immigrants. In S. R. Goldman & K. Trueva (Eds.), *Becoming literate in English as a second language.* Norwood, NJ: Ablex.

Dunning, D., & Mason, J. (1984). *An investigation of kindergarten children's expressions of story character intentions.* Paper presented at the 34th annual meeting of the National Reading Conference, S. Petersburg, FL.

Elley, W. B., & Mungubhai, F. (1983). The impact of reading on second language reading. *Reading Research Quarterly, 19,* 53–67.

Feitleson, D., Kita, B., & Goldstein, Z. (1986). Effects of listening to series stories on first graders' comprehension and use of language. *Research in the Teaching of English, 20,* 339–356.

Fielding, L. G., Wilson, P. T., & Anderson, R. C. (1989). A new focus on free reading: The role of trade books in reading instruction. In T. E. Raphael & R. Reynolds (Eds.), *Contexts of literacy*. New York: Longman.

Flood, J., & Lapp, D. (1994). Broadening the lens: Toward an expanded conceptualization of literacy. In K. Hinchman, D. Hinchman, D. Leu, & C. Kinzer (Eds.), *Perspectives on literacy research and practice: Forty-fourth yearbook of the National Reading Conference* (Vol.44, pp. 1-16). New York: MacMillan.

Ford, M. E. (1992). *Motivating humans: Goals, emotions, and personal agency beliefs*. Newbery Park, CA: Sage.

Fracter, J. S., Woodruff, M. C., Martinez, M. G., & Teale, W. H. (1993). Let's not miss opportunities to promote voluntary reading in the elementary school. *The Reading Teacher, 46,* 476-484.

Gambrell, L. B., Almasi, J. F., Xie, Q., & Heland, V. (1994). Helping first-graders get off to a running start in reading: A home-school-community program that enhances family literacy. In L. M. Morrow (Ed.), *Family literacy: Multiple perspectives to enhance literacy development*. Newark, DE: International Reading Association.

Gambrell, L. B., Palmer, B. M., & Codling, R. M. (1993). *Motivation to read*. Washington, DC: Office of Educational Research and Improvement.

Gerla, J. P. (1996). Response-based instruction: At-risk students engaging in literature. *Reading and Writing Quarterly: Overcoming Learning Difficulties, 12*(2), 195-214.

Goatley, V. J., Brock, C. H., & Raphael, T. E. (1995). Diverse learners participating in regular education "Book Clubs." *Reading Research Quarterly, 30*(3), 352-380.

Goatley, V. J., & Raphael, T. E. (1992). *Non-traditional learners' written and dialogic response to literature: Fortieth yearbook of the National Reading Conference* (Vol. 40, pp. 313-322). Chicago: National Reading Conference.

Greaney, V. (1980). Factors related to amount and type of leisure reading. *Reading Research Quarterly, 15,* 337-357.

Greaney, V., & Hegarty, M. (1985). *Correlates of leisure-time reading*. Unpublished paper, St. Patricks College, Educational Research Centre. Dublin, Ireland.

Greaney, V., & Hegarty, M. (1987). Correlates of leisure-time reading. *Journal of Research in Reading, 10,* 3-20.

Green, J. L., & Harker, J. O. (1982). Reading to children: A communicative process. In J. A. Langer & M. T. Smith-Burke (Eds.), *Reder meets author/bridging the gap: A psycho-linguistic perspective* (pp. 196-221). Newark, DE: International Reading Association.

Guthrie, J. T., Van Meter, P. et al. (1997). Growth of literacy engagement: Changes in motivation and strategies during concept-oriented reading instruction. *Reading Research Quarterly, 31,* 306-333.

Guthrie, J. T., & Wigfield, A. (Eds.). (1997). *Reading engagement: Motivating readers through integrated instruction*. Newark, DE: International Reading Association.

Hall, M. (1971). Literature experiences provided by cooperating teachers. *Reading Teacher, 24,* 425-431.

Heath, S. B. (1982). What no bedtime story means: Narrative skills at home and school. *Language in Society, 11,* 49-76.

Hickman, J. (1983). Classrooms that help children like books. In N. Rosen & M. Frith (Eds.), *Children's choices. Teaching with books children like* (pp. 1-11). Newark, DE: International Reading Association.

Holdaway, D. (1979). *The foundations of literacy*. New York: Ashton Scholastic.

Holdaway, D. (1986). The structure of natural learning as a basis for literacy instruction. In M. Samson (Ed.), *The pursuit of literacy: Early reading and writing*. Dubuque, IA: Kendall/Hunt.

Huck, S. (1976). *Children's literature in the elementary school* (3rd ed.). New York: Holt, Rinehart & Winston.

Ingham, J. L. (1981). *Books and reading development: The Bradford books flood experiment*. Exeter, NH: Heinemann.

Irving, A. (1980). *Promoting voluntary reading for children and young people*. Paris: UNESCO.

Jones, H. J., Coombs, W. T., & McKinney, C. W. (1994). A themed literature unit versus a textbook: A comparison of the effects on content acquisition and attitudes in elementary social studies. *Reading Research and Instruction, 34*(2), 85-96.

Koch, A., & Peden, W. (Eds.). (1944). *The life and selected writings of Thomas Jefferson,* New York: Random House.

Krashen, S. (1994). An answer to the literacy crisis: Free voluntary reading. *School Library Media Annual, 12,* 113-122.

Lomax, L. M. (1976). Interest in books and stories at nursery school. *Educational Research, 19,* 100-112.

Maehr, M. L. (1976). Continuing motivation: An analysis of a seldom considered educational outcome. *Review of Educational Research, 46,* 443-462.

Manley, M. A., & Simon, E. A. (1980). A reading celebration from K to 8. *The Reading Teacher, 33,* 552-554.

Manning, G. L., & Manning, M. (1984). What models of recreational reading make a difference? *Reading World, 23,* 375-380.

McCombs, B. L. (1989). Self-regulated learning and academic achievement: A phenomenological view. In B. J. Zimmerman & D. H. Schunck (Eds.), *Self-regulated learning and academic achievement: Theory, research, and practice* (pp. 51-82). New York: Springer-Verlag.

McKenna, M. C., Kear, D. J., & Ellsworth, R. A. (1995). Children's attitudes toward reading: A national survey. *Reading Research Quarterly, 30*(4), 934-955.

McKenna, M. C., Stratton, B. D., Grindler, M. C., & Jenkins, S. J. (1995). Differential effects of whole language and traditional instruction on reading attitudes. *Journal of Reading Behavior, 27*(1), 19-44.

Morrow, L. M. (1982). Relationships between literature programs, library corner designs and children's use of literature. *Journal of Educational Research, 75,* 339-344.

Morrow, L. M. (1983). Home and school correlates of early interest in literature. *Journal of Educational Research, 76,* 221-230.

Morrow, L. M. (1985a). *Promoting vocabulary reading at school and at home*. Bloomington, IN: Phi Delta Kappa Educational Foundation.

Morrow, L. M. (1985b). Retelling stories: A strategy for improving young children's comprehension concept of story structure, and oral language complexity. *The Elementary School Journal, 85,* 647-661.

Morrow, L. M. (1986). Voluntary reading: Forgotten goal. *Educational Forum, 50,* 159-168.

Morrow, L. M. (1987). Promoting inner city children's recreational reading. *Reading Teacher, 41,* 266-274.

Morrow, L. M. (1991). Promoting voluntary reading. In J. Flood, J. M. Jensen, D. Lapp, & J. R. Squire (Eds.), *Handbook of research on teaching the English language arts* (pp. 681-690). New York: MacMillan.

Morrow, L. M. (1992). The impact of a literature-based program on literacy achievement, use of literature, and attitudes of children from minority backgrounds. *Reading Research Quarterly, 27,* 250-275.

Morrow, L. M. (1997). *Literacy development in the early years: helping children read and write* (3rd ed.). Needham Heights, MA: Allyn & Bacon.

Morrow, L. M., Pressley, M., Smith, J. K., & Smith, M. (1997). The effect of a literature-based program integrated into literacy and science instruction with children from diverse backgrounds. *Reading Research Quarterly, 32*(1), 54-76.

Morrow, L. M., & Weinstein, C. S. (1982). Increasing children's use of literature through program and physical design changes. *Elementary School Journal, 83,* 131-137.

Morrow, L. M., & Weinstein, C. S. (1986). Encouraging voluntary reading. The impact of a literature program on children's use of library centers. *Reading Research Quarterly, 21,* 330–346.

National Assessment of Educational Progress. (1996). *Reading report card: Findings for the nation and the states.* U.S. Department of Education-OERI.

Neuman, S. B. (1981). Television: Its effects on reading and school achievement. *The Reading Teacher,* 801–805.

Neuman, S. B. (1986). The home environment and fifth grade students' leisure reading. *Elementary School Journal, 86,* 335–342.

Neuman, S. (1991). *Literacy in the television age: The myth of the TV effect.* Norwood, NJ: Ablex.

Ninio, A. (1980). Picture-book reading in mother–infant dyads belonging to two subgroups in Israel. *Child Development, 51,* 587–590.

Oberlin, K. J., & Shugarman, S. L. (1989). Implementing the reading workshop with middle school LD readers. *Journal of Reading, 32*(8), 682–687.

Oldfather, P. (1993). What students say about motivating experiences in a whole language classroom. *The Reading Teacher, 46,* 672–681.

Pellegrini, A., & Galda, L. (1982). The effects of thematic-fantasy play training on the development of children's story comprehension. *American Educational Research Journal, 19,* 443–452.

Pressley, M., Rankin, J., & Yokoi, L. (1996). A survey of the instructional practices of outstanding primary level literacy teachers. *Elementary School Journal, 96,* 363–384.

Purcell-Gales, V. (1996). Stives, coupons, & the "TV Guide": Relationships between home literacy, experiences and emergent literacy knowledge. *Reading Research Quarterly, 31,* 406–428.

Richeck, M. A., & McTague, B. K. (1988). The "Curious George" strategy for students with reading problems. *The Reading Teacher, 42,* 220–226.

Rosler, F. (1979). Spring reading campaign. *The Reading Teacher, 32,* 397–398.

Shavelson, R. J., & Borko, H. (1979). Research on teacher's pedagogical thoughts, judgments, decisions, and behaviors. *Review of Educational Research, 51,* 455–498.

Smith, J. A. (1993). Content learning: A third reason for using literature in teaching reading. *Reading Research and Instruction, 32*(3), 64–71.

Smith, N. B. (1934). *American reading instruction.* New York: Silver, Burdett.

Snow, C. E. (1983). Literacy and language: Relationship during the preschool years. *Harvard Educational Review, 53,* 165–189.

Spaulding, C. I. (1992). The motivation to read and write. In J. W. Irwin & M. A. Doyle (Eds.), *Reading/writing connections: Learning from research* (pp. 177–201). Newark, DE: International Research Association.

Speigel, D. L. (1981). *Reading for pleasure: Guidelines.* Newark, DE: International Reading Association.

Spielberg, S. (1987). Acceptance speech at the Academy Awards, Los Angeles.

Stahl, S. A., McKenna, M. C., & Pagnucco, J. (1994). The effects of whole language instruction: An update and reappraisal. *Educational Psychologist, 29*(4), 175–185.

Stewart, R. A., Paradis, E. E., Ross, B. D., & Lewis, M. J. (1996). Student voices: What works in literature-based developmental reading. *Journal of Adolescent and Adult Literacy, 39*(6), 468–477.

Stewig, J. W., & Sebesta, S. (Eds.). (1978). *Using literature in the elementary classroom.* Urbana, IL: National Council of Teachers of English.

Sutfin, H. (1980). *The effects on children's behavior of a change in the physical design of a kindergarten classroom.* Unpublished doctoral dissertation, Boston University, Boston.

Taylor, D. (1983). *Family literacy: Young children learn to read and write.* Exeter, NH: Heinemann.

Taylor, D., & Dorsey-Gaines, G. (1988). *Growing up literate: Learning from inner city families.* Portsmouth, NH: Heinemann.

Taylor, D. Frye, & Marigamu. (1990). Time spent reading and reading growth. *American Educational Research Journal, 27,* 351–362.

Teale, W. (1978). Positive environments for learning to read: What studies of early readers tell us. *Language Arts, 55,* 922–932.

Teale, W. (1984). Reading to young children: Its significance for literacy development. In H. Goelman, A. Oberg, & F. Smith (Eds.), *Awakening to literacy.* London: Heinemann Educational Books.

Teale, W. H. (1982). Parents reading to their children: What we know and need to know. *Language Arts, 59,* 555–570.

Teale, W. H., & Sulzby, E. (1987). Literacy acquisition in early childhood: The roles of access and mediation in storybook readings. In D. A. Wagner (Ed.), *The future of literacy in a changing world.* Tarrytown, NY: Pergamon.

Turner, J. C. (1992, April). *Identifying motivation for literacy in first grade: An observational study.* Paper presented at the annual meeting of the American Educational Research Association, San Francisco.

Vygotsky, L. S. (1981). The genesis of higher mental functions In J. V. Wetsch (Ed.), *The concept of activity in society psychology.* White Plains, NY: Sharpe.

Walberg, H. J., & Tsai, S. (1984). Reading achievement and diminishing returns to time. *Journal of Educational Psychology, 76*(3), 442–451.

Wittrock, M. C. (Ed.). (1986). *Handbook of research on teaching* (3rd ed.). New York: Macmillan.

Witty, P. (1967). Children of the television era. *Elementary English, 44,* 528–535, 554.

Woiwode, L. (1992). Television: The cyclops that eats books. *Imprimis, 21*(2), 1.

Yatvin, J. (1977). Recreational reading for the whole school. *The Reading Teacher, 31,* 185–188.

# REFLECTIONS AND REFRACTIONS OF MEANING: DIALOGIC APPROACHES TO READING WITH CLASSROOM DRAMA

## Brian Edmiston and Patricia E. Enciso
### Ohio State University

In her groundbreaking research on children's use of popular culture in writing and story performances, Dyson (1998) argued that as young children represent characters, actions, and one another, their texts reflect and refract "the children's professed values, interests, and beliefs about human relations" (p. 152). The terms *reflect* and *refract* are borrowed from Volosinov (1986) and Bakhtin (1981), who were concerned with the social and ideological forces of language in everyday events. When children write about and build performances of their worlds, their words, intonations, and gestures contain and reflect fragments of the relationships, identities, and ideas they value. As their words become increasingly public, they also become contested and transformed—refracted—across the dynamic identities and social relationships in the classroom. Similarly, when students and teachers read and discuss texts in school, their interpretations reflect and refract the students' values, interests, and beliefs about social relations (Beach, 1993; Enciso, 1994; 1997a, 1997b, 1998; Enciso & Edmiston, 1997; Lewis, 1993, 1997; Rogers & O'Neill, 1993). The problem for researchers and teachers is to understand what is reflected and refracted through the public interpretation of texts and to understand how classroom drama, a public art form, can enable all students to persist in finding and exploring the consequences of multiple, often conflicting values, interests, and beliefs.

This chapter focuses on research and teaching practices that show how drama can be used to create forums for text interpretation as it also exposes and mediates students' diverse beliefs about social relations. The first section compares "monologic" and "dialogic" approaches to classroom drama and reading. These terms are drawn from Bakhtin's theory of dialogism

(1981, 1984, 1986, 1990, 1993), and the basic understanding that texts and relationships can be considered on a continuum between those that are highly monologic and those that are highly dialogic. Texts and relations that tend toward the monologic are more singular and static, holding authoritative uncontested meanings, whereas more dialogic texts and relations allow for a dynamic interplay of contested, yet interrelated, beliefs and interests with the potential for continual transformation of meaning. A dialogic approach to drama is based on an understanding of drama practice that relies on nonnaturalistic drama conventions to promote an interplay of meaning among teachers and students across the shifting social positions they explore and present through drama. Examples of drama with children will help illustrate this approach.

The second section provides a review of discourse theory and research related to drama as a dialogic practice. The third section offers an overview of promising directions in research and practice for drama and literacy education. We are particularly interested in teacher-practitioner research that highlights teachers' responsiveness to students' specific questions and points of view.

## MONOLOGIC AND DIALOGIC CONCEPTIONS OF CLASSROOM DRAMA

Classroom drama is subject to misconstrual and is likely to promote superficial interpretations when practitioners assume that students should interpret texts as though they have only one meaning, when drama is seen as a linear sequence of

TABLE 64.1. Monologic Versus Dialogic Approaches
to Classroom Drama

| Monologic Approaches | Dialogic Approaches |
| --- | --- |
| Confrontations between people | Conflicting interrelated discourses |
| Linear sequencing | Dialogic sequencing |
| Naturalistic representations | Nonnaturalistic representations |
| Explanation | Evaluation |
| Role | Positioning |

students' experiences of confrontation between characters, when naturalism is regarded as the primary or sole mode of representation, and when students and/or teachers are expected through the use of "role" to create fully realized, sustained performances of characters that merely explain events. All of these pitfalls are associated with the misconception that drama is monologic—a product and performance of "the" text rather than a process or tool in children's literacy education through which multiple meanings are evoked and problematized.

We argue that if teachers want to engage students in reading and extend their interpretations, they will do so more effectively by using dialogic approaches to drama. As Table 64.1 shows, such approaches require teachers and students to set multiple meanings in motion in which conflict between discourses (rather than people) are experienced. Rather than a linear attention to plot we advocate dialogic sequencing of experiences. Instead of a reliance on naturalistic drama conventions we illustrate the value of nonnaturalistic conventions. Finally, we extend conceptions of role, to include an attention to social positioning through which students are placed at the crossroads of different discourses, across time, and place and in relation to one another. Through these positionings, which are negotiated and improvised with the teacher and their peers, students are seen as responsible for evaluating (rather than only explaining) meaning.

This is not to say that drama should be all process with no discernible experience of presentation. On the contrary, drama is engaging and significant not only because students imagine themselves in other times, places, and social positions, but also because they are able to put ideas into action in a public space where others can view and consider their meaning. As Bolton (1999) noted, drama has two broad interrelated functions: (a) making meaning, when students are not concerned with being watched; and (b) presenting meaning (whether in classroom performances or as part of ongoing improvised drama work) so that interpretations can be evaluated.

## Making and Presenting Meaning

An earlier analysis of classroom drama and literacy education (Wolf, Edmiston, & Enciso, 1997) described two distinct uses of text and drama. The first, "text-centered drama," relies on children's close reading and representations of the author's narrative. However, unlike the making of a teacher-directed class play, the text becomes a shared source for narrative direction around which children are able to improvise on characters' intonations, actions, and interactions by drawing on their

knowledge of stories, human emotion, and relationships. As they follow the text, students evaluate the text's *potential* meanings in relation to their own representations. These dramatizations of texts may take the form of readers theater, classroom theater, or story theater. Wolf's research (1994) indicated that children who participate in text performance as a medium for reading instruction, also discuss and improvise on their personal stories and perspectives through their representations of characters. The more students are invited to draw on multiple experiences, knowledge of contexts, and positions of relationship to characters, the more dialogic their presentations of meaning will become.

Readers theater, and chamber theater (Heathcote & Bolton, 1995) in particular, embrace the use of multiple drama conventions insofar as the participants must create a context that is minimal, but also coherent, for the text's narration and dialogue. Participants are also encouraged to interpret beyond literal actions or meanings in order to create their own realization of the narrator and characters' views and attitudes. Given the students' ongoing reference to the text, it is likely that the interpretation will be relatively more chronologically sequenced, scripted, and performed than other dialogic drama practices. However, if the text is fairly "open" and thus ambiguous in its context and referents, students' performances will necessarily be preceded by discussions and improvisations of implied events and viewpoints as they sort through possible meanings, voices, and settings.

Research suggests that as children participate in reading and reflecting on texts before, during, and after their performances, they develop more elaborated understanding of reading as an interpretive activity (Wolf, 1998), their attitudes toward reading are more positive (J. T. Jackson, 1993; Wolf, 1998), and in some cases reading comprehension, measured by standardized tests, is significantly greater (Gourgey, Bosseau, & Delgado, 1985; Knudson, 1970). Drama that is "text-centered" and dialogized offers teachers and students the opportunity to read with a sense of audience and purpose, and it also engages children's personal and cultural resources (related life experience, language, music, gesture, and image) as symbol systems for meaning making (Garcia, 1998). Text-centered drama seems to be particularly well suited to students' interpretations of literary excerpts, short stories, and picture books that portray clear action and characterization.

A second approach to drama can be described as "text-edged" (Wolf et al., 1997), because the text creates the basis for a shared context from which multiple *implied* events, characters, and conversations can be imagined, represented, and interpreted. As an illustration we expand a previous example (Wolf et al., 1997).

## Dr. De Soto: A Dialogic Approach to Drama and Reading

Children might read the opening pages of William Steig's *Dr. De Soto* (1982) and learn that a deceitful fox wants a kindly mouse dentist to repair his aching tooth, but the fox fully intends to eat the mouse as soon as the procedure is completed. At this point in the story, the teacher might ask the children to imagine themselves as dentists and to discuss their perception of the fox. Although Steig narrated Dr. De Soto's skepticism, the text leaves room for further speculation and interpretation, which the children can provide. The teacher could also ask the children to imagine that they were other animals previously tended by the dentist; in turn, the children, from the position of animal patients, could describe their understanding of "the rules" for behavior and service in a dentist's office, like Dr. De Soto's, which was dedicated to the treatment of all animals in need. Working in small groups, the children could use their bodies to create and then present "photographs" of before and after their treatment, and add the "inner voices" of how their lives had been changed. From the position of receptionists in the dentist's office they could look at potential clients through "surveillance cameras" and then interview them by "phone" in order to screen those who seem to be too dangerous to be treated by the dentist. Finally, from the position of fellow dentists, they could discuss plans for how they could manage to treat the fox, despite his likely sinister intentions.

All of these inventions of dialogue, interactions, presentations, and plans enable children to participate in the authoring of the text. As they invent and elaborate on the text's potential, they generate multiple perspectives based on their knowledge of stories and life. Rather than moving through the text in a linear, literal, and ultimately monologic manner, the text's narrative is reshaped to make room for additional narrative pathways, perspectives, images, and positions. These pathways enable the teacher to actively engage children with the problems of conflicting viewpoints and discourses without taking children directly to enactment of the moment of conflict when Dr. De Soto and his wife begin their repairs on the fox's tooth.

If and when the children do eventually want to face that moment, they will bring a more fully elaborated understanding of the decisions and worries accompanying the action. Indeed, to promote a more dialogic relationship with the text, the teacher could ask the students to view a similar operation from the position of dentists in training who are viewing a "video" of a dentist at work on a potentially dangerous patient. Students could work together in small groups to create and then represent sections from the "video" for everyone to watch. Given the lens which this nonnaturalistic convention provides, the children could watch this tense encounter with a highly critical, evaluative purpose that would make it quite reasonable for the teacher to show the film in slow motion or to repeat sections so that children could view particularly worrisome fox gestures and the doctor's skillful responses. Later, the children might want to talk with the doctor or his assistant (who could be represented by teacher or students) about their perceptions of the procedure and their evaluation of the problems in balancing danger with service.

The *Dr. De Soto* example illustrates the five ways we propose classroom drama can be reconceptualized. Across their conversations and interactions in and around Dr. De Soto's office, the children are focusing not on confrontation between people but rather on *conflicting discourses* (e.g., a discourse of professional service balanced with a discourse that recognizes the need to take individual care in potentially dangerous situations). Rather than create a linear dramatization of the story, teacher and students *sequence events dialogically* to create dialogue in which discourses come into conflict and meanings can be problematized. Instead of attempting to realistically recreate the setting, events, and images in the text, children are invited to use drama conventions to create *nonnaturalistic representations* such as "photographs," "inner thoughts," events on "camera," "telephones," and watching events depicted on "video." These are not performed in a naturalistic way but instead are presented as glimpses of moments and dialogue to be evaluated both from the fictional positions of characters from the text and from the actual positions of students, everyday understandings. The drama work involves movement back and forth in time, and in and out of different spaces, in order to create a cumulative representation and evaluation of beliefs, values, actions, and relations.

This work with Steig's (1982) book also suggests that the reading goals are dialogic in nature. Students are not expected to simply explain the story, rather the students are asked to complicate the apparent perspectives of characters and *evaluate* the consequences of their actions. Finally, in this example, it is evident that the children are not acting or simply taking on static social roles; rather, they are shifting among multiple *positions* that require them to articulate and represent a wide range of viewpoints. By moving across positions, space, and time, rather than establishing roles that each child sustains, students are asked to present multiple views so that one discourse's beliefs and values are located within and across contexts and differing views are heard in relation to one another. As each context and discourse is made visible, its meanings reflect and refract the previous presentations, thus highlighting new tensions and new possibilities for interpretation. As we discuss in the following section, this kind of interplay of meanings creates what Bakhtin (1981) terms "dialogized discourses" (p. 324). It is up to the teacher to recognize the potential discourses emerging in the text and students' ideas and to make these visible through drama conventions so that meanings will be dialogized in subsequent presentations and readings. In the next section, the five dimensions of a dialogic approach to classroom drama, briefly illustrated here, are described and discussed in greater depth through a focus on related theory and practice.

## THEORIZING DRAMA AS A DIALOGIC PRACTICE

In proposing a dialogic approach to classroom drama we rely on the theories of Bakhtin (1981, 1984, 1986, 1990, 1993). Bakhtin's theory of dialogism extends far beyond a concern with verbal exchanges. Bakhtin viewed consciousness, understanding, texts, reading, relationships, and life itself as dialogic and thus fundamentally dynamic, social, and cultural. "To live means to participate in dialogue: to ask questions, to heed, to respond, to agree, and so forth. In this dialogue a person participates wholly and throughout his [or her] whole life" (Bakhtin, 1984, p. 293). In contrast, a monologic approach to classroom drama relies on the prevalent but limited view of dialogue as a sequence of one-way verbal interactions and of understanding as a largely individual response to the world.

According to Bakhtin and other discourse analysts (Gee, 1990; Hodge & Kress, 1993), the words we use in everyday interactions do more than state our meaning. As "discourse," our words also express our social, cultural, ideological, and ethical positions about social relations, whether those relations are very intimate and close to our lives or distant from our immediate experience. For Bakhtin, discourse is always highly social and contextualized; it must always be understood as being about the social relations among particular people and recognized as uttered by specific people with particular social status or authority relative to those who are being addressed. Thus, we are never alone when we use language, because our language is always addressed to someone. Furthermore, our use of language is informed by all the ways we have heard language in use among others. As Bakhtin (1981) described it, language is "half-ours, half-someone else's" (p. 293). All of "my" understandings have been formed in dialogue with others who have themselves formed understandings in previous dialogues.

In dialogized forms of drama and reading it is crucial that apparently singular or monologic meanings be given social meaning as they are moved into social action. To avoid monologic discourse and static relations with others, discourses must be "dialogized" or "double-voiced" (Bakhtin, 1984, p. 199). In other words, we need to place one discourse in dialogue with other discourses. When we experience one discourse "through" another then, for Bakhtin, a discourse is internally dialogized or double-voiced. Ideally, as discourses are experienced in action and in relation to one another, participants recognize the "interillumination" of meaning and their ideas and meanings become more complex or changed. As Bakhtin (1986) argued, "In the act of understanding, a struggle occurs that results in mutual change and enrichment" (p. 143). Thus, a dialogic approach to classroom drama positions students to experience multiple discourses and assumes that there will be resulting struggles for meaning.

## Conflicting Interrelated Discourses

A dialogic approach to drama focuses on the conflict between discourses not merely on the conflicts between people. Rather than create or dwell in a monologic experience of conflict from a single position it is critical that students experience discourse from more than one position. When students have opportunities to view one discourse through another then they are likely to dialogize their discourse.

When we used drama to read Karen Hesse's (1997) novel, *Out of the Dust*, with 9- and 10-year olds, and again with 13- and 14-year old students, we did not dramatize any of the confrontations described or implied in the story between bankers and farmers, or between people determined to stay in Oklahoma versus those determined to leave for California (Edmiston, Long, & Enciso, 1998). Nor did we enact scenes from the book. Instead, we examined the emotions and conflicting meanings associated with multiple discourses related to peoples' decisions and dilemmas during the dust bowl of the 1930s. Hesse's free-verse

poetry suggests that people held conflicting beliefs about self-sufficiency, financial security, and commitments to the land. Early in our use of drama, many children expressed the assumption that any one of these dilemmas could be easily resolved: "They should just move!" "I'd leave." Students' statements were monological insofar as they were based on the simplistic view that "the right thing to do" was self-evident and not subject to contestation. Using drama conventions, our consideration of different social positionings, along with a selection of photographs showing the desolation of the dust bowl, we worked to place their monologic, self-evident interpretations of Hesse's words into action and in relation to other conflicting ways of thinking about people's relations to one another, to the banks, and to the land.

After students looked at photographs from the period and read several of the poems from the book, we talked about words from the poem "The Path of Our Sorrow" in Hesse's (1997) book. We wondered how we could understand Hesse's poetry that offers a double-voiced history of the region through the *narrator's* reflections on her *teacher's* explanations of the farmers' and bankers' gains and ultimate losses:

'. . .
Such a sorrow doesn't come suddenly,
there are a thousand steps to take
before you get there.'
But now,
sorrow climbs up our front steps,
big as Texas, and we didn't even see it coming,
even through it'd been making its way straight for us
all along. (Hesse, 1997, p. 84)

To begin our work with this text, we read a letter, invented by the teachers, as if written by Dorothea Lange to journalists at *Life* magazine. The letter asked the journalists to research and write a story on what was happening in Oklahoma. In this letter, a fictionalized Lange enclosed some of her photographs (we photocopied several evocative ones) and some poems she had seen published in a newspaper (they were poems, extracted from the novel). We asked the students if they were interested in imagining what photographs they might have taken if they had been those journalists. They were prepared to go along with the idea that they were photojournalists who were willing to be responsible for documenting a community's experience of the dust bowl.

Students talked about and then carried their ideas into actions by imagining and depicting photographs that could have been taken at the time, showing people in Oklahoma who had "sorrow climbing up their front steps." One group depicted a person receiving a foreclosure notice from the bank, another group showed a family looking at a charred farmhouse, another represented a family on the road headed west. As these depictions were shared, the students talked about why the sorrows had happened, why the people kept struggling, and how journalists, in their writing, might acknowledge the complexity of the story. Now the students were imagining and acting from inside multiple discourses, with a responsibility, as journalists, to reject simple solutions or explanations.

## Dialogic Sequencing

A person can experience discourses as dialogized when drama activities are sequenced dialogically (Edmiston, 1994, 1998; Edmiston & Wilhelm, 1998b); that is, discourses are first made visible and then evaluated in a recurring, interrelated practice of presentation and interpretation. In our experiences, discourses become more visible in action. Although talk can be significant, the ideological and ethical assumptions underlying discourse are more likely to become visible in action because those actions are seen to have consequences for others. Talk can easily remain abstract and generalized. What Bakhtin (1981) said of novels applies to fictional enactment in classroom drama: "The action and individual act of a character in a novel are essential in order to expose—as well as to test—his ideological position, his discourse" (p. 334).

In action, discourse becomes "an object to be perceived, reflected upon, or related to" (Bakhtin, 1981, p. 286). This is the case whether action is actual or imagined. Drama allows students the opportunity to experience the consequences of actions which are enacted in an imagined context. The sort of action and reflection that Bakhtin thought was largely only possible for artists, especially novelists, is made possible for students in classrooms. As an "author" of the fiction being created, students "step back and objectify" the "quarrels between characters." Rather than being trapped inside one single viewpoint, students begin to present and interrelate competing discourses and their consequences in action.

Having presented discourses and moved "outside" them, as students began to do when they took up the positions of both Oklahomans and journalists, they might then be able to evaluate discourses (Bakhtin, 1986, p. 7). Discourses, then, become double-voiced and multilayered as one position, made visible in action, illuminates another.

For example, the students reading *Out of the Dust* (Hesse, 1997) depicted the discourses and consequences related to peoples' beliefs about financial responsibility. Students composed a foreclosure letter from the bank; then they presented its meaning through drama conventions including a frozen moment when the letter was received, an overheard dialogue between the banker and an assistant, and a dream depicting the farm family's hopes for their land and future. When students returned to their letter and reflected on its implications, the abstract words illuminated different discourses about life on the land: "We regret to inform you that ... because you failed to make payment on ... [y]ou must vacate the property on ..." The students felt the letter was not only ending a way of life, it was also questioning people's previous judgments, their future ability to earn money, and undermining a family's belief in the American dream. The financial trap created by federal farming policies, described in Hesse's "The Path of Our Sorrow" were no longer someone else's words. In Bakhtin's (1981) terms, they were half the students' and half the diverse people's and positions' coexisting in Oklahoma during the dust bowl. Two broad discourses of the American dream and the paths of sorrow were interilluminated through a spiraling sequence of presentation and evaluation of discourses.

## Nonnaturalistic Representations

The aim of naturalistic conventions, like role playing, is to represent people interacting as "rounded characters" and to simulate actions and events as if they were actually happening. Role playing is most often used to represent life-rate talk, the linear passage of time and naturalistic contexts. However, as in everyday interactions, when all of our surroundings are equally "real" and when time moves along without interruption, it is difficult to highlight specific aspects of discourses or their implications.

In contrast, use of nonnaturalistic conventions makes it easier to focus on the particularities of discourses and their consequences for other people. Time can be slowed down, speeded up, repeated, or even reversed. In one space, different events can be represented concurrently or in a variety of sequences. Language and meanings are also made more significant when particular words and related gestures can be thoughtfully selected and presented in multiple ways instead of "played" to give the appearance of naturally flowing dialogue.

Heathcote (1980) provided the first and most complete classification of the range of drama conventions. Her comprehensive list has been further adapted and extended by a number of drama educators across the world (Ball & Ayers, 1995; Neelands, 1990; O'Neill, 1995; Owens & Barber, 1997). Heathcote's 33 nonnaturalistic drama conventions are forms of representation that offer variations on "still image," "tableau," or "depiction." Table 64.2 provides an overview of modes of communication often used in film and drama to make relations, language, attitude, and selected information both more visible and significant.

The students reading *Out of the Dust* (Hesse, 1997) used several nonnaturalistic conventions. The farming families were seen in full-size "photographs" and overheard speaking their inner hopes and fears; they also interacted and spoke out of their surreal nightmares and hopeful dreams for the future. In

TABLE 64.2. Modes of Communication Used in Film and Drama

| Nonnaturalistic Convention | Examples |
| --- | --- |
| People seen ... | in photographs |
|  | in dreams |
|  | in paintings |
|  | in statues |
|  | in video clips |
|  | through binoculars |
|  | through a two-way mirror |
| People heard ... | on the telephone |
|  | recorded on audio or video tape |
|  | speaking inner thoughts |
|  | when paintings or statues are brought to life |
|  | overheard talking to others |
| People represented abstractly ... | in writing |
|  | in drawings |
|  | by clothing |
|  | by personal possessions |

addition, the people were represented in letters and drawings and by possessions people left behind when they began their journeys to California. The banker was overheard talking on the phone then viewed as if in a portrait; the portrait was then brought to life and asked specific questions. All these conventions were presented and interpreted in relation to Hesse's poetry, which presents the dust bowl's effects through the diary of a 13-year-old girl whose family barely survived drought, dust, and devastation.

## Evaluation

Bakhtin (1986) made clear that explanation is limited in its meaning-making potential, whereas evaluations are dialogic as they place one possible interpretation in relation with another: "With explanation there is only one consciousness, one subject. With comprehension [and evaluation] there are two consciousnesses and two subjects . . . Understanding is always dialogic to some degree. . . . Understanding is impossible without evaluation" (pp. 111, 143). Reflections that lead to literal, factual, and uncontested explanations of actions tend to be monologic. Through this kind of reflection, students are likely either to avoid ethical evaluations or offer opinions and finalizing comments which are not themselves tested in action.

In contrast, when students create depictions of actions and consequences using drama conventions they witness and participate in discourses as they carry differing, conflicting beliefs into action and relationships. They make value judgments as they choose what to represent and they evaluate those choices when they wonder whether or not a character should have taken a particular action. Bolton's (1999) classification of drama activities into two broad categories of students' relationship to meaning are useful for recognizing moments of evaluation in drama. He argued that when activities focus on "*making* meaning," students are not concerned with being watched. In contrast, if students are aware of being watched then they are "*presenting* meaning" for others to evaluate.

Students might make meaning through any number of drama conventions described above, through whole group, small group, and pair participation in ongoing activities. However, if drama work only involves enactments there will be little opportunity for reflection and no chance for teacher and students to step outside the action to consider the consequences of meanings and actions. To dialogize the discourses which students explore as they make meaning there must be both a presentation of meaning and a concurrent or subsequent evaluation.

Critical to evaluation is teacher questioning. Evaluation will not occur if teachers focus on students' literal and factual explanations and on uncontested opinions rather than ongoing dialogue. Morgan and Saxton (1994) wrote an invaluable resource that lays out in detail different types, styles, and considerations of many aspects of teacher questioning. Lewis (1999) analyzed how the quality of a teacher's questions can promote students' awareness of the constructed nature of texts, their resistance to accepting without question authors' assumptions about what is "natural," their critical awareness of a text's social, cultural, and

historical complexity, and an examination of why people might hold certain beliefs.

The students reading *Out of the Dust* (Hesse, 1997) both made meaning and presented meaning for evaluation. Their depictions of people at the time of the dust bowl came to life as the students imagined their actions, their thoughts, their hopes and fears, and their reactions to events like foreclosure and the actions of other people like bankers. As the students observed one another's depictions they evaluated. We asked open-ended, though pointed, questions such as "I wonder how the people lived with such sorrow and yet continued to help each other?" Some of the students' evaluations were initially detached and prescriptive, as when they argued, "They should have paid their bills." However, as students became more engaged and discourses were dialogized, evaluations became more double-voiced: "I don't trust those flyers about California, but if we stay we might not all survive another summer." With these words, this student expresses an evaluation of meaning that refers to yet another text, and she also assesses the tensions in her own and an Oklahoman's troubled situation. She and other students could begin to understand the discourses and dilemmas that led to the enormous weight of Hesse's (1997) words, "[S]orrow climbs our front steps . . . and we didn't even see it coming" (p. 84).

## Positioning

For Bakhtin (1981), the struggle for understanding occurs not only among people but also within each of us. "He imagines the self as a conversation, often a struggle, of discrepant voices with each other, voices (and words) speaking from different positions and invested with different degrees and kinds of authority" (Morson & Emerson, 1990, p. 218). Drama can make internal and external struggles more visible and more productive through students' experience of internally competing meanings, represented through different social positions in relation to others. In contrast, the term *role* connotes the presentation of a singular voice that does not shift across beliefs or values within itself or across relations with others. A role is "in place" to be stood up and propelled forward in relation to another role. In contrast, a social position is in dynamic relationship to others as multiple discourses, expressed both internally and externally, compete for significance.

For example, a mother living during the dust bowl might have had to struggle with the competing, internal positions of a dutiful and doubtful partner who wants to support the farm business and her children's future. Neither of these positions can be simply ignored; they must be brought into dialogue and action through her relations with others across numerous different contexts. Students role-playing the dust bowl period might imagine and enact only one of these positions, yet it is crucial to the experience of that time to appreciate the struggle among competing discourses embedded in different social positions.

According to the theory of positioning, we position ourselves and others and are, in turn, positioned by them as we move in and out of social situations (Davies & Harré, 1990; Harré & Langehove, 1998). Across these situations, we encounter and express varying degrees of social status and authority in our relative positions. For example, a banker might use his status to question a farmer's integrity. Because status differentials restrict the range of discourses we anticipate and express, and because our positions *appear* to be "fixed" it is difficult for the banker or the farmer to reject their status and related ways of seeing one another. However, when these positions become visible and made more dynamic, as they can be through drama, it is possible to imagine and enact new terms for interpreting oneself and others—and our mutual dilemmas.

When students position themselves and others in drama they do not "become" someone else. As Warner (1995) discovered, students' engagement in drama is marked by movement across social positions, personal experiences, and anticipation of responsibilities. Much like the findings in Enciso's (1990) research on engagement in reading, students' drama engagement is highly active, visual, and social. As Arnold (1998) insisted, drama is as much about affective response as it is about cognitive understanding. However, students do not empathize to the extent that they stop thinking as themselves; instead, they use their own value systems to understand their temporary positions while they simultaneously evaluate actions from the conflicting positions of others who must interpret their particular circumstances and social relations. Drama allows students to experience what Bakhtin (1993) called "aesthetic emphathizing" (p. 17). In dialogized drama work, students "bring into interaction both perspectives simultaneously and create a . . . vision reduceable to neither" (Morson & Emerson, 1990, p. 54).

The students reading *Out of the Dust* (Hesse, 1997) did not simply play out the roles of family farmers and bankers; instead, they positioned one another using discourses from the novel. In doing so, the students engaged in struggles for understanding. When students imagined that they were people who lived during the time of the dust bowl, they drew on their own knowledge and values ("We should help each other"). They also made social, cultural, and ethical assumptions about the period based on their own life experiences and their interpretation of Hesse's novel, photographs, and other sources. Discourses became more double-voiced when they came into conflict as students positioned themselves and each another. What at first seemed straightforward for some students gradually became more complex. The "sorrow" that "climbed their front steps" was no longer seen as simply caused by a letter from an individual banker. Students began to understand how the sorrow of events were the result of many social, political, and cultural beliefs implied in the discourses and decisions of journalists, historians, and politicians.

## PROMISING DIRECTIONS IN DRAMA RESEARCH AND PRACTICE

As a field of study classroom drama (also known as drama in education, educational drama, drama education, creative drama, process drama, teaching and learning with drama, or just drama) encompasses a worldwide network of researchers and practitioners whose concerns range from community development through drama to the analysis of teachers' involvement in

young children's spontaneous play (see in particular O'Toole & Donelan, 1996; Saxton & Miller, 1998; P. Taylor & Hoepper, 1995). All of these researchers and practitioners use texts to interrogate and represent meanings, whether the texts are generated from participants' lives or selected from canonical or other literature. For an extensive and detailed review of research in drama and the language arts, we direct readers to Wagner's (1998) edited volume, *Educational Drama and Language Arts: What Research Shows*.

A review of drama research and analyses of practice from the past 5 years indicates that many scholars and practitioners of drama have been influenced by research methods that allow them to examine their own participation and decision making as they also document the contexts of and participants' responses to planning and implementing drama work. In particular, teacher researchers using drama in classrooms and communities have been encouraged to use the stance of reflective practitioner to describe and analyze their work with children, adults, and texts (P. Taylor, 1996). Rather than provide an exhaustive overview of research and practice, we choose instead to focus selectively on those teacher-researcher and ethnographic studies that we believe present researchers with new "dialogic" directions for the analysis and practice of classroom drama.

The studies we review are divided into three sections according to the ways texts are made and read: (a) *emergent texts*, evolved from a briefly stated premise that is negotiated and moved into action by all participants; (b) pre-texts, including extensive historical documents and other narratives already partially known and presented by teachers (or "drama leaders") then extended into action and reflection by participants; and (c) *extant texts*, usually novels or poetry, read and retrospectively interrogated through drama by participants, with the direction of a drama leader.

### Research and Practice With Emergent Texts

Heathcote's pioneering work in classroom drama provides a complex and detailed exposition of the use of drama to generate and transform events based on the multiple, interrelated texts of participants' lives (Bolton & Heathcote, 1999; Johnson & O'Neill, 1984; Heathcote & Bolton, 1995; Wagner, 1999b). In a sense, Heathcote's practice is comparable to the work of a novelist, or, in her terms, a playwright, who is able to construct interactions and reflective moments with children as she negotiates who is speaking to whom, from what social positions, in what times and places, from what frame of reference, and under what constraints. In this respect, Heathcote's work is very much an enactment of Bakhtin's theory of dialogism. The texts, and the associated discourses, that emerge through drama are presented by people who are socially situated as they face the dilemmas of their particular crossroads. All of these social positions and crossroads are infused with beliefs, interests, and values; in short, social ideologies that become reflected and refracted back to the participants as their interpretations are presented and evaluated.

The use of drama to situate social relations and dilemmas, without the support of a written text can be the most complex form of drama work to plan and implement. However, it is important to recognize that even without a written text, the drama evolves in response to participants' personal, popular, and cultural knowledge—all texts (and all discourses) of one sort or another that have the potential to be presented as related meaning in the unfolding drama.

Many drama educators have been influenced by the vision of Freire (1970) and Boal (1979), who urge community leaders to assist participants toward representations and critiques of the realities and oppression of their worlds. For example, the South African community activist Doësebs (1998) argued that among people living during a period of extreme violence in KwaZulu-Natal, it was crucial that "events and past experiences" (p. 179) become the texts for teaching. Indeed, through the telling of a community-based story, members of a village not only participated in representing the people of the story but also transforming its relationships and consequences so that their own divided relationships could begin to heal. Arguing that this work with emerging beliefs and events requires that teachers build their own capacity for personal change, Doësebs (1998) wrote:

We need to question our own motives and the methodologies we use in facilitating [community] development and be open to new ideas that instigate real change.... The ghost of apartheid still haunts—within institutions, communities and classrooms, in our churches, our kitchens, our bedrooms and in our boardrooms and more importantly, *in our minds* [italics added]. (p. 179)

Community work, like Heathcote's early explorations of classroom drama (see Wagner, 1999b), requires teachers to listen carefully to how participants bring their social positions, knowledge, and experience into public forums. In this and all educational work, it is essential that teachers become aware of their own socially situated perspectives, biases, and beliefs so that these can also be made a part of the group's explorations and presentations of meaning. For example, Edmiston (1993) analyzed his teaching with third-graders and described the range of structures he used to facilitate his and the children's reflections on their contributions to the drama's emerging text and discourses. Similarly, Gonzalez (1999) described and analyzed her viewpoints and expectations of power relations as she and her students improvised on the meanings in a script and rehearsed for a play.

In her consideration of the teacher's function in developing drama texts with students, O'Neill (1995) stressed the artistic nature of drama in arguing that drama teachers should use "creative structure" to shape experiences. However, she cautioned:

Any creative structure will contain unknown variables, which must be accommodated. The artist works in a kind of open possibility, as does the leader in process drama.... The craftsperson uses skills to achieve a predetermined end, but the artist uses skills to discover ends through action. (O'Neill, 1995, p. 65)

As discussed throughout this chapter, "Each of the participants in process drama will be not just an actor, but also both playwright and spectator" (O'Neill, 1995, p. 65).

This characterization of drama as equivalent to the work of actors, playwrights, and spectators is applicable to Dyson's (1998) descriptions of young children making new texts and dramatizations of the multiple, intersecting texts they encounter through television, music, home relations, and school relations. Although their forums for presentation of meaning are only minimally guided by an adult leader or teacher, they are quite heavily directed by the children themselves. What emerges, in Dyson's view, are transformations of texts that reflect and refract the discourses children use to position their own and others' identities in a complex classroom and society. The children's group-generated texts are based on what Dyson calls the "ideological gaps" (p. 149) in classroom life. Her research highlighted the tensions in belief systems among children as they transform popular cultural images and narratives in their classroom writing and dramatizations. Dyson (1998) argued:

"These ideological gaps reveal larger societal fault lines, including those related to gender, class, and race. Children struggle to use written signs to bring order to their inner thoughts and simultaneously to reach out to address others, but their signs are themselves symbols of societal order.... Through the dramatic enactment of texts on a community stage, those tensions [between signs and social relations] may be revealed and, moreover they may become the basis for public deliberation." (p. 149)

Dyson's analytic lenses and careful documentation of children's talk during play and text development offer important directions for further research in classroom drama.

## Research and Practice With Pre-Texts

Although a pre-text can be understood to be a premise or beginning point, O'Neill (1995) argued that a pre-text is much more than the stimulus for an idea:

The function of the pre-text is to activate the weaving of the text of the process drama.... [T]he pre-text operates, first of all, to define the nature and limits of the dramatic world, and second, to imply roles for the participants. Next, it switches on expectation and binds the group together in anticipation." (1995, p. 20)

She continued, "An effective pre-text... suggests a will to be read, a task to be undertaken, a decision to be made, a puzzle to be solved, a wrong-doer to be discovered, a haunted house to be explored" (p. 20). In O'Neill's analysis of her own and others' drama work, she made clear that a pre-text is quite different from the emergent text of the drama: "The pre-text that is the source of the work... remains as an outline, a trace, in the memories of the participants after the event. The [text generated by the process] is an outcome, a product" (p. 20).

Any number of pre-texts have been used to establish drama world parameters and participants' social positions. Often, the pre-text is taken from literary sources as in many of the examples of drama work described in *Dreamseekers: Creative approaches to the African American Heritage* (Manley & O'Neill, 1997). This same edited collection also includes examples of historical documents used as pre-texts. For example,

Tyson (1997) described her use of the persona "Hattie," a time traveler from the 1860s, as both a pre-text herself and as a vehicle for introducing children to stories from the history of enslavement in the United States. In other descriptions, teachers used photographs or song (Douglas, 1997; Manley, 1997) to establish a time period and students' relationship to events. Books by Swartz (1996) and Saldaña (1995) present stories or excerpts from folktales, picture books, and novels along with outlines of drama strategies that enable students and their teachers to present and interpret meanings from multiple perspectives. Montgomerie and Ferguson (1999) read stories with 4–8 year old children and then used the stories as pre-texts for drama work that explored possible meanings.

P. Taylor (1998) conducted a detailed teacher researcher study of the use of drama to enliven and deepen his middle school students' engagement with history. His students investigated primary source materials, created and transformed historically based episodes, and wrote extensively in journals as they were placed in the roles of Revolutionary War era patriots, traitors, and politicians. Alongside his descriptions of his plans and actions in the classroom, Taylor analyzed his authority and students' rights to negotiate the curriculum through drama. Similarly, the historian Fines (Fines, 1997; Fines & Verrier, 1974) described in eloquent prose his understanding of the role of selective signing for and positioning with students so that they would have a fuller range of authority over the materials they read and interpreted through dramatic structures and conventions. Fines' work is marked by his use of drama to present students with multiple social positions, besides the singular authority of the teacher, in order to provoke and facilitate students' multifaceted and often provocative inquiry.

Booth (1998) described the work of Nancy Steele, who used a letter of invitation to establish the context and relationship of her eighth-grade students to their study of the Holocaust. The letter invites the students to become "filmmakers" who will create a documentary showing people's willingness to forget the past and move on. Through this letter, the teacher not only established a purpose for and relationship to their study but also conflicting discourses (stances that advocate forgetting the past or remembering horrors) that would soon be interrogated as students discovered what it might mean if people were to forget the Holocaust. Booth's adamance about the importance of evaluation and critique in drama work is evident in his contention that "[w]e need to direct the attention of students not just to the subject of discussion, but to the very language they are using in drama" (p. 69). Booth's own teaching, which used an extract from a history textbook as a pre-text, was analyzed by Hume and Wells (1999). They emphasized that the students explored multiple perspectives on the topic of "Westward expansion" in 19th-century Canada (from railroad managers to Chinese immigrant laborers to their families in China), perspectives that were experienced affectively as well as intellectually.

Another form of drama, named "mantle of the expert," uses pre-texts to establish a relationship to and purpose for learning, but it is carefully sequenced to engage students in close readings of and reflections on an ongoing presentation of documents, events, tasks, and perspectives that can be directly tied to an academic course of study. According to Heathcote (Heathcote & Bolton, 1995) who originated this use of text and relationship to the world through drama, the term *mantle* is used because people "wear their 'mantle' (i.e., express their interests, habits, and style) . . . [and t]hey use their expertise and knowledge to move along different highways" (p. 194). Heathcote and Bolton discussed the overlap between theatre and mantle-of-the-expert. They wrote that this work grew out of the intersection of two ideas:

1. Actors need a vast amount of knowledge in creating their roles and interpreting the life-style and period of the plays they interpret and perform.
2. Students come to school to learn; drama and theater provide contextual parameters that invite and require research. (p. 194)

Thus, mantle-of-the-expert work requires teachers to establish contextual parameters so that students might find both intellectual and emotional links with the worlds and texts they study.

This work is extraordinary when planned and developed with a clear understanding of the domains of knowledge and skill children will be expected to present. Texts must be carefully selected for children's use so that information is made available in highly significant forms, causing students to reach for possibilities and imagine relations and connections as they solve problems. The coauthored text *Drama for Learning: Dorothy Heathcote's mantle of the expert approach to education* (Heathcote & Bolton, 1995) and *Interactive Research in Drama in Education*, edited by Davies (1997), are invaluable sources for beginning inquiry into this approach to teaching and learning. Towler-Evans (1997) provided a usable succinct analysis of some of Heathcote's guiding principles. Edmiston and Wilhelm (1998a) provided a description and analysis of how mantle-of-the-expert work was begun with sixth-grade students studying history, using documentary and historical material as pre-texts.

Several exemplars of teacher-researcher studies also provide useful descriptions and analyses of structures and pre-texts used to endow students with the authority to investigate, report on, and present their understanding. Maine educator, Housum-Stevens (1998), initiating mantle-of-the-expert work for the first time, invited her middle school students to create a museum focusing on ancient peoples around the world. She wrote:

I simultaneously used smaller dramas [i.e., drama strategies and conventions] to open kids to different viewpoints, and introduced them to the extended drama framework that would ultimately allow us to get the big museum work done. Both gave us structure and purpose, the *context*, for everything else that came after—the month of research, the weeks of planning and creating exhibits, the efforts to understand other cultures and to connect with the people who created them, the public presentation of the learning. (p. 21)

Sylvia Jackson (1997) described similar structures and movement across drama episodes as she engaged her younger students in a study of African Americans' participation in the science and ethics associated with inventions and patent laws.

Edmiston (1998) also described work with middle school students who needed to complete social studies reports related to famous people and events. Working with students in small groups, Edmiston shifted the students away from the usual "student doing a report" monologic relation to their subjects. As he heard their key questions, he gave students tasks and positions *within* the situations they were exploring so they would experience and imagine the interrelated ethical dilemmas people faced in their particular circumstances. As a result of their brief drama work, students' thinking became far more dialogic. One young man stated, for example, "I'm kind of more open to that there are other opinions that are strong and stuff even though you might disagree [with those other opinions]" (1998, p. 103).

## Research and Practice With Extant Texts: Plays and Literature

Many educators and researchers have considered the problem of "slowing down" reading so that students will critically reflect on the meanings and implications of both the author's form and the dilemmas described in a text. Certainly, theater teachers, who direct students in script reading and performance, must be able to draw on a wide range of conventions and strategies to assist students in their interpretations and presentations of meaning. An award-winning teacher-researcher study by Gonzalez (1999) highlighted the importance of students' investment in the interpretation of a play; at the same time, Gonzalez recognized and explored the politics of negotiating students' versus the director's vision of a play's meaning. Her work reveals the high degree of skepticism students often hold when the teacher professes a commitment to democratic negotiations among a community of players. Studies such as Gonzalez's are especially valuable for their insights into both the teacher's complex goals and the students' desire to understand plays as a text and as a dramatic artform.

Heathcote and Bolton (1995, pp. 213–217) developed an approach to the reading and dramatization of texts based on Robert Breen's (1987) "chamber theatre." The appeal of chamber theater, according to Heathcote and Bolton (1995), lies in the possibility of *showing* a story: "The *narrator* tells and holds the form [of the story], while the showing involves the actors [students] in the demonstration of action" (p. 213). Although this may seem a very simplistic approach to dramatization, it actually requires a high degree of inference and imagination so that each action, stillness, and sign carries significance. Furthermore, because the narrator *tells* the feelings and motivations of the characters, the actors do not have to invent or "enact" an emotional response: "All they are required to do is give a crude "sign" of what the feelings might be" (p. 213). Heathcote and Bolton explained that chamber theater achieves goals for reading and interpretation that are often very difficult to access or sustain through other approaches to drama:

[T]he primary value of chamber theater lies in the way participants must scrutinize the written text in order to clarify what parts represent action and talk and attitude. Because the action part of the narrative will be demonstrated by people moving in space and immediate time, it is essential that they decide by careful reading of the text *who is the narrator* and what is that person's *investment in telling the account.* (p. 214)

These two key questions asked of the narrator, call attention to the dialogic potential of drama in education. Heathcote and Bolton (1995) recognized the dramatic and educational possibilities in situating people in very specific relationships with an account, or "telling." The narrator's investment is crucial to the creation of a context, which, in turn, is linked with implied and explicit discourses, actions, and interactions that actors/students will invent and present while holding firmly to the written text. Although this approach to text through drama is only briefly described in *Drama for Learning* (Heathcote & Bolton, 1995), it is a practice that warrants considerable attention and development among educators and researchers.

Salvio (1999) used drama conventions similar to chamber theater to mediate and represent and also to complicate the meaning of some of "the unspeakable" facets of response to "testimonial" literature, in this case accounts of massacre and terrorism. With student teachers taking a Foundations of Reading Instruction class she read *Krik? Krak!* a collection of non-naturalistic "magic realism" short stories written by Edwidge Danticat (1991), a Haitian American writer. Together they considered which different perspectives in and on the narrative would be privileged (and which would be silenced). She introduced the students to the nonverbal aspects of several drama conventions (e.g., relationships among people represented abstractly by objects in a collage). The class began to take up positions of witnesses to the events as they used these conventions, which became integral to performative readings of extracts. In doing so, the students explored the gaps in words and validated responses that had been previously composed from their half-perceived ideas.

Teacher researchers, working outside of theater programs, have described their use of drama with novels and poetry (for multiple examples, see Manley & O'Neill, 1997). Typically, their descriptions focus on a series of drama conventions that enable students to visualize and elaborate on characters' perspectives (Swartz, 1996; Wilhelm, 1998). Other teachers use drama, discussion, and writing to support students' review and analysis of an entire text, as was the case in Warner's (1997) work with *Roll of Thunder, Hear My Cry* (M. D. Taylor, 1977). Warner's sequence of drama conventions and discussions enabled students to build their understanding of the characters' integrity as they faced multiple injustices. Furthermore, she described a highly abstract yet affecting sequence of structures that connect the novel's events to the author's and characters' deep relationship with the land. In the same volume, Thomas (1997) described her use of several poems and music to both evoke students' empathy and provide multiple shifts in their perspectives as they represented and reflected on the terror and loss associated with lynchings in the United States.

Enciso and Edmiston (1997) described the structures and nonnaturalistic conventions they used to engage students in a careful reading and rereading of *The True Story of the Three Little Pigs* (Scieszka, 1989). The students, in the role of police officers, were asked to view a "video" of A. Wolf delivering his sworn testimony, which was the full text of the book. Children were also given typewritten copies of the testimony, which they read and underlined as they prepared for the actions and questioning they would need to pursue to gather evidence that would confirm or disconfirm the wolf's story. Through drama conventions, they not only encountered witnesses but also took up the perspectives of those witnesses; and as they encountered evidence, they had to first stop and reenact the steps leading to the making and placing of the evidence. In effect, the children read the text multiple times, in and out of sequence, from numerous social positions, with different purposes and critical concerns in mind. As their reading and drama work concluded, children were keenly aware that "the truth" is not a simple statement of facts; the truth can be hidden or distorted by language, social status, and institutionalized procedures.

## CONCLUSION

This chapter provides a theoretical frame for interpreting drama as a practice for dialogizing discourses. We described drama practices that dialogize the discourses of literary texts, community texts, students' lives, and teachers' curricular goals. Although many resources exist for understanding the practice of drama in relation to reading, we believe that this chapter opens up new directions for studying and planning for drama that is explicitly interested in the problem of developing students' insights about themselves and others in the world. Our work, then, is informed by and aligned with the teaching Dorothy Heathcote has been developing for 3 decades. We close with one of her extraordinary insights about the purpose of education:

We have to set up a situation in our schools where all the time, every time, we introduce a new element to children, it has the effect of cracking all the previous understanding into new awareness, new understanding. This is what growing older is about. This is what being more mature is about. This is what being educated is about. The moment whereby all the understanding you had before is sharpened into a new juxtaposition. Drama is about shattering the human experience into new understanding. (Heathcote, 1976, p. 122)

## References

Arnold, R. (1998). The drama in research and articulating dynamics—A unique theatre. In J. Saxton & C. Miller (Eds.), *The research of practice, the practice of research* (pp. 110-131). Víctoría, Canada: IDEA.

Bakhtin, M. M. (1981). *The dialogic imagination.* Austin: University of Texas Press.

Bakhtin, M. M. (1984). *Problems of Dostoevsky's poetics.* Minneapolis: University of Minnesota Press.

Bakhtin, M. M. (1986). *Speech genres and other late essays.* Austin: University of Texas Press.

Bakhtin, M. M. (1990). *Art and answerability.* Austin: University of Texas Press.

Bakhtin, M. M. (1993). *Toward a philosophy of the act.* Austin: University of Texas Press.

Ball, C., & Ayres, J. (1995). *Taking time to act: A guide to cross-curricular drama.* Portsmouth, NH: Heinemann.

Beach, R. (1993). *A teacher's introduction to reader-response theories.* Urbana, IL: National Council of Teachers of English.

Boal, A. (1979). *Theatre of the oppressed.* New York: Theatre Communications Group.

Booth, D. (1998). Language power through working in role. In B. J. Wagner (Ed.), *Educational drama and language arts: What research shows* (pp. 57-76). Portsmouth, NH: Heinemann.

Bolton, G. (1999). *Acting in classroom drama: A critical analysis.* Portland, ME: Calendar Island.

Bolton, G., & Heathcote, D. (1999). *So you want to use role play?* Staffordshire, England: Trentham.

Breen, R. S. (1987). *Chamber theatre.* England, Cliffs, NJ: Prentice-Hall.

Danticat, D. (1991). *Krik? Krak!* New York: Soho Press.

Davies, D. (Ed.) (1997). *Interactive research in drama in education.* Staffordshire, England: Trentham.

Davies, B., & Harré, R. (1990). Positioning: The discursive production of selves. *Journal for the Theory of Social Behaviour, 20*(1), 43-63.

Doësebs, V. (1998). Lay down your arms: Drama as an efficacious remedy in South Africa. *Research in Drama Education, 3*(2), 167-180.

Douglas, R. (1997). Democracy and empowerment: The Nashville student sit-ins of the 1960s. In A. Manley & C. O'Neill (Eds.), *Dreamseekers: Creative approaches to the African-American heritage* (pp. 69-84). Portsmouth, NH: Heinemann.

Dyson, A. H. (1998). The children's forum: Linking writing, drama, and the development of community in an urban classroom. In B. J. Wagner (Ed.), *Educational drama and language arts: What research shows* (pp. 148-172). Portsmouth, NH: Heinemann.

Edmiston, B. (1993). Structuring drama for reflection and learning: A teacher-researcher study. *Youth Theatre Journal, 7*(3), 3-11.

Edmiston, B. (1994). More than talk: A Bakhtinian perspective on drama in education and change in understanding. *The NADIE Journal, 18*(2), 25-36.

Edmiston, B. (1998). Drama as inquiry: Students and teachers as co-researchers. In J. Wilhelm & B. Edmiston (Eds.), *Imagining to learn: Inquiry, ethics, and integration through drama* (pp. 103-108). Portsmouth, NH: Heinemann.

Edmiston, B., Long, T., & Enciso, P. (1998). *Using drama to teach* Out of the dust. Unpublished manuscript.

Edmiston, B., & Wilhelm, J. (1998a). Exploring castles: Authentic teaching and learning through drama. In J. Wilhelm & B. Edmiston (Eds.), *Imagining to learn: Inquiry, ethics, and integration through drama* (pp. 1-27). Portsmouth, NH: Heinemann.

Edmiston, B., & Wilhelm, J. (1998b). Repositioning views/reviewing positions. In B. J. Wagner (Ed.), *Educational drama and language arts: What research shows* (pp. 99-117). Portsmouth, NH: Heinemann.

Enciso, P. (1990). *The nature of engagement in reading: Case studies of fourth and fifth grade students' engagement strategies and stances.* Unpublished doctoral dissertation, Ohio State University, Columbus.

Enciso, P. (1994). Cultural identity and response to literature: Running lessons from Maniac Magee. *Language Arts, 71,* 524-533.

Enciso, P. (1997a, September 25). *Learning to be/read together: A sociocultural analysis children's reading, art and relationships.* Paper presented at the fall meeting of the National Academy of Education, Boulder, CO.

Enciso, P. (1997b). Negotiating the meaning of difference: Talking back to multicultural literature. In T. Rogers & A. Soter (Eds.), *Reading across cultures* (pp. 13-41). New York: Teachers College Press.

Enciso, P. (1998). Good/bad girls read together: Young girls co-authorship of subject positions during a shared reading event. *English Education, 30,* 44-62.

Enciso, P., & Edmiston, B. (1997). Drama and response to literature: reading the text and re-reading the truth. In N. Karolides (Ed.), *Reader response in elementary classrooms: Quest and discovery* (pp. 69–94). Mahwah, NJ: Lawrence Erlbaum Associates.

Fines, J. (1997). Truth and the imagination—A little investigation in three fits. In D. Davis (Ed.), *Interactive research in drama in education* (pp. 41–57). Staffordshire, England: Trentham.

Fines, J., & Verrier, R. (1974). *The drama of history.* London: New University Education.

Freire, P. (1970). *Pedagogy of the oppressed.* New York: Herder & Herder.

Garcia, L. (1998). Creating community in a university production of *Bocon! Research in Drama Education, 3*(2), 155–166.

Gee, J. (1990). *Social linguistics and literacies: Ideology in discourses.* New York: Falmer Press.

Gonzalez, J. B. (1999). Directing high school theater: the impact of student empowerment strategies and unconventional staging techniques on actors, director, and audience, *Youth Theatre Journal, 13,* 4–23.

Gourgey, A., Bosseau, J., & Delgado, J. (1985). The impact of an improvisational dramatics program on students attitudes and achievement. *Children's Theatre Review, 34*(3), 9–14. (ERIC Document Reproduction Service, No. ED 244245)

Harré, R., & Langehove, V. (1998). *Positioning theory: Moral contexts of international action.* Malden, MA: Blackwell.

Heathcote, D. (1980). Signs and portents. In L. Johnson & C. O'Neill (Eds.) (1984) *Dorothy Heathcote: Collected writings on education and drama* (pp. 18–25). Evanston, IL: Northwestern University Press.

Heathcote, D. (1976). Drama as a process for change. In L. Johnson & C. O'Neill (Eds.), *Dorothy Heathcote: Collected writings on education and drama* (pp. 114–125). Evanston, IL: Northwestern University Press.

Heathcote, D., & Bolton, G. (1995). *Drama for learning. Dorothy Heathcote's mantle of the expert approach to education.* Portsmouth, NH: Heinemann.

Hesse, K. (1997). *Out of the Dust.* New York: Scholastic.

Hodge, R., & Kress, G. (1993). *Language as ideology* (2nd ed.). New York: Routledge.

Housum-Stevens, J. B. (1998). Performance possibilities: Curating a museum. *Voices from the middle, 6*(2), 19–27.

Hume, K., & Wells, G. (1999). Making lives meaningful: Extending perspectives through role-play. In B. J. Wagner (Ed.), *Building moral communities through educational drama* (pp. 63–87). Stamford, CT: Ablex.

Jackson, J. T. (1993). The effects of creative dramatics participation on the reading achievement and attitudes in elementary level children with behavioral disorders. *Dissertation Abstracts International, 53*(10), 3412A.

Jackson, S. (1997). Everybody's history. In A. Manley & C. O'Neill (Eds.), *Dreamseekers: Creative approaches to the African-American heritage* (pp. 23–34). Portsmouth, NH: Heinemann.

Knudson, F. L. (1970). *The effect of pupil-prepared videotaped drama on the language development of selected children.* Unpublished doctoral dissertation, Boston University.

Lewis, C. (1993). "Give people a chance": Acknowledging social differences in reading. *Language Arts, 70,* 454–461.

Lewis, C. (1997). The social drama of literature discussions in a fifth/sixth-grade classroom. *Research in the Teaching of English, 31*(2), 163–204.

Lewis, C. (1999). The quality of the question: Probing culture in literature-discussion groups. In C. Edelsky (Ed.), *Making justice our project: Teachers working toward critical whole language practice.* Urbana, IL: National Council of Teachers of English.

Manley, A. (1997). Incredible journeys: From manicles of oppression to mantles of hope. In A. Manley, C. O'Neill, etc. from next citation (pp. 1–13).

Manley, A., & O'Neill, C. (1997). *Dreamseekers: Creative approaches to the African American heritage.* Portsmouth, NH: Heinemann.

Montgomerie, D., & Ferguson, J. (1999). Bears don't need phonics: An examination of the role of drama in laying the foundations for critical thinking in the reading process, *Research in drama education, 4*(1), 11–20.

Morgan, N., & Saxton, J. (1994). *Asking better questions.* Markham, Canada: Pembroke.

Morson, G. S., & Emerson, C. (1990). *Mikhail Bakhtin: Creation of a prosaics.* Stanford, CA: Stanford University Press.

Neelands, J. (1990). *Structuring drama work.* Cambridge, England: Cambridge University Press.

O'Neill, C. (1995). *Drama worlds: A Framework for process drama.* Portsmouth, NH: Heinemann.

O'Toole, J., & Donelan, K. (1996). *Drama, culture, and empowerment: The IDEA dialogues.* Brisbane, Australia: IDEA.

Owens, A., & Barber, K. (1997). *Dramaworks.* Carlisle, England: Carel Press.

Rogers, T., & O'Neill, C. (1993). Creating multiple worlds: Drama and literary response. In G. Newall & R. Durst (Eds.), *Exploring texts: The role of discussion and writing in the teaching and learning of literature.* Norwood, MA: Christopher-Gordon.

Saldaña, J. (1995). *Drama of color: Improvisation with multiethnic folklore.* Portsmouth, NH: Heinemann.

Salvio, P. (1999). Reading in the age of testimony. In B. J. Wagner (Ed.), *Building moral communities through educational drama* (pp. 39–62). Stamford, CT: Ablex.

Saxton, J., & Miller, C. (Eds.) (1998). *The Research of practice, the practice of research.* Victoria, Canada: IDEA.

Sciezcka, J. (1989). *The true story of the three little pigs.* New York: Viking.

Steig, W. (1982). *Dr. De Soto.* New York: Scholastic.

Swartz, L. (1996). *Dramathemes.* Markham, Canada: Pembroke.

Taylor, M. D. (1977). *Roll of thunder, Hear my cry.* New York: Bantam.

Taylor, P. (Ed.) (1996). *Researching drama and arts education: Paradigms and possibilities.* London: Falmer Press.

Taylor, P. (1998). *Redcoats and patriots: Reflective practice in drama and social studies.* Portsmouth, NH: Heinemann.

Taylor, P., & Hoepper, C. (Eds.) (1995). *Selected readings in drama and theatre education: The IDEA '95 papers* (pp. 114–125). Brisbane, Australia: NADIE.

Thomas, E. (1997). Postcards of the hanging: 1869 African-American poetry, drama, and interpretation. In A. Manley & C. O'Neill (Eds.), *Dreamseekers: Creative approaches to the African-American heritage* (pp. 47–58). Portsmouth, NH: Heinemann.

Towler-Evans, I. (1997). "It's not your everyday lesson is it?" In search of the quality of learning operating in mantle of the expert. In D. Davis (Ed.), *Interactive research in drama in education* (pp. 105–116). Staffordshire, England: Trentham.

Tyson, C. (1997). Meeting "Hattie." In A. Manley & C. O'Neill (Eds.), *Dreamseekers: Creative approaches to the African-American heritage* (pp. 15–22). Portsmouth, NH: Heinemann.

Volosinov, V. N. (1986). *Marxism and the philosophy of language.* Cambridge, MA: MIT Press.

Wagner, B. J. (1998). *Educational drama and language arts: What research shows.* Portsmouth, NH: Heinemann.

Wagner, B. J. (Ed.) (1999a). *Building moral communities through educational drama.* Stamford, CT: Ablex.

Wagner, B. J. (1999b). *Dorothy Heathcote: Drama as a learning medium* (rev. ed.). Portland, ME: Calendar Island.

Warner, C. (1995). *The nature of engagement in drama*. Unpublished doctoral dissertation, Ohio State University, Columbus.

Warner, C. (1997). The struggle for justice: responding to *Roll of thunder hear my cry*. In A. Manley & C. O'Neill (Eds.), *Dreamseekers: Creative approaches to the African-American heritage* (pp. 143–148). Portsmouth, NH: Heinemann.

Wilhelm, J. (1998). Drama and reading: Experiencing and learning from text. In J. Wilhelm & B. Edmiston (Eds.), *Imagining to learn: Inquiry, ethics, and integration through drama* (pp. 27–54). Portsmouth, NH: Heinemann.

Wolf, S. A. (1994). Learning to act/Acting to learn: Children as actors, characters, and critics in classroom theatre. *Research in the Teaching of English, 28*(1), 7–44.

Wolf, S. A. (1998). The flight of reading: Shifts in instruction, orchestration, and attitudes through classroom theatre. *Reading research quarterly, 33,* 382–415.

Wolf, S. A., Edmiston, B., & Enciso, P. (1997). Drama worlds: Places of the heart, head, voice and hand in dramatic interpretation. In J. Flood, S. B. Heath, & D. Lapp (Eds.), *The handbook for literacy educators: Research on teaching the communicative and visual arts* (pp. 492–505). New York: Simon & Schuster Macmillan.

# ·65·

# ORAL LANGUAGE: SPEAKING AND LISTENING IN ELEMENTARY CLASSROOMS

## Gay Su Pinnell
### Ohio State University

## Angela M. Jaggar
### New York University

As intensively now as at any time in history, national attention is focused on literacy learning. Skill in using written language, writing it and reading it, is the coin of the realm, the treasure that politicians call for and high-stakes tests measure. No one would dispute that literacy is important, even "basic," to a quality life. We have spent much of our own professional careers studying, teaching, and promoting literacy. We recently served as members of the New Standards Primary Literacy Committee, charged with generating standards for early literacy achievement. The committee's work did not include standards for oral language, which would be a difficult task indeed; and the committee's report (New Standards Primary Literacy Standards Committee, 1999) gave little attention to oral language. However, the work of committee members and the conversations that surrounded their work underscored the vital role that educational systems play in developing children's oral language capabilities. Therefore, in this chapter, we turn our thinking to something even more "basic," or "fundamental," than literacy. Oral language is the foundation not only of learning and schooling but of our living together as people of the world.

Daily life is conducted in spoken language—listening and speaking. Human beings constantly converse, negotiate, discuss, and debate the issues and decisions of their lives; the ability to speak and listen effectively often makes the critical difference between success or failure. Speaking and listening, traditionally treated as separate areas of the curriculum, together constitute the oral language arts. Should speaking and listening be taught in school? The answer must be yes; a better question is *how*?

Research on the teaching of oral language in elementary schools must ultimately address that question.

Our review was undertaken within a framework suggesting that language is communication, that it is social, and that it is a tool for learning. As Vygotsky (1978) wrote, language is a primary mediator of learning that has both intellectual and social significance. Language is learned through use, first in the home, family, and social community and then in the social context of the classroom and school. Moreover, in both formal and informal social contexts, speaking and listening are not separate processes. Instead, they are interrelated as participants engage in the give and take of oral communication. The processes of speaking (producing messages) and listening (comprehending messages) require the same underlying knowledge of language, including knowledge of the linguistic structures and the social rules that determine how language is used in context. Throughout the elementary years, students participate in an ever-widening world that requires new ways of interacting and expands their oral language competencies. Even as adults, we learn to adjust to new social contexts or to talk about newly acquired knowledge. As social beings, we are always expanding our oral language skills.

Oral language development is inextricably related to literacy development. Children do not learn everything there is to know about talking before they begin to understand important concepts about literacy. Processes for understanding and using oral and written language occur in connected ways, often simultaneously. A large body of research on emergent literacy (Adams,

1990; Chaney, 1992; Clay, 1991; Teale, Hiebert, & Chittenden, 1987; Teale & Sulzby, 1986) indicates that children, given exposure, learn important concepts about literacy beginning very early in their lives. As they participate in literacy-related experiences, for example, "bedtime stories," they simultaneously develop language and literacy abilities. Oral language development is enhanced by learning about written language, and this reading/writing relationship continues throughout life. For example, Sénéchal, LeFevre, Thomas, & Daley, 1998) recently found that storybook exposure at home contributed significantly to children's oral language vocabulary, listening comprehension, and phoneme awareness (also see Debaryshe, 1993; Dickinson & Snow, 1987; Dickinson & Tabors, 1991; P. A. Edwards, 1991).

Students talk about what they read and write. Through oral discussion, they inquire into the ideas, language structures, social issues, human feelings, experiences, and information that they encounter through reading and extend through writing. In the process, they acquire new vocabulary and new ways of talking. All of this means teachers at all levels must create classroom environments that foster a variety of talk, enable students to act on written texts through oral language; and interact with students in ways that will help them to develop and effectively use oral language as a tool for communication and learning?

First, to provide historical perspective, we begin with a review of the traditional lines of research treating listening and speaking as separate areas of study. We then review the important trend treating speaking and listening as an integrated system, with emphasis on communicative competence and on the role of talk in learning. The remainder of the chapter contains an overview of the literature in four areas:

1. Communicative competence, surveying findings on children's language functions, interactional skills, and discourse development.
2. Comparisons of home and school language, including issues related to diversity.
3. The nature of classroom talk and its impact on students communication development and learning.
4. The expansion of oral language through inquiry.

Finally, the implications of the research will be discussed in terms of principles for teaching oral language in classrooms.

## INSTRUCTION IN SPEAKING AND LISTENING

Historically, listening and speaking have been considered as separable processes. Thirty years ago, a joint statement (Mackintosh, 1964) by the National Council of Teachers of English and other professional organizations confirmed the importance of oral language for social development and for learning, and presented suggestions for instruction and evaluation. The authors of this document summed up their position, saying:

We share with all educators the concern about written communication and the recognition that reading skills are basic to all learning. But we have voiced the need for equal concern about educating all children to be effective speakers and listeners. . . . [T]he ability to speak and listen

effectively is probably the most important asset that he can acquire and maintain throughout a lifetime (p. 36).

A supplementary document (Petty, 1967) presented research-based articles by noted educators. Those scholars examined what was known about the relationship of oral language to areas such as personal and social development, reading, writing, home environment, sex differences, classroom context, and teacher behavior. The articles suggested the interrelatedness of speaking and listening; but the two areas were discussed in separate chapters, and different conceptual models were used to describe them. In one of the statements on needed research, Strickland, Blake, and Amato and Petty in the mid 1960s reported they had found an almost complete void of studies on oral language. They called for greater attention to research related to defining and teaching oral communication skills and for more investigation into the relations between speaking and listening, and among all the language arts.

Research on oral language development increased during the 1960s. Findings from this research challenged the highly structured traditional approach to language teaching that dominated instruction in both the United States and Britain. This approach emphasized learning of "correct" form and rules of grammar through exercises and drills that would, it was assumed, improve reading, writing, and speaking (Czerniewska, 1981). Language development research suggested, however, that by the time children entered school, they already know the basic patterns and "have mastered the fundamental rules of their native language, rather than being empty vessels into which teachers somehow pour language" (Hendricks, 1980, p. 366). Many educators began to reject exercises in favor of creative and individual activities that could tap the child's language resources. "Teachers began to use real-life contexts, instead of lists of abstract rules, as starting points for language work. . . . The teacher merely supplies the stimulus—from seashells to poetry—and the child is left the freedom to respond in the form of language of his choosing" (Czerniewska, 1981, pp. 168–169).

This shift in language teaching was part of a shift in the approach to education as a whole during the 1960s, with the former subject-centered approach being replaced by a child-centered approach (Czerniewska, 1981). In the field of English education, a surge of activity led to the Anglo-American Seminar held in Dartmouth, New Hampshire, in 1966 and to the book *Growth Through English* by John Dixon (1967) that described the personal growth model of English teaching supported by many seminar participants. "Basically the assumption of this model is that the individual learner should be the focus. He develops in no small measure through language: by language he is able to understand his world" (A. M. Wilkinson, Barnsley, Hanna, & Swan, 1980, p. 7). For an interesting discussion of the impact of the Seminar in Dartmouth, see D. Allen (1980).

Throughout the 1970s, 1980s, and 1990s, language arts and literacy education endured constant tension between the child-centered approach, supported by language development research, and a "basic skills" approach, promoted by mounting concern about the quality of education in the United States generally. In 1978, the federal government amended Title II of the Elementary and Secondary Act of 1965 to include, for the first time, speaking and listening as "basic skills" along with reading and writing. This legislation, Public Law 95–561, called on federal, state, and local authorities to reevaluate their curricula so that all children are able to master the basic skills of effective communication, written and *spoken*, and to either restructure or create new programs that placed greater emphasis on oral language skills. In the 1980s, statements from the National Council of Teachers of English, the National Commission on Excellence in Education (1983), the College Entrance Examination Board (1983) further supported oral language instruction as essential so that students could develop the ability to use language to communicate and think effectively. In addition, a number of state and local education agencies began to accept speaking and listening as basic skills (Van Rheenan, McClure, & Backlund, 1984).

Undertaken to identify the most fruitful directions for the development of speech communication programs in the school, the final report of the Speech Communication Association's National Project on Speech Communication Competencies, reviewed over 1,000 studies considered pertinent to communication development. The report listed of the communication competencies derived from the literature review. Two convictions held widely by communication scholars and educators were that (a) functional communication behaviors are of such crucial significance that they must be emphasized progressively and continuously throughout the school experience and (b) our nation's schools have largely ignored the functional communication needs of children and youth (Allen & Brown, 1976, p. 3). Based on the report, the Speech Communication Association and the American Speech-Language Hearing Association issued *Standards for Effective Oral Communication Instruction* (see Lieb-Brilhart, 1982), defining oral communication as the process of interacting through heard and spoken messages in a variety of situations. The definitions stressed the interrelatedness of the two processes, depicting communication as a transactional process wherein speakers and listeners exchange roles in the course of interacting.

With passage of the new basic skills legislation, speech communication and English language arts educators undertook a number of projects to disseminate research on the processes involved in oral communication development and to translate theory and research into useful suggestions for classroom practice. Examples of this work include Book (1978); Brown (1984); Brown, Burnett, Jones, Matsumoto, Langford, and Pacheco (1981); Friedrich (1981); Holdzkom, Reed, Porter, and Rubin (1982); Hopper and Wrather, 1978; Parkay, O'Bryan, and Hennessy (1984); Thaiss and Suhor (1984); and Wood (1977a, 1977b, 1981). Because evaluation is an essential part of the education process, several other projects were undertaken to review and critique procedures for assessing oral communication skills and to suggest research and development priorities for the 1980s. For examples, see Larson (1978), Larson, Backlund, Redmond, and Barbour (1978), Powers (1984), Rubin and Mead (1984), and Stiggins (1981).

At the beginning of the 1990s, English educators at all levels again focused on ways to further the development of students spoken language abilities as evidenced in *The Coalition Conference: Democracy Through Language* (Lloyd-Jones & Lundsford,

1989). Recognizing the centrality of talk in both communication and learning, researchers and educators searched for more effective approaches to developing students' "oracy" skills. Back in the 1960s, A. M. Wilkinson (1965) had coined the term *oracy*, analogous to *literacy*, to denote abilities related to speaking and listening.

Throughout the 1980s and 1990s, the concept of oracy received much attention in the United States and Britain. There were two views of oracy, each with different implications for practice (MacLure, 1988; Rubin, 1985). One view defined oracy as communicative competence and called for programs directed at teaching and assessing oral skills and competencies in their own right (MacLure, 1988). This view of oracy found support among members of the Speech Communication Association and others who advocated a deliberate approach to the teaching of specific oral communication competencies.

Speech communication educators have advocated a deliberate approach to the teaching of oral communication (see Allen & Brown, 1976; Allen, Brown, & Yatvin, 1986; Rubin, 1985; Rubin & Kantor, 1984, Wood, 1977a, 1977b, 1984). This view suggests that the curriculum should comprise activities that give students opportunities to practice different language functions and communication skills in specifically planned situations. The purpose of instruction is to help students learn a repertoire of strategies for using language appropriately and effectively in different social situations.

Advocates of this functional approach to oral communication suggest that students should be aware that they are studying speech communication, just as they might know they are studying biology (Rubin, 1985). This view of language teaching holds that, while communication skills and functions of language can be developed within any subject matter area, it is also necessary to have an explicitly defined curriculum for teaching speaking and listening skills and to focus on that specifically at certain times each day (Rubin, 1985).

British educators MacLure (1988), Barnes (1992), and others have argued that the functional approach, also evident in the United Kingdom, is based on a narrow concept of oracy, which calls "oracy as communication." The assumption is that oracy is an aspect of communicative competence and teachers have the obligation to teach children to speak and listen, just as they have the responsibility to teach them to read and write. "In this view, oracy tends to be seen as primarily the concern of English teachers and language specialists; and oral *assessment* means the assessment of oral skill and competencies in their own right, rather than as a vehicle or expression of learning in other curriculum subjects" (p. 5).

MacLure (1988) and others call for a view of "oracy as a tool for learning." Those who hold this view (Barnes, 1992; Britton, 1970, 1971; Corson, 1988; Jones, 1988; Marland, 1977; Tarleton, 1988; Thaiss, 1986; A. M. Wilkinson, 1970) advocate an indirect approach to fostering development of students' oral language abilities. In this view, oracy is the medium for learning in every subject area of the curriculum, not just English language arts. All teachers are seen as language teachers. These theorists argue that students in elementary and in secondary schools should be involved in settings and circumstances across the curriculum that regularly require them to actively learn by talking. The assumption is that through talking students construct their knowledge of the content and, at the same time, develop skill in different modes of discourse (exploratory, transactional, and poetic), become aware of the contextual constraints on language, and learn how to modify their language depending on the setting, audience, topic, and purpose. As appropriate, the teacher may hold up language for explicit examination or instruction; most of the time, however, the teaching is indirect.

The view of oracy as a tool for learning was the basis for programs that would give students many opportunities to talk for learning across the curriculum (Bullock, 1975; MacLure, 1988; Marland, 1977; Corson, 1988). This view of oracy found support in the "language across the curriculum" movement in both countries and particularly in the "Whole Language" philosophy which gained widespread popularity throughout this 20-year period in the United States.

Based on the body of research showing the critical relations between language knowledge and school success, some scholars (F. Christie, 1985a, 1985b, 1987) have called for greater attention to the forms of discourse students will need in order to participate successfully in discourse required by the subject areas. For example, F. Christie (1985b) argued that successful participation in any context or situation requires the ability to recognize and use the relevant discourse patterns or generic structures. This knowledge is important in two ways: in production and in comprehension. Thus, the same knowledge is needed by speaker/listener in order to successfully engage in discourse in a particular situation.

F. Christie (1985b) stated that learning in any "content area—math, science, history—is "primarily a matter of learning language: a matter, that is, of learning," not only the vocabulary or lexical items, "but the discourse patterns or genre . . . which are characteristic of the different subjects" (p. 37). Both the content and the ways of working together, the methods of inquiry, find expression in the discourse patterns that are characteristic of the field. F. Christie emphasized the importance of exploratory talk in learning but proposed that more attention be paid to the forms of discourse students need to learn in order to talk, write, and read successfully in the different content areas. When planning, she suggested:

Whatever the age group and whatever the subject matter, teachers need to consider two questions:

What do my students need to be able to do in language in order to be successful in mastering this content?

What kind of context of situation for working and learning should be generated in order that the students will be assisted to master the required language patterns?" (1985b, p. 31).

The focus on speaking and listening as basic competencies stimulated interest in oral language instruction; however, these projects seem to have had little impact on practice. The status of instruction in speaking and listening still has not changed much despite their designation as basic skills and the initial availability of federal fund to support curriculum improvement in oral communication. In both elementary and secondary education, listening (Devine, 1982; Strother, 1987) as well as speaking (Backlund, Booth, Moore, Parks, & Van Rheenan, 1982; Hendricks, 1980; Rubin, 1985) are still not priorities.

The current research guiding the federal agenda is reviewed in *Preventing Reading Difficulties in Young Children* (Snow, Burns, & Griffin, 1998). Of particular concern in that volume is language development related to literacy learning. The editors, reporting the findings of a national committee, discuss children's growing "metalinguistic" knowledge. Throughout early childhood, children growing increasingly more sophisticated in their vocabulary (Nagy & Herman, 1987) as well as their use of basic syntactic structures (P. Bloom, Barss, Nicol, & Conway, 1994). They learn how to use language effectively in a variety of contexts (Ninio & Snow, 1996). While learning language, however, they also learn *about* language; that is, children learn to treat language as an object that they can think and talk about.

Of particular interest to the committee was children's ability to notice the phonological structure of words. In other words, children may learn the sounds of language in that they can distinguish words when they hear them and connect them to appropriate meanings. Phonological awareness, however, is metalinguistic, in that students are able to analyze and manipulate sounds in words—for example, taking the /k/ away from *cat* to make *at*. Canadian researchers (Malicky & Norman, 1999) report that the relationship between phonological awareness and reading is both more complex and less direct than expected. The skill does not guarantee that children will learn to read. Reading programs that fail to make explicit the connection between oral and written language may fail.

Committee members were also interested to note that many basic cognitive processes are shared between listening and reading. They cited the high correlations between listening comprehension and reading comprehension (Gernsbacher, Varner, & Faust, 1990; Sticht & James, 1984), pointing out that these high correlations occur after readers have developed decoding skills and that the gap between listening and reading comprehension can be large (Snow et al., 1998).

The interest in language development here is primarily because of the high correlation between oral language and reading. This high profile document is guiding federal policy, and it illustrates the current view of oral language—language competency has value for learning how to master the alphabetic principle, decode words, learn the meaning of words, spell words, understand the relationship between the syntactic system and reading and writing, and using prior knowledge to comprehend. This research offers valuable insights. Oral language is critical in the process of literacy development. It also provides evidence that oral language continues to be neglected in modern classrooms. As observed more than 30 years ago (Petty, 1967), instruction in oral language continues to take a back seat to reading and writing. Even where oral language skills are emphasized, there is generally not a strong conceptual base for the curriculum.

## LISTENING AND SPEAKING AS SEPARATE AREAS OF INQUIRY: A HISTORICAL SKETCH

Traditionally, research and pedagogy have treated listening and speaking as separate areas of study. To provide historical perspective, this section sketches some directions research has taken in these two areas and discusses the implications for practice that have been drawn from that work.

## Listening

The words *ignored* and *neglected* frequently appear in the literature on listening (Landry, 1969; Pearson & Fielding, 1982; Schaudt, 1983; Strother, 1987). Although reading research began in the 1880s, research on listening was not published until the 1920s. By 1948, only three research reports had been published on listening; although over 3,000 studies had been published on reading (Anderson, 1952). The *Encyclopedia of Educational Research* did not include the entries "Listening: Teaching of" and "Tests of" until 1960; and in 1969, Landry described listening as being "crowded out" by reading, and that is still true today.

One wonders why listening has been so neglected considering how much time students spend listening in school. In an often cited study, Wilt (1950) discovered that elementary school-age children were expected to listen $2^1/_2$ hours per day, more than 60% of the time they were in the classroom and more time than on any other activity. Moreover, for most of that time, students listened to the teacher talk; yet teachers appeared to be unaware of the amount of time children were expected to listen, estimating only 74.3 minutes per day. Wilt suggested that teachers need to become more aware of listening as a factor in learning. Her findings on time spent listening in classrooms were comparable to Rankin's (1928) much earlier study. He brought attention to the importance of listening in everyday life when he discovered people devote 45% of their time to listening, 30% to speaking, 16% to reading, and only 9% to writing.

With the recognition that students were engaged in listening for much of their school day, researchers began to investigate the relations between listening ability and other areas of school achievement. For example, R. Ross (1964) found high correlations between poor listening and poor school achievement. Early studies (R. P. Larson & Feder, 1940; W. E. Young, 1936) reported relationships between listening and reading; later studies (reviewed in more detail in Devine, 1978; Duker, 1961, 1966, 1969; Lundsteen, 1979; Sticht, Beck, Hauke, Kleiman, & James, 1974) found substantial correlations between listening comprehension, reading comprehension, and reading achievement. In addition, studies of the relationship between listening comprehension and reading comprehension (Hampleman, 1958) suggested that listening is an important vehicle for learning, particularly in elementary school and particularly for students who are slower.

Another line of research during the 1950s and 1960s focused on the effects of instruction in listening. This research addressed the question: Does listening skill develop "naturally," or can it be taught directly? Studies showed that direct instruction in listening (Canfield, 1961; Hollow, 1955; Lundsteen, 1964, 1965; Pratt, 1956; Trivette, 1961) led to measurable gains in listening comprehension. Lundsteen's (1964, 1971) influential studies of critical listening suggested the direct teaching of critical thinking skills is related to an improvement in listening comprehension. Lundsteen (1971) recommended that students be given

experience in critical listening and that researchers work to identify hierarchies of skills in this area. Lundsteen (1979) provided a suggested hierarchy that could be used for instructional purposes.

In their review of listening research, Pearson and Fielding (1982) concluded that by the 1960s there was "considerable proof that elementary children can improve in listening comprehension through training" (p. 619). Though the training methods used in the studies "generally focused on skills commonly taught in reading, such as getting the main idea, sequencing, summarizing and remembering facts," the important thing is that "the instruction occurred in listening, *not* in reading, and that the children were aware that they were receiving listening instruction (p. 619). Pearson and Fielding reviewed some more recent studies and suggest that "one promising approach to listening comprehension may lie in combining listening with oral responses from the listeners" (p. 620). Active involvement following listening activities may help more than do passive activities.

Following the work on the relations between listening and other areas, particularly reading comprehension, investigations into the nature and attributes of listening took a new direction. According to Horrworth (1966), the research suggested that listening is not a discrete skill or a generalized ability but rather a cluster of specific abilities closely related to those needed in the reading task (Russell, 1964). Caffrey (1955) and later Spearritt (1962), reported in Duker (1968), sought to define this cluster of abilities and suggested that there may be factors in listening ability, or "auding," that are different from those involved in reading. Based on this work, Horrworth (1966) defined auding as "the gross process of listening to, recognizing, and interpreting spoken symbols. This definition is holistic in nature and embraces the hearing act, the listening act, and the comprehending act" (p. 857). The expressed this definition as a paradigm: Auding = Hearing + Listening + Cognizing.

Though Horrworth (1966) considered listening as a part of a cluster of abilities, new research followed that attempted to further integrate listening and overall comprehension. Sticht et al.'s (1974) work challenged the idea of a special "listening comprehension" different from other language abilities. Their model of the reading–writing, auding–speaking process assumed that reading and auding access the same language and conceptual bases. in other words, people use the same basic kinds of adaptive processes to build cognitive competence and acquire language skill, first in auding and speaking and then later in reading and writing, with additional competencies added to enable the decoding of print (Sticht, 1972).

Using recordings that artificially compressed speech into a shorter time period, Sticht (Foulke & Sticht, 1969; Sticht et al., 1974) and several other researchers (Orr, Friedman, & Williams, 1965; Zemlin, Daniloff, & Shriner, 1968) investigated the rate at which individuals could track and process information presented orally. Spoken discourse usually ranges from 125 to 200 words per minute, with maximum listening rate appeared to be about 300 words per minute (Goldstein, 1940; Sticht et al., 1974). When speech was presented at a faster rate, comprehension was severely diminished, although intelligible was less affected. In other words, intelligibility scores fell off less rapidly than comprehension scores when the rate of listening was increased (Foulke & Stitch, 1969).

Experiments with compressed speech also indicated that short phrases were more intelligible than isolated words; common words were more intelligible than less common words; and, as in reading, words presented in context were more intelligible than the same words presented in isolation. Sticht (1972) interpreted the results of these experiments as evidence of a reciprocal relationship between intelligibility and understanding. The listener makes predictions about what the input of the messages should be and then checks out the elements only as thoroughly as needed to confirm the predictions. Not only does the intelligibility of the message affect comprehension, but the listener's knowledge and comprehension also affect intelligibility. His work challenged the idea that reading problems were isolated as a barrier to learning and suggested that simply converting reading tasks to "listening" tasks (for example reading to children to putting books on tape) would not necessarily increasing comprehension.

In both listening and reading, greater learning may be achieved with the use of advanced organizers (Ausubel, 1960; Ausubel & Robinson, 1969). The idea is that learning new material is facilitated when the learner already has the concepts within which to integrate the new information. This "frame of reference," if effective in reading, should also be helpful in listening. Sticht argued that both listening and reading are part of a larger and more general language ability. Teaching listening, then, really means teaching "learning (comprehending) by listening" and should include the same kinds of practices suggested for helping students "read to learn." He proposed attention to the acoustic, linguistic, and semantic features of listening. Pearson and Fielding (1982) found Sticht's line of research important because it suggests that "once lower level reading skills are mastered, both reading and listening are controlled by the same set of cognitive processes" (p. 623). They called for more investigations into the implications of schema theory and models of text comprehension or listening comprehension curricula.

In the early 1970s, Wilt (1973) expressed concern that the field of listening research had progressed little since the 1950s, claiming that studies had been based on narrow definitions of listening and had come out with limited results applicable only to small populations. Wilt suggested that listening research may have been based on faulty notions of the nature of listening and warned that listening must be considered as part of a much larger whole and argued that speaking, listening, reading, and writing cannot be taught as discrete lessons. The task of improving listening is one of expanding the child's thinking and learning, according to Wilt (1973), the "efficacy of listening will need to be found in observation of a person's ability to interact in a communication situation with all of its ramifications rather than in whether an individual can remember facts he hears" (p. 69).

Much listening research is open to criticism for using artificial rather than naturalistic situations, and employing inadequate measurement techniques (Kelly, 1971; Rubin & Mead, 1984; Wilt, 1973). Back in 1955, Wilt observed that techniques such as observational checklists (Farrell & Flint, 1967) and standardized tests like the *Durrell Listening–Reading Series* (1969)

measured only a minute aspect of listening. Fifteen years later, Wilt (1973) proposed that real assessment of listening must take into account the complex combination of understandings and behaviors that make up effective listening in various social situations. More recent reviews of assessment procedures ( see, e.g., Rubin & Mead, 1984) suggested little progress in the development and use of naturalistic techniques for assessing listening. To this day, most listening assessment takes the form of pencil-and-paper tests that typically resemble reading comprehension tests.

Another facet of listening is to consider listening as an active process within dialogue. Research on both first language learning (Nelson, 1973) and second language learning (Fillmore, 1983) highlights the intensive nature of active listing as a strategy for comprehension. In other words, listening is not simply a receptive or passive act. According to Bakhtin (1986), listening is active interpretation and it is the listener's understanding, as much as the speaker's, that is as important to the creation of shared meaning in dialogue (Clark & Holquist, 1984).

The importance of listening in school success is widely accepted, but listening is largely ignored in instruction. Research over the years has spanned from considering listening as an isolated activity so the more recent view that listening is intertwined with the child's overall communication development. Certainly much more theory and research, especially naturalistic studies, are needed on the linguistic, cognitive, and social processes involved in listening; the course of listening development; the factors that affect that development; and on ways teaching can further the development of listening as a tool for communication and learning.

## Speaking

Prior to the 1900s, elocution was considered an essential part of competence, but the emphasis on oral expression declined in the 1920s and 1930s when research and practice shifted its focus to silent reading. Since the 1940s, emphasis on oral skills in the language arts curriculum has increased, although assessment practices have contributed to maintaining the primary focus on literacy. In summarizing trends in oral communication instruction at the secondary level, Lieb-Brilhart (1984) claimed that "the use of silent reading . . . and the emphasis on literature and composition helped foster the view of oral communication as 'speech arts,' reducing it to an elective or extra curricula activity in the English curriculum" (p. 69).

Although speaking does not receive large amounts of instructional time (DeLawter & Eash, 1966; Rubin, 1985), educators believe that the ability to speak effectively is an important fundamental skill that is necessary for success in school. At the surface level, teachers are still concerned with distinct articulation, enunciation, and pronunciation. Beyond that, they recognize that children need to be able to organize and present ideas, give clear directions, and display their knowledge.

During the 1960s, studies of oral expression focused on the use of structures and on developmental changes in speech patterns. For example, O'Donnell, Griffin, and Norris (1967) studied the oral language of kindergarten, first-, second-, third-, fifth-, and seventh-grade students and found increasing complexity in use of syntax between kindergarten and 1st-year students and between fifth- and seventh-grade students. It was not until fifth grade that the syntax of written language compositions began to overtake oral language in complexity. Thus, for younger children, using oral language means expressing ideas in complex language, and as indicated by C. Chomsky's (1969) research, school-age children are still developing the use of new structures in their oral language throughout the elementary school years.

Studies of oral expression (e.g., Loban, 1963, 1976; Ruddell 1965, 1966; R. G. Strickland, 1962) have demonstrated the close relationship between sentence patterns, vocabulary, and speech rhythms of oral language and the speaker's proficiency in reading and writing. Loban's (1963, 1976) longitudinal work indicated that children who were advanced in language ability at the kindergarten level used language in flexible ways. They could take "movables," that is, parts of a sentence that may occur several different places, and distribute them in various ways. According to Loban, such skill represented control over language, and children who could demonstrate such oral skill eventually scored higher in reading achievement. Differences in this skill between high and low reading groups increased from year to year.

The research described above focused on children's use of language structure and on developmental changes in speech patterns and their relations to reading achievement. At the same time, other studies focused on how to help students better express themselves. For example, in an analysis of children's recorded interviews after hearing unfinished stories, DeLawter and Eash (1966) noted errors that signaled a lack of the skill they claimed was critical for mature listening and should be used to plan oral language curricula. These areas of need included failure to focus and to clarify questions, poor organization of ideas, lack of supporting ideas and appropriate subordination of ideas, stereotyped vocabulary, and inadequate descriptions. To help students overcome such errors, DeLawter and Eash (1966) recommended greater use of small-group discussion to give children practice, the use of devices such as tape recorders to help students evaluate their own oral speech, and integration of speaking with the other language arts.

Just as in listening studies, much early research on the effects of spoken language instruction involved use of contrived situations that do not tap students' true language abilities; however, during the 1960s researchers and English teachers at all levels began to recognize the power of learning language while using it in more realistic social situations. They advocated that the traditional approach to language teaching, which emphasized learning of skills through exercises and drills, be replaced by more creative oral language activities, such as storytelling, discussion, and creative dramatics. They found support for this approach in the linguistic studies that seemed to show children learn linguistic rules and structures before they enter kindergarten and that speaking and listening are learned "naturally" and required no further direct instruction from the teacher (Czerniewska, 1981; Hendricks, 1980; Lieb-Brilhart, 1984).

With the designation of speaking and listening as basic skills in the 1970s, many speech communication and English language

arts educators called for more deliberate teaching of oral communication skills. Based on an extensive survey of the research on the development of children's oral communication available at the time (see Allen & Brown, 1976), they advocated that the popular activities approach be replaced by a more deliberate approach to teaching listening and speaking. These researchers (e.g., Brown, 1984; Brown et al., 1981; Hopper & Wrather, 1978; Lieb-Brilhart, 1984; Rubin & Kantor, 1984; and Wood, 1977a, 1977b, 1981, 1984) attempted to define oral communication competence, specified the goals of instruction, identified the skills to be taught, and outlined programs for elementary and secondary education that were based on a functional approach to oral communication. According to Brown (1984), instruction in this approach focuses on using language for five major functions identified by Wells (1973). Experience with each of the five functions is gained through games, simulations, and problem situations that are "designed to help students (a) develop a wide repertoire of communication strategies and skills, (b) select skills which seem appropriate to the situation, (c) implement the skills through practice, and (d) evaluate the effectiveness and the appropriateness of the skills employed" (Brown et al., 1981, pp. 79–80).

The functional approach received a great deal of attention in language arts and speech communication publications in the late 1970s and early 1980s; however, little recognized research establishes the effects of the approach on students' speaking and listening abilities. In addition, several researchers (Hendricks, 1980; McCrosky, 1982; Weimann & Backlund, 1980; and others) have questioned the approach for equating competence and performance and for being too behavioristic in tone. They suggested that definitional problems and theoretical issues about what knowledge, abilities, and factors are involved in communicative competence must be resolved before conceptually sound pedagogy can be designed.

Given the continuing priority placed on literacy and the problems in defining oral communication competence as a pedagogical objective, it is not surprising that surveys show oral language curricula in the United States have changed little since the 1960s. Oral language curricula at the elementary and at the secondary level tend to emphasize performance rather than the natural uses of language needed to use language effectively in a variety of different social and academic settings.

In the elementary schools, listening and speaking are learned as children engage in language activities designed to strengthen not only oral language skills but to enhance reading and writing (Brown, 1984; Brown et al., 1981; Cochran-Smith, 1984; Graves, 1983; Harste & Short, 1988). Oral language could be seen as a means to an end, because evaluation and testing practices tend to emphasize written language skills, much of the value attached to listening and speaking lessons at the elementary level has been associated with developing the foundation for literacy. In the 1980s, some researchers were even beginning to express doubt about the assumed relationship between oral language competency and school performance in reading and writing. Reviews (Gray, Sasky, McEntire, & Larsen, 1980) of a large number of studies conducted in the 1960s and 1970s revealed that the correlations between specific oral language skills (e.g, grammatical usage) and measures of reading and writing were generally low, suggesting that achievement in written language may not be related to oral language proficiency. However, as in all such studies, low correlations may reflect problems associated with the validity of the measures used to investigate the constructs assumed to be under study.

Defining and assessing competence in speaking presents problems for both educators and researchers. If the organized instructional program "neglects" speaking, it may be because competence in this area cannot be measured through group standardized pencil-and-paper measures. Teachers can use tape recorded samples and checklists to evaluate student progress and assess group discussions and other oral activities using observation guides and checklists or participation charts (Rubin & Mead, 1984). However, valid assessment of students speaking abilities must include facility in using spoken language in a variety of social/academic context and for a range of different purposes (see Barnes, 1992; Gorman, 1985; A. M. Wilkinson, 1965).

## ORAL LANGUAGE USE AND COMMUNICATIVE DEVELOPMENT

Over several decades, language research confirmed the importance of oral communication in the child's social and cognitive development, and provided the impetus not only to integrate speaking and listening but also to define competence in new ways, this time with emphasis on the interactive nature of communication and on contextual factors that influence such communication. This research provided the evidence necessary for new directions in practice. First, language research (King, 1984) confirmed the human potential to construct meaning through and to use language to learn. Second, language research (Cazden, John, & Hymes, 1972) brought attention to the functions of language and to communicative competence within the social context of the classroom. Third, it lead to new definitions of competence to account for the complexities of human learning and provide the basis for an integrated language-arts curriculum that acknowledged the interrelatedness of the social and intellectual functions of language.

### Shifting Views of Oral Language Development

Linguists in the 1940s and 1950s studied the structure of language. They were concerned with describing the phonology, morphology, and syntax of the language. These studies of language form and structure provided accurate information about the nature of language and generated a concept of what must be learned. At the same time studies of language development concentrated on establishing norms for language learning. Educators and language development scholars focused on when, and in what sequence, children learned the forms of language. They established milestones that allowed for comparisons between groups and for evaluation of individuals, but they did not take into account the social, cultural, and contextual factors that

may have influenced language development or the role of the child in that development (L. Bloom, 1975).

By the 1960s, researchers realized that children were not just acquiring collections of words; instead, they were abstracting systems of rules that they could use to generate their own language structures. This research revealed that all children appear to have this ability so learn and use a system for language. This linguistic competence (N. A. Chomsky, 1957, 1965) is made up of their acquired knowledge of the forms of language and of the rules for generating those forms. (For reviews of this early work on children's language development, see L. Bloom, 1975; DiVesta & Palermo, 1974). In the 1960s, scholars also recognized that all dialects and varieties of a language are systematic and rule governed, complex, and useful as a tool for cognitive and social development (e.g., Labov, 1969) and that language learning could be studied across languages and cultural groups. (See Wells & Nicholls, 1985, for interesting discussions of the major issues in language research in both Britain and the United States during this period.) In 1988 advice to the British government, *The Kingman Report* offered a model of language and language development "as inherently variable, with the standard variety being only one kind, and with different varieties of language revealed through specific uses in certain contexts" (Department of Education and Science, 1988).

By the 1970s, research on language, particularly children's language learning, had shifted from concern with form and structure to the study of language in use. Linguists, sociolinguists, and ethnographers began to focus on larger units of language and to give attention to the context in which language is used and developed. (This gradual development of language knowledge, from phonology to morphology to syntax to discourse, paralleled by a gradual development from form to function, now places language knowledge in a position to be most helpful to educators and students alike" (Shuy, 1984, p. 168). That advice, offered in 1984, has yet to be heeded in typical classrooms; however, researchers continued to offer counsel to policymakers.

### Communicative Competence

The new views of language signaled a new definition of competence. To use language effectively, one must know more than the complex or "mature" linguistic structures identified in previous research. As researchers examined language use in naturalistic contexts, it became clear that one must know how to use language as a social instrument. This shift in focus is illustrated by the difference between N. A. Chomsky's (1957, 1965) notion of linguistic competency (knowledge of the system) and Hymes' (1972) notion of communicative competence (a repertoire of language strategies that are appropriate for different context).

Hymes (1971) introduced the concept, saying that communicative competence meant "the most general term for speaking and hearing capabilities of a person. . . . Competence is understood to be dependent on two things: (tacit) passive knowledge and (ability for) use" (p. 16). It is the totality of knowledge that enables a speaker to produce speech that is socially appropriate as well as grammatical in culturally determined contexts, and to understand the speech of others in those context (Gumperz & Hymes, 1964; Hymes, 1971). This knowledge is used in both the production and comprehension of language.

The purpose of instruction, then, should be to help students develop a repertoire of strategies (forms) for different functions of language that would enable them to select particular strategy in a given context, to communicate using that strategy, to evaluate the effectiveness of that strategy and modify it, if necessary, and to do so while simultaneously engaged in social dialogue. In an analysis of the 1988 *Kingman Report* (Department of Science and Education, 1988), Raban (1999) noted that language is seen here to relate to intellectual and social development as well as to personal and aesthetic need. Language was acknowledged to express identity, enable cooperation, and confer freedom on those who have access to and control over a wide repertoire of language strategies" (p. 101). Current research on children's language development provides important information that can be used to design classroom situations that will foster rather than hinder this development. This research is reviewed in the next section.

## Language Functions and Interactional Competence

Piaget (1959) considered young children under 7 or 8 years old to be "egocentric," that is, unable to consider the listener's viewpoint. Children may be better described as "sociocentric." Apparently, even infants are interested in their peers (Vandell & Mueller, 1980), and even very young children seek social interaction (Genishi & Dyson, 1984). Evidence from studies of caregivers (Bates, 1976; Nelson, 1973; Snow, 1977; Snow & Ferguson, 1977) shows that for young children, and older children (H. S. Ross & Goldman, 1976), interaction with adults appears to promote language development, especially when the child's utterances are treated as meaningful (Wells, 1981).

In the late 1960s and the 1970s, studies of young children's language learning (L. Bloom, 1970; Dore, 1974, 1979; Ervin-Tripp, 1973; Halliday, 1973, 1975; Weeks, 1979) suggested that function precedes form. Children use language for a wide range of social functions before they enter school. Through this intentional use of language, children increase their repertoire of forms and language strategies. In a study of preschool children's everyday motives for talking, Schachter, Kirshner, Klips, Friedricks, and Sanders (1974) used an observational checklist to score children's functional use of language. The analysis of data revealed that children from 2 to 5 years old gradually moved toward using more sophisticated speech in addressing adults and in adapting their forms of speech to the needs of the listener depending on their intention.

Studies of children's language use (variously called developmental pragmatics or discourse analysis) provide insights about how listening and speaking abilities develop. The following is a review of selected research on a range of social functions and interactional skills needed to use language effectively in context. (For comprehensive reviews, see Lindfors, 1987; McTear, 1985; Menyuk, 1988; Romaine, 1984. See Franklin & Barten, 1988, for a collection of studies that represent significant areas

in which there is ongoing theoretical controversy and productive research. Also see chapters in this volume.)

*Conversational discourse.* Conversation has been one of the most studied forms of discourse. Researchers have been interested to learn how children develop their sense of the structure and design of a conversation, and how those structures and designs vary accordingly to culture (Tannen, 1982, 1985). Studies of infants and caregivers (Snow, 1977; Stern, 1977; Stern, Jaffe, Beebe, & Bennett, 1975; Whiten, 1977) reveal the beginnings of children's knowledge about the social processes involved in oral language interaction. In these "protoconversations" (McTear, 1984, 1985) adults and infants apparently engage in patterns of behavior such as turn taking (Snow, 1977; Whiten, 1977), and sometimes the infant takes the lead (Foster, 1979; Trevarthen, 1979). Gestures are related to intentions, such as requests and imperatives, and form the basis for later verbalizations (Bates, Camaioni, & Volterra, 1975). Mothers tend to treat infants as if they are conversing, and they build a structure around the child's responses as if they were engaged in turn taking, with the mother gradually decreasing her role, while the child develops more extensive contributions (Snow, 1977). In a study of the development of dialogue strategies among preschool children, McTear (1984) video recorded and analyzed freeplay conversations. He found that in the early stages interactions are usually closed and do not develop into sustained dialogue. In later stages, however, children learn to link exchanges topically and to sustain talk, an important feature of, mature conversation.

*Sensitivity to audience.* Part of what must be learned in the communication situation is how to adjust language according to the characteristics of one's audience. People talk differently to others based on factors such as age and previous knowledge. Even young children appear to practice conversational rules, including the adjustment of speech to their audience. For example, they may vary length of utterances and number or pattern of pausing. This evidence suggests that even young children are aware of the cooperative principles (Grice, 1975) required for social interaction and improve as they get older (Garvey & BenDebba, 1974; Shatz & Gelman, 1973; Welkowitz, Cariffe, & Feldstein, 1976).

*Arguing, persuading and controlling others.* Eisenberg and Garvey (1981) studied argument and the resolution of conflict in conversations among 3- to 5-year-olds playing in pairs in laboratory settings. The results indicated that preschool children were able to use complex strategies such as giving reasons and requesting explanations or justifications for behavior. When preschool children's arguing strategies were recorded in more naturalistic settings, however, results demonstrated the powerful influence of the social context on the kinds of strategies children employed (Genishi & DiPaolo, 1982). These findings indicated that children in a preschool setting could be distracted by the activity around them and generally argued to establish their own authority rather than to resolve conflicts by reasoning or compromising. They did not necessarily need to resolve conflict to continue in their interaction with others.

Studies of children's arguments in preschool settings (Genishi & DiPaolo, 1982) provided evidence that although children's frequently occurring arguments were simple in structure, the children had internalized knowledge of a particular form and the social rules for engaging in that form of discourse. Children were learning to establish their relative status and defend themselves. In a study of interaction within first-grade reading classrooms, L. C. Wilkinson and Dollaghan (1979) found that children were consistently engaged in a kind of trial and error process for communication strategies. Another first-grade study by Ervin-Tripp (1982) focused on children's ability to control others and get what they wanted. Children demonstrated a repertoire of strategies and selected from that repertoire based on an awareness of factors such as closeness and familiarity of partners and status differences. Wood's (1981) study of directives indicated that children appeared to move from simple, direct requests to subtle directives that included more complex, adultlike forms such as hints. The ability to use a range of control strategies, including hints, indicated a sensitivity to contextual factors that influenced the structure of their conversation.

Studies of persuasive strategies (see Delia & Clark, 1977) demonstrate children's ability to analyze and have impact on listeners. Specific stages were identified (Delia & Clark, 1977; Delia, Kline, & Burleson, 1979). Delia and Clark's studies of 6-, 8-, 10-, and 12-year-olds and Alvy's (1973) studies of children from varying social backgrounds showed that children could use persuasive strategies and that those strategies became more effective as children got older. Perspective taking appears to be the underlying cognitive skill that is developed in this trial and error process. These findings suggest that children need the opportunity to use persuasive talk in a variety of different situations; for example, dramatic play was found to be a particularly rich situation by both Pinnell (1975) and Black (1979a, 1979b).

***Making requests and asking for information.*** As children explore alternative ways of expressing their intentions, they are obliged to respond to elements of the social system. This process is illustrated by Ervin-Tripp's (1974) study of the comprehension and production of requests by children. She found that by the middle of the 3rd year, children had a variety of alternative ways to produce requests. For example, they could make requests through questions, statements of need, direct requests, or persuasive rhetoric. She also found that children showed a systematic social distribution in the forms of requests they used. Even among 2-year-olds there were systematic differences between requests made to children and those made to adults. Moreover, their requests of adults differed depending on a variety of factors. Children in nursery schools appeared to give negative requests and imperatives more often to children than to adults. They addressed their need statements and general condition statements more often to adults. At age 4, children addressed embedded imperatives and permission-request forms more often to adults than peers. Even very young children seem to be aware of questions (Halliday, 1975), although they might not be able to provide an appropriate response (Dore, 1977). Studies of response to questions indicate that there is change between ages 1 and 6 (Ervin-Tripp, 1970), and that children grow

in ability to more directly answer their questioners (McTear, 1984).

***Informing.*** Much research on functions of children's language has concentrated on referential communication or the informing function (see Dickson, 1981; Flavell, Speer, Green, & August, 1981; Glucksberg & Krauss, 1967) and has focused on school-age children. For example, in a sociolinguistic study, Cook-Gumperz (1977) recorded fifth-grade children who were engaged in instruction and direction-giving situations that were subject to constraints similar to testing. Children were required to lexicalize the details of the activities and their own interpretations. Pairs of children were asked to make a tinkertoy model, with one child as the blindfolded builder and the other as instructor. Differences in success were related to differing strategies of "doing instruction-giving." The researchers identified two main patterns in the interaction between instructor and builder: (a) cooperative and based on dialogue and (b) controlling and taking the form of a monologue. Children tended to use direct imperatives and relied on prosodic features to convey information, strategies that were efficient in this situation but resulted in a reduced amount of lexicalized information.

Dickson (1981) wrote that research done from two separate perspectives, experimental research on referential communication skills and sociolinguistic approaches to the study of communicative competence in natural settings, "portrays an optimistic view of children's ability to communicate, both in the sense of specific communication skills such as speaking and listening and in the broader aspects of communicative competence" (pp. xiii). Careful study of children in natural settings has revealed many instances in which children are highly competent communicators. The experimental studies show, however, that "children can [also] be taught to encode more informative measures and to ask for more information when given inadequate messages. In addition, children can be taught that communication is a two-person activity, and that successful communication depends on the efforts of both" (p. xiv). Dickson (1982) also discussed how experimental referential training tasks might be translated into communication games to improve speaking and listening in the classroom.

***Imagining.*** Irwin's (1975) study of dramatic play of children aged 2 to 7 indicated that children used words to symbolize their feelings and thoughts, suggesting that language use in such situations can play an important role in children's social and intellectual development. Imagining has been shown to arise from play (Garvey, 1977). In their play, even very young children vary their speech patterns as they take on various roles. Role taking is an important skill in mature communication, indicating that social and dramatic play for young children, improvisation, and more structured forms of drama for older children are effective means of facilitating growth in communicative competence. According to Garvey (1974), Genishi and Dyson (1984), and others, participation in social play and drama requires, among other things, that children abstract the conversational rules (e.g., turn taking) for structuring the play and that they be able to select and use linguistic features that are appropriate to the roles played.

Galda (1984) proposed that children's play in the narrative mode (narrative play) is also related to narrative development. She reviewed several studies and concluded that, although the studies had methodological flaws, dramatic play does seem to be an effective facilitator of narrative competence. In a subsequent study, Pellegrini and Galda (1988) documented ways children use personal narratives under two conditions and found that use of narrative language was related to age and the context of the situation; children more often generated personal narratives in ambiguous and more natural peer-play situations than in explicit storytelling situations. They concluded that the "formality of the storytelling interview may have may have suppressed children's narrative competence. it may be that other more natural contexts, such as dramatic play, may be more appropriate for eliciting children's narratives" (p. 188).

Through the 1990s, dramatic play has received attention because of its connections to literacy learning (J. F. Christie, 1991). Rowe (1998) has observed that children create direct linkages between their oral dramatic play and their literacy experiences and found that book-related play served as a means of inquiry.

***Telling stories: development of narrative discourse.***
Children's stories, both oral and written, have been the subject of important research on the development of children's ability to construct coherent texts (e.g., Haslett, 1983; King & McKenzie, 1988; Rentel & King, 1983; Stenning & Michell, 1985). Storytelling is probably the first situation in which the child must sustain a monologue without the support of a conversational partner. Stories also have a defined structure and require complex cognitive processes such as the use of explanation; however, even very young children have been shown to display story sense through paralinguistic features before syntactic and lexical systems are in place (Wade, 1983).

To tell a story, children must learn, among other things, how narratives are structured. A number of researchers (Hasan, 1984a, 1984b, 1984c; Johnson & Mandler, 1980; Labov, 1972; Stein & Glenn, 1979) have identified the overall structure of narrative discourse. Developing a "sense of story" means learning this "story grammar" and being able to produce it (Applebee, 1978; Botvin & Sutton-Smith, 1977, Westby, 1984). Bower (1976) and Thorndyke (1977) indicated that structure is also important in listening comprehension; a coherent story is remembered better than a series of unrelated events. The issue is that each type of discourse has its own structure or "script" (Mandler, 1984; Nelson, 1986). It is this structure (mental schema) that must be learned and used in producing (speaking and writing) and understanding (listening and reading) a particular form of discourse.

Research on children's narrative competence has focused mainly on primary grade children. For example, using a Piagetian framework, Applebee (1978) found that children's concept of story and ability to maintain a different point of view developed with maturity. He found that children's use of conventions, attitudes toward story, and organizational patterns reflected general cognitive developmental trends. King and Rentel (1981) studied structural features of children's told (dictated) and retold stories. They analyzed story structure and cohesion using procedures developed by Propp (1968) and Halliday and Hasan (1976),

respectively. Their findings show that children's narratives became increasingly complex as they progressed from the end of first through the second grade. As the children matured, their narratives contained more elements of story structure, such as conflict, character development, and definite endings. In addition, students were also better able to use language that was not context bound. Very young storytellers believed that their audiences knew all the things that they knew, but as the children matured and developed a better sense of audience, they provided information a listener needed to understand. Furthermore, the type of cohesive devices in their narratives changed as they grew older. They increased their use of lexical cohesion and conjunctions and decreased their use of exophoric reference, thereby showing increasing sensitivity to audience.

Many recent studies have shown that as young children hear stories told and read, children learn the structure as well as the linguistic features of narrative discourse (Cox & Sulzby, 1984; King & Rentel, 1981; Pappas, 1985). They often display their knowledge by "talking like a book" when they reenact or pretend to read their favorite stories (Butler, 1980; Cochran-Smith, 1984; Doake, 1985; Fox, 1985, 1988; Heath, 1983; King & McKenzie, 1988; Pappas & Brown, 1987; Schickedanz & Sullivan, 1984; Sulzby, 1985; Taylor, 1983). These studies suggest that reading aloud to children facilitates the development of narrative competence, particularly literate narrative.

Descriptions of narrative discourse have arisen in several different fields and have shown to be highly related to cultural factors (Labov, 1972). Tannen (1982) claimed that oral discourse can be sorted into oral and literate categories. For example, in storytelling, some adults dramatize rather than state the point of the story, or they utilize exaggerated paralinguistic features to convey meaning, a style Tannen labeled as more "oral," within which there is a scarcity of explicit verbal information. Tannen (1985) further suggested that the differences between oral and literate traditions lie in the focus, whether it is on interpersonal involvement or on information and explicit messages.

"Sharing time" is a common discourse activity in primary school classrooms. Analyses of "sharing time" (Michaels, 1981, 1984, 1985, 1986; Michaels & Cook-Gumperz, 1979; Michaels & Foster, 1985) provide evidence as groups, African American and White children differed in their performance, the reinforcement they received from the teacher, and the practice in literate-style discourse they received during the event. Teachers appeared to have difficulty recognizing tile special intonation patterns that some African American children, who came from backgrounds different from the teachers, used to emphasize points or create cohesion in messages. In another study, Michaels and Collins (1984) were able to identify oral-based and literate-based strategies in spoken narratives. Children's narratives, produced in response to a short film, were used to characterize children as literate-style or oral style speakers. These two groups both attempted to establish cohesion, but they used different strategies to do so. Oral-style children relied on context, paralinguistic cues, and audience involvement more than on lexicalization, the strategy used more by the literate-style children. Michaels' work indicates that children learn the narrative structures used in their families communities; but when they attempt to use the structure they know in social settings, they may encounter another concept of the structure of narrative. Stories are related to culture, context, and purpose, and assessment of children's narrative knowledge should be based on performance in several different contexts (Pappas, 1981, 1985).

***The language of inquiry.*** As children learn language, they use language to express themselves as individuals; connect with others, and make sense of the world. In the beginnings of language expression even very young children reveal their individuality (Nelson, 1981; Wolf & Gardner, 1979). Early studies of mothers and children (Schaffer, Collis, & Parsons, 1977; Trevarthen, 1977, 1992) show that even infants prefer to interact with human rather than objects and exhibit aspects of dialogue in their interactions with caregivers. Infant games such as "peekaboo" count as linguistic rituals that are part of ushering the child into dialogue (Bruner, 1978, 1981; Cazden, 1979; Trevarthen, 1992).

Language behavior stands as evidence that infants and young children are inherently curious and that they are constantly working to make sense of their world (Britton, 1973; Donaldson, 1979). Lindfors (1999) argued that all three of these broad language uses (personal, social, and intellectual) are present in the beginnings of acts of inquiry. Paralleling Clay's (1991; Sulzby & Teale, 1991) concept of "emergent literacy," Lindfors (1999) described "emergent inquiry" as beginning at birth and continuing into and beyond the school years. Lindfors saw "the emergent inquirer as actively and continuously engaged in constructing her understanding of inquiry acts: purposes, expression, participants, contexts (p. 49).

This view of inquiry recognizes the interconnectedness of speaking and listening with intention, social context, and focus of the content. Vygotsky (1986) spoke of children's "inner speech" as a tool for problem solving, an internal dialogue that permits the individual to reflect and analyze. This internal dialogue is nourished and mediated by social speech. Others within the sociocultural setting for language form an integral part of acts of inquiry. Rogoff (1990) provided evidence that "guided participation," that is, the ways community members demonstrate to children and engage them in the activities of daily life, are universal across cultures. Through conversation that accompanies acts of daily life, members of a community share the world with children. They reveal perspectives and demonstrate how to identify properties and relationships of experience. Every day involves lessons in how to talk about the world. Children see many demonstrations of acts of inquiry that occur within the social context and they are daily engaged in these acts of inquiry. Feelings, too, are integral to language users' talk about the world and what it means. Thus, making sense of the world through inquiry is a natural part of the child's construction of knowledge and oral language is inherent in the process.

***Pedagogical significance of child language research.*** Research on children's oral language learning shows that by the time children go off to school they know a great deal about their native language as well as how to use that language to communicate with others. Although not specifically related to teaching oral language in the classroom, the studies provide important

insights about the basic processes involved in language learning. The studies illustrate the following:

1. While they are learning language, children learn to use language in personal, social, and intellectual ways.
2. Children learn language by using it for real purposes within social situations.
3. Factors in the social context heavily influence language use and learning.
4. Children use language as acts of inquiry.

Studies show that children do become increasingly sophisticated at using spoken language for a variety of functions (making requests, asking for information, controlling others, informing, imagining, and telling stories) and different forms of discourse (conversation, argument, narrative), and in monitoring and adjusting their language to the context of the situation (setting, audience, task). Whether or how these competencies can be further developed in the classroom, remains an open question.

Development of communicative competence is a complex process. Children need to learn the functions of language, the rules that govern social interaction, and the structure of various forms of discourse in order to use language effectively in both speaking and listening. The three aspects of communicative competence are interrelated in language use and learning and are also related to literacy development (for discussions of the potential relationships, see Dickinson, 1987; Fitzgerald, 1989, Kretschmer, 1989; Myers, 1987; Torrence & Olson, 1984). Although more research is needed to describe and explain the process and to determine the conditions that will promote learning, the research does suggest that "communicative competence in the classroom cannot be broken down into fragments out of context, without destroying the essence of the process" (L. C. Wilkinson & Spinelli, 1982, p. 327).

## FROM HOME TO SCHOOL

When children enter school, they encounter a new language environment; and for many, it is an environment greatly different from their homes. An aspect of learning to be a pupil is the mastery of a code of oral language interactions, including rules that are rarely made explicit by teachers. Willes (1983) found that teachers who taught children entering school for the first time took a great deal for granted about children's knowledge of this system of rules. Teachers frequently assumed that instructions would be understood by pupils who did not understand the context to which those instructions referred and who had not been provided with relevant explanations of procedures. Because this was the children's first school experience, it might have been reasonable to expect teachers to ease the transition from home to school, including explanations, demonstrations, and time to practice the ways of talking and behaving that are important in school settings. Instead, the whole process of acquiring competence as a student is somewhat haphazard and left to chance. According to Willes, many children receive far less support than they need. Children do not start at a common level of experience in school-like settings; the required knowledge is not easily communicated through direct instruction, Some children remain "baffled and silent."

Through detailed studies of children in both home and school settings, Wells (1985, 1986a, 1986b; Wells & Wells, 1984) discovered that young children's home environments provide interactions characterized by collaboration in the negotiation of meaning and intention. Wells' data were collected through recording language in naturalistic settings and then systematically analyzing the transcribed data. A total of 128 children were recorded at intervals over $2\frac{1}{2}$, with a subgroup followed through primary school. Wells was able to observe children in both home and school settings and to note differences among children and between the settings.

School language was basically teacher dominated. Compared with the home setting, children initiated fewer interactions, played a much more passive role in conversations, took fewer turns, and asked fewer questions. Children in school produced syntactically less complex utterances with a narrower range of meaning content than in home settings. Teachers were twice as likely to develop their own meanings as they were to respond to children's meanings, while parents were twice as likely to respond to children's contributions. Wells (1985, 1986a, 1986b; Wells & Wells, 1984) explained the "impoverished" talk between teachers and pupils by proposing that teachers probably do not believe that pupils' own talk has value in their learning.

Wells (1985, 1986a, 1986b; Wells & Wells, 1984) suggested that homes tended to provide richer oral language environments than did classrooms. Educators have assumed that children's lack of language skills, resulting from deficient home environments, contributes to a lack of success in school. Wells' research raises doubts about this assumption and suggests that schools do not provide a context that demands children use language in new ways. Classrooms may not provide opportunities for children to learn through talk and, at the same time, to expand their repertoire for talking in different ways.

Tizard and Hughes (1984) drew similar conclusions from their comparisons of 4-year-olds in conversations with their mothers and in conversations with their teachers at nursery school. The conversations at home revealed children to be persistent and logical thinkers, puzzling to grasp new ideas. The children's talk with teachers lacked such richness, depth, and variety. There was not the same sense of intellectual struggle and mutual attempt to communicate the researchers found in homes. DeStefano and Kantor (1988) had similar findings in their study of the differences between the language used at home and that used in school with Appalachian children.

Heath (1983) studied aspects of learning behavior in southern U.S. African American and White communities. She found that each community had its own values and conventions for instructional encounters. Strategies that outside observers might label as dysfunctional behaviors were actually firmly grounded in the interactive practices and learning styles of the home. These differences in discourse patterns had consequences for children's ability to profit from instruction in the school classroom. Heath concluded that educators must account for variations in interactive norms and continuously seek to be sure that information is conveyed to students. Accomplishing this goal would mean viewing teaching and learning as interactive processes.

These and other studies (Philips, 1972) of the differences between conversations at home and in school and among different cultural groups throw doubt on the theory that some children underachieve at school because of a language deficit at home, and raise serious issues about how schools affect students of different sociocultural and economic backgrounds. Tizard and Hughes (1984) concluded:

The schools' problem, as we see it, is how to foster the interest and curiosity which children show at home. An environment is required that will allow the "puzzling" to flourish, and which will help the young child . . . develop her intellectual and communication skills (p. 261).

The studies reviewed above focus on differences in patterns of language use that are the result of differences in the social system, the rules that govern a speaker's interactions with others. Differences in language structure (e.g., phonology and syntax) are also potential sources of interference in communication and learning. Many teachers, though aware of the differences, still hold the view that children who speak a language that is different from the accepted standard are poor language users (Goodman, Smith, Meredith, & Goodman, 1987). In fact, every version of a language is appropriate and useful for the culture within which it is constructed (DeStefano, 1973; Labov, 1969).

Goodman et al. (1987) cautioned that educators must not ignore dialect differences because they might make unconscious assumptions about language and text that will cause problems in instruction, such as presenting rhyming words that do not rhyme for the divergent speaker. All children, as they encounter new situations, must learn to expand their ability to use language in different ways. The teacher, however, must not subvert this expansion process by rejection or negative attitude towards children's own speech (Kiefer & DeStefano, 1985). Children who experience such rejection may be reluctant to risk speaking in new ways, and they may not make full use of their language resources in the learning situation.

As mentioned earlier, *the Kingman Report* from Britain (Department of Education and Science 1988) recognized the great variety of language, standard variety being only one kind (as cited in Raban, 1999). It is through use that children extend, expand and enrich the varieties of language that make up their competence. Wolfram's (1998) research on American dialects led to a proposal for helping students explore language differences. His work has led to instructional programs that involve students in investigations of dialect differences. Such curricular approaches show promise for helping students make conscious choices about the expansion of their language.

Language variety is endless; and children entering our schools represent the full range. They may speak different idiolects, different regional or social dialects of the same language, or different languages. They may even be hard of hearing and use the sign language of the deaf as a primary communication system. Research has provided evidence that there are culturally distinct ways of using language (Heath, 1982a, 1982b, 1983). Educators have learned to value diversity and cultural differences (Edelsky, 1991; Lindfors, 1986, 1987; Smitherman,

1977) and to create classroom contexts that allow children to use the language strengths that they bring from their homes (Au, 1980; Hudelson, 1989, 1994). By expanding their awareness of children's language, sensitive teachers can adjust their own language patterns in ways that will invite children into the process of inquiry. Issues related to diversity underscore the arguments in favor of oral language that teachers notice characteristics of divergent speech, and it is through oral language that teachers can help children constantly expand their language repertoires.

## RESEARCH ON ORAL LANGUAGE IN THE CLASSROOM

Research on classroom language has provided important information about the uses of oral language in schools, the characteristic features of classroom discourse, and the potential consequences of students' oral language development and learning. This section describes three perspectives from which classroom discourse has been studied: one that developed in the United States and dominated classroom research for years, another that developed in Britain and focuses on the role of talk in learning, and a third that focuses on classrooms as contexts for social interaction and has had a significant impact on classroom research in both countries. The subsequent section reviews the results of classroom language research for insights about the state of practice.

### U.S. Tradition: Analyzing the Structure of Classroom Talk

During the 1960s and 1970s, almost all the classroom research in the United States, and some in Britain, involved the creation and use of coding approaches for analyzing classroom social systems. As reviewed in Dunkin and Biddle (1974), the systematic tradition, stemming from psychology, resulted in a large number of studies designed to provide clues to the kinds of social interactions and social systems that were related to higher achievement or positive outcomes in education. Studies of social interaction rose from three sources: (a) educators who were concerned with conditions for learning, (b) psychologists concerned with mental health in schools, and (c) social scientists studying the behavior of groups in social settings such as the classroom (Withall & Lewis, 1971).

To quickly and efficiently code classroom talk into quantifiable data, a large number of techniques were designed (Amidon & Hunter, 1967; Flanders, 1966; Simon & Boyer, 1974). As indicated in one review (Dunkin & Biddle, 1974), these methods were "systematic." They used instruments for noting or measuring events and used them consistently for a number of observations. These investigators systematically observed what happened in classrooms and quantified those observations for descriptive and correlational studies.

The results of these observational studies suggested that "the majority of classrooms are dominated by a style of teaching that has remained virtually unchanged since the beginning of modern schooling in the nineteenth century, and probably since the beginning of the age-graded school class" (R. Young & Watson, 1981, p. 82). Teachers do most of the talking, estimates go as high as 72% to 75%. Moreover, teachers ask almost all the questions in classrooms (90% to 95%), and the recitation pattern (with teachers' instructions, questions, and reactions to student responses making up 70% to 75% of the talk, and student responses constituting 25% to 30%) dominates classroom discourse in studies done across different levels and areas of the curriculum, including English and language-arts instruction (R. Young & Watson, 1981).

Although these systematic studies offer educators information about classroom language, they were criticized by English educators (Barnes, 1972) and by language researchers working in other disciplines (Delamont, 1976, 1981; Delamont & Hamilton, 1984; A. D. Edwards & Furlong, 1978; A. D. Edwards & Westgate, 1987; Gumperz, 1986; Hammersley, 1986b; Mehan, 1981; Sevigny, 1981). Critics claimed, among other things, that the coders/observers were subject to cultural blinders, ignored the perspectives and intentions of the participants involved in the interactions, did not record actual data for more systematic and reliable analysis, and, as a result, failed to see the complexity and patterns of interaction in classroom discourse, Evertson and Green (1986) identified many common sources of error in this research and note that these problems need attention if one is to observe accurately in classrooms.

Delamont and Hamilton (1984) criticized prespecified coding schemes because:

1. Such schemes seek to produce only numerical and normative data.
2. Procedures tend to ignore the context in which data are gathered.
3. The coding schemes are usually concerned-only with overt, observable behavior, and not with the intentions behind the behavior.
4. They focus on things that can be categorized and measured, and distort or ignore the qualitative features.
5. The systems focus on small bits of behavior rather than global concepts.
6. Categories are prespecified and thus may assume rather than explain social processes; and
7. Arbitrary boundaries are pre-established, thus creating an initial bias that "freezes" reality (pp. 8–10).

Despite these problems, research using interactional analysis systems provided important information about language use in classrooms. These studies created the notion of objective feedback to assist teachers in becoming aware of their own language as a means of improving their teaching (Good & Brophy, 1987). Furthermore, the results raised issues for English educators and researchers in Britain and the United States who were already concerned about the impact of classroom language on students' learning and communication development (e.g., R. R. Allen & Brown, 1976; Barnes, 1972; Barnes, Britton, & Rosen, 1971; Dixon, 1967; Moffett, 1968).

## British Approach: Recognizing the Role of Oral Language

In the 1960s and 1970s, research emerging in the United Kingdom brought increased attention to the development of oral language in school settings. Exemplified by the new term *oracy*, coined to parallel *literacy* that at the time dominated the curriculum (A. M. Wilkinson, 1965, 1970), a new scholarly direction emphasized the integrated nature of listening and speaking and the importance of talking in learning.

Seminal studies of talk in primary and secondary classrooms were produced by Barnes (1976), Barnes et al. (1971), and Rosen and Rosen (1973). These studies were important because they provided pictures of what classrooms were and could be like and had implications that seemed sensible and real to teachers on both sides of the Atlantic. These researchers tended not to focus on language itself, but to view language as providing a window on students' learning and social development.

A major policy document, Bullock's (1975), *A Language for Life,* presented a forward-looking language policy that would create what Marland (1977) called "a 'virtuous circle': if a school devotes thought and time to assisting language development, learning in all areas will be helped; if attention is given to language in the content and skill subjects, language development will be assisted powerfully by the context and purpose of those subjects" (p. 3). Though the report focused on secondary schools, the ideas were equally applicable to education in primary schools.

The climate was right for this report, being already influenced by the "language across the curriculum movement" advocated by the National Association for the Teaching of English (1976). The origin of the movement could be traced to an interest in theories of language and learning derived from the work of Bruner (1975), Kelly (1955), Piaget (1959), and Vygotsky (1978). The work by Barnes (1971, 1972, 1973); Barnes et al. (1971); Britton (1970, 1971); Doughty, Pearce, and Thornton (1972); Halliday (1969, 1971, 1973, 1975, 1978); A. M. Wilkinson (1971, 1972, 1975); A. M. Wilkinson, Stratta, and Dudley (1974) provided theoretical foundations for the movement. In their work, they addressed such issues as the functions of language, language as part of the social system, the relations between language and situation, classroom environments for language use, and the relations between talking and learning. Others attempted to translate theory into teachers' guides for language work in the school. For example, in *Language in Use*, Doughty, Pearce, and Thornton (1971), developed Halliday's ideas into a set of classroom activities that would allow secondary students to explore, discover, and experiment with the variety of uses of language.

Moreover, following Barnes' (1972) criticism of the systematic approach to investigating classrooms and his call for more naturalistic studies, English educators (Barnes, 1976; Jones & Mulford, 1971; Mallet & Newsome, 1977; Martin, D'Arcy, Newton, & Parker, 1976; Martin, Williams, Wilding, Hemmings, & Medway, 1976; Rosen & Rosen, 1973; Torbe & Protherough, 1976) published case studies and anecdotal reports that provided powerful descriptive portraits of how language use shares learning when primary and secondary students are given opportunities to use language—talk and write, read and listen—to learn across the curriculum.

These British scholars had a significant impact on views of oral language competence and moved language teaching into the future by envisioning a curriculum for listening and speaking based on broad communicative competence. In a volume titled *An Introduction to Oracy* (Holderness & Lalljee, 1998), Lalljee laid out a startling list of speaking and listening skills: "announcing, persuading, clarifying, reporting, evaluating, exploring, speculating, instructing, describing, narrating, explaining, criticizing, reflecting, finding out, interpreting, predicting, summarizing, analyzing, expressing, presenting, communicating, questioning, comparing, reviewing, demonstrating, investigating, selecting, organizing, problem-solving, responding, arguing a case." Promoters of oracy suggested that when engaged in the process of "languaging," a speaker looks outward, towards the audience, as well as inward, at his/her own linguistic resources. Competence is an individual's ability to select and use language in a way that communicates what he/she wants to "mean" in that context (Halliday, 1973, 1975). Competence, then, is a mediating factor between the speaker's potential for making meanings and the demands of the situation.

This view of competence suggests that students who perform poorly may have considerable "meaning potential" and resources, but may lack experience using language in the contexts concerned. The task for the curriculum, then, is to provide experiences in the classroom that require the growth of this competence. Variety in learning situations is necessary; these must constantly change and should demand a range of oral language use (Britton, 1970, 1971; Halliday, 1969, 1973, 1978). This view suggests that language is inseparable from meaning making. Sapir (1949) wrote of language as a tool not just for communicating existing meanings but for generating new meanings. This view is consistent with that of Vygotsky (1962) and Bruner (1966) in that language is seen as a way that we become a part of our culture and interpret it for ourselves, thus making the meanings that guide our lives.

Both kinds of classroom research—systematic observation and naturalistic case studies—have provided important information on the uses of oral language in the classroom; however, still another line of research sprang from theories of classroom discourse emerging in the fields of educational sociology, linguistics, sociolinguistics, and anthropology (Cicourel et al., 1974; Coulthard, 1977; Delamont, 1983; Erickson & Shultz, 1977; Gumperz & Hymes, 1972; Hymes, 1962, 1967, 1972, 1974; Mehan, 1979, 1981; Sinclair & Coulthard, 1975; Stubbs, 1983; Stubbs & Delamont, 1976; M. F. D. Young, 1971). These new theories influenced the direction of classroom research in the United States and the United Kingdom.

## Classrooms as Contexts for Social Interaction: An Ethnographic Perspective

Sociologists who studied schools in the 1960s found that children previously thought unresponsive and lacking in verbal ability were actually skilled communicators in peer group situations (Labov, 1969). Their speech showed reflection of underlying grammatical rules and indicated the use of complex cognitive abilities. It was still unclear, however, how language entered into the social environment of the school.

In 1962, Hymes called for an ethnography of communication that signaled the blending of different perspectives to study language use in social contexts. Techniques from anthropology, sociology, linguistics, and sociolinguistics were used to create detailed observations of the ways language is used in different speech communities (Hymes, 1962, 1967), including the classroom (Gumperz, 1981, 1986). Hymes' work was given greater attention with the publication of *Functions of Language in the Classroom* (Cazden et al., 1972). In the introduction to that volume, Hymes (1972) restated his previous position concerning the way language should be studied. He maintained that it must be studied in the social context and in terms of the way it is organized to meet social needs. Accepting each child's culture, language, and ways of using language was a primary theme of the volume. The educative process is based on what the child brings to the situation and on the relationship between ways of using language and ways of learning in the classroom.

The early work, in particular, focused on the discrepancy between language use at home among various cultural and socioeconomic groups and use at school (see Bernstein, 1971, 1973, 1974; Boggs, 1972; Philips, 1972). Subsequent work included research by Au (1980); Erickson & Mohatt (1982); and Heath (1983). Recognition of the relations between language and culture contributed significantly to knowledge of oral language use in classrooms. In the search for ways to understand cultural differences, researchers in a number of disciplines began to study the classroom as a social system and developed new ways to analyze communication in this speech community (Hymes, 1967).

Communication is a critical component of classroom teaching and learning; it is important because of its role in social interaction and in gaining and displaying knowledge. As Mehan (1979) stated:

Students not only must know the content of academic subjects, they must learn the appropriate form in which to cast their knowledge. That is, competent membership in the classroom community involves employing interactional skills and abilities in the display of academic knowledge. They must know with whom, when, and where they can speak and act, and they must provide the speech and behavior that are appropriate for a given classroom situation. (p. 133)

(For more comprehensive reviews of this work see Cazden, 1986, 1988; A. D. Edwards & Furlong, 1978; A. D. Edwards & Westgate, 1987; D. Edwards & Mercer, 1987; Green, 1983; Green & Smith, 1983. For collections of representative studies see Gilmore & Glatthorn, 1982; Green, 1979; Green & Wallat, 1981a; Hammersley, 1986a; Trueba, Guthrie, & Au, 1981; and L. C. Wilkinson, 1982. Findings from research on the nature of classroom discourse and on the role of talk in learning have provided significant information about the state of practice and the nature of classrooms as contexts for communication development and learning.

# CLASSROOMS AS CONTEXTS FOR COMMUNICATION AND LEARNING: THE STATE OF PRACTICE

Many researchers have explored the communication demands of the classroom. They have studied the functions of language and various features of the discourse used in urban and suburban schools, across grade levels (K–12), in whole-class and small-group instruction, in various activities (free play, role-play, lessons, discussions), and in different curriculum areas (reading, math, science, social studies, English, and the humanities). The results provide important insights about the kinds talking and learning that take place in elementary and secondary classrooms.

## Functions of Language in the Classroom

Language is functional; it serves important purposes in people's lives, it is used to establish and maintain relationships, influence others, tell stories, ask questions and give information, and analyze and speculate about the world. Its primary function is for communication, but it is also a tool for learning. The study of the functions of language, then, focuses on what people do with language.

Various approaches have been used to study the functions of oral language in classrooms. The particular approach depends on the researcher's purpose and the way that language is conceptualized. For example, Halliday (1973, 1978) conceptualized language as "meaning potential," which is actualized in various social situations through communication. He argued that language development is a process of "learning how to mean," that is, learning what one can do with language in interaction with others. For Halliday, then, meaning is defined in terms of function.

Halliday (1969, 1973) identified seven models or social functions of language. Halliday (1975) found that these functions evolve over time, but that children use language for all of these functions before they enter school. He found that children's language initially expresses:

1. An *instrumental* function to satisfy basic needs.
2. A *regulatory* function to influence the behavior of others.
3. An *interactional* function to mediate relationships with others.
4. A *personal* function to express self.
5. A *heuristic* function to explore and find out about the environment.
6. An *imaginative* function to pretend and explore an imagination world and, finally.
7. An *informative*, or *representational*, function to inform or communicate information to others.

Halliday (1975, 1978) also argued that these seven functions, which are discrete and independent language uses in young children, merge into three more general functions that characterize adult language. These include: the *pragmatic*, or *interpersonal*, function that has to do with maintaining social relationships; the *mathetic*, or *ideational*, function that has to do with reflecting on personal experience and exploring the environment, and the *textual* function that involves the use of language resources to construct oral texts (e.g., stories, conversation) that are coherent within themselves and within the context of the situation. In adult language, all three of these functions are used simultaneously.

Halliday (1969, 1978) stressed the importance of children experiencing the full range of language functions in the classroom. Pinnell (1975) used Halliday's framework to study first grade learning environments and concluded that "even in the best of educational situations, encouragement for talking and an array of materials are not enough. Teachers' . . . subtle communication through which they invite children to use language for a variety of purposes makes the critical difference" (p. 325). Although it is important for teachers to accept and appreciate the language children have when they come to school, it is also important for them to provide the conditions whereby children can increase their range of competence.

The way young children use language in educational settings has been the subject of Tough's (1973, 1977a) work in England. Her studies of the language of 3-, 4-, and 5-year-old children provide evidence that when children come to the school situation they have already established certain orientations to language and expectations about ways of using it. Tough agreed with Halliday (1973) and Bernstein (1971, 1973, 1975) that differences in children's language use may reflect differences in the set of meanings they hold. As they attempt to deal with the new experiences of the school situation, they must refer to the set of meanings developed through prior experience. For some, this task is relatively simple because the school requires using language in many of the same ways they have used it at home. For others, school may mean adjustment to many unaccustomed ways of using language. Tough concluded that the socially disadvantaged group talked as much and had the same general knowledge and language resources as the advantaged group; however, they were inexperienced in the ways schools expect students to verbalize thought. Tough (1976, 1977b, 1979) then proposed procedures teachers could use to provide more supportive and demanding contexts for language development. Tough's work has been criticized (Shuy, 1984) for being "reductionist"; that is, she reduced her analysis to sets of categories rather than probing responses within each interaction; but her close look at children's development of language functions in classroom settings revealed powerful "under the surface" factors in children's oral language learning.

Britton (1970, 1971) developed a theory of language functions based on a continuum of language roles. He emphasized the importance of "starting where the child is" and gradually developing the differences in language use by refining the various language roles into which children enter. He created a continuum from the participant role in which the speaker uses language for practical matters such as informing, persuading, and explaining, to the spectator role in which the speaker uses language to daydream, chat about experiences, contemplate events, tell stories, and preserve delight in utterance. These roles are seen to cover all uses of language: the transactional or informative uses at the participant end of the continuum, the expressive uses in the middle, and the poetic uses at the spectator end.

Britton (1970, 1971) proposed that the young child's language is primarily expressive, but with experience it gradually moves outward toward the kinds of language used in both the participant (transactional) or spectator (poetic) roles in response to different contexts. However, expressive language, out of which the other two functions grow, continues to be important for learners of all ages. Britton (1971) argued that expressive speech is not only the means by which we get to know one another; it is the means by which we "rehearse the growing points of our formulation and analysis of experience. . . . It is our principal means of exchanging opinions, attitudes, and beliefs in face-to-face situations" (pp. 207–208). Thus, expressive language is used to speculate and to explore new ideas and, as such, plays a central role in learning.

Britton's (1970, 1971) framework of expressive, transactional, and poetic functions was initially developed to analyze written language (Britton, Burgess, Martin, Mcleod & Rosen, 1975); nevertheless, it is equally applicable to spoken and written discourse. Britton (1971) saw the scheme as providing a framework for planning language activities across the curriculum that engage students in roles where they have opportunities to use language-spoken and written-for the full range of functions. "We hope, for instance, the expressive language may be increasingly seen to play a role in all learning (even the most subject oriented) as well as in learning to use language; and that the educational value of spectator activities may come to be better understood and more convincingly argued" (p. 218).

In his now classic survey of secondary classrooms, Barnes et al. (1971) found little or no exploratory talk during formal lessons in the general area of the humanities and in science subjects, areas where one would expect to find students engaged in inquiry. Instead, teachers did most of the talking; students were cast in a passive role. In another study, Barnes (1976) analyzed relatively unstructured peer conversations and found students more frequently used exploratory talk in their discussions of science, history, and poetry. Based on close analysis of language use in small-group student discussions, Barnes and Todd (1977) and other investigators (Chilver & Gould, 1982; Phillips, 1985) advocate use of small-group discussions without a teacher as a way to avoid the constraints placed on talk and learning in teacher-led lessons. Recent reviews of research indicate, however, that true discussion is rare in classrooms (Dillon, 1984). Based on her study of secondary English classrooms, Alverman (1986) called discussion the "forgotten language art."

Whole-class, teacher-led "discussions" predominate, particularly at the secondary level, in the United States as well as other countries. Watson (1987) suggested that alternatives are needed to the teacher-dominated patterns of whole-class lessons, patterns that will give students more activity and opportunities to explore through language. Watson (1980) found such patterns in a study of 90 English lessons in New South Wales. He observed three distinct types of whole-class discussion, each characterized by a different kind of conversational control (Stubbs, 1976). The first type (60% of lessons) was a classroom in which closed questions predominated and teachers were content with one-word or very brief answers. The discourse in these lessons was similar to what Barnes (1973) described as a transmission model of teaching. The second (30% of lessons) was a class in which the teacher still retained conversational control over choice of topic, and who and when students could speak, but there were more open questions and the teacher responded to students' replies instead of simply evaluating them. In this type of classroom, students were encouraged to engage in some exploratory talk (Barnes, 1976). In the third type (observed in four to five lessons), Watson (1980) found less conversational control. Pupil-initiated responses were more common and teachers generally used open questions and did not demand that all comments be funneled through the teacher. Watson described the second and third types as more conducive to critical thinking. The discourse in these classrooms was more reflective of Barnes' (1973) interpretational style of teaching. Follow-up interviews revealed that teachers in the first category believed that they were encouraging pupils to develop their answers and were responding rather than simply evaluating. They tended to exaggerate the involvement of pupils in the discussion. Because whole-class discussion appears to be the predominate mode of instruction in most of the upper grades, teachers need to be more aware of the effects of conversational control and of their own tendency to deceive themselves about the nature of students' experiences.

Many researchers have used Britton's framework to study classroom talk. Several (Barr, D'Arcy & Healey, 1982; Berrill, 1988; Hickman & Kimberley, 1988; Mallet & Newsome, 1977; Martin, 1983; Martin, D'Arcy et al., 1976; Martin, Williams et al., 1976; Robertson, 1980; Torbe & Medway, 1981; Torbe & Protherough, 1976) have shown how students, given the opportunities to talk and listen, can and do use spoken language in productive ways to learn in all areas of the curriculum. These studies highlight the kinds of curriculum activities, learning tasks, and conditions that are likely to encourage students to use language to learn and, in the process, learn how to use language.

Research on language use in the classroom points to the fact that language, even for young children, is functionally complex and that any segment of talk can serve many purposes (Halliday, 1973, 1975). It has also demonstrated that language use is related to the type of activities students engaged in (Genishi & Dyson, 1984; Pinnell, 1975; Shure, 1963). For example, language used in dramatic play has been found to be unusually rich and productive, as evidenced in Black's (1979b) comparisons of young children's language during play and test situations. Other studies have shown that language use is related to physical arrangements and materials (Doke & Risley, 1972) and to group size and/relationship (Berk, 1973; Schachter et al., 1974).

The research reviewed here also points to the need for teachers to be aware of how oral language is used in their classrooms. In the early 1980s, Cahir and Kovac developed sets of materials to help teachers become more aware of student's uses for language as well as their own. Others (e.g., R. R. Allen et al., 1986; Doughty & Doughty, 1974; Doughty, Pearce, & Thornton, 1971; Gorman, 1985; Klein, 1977, 1979; Lund & Duchan, 1988; Moffett, 1968; Moffett & Wagner, 1973, 1983; Pinnell, 1985; Shafer, Staab, & Smith, 1983; A. M. Wilkinson, 1975; A. M. Wilkinson et al., 1980; Wood, 1977a, 1977b) explored theory and research on functions of language and suggested ways teachers can use various category systems to observe and assess students' use of spoken language and to design curriculum activities that provide practice in talking and listening for a full range of social and intellectual functions.

## Classroom Communication and Learning: A Sociolinguistic Perspective

Much current research focuses on classroom communication processes and is framed from a sociolinguistic perspective. This research draws on methodologies and interpretive frameworks from a variety of disciplines (Cazden, 1986; Green, 1983; Green & Harker, 1988; Wilkinson, 1982). Sociologists, linguists, and sociolinguists are interested in the classroom as a social context for language use because it has recognizable and well defined roles and traditions (A. D. Edwards, 1979; Gumperz, 1986; Gumperz & Herasimchuk, 1975; Hymes, 1972; Sinclair & Coulthard, 1975). Language is seen as a window to provide information on learning and social development; however, researchers also find it valuable to focus on the window itself, to learn about how people learn to communicate and use language in classroom contexts.

This research has revealed the special characteristics of speech routines that occur in classroom situations. These routines are similar across classroom contexts and serve as "speech events" for study (Gumperz, 1986). In general, this research shows that teachers and children in classrooms interact in very patterned, rule-governed ways. These rules or norms for behavior are continually monitored, signaled, and interpreted by the people involved, and part of learning is finding out how to read cues and make inferences necessary to be successful in classrooms (Gilmore & Glatthorn, 1982; Green & Wallat, 1981b). This process is complex because expectations vary by situational factors (Gumperz, 1981), such as the background of people involved. Also, the context constantly changes as signals interact with the background experiences and assumptions of participants, and they are often interpreted differently.

Many of the sociolinguistic studies of classroom communication have focused on the nature of the social relationships underlying the distinctive discourse produced in the spoken language of the classroom. Primarily two kinds of relationships exist within any K–12 classroom: relationships between teachers and students, and between students and students.

***Teacher and student talk: studying classroom lessons.*** According to A. D. Edwards (1979), classroom talk typically consists of working out the power relationships between teacher and students. Classrooms seem to be environments in which teachers place severe functional constraints upon what students say. Knowledge is framed by the teacher and communicated by the authority to the pupils (A. D. Edwards, 1979). In some classroom environments, "elaborated codes" (Bernstein, 1964, 1975) predominate. Students who are not accustomed to reconstructing their knowledge and expressing it explicitly may find themselves at a disadvantage and teachers may view them as inferior in learning ability. Studies of teacher and student talk reveal that not only must students learn the content of school lessons, they must learn the behaviors and language teachers connect with successful students (Cazden, 1988; A. D. Edwards, 1981; Mehan, 1979).

A fruitful area of investigation in sociolinguistic studies of classroom language has been the teacher-led lesson that, as documented in many studies (Bellack, Kliebard, Hyman, & Smith, 1966; Mehan, 1979; Sinclair & Coulthard, 1975; Griffin & Shuy, 1978), takes place in an orderly and patterned way. The basic lesson structure includes a three-part sequence of turns in which the teacher asks a question that requires a response, a student responds, and the teacher comments on the response, evaluating or reformulating the student's response (Mehan, 1979). This has become known as the recitation pattern. Shavelson and Stern (1981) found that when teachers prepare lessons they follow implicit "scripts" that guide the lesson and determine the overall structure and flow of the action.

Lessons provide a predictable environment, within which, once established, the teacher can use simple utterances that would be ambiguous without knowledge of the context (Mehan, 1979). In a year-long study of a first-grade classroom, Gumperz (1986) found that the manner of articulation is more important than the actual content of lessons. The teacher used phrases and intonation to set up a predictable structure within which children could understand what was expected. Erickson and Shultz (1977) suggest that the teacher "sets them up" for prediction through the words and phrases used in the lesson (Erickson & Schultz, 1977).

Lessons are different from ordinary conversation. In everyday conversation, speakers share responsibility and they negotiate turns. In situations in which it is very difficult to get a turn, speakers often reform into smaller groups. In classrooms, however, the number of speakers are contained in one space for a long period of time. The teacher is pressed to keep order so that information can be transmitted; as a result, teachers control turns (A. D. Edwards, 1979). There is one speaker at a time, to which everyone is supposed to listen, few gaps in conversation, and little overlap of speakers. Teachers usually speak between each turn. The teacher allocates turns, monitors what is said, repairs breakdowns, and sums up, thereby having complete control of who speaks, and what and how much is said (A. D. Edwards, 1979). Based on what he observed in secondary English classrooms, Stubbs (1976) described classroom talk as "asymmetrical . . . almost never used by pupils and, when it is, it is a sign that an atypical teaching situation has arisen" (p. 162).

In the classroom situation, questions are asked by a person who already knows the answer (Cazden, 1988; A. D. Edwards, 1979). This particular circumstance means that the person asking the question retains the power to evaluate the response (Sinclair & Coulthard, 1975). When teachers ask questions, students are obligated to respond, to wait for an assessment of what they say, and to look for cues as to how they should modify their responses (Hammersley, 1977; Mehan, 1978, 1979). As A. D. Edwards (1979) explained, the teacher in the classroom "owns" instructional talk, with the prerogative to direct speakership and to make at least most of the decisions concerning

duration, and content of the talk. The critical element in the pattern is the teacher's prior knowledge that is to be transmitted to the students. The teacher retains the preallocated rights of the "expert" and the students are assumed to be unknowing; thus, the teacher's questions function as "tests"; the pupil's meanings are defined in relationship to the body of knowledge that defines what is relevant and irrelevant. This pattern of interaction is not unique to the classroom. It is typical of any hierarchical relationship in which one person holds the knowledge and power and attempts to instruct another.

Given this constrained view of classroom discourse, it appears that the gap between middle-class and lower class children's ability to cope with school is not so much being able to be explicit or talk in elaborated ways as it is knowing how and when to talk and how to display knowledge in talk. A. D. Edwards (1979) suggested that middle-class children, who seem to have more experience with adults in tutorial roles, may be more successful in school situations where information exchange and knowledge testing are primary. "They seem to be more accustomed to having their knowledge tested, more concerned with getting their answers right, more constrained by what they perceive as being relevant to the adult listener, and more experienced in . . . drills which prepare them to ignore verbally the fact that the questioner already knows" (p. 251).

D. Dillon and Searle (1981) conducted an ethnographic study of a first-grade class that supported Edwards' description of classroom language as constrained. They observed one teacher judged as "good," and six children considered "successful" at home and at school. Out of school, children were more likely to be partners with adults in conversations, resembling Bernstein's (1964) "elaborated" code. In school, however, a "restricted" code was more likely to be the norm. Their findings are similar to those of Wells (1981) and Tizard and Hughes (1984) who also found the home a richer context for communication and learning.

In a review of 10 studies funded by National Institute of Education in the late 1970s, Green and Smith (1983) provided a list of constructs that define teaching and learning as linguistic processes. These same constructs represent basic assumptions pertinent to the study of speaking and listening as integrated oral language actions. Their list included the following:

1. Classrooms are communicative environments.
2. Communication is a rule-governed activity.
3. Inferencing is required for conversational comprehension.
4. Meaning is context-specific.
5. Contexts are constructed during interaction.

Teachers appear to provide contextualization cues to help students understand the classroom language. These contextualization cues and students' ability to understand and use them are critical to the transmission and construction of meaning in the classroom (Green & Smith, 1983).

In a comprehensive study of classroom processes, one that combined examination of recorded language, interviews to gain perspective, and achievement data, Morine-Dershimer (1985) found that achievement seemed to be related to a close "fit" between pupil perspectives and interpretations and the teacher's use of classroom language. Morine-Dershimer concluded that teachers were confirming and acknowledging pupils' understandings about the rules for discourse in the classroom. Thus, learning was a complex interaction of teachers' use of contextualization cues and pupils' belief systems about the nature of how to learn in classrooms. This study provided an example of the complexity of contextual variables in classroom communication processes. The context is affected by all past experiences participants bring into the setting and is constantly built in a dynamic way on everything that went before (Green, 1983).

Studies such as Morine-Dershimer's (1985) illustrated that tasks and activities do not necessarily structure the learning that goes on. Acting together on tasks and on each others' messages and behaviors, teachers and children construct the learning that takes place (Erickson & Shultz, 1977; Green & Wallat, 1981b; Gumperz, 1981). Students must not only acquire academic knowledge; they must learn how and when to display it (Bloome & Theodorou, 1988; Mehan, 1979, 1981). This goal requires that educators reexamine language use in the classroom. They must be alert to the hidden curriculum that implicitly "teaches" students to present themselves through speech as "good students."

Classroom talk appears to be a series of "scripts," (Hatch, 1992; Padak, 1986) in which participants play ritualized and highly predictable roles. These scripts are played out in the oral language that surrounds educational experiences. In elementary classrooms, teachers interact with the students as a whole group, with some students as a small group, with students working independently and approaching the teacher for help, or with group work that students conduct on their own. All of these settings require different types of discourse or "scripts." Classroom lessons also have the structure of scripts (Sinclair & Coulthard, 1975). Holderness and Lalljee (1998) emphasized the need to structure classrooms instruction to put children together in different ways, extending their language use as they work with different individuals and in different configurations.

The predominant voice in the classroom is that of the teacher. Through questioning the teacher elicits forms of language from students. Research has revealed that teachers use their questions to serve a wide variety of purposes, for example, to direct and manage student behavior and the routines of instruction, to focus students' attention and have them engage in reflection or evaluation, and to assess their understanding (J. T. Dillon, 1983, 1988a, 1988b, 1994). Research provides evidence that questions can play an important role in student learning if they are open-ended to encourage student thinking (J. T. Dillon, 1994, Hunkins, 1995) or if they are sequenced in a way that will help students expand to more complex understandings (Christianbury & Kelly, 1983; Wilen, 1991). The work of Palinscar and Brown (1984) involved explicit modeling of questions by teachers. Barnes (1992) advocated a tentative questioning style, modeled by the teacher and taken up by students in use with each other. Expressing both questions and statements tentatively (e.g., "I suppose . . ." or "Could it be . . ." or "It might be . . .") keep discussion going because they do not bring closure. They also invite divergent thinking.

Lindfors (1999) has turned our thinking toward real or honest questions. As human beings, teachers can, with authenticity,

model questions that seek information or investigate matters to which they do not know the answers (Albritton, 1992). Teacher questioning still exists for functions like assessment, management, and informing students of what they nerd to know, but a major shift toward inquiry is indicated in the literature (Lindfors, 1999). It is still true that teacher language is key to student learning; if we are serious about creating students who can take charge of their own learning, teachers' questions can demonstrate the purposes and process of genuine inquiry.

***Student talk: child-to-child interactions.*** A number of researchers have studied how students talk with peers in situations where the teacher is not present. Some researchers focused on the potential benefits of peer interaction for communication or social development, while others were interested in the benefits for students' learning and cognitive growth.

Most research on peer-peer interaction among school-age children has focused on students in the lower grades and points to the value of these situations for students' social development. For example, Lazarus (1984) recorded kindergarten pupils in peer interactions in informal settings and more formal settings with the teacher. She found children are aware of regularities in language use in classrooms, including address forms, greetings, and norms of interaction. She also found that young children are able to announce their learning confusions, solicit help from peers or teacher, and adjust their strategies depending on the audience.

Black (1979a) and D. D. Ross (1983) found that kindergarten children use a wide range of language strategies to deal with problems in situations away from adult supervision. These studies indicated the value of such situations for learning the social skills necessary for working together. Children develop understandings of cooperation, independence, and competition that are learned not so much through formal instruction as through opportunities to engage in peer interaction. Through oral language activities, children learn to maintain their own relative status with peers and to engage in learning situations in cooperation with others. Black emphasized the importance of teachers focusing on communicative, rather than linguistic, competence and proposed that the opportunity for children to practice and use language with peers as they work and play in the natural classroom environment could be the most effective language program.

Cooper, Marquis and Ayers-Lopez (1982) studied the roles children assume, the developmental trends, and the discourse patterns in spontaneous peer-peer learning situations in kindergarten, first- and second-grade classrooms. They found wide variation in children's competence to take on roles related to forming working relationships and accomplishing tasks in peer learning situations. They also found evidence of developmental differences. Second-graders formed more long-lasting relationships with others in their class, whereas kindergarten children had more transitory contacts with peers. Older children were more successful at asking for help, getting and giving information, managing others' behavior, engaging the listener's attention, and participating in collaborative learning groups, though there continued to be varying degrees of social competence within grades and across peer learning situations.

In a series of studies (L. C. Wilkinson, 1984; L. C. Wilkinson & Calculator, 1982; L. C. Wilkinson & Dollaghan, 1979), Wilkinson focused on first through third-grade children's use of requests for action and requests for information in small peer reading and math groups. The results revealed that children's skills in using language effectively to obtain responses in peer learning situations improve as they get older. The research showed that the effective communicators are those students who produce requests that are direct, sincere, on task, and directed to a specific peer, and who can revise their requests if not initially successful. L. C. Wilkinson (1984) also found that the way children talk in peer groups is related to achievement in reading and math. This research points to the value of small group, peer-peer interaction for promoting academic and social learning.

In addition to the opportunity for social development, so necessary in a pluralistic society, Cazden (1988, pp. 123–135) identified four potential cognitive benefits of discourse among peers that apply to all ages and cites studies that support each. The benefits include discourse as:

1. *A relationship with an audience* in which an orientation to Other is achieved in speech when immediate feedback is available (Heap, 1986).
2. *Enactment of complementary rules* through which peers scaffold one another to perform tasks together when they would not be able to do so alone (Forman, 1981).
3. *Catalyst for development of logical reasoning skills* in which students hear different points of view and collaborate to solve problems (Paley, 1981).
4. *Exploratory talk* in which the learner can "rehearse" knowledge before formalizing it into a "final draft," such as an oral presentation or report (Barnes, 1976).

Barnes suggested that exploratory small-group talk supports forms of learning that rarely take place in full group, teacher-led discussions.

Several maxims (Grice, 1975) or social rules guide human interaction and make effective communication possible. One is the "cooperative principle" that consists of a willingness to believe that the statements of those with whom we interact mean something and that our job as listeners is to discern that meaning. Grice also listed "quantity," which involves providing what is required but no more than needed; "relevance," making contributions that are related to ongoing conversation; and "manner," being clear rather than ambiguous and wordy. Listeners, they scan talk and context in search of meaning and test our interpretations in various ways as they negotiate our way through a conversation. As they attempt to persuade others or to explain to others, they hear themselves say what they think and in the process organize their thinking. This process of "talking things through" provides the basis for developing the internalization (Vygotsky, 1962) that support cognitive processes.

All teachers, elementary or secondary, English language arts or subject matter specialists, can take advantage of the social and cognitive benefits derived from peer-peer learning by creating classroom situations that foster interaction around tasks, issues, and problems that are meaningful to their students. In such contexts, students are more likely to assume greater responsibility for their own learning.

## The Constructivist Perspective: Using Language for Inquiry

Researchers have described language as an interactive system that integrates speaking and listening in socially defined ways. Oral language is social; it means conversation, based on communicative purpose. Language has been described as "the seamless union of four aspects: communication *purpose* (or intention), *expression* (of purpose, of content, of stance), *participants*, *context*" (Lindfors, 1999, p. 3). These for elements are woven through every kind of language event. "To use language at all—to speak to write or sign—in conscious awareness of another's presence is to engage in an act of connection" (Lindfors, p. 11). Researchers in the 1990s emphasized the uses of language in the process of inquiry. A constructivist perspective involves inquiry that arises from and contributes to socially shared meanings (Bakhtin, 1981; Vygotsky, 1986). Although people have unique meanings, born of their individual experiences, they also have socially shared meanings, born of communicating individual meanings through language and of common experiences, supported through the oral language that accompanies learning. Inquiry, or the investigation that results in new learning, rests on this combination of individual and sharing meanings.

Using language for inquiry involves making connections with others in an attempt to build understanding, or to learn. Lindfors (1999) described two broadly defined types of inquiry acts: (a) *information seeking*, which involves utterances designed to seek clarification, explanation, justification or confirmation; and (b) *wondering*, utterances that involve others in reflecting, predicting, exploring, considering possibilities. Information seeking is bounded and seeks closure; wondering is open, exploratory. Using language in an information seeking way deals with the "actual world," but wondering deals in "possible worlds" (Bruner, 1996).

Whatever the content, inquiry means active investigation on the part of learners. The study of literature, for example, may be framed as inquiry. Barnes (1992) spoke of children "making sense of a poem by talking their way into it" (p. 25). As students discuss books they are reading, what is happening may look like simple conversation; the stance, however is one of inquiry. "They turn toward one another and toward their topics in uncertainty and invitation" (Lindfors, 1999, p. 118). Through the conversational turns of the discussion, they deepen their own understandings and others' and come to know the text in new ways.

Active listening is especially important in inquiry dialogue because "one partner explicitly *seeks* verbal response of a particular kind and thus he acutely tunes into that response; whereas the other partner is one from whom the verbal response is being *sought* and thus he is accurately attuned to the elicitation" (Lindfors, 1999, p. 147). In inquiry, speaking and listening are simultaneous, related processes that come together. Paley (1981) and Gallas (1995) provided richly documented examples of classrooms that are characterized by layers of collaborative inquiry. The teachers, in fact frame their work with children as ongoing inquiry with a focus on children's learning; children collaborate with each other to investigate ongoing questions in the full range of interesting content. In such classrooms, children's language provides evidence that they see learning as ongoing questioning, the gathering of information, and the forming of conclusions, but knowing that those conclusions are open to revision. Answers give rise to new questions. In the process, there is not mere understanding of the information provided, but interpretation that creates shared meaning and new understandings.

Classroom approaches that follow constructivist principles engage students in using language for inquiry. There is increasing awareness that the ability to engage in inquiry is fundamental to learning and curricular approaches are directed towards this goal. Engaging students in investigation is not a simple matter of getting students to ask questions, although much research has focused on children's developing ability to ask different kinds of questions (L. Bloom, Merkin, & Wootten, 1982; Piaget, 1955).

Reciprocal teaching (Palinscar & Brown, 1984) for example, focuses on teaching strategies that will help students monitor and expand their own comprehension of texts. The idea is to explicitly teach students ways to summarize ideas, ask questions, provide clarifications, and make predictions. These sophisticated language uses are modeled for students and practiced with teacher support. Students learn to make their language much more precise as they use it for inquiry.

Barnes (1992) took a different view of the language of inquiry. Instead of the forms of language, he looked to the functions. In the second edition of his classic text *From Communication to Curriculum*, he discussed "exploratory talk," describing it as tentative, marked by hesitations, false starts, restating, and changes of direction. Barnes called this kind of talk "groping towards a meaning" (1992, p. 28). His descriptions provide a contrast to the language precision that is the goal of reciprocal teaching. It may be that students need a great deal of time working on authentic investigations, during which they are allowed to engage in exploratory talk before they begin to refine their language in a formal way.

Reciprocal teaching has increased students' ability to perform as language users within instructional events of the classroom, but Lindfors (1999) cautioned that these dialogues may provide for students to ask questions simply to satisfy the teacher's requirements rather than posing authentic questions for their own intentions. Expert readers, she said, engage in acts of inquiry. In reciprocal teaching, students are enabled to demonstrate comprehension in the way that reading skills are measured and evaluated. Students are working to perfect a skill. Lindfors (1999) recommended the use language in more varied ways, describing teachers' work with children as invitations to students to engage in acts of wondering.

## IMPLICATIONS OF RESEARCH FOR TEACHING ORAL LANGUAGE

The conclusion to this chapter is organized around five principles for oral language teaching that are worth pondering.

Researchers are still developing good descriptions of classroom processes and gaining insights into how spoken language is used to form social relationships, to communicate, and to learn. The implications of current research are so powerful, however, that educators must begin to interpret the findings and to define new directions for practice. This goal is particularly important when we consider the current state of oral language teaching.

With regard to elementary classrooms, research points to the neglect of oracy in favor of teaching reading and writing. Students are still expected to spend most of their time listening to teacher-talk, and major gaps still exist between the home and school language some young children face when they enter school. Many children have difficulty because of differences between their home and school environments and these difficulties are sometimes so severe that children are restricted in using their language skills and competencies to help them in school learning.

As students advance through the grades, opportunities for them to use oral language in the classroom appear to decrease. Students are programmed for input, not output. Whole-class teaching still predominates in elementary and secondary schools in the United States and other countries. Research shows that the patterns of discourse in this style of teaching severely restrict students' use of talking, thus ignoring the learning potential of students' own spoken language. In 1999, researchers were still attempting to draw policymakers' and educators' attention to the development of a wide variety of talk (Raban, 1999).

The research reviewed in this chapter indicates that the situation must change for both elementary and secondary school students. From simple descriptions of classroom interaction to complex mappings of the sociolinguistic context, research supports the integration of speaking and listening, and the development of language curricula that provide students with opportunities to use language (i.e., talk) for a wide variety of purposes, in different situations, and with different audiences.

*The English language arts classroom must engage students in talk.* Children learn language and how to use it through social interaction in situations where spoken language serves genuine purposes for them and those around them. Through interaction with others, children learn the functions of language, the structure of different forms of spoken discourse, and the social rules that govern how language is used in different contexts.

The goal of oral language education is to help students use language as tool for learning, to help them shape knowledge. Barnes (1992) asserted that this knowledge is not necessarily the kind of information that students are expected to memorize and feed back to the teacher. The goal of language teaching, or "oracy," is to enable children to learn principles that they can use in constructing new knowledge or reconstructing their current knowledge.

*Classroom contexts must provide a wide range of learning contexts that require the development and use of a wide range of language.* The knowledge and skills needed for speaking and listening are inextricably intertwined, and therefore the two should not be treated as separate from one another, or separate from reading and writing. All four processes are language processes; experiences that enhance development in one area should benefit development in the others areas. Nor can the skills and knowledge needed to use language effectively be taught through narrow lessons, or isolated drills and exercises; instead, the school experience should help students learn how to use language (i.e., talk and listen) effectively in real life circumstances. The most effective techniques for promoting oral language development are small-group student discussions and project work, informal conversations between students and their peers and teachers, language games, storytelling, creative dramatics, role-playing, improvisation, and, for older students, more formal drama.

One issue that remains, however, is how to organize and sequence oral language activities to form a coherent and developmentally sound K–12 curriculum. The student-centered, "activities approach" of the late 1960s and 1970s, which remains popular at the elementary level and in some junior high and high schools, is considered by many to be haphazard, fragmented, and inadequate. Czerniewska (1981), Watson (1987), and others discuss the limitations of the activities approach and suggest alternative ideas.

There are cautions also against as linear approach requiring that one skill be developed before another. According to Raban (1999), analyzing the model presented in *The Kingman Report* (Department of Education and Science, 1988), "language learning is considered recursive in the sense that through active use, language is extended, enriched, and restructured, not necessarily in any linear fashion." According to Howe (1989), talk will be related to the roles that students have the opportunity to take, experiencing the role of "expert" will elicit more precise language as students work to make explanations clear.

Watson (1987) examined the strengths of a thematic approach to teaching secondary English that engages students in a wide variety of language activities around a given topic or theme. The approach provides for sustained, serious "explorations of the given theme or topic, as well as purposeful speaking, listening, reading and writing" (p. 99). Thus, the approach is a means of integrating the language arts. D. S. Strickland (1989), Gamberg, Kwak, Hutchings, and Altheim (1988), and other whole-language specialists see the same advantages for younger children and, therefore, advocate an integrated thematic approach to teaching language arts in the early childhood and elementary years. Moffetts' (1968) familiar theory of teaching the universe of discourse offers another approach to organizing and sequencing language activities. Others, however, propose functional approaches to language teaching.

According to Barnes (1992), the learner's opportunities depend on the patterns of communication that are characteristic of the classroom. The relationships within the classroom and the way discourse is supported, encouraged, and controlled create the opportunities for talk and thus affect the opportunities for the student to learn and practice forms of discourse. Children's participation depends not only on their own abilities and experience but also on how effective they are at masking sense of what the teacher wants and values. Teachers who use observation skillfully can create more opportunities for students by the way they listen to them, encourage them to use their own knowledge and strengths, recognize the value of their personal styles and determine ways to help students expand their ability to ask questions, clarify, wonder, and explain.

*Education should expand the intellectual, personal, and social purposes for which children use language.* Based on current research and theories of language use and learning, many language arts and speech communication educators advocate a functional approach to language learning. Curriculum based on this view would challenge students with the study and practice of various forms of discourse. Such practice may indeed be necessary so that students can require the more formal approaches to the display of knowledge. This view assumes that oracy is communication. A broader concept of "oracy as a tool for learning" assumes that oral language is the medium for learning in every subject matter area, not just language arts. Students would focus on the content they are exploring; at the same time, they develop critical skills because of they way they use language. The teaching is indirect. The concept of oracy as a tool for learning is related to the constructivist view, explained next.

*A constructivist view of learning requires a curriculum that involves language interactions of many different kinds.* In a constructivist curriculum, students engage in a learning process that is surrounded by talk. Their focus is on the content of interest but the process, inherently fosters language development. This instructional model involves a range of teaching and learning contexts. Bybee's outline from the mid 1990s of several stages offers an example of the range of language that accompanies constructivist learning:

1. Students engage in learning by focusing on something of interest, which might be an object, an event, or a problem. They ask questions and express interest.
2. Students explore ideas through common concrete experiences during which they describe, make and test predictions, discuss and try alternatives, and summarize findings in oral and written language.
3. Teachers provide clear demonstrations and explanations through which students expand their concepts and ideas so that they can express them language. They develop a common language for exploratory purposes that allows them to share meanings and provide many explanations for each other.
4. Through elaboration, students extend their understandings of concepts processes and skills developed through inquiry.
5. Through evaluation, students receive feedback on oral and written efforts, testing their explanations and solutions.

An educational program based on the construction of knowledge through inquiry is a language laboratory that continually offers opportunity for students to expand oral language across content and also in terms of high level intellectual functions (Champagne, 1987; Lindfors, 1999).

*Context plays a central role in oral language learning.* Oral language is the primary medium through which the business of learning is carried out (Cazden, 1986) in the classroom. As this review of research indicates, the classroom context can have a significant impact on language use and learning. Teachers must be aware of the language environment in their classrooms and understand the conditions that may foster or hinder oracy development. Several theorists provide models or frameworks that teachers and curriculum developers can use to identify and observe situational factors (e.g., audience, setting, task) that affect language use in the classroom.

For example, Halliday's (1978) concepts of field, tenor, and mode of discourse provide a useful framework for understanding the complex ways that classrooms vary as language learning environments. He proposed three components of any situation that influence language use:

1. The *field of discourse* refers to the activity participants are engaged in and the topic or subject matter of their talk that affects language use, not just the vocabulary but also the ways of expressing concepts and relationships between phenomenon in the field.
2. The *tenor of the discourse* refers to the role relationships among the participants and affects the style of discourse.
3. The *mode of discourse* refers to the medium (spoken/written) and to the distance among the participants (e.g., close as in conversation or distant as in writing). Mode interacts with the speaker's purpose to determine, in large measure, the genre or form of discourse used (e.g., story, conversation, discussion.)

In a study of rich classroom environments, Platt (1984) found that children's oral and written language varied according to the nature of the interpersonal situation (tenor) and the content (field). Learning oral and written language was scaffolded through both peer and teacher interaction that helped children to make connections between the familiar and the new. Content was integrated across subject matter lines and first experiences were both exploratory and concrete. Gradually children moved toward more formal categories of knowledge and representations of knowledge in oral and written language. Classroom descriptions such as those provided by Platt (1984), illustrate Barnes' (1973) earlier assertion that children need a rich classroom experience and high-quality interactions with a knowledgeable adult. Those who believe students should bring their own knowledge to the new learning will base instruction on the assumption that students do have knowledge, and quite different forms of discourse may be the result (A. D. Edwards, 1979).

*Oral language is a means to learning.* Studies of classroom processes (Delamont, 1983; Green & Wallat, 1981a) have made it clear that oral language functions in subtle, yet immensely important, ways to give students access to learning. Oral language is subtly evaluated by teachers and other students as students attempt to display what they know in classroom lessons. Teachers' awareness of these processes is the first step toward finding ways to provide greater access for and participation from all students.

## Final Thoughts

The research on speaking and listening justifies the present interest in developing school curricula to help all students become more competent oral language users. In light of current assessment practices and the continued emphasis on reading and writing, it is difficult to keep oral language in the forefront of curriculum development. However, the accumulating body of evidence, from diverse perspectives and different fields, indicates the centrality of talking and listening in students' learning.

Having now entered the 21st century, children in elementary schools today will need an unprecedented level of "oracy" to meet the challenges of the new century. The revisions required may not lend themselves to packaged programs or written materials. Oral language skills and concepts are best developed in situations that imitate life. Constructing such learning experiences will not be easy and will require extensive study, and development on the part of teachers. With that in mind, it appears that an immediate start is warranted.

## References

Adams, M. J. (1990). *Beginning to read: Thinking and learning about print.* Cambridge, MA: MIT Press.

Albritton, T. (1992). Honest questions and the teaching of English. *English Education, 24*(2), 91–100.

Allen, D. (1980). *English teaching since 1965: How much growth?* London: Heinemann Educational Books.

Allen, R. R., & Brown, K. L. (Eds.) (1976). *Developing communication competence in children.* Skokie, IL: National Textbook.

Allen, R. R., Brown, K. L., & Yatvin, J. (1986). *Learning language through communication.* Belmont, CA: Wadsworth.

Alverman, D. E. (1986). *Discussion: The forgotten art: Becoming literate in the secondary school.* Paper presented at the annual meeting of the American Educational Association, San Francisco. (ERIC Document Reproduction Service No. 269 717)

Alvy, K. T. (1973). The development of listener adapted communications in grade-school children from different social-class backgrounds. *Genetic Psychology Monograph, 87,* 33–104.

Amidon, E. J., & Hunter, E. (1967). *Improving teaching: The analysis of verbal interaction.* New York: Holt, Rinehart & Winston.

Anderson, H. A. (1952). Needed research in listening. *Elementary English, 29,* 215–224.

Applebee, A. (1978). *The child's concept of story.* Chicago: University of Chicago Press.

Au, K. H. (1980). On participation structure in reading lessons. *Anthropology and Education Quarterly, 11,* 91–115.

Ausubel, D. P. (1960). The use of advance organizers in the learning and retention of meaningful verbal material. *Journal of Educational Psychology, 51,* 267–272.

Ausubel, D. P., & Robinson, F. G. (1969). *School learning: An introduction to educational psychology.* New York: Holt, Rinehart and Winston.

Backlund, P., Booth, J., Moore, M., Parks, A. M., & Van Rheenan, D. (1982). A national survey of state practices in speaking and listening skill assessment. *Communication Education, 31,* 125–130.

Bakhtin, M. M. (1981). *The dialogic imagination.* Austin: University of Texas Press.

Bakhtin, M. M. (1986). *Speech genres and other late essays.* Austin: The University of Texas Press.

Barnes, D. (1971). Classroom contexts for language and learning. *Educational Review, 23,* 235-248.

Barnes, D. (1972). Language and learning in the classroom. In *Language in education: A source book* (pp. 112-118). London: Routledge & Kegan Paul in association with Open University, Press.

Barnes, D. (1973). Styles of communication and thinking in the classroom. In *Language in the classroom* (pp. 14-17). Ed. 262, Block 4, Milton Keynes, England: Open University Press.

Barnes, D. (1976). *From communication to curriculum.* Hammondsworth, England: Penguin.

Barnes, D. (1980). Situated speech strategies: Aspects of the monitoring of oracy. *Educational Review, 32,* 123-131.

Barnes, D. (1992). From communication to *Curriculum* (2nd ed.). Portsmouth, NH: Boynton/Cook Heinemann.

Barnes, D., Britton, J., & Rosen, H. (1971). *Language, the learner and the school.* Hammondsworth, England: Penguin.

Barnes, D., & Todd, F. (1977). *Communication and learning in small groups.* London: Routledge & Kegan Paul.

Barr, M., D'Arcy, P., & Healy, M. K. (1982). *What's going on: Language episodes in British and American classrooms, grades 4-13.* Montclair, NJ: Boynton/Cook.

Bates, E. (1976). *Language and context: The acquisition of pragmatics.* New York: Academic Press.

Bates, E., Camaioni, L., & Volterra, V. (1975). The acquisition of performatives prior to speech. (Rev. ed.). *Merrill-Palmer Quarterly, 21,* 205-224.

Bellack, A. A., Kliebard, H. M., Hyman, R. T., & Smith, F. L. (1966). *The language of the classroom.* New York: Teachers College Press.

Berk, L. E. (1973). *An analysis of activities in preschool settings* (Final report). Washington, DC: National Center for Educational Research and Development. (ERIC Document Reproduction Service No. ED 099 131)

Bernstein, B. (1964). Elaborated and restricted codes: Their social origins and some consequences. In J. J. Gumperz & D. Hymes (Eds.), The ethnography of communication. *American Anthropology, 66,* 55-69.

Bernstein, B. (1971). *Class, codes, and control: Vol. I. Theoretical studies toward a sociology of language.* London: Routledge & Kegan Paul.

Bernstein, B. (1973). *Class, codes, and control: Vol. II. Applied studies towards a sociology of language.* London: Routledge & Kegan Paul.

Bernstein, B. (1974). *Class, codes and control* (2nd rev. ed.). New York: Schocken.

Bernstein, B. (1975). Class, codes, and control: Vol. III. *Towards a theory of educational transmissions.* London: Routledge & Kegan Paul.

Berrill, D. P. (1988). Anecdote and the development of oral argument in sixteen-year-olds. In M. MacLure, T. Phillips, & A. Wilkinson (Eds.), *Oracy matters* (pp. 57-68). Milton Keynes, England: Open University Press.

Black, J. (1979a). Assessing kindergarten children's communication competence. In O. K. Garnica & M. L. King (Eds.), *Language, children and society* (pp. 37-52). Oxford, England: Pergamon.

Black, J. (1979b). Formal and informal means of assessing the communicative competence of kindergarten children. *Research in the Teaching of English, 13,* 49-68.

Bloom, L. (1975). Language development. In F. D. Horowitz (Ed.), *Review of child development research, 4,* (pp. 245-303). Chicago: University of Chicago Press.

Bloom, L. (1970). *Language development: Form and function in emerging grammars.* Cambridge, MA: MIT Press.

Bloom, L., Merkin, S., & Wootten, J. (1982). *Wh*-questions: Linguistic factors that contribute to the sequence of acquisition. *Child Development, 53,* 1084-1092.

Bloom, P., Barss, A., Nicol, J., & Conway, L. (1994). Children's knowledge of binding and conference: Evidence from spontaneous __. *Language, 70*(1), 53-71.

Bloome, D., & Theodorou, E. (1988). Analyzing teacher-student and student-student discourse, In J. L. Green & J. O. Harker (Eds.), *Multiple perspective analyses of classroom discourse* (pp. 217-248). Norwood, NJ: Ablex.

Boggs, S. T. (1972). The meaning of questions and narratives to Hawaiian children. In C. B. Cazden, V. P. John, & D. Hymes (Eds.), *Functions of language in the classroom* (pp. 299-327). New York: Teachers College Press.

Book, C. L. (1978). Teaching functional communication skills in the secondary classroom. *Communication Education, 27,* 322-327.

Botvin, G., & Sutton-Smith, B. (1977). The development of structural complexity in children's fantasy narratives. *Developmental Psychology, 13,* 377-388.

Bower, G. H. (1976). Experiments on story understanding and recall. *Quarterly Journal of Experimental Psychology, 28,* 511-534.

Britton, J. (1970). *Language and learning.* London: Penguin.

Britton, J. (1971). What's the use? A schematic account of language functions. *Educational Review, 23,* 205-219.

Britton, J. (1973). *Language and learning.* Hammondsworth, England: Pelican.

Britton, J., Burgess, T., Martin, N., McLeod, A., & Rosen, H. (1975). *The development of writing abilities* (11-18). London: Schools Council Publications & Macmillan.

Brown, K. L. (1984). Teaching and assessing oral language. In F. W. Parkay, S. O'Bryan, & M. Hennessy (Eds.), *Quest for quality: Improving basic skills instruction in the 1980's* (pp. 78-87). Lanham, MD: University Press of America.

Brown, K. L., Burnett, N., Jones, G. Matsumoto, S., Langford, N. J., & Pacheco, M. (1981). *Teaching speaking and listening skills in the elementary and secondary schools.* Boston: Massachusetts Department of Education.

Bruner, J. S. (1966). *Toward a theory of instruction.* Cambridge, MA: Belknap Press.

Bruner, J. S. (1975). Language as an instrument of thought. In A. Davies (Ed.), *Problems of language and learning* (pp. 61-81). London: Heinemann.

Bruner, J. S. (1983). *Child's talk: Learning to use language.* London: Norton.

Bruner, J. S. (1978). From communication to language: A psychological perspective. In I. Markova (Ed.), *The social context of language* (pp. 17-48). New York: Wiley.

Bruner, J. S. (1981). The pragmatics of acquisition. In W. Deutsch (Ed.), *The child's construction of language* (pp. 39-55). New York: Academic Press.

Bruner, J. S. (1996). *Actual minds, possible worlds.* Cambridge, MA: Harvard University Press.

Bullock, A. (1975). *A language for life.* London, Department of Education and Science, Her Majesty's Stationary Office.

Butler, D. (1980). *Cushla and her books.* Boston: Horn Book.

Caffrey, J. (1955). Auding. *Review of Educational Research, 25,* 121-132.

Canfield, R. G. (1961). How useful are lessons for listening? *Elementary School Journal, 62,* 147-151.

Cazden, C. (1979). Peekaboo as an instructional model: Discourse development at home and at school. *Papers and Reports on Child Development, 17,* 1-29.

Cazden, C. (1986). Classroom discourse. In M. C. Wittrock (Ed.), *Handbook of research on teaching* (3rd ed., pp. 432-463). New York: Macmillan.

Cazden, C. (1988). *Classroom discourse: The language of teaching and learning*. Portsmouth, NH: Heinemann.

Cazden, C., John, V. P., & Hymes, D. (1972). *The functions of language in the classroom*. New York: Teachers College Press.

Champagne, A. B. (1987). *This year in school science, 1987: students and science learning*. Washington, DC: American Association for the Advancement of Science.

Chaney, C. (1992). Language development, metalinguistic skills, and print awareness in 3-year-old children. *Applied Psycholinguistics, 13*, 485–514.

Chilver, P., & Gould, G. (1982). *Learning and language in the classroom*. Oxford, England: Pergamon.

Chomsky, C. (1969). *The acquisition of syntax in children from 5 to 10*. Cambridge, MA: MIT Press.

Chomsky, N. A. (1957). *Syntactic structures*. The Hague: Netherlands: Mouton.

Chomsky, N. A. (1965). *Aspects of the theory of syntax*. Cambridge, MA: MIT Press.

Christianbury, L., & Kelly, P. P. (1983). *Questioning: A path to critical thinking*. Urbana, IL: National Council of Teachers of English.

Christie, F. (1985a). Language and schooling. In S. N. Tchudi (Ed.), *Language, schooling and society* (pp. 21–40). Montclair, NJ: Boynton/Cook.

Christie, F. (1985b). *Language education*. Victoria, Australia: Deakin University.

Christie, F. (1987). Young children's writing: From spoken to written genre. *Language and Education, 1*, 3–13.

Christie, J. F. (1991). Psychological research on play: Connections with early literacy development. In J. Christie (Ed.), *Play and early literacy development* (pp. 27–43). Albany: State University of New York Press.

Cicourel, A. V., Jennings, K. H., Jennings, S. H. M., Leiter, K. C. W., MacKay, R., Mehan, H., & Roth, D. R. (1974). *Language use and school performance*. New York: Academic Press.

Clark, K., & Holquist, M. (1984). *Mikhail Bakhtin*. Cambridge, MA: Harvard University, Belknap Press.

Clay, M. M. (1991). *Becoming literate: The construction of inner control*. Portsmouth, NH: Heinemann.

Cochran-Smith, M. (1984). *The making of a reader*. Norwood, NJ: Ablex.

College Entrance Examination Board. (1983). *Academic preparation for college: What students need to know and be able to do*. New York: Author.

Cook-Gumperz, J. C. (1977). Situated instructions: Language socialization of school age children. In S. Ervin-Tripp & C. Mitchell-Kernan (Eds.), *Child discourse* (pp. 103–124). New York: Academic Press.

Cooper, C. R., Marquis, A., & Avers-Lopez, S. (1982). Peer learning in the classroom. Tracing developmental patterns and consequences of children's spontaneous interactions. In L. C. Wilkinson (Ed.), *Communicating in the classroom* (pp. 69–84). New York: Academic Press.

Corson, D. (1988). *Oral language across the curriculum*. Clevedon, England, and Philadelphia: Multilingual Matters.

Coulthard, M. (1977). *An introduction to discourse analysis*. London: Longman.

Cox, B., & Sulzby, E. (1984). Children's use of reference in told, dictated, and handwritten stories. *Research in the Teaching of English, 18*, 345–365.

Czerniewska, P. (1981). Teaching children language. In N. Mercer (Ed.), *Language in school and community* (pp. 161–178). London: Edward Arnold.

Debaryshe, A. D. (1976). *Language in culture and class*. London: Heinemann Educational Books.

Debaryshe, B. (1993). Joint picture-book reading correlates of early oral language skill. *Journal of child language, 20*, 455–461.

Delamont, S. (1976). Beyond Flanders fields: The relationship of subject matter and individuality to classroom style. In M. Stubbs & S. Delamont (Eds.), *Explorations in classroom observation* (pp. 101–131). London: John Wiley.

Delamont, S. (1981). All too familiar: A decade of classroom research, *Educational Analysis, 3*, 69–83.

Delamont, S. (1983). *Interaction in the classroom: Contemporary sociology of the school* (2nd ed.). London: Methuen.

Delamont, S., & Hamilton, D. (1984). Revisiting classroom research: A cautionary tale. In S. Delamont (Ed.), *Readings on interaction in the classroom* (pp. 3–38). London: Methuen.

DeLawter, J. A., & Eash, M. J. (1966). Focus on oral communication. *Elementary English, 43*, 880–883.

Delia, J. D., & Clark, R. A. (1977). Cognitive complexity, social perception, and the development of listener-adapted communication in six-, eight-, ten-, and twelve-year-old boys. *Communication Monographs, 44*, 236–245.

Delia, J. D., Kline, S. L., & Burleson, B. R (1979). The development of persuasive communication strategies in kindergarteners through twelfth graders. *Communication Monographs, 46*, 241–256.

Department of Education and Science. (1988). *The Kingman report. Report of the Committee of Inquiry Into the Teaching of English Language*. London: Her Majesty's Stationery Office.

DeStefano, J. S. (Ed.) (1973). *Language, society and education: A profile of Black English*. Worthington, OH: Jones.

DeStefano, J. S., & Kantor, R. (1988). Cohesion in spoken and written dialogue: An investigation of cultural and textual constraints. *Linguistics and Education, 1*, 105–124.

Devine, T. G. (1978). Listening: What do we know after fifty years of research and theorizing? *Journal of Reading, 21*, 269–304.

Devine, T. G. (1982). *Listening skills schoolwide*. Urbana, IL: ERIC Clearinghouse on Reading and Communication Skills and the National Council of Teachers of English.

Dickinson, D. K. (1987). Oral language, literacy skills, and response to literature. In J. R. Squire (Ed.), *The dynamics of literacy learning: Research in reading and English* (pp. 147–183). Urbana, IL: ERIC Clearinghouse on Reading and Communication Skills and National Conference on Research in English.

Dickinson, D. K., & Snow, C. E. (1987). Interrelationshipos among prereading and oral-language skills in kindergartners from two social classes. *Early Childhood Research Quarterly, 2*, 1–25.

Dickinson, D. K., & Tabors, P. O. (1991). Early literacy. *Journal of Research in Childhood Education, 6*, 30–46.

Dickson, W. P. (Ed.) (1981). *Children's oral communication skills*. New York: Academic Press.

Dickson, W. P. (1982). Creating communication-rich classrooms: Insights from sociolinguistic and referential traditions. In L. C. Wilkinson (Ed.), *Communicating in the classroom* (pp. 131–152). New York: Academic Press.

Dillon, D., & Searle, D. (1981). The role of language in one first grade classroom. *Research in the Teaching of English, 15*, 311–328.

Dillon, J. T. (1983). *Teaching and the art of questioning*. Bloomington, IN: Phi Delta Kappa Educational Foundation.

Dillon, J. T. (1984). Research on questioning and discussion. *Educational Leadership, 42*, 50–56.

Dillon, J. T. (1988a). *Questioning and discussion: A multidisciplinary study*. Norwood, NJ: Ablex.

Dillon, J. T. (1988b). *Questioning and teaching: A manual of practice*. New York: Teachers College Press.

Dillon, J. T. (1994). *Using discussion in classrooms*. Philadelphia: Open University Press.

DiVesta, F. J., & Palermo, D. S. (1974). Language development. In F. N. Kerlinger & J. B. Carroll (Eds.), *Review of research in education* (pp. 55–107). Itasca, IL: Peacock.

Dixon, J. (1967). *Growth through English*. London: Oxford University Press.

Doake, D. B. (1985). Reading-like behavior: Its role in learning to read. In A. Jaggar & M. T. Smith-Burke (Eds.), *Observing the language learner* (pp. 82–98). Newark, DE International Reading Association, Urbana, IL: National Council of Teachers of English.

Doke, L. A., & Risley, T. R. (1972). The organization of day-care environments: Required versus optional activities. *Journal of Applied Behavior Analysis, 5,* 205–420.

Donaldson, M. (1979). *Children's minds*. New York: Norton.

Dore, J. (1974). A description of early language development. *Journal of Psycholinguistic Research, 4,* 423–430.

Dore, J. (1977). "Oh them sheriff": A pragmatic analysis of children's responses to questions. In S. Ervin-Tripp & C. Mitchell-Kernan (Eds.), *Child discourse* (pp. 139–164). New York: Academic Press.

Dore, J. (1979). Conversation and preschool language development. In P. Fletcher & M. Garman (Eds.), *Language acquisition: Studies in first language development* (pp. 337–362). Cambridge, England: Cambridge University Press.

Doughty, A., & Doughty, P. (1974). *Using language in use: A teacher's guide to language work in the classroom*. London: Edward Arnold.

Doughty, P., Pearce, J., & Thornton, G. (1971). *Language in use*. London: Edward Arnold.

Doughty, P., Pearce, J., & Thornton, G. (1972). *Exploring language*. London: Edward Arnold.

Duker, S. (1961). Listening. *Review of Educational Research, 31,* 145–151.

Duker, S. (1966). *Listening: Readings*. Metuchen, MA: Scarecrow Press.

Duker, S. (1968). *Listening bibliography*. Metuchen, MA: Scarecrow Press.

Duker, S. (1969). Listening. In R. L. Ebel (Ed.), *Encyclopedia of educational research* (4th ed.). London: Collier-Macmillan.

Dunkin, M. J., & Biddle, B. J. (1974). *The study of teaching*. New York: Holt, Rinehart & Winston.

*Durrell listening–reading series*. (1969). New York: Harcourt, Brace & World.

Edelsky, C. (1991). *With literacy and justice for all: Rethinking the social in language and education*. New York: Falmer Press.

Edwards, A. D. (1979). Patterns of power and authority in classroom talk. In P. Woods (Ed.), *Teacher strategies: Explorations in the sociology of the school* (pp. 237–253). London: Croom Helm.

Edwards, A. D. (1981). Analyzing classroom talk. In P. French & M. MacLure (Eds.), *Adult-child conversation* (pp. 291–308). London: Croom Helm.

Edwards, A. D., & Furlong, V. J. (1978). *The language of teaching: Meaning in classroom interaction*. London: Heinemann.

Edwards, A. D., & Westgate, D. P. G. (1987). *Investigating classroom talk*. London: Falmer Press.

Edwards, D., & Mercer, N. (1987). *Common knowledge: The development of understanding in the classroom*. London: Methuen.

Edwards, P. A. (1991). Fostering early literacy through parent coaching. In E. H. Hiebert (Ed.), *Literacy for a diverse society: Perspectives, practices, and policies* (pp. 199–213). New York: Teachers College Press.

Eisenberg, A., & Garvey, C. (1981). Children's use of verbal strategies in resolving conflict. *Discourse Processes, 4,* 149–170.

Erickson, F., & Mohatt, G. (1982). Cultural organization of participant structures in two classrooms of Indian students. In G. Spindler (Ed.), *Doing the ethnography of schooling: Educational anthropology in action* (pp. 132–174). New York: Holt, Rinehart & Winston.

Erickson, F., & Schultz, J. (1977). When is a context? Some issues and methods in the analysis of social competence. *Quarterly Newsletter for Comparative Human Development, 1,* 5–10.

Ervin-Tripp, S. (1970). Discourse agreement: How children answer questions. In J. R. Hayes (Ed.), *Cognition and the development of language* (pp. 79–108). New York: Wiley.

Ervin-Tripp, S. (1973). *Language acquisition and communicative chance*. Palo Alto, CA: Stanford University Press.

Ervin-Tripp, S. (1974). The comprehension and production of requests by children. In *Papers and reports on child language development* (Special issue, pp. 188–195). Stanford, CA: Sixth Child Language Research Forum.

Ervin-Tripp, S. (1982). Structures of control. In L. C. Wilkinson (Ed.), *Communicating in the classroom* (pp. 27–48). New York: Academic Press.

Evertson, C. M., & Green, J. L. (1986). Observation as inquiry and method. In M. C. Wittrock (Ed.), *Handbook of research on teaching* (3rd ed., pp. 162–213). New York: Macmillan.

Farrell, M., & Flint, S. H. (1967). Are they listening? *Childhood Education, 43,* 528–529.

Fillmore, L. W. (1983). The language learner as an individual: Implications of research on individual differences for the ESL teacher. In J. Hamscombe & M. Clarke (Eds.), *On TESOL '82: Pacific perspectives on language learning and teaching* (pp. 157–173). Washington, DC: Teachers of English to Speakers of Other Languages.

Fitzgerald, J. (1989). Research on stories: Implications for teachers. In K. D. Muth (Ed.), *Children's comprehension of text: Research into practice* (pp. 2–36). Newark, DE: International Reading Association.

Flanders, N. A. (1966). *Interaction analysis in the classroom: A manual for observers* (Rev. ed.). Ann Arbor: University of Michigan, School of Education.

Flavell, J. H., Speer, J. R., Green, F. L., & August, D. L. (1981). The development of comprehension monitoring and knowledge about communication. *Monographs of the Society for Research in Child Development, 46* (5, Serial No. 192).

Forman, E. A. (1981). *The role of collaboration in problem solving in children*. Unpublished doctoral dissertation, Harvard University, Cambridge, MA.

Foster, S. (1979). *From non-verbal to verbal communication: A study of the development of topic initiation strategies during the first two-and-a-half years*. Unpublished doctoral dissertation, University of Lancaster, Lancaster, England.

Foulke, E., & Sticht, T. (1969). Review of research on the intelligibility and comprehension of accelerated speech. *Psychological Bulletin, 72,* 50–62.

Fox, C. (1985). Talking like a book: Young children's oral monologues. In M. Meek (Ed.), *Opening moves: Work in progress in the study of children's language development* (pp. 12–25). University of London, London: Institute of Education.

Fox, C. (1988). "Poppies will make them grant.' In M. Meek & C. Mills (Eds.), *Language and literacy in the primary school* (pp. 53–68). East Sussex, England: Falmer Press.

Franklin, M. B., & Barten, S. S. (1988). *Child language: A reader*. Oxford, England: Oxford University Press.

Friedrich, G. W. (Ed.) (1981). *Education in the 80's: Speech communication*. Washington, DC: National Education Association.

Galda, L. (1984). Narrative competence: Play, storytelling, and story comprehension. In A. D. Pellegrini & T. Yawkey (Eds.), *The development of oral and written language in social contexts* (pp. 105–117). Norwood, NJ: Ablex.

Gallas, K. (1995). *Talking their way into science*. New York: Teachers College Press.

Gamberg, R., Kwak, W., Hutchings, M., & Altheim, A. (1988). *Learning and loving it: Theme studies in the classroom*. Portsmouth, NH: Heinemann.

Garvey, C. (1974). Some properties of social play. *Merrill-Palmer Quarterly, 20,* 163–180.

Garvey, C. (1977). Play with language and speech. In S. Ervin-Tripp & C. Mitchell-Kernan (Eds.), *Child Discourse* (pp. 27–47). New York: Academic Press.

Garvey, C., & BenDebba, M. (1974). Effects of age, sex, and partner on children's dyadic speech. *Journal of Child Development, 45,* 1159–1161.

Genishi, C., & DiPaolo, M. (1982). Learning through argument in a preschool. In L. C. Wilkinson (Ed.), *Communicating in the classroom* (pp. 49–68). New York: Academic Press.

Genishi, C., & Dyson, A. H. (1984). *Language assessment in the early years*. Norwood, NJ: Ablex.

Gernsbacher, M. A., Varner, K. R., & Foust, M. E. (1990). Investigating difference in general comprehension skill. *Journal of Experimental Psychology: Learning, Memory and Cognition 16,* 430–445.

Gilmore, P., & Glatthorn, E. (1982). *Children in and out of school*. Washington, DC: Center for Applied Linguistics.

Glucksberg, S., & Krauss, R. (1967). What do people say after they have learned how to talk? Studies of the developmental of referential communication. *Merrill Palmer Quarterly, 13,* 309–316.

Goldstein, H. (1940). *Reading and listening comprehension at various controlled rates*. New York: Teachers College Press.

Good, T. L., & Brophy, J. E. (1987). *Looking in classrooms* (4th ed.). New York: Harper & Row.

Goodman, K. S., Smith, E. B., Meredith, R., & Goodman, Y. M. (1987). *Language and thinking in school* (3rd ed.). New York: Owen.

Gorman, T. (1985). Language assessment and language teaching: Innovation and interaction. In G. Wells & J. Nicholls (Eds.), *Language and learning: An interactional perspective* (pp. 125–134). London: Falmer Press.

Graves, D. H. (1983). *Writing: Teachers and children at work*. Exeter, NH: Heinemann.

Gray, R. A., Saski, J., McEntire, M. E., & Larsen, S. C. (1980). Is proficiency in oral language a predictor of academic success? *The Elementary School Journal, 80,* 260–268.

Green, J. L. (Ed.) (1979). Communicating with young children. *Theory Into practice, 18.*

Green, J. L. (1983). Research on teaching as a linguistic process: A state of the art. *Review of Research in Education, 10,* 151–252.

Green, J. L., & Harker, J. O. (Eds.) (1988). *Multiple perspective analyses of classroom discourse* (pp. 11–47). Norwood, NJ: Ablex.

Green, J. L., & Smith, D. (1983). Teaching and learning: A linguistic perspective. *The Elementary School Journal, 83,* 353–391.

Green, J. L., & Wallat, C. (Eds.) (1981a). *Ethnography and language in educational settings*. Norwood, NJ: Ablex.

Green, J. L., & Wallat, C. (1981b). Mapping instructional conversations: A sociolinguistic ethnography. In J. L. Green & C. Wallat (Eds.), *Ethnography and language in educational settings* (pp. 161–205). Norwood, NJ: Ablex.

Grice, H. P. (1975). Logic and conversation. In P. Cole & J. Morgan (Eds.), *Syntax and semantics: Vol. 3. Speech acts* (pp. 41–58). New York: Academic Press.

Griffin, P., & Shuy, R. W. (1978). *Children's functional language and education in the early years*. Final report to Carnegie Corporation of New York. Arlington, VA: Center for Applied Linguistics.

Gumperz, J. J. (1981). Conversational inference and classroom learning. In J. L. Green & C. Wallat (Eds.), *Ethnography and language in educational settings* (pp. 3–24). Norwood, NJ: Ablex.

Gumperz, J. J. (1986). Interactional sociolinguistics in the study of schooling. In J. Cook-Gumperz (Ed.), *The social construction of literacy* (pp. 45–68). London: Cambridge University Press.

Gumperz, J. J., & Herasimchuk, E. (1975). The conversational analysis of social meaning: A study of classroom interaction. In M. Sanches & B. Blount (Eds.), *Sociocultural dimensions of language use* (pp. 81–116). New York: Academic Press.

Gumperz, J. J., & Hymes, D. (1964). The ethnography of communication (Pt. 2). *American Anthropology, 66.*

Gumperz, J. J., & Hymes, D. (Eds.) (1972). *Directions in sociolinguistics: The ethnography of communication*. New York: Holt, Rinehart & Winston.

Halliday, M. A. K. (1969). Relevant models of language. *Educational Review, 22,* 26–37.

Halliday, M. A. K. (1971). Language in a social perspective. *Educational Review, 23,* 165–188.

Halliday, M. A. K. (1973). *Explorations in the functions of language*. London: Edward Arnold.

Halliday, M. A. K. (1975). *Learning how to mean: Explorations in the development of language*. London: Edward Arnold.

Halliday, M. A. K. (1978). *Language as social semiotic: The social interpretation of language and meaning*. London: Edward Arnold.

Halliday, M. A. K., & Hasan, R. (1976). *Cohension in English*. London: Longman.

Hammersley, M. (1977). School learning: The cultural responses required by pupils to answer a teacher's question. In P. Woods & M. Hammersley (Eds.), *School experience: Explorations in the sociology of education* (pp. 57–86). New York: St. Martin's Press.

Hammersley, M. (Ed.) (1986a). *Case studies in classroom research*. Philadelphia and Milton Keynes, England: Open University Press.

Hammersley, M. (Ed.) (1986b). *Controversies in classroom research*. Philadelphia and Milton Keynes, England: Open University Press.

Hampleman, R. S. (1958). Comparison of listening and reading comprehension ability of fourth and sixth grade pupils. *Elementary English, 35,* 49–53.

Harste, J., & Short, K. G. (1988). *Creating classrooms for authors: The reading-writing connection*. Portsmouth, NH: Heinemann.

Hasan, R. (1984a). Coherence and cohesive harmony. In J. FLood (Ed.), *Understanding reading comprehension: Cognition, language, and the structure of prose* (pp. 181–219). Newark, DE: International Reading Association.

Hasan, R. (1984b). The nursery tale as a genre. *Nottingham Linguistic Circular, 13,* 71–102.

Hasan, R. (1984c). The structure of the nursery tale: An essay in text typology. *Proceedings of the 15th Congress of S.L.I.*

Haslett, B. (1983). Children's strategies for maintaining cohesion in their written and oral stories. *Communication Education, 32,* 91–106.

Hatch, E. (1992). *Discourse and language education*. New York: Cambridge University Press.

Heap, J. L. (1986). Sociality and cognition in collaborative computer writing. In D. Bloome (Ed.), Classrooms and literacy (pp. 135–158). Norwood, NJ: Ablex.

Heath, S. B. (1982a). Questioning at home and at school: A comparative study. In G. Spindler (Ed.), *Doing the ethnography of schooling: Educational anthropology in action* (pp. 104–131). New York: Holt, Rinehart, & Winston.

Heath, S. B. (1982b). What no bedtime story means: Narrative skills at home and school. *Language in Society, 11*(2), 49–76.

Heath, S. B. (1983). *Ways with words: Language, life, and work in communities and classrooms*. Cambridge, England: Cambridge University Press.

Hendricks, B. L. (1980). The status of elementary speech communication education. *Communication Education, 29,* 364–369.

Hickman, J., & Kimberley, K. (1988). *Teachers, language and learning.* London: Routledge.

Holderness, J., & Lalljee, B. (Eds.) (1998). *An introduction to oracy*: Frameworks for talk. Cassell.

Holdzkom, D., Reed, L. J., Porter, E. J., & Rubin, D. L. (1982). *Research within reach*: Oral and written communication: A research-guided response to the concerns of educators. St Louis, MO: CEMREL.

Hollow, M. K., Sr. (1955). Listening comprehension at the intermediate grade level. *The Elementary School Journal, 56,* 158-161.

Hopper, R., & Wrather, N. (1978). Teaching functional communication skills in the elementary classroom. *Communication Education, 27.*

Horrworth, G. I. (1966). Listening: A facet of oral language. *Elementary English, 43,* 856-864, 868.

Howe, A. (1989). *Expanding horizons.* Sheffield, England: National Association for Teachers of English.

Hudelson, S. (1989). *Write on: Children's writing in ESL.* Englewood, Cliffs, NJ: Prentice-Hall.

Hudelson, S. (1994). Literacy development of second language children. In F. Genesee (Ed.), *Educating second language children: The whole child, the whole curriculum, the whole community.* New York: Cambridge University Press.

Hunkins, F. P. (1995). *Teaching thinking through effective questioning* (2nd ed.). Norwood, MA: Christopher-Gordon.

Hymes, D. (1962). The ethnography of speaking. In T. Gladwin & W. C. Sturtevant (Eds.), *Anthropology and human behavior* (pp. 15-33). Washington: Anthropological Society of Washington.

Hymes, D. (1967). Models of the interaction of language and social setting. *Journal of Social Issues, 23,* 8-29.

Hymes, D. (1971). Competence & performance in linguistic theory. In R. Huxley & E. Ingram (Eds.), *Language Acquisition. Models and methods* (pp. 3-24). New York: Academic Press.

Hymes, D. (1972). Introduction. In C. Cazden, V. P. John, & D. Hymes (Eds.), *Functions of language in the classroom* (pp. xi-liv). New York: Teachers College Press.

Hymes, D. (1974). *Foundations in sociolinguistics: An ethnographic approach.* Philadelphia: University of Pennsylvania Press.

Irwin, E. C. (1975). Play and language development. *Speech Teacher, 24,* 15-23.

Johnson, N. S., & Mandler J. M. (1980). A tale of two structures: Underlying and surface forms in stories. *Poetics, 9,* 51-86.

Jones, P. (1988). *Lipservice. The story of talk in schools.* Milton Keynes, England: Open University Press.

Jones, A., & Mulford, J. (Eds.) (1971). *Children using language: An approach to English in the primary school.* London: Oxford University Press.

Kelly, C. M. (1971). Listening: Compex of activities—And a unitary skill? In S. Duker (Ed.), *Listening: Readings* (Vol. 2, pp. 213-229). Metuchen, NJ: Scarecrow Press.

Kelly, G. A. (1955). *The psychology of personal constructs.* New York: Norton.

Kiefer, B. Z., & DeStefano, J. S. (1985). Cultures together in the classroom: "What you saying?" In A. Jaggar & M. T. Smith-Burke (Eds.), *Observing the language learner* (pp. 159-172). Newark, DE: International Reading Association, Urbana, IL: National Council of Teachers of English.

King, M. L. (1984). Language and school success: Access to meaning. *Theory Into Practice, 23,* 175-182.

King, M. L., & McKenzie, M. G. (1988). Research currents: Literary discourse from the child's perspective. *Language Arts, 65,* 304-314.

King, M. L., & Rentel, V. (1981). Research Update: Conveying meaning in written texts. *Language Arts, 58,* 721-728.

Klein, M. L. (1977). *Talk in the language arts classroom.* Urbana, IL: ERIC Clearinghouse on Reading and Communication and National Council of Teachers of English.

Klein, M. L. (1979). Designing a talk environment for the classroom. *Language Arts, 56,* 647-656.

Kretschmer, R. E. (1989). Pragmatics, reading, and writing: Implications for hearing impaired individuals. *Topics in Language Disorders, 9,* 17-32.

Labov, W. (1969). The logic of non-standard English. In J. Alatis (Ed.), *Linguistics and the teaching of standard English to speakers of other languages* (pp. 1-44). Washington, DC: Georgetown University Press.

Labov, W. (1972). *Language in the inner city.* Philadelphia: University of Pennsylvania Press.

Landry, D. L. (1969). The neglect of listening. *Elementary English, 46,* 599-605.

Larson, C. (1978). Problems in assessing functional communication. *Communication Education, 27,* 304-309.

Larson, C., Backlund, P., Redmond, M., & Barbour, A. (1978). *Assessing functional communication.* Urbana, IL ERIC Clearinghouse on Reading and Communication Skills, Falls Church, VA: Speech Communication Association.

Larson, R. P., & Feder, D. D. (1940). Common and differential factors in reading and hearing comprehension. *Journal of Educational Psychology, 31,* 241-252.

Lazarus, P. G. (1984). What children know and teach about language competence. *Theory Into Practice, 23,* 225-231.

Lieb-Brilhart, B. (1982). Standards for effective oral communication programs. In I. Reed & S. Ward (Eds.), *Basic skills, issues and choices* (Vol. 2). St. Louis, MO: CEMREL.

Lieb-Brilhart, B. (1984). Oral communication instruction: Goals and teacher needs. In F. W. Parkay, S. O'Bryan, & M. Hennessy (Eds.), *Quest for quality: Improving basic instruction in the 1980's* (pp. 69-77). Lanham, MD: University Press of America.

Lindfors, J. (1999). *Children's inquiry: Using language to make sense of the world.* New York: Teachers' College Press, Language and Literacy Series.

Lindfors, J. W. (1986). English for everyone. *Language Arts, 63*(1).

Lindfors, J. W. (1987). *Children's language and learning* (2nd ed.). Englewood Cliffs, NJ: Prentice-Hall.

Lloyd-Jones, R., & Lunsford, A. A. (Eds.) (1989). *The English coalition conference: Democracy through language.* Urbana, IL: National Council of Teachers of English.

Loban, W. D. (1963). *The language of elementary school children* (National Council of Teachers of English Research Report No. 1). Urbana, IL: National Council of Teachers of English.

Loban, W. D. (1976). *Language development: Kindergarten through grade twelve* (National Council of Teachers of English Research Report No. 18). Urbana, IL: National Council of Teachers of English.

Lund, N. J., & Duchan J. F. (1988). *Assessing children's language in naturalistic contexts* (2nd ed.). Englewood Cliffs, NJ: Prentice-Hall.

Lundsteen, S. W. (1964). Teaching and testing critical listening in the fifth and sixth grades. *Elementary English, 41,* 743-747, 752.

Lundsteen, S. W. (1965). Critical listening—permanency and transfer of gains made during and experiment in fifth and sixth grades. *California Journal of Educational Research, 16,* 210-216.

Lundsteen, S. W. (1971). Critical listening and thinking: A recommended goal for future research. In S. Duker (Ed.), *Listening: Readings* (Vol. 2, pp. 233-248). Metuchen, NJ: Scarecrow Press.

Lundsteen, S. W. (1979). *Listening: Its impact on reading and the other language arts* (Rev. ed.). Urbana, IL: National Council of Teachers of English and ERIC Clearinghouse on Reading and Communication.

Mackintosh, H. K. (1964). *Children and oral language. A joint statement of the Association for Childhood Education International,*

*Association for Supervision and Curriculum Development.* Urbana, IL: International Reading Association, National Council of Teachers of English.

MacLure, M. (1988). Introduction oracy: Current trends in context. In M. MacLure, T. Phillips, & A. Wilkinson (Eds.), *Oracy matters.* Philadelphia Milton Keynes, England: Open University Press.

Malicky, G. V., & Norman, C. A. (1999). Phonological awareness and reading. An alternative interpretation of the literature from a clinical perspective. *The Alberta Journal of Educational Research, 45,* 18–34.

Mallett, M., & Newsome, B. (1977). *Talking, writing and learning 8-13.* London: Evans/Methuen.

Mandler J. M. (1984). *Stories, scripts, and scenes: Aspects of schema theory.* Hillsdale, NJ: Lawrence Erlbaum Associates.

Marland, M. (1977). *Language across the curriculum.* London: Heinemann Educational Books.

Martin, N. (1983). *Mostly about writing: Selected essays.* Montclair, NJ: Boynton/Cook.

Martin, N., D'Arcy, P., Newton, B., & Parker, R. (1976). *Writing and learning across the curriculum 11-16.* London: Schools Council Publications.

Martin, N., Williams, P., Wilding J., Hemmings, S., & Medway, P. (1976). Understanding children talking. Hammondsworth, England: Penguin.

McCrosky, J. M. (1982). Communication competence and performance: A research and pedagogical perspective. *Communication Education, 31,* 1–7.

McTear, M. G. (1984). Structure and process in children's conversational development. In S. A. Kuczaj (Ed.), *Discourse development: Progress in cognitive development research* (pp. 37–76). New York: Springer-Verlag.

McTear, M. G. (1985). *Children's conversations.* Oxford, England: Blackwell.

Mehan, H. (1978). Structuring school structure. *Harvard Educational Review, 48,* 32–64.

Mehan, H. (1979). *Learning lessons: Social organization in the classroom.* Cambridge, MA: Harvard University Press.

Mehan, H. (1981). Ethnography of bilingual education. In H. T. Trueba, G. P. Guthrie, & K. H. Au (Eds.), *Culture and the bilingual classroom: Studies in classroom ethnography* (pp. 36–55). Rowley, MA: Newbury House.

Menyuk, P. (1988). *Language development: Knowledge and use.* Glenview, IL: Scott, Foresman.

Michaels, S. (1981). "Sharing time": Children's narrative styles and differential access to literacy. *Language in Society, 10.*

Michaels, S. (1984). Listening and responding: Hearing the logic in children's classroom narratives. *Theory Into Practice, 23,* 218–224.

Michaels, S. (1985). Hearing the connections in children's oral and written discourse. *Journal of Education, 167,* 36–56.

Michaels, S. (1986). Narrative presentations: An oral preparation for literacy with first graders. In J. Cook-Gumperz (Ed.), *The social construction of literacy* (pp. 94–116). London: Cambridge University Press.

Michaels, S., & Collins, J. (1984). Oral discourse style: Classroom interaction and the acquisition of literacy. In D. Tannen (Ed.), *Coherence in spoken and written discourse* (pp. 219–244). Norwood, NJ: Ablex.

Michaels, S., & Cook-Gumperz, J. (1979). A study of sharing time with first grade students: Discourse narratives in the classroom. *Proceedings of the Fifth Annual Meeting of the Berkeley Linguistics Society* (pp. 51–80).

Michaels, S., & Foster, M. (1985). Peer-peer learning: Evidence from a student run sharing time. In A. Jaggar & M. T. Smith-Burke (Eds.), *Observing the language learner* (pp. 143–158). Newark, DE

International Reading Association, Urbana, IL: National Council of Teachers of English.

Moffett, J. M. (1968). *Teaching the universe of discourse.* New York: Houghton Mifflin.

Moffett, J. M., & Wagner, B. J. (1973). *Student-centered language arts and reading, K-13.* Boston: Houghton Mifflin.

Moffett, J. M., & Wagner, B. J. (1983). *Student-centered language arts and reading, K-13* (3rd ed.). Boston: Houghton Mifflin.

Morine-Dershimer, G. (1985). *Talking, listening, and learning in elementary classrooms.* New York: Longman.

Myers, M. (1987). The shared structure of oral and written language and the implications for teaching writing, reading, and literature. In J. R. Squire (Ed.), *The dynamics of language learning: Research in reading and English* (pp. 121–146). Urbana, IL: ERIC Clearinghouse on Reading and Communication Skills and National Conference on Research in English.

Nagy, W. P., & Herman, P. S. (1987). Breadth and depth of vocabulary knowledge: Implications for acquisition. In M. McKeown & M. Curtis (Eds.), *The nature of vocabulary acquisition* (pp. 19–35). Hillsdale, NJ: Lawrence Erlbaum Associates.

National Association for the Teaching of English (1976). *Language across the Curriculum. Guidelines for schools.* London: Ward Lock.

National Commission on Excellence in Education (1983). *A nation at risk: The imperative for educational reform.* Washington, DC: U.S. Government Printing Office.

Nelson, K. (1973). Structure and strategy in learning to talk. *Monographs of the Society for Research in Child Development, 149* (38 Pt. 1, 2).

Nelson, K. (1981). Individual differences in language development: Implications for development and language. *Developmental Psychology, 17,* 170–187.

Nelson, K. (1986). *Event knowledge: Structure and function in development.* Hillsdale, NJ: Lawrence Erlbaum Associates.

New Standards Primary Literacy Standards Committee (1999). *Reading and writing grade by grade: Primary literacy standards for kindergarten through third grade.* Washington, DC: National Center on Education and the Economy.

Ninio, A., & Snow, C. E. (1996). *Pragmatic development.* Boulder, CO: Westview.

O'Donnell, R. C., Griffin, W. J., & Norris, R. C. (1967). *Syntax of kindergarten and elementary school children: A transformational analysis* (National Council of Teachers of English Research Report No. 8). Urbana, IL: National Council of Teachers of English.

Orr, D. B., Friedman, H. L., & Williams, J. C. (1965). Trainability of listening comprehension of speeded discourse. *Journal of Educational Psychology, 56,* 148–156.

Padak, N. (1986). Teachers' verbal behaviors: A window to the teaching process. In J. A. Niles & R. V. Lalik (Eds.), *Solving problems in literacy: Learners, teachers, and researchers: Thirty-fifth yearbook of the National Reading Conference* (Vol. 35, pp. 185–191).

Paley, V. G. (1981). *Wally's stories.* Cambridge, MA: Harvard University Press.

Palinscar, A. S., & Brown, A. L. (1984). Reciprocal teaching of comprehension-fostering and comprehension-monitoring activities. *Cognition and Instruction, 1*(2), 117–175.

Pappas, C. C. (1981). *The development of narrative capabilities within a synergistic, variable perspective of language development: An examination of cohesive harmony of stories produced in three contexts—Retelling, dictating, and writing.* Unpublished doctoral dissertation, Ohio State University, Columbus.

Pappas, C. C. (1985). The cohesive harmony and cohesive density of children's oral and written stories. In J. D. Benson & W. S. Greaves (Eds.), *Advances in discourse processes* (Vol. 16). Systematic perspectives on discourse Selected applied papers from the ninth international systemic workshop (Vol. 2, pp. 169-186). Norwood, NJ: Ablex.

Pappas, C. C., & Brown, E. (1987). Learning to read by reading: Learning how to extend the functional potential of language. *Research in the Teaching of English, 21,* 160-184.

Parkay, F. W., O'Bryan, S., & Hennessy, M. (Eds.) (1984). *Quest for quality: Improving basic skills instruction in the 1980's.* Lanham, MD: University Press of America.

Pearson, P. D., & Fielding, L. (1982). Research update: Listening comprehension. *Language Arts, 59,* 617-629.

Pellegrini, A. D., & Gaida, L. (1988). The effects of age and context on children's use of narrative language. *Research in the Teaching of English, 22,* 183-195.

Petty, W. T. (1967). *Research in oral language* [A Research Bulletin]. Urbana, IL: National Council of Teachers of English.

Philips, S. (1972). Participant structures and communicative competence: Warm Springs children in community and classroom. In C. Cazden, V. P. John, & D. Hymes (Eds.), *Functions of language in the classroom* (pp. 370-394). New York: Teachers College Press.

Phillips, T. (1985). Beyond lip-service: Discourse development after the age of nine. In G. Wells & J. Nicholls (Eds.), *Language & learning: An interactional perspective* (pp. 59-82). London Falmer Press.

Piaget, J. (1955). *The language and thought of the child.* New York: Meridian.

Piaget, J. (1959). *The language and thought of the child.* London: Routledge & Kegan Paul.

Pinnell, G. S. (1975). Language in primary classrooms. *Theory Into Practice, 24,* 318-327.

Pinnell, G. S. (1985). Ways to look at the functions of children's language. In A. Jaggar & M. Trika Smith-Burke (Eds.), *Observing the language learner* (pp. 57-72). Newark, DE: International Reading Association; Urbana, IL: National Council of Teachers of English.

Platt, N. G. (1984). How one classroom gives access to meaning. *Theory Into Practice, 23,* 239-245.

Powers, D. F. (1984). *Considerations for developing measures of speaking and listening.* New York: College Entrance Examination Board.

Pratt, E. (1956). Experimental evaluation of a program for the improvement of listening. *Elementary School Journal, 56,* 315-320.

Propp, V. (1968). *Morphology of the folktale* (L. Scott, Trans.). Austin: University of Texas Press.

Raban, B. (1999). Language and literacy as epistemology. In J. S. Gaffney & B. J. Askew (Eds.), *Stirring the waters: The influence of Marie Clay* (pp. 99-112). Portsmouth, NH: Heinemann.

Rankin, P. T. (1928). The importance of listening ability. *English Journal* (College ed.), *17,* 623-630.

Rentel, V., & King, M. L. (1983). Present at the beginning. In P. Mosenthal, L. Tamor, & S. Walmsley (Eds.), *Research on Writing: Principles and methods* (pp. 139-176). New York: Longman.

Robertson, I. (1980). *Language across the curriculum: Four cast studies.* London: Metheun.

Rogoff, B. (1990). *Apprenticeship in thinking: Cognitive development in social context.* New York: Oxford University Press.

Romaine, S. (1984). *The language of children and adolescents: The acquisition of communicative competence.* Oxford, England: Blackwell.

Rosen, C., & Rosen, H. (1973). *The language of primary school children.* London: Schools Council Publications, Penguin.

Ross, D. D. (1983). *Competence, relational status, and identity work: A study of the social interactions of young children.* Paper presented at annual conference of National Association for the Education of Young Children, Washington, DC.

Ross, H. S., & Goldman, B. M. (1976). Establishing new social relationships in infancy. In T. Alloway, L. Krames, & P. Pliner (Eds.), *Advances in communication and affect* (Vol. 4). New York: Plenum.

Ross, R. (1964). A look at listeners. *The Elementary School Journal, 64,* 369-372.

Rowe, D. W. (1998). The literate potentials of book-related dramatic play. *Reading Research Quarterly, 33,* 10-35.

Rubin, D. L. (1985). Instruction in speaking and listening: Battles and options. *Educational Leadership, 42,* 31-36.

Rubin, D. L., & Kantor, K. (1984). Talking and writing: Building communication competence. In C. Thaiss & C. Suhor (Eds.), *Speaking and writing K-12* (pp. 29-73). Urbana, IL: National Council of Teachers of English.

Rubin, D. L., & Mead, N. A. (1984). *Large scale assessment of oral communication skills: Kindergarten through grade 12.* Urbana, IL, and Annandale, VA: ERIC Clearinghouse on Reading and Communication Skills and Speech Communication Association.

Ruddell, R. B. (1965). Effect of the similarity of oral and written patterns of language structure on reading comprehension. *Elementary English, 42,* 403-410.

Ruddell, R. B. (1966). Oral language and the development of other language skills. *Elementary English, 43,* 489-498.

Russell, D. H. (1964). A conspectus of recent research on listening abilities. *Elementary English, 41,* 262-267.

Sapir, E. (1949). *Selected writings in language, culture and personality.* San Francisco, CA: University of California Press.

Schachter, F. F., Kirshner, K., Klips, B., Friedricks, M., & Sanders, K. (1974). Everyday preschool interpersonal speech usage: Methodological, developmental, and sociolinguistics studies. *Monograph of the Society for Research in Child Development, 39* (3, Serial No. 156).

Schaffer, H. R., Collis, G. M., & Parsons, G. (1977). Vocal interchange and visual regard in verbal and pre-verbal children. In H. R. Schaffer (Ed.), *Studies in mother-infant interaction* (pp. 291-324). New York: Academic Press.

Schaudt, B. A. (1983). *Relationships between listening and reading: A historical survey.* Paper presented at the annual meeting of the Great Lakes Regional conference of the International Reading Association, Springfield, IL. (ERIC Document Reproduction Service No. ED 240 544)

Schickedanz, J. A., & Sullivan, M. (1984). Mom, what does U-F-F spell? *Language Arts, 61,* 7-17.

Sénéchal, M., LeFevre, J., Thomas, E. M., & Daley, K. E. (1998). Differential effects of home literacy experiences on the development of oral and written language. *Reading Research Quarterly, 33,* 96-116.

Sevigny, M. J. (1981). Triangulated inquiry: A methodology for the analysis of classroom interaction. In J. Green & C. Wallat (Eds.), *Ethnography and language in educational settings* (pp. 65-86). Norwood, NJ: Ablex.

Shafer, R. E., Staab, C., & Smith, K. (1983). *Language functions and school success.* Glenview, IL: Scott, Foresman.

Shatz, M., & Gelman, R. (1973). The development of communication skills: Modifications in the speech of young children as a function of listeners. *Monograph of the Society for Research in Children's Development, 38,* 55.

Shavelson, R. J., & Stern P. (1981). Research on teachers' pedagogical thoughts, judgments, decisions, and behavior. *Review of Educational Research, 51,* 455-498.

Shure, M. B. (1963). Psychological ecology of a nursery school. *Child Development, 34,* 979-992.

Shuy, R. (1984). Language as a foundation for education: The school context. *Theory Into Practice, 23,* 167-174.

Simon, A., & Boyer, B. G. (Eds.) (1974). *Mirrors for behavior III: An anthology of observation instruments.* Wyncote, PA: Communications Materials Center.

Sinclair, J. M., & Coulthard, M. (1975). *Towards an analysis of discourse: The English used by teachers and pupils*. London: Oxford University Press.

Smitherman, G. (1977). *Talkin and testifyin*. Boston: Houghton Mifflin.

Snow, C. (1977). The development of conversation between mothers and babies. *Journal of Child Language, 4*, 1-22.

Snow, C. E., Burns, M., & Griffin, S. (Eds.) (1998). Preventing reading difficulties in young children. Washington, DC: Committee on the Prevention of Reading Difficulty in Young Children, Commission on Behavioral and Social Sciences and Education, National Research Council.

Snow, C., & Ferguson, C. (Eds.) (1977). *Talking to children: Language input and acquisition*. New York: Cambridge University Press.

Spearritt, D. (1962). *Listening comprehension: A factoral analysis* (Australian Council for Educational Research, Research Series No. 76). Melbourne, Australia: Green.

Stein, N., & Glenn, C. (1979). An analysis of story comprehension in elementary school children. In R. Freedle (Ed.), *New directions in discourse processing* (Vol. 2, pp. 53-120). Norwood, NJ: Ablex.

Stenning, K., & Michell, L. (1985). Learning how to tell a good story: The development of content and language in children's telling of one tale. *Discourse Processes, 8*, 261-279.

Stern, D. (1977). *The first relationship: Infant and mother*. London: Open Books.

Stern, D., Jaffe, J., Beebe, B., & Bennett, S. (1975). The infant's stimulus world during social interactions. In H. R. Schaffer (Ed.), *Studies of mother-infant interactions*. New York: Academic Press.

Sticht, T. (1972). Learning by listening. In R. O. Freedle & J. B. Carroll (Eds.), *Language comprehension and the acquisition of knowledge* (pp. 285-314). Washington, DC: Winston.

Sticht, T., Beck, L., Hauke, R., Kleiman, G., & James, J. (1974). *Auding and reading: A developmental model*. Alexandria, VA: Human Resources Research Organization.

Sticht, T. G., & James, J. H. (1984). Listening and reading. In P. D. Pearson (Ed.), *Handbook of Reading Research* (pp. 293-317). New York: Longman.

Stiggins, R. J. (Ed.) (1981). *Perspectives on oral communication assessment in the 80's*. Portland, OR: Northwest Regional Educational Laboratory.

Strickland, D. S. (1989). A model for change: Framework for an emergent literacy program. In D. S. Strickland & L. M. Morrow (Eds.), *Emerging literacy: Young children learn to read and write* (pp. 135-146). Newark, DE: International Reading Association.

Strickland, R. G. (1962). The language of elementary school children: Its relationship to the language of reading textbooks and the quality of reading of selected children. *Bulletin of the School of Education, 38*(4). Bloomington: Bureau of Educational Studies and Testing, School of Education, Indiana University.

Strother, D. B. (1987). Practical applications of research: On listening. *Phi Delta Kappan, 68*, 625-628.

Stubbs, M. (1976). *Language, schools and classrooms*. London: Methuen.

Stubbs, M. (1983). *Discourse analysis: The sociolinguistic analysis of natural language*. Oxford, England: Blackwell.

Stubbs, M., & Delamont, S. (Eds.) (1976). *Explorations in classroom observation*. London and New York: Wiley.

Sulzby, E. (1985). Children's emergent reading of favorite storybooks: A developmental study. *Reading Research Quarterly, 20*, 458-481.

Sulzby, E., & Teale, W. (1991). Emergent literacy. In R. Barr, M. L. Kamil, P. B. Mosenthal, & P. D. Pearson (Eds.), *Handbook of reading research* (Vol. 2, pp. 727-757). New York: Longman.

Tannen, D. (1982). Oral and literate strategies in spoken and written narrative. *Language Arts, 58*, 1-21.

Tannen, D. (1985). Relative focus on involvement in oral and written discourse. In D. R. Olson, N. Torrance, & A. Hildyard (Eds.), *Literacy, language and learning: The nature and consequences of reading and writing* (pp. 124-147). New York: Cambridge University Press.

Tarleton, R. (1988). *Learning and talking: A practical guide to oracy across the curriculum*. New York: Routledge.

Taylor, D. (1983). *Family literacy*. Exeter, NH: Heinemann.

Teale, W. H., Hiebert, E. H., & Chittenden, E. A. (1987). Assessing young children's literacy development. *The Reading Teacher, 40*, 772-777.

Teale, W. H., & Sulzby, E. (Eds.) (1986). *Emergent literacy: Writing and reading*. Norwood, NJ: Ablex.

Thaiss, C. (1986). *Language across the curriculum in elementary grades*. Urbana, IL: National Council of Teachers of English.

Thaiss, C., & Suhor, C. (Eds.) (1984). *Speaking and writing K-12*. Urbana, IL: National Council of Teachers of English.

Thorndyke, P. W. (1977). Cognitive structures in comprehension and memory in of narrative discourse. *Cognitive Psychology, 9*, 77-110.

Tizard, B., & Hughes, M. (1984). *Young children learning: Talking and thinking at home and at school*. London: Fontana Press.

Torbe, M., & Medway, P. (1981). *The climate for learning*. Montclair, NJ: Boynton/Cook.

Torbe, M., & Protherough, R. (Eds.) (1976). *Classroom encounters: Language and English teaching*. London: Ward Lock in association with the National Association for the Teaching of English.

Torrence, N., & Olson, D. R. (1984). Oral language competence and the acquisition of literacy. In A. D. Pellegrini & T. Yawkey (Eds.), *The development of oral and written language in social contexts* (pp. 167-181). Norwood, NJ: Ablex.

Tough, J. (1973). *Focus on meaning: Talking to some purpose with young children*. London: Allen & Unwin.

Tough, J. (1976). *Listening to children talking: A guide to the appraisal of children's use of language*. London: Ward Lock.

Tough, J. (1977a). *The development of meaning: A study of children's use of language*. London: Allen & Unwin.

Tough, J. (1977b). *Talking and learning: A guide to fostering communication skills in nursery and infant schools*. London: Ward Lock.

Tough, J. (1979). *Talk for teaching and learning*. London: Ward Lock.

Trevarthen, C. (1977). Descriptive analyses of infant communicative behaviour. In H. R. Schaffer (Ed.), *Studies in mother-infant interaction* (pp. 227-270). New York: Academic Press.

Trevarthen, C. (1979). Communication and cooperation in early infancy: A description of primary intersubjectivity. In M. Bullowa (Ed.), *Before speech: The beginning of interpersonal communication* (pp. 321-347) Cambridge, England: Cambridge University Press.

Trevarthen, C. (1992). An infant's motives for speaking and thinking in the culture. In A. H. Wold (Ed.), *The dialogical alternative: Towards a theory of language and mind* (pp. 99-137). Oslo, Norway: Scandinavian University Press.

Trivette, S. E. (1961). The effect of training in listening for specific purposes. *Journal of Educational Research, 54*, 276-277.

Trueba, H. T., Guthrie, G. P., & Au, K. H. (1981). *Culture and the classroom: Studies in classroom ethnography*. Rowley, MA: Newbury House.

Vandell, D. L., & Mueller, E. (1980). Peer play and friendships during the first two years. In H. C. Foot, A. J. Chapman, & J. R. Smith (Eds.), *Friendship and social relations in children*. New York: Wiley.

Van Rheenan, D., McClure, E., & Backlund, P. (1984). *State policies in speaking and listening skill assessment through 1983*. Orono: University of Maine, Department of Speech Communication.

Vygotsky, L. (1962). *Thought and language*. Cambridge, MA: MIT Press.

Vygotsky, L. (1978). *Mind in society: The development of higher psychological processes* (M. Cole, V. John-Steiner, S. Scribner, & E. Souberman, Trans.). Cambridge, MA: Harvard University Press.

Vygotsky, L. S. (1986). *Thought and language* (A. Kozulin, Ed.). Cambridge, MA: MIT Press.

Wade, B. (1983). Story and intonation features in young children: A case study. *Educational Review, 35,* 175-186.

Watson, K. (1980). A close look at whole class-discussion. *English in Education, 14,* 39-44.

Watson, K. (1987). *English teaching in perspective* (2nd ed.). Milton Keynes, England: Open University Press.

Weeks, T. E. (1979). *Born to talk.* Rowley, MA: Newbury House.

Weimann, J. M., & Backlund, P. (1980). Current theory and research in communicative competence. *Review of Educational Research, 50,* 185-199.

Welkowitz, J., Cariffe, G., & Feldstein, S. (1976). Conversational congruence as a criterion of socialization in children. *Child Development, 47,* 269-272.

Wells, G. (1973). *Coding manual for the description of child speech.* Bristol, England: University of Bristol School of Education.

Wells, G. (1981). *Learning through interaction: The study of language development.* Cambridge England: Cambridge University Press.

Wells, G. (1985). *Language, learning and education.* England: NFER-NELSON.

Wells, G. (1986a). The language experience of five-year-old children at home and at school. In J. Cook-Gumperz (Ed.), *The social construction of literacy* (pp. 69-93). London: Cambridge University Press.

Wells, G. (1986b). *The meaning makers: Children learning language and using language to learn.* Portsmouth, NH: Heinemann.

Wells, G., & Nicholls, J. (Eds.) (1985). *Language and learning: An interactional perspective* (pp. 18). London: Falmer Press.

Wells, G., & Wells, J. (1984). Learning to talk and talking to learn. *Theory Into Practice, 23,* 190—197.

Westby, C. (1984). Development of narrative language abilities. In G. Wallach & K. Butler (Eds.), *Language learning disabilities in school-age children* (pp. 347-374). Baltimore, MD: Williams & Wilkins.

Whiten, A. (1977). Assessing the effects of perinatal events on the success of the mother-infant relationship. In H. R. Schaffer (Ed.), *Studies in mother-infant interaction.* New York: Academic Press.

Wilen, W. W. (1991). *Questioning skills for teachers* (3rd ed.). Washington, DC: National Education Association.

Wilkinson, A. M. (with Davies, A., & Atkinson, D.). (1965). *Spoken English,* Birmingham, England: University of Birmingham.

Wilkinson, A. M. (1970). The concept of oracy. *English Journal, 59,* 70-77.

Wilkinson, A. M. (1971). *The foundations of language: Talking and reading in young children.* Oxford, England: Oxford University Press.

Wilkinson, A. M. (1972). Total communication. *English in Education, 6,* 55-62.

Wilkinson, A. M. (1975). Language and education. Oxford, England: Oxford University Press.

Wilkinson, A. M., Barnsley, G., Hanna, P., & Swan, M. (1980). *Assessing language development.* Oxford, England: Oxford University Press.

Wilkinson, A. M., Stratta, L., & Dudley, P. (1974). *The quality of listening.* England: Schools Council Research Study, Macmillan.

Wilkinson, L. C. (Ed.) (1982). *Communicating in the classroom.* New York: Academic Press.

Wilkinson, L. C. (1984). Research currents: Peer group talk in elementary school. *Language Arts, 61,* 164-169.

Wilkinson, L. C., & Calculator, S. (1982). Effective speakers: Students' use of language to request and obtain information and action in the classroom. In L. C. Wilkinson (Ed.), *Communicating in the classroom* (85-99). New York: Academic Press.

Wilkinson, L. C., & Dollaghan, C. (1979). Peer communication in first-grade reading groups. *Theory into Practice, 18,* 267-274.

Wilkinson, L. C., & Spinelli, F. (1982). Conclusion: Application for education. In L. C. Wilkinson (Ed.), *Communicating in the classroom* (pp. 323-327). New York: Academic Press.

Willes, M. (1983). *Children into pupils.* London: Routledge & Kegan Paul.

Wilt, M. E. (1950). A study of teacher awareness of listening as a factor in elementary education. *Journal of Educational Research, 43,* 626-636.

Wilt, M. E. (1955). Children's experiences in listening. In V. E. Herrick & L. B. Jacobs (Eds.), *Children and the language arts.* Englewood Cliffs, NJ: Prentice-Hall.

Wilt, M. E. (1973). Listening! What's new? In M. L. King, R. Emans, & P. J. Cianciolo (Eds.), *A forum for focus* (pp. 63-72). Urbana, IL: National Council of Teachers of English.

Withall, J., & Lewis, W. W. (1971). *Social interaction in the classroom.* In A. H. Yee (Ed.), *Social interaction in educational settings* (pp. 25-57). Englewood Cliffs, NJ: Prentice-Hall.

Wolf, D., & Gardner, H. (1979). Style and sequence in early symbolic play. In N. R. Smith & M. B. Franklin (Eds.), *Symbolic functioning in childhood* (pp. 117-138). Hillsdale, NJ: Lawrence Erlbaum Associates.

Wolfram, W. (1998). Dialect awareness and the study of language. In A. Egan-Robertson & D. Bloome (Eds.), *Students as researchers of culture and language in their own communities* (pp. 167-190). Creskill, NJ: Hampton Press.

Wood, B. S. (Ed.) (1977a). *The development of functional communication competencies: Grades* 7-12. Urbana, IL: ERIC Clearinghouse on Reading and Communication Skills. (ERIC Document Reproduction Service No. ED 137 859)

Wood, B. S. (Ed.) (1977b). *The development of functional communication competencies:* Pre-K through grade 6. Urbana, IL: ERIC Clearinghouse on Reading and Communication Skills.

Wood, B. S. (1981). *Children and communication: Verbal and nonverbal language development* (2nd ed.). Englewood Cliffs, NJ: Prentice Hall.

Wood, B. S. (1984). Oral communication in the elementary classroom. In C. Thaiss & C. Suhor (Eds.), *Speaking and writing, K-12* (pp. 104-125). Urbana, IL: National Council of Teachers of English.

Young, M. F. D. (1971). An approach to the study of curricula as socially organized knowledge. In M. F. D. Young (Ed.), *Knowledge and control.* London: Collier-Macmillan.

Young, R., & Watson, K. (1981). Verbal communication: The nature of classroom discourse. In Deakin University, *Classroom communication: Classroom processes* (pp. 81-100). Victoria, Australia: Deakin University Press.

Young, W. E. (1936). The relation of reading comprehension and retention to hearing comprehension and retention. *Journal of Experimental Education, 5,* 30-39.

Zemlin, W. R., Daniloff, R. G., & Shriner, T. H. (1968). The difficulty of listening to time-compressed speech. *Journal of Speech and Hearing Research, 11,* 869-874.

# READING: CHILDREN'S DEVELOPING
# KNOWLEDGE OF WORDS

## Jana M. Mason
### University of Illinois, Urbana-Champaign

## Steven A. Stahl
### University of Georgia

## Kathryn H. Au and Patricia A. Herman
### Kamehameha Schools

Over time, research on the acquisition of knowledge about words and an understanding of the larger process of reading for meaning has led to changes in views of reading and its development. In this chapter, we review research on two aspects of beginning reading: word identification and vocabulary knowledge are critical in the sense that reading for meaning cannot take place n their absence. We do not intend this to mean that other aspects of reading such as knowledge of the functions of literacy (Heath, 1983) or concepts about print (Clay, 1985) or story forms (Yussen & Ozcan, 1996) are unimportant. It would be inaccurate to speak of word identification and vocabulary knowledge as the only skills basic to reading. (We use the terms *word recognition* and *word identification* to refer to a person's identification of the visual form of words that he or she knows the meaning of, and *vocabulary* to refer to a person's store of word meanings.)

In fact, one of the major themes in this chapter is that children's understanding of words is best understood from the perspective of developing sensitivities to the English language. In the case of word identification, for example, experiences in writing, spelling, and reading words make a significant contribution. Vocabulary knowledge takes place through word play and talk about language as well as through wide-ranging opportunities to express, hear, and read new words in meaningful contexts.

A second major theme is that acquisition of word identification skills and vocabulary knowledge centers on discovery of the regularity of the language. Of course, the English language is quite complex, so the process of discovery is not simple. In some cases words may be identified or their meanings interpreted through the application of rather simple understandings. In other cases, though, more complicated understandings must be invoked.

The first section of this chapter deals with word identification and the second with vocabulary knowledge. We decided not to address the two topics in a strictly parallel manner. Research conducted with adults receives much less attention in the section on word identification than in the section on vocabulary. The reason for this difference is that children's learning of word identification involves striking developmental changes. Children typically shift from identifying words one by one, in piecemeal fashion, to identifying words using a variety of approaches based on extensive knowledge of context, letter sounds, and syllable patterns. A similar shift in approaches does not seem to occur with acquisition of vocabulary knowledge. Thus, research conducted with adults may be less informative in the case of word identification than in the case of vocabulary knowledge, especially when it comes to instructional implications.

The research reviewed in this chapter presents a synthesis of information from both qualitative and quantitative studies. The literature on word identification and vocabulary development is vast, go the studies cited here should be considered illustrative. These studies stem from different theoretical, as well as methodological, orientations. Nevertheless, it appears that the patterns of findings in both bodies of research are gradually converging and tend to provide support for many of the same conclusions. It is these patterns that we have tried to convey.

## WORD IDENTIFICATION

The typical 4-year-old relies on idiosyncratic cues to identify words. For example, a child might recognize the word *monkey* because there is a tail on the *y* (Gates & Bocker, 1923) or the word *look* because it seems to have two eyes in the middle. In a word learning study, Gough, Juel, and Griffith (1992) even found that young children were more likely to notice and rely on a thumb print on a word card than on the letter information. These examples make the point that children do not intuitively make use of letter–sound information to recognize words. By the end of the elementary school years, however, children can usually read and understand words using a vast array of information about letter–sound patterns, clusters of letters, and syllables. Children can then identify words quickly and with little effort. They are better able to place word identification in the background and focus on comprehension. Children with inadequate word identification skills, however, continue to rely principally on context cues and are almost invariably poor readers (Simon & Leu, 1987; Stanovich, 1993–94).

Clearly, proficiency in word identification is central to the reading act. How might proficient word identification be characterized? What course do children generally follow in developing the ability to identify words? What types of classroom experiences appear most valuable for strengthening children's ability to identify words? We address these questions next.

### Proficient Word Identification

Skilled readers have the ability to identify words fluently and effortlessly. According to McConkie and Zola (1987), reading is carried out

"by making a series of eye fixations, each of which exposes the processing system to a large and complex stimulus array.... During reading these displaced views of the text occur four times per second, on the average. Thus, about every quarter of a second the reader selects from the stimulus array the information that is needed to further an understanding of the text" (p. 385).

The processes of identifying words become subservient to text meaning and overall understanding.

Many of the difficulties in identifying English words come from the nature of the English language. English is not just phonetic but morphophonemic in its structure (Byrne, 1999). That is, words in English represent not only phonemes, but also morphemes. For example, the regular English plural can be /s/ or /z/ (or /ez/), but is encoded with an *s*. This preserves the morphology, but violates the phonology. In addition, English varies in terms of how phonological relations are encoded. The "long *a*" can be encoded as *ai, aigh, eigh, ay,* or *a_e,* depending on the word. A person needs to have specific word knowledge, above and beyond sound-symbol knowledge, to recognize words. As children learn to recognize words, they use these three sources of knowledge—morphological, phonological, and orthographic—interactively. These particular sources of knowledge develop in spelling as well as in word recognition (Treiman & Caesar, 1997).

Some have argued for two mechanisms for the word identification process (e.g., Rayner & Pollatsek, 1989). One mechanism, a direct route, involves rapid or automatic recognition of words and their pronunciation and meaning. Most common words, words that appear frequently in texts such as pronouns, articles, and frequently read nouns and verbs, are recognized rapidly by skilled readers. Less common words and words never before seen cannot be recognized by this process. The other mechanism seems to operate through an ongoing construction process of plausible pronunciations. Words are recognized through a process of similarity or analogy to known words and by knowing spelling pattern rules. One might pronounce *barbet,* for example, through analogy to other known words, such as *barber* or *sherbet.* One would not think that it is pronounced like *ba-rbet* because *rbet* is not a legitimate syllable in English. One usually can make appropriate generalizations to new words based on this sort of extensive knowledge of words and word patterns.

Others have argued that sight word recognition and reading of regular words use the same underlying mechanisms. Plaut (1997) and Plaut, McClelland, and Seidenberg (1995) used computer simulations using parallel distributed processing (PDP; see Adams, 1990) to suggest that at least a computer simulation can recognize both types of words using the same underlying mechanisms. In their simulations, computers have been able to achieve near human levels of accuracy in reading both types of words. In the PDP model, the underlying knowledge is a rich knowledge of spellings. Ehri (1995, 1998) comes to the same conclusion from a different angle. Examining the correlations between alphabetic knowledge, phonological awareness, and recognition of both regular and irregular words, she also suggested that sight word recognition is the result of rich connections between knowledge of graphemes and phonemes in children's lexicons.

Whether there is one mechanism or two, this picture of skilled reading indicates that children need to be able to identify common words effortlessly and to figure out less common words through knowledge of word structures. How do most children arrive at this point? The beginnings of word identification can be traced back to children's early experiences with literacy. If one follows development from that period through the primary grades, one can see how word identification develops systematically and can be related to instruction.

### Development of Word Identification Skills

Becoming literate builds on the production and understanding of speech but also goes far beyond. Literacy requires an awareness that the words in books, on signs, and in other places are intended to convey a message that may be interesting, amusing, or important (Mason & Au, 1990). Literacy also involves an ability to separate oneself from meaning, that is, to take a distant or analytic position, to judge as well as to understand text information, and to think of language as a tool (Egan, 1987; Olson, 1984).

Children first become aware that language can be observed and analyzed into words and letters by seeing its written form in familiar contexts. For example, while looking at an alphabet book with a parent, the young child may see the word *apple* accompanied by the capital letter *A* and a picture of an apple. At breakfast there may be Special K cereal with an oversized *K* on the box. On outings, the child visits a McDonald's restaurant and sees the sign with the golden arches. These early experiences with environmental print may play a role in children's early understanding of words by helping children view printed words as meaningful representations of objects, unchanging in their context (Mason, 1980).

A further contribution of these experiences to later word identification, however, has not been clearly established. Masonheimer, Drum, and Ehri (1984), for example, found that many children noticed nothing different about the Pepsi logo when the letters were changed to read Xepsi. Nonetheless, although children are not processing all letter information, their responses suggest that they are gaining an understanding of the function of familiar environmental print. Those children who were able to notice the changes in the print also were those who recognized a significant number of letters, or who were already beginning to read (see also Stahl & Murray, 1993). Mason and Stewart (1988) found in testing preschool children's understanding of print that they were likely to give the response "stop sign" when asked to read the word *stop* when it was painted on the familiar octagon-shaped sign. This erroneous response was only a temporary stage in their reading development.

It may be, then, that environmental print serves to make children aware of some words and helps to illustrate some of the purpose served by print. Having a sense of these purposes would also make the print more meaningful and thus more memorable (Doake, 1985), and it could help motivate children to begin attending more closely to print.

Another indication that word identification has its roots in children's general understandings of print is provided by the work of Peterman and Mason (1984). They showed kindergarten children labeled pictures. They found that some children could point to the print when asked where there is something to read but then would ignore the print when asked to read what it says. That is, children knew that reading involved print, but had the idea that they could read without using the letter information. Children further along realized that they should attend both to pictures and print when trying to identify the labeled pictures or when trying to recall a page of text that had been read to them. Even then, however, many children were uncertain about where a word ended or where to begin and stop reading. For example, when shown the phrase *wood blocks* and asked how many words there were, some children did not distinguish letters from words and counted the letters instead.

As children have more opportunities to watch others read and try to read by themselves, they come to the realization that printed words can be differentiated on a page. They might try to remember words by the initial letter, especially if a word begins with the same letter as their name. They might overuse letter names when they write, spelling *are* as *R*, and *you* as *U*, indicating that they cannot yet break words into letter sounds.

As part of becoming literate in English, though, children must come to realize that words can be further analyzed and that there are predictable patterns of letters and sounds. That is, they must understand the regularity of spelling-to-sound correspondence (Ehri, 1995, 1998). As with learning about the visual properties of print, initial learning about the relationships between letters and sounds often begins through home literacy activities. A variety of experiences appear to support the development of these concepts: hearing nursery rhymes, stories, and interesting words; discussing words pointed out in context (Bissex, 1980; D. Taylor, 1983). Maclean, Bryant, and Bradley (1987) determined that knowledge of nursery rhymes at age 3 was strongly related to early reading performance.

Burgess (in press) examined 4- and 5-year-old children on a variety of measures one year apart and found that once phonological awareness at the first testing was factored out, only home literacy variables contributed to phonological awareness a year later. The variables examined by Burgess included resources available for literacy, the child's opportunities to interact with those resources, parental interest, and parental motivation for literacy.

One key activity might be the reading of alphabet books. Yaden, Smolkin, and MacGillivray (1993) analyzed children's reading of alphabet books. They found that until a child had a basic understanding that words can be broken into sounds, such statements as "*M* is for mouse" made no sense. In the process of reading alphabet books, the child they studied came to understand why *M* was for *mouse*, a key understanding in phonological awareness. Murray, Stahl, and Ivey (1996) found that reading alphabet books for 10 minutes a day to 4-year-olds appeared to improve their phonological awareness, even without special instruction.

Before making much use of spelling-to-sound regularities in English words, children tend to use other types of information. Context cues provided by pictures and sentences make it easier for beginning readers to identify words. When these cues are unavailable, beginners generally experience much more difficulty. Less advanced first graders, for example, find words easier to identify if they are presented in the sentences in which they were learned than in other sentences or lists (Francis, 1977). Beginning readers are likely to make oral reading errors that are consistent with sentence context but not with spelling-to-sound information (Stanovich, Cunningham, & Feeman, 1984; Underwood, 1985). According to a compensatory model of reading performance, it is said that beginners are compensating for their limitations in using spelling-to-sound correspondence by relying heavily on context cues (Stanovich, 1984).

Considerable research has verified that an ability to break the sounds of words into phonemes, or phonemic awareness, is the initial step in lessening the importance of context. Phonemes are the sounds of letters and letter groups in words (e.g., *m-ea-t, g-r-i-pe, sh-e-ll-s*). Early on, children are not aware of phonemes. Rather, they seem first to recognize the syllables as a unit, and then notice that a syllable has two major subunits, called the onset and the rime (Treiman, 1992). The onset is the initial portion of the syllable (e.g., m in *meat*, gr in *gripe*, or sh in *shells*). The rime includes the vowel and ending consonants (e.g., *eat* in *meat*, *ipe* in *gripe*, *ells* in *shells*). Treiman found that young children could analyze spoken syllables into onsets and rimes before they could identify phonemes. This suggests that children can be helped to hear syllables in words, then onset/rimes, and then individual phonemes. Instructionally, it suggests that breaking spoken words into syllables by clapping could be a useful beginning step. Initial sounds of words could be introduced through ABC books, where the first letter in a word is highlighted, and ending sounds of words could be presented through rhymes.

After children can distinguish onset/rime units in words, they will be able to separate other phonemes in words and to manipulate phonemes. Bissex (1980), for example, reported her son's discovery that he could remove the *l* from please and have the word *peas(e)*. With these and related discoveries, children begin to understand the regularities in spelling-to-sound patterns. They begin to figure out words that they have never seen in print before, based on their knowledge. This hypothesis has been tested with various word and letter-sound analysis tasks, which Stanovich, Cunningham, and Cramer (1984), and Yopp (1988) have shown are all highly correlated.

More generally, word and letter-sound analysis ability is significantly related to later reading achievement (e.g., Calfee, Lindamood, & Lindamood, 1973) An ability to analyze word into letter sounds appears to allow children to discover and exploit the alphabetic principle of spelling-to-sound regularities. Understanding this aspect of written language structure provides "a basis for constructing a large and expandable set of words—all the words that ever were, are and will be—out of two or three dozen signal elements (phonemes)" (Liberman & Shankweiler, 1985, p. 9).

Can children be taught an awareness of phonemes in words? Apparently yes. Two studies have shown that phonemic awareness training in kindergarten benefits children's later reading. Bradley and Bryant (1983) worked with children who had obtained low scores on a test of phonemic awareness. One treatment group was given 40 individual tutoring sessions on identifying beginning, middle, and final sounds in words and connecting sounds to letters. Those in comparison and control groups did not fare as well as this group in reading in later school years. Lundberg, Frost, and Peterson (1988) found that children's reading and spelling benefited from metalinguistic training given in daily, whole-class lessons during the kindergarten year. Teachers provided the following types of activities in approximately this sequence: listening to nonverbal and verbal sounds; nursery rhymes and stories and games for rhyming production; segmentation of sentences into words; segmentation of words into syllables (clapping, marching, dancing, walking followed by use of plastic markers and games using puppets); segmentation of initial letters of words from remainder; and segmentation of two-letter words into phonemes.

Recent meta-analyses of the effects of phonological awareness training found that phonological awareness training to transfer to beginning reading. Ehri found that phonological awareness training had strong and significant effects on phonological awareness, reading and spelling measures. She found that teaching children to manipulate letters while learning to associate them with phonemes created effect sizes nearly twice as large as training without letters on both reading and spelling, although the effect dissipated on follow-up tests of spelling. Even the training without letters, however, had significant effects on reading and spelling measures. She also found that phonological awareness training was most effective when given in small groups, and that longer training periods seemed to produce diminished effects. This may be because phonological awareness is an insight, which is learned in a nearly all-or-none manner, or because the more difficult-to-teach children were given longer treatments. The effects of phonological awareness training were consistent across grade levels (preschool, kindergarten, first grade, or second grade and up) on reading measures, but effects were stronger for preschool and kindergarten students on measures of spelling.

Thus, phonological awareness training does seem to influence reading and spelling acquisition, a strong argument for a causal relation between phonological awareness and at least word recognition. The most successful training, however, seems to involve children working with letters as well as sounds, in an integrated manner. Furthermore, phonological awareness training seems be most important in preschool and kindergarten, at least for spelling development.

## How Word Recognition Develops

There is a series of stages through which children pass as they learn to recognize words (Ehri, 1998). They first recognize words holistically, as a single logograph. Children at this stage may recognize words like *look* through the two "eyes" in the middle or the word *monkey* by its "tail." This is a prealphabetic stage (Ehri, 1995), because children are not using letters and sounds but are instead using the look of each word. As children develop phonological awareness, they may begin to use some partial sound information in the word, such as an initial or final sound. Ehri called this stage phonetic cue reading. In this stage, a child might substitute a word that begins with the same letter, such as *bird* for *bear*, when reading words in text or in lists. As children learn more words, phonetic cue reading becomes less efficient and children analyze the word more deeply. In the cipher or full alphabetic stage (Ehri, 1995), children use all the letters and sounds. At this stage, children's reading can still be labored, relying on sounding out the word or other, less efficient strategies. At this point, they are either "sounding the word out" or using analogies to identify the whole word. Following this stage, children move to automatic word recognition, where they are able to identify the word seemingly as a whole or through rapid recognition of chunks within the word. At this point, children are free to put all of their attention toward comprehension, for word recognition has become fluent and transparent. With greater practice, children will develop automatic word recognition so that they do not have to think about the words in a text and can concentrate fully on the meaning of the text (Ehri, 1995).

Ehri and her colleagues have used a number of different paradigms to study this development. For example, Ehri and Wilce (1985) found that children in the prealphabetic phase were better at learning sight words that were visually distinct but not related phonologically to their referent (e.g., WcB for *elephant*), but children who were phonetic cue readers were better at learning sight words that were phonetically related to their referent (e.g., LFT for *elephant*). Children were classified on the basis of their ability to read preprimer- and primer-level words. Children who could not read any words were considered nonreaders and, by inference, as visual cue learners; children who could identify a few words were considered novices, and, again by inference, as phonetic cue readers. Ehri and Wilce (1987) classified as phonetic cue readers those children who could name or give sounds for letters but could neither spell nonsense words nor read any of the words to be taught in the study. They found that teaching these children how to spell words improved their ability to read words as well. They suggested that the spelling training improved the children's ability to use phonetic cues, which enabled them to better remember taught words.

Neither of these approaches to classifying children directly assesses the nature of phonetic cue reading. Ehri and Wilce (1985, 1987) inferred children's ability to use phonetic cues by how well they performed on reading and/or spelling tasks. Without disputing the classification, it would be preferable to use more direct measures of children's ability to use phonetic cues in word recognition.

## How Spelling Develops

Children pass through a similar set of stages with respect to how they invent spellings for words (see Bear & Barone, 1989; Gillet & Temple, 1990; Zutell & Rasinkski, 1989). Initially, a child may spell a word by drawing a picture or scribbling something that looks like writing (Harste, Burke, & Woodward, 1982). As children learn that words need letters, they may use random letters to represent a word. At this point, the writers themselves are the only ones who can read what they have written. As children begin to think about sounds in words, their spelling may represent only one sound in a word, usually an initial sound, and occasionally a final sound. Sometimes they represent a word with a single letter, or pair of letters, but often they represent a word with the correct initial letter followed by some random letters. For example, one child in our reading clinic wrote *fish* with an initial *f* and continued by adding an additional six letters, stating that "words that begin with *f* have a lot of letters in them." As children analyze words further, they may use the names of letters to represent sounds. At this stage, they represent at least all of the consonants in a word, often not using vowels. For example, they might spell *girl* as *grl* or *ten* as *tn*. As children learn more about how words are spelled, they use vowels, and the words they write resemble the actual word, like *dragun* for *dragon*. However, children in this stage many not always use conventional spellings.

A number of different scales have been proposed to capture this development (e.g., Bear & Barone, 1989; Bear, Invernizzi, Templeton, & Johnston, 2000; Gillet & Temple, 1990; Zutell & Rasinkski, 1989). Many of these concentrate on early emergent spellings. Bear et al. provided a 15-point scale from prephonetic spellings to sophisticated knowledge of the morphemic structure of derived words.

These scales, however, confound the development of phonological, orthographic, and morphemic knowledge. As Treiman and Caesar (1997) pointed out, these knowledge sources develop independently. Scales such as these combine the various aspects of development into one omnibus scale. A more accurate view of spelling development might separate the various aspects.

***Reading and spelling.*** Although there are similarities in the general trends between reading and spelling, there are some important differences. Ehri's (1998) stages concentrated on the use of consonants. Her first movement is from no use of consonants to the use of initial or final consonants. The second movement is from the use of only consonants to the use of consonants and vowels. Bear et al.'s (2000) spelling stages also contain movement from the use of no phonological information to the use of initial and then final consonants. However, much of the development documented by Bear et al. involves increased sophistication in the use of vowels. Understanding that there is a vowel sound between consonants involves phonological knowledge, but understanding that a long vowel is coded differently (through the silent e convention or with a vowel digraph) involves orthographic knowledge. So, after children understand the function of vowels, their development in the use of vowels grows as they learn more spelling patterns. Although the development of reading and spelling have been contrasted in the literature spelling involves much more than reading and the two paths may diverge after the beginning stages.

***Writing and spelling.*** Writing and spelling are coordinated with reading because all three aspects of literacy require similar knowledge about the written language (e.g., Bear & Barone, 1989; Brugelmann, 1986). Children's writing moves from aimless traces, beginning with toddlers who might experiment by touching pencil to paper, and then to directed scribbling, such as zigzags across the page. Next, children imitate letter shapes, constructing letterlike scribbles, then single letters, and then multiple letters. Finally, recognizing that the letters can form words and phrases, they construct letters that are connected. Just as writing develops from scribbles, so spelling develops from drawings that are intended to represent words, and then letters are added arbitrarily to the drawings. Next, letters that represent particular words are used, such as *R* for the word *are*. A sound-oriented shorthand, an invented spelling, is then developed to represent the sounds the child hears in words. A child might spell *kite* as *kt*. Children eventually replace invented spellings with specific learned spellings, filling in the vowels and applying learned orthographic patterns. Earliest aspects of reading are listening to stories and telling stories. Then, mock or pretend reading, imitations of being read to, occur. Lartz and Mason (1988), for example, showed how a 4-year-old child could say a substantial part of a story from remembering what was read to her and with the aid of the illustrations on successive pages. For all three aspects of literacy, context is used, and then gradually superseded by attention to letter–sound information and more complex patterns of English.

***Spelling-to-sound patterns.***  When children first turn to the use of spelling-to-sound information, the presence of the more consistent or regular spelling-to-sound patterns (as in words such as *pat, paid, pave*) becomes important. For a short time, children might even have more difficulty identifying words that form inconsistent patterns or are exceptions to regular patterns (e.g., *put, said, have*). Gradually though, they recognize words directly. Recognition of less common words builds on an understanding of regular word patterns and may lead to recognition through a second word identification mechanism (Tumner, Herriman, & Nesdale, 1988).

This means that knowledge of spelling-to-sound correspondence not only enables readers to recognize words they know but also to identify words never encountered previously. Glushko (1981) showed that adults use their knowledge of common, regular words to identify unknown words by using familiar, analogous words. Goswami (1998) suggested that even beginning readers figure out new words by analogy, that is, by thinking of similar (rhyming of alliterative) words. For example, a child may recognize a new word, *peak*, by recalling the pronunciation of the analogous word, *beak*. Goswami found that children who had acquired letter-sound knowledge used decoding by analogy both when reading words in lists and when the new words were in connected texts. In a second study, she found that children who were taught words with regular patterns (e.g., *beak*) made more analogies than children who were taught words inconsistent in pattern (e.g., *break*). Goswami pointed out that these results are congruent with Treiman's view that "phonemic awareness progresses from an analysis of syllable into onsets and rimes, and only subsequently to the ability to analyze onsets and rimes into phonemes" (p. 41). Similarly, in an unpublished study, Mason found that a number of second-grade children figured out how to pronounce pseudowords by analogy, for example, explaining that they could pronounce *moke* by taking the *s* off from *smoke*.

Ehri (1998; Ehri & Robbins, 1992) found that children need to have some knowledge of the alphabetic principle in order to read words by analogy. Unlike Goswami (1998), Ehri found that children who did not know sound–symbol correspondences were unable to use analogies. The difference between the results might lie in the difference between her tasks and those of Goswami. In Goswami's task, children had the analogous word in front of them; in Ehri and Robbins' task, the children had to come up with the analogue from memory. Ehri suggested that children have to learn words well before they can be used as analogues. She incorporated this insight into a revision of the Benchmark Reading Program (Gaskins, Ehri, Cress, O'Hara, & Donnelly, 1996).

Knowledge that letters form predictable sequences is also important, beginning at about second grade (Adams, 1990). Children find it easier to identify words containing commonly occurring letter sequences. For example, words such as *ten* and *the* will be easier to identify then *tsar* or *two* because *t* as the first letter of a word is more likely to be followed by *e* or *h* than *s* or *w*. Children gradually become knowledgeable about the predictability of letter sequences, and at about fourth grade they can use this knowledge to recognize syllable patterns and boundaries in multisyllable words. They can determine where breaks between syllables are likely to occur and how the syllables might be pronounced (e.g., *mon-key* rather than *mo-nkey* because *nkey* is not a legitimate syllable; *fa-ther* rather than *fat-her* because *th* is a letter sequence that usually appears in the same syllable).

In brief, by the end of first grade, many children are reading easy texts fluently, and some have even gained the ability to identify common syllable patterns. At this point, most children are well on their way to becoming effective word readers, able to make good use of common and less common patterns in written English. By the end of third or fourth grade, only uncommon multisyllable words are difficult for most children to recognize.

## Connecting Word Recognition Development to Other Aspects of Literacy

Recent developmental models of reading connect early with more skilled reading and introduce an interplay between word identification and text comprehension. A number of different models suggest that reading emerges from two related but separate roots (Carver, 1993; Gough & Tumner, 1986). One, word recognition, is related to phonology, and the other is related to comprehension. When learning to read, children use internal representations of words from their own language to begin the analysis of written words. Children begin reading using highly contextualized skills and then move on to relatively decontextualized skills. Book reading, listening to stories an early age, and learning to read easy stories appear to contribute to effective reading development.

## Instructional Implications

Children face a major cognitive challenge to understand the regularity of written English for identifying, writing, and spelling words effortlessly. Word recognition research points to the complexity of the learning children must do to become proficient word identifiers. They must develop phonemic awareness, come to an understanding of spelling-to sound correspondence, and then progress to applying knowledge of letter patterns and syllables.

It is not surprising, then, that research supports the importance of systematic instruction in spelling-to-sound correspondences during the early grades (Anderson, Hiebert, Wilkinson, & Scott, 1985). Early studies tended to pit approaches incorporating systematic phonics instruction against approaches that emphasized text reading and relied on children's learning of words as wholes. We believe this tendency had the inadvertent effect of creating a false dichotomy. It seemed to lead some educators to infer that reading programs including systematic instruction in spelling-to-sound regularities should minimize comprehension, book reading, and writing. At times, this led to the implementation of beginning reading programs in which book reading played little or no role, and children received lesson after lesson on letter-sound-relationships (Mason, 1984). Other educators, in turn, rejected what they viewed as an overemphasis on phonics instruction and tried to promote programs that emphasized book reading, writing, and the development of positive attitudes toward literacy (Allen, 1989).

In our view, an integrated reading and writing program and systematic instruction in spelling-to-sound regularities need not be diametrically opposed, because word recognition and comprehension may share common roots in children's early experiences with story book reading and other home experiences involving print (Baker, Fernandez-Fein, Scher, & Williams, 1998). Current approaches to teaching sound–symbol correspondences stress the integration of skills teaching with the reading of connected text (e.g., Fountas & Pinnell, 1996). B. Taylor, Pearson, Clark, and Walpole (1999) found, for example, that the most effective teachers in their study not only taught sound–symbol correspondences directly but also scaffolded children's use of these correspondences during the reading of connected text. Other successful approaches integrate spelling and word recognition instruction (e.g., Bear, Invernizzi, Templeton, & Johnston, 2000; for a review, see S. A. Stahl, Duffy-Hester, & K. A. D. Stahl, 1998). Moreover, because reading and spelling can support the development of the other skills (Clarke, 1988; Dobson, 1989), they will foster word recognition if taught together. Let us be more specific about how systematic instruction in spelling-to-sound regularities and holistic approaches could work in concert.

Research on children's reading development suggests that essential concepts about word identification can be acquired informally at home in the context of meaningful reading and writing activities. School programs for introducing written words would be more supportive if children could experience reading and writing informally. A number of new kindergarten programs are moving in this direction. There are successful ways to provide instruction as well as child-directed activity (Allen & Mason, 1989; Crowell, Kawakami, & Wong, 1986). In these programs, literacy goals are accomplished through activities that are staged by teachers. Directed activities might include having children talk about and learn to recite or read books that were read aloud to them, having them play letter-and-word sound games, having them write and analyze words in a teacher-written message, shared reading and writing, and reading aloud to children. Child-directed activities might include reading and writing, story listening centers that are changed weekly to include inviting new materials, and dramatic and block play centers in which reading and writing material are available and become part of the situations that children create.

If children can begin reading by using a variety of context-supported materials, they will be less likely to lose the sense of text meaning and will know to rely on pictures as well as letter and sentence information to begin reading (Clay, 1993). As letter and sound cues in words become more apparent, children will use their knowledge of context in conjunction with spelling patterns to become more proficient readers.

An integrated reading and writing instructional program should extend beyond kindergarten into the primary grades, and there should still be both systematic and informal opportunities for children to learn about word identification. Phonics instruction alone is not sufficient for building proficient word identification skills, a conclusion that is also supported by phonics advocates. Phonics instruction supports only one strategy for word identification, namely, analysis of words into their constituent phonemes. To avoid giving the impression that phonetic analysis is the only way to identify words, teachers should encourage children to decode words by analogy. Moreover, because early growth in word reading is linked with opportunities to read connected text (Anderson et al., 1985), teachers should provide opportunities for children to listen to stories and read and write on their own.

Creative writing is an example of an informal activity that will support the development of other word identification strategies. In a study comparing first graders who used conventional spelling with those who invented their own spellings of words, Clarke (1988) found that allowing children to invent word spellings in their creative writing assignments led to longer pieces, knowledge of more written words, and superior spelling and phonetic analysis skills.

There are a number of supports for reading instruction balanced between decoding and contextual reading. Studies of effective teachers have found that exemplary primary grade teachers have found that effective teachers combine direct instruction in decoding with a great deal of text reading. Taylor and Pearson found that exemplary teachers often provide scaffolded decoding support during text reading, extending the lessons into authentic texts. Other successful approaches, such as the "Four Blocks" approach, incorporate both directed decoding instruction and literature-oriented instruction (Cunningham, Hall, & DeFee, 1991, 1998).

It is hard to learn to identify words in our language. As a result, developmental change in word identification involves an understanding of many subtle concepts. What must be learned cannot be completely taught or satisfactorily supervised by teachers. Thus, we recommend that teachers keep children's meaningful text reading as the primary goal and encourage them to apply more inductive word identification approaches. If teachers coach children to use word identification strategies in meaningful contexts and encourage them to use more than one strategy, children will learn how to navigate independently and find their own way through the thicket of letters and sounds, word patterns and irregularities, phrases and text context. As Clay (1985) directed, children need to learn how to monitor their own reading, use strategies involving letter information, word patterns, and text interpretation, and cross-check for meaningful renditions of the text. Practicing with complete texts—stories, informative text, and children's own writings—is probably the best approach.

These conclusions point to the need for significant changes in typical kindergarten and primary grade reading lessons. Among the changes are the following:

1. A shift from assuming that learning to read and write is initiated in elementary school to the notion that literacy can and often does begin to develop informally at home and in preschool and can be fostered with context-supported reading and writing activities in kindergarten.

2. A shift from teaching word recognition as isolated words and skills to teaching them in the context of a wide range of meaningful reading and writing activities.

3. A realization that word identification skills are acquired over a period of years, and that new literacy concepts should be built on those already learned and understood.

4. An understanding that children need a range of word-reading experiences in order to acquire word identification processing mechanisms that lead to accurate, rapid access to common words and analyses of letters and word patterns in other words.

## Word Identification Summary

The instructional changes we advocate are in keeping with the two major themes of this chapter, one being that children learn to identify words more effectively if they are presented within a larger, more meaningful context, whether it be a story, sentence, picture book, phrase, or advertisement. Extensive opportunities to read and listen to texts of all sorts are recommended. If words are learned in context, children will be able to keep the goal of understanding in mind as they see, learn, and figure out new words. Teachers will then find it easier to model the act of reading for children, which in turn will aid children to better understand both the processing steps of word identification and the purposes for reading and learning words.

The second theme in this chapter is that the very complexity of written English requires children to develop a number of different strategies for learning to identify words. Children need to supplement the instruction they receive in school with their own discoveries about language patterns. To that end, we recommend systematic instruction that encourages phonemic awareness and then leads children to knowledge of spelling-to-sound correspondences. We also recommend that the teacher establish opportunities in the classroom for children to read and write informally. Children can learn to read and write accurately and fluently if they are allowed to experience invented spelling, approximations to conventional text reading, and story rereadings.

## VOCABULARY KNOWLEDGE

Knowledge of word meanings is related to word identification. Adams (1990) suggested that the proficient reader's identification of words is the result of the interaction of orthographic, phonological, semantic, and contextual knowledge. Semantic knowledge is involved because readers tend to use their knowledge of word meanings to help identify orthographic strings. A group of letters is more easily identified if it is meaningful and in the reader's lexicon than it is if it is a nonsense word or not in the reader's lexicon. This effect is stronger with younger children than with more proficient readers (Stanovich, 1984).

Carroll (1964) argued that the most effective approaches to teaching word meanings must mimic natural processes of learning word meanings, but do so in a more efficient manner. In other words, to teach word meanings effectively one must produce the same type of knowledge that natural processes produce. Thus, to understand how to teach word meanings, one must understand how vocabulary is acquired.

## Most Words are Learned From Context

Although vocabulary instruction does improve children's store of word meanings and comprehension abilities (Stahl & Fairbanks, 1986), most words are learned from repeated exposures in context rather than through direct teaching. If an average high school senior knows 45,000 words, as according to one estimate (Nagy & Anderson, 1984), then it might not be possible to teach someone all the words they need to know through direct instruction. (If the estimate is closer to 17,000, as other authors have suggested [D'Anna, Zechmeister, & Hall, 1991], or even 5,000 [Hirsh & Nation, 1992], then direct teaching might play a more important role. This may be especially true for speakers of other languages who are learning English.) Studies (e.g., Stanovich & Cunningham, 1992) have found that amount of print exposure to be related to vocabulary, even when intelligence is controlled. Thus, the more a person reads, the more word meanings that person is likely to know.

## Words in Texts

Although estimates vary widely as to how many total words there are in English (unabridged dictionaries can have between 250,000 and 500,000 entries, depending on what they allow as entries), there are sound data about the number of words in books used by elementary and secondary students. The best estimate, taken from Nagy and Anderson (1984), is that there are roughly 88,700 "word families" used in books up to 12th grade. A word family is defined by Nagy and Anderson as a groups of words in which someone knowing one of the words in the set could guess or infer the meaning of the others when encountering it in context while reading. An example would be the family that includes the words *add, addition, additive, adding*, and so on.

About half the texts one reads consist of the 107 most common words. Another 5,000 words account for the next 45%, so that 95% of the texts we read consist of about 5,100 different words (Adams, 1990). The rest of the texts one reads consist of the remaining 83,000 or so words (Nagy & Anderson, 1984). If this is so, then why not just teach students the 5,100 most common words and not worry about the relatively rare words? There are two problems with this logic. The first is that these rare or uncommon words are not so rare at all. They are words that every literate adult should know and assumes that other literate adults do know. Words in this group might include *beneficial, advocate, accountant, cancer* and so on. The second problem is that these rare words are just the words that carry most of the content of texts. Many, but not all, of the uncommon words have to do with the particular topic of the text. This is especially true in the content areas. Words such as *abiotic, ecosystem,* and *niche* may be relatively uncommon, but they are also useful, and perhaps necessary, to a full understanding of ecology.

It is useful to look at the number of words in texts students read, but this does not tell us how many words an average student knows. Researchers do know that this number is considerably less than 88,700, but it is not clear how much less. Early estimates varied wildly, from 17,000 to more than 200,000 words estimated as known by university undergraduates, or from 2,562 to 26,000 words estimated as known by first graders (Lorge & Chall, 1963). Because one cannot ask a person about every word possibly known, tests need to be based on samples. But the larger the dictionary from which the sample is taken, the larger the estimate of a person's word knowledge; thus, dictionaries of varying sizes are partly responsible for these differences (see Lorge & Chall, 1963, for an explanation).

Even with a low estimate of 17,000 words, a researcher cannot simply ask students to define every word they supposedly should know. Even a test of 100 words is likely to be so fatiguing as to yield inaccurate results. Thus every study that estimates the number of words known uses a sample. Usually this sample comes from a dictionary, possibly the fifth word from every fortieth page.

The differing estimates of vocabulary knowledge are crucial to making decisions about vocabulary instruction. Because the experience of Stahl and his colleagues suggested that 300 to 500 words per year can reasonably be taught through direct instruction (8–10 words per week, 50 weeks a year), the figure accepted is important in determining how to plan for vocabulary growth. If a teacher accepts Nagy and Anderson's (1984) estimate that there are 88,700 word types in English and that students learn about half of them, this suggests that the average child learns about 3,000 new words each year. (There is other independent evidence that indeed children do learn about 3,000 new words per year [White, Graves, & Slater, 1990; but see Nation & Waring, 1997]). Even doubling or tripling our estimate for direct vocabulary teaching, one cannot reach 3,000 words per year through direct teaching alone. Most of these words learned must come from reading them in context (Sternberg, 1987). However, if a lower figure is accepted, such as the 17,000 words suggested by D'Anna et al. (1991), or about 1,000 new words per year, then it may be possible to teach all the words that a person needs to learn. This distinction is especially important in teaching English as a second language (Gouldman, Nation, & Read, 1990). Students learning English as a second language rely more heavily on direct instruction than native speakers, because they typically need to be acquiring new vocabulary at a faster pace in order to keep up with their peers.

If one takes a higher estimate for the number of words that children learn each year, will contextual reading be adequate to the task of learning of 3,000 words per year? This is a monumental task, requiring the learning of about 8 words a day, every day, and twice that many if word learning occurs only on school days. William Nagy and his colleagues (Nagy, Anderson, & Herman, 1987; Nagy, Herman, & Anderson, 1985) calculated that much of this annual growth in reading can come from incidental learning of word meanings. Their argument goes as follows:

If, for example, it can be assumed that a fifth-grade child reads for an hour per day (in and out of school) at a rate of 150 words per minute (a conservative estimate; see Harris & Sipay, 1990), 5 days a week, then the child will have encountered 2,250,000 words in the course of all this reading. If 2% to 5% of those words are unknown (as in instructional level text), the child will have encountered from 45,000 to 112,500 unknown words. From other research, it is known that children will learn between 5% and 10% of previously unknown words from a single reading (Nagy & Herman, 1987). This would account for at least 2,250 new words learned from context each year. Making all the estimates as conservative as possible, the 2,250 new words is close enough to 3,000 to suggest that context can be a powerful influence on students' vocabulary growth. This suggests that one of the most powerful things we can do to increase children's vocabulary is to encourage them to read as widely as possible.

However, what if one accepts the lower estimate of 1,000 words per year? Although our estimates show that children usually can be taught 300 to 400 words per year (8–10 words per week, 40 weeks a year), this total could be doubled with more intensive vocabulary instruction. Thus, one might be able to teach nearly all the words an average child learns in a year through direct instruction.

## Differences in Word Knowledge

Either set of estimates to determine children's knowledge of word meanings is only an average. Averages can hide some fairly large differences in word learning. One study estimated that fifth-graders learned from 1,000 to nearly 5,000 new word meanings per year (White et al., 1990). This is a fairly large spread, with the most able learner learning five times as many new word meanings as the less able learners.

Why is there such a difference? One explanation is that good readers are better able to derive word meanings from context than poorer readers (Sternberg & Powell, 1983). This explanations seems to hold true to some extent, although reading ability appears to be less of a factor than grade level and method of assessment (whether partial word knowledge is counted) (Swanborn & Glopper, 1999). Two types of studies have been used to examine children's learning from context. The first set of studies had students derive a word's meaning from context. That is, students would be given a sentence such as "We needed to close the kloptics so the drapes would not fade" and were asked to determine what *kloptic* meant. In this task, more able students were better able to define the unknown word (Elshout-Mohr & van Daalen-Kapteijns, 1987; McKeown, 1985). However, the real task of word learning does not involve giving students sentences and having them derive these meanings. Instead, words are learned through chance encounters in text. Unknown words are not signaled, nor are readers asked to come up with a definition immediately after reading. Instead, words are accumulated over time, through exposure and gradual learning (Schwanenflugel, Stahl, & McFalls, 1997).

## How are Words Learned in Context

The task of deriving a word's meaning may be a different task from ordinary learning from context. Studies suggest that readers often have no conscious awareness of unknown words during reading (e.g., Baker & Brown, 1984; Stahl, Rinehart, & Erickson, 1986). Without conscious awareness, it is difficult to posit a conscious derivation process. Instead, the process of learning from context seems ordinarily to be subconscious.

***Definitional and contextual knowledge.*** Although an exact understanding of what it means to know a word is currently being debated (cf. Carey, 1982), knowing a word clearly involves possessing a fleshed out understanding of the concept itself, and understanding how that concept fits with related groups of words—words related by topic, morphology, or function. "A vocabulary is a coherent, integrated system of concepts" (Miller, 1986, p. 175). These two aspects of word meaning can be called "definitional knowledge" or the relations between a word and other words and "contextual knowledge" or how the word's core meaning changes in different contexts (Stahl & Fairbanks, 1986).

After an initial encounter with a word, the child picks up basic information about these two dimensions of word meaning. Research with young children suggests that children at first associate the word with the entire context. That is, the child may associate the word *dog* not only with the animal but also with the situation in which the word was first labeled. Through repeated encounters, the child learns to separate the concept from the context. However, various aspects of the context are maintained. Ellis (1997) suggested that words vary in terms of the number of contexts in which they are found in. That is, some words are found in only a few phrases, and others are found in innumerable contexts. The word *joust* implies *knights*, the word *infarction* implies *cardiac*, and so on. Although *joust* and *infarction* are potentially definable, in reality they rarely occur in other contexts.

Other words are polysemous, or have multiple meanings. This is not only true of words with two or more clearly different meanings, such as "line" (as in _____ and in "line one's pockets") but also in common words. Anderson and Nagy (1991) suggested that most words are at least mildly polysemous. To *give* means something different in the following sentences:

John gave Frank five dollars.
John gave Mary a kiss.
The doctor gave the child an injection.
The orchestra gave a stunning performance. (Anderson & Nagy, 1991, p. 700)

Although all senses of *give* involve transferring, the nature of *give* seems to change due to the nature of what was transferred.

***Definitional knowledge.*** A number of scholars (Brown, Collins, & Duguid, 1989; Fodor, Garrett, Walker, & Parkes, 1980) have argued that definitions cannot capture word meanings because meanings are inherently context-bound, varying in different contexts. We suggest that definitions do capture part of what is known about a word, its relation to other words.

There is evidence that words are stored, at least partly, with other words with similar meanings, or in rough categories (Smith & Medin, 1981). Furthermore, when children encounter a word for the first time, they engage in "fast mapping" (Heibeck & Markman, 1987; Rice, Buhr, & Nemeth, 1990) or assigning a general category to a new word. Fast mapping may allow a child to decide a word is a "color" or that it "moves." This rough definition may allow the child to make sense of the overall context, thus allowing comprehension to progress.

Fast mapping may relate to what Scott and Nagy (2000) called a word schema. In addition to and in conjunction with well-developed systems of words, people with good vocabulary knowledge have a rich understanding of how systematically the English language operates (Nagy & Gentner, 1987; Nagy, Scott, Schommer, & Anderson, 1987). Such knowledge encompasses what people know "about words as words, about how words and their meanings are put together, and how they are used in text" (Nagy et al., 1987, p. 3).

Much of what people know about words as words, or patterns of word meaning, is at the unconscious level. "For example, [people] know, at least implicitly, that English verbs of motion typically tell something about the way an object moves (e.g., slide, wobble, plunge, spin), but not, for example, what shape it is . . . people have to have rich word schemas—expectations about what words are like and constraints on what types of information can be encoded in words" (Nagy et al., 1987, pp. 2–3). Nonetheless, such tacit knowledge is an integral part of a person's vocabulary knowledge and plays an important role in constraining word meanings (Nagy et al., 1987).

The English language depends heavily on word order to communicate meaning. Words are positioned as English grammar (syntax) dictates. Such syntactic structure enables people to know that the three missing words in the sentences below must be a noun, verb, and an adjective (Johnson & Pearson, 1978):

The _____ went to the game.
We tried to _____ the table.
She blew up the big _____ balloon. (p. 116)

Again, proficient word users apply their understanding of English grammar so automatically that they are little aware of its role in their construction of meaning (Nagy & Gentner, 1987).

An integral part of vocabulary knowledge is an extensive understanding of appropriate usage of words. A key expectation is that words appear in contexts that make sense. People with vast vocabulary knowledge are likely to have read many books (Anderson, Wilson, & Fielding, 1988) and, over the course of time, to have developed expectations about what kind of words authors are prone to use. Therefore, one might expect to find *putative* in a scholarly article but not in a romance novel or in most conversations. Much of this systematic knowledge apparently operates so automatically that people are not aware of its role in constructing meaning unless an anomaly arises (as, for example, if we were to insert, "What's up Doc?" in this chapter).

In summary, people with well-developed vocabulary knowledge possess rich, interconnecting networks of concepts with words to label much of that knowledge rather than long lists of dictionary-like definitions in their heads (Miller, 1986). Woven into such understanding is a keen sense of how the English language operates and a set of expectations about appropriate uses. Much of this knowledge is processed so interactively and automatically that people are rarely, if ever, aware of the role of any one part in constructing meaning. Like word identification, then, application of vocabulary knowledge during reading involves sophisticated, instantaneous use of regular patterns and meaningful connections among words.

For example, while reading a text on the development of river systems, suppose a new term, *rills*, is encountered in the following text excerpt: "A river system has several parts. Small rills form first. They join to form creeks, which join to form streams." The reader senses the importance of this word because it initiates a description of the topic. The reader then draws on the meaning envisioned from the text so far, automatically notices from context that *rills* is a plural noun with some tangible properties and assumes that it is connected to river systems. After this fairly rapid initial mapping, the reader makes a hypothesis about the meaning of *rills* and forms a mental model of the word/concept (Elshout-Mohr & van Daalen-Kapteijns, 1987). The reader continues through the text and gains more information about the word, consciously adjusting the model within the framework of river systems concepts or schema and unconsciously within the constraints of the English language. The reader may end up with a fairly well fleshed out understanding of rills or, as is often the case, may end up with some level of partial knowledge, such as: Rills are small waterways. Fuller understanding, such as how rills fits into the entire river system schema, may be mapped out more slowly as further encounters with rills occur over time.

***Understanding new words.*** Persons who have depth of vocabulary knowledge have efficient procedural knowledge for gaining an understanding of new words. Such people are competent comprehenders (e.g., Anderson & Freebody, 1981; Davis, 1944, 1968) and monitor information-bearing contexts for sense (Brown, 1985). When they detect an unfamiliar word that is important to their continued construction of meaning, they bring to bear their knowledge of integrated word meaning systems, how words fit in text contexts, problem-solving skills, and a compelling motivation to figure it out.

## Instructional Implications for Developing Vocabulary Knowledge

With the foregoing picture of extensive, well-developed vocabulary knowledge, what can be said about how children might acquire vocabulary knowledge? First, it is not possible to teach children as many words a year as the 3,000 they typically learn. Moreover, because teachers usually introduce far fewer words a year, most words students learn over the course of a year cannot be acquired from direct instruction (Nagy & Herman, 1987). Instead, words must be acquired informally and outside of school, principally through voluntary reading. Incidental word learning is possible because we know that children are able to learn something about the meaning of a new word from a single exposure if the word is embedded in a context that is meaningful to students (Carey, 1982; Markman, 1984; Nagy, et al., 1985). For example,

some concepts about new words could be acquired through conversations about dinosaurs at an exhibit, from listening to a dramatic reading of *Julius Caesar*, or by reading an article about baseball. In fact, students who engage in a wide range of reading and other experiences encounter thousands of words in meaningful contexts and acquire partial knowledge for hundreds of them—one of the most profitable avenues for acquiring vocabulary knowledge (Nagy et al., 1985; Nagy, Anderson, & Herman, 1987). Therefore, it makes pedagogical sense to encourage voluntary reading and to provide instruction that enhances the likelihood that students will acquire more vocabulary knowledge on their own. Research does not show the superiority of any one particular approach to teaching students how to derive word meanings from context. Rather, what seems important is that students have ample opportunities to practice whatever strategies they are taught (Kuhn & Stahl, 1998).

By contrast, consider the common types of school activities that are meant to teach vocabulary: words and meanings to match on workbook pages, packaged programs that drill on lists of unrelated words, guessing a word meaning by reading a sentence or two, looking up lists of words in the dictionary, and brief introductions of words before students read. If the words are already known, these activities are of no help; they are busy work. If the words are not known, much more support for learning is needed. None of the activities listed above produces the kind of vocabulary knowledge that affects overall comprehension (e.g., Ahlfors, 1979; Tuinman & Brady, 1974), although some level of partial knowledge may be gained when these activities are repeated with a small number of words (Beck & McKeown, 1985; Graves, 1986). Graves and Prenn (1986) suggest that even a little knowledge may be enough for certain tasks.

Stahl (1999) suggested that how you teach a word depends on whether the word is a complex concept in itself (such as *photosynthesis* or *legislature*) or the word is a synonym for or elaboration of other, known concepts (such as *consumption* or *murmur*). For new concepts, one must engage in systematic concept building, such as providing examples and nonexamples, categories that the concept belongs in, and significant features which distinguish this concept from other members of the category. For example, for the word *legislature*, examples might include the U.S. Congress, the state legislature, the British House of Commons, and so on. Nonexamples might include a king's court or the president's Cabinet. *Legislature* belongs to the category "government bodies" or "lawmaking groups," but it is different from other government bodies because it makes laws and different from other law-making groups because it is usually elected. This can be done in class with extensive discussion. Wixson (1986) and Schwartz and Raphael (1985) both found variations of this concept-development approach to be effective.

A well-researched variation of this concept-development approach is semantic mapping (e.g., Johnson, Pittelman, Toms-Bronowski, & Levin, 1984; Johnson, Toms-Bronowski, & Pittelman, 1982; Stahl & Vancil, 1986). In semantic mapping, a class might begin by brainstorming what they know about a topic. The teacher would introduce target words in the process of this discussion. The words that are generated, both known and new, are put into a semantic map, organizing the words into categories and subcategories. Semantic feature analysis uses a grid instead of a map, but similarly forces students to classify new and known words (e.g., Johnson et al., 1982). "Possible sentences" (Stahl & Kapinus, 1991) has students generate possible sentences that might appear in a passage about a given topic using two target words.

All of these approaches involve teaching words in semantically related groups. The rationale for grouping words in semantic categories comes from studies of adult's knowledge of concepts, which suggests that words are stored in long-term semantic memory in networks (e.g., Collins & Loftus, 1975). In these models of memory, concepts are stored in nodes, which are connected to other nodes by various links, including logical relations. So a concept like *shark* might be connected to *fish*, as well as to related concepts such as *man-eating, hammerhead*, the movie *Jaws*, and so on. One can answer questions such as "Do sharks have gills?" through one's knowledge that sharks are fish, even if one does not know for a fact that sharks do have gills. Although these successful approaches all use semantic groups, there is little evidence that teaching words in groups is more effective than teaching words individually. One technique for assessing background knowledge is brainstorming and visually displaying what students know about key words/concepts (Carr, 1985; Heimlich & Pittelman, 1986). Often students know bits and pieces related to a schema (Anderson & Pearson, 1984) and have limited understanding of its scope (Bransford & Nitsch, 1978). Once students' background knowledge has been assessed, the teacher can initiate a discussion to show students how these pieces fit together and to broaden their understanding of how words/concepts belong to larger schemata (Stahl & Vancil, 1986; see Marzano & Marzano, 1988, for examples of word clusters). For example, students can be led to see how *frenzy* relates to *hysterical, excitement, calmness*, and to the more general concept of emotions in a novel; how veins not only relates to arteries, carbon dioxide, and so on, but also to the circulatory system schema in a science unit.

## Three Principles of Vocabulary Development

Because vocabulary instruction is an ongoing process, a teacher needs to be able to vary the delivery of that instruction. This involves using a variety of different approaches during the school year. Our model of effective vocabulary instruction suggests vocabulary instruction that (a) includes both definitional information and contextual information about each word's meaning, (b) involves children more actively in word learning, and (c) provides multiple exposures to meaningful information about the word. Each as discussed in turn.

***Include both definitional and contextual information.*** As noted earlier, our knowledge of a word's meaning involves more than knowing a definition. People also need to know how a word functions in different contexts. Stahl and Fairbanks (1986) found that approaches providing only definitional information did not significantly affect children's reading comprehension. In contrast, methods that provided both definitional and contextual information did significantly improve comprehension.

Some things that a teacher might do to provide definitional information include teaching synonyms, antonyms, rewriting definitions, or discussing the difference between the new word and related, known words. Despite their ubiquity, definitions themselves are problematic for vocabulary learning. Children have a difficult time understanding conventional definitions (McKeown, 1993; J. A. Scott & Nagy, 1997), so giving children a list of words to define is more likely to produce misunderstandings than accurate knowledge (Miller & Gildea, 1987). This "definition-first" strategy has not been proven effective in improving comprehension (Stahl & Fairbanks, 1986). The way dictionaries are conventionally used, looking up words encountered in a text, has been found to be an effective strategy. Nist and Olejnik (1995) found that providing an adequate definition after a student reads a word in context was effective in teaching word meanings.

A teacher could provide contextual information by having students create sentences containing the target word, discussing the meaning of the same word in different sentences (Stahl, 1983), "Silly questions" (Beck, Perfetti, & McKeown, 1982) which involve pairing the words being taught and creating a question out of each pair, and so on.

***Involve children in actively processing new word meanings.*** A second principle of effective vocabulary instruction relates to how active students are at constructing links between new information and previously known information. Children remember more information when they are performing cognitive operations on that information (Craik & Tulving, 1975). Such operations might include relating it to known information, transforming it in their own words, generating examples, nonexamples, antonyms, synonyms, and so forth. Stahl and Fairbanks (1986) developed a scale of processing useful for evaluating vocabulary instructional programs:

Association processing involves the rote memorization of an association between a word and its meaning or between a word and a single context.

Comprehension processing in which the child demonstrates comprehension of an association by reading it in a sentence or by doing something with the definitional information, such as finding an antonym, classifying words, etc.

Generative processing in which the child takes the information learned and creates a new product or a novel response to the word, including creating a sentence which fully expresses the word's meaning, restating a definition in one's own words, etc.

This product could be written or oral. Stahl and Fairbanks (1986) found that generative processing led to better retention of word meanings, but the effects on comprehension were not as clear. Generative processing did lead to improvements in comprehension but only when children were given multiple exposures to different information about word meanings.

A series of studies examining the effects of generative processing with multiple exposures was conducted by Beck and her colleagues (Beck et al., 1982; McKeown, Beck, Omanson, & Perfetti, 1983; McKeown, Beck, Omanson, & Pople, 1985).

Lessons in the Beck et al. (1982) study, for example, were conducted in a 5-day cycle. On the 1st day, words were defined. Then students discussed how each word was used in context. This discussion could take a number of different forms, including discussion of examples and nonexamples, pantomimes, or having students say "Yea" if the word was used correctly in a sentence or "Boo" if it was not. On the 2nd day, after a review of the definitions, students might work on log sheets, completing sentences for each word. On the 3rd day, students would complete another worksheet with the vocabulary words and then work on a Ready, Set, Go activity. This was a timed activity in which pairs of students attempted to match the words with their definitions in the shortest amount of time. This activity was repeated on the 4th day. After completion of the second Ready, Set, Go activity, students were asked silly questions pairing two of the concepts together such as "Can a virtuoso also be a rival?" On the 5th day, students took a posttest.

These are only examples of activities, which varied somewhat with different units. Students also completed a "Word Wizard" activity each day. They were given credit toward becoming a Word Wizard by finding examples of each word used outside of class.

This program, or variations of it, was found to significantly improve student's comprehension of text containing words that were taught. In addition, McKeown et al. (1985) found that 12 encounters with a word reliably improved comprehension, but 4 encounters did not. They also found that their approach, which involved active processing of each word's meaning, had significantly greater effects than the definition-only approach on measures of comprehension but not on measures involving the recall of definitions. Thus, their research suggest that vocabulary instruction can improve comprehension, but only if the instruction is rich and extensive, and includes a great many encounters with to-be-learned words.

***Use discussion to actively teach word meanings.*** Discussion adds an important dimension to vocabulary instruction. First of all, children benefit from the contributions of other children. It is our experience that children who enter a vocabulary lesson without any knowledge of a target word seem to learn a great deal from their peers, who may have partial or even fairly good knowledge of the word. We have found that in open discussions, children are often able to construct a good idea of a word's meaning from the partial knowledge of the class as a whole. (When the class as a whole does not know much about a word, however, we have had to interject some information about the word, such as a quick definition.)

Discussion can clarify misunderstandings, by making them public. For words that a child partially knows, or knows in one particular context, a give-and-take discussion can clarify meanings. When misunderstandings are public, the teacher can correct these notions and move understanding toward conventional meaning.

In addition, discussion seems to involve children in other ways. While waiting to be called on, students practice or prepare a response to themselves. Even though only one child is called upon, many children anticipate having to come up with an answer. Because many children are practicing a response covertly, discussion seems to lead to increased vocabulary learning (Stahl & Clark, 1987). Because of the importance of having all children expect that they may be called on, teachers should allow all children in the class some think time before calling on one individual. Also, a teacher should be sensitive to his or her patterns of calling on children, avoiding just calling on the "fast" students. If a child does not think that he or she will be called on, that child will not practice a response. Without the practiced response, discussion is not as valuable a learning experience (see Alvermann, Dillon, & O'Brien, 1987).

### Limitations

Although vocabulary instruction does seem to significantly improve comprehension, at least when the words being taught are in the text, there are some limitations. Teaching vocabulary can, under certain circumstances, distract a reader from the main ideas in the text. One study found that teaching words that were associated with low level information encouraged students to focus on that information. Because students were focusing on unimportant details, they were not as good at recalling important information as students who did not receive vocabulary instruction (Wixson, 1986). Thus, it is important that a teacher choose words important to the ideas in a text, rather than words that may be interesting but not central to the main ideas of a story or passage.

The final instructional principle is that not all words in a text can or should be taught. Students must have the opportunity to apply what they understand about the topic at hand and aspects of the English language just outlined to figure out meanings of unfamiliar words in meaningful contexts. One such context is after reading a story. Students look back, identify a new word and, under the guidance of the teacher, reason about its meaning (for an example, see Duffy, Roehler, & Rackliffe, 1986; Herman & Dole, 1988 ).

Above all, students who have become infected with a love for and fascination with words possess a key ingredient in continuing to develop vocabulary knowledge (Deighton, 1960; McKeown et al., 1983). In fact, "establishing motivation and desire to acquire new vocabulary is at the very heart of vocabulary acquisition" (Ruddell, 1986, p. 587) and within the inspirational power of teachers.

## CONCLUSION

Implications of current research on the topics of word identification and vocabulary knowledge have two characteristics in common. The first is that children's learning should be viewed in the context of their overall development in literacy. Learning is cumulative and interrelated, not disjointed. Young children's understanding affects later acquisition, and acquisition generally takes place in informal as well as formal instructional settings, proceeding best when reading and writing activities are meaningful. In our view, the research supports instructional activities with a broad focus rather than a narrow one, so children can read or attempt to read and understand many words in a number of text contexts and learn to apply varying strategies for recognition and understanding.

The second characteristic is that word identification ability and vocabulary knowledge involve an appreciation of the regularity of the English language. We hope we have succeeded in communicating that understanding the systematic nature of English is not a trivial task. Many strategies are needed for identifying words and for building vocabulary knowledge. Simple processes of memorization, letter–sound associations, or word meanings are not sufficient and cannot form the basis for skilled performance. It follows, then, as the research shows and as we have portrayed in this chapter, that instruction must also be better tuned to children's existing knowledge than was previously assumed. Quite varied formal as well as informal instruction is required so that children have opportunities to rely on lower and higher order thinking skills, including rapid recognition of printed words and inference of their meanings, analysis and synthesis of words into sounds and morphemes, rule-constructing and generalization of those rules to new and related words. Word identification and vocabulary knowledge may be "basic" skills, but they are far from being simple or simply taught.

# References

Adams, M. J. (1990). *Beginning to read: Thinking and learning about print.* Cambridge, MA: MIT Press.

Ahlfors, G. (1979). *Learning word meanings: A comparison of three instructional procedures.* Unpublished doctoral dissertation, University of Minnesota.

Allen, J. B. (1989). Reading and writing development in whole language kindergartens. In J. Mason (Ed.), *Reading and writing connections* (pp. 121–146). Needham Heights, MA: Allyn & Bacon.

Allen, J. B., & Mason, J. (1989). *Risk makers, risk takers, risk breakers: Reducing the risks for young literacy learners.* Portsmouth, NH: Heinemann.

Alvermann, D. E., Dillon, D. R., & O'Brien, D. G. (1987). *Using discussion to promote reading comprehension.* Newark, DE: International Reading Association.

Anderson, R. C., & Freebody, P. (1981). Vocabulary knowledge. In J. T. Guthrie (Ed.), *Comprehension and teaching: Research reviews* (pp. 77–117). Newark, DE: International Reading Association.

Anderson, R. C., Hiebert, E. F., Wilkinson, I. A. G., & Scott, J. (1985). *Becoming a nation of readers.* Champaign, IL: National Academy of Education and Center for the Study of Reading.

Anderson, R. C., & Nagy, W. E. (1991). Word meanings. In R. Barr, M. L. Kamil, P. Mosenthal, & P. D. Pearson (Eds.), *Handbook of Reading Research* (Vol. 2). White Plains, NY: Longman.

Anderson, R. C., & Pearson, P. D. (1984). A schema-theoretic view of basic processes in reading. In P. D. Pearson (Ed.), *Handbook of reading research* (pp. 255–292). White Plains, NY: Longman.

Anderson, R. C., Wilson, P. T., & Fielding, L. G. (1988). Growth in reading and how children spend their time outside of school. *Reading Research Quarterly, 23*, 285–303.

Baker, L., & Brown, A. L. (1984). Metacognitive skills and reading. In P. D. Pearson (Ed.), *Handbook of reading research* (pp. 353–394). White Plains, NY: Longman.

Baker, L., Fernandez-Fein, S., Scher, D., & Williams, H. (1998). Home experiences related to the development of word recognition. In J. Metsala & L. Ehri (Eds.), *Word recognition in beginning literacy* (pp. 263–287). Mahwah, NJ: Lawrence Erlbaum Associates.

Bear, D. R., & Barone, D. (1989). Using children's spellings to group for word study and directed reading in the primary classroom. *Reading Psychology, 10*, 275–292.

Bear, D. R., Invernizzi, M., Templeton, S., & Johnston, F. (2000). *Words their way: Word study for phonics, vocabulary and spelling instruction* (2nd ed.). Upper Saddle River, NJ: Merrill.

Beck, I. L., & McKeown, M. G. (1985). Teaching vocabulary: Making the instruction fit the goal. *Educational Perspectives, 23*, 11–15.

Beck, I. L., Perfetti, C. A., & McKeown, M. G. (1982). Effects of long-term vocabulary instruction on lexical access and reading comprehension. *Journal of Educational Psychology, 74*, 506–521.

Bissex, G. L. (1980). *GYNS at work: A child learns to read and write.* Cambridge, MA: Harvard University Press.

Bradley, L., & Bryant, P. E. (1983). Categorizing sounds and learning to read—A causal connection. *Nature, 301*, 419–421.

Bransford, J. D., & Nitsch, K. (1978). Coming to understand things we could not previously understand. In J. Kavanaugh & W. Strange (Eds.), *Speech and language in the laboratory, school, and clinic* (pp. 267–327). Cambridge, MA: MIT Press.

Brown, A. L. (1985). *Teaching students to think as they read: Implications for curriculum reform* (Reading Education Rep. 58). Champaign: University of Illinois, Center for the Study of Reading.

Brown, J. S., Collins, A., & Duguid, P. (1989). Situated cognition and the culture of learning. *Educational Researcher, 18*(1), 32–42.

Brugelmann, H. (1986). *No future for graded reading schemes.* Paper presented at the 11th International Reading Association World Congress, London.

Burgess, S. (in press). The relationships between phonological sensitivity, home environment, and early reading behaviors. *Reading and Writing: An Interdisciplinary Journal.*

Bus, A. G. (1999). Phonological awareness and early reading: A meta-analysis of experimental training studies. *Journal of Educational Psychology, 91*, 403–414.

Byrne, B. (1999). *The foundation of literacy: The child's acquisition of the alphabetic principle.* East Sussex, England: Psychology Press.

Calfee, R. C., Lindamood, P., & Lindamood, C. (1973). Acoustic-phonetic skills and reading: Kindergarten through twelfth grade. *Journal of Educational Psychology, 64*, 293–298.

Carey, S. (1982). Semantic development: The state of the art. In W. Wanner & L. Gleitman (Eds.), *Language acquisition: The state of the art* (pp. 345–489). New York: Cambridge University Press.

Carr, E. (1985). The vocabulary overview guide: A metacognitive approach to improve vocabulary, comprehension, and retention. *Journal of Reading, 28*, 588–595.

Carroll, J. B. (1964). Words, meanings, and concept. *Harvard Educational Review, 34*(2), 178–202.

Carver, R. P. (1993). Merging the simple view of reading with rauding theory. *Journal of Reading Behavior, 25*, 439–455.

Chall, J. S. (1996). *Stages of reading development* (2nd ed.). Fort Worth, TX: Harcourt-Brace.

Clarke, L. K. (1988). Encouraging invented spelling in first graders' writing: Effects on learning to spell and read. *Research in the Teaching of English, 22*, 281–309.

Clay, M. M. (1985). *The early detection of reading difficulties.* Portsmouth, NH: Heinemann.

Clay, M. M. (1993). *An observation survey of early literacy achievement*. Portsmouth, NH: Heinemann.

Collins, A. M., & Loftus, E. E. (1975). A spreading activation theory of semantic processing. *Psychological Review, 82,* 407-428.

Craik, F. I. M., & Tulving, E. (1975). Depth of processing and the retention of words in episodic memory. *Journal of Experimental Psychology: General, 104,* 268-294.

Crowell, D., Kawakami, A., & Wong, J. (1986). Emerging literacy: Experiences in a kindergarten classroom. *The Reading Teacher, 40,* 144-149.

Cunningham, P. M., Hall, D. P., & Defee, M. (1991). Non-ability grouped, multilevel instruction: a year in a first grade classroom. *The Reading Teacher, 44,* 566-571.

Cunningham, P. M., Hall, D. P., & Defee, M. (1998). Nonability-grouped, multimethod instruction: Eight years later. *The Reading Teacher, 51,* 652-664.

D'Anna, C. A., Zechmeister, E. B., & Hall, J. W. (1991). Toward a meaningful definition of vocabulary size. *Journal of Reading Behavior, 23,* 109-122.

Davis, F. B. (1944). Fundamental factors of comprehension in reading. *Psychometrika, 9,* 185-197.

Davis, F. B. (1968). Research on comprehension in reading. *Reading Research Quarterly, 3,* 499-544.

Deighton, L. (1960). Developing vocabulary: Another look at the problem. *English Journal, 49,* 82-87.

Doake, D. (1985). Reading-like behavior: Its role in learning to read. In A. Jaggar & M. T. Smith-Burke (Eds.), *Observing the language learner* (pp. 82-98). Newark, DE: International Reading Association.

Dobson, L. (1989). Connections in learning to write and read: A study of children's development through kindergarten and first grade. In J. Mason (Ed.), *Reading and writing connections* (pp. 83-104). Needham Heights, MA: Allyn & Bacon.

Duffy, G., Roehler, L., & Rackliffe, G. (1986). How teachers' instructional talk influences students' understanding of lesson content. *Elementary School Journal, 87,* 3-16.

Durkin, D. (1978-79). What classroom observations reveal about reading comprehension instruction. *Reading Research Quarterly, 14,* 481-533.

Egan, K. (1987). Literacy and the oral foundations of education. *Harvard Educational Review, 57,* 445-472.

Ehri, L. (2000). Alphabetics, *Report of the National Reading Panel*. Washington, DC: National Reading Panel.

Ehri, L. C. (1995). Phases of development in learning to read words by sight. *Journal of Research in Reading, 18,* 116-125.

Ehri, L. C. (1997). Learning to read and learning to spell are one and the same, almost. In C. A. Perfetti & L. Rieben (Eds.), *Learning to spell: Research, theory, and practice across languages* (pp. 237-268). Mahwah, NJ: Lawrence Erlbaum Associates.

Ehri, L. C. (1998). Grapheme-Phoneme knowledge is essential for learning to read words in English. In J. L. Metsala & L. C. Ehri (Eds.), *Word recognition in beginning literacy* (pp. 3-40). Mahwah, NJ: Lawrence Erlbaum Associates.

Ehri, L. C., & Robbins, C. (1992). Beginners need some decoding skill to read words by analogy. *Reading Research Quarterly, 27,* 12-26.

Ehri, L. C., & Wilce, L. S. (1985). Movement into reading: Is the first stage of printed word learning visual or phonetic? *Reading Research Quarterly, 20,* 163-179.

Ehri, L. C., & Wilce, L. S. (1987). Does learning to spell help beginners learn to read words? *Reading Research Quarterly, 22,* 47-65.

Ellis, N. C. (1997). Vocabulary acquisition: Word struccture, collocation, word-class, and meaning. In N. Schmitt & M. McCarthy (Eds.), *Vocabulary: Description, acquisition and pedagogy* (pp. 122-139). Cambridge, England: Cambridge University Press.

Elshout-Mohr, M., & van Daalen-Kapteijns, M. M. (1987). Cognitive processes in learning word meanings. In M. G. McKeown & M. E. Curtis (Eds.), *The nature of vocabulary acquisition* (pp. 53-72). Hillsdale, NJ: Lawrence Erlbaum Associates.

Fodor, J. A., Garrett, M. F., Walker, E. C., & Parkes, C. H. (1980). Against definitions. *Cognition, 8,* 283-367.

Fountas, I. C., & Pinnell, G. S. (1996). *Guided reading: Good first teaching for all children*. Portsmouth, NH: Heinemann.

Francis, H. (1977). Reading abilities and disabilities: Children's strategies in learning to read. *British Journal of Educational Psychology, 47,* 117-125.

Gaskins, I. W., Ehri, L. C., Cress, C., O'Hara, C., & Donnelly, K. (1996). Procedures for word learning: Making discoveries about words. *The Reading Teacher, 50,* 312-328.

Gates, A., & Bocker, E. (1923). A study of initial stages in reading by preschool children. *Teacher's College Record, 24,* 469-688.

Gillet, J. W., & Temple, C. (1990). *Understanding reading problems* (3rd ed.). Glenview, IL: Scott, Foresman.

Glushko, R. J. (1981). Principles for pronouncing print: The psychology of phonology. In A. Lesgold & C. Perfetti (Eds.), *Interactive processes in reading* (pp. 61-84). Hillsdale, NJ: Lawrence Erlbaum Associates.

Goswami, U. (1998). The role of analogies in the development of word recognition. In J. Metsala & L. Ehri (Eds.), *Word recognition in beginning literacy* (pp. 41-64). Mahwah, NJ: Lawrence Erlbaum Associates.

Gough, P. B., Juel, C., & Griffith, P. L. (1992). Reading, spelling, and the orthographic cipher. In P. B. Gough, L. C. Ehri, R. Treiman (Eds.), *Reading acquisition* (pp. 35-48). Hillsdale, NJ: Lawrence Erlbaum Associates.

Gough, P. B., & Tumner, W. E. (1986). Decoding, reading, and reading disability. *Remedial and Special Education, 7,* 6-10.

Gouldman, R., Nation, P., & Read, J. (1990). How large can a receptive vocabulary be? *Applied Linguistics, 11,* 341-363.

Graves, M. F. (1986). Vocabulary learning and instruction. In E. Z. Rothkopf (Ed.), *Review of Research in Education* (Vol. 13, pp. 49-91). Washington, DC: American Educational Research Association.

Graves, M. F., & Prenn, M. C. (1986). Costs and benefits of various methods of teaching vocabulary. *Journal of Reading, 29,* 596-602.

Harris, A. J., & Sipay, E. (1990). *How to increase reading ability* (10th ed.). White Plains, NY: Longman.

Harste, J. C., Burke, C. L., & Woodward, V. A. (1982). Children's language and world: Initial encounters with print. In J. A. Langer & M. T. Smith-Burke (Eds.), *Reader meets author/Bridging the gap* (pp. 105-131). Newark, DE: International Reading Association.

Heath, S. B. (1983). *Ways with words*. Cambridge, England: Cambridge University Press.

Heibeck, T. H., & Markman, E. M. (1987). Word learning in children: An examination of fast mapping. *Child Development, 58,* 1021-1034.

Heimlich, J. E., & Pittelman, S. D. (1986). *Semantic mapping: Classroom applications*. Newark, DE: International Reading Association.

Herman, P. A., & Dole, J. (1988). Theory and practice in vocabulary learning. *Elementary School Journal, 89,* 41-52.

Herman, P. A., & Weaver, R. (1988). *Contextual strategies for learning word meanings: Middle grade students look in, look out*. Paper presented at annual meeting of the National Reading Conference. Tucson, AZ.

Hirsh, D., & Nation, P. (1992). What vocabulary size is needed to read unsimplified texts for pleasure? *Reading in a Foreign Language, 8,* 689-696.

Johnson, D. D., & Pearson, P. D. (1978). *Teaching reading comprehension*. New York: Holt, Rinehart, & Winston.

Johnson, D. D., Pittelman, S. D., Toms-Bronowski, S., & Levin, K. M. (1984). An investigation of the effects of prior knowledge and vocabulary acquisition on passage comprehension (Program Report 84-5). Madison, WI: University of Wisconsin, Wisconsin Center for Educational Research.

Johnson, D. D., Toms-Bronowski, S., & Pittelman, S. D. (1982). *An investigation of the effectiveness of semantic mapping and semantic feature analysis with intermediate grade children (Program Report 83-3).* Madison, WI: University of Wisconsin, Wisconsin Center for Educational Research.

Kuhn, M. R., & Stahl, S. A. (1998). Teaching children to learn word meanings from context: A synthesis and some questions. *Journal of Literacy Research, 30,* 119-138.

Lartz, M., & Mason, J. (1988). Jamie: One child's journey from oral to written language. *Early childhood Research Quarterly, 3,* 193-208.

Liberman, I., & Shankweiler, D. (1985). Phonology and the problems of learning to read. *Remedial and Special Education, 6*(6), 8-17.

Lorge, I., & Chall, J. S. (1963). Estimating the size of vocabularies of children and adults: An analysis of methodological issues. *Journal of Experimental Education, 32*(2), 147-157.

Lundberg, I., Frost, J., & Peterson, O.-P. (1988). Effects of an extensive program for stimulating phonological awareness in preschool children. *Reading Research Quarterly, 23,* 263-284.

Maclean, M., Bryant, P., & Bradley, L. (1987). Rhymes, nursery rhymes, and reading in early childhood. *Merrill-Palmer Quarterly, 33,* 255-281.

Markman, E. M. (1984). *How children constrain the possible meanings of words.* Unpublished manuscript, Stanford University, Stanford, CA.

Marzano, R., & Marzano, J. (1988). *A cluster approach to elementary vocabulary instruction.* Newark, DE: International Reading Association.

Mason, J. (1980). When do children begin to read? *Reading Research Quarterly, 15,* 203-227.

Mason, J. (1984). A question about reading comprehension instruction. In G. Duffy, L. Roehler, & J. Mason (Eds.), *Comprehension instruction: Perspectives and suggestions* (pp. 39-56). New York: Longman.

Mason, J., & Au, K. (1990). *Reading instruction for today.* Glenview, IL: Scott, Foresman.

Mason, J., & Stewart, J. (1989). Testing emergent literacy in kindergarten. In L. Morrow & J. Smith (Eds.), *Assessment for instruction in early literacy* (pp. 155-175). Englewood Cliffs, NJ: Prentice-Hall.

Masonheimer, P. E., Drum, P. A., & Ehri, L. C. (1984). Does environmental print identification lead children into word reading? *Journal of Reading Behavior, 16,* 257-271.

McConkie, G., & Zola, D. (1987). Visual attention during eye fixations while reading. In M. Coltheart (Ed.), *Attention and performance XII: The psychology of reading.* Hillsdale, NJ: Lawrence Erlbaum Associates.

McKeown, M. G. (1985). The acquisition of word meaning from the context by children of high and low ability. *Reading Research Quarterly, 20,* 482-496.

McKeown, M. G. (1993). Creating effective definitions for young word learners. *Reading Research Quarterly, 27,* 16-31.

McKeown, M. G., Beck, I. L., Omanson, R. C., & Perfetti, C. A. (1983). The effects of long-term vocabary instruction on reading comprehension: A replication. *15*(1), 3-18.

McKeown, M. G., Beck, I. L., Omanson, R. C., & Pople, M. T. (1985). Some effects of the nature and frequency of vocabulary instruction on the knowledge and use of words. *20,* 522-535.

Miller, G. (1986). Dictionaries in the mind. *Language and Cognitive Processes, 1,* 171-185.

Miller, G., & Gildea, P. (1987). How children learn words. *Scientific American, 257*(3), 94-99.

Murray, B. A., Stahl, S. A., & Ivey, M. G. (1996). Developing phoneme awareness through alphabet books. *Reading and writing: An interdisciplinary Journal, 8,* 307-322.

Nagy, W. E. (1988). *Teaching vocabulary to improve reading comprehension.* Newark, DE: International Reading Association.

Nagy, W. E., & Anderson, R. C. (1984). How many words are there in printed school English? *Reading Research Quarterly, 19,* 304-330.

Nagy, W. E., Anderson, R. C., & Herman, P. A. (1987). Learning word meanings from context during normal reading. *American Educational Research Journal, 24,* 237-270.

Nagy, W. E., & Gentner, D. (1987). *Semantic constraints on lexical categories* (Tech. Rep. 413): Champaign: University of Illinois, Center for the Study of Reading.

Nagy, W. E., & Herman, P. A. (1987). Breadth and depth of vocabulary knowledge: Implications for acquisition and instruction. In M. G. McKeown & M. E. Curtis (Eds.), *The nature of vocabulary acquisition* (pp. 19-36). Hillsdale, NJ: Lawrence Erlbaum Associates.

Nagy, W. E., Herman, P. A., & Anderson, R. C. (1985). Learning words from context. *Reading Research Quarterly, 20,* 233-253.

Nagy, W. E., Scott, J., Schommer, M., & Anderson, R. C. (1987). *Word schemas: What do people know about words they don't know?* Paper presented at the National Reading Conference, St. Petersburg Beach, FL.

Nation, P., & Waring, R. (1997). Vocabulary size, text coverage, and word lists. In N. Schmitt & M. McCarthy (Eds.), *Vocabulary: Description, acquisition and pedagogy* (pp. 6-19). Cambridge, England: Cambridge University Press.

Nist, S. L., & Olejnik, S. (1995). The role of context and dictionary definitions on varying levels of word knowledge. *Reading Research Quarterly, 30,* 172-193.

Olson, D. (1984). "See! Jumping!" Some oral language antecedents of literacy. In H. Goelman, A. Oberg, & F. Smith (Eds.), *Awakeing to literacy* (pp. 185-192). Portsmouth, NH: Heinemann.

Peterman, C., & Mason, J. (1984). *Kindergarten children's perceptions of the forms of print in labelled pictures and stories.* Paper presented at the National Reading Conference, St. Petersburg, FL.

Plaut, D. C. (1997). Structure and function in the lexical system: Insights from distributed models of word reading and lexical decision. *Language and Cognitive Processes, 12*(5-6), 765-805.

Plaut, D. C., McClelland, J. C., & Seidenberg, M. S. (1995). Reading exception words and pseudowords: Are two routes really necessary? In J. P. Levy & D. Bairaktaris (Eds.), *Connectionist models of memory and language* (pp. 145-159). London: Ucl Press.

Pressley, M., Wharton-McDonald, R., & Mistretta, J. (1998). Effective beginning literacy instruction: Dialectical, scaffolded, and contextualized. In J. Metsala & L. Ehri (Eds.), *Word recognition in beginning literacy* (pp. 357-373). Mahwah, NJ: Lawrence Erlbaum Associates.

Rayner, K., & Pollatsek, A. (1989). *The psychology of reading.* Englewood Cliffs, NJ: Prentice-Hall.

Rice, M. L., Buhr, J. C., & Nemeth, M. (1990). Fast mapping word-learning abilities of language-delayed preschoolers. *Journal of Speech and Hearing Disorders, 55,* 33-42.

Ruddell, R. (1986). Vocabulary learning: A process model and criteria for evaluating instructional strategies. *Journal of Reading, 29,* 581-587.

Schwanenflugel, P. J., Stahl, S. A., & McFalls, E. L. (1997). *Partial word knowledge and vocabulary growth during reading comprehension.* Athens, GA: National Reading Research Center.

Schwartz, R. M., & Raphael, T. (1985). Concept of definition: A key to improving students' vocabulary. *The Reading Teacher, 39,* 198-203.

Scott, J., & Nagy, W. E. (2000). Vocabulary development. In M. Kamil, R. Barr, P. Mosenthal, & P. D. Pearson (Eds.), *Handbook of reading research* (Vol. 3). Mahwah, NJ: Lawrence Erlbaum Associates.

Scott, J. A., & Nagy, W. E. (1997). Understanding the definitions of unfamiliar verbs. *Reading Research Quarterly, 32,* 184-200.

Simon, H., & Leu, D. (1987). The use of contextual and graphic information in word recognition by second-, fourth- and sixth-grade readers. *Journal of Reading Behavior, 19,* 33-47.

Smith, E. E., & Medin, D. (1981). *Categories and concepts.* Cambridge, MA: Harvard University Press.

Stahl, S. A. (1983). Differential word knowledge and reading comprehension. *Journal of Reading Behavior, 15*(4), 33-50.

Stahl, S. A. (1999). *Vocabulary development.* Cambridge, MA: Brookline.

Stahl, S. A., Burdge, J. L., Machuga, M. B., & Stecyk, S. (1992). The effects of semantic grouping on learning word meanings. *Reading Psychology, 13,* 19-35.

Stahl, S. A., & Clark, C. H. (1987). The effects of participatory expectations in classroom discussion on the learning of science vocabulary. *American Educational Research Journal, 24,* 541-556.

Stahl, S. A., Duffy-Hester, A. M., & Stahl, K. A. D. (1998). Everything you wanted to know about phonics (but were afraid to ask). *Reading Research Quarterly, 35,* 338-355.

Stahl, S. A., & Fairbanks, M. M. (1986). The effects of vocabulary instruction: A model-based meta-analysis. *Review of Educational Research, 56*(1), 72-110.

Stahl, S. A., & Kapinus, B. A. (1991). Possible sentences: Predicting word meanings to teach content area vocabulary. *The Reading Teacher, 45,* 36-45.

Stahl, S. A., & Murray, B. A. (1993). Environmental print, phonemic awareness, letter recognition, and word recognition. In *Forty-second yearbook of the National Reading Conference* (Vol. 42, pp. 227-233).

Stahl, S. A., & Murray, B. A. (1994). Defining phonological awareness and its relationship to early reading. *Journal of Educational Psychology, 86,* 221-234.

Stahl, S. A., Rinehart, S. D., & Erickson, L. G. (1986). Detection of inconsistencies by above and below average reflective and impulsive sixth graders. *Journal of Educational Research, 79*(3), 185-189.

Stahl, S. A., & Vancil, S. J. (1986). Discussion is what makes semantic maps work. *The Reading Teacher, 40,* 62-67.

Stanovich, K. E. (1984). The interactive-compensatory model of reading: A confluence of developmental, experimental, and educational psychology. *Remedial and Special Education, 5*(3), 11-19.

Stanovich, K. E. (1993-94). Romance and reality. *The Reading Teacher, 47,* 280-291.

Stanovich, K. E., & Cunningham, A. (1992). Studying the consequences of literacy within a literate society: The cognitive correlates of print exposure. *Memory and Language, 20,* 51-88.

Stanovich, K. E., Cunningham, A., & Cramer, B. (1984). Assessing phonological awareness in kindergarten children: Issues of task compatitibity. *Journal of Experimental Child Psychology, 38,* 175-190.

Stanovich, K. E., Cunningham, A., & Feeman, D. (1984). Relation between early reading acquisition and word decoding with and

without context: A longitudinal study of first-grade children. *Journal of Educational Psychology, 76,* 668-677.

Sternberg, R. J. (1987). Most words are learned from context. In M. G. McKeown & M. E. Curtis (Eds.), *The acquisition of word meanings* (pp. 89-106). Hillsdale, NJ: Lawrence Erlbaum Associates.

Sternberg, R. J., & Powell, J. S. (1983). Comprehending verbal comprehension. *American Psychologist, 38,* 878-893.

Swanborn, M. S. L., & Glopper, K. D. (1999). Incidental word learning while reading: A meta-analysis. *Review of Educational Research, 69,* 261-285.

Taylor, B., Pearson, P. D., Clark, K., & Walpole, S. (1999). *Schools that beat the odds* (Research Report 2-008). Ann Arbor: University of Michigan, Center for the Improvement of Early Reading Achievement.

Taylor, D. (1983). *Family literacy.* Exeter, NH: Heinemann.

Treiman, R. (1992). The role of intersyllabic units in learning to read and spell. In P. B. Gough, L. C. Ehri, & R. Treiman (Eds.), *Reading Acquisition* (pp. 85-106). Hillsdale, NJ: Lawrence Erlbaum Associates.

Treiman, R., & Caesar, M. (1997). Spelling acquisition in English. In C. A. Perfetti, L. Rieben, & M. Fayol (Eds.), *Learning to Spell: Research, theory, and practice across languages* (pp. 61-80). Mahwah, NJ: Lawrence Erlbaum Associates.

Tuinman, J., & Brady, M. (1974). How does voabulary account fo variance on reading comprehension tests: A preliminary instructional analysis. *Twenty-third yearbook of the National Reading Conference* (Vol. 23). Clemson, SC: National Reading Conference.

Tumner, W. E., Herriman, M. L., & Nesdale, A. R. (1988). Metalinguistic abilities and beginning reading. *Reading Research Quarterly, 23,* 134-158.

Underwood, G. (1985). Information porcessing in skileld readers. In G. MacKinnon & T. G. Waller (Eds.), *Reading reserach, advances in theory and practice* (Vol. 4, pp. 139-181). New York: Academic Press.

Wharton-McDonald, R., Pressley, M., & Hampston, J. M. (1998). Literacy instruction in nine first-grade classrooms: Teacher characteristics and student achievement. *Elementary School Journal, 99,* 101-128.

White, T. G., Graves, M. F., & Slater, W. H. (1990). Growth of reading vocabulary in diverse elementary schools: Decoding and word meaning. *Journal of Educational Psychology, 82,* 281-290.

Wixson, K. K. (1986). Vocabulary Instruction and Children's Comprehension of Basal Stories. *Reading Research Quarterly, 21*(3), 317-329.

Yaden, D. B., Smolkin, L. B., & MacGillivray, L. (1993). A psychogenetic perspective on children's understanding about letter associations during alphabet book readers. *Journal of Reading Behavior, 25,* 43-68.

Yopp, H. K. (1988). The validity and reliability of phonemic awareness tests. *Reading Research Quarterly, 23,* 159-177.

Yussen, S. R., & Ozcan, N. M. (1996). The development of knowledge about narratives. *Issues in Education, 2,* 1-68.

Zutell, J., & Rasinkski, T. (1989). Reading and spelling connections in third and fifth grade students. *Reading Psychology, 10,* 137-155.

# READING COMPREHENSION INSTRUCTION

## James Flood, Diane Lapp, and Douglas Fisher
### San Diego State University

In the past few years, a great deal has been written about "state-of-the-art" reading comprehension instructional practices (Ezell, Hunsicker, Quinque, & Randolph, 1996; Kamhi, 1997; Keene & Zimmermann, 1997; Klinger, Vaughn, & Schumm, 1998; Kincade, 1996; Rasinski & Padak, 1998). During this same time, the curriculum has been challenged, expanded, and broadened. Changes such as literature-based social studies and science (e.g., McGowan & Guzzetti, 1991), issues-centered curriculum (e.g., Evans, 1997), and thematic units (e.g., Lapp & Flood, 1994) have become significant foci in the field. Teachers have been challenged to develop interdisciplinary units and access numerous narrative and nonnarrative texts while responding to district and state standards. Regardless of the curriculum, teachers want students to gain information from texts and use that knowledge in a variety of ways.

Researchers in the area of reading comprehension generally maintain that comprehension instruction is dependent on the interaction of four sets of critical variables: (a) reader variables (age, ability, affect, motivation), (b) text variables (genres, type, features, considerateness), (c) educational-context variables (environment, task, social grouping, purpose), and (d) teacher variables (knowledge, experience, attitude, and pedagogical approach). Without taking each of these key variables into consideration, an adequate explanation of effective comprehension instruction is impossible.

In this chapter, each of these sets of variables are discussed as they relate to researchers' most current understanding of effective comprehension instruction. The chapter is divided into two major sections: (a) what researchers know about the competent comprehender and (b) what researchers know about instructing for competent comprehension.

## WHAT RESEARCHERS KNOW ABOUT THE COMPETENT COMPREHENDER

Although research in reading comprehension instruction is incomplete and still developing, most educators agree that competent comprehenders exhibit a set of discernible characteristics. Researchers have found that competent readers actively construct meaning through an integrative process in which they "interact" and "transact" with the words on the page, integrating new information with preexisting knowledge structures (Fielding & Pearson, 1994; Kucan & Beck, 1997; Lapp & Flood, 1992; Rosenblatt, 1938, 1982; see also Chapter 7, this volume). Furthermore, a reader's prior knowledge, experience, attitude, and perspective determine the ways that information is perceived, understood, valued, and stored (Emery, 1996; Gaskins, 1996; Gavelek & Raphael, 1996; Squire, 1983).

### The Competent Comprehender: A Strategic Reader

Good readers are strategic readers who actively construct meaning as they read; they are self-motivated and self-directed; they monitor their own comprehension by questioning, reviewing, revising, and rereading to enhance their overall comprehension (Beck, McKeown, Sandora, Kukan, & Worthy, 1996; Bryant, Uygel, Thompson, & Hamff, 1999; Lin, Zabrucky, & Moore, 1997; Loranger, 1997). Good readers have learned that it is the *reader* in the reading process who creates meaning, not the text or even the author of the text. As Rosenblatt (1938) noted:

The same text will have a very different meaning and value to us at different times or under different circumstances. Some state of mind, a worry, a temperamental bias, or a contemporary social crisis may make us either especially receptive or especially impervious to what the work offers. Without an understanding of the reader, one cannot predict what particular text may be significant to him or what may be the special quality of his experience. (p. 35)

There is some agreement among contemporary researchers about the mental processes that readers engage in while reading. Most agree that reading is essentially a thinking activity in which the reader engages in a series of complex processes (Anderson & Roit, 1996; Chan, 1996; Crain-Thoreson, Lippman,

& McClendon-Magnuson, 1997). First the reader previews the text by noting its general features (print size, pictures, headings); then, as reading begins, five different kinds of knowledge are used by the reader to process the information of the text, including:

1. Knowledge of letters and sound correspondences.
2. Knowledge of words and word forms.
3. Knowledge of syntax, i.e., the grammatical structures of sentences and their functions.
4. Knowledge of meanings and semantic relations.
5. Knowledge of the social ways in which language is used.

Throughout, the reader uses metacognitive processes to monitor, control, and advance the search for meaning. Flavell (1992) suggested that there were at least four components of metacognitive monitoring that readers use as they process texts:

1. They establish learning goals;
2. They generate cognitive associations to achieve these goals;
3. They evaluate their own metacognitive experiences through questioning and reflections; and
4. They use their own metacognitive knowledge to monitor their own understanding.

There is also consensus among researchers that good readers—competent comprehenders—have a plan for comprehending and they use their metacognitive knowledge in an orderly way to implement their plan. Although each reader's plan varies for each text and task, the following steps seem to be part of the competent reader's generalizable plan for many different kinds of texts. Before reading, the strategic reader:

1. *Previews* the text by looking at the title, the pictures, and the print in order to evoke relevant thoughts and memories.
2. *Activates appropriate prior knowledge* through self-questioning about what he/she already knows about the topic (or story), the vocabulary, and the form in which the topic (or story) is presented.
3. *Sets purpose* for reading by asking questions about what he/she wants to learn (know) during the reading episode.

During reading, the strategic reader:

1. *Checks understanding* of the text by paraphrasing the author's words.
2. *Monitors Comprehension* by using context clues to figure out unknown words and by imaging, imagining, inferencing, and predicting.
3. *Integrates* new concepts with existing knowledge; continually revising purposes for reading.
4. *Obtains appropriate help* by adjusting pace, taking notes, creating a concept map, reading less difficult texts on the same topic, uses the dictionary, or asks teachers, parents or peers.

After reading, the strategic reader:

1. *Summarizes* what has been read by retelling the plot of the story or the main idea of the text.

2. *Evaluates* the ideas contained in the text against background or prior knowledge.
3. *Applies* the ideas in the text to unique situations, extending the ideas to broader perspectives.

Many researchers have discussed the similarity of the writing process to the reading process. It has been argued that in reading the student constructs meaning, whereas in writing the student reconstructs meaning (Dahl & Farnan, 1998; Fearn & Farnan, 1998; Flood & Lapp, 1987; Tierney & Pearson, 1984). Jensen (1984) explained that "both reading and writing processes require similar abilities, similar analysis and synthesis—comparing and contrasting, connecting and reevaluating—the same weighting and judging of ideas" (p. 4).

## WHAT WE KNOW ABOUT READING COMPREHENSION INSTRUCTION

If the preceding section accurately reflects the processes that the competent comprehender engages in, one might wonder, Is there a role for the teacher or does comprehension ability merely occur as a result of practice, of extensive and frequent reading?

### Can Comprehension Be Taught?

Carver (1987), in an article titled "Should Reading Comprehension Skills Be Taught?" argued that the evidence for teaching comprehension was "weak, nonexistent, or directly counter (to the data)." After reviewing several of the seminal studies that served as the basis for maintaining that reading comprehension can be taught and has been taught and learned effectively, Carver stated, "It makes more sense to regard comprehension skills as study skills in disguise, and teaching them to unskilled readers is a questionable practice" (p. 125).

Carver (1987) argued that the question "Can comprehension skills be taught?" was answered with a resounding no. However, Haller, Child, and Walberg (1988) argued in their article titled "Can Comprehension Be Taught? A Quantitative Synthesis of Metacognitive Studies" that comprehension can be taught; their data suggested that sufficient evidence existed for encouraging teachers to instruct their students in reading comprehension.

It seems that the real answer to this question is not a simple yes or no, but a qualified one that clearly explains definition and purpose (e.g., Loranger, 1997). All of the studies cited in both Carver's (1987) study and the series of studies examined by Haller et al. (1988) are dependent on their own kind of comprehension measurement for legitimacy. In almost all of these cases, comprehension was assessed and determined by measures of understanding elements included in or derivable from a specific text, either through a formal norm-referenced test or an informal reading–writing measure. All of the studies used measures that tested how well the student performed on one text. None used longitudinal data, collected over the course of many years, to examine other aspects of comprehension, like reading freely and reading widely. Although the purpose of these studies was to directly and immediately assess the instruction students received for specific texts, clearly, these broader purposes need to be taken into consideration when attempting to ultimately answer the question of whether comprehension can be taught and whether such teaching is effective. In asking the question "Can comprehension be taught?" one has to be careful to qualify "comprehension of what, by whom, under what conditions, and for what purposes?"

Although one has to attend to the possibility that the question is still open, there is ample and ever increasing evidence that comprehension instruction has been effective in many different studies. The purpose of this chapter is to review representative samples of these studies to determine elements of comprehension instruction that seem generalizable and useful for teachers at various grade levels in various settings. Naturally not all relevant studies can be included in this chapter; rather, only a modest number will be included as illustrations of what researchers currently know about comprehension instruction.

Such a listing and review of the studies that point to the effectiveness of comprehension instruction would not be particularly useful without placing the studies within a framework that evolves into a specific approach that capitalizes on students' current reading fluency levels as well as their experiences, knowledges, and values. In order to provide this framework, a brief historical review of comprehension instruction in the United States is presented.

## Historical Perspectives on Teaching Reading Comprehension in the United States

The history of reading comprehension instruction in the United States is actually very brief. The term *comprehension* seems first to have been used by J. Russell Webb in the third reader of his series, *Normal Readers* in 1856 (Smith, 1965). Prior to that time, comprehension per se was not discussed—one presumes it was thought about but not researched or reported. Although it is dangerous to try to guess what our predecessors thought, there does seem to be evidence that comprehension was not included as a major thrust in reading instruction in the early years because it was thought to be a logical by-product of learning to read (Smith, 1965).

In the 19th century, the term *meaning* came into use, and in the early 20th century it evolved into *understanding what one reads*. The definition of comprehension in the late 19th century was one in which comprehension was thought to be the product of reading; the aggregated total of comprehending many small units. Perhaps the most significant shift in emphasis in reading comprehension instruction that is observable from published research reports occurred in the early part of the 20th century during which time educators shifted their emphasis from the improvement of oral reading as a means for "getting meaning" to an emphasis on improving comprehension during silent reading (Mathews, 1966; Roser, 1984; Smith, 1965).

This movement seems to have signaled (and foreshadowed) a growing interest in contemporary efforts that encourage students to be in control of their own comprehension processes. This early 20th century movement seems to have resulted in a contemporary concern to move the focus of learning from external control of comprehension (prescribed materials and predetermined activities) to internal control in which students generate their own perspectives, interpretations, and understandings.

Another gradual shift in comprehension instruction was the movement away from "subskills" approaches, in which students were taught isolated skills in the belief that the accumulation of these skills would result in comprehension, to holistic strategic approaches in which students are taught about the what, how, and when of comprehension.

Farr (1971) referred to the period between 1940 and 1980 as the period of subskill proliferation. In one of the earliest attempts to isolate specific subskills that affect comprehension, Davis (1944), using factor analysis techniques, found five skills that contributed to reading comprehension performance:

1. Knowledge of word meaning.
2. Reasoning in reading.
3. Concentration on literal sense meaning.
4. Following the structure of a passage.
5. Recognizing the mood and literary techniques of a writer.

The first two, word knowledge and reasoning, accounted for 89% of the variance in this study. Although there were criticisms of the factor analysis techniques he used, Davis' (1968) later work continued to demonstrate that reading comprehension can be affected by specific skills.

Many attempts to isolate the "skills" of comprehension based on Davis' (1944) findings followed to the point where long lists of comprehension skills were developed. Simons (1971) found that some checklists contained more than 200 separate comprehension skills. Roser (1984) explained that attempts to systematically organize these skills (sometimes discussed as taxonomies) were not successful for three basic reasons:

1. The skills identified in the list were ambiguous and confusing; there was no logic for their grouping. Some of these skills described "uses" of comprehension, some described instructional practices, and some described cognitive processes.
2. Each skill could be listed under a variety of labels.
3. The lists or taxonomies suggested greater scientific precision than they actually had.

Although some studies have examined the beneficial effects of training in individual skills on overall comprehension, many current theorists suggest that comprehension is a unitary phenomenon. Although the debate of whether comprehension is best understood as a unitary process or a set of discernible skills will rage on for the foreseeable future, Roser (1984) suggested a practical explanation: It may be both. She maintains that an endorsement of this explanation gives credence "to the efforts of the cognitive psychologists as they search for ways to explain the unity, as well as the efforts of the practitioners who must interpret the whole into transferable good" (p. 58).

A final major movement in comprehension instruction is the movement toward the explicit teaching of comprehension strategies with guided and independent practice. Evidence appears to be mounting that explicit instruction in comprehension increases reading comprehension ability for specific texts (e.g., Dole, Brown, & Trathen, 1996). In several frequently cited studies that examined the effectiveness of explicit instruction at various grade levels, it has been demonstrated that explicit instruction results in enhanced understanding of texts (Baumann, 1983, 1986; Rosenshine & Stevens, 1984). Successful explicit reading comprehension instruction usually includes four stages in which responsibility gradually shifts from the teacher to the students:

1. *Setting Purposes for Reading.* The teacher uses a structured overview to introduce the students to the task, including the purpose for the lesson. The teacher assumes the major responsibility for this part of the instruction.
2. *Modeling.* The teacher tells, shows, or demonstrates *how* comprehension occurs. The teacher again assumes the greatest responsibility for this part of the lesson.
3. *Guided Practice.* The students attempt to follow the model provided by the teacher; feedback and conferencing are an integral part of this step. Students and teachers share the responsibility during this stage.
4. *Independent Practice.* The student practices independently with "novel" materials. The student accepts the major share of the responsibility for this part of the instruction.

These shifts in practice over the years seem to reflect a growing understanding of the mental processes that are involved in comprehension and an understanding that these processes can be acquired and developed through instruction and practice. These radical changes over the years acknowledge the changing perspective of the teacher's role in fostering comprehension and the learner's role in controlling his or her own comprehension. Appropriately, from a historical perspective, there does not seem to be a single model for comprehension instruction that can be immediately implemented in every classroom. Rather, many models, approaches, methods, heuristics, and practices seem to hold promise for helping students develop their own comprehension (e.g., Beck et al., 1996; Chan, 1996; Emery, 1996; Kraft-Robey, 1996).

The framework that seems most appropriate after reviewing the evidence from many studies attempting to find the "best practices in reading comprehension instruction research" seems to favor a process approach that builds upon what we know about the ways that students read and learn.

## Instructional Methods in Reading Comprehension

Three methods that have been particularly successful in helping to develop competent comprehension strategies will be reviewed. The first method, reader response to literature, is generally thought to be a method used for instruction with literary texts (narratives, poetry, drama), but it can also be used in some instances with certain forms of information texts. The second method, reciprocal teaching, has sometimes been classified as an instructional activity rather than a method of teaching. For our purposes in this review, we will classify it as a method because it is a comprehensive way to instruct students through an entire text. Reciprocal teaching has also sometimes been

thought to be a method of instruction to be used with information texts exclusively. However, evidence suggests that it can be used effectively with many different forms of texts, including narrative pieces. The third method, intermediality, is a relatively new way to organize instruction. Many teachers see intermediality as a way to organize instruction, so we classify it as a method as well.

***Reader response method for teaching literature.*** As early as 1938, Rosenblatt proposed a "new" method for teaching literature; an essentially reader-based method that attended directly to what "real" readers thought of the literature they were reading. In more recent years, this method has become known as reader response. She argued that reader response instruction, in which readers' personal interpretations of texts were of primary importance, would provide for more meaningful and effective teaching than the critical interpretative methods that were traditionally used (Flood & Langer, 1994).

A reader-response-based method of teaching literature is a fundamental shift from the viewpoint that literary interpretation is a right–wrong entity to a view that perceives literary interpretation as a transaction between the reader and the text. Four basic assumptions underlie a response-based approach:

1. Literary meaning is a "transaction" between the reader and the text.
2. The meaning of literature is not contained in a static text.
3. Readers comprehend differently because every reader is unique.
4. Readers' personal responses to text are a critical element in meaning making.

In arguing for a shift to a reader response approach to the teaching of literature, which is essentially a constructivist process approach, Blau (1994) argued that such a change will take tremendous support because of the powerful and lasting effects of New Criticism on teaching and learning theory. In New Criticism theory, it is argued that meaning resides principally in the text, and students must be taught a great deal *about* literature before they can appropriately interpret a text. In advocating a reader response methodology, researchers are essentially arguing for a fundamental change in thinking and in teaching. Educators are being asked to alter their belief that each text has one, true accurate meaning to accepting what Rosenblatt (1982) and others (e.g., Commeyras & Sumner, 1998; Garber, 1999; Sipe, 1998) called transaction, or interrogation between text and reader.

Reader response methodology is not a new phenomenon; it has its roots in the work of Richards (1929) who believed that reader response was the only powerful route to literature teaching because readers are unique and their responses will always be individualistic, unique, and idiosyncratic. He believed in a process that allowed readers to interpret any way they want (provided that their responses adhere to principles of logical thought). Reader response has been investigated in many areas and it has been found to be affected by age, ability level, sex, and type of text that is read (Farnan & Kelly, 1993; Laframboise & Griffith, 1998; Sipe, 1997; Spiegel, 1998; Totten, 1998).

For example, in Applebee's (1978) seminal study, he found that children at Piaget's preoperational stage (2 to 6 years of age) displayed step-by-step retellings; at the concrete stage (6 to 11 years of age) children used summarizations; at the formal stage, Level I, (1 to 15 years of age) children displayed empathy in their responses and at Level II (16 years of age to adulthood) students were able to make generalizations.

The results of these studies taken collectively argue for the effectiveness of a response-based approach, but the researchers associated with these studies caution that there are factors that will impinge upon the effectiveness of the approach at various age levels, with various students and with various types of texts.

***Reciprocal teaching.*** Palincsar and Brown (1985) and Palincsar (1982, 1984, 1986) have developed a paradigm that has been effective for developing constructivist, process-oriented reading comprehension abilities. In their methodology, students and teachers take turns assuming the role of the teacher through a structured dialogue. The teacher models four distinct comprehension strategies and the students have opportunities to practice these strategies. Students are asked to (a) summarize the paragraph that was read in a simple sentence, (b) generate a question about the paragraph that was read to ask a fellow student, (c) ask for clarity (or resolution) of anything in the text that was unclear, and (d) make a prediction about what will happen next in the text. In their studies, students were shown how to do this by teacher modeling; adult support was withdrawn gradually as students exhibited their ability to perform the task independently.

Palincsar and Brown's (1985) original formulation was based on Vygotsky's notions about the zone of proximal development, which he described as "the distance between the actual developmental level as determined by independent problem solving and the level of potential development as determined through problem solving under adult guidance or in collaboration with more capable peers" (p. 117).

The foundation of reciprocal teaching rests on the premise that children can be taught to internalize rules for comprehending over a period of time through the gradual removal of supportive scaffolds (Alfassi, 1998; Klinger & Vaughn, 1996; Palincsar, 1984, 1986). This notion rests on the assumption that scaffolds are adjustable as well as temporary and that learning is a natural interactive process because it occurs in social contexts (King & Parent-Johnson, 1999). It is highly dependent upon discussions between students and teachers and relies on an interactive model as readers learn new information (Carter, 1997; Dermody & Speaker, 1999).

***Intermediality.*** Increased reliance on media and technology has led to new understandings of literacy and learning (Reinking, McKenna, Labbo, & Kieffer, 1998). Flood and Lapp (1995) proposed a "broader conceptualization in which literacy is defined as the ability to function competently in the 'communicative arts,' which include the language arts as well as the visual arts of drama, art, film, video, and television" (p. 1). These new forms of visual and information literacy are changing the very nature of schooling (Dahl & Farnan, 1998; Messaris, 1994). For example, one new area of inquiry focuses on accessing information through multiple forms of media—intermediality (Semali & Pailliotet, 1999). Although a consensus definition of intermediality has yet to emerge, generally speaking it involves multiple forms of both text and media, including books, videos, life experiences, Web sites, films, posters, CD-ROMs, illustrations, and the like. These multiple forms of media are significantly influenced by advances in technology.

With the widespread attention being given to the integration of literacy across the curriculum, many teachers who use the textbook as a resource supplement it with literature selections and other forms of media (Combs & Beach, 1994; N. M. Johnson & Ebert, 1992; Lapp, Flood, & Fisher, 1999; Moss, 1991). Intermediality is believed to have a positive effect on comprehension, detail, and across-text comparisons (Flood, Heath, & Lapp, 1997; Koretz, 1999; Semali & Pailliotet, 1999). For example, the use of video appears to have a positive impact on the readers' stance toward a book as well as one's level of personal understanding (Cox, 1991). Frey (1998) reported increased levels of understanding and more frequent responses at the aesthetic level when fourth-graders had access to multiple information sources. Similarly, Massich and Munoz (1996) described the success they experienced with their middle school students, especially English language learners, as they taught a Civil War unit with multiple information sources, including visuals, realia, music, documents, and diaries.

## Instructional Activities That Foster Comprehension

In addition to the three methods reviewed above, several teaching and learning activities are believed to lead to the development of comprehension abilities. These activities are based on the premise that comprehension is a gradual, emerging process in which readers grow in comprehension abilities by processing texts in a generative manner, building on their own experiences, knowledges, and values. Eight categories of activities that have proven to be successful in helping students develop their comprehension abilities are discussed:

1. Preparing for reading activities.
2. Developing vocabulary activities.
3. Understanding and using text structure knowledge activities.
4. Questioning activities.
5. Information-processing activities.
6. Summarizing activities.
7. Note-taking activities.
8. Voluntary or recreational reading activities.

***Preparing for reading.*** Three activities that help students ready themselves for reading will be discussed. These include Prereading Plan (PreP), previewing, and anticipation guides.

Many of these activities have been used by teachers for generations. Although most of these have been practiced in classrooms around the world for some time, the successful research base for some of them has only been recently established, although others have a long historical research base. The research study references that are included with these activities are selective, tending to be recent studies because space limits a historical review of the research base of all of these activities. It is in no way our intent to suggest that these are new ideas. Rather, we hope to show that effective instructional activities sustain themselves and remain in practice over time with modifications, revisions, and additions precisely because they help students to construct meaningful understandings of texts.

***Prereading Plan (PreP).*** Langer (1982, 1984) proposed an activity that prepares students for reading by activating their prior knowledge that is relevant to the text through a series of prompt questions. She proposed three stages to PreP—initial associations' reflections about initial associations and reformulation of knowledge. In the initial association stage, the teacher selects a word, phrase, or picture about the key concept in the text and initiates a discussion to induce concept-related associations. For example, in teaching a lesson about the American Revolution, the teacher might ask "What comes to mind when you hear the term *Revolutionary War*?" During the reflection stage, students are asked to explain their associations, for example, "Why do those ideas come to mind?" Langer (1984) found that the social context of this activity advanced students understanding—they expanded or revised their knowledge through listening to and interacting with their peers. In the final stage, reformulation of knowledge, students might be asked, "Have you gained any new ideas of the Revolutionary War?" She found that students' knowledge was expanded through the generative processes in which they were engaged. She found that students' responses changed from remotely related personal experiences to an understanding of relations between pieces of knowledge. In this stage, responses consisted of superordinate concepts with characteristics, traits, and examples as well as analogies. Prereading has also been used by secondary school teachers as one of the instructional strategies employed in nontracked English classrooms to teach complex literary texts (Adams, 1995).

***Previewing.*** Graves, Penn, and Cooke (1985) tested a procedure in which students listened to a lengthy preview of the assigned text. The preview was prepared by the teacher and had as its purpose to motivate students by (a) activating prior personal experiences that are relevant to the text, (b) building necessary background knowledge for the text, and (c) establishing an organizational framework for the text that is consistent with the framework the author used to present information. Students who listen to the previews before reading the text often significantly outperform students who do not have previews on several measures of comprehension (Cheney, 1990; Mastropieri, Leinart, & Scruggs, 1999). Previewing is also an effective reading and comprehension strategy for use with English language learners (Chen & Graves, 1998).

***Anticipation–reaction guides.*** Herber (1978) designed a previewing guide in which students were encouraged to predict the information they expected to encounter in the text. As they read the text, their predictions were compared with the information that was actually contained in the text. This active form of processing text helped children develop effective comprehension strategies. Readance, Bean, and Baldwin (1989) expanded anticipation guides to include reactions to text. Poindexter (1994, 1995) has focused on the use of anticipation-reaction guides as one instructional method that encourages secondary school teachers to overcome their reluctance to teach reading in content areas.

***Developing vocabulary.*** Nagy (1988) documented the relationship between word knowledge and reading comprehension, cogently arguing that one cannot understand oral and written language without knowing what most words mean. The extent of one's vocabulary (receptive and/or expressive) has been considered to be a measure of one's world knowledge and one' active ability to comprehend (Harmon, 1999; Nagy, 1988; Nagy & Herman, 1987). In several reviews of effective vocabulary instruction, Beck, McKeown, and Omanson (1987) and McKeown and Beck (1988) found that vocabulary needed to be taught in semantically and topically related networks in order to improve overall comprehension. Several researchers have found that vocabulary instruction that is not tied to building board background knowledge relevant to the text will not result in vocabulary or comprehension growth (Ewers & Brownson, 1999; Lapp, Jacobson, Fisher, & Flood, 2000).

***Semantic mapping.*** Anders and Bos (1986), Flood and Lapp (1988), D. Johnson and Pearson (1978), and Webster (1998) found that vocabulary words that were taught and learned in networks were better learned than words that were taught through contextual approaches. In addition to specific vocabulary development, semantic mapping has been used to increase reading comprehension by identifying such structures as whole–part relationships, characteristics, and temporal–spatial relationships (Lapp, Flood, & Hoffman, 1996; Lipson, 1995; Miholic, 1990).

***Semantic feature analysis.*** Anders and Bos (1986), Beck et al. (1987), and Pikulski (1989) found that students who were taught vocabulary words through a semantic feature analysis paradigm learned the words more thoroughly than students who learned the target words in other ways. More specifically, "Semantic feature analysis (SFA) is an instructional strategy that capitalizes on the way information is stored by category in memory" (Pittelman, Heimlich, Berglund, & French, 1991, p. 1). The SFA grid provides students a visual representation of characteristics and examples of the target word (Tarquin & Walker, 1996).

***Understanding and using text structure knowledge.*** In recent years, there has been a great deal of attention given to the role that understanding of text structure plays in students' comprehension. Understanding the organizational structure of the text is likely one of the predictors of comprehension (Lapp, Flood, & Farnan, 1996).

***Narrative texts.*** Some researchers have argued that explicit instruction of story structure is unnecessary because students will automatically acquire this knowledge indirectly as a by-product of story listening or viewing (e.g., Moffett, 1983). Schmitt and O'Brien (1986) argued against instruction in narrative structure, suggesting that this form of instruction was both unnecessary and counterproductive; it emphasized only one piece of a story and deemphasized story content. However, there are other researchers who have found that instruction in narrative structure positively affects students reading and comprehension (Lapp & Flood, 1992; McMackin, 1998; Pershey, 1998).

***Information texts.*** Many researchers have reported that students at all grade levels can be taught the structures that underlie expository texts (Berkowitz, 1986; Mueller, 1997; Schallert & Roser, 1996; Slater, Graves, & Piche, 1985; Walpole, 1998–99) and these students have opinions about text structure (Lester & Cheek, 1997–98). It has also been discovered that students who consistently use their knowledge of text structure while they are processing texts recall and comprehend more than students who do not know or use text structure knowledge (Armbruster, Anderson, & Ostertag, 1987). Furthermore, students who had the knowledge but did not use it were more negatively affected when reading texts with unfamiliar material than texts with familiar material (Taylor & Beach, 1984).

***Questioning.*** Question–answer relationship (QAR) and inference training activities have been found to improve reading comprehension for students at several different grade levels.

*Question–Answer Relationships (QARs).* In several studies, Raphael (1982, 1986) and others (e.g., Marzola, 1988; McIntosh & Draper, 1996) demonstrated that students were capable of generating and answering questions that enhanced their comprehension and led to independent processing. Four types of QARs were designed, tested, and found to be successful in helping students to comprehend:

1. Text-based QARs in which the answers are "right there" explicitly stated in the text.
2. Text-based QARs in which the student has to "think and search" for relevant information throughout the text.
3. Knowledge-based QARs in which the reader has to read the text to understand the question, but the answer is not in the text.
4. Knowledge-based QARs in which the student can answer the question without reading the text.

In the beginning stage of this process, the teacher accepts total responsibility for the five key elements of the activity: (a) assigning the text, (b) generating the questions, (c) providing answers, (d) identifying the QAR, and (e) providing a justification for the QAR identified. Eventually, control is released to the student after guided practice is offered to the student. Students who were trained in the QAR activity demonstrated significant gains in comprehension.

***Information processing.***

***K-W-L: what we know, what we want to find out, what we learn and still need to learn.*** The K-W-L procedure (Carr & Ogle, 1987; McAllister, 1994; Ogle, 1986) rests on constructivist

principles: it is the reader who ultimately must create meaning. The emphasis of responsibility in this activity is on the students' deciding what is known and what needs to be learned. Initially, the student is shown how to use the guide. This is followed by the teacher's question "How do you know that?" which reminds the student to seek evidence from the text or from previous knowledge. This procedure is intended to activate, review, and develop background knowledge, and to set useful purposes that will enable the student to be an active independent learner.

***Analogies.*** Several researchers have demonstrated the effectiveness of using analogies to enhance comprehension (Glynn, 1996; Moreno & DiVesta, 1994; Pittman, 1999). Bean, Singer, and Cowen (1985) developed an analogical study guide to help students in biology understand the concepts they were learning. In their study, they used the analogy of a factory functioning to understand the working of cells in the human body. Students who were given the analogical guide outperformed students who were taught the information in more traditional ways.

***Summarizing.*** A renewed interest in summarization as a means for improving reading comprehension has occurred during the past few years. Much of this contemporary interest has been a result of Kintsch and Van Dijk's (1978) work that tied summarization ability to reading comprehension, and this renewed interest is documented and detailed in Hidi and Anderson's (1986) report in *Review of Educational Research.* The antecedents to this contemporary work can be found in a series of research studies conducted in the 1920s and 1930s. In the 1930s, Salisbury reported on the efficacious results of using outlines as the basis for summaries that positively affected reading comprehension.

In its more recent development, summary writing has been difficult to describe because the summary itself has no universally accepted definition. Therefore, appropriate instruction that results in informal summaries is often difficult to describe. However, even with that caveat, summary writing in its various forms still seem to be one of the best vehicles available for implementing a constructivist, process-oriented approach to teaching reading comprehension (Bromley & McKeveny, 1986; Guido & Colwell, 1987; Wood, Winne, & Carney, 1995). As Annis (1985) explained there are three cognitive/linguistic requirements for comprehending prose: (a) orientation of attention toward task, (b) recording the information in the text into one's own words, and (c) making connections between the new material and one's prior knowledge. As readers work through these three requirements, they are building summaries of the text.

***Note taking.*** Although the studies on the effectiveness of notetaking as an aid to comprehension and learning have yielded results, Lapp and Flood (1992) argued that note taking is essentially a complex task of rehearsal that requires time for the reader to learn how to select and practice strategies that lead to information acquisition. In the studies in which note taking has been found to be an aid to comprehension and learning, it has been argued that performance increases because the reader is directed to specific text ideas and permitted to reflect on these ideas that have been presented in a meaningful context (Seitz, 1997; Tomlinson, 1997).

***Voluntary or recreational reading.*** One contemporary approach to addressing the problems associated with aliteracy (those who can read but do not) has been the use of voluntary reading programs within and outside school. These programs forward the tenets of a constructivist approach to developing reading comprehension because they foster self-selection by the student that in turn encourages personal meaning making by the student. When students select their own literature, they are taking a first step toward being responsible for their own comprehension development (Beck & McKeown, 1999).

Several studies that examined the effectiveness of voluntary reading programs, in which classrooms were filled with high quality trade books, reported success in overall reading comprehension as well as improved attitudes toward reading (Hertz & Swanson, 1999; Krashen, 1994, 1997; Ross, 1997).

## SUMMARY

The story of reading comprehension instruction has moved from a period of no awareness of the importance of instruction to a period of emphasis on the subskills that were thought to be the underpinnings of comprehension to the present that views comprehension as a gradual, emerging process in which the reader constructs meaning through a transaction with the text.

Contemporary trends suggest that instructional activities need to be based on basic constructivist principles that acknowledge the reader as the meaning maker. The activities need to be conducted in such a way that readers are encouraged to build meaning based on their experiences and knowledge. Assessment techniques, which have always driven the ways in which comprehension has been perceived as a construct and the ways in which it has been taught (or not taught), are gradually changing. More change is needed to help teachers and students understand that comprehension is a complex phenomenon that cannot be easily measured, and it almost certainly cannot be measured with a single instrument.

Finally, there are still many unanswered questions and many questions unframed and unasked. In the future, teachers will need to know more about the delicate instructional balances between preparing for reading and reading, guided reading and independent reading, reading and writing, reading and discussing, reading primary and secondary text sources, vocabulary knowledge and reading, and language variation and reading.

The current climate in education argues well for continued research in comprehension because most educators now agree that the fundamental purpose for reading instruction is to help develop lifelong, independent readers.

## References

Adams, P. E. (1995). Teaching "Romeo and Juliet" in the nontracked English classroom. *Journal of Reading, 38,* 424-432.

Alfassi, M. (1998). Reading for meaning: The efficacy of reciprocal teaching in fostering reading comprehension in high school students in remedial reading classes. *American Educational Research Journal, 35,* 309-332.

Anders, P. L., & Bos, C. S. (1986). Semantic feature analysis: An interactive strategy for vocabulary development and text comprehension. *Journal of Reading, 29,* 610-616.

Anderson, V., & Roit, M. (1996). Linking reading comprehension instruction to language development for language-minority students. *Elementary School Journal, 96,* 295-309.

Annis, L. F. (1985). Student-generated paragraph summaries and the information-processing theory of prose learning. *Journal of Experimental Education, 54,* 4-10.

Applebee, A. N. (1978). *The child's concept of story: Ages 2 to 17.* Chicago: University of Chicago Press.

Armbruster, B. B., Anderson, T. H., & Ostertag, J. (1987). Does text structure/summarization instruction facilitate learning from expository text? *Reading Research Quarterly, 21,* 331-346.

Baumann, J. F. (1983). A generic comprehension instruction strategy. *Reading World, 22,* 284-294.

Baumann, J. F. (1986). Teaching third grade students to comprehend anaphoric relationships. The application of a direct instruction model. *Reading Research Quarterly, 21,* 70-90.

Bean, T. W., Singer, H., & Cowen, S. (1985). Acquisition of a topic schema in high school biology through an analogical study guide. In J. A. Niles & R. V. Lalik (Eds.), *Issues in literacy: A research perspective: Thirty-fourth yearbook of the National Reading Conference* (Vol. 34). Rochester, NY: National Reading Conference.

Beck, I. L., & McKeown, M. G. (1999). Comprehension: The sine qua non of reading. *Teaching and Change, 6,* 197-211.

Beck, I. L., McKeown, J. G., & Omanson, R. C. (1987). The effects and uses of diverse vocabulary instructional techniques. In M. G. McKeown & M. E. Curtin (Eds.), *The nature of vocabulary acquisition.* Hillsdale, NJ: Lawrence Erlbaum Associates.

Beck, I. L., McKeown, M. G., Sandora, C., Kucan, L., & Worthy, J. (1996). Questioning the author: A yearlong classroom implementation to engage students with text. *Elementary School Journal, 96,* 385-414.

Berkowitz, S. J. (1986). Effects of instruction in text organization on sixth grade students' memory for expository reading. *Reading Research Quarterly, 21,* 161-178.

Blau, S. (1994). Transactions between theory and practice in the teaching of literature. In J. Flood & J. A. Langer (Eds.), *Literature instruction: Practice and policy* (pp. 19-52). New York: Scholastic.

Bromley, K. D., & McKeveny, L. (1986). Precis writing: Suggestions for instruction in summarizing. *Journal of Reading, 2,* 392-395.

Bryant, D. P., Ugel, N., Thompson, S., & Hamff, A. (1999). Instructional strategies for content-area reading instruction. *Intervention in School and Clinic, 34,* 293-302.

Carr, E., & Ogle, D. (1987). K-W-L plus: A strategy for comprehension and summarization. *Journal of Reading, 30,* 626-631.

Carter, C. J. (1997). Why reciprocal teaching? *Educational Leadership, 54*(6), 64-68.

Carver, R. (1987). Should reading comprehension skills be taught? In J. E. Readence & R. S. Baldwin (Eds.), *Research in literacy: Merging perspectives: Thirty-sixth yearbook of the National Reading Conference* (Vol. 36). Rochester, NY: National Reading Conference.

Chan, L. K. S. (1996). Combined strategy and attributional training for seventh grade average and poor readers. *Journal of Research in Reading, 19,* 111–127.

Chen, H. S., & Graves, M. F. (1998). Previewing challenging reading selections for ESL students. *Journal of Adolescent and Adult Literacy, 41,* 570–571.

Cheney, K. (1990). Ten seconds for a preview. *Journal of Reading, 34,* 67.

Combs, M., & Beach, J. D. (1994). Stories and storytelling: Personalizing the social studies. *The Reading Teacher, 47,* 464–471.

Commeyras, M., & Sumner, G. (1998). Literature questions children want to discuss: What teachers and students learned in a second-grade classroom. *Elementary School Journal, 99,* 129–152.

Cox, C. (1991). The media arts and English language arts teaching and learning. In J. Flood, J. M. Jensen, D. Lapp, & J. R. Squire (Eds.), *Handbook of research on teaching the English language arts* (pp. 542–548). New York: Macmillan.

Crain-Thoreson, C., Lippman, M. Z., & McClendon-Magnuson, D. (1997). Windows on comprehension: Reading comprehension processes as revealed by two think-aloud procedures. *Journal of Educational Psychology, 89,* 579–591.

Dahl, K. L., & Farnan, N. (1998). *Children's writing: Perspectives from research.* Newark, DE: International Reading Association and National Reading Conference.

Davis, F. B. (1944). Fundamental factors of comprehension. *Reading Psychometrika, 9,* 185–197.

Davis, F. B. (1968). Research in comprehension. *Reading Research Quarterly, 3,* 499–545.

Dermody, M. M., & Speaker, R. B., Jr. (1999). Reciprocal strategy training in prediction, clarification, question generating and summarization to improve reading comprehension. *Reading Improvement, 36,* 16–23.

Dole, J. A., Brown, K. J., & Trathen, W. (1996). The effects of strategy instruction on the comprehension performance of at-risk students. *Reading Research Quarterly, 31,* 62–88.

Duffy, G. G., & Roehler, L. R. (1987). *Characteristics of responsive elaboration which promote the mental processing associated with strategy use.* Paper presented at annual meeting, National Reading Conference, St. Petersburg Beach, FL.

Emery, D. W. (1996). Helping readers comprehend stories from the characters' perspective. *Reading Teacher, 49,* 543–541.

Evans, R. W. (1997). Teaching social issues: Implementing an issues-centered curriculum. In E. W. Ross (Ed.), *The social studies curriculum: Purposes, problems, and possibilities* (pp. 197–212). Albany: State University of New York Press.

Ewers, C. A., & Brownson, S. M. (1999). Kindergartners' vocabulary acquisition as a function of active vs. passive storybook reading, prior vocabulary, and working memory. *Reading Psychology, 20,* 11–20.

Ezell, H. L., Hunsicker, S. A., Quinque, M. M., & Randolph, E. (1996). Maintenance and generalization of QAR reading comprehension strategies. *Reading Research and Instruction, 36,* 64–81.

Farnan, N., & Kelly, P. R. (1993). Response-based instruction at the middle level: When student engagement is the goal. *Middle School Journal, 25,* 46–49.

Farr, R. (1971). Measuring reading comprehension: A historical perspective. In F. Greene (Ed.), *Reading: The right to participate: Twentieth yearbook of the National Reading Conference* (Vol. 20).

Fearn, L., & Farnan, N. (1998). *Writing effectively: Helping children master the conventions of writing.* Boston: Allyn & Bacon.

Fielding, L. G., & Pearson, P. D. (1994). Reading comprehension: What works. *Educational Leadership, 51*(5), 62–68.

Flavell, J. H. (1992). Cognitive development: Past, present, and future. *Developmental Psychology, 28,* 998–1005.

Flood, J., Heath, S. B., & Lapp, D. (1997). *Handbook of research on teaching literacy through the communication and visual arts.* New York: Macmillan.

Flood, J., & Langer, J. A. (Eds.) (1994). *Literature instruction: Practice and policy.* New York: Scholastic.

Flood, J., & Lapp, D. (1987). Reading and writing relations: Assumptions and directions. In J. Squire (Ed.), *The dynamics of language learning.* Urbana, IL: National Conference on Research in English.

Flood, J., & Lapp, D. (1988). Using conceptual mapping for improving comprehension. *The Reading Teacher, 41,* 780–783.

Flood, J., & Lapp, D. (1995). Broadening the lens: Toward an expanded conceptualization of literacy. In K. A. Hinchman, D. J. Leu, & C. K. Kinzer (Eds.), *The Forty-fourth yearbook of the National Reading Conference* (Vol. 44, pp. 1–16). Chicago: National Reading Conference.

Frey, J. (1998). *Maximizing reader response through films and videos.* Unpublished master's thesis, San Diego State University, San Diego, CA.

Garber, S. (1999). Diamonds of thought: A reflection. *Language Arts, 76,* 401–403.

Gaskins, R. W. (1996). "That's just how it was": The effect of issue-related emotional involvement on reading comprehension. *Reading Research Quarterly, 31,* 386–405.

Gavelek, J. R., & Raphael, T. E. (1996). Changing talk about text: New roles for teachers and students. *Language Arts, 73,* 182–192.

Glynn, S. (1996). Teaching with analogies: Building on the science textbook. *The Reading Teacher, 49,* 490–492.

Graves, M. F., Penn, M. C., & Cooke, C. L. (1985). The coming attraction: Previewing short stories. *Journal of Reading, 28,* 594–598.

Guido, B., & Colwell, C. G. (1987). A rationale for direct instruction to teach summary writing following expository text reading. *Reading Research and Instruction, 26,* 89–98.

Haller, E. P., Child, D. A., & Walberg, H. J. (1988). Can comprehension be taught? A quantitative synthesis of "metacognitive" studies. *Educational Researcher, 17,* 5–8.

Harmon, J. M. (1999). Initial encounters with unfamiliar words in independent reading. *Research in the Teaching of English, 33,* 304–338.

Herber, H. (1978). *Teaching reading in content areas* (2nd ed.). Englewood Cliffs, NJ: Prentice-Hall.

Hertz, M., & Swanson, K. L. (1999). We love to read—A collaborative endeavor to build the foundation for lifelong readers. *Reading Horizons, 39,* 209–229.

Hidi, S., & Anderson, V. (1986). Producing written summaries: Task demands, cognitive operations, and implications for instruction. *Review of Educational Research, 56,* 473–493.

Jensen, J. (1984). *Composing and comprehending.* Urbana, IL: ERIC Clearinghouse.

Johnson, D., & Pearson, P. D. (1978). *Teaching reading vocabulary.* New York: Holt, Rinehart & Winston.

Johnson, N. M., & Ebert, M. J. (1992). Time travel is possible: Historical fiction and biography—Passport to the past. *The Reading Teacher, 45,* 488–495.

Kamhi, A. G. (1997). Three perspectives on comprehension: Implications for assessing and treating comprehension problems. *Topics in Language Disorders, 17*(3), 62–74.

Keene, E. O., & Zimmermann, S. (1997). *Mosaic of thought: Teaching comprehension in a reader's workshop.* Portsmouth, NH: Heinemann.

Kincade, K. M. (1996). Improving reading comprehension through strategy instruction. *Reading Psychology, 17,* 273–281.

King, C. M., & Parent-Johnson, L. M. (1999). Constructing meaning via reciprocal teaching. *Reading Research and Instruction, 38,* 169-186.

Kintsch, W., & Van Dijk, T. A. (1978). Toward a model of text comprehension and production. *Psychological Review, 85,* 363-394.

Klinger, J. K., & Vaughn, S. (1996). Reciprocal teaching of reading comprehension strategies for students with learning disabilities who use English as a second language. *Elementary School Journal, 96,* 275-293.

Klinger, J. K., Vaughn, S., & Schumm, J. S. (1998). Collaborative strategic reading during social studies in heterogeneous fourth-grade classrooms. *Elementary School Journal, 99,* 3-22.

Koretz, S. (1999). *A study of fourth grade students reading and thinking behaviors during social studies class when using multiple sources strategies.* Unpublished master's Thesis, San Diego State University, San Diego, CA.

Kraft-Robey, E. (1996). Letting fourth graders design reading questions. *Teaching and Change, 4,* 35-49.

Krashen, S. (1994). An answer to the literacy crisis: Free voluntary reading. *School Library Media Annual, 12,* 113-122.

Krashen, S. (1997). Does free voluntary reading lead to academic language? *Journal of Intensive English Studies, 11,* 1-18.

Kucan, L., & Beck, I. L. (1997). Thinking aloud and reading comprehension research: Inquiry, instruction, and social interaction. *Review of Educational Research, 67,* 271-299.

Laframboise, K. L., & Griffith, P. L. (1998). Literature case studies: Case method and reader response come together in teacher education. *Journal of Adolescent and Adult Literacy, 41,* 364-375.

Langer, J. A. (1982). Facilitating text processing: The elaboration of prior knowledge. In J. A. Langer & M. T. Smith-Burke (Eds.), *Reader meets author/bridging the gap: A psycholinguistic and sociolinguistic perspective.* Newark, DE: International Reading Association.

Langer, J. A. (1984). Examining background knowledge and text comprehension. *Reading Research Quarterly, 19,* 468-481.

Lapp, D., & Flood, J. (1992). *Teaching students to read* (3rd ed.). New York: Macmillan.

Lapp, D., & Flood, J. (1994). Integrating the curriculum: First steps. *The Reading Teacher, 47,* 416-419.

Lapp, D., Flood, J., & Farnan, N. (Eds.) (1996). *Content area reading and instruction: Instructional strategies.* Boston: Allyn & Bacon.

Lapp, D., Flood, J., & Fisher, D. (1999). Intermediality: Multiple media makes learning memorable. *The Reading Teacher, 52,* 776-780.

Lapp, D., Flood, J., & Hoffman, R. P. (1996). Using concept mapping as an effective strategy in content area instruction. In D. Lapp, J. Flood, & N. Farnan (Eds.), *Content area reading and instruction: Instructional strategies* (pp. 291-305). Boston: Allyn & Bacon.

Lapp, D., Jacobson, J., Fisher, D., & Flood, J. (2000). Tried and true word study and vocabulary practices. *The California Reader, 33*(2), 25-30.

Lester, J. M., & Cheek, E. H. (1997-98). The "real" experts address textbook issues. *Journal of Adolescent and Adult Literacy, 41,* 282-291.

Lin, L., Zabrucky, K., & Moore, D. (1997). The relations among interest, self-assessed comprehension, and comprehension performance in young adults. *Reading Research and Instruction, 36,* 127-139.

Lipson, M. (1995). The effect of semantic mapping instruction on prose comprehension of below-level college readers. *Reading Research and Instruction, 34,* 367-378.

Loranger, A. L. (1997). Comprehension strategies instruction: Does it make a difference? *Reading Psychology, 18,* 31-68.

Marzola, E. S. (1988). Interrogating the text: Questioning strategies designed to improve reading comprehension. *Journal of Reading,*

Writing, and Learning Disabilities International, 4, 243-258.

Massich, M., & Munoz, E. (1996). Utilizing primary sources as building blocks for literacy. *Social Studies Review, 36*(1), 52-57.

Mastropieri, M. A., Leinart, A., & Scruggs, T. E. (1999). Strategies to increase reading fluency. *Intervention in School and Clinic, 34,* 278-283, 292.

Mathews, M. (1966). *Teaching to read: Historically considered.* Chicago: University of Chicago Press.

McAllister, P. J. (1994). Using K-W-L for informal assessment. *The Reading Teacher, 47,* 521-511.

McGowan, T., & Guzzetti, B. (1991). Promoting social studies understanding through literature-based instruction. *The Social Studies, 82,* 16-21.

McIntosh, M. E., & Draper, R. J. (1996). Using the question-answer relationship strategy to improve students' reading of mathematics texts. *Clearing House, 69,* 154-162.

McKeown, M. G., & Beck, I. L. (1988). Learning vocabulary: Different ways for different goals. *Remedial and Special Education, 9,* 42-46.

McMackin, M. C. (1998). Using narrative picture books to build awareness of expository text structure. *Reading Horizons, 39,* 7-20.

Messaris, P. (1994). *Visual literacy: Image, mind, & reality.* Boulder, CO: Westview.

Miholic, V. (1990). Constructing a semantic map for textbooks. *Journal of Reading, 33,* 464-465.

Moffett, J. (1983). *Teaching the universe of discourse.* Boston: Houghton Mifflin.

Moreno, V., & DiVesta, F. J. (1994). Analogies (adages) as aids for comprehending structural relations in text. *Contemporary Educational Psychology, 19,* 179-198.

Moss, B. (1991). Children's nonfiction trade books: A complement to content area texts. *The Reading Teacher, 45,* 26-32.

Mueller, M. E. (1997). Using metacognitive strategies to facilitate expository text mastery. *Educational Research Quarterly, 20,* 41-65.

Nagy, W. E. (1988). *Vocabulary instruction and reading comprehension* (Tech. Rep. No. 431). Champaign, IL: University of Illinois, Center for the Study of Reading.

Nagy, W. E., & Herman, P. A. (1987). Breadth and depth of vocabulary knowledge: Implications for acquisition and instruction. In M. G. McKeown & M. E. Curtis (Eds.). *The nature of vocabulary acquisition.* Hillsdale, NJ: Lawrence Erlbaum Associates.

Ogle, D. (1986). K-W-L: A teaching model that develops active reading of expository text. *The Reading Teacher, 39,* 564-570.

Palincsar, A. S. (1982). Improving the reading comprehension of junior high students through the reciprocal teaching of comprehension-monitoring strategies. *Dissertation Abstracts International, 43,* 3744A.

Palincsar, A. S. (1984). Reciprocal teaching of comprehension fostering and comprehension monitoring activities. *Cognition and Instruction, 2,* 117-175.

Palincsar, A. S. (1986). The role of dialogue in providing scaffolded instruction. *Educational Psychologist, 21,* 73-98.

Palincsar, A. S., & Brown, A. L. (1985). Reciprocal teaching activities to promote reading with your mind. In E. J. Cooper (Ed.), *Reading, thinking, and concept development: Interactive strategies for the class.* New York: The College Board.

Pershey, M. G. (1998). Teaching children to identify and respond to pragmatic language functions in narrative text. *Reading Improvement, 35,* 146-166.

Pikulski, J. J. (1989). Questions and answers. *The Reading Teacher, 42,* 429.

Pittelman, S. D., Heimlich, J. E., Berglund, R. L., & French, M. P. (1991). *Semantic feature analysis: Classroom applications*. Newark, DE: International Reading Association.

Pittman, K. M. (1999). Student-generated analogies: Another way of knowing? *Journal of Research in Science Teaching, 36,* 1-22.

Poindexter, C. C. (1994). Classroom strategies that convinced content area teachers they could teach reading, too. *Journal of Reading, 38,* 134.

Poindexter, C. C. (1995). Applying effective reading techniques in content area classes. *Reading Horizons, 35,* 244-249.

Raphael, T. (1982). Question-answering strategies for children. *The Reading Teacher, 36,* 186-190.

Raphael, T. (1986). Teaching question answer relationships, revisited. *The Reading Teacher, 39,* 516-522.

Rasinski, T. V., & Padak, N. D. (1998). How elementary students referred for compensatory reading instruction perform on school-based measures of word recognition, fluency, and comprehension. *Reading Psychology, 19,* 185-216.

Readance, J., Bean, T., & Baldwin, S. (1989). *Content area reading: An integrated approach*. Dubuque, IA: Kendall-Hunt.

Reinking, D., McKenna, M. C., Labbo, L. D., & Kieffer, R. D. (Eds.) (1998). *Handbook of literacy and technology: Transformations in a posttypographic world*. Mahwah, NJ: Lawrence Earlbaum Associates.

Richards, I. A. (1929). *Practical criticism: A study of literary judgement*. New York: Harcourt, Brace & World.

Rosenblatt, L. M. (1938). *Literature as exploration*. New York: Noble & Noble.

Rosenblatt, L. M. (1982). The literary transaction: Evocation and response. *Theory Into Practice, 21,* 268-277.

Rosenshine, B., & Stevens, R. (1984). Classroom instruction in reading. In P. D. Pearson, R. Barr, M. Kamil, & P. Mosenthal (Eds.), *Handbook of reading research*. New York: Longman.

Roser, N. (1984). Teaching and testing reading comprehension: A historical perspective on instructional research and practices. In J. Flood (Ed.), *Promoting reading comprehension* (pp. 48-60). Newark, DE: International Reading Association.

Ross, C. (1997). Reading the covers off Nancy Drew: What readers say about series books. *Emergency Librarian, 24,* 19-22.

Schallert, D. L., & Roser, N. L. (1996). The role of textbooks and tradebooks in content area instruction. In D. Lapp, J. Flood, & N. Farnan (Eds.), *Content area reading and instruction: Instructional strategies* (pp. 27-38). Boston: Allyn & Bacon.

Schmitt, M. C., & O'Brien, D. (1986). Story grammars: Some cautions about the translation of research into practice. *Reading Research and Instruction, 26,* 1-8.

Seitz, E. A. (1997). Using media presentations to teach notetaking, main idea, and summarization skills. *Journal of Adolescent and Adult Literacy, 40,* 562-562.

Semali, L. M., & Pailliotet, A. W. (1999). *Intermediality: The teachers' handbook of critical media literacy*. Boulder, CO: Westview.

Simons, H. (1971). Reading comprehension: The need for a new perspective. *Reading Research Quarterly, 6,* 338-363.

Sipe, L. R. (1997). Children's literature, literacy, and literary understanding. *Journal of Children's Literature, 23,* 6-19.

Sipe, L. R. (1998). Individual literary response styles of first and second graders. *National Reading Conference Yearbook, 47,* 76-89.

Slater, W. H., Graves, J. F., & Piche G. L. (1985). Effects of structural organizers on ninth grade students' comprehension and recall of four patterns of expository text. *Reading Research Quarterly, 20,* 189-202.

Smith, N. B. (1965). *American reading instruction*. Newark, DE: International Reading Association.

Spiegel, D. L. (1998). Reader response approaches and the growth of readers. *Language Arts, 76,* 41-48.

Squire, J. R. (1983). Composing and comprehending: Two sides of the same basic process. *Language Arts, 60,* 581-589.

Tarquin, P., & Walker, S. (1996). *Creating success in the classroom!: Visual organizers and how to use them*. New York: Libraries Unlimited.

Taylor, B. M., & Beach, R. W. (1984). The effects of text structure instruction on middle grade students' comprehension and production of expository text. *Reading Research Quarterly, 19,* 134-146.

Tierney, R., & Pearson, P. D. (1984). Toward a composing model of reading. In J. Jensen (Ed.), *Composing and comprehending*. Urbana, IL: ERIC Clearinghouse. (ED 243 139)

Tomlinson, L. M. (1997). A coding system for notetaking in literature: Preparation for journal writing, class participation, and essay tests. *Journal of Adolescent and Adult Literacy, 40,* 468-476.

Totten, S. (1998). Using reader-response theory to study poetry about the Holocaust with high school students. *Social Studies, 89,* 30-34.

Walpole, S. (1998-99). Changing texts, changing thinking: Comprehension demands of new science textbooks. *The Reading Teacher, 52,* 358-369.

Webster, J. P. (1998). Semantic maps. *TESOL Journal, 7*(5), 42-43.

Wood, E., Winne, P. H., & Carney, P. A. (1995). Evaluating the effects of training high school students to use summarization when training includes analogically similar information. *Journal of Reading Behavior, 27,* 605-626.

# STUDYING: SKILLS, STRATEGIES, AND SYSTEMS

*Thomas G. Devine*
*University of Lowell*

*John S. Kania*

The term *studying* implies a deliberate effort by the student to understand, remember, and use specified knowledge or procedures. Although often associated with reading, it is not the same. Studying frequently occurs in a variety of nonverbal contexts (as when one deliberately tries to play a musical passage on an instrument, develop computational skills, or master intricate physical maneuvers in basketball or a similar activity). Studying is also unlike reading in its emphasis on memory and the later use of studied material; that is, students study to remember and demonstrate at another time some competence or understanding (through performance, test taking, or writing). Students may read but not study and study but not read.

The term *study skills* has come to embrace a wide variety of competencies associated with academic learning, from alphabetizing to using a table of contents and index, from taking lecture notes to writing a library research paper. Many study skills textbooks and programs, from elementary school through college levels, aim to introduce students to a vast array of discrete and often unrelated skills. However, some of the skills described in popular student guides and textbooks appear to be distinctly peripheral to the central purposes of study (to understand, remember, and use knowledge or procedures), and overemphasis on their acquisition may be uneconomical in terms of teacher and student time and energy. A smaller number of these skills may be better viewed as *study strategies* that directly promote comprehension, retention in memory, and the ability to demonstrate learning. Teachers and researchers have combined two or more of these specific strategies as *study systems* on the grounds that related strategies when used together somehow become more effective. All three—study skills, study strategies, and study systems—are bound by a common goal: Each is intended to assist students to learn on their own. They are suggested as aids for independent learning, for student rather than teacher use.

Reasons for providing instruction in study skills, strategies, and systems are evident. Students clearly benefit from the competencies included in traditional study skills programs (that is, using a table of contents, library reference systems, a glossary, and so on). They obtain even greater benefits, however, from the use of specific study strategies, such as defining and previewing an assignment, taking effective notes, outlining, self-recitation, or summarizing, as well as the ability to use specific study systems such as SQ3R (survey, question, read, recite, review) or PORPE (predict, organize, rehearse, practice, and evaluate). Instruction in how to study can help learners recognize their own cognitive capabilities, realize how to define and analyze study tasks, and be aware of the array of learning methods available to them. Although teachers need to better understand and use available tools for improving teaching (such as lesson frameworks, effective study guides, and various instructional strategies), it is important that they also understand and promote those tools that will allow students to strike out on their own.

Many useful books and guides have long been available to promote independent learning at all levels (see, e.g., Bragstad & Stumpf, 1987; Devine, 1987; Fry, 1996), as are countless informative articles (e.g., Hoover, 1993; Pearson & Santa, 1995). Although several present information about research and theory, most focus on study skills and strategies and suggest ways that teachers may develop them in students. This chapter examines research findings underlying several widely used study strategies and often recommended study systems, and concludes with discussion of instructional issues.

## SPECIFIC STUDY STRATEGIES

Research findings on specific study strategies, though sometimes anfractuous and equivocal, tend to support the belief that students may be given tools to help them better understand, remember, and apply knowledge and procedures that are new to them. Several widely used strategies are examined here, particularly those that seem to promote deep processing tactics, such as those noted by Winne (1985): retrieving related concepts and ideas relevant to material currently being studies, monitoring relationships between new information and prior knowledge, assembling propositions into elaborated structures, rehearsing and transforming information into meaningful schemata, and metacognitively monitoring and adapting learning tactics according to the requirements of a task.

## Defining Study Tasks

Students who know exactly what they are supposed to learn tend to outperform those who simply "study." Although some teachers continue to tell students "Study Chapter 8" or "Learn the causes of the American Revolution," research findings suggest that such assignments handicap students. R. C. Anderson and Biddle (1975), for example, noted in a review of 14 studies that students given information, while studying, about the questions to be asked at the conclusion of a reading assignment tended to do significantly better on tests than students who were not given such information. Further studies by T. H. Anderson (1980) and Glynn (1978) suggested that the more specific the knowledge provided, the better the performance. After examining studies done since the 1930s, T. H. Anderson and Armbruster (1984) noted that several lines of research suggest that "the more specific the knowledge about the criterion event, the greater the effectiveness of studying" (p. 660), especially when students realize that modifying their study habits to conform to the task will result in better performance. More recent studies of *task impression*, or *task definition* (e.g., Flower, 1990; McMackin, 1994; Nelson, 1990) also support the belief that time spent with students, whether in elementary school or college, in defining the task so that they understand what is expected of them is evidently time well spent. Other studies, too, seem to indicate that defining the study task promotes student ability to better manage study time, a major key to school success (Cormier, 1995; Davey, 1993; Dickinson & O'Connell, 1990; Hadwen & Winne, 1996). After repeated experiences under teacher guidance, task definition may become a study strategy for students to use independently so that they can, on their own, try to spell out the goals and parameters of an assignment and see the ways it relates to course and curriculum objectives.

## Previewing

Related to task definition is previewing (sometimes also called *overviewing*, or *surveying*). Previewing an assignment helps students see its purpose, the lines of demarcation separating it from other study tasks, and how its components fit into a larger task. In addition, previewing before study can activate relevant background knowledge and may enrich and refine new schemata.

Research on various forms of previewing tends to be positive, although most has focused on previewing as an instructional rather than a study strategy. Many studies have examined the value of previewing as means of activating or providing prior knowledge: Graves and colleagues (Graves & Cooke, 1980; Graves, Cooke, & LaBerge, 1983; Graves & Palmer, 1981), for example, used previews in story reading and found that building background knowledge increased learning by significant amounts; Stevens (1982) also found previewing and providing relevant background knowledge helped 10th-grade students better understand passages in a history textbook; Hayes and Tierney (1982) discovered that giving students information about the topic treated in the text prior to reading helped readers learn more from the text.

Informal types of previewing have long been used by many teachers as instructional strategies: class discussions, informal lectures, examination of illustrations, viewing appropriate films, reading outlines, and so on. Some teachers have also used more structured previews. *Advance organizers*, for example, were first suggested by Ausubel (1960) as "introductory material at a higher level of abstraction, generality and inclusiveness than the learning passage itself" (Ausubel, 1978, p. 252). They are intended to serve as ideational scaffolding for the incorporation of new material. Some research indicates that they are effective (Corkill, Bruning, & Glover, 1988; Tudor, 1986). Studies by Glover, Bullock, and Dietzer (1990) and Rinehart and Welker (1992) found that advanced organizers enhanced recall of material. Other research, however, is less conclusive (Tierney & Cunningham, 1984). *Structured overviews* are designed to serve the same purpose but present visual overviews of the concepts and relationships in the text (Wolfe & Lopez, 1993). *Structural organizers* (Slater, Graves, & Piche, 1985) focus student attention on the ways a text is organized: before they read, they are given its basic rhetorical framework, such as cause-effect, claim-support-conclusion, problem solution, and so on, with paragraph plans, main idea sentences, and signal words and phrases highlighted.

Previewing as a study strategy rather than a teaching approach has not been carefully examined by researchers. Clearly, previewing can be—and is—used independently by many students. They have learned to examine illustrations prior to reading to get a notion of the assignment; many read chapter summaries first, others study an available outline before they read, and still others have learned to check typographical aids or even the first sentences of paragraphs before beginning to read and study an assignment. Previewing to create questions to be answered during reading is a strategy developed by many teachers as a result of frequent experience with the study system SQ3R (see the section Study Systems that appears later in the chapter): They have internalized an approach recommended and used by their teachers. Many of the highly structured previewing strategies used by teachers may also, in time, become internalized by students to become part of their personal study strategy repertoires. Teachers should probably encourage students to make classroom previewing strategies their own by regularly reminding them to check titles, subtitles, and headings; look at typographical aids; study illustrations, maps, charts, and graphs prior to reading; examine ends of previous chapters and beginnings of subsequent ones; note any study material provided; read summaries first; create their own guide questions; and so on.

## Questioning

Questioning, as a study strategy, may take at least three forms:

1. Students may use teacher or textbook questions to guide them through a reading assignment or lecture.
2. They may generate their own questions for the same purpose.
3. They may use other- or self-generated questions for self-recitation and/or review.

The values of teacher and textbook prequestions have been fairly well established. They can, for example, focus student attention on key points, thus better defining the study task. In one study, Wade and Trathen (1989) found that prereading questions seemed to reduce the amount of unimportant information subjects noted and that, particularly, they also improved the recall of important information for lower ability groups. In another study, Rickards and McCormick (1988) found that conceptual prequestions in a lecture situation seemed to encourage more elaborate processing. Prequestions by teachers and others, however, fall in the category of instructional, not learner, strategies. What evidence supports the belief that student-generated prequestions are effective? Unfortunately, most studies on student-generated questioning have focused on questioning during, not before, study. In his examination of the SQ3R study system, Martin (1985) attributed the effectiveness of the system to its structure of which self-generated prequestioning is an intrinsic component. (He also discovered that self-questioning *during* reading was not significantly superior to SQ3R). Studies of self-generated questioning during reading have sometimes been negative (King, Biggs, & Lipsky, 1984; Morse, 1975), sometimes positive. Duell (1978) found that college students who developed their own questions from instructional objectives outperformed those who simply studied the material with knowledge of the objectives. Frase and Schwartz (1975) found that students who wrote out questions while studying did better than those in control groups who read only. As T. H. Anderson and Armbruster (1984) noted, "It seems plausible that when student questioning is effective, it is so because students are forced to encode the information more than they might if they simply read it" (p. 672). They also noted that the actual writing of questions required students to paraphrase or perform some other transformation of the text, thus entailing processing.

The research on self-recitation, or self-testing, goes back more than 80 years (Gates, 1917). It seems to be one of the most-used as well as oldest of study strategies. Recall during practice (i.e., reciting to oneself as material is studied) clearly increases the chances of retention of material being studied. When based on teacher-prepared questions and lists, it is especially effective, because usually the teacher develops the questions or lists with the test in mind. Thus, the problem of task definition is minimized if not resolved in advance of study. When material to be studied is generated by students, they may select inappropriate material unless they are competent in task definition.

However, enough research support of student-generated questions exists (as previously noted) to encourage students to continue self-recitation. They need to be shown such activities as:

1. The use of 3- × 5-inch "flip" cards (with questions on one side and answers on the back),
2. The self-test in which they write out answers to their own questions.
3. Matching puzzles to connect names and dates with events and so on.
4. The use of charts, graphs, and maps to be filled in to verify their learning, and similar self-recitation devices.

Self-recitation remains a viable study strategy. When coupled with guidance in task definition, it seems an especially powerful study tool.

## Underlining

Underlining (also called *underscoring* or *highlighting*) seems to be the most popular study strategy. It probably owes its effectiveness to the Von Restoff effect, a laboratory finding that the isolation, or highlighting, of one item from a homogeneous background leads to increased recall of that item (McAndrew, 1983). For example, when a word or phrase is printed in a different color or type from others on a list, viewers tend to remember it better than other items. Although some studies show positive results from underlining texts (e.g., Rickards & August, 1975; Schell & Rocchio, 1975), others indicate that it is no more effective than other study approaches (for a summary, see T. H. Anderson & Armbruster, 1984, p. 665). Some do not consider it a study strategy (Hadwen & Winne, 1996).

In a study of its use at the college level, Policastro (1975) noted:

1. Students usually underline too much. The average textbook runs to 400 pages. If just 20 percent of each page were underlined, it would result in 80 pages of rereading (while turning all 400) for a review in preparation for an exam.
2. The underlined section will often lose some, it not all, of its significance when reread at some future time. The student then has to reread surrounding material in order to reconstruct the original meaning, requiring extra time and effort.
3. Underlining is a comparatively passive activity and has the effect of psychologically deferring the active (learning) process to some future point. Often a student will underline something that is assumed (rightly or not) to be important, though not fully understood, with the intention of rereading the item at a more "opportune" time in order to discover the complete meaning. (pp. 372–375)

In another study at the college level, Nist and Hogrebe (1987) investigated opposing theoretical viewpoints as explanations of the effect of underlining. Four groups of provisionally admitted college freshmen were given preunderlined material (a passage from a "typical" college textbook on American government). Group 1 received the passage with information marked that was considered important by a panel of experts. Group 2 received the same markings but with accompanying annotation. Group 3 received the passage with underlining under information that was not selected unanimously by the panel of experts. Group 4 received the same underlining as Group 3 but with accompanying annotation. Group 5 participants were instructed to generate their own underlining. All students took a test of prior knowledge, read the assigned passage, and took a 24-item multiple-choice test consisting of 12 high-relevant and 12 low-relevant questions. Data analysis indicated that when text material was underlined or underlined and annotated, students directed their attention to the information highlighted, thus supporting the operation of the Von Rostoff effect. Students in Groups 1 and 2 correctly answered more questions about information deemed important by the experts. Students in Groups 3 and 4 answered correctly more of the questions about information not considered important by the experts. Nist and Hogrebe noted, "These results suggest that text material which had been marked by the researchers, regardless of the quality of that marking, had a rather strong influence on directing the reader's attention to certain parts of the text" (p. 22). (Students who generated their own underlining did not perform significantly better than those who were given experimenter-generated underlining.) In a recent study, however, Silvers and Kreiner (1997) found that preexisting inappropriate highlighting (used textbooks bought by college students already highlighted) reduces reading comprehension of that text. Highlighted appropriate material seems not to interfere with retention of reading material, but students given prior warning of inappropriate highlighted material were unable to ignore it.

Probably better than underlining are *marginal comments* and *personal coding systems*. Writing their own questions, rephrasing difficult sentences, defining unfamiliar words indicate that the student is more engaged in the process of learning than when tracing lines across the page. Coding systems involving colored symbols for key ideas, lines drawn from main ideas to supporting examples, arrows to show relationships, boxes containing related ideas, marginal numbers indicating chronological patterns, question marks noting unsupported references, hearts and flowers to signal emotional language, and so on also tend to encourage active processing of new information. Simple underlining may be more effective than passive reading, but marginal comments and/or personal coding systems involve students more directly with the text.

## Note Taking

The value of note taking seems clear. It assists students in focusing attention and processing new material. It aids in memory retention and provides students with a record for later review and study. More specifically, it allows students to record in their own words what may be their own more deeply processed version of the text. Studies on notetaking, however, have generally produced mixed results.

Some studies (e.g., Arnold, 1942; Poppleton & Austwick, 1964; Schultz & DiVesta, 1972; Todd & Kessler, 1971) showed note taking to be only as effective as rereading, underlining,

or making marginal comments. Other studies indicated positive effects. Kulhavy, Dyer, and Silver (1975) compared note taking with reading only and underlining, and found students in their note-taking group outperformed students in the other two groups. In an older study, Mathews (1938) compared groups who reread, took marginal notes, and outlined, and found that although there were no significant differences on test scores for the three groups, the outlining group scored better when required to give back information in outline form. Bizinkauskas (1970) compared outlining with underlining, reading only, and tape recording key ideas and words; he found note taking in outlines superior.

Other aspects of note taking have been examined. Kiewra, Dubois, Christian, and McShane (1988), for example, showed college students a videotaped lecture but did not allow them to take any kinds of notes. They then provided the students with one of three forms of notes for review: a complete text, a linear outline including all 121 key ideas of the lecture, and a matrix with the 121 ideas arranged in organized cells. Another group of students in a control group were given no notes and asked to review mentally. Posttesting indicated that students using any of the three forms of preprepared notes outperformed those who reviewed mentally and that outline and matrix notes were more effective than no notes. In another study, Rickards and McCormick (1988) found that note taking alone resulted in "more shallow, literal, or paraphrased listing of passage material" (p. 592) than note taking guided by questions inserted at intervals to guide note taking. Kiewra and Frank (1988) compared personal notes, completed forms of detailed instructor's notes, and skeletal forms of instructor's notes and found that detailed instructor's notes provided for better review. Shrager and Mayer (1989) instructed college students to take notes or not take notes during a videotaped lecture. They found that note takers outperformed non–note takers for students with low prior knowledge of the topic but not for students with high prior knowledge of the topic.

Sometimes study results vary because student note-taking varies. Some students jot down single words, phrases, sentences, dates, or computations; other try to copy verbatim, from both books and lectures. Some students paraphrase, draw illustrations, make up questions, summarize as they go along, add personal examples, and so on. Clearly, copiousness, quality, and character of notes affect their value. Some research suggests a relationship between copiousness and achievement on examinations. Kiewra (1984) found that students who were not permitted to review their study notes nevertheless recalled up to 78% of the material they had recorded but only from 5% to 34% of that they did not record. Some of the benefits of note taking results evidently from greater attention to the material noted, as well as deeper processing of it (Kierwa & Fletcher, 1983). Indeed, any note taking that maximizes processing (such as paraphrasing, summarizing, elaborating, or personalizing) seems to help. (See, e.g., Barnett, Divester, & Rogozinski, 1981; Einstein, Morris, & Smith, 1985). Bretzing and Kulhavy (1979) compared high school groups who took verbatim notes with groups who wrote summaries, paraphrased main ideas, and simply wrote down words that began with uppercase letters. On tests requiring integration of information, students who wrote summaries or paraphrased main ideas outperformed those who took verbatim notes or simply copied certain words. In another study, Bretzing and Kulhavy (1981) compared groups of college students who read only, took notes to deliver a lecture to other students, and took notes to lecture professionals. On tests, both groups of note takers did significantly better than students who read only. Many recent studies tend to support the effectiveness of notetaking. Kierwa et al. (1991) found that encoding plus storage (taking notes and reviewing notes) was superior to just encoding (taking them but not reviewing them) or external storage (that is, reviewing borrowed notes). They also noted that college students actively assess and shift learning strategies each time a lecture is repeated in what Kierwa et al. called successive differentiation—students focus on top-level information first and then, when the lecture is repeated, search out the next level of information to write notes on. In another study, Kierwa, Benton, Kim, Risch, and Christensen (1995) studied note-taking formats and found that outline note takers performed best over conventional and matrix note takers. Laidlaw, Skok, and McLaughlin (1993) found that the combination of notetaking and self-questioning was a superior strategy for teaching science to intermediate students. Hughes and Suritsky (1993) studied AWARE, a note-taking strategy. They found that college students with learning disabilities could take organized notes if taught to *arrange* to take notes, *write* quickly using shorthand, *attend* to cues, and then *review* and *edit*.

## Outlining, Traditional and Free Form

Both traditional outlining and forms of diagrammatic outlining need further research. Traditional outlining encourages students to read texts carefully enough to note main ideas, distinguish between main and subordinate points, locate and list supporting examples and details, be aware of sequence and use of traditional elements, note patterns of organization, and, usually, rewrite material in their own words. Traditional outlining, therefore, appears to be a powerful study strategy, and, indeed, studies lend support to this view. Barton (1930), Salisbury (1935), Mathews (1938), Bisinkauskas (1970) and others found that students who outlined texts outperformed others. On the other hand, other studies (e.g., Arnold, 1942; Todd & Kessler, 1971; Willmore, 1966) found outlining to be less, or no more, effective than other study strategies. An important point to note, however, is that traditional outlining, with its highly structured and codified format, demands instruction. As Courtney (1965) pointed out, the ability to recognize organization in spoken or printed texts is rarely a natural accomplishment nor a quality of native intelligence (p. 78). To realize the full potential of traditional outlining as a study tool, it must be taught, probably in early grades with regular review and further application through secondary school and college. Lazarus (1996), for example, used a skeleton outline that later becomes guided notes for adolescents with mild disabilities to use during lectures or text reading but provides instruction on the development, practice, and use of these flexible skeleton notes. Three questions need to be asked about outlining: When should instruction begin? How much is required? What approaches to instruction are most effective?

Variations of traditional outlining have been studied and found effective. *Mapping* (sometimes called *graphing* or *networking*) allows students to note text relationships visually, in a nonlinear rather than linear way. Rather than list main and subordinate ideas and supporting examples or details consecutively as found in the printed text, students may indicate relationships in circles, constellations, or other ways. Czuchry and Dansereau (1996) found that *node-link mapping*, a spatial-verbal mapping technique, was a viable alternative to traditional writing assignments for undergraduate psychology students who found the technique to be very helpful in organizing and remembering information taught in the course. *Array outlining* (Hansell, 1978) has students identify key points in an assignment, copy these onto small pieces of paper, and arrange the pieces on their desktops in some order. After discussion with other students and teacher, students then copy their arrangements, or outlines, onto a larger sheet for study and review. *Pyramid outlines* (Walker, 1979) are drawings students prepare with key ideas at the top of a pyramid and with subordinate ideas arranged below. In a review of empirical studies in postsecondary settings, *concept mapping* (when nodes of information are linked, often in the form of a flow chart), was singled out by Hadwen and Winne (1996) as one of the most "potentially effective" study tactics and strategies (p. 702).

Research on graphic organizers (Hawks, McLeod, & Jonassen, 1985) has led to the use of *structured note taking* (Smith & Tompkins, 1988). Structured overviews and structural organizers (discussed earlier) are explained to students who are then given extensive practice in their use. Once students understand that such organizers represent text structures pictorially, they are encouraged to work collaboratively to prepare their own graphic organizers and then to use these as notetaking strategies. They learn to outline textual material diagrammatically and, with further practice, apply the strategy to both lecture note taking and the development of their own written compositions.

Recently, the use of semantic webbing, concept mapping, and similar forms of nonlinear note taking have been successfully used in the classroom to increase reading comprehension and develop writing skills, as well as promote and guide note taking. Avery, Baker, and Gross (1996) found in high school social studies classes that semantic webs can be used prior to instruction to assess what students know, during instruction to promote and guide note taking, as well as to assess gains made, and as a postassessment activity to evaluate what has been learned. Boyle (1996) found that teaching learning-disabled students the cognitive mapping strategy TRAVEL (topic, read, ask, verify, examine, and link) helped learning-disabled students with both literal and inferential comprehension of text. Bulgren and Scanlon (1998) found learning-disabled students gained from learning strategies such as CONCEPT, COMPARING, and a two-step strategy, ORDER. Ellis (1994) found that graphic organizers helped students comprehend content area material and recommended both teacher and student constructed graphic organizers. A meta-analysis by Horton et al. (1993), which reviewed 19 studies on concept mapping, found generally positive effects on both student achievement and attitudes whether the concept maps were teacher or student prepared. Spiegel and Barufaldi (1994) found that students who used graphic postorganizers of the text structure recalled more content than students who simply underlined and suggest graphic organizers as a way for science students to be more self-regulating in their learning when used flexibly to represent text structure. More recently, Hoover and Rabideau (1995) suggested using semantic webs as a tool for directly teaching and developing study skills, suggesting students construct semantic webs on topics such as test taking or note taking/outlining to activate prior knowledge on the particular study skill, its use, and its application.

Diagrammatic outlining offers many of the advantages of traditional outlining and, unlike traditional outlining, may be used to take lecture notes when lecturers fail to follow standard outline form. Again, more studies need to be done on both linear and nonlinear outlining, especially on variations of nonlinear.

## Summarizing

Many studies have examined the value of summarizing as a study strategy. Some have found that is seems to improve both retention and recall (Brown, Campione, & Day, 1980; Davis & Hult, 1997); reading comprehension (Palincsar & Brown, 1983; Wittrock & Alesandrini, 1990); and written summaries (Hare & Borchardt, 1984; McNeil & Donant, 1982).

Summarizing actually is a series of separate operations. Students must decide what to include or eliminate (evaluation), what to combine (condensation), and what language to use (transformation) (Hidi & Anderson, 1986). At least two sets of cognitive operations seem to be necessary: a selection process in which conscious judgments are continuously made of what is important and what is not and a reduction process in which ideas are deliberately condensed through a variety of high-order transformations. In the classroom, summarizing encourages students to:

1. Identify the writer's main ideas.
2. Recognize the purpose or intent of the selection.
3. Distinguish between relevant and irrelevant material.
4. Note the key evidence offered in support of a thesis or main idea.
5. See the underlying structure of organization.
6. Note the transitional, or signal, expressions used in the text.
7. Follow the sequence of the material. (Devine, 1986)

Specific rules for summarizing have been described by McNeil and Donant (1982):

1. Delete unnecessary or trivial material.
2. Delete material that is important but redundant.
3. Substitute a superordinate term for a list of terms.
4. Substitute a superordinate term for components of an action.
5. Select a topic sentence.
6. Invent a topic sentence when there is not one.

In addition to such rule-governed approaches to instruction, Cunningham (1982) suggested a more intuitive strategy called GIST (for generating interactions between schema and text), which restricts students' summaries to 15 blanks: As they read, they must delete all trivial propositions and select macrolevel ideas. In another approach, Laflamme (1998) devised the LiST summary technique, a six-step procedure that focused on story

structure and found that it was effective with high school students in comprehending complex short stories.

Is summarizing an effective study strategy? Its values seem apparent: It forces students to more carefully examine texts and record their reworked versions in their own language; it assists retention and is readily adoptable in a variety of classroom situations. Clearly, summarization training makes students more aware of the structure of ideas within the reading assignment and how the individual ideas relate to each other. In addition, such training causes students to spend more time with reading assignments, and, as has been frequently noted (see, e.g., Rinehart, Stahl, & Erickson, 1986), time spent on reading correlates highly to reading achievement. Study findings in general suggest that summarizing can be a powerful study tool. However, to be effective, it requires some instruction: children do not summarize naturally.

Skillful mature readers discriminate among portions of a text as they summarize, basing their choices of summary material on their knowledge of the content and their understanding of the author's intentions and the textual structure. Children, on the other hand, tend to overlook textual clues and make decisions about what to include or eliminate on a sentence-by-sentence basis (Hare & Borchardt, 1984). They also tend to include material they consider interesting or outstanding, sometimes disregarding topic sentences and implicit main ideas (Brown & Day, 1983). In one study, Winograd (1984) found poorer readers unable to select the same material as adult and better readers. Without guidance, eighth-graders in the study seemed to have difficulty using textual clues. In another study (Pichert, 1979), third-graders were able to rate the relative importance of a passage's idea units but only after they had received instruction.

Instruction does seem to pay dividends. Summarization training has been found to improve written summaries (Brown, Campione, & Day, 1981; Hare & Borchardt, 1984; Palincsar & Brown, 1983). Baumann (1984) found the reading comprehension of sixth-graders improved through summarization training. Bean and Steenwyk (1984) used two different methods of teaching summarization to sixth-grade students: a rule-governed approach (see McNeil & Donant, 1982, noted earlier) and the intuitive GIST approach (Cunningham, 1982, also described earlier). They found that both treatment groups significantly outperformed the control group on both paragraph summarization measures and a standardized reading comprehension test. A study at the college level (King et al., 1984) also found that students trained in summary writing not only wrote better summaries but achieved higher scores on a reading comprehension test than students in a control group that received no training.

## Writing to Learn

Related to summarizing, particularly the writing of summaries, is writing as a study approach or strategy. As Emig (1977) pointed out more than 20 years ago, "Writing serves learning uniquely because writing as process-and-product possesses a cluster of attributes that correspond uniquely to certain powerful learning strategies." Clearly, writing can make students aware of what they know and do not know, thus serving to monitor learning. In addition, the active researching that takes place before and during writing may add to students' knowledge, while the writing itself helps them discover meanings for themselves.

Evidence exists that students may use written summaries as a means of retaining new content area knowledge in memory (Dansereau et al., 1974; Davis & Hult, 1997; Vacca & Linek, 1992), especially after they have received training in how to write a summary. Further evidence seems to indicate that personal (learner-oriented) summaries, used by students to facilitate and monitor their own learning, are more effective than those prepared for teachers and others (audience-oriented summaries) (Hidi & V. Anderson, 1986; Jenkins, 1979). Evidence exists, too, that the writing of analytic essays aids student's learning. In studies by Langer (1986) and Newell (1984), high school students were asked to read a selection and respond in one of three ways: answer questions, take notes, or write an analytic essay that applied the new ideas to a new situation. Newell found the writing group produced a more abstract set of associations for key ideas in the selection; Langer found that content area knowledge increased most from essay writing (with note taking next and questioning–answering last). They both concluded that writing analytic seems to require students to be less bound by the text in front of them and more involved in organizing, integrating, and assimilating new ideas and information. Simpson, Hayes, Stahl, Connor, and Weaver (1988) attempted to structure essay writing in a study system called PORPE (see the section Study Systems that appears later) and reported that students trained in this writing approach tended to write significantly more organized and coherent essays. They concluded that this writing approach led to an efficient independent study strategy.

Feathers (1987) found that journal writing also seemed to facilitate learning and study. College students were encouraged to predict, underline, make notes, prepare maps, charts and written summaries, as well as generate their own questions. While studying chapters from college-level textbooks, they kept journals, writing four times a week. Analysis of the journals revealed that students not only learned the study strategies they were being taught but also grew in their metacognitive awareness of learning. Students demonstrated an understanding of the textbook material and alternative ways of studying it. Other recent studies support the value of journal writing. DeAngelis (1994) found college students who kept journals of lectures more successful on course examinations. Sweidel (1996) used journal writing as part of a project called study strategy portfolios, in which college students kept journals to encourage self-monitoring and self-reflection concerning studying. Sweidel found that it helped some students develop time management skills, learn new study strategies, and evaluate their use of strategies and their plan for study.

## STUDY SYSTEMS

Study systems are combinations of specific strategies, joined to increase their effectiveness. Among the oldest and most often recommended is SQ3R (Robinson, 1970). Using this approach, students first *survey* the assignment to get a general idea of what the passages are about; then they make up their own *questions* (often from headings and subtitles in the text). They next *read* to discover answers to their own questions, *recite* (in writing or aloud) these answers and, finally, *review* by rereading parts of the assignment to verify their answers. Clearly, SQ3R provides students with both an overview and opportunity to better define the study task, as well as opportunities for notetaking and self-recitation. Since Francis Robinson first described this system in the early 1940s, SQ3R has been widely used by teachers and students at all grade levels and has stimulated the development of many similar systems: PORST (preview, question, read, state, test; Staton, 1954), the Triple S Technique (scan, search, and summarize; Farquhar, Krumboltz, & Wrenn, 1960), OARWET (overview, achieve, write, evaluate, test; Norman & Norman, 1968), OK5R (overview, key idea, read, record, recite, review, reflect; Pauk, 1974), PQ4R (preview, question, read, reflect, recite, review; Thomas & Robinson, 1972), S4R (survey, read, recite, record, review; Stetson, 1981), and PQ5R (preview, question, read, record, recite, review, reflect; as cited in Graham & Robinson, 1984).

Bailey (1988) described a variation of SQ3R devised for college students; in SRUN, students survey, read, underline, and take notes. In HEART, Santeusanio (1988) has students ask "*How much do I know about this topic?*," *establish* a purpose for study, *ask* questions as they study, *record* their answers, and, finally, *test* themselves. The PORPE (for predict, organize, rehearse, practice, and evaluate) method was also developed for college students (Simpson et al., 1988). Students are asked to predict possible essay questions, organize key ideas pertinent to the questions, rehearse through self-recitation, practice by actually writing an essay, and evaluate their work for completeness and accuracy. The PSRT approach (Simons, 1989) has students prepare, structure, read, and think, with preparation focusing on activating prior knowledge, structure on noting how the text is organized, and thinking as summarizing and developing thought-provoking questions. The SPIN technique (Aylward, 1990) has students summarize, predict, infer, and take notes. New systems are regularly being developed for specific aspects of study; for example, POSSE (Englert & Mariage, 1991), PLANS (Graham, McArthur, Schwartz, & Page-Roth, 1992), and AWARE (Hughes & Suritsky, 1993).

Do study systems work? The individual components of most study systems rest on some research base. Defining study tasks, overviewing, notetaking, summarizing, and others (see previous section) are supported by study findings (although findings are in some instances equivocal or open to various interpretations). Study systems themselves usually are recommended by teachers who have devised and used them successfully but not tested them in controlled studies. Many are known primarily because of a single article in a professional journal or advocacy in a textbook or program.

SQ3R is a notable exception. Since its first promotion as an effective tool for studying expository text, many studies have been conducted on its usefulness (Chastain & Thurber, 1989; Gustafson & Pederson, 1985; McCormick & Cooper, 1991). Johnson (1973) reviewed the research on SQ3R and concluded that research evidence did not support its widespread use but that the value of its component parts is generally substantiated. Spencer (1978) reviewed the research and concurred with Harris (1971) that SQ3R "seems to be well grounded in the experimental psychology of learning, but has not been subjected to much experimentation" (p. 440). Johns and McNamara (1980) noted that its wide use stems less from controlled studies than endorsements by reading educators. Maxwell (1980) noted, too, that although studies support the separate components, SQ3R needs further research as a total method. She also pointed out, "For the fearful student, faced with a long, difficult text to read, the SQ3R method provides a technique for getting started." Moreover, she noted, "[I]t makes explicit the steps that a skilled learner automatically follows' (p. 306). Santeusanio (1983) found a lack of specific research evidence to support SQ3R but recommended its continued use as a study tool.

Martin (1985) focused on the self-questioning aspect of SQ3R. College freshmen in three groups were trained in SQ3R, self-questioning, and the REAP study system (Eanet & Manzo, 1976). Selected because it does not include a self-questioning component, it requires students to read the passage, encode the meaning in the reader's language, annotate the meaning by writing personal notes, and then ponder the passage's meaning, now in annotated form, either through internal "dialectic thinking" or through discussion with others. (In the annotation stage, the reader is expected to "discriminate and synthesize the ideas presented by the writer, translate these into his own language, and crystallize the result in writing"; Eanet & Manzo, 1976). After 6 weeks of practice students were given an unfamiliar passage and told to apply the specific approach they had learned. Two weeks later, students were again tested to determine the effects of the treatment on longer term retention. Students who used SQ3R significantly outperformed those who used REAP. However, the SQ3R group did not significantly outperform the self-questioning group, although self-questioning was not significantly superior to SQ3R. Martin concluded that SQ3R owes its effectiveness to its step-by-step structured procedure. Evidently, it does help students concentrate upon those areas of a passage that could be of most importance: "By surveying headings and subheadings, and converting them into questions, subjects are better able to focus in on the important information" (p. 78). However, after surveying recent studies, Hadwen and Winne (1996) concluded that "there is *very* meager evidence" in support of SQ3R (p. 694).

Two other studies of study systems are described here. The PORPE approach was developed as an integrated study system that focuses on writing, particularly on writing as a postreading strategy to assist students in the assimilation and synthesis of concepts (Simpson et al., 1988). In their study, the researchers wanted to determine the extent which writing as an integrated component of a study system improved the learning of content area material. Predicting possible essay questions, they believed, would promote self-generated questions to encourage active and elaborative processing and act as a catalyst for the subsequent steps in the system: organizing key ideas would help students plan and arrange information for later writing much as they would do in the drafting stage of writing. Rehearsing would engage them in active self-recitation and self-testing,

thus helping them to monitor and question themselves and take corrective actions when needed; practicing would help students create from memory their own text which would answer their self-predicted essay questions, and evaluating would help them check whether they had created meaningful text that demonstrated their understanding of the content. Sixty-five college freshmen were trained over a 3-week period to use either a question-answer recitation format or PORPE. All students took both prestudy and poststudy essay and multiple-choice tests. The results indicated that the students trained in the PORPE system scored significantly higher than students using a recitation format with questions similar to those found in textbooks or usually used by teachers. They scored higher on both recall and recognition items on the multiple-choice tests and on an essay scored for content, organization, and cohesion. It was concluded that PORPE can be a potent, durable, and efficient study strategy for college students in their efforts to learn content area concepts" (p. 149).

In SPIN, Aylward (1990) focused on summarizing, predicting, inferencing, and note taking. Using summary rules suggested by Brown and Day (1983), 50 eighth-grade students were trained to summarize and take notes. Through teacher modeling and worksheets they were given practice in predicting and making inferences about stories and content area materials. These students were given 10 weeks of continued practice in the use of SPIN in content area classes; an equated control group studied the same material without instruction in SPIN. A comparison of pretest and posttest scores on measures of content indicated that students in the SPIN group scored significantly higher in knowledge of content as well as in ability to summarize, predict, infer, and take notes. SPIN differs from other study systems in that students are not advised to use the separate study strategies in sequence; that is, there are no "stages"—they are not told to, first, predict, then read, and then, infer and take notes, and, finally, summarize. Instruction stresses all four strategies and encourages students to use them together.

Study systems such as SQ3R, PORPE, or SPIN, should not be confused with teacher-directed lesson frameworks. Lesson frameworks help teachers structure and control learning in the classroom. In the directed reading activity, or DRA, for example, Betts (1955) suggested stages in a reading lesson: exploring and building background knowledge, reading, discussion, and extension. By moving sequentially through the stages, teachers are better able to control student learning. The directed reading-thinking activity, or DR-TA (Stauffer, 1969), moves students through prediction and verification to considered judgments in five steps. The guided reading procedure, or GRP (Manzo, 1975), has eight steps to guide students, under the teacher's direction, from prereading to evaluation. The K-W-L Plus method (Carr & Ogle, 1987) has students recall what they *know* about the topic of a passage, decide what they *want* to learn from reading, and then identify what they have *learned*, using both mapping and summarizing. Such approaches may in time be internalized by students and become personal study systems for them, but their primary intent is to aid teachers. Another framework includes FLIP (Schumm & Mangrum, 1991).

## IMPROVEMENT OF STUDY: FURTHER CONSIDERATIONS

At the present time, the convergence of a number of research areas seem to promise fresh insights into how students learn. Studies in learning theory, cognitive psychology, cognitive styles, reading, the writing process, and other areas are revealing interconnections between areas that point to new understandings about ways to improve study. Different theories and data lead to different data and theories; all lead to different ways of looking at learning. However, several concerns, questions, and issues, although certainly affected by research findings, need to be addressed less in terms of statistical analysis and measures and more in terms of professional considerations. Four such concerns are examined here.

First, students need a repertoire of study tools. Although enthusiastic advocates regularly promote one specific type of, say, note taking, the latest version of SQ3R, or some particular strategy as a panacea, no single study skill, strategy, or system is demonstrably superior to others. The quick-and-easy ones often work only at certain times, for certain students, in certain situations. Those that do seem to focus attention effectively and promote deeper understanding often demand great expenditures of time and effort on the part of students. In addition, the tools that show great promise—such as summarizing and both linear and diagrammatic outlining—usually require considerable training. Some study tools have demonstrated power but only in specific contexts, with students of a certain age, in one content area but not in another, with one kind of materials but not with others, and so on. To complicate matters further, not enough is yet known about cognitive styles to generalize about the best strategies for independent learning. Due to these reasons and the fact that some research questions remain unaddressed while other are equivocal, it seems appropriate to introduce students to a wide array of study tools and encourage them to experiment to discover those that work most effectively for them in various situations.

Second, students need help in test taking. Study skills, strategies, and systems are developed in school settings where achievement is measured by tests. Many teachers have suggested, therefore, that test-taking skills need to be developed along with study tools. They cite the positive relationship between test performance and the skills required to take tests and note the value to students of knowledge of test characteristics and formats to improve performance. Many teachers show students how to prepare for tests by defining the content area to be studied, noting specialized vocabulary, as well as ideas and information stressed in class, and examining previous exams, study guides, outlines, notes, and assignments. They have encouraged students to generate their own questions for study, summarize difficult points, check other sources, and given tips about controlling test anxiety. In addition, many teachers at all levels have shared with students specific information about test formats, pacing during exams, writing essay tests, dealing with multiple-choice items, and so on. A variety of articles and handbooks are available to assist teachers in showing students how to take tests (see, e.g., Devine & Meagher, 1989; Flippo,

2000; Pauk, 1984). Many teachers use specific strategies such as SCORER (for schedule your time; *check* clue words; *omit* difficult questions; *read* carefully; *estimate* your answer; *review* your work). Devised by Carman and Adams (1972) the strategy has been further developed and used in several studies (see Lee & Alley, 1981; Ritter & Idol-Maestas, 1983). Ritter and Idol-Maestas (1986) found that the SCORER strategy worked successfully with both poor and above-average comprehenders and recommended such a test-taking strategy to help students earn optimal scores on tests.

Although there may be ethical concerns about test coaching, which is specific to the content being examined, test wiseness (or test sophistication) seems a reasonable objective of any program designed to improve independent study. Flippo (2000) addressed this question by providing strategies in handling test panic, test-study techniques, test format, and test taking. In addition, Flippo, Becker, and Wark (2000) addressed test wiseness on the college level.

Third, students should be encouraged by teachers to look at a number of materials and resources in their quest to learn various study skills strategies. Technology, especially computer-aided instruction, may provide students with an engaging and effective way to learn study skills. For example, computers can be used to help students understand text organization and structure: Anderson-Inman (1996), Anderson-Inman, Redekopp, and Adams (1992), and Tenny (1992) all advocated the use of computer-assisted outlining in the creation of both traditional outlines and graphic organizers for use as notes or for recording and synthesizing material for a report. Current *hypertext* (those programs that focus on text only) and *hypermedia* (applications of text, music, graphics and so on) offer students the possibility to learn without interruption, especially those students that have difficulty with text. Boone and Higgins (1992) used hypermedia applications to construct computer study guides for students with reading difficulties and found that these guides were as effective as teacher lectures at the high school level. MacArthur and Haynes (1996) worked with SALT (student assistant for learning text), a hypermedia reading aid that allowed low achieving students access to text with typical textbook features (graphics, outline, glossary and text questions) and nontypical features such as a note-taking area, speech synthesis, highlighting of main ideas, and summarizing capabilities. Students who used this hypermedia program gained in comprehension of text and attitude in learning. Anderson-Inman, Horney, Chen, and Lewin (1994) used hypertext literacy in the Electrotext Project with middle school students and found that some students benefited from the use of text when students had notetaking and graphic organizer options built into the program.

Fourth, students need study help in *all* classses. In many schools, guidance in independent learning is often relegated to special classes or courses taught by special teachers. Instructional programs in elementary and secondary schools (especially middle schools) meet one, two, or three times a week to introduce students to basic strategies; a study system, usually SQ3R; and a variety of so-called study skills, ranging from alphabetizing to using the card catalog. Such arrangements may make students more aware of the need to study, help foster positive study habits and attitudes, and introduce important study skills, strategies, and systems. However, no evidence exists that these arrangements lead to transfer or further growth. Most college level programs have been similarly arranged: Students, usually freshmen, meet one, two, or three times a week with a specialist who introduces basic skills, explains time management, encourages the use of assignment books, and so on (Reed, 1986; Sherman, 1985). Again, no evidence exists that students transfer such learning to other college courses. Another point of view about the improvement of independent study has gained

prominence in recent years (Devine, 1989). It suggests that instruction in how to study begins in the primary grades and continues through to the final college years and that it takes place in content area classes under the guidance of content area teachers and administrators who suggest that study techniques be taught not in separate freshmen year courses by specialists but by all college teachers (Donohoe, 1989). Learning how to learn on one's own may be too important to be the exclusive concern of specialists. It is the core of education.

# References

Anderson, R. C., & Biddle, W. B. (1975). On asking people questions about what they are reading. In G. H. Bower (Ed.), *The psychology of learning and motivation* (Vol. 9, pp. 89-132). New York: Academic Press.

Anderson, T. H. (1980). Study strategies and adjunct aids. In R. J. Spiro, B. C. Bruce, & W. F. Brewer (Eds.), *Theoretical issues in reading comprehension* (pp. 483-502). Hillsdale, NJ: Lawrence Erlbaum Associates.

Anderson, T. H., & Armbruster, B. B. (1984). Studying. In P. D. Pearson (Ed.), *Handbook of reading research* (pp. 657-679). New York: Longman.

Anderson-Inman, L. (1996). Computer-assisted outlining: Information organization made easy. *Journal of Adolescent and Adult Literacy, 39,* 316-320.

Anderson-Inman, L., Horney, M. A., Chen, D. T., & Lewin, L. (1994). Hypertext Literacy: Observations from the electrotext project. *Language Arts, 71,* 279-287.

Anderson-Inman, L., Redekopp, R., & Adams, V. (1992). Electronic studying: Using computer-based outlining programs as study tools. *Reading and Writing Quarterly: Overcoming Learning Disabilities, 8,* 337-358.

Arnold, H. F. (1942). The comparative effectiveness of certain study techniques in the field of history. *Journal of Educational Pyschology, 33,* 449-457.

Ausubel, D. P. (1960). The use of advance organizers in the learning and retention of meaningful verbal material. *Journal of Educational Psychology, 51,* 267-272.

Ausubel, D. P. (1978). In defense of advance organizers: A reply to critics. *Review of Educational Research, 48,* 251-257.

Avery, P. G., Baker, J., & Gross, S. H. (1996). "Mapping learning at the secondary level. *The Social Studies,* 217-223.

Aylward, M. (1990). *The SPIN reading/study skills system.* Unpublished doctoral dissertation, Lowell, MA: University of Lowell.

Bailey, N. S. (1988). S-RUN: Beyond SQ3R. *Journal of Reading, 32,* 170-171.

Barnett, J. E., Divester, F. J., & Rogozinski, J. T. (1981). What is learned in notetaking? *Journal of Educational Psychology, 73,* 181-192.

Barton, W. A. (1930). *Outlining as a study procedure.* New York: Teachers College, Columbia University.

Baumann, R. (1984). The effectiveness of a direct instruction paradigm for teaching main idea comprehension. *Reading Research Quarterly, 20,* 93-115.

Bean, T. W., & Steenyk, F. L. (1984). The effect of three forms of summarization instruction on sixth grader's summary writing and comprehension. *Journal of Reading Behavior, 16,* 297-307.

Betts, E. (1955). Reading as a thinking process. *The National Elementary Principal, 35,* 90-99.

Bizinkauskas, P. A. (1970). *An evaluation of the effectiveness of tape-recorded note-taking versus written note-taking versus rereading as a study technique.* Unpublished doctoral dissertation, Boston: Boston University.

Boone, R., & Higgins, K. (1992). Hypermedia applications for content-area study guides. *Reading and Writing Quarterly: Overcoming Learning Difficulties, 8,* 379-393.

Boyle, J. R. (1996). The effects of a cognitive mapping strategy on the literal and inferential comprehension of students with mild disabilities. *Learning Disability Quarterly, 19,* 86-98.

Bragstad, B. J., & Stumpf, S. M. (1987). *A guidebook for teaching study skills and motivation.* Needham, MA: Allyn & Bacon.

Bretzing, B. B., & Kulhavy, R. W. (1979). Note taking and depth of processing. *Contemporary Educational Psychology, 4,* 145-153.

Bretzing, B. B., & Kulhavy, R. W. (1981). Notetaking and passage style. *Journal of Educational Psychology, 73,* 242-250.

Brown, A. L., Campione, J. C., & Day, J. D. (1980). *Learning to learn: On training students to learn from texts.* (Rep. No. CS 006 135). Cambridge, MA: Bolt, Beranek & Newman. (ERIC Document Reproduction Service No. ED 203 297)

Brown, A. L., Campione, J. C., & Day, J. D. (1981). Learning to learn: On training students to learn from texts. *Educational Researcher, 10,* 14-21.

Brown, A. L., & Day, J. D. (1983). Macrorules for summarizing texts: The development of expertise. *Journal of Verbal Learning and Verbal Behavior, 22,* 1-14.

Bulgren, J., & Scanlon, D. (1998). Instructional routines and learning strategies that promote understanding of content area concepts. *Journal of Adolescent and Adult Literacy, 41*(4), 292-301.

Carman, R. A., & Adams, W. R. (1972). *Study skills: A student's guide for survival.* New York: Wiley.

Carr, E., & Ogle, D. (1987). K-W-L Plus: A strategy for comprehension and summarization. *Journal of Reading, 30,* 626-631.

Chastian, G., & Thurber, S. (1989). The SQ3R study technique enhances comprehension of an introductory psychology textbook. *Reading Improvement, 26,* 94-96.

Corkill, A. J., Bruning, R. H., & Glover, J. A. (1988). Advance organizers: Concrete versus abstract. *Journal of Educational Research, 82,* 76-81.

Cormier, P. (1995). *The effects of instruction in selected study procedures on student achievement and attitude.* Unpublished doctoral dissertation, Lowell, MA: University of Massachusetts, Lowell.

Courtney, L. (1965). Organization produced. In H. L. Herber (Ed.), *Developing study skills in secondary schools* (pp. 77-96), Newark, DE: International Reading Association.

Cunningham, J. R. (1982). Generating interaction between schemata and text. In J. A. Niles & L. A. Harris (Eds.), *New inquiries in reading research and instruction* (pp. 42-47). Rochester, NY: National Reading Conference.

Czuchry, M., & Dansereau, D. F. (1996). Node-link mapping as an alternative to traditional writing assignments in undergraduate psychology courses. *Teaching of Psychology, 23,* 91-96.

Dansereau, D. F., McDonald, B. A., Long, G. L., Atkinson, T. R., Ellis, A. M., Collins, K. W., Williams, S., & Evans, S. H. (1974). *The development and assessment of an effective learning strategy program.* (Rep. No. 3). Fort Worth: Texas Christian University.

Davey, B. (1993). Helping middle school learners succeed with reading assignments: A focus on time planning. *Journal of Reading, 37*(3), 170-173.

Davis, M., & Hult, R. E. (1997). Effects of writing summaries as a generative learning activity during notetaking. *Teacher of Psychology, 24*(1), 47-49.

DeAngelis, V. G. (1994). *Effects of selected expressive writing activities on college learning.* Unpublished doctoral dissertation, Lowell, MA: University of Massachusetts, Lowell.

Devine, T. G. (1986). *Teaching reading comprehension: From theory to practice.* Needham, MA: Allyn & Bacon.

Devine, T. G. (1987). *Teaching study skills: A guide for teachers* (Rev. ed.). Needham, MA: Allyn & Bacon.

Devine, T. G. (1989). Not just reading—Study skills, too. *New England Reading Association Journal, 25,* 7-14.

Devine, T. G., & Meagher, L. D. (1989). *Mastering study skills: A student guide.* Englewood Cliffs, NJ: Prentice-Hall.

Dickinson, D. J., & O'Connell, D. Q. (1990). Effect of quality and quantity of study on student grades. *Journal of Educational Research, 83,* 227-231.

Donohoe, J. S. (1989). *The impact of faculty participation in a college study skills program.* Unpublished doctoral dissertation, Boston: Northeastern University.

Duell, O. K. (1978). Overt and covert use of objectives of different cognitive levels. *Contemporary Journal of Educational Psychology, 3,* 239-245.

Eanet, M. G., & Manzo, A. V. (1976). REAP—A strategy for improving reading/writing/study skills. *Journal of Reading, 19,* 647-652.

Einstein, G. O., Morris, J., & Smith, S. (1985). Notetaking, individual differences, and memory for lecture information. *Journal of Educational Psychology, 77,* 522-532.

Ellis, E. S. (1994). Integrating writing strategy instruction with content-area instruction: Part I. Orienting students to organizational devices. *Intervention in School and Clinic, 29,* 169-179.

Emig, J. (1977). Writing as a mode of learning. *College Composition and Communication, 28,* 122-128.

Englert, C. S., & Mariage, T. V. (1991). Making students partners in the comprehension process: Organizing the reading "POSSE." *Learning Disabilities Quarterly, 14,* 123-138.

Farquhar, W. W., Krumboltz, J. D., & Wrenn, C. G. (1960). *Learning to study.* New York: Ronald Press.

Feathers, K. M. (1987). Learning to learn: Case studies of the process. *Reading Research and Instruction, 26,* 264-274.

Flippo, R. F. (2000). *TestWise: Strategies for success in taking tests* (2nd ed.). Torrance, CA: Good Apple/Frank Schaffer.

Flippo, R. F., Becker, M. J., & Wark, D. M. (2000). Preparing for and taking tests. In R. F. Flippo & D. C. Caverly (Eds.), *Handbook of college reading and study strategy research* (pp. 221-260). Mahwah, NJ: Lawrence Erlbaum Associates.

Flower, L. (1990). The role of task representation in reading-to-write. In L. Flower, V. Stein, J. Ackerman, M. Kantz, K. McCormick, & W. Peck. *Reading to Write: Exploring a Cognitive and Social Process* (pp. 35-75). New York: Oxford University Press.

Frase, L. T., & Schwartz, B. J. (1975). Effect of question production and answering on prose recall. *Journal of Educational Psychology, 67,* 628-635.

Fry, R. W. (1996). *How to study* (4th ed.). Franklin Lakes, NJ: Career Press.

Gates, A. I. (1917). Recitation as a factor in memorizing. *Archives of Psychology, 40.*

Glover, J. A., Bullock, R. G., & Dietzer, M. L. (1990). Advance organizers: Delay hypotheses. *Journal of Educational Psychology, 82,* 291-297.

Glynn, S. M. (1978). Capturing reader's attention by means of typographic cueing strategies. *Educational Technology, 18,* 7-12.

Graham, S., MacArthur, C., Schwartz, S., & Page-Roth, R. (1992). Improving the Composition of students with learning disabilities using a strategy involving product and process goal setting. *Exceptional Children, 58,* 322-334.

Graham, K. G., & Robinson, H. A. (1984). *Study skills handbook: A guide for all teachers.* Newark. DE: International Reading Association.

Graves, M. F., & Cooke, C. L. (1980). Effects of previewing difficult short stories for high school students. *Research on Reading in Secondary Schools, 6,* 38-54.

Graves, M. F., Cooke, C. L., & LaBerge, M. J. (1983). Effects of previewing difficult short stories in low ability junior high school students' comprehension, recall, and attitude. *Reading Research Quarterly, 18,* 262-276.

Graves, M. F., & Palmer, R. J. (1981). Validating previewing as a method of improving fifth and sixth grade students' comprehension of short stories. *Michigan Reading Journal, 15,* 1-3.

Gustafson, D. J., & Pederson, J. E. (1985). SQ3R: Surveying and questioning relevant, recent (and not so recent) research. (Rep. No. CS 008 436). Miwaukee, WI: Great Lakes Regional Conference of the International Reading Association. (ERIC Document Reproduction Service No. ED 269 736)

Hadwen, A. F., & Winne, P. H. (1996). Study strategies have meager support: A review with recommendations for implementation. *Journal of Higher Education, 67*(6), 692-715.

Hansell, T. S. (1978). Stepping up to outlining. *Journal of Reading, 22,* 248-252.

Hare, V. C., & Borchardt, K. M. (1984). Direct Instruction of summarization skills. *Reading Research Quarterly, 20,* 62-78.

Harris, A. J. (1971). *How to increase reading abilities* (5th ed.). New York: McKay.

Hawks, P., McLeod, N. P., & Jonassen, D. H. (1985). Graphic organizers in texts, courseware, and supplementary materials. In D. H. Jonassen (Ed.), *Technology of text* (Vol. 2, pp. 250-262). Englewood Cliffs, NJ: Educational Technology.

Hayes, D. A., & Tierney, R. J. (1982). Developing readers' knowledge through analogy. *Reading Research Quarterly, 17,* 256-280.

Hidi, S., & Anderson, V. (1986). Producing written summaries: Task demands, cognitive operations, and implications for instruction. *Review of Educational Research, 56,* 473-493.

Hoover, J. J. (1993). Helping parents develop a home-based study skills program. *Intervention in School and Clinic, 28*(4), 238-245.

Hoover, J. J., & Rabideau, D. K. (1995). Semantic webs and study skills. *Intervention in School and Clinic, 30,* 292-296.

Horton, P. B., McConney, A. A., Gallo, M., Woods, A. L., Senn, G. J., & Hamelin, D. (1993). An investigation of the effectiveness of concept mapping as an instructional tool. *Science Education, 77,* 95-111.

Hughes, C. A., & Suritsky, S. K. (1993). Notetaking skills and strategies for students with learning disabilities. *Preventing School Failure, 38,* 7-11.

Jenkins, J. J. (1979). Four points to remember: A tetrahedral model and memory experiments. In L. S. Cermak & F. I. M. Craik (Eds.), *Levels of processing in human memory* (pp. 429-446). Hillsdale, NJ: Lawrence Erlbaum Associates.

Johns, J. L., & McNamara, L. P. (1980). The SQ3R technique: A forgotten research target. *Journal of Reading, 23*, 705-708.

Johnson, S. (1973). A system for the diagnosis and treatment of test study problems. In G. Kerstiens (Ed.), *Proceedings of the sixth annual conference of the Western College Reading Association*. Santa Fe Springs, CA: Western College Reading Association.

Kierwa, K. A. (1984). Acquiring effective notetaking skills: An alternative to professional notetaking. *Journal of Reading, 27*, 299-302.

Kierwa, K. A., Benton, S. L., Kim, S. I., Risch, N., & Christensen, M. (1995). Effects of notetaking and study technique on recall and relational performance. *Contemporary Educational Psychology, 20*, 172-187.

Kiewra, K. A., DuBois, N. F., Christian, D., & McShane, A. (1988). Providing study notes: Comparison of three types of notes for review. *Journal of Educational Psychology, 80*, 595-597.

Kiewra, K. A., DuBois, N. F., Christian, D., McShane, A., Meyerhoffer, M., & Roskelley, D. (1991). Note-taking functions and techniques. *Journal of Educational Psychology, 83*, 240-245.

Kiewra, K. A., & Fletcher, H. J. (1983). *A levels of processing approach for determining the relationship between note encoding and achievement*. Paper presented at the Southwest Psychological Association, San Antonio, TX.

Kiewra, K. A., & Frank, B. M. (1988). Encoding and external-storage effects of personal lecture notes, skeletal notes, and detailed notes for field-independent and field-dependent learners. *Journal of Educational Research, 81*, 143-148.

Kiewra, K. A., Mayer, R. E., Christensen, M., Kim, S., & Risch, N. (1991). Effects of repetition on recall and note-taking: Strategies for learning from lectures. *Journal of Educational Psychology, 83*, 120-123.

King, J. R., Biggs, S., & Lipsky, S. (1984). Students' self questioning and summarizing as reading-study strategies. *Journal of Reading Behavior, 16*, 205-218.

Kulhavy, R. W., Dyer, J. W., & Silver, L. (1975). The effects of note-taking and test expectancy on the learning of text material. *Journal of Educational Research, 68*, 363-365.

Laflamme, J. G. (1998). *An evaluation of an experimental technique, the LiST summary, to improve the comprehension of short stories*. Unpublished doctoral dissertation, Lowell, MA: University of Massachusetts.

Laidlaw, E. N., Skok, R. L., & McLaughlin, T. F. (1993). The effects of notetaking and self-questioning on quiz performance. *Science Education, 77*, 75-82.

Langer, J. A. (1986). Learning through writing: Study skills in the content areas. *Journal of Reading, 29*, 400-406.

Lazarus, B. D. (1996). Flexible skeletons: Guided notes for adolescents with mild disabilities. *Teaching Exceptional Children*, 36-40.

Lee, P., & Alley, G. G. (1981). *Training junior high LD students to use a test-taking strategy* (Research Rep. No. 38). Lawrence: University of Kansas, Institute for Research in Learning Disabilities.

MacArthur, C. A., & Haynes, J. B. (1995). Student assistant for learning from text (SALT): A hypermedia reading aid. *Journal of Learning Disabilities, 28*, 150-159.

Manzo, A. (1975). Guided reading procedures. *Journal of Reading, 18*, 287-291.

Martin, M. A. (1985). Students' applications of self-questioning study techniques: An investigation of their efficiency. *Reading Psychology, 6*, 69-83.

Mathews, C. O. (1938). Comparison of methods of study for immediate and delayed recall. *Journal of Educational Psychology, 29*, 101-106.

Maxwell, M. (1980). *Improving student learning skills*. San Francisco, CA: Jossey-Bass.

McAndrew, D. A. (1983). Underlining and notetaking: Some suggestions from research. *Journal of Reading, 27*, 103-108.

McCormick, S., & Cooper, J. O. (1991). Can SQ3R facilitate secondary learning disabled students' literal comprehension of expository text? *Reading Psychology, 12*, 239-271.

McMackin, M. C. (1994). *Discourse synthesis: The role of task impression, goal setting, organization, and creativity when writing from sources*. Unpublished doctoral dissertation, Lowell, MA: University of Massachusetts.

McNeil, J., & Donant, L. (1982). Summarization strategy for improving reading comprehension. In J. A. Niles & L. A. Harris (Eds.), *New inquiries in reading research and instruction*. Rochester, NY: National Reading Conference.

Morse, J. M. (1975). The effects of question generation, question answering, and reading on prose learning (Doctoral dissertation, University of Oregon). *Dissertation Abstracts International, 37*, 5709A-5710A. (University Microfilms No. 77-4750)

Nelson, J. (1990). This was an easy assignment: Examining how students interpret academic writing tasks. *Research in Teaching English, 24*(4), 363-396.

Newell, G. E. (1984). Learning from writing in two content areas: A case/study protocol analysis. *Research in the Teaching of English, 18*, 265-285.

Nist, S. L., & Hogrebe, M. C. (1987). The role of underlining and annotating in remembering textual information. *Reading Research and Instruction, 27*, 12-25.

Norman, M. H., & Norman, E. S. (1968). *Successful reading*. New York: Holt, Rinehart & Winston.

Palinscar, A. S., & Brown, A. L. (1983). *Reciprocal teaching of comprehension-monitoring activities* (Tech. Rep. No. 269). Champaign, IL: University of Illinois, Center for the Study of Reading. (ERIC Document Reproduction Service No. ED 225 135)

Pauk, W. (1974). *How to study in college* (2nd ed.). Boston: Houghton Mifflin.

Pauk, W. (1984). Preparing for exams. *Reading World, 23*, 386-387.

Pearson, J. W., & Santa, C. M. (1995). Students as researchers of their own learning. *Journal of Reading, 38*(6), 462-469.

Pichert, J. W. (1979). *Sensitivity to what is important in prose* (Rep. No. CS 005 172). Cambridge, MA: Bolt, Beranek & Newman. (ERIC Document Reproduction Service No. ED 179 946)

Policastro, M. (1975). Notetaking: The key to college success. *Journal of Reading, 18*, 372-375.

Poppleton, P. K., & Austwick, K. (1964). A comparison of programmed learning and note-taking at two age levels. *British Journal of Educational Psychology, 34*, 43-50.

Reed, M. E. B. (1986). Management strategies to assist students in improving learning skills. *Journal of Developmental Education, 9*, 2-4.

Rickards, J. P., & August, G. J. (1975). Generative underlining strategies in prose recall. *Journal of Educational Psychology, 67*, 860-865.

Rickards, J. P., & McCormick, C. B. (1988). Effect of interspersed conceptual prequestions on note-taking in listening comprehension. *Journal of Educational Psychology, 80*, 592-594.

Rinehart, S. D., Stahl, S. A., & Erikson, L. G. (1986). Some effects of summarization training on reading. *Reading Research Quarterly, 21*, 422-436.

Rinehart, S. D., & Welker, W. A. (1992). Effects of advance organizers on level and time of text recall. *Reading Research and Instruction, 32*, 77-86.

Ritter, S. A., & Idol-Maestas, L. (1983). *Training EMH senior high school students to use a test-taking strategy*. Unpublished manuscript, University of Illinois, Department of Special Education, Urbana-Champaign.

Ritter, S. A., & Idol-Maestas, L. (1986). Teaching middle school students to use a test-taking strategy. *Journal of Educational Research, 79,* 350-357.

Robinson, F. (1970). *Effective study* (4th ed.). New York: Harper & Row.

Salisbury, R. (1935). Some effects of training in outlining. *English Journal, 24,* 111-116.

Santeusanio, R. P. (1983). *A practical approach to content area reading.* Reading, MA: Addison-Wesley.

Santeusanio, R. P. (1988). *Study skills and strategies.* Baltimore, MD: College Skills Center.

Schell, T. R., & Rocchio, D. (1975). A comparison of underlining strategies for improving reading comprehension and retention. In G. H. McNinch & W. D. Miller (Eds.), *Reading: Convention and inquiry* (pp. 391-399). Clemson, SC: National Reading Conference.

Sherman, T. M. (1985). Learning improvement programs: A review of controllable influences. *Journal of Higher Education, 56,* 85-100.

Shrager, L., & Mayer, R. E. (1989). Note-taking fosters generative learning strategies in novices. *Journal of Educational Psychology, 81,* 263-264.

Schultz, C. B., & DiVesta, F. J. (1972). Effects of passage organization and note-taking on the selection of clustering strategies and on recall of textual material. *Journal of Educational Psychology, 63,* 244-252.

Schumm, J. S., & Mangrum, C. T. (1991). FLIP: A framework for content area reading. *Journal of Reading, 35*(2), 120-124.

Silvers, V. L., & Kreiner, D. S. (1997). The effects of pre-existing inappropriate highlighting on reading comprehension. *Reading Research and Instruction, 36,* 217-223.

Simons, S. M. (1989). PSRT—A reading comprehension strategy. *Journal of Reading, 32,* 419-427.

Simpson, M. L., Hayes, C. G., Stahl, N., Connor, R. T., & Weaver, D. (1988). An initial validation of a study strategy system. *Journal of Reading Behavior, 20,* 149-180.

Slater, W. H., Graves, M., & Piche, G. L. (1985). Effects of structural organizers on ninth-grade students' comprehension and recall of four patterns of expository prose. *Reading Research Quarterly, 20,* 189-202.

Smith, P. L., & Tompkins, G. E. (1988). Structured notetaking: A new strategy for content area readers. *Journal of Reading, 32,* 46-53.

Spencer, F. (1978). SQ3R: Several queries regarding relevant research. In J. L. Vaughan & P. J. Gaus (Eds.), *Research on reading in secondary schools* (pp. 285-293). Tucson: University of Arizona.

Spiegel, G. F., & Barufaldi, J. P. (1994). The effects of a combination of text structure awareness and graphic postorganizers on recall and retention of science knowledge. *Journal of Research in Science Teaching, 31,* 913-932.

Staton, T. H. (1954). *How to study.* Nashville, TN: McQuiddley.

Stauffer, R. G. (1969). *Directing reading maturity as a cognitive process.* New York: Harper & Row.

Stetson, E. G. (1981). Improving textbook learning with S4R: A strategy for teachers, not students. *Reading Horizons, 22,* 129-135.

Stevens, K. C. (1982). Can we improve reading by teaching background information? *Journal of Reading, 25,* 326-329.

Stewart-Dore, N. (1982, July). *Where is the learning we have lost in information? Strategies for effective reading in content areas.* Paper presented at the Ninth World Congress in Reading, International Reading Association, Dublin, Ireland. (ED 322 138)

Sweidel, G. B. (1996). Study strategy portfolio: A project to enhance study skills and time management. *Teaching of Psychology, 23,* 246-248.

Tenny, J. L. (1992). Computer-supported study strategies for purple people. *Reading and Writing Quarterly: Overcoming Learning Disabilities, 8,* 359-377.

Thomas, E., & Robinson, H. A. (1972). *Improving reading in every classroom.* Boston: Allyn & Bacon.

Tierney, R. J., & Cunningham, J. W. (1984). Research in teaching reading comprehension. In P. D. Pearson (Ed.), *Handbook of reading research* (pp. 609-655). New York: Longman.

Todd, W., & Kessler, C. C. (1971). Influence of response mode, sex, reading ability and level of difficulty as four measures of recall of meaningful written material. *Journal of Educational Psychology, 62,* 229-234.

Tudor, I. (1986). Advance organizers as adjuncts to L2 reading comprehension. *Journal of Research in Reading, 9,* 103-115.

Vacca, R. T., & Linek, W. M. (1992). Writing to Learn. In J. W. Spiro & M. A. Doyle (Eds.), *Reading/writing connections: Learning from research* (pp. 145-159). Newark, DE: International Reading Association.

Wade, S. E., & Trathen, W. (1989). Effect of self-selected study methods on learning. *Journal of Educational Psychology, 81,* 40-47.

Walker, J. (1979). Squeezing study skills (into, out of) content areas. In R. T. Vacca & J. A. Meagher (Eds.), *Reading through content* (pp. 137-148). Storrs: University of Connecticut.

Willmore, D. J. (1966). *A comparison of four methods of studying a textbook.* Unpublished doctoral dissertation, Minneapolis: University of Minnesota.

Winne, P. H. (1985). Steps toward promoting cognitive achievement. *Elementary School Journal, 85,* 673-693.

Winograd, P. N. (1984). Strategic difficulties in summarizing texts. *Reading Research Quarterly, 19,* 404-425.

Wittrock, M. C., & Alesandrini, K. (1990). Generation of summaries and analogies and analytic and holistic abilities. *American Educational Research Journal, 27,* 489-502.

Wolfe, R., & Lopez, A. (1993). Structured overviews for teaching science concepts and terms. *Journal of Reading, 36,* 315-317.

# BALANCED LITERACY INSTRUCTION: IMPLICATIONS FOR STUDENTS OF DIVERSE BACKGROUNDS

## Kathryn H. Au
### University of Hawaii

Few topics, if any, in the field of language arts have been as contentious as beginning reading. In the 1960s, Chall (1967) used the phrase *great debate* to characterize the disagreements between proponents of code-emphasis versus meaning-emphasis approaches. In the 1990s, the popular press used the phrase *reading wars* to describe the arguments between proponents of phonics versus whole language (Collins, 1997). Continuing press coverage of the so-called reading wars served to obscure the fact that the majority of classroom teachers and literacy researchers did not fall into either of the extreme camps. For example, results of a large-scale survey indicated that 89% of elementary teachers held a balanced or eclectic philosophy, as reflected in the statement, "I believe in a balanced approach to reading instruction which combines skills development with literature and language-rich activities" (Baumann, Hoffman, Moon, & Duffy-Hester, 1998, p. 642). Prominent researchers agreed that emphasizing only phonics instruction would make learning to read difficult and that children should read and discuss a wide variety of texts (Flippo, 1998). By the mid-1990s, this seldom heard majority had begun to articulate a position known as balanced literacy instruction.

My purpose in this chapter is to present a perspective on balanced literacy instruction that I hope will be especially helpful to those who work, as I do, with students of diverse cultural and linguistic backgrounds. I begin by looking at different dimensions of balance in literacy instruction. Then I examine the intersection of three topics that have figured prominently

in recent debates about literacy instruction: constructivist approaches to literacy instruction, phonics and skills, and the literacy learning of students of diverse backgrounds.

---

## BACKGROUND

### Balanced Literacy Instruction

Pearson and Raphael (1999) provided a comprehensive discussion of balance, unpacking the term by referring to continua in the context and content of literacy instruction. In the context of literacy instruction, the first continuum is authenticity, with the need to achieve a balance between "doin' school" and "doin' life." The second continuum is classroom discourse, with the need to achieve a balance between the rights of teachers and of children to determine the topics discussed and the patterns of classroom talk. The third continuum is the teacher's role, which can range from minimal (the teacher joins the students in participating in a literacy activity such as sustained silent reading) to maximum (the teacher uses explicit instruction). The final context continuum is curricular control, with the need to achieve a balance between local control by educators in the classroom and distant control at the state or national level.

Pearson and Raphael (1999) highlighted three continua in the area of content. Skill contextualization refers to maintaining a balance between a predetermined curriculum of skill

---

An earlier version of this paper was presented as the presidential address to the National Reading Conference, December 1997.

instruction and the teaching of skills as teachable moments are provided by texts and tasks. Text genres refers to maintaining a balance between the reading of narrative as opposed to informative texts, as well as a balance between the reading of texts written to support the practice of beginning reading skills versus authentic texts, such as children's literature. The final continuum, response to literature, refers to maintaining a balance between conventional or canonical interpretations and students' personal interpretations. In short, these authors suggested that the concept of balanced literacy instruction has at least seven dimensions.

As the analysis by Pearson and Raphael (1999) suggested, balanced literacy instruction is a complex concept. Furthermore, other dimensions can easily be added. For example, Strickland (1994–95) addresses the dimensions of ability versus heterogeneous grouping and standardized versus ongoing classroom assessment. Spiegel (1998) emphasized the role of the teacher as a reflective practitioner and decision maker in finding the best way to help each child become a better reader and writer. Freppon and Dahl (1998) pointed out that although there is wide agreement on the benefits of phonics instruction, there is no consensus on how this instruction should take place. They found that "[s]everal balanced literacy researchers repeatedly emphasize the importance of phonics teaching and learning within integrated language-based instruction; however, others argued for separating phonics teaching and learning" (p. 247).

I call here for consideration of still another dimension of balance, and that is between the demands of the mainstream language arts curriculum and the needs in learning to read and write of children of diverse cultural and linguistic backgrounds. This dimension intersects all of the continua proposed by Pearson and Raphael (1999) and brings to the fore issues of authenticity, classroom discourse, curricular control, and response to literature. However, the predominate continuum of balance in my discussion will be skill contextualization. In keeping with the issue raised by Freppon and Dahl (1998) about how phonics instruction should take place, I argue that such instruction is more likely to be effective for many children of diverse backgrounds when it is integrated into language-based instruction.

## Research With Hawaiian Children

My perspective on balanced literacy instruction has been shaped by the 24 years that I spent working at the Kamehameha Elementary Education Program (KEEP) in Hawaii. The purpose of KEEP was to improve the literacy achievement of students of Hawaiian ancestry enrolled in public schools. These students typically came from low-income families, grew up speaking Hawai'i Creole English (a nonmainstream variety of English), and, as a group, scored in the lowest quartile on standardized tests of reading achievement. I do not support a narrow focus on "back to basics" instruction because my research with Hawaiian students has shown me that phonics is just one part of children's literacy learning during the early years of elementary school. It is an essential part but, as I will explain, neither the starting point nor the most important element.

In this chapter I draw on three sources of information. The first is the research at KEEP on a constructivist literacy curriculum. The Kamehameha Elementary Education Program was the nation's longest running research and development project dedicated to improving the educational opportunities of underprivileged students of a particular ethnic group. From 1989 to 1995 (KEEP was closed in 1995), my colleagues and I conducted research on a constructivist literacy curriculum, centered on writers' and readers' workshops. The second source of information is the larger body of research conducted by others, and the third is the experience of the teachers with whom I have worked.

## Definition of Terms

*Constructivist approaches to literacy instruction* refers to approaches based on the idea that students create their own understandings of literacy in the context of the various aspects of their lives (Spivey, 1997). The assumption in these approaches is that learning takes place through social interaction with peers as well as the teacher. The teacher initiates instruction by getting students interested and involved in the full processes of reading and writing, and skills are taught as part of students' engagement with meaningful literacy activities. Constructivist approaches to literacy instruction include the process approach to writing (Calkins, 1994; Graves, 1983, 1994), literature-based instruction (Raphael & Au, 1998; Roser & Martinez, 1995), whole language (Goodman, 1986; Weaver, 1990), and balanced literacy instruction (Au, Carroll, & Scheu, 1997; Strickland, 1994–95). These approaches and philosophies are consistent with a constructivist or interpretivist paradigm (Guba & Lincoln, 1994; Spivey, 1997) and the sociocultural or sociohistorial perspective, as exemplified in the work of (Vygotsky, 1978) and extended to literacy research and education by Applebee (1991), Brock and Gavelek (1998), Cole and Griffin (1983), Moll (1990), Raphael and Hiebert (1996), and others.

*Phonics* refers to the teaching of letter–sound correspondences. The term is also commonly used to refer to the letter–sound correspondences themselves, as in the phrase "phonics instruction" or in the statement "Children need to know phonics." Phonics is valuable because English is an alphabetic language, and knowledge of letter–sound correspondences helps students to decode words. However, phonics is not the only type of word identification instruction that students should receive. Students also need to learn to recognize words that are not decodable (a category that includes many of the most frequently occurring words), to analyze multisyllabic words, and to make use of base words and affixes.

The phrase *students of diverse backgrounds*, used in the context of the United States, refers to students who are African American, Asian American, Latino, or Native American in ethnicity. These students speak a first language other than standard American English, and they come from low-income families.

Constructivist approaches provide us with many powerful ways to improve the literacy instruction of students of diverse backgrounds. I have written elsewhere about my reasons for recommending a constructivist, process approach to writing, in the form of the writers' workshop, as the starting point for literacy instruction in classrooms with students of diverse backgrounds (Au, 1997a). Here I focus primarily on a constructivist approach to the teaching of reading and literature-based instruction. This information is organized according to six understandings I have gained about these issues, drawing from my own research as well as the research of others.

## FINDINGS FROM RESEARCH

### Ownership of Literacy as the Overarching Goal

The first understanding has to do with the breadth of the elementary language arts curriculum and the shift from reading, narrowly defined, to literacy, broadly defined. As shown in Fig. 69.1, The researchers at KEEP worked with a curriculum with six aspects of literacy: ownership, the writing process, reading comprehension, vocabulary development, word reading and spelling strategies, and voluntary reading (Au, Scheu, Kawakami, & Herman, 1990). This curriculum recognized the connections between reading and writing and the importance of affective dimensions of literacy as well as cognitive ones.

Perhaps the most important discovery was that ownership of literacy needed to be the overarching goal of the curriculum. Ownership may be defined as students' valuing of literacy (Au, 1997b). Ownership is seen when students not only have positive attitudes about literacy but make it a part of their everyday lives, at home as well as in school. Students demonstrate ownership by reading books of their own choosing, keeping journals, and sharing books with one another, even when these activities are not assigned by the teacher. They use reading and writing for purposes they have set for themselves. Winograd and Paris (1988) espoused a similar view when they wrote about students needing to have the will as well as the skill to use literacy. Dahl and Freppon (1995) suggested that acquiring a "disposition for learning" and thinking of oneself as a reader and writer may be a critical occurrence during inner-city children's beginning years in school. The importance of ownership is supported in recent research on the engagement perspective by Guthrie and Alvermann (1999) and their colleagues. The engagement perspective looks beyond the question of *how* people read to the question of *why* someone would want to read in the first place.

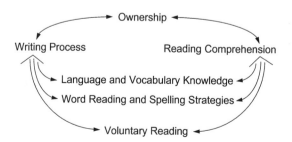

FIGURE 69.1. The Kamehameha Elementary Education Program (KEEP) literacy curriculum.

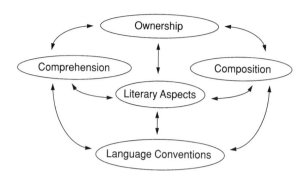

FIGURE 69.2. The current literacy curriculum. From "Curriculum and Teaching in Literature-Based Programs," by K. H. Au and T. E. Raphael, 1998, in *Literature-Based Instruction: Reshaping the Curriculum* (p. 128), edited by T. E. Raphael and K. H. Au, Norwood, MA: Christopher-Gordon. Copyright 1998. Reprinted with permission.

The view of the literacy curriculum reflected in the six aspects of literacy is largely process oriented, which I believe is typical of constructivist language arts curricula developed in the late 1980s and early 1990s. Views of the literacy curriculum have now shifted somewhat, as shown in Fig. 69.2

Two differences between Figs. 69.1 and 69.2 should be noted. First, the label *literary aspects* in Fig. 69.2 represents a recognition that the literacy curriculum must address content, not just process. Literary aspects include the themes developed through literature, or the ideas that hold the story together and that will be remembered long after details of the plot and setting have faded from memory (Lukens, 1990). The value of themes in literature-based instruction has been discussed in work by Peters and Wixson (1998) and Valencia and Lipson (1998). Literary elements also include point of view, plot, and characters. Of course, the purpose of addressing literary aspects is to enhance the reader's response to the literature, whether that response is personal, creative, or critical.

Second, the label *language conventions* in Fig. 69.2 reflects the idea that literacy is a social process requiring interactional skills, not just text-based skills and strategies. This element encompasses the aspects of literacy represented in the KEEP framework in Fig. 69.1 by the labels *language and vocabulary knowledge* and *word reading and spelling strategies*. Besides addressing the traditional skill areas of vocabulary, word identification, grammar, punctuation, and other mechanics, this area deals with the conventions of interaction students must know in order to participate appropriately in literacy events. These conventions come into play in all literacy events but may be particularly complex in activities directed by the students themselves, such as literature discussion groups during the readers' workshop or peer conferences during the writers' workshop. Many of these language conventions may be more familiar to mainstream students than to students of diverse backgrounds.

In short, current research shows the breadth of the literacy curriculum. Many studies document the importance of all of these curriculum elements in students' development as readers and writers (Guthrie & Alvermann, 1999; Raphael & Au, 1998).

What is the place of phonics in this picture? Phonics is part of one of the five elements in the contemporary literacy curriculum. Phonics cannot be neglected, but there is no evidence to suggest that it can or should be the whole of reading, even at the kindergarten and first grade levels. As I explain, research conducted at KEEP indicates that students of diverse backgrounds may develop greater proficiency in word identification when instruction begins by promoting ownership and not just skills (Au, 1994).

## Improvement of Word Identification and Higher-level Thinking

The second understanding concerns the importance of providing students at all grades with instruction in comprehension and composition, complex literacy processes requiring higher level thinking. In our initial work with the constructivist curriculum at KEEP, we made an interesting discovery. The results shown in Table 69.1 illustrate the pattern we observed for 2 consecutive years with nearly 2,000 students in six schools in Grades 1 through 3, as measured by a portfolio assessment system anchored in grade-level benchmarks (Au, 1994). We saw better achievement results in some aspects of literacy than in others. The results for these aspects of literacy are shown above the heavy line in the table, and they are ownership of literacy, voluntary reading, and word reading strategies. This is what seems to have happened. Teachers with KEEP focused on promoting students' ownership of literacy, and they encouraged students to read books at home as well as at school. They set aside time daily for sustained silent reading, and the vast majority of students developed the habit of daily reading. Because of this increase in independent reading, students' fluency and accuracy in word identification improved, as indicated in individually administered running records (Clay, 1985). We were particularly surprised to find 39% of the second-graders performing above grade level, which in this case meant that they could accurately decode texts at the 3.2 (third grade, second semester) reading level. Achievement lagged in the other three aspects of literacy: the writing process, reading comprehension, and language and vocabulary knowledge.

These initial results show that gains in word identification were somewhat easier to obtain with constructivist curricula than gains in the more complex literacy processes—composition, comprehension, and the learning of concepts and vocabulary. With the KEEP students, and very likely with other students of diverse backgrounds, word identification was neither as difficult for teachers to teach nor as difficult for students to learn, as these more complex processes. In other words, our findings at KEEP contradict the impression that constructivist approaches are somehow detrimental to students' development of word identification ability. In our last 2 years of work with the constructivist curriculum at KEEP, we focused specifically on improving students higher level thinking about text, particularly in the writing process. We learned that a constructivist curriculum could be effective in improving students' achievement in these areas but only when teachers fully implemented the curriculum (Au & Carroll, 1997). Narrowly focused basic skill instruction, unlike constructivist approaches, ignores the more complex literacy processes and therefore cannot lead to improvement in these processes.

Our research findings at KEEP will come as no surprise to those familiar with the extensive research base on comprehension instruction developed during the 1980s. We learned early on, most notably from a study conducted by Anderson, Mason, and Shirey (1984), that comprehension does not result naturally as a consequence of students being able to decode every word in a text. Researchers looked at the different kinds of challenges comprehension posed for students, and at how students might be taught to meet these challenges. They demonstrated that strategy instruction could improve students' comprehension, in terms of their ability to make inferences (Hansen & Pearson, 1983), identify the main idea (Baumann, 1984), or summarize a text (Taylor, 1982). Other studies pointed to the benefits of students being able to monitor their own comprehension—to know when they didn't know (Palincsar & Brown, 1984). This research on comprehension strategy instruction is ably summarized by Dole, Duffy, Roehler, and Pearson (1991). Work by Beck, McKeown, Sandora, Kucan, and Worthy (1996), in which students are taught to "question the author," built on this foundation.

Concepts of comprehension have been enriched with the growing interest in literature-based instruction, which has its theoretical basis in reader response theory. Rosenblatt's (1978) work established the distinction between the aesthetic and efferent stances and argued persuasively for the predominance of the aesthetic stance in the reading of literature. Our views of what it means to comprehend have been broadened to encompass personal response, which includes the emotions called forth by the literature and the ability to see connections between the literature and one's own life.

## The Timing of Phonics

The third understanding recognizes that although phonics has its place, it cannot be the first or only focus for beginning readers, particularly for young children of diverse backgrounds who have limited experienced with family storybook reading or other mainstream literacy events. The timing of phonics instruction for these children is critical. In fact, in kindergarten and first grade, an overemphasis on phonics instruction, to the exclusion of other literacy activities, may prevent these children from developing the concepts and background necessary for the later development of word identification ability.

TABLE 69.1. Initial Results: Grade 2

| Aspect of Literacy | % Above | % At | % Below | Missing Data |
|---|---|---|---|---|
| Ownership | 30 | 19 | 46 | 5 |
| Voluntary reading | 71 | 24 | 5 | 0 |
| Word reading strategies | 39 | 20 | 38 | 2 |
| Writing process | 0 | 33 | 55 | 11 |
| Reading comprehension | 5 | 31 | 59 | 5 |
| Language and vocabulary | 3 | 37 | 54 | 6 |

This point is made clear in a discussion by Stahl (1997). Citing common findings in the work of a number of researchers (Biemiller, 1970; Chall, 1983; Frith, 1985; Lomax & McGee, 1987; McCormick & Mason, 1986), Stahl noted that children go through three broad stages in learning to identify words: awareness, accuracy, and automaticity.

In the first stage, awareness, children are developing a conceptual understanding of the nature of written language and its relationship to spoken language. This understanding covers four areas. The first, functions of print, involves understanding, for example, that print can be used to tell stories. The second, conventions of print, includes knowing that one reads from left to right and from the top of the page to the bottom. The third, forms of print, encompasses the letters of the alphabet. The fourth, awareness of phonemes, entails the notion that spoken words can be broken into separate sounds or phonemes, an understanding central to the later learning of letter–sound correspondences. Stahl (1997) asserted that these four aspects of the relationship between written and spoken language serve as the foundation for children's later development as readers, and that children will experience difficulty in learning to read if they lack any of these aspects.

In the second stage, accuracy, children learn to decode words accurately. They are focused on print and working to identify words correctly. Sulzby (1985) described this as a time when children, who previously freely retold stories from familiar books, will refuse to do so, stating, "I don't know the words." Children read text aloud in a laborious, choppy, word-by-word fashion, a phenomenon usually termed "word calling." Stahl (1997) noted that this stage is generally short-lived, leading quickly into the third stage, automaticity, in which children come to recognize words automatically. The transition from accuracy to automaticity usually occupies the time from the end of first grade to the end of third grade, although it may be prolonged for struggling readers. The rapid, automatic recognition of words is, of course, necessary to free up information processing capacity for comprehension of the text.

This overview of the development of word identification ability suggests that phonics instruction should be emphasized when children are in the accuracy phase, not when they are in the awareness phase and not when they are in the automaticity phase. Phonics plays a crucial but temporary role, and phonics instruction must be properly timed to achieve its optimal effect. Phonics cannot be seen as a blanket approach to beginning reading instruction, because knowledge of letter–sound correspondences is not the first or the only thing that children need to learn as they develop the ability to identify words.

In a conversation about research on emergent literacy in the *Reading Research Quarterly*, Purcell-Gates (McGee & Purcell-Gates, 1997) drew a conclusion that is not new but often forgotten in current debates: "Children learn to read and write successfully if their teachers accommodate their instruction *to* the children, and they struggle if they do not" (p. 312). This statement certainly applies to young Hawaiian children, who are in the awareness stage when they first arrive in kindergarten. At KEEP we administered emergent literacy tasks (based on the work of Mason & Stewart, 1989) to children entering kindergarten. The typical child could name perhaps one to three letters

of the alphabet, often letters that appeared in his or her name but could not use magnetic letters to represent the first or last sounds of any words. When shown the page of a simple book and asked where there was something to read, the typical child pointed to the illustration, not to the print. Clearly, the typical child was not yet attending to print. Many KEEP kindergarteners had little or no experience with family storybook reading, and most had not attended preschool.

Unless there is good evidence that kindergarten children are already in or near the accuracy stage, it appears harmful to their overall literacy development to begin with an emphasis on the teaching of phonics in isolation. Some kindergarten teachers insist on drilling children on letter names and sounds in isolation, a form of teaching that is too abstract for many children. This type of teaching cannot replace instructional activities, such as shared reading or the writing of their own stories, that provide children with meaningful contexts for the learning of letter–sound correspondences. These activities allow children to develop understandings of the four aspects of written-spoken language relationships that form the foundation for later acquisition of letter–sound correspondences. Phonics instruction can certainly be introduced as part of shared reading and children's writing of their own stories, as I describe next, but phonics should not be taught apart from these meaningful literacy activities.

## The Importance of Writing to Children's Learning of Letter–Sound Correspondences

The fourth understanding concerns the contributions of writing, specifically invented spelling, to children's learning of phonics. In KEEP primary-grade classrooms, teachers conducted a writers' workshop four or five times a week. They introduced the writers' workshop as soon as possible, sometimes during the first day of school. This introduction required courage and faith on the part of teachers, especially in kindergarten classrooms. In September, most of these kindergarten students were drawing, and just a few were scribbling or using letterlike forms. In classrooms in rural schools, there was often a child who had not had the experience of holding a pencil or crayon and drawing with it.

During the writers' workshop, kindergarten teachers promoted children's understandings of print in many ways. They modeled writing during the morning message, asking children to help them spell the words, and had children make observations about the print in the message (Crowell, Kawakami, & Wong, 1986). They taught mini-lessons showing children how to say words slowly and isolate the sounds. They introduced children to the sounds and letters of the alphabet, through lessons in which children associated letters with the names of their classmates or familiar objects. They created word walls and posted charts to which the children could refer, including lists of people (*mommy, brother, cousin*) and actions (*planting, surfing, roller blading*). Gradually, teachers identified children who could use invented spelling to label objects in their drawings. During individual or small group writing conferences, they assisted these children with labeling and then taught them how to use initial consonants to draft short sentences. By the spring semester, most of the children in these kindergarten classrooms were able to draft several sentences each day during the writers' workshop, using at least initial consonants to represent words.

In my experience, the writers' workshop provides the best context in which to teach children letter–sound correspondences—phonics—in a manner that makes that knowledge useful and ensures its application. The following summary of my observations in a kindergarten classroom provides a sense of how phonics fits within the larger context of meaningful literate activity in the writers' workshop. In this classroom the teacher had the children keep four questions in mind when they wrote their stories:

1. Who is in my story?
2. What is happening in my story?
3. Where is my story taking place?
4. What else happened?

She did not use the terms characters, events, and setting, but the children clearly understood these concepts. I observed a girl drafting the sentence, "I am popping firecrackers with my friends at home." The teacher had taught the children to isolate the first sound in the word and write that letter. Then they were to say the word slowly, listen for other sounds, and add those letters. For example, the girl who wanted to write *popping* isolated the initial *p* sound, said, "Puh-puh-puh" to herself, and wrote the letter *p*. As this example shows, children in primary classrooms with writers' workshops create their own phonics exercises because of the stories they want to write. The teacher in this classroom, as well as many others, have told me words to this effect: "I have taught letter sounds in isolation, and this way, through invented spelling, is much faster and more effective."

My observations in classrooms with Hawaiian children are consistent with a growing body of studies pointing to the benefits of invented spelling in children's long-term development as readers and writers (Ehri, 1987; Wilde, 1989). These studies suggest that children who have the opportunity to use invented spelling eventually become better spellers than children who are taught spelling by rote memorization and never have the opportunity to infer for themselves how the English spelling system works. In the case of both spelling and phonics, it is not just a matter of learning skills but of applying these skills in the context of real reading and writing. Teachers commonly observe that students misspell words they wrote correctly on recent spelling tests. Similarly, it is likely that many children who learn phonics in isolation do not use these skills when they read (Shannon, 1989), and by fourth grade, students' reading problems are related to a lack of automaticity rather than to the absence of basic reading skills (Campbell & Ashworth, 1995).

## A Multipronged Approach to Phonics

There does not appear to be one best way to teach phonics and beginning reading (Allington, 1997). This assertion is supported by the fact that, for every method studied, some children learned to read well while others experienced considerable difficulty (International Reading Association, 1999). It

can be concluded, then, that students of diverse backgrounds will benefit from a multipronged approach that shows them the usefulness of letter–sound correspondences during both reading and writing. Our research at KEEP supports this contention. Decoding by analogy is an approach to word identification, demonstrated to be effective (Gaskins, Gaskins, & Gaskins, 1991) that has undergone continual refinement (Gaskins, Ehri, Cress, O'Hara, & Donnelly, 1997). At KEEP we asked Pat Cunningham to provide workshops to our teachers on decoding by analogy, and KEEP teachers taught lessons incorporating word walls (Cunningham, 1991). The relative importance of onset-rime segmentation and phonemic segmentation in children's development of word reading and spelling ability continues to be explored in the experimental literature (e.g., Nation & Hulme, 1997). However, the KEEP students seemed to benefit both from learning decoding by analogy, which requires onset-rime segmentation, and from learning invented spelling, which led them to employ phonemic segmentation.

Although research suggests that there is no single best way to teach phonics, there do appear to be two principles that underlie effective phonics instruction for Hawaiian students and others of diverse backgrounds. The first principle is that phonics instruction should be explicit. In two controversial and widely cited articles in the *Harvard Educational Review*, Delpit (reprinted in Delpit, 1995) presented a convincing case for the explicit instruction of skills within constructivist approaches for students of diverse backgrounds. Delpit stated that, unlike their mainstream, middle-class peers, students of diverse backgrounds generally did not have the opportunity outside of the classroom to acquire the codes of the culture of power. These codes include such skills as phonics and standard English grammar. According to Delpit, teachers handicap students of diverse backgrounds when they fail to provide explicit instruction in these skills. As indicated above, teachers in KEEP classrooms provided students with explicit instruction in phonics through a wide variety of activities. Delpit described herself as a progressive educator, with a commitment to the process approach to writing, but she argued that explicit skill instruction should be a part of the process approach. Delpit (1988) added this caveat, with which I agree: "I am not an advocate of a simplistic 'basic skills' approach for children outside the culture of power. It would be (and has been) tragic to operate as if these children were incapable of critical and higher-order thinking and reasoning" (p. 286).

I hesitate to use the word *systematic* along with *explicit* because of the many misunderstandings of what *systematic* might mean when it comes to phonics instruction. There is no evidence for the effectiveness of phonics that is thought to be systematic because the teacher follows a set sequence of skill lessons. As Allington (1997) put it, "There simply is no 'scientifically' validated sequence of phonics instruction" (p. 15). This rigid concept should be replaced by one in which phonics is understood to be systematic because the teacher provides instruction based on ongoing assessment of the children's needs as readers and writers. Phonics should also be systematic in the sense that teachers devote considerable time and attention to it on a daily basis, when ongoing assessment indicates that such instruction will be beneficial to children.

The second principle is that this explicit phonics instruction should take place in meaningful contexts in which the reasons for learning letter–sound correspondences can readily be understood by children. In the writers' workshop, described earlier, children understand that they need knowledge of letter–sound correspondences to put their stories down on paper for communication to others. In shared reading and guided reading, children understand that knowledge of letter–sound correspondences enables them to read the words in books for themselves. Children are pursuing certain purposes through literacy and can see the value of knowledge of letter–sound correspondences in achieving these purposes.

McGee (in McGee & Purcell-Gates, 1997) presented a thoughtful discussion of these issues. She noted that "any understandings constructed about phonemic awareness, or any other of the processes and understandings associated with reading and writing, are always embedded with and connected with all the other processes operating in concert" (pp. 313–314). She emphasized that it is the richness of these embedded and interconnected understandings that supports children's literacy learning. Children who have had many opportunities to learn about reading and writing through interactions in a variety of literacy events develop a deeper and qualitatively different kind of understanding from children whose understandings have developed largely through training—especially if that training has focused on the teaching of letter–sound correspondences or other skills in the absence of a purpose drawn from a larger, meaningful activity. McGee did not object to the gamelike activities in these training programs, because children on their own do play with language. (Also, as described earlier, children create "phonics exercises" for themselves when engaged in invented spelling.) What is at issue is the connections made for children between these activities and their purposeful engagement in the full processes of reading and writing. McGee concluded:

I would suggest that for children who have *not* developed a rich, sophisticated phonemic awareness—and many children do not—we should instead examine our instruction to see whether it does provide opportunities to develop these kinds of understandings. If not, we should build more explicit attention within the more natural activities. (p. 314)

## Supporting Literacy Learning With a Continuum of Instructional Approaches

The sixth understanding centers on a continuum of instructional approaches for promoting students' learning to read during the elementary school grades. I have observed the use of these strategies in the classrooms of teachers whose success in promoting the literacy of Hawaiian students was well documented (Au & Carroll, 1997). These instructional approaches are presented in Fig. 69.3. Two instructional approaches are shown to be appropriate to all grades: teacher read-alouds and sustained silent reading. The other four instructional approaches are arranged in the order in which they would often be judged appropriate, given students' progress in learning to read. Beginning at kindergarten and moving up the grades, these are

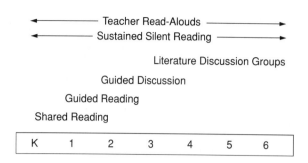

FIGURE 69.3. Continuum of instructional approaches.

shared reading, guided reading, guided discussion, and literature discussion groups. The use of these approaches is not linear. Teachers may use some combination of these approaches with a particular group of students, for example, adding opportunities for extended discussion to shared reading and guided reading. The nature of the text may also influence the teacher's choice of approach. For example, a teacher may plan to have students engage in a literature discussion group. However, if the novel proves particularly challenging for students, she may decide instead to use guided discussion, to provide students with more scaffolding.

Although this sequence indicates a rough time line for many students, there are, of course, those who are progressing more rapidly or more slowly. In most second grade classrooms in schools in low-income Hawaiian communities, I can usually identify a group of about four students whose literacy is still emergent and for whom shared reading is the appropriate instructional approach at the beginning of the school year. In other words, these instructional approaches are less tied to grade levels and more tied to students' needs in learning to read.

***Literature discussion groups.*** I comment first on literature discussion groups, because this is the newest instructional approach in my repertoire as a teacher educator and the one that caused me seriously to rethink my views of reading instruction. Literature discussion groups may also be called book clubs (Raphael & McMahon, 1994) or literature circles (Short & Pierce, 1990). Literature discussion groups promote students' ownership of literacy by giving them the opportunity to shape their own conversations about literature. Talk does not follow the typical pattern of classroom recitation driven by the teacher's quizzing. Rather, as Atwell (1987) put it, these are conversations around the dining room table, or in the words of Eeds and Wells (1989), "grand conversations," the kinds of conversations that adults might have in the real world when discussing books with family, friends, and colleagues.

In workshops on literature-based instruction, I try to give teachers the opportunity to engage in such conversations. I begin these workshops by having teachers read and write in response to a poem, then share their responses in a literature discussion group. I always choose a poem that appears to offer room for a number of different yet plausible interpretations. "Riding the San Francisco Train" by Diane O'Hehir (1988) is a good example of such a poem. Readers usually agree that this poem conveys feelings of guilt, but they differ widely in their views of the probable source of the guilt. Participants think that the individual is gay, has just been released from prison, or has left an abusive relationship, and they are always able to support their views by referring to particular lines in the poem. Most teachers are surprised by the extent to which literature discussion groups capture their interest and attention, and they contrast this experience with that of typical school discussions of literature, in which the student's goal is to arrive at the canonical interpretation or that favored by the teacher. This brief experience with literature discussion groups often helps teachers to gain insights about the differences between literature-based instruction, rooted in reader response theory (Rosenblatt, 1991), and other ways of teaching reading.

Many teachers are quick to see the value of having their students participate in literature discussion groups. For teachers in the primary grades, the question arises: If students are to gain the background needed for them to participate in and benefit from literature discussion groups, how do we prepare them for this experience? To address this question, I briefly discuss my views of the other instructional approaches in the continuum, beginning with shared reading.

***Shared reading.*** Shared reading developed from the shared book experience, as Holdaway (1979) described it. Holdaway had the insight that the benefits of family storybook reading could be brought into the classroom through the shared reading of enlarged texts, or what are now called big books. As mentioned earlier, many Hawaiian children in low-income communities enter kindergarten without having participated in family storybook reading. Shared reading, in conjunction with the reading aloud of picture storybooks, provides the teacher with a prime opportunity to introduce these children to the joys of reading and of books.

When they enter kindergarten, many young Hawaiian children are in the awareness stage in their development of word identification ability. Shared reading is beneficial because it provides teachers with opportunities to promote all four of the understandings about the relationships between spoken and written language that develop during this stage. Teachers can help children gain knowledge of an important function of print, that print can be used to communicate stories. Teachers can model how readers observe conventions of print, such as directionality. Teachers can call children's attention to the forms of print, including letters of the alphabet and punctuation. Teachers can develop children's phonemic awareness, by pointing out or having children identify words that rhyme, or words that begin or end with the same sounds.

In terms of the development of word identification ability, shared reading serves the crucial function of moving children from paying attention only to pictures to paying attention to print. As Sulzby's (1985) work on young children's storybook reading demonstrated, this shift is a major landmark in literacy development. Teachers worry that children memorize the texts of big books, and they question whether children are actually referring to print. In my observations of young Hawaiian children, I have seen that memorization of the text plays an important role in their development as readers. The ability to associate certain exact words with each page signals their understanding that

the text of a book is stable and unchanging. This understanding leads to another, that the memorized words they recite can be matched with the print on the page. Teachers can guide children to slow down their recitation of the text and to point to each word as they say it. In this way, memorization of the big book text contributes to development of the children's ability to track print. At this point, the children cannot yet use letter information to identify words, but they have progressed from attending only to pictures to attending to print.

Even during the introductory stage with a big book, Holdaway noted that teachers should "induce sound strategies of word solving by encouraging and discussing suggestions, at an appropriate skill level and without unduly interrupting the story" (p. 72). One activity used during rereading is the masking of individual words in the big book. The teacher uses a sliding mask to reveal the letters in the word, one at a time, for the children's study. In another activity, the teacher copies the text of the big book on an overhead transparency. The words are covered with strips of paper and progressively unmasked, letter by letter. When teachers unmask words, they model for children how good readers look at each letter of a word in order, moving from left to right. Many teachers copy the text of the big book on sentence strips or word cards. They involve children in activities that require the reading and arranging of the words in pocket charts. A critical feature of all of these activities is the requirement that children attend closely to print and break away from a reliance on pictures. Shared reading lays the foundation for the independence in word identification furthered through guided reading.

***Guided reading.*** A major focus of guided reading is to teach children to use reading strategies—particularly strategies of word identification—independently. A comprehensive treatment of guided reading, based on the research of Clay (1991), is provided by Fountas and Pinnell (1996). As described by these authors, the strategies promoted through guided reading include those for maintaining fluency, for detecting and correcting errors, and for problem solving with new words.

Guided reading may be introduced when children are moving from the awareness stage to the accuracy stage. While shared reading is usually conducted with the whole class, guided reading takes place with a small group of children whose reading processes are at a similar level. The teacher introduces a previously unseen little book to this small group, and the children read the book on their own with a minimum of help from the adult. The teacher takes great care in selecting the text. It must be difficult enough to allow children to improve their strategies for problem solving with text, but not so difficult that children cannot read it themselves.

For many Hawaiian children, the move from shared reading to guided reading is quite a leap. For one thing, they must track the print on their own, as they are now looking at their own individual copies of the book, not at a big book in which the teacher is tracking the print for them. Also, they are expected to read through a text that has not previously been read aloud to them. I see teachers providing scaffolding as children make the transition from shared reading to guided reading. For example, the teacher may have the children look at her copy of the book.

She remains silent but tracks the print as the children read along for a page or two. Then she has the children continue independently in their own books.

During guided reading, the central activity is the children's own independent reading of the text. As the children read the text on their own, the teacher monitors their performance. She encourages children's problem-solving efforts and provides assistance as it is needed. Based on her work with individual children, the teacher usually discovers a point or two that could profitably be discussed with the whole group. "Brief detours" is how Fountas and Pinnell (1996, p. 4) described the problem-solving assistance given by the teacher when children need help. They cautioned teachers to be very quick about individual interventions, so that children can immediately return to their efforts at meaning construction with text. This view echoes Holdaway's (1979) concern that the teacher not "unduly interrupt" the flow of the story during shared reading. By conducting a mini-lesson after the children have finished reading, the teacher can address the points of difficulty identified earlier.

***Guided discussion.*** As children gain proficiency in word identification, they are able to read more complex texts. These texts include picture storybooks, such as *Halmoni and the Picnic* by Choi (1993), that contain such elements as a theme, memorable characters, and a plot with a problem and solution. These books offer the possibility for in-depth, guided discussion. In guided discussion, the teacher uses questioning to sharpen students' understanding of the theme and other story elements and to help them make personal connections to the text (Au, 1992). Guided discussion enhances students' comprehension ability and creates opportunities for students to see connections between the texts they read and their own lives.

Teachers at KEEP used the form of guided discussion known as the experience-text-relationship, or ETR approach (Au, Carroll, 1997). Lessons of about 20 minutes are taught to small groups of children, and the lessons on a particular story usually take from 3 to 5 days. As in guided reading, these are children whose reading processes are at a similar level. The teacher selects a text the students will be able to read largely on their own, on a topic likely to be of interest, and she identifies a possible theme for the text. In the experience, or E, phase, the teacher introduces the story and has the students discuss their experiences which relate to the possible theme. As the lesson enters the text, or T, phase, the teacher has the students read the first segment of the story silently. As in guided reading, she assists students who encounter a problem while reading. After reading, the students discuss this part of the text, with the teacher guiding discussion to focus on key points, such as the characters and events, as well as the emerging theme. The lesson alternates between silent reading and discussion until students have finished reading the text. In the relationship, or R, phase, the teacher helps the students to draw relationships between their own experiences and the ideas in the story. It is not uncommon for the students to construct their own theme for the story, rather than assenting to the theme planned by the teacher (Au, 1992).

The teacher may focus on one or two teaching points near the end of the 20-minute lesson. As in shared and guided reading,

the idea is that skill instruction should intrude as little as possible upon students' ongoing efforts at constructing meaning from text. The teacher has the students return to the text and reread the passage containing the target word, and she and the students discuss how the word might be identified and what it might mean. Often, especially as students reach the third grade, they are beginning to encounter multisyllabic words, such as *richochet* or *coincidence*, that may not be part of their speaking vocabularies. The need at this point is not usually for phonics but for other strategies useful in identifying and deriving the meaning of unfamiliar words. One of these strategies is decoding by analogy, which involves comparison of the new word with words already known (Gaskins et al., 1991). Another is the look in, look around strategy (Herman & Weaver, 1988), which involves looking in the word to find a base word and affixes, and around the passage to gain a sense of what the word might mean.

For many Hawaiian students, guided discussion provides the background necessary for later participation in literature discussion groups. Teachers encourage students to read carefully and thoughtfully, in preparation for sharing their ideas with others. In the process, teachers familiarize students with traditional comprehension skills such as identifying the sequence of events and with literary elements such as character development, flashbacks, point of view, and theme. Students engage in in-depth discussions of literature, under the teacher's guidance, and present justifications for their interpretations. Perhaps most important, guided discussion can contribute to students' ownership of literacy, as they learn to make personal connections to books and to see that books can have themes of relevance to their lives.

***Read-alouds and sustained silent reading.*** In classrooms with Hawaiian students from low-income communities, read alouds serve the important function of allowing teachers to act as literate role models and to convey their own love of books and reading. This function is particularly important in these classrooms, because few such role models may be available to students.

The reading aloud of picture storybooks in kindergarten and first grade, when shared reading and guided reading are the principal instructional approaches, appears to play a critical role in the literacy development of Hawaiian children. The reason is that the majority of texts children can read on their own in these grades are not likely to be high quality works of children's literature or to have many ideas worth discussing at length. Children delight in books with simple but clever texts, such as *Mrs. Wishy-washy* (Cowley, 1990), and these texts help them to acquire a sense of what it is like to be a reader, to develop strategies for identifying words, and to gain confidence. At the same time, the children's development as readers is greatly enriched if the teacher reads aloud picture storybooks, such as *Mufaro's Beautiful Daughters* by Steptoe (1987), which are too difficult for the children to read on their own. Many Hawaiian children will not be able to read such meaty texts independently until they are in the second or third grades. Picture storybooks give the teacher the opportunity to engage children in thoughtful discussions of literature. They allow teachers to encourage comprehension and personal connections to literature, at a depth seldom possible with simpler texts. As I have argued, attention to comprehension and other complex literacy processes is required even at the earliest grades.

Teachers effective in teaching reading to young Hawaiian children often put limits on the books that children may read during the time set aside for sustained silent reading (which in kindergarten and first grade is usually not particularly sustained or silent). One first grade KEEP teacher marked books according to difficulty, giving each book a blue, yellow, or red dot, and the children in her class knew which books they should be reading. The teacher justified her system to me in these words: "The reason I do that is because I don't want them to start working with books and just read the pictures. I know they can read the pictures already" (personal communication, J. Oshiro, March 15, 1995).

She wanted to be sure her students were focused on print. If children were interested in books they could not yet read on their own, they could take these books home and have their parents read them aloud. A similar insistence on students' independent reading of books at an appropriate level of difficulty is observed at Benchmark School, which has a record of success in assisting struggling readers (Center for the Study of Reading, 1991). In both cases, students have a choice of numerous books, but these books must be those that they can read on their own, so that independent reading contributes to students' application of effective reading strategies.

As this overview of the continuum of six instructional approaches shows, Hawaiian students and others of diverse backgrounds are not expected magically to develop the reading ability that will enable them to engage in thoughtful conversations in literature discussion groups and to comprehend, learn from, and interpret text, informative as well as narrative. Rather, students are systematically guided to this point through the conscientious use of instructional approaches, consistent with a constructivist perspective, that enable them to understand the functions of literacy, to identify words and to read them in a fluent and accurate manner, to comprehend text, to construct themes, and to develop personal responses to text.

## CONCLUSION

I began with a discussion of the concept of balance in literacy instruction, and it seems fitting in closing to return to that concept. My focus has been on skill contextualization as a dimension of balance and on the importance of integrating phonics instruction into meaningful literacy activities involving the full processes of reading and writing. Proficiency is an essential goal for the literacy achievement of students of diverse backgrounds, and knowledge of phonics is, of course, necessary for proficiency in reading. However, the first task a teacher faces with young Hawaiian children from low-income communities, or other children of diverse backgrounds, is not the teaching of phonics. Instead, the task is to make sure that students are engaged in meaningful literacy activities, so they realize that literacy can serve real purposes in their own lives.

One of the most compelling purposes for reading is the joy of becoming "lost in a book." Another is the understanding of one's own life that can grow from writing personal narratives. Both these reasons are readily grasped by students of diverse backgrounds when they experience literature-based instruction and the readers' workshop, and the process approach to writing and the writers' workshop. When teaching classes of preservice teachers, I find it helps to capture these ideas in simple terms. What you are trying to do, I say, is to help your students to fall in love with books and to write from the heart.

Students of diverse backgrounds readily learn phonics and other skills when systematic instruction in these skills is integrated into the reading of books and the composing of messages that have meaning to them. In short, balanced literacy instruction should give students of diverse backgrounds the best of both worlds: motivation to use literacy in everyday life, for the purposes they set for themselves, and proficiency in the literacy skills and strategies necessary to accomplish these purposes.

## References

Allington, R. L. (1997). Overselling phonics. *Reading Today*, 15-16.

Anderson, R. C., Mason, J., & Shirey, L. (1984). The reading group: An experimental investigation of a labyrinth. *Reading Research Quarterly, 20*(1), 6-38.

Applebee, A. N. (1991). Environments for language teaching and learning: Contemporary issues and future directions. In J. Flood, J. M. Jensen, D. Lapp, & J. R. Squire (Eds.), *Handbook of research on teaching the English language arts* (pp. 549-556). New York: Macmillan.

Au, K. H. (1992). Constructing the theme of a story. *Language Arts, 69*(2), 106-111.

Au, K. H. (1994). Portfolio assessment: Experiences at the Kamehameha Elementary Education Program. In S. W. Valencia, E. H. Hiebert, & P. P. Afflerbach (Eds.), *Authentic reading assessment: Practices and possibilities* (pp. 103-126). Newark, DE: International Reading Association.

Au, K. H. (1997a). Literacy for all students: Ten steps toward making a difference. *The Reading Teacher, 51*(3), 186-194.

Au, K. H. (1997b). Ownership, literacy achievement, and students of diverse cultural backgrounds. In J. T. Guthrie & A. Wigfield (Eds.), *Reading engagement: Motivating readers through integrated instruction* (pp. 168-182). Newark, DE: International Reading Association.

Au, K. H., & Carroll, J. H. (1997). Improving literacy achievement through a constructivist approach: The KEEP Demonstration Classroom Project. *Elementary School Journal, 97*(3), 203-221.

Au, K. H., Carroll, J. H., & Scheu, J. A. (1997). *Balanced literacy instruction: A teacher's resource book*. Norwood, MA: Christopher-Gordon.

Au, K. H., & Raphael, T. E. (1998). Curriculum and teaching in literature-based programs. In T. E. Raphael & K. H. Au (Eds.), *Literature-based instruction: Reshaping the curriculum* (pp. 123-148). Norwood, MA: Christopher-Gordon.

Au, K. H., Scheu, J. A., Kawakami, A. J., & Herman, P. A. (1990). Assessment and accountability in a whole literacy curriculum. *The Reading Teacher, 43*(8), 574-578.

Baumann, J. F., Hoffman, J. V., Moon, J., & Duffy-Hester, A. M. (1998). Where are teachers' voices in the phonics/whole language debate? Results from a survey of U.S. elementary classroom teachers. *The Reading Teacher, 51*(8), 636-650.

Beck, I. L., McKeown, M. G., Sandora, C., Kucan, L., & Worthy, J. (1996). Questioning the author: A yearlong classroom implementation to engage students with text. *Elementary School Journal, 96*(4), 385-414.

Biemiller, A. (1970). The development of the use of graphic and contextual information as children learn to read. *Reading Research Quarterly, 6*, 75-96.

Brock, C. H., & Gavelek, J. R. (1998). Fostering children's engagement with text: A sociocultural perspective. In T. E. Raphael & K. H. Au (Eds.), *Literature-based instruction: Reshaping the curriculum* (pp. 72-94). Norwood, MA: Christopher-Gordon.

Calkins, L. M. (1994). *The art of teaching writing* (2nd ed.). Portsmouth, NH: Heinemann.

Campbell, J. R., & Ashworth, K. P. (Eds.) (1995). *A synthesis of data from NAEP's 1992 integrated reading performance record at Grade 4.* Washington, DC: U.S. Department of Education, Office of Educational Research and Improvement.

Center for the Study of Reading (1991). *Teaching word identification* [Videotape]. (Available from the International Reading Association, 800 Barksdale Road, Newark, DE 19714-8139 USA).

Chall, J. (1967). *Learning to read: The great debate.* New York: McGraw-Hill.

Chall, J. (1983). *Stages of reading development.* New York: McGraw-Hill.

Choi, S. N. (1993). *Halmoni and the picnic.* Boston: Houghton Mifflin.

Clay, M. M. (1985). *The early detection of reading difficulties* (3rd ed.). Portsmouth, NH: Heinemann.

Clay, M. M. (1991). *Becoming literate: The construction of inner control.* Portsmouth, NH: Heinemann.

Cole, M., & Griffin, P. (1983). A socio-historical approach to re-mediation. *The Quarterly Newsletter of the Laboratory of Comparative Human Cognition, 5*(4), 69-74.

Collins, J. (1997). How Johnny should read. *Time, 150,* September 15, 1999. Retrieved from www.pathfinder.com/time/magazine/1997/dom971047/box3.html

Cowley, J. (1990). *Mrs. Wishy-washy.* Bothell, WA: Wright Group.

Crowell, D. C., Kawakami, A. J., & Wong, J. L. (1986). Emerging literacy: Reading-writing experiences in a kindergarten classroom. *The Reading Teacher, 40*(2), 144-149.

Cunningham, P. M. (1991). *Phonics we use: Words for reading and writing.* Glenview, IL: Scott Foresman.

Dahl, K., & Freppon, P. (1995). A comparison of innercity children's interpretations of reading and writing instruction in the early grades in skills-based and whole language classrooms. *Reading Research Quarterly, 30,* 50-74.

Delpit, L. (1988). The silenced dialogue: Power and pedagogy in educating other people's children. *Harvard Educational Review, 58,* 280-298.

Delpit, L. (1995). *Other people's children: Cultural conflict in the classroom.* New York: New Press.

Dole, J. A., Duffy, G. G., Roehler, L. R., & Pearson, P. D. (1991). Moving from the old to the new: Research on reading comprehension instruction. *Review of Educational Research, 61*(2), 239-264.

Eeds, M., & Wells, D. (1989). Grand conversations: An exploration of meaning construction in literature study groups. *Research in the Teaching of English, 23,* 4-29.

Ehri, L. C. (1987). Learning to read and spell words. *Journal of Reading Behavior, 19*(1), 5-31.

Flippo, R. (1998). Points of agreement: A display of professional unity in our field. *The Reading Teacher, 52*(1), 30-40.

Fountas, I. C., & Pinnell, G. S. (1996). *Guided reading: Good first teaching for all children.* Portsmouth, NH: Heinemann.

Freppon, P. A., & Dahl, K. L. (1998). Balanced instruction: Insights and considerations. *Reading Research Quarterly, 33*(2), 240-251.

Frith, U. (1985). Beneath the surface of developmental dyslexia. In K. E. Patterson, J. C. Marshall, & M. Colheart (Eds.), *Surface dyslexia: Neurophysiological and cognitive studies of phonological reading.* Hillsdale, NJ: Lawrence Erlbaum Associates.

Gaskins, I. W., Ehri, L. C., Cress, C., O'Hara, C., & Donnelly, K. (1997). Analyzing words and making discoveries about the alphabetic system: Activities for beginning readers. *Language Arts, 74*(3), 172-184.

Gaskins, R. W., Gaskins, J. C., & Gaskins, I. W. (1991). A decoding program for poor readers—And the rest of the class, too! *Language Arts, 68*(3), 213-225.

Goodman, K. (1986). *What's whole in whole language?* Portsmouth, NH: Heinemann.

Graves, D. (1983). *Writing: Teachers and children at work.* Exeter, NH: Heinemann.

Graves, D. (1994). *A fresh look at writing.* Portsmouth, NH: Heinemann.

Guba, E. G., & Lincoln, Y. S. (1994). Competing paradigms in qualitative research. In N. K. Denzin & Y. S. Lincoln (Eds.), *Handbook of qualitative research* (pp. 105-117). Thousand Oaks, CA: Sage.

Guthrie, J. T., & Alvermann, D. E. (Eds.) (1999). *Engagement in reading: Processes, practices, and policy implications.* New York: Teachers College Press.

Hansen, J., & Pearson, P. D. (1983). An instructional study: Improving the inferential comprehension of fourth-grade good and poor readers. *Journal of Educational Psychology, 75*(6), 821-829.

Herman, P. A., & Weaver, C. R. (1988, December). *Contextual strategies for learning word meanings.* Paper presented at the National Reading Conference, Tucson, AZ.

Holdaway, D. (1979). *The foundations of literacy.* Sydney, Australia: Ashton Scholastic.

International Reading Association (1999). *Using multiple methods of beginning reading instruction: A position statement of the International Reading Association.* Newark, DE: International Reading Association.

Lomax, R. G., & McGee, L. M. (1987). Young children's concepts about print and reading: Toward a model of word reading acquisition. *Reading Research Quarterly, 22*(2), 237-256.

Lukens, R. J. (1990). *A critical handbook of children's literature* (4th ed.). Glenview, IL: Scott, Foresman.

Mason, J. M., & Stewart, J. P. (1989). *CAP early childhood screening/diagnostic tests* (pilot version). Iowa City, IA: American Testronics.

McCormick, C. E., & Mason, J. M. (1986). Intervention procedures for increasing preschool children's interest in and knowledge about reading. In W. H. Teale & E. Sulzby (Eds.), *Emergent literacy: Writing and reading.* Norwood, NJ: Ablex.

McGee, L. M., & Purcell-Gates, V. (1997). "So what's going on in research on emergent literacy?" *Reading Research Quarterly, 32*(3), 310-318.

Moll, L. C. (1990). Introduction. In L. C. Moll (Ed.), *Vygotsky and education: Instructional implications and applications of sociohistorical psychology* (pp. 1-27). Cambridge, England: Cambridge University Press.

Nation, K., & Hulme, C. (1997). Phonemic segmentation, not onset-rime segmentation, predicts early reading and spelling skills. *Reading Research Quarterly, 32*(2), 154-167.

O'Hehir, D. (1988). *Home free*. New York: Atheneum.

Palincsar, A. S., & Brown, A. L. (1984). Reciprocal teaching of comprehension-fostering and comprehension-monitoring activities. *Cognition and Instruction, 2,* 117-175.

Pearson, P. D., & Raphael, T. E. (1999). Toward a more complex view of balance in the literacy curriculum. In W. D. Hammond & T. E. Raphael (Eds.), *Early literacy instruction for the new millennium* (pp. 1-21). Grand Rapids: Michigan Reading Association and Center for the Improvement of Early Reading Achievement.

Peters, C. W., & Wixson, K. W. (1998). Aligning curriculum, instruction, and assessment in literature-based approaches. In T. E. Raphael & K. H. Au (Eds.), *Literature-based instruction: Reshaping the curriculum* (pp. 261-284). Norwood, MA: Christopher-Gordon.

Raphael, T. E., & Au, K. H. (Eds.) (1998). *Literature-based instruction: Reshaping the curriculum*. Norwood, MA: Christopher-Gordon.

Raphael, T. E., & Hiebert, E. H. (1996). *Creating an integrated approach to literacy instruction*. Fort Worth, TX: Harcourt Brace.

Raphael, T. E., & McMahon, S. I. (1994). Book Club: An alternative framework for reading instruction. *The Reading Teacher, 48*(2), 102-116.

Rosenblatt, L. (1978). *The reader, the text, the poem: The transactional theory of the literary work*. Carbondale: Southern Illinois University Press.

Rosenblatt, L. M. (1991). Literary theories. In J. Flood, J. M. Jensen, D. Lapp, & J. R. Squire (Eds.), *Handbook of research on teaching the English language arts*. New York: Macmillan.

Roser, N. L., & Martinez, M. G. (Eds.) (1995). *Book talk and beyond: Children and teachers respond to literature*. Newark, DE: International Reading Association.

Shannon, P. (1989). *Broken promises: Reading instruction in twentieth-century America*. New York: Bergin & Garvey.

Short, K. G., & Pierce, K. M. (1990). *Talking about books: Creating literate communities*. Portsmouth, NH: Heinemann.

Spiegel, D. L. (1998). Silver bullets, babies, and bath water: Literature response groups in a balanced literacy program. *The Reading Teacher, 52*(2), 114-124.

Spivey, N. N. (1997). *The constructivist metaphor: Reading, writing, and the making of meaning*. San Diego: Academic Press.

Stahl, S. A. (1997). Instructional models in reading: An introduction. In S. A. Stahl & D. A. Hayes (Eds.), *Instructional models in reading* (pp. 1-29). Mahwah, NJ: Lawrence Erlbaum Associates.

Steptoe, J. (1987). *Mufaro's beautiful daughters*. New York: Lothrop, Lee & Shepard.

Strickland, D. S. (1994-95). Reinventing our literacy programs: Books, Basics, balance. *The Reading Teacher, 48*(4), 294-302.

Sulzby, E. (1985). Children's emerging reading of favorite storybooks: A developmental study. *Reading Research Quarterly, 20*(4), 458-481.

Taylor, B. M. (1982). A summarizing strategy to improve middle grade students' reading and writing skills. *The Reading Teacher, 36,* 202-205.

Valencia, S. W., & Lipson, M. Y. (1998). A quest for challenging ideas and meaningful learning. In T. E. Raphael & K. H. Au (Eds.), *Literature-based instruction: Reshaping the curriculum* (pp. 96-122). Norwood, MA: Christopher-Gordon.

Vygotsky, L. S. (1978). *Mind in society: The development of higher psychological processes* (M. Cole, Trans.). Cambridge, MA: Harvard University Press.

Weaver, C. (1990). *Understanding whole language: Principles and practices*. Portsmouth, NH: Heinemann.

Wilde, S. (1989). Looking at invented spelling: A kidwatcher's guide to spelling, part I. In K. Goodman, Y. Goodman, & W. Hood (Eds.), *The whole language evaluation book*. Portsmouth, NH: Heinemann.

Winograd, P., & Paris, S. G. (1988). A cognitive and motivational agenda for reading instruction. *Educational Leadership, 46*(4), 30-36.

# ·70·

# WRITING

## Anne Haas Dyson and Sarah Warshauer Freedman
### University of California, Berkeley

Five-year-old Sharon had been standing a few feet from the classroom writing center, observing her friends at work. Anxious to involve Sharon in the writing, the adult observer inquired, "You gonna write today too, Sharon?"

"Well," said Sharon, "how do you do it?" (Dyson, 1981, p. 776).

Although few students are as straightforward as Sharon, most expect their teachers to help them answer the "How do you do it?" question. Despite the deceptively simple nature of the question, providing supportive answers is a complex challenge.

Some of the complexity of teaching writing comes from the nature of writing itself. As we illustrate in this chapter, writing can be an avenue for individual expression, and, at the same time, it can serve to construct or proclaim the individual author's membership in a social group. Furthermore, writing is conceived of as a skill, and yet, at the same time, that skill is itself a process dependent on a range of other skills and, moreover, a process that is kaleidoscopic, shaped by the author's changing purposes for writing.

Some of the complexity of teaching writing comes from the nature of classrooms as educational settings. Teachers negotiate between the class as a social group and individual students in that group, a challenging task when individuals number in the 20s and 30s or more and when social membership is diverse. Moreover, teachers often negotiate between their desires to teach writing as a purposeful process and to teach the varied "skills" conceived of as integral to that process, skills differentially controlled by their students. This negotiating is more urgent in a political climate of high-stakes tests that may determine individuals' access to future educational opportunities (Strickland, Bodino, Buchan, Jones, Nelson, & Rosen, in press).

To manage this complex teaching act, teachers of all levels must become comfortable with and careful observers of writers and of writing, seeking the sort of information about children that helps them respond to the questions—the challenges—inherent in students' efforts. In the following three sections of this chapter, we review the kinds of interrelated research knowledge about writing that may inform teachers' observations of their students and their decisions about how to best support their students' efforts.

First, because ways of using written language vary with different social situations, we review research on how literacy functions in varied communities, including both the classroom itself and the larger communities students inhabit outside the classroom. This research may support teachers' efforts to broaden and deepen their literacy curricula, allowing individuals to build on the foundation of their literacy experiences and allowing the classroom community to experience new forms of agency through writing.

Second, because writing is a complex process, one involving the orchestration of many kinds of skills, we review research on the composing process. Such knowledge may support teachers' efforts to observe individual writers' ways of composing, including their successes and challenges. On the basis of such observations, teachers may help writers overcome difficulties that cannot be seen on the page, ward off problems before they occur in print, and ease students' ways into writing.

Finally, because writing is a developmental process, one in which today's ways of composing change in complex ways into tomorrow's, we review research on the development of writing. Such knowledge may help teachers appreciate the diversity of students' resources for composing and, further, to note the signs of future growth that may be hidden in students' tangled texts and scratch-outs. Too, such knowledge may support teachers' efforts to understand the questions students cannot articulate and to appreciate the answers they figure out for themselves. Finally, knowledge about developmental processes may guide teachers to see and to provide the kinds of support individual students might find most helpful.

The research we review can provide support for teachers, but it can not provide prescriptions to follow, techniques proven to "work" for all learners. Rather, it can provide information that might help focus teacher observations, deepen insights, and, in the end, inform the crucial decision making that is the daily work of all teachers—when to push a student for more, when to praise what may seem to be "errors," when to encourage students to write collaboratively, when to call a parent in.

As suggested by our review, this decision making is informed by observations of both the classroom community and individual class members. Each student has a unique rhythm, a particular pitch, but that individual quality is a part of, and is shaped by, the rhythm and pitch—the communal quality—of the classroom as a whole. Just as musical notes play differently in varied compositions, so do our students reveal themselves differently in different combinations of others. We, then, aim through this review to contribute to educators' understanding of writing's compositional possibilities, of each student's challenges and promise, and of their own potential as teachers to further literacy growth in their classrooms.

## THE USES OF WRITING

Five-year-old Sharon's "How do you do it?" question is difficult to answer, in part, because the hows are shaped by the whys, whos, and whats: Who wants to write, to or for whom, about what, and why? Indeed, in the lives of children, as in the lives of whole communities, literacy prospers if and when compelling reasons exist for writing and when the information conveyed through that writing is a valued part of the social network— when it helps people mediate relationships with other people and reflect on their own lives (Farr, 1994; Heath, 1986; B. J. Moss, 1994; Schieffelin & Cochran-Smith, 1984; Street, 1995; Taylor & Dorsey-Gaines, 1988).

In fact, children like Sharon are usually introduced to literacy within their homes and communities and within the social and emotional context of relationships. For example, in their families, list making may be at the center of family planning for a shopping trip; an illegible phone message or returned check may be surrounded by a family argument; a note from a teacher may elicit parental confusion, pride, or anger, whereas an "I love you" note from a child might evoke an oral response and a hug. Within the context of familial occasions, things happen around and through particular kinds of print (Heath, 1983; McNaughton, 1995; Taylor, 1983).

Writing, then, like speech, is a communicative tool that members of a society use to carry on their lives together and that they pass on to their children (Scribner & Cole, 1981). Unlike speech, however, writing is a cultural invention and consciously learned, and its learning is inextricably linked not only to individuals' efforts but also to relational contexts and broader social and institutional structures (Barton, Hamilton, & Ivanic, 2000; Luke, 1995).

### Variation in Writing's Functions and Forms

The tool of writing is viewed by many scholars as contributing to human cultures in unique ways (Goody, 1968; Goody & Watt, 1963; Olson, 1977; Ong, 1982). For example, Goody (1968) argued:

The importance of writing lies in its creating a new medium of communication between [people]. Its essential service is to objectify speech, to provide language with a material correlative, a set of visible signs. In this material form, speech can be transmitted over space and preserved over time; what people say and think can be rescued from the transitoriness of oral communication. (1968, pp. 1-2)

In the last 2 decades anthropologists, linguists, and psychologists have tried to specify writing's varied functions and forms—its usefulness—in a range of situations. Some scholars have worked to characterize the features of written language that make it such a potentially powerful medium of communication in particular situations. In this work, written language is contrasted with oral language. Written language, researchers and theorists argue, can be constructed so that it is ultimately less dependent upon a specific context. Authors can pack much meaning onto the printed page, weaving words together tightly through such linguistic features as subordinate clauses, prepositional phrases, and adjective phrases (Chafe, 1982, 1985; Johnston, 1979; Tannen, 1982, 1984a, 1984b). By tightly structuring words, meanings are made explicit; that is, the connections between ideas and the qualifications of those ideas are deliberately put into words. "On the other hand," "however," "despite this" are the sorts of phrases that weave together written essays. Some scholars argue that the development of writing had intellectual consequences in the history of humankind, leading to the development of abstract, logical reasoning (Goody & Watt, 1963; Olson, 1977).

However, this vision of writing as explicit—as able to exist on its own, meaningful for anyone in any situation—contrasts sharply with the sorts of cozy home literacy scenes just discussed. Clearly there are varied styles of written language, just as there are varied styles of oral language (Chafe & Danielewicz, 1987). Moreover, activities involving *oral language* provide the context for most instances of *written language* use. "Even in the most seemingly literate of environments, such as the law court, a schoolroom, or a university office, most of the conventions of how to act and what to do [with and through texts] are passed on orally" (Barton, 1994, p. 90). Ways of using both oral and written language are interrelated with each other and with ways of living—historical and geographical conditions; social and economic resources and opportunities; religious beliefs, values, and motivations (Farr, 1994; Finnegan, 1988; Hamilton, Barton, & Ivanic, 1994; Heath, 1983; Philips, 1975; Scribner & Cole, 1981; Street, 1995). In this sense, written language is always "embedded"; it always figures into particular kinds of communicative events. Its form varies depending on its uses.

Many scholars have investigated how writing varies from situation to situation. For example, the study of literature and rhetoric has produced taxonomies of textual types (e.g., Kinneavy, 1971; Lundsford & Ede, 1984; Winterowd, 1975). And authors concerned with the teaching of writing have produced other categories (Britton, Burgess, Martin, McLeod, & Rosen, 1975; Emig, 1971). They distinguish kinds of writing according to the purpose for writing (e.g., to persuade or to inform) and the features associated with those purposes. (For a review of ways of categorizing writing in educational research, see Applebee, 2000.)

Another way to investigate how writing varies across situations is to consider how the activity of writing is socially organized within the ongoing life of particular groups (Basso, 1974; B. J. Moss, 1994; Szwed, 1981). Researchers working within this tradition are called "ethnographers of communication" (Gumperz & Hymes, 1972; Hymes, 1962). They study social activities that are centered around reading or writing, activities often termed "literacy events" (Heath, 1982; Teale, Estrada, & Anderson, 1981). Like "speech events" (Hymes, 1972), literacy events are characterized by varied components, including setting, participants (e.g., senders, recipients), purposes and goals, message form, content, channel, key or tone, and rules governing the sort of writing and talking that should occur (Basso, 1974). For example, informal letter-writing events differ from joint committee-report-writing events, which differ from list-making events.

Both the social and the cognitive "consequences" of written language, then, depend on the specific nature of the written language events within which that language is used, including the goals and the cognitive processes those events entail. In other words, it is not writing per se but the sorts of social situations in which writing is embedded that determines its ultimate human effects. For example, writing to memorize texts may influence individuals' rote memory, but such literacy use would not affect performance on a logical reasoning task (Scribner & Cole, 1981). From a sociocultural point of view, a person who finds writing a letter to a relative a comfortable use of literacy may not also be socially comfortable writing an academic essay—such impersonal writing for an unknown audience may be contrary to that individual's sense of self in relationship to other people (Scollon & Scollon, 1981).

Furthermore, even within what may be considered one kind of genre or literacy event, individuals' comfort and expertise may vary. For example, in many cultural contexts, children may collaborate orally to compose a written letter with their parents. However, across letter writing events, literacy expertise may be distributed quite differently among child and adult participants because of their respective knowledge of written graphics, genre conventions, audience expectations, and/or linguistic code (e.g., control over a standard English). These differences may engender nontraditional family dynamics (e.g., children guiding adults), and thus they may have ramifications for both social and language learning (e.g., Schieffelin & CochranSmith, 1984; Vasquez, Pease-Alvarez, & Shannon, 1994).

Even within the negotiation of a single literacy event, expertise may be differentially negotiated. Kalman (1996) provided a vivid illustration through her study of the work world of Mexican scribes. The scribes earn their livelihood composing letters for clients, who come to them for assistance in varied legal, workplace, and family matters. Because the distribution of relevant expertise varies between scribes and clients, the scribes' composing events entail complex oral negotiating. In Kalman's words, "Any use of writing and written texts implies understanding how convention, purpose, knowledge, and power are negotiated to produce a particular piece of writing" (p. 215). Moreover, given new social circumstances for writing (e.g., new institutional contexts, new relationships), any "expert" can become a "novice."

Heath (1983) provided a seminal study of the complex oral and written configurations of literacy use in American communities. She studied oral and written language use in two working class communities and in the homes of middle-class teachers in the Piedmont Carolinas. Individuals in all three settings were literate, in that all made some use of written language, but only the middle-class community used written language—and talked about written language—in ways compatible with the literacy models used in school. For example, people in all communities made lists and wrote notes, but only those in the middle-class neighborhood would bring home expository sorts of writing tasks, such as writing summaries or reports.

Heath (1980) worked with teachers to develop strategies for making school ways of using and talking about written language sensible to students from the working-class communities (one of African American heritage, the other, European American) as well as to those from the middle-class community (which included both heritages). For example, a primary grade teacher incorporated environmental print (e.g., labels on cans and boxes, street signs, store advertisements and price tags) into her classroom. Heath (1980) described the philosophy of this teacher:

Reading and writing are things you do all the time—at home, on the bus, riding your bike, at the barber shop. You can read, and you do everyday before you ever come to school. You can also play baseball and football at home, at the park, wherever you want to, but when you come to school or go to a summer program at the Neighborhood Center, you get help on techniques, the gloves to buy, the way to throw, and the way to slide. School does that for reading and writing. We all read and write a lot of the time, lots of places. School isn't much different except that here we work on techniques, and we practice a lot—under a coach. I'm the coach. (pp. 130–131)

An intermediate grade teacher helped her students become ethnographers, who talked, read, and wrote about the folk concepts about agriculture in their local community and the relationship of those concepts to "scientific" concepts. A high school teacher encouraged students to create documents and videos explaining to senior citizen groups the meanings of complex written forms, like housing regulations and warranties. At all levels, students talked about differences in how people used oral and written language, thereby developing their comfort with the talk about oral and written language so prevalent in schools as well as developing their capacity to deliberately manipulate language to suit different social occasions.

Studies, like Heath's (1980, 1983), of literacy in varied cultural groups are helpful, sensitizing us to the rich diversity of literacy use in our society. However, teachers cannot all do extensive studies in the homes of students. Still, teachers can provide curricular time and space for students to talk about their out of school lives, and, given adequate institutional support, they can build positive relationships with children's families and communities; in these ways they can gain insight into possible ways of building bridges, making connections (Dyson, 1997a; Edwards, 1999; Hymes, 1980; Moll, Amanti, Neff, & Gonzalez, 1992).

Moreover, teachers can learn a great deal about the breadth of students' literacy experiences beyond the school walls by observing and discussing with students the kinds of textual knowledge that inform their actions within those walls. For writing (and reading) may be a key tool in students' construction of their own unofficial or student-controlled school spaces, from the very beginning of schooling. In these spaces, students may use a repertoire of genres or familiar ways of using language learned in varied institutions, including homes, churches, the popular media, and local peer cultures themselves (e.g., Blake, 1997; Camitta, 1993; Dyson, 1993, 1997b; Fiering, 1981; Finders, 1996; Gilmore, 1983; Sola & Bennett, 1985). These diverse genres too, often involving varied semiotic tools, can potentially broaden the scope of concern of traditional language arts classrooms (for theoretical discussion, see the New London Group, 1996; for an elementary-focused discussion of incorporating media into the literacy curriculum, see Kavanagh, 1997; for secondary-focused discussions, see Buckingham & Sefton-Green, 1994).

In sum, the variability of writing's forms and functions suggests that the formal school curriculum recognize variable functions and forms (Comber, Thomson, & Wells, in press; Dyson, 1993; Florio & Clark, 1982; Moll & Whitmore, 1993; Newkirk, in press). Defining writing more broadly might allow more children to see themselves officially as writers and would allow teachers more footholds from which to build—more ways of engaging children in classroom literacy events.

## Literacy in the Classroom Community

A "literacy community" is not synonymous with a "cultural community" (Teale et al., 1981). Just as speech communities (Gumperz, 1971) may be occupational or interest specific, so may literacy communities. The classroom itself can be considered a literacy community, one with special ways of using and talking about written language. Thus, the classroom can create or restrict the sorts of opportunities students have to become literate. In this section, we look closely at the nature of the classroom as a context for writing.

In trying to understand how literacy functions in the classroom community, a basic question is, what is the nature of the kinds of literacy activities that occur there? This kind of question can allow teachers insight into the sorts of supportive linkages they are allowing children to make between school literacy and literacy use in homes, communities, and workplaces (Gundlach, Farr, & Cook-Gumperz, 1989). In addition, it can allow teachers to evaluate the ways in which literacy becomes meaningful inside classrooms.

For example, Applebee (1981), at the secondary school level, and Florio and Clark (1982; Clark & Florio, 1981), at the elementary school level, documented how many school writing opportunities restrict children from intellectually and socially engaging in the writing process. Writing's format and much of its content might be provided by a commercial publisher on a worksheet or by the teacher, as in boardwork; in such cases, students do not have to formulate their own thoughts. As Hudson (1988) illustrated, the more students control the form and content of their writing, the more likely they may be to perceive even assigned writing as their own.

To look in more fine-grained ways at classroom writing events—to begin to understand exactly how teachers and students interactively construct them—we must step back and consider how teachers and students interactively construct schooling itself. The concept of the classroom as a social system jointly constructed by teachers and students has been dramatized by studies that began in the fifties (Henry, 1955, 1963; Jackson, 1968; Leacock, 1969; Rist, 1970, 1973).

In the 1970s, researchers began to focus specifically on the language of the classroom, arguing that it was, after all, through language that teaching and learning occurred and thus through language that insight could be gained into the social context of learning (for a review, see Cazden, 1988). This research, much of which has been conducted in elementary classrooms, has revealed the varied demands made by classroom activities. It is not enough for students to know in an academic sense—they must know how to display what they know through appropriate talk (e.g., Bremme & Erickson, 1977; Greene & Wallat, 1979; Mehan, 1979; Merritt, 1982; Philips, 1972). That is, they must be familiar and comfortable with the kinds of questions that teachers ask, with the ways people take turns speaking, or with the sorts of relationships expected among the children themselves (relationships that are often competitive rather than cooperative).

In the schools, writing is taught as teachers and students talk about writing. Thus, the literature on classroom language can inform teachers' efforts to take advantage of the rich interactional potential of the classroom. During the 1980s, researchers interested in talk and writing were inspired by a newly available book of Vygotskian theory (Vygotsky, 1934/1978) and by research on parent–child interaction in language learning (e.g., Cross, 1975). They focused heavily on dyadic encounters between students and teachers about their texts. From this perspective, experts "loan" children their consciousness about language and language use (Bruner, 1986, p. 175); they thus negotiate the developmental gap—the "zone of proximal development" (Vygotsky, 1934/1978, p. 84)—between what children can do on their own and with help. That is, they help children to choose, encode, and reflect on their written choices. In these "scaffolding" interactions, teachers, like their caregiver counterparts (Ninio & Bruner, 1978), orally support children's language.

Consistent with this viewpoint, Wells (1986) discussed the instructional implications of his study of parent–child interaction during first language acquisition; he stressed the importance of teachers, like parents, responding to students' written initiatives, helping them develop their ideas, an emphasis compatible with a pedagogical emphasis on dialogue journals (Staton, Shuy, Peyton, & Reed, 1988) and on teacher–student writing conferences (e.g., Applebee, 1984; Calkins, 1983, 1986; Graves, 1983; S. Freedman, 1987b), discussed in a later section.

Despite the usefulness of the scaffolding metaphor, it is not adequate for capturing the complexity of learning in classroom communities. Unlike the middle-class caregivers and their singular charges studied in language development research, classroom teachers have 20 to 30 children or more, and those children do not necessarily share similar sociocultural backgrounds with each other or with their teachers. More recently, researchers have focused on the network of oral and written events that constitute the official learning community (for a review, see Langer & Flihan, 2000). As Moll and Whitmore (1993) suggested, this network is not a dyadic zone of proximal development but rather a "collective" zone, formulated by diverse events in varied units of study. Children's talk about and use of text is guided, then, not only by scaffolding interactions but also by their evolving understanding of event purposes, social relations, and textual expectations—understanding gained from, and negotiated by, oral participation. Over the school years, as the curriculum differentiates into disciplines, children's participation in literacy events and their associated genres becomes a means for participation in, and development of, both disciplinary and literacy knowledge and skill (Applebee, 1996; A. Freedman & Medway, 1994).

Some researchers have focused specific attention on the interplay between classroom discourse and student writing (e.g., Applebee, 1996; Gutierrez, 1992; Larson & Maier, 2000; Losey, 1997; Nystrand, 1997; Sperling & Woodlief, 1997). A consistent finding of such work is that the "default" teacher–student interaction pattern, to use Cazden's term (1988, p. 53), predominates in our classrooms and, moreover, that that pattern provides minimal support for student composing. As Cazden discussed, to enact this familiar interactional rhythm, teachers ask testing questions, students provide minimal responses, and teachers evaluate those responses. This interactional mode is very well suited to "assembling factual information" that can be provided in "short answers" (p. 50) but not well suited at all to interactively guided composing, in which ideas are exchanged, elaborated, and integrated.

Moreover, it is not just the kind of talk during composing instruction that shapes learning but the way in which classroom discourse throughout all curricular activities helps shape a classroom epistemology and the literacy practices through which it is enacted (Many, Fyfe, Lewis, & Mitchell, 1996; Nystrand & Graff, in press). For example, Nystrand and Graff (in press) analyzed a middle school teacher's' efforts to teach argumentative writing through state-of-the-art writing process pedagogy; they argued that a rhetorical emphasis on reporting information couched all literacy activities and thus worked against the teacher's efforts to promote sophisticated written interpretations and analyses.

Even given the best laid teacher plans for productive writing activities and the most thoughtfully enacted curricular context, students inevitably have their own interpretations of those activities, shaped by complex social, developmental, and cultural factors. Students may differ in their social interpretations of the events (e.g., who in fact the audience is, what the actual purpose of the event is, what the evaluative standards are) (Clark & Florio, 1981; Dyson, 1985, 1993; S. Freedman, 1987b; Reyes, 1991; Sperling & S. Freedman, 1987). They may also have differing conceptions about writing and written language than those underlying an activity planned by the teacher. For example, they may not assume the analytic approach to language that underlies and is taken for granted by many beginning literacy programs (Dyson, 1999b). They may have differing notions of how narratives are structured or even what stories are (Cazden, 1988; Heath, 1983; Michaels & Cook-Gumperz, 1979). Indeed, they

may question whether or not a teacher is actually teaching, particularly given the emphasis on teachers responding conversationally (rather than prescriptively) to students' efforts (Delpit, 1995; Newkirk, 1995; Walker, 1992).

One particularly potent source of tension between teachers and students is the relationship among students themselves that is expected in the classroom. Although teachers organize and guide communicative activities, students' actions and interactions are inevitably influenced by the social concerns, relationships, and energy among the students themselves. Peer relationships are not necessarily always positive or productive (Lensmire, 1993), and, as experienced teachers attest, they too require active monitoring and guidance (Dyson, 1997a). Moreover, if peer group values conflict with classroom values, children may reject academic demands; among those aspects of school life most often cited as divisive are those that touch on children's relationships with each other—children having to work silently, to value adult more than self and peer approval, to compete with friends for that adult approval (Gilbert & Gay, 1985; Gilmore, 1983; Labov, 1982; Philips, 1972; Tharp et al., 1984). In writing classrooms in particular, students having to evaluate each other's work can generate tension (S. Freedman, 1987a).

Nonetheless, students' peer relationships do have the potential, even when conflict-ridden, to support student's writing. Peers have the potential to be effective teachers and collaborative learners (Cooper, Marquis, & Ayers-Lopez, 1982; Daiute, 1989, 1993; Gere, 1987). Through their informal talk during writing times, young children may learn how it is that writing figures into human relationships, as peers respond both critically and playfully to their efforts (Dyson, 1989). Through co-constructed writing in collaboratively enacted whole class events (Larson & Maier, 2000) and through peer conferences in dyads and small-group sessions (Bruce, 1987; Gere, 1987; Graves, 1983; Nystrand, 1986; Sowers, 1985), students across the grades may be guided to attend to each other's writing in particular ways. Tensions among students in their preferences for varied kinds of genres and text content, for kinds of social spaces for writing response, and for particular kinds of feedback can become the focus of critical classroom reflection (Dyson, 1993, 1997b; Finders, 1996; for a review of related issues, see Dahl & Farnan, 1998). Students also can use written language to establish relationships with students in other grade levels, other schools, cities, or states, or even other countries (e.g., S. Freedman, 1994; S. Freedman & McLeod, 1988; Greene, 1985; Heath & Branscombe, 1985), relationships that can provide them with engaging but potentially demanding audiences.

No doubt we have much to learn about how particular kinds of relationships between teachers and students and among students themselves—and the sorts of talk that enact those relationships—influence students' learning in our very diverse society. As we explore the characteristics of varied classrooms serving students from varied backgrounds we may be able to articulate better the sorts of experiences that are critical for writing growth (e.g., opportunity to talk about, reflect on writing in particular ways) from the particular shapes that critical experience can take (the variety of ways such opportunities can be provided).

## Writing and the Transformation of Community

The emphasis of most research on writing and the classroom community is on how the social organization and enacted relations of that community socialize students as writers. Building especially on the critical pedagogy of Freire (1970), there has been some research interest in examining the nature of classroom conditions and processes through which children and youth can use writing to transform or reconstruct community relations themselves, both within the classroom and in the wider community. This research tends to foreground the phrase *writing practice*, in contrast to the phrase *writing event*; unlike the latter, the former phrase highlights the ideological aspects of literacy use (see, especially, Luke, 1995; Street, 1995). *Critical literacy practices*, then, involve talk that helps participants reflect on given words—and potentially change their ways of acting on and with those words in given social worlds.

In the classroom, interactions for critical transformation of the community itself are meant to articulate and examine, not just experiential gaps in writing skill or interactional gaps in author intention and audience comprehension, but sociopolitical gaps that are existent in any human community. For example, Dyson (1997b) examined a writing class in an urban primary classroom organized around an "author's theater," in which children dramatized compositions, many of which were based on the popular media. Ideologies of gender, class, and race were visible in children's decisions to write (or not write) certain kinds of stories (e.g., superhero ones), in their selection of child actors for varied character roles, and in audience response to the social worth and textual clarity of stories and to the sensibleness of choice of actors. By helping the children articulate the views behind their giggles, sour faces, scrunched noses, and cries of "That's not fair," the teacher helped the children link authorial decisions about character and plot to social and ideological issues in their relations to each other. (Volosinov, 1973, provided a clear theoretical link between language use and ideological awareness.)

To provide an example from a secondary school, G. Moss (1989) described her efforts to help secondary students articulate their pleasures in, and reservations about, what she terms the "un/popular" fictions of teenage romance stories and comic book adventures; in so doing, she revealed the complex authorial processes—decisions about the portrayal of love, power, gender roles—that lie behind a seemingly simplistic text. (For further discussions of gender-related issues, see Gilbert, 1989, 1994.) And, in a powerful piece, poet June Jordan (1988) described her African American college students' talk about writing—especially their talk about the kind of *talk in writing*—as she helped them (to use Freire's words) "separate themselves from their own activity [their own speech]" and to reflect on the "historical dimensions" of the negative evaluations they had appropriated uncritically about African American vernaculars (Freire, 1970, p. 80). (For a moving analysis of critical literacy as enacted in an adult women's writing group, see Heller, 1997.)

Underlying studies of in-classroom interactions is a desire to help students realize their authoring possibilities, not only in texts, but in their communities. There have been efforts to document and analyze the kinds of teacher actions and classroom practices that further children's and youth's efforts to enact such agency. For example, in a series of papers, Comber and colleagues (e.g., Comber, 1999; Comber et al., in press; Comber & Nixon, 1999) illustrate that critical literacy is not a gloomy imposition of world problems on innocent children (a common myth). At its best, critical literacy entails teacher attentiveness to issues embedded in students' everyday talk, issues that teachers may help link to larger societal issues. Moreover, it can be engaging and, indeed, fun, to take action, to be a participant the larger world. In enacting critical literacy practices, teachers may need to begin with students' familiar symbolic tools and practices (e.g., drawing pictures, audiotaping interviews), introducing new tools and practices into student repertories, particularly those involving research strategies and informational and persuasive writing. Finally, teacher intentions may have unintended consequences, realized in resistant or resentful students; critical literacy practices not only are new for teachers, they are new for students, and, moreover, as already noted, classroom communities are not ideologically homogeneous, any more than they are academically so. As Blake (1997) noted in her ethnography of writing among fifth grade urban girls, private writing contexts may be necessary for exploring sensitive topics, especially if the larger classroom public is, itself, viewed as unsafe.

In this technologically shrinking world, critical literacy practices can affect change in and out of the classroom, when teachers in different geographic areas collaborate through electronic media, like e-mail, to exchange information about, and explore, local ways of living and to jointly address global concerns (e.g., conditions for children in refugee camps, conservation projects; for documentation and analyses of many such examples, see Cummins & Sayers, 1995). Still, it is important to remember, as Sahni (1994) noted, that an act as simple as writing a letter to one's teacher can transform power relationships in many classrooms; although Sahni was discussing an authoritarian school in rural India, her appreciation for children's desires for transforming their relational worlds is relevant for many classrooms.

## THE EVALUATION OF WRITTEN LANGUAGE

In any classroom community, a learner's query like Sharon's "How do you do it?" may soon be overshadowed by a teacher's inquiry, "How well can *you* do it?" For a major educational issue is determining how well the writing of individual students, whole classes, whole school districts, indeed whole countries is progressing. How can student progress be measured? How can successful instruction be identified? An even more basic question is, What is "good" writing? As is discussed later in the section The Development of Writing, there is no one description of what writing progress looks like throughout the school years. Still, there are ways to document progress, ways which we discuss here.

***Inside classrooms.*** The most common classroom practices for evaluating student writing have proven problematic: writing comments on student papers and, particularly for intermediate and secondary school students, grading (Searle & Dillon, 1980;

Tchudi, 1997). Comments on mechanics (spelling, handwriting, grammar) may overshadow any comment on students' ideas (Petty & Finn, 1981). In addition, when papers are graded, comments may serve primarily to justify the grade rather than to help students learn; furthermore, written comments tend to be phrased so generally that they carry little meaning (Butler, 1980; Hahn, 1981; Sommers, 1982; Sperling & S. Freedman, 1987). When every piece of writing is commented on by the teacher, students have little opportunity to practice evaluating their own progress, an activity critical to student growth (Graves, 1983; Hilgers, 1986; Hillocks, 1986; Wolf, 1988). To become reflective writers, students must take communication, not grades, as their end goal (Applebee, 1984; Britton et al., 1975; S. Freedman, 1987b; Tchudi, 1997).

An alternative to comments and grades, one applicable across all levels of schooling, is informal assessment based on teacher observation and careful record keeping (e.g., anecdotal records, folders of children's work samples, portfolios). Through such techniques, student progress is revealed by patterns in behaviors over time (British National Writing Project, 1987; Calfee & Perfumo, 1996; Dixon & Stratta, 1986; Genishi & Dyson, 1984; Graves, 1983; Jaggar & Smith-Burke, 1985; Murphy & Underwood, 2000; M. W. Nelson, 1997; Newkirk & Atwell, 1988; Valdes & Sanders, 1999). These patterns are not likely to display smooth forward motion but rather will be characterized by ups and downs. Some kinds of writing activities pose more difficulties than others, and, too, students themselves sometimes take on more challenges when they write than they do at other times (Flower, 1988; Lucas, 1988a, 1988b; Ruth & Murphy, 1988). Finally, the challenges students take on vary depending on the language experience students bring (Cooper & Odell, 1999).

As teachers move toward keeping folders or portfolios of their students' writing, perhaps giving a grade to the entire portfolio or to selected pieces, they may involve students in the evaluation process. Teachers can ask students to discuss their ways of writing and their products, articulating changes in processes and products over time and across kinds of writing activities; students are thus helped to formulate concepts about "good" writing, including the variability of "good" writing across situations and audiences (Camp, 1992; Gere & Stevens, 1985; Knoblauch & Brannon, 1984; Murphy & Underwood, 2000). As part of their portfolio evaluation, students can select for evaluation pieces they feel most proud of and explain specifically why they like those pieces better than others (Burnham, 1986; Calfee & Freedman, 1996; Camp, 1992; Graves, 1983; Murphy & Underwood, 2000).

***In schools, districts, and states.*** Outside the classroom, writing evaluation plays a major role in the educational decision making of the school, the school district, and the state. For example, writing programs within a school or a district must be evaluated, and students must be assessed for placement in courses or schools or even for promotion and certification. Moreover, through an evaluation procedure, teachers may be brought together to develop community standards for "good" writing.

In the 1970s and 1980s, the most popular large-scale assessments of writing were modeled after the evaluations developed and commonly used by the Educational Testing Service (Davis, Scriven, & Thomas, 1987; Diederich, 1974; Myers, 1980; White, 1985). In these evaluation procedures, students wrote on an assigned topic, in a relatively short time, and in a testing situation. Teachers were then brought together to rate the papers, giving a single score to each paper. The teachers discussed their rating standards, and more than one teacher rated each paper, to be certain that raters agreed. When the goal is to make judgments about individuals, evaluators advise that more than one writing sample be gathered from each writer.

These "holistic" evaluation procedures were a major advance over older methods of judging writing that were based on multiple-choice grammar tests, and they were also very useful for helping communities of teachers develop standards together. However, there are serious problems with holistic assessments (Brown, Palincsar, & Purcell, 1986; Lucas, 1988a, 1988b). Writing for a test has little function for the student writers other than for them to be evaluated. Students also must write on topics they have not selected and may not be interested in. Furthermore, they are not given sufficient time to engage in the elaborated processes that, as is soon discussed, are fundamental to how good writers write.

In the mid-1980s an alternative emerged that built on the in-classroom portfolio evaluation just discussed. This alternative moved portfolios into the realm of more standardized, large-scale testing (Calfee & Perfumo, 1996; S. W. Freedman, 1993; Murphy & Underwood, 2000). In most of these early large-scale portfolio assessments, students and their teachers submitted a folder of student work, created as part of normal instructional activity, to be evaluated in a formal evaluation setting (Camp, 1985; Camp & Belanoff, 1987; Elbow, 1986; Elbow & Belanoff, 1986). This alternative, although less controlled and standardized than a single writing sample produced under timed conditions, can provide a more accurate picture of individual writers and writing programs than the timed, single sample assessments. Also, as teachers work together to analyze portfolios, they may develop analytic tools that may prove useful in their teaching.

By the early 1990s, 20 states were considering, if not implementing, some kind of portfolio assessment (Aschbacher, 1991; Calfee & Perfumo, 1992; Gentile, Martin-Rehrmann, & Kennedy, 1995). At the close of the decade, Vermont and Kentucky had implemented systems that still continue in some form today. The other states either never got past the experimentation stage or went back to more traditional forms of testing. Underwood (1999) chronicled the story of California's return to multiple choice testing. Murphy and Underwood (2000) pointed out that "although accountability issues continue to dominate the discourse of policymakers as we end the decade of the 1990s, political interest in mandating portfolio assessment for large-scale programmatic purposes has clearly diminished" (p. 2).

At the district and school level, portfolio implementation has taken a number of forms. Murphy and Underwood (2000) provided detailed descriptions of the most interesting of these. Although many policymakers and educators (e.g., Cooper, 1981; Cooper & Odell, 1977; Diederich, 1974; Mellon, 1975; Myers, 1980; Resnick & Resnick, 1990) expect assessment systems to affect classroom practices, at the state level the trend is toward a greater disjunction between large-scale assessment systems and what is known about how students write best and how they learn to write. Even the remaining state-level portfolio systems have become less sensitive to classroom issues as they have bent to the demands of testers for increased standardization. As Underwood (1999) showed, what happens at the state level affects what happens at the district and school levels.

***In the nation.*** In the United State, there are two ongoing national assessments of writing: the writing portion of the National Assessment of Educational Progress (NAEP), for 9-, 13-, and 17-year-olds (Ballator, Farnum, & Kaplan, 1999; Greenwald, Persky, Campbell, & Mazzeo, 1999; NAEP, 1990), and the College Entrance Examination Board's Achievement Test in English Composition given to a select population of high school seniors. In addition, in the early 1980s, the International Writing Assessment collected writing samples in 14 countries from students in elementary school, at the end of compulsory secondary education and at the end of academic secondary education (Gorman, Purves, & Degenhart, 1988; Gubb, Gorman, & Price, 1987; Purves, 1988).

These national writing assessments all evaluate relatively short samples of writing collected under formal testing conditions. Thus, the samples present the same validity problems as the impromptu writing scored for school, district, and state assessments. Only the NAEP has published claims about the status of writing in our nation, and these claims must be interpreted with great caution, given that their conclusions are based on students' performance on impromptu writing completed in 15 minutes (S. W. Freedman, 1993; Mellon, 1975; Nold, 1981; Silberman, 1989).

The NAEP, responding to complaints about the validity of their conclusions, experimented with a national portfolio study (Gentile, 1992; Gentile et al., 1995). Although national portfolios have never been used for national evaluation purposes in the United State, they were used in England in the 1980s (Dixon & Stratta, 1986). As is the case in the United States, trends in England have also moved away from portfolios or what the British called "coursework-only assessment," toward more tightly constrained testing systems.

The concerns discussed in this opening section of our review, on the uses of literacy, will be echoed in our succeeding two sections, The Process of Writing and The Development of Writing, respectively. Even as we focus in to look at how individual students engage with writing—and how their engagement changes over time—we must bear in mind the purposes and situations that are couching their efforts, including the people among whom and for whom they are writing. As we have argued, the meaning of writing for individual students, like that of individual notes, is best revealed in composition with others.

## THE PROCESSES OF WRITING

Sharon's "How do you do it?" question is central to research on writing processes, not just for 5-year-olds but also for older writers, their teachers, and researchers. All involved want to know how writers write—what problems writers face, how they solve their problems, and what support they need along their journey from first idea to final version.

In the past 2 decades researchers shifted their attention from studies of pieces of writing, the written products, to studies of "how you do it," of writers' composing processes. They investigate what writers think about and the decisions they make, in essence how they manage the complex task of putting thoughts on paper. This shift from studying writing itself to studying how writers write has been accompanied by a similar shift in the orientation of many classroom teachers (Applebee, 2000; Applebee, Langer, & Mullis, 1986a, 1986b; S. Freedman, 1987b; Greenwald et al., 1999; Hairston, 1982). Still, process approaches in actual classroom practice have not been universally successful (Applebee, 1981, 1984; S. Freedman, 1987b; Hillocks, 1986; Langer & Applebee, 1987; Swanson-Owens, 1986). One difficulty is that there is no "writing process," but a flexible process, one influenced by the kind of writing being attempted, the writer's purpose and the situational conditions—by, in other words, the complex dimensions of literacy events discussed in our first section. Thus, process research, like all research, does not offer any simple prescriptions for practice, but it can offer a vocabulary for talking about the nature of writing—planning, revising, editing—and insight into how these processes work for particular writers in particular situations.

### Describing Writers at Work

Research on how writers write began with Emig's (1971) case studies of 12th-graders. She pioneered the think-aloud protocol as a way of studying how writers compose. These protocols consist of what writers say they are thinking about while they are actually in the process of writing. Protocols, then, give researchers some access to the thinking processes of teenage and adult writers who do not naturally talk as they write. Emig, though, not only used protocols; she used many sources of data, of information, to understand her students' writing, including, in addition to the think-aloud protocols, extensive interviews with the students about their experiences with school writing and analysis of their written products.

Emig (1971) learned that the highly successful, middle-class, 12th-grade students she studied found school-assigned writing generally unengaging; they spent little time planning what they would say and less time revising it. In essence, school writing was a well-learned, fairly routinized, mechanical activity; its purpose for the students was not to communicate to someone about something or to help them grapple with difficult new material. By contrast, the story and poetry writing these students did for themselves, outside of school, engaged their interest; on such writing, they spent substantial amounts of time writing, planning, and revising.

Since Emig (1971), many researchers have studied students' writing processes. Some have used Emig's case study methods (Perl, 1979; Pianko, 1979; Stallard, 1979). Others have used protocols but from a somewhat different research tradition, most notably, Flower and Hayes (1981a, 1981b, 1981c, 1983) from rhetoric and cognitive psychology. Others have observed writers' behaviors while they write, most notably examining when writers pause and when they write fluently (Chafe, 1982, 1985; Matsuhashi, 1981).

## A Model of Adult Composing

While trying to understand how writers compose, some researchers have worked toward a model of a prototypical expert adult's composing process (de Beaugrande, 1984; Bracewell, Fredericksen, & Fredericksen, 1982; Cooper & Matsuhashi, 1983; Hayes, 2000; Hayes & Flower, 1980; Kintsch & van Dijk, 1978; Nold, 1981; Witte, 1985, 1987). This model construction has involved much research on the composing processes of adults, usually mainstream college students and sometimes high school students and has suggested widely accepted characteristics of the adult model.

First, writing is viewed as consisting of several main processes—planning, transcribing text, reviewing—that do not occur in any fixed order. Thought in writing is not linear but jumps from process to process in an organized way which is largely determined by the individual writer's goals. Britton et al. (1975) and Emig (1971) fully described these processes, although their descriptions are more linear than more recent researchers. Flower and Hayes (1980, 1981a), along with many other researchers (de Beaugrande, 1984; Bridwell, 1980; Daiute, 1981; Faigley & Witte, 1981; Matsuhashi, 1981; Perl, 1979; Sommers, 1980; Witte, 1983, 1985, 1987), defined these processes recursively, showing how the subprocesses interrupt each other.

If the subprocesses of writing are recursive, any classroom structures that demand that all students plan, write, and revise on cue or in that order are likely to run into difficulty. Writers need flexibility, and they need time to allow the subprocesses to cycle back on each other.

A second characteristic of the adult model describes writing as a hierarchically organized, goal-directed, problem-solving process. Whatever one writes poses an intellectual problem to be solved on multiple levels, with some goals overarching others (Bereiter & Scardamalia, 1980; Collins & Gentner, 1980; Flower & Hayes, 1981b; Hayes & Flower, 1980). For many kinds of school writing, writers try to achieve the more global goal of communicating an intended message to a reader by setting up that goal as the overriding problem to be solved. To solve that problem, the writer sets up subgoals and solves subproblems. For example, when writing an essay in school, the writer must solve the subproblems of how to form letters, how to punctuate and spell, how to construct felicitous written sentences, how to get ideas, how to order those ideas, and so on. Some of these processes become quite automatic and unconscious as the writer matures, whereas others take time, attention, and skill, even for experienced adults.

Thinking about writing as problem solving can be helpful for teachers, guiding them to attend to the particular problems their student writers are grappling with. As is further discussed in a later section, teachers' help is more likely to be effective if it is directed toward specific difficulties students are facing.

## Novice–Expert Differences

Another key strand of research on composing shows that "experts" and "novices" solve the problems posed by the task of writing differently. The concept of the novice has been used to include (a) students at all levels whose skills are developing, (b) basic writers who are behind their peers or age group, and (c) young writers or children. Each group, however, is distinctive, having differing characteristics and needs. Moreover, all writers, even the "experts," may continually develop, as they pose new problems and thus meet new challenges.

When college-age experts write essays, they write what Flower (1979) called "reader-based prose." Their less-skilled peers, on the other hand, often create what Flower called "writer-based prose." They are described as not consciously attending to, and Flower and Hayes (1977) concluded they do not think about, their reader while they are writing; instead, they are most concerned with the text. Thinking about the reader seems to help the experts plan their essays and generate ideas.

Findings from other expert–novice studies show that secondary, college-age, and adult experts who are given the same task as novices make global revisions while novices revise mostly on the word level (Bridwell, 1980; Sommers, 1980). Sommers compared the changes adult student and expert writers made as they revised their written work. In analyzing interviews with the writers about their revision process, she found that expert writers revised on the discourse level and made changes in meaning, whereas student writers revised mostly on the word level and made changes in form. Bridwell came to similar conclusions on the basis of her comparisons of the revision process of more and less competent 12th-graders.

Differences in what writers revise are related to how they detect and diagnose problems. Hayes, Flower, Schriver, Stratman, and Carey (1987), in describing the cognitive processes of revision, found that professionals detected more problems than did instructors, who detected more than students. Similarly, professionals displayed a larger repertoire of revision strategies than instructors, who displayed more strategies than students for solving local and global problems. Students attempted to solve problems simply by rewriting, without analyzing them.

Witte's (1987) studies, however, suggested caution in drawing conclusions about the extensiveness and meaning of writers' revisions by only looking at the marks made on the page. His work has allowed insight into the words in adult writers' heads before the words appear on the page, what he calls "pre-text," and thus demonstrates that much revision may occur mentally, before anything is written on the page.

The ability to revise demands flexibility as a writer, a willingness to reconsider, to try again. Rose (1980) discovered that writers who suffer from writer's block may follow rigid rules and have inflexible plans. Students who have this type of writing difficulty are stymied because they apply rules rigidly to situations where the rules do not apply. Unblocked writers work with flexible plans rather than rigid rules.

Basic college-age writers may have difficulty following through on their plans; they may lose their train of thought because they spend so much of their energy during composing attending to mechanical concerns (Perl, 1979). Too, basic writers may have a different grammar of written language, an intermediate grammar between speech and writing (Bartholomae, 1980; de Beaugrande, 1982; Shaughnessy, 1977); thus, they may be less able than more expert writers to attune to the "flow" of their text, that is, to detect errors by relying on their sense of the sounds of written text (Hull, 1987).

## Relating What One Writes to How One Writes

Another line of research on composing examines how the nature of the writing task affects the writer's strategies. Researchers have demonstrated the effects of different modes of discourse or types of writing on parts of the composing process, be it the amount of attention to audience or engagement with the task itself (Applebee et al., 1984; Britton et al., 1975; Chafe, 1982; Durst, 1987; Emig, 1971; Hidi & Hildyard, 1984; Kroll, 1978; Langer, 1986; Marshall, 1987; Perron, 1974; Tannen, 1982). For example, as writers see their topics as more abstract, they spend more time planning. Writers tend to pause more when writing pieces that require generalizations than when writing reports; furthermore, writers tend to pause more before abstract than concrete sentences (Matsuhashi, 1981).

Even given the same writing assignment, different college students will interpret it differently and thus will pose qualitatively different writing problems to themselves (Flower, 1987; J. Nelson & Hayes, 1988). Flower found that students show only minimal awareness that they and others in their class may be solving very different writing problems. J. Nelson and Hayes demonstrated that college students expend significantly more effort and tackle more difficult tasks when their teachers monitor and support them throughout their writing processes, giving them guidance on references and asking them questions along the way. College students also stretch themselves more when they must present their work orally to the class as well as in written form to the teacher.

## The Writing Process in the Classroom

We began this review of process research by pointing out that many teachers use "the process approach," an approach to teaching writing that recognizes the many kinds of activities writers may engage in, including planning, drafting, revising, editing, and publishing. Although there is at least some indication from the latest NAEP results that drafting processes are correlated with higher test scores for middle and secondary students (Greenwald et al., 1999), it is difficult to evaluate the degree to which the approach in the country as a whole has improved students' writing. Indeed, there seems to be confusion over exactly what a process approach is. In his meta-analysis of the effects of different classroom approaches, Hillocks (1984, 1986) equated the process approach with "the natural process approach." As he described it, teachers following this tack are concerned with having their students "go through a process" or essentially follow a set of procedures that include planning and revising, something more than just transcribing words onto paper. This approach, outlined in some detail in the *California Handbook for Planning an Effective Writing Program* (1986), may yield a set of unconnected "process" activities that fit well into the usual organizational structure of the school—and that do not require teacher decision making to put into place.

Thus, many instructional leaders have expressed concern that the writing process may become a rigid set of activities in the school week: "Monday we plan; Tuesday we draft; Wednesday we respond to drafts; Thursday we revise," and so on (for an example of such concern, see introduction to Newkirk & Atwell, 1988). Viewing writing as a problem-solving process demands flexibility and room for a recycling through its various subprocesses. Students may not always need to revise, for example, or they may not benefit from response on the day response is scheduled (DiPardo & S. Freedman, 1988; S. Freedman, 1987b).

Furthermore, Australian educators in particular raised concerns that the process approach took for granted a knowledge of structural features of varied genre forms, to the detriment particularly of nonmainstream students (e.g., Cope & Kalantzis, 1993; for a thoughtful review, see Hicks, 1997). Researchers in the United States have stressed a more fluid sense of genre as kinds of social actions, not set forms (see, e.g., Miller, 1984), but there is evidence that, in the context of process writing activities, middle and secondary school students in particular may benefit from explicit teaching of heuristics for composing genre forms (e.g., Hillocks, 1995; Yeh, 1998).

Moreover, there has been relatively little attention to the varied language situations of writers in our classrooms. For example, nonnative speakers of English and bilinguals may use more than one language as they compose, with their oral and written language development intertwined in patterned ways, influenced in part by their levels of proficiency in the language in which they are writing (Valdes, 1988, who suggested needed future research). Indeed, as Moll, Saez, and Dworin (in press) illustrated, given certain classroom conditions, writing events may support children's growth as bilingual and bicultural people, as they may draw differentially on their languages as tools for talking, reading, notetaking, and composing across the curriculum; in a dialectic fashion, children's resources as bilingual and bicultural people may support their growth as writers and as participants in the intellectual life of the classroom.

In summary, taken alone, knowledge about how adult writers compose provides an inadequate theoretical base for reforming instruction. Because the research on writing processes reveals something about how individuals write, its best use seems to be to help individual teachers better understand the writing processes of their individual students. This teacher knowledge, coupled with an understanding of how writing functions for and is used by writers, can lead to suggestions for reforming the teaching and learning of writing.

Needed as well, though, is an understanding of how writing develops, for the writing process varies, not only across contexts, but also over time. Children do not develop as writers by simply imitating "experts." Many educators have offered insight into the potential of child writers when not stymied by overemphasis on handwriting and spelling (e.g., Ashton-Warner, 1963; Britton, 1970; Burrows, 1959; Evertts, 1970; Rosen & Rosen, 1973). Beginning most notably during the mid-1970s, though, formal studies of young writers began to yield visions of writing that looked very different from those of adults. In her research, Clay (1975) introduced 5-year-olds who clearly did not plan in any adultlike way, hence the title of her book, *What Did I Write?* Graves (1973) described second-graders whose processes involved much talk to themselves and much drawing as well—neither critical variables in the adult writing literature. Development, then, takes its own course and must be examined as it unfolds, from children's points of view and within the contexts of children's lives, not from the viewpoints and literacy contexts of adult lives. For this reason, we now turn to a discussion of children's writing development.

## THE DEVELOPMENT OF WRITING

When kindergartner Sharon finally decided to have a go at writing, she filled her paper with letters and letterlike shapes, hoping that indeed she had succeeded in "doing" writing but not at all sure of what exactly she had done. Over the last 25 years, language arts educators have gained an appreciation of both young children's ability to "explore with a pencil," to use Marie Clay's (1977) words, and of the ways students' writing may change over time. As they do in learning other symbol systems (Werner, 1948), children experiment and approximate, gradually becoming aware of the specific features of written language and the relationships between meanings and symbols and between symbol makers and symbol receivers in the recurrent literacy practices of their daily lives in and out of school.

Written language learning, like oral language learning, is complex, for written language too is a "complex of interconnecting systems," including phonological (more accurately for writing, orthographic), syntactic, semantic, and discourse rule systems (K. E. Nelson & K. Nelson, 1978, p. 225). The complexity of the written language system is reflected in the diverse perspectives of the literature on writing development. Some researchers have focused on children's exploration of the visual features of print, for example, its directionality and arrangement on a page (e.g., Clay, 1975). Others have studied how both monolingual (e.g., Ferreiro & Teberosky, 1982; Read, 1975; Treiman, 1993) and bilingual children (e.g., Edelsky, 1986; Silva, 1998) come to understand the orthographic encoding system and the intricacies of graphic segmentation and punctuation (e.g., Cazden, Cordeiro, & Giacobbe, 1985; Edelsky, 1983), tracing the evolution from early forms, like a 5-year-old's "ILVBS" to the more conventional, "I love (ILV) spaghetti" (pronounced "'basghetti," hence "BS").

Still others have examined such text-level features as the changing structural organization of children's stories or reports (e.g., Applebee, 1978; Kamberelis, 1999; King & Rentel, 1981; Langer, 1986; Newkirk, 1987), the expanding genre repertoire evident in their efforts in classroom contexts (e.g., Chapman, 1995; Dyson, 1999a), or changes in children's control of the varied processes involved in forming texts (e.g., Bereiter & Scadamalia, 1987; Graves, 1975, 1983; Perl, 1979).

Within each area or strand of written language, general patterns in how children perform particular sorts of writing tasks can be identified. Often researchers and educators talk about what "developmental stage" of writing particular children are in by "stage," they have in mind one aspect of written language use. For example, in the literature on young children's writing, "stage" is most often used in reference to spelling. When we look at a child like Sharon, however, with consideration for the whole of her development as a symbol maker, commenting on what "stage" *she* is in is quite a different matter.

Although writing can be logically analyzed into its varied aspects, a learner comes as a whole, not displaying knowledge of these aspects in neat sequential order, but in clumps that the researcher and the teacher (not the learner) must separate into neatly organized categories. Furthermore, written language, like oral, is an independent entity but is subject to the demands of the situation. Like a kaleidoscope, its parts are ever newly arranged, newly revealed. Finally, the person controlling the kaleidoscope has his or her own intentions and style, his or her own sense of what's interesting; thus individuals who share similar knowledge about written language may have different stylistic preferences for organizing and using that knowledge for acting, thinking, and expressing meaning (Bussis, Chittenden, Amarel, & Klausner, 1985). In brief, the nature of the individual learner, the nature of the situational context, and the complex nature of the writing system itself all interact in written language growth, just as they do in oral language growth (Clay, 1998; Dyson, 1987).

The interplay of these factors suggests that we cannot offer a one-dimensional description of writing development that can serve as a template for all learners. However, educators can ask varied kinds of broad questions that will inform our decisions about the challenges facing and the potential sources of support for students. For example, they can ask how young children as symbolizers—ones virtually blooming with symbolic capacity in the preschool and early school years—approach this relatively more difficult form of symbolization (e.g., Ballenger, 1999; Donaldson, 1984; Dyson, 1989, in press-b; Ferreiro & Teberosky, 1982; Genishi, Stires, & Yung-Chan, 2001; Gundlach, 1982). How do other symbol systems, like those of drawing or of talk, support written language growth? How do they pose tensions, challenges to be resolved?

Educators can also ask, within a developing strand of the system, what sorts of patterns of change have been observed. How do those developmental patterns relate to broader patterns of cognitive, linguistic, and social development (e.g., Bartlett, 1981; Bereiter & Scardamalia, 1982; Edelsky, 1986; Graves, 1975)? Educators can offer insight into the varied ways these developmental strands may be interwoven as individual learners grow and change: What qualities (of individual styles, linguistic resources, and situational contexts) influence the ways in which students orchestrate these varied dimensions of writing (Bussis et al., 1985; Dyson, 1987; Edelsky, 1986; Moll et al., in press; Perez, 1998; Smitherman, 1994)?

More broadly, educators can ask how students' participation in their everyday communicative practices outside of school function as meaningful frames and as sources of cultural material for their literacy learning in school. As already noted, for children, school exists in a configuration of other social worlds, including those of family, neighborhood, and peers. In those social worlds too, children are active participants in varied kinds of communicative events through the use of a range of symbolic tools, including, potentially, different languages. In many recent studies of learning of varied kinds, not just writing, researchers have turned to these familiar, everyday cultural practices as the basis for development, providing resources and the social agency and guidance to strategically use those resources (for discussion, see Goodnow, 2000). Thus, in research on writing development, educators can ask how children recontextualize their communicative resources in school, and they can ask about the developmental challenges they face in negotiating boundaries of symbol systems and social practices (Dyson, 1999b, 2001; Moll et al., in press; Perez, 1998). Ideally, children reconfigure, rearrange, and rearticulate their resources, as they collaboratively construct and participate in new communicative practices (Dyson, 2000).

In the following sections, we selectively review the developmental literature, intending to capture a sense of development, as children's writing possibilities evolve and expand into new practices. We aim too to illustrate the kinds of social and symbolic resources that support development. Because other chapters in this volume discuss students' developing control of conventions, we emphasize here changes in their ways of composing text worlds. For example, in a Vygotskian sense, what sorts of collaborations with others guide children's learning? In a Piagetian sense, how do productive tensions, between self and others, between meaning intended and meaning formed, get set into motion? To harken back to an earlier theme, in a socioideological sense, what qualities of classroom communities allow students' sociocultural and linguistic resources to be made visible and relevant to school learning? We join here with the work of the many teachers who have shared their insight into the workings and unfoldings of writing in their particular environments (e.g., S. Freedman, Simons, & Kalnin, 1999; Hillocks, 1995; Newkirk & Atwell, 1988; for a review of instructional practices and students writing, with an emphasis on teacher inquiry, see Dahl & Farnan, 1998).

## The Nature of Writing Development

***Children's early ways of writing.*** Although children may be initiated into the use of written symbols during infancy, they control first-order symbols systems, like speech and drawing, before they control second-order systems like written language (systems in which one symbol stands for another, as the written graphics stand for the spoken word). Researchers have pointed out that children use drawing, talk, and other symbolic forms to support their early exploration of and use of print (Dyson, 1982, 1989; Genishi et al., in press; Graves, 1981; Gundlach, 1981).

Children themselves make clear this linking, as they declare their interest in "writing houses and stuff." They understand that writing, like drawing, is a way of representing experiences. Children may, in fact, initially view writing as similar to drawing in the way that meaning is encoded in both. That is, they may view writing as direct symbolism: Children may not form letters to represent speech but to directly represent known people or objects or the names of those figures (Ferreiro & Teberosky,

FIGURE 70.1. Sance's writing and drawing.

1982). In their view, readers may then elaborate on, talk about, the written names (Dyson, 1983).

For example, 5-year-old Sance's piece, produced in an open-ended writing center, is similar to many products by young children in which they inventory some of their important symbols (Fig. 70.1)

Following are Sance's comments on her graphics:

That's my Mama's name [Patty]. That's my phone number [1626]. That's my house. That's a whale. That's grass.

This is my name. HBO. That's my neighbor. That's my brother's name [Troy]. That's love. And that's my dog.

Sance graphically depicted figures with letters or with drawings, and then she talked about these important people and things. As her piece suggests, children's first conventionally written words are usually their own names, and, from those names, they reach out to learn more about written language: For example, 5-year-old Mark commented, "That's me," pointing to the letter *M*; his peer Rachel remarks, "That goes in Brian's name," when she spots a *B*.

Children's early behavior reflects the complex and hierarchical nature of the symbol system, for they seem to initially explore all aspects of written language (Clay, 1975; Hiebert, 1981). In addition to finding personally meaningful connections with these new symbol systems, they often explore the medium itself, with no concern for a specific message; in their exploring, they play with print's basic graphic features, for example, its linearity and the arrangement of print lines on the page (Clay, 1975). Children also repeat for pragmatic or exploratory purposes familiar sentence or phrase routines ("I love you"), and they may even write whole texts (stories); these extended texts may be written with children's least sophisticated encoding procedures (e.g., cursive writing) (Dyson, 1981; Sulzby, 1985). Their efforts to write for immediate audiences, as in letters and cards, may result in more conventional words than their writing for less specific audiences (as in book writing) (Lamme & Childers, 1983).

Once children gain some initial understanding of the unique nature of the symbol system, including its alphabetic nature— that precisely what is read depends on precisely what letters are written and that particular oral/written relationships define the precise letters—writing may become more difficult. Children may be less willing to randomly put down well-known letters, or to simply trust that a reader will find a message in their printed graphics (Clay, 1975). They must work hard to orchestrate the complex message creating and encoding process of writing. In so doing, they lean on other people, other symbol systems, and their understanding of the sort of activity they are participating in (i.e., their knowledge of the kind of writing expected in any particular situation).

***Patterns in structural development.*** Children's early writing often consists of well-known words, simple statements, or repetitive sentence structures (Clay, 1975; Edelsky, 1986; McCaig, 1981; Sowers, 1981). The text is often just a reference point for an experience, which may well have been recorded more fully elsewhere, in talk or, less ephemerally, in drawing. Depending on the child's intentions, a label could be the written tip of an imaginary world (Dyson, 1983, 1989) or the seedling of an essay on a topic of interest (Newkirk, 1987). Thus, to gain insight into children's efforts—and to help them reflect on what exactly they have done—teachers may have to listen to children's talk during the drawing and writing as well as "read" both their pictures and their text.

Children's early written texts, like their spelling (Henderson, 1981; Read, 1975) and syntax (Loban, 1976; O'Donnell, Griffin, & Norris, 1967) undergo transformations during the school years (Gundlach, 1981). They not only become longer, they also become more coherent and internally cohesive. For example, children become less likely to make references outside the texts themselves (e.g., to begin texts with "This is") or to use pronouns without references (e.g., to use "He is" when who "he" actually "is" is not clear). Still, even middle school children have difficulties making clear these internal connections in particular situations, for example in disambiguating two "he's" when a text involves two same-sex characters (Bartlett, 1981).

In addition to changes in length and internal connectedness, the global structure of children's texts becomes more complex over time. Even preschoolers are aware of differences in text structures or genres. Through their experiences with the print world surrounding them, they come to realize that surface forms of letters, maps, and stories, for example, may all vary (Harste, Woodward, & Burke, 1984). Yet, as just discussed, children's initial authoring, their stories and reports in school, may consist of statements and labels.

A number of researchers have traced the increasing complexity and structural integrity of children's texts, particularly their written stories. By the time they begin formal schooling, young children generally display an understanding of many underlying features of narratives, that is, of their culture's way of storytelling (Applebee, 1978; Leondar, 1977; Stein & Glenn, 1979; Wolf, 1985). Children can often tell stories with recognizable characters engaged in simple plots, with beginnings, middles, and ends. They know the conventional "once upon a time"

beginning and, less often, the "happily ever after" ending, and they place intervening events in the past tense.

King and Rentel (1981, 1982) illustrated how, over the course of the first 2 years of schooling, children's written stories acquired the structural complexity evident from the very beginning of school in their orally told stories. This progress in writing was less evident for non-middle class than middle class children in their study; the former children began with less knowledge of written languagelike story structures, but, in addition, they had fewer opportunities in their school to hear, produce, and talk about stories.

Although basic narrative knowledge is evident quite early, it does continue to develop throughout the school years. For example, it is not until the middle school years that detailed information about characters' motivations and reactions is regularly included in students' stories. Similarly, elaborate accounts of how events unfolded are not consistently given until the middle and junior high years (Bartlett, 1981). Indeed, even fluent adolescent writers may be far from skilled in embedding the quality of an experience in textual description and narration of actors and their actions (Dixon & Stratta, 1986); secondary students, like elementary ones, may discover that, in visualizing and dramatizing their stories (in making use of other media), characters' unarticulated emotions emerge in facial expressions, gestures, movement and dialogue—all aspects of the living "text" that may be translated into words (Wagner, 1998) or, perhaps, remain fully realizable only in alternative symbolic forms (Smagorinksy, 1995).

There is less information available on the development of expository prose, but what is available suggests a more gradual development. Young children do use exposition (Bissex, 1980; Kamberelis, 1999; Langer, 1986; Newkirk, 1984; Taylor, 1983), but research has emphasized how even middle and junior high students grapple with nonfictional forms (e.g., Bereiter, 1980; Nystrand & Graff, 2001; Scardamalia, 1981). Bereiter and Scardamalia suggested that students' difficulty with these forms has to do with their general cognitive development; that is, students have difficulty integrating the multiple ideas contained in exposition into an orderly whole. However, students may simply have less exposure to models of expositions and, in the primary grades, fewer opportunities for practice (Langer, 1986).

From the work of Newkirk (1987) with primary grade children and Langer (1986) with intermediate and middle school children comes a sense of how children's expository writing may be gradually transformed. Without claiming that there is a rigid developmental sequence, Newkirk presents a general progression of structural complexity in children's texts. Simple written labels for pictures may evolve into a series of labels or linked information statements, attributes, or reasons. For example, an early label like *bird* or a simple listing of figure names (*bird, dog, house, flower*) may appear before two-unit clauses— "couplets"— which can link the "litany-like repetition," for example:

> This is my kneaf My knife is sharp [one couplet]
> This is a bowy knife Bowie knifs are sharp [another couplet]
> (Newkirk, 1987, pp. 131, 133)

Still more complex are texts containing paragraphs in which the statements are in some kind of logical order, even though paragraphs themselves may not yet be ordered.

Like Newkirk's, Langer's (1986) findings also suggested that students gradually transform structures they already control. For example, as late as ninth grade, students did not regularly use such complex expository forms as problem/solution, causality, or comparison of alternatives to globally organize their texts. However, when she examined lower level, more circumscribed structures, Langer found that indeed more complex expository structures did gradually appear across the school years (see also Durst, 1984).

As just illustrated, text structures, like children's drawing schemata (Goodnow, 1977) and grammatical structures (Slobin, 1979), undergo gradual transformations. Rather than adopting wholly new structures, students seem to solve new text-forming problems by gradually adapting forms already controlled. This transformation process is conservative; text features are added on before internal restructuring occurs (Bartlett, 1981).

Similarly, the very process of rethinking—revising—texts develops conservatively. With Sowers (1985) and Calkins (1980), Graves (1983) studied 16 elementary school children (Grades 1 through 4) in a middle class community school over a 2-year period. One of the researchers' major means for studying the children—which became a major means for teaching them as well—was the "workshop" conference in which researchers and teachers talked to individual children about their writing processes and products. The children's responses to these conferences illustrated a gradual development of an awareness of text malleability and of the means to deliberately act on that awareness.

For example, children seemed willing to change spelling and handwriting earlier than they did structure and content. Indeed, they might find abandoning drafts easier than reworking them (Calkins, 1980). Children may find little use for revision unless they are grappling with ordering ideas (Graves, 1983)—a list of names or statements makes sense in any arrangement—or unless they are actively working toward some social end requiring a heightened attention to chosen words (e.g., a rhyme, a horror story; Dyson, 1993, 2000). In the latter case, revision may not occur in a formal phase of the writing curriculum (i.e., after a conference) but in the course of composing itself. Working collaboratively, and playfully, with a peer may increase such attention to writing decisions (Daiute, 1993).

The research reviewed on discourse forms, and the insight it offers into students' ways of structuring texts, may help teachers respond in helpful ways to possibilities present in individuals' work. That is, by looking analytically at students' efforts, teachers may find new structures in their products, structures that can be talked about and built upon (e.g., "You know how you arranged the sentences in that paragraph? I wonder if the paragraphs themselves should be rearranged.").

As argued throughout this section, developmental changes in students' writing processes and products are linked not only to changes in writing itself but also to changes in how students use writing vis à vis other symbol systems, particularly drawing and speech. For example, Dyson (1989) examined the changing role of writing in the symbol making of eight primary (kindergarten through Grade 3) children in an urban magnet school. In the observed classrooms, children wrote but, in the very same composing event, also wove their symbolic productions by drawing, singing, playing, and above all, talking. Indeed, the social functions of composing time were accomplished primarily through talking and drawing; through those media, children not only represented imaginative worlds, but they also connected with their friends, as peers talked about, critiqued, and at times playfully dramatized each others' texts.

The children's multimedia texts, however, were unstable, generative of potentially productive tensions. For example, the space–time frames of drawn pictures, enacted dramas, and written texts did not fit neatly together, nor did the dull black-and-white print hold the same semiotic capacities as other, more accessible and, in one child's words, "prettier" media. Moreover, the social events themselves were unstable. The overlapping symbolic worlds of text, talk, and pictures; the ongoing social world; and the wider world of experiences all exist in different space–time structures; tensions among these structures were evident in the children's talk during writing and also in their texts (e.g., in shifts of tense and of person). That is, children's often awkward texts, with their unstable time frames and points of view, result not only from children's grappling with discourse forms—with textual worlds—but from their grappling with multiple worlds. For example, consider second-grader Jake's piece, written as he played inside—and outside—his text with his friend Manuel:

Once there was a boy that is named Manuel. Manuel is going to fly the fastest jet and I am going to fly the the jet too. But Manuel's headquarters is going to blow up But I am OK. But I don't know about Manuel but I am going to find Manuel [and on the story goes as Jake finds Manuel, assures himself of his safety (Manuel are you OK? Yes I am OK.) and then saves him by shooting the bad guys "out of the universe."]

"Simple" narrations, then, are not so simple (cf. Perera, 1984), considering the different media and different "worlds" writers move among. Nonetheless, the tensions between intentional composers and curious if confused audience members, between an imagined world and the symbolically fragmented product others may experience, may become the focus of productive talk among students and teachers. Indeed, students may be able to support the development of more coherent written forms by deliberately supplementing their efforts with, or examining them from the standpoint of, other media forms and other participants (e.g., drawings, dramatic play, Dyson, 1989, 1997b; Paley, 1980; Smagorinsky, 1995; Wagner, 1998). Thus, with guidance and experience, students may manipulate straightforward chronologies into time expansions and condensations, foreshadowing and remembering (Dixon & Stratta, 1986; Graves, 1983), as they develop new ways of structuring experiences—and connecting with readers.

***Recontextualization: development as repertoire expansion.*** Recently, researchers have called attention to the narrow scope of genre forms considered in school, relative both to the expanding and increasingly multimodal genres used in contemporary times and to the predominant role of popular genres in children's and youth cultures (e.g., Alvermann, Moon, Hagood, 1999; Buckingham & Sefton-Green, 1994; Dyson, 1997b, 1999a; Luke, 1995; Marsh, 1999; New London Group, 1996). In this literature, genre is viewed not as a typified text form but instead as a kind of social participation (Bakhtin, 1986) or communicative practice (Hanks, 1996).

Most relevant to this subsection of the review is, first, the realization that students' ways of structuring texts may differ from those expected, not because of some general developmental difficulty but because, in fact, the students are participating in a different kind of practice, and producing a different genre form, than that assumed by the school. These differences may be attributable not only to ethnic cultures but to students' participation in local forms of popular culture (e.g., Dyson, 1993, 1997b; G. Moss, 1989; Newkirk, in press). For example, children may be informed by visually driven media forms, like superhero or action adventure movies, or by relationship-driven narratives, like romances.

Second, the diversity of students' potential communicative practices suggests the social and political complexity of classrooms themselves, as earlier discussed; students' social orientations to goals and audience, and their sense of rhetorical effectiveness (or ineffectiveness), are informed and guided by relations, tastes, and values that mark their membership or distance from complex peer worlds.

Finally, children's strikingly varied communicative experiences in families, communities, and peer groups situate literacy learning within a diversity of developmental pathways (Clay, 1998). The developmental cliché that children build from what they know has been central to the literature on writing since the 1970s, but children themselves have been treated generically and the developmental pathway imagined as a singular route.

Seminal research emphasizing children's dependence on communicative experience, and the gradual expansion of their communicative repertoire, was done by Britton (1970) and Britton et al. (1975). For example, in a study of the written products produced in school by secondary students, Britton et al. found a predominance of "transactional" writing, writing to accomplish some practical aim in the world (e.g., giving information). They argued that students may become more comfortable and fluent as writers—and be better able to reflect on their experiences—when initially allowed to write "expressively," that is, in a relaxed, conversational way. To illustrate, the authors presented a number of student texts, including the following text by a young girl:

It is quite easy to make oxygen if you have the right equipment necessary. You will need a test tube (a large one), a stand with some acid in it. You will need also a Bunston burner. Of course you must not forget a glass tank too. A thin test tube should fix neatly in its place. When you have done that fill the glass tank and put the curved end upwards. Put the glass tank on the table and fill with water. Very soon you will find that you have made oxygen and glad of it. (Britton et al., 1975, p. 196)

Moffett (1968; Moffett & Wagner, 1983) also wrote persuasively about the importance of writing that is infused, like the above science report, with the writer him or herself. Indeed, many successful writing programs have followed this dictate; students begin by writing about familiar subjects for known others (for example, see earlier discussion on Heath's (1980) work with teachers), gradually expanding their textual repertoire, that is, their understanding of how text forms and functions position authors in particular stances toward the experienced world and toward anticipated readers (Bakhtin, 1986).

It is developmentally sensible that control of formal discourse forms will happen gradually and that many students will build from more comfortable conversational forms. Indeed, it is this concept that underlies "dialogue journal" programs, which have been used to help students from varied backgrounds learn to write (Staton et al., 1988, see also Fulwiler, 1987). However, the emphasis on conversational writing predated the more recent emphasis on young children's early writing, which is decidedly unlike speech. Moreover, the research underestimated students' interest in, and experience with, varied kinds of writing, just as it underestimated the tremendously diverse roles writing may play in the lives of individuals as members of diverse discourse communities (Luke, 1995). Students' familiarity with particular genres, and thus their "comfort" with them, varies. They may use genre forms inappropriately (e.g., a personally expressive piece for a task requiring an informative stance, a summary for one requesting a persuasive piece) not because they are at some earlier developmental stage in discourse production but because they do not understand the particular disciplinary conversation they are entering (Applebee, 1996).

Therefore, there is not a singular developmental pathway through which students progress on their way to a textual pinnacle. Students must make sense of school literacy tasks, and the written medium itself, in the context of their experiences with other texts, some of which are not, and undoubtedly will not be, central to school literacy curricula. For example, Dyson (1999a, 2000, in press-a, in press-b) focused on urban primary school children's appropriations from out-of-school cultural and textual practices, particularly the materials of popular culture. Analysis of ethnographic data revealed that children drew deeply on nonacademic social worlds to negotiate their entry into school literacy; those worlds provided them with agency and meaningful symbols, including those from popular music, films, animated shows, and sports media. The children's use of this material was developmentally useful, in part because it provided them with conceptual content, functional genres, models of textual structures and elements, and a pool of potential characters, plots, and themes.

Moreover, the use of media material also posed useful developmental challenges in differentiating symbol systems and social practices. For example, information about games results is arranged differently on a television screen during a sports news show than it would be in a prose report; popular music themes are "too fast" for children and may best be written surreptitiously; and animated characters' interactive style is more visual, more physical than the dialogue that provides the substance of young children's early reading books. Thus, at the very same time that children were differentiating the elements of the written symbol system, they were also differentiating the new social practices of school and their underlying ideological values. Indeed, becoming socioculturally and politically astute in the use of written language is a potential, and important, developmental outcome in contemporary times.

This section closes with a return to the earlier introduced concept of orchestration (Bussis et al., 1985). Students cannot control all aspects of the written system at once (Graves, 1982; Jacobs, 1985; Weaver, 1982). There are individual differences, stylistic differences, in how students get a handle on the process, that is, in which aspects of the process they do or do not attend to at any given writing moment. Moreover, to this orchestration, students bring varied resources—different understandings of the encoding system, of text structure, and of literacy's purposes—and they bring diverse ways of interacting with other people and with other symbolic media (Dyson, 1987).

The task of supporting students—the task of teaching—is therefore also very complex. In Applebee's (1996) words, classroom "literacy events will be shaped by . . . [diverse] discourses, not just by that of the academic tradition. And the teacher's ability to mediate among these traditions, drawing from rather than fighting against them, will have a substantial impact on the learning that occurs" (p. 101). Teachers are supported in their efforts by their understandings of the nature of writing and of the developmental challenges inherent in writing. They are supported as well by their ability to observe in students' processes and products signs of what students are grappling with and by their understanding and ability to make use of the resources available to them in the classroom environment. The most important of those resources are the human ones—themselves and their students.

## The Support System for Writing Development

Understandings of the social support for learning to write have been influenced by the theoretical ideas of Vygotsky and, more specifically, by research on children's acquisition of language. Vygotsky (1934/1978) argued that learning is a social process; children are initiated into the use of their culture's signs and tools, such as written language, by their interactions with other people:

From the very first days of the child's development, his activities acquire a meaning of their own in a system of social behavior and, being directed towards a definite purpose, are refracted through the prism of the child's environment. (p. 30)

Children, then, grow and learn as they join in ongoing social activities, engaging in problem solving with others. Gradually, they begin to internalize—take over internally—the processes they initially performed collaboratively. Just as a symphony gives meaning to the individual notes it contains, the social system in which children participate shapes the cognitive development of individuals (Rogoff, 1990; Rogoff & Lave, 1984).

Schools, therefore, can promote development best if they are very social places, places where students have ample opportunities to interact with one another and with their teacher. Schools can maintain order and organization, but they cannot remain halls of silence. Although the emphasis here is on teachers' efforts in classroom settings, efforts to build interactive classroom communities will be influenced by institutional qualities of schools themselves. For example, in her study of secondary school classrooms in Great Britain and the United States, S. Freedman (1994) analyzed school-level support for teachers' efforts to create learning communities, support that was much stronger for British than U.S. teachers. All the British schools allowed teachers longer time spans to work with and get to know the same group of children; they also subdivided the school itself into smaller working units and, within those units, offered smaller classes. Moreover, the schools organized academic departments that allowed substantive interaction among teachers themselves. These school-level supports, which were not the norm for U.S. schools, were related to the general nature of communities teachers envisioned and enacted and, moreover, to the depth of student involvement in the intellectual life of the classroom.

It is to the nature of involvement itself, and its relationship to learning, that we now turn. In so doing, we circle back here, in the closing pages of this chapter, to the concepts discussed earlier in the section Literacy in the Classroom Community. Because writing research has placed much theoretical and pedagogical emphasis on dyadic encounters between individual students and their teachers, we begin by highlighting these encounters. However, ultimately, the social support system for writing is found in the qualities of the classroom community as a whole.

***The role of interaction in development.*** Vygotsky (1934/1978) suggested that social interaction leads a child's development forward in the context of specific, culturally valued activity. Learning does not wait upon but in fact leads development, as the instructor aims for the learner's "zone of proximal development . . . the distance between the actual developmental level as determined by independent problem solving and the level of potential development as determined through problem solving under adult guidance or in collaboration with peers" (p. 86). A child's learning, then, is dependent on the nature of the social activity, which reveals and extends (or does not) that child's relevant knowledge and skill. As Lee and Smagorinsky (2000a) commented, in Vygotskian-inspired studies, "context and capacity are intertwined" (p. 2).

Researchers have focused on understanding more precisely how thinking is influenced by social interaction in a variety of home, work, and school settings (e.g., Goodnow, Miller, & Kessel, 1995; Haneda & Wells, 2000; Lee & Smagorinksy, 2000b). In daily life, teachers do not simply direct learners' performance but, rather, collaborate with them; teachers model both problem-solving processes and involve learners in those processes.

The following classroom example illustrates a collaborative social interaction about a piece of writing between Art Peterson and his ninth-grade student, Gina. In this example, Peterson and Gina discussed a draft of a paper that she had written about her friend Dianne. After reading Gina's draft, Peterson modeled how Gina might go back and forth between generalization and support for her generalizations:

Peterson: All right. . . . What . . . is Dianne's main quality as you see it?

Gina: Uhm, well, she is pretty phony.

Peterson: Phony.

Gina: . . . That's the main word. Phony. Uhm . . . she has a lot of money and she uses it to get people to like her. She thinks that . . . her money is the only thing that's . . . in her that's worth anything. So in a lot of ways she's very uhm—

Peterson: Insecure.

Gina: Insecure. Well she's also secure in that . . . she tries to act as if she is secure. You can really see through that after you get to know her. . . . She uses her friends as a sort of shield. If she wants to do something, and because of her insecurity she feels bad about it, she tells her friend, "Go do this for me." For example, if she wants to uh ask somebody to do something for her . . . Her friend said she wanted me to go to the movies with her. She was insecure about me saying "yes" or "no," whether or not I liked her. So she asked her friend to ask me.

Peterson: Okay. Okay. So you've got this insecure person, but she has certain uh uhm . . .

Gina: But she tells people in a lot of ways. A lot of people think that she is the most secure person that they've ever seen.

Peterson: Yeah. Because she has these little uh tricks or devices, one of which is money.

Gina: Yeah. Uh hum.

Peterson: Another, another, another . . .

Gina: She has lots of clothes, her tennis ability, her skiing ability. That stuff.

Peterson: Okay, and then she has all these other little manipulative techniques.

Gina: Yeah. She uses her friends.

Peterson: Yeah right.

Gina: Yeah.

Peterson: Okay. So that's good. You've got a person who is basically insecure, but is able to cover it up. Of course you've got to establish her insecurity. You can't just say she's insecure.

Gina: Uh hum.

Peterson: I mean you've got to [unclear] give me some examples of how this shows through sometimes. Uh hum. But then, you get in to the way you, these little techniques that she uses. That could be good.
(S. Freedman, 1987b)

Peterson's questions allowed Gina to articulate her essential understanding of Dianne. Through this collaborative problem solving with her teacher, Gina comes to new understandings of Dianne's insecurity, as she sorts out the appearance from the reality. Gina moved from describing Dianne as phony, to insecure, to apparently secure. Peterson did not impose his ideas; after all, he has never met Dianne. Instead, playing the roles of an interested listener and reader, as well as teacher, he drew an inference from what Gina had said about Dianne, gave Gina opportunity to elaborate on the reasons others perceive Dianne as

secure, coached Gina in synthesizing her thoughts by taking one of her judgments (Dianne appears secure although she is really insecure), modeled the process of supporting a generalization by adding a piece of support from what Gina has already said (Dianne's use of money), and then asked Gina to independently add further elaboration and thereby show that she understood the process he had just modeled. Finally, he summarized what he and Gina had constructed, what would become the essence of Gina's paper: "You've got a person who is basically insecure, but is able to cover it up." Peterson led Gina to verbalize more than the surface phoniness, to understand its source and its effects. Gina used oral language in the form of a student-teacher conversation to bring her thoughts together (S. N. Freedman, 1987b).

As Peterson illustrated, teachers need to be sensitive to their students' current skills and understandings and provide collaborative support to help them move along (Cole & Griffin, 1980; Wertsch et al., 1980). "In instruction using the zone of proximal development, the adult oversees the construction of an instructional context by establishing references to what the child already knows. This context allows the child to build new information or skills into the existing knowledge structure" (Rogoff & Gardner, 1984, p. 100).

***Instructional procedures.*** In 1979, Cazden summarized research on discourse learning and proposed Bruner's studies of mother–infant interaction as a starting point for instructional models, which indeed were developed (e.g., Applebee & Langer, 1983; Brown et al., 1986; Langer & Applebee, 1984; Palincsar & Brown, 1984). It was Bruner and his colleagues who characterized the adult role as one of "scaffolding" early language learning (Bruner, 1978; Ninio & Bruner, 1978; Ratner & Bruner, 1978). This scaffolding involved familiar and routinized situations, such as peekaboo games and storytime rituals, which serve both as immediate ends in themselves and as contexts within which children gradually learn more sophisticated language functions: Mothers "would introduce a new procedure and gradually 'hand it over' to the child as his skills for executing it developed" (Bruner, 1983, p. 60).

These efforts to apply the concept of scaffolding to teaching and learning in schools are appealing. However, as earlier discussed, the scaffolding metaphor oversimplifies the professional challenge of establishing truly dialogic relationships between teachers and students (McCarthy, 1994; Nystrand, 1997), of actually being able to establish "references to what the child already knows," to return to Rogoff and Gardner's confident phrase (1984, p. 100). In classrooms, there is no generic "the child"; children may not share teachers' assumptions about what sort of text is being collaboratively produced, nor even about how teacher-student interaction should proceed (e.g., Delpit, 1995; Dyson, 1993; Reyes, 1991; Walker, 1992). Indeed even the scaffolding Bruner described may unfold in very different ways in different cultures (Heath, 1983; Schieffelin, 1979).

In assisting developing writers, teachers can provide a variety of kinds of social interaction around writing—including teacher-guided class collaborations, teacher conferences with individuals or small groups, and formal and informal interactions among the students themselves (see, e.g., Flood & Lapp, 2000; Larson & Maier, 2000; Moll & Whitmore, 1993; Putney, Green, Dixon, Duran, & Yeager, 2000). Indeed, as Larson (1999) noted, in interactive composing events, the responsibilities of adults and children can be quite fluid, as participants shift among the roles of, and overlap their actions as, teachers, authors, coauthors, and overhearers of others' efforts.

Student interaction itself can take many forms. In classrooms, writers may talk to one another about their writing informally as they work side by side on their individual papers (Dyson, 1989) or as they collaborate on a joint piece (Daiute, 1989, 1993). As Daiute (1993) argued, the informal and playful talk of elementary school children sounds quite different from more formal teacher–student conferences. However, its playfulness—its childlikeness—is in fact its value, for language play involves modeling, exploring, and negotiating the sounds and meanings of language. Students, particularly secondary school students, may also interact in highly structured peer response groups (Berkenkotter, 1984; S. Freedman, 1984, 1987b; Gere & Abbott, 1985; Gere & Stevens, 1985; Healy, 1980; Macrorie, 1970, 1984; Moffett, 1968; Newkirk, 1984), in special peer tutoring programs (Bruffee, 1973, 1978, 1984, 1985; Hawkins, 1976), in classrooms organized specifically to allow for peer writing groups (Elbow, 1973; Murray, 1984; Nystrand, 1986), and even in writing groups that are based in communities rather than schools (Gere, 1987; Heller, 1997).

In working toward interactive classroom communities and, particularly, in their efforts to establish common frames of reference with their students, teachers have engaged with children's families and communities outside the classroom (e.g., Edwards, 1999; McCaleb, 1994; Moll et al., 1992). Within the classroom, they have orchestrated a curriculum of thematically interrelated events on which both they and their students can draw (e.g., Putney et al., 2000). Furthermore, teachers have organized classroom practices in which to learn from and with children about the textual practices—including those influenced by the popular media—that inform their composing efforts; such practices help teachers and students enact "permeable curricula" (Dyson, 1993), in which they allow for students' social and textual knowledge, for class members to learn from each other, and for their own provision of analytic language to help students name and discuss the diversity of textual and media practices that may be unanticipated by the curriculum but critical to contemporary society (see also Edelsky, 1999).

In the end, for teachers or peers to provide meaningful support to developing writers, they must work in environments that are flexible, where they can be attentive to the highly varied needs of individual writers. Indeed, writers and teachers of writing will need to become "members of a diversified community of learners—dynamically interacting and, like the business of becoming a writers, forever in process" (DiPardo & S. Freedman, 1988, p. 145).

## CONCLUSION

Sharon's task is complex, but she has many years, indeed a lifetime, in which to build a repertoire of skills that will enable her to create the music of her written language portfolio. She will need the help and encouragement of many people along her way—members of her community and of her family, teachers, friends, and classmates.

As she grows up, Sharon's developmental path may take different directions from the paths of some of her other 5-year-old friends. The challenge for the schools is to understand Sharon's needs and the needs of Sharon's friends and to provide the support they all will need throughout their years in the classroom. Through supportive and responsive classroom environments, schools may best help each generation grow into literacy in ways that enable them to use written language productively and fulfillingly throughout their lives.

## ACKNOWLEDGMENTS

This chapter is a significant revision of the original 1991 chapter; the first author thanks Soyoung Lee and Sheila Shea, who provided critical assistance in accomplishing this revision.

The 1991 chapter was itself a major revision of S. Freedman, S. Warshauer, A. Haas Dyson, L. Flower, and W. Chafe, *Research in Writing: Past, Present, and Future* (Tech. Rep. No. 1) of the Center for the Study of Writing, University of California, Berkeley. That report was based on the mission statement from "A Proposal to Establish a Center for Study of Writing" submitted to the National Institute of Education by the University of California at Berkeley in collaboration with Carnegie Mellon University in March 1985. In parts of the process of writing that mission statement, we worked closely with Arthur Applebee, Shirley Brice Heath, and Judith Langer at Stanford University. They deserve credit for their contributions to many of the ideas behind the Mission Statement. In addition, Peg Griffin, Luis Moll, and Michael Cole of the University of California at San Diego assisted at many points in its development.

## *References*

Alvermann, D. E., Moon, J. S., & Hagood, M. (1999). *Popular culture in the classroom*. Newark, DE: International Reading Association; Chicago: National Reading Conference.

Applebee, A. N. (1978). *The child's concept of story: Ages two to seventeen*. Chicago: University of Chicago Press.

Applebee, A. N. (1981). *Writing in the secondary school: English and the content areas* (NCTE Research Rep. No. 21). Urbana, IL: National Council of Teachers of English.

Applebee, A. N. (1984). Writing and reasoning. *Review of Educational Research, 54*(4), 577–596.

Applebee, A. N. (1996). *Curriculum as conversation: Transforming traditions of teaching and learning*. Chicago: University of Chicago Press.

Applebee, A. N. (2000). Alternative models of writing development. In R. Indrisano & J. R. Squire (Eds.), *Perspectives on writing: Research, theory and practice* (pp. 90–111). Newark, DE: International Reading Association.

Applebee, A. N., & Langer, J. A. (1983). Instructional scaffolding: Reading and writing as natural language activities. *Language Arts, 60,* 168–175.

Applebee, A. N., Langer, J. A., Durst, R. K., Butler-Nalin, K., Marshall, J. D., & Newell, G. E. et al. (1984). *Contexts for learning to write: Studies of secondary school instruction*. Norwood, NJ: Ablex.

Applebee, A. N., Langer, J. A., & Mullis, I. (1986a) *The writing report card: Writing achievement in American schools*. Princeton, NJ: National Assessment of Educational Progress, National Testing Service.

Applebee, A. N., Langer, J. A., & Mullis, I. (1986b). *Writing: Trends across the decade: 1974–1984*. Princeton, NJ: National Assessment of Educational Progress, National Testing Service.

Aschbacher, P. (1991). Performance assessment: State activity, interest and concerns. *Applied Measurement in Education, 4*(4), 275–288.

Ashton-Warner, S. (1963). *Teacher*. New York: Simon & Schuster.

Bakhtin, M. (1986). *Speech genres and other late essays*. Austin: University of Texas Press.

Ballator, N., Farnum, M., & Kaplan, B. (1999). *NAEP 1996 trends in writing: Fluency and writing conventions*. Washington, DC: U.S. Department of Education.

Ballenger, C. (1999). *Teaching other people's children: Literacy and learning in a bilingual classrooom*. New York: Teachers College Press.

Bartholomae, D. (1980). The study of error. *College Composition and Communication, 31*(3), 253–269.

Bartlett, E. J. (1981). *Learning to write: Some cognitive and linguistic components*. Washington, DC: Center for Applied Linguistics.

Barton, D. (1994). *Literacy: An introduction to the ecology of written language*. London: Blackwell.

Barton, D., Hamilton, M., & Ivanic, R. (Eds.) (2000). *Situated literacies: Reading and writing in context*. London: Routledge.

Basso, K. (1974). The ethnography of writing. In R. Bauman & J. Sherzer (Eds.), *Explorations in the ethnography of speaking* (pp. 425–432). Cambridge, England: Cambridge University Press.

Bereiter, C. (1980). Development in writing. In L. W. Gregg & E. R. Steinberg (Eds.), *Cognitive processes in writing* (pp. 73–93). Hillsdale, NJ: Lawrence Erlbaum Associates.

Bereiter, C., & Scardamalia, M. (1980). *Fostering the development of self-regulation in children's knowledge processing*. Paper presented at the NIE-LRDC Conference on Thinking and Learning Skills, Pittsburgh, PA.

Bereiter, C., & Scardamalia, M. (1982). From conversation to composition. In R. Glaser (Ed.), *Advances in instructional psychology* (Vol. 2, pp. 1–64). Hillsdale, NJ: Lawrence Erlbaum Associates.

Bereiter, C. & Scardamalia, M. (1987). Cognitive coping strategies and the problem of "inert knowledge." In S. Chipman et al. (Eds.), *Thinking and learning skills* (pp. 65–80). Hillsdale, NJ: Lawrence Erlbaum Associates.

Berkenkotter, C. (1984). Student writers and their sense of authority over text. *College Composition and Communication, 34,* 312–319.

Bissex, G. L. (1980). *Gnys at wrk*. Cambridge, MA: Harvard University Press.

Blake, B. E. (1997). *He say/she say: Urban girls write their lives*. Albany: State University of New York Press.

Bracewell, R. J., Frederiksen, C. H., & Frederiksen, J. D. (1982). Cognitive processes in composing and comprehending discourse. *Educational Psychologist, 17,* 146–164.

Bremme, D. W., & Erickson, F. (1977). Relationships among verbal and nonverbal classroom behaviors. *Theory Into Practice, 16,* 153–161.

Bridwell, L. (1980). Revising strategies in twelfth grade students' transactional writing. *Research in the Teaching of English, 3,* 197–222.

British National Writing Project (1987). *Ways of looking at children's writing: The National Writing Project response to the task group on assessment and testing* (Occasional Paper No. 8). London: School Curriculum Development Committee Publications.

Britton, J. (1970). *Language and learning*. Hammondsworth, England: Penguin.

Britton, J., Burgess, T., Martin, N., McLeod, A., & Rosen, H. (1975). *The development of writing abilities: 11–18*. London: Macmillan.

Brown, A. L., Palinscar, A. S., & Purcell, L. (1986). Poor readers: Teach, don't label. In U. Neisser (Ed.), *The academic performance of minority children: A new perspective* (pp. 105–144). Hillsdale, NJ: Lawrence Erlbaum Associates.

Bruce, B. C. (1987). An examination of the role of computers in teaching language and literature. In J.R. Squire (Ed.), *The dynamics of language learning: Research in reading and English* (pp. 277–293). Urbana, IL: National Council of Teachers of English.

Bruffee, K. (1973). Collaborative learning: Some practical models. *College English, 34*(5), 579–586.

Bruffee, K. (1978). The Brooklyn plan: Attaining intellectual growth through peer-group tutoring. *Liberal Education, 64,* 447–468.

Bruffee, K. (1984). Peer tutoring and the "conversation of mankind." *College English, 56*(7), 635–652.

Bruffee, K. (1985). *A short course in writing* (3rd ed.). Boston: Little, Brown.

Bruner, J. (1978). The role of dialogue in language acquisition. In A. Sinclair (Ed.), *The child's conception of language* (pp. 241–256). New York: Springer-Verlag.

Bruner, J. (1983). *Child's talk: Learning to use language*. London: Oxford University Press.

Bruner, J. (1986). *Actual minds, possible worlds*. Cambridge, MA: Harvard University Press.

Buckingham, D., & Sefton-Green, J. (1994). *Cultural studies goes to school.: Reading and teaching popular media*. London: Taylor & Francis.

Burnham, C. (1986). Portfolio evaluation: Room to breathe and grow. In C. Bridges (Ed.), *Training the teacher of college composition* (pp. 125–138). Urbana, IL: National Council of Teachers of English.

Burrows, A. T. (1959). *Teaching composition: What research says to the classroom teacher*. Washington, DC: National Education Association.

Bussis, A. M., Chittenden, E. A., Amarel, M., & Klausner, E. (1985). *Inquiry into meaning: An investigation of learning to read*. Hillsdale, NJ: Lawrence Erlbaum Associates.

Butler, J. (1980). Remedial writers: The teacher's job as corrector of papers. *College Composition and Communication, 31,* 270–277.

Calfee, R., & Freedman, S. W. (1996). Classroom writing portfolios: Old, new, borrowed, blue. In R. Calfee & P. Perfumo (Eds.), *Writing Portfolios in the Classroom: Policy and Practice, Promise and Peril* (pp. 3–26). Mahwah, NJ: Lawrence Erlbaum Associates.

Calfee, R., & Perfumo, P. (1992). *A survey of portfolio practices*. Berkeley: University of California, Center for the Study of Writing.

Calfee, R., & Perfumo, P. (Ed.) (1996). *Writing portfolios in the classroom*. Mahwah, NJ: Lawrence Erlbaum Associates.

*California handbook for planning an effective writing program* (1986). Sacramento: California State Department of Education.

Calkins, L. M. (1980). Children's rewriting strategies. *Research in the Teaching of English, 14,* 331-341.

Calkins, L. M. (1983). *Lessons from a child on the teaching of writing.* Exeter, NH: Heinemann.

Calkins, L. M. (1986). *The art of teaching writing.* Portsmouth, NH: Heineman.

Camitta, M. (1993). Vernacular writing: Varieties of literacy among Philadelphia high school students. In B. Street (Ed.), *Cross-cultural approaches to literacy* (pp. 228-246). New York: Cambridge University Press.

Camp, R. (1985). The writing folder in post-secondary assessment. In P. J. A. Evans (Ed.), *Directions and misdirections in English evaluation* (pp. 91-99). Ottowa, Canada: The Canadian Council of Teachers of English.

Camp, R. (1992). Portfolio reflections in middle and secondary classrooms. In K. B. Yancey (Ed.), *Portfolios in the writing classroom: An introduction.* Urbana, IL: National Council of Teachers of English.

Camp, R., & Belanoff, P. (1987). Portfolios as proficiency tests. *Notes from the National Testing Network in Writing, 7*(8).

Cazden, C. (1979). Peekaboo as an instructional model: Discourse development at home and at school. *Papers and Reports on Child Language Development, 17,* 1-19.

Cazden, C. (1988). *Classroom discourse: The language of teaching and learning.* Portsmouth, NH: Heinemann.

Cazden, C., Cordeiro, P., & Giacoabbe, M. E. (1985). Spontaneous and scientific concepts: Young children's learning of punctuation. In G. Wells & J. Nicholls (Eds.), *Language and learning: An interactional perspective* (pp. 107-124). Philadelphia: Falmer Press.

Chafe, W. (1982). Integration and involvement in speaking, writing, and oral literature. In D. Tannen (Ed.), *Spoken and written language: Exploring orality and literacy* (pp. 35-54). Norwood, NJ: Ablex.

Chafe, W. (1985). Linguistic differences produced by differences between speaking and writing. In D. Olson, A. Hildyard, & Torrance (Eds.), *Language, literacy, and education* (pp. 105-123). Cambridge, England: Cambridge University Press.

Chafe, W., & Danielewicz, J. (1987). Properties of spoken and written language. In R. Horowitz & J. Samuels (Eds.), *Comprehending written language* (pp. 83-113). New York: Academic Press.

Chapman, M. L. (1995). The sociocognitive construction of written genres in first grade. *Research in the Teaching of English, 29,* 164-192.

Clark, C. M., & Florio, S. (1981). *Diary time: The life history of an occasion for writing.* East Lansing, MI: Institute for Research on Teaching.

Clay, M. (1975). *What did I write?* Auckland: Heinemann.

Clay, M. (1977). Exploring with a pencil. *Theory Into Practice, 16,* 334-341.

Clay, M. (1998). *By different paths to common outcomes.* York, ME: Stenhouse.

Cole, M., & Griffin, P. (1980). Cultural amplifiers reconsidered. In D. R. Olson (Ed.), *The social foundations of language and thought* (pp. 343-364). New York: Norton.

Collins, A., & Gentner, D. (1980). A framework for a cognitive theory of writing. In L. Gregg & E. Steinberg (Eds.), *Cognitive processes in writing* (pp. 51-72). Hillsdale, NJ: Lawrence Erlbaum Associates.

Comber, B. (1999). *Critical literacies: Negotiating powerful and pleasurable curricula: How do we foster critical literacy through English language arts?* Paper presented at the annual convention of the National Council of Teachers of English. Denver, CO.

Comber, B., & Nixon, H. (1999). In C. Edelsky (Ed.), *Making justice our project* (pp. 316-154). Urbana, IL: National Council of Teachers of English.

Comber, B., Thomson, P., & Wells, M. (2001). Critical literacy finds a "place": Writing and social action in a neighborhood school. *Elementary School Journal.*

Cooper, C. R. (Ed.) (1981). *The nature and measurement of competency in English.* Urbana, IL: National Council of Teachers of English.

Cooper, C. R., Marquis, A., & Ayer-Lopez, S. (1982). Peer learning in the classroom: Tracing developmental patterns and consequences of children's spontaneous interactions. In L. C. Wilkinson (Ed.), *Communicating in the classroom* (pp. 69-84). New York: Academic Press.

Cooper, C. R., & Matsuhashi, A. (1983). A theory of the writing process. In M. Martlew (Ed.), *The psychology of written language* (pp. 3-39). London: Wiley.

Cooper, C. R., & Odell, L. (Eds.) (1977). *Evaluating writing: Describing, measuring, judging.* Urbana, IL: National Council of Teachers of English.

Cooper, C., & Odell, L. (Ed.) (1999). *Evaluating writing: The role of teachers' knowledge about text, learning, and culture.* Urbana, IL: National Council of Teachers of English.

Cope, B., & Kalantzis, M. (Eds.) (1993). *The powers of literacy: A genre approach to teaching writing.* London: Falmer Press.

Cross, T. (1975). Some relationships between mothers and linguistic levels in accelerated children. *Papers and reports on child language development* (Vol. 10). Stanford, CA: Stanford University.

Cummins, J., & Sayers, D. (1995). *Brave new schools: Challenging cultural illiteracy through global learning networks.* New York: St. Martin's Press.

Dahl, K. L., & Farnan, N. (1998). *Children's writing: Perspectives from research.* Newark, DE: International Reading Association.

Daiute, C. (1981). Psycholinguistic foundations of the writing process. *Research in the Teaching of English, 15,* 5-22.

Daiute, C. (1989). Play as thought: Thinking strategies of young writers. *Harvard Educational Review, 59,* 1-23.

Daiute, C. (Ed.) (1993). *The development of literacy through social interaction.* San Francisco: Jossey Bass.

Davis, B., Scriven, M., & Thomas, S. (1987). *The evaluation of composition instruction* (2nd ed.). New York: Teachers College Press.

de Beaugrand, R. (1982). Psychology and composition: Past, present and future. In M. Nystrand (Ed.), *What writers know: The language process and structure of written discourse* (pp. 211-268). New York: Academic Press.

de Beaugrande, R. (1984). *Advances in discourse processes: Vol. 11. Text production: Toward a science of composition.* Norwood, NJ: Ablex.

Delpit, L. (1995). *Other people's children: Cultural conflict in the classroom.* New York: New Press.

Diederich, P. (1974). *Measuring growth in English.* Urbana, IL: National Council of Teachers of English.

DiPardo, A., & Freedman, S. (1988). Peer response groups in the writing classroom: Theoretical foundations and new directions. *Review of Educational Research, 58,* 119-143.

Dixon, J., & Stratta, L. (1986). *Writing narrative—And beyond.* Upper Montclair, NJ: Boynton/Cook.

Donaldson, M. (1984). Speech and writing as modes of learning. In H. Goelman, A. A. Oberg, & F. Smith (Eds.), *Awakening to literacy* (pp. 174-184). Portsmouth, NH: Heinemann.

Durst, R. (1984). The development of analytic writing. In A. N. Applebee (Ed.), *Contexts for learning to write* (pp. 79-102). Norwood, NJ: Ablex.

Durst, R. (1987). Cognitive and linguistic demands of analytic writing. *Research in the Teaching of English, 21*(4), 347-376.

Dyson, A. H. (1981). Oral language: The rooting system for learning to write. *Language Arts, 58,* 776-784.

Dyson, A. H. (1982). The emergence of visible language: Interrelationships between drawing and early writing. *Visible Language, 6,* 360-381.

Dyson, A. H. (1983). The role of oral language in early writing processes. *Research in the Teaching of English, 17,* 1-30.

Dyson, A. H. (1985). Individual differences in emerging writing. In M. Farr (Ed.), *Advances in writing research: Vol. 1. Children's early writing development* (pp. 59-126). Norwood, NJ: Ablex.

Dyson, A. H. (1987). Individual differences in beginning composing: An orchestral vision of learning to compose. *Written Communication, 4,* 411-442.

Dyson, A. H. (1989). *Multiple worlds of child writers: Friends learning to write.* New York: Teachers College Press.

Dyson, A. H. (1993). *Social worlds of children learning to write in an urban primary school.* New York: Teachers College Press.

Dyson, A. H. (with Bennett, A. et al.). (1997a). *What differences does difference make? Teacher perspectives on diversity, literacy, and the urban primary school.* Urbana, IL: National Council of Teachers of English.

Dyson, A. H. (1997b). *Writing superheroes: Contemporary childhood, popular culture, and classroom literacy.* New York: Teachers College Press.

Dyson, A. H. (1999a). Coach Bombay's kids learn to write: Children's appropriation of media material for school literacy. *Research in the Teaching of English, 33,* 367-402.

Dyson, A. H. (1999b). Transforming transfer: Unruly children, contrary texts, and the persistence of the pedagogical order. In A. Iran-Nejad & P. D. Pearson (Eds.). *Review of research in education: Vol. 24.* Washington, DC: American Educational Research Association.

Dyson, A. H. (2000). On reframing children's words: The perils, promises, and pleasures of writing children. *Research in the Teaching of English, 34,* 352-367.

Dyson, A. H. (in press-a). Donkey Kong in Little Bear Country: Examining composing development in the media spotlight. *Elementary School Journal.*

Dyson, A. H. (in press-b). Writing and children's symbolic repertories: Development unhinged. In S. Neuman & D. Dickinson (Eds.), *Handbook on research in early literacy for the 21st century.* New York: Guilford.

Edelsky, C. (1983). Segmentation and punctuation: Developmental data from young writers in a bilingual program. *Research in the Teaching of English, 17,* 135-156.

Edelsky, C. (1986). *Writing in a bilingual program: Habia una vez.* Norwood, NJ: Ablex.

Edelsky, C. (Ed.) (1999). *Making justice our project : teachers working toward critical whole language practice.* Urbana, IL: National Council of Teachers of English.

Edwards, P. (1999). *A path to follow: Learning to listen to parents.* Portsmouth, NH: Heinemann.

Elbow, P. (1973). *Writing without teachers.* London: Oxford University Press.

Elbow, P. (1986). Portfolio assessment as an alternative in proficiency testing. *Notes from the National Testing Network in Writing, 6, 3,* 12.

Elbow, P., & Belanoff, P. (1986). Using portfolios to judge writing proficiency at SUNY Stony Brook. In P. Connolly & T. Vilardi (Eds.), *New directions in college writing programs* (pp. 95-105). New York: Modern Language Association.

Emig, J. (1971). *The composing processes of twelfth graders* (Research Rep. No. 13). Urbana, IL: National Council of Teachers of English.

Evertts, E. (1970). *Explorations in children's writing.* Urbana, IL: National Council of Teachers of English.

Faigley, L., & Witte, S. (1981). Analyzing revisions. *College Composition and Communication, 32,* 400-414.

Farr, M. (1994). En los dos idiomas: Literacy practices among Chicano Mexicanos. In B. J. Moss (Ed.), *Literacy across communities* (pp. 9-48). Cresskill, NJ: Hampton Press.

Ferreiro, E., & Teberosky, A. (1982). *Literacy before schooling.* Exeter, NH: Heinemann.

Fiering, S. (1981). Commodore School: Unofficial writing. In D. H. Hymes (Ed.), *Ethnographic monitoring of children's acquisition of reading/language arts skills in and out of the classroom* (Final report to the National Institute of Education).

Finders, M. (1996). Just girls: Hidden literacies and life in junior high. *Written Communication, 13,* 93-129.

Finnegan, R. (1988). *Literacy and orality.* Oxford, England:Blackwell.

Flood, J., & Lapp, D. (2000). Teaching writing in urban schools: Cognitive processes, curriculum resources, and the missing links—Management and grouping. In R. Indrisano & J. R. Squire (Eds.), *Perspectives on writing: Research, theory, and practice* (pp. 233-250). Newark, DE: International Reading Association.

Florio, S., & Clark, C. (1982). The functions of writing in an elementary classroom. *Research in the Teaching of English, 16,* 115-129.

Flower, L. (1979). Writer-based prose: A cognitive basis for problems in writing. *College English, 41,* 19-37.

Flower, L. (1987). Interpretive acts: Cognition and the construction of discourse. *Poetics, 16,* 109-130.

Flower, L. (1988). Taking thought: The role of conscious processing in the making of meaning. In E. Maimon, B. Nodine, & F. O'Connor (Eds.), *Thinking, reasoning, and writing.* New York: Longman.

Flower, L., & Hayes, J. R. (1977). Problem-solving strategies and the writing process. *College English,* 449-461.

Flower, L., & Hayes, J. R. (1980). Identifying the organization of writing processes. In L. W. Gregg & E. R. Steinberg (Eds.), *Cognitive processes in writing.* Hillsdale, NJ: Lawrence Erlbaum Associates.

Flower, L., & Hayes, J. R. (1981a). A cognitive process theory of writing. *College Composition and Communication, 32,* 365-387.

Flower, L., & Hayes, J. R. (1981b). Plans that guide the composing process. In C. H. Frederiksen & J. F. Dominic (Eds.), *Writing: Process, development and communication* (pp. 39-58). Hillsdale, NJ: Lawrence Erlbaum Associates.

Flower, L., & Hayes, J. R. (1981c). The pregnant pause: An inquiry into the nature of planning. *Research in the Teaching of English, 15,* 229-243.

Flower, L., & Hayes, J. R. (1983). Uncovering cognitive processes in writing: An introduction to protocol analysis. In P. Mosenthal, L. Tamor, & S. Walmsley (Eds.), *Research on written language: Principals and methods* (pp. 206-219). New York: Guilford Press.

Freedman, A., & Medway, P. (Eds.) (1994). *Learning and teaching genre.* Portsmouth, NH: Boynton/Cook.

Freedman, S. (1984). *Response to and evaluation of writing: A review.* Paper presented at the Annual Meeting of the American Educational Research Association, New Orleans (ERIC Document Reproduction Service No. ED 247 605).

Freedman, S. (1987a). *Peer Response Groups in Two Ninth-Grade Classrooms* (Tech. Rep. No. 12). Berkeley: University of California, Center for the Study of Writing.

Freedman, S. (with Greenleaf, C., & Sperling, M.) (1987b). *Response to student writing* (Research Rep. No. 23). Urbana, IL: National Council for the Teachers of English.

Freedman, S. (1994). *Exchanging writing: Exchanging cultures.* Cambridge, MA: Harvard University Press.

Freedman, S., & McLeod, A. (1988). *National surveys of successful teachers of writing and their students: The United Kingdom and the United States* (Tech. Rep. No. 14). Berkeley: University of California, Center for the Study of Writing.

Freedman, S., Simons, E. R., & Kalnin, J. S. (1999). *Inside city schools: Investing literacy in multicultural classrooms*. New York: Teachers College Press.

Freedman, S. W. (1993). Linking large-scale testing and classroom portfolio assessments of student writing. *Educational Assessment, 1*(1), 27–52.

Freire, P. (1970). *Pedagogy of the oppressed*. New York: Continuum.

Fulwiler, T. (Ed.) (1987). *The journal book*. Portsmouth, NH: Heinemann.

Genishi, C., & Dyson, A. H. (1984). *Language assessment in the early years*. Norwood, NJ: Ablex.

Genishi, C., Stires, S., & Yung-Chan, D. (in press). Writing in an integrated curriculum: Prekindergarten English language learners as symbol-makers. *Elementary School Journal*.

Gentile, C. (1992). *Exploring new methods for collecting school-based writing: NAEP's 1990 portfolio study*. Washington, DC: U.S. Government Printing Office.

Gentile, C., Martin-Rehrmann, J., & Kennedy, J. (1995). *Windows into the classroom: NAEP's 1992 writing portfolio study*. Washington, DC: U.S. Department of Education.

Gere, A. (1987). *Writing groups: History, theory, and implications*. Carbondale: Southern Illinois University Press.

Gere, A., & Abbott, R. (1985). Talking about writing: The language of writing groups. *Research in the Teaching of English, 19*(4), 362–86.

Gere, A., & Stevens, R. (1985). The language of writing groups: How oral response shapes revision. In S. W. Freedman (Ed.), *The acquisition of written language: Response and revision* (pp. 85–105). Norwood, NJ: Ablex.

Gilbert, S. H. (1989). *Writing, schooling, and deconstruction: From voice to text in the classroom*. London: Routledge.

Gilbert, S. H. (1994). "And they lived happily ever after": Cultural storylines and the construction of gender. In A. H. Dyson & C. Genishi (Eds.), *The need for story: Cultural diversity in the classroom and community* (pp. 124–144). Urbana, IL: National Council of Teachers of English.

Gilbert, S. H., & Gay, G. (1985). Improving the success in school of poor black children. *Phi Delta Kappan, 67*(2), 133–137.

Gilmore, P. (1983). Spelling "Mississippi": Recontextualizing a literacy-related speech event. *Anthropology & Education Quarterly, 14*(4), 235–256.

Goodnow, J. (1977). *Children drawing*. Cambridge, MA: Harvard University Press.

Goodnow, J. (2000). Combining analysis of culture and of cognition. *Human Development, 43*, 115–125.

Goodnow, J., Miller, P. J., & Kessel, J. (Eds.) (1995). *Cultural practices as contexts for development*. San Francisco: Jossey-Bass.

Goody, J. (1968). *Literacy in traditional societies*. Cambridge, England: Cambridge University Press.

Goody, J., & Watt, I. (1963). The consequences of literacy. *Comparative Studies in Society and History, 5*, 304–326, 332–345.

Gorman, T., Purves, A., & Degenhart, R. E. (Eds.) (1988). *The international writing tasks and scoring scales: International study of achievement in writtten composition* (Vol. 1). Tarrytown, NY: Pergamon.

Graves, D. (1973). *Children's writing: Research directions on hypotheses based upon an examination of the writing process of seven-year-old children*. Unpublished doctoral dissertation, State University of New York, Buffalo.

Graves, D. (1975). An examination of the writing processes of seven year old children. *Research in the Teaching of English, 9*, 227–241.

Graves, D. (1981). *A case study observing the development of primary children's composing, spelling and motor behaviors during the writing process* (Final report to the National Institute of Education). Durham: University of New Hampshire.

Graves, D. (1982). Patterns of child control of the writing process. In R. D. Walsh (Ed.), *Donald Graves in Australia*. Exeter, NH: Heinemann.

Graves, D. (1983). *Writing: Teachers and children at work*. Exeter, NH: Heinemann.

Greene, J. (1985). Children's writing in an elementary postal system. In M. Farr (Ed.), *Advances in writing: Vol. 1. Children's early writing development* (pp. 201–296). Norwood, NJ: Ablex.

Greene, J., & Wallat, C. (1979). What is an instructional context? An exploratory analysis of conversational shifts over time. In O. Garnica & M. King (Eds.), *Language, children, and society* (pp. 159–188). Tarrytown: Pergamon.

Greenwald, E., Persky, H., Campbell, J., & Mazzeo, J. (1999). *NAEP 1998 writing report card for the nation and the states*. Washington, DC: U.S. Department of Education.

Gubb, J., Gorman, T., & Price, E. (1987). *The study of written composition in England and Wales*. Windsor, England: NFER-NELSON.

Gumperz, J. (Ed.) (1971). *Language in social groups*. Stanford: Stanford University Press.

Gumperz, J., & Hymes, D. H. (Eds.) (1972). *Directions in sociolinguistics: The ethnography of communication*. Oxford, England: Blackwell.

Gundlach, R. (1981). On the nature and development of children's writing. In C. Fredericksen & J. Dominic (Eds.), *Writing: The nature, development and teaching of written communication: Vol. 2. Writing: Process, development and communication* (pp. 133–152). Hillsdale, NJ: Lawrence Erlbaum Associates.

Gundlach, R. (1982). Children as writers: The beginnings of learning to write. In M. Nystrand (Ed.), *What writers know* (pp. 129–148). New York: Academic Press.

Gundlach, R., Farr, M., & Cook-Gumperz, J. (1989). Writing and reading in the community. In A. Haas Dyson (Ed.), *Collaborating through writing and reading: Exploring possibilities* (pp. 91–130). Urbana, IL: National Council of Teachers of English.

Guttierez, K. (1992). A comparison of instructional contexts in writing process classrooms with Latino children. *Education in Urban Society, 24*, 244–262.

Hahn, J. (1981). Students' reactions to teachers' written comments. *National Writing Project Network Newsletter, 4*, 7–10.

Hairston, M. (1982). The winds of change: Thomas Kuhn and the revolution in the teaching of writing. *College Composition and Communication, 33*(1), 76–88.

Hamilton, M., Barton, D., & Ivanic, R. (Eds.) (1994). *Worlds of literacy*. Toronto, Canada: Institute for Studies in Education.

Haneda, M., & Wells, G. (2000). Writing in knowledge-building communities. *Research in the Teaching of English, 34*, 396–431.

Hanks, W. F. (1996). *Language and communicative practices*. Boulder, CO: Westview Press.

Harste, J. C., Woodward, V. A., & Burke, C. L. (1984). *Language stories & literacy lessons*. Portsmouth, NH: Heinemann.

Hawkins, T. (1976). *Group inquiry techniques for teaching writing*. Urbana, IL: National Council of Teachers of English and ERIC.

Hayes, J. R. (2000). A new framework for understanding cognition and affect in writing. In R. Indrisano & J. R. Squire (Eds.), *Perspectives on writing: Research, theory and practice* (pp. 6–44). Newark, DE: International Reading Association.

Hayes, J. R., & Flower, L. S. (1980). Identifying the organization of writing processes. In L. W. Gregg & E. R. Steinberg (Eds.), *Cognitive processes in writing* (pp. 3-30). Hillsdale, NJ: Lawrence Erlbaum Associates.

Hayes, J. R., Flower, L., Schriver, K., Stratman, J., & Carey, L. (1987). Cognitive processes in revision. In Rosenberg, S. (Ed.), *Advances in applied psycholinguistics: Reading, writing, and language processing* (pp. 176-240). Cambridge, England: Cambridge University Press.

Healy, M. K. (1980). *Using student writing response groups in the classroom*. Berkeley: University of California, Bay Area Writing Project.

Heath, S. B. (1980). The functions and uses of literacy. *Journal of Communication, 30*, 123-133.

Heath, S. B. (1982). Protean shapes in literacy events: Evershifting oral and literate traditions. In D. Tannen (Ed.), *Spoken and written language: Exploring orality and literacy* (pp. 91-118). Norwood, NJ: Ablex.

Heath, S. B. (1983). *Ways with words: Language, life, and work in communities and classrooms*. Cambridge, England: Cambridge University Press.

Heath S. B. (1986). Taking a cross-cultural look at narratives. *Topics in Language Disorders, 7*(1), 84-94.

Heath, S., & Branscombe, A. (1985). "Intelligent writing" in an audience community: Teacher, students and researchers. In S. W. Freedman (Ed.), *The acquisition of written language: Response and revision* (pp. 3-32). Norwood, NJ: Ablex.

Heller, C. (1997). *Until we are strong together*. New York: Teachers College Press.

Henderson, E. H. (1981). *Learning to read and spell: The child's knowledge of words*. DeKalb: Northern Illinois University Press.

Henry, J. (1955). Docility or giving teacher what she wants. *The Journal of Social Issues, 11*(2), 33-41.

Henry, J. (1963). *Culture against man*. New York: Random House.

Hicks, D. (1997). Working through discourse genres in school. *Research in the Teaching of English, 31*, 459-485.

Hidi, S., & Hildyard, A. (1984). The comparison of oral and written productions in two discourse modes. *Discourse Processes, 6*, 91-105.

Hiebert, E. H. (1981). Developmental patterns and interrelationships of preschool children's print awareness. *Reading Research Quarterly, 49*, 1231-1234.

Hilgers, T. L. (1986). How children change as critical evaluators of writing: Four three-year case studies. *Research in the Teaching of English, 20*, 36-55.

Hillocks, G., Jr. (1984). What works in teaching composition: A meta-analysis of experimental treatment studies. *American Journal of Education, 93*(1), 107-132.

Hillocks, G., Jr. (1986). *Research on written composition: New directions for teaching*. Urbana, IL: ERIC Clearinghouse on Reading and Communication Skills.

Hillocks, G., Jr. (1995). *Teaching writing as reflective practice*. New York: Teachers College Press.

Hudson, S. A. (1988). Children's perceptions of classroom writing: Ownership in a continuum of control. In B. Rafoth & D. Rubin (Eds.), *The social construction of written language* (pp. 37-69). Norwood, NJ: Ablex.

Hull, G. (1987). The editing process in writing: A performance study of more skilled and less skilled college writers. *Research in the Teaching of English, 21*(1), 8-29.

Hymes, D. H. (1962). The ethnography of speaking. In T. Gladwin & W. C. Sturtevant (Eds.), *Anthropology and human behavior* (pp. 13-53). Washington, DC: Anthropology Society of Washington.

Hymes, D. H. (1972). Models of the interaction of language and social life. In J. J. Gumperz & D. Hymes (Eds.), *Directions in sociolinguistics* (pp. 35-71). New York: Holt, Rinehart & Winston.

Hymes, D. H. (with Cazden, C.) (1980). Narrative thinking and storytelling rights: A folklorist's clue to a critique of education. In D. Hymes, *Language in education* (pp. 126-138). Washington, DC: Center for Applied Linguistics.

Jackson, P. (1968). *Life in classrooms*. New York: Holt, Rinehart & Winston.

Jacobs, S. E. (1985). The development of children's writing: Language acquisition and divided attention. *Written Communication, 2,* 414-433.

Jaggar, A., & Smith-Burke, T. (1985). *Observing the language learner*. Urbana, IL: National Council of Teachers of English.

Johnston, R. (1979). Development of a literary mode in the language of nonliterary communities. In S. A. Wurm (Ed.), *New Guinea and neighboring areas: A sociolinguistic laboratory* (pp. 129-155). The Hague, Netherlands: Mouton.

Jordan, J. (1988). Nobody mean more to me than you and the future life of Willie Jordan. *Harvard Educational Review, 58*, 363-374.

Kalman, J. (1996). Joint composition: The collaborative letter writing of a scribe and his client in Mexico. *Written Communication, 13,* 190-220.

Kamberelis, G. (1999). Genre development and learning: Children writing stories, science reports and poems. *Research in the Teaching of English, 33*(4), 403-460.

Kavanagh, K. (1997). *Texts on television: School literacies through viewing in the first years of school*. Henley Beach, Australia: South Australian Department of Education and Children's Services.

King, M., & Rentel, V. (1981). *How children learn to write: A longitudinal study*. Columbus: Ohio State University.

King, M., & Rentel, V. (1982). *Transition to writing*. Columbus: Ohio State University.

Kinneavy, J. (1971). *A theory of discourse*. New York: Norton.

Kinstch, W., & van Dijk, T. (1978). Toward a model of text comprehension and production. *Psychological Review, 85*, 363-394.

Knoblauch, C., & Brannon, L. (1984). *Rhetorical traditions and the teaching of writing*. Upper Montclair, NJ: Boynton/Cook.

Kroll, B. (1978). Cognitive egocentrism and the problem of audience awareness in written discourse. *Research in the Teaching of English, 12*, 269-281.

Labov, W. (1982). Competing value systems in inner-city schools. In P. Gilmore & A. A. Glatthorn (Eds.), *Children in and out of school* (pp. 148-171). Washington, DC: Center for Applied Linguistics.

Lamme, L., & Childers, N. (1983). The composing processes of three young children. *Research in the Teaching of English, 17,* 31-50.

Langer, J. (1986). *Children reading and writing: Structures and strategies*. Norwood, NJ: Ablex.

Langer, J. A., & Applebee, A. N. (1984). Language, learning, and interaction: A framework for improving the teaching of writing. In A. Applebee (Ed.), *Contexts for learning to write: Studies of secondary school instruction* (pp. 169-182). Norwood, NJ: Ablex.

Langer, J. A., & Applebee, A. N. (1987). *How writing shapes thinking: A study of teaching and learning* (Research Rep. No. 22). Urbana, IL: National Council of Teachers of English.

Langer, J. A., & Flihan, S. (2000). Writing and reading relationships: Constructive tasks. In R. Indrisano & J. R. Squire. (Eds.), *Perspectives on writing: Research, theory and practice* (pp. 112-139). Newark, DE: International Reading Association.

Larson, J. (1999). Analyzing participation frameworks in kindergarten writing activity: The role of overhearer in learning to write. *Written Communication, 16*(2), 225-257.

Larson, J., & Maier, M. (2000). Co-authoring classroom texts: Shifting participant roles in writing activity. *Research in the Teaching of English, 34,* 468-498.

Leacock, E. (1969). *Teaching and learning in city schools*. New York: Basic Books.

Lee, C. D., & Smagorinsky, P. (2000a). Introduction: Constructing meaning through collaborative inquiry. In C. D. Lee & P. Smagorinsky (Eds.), *Vygotskian perspectives on literacy research: Constructing meaning through collaborative inquiry* (pp. 1-18). Cambridge, England: Cambridge University Press.

Lee, C. D., & Smagorinsky, P. (Eds.) (2000b). *Vygotskian perspectives on literacy research: Constructing meaning through collaborative inquiry*. Cambridge, England: Cambridge University Press.

Lensmire, T. (1993). *When children write: Critical revisions of the writing workshop*. New York: Teachers College Press.

Leondar, B. (1977). Hatching plots: Genesis of storymaking. In D. Perkins & B. Leondar (Eds.), *Arts and cognition* (pp. 172-191). Baltimore, MD: Johns Hopkins University Press.

Loban, W. (1976). *Language development: Kindergarten through grade twelve*. Urbana, IL: National Council of Teachers of English.

Losey, K. (1997). *Listen to the silences: Mexican American interaction in the composition classroom and the community*. Norwood, NJ: Ablex.

Lucas, C. K. (1988a). Recontextualizing literacy assessment. *The Quarterly, 10*, 4-10.

Lucas, C. K. (1988b). Toward ecological evaluation. *The Quarterly, 10*, 1-3, 12-17.

Luke, A. (1995). Text and discourse in education: An introduction to critical discourse analysis. In M. W. Apple (Ed.), *Review of Research in Education, 21* (pp. 3-48). Washington, DC: American Educational Research Association.

Lundsford, A., & Ede, L. (1984). Classical rhetoric, modern rhetoric, and contemporary discourse studies. *Written Communication, 1*, 78-100.

Macrorie, K. (1970). *Uptaught*. New York: Hayden.

Macrorie, K. (1984). *Twenty teachers*. New York: Oxford University Press.

Many, J. E., Fyfe, R., Lewis, G. L., & Mitchell, E. (1996). Traversing the topical landscape: Exploring students' self-directed reading-writing-research processes. *Reading Research Quarterly, 31*(1), 12-35.

Marsh, J. (1999). Batman and Batwoman go to school: Popular culture in the literacy curriculum. *International Journal of Early Years Education, 7*, 117-131.

Marshall, T. (1987). The effects of writing on students' understanding of literary texts. *Research in the Teaching of English, 21*(1), 30-63.

Matsuhashi, A. (1981). Pausing and planning: The tempo of written discourse. *Research in the Teaching of English, 15*, 113-134.

McCaig, R. (1981). A district-wide plan for the evaluation of student writing. In S. Haley-James (Ed.), *Perspectives on writing in grades 1-8* (pp. 73-92). Urbana, IL: National Council of Teachers of English.

McCaleb, S. P. (1994). *Building communities of learners: A collaboration among teachers, students, families and community*. New York: St. Martin's Press.

McCarthy, S. J. (1994). Authors, text, and talk. The internalization of dialogue from social interaction during writing. *Reading Research Quarterly, 29*, 210-231.

McNaughton, S. (1995). Developmental diversity and beginning literacy instruction at school. In J. S. Gaffney & B. J. Askew (Eds.), *Stirring the waters: The influence of Marie Clay* (pp. 3-16). Portsmouth, NH: Heinemann.

Mehan, H. (1979). "What time is it, Denise?": Asking known information questions in classroom discourse. *Theory into Practice, 28*, 285-294.

Mellon, J. C. (1975). *National assessment and the teaching of writing*. Urbana, IL: National Council of Teachers of English.

Merritt, M. (1982). Distributing and directing attention in primary classrooms. In L. C. Wilkinson (Ed.), *Communicating in the classroom* (pp. 223-244). New York: Academic Press.

Michaels, S., & Cook-Gumperz, J. (1979). A study of sharing time with first grade students: Discourse narratives in the classroom. *Proceedings of the Fifth Annual Meeting of the Berkeley Linguistics Society*, Berkeley, CA.

Miller, C. R. (1984). Genre as social action. *Quarterly Journal of Speech, 70*, 151-167.

Moffett, J. (1968). *Teaching the universe of discourse*. Boston: Houghton Mifflin.

Moffett, J., & Wagner, B. J. (1983). *Student-centered language arts and reading, K-13: A handbook for teachers* (3rd ed.). Boston: Houghton Mifflin.

Moll, L., Amanti, C., Neff, D., & Gonzalez, N. (1992). Funds of knowledge for teaching. *Theory Into Practice, 31*, 132-141.

Moll, L., Saez, R., & Dworin, J. (in press). Exploring biliteracy. *Elementary School Journal*.

Moll, L., & Whitmore, K. (1993). Vygotsky in classroom practice: Moving from individual transmission to social transaction. In E. Forman, N. Minick, & C. A. Stone (Eds.), *Contexts for learning: Sociocultural dynamics in children's development* (pp. 19-42). New York: Oxford University Press.

Moss, B. J. (Ed.) (1994). *Literacy across communities*. Cresskill, NJ: Hampton Press.

Moss, G. (1989). *Un/Popular Fictions*. London: Virago.

Murphy, S., & Underwood, T. (2000). *Portfolio practices: Lessons from schools, districts and states*. Norwood, MA: Christopher-Gordon.

Murray, D. (1984). *A writer teaches writing* (2nd ed.). Boston: Houghton Mifflin.

Myers, M. (1980). *A procedure for writing assessment and holistic scoring*. Urbana, IL: National Council of Teachers of English.

National Assessment of Educational Progress (1990). *The writing report card, 1984-88: Findings from the nation's report card*. Princeton, NJ: Educational Testing Service.

Nelson, J., & Hayes, J. (1988). *How the writing context shapes college students' strategies for writing from sources* (Tech. Rep. No. 16). Berkeley: University of California, Center for the Study of Writing.

Nelson, K. E., & Nelson, K. (1978). Cognitive pendulums and their linguistic realization. In K. E. Nelson (Ed.), *Children's language* (Vol. 1, pp. 233-285). New York: Gardner.

Nelson, M. W. (1997). Growth-biased assessing of writers—A more democratic choice. In S. Tchudi (Eds.), *Alternatives to grading student writing*. Urbana, IL: National Council of Teachers of English.

Newkirk, T. (1984). How students read student papers: An exploratory study. *Written Communication, 3*, 283-305.

Newkirk, T. (1987). The non-narrative writing of young children. *Research in the Teaching of English, 21*, 121-145.

Newkirk, T. (1995). The writing conference as performance. *Research in the Teaching of English, 29*, 193-215.

Newkirk, T. (in press). The revolt against realism: The attraction of fiction for young writers. *Elementary School Journal*.

Newkirk, T., & Atwell, N. (Eds.) (1988). *Understanding writing* (2nd ed.). Portsmouth, NH: Heinemann.

New London Group (1996). A pedagogy of multiliteracies: Designing social futures. *Harvard Educational Review, 61*, 60-92.

Ninio, A., & Bruner, J. (1978). The achievement and antecedents of labeling. *Journal of Child Language, 5*, 1-15.

Nold, E. (1981). Revising. In C. H. Fredericksen & J. F. Dominic (Eds.), *Writing: The nature, development, and teaching of written communication: Vol. 2. Process, development, and communication* (pp. 67-80). Hillsdale, NJ: Lawrence Erlbaum Associates.

Nystrand, M. (1986). Learning to write by talking about writing: A summary of research on intensive peer review in expository writing instruction at the University of Wisconsin-Madison. In M. Nystrand (Ed.), *The structure of written communication* (pp. 179–211). Orlando, FL: Academic Press.

Nystrand, M. (1997). *Opening dialogue: Understanding the dynamics of language and learning in the English classroom.* New York: Teachers College Press.

Nystrand, M., & Graff, N. (2001). Report in argument's clothing: An ecological perspective on writing instruction. *Elementary School Journal.*

O'Donnell, R. C., Griffin, W. J., & Norris, R. C. (1967). *Syntax of kindergarten and elementary school children: A transformational analysis.* Urbana, IL: National Council of Teachers of English.

Olson, D. (1977). From utterance to text. *Harvard Educational Review, 47,* 257–279.

Ong, W. (1982). *Orality and literacy: The technologizing of the word.* London: Methuen.

Paley, V. (1980). *Wally's stories.* Cambridge, MA: Harvard University Press.

Palinscar, A. S., & Brown, A. L. (1984). Reciprocal teaching of comprehension-fostering and monitoring activities. *Cognition and Instruction, 1*(2), 117–175.

Perera, K. (1984). *Children's writing and reading.* Oxford: Blackwell.

Perez, B. (Ed.) (1998). *Sociocultural contexts of language and literacy.* Mahwah, NJ: Lawrence Erlbaum Associates.

Perl, S. (1979). The composing processes of unskilled college writers. *Research in the Teaching of English, 13,* 317–336.

Perron, J. (1974). *An exploratory approach to extending the syntactic development of fourth-grade students through the use of sentence-combining methods.* Bloomington: Indiana University Press.

Petty & Finn (1981). Classroom teachers' reports on teaching composition. In S. Haley-James (Ed.), *Perspectives on writing in grades 1–8* (pp. 19–34). Urbana, IL: National Council of Teachers of English.

Perez, B. (1998). *Sociocultural contexts of language and literacy.* Mahwah, NJ: Lawrence Erlbaum Associates.

Philips, S. U. (1972). Participant structure and communicative competence: Warm Springs children in community and classroom. In C. B. Cazden, V. P. John, & D. Hymes (Eds.), *The functions of language in the classroom* (pp. 370–393). New York: Teachers College Press.

Philips, S. U. (1975). Literacy as a mode of communication on the Warm Springs Indian Reservation. In E. H. Lenneberg & E. Lenneberg (Eds.), *Foundations of language development* (pp. 367–381). New York: Academic Press; Paris: UNESCO.

Pianko, S. (1979). A description of the composing process of college freshman writers. *Research in the Teaching of English, 13,* 5–22.

Purves, A. (Ed.) (1988). *Written Communication Annual: Vol. 2. Writing across languages and cultures: Issues in contrastive rhetoric.* Newbury Park: Sage.

Putney, L. G., Green, J., Dixon, C., Duran, R., & Yeager, B. (2000). Consequential progressions: Exploring collective-individual development in a bilingual classroom. In C. D. Lee & P. Smagorinsky (Eds.), *Vygotskian perspectives on literacy research* (pp. 86–126). Cambridge, England: Cambridge University Press.

Ratner, N., & Bruner, J. (1978). Games, social exchange and the acquisition of language. *Journal of Child Language, 5,* 391–401.

Read, C. (1975). *Children's categorizations of speech sounds in English.* Urbana, IL: National Council of Teachers of English.

Resnick, L., & Resnick, D. (1990). Tests as standards of achievement in schools. In J. Pfleiderer (Eds.), *The uses of standardized tests in American education: Proceedings of the 1989 Educational Testing Service Invitational Conference.* Princeton, NJ: Educational Testing Service.

Reyes, M. (1991). A process approach to literacy using dialogue journals and literature logs with second language learners. *Research in the Teaching of English, 25,* 291–312.

Rist, R. C. (1970). Student social class and teach expectations: The self-fulfilling prophesy in ghetto education. *Harvard Educational Review, 40*(3), 411–451.

Rist, R. C. (1973). *The urban school: A factory for failure.* Cambridge, MA: MIT Press.

Rogoff, B. (1990). *Apprenticeship in thinking: Cognitive development in social context.* New York: Oxford University Press.

Rogoff, B., & Gardner, W. (1984). Adult guidance of cognitive development. In B. Rogoff & J. Lave (Eds.), *Everyday cognition: Its development in social context* (pp. 95–116). Cambridge, MA: Harvard University Press.

Rogoff, B., & Lave, J. (Eds.) (1984). *Everyday cognition: Its development in social context.* Cambridge, MA: Harvard University Press.

Rose, M. (1980). Rigid rules, inflexible plans, and the stifling of language: A cognitive analysis of writer's block. *College Composition and Communication, 31,* 389–401.

Rosen, C., & Rosen, H. (1973). *The language of primary school children.* Hammonsworth, England: Penguin.

Ruth, L., & Murphy, S. (1988). *Designing writing tasks for the assessment of writing.* Norwood, NJ: Ablex.

Sahni, U. (1994). *Building circles of mutuality: A socio-cultural analysis of literacy in a rural classroom in India.* Unpublished doctoral dissertation, University of California, Berkeley.

Scardamalia, M. (1981). How children cope with the cognitive demands of writing. In C. H. Frederiksen & J. F. Dominic (Eds.), *Writing: The nature, development, and teaching of written communication: Vol. 2. Process, development, and communication* (pp. 81–104). Hillsdale, NJ: Lawrence Erlbaum Associates.

Schieffelin, B. B. (1979). Getting it together: An ethnographic approach to the study of the development of communicative competence. In E. Ochs & B. B. Schieffelin (Eds.), *Developmental pragmatics* (pp. 73–108). New York: Academic Press.

Schieffelin, B. B., & Cochran-Smith, M. (1984). Learning to read culturally: Literacy before schooling. In H. Goelman, A. A. Oberg, & F. Smith (Eds.), *Awakening to literacy* (pp. 3–23). Portsmouth, NH: Heinemann.

Scollon, R., & Scollon, S. B. K. (1981). *Narrative, literacy, and face in interethnic communication.* Norwood, NJ: Ablex.

Scribner, S., & Cole, M. (1981). *The psychology of literacy.* Cambridge, MA: Harvard University Press.

Searle, D., & Dillon, D. (1980). The message of marking: Teacher written responses to student writing at intermediate grade levels. *Research in the Teaching of English, 14*(3), 233–242.

Shaughnessy, M. P. (1977). *Errors and expectations: A guide for the teacher of basic writing.* New York: Oxford University Press.

Silberman, A. (1989). *Growing up writing: Teaching children to write, think, and learn.* New York: Times Books.

Silva, A. D. de (1998). Emergent Spanish writing of a second grader in a whole language classroom. In B. Perez (Ed.), *Sociocultural contexts of language and literacy* (pp. 223–250). Mahwah, NJ: Lawrence Erlbaum Associates.

Slobin, D. (1979). *Psycholinguistics.* Glenview, IL: Scott, Foresman.

Smagorinsky, P. (1995). Constructing meaning in the disciplines: Reconceptualizing writing across the curriculum as composing across the curriculum. *American Journal of Education, 103,* 160–184.

Smitherman, G. (1994). *Black talk: Words and phrases from the hood to the Amen Corner.* Boston: Houghton Mifflin.

Sola, M., & Bennett, A. (1985). The struggle for voice: Narrative, literacy, and consciousness in an East Harlem school. *Journal of Education, 167,* 88–110.

Sommers, N. (1980). Revision strategies of student writers and experienced adult writers. *College Composition and Communication, 31,* 378-388.

Sommers, N. (1982). Responding to student writing. *College Composition and Communication, 33,* 148-156.

Sowers, S. (1981). Young writers' preference for non-narrative modes of composition. In D. H. Graves (Ed.), *A case study observing the development of primary children's composing, spelling, and motor behavior during the writing process, final report* (pp. 189-206). Durham, NH: University of New Hampshire.

Sowers, S. (1985). Learning to write in a workshop: A study in grades one through four. In M. F. Whiteman (Ed.), *Advances in writing research: Vol. 1. Children's early writing development* (pp. 297-342). Norwood, NJ: Ablex.

Sperling, M., & Freedman, S. (1987). A good girl writes like a good girl: Written response and clues to the teaching/learning process. *Written Communication, 4,* 343-369.

Sperling, M., & Woodlief, L. (1997). Two classrooms, two writing communities. *Research in the Teaching of English, 31.*

Stallard, C. (1979). An analysis of the writing behavior of good writers. *Research in the Teaching of English, 8,* 206-218.

Staton, J., Shuy, R., Peyton, J., & Reed, L. (1988). *Dialogue journal communication.* Norwood, NJ: Ablex.

Stein, N. L., & Glenn, C. G. (1979). An analysis of story comprehension in elementary school children. In R. O. Freedle (Ed.), *New directions in discourse processing II* (pp. 53-120). Norwood, NJ: Ablex.

Street, B. (1995). *Social literacies: Critical approaches to literacy in development, ethnography, and education.* London: Longman.

Strickland, D., Bodino, A., Buchan, K., Jones, K., Nelson, A., & Rosen, M. (in press). Teaching writing in a time of reform. *Elementary School Journal.*

Sulzby, E. (1985). Kindergartners as writers and readers. In M. Farr (Ed.), *Advances in writing research: Vol. 1. Children's early writing development* (pp. 127-200). Norwood, NJ: Ablex.

Swanson-Owens, D. (1986). Identifying natural sources of resistance: A case study of implementing writing across the curriculum. *Research in the Teaching of English, 20*(1), 68-97.

Szwed, John F. (1981). The ethnography of literacy. In M. F. Whiteman (Ed.), *Writing: The nature, development, and teaching of written communication: Vol. 2. Variation in writing: Functional and linguistic-cultural differences* (pp. 13-24). Hillsdale, NJ: Lawrence Erlbaum Associates.

Tannen, D. (1982). Oral and literate strategies in imaginative fiction: A comparison of spoken and written narratives. *Language, 58,* 1-22.

Tannen, D. (1984a). *Coherence in spoken and written discourse.* Norwood, NJ: Ablex.

Tannen, D. (1984b). *Conversational style: Analyzing talk among friends.* Norwood, NJ: Ablex.

Taylor, D. (1983). *Family literacy: Young children learning to read and write.* Exeter, NH: Heinemann.

Taylor, D., & Dorsey-Gaines, C. (1988). *Growing up literate: Learning from inner-city families.* Portsmouth, NH: Heinemann.

Tchudi, S. (Ed.) (1997). *Alternatives to grading student writing.* Urbana, IL: National Council of Teachers of English.

Teale, W. H., Estrada, E., & Anderson, A. B. (1981). How preschoolers interact with written communication. In M. L. Kamil (Ed.), *Directions in reading: Research and instruction: Thirtieth yearbook of the National Reading Conference* (Vol. 30, pp. 257-265). Washington, DC: National Reading Conference.

Tharp, R., Jordan, C., Speidel, G. E., Au, K., Klein, T., Calkins, R., Sloat, K., & Gallimore, R. (1984). Product and process in applied developmental research: Education and the children of a minority. In M. E. Lamb, A. L. Brown, & B. Rogoff (Eds.), *Advances in developmental psychology* (pp. 91-144). Hillsdale, NJ: Lawrence Erlbaum Associates.

Treiman, R. (1993). *Beginning to spell : a study of first-grade children.* New York: Oxford University Press.

Underwood, T. (1999). *The portfolio project: A study of assessment, instruction, and middle school reform.* Urbana, IL: National Council of Teachers of English.

Valdes, G. (1988). *Identifying priorities in the study of writing of Hispanic background students.* Final Report to the Office of Educational Research and Improvement. Berkeley: University of California, Center for the Study of Writing.

Valdes, G., & Sanders, P. (1999). Latino ESL students and the development of writing abilities. In C. Cooper & L. Odell (Eds.), *Evaluating writing: The role of teachers' knowledge about text, learning, and culture.* Urbana, IL: National Council of Teachers of English.

Vasquez, O., Pease-Alvarez, L., & Shannon, S. (1994). *Pushing boundaries: Language and culture in a Mexicano community.* New York: Cambridge University Press.

Volosinov, V. N. (1973). *Marxism and the philosophy of language* (L. Matejka & I.R. Titunik, Trans.). New York: Seminar Press.

Vygotsky, L. S. (1978). *Mind in society.* Cambridge, MA: Harvard University Press. (Original work published 1934)

Wagner, B. J. (Ed.) (1998). *Educational drama and language arts: What research shows.* Portsmouth, NH: Heinemann.

Walker, E. V. S. (1992). Falling asleep and failure among African-American students: Rethinking assumptions about process teaching. *Theory Into Practice, 31,* 321-328.

Weaver, C. (1982). Welcoming errors as signs of growth. *Language Arts, 59,* 438-444.

Wells, G. (1986). Variation in child language. In P. Fletcher & M. Garman (Eds.), *Language acquisition* (2nd ed., pp. 109-140). Cambridge, England: Cambridge University Press.

Werner, H. (1948). *Comparative psychology of mental development.* New York: International Universities Press.

Wertsch, J. V., McNamee, G. W., McLane, J. B., & Budwig, N. A. (1980). The adult–child dyad as a problem-solving system. *Child Development, 51,* 1215-1221.

White, E. (1985). *Teaching and assessing writing.* San Francisco: Jossey-Bass.

Winterowd, R. (1975). *Contemporary rhetoric: A conceptual background with readings.* New York: Harcourt Brace Jovanovich.

Witte, S. (1983). Topical structure and revision: An exploratory study. *College Composition and Communication, 34,* 313-341.

Witte, S. (1985). Revising, composing theory and research design. In S. W. Freedman (Ed.), *The acquisition of written language: Response and revision* (pp. 250-284). Norwood, NJ: Ablex.

Witte, S. (1987). Composing and pre-text. *College Composition and Communication, 38,* 297-425.

Wolf, D. P. (1985). Ways of telling: Text repertoires in elementary school children. *Journal of Education, 167,* 71-87.

Wolf, D. P. (1988). Opening up assessment. *Educational Leadership,* 24-29.

Yeh, S. (1998). Empowering education: Teaching argumentative writing to cultural minority middle-school students. *Research in the Teaching of English, 33,* 49-83.

# CHILDREN'S WRITING: RESEARCH AND PRACTICE

*Nancy Farnan*
San Diego State University

*Karin Dahl*
The Ohio State University

Inside the Educational Resource Information Center (ERIC) database are over 950,000 articles and documents. Our search of ERIC revealed 63,480 articles and documents on the subject of writing. In contrast, a similar search on the subject of reading revealed 116,621 articles and documents, nearly twice the number found in writing. Clearly, there has been extensive interest in reading research and practice that predates a similar interest in writing. This early interest in reading instruction is not surprising. Dating back to colonial America, society placed a high priority on reading. The reading of religious works was central to an individual's eternal salvation. Writing instruction came after children learned to read. Writing was considered an advanced skill and was not critical in religious education. When writing instruction did enter the curriculum, it emphasized penmanship and transcription of what had already been written. Additionally, writing was not a priority in the instruction of girls because it was considered necessary only if one planned to go to college or work outside the home. (For a history of reading and writing instruction, see Nelson & Calfee, 1998). In the last 10 years the disparity between interest in reading and writing has narrowed. Since 1990, 24,831 documents and articles have been catalogued under reading, and 22,941 were catalogued under writing. In this chapter we explore research that has implications for classroom practices and the teaching of writing. The central questions are, What do we know? about writing process, the role of writing in learning, the effect of technology on writing, writing assessment and interactions between writing and reading; we conclude by posing questions about what we still have to learn.

## WRITING–READING INTERACTIONS

The term *interactions* in the heading above is purposeful because we focus on the *interactive* nature of writing and reading (Fearn & Farnan, 2001). It is not on what is often called *integration* of the language arts, that is, putting writing and reading together in the same time and place and using both in the context of a lesson. This section is about writing and reading as naturally interacting language skills and on how the interaction can enhance development in both.

### How Writing Influences Reading

Marie Clay coined the term *emergent literacy* in 1966. In her work with young children, she observed that "writing plays a significant part in the early reading process" (Clay, 1975, p. 70), concluding that "if a child knows how to scan, how to study a word in order to reproduce it, and how to organize his writing of that word, he has the skills to deal with the detail of print" (p. 71). Her research showed that as children write, they develop certain skills and abilities: how to pay attention to print, organize their thinking as they explore print forms, develop a left–right orientation, analyze letters and sounds visually, understand what is important in a word in order to produce it in writing, and organize their behaviors to carry out a specific sequence of movements. She commented, "In the child's early contact with written language, writing behaviours seem to play the role of organizers of reading behaviours. . . . [which] appear to help the child to come to grips with learning to attend to the significant details of written language" (p. 3).

Clay (1975) isolated seven factors that emergent writers pay attention to in their writing:

1. *Copying Principle.* Early in their writing development, children attempt to copy words, demonstrating that they already know some words.
2. *Flexibility Principle.* Children experiment with letters and words to show their developing understandings of print (e.g., children's phases of invented or temporary spelling as they move toward using conventional print forms, Henderson, 1990).
3. *Recurring Principle.* Children often display their ability to use print by repeating words and letters in their early writing.
4. *Directional Principle.* As children learn to sequence letters one after another on a line, they display their learning of left–right directionality, important for reading and writing.
5. *Space Principle.* As children develop print awareness through reading and writing, they learn that part of the meaning making involves spaces between words.
6. *Generating Principle.* Children may begin early writing by simply having fun making marks on paper or whatever might be handy, but with experience in reading and writing they learn that the marks must be formed in certain ways and that they make meaning.
7. *Inventory Principle.* Children often pay attention to their own learning in systematic ways. For instance, they may write all the letters or all the words they know.

As Clay was doing her research in the 1970s in New Zealand, Chomsky (1976) was studying children in the United States Chomsky documented children's emergent writing and concluded that it contributed to their understandings of print. She found that children would attempt to write words based on their sounds before they could actually read. Chomsky suggested that for some children, writing might be a way into reading: "The printed word 'belongs' to the spontaneous speller far more directly than to children who have experienced it only ready made" (p. 64). Chomsky found that when children began writing without formal instruction in either reading or writing, the children knew some letters and sounds. They could also write their name and had a sense of linear sequencing of letters to make words. In addition, the adults around them were enthusiastic about children's language development and responded positively to what they wrote.

Hansen (1987) described writing's effect on reading: "Writing is the foundation of reading. . . . When our students write, they learn how reading is put together because they do it. They learn the essence of print" (pp. 178–79). Avery (1993) conducted research in her first-grade classroom and described how her students' reading and writing skills developed in mutually supporting ways. She noted that "children naturally incorporate context, visual, and phonetic clues to decipher their own writing, then transfer these strategies to the reading of books by professional authors" (p. 381). Over the past 35 years, research consistently points to the importance of the writing-reading interaction and its effect on reading development.

## How Reading Influences Writing

Smith (1983) wrote about "reading like a writer" and commented that "to read like a writer we engage with the author in what the author is writing" (p. 563). Readers notice the way words are spelled, the way the authors uses a phrase or sentence to create an image, how a certain word conveys the right connotation, and how a writer leads readers through a clear explanation of a complex process. Smith cautioned that although experienced readers often find themselves being aware of a text through a writer's eyes, novice readers may experience that phenomenon less frequently. If a novice reader is struggling with understanding words and constructing meaning, then that reader's attention is focused on the struggles rather than a writer's perspective.

In 1983, Eckhoff examined the effect of second-graders' reading on their writing. She conducted research in two schools, each using a different basal reading program, hypothesizing that what students read might have a powerful effect on their writing. One classroom used a basal reader in which the text was what Eckhoff referred to as "literary prose" (p. 611). It included longer sentences, often with complex structures. The text did not use controlled vocabulary or repetitive words and phrases. The other basal text, in contrast, included shorter, simple sentences and repetition of vocabulary. Children who read the simpler basal text used less elaboration, wrote one sentence per line, as was modeled in the text, and often began sentences with "And" and ended them with "too," patterns used in the text but that did not add linguistic complexity to their sentences. Students reading literary prose included complex verb forms, complex sentences, and infinitive and participial phrases. Although Eckhoff cautioned that her study was only exploratory, we agree with her that "the findings are striking and merit further investigation" (p. 615), taking into account such things as the way teachers teach writing and children's linguistic abilities.

In 1990, Dressel conducted similar research with fifth-graders. She read aloud three short detective novels to two groups of students. One set of books had been judged by experts in children's literature to be high-quality literature, whereas the books read to the other class were judged to be of lesser quality. Part of each read-aloud process included Dressel's drawing attention to reading like a writer. She highlighted what the author did to create the story and its genre features. After conducting the three read-alouds in each class, students were asked to write their own detective stories. Dressel found that those who heard the higher quality stories wrote stories that were judged to be better on literary elements of plot development, setting, character development, literary style, and mood.

Lancia (1997) conducted classroom action research with second-graders. The second-grade literacy curriculum included independent reading, guided reading, read-alouds, shared reading, teacher–student conferencing, and writing workshops. He found that students' "literary borrowings" (p. 474) were numerous and included using plot ideas from stories they read, characters, conflicts, plot devices, and genre characteristics. Lancia concluded that students' borrowings from literature "illustrate a lively interaction between reading and writing" (p. 471) and that "children made natural connections between their reading and writing through their daily interactions with books, as well as their conversations with fellow authors" (p. 475).

## The Writing-Reading Interaction in Book Clubs

McMahon and Raphael (1997) began working with book clubs because they wanted to develop a reading program that would engage students in reading and talking about books and that would motivate them to read. They began with certain assumptions: oral language and writing are a foundation for language acquisition and development; authentic reading (including use of quality literature), writing, and oral language activities are critical for language acquisition and development; the social aspect of reading and language development is an important element of a reading program, as individuals learn through interactions with one another; and learners must actively construct meaning through reading, writing, and talking about texts. Four essential elements emerged. One is that ideas from small-group discussions, the book clubs, should be shared with the larger reading community, such as an entire class. Two elements are reading and writing: reading a variety of texts, building reading skills, and writing, wherein writing supports a reader's thinking about the text. The fourth element is the book club itself, where readers meet in groups of three to five to discuss something commonly read.

Rocha (as cited in Fearn & Farnan, 2001) conducted research in a middle school classroom, asking students to write a one-page reflection after reading and before coming to the book club discussion. They were directed as a group to decide on a topic on which to focus their reflection, such as writing about characters' motivations or what students noticed as important. Rocha found that when students wrote prior to their conversations, their discussions were higher in categories of interpretation and evaluation, in which they cited reasons for their judgments. When groups neglected to write before coming to the book club, they tended to retell what they read and focus on details and literal information. They also reported that it was more difficult to contribute when they had not written beforehand and that they had difficulty staying on task.

## RESEARCH ON WRITING PROCESSES

Writing is process or, rather, a set of mental processes writers use when they write. *Process writing* is a redundant term because there is no such thing as *nonprocess writing*. Writing is process (Tobin, 1994), as are all complex behaviors. We speculate that the term *process writing* was coined as a reaction to the days when writing instruction consisted of three components: assign, write, and assess. The teacher assigned a work to write; students wrote something they thought would garner a high grade; and the teacher assessed the writing, with comments and corrections penned in red ink. Typically, another assignment followed, and the cycle began again. Writing instruction, most often labeled *composition*, worked for those for

whom the teachers' comments were instructive. "It was also a system that paid little attention to what young writers thought, valued, or did when they wrote" (Fearn & Farnan, 2001, p. 182). Information on writing processes comes from two sources: researchers and writers themselves.

In the 1970s, a revolution occurred in writing instruction, fueled by researchers such as Janet Emig (1971). Emig began with a creative process described by Wallas (1926), which included four stages: preparation, incubation, illumination, and verification. Emig connected those stages to Cowley's (1958), four stages in the composition of a story: germination of the story, conscious mediation, draft, and revision. From there, Emig theorized a four-stage description of writing process. It turned out, however, that Emig's subjects, eight 12th-graders, did not follow a linear, stage-bound process inferred in her theory. Instead, students' processes included hesitations and reformulations as they wrote, and she used the term *recursive* (meaning "to go back") to describe what she observed. She also suggested that at times the subjects seemed to exhibit forward thinking, or coming from "the foreconsciousness of the writer" (p. 58). Emig's research helped focus attention on the processes of writing. What had been viewed as product-oriented writing became process writing (Marshall, 1994).

Flower and Hayes (1980, 1981) proposed a model, generated from their research on think-alouds of college-age writers, that offered a complex look at writing processes and subprocesses. Their model illustrates the recursive and interactive nature of writing processes and consisted of three elements: (a) *planning*, setting goals and generating and organizing ideas; (b) *translating*, or attending to audience, tone, style and syntax, as well as to the motor demands of producing letters and words; and (c) *reviewing*, or evaluating and revising the text. These processes interact with the *task environment*, which includes the topic, audience, purpose for writing, and the text as it is produced. The processes also interact throughout writing with the *monitor*, which represents a writer's decisions about such things as generating and organizing ideas and deciding when to review. According to this model, writing processes do not occur in a linear progression; rather, they consist of complex subprocesses that occur interactively as writers work their way from the beginning of a writing to its culmination. The stage-bound model, then, that follows a progression of prewrite-write-revise/edit-publish, though seeming to provide a convenient instructional scheme for writing, is not a valid representation of how writing processes actually work.

Research by Bereiter and Scardamalia (1987) corroborated Flower and Hayes' (1980, 1981) model by suggesting that multiple demands compete for a writer's attention. They noted that the complexity of writing rests on "the interdependency of components, which requires that a number of elements be coordinated or taken into account jointly" (p. 133). Murray (1985) highlighted this complexity when he examined the role of the writing task itself in shaping a writer's processes. For example, the demands of a 15-minute quick-write relating an autobiographical incident would be quite different from writing a biographical sketch over several days, during which time the writer received input and feedback from a variety of sources. Influenced by more than the mental processes associated with producing a text, a writer is also affected by the task itself, which the Flower and Hayes model (1980, 1981) referred to as the task environment.

Interested in examining children's writing processes in a classroom context, Schneider (1997) conducted research on the writing strategies of five second- and third-grade children. Across an academic year, she examined the relationship between the children's writing strategies and the instructional contexts the teacher created. She found that each child made decisions about his or her writing and writing strategies in individual ways; each child's decision–making and strategy use varied with the instructional context and genre.

Underlying the teacher's writing instruction was the philosophy that children needed to use language and writing to explore and discover. Therefore, Schneider (1997) did not overlay a set of rigid guidelines on students' writing. For example, although story plans were available to help children plan stories, one child preferred and was encouraged to create stories in her head. Children were allowed to stop writing a piece if they felt they did not want to continue that particular work. As a result of documenting the interplay between the children's own writing processes and the instructional environment, Schneider concluded that "researchers need to reconceptualize child writers so that we are able to view them as individuals who are communicating thoughts, not writers performing a series of tasks" (p. 28). She also concluded that "teachers need instructional processes that complement children's idiosyncratic processes and build upon their understanding of written communication, not methods that force children into molds" (p. 7). The molds to which she referred included "contrived writing behaviors" (p. 5) such as students writing for the sake of pleasing the teacher and writing in predetermined procedural steps.

The Flower and Hayes model (1980, 1981), however, does not necessarily represent all of the components influencing writing processes. Cooper and Holzman (1989) were critical of the fact that the model did not account for the effect of social structures and classroom dynamics. They also questioned the value of using only think-aloud protocols to document writing processes. They preferred, as Schneider did (1997), to conduct research in an authentic, situated setting that considered both classroom activities and writers' processes.

Research on children's actions during composing shows that children are accomplishing specific kinds of social goals as they write. Composing is a ticket to social status, to inclusion in the group, or to defining one's writing identity within the classroom (Dyson, 1993). Children think about what is valued by the group and what has status in the writing community (Hudson, 1986; Dyson, 1993). They develop characters and personal topics that meet the social demands of their peer group (Finders, 1996; Schultz, 1994).

Research on writing processes seems to point to what Hillocks (1986) stated: [R]esearch demands that that we view composing as involving a variety of plans and subprocesses which are brought to bear throughout the composing process as they are needed. The evidence they present clearly contradicts textbook approaches, which often suggest arbitrary, discrete steps in composing: formulate a thesis, develop an outline, and write (p. 27).

He noted that research has established the importance of generating ideas prior to and during a writing, of engaging in goal setting, and of having criteria by which writers judge their texts and those of others, criteria that may "serve not simply to 'judge the text' but to guide its generation" (p. 24). Research suggests that these strategies are amenable to instruction. Scardamalia, Bereiter, and Goelman (1982) asked children to write on a topic as much as they could. When they stopped, they were given "contentless prompts," urging them to continue writing; and the children continued writing. When they stopped responding to the "contentless prompts," topic-specific questioning caused them to write even more. These focused prompts helped children access more information for writing, supporting the role of conferencing and collaboration in helping novice writers select information for a writing. Although writing comprises complex interactions among cognitive processes, sociocultural contexts, the task, the genre, and mode of writing, it appears that various instructional strategies can support young writers as they move from being novices to experienced writers.

## Composing Processes of Children in the Primary Grades

Several studies of composing in the primary grades show the playful nature of children's early writing efforts. Writing as play includes children discovering their intended meanings as they work with art media and as they experiment with the forms and functions of written language. Children may impulsively write a label on their picture or scatter words within their drawings. Stories may emerge in speech bubbles or phrases at the bottom of pictures. Often an early story may include several dimensions: talk about the story action, artwork produced while talking, and words actually written. When Graves (1981) conducted his landmark research on primary-grade writers, he observed children as they wrote, interviewed them before, during, and after writing, and took notes as children and teachers worked together. His conclusions were that the writing process for these young writers included a number of subprocesses associated with writing. These included topic selection, rehearsing, accessing information, paying attention to spelling and handwriting, reading, organizing, editing and revising. He noted that the youngest children playfully experiment with letters, words, spacing, and ways to use writing materials. Their activities are overt as they talk their way through writing, laboring over which letters to select and what to write next. Young children reread aloud what they have written as though they were cycling back to check meaning and get a running start into the writing that will come next.

Another source of writing research is Dyson's (1989, 1991, 1993) documentation of primary-grade writers over time. Her classroom-based case studies of primary-grade writers indicated that children take widely divergent paths as writers and are influenced by social relationships with their peers (Dyson, 1989). Her research documented the tensions between children's imaginations and experiences and the conventions of written language needed to communicate their meanings. Children grapple with the symbolic function of written language (How do I show my meaning?) while experimenting with its social function (Will my friends like this story?).

Dyson's (1993) research also described the social and cultural dimensions of children's writing development. Children use the cultural information they know from movies, television, cartoons, videos and neighborhood observations in their writing. Cultural material from the media is subject matter for writing (Dyson, 1999). Children respond to social pressures, even in the primary grades, to write in peer-accepted gender roles in order to place themselves within the child collective through their writing (Dyson, 1994).

## Composing Processes of Intermediate- and Middle-Grade Children

In the intermediate and middle grades a number of significant changes occur both in children's sense of the functions of writing and in their composing processes. McGinley and Kamberelis (1996) studied third- and fourth-graders at work in various writing activities and interviewed students and teachers. Their study found that as children expand their writing repertoires, they write mostly about personal experience and use writing to imagine possible selves, think about personal interests, and participate in the worlds of imaginary characters. Writing functioned for intermediate grade children as an arena for personal exploration and growth as children wrote about their own identities and possible social actions.

Research by Langer (1986) showed important shifts in children's composing processes during these years. She examined the strategies and structures of children's writing and reading at ages 8, 11, and 14 and analyzed children's think-alouds during composing. Her findings showed that intermediate-grade children focus on content, the ideas and concepts in their writing. Their think-alouds showed concern for what to include in writing and awareness of strategies used to get at meaning. Writing strategies for intermediate-grade children include four categories of activity:

1. *Generating Ideas*. Children are aware of relevant ideas and the processes needed to organize them.
2. *Formulating Meaning*. Children are developing their message with an eye to the needs of the audience as well as monitoring the language used to connect concepts.
3. *Evaluating*. Children are monitoring and reviewing the message constructed.
4. *Revising*. Children engage in thinking again about the meaning and structure of their writing.

## Composing Processes of Novice and Experienced Writers

Bereiter and Scardamalia (1987) found that one difference between novice and experienced writers lies in how they generate and interact with texts. In the knowledge-telling model, found with novice writers, writing processes are affected by the writer's knowledge and experiences. The writer begins with a task and topic ideas, and retrieves information that reflects "the straight-ahead form of oral language production and requires no significantly greater amount of planning or goal setting than does ordinary conversation" (p. 9). The researchers offered a self-report from a 12-year-old boy: "I have a whole bunch of ideas and write down until my supply of ideas is exhausted. Then I might try to think of more ideas up to the point when you can't get any more ideas that are worth putting down on paper and then I would end it" (p. 9). Bereiter and Scardamalia referred to this as the "what next" strategy.

The knowledge-transforming model represents a phenomenon experienced by more expert writers. According to this model, a writer's knowledge and the text interact, creating a problem-solving process in which knowledge is transformed during the thinking and writing; writing processes involve a "two-way interaction between continuously developing knowledge and continuously developing text" (Bereiter & Scardamalia, 1987, p. 13). In this model, writing processes function in such a way that text produced is based on what a writer already knows and also on ideas and knowledge that are generated as text is created.

Bereiter and Scardamalia (1987) found these models highlighted the different ways novice and experienced writers planned writing. Regardless of the time allowed, elementary-age children tended to begin writing almost immediately and stopped when they ran out of ideas. Tenth-graders behaved similarly, but did vary their start-up times somewhat when the length requirement for a writing increased. Adults, however, altered their writing processes considerably when given more time to write and the length requirement increased. The researchers' assumption was that more experienced writers were planning, particularly when writing longer pieces. They cautioned, however, that the exact nature of the thinking and planning were not evident in their observations.

Evidence suggests that planning is strongly shaped by development. Bereiter and Scardamalia (1987) presented novice and expert writers with a strategy for planning. Students were directed to take notes on their ideas before writing but not actually write the text. Younger writers tended to simply transcribe their notes later directly as the text while adolescents seemed to work at a more global abstract level, planning before writing. These results seemed to hold for other investigations and other specific strategy interventions outside the classroom including comparisons of novice and expert writers. Bereiter and Scardamalia (1987) concluded that through early adolescence children did not seem to be able to separate their planning from actual text writing; their plans simply became the texts.

## Learning From Experienced Writers

Numerous texts document experienced writers, self-reports of their writing, among which are texts edited by Lloyd (1987), Murray (1990), and Plimpton (1989). In addition, well-known children's authors have written about their lives as writers, including Katherine Paterson (1989) and Helen Lester (1997), whose self-report is in the form of a picture book written for children. These self-reports illustrate the idiosyncratic nature of writing and the way individuals mobilize their writing processes. Lloyd (1987) and Murray (1990) group writers' self-reports around themes, such as why writers write and where they get their ideas for writing. Murray noted that writers contradict one another as they talk about writing tasks. Roald Dahl reported that writing is rewriting, and William Styron reported that he perfects each sentence and paragraph as he goes along (Murray, 1990). At the other extreme, Frank O'Connor attempted simply to get anything down on paper, even if it's "rubbish," which gives him something with which to work. Lloyd Alexander described the research he does before writing fiction (Lloyd, 1987). However, he puts the information aside when he begins to write. He has absorbed so much information that he does not need his notes. Jane Yolan, on the other hand, reported her planning process differently:

I actually physically write for only an hour a day, but I'm writing my story all the time—when I'm driving the car, or taking a shower; when I first wake up in the morning, or when I am about to fall asleep. I'm thinking about ideas and processing them, and that's all part of the writing. (Lloyd, 1987, p. 97)

Individual writers are influenced, as Flower and Hayes' model (1980, 1981) suggested, by knowledge and experiences, by the task, and by the environment. (For more information and a comprehensive bibliography on writers' self reports, see Fearn & Farnan, 2001.)

## TEACHING THE CRAFT OF WRITING

In our view, the craft of writing includes the specific work of thinking about and generating the text itself—word choices, spelling, sentencing, organization, and strategies to address audience. It also includes more global matters associated with revising and understanding genre. Finally, we include, as a craft matter, some of the instructional concerns of the writing classroom: what happens in writing conferences, in collaborations between writers, and in writers workshops as teachers and students work together.

### The Role of Audience in Craft Development

Our interest in audience awareness is a developmental one. We recognize that writers often use their sense of audience to make decisions about what to include and how to present ideas. The critical issue seems to be the role that development plays in children's awareness of audience and whether young children are simply too egocentric to think of audience while writing. Langer (1986) addressed this developmental issue by asking children in Grades 3, 6, and 9 to answer questions about their writing and talk about audience. She found that although younger writers knew their role was to communicate meaning to an audience, they were more concerned about the neatness and length of their writing than with audience. Older writers in this study showed awareness of audience and were concerned whether their audience would find their writing boring or too difficult.

In a more recent investigation by Frank (1992), fifth-graders were asked to revise an advertisement to communicate effectively with two different audiences, a third-grade reader and an adult. This study showed that fifth-grade children were able to target the audience groups and write effectively for each. The conclusion was that elementary students need the experience of writing for audiences outside their own classrooms as they learn to communicate effectively.

### Understanding of Genres

Recent research on genres broadens and reshapes traditional notions. Chapman (1999) argued that we need to move beyond form and structure, seeing genres as social, situated, and thereby responsive to the setting in which they are experienced and actively learned by doing. Her recommendations were to expand children's genre learning across subject areas by using writing for a broader range of functions. These included writing to manage and organize activities, writing description in science observations, using narrative as a tool for extending social studies (biographical accounts), and seeing that narrative in language arts is not the only genre worthy of study. Chapman's research on the genres with first-grade children showed a close connection between the classroom context, specifically the works chosen by the teacher, and the writing of children. Her analyses also showed that first-graders produce writings with the focus on objects rather than events (Chapman, 1995). Their writing includes lists, labels, attribute series (e.g., I like dogs, I like cats, I like birds), verse, and word plays. Chapman's research supported earlier findings by Newkirk (1987), in which nonnarrative forms of writing in the early grades were studied. Newkirk found that the expository forms evident in first grade (list and label) were not used as frequently by writers in the third grade. He noted that these first-grade efforts were related to sorting and display of information and concluded that "exposition may well begin not as speech written down, but as the appropriation and extension of dominant literate forms—the list and the label" (p. 141).

More recent genre research has looked at genre learning and the influence of specific scaffolds on children's writing. Kamberelis and Bovino (1999) examined stories and biology reports about animals written by children in kindergarten, and first and second grades. Participants wrote stories and animal reports on their own and were also asked to recall a well-known fictional story and factual science report and write down the texts from memory. The authors anticipated that the recalled (scaffolded) writing would contain richer language and more complete genre structures than the stories and reports written in the unscaffolded condition. The findings were that children in these early grades have a "good grip on the cultural convention of narrative discourse genres, but a more nascent sense of the cultural conventions of informational genres" (p. 161). The authors concluded that children's understandings of genre are emerging in these early grades and are supported by genre experiences. Most children in this study produced more well formed texts in the scaffolded condition in which they were recalling and writing a text they already knew.

These findings for children in the early grades are closely related to research addressing genre knowledge in older children. Langer (1986) investigated genre knowledge across third-, sixth-, and ninth-grade writers. Her analysis showed a developmental gap between children's facility with stories and with reports. For third-graders, story structures in writing are already in place, with time orderings often shaping the overall story structures that children use. In contrast, children's ways of structuring reports change radically among third-, sixth-, and ninth-graders. Although third-graders' reports show simple thesis and elaboration structures, sixth- and ninth-graders show more organizational facility with reports. They are able to embed multiple pieces of information, and to elaborate. Factors that seem to influence genre writing across this array of studies include purpose and social context, children's sense of the writing task, including the instruction, as well as their reading experiences and maturation.

## Revision in Children's Writing

In our view, the critical information about children's knowledge of revision involves three issues: (a) understanding the influences of age and expertise on children's revisions so that effective information can be demonstrated in classrooms and supported in classroom writing programs, (b) determining whether there are support systems or writing experiences that can successfully facilitate children's revisions, and (c) figuring out the young writer's perspective on revising in relation to the writing event. The body of research on revision in children's writing is mostly about writing with paper and pen, though a few studies address computer revisions. We have yet to experience a generation of children whose main writing tool is the computer and whose revision strategies include such computer manipulations as merging drafts, moving text, deleting, and printing out alternative versions.

We know that primary-grade children begin to revise as soon as they begin to write. They cross out words and erase others, add new words within the text, and write new text at the end of their pieces. (See Fitzgerald, 1987, for a comprehensive review of revision research). Many writers in the primary grades view revision as a process of copying the whole text over and are resistant to the need for change. Early case study research by Calkins (1983) showed that within a rich instructional environment that includes individual conferences, sustained writing activity, and demonstrations, a young writer in third and fourth grade can produce increasingly complex revisions. These revisions include, among others, thinking through alternative leads as an internalized process, identifying parts of an initial draft to expand with details in a subsequent draft (circle and expand), and using a dividing-line strategy for eliminating story sections.

A number of studies address revision by presenting specific kinds of procedural support. A line of research by Bereiter and Scardamalia (1987) involved work with fourth-, sixth-, and eighth-grade children who are taught specific revision routines, such as compare, diagnose, and choose, in order to analyze and revise text. Their work shows that children can use these executive routines for evaluating and revising their writing. Some computer-based research involves specific programs that prompt children to look at particular aspects of a draft. The results of research on these revision-prompting programs indicate that children using them tend to make more global revisions than writers composing on their own (Diaute, 1986).

Among the reference materials focusing on revision instruction and the revision problems at the elementary level is *After the End: Teaching and Learning Creative Revision*, in which Lane (1993) presented lessons that show revision strategies and includes specific writing activities to be used in instruction.

## Instructional Concerns for the Writing Classroom

Although many topics could be addressed as instructional concerns in the elementary writing program, for the purpose of this chapter we select three that are of particular interest: what happens in writing conferences, what we're learning about writing collaborations, and what new directions are occurring in writing workshop programs.

A study of small-group writing conferences (Fitzgerald & Stamm, 1992) used fixed questions to guide children's discussions of each other's writing: What was the piece about? What did you like about it? What comments or suggestions do you have for the author? The teacher contributed suggestions for revision along with those made by children within the conference. Researchers kept track of revisions made in relation to conference activity and found that the less experienced writers tended to follow conference suggestions for revisions. The group conferences provided a specific direction for change and indicated ideas for revision. Interestingly, the most knowledgeable young writer in this study tended to ignore revision suggestions by the small group and by the teacher. Instead he engaged in his own flurry of revisions. This study pointed up the value of the group conference as a scaffold and the complexity of children's revision decisions. Ownership of writing and at-the-moment interests are both factors shaping children's decisions.

Within the research on individual writing conferences is a particularly controversial study (McCarthey, 1994) that looked closely at one teacher's conferencing along two dimensions: how in tune conference participants were with each other (synchrony) and how productive the conferences were in terms of helping writers learn to make changes. After observing and videotaping conferences, the analysis focused on the match between teacher recommendations and student revisions. As would be expected, most of the children studied used the teacher's ideas about writing and even drew on them later in their own conferences with younger children. They demonstrated a synchronous relation to the teacher. The child who did not conform to this pattern was new to writing workshop routines and produced work that was not viewed as good writing by the teacher. The conferences with this child were marked with conflict, and teacher recommendations presented a dilemma for this writer. The difficulty was how to please the teacher yet not write about the painful subject that the teacher suggested as an alternative writing topic. A number of key questions were provoked by this investigation: What is the relation between the teacher's image of a good text and an emerging writer's ideas? What provisions are there for children who for one reason or another are not adept at thinking and talking about writing processes and their own strategies for writing? The need for classroom research about these aspects of teaching is critical as teachers attempt to work effectively in conferences with individual learners.

The research on writers working together addresses whether children can provide real help for one another and whether they will stay on task. A number of studies show that the social context of the writing classroom and influence of writers on each other can be a positive force (Dyson, 1989, Schultz, 1994). Gere and Abbott (1985) investigated writing groups at 5th, 8th, and 11th grade and found that peers stayed on task and talked about both content and process. The authors suggested that this productive talk among peers could enable writers to be more aware of their choices and processes as writers.

The counterargument, however, surfaced in a study of third-graders (Lensmire, 1994). He noted that social outliers of the group were mistreated by peers in the workshop setting. Conferences contained peer cruelty, and fictionalized writings became not-so-veiled attacks on less popular students. Lensmire recommended close monitoring of conferences and suggested alternatives to sole reliance on an audience of peers. This cautionary trend was echoed in research with junior high girls (Finders, 1996). Her research traced the literate underlife of girls by looking at writing activities and peer talk within social cliques. In this study, peer pressures shaped the ways that girls wrote and shared their work. Because the peer group ethic privileged the private and marginalized the public, group conferencing and sharing in writing workshop became problematic. This research alerts us to the differences between student and adult perspectives and the need to look closely at classroom practices.

Writing workshop programs are the focus of a number of suggested new instructional directions. Graves (1944), a decade after publishing *Writing: Teachers and children at work* (1983), revised his original notions of writing workshop by giving a less central role to writing conferences and noting that significant instruction comes through the social interactions of the writing classroom. He also noted that "although listening to children is still the heart of the book, I think we know better when to step in, when to teach, and when to expect more of our students" (1994, p. xvi).

Other shifts in writing workshop programs include more comprehensive genre studies where children are immersed in reading, studying, and writing in specific genres over time (Calkins, 1994) and more elaborated roles for writing in connection with the literature program (Harwayne, 1992).

Recent works written for teachers also show an expansion of information about the craft of writing and teaching young writers in writing workshops. These classroom-based books are rich in materials about what writers at particular grade levels do, what issues they grapple with, and how instruction can be conducted in workshop programs (Avery, 1993; Fraser & Skolnick, 1994; Rief, 1992; Routman, 2000).

## RESEARCH ON WRITING TO LEARN

Research highlights the role writing plays in learning across the curriculum. The writing-to-learn process is based on constructivist principles (Newell, 1998), which have as a foundation the deceptively simple idea that knowledge is actively constructed by a learner. Although the concept may seem simple, processes associated with knowledge construction are not. Constructivist theorists, including Jean Piaget (1970), Lev Vygotsky (1986), and Jerome Bruner (1966), described learners as active constructors of meaning and knowledge. They described the complex interplay between an individual's prior knowledge and experience and new experiences, resulting in new learning.

The following are assumptions of constructivist instruction: (a) Learning occurs through learners' active construction of knowledge; (b) learners are constantly weighing new information against previous understandings; and (c) learners work through discrepancies and confusions on their own and with others, coming to new understandings (Brooks & Brooks, 1993). Brooks and Brooks (1993) described the constructivist paradigm this way: "Constructivist teaching practices . . . help learners to internalize and reshape, or transform, new information. . . . Deep understanding occurs when the presence of new information prompts the emergence or enhancement of cognitive structures that enable us to rethink our prior ideas" (p. 15). Images of the engaged learner, hands-on instruction, and project-based learning are directly connected to a constructivist view of learning.

Britton (1970) talked about the pivotal role language plays in they way we shape or interpret experiences. He described the role of writing as a way for learners to reflect on and "wrestle with" their thoughts as they work to understand and clarify. Compared with research in other areas of literacy development (e.g., spelling, emergent reading and writing, oral language development, and use of reading strategies), research on the writing-to-learn process has been relatively scarce. However, some research has been conducted.

Connolly and Vilardi (1989) edited a collection of research reports about science and mathematics instructors who used the writing-to-learn process in their classrooms. As Gopen and Smith (1989) incorporated writing into a calculus class, they concluded the following: Writing can be incorporated into mathematics classes. Thinking and the expression of thoughts are so intertwined that one cannot be good unless the other is, as well. If students did not have the language needed to reflect on a concept and could not clearly express ideas associated with it, that was an indication of the quality of their thinking about the concept. Writing can help students better understand mathematics (in this case, calculus).

Although writing can assist learning (Cooper & Odell, 1999), Langer and Applebee's (1987) research illustrated that not all writing has the same effect on learning. When teachers ask students to write short responses to questions, students tend not to do a lot of rethinking or reflecting on content. Instead, they look for the information needed to answer a question in texts they are reading and copy that information. The task does not require students to think about relationships among ideas and extend those ideas in any way. In contrast, writing tasks can cause learners to explore ideas, rethink and reflect on what they are learning, explain, and clarify. These are analytic writing tasks "that require students to compare and contrast, evaluate, explain, and draw conclusions. In other words, students are not asked simply to restate information and ideas, but to think about them" (Dahl & Farnan, 1998, p. 73).

Langer and Applebee (1987) collaborated with 23 science, home economics, English, and social studies teachers who wanted to incorporate more writing into their content areas. The researchers concluded that "different kinds of writing activities lead students to focus on different kinds of information, to think about that information in different ways, and . . . to take different kinds of knowledge away from their writing experiences" (p. 135). Short-answer study questions lead to short-term recall of information, with little or no reflection on a text, and no consideration of relationships among ideas. Writing tasks that require learners to manipulate ideas lead to less memorization of information but to more in-depth understanding. This is critical for learning, as memory for ideas is long term, as are understandings about relationships among ideas and concepts. Analytic writing requires learners to compare and contrast, evaluate, explain and elaborate, and draw conclusions. Learners are not asked just to restate ideas but to think about them. Research indicates that if writing tasks are going to support learning, they must require students to think about content (Langer & Applebee, 1987). The researchers also concluded that students must have specific understandings in relation to writing tasks across the curriculum (Langer & Applebee, 1987). For example, it is important for learners to understand why the task is valuable and how it will support their learning, so they may see writing as a natural part of the learning process. It is also important that learners have the knowledge and skills to complete the writing task and that teachers provide modeling and feedback for the writing-to-learn process.

Rosenshine, Meister, and Chapman (1996) reviewed intervention studies that examined the value of summary writing to support learning. They discovered that the power of writing a summary lay in the fact that it requires readers to evaluate information and make decisions regarding what represents important ideas and what are supporting or descriptive details. Summary writing requires that learners arrange those ideas in a way that reconstructs the main points clearly and logically. The researchers found, however, that it is not sufficient to ask students to write a summary. They must be taught how to do it.

## RESEARCH ON WRITING ASSESSMENT

Research on writing assessment provides critical input for classrooms, schools, and school districts. Spandel and Stiggins (1997) made the statement that "assessment—good assessment—has *very* little to do with grades. Assessment feeds and supports our grading system, but that is far from its most important function" (p. 23). Cooper and Odell (1999) elaborated: "A grade or numerical ranking represents simply a final judgment about how

well or poorly one has written a particular piece. . . . Evaluation, by contrast . . . specifically addresses all the issues that a grade or numerical score cannot" (p. viii). Research on writing assessment is about the efficacy of writing assessments that exist for the purpose of documenting learners' achievement, of addressing issues that can directly inform curriculum and instruction.

### Validity and Reliability of Writing Assessments

As with other kinds of assessments, writing assessment must be reliable and valid. Assessment in writing is often viewed as subjective, that is, subject to an individual's (i.e., a teacher's) judgment during the process of scoring (Spandel & Stiggins, 1997), and therefore not trustworthy. This is in contrast to assessments that are considered to be objective, such as multiple-choice tests. However, Spandel and Stiggins (1997) pointed out that objectivity and fairness are not synonymous. Just because an assessment is objective does not mean that it accurately measures what it purports to measure. A multiple-choice test about writing would not reflect a writer's ability to compose an effective persuasive essay. In addition, objectivity itself is a myth, given that someone, somewhere, created the multiple-choice items based on his or her own, or a group's, judgments and decisions.

Assessments driven by individual judgment may be subjective, but that does not rule out reliability and validity. In writing assessment, *reliability* refers to raters' judgments being applied consistently across papers and across time. *Validity* refers to whether assessment actually assesses the skills and abilities valued in effective writing (face validity). It also refers to whether an assessment will predict the way an individual would perform on another assessment conducted for the same purpose (concurrent validity) and predict similar performance in a different situation (e.g., performance in a writing course). Finally, it refers to whether an assessment measures skills and abilities that are considered essential to being an effective writer (construct validity) (Spandel & Stiggins, 1997). Researchers have examined the reliability and validity of two common assessment processes in writing: holistic evaluation and portfolio assessment.

Holistic assessment is a criteria-driven procedure whose purpose is to rank or sort written work (Cooper & Odell, 1977). Based on this definition, a rater assesses a piece of writing by doing one or more of the following: (a) matching it with another piece in a graded series of pieces, (b) scoring it for the prominence of certain features important to that kind of writing, or (c) assigning it a letter of number grade (Cooper & Odell, 1977, p. 3). Raters often use a rubric as a guideline that provides a set of criteria by which to judge a writing. On the rubric, points are assigned to the criteria and papers are given a score.

Cooper and Odell (1977) reviewed research on holistic scoring and concluded that reliability can be a problem. There are likely to be wide differences in the scoring of a piece of writing across a group of raters, even if they are experienced teachers. Cooper (1977), however, found that holistic scoring can become reliable when raters have similar backgrounds and expertise and when, through training, they hold similar views regarding what represents quality work when judged against specific criteria. He cited research conducted nearly 60 years ago that found raters' reliability on scoring could be increased "from a range of .30 to .75 before training to a range of .73 to .98 after training" (p. 18). Cooper explained that when inter-rater reliability approaches the .90 level, scores can be considered useful for program evaluation and for assessing individual growth in writing.

It appears that if holistic assessment is to be useful, time must be devoted to training raters, who not only should have experience reading many papers but who also must collaborate with other raters to ensure similar perspectives to guide their judgments. Cooper (1977) also recommended that in order to reliably assess a writer's performance, at least two papers from that individual should be scored because writers can vary in their writing performance. Another caution centers on the scoring of papers for items related to grammar, capitalization, and punctuation. Although these items may be a component of a holistic scoring rubric, when raters are not properly trained in the use of scoring guidelines, raters tend to overemphasize the mechanics, compared with considerations for other important components, such as organization, use of detail and elaboration, and clarity of purpose.

Another form of writing assessment, the portfolio, has emerged recently. Although there are various ways to define and structure portfolios (Camp, 1993; Paulsen & Paulsen, 1994), when they are used for assessment purposes, reliability and validity again become important issues. Herman and Winter (1994) reviewed 89 articles on portfolios and found only seven that provided data regarding the technical quality of portfolios, including reliability and validity. Rater reliability is critical, as with holistic scoring, particularly if portfolio results are to be used to make program or learner decisions. Herman and Winter reported that ratings could be considered useful indicators of student work only in districts where teachers had training as evaluators and collaborated with their peers. The researchers concluded that certain factors were associated with reliable scoring of portfolios. Those included having specific and clear criteria for portfolio development and evaluation and having evaluators with a high degree of expertise regarding student performance.

Another indicator of effective portfolio assessment is what Spandel and Stiggins (1997) refer to as concurrent validity. In their work through the National Center for Research on Evaluation, Standards, and Student Testing, Gearhart, Herman, Baker, and Whittaker (1992) found little relationship between students' portfolio ratings and their scores on a standardized writing assessment. In addition, when portfolios were scored two ways, one a holistic score of the entire portfolio and the other an average of the individual portfolio pieces, the general portfolio scores tended to be higher. Half of the students who had been judged as "masters" on the general score were placed in a lower classification when their individual portfolio writings' scores were averaged. These results call into question the validity of portfolio assessment.

## Research on Assessment of Writing Conventions and on Teachers' Comments

Little research has been done on the effect of assessing writing conventions in student writing, but what has been done indicates that it has little direct influence on students' writing achievement. Thirty years ago, Adams (1971) studied two 12th-grade classrooms, one of which placed little emphasis on grammar and mechanics. Instead, the teacher emphasized students' creativity and freewriting. In the other classroom, the teacher used a more formal instructional approach to writing and heavily emphasized grammar and mechanics. In this classroom, every error in students' compositions was marked and returned for student correction. Although Adams found no gain in students' writing achievement in the more informal classroom, in the classroom where students focused on every error in every composition, the quality of their writing decreased. Other studies have also failed to find positive effects of such assessment and instruction on the quality of student writing (Elley, Barham, Lamb, & Wyllie, 1976; Fry, 1972; Goddin, 1969).

In Hillocks' (1986) extensive review of writing research, he reported on various assessment processes and their effect on writing quality. Regarding teacher comments on student papers, research indicates that they do little to improve writing. Hillocks reported no difference, whether the comments were negative or positive. However, consistently negative comments frustrate young writers and make them feel negative about themselves as writers. Perhaps teacher comments have not been effective because of another element reported in Hillocks' review. In their comments on students' papers, teachers tended to comment on everything—from spelling, grammar, mechanics, organization, clarify, and word choice. On the other hand, when comments focused on a particular issue (e.g., use of description, sentence structure), whether the comments were positive or represented corrective feedback, they often resulted in improvement in writing quality. This effect was enhanced when classroom instruction addressed issues related to the corrective feedback.

Straub (1997) examined 142 first-year college students' reactions to teacher comments on their writings. He reviewed research on teacher response to student writing and identified principles of effective response. Students were shown a sample paper, on which 20 expert teachers made comments, using an emerging theory of teacher response as their guide. The college students then responded to a 40-item questionnaire about their preferences for teacher comments. Students were equally interested in receiving comments on content, purpose, organization, sentencing, wording, and mechanics. However, they did not like negative comments in which the teacher criticized the writer's ideas. The students disliked comments that sounded like sarcasm or advice that indicated the teacher's beliefs or ideas were superior to the student's. Straub found that students appreciate praise but appreciate even more comments that are detailed, instructive, and corrective, as long as they focus on making the writing better. Straub reported that these students' views of teacher comments were similar to those found in previous research.

# THE EFFECT OF TECHNOLOGY ON WRITING

Questions about the effect of technology on writing evolve as the technology evolves; concerns arise now that 5 years ago would not have been considered. Word processing affects not only how we write but what we write. In addition, other forms of technology have influenced the composition–technology interaction. There was a time when the computer had two basic uses in education. It served a word processing function, and it functioned as an electronic workbook, where students clicked on the correct multiple-choice item in response to a question. It was assumed that once writers had a degree of keyboard expertise, the computer would replace pen-and-paper writing, circumventing the need for handwriting skills and making revision and editing easier. It was not until the 1980s that researchers began to explore the relationship between writing and technology and concluded that technology may transform our ways of thinking, knowing, and communicating (McDaniel, 1987; Ong, 1982).

LeBlanc (1993) gave an example of computer-assisted communication software affecting processes of writing. He offered as an example Anne and Mike DiPardo's HyperCard-based system, which allows users to make complex links among ideas, where students "write essays with build-in buttons which open up windows that would include students' asides, further explanations, and other information they wish to link out from the text" (LeBlanc, 1993, p. 74). Also, links to certain screens contain suggestions for writers, encouraging them to reread and reflect on their ideas and brainstorm, as well as provide suggestions for introductions and conclusions. By encouraging certain processes and activities, the software can affect how writers think about their writing and use writing processes. LeBlanc argued that teachers should have a voice in creating software that writers might use, in order to ensure that the interaction between writing and technology is productive.

Baker and Kinzer (1998) conducted research "to better understand its [technology's] benefits and areas where caution is warranted" (p. 429). They particularly focused on the effects on children's writing processes in classrooms where technology was in the classroom as part of the classroom routine. They also were interested in examining children's multimedia compositions as part of their writing processes.

The computer made writing and revisions easier because, according to the students who had some keyboarding skills, typing was easier than learning cursive. The researchers also concluded that when using a computer, students' writing processes were dynamic and nonsequential. The researchers speculated that teachers' perceptions of paper-and-pencil composing as being a linear process might affect the teaching of writing and that "technology may require teachers to allow and expect students to draft before they brainstorm, to revise an already published composition, and to revisit the 'steps' of the writing process as a dynamic rather than a sequential process" (Baker & Kinzer, 1998, p. 435). The researchers observed that when composing with a computer, students rarely considered a composition finished. They often went back to files to update and work on products they had previously "completed" or that were works in progress.

Baker and Kinzer (1998) also found that student collaboration seems to happen more frequently when compositions are accessible for reading on computer screens. In this context, peers read one another's compositions and give feedback, whether solicited or not. Similarly, other researchers have found that spontaneous peer feedback increased when students' writing was publicly displayed on a computer screen (Bruce, Michaels, & Watson-Geogeo, 1985; Dickinson, 1986). In these studies, it was observed that students frequently worked together to compose on the computer.

Interestingly, Baker and Kinzer (1998) discovered that technology tended to foster a product-oriented approach toward writing, as students worked on ways to present their work to their peers. Although the composing was facilitated by the use of video, animation, narration, and sound effects, students tended to focus more on the clip art choices, or what they might scan in to make the product attractive, than on the content. This was true even when students became proficient at using the technology, such as PowerPoint presentation software and hypertext and hypermedia software, and even after the novelty of it had worn off. A work presented may look impressive and sophisticated because of its use of graphics, video, and so forth; but the teacher often had to work with students to ensure the content was substantive.

The researchers concluded that there were concerns associated with the technology. Sometimes students were frustrated with the software and therefore gave up on a particular writing task. Hawisher (1986) found, similarly, that when composing at a computer, students were frustrated by only being able to read the text on the screen. She suggested that perhaps it would be useful for writers to print out their work occasionally, in order to see and evaluate their text globally. Baker and Kinzer (1998) discovered that another problem with the technology–writing interaction was students' frustration with software when, for example, they realized they could not revise a page or line of text that was saved as a graphic; it could only be deleted or replaced. Students also found the computer limiting when they wanted to take notes or brainstorm in the midst of a composition, so they often used the technology in conjunction with paper and pencil.

Haas (1990) found that the kinds of notes writers made were different when they composed on a computer. Writers who used pencil and paper tended to make more elaborate notes that contained arrows and other graphics that helped them think about the structure and organization of their writing. When they used a computer, their notes tended to be more textlike and to be focused almost exclusively on content, not on organization. Haas concluded that perhaps the best situation would be to combine the use of pencil and paper with use of the computer when composing or that computer software should routinely contain features that would help writers plan and organize their ideas.

Cochran-Smith, Kahn, and Paris (1991) found that many variables affect the relationship between computers and writing, including writers' keyboarding skills, teachers' instructional goals and attitudes toward computers, and organization of the classroom. The researchers concluded that students who used computers for writing tended to revise more, write longer compositions, and produce text that was freer of surface errors related to the conventions of writing compared to those who used pencil and paper. In his review of 32 studies, Bangert-Downs (1993) found similar results. Students using computers tended to write longer compositions that were judged to be of higher quality than compositions written with pencil and paper. He also reported that word processing itself does not necessarily result in better compositions but that the teacher's learning goals, the type of instruction, and opportunities for practice all affected outcomes of writing.

Jones and Pellegrini's (1996) research with first-graders' writing and use of computers found that students' narratives were more cohesive when composing with the computer and that students paid more attention to word choice and putting ideas together. Based on similar findings, Cochran-Smith, Kahn, and Paris (1990) concluded that with the technology, children were freer to think about writing as "verbal composition" (p. 240)— that is, to think about words and ideas.

In a study of middle school students' expository writing, Owston, Murphy, and Wideman (1992) found that the essays were of higher quality but not significantly longer than when using paper and pen. To find out what made the writings better, they looked at spelling differences between word processed and handwritten papers. They found no significant spelling differences. They did discover that when using word processing, students revised throughout their writing. Furthermore, students tended to do the most revising during the initial drafting of a writing, before their texts were considered finished. This is similar to Baker and Kinzer's (1998) research, in which they concluded that students used their writing processes interactively when using technology. Owston et al.'s (1992) found that the revisions students made tended to be small changes within sentences and paragraphs, rather than large structural changes and reorganization.

When Daiute (1986) looked at middle school students' revisions as they used word processing, she found that they corrected more errors than when using pen and paper. Their revisions were also noticeably different. Students tended to add to their writing more often with word processing, especially at the end of a writing. She found that initial drafts tended to be shorter with word processing than with pen and pencil, but that their final papers tended to be longer. She also found that students' revisions tended to be at the micro level. However, when the word processing software prompted students to reflect on their thinking and writing, the revisions were more apt to include significant changes in organization.

Technology seems to be a promising tool for writing for children with learning disabilities. The technology has been found to be especially useful when it provides aids for thinking and writing, such as prompts to support reflection, instructions on procedures for writing, and spelling and grammar checkers. Using such software, students were better able to work with their texts and do such things as add and delete ideas (Morocco, 1987; Morocco, Dalton, & Tivnan, 1992).

Lewis, Graves, Kieley, and Ashton (1998) conducted a study to discover whether the keyboard itself represented an obstacle for students with special needs. When compared with students writing by hand, they found that using word processing lowered students' fluency rate of text entry by about 50%. However, different technologies seemed to have different effects on students' fluency. The researchers looked at five groups of students. One group, without instruction in its use, used the standard QWERTY keyboard. Another received instruction in keyboarding. A third used an alternate keyboard with keys arranged alphabetically. The fourth group used a word prediction program, Co:Writer, to enter text; and, finally, a fifth group used this same word prediction program with the speech synthesis feature activated. The researchers found that the fourth group had the highest rate of text entry and also showed improvement in writing quality. The next most effective strategy was using the QWERTY keyboard along with keyboarding instruction, and here students showed the greatest improvement in writing.

Finally, it is important to look at other forms of writing that have emerged with technology, specifically, networked discourse, or computer-mediated communication (CMC). Computer-mediated communication listservs, bulletin boards, chat rooms, and newsgroups. Beach and Lundell (1998) conducted a study with 12 seventh-graders who used CMC for 3 months. Students communicated in groups of four, each sitting at separate computers. In these synchronous exchanges, students wrote and received immediate responses from their peers. One student commented, "If you have something important to say, then you don't get interrupted" (p. 96).

Beach and Lundell (1998) saw greater equity among students in their participation, when compared to classroom discussions. Shy students who were intimidated by face-to-face interactions felt more secure. As they shared their responses to stories they were reading, students posed questions for each other and offered ideas for the purpose of eliciting a response. Students felt left out or ignored if they posed an idea that was not addressed in subsequent interchanges among the group members. The focus in their interchanges was always on the evolving message, their agreements and disagreements, but not on a finished product. The researchers concluded that in this classroom, CMC centered on specific reasons for communicating, such as establishing social relationships, sharing reactions to a text, debating an issue, brainstorming ideas, collaborating on a project, and providing feedback to one another on their writing.

Beach and Lundell (1998) offered several insights regarding use of CMC in the classroom: Provide time for students to play and experiment with the technology so that the novelty will wear off, allowing them to be able to concentrate on communication. Keep CMC groups small so that conversations are manageable. Model for students the various response modes. For example, show students how to briefly restate the message they're responding to and how to disagree while being sensitive to others' perspectives. Students must understand that when communication is not face to face, misunderstandings can easily occur, which in CMC is referred to as "flaming," defined as using language in a way that is hurtful or insulting to another person, even if it is unintentional. The researchers also recommend using printouts of chat transcripts to help students reflect on their conversations, by recalling ideas shared, evaluating the appropriateness of social roles and their participation, and generating questions based on the conversations. Beach and Lundell reported that "through participation in CMC exchanges, students are being transformed as readers and writers. They can evaluate those transformations as part of a portfolio self-reflection by reviewing transcripts from the beginning, middle, and end of a course" (1998, p. 108).

## QUESTIONS THAT REMAIN

Although a body of research may begin to respond to some questions and reveal trends, research also raises questions. In this final section of the chapter, we raise what we think are some relevant questions and directions for future research in the area of writing:

1. How does the writing–reading interaction change as children's reading and writing skills develop? What best practices take advantage of the writing–reading interaction?

2. What instructional processes best support novice writers' writing processes? What is the effect of such support on a novice's writing development?

3. How do conferences best support students' writing development and bolster student independence?

4. What is the role of metacognition and an individual's understanding of his or her writing processes affect that individual's thinking about writing and writing development?

5. Literacy across the content areas includes a focus on the interaction between writing and content area reading and learning. What practices, regarding the role of this interaction, best support reading and learning in all content areas?

6. Does facilitating composing with images and other modalities and sign systems promote literacy or illiteracy, "as traditionally defined" (Baker & Kinzer, 1998, p. 435). What new definitions of written literacy emerge with the technology-writing interaction? Does traditional composition suffer, by traditional standards, or it enhanced? What is gained or lost?

7. What is the role of facilitative devices associated with word processing on students' writing processes and writing quality?

8. Strong emphasis on the assessment and instruction of grammar and mechanics has not had a positive effect on writing achievement. Is the problem the result of overemphasis on grammar and mechanics in writing by marking every item on every paper, is it because of the type of instruction designed to address this aspect of writing, or is it a combination of these issues? What ways of assessing and designing instruction to address grammar and mechanics might have a positive influence on writing achievement?

9. What types of assessment processes provide valid and reliable judgments regarding writing quality? How can writing assessment be designed to ensure that students, teachers, parents, administrators, and the general public receive useful and trustworthy data regarding writing quality at the individual, classroom, school, state, and national levels?

10. What effects do teacher comments have on students' thinking about their writing and on their writing achievement?

## *References*

Adams, V. A. (1971). *A study of the effects of two methods of teaching composition to twelfth graders.* Unpublished doctoral dissertation. Illinois, Champaign-Urbana.

Avery, C. (1993). *. . . And with a light touch: Learning about reading, writing, and teaching with first graders.* Portsmouth, NH: Heinemann.

Baker, E., & Kinzer, C. K. (1998). Effects of technology on process writing: Are they all good? In T. Shanahan & F. V. Rodriguez-Brown (Eds.), *Forty-seventh yearbook of the National Reading Conference* (Vol. 47, pp. 428–440). Chicago, IL: National Reading Conference.

Bangert-Downs, R. L. (1993). The word processor as an instructional tool: A meta-analysis of word processing in writing instruction. *Review of Educational Research, 63,* 69–93.

Beach, R., & Lundell, D. (1998). Early adolescents' use of computer-mediated communication in writing and reading. In D. Reinking, M. C. McKenna, L. D. Labbo, & R. D. Kieffer (Eds.), *Handbook of literacy and technology: Transformations in a post-typographic world* (pp. 93–112). Mahwah, NJ: Lawrence Erlbaum Associates.

Bereiter, C., and Scardamalia, M. (1987). *The psychology of written composition.* Hillsdale, NJ: Lawrence Erlbaum Associates.

Britton, J. (1970). *Language and learning.* New York: Penguin.

Brooks, J. G., & Brooks, M. G. (1993). *In search of understanding: The case for constructivist classrooms.* Alexandria, VA: Association for Supervision & Curriculum Development.

Bruce, B., Michaels, S., & Watson-Geogeo, K. (1985). How computers change the writing process. *Language Arts, 62,* 143–149.

Bruner, J. (1966). *Toward a theory of instruction.* New York: W.W. Norton.

Calkins, L. M. (1983). *Lessons from a child.* Portsmouth, NH: Heinemann.

Calkins, L. M. (1994). *The art of teaching writing.* Portsmouth, NH: Heinemann.

Camp, R. (1993). The place of portfolios in our changing views of writing assessment. In R. Bent & W. Ward (Eds.), *Construction versus choice in cognitive measurement: Issues in constructed response, performance testing, and portfolio assessment* (pp. 136–152). Hillsdale, NJ: Lawrence Erlbaum Associates.

Chapman, M. (1995). The sociocognitive construction of written genres in first grade. *Research in the Teaching of English, 29,* 164–191.

Chapman, M. (1999). Situated, social, active: Rewriting genre in the elementary classroom. *Written Communication, 6,* 461–490.

Chomsky, C. (1976, May). *Approaching reading through invented spelling.* Paper presented at the Theory and Practice of Beginning Reading Instruction. University of Pittsburgh, Learning and Research Development Center. (ERIC Document Reproduction Service No. 15 5630)

Clay, M. M. (1966). *Emergent reading behavior.* Unpublished doctoral dissertation, University of Auckland, New Zealand.

Clay, M. M. (1975). *What did I write?* Portsmouth, NH: Heinemann.

Cochran-Smith, M., Kahn, J., and Paris, C. L. (1990). Writing with a felicitous tool. *Theory Into Practice, 29,* 235–247.

Connolly, P., & Vilardi, T. (Eds.) (1989). *Writing to learn: Mathematics and science*. New York: Teachers College Press.

Cooper, C. (1977). Holistic evaluation of writing. In C. R. Cooper & L. Odell (Eds.), *Evaluating writing: Describing, measuring, judging* (pp. 3-31). Urbana, IL: National Council of Teachers of English.

Cooper, C. R., & Odell, L. (Eds.) (1977). *Evaluating writing: Describing, measuring, judging*. Urbana, IL: National Council of Teachers of English.

Cooper, C. R., & Odell, L. (Eds.) (1999). *Evaluating writing: The role of teachers' knowledge about text, learning, and culture*. Urbana, IL: National Council of Teachers of English.

Cooper, M., & Holzman, M. (1989). *Writing as social action*. Portsmouth, NH: Boynton/Cook.

Cowleg, M. (Ed.) (1958). *Writers at work: The Paris review interviews*. New York: Penguin Books.

Dahl, K., & Farnan, N. (1998). *Children's writing: Perspectives from research*. Newark, DE: International Reading Association.

Daiute, C. (1986). Physical and cognitive factors in revising: Insights from studies with computers. *Research in the Teaching of English, 20,* 141-159.

Dressel, J. H. (1990). The effects of listening to and discussing different qualities of children's literature on the narrative writing of fifth graders. *Research in the Teaching of English, 24,* 397-414.

Dyson, A. H. (1989). *Multiple worlds of child writers: Friends learning to write*. New York: Teachers College Press.

Dyson, A. H. (1991). Viewpoints: The word and the world— Reconceptualizing written language development or, do rainbows mean a lot to little girls? *Research in the Teaching of English, 25,* 97-123.

Dyson, A. H. (1993). *Social worlds of children learning to write in an urban primary school*. New York: Teachers College Press.

Dyson, A. H. (1994). The ninjas, the X-men, and the ladies: Playing with power and identity in an urban primary school (Tech. Rep. No. 70). Berkeley, CA: Center for the Study of Writing.

Dyson, A. H. (1999). Coach Bombay's kids learn to write: Children's appropriation of media material for school literacy. *Research in the Teaching of English, 33,* 367-402.

Eckhoff, B. (1983). How reading affects children's writing. *Language Arts, 60,* 607-616.

Elley, W. B., Barham, I. H., Lamb, H., & Wyllie, M. (1976). The role of grammar in a secondary school English curriculum. *Research in the Teaching of English, 10,* 5-21.

Emig, J. (1971). *The composing processes of twelfth graders*. Urbana, IL: National Council of Teachers of English.

Fearn, L., & Farnan, N. (2001). *Interactions: Teaching writing and the language arts*. Boston: Houghton Mifflin.

Finders, M. (1996). "Just girls": Literacy and allegiance in junior high school. *Written Communication, 13,* 93-129.

Fitzgerald, J. (1987). Research on revision in writing. *Review of Educational Research, 57,* 481-506.

Fitzgerald, J., & Stamm, C. (1992). Variation in writing conference influence on revision: Two cases. *Journal of Reading Behavior, 24,* 21-49.

Flower, L. S., & Hayes, J. R. (1980). Identifying the organization of writing processes. In L. W. Gregg & E. R. Steinberg (Eds.). *Cognitive processes in writing* (pp. 3-30). Hillsdale, NJ: Lawrence Earlbaum Associates.

Flower, L. S., & Hayes, J. R. (1981). A cognitive process theory of writing. *College composition and communication, 32,* 365-387.

Frank, L. A. (1992). Writing to be read: Young writers' ability to demonstrate audience awareness when evaluated by their readers. *Research in the Teaching of English, 26*(3), 277-298.

Fraser, J., & Skolnick, D. (1994). *On their way: Celebrating second graders as they read and write*. Portsmouth, NH: Heinemann.

Fry, D. J. W. (1972). The effects of transformational grammar upon the writing performance of students of low socioeconomic backgrounds. *Dissertation Abstracts International, 32,* 4835-A.

Gearhart, M., Herman, J. L., Baker, E. L., & Whittaker, A. K. (1992). *Writing portfolios: Potential for large-scale assessment*. Los Angeles: National Center for Research on Evaluation, Standards, and Student Testing. (ERIC Document Reproduction Service No. ED 350312)

Gere, A. R., & Abbott, R. (1985). Talking about writing: The language of writing groups. *Research in the Teaching of English, 19,* 362-381.

Goddin, M. A. P. (1969). A comparison of the effect on student achievement of a generative approach and a traditional approach to the teaching of English grammar at grades three and seven. *Dissertation Abstracts International, 29,* 3522A.

Gopen, G. D., & Smith, D. A. (1989). What's an assignment like you doing in a course like this? Writing to learn mathematics. In P. Connolly & T. Vilardi (Eds.), *Writing to learn mathematics and science* (pp. 209-230). New York: Teachers College Press.

Graves, D. (1981). *A case study observing the development of primary children's composing, spelling and motor behaviors during the writing process* (Final report, NIE Grant No. G-78-0174. ED218-653). Durham: University of New Hampshire.

Graves, D. (1994). *A Fresh look at writing*. Portsmouth, NH: Heinemann.

Graves, D. (1983). *Writings: Teachers and children at work*. Exeter, NH: Heinemann.

Hansen, J. (1987). *When writers read*. Portsmouth, NH: Heinemann.

Harwayne, S. (1992). *Lasting impressions: Weaving literature into the writing workshop*. Portsmouth, NH: Heinemann.

Haas, C. (1990). Composing in technological contexts: A study of notemaking. *Written Communication, 7,* 512-547.

Hawisher, G. (1986). Studies in word processing. *Computers and composition, 4,* 6-31.

Henderson, E. H. (1990). *Teaching spelling* (2nd ed.). Boston: Houghton Mifflin.

Herman, J. L., & Winters, L. (1994). Portfolio research: A slim collection. *Educational Leadership, 52,* 48-55.

Hillocks, G., Jr. (1986). *Research on written composition: New directions for teaching*. Urbana, IL: ERIC Clearinghouse on Reading and Communication Skills.

Hudson, S. (1986). Context and children's writing. *Research in the Teaching of English, 20,* 294-316.

Jones, I., & Pellegrini, A. D. (1996). The effects of social relationships, writing media, and microgenetic development of first-grade students' written narratives. *American Educational Research Journal, 33,* 691-718.

Kamberelis, G., & Bovino, T. (1999). Cultural artifacts as scaffolds for genre development. *Reading Research Quarterly, 34*(2), 138-170.

Lancia, P. (1997). Literary borrowing: The effects of literature on children's writing. *The Reading Teacher, 50,* 470-475.

Lane, B. (1993). *After the end: Teaching and learning creative revision*. Portsmouth, NH: Heinemann.

Langer, J. A. (1986). *Children reading and writing: Structures and strategies*. Norwood, NJ: Ablex.

Langer, J. A., & Applebee, A. N. (1987). *How writing shapes thinking*. Urbana, IL: National Council of Teachers of English.

LeBlanc, P. (1993). *Writing teachers/writing software: Creating our place in the electronic age*. Urbana, IL: National Council of Teachers of English.

Lester, H. (1997). *Author: A true story*. Boston: Houghton Mifflin.

Lewis, R. B., Graves, A. W. Kieley, C. L., and Ashton, T. M. (1998). Word processing tools for students with learning disabilities: A comparison of strategies to increase text entry speed. *Learning Disabilities Research and Practice, 13,* 95-108.

Lensmire, T. (1994). When children write: Critical re-visions of the writing workshop. New York: Teachers College Press.

Lloyd, P. (Ed.) (1987). *How writers write.* Portsmouth, NH: Heinemann.

Marshall, J. (1994). Of what does skill in writing really consist? The political life of the writing process movement. In L. Tobin & T. Newkirk (Eds.), *Taking stock: The writing process movement in the '90s* (pp. 45-56). Portsmouth, NH: Heinemann.

McCarthey, S. J. (1994). Authors, text, and talk: The internalization of dialogue from social interaction during writing. *Reading Research Quarterly, 29,* 200-231.

McDaniel, E. (1987). Bibliography of text-analysis and writing-instruction software. *Journal of Advanced Composition, 7,* 139-169.

McGinley, W., & Kamberelis, G. (1996). Maniac Magee and Ragtime Trumpie: Children negotiating self and world through reading and writing. *Research in the Teaching of English, 30,* 75-113.

McMahon, S. I., & Raphael, T. E. (1997) (Eds.). *The book club connection: Literacy learning and classroom talk.* New York: Teachers College Press; Newark, DE: International Reading Association.

Morocco, C. (1987). *Final report to the US Office of Education.* Washington, DC: Special Education Programs, Educational Development Center.

Morocco, C., Dalton, B., & Tivnan, T. (1992). The impact of computer-supported writing instruction on 4th grade students with and without learning disabilities. *Reading and Writing Quarterly: Overcoming Learning Disabilities, 8,* 87-113.

Murray, D. M. (1985). *A teacher teaches writing* (2nd ed.). Boston: Houghton Mifflin.

Murray, D. M. (Ed.) (1990). *Shoptalk: Learning to write with writers.* Portsmouth, NH: Heinemann.

Nelson, N., & Calfee, R. C. (Eds.) (1998). *The reading-writing connection: Ninety-seventh yearbook of the National Society for the Study of Education* (Vol. 97). Chicago: University of Chicago Press.

Newell, G. (1998). "How much are we the wiser?" Continuity and change in writing and learning. In N. Nelson & R. C. Calfee (Eds.), *The reading-writing connection: Ninety-seventh yearbook of the National Society for the Study of Education* (Vol. 97, pp. 178-202). Chicago: University of Chicago Press.

Newkirk, T. (1987). The non-narrative writing of young children. *Research in the Teaching of English, 21,* 121-144.

Ong, W. J. (1982). *Orality and literacy: The technologizing of the world.* New York: Methuen.

Owston, P. D., Murphy, S., & Wideman, H. H. (1992). The effects of word processing on students' writing quality and revision strategies. *Research in the Teaching of English, 26,* 249-276.

Paterson, K. (1989). *The spying heart: More thoughts on reading and writing books for children.* New York: E. P. Dutton.

Paulsen, F., & Paulsen, P. (1994). *A guide for judging portfolios.* Portland, OR: Multnomah Education Service District.

Piaget, J. (1990). The science of education and the psychology of the child. New York: Orion Press.

Plimpton, G. (Ed.) (1989). *The writer's chapbook: A compendium of fact, opinion, wit, and advice from the 20th Century's preeminent writers.* New York: Viking.

Rief, L. (1993). *Seeking diversity.* Portsmouth, NH: Heinemann.

Rosenshine, B., Meister, C., & Chapman, S. (1996). Teaching students to generate questions: A review of the intervention studies. *Review of Educational Research, 66,* 181-221.

Routman, R. (2000). *Conversations.* Portsmouth, NH: Heinemann.

Scardamalia, M., Bereiter, C., & Goelman H. (1982). The role of production factors in writing ability. In M. Nystrand (Ed.). *What writers know: The language, process, and structure of written discourse* (pp. 173-210). New York: Academic Press.

Schneider, J. J. (1997). *Undoing "the" writing process: Supporting the idiosyncratic strategies of children.* Paper presented at the annual meeting of the 47th National Reading Conference (December). Scottsdale, AZ. (ERIC Document Reproduction Service No. ED 417 425)

Schultz, K. (1994). "I want to be good; I just don't get it": A fourth grader's entrance into a literacy community. *Written Commnunication, 11,* 381-413.

Smith, F. (1983). Reading like a writer. *Language Arts, 60,* 558-567.

Spandel, V., & Stiggins, R. J. (1997). *Creating writers: Linking writing assessment and instruction* (2nd ed.). New York: Longman.

Straub, R. (1997). Students' reactions to teacher comments: An exploratory study. *Research in the Teaching of English, 31,* 91-119.

Tobin, L. (1994). Introduction: How the writing process was born— And other conversion narratives. In L. Tobin & T. Newkirk (Eds.), *Taking stock: The writing process movement in the '90s* (pp. 3-11). Portsmouth, NH: Heinemann.

Vygotsky, L. (1986). *Thought and Language.* Cambridge: MIT Press.

Wallas, G. (1926). *The art of thought.* New York: Harcourt Brace Jovanovich.

# IMAGINATIVE EXPRESSION

## Betty Jane Wagner
### National-Lewis University

The focus of this chapter is research on oral and written discourse that is primarily imaginative. One could argue, of course, that all expressive discourse, or even all discourse for that matter, is at least partly imaginative. Certainly all writing at its best in all genres, expository as well literary, captures personal voice and creative perspective. On the other hand, poetry, as well as fiction, can serve a wide range of expository aims, in addition to literary ones. However, to limit the scope of this chapter, imaginative discourse is confined to educational drama, performing texts, and the writing of poems, fictional narratives, and plays—the aim of discourse Britton (1970) termed poetic. This includes the whole "let's pretend" function as Halliday (1977) distinguished it from his other six functions of language. "The imaginative function of language . . . is the [one] whereby the child creates an environment of his own . . . a world initially of pure sound, but which gradually turns into one of story and make-believe and let's pretend, and ultimately into the realm of poetry and imaginative writing" (p. 20). This imaginative function often co-occurs with others, of course, so the scope of this chapter unavoidably overlaps with most of the material in the chapters in this Part of this *Handbook*. The focus on imaginative discourse in a separate chapter highlights its importance and provides a place to consider educational drama, which is not a part of other chapters.

The term *educational drama* refers to any informal, improvisational group role-playing, almost always under a teacher's leadership, for the purpose of learning. Oral interpretation, storytelling, or choral reading are included in this chapter as responses to literature, but no other responses to reading imaginative discourse are covered since they are reviewed elsewhere in this volume. Also omitted from this chapter is a consideration of writing solely to express personal feeling, opinion, or actual experience as well as such expressive discourse as freewriting, brainstorming, listing, clustering, or making journal entries as prewriting for informative or persuasive discourse.

First, a caveat: By separating a discussion of imaginative expression from chapters on language, literature, speaking, listening, reading, and writing, this *Handbook* might suggest a view of the field of language arts as a set of separate skills strands rather than as an integrated interweaving of all of them. However, the editors' goal is a practical one: For the purposes of clarity and analysis, the focus in each chapter is on a separate goal of language arts and English. Therefore, it is only the organization of this book that does not represent the constructivist view that sees language as a vehicle for thinking and learning of all subjects. One should never forget that the fountain of imaginative expression should splash over all of the whole curriculum.

In this discussion of imaginative expression, claims for the centrality of this type of discourse come first. Then follow discussions of effective teaching strategies, the effects of educational drama on language arts, and examples of effective and ineffective instructional strategies for the development of imaginative writing.

## CLAIMS AND PERSPECTIVES

Major theorists have asserted that imaginative discourse is central to language arts development: Barnes (1968), Britton (1970), Moffett & Wagner (1983), not to overlook the guiding philosopher of the early decades of this century, Dewey (1959). Moreover, Piaget (1945/1962), Vygotsky (1967), and Bruner (1983) showed how pretend play, especially the use of objects in an on-literal fashion, parallels cognitive development.

Most English teachers were lured into their profession in the first place by imaginative discourse, what Dryden (1998) termed that "fairy kind of writing which depends only upon the force of imagination" (*King Arthur*, Dedication). However, this profession seems to need continual reminders to "reclaim the imagination" (Berthoff, 1984) and to recognize Susanne K. Langer's insight: "Imagination is the primary talent of the human mind, the activity in whose service language was evolved."

Despite repeated calls to imaginative expression and English for personal growth, there worthy goals get shoved back in public perception until the nurturing of imaginative expression is seen as a luxury society can ill afford. At best, imaginative expression in school is justified as simply a way to develop fluency in preparation for the sterner stuff that is the real business of school. In some quarters, policymakers with this narrower view of schooling relegate imaginative discourse to early elementary grades, elective options, or programs for the gifted and talented. The rest of the students, it is argued, especially those in schools with low standardized test scores, need a narrower curriculum, one geared toward test preparation and low-level skill development. Thus, the very children who most need the stimulation and inspiration that comes from imaginative expression are the least likely to receive it. Instead, they are all too often subjected only to direct instruction. This view reflects, of course, the larger society's focus on global competition in the marketplace and the misperception that higher academic standards mean more skill and drill. The creative, socially adept, and morally responsible workers the society needs will, of course, be more likely to emerge from schools that nurture students' imaginations and spirits as well as their intellects—a view that has always been a part of US educational theory at least since the Report of the Committee of Ten in 1894 (Kantor, 1975). As Howell (1982) noted, "the place given to 'creative expression' in the curriculum is a barometer of the society's attitudes towards spontaneity, freedom, and individuality" (p. 16).

The apex of commitment to imaginative expression was in the 1920s and 1930s. The Progressive movement in education reflected the larger society's values. Creative expression received a powerful shot in the arm from the Anglo-American Conference at Dartmouth College in 1966, after which there was a flurry of activity in response to the call for more imaginative expression in schools. Innovative materials for the classroom were bodied forth, such as Moffett's *Interaction* in the early 1970s, a widely acclaimed but short-lived language arts and reading curriculum, which emphasized educational drama and expressive writing.

A few current signs point to a resurgence of public affirmations advocating more literature and dramatic art in the schools, such as publications like the National Endowment for the Arts' (1988) *Toward Civilization*, and standards for the arts that many states are incorporating into their state academic standards. Advocates for imaginative expression argue that what makes a difference in students' lives is not just "cultural literacy," as defined by E. D. Hirsch (1984) among others, but cultural *renewal*. Through imaginative expression, students make a cultural heritage their own, first by choosing among what should be available to them—a rich array of attractive alternatives—and by creatively transforming what they select into something that is personally meaningful.

Few studies have been reported of effective teaching strategies that focus solely on imaginative expression—either in educational drama or in writing poems, fiction, or play scripts. This is not surprising in light of the fact that the goal of such discourse is divergent, not convergent, thinking, and so does not lend itself to easy measurement of either student achievement or teacher effectiveness.

Furthermore, when the effect of educational drama or creative writing is assessed, too often the measuring tool is not apt. Piaget's (1945/1962) stages of development are not appropriate for measuring growth in imaginative expression because the cognitive end state he posits, although comparatively easy to measure, is not the same end-state as the goal of imaginative expression. Bruner (1986) recognized that the world of the humanities is a separate one from that of science, and therefore has a different end state as a goal. This means that students engaging in educational drama or imaginative writing are not following a mode of problem solving familiar to scientists, nor is it appropriate to measure their achievement by the same standards. This view is increasingly gaining favor largely due to the advances in cognitive psychology and the widespread respect for a constructivist theory of learning. Educational psychology is finally moving beyond the society Moffett (1979) viewed in the 1970s as out of balance with its overemphasis on linear, analytic thinking which skews schooling (p. 115). The postmodernist shift to multiple perspectives and personal meaning making has reenergized teachers and scholars in the disciplines of the humanities and the arts.

## Development of Imaginative Expression

When a teacher aims for imaginative expression, he or she is inevitably drawn into a consideration of the development of artistic sensibility. The teacher's work at least in part must be to help students become artists. Such a teacher must enable students to learn how to grapple with material, reorder it, *reconstruct* it, as Dewey (1959) or Kelley (1984) would say, or to make of it an object of *personal knowledge*, in Polyani's (1962) words. Archambault (1968) and Heathcote (Wagner, 1976) saw the teacher as primarily a catalyst for students' artistic as well as academic development. Students are improvisational players—making something of their own by and mixing their labor with the inspiration the teacher gives and discipline he or she imposes. What is artistic growth in imaginative expression, and what are its stages of development?

Imaginative expression begins even before a child can use language. Examples are popular infant games like peekaboo and deliberate child-initiated fantasy such as the "play-face" mode of interaction as that Britton's (1983) granddaughter adopted even when she could say only a few words. When she hunched up one shoulder and looked slightly askance with a gleam of mischief in her eye, she felt free to pretend to misbehave. This play-face behavior disappeared when she was a little older and could understand and tell stories. Before they are three, many children can tell surprisingly complete imaginative stories (Applebee, 1978; Pitcher & Prelinger, 1973; Scollon & Scollon, 1981). Preschoolers characteristically engage in highly imaginative play and enjoy hearing, telling, and enacting fantasies (Paley, 1987). Emergent literacy studies document the vitality of imaginative discourse in kindergarten and first grade (Dyson, 1986; Harste, Woodward, & Burke, 1984). Many teachers report their primary children much prefer the imaginative to the transactional or nonfiction aims of discourse.

To assess the effectiveness of teaching strategies to develop imaginative expression, inasmuch as it differs from teaching other areas of the curriculum, one needs to understand how imaginative expression develops. Such research has only recently begun to emerge. Comprehensive longitudinal studies are needed to determine and to chronicle stages in the growth of the divergent thinking and artistic creation that is the goal of imaginative expression. Such developmental research will depend on the collaboration of educators, developmental psychologists, and artists—poets, fiction writers, actors, and playwrights. The end state for the artist is verisimilitude and evocative power; this is not the same ideal as the end-state for the scientist. Each operates in a different possible world (Bruner, 1986).

Moreover, the kind of intelligence required to develop as an artist differs from that of the scientist. H. Gardner's (1983, 1985) theory of multiple intelligences has a rich heuristic value for researchers in language arts. By positing appropriate end states of development that are different for each of his different intelligences, he provided those who study or teach English with a new way to envision their purview. If students are progressing toward an end state of *dramatic* or *linguistic* artistry, then their teacher is effective.

For example, an actor needs to have several highly developed intelligences: linguistic, interpersonal, and bodily kinesthetic. Dramatic competence encompasses the ability to represent with gesture, to have a facial expression or movement stand for something else. Thus, pantomime development can be seen as moving from a preschool child's spreading his arms wide and swooping with abandon about the room as a jet plane in spontaneous fantasy play to the precise gesturing of Marcel Marceau's pensive plucking of a petal from an imaginary daisy.

Colby's (1988) work in describing the development of dramatic intelligence as a U-shaped trajectory is a provocative extension of H. Gardner's (1983, 1985) work, one that could guide future studies of growth in dramatic or linguistic expression and of appropriate teaching strategies for each stage. Colby posited successive reorganizations of understanding that account for, for example, growth from the preschool stage of *being* a character to the middle childhood stage of *playing* a character, to the adolescent stage of returning to the "notion of *being* a character, but on a higher level and with the discoveries of the previous stages available" (p. 183).

Interestingly, Colby's (1988) U-shaped trajectory in development for school-age students is inverted in the growth of the spontaneous pretend play of early childhood. Cognitive psychologists have found that of all the types of play young children spontaneously engage in (functional, constructive, pretend, and games with rules), the proportion of time spent in pretend play increases steadily from the 2nd year of life until around 7 years; then it declines, largely because games with rules replace it. Spontaneous pretend play moves from solitary to social or interactive pretense. Children who have drama instruction in school often begin their study at about age 7, so for them the spontaneous play of the preschool years is replaced by teacher-led drama. Colby characterizes this middle childhood stage as that of *playing* a character. It is as if children see acting as a game with rules, which is their predominant mode of play at this age. Only later do they return to a greater identification with a character.

Similar developmental studies of imaginative writing need to be conducted. H. Gardner (1985) posited the poet as the epitome of what he terms a person with *linguistic intelligence*. Development of imaginative expression in language is toward an ever greater sensitivity to style, composition, balance, cadence of sound, and grace as well as an ever greater power to embody experience in language.

## Implications for Teaching

If the end state of linguistic or dramatic intelligence is different from the end state of other intelligences, then perhaps teachers of imaginative expression must themselves be aware of and capable of using strategies central to growth in dramatic arts or language. They need to show students what dramatic and linguistic craft looks like, engaging with them more like masters modeling imaginative expression for apprentices than like presenters of completed products. The more transparent they can make their own creative processes, the more their apprentices will be able to experiment with the teacher's strategies for their own ends. The masters are not building a scaffold, to use a currently popular metaphor, for students to stand on as they are led step by step to solve the same problems the teacher has long since mastered. Rather, the teachers are publicly struggling anew with their material with the goal of creating a product unique in the world. Teachers need to model the way an artist works, taking risks and facing new challenges in front of their students. For example, when a teacher and students together improvise a drama, both "engage in problem solving in a deep personal way through the fictional present" (Courtney, 1985, p. 49). When students write imaginatively, subject and object distinctions blur. Through the imagination, they create a new entity out of the many different elements of their experience.

In both improvisational educational drama and in writing, the individual is intuitively aware of the relatedness of the self and the object of creation. The process of imagining generates feeling and enables students to align feeling with ideas, images, and action. Teachers need to model this imaginative process.

Thus, teaching for growth along an artistic spectrum is somewhat different from teaching to achieve other goals of the English curriculum. A presentation or transmission lesson may actually inhibit rather than foster the growth of imaginative expression. As Peters (1987) put it, "Direct instruction and similar strategies that have successfully improved basic skills may not be as effective as other strategies for creativity, complex problem solving, or independent thinking" (p. 36). In a Rand report, Wise, Darling-Hammond, McLaughlin, and Bernstein (1984) noted that no one unidimensional construct called effective teaching exists. The more complex and variable one considers the educational environment, the more one relies on teacher judgment to guide the activities of classroom life, and the less one relies on generalized rules for teacher behavior (pp. 10–11). It follows that the more varied human intelligences and their ideal end states are, the more varied are effective teaching strategies.

What kind of teacher judgment can most aptly guide students' growth in imaginative expression, and how can it be described? Harris (1973) found that students increase their own creative behavior if their teacher is flexible, divergent, or creative—in contrast to students whose teachers do not have these characteristics. Witkin (1974) was convinced that teachers need to understand the praxis of creative expression and must "enter the creative process at the outset" (p. 69). He contended that teacher involvement is essential to the setting, making, holding, and resolving of expressive acts.

In summary, although claims for the centrality of imaginative expression in the school curriculum are solid, few studies exist of effective teaching strategies to foster its growth. Studies of the stages in the development of dramatic and linguistic intelligence need to be done so an understanding of effective teaching can be grounded in this knowledge. The rest of this chapter is a summary of recent studies of educational drama and imaginative writing.

## EDUCATIONAL DRAMA

Educational drama in the classroom is a type of oral imaginative expression through which students work together in a fictive enterprise. The purpose is to learn through drama, not to produce a play for an audience, and in this way it differs from theater programs in schools. By its nature, educational drama is a social medium. It is not exclusively imaginative, however. Some social dramatic play, especially in infants and toddlers, is merely a ritualistic reenactment of real-world scripts. In the elementary, as opposed to the preschool classroom, educational drama is usually led by a teacher either in or out of role. Such drama builds on the experience of informal pretend play that usually arises spontaneously in early childhood.

In this section are claims for educational drama and an overview of major studies of its effectiveness on oral language, reading, and writing. Studies of educational drama have shown its effect on skills of recognized value outside the field of drama, such as oral language and literacy. Presenting arguments to justify drama in the schools is not new, however; in 16th-century Europe, schoolboys' performance of plays was defended as an aid to the study of the art of rhetoric and classical drama.

Despite the claims for and research supporting it, however, very little informal classroom drama is actually taking place in schools. This section concludes with a report of surveys of educational drama in schools and suggestions for further study.

### Claims

Oral language is commonly held to be the seedbed for later growth in literacy. Drama particularly has been advocated as a way to develop not only oral language facility but also reading and writing as well (Barnes, 1968; Britton, 1970; Britton, Burgess, Martin, McLeod, & Rosen, 1975; Creber, 1965; Dixon, 1975; Heathcote, 1981; Hoetker, 1969; Moffett & Wagner, 1983; Verriour, 1986; Wagner, 1976, 1990). Both observational and empirical studies appear to be consistent with these claims, although many of the existing studies are not comparable or are faulty in method (Galda, 1984).

### Effects on Oral Language

Studies show that educational drama can offer a range of different language contexts, each of which calls forth a different mode of expression and thus enhance language growth (Benson, 1990; Byron, 1986; and others). In drama, children also use language for a wider range of purposes than in typical classroom talk (Carroll, 1988; Felton, Little, Parsons, & Schaffner, 1984). Drama also "appears to have an extremely beneficial effect on role taking ability," which shows an awareness of audience and is usually associated with growth in effective communication (Kardash & Wright, 1987, p. 17).

During their dramatic play, even preschoolers are able to negotiate meanings using metacommunication. In the process of maintaining the "let's pretend" frame, they use language in a highly sophisticated way, cueing their fellow players that they expect them to respond appropriately to the pretend world they are creating together (Giffin, 1994).

Pellegrini (1980, 1982) and his colleagues did a series of studies with lower socioeconomic children in kindergarten through second grade to examine the effect of dramatic play on a wide range of language and cognitive skills. They show that children engaging in symbolic play use literate language and thus are doing orally what they will later need to transfer to writing. They tend to delineate roles and props precisely at the beginning of play episodes, typically defining pronouns linguistically, introducing topics explicitly, and clarifying roles when they are ambiguous. Because drama involves explicitly separating symbols from the concepts they stand for, Pellegrini (1984) suggested it may facilitate the use of explicit language.

Dialogue within a drama challenges participants to use language in new ways. The frustration of an obstacle can lead a child to sharpen the edges of the words he has heard but not yet used. He learns the effect of his words by trying them out on others. Rhetorical style is honed on the whetstone of response. Like actual conversation, improvised drama provides feedback and pressure to reshape an utterance to achieve the desired effect.

Twenty-five of 32 quasi-experimental or correlational studies of the effects of drama on oral language development found in the literature show drama improves or correlates with improvement of oral language (Brown, 1992; McIntyre, 1957; Norton, 1973; Paley, 1987; Smilansky, 1968; Smith & Syddal, 1978; Snyder-Greco, 1983; Stewig & Young, 1978; Vitz, 1984). Seven studies show no significant improvement in oral language after drama (Dunn, 1977; Kassab, 1984; Stewig & Vail, 1985; Youngers, 1977).

What follows are results of some of the most important studies. Smilansky's (1968) pioneering research on the effects of drama training by adults on oral language and on other areas of the cognitive and social development of disadvantaged Israeli 3- to 6-year-olds shows significant improvement in both oral language and social behavior. Snyder-Greco (1983) showed that kindergarten to third-grade language-disordered children who engage in drama make a significant gain in the number of words spoken and in projective language, language that forecasts events, anticipates consequences of actions or events, surveys possible alternatives, and recognizes problems and predicts solutions (pp. 10–11). Other studies of preschoolers and kindergarteners have shown that creative drama contributes significantly to the development of language and verbal fluency. In the early 1970s, Neidermeyer and Oliver found drama significantly improved kindergarteners' and first-graders' extemporaneous speaking and other drama skills.

Norton (1973) found that after drama second-graders' oral communication was significantly more flexible, original, coherent, and fluent. In 1990, Rosen and Koziol examined the relationship of oral reading, dramatic activities, and theatrical production to the improvement of oral communication skills, knowledge, comprehension, and attitudes. They found that informal drama had more influence on oral communication skills and self-esteem whereas theater production had a somewhat greater influence on knowledge and comprehension of the play.

Numerous studies noted that spontaneous dramatic play correlates with the level of language. In the early 1990s, Lim found preschoolers who engaged in more sociodramatic play had longer utterances and improved vocabulary. In the early 1970s Lewis had also found that kindergarten children who did well in unstructured dramatics also had greater syntactic maturity, fluency, and language organization. Paley, in the late 1970s, in interpretive drama sessions, observed an increase the quality of oral language in kindergartners with low verbal skills, which confirmed Rice's early 1970s' findings. Ravich also early 1970s, like many drama teachers, observed increased competency in oral speaking following participation in dramatics activities by a group of ten teenage dropouts in a reading program at the University of Alabama.

Other studies showed that drama is effective with special populations. In the mid 1990s, De la Cruz showed that children with learning disabilities significantly improve their oral expressive language and social skills after a 12-week creative drama program. Both McIntyre's studies in the 1950s and Woolf and Meyers' studies in the 1960s found that creative drama helps students with speech disorders. Several studies show significant improvement in language acquisition when sign language is incorporated into the curriculum of children with language disabilities. In the 1980s, Timms found that eight profoundly deaf residential students increased their knowledge of story structure after drama and other activities in both English and American Sign Language–based language systems. In addition to these studies, qualitative studies in 1995 show how Heathcote's teacher-in-role and mantle-of-the-expert strategies are powerful in evoking language for severe to profound hearing-impaired students as well as for normal ones.

Students do not have to be deaf, however, to benefit from sign language instruction. Brown (1992) found that a year of teacher-directed activities in drama and sign language with nondeaf Head Start children resulted in significant improvement in language. Brown suggested that the key factor in the children's improvement may be the fact that both sign language and drama provide alternative symbol systems for conveying information. Because sign language makes fewer information-processing demands than does spoken language (Brown, 1992, p. 3), it & drama are easier for children to master than the more abstract symbol system of language. Both are more concrete (Brown, 1992, p. 6).

In summary, both observational and empirical studies show that drama challenges students to use language more explicitly and unambiguously, in a wide range of registers and styles, and for a much broader range of purposes than customary school dialogues. New studies need to describe more fully the structure of drama teaching to determine which instructional strategies and interactions with the students are critical to expanding the range and raising the level of the children's oral language and thus might account for the differences in the results of the studies reported here.

## Effect on Reading

Piaget (1962), Vygotsky (1967), and others provided a strong theoretical foundation for the relationship of pretend play to the development of literacy. Piaget showed the child moving from egocentric symbolic play to social symbolic play. Through play and imitation, the child learns to separate signifiers from the signified, and to attach meanings to symbols, using experiences from the real world to engage in object substitutions and decontextualized behavior. Vygotsky saw play, which for him was synonymous with pretense, as part of the process of learning to engage in symbol manipulation.

Children in dramatic play often use symbols or signs to represent objects that are absent, and almost always use language, the signifier par excellence (Galda, 1984, p. 106). In drama, language transforms roles, objects, and situations from their real to a pretense function (p. 107). As children get older, they are increasingly apt to use explicit language to define what the object stands for (Pellegrini, 1985). This use of decontextualized language and enactment of role-appropriate behavior in a make-believe situation represents a major step toward literacy, or what Vygotsky termed second-rather than first-order symbolism. In reading and writing, children engage in a form of conscious symbolization; they assign meaning to arbitrary forms (letters) just as they do to objects in drama (Clay, 1975; Moffett & Wagner, 1983).

Five literature reviews conclude that drama seems to be effective in promoting literacy (Christie, 1991; Kardash & Wright, 1987; Isenberg & Jacob, 1983; Pellegrini, 1985). Three of the studies in Kardash and Wright's (1987) meta-analysis that examined effects on diverse populations show that "creative drama appears to have extremely beneficial effects for gifted children, a very small effect for remedial readers, and a moderate, positive effect on learning disabled students" (p. 16).

Isenberg and Jacob (1983) concluded that dramatic play fosters literacy development in two ways: (a) Children's use of representational skills serves as a basis for representation in literacy, and (b) dramatic play provides a safe environment for practicing "the skills and social behaviors associated with literacy activities" (p. 272).

Observational studies show that both drama and reading involve similar mental processes: decontextualized language and narrative sequencing (Pellegrini, 1985). Nursery school and kindergarten children often incorporate into their drama social activities associated with specific uses of print (Hall, 1988; Isenberg & Jacob, 1983). Durkin (1966) observed that children who read early often play "school" with older siblings; and Wolfgang (1973) noted that first-grade boys who are not at a high level in dramatic play also have difficulty in reading (p. 273).

Eighteen out of 29 quasi-experimental studies showed that drama improves story recall, comprehension, and/or vocabulary (including Adamson, 1981; Backstrom, 1988; Bush, 1985; Carlton & Moore, 1966; Bosseau & Delgado, 1985; Henderson & Shanker, 1978; Pate, 1974; Saltz, Dixon, & Johnson, 1977; Strickland, 1973; Tucker, 1971). In contrast to these studies, 11, representing almost all grade levels, did not show that drama has a positive effect on reading (including Allen, 1968; Amato, Emans, & Ziegler, 1973; Aoki, 1978; O. G. Bennett, 1982; Burke, 1980; Youngers, 1977).

Pellegrini concluded that studies with kindergarteners and 1st graders that attempt to show that drama facilitates literate behavior are not particularly supportive, but that drama convincingly *correlates* with literacy skills (Pellegrini, 1980; Wolfgang, 1973). Pellegrini (1980) found among kindergarteners a significant relationship between symbolic play and reading achievement, this in contrast to sex and socioeconomic background, which are not significantly correlated. Children who spontaneously engage primarily in social symbolic play have significantly higher scores in word comprehension and in understanding a variety of syntactic structures than other children.

In the 1980s, Pellegrini and Galda found that adult-directed drama is significantly more effective in promoting recall of literal details than either discussion or drawing for kindergarten to second-grade children, and more for younger than for older ones. However, a later study (Pellegrini, 1985) showed a significant effect only when the children are measured right after the dramatic enactment, but not when measured a week later.

Part of the problem of assessing the effects of drama on reading is the use of standardized reading tests, which are not sensitive to the kinds of language gain that facilitates deep understanding of a text and empathy with characters (Vitz, 1984). For example, when drama is used as response to literature, readers are better able to imaginatively create a story world, including the multiple perspectives of minor characters in a novel who have their own reasons for acting in ways that create problems for a protagonist. Galda (1984) found that for second-graders dramatizing a story "seems to result in a greater understanding of cause and effect and the motivations and emotional responses of the characters" (p. 114). It probably helps children shift from a focus on physical to a focus on character or on psychological events. Other studies found a significant positive relationship between dramatic activities and general cognition, response to literature, language, empathy for characters, and comprehension (Conner, 1974; Demmond, 1977; Galda, 1984; Green, 1974).

## Effect on Writing

If Bereiter and Scardamalia's (1982) conclusion from evidence is valid, namely, that children's main problem in writing is accessing and giving order to what they know (p. 17), then drama should help them discover and shape their ideas. The kinesthetic element of assuming an appropriate posture and using apt gestures should enable students to access not only oral but also written persuasive competence. Moffett and Wagner (1983) posited that experience is first coded by the muscles, then by the senses, then by memory, and, finally, by reason (p. 530). Vygotsky (1978) provided the theoretical foundation for the assumption that gesture is akin to writing. Both, like drawing, are accomplished with the hand, and their significance lies in what the gesture symbolizes. As Emig (1978) implied, writing may be even closer to gesture than to speech, and, if so, giving students an opportunity to use gesture in drama may help them kinesthetically identify with a particular posture and stance, and to produce the natural language that goes with it.

Emergent literacy studies (Calkins, 1980; Cioffi, 1984; work by Dyson; Graves, 1982, 1983; Sowers, 1979) show that children give their early writing a multimodality associated with gesture and graphics. Monson (1986) described several ways that drama serves as an effective prewriting strategy, clarifying for children concepts they might want to explore through writing.

Recent observational studies report remarkable maturity in student writing that emerges from drama (Booth, 1998; 1996; Wagner, 1976, 1990; among others). In 1990s Dunnagan's case study of six seventh-graders shows that there are significant shifts in audience awareness before, during, and after participation in drama. The writing produced in role shows more attention to sensory imagery, second-person narrative voice (addressing the reader), insight into characters' feelings and empathy, and the need to clarify information and to disclose it selectively; but less attention to the setting, first- or third-person narrative voice, descriptive language, and closure.

Several studies point to confirming the claims that drama improves writing (including Pellegrini, 1984; Ridel, 1975; Roubicek, 1983; Troyka, 1973; Wagner, 1986). Pellegrini (1984) showed that drama is significantly correlated with word-writing fluency in kindergarten. However, because children were writing single dictated words, the results may have more to do with transcription skills than with composition. This finding, however, suggested to Pellegrini that pretend play is a powerful predictor of writing achievement in kindergarten.

Although word writing is only the beginning of sustaining a monologue using graphic symbols, both it and drama demand moving from the here-and-now perceptions of the moment to displaying internal mental constructions. With growth, a child shows an increasing independence from the limitations of current stimuli and an increasing control of self through internal direction. When children engage in social symbolic or fantasy play, they need to define their symbolic representations socially just as they do when they write words. Both pretend play and word writing "may be related to the child's general representational competence" (Pellegrini, 1984, p. 276).

In the 1990s McNaughton compared two sets of writing of two groups of primary children. In 17 of the 20 sets of writing, the drama group wrote slightly better than the discussion group, which served as a control, and they wrote 24.5% more.

Further studies in the 1990s by Moore and Caldwell found that for second- and third-graders, 15 sessions of either drama or drawing were more effective forms of rehearsal for story writing than traditional planning using discussion. The experimental group wrote stories that were better in overall impression, organization, ideas, context, and style. Drama stimulates writers to explore in several directions without the constraints of linear structure. They can shape their ideas into a more fully conceived whole, and then later revise them in relation to this vision. Roubicek (1983) found that, among fifth-graders, acting out a story is significantly more effective than a structured discussion for improving subsequent writing. The children's compositions show significant differences from the control group in elaboration, and in the "ideas" and "flavor" features on the Diederich Writing Assessment Scale.

Wagner (1986) found role-playing to be significantly effective in improving the persuasive letter writing of fourth- and eighth-graders when compared to either a presentation of models and rules for persuasive letters or to no instruction. The writing samples were scored for their level of target orientation, or tailoring of the persuasion to its audience. Ridel (1975) showed that ninth-graders write more original creative stories after a creative drama program based on theater games. Troyka (1973) showed an effect of drama on writing of .75 for the persuasive essays of remedial college freshmen. Cohen (1977) defined .10 as a small effect size as medium and .40 as large (p. 348).

These six studies show dramatic play in kindergarten correlates with word-writing fluency, and educational drama under a teacher's guidance is effective in improving subsequent writing in studies at second-, third-, fourth-, fifth-, eighth-, and ninth-grade levels and at the remedial college freshmen level.

## Surveys

For 3 decades major leaders in the English and language arts fields have been advocating a greater role for drama in the curriculum. Three major recommendations came out of the 1966 Dartmouth Conference, that seminal meeting of British and American educators: (a) more writing in schools, (b) reader response to literature, instead of prescribed mastery of a text, and (c) more drama in English classrooms. The first two recommendations have had a wide impact and have transformed the language arts profession, but the third has yet to take hold. To the well-respected Writing Across the Curriculum movement, there has not been a corresponding "drama across the curriculum" movement. However, to read accounts by Dartmouth Conference participants, one of the most readily accepted resolutions was that drama should be made an integral part of the English curriculum from beginning to end because of its rich potentialities and by virtue of its roots in the ritual and play going far back in man's history, as well as in the dramatic play of children. At the time of the Dartmouth Conference, British students devoted 20% to 25% of class time to drama.

Despite all the passionate and well-argued pleas (Barnes, 1968; work by Moffett), and despite research that shows classroom drama helps students achieve some very important language arts goals, surveys suggest that only very recently has educational drama become a regular part of even the best of language arts programs. Stewig's (1986) interviews with building principals in eight metropolitan school districts revealed that educational drama was not widely used in the 1980s on a regular (more than once a month) basis. Many of the principals were not aware of the differences between informal classroom drama and the more traditional scripted plays. Because most school districts do not have a team of drama specialists, the future of drama in the classroom lies increasingly with regular classroom teachers, most of whom have never had even a single course in educational drama.

The situation seems to be changing in this decade, however. A study in 1993 by Kaaland-Wells surveyed the extent to which 224 elementary classroom teachers in a large urban school district used seven different dramatic forms (improvisation, story dramatization, dramatic play, puppetry, pantomime, storytelling, and readers theater). On the basis of a questionnaire, she found that 84% supported the use of drama, 77% reported a high rate of success in using drama through improvisation, 75% in using story dramatization, 65% in dramatic play, 62% in puppetry, 45% in pantomime, and 37% in readers theater. Six percent used some form of drama at least once a day, 25% at least once a week, 27% once a month, and 32% once a year; 10% never used it. They saw lack of time and space as their biggest obstacles to the use of drama. In 1984, in a similar survey, Stewig found that most teachers saw "too much prescribed curriculum" as their chief obstacle. At least half of the teachers in Kaaland-Wells' survey did not think drama takes vital time away from learning basic subjects, but they were divided on whether or not it tooks more or the same time to teach lessons using drama rather than conventional lessons. In 1994, Kaaland-Wells compared the results of her study with those of Stewig. She found more teachers had been exposed to drama than in the previous decade:

Over half of the teachers had exposure to drama, though only 31% had taken a college creative drama course against 14% of Stewig's teachers. Over half (55%) had taken a college course which included some creative drama, similar to 47% of Stewig's teachers who had taken a language arts course which spent one to fifteen or more hours on drama. Over half (52%) had attended an inservice or conference which included drama, more than Stewig's teachers . . . (20%).

Those teachers who had a college drama course were more likely than the others to feel it should be a part of all teacher training and they were more likely to view it as effective. Charles Leonhard's national survey in 1991 showed that 85% of elementary classroom teachers used drama as an instructional approach. This experimentation with drama goes on despite limited financial resources and a lack of drama specialists and/or state-mandated standards, curricula, or assessments. The use of drama seems to spring from the initiative of individual teachers.

## Observational Explorations

Those who have led groups of children or have heard them interact in role in a classroom drama have often marveled at their depth of understanding and maturity of expression. Surely this is the quality of language that should be fostered. What both the research community and teachers need are more richly detailed observations like these, descriptions that capture the immediacy and power of the student's struggle to make meaning. Publishing long verbatim quotations of students' written output can help build a case for drama just as Hughes Mearns did in the 1920s and 1930s and James Moffett did in the 1980s by publishing children's literary pieces and thus showing the larger society that students are capable of powerful imaginative writing. Researchers and teachers also need the analytical insight that Dyson (1981), Florio and Clark (1982), Giffin (1984), Hall (1988), and Paley (1987, 1994) provided for preschool spontaneous pretend play, emergent literacy events, and classroom interaction. Their thick descriptions have powerful implications for classroom instruction.

The whole premise on which quasi-experimental studies are based is that the effect of a particular instructional strategy can be determined on the basis of some sort of test, usually with paper and pencil. This premise is embedded in a positivist view, one that assumes learning experiences are replicable and can be generalized to all situations. This paradigm is a mismatch with the phenomenon that is being investigated. Teachers whose goal is imaginative expression know that no single experience can apply to all classroom communities, and thus they need instead to understand not which instructional strategies have been "proven" to be effective, but rather which heuristics are the most likely to produce the divergent thinking, deep understanding, and creative response they are seeking. The need to know how experiences unfold in all their complexity, how to respond to the surprises of the responses of engaged students, and how to celebrate imaginative expression. This they will not find in quasi-experimental studies. In contrast to the varied research methods reflected in Part II of this *Volume*, most studies of educational drama have been quasi-experimental, and only in the last decade have there been a few descriptive investigations of teaching strategies.

Because of the limited methods used in drama research, the teaching profession knows too little about what actually goes on in an effective lesson. What are the teacher's goals and how does he or she achieve them? What types of student response indicate growth? What kind of cognitive processing takes place? To answer such questions, teachers need descriptions focusing on drama teaching in its classroom context. Researchers also need to examine the oral texts students produce in role as Beach and Anson (1988) did with texts written in role and analyze them systematically to document qualitative differences. Teachers would benefit both from longitudinal studies identifying stages in dramatic growth such as Colby's (1988) work and from participant–observer and ethnographic field studies, in which trained observers code categories of teacher–student interaction and participant behaviors. A combination of cognitive and ethnomethodological perspectives could enlighten the field.

In the next section, the dramatic rendering of texts is discussed. In this type of drama work, participants are constrained by a text, Which makes it different from the educational drama discussed so far, in which the oral text as well as the action is generated by the participants.

## PERFORMING TEXTS

Frequent calls for more oral reading of poems and telling and reading of stories by both teachers and students has characterized the profession for decades. If narrative and poetry are to be nurtured, the sound of language as well as its sense must be valued. Educators are rediscovering the power of modeling expressive oral reading, choral reading, and individual performing of longer texts (Hoffman, 1987). Very few studies have been done of the effect of classroom performances of texts; but common sense suggests that interpreting literature orally should aid enjoyment and comprehension.

Children respond enthusiastically to the entertainment of a well-told story. Even college students who rank their teachers as effective perceive them to tell more stories in the classroom than teachers ranked as less effective (Holladay, 1987). Speech communication researchers who have analyzed storytelling view it as a dense achievement sustained through the interactional cooperation of both tellers and recipients, one that has the effect of bonding group participants.

Orally presented stories show significant effects on the learning of young children. Milner (1982) found that preschool teachers who base their curriculum on orally presented fairy tales have children who are significantly higher than a control group in level of empathy, reading readiness, oral language, and concept of story. Pelias (1979) showed that a course in oral interpretation improves the perspective-taking abilities of college undergraduates.

Telling stories as opposed to reading them aloud is also advocated (Rosen, 1986). Storytelling is like all other types of imaginative expression: a creative art. It depends on the same two abilities on which creativity depends: divergent production and transformation. Teachers who ask children to tell stories need to be sensitive to diverse ethnic and cultural patterns of oral storytelling. For example, instead of a sustained monologue, a cooperative, conversational "talk story" is the conventional pattern in the Athabaskan (Scollon & Scollon, 1981) and Hawaiian cultures (Au & Kawakami, 1985).

Story dramatization is another form of text presentation that has a long history of claims for its value. Page (1983) compared the effects of story dramatization with storytelling on primary children. First-graders, particularly low readers, comprehend more after drama, but interesting differences emerge. Drama is more effective for building understanding of enacted words and details, whereas storytelling is more effective for understanding descriptive details and words. Drama is better for facilitating comprehension of main idea, character motivation, and identification; storytelling, for inference. To help children empathize with a character and bring to a story their own experience, dramatizing is better, taking a particular moment in time and living it at life rate, tearing the story apart and exploding it into its twisted moments. On the other hand, to make literary forms familiar, to help children internalize story schema, and to stimulate reflection and evaluation of the universal theme inherent in a tale, storytelling is the better medium.

Readers theater, a group form of oral interpretation, is another oral mode of performance that has strong support among reading and English educators (Bacon, 1972; Coger & White, 1973; Moffett & Wagner, 1983, Post, 1974; Winegarden, 1980). Mayberry (1975) compared the effect of readers theater and solo performance with silent reading. He found that for both comprehension and appreciation, readers theater and solo performance are more effective than silent reading, with readers theater the most powerful in effect: Means are 7.40, 7.09, and 6.43.

The Arizona State University Seven-Year Longitudinal Study shows that regularly scheduled classroom creative drama sessions *and* frequent theater viewing have a measurable effect on the way children perceive and respond to theater as compared to a control group (Saldaña, 1987). Almost no research exists on the effects on students of high school theater programs and on successful teaching or coaching strategies for such programs.

The focus of the final section of this chapter is on teaching strategies to foster student writing of poems, fiction, and plays. The chapter ends with surveys of imaginative writing in schools.

## WRITTEN IMAGINATIVE EXPRESSION

In recent years, techniques of teaching writing have received increasing attention, but little of this focuses specifically on the writing of literary forms. For the past 3 decades writing projects as part of the 160-site National Writing Project network have provided forums for teachers to hone their own writing skill and develop strategies for teaching all types of writing. Many teachers in these projects find to their surprise they can write in genres they may not have tried before—poetry, fiction, or drama, and can help their students do the same.

Shumaker (1982) found that imaginative writing can improve growth in language arts. Sixth-graders taught expressive writing three times a week improve significantly more than students who follow a textbook language arts program. The differences are significant in word knowledge, reading, language, and creative writing, but not spelling and mechanics.

### Ideology of Teachers

Several studies have identified general characteristics of effective teachers. Students whose teachers teach reading in an open-ended manner produce better imaginative writing. Mosenthal (1984; Mosenthal, Conley, Colella, & Davidson-Mosenthal, 1985) found what they termed a cognitive-developmental ideology to be significantly more effective than an academic ideology in improving fourth-graders' ability to draw on a variety of meaning sources in writing stories. The students of teachers with a cognitive-developmental ideology tend to generate stories with more developed motive structures and appropriate goals. Such teachers are most likely to improvise rather than follow a basal reader guide exactly, to ask reconstructive questions and give reconstructive directives, and to accept or prompt plausibly correct responses rather than to insist that responses be based only on the book the children are currently reading (Mosenthal, 1984, p. 683). Teachers reflecting an academic ideology are those most likely to reproduce the basal reader guide, to ask reproductive questions and give reproductive directives, and to reject plausibly correct responses drawn from sources other than the current text (1984, p. 683).

Calkins (1986), Florio and Clark (1982), and Graves (1973) found that for all types of writing, not just imaginative, the most effective teaching strategies are those that:

1. Create an informal environment and climate of risk taking.
2. Encourage students to generate their own topics.
3. Provide stimulating prewriting experiences.
4. Recognize and allow for individual and sometimes unique processes of writing.
5. Set up real purposes and real audiences.
6. Provide conferences during the writing process in a nondirective way to facilitate the writer's achieving his or her own intentions.

In contrast to the findings of Mosenthal (1984), Calkins (1986), Florio and Clark (1982), and Graves (1973), N. Bennett (1976) found no significant differences between imaginative essays written by British primary children whose teachers were "formal" and those who were "informal."

### Teachers Accomplished at Linguistic Craft

In this section are descriptions of five teachers, each of whom is an exemplar of the writing craft he is teaching. Three of these were successful in stimulating student writing, but the other two met with less than complete success because their stimuli and modeling did not carry over into student efforts. Thus, although a teacher's ability to demonstrate the craft he or she teaches is a highly desirable attribute, it is by no means the only critical element in successful teaching.

The first three reports show the variety of ways teacher nurturing and response to student writing can foster development. The first two are ethnographic studies of high school creative writing teachers noted for their effectiveness in motivating student writing, and the third is a self-report. The last two cases show teaching strategies that are not particularly effective.

In the first study (Dunn, Florio-Ruane, & Clark, 1985), the teacher is himself a poet; in the second (Kantor, 1984), the teacher is a story writer. The success of these two teachers suggests that the teaching of imaginative writing by a teacher who is a linguistic craftsman may be qualitatively different from other teaching. Teachers who represent the end state toward which students are striving may be, as suggested earlier, assuming a role more like a master with apprentices than like an explicit lesson giver.

Dunn et al. (1985) closely observed a teacher in a multigrade elective creative writing class in a suburban high school. The teacher was concerned that the students' commitment to academic writing might make them reluctant to take the risk of engaging in more personally meaningful writing. To get his students to write evocative haiku poetry, he carefully modulated the roles he assumed. At some times he stimulated ideas; at others, he modeled; at still others, he coached; and, most important, perhaps, he provided a real-world audience not only in the classroom but also outside in the writing contests he urged his students to enter.

He sufficiently distanced himself "from the putative role of 'teacher as evaluator' to enable his students to take greater power and responsibility for their roles as authors" (Dunn et al., 1985, p. 39). The role the teacher chose at any particular time depended on his instructional purpose and also on a sensitive response to context, which meant frequently negotiating his role with the students. His classroom walls were laden with his own photographs and paintings, as well as charcoal sketches, airbrush designs, and oil paintings done by his students. When introducing a new poetry topic, he read aloud the poetry of other authors, played recordings of poems set to music, presented slides and photographs, and provided a rich array of stimulating books. To help students see how visual images could make statements about the world, he had them do photo montages. He shared montages done by former students. He also advised them to write frequently by suggesting that his own photography and poetry efforts often failed, but that successive trials paid off. As he wrote in his teacher journal, his goal was "to get people into spaces where they are really thinking about what they have to say and are being honest" (p. 44). One of his students wrote in his journal: "The spaces my teacher talks of can only be entered when I feel like writing true feelings and not what people want to read" (p. 44).

Kantor (1984) documented the effectiveness of providing students with an opportunity to write for their peer communities as a way to allow writing to intersect personal and social spheres. He also showed how much can be learned from an examination of instruction in imaginative writing that includes not only teaching strategies but also a thick description of the conditions under which students write and of the personalities, attitudes, and interpersonal styles of both the students and the teacher. His description of one teacher's work with a group of bright and academically successful 12th-graders in a creative writing class highlights the effectiveness of nondirective teaching with such a group. Kantor described how the teacher helped students become more comfortable and willing to take risks in a situation unfamiliar to them. The teacher encouraged them to choose their own topics and modes of discourse; he gave no grades until the end of the quarter.

A short-story writer himself, the teacher assumed the role of responder and fellow writer, and he carried on the class discussion in a low-keyed and informal manner. He, the students, and the participant observer, Kantor, sat in a circle. All of them wrote and shared their writing with the group. The teacher tried to read each student's piece on the author's terms, not his own. He was unfailingly encouraging, patient, and accepting, effectively helping the students move from a perception of him as authority to one of trusted adult. He admitted his difficulties with writing and showed his own processes—how he dealt with blocks and how he revised. He read them statements by various professional writers and shared how he had come to see writing as a discovery process and to trust his own writing intuitions. He modeled the way he wanted students to receive one another's work by responding spontaneously after a student read a finished or unfinished piece, making suggestions but avoiding formulas. Occasionally he gave them what he called a "sermonette," providing advice, such as the value of using concrete and sensory detail. The teacher encouraged social interactions, engendering camaraderie and solidifying community as well as contributing to the richness and vividness of the writing. Student writing grew toward using stronger sensory details, revealing feeling and personal voice, experimenting with new genres, becoming more aware of the appropriateness of a particular genre

for an individual writer, expressing greater imagination and humor, and using a wider range of revising strategies.

A third example of successful teaching is Hirsch's (1984) description of his own experience, as Artist in the Schools, with a ninth-grade creative writing class. He described his reluctance to "show off" his own writing efforts for fear that would inhibit his students. He started the class by having them remember a traumatic or life-changing experience in their past, and then day by day he went through a series of suggestions for fictionalizing and expanding that incident into a story. Because he deliberately went for the most personal of experiences, he sensed that students would be reluctant to share with one another, just as the students were in the classroom described below. However, instead of forcing the issue as the unsuccessful teacher in Perl and Wilson's (1986) study did, he invited them to turn in their papers to him, clipping each successive draft to the preceding ones. His first responses were invariably encouraging. By the end of the 8-week session, some of the students were willing to own and share their by now fairly fictionalized stories, not only with the teacher and each other, but with an outside observer as well.

To be a linguistic craftsman, however, is not all that is needed. Even when they themselves have refined their own skill and can provide good models of an end state of a writer, teachers do not always find it easy to effect student development of the craft of imaginative writing. Perl and Wilson (1986) documented a painful failure by a usually effective eighth-grade teacher who one year simply could not connect with his students. Although he was considered a successful teacher, using many of the strategies one or more of the three high school teachers described above did, his students did not respond well. He provided a model by reading his own poems to the class, and his walls were covered with stimulating posters on popular culture or environmental issues. He had handy an impressive array of media equipment. He began the year by asking the students to engage in ten minutes of uninterrupted writing, and he wrote with them. Perhaps what he lacked was the patience Kantor's (1984) teacher showed. Perl first observed this when instead of inviting students to read their 10-minute freewriting samples, he volunteered to go first, and then, when no one volunteered to read next, he called on the students. He was fairly directive in what would be expected of them—to memorize and recite a poem, to keep all drafts of their writing, to keep a process journal and a social studies journal, and to bring to class a notebook for in-class writing and "a writing implement" (p. 122).

Although this teacher's room had dramatic appeal, he was the one who usually took center stage. He composed out loud in front of the students and asked them to notice how he wrote. When one of the students noticed, "You use the biggest vocabulary I ever heard" (Perl & Wilson) and others agreed they could not write like that, the teacher got up from his chair in the center of the group and moved to the chalkboard, saying, "What you are talking about now is ownership. This is the vocabulary I've become comfortable with." The teacher continued to be, in his terms, "the educational leader in the classroom . . . the driving force behind what happens" (p. 124), but at the same time, outside of class, he began to wonder if he were too strong a writer and too forceful in a discussion. Indeed, such fears were well founded; he lacked patience with students. Although he continued to write verses and parodies to commemorate school events, his own joy of performance did just the opposite of what he had hoped. Unlike the first two teachers described above, this teacher's willingness to share his own writing made the students feel less able rather than empowered. This teacher felt afraid that when the small writing groups met, they might not be doing what they were supposed to do. He did not feel comfortable with the feeling of not being "in charge." Whenever he found students who seemed to be wasting time, he scolded them and got mad at himself for not having structured the task more clearly. He felt that because he was not giving them grades the students were doing rushed, sloppy work.

By midyear, the students were resisting; except for a few dutiful ones, they didn't volunteer to read their writing aloud or share their observations and ideas about their writing processes. Stalemates continued, followed by outright hostility on both sides. Perhaps this teacher was confusing his artistic role as a poet who carefully controls and crafts language with his less satisfying (for him) role of enabler of student growth. In any case, his efforts to control the class and force their output became increasingly difficult, and he became more and more tense and depressed. The students also sensed something was wrong. When a multimedia show his social studies class was rehearsing became hopelessly bogged down, the teacher asked the students to write letters about what had happened, their feelings, and what he should do to improve (p. 136). One girl captured not only how the students felt about this show but what might have been at the source of their resistance in the creative writing class as well: "We (some of us) don't feel that the show is ours anymore. You do everything (well almost everything). It's sort of like you are taking over" (p. 137).

In this example, the master was perceived as one who did not relish apprentices; their limitations irritated him. His modeling was not firing student energy; it was dampening it.

One final report is that of Lopate (1978), a widely published author of poetry and fiction. He observed that an interesting discussion or a collaborative composition with an elementary-school class does not necessarily serve as a model to improve the quality of children's individual poems, as he had hoped. He found that although some children pick up on the visual model of modern verse they and the teacher have created as a class poem, most of them return to their usual style when they write individually. "Certainly the reckless tempo, linguistic freedom, and subject leaps which characterize the collaborative class poem rarely carry over to the individual student's work" (p. 138). Lopate advised teachers to let the writer choose his or her own moment to compose. He believed that the process of serious creative writing requires withdrawal and learning to be alone.

## Specific Teaching Strategies

A few studies have assessed the effectiveness of particular heuristics for developing imaginative expression. Several descriptive studies confirm Lopate's observation that success in evoking poetry and stories is largely a by-product of allowing students to choose their own topics and their own time to write

(Calkins, 1986; Emig, 1971; Graves, 1973; McClure, 1985; Perl & Wilson, 1986). These studies describe some of the same qualities of successful teaching that Dunn et al. (1985) and Kantor (1984) identified and described.

McLure (1985) described a supportive context that was critical to developing mature responses to poetry and experimentation in writing poems by a group of intermediate children. The teacher sanctioned peer interaction, gave focused praise and feedback, acknowledged frustration, had clear expectations, allowed flexibility in time and space, and helped the children create a strong social network. The children generally enjoyed reading and writing poetry, and developed preferences for more complex and challenging poems as they continued to enjoy light humorous pieces. Perl and Wilson (1986) described the teaching of a fourth-grade/fifth-grade teacher and an eighth-grade teacher, both of whom were successful in evoking poetry and stories, largely as a by-product of allowing students to choose their own topics. Although neither of these teachers was an accomplished writer, their students often burst into imaginative expression and produced some carefully crafted pieces. What characterized the classrooms of these two successful teachers was that they were no longer the sole sources of knowledge. Students wrote for and learned from each other. When freed from "the need to write merely to please their teachers, some students, some of the time, discovered a freedom and depth of expression they had rarely known before" (p. 251).

Scardamalia and Bereiter (1986), in their review of the literature on writing instruction, noted the common view that much of what students learn about writing has to come from exposure to examples. The next three studies focus on the texts primary children read and their influence on the stories and poems they write.

***Basal readers.*** Phillips (1986) found first-graders whose teachers read and discuss poems and stories rather than use basal readers write significantly more and better than control groups. Their stories and poems are more original and show such elements as simile, metaphor, personification, exaggeration, and repetition. The vocabulary is more richly figurative and sensory. Burton (1985) found third- and fourth-graders in an open classroom borrow and improvise on the language of the classroom literature. Children's literature provides a necessary source of authentic experience for the writers. Eckhoff (1983) found second-graders who read basal reading texts that have unelaborated stories with simple sentences and one sentence per line write that way, whereas those reading a basal text that has more elaborate structures write more elaborated and mature sentences. All too often when children start handwriting and encoding practice in workbooks in school, they halt the progress they have made as preschoolers in creative and innovative explorations into producing printed language (Bissex, 1981; Dyson, 1982).

***Story elements.*** Although the quality of the imaginative literature children read seems to influence their writing, direct teaching of models is not the most effective way to improve writing (Hillocks, 1986). Instead, teaching specific knowledge about the structure or schema, based on Stein's (1983, 1984,

1986) work on story comprehension, seems to improve story-writing skills.

Fitzgerald, Spiegel, and Teasley (1987) showed that story structure instruction to poor-reading fourth-graders improved the overall quality and organization of written stories, but not coherence and creativity. Reynolds (1982) found a similar effect with low-achieving high school students (mostly sophomores); they wrote significantly better stories after 12 weeks of "traditional" writing instruction than after 12 weeks of expressive writing instruction. However, high-achieving students did not. Traditional instruction, as Reynolds defined it, includes an overview of story elements and then presentations of the different characteristics of four types of fiction: gothic, romance, hero, and mystery. The teacher spells out the different audiences for and structures of each of these types of literature, and students choose a story type and answer a set of questions such as "How was the evil unleashed?" before they write their story. Then they outline the scenes. In the expressive writing condition, they choose their own topics, engage in freewriting, brainstorming, listing, etc.

Direct teaching of story elements is not always effective, however. Scardamalia and Bereiter (1986) reported that when third- and seventh-graders are exposed to instruction and/or a model suspense story, they do not, when asked to do so, revise a suspenseful story they have written earlier to make it more suspenseful.

***Stimuli for elaborative thinking.*** Hillocks (1986), in his meta-analysis of 60 studies of writing instruction, included a few that are of imaginative expression (as defined in this chapter). However, he did not report these separately from other modes of writing. He found the instruction he categorized as "environmental" had the greatest power for effecting student improvement in a variety of types of writing, largely because it stimulates elaboration. Although Hillocks distinguished the environmental mode of instruction from what he terms natural process, it is actually structured process, a version of a process-oriented approach, one that, as Applebee (1986) noted, "draws on the panoply of techniques [Hillocks] . . . seems to be attacking" (p. 105).

One of the effective environmental instructional modes for imaginative writing Hillocks (1986) described is Sager's (1973). Teachers gave inner city sixth-graders a set of scales for evaluating compositions. For example, experimental subjects were asked to read an unelaborated story on "The Green Martian Monster" and then asked to do a series of tasks such as quickly listing "all the reasons why a mouthless, green Martian monster might land in the USA" (Hillocks, 1986, p. 123). They worked with scales that focused on elaboration, vocabulary, organization, and structure. After 8 weeks the experimental control effect size was .93, nearly a full standard deviation, but there were inadequate teacher controls. Coleman (1982) confirmed Sager's results with second- and third-grade gifted students. Thibodeau (1974) presented sixth-graders with problems involving elaborative thinking. They worked in pairs or small groups to list, for example, all the reasons a diver might suddenly realize he must fight his way back to the surface. The effect size of this instruction is .35.

Bereiter and Scardamalia (1982) found that when sixth-graders are given the task of composing a story to fit with an ending sentence, they discuss the problem of how to develop the story in a manner that reflects the flavor of adult planning (p. 24). In the early 1980s, Hilyard and Hidi found when they gave third- and fifth-graders two inconsistent sentences—one for the story beginning sentence and the second for the ending—children were about twice as likely to resolve the inconsistency than if they are given the same two sentences as the beginning of the story (Bereiter & Scardamalia, 1982, p. 27).

In contrast to these findings, Kelley (1984) found that a flexible six-step (aiming, extending, organizing, expressing, refining, and communicating) creative approach for teaching story writing is not significantly more effective than a sentence–paragraph structure approach in improving the story-writing ability of sixth-graders but is significantly more effective than an equivalent amount of time in sustained silent reading.

Roubicek (1983) and Ridel (1975) found creative drama improves creative writing as noted in the discussion above of the effects of improvisational drama. These studies suggest that any strategies that stimulate elaboration or problem solving are likely to foster better story writing.

***Visual stimuli.*** Two researchers examined the effect of visual stimuli on story writing. Golub (1983) found that third- through sixth-grade children tend to see the narrative-descriptive possibilities in concrete black-and-white pictures and write more, in contrast to three other types of pictures: abstract black-and-white, concrete color, or abstract color. Children responding to concrete black and white pictures use more subordinate adverbial clauses, more adverbs other than time, place, and manner modifiers, and more medial adverbs. They also tend to tell a story rather than simply describe what they see (p. 111). Golub concluded that black and white concrete pictures provide enough stimulus to energize and direct the student's creative and linguistic imagination. Kafka (1971) found that intermediate-grade children write significantly worse narratives after auditory and tactile stimuli than with no stimuli. Visual stimuli produces better compositions than auditory or tactile but not significantly better.

***Mental imagery.*** Gambrell (1982) found induced mental imagery to be more effective with third-graders than instructions to "think about" what was read. The children in the imagery group wrote more words than the other group. Gambrell suggested that "mental imagery encourages reflection and contemplation" (p. 8), which have been shown to play a significant role in the composing process (Graves, 1978; King, 1978; Stallard, 1974).

A final important method of teaching imaginative expression, one that has shown astonishing improvement in the writing of open-admissions college students, is the story workshop technique (Schultz, 1982). High school teachers who use it report similar results. The highly prescribed technique incorporates oral word association, oral telling, oral reading, writing, and recall exercises, with the emphasis on seeing an image in the mind, using precise gesture, and addressing a present audience.

## Surveys and Assessments

Just how much imaginative writing actually goes on, and how much do their teachers value it? Even the National Assessment of Educational Progress (NAEP) did not include imaginative writing in its assessment of writing until its second round in 1973 to 1974. Some NAEP evidence suggests that outside of school, students are engaging in imaginative writing. According to the 1984 NAEP survey of writing achievement, students reported they wrote stories or poems that were not schoolwork; the percentage declined after fourth grade: 27% at 4th grade, 11.2% at 8th grade, and 12.8% at 11th grade (Applebee, Langer, & Mullis, 1986). Applebee, Langer, Mullis, Latham, and Gentile (1994) reported the same pattern of decline across grade levels in the 1992 NAEP assessment occurs in school with narrative writing, which includes both non-fictional and fictional stories. Eighty-two percent of 4th-graders are assigned to write a story at least once a month; by 8th grade, this declines to 75%, and by 12th grade, this declines to 62% (pp. 136–137).

Despite the effect writing projects may be having on some teachers, a large number of high school teachers still neither embrace the so-called process approach to writing nor foster imaginative expression in their classrooms. Applebee's (1984) analysis pinpointed the major factor that works against widespread acceptance of more open-ended strategies for teaching writing: the real threat such teaching poses "to the teachers' conception of their instructional role. To implement such activities effectively, the teacher must shift from a position of knowing what the students response should be to a less secure position in which there are no clear right or wrong answers" (p. 187). Such a shift is essential if the goal is student production of a unique piece of imaginative discourse, one the teacher cannot sketch ahead of time. S. Gardner's (1985) findings confirmed those of Applebee. She found that secondary teachers who feel less threatened will risk letting students assume more control of their learning. Those who are uncertain about what students are capable of doing are those who exert more control and are more cynical about student abilities. A second reason some teachers do not teach writing as a process is rooted in the fact that teachers are uncomfortable with writing themselves and have never enjoyed the satisfaction of producing their own compositions.

For whatever reasons, one thing is certain: In school, high school students do not write much fiction, poetry, or drama. In Applebee's (1981) nationwide survey of 754 high school teachers, he found that students in English classes spent only 10% of their class time generating "extended writing," a paragraph or more. One can guess that this 10% did not include much imaginative writing. Applebee's finding is all the more disheartening because the survey included only "good teachers," those nominated by their building principals as representing "good practice."

Freedman and McLeod (1988) used the same survey for 560 teachers selected as the most successful in their communities by National Writing Project directors throughout the country. They found more than Applebee found of high school teachers (42.2% compared to 30%) who chose "to share

imaginative experiences" as one of their two most important reasons for asking students to write. They also found significantly more elementary (68.8%) than high school teachers who chose imaginative experiences. Freedman and McLeod (1988) did a comparable survey of teachers in the United Kingdom. They were designated as especially capable by members of the executive board of the National Association of English Advisors. In contrast to their U.S. counterparts, 67.8% of the secondary and 84.4% of the elementary teachers in the United Kingdom selected "to share imaginative experiences" as one of the two most important reasons to ask students to write.

Even in the United Kingdom, however, where imaginative writing has assumed a larger part of the English curriculum than in the United States, some reports suggest that the recent development of the national curriculum has led to a devaluing of imaginative expression. This reflects the view of a group of teachers, cited in the Bullock's (1975) report who believed that overemphasis on creative, personal, or freewriting has meant, in actuality, artificially stimulated colorful or fanciful language at the expense of ordinary language with vivid imagery.

Applebee (1984) also surveyed U.S. secondary school textbooks and found significantly more imaginative writing assignments in literature anthologies than in any of the other textbooks he examined. The assignments, however, "are either very abrupt, with little development, or very analytic, asking students to examine the workings of a selection very closely, and then to imitate its content or form" (p. 26). Perhaps not surprisingly, on the 1984 NAEP assessment of writing achievement of American schoolchildren, "students found it moderately difficult to write well-developed stories" (Applebee et al., 1986, p. 9). An adequate story is one "with clear evidence of the storyteller's obligation to structure a plot and provide it with appropriate details" (p. 38). About 48% of the 11th-graders and 33% of the 8th-graders wrote stories that were at least adequate; fewer than 9% of the 4th-graders wrote stories at or above the adequate level.

---

## SUMMARY

The best teacher of imaginative writing is one who is not only a master of the craft but also one who can create an appropriately safe and supportive climate for risk taking, can introduce a wide array of stimuli and models without overwhelming the students or without teaching the models directly, and can set up a real-world audience without inhibiting the privacy needed for what Lopate (1978) referred to as that type of writing that dives into the deepest part of oneself. A good teacher of imaginative writing needs a well-tuned sensitivity to each student's own inner ripeness for writing, a flexibility that enables the teacher to negotiate his or her role with the students, and an ability to enable students to get started in the process and at the same time encourage their own selection of material to write about.

The successful teacher must be a patient respondent who acknowledges writing difficulties but enables movement out of a morass and becomes an adviser and information giver when the time is right. Indirect but engaged teaching, an ability to let the students have center stage, a capacity for stimulating mental imagery, elaborative and divergent thinking, and problem solving all are effective. Somehow a good imaginative writing teacher must provide literature that fosters at least an unconscious awareness of schema and form, and at the same time allow students to ignore or transcend such models. A flexible teacher improvises and conferences with students during their writing in a nondirective way to enable them to realize their own intentions. The order is a tall one; it is a wonder any teachers ever realize it. A number of studies and reports of classroom observers show that many of them do. However, after fourth grade, imaginative writing declines, and very little writing of fiction, poetry, or drama goes on in U.S. high schools.

## CONCLUSION

Effective teaching of imaginative expression calls for a special commitment to artistry in addition to the informal instructional strategies and styles that are effective for the rest of the English curriculum. If teachers are to enable students to call into existence something new in the world, to draw out of their kinesthetic knowing, their sensory experience, and their memories authentic expressions wrought into verbal symbols, their teachers need to know how to inspire and challenge them for this bracing task. If the flexible and holistic teaching strategies described in this chapter are central to success, then what is currently known about the development of imaginative expression and effective ways to foster it in the classroom points to a holistic, integrated curriculum.

## References

Adamson, D. O. (1981). Dramatization of children's literature and visual perceptual kinesthetic intervention for disadvantaged beginning readers (Doctoral dissertation, Northwestern State University of Louisiana). *Dissertation Abstracts International, 42/06-A,* 2481.

Allen, E. G. (1968). *An investigation of change in reading achievement, self-concept, and creativity of disadvantaged elementary school children experiencing three methods of training* (Doctoral dissertation, University of Southern Mississippi). (University Microfilms No. 69-4683)

Amato, A. R., Emans, R., & Ziegler, E. (1973). The effectiveness of creative dramatics and storytelling in a library setting. *Journal of Educational Research, 67*(4), 161-162, 181.

Aoki, E. M. (1978). The effects of active student-initiated responses on literal and non-literal reading comprehension and attitudes toward reading of third-grade students (Doctoral dissertation, University of Washington). *Dissertation Abstracts International, 39/05-A,* 2714.

Applebee, A. N. (1978). *The child's concept of story.* Chicago: University of Chicago Press.

Applebee, A. N. (1981). *Writing in the secondary school: English and the content area.* Urbana, IL: National Council of Teachers of English.

Applebee, A. N. (Ed.) (1984). *Contexts for learning to write: Studies of secondary school instruction.* Norwood, NJ: Ablex.

Applebee, A. N. (1986). Problems in process approaches: Toward a reconceptualization of process instruction. In A. Petrosky & D. Bartholomae (Eds.), *The teaching of writing* (pp. 95-113). Urbana, IL: National Council of Teachers of English.

Applebee, A. N., Langer, J. A., & Mullis, I. V. S. (1986). *The writing report card: Writing achievement in American schools.* Princeton, NJ: Educational Testing Service.

Applebee, A. N., Langer, J. A., & Mullis, I. V. S., Latham, A. S., & Gentile, C. A. (1994). *NAEP 1992 writing report card.* Washington, DC: U.S. Government Printing Office.

Archambault, R. D. (1968). Education and creativity. In L. V. Kosinski (Ed.), *Readings on creativity and imagination in literature and language* (pp. 37-49). Champaign, IL: National Council of Teachers of English.

Au, K., & Kawakami, A. J. (1985). Research currents: Talkstory and learning to read. *Language Arts, 62,* 406-411.

Backstrom, E. L. (1989). The effects of creative dramatics on student behaviors and attitudes in literature and language arts (Doctoral dissertation, University of California, Los Angeles, 1988). *Dissertation Abstracts International, 49/11-A,* 3243.

Bacon, W. (1972). *The art of interpretation* (3rd ed.). New York: Holt, Rinehart & Winston.

Barnes, D. (1968). *Drama in the English classroom.* Urbana, IL: National Council of Teachers of English.

Beach, R., & Anson, C. M. (1988). The pragmatics of memo writing: Developmental differences in the use of rhetorical strategies. *Written Communication, 5*(2), 157-183.

Bennett, N. (1976). *Teaching styles and pupil progress.* Cambridge, MA: Harvard University Press.

Bennett, O. G. (1982). *An investigation into the effects of a creative experience in drama on the creativity, self-concept, and achievement of fifth and sixth grade students.* Unpublished doctoral dissertation, Georgia State University, Atlanta.

Benson, M. S. (1990). Narration in pretend play and storytelling: An analysis of two modes of event representation (Doctoral dissertation, Pennsylvania State University). *Dissertation Abstracts International, 51/06-A,* 259.

Bereiter, C., & Scardamalia, M. (1982). From conversation to composition: The role of instruction in a developmental process. In R. Glaser (Ed.), *Advances in instructional psychology* (Vol. 2, pp. 1-64). Hillsdale, NJ: Lawrence Erlbaum Associates.

Berthoff, A. E. (1984). *Reclaiming the imagination.* Upper Montclair, NJ: Boynton/Cook.

Bissex, G. L. (1981). *Gns at wrk.* Cambridge, MA: Harvard University Press.

Booth, D. H. (1987). *Drama worlds: The role of drama in language growth.* Toronto, Canada: Language Study Centre, Toronto Board of Education.

Booth, D. H. (1994a). Entering the story cave. *National Association for Drama in Education Journal* (Australia), *18*(2), 67-77.

Booth, D. H. (1994b). *Story drama.* Markhamon, ON: Pembroke.

Booth, D. H. (1998). Language power through working in role. In B. J. Wagner, *Educational drama and language arts: What research shows* (pp. 57-76). Portsmouth, NH: Heinemann.

Britton, J. N. (1970). *Language and learning.* Baltimore, MD: Penguin.

Britton, J. N. (1983). Writing and the story world. In B. M. Kroll & G. Wells (Eds.), *Explorations in the development of writing* (pp. 3-30). New York: John Wiley & Sons.

Britton, J. N., Burgess, T., Martin, N., McLeod, A., & Rosen, H. (1975). *The Development of Writing Abilities (11-18)*. Urbana, IL: National Council of Teachers of English.

Brown, V. (1992). Drama and sign language: A multisensory approach to the language acquisition of disadvantaged preschool children. *Youth Theatre Journal, 6*(3), 3-7.

Bruner, J. S. (1983). *Child's talk: Learning to use language*. New York: Norton.

Bruner, J. S. (1986). *Actual minds, possible worlds*. Cambridge, MA: Harvard University Press.

Bullock, A. L. C. (1975). *A language for life: Report of the Committee of Inquiry appointed by the Secretary of State for Education and Science under the Chairmanship of Sir Alan Bullock*. London: Her Majesty's Stationery Office.

Burke, J. J., Jr. (1980). The effect of creative dramatics on the attitudes and reading abilities of seventh grade students (Doctoral dissertation, Michigan State University). *Dissertation Abstracts International, 41/12-A*, 4887. (University Microfilms No. D81-12,054)

Burton, F. R. (1985). The reading-writing connection: A one-year teacher-as-researcher study of third-fourth grade writers and their literary experiences (Doctoral dissertation, Ohio State University). *Dissertation Abstracts International, 46/12-A*, 3595. (University Microfilms No. DA8-02,976)

Bush, B. J. (1985). Effects of creative drama instruction on the story grammar knowledge of field-dependent and field-independent primary grade students (cognitive style) (Doctoral dissertation, University of Missouri). *Dissertation Abstracts International, 46/05-A*, 1234. (University Microfilms No. 85-14,608)

Byron, K. (1986). *Drama in the English classroom*. New York: Methuen.

Calkins, L. M. (1980). Children's rewriting strategies. *Research in the Teaching of English, 14*, 331-341.

Calkins, L. M. (1986). *The art of teaching writing*. Portsmouth, NH: Heinemann.

Carlton, L., & Moore, R. (1966). The effects of self-directive dramatization on reading achievement and self-concept of culturally disadvantaged children. *The Reading Teacher, 20*(2), 125-130.

Carroll, J. (1988). Taking the initiative: The role of drama in pupil/teacher talk (Doctoral dissertation, University of Newcastle Upon Tyne, England). *Dissertation Abstracts International, 49/016-A*, 422.

Christie, J. F. (Ed.) (1991). *Play and early literacy development*. Albany: State University of New York Press.

Cioffi, G. (1984). Observing composing behaviors of primary-age children: The interaction of oral and written language. In R. Beach & L. Bridwell (Eds.), *New directions in composition research* (pp. 171-190). New York: Guilford.

Clay, M. M. (1975). *What did I write?* Exeter, NH: Heinemann.

Coger, L. I., & White, M. R. (1973). *Readers theatre handbook: A dramatic approach to literature* (Rev. ed.). Glenview, IL: Scott, Foresman.

Cohen, J. (1977). *Statistical power analysis in the behavioral sciences* (Rev. ed.). New York: Academic Press.

Colby, R. W. (1988). *On the nature of dramatic intelligence: A study of developmental differences in the process of characterization by adolescents* (Unpublished doctoral dissertation, Harvard University). *Dissertation Abstracts International, 49/06B*, 239.

Coleman, D. R. (1982). *The effects of pupil use of a creative writing scale as an evaluative and instructional tool by primary gifted students* (Unpublished doctoral dissertation, Kansas State University). *Dissertation Abstracts International, 42*, 3409-A. (University Microfilms No. 81278860)

Conner, M. C. (1974). *An investigation of the effects of selected educational dramatics techniques on general cognitive abilities* (Unpublished doctoral dissertation, Southern Illinois University). *Dissertation Abstracts International, 34*, 6162A. (University Microfilms No. 74-6189, 119)

Courtney, R. (1985). The dramatic metaphor and learning. In J. Kase-Polisini (Ed.), *Creative drama in a developmental context*. New York: University Press of America.

Creber, J. W. P. (1965). *Sense and sensitivity*. London: University of London Press.

Demmond, J. (1977). *The use of role-playing, improvisation and performance in the teaching of literature* (Unpublished doctoral dissertation, Georgia State University). *Dissertation Abstracts International, 38/07A*, 3906.

Dewey, J. (1959). *Art as experience*. New York: Putnam.

Dixon, J. (1975). *Growth in English*. Urbana, IL: National Council of Teachers of English.

Dunn, J. (1977). *The effect of creative dramatics on the oral language abilities and self-esteem of Blacks, Chicanos, and Anglos in the second and fifth grades* (Unpublished doctoral dissertation, University of Colorado). *Dissertation Abstracts International, 38/07-A*, 3907. (University Microfilms No. 77-29908)

Dunn, S., Florio-Ruane, S., & Clark, C. M. (1985). The teacher as respondent to the high school writer. In S. W. Freedman (Ed.), *The acquisition of written language* (pp. 33-50). Norwood, NJ: Ablex.

Durkin, D. (1966). *Children who read early*. New York: Teachers College Press.

Dyson, A. H. (1981). Oral language: The rooting system for learning to write. *Language Arts, 58*, 776-784.

Dyson, A. H. (1982). Teachers and young children: Missed connections in teaching learning to write. *Language Arts, 59*, 674-680.

Dyson, A. H. (1986). The imaginary worlds of childhood: A multimedia presentation. *Language Arts, 63*, 799-808.

Eckhoff, B. (1983). How reading affects children's writing. *Language Arts, 60*, 607-616.

Emig, J. (1971). *The composing process of twelfth graders*. (Research Report No. 13). Urbana, IL: National Council of Teachers of English.

Emig, J. (1978). Hand, eye, brain: Some "basics" in the writing process. In C. R. Cooper & L. Odell (Eds.), *Research on composing: Points of departure* (pp. 59-71). Urbana, IL: National Council of Teachers of English.

Fitzgerald, J., Speigel, D. L., & Teasley, A. B. (1987). Story structure and writing. *Academic Therapy, 22*, 255-263.

Florio, S., & Clark, C. M. (1982). What is writing for? Writing in the first weeks of school in a second-third-grade classroom. In L. C. Wilkinson (Ed.), *Communicating in the classroom* (pp. 265-282). New York: Academic Press.

Freedman, S. W., & McLeod, A. (1988). *National surveys of successful teachers of writing and their students: The United Kingdom and the United States* (Tech. Rep. No. 14). Berkeley, CA: Center for the Study of Writing.

Galda, L. (1984). Narrative competence: Play, storytelling, and story comprehension. In A. Pellegrinl & T. Yawkey (Eds.), *The development of oral and written language in social contexts* (pp. 105-117). Norwood, NJ: Ablex.

Gambrell, L. B. (1982). *Induced mental imagery and the written language expression of young children*. Paper presented at the annual meeting of the National Reading Conference, Clearwater, FL.

Gardner, H. (1983). *Frames of mind: The theory of multiple intelligences*. New York: Basic Books.

Gardner, H. (1985). Towards a theory of dramatic intelligence. In J. Kase-Polisini (Ed.), *Creative drama in a developmental context*. New York: University Press of America.

Gardner, S. (1985). *The teaching of writing from the perspective of secondary English teachers* (Unpublished doctoral dissertation, University of Michigan). *Dissertation Abstracts International, 46/04-A,* 915. (University Microfilms No. DA85-12409)

Giffen, H. (1984). Coordination of meaning in shared make believe. In I. Bretherton (Ed.), *Symbolic play: The development of social understanding.* New York: Academic Press.

Golub, L. S. (1983). Stimulating and receiving children's writing: Implications for an elementary writing curriculum. In M. Myers & J. Gray (Eds.), *Theory and practice in the teaching of composition: Processing, distancing, and modeling* (pp. 103–115). Urbana, IL: National Council of Teachers of English.

Graves, D. H. (1973). *Children's writing: Research directions and hypotheses based upon an examination of the writing processes of seven-year-old children.* Unpublished doctoral dissertation, State University of New York at Buffalo. *Dissertation Abstracts International, 34/10-A,* 6255. (University Microfilms No. 74-8375)

Graves, D. H. (1978). Balance the basics: Let them write. *Learning, 6,* 30–33.

Graves, D. H. (1982). *A case study observing the development of primary children's composing, spelling, and motor behaviors during the writing process* (Final report, September 1, 1978–August 31, 1981). Durham, NH: Department of Education. (ERIC Document Reproduction Service No. ED 218 653)

Graves, D. H. (1983). *Writing: Teachers and children at work.* Exeter, NH: Heinemann.

Green, B. T. (1974). *The effects of dramatic techniques on selected learning outcomes* (Unpublished doctoral dissertation, Clark University). *Dissertation Abstracts International, 35/05-A,* 2767. (University Microfilms No. D74-24186)

Hall, N. (1988). Playing at literacy. *London Drama, 7*(5), 11–15.

Halliday, M. A. K. (1977). *Learning how to mean: Explorations in the development of language.* New York: Elsevier.

Harris, M. B. (1973). Modeling and flexible problem-solving. *Psychological Reports, 33*(1), 19–23.

Harste, J., Woodward, V. A., & Burke, C. (1984). *Language stories and literacy lessons.* Portsmouth, NH: Heinemann.

Heathcote, D. (1981). Drama as education. In Nellie McCaslin (Ed.), *Children and drama* (2nd ed., pp. 78–90). New York: Longman.

Henderson, L. C., & Shanker, J. L. (1978). The use of interpretative dramatics versus basal reader workbooks for developing comprehension skill. *Reading World, 17,* 239–243.

Hillocks, G. (1986). *Research on written composition: New directions for teaching.* Urbana, IL: National Conference on Research in English.

Hirsch, S. C. (1984). Understanding fiction through writing it. *English Journal, 73*(5), 77–81.

Hoetker, J. (1969). *Dramatics and the teaching of literature.* Champaign, IL: National Council of Teachers of English.

Hoffman, J. V. (1987). Rethinking the role of oral reading in basal instruction. *The Elementary School Journal, 87,* 367–373.

Holladay, S. J. (1987). *Narrative activity and teacher effectiveness: An investigation of the nature of storytelling in the classroom.* Paper presented at the annual meeting of the Speech Communication Association, Boston.

Howell, S. (1982). *The role of expressive writing in the writing program* (Unpublished doctoral dissertation, Southern Illinois University). *Dissertation Abstracts International, 43/05-A,* 1454. (University Microfilms No. DA82-21940)

Isenberg, J., & Jacob, E. (1983). Literacy and symbolic play: A review of the literature. *Childhood Education, 59,* 272–276.

Kafka, T. T. (1974). *A study of the effectiveness of four motivational stimuli on the quality of composition of intermediate students in one school district* (Unpublished doctoral dissertation, St. John's University). *Dissertation Abstracts International, 32,* 2549A. (University Microfilms No. D71-30213)

Kantor, K. J. (1975). Creative expression in the English curriculum: An historical perspective. *Research in the Teaching of English, 9,* 5–29.

Kantor, K. J. (1984). Classroom contexts and the development of writing intuitions: An ethnographic case study. In R. Beach & L. S. Bridwell (Eds.), *New directions in composition research.* New York: Guilford.

Kardash, C. A. M., & Wright, L. (1987). Does creative drama benefit elementary school students: A meta-analysis. *Youth Theater Journal, 2*(1), 11–18.

Kassab, L. J. (1984). *A poetic/dramatic approach to facilitate oral communication (oral interpretation, reticence).* Unpublished doctoral dissertation, Pennsylvania State University. *Dissertation Abstracts International, 45/10-A,* 3026. (University Microfilms No. D84-29098)

Kelley, K. R. (1984). *The effect of writing instruction on reading comprehension and story writing ability.* Unpublished doctoral dissertation, University of Pittsburgh. *Dissertation Abstracts International, 45/06-A,* 1703. (University Microfilms No. D84-21346)

King, M. (1978). Research in composition: A need for theory. *Research in the Teaching of English, 12,* 193–202.

Lopate, P. (1978). Helping young children start to write. In C. R. Cooper & L. Odell (Eds.), *Research on composing: Points of departure* (pp. 135–149). Urbana, IL: National Council of Teachers of English.

Mayberry, D. R. (1975). *A comparison of three techniques of teaching literature: Silent reading, solo performance, and readers theatre* (Unpublished doctoral dissertation, North Texas State University). *Abstract in I.D. Newsletter, 16,* 10.

McIntyre, B. M. (1957). *The effect of a program of creative activities upon the consonant articulation skills of adolescent and preadolescent children with speech disorders* (Unpublished doctoral dissertation, University of Pittsburgh). *Dissertation Abstracts International, 17/05,* 1152. (University Microfilms No. DOO-21006)

McLure, A. A. (1985). *Children's responses to poetry in a supportive literary context* (Unpublished doctoral dissertation, Ohio State University). *Dissertation Abstracts International, 46/09-A,* 2603. (University Microfilms No. DA85-26218)

Milner, S. C. (1982). *Effects of a curriculum intervention program using fairy tales on preschool children's empathy level, reading readiness, oral language development and concept of a story* (Unpublished doctoral dissertation, University of Florida). *Dissertation Abstracts International, 44/2,* 430-A. (University Microfilms No. DA83-13664)

Moffett, J. (1979). Commentary: The word and the world. *Language Arts, 56,* 115–116.

Moffett, J., & Wagner, B. J. (1983). *Student-centered language arts and reading, K–13: A handbook for teachers.* Boston: Houghton Mifflin.

Monson, D. (1986). Drama and narrative. The link to literature and composition in the elementary school. In J. Kase-Polisini (Ed.), *Children's theater: Creative drama and learning.* New York: University Press of America.

Mosenthal, P. B. (1984). The effect of classroom ideology on children's production of narrative text. *American Educational Research Journal, 21,* 679–689.

Mosenthal, P. B., Conley, M. W., Colella, A., & Davidson-Mosenthal, R. (1985). The influence of prior knowledge and teacher lesson structure on children's production of narratives, *The Elementary School Journal, 85,* 621–634.

National Endowment for the Arts (1988). *Toward civilization*. Washington, DC: Public Information Office.

Norton, N. J. (1973). *Symbolic arts: The effect of movement and drama upon the oral communication of children in grade two* (Unpublished doctoral dissertation, Boston University). *Dissertation Abstracts International, 34/04-A,* 1491. (University Microfilms No. 73-23589)

Page, A. (1983). *Children's story comprehension as a result of storytelling and story dramatization: A study of the child as spectator and as participant* (Unpublished doctoral dissertation, University of Massachusetts). *Dissertation Abstracts International, 44/04-A,* 985. (University Microfilms No. DA83-17447)

Paley, V. (1987). *Wally's stories: Conversations in the kindergarten*. Cambridge: Harvard University Press.

Pellegrini, A. D. (1980). The relationship between kindergarteners' play and achievement in prereading, language, and writing. *Psychology in the Schools, 17,* 530-535.

Pellegrini, A. D. (1982). The construction of cohesive text by preschoolers in two play contexts. *Discourse Processes, 5*(1), 101-108.

Pellegrini, A. D. (1984a). The effect of dramatic play on children's generation of cohesive text. *Discourse Processes, 7*(1), 57-67.

Pellegrini, A. D. (1984b). Symbolic functioning and children's early writing: The relations between kindergarteners' play and isolated word-writing fluency. In R. Beach & L. S. Bridwell (Eds.), *New directions in composition research* (pp. 274-284). New York: Guilford.

Pellegrini, A. D. (1985). The relations between symbolic play and literate behavior: A review and critique of the empirical literature. *Review of Educational Research, 55*(1), 107-121.

Pelias, R. J. (1979). *Oral interpretation as a method for increasing perspective-taking abilities* (Unpublished doctoral dissertation, University of Illinois at Urbana-Champaign). *Dissertation Abstracts International, 40/10-A,* 5248. (University Microfilms No. 80-09127)

Perl, S., & Wilson, N. (1986). *Through teachers' eyes*. Portsmouth, NH: Heinemann.

Peters, W. H. (1987). Research on teaching: Presage variables. In W. H. Peters & Conference on English Education Commission on Research in Teachers Effectiveness (Eds.), *Effective English teaching*. Urbana, IL: National Council of Teachers of English.

Piaget, J. (1962). *Play, dreams, and imitation in childhood*. New York: Norton. (Original work published 1945)

Pitcher, E., & Prelinger, E. (1973). *Children tell stories*. New York: International Universities Press.

Polyani, M. (1962). *Personal knowledge: Towards a post-critical philosophy*. Chicago: University of Chicago Press.

Post, R. M. (1974). Readers theatre as a method of teaching literature. *English Journal, 63*(6), 69-72.

Ridel, S. J. H. (1975). *An investigation of the effects of creative dramatics on ninth grade students* (Unpublished doctoral dissertation, Florida State University). *Dissertation Abstracts International, 36/06-A,* 3551-A. (University Microfilms No. 75-26, 811, 238)

Rosen, H. (1986). The importance of story. *Language Arts, 63,* 226-237.

Roubicek, H. L. (1983). *An investigation of story dramatization as a pre-writing activity* (Unpublished doctoral dissertation, University of Maryland). *Dissertation Abstracts International, 45/02-A,* 403. (University Microfilms No. 84-12051)

Sager, C. (1973). *Improving the quality of written composition through pupil use of rating scale* (Unpublished doctoral dissertation, Boston University). *Dissertation Abstracts International, 34,* 1496-A.

Saldaña, J. (1987). Statistical results in progress for the theatre for children component of the ASU longitudinal study. *Youth Theatre Journal, 2*(2), 14-27.

Saltz, E., Dixon, D., & Johnson, J. (1977). Training disadvantaged preschoolers on various fantasy activities: Effects on cognitive functioning and impulse control. *Child Development, 48,* 367-380.

Scardamalia, M., & Bereiter, C. (1986). Research on written composition. In M. C. Wittrock (Ed.), *Handbook of research on teaching* (3rd eds., pp. 778-803). New York: Macmillan.

Schultz, J. (1982). *Writting: From start to finish*. Portsmouth, NH: Heinemann Boynton/Cook.

Scollon, R., & Scollon, B. K. S. (1981). *Narrative, literacy, and face in interethnic communication*. Norwood, NJ: Ablex.

Shumaker, C. L. (1982). *A study to determine if planned weekly instruction in expressive writing in grade six improves pupils' language arts achievement scores* (Unpublished doctoral dissertation, Temple University). *Dissertation Abstracts International, 43/03-A,* 709. (University Microfilms No. DA82-17798)

Smilansky, S. (1968). *The effects of sociodramatic play on disadvantaged preschool children*. New York: Wiley.

Snyder-Greco, T. (1983). The effects of creative dramatic techniques on selected language functions of language disorders children. *Children's Theatre Review, 32,* 9-13.

Sowers, S. A. (1979). A six year old's writing process: The first half of first grade. *Language Arts, 56,* 829-835.

Stallard, C. K. (1974). An analysis of the writing behavior of good student writers. *Research in the Teaching of English, 8,* 207-218.

Stein, N. (1983). On the goals, functions, and knowledge of reading and writing. *Contemporary Educational Psychology, 8,* 261-292.

Stein, N. (1984). Critical issues in the development of literacy education: Toward a theory of issues and instruction. *American Journal of Education, 93*(1), 171-197.

Stein, N. (1986). Knowledge and process in the acquisition of writing skills. In E. Z. Rothkopf (Ed.), *Review of research in education* (Vol. 3, pp. 225-258). Washington, DC: American Educational Research Association.

Stewig, J. W. (1986a). The classroom connection: Elementary school principals and creative drama. *Youth Theater Journal, 1*(2), 15-18.

Stewig, J. W. (1986b). NCTE Centers of Excellence: A place for drama. *Youth Theater Journal, 1*(2), 25-27.

Stewig, J. W., & Vail, J. (1985). The relation between creative drama and oral language growth. *Clearing House, 58,* 261-264.

Stewig, J. W., & Young, L. (1978). An exploration of the relations between creative drama and language growth. *Children's Theatre Review, 27*(2), 10-12.

Strickland, D. S. (1973). A program for linguistically different Black children. *Research in the Teaching of English, 7,* 79-86.

Thibodeau, A. L. (1974). *A study of the effects of elaborative thinking and vocabulary enrichment exercises on written composition* (Unpublished doctoral dissertation, Boston University). *Dissertation Abstracts International, 25/04-A,* 2388. (University Microfilms No. D64-04041)

Troyka, L. Q. (1973). *A study of the effect of simulation-gaming on expository prose competence of college remedial English composition students* (Unpublished doctoral dissertation, New York University). *Dissertation Abstracts International, 34,* 4092-A. (University Microfilms No. 73-30, 136) (ERIC Document Reproduction Service No. ED 090 541)

Tucker, J. K. (1971). *The use of creative dramatics as an aid in developing reading readiness with kindergarten children* (Unpublished doctoral dissertation, University of Wisconsin). *Dissertation Abstracts International, 32/06-A,* 3471. (University Microfilms No. 71-25508)

Vitz, K. (1984). The effects of creative drama in English as a second language. *Children's Theatre Review, 33,* 23-26, 33.

Vygotsky, L. S. (1967). Play and its role in the mental development of the child. *Soviet Psychology, 12,* 62-76.

Vygotsky, L. S. (1978). *Mind in society: The development of higher psychological processes.* (M. Cole, V. John-Steiner, S. Scribner, & E. Souberman, Eds.). Cambridge, MA: Harvard University Press.

Wagner, B. J. (1976). *Dorothy Heathcote: Drama as a learning medium.* Washington, DC: National Education Association.

Wagner, B. J. (1986). *The effects of role playing on written persuasion: An age and channel comparison of fourth and eighth graders* (Unpublished doctoral dissertation, University of Illinois at Chicago). *Dissertation Abstracts International, 47/11-A,* 4008. (University Microfilms No. 87-05196)

Wagner, B. J. (1990). Dramatic improvisation in the classroom. In D. L. Rubin & S. Hynds (Eds.), *Perspective on talk and learning.* Urbana, IL: National Council of Teachers of English.

Winegarden, A. D. (1980). The value of readers theatre: Claims, programs, and research. *Research in Education.* (ERIC Document Reproduction Service No. ED 182 793)

Wise, A. E., Darling-Hammond, L., McLaughlin, M. W., & Bernstein, H. T. (1984). *Teacher evaluation: A study of effective practices.* Santa Monica, CA: Rand Corporation. (ERIC Document Reproduction Service No. ED 246 559)

Witkin, R. W. (1974). *The intelligence of feeling.* London: Heinemann.

Wolfgang, C. H. (1973). *An exploration of the relationship between reading achievement and selected development aspects of children's play* (Unpublished doctoral dissertation, University of Pittsburgh). *Dissertation Abstracts International, 34/08-A.*

Youngers. J. S. (1977). *An investigation of the effects of experiences in creative dramatics on creative and semantic development in children* (Vols. I and II) (Unpublished doctoral dissertation, University of Iowa). *Dissertation Abstracts International, 39/117-A.* (University Microfilms No. 7810 405, 922)

# THE LANGUAGE ARTS INTERACT

## Jane Hansen
### University of New Hampshire

Whether teachers teach kindergarten children or Ph.D. students, a dilemma about language arts instruction faces them. Various definitions of literacy lead to alternative forms of pedagogy. One school of thought defines literacy as the ability to read and write, with the two taught as separate subjects. Others define literate persons as those whose actions reveal an understanding of ways to better the condition of humanity. Countless variations dwell between the two poles.

Researchers, whether they research their own teaching or that of others, face a similar dilemma when they study the language arts. Those who rest research results on test scores may believe that literate persons are those who perform well on tests, regardless of what use they make of their literacy. Students with high scores on tests of factual information can be judged successful within this view of literacy.

On the other hand, researchers who look to social behaviors in the workplace, home, school, classroom, community, and beyond as necessary components of literacy evaluate students in terms of their use of knowledge for purposes worthwhile to their culture. They not only read and write to satisfy their quests, they consider art and talk to be important learning modes. They also listen—to everyone, not only to authorities.

As author of this chapter, I have my belief system. To me, literate persons seek and find purposes for which they use their literacy. Whereas this may sound obvious to researchers who typically set their own agendas, elementary and secondary teachers are often in positions where they do not establish their own goals. They often feel compelled to use teaching procedures prescribed by administrators. Literate teachers, however, strive to set their own agendas for their professional growth.

Similarly, these teachers strive to create classrooms in which they teach their students to set their own agendas for themselves as learners. Actually, they typically negotiate these with their teachers, and the teachers, in turn, consider their students' purposes when they plan. These literate teachers consider it their responsibility to teach students how to find purposes for reading, writing, art, life, talk, and listening. These students try

to find situations in which their learning will have meaning for them. They do not use language in mechanistic ways. Literate students are engaged.

In this chapter, I show where and how the various language arts (reading, writing, art, talking, and listening) take on significance in the lives of literate researchers, teachers, and students. I use the following format to show purposeful uses of the language arts by these persons. First, I examine ways they use language to initiate and maintain interactions with others. Second, I examine uses of the language arts to learn information, processes, and skills. Third, I show ways to use language to accomplish actions, and, finally, I focus on purposeful uses of language for enjoyment.

## PURPOSEFUL USES OF THE LANGUAGE ARTS TO INITIATE AND MAINTAIN INTERACTIONS WITH OTHERS

To value the influence of everyone who affects students—in their homes, community, school, and beyond—has become necessary in our diverse culture. The consideration of students' overall lives underlies the question of how to teach the language arts as interdependent ways of learning. Families are minisocieties in which children learn social values and ways to interact. They use many kinds of language patterns in their homes and communities, and bring this knowledge with them when they enter school. Many schools, however, do not build upon the skills children bring with them (Heath, 1983). Conflict can arise very soon if the interaction patterns children have learned are not understood and valued by schools. Thus, knowledge of the influences of home and community is crucial to the teaching of the language arts.

Gundlach, McLane, Stott, & McNamee (1985) found that children's interaction with their siblings and neighborhood playmates can provide guidelines for instruction. One 5-year-old girl learned from, with, and despite her 7-year-old sister. One day when they had fun making a magic potion, they spontaneously wrote a list of their ingredients and this activity stretched the younger sister's writing ability.

On another occasion, however, the older sister did not want to include the younger, but the neighborhood children overrode the older sister and, thus, the younger one became involved in a group writing game that helped her writing skills. In both situations, the younger sister did not get better on her own. Interactions with others contribute to children's learning. This aspect of an effective learning environment informs educators. Teachers who are comfortable with scenes of interaction among students are those who realize that persons' learning may be limited if they primarily interact with one person—even if that person is a teacher.

In programs for the children of the northern Cheyenne Indian tribe and of Spanish-speaking migrant families in a border area in Texas, very low success rates in school changed when interaction between the community and classrooms became a reality (McConnell, 1989). When local leaders managed programs and parents became part of the teaching staff, rather than all the teachers being outsiders, the children's tests scores rose significantly. The hiring of teachers from ethnic and language-minority groups

minimized the cultural shock for the children. . . . If the adults in the school are more like the adults at home there is less shock than if the children encounter someone . . . using . . . a different manner of relating to other people, insofar as these patterns are culturally determined. (McConnell, 1989)

Scollon and Scollon (1981) studied the nature of Athabaskan's responses and learned how their unique communication system can help us with insights into our own. They learned the value of reserving judgment, and coined the term *deferred politeness*, as the Athabaskan practice of bringing about a cohesive community. People who practice deferred politeness listen carefully to others in order to understand their point of view, but not necessarily to accept it. This contrasts with the notion that it is necessary to agree in order to maintain a close-knit community. With a deferred politeness model, people listen in order to give the other person room.

Cultures vary, and so must classrooms. Whereas it is extremely important for children to learn in a language-friendly environment, Halliday (1979) revealed the necessity of an interactive stance toward social class and language. Not only do students need to interact with persons of their own culture, they need to interact with language users whose dialect is different from theirs, and whose register is different.

The dialect of a language user reveals class, and register (the variation in talk depending upon whether a person talks to the retired gentleman next door or the lively toddler across the street) shows the variations used within a dialect. If people cannot adjust, then those to whom they talk get confused. A situation determines the dialect and register people use, and affects their ability to make meaning in, and of, an event. The more diverse someone's language experiences are the greater is the person's chance to use and understand language effectively.

Schools, however, sometimes structure talk so that it does not foster varied interactions. Shannon (1998) showed patterns teachers use when they respond to various students and says these patterns often reflect our country's stratified society. In other words, the classroom society is often divided into groups that have less than equal status and the teacher uses different language with the various groups; the teacher's expansive language with top groups serves to expand their learning whereas the narrow language used with low groups pinpoints those children's thinking toward specific bits of information. Differentiation among social groups is perpetuated rather than blurred in these classrooms.

When Collins (1982) collected data in schools with homogenous groups, the high groups "improved dramatically during the year and the low groups improved little." Teachers interrupt children in low reading groups (Moll & Diaz, 1987). The teachers want to break the subject matter down into simple components within the grasp of the poor students, but such practices underestimate and constrain what children learn. This instructional process perpetuates differences between high- and low-group students; the low-group students do not interact with what they read in meaningful ways.

Grouping helps to ensure the failure of low students (Oakes, 1985). Educators establish groups to give additional help under the false assumption that success gained in a low group will increase students' desire to learn. This belief overlooks the overriding effect of the socialization modeled when professionals make it their practice to put someone down. Being in a bottom group every day does not increase students' sense of their possibility.

Similarly, when students spend their language arts time in a resource room, they often suffer. Wansart (1988) described the benefits to children who learn in ways different from the mainstream when they interact with normal children for reading and writing. His findings showed results that learning disabilities research failed to document when resource rooms focused on the isolation of skills from a context of real writing and reading, separated those skills into discrete units arranged into a hierarchy, and isolated coded children from normal children. In Wansart's study of one learning-disabled child in a fourth-grade classroom, the

community milieu of the classroom supported the idea that writing is hard work for everyone. This allowed the student with disabilities to become integrated into the classroom learning process and to feel a connection with other students, rather than feeling isolated and incapable. (Wansart, 1988)

The child with problems could not only admit to having a question but could ask for and receive help. She acquired, over a period of several months, the local knowledge (Geertz, 1983) she needed to interact appropriately with her Grade 4 classmates. All groups have personalities and codes of behavior, but Jessica, because she had always gone to the resource room for reading and writing, did not initially possess the language patterns the other children used. In time, she learned how to respond to others and initiate reading–writing conversations.

Because "speech unites the cognitive and the social" (Cazden, 1986), educators consider many contexts when bringing the notion of interaction into classrooms. Who speaks to whom, about what, when, and for what purposes sets the groundwork on which language instruction rests. "Interaction among the language arts" takes on a particular meaning for teachers who value what they learn when they listen to students and what the students learn when they talk and listen to each other.

An atmosphere in which talk flourishes, rather than one which keeps students apart, underlies whether the language arts will ever come together. In the late 1980s, a high school English teacher and her class researched reading and started to question the beliefs about reading that they had inherited from their former teachers. They had been taught that reading was a solitary activity, as opposed to an activity that may bring people together. Their former teachers convinced these students that reading is not a social act.

However, via these insights teachers started to think about the possibility of book-talk as a social bond. The probability that reading could serve as an interpersonal glue was the only hope for the survival of reading; their peer network was more influential than anything else in most of their lives. These students' emerging beliefs in the social nature of reading started to bring reading into the center of their lives.

This type of change in language arts teachers' understanding of pedagogy has started to drastically influence the types of interaction they encourage. Many students do not sit quietly, listening to a teacher who thinks students learn best by listening to her language (Glover, 1993; Hindley, 1996). Often, they meet to discuss a variety of books they have individually chosen to read (Avery, 1993; Von Dras, 1995), and they are aware of various processes they use as readers (Keene & Zimmermann, 1997). They excitedly construct meaning for themselves as they interact with both adults and other children.

## PURPOSEFUL USES OF THE LANGUAGE ARTS TO LEARN INFORMATION, PROCESSES, AND SKILLS

In Goodlad's (1984) *A Place Called School*, he described the emotions, atmosphere, and environments of schools as "flat." Many students do not commit energy to their work; they do not care. He advocated change.

Ivey's (1999) case studies of three sixth-grade readers supported, 15 years after Goodlad, the still-present need for change. Ivey learned of students' incredible variability but also of the narrowness present in much curriculum. When students, regardless of their proficiency as readers, have a felt purpose for reading a particular book, poem, or article, they become engaged. Because learning purposes vary so much from person to person, task to task, and situation to situation, effective middle school educators interact with their students, find out what is of interest to them, negotiate if necessary, and create reading workshops in which students read from materials they deem worthwhile.

Duthie (1996) found this same variability of interests and awareness of purpose in her first-grade children. They know what they want to learn and pursue nonfiction to those ends. Her students start to write nonfiction by composing entire thoughts and learn to find information in books. They do not learn to read and then read to learn, a belief espoused by our profession in earlier decades; they learn to read as they purposefully search for information. Similarly when young children write, they compose messages.

Graves (1983) espoused the importance of children's and teachers' initial focus on information rather than on mechanics. In addition, the writing teachers he studied knew it was unwise for them to frequently assign topics or give story starters. Those devices rest on the assumption that the writer does not already have an idea to explore, but students do come to school with strong opinions, desires, and interests in various kinds of knowledge.

Writing teachers set aside time for students to write about what they wonder about, whether it is Hurricane Dennis or Uncle Herbert. When the teachers respond to the children's writing, they begin by listening. Mr. Metson, a third-grade teacher, heard some facts and feelings about Hurricane Dennis when Amy told him about her writing. He wondered about supportive details, so he asked, "Amy, if Floyd was the largest hurricane ever, how large was he?"

A teacher's meaning-based questions are specific, honest queries to which he does not know the answers. Amy will decide whether to find and incorporate the answer to Mr. Metson's question, whether she wants to read newspapers and magazines for other additional data; whether her draft contains any irrelevant or incorrect information; whether it needs sequencing, characters, or both; with whom to share it; when it needs to be edited and when it is in final draft form. Writers have many decisions to make, all of which center around their desire to create a clear message written in their own, distinctive voice.

These students turn hierarchical theories upside down; they do not move from simple to complex. Even first-grade writers make these decisions. Primary children use all the thinking skills of adults (Donaldson, 1977).

Goodman (1996), in extending her work with miscue analysis, realized the roles students can play. Whereas miscue analysis was originally employed as a technique for teachers to use to evaluate students' strengths and specific needs, it is now known that students can analyze their own reading. Children's reflections are important to their growth. With experience, they become articulate about what they can do to address their miscues.

When learners evaluate themselves (Hansen, 1998; in press), they become increasingly able to positively influence their engagement in their learning. This, however, is not necessarily easy for students to see, nor for teachers to arrange. Students sometimes come to class academic histories and complex life roles that appear to interfere with the completion of their assignments. In the classrooms in which Hansen served as a researcher, the teachers and students studied themselves, which led to an appreciation for self, others, and their work.

Lehr (1988) studied the benefits to children's reading when complexity was the hallmark of the class. She analyzed children's sense of theme in literature and her students surpassed those in other studies. She hypothesized that this was because her students used real books. In previous research on children's sense of theme, researchers used artificially created text, sometimes simplified. "None of the former studies used book-length texts with extended plot, setting, characterization and multiple themes (and) none had been conducted in naturalistic settings where children were allowed to see and touch the actual books as they were read aloud" (Lehr, 1988).

When Lehr's (1988) kindergarten, second-, and fourth-grade children responded to books such as *The Carrot Seed* by Pat Hutchins, *The Hating Book* by Charlotte Zolotow, and *When I Was Young in the Mountains* by Cynthia Rylant, they often generated themes that reflected knowledge of more than one book. The setting in which they discussed the books and the multifaceted plots and characterizations helped the children see the complex relationships among them. When researchers simplify texts, they remove the interactions typically found in realistic fiction, and these simplifications interfere with children's ability to purposefully construct meanings for literature.

Cochran-Smith (1984) documented nursery school teachers' story-reading sessions and heard them build on what the children noticed in the text and pictures. She observed "Storyreading was not a recitation of set reader-questions and listener-responses." The discussions were negotiated, nonfocused interactions. The teachers were aware of the sense making of the children and two readings of the same book did not bring forth the same thoughts. The cooperative negotiation of the story depended on what the children said; the teachers wanted to know what the children heard in the books. They reinforced and extended the meaning the group seemed to make of the stories.

This viewpoint is possible when the teacher believes there is more than one valid interpretation of a piece of literature. In the last 2 decades, the education profession has learned more about literature as an art, and art "opens us to dilemmas, to the hypothetical, to the range of possible worlds that a text can refer to . . ." (Bruner, 1986). This notion frightens many parents and educators who wonder, "Where does the range of possible worlds end?" Certainly there must be some limit to what is acceptable and what is not. When teachers open their classrooms to discussions in which they and their students express their values, boredom may no longer reign. "Literature, in this spirit, is an instrument of freedom, lightness, imagination, and, yes, reason. It is our only hope against the long gray night" (Bruner, 1986).

Thus, literature helps us mediate our place in society. A sociohistorical look at written language helps us understand the concept of reading as a process of mediation, and thus, to look at what could be the heart of remediation. As a process of mediation, reading is a means by which readers mediate their world. Thus, when students do not use reading to help them understand their world, they need help, or remediation. At the core of this assistance are strategies to help readers see relationships between themselves and others, as happens in Cora Five's fifth-grade class (Five, 1992).

The sharing and caring of children who support each other promote a group belief where their "affective identity" is an "effective identity" (Turnbull, 1983). The anthropological view of Turnbull highlights the benefits of learning in society rather than in isolation. Brady and Jacobs (1994) write about Brady's fifth-grade classroom in which the students teach each other and learn a great deal in the process of doing so.

Historically, children were not teachers. They were not considered sources of information in classrooms, but letters author Jane Yolen (1985) received from her young readers showed her the impossibility of stating *the* one meaning that resides in any of the books she authors. Wells (1986) said that educators must reconsider what it means to be a teacher: "The conception of teaching as transmission must be a mistaken one. First, it is not possible, simply by telling, to cause students to come to have the knowledge that is in the mind of the teacher. Knowledge cannot be transmitted." It is, instead, constructed, and it must be constructed by each individual.

Whether child or adult, any person who comes across new information will make sense of it based on the

learner's existing internal model of the world. The process (of learning) is therefore essentially interactional in nature, both within the learner and between the learner and the teacher, and calls for the negotiation of meaning, not its unidirectional transmission. . . . For those of us who are . . . teachers—the responsibility is clear: to interact with those in our care in such a way as to foster and enrich their meaning making. (Wells, 1986)

Teachers build on what children say. Wells. (1986) gave the following example to show how a teacher's questions can create in children a sense that they know something, and, therefore, can learn more:

Amanda: Mrs. M, if he put this bit in the belt and this bit in the back with the oxygen, it might look like a real diver.

Matthew: That's what I'm going to do.

Teacher: Do you think it looks like a real diver at the moment?

Matthew: No.

Amanda: No.

Maxine: Not much. It hasn't got the equipment on it.

Amanda: Yes, but if you put the feet too small, it could easily fall down.

Teacher: How do you know about a real diver, Matthew?

Matthew: I read a lot about it.

Maxine: Why? Have you got a book about divers?

Matthew: Two. Two great big annuals of divers at home and I read 'em . . . every night 'fore I go to bed. But I'm in—I'm in the middle of book one and in book two it tells you about deep-sea divers. In book one it tells you about frogmen.

Maxine: How to make it?

Matthew: Not how to make 'em.

Teacher: What's the difference between frogmen and deep-sea divers?

Matthew: 'Cos deep-sea divers aren't like frogmen—deep-sea divers haven't got flippers and—and they have different kinds of—Frogmen don't have helmets, but deep-sea divers do. So frogmen are quite different, 'cos they haven't got helmets.

The teacher asks questions to learn, more so than to check the child's knowledge; these questions set a tone of support for the student.

However, a more common model of interaction between teacher and students follows this form: Initiate, respond, evaluate (Goodwin, 1981). The teacher begins, the students respond, and the teacher evaluates. Ms. Jones asks, "What was the main idea of the story?" Fred responds, "That successful people aren't always happy." Ms. Jones evaluates, "Right! Good thinking!"

Teachers and students learn their lines for these parts very well, and for changes in these roles to continue to evolve, the parts everyone plays must be carefully critiqued. It is what is conveyed by this exchange pattern that has a significant effect on what is learned in classrooms. Even though teachers may have created this pattern because they think it is the best way to teach comprehension, it is not consistent with what we now know about reading.

Readers must learn to set their own purposes and decide for themselves whether they've understood a text to their satisfaction. If not, they may ask someone questions for clarification. Children, as well as teachers, can initiate. Because language use in the real world bounces back and forth between at least two participants, children must learn to play both roles. The social nature of learning implies that, because each context is different, participants must always evaluate what to say, consider options, and make choices.

The reciprocity and mutual responsibility that can exist between teacher and student may be the core of thinking (John-Steiner, 1985). John-Steiner's interviewed renowned thinkers and finds a triangle of results about the nature of learning, all of which inform education. In general, thinking results from various interactions, all of which a mentor supports in a young learner. One interaction is a back-and-forth movement between known concepts and new, which is different from a prevailing notion in literacy education where we more frequently hear about the necessity of building new information on old. However, exceptional learners zigzag from new to known when they regularly test and reaffirm their knowledge.

Another characteristic of thinkers is their bursts of exploration followed by long-term study. They dash after new "I wonders" and then stay for endless periods of time on one idea. Their inner drives to move ahead and to rehash familiar data need the support of a mentor who can reflect and stretch the learner's thoughts. The mentor is sensitive to whether the learner is on a plateau or shooting forward.

Finally, intensity is the overriding feature of creative thinkers. John-Steiner (1985) found no well-known thinkers who spent isolated periods of time on many barely related, short-term tasks in which they were only minimally involved. Her research encourages us to serve as mentors for our students as they become more intense people who may pursue, under our guidance, concentrated areas of study that are important to them. Learning occurs in these risks into the unknown (Cook-Gumperz, 1986).

Thus, it is up to the adult to find out what the child needs or wants. To sense what it is that children are on the verge of knowing is what teachers listen for when children talk about their interests, books, drawings, and writing. The teacher wants to know what to teach and wants her teaching to hit the mark as

often as possible. Wertsch (1984) wrote about this in relation in relation to Vygotsky's (1978) notion of the zone of proximal development (ZPD). Children learn best when they interact with adults at the point where the child is. This information, process, or skill is what is most learnable; it lies within the ZPD. When instruction reinforces, stretches, and excites a learner's passion, it is well timed.

## PURPOSEFUL USES OF THE LANGUAGE ARTS TO ACCOMPLISH ACTIONS

In 1971, Janet Emig wrote:

In this inquiry we have seen that the most significant others in the writing of twelfth graders are peers. . . . American high schools and colleges must seriously and immediately consider that the teacher-centered presentation of composition, like the teacher-centered presentation of almost every other segment of a curriculum, is pedagogically, developmentally, and politically an anachronism.

So ends Emig's book. She certainly wants action.

Emig (1971) slammed the five-paragraph essay, and, when she hypothesizes about its existence in instruction, she wonders if teachers read and assumes not. Because teachers are not well read in current and classic literature, they do not realize that the five-paragraph essay is not a form used by real writers. It is something created only for students and has no purpose. However, if teachers possessed substantial knowledge about reading and writing, they would realize the emptiness of the five-paragraph form.

When writing, as Emig (1971) hypothesized, is divorced from reading, it becomes nonsense. Reading and writing cannot interact for students if they do not interact for teachers. Teachers cannot teach something they do not do. Besides not reading, teachers do not write.

They have no recent, direct experience with a process they purport to present to others. . . . [B]ecause they have no direct experience with composing, teachers of English err in important ways. They underconceptualize and oversimplify the process of composing. Planning degenerates into outlining; reformulating becomes the correction of minor infelicities. (Emig, 1971)

Teaching goes awry when someone simplifies it.

Young children learn written language as they learn oral language, by acquiring a sense of the context, by determining what they want, and by trying a form of imposition (Lindfors, 1999). Learners inquire, and those who know how to pose their questions in effective ways learn the most. As toddlers they lived a life immersed in the oral language of a variety of people from whom they learned to talk and act in different ways.

Oral language may underlie success in both writing and reading (Tannen, 1985); children know that their talk gets them something, or, at times, fails. Thus, they learn from oral language that words have a purpose and that the better one puts those words together, the better off one is. They also know that talk does not exist in a vacuum. When someone talks, someone else is present, and, hopefully, listens.

Glenda Bissex's son Paul caught her attention one day when she was engrossed in a book (Bissex, 1980). He wrote *RUDF* on a scrap of paper and shoved it between her eyes and her book. "Are you deaf?" she read, closed her book, and paid attention. Paul felt the significance of words before he wrote, but when this, his first demanding piece of writing brought action, he knew the power of words.

Literate people strive to use words to their advantage, but sometimes experience difficulty. Inability to initiate positive interactions with others can interfere with learning, but our profession sometimes does not take such interferences seriously. At a special education placement meeting, this comment was considered irrelevant, "Johnny has been a problem on the playground ever since first grade" (Poplin, 1987). Contrary to the special education team's belief, Johnny's ability to get along with his peers is relevant. His inability to use language to accomplish playground actions may be at the heart of his learning difficulties.

Booth (1974) wrote about the two major bases for all teaching, one being the only clear value he believed everyone shares:

It is always good to maintain and improve the quality of our symbolic exchange with our fellow "selves"—to sharpen our symbolic powers so that we can understand and be understood, "taking in" other selves and thus expanding our own. What we say matters, and it matters how we say it.

People live in a world threatened by alienation and the loss of caring. Thus, Booth's (1974) second premise comes into being. He wanted to belong to a "community of those who want to discover good reasons together." Children who work together in schools, on playgrounds, and in classrooms where their goal is to find worth in each other's contributions, tend to become thoughtful, but formal evaluation measures typically value something other than the child's interpretation of a situation or ability to use language to mediate social situations. High scores on a single dimension can determine a child's future. Brown (1987) worried about this and pushes for change in schools. He noted:

[M]any of us are captivated by theories of teaching and learning that tell us to break knowledge into discrete pieces and to teach and test these pieces one by one, starting with the simplest elements. We then find that knowledge can be broken into so many pieces that we wind up spending all our time covering the simple elements and never get to the more complicated stuff....

... [A] reason we attend so faithfully to minimums and basics is that policy makers hold us accountable for them. It is the policy makers' job to establish minimum standards in housing, health matters, prison conditions, building codes, and so forth.

The problem with a policy that is minimum-oriented, however, is that it requires a free market or some other such device to push it toward excellence. Take health codes in the restaurant business, for example.... [They] greatly boost my confidence in dining out. But...the marketplace serves to promote excellence and run mediocrity out of business.

Education policy has been strong on enforcing minimums, but it has had no system of comparable strength to push for maximum....

If we want an accountability system that will gather data for maintaining minimum standards without thwarting constructive growth and change, we will have to redesign the existing system.

Such wholesale restructuring has happened before. Testing as we know it today became a part of schooling at a time when great demands were being placed on the educational system to absorb large numbers of people who had not previously sought schooling. A national need to sort people and a desire to do so "objectively" ran head-on into the long-established practice of "subjective" evaluation. Slowly but surely, subjectivity was driven to the margins....

The best way to restore balance would be to create a strong counter-culture within the system that values inquiry and thoughtfulness above all else.... Since we have not yet made a strong commitment to the proposition that all students can learn—and can learn a great deal more than they do today—we do not really know what our educational system can do.

Rousseau (1762, 1979), years ago, cautioned educators against simplifying and impoverishing the human experience. It is the task of building a oneness for self that preoccupies people throughout their lives, and it is the task of teachers to help children with this goal. This places great demands on teachers to help children create harmony among beauty, anger, and goodness.

Victoria Koivu-Rybicki is a teacher of 8- and 9-year-old students who does this. In *The Writing Lives of Children* (Madigan & Koivu-Rybicki, 1997), she and Dan Madigan write about 10 of her students who live complex live and use writing to try to figure out who they are. Jakeem wrote about a day when his brother shot into their house. The response Jakeem received from his classmates when he shared his writing helped him realize that this piece of writing served as the "mean face" he once adopted to scare away bullies. By sharing this shocking piece of writing, he became more daring, adventurous, and fearless. Jakeem gained confidence; he could more readily seek to control events rather than be controlled by them.

Literacy includes knowledge of society's expectations, and the realization that changes come about because people sense the necessity to go beyond existing social rules (de Castell, Luke, & Egan, 1986). Students and teacher go beyond print to explore the ideas it gives them about how to make their own world, this entire world, a better place. Teachers purposefully create the confidence students need to initiate change.

The high school in which Flores-González (1999) collected her data created a safe environment for high-achieving Puerto Rican students. They could outwardly live the lives of good students, and didn't need to compromise their Puerto Rican identity; it was good to be a smart Puerto Rican. In a school of much hostility those known as academics were immune from harassment. They could be students, take part in extra-curricular activities, and meet the demands of home without conflict, whereas low achievers felt themselves dragged down by the multiple roles they needed to play to juggle jobs, child care, gang membership, and studies.

Uttech (1997), distraught by the growing hostility toward the Mexican immigrant population in her area, decided to study one family. The intended to use her newly gained information to take action—to do what she could to create positive approaches to the these students, who constituted the majority of her class. She learned a great deal about the importance of respect for friends, elders, and other family members in her student's household and advocated for classrooms in which caring for all mitigated the prevailing emphasis on individualism that reigns in many schools.

When Purcell-Gates (1997) studied the family and community of the woman and child she tutored, the power of forces beyond the individuals shouted. The child appeared to need to choose between his two parents, and father did not favor literacy. The entire family must consider their extended family and community, neither of which necessarily felt the need for universal literacy. In a community various members play various roles and all don't need to be able to read telephone bills. People help each other.

Educators who collect data feel more certain of their surroundings, and more secure about changes they advocate. Fenstermacher (1986) argued that research will only make a difference if it rests on the practical arguments in the minds of teachers. Much data collected within the paradigm of natural scientists (Poplin, 1987) stripped problems from their context and the results of that research, though statistically significant, often fell on deaf ears in schools. When many aspects of classrooms are not included in a research project, results may be unrealistic. Learning is part of a social system and to isolate it from its context distorts its character.

Every aspect of children strives to develop, and needs a complex environment in order to do so. The confidence to move forward arises from and is fostered by the support of others. Development in the ability to move one's self forward, as well as promote the strengths of others, is difficult and inherently uneven. Unfortunately, educators often view unevenness in any form as indication of something wrong and focus on the perceived weakness rather than the harmony of development. This is the eternal mistake of pedagogical theories.

Focusing on one part of a child is especially detrimental if teachers let a child come to believe that the activity of learning is not a valued pursuit (Papert, 1980). Educators forget that when people are learning, they are trying something new. They do not know how to do it, and will make mistakes. Errors are a sign of trying new things, of taking risks—the hallmarks of learners. How educators respond to people's mistakes influences their willingness to try again and their enthusiasm for even the things they cannot do well.

Harste, Woodward, & Burke (1984) urged educators to listen carefully to students' stories so we know what to do as teachers. A child who fills a page with rows of scribbles and sweeps her hand from left to right as she tells a story, knows a great deal. She is not a nonwriter. For her to be a part of literacy lessons in which the teacher writes and sweeps her hand across the paper as she reads, supports what she knows—and extends her knowledge. She sees words on the teacher's chart, not scribbles. Driven by her continued desire to place her own voice on paper, and with her teacher's instruction she will grow as a writer.

## PURPOSEFUL USES OF THE LANGUAGE ARTS TO LIVE ENRICHED LIVES

Some students will never love to read and write, and that is as it should be; some prefer art, math, physical engagements, and oral interaction. In this century, literacy is more than reading and writing—it is a person's ability to thoughtfully identify, gather, analyze and use information so they can control the decisions they make in their lives. Educators must be responsible for enabling students to enjoy the literacy process.

Gallas (1998) wrote, as a teacher researcher, about the girls in one class, led by Sophia, who loved to tell stories at sharing time, and the class, including Karen, savored these oral dramas. Intended as power plays, the girls' stories tended to lead class members to think they could do anything. Whereas these tales served a very serious need of the children for power, they show the students' simultaneous use of language for enjoyment. When they sat in the teacher's chair, nothing could diminish their performance, nor their love for all. On May 2, Sophia told this story.

Once upon a time in a far, far town in a far, far city, there lived a mommy and a daddy, and another mommy and daddy. And they had babies: Sophia and Barbara.... [B]ut one day they decided to run away. They got a boat and set sail down a river. They saw a Violet in the river. "Stop the boat!" said Sophia.

They stopped and jumped into the river and followed the Violet to a secret hole. And the one Violet led them to a secret place. There was a mountain of Violets! A volcano of Violets! Sophia threw a rock into the volcano. The volcano erupted! And Violets came out of the volcano! They could only choose one. Every Violet put on the cutest face, so they had to take all the Violets. (Gallas, 1998, p. 147)

Dyson (1997), with the teachers of a study group, wrote about "the very strength of childhood, that is, the inclination to play, to turn the world on its head" (p. 93). Children not only use language to turn their own world on its head, but they frequently confuse their teachers, who, in turn, strive to figure out the children's viewpoint. Sometimes, when freedom of language leads to offensive portrayals of others, teachers step in to help children imagine new possibilities. The classroom becomes a place in which multiple perspectives arise and someone may question a child's familiar worlds and words, but the positiveness of difference reigns in these classrooms.

In culturally sensitive classrooms (Diamond & Moore, 1995), students' interests foster the development of their literacy skills. They construct meaning for multicultural literature through their own personal experiences as they talk, create art, and write about themselves, their communities, and print. The students do not feel alienated; they feel comfortable in this place called school.

Ladson-Billings (1994) wrote about the power of caring in classrooms of successful teachers of African American students. Their ideologies vary and the outward appearance of their classrooms differ, but they care about their students, both in and beyond the classroom. They students know their teachers care for them and believe in caring, as they create classrooms in which students cheer for each other.

When Suzanne McCotter's and Sara Glickman's class (McCotter, 1999) planned for their 1st year as teaching partners, they wanted to deal with racism overtly and honestly. As they set more specific goals they wanted a classroom in which students felt safe to question, studied a rigorous curriculum, and had fun. These teachers created a format for daily team meetings in which students celebrated and raised concerns. This reserved time in which their voices were valued spilled over, in effect, into their entire day. As they learned to work in democratic groups in social studies, for example, they became actively involved and excited. As the teachers, said, "The key is making a philosophical commitment to sharing power with kids; the rest is following through" (p. 116).

The high school, student researchers (Oldfather et al., 1999) who studied the notion of motivation did so because they felt unheard in many of their classrooms. They each chose a teacher who did appear to be motivated and valued students' motivations, and became increasingly convinced of the importance of each person's voice, both in discussions and in writing. When Forencia's classrooms provided her with decreased opportunities for self-expression, she said, "I felt like they took away the paper, and my mind went blank" (p. 204). As the students analyzed their various forms of data, the possibilities for transformations in pedagogy emerged. Students and teachers can plan school together.

When Parker (1997) structured her primary classroom, she wanted her students to have a say in what they did and how. She faced a particular joy and challenge in the placement of Jamie, a child with spinal atrophy, in her class from kindergarten through second grade. Jamie, a delightful, strong-willed, helpful girl brought other children into literacy when they witnessed her pleasure with books. Children watched her as she turned pages, smiled, and chuckled to herself. Curious, they moved closer, and invited her to read with them. Soon, they all started to laugh and enjoy themselves as they talked about books.

Ostrow (1995) created a huge span of opportunities in her multi-age primary classroom. Frequent interaction among the learners (the teacher is one of the learners) help everyone learn about various processes, kinds of information, and useful skills.

They create art, talk, and write in genres that serve their various pursuits about islands or weather and read a huge range of materials (Hubbard, 1996). They learn, and the language arts serve them.

Ernst's (1994) art students use writing and talk to enrich their experiences with paint and clay. As Ernst circulated among them in their artists' workshop, she paused beside various artists, "What are you working on?" She did not assign particular media or topics, and she did not know why students had chosen their materials. She truly wanted to know what they were doing. The assumption on both her part and theirs is that when individuals draw, read, or write, they do so with a purpose in mind, and they are mindful of that purpose.

Language arts teacher Rief (1999) and the music teacher with whom she collaborated use meaning, purpose, and enrichment as their guiding principles when their seventh-graders created an original musical. When students make intellectual and emotional connections, the musical, the books they read, their writings, and drawings become meaningful. Their purposes lead the middle schoolers from one meaning to another as they find the depth and concentric layers of possibilities in a person, song, piece of information, or event. Students and teachers feel electricity jaggle up their spines when their interactive language arts experiences enrich their lives.

The education profession has only begun to realize the possibilities of the arts and the various forms of language. Educators have only begun to value the many ways their students reach out for meaning. When students use classrooms to search for answers to the big question, "What am I hear for?" the language arts allow visions to emerge, and language arts teachers take on the responsibility of teaching students ways to catch glimpses of who they are.

## References

Avery, C. (1993). . . . And with a light touch: Learning about reading, writing, and teaching with first graders. Portsmouth, NH: Heinemann.

Bissex, G. (1980). GNYS AT WRK: A child learns to write and read. Cambridge, MA: Harvard University Press.

Booth, W. C. (1974). Modern dogma and the rhetoric of assent. Notre Dame, IN: University of Notre Dame Press.

Brady, S., & Jacobs, S. (1994). Mindful of others: Teaching children to teach. Portsmouth, NH: Heinemann.

Brown, R. (1987). Who is accountable for "thoughtfulness"? Phi Delta Kappan, 694-52.

Bruner, J. (1986). Actual minds, possible worlds. Cambridge, MA: Harvard University Press.

Cazden, C. B. (1986). Classroom discourse. In M. C. Wittrock (Ed.), Handbook of research on teaching (3rd ed.). New York: Macmillan.

Cochran-Smith, M. (1984). The making of a reader. Norwood, NJ: Ablex.

Collins, J. (1982). Discourse style, classroom interaction and differential treatment. Journal of Reading Behavior, 14, 429-438.

Cook-Gumperz, J. (1986). The social construction of literacy. Cambridge, England: Cambridge University Press.

de Castell, S., Luke, A., & Egan, K. (Eds.) (1986). Literacy, society, and schooling: A reader. Cambridge, England: Cambridge University Press.

Diamond, B. J., & Moore, M. A. (1995). Multicultural literacy: Mirroring the reality of the classroom. White Plains, New York: Longman.

Donaldson, M. (1977). Children's minds. New York: Norton.

Duthie, C. (1996). True stories: Nonfiction literacy in the primary classroom. York, ME: Stenhouse.

Dyson, A. H. (with the San Francisco East Bay Teachers Study Group). (1997). What difference does difference make? Teacher reflections on diversity, literacy, and the urban primary school. Urbana, IL: National Council of Teachers of English.

Emig, J. (1971). The composing processes of twelfth graders (NCTE Research Rep. No. 13). Urbana, IL: National Council of Teachers of English.

Ernst, K. (1994). Picturing learning: Artists and writers in the classroom. Portsmouth, NH: Heinemann.

Fenstermacher, G. D. (1986). Philosophy of research on teaching: Three aspects. In M. C. Wittrock (Ed.), Handbook of research on teaching. New York: Macmillan.

Five, C. (1992). Special voices: Teaching children with special needs in the regular classroom. Portsmouth, NH: Heinemann.

Flores-González, N. (1999). Puerto Rican high achievers: An example of ethnic and academic identity compatibility. Anthropology and Education Quarterly, 30(3), 343-362.

Gallas, K. (1998). "Sometimes I can be anything": Power, gender and identity in a primary classroom. New York: Teachers College Press.

Geertz, C. (1983). *Local knowledge: Further essays in interpretive anthropology*. New York: Basic Books.

Glover, M. K. (1993). *Two years: A teacher's memoir*. Portsmouth, NH: Heinemann.

Goodlad, J. (1984). *A place called school*. New York: McGraw.

Goodman, Y. (1996). Revaluing readers while readers revalue themselves: Retrospective Miscue Analysis. *The Reading Teacher, 49*(8), 600–609.

Goodwin, C. (1981). *Conversational organization: Interaction between speakers and hearers*. San Diego: Academic Press.

Graves, D. (1983). *Writing: Teachers and children at work*. Portsmouth, NH: Heinemann.

Gundlach, R., McLane, J. B., Stott, F. M., & McNamee, G. D. (1985). The social foundations of children's early writing development. In M. Farr (Ed.), *Advances in writing research: Vol. 1. Studies in children's writing development*. Norwood, NJ: Ablex.

Halliday, M. A. K. (1979). *Language as social semiotic: The social interpretation of language and meaning*. London: Edward Arnold.

Hansen, J. (1998). *When learners evaluate*. Portsmouth, NH: Heinemann.

Hansen, J. (in press). *When writers read* (2nd ed.). Portsmouth, NH: Heinemann.

Harste, J. C., Woodward, V., & Burke, C. (1984). *Language stories and literacy lessons*. Portsmouth, NH: Heinemann.

Heath, S. B. (1983). *Ways with words*. Cambridge, England: Cambridge University Press.

Hindley, J. (1996). *In the company of children*. York, ME: Stenhouse.

Hubbard, R. S. (1996). *Workshop of the possible: Nurturing children's creative development*. York, ME: Stenhouse.

Ivey, G. (1999). A multicase study in the middle school: Complexities among young adolescent readers. *Reading Research Quarterly, 3*(2), 172–192.

John-Steiner, V. (1985). *Notebooks of the mind*. Albuquerque: University of New Mexico Press.

Keene, E. O., & Zimmermann, S. (1997). *Mosaic of thought: Teaching comprehension in a reader's workshop*. Portsmouth, NH: Heinemann.

Ladson-Billings, G. (1994). *The dreamkeepers: Successful teachers of African American children*. San Francisco: Jossey-Bass.

Lehr, S. (1988). The child's developing sense of theme as a response to literature. *Reading Research Quarterly, 23*(3), 337–357.

Lindfors, J. W. (1999). *Children's inquiry: Using language to make sense of the world*. New York: Teachers College Press; Urbana, IL: National Council of Teachers of English.

Madigan, D., & Koivu-Rybicki, V. (1997). *The writing lives of children*. York, ME: Stenhouse.

McConnell, B. (1989). Education as a cultural process: The interaction between community and classroom in fostering learning. In J. Allen & J. Mason (Eds.), *Risk makers, risk takers, risk breakers: Reducing the risks for young literacy learners* (pp. 201–221). Portsmouth, NH: Heinemann.

McCotter, S. S. (1999). Team meetings, integrated curriculum, and literature groups: Forums for democratic decision-making. In J. Allen (Ed.), *Class actions: Teaching for social justice in elementary and middle school*. New York: Teachers College Press.

Moll, L. C., & Diaz, S. (1987). Change as the goal of educational research. *Anthropology and Education Quarterly, 18*(4), 300–311.

Oakes, J. (1985). *Keeping track: How schools structure inequality*. New Haven, CT: Yale University Press.

Oldfather, P., Thomas, S., Eckert, L., Garcia, F., Grannis, N., Kilgore, J. Newman-Gonchar, A., Petersen, B., Rodriguez, P., & Tjioe, M. (1999). The nature and outcomes of students' longitudinal participatory research on literacy motivations and schooling. *Research in the Teaching of English, 34*, 281–320.

Ostrow, J. (1995). *A room with a different view: First through third graders build community and create curriculum*. York, ME: Stenhouse.

Papert, S. (1980). *Mindstorms*. New York: Basic Books.

Parker, D. (1997). *Jamie: A literacy story*. York, ME: Stenhouse.

Poplin, M. S. (1987). Self-imposed blindness: The scientific method in education. *Remedial and Special Education, 8*(6), 31–37.

Purcell-Gates, V. (1997). *Other people's words: The cycle of low literacy*. Cambridge: Harvard University Press.

Rief, L. (1999). *Vision and voice: Extending the literacy spectrum*. Portsmouth, NH: Heinemann.

Rousseau, J. J. (1979). *Emile, or, On education*. (A. Bloom, Trans.) New York: Basic Books. (Original work published 1762)

Scollon, R., & Scollon, S. B. K. (1981). *Narrative, literacy and face in interethnic communication*. Norwood, NJ: Ablex.

Shannon, P. (1998). *Reading poverty*. Portsmouth, NH: Heinemann.

Tannen, D. (1985). Relative focus on involvement in oral and written discourse. In D. R. Olson, N. Torrance, & A. Hildyard (Eds.), *Literacy, language, and learning: The nature and consequences of reading and writing* (pp. 124–147). Cambridge, England: Cambridge University Press.

Turnbull, C. (1983). *The human cycle*. New York: Simon & Schuster.

Uttech, M. (1997). Vale la pena: Advocacy along the borderlands. In D. Taylor, D. Coughlin, & J. Morasco (Eds.), *Teaching and advocacy*. York, ME: Stenhouse.

Von Dras, J. (1995). Will the real teacher please stand up? *Primary Voices K–6, 3*(1), 30–37.

Vygotsky, L. S. (1978). *Mind in society: The development of higher psychological processes*. Cambridge, MA: Harvard University Press.

Wansart, W. (1988). The student with learning disabilities in a writing process classroom: A case study. *Journal of Reading, Writing, and Learning Disabilities International, 4*, 311–319.

Wells, G. (1986). *The meaning makers: Children learning language and using language to learn*. Portsmouth, NH: Heinemann.

Wertsch, J. V. (1984). The zone of proximal development: Some conceptual issues. In B. Rogoff & J. V. Wertsch (Eds.), *Children's learning in the "zone of proximal development"* (New Directions for Child Development, No. 24). San Francisco, Jossey-Bass.

Yolen, J. (1985). The story between. *Language Arts, 62*(6), 590–592.

# CURRICULUM INTEGRATION TO PROMOTE LITERATE THINKING: DILEMMAS AND POSSIBILITIES

## Donna M. Ogle and Susan I. McMahon
### National-Louis University

The language arts—reading, writing, speaking, and listening are unique among the disciplines in that they are most fundamentally the foundation for all learning. The traditional disciplinary orientation of schools, however, separates that foundation from the content to be learned. This artificial separation continues to create tensions in how we organize and develop students' competence as language users. Making the instructional issues even more complicated is the fact that the disciplines themselves are artificial and do not represent the requirements for knowledge and conceptual use in most of life beyond academic situations in schools.

Discussions with practicing teachers about how they can best foster learning often lead to talk about "integrating" curriculum. They explain that it makes the real relationships across school subjects practical for students. They express beliefs that such forms of curriculum are more motivational for learners, promote deeper understandings, and result in higher achievement. Although educators have a variety of ways of talking about how to incorporate the content of one school subject into another (such as thematic, integrated, or interdisciplinary), one prevalent notion is that children will learn better if we break down existing content boundaries. Examination of practice will reveal this belief system at elementary, secondary, and university settings. Furthermore, many publishers provide materials to help teachers implement integrated units. In addition to those perspectives of the practitioner, many educational theorists have also provided reasonable arguments supporting more connections across content areas. Thus, a strong perception exists that such instruction is beneficial. Although prevalent in belief systems and practice, integration has not been sufficiently

studied systematically to demonstrate (a) what specific benefits it provides to learners, (b) what should be integrated, (c) how to do so effectively, or (d) when content should be connected and/or when it may be better taught more discretely.

Real are the dilemmas educators face in organizing and structuring schooling so that students develop the knowledge and skills they need, as well as the awareness of how to use these meaningfully in varied situations and to solve authentic problems. Attempts to bridge these artificial distinctions have led to many different innovations and currently focus on various forms of integrated curriculum. Research on integrated instruction should provide a valuable guide for teachers and schools. Unfortunately, there is little available on ways language arts enhances learning of content, the development of literacy within such contexts, and the support teachers need to develop and implement such curriculum. Finally, the increased focus on content standards and standardized tests that measure knowledge within the content areas also presents reason for a thorough exploration of the issues related to connecting curriculum in new ways.

When describing the combining of curriculum areas in this chapter, we use the term *integrated* to apply to several models. Although we recognize that this chunking of various types of integrated learning may blur some important distinctions, it will provide a general concept label for our discussion. Recognizing there are several ways to conceive of integration, we are going to focus our discussion primarily on integration that involves conscious attention to the language arts. Therefore, research focused basically on science and mathematics, for example, will not be included. This review is limited to how literacy functions as a tool for learning in integrated curriculum experiences.

## THEORETICAL PERSPECTIVES

Educators have long argued that connecting curriculum will facilitate students' learning. Dewey (1956) reasoned that school subjects need to be taught in ways that connect the ideas to the child's prior experiences and daily life. Thus, instead of content organized from the standpoint of an adult and divided into content areas, Dewey asserted teachers should begin with the learners and their experiences to plan content that is relevant to them. Such ideas were embraced by those associated with Dewey's progressive education movement leading to the notion of "core" curriculum (Lounsbury & Vars, 1978; Oberholzer, 1988). Further, Tyler (1949) proposed that integration provides educators a cohesive way to plan and implement instruction. If the curriculum is organized around conceptual frameworks that do not need to be divided into school subjects, then all the content areas can be merged. Once school subjects are integrated, learners can more easily see the relationships across areas. Other scholars contribute to the discussion, noting the importance of inquiry-based learning (Bloom, 1958) and making connections across contents (Bruner, 1986).

Considering the language arts specifically, there has long been a tension about how to teach the components of language arts, whether separately (as the National Writing Project still argues is needed for writing), in an integrated way (whole-language instruction), or by making the connections and applications within other content areas or units of study. (Content area reading and writing across the curriculum movements are a good example of this orientation.) Britton, Burgess, Martin, McLeod, and Rosen (1975) created the concept of language across the curriculum nearly 30 years ago to emphasize that language processes are really tools for thinking about significant content and thus should be taught throughout the curriculum. Fulwiler's (1987) work is a North American extension of these ideas.

Other scholars enlarge the discussion, noting the importance of inquiry-based learning (Beane, 1995; Bloom, 1958; Short & Harstee, 1996), the assumption being that if learners pursue topics of interest they will be more motivated and will learn content in ways that are applicable to life beyond the classroom. All these scholars present compelling arguments for integrating curriculum to foster enhanced learning. Contemporary thought expands the argument further as scholars learn more about the processes of thinking. That is, recent research in cognition has focused attention on understanding the development of knowledge and the differentiation of lower from higher order thinking (Mathison & Freeman, 1998). Goleman's (1995) work with emotional intelligence also argued that the more students can personally and emotionally connect with learning experiences, the more likely the brain is to receive and build extended networks to make those experiences memorable. This emphasis on thought processes, as well as earlier considerations concerning how to make the language arts most applicable to reading

tasks has led many educators to the works of Vygotsky (1978), whose ideas are gaining acceptance as a way of rethinking existing practices, including modifications of curriculum organization and instruction. Three Vygotskian notions are of key importance when considering support for integrated curriculum: (a) language develops thinking, (b) learning occurs on a social plane before being internalized, and (c) learning is facilitated through a knowledgeable other working within the learner's zone of proximal development.

### Language Develops Thinking

Vygotsky (1978) argued that the use of language and other sign systems develops higher order thinking. That is, humans mediate the learning of the young through the use of multiple signs, both verbal and nonverbal. The learner synthesizes the knowledge by connecting it to what she already knows, thus constructing a new understanding. The language of the adult should facilitate such a synthesis. That is, language use that creates relationships in content will be more likely to foster cohesive thinking. Moreover, each discipline has its own discourse that participants within that community use and understand (Kuhn, 1970). These ways of interaction are not formed in isolation, but are, instead, more integrative of multiple aspects of knowledge. For learners to truly understand the discourses, interactions in classrooms should also relate to those oral and written texts reproduced within the disciplines (O'Flahaven & Tierney, 1996) on which school subjects are built. Therefore, if we want learners to construct more relationships across ideas and synthesize these in ways that promote higher order thinking, then those adults responsible for teaching children need to implement language and sign systems that foster connections and help students understand the similarities and differences within and across disciplinary boundaries. Thus, Vygotsky's idea that language develops higher order thinking can support integrated curriculum because existing practice that divides school subjects artificially leads to discourses that separate concepts. Instead of segmenting discourses so that they "fit" existing school content, teachers may foster enhanced learning if they find ways to integrate those discourses which overlap and create an environment in which students experience engaged inquiry. Vygotsky's ideas about the centrality of language for thinking have served as the theoretical basis for much of the current attempt to teach language within meaningful learning experiences so students develop the tools to work within and across disciplines and discourse communities. In addition, they have supported the practical focus on cooperative learning and student talk in the classroom.

### Learning on a Social Plane Prior to Internalization

Another of Vygotsky's (1978) ideas that assists thinking about the organization of curriculum is his position that learning occurs first on a social plane before being internalized. If children learn through the language and sign systems of the adult world, then they learn in a social context. It is only through multiple experiences in this social world that learners begin to internalize these systems as part of their own thinking. Gee (1996) maintained that learners come to school having developed ways of building knowledge based on their home and community experiences. Furthermore, these knowledge bases and ways of communicating are socially constructed over time and reflect people's memberships in particular social groups. Because children move between various communities, they acquire the use of multiple ways of interacting that fit the needs of different contexts. Gallas and her colleagues (1996) referred to this as a "language kit of discourses."

Like other social discourse groups, scholars studying particular disciplines also develop communities (Kuhn, 1970) with language kits of discourse. As participants in these social groups, discipline specialists formulate hypotheses, engage in inquiry, and construct knowledge. This knowledge then becomes the source of content for school textbooks. Teachers, too, are members of discourse communities with particular identities. However, unlike participants within disciplinary communities who are perceived as constructors of knowledge, teachers often are treated as transmitters of information and processes deemed as valuable by experts in the disciplines. In addition, the age of the prospective learner also contributes to preparations for very different approaches to teaching. That is, many elementary teachers are educated to focus on the processes, skills, and strategies associated with learning, secondary teachers emphasize content identified as important to know. Thus, teachers participate in discourse communities that vary considerably from those of content specialists and even within different communities based on the grade level they teach. Like teachers, learners also a members of very different communities.

One community in which children aged 5 and older spend a significant amount of time is the classroom. This social context varies considerably from all others in which the learner participates. For example, it is probably the only one in which the child is one of 20 or more who are the same age. Furthermore, there is only one adult to mediate the learning of all the children. Another way the classroom is distinctively different from other experiences of children is that the social context of the traditional classroom is divided into segments to facilitate management, such as dividing content into school subjects to ease the task of measuring student knowledge about discrete skills and strategies. In contrast, in contexts beyond school, all discourse is focused on communicating meaning related to the event. Thus, the social context of the traditional, transmission-oriented classroom emphasizes disconnected facets of learning, so this is what learners internalize. Instead of the synthesized knowledge constructed in ways that foster higher order thinking, students learn isolated facts, ideas, and processes. Such instructional practice is predicated on the belief that learners will synthesize and transfer this information themselves. However, Vygotsky's (1978) ideas about the important role the social context plays brings this assumption into question and supports the development of a social context that promotes learners' efforts to construct their own understandings, synthesize their learning, and apply it appropriately. Such a context can facilitate the internalization of conceptual development by emphasizing the integration of ideas.

## The Support of the Knowledgeable Other

Vygotsky (1978) also proposed that children learn through the support of a more knowledgeable other who understands the learning process of each child. To explain this, Vygotsky used the notion of the zone of proximal development. This zone is defined by whatever the learner can do with the help of a more knowledgeable one (Wertsch, 1985). In classrooms, the teacher most frequently fulfills this role. When considering this idea in relation to integrated curriculum, it seems essential that the teacher be knowledgeable about where the language and sign systems of school subjects overlap. If teachers understand school subjects only as discrete entities, then they can only support learning that perpetuates this way of thinking. In contrast, teachers whose knowledge base includes an integrated comprehension of content areas and an understanding of processes and language uses will be better able to foster such connected learning. Developing such teachers is not easy, however. Elementary teachers are trained as generalists and secondary teachers as content specialists. Therefore, when thinking of ways teachers can competently create integrated learning opportunities for students, these different orientations must be acknowledged and taken into account.

Most elementary teachers teach all subjects to their students and do not consider themselves "experts" in particular content fields. They focus on learning and development and approach children by holistically responding to their needs in a variety of academic and social areas. An advantage of being a generalist is that the elementary teacher can more easily build a bridge between the language arts and the content areas for novice learners than can the expert who has forgotten the large amount of information and conceptual knowledge that provides the foundation for the discipline. Thus, the goals of integrated curriculum that focus on developing students' ability to engage in inquiry ("literate discourse" in a general sense) and use language processes to learn and share the results come more easily to the generalist. Elementary teachers may use more exploratory language and engage students as they "think aloud" about how to understand disciplinary concepts. Furthermore, given their acceptance of their role as a generalist, they may be more open to including multiple knowledgeable others in their teaching. That is, when teachers conceive of their role as helping novice learners explore issues and topics in a more integrated way, they may be more likely to draw on a wider variety of expert resources, including other adults and more capable peers, who then enrich the scaffolding opportunities within the school classroom. The more knowledgeable adults who are engaged with children in learning experiences, the more scaffolding opportunities for children to appropriate the language and thinking of "experts" occurs. Because elementary teachers understand they are educated as generalists, they may be more likely to seek out additional people who are more expert and can serve to link the classroom to "expert" explanations and discourse. Therefore, having more open integrated units of instruction may facilitate the use of a variety of resources and thus open more authentic content discourse for young learners. The challenge posed by integration for elementary teachers is how to best help students build content knowledge and concepts and to help students differentiate how language and sign systems vary by content areas.

Secondary teachers have training as content specialists. Thus, they are more able to introduce students to the "literate discourse" of their particular field and provide scaffolding for specific disciplinary ways of thinking and representing knowledge than are elementary teachers. By knowing their area well, they can distinguish among different subjects and help students find the particular language and sign system of their discipline. However, two issues face secondary teachers engaged in forms of integrated curriculum. First, although they are knowledgeable, they do not often engage students as members of their academic community in the development of ideas but rather act as transmitters of disciplinary knowledge. Second, because they know their content so intimately, they struggle with how to provide the scaffolding of literate processes that permits students to learn effectively. They have developed such expertise in their field that they have often forgotten the foundational knowledge and take for granted their sophisticated understanding of the content area. They often do not know how to build bridges to their students so they can gain confidence as learners. Further, because they perceive themselves as content specialists, they are less likely to enlist the support of others knowledgeable about the content.

Therefore, from a Vygotskian perspective, the role of the knowledgeable other is important to learning. At the same time, this notion of what constitutes the requisite knowledge when thinking about integrating curriculum is complicated by the current expectations for teachers. To successfully integrate multiple content areas, teachers must understand various discourse communities; ways of constructing meaning; ways of planning, implementing and evaluating curriculum; and the various backgrounds and needs of their learners. In addition, they must understand how to integrate all of this into meaningful, engaging lessons.

## LITERACY AS DISCOURSE OF THOUGHT AND DISCIPLINES

In addition to theoretical arguments supporting the development of the relationships across the disciplines to facilitate student learning, some scholars argue that literacy is the key bridge between and across school subjects. That is, literacy is the foundation of communication and meaning construction within each discipline. In addition, it is also the means through which we learn. Therefore, it is essential that no matter what content is being taught, the literacy and oracy processes and skills must also be developed by teachers. Learning depends on language.

Wells (1990) argued that to be fully literate . . . "is to have the disposition to engage appropriately with texts of different types

in order to empower action, feeling, and thinking in the context of purposeful social activity" (1990, p. 14). McKay (1994) proposed a similar stance. Citing Harste, McKay argued that the disciplines themselves are forms of literacy. Shanahan (1997) echoed similar concepts by positing that literacy is a way of thinking about the world. This position seems reminiscent of Kuhn's (1970) thesis that each discipline has its own discourse community. Thus, from this perspective, reading and writing are the means through which to incorporate thinking related to each discipline. Wells (1990) expanded this position by noting that, for children to learn most effectively, they must participate in "joint" activities, collaborating with others. Gavelek, Raphael, Biondo, and Wang (2000) furthered this perspective, noting that language facilitates the development of knowledge and serves as a basis for the development of a community.

Some scholars argue that although literacy is the foundation for learning, by the secondary grades, students need to be introduced to disciplinary communities and their specific ways of thinking and learning. For example, O'Flahaven and Tierney (1996), in writing to middle and high school teachers, argued that rather than be taught distilled content, students should be introduced to the disciplinary ways of constructing knowledge. Moreover, they argued that instead of emphasizing reading and writing across the curriculum, educators should focus on discipline-based inquiry. Smagorinsky (1995) supported this, noting that educators should no longer emphasize writing across the curriculum but should encourage students to engage in the construction of meaning in a variety of forms. Such a process mirrors the meaning-making processes in many of the discipline-based discourse communities. This position is reflective of Kuhn's (1970) thesis that discourse within the disciplines varies and provides a means of entering the community. Although the argument appears rationale, it is problematic when considering classroom teachers who are prepared as either content specialists, as in the case of secondary teachers, or generalists, as with elementary teachers. That is, teachers are not members of these discourse communities themselves so may not have knowledge of the discourses adopted within them.

Thus, it seems that agreement exists that literacy is key to learning and provides the foundation for disciplinary inquiry. However, the means through which to develop these abilities is debatable, so questions emerge regarding how much to focus on general literacy development or learning and how much to emphasize particular disciplinary ways of thinking and learning. Can students learn general modes of inquiry using language? Is there a difference in what elementary teachers ought to do and what secondary educators, who are much more discipline based, should do? How do middle grades fit in this discussion?

Consequently, as scholars consider the role of literacy in integrating content areas, significant questions are raised; however, despite these issues to be resolved, commonalities exist. For example, one common understanding is that reading, writing, and oral language are the means through which thinking develops and through which novice learners can become part of a literate discourse community, not simply passive recipients of developed knowledge. Second, students need to become engaged as learners asking real questions and learning to use language to address them. None of these positions accept the transmission of distilled knowledge as adequate to prepare students to think—whether within a discipline or across them.

## RESEARCH INTO INTEGRATED CURRICULUM

Despite the powerful arguments supporting integrated curriculum and despite the theoretical grounding for research and practice related to it, there is little research investigating this instructional approach. Recent reviews of integration are easily available (see Adler & Flihan, 1997; Gavelek et al., 2000; Mathison & Freeman, 1998; St. Clair & Hough, 1992); therefore, rather than repeat this extant work, we want to build on it by synthesizing their findings, adding some additional case studies about classroom integration, and raising issues for essential additional steps from the perspective of the language arts.

In a review of the literature, St. Clair & Hough (1992) defined interdisciplinary teaching broadly as the integration of two or more disciplines. They addressed the other terminology (e.g., multidisciplinary, transdisciplinary, thematic teaching, integrated learning) as synonymous. These authors maintained that even though there are few studies dealing with student learning while participating in integrated lessons, a good deal of related research suggests interdisciplinary approaches are promising because such instruction can make the subject matter relevant to real life and thus engage students in the learning process. Finally, they concluded that further research is necessary but may be very complex, noting two major problems when designing studies investigating the impact interdisciplinary teaching has on student learning: unclear definition of the term interdisciplinary teaching and inabilities to isolate interdisciplinary teaching from other, closely related, variables that affect student learning. Isolating the integration of curriculum to evaluate its effectiveness may not be possible, so, they argued, researchers

may need to rely on multiple variable constructs and use structural model equations to interpret the complex relationships among the variables that impact student learning. Despite their 1992 call for additional studies investigating integration, three recent reviews (Adler & Flihan, 1997; Gavelek et al., 2000; Mathison & Freeman, 1998) continued to note the paucity of research.

When trying to synthesize existing research related to connected curriculum, Alder and Flihan (1997) attempted to examine the perspectives on how knowledge is reflected in secondary classrooms that adopt an interdisciplinary approach. These authors selected the term *interdisciplinary* ("the study of relationships among the disciplines," p. 4, 1997) over *integrated* because they believed it is more distinctly descriptive of educative practices. Through this work, they developed an "interdisciplinary continuum" that helped organized the varied perspectives within the literature. This continuum consists of three major categories: correlated knowledge, shared knowledge, and reconstructed knowledge (Table 74.1). Among these include the prevalence of integrating two disciplines, primarily English and history/social studies. Furthermore, they found that most of the program designs could be described as thematic, interdisciplinary, integrated, or broad-field curriculum.

Alder and Flihan (1997) then focused on the curriculum in practice. They found that although there is considerable self-reported success with "interdisciplinary" methods, research examining this instruction at the middle and high school level is lacking, one reason being the complexity involved in examining such practices. Thus, by implicitly acknowledging the same complexity in research St. Clair and Hough (1992) noted, Alder and Flihan limited their review to research-based descriptions of secondary classrooms, particularly those combining English and history. Their review examines the curriculum, pedagogy, assessment and outcomes. Regarding curriculum, they found that frequently one content area tends to drive decisions within

TABLE 74.1. The Interdisciplinary Continuum

| Correlated Knowledge | Shared Knowledge | Reconstructed Knowledge |
|---|---|---|
| Represented as: | Represented as: | Represented as: |
| Multidisciplinary<br>Complementary<br>Juxtaposed<br>Parallel, sequenced<br>Thematic (passive)<br>Webbed | Thematic (active)<br>Interdisciplinary<br>Integrated<br>Broad-field curriculum | Synthesized<br>Blended, fused<br>Core curriculum<br>Problem centered<br>Integrated/ive |
| Characterized by: → | Characterized by: → | Characterized by: |
| Related concepts | Preserving disciplinary boundaries<br>Overlapping concepts<br>Emergent patterns<br>Disciplines mutually supported | Eliminating disciplinary boundaries |
| | Disciplines most distinct ⟶ Disciplines most blended | |

Note. From *Reconciling Theory, Research and Practice* (Report Series 2.36, p. 5), by M. Adler and S. Flihan, 1997, Albany, NY: Center on English Learning & Achievement. Copyright 1997. Reprinted with permission.

the other. For example, history topics dictated the literature read. Furthermore, they found that even though the teachers in these studies tended to include final projects and student discussions as a means of fostering learning, the emphasis on what students should learn varied. In addition, they found assessment virtually missing from the research, causing them to question the outcomes of interdisciplinary units regarding student learning. Finally, the review noted that instruction integrating language arts and history did, indeed, seem to elevate the study of history and writing; however, the impact on the study of English was unclear. In concluding, they argued that future research can have a significant influence if it can reflect the more fluid approaches to content that exists in many classrooms. Such research will facilitate the development of more common language.

In another review of research into integrated curriculum, Mathison and Freeman (1998) also needed to develop a framework within which to understand its status. Instead of a continuum, these scholars developed what they termed "levels of integration." In their structure, Mathison and Freeman listed five categories: intradisciplinary discipline field, cross-disciplinary correlated, interdisciplinary, integrated, and integrative (Table 74.2). These levels range from merely enhancing linkages within disciplines (intradisciplinary discipline field) to an inquiry-based approach in which the distinctions between the disciplines are lost. Common across the top three approaches (interdisciplinary, integrated, integrative) is the attempt to foster meaningful learning that is connected to life. Mathison and Freeman continued by listing the following supporting arguments for these top three approaches:

- Increased understanding, retention and application of general concepts.
- Better comprehension of global interdependencies and development of multiple perspectives.
- Increased ability in problem solving, critical thinking, creativity, and synthesis of knowledge.
- Increased ability in identification, assessment, and transference of important knowledge when problem solving.

- Promotion of cooperative learning, positive self-concept, and being a productive member of a community.
- Increased motivation.

Mathison and Freeman (1998) then focus the review on the process of integration, noting that one model may not be better than another but that the tendency is to work within a framework that does not require significant changes from traditional pedagogical or curricular approaches. In part, this is because teachers find it difficult to take the risks associated with more consequential modifications. In fact, they noted Drake's 1991 (as cited in Mathison & Freeman, 1998) position that perhaps models that allow for less drastic modifications are a necessary stage toward more truly integrated instruction. They concluded by echoing other reviews and stating that although there is general belief that integration leads to positive outcomes, there is no solid research base that proves this.

Although these two reviews of existing research identified different frameworks to help understand the current practice as described through research, these models reveal similar patterns. Both acknowledge that in some situations the merging of the disciplines is less distinct. Instead, school subjects maintain their prevalent characteristics. Moreover, they noted that at the other extreme the boundaries between the disciplines are lost, providing a true integration of concepts, skills, and knowledge.

In addition, these reviewers also agree that there are several problems across research investigating such curriculum. One noted problem is the lack of consistent meanings for terms. For example, the words *integrated* and *interdisciplinary* are often used interchangeably in both research and practice. Furthermore, these scholars noted a paucity of research investigating the development of such curriculum and little research on how teachers interpret these concepts as they plan and implement instruction.

The issue of no consistent meaning for terms is clearly problematic, particularly from a Vygotskian perspective. That is, if language develops higher order thinking, then inexact terminology results in a lack of understanding of the concept. Thus, researchers and practitioners are operating from indistinct ideas,

TABLE 74.2. Levels of Integration

| | |
|---|---|
| Intradisciplinary discipline-field | • Enhances connections within disciplines<br>• Promotes success for all students |
| Cross-disciplinary correlated | • Coordinated themes/content across separate subjects<br>• Emphasis of certain skills across disciplines |
| Interdisciplinary | • Processes, concepts, skills, or elements of two or more disciplines together<br>• Common themes or modes of inquiry from interdisciplinary connections<br>• Inquiry skills and discipline content enhanced |
| Integrated | • Disciplines lost in global perspective<br>• Theme or issue oriented<br>• Inquiry oriented |
| Integrative | • Disciplines lost in global perspective<br>• Student–teacher negotiated themes and issues directed<br>• Inquiry oriented |

Note. From *The Logic of Interdisciplinary Studies* (Report Series 2.33, p. 7), by S. Mathison and M. Freeman, 1998, Albany, NY: Center on English Learning and Achievement. Copyright 1998. Reprinted with permission.

not uniform understanding. This is problematic when considering research findings and assessing teacher reports of success. Without explicit understandings of the concepts conveyed by the terms *thematic, integrated, interdisciplinary*, and so on, researchers and practitioners may or may not be discussing the same things.

Finally, these two reviews agree that additional research is necessary to support the belief that such practices lead to greater student achievement.

In another recent review, Gavelek et al. (2000) supported many of the findings in the other two reviews. However, they presented an additional contribution—the clarification of three different conceptualizations of integration when considering language arts. (a) the integration of the language arts (see this volume; Lipson, Valencia, Wixson, & Peters, 1993; Raphael & Hiebert, 1996); (b) the integration of curriculum, which includes other school subjects; and (c) the integration of in-school and out-of-school learning. This chapter focuses on the second classification.

Integration of curriculum was defined by Gavelek et al. (2000) as the union of school subjects through "overlapping skills, concepts and attitudes" (p. 591, citing Fogarty, 1991). They noted that such approaches either stress the connections between the language arts and other content areas or emphasize problem-centered teaching and learning. Although they also documented the lack of a solid research base, they noted that within existing research the dominant instructional practice is to maintain disciplinary boundaries. Within this reviewed research, one finding seems relevant. When literature or literacy processes were included to teach history, children remembered more and developed greater conceptual understandings. They concluded their review by noting the difficulty of planning and implementing such instruction and the need for a theoretical grounding of the research. Such a theoretical lens is essential when trying to understand these practices because integrated curriculum is multifaceted. As such, without a lens, researchers may flounder when trying to identify important components to study and may not ask significant questions. They also noted that some scholars (e.g., Alleman & Brophy, 1993, 1994) cautioned against this tendency toward integration because it may threaten one content area to serve another, just as Adler and Flihan (1997) found in their review. They concluded that instead of asking whether to integrate, research should be investigating what to integrate—and when, how, why, and for whom.

## THE IMPORTANCE OF ORAL LANGUAGE IN INTEGRATED CURRICULUM

As described above, language use is key to thought and learning. Although the role of reading and writing as tools for thinking and learning has long been valued in schools, the role of oral language, except perhaps among children in preschool and the primary grades, has been taken for granted. However, if language does indeed develop thinking and create communities, then oral language use is essential in any classroom. Not only does it provide teachers windows into the thought processes of the learners, but it also helps students understand their own

learning processes. Further, if learning occurs first on a social plane (Vygotsky, 1978), then oral discourse is an essential component of that social plane. Therefore, we argue that oral language is so important to learning that is must assume a more valued place in classrooms integrating the language arts with other content areas.

### Support for an Increased Emphasis on Oral Language

Barnes (1993) created a strong argument for why teachers should include more occasions for oral talk at all levels by identifying two types of talk: language of performance and exploratory language. Language of performance is the oral equivalent of the written final draft. It is clear, concise, and accurate. Although such oral discourse serves a necessary function in classrooms, it should not be the sole type students practice. In contrast, exploratory language is more like the rough draft of our written work. It is where we experiment with ideas, expanding those that seem relevant and omitting others. Exploratory talk is essential for two reasons. First, it enables learners to explore their own thinking. Second, it makes their thought processes more visible to the teacher. When considering the role language arts plays in learning content, then the purposes for both types of oral discourse seems apparent. Students need opportunities to explore their developing thinking about the content areas. Moreover, they also need circumstances in which to develop, refine, and share their knowledge in a more concise, clear and accurate format. Although many classrooms allow for this through written forms, students' opportunities for this in oral discourse are much more limited.

Several studies over the years have integrated the written language processes of reading and writing in content instruction. More recently with the sociocultural orientation, much more attention is now being focused on the way talk and discussion function in classroom content learning. It is interesting how a theoretical orientation can help us look more deeply at practice, especially the long overlooked area of oral language. Work with oral language has not emerged from an interest in "language across the curriculum" as it did in England after James Britton et al.'s (1975) national report. Rather, it has come from the shift to more sociocultural and sociocognitive classroom practices of small-group work, discussion, and cooperative learning. None of these have been areas of much attention in language arts instruction, although they could have productively been given more priority and students might have experienced more success using these tools to learn.

Now, with the interest in the social construction of knowledge and Vygotsky's (1978) concept of learning being first in the social plane before being internalized, much more attention is given to classroom discussions as a part of learning. (see this volume, for a review of the role of discussion in language arts learning.) Researchers have identified several difficulties in communication when looking closely at the exchanges that occur when students are engage in small group work. For example, Alvermann (1995–96) found that power relations operated with adolescents in the honors class she studied and females were intimidated to engage in an active meaning construction with their male peers. Evans (1996) found similar influences related to gender in elementary students' discussions of literature. Sperling and Freedman (1992) addressed these issues in writing process classes where peers are to provide feedback and guidance for others. Finally, one model of literature discussions, Book Club (McMahon & Raphael, 1997), found evidence that students need instructional support emphasizing not only what to discuss but how to do so within a peer group.

In the research that is being conducted outside the language arts, especially in science, issues of how group discussions function in helping students acquire literate discourse are instructive and add to these findings. Researchers (Anderson, Holland, & Palincsar, 1997) have identified several difficulties in communication when looking closely at the exchanges that occur when students are engaged in small group work. They found that many times the scientific inquiry and thinking lost priority to the small group attention to the completion of the tasks that were assigned and to the social interactions among group members. The researchers' choice of three focuses from which to analyze groups provided a framework from which the tensions students face when asked to collaborate can be analyzed. These three focal points are scientific activity (i.e., content), task requirements, and interpersonal relationships, and all can be useful in studies of integrated instruction.

These authors concluded:

At best, teachers help students to combine [these] personal agendas with their scientific activities and with the development of arguments based on theory and evidence. They also help students to develop a collective discourse of functional scientific literacy that includes characteristic activities, purposes, ways of using language, values, and patterns of relationships among participants, not just ways of knowing and using canonical knowledge. (Anderson et al., 1997, p. 381)

In a similar way, Dyson (1992) explained that the way children as literacy users or authors position themselves with a certain social space is contingent on authority (e.g., a disciplinary community's conventions for inquiry, the instruction of school, of a writer's expertise), the purposes that bring writers together within a particular social forum, and the topic of their discourse or task at hand.

As each of the disciplines within language arts and beyond to science and social sciences considers the goals of creating students who have not just memorized information but who have learned to participate in the thinking and dialog within particular discourse communities, the priority for conducting research on both the ways classrooms are organized to promote talk and on the nature and quality of talk that occurs as students work together in constructing understanding become more essential. Already there are interesting and promising approaches being taken in the study of language. With the language arts, scholars (Freemen & Sperling, 1992; Sperling, 1990, 1995, 1996) have looked closely as the nature of the exchanges that occur between teachers and students and among students as they engage in writing process conferences. So, too, the attention in reading has shifted somewhat to the nature and quality of student talk around text and topics of study (e.g., Eeds & Wells, 1989; Gambrel & Almasi, 1996; McMahon & Raphael, 1997). The

results of these investigations raise more questions than they answer in many ways. Talk as exploration of ideas does not come easily to children in school settings (Almasi, 1995; Alvermann 1995–96; Anderson et al., 1997; Hauschildt & McMahon, 1996; King, 1989, 1990; Webb & Farivar, 1999).

Additionally, some data suggest that teachers may move too prematurely into using small groups to stimulate social construction of knowledge. The assumptions that middle class teachers make about how student engage productively in discussion and peer talk have been found to be highly related to cultural conventions. As Heath's (1983) groundbreaking study revealed, children from difference social communities often have different norms for roles and structures of oral engagement. Delpit (1996) argued that these differences should lead to adaptations in the ways teachers provide instructional supports to students. She challenged middle class Anglo preferences for an indirect, process approach to teaching literacy skills. Other researchers have also documented cultural differences in assumptions about talk (Au, 1993; Anderson et al., 1997). These studies from literacy classrooms and content-oriented classrooms raise questions about how teachers can best engage students in more shared oral construction of meaning. Much sensitivity and scaffolding will be needed if the theoretically sound use of oral discourse as a tool to socially construct shared meaning is to include all students successfully.

The research on both the nature of and ways to enhance discussion and small-group interaction challenges our own field of language arts. Oracy had been overlooked for years as we focused on the written aspects of language arts. Most of the early work on using talk and small-group processes took place outside the field of language arts, particularly the work at the elementary level. The early models for cooperative group work came from Slavin (1990) and Johnson, Johnson, and Holubec (1988). Current attention to ways to explicitly teach students how to function within groups also seems more highly developed beyond language arts (Anderson et al., 1997; King, 1989, 1990; Webb & Farivar, 1999). This seems particularly interesting in contrast to the more extensive research and curricular guidelines that are available within the language arts community on writing across the curriculum and reading in the content areas. Given the dominant socioconstructivist theoretical orientation held across content areas, there is a challenge for more participation from language arts researchers so that integration within research communities can be actualized (see Bloome & Egan-Robertson, 1993). Concerns for status and gender issues (Henkin, 1997; Hynds, 1997; Noddings, 1984), the ways children from different cultures understand participation in discussion and talk in classrooms (Ladson-Billings, 1997), the ways various discourse communities function (see Mathison & Freeman, 1998), and the goal of talk across the disciplines within authentic inquiry may all lead to needed areas of research.

Anderson et al. (1997) expressed such ideas as they explained, that, from a sociocultural perspective, acquiring functional scientific literacy is not simply a matter of mastering and using a canon. It requires "appropriating scientific discourse" (Rosebery, Warren, & Conant, 1992). That is, "Learning to use language, think and act in ways that identify one as a member of the community of scientifically literate people and enable one to participate fully in the activities of that community" (p. 364). Rosebery et al. go on to raise the question of how to best scaffold for students from different cultural backgrounds, suggesting that scientific literacy "embodies a peculiarly western, middle-class way of understanding the world". Students from other cultures are thus put at a disadvantage in learning science because they are not part of the discourse community. Given the increasing numbers of immigrants and students of color in our schools, this issue has ramifications for both research and teaching. That is, teachers need to become more knowledgeable about how to address the needs of all the students in their classes regardless of race or class. In addition, it is important that research address issues surrounding the development of literate discourse regarding all content areas, in a conscious way, so that all students can benefit.

## CASE STUDIES OF PRACTICING TEACHERS

Because the reviews of integrated curriculum note the lack of a solid research base and because there still appears to be a belief among practitioners that integrating the language arts into the instruction of the other content areas promotes greater student achievement (National Board Certification for Generalist Teachers requires development of integrated instructional units), we include a few case studies of teachers who integrate their language arts with another content area. These case studies may be enlightening because some of the complexities teachers consider when developing integrated curriculum may be exactly the issues that make such research difficult (St. Clair & Hough, 1992). Therefore, we include this section to provide a mirror from which research can be considered. Before discussing these, however, we must clarify the variations in conceptual approaches to planning and implementing integrated curriculum teachers appear to adopt.

### Conceptualizing Integration of the Language Arts With Other Content Areas

The reviews cited above noted that researching the integration of school subjects is complex. This complexity derives from the number of factors that influence modifications of the curriculum, the planning and implementation of instruction, and the assessment of student learning. Because of this complexity, teachers need to identify a reasonable way to begin the process of moving from a traditional approach to curriculum and instruction. Many of the reviewed studies emphasized the combination of content with processes. Certainly these are essential elements to ponder when reviewing the merging of school subjects, particularly with the language arts, because they encompass several mental processes. However, when examining teacher practices and self-reports, we have found that they consider other issues when planning their instruction: content, processes, activities, content standards, and literate discourse (Fig. 74.1). As the following case studies demonstrate, teachers begin modifying their curriculum by thinking about one of these factors. We include

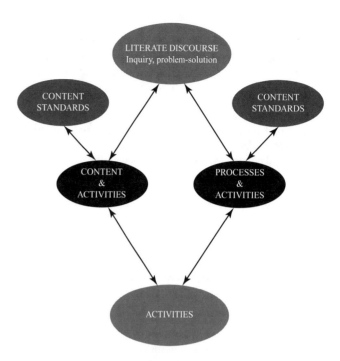

FIGURE 74.1. Means through which teachers begin planning for integrated units.

these cases to provide concrete examples for the reader about the multiple approaches to integrated curriculum that exist in practice and are noted in the review of research. As examples of practice, they are presented to help illuminate the complexity of both the planning and implementation of such instruction and the difficulty for researchers to identify specifically which aspect of the process to research.

***Standards as the entrance to integrated curriculum.*** One case study exploring a relatively new teacher's evolving thinking regarding the planning, implementation, and assessment of integrated language arts and social studies curriculum described the role the standards played (McMahon, Gordy, & Strop, 1998). The teacher in this study, "Doris," was in her 5th year of teaching and reported that the district's standards helped her identify her instructional goals whenever she planned. The language arts document listed six standards with supporting "proficiencies," each emphasizing language processes and reading skills/strategies. However, only one stressed the higher order thinking associated with literate thought. Furthermore, because the district's social studies committee had not yet finalized their version of the standards, Doris used the 10 standards developed by the National Council for the Social Studies (NCSS, 1994) and identified three as relevant for her integrated unit on Native Americans: (a) cultures; (b) time, continuity, and change; and (c) people, places, and environments. As a result of using the standards as an influential basis of entry into an integrated unit, Doris developed a unit that emphasized language arts processes to teach social studies content. That is, her instruction emphasized language arts skills, strategies, and processes but did not focus on analysis, evaluation, and synthesis of the texts read. In addition, she did not stress literary understanding and critical thinking associated with the literature she had children read. Instead, the literature served as a means of understanding the history content. Moreover, her instruction accentuated the concepts associated with the historical aspect of the unit but did not stress social studies skills, strategies and processes. When assessing student achievement, researchers found that students' writing and oral presentation of information improved over time, as did their understanding of history content. At the same time, students did not demonstrate an increased understanding of the literature read or of the social studies processes involved with the construction of historical documents. Although no individual unit can teach everything, these omissions seemed problematic because the novels were historical fiction and students appeared to merge the fiction in the books to the "facts" presented in other documents. Some additional instructional focus on the differences in genres may have furthered students' thinking about both the development of literature and the process of documenting actual events. Thus, analysis of Doris's instruction and students' learning indicated that there seemed to be a lack of balanced when considering the two content areas. This imbalance is not like any described in the reviews of existing research.

The use of standards as a means of entering integrated instruction can be found in another case study, this one of "Darcy" (Goatley & McMahon, 1999). Darcy, a teacher with 33 years of classroom experience, focused her instruction on the state standards as well, but, unlike Doris, she also emphasized conceptual issues, drawing on professional books such as *Doing History* (Levstik & Barton, 1997). Her use of "powerful ideas" through integrated instruction was designed to meet state standards but also to facilitate students' efforts to understand larger issues. As a result, Darcy made instructional decisions that moved her students' learning beyond the minimal standards to making connections across content areas. Therefore, her approach to beginning an integrated unit by consulting the standards created a solid initiating point but did not constitute the only guidelines she used. Darcy, perhaps because of her extensive experience, moved beyond the basics provided by the standards to include learning she knew was also important.

Terry Lindquist (1997), another veteran elementary teacher who used the standards as an entry into integration, explained her approach in the book she wrote for young teachers entering the field. Having seen many novice teachers struggle with how to manage the many curriculum demands and loose the excitement of teaching through a skills focus, she elaborated on her philosophy and explained her thinking and instructional planning. Two themes came through strongly: She no longer teaches language arts as a separate block of time but develops and applies skills through the social studies, and she uses the standards as a focal point in her instructional planning. For her, the standards provided a frame from which she develops integrated units—units that expand or contract depending on the needs and interests of the students. She organized the chapters of the book around social studies standards and explained how she develops rich, varied exploratory activities to engage students actively in learning. According to Lindquist, the involvement of students in learning is most important: How they learn is as important to her as what they learn. Therefore, she encouraged

students' exploration and looked forward to the end of units that have elicited more questions from students than those they had initially. She wanted students to think critically, not just focus on what happened but to ask who explained it and what was the point of view. Developing a learning environment in the classroom that nurtures students' inquiry was her goal.

Lindquist (1997) provided several examples of integrated units based on social studies standards. Like Doris, she discovered that the basic themes of social studies seemed to provide rich opportunities for using language arts—reading historical fiction, creating dramatic presentation from other cultures (shadow theater), and varied forms of writing (cooperative biography). Like Darcy, she often used historical fiction as a hook to introduce an issue to illuminate a time period so that students could gain a deeper engagement with the unit. By providing this shared experience with the whole class, she could move into small group project work and still have a grounding experience the whole class shares. Lindquist saw her classroom as open and used the community as an important resource. When students completed their study of a particular issue, they would culminated their work with a form of sharing, a "peak experience" that involved the students communicating their ideas to a larger audience. This seasoned, master teacher had a clear grasp on what students need to learn and finds integration of curriculum a powerful way to engage her classes as a "discourse community." Each year, Lindquist reported, she modifies her units to meet the students' interests and needs.

Many issues emerge when teachers use content standards to guide initial planning for integrated units. First, teachers may have several standards documents available. The teacher's experience may influence the decisions she makes about which standards to select. For example, Doris had district, state, and national standards at hand. Because the district was the most immediate, she selected these when possible. However, unlike some of the state standards, which were more conceptual, the district standards attempted to identify specific skills, strategies, and processes for each grade level. In many ways, this created a situation in which Doris could "see the trees but not the forest" when planning her language arts curriculum. In contrast, because the district had not yet developed social studies standards, Doris needed to consult another source. She decided to use the more global NCSS standards. The extreme differences between the particulars of the district's language arts document combined with the abstract nature of the NCSS standards led Doris to plan a unit reflecting this imbalance. With more experience, she may be better able to differentiate standards developed within a district to address more immediate and, perhaps narrow needs for accountability, from state or content standards which focus on bigger ideas. When understanding the varied audiences for each set of standards, a teacher may be better able to make choices about which ones to use as a guideline for planning and which ones may influence specific assessments.

In contrast, Darcy and Lindquist (1997) approached the use of standards in a completely different and more flexible way. These two teachers began planning with the standards documents but did not allow them to completely influence their instructional decisions. Instead, they consulted standards documents as guidelines but moved beyond them to the more conceptual ideas they wanted students to learn. Thus, as these case studies demonstrate, using standards documents as a guideline for planning an integrated unit can be beneficial if teachers move beyond the standards to stressing higher order thinking.

Perhaps the ability to move beyond the standards is related to differences in how these three teachers perceived them. In a study of several teacher's reactions to standards, (McGill-Franzen, Goatley, & Machoda, 1998) found that teachers tended either to accept a personal accountability to use the standards to guide their own teaching or to perceive the standards as a mandate from an external authority. The first group tended to work toward understanding the standards documents to inform their teaching; the second group perceived the standards as outside their responsibility. Perhaps Doris saw the standards as finalized requirements outside her control whereas Darcy and Terry viewed them as a way to guide their practice but not dictate it. As these cases reveal, the standards documents may facilitate teachers' efforts to integrate their curriculum, but these documents were developed as frameworks for content understanding, and, as such, they need to be integrated as well if they are to help teachers modify their own curriculum and instruction. Therefore, if teachers perceive them as flexible guidelines instead of objectives to be checked off at the end of a unit, standards may facilitate planning, implementation, and evaluation of instruction.

***Activities as the entrance to integrated curriculum.*** In contrast to the three teachers above, "Jelisa" (Goatley & McMahon, 1999; McMahon, Strop, & Gordy, 2000), a beginning teacher, accessed integration through the activities she wanted her students to participate. In part, this decision was grounded within her belief that students are more likely to learn when actively creating something they can engage in, not when they are expected to articulate the information the teacher emphasizes. Thus, she agreed with Dewey (1956) that students learn better when the teacher begins instruction in school content with real world experiences. Furthermore, her ideas are congruent with other social studies educators who argue for activities as a way for learners to understand the connectedness across. Therefore, her planning began with the activities that would enable students to simulate events in history.

When studying the civil rights movement of the 1960s, Jelisa had students adopt various identities representing multiple races, genders, and socioeconomic classes to act out their role within the historical period. For example, she projected a picture of a lunch counter sit-in on the wall and asked students to put themselves in the picture over one of the participants in the demonstration. Then she asked them to talk about what they were thinking and feeling. In another unit, she asked students to participate in town meetings, discussing issues that were historically important in their city. Thus, for the bulk of these early units, students acted out roles based on the teacher's and other students' oral presentations of information and reading aloud from relevant texts. As a novice teacher, Jelisa believed that role playing and class discussions would be sufficient ways for students to develop important concepts. With experience, however, she added more to her instructional plans. For example, in later units, Jelisa began including more reading and

writing activities. In particular, she incorporated more examples of children's literature that related to the topic of study, daily response journals for students to record their reactions to the texts, and small group discussion time. As students read about events during this time period, Jelisa asked them to reflect on the events from their assumed identity.

When analyzing Jelisa's early units, researchers noted that even though she emphasized activities in her instruction, she did not ignore the content. At the same time, her decisions were initially influenced by the activities, so her approach to learning seemed to be inquiry based and one that tried to build on students' experiences outside school. She consulted content standards only periodically because she was confident in her ability to teach social studies. Because of her confidence within social studies, this aspect of her program was dominant. In contrast, she expressed a lack of confidence in teaching the language arts. Therefore, she initially adhered to published worksheets to teach much of her language arts. Over time, though, she shifted the attention from worksheets to journals and reading historic fiction. However, because she was still learning ways to help children make explicit connections between the journals, the literature, and the civil rights movement, her students' reading and writing abilities remained relatively stable over her first years of teaching.

***Process as the entrance to integration.*** Another approach described in case study research into integrated units is to begin the planning and implementation process by considering the processes students use to accumulate information and report their learning. This method stresses reading and writing as tools for learning. McMahon (2001) described the case study of "Carol," a fifth-grade teacher, and her uses of reader's and writer's workshop to encourage students to research and report some aspect of science or history. Carol provided the necessary modeling and scaffolding so that students could use literacy processes as they research a self-selected topic. Although she guided their selection (e.g., when researching biographies students had to select someone who had historical significance and, when reporting on a science topic, students had to write about a general topic such as the habitat and life experiences of an animal), Carol did not identify particular historic periods or scientific concepts that all students had to research. Students in this classroom had an impressive knowledge of their topics, which they related well both orally and in writing. At the same time, the scientist or social scientist may question whether students left Carol's classroom with a body of "core" knowledge that other fifth- and sixth-graders had. That is, her students in fifth grade did not study key periods in U.S. history either together or individually.

Although the above cases came from teachers who used social studies as a framework for integration of language arts and content, Robert Tierney (1996) and Judy McKee (Ogle & McKee, 1996) presented evidence of how to integrate science with language arts. Like Carol, these two teachers began their planning for integrating instruction by thinking about the literacy processes they wanted to emphasize.

Tierney (1996), as a result of participation in the Bay Area Writing Project, wrote a book published by the National Science

Teachers Association explaining how he integrated writing with science. He explained that key to his use of writing in his science teaching was his desire that students become more engaged with the scientific process of discovery. He wanted his students to have "the exhilaration of their own discovery" (p. 2). Therefore, expressive writing became an integral part of his science teaching. He entered integration then from the desire for his students to participate in literate discourse. Rather than transmitting scientific facts and information, he wanted a way for students to become more like real scientists. In each of his units, students began by observing and recording what they see and know. Tierney carefully crafted activities and lessons that enabled students to document, revise, and track the development of their own thinking. For example, they "search for truth" by writing one sentence they know to be true and sharing it with the class. From there, they develop questions; gain new knowledge from lecture, lab, and writing; and reflect and review through writing. Thus, students continually documented their own learning process and reflected on it.

In her second-grade classroom, Judy McKee (Ogle & McKee, 1996) also wanted her students to be part of an exploratory community, using science as a way to involve students actively in learning. As a veteran teacher, she balanced both the teaching of literacy processes with the excitement she generated around the units in science she created for the young children. Her science content was what the district curriculum outlines; her literacy activities developed the skills and competencies that the district and state required, too. Like Tierney (1996), McKee wanted students to be engaged in discovery and possess the literacy tools for success. She used science journals as the thread to help students become aware of their own learning process and form their own conclusions about what they observe in experiments and about research they conduct from books and authorities. She did a great deal of modeling to help her students learn to record accurately and to create illustrations and graphic depictions to accompany their words. Her goal was for students to use literacy to become independent learners. The science journal provided a concrete way for both teacher and students to assess growth in their knowledge and their literacy processes. Students prized these journals and kept returning to them over the year.

***Content as the entrance to integrated curriculum.*** Yet another way to begin planning integrated curriculum is through the content teachers want taught. Because they are faced with so much content, teachers need to find a way of organizing it in a coherent way. They often do this by the development of a theme (Lapp & Flood, 1994; Peters & Wixson, 1998), a concept (Guthrie, Bennett, & McGough, 1994), a guiding question (Levstik & Barton, 1997), or a problem to be solved. Although there were no case studies using such approaches as entries into planning for integrated curriculum, this is one of the most commonly advocated formats in the literature and one often voiced by teachers. In our review there were units that teachers developed that were organized around themes, but these generally had a more specific grounding in "themes" included in the social studies standards, such as with Doris described above. Because it was not the teachers' own selection of "theme" but rather

their use of standards-determined themes, these case studies fall under that category.

Thematic teaching is not necessarily the same thing as integrated curriculum. For example, social studies content standards are defined by themes but do not necessarily imply an integrated approach. Many teachers use "themes" as a way to define their units, but we have found through our case study review that there are deeper reasons that guide their planning, basically the teacher's desire to teach core literacy and inquiry processes or content.

## SUMMATIVE IDEAS

These case studies were included to demonstrate the complexity teachers face when trying to integrate their language arts instruction with other content areas. Because of the complexity acknowledged by reviews of the research on integration (St. Clair & Hough, 1992; Adler & Flihan, 1997), teachers must enter their planning from one of the many possible perspectives. That is, they may initiate their shaping of new curriculum and instruction by considering the content, processes, activities, or discourses in which they want students to learn or participate. Given the maze of the potential skills, strategies, processes and content that could be included, teachers make choices. As in the case studies described above, the resulting lessons meet some of the needs of students but may omit others. No single unit can meet all learners' needs so this may not be problematic if across the year or across a child's experiences in school all these learning needs are met. On the other hand, it is problematic if many of these essentials are left out or included haphazardly. Therefore, it may be helpful if educators have a model to facilitate their decision-making process (Fig. 74.2).

Evidence from research and the case studies described above indicate that teachers make choices that appear to be from four major categories: (a) content/content standards, (b) processes, (c) activities, and (d) literate discourse. In every case described above, the teacher entered the planning stage through one of these. Depending on the teacher's experience, knowledge of the content areas and dispositions, each moved from the entry point to develop integrated units. The more experienced teachers were more likely to include aspects of all four within their instruction. This probably indicates their knowledge of how to incorporate all of these components when applicable across

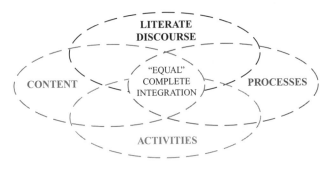

FIGURE 74.2. Balanced integrated curriculum.

the year. Novice teachers do not have this depth of understanding yet, so their instruction may be less balanced. What is clear from these cases is that designing integrated instruction is complicated and can result in an imbalance when implemented. Therefore, teachers may benefit from having a model to facilitate their thinking when planning integrated instruction that is purposeful. By purposeful, we mean a unit of study that integrates content, processes, activities, and discourses that promote higher order thinking through the development of concepts that meet learning goals. Omitting any one of these four components may result in an instructional unit that is representing only part of the complete picture and result in learning that is less powerful than it potentially could be. In the case of elementary teachers, their tendency is to shift away from content to stress learning processes and activities. In contrast, secondary teachers may emphasize content over processes and activities that meet the learners' needs and scaffold their meaning construction. Although some of these shifts in emphasis are necessary, they should be made only after considering the needs of learners and the ultimate goals for education.

## POINTS TO PONDER

As we reviewed the research, our own research and work with teachers, and our interactions with teachers in our classes, we realized that there are several complex issues that influence the development and progress of educators' efforts to develop and study the integrating of language arts into other content areas. Although there are many of these, we identified four that seemed the most salient: (a) how to "honor" the disciplines and transcend them; (b) how assessment and standards may seem to work against integrating curriculum; (c) how university and college preparation programs may need to adjust to educate future teachers in ways that enable them to integrate their curriculum better; and (d) how the product orientation of integrated units may lose a focus on the skills and strategies that students need to become more independent, literate learners. We now expand on each of these.

### How to "Honor" the Disciplines and Transcend Them

As noted in the reviews of the existing research, there appears to be a continuum or hierarchy of approaches to integration. Although many educators argue that we need to transcend the boundaries between school subjects because they do not reflect the "real world" of scholars within the disciplines, others refute this, noting that students are learners. As such, they do not have the foundation on which to build an integrated knowledge base. Without this foundation, they cannot engage in grounded, literate thinking. Instead of integration, they argue for discrete content emphasis until students have developed this foundation. This basis can be developed through the content standards and assessment that measures the resulting knowledge.

When we consider the language arts this position creates a dilemma. On one hand, if we consider the processes of literacy, we must debate this position. After all, literacy is a means of thinking and learning, and, as such, it cannot occur within a vacuum. Instead of decontextualized instruction on processes, skills, and strategies, embedding these within the context of authentic learning in content areas is more desirable. Thus, the process of literacy may indeed benefit from being integrated with other content areas.

On the other hand, the discipline of literature studies presents another perspective which causes us to understand the need to focus on particular content, perhaps outside the parameters of an integrated unit because there are particular literary elements that are important for students to understand. For example, without comprehending story structure or literary language, readers struggle with interpreting literature. Furthermore, we can support the need for learners to read and appreciate a number of different genres—ones that do not easily "fit" integrated units. If indeed the dominant practice is integrating the language arts with history, then the major genre of study is historic fiction. Although this may facilitate a stronger understanding of historic events, what about other literary genres? Where is their place in the curriculum?

Thus, it seems that educators need to approach the notion of integration with some reservations. Even with the language arts—the primary means of learning and thinking—there are concerns about what "gets lost" with integration. Therefore, some aspects of the language arts may be best taught discretely, without having another content area refocus teachers' decision making about genres and topics for instruction.

### Assessment/Standards May Seem to Work Against Integrating Curriculum

At the same time that a social constructivist perspective has provided strong support for curriculum that emphasizes integrated forms of learning, the discipline-based standards movement has also evolved. Forty-nine states have established learning or performance standards for student achievement and to varying degrees are using them as the foundation for what is considered important for teaching and learning. Professional organizations, particularly the National Council of Teachers of Mathematics, led the way by developing their own disciplinary area standards and the other professional organizations have continued to develop and revise their own standards documents. Despite many preliminary statements in the professional organization and in-state documents affirming the need to integrate and teach the targeted content in authentic contexts, the result has often been a return to "basics" teaching. (For example, Illinois Foundations for Learning affirm the need for problem solving, integrating across discipline, etc. These statements are overlooked as districts focus on the disciplinary content standards, particularly those included on the state test.) Thus, just as integration was making some headway, the standards focus has turned attention again to the individual disciplines. Combining the standards with high stakes or at least publicly reported assessment has led, in the short term at least, to teacher shifting energies to items found on the state's mandated assessments. In some schools, teachers spend a major part of their instructional time preparing students for these assessments. This fear of acceptability can have a pernicious effect in many ways, but for our purposes in looking at integrated learning, it certainly has worked against teachers seeing the larger picture of teaching for thinking and problem solving that leads to literate thinking and discourse.

Two notable exception to this can be identified. The first is the Michigan English Language Arts Framework, described by Peters and Wixson (1998). This framework is designed to help teachers develop integrated curriculum that provides balance of content and processes. The second is found in the state of Maryland where the Maryland School Performance Assessment Program (MSPAP) models authentic thinking and learning. The assessment program takes a problem that students both together and individually work on over a week. Teachers introduce the problem and provide the tools needed for students' work. Each assessment combines at least two curricular areas—for example, sciences and language or mathematics and social studies—and scores are derived for each of the targeted tasks. A unique and problematic feature of the assessment system is that individual scores are not reported; rather, schools are scored (see discussion by the state Superintendent of Education in Grasmick, 2000; Kapinus, Collier, & Kruglanski, 1994.) The MSPAP has served as a catalyst for many schools to rethink their instruction, refocus so that students learn to think about issues, and then design instructional opportunities that draw on authentic uses of language to solve problems with various "contents."

## Implications for Teacher Preparation

Despite the paucity of research to support or refute beliefs about the strengths of integrating the language arts with other content areas, one common trend in existing research is the complexity of such approaches. This additional entanglement of content and processes with a focus on higher order thinking clearly increases the demands on teachers. As students, they learned content in more traditional ways with distinct divisions. Moreover, as Shulman (1987) argued, teaching already requires several different types of knowledge on which every teacher must draw. In addition, some scholars (e.g., Wilson & Ball, 1996; Wilson & Wineburg, 1988) documented the important role knowledge of the disciplines plays in teaching content. Teacher preparation programs are already filled with courses trying to facilitate the building of knowledge that can foster better instruction. If the expectation is for teachers to present instruction that integrates the language arts with other content areas, then novice and practicing teachers must reexamine not just their teaching but also the way they think about school subjects. Furthermore, they may need to fortify their existing knowledge so that they too have conceptual understandings of the disciplines to see better the connections and a strong sense of the diversity of their learners and their needs to construct foundational knowledge on which to build. For secondary teachers, an understanding of the disciplines may be less of an issue because they are content specialists already. However, they may benefit from a greater understanding how the discourse communities of their disciplines interact. In addition, they may need support in understanding more about their learners. For those teachers in elementary who must teach a variety of content areas, the answer may be

to provide a wide spectrum of other resources and experts in the community to help them develop better understandings of the disciplines and their related discourse communities.

## Product Orientation May Lose Focus on Important Skills and Strategies

As we alluded above when discussing the problem of integrating all content, some aspects of the language arts and the other content areas may get "lost" in an integrated unit. In addition to this, the product orientation of many integrated units may create an illusion of instruction in and learning of particular skills, strategies, and content that may not indeed be occurring. For learners to become better readers, writers, speakers, and thinkers, they must have explicit instruction on those skills and strategies that can enhance the meaning-making process. When the language arts are integrated within other content areas, teachers may not engage in explicit instruction on reading, writing skills, and strategies. Students read texts "at their level" to complete a project but do not necessarily become more skilled at either reading or writing because the emphasis is on the content reflected in the project. Teachers may assume that because students are capable of completing the final project—which requires reading, writing, and speaking—that students are becoming more skilled. Indeed, practice with reading, writing, and speaking can improve one's literacy development. At the same time, these are novices who can benefit from the guidance of a more knowledgeable other (Vygotsky, 1978) who guides the process and provides instruction within the learner's zone (Wertsch, 1985). For example, research indicates that for students to become more strategic readers they need explicit instruction on these strategies (e.g., Dole, 2000). However, through the use of integrated units, teachers may omit such instruction because they know their learners are motivated, or they perceive such instruction as contradictory to their beliefs about integrated instruction. As a result, students may experience success as measured by the goals of the integrated unit but may not be developing a larger repertoire of skills and strategies to transfer to other learning contexts. One may propose that if students can meet the objects of an integrated unit, then they have the necessary skills. One must counter this however when considering the existing research. As the reviews document, often the language arts become the vehicle for understanding other content areas. As such, their importance is secondary to content. Moreover, reviewers have noted that many studies have not adequately assessed students' learning. Thus, some important skills, strategies, competencies, processes, and content may not be taught, learned, or evaluated.

## CONCLUSION

The rationale for integrating the language arts with other content areas is that language is central to the meaning making process both within schools and within other communities. Therefore, integration fosters a more authentic context for learning. Putting students into settings where they use language to explore and learn about topics or problems of interest stimulates their interest in and development of language abilities. Both exploratory and performance oriented talk are essential in units where students begin framing questions, observing, collecting data, and constructing meaning together. Language functions both for meaningful exchanges among peers, for scaffolded and guided exploration by the teacher, and in individual meaning construction by each student during the learning process. The context of integrated units that generally extend over significant periods of time and permit exploration of issues from multiple perspectives encourages such uses of language. The research challenges educators to look more closely at how students can be guided to using language more effectively in learning, especially now with a wider population of children of color and second-language learners for whom the general school discourse community is unfamiliar. The challenge comes also as we find how power structures among students and verbal competence influence the effectiveness of group learning activities in classrooms.

The more we focus our research lens on ways communities of learners construct meaning, the more the dilemma of specific content versus integrated content emerges. As the case studies demonstrate, teachers must make choices about what to include and how. Such decisions do not solve problems but manage dilemmas (Lampert, 1985). When selecting among options, teachers draw on multiple reasons grounded in their own educational preparation, sometimes with unclear outcomes. Research can support teachers' efforts in this process and inform the educational community about which alternatives to choose and under which circumstances. Some questions for research are, Which discourse community or communities do we prepare students to enter? Do elementary students need a more general introduction to exploration and inquiry? How do teachers help secondary students build on their general use of language skills to learn and also introduce them to specific disciplinary communities? How much do the traditional "discourse communities" even serve students now? Should the old boundaries be transcended in truly integrated learning? Many challenges face educators when the goals of educating young students for a changing world are considered. Perhaps we need to think more creatively about what integration and language for learning can be in this new millennium.

# References

Adler, M., & Flihan, S. (1997). *The interdisciplinary continuum: Reconciling theory, research and practice* (Report Series 2.36). Albany, NY: Center on English Learning & Achievement.

Alleman, J., & Brophy, J. (1993, October). Is curriculum integration a boon or a threat to social studies? *Social Education,* 287-291.

Alleman, J., & Brophy, J. (1994). Trade-offs embedded in the literary approach to early elementary social studies. *Social Studies and the Young Learner, 6*(3), 6-8.

Almasi, J. F. (1995). The nature of 4th graders' sociocognitive conflicts in peer-led and teacher-led discussions of literature. *Reading Research Quarterly, 30*(3), 314-351.

Alvermann, D. E. (1995-96). Peer-led discussions: Whose interests are served? *Journal of Adolescent and Adult Literacy, 39,* 282-289.

Anderson, C. W., Holland, J. D., & Palincsar, A. S. (1997). Canonical and sociocultural approaches to research and reform in science education: The story of Juan and his group. *The Elementary School Journal, 97*(4), 359-382.

Au, K. (1993). *Literacy instruction in multicultural settings.* New York: Harcourt, Brace Jovanovich.

Barnes, D. (1993). Supporting exploratory talk. In A. M. Pierce & C. J. Gilles (Eds.), *Cycles of meaning* (pp. 17-35). Portsmouth, NH: Heinemann.

Beane, J. A. (Ed.) (1995). *Toward a coherent curriculum: The 1995 ASCD Yearbook.* Alexandria, VA: Association for Supervision and Curriculum Development.

Bloom, B. S. (1958). Ideas, problems, and methods of inquiry. In N. B. Henry (Ed.), *The integration of educational experiences*: Fifty-seventh *yearbook for the National Society for the Study of Education* (Pt. 3, pp. 84-104). Chicago: University of Chicago Press.

Bloome, D., & Egan-Robertson, A. (1993). The social construction of intertextuality in classroom reading and writing lessons. *Reading Research Quarterly, 28,* 305-333.

Britton, J., Burgess, A., Martin, N., McLeod, A., & Rosen, H. (1975). *The development of writing abilities.* London: Macmillan.

Bruner, J. (1986). *Actual minds, possible worlds.* Cambridge, MA: Harvard University Press.

Delpit, L. (1996). *Other people's children: Cultural conflict in the classroom.* New York: New Press.

Dewey, J. (1956). *Experience and education.* New York: Macmillan.

Dole, J. A. (2000). Explicit and implicit instruction in comprehension. In B. M. Taylor, M. F. Graves, & Van Den Broek (Eds.), *Reading for meaning* (pp. 52-69). New York: Teachers College Press.

Dyson, A. H. (1992). Whistles for Willie, lost puppies & cartoon dogs: the sociocultural dimensions of young children. *Journal of Reading Behavior, 24,* 433-462.

Eeds, M., & Wells, D. (1989). Grand conversations: An explanation of meaning construction in literature study groups. *Research in the Teaching of English, 23*(1), 4-29.

Evans, K. (1996). A closer look at literature discussion groups: The influence of gender on student response and discourse. *The New Advocate, 9*(3), 183-196.

Fogarty, R. (1991). Ten ways to integrate curriculum. *Educational Leadership, 49*(2), 61-65.

Fulwiler, T. (1987). *The journal book.* Montclair, NJ: Boynton/Cook.

Gallas, K., Anton-Oldenburg, M., Ballenger, C., Beseler, C., Griffin, S., Pappenheimer, R., & Swaim, J. (1996). Talking the talk and walking the walk: Researching oral language in the classroom. *Language Arts, 73,* 608-617.

Gambrell, L. B., & Almasi, J. F. (1996). *Creating classroom cultures that foster discussion, interpretation, and comprehension of text.* Newark, DE: International Reading Association.

Gavelek, J. R., Raphael, T. E., Biondo, S. M., & Wang, D. (2000). Integrated literacy instruction. In M. L. Kamil, P. B. Mosenthal, & P. D. Pearson (Eds.), *Handbook of reading research* (Vol. 3, pp. 587-608). New York: Lawrence Erlbaum Associates.

Gee, J. P. (1996). *Social linguistics and literacies: Ideology in discourses.* New York: Taylor & Francis.

Goatley, V. J., & McMahon, S. I. (1999, December). *Making decisions about integrated instruction: Two case studies of classroom teachers.* Paper presented at the annual meeting of the National Reading Conference, Orlando, FL.

Goleman, D. (1995). *Emotional intelligence.* New York: Bantam.

Grasmick, N. S. (2000). How Maryland communities change. *Educational Leadership, 57*(7), 44-47.

Green, J. L., & Dixon, C. (1993). Talking knowledge into being: Discursive and social practices in classrooms. *Lingustics and Education, 5*(3-4), 231-239.

Guthrie, J. T., Bennett, L., & McGough, K. (1994). *Concept-oriented reading instruction: An integrated curriculum to develop motivations and strategies for reading* (Report No. 10). National Reading Research Center, Universities of Georgia and Maryland. Athens, GA: National Reading Research Center.

Hauschildt, P., & McMahon, S. I. (1996, December). Reconceptualizing "resistant" learners and rethinking instruction: Risking a trip to the swamp. *Language Arts, 73*(8), 576-586.

Heath, S. B. (1983). *Ways with words: Language, life, and work in communities and classrooms.* Cambridge, England: Cambridge University Press.

Henkin, R. (1997). *Who's invited to share.* Portsmouth, NH: Heinemann.

Hynds, S. (1997). *One the brink: negotiating literature and life with adolescents.* New York. Teachers College Press; London: International Reading Association.

Johnson, D. W., Johnson, R. T., & Holubec, E. J. (1988). *Cooperation in the classroom* (Rev. ed.). Edina, MN: Interaction Book.

Kapinus, B. A., Collier, G. V., & Kruglanski, H. (1994). The Maryland School Performance Assessment Program: A new view of assessment. In S. W. Valencia, E. H. Hiebert, & P. P. Afflerbach (Eds.), *Authentic reading assessment: Practices and possibilities* (pp. 255-276). Newark, DE: International Reading Association.

King, A. (1989). Verbal interaction and problem-solving within computer-assisted cooperative learning groups. *Journal of Educational Computing Research, 5*, 1-15.

King, A. (1990). Enhancing peer interaction and learning in the classroom through reciprocal questioning. *American Educational Research Journal, 27*, 664-687.

Kuhn, T. S. (1970). *The structure of scientific revolutions.* Chicago: University of Chicago Press.

Ladson-Billings, G. (1997). *The dreamkeepers: Successful teachers of African-American children.* New York: Jossey-Bass.

Lampert, M. (1985). How do teachers manage to teach: Perspectives on problems in practice. *Harvard Education Review, 55*(2), 178-194.

Lapp, D., & Flood, J. (1994). Integrating the curriculum: First steps. *Reading Teacher, 47*(5), 416-419.

Levstik, L. S., & Barton, K. C. (1997). *Doing History: Investigating with children in elementary and middle schools.* New York: Lawrence Erlbaum Associates.

Lindquist, T. (1997). *Ways that work: Putting social studies standards into practice.* Portsmouth, NH: Heinemann.

Lipson, M. Y., Valencia, S. W., Wixson, K. K., & Peters, C. W. (1993). Integration and thematic teaching: Integration to improve teaching and learning. *Language Arts, 70*(4), 252-263.

Lounsbury, J. H., & Vars, G. F. (1978). *A curriculum for the middle school grades.* New York: Harper & Row.

Mathison, S., & Freeman, M. (1998). *The logic of interdisciplinary studies* (Report Series 2.33). Albany, NY: Center on English Learning & Achievement.

McKay, R. (1994). Social studies as a form of literacy: Beyond language across the curriculum. *Canadian Social Studies, 29*(1), 11-12.

McGill-Franzen, A., Ward, N., Goatley, V., & Machado, V. (1998). *Teachers' use of new standards, frameworks, and assessments: Local cases of NYS elementary grade teachers.* Reading Research and Instruction.

McMahon, S. I. (in progress). *Carol, a study of a fifth-grade, process-oriented integrated classroom.*

McMahon, S. I. (December, 2001). Integrated language arts & social studies in a process-oriented fifth-grade classroom. Paper presented at the annual meeting of the National Reading Conference, San Antonio, TX.

McMahon, S. I., Gordy, L. M., & Strop, J. J. (1998, December). *Constructing and maneuvering the integrated curriculum: An example from one classroom.* Paper presented at the annual meeting of the National Reading Conference, Austin, TX.

McMahon, S. I., Gordy, L. M., & Strop, J. J. (2000, December). *Increasing literacy in integrated curriculum: One teacher's change over time.* Paper presented at the annual meeting of the National Reading Conference, Scottsdale, AZ.

McMahon, S. I., & Raphael, T. E. (Eds.) (1997). *The Book Club Connection: Literacy learning and classroom talk.* New York: Teachers College Press.

NCSS STANDARDS (1994). Expectation of Excellence: Curriculum Standards for Social Studies. *Social Education, 58*(6), 365-368.

Noddings, B. (1984). *Caring: A feminine approach to ethics and moral education.* Berkeley, CA: University of California Press.

Oberholzer, E. E. (1988). Similarities between history-social science framework and English-language arts framework: What it means for elementary teachers. *Social Studies Review, 28*(1), 48-52.

O'Flahaven, J., & Tierney, R. J. (1996). Moving beyond reading and writing in the content areas to discipline-based inquiry. In D. Lapp, J. Flood, & N. Farnan (Eds.), *Content area reading and learning: Instructional strategies.* Needham Heights, MA: Allyn Bacon.

Ogle, D., & McKee, J. (1996). Science journals in an integrated 2nd grade classroom. *Illinois Reading Council Journal, 2*, 7-22.

Peters, C. W., & Wixson, K. K. (1998). Aligning curriculum, instruction and assessment in literature-based approaches. In T. E. Raphael & K. H. Au (Eds.), *Literature-based instruction: Reshaping the curriculum* (pp. 261-284). Norwood, MA: Christopher-Gordon.

Raphael, T. E., & Hiebert, E. H. (1996). *Creating an integrated approach to literacy instruction.* New York: Harcourt Brace.

Rosebery, A., Warren, B., & Conant, F. (1992). Appropriate scientific discourse: Findings from language minority classrooms. *Journal of the Learning Sciences, 2*(1), 61-94.

Shanahan, T. (1997). Reading-writing relationships, thematic units, inquiry learning . . . In pursuit of effective integrated literacy instruction. *The Reading Teacher, 51*(1), 12-19.

Short, K. G., & Harste, J. C. (1996). *Creating classrooms for authors and inquirers.* Portsmouth, NH: Heinemann.

Shulman, L. S. (1987, February). Knowledge and teaching: Foundation of the New Reform. *Harvard Education Review, 57*(1), 1-22.

Slavin, R. (1990). *Cooperative learning: Theory, research and practice.* Englewood Cliffs, NJ: Prentice-Hall.

Smagorinsky, P. (1995, February). Constructing meaning in the disciplines: Reconceptualizing, writing across the curriculum as composing across the curriculum. *American Journal of Education, 103,* 160-184.

Sperling, M. (1990). I want to talk to each of you: Collaboration and the teacher-student writing conference. *Research in the Teaching of English, 24,* 279-321.

Sperling, M. (1995). Uncovering the role of role in writing and learning to write. One day in an inner-city classroom. *Written Communication, 12*(1), 93-133.

Sperling, M. (1996). Revisiting the writing-speaking connection: Challenges for research on writing and writing instruction. *Review of Educational Research, 66*(1), 53-86.

Sperling, M., & Freedman, S. W. (1992). *Research on writing.* University of California, Berkeley.

St. Clair, B., & Hough, D. L. (1992). *Interdisciplinary teaching: A review of the literature.* Springfield: Southwest Missouri State University. (ERIC Document Reproduction Service No. ED 373 056)

Tyler, R. W. (1949). *Basic principles of curriculum and instruction.* Chicago: University of Chicago Press.

Tierney, B. (1996). *How to write to learn science.* Arlington, VA: National Science Teachers Association.

Vygotsky, L. S. (1978). *Mind in society: The development of higher mental psychological processes.* Cambridge, MA: Harvard University Press.

Webb, N. M., & Farivar, S. (1999). Developing productive group interaction in middle school mathematics. In A. M. O'Donnell & A. King, *Cognitive perspectives on peer learning* (pp. 117-150). Mahwah, NJ: Lawrence Erlbaum Associates.

Wells, G. (1990). Creating the conditions to encourage literate thinking. *Educational Leadership, 13-17.*

Wertsch, J. V. (1985). *Vygotsky and the social formation of mind.* Cambridge, MA: Harvard University Press.

Wilson, S. M., & Ball, D. L. (1996). Helping teachers meet the standards: New challenges for teacher educators. *The Elementary School Journal, 97*(2), 121-138.

Wilson, S. M., & Wineburg, S. S. (1988). Peering at history through different lenses: The role of disciplinary perspectives in teaching history. *Teachers College Record, 89*(4), 525-539.

# ·75·

# THE CONVENTIONS OF WRITING

## Richard E. Hodges
### University of Puget Sound

This chapter examines research concerning teaching *conventions of writing*, a component of general written language instruction that includes spelling, handwriting, and typographical elements including capitalization, segmentation, and punctuation. Spelling and handwriting once held prominent positions in the school curriculum, whereas the teaching of other writing conventions traditionally has been subsumed within spelling and composition instruction. As a result, punctuation and capitalization are, for the most part, auxiliary footnotes in an extensive English language arts literature.

A review of the literature covering the conventions of writing reveals a decline in the past 30 years in the number of investigations into the nature and teaching of handwriting. Such has not been the situation for spelling, however. Spelling continues to be a source of considerable interest for researchers, especially for those looking into the general acquisition of written language, because orthographic skills are involved in both writing and reading. It is also the case that in the more recent work on spelling development, punctuation, segmentation, and capitalization are becoming objects of study in view of their relevance in understanding the development of general print literacy.

Many decades have elapsed since B. C. Gregory, superintendent of schools in Chelsea, Massachusetts, observed that

Of all the blind teaching we teachers do, the teaching of spelling is the blindest. It is empirical in most cases; reason (much less psychology) enters very little into our methods. We differ as to oral and written spelling, we differ as regards the use of spelling-books and the degree of difficulty of words used; but why we differ, or what is the psychological basis of this or that method, few of us can say. (Gregory, 1907–1908)

Much has been accomplished in the intervening years to allay Superintendent Gregory's concern. In many respects, spelling has been one of the most studied areas of the school curriculum. This is not to suggest that consensus has been achieved regarding the nature of spelling ability or the instructional practices that are believed to foster this ability. On the contrary, spelling

remains a subject about which widely divergent views are held regarding both theory and practice.

A primary purpose of this chapter is a consideration of teaching practices in spelling, although, modern research has centered largely on the nature and development of spelling ability rather than on instructional issues (Read & Hodges, 1982). This emphasis is not typical of the traditional spelling research literature that prior to 1970 was concerned largely with curriculum and method (Horn, 1941, 1950, 1960; T. Horn, 1969; Sherwin, 1969).

In addition, spelling research has seldom been extended beyond the elementary school years, in large part because direct instruction in spelling is uncommon past eighth grade. Interestingly, studies of spelling sometimes reappear at the college level, usually to identify and remediate spelling difficulties (Shaughnessy, 1977; Fischer, Shankweller, & Liberman, 1985). Given the dearth of research on spelling during the high school years, the picture of spelling development from its onset to maturity remains incomplete.

## HISTORICAL FRAMEWORK

Spelling has maintained a secure position as a subject in the school curriculum (Hanna & Hanna, 1959; Hodges, 1977, 1987; Towery, 1979; Venezky, 1980), mainly because of the importance attributed to correct spelling by the larger society. The first large-scale American scientific study of classroom learning, for instance, included an appraisal of the outcome of spelling instruction as a measurement of school effectiveness (Rice, 1987; Venezky, 1980).

Contemporary spelling instruction still reflects the brunt of two forces—one societal, the other psychological—that altered the traditional school curriculum in the early twentieth century. An intensified sense of the social purposes that schooling plays led to a new guide for the selection of content—*the principle of social utility*—a principle that proposed that what is learned in school should have utility in life outside of school (McKee, 1939). At the same time, views of learning also changed as mental discipline gave way to the formation of bonds between stimulus and behavior (Thorndike, 1929).

The principle of social utility and behavioral psychology affected the spelling curriculum through a number of influential publications devoted to explicating new views of spelling theory and practice, especially those set forth by Ernest Horn (Horn, 1919, 1926) whose influence is still felt (c.f. Fitzsimmons & Loomer, 1974; Graham, 1983; Johnson, Langford, & Quorn, 1981; Sherwin, 1969).

## Traditional Research and Its Implications

A basic question early spelling researchers asked was "What words should be learned?" In response, the approach taken was investigations of the frequencies of words that writers use (Ayres, 1913; Bauer, 1916; Buckingham & Dolch, 1936; Chancellor, 1910; Dolch, 1927; Fitzgerald, 1951; Hillerich, 1978; Horn, 1926; Jones, 1913; Rinsland, 1945; Tidyman, 1926) and investigations of the words that writers have the most difficulty spelling (Bauer, 1916; Brittain & Fitzgerald, 1942; Fitzgerald, 1932, 1938; Furness & Boyd, 1958; Gates, 1937; Johnson, 1950; Pollack, 1953).

Hanna and Hanna (1959) reported that more than 600 such studies were undertaken up to 1940. The number may be excessive, but these inquiries had lasting effects on spelling instruction and established an ongoing examination of the frequency distributions of words (c.f. Carroll, Davis, & Richman, 1971; Kucera & Francis, 1967). What have studies such as these revealed? The answer is perhaps most succinctly stated by J. A. H. Murray, founding editor of the *Oxford English Dictionary*, who observed that the "English language has a well-defined center but no discernible circumference" (Horn, 1938).

Studies to determine optimal instructional methods in spelling paralleled those that were intended to determine utilitarian word lists. Spelling became one of the most thoroughly researched school subjects, leading Horn (1919) to conclude that ample experimental data were available to develop a definitive course of study and to prepare a list of 41 instructional principles that set the course of spelling instruction for nearly the next half century.

## CURRENT UNDERSTANDING

### Orthography

English orthography has a widely held reputation as an inadequate writing system with unstable correspondences between letters and sounds. Were it a true alphabetic writing system, its critics assert, English orthography would include only as many letters as are needed to represent the number of speech sounds of spoken language. Such a one-to-one correspondence would make learning to spell and read a relatively simple matter (Hodges, 1972).

Proposals to reform the alphabetic vagaries of English orthography date at least as far back as the thirteenth century (Hodges, 1964; Venezky, 1980). Like the language that it represents, an orthography is an instrument that is influenced and shaped by cultural forces and events. Invasions by Danes and Normal French, a rebirth of classical studies during the Renaissance, Gutenberg's printing press, interactions with other cultures and languages, changes in English phonology over time, and Samuel Johnson's dictionary are among the significant forces and events that have shaped present-day English orthography (Scragg, 1974).

Despite the orthography's apparently erratic nature and calls for its reform (c.f. Dewey, 1971; Pitman & St. John, 1969; Yule, 1986), it is worth noting that in-depth investigations and analyses of the nature of English orthography have primarily taken place within the past 35 years (Adams, 1981; Albrow, 1972; Hodges, 1972; Becker, Dixon, & Anderson-Inman, 1980; Chomsky & Halle, 1968; Gleitman & Rozin, 1977; Hall, 1961; Hanna, Hanna, Hodges, & Rudorf, 1966; Henderson, 1982; Reed, 1969; Russell, 1975; Smith, 1968; Stubbs, 1980; Venezky, 1967, 1970). These investigations revealed that English orthography is more complex than its surface appearance suggests. The English writing system is more than an apparently flawed graphic transcription of phonology; it also represents lexical, grammatical, and semantic features of language (Chomsky & Halle, 1968; Venezky, 1970).

The findings of these orthographic studies have significance for the spelling curriculum. If the orthography is a closer representation of language than a surface inspection suggests, then a spelling course of study can emphasize an examination of structural relationships among written words rather than treating the spelling of each word as a specific act of learning.

### Models of Spelling

Several attempts have been made to devise models of spelling behavior that explain what transpires in people's minds as they spell. Such models reflect theorists' conceptions of the nature of language and the nature of learning. Simon and Simon (1973) and Simon (1976) proposed an information-processing model of spelling behavior composed of word recognition memory and phonetic knowledge. Nicholson and Schacter (1979) developed a three-tiered model in which spelling ability grows out of general language knowledge, visual associations, and internalized orthographic rules. Nelson (1980) described two routes to spelling achievement, one that translates the phonemic elements of words into graphemes and one that moves directly front word meaning to spelling.

Ehri (1987b) proposed that spellings of specific words systematically accumulate in memory through a process that assimilates the spellings of known words into memories of their meanings and pronunciations, especially when those spellings conform to known orthographic regularities. In Ehri's "amalgamation" model, spelling and reading development are closely related. Her model contained three knowledge sources: alphabetic letters; the orthographic system; and memory of spellings of specific words, including their visual configurations and such features as letter symbolizations of phonemes and morphemes.

Yellin (1986) placed learning to spell within a context of general written language literacy and attempted to classify spelling processes and practices in terms of "bottom-up," "top-down," and "interactive-compensatory" models. Bottom-up models, according to Yellin, describe texts and teachers as controllers of student learning. Such models emphasize rules, word lists, and rote memory in spelling instruction with little connection with actual writing (Fitzsimmons & Loomer, 1974). Top-down models, on the other hand, describe students as controllers of their own learning. These models emphasize the development of generalizations about the nature of the writing system that emerge during the course of active involvement in writing and reading (Gentry, 1984; Henderson & Beers, 1980; Read, 1986). Interactive compensatory models describe spelling behavior in terms of phonological information and higher level processing skills (Jorm, 1983).

A provocative spelling model is that proposed by Bouffler (1984) who viewed language as functional, social, and contextual. In her socio-psycholinguistic (semiotic) model, children learn to spell as needs arise for writing. Bouffler maintained that developmental stage theory is incorrect because it posits an endpoint—adult language—toward which learners strive. She countered this view with one in which children draw upon many of the same strategies that adults employ in writing (including spelling), although lacking knowledge of the full range of the language system to draw upon because of less experience with language.

Recent models of spelling share a common foundation that learning to spell is a complex cognitive undertaking to which formal instruction and reading and writing in daily life contribute. As Frith (1980a) noted, learning to spell is richer in intellectual texture than commonly pictured.

## Spelling–Reading Relationships

That spelling ability grows in context with the development of other written language abilities is not a new idea (Cornman, 1902; Thorndike, 1929). Spelling and reading instruction, for example, were at one time directly linked, becoming separate subjects during the nineteenth century (Hodges, 1987).

At the same time, it should be recognized that the processes of reading and spelling differ in some significant ways. Spelling in English orthography is a more complex process than reading because spelling requires an accurate reproduction of all the letters of words, many of which have complex links to phonology. Spelling requires that the writer pay close attention to the fine details of printed words, a process that hinders efficient reading. Such differences suggest that good readers who are poor spellers appear to have developed very functional sampling strategies for reading but ill-defined strategies for looking at words in detail for spelling (Frith, 1978, 1980b).

Both reading and spelling behavior rely on the concept of the *orthographic word*, that spoken words can be represented graphically. Orthographic words provide a visual and spatial form that facilitates word memory (Ehri, 1987a, 1987b; Templeton, 1979b), both in recognizing words when reading and in recalling words when writing (Invernizzi, 1984). A knowledge of orthographic words develops from numerous, varied interactions with written language—being read to, observing print in the environment, exploring books, and writing (Ehri, 1980; Fearing, 1983).

R. S. Thompson (1930) observed that "Theorists who have been fortunate in a special aptitude (for spelling), or have forgotten their early struggles with the subject, have sometimes been disposed to consider the matter a simple one" (p. 1). Thompson's admonition has not been lost on contemporary spelling researchers. Their descriptions of the development of spelling ability and how it emerges in concert with maturing intellectual processes, word knowledge, and functional experiences with written language in various social contexts reveal the complex nature of spelling behavior (Henderson, 1981; Templeton, 1986).

That young learners view the world differently than adults has special consequence for understanding spelling development. Read's (1971, 1975) groundbreaking observations of young children's early spelling strategies and their invented spellings set the stage for a wealth of studies that in aggregate describe the active roles learners play in developing knowledge about the nature and uses of written language.

Young learners' acquaintance with written language begins with a kind of global understanding, a *gestalt*, of its nature and purposes (Wood, 1982), for example, that writing is a graphic representation of meaning and that orthography contains some basic attributes, such as directionality and linearity (Clay, 1975; Ferreiro & Teberosky, 1982). A child's scribbling, for instance, globally represents an intended meaning (Harste, Woodward, & Burke, 1984; Heald-Taylor, 1984). Random letters and other graphic markers used in early writing attempts represent various semantic units such as paragraphs, sentences, and phrases (Hall & Hall, 1984). Children's early writing, in short, reveals the emergent beginnings of literacy.

The initial phase of spelling development has been variously termed as *precommunicative* (Gentry, 1982) and *preliterate* (Henderson & Templeton, 1986), the latter term more appropriate because early writing has a communicative function, however primitive. Although preliterate spelling demonstrates a young child's awareness of the purposes of writing, it also demonstrates that a concept of *word* is lacking and that words can be segmented into phonemes (Read, 1986). Later use of letter-name spellings more nearly approximates true spelling as children associate letters to sounds based on shared phonetic features (Read, 1971, 1975).

Several investigators have described the transition from a phonetic letter-name spelling strategy to a phonemic spelling strategy in which conventional spellings begin to appear (Beers, 1980; Beers & Henderson, 1977; Bissex, 1980; Gentry, 1978). These *transitional* spellings (Gentry, 1984) are illustrative of a young child's recognition of important orthographic features, such as vowel spellings, *e*-markers and vowel digraph patterns, orthographic inflectional patterns, and frequently used letter sequences. The use of these features is indicative of a child's growing visual memory of spelling patterns within *words* (Fearing, 1983; Ehri, 1980; Sloboda, 1980) where more abstract (and more powerful) orthographic relationships are to be found.

Morton Hunt (1982) pointed out that "The human mind makes order out of its experiences not only by grouping them into categories but by noticing patterns or regularities in the way things happen" (p. 177). For developing spelling ability, an awareness of orthographic patterns within words mark an important advance (Schlagal, 1982). Yet, many riddles abound for young spellers to solve as they understand English spelling and move beyond the limitations of sound–letter relationships and toward the orthographic nature of words—riddles about letter constraints and ways that syllables, bases, prefixes, and suffixes are joined in polysyllabic words (Beers & Henderson, 1977; Beers, Beers, & Grant, 1977; J. Gentry, 1981; Marino, 1979; Schwartz & Doehring, 1977; Schlagal, 1982; Thomas, 1982; Wilde, 1986; Zutell, 1979).

A significant strategy emerges in the elementary school years for most developing spellers, as early as second grade for some (Beers & Beers, 1980). This is an *analogical* spelling strategy in which orthographic knowledge of known words is used to spell other words whose spellings have not been secured in memory (Baron, 1978; Marsh, Friedman, Welsh, & Desberg, 1980; Nolen & McCartin, 1984; Phillips, 1980; Radebaugh, 1985). Analogical spelling is a high-order strategy that draws on a writer's knowledge of orthographic relationships among related words, requires a well-stocked memory store of words, and emphasizes visual strategies over phonological ones (Marsh, Friedman, Welsh, & Desberg, 1980).

Another important orthographic strategy involves the spellings of words with shared roots and bases (Chomsky & Halle, 1968; Venezky, 1970) in which the root spellings remain essentially the same, even when the words are differently pronounced. Awareness of this strategy makes it possible for spellers to break words with unfamiliar spellings into morphemic segments and to seek analogies to morphemically related words they do know that will help in spelling the unfamiliar ones (Hodges, 1982; Radebaugh, 1985).

Using morphemic representations in orthography is one of the later spelling strategies to develop (Thomas, 1982; Zutell, 1979). Children before fourth grade exhibit little control over derivational spelling patterns (Marino, 1979; Zutell, 1979). Although derivational spelling strategies are displayed by some fifth and sixth graders (Invernizzi, 1984; Templeton, 1979a, 1979b, 1986), the development of this strategy usually continues into maturity (Baker, 1980; Fischer, Shankweiler, & Liberman, 1985; Read, 1986).

Few studies have examined the spelling behaviors of high school students. Templeton (1979b) compared sixth, eighth, and tenth graders in their abilities to pronounce and spell derived words. Templeton and Scarborough-Franks (1985) looked at the ability of sixth and tenth graders to produce orthographic and phonetic derivatives of three vowel alternation patterns found in derived words. The results of both studies indicated that many students are more knowledgeable of the orthography than of the phonology of derived words.

A few investigations of the spelling behaviors of adults suggested inferences about spelling development in later school years. Fischer, Shankweiler, and Liberman (1985) found in comparing college-level good and poor spellers that although poor spellers were deficient at all levels (phonetic, orthographic rules, morphophonemic/derived), they mostly lacked a knowledge of morphophonemic structure. Bookman (1984) compared college-level poor spellers' performance on the spelling section of the WRAT with those of fifth graders on the same test and found that the adult poor spellers who read poorly performed much like the fifth graders when analyzed in a developmental framework. Marcel (1980) compared the spelling behavior of adults in a literacy class, a dysphasic/dysgraphic adult patient, and eight- and nine-year-old children and found developmental similarities among the three groups.

Studies such as these demonstrated that older students with spelling difficulties have a limited knowledge of the multilevel nature of English orthography and a limited apprehension of word structure (Anderson, 1985). It seems in learning to spell, as Shipley remarked about the lexicon in general, that "words repay the attention they are accorded" (1977, p. 52).

## Analyses of Spelling Errors

Investigations of spelling behavior from a developmental perspective provide a significant observation: Spelling errors are graphic expressions of a writer's knowledge of linguistic/orthographic reality. Individuals make few random spelling errors in their writing (Hodges, 1981).

The first extensive study of spelling errors took place in 1918 (Hollingsworth, 1918). Numerous studies followed, usually in hope of determining causes of spelling difficulties that would suggest ways to group words to facilitate their learning (c.f. Book & Harter, 1929; Carroll, 1930; Foran, 1934; Gates, 1937; Masters, 1927; Mendenhall, 1930; Robinson, 1940; Spache, 1940a, 1940b, 1940c).

Spelling errors have been variously classified but usually on the basis of *word difficulty* (Johnson, 1950; Fitzgerald, 1932, 1938; Jones, 1913); *word frequency* (Brittain & Fitzgerald, 1942; Goyen & Martin, 1977; Johnson, 1970; Pollack, 1953): *word meaningfulness* (Bloomer, 1961; Mangieri & Baldwin, 1979); *serial-position effects* (Jensen, 1962; Mendenhall, 1930); and *phonetic factors* (Petty, 1957), (c.f. Cahen, Craun, & Johnson, 1971, for a comprehensive discussion of spelling difficulties).

Spelling error classifications have focused mainly on surface characteristics such as letter omissions, additions, substitutions, and transpositions. Following Read's exploration of underlying causes of invented spellings (1971, 1975), however, attention has been turned to identifying perceptual, linguistic, and cognitive factors involved in spelling that errors reveal (Bouffler, 1984; Frith, 1980b; Ganschow, 1984; Henderson, 1981; c.f. Henderson & Beers, 1980; Invernizzi, 1984; Marino, 1981; Nelson, 1980; Schlagal, 1982; Weiner, 1980; Wilde, 1986, 1987) and that focus more on the writer's own contributions to spelling performance than on the effects of various instructional methods and materials (Francis, 1984).

Spelling errors provide clues to a writer's personal system of orthographic rules that is drawn upon when spelling (Zutell, 1979) and reveal a developmental progression of the logical processes involved (Francis, 1984; Marino, 1981). It seems, as John Dryden observed, "Errors like straws upon the surface flow; He who would search for pearls must dive below" (1972, p. 27).

## Differences Between Good and Poor Spellers

Spelling remains, of course, a difficulty for many writers. A developmental perspective helps to clarify some of the reasons. Unlike reading, as noted earlier, a thorough knowledge of orthographic word structures is inherent in correct spelling (Ehri, 1987c). However, although poor spellers' misspellings are more diverse and deviant than misspellings of typical spellers (Manolakes, 1975; Schlagal, 1982), the misspellings approximate those made by typical spellers at earlier developmental phases. Similar findings have been reported for mentally retarded spellers (Holmes & Peper, 1977) and for learning disabled spellers whose error patterns are analogous to those of writers three to four years younger (Gerber, 1984). The profiles of dyslexic spellers also have been found to be similar to those of normal spellers in early stages of writing (Moats, 1983). What emerges from an accumulation of research into spelling difficulty is a picture of spellers who, for whatever reason, have incomplete information about the orthographic structures of words (Drake & Ehri, 1984).

Poor spellers who are poor readers, for example, appear to have little knowledge of phoneme-grapheme relationships, as well as a diminished word memory (Drake & Ehri, 1984; Fox & Routh, 1983; Frith, 1980b; Perin, 1982). Better readers who are yet poor spellers, however, make misspellings that more closely correspond to plausible phoneme-grapheme patterns (Frith, 1980b). Nevertheless, they tend to stay with a phonological strategy, even when there is insufficient knowledge about the sound structure of a word (Frith & Frith, 1980). They also tend to spell phoneme-by-phoneme, as though naive about word structure (Radebaugh, 1985).

Poor spellers who are further along the developmental path appear to have a limited, poorly organized knowledge about word structure and orthography that is not easily accessed when needed (Gerber, 1984). They are less able than typical spellers to determine whether nonsense words approximate standard English spelling (Wallace, Klein, & Schneider, 1968). They lack knowledge of morphographic root patterns (Drake & Ehri, 1984), and they have difficulty identifying misspelled segments of text (Ormrod, 1985).

## Proofreading

Being able to detect and correct misspelled words, however, is not readily achieved by average spellers. Part of the difficulty is that strategies used for reading mitigate against proofreading. Proficient readers do not usually read word by word, nor, for that matter, do they delve into the structures of words unless it becomes necessary to do so. Yet, proofreading requires both of these operations. In addition, having once written some text, that text is highly predictable to the writer (Bouffler, 1984). It is for this reason that errors are more likely to be detected when a text is set aside for a period of time after it is written.

Being able to detect and correct one's spelling errors is a necessary aspect of spelling behavior. Yet, few inquiries have

been made into the manner in which proofreading skills develop (Lydiatt, 1984) or into the kinds of proofreading strategies that appear to be most effective (Personke & Knight, 1967). The scant available research evidence indicates that text familiarity enhances proofreading, because attention can be focused on the proofreading task (Levy & Begin, 1984); that it is easier to detect spelling errors that both look wrong and sound wrong (Cohen, 1980); and that poor spellers have difficulty identifying and reading their own misspellings (Frith, 1978).

Common wisdom often has advocated reading text backward (to obscure meaning and highlight word analysis), subvocalizing or reading text out loud (to relate orthographic words with spoken ones), allowing a "cooling off" period before proofreading new written material, exchanging papers with others, and reading text aloud while another student proofreads as effective proofreading techniques. Riefer (1987), however, reported that reading through a text more than once is a more effective proofreading procedure than reading text backward. Lydiatt (1984) described several proofreading strategies based on assumptions that effective proofreading is a function of a reader's sensitivity to the existence of errors and the extent of certainty in making a judgment that a word is incorrectly spelled. Drake and Ehri (1984) suggested convening spelled words to their spoken forms to see if the spelling conforms to correct pronunciation. Whatever techniques are taught, direct instruction of proofreading techniques appears to have a positive outcome (Frasch, 1965; Personke & Knight, 1967).

## Punctuation, Segmentation, and Capitalization

Although the emphasis of this chapter has been on spelling, writers also need to be conversant with other graphic features that make up written language, namely, punctuation, segmentation, and capitalization. Wilde (1986) described the important functions of these writing conventions. Punctuation sets apart syntactic units, and provides intonational cues and semantic information. Segmentation (the spaces between words in print) identifies word boundaries. In conjunction with periods, capital letters have both semantic and syntactic uses in indicating proper names and sentence boundaries.

Instruction in the uses of these graphic conventions has long been a part of teaching spelling and composition (Cronnell, 1980; L. Gentry, 1980, 1981). Yet, how young writers conceptualize those uses has only recently become a subject of empirical investigation (Wilde, 1986, 1987).

Knowledge of the functions of various punctuation markers progresses slowly, even with instruction (Cordeiro, 1986; Cordeiro, Giacobbe, & Cazden, 1983). Milz (as cited in Wilde, 1986) reported that some first graders are likely to omit punctuation altogether, except a period, which might be placed at the end of every line, or at the end of a written discourse (Edelsky, 1983). Some young writers even invent their own punctuation marks (Calkins, 1980; Cordeiro, Giacobbe, & Cazden, 1983). The idiosyncratic use of periods and other punctuation marks is most likely a consequence of an absence of simple rules that would explain their functions to young writers (Edelsky, 1983).

Gradually, however, knowledge about the use of graphic conventions stabilizes, probably as much from using them in functional writing as from formal instruction and practice, especially if functional writing is frequent (Calkins, 1980; Edelsky, 1983; Harste, Woodward, & Burke, 1984). At the present state of understanding, it appears clear that the growth of knowledge of functional uses of punctuation, capitalization, and segmentation can be accounted for within the context of the development of general written language ability.

## Handwriting

The importance that is attributed to correct spelling in school and in the larger society was pointed out previously, and legible handwriting has also had a share of that importance. The quality of a student's handwriting, for example, can influence raters' judgments of the quality of content of compositions (Marschall & Powers, 1969).

Handwriting enjoyed a featured place in the common school curriculum as a separate subject until the early 1930s when it began to be taught in connection with spelling and composition. Other subjects moved into the curriculum to take its place and less attention was given to methods of teaching handwriting in teacher preparation (Currie, 1981). Systematic handwriting instruction became largely relegated to the early school years (Sassoon, 1983).

Numerous surveys of existing handwriting research and practices have been published (c.f. Askov & Peck, 1982; Graham & Miller, 1980; Masters, 1987; Peck, Askov, & Fairchild, 1980). Yet, perhaps more than any other subject, handwriting instruction has been largely guided by tradition and pragmatic factors, with considerable reliance on commercial materials as vehicles of instruction (Froese, 1981).

Summaries of current practices indicate that handwriting instruction is fairly uniform throughout the United States, typically beginning with manuscript writing in the first grade, with a transition to cursive writing sometime in the third grade. Direct handwriting instruction is commonly a whole-class activity, nearly a third of the classes use commercial workbooks, most often for copying practice. Teacher observation rather than some uniform scale remains the predominant form of handwriting assessment (Masters, 1987). Legibility (well proportioned, uniformly arranged, letters and words) and fluency (rate of writing) are critical criteria in determining handwriting quality. Freeman's (1959) legibility classification scheme is the most commonly used; namely, letter form, uniformity of slant, letter alignment, quality of line, and spacing between letters and words. Writing speed is sometimes considered in assessing handwriting skill, especially in activities where speed may be a factor, such as notetaking and timed practices (Graham & Miller, 1980). Phelps, Stempel, and Speck (1985) reported that writing speed is perceived as a bigger problem than legibility for many children.

The preferred form of writing—cursive or manuscript—has generated considerable debate among handwriting specialists since 1920 when manuscript writing was transplanted to

the United States from Great Britain. Yet, by 1962 nearly 86% of American schools taught manuscript as an initial writing device, followed by a transition to cursive (Froese, 1981), even though evidence was sparse to show that cursive was faster to write or more legible to read (Koenke, 1986; Peck, Askov, & Fairchild, 1980). Research evidence is similarly equivocal concerning the superiority of particular approaches of commercial systems to ease the transition from manuscript to cursive. If even necessary, it should be an individual decision; and, if so, research indicates that both writing forms should be maintained (Peck, Askov, & Fairchild, 1980).

Evidence is also inconclusive with respect to superiority of styles of writing (e.g., italic, cursive, D'Nealian). In general, proponents of respective writing styles have found their own system to be the most beneficial. One is reminded of Bruner's comment that "common sense (and scientific puritanism) warns against: Better not to know too early at the start of what you are looking for lest you find it" (1983, p. 3).

Finally, literature on handwriting provides only limited insights into successful teaching practices (Askov & Peck, 1982; Masters, 1987). What appears to be important in the development of handwriting is the amount of emphasis teachers place on legible, neat writing (Koenke, 1986; Milone & Wasylyk, 1981; Peck, Askov, & Fairchild, 1980), and also the presence in the classroom of good handwriting models (Milone & Wasylyk, 1981).

## CURRICULAR AND INSTRUCTIONAL IMPLICATIONS

This chapter began with an observation made by a Massachusetts school superintendent who early in the present century deplored the absence of a sensible rationale for teaching spelling (Gregory, 1907–1908). The remainder of the chapter has centered on an examination of current understandings of the nature and functions of spelling development other conventions of writing from which such a rationale might be established.

Perhaps the most significant insight stemming from this examination is a recognition of the active involvement of developing writers in their own learning as they extract fundamental characteristics about the conventions of writing from an orthography whose surface appearance belies the existence of an underlying rationale. Bissex's (1980) illuminating description of her son's emergence as a mature writer concludes with the comment that "The logic by which we teach is not always the logic by which children learn" (1981, p. 199). What, then, might be concluded from the areas of research that have been reviewed here that places the logic of instruction in closer proximity with the logic of the learner?

It is evident that learning about the conventions of writing is a part of a process in which general written literacy develops from experiences both in and out of school. Ferreiro and Teberosky (1982), among others reported elsewhere in this *Handbook* have described how many young learners access the print environment in which they live in formulating early conceptions of the nature and purposes of written language.

For such children, school becomes a place in which these conceptions are expanded and refined.

One study (Clarke, 1988), for example, in which first-grade children who were encouraged to use invented spelling in creative writing were compared with other first graders who were prompted to use correct spellings reveals that more of the inventive spellers were able to write independently early in the school year. Significant differences favoring the inventive spellers were also found with respect to text length and variety of words used. Moreover, the children using invented spelling scored higher on subsequent posttests of spelling and word recognition, although their written productions showed no increase in the percentage of correct spelling over the term of the study. Clearly, these young writers were expanding their understandings of the nature and functions of spelling, even in the absence of direct instruction.

Herein lies a basic issue concerning the treatment of spelling and other writing conventions in the English language arts curriculum in the years ahead, namely, whether students' control over the conventions of writing is most effectively achieved by teacher-directed instruction using texts and other prepared materials or whether such control grows incidentally out of students' use of these conventions in natural writing. The issue is not a trivial one. At its heart lie basically different views about the nature and purposes of the English language arts curriculum (and curriculum in general), views that provide fuel to a general ongoing debate concerning the merits of "student-centered" versus "teacher-centered" approaches to curriculum development.

In support of student-centered approaches, numerous reports call attention to how teachers' utilization of children's invented spellings in daily writing can provide opportunities to help young students extend their emerging knowledge of English orthography (c.f. Anderson, 1985; DiStefano & Hagerty, 1985; Lehr, 1986; Lutz, 1986; Wilde, 1989). These and other reports cited in this chapter point out students' active roles in determining the nature and uses of writing conventions through reading and writing and how they develop strategies for coping with a complex orthography. In this regard, Wilde (1990) set forth a rationale for a student-centered spelling curriculum that is predicated on these finding, one in which the pace and direction of learning about English spelling are determined primarily by students themselves.

Conversely, others (c.f. Henderson, 1985; Henderson & Templeton, 1986; Morris, Nelson, & Perney, 1986) have drawn upon developmental spelling research data to describe spelling programs in which formal, direct instruction using textual material provides the basis for student learning. In either case, the research base concerning the nature and development of spelling ability is now sufficiently rich to focus once again on investigations of instructional methods and on the development of materials that draw upon this research base to promote spelling literacy throughout the school years.

Regardless of which instructional approaches are advocated, the research reviewed in this chapter points to an important conclusion that learning about and using the conventions of writing is an *intellectual* process. Providing for spelling instruction as though the ability to spell is only a product of memorizing specific words fails to acknowledge that like the acquisition of other language behavior, much of what is learned about spelling is gained by noticing recurring patterns encountered in functional settings and trying out and revising hypotheses about these patterns in other writing situations.

That the orthography operates at more abstract levels than sound–letter correspondence has been cogently pointed out elsewhere (Bookman, 1984; Read, 1975). These levels are revealed when groups of words are associated by their phonological, lexical, syntactic, and semantic relationships—relationships that many students make intuitively (Radebaugh, 1985; Schlagal, 1982; Thomas, 1982), and that creative instruction can foster for others (Chomsky, 1979). The more information about the logic of word structure to which students become sensitive, the more sophisticated and responsive become their uses of this knowledge in spelling word (Hodges, 1982, Templeton, 1979a, 1979b). The discovery of relationships among words of similar structure, then, is an important step in advancing the development of useful spelling strategies (Elliott, 1982; Zutell, 1979).

Learning to spell, after all, is learning about the structures and uses of words in written language. Wide reading in a variety of contexts contributes to the development of a word reservoir that can be used as a database for exploring orthographic relationships (Zutell, 1979) and that makes possible an analogical spelling strategy. Instructional strategies such as word sorts (Gillet & Kita, 1979) and semantic mapping (Johnson & Pearson, 1984) further help in the formation of analogies among related words.

Students' spelling and their use of other writing conventions in functional writing provide the discerning teacher with important information about their orthographic knowledge. A qualitative analysis of spelling errors reveals the different levels of word knowledge and learning rates that exist in classrooms and provides information that makes it more likely that instruction can be matched to learners' levels of understanding (Marcel, 1980; Schlagal, 1982), both for individual students (Ganschow, 1981, 1984; Marino, 1981; Wilde, 1989) and for students who are grouped at similar instructional levels (Morris, Nelson, & Perney, 1986).

In a 1930 review of spelling instruction, R. S. Thompson made the following observation:

"Neither more nor better methods of drill, nor the most ingenious methods of individual and specific attack on words will make up for the ignorance of exactly how the learning of spelling goes on, incidentally and within the spelling, period." (p. 1)

The aim of this chapter has been to consider the extent to which such ignorance has been supplanted by recent understanding which has been gained about the nature and function of spelling behavior and other writing conventions—understanding that may shed light on how using these fundamental writing tools can effectively be presented in English language arts. At the least, curriculum makers and teachers should be constantly mindful of the contributions that students make to their own learning, and in doing so, create instructional settings and materials that promote students' active exploration of the conventions of writing.

# References

Adams, M. J. (1981). What good is orthographic redundancy? In J. L. Tzeng & H. Singer (Eds.), *Perception in print: Reading research in experimental psychology* (pp. 197-221). Hillsdale, NJ: Lawrence Erlbaum Associates.

Albrow, K. H. (1972). *The English Writing System: Notes towards a description*. London: Longman.

Anderson, K. F. (1985). The development of spelling ability and linguistic strategies. *The Reading Teacher, 39,* 140-147.

Askov, E. N., & Peck, M. (1982). Handwriting. In H. E. Mitzel (Ed.), *Encyclopedia of educational research* (5th ed., pp. 764-769). New York: Macmillan.

Ayres, I. P. (1913). *The spelling vocabularies of personal and business letters.* New York: Russell Sage Foundation.

Baker, R. G. (1980). Orthographic awareness. In U. Frith (Ed.), *Cognitive processes in spelling* (pp. 51-68). London: Academic Press.

Baron, J. (1978). Using spelling-sound correspondences without trying to learn them. *Visible Language, 12,* 55-70.

Bauer, N. (1916). *The New Orleans public school spelling list.* New Orleans, LA: F. F. Hansell & Bros.

Becker, W. C., Dixon, R., & Anderson-Inman, L. (1980). *Morphographic and root word analysis of 26,000 high frequency words* (Technical report 1980-1). Eugene: University of Oregon Follow Through Protect.

Beers, J. W. (1980). Developmental strategies of spelling competence in primary school children. In E. H. Henderson & J. W. Beers (Eds.), *Developmental and cognitive aspects of learning to spell* (pp. 36-45). Newark, DE: International Reading Association.

Beers, J. W., & Beers, C. S. (1980). Vowel spelling strategies among first and second graders: A growing awareness of written words. *Language Arts, 57,* 166-172.

Beers, J. W., Beers, C. S., & Grant, K. (1977). The logic behind children's spelling. *The Elementary School Journal, 77,* 238-242.

Beers, J. W., & Henderson, E. H. (1977). A study of developing orthographic concepts among first graders. *Research in the English Language, 17,* 133-148.

Bissex, G. L. (1980). *Gyns at wrk: A child learns to read and write.* Cambridge, MA: Harvard University Press.

Bloomer, R. H. (1961). Concepts of meaning and the reading and spelling difficulty of words. *Journal of Educational Research, 54,* 178-182.

Book, W. F., & Harter, R. S. (1929). Mistakes which pupils make in spelling. *Journal of Educational Research, 19,* 106-118.

Bookman, M. O. (1984). Spelling as a cognitive-developmental linguistic process. *Academic Therapy, 20,* 21-32.

Bouffler, C. M. (1984). *Case study explorations of functional strategies in spelling.* Unpublished doctoral dissertation. Indiana University.

Brittain, F. J., & Fitzgerald, J. A. (1942). The vocabulary and spelling errors of second-grade children's themes. *Elementary English Review, 19,* 43-50.

Bruner, J. S. (1983). *In search of mind: Essays in autobiography.* NY: Harper & Row.

Buckingham, B. R., & Dolch, E. W. (1936). *A combined word list.* Boston: Ginn.

Cahen, L. S., Craun, M. J., & Johnson, S. K. (1971). Spelling difficulty: A survey of the research. *Review of Educational Research, 41,* 281-301.

Calkins, L. M. (1980). Research update—When children want to punctuate: Basic skills belong in context. *Language Arts, 57,* 567-573.

Carroll, H. E. (1930). *Generalization of bright and dull children: A comparative study with special reference to spelling.* NY: Teachers College, Columbia University, Contributions to Education, No. 439.

Carroll, J. A., Davies, P., & Richman, B. (1971). *The American heritage word frequency book.* NY: Houghton Mifflin and American Heritage Publishing.

Chancellor, W. E. (1910). Spelling: 1000 words. *Journal of Education, 71,* 488-489, 517, 522, 545-546, 573, 578, 607-608.

Chomsky, C. (1979). Approaching reading through invented spelling. In L. B. Resnick & P. Weaver (Eds.), *Theory and practice in early reading* (Vol. 11, pp. 43-65). Hillsdale, NJ: Lawrence Erlbaum Associates.

Chomsky, N., & Halle, M. (1968). *The sound pattern of English.* NY: Harper & Row.

Clarke, L. K. (1988). Invented versus traditional spelling in first grades' writings: Effects on learning to spell and read. *Research in the Teaching of English, 22,* 281-309.

Clay, M. M. (1975). *What did I write?* London: Heinemann.

Cohen, G. (1980). Reading and searching for spelling errors. In U. Frith (Ed.), *Cognitive processes in spelling* (pp. 135-155). London: Academic Press.

Cordeiro, P. A., (1986). Punctuation in a third grade class: An analysis of errors in period placement. *Dissertation Abstracts International, 47,* 05A. (University Microfilms No. 86-16, 763)

Cordeiro, P. A., Giacobbe, M. E., & Cazden, C. (1983). Apostrophes, quotation marks, and periods: Learning punctuation in the first grade. *Language Arts, 60,* 323-332.

Corrnman, O. P. (1902). *Spelling in the elementary school.* NY: Ginn.

Cronnell, B. (1980). *Punctuation and capitalization: A review of the literature.* Los Alamitos, CA: Southwest Regional Laboratory for Educational Research and Development. (ERIC Document Reproduction Service No. ED 208 404)

Currie, A. B. (1981). *Instruction in handwriting in Ontario schools.* Toronto, Canada: Ontario Department of Education. (ERIC Document Reproduction Service No. ED 205 983)

Dewey, G. (1971). *English spelling: Roadblock to reading.* NY: Teachers College Press.

DiStefano, P. P., & Hagerty, P. J. (1985). Teaching spelling at the elementary level: A realistic perspective. *The Reading Teacher, 38,* 372-377.

Dolch, E. W. (1927). Grade vocabularies. *Journal of Educational Research, 16,* 16-26.

Drake, O. A., & Ehri, L. C. (1984). Spelling acquisition: Effects of pronouncing words on memory for their spellings. *Cognition and Instruction, 1,* 297-320.

Dryden, J. (1972). *All for love.* D. M. Veith (Ed.), Lincoln, NE: University of Nebraska Press. (Original work published in 1678)

Edelsky, C. (1983). Segmentation and punctuation: Developmental data from young writers in a bilingual program. *Research in the Teaching of English, 17,* 135-136.

Ehri, L. C. (1980). The development of orthographic images. In U. Frith (Ed.), *Cognitive processes in spelling* (pp. 311-338). London: Academic Press.

Ehri, L. C. (1987a). Does learning to spell help beginners learn to read words? *Reading Research Quarterly, 22,* 47-65.

Ehri, L. C. (1987b). Learning to read and spell. *Journal of Reading Behavior, 19,* 5-31.

Ehri, L. C. (1987c). Sources of difficulty in learning to spell and read. In M. L Wolraich & D. K. Routh (Eds.), *Advances in developmental and behavioral pediatrics* (Vol. 8, pp. 5591-5666). Greenwich, CT: JAI Press.

Elliott, I. (1982). *Learning to spell: Children's development of phoneme grapheme relationships* (Research report 4/82). Carlton, Victoria: Curriculum Services Unit, Education Department of Victoria.

Fearing, H. (1983). *Learning to spell: The role of visual memory* (Research report 1/83). Carlton, Victoria: Curriculum Services Unit, Education Department of Victoria.

Ferreiro, E., & Teberosky, A. (1982). *Literacy before schooling.* Exeter, NH: Heinemann.

Fischer, F. W., Shankweiler, D., & Liberman, I. (1985). Spelling proficiency and sensitivity to word structure. *Journal of Memory and Language, 24,* 423–441.

Fitzgerald, J. A. (1932). Words misspelled most frequently by children of the fourth, fifth, and sixth grade levels in life outside the school. *Journal of Educational Research, 26,* 213–218.

Fitzgerald, J. A. (1938). The vocabulary and spelling errors of third-grade children's life-letters. *The Elementary School Journal, 38,* 518–527.

Fitzgerald, J. A. (1951). *A basic life spelling vocabulary.* Milwaukee, WI: The Bruce Publishing Co.

Fitzsimmons, R. J., & Loomer, B. M. (1974). *Improved spelling through scientific investigation.* Des Moines and Iowa City, IA: Iowa State Department of Public Instruction and Iowa Center for Research in School Administration, University of Iowa.

Foran, G. T. (1934). *The psychology and teaching of spelling.* Washington, DC: The Catholic Education Press.

Fox, B., & Routh, D. K. (1983). Reading disability, phonemic analysis and sysphonetic spelling: A follow-up study. *Journal of Clinical Child Psychology, 72,* 28–32.

Francis, K. (1984). Children's knowledge of orthography in learning to read. *British Journal of Educational Psychology, 54,* 8–23.

Frasch, D. K. (1965). How well do sixth-graders proofread for spelling errors? *The Elementary School Journal, 65,* 381–385.

Freeman, F. (1959). New handwriting scale. *The Elementary School Journal, 35,* 366–372.

Frith, U. (1978). Annotation: Spelling difficulties. *Journal of Child Psychology and Psychiatry, 19,* 279–285.

Frith, U. (Ed.). (1980a). *Cognitive processes in spelling.* London: Academic Press.

Frith, U. (1980b). Unexpected spelling problems. In U. Frith (Ed.). *Cognitive processes in spelling* (pp. 499–515). London: Academic Press.

Frith, U., & Frith, C. (1980). Relationships between reading and spelling. In J. F. Kavanaugh & R. I. Venezky (Eds.), *Orthography, reading, and dyslexia* (pp. 287–295). Baltimore: University Park Press.

Froese, V. (1981). Handwriting: Practice, pragmatism, and progress. In V. Froese & S. B. Straw (Eds.), *Research in the language arts: Language and schooling* (pp. 227–243). Baltimore: University Park Press.

Furness, E. I., & Boyd, G. A. (1958). Real spelling demons for high school students. *The English Journal, 47,* 267–270.

Ganschow, L. (1981). Discovering children's learning strategies for spelling through error analysis. *The Reading Teacher, 34,* 676–680.

Ganschow, L. (1984). Analyze error patterns to remediate severe spelling difficulties. *The Reading Teacher, 38,* 288–293.

Gates, A. I. (1937). *Spelling difficulties of 3876 words.* New York: Bureau of Publications, Teachers College, Columbia University.

Gentry, J. R. (1978). Early spelling strategies. *The Elementary School Journal, 79,* 88–92.

Gentry, J. R. (1981). Learning to spell developmentally. *The Reading Teacher, 34,* 378–381.

Gentry, J. R. (1982). Developmental spelling: Assessment. *Diagnostique, 8,* 52–61.

Gentry, J. R. (1984). Developmental aspects of learning to spell. *Academic Therapy, 20,* 11–19.

Gentry, L. A. (1980). *Capitalization instruction in elementary school textbooks* (Technical Note TN 2-81-01). Los Alamitos, CA: Southwest Regional Laboratory for Educational Research and Development. (ERIC Document Reproduction Service No. ED 199 756)

Gentry, L. A. (1981). *Punctuation instruction in elementary school textbooks.* Los Alamitos, CA: Southwest Regional Laboratory for Educational Research and Development. (ERIC Document Reproduction Service No. ED 199 757)

Gerber, M. M. (1984). Orthographic problem-solving ability of learning disabled and normally achieving students. *Learning Disability Quarterly, 7,* 157–164.

Gillet, J. W., & Kita, M. J. (1979). Words, kids and categories. *The Reading Teacher, 32,* 538–542.

Gleitman, L. L., & Rozin, P. (1977). The structure and acquisition of reading 1. Relations between orthographies and the structure of language. In A. S. Reber & D. L. Scarborough (Eds.), *Toward a psychology of reading: The proceeding of the CUNY Conference* (pp. 1–53). Hillsdale, NJ: Lawrence Erlbaum Associates.

Goyen, J. D., & Martin, M. (1977). The relation of spelling errors to cognitive variables and word type. *British Journal of Educational Psychology, 47,* 268–273.

Graham, S. A. (1983). Effective spelling instruction. *The Elementary School Journal, 83,* 560–567.

Graham, S. A., & Miller, L. (1980). Handwriting research and practice: A unified approach. *Focus on Exceptional Children, 13,* 1–15.

Gregory, B. C. (1907-1908). The rationale of spelling. *The Elementary School Teacher, 8,* 40–55.

Hall, R. A., Jr. (1961). *Sound and spelling in English.* Philadelphia and New York: Chilton.

Hall, S., & Hall, C. (1984). It takes a lot of letters to spell 'Erz'. *Language Arts, 61,* 822–827.

Hanna, P. R., & Hanna, J. S. (1959). Spelling as a school subject: A brief history. *National Elementary Principal, 38,* 8–23.

Hanna, P. R., Hanna, J. S., Hodges, B. F., & Rudorf, E. H. (1966). *Phoneme-grapheme correspondences as cues to spelling improvement.* Washington, DC: U.S. Government Printing Office, U.S. Office of Education.

Harste, I. C., Woodward, V. A., & Burke, C. I. (1981). *Language stories and literacy lessons.* Portsmouth, NH: Heinemann.

Heald-Taylor, B. G. (1984). Scribble in first grade writing. *The Reading Teacher, 38,* 4–8.

Henderson, E. H. (1981). *Learning to read and spell: The child's knowledge of words.* Dekalb, IL: Northern Illinois University Press.

Henderson, E. H. (1985). *Teaching and spelling.* Boston: Houghton Mifflin.

Henderson, E. H., & Beers, J. W. (Eds.). (1980). *Developmental and cognitive aspects of learning to spell: A reflection of word knowledge.* Newark, DE: International Reading Association.

Henderson, E. H., & Templeton, S. (1986). A developmental perspective of formal spelling instruction through alphabet, pattern, and meaning. *The Elementary School Journal, 86,* 304–316.

Henderson, L. C. (1982). *Orthography and word recognition in reading.* London: Academic Press.

Hillerich, H. L. (1978). *A writing vocabulary of elementary children.* Springfield, IL: Charles C. Thomas.

Hodges, R. E. (1964). A short history of spelling reform in the United States. *Phi Delta Kappan, 45,* 330–332.

Hodges, R. E. (1972). Theoretical frameworks of English orthography. *Elementary English, 49,* 1089–1097, 1105.

Hodges, R. E. (1977). In Adam's fall: A brief history of spelling instruction in the United States. In H. A. Robinson (Ed.), *Reading and writing instruction in the United States: Historical trends* (pp. 1-16). Urbana, IL and Newark, DE: ERIC Clearinghouse on Reading and Communication Skills and the International Reading Association.

Hodges, R. E. (1981). *Learning to spell*. Urbana, IL: ERIC Clearinghouse on Reading and Communication Skills and the National Council of Teachers of English.

Hodges, R. E. (1982). *Improving spelling and vocabulary in the secondary school*. Urbana, IL: ERIC Clearinghouse on Reading and Communication Skills and the National Council of Teachers of English.

Hodges, R. E. (1987). American spelling instruction: Retrospect and prospect. *Visible Language, 21*, 215-235.

Hollingsworth, L. S. (1915). *The psychology of special disability in spelling*. NY: Teachers College, Columbia University. Contributions to Education, No. 88.

Holmes, D. L., & Peper, R. J. (1977). Evaluation of the use of spelling error analysis in the diagnosis of reading disabilities. *Child Development, 48*, 1708-1711.

Horn, E. (1919). Principles of teaching spelling, as derived from scientific investigation. In G. M. Whipple (Ed.), *Fourth Report of Committee on Economy of Time in Education* (pp. 52-77) (Eighteenth Yearbook of the National Society for the Study of Education, Part 2). Bloomington, IL: Public School Publishing Co.

Horn, E. (1926). *A basic writing vocabulary: 10,000 words most commonly used in writing* (University of Iowa Monographs in Education No. 4). Iowa City, IA: College of Education, University of Iowa.

Horn, E. (1938). Contributions of research to special methods: Spelling. In F. N. Freeman (Ed.), *The Scientific Movement in Education* (pp. 107-114) (Thirty-seventh Yearbook of the National Society for the Study of Education, Part 2). Chicago: University of Chicago Press.

Horn, F. (1950). Spelling. In W. S. Monroe (Ed.), *Encyclopedia of Educational Research* (Rev. ed., pp. 1247-1264). New York: Macmillan.

Horn, F. (1960). Spelling. In C. W. Harris (Ed.), *Encyclopedia of Educational Research* (3rd ed., pp. 1337-1354). New York: Macmillan.

Horn, H. (1941). Spelling. In W. S. Monroe (Ed.), *Encyclopedia of Educational Research* (pp. 1166-1185). New York: Macmillan.

Horn, T. D. (1969). Spelling. In R. L. Ebel (Ed.), *Encyclopedia of Educational Research* (4th ed., pp. 1282-1299). New York: Macmillan.

Hunt, M. (1982). The universe within: A new science explores the human mind. New York: Simon & Schuster.

Invernizzi, M. (1984). *Memory for word elements in relation to stages of spelling power*. Paper presented at annual meeting of the International Reading Association, Atlanta.

Jensen, A. (1962). Spelling errors and the serial-position effect. *Journal of Educational Psychology, 53*, 105-109.

Johnson, D. D., & Pearson, P. D. (1984). *Teaching reading vocabulary* (2nd ed.). NY: Holt, Rinehart, & Winston.

Johnson, J. B. (1970). *An analysis of spelling difficulties of common words used with high frequency*. Unpublished doctoral dissertation, University of Wyoming, Laramie.

Johnson, L. W. (1950). One hundred words most often misspelled by children in the elementary grades. *Journal of Educational Research, 44*, 54-55.

Johnson, T. D., Langford, K. G., & Quorn, K. C. (1981). Characteristics of an effective spelling program. *Language Arts, 58*, 581-514.

Jones, W. F. (1913). *Concrete investigation of the material of spelling*. Vermillion, SD: University of South Dakota.

Jorm, A. F. (1983). *The psychology of reading and spelling disabilities*. London: Routledge & Kegan Paul.

Koenke, K. (1986). Handwriting instruction: What do we know? *The Reading Teacher, 40*, 214-216.

Kucera, H., & Francis, W. N. (1967). *Computational analysis of present-day American English*. Providence, RI: Brown University Press.

Kuni, B. Y., Schuta, B. H., & Baker, R. L. (1965). Spelling errors and the serial position effect. *Journal of Educational Psychology, 6*, 334-336.

Lehr, F. (1986). Invented spelling and language development. *The Reading Teacher, 39*, 452-454.

Levy, B. A., & Begin, J. (1984). Proofreading familiar text: Allocating resources to perceptual and conceptual processes. *Memory and Cognition, 12*, 621-632.

Lutz, E. (1986). Invented spelling and spelling development. *Language Arts, 63*, 742-744.

Lydiatt, S. (1984). Error detection and correction in spelling. *Academic Therapy, 20*, 33-40.

Mangierri, J. N., & Baldwin, R. S. (1979). Meaning as a factor in predicting spelling difficulty. *Journal of Educational Research, 72*, 285-287.

Manolakes, G. (1975). The teaching of spelling: A pilot study. *Elementary English, 52*, 243-247.

Marcel, T. (1980). Phonological awareness and phonological representation: Investigation of a specific spelling problem. In U. Frith (Ed.), *Cognitive processes in spelling* (pp. 373-403). London: Academic Press.

Marino, J. L. (1979). *Children's use of phonetic, graphemic, and morphophonemic cues in a spelling task*. Unpublished paper. (ERIC Document Reproduction Service No. ED 188 235)

Marino, J. L. (1981). Spelling errors: From analysis to instruction. *Language Arts, 58*, 567-572.

Marschall, J. C., & Powers, J. M. (1969). Writing neatness, composition errors, and essay grades. *Journal of Educational Measurement, 6*, 72-101.

Marsh, G., Friedman, M., Welch, V., & Desberg, P. (1980). The development of strategies in spelling. In U. Frith (Ed.), *Cognitive processes in spelling* (pp. 339-353). London: Academic Press.

Masters, D. G. (1987). *Handwriting* (English Language Arts Concept Paper, No. 2). Salem, OR: Oregon State Department of Education. (ERIC Document Reproduction Service No. ED 284 265)

Masters, H. V. (1927). *A study of spelling errors* (Studies in Education, No. 4). Iowa City, IA: University of Iowa.

McKee, P. (1939). *Language in the elementary school: Composition, spelling, writing*. Boston: Houghton Mifflin.

Mendenhall, J. E. (1930). *An analysis of spelling errors: A study of factors associated with word difficulty*. New York: Bureau of Publications, Teachers College, Columbia University.

Milone, M. N. Jr., & Wasylyk, T. M. (1981). Handwriting in special education. *Teaching Exceptional Children, 14*, 58-61.

Moats, L. C. (1983). A comparison of spelling errors of older dyslexic and second-grade normal children. *Annals of Dyslexia, 33*, 121-411.

Morris, D., Nelson, L., & Perney, J. (1986). Exploring the concept of spelling instructional level through analysis of error types. *The Elementary School Journal, 17*, 181-211.

Nelson, H. E. (1980). Analysis of spelling errors in normal and dyslexic children. In U. Frith (Ed.), *Cognitive processes in spelling* (pp. 475-493). London: Academic Press.

Nicholson, T., & Schacter, S. (1979). Spelling skill and teaching practice: Putting them back together again. *Language Arts, 56*, 804-809.

Nolen, P., & McCartin, K. (1984). Spelling strategies on the Wide Range Achievement Test. *The Reading Teacher, 38*, 148-158.

Ormrod, J. (1985). Proofreading the cat in the hat: Evidence for different reading styles of good and poor spellers. *Psychological Reports, 57*, 863-867.

Peck, M., Askov, E. N., & Fairchild, S. H. (1980). Another decade research in handwriting: Progress and prospect in the 1970s. *The Journal of Educational Research, 73,* 293-298.

Perin, D. (1982). Spelling strategies in good and poor readers. *Applied Psycholinguistics, 3,* 1-14.

Personke, C., & Knight, L. (1967). Proofreading and spelling: A report and a program. *Elementary English, 44,* 768-774.

Petty, W. (1957). Phonetic elements as factors in spelling difficulty. *Journal of Educational Research, 51,* 209-214.

Phelps, J., Stempel, L., & Speck, G. (1985). The children's handwriting scale: A new diagnostic tool. *Journal of Educational Research, 79,* 46-50.

Phillips, L. P. (1980). *Strategies children use in spelling.* Unpublished doctoral dissertation, University of Denver, Denver, CO.

Pitman, J., & St. John, J. (1969). *Alphabets and reading: The initial teaching alphabet.* New York: Pitman.

Pollack, T. C. (1953). *Words most frequently misspelled in the seventh and eighth grades* (In Teachers Service Bulletin in English). New York: Macmillan.

Radebaugh, M. H. (1985). Children's perceptions of their spelling strategies. *The Reading Teacher, 38,* 532-536.

Read, C. (1971). Pre-school children's knowledge of English phonology. *Harvard Educational Review, 42,* 1-34.

Read, C. (1975). *Children's categorizations of speech sounds in English* (Research Report No. 17). Urbana, IL: National Council of Teachers of English.

Read, C. (1986). *Children's creative spelling.* London: Routledge & Kegan Paul.

Read, C., & Hodges, R. E. (1982). Spelling. In H. Mitzel (Ed.), *Encyclopedia of Educational Research* (5th ed., pp. 1758-1767). New York: Macmillan.

Reed, D. W. (1969). A theory of language, speech, and writing. In H. Singer & R. B. Ruddell (Eds.), *Theoretical models and processes of reading* (pp. 219-228). Newark, DE: International Reading Association.

Rice, J. M. (1897). The futility of the spelling grind. *The Forum, 23,* 163-172, 109-419.

Riefer, D. M. (1987). Is 'backwards reading' an effective proofreading strategy? (ERIC Document Reproduction Service No. ED 281 175)

Rinsland, H. D. (1945). *A basic vocabulary of elementary-school children.* New York: Macmillan.

Robinson, F. P. (1940). Misspellings are intelligent. *Educational Research Bulletin, 12,* 136-442.

Russell, P. (1975). *An outline of English spelling* (Technical Report No. 55). Los Alamitos, CA: Southwest Regional Laboratory for Educational Research and Development.

Sassoon, R. (1983). *The practical guide to children's writing.* London: Thames & Hudson.

Schafer, J. C. (1988). Invented spelling and teacher preparation. *English Education, 20,* 97-108.

Schlagal, R. C. (1982). A qualitative inventory of word knowledge: A developmental study of spelling, grades one through six. Unpublished doctoral dissertation, University of Virginia, Charlottesville. *Dissertation Abstracts International, 47,* 915A.

Schwartz, S., & Doehring, D. G. (1977). A developmental study of children's ability to acquire knowledge of spelling pattern. *Developmental Psychology, 13,* 419-420.

Scragg, D. G. (1974). *A history of English spelling.* Manchester: Manchester University Press.

Shaughnessy, M. (1977). *Errors and expectations.* New York: Oxford University Press.

Sherwin, S. J. (1969). *Four problems in teaching English: A critique of research.* Scranton, PA: International Textbook Co.

Shipley, J. T. (1977). *In praise of English.* New York: New York Times Books.

Simon, D. P. (1976). Spelling: A task analysis. *Instructional Sciences, 5,* 277-302.

Simon, D. P., & Simon, H. A. (1973). Alternative uses of phonemic information in spelling. *Review of Educational Research, 43,* 115-137.

Sloboda, J. A. (1980). Visual imagery and individual differences in spelling. In U. Frith (Ed.), *Cognitive processes in spelling* (pp. 231-248). London: Academic Press.

Smith, H. L., Jr. (1968). *English morphophonics: Implications for the teaching of reading Monograph No. 10.* New York State English Council.

Spache, G. (1940a). A critical analysis of various methods of classifying spelling errors. *Journal of Educational Psychology, 31,* 111-134.

Spache, G. (1940b). Validity and reliability of the proposed classification of spelling errors, II. *Journal of Educational Psychology, 31,* 204-214.

Spache, G. (1940c). Spelling disability correlates 1-Factors probably causal in spelling disability. *Journal of Educational Research, 34,* 561-586.

Stubbs, M. (1980). *Language and literacy: The sociolinguistics of reading and writing.* London: Routledge & Kegan Paul.

Templeton, S. (1979a). The circle game of spelling: A reappraisal for teachers. *Language Arts, 56,* 789-797.

Templeton, S. (1979b). Spelling first, sound later: The relationship between orthography and higher order phonological knowledge in older students. *Research in the Teaching of English, 13,* 255-264.

Templeton, S. (1986). Synthesis of research on the learning and teaching of spelling. *Educational Leadership, 43,* 73-78.

Templeton, S., & Scarborough-Franks, L. (1985). The spelling's the thing: Knowledge of derivational morphology in orthography and phonology among older students. *Applied Psycholinguistics, 6,* 371-390.

Thomas, V. (1982). *Learning to spell: The way children make use of morphemic information* (Research Project 1/82). Carlton, Victoria: Curriculum Services Unit, Education Department of Victoria.

Thompson, R. S. (1930). *The effectiveness of modern spelling instruction.* New York: Bureau of Publications, Teachers College, Columbia University, Contributions to Education No. 436.

Thorndike, F. L. (1929). The need of fundamental analysis of methods of teaching. *The Elementary School Journal, 30,* 189-191.

Tidyman, W. F. (1926). *The teaching of spelling.* Yonkers. NY: World Book.

Towery, G. (1979). Spelling instruction through the nineteenth century. *English Journal, 68,* 22-27.

Vachek, J. (1973). *Written language.* The Hague: Mouton.

Venezky, R. L. (1967). English orthography: Its graphical structure and its relation to sound. *Reading Research Quarterly, 2,* 75-105.

Venezky, R. L. (1970). *The structure of English orthography.* The Hague: Mouton.

Venezky, R. I. (1980). From Webster to Rice to Roosevelt: The formative years for spelling instruction and spelling reform in the USA. In U. Firth (Ed.), *Cognitive Processes in spelling* (pp. 9-30). London: Academic Press.

Wallace, J., Klein, R., & Schneider, P. (1968). Spelling ability and probability structure of English. *Journal of Educational Research, 61,* 315-319.

Weiner, E. S. (1980). Diagnostic evaluation of writing skills. *Journal of Learning Disabilities, 13,* 48-53.

Wilde, S. (1986). An analysis of the development of spelling and punctuation in selected third and fourth grade children. Unpublished doctoral dissertation, University of Arizona, Tucson. *Dissertation Abstracts International.*

Wilde, S. (1987). *Spelling and punctuation development in selected third and fourth grade children* (Occasional Paper No. 17). Arizona Center for Research and Development, University of Arizona, Tucson.

Wilde, S. (1989). Looking at invented spelling: A kidwatcher's guide to spelling, Part 1. In K. S. Goodman, Y. M. Goodman, & W. J. Hood (Eds.), *The whole language evaluation book* (pp. 213-226). Portsmouth, NH: Heinemann.

Wilde, S. (1990). A proposal for a new spelling curriculum. *The Elementary School Journal, 90*, 275-289.

Wood, M. (1982). Invented spelling. *Language Arts, 59*, 707-717.

Yellin, D. (1986). Connecting spelling instruction to reading and writing. Paper presented at the annual meeting of Southwest Regional Conference of the International Reading Association (ERIC Document Reproduction Service No. ED 268 486), San Antonio.

Yule, V. (1986). The design of spelling to match needs and abilities. *Harvard Educational Review, 56*, 278-297.

Zutell, J. (1978). Some psycholinguistic perspectives on children's spelling. *Language Arts, 55*, 844-850.

Zutell, J. (1979). Spelling strategies of primary school children and their relationships to Piaget's concept of decentration. *Research in the Teaching of English*.

# AUTHOR INDEX

# SUBJECT INDEX

## A

AAA, *see* American Anthropology Association
AASL, *see* American Association of School
    Librarians (AASL)
Ability grouping
    alternatives to, 568-569
    versus cooperative learning, 567-568
    research findings, 566-567
    secondary classrooms, 519-521
    social interaction, 569-570
    students' perceptions of, 570
Accelerated Reader, 75
Accountability
    in California, 102-103
    definition of literacy and, 146
    effect on instruction, 76
    history, 9-10
    legislation, 102-103
    state takeovers, 76
Acquisition, language, *see also* Linguistics
    communicative interaction, 26
    developmental influences, 26-27
    impact on classroom instruction, 348
    literature use, 642
    metaprocessing, 26
    model of, 26-27
    print awareness studies, 174-175
    process, 26-27
    theories, 24-26
Acquisition, oral language, *see also* Speaking
    classroom talk, 894-895
    effects of drama on, 1011-1012
    of elementary students, 340-344
    emergent literacy and, 306-307
    of ESL students, 423-424, 427
    overview, 881-882
    policy making, 882-884
    research history, 47, 306-307, 882-888
    views of, 47-48, 306-307, 888
Acquisition, reading
    alphabetic knowledge, 182
    elementary students, 349-350
    kindergarten students, 346-347
    longitudinal research, 178-183
    phonemic awareness, 671-672
    research history, 48
    teachers' views of, 48
    technology and, 187
Acquisition, written language
    culture, 981
    elementary students, 344-346, 347-349,
      350-351, 979-980
    home factors, 981-982

kindergarten students, 345-346
preschool students, 978-979
studies of, 48, 175, 176-179
symbolic play and, 176
technology and, 187
Action research, 134
Active engagement, 25, 426
Admission tests, 482
Adolescents
    after-school jobs, 290
    birth rates, 290
    boredom with school, 75
    case studies of, 196
    drugs and, 291
    high-risk behavior, 364-365
    homosexuality, 364
    longitudinal studies of, 186
    reading preferences, 840-841
Adults
    barriers to reading, 408
    case studies of, 196-197
    cognitive development, 406-407
    developmental models, 407-408
    fluency, 410
    problem solving, 410
    processing problems, 408
    reading improvement, 409-410
    vocabulary acquisition, 410
    writing process, 975
Advanced Placement program, 20
Advocacy-oriented research, 134
AERA, *see* American Educational Research
    Association (AERA)
Affect, 701-703
Aims of rhetoric, 793-795
Alabama, 107
Alphabetic knowledge, 182
American Anthropology Association (AAA),
    54n.2
American Association for Applied Linguistics,
    117
American Association of School Librarians
    (AASL), 12
American Dialect Society, 117
American Educational Research Association
    (AERA), 135
American Federation of Teachers, 12
Analogies, 937
Analysis of variance, 167
Anecdotal records, 605
Anecdote, 121-122
Anglo-American Dartmouth Seminar, 10, 12,
    80, 114
Anthologies, 8, 19

Anthroethnography, 201
Anthropology
    cognitive anthropology, 55
    constructs of, 54
    culture and, 55-56
    current debates in, 53-54
    education and, 56-57
    educational researchers in, 54
    functionalism, 55
    influence on research, 54
    language and, 57-58
    learning and, 61-62
    linguistic anthropology, 55
    literacy and, 58-60
    literature and, 60-61
    obstacles to educational research, 62
    psychological anthropology, 55
    research contributions of, 53
    speech community and, 58
    symbolic analysis, 55
    teaching and, 61
Anticipation-reaction guides, 936
Anxiety, 34
Appeals of rhetoric, 791-793
Appropriateness of instruction, 683
Arizona, 118
Assembly Bill 1086 (California, 1997), 102
Assessment
    in California, 100, 101, 385-386
    current purposes of, 104
    curriculum-driven, 594-595
    elementary students, 595-596
    emphasis on passing, 105-106
    in Florida, 385-386
    of high school students, 395-396
    history, 9-10
    holistic, 621-622
    impact of standardized tests, 627-628
    informal versus formal, 590-591
    integrated curriculum, 1047-1048
    International Reading Association, 95, 383
    issues with, 597
    kindergarten students, 595-596
    literacy in hypermedia, 559
    litigation about, 98-99
    male versus female performance, 396
    in mastery learning model, 79
    middle school students, 381-387
    National Council of Teachers of English, 95,
      383
    overview, 590
    of phonics instruction, 328
    policy making and, 104-106
    preparation for, 105-106